D1312443

...AN...

Exposition of the Bible

A SERIES OF EXPOSITIONS COVERING ALL THE BOOKS OF THE OLD AND NEW TESTAMENT . . . .

BY

Marcus Dods, D. D.,
R. A. Watson, D. D.,
Dean F. W. Farrar, D. D.,
Alexander MacLaren, D. D.,
S. H. Kellogg, D. D.,
J. Monro Gibson, D. D.,
H. C. G. Moule, D. D.,
Robert Rainy, D. D.,
J. R. Lumby, D. D.,
G. A. Chadwick, D. D.,
Andrew Harper, D. D.,
W. H. Bennett, M. A.,
R. F. Horton, D. D.,
C. J. Ball, M. A.,
Henry Burton, M. A.,
James Denney, D. D.,
A. Plummer, D. D.,
W. Alexander, D. D.,
George Adam Smith, D.D., LL.D.,
W. G. Blaikie, D. D., LL.D.,
W. F. Adeney, M. A.,
Samuel Cox, D. D.,
John Skinner, M. A.,
G. T. Stokes, D. D.,
G. G. Findlay, D. D.,
T. C. Edwards, D. D.,
W. Milligan, D. D.

Vol. IV.

JEREMIAH—ST. MARK.

PRINTED INDEPENDENTLY OF THE ENGLISH EDITORS AND OF OTHER PUBLISHERS
BY AND FOR
THE S. S. SCRANTON CO.,
HARTFORD, CONN.
1914.

THE PROPHECIES OF JEREMIAH.

CONTENTS.

THE PROPHECIES OF JEREMIAH.

BY THE REV. C. J. BALL, M. A.

PRELIMINARY SKETCH OF THE LIFE AND TIMES OF JEREMIAH.

A PRIEST by birth, Jeremiah became a prophet by the special call of God. His priestly origin implies a good literary training, in times when literature was largely in the hands of the priests. The priesthood, indeed, constituted a principal section of the Israelitish nobility, as appears both from the history of those times, and from the references in our prophet's writings, where kings and princes and priests are often named together as the aristocracy of the land (i. 18, ii. 26, iv. 9); and this fact would ensure for the young prophet a share in all the best learning of his age. The name of Jeremiah, like other prophetic proper names, seems to have special significance in connection with the most illustrious of the persons recorded to have borne it. It means "Iahvah foundeth," and, as a proper name, The Man that Iahvah foundeth; a designation which finds vivid illustration in the words of Jeremiah's call: "Before I moulded thee in the belly, I knew thee; and before thou camest forth from the womb, I consecrated thee: a spokesman to the nations did I make thee" (i. 5). The not uncommon name of Jeremiah—six other persons of the name are numbered in the Old Testament—must have appeared to the prophet as invested with new force and meaning, in the light of this revelation. Even before his birth he had been "founded" * and predestined by God for the work of his life.

The Hilkiah named as his father was not the high priest of that name,† so famous in connection with the reformation of king Josiah. Interesting as such a relationship would be if established, the following facts seem decisive against it. The prophet himself has omitted to mention it, and no hint of it is to be found elsewhere. The priestly family to which Jeremiah belonged was settled at Anathoth (i. 1, xi. 21, xxix. 27). But Anathoth in Benjamin (xxxvii. 12), the present *'Anâtâ*, between two and three miles N. N. E. of Jerusalem, belonged to the deposed line of Ithamar (1 Chron. xxiv. 3; comp. with 1 Kings ii. 26, 35). After this it is needless to insist that the prophet, and presumably his father, resided at Anathoth, whereas Jerusalem was the usual residence of the high priest. Nor is the identification of Jeremiah's family with that of the ruling high priest helped by the observation that the father of the high priest was named Shallum (1 Chron. v. 39), and that the prophet had an uncle of this name (Jer. xxxii. 7). The names Hilkiah‡ and Shallum are too common to justify any conclusions from such data. If the prophet's father was head of one of the twenty-four classes or guilds of the priests, that might explain the influence which Jeremiah could exercise with some of the grandees of the court. But we are not told more than that Jeremiah ben Hilkiah was a member of the priestly community settled at Anathoth. It is, however, a gratuitous disparagement of one of the greatest names in Israel's history, to suggest that, had Jeremiah belonged to the highest ranks of his caste, he would not have been equal to the self-renunciation involved in the assumption of the unhonoured and thankless office of a prophet.* Such a suggestion is certainly not warranted by the portraiture of the man as delineated by himself, with all the distinctive marks of truth and nature. From the moment that he became decisively convinced of his mission, Jeremiah's career is marked by struggles and vicissitudes of the most painful and perilous kind; his perseverance in his allotted path was met by an ever increasing hardness on the part of the people; opposition and ridicule became persecution, and the messenger of Divine truth persisted in proclaiming his message at the risk of his own life. That life may, in fact, be called a prolonged martyrdom; and, if we may judge of the unknown by the known, the tradition that the prophet was stoned to death by the Jewish refugees in Egypt is only too probable an account of its final scene. If "the natural shrinking of a somewhat feminine character" is traceable in his own report of his conduct at particular junctures, does not the fact shed an intenser glory upon the man who overcame this instinctive timidity, and persisted, in face of the most appalling dangers, in the path of duty? Is not the victory of a constitutionally timid and shrinking character a nobler moral triumph than that of the man who never knew fear—who marches to the conflict with others, with a light heart, simply because it is his nature to do so—because he has had no experience of the agony of a previous conflict with self? It is easy to sit in one's library and criticise the heroes of old; but the modern censures of Jeremiah betray at once a want of historic imagination, and a defect of sympathy with the sublime fortitude of one who struggled on in a battle which he knew to be lost. In a protracted contest such as that which Jeremiah was called upon to maintain, what wonder if courage sometimes flags, and hopelessness utters its forsaken cry? The moods of the saints are not always the same; they vary, like those of common men, with the stress of the hour. Even our Saviour could cry from the cross, "My God, My God, why hast hast Thou forsaken Me?" It is not by passing expressions, wrung from their torn hearts by the agony of the hour, that men are to be judged. It is the issue of the crisis that is all-important; not the cries of pain, which indicate its overwhelming pressure.

"It is sad," says a well-known writer, with reference to the noble passage, xxxi. 31-34, which he justly characterises as "one of those which best deserve to be called the Gospel before Christ," "It is sad that Jeremiah could not always keep his spirit under the calming influence of these high thoughts. No book of the Old Testament, except the book of Job and the

* The same root is used in the Targ. on i. 15 for *setting* or fixing thrones, *cf.* Dan. vii. 9: (רְמִיו)

† Clem. Alex., "Strom.," I. § 120.

‡ At least seven times.

* Hitzig.

Psalms, contains so much which is difficult to reconcile with the character of a self-denying servant of Jehovah. Such expressions as those in xi. 20, xv. 15, and especially xviii. 21-23, contrast powerfully with Luke xxiii. 34, and show that the typical character of Jeremiah is not absolutely complete." Probably not. The writer in question is honourably distinguished from a crowd of French and German critics, whose attainments are not superior to his own, by his deep sense of the inestimable value to mankind of those beliefs which animated the prophet, and by the sincerity of his manifest endeavours to judge fairly between Jeremiah and his detractors. He has already remarked truly enough that "the baptism of complicated suffering," which the prophet was called upon to pass through in the reign of Jehoiakim, "has made him, in a very high and true sense, a type of One greater than he." It is impossible to avoid such an impression, if we study the records of his life with any insight or sympathy. And the impression thus created is deepened, when we turn to that prophetic page which may be called the most "appealing" in the entire range of the Old Testament. In the 53d of Isaiah the martyrdom of Jeremiah becomes the living image of that other martyrdom, which in the fulness of time was to redeem the world. After this, to say that "the typical character of Jeremiah is not absolutely complete," is no more than the assertion of a truism; for what Old Testament character, what character in the annals of collective humanity, can be brought forward as a perfect type of the Christ, the Man whom, in His sinlessness and His power, unbiassed human reason and conscience instinctively suspect to have been also God? To deplore the fact that this illustrious prophet "could not always keep his spirit under the calming influence of his highest thoughts," is simply to deplore the infirmity that besets all human nature, to regret that natural imperfection which clings to a finite and fallen creature, even when endowed with the most splendid gifts of the spirit. For the rest, a certain degree of exaggeration is noticeable in founding upon three brief passages of so large a work as the collected prophecies of Jeremiah the serious charge that "no book of the Old Testament, except the book of Job and the Psalms, contains so much which is difficult to reconcile with the character of a self-denying servant of Jehovah." The charge appears to me both ill-grounded and misleading. But I reserve the further consideration of these obnoxious passages for the time when I come to discuss their context, as I wish now to complete my sketch of the prophet's life. He has himself recorded the date of his call to the prophetic office. It was in the thirteenth year of the good king Josiah, that the young* priest was summoned to a higher vocation by an inward Voice whose urgency he could not resist.† The year has been variously identified with 629, 627, and 626 B. C. The place has been supposed to have been Jerusalem, the capital, which was so near the prophet's home, and which, as Hitzig observes, offered the amplest scope and numberless occasions for the exercise of prophetic activity. But there appears no good reason why Jeremiah should not have become known locally as one whom God had specially chosen, before he abandoned his native place for the wider sphere of the capital. This, in truth, seems to be the likelier supposition, considering that his reluctance to take the first decisive step in his career excused itself on the ground of youthful inexperience: "Alas, my Lord Iahvah! behold, I know not (how) to speak; for I am but a youth."* The Hebrew term may imply that he was but about eighteen or twenty: an age when it is hardly probable that he would permanently leave his father's house. Moreover, he has mentioned a conspiracy of his fellow-townsmen against himself, in terms which have been taken to imply that he had exercised his ministry among them before his removal to Jerusalem. In chap. xi. 21, we read: "Therefore thus said Iahvah Sabaoth upon the men of 'Anathoth that were seeking thy life, saying, Prophesy not in the name of Iahvah, that thou die not by our hand! Therefore thus said Iahvah Sabaoth: Behold I am about to visit it upon them: the young men shall die by the sword; their sons and their daughters shall die by the famine. And a remnant they shall have none; for I will bring evil unto the men of 'Anathoth, (in) the year of their visitation." It is natural to see in this wicked plot against his life the reason for the prophet's departure from his native place (but *cf.* p. **74**). We are reminded of the violence done to our Lord by the men of "His own country" (ἡ πάτρις αὐτοῦ), and of His final and, as it would seem, compulsory departure from Nazareth to Capernaum (St. Luke iv. 16-29; St. Matt. iv. 13). In this, as in other respects, Jeremiah was a true type of the Messias.

The prophetic discourses, with which the book of Jeremiah opens (ii. 1-iv. 2), have a general application to all Israel, as is evident not only from the ideas expressed in them, but also from the explicit address, ii. 4: "Hear ye the word of Iahvah, O house of Jacob, and all the clans of the house of Israel!" It is clear enough, that although Jeremiah belongs to the southern kingdom, his reflections here concern the northern tribes as well, who must be included in the comprehensive phrases "house of Jacob," and "all the clans of the house of Israel." The fact is accounted for by the circumstance that these two discourses are summaries of the prophet's teaching on many distinct occasions, and as such might have been composed anywhere. There can be no doubt, however, that the principal contents of his book have their scene in Jerusalem. In chap. ii. 1, 2, indeed, we have what looks like the prophet's introduction to the scene of his future activity. "And there fell a word of Iahvah unto me, saying, Go and cry in the ears of Jerusalem." But the words are not found in the LXX., which begins chap. ii. thus: "And he said, These things saith the Lord, I remembered the lovingkindness (ἔλεος) of thy youth, and the love of thy espousals (τελείωσις)." But whether these words of the received Hebrew text be genuine or not, it is plain that if, as the terms of the prophet's commission affirm, he was to be "an embattled city, and a pillar of iron, and walls of bronze . . . to the kings of Judah, to her princes, to her priests," as well as "to the country folk" (i. 18), Jerusalem, the residence of kings and princes and chief priests, and the centre of the land, would be the natural

* i. 6.

† i. 2, xxv. 3.

* נער *puer*; (1) Ex. ii. 6, of a three months' babe; (2) of a young man up to about the twentieth year, Gen. xxxiv. 19, of Shechem ben Hamor; 1 Kings iii. 7, of Solomon, as here.

sphere of his operations. The same thing is implied in the Divine statement: "A *nabî* to 'the nations' have I made thee" (i. 5). The prophet of Judea could only reach the "gôyîm"—the surrounding foreign peoples—through the government of his own country, and through his influence upon Judean policy. The leaving of his native place, sooner or later, seems to be involved in the words (i. 7, 8): "And Iahvah said unto me, Say not, I am a youth: for upon whatsoever (journey) I send thee, thou shalt go (Gen. xxiv. 42); and with whomsoever I charge thee, thou shalt speak (Gen. xxiii. 8). Be not afraid of them!" The Hebrew is to some extent ambiguous. We might also render: "Unto whomsoever I send thee, thou shalt go; and whatsoever I charge thee, thou shalt speak." But the difference will not affect my point, which is that the words seem to imply the contingency of Jeremiah's leaving Anathoth. And this implication is certainly strengthened by the twice-given warning: "Be not afraid of them!" (i. 8), "Be not dismayed at them, lest I dismay thee (indeed) before them!" (17). The young prophet might dread the effect of an unpopular message upon his brethren and his father's house. But his fear would reach a far higher pitch of intensity, if he were called upon to confront with the same message of unwelcome truth the king in his palace, or the high priest in the courts of the sanctuary, or the fanatical and easily excited populace of the capital. Accordingly, when after his general prologue or exordium, the prophet plunges at once "into the agitated life of the present,"* it is to "the men of Judah and Jerusalem" (iv. 3), to "the great men" (v. 5), and to the throng of worshippers in the temple (vii. 2), that he addresses his burning words. When, however (v. 4), he exclaims: "And for me, I said, They are but poor folk; they *do* foolishly (Num. xii. 11), for they know not the way of Iahvah, the rule (*i. e., religion*) of their God (Isa. xlii. 1): I will get me unto the great men, and will speak with them; for *they* know the way of Iahvah, the rule of their God:" he again seems to suggest a prior ministry, of however brief duration, upon the smaller stage of Anathoth. At all events, there is nothing against the conjecture that the prophet may have passed to and fro between his birthplace and Jerusalem, making occasional sojourn in the capital, until at last the machinations of his neighbours (xi. 19 *seq.*), and as appears from xii. 6, his own kinsmen, drove him to quit Anathoth for ever. If Hitzig be right in referring Psalms xxiii., xxvi.-xxviii. to the prophet's pen, we may find in them evidence of the fact that the temple became his favourite haunt, and indeed his usual abode. As a priest by birth, he would have a claim to live in some one of the cells that surrounded the temple on three sides of it. The 23d Psalm, though written at a later period in the prophet's career—I shall refer to it again by-and-by—closes with the words, "And I will return unto (Ps. vii. 17; Hos. xii. 7) the house of Iahvah as long as I live," or perhaps, "And I will return (and dwell) in," etc., as though the temple were at once his sanctuary and his home. In like manner, Ps. xxvi. speaks of one who "washed his hands, in innocency" (*i. e.*, in a state of innocency; the symbolical action corresponding to the real state of his heart and conscience), and so "compassed the altar of Iahvah"; "to proclaim with the sound of a psalm of thanksgiving, and to rehearse all His wondrous works." The language here seems even to imply (Ex. xxx. 19-21) that the prophet took part, as a priest, in the ritual of the altar. He continues: "Iahvah, I love the abode of thine house, And the place of the dwelling of Thy glory!" and concludes, "My foot, it standeth on a plain; In the congregations I bless Iahvah," speaking as one continually present at the temple services. His prayers "Judge me," *i. e.*, Do me justice, "Iahvah!" and "Take not away my soul among sinners, Nor my life among men of bloodshed!" may point either to the conspiracies of the Anathothites, or to subsequent persecutions at Jerusalem. The former seem to be intended both here, and in Ps. xxvii., which is certainly most appropriate as an Ode of Thanksgiving for the prophet's escape from the murderous attempts of the men of Anathoth. Nothing could be more apposite than the allusions to "evil-doers drawing near against him to eat up his flesh" (*i. e.*, according to the common Aramaic metaphor, to slander him, and destroy him with false accusations); to the "lying witnesses, and the man (or men) breathing out (or panting after) violence" (ver. 12); and to having been forsaken even by his father and mother (ver. 10). With the former we may compare the prophet's words, chap. ix. 2 *sqq.*, "O that I were in the wilderness, in a lodge of wayfaring men; that I might forsake my people, and depart from among them! For all of them are adulterous, an assembly of traitors. And they have bent their tongue, (as it were) their bow for lying; and it is not by sincerity that they have grown strong in the land. Beware ye, every one of his friend, and have no confidence in any brother: for every brother will assuredly suppliant" (עקוב יעקב a reference to Jacob and Esau), "and every friend will gad about for slander. And each will deceive his friend, and the truth they will not speak: they have taught their tongue to speak lies; with perverseness they have wearied themselves. Thy dwelling is in the midst of deceit. . . . A murderous arrow is their tongue; deceit hath it spoken; with his mouth one speaketh peace with his neighbour, and inwardly he layeth an ambush for him." Such language, whether in the psalm or in the prophetic oration, could only be the fruit of bitter personal experience. (*Cf.* also xi. 19 *sqq.*, xx. 2 *sqq.*, xxvi. 8, xxxvi. 26, xxxvii. 15, xxxviii. 6). The allusion of the psalmist to being forsaken by father and mother (Ps. xxvii. 10) may be illustrated by the prophet's words, chap. xii. 6.

Jeremiah came prominently forward at a serious crisis in the history of his people. The Scythian invasion of Asia, described by Herodotus (i. 103-106), but not mentioned in the biblical histories of the time, was threatening Palestine and Judea. According to the old Greek writer, Cyaxares the Mede, while engaged in besieging Nineveh, was attacked by a great horde of Scythians, under their king Madyes, who had entered Asia in pushing their pursuit of the Cimmerians, whom they had expelled from Europe.* The Medes lost the battle, and the barbarous victors found themselves masters of Asia. Thereupon they marched for Egypt, and had made their way past Ascalon, when they were

* Hitzig, *Vorbemerkungen.*

* The Cimmerians are the Gomer of Scripture, the Gimirrâ'a of the cuneiform inscriptions.

met by the envoys of Psammitichus I. the king of Egypt, whose "gifts and prayers," induced them to return. On the way back, some few of them lagged behind the main body, and plundered the famous temple of Atergatis-Derceto, or as Herodotus calls the great Syrian goddess, Ourania Afrodite, at Ascalon (the goddess avenged herself by smiting them and their descendants with impotence—*θήλειαν νοῦσον*, *cf.* I Sam. v. 6 *sqq.*). For eight and twenty years the Scythians remained the tyrants of Asia, and by their exactions and plundering raids brought ruin everywhere, until at last Cyaxares and his Medes, by help of treachery, recovered their former sway. After this, the Medes took Nineveh, and reduced the Assyrians to complete subjection; but Babylonia remained independent. Such is the story as related by Herodotus, our sole authority in the matter. It has been supposed * that the 59th Psalm was written by king Josiah, while the Scythians were threatening Jerusalem. Their wild hordes, ravenous for plunder, like the Gauls who at a later time struck Rome with panic, are at any rate well described in the verse

"They return at eventide
They howl like the dogs,

the famished pariah dogs of an eastern town—

And surround the city."

But the Old Testament furnishes other indications of the terror which preceded the Scythian invasion, and of the merciless havoc which accompanied it. The short prophecy of Zephaniah, who prophesied "in the days of Josiah ben Amon king of Judah," and was therefore a contemporary of Jeremiah, is best explained by reference to this crisis in the affairs of Western Asia. Zephaniah's very first word is a startling menace. "I will utterly away with everything from off the face of the ground, saith Iahvah." "I will away with man and beast, I will away with the birds of the air, and the fishes of the sea, and the stumblingblocks along with the wicked (*i. e.*, the idols with their worshippers); and I will exterminate man from off the face of the ground, saith Iahvah." The imminence of a sweeping destruction is announced. Ruin is to overtake every existing thing; not only the besotted people and their dumb idols, but beasts and birds and even the fish of the sea are to perish in the universal catastrophe. It is exactly what might be expected from the sudden appearance of a horde of barbarians of unknown numbers, sweeping over a civilised country from north to south, like some devastating flood; slaying whatever crossed their path, burning towns and temples, and devouring the flocks and herds. The reference to the fishes of the sea is explained by the fact that the Scythians marched southward by the road which ran along the coast through Philistia. "Gaza," cries the prophet, "shall be forsaken,"—there is an inimitable paronomasia in his words †—"And Ascalon a desolation: as for Ashdod, at noonday they shall drive her into exile; and Ekron shall be rooted up. Alas for the dwellers by the shore line, the race of the Cherethites! The word of Iahvah is against you, O Canaan, land of the Philistines! And I will destroy thee, that there shall be no inhabitant." It is true that Herodotus relates that the Scythians, in their retreat, for the most part marched past Ascalon without doing any harm, and that the plunder of the temple was the work of a few stragglers. But neither is this very probable in itself, nor does it harmonise with what he tells us afterwards about the plunder and rapine that marked the period of Scythian domination. We need not suppose that the information of the old historian as to the doings of these barbarians was as exact as that of a modern state paper. Nor, on the other hand, would it be very judicious to press every detail in a highly wrought prophetic discourse, which vividly sets forth the fears of the time, and gives imaginative form to the feelings and anticipations of the hour; as if it were intended by the writer, not for the moral and spiritual good of his contemporaries, but to furnish posterity with a minutely accurate record of the actual course of events in the distant past.

The public danger, which stimulated the reflection and lent force to the invective of the lesser prophet, intensified the impression produced by the earlier preaching of Jeremiah. The tide of invasion, indeed, rolled past Judea, without working much permanent harm to the little kingdom, with whose destinies were involved the highest interests of mankind at large. But this respite from destruction would be understood by the prophet's hearers as proof of the relentings of Iahvah towards His penitent people; and may, for the time at least, have confirmed the impression wrought upon the popular mind by Jeremiah's passionate censures and entreaties. The time was otherwise favourable; for the year of his call was the year immediately subsequent to that in which the young king Josiah "began to purify Judah and Jerusalem from the high places and the Asherim, and the carven images and the molten images," which he did in the twelfth year of his reign, *i. e.*, in the twentieth year of his age, according to the testimony of the Chronicler (2 Chron. xxxiv. 3), which there is no good reason for disallowing. Jeremiah was probably about the same age as the king, as he calls himself a mere youth (na'ar). After the Scythians had retired—if we are right in fixing their invasion so early in the reign—the official reformation of public worship was taken up again, and completed by the eighteenth year of Josiah, when the prophet might be about twenty-five. The finding of what is called "the book of the Law," and "the book of the Covenant," * by Hilkiah the high priest, while the temple was being restored by the king's order, is represented by the histories as having determined the further course of the royal reforms. What this book of the Law was, it is not necessary now to discuss. It is clear from the language of the book of Kings, and from the references of Jeremiah, that the substance of it, at any rate, closely corresponded with portions of Deuteronomy. It appears from his own words (chap. xi. 1-8) that at first, at all events, Jeremiah was an earnest preacher of the positive precepts of this book of the Covenant. It is true that his name does not occur in the narrative of Josiah's reformation, as related in Kings. There the king and his counsellors inquire of Iahvah through the prophetess Huldah (2 Kings xxii. 14). Supposing the account to be both complete and correct, this only shows that five years after his

* Ewald, "Die Psalmen," 165.

† Zeph. ii. 4 *sqq.*, עזה עזובה תהיה . . . . עקרון תעקר

* ספר התורה, 2 Kings xxii. 8; ספר הברית, 2 Kings xxiii. 2.

call, Jeremiah was still unknown or little considered at court. But he was doubtless included among the "prophets," who, with "the king and all the men of Judah and all the inhabitants of Jerusalem," "and the priests . . . and all the people, both small and great," after the words of the newfound book of the Covenant had been read in their ears, bound themselves by a solemn league and covenant, "to walk after Iahweh, and to keep His commandments, and His laws, and His statutes, with all the heart, and with all the soul" (2 Kings xxiii. 3). It is evident that at first the young prophet hoped great things of this national league and the associated reforms in the public worship. In his eleventh chapter he writes thus: "The word that fell to Jeremiah from Iahvah, saying: Hear ye the words of this covenant"—presumably the words of the new-found book of the Torah—"And speak ye to the men of Judah, and to the inhabitants of Jerusalem. And thou shalt say unto them"—the change from the second plural "hear ye," "speak ye," is noticeable. In the first instance, no doubt, the message contemplates the leaders of the reforming movement generally; the prophet is specially addressed in the words, "And *thou* shalt say unto them, Thus said Iahvah, the God of Israel, Cursed is the man that will not hear the words of this covenant, which I commanded your fathers, in the day when I brought them forth from the land of Egypt, from the iron furnace, saying, Hearken to My voice, and do them, according to all that I command you; and ye shall become to Me a people, and I—I will become to you Elohim: in order to make good the oath that I sware to your fathers, to give them a land flowing with milk and honey, as at this day.

"And I answered and said, So be it, Iahvah!

"And Iahvah said unto me, Proclaim all these words in the cities of Judah and in the streets of Jerusalem, saying, Hear ye the words of this covenant, and do them. For I solemnly adjured your fathers, at the time when I brought them up out of the land of Egypt, (and) unto this day, with all earnestness [earnestly and incessantly], saying, Hearken ye to My voice. And they hearkened not, nor inclined their ear, and they walked individually in the stubbornness of their evil heart. So I brought upon them all the words of this covenant"—*i. e.*, the curses, which constituted the sanction of it: see Deut. iv. 25 *sqq.*, xxviii. 15 *sqq.*—"(this covenant) which I commanded them to do, and they did it not." [Or perhaps, "Because I bade them *do* and they *did* not;" implying a general prescription of conduct, which was not observed. Or, "I who had bidden them do, and they did not"—justifying, as it were, God's assumption of the function of punishment. *His* law had been set at naught; the national reverses, therefore, were *His* infliction, and not another's.] This, then, was the first preaching of Jeremiah. "Hear ye the words of this covenant!"—the covenant drawn out with such precision and legal formality in the new-found book of the Torah.

Up and down the country, "in the cities of Judah" and "in the streets of Jerusalem," everywhere within the bounds of the little kingdom that acknowledged the house of David, he published this panacea for the actual and imminent evils of the time, insisting, we may be sure, with all the eloquence of a youthful patriot, upon the impressive warnings embodied in the past history of Israel, as set forth in the book of the Law. But his best efforts were fruitless. Eloquence and patriotism and enlightened spiritual beliefs and lofty purity of purpose were wasted upon a generation blinded by its own vices and reserved for a swiftly approaching retribution. Perhaps the plots which drove the prophet finally from his native place were due to the hostility evoked against him by his preaching of the Law. At all events, the account of them immediately follows, in this eleventh chapter (vers. 18 *sqq.*). But it must be borne in mind that the Law-book was not found until *five* years after his call to the office of prophet.

In any case, it is not difficult to understand the popular irritation at what must have seemed the unreasonable attitude of a prophet, who, in spite of the wholesale destruction of the outward symbols of idolatry effected by the king's orders, still declared that the claims of Iahweh were unsatisfied, and that something more was needed than the purging of Judah and Jerusalem from the high places and the Asherim, if the Divine favour were to be conciliated, and the country restored to permanent prosperity. The people probably supposed that they had sufficiently fulfilled the law of their God, when they had not only demolished all sanctuaries but His, but had done away with all those local holy places where Iahvah was indeed worshipped, but with a deplorable admixture of heathenish rites. The law of the one legal sanctuary, so much insisted upon in Deuteronomy, was formally established by Josiah, and the national worship was henceforth centralised in Jerusalem, which from this time onward remained in the eyes of all faithful Israelites "the place where men ought to worship." It is entirely in accordance with what we know of human nature in general, and not merely of Jewish nature, that the popular mind failed to rise to the level of the prophetic teaching, and that the reforming zeal of the time should have exhausted itself in efforts which effected no more than these external changes. The truth is that the reforming movement began from above, not from below; and however earnest the young king may have been, it is probable that the mass of his subjects viewed the abolition of the high places, and the other sweeping measures, initiated in obedience to the precepts of the book of the Covenant, either with apathy and indifference, or with feelings of sullen hostility. The priesthood of Jerusalem were, of course, benefited by the abolition of all sanctuaries, except the one wherein they ministered and received their dues.

The writings of our prophet amply demonstrate that, whatever zeal for Iahvah, and whatever degree of compunction for the past may have animated the prime movers in the reformation of the eighteenth of Josiah, no radical improvement was effected in the ordinary life of the nation. For some twelve years, indeed, the well-meaning king continued to occupy the throne; years, it may be presumed, of comparative peace and prosperity for Judah, although neither the narrative of Kings and Chronicles nor that of Jeremiah gives us any information about them. Doubtless it was generally supposed that the nation was reaping the reward of its obedience to the law of Iahvah.

But at the end of that period, *circ.* B. C. 608, an event occurred which must have shaken this faith to its foundations. In the thirty-first year of his reign, Josiah fell in the battle of Megiddo, while vainly opposing the small forces at his command to the hosts of Egypt. Great indeed must have been the "searchings of heart" occasioned by this unlooked-for and overwhelming stroke. Strange that it should have fallen at a time when, as the people deemed, the God of Israel was receiving His due at their hands; when the injunctions of the book of the Covenant had been minutely carried out, the false and irregular worships abolished, and Jerusalem made the centre of the cultus; a time when it seemed as if the Lord had become reconciled to His people Israel, when years of peace and plenty seemed to give demonstration of the fact; and when, as may perhaps be inferred from Josiah's expedition against Necho, the extension of the border, contemplated in the book of the Law, was considered as likely to be realised in the near future. The height to which the national aspirations had soared only made the fall more disastrous, complete, ruinous.

The hopes of Judah rested upon a worldly foundation; and it was necessary that a people whose blindness was only intensified by prosperity, should be undeceived by the discipline of overthrow. No hint is given in the meagre narrative of the reign as to whether the prophets had lent their countenance or not to the fatal expedition. Probably they did; probably they too had to learn by bitter experience that no man, not even a zealous and godfearing monarch, is *necessary* to the fulfilment of the Divine counsels. And the agony of this irretrievable disaster, this sudden and complete extinction of his country's fairest hopes, may have been the means by which the Holy Spirit led Jeremiah to an intenser conviction that illicit modes of worship and coarse idolatries were not the only things in Judah offensive to Iahvah; that something more was needed to win back His favour than formal obedience, however rigid and exacting, to the letter of a written code of sacred law; that the covenant of Iahvah with His people had an inward and eternal, not an outward and transitory significance; and that not the letter but the spirit of the law was the thing of essential moment. Thoughts like these must have been present to the prophet's mind when he wrote (xxxi. 31 *sqq.*): "Behold, a time is coming, saith Iahvah, when I will conclude with the house of Israel and with the house of Judah a fresh treaty, unlike the treaty that I concluded with their forefathers at the time when I took hold of their hand, to bring them out of the land of Egypt; when they, on their part, disannulled my treaty, and I—I disdained them, saith Iahvah. For this is the treaty that I will conclude with the house of Israel after those days [*i. e.*, in due time], saith Iahvah: I will put my Torah within them and upon their heart will I grave it; and I will become to them a God, and they—they shall become to me a people."

It is but a dull eye which cannot see beyond the metaphor of the covenant or treaty between Iahvah and Israel; and it is a strangely dark understanding that fails to perceive here and elsewhere a translucent figure of the eternal relations subsisting between God and man. The error is precisely that against which the prophets, at the high-water mark of their inspiration, are always protesting—the universal and inveterate error of narrowing down the requirements of the Infinitely Holy, Just, and Good, to the scrupulous observance of some accepted body of canons, enshrined in a book and duly interpreted by the laborious application of recognised legal authorities. It is so comfortable to be sure of possessing an infallible guide in so small a compass; to be spared all further consideration, so long as we have paid the priestly dues, and kept the annual feasts, and carefully observed the laws of ceremonial purity! From the first, the attention of priests and people, including the official prophets, would be attracted by the ritual and ceremonial precepts, rather than by the earnest moral teaching of Deuteronomy. As soon as first impressions had had time to subside, the moral and spiritual element in that noble book would begin to be ignored, or confounded with the purely external and mundane prescriptions affecting public worship and social propriety; and the interests of true religion would hardly be subserved by the formal acceptance of this code as the law of the state. The unregenerate heart of man would fancy that it had at last gotten that for which it is always craving—something final—something to which it could triumphantly point, when urged by the religious enthusiast, as tangible evidence that it was fulfilling the Divine law, that it was at one with Iahvah, and therefore had a right to expect the continuance of His favour and blessing. Spiritual development would be arrested; men would become satisfied with having effected certain definite changes bringing them into external conformity with the written law, and would incline to rest in things as they were. Meanwhile, the truth held good that to make a fetish of a code, a system, a holy book, is not necessarily identical with the service of God. It is, in fact, the surest way to forget God; for it is to invest something that is not He, but, at best, a far-off echo of His voice, with His sole attributes of finality and sufficiency.

The effect of the downfall of the good king was electrical. The nation discovered that the displeasure of Iahvah had not passed away like a morning cloud. Out of the shock and the dismay of that terrible disillusion sprang the conviction that the past was not atoned for, that the evil of it was irreparable. The idea is reflected in the words of Jeremiah (xv. 1): "And Iahvah said unto me, If Moses were to stand before Me (as an intercessor), and Samuel, I should not incline towards this people: dismiss them from My presence, and let them go forth! And when they say unto thee, Whither are we to go forth? thou shalt say unto them, Thus said Iahvah, They that are Death's to death; and they that are the Sword's to the sword; and they that are Famine's to famine; and they that are Captivity's to captivity. And I will set over them four families, saith Iahvah; the sword to slay, and the dogs to draw (2 Sam. xvii. 13), and the birds of the air, and the beasts of the earth, to devour and to destroy. And I will give them for worry (Deut. xxviii. 25) to all the realms of earth: 'because of (Deut. xv. 10, xviii. 12; בגלל) Manasseh ben Hezekiah king of Judah, for what he did in Jerusalem.'" In the next verses we have what seems to be a reference to the death of Josiah (ver. 7). "I fanned them with a fan"—the fan by which the husbandman separates wheat from chaff in the threshingfloor —"I fanned them with a fan, in the gates of the land"—at Megiddo, the point where an enemy marching along the maritime route might enter the land of Israel; "I bereaved, I ruined my people (ver. 9). She that has borne seven, pined away; she breathed out her soul; 'her sun went down while it was yet day.'" The national mourning over this dire event became proverbial, as we see from Zech. xii. 11: "In that day, great shall be the mourning in Jerusalem; like the mourning of Hadadrimmon in the valley of Megiddo."

The political relations of the period are certainly obscure, if we confine our attention to the biblical data. Happily, we are now able to supplement these, by comparison with the newly recovered monuments of Assyria. Under Manasseh, the kingdom of Judah became tributary to Esarhaddon; and this relation of dependence, we may be sure, was not interrupted during the vigorous reign of the mighty Ashurbanipal, B. C. 668-626. But the first symptoms of declining power on the side of their oppressors would undoubtedly be the signal for conspiracy and rebellion in the distant parts of the loosely amalgamated empire. Until the death of Ashurbanipal, the last great sovereign who reigned at Nineveh, it may be assumed that Josiah stood true to his fealty. It appears from certain notices in Kings and Chronicles (2 Kings xxiii. 19; 2 Chron. xxxiv. 6) that he was able to exercise authority even in the territories of the ruined kingdom of Israel. This may have been due to the fact that he was allowed to do pretty much as he liked, so long as he proved an obedient vassal; or, as is more likely, the attention of the Assyrians was diverted from the West by troubles nearer home in connection with the Scythians or the Medes and Babylonians. At all events, it is not to be supposed that when Josiah went out to oppose the Pharaoh at Megiddo, he was facing the forces of Egypt alone. The thing is intrinsically improbable. The king of Judah must have headed a coalition of the petty Syrian states against the common enemy. It is not necessary to suppose that the Palestinian principalities resisted Necho's advance, in the interests of their nominal suzerain Assyria. From all we can gather, that empire was now tottering to its irretrievable fall, under the feeble successors of Ashurbanipal. The ambition of Egypt was doubtless a terror to the combined peoples. The further results of Necho's campaign are unknown. For the moment, Judah experienced a change of masters; but the Egyptian tyranny was not destined to last. Some four years after the battle of Megiddo, Pharaoh Necho made a second expedition to the North, this time against the Babylonians, who had succeeded to the empire of Assyria. The Egyptians were utterly defeated in the battle of Carchemish, *circ.* B. C. 606-05, which left Nebuchadrezzar in virtual possession of the countries west of the Euphrates (Jer. xlvi. 2). It was the fourth year of Jehoiakim, son of Josiah, king of Judah, when this crisis arose in the affairs of the Eastern world. The prophet Jeremiah did not miss the meaning of events. From the first he recognised in Nebuchadrezzar, or Nabucodrossor, an instrument in the Divine hand for the chastisement of the peoples; from the first, he predicted a judgment of God, not only upon the Jews, but upon all nations, far and near. The substance of his oracles is preserved to us in chapters xxv. and xlvi.-xlix. of his book. In the former passage, which is expressly dated from the fourth year of Jehoiakim, and the first of Nebuchadrezzar, the prophet gives a kind of retrospect of his ministry of three-and-twenty years, affirms that it has failed of its end, and that Divine retribution is therefore certain. The "tribes of the north" will come and desolate the whole country (ver. 9), and "these nations"—the peoples of Palestine—"shall serve the king of Babel seventy years" (ver. 11). The judgment on the nations is depicted by an impressive symbolism (ver. 15). "Thus said Iahvah, the God of Israel, unto me, Take this cup of wine, the (Divine) wrath, from My hand, and cause all the nations, unto whom I send thee, to drink it. And let them drink, and reel, and show themselves frenzied, because of the sword that I am sending amongst them!" The strange metaphor recalls our own proverb: *Quem Deus vult perdere, prius dementat.* "So I took the cup from the hand of Iahvah, and made all the nations drink, unto whom Iahvah had sent me." Then, as in some list of the proscribed, the prophet writes down, one after another, the names of the doomed cities and peoples. The judgment was set for that age, and the eternal books were opened, and the names found in them were these (ver. 18): "Jerusalem, and the cities of Judah, and her kings, and her princes. Pharaoh, king of Egypt, and his servants, and his princes, and all his people. And all the hired soldiery, and all the kings of the land of Uz, and all the kings of the land of the Philistines, and Ashkelon, and Gaza, and Ekron, and the remnant of Ashdod. Edom, and Moab, and the benê Ammon. And all the kings of Tyre, and all the kings of Sidon, and the kings of the island (*i. e.*, Cyprus) that is beyond the sea. Dedan and Tema and Buz and all the tonsured folk. And all the kings of Arabia, and all the kings of the hired soldiery, that dwell in the wilderness. And all the kings of Zimri, and all the kings of Elam, and all the kings of Media. And all the kings of the north, the near and the far, one with another; and all the kingdoms of the earth that are upon the surface of the ground."

When the mourning for Josiah was ended (2 Chron. xxxv. 24 *sqq.*), the people put Jehoahaz on his father's throne. But this arrangement was not suffered to continue, for Necho, having defeated and slain Josiah, naturally asserted his right to dispose of the crown of Judah as he thought fit. Accordingly, he put Jehoahaz in bonds at Riblah in the land of Hamath, whither he had probably summoned him to swear allegiance to Egypt, or whither, perhaps, Jehoahaz had dared to go with an armed force to resist the Egyptian pretensions, which, however, is an unlikely supposition, as the battle in which Josiah had fallen must have been a severe blow to the military resources of Judah. Necho carried the unfortunate but also unworthy king (2 Kings xxiii. 32) a prisoner to Egypt, where he died (*ibid.* 34). These events are thus alluded to by Jeremiah (xxii. 10-12): "Weep ye not for one dead (*i. e.*, Josiah), nor make your moan for him: weep ever for him that is going away; for he will not come back again, and see his native land! For thus hath Iahvah said of Shallum (*i. e.*, Jehoahaz, 1 Chron. iii. 15) ben Josiah, king of

Judah, that reigned in the place of Josiah his father, who had gone forth out of his place (*i. e.*, Jerusalem, or the palace, ver. 1), He will not come back thither again. For in the place whither they have led him into exile, there he will die; and this land he will not see again." The pathos of this lament for one whose dream of greatness was broken for ever within three short months, does not conceal the prophet's condemnation of Necho's prisoner. Jeremiah does not condole with the captive king as the victim of mere misfortune. In this, as in all the gathering calamities of his country, he sees a retributive meaning. The nine preceding verses of the chapter demonstrate the fact.

In the place of Jehoahaz, Necho had set up his elder brother Eliakim, with the title of Jehoiakim (2 Kings xxiii. 34). This prince also is condemned in the narrative of Kings (ver. 37), as having done "the evil thing in the eyes of Iahvah, according to all that his forefathers had done;" an estimate which is thoroughly confirmed by what Jeremiah has added to his lament for the deposed king his brother. The pride, the grasping covetousness, the high-handed violence and cruelty of Jehoiakim, and the doom that will overtake him, in the righteousness of God, are thus declared: "Woe to him that buildeth his house by injustice, and his chambers by iniquity! that layeth on his neighbour work without wages, and giveth him not his hire! That saith, I will build me a lofty house, with airy chambers; and he cutteth him out the windows thereof, panelling it with cedar, and painting it with vermilion. Shalt thou *reign*, that thou art hotly intent upon cedar?" (Or, according to the LXX. Vat., thou viest with Ahaz—LXX. Alex., with Ahab; perhaps a reference to "the ivory house" mentioned in 1 Kings xxii. 39). "Thy father, did he not eat and drink and do judgment and justice? Then it was well with him. He judged the cause of the oppressed and the needy: then it was well. Was not this to know Me? saith Iahvah. For thine eyes and thine heart are set upon nought but thine own lucre (thy plunder), and upon the blood of the innocent, to shed it, and upon extortion and oppression to do it. Therefore, thus hath Iahvah said of Jehoiakim ben Josiah, king of Judah: They shall not lament for him with Ah, my brother! or Ah, sister! They shall not lament for him with Ah, lord! or Ah, his majesty! With the burial of an ass shall he be buried; with dragging and casting forth beyond the gates of Jerusalem!"

In the beginning of the reign of this worthless tyrant, the prophet was impelled to address a very definite warning to the throng of worshippers in the court of the temple (xxvi. 4 *sqq.*). It was to the effect that if they did not mend their ways, their temple should become like Shiloh, and their city a curse to all the nations of the earth. There could be no doubt of the meaning of this reference to the ruined sanctuary, long since forsaken of God (Ps. lxxviii. 60). It so wrought upon that fanatical audience, that priests and prophets and people rose as one man against the daring speaker; and Jeremiah was barely rescued from immediate death by the timely intervention of the princes. The account closes with the relation of the cruel murder of another prophet of the school of Jeremiah, by command of Jehoiakim the king; and it is very evident from these narratives that, screened as he was by powerful friends, Jeremiah narrowly escaped a similar fate.

We have reached the point in our prophet's career when, taking a broad survey of the entire world of his time, he forecasts the character of the future that awaits its various political divisions. He has left the substance of his reflections in the 25th chapter, and in those prophecies concerning the foreign peoples, which the Hebrew text of his works relegates to the very end of the book, as chapters xlvi.-li., but which the Greek recension of the Septuagint inserts immediately after chapter xxv. 13. In the decisive battle at Carchemish, which crippled the power of Egypt, the only other existing state which could make any pretensions to the supremacy of Western Asia, and contend with the trans-Euphratean empires for the possession of Syria-Palestine, Jeremiah had recognised a signal indication of the Divine Will, which he was not slow to proclaim to all within reach of his inspired eloquence. In common with all the great prophets who had preceded him, he entertained a profound conviction that the race was not necessarily to the swift, nor the battle to the strong; that the fortune of war was not determined simply and solely by chariots and horsemen and big battalions; that behind all material forces lay the spiritual, from whose absolute will they derived their being and potency, and upon whose sovereign pleasure depended the issues of victory and defeat, of life and death. As his successor, the second Isaiah, saw in the polytheist Cyrus, king of Anzan, a chosen servant of Iahvah, whose whole triumphant career was foreordained in the counsels of heaven; so Jeremiah saw in the rise of the Babylonian domination, and the rapid development of the new empire upon the ruins of the old, a manifest token of the Divine purpose, a revelation of a Divine secret. His point of view is strikingly illustrated by the warning which he was directed to send a few years later to the kings who were seeking to draw Judah into the common alliance against Babylon (chap. xxvii. 1 *sqq.*). "In the beginning of the reign of Zedekiah * ben Josiah, king of Judah, fell this word to Jeremiah from Iahvah. Thus said Iahvah unto me, Make thee thongs and poles, and put them upon thy neck; and send them to the king of Edom, and to the king of Moab, and to the king of the benê Ammon, and to the king of Tyre, and to the king of Zidon, by the hand of the messengers that are come to Jerusalem, unto Zedekiah the king of Judah. And give them a charge unto their masters, saying, Thus said Iahvah Sabaoth, the God of Israel, Thus shall ye say to your masters: I it was that made the earth, mankind, and the cattle that are on the face of the earth, by My great strength, and by Mine outstretched arm; and I give it to whom it seemeth good in My sight. And now, I will verily give all these countries into the hands of Nebuchadrezzar king of Babel, My servant; and even the wild creatures of the field will I give unto him to serve him."

Nebuchadrezzar was invincible, and the Jewish prophet clearly perceived the fact. But it must not be imagined that the Jewish people generally, or the neighbouring peoples, enjoyed a similar degree of insight. Had that been so, the battle of Jeremiah's life would never have been fought out under such cruel, such hopeless conditions. The prophet saw the truth, and pro-

* So rightly the Syriac, for Jehoiakim.

claimed it without ceasing in reluctant ears, and was met with derision, and incredulity, and intrigue, and slander, and pitiless persecution. By-and-by, when his word had come to pass, and all the principalities of Canaan were crouching abjectly at the feet of the conqueror, and Jerusalem was a heap of ruins, the scattered communities of banished Israelites could remember that Jeremiah had foreseen and foretold it all. In the light of accomplished facts, the significance of his prevision began to be realised; and when the first dreary hours of dumb and desperate suffering were over, the exiles gradually learned to find consolation in the few but precious promises that had accompanied the menaces which were now so visibly fulfilled. While they were yet in their own land, two things had been predicted by this prophet in the name of their God. The first was now accomplished; no cavil could throw doubt upon actual experience. Was there not here some warrant, at least for reasonable men, some sufficient ground for trusting the prophet at last, for believing in his Divine mission, for striving to follow his counsels, and for looking forward with steadfast hope out of present affliction, to the gladness of the future which the same seer had foretold, even with the unwonted precision of naming a limit of time? So the exiles were persuaded, and their belief was fully justified by the event. Never had they realised the absolute sovereignty of their God, the universality of Iahvah Sabaoth, the shadowy nature, the blank nothingness of all supposed rivals of His dominion, as now they did, when at length years of painful experience had brought home to their minds the truth that Nebuchadrezzar had demolished the temple and laid Jerusalem in the dust, not, as he himself believed, by the favour of Bel-Merodach and Nebo, but by the sentence of the God of Israel; and that the catastrophe, which had swept them out of political existence, occurred not because Iahvah was weaker than the gods of Babylon, but because He was irresistibly strong; stronger than all powers of all worlds; stronger therefore than Israel, stronger than Babylon; stronger than the pride and ambition of the earthly conqueror, stronger than the selfwill, and the stubbornness, and the wayward rebellion, and the fanatical blindness, and the frivolous unbelief, of his own people. The conception is an easy one for us, who have inherited the treasures both of Jewish and of Gentile thought; but the long struggle of the prophets, and the fierce antagonism of their fellow-countrymen, and the political extinction of the Davidic monarchy, and the agonies of the Babylonian exile, were necessary to the genesis and germination of this master-conception in the heart of Israel, and so of humanity.

To return from this hasty glance at the remoter consequences of the prophet's ministry, it was in the fourth year of Jehoiakim, and the first of Nebuchadrezzar (xxv. 1) that, in obedience to a Divine intimation, he collected the various discourses which he had so far delivered in the name of God. Some doubt has been raised as to the precise meaning of the record of this matter (xxxvi.). On the one hand, it is urged that "An historically accurate reproduction of the prophecies would not have suited Jeremiah's object, which was not historical but practical: he desired to give a salutary shock to the people, by bringing before them the fatal consequences of their evil deeds:" and that "the purport of the roll (ver. 29) which the king burned was (only) that the king of Babylon should 'come and destroy this land,' whereas it is clear that Jeremiah had uttered many other important declarations in the course of his already long ministry." And on the other hand, it is suggested that the roll, of which the prophet speaks in chap. xxxvi., contained no more than the prophecy concerning the Babylonian invasion and its consequences, which is preserved in chap. xxv., and dated from the fourth year of Jehoiakim.

Considering the unsatisfactory state of the text of Jeremiah, it is perhaps admissible to suppose, for the sake of this hypothesis, that the second verse of chap. xxv., which expressly declares that this prophecy was spoken by its author "to all the people of Judah, and to all the inhabitants of Jerusalem," is "a loose inaccurate statement due to a later editor;" although this inconvenient statement is found in the Greek of the LXX. as well as in the Massoretic Hebrew text. But let us examine the alleged objections in the light of the positive statements of chap. xxxvi. It is there written thus: "In the fourth year of Jehoiakim ben Josiah king of Judah, this word fell to Jeremiah from Iahvah. Take thee a book-roll, and write on it all the words that I have spoken unto thee, concerning Israel and Judah and all the nations, from the day when I (first) spake unto thee,—from the days of Josiah,—unto this day." This certainly seems plain enough. The only possible question is whether the command was to collect within the compass of a single volume, a sort of author's edition, an indefinite number of discourses preserved hitherto in separate MSS. and perhaps to a great extent in the prophet's memory; or whether we are to understand by "all the words" the *substance* of the various prophecies to which reference is made. If the object was merely to impress the people on a particular occasion by placing before them a sort of historical review of the prophet's warnings in the past, it is evident that a formal edition of his utterances, so far as he was able to prepare such a work, would not be the most natural or ready method of attaining that purpose. Such a review for practical purposes might well be comprised within the limits of a single continuous composition, such as we find in chap. xxv., which opens with a brief retrospect of the prophet's ministry during twenty-three years (vers. 3-7), and then denounces the neglect with which his warnings have been received, and declares the approaching subjugation of all the states of Phenicia-Palestine by the king of Babylon. But the narrative itself gives not a single hint that such was the sole object in view. Much rather does it appear from the entire context that, the crisis having at length arrived, which Jeremiah had so long foreseen, he was now impelled to gather together, with a view to their preservation, all those discourses by which he had laboured in vain to overcome the indifference, the callousness, and the bitter antagonism of his people. These utterances of the past, collected and revised in the light of successive events, and illustrated by their substantial agreement with what had actually taken place, and especially by the new danger which seemed to threaten the whole West, the rising power of Babylon, might certainly be expected to produce a powerful impression by their coincidence with the national apprehensions; and the prophet might even hope that warnings, hitherto disregarded, but now visibly justified by events in course of development, would at last bring "the house of Judah" to consider seriously the evil that, in God's Providence, was evidently impending, and "return every man from his evil way," that even so late the consequences of their guilt might be turned aside. This doubtless was the immediate aim, but it does not exclude others, such as the vindication of the prophet's own claims, in startling contrast with those of the false prophets, who had opposed him at every step, and misled his countrymen so grievously and fatally. Against these and their delusive promises, the volume of Jeremiah's past discourses would constitute an effective protest, and a complete justification of his own endeavours. We must also remember that, if the repentance and salvation of his own contemporaries was naturally the first object of the prophet in all his undertakings, in the Divine counsels prophecy has more than a temporary value, and that the writings of this very prophet were destined to become instrumental in the conversion of a succeeding generation.

Those twenty-three years of patient thought and earnest labour, of high converse with God, and of agonised pleading with a reprobate people, were not to be without their fruit, though the prophet himself was not to see it. It is a matter of history that the words of Jeremiah wrought with such power upon the hearts of the exiles in Babylonia, as to become, in the hands of God, a principal means in the regeneration of Israel, and of that restoration which was its promised and its actual consequence; and from that day to this, not one of all the goodly fellowship of the prophets has enjoyed such credit in the Jewish Church as he who in his lifetime had to encounter neglect and ridicule, hatred and persecution, beyond what is recorded of any other.

"So Jeremiah called Baruch ben Neriah; and Baruch wrote, from the mouth of Jeremiah, all the words of Iahvah, that He had spoken unto him, upon a book-roll" (ver. 4). Nothing is said about time; and there is nothing to indicate that what the scribe wrote at the prophet's dictation was a single brief discourse. The work probably occupied a not inconsiderable time, as may be inferred from the datum of the ninth verse (*vid. infra*). Jeremiah would know that haste was incompatible with literary finish; he would probably feel that it was equally incompatible with the proper execution of what he had recognised as a Divine command. The prophet hardly had all his past utterances lying before him in the form of finished compositions. "And Jeremiah commanded Baruch, saying: I am detained (or confined); I cannot enter the house of Iahvah; so enter *thou*, and read in the roll, that thou wrotest from my mouth, the words of Iahvah, in the ears of the people, in the house of Iahvah, upon a day of fasting: and also in the ears of all Judah (the Jews), that come in (to the temple) from their (several) cities, thou shalt read them. Perchance their supplication will fall before Iahvah, and they will return, every one from his evil way; for great is the anger and the hot displeasure that Iahvah hath spoken (threatened) unto this people. And Baruch ben Neriah did according to all that Jeremiah the prophet commanded him, reading in the book the words of Iahvah in Iahvah's house." This last sentence might be regarded as a general statement, anticipative of the detailed account that follows, as is often the case in Old Testament narratives. But I doubt the application of this well-known exegetical device in the present instance. The verse is more likely an interpolation; unless we suppose that it refers to divers readings of which no particulars are given, but which preceded the memorable one described in the following verses. The injunction, "And also in the ears of all Judah that come out of their cities thou shalt read them!" might imply successive readings, as the people flocked into Jerusalem from time to time. But the grand occasion, if not the only one, was without doubt that which stands recorded in the text. "And it came to pass in the *fifth* year of Jehoiakim ben Josiah king of Judah, in the *ninth* month, they proclaimed a fast before Iahvah,—all the people in Jerusalem and all the people that were come out of the cities of Judah into Jerusalem. And Baruch read in the book the words of Jeremiah, in the house of Iahvah, in the cell of Gemariah ben Shaphan the scribe, in the upper (inner) court, at the entry of the new gate of Iahvah's house, in the ears of all the people." The dates have an important bearing upon the points we are considering. It was in the fourth year of Jehoiakim that the prophet was bidden to commit his oracles to writing. If, then, the task was not accomplished before the *ninth* month of the *fifth* year, it is plain that it involved a good deal more than penning such a discourse as the twenty-fifth chapter. This datum, in fact, strongly favours the supposition that it was a record of his principal utterances hitherto, that Jeremiah thus undertook and accomplished. It is not at all necessary to assume that on this or any other occasion Baruch read the entire contents of the roll to his audience in the temple. We are told that he "read *in* the book the words of Jeremiah," that is, no doubt, some portion of the whole. And so, in the famous scene before the king, it is not said that the entire work was read, but the contrary is expressly related (ver. 23): "And when Jehudi had read *three columns or four*, he (the king) began to cut it with the scribe's knife, and to cast it into the fire." Three or four columns of an ordinary roll might have contained the whole of the twenty-fifth chapter; and it must have been an unusually diminutive document, if the first three or four columns of it contained no more than the seven verses of chap. xxv. (3-6), which declare the sin of Judah, and announce the coming of the king of Babylon. And, apart from these objections, there is no ground for the presumption that "the purport of the roll which the king burnt was (only) that the king of Babylon should 'come and destroy this land.'" As the learned critic, from whom I have quoted these words, further remarks, with perfect truth, "Jeremiah had uttered many other important declarations in the course of his already long ministry."

That, I grant, is true; but then there is absolutely nothing to prove that this roll did not contain them all. Chap. xxxvi. 29, cited by the objector, is certainly not such proof. That verse simply gives the angry exclamation with which the king interrupted the reading of the roll, "Why hast thou written upon it, The king of Babylon shall surely come and destroy this land, and cause to cease from it man and beast?"

This may have been no more than Jehoiakim's very natural inference from some one of the many allusions to the enemy "from the north," which occur in the earlier part of the Book of Jeremiah. At all events, it is evident that, whether the king of Babylon was directly mentioned or not in the portion of the roll read in his presence, the verse in question assigns, not the sole import of the entire work, but only the particular point in it, which, at the existing crisis, especially roused the indignation of Jehoiakim. The 25th chapter may of course have been contained in the roll read before the king.

And this may suffice to show how precarious are the assertions of the learned critic in the "Encyclopædia Britannica" upon the subject of Jeremiah's roll. The plain truth seems to be that, perceiving the imminence of the peril that threatened his country, the prophet was impressed with the conviction that now was the time to commit his past utterances to writing; and that towards the end of the year, after he had formed and carried out this project, he found occasion to have his discourses read in the temple, to the crowds of rural folk who sought refuge in Jerusalem before the advance of Nebuchadrezzar. So Josephus understood the matter ("Ant.," x. 6, 2).

On the approach of the Babylonians, Jehoiakim made his submission; but only to rebel again, after three years of tribute and vassalage (2 Kings xxiv. 1). Drought and failure of the crops aggravated the political troubles of the country; evils in which Jeremiah was not slow to discern the hand of an offended and alienated God. "How long," he asks (xii. 4), "shall the country mourn, and the herbage of the whole field wither? From the wickedness of them that dwell therein the beasts and the birds perish." And in chap. xiv. we have a highly poetical description of the sufferings of the time.

"Judah mourneth, and her gates languish;
They sit in black on the ground;
And the outcry of Jerusalem hath gone up.
And their nobles, they sent their menial folk for water;
They came to the pits, they found no water;
They returned with their vessels empty;
They were ashamed and confounded and covered their head.
On account of ye ground that is chapt,
For rain hath not fallen in the land,
The ploughmen are ashamed—they cover their head.
For even the hind in the field—
She calveth and forsaketh her young;
For there is no grass.
And the wild asses, they stand on the scaurs;
They snuff the wind * like jackals;
Their eyes fail, for there is no herbage."

And then, after this graphic and almost dramatic portrayal of the sufferings of man and beast, in the blinding glare of the towns, and in the hot waterless plains, and on the bare hills, under that burning sky, whose cloudless splendours seemed to mock their misery, the prophet prays to the God of Israel.

"If our misdeeds answer against us,
O Iahvah, work for Thy name sake!
Verily, our fallings away are many;
Towards thee we are in fault.
Hope of Israel, that savest him in time of trouble!
Why shouldst thou be as a sojourner in the land,
And as a traveller, that turneth aside to pass the night?
Why shouldst thou be as a man stricken dumb,
As a champion that cannot save?
Yet Thou art in our midst, O Iahvah,
And Thy name is called over us:
Leave us not!"

* *i. e.*, to scent food afar off, like beasts of prey There was no occasion to alter A. V.

And again, at the end of the chapter,

"Hast Thou wholly rejected Judah?
Hath Thy soul loathed Zion?
Why hast Thou smitten us,
That there is no healing for us?
We looked for welfare, but bootlessly,
For a time of healing, and behold terror!
We know, Iahvah, our wickedness, the guilt of our fathers:
Verily, we are in fault toward Thee!
Be not scornful, for Thy name's sake!
Dishonour not Thy glorious throne! [*i. e.*, Jerusalem.]
Remember, break not Thy covenant with us!
Among the Vanities of the nations are there indeed raingivers?
Or the heavens, can they yield showers?
Art not Thou He (that doeth this), Iahvah our God?
And we wait for Thee,
For 'tis Thou that madest all this world."

In these and the like pathetic outpourings, which meet us in the later portions of the Old Testament, we may observe the gradual development of the dialect of stated prayer; the beginnings and the growth of that beautiful and appropriate liturgical language in which both the synagogue and the church afterwards found so perfect an instrument for the expression of all the harmonies of worship. Prayer, both public and private, was destined to assume an increasing importance, and, after the destruction of temple and altar, and the forcible removal of the people to a heathen land, to become the principal means of communion with God.

The evils of drought and dearth appear to have been accompanied by inroads of foreign enemies, who took advantage of the existing distress to rob and plunder at will. This serious aggravation of the national troubles is recorded in chap. xii. 7-17. There it is said, in the name of God, "I have left My house, I have cast off My heritage; I have given the Darling of My soul into the hands of her enemies." The reason is Judah's fierce hostility to her Divine Master: "Like a lion in the forest she hath uttered a cry against Me." The result of this unnatural rebellion is seen in the ravages of lawless invaders, probably nomads of the desert, always watching their opportunity, and greedy of the wealth, while disdainful of the pursuits of their civilised neighbours. It is as if all the wild beasts, that roam at large in the open country, had concerted a united attack upon a devoted land; as if many shepherds with their innumerable flocks had eaten bare and trodden down the vineyard of the Lord. "Over all the bald crags in the wilderness freebooters (Obad. 5) are come; for a sword of Iahweh's is devouring: from land's end to land's end no flesh hath security" (ver. 12). The rapacious and heathenish hordes of the desert, mere human wolves intent on ravage and slaughter, are a sword of the Lord's, for the chastisement of His people; just as the king of Babylon is His "servant" for the same purpose.

Only ten verses of the Book of Kings are occupied with the reign of Jehoiakim (2 Kings xxiii. 34-xxiv. 6); and when we compare that flying sketch with the allusions in Jeremiah, we cannot but keenly regret the loss of that "Book of the Chronicles of the Kings of Judah," to which the compiler of Kings refers as his authority. Had that work survived, many things in the prophets, which are now obscure and baffling, would have been clear and obvious. As it is, we are often obliged to be content with surmises and probabilities, where certainty would be right welcome. In the present instance, the facts alluded to by the prophet appear to be included in the statement that the Lord sent against Jehoiakim bands of Chaldeans, and bands of Arameans, and bands of Moabites, and bands of benê Ammon. The Hebrew term implies marauding or predatory bands, rather than regular armies, and it need not be supposed that they all fell upon the country at the same time or in accordance with any preconcerted scheme. In the midst of these troubles, Jehoiakim died in the flower of his age, having reigned no more than eleven years, and being only thirty-six years old (2 Kings xxiii. 36). The prophet thus alludes to his untimely end: "Like the partridge that sitteth on eggs that she hath not laid, so is he that maketh riches, and not by right: in the midst of his days they leave him; and in his last end he proveth a fool" (xvii. 11). We have already considered the detailed condemnation of this evil king in the 22d chapter. The prophet Habakkuk, a contemporary of Jeremiah, seems to have had Jehoiakim in his mind's eye, when denouncing (ii. 9) woe to one that "getteth an evil gain for his house, that he may set his nest on high, that he may escape from the hand of evil!" The allusion is to the forced labour on his new palace, and on the defences of Jerusalem, as well as to the fines and presents of money, which this oppressive ruler shamelessly extorted from his unhappy subjects. "The stone out of the wall," says the prophet, "crieth out; and the beam out of the woodwork answereth it."

The premature death of the tyrant removed a serious obstacle from the path of Jeremiah. No longer forced to exercise a wary vigilance in avoiding the vengeance of a king whose passions determined his conduct, the prophet could now devote himself heart and soul to the work of his office. The public danger, imminent from the north, and the way to avert it, is the subject of the discourses of this period of his ministry. His unquenchable faith appears in the beautiful prayer appended to his reflections upon the death of Jehoiakim (xvii. 12 *sqq.*). We cannot mistake the tone of quiet exultation with which he expresses his sense of the absolute righteousness of the catastrophe. "A throne of glory, a height higher than the first (?), (or, higher than any before) is the place of our sanctuary." Never before in the prophet's experience has the God of Israel so clearly vindicated that justice which is the inalienable attribute of His dread tribunal.

For himself, the immediate result of this renewal of an activity that had been more or less suspended, was persecution, and even violence. The earnestness with which he besought the people to honestly keep the law of the Sabbath, an obligation which was recognised in theory though disregarded in practice; and his striking illustration of the true relations between Iahvah and Israel as parallel to those that hold between the potter and the clay (chap. xvii. 19 *sqq.*), only brought down upon him the fierce hostility and organised opposition of the false prophets, and the priests, and the credulous and self-willed populace, as we read in chap. xviii. 18 *sqq.* "And they said, Come, and let us contrive plots against Jeremiah. . . Come, and let us smite him with the tongue, and let us not listen to any of his words. Should evil be repaid for good, that they have digged a pit for my life?" And after his solemn testimony before the elders in the valley of Ben-Hinnom, and before the people generally, in the court of the Lord's house (chap. xix.), the prophet was seized by order of Pashchûr, the commandant of the temple, who was himself a leading false prophet, and cruelly beaten, and set in the stocks for a day and a night. That the spirit of the prophet was not broken by this shameful treatment is evident from the courage with which he confronted his oppressor on the morrow, and foretold his certain punishment. But the apparent failure of his mission, the hopelessness of his life's labour, indicated by the deepening hostility of the people, and the readiness to proceed to extremities against him thus evinced by their leaders, wrung from Jeremiah that bitter cry of despair, which has proved such a stumbling-block to some of his modern apologists.

Soon the prophet's fears were realised, and the Divine counsel, of which he alone had been cognisant, was fulfilled. Within three short months of his accession to the throne, the boy-king Jeconiah (or Jehoiachin or Coniah), with the queen-mother, the grandees of the court, and the pick of the population of the capital, was carried captive to Babylon by Nebuchadrezzar (2 Kings xxiv. 8 *sqq.*; Jer. xxiv. 1).

Jeremiah has appended his forecast of the fate of Jeconiah, and a brief notice of its fulfilment, to his denunciations of that king's predecessors (xxii. 24 *sqq.*). "As I live, saith Iahvah, verily, though Coniah ben Jehoiakim king of Judah be a signet ring upon My own right hand, verily thence will I pluck thee away! And I will give thee into the hand of them that seek thy life, and into the hand of those of whom thou art afraid; and into the hand of Nebuchadrezzar king of Babel, and into the hand of the Chaldeans. And I will cast thee forth, and thy mother that bare thee, into the foreign land, wherein ye were not born; and there ye shall die. But unto the land whither they long to return, thither shall they not return. Is this man Coniah a despised broken vase, or a vessel devoid of charm? Why were he and his offspring cast forth, and hurled into the land that they knew not? O land, land, land, hear thou the word of Iahvah. Thus hath Iahvah said, Write ye down this man childless, a person that shall not prosper in his days: for none of his offspring shall prosper, sitting on the throne of David, and ruling again in Judah."

No better success attended the prophet's ministry under the new king Zedekiah, whom Nebuchadrezzar had placed on the throne as his vassal and tributary. So far as we can judge from the accounts left us, Zedekiah was a well-meaning but unstable character, whose weakness and irresolution were too often played upon by unscrupulous and scheming courtiers, to the fatal miscarriage of right and justice. Soon the old intrigues began again, and in the fourth year of the new reign (xxviii. 1) envoys from the neighbour-states arrived at the Jewish court, with the object of drawing Judah into a coalition against the common suzerain, the king of Babylon. This suicidal policy of combination with heathenish and treacherous allies, most of whom were the heirs of immemorial feuds with Judah, against a sovereign who was at once the most powerful and the most enlightened of his time, called forth the prophet's immediate and strenuous opposition. Boldly affirming that Iahvah had conferred universal dominion upon Nebuchadrezzar, and that consequently all resistance was futile, he warned Zedekiah himself to bow his neck to the yoke, and dismiss all thought of rebellion. It would seem that about this time (*circ.* 596 B. C.) the empire of Babylon was passing through a serious crisis, which the subject peoples of the West hoped and expected would result in its speedy dissolution. Nebuchadrezzar was, in fact, engaged in a life-and-death struggle with the Medes; and the knowledge that the Great King was thus fully occupied elsewhere, encouraged the petty princes of Phœnicia-Palestine in their projects of revolt. If chaps. l., li., are genuine, it was at this juncture that Jeremiah foretold the fall of Babylon; for, at the close of the prophecy in question (li. 59), it is said that he gave a copy of it to one of the princes who accompanied Zedekiah to Babylon "in the fourth year of his reign," *i. e.*, in 596 B. C. But the style and thought of these two chapters, and the general posture of things which they presuppose, are decisive against the view that they belong to Jeremiah. At all events the prophet gave the clearest evidence that he did not himself share in the general delusion that the fall of Babylon was near at hand. He declared that all the nations must be content to serve Nebuchadrezzar, and his son, and his son's son (xxvii. 7); and as chap. xxix. shows, he did his best to counteract the evil influence of those fanatical visionaries who were ever promising a speedy restoration to the exiles who had been deported to Babylon with Jeconiah. At last, however, in spite of all Jeremiah's warnings and entreaties, the vacillating king Zedekiah was persuaded to rebel; and the natural consequence followed—the Chaldeans appeared before Jerusalem. King and people had refused salvation, and were now no more to be saved.

During the siege the prophet was more than once anxiously consulted by the king as to the issue of the crisis. Although kept in ward by Zedekiah's orders, lest he should weaken the defence by his discouraging addresses, Jeremiah showed that he was far above the feeling of private ill-will, by the answers he returned to his sovereign's inquiries. It is true that he did not at all modify the burden of his message; to the king as to the people he steadily counselled surrender. But strongly as he denounced further resistance, he did not predict the king's death; and the tone of his prophecy concerning Zedekiah is in striking contrast with that concerning his predecessor Jehoiakim. It was in the tenth year of Zedekiah and the eighteenth of Nebuchadrezzar, that is to say, *circ.* 589 B. C., when Jeremiah was imprisoned in the court of the royal guard, within the precincts of the palace (xxxii. 1 *sqq.*): when the siege of Jerusalem was being pressed on with vigour, and when of all the strong cities of Judah, only two, Lachish and Azekah, were still holding out against the Chaldean blockade; that the prophet thus addressed the king (xxxiv. 2 *sqq.*): "Thus hath Iahvah said, Behold, I am about to give this city into the hand of the king of Babel, and he shall burn it with fire. And thou wilt not escape out of his hand; for thou wilt certainly be taken, and into his hand thou wilt be given. And thine eyes shall see the king of Babel's eyes, and his mouth shall speak with thy mouth, and to Babel wilt thou come. But hear thou Iahvah's word, O Zedekiah king of Judah! Thus hath Iahvah said upon thee, Thou wilt not die by the sword. In peace wilt thou die; and with the burnings of thy fathers, the former kings that were before thee, so will men burn (spicery) for thee, and with Ah, Lord! will they wail for thee; for a promise have *I* given, saith Iahvah." Zedekiah was to be exempted from the violent death, which then seemed so probable; and was to enjoy the funeral honours of a king, unlike his less worthy brother Jehoiakim, whose body was cast out to decay unburied, like that of a beast. The failure of Jeremiah's earnest and consistent endeavours to bring about the submission of his people to what he foresaw to be their inevitable destiny, is explained by the popular confidence in the defences of Jerusalem, which were enormously strong for the time, and were considered impregnable (xxi. 13); and by the hopes entertained that Egypt, with whom negotiations had long been in progress, would raise the siege ere it was too late. The low state of public morals is vividly illustrated by an incident which the prophet has recorded (chap. xxxiv. 7 *sqq.*). In the terror inspired by the approach of the Chaldeans, the panic-stricken populace of the capital bethought them of that law of their God which they had so long set at naught; and the king and his princes and the entire people bound themselves by a solemn covenant in the temple, to release all slaves of Israelitish birth, who had served six years and upwards, according to the law. The enfranchisement was accomplished with all the sanctions of law and of religion; but no sooner had the Chaldeans retired from before Jerusalem in order to meet the advancing army of Egypt, than the solemn covenant was cynically and shamelessly violated, and the unhappy freedmen were recalled to their bondage. After this, further warning was evidently out of place; and nothing was left for Jeremiah but to denounce the outrage upon the majesty of heaven, and to declare the speedy return of the besiegers and the desolation of Jerusalem. His own liberty had not yet been restricted (xxxvii. 4) when these events happened; but a pretext was soon found for venting upon him the malice of his enemies. After assuring the king that the respite was not to be permanent, but that Pharaoh's army would return to Egypt without accomplishing any deliverance, and that the Chaldeans would "come again, and fight against the city, and take it, and burn it with fire" (xxxvii. 8), Jeremiah availed himself of the temporary absence of the besieging forces, to attempt to leave his City of Destruction; but he was arrested in the gate by which he was going out, and brought before the princes on a charge of attempted desertion to the enemy. Ridiculous as was this accusation, when thus levelled against one whose whole life was conspicuous for sufferings entailed by a lofty and unflinching patriotism and a devotion, at the time almost unique, to the sacred cause of religion and morality; it was at once received and acted upon. Jeremiah was beaten and thrown into a dungeon, where he languished for a long time in subterranean darkness and misery, until the king desired to consult him again. This was the saving of the prophet's life; for after once more declaring his unalterable message, בְּיַד מֶלֶךְ בָּבֶל תִּנָּתֵן, "Into the king of Babel's hand thou wilt be given!" he made indignant protest against his cruel wrongs, and obtained from Zedekiah some mitigation of his sentence. He was not sent back to the loathsome den under the house of Jonathan the scribe, in whose dark recesses he had well-nigh perished (xxxvii. 20), but was detained in the court of the guard, receiving a daily dole of bread for his maintenance. Here he appears to have still used such opportunity as he had, in dissuading the people from continuing the defence. At all events, four of the princes induced the king to deliver him into their power, on the ground that he "weakened the hands of the men of war," and sought not the welfare but the hurt of the nation (xxxviii. 4). Unwilling for some reason or other, probably a superstitious one, to imbrue their hands in the prophet's blood, they let him down with cords into a miry cistern (בּוֹר) in the court of the guard, and left him there to die of cold and hunger. Timely help sanctioned by the king rescued Jeremiah from this horrible fate; but not before he had undergone sufferings of the severest character, as may easily be understood from his own simple narrative, and from the indelible impression wrought upon others by the record of his sufferings, which led the poet of the Lamentations to refer to this time of deadly peril, and torture both mental and physical, in the following terms:

"They chased me sore like a bird,
They that were my foes without a cause.
They silenced my life in the pit,
And they cast a stone upon me.
Waters overflowed mine head;
Methought, I am cut off.
I called Thy name, Iahvah,
Out of the deepest pit.
My voice Thou heardest (saying),
'Hide not Thine ear at my breathing, at my cry.'
Thou drewest nearer when I called Thee;
Thou saidst, 'Fear not'!
Thou pleadedst, O Lord, my soul's pleadings;
Thou ransomedst my life."

After this signal escape, Jeremiah's counsel was once more sought by the king, in a secret interview, which was jealously concealed from the princes. But neither entreaties, nor assurances of safety, could persuade Zedekiah to surrender the city. Nothing was now left for the prophet but to await, in his milder captivity, the long foreseen catastrophe. The form now taken by his solitary musings was not anxious speculation upon the question whether any possible resources were as yet unexhausted, whether by any yet untried means king and people might be convinced, and the end averted. Taking that end for granted, he looks forth beyond his own captivity, beyond the scenes of famine and pestilence and bloodshed that surround him, beyond the strife of factions within the city, and the lines of the besiegers without it, to a fair prospect of happy restoration and smiling peace, reserved for his ruined country in the far-off yet ever-approaching future (xxxii., xxxiii.).

Strong in this inspired confidence, like the Roman who purchased at its full market value the ground on which the army of Hannibal lay encamped, he did not hesitate to buy, with all due formalities of transfer, a field in his native place, at this supreme moment, when the whole country was wasted with fire and sword, and the artillery of the foe was thundering at the walls of Jerusalem. And the event proved that he was right. He believed in the depth of his heart that God had not finally cast off His people. He believed that nothing, not even human error and revolt, could thwart and turn aside the Eternal purposes. He was sure—it was demonstrated to him by the experience of an eventful life—that, amid all the vicissitudes of men and things, one thing stands immutable, and that is the will of God. He was sure that Abraham's family had not become a nation merely in order to be blotted out of existence by a conqueror who knew not Iahvah; that the torch of a true religion, a spiritual faith, had not been handed on from prophet to prophet, burning in its onward course with an ever clearer and intenser flame, merely to be swallowed up before its final glory was attained, in utter and eternal darkness. The covenant with Israel would no more be broken than the covenant of day and night (xxxiii. 20). The laws of the natural world are not more stable and secure than those of the spiritual realm; for both have their reason and their ground of prevalence in the Will of the One Unchangeable Lord of all. And as the prophet had been right in his forecast of the destruction of his country, so did he prove to have been right in his joyful anticipation of the future renascence of all the best elements in Israel's life. The coming time fulfilled his word; a fact which must always remain unaccountable to all but those who believe as Jeremiah believed.

After the fall of the city special care was taken to ensure the safety of Jeremiah, in accordance with the express orders of Nebuchadrezzar, who had become cognisant of the prophet's consistent advocacy of surrender, probably from the exiles previously deported to Babylonia, with whom Jeremiah had maintained communications, advising them to settle down peaceably, accepting Babylon as their country for the time being, and praying for its welfare and that of its rulers. Nebuzaradan, the commander-in-chief, further allowed the prophet his choice between following him to Babylon, or remaining with the wreck of the population in the ruined country. Patriotism, which in his case was identified with a burning zeal for the moral and spiritual welfare of his fellow-countrymen, prevailed over regard for his own worldly interests; and Jeremiah chose to remain with the survivors—disastrously for himself, as the event proved (xxxix. 11, xl. 1).

An old man, worn out with strife and struggle, and weighed down by disappointment and the sense of failure, he might well have decided to avail himself of the favour extended to him by the conqueror, and to secure a peaceful end for a life of storm and conflict. But the calamities of his country had not quenched his prophetic ardour; the sacred fire still burnt within his aged spirit; and once more he sacrificed himself to the work he felt called upon to do, only to experience again the futility of offering wise counsel to head-strong, proud, and fanatical natures. Against his earnest protestations, he was forced to accompany the remnant of his people in their hasty flight into Egypt (xlii.); and, in the last glimpse afforded us, we see him there among his fellow-exiles making a final, and alas! ineffectual protest against their stubborn idolatry (xliv.). A tradition mentioned by Tertullian and St. Jerome which may be of earlier and Jewish origin, states that these apostates in their wicked rage against the prophet stoned him to death (*cf.* Heb. xi. 37).

The last chapter of his book brings the course of events down to about 561 B. C. The fact has naturally suggested a conjecture that the same year witnessed the close of the prophet's life. In that case, Jeremiah must have attained to an age of somewhere about ninety years; which, taking all the circumstances into consideration, is hardly credible. A celibate life is said to be unfavourable to longevity; but however that may be, the other conditions in this instance make it extremely unlikely. Jeremiah's career was a vexed and stormy one; it was his fate to be divided from his kindred and his fellow-countrymen by the widest and deepest differences of belief; like St. Athanasius, he was called upon to maintain the cause of truth against an opposing world. "Woe's me, my mother!" he cries, in one of his characteristic fits of despondency, which were the natural fruit of a passionate and almost feminine nature, after a period of noble effort ending in the shame of utter defeat; "Woe's me, that thou gavest me birth, a man of strife, and a man of contention to all the land! Neither lender nor borrower have I been; yet all are cursing me" (xv. 10). The persecutions he endured, the cruelties of his long imprisonment, the horrors of the protracted siege, upon which he has not dwelt at length, but which have stamped themselves indelibly upon his language (xviii. 21, 22, xx. 16), would certainly not tend to prolong his life. In the 71st Psalm, which seems to be from his pen, and which wants the usual heading "A Psalm of David," he speaks of himself as conscious of failing powers, and as having already reached the extreme limit of age. Writing after his narrow escape from death in the miry cistern of his prison, he prays

"Cast me not off in the time of old age ;
Forsake me not, when my strength faileth."

And again,

"Yea, even when I am old and grey-headed,
O God forsake me not!"

And, referring to his signal deliverance,

"Thou that shewedst me many and sore troubles,
Thou makest me live again ;
And out of the deeps of the earth again Thou bringest me up."

The allusion in the 90th Psalm, as well as the case of Barzillai, who is described as extremely old and decrepit at fourscore (2 Sam. xix. 33), proves that life in ancient Palestine did not ordinarily transcend the limits of seventy to eighty years. Still, after all that may be urged to the contrary, Jeremiah may have been an exception to his contemporaries in this, as in most other respects. Indeed, his protracted labours and sufferings seem almost to imply that he was endowed with constitutional vigour and powers of endurance above the average of men; and if, as some suppose, he wrote the book of Job in Egypt, to embody the fruits of his life's experience and reflection, as well as arranged and edited his other writings, it is evident that he must have sojourned among the exiles in that country for a considerable time.

The tale is told. In meagre and broken outline I have laid before you the known facts of a life which must always possess permanent interest, not only for the student of religious development, but for all men who are stirred by human passion and stimulated by human thought. And fully conscious as I am of failure in the attempt to reanimate the dry bones of history, to give form and colour and movement to the shadows of the past; I shall not have spent my pains for naught, if I have awakened in a single heart some spark of living interest in the heroes of old; some enthusiasm for the martyrs of faith; some secret yearning to cast in their own lot with those who have fought the battle of truth and righteousness, and to share with the saints departed in the victory that overcometh the world. And even if in this also I have fallen short of the mark, these desultory and imperfect sketches of a good man's life and work will not have been wholly barren of result, if they lead any one of my readers to renewed study of that truly sacred text which preserves to all time the living utterances of this last of the greater prophets.

CHAPTER I.

THE CALL AND CONSECRATION.

In the foregoing pages we have considered the principal events in the life of the prophet Jeremiah, by way of introduction to the more detailed study of his writings. Preparation of this kind seemed to be necessary, if we were to enter upon that study with something more than the vaguest perception of the real personality of the prophet. On the other hand, I hope we shall not fail to find our mental image of the man, and our conception of the times in which he lived, and of the conditions under which he laboured as a servant of God, corrected and perfected by that closer examination of his works to which I now invite you. And so we shall be better equipped for the attainment of that which must be the ultimate object of all such studies; the deepening and strengthening of the life of faith in ourselves, by which alone we can hope to follow in the steps of the saints of old, and like them to realise the great end of our being, the service of the All-Perfect.

I shall consider the various discourses in what appears to be their natural order, so far as possible, taking those chapters together which appear to be connected in occasion and subject. Chap. i. evidently stands apart, as a self-complete and independent whole. It consists of a chronological superscription (vv. 1-3), assigning the temporal limits of the prophet's activity; and secondly, of an inaugural discourse, which sets before us his first call, and the general scope of the mission which he was chosen to fulfil. This discourse, again, in like manner falls into two sections, of which the former (vv. 4-10) relates how the prophet was appointed and qualified by Iahvah to be a spokesman for Him; while the latter (vv. 11-19), under the form of two visions, expresses the assurance that Iahvah will accomplish His word, and pictures the mode of fulfilment, closing with a renewed summons to enter upon the work, and with a promise of effectual support against all opposition.

It is plain that we have before us the author's introduction to the whole book; and if we would gain an adequate conception of the meaning of the prophet's activity both for his own time and for ours, we must weigh well the force of these prefatory words. The career of a true prophet, or spokesman for God, undoubtedly implies a special call or vocation to the office. In this preface to the summarised account of his life's work, Jeremiah represents that call as a single and definite event in his life's history. Must we take this in its literal sense? We are not astonished by such a statement as "the word of the Lord came unto me;" it may be understood in more senses than one, and perhaps we are unconsciously prone to understand it in what is called a natural sense. Perhaps we think of a result of pious reflection pondering the moral state of the nation and the needs of the time: perhaps of that inward voice which is nothing strange to any soul that has attained to the rudiments of spiritual development. But when we read such an assertion as that of ver. 9, "Then the Lord put forth His hand, and touched my mouth," we cannot but pause and ask what it was that the writer meant to convey by words so strange and startling. Thoughtful readers cannot avoid the question whether such statements are consonant with what we otherwise know of the dealings of God with man; whether an outward and visible act of the kind spoken of conforms with that whole conception of the Divine Being, which is, so far as it reflects reality, the outcome of His own contact with our human spirits. The obvious answer is that such corporeal actions are incompatible with all our experience and all our reasoned conceptions of the Divine Essence, which fills all things and controls all things, precisely because it is not limited by a bodily organism, because its actions are not dependent upon such imperfect and restricted media as hands and feet. If, then, we are bound to a literal sense, we can only understand that the prophet saw a vision, in which a Divine hand seemed to touch his lips, and a Divine voice to sound in his ears. But *are* we bound to a literal sense? It is noteworthy that Jeremiah does not say that Iahvah Himself appeared to him. In this respect, he stands in conspicuous contrast with his predecessor Isaiah, who writes (vi. 1), "In the year that king Uzziah died, I saw the Lord sitting upon a throne, high and lifted up;" and with his successor Ezekiel, who affirms in his opening verse (i. 1) that on a certain definite occasion "the heavens opened," and he saw "visions of God." Nor does Jeremiah use that striking phrase of the younger prophet's, "The hand of Iahvah was upon me," or "was strong upon me." But when he says, "Iahvah put forth His hand and touched my mouth," he is evidently thinking of the seraph that touched Isaiah's mouth with the live coal from the heavenly altar (vi. 7). The words are identical (על פי ויגע), and might be regarded as a quotation. It is true that, supposing Jeremiah to be relating the experience of a trance-like condition or ecstasy, we need not assume any conscious imitation of his predecessor. The sights and sounds which affect a man in such a condition may be partly repetitions of former experience, whether one's own or that of others; and in part wholly new and strange. In a dream one might imagine things happening to oneself, which one had heard or read of in connection with others. And Jeremiah's writings generally prove his intimate acquaintance with those of Isaiah and the older prophets. But as a trance or ecstasy is itself an involuntary state, so the thoughts and feelings of the subject of it must be independent of the individual will, and as it were imposed from without. Is then the prophet describing the experience of such an abnormal state—a state like that of St. Peter in his momentous vision on the housetop at Joppa, or like that of St. Paul when he was "caught up to the third heaven," and saw many wonderful things which he durst not reveal? The question has been answered in the negative on two principal grounds. It is said that the vision of vv. 11, 12, derives its significance not from the visible thing itself, but from the name of it, which is, of course, not an object of sight at all; and consequently, the so-called vision is really "a well-devised and ingenious product of cool reflection." But is this so? We may translate the original passage thus: "And there fell a word of Iahvah unto me, saying, What seest thou, Jeremiah? And I said, A rod of a wake-tree" (*i. e.*, an almond) "is what I see. And Iahvah said unto me, Thou hast well seen; for wakeful am I over My word, to do it." Doubtless there is here one of those plays on words which are so well known a feature of the prophetic style; but to admit this is by no means tantamount to an admission that the vision derives its force and meaning from the "invisible name" rather than from the visible thing. Surely it is plain that the significance of the vision depends on the fact which the name implies; a fact which would be at once suggested by the sight of the tree. It is the well-known characteristic of the almond tree that it wakes, as it were, from the long sleep of winter before all other trees, and displays its beautiful garland of blossom, while its companions remain leafless and apparently lifeless. This quality of early wakefulness is expressed by the Hebrew name of the almond tree; for *shāqēd* means *waking* or *wakeful*. If this tree, in virtue of its remarkable peculiarity, was a proverb of watching and waking, the sight of it, or of a branch of it, in a prophetic vision would be sufficient to suggest that idea, independently of the name. The allusion to the name, therefore, is only a literary device for expressing with inimitable force and neatness the sigificance of the visible symbol of the "rod of the almond tree," as it was intuitively apprehended by the prophet in his vision.

Another and more radical ground is discovered in the substance of the Divine communication. It is said that the anticipatory statement of the contents and purpose of the subsequent prophesyings of the seer (ver. 10), the announcement beforehand of his fortunes (vv. 8, 18, 19), and the warning addressed to the prophet personally (ver. 17), are only conceivable as results of a process of abstraction from real experience, as prophecies conformed to the event (*ex eventu*). "The call of the prophet," says the writer whose arguments we are examining, "was the moment when, battling down the doubts and scruples of the natural man (vv. 7, 8), and full of holy courage, he took the resolution (ver. 17) to proclaim God's word. Certainly he was animated by the hope of Divine assistance (ver. 18), the promise of which he heard inwardly in the heart. More than this cannot be affirmed. But in this chapter (vv. 17, 18), the measure and direction of the Divine help are already clear to the writer; he is aware that opposition awaits him (ver. 19); he knows the content of his prophecies (ver. 10). Such knowledge was only possible for him in the middle or at the end of his career; and therefore the composition of this opening chapter must be referred to such a later period. As, however, the final catastrophe, after which his language would have taken a wholly different complexion, is still hidden from him here; and as the only edition of his prophecies prepared by himself, that we know of, belongs to the fourth year of Jehoiakim (xxxvi. 45); the section is best referred to that very time, when the posture of affairs promised well for the fulfilment of the threatenings of many years (*cf.* xxv. 9 with vv. 15, 10; xxv. 13 with vv. 12-17; xxv. 6 with ver. 16. And ver. 18 is virtually repeated, chap. xv. 20, which belongs to the same period)."

The first part of this is an obvious inference from the narrative itself. The prophet's own statement makes it abundantly clear that his conviction of a call was accompanied by doubts and fears, which were only silenced by that faith which moves mountains. That lofty confidence in the purpose and strength of the Unseen, which has enabled weak and trembling humanity to endure martyrdom, might well be sufficient to nerve a young man to undertake the task of preaching unpopular truths, even at the risk of frequent persecution and occasional peril. But surely we need not suppose that, when Jeremiah started on his prophetic career, he was as one who takes a leap in the dark. Surely it is not necessary to suppose him profoundly ignorant of the subject-matter of prophecy in general, of the kind of success he might look for, of his own shrinking timidity and desponding temperament, of "the measure and direction of the Divine help." Had the son of Hilkiah been the first of the prophets of Israel instead of one of the latest; had there been no prophets before him; we might recognise some force in this criticism. As the facts lie, however, we can hardly avoid an obvious answer. With the experience of many notable predecessors before his eyes; with the message of a Hosea, an Amos, a Micah, an Isaiah, graven upon his heart; with his minute knowledge of their history, their struggles and successes, the fierce antagonisms they roused, the cruel persecutions they were called upon to face in the discharge of their Divine commission; with his profound sense that nothing but the good help of their God had enabled them to endure the strain of a lifelong battle; it is not in the least wonderful that Jeremiah should have foreseen the like experience for himself. The wonder would have been, if, with such speaking examples before him, he had not anticipated "the measure and direction of the Divine help"; if he had been ignorant "that opposition awaited him"; if he had not already possessed a general knowledge of the "contents" of his own as of all prophecies. For there is a substantial unity underlying all the manifold outpourings of the prophetic spirit. Indeed, it would seem that it is to the diversity of personal gifts, to differences of training and temperament, to the rich variety of character and circumstance, rather than to any essential contrasts in the substance and purport of prophecy itself, that the absence of monotony, the impress of individuality and originality is due, which characterises the utterances of the principal prophets.

Apart from the unsatisfactory nature of the reasons alleged, it is very probable that this opening chapter was penned by Jeremiah as an introduction to the first collection of his prophecies, which dates from the fourth year of Jehoiakim, that is, *circ.* B. C. 606. In that case, it must not be forgotten that the prophet is relating events which, as he tells us himself (chap. xxv. 3), had taken place three and twenty years ago; and as his description is probably drawn from memory, something may be allowed for unconscious transformation of facts in the light of after experience. Still, the peculiar events that attended so marked a crisis in his life as his first consciousness of a Divine call must, in any case, have constituted, cannot but have left a deep and abiding impress upon the prophet's memory; and there really seems to be no good reason for refusing to believe that that initial experience took the form of a twofold vision seen under conditions of trance or ecstasy. At the same time, bearing in mind the Oriental passion for metaphor and imagery, we are not perhaps debarred from seeing in the whole chapter a figurative description, or rather an attempt to describe through the medium of figurative language, that which must always ultimately transcend description—the communion of the Divine with the human spirit. Real, most real of real facts, as that communion was and is, it can never be directly communicated in words; it can only be hinted and suggested through the medium of symbolic and metaphorical phraseology. Language itself, being more than half material, breaks down in the attempt to express things wholly spiritual.

I shall not stop to discuss the importance of the general superscription or heading of the book, which is given in the first three years. But before passing on, I will ask you to notice that, whereas the Hebrew text opens with the phrase "Dibrê Yirmeyáhu (דִּבְרֵי יִרְמְיָהוּ), "The words of Jeremiah," the oldest translation we have, viz., the Septuagint, reads: "The word of God which came to Jeremiah" (τὸ ῥῆμα τοῦ Θεοῦ ὃ ἐγένετο ἐπὶ Ἰερεμίαν. It is possible, therefore, that the old Greek translator had a Hebrew text different from that which has come down to us, and opening with the same formula which we find at the beginning of the older prophets Hosea, Joel, and Micah. In fact, Amos is the only prophet, besides Jeremiah, whose book begins with the phrase in question דברי עמוס—Λόγοι Ἀμώς); and although it is more appropriate there than here, owing to the continuation "And he said," it looks suspicious even there, when we compare Isaiah i. 1, and observe how much more suitable the term "vision" (חֲזוֹן) would be. It is likely that the LXX. has preserved the original reading of Jeremiah, and that some editor of the Hebrew text altered it because of the apparent tautology with the opening of ver. 2: "To whom the word of the Lord" (LXX. τοῦ Θεοῦ) "came" in the "days of Josiah."

Such changes were freely made by the scribes in the days before the settlement of the O. T. canon; changes which may occasion much perplexity to those, if any there be, who hold by the unintelligent and obsolete theory of verbal and even literal inspiration, but none at all to such as recognise a Divine hand in the facts of history,* and are content to believe that in holy books, as in holy men, there is a Divine treasure in earthen vessels. The textual difference in question may serve to call our attention to the peculiar way in which the prophets identified their work with the Divine will, and their words with the Divine thoughts; so that the words of an Amos or a Jeremiah were in all good faith held and believed to be self-attesting utterances of the Unseen God. The conviction which wrought in them was, in fact, identical with that which in after times moved St. Paul to affirm

* Even in the history of the transmission of ancient writings.

the high calling and inalienable dignity of the Christian ministry in those impressive words, "Let a man so account of us as of the ministers of Christ, and stewards of the mysteries of God."

Vv. 5-10, which relate how the prophet became aware that he was in future to receive revelations from above, constitute in themselves an important revelation. Under Divine influence he becomes aware of a special mission. "Ere I began to form" (mould, fashion, יצר, as the potter moulds the clay) "thee in the belly, I knew thee; and ere thou begannest to come forth from the womb,* I had dedicated thee, not 'regarded' thee as holy," Isa. viii. 13; nor perhaps "'declared' thee holy," as Ges.; but "'hallowed' thee," *i. e.*, dedicated thee to God (Judg. xvii. 3; 1 Kings ix. 3; especially Lev. xxvii. 14; of money and houses. The pi. of "consecrating" priests, Ex. xxviii. 41; altar, Ex. xxix. 36, temple, mountain, etc.); perhaps also, "'consecrated' thee" for the discharge of a sacred office. Even soldiers are called "consecrated" (מקדשים Isa. xiii. 3), as ministers of the Lord of Hosts, and probably as having been formally devoted to His service at the outset of a campaign by special solemnities of lustration and sacrifice; while guests bidden to a sacrificial feast had to undergo a preliminary form of "consecration" (1 Sam. xvi. 5; Zeph. i. 7), to fit them for communion with Deity.

With the certainty of his own Divine calling, it became clear to the prophet that the choice was not an arbitrary caprice; it was the execution of a Divine purpose, conceived long, long before its realisation in time and space. The God whose foreknowledge and will direct the whole course of human history—whose control of events and direction of human energies is most signally evident in precisely those instances where men and nations are most regardless of Him, and imagine the vain thought that they are independent of Him (Isa. xxii. 11, xxxvii. 26)—this sovereign Being, in the development of whose eternal purposes he himself, and every son of man was necessarily a factor, had from the first "known him,"—known the individual character and capacities which would constitute his fitness for the special work of his life;—and "sanctified" him; devoted and consecrated him to the doing of it when the time of his earthly manifestation should arrive. Like others who have played a notable part in the affairs of men, Jeremiah saw with clearest vision that he was himself the embodiment in flesh and blood of a Divine idea; he knew himself to be a deliberately planned and chosen instrument of the Divine activity. It was this seeing himself as God saw him which constituted his difference from his fellows, who only knew their individual appetites, pleasures, and interests, and were blinded, by their absorption in these, to the perception of any higher reality. It was the coming to this knowledge of "himself," of the meaning and purpose of HIS individual unity of powers and aspirations in the great universe of being, of his true relation to God and to man, which constituted the first revelation to Jeremiah, and which was the secret of his personal greatness.

This knowledge, however, might have come to him in vain. Moments of illumination are not always accompanied by noble resolves and corresponding actions. It does not follow that, because a man sees his calling, he will at once renounce *all*, and pursue it. Jeremiah would not have been human, had he not hesitated a while, when, after the inward light, came the voice, "A spokesman," or Divine interpreter (נביא), "to the nations appoint I thee." To have passing flashes of spiritual insight and heavenly inspiration is one thing; to undertake *now*, in the actual present, the course of conduct which they unquestionably indicate and involve, is quite another. And so, when the hour of spiritual illumination has passed, the darkness may and often does become deeper than before.

"And I said, Alas! O Lord Iahvah, behold I know not how to speak; for I am but a youth." The words express that reluctance to begin which a sense of unpreparedness, and misgivings about the unknown future, naturally inspire. To take the first step demands decision and confidence; but confidence and decision do not come of contemplating oneself and one's own unfitness or unpreparedness, but of steadfastly fixing our regards upon God, who will qualify us for all that He requires us to do. Jeremiah does not refuse to obey His call; the very words "My Lord Iahvah"—'Adonai, Master, or my Master—imply a recognition of the Divine right to his service; he merely alleges a natural objection. The cry, "Who is sufficient for these things?" rises to his lips, when the light and the glory are obscured for a moment, and the reaction and despondency natural to human weakness ensue. "And Iahvah said unto me, Say not, I am but a youth; for unto all that I send thee unto, thou shalt go, and all that I command thee thou shalt speak. Be not afraid of them; for with thee am I to rescue thee, is the utterance of Iahvah." "Unto all that I send thee unto"; for he was to be no local prophet; his messages were to be addressed to the surrounding peoples as well as to Judah; his outlook as a seer was to comprise the entire political horizon (ver. 10, xxv. 9, 15, xlvi. *sqq.*). Like Moses (Ex. iv. 10), Jeremiah objects that he is no practised speaker; and this on account of youthful inexperience. The answer is that his speaking will depend not so much upon himself as upon God: "All that I command thee, thou shalt speak." The allegation of his youth also covers a feeling of timidity, which would naturally be excited at the thought of encountering kings and princes and priests, as well as the common people, in the discharge of such a commission. This implication is met by the Divine assurance: "Unto all"—of whatever rank—"that I send thee unto, thou shalt go"; and by the encouraging promise of Divine protection against all opposing powers: "Be not afraid of them; for with thee am I to rescue thee." *

"And Iahvah put forth His hand and touched my mouth: and Iahvah said unto me, Behold I have put My words in thy mouth!" This word of the Lord, says Hitzig, is represented as a corporeal substance; in accordance with the Oriental mode of thought and speech, which invests everything with bodily form. He refers to a passage in Samuel (2 Sam. xvii. 5) where Absalom says, "Call now Hushai the Archite, and let us hear *that which is in his mouth* also;" as if what the old counsellor had to say were something *solid* in more senses than one. But we need not press the literal force of the language. A prophet who could write (v. 14): "Behold I am about to make my words in thy

* Isa. xliv. 24, יוֹצֶרְךָ מִבָּטֶן, xlix. 5, יֹצְרִי מִבֶּטֶן לְעֶבֶד לוֹ

* For the words of this promise, *cf.* ver. 19 *infra*, xv. 20, xlii. 11.

mouth fire and this people logs of wood; and it shall devour them;" or again (xv. 16), "Thy words were found, and I did eat them; and Thy word became unto me a joy and my heart's delight," may also have written, "Behold I have put My words in thy mouth!" without thereby becoming amenable to a charge of confusing fact with figure, metaphor with reality. Nor can I think the prophet means to say that, although, as a matter of fact, the Divine word already dwelt in him, it was now "put in his mouth," in the sense that he was henceforth to utter it. Stripped of the symbolism of vision, the verse simply asserts that the spiritual change which came over Jeremiah at the turning point in his career was due to the immediate operation of God; and that the chief external consequence of this inward change was that powerful preaching of Divine truth by which he was henceforth known. The great Prophet of the Exile twice uses the phrase, "I have set My words in thy mouth" (Isa. li. 16, lix. 21) with much the same meaning as that intended by Jeremiah, but without the preceding metaphor about the Divine hand.

"See I have this day set thee over the nations and over the kingdoms, to root out and to pull down, and to destroy and to overturn; to rebuild and to replant." Such, following the Hebrew punctuation, are the terms of the prophet's commission; and they are well worth consideration, as they set forth with all the force of prophetic idiom his own conception of the nature of that commission. First, there is the implied assertion of his own official dignity: the prophet is made a *paqîd* (Gen. xli. 34, "officers" set by Pharaoh over Egypt; 2 Kings xxv. 19 a military prefect) a prefect or superintendent of the nations of the world. It is the Hebrew term corresponding to the ἐπίσκοπος of the New Testament and the Christian Church (Judg. ix. 28; Neh. xi. 9). And secondly, his powers are of the widest scope; he is invested with authority over the destinies of all peoples. If it be asked in what sense it could be truly said that the ruin and renascence of nations were subject to the supervision of the prophets, the answer is obvious. The word they were authorised to declare was the word of God. But God's word is not something whose efficacy is exhausted in the human utterance of it. God's word is an irreversible command, fulfilling itself with all the necessity of a law of nature. The thought is well expressed by a later prophet: "For as the rain cometh down, and the snow from heaven, and returneth not thither, but watereth the earth, and maketh it bring forth and spring; and yieldeth seed to the sower and bread to the eater: so shall My word become, that goeth forth out of My mouth; it shall not return to Me empty (ריקם), but shall surely do that which I have willed, and shall carry through that for which I sent it" (or "shall prosper him whom I have sent," Isa. lv. 10, 11). All that happens is merely the self-accomplishment of this Divine word, which is only the human aspect of the Divine will. If, therefore, the absolute dependence of the prophets upon God for their knowledge of this word be left out of account, they appear as causes, when they are in truth but instruments, as agents when they are only mouthpieces. And so Ezekiel writes, "when I came to destroy the city" (Ezek. xliii. 3), meaning when I announced the Divine decree of its destruction. The truth upon which this peculiar mode of statement rests—the truth that the will of God must be and always is done in the world that God has made and is making—is a rock upon which the faith of His messengers may always repose. What strength, what staying power may the Christian preacher find in dwelling upon this almost visible fact of the self-fulfilling will and word of God, though all around him he hear that will questioned, and that word disowned and denied! He knows—it is his supreme comfort to know—that, while his own efforts may be thwarted, that will is invincible; that though *he* may fail in the conflict, that word will go on conquering and to conquer, until it shall have subdued all things unto itself.

CHAPTER II.

THE TRUST IN THE SHADOW OF EGYPT.

JEREMIAH ii. 1-iii. 5.

THE first of the prophet's public addresses is, in fact, a sermon which proceeds from an exposure of national sin to the menace of coming judgment. It falls naturally into three sections, of which the first (ii. 1-13) sets forth Iahvah's tender love to His young bride Israel in the old times of nomadic life, when faithfulness to Him was rewarded by protection from all external foes; and then passes on to denounce the unprecedented apostasy of a people from their God. The second (14-28) declares that if Israel has fallen a prey to her enemies, it is the result of her own infidelity to her Divine Spouse; of her early notorious and inveterate falling away to the false gods, who are now her only resource, and that a worthless one. The third section (ii. 29-iii. 5) points to the failure of Iahvah's chastisements to reclaim a people hardened in guilt, and in a self-righteousness which refused warning and despised reproof; affirms the futility of all human aid amid the national reverses; and cries woe on a too late repentance. It is not difficult to fix the time of this noble and pathetic address. That which follows it, and is intimately connected with it in substance, was composed "in the days of Josiah the king" (iii. 6), so that the present one must be placed a little earlier in the same reign; and, considering its position in the book, may very probably be assigned to the thirteenth year of Josiah, *i. e.*, B. C. 629, in which the prophet received his Divine call. This is the ordinary opinion; but one critic (Knobel) refers the discourse to the beginning of the reign of Jehoiakim, on account of the connection with Egypt which is mentioned in vv. 18, 36, and the humiliation suffered at the hands of the Egyptians which is mentioned in ver. 16; while another (Graf) maintains that chaps. ii.-vi. were composed in the fourth year of Jehoiakim, as if the prophet had committed nothing to writing before that date—an assumption which seems to run counter to the implication conveyed by his own statement, chap. xxxvi. 2. This latter critic has failed to notice the allusions in chaps. iv. 14, vi. 8, to an approaching calamity which may be averted by national reformation, to which the people are invited;—an invitation wholly incompatible with the prophet's attitude at that hopeless period. The series of prophecies beginning at chap. iv. 3 is certainly later in time than the discourse we are now considering; but as certainly belongs to the immediate subsequent years.

It does not appear that the first two of Jeremiah's addresses were called forth by any striking event of public importance, such as the Scythian invasion. His new-born consciousness of the

Divine call would urge the young prophet to action; and in the present discourse we have the firstfruits of the heavenly impulse. It is a retrospect of Israel's entire past and an examination of the state of things growing out of it. The prophet's attention is not yet confined to Judah; he deplores the rupture of the ideal relations between Iahvah and His people as a whole (ii. 4; *cf.* iii. 6). As Hitzig has remarked, this opening address, in its finished elaboration, leaves the impression of a first outpouring of the heart, which sets forth at once without reserve the long score of the Divine grievances against Israel. At the same time, in its closing judgment (iii. 5), in its irony (ii. 28), in its appeals (ii. 21, 31), and its exclamations (ii. 12), it breathes an indignation stern and deep to a degree hardly characteristic of the prophet in his other discourses, but which was natural enough, as Hitzig observes, in a first essay at moral criticism, a first outburst of inspired zeal.

In the Hebrew text the chapter begins with the same formula as chap. i. (ver. 4): "And there fell a word of Iahvah unto me, saying." But the LXX. reads: "And he said, Thus saith the Lord," (καὶ εἶπε, τάδε λέγει κύριος); a difference which is not immaterial, as it may be a trace of an older Hebrew recension of the prophet's work, in which this second chapter immediately followed the original superscription of the book, as given in chap. i. 1, 2, from which it was afterwards separated by the insertion of the narrative of Jeremiah's call and visions (וַיֹּאמֶר: *cf.* Amos i. 2). Perhaps we may see another trace of the same thing in the fact that whereas chap. i. sends the prophet to the rulers and people of Judah, this chapter is in part addressed to collective Israel (ver. 4); which constitutes a formal disagreement. If the reference to Israel is not merely retrospective and rhetorical,—if it implies, as seems to be assumed, that the prophet really meant his words to affect the remnant of the northern kingdom as well as Judah,—we have here a valuable contemporary corroboration of the much disputed assertion of the author of Chronicles, that king Josiah abolished idolatry "in the cities of Manasseh and Ephraim and Simeon even unto Naphtali, to wit, in their ruins round about" (2 Chron. xxxiv. 6), as well as in Judah and Jerusalem; and that Manasseh and Ephraim and "the remnant of Israel" (2 Chron. xxxiv. 9 *cf.* 21) contributed to his restoration of the temple. These statements of the Chronicler imply that Josiah exercised authority in the ruined northern kingdom, as well as in the more fortunate south; and so far as this first discourse of Jeremiah was actually addressed to Israel as well as to Judah, those disputed statements find in it an undesigned confirmation. However this may be, as a part of the first collection of the author's prophecies, there is little doubt that the chapter was read by Baruch to the people of Jerusalem in the fourth year of Jehoiakim (chap. xxxvi. 6).

"Go thou and cry in the ears of Jerusalem: Thus hath Iahvah said" (or "thought:" This is the Divine thought concerning thee!) "I have remembered for thee the kindness of thy youth, the love of thine espousals; thy following Me" (as a bride follows her husband to his tent) "in the wilderness, in a land unsown. A dedicated thing" (קֹדֶשׁ: like the high priest, on whose mitre was graven קֹדֶשׁ לַיהוָה) "was Israel to Iahvah, His first fruits of increase; all who did eat him were held guilty, ill would come to them, saith Iahvah" (vers. 2, 3).—"I have remembered for thee," *i. e.*, in thy favour, to thy benefit—as when Nehemiah prays, "Remember in my favour, O my God, for good, all that I have done upon this people," (Neh. v. 19)—"the kindness"—חֶסֶד—the warm affection of thy youth, "the love of thine espousals," or the charm of thy bridal state (Hos. ii. 15, xi. 1); the tender attachment of thine early days, of thy new born national consciousness, when Iahvah had chosen thee as His bride, and called thee to follow Him out of Egypt. It is the figure which we find so elaborately developed in the pages of Hosea. The "bridal state" is the time from the Exodus to the taking of the covenant at Sinai (Ezek. xvi. 8), which was, as it were, the formal instrument of the marriage; and Israel's young love is explained as consisting in turning her back upon "the flesh-pots of Egypt" (Ezek. xvi. 3), at the call of Iahvah, and following her Divine Lord into the barren steppes. This forsaking of all worldly comfort for the hard life of the desert was proof of the sincerity of Israel's early love. [The evidently original words "in the wilderness, a land unsown," are omitted by the LXX., which renders: "I remembered the mercy of thy youth, and the love of thy nuptials τελειώσις, consummation), so that thou followedst the Holy One of Israel, saith Iahvah."] Iahvah's "remembrance" of this devotion, that is to say, the return He made for it, is described in the next verse. Israel became not "holiness," but a holy or hallowed thing; a dedicated object, belonging wholly and solely to Iahvah, a thing which it was sacrilege to touch; Iahvah's "firstfruits of increase" (Heb. ראשית תבואתה). This last phrase is to be explained by reference to the well-known law of the firstfruits (Ex. xxiii. 19; Deut. xviii. 4, xxvi. 10), according to which the first specimens of all agricultural produce were given to God. Israel, like the firstlings of cattle and the firstfruits of corn and wine and oil, was קדש ליהוה consecrated to Iahvah; and therefore none might eat of him without offending. "To eat" or devour is a term naturally used of vexing and destroying a nation (x. 25, l. 7; Deut. vii. 16, "And thou shalt eat up all the peoples, which Jehovah thy God is about to give thee;" Isa. i. 7; Ps. xiv. 4, "Who eat up My people as they eat bread"). The literal translation is, "All his eaters become guilty (or are treated as guilty, punished); evil cometh to them;" and the verbs, being in the imperfect, denote what happened again and again in Israel's history; Iahvah suffered no man to do His people wrong with impunity. This, then, is the first count in the indictment against Israel, that Iahvah had not been unmindful of her early devotion, but had recognised it by throwing the shield of sanctity around her, and making her inviolable against all external enemies (vv. 1-3). The prophet's complaint, as developed in the following section (vv. 4-8), is that, in spite of the goodness of Iahvah, Israel has forsaken Him for idols. "Hear ye the word of Iahvah, O house of Jacob, and all the clans of the house of Israel!" All Israel is addressed, and not merely the surviving kingdom of Judah, because the apostasy had been universal. A special reference apparently made in ver. 8 to the prophets of Baal, who flourished only in the northern kingdom. We may compare the word of Amos "against *the whole clan*," which Iahvah "brought up from the land of Egypt" (Amos iii. 1), spoken at a time when Ephraim was yet in the heyday of his power.

"Thus hath Iahvah said, What found your fathers in Me, that was unjust, (עָוֶל a single act of injustice, Ps. vii. 4; not to be found in Iahvah, Deut. xxxii. 4) that they went far from Me and followed the Folly and were befooled (or 'the Delusion and were deluded')" (ver. 5). The phrase is used 2 Kings xvii. 15 in the same sense; הַהֶבֶל "the (mere) breath," "the nothingness" or "vanity," being a designation of the idols which Israel went after (*cf.* also chap. xxiii. 16; Ps. lxii. 11; Job xxvii. 12); much as St. Paul has written that an "idol is nothing in the world" (1 Cor. viii. 4), and that, with all this boasted culture, the nations of classical antiquity "became vain," or were befooled "in their imaginations" (ἐματαιώθησαν=ויהבלו), "and their foolish heart was darkened" (Rom. i. 21). Both the prophet and the apostle refer to that judicial blindness which is a consequence of persistently closing the eyes to truth, and deliberately putting darkness for light and light for darkness, bitter for sweet, and sweet for bitter, in compliance with the urgency of the flesh. For ancient Israel, the result of yielding to the seductions of foreign worship was, that "They were stultified in their best endeavours. They became false in thinking and believing, in doing and forbearing, because the fundamental error pervaded the whole life of the nation and of the individual. They supposed that they knew and honoured God, but they were entirely mistaken; they supposed they were doing His will, and securing their own welfare, while they were doing and securing the exact contrary" (Hitzig). And similar consequences will always flow from attempts to serve two masters; to gratify the lower nature, while not breaking wholly with the higher. Once the soul has accepted a lower standard than the perfect law of truth, it does not stop there. The subtle corruption goes on extending its ravages farther and farther; while the consciousness that anything is wrong becomes fainter and fainter as the deadly mischief increases, until at last the ruined spirit believes itself in perfect health, when it is, in truth, in the last stage of mortal disease. Perversion of the will and the affections leads to the perversion of the intellect. There is a profound meaning in the old saying that, Men make their gods in their own likeness. As a man is, so will God appear to him to be. "With the loving Thou wilt shew Thyself loving; With the perfect, Thou wilt shew Thyself perfect; With the pure, Thou wilt shew Thyself pure; And with the perverse, Thou wilt shew Thyself froward" (Ps. xviii. 25 *sq.*). Only hearts pure of all worldly taint see God in His purity. The rest worship some more or less imperfect semblance of Him, according to the varying degrees of their selfishness and sin.

"And they said not, Where is Iahvah, who brought us up out of the land of Egypt, that guided us in the wilderness, in a land of wastes and hollows (or desert and defile), in a land of drought and darkness (dreariness צלמות), in a land that no man passed through, and where no mortal dwelt" (ver. 6). "They said not, Where is Iahvah, who brought us up out of the land of Egypt." It is the old complaint of the prophets against Israel's black ingratitude. So, for instance, Amos (ii. 10) had written: "Whereas I—I brought you up from the land of Egypt, and guided you in the wilderness forty years;" and Micah (vi. 3 *sq.*): "My people, what have I done unto thee, and how have I wearied thee? Answer against Me. For I brought thee up from the land of Egypt, and from a house of bondmen redeemed I thee." In common gratitude, they were bound to be true to this mighty Saviour; to enquire after Iahvah, to call upon Him only, to do His will, and to seek His grace (*cf.* xxix. 12 *sq.*). Yet, with characteristic fickleness, they soon forgot the fatherly guidance, which had never deserted them in the period of their nomadic wanderings in the wilds of Arabia Petræa; a land which the prophet poetically describes as "a land of waste and hollows"—alluding probably to the rocky defiles through which they had to pass—and "a land of drought and darkness;" * the latter an epithet of the Grave or Hades (Job x. 21), fittingly applied to that great lone wilderness of the south, which Israel had called "a fearsome land" (xxi. 1), and "a land of trouble and anguish" (xxx. 6), whither, according to the poet of Job, "The caravans go up and are lost" (vi. 18).

"And I brought you into the garden land, to eat its fruits and its choicest things (טוּבָהּ Isa. i. 19; Gen. xlv. 18, 20, 23); and ye entered and defiled My land, and My domain ye made a loathsome thing!" (ver. 7). With the w lderness of the wanderings is contrasted the "land of the *carmel*," the land of fruitful orchards and gardens, as in chap. iv. 26; Isa. x. 18, xvi. 10, xxix. 17. This was Canaan, Iahvah's own land, which He had chosen out of all countries to be His special dwelling-place and earthly sanctuary; but which Israel no sooner possessed, than they began to pollute this holy land by their sins, like the guilty peoples whom they had displaced, making it thereby an abomination to Iahvah (Lev. xviii. 24 *sq.*, *cf.* chap. iii. 2).

"The priests they said not, Where is Iahvah? and they that handle the law, they knew (*i. e.*, regarded, heeded) Me not; and as for the shepherds (*i. e.*, the king and princes, ver. 26), they rebelled against Me, and the prophets, they prophesied by (through) the Baal, and them that help not (*i. e.*, the false gods) they followed" (ver. 8). In the form of a climax, this verse justifies the accusation contained in the last, by giving particulars. The three ruling classes are successively indicted (*cf.* ver. 26, ch. xviii. 18). The priests, part of whose duty was to "handle the law," *i. e.*, explain the Torah, to instruct the people in the requirements of Iahvah, by oral tradition and out of the sacred law-books, gave no sign of spiritual aspiration (*cf.* ver. 6); like the reprobate sons of Eli, "they knew not" (1 Sam. ii. 12) "Iahvah," that is to say, paid no heed to Him and His will as revealed in the book of the law; the secular authorities, the king and his counsellors ("wise men," xviii. 18),

* עַלְמָוֶת, so far as the punctuation suggests that the term is a compound, meaning "shadow of death," is one of the fictions of the Masorets, like לִגְאֵיוֹנִים and חֵלְכָּאִים and חֵלְכָה in the Psalms.

not only sinned thus negatively, but positively revolted against the King of kings, and resisted His will; while the prophets went further yet in the path of guilt, apostatising altogether from the God of Israel, and seeking inspiration from the Phœnician Baal, and following worthless idols that could give no help. There seems to be a play on the words Baal and Belial, as if Baal meant the same as Belial, "profitless," "worthless" (*cf.* 1 Sam. ii. 12: "Now Eli's sons were sons of Belial; they knew not Iahvah." The phrase לֹא־יוֹעִלוּ "they that help not," or "cannot help," suggests the term בְּלִיַּעַל Belial; which, however, may be derived from בְּלִי "not," and עַל "supreme," "God," and so mean "not-God," "idol," rather than "worthlessness," "unprofitableness," as it is usually explained). The reference may be to the Baal-worship of Samaria, the northern capital, which was organised by Ahab, and his Tyrian queen (chap. xxiii. 13).

"Therefore"—on account of this amazing ingratitude of your forefathers,—"I will again plead (reason, argue forensically) with you (the present generation in whom their guilt repeats itself) saith Iahvah, and with your sons' sons (who will inherit your sins) will I plead." The nation is conceived as a moral unity, the characteristics of which are exemplified in each successive generation. To all Israel, past, present, and future, Iahvah will vindicate his own righteousness. "For cross" (the sea) "to the coasts of the Citeans" (the people of Citium in Cyprus) "and see; and to Kedar" (the rude tribes of the Syrian desert) "send ye, and mark well, and see whether there hath arisen a case like this. Hath a nation changed gods—albeit they are no-gods? Yet My people hath changed his" (true) "glory for that which helpeth not" (or is worthless). "Upheave, ye heavens (שֹׁמּוּ שָׁמַיִם, a fine paronomasia), "at this, and shudder (and) be petrified" חָרְבוּ מְאֹד Ges., "be sore amazed" =שׁמם; but Hitzig "be dry" = stiff and motionless, like syn. יבשׁ in 1 Kings xiii. 4), "saith Iahvah; for two evil things hath My people done: Me they have forsaken—a Fountain of living water—to hew them out cisterns, broken cisterns, that cannot (imperf. = potential) "hold water" (Heb. *the* waters: generic article) (vv. 9-13). In these five verses, the apostasy of Israel from his own God is held up as a fact unique in history—unexampled and inexplicable by comparison with the doings of other nations. Whether you look westward or eastward, across the sea to Cyprus, or beyond Gilead to the barbarous tribes of the Cedrei (Ps. cxx. 5), nowhere will you find a heathen people that has changed its native worship for another; and if you did find such, it would be no precedent or palliation of Israel's behaviour. The heathen in adopting a new worship simply exchanges one superstition for another; the objects of his devotion are "non-gods" (ver. 11). The heinousness and the eccentricity of Israel's conduct lies in the fact that he has bartered truth for falsehood; he has exchanged "his Glory"—whom Amos (viii. 7) calls the Pride (A. V. Excellency) of Jacob—for a useless idol; an object which the prophet elsewhere calls "The Shame" (iii. 24, xi. 13), because it can only bring shame and confusion upon those whose hopes depend upon it. The wonder of the thing might well be supposed to strike the pure heavens, the silent witnesses of it, with blank astonishment (*cf.* a similar appeal in Deut. iv. 26, xxxi. 28, xxxii. 1, where the earth is added). For the evil is not single but twofold. With the rejection of truth goes the adoption of error; and both are evils. Not only has Israel turned his back upon "a fountain of living waters;" he has also "hewn him out cisterns, broken cisterns, that cannot hold water." The "broken cisterns" are, of course, the idols which Israel made to himself. As a cistern full of cracks and fissures disappoints the wayfarer, who has reckoned on finding water in it; so the idols, having only the semblance and not the reality of life, avail their worshippers nothing (vv. 8. 11). In Hebrew the waters of a spring are called "living" (Gen. xxi. 19), because they are more refreshing and, as it were, life-giving, than the stagnant waters of pools and tanks fed by the rains. Hence by a natural metaphor, the mouth of a righteous man, or the teaching of the wise, and the fear of the Lord, are called a fountain of life (Prov. x. 11, xiii. 14, xiv. 27). "The fountain of life" is with Iahvah (Ps. xxxvi. 10); nay, He is Himself the Fountain of living waters (Jer. xvii. 13); because all life, and all that sustains or quickens life, especially spiritual life, proceeds from Him. Now in Ps. xix. 8 it is said that "The law of the Lord—or, the teaching of Iahvah—is perfect, reviving (or restoring) the soul" (*cf.* Lam. i. 11; Ruth iv. 15); and a comparison of Micah and Isaiah's statement that "Out of Zion will go forth the law, and the word of the Lord from Jerusalem" (Isa. ii. 3; Mic. iv. 2), with the more figurative language of Joel (iii. 18) and Zechariah (xiv. 8), who speak of "a fountain going forth from the house of the Lord," and "living waters going forth from Jerusalem," suggests the inference that "the living waters," of which Iahvah is the perennial fountain, are identical with His law as revealed through priests and prophets. It is easy to confirm this suggestion by reference to the river "whose streams make glad the city of God" (Ps. xlvi. 4); to Isaiah's poetic description of the Divine teaching, of which he was himself the exponent, as "the waters of Shiloah that flow softly" (viii. 6), Shiloah being a spring that issues from the temple rock; and to our Lord's conversation with the woman of Samaria, in which He characterises His own teaching as "living waters" (St. John iv. 10), and as "a well of waters, springing up unto eternal Life" (*ibid.* 14).

"Is Israel a bondman, or a homeborn serf? Why hath he become a prey? Over him did young lions roar; they uttered their voice; and they made his land a waste; his cities, they are burnt up" (or "thrown down), so that they are uninhabited. Yea, the sons of Noph and Tahpan(h)es, they did bruise thee on the crown. Is not this what" (the thing that) "thy forsaking Iahvah thy God brought about for thee, at the time He was guiding thee in the way?" (vv. 14-17). As Iahvah's bride, as a people chosen to be His own, Israel had every reason to expect a bright and glorious career. Why was this expectation falsified by events? But one answer was possible, in view of the immutable righteousness, the eternal faithfulness of God. "The ruin of Israel was Israel's own doing." It is a truth which applies to all nations, and to all individuals capable of moral agency, in all periods and places of their existence. Let no man lay his failure in this world or in the world to come at the door of the Almighty. Let none venture to repeat the thoughtless blasphemy which charges the All-Merciful with sending frail human beings to expiate their offences in an everlasting hell! Let none dare to say or think, God might have made it otherwise, but He would not! Oh, no; it is all a monstrous misconception of the true relations of things. You and I are free to make our choice now, whatever may be the case hereafter. We may choose to obey God, or to disobey; we may seek His will, or our own. The one is the way of life; the other, of death, and nothing can alter the facts; they are part of the laws of the universe. Our destiny is in our own hands, to make or to mar. If we qualify ourselves for nothing better than a hell—if our daily progress leads us farther and farther from God and nearer and nearer to the devil—then hell will be our eternal home. For God is love, and purity, and truth, and glad obedience to righteous laws; and these things, realised and rejoiced in, are heaven. And the man that lives without these as the sovereign aims of his existence—the man whose heart's worship is centred upon something else than God—stands already on the verge of hell, which is "the place of him that knows not (and cares not for) God." And unless we are prepared to find fault with that natural arrangement whereby like things are aggregated to like, and all physical elements gravitate towards their own kind, I do not see how we can disparage the same law in the spiritual sphere, in virtue of which all spiritual beings are drawn to their own place, the heavenly-minded rising to the heights above, and the contrary sort sinking to the depths beneath.

The precise bearing of the question (ver. 14), "Is Israel a bondman, or a homeborn slave?" is hardly self-evident. One commentator supposes that the implied answer is an affirmative. Israel *is* a "servant," the servant, that is, the worshipper of the true God. Nay, he is more than a mere bondservant; he occupies the favoured position of a slave born in his lord's house (*cf*. Abraham's three hundred and eighteen young men, Gen. xiv. 14), and therefore, according to the custom of antiquity, standing on a different footing from a slave acquired by purchase. The "home" or house is taken to mean the land of Canaan, which the prophet Hosea had designated as Iahvah's "house" (Hosea ix. 15, *cf*. 3); and the "Israel" intended is supposed to be the existing generation born in the holy land. The double question of the prophet then amounts to this: If Israel be, as is generally admitted, the favourite bondservant of Iahvah, how comes it that his lord has not protected him against the spoiler? But, although this interpretation is not without force, it is rendered doubtful by the order of the words in the Hebrew, where the stress lies on the terms for "bondman" and "homeborn slave"; and by its bold divergence from the sense conveyed by the same form of question in other passages of the prophet, *e. g.*, ver. 31 *infra*, where the answer expected is a negative one (*cf*. also chap. viii. 4, 5, xiv. 19. xlix. 1. The formula is evidently characteristic). The point of the question seems to lie in the fact of the helplessness of persons of servile condition against occasional acts of fraud and oppression, from which neither the purchased nor the homebred slave could at all times be secure. The rights of such persons, however humane the laws affecting their ordinary status, might at times be cynically disregarded both by their masters and by others (see a notable instance, Jer. xxxiv. 8 *sqq.*). Moreover, there may be a reference to the fact that slaves were always reckoned in those times as a valuable portion of the booty of conquest; and the meaning may be that Israel's lot as a captive is as bad as if he had never known the blessings of freedom, and had simply exchanged one servitude for another by the fortune of war. The allusion is chiefly to the fallen kingdom of Ephraim. We must remember that Jeremiah is reviewing the whole past, from the outset of Iahvah's special dealings with Israel. The national sins of the northern and more powerful branch had issued in utter ruin. The "young lions," the foreign invaders, had "roared against" Israel properly so called, and made havoc of the whole country (*cf*. iv. 7). The land was dispeopled, and became an actual haunt of lions (2 Kings xvii. 25), until Esarhaddon colonised it with a motley gathering of foreigners (Ezra iv. 2). Judah too had suffered greatly from the Assyrian invasion in Hezekiah's time, although the last calamity had then been mercifully averted (Sanherib boasts that he stormed and destroyed forty-six strong cities, and carried off 200,000 captives, and an innumerable booty). The implication is that the evil fate of Ephraim threatens to overtake Judah; for the same moral causes are operative, and the same Divine will which worked in the past is working in the present, and will continue to work in the future. The lesson of the past was plain for those who had eyes to read and hearts to understand it. Apart from this prophetic doctrine of a Providence which shapes the destinies of nations, in accordance with their moral deserts, history has no value except for the gratification of mere intellectual curiosity.

"Aye, and the children of Noph and Tahpanhes they bruise (? used to bruise; are bruising:" the Heb. ירעו may mean either) "thee on the crown" (ver. 16). This obviously refers to injuries inflicted by Egypt, the two royal cities of Noph or Memphis, and Tahpanhes or Daphnæ, being mentioned in place of the country itself. Judah must be the sufferer, as no Egyptian attack on Ephraim is anywhere recorded; while we do read of Shishak's invasion of the southern kingdom in the reign of Rehoboam, both in the Bible (1 Kings xiv. 25), and in Shishak's own inscriptions on the walls of the temple of Amen at Karnak. But the form of the Hebrew verb seems to indicate rather some contemporary trouble; perhaps plundering raids by an Egyptian army, which about this time was besieging the Philistine stronghold of Ashdod (Herod., ii. 157). "The Egyptians are bruising (or crushing) thee" seems to be the sense; and so it is given by the Jewish commentator Rashi (ירצצו diffringunt). Our English marginal rendering "fed on" follows the traditional pronunciation of the Hebrew term (יִרְעוּ) which is also the case with the Targum and the Syriac versions; but this can hardly be right, unless we suppose that the Egyptians infesting the frontier are scornfully compared to vermin (read יְרֹעוּ with J. D. Mich.) of a sort which, as Herodotus tells us, the Egyptians particularly disliked (but *cf*. Mic. v. 5; Ges., depascunt, "eating down.")

The A. V. of ver. 17 presents a curious mistake which the Revisers have omitted to correct. The words should run, as I have rendered them, "Is not *this*"—thy present ill fortune—"the thing that thy forsaking of Iahvah thy God did for thee—at the time when He was guiding thee in the way?" The Hebrew verb does not admit of the rendering in the perf. tense, for it is an impf., nor is it a 2d pers. fem. (תעשה not תעשי) but a 3d. The LXX. has it rightly (*οὐχὶ ταῦτα ἐποίησέ σοι τὸ καταλιπεῖν σε ἐμέ;*), but leaves out the next clause which specifies the time. The words, however, are probably original; for they insist, as vv. 5 and 31 insist, on the groundlessness of Israel's apostasy. Iahvah had given no cause for it; He was fulfilling His part of the covenant by "guiding them in the way." Guidance or leading is ascribed to Iahvah as the true "Shepherd of Israel" (chap. xxxi. 9; Ps. lxxx. 1). It denotes not only the spiritual guidance which was given through the priests and prophets; but also that external prosperity, those epochs of established power and peace and plenty, which were precisely the times chosen by infatuated Israel for defection from the Divine Giver of her good things. As the prophet Hosea expresses it, ii. 8 *sq.*, "She knew not that it was I who gave her the corn and the new wine and the oil; and silver I multiplied unto her, and gold, which they made into the Baal. Therefore will I take back My corn in the time of it, and My new wine in its season, and will snatch away My wool and My flax, which were to cover her nakedness." And (chap. xiii. 6) the same prophet gives this plain account of his people's thankless revolt from their God: "When I fed them, they were sated; sated were they, and their heart was lifted up: therefore they forgot Me." It is the thought so forcibly expressed by the minstrel of the Book of the Law (Deut. xxxii. 15) first published in the early days of Jeremiah: "And Jeshurun waxed fat and kicked; Thou waxedst fat, and gross and fleshy! And he forsook the God that made him, And made light of his protecting Rock." And, lastly, the Chronicler has pointed the same moral of human fickleness and frailty in the case of an individual, Uzziah or Azariah, the powerful king of Judah, whose prosperity seduced him into presumption and profanity (2 Chron. xxvi. 16): "When he grew strong, his heart rose high, until he dealt corruptly, and was unfaithful to Iahvah his God." I need not enlarge on the perils of prosperity; they are known by bitter experience to every Christian man. Not without good reason do we pray to be delivered from evil "In all time of our wealth;" nor was that poet least conversant with human nature who wrote that "Sweet are the uses of adversity."

"And now"—a common formula in drawing an inference and concluding an argument—"what hast thou to do with the way of Egypt, to drink the waters of Shihor" (the Black River, the Nile); "and what hast thou to do with the way to Assyria, to drink the waters of the River? (*par excellence, i. e.*, the Euphrates). "Thy wickedness correcteth thee, and thy revolts it is that chastise thee. Know then, and see that evil and bitter is thy forsaking Iahvah thy God, and thine having no dread of Me, saith the Lord Iahvah Sabaoth" (vv. 18, 19). And now—as the cause of all thy misfortunes lies in thyself—what is the use of seeking a cure for them abroad? Egypt will prove as powerless to help thee now, as Assyria proved in the days of Ahaz (ver. 36 *sq.*). The Jewish people, anticipating the views of certain modern historians, made a wrong diagnosis of their own evil case. They traced all that they had suffered, and were yet to suffer, to the ill will of the two great Powers of their time; and supposed that their only salvation lay in conciliating the one or the other. And as Isaiah found it necessary to cry woe on the rebellious children, "that walk to go down into Egypt, and have not asked at My mouth; to strengthen themselves in the strength of Pharaoh, and to trust in the shadow of Egypt!" (Isa. xxx. 1 *sq.*), so now, after so much experience of the futility and positive harmfulness of these unequal alliances, Jeremiah has to lift his voice against the same national folly.

The "young lions" of ver. 15 must denote the Assyrians, as Egypt is expressly named in ver. 16. The figure is very appropriate, for not only was the lion a favourite subject of Assyrian sculpture; not only do the Assyrian kings boast of their prowess as lion-hunters, while they even tamed these fierce creatures, and trained them to the chase; but the great strength and predatory habits of the king of beasts made him a fitting symbol of that great empire whose irresistible power was founded upon and sustained by wrong and robbery. This reference makes it clear that the prophet is contemplating the past; for Assyria was at this time already tottering to its fall, and the Israel of his day, *i. e.*, the surviving kingdom of Judah, had no longer any temptation to court the countenance of that decaying if not already ruined empire. The sin of Israel is an old one; both it and its consequences belong to the past (ver. 20 compared with ver. 14); and the national attempts to find a remedy must be referred to the same period. Ver. 36 makes it evident that the prophet's contemporaries concerned themselves only about an Egyptian alliance.

It is an interesting detail that for "the waters of Shihor," the LXX. gives "waters of Gihon" (*Γηῶν*), which it will be remembered is the name of one of the four rivers of Paradise, and which appears to have been the old Hebrew name of the Nile (Ecclus. xxiv. 27; Jos., "Ant.," i. 1, 3). Shihor may be an explanatory substitute. For the rest, it is plain that the two rivers symbolise the two empires (*cf.* Isa. viii. 7; chap. xlvi. 7); and the expression "to drink the waters" of them must imply the receiving and, as it were, absorption of whatever advantage might be supposed to accrue from friendly relations with their respective countries. At the same time, a contrast seems to be intended between these earthly waters, which could only disappoint those who sought refreshment in them, and that "fountain of living waters" (ver. 13) which Israel had forsaken. The nation sought in Egypt its deliverance from self-caused evil, much as Saul had sought guidance from witches when he knew himself deserted by the God whom by disobedience he had driven away. In seeking thus to escape the consequences of sin by cementing alliances with heathen powers, Israel added sin to sin. Hence (in ver. 19) the prophet reiterates with increased emphasis what he has already suggested by a question (ver. 17): "Thy wickedness correcteth thee, and thy revolts it is that chastise thee. Know then, and see that evil and bitter is thy forsaking of Iahweh thy God, and thine having no dread of Me!" Learn from these its bitter fruits that the thing itself is bad (Read פַּחְדְּתִי אֵלַי as a 2d pers. instead of פַּחְדָּתִי. Job xxi. 33, quoted by Hitzig, is not a real parallel; nor can the sentence, as it stands, be rendered, "Und dass die Scheu vor mir nicht an dich kam"); and renounce that which its consequences declare to be an evil course, instead of aggravating the evil of it by a new act of unfaithfulness.

"For long ago didst thou break thy yoke, didst thou burst thy bonds, and saidst, I will not serve: for upon every high hill, and under each evergreen tree thou wert crouching in fornication" (vv. 20-24). Such seems to be the best way of taking a verse which is far from clear as it stands in the Masoretic text. The prophet labours to bring home to his hearers a sense of the reality of the national sin; and he affirms once more (vv. 5, 7) that Israel's apostasy originated long ago, in the early period of its history, and implies that the taint thus contracted is a fact which can neither be denied nor obliterated (The punctuators of the Hebrew text, having pointed the first two verbs as in the 1st pers. instead of the 2d feminine, were obliged, further, to suggest the reading לֹא אֶעֱבוֹר, "I will not transgress," for the original phrase לא אעבוד "I will not serve;" a variant which is found in the Targum, and many MSS. and editions. "Serving" and "bearing the yoke" are equivalent expressions (xxvii. 11, 12); so that, if the first two verbs were really in the 1st pers., the sentence ought to be continued with, "And *I* said, *Thou* shalt not serve." But the purport of this verse is to justify the assertion of the last, as is evident from the introductory particle "for," כִּי. The Syriac supports אעבוד; and the LXX. and Vulg. have the two leading verbs in the 2d pers., (iv. 19.). The meaning is that Israel, like a stubborn ox, has broken the yoke imposed on him by Iahvah; a statement which is repeated in v. 5: "But these have altogether broken the yoke, they have burst the bonds" (*cf.* ver. 31, *infra*; Hos. iv. 16; Acts xxvi. 14).

"Yet I—I planted thee with" (or, "as") noble vines, all of them genuine shoots; and how hast thou turned Me thyself into the wild offshoots of a foreign vine?" (ver. 21). The thought seems to be borrowed from Isaiah's Song of the Beloved's Vineyard (Isa. v. 1 *sqq.*). The nation is addressed as a person, endowed with a continuity of moral existence from the earliest period. "The days of the life of a man may be numbered; but the days of Israel are innumerable" (Ecclus. xxxvii. 25). It was with the true seed of Abraham, the real Israel, that Iahvah had entered into covenant (Ex. xviii. 19; Rom. ix. 7); and this genuine offspring of the patriarch had its representatives in every succeeding generation, even in the worst of times (1 Kings xix. 18). But the prophet's argument seems to imply that the good plants had reverted to a wild state, and that the entire nation had become hopelessly degenerate; which was not far from the actual condition of things at the close of his career. The culmination of Israel's degeneracy, however, was seen in the rejection of Him to whom "gave all the prophets witness." The Passion of Christ sounded a deeper depth of sacred sorrow than the passion of any of His forerunners. "O Jerusalem, Jerusalem! Thou that killest the prophets, and stonest them that are sent unto thee!"

"Then on My head a crown of thorns I wear;
For these are all the grapes Sion doth bear,
Though I My vine planted and watered there:
Was ever grief like Mine?"

"For if thou wash with natron, and take thee much soap, spotted (crimsoned; Targ. Isa. i. 18: or written, recorded) is thy guilt before Me, saith My Lord Iahvah." Comparison with Isa. i. 18, "Though thy sins be as scarlet . . . though they be red like crimson," suggests that the former rendering of the doubtful word (נִכְתָּם) is correct; and this idea is plainly better suited to the context than a reference to the Books of Heaven, and the Recording Angel; for the object of washing is to get rid of spots and stains.

"How canst thou say, I have not defiled myself; after the Baals I have not gone: See thy way in the valley, know what thou hast done, O swift she-camel, running hither and thither" (literally, intertwining or crossing her ways) (ver. 23). The prophet anticipates a possible attempt at self-justification; just as in ver. 35 he complains of Israel's self-righteousness. Both here and there he is dealing with his own contemporaries in Judah; whereas the idolatry described in ver. 20 *sqq.* is chiefly that of the ruined kingdom of Ephraim (ch. iii. 24; 2 Kings xvii. 10). It appears that the worship of Baal proper only existed in Judah for a brief period in the reign of Ahaziah's usurping queen Athaliah, side by side with the worship of Iahvah (2 Chron. xxiii. 17); while on the high places and at the local sanctuaries the God of Israel was honoured (2 Kings xviii. 22). So far as the prophet's complaints refer to old times, Judah could certainly boast of a relatively higher purity than the northern kingdom; and the manifold heathenism of Manasseh's reign had been abolished a whole year before this address was delivered (2 Chron. xxxiv. 3 *sqq.*). "The valley" spoken of as the scene of Judah's misdoings is that of Ben-Hinnom, south of Jerusalem, where, as the prophet elsewhere relates (vii. 31, xxxii. 35; 2 Kings xxiii. 10), the people sacrificed children by fire to the God Molech, whom he expressly designates as a *Baal* (xix. 5, xxxii. 35), using the term in its wider significance, which includes all the aspects of the Canaanite sun-god. And because Judah betook herself now to Iahvah, and now to Molech, varying, as it were, her capricious course from right to left and from left to right, and halting evermore between two opinions (1 Kings xviii. 21), the prophet calls her "a swift young she-camel," (swift, that is, for evil) intertwining, or crossing her ways." The hot zeal with which the people wantonly plunged into a sensual idolatry is aptly set forth in the figure of the next verse. A "wild ass, used to the wilderness (Job xxiv. 5), in the craving of her soul she snuffeth up (xiv. 6) the wind" (not "lässt sie kaum Athem genug finden, indem sie denselben vorweg vergeudet," as Hitzig; but, as a wild beast scenting prey, *cf.* xiv. 6, or food afar off, she scents companions at a distance); "her greedy lust, who can turn it back? None that seek her need weary themselves; in her month they find her." While passion rages, animal instinct is too strong to be diverted from its purpose; it is idle to argue with blind appetite; it goes straight to its mark, like an arrow from a bow. Only when it has had its way, and the reaction of nature follows, does the influence of reason become possible. Such was Israel's passion for the false gods. They had no need to seek her (Hos. ii. 7; Ezek. xvi. 34); in the hour of her infatuation she fell an easy victim to their passive allurements. (The "month" is the season when the sexual instinct is strong.) Warnings fell on deaf ears. "Keep back thy foot from bareness, and thy throat from thirst!" This cry of the prophets availed nothing: "Thou saidst, It is vain! (*sc.* that thou urgest me.) No, for I love the strangers and after them will I go!" The meaning of the admonition is not very clear. Some (*e. g.*, Rosenmüller) have understood a reference to the shameless doings and the insatiable cravings of lust. Others (as Gesenius) explain the words thus: "Do not pursue thy lovers in such hot haste as to wear thy feet bare in the wild race!" Others, again, take the prohibition literally, and connect the barefootedness and the thirst with the orgies of Baal-worship (Hitz.), in which the priests leaped or rather limped with bare feet (what proof?) on the blazing altar, as an act of religious mortification, shrieking the while till their throats were parched and dry (Ps. lxix. 4, נִחַר גְּרוֹנִי in frenzied appeal to their lifeless god (*cf.* Ex. iii. 5; 2 Sam. xv. 30; 1 Kings xviii. 26). In this case the command is, Cease this self-torturing and bootless worship! But the former sense seems to agree better with the context.

"Like the shame of a thief, when he is detected, so are the house of Israel ashamed—they, their kings, their princes, and their priests, and their prophets; in that they say (are ever saying) to the wood (iii. 9 in Heb. masc.), Thou art my father! (iii. 4) and to the stone (in Heb. fem.), Thou didst bring me forth! For they (xxxii. 33) have turned towards Me the back and not the face; but in the time of their trouble they say (begin to say), O rise and save us! But where are thy gods that thou madest for thyself? Let them arise, if they can save thee in the time of thy trouble; for numerous as thy cities are thy gods become, O Judah!" (vv. 26-28). "The Shame" (הבשת) is the well-known title of opprobrium which the prophets apply to Baal. Even in the histories, which largely depend on prophetic sources, we find such substitutions as Ishbosheth for Eshbaal, the "Man of Shame" for "Baal's Man." Accordingly, the point of ver. 26 *sqq.* is, that as Israel has served the Shame, the idol-gods, instead of Iahvah, shame has been and will be her reward: in the hour of bitter need, when she implores help from the One true God, she is put to shame by being referred back to her senseless idols. The "Israel" intended is the entire nation, as in ver. 3, and not merely the fallen kingdom of Ephraim. In ver. 28 the prophet specially addresses Judah, the surviving representative of the whole people. In the book of Judges (x. 10-14) the same idea of the attitude of Iahvah towards His faithless people finds historical illustration. Oppressed by the Ammonites they "cried unto the Lord, saying, We have sinned against Thee, in that we have both forsaken our own God, and have **served** the Baals;" but Iahvah, after reminding them of past deliverances followed by fresh apostasies, replies: "Go, and cry unto the gods which ye have chosen; let *them* save you in the time of your distress!" Here also we hear the echoes of a prophetic voice. The object of such ironical utterances was by no means to deride the self-caused miseries in which Israel was involved; but, as is evident from the sequel of the narrative in Judges, to deepen penitence and contrition, by making the people realise the full flagrancy of their sin, and the suicidal folly of their desertions of the God whom, in times of national distress, they recognised the only possible Saviour. In the same way and with the same end in view, the prophetic psalmist of Deut. xxxii. represents the God of Israel as asking (ver. 37) "Where are their gods: the Rock in which they sought refuge? That used to eat the flesh of their sacrifices, that drank the wine of their libation? Let them arise and help you; let them be over you a shelter!" The purpose is to bring home to them a conviction of the utter vanity of idol-worship; for the poet continues: "See *now* that I even I am He (the One God) and there is no god beside Me (with Me, sharing My sole attributes); 'Tis I that kill and save alive; I have crushed, and *I* heal." The folly of Israel is made conspicuous, first by the expression "Saying to the wood, Thou art my father, and to the stone, Thou didst bring me forth;" and secondly, by the statement, "Numerous as thy cities are thy gods become, O Judah!" In the former we have a most interesting glimpse of the point of view of the heathen worshipper of the seventh century B. C., from which it appears that by a *god* he meant the original, *i. e.*, the real author of his own existence. Much has been written in recent years to prove that man's elementary notions of deity are of an altogether lower kind than those which find expression in the worship of a Father in heaven; but when we see that such an idea could subsist even in connection with the most impure nature-worships, as in Canaan, and when we observe that it was a familiar conception in the religion of Egypt several thousand years previously, we may well doubt whether this idea of an Unseen Father of our race is not as old as humanity itself.

The sarcastic reference to the number of Judah's idols may remind us of what is recorded of classic Athens, in whose streets it was said to be easier to find a god than a man. The irony of the prophet's remark depends on the consideration that there is, or ought to be, safety in numbers. The impotency of the false gods could hardly be put in a stronger light in words as few as the prophet has used. In chap. xi. 13 he repeats the statement in an amplified form: "For numerous as thy cities have thy gods become, O Judah; and numerous as the streets of Jerusalem have ye made altars for The Shame, altars for sacrificing to the Baal." From this passage, apparently, the LXX. derived the words which it adds here: "And according to the number of the streets of Jerusalem did they sacrifice to the (image of) Baal" (ἔθυον τῇ Βάαλ).

"Why contend ye with Me? All of you have rebelled against Me, saith Iahvah. (LXX. ἠσεβήσατε, καὶ πάντες ὑμεῖς ἠνομήσατε εἰς ἐμέ. "Ebenfalls authentisch" says Hitzig). In vain have I smitten your sons; correction they (*i. e.*, the people; but LXX. ἐδέξασθε may be correct), received not! your own sword hath eaten up your prophets, like a destroying lion. Generation that ye are! See the word of Iahvah! Is it a wilderness that I have been to Israel, or a land of deepest gloom? Why have My people said, We are free; we will come no more unto Thee? Doth a virgin forget her ornaments, a bride her bands (or garlands, Rashi)? yet My people hath forgotten Me days without number" (vv. 29-32). The question "Why contend, or dispute ye תריבו or, as the LXX. has it, talk ye (תדברו) towards or about Me (אלי) implies that the people murmured at the reproaches and menaces of the prophet (ver. 26 *sqq.*). He answers them by denying their right to complain. Their rebellion has been universal; no chastisement has reformed them; Iahvah has done nothing that can be alleged in excuse of their unfaithfulness; their sin is, therefore, a portentous anomaly, for which it is impossible to find a parallel in ordinary human conduct. In vain had "their sons," the young men of military age, fallen in battle (Amos iv. 10); the nation had stubbornly refused to see in such disasters a sign of Iahvah's displeasure; a token of Divine chastisement; or rather, while recognising the wrath of heaven, they had obstinately persisted in believing in false explanations of its motive, and refused to admit that the purpose of it was their religious and moral amendment. And not only had the nation refused warning, and despised instruction, and defeated the purposes of the Divine discipline. They had slain their spiritual monitors, the prophets, with the sword; the prophets who had founded upon the national disasters their rebukes of national sin, and their earnest calls to penitence and reform (1 Kings xix. 10; Neh. ix. 26: St. Matt. xxiii. 37). And so when at last the long deferred judgment arrived, it found a political system ready to go to pieces through the feebleness and corruption of the ruling classes; a religious system, of which the spirit had long since evaporated, and which simply survived in the interests of a venal priesthood, and its intimate allies, who made a trade of prophecy; and a kingdom and people ripe for destruction.

At the thought of this crowning outrage, the prophet cannot restrain his indignation. "Generation that ye are!" he exclaims, "behold the word of the Lord. Is it a wilderness that I have been to Israel, or a land of deepest gloom?" Have I been a thankless, barren soil, returning nothing for your culture? The question is more pointed in Hebrew than in English; for the same term (עבד 'abad) means both to till the ground, and to serve and worship God. We have thus an emphatic repetition of the remonstrance with which the address opens: Iahvah has not been unmindful of Israel's service; Israel has been persistently ungrateful for Iahvah's gracious love. The cry "We are free!" (רדנו) implies that they had broken away from a painful yoke and a burdensome service (*cf.* ver. 20); the yoke being that of the Moral Law, and the service that perfect freedom which consists in subjection to Divine Reason. Thus sin always triumphs in casting away man's noblest prerogative; in trampling under foot that loyalty to the higher ideal which is the bridal adornment and the peculiar glory of the soul.

"Why hurriest thou to seek thy love?" (Lit. "why dost thou make good thy way?" somewhat as we say, "to make good way with a thing") (ver. 33). The key to the meaning here is supplied by ver 36: "Why art thou in such haste to change thy way? In (Of) Egypt also shalt thou be disappointed, as thou wert in Assyria." The "way" is that which leads to Egypt; and the "love" is that apostasy from Iahvah which invariably accompanies an alliance with foreign peoples (ver. 18). If you go to Assyria, you "drink the waters of the Euphrates," *i. e.*, you are exposed to all the malign influences of the heathen land. Elsewhere, also (iv. 30), Jeremiah speaks of the foreign peoples, whose connection Israel so anxiously courted, as her "lovers"; and the metaphor is a common one in the prophets.

The words which follow are obscure. "Therefore the evil things also hast thou taught thy ways." What "evil things"? Elsewhere the term denotes "misfortunes, calamities." (Lam. iii. 38); and so probably here (*cf.* iii. 5). The sense seems to be: Thou hast done evil, and in so doing hast taught Evil to dog thy steps! The term *evil* obviously suggests the two meanings of sin and the punishment of sin; as we say, "Be sure your *sin* will find you out!" Ver. 34 explains what was the special sin that followed and clung to Israel: "Also in thy skirts (the borders of thy garments) are they (the evil things) found (viz.), the life-blood of innocent helpless ones; not that thou didst find them house-breaking, (and so hadst excuse for slaying them) (Exod. xxii. 2); but for all these (warnings or, because of all these apostasies and dallyings with the heathen, which they denounced) (*cf.* iii. 7), thou slewest them." The murder of the prophets (ver. 30) was the unatoned guilt which clung to the skirts of Israel.

"And thou saidst, Certainly I am absolved! Surely His wrath is turned away from me! Behold I will reason with thee, because thou sayest, I sinned not!" (ver. 35). This is what the people said when they murdered the prophets. They, and doubtess their false guides, regarded the national disasters as so much atonement for their sins. They believed that Iahvah's wrath had exhausted itself in the infliction of what they had already endured, and that they were now absolved from their offences. The prophets looked at the matter differently. To them, national disasters were warnings of worse to follow, unless the people would take them in that sense, and turn from their evil ways. The people preferred to think that their account with Iahvah had been balanced and settled by their misfortunes in war (ver. 30). Hence they slew those who never wearied of affirming the contrary, and threatening further woe, as false prophets (Deut. xviii. 20). The saying, "I sinned not!" refers to these cruel acts; they declared themselves guiltless in the matter of slaying the prophets, as if their blood was on their own heads. The only practical issue of the national troubles was that instead of reforming, they sought to enter into fresh alliances with the heathen, thus, from the point of view of the prophets, adding sin to sin. "Why art thou in such haste to change thy way? (*i. e.*, thy course of action, thy foreign policy). Through Egypt also shalt thou be shamed, as thou hast been shamed through Assyria. Out of this affair also (or, from him, as the country is perhaps personified as a lover of Judah;) shalt thou go forth with thine hands upon thine head (in token of distress, 2 Sam. xiii. 19: Tamar); for Iahvah hath rejected the objects of thy trust, so that thou canst not be successful regarding them" (vv. 36, 37). The Egyptian alliance, like the former one with Assyria, was destined to bring nothing but shame and confusion to the Jewish people. The prophet urges past experience of similar undertakings, in the hope of deterring the politicians of the day from their foolish enterprise. But all that they had learnt from the failure and loss entailed by their intrigues with one foreign power was, that it was expedient to try another. So they made haste to "change their way," to alter the direction of their policy from Assyria to Egypt. King Hezekiah had renounced his vassalage to Assyria, in reliance, as it would seem, on the support of Taharka, king of Egypt and Ethiopia (2 Kings xviii. 7; *cf.* Isa. xxx. 1-5); and now again the nation was coquetting with the same power. As has been stated, an Egyptian force lay at this time on the confines of Judah, and the prophet may be referring to friendly advances of the Jewish princes towards its leaders.

In the Hebrew, ch. iii. opens with the word "saying" (לֵאמֹר). No real parallel to this can be found elsewhere, and the Sept. and Syriac omit the term. Whether we follow these ancient authorities, and do the same, or whether we prefer to suppose that the prophet originally wrote, as usually, "And the Word of Iahvah came unto me, saying," will not make much difference. One thing is clear; the division of the chapters is in this instance erroneous, for the short section, iii. 1-5, obviously belongs to and completes the argument of ch. ii. The statement of ver. 37, that Israel will not prosper in the negotiations with Egypt, is justified in iii. 1 by the consideration that prosperity is an outcome of the Divine favour, which Israel has forfeited. The rejection of Israel's "confidences" implies the rejection of the people themselves (vii. 29). "If a man divorce his wife and she go away from him (מֵאִתּוֹ), *de chez lui*), and become another man's, doth he (her former husband) return unto her again? Would not that land be utterly polluted?" It is the case contemplated in the Book of the Law (Deut. xxiv. 1-4), the supposition being that the second husband may divorce the woman, or that the bond between them may be dissolved by his death. In either contingency, the law forbade reunion with the former husband, as "abomination before Iahvah;" and David's treatment of his ten wives, who had been publicly wedded by his rebel son Absalom, proves the antiquity of the usage in this respect (2 Sam. xx. 3). The relation of Israel to Iahvah is the relation to her former husband of the divorced wife who has married another. If anything it is worse. "And thou, thou hast played the harlot with many paramours; and shalt thou return unto Me? saith Iahvah." The very idea of it is rejected with indignation. The author of the law will not so flagrantly break the law. (With the Heb. form of the question, *cf.* the Latin use of the infin. "Mene incepto desistere victam?") The details of the unfaithfulness of Israel—the proofs that she belongs to others and not to Iahvah—are glaringly obvious; contradiction is impossible. "Lift up thine eyes upon the bare fells, and see!" cries the prophet; "where hast thou not been forced? By the roadsides thou satest for them like a Bedawi in the wilderness, and thou pollutedst the land with thy whoredom and with thine evil" (Hos. vi. 13). On every hilltop the evidence of Judah's sinful dalliance with idols was visible; in her eagerness to consort with the false gods, the objects of her infatuation, she was like a courtesan looking out for paramours by the wayside (Gen. xxxviii. 14), or an Arab lying in wait for the unwary traveller in the desert. (There may be a reference to the artificial *bamoth*, or "high places" erected at the top of the streets, on which the wretched women, consecrated to the shameful rites of the Canaanite goddess Ashtoreth, were wont to sit plying their trade of temptation: 2 Kings xxiii. 8; Ezek. xvi. 25). We must never forget that, repulsive and farfetched as these comparisons of an apostate people to a sinful woman may seem to us, the ideas and customs of the time made them perfectly apposite. The worship of the gods of Canaan involved the practice of the foulest impurities; and by her revolt from Iahvah, her lord and husband, according to the common Semitic conception of the relation between a people and their god, Israel became a harlot in fact as well as in figure. The land was polluted with her "whoredoms," *i. e.*, her worship of the false gods, and her practice of their vile rites; and with her "evil," as instanced above (ii. 30, 35) in the murder of those who protested against these things (Num. xxxv. 33; Ps. cvi. 38. As a punishment for these grave offences, "the showers were withholden, and the spring rains fell not;" but the merciful purpose of this Divine chastisement was not fulfilled; the people were not stirred to penitence, but rather hardened in their sins: "but thou hadst a harlot's forehead; thou refusedst to be made ashamed!" And now the day of grace is past, and repentance comes too late. "Hast thou not but now called unto Me, My Father! Friend of my youth wert Thou? Will He retain His wrath for ever? or keep it without end?" (vv. 3, 5). The reference appears to be to the external reforms accomplished by the young king Josiah in his twelfth year—the year previous to the utterance of this prophecy; when, as we read in 2 Chron. xxxiv. 3, "He began to purge Judah and Jerusalem from the high places, and the Asherim, and the carven images, and the molten images." To all appearance, it was a return of the nation to its old allegiance; the return of the rebellious child to its father, of the erring wife to the husband of her youth. By those two sacred names which in her inexcusable fickleness and ingratitude she had lavished upon stocks and stones, Israel now seemed to be invoking the relenting compassion of her alienated God (ii. 27, ii. 2). But apart from the doubt attaching to the reality of reformations to order, carried out in obedience to a royal decree; apart from the question whether outward changes so easily and rapidly accomplished, in accordance with the will of an absolute monarch, were accompanied by any tokens of a genuine national repentance; the sin of Israel had gone too far, and been persisted in too long, for its terrible consequences to be averted. "Behold,"—it is the closing sentence of the address; a sentence fraught with despair, and the certainty of coming ruin;—"Behold, thou hast planned and accomplished the evil (ii. 33); and thou hast prevailed!" The approaches of the people are met by the assurance that their own plans and doings, rather than Iahvah's wrath, are the direct cause of past and prospective adversity; ill doing is the mother of ill fortune. Israel inferred from her troubles that God was angry with her; and she is informed by His prophet that, had she been bent on bringing those troubles about, she could not have chosen any other line of conduct than that which she had actually pursued. The term "evils" again suggests both the false and impure worships, and their calamitous moral consequences. Against the will of Iahvah, His people "had wrought for its own ruin," and had prevailed.

And now let us take a farewell look at the discourse in its entirety. Beginning at the beginning, the dawn of his people's life as a nation, the young prophet declares that in her early days, in the old times of simple piety and the uncorrupted life of the desert, Israel had been true to her God; and her devotion to her Divine spouse had been rewarded by guidance and protection. "Israel was a thing consecrated to Iahvah; whoever eat of it was held guilty, and evil came upon them" (ii. 1-3). This happy state of mutual love and trust between the Lord and His people began to change with the great change in outward circumstances involved in their conquest of Canaan and settling among the aboriginal inhabitants as the ruling race. With the lands and cities of the conquered, the conquerors soon learned to adopt also their customs of worship, and the licentious merriment of their sacrifices and festivals. Gradually they lost all sense of any radical distinction between the God of Israel and the local deities at whose ancient sanctuaries they now worshipped Him. Soon they forgot their debt to Iahvah; His gracious and long-continued guidance in the Arabian steppes, and the loving care which had established them in the goodly land of orchards and vineyards and cornfields. The priests ceased to care about ascertaining and declaring His will; the princes openly broke His laws; and the popular prophets spoke in the name of the popular Baals (vv. 4-8). There was something peculiarly strange and startling in this general desertion of the national God and Deliverer; it was unparalleled among the surrounding heathen races. *They* were faithful to gods that were no gods; Israel actually exchanged her Glory, the living source of all her strength and well-being, for a useless, helpless idol. Her behaviour was as crazy as if she had preferred a cistern, all cracks and fissures, that could not possibly hold water, to a never failing fountain of sweet spring water (vv. 9-13). The consequences were only too plain to such as had eyes to see. Israel, the servant, the favoured slave of Iahvah, was robbed and spoiled. The "lions," the fierce and rapacious warriors of Assyria, had ravaged his land, and ruined his cities; while Egypt was proving but a treacherous friend, pilfering and plundering on the borders of Judah. It was all Israel's own doing; forsaking his God, he had forfeited the Divine protection. It was his own apostasy, his own frequent and flagrant revolts which were punishing him thus. Vain, therefore, utterly vain were his endeavours to find deliverance from trouble in an alliance with the great heathen powers of South or North (vv. 14-19). Rebellion was no new feature in the national history. No; for of old the people had broken the yoke of Iahvah, and burst the bonds of His ordinances, and said, I will not serve! and on every high hill, and under every evergreen tree, Israel had bowed down to the Baalim of Canaan, in spiritual adultery from her Divine Lord and Husband. The change was a portent; the noble vine-shoot had degenerated into a worthless wilding (vv. 20-21). The sin of Israel was inveterate and ingrained: nothing could wash out the stain of it. Denial of her guilt was futile; the dreadful rites in the valley of Hinnom witnessed against her. Her passion for the foreign worships was as insatiable and headstrong as the fierce lust of the camel or the wild ass. To protests and warnings her sole reply was: "It is in vain! I love the strangers, and them will I follow!" The outcome of all this wilful apostasy was the shame of defeat and disaster, the humiliation of disappointment, when the helplessness of the stocks and stones, which had supplanted her Heavenly Father, was demonstrated by the course of events. Then she bethought her of the God she had so lightly forsaken, only to hear in His silence a bitterly ironical reference to the multitude of her helpers, the gods of her own creation. The national reverses failed of the effect intended in the counsels of Providence. Her sons had fallen in battle; but instead of repenting of her evil ways, she slew the faithful prophets who warned her of the consequences of her misdeeds (vv. 20-30). It was the crowning sin; the cup of her iniquity was full to overflowing. Indignant at the memory of it, the prophet once more insists that the national crimes are what has put misfortune on the track of the nation; and chiefly, this heinous one of killing the messengers of God like housebreakers caught in the act; and then aggravating their guilt by self-justification, and by resorting to Egypt for that help which they despaired of obtaining from an outraged God. All such negotiations, past or present, were doomed to failure beforehand; the Divine sentence had gone forth, and it was idle to contend against it (vv. 31-37). Idle also it was to indulge in hopes of the restoration of Divine favour. Just as it was not open to a discarded wife to return to her husband after living with another; so might not Israel be received back into her former position of the Bride of Heaven, after she had "played the harlot with many lovers." Doubtless of late she had given tokens of remembering her forgotten Lord, calling upon the Father who had been the Guide of her youth, and deprecating the continuance of His wrath. But the time was long since past when it was possible to avert the evil consequences of her misdoings. She had, as it were, steadily purposed and wrought out her own evils; both her sins and her sufferings past and to come: the iron sequence could not be broken; the ruin she had courted lay before her in the near future: she had "prevailed." All efforts such as she was now making to stave it off were like a deathbed repentance; in the nature of things, they could not annihilate the past, nor undo what had been done, nor substitute the fruit of holiness for the fruit of sin, the reward of faithfulness and purity for the wages of worldliness, sensuality, and forgetfulness of God.

Thus the discourse starts with impeachment, and ends with irreversible doom. Its tone is comminatory throughout; nowhere do we hear, as in other prophecies, the promise of pardon in return for penitence. Such preaching was necessary, if the nation was to be brought to a due sense of its evil; and the reformation of the eighteenth of Josiah, which was undoubtedly accompanied by a considerable amount of genuine repentence among the governing classes, was in all likelihood furthered by this and similar prophetic orations.*

* Perhaps, too, the immediate object of the prophet was attained, which was, as Ewald thinks, to dissuade the people from alliance with Psammitichus, the vigorous monarch who was then reviving the power and ambition of Egypt. Jeremiah dreaded the effects of Egyptian influence upon the religion and morals of Judah. Ewald notes the significant absence of all reference to the enemy from the north, who appears in all the later pieces.

CHAPTER III.

ISRAEL AND JUDAH; A CONTRAST.

JEREMIAH iii. 6-iv. 2.

THE first address of our prophet was throughout of a sombre cast, and the darkness of its close was not relieved by a single ray of hope. It was essentially a comminatory discourse, the purpose of it being to rouse a sinful nation to the sense of its peril, by a faithful picture of its actual condition, which was so different from what it was popularly supposed to be. The veil is torn aside; the real relations between Israel and his God are exposed to view; and it is seen that the inevitable goal of persistence in the course which has brought partial disasters in the past, is certain destruction in the imminent future. It is implied, but not said, that the only thing that can save the nation is a complete reversal of policies hitherto pursued, in Church and State and private life; and it is apparently taken for granted that the thing implied is no longer possible. The last word of the discourse was: "Thou hast purposed and performed the evils, and thou hast conquered" (iii. 5). The address before us forms a striking contrast to this dark picture. It opens a door of hope for the penitent. The heart of the prophet cannot rest in the thought of the utter rejection of his people; the harsh and dreary announcement that his people's woes are self-caused cannot be his last word. "His anger was only love provoked to distraction; here it has come to itself again," and holds out an offer of grace first to that part of the whole nation which needs it most, the fallen kingdom of Ephraim, and then to the entire people. The all Israel of the former discourse is here divided into its two sections, which are contrasted with each other, and then again considered as a united nation. This feature distinguishes the piece from that which begins chap. iv. 3, and which is addressed to "Judah and Jerusalem" rather than to Israel and Judah, like the one before us. An outline of the discourse may be given thus. It is shown that Judah has not taken warning by Iahvah's rejection of the sister kingdom (6-10); and that Ephraim may be pronounced less guilty than Judah, seeing that she had witnessed no such signal example of the Divine vengeance on hardened apostasy. She is, therefore, invited to repent and return to her alienated God, which will involve a return from exile to her own land; and the promise is given of the reunion of the two peoples in a restored Theocracy, having its centre in Mount Zion (11-19). All Israel has rebelled against God; but the prophet hears the cry of universal penitence and supplication ascending to heaven; and Iahvah's gracious answer of acceptance (iii. 20-iv. 2).

The opening section depicts the sin which had brought ruin on Israel, and Judah's readiness in following her example, and refusal to take warning by her fate. This twofold sin is aggravated by an insincere repentance. "And Iahvah said unto me, in the days of Josiah the king, Sawest thou what the Turncoat or Recreant Israel did? she would go up every high hill, and under every evergreen tree, and play the harlot there. And methought that after doing all this she would return to Me; but she returned not; and the Traitress, her sister Judah saw it. And I * saw that when for the very reason that she, the Turncoat Israel, had committed adultery, I had put her away, and given her her bill of divorce, the Traitress Judah, her sister, was not afraid, but she too went off and played the harlot. And so, through the cry (*cf.* Gen. iv. 10, xviii. 20 *sq.*) of her harlotry (or read רב for קל, script. defect. through her manifold or abounding harlotry) she polluted the land וַתֶּחֱנַף ver. 2), in that she committed adultery with the Stone and with the Stock. And yet though she was involved in all this guilt (lit. and even in all this. Perhaps the sin and the penalties of it are identified; and the meaning is: "And yet for all this liability:" *cf.* Isa. v. 25), the Traitress Judah returned not unto Me with all her heart (with a *whole* or *undivided* heart, with entire sincerity †) but in falsehood, saith Iahvah." The example of the northern kingdom is represented as a powerful influence for evil upon Judah. This was only natural; for although from the point of view of religious development Judah is incomparably the more important of the sister kingdoms; the exact contrary is the case as regards political power and predominance. Under strong kings like Omri and Ahab, or again, Jeroboam II., Ephraim was able to assert itself as a first-rate power among the surrounding principalities; and in the case of Athaliah, we have a conspicuous instance of the manner in which Canaanite idolatry might be propagated from Israel to Judah. The prophet declares that the sin of Judah was aggravated by the fact that she had witnessed the ruin of Israel, and yet persisted in the same evil courses of which that ruin was the result. She sinned against light. The fall of Ephraim had verified the predictions of her prophets; yet "she was not afraid," but went on adding to the score of her own offences, and polluting the land with her unfaithfulness to her Divine Spouse. The idea that the very soil of her country was defiled by Judah's idolatry may be illustrated by reference to the well-known words of Ps. cvi. 38: "They shed innocent blood, even the blood of their sons and their daughters whom they sacrificed unto the idols of Canaan; and the land was defiled with the bloodshed." We may also remember Elohim's words to Cain: "The voice of thy brother's blood is crying unto Me from the ground!" (Gen. iv. 10). As Iahvah's special dwelling-place, moreover, the land of Israel was holy; and foreign rites desecrated and profaned it, and made it offensive in His sight. The pollution of it cried to heaven for vengeance on those who had caused it. To such a state had Judah brought her own land, and the very city of the sanctuary; "and yet in all this"—amid this accumulation of sins and liabilities—she turned not to her Lord with her whole heart. The reforms set on foot in the twelfth year of Josiah were but superficial and half-hearted; the people merely acquiesced in them, at the dictation of the court, and gave no sign of any inward change or deep-wrought repentance. The semblance without the reality of sorrow for sin is but a mockery of heaven, and a heinous aggravation of guilt. Hence the sin of

* *She* saw: Pesh. This may be right. And the Traitress, her sister, Judah, "saw it: yea, saw that even because the Turncoat Israel had committed adultery, I put her away. . . . And yet the Traitress Judah, her sister, was not afraid, etc."

† 1 Kings ii. 4, בְּכָל־לְבָבָם=בֶּאֱמֶת.

Judah was of a deeper dye than that which had destroyed Israel. "And Iahvah said unto me, The Turncoat *or* Recreant Israel hath proven herself more righteous than the Traitress Judah." Who could doubt it, considering that almost all the prophets had borne their witness in Judah; and that, in imitating her sister's idolatry, she had resolutely closed her eyes to the light of truth and reason? On this ground, that Israel has sinned less and suffered more, the prophet is bidden to hold out to her the hope of Divine mercy. The greatness of her ruin, as well as the lapse of years since the fatal catastrophe, might tend to diminish in the prophet's mind the impression of her guilt; and his patriotic yearning for the restoration of the banished Ten Tribes, who, after all, were the near kindred of Judah, as well as the thought that they had borne their punishment, and thus atoned for their sin (Isa. xl. 2), might coöperate with the desire of kindling in his own countrymen a noble rivalry of repentance, in moving the prophet to obey the impulse which urged him to address himself to Israel. "Go thou, and cry these words northward (toward the desolate land of Ephraim), and say: Return, Turncoat *or* Recreant Israel, saith Iahvah; I will not let My countenance fall at the sight of you (lit. against you, *cf.* Gen. iv. 5); for I am loving, saith Iahvah, I keep not anger for ever. Only recognise thy guilt, that thou hast rebelled against Iahvah thy God, and hast scattered (or lavished: Ps. cxii. 9) thy ways to the strangers (hast gone now in this direction, now in that, worshipping first one idol and then another; *cf.* ii. 23; and so, as it were, dividing up and dispersing thy devotion) under every evergreen tree; but My voice ye have not obeyed, saith Iahvah." The invitation, "Return Apostate Israel!"—'שובה משבה יש*— contains a play of words which seems to suggest that the exile of the Ten Tribes was voluntary, or self-imposed; as if, when they turned their backs upon their true God, they had deliberately made choice of the inevitable consequence of that rebellion, and made up their minds to abandon their native land. So close is the connection, in the prophet's view, between the misfortunes of his people and their sins.

"Return, ye apostate children" (again there is a play on words—שובו בנים שובבים—"Turn back, ye back-turning sons," or "ye sons that turn the back to Me) "saith Iahvah; for it was I that wedded you" (ver. 14), and am, therefore, your proper lord. The expression is not stranger than that which the great prophet of the Return addresses to Zion: "Thy sons shall marry thee." But perhaps we should rather compare another passage of the Book of Isaiah, where it is said: "Iahvah, our God! other lords beside Thee have had dominion over us" (בְּעָלוּנוּ Isa. xxvi. 13), and render: "For it is I that will be your lord;" or perhaps, "For it is I that have mastered you," and put down your rebellion by chastisements; "and I will take you, one of a city and two of a clan, and will bring you to Zion." As a "city" is elsewhere spoken of as a "thousand" (Mic. v. 1), and a "thousand" (אלף) is synonymous with a "clan" (משפחה), as providing a thousand warriors in the national militia, it is clear that the promise is that one or two representatives of each township in Israel shall be restored from exile to the land of their fathers. In other words, we have here Isaiah's doctrine of the remnant, which he calls a "tenth" (Isa. vi. 13), and of which he declared that "the survivors of the house of Judah that remain, shall again take root downwards, and bear fruit upwards" (Isa. xxxvii. 31). And as Zion is the goal of the returning exiles, we may see, as doubtless the prophets saw, a kind of anticipation and foreshadowing of the future in the few scattered members of the northern tribes of Asher, Manasseh, and Zebulun, who "humbled themselves," and accepted Hezekiah's invitation to the passover (2 Chron. xxx. 11, 18); and, again, in the authority which Josiah is said to have exercised in the land of the Ten Tribes (2 Chron. xxxiv. 6; *cf.* 9). We must bear in mind that the prophets do not contemplate the restoration of every individual of the entire nation; but rather the return of a chosen few, a kind of "firstfruits" of Israel, who are to be a "holy seed" (Isa. vi. 13), from which the power of the Supreme will again build up the entire people according to its ancient divisions. So the holy Apostle in the Revelation hears that twelve thousand of each tribe are sealed as servants of God (Rev. vii.).

The happy time of restoration will also be a time of reunion. The estranged tribes will return to their old allegiance. This is implied by the promise, "I will bring you to Zion," and by that of the next verse: "And I will give you shepherds after My own heart; and they shall shepherd you with knowledge and wisdom." Obviously, kings of the house of David are meant; the good shepherds of the future are contrasted with the "rebellious" ones of the past (ii. 8). It is the promise of Isaiah (i. 26): "And I will restore thy judges as at the first, and thy counsellors as at the beginning." In this connection, we may recall the fact that the original schism in Israel was brought about by the folly of evil shepherds. The coming King will resemble not Rehoboam but David. Nor is this all; for "It shall come to pass, when ye multiply and become fruitful in the land, in those days, saith Iahvah, men shall not say any more, The ark of the covenant of Iahvah," (or, as LXX., "of the Holy One of Israel; nor shall it" (the ark) "come to mind; nor shall men remember it, nor miss it; nor shall it be made any more" (pointing יֵעָשֶׂה although the verb may be impersonal. I do not understand why Hitzig asserts "Man wird keine andere machen" (Movers) oder; "sie wird nicht wieder gemacht" (Ew., Graf) "als wäre nicht von der geschichtlichen Lade die Rede, sondern von ihr begrifflich, können die Worte nicht bedeuten." But *cf.* Exod. xxv. 10; Gen. vi. 14; where the same verb עשה is used. Perhaps, however, the rendering of C. B. Michaelis, which he prefers, is more in accordance with what precedes: "nor shall all that be done any more," Gen. xxix. 26, xli. 34. But פקד does not mean "nachforschen:" *cf.* 1 Sam. xx. 6, xxv. 15). "In that time men will call Jerusalem the throne of Iahvah; and all the nations will gather into it" (Gen. i. 9), "for the name of Iahvah (at Jerusalem:" LXX. om.); "and they" (the heathen) "will no longer follow the stubbornness of their evil heart" vii. 24; Deut. xxix. 19).

In the new Theocracy, the true kingdom of God, the ancient symbol of the Divine presence

*As if "Turn back, back-turning Israel!" *i. e.*, Thou that turnedst thy back upon Iahvah, and, therefore, upon His pleasant land.

will be forgotten in the realisation of that presence. The institution of the New Covenant will be characterised by an immediate and personal knowledge of Iahvah in the hearts of all His people (xxxi. 31 *sq.*). The small object in which past generations had loved to recognise the earthly throne of the God of Israel, will be replaced by Jerusalem itself, the Holy City, not merely of Judah, nor of Judah and Israel, but of the world. Thither will all the nations resort "to the name of Iahvah;" ceasing henceforth "to follow the hardness (or callousness) of their own evil heart." That the more degraded kinds of heathenism have a hardening effect upon the heart; and that the cruel and impure worships of Canaan especially tended to blunt the finer sensibilities, to enfeeble the natural instincts of humanity and justice, and to confuse the sense of right and wrong, is beyond question. Only a heart rendered callous by custom, and stubbornly deaf to the pleadings of natural pity, could find genuine pleasures in the merciless rites of the Molech-worship; and they who ceased to follow these inhuman superstitions, and sought light and guidance from the God of Israel, might well be said to have ceased "to walk after the hardness of their own evil heart." The more repulsive features of heathenism chime in too well with the worst and most savage impulses of our nature; they exhibit too close a conformity with the suggestions and demands of selfish appetite; they humour and encourage the darkest passions far too directly and decidedly, to allow us to regard as plausible any theory of their origin and permanence which does not recognise in them at once a cause and an effect of human depravity (*cf.* Rom. i.).

The repulsiveness of much that was associated with the heathenism with which they were best acquainted, did not hinder the prophets of Israel from taking a deep spiritual interest in those who practised and were enslaved by it. Indeed, what has been called the universalism of the Hebrew seers—their emancipation in this respect from all local and national limits and prejudices—is one of the clearest proofs of their divine mission. Jeremiah only reiterates what Micah and Isaiah had preached before him; that "in the latter days the mountain of Iahvah's House shall be established as the chief of mountains, and shall be exalted above the hills; and all the nations will flow unto it" (Isa. ii. 2). In chap. xvi. 19 *sq.* our prophet thus expresses himself upon the same topic. "Iahvah, my strength and my stronghold, and my refuge in the day of distress! unto Thee shall nations come from the ends of the earth, and shall say: Our forefathers inherited naught but a lie, vanity, and things among which is no helper. Shall a man make him gods, when they are no gods?" How largely this particular aspiration of the prophets of the seventh and eighth centuries B. C. has since been fulfilled in the course of the ages is a matter of history. The religion which was theirs has, in the new shape given it by our Lord and His Apostles, become the religion of one heathen people after another, until at this day it is the faith professed, not only in the land of its origin, but by the leading nations of the world.

So mighty a fulfilment of hopes, which at the time of their first conception and utterance could only be regarded as the dreams of enthusiastic visionaries, justifies those who behold and realise it in the joyful belief that the progress of true religion has not been maintained for six and twenty centuries to be arrested now; and that these old-world aspirations are destined to receive a fulness of illustration in the triumphs of the future, in the light of which the brightest glories of the past will pale and fade away.

The prophet does not say, with a prophet of the New Covenant, that "all Israel shall be saved" (Rom. xi. 26). We may, however, fairly interpret the latter of the true Israel, "the remnant according to the election of grace," rather than of "Israel according to the flesh," and so both will be at one, and both at variance with the unspiritual doctrine of the Talmud, that "All Israel," irrespective of moral qualifications, will have "a portion in the world to come," on account of the surpassing merits of Abraham, Isaac, and Jacob, and even of Abraham alone (*cf.* St. Matt. iii. 9; St. John viii. 33).

The reference to the ark of the covenant in the sixteenth verse is remarkable upon several grounds. This sacred symbol is not mentioned among the spoils which Nebuzaradan (Nabû-zir-iddin) took from the temple (lii. 17 *sqq.*); nor is it specified among the treasures appropriated by Nebuchadrezzar at the surrender of Jehoiachin. The words of Jeremiah prove that it cannot be included among "the vessels of gold" which the Babylonian conqueror "cut in pieces" (2 Kings xxiv. 13). We learn two facts about the ark from the present passage: (1) that it no longer existed in the days of the prophet; (2) that people remembered it with regret, though they did not venture to replace the lost original by a new substitute. It may well have been destroyed by Manasseh, the king who did his utmost to abolish the religion of Iahvah. However that may be, the point of the prophet's allusion consists in the thought that in the glorious times of Messianic rule the idea of holiness will cease to be attached to things, for it will be realised in persons; the symbol will become obsolete, and its name and memory will disappear from the minds and affections of men, because the fact symbolised will be universally felt and perceived to be a present and self-evident truth. In that great epoch of Israel's reconciliation, all nations will recognise in Jerusalem "the throne of Iahvah," the centre of light and source of spiritual truth; the Holy City of the world. Is it the earthly or the heavenly Jerusalem that is meant? It would seem, the former only was present to the consciousness of the prophet, for he concludes his beautiful interlude of promise with the words: "In those days will the house of Judah walk beside the house of Israel; and they will come together from the land of the North" ("and from all the lands:" LXX add. *cf.* xvi. 15) "unto the land that I caused your fathers to possess." Like Isaiah (xi. 12 *sqq.*) and other prophets his predecessors, Jeremiah forecasts for the whole repentant and united nation a reinstatement in their ancient temporal rights, in the pleasant land from which they had been so cruelly banished for so many weary years.

"The letter killeth, but the spirit giveth life." If, when we look at the whole course of subsequent events, when we review the history of the Return and of the narrow religious commonwealth which was at last, after many bitter struggles, established on mount Sion; when we consider the form which the religion of Iahvah assumed in the hands of the priestly caste, and the half-religious, half-political sects, whose intrigues and conflicts for power constitute almost all we know of their period; when we reflect upon the character of the entire post-exilic age down to the time of the birth of Christ, with its worldly ideals, its fierce fanaticisms, its superstitious trust in rites and ceremonies; if, when we look at all this, we hesitate to claim that the prophetic visions of a great restoration found fulfilment in the erection of this petty state, this paltry edifice, upon the ruins of David's capital; shall we lay ourselves open to the accusation that we recognise no element of truth in the glorious aspirations of the prophets? I think not.

After all, it is clear from the entire context that these hopes of a golden time to come are not independent of the attitude of the people towards Iahvah. They will only be realised, if the nation shall truly repent of the past, and turn to Him with the whole heart. The expressions "at that time," "in those days" (vv. 17, 18), are only conditionally determinate; they mean the happy time of Israel's repentance, "if such a time should ever come." From this glimpse of glorious possibilities, the prophet turns abruptly to the dark page of Israel's actual history. He has, so to speak, portrayed in characters of light the development as it might have been; he now depicts the course it actually followed. He restates Iahvah's original claim upon Israel's grateful devotion (ii. 2), putting these words into the mouth of the Divine Speaker: "And I indeed thought, How will I set thee among the sons" (of the Divine household), "and give thee a lovely land, a heritage the fairest among the nations! And methought, thou wouldst call Me 'My Father,' and wouldst not turn back from following Me." Iahvah had at the outset adopted Israel, and called him from the status of a groaning bondsman to the dignity of a son and heir. When Israel was a child, He had loved him, and called His son out of Egypt (Hos. xi. 1), to give him a place and a heritage among nations. It was Iahvah, indeed, who originally assigned their holdings to all the nations, and separated the various tribes of mankind, "fixing the territories of peoples, according to the number of the sons of God" (Deut. xxxii. 8 Sept.). If He had brought up Israel from Egypt, He had also brought up the Philistines from Caphtor, and the Arameans from Kir (Amos ix. 7). But He had adopted Israel in a more special sense, which may be expressed in St. Paul's words, who makes it the chief advantage of Israel above the nations that "unto them were committed the oracles of God" (Rom. iii. 2). What nobler distinction could have been conferred upon any race of men than that they should have been thus chosen, as Israel actually was chosen, not merely in the aspirations of prophets, but as a matter of fact in the divinely-directed evolution of human history, to become the heralds of a higher truth, the hierophants of spiritual knowledge, the universally recognised interpreters of God? Such a calling might have been expected to elicit a response of the warmest gratitude, the most enthusiastic loyalty and unswerving devotion. But Israel as a nation did not rise to the level of these lofty prophetic views of its vocation; it knew itself to be the people of Iahvah, but it failed to realise the moral significance of that privilege, and the moral and spiritual responsibilities which it involved. It failed to adore Iahvah as the Father, in the only proper and acceptable sense of that honourable name, the sense which restricts its application to one sole Being. Heathenism is blind and irrational as well as profane and sinful; and so it does not scruple to confer such absolutely individual titles as "God" and "Father" upon a multitude of imaginary powers.

"Methought thou wouldst call Me 'My Father,' and wouldst not turn back from following Me. But" (Zeph. iii. 7) "a woman is false to her fere; so were ye false to Me, O house of Israel, saith Iahvah." The Divine intention toward Israel, God's gracious design for her everlasting good, God's expectation of a return for His favour, and how that design was thwarted so far as man could thwart it, and that expectation disappointed hitherto; such is the import of the last two verses (19, 20). Speaking in the name of God, Jeremiah represents Israel's past as it appears to God. He now proceeds to show dramatically, or as in a picture, how the expectation may yet be fulfilled, and the design realised. Having exposed the national guilt, he supposes his remonstrance to have done its work, and he overhears the penitent people pouring out its heart before God. Then a kind of dialogue ensues between the Deity and His suppliants. "Hark! upon the bare hills is heard the weeping of the supplications of the sons of Israel, that they perverted their way, forgot Iahvah their God." The treeless hill-tops had been the scene of heathen orgies miscalled worship. There the rites of Canaan performed by Israelites had insulted the God of heaven (vv. 2 and 6). Now the very places which witnessed the sin, witness the national remorse and confession. (The 'high places' are not condemned even by Jeremiah as places of worship, but only as places of heathen and illicit worships. The solitude and quiet and purer air of the hill-tops, their unobstructed view of heaven and suggestive nearness thereto, have always made them natural sanctuaries both for public rites and private prayer and meditation: *cf.* 2 Sam. xv. 32; and especially St. Luke vi. 12.

In this closing section of the piece (iii. 19–iv. 2) "Israel" means not the entire people, but the northern kingdom only, which is spoken of separately also in iii. 6-18, with the object of throwing into higher relief the heinousness of Judah's guilt. Israel—the northern kingdom—was less guilty than Judah, for she had no warning example, no beacon-light upon her path, such as her own fall afforded to the southern kingdom; and therefore the Divine compassion is more likely to be extended to her, even after a century of ruin and banishment, than to her callous, impenitent sister. Whether at the time Jeremiah was in communication with survivors of the northern Exile, who were faithful to the God of their fathers, and looked wistfully toward Jerusalem as the centre of the best traditions and the sole hope of Israelite nationality, cannot now be determined. The thing is not unlikely, considering the interest which the prophet afterwards took in the Judean exiles who were taken to Babylon with Jehoiachin (chap. xxix.) and his active correspondence with their leaders. We may also remember that "divers of Asher and Manasseh and Zebulun humbled themselves" and came to keep passover with king Hezekiah at Jerusalem. It cannot, certainly, be supposed, with any show of reason, that the Assyrians either carried away the entire population of the northern kingdom, or exterminated all whom they did not carry away. The words of the Chronicler who speaks of "a remnant . . . escaped out of the hand of the kings of Assyria," are themselves perfectly agreeable to reason and the nature of the case, apart from the consideration that he had special historical sources at his command (2 Chron. xxx. 6, 11). We know that in the Maccabean and Roman wars the rocky fastnesses of the country were a refuge to numbers of the people, and the history of David shows that this had been the case from time immemorial (*cf.* Judg. vi. 2). Doubtless in this way not a few survived the Assyrian invasions and the destruction of Samaria (B. C. 721). But to return to the text. After the confession of the nation that they have "perverted their way" (that is, their mode of worship, by adoring visible symbols of Iahvah, and associating with Him as His compeers a multitude of imaginary gods, especially the local Baalim, ii. 23, and Ashtaroth), the prophet hears another voice, a voice of Divine invitation and gracious promise, responsive to penitence and prayer: "Return, ye apostate sons, let Me heal your apostasies!" or "If ye return, ye apostate sons, I will heal your apostasies!" It is an echo of the tenderness of an older prophet (Hos. xiv. 1, 4). And the answer of the penitents quickly follows: "Behold us, we are come unto Thee, for Thou art Iahvah our God." The voice that now calls us, we know by its tender tones of entreaty, compassion, and love to be the voice of Iahvah our own God; not the voice of sensual Chemosh, tempting to guilty pleasures and foul impurities, not the harsh cry of a cruel Molech, calling for savage rites of pitiless bloodshed. Thou, Iahvah—not these nor their fellows—art our true and only God.

"Surely, in vain" (for naught, bootlessly, 1 Sam. xxv. 21; chap. v. 2, xvi. 19) "on the hills did we raise a din" (lit. "hath one raised"; reading בַּגְּבָעוֹת and הֵרִים ; "surely in Iahvah our God is the safety of Israel!" The Hebrew cannot be original as it now stands in the Masoretic text, for it is ungrammatical. The changes I have made will be seen to be very slight, and the sense obtained is much the same as Ewald's "Surely in vain from the hills is the noise, from the mountains" (where every reader must feel that "from the mountains" is a forcible-feeble addition which adds nothing to the sense). We might also perhaps detach the *mem* from the term for "hills," and connect it with the preceding word, thus getting the meaning: "Surely, for Lies are the hills, the uproar of the mountains!" (הָרִים לַשְּׁקָרִים . . . הֲמוֹן) that is to say, the high places are devoted to delusive nonentities, who can do nothing in return for the wild orgiastic worship bestowed on them; a thought which contrasts very well with the second half of the verse: "Surely, in Iahvah our God is the safety of Israel!"

The confession continues: "And as for the Shame"—the shameful idol, the Baal whose worship involved shameful rites (chap. xi. 13; Hos. ix. 10), and who put his worshippers to shame, by disappointing them of help in the hour of their need (ii. 8, 26, 27)—"as for the Shame"—in contrast with Iahvah, the Safety of Israel, who gives all, and requires little or nothing of this kind in return—"it devoured the labour of our fathers from our youth, their flocks and their herds, their sons and their daughters." The allusion is to the insatiable greed of the idol-priests, and the lavish expense of perpetually recurring feasts and sacrifices, which constituted a serious drain upon the resources of a pastoral and agricultural community; and to the bloody rites which, not content with animal offerings, demanded human victims for the altars of an appalling superstition. "Let us lie down in our shame, and let our infamy cover us! for toward Iahvah our God we trespassed, we and our fathers, from our youth even unto this day, and obeyed not the voice of Iahvah our God." A more complete acknowledgment of sin could hardly be conceived; no palliating circumstances are alleged, no excuses devised, of the kind with which men usually seek to soothe a disturbed conscience. The strong seductions of Canaanite worship, the temptation to join in the joyful merriment of idol-festivals, the invitation of friends and neighbours, the contagion of example,—all these extenuating facts must have been at least as well known to the prophet as to modern critics, but he is expressively silent on the point of mitigating circumstances in the case of a nation to whom such light and guidance had come as came to Israel. No, he could discern no ground of hope for his people except in a full and unreserved admission of guilt, an agony of shame and contrition before God, a heartfelt recognition of the truth that from the outset of their national existence to the passing day they had continually sinned against Iahvah their God and resisted His holy Will.

Finally, to this cry of penitents humbled in the dust, and owning that they have no refuge from the consequences of their sin but in the Divine Mercy, comes the firm yet loving answer: "If thou wilt return, O Israel, saith Iahvah, unto Me wilt return, and if thou wilt put away thine Abominations" ("out of thy mouth and," LXX.) "out of My Presence, and sway not to and fro" (1 Kings xiv. 15), "but wilt swear 'By the Life of Iahvah!' in good faith, justice, and righteousness; then shall the nations bless themselves by Him, and in Him shall they glory" (iv. 1, 2). Such is the close of this ideal dialogue between God and man. It is promised that if the nation's repentance be sincere—not half-hearted like that of Judah (iii. 10; 2 Chron. xxxiv. 33)—and if the fact be demonstrated by a resolute and unwavering rejection of idol-worship, evinced by the disuse of their names in oaths, and the expulsion of their symbols "from the Presence," that is, out of the sanctuaries and domain of Iahvah, and by adhering to the Name of the God of Israel in oaths and compacts of all kinds, and by a scrupulous loyalty to such engagements (Ps. xv. 4; Deut. x. 20; Isa. xlviii. 1); then the ancient oracle of blessing will be fulfilled, and Israel will become a proverb of felicity, the pride and boast of mankind, the glorious ideal of perfect virtue and perfect happiness (Gen. xii. 3; Isa. lxv. 16). Then, "all the nations will gather together unto Jerusalem for the Name of Iahvah" (iii. 17); they will recognise in the religion of Iahvah the answer to their highest longings and spiritual necessities, and will take Israel for what Iahvah intended him to be, their example and priest and prophet.

Jeremiah could hardly have chosen a more extreme instance for pointing the lesson he had to teach than the long-since ruined and depopulated kingdom of the Ten Tribes. Hopeless as their actual condition must have seemed at the time, he assures his own countrymen in Judah and Jerusalem that even yet, if only the moral requirements of the case were fulfilled, and the heart of the poor remnant and of the survivors in banishment aroused to a genuine and permanent repentance, the Divine promises would be accomplished in a people whose sun had apparently set in darkness for ever. And so he passes on to address his own people directly in tones of warning, reproof, and menace of approaching wrath (iv. 3–vi. 30).

CHAPTER IV.

THE SCYTHIANS AS THE SCOURGE OF GOD.

JEREMIAH iv. 3–vi. 30.

IF we would understand what is written here and elsewhere in the pages of prophecy, two things would seem to be requisite. We must prepare ourselves with some knowledge of the circumstances of the time, and we must form some general conception of the ideas and aims of the inspired writer, both in themselves, and in their relation to passing events. Of the former, a partial and fragmentary knowledge may suffice, provided it be true so far as it goes; minuteness of detail is not necessary to general accuracy. Of the latter, a very full and complete conception may be gathered from a careful study of the prophetic discourses.

The chapters before us were obviously composed in the presence of a grave national danger; and what that danger was is not left uncertain, as the discourse proceeds. An invasion of the country appeared to be imminent; the rumour of approaching war had already made itself heard in the capital; and all classes were terror-stricken at the tidings.

As usual in such times of peril, the country people were already abandoning the unwalled towns and villages, to seek refuge in the strong places of the land, and, above all, in Jerusalem, which was at once the capital and the principal fortress of the kingdom. The evil news had spread far and near; the trumpet-signal of alarm was heard everywhere; the cry was, "Assemble yourselves, and let us go into the fenced cities!" (iv. 5).

The ground of this universal terror is thus declared: "The lion is gone up from his thicket, and the destroyer of nations is on his way, is gone forth from his place; to make thy land a desolation, that thy cities be laid waste, without inhabitant" (ver. 7). "A hot blast over the bare hills in the wilderness, on the road to the daughter of my people, not for winnowing, nor for cleansing; a full blast from those hills cometh at My beck" (ver. 11). "Lo, like clouds he cometh up, and, like the whirlwind, his chariots; swifter than vultures are his horses. Woe unto us! We are verily destroyed" (ver. 13). "Besiegers" (lit. "watchmen," Isa. i. 8) "are coming from the remotest land, and they utter their cry against the cities of Judah. Like keepers of a field become they against her on every side" (vv. 16-17). At the same time, the invasion is still only a matter of report; the blow has not yet fallen upon the trembling people. "Behold, I am about to bring upon you a nation from afar, O house of Israel, saith Iahvah; an inexhaustible nation it is, a nation of old time it is, a nation whose tongue thou knowest not, nor understandest (lit. 'hearest') what it speaketh. Its quiver is like an opened grave; they all are heroes. And it will eat up thine harvest and thy bread, which thy sons and thy daughters should eat; it will eat up thy flock and thine herd; it will eat up thy vine and thy figtree; it will shatter thine embattled cities, wherein thou art trusting, with the sword" (v. 15-17). "Thus hath Iahvah said: Lo, a people cometh from a northern land, and a great nation is awaking from the uttermost parts of earth. Bow and lance they hold; savage it is, and pitiless; the sound of them is like the sea, when it roareth; and on horses they ride; he is arrayed as a man for battle, against thee, O daughter of Zion. We have heard the report of him; our hands droop; anguish hath taken hold of us, throes, like hers that travaileth" (vi. 22 *sq.*). With the graphic force of a keen observer, who is also a poet, the priest of Anathoth has thus depicted for all time the collapse of terror which befell his contemporaries, on the rumoured approach of the Scythians in the reign of Josiah. And his lyric fervour carries him beyond this; it enables him to see with the utmost distinctness the havoc wrought by these hordes of savages; the surprise of cities, the looting of houses, the flight of citizens to the woods and the hills at the approach of the enemy; the desertion of the country towns, the devastation of fields and vineyards, confusion and desolation everywhere, as though primeval chaos had returned; and he tells it all with the passion and intensity of one who is relating an actual personal experience. "In my vitals, my vitals, I quake, in the walls of my heart! My heart is murmuring to me; I cannot hold my peace; for my soul is listening to the trumpet-blast, the alarm of war! Ruin on ruin is cried, for all the land is ravaged; suddenly are my tents ravaged, my pavilions in a moment! How long must I see the standards, must I listen to the trumpet-blast?" (iv. 19-21). "I look at the earth, and lo, 'tis chaos: at the heavens, and their light is no more. I look at the mountains, and lo, they rock, and all the hills sway to and fro. I look, and lo, man is no more, and the birds of the air are gone. I look, and lo, the fruitful soil is wilderness, and all the cities of it are overthrown" (iv. 23-26). At the noise of horseman and archer all the city is in flight! They are gone into the thickets, and up the rocks they have clomb: all the city is deserted" (ver. 29). His eye follows the course of devastation until it reaches Jerusalem: Jerusalem, the proud, luxurious capital, now isolated on her hills, bereft of all her daughter cities, abandoned, even betrayed, by her foreign allies. "And thou, that art doomed to destruction, what canst thou do? Though thou clothe thee in scarlet, though thou deck thee with decking of gold, though thou broaden thine eyes with henna, in vain dost thou make thyself fair; the lovers have scorned thee, thy life are they seeking." * The "lovers"—

* The modern singer has well caught the echo of this ancient strain.

"Wilt thou cover thine hair with gold, and with silver thy feet?
Hast thou taken the purple to fold thee, and made thy mouth sweet?
Behold, when thy face is made bare, he that loved thee shall hate:
Thy face shall be no more fair at the fall of thy fate."
—"*Atalanta in Calydon.*"

the false foreigners—have turned against her in the time of her need; and the strange gods, with whom she dallied in the days of prosperity, can bring her no help. And now, while she witnesses, but cannot avert the slaughter of her children, her shrieks ring in the prophet's ear: "A cry, as of one in travail, do I hear; pangs as of her that beareth her firstborn; the cry of the daughter of Zion, that panteth, that spreadeth out her hands: Woe's me! my soul swooneth for the slayers!" (vv. 30, 31).

Even the strong walls of Jerusalem are no sure defence; there is no safety but in flight. "Remove your goods, ye sons of Benjamin, from within Jerusalem! And in Tekoah" (as if Blaston or Blowick or Trumpington) "blow a trumpet-blast and upon Beth-hakkérem raise a signal (or 'beacon')! for evil hath looked forth from the north, and mighty ruin" (vi. 1, 2). The two towns mark the route of the fugitives, making for the wilderness of the south; and the trumpet-call, and the beacon-light, muster the scattered companies at these rallying points or haltingplaces. "The beautiful and the pampered one will I destroy—the daughter of Sion." (Perhaps: "The beautiful and the pampered woman art thou like, O daughter of Sion!" 3d fem. sing. in *-i*.) "To her come the shepherds and their flocks; they pitch the tents upon her round about; they graze each at his own side" (*i. e.*, on the ground nearest him). The figure changes, with lyric abruptness, from the fair woman, enervated by luxury (ver. 2) to the fair pasture-land, on which the nomad shepherds encamp, whose flocks soon eat the herbage down, and leave the soil stripped bare (ver. 3); and then, again, to an army beleaguering the fated city, whose cries of mutual cheer, and of impatience at all delay, the poet-prophet hears and rehearses. "Hallow ye war against her! Arise ye, let us go up" (to the assault) "at noontide! Unhappy we! the day hath turned; the shadows of eventide begin to lengthen! Arise ye, and let us go up in the night, to destroy her palaces!" (vv. 4, 5).

As a fine example of poetical expression, the discourse obviously has its own intrinsic value. The author's power to sketch with a few bold strokes the magical effect of a disquieting rumour; the vivid force with which he realises the possibilities of ravage and ruin which are wrapped up in those vague, uncertain tidings; the pathos and passion of his lament over his stricken country, stricken as yet to his perception only; the tenderness of feeling; the subtle sweetness of language; the variety of metaphor; the light of imagination illuminating the whole with its indefinable charm; all these characteristics indicate the presence and power of a master-singer. But with Jeremiah, as with his predecessors, the poetic expression of feeling is far from being an end in itself. He writes with a purpose to which all the endowments of his gifted nature are freely and resolutely subordinated. He values his powers as a poet and orator solely as instruments which conduce to an efficient utterance of the will of Iahvah. He is hardly conscious of these gifts as such. He exists to "declare in the house of Jacob and to publish in Judah" the word of the Lord.

It is in this capacity that he now comes forward, and addresses his terrified countrymen, in terms not calculated to allay their fears with soothing suggestions of comfort and reassurance, but rather deliberately chosen with a view to heightening those fears, and deepening them to a sense of approaching judgment. For, after all, it is not the rumoured coming of the Scythian hordes that impels him to break silence. It is his consuming sense of the moral degeneracy, the spiritual degradation of his countrymen, which flames forth into burning utterance. "Whom shall I address and adjure, that they may hear? Lo, their ear is uncircumcised, and they cannot hearken; lo, the word of Iahvah hath become to them a reproach; they delight not therein. And of the fury of Iahvah I am full; I am weary of holding it in." Then the other voice in his heart answers: "Pour thou it forth upon the child in the street, and upon the company of young men together!" (vi. 10, 11). It is the righteous indignation of an offended God that wells up from his heart, and overflows at his lips, and cries woe, irremediable woe, upon the land he loves better than his own life.

He begins with encouragement and persuasion, but his tone soon changes to denunciation and despair (iv. 3 *sq.*). "Thus hath Iahvah said to the men of Judah and to Jerusalem, Break you up the fallows, and sow not into thorns! Circumcise yourselves to Iahvah, and remove the foreskins of your heart, ye men of Judah, and ye inhabitants of Jerusalem! lest My fury come forth like fire, and burn with none to quench it, because of the evil of your doings." Clothed with the Spirit, as Semitic speech might express it, his whole soul enveloped in a garment of heavenly light—a magical garment whose virtues impart new force as well as new light—the prophet sees straight to the heart of things, and estimates with God-given certainty the real state of his people, and the moral worth of their seeming repentance. The first measures of Josiah's reforming zeal have been inaugurated; at least within the limits of the capital, idolatry in its coarser and more repellent forms has been suppressed; there is a show of return to the God of Israel. But the popular heart is still wedded to the old sanctuaries, and the old sensuous rites of Canaan; and, worse than this, the priests and prophets, whose centre of influence was the one great sanctuary of the Book of the Law, the temple at Jerusalem, have simply taken advantage of the religious reformation for their own purposes of selfish aggrandisement. "From the youngest to the oldest of them, they all ply the trade of greed; and from prophet to priest, they all practise lying. And they have repaired the ruin of (the daughter) of my people in light fashion, saying, It is well, it is well! though it be not well" (vi. 13, 14). The doctrine of the one legitimate sanctuary, taught with disinterested earnestness by the disciples of Isaiah, and enforced by that logic of events which had demonstrated the feebleness of the local holy places before the Assyrian destroyers, had now come to be recognised as a convenient buttress of the private gains of the Jerusalem priesthood and the venal prophets who supported their authority. The strong current of national reform had been utilised for the driving of their private machinery; and the sole outcome of the self-denying efforts and sufferings of the past appeared to be the enrichment of these grasping and unscrupulous worldlings who sat, like an incubus, upon the heart of the national church. So long as money flowed steadily into their coffers, they were eager enough to reassure the doubting, and to dispel all misgivings by their deceitful oracle that all was well. So long as the sacrifices, the principal source of the priestly revenue, abounded, and the festivals ran their yearly round, they affirmed that Iahweh was satisfied, and that no harm could befall the people of His care. This trading in things Divine, to the utter neglect of the higher obligations of the moral law, was simply appalling to the sensitive conscience of the true prophet of that degenerate age. "A strange and a startling thing it is, that is come to pass in the land. The prophets, they have prophesied in the Lie, and the priests, they tyrannise under their direction; and My people, they love it thus; and what will ye do for the issue thereof?" (v. 30, 31.). For such facts must have an issue; and the present moral and spiritual ruin of the nation points with certainty to impending ruin in the material and political sphere. The two things go together; you cannot have a decline of faith, a decay of true religion, and permanent outward prosperity; *that* issue is incompatible with the eternal laws which regulate the life and progress of humanity. One sits in the heavens, over all things from the beginning, to whom all stated worship is a hideous offence when accompanied by hypocrisy and impurity and fraud and violence in the ordinary relations of life. "What good to me is incense that cometh from Sheba, and the choice calamus from a far country? your burnt offerings" (holocausts) "are not acceptable, and your sacrifices are not sweet unto Me." Instead of purchasing safety, they will ensure perdition: "Therefore thus hath Iahvah said: Lo, I am about to lay for this people stumblingblocks, and they shall stumble upon them, fathers and sons together, a neighbour and his friend; and they shall perish" (vi. 20 *sq.*).

In the early days of reform, indeed, Jeremiah himself appears to have shared in the sanguine views associated with a revival of suspended orthodoxy. The tidings of imminent danger were a surprise to him, as to the zealous worshippers who thronged the courts of the temple. So then, after all, "the burning anger of Iahvah was not turned away" by the outward tokens of penitence, by the lavish gifts of devotion; this unexpected and terrifying rumour was a call for the resumption of the garb of mourning and for the renewal of those public fasts which had marked the initial stages of reformation (iv. 8). The astonishment and the disappointment of the man assert themselves against the inspiration of the prophet, when, contemplating the helpless bewilderment of kings and princes, and the stupefaction of priests and prophets in face of the national calamities, he breaks out into remonstrances with God. "And I said, Alas, O Lord Iahvah! of a truth, Thou hast utterly beguiled this people and Jerusalem, saying, It shall be well with you; whereas the sword will reach to the life." The allusion is to the promises contained in the Book of the Law, the reading of which had so powerfully conduced to the movement for reform. That book had been the text of the prophet-preachers, who were most active in that work; and the influence of its ideas and language upon Jeremiah himself is apparent in all his early discourses.

The prophet's faith, however, was too deeply rooted to be more than momentarily shaken; and it soon told him that the evil tidings were evidence not of unfaithfulness or caprice in Iahvah, but of the hypocrisy and corruption of Israel. With this conviction upon him he implores the populace of the capital to substitute an inward and real for an outward and delusive purification. "Break up the fallows!" Do not dream that any adequate reformation can be superinduced upon the mere surface of life: "Sow not among thorns!" Do not for one moment believe that the word of God can take root and bear fruit in the hard soil of a heart that desires only to be secured in the possession of present enjoyments, in immunity for self-indulgence, covetousness, and oppression of the poor. "Wash thine heart from wickedness, O Jerusalem! that thou mayst be saved. How long shall the schemings of thy folly lodge within thee? For hark! one declareth from Dan, and proclaimeth folly from the hills of Ephraim" (iv. 14 *sq.*). The "folly" (*'awen*) is the foolish hankering after the gods which are nothing in the world but a reflection of the diseased fancy of their worshippers; for it is always true that man makes his god in his own image, when he *does* make him, and does not receive the knowledge of him by revelation. It was a folly inveterate and, as it would seem, hereditary in Israel, going back to the times of the Judges, and recalling the story of Micah the Ephraimite and the Danites who stole his images. That ancient sin still cried to heaven for vengeance; for the apostatising tendency, which it exemplified, was still active in the heart of Israel.* The nation had "rebelled against" the Lord, for it was foolish and had never really known Him; the people were silly children, and lacked insight; skilled only in doing wrong, and ignorant of the way to do right (iv. 22). Like the things they worshipped, they had eyes, but saw not; they had ears, but heard not. Enslaved to the empty terrors of their own imaginations, they, who cowered before dumb idols, stood untrembling in the awful presence of Him whose laws restrained the ocean within due limits, and upon whose sovereign will the fall of the rain and increase of the field depended (v. 21-24). The popular blindness to the claims of the true religion, to the inalienable rights of the God of Israel, involved a corresponding and ever-increasing blindness to the claims of universal morality, to the rights of man. Competent observers have often called attention to the remarkable influence exercised by the lower forms of heathenism in blunting the moral sense; and this influence was fully illustrated in the case of Jeremiah's contemporaries. So complete, so universal was the national decline that it seemed impossible to find one good man within the bounds of the capital. Every aim in life found illustration in those gay, crowded streets, in the bazaars, in the palaces, in the places by the gate where law was administered, except the aim of just and righteous and merciful dealing with one's neighbour. God was ignored or misconceived of, and therefore man was wronged and oppressed. Perjury, even in the Name of the God of Israel, whose eyes regard faithfulness and sincerity, and whose favour is not to be won by professions and presents; a self-hardening against both Divine chastisement and prophetic admonition; a fatal inclination to

* The second *'awen*, however, probably means "trouble," "calamity," as in Hab. iii. 7. The Sept. renders πόνος, and this agrees with the mention of Dan in viii. 16. As Ewald puts it, "from the north of Palestine the misery that is coming from the further north is already being proclaimed to all the nations in the south (vi. 18)."

the seductions of Canaanite worship and the violations of the moral law, which that worship permitted and even encouraged as pleasing to the gods; these vices characterised the entire population of Jerusalem in that dark period. "Run ye to and fro in the streets of Jerusalem, and see now, and know, and seek ye in the broad places thereof, if ye can find a man, if indeed there be one that doeth justice, that seeketh sincerity; that I may pardon her. And if they say, By the life of Iahvah! Even so they swear falsely. Iahvah, are not thine eyes toward sincerity? Thou smotest them, and they trembled not; Thou consumedst them, they refused to receive instruction; they made their faces harder than a rock, they refused to repent. And for me, I said" (methought), "These are but poor folk; they behave foolishly, because they know not the way of Iahvah, the justice" (ver. 1) "of their God: let me betake myself to the great, and speak with them; for they at least know the way of Iahvah, the justice of their God: but these with one consent had broken the yoke, had burst the bonds in sunder" (v. 1-5).

Then, as now, the debasement of the standard of life among the ruling classes was a far more threatening symptom of danger to the commonwealth than laxity of principle among the masses, who had never enjoyed the higher knowledge and more thorough training which wealth and rank, as a matter of course, confer. If the crew turn drunken and mutinous, the ship is in unquestionable peril; but if they who have the guidance of the vessel in their hands follow the vices of those whom they should command and control, wreck and ruin are assured.

The profligacy allowed by heathenism, against which the prophets cried in vain, is forcibly depicted in the words: "Why should I pardon thee? Thy sons have forsaken Me, and have sworn by them that are no gods: though I had bound them" (to Me) "by oath,* they committed" (spiritual) "adultery, and into the house of the Fornicatress" (the idol's temple, where the harlot priestess sat for hire) "they would flock. Stallions roaming at large were they; neighing each to his neighbour's wife. Shall I not punish such offences, saith Iahvah; and shall not My soul avenge herself on such a nation as this?" The cynical contempt of justice, the fraud and violence of those who were in haste to become rich, are set forth in the following: "Among My people are found godless men; one watcheth, as birdcatchers lurk; they have set the trap, they catch men. Like a cage filled with birds, so are their houses filled with fraud: therefore they are become great, and have amassed wealth. They are become fat, they are sleek; also they pass over" Isa. xi. 27) cases (Ex. xxii. 9, xxiv. 14; *cf.* also 1 Sam. x. 2) "of wickedness —neglect to judge heinous crimes; the cause they judge not, the cause of the fatherless, to make it succeed; and the right of the needy they vindicate not" (v. 26-28).

"She is the city doomed to be punished! she is all oppression within. As a spring poureth forth its waters, so she poureth forth her wickedness; violence and oppression resound in her; before Me continually is sickness and wounds" (vi. 6, 7). There would seem to be no hope for such a people and such a city. The prophet, indeed, cannot forget the claims of kindred, the thousand ties of blood and feeling that bind him to this perverse and sinful nation. Thrice, even in this dark forecast of destruction, he mitigates severity with the promise, "yet will I not make a full end." The door is still left open, on the chance that some at least may be won to penitence. But the chance was small. The difficulty was, and the prophet's yearning tenderness towards his people could not blind him to the fact, that all the lessons of God's providence were lost upon this reprobate race: "They have belied the Lord, and said, it is not He; neither shall evil come upon us; neither shall we see sword and famine." The prophets, they insisted, were wrong both in the significance which they attributed to occasional calamities, and in the disasters which they announced as imminent: "The prophets will become wind, and the Word of God is not in them; so will it turn out with them." It was, therefore, wholly futile to appeal to their better judgment against themselves: "Thus said Iahvah, Stop on the ways, and consider, and ask after the eternal paths, where is the good way, and walk therein, and find rest for your soul: and they said, We will not walk therein. And I will set over you watchmen" (the prophets); "hearken ye to the call of the trumpet!" (the warning note of prophecy) "and they said We will not hearken." For such wilful hardness and impenitence, disdaining correction and despising reproof, God appeals to the heathen themselves, and to the dumb earth, to attest the justice of His sentence of destruction against this people: "Therefore, hear, O ye nations, and know, and testify what is among them! Hear, O earth! Lo, I am about to bring evil upon this people, the fruit of their own devisings; for unto My words they have not hearkened, and as for Mine instruction, they have rejected it." Their doom was inevitable, for it was the natural and necessary consequence of their own doings: "Thine own way and thine Own deeds have brought about these evils for thee; this is thine own evil; verily, it is bitter, verily, it reacheth unto thine heart." The discourse ends with a despairing glance at the moral reprobation of Israel. "An assayer did I make thee among My people, a refiner" (reading ***meçārēf***, Mal. iii. 2, 3), "that thou mightest know and assay their kind" (lit. *way*). Jeremiah's call had been to "sit as a refiner and purifier of silver" in the name of his God: in other words, to separate the good elements from the bad in Israel, and to gather around himself the nucleus of a people "prepared for Iahvah." But his work had been vain. In vain had the prophetic fire burnt within him; in vain had the vehemency of the spirit fanned the flame; the Divine word—that solvent of hearts—had been expended in vain; no good metal could come of an ore so utterly base. "They are all the worst" (1 Kings xx. 43) "of rebels" (or, "deserters to the rebels"), "going about with slander; they are brass and iron; they all deal corruptly.* The bellows blow; the lead" (used for fining the ore) "is consumed by the fire; in vain do they go on refining" (or, "does the refiner refine"*); "and the wicked are not separated. Ref-

* With a different point: "When I had fed them to the full" (*cf.* Hos. xiii. 6).

* This term—*mashchîthîm*—is certainly not the plur. of the *mashchîth*, "pitfall" or "trap," of v. 26. The meaning is the same as in Isa. i. 4. The original force of the root *shachath* is seen in the Assyrian *shachâtu*, "to fall down."

† The form—*çārōf*—is like *bāchōn*, "assayer," in ver. 27.

use silver are they called, for Iahvah hath refused them."

CHAPTER V.

POPULAR AND TRUE RELIGION.

JEREMIAH vii.-x., xxvi.

IN the four chapters which we are now to consider we have what is plainly a finished whole. The only possible exception (x. 1-16) shall be considered in its place. The historical occasion of the introductory prophecy (vii. 1-15), and the immediate effect of its delivery, are recorded at length in the twenty-sixth chapter of the book, so that in this instance we are happily not left to the uncertainties of conjecture. We are there told that it was "in the beginning of the reign of Jehoiakim son of Josiah, king of Judah," that Jeremiah received the command to stand in the fore-court of Iahvah's house, and to declare "to all the cities of Judah that were come to worship" there, that unless they repented and gave ear to Iahvah's servants the prophets, He would make the temple like Shiloh, and Jerusalem itself a curse to all the nations of the earth. The substance of the oracle is there given in briefer form than here, as was natural, where the writer's object was principally to relate the issue of it as it affected himself. In neither case is it probable that we have a verbatim report of what was actually said, though the leading thoughts of his address are, no doubt, faithfully recorded by the prophet in the more elaborate composition (chap. vii.). Trifling variations between the two accounts must not, therefore, be pressed.

Internal evidence suggests that this oracle was delivered at a time of grave public anxiety, such as marked the troubled period after the death of Josiah, and the early years of Jehoiakim. "All Judah," or "all the cities of Judah" (xxvi. 2), that is to say, the people of the country towns as well as the citizens of Jerusalem, were crowding into the temple to supplicate their God (vii. 2). This indicates an extraordinary occasion, a national emergency affecting all alike. Probably a public fast and humiliation had been ordered by the authorities, on the reception of some threatening news of invasion. "The opening paragraphs of the address are marked by a tone of controlled earnestness, by an unadorned plainness of statement, without passion, without exclamation, apostrophe, or rhetorical device of any kind; which betokens the presence of a danger which spoke too audibly to the general ear to require artificial heightening in the statement of it. The position of affairs spoke for itself" (Hitzig). The very words with which the prophet opens his message, "Thus said Iahvah Sabaoth, the God of Israel, Make good your ways and your doings, that I may cause you to dwell (permanently) in this place!" (ver. 3, *cf.* ver. 7) prove that the anxiety which agitated the popular heart and drove it to seek consolation in religious observances, was an anxiety about their political stability, about the permanence of their possession of the fair land of promise. The use of the expression "Iahvah Sabaoth" "Iahvah (the God) of Hosts" is also significant, as indicating that war was what the nation feared; while the prophet reminds them thus that all earthly powers, even the armies of heathen invaders, are controlled and directed by the God of Israel for His own sovereign purposes. A particular crisis is further suggested by the warning: "Trust ye not to the lying words, 'The Temple of Iahvah, the Temple of Iahvah, the Temple of Iahvah, is this!'" The fanatical confidence in the inviolability of the temple, which Jeremiah thus deprecates, implies a time of public danger. A hundred years before this time the temple and the city had really come through a period of the gravest peril, justifying in the most palpable and unexpected manner the assurances of the prophet Isaiah. This was remembered now, when another crisis seemed imminent, another trial of strength between the God of Israel and the gods of the heathen. Only part of the prophetic teachings of Isaiah had rooted itself in the popular mind—the part most agreeable to it. The sacrosanct inviolability of the temple, and of Jerusalem for its sake, was an idea readily appropriated and eagerly cherished. It was forgotten that all depended on the will and purposes of Iahvah himself; that the heathen might be the instruments with which He executed his designs, and that an invasion of Judah might mean, not an approaching trial of strength between His omnipotence and the impotency of the false gods, but the judicial outpouring of His righteous wrath upon His own rebellious people.

Jeremiah, therefore, affirms that the popular confidence is ill-founded; that his countrymen are lulled in a false security; and he enforces his point, by a plain exposure of the flagrant offences which render their worship a mockery of God.

Again, it may be supposed that the startling word, "Add your burnt-offerings to your" (ordinary) "offerings, and eat the flesh (of them)" (vii. 21), implies a time of unusual activity in the matter of honouring the God of Israel with the more costly offerings of which the worshippers did not partake, but which were wholly consumed on the altar; which fact also might point to a season of special danger.

And, lastly, the references to taking refuge behind the walls of "defenced cities" (viii. 14; x. 17), as we know that the Rechabites and doubtless most of the rural populace took refuge in Jerusalem on the approach of the third and last Chaldean expedition, seem to prove that the occasion of the prophecy was the first Chaldean invasion, which ended in the submission of Jehoiakim to the yoke of Babylon (2 Kings xxiv. 1). Already the northern frontier had experienced the destructive onslaught of the invaders, and rumour announced that they might soon be expected to arrive before the walls of Jerusalem (viii. 16, 17).

The only other historical occasion which can be suggested with any plausibility is the Scythian invasion of Syria-Palestine, to which the previous discourse was assigned. This would fix the date of the prophecy at some point between the thirteenth and the eighteenth years of Josiah (B. C. 629-624). But the arguments for this view do not seem to be very strong in themselves, and they certainly do not explain the essential identity of the oracle summarised in chap. xxvi. 1-6, with that of vii. 1-15. The "undisguised references to the prevalence of idolatry in Jerusalem itself (vii. 17; *cf.* 30, 31), and the unwillingness of the people to listen to the prophet's teaching (vii. 27)," are quite as well accounted for by supposing a religious or rather an irreligious reaction under Jehoiakim—which is every way probable considering the bad character of that king (2 Kings xxiii. 37; Jer. xxii. 13 *sqq.*), and the serious blow inflicted upon the reforming party by the death of Josiah; as by assuming that the prophecy belongs to the years before the extirpation of idolatry in the eighteenth year of the latter sovereign.

And now let us take a rapid glance at the salient points of this remarkable utterance. The people are standing in the outer court, with their faces turned toward the court of the priests, in which stood the holy house itself (Ps. v. 7). The prophetic speaker stands facing them, "in the gate of the Lord's house," the entry of the upper or inner court, the place whence Baruch was afterwards to read another of his oracles to the people (xxxvi. 10). Standing here, as it were between his audience and the throne of Iahvah, Jeremiah acts as visible mediator between them and their God. His message to the worshippers who throng the courts of Iahvah's sanctuary is not one of approval. He does not congratulate them upon their manifest devotion, upon the munificence of their offerings, upon their ungrudging and unstinted readiness to meet an unceasing drain upon their means. His message is a surprise, a shock to their self-satisfaction, an alarm to their slumbering consciences, a menace of wrath and destruction upon them and their holy place. His very first word is calculated to startle their self-righteousness, their misplaced faith in the merit of their worship and service. "Amend your ways and your doings!" Where was the need of amendment? they might ask. Were they not at that moment engaged in a function most grateful to Iahvah? Were they not keeping the law of the sacrifices, and were not the Levitical priesthood ministering in their order, and receiving their due share of the offerings which poured into the temple day by day? Was not all this honour enough to satisfy the most exacting of deities? Perhaps it was, had the deity in question been merely as one of the gods of Canaan. So much lip-service, so many sacrifices and festivals, so much joyous revelling in the sanctuary, might be supposed to have sufficiently appeased one of the common Baals, those half-womanish phantoms of deity whose delight was imagined to be in feasting and debauchery. Nay, so much zeal might have propitiated the savage heart of a Molech. But the God of Israel was not as these, nor one of these; though His ancient people were too apt to conceive thus of Him, and certain modern critics have unconsciously followed in their wake.

Let us see what it was that called so loudly for amendment, and then we may become more fully aware of the gulf that divided the God of Israel from the idols of Canaan, and His service from all other service. It is important to keep this radical difference steadily before our minds, and to deepen the impression of it, in days when the effort is made by every means to confuse Iahvah with the gods of heathendom, and to rank the religion of Israel with the lower surrounding systems.

Jeremiah accuses his countrymen of flagrant transgression of the universal laws of morality. Theft, murder, adultery, perjury, fraud, and covetousness, slander and lying and treachery (vii. 9, ix. 3-8), are charged upon these zealous worshippers by a man who lived amongst them, and knew them well, and could be contradicted at once if his charges were false.

He tells them plainly that, in virtue of their frequenting it, the temple is become a den of robbers.

And this trampling upon the common rights of man has its counterpart and its climax in treason against God, in "burning incense to the Baal, and walking after other gods whom they know not" (vii. 9); in an open and shameless attempt to combine the worship of the God who had from the outset revealed Himself to their prophets as a "jealous," *i. e.*, an exclusive God, with the worship of shadows who had not revealed themselves at all, and could not be "known," because devoid of all character and real existence. They thus ignored the ancient covenant which had constituted them a nation (vii. 23).

In the cities of Judah, in the streets of the very capital, the cultus of Ashtoreth, the Queen of Heaven, the voluptuous Canaanite goddess of love and dalliance, was busily practised by whole families together, in deadly provocation of the God of Israel. The first and great commandment said, Thou shalt love Iahvah thy God, and Him only shalt thou serve. And they loved and served and followed and sought after and worshipped the sun and the moon and the host of heaven, the objects adored by the nation that was so soon to enslave them (viii. 2). Not only did a worldly, covetous, and sensual priesthood connive in the restoration of the old superstitions which associated other gods with Iahvah, and set up idol symbols and altars within the precincts of His temple, as Manasseh had done (2 Kings xxi. 4-5); they went further than this in their "syncretism," or rather in their perversity, their spiritual blindness, their wilful misconception of the God revealed to their fathers. They actually confounded HIM—the Lord "who exercised lovingkindness, justice, and righteousness, and delighted in" the exhibition of these qualities by His worshippers (ix. 24)—with the dark and cruel sun-god of the Ammonites. They "rebuilt the high places of the Tophet, in the valley of ben Hinnom," on the north side of Jerusalem, "to burn their sons and their daughters in the fire;" if by means so revolting to natural affection they might win back the favour of heaven —means which Iahvah "commanded not, neither came they into His mind" (vii. 31). Such fearful and desperate expedients were doubtless first suggested by the false prophets and priests in the times of national adversity under king Manasseh. They harmonised only too well with the despair of a people who saw in a long succession of political disasters the token of Iahvah's unforgiving wrath. That these dreadful rites were not a "survival" in Israel, seems to follow from the horror which they excited in the allied armies of the two kingdoms, when the king of Moab, in the extremity of the siege, offered his eldest son as a burnt-offering on the wall of his capital before the eyes of the besiegers. So appalled were the Israelite forces by this spectacle of a father's despair, that they at once raised the blockade, and retreated homeward (2 Kings iii. 27). It is probable, then, that the darker and bloodier aspects of heathen worship were of only recent appearance among the Hebrews, and that the rites of Molech had not been at all frequent or familiar, until the long and harassing conflict with Assyria broke the national spirit and inclined the people, in their trouble, to welcome the suggestion that costlier sacrifices were demanded, if Iahvah was to be propitiated and His wrath appeased. Such things were not done, apparently, in Jeremiah's time; he mentions them as the crown of the nation's past offences; as sins that still cried to heaven for vengeance, and would surely entail it, because the same spirit of idolatry which had culminated in these excesses, still lived and was active in the popular heart. It is the persistence in sins of the same character which involves our drinking to the dregs the cup of punishment for the guilty past. The dark catalogue of forgotten offences witnesses against us before the Unseen Judge, and is only obliterated by the tears of a true repentance, and by the new evidence of a change of heart and life. Then, as in some palimpsest, the new record covers and conceals the old; and it is only if we fatally relapse, that the erased writing of our misdeeds becomes visible again before the eye of Heaven. Perhaps also the prophet mentions these abominations because at the time he saw around him unequivocal tendencies to the renewal of them. Under the patronage or with the connivance of the wicked king Jehoiakim, the reactionary party may have begun to set up again the altars thrown down by Josiah, while their religious leaders advocated both by speech and writing a return to the abolished cultus. At all events, this supposition gives special point to the emphatic assertion of Jeremiah, that Iahvah had *not* commanded nor even thought of such hideous rites. The reference to the false labours of the scribes (chap. viii. 8) lends colour to this view. It may be that some of the interpreters of the sacred law actually anticipated certain writers of our own day, in putting this terrible gloss upon the precept, "The firstborn of thy sons shalt thou give unto Me" (Ex. xxii. 29).

The people of Judah were misled, but they were willingly misled. When Jeremiah declares to them, "Lo, ye are trusting, for your part, upon the words of delusion, so that ye gain no good!" (vii. 8) it is perhaps not so much the smooth prophecies of the false prophets as the fatal attitude of the popular mind, out of which those misleading oracles grew, and which in turn they aggravated, that the speaker deprecates. He warns them that an absolute trust in the "præsentia Numinis" is delusive; a trust, cherished like theirs independently of the condition of its justification, viz., a walk pleasing to God. "What! will ye break all My laws, and then come and stand with polluted hands before Me in this house (Isa. i. 15), which is named after Me 'Iahvah's House' (Isa. iv. 1), and reassure yourselves with the thought, We are absolved from the consequences of all these abominations?" (vv. 9-10. Lit. "We are saved, rescued, secured, with regard to having done all these abominations:" *cf.* ii. 35. But perhaps, with Ewald, we should point the Hebrew term differently, and read, "Save us!" "to do all these abominations," as if that were the express object of their petition, which would really ensue, if their prayer were granted: a fine irony. For the form of the verb, *cf.* Ezek. xiv. 14). They thought their formal devotions were more than enough to counterbalance any breaches of the decalogue; they laid that flattering unction to their souls. They could make it up with God for setting His moral law at naught. It was merely a question of compensation. They did not see that the moral law is as immutable as laws physical; and that the consequences of violating or keeping it are as inseparable from it as pain from a blow, or death from poison. They did not see that the moral law is simply the law of man's health and wealth, and that the transgression of it is sorrow and suffering and death.

"If men like you," argues the prophet, "dare to tread these courts, it must be because you believe it a proper thing to do. But that belief implies that you hold the temple to be something other than what is really is; that you see no incongruity in making the House of Iahvah a meeting-place of murderers ("spelunca latronum:" Matt. xxi. 13). That you have yourselves made it, in the full view of Iahvah, whose seeing does not rest there, but involves results such as the present crisis of public affairs; the national danger is proof that He has seen your heinous misdoings." For Iahvah's seeing brings a vindication of right, and vengeance upon evil (2 Chron. xxiv. 22; Ex. iii. 7). He is the watchman that never slumbers nor sleeps; the eternal Judge, Who ever upholds the law of righteousness in the affairs of man, nor suffers the slightest infringement of that law to go unpunished. And this unceasing watchfulness, this perpetual dispensation of justice, is really a manifestation of Divine mercy; for the purpose of it is to save the human race from self-destruction, and to raise it ever higher in the scale of true well-being, which essentially consists in the knowledge of God and obedience to His laws.

Jeremiah gives his audience further ground for conviction. He points to a striking instance in which conduct like theirs had involved results such as his warning holds before them. He establishes the probability of chastisement by an historical parallel. He offers them, so to speak, ocular demonstration of his doctrine. "I also, lo, I have seen, saith Iahvah!" Your eyes are fixed on the temple; so are Mine, but in a different way. You see a national palladium; *I* see a desecrated sanctuary, a shrine polluted and profaned. This distinction between God's view and yours is certain: "for, go ye now to My place which was at Shiloh, where I caused My Name to abide at the outset" (of your settlement in Canaan); "and see the thing that I have done to it, because of the wickedness of My people Israel" (the northern kingdom). *There* is the proof that Iahvah seeth not as man seeth; there, in that dismantled ruin, in that historic sanctuary of the more powerful kingdom of Ephraim, once visited by thousands of worshippers like Jerusalem to-day, now deserted and desolate, a monument of Divine wrath.

The reference is not to the tabernacle, the sacred Tent of the Wanderings, which was first set up at Nob (1 Sam. xxi. 22) and then removed to Gibeon (2 Chron. i. 3), but obviously to a building more or less like the temple, though less magnificent. The place and its sanctuary had doubtless been ruined in the great catastrophe, when the kingdom of Samaria fell before the power of Assyria (721 B. C.).

In the following words (vv. 13-15) the example is applied. "And now"—stating the conclusion —"because of your having done all these deeds" ("saith Iahvah," LXX. omits), "and because I spoke unto you" ("early and late," LXX. omits), "and ye hearkened not, and I called you and ye answered not" (Prov. i. 24): "I will do unto the house upon which My Name is called, wherein ye are trusting, and unto the place which I gave to you and to your fathers—as I did unto Shiloh."

Some might think that if the city fell, the holy house would escape, as was thought by many like-minded fanatics when Jerusalem was beleaguered by the Roman armies seven centuries later: but Jeremiah declares that the blow will fall upon both alike; and to give greater force to his words, he makes the judgment begin at the house of God. (The Hebrew reader will note the dramatic effect of the disposition of the accents. The principal pause is placed upon the word "fathers," and the reader is to halt in momentary suspense upon that word, before he utters the awful three which close the verse: "as I—did to—Shiloh." The Massorets were masters of this kind of emphasis.)

"And I will cast you away from My Presence, as I cast" ("all:" LXX. omits *) "your kinsfolk, all the posterity of Ephraim" (2 Kings xvii. 20). Away from My Presence: far beyond the bounds of that holy land where I have revealed Myself to priests and prophets, and where My sanctuary stands; into a land where heathenism reigns, and the knowledge of God is not; into the dark places of the earth, that lie under the blighting shadow of superstition, and are enveloped in the moral midnight of idolatry. "Projiciam vos a facie mea." The knowledge and love of God—heart and mind ruled by the sense of purity and tenderness and truth and right united in an Ineffable Person, and enthroned upon the summit of the universe—these are light and life for man; where these are, there is His Presence. They who are so endowed behold the face of God, in Whom is no darkness at all. Where these spiritual endowments are nonexistent; where mere power, or superhuman force, is the highest thought of God to which man has attained; where there is no clear sense of the essential holiness and love of the Divine Nature; there the world of man lies in darkness that may be felt: there bloody rites prevail; there harsh oppression and shameless vices reign: for the dark places of the earth are full of the habitations of cruelty.

"And thou, pray thou not for this people" (xviii. 20), "and lift not up for them outcry nor prayer, and urge not Me, for I hear thee not. Seest thou not what they do in the cities of Judah and in the streets of Jerusalem? The children gather sticks, and the fathers light the fire, and the women knead dough, to make sacred buns" (xliv. 19) "for the Queen of Heaven, and to pour libations to other gods, in order to grieve Me" (Deut. xxxii. 16, 21). "Is it Me that they grieve? saith Iahvah; is it not themselves" (rather), "in regard to the shame of their own faces" (16-19).

From one point of view, all human conduct may be said to be "indifferent" to God; He is αὐτάρκης, self-sufficing, and needs not our praises, our love, our obedience, any more than He needed the temple ritual and the sacrifices of bulls and goats. Man can neither benefit nor injure God; he can only affect his own fortunes in this world and the next, by rebellion against the laws upon which his welfare depends, or by a careful observance of them. In this sense, it is true that wilful idolatry, that treason against God, does not "provoke" or "grieve" the Immutable One. Men do such things to their own sole hurt, to the shame of their own faces: that is, the punishment will be the painful realisation of the utter groundlessness of their confidence, of the folly of their false trust; the mortification of disillusion, when it is too late. That Jeremiah should have expressed himself thus is sufficient answer to those who pretend that the habitual anthropomorphism of the prophetic discourses is anything more than a mere accident of language and an accommodation to ordinary style.

In another sense, of course, it is profoundly true to say that human sin provokes and grieves the Lord. God is Love; and love may be pained to its depths by the fault of the beloved, and stirred to holy indignation at the disclosure of utter unworthiness and ingratitude. Something corresponding to these emotions of man may be ascribed, with all reverence, to the Inscrutable Being who creates man "in His own image," that is, endowed with faculties capable of aspiring towards *Him*, and receiving the knowledge of His being and character.

"Pray not thou for this people . . . for I hear thee not!" Jeremiah was wont to intercede for his people (xi. 14, xviii. 20, xv. 1; *cf.* 1 Sam. xii. 23). The deep pathos which marks his style, the minor key in which almost all his public utterances are pitched, proves that the fate which he saw impending over his country grieved him to the heart. "Our sweetest songs are those which tell of saddest thought;" and this is eminently true of Jeremiah. A profound melancholy had fallen like a cloud upon his soul; he had seen the future, fraught as it was with suffering and sorrow, despair and overthrow, slaughter and bitter servitude; a picture in which images of terror crowded one upon another, under a darkened sky, from which no ray of blessed hope shot forth, but only the lightnings of wrath and extermination. Doubtless his prayers were frequent, alive with feeling, urgent, imploring, full of the convulsive energy of expiring hope. But in the midst of his strong crying and tears, there arose from the depths of his consciousness the conviction that all was in vain. "Pray not thou for this people, for I will not hear thee." The thought stood before him, sharp and clear as a command; the unuttered sound of it rang in his ears, like the voice of a destroying angel, a messenger of doom, calm as despair, sure as fate. He knew it was the voice of God.

In the history of nations as in the lives of individuals there are times when repentance, even if possible, would be too late to avert the evils which long periods of misdoing have called from the abyss to do their penal and retributive work. Once the dike is undermined, no power on earth can hold back the flood of waters from the defenceless lands beneath. And when a nation's sins have penetrated and poisoned all social and political relations, and corrupted the very fountains of life, you cannot avert the flood of ruin that must come, to sweep away the tainted mass of spoiled humanity; you cannot avert the storm that must break to purify the air, and make it fit for men to breathe again.

"Therefore"—because of the national unfaith-

* The omissions of the Septuagint are not always intelligent. The repetition of the "all" here intensifies the idea of the *totality* of the ruin of the northern kingdom. The two clauses balance each other: "all your brethren—all the seed of Ephraim." The objection that Edom was also a "brother" of Israel (Deut. xxiii. 8; Amos i. 11) shows a want of rhetorical sense.

In vii. 4 the Septuagint tastelessly omits the third "The Temple of Iahvah!" upon which the rhetorical effect largely depends: *cf.* chap. xxii. 29: Isa. vi. 3.

fulness—"thus said the Lord Iahvah, Lo, Mine anger and My fury are being poured out toward this place—upon the men, and upon the cattle, and upon the trees of the field, and upon the fruit of the ground; and it will burn, and not be quenched!" (vii. 20). The havoc wrought by war, the harrying and slaying of man and beast, the felling of fruit trees and firing of the vineyards, are intended; but not so as to exclude the ravages of pestilence and droughts (chap. xiv.) and famine. All these evils are manifestations of the wrath of Iahvah. Cattle and trees and "the fruit of the ground," *i. e.*, of the cornlands and vineyards, are to share in the general destruction (*cf.* Hos. iv. 3), not, of course, as partakers of man's guilt, but only by way of aggravating his punishment. The final phrase is worthy of consideration, because of its bearing upon other passages. "It will burn and not be quenched," or "it will burn unquenchably." The meaning is not that the Divine wrath once kindled will go on burning for ever; but that once kindled, no human or other power will be able to extinguish it, until it has accomplished its appointed work of destruction.

"Thus said Iahvah Sabaoth, the God of Israel: Your holocausts add ye to your common sacrifices, and eat ye flesh!" that is, Eat flesh in abundance, eat your fill of it! Stint not yourselves by devoting any portion of your offerings wholly to Me. I am as indifferent to your "burnt-offerings," your more costly and splendid gifts, as to the ordinary sacrifices, over which you feast and make merry with your friends (1 Sam. i. 4, 13). The holocausts which you are now burning on the altar before Me will not avail to alter My settled purpose. "For I spake not with your fathers, nor commanded them, in the day that I brought them forth out of the land of Egypt, concerning matters of holocaust and sacrifice, but this matter commanded I them, 'Hearken ye unto My voice, so become I God to you, and you—ye shall become to Me a people; and walk ye in all the way that I shall command you, that it may go well with you!" (22-23) *cf.* Deut. vi. 3. Those who believe that the entire priestly legislation as we now have it in the Pentateuch is the work of Moses, may be content to find in this passage of Jeremiah no more than an extreme antithetical expression of the truth that to obey is better than sacrifice. There can be no question that from the outset of its history. Israel, in common with all the Semitic nations, gave outward expression to its religious ideas in the form of animal sacrifice. Moses cannot have originated the institution, he found it already in vogue, though he may have regulated the details of it. Even in the Pentateuch, the term "sacrifice" is nowhere explained; the general understanding of the meaning of it is taken for granted (see Ex. xii. 27, xxiii. 18). Religious customs are of immemorial use, and it is impossible in most cases to specify the period of their origin. But while it is certain that the institution of sacrifice was of extreme antiquity in Israel as in other ancient peoples, it is equally certain, from the plain evidence of their extant writings, that the prophets before the Exile attached no independent value either to it or to any other part of the ritual of the temple. We have already seen how Jeremiah could speak of the most venerable of all the symbols of the popular faith (iii. 16). Now he affirms that the traditional rules for the burnt-offerings and other sacrifices were not matters of special Divine institution, as was popularly supposed at the time. The reference to the Exodus may imply that already in his day there were written narratives which asserted the contrary; that the first care of the Divine Saviour after He had led His people through the sea was to provide them with an elaborate system of ritual and sacrifice, identical with that which prevailed in Jeremiah's day. The important verse already quoted (viii. 8) seems to glance at such pious fictions of the popular religious teachers: "How say ye, We are wise, and the instruction" (A. V. "law") "of Iahvah is with us? But behold for lies hath it wrought—the lying pen of the scribes!"

It is, indeed, difficult to see how Jeremiah or any of his predecessors could have done otherwise than take for granted the established modes of public worship, and the traditional holy places. The prophets do not seek to alter or abolish the externals of religion as such; they are not so unreasonable as to demand that stated rites and traditional sanctuaries should be disregarded, and that men should worship in the spirit only, without the aid of outward symbolism of any sort, however innocent and appropriate to its object it might seem. They knew very well that rites and ceremonies were necessary to public worship; what they protested against was the fatal tendency of their time to make these the whole of religion, to suppose that Iahvah's claims could be satisfied by a due performance of these, without regard to those higher moral requirements of His law which the ritual worship might fitly have symbolised but could not rightly supersede. It was not a question with Hosea, Amos, Micah, Isaiah, Jeremiah, whether or not Iahvah could be better honoured with or without temples and priests and sacrifices. The question was whether these traditional institutions actually served as an outward expression of that devotion to Him and His holy law, of that righteousness and holiness of life, which is the only true worship, or whether they were looked upon as in themselves comprising the whole of necessary religion. Since the people took this latter view, Jeremiah declares that their system of public worship is futile.

"Hearken unto My voice": not as giving regulations about the ritual, but as inculcating moral duty by the prophets, as is explained immediately (ver. 25), and as is clear also from the statement that "they walked in the schemes of their own evil heart" (omit: "in the stubbornness," with LXX., and read "mô'açôth" stat. constr.), "and fell to the rear and not the front." As they did not advance in the knowledge and love of the spiritual God, who was seeking to lead them by His prophets, from Moses downwards (Deut. xviii. 15), they steadily retrogaded and declined in moral worth, until they had become hopelessly corrupt and past correction. (Lit. "and they became back and not face," which may mean, they turned their backs upon Iahvah and His instruction.) This steady progress in evil is indicated by the words, "and they hardened their neck, they did worse than their fathers" (ver. 26). It is implied that this was the case with each successive generation, and the view of Israel's history thus expressed is in perfect harmony with common experience. Progress, one way or the other, is the law of character; if we do not advance in goodness, we go back, or, what is the same thing, we advance in evil.

Finally, the prophet is warned that his mission

also must fail, like that of his predecessors, unless indeed the second clause of ver. 27, which is omitted by the Septuagint, be really an interpolation. At all events, the failure is implied if not expressed, for he is to pronounce a sentence of reprobation upon his people. "And thou shalt speak all these words unto them" ("and they will not hearken unto thee, and thou shalt call unto them, and they will not answer thee:" LXX. omits). "And thou shalt say unto them, This is the nation that hearkened not unto the voice of Iahvah its God, and received not correction: Good faith is perished and cut off from their mouth" (*cf.* ix. 3 *sq.* The charge is remarkable. It is one which Jeremiah reiterates: see ver. 9, vi. 13, vii. 5, ix. 3 *sqq.*, xii. 1. His fellow-countrymen are at once deceivers and deceived. They have no regard for truth and honour in their mutual dealings; grasping greed and lies and trickery stamp their everyday intercourse with each other; and covetousness and fraud equally characterise the behaviour of their religious leaders. Where truth is not prized for its own sake, there debased ideas of God and lax conceptions of morality creep in and spread. Only he who loves truth comes to the light; and only he who does God's will sees that truth is divine. False belief and false living in turn beget each other; and as a matter of experience it is often impossible to say which was antecedent to the other.

In the closing section of this first part of his long address (vv. 29-viii. 3), Jeremiah apostrophises the country, bidding her bewail her imminent ruin. "Shear thy tresses" (coronal of long hair) "and cast them away, and lift upon the bare hills a lamentation!"—sing a dirge over thy departed glory and thy slain children, upon those unhallowed mountain-tops which were the scene of thine apostasies (iii. 21); "for Iahvah hath rejected and forsaken the generation of His wrath." The hopeless tone of this exclamation (*cf.* also vv. 15, 16, 20) seems to agree better with the times of Jehoiakim, when it had become evident to the prophet that amendment was beyond hope, than with the years prior to Josiah's reformation. His own contemporaries are "the generation of Iahvah's wrath," *i. e.*, upon which His wrath is destined to be poured out, for the day of grace is past and gone; and this, because of the desecration of the temple itself by such kings as Ahaz and Manasseh, but especially because of the horrors of the child-sacrifices in the valley of ben Hinnom (2 Kings xvi. 3, xxi. 3-6), which those kings had been the first to introduce in Judah. "Therefore behold days are coming, saith Iahvah, and it shall no more be called the Tophet" (an obscure term, probably meaning something like "Pyre" or "Burning-place:" *cf.* the Persian *tab-idan* "to burn," and the Greek θάπτω, ταφ-εῖν, "to bury," strictly "to burn" a corpse; also τύφω, "to smoke," Sanskrit *dhûp:* to suppose a reproachful name like "Spitting" = "Object of loathing," is clearly against the context: the honourable name is to be exchanged for one of dishonour), "and the Valley of ben Hinnom, but the Valley of Slaughter, and people shall bury in (the) Tophet for want of room (elsewhere)"! A great battle is contemplated, as is evident also from Deut. xxviii. 25, 26, the latter verse being immediately quoted by the prophet (ver. 33). The Tophet will be defiled for ever by being made a burial place; but many of the fallen will be left unburied, a prey to the vulture and the jackal. In that fearful time, all sounds of joyous life will cease in the cities of Judah and in the capital itself, "for the land will become a desolation." And the scornful enemy will not be satisfied with wreaking his vengeance upon the living; he will insult the dead, by breaking into the sepulchres of the kings and grandees, the priests and prophets and people, and haling their corpses forth to lie rotting in face of the sun, moon, and stars, which they had so sedulously worshipped in their lifetime, but which will be powerless to protect their dead bodies from this shameful indignity. And as for the survivors, "death will be preferred to life in the case of all the remnant that remain of this evil tribe, in all the places whither I shall have driven them, saith Iahvah Sabaoth" (omit the second "that remain," with LXX. as an accidental repetition from the preceding line, and as breaking the construction). The prophet has reached the conviction that Judah will be driven into banishment; but the details of the destruction which he contemplates are obviously of an imaginative and rhetorical character. It is, therefore, superfluous to ask whether a great battle was actually fought afterwards in the valley of ben Hinnom, and whether the slain apostates of Judah were buried there in heaps, and whether the conquerors violated the tombs. Had the Chaldeans or any of their allies done this last, in search of treasure for instance, we should expect to find some notice of it in the historical chapters of Jeremiah. But it was probably known well enough to the surrounding peoples that the Jews were not in the habit of burying treasure in their tombs. The prophet's threat, however, curiously corresponds to what Josiah is related to have done at Bethel and elsewhere, by way of irreparably polluting the high places (2 Kings xxiii. 16 *sqq.*); and it is probable that his recollection of that event, which he may himself have witnessed, determined the form of Jeremiah's language here.

In the second part of this great discourse (viii. 4-23) we have a fine development of thoughts which have already been advanced in the opening piece, after the usual manner of Jeremiah. The first half (or strophe) is mainly concerned with the sins of the nation (vv. 4-13), the second with a despairing lament over the punishment (14-23 = ix. 1). "And thou shalt say unto them: Thus said Iahvah, Do men fall and not rise again? Doth a man turn back, and not return? Why doth Jerusalem make this people to turn back with an eternal" (or perfect, utter, absolute) "turning back? Why clutch they deceit, refuse to return?" (The LXX. omits "Jerusalem," which is perhaps only a marginal gloss. We should then have to read שׁוֹבָב "shobab" for שׁוֹבֵבָה "shobebah," as "this people" is masc. The "He" has been written twice by inadvertence. The verb, however, is transitive in l. 19; Isa. xlvii. 10, etc.; and I find no certain instance of the intrans. form besides Ezek. xxxviii. 8, participle.) "I listened and heard; they speak not aright" (Ex. x. 29; Isa. xvi. 6); "not a man repenteth over his evil, saying (or think-

NOTE ON vii. 25.—The word answering to "daily" in the Heb. simply means "day," and ought to be omitted, as an accidental repetition either from the previous line, or of the last two letters of the preceding word "prophets." *Cf.* ver. 13, where a similar phrase, "rising early and speaking," occurs in a similar context, but without "daily."

ing), 'What have I done?' They all" (lit. "all of him," *i. e.*, the people) "turn back into their courses" (plur. Heb. text; sing. Heb. marg.), "like the rushing horse into the battle."

There is something unnatural in this obstinate persistence in evil. If a man happens to fall he does not remain on the ground, but quickly rises to his feet again; and if he turn back on his way for some reason or other, he will usually return to that way again. There is a play on the word "turn back" or "return," like that in iii. 12, 14. The term is first used in the sense of turning back or away from Iahvah, and then in that of returning to Him, according to its metaphorical meaning "to repent." Thus the import of the question is: Is it natural to apostatise and never to repent of it? (Perhaps we should rather read, after the analogy of iii. 1, "Doth a man 'go away' (הֲיֵלֵךְ) on a journey, and not return?")

Others interpret: "Doth a man return, and not return?" That is, if he return, he does it, and does not stop midway; whereas Judah only pretends to repent, and does not really do so. This, however, does not agree with the parallel member, nor with the following similar questions.

It is very noticeable how thoroughly the prophets, who, after all, were the greatest of practical moralists, identify religion with right aims and right conduct. The beginning of evil courses is turning away from Iahvah; the beginning of reform is turning back to Iahvah. For Iahvah's character as revealed to the prophets is the ideal and standard of ethical perfection; He does and delights in love, justice, and equity (ix. 23). If a man look away from that ideal, if he be content with a lower standard than the Will and Law of the All-Perfect, then and thereby he inevitably sinks in the scale of morality. The prophets are not troubled by the idle question of mediæval schoolmen and sceptical moderns. It never occurred to them to ask the question whether God is good because God wills it, or whether God wills good because it is good. The dilemma is, in truth, no better than a verbal puzzle, if we allow the existence of a personal Deity. For the idea of God is the idea of a Being who is absolutely good, the *only* Being who is such; perfect goodness is understood to be realised nowhere else but in God. It is part of His essence and conception; it is the aspect under which the human mind apprehends Him. To suppose goodness existing apart from Him, as an independent object which He may choose or refuse, is to deal in empty abstractions. We might as well ask whether convex can exist apart from concave in nature, or motion apart from a certain rate of speed. The human spirit can apprehend God in His moral perfections, because it is, at however vast a distance, akin to Him—a "divinæ particula auræ;" and it can strive towards those perfections by help of the same grace which reveals them. The prophets know of no other origin or measure of moral endeavour than that which Iahvah makes known to them. In the present instance, the charge which Jeremiah makes against his contemporaries is a radical falsehood, insincerity, faithlessness: "they clutch" or "cling to deceit, they speak what is not right" or "honest, straightforward" (Gen. xlii. 11, 19). Their treason to God and their treachery to their fellows are opposite sides of the same fact. Had they been true to Iahvah, that is, to His teachings through the higher prophets and their own consciences, they would have been true to one another. The forbearing love of God, His tender solicitude to hear and save, are illustrated by the words: "I listened and heard . . . not a man repented over his evil, saying, What have I done?" (The feeling of the stricken conscience could hardly be more aptly expressed than by this brief question.) But in vain does the Heavenly Father wait for the accents of penitence and contrition: "they all return"—go back again and again (Ps. xxiii. 6)—"into their own race" or "courses, like a horse rushing" (lit. "pouring forth:" of rushing waters, Ps. lxxviii. 20) "into the battle." The eagerness with which they follow their own wicked desires, the recklessness with which they "give their sensual race the rein," in set defiance of God, and wilful oblivion of consequences, is finely expressed by the simile of the warhorse rushing in headlong eagerness into the fray (Job xxxix. 25). "Also" (or "even") "the stork in the heavens knoweth her appointed times, and turtledove, swift and crane observe the season of their coming; but My people know not the ordinance of Iahvah"—what He has willed and declared to be right for man (His Law; "jus divinum, relligio divina"). The dullest of wits can hardly fail to appreciate the force of this beautiful contrast between the regularity of instinct and the aberrations of reason. All living creatures are subject to laws upon obedience to which their well-being depends. The life of man is no exception; it too is subject to a law—a law which is as much higher than that which regulates mere animal existence as reason and conscience and spiritual aspiration are higher than instinct and sexual impulse. But whereas the lower forms of life are obedient to the laws of their being, man rebels against them, and dares to disobey what he knows to be for his good; nay, he suffers himself to be so blinded by lust and passion and pride and self-will that at last he does not even recognise the Law—the ordinance of the Eternal—for what it really is, the organic law of his true being, the condition at once of his excellence and his happiness.

The prophet next meets an objection. He has just alleged a profound moral ignorance—a culpable ignorance—against the people. He supposes them to deny the accusation, as doubtless they often did in answer to his remonstrances (*cf.* xvii. 15, xx. 7 *sq.*) "How can ye say, 'We are wise'"—morally wise—"'and the teaching of Iahvah is with us!'" ("but behold:" LXX. omits: either term would be sufficient by itself) "for the Lie hath the lying pen of the scribes made it!" The reference clearly is to what Jeremiah's opponents call "the teaching (or 'law: torah') of Iahvah"; and it is also clear that the prophet charges the "scribes" of the opposite party with falsifying or tampering with the teaching of Iahvah in some way or other. Is it meant that they misrepresent the terms of a written document, such as the Book of the Covenant, or Deuteronomy? But they could hardly do this without detection, in the case of a work which was not in their exclusive possession. Or does Jeremiah accuse them of misinterpreting the sacred law, by putting false glosses upon its precepts, as might be done in a legal document wherever there seemed room for a difference of opinion, or wherever conflicting traditional interpretations existed side by side? (*Cf.* my remarks on vii. 31). The Hebrew may indicate this, for we may translate: "But lo, into the lie the lying pen of the scribes hath made it!" which recalls St. Paul's description of the heathen as changing the truth of God into a lie (Rom. i. 26). The construction is the same as in Gen. xii. 2; Isa. xliv. 17. Or, finally, does he boldly charge these abettors of the false prophets with forging supposititious law-books, in the interest of their own faction, and in support of the claims and doctrines of the worldly priests and prophets? This last view is quite admissible, so far as the Hebrew goes, which, however, is not free from ambiguity. It might be rendered, "But behold, in vain," or "bootlessly" (iii. 23) "hath the lying pen of the scribes laboured;" taking the verb in an absolute sense, which is not a common use (Ruth ii. 19). Or we might transpose the terms for "pen" and "lying," and render, "But behold, in vain hath the pen of the scribes fabricated falsehood." In any case, the general sense is the same: Jeremiah charges not only the speakers, but the writers, of the popular party with uttering their own inventions in the name of Iahvah. These scribes were the spiritual ancestors of those of our Saviour's time, who "made the word of God of none effect for the sake of their traditions" (Matt. xv. 6). "For the Lie" means, to maintain the popular misbelief. (It might also be rendered, "for falsehood, falsely," as in the phrase "to swear falsely," *i. e.*, for deceit; Lev. v. 24.) It thus appears that conflicting and competing versions of the law were current in that age. Has the Pentateuch preserved elements of both kinds, or is it homogeneous throughout? Of the scribes of the period we, alas! know little beyond what this passage tells us. But Ezra must have had predecessors, and we may remember that Baruch, the friend and amanuensis of Jeremiah, was also a scribe (xxxvi. 26).

"The 'wise' will blush, they will be dismayed and caught! Lo, the word of Iahvah they rejected, and wisdom of what sort have they?" (vi. 10). The whole body of Jeremiah's opponents, the populace as well as the priests and prophets, are intended by "the wise," that is, the wise in their own conceits (ver. 8); there is an ironical reference to their own assumption of the title. These self-styled wise ones, who preferred their own wisdom to the guidance of the prophet, will be punished by the mortification of discovering their folly when it is too late. Their folly will be the instrument of their ruin, for "He taketh the wise in their own craftiness" as in a snare (Prov. v. 22).

They who reject Iahvah's word, in whatever form it comes to them, have no other light to walk by; they must needs walk in darkness, and stumble at noonday. For Iahvah's word is the only true wisdom, the only true guide of man's footsteps. And this is the kind of wisdom which the Holy Scriptures offer us; not a merely speculative wisdom, not what is commonly understood by the terms science and art, but the priceless knowledge of God and of His will concerning us; a kind of knowledge which is beyond all comparison the most important for our well-being here and hereafter. If this Divine wisdom, which relates to the proper conduct of life and the right education of the highest faculties of our being, seem a small matter to any man, the fact argues spiritual blindness on his part; it cannot diminish the glory of heavenly wisdom.

Some well-meaning but mistaken people are fond of maintaining what they call "the scientific accuracy of the Bible," meaning thereby an essential harmony with the latest discoveries, or even the newest hypotheses, of physical science. But even to raise such a preposterous question, whether as advocate or as assailant, is to be guilty of a crude anachronism, and to betray an incredible ignorance of the real value of the Scriptures. That value I believe to be inestimable. But to discuss "the scientific accuracy of the Bible" appears to me to be as irrelevant to any profitable issue, as it would be to discuss the meteorological precision of the Mahabharata, or the marvellous chemistry of the Zendavesta, or the physiological revelations of the Koran, or the enlightened anthropology of the Nibelungenlied.

A man may reject the word of Iahvah, he may reject Christ's word, because he supposes that it is not sufficiently attested. He may urge that the proof that it is of God breaks down, and he may flatter himself that he is a person of superior discernment, because he perceives a fact to which the multitude of believers are apparently blind. But what kind of proof would he have? Does he demand more than the case admits of? Some portent in earth or sky or sea, which in reality would be quite foreign to the matter in hand, and could have none but an accidental connection with it, and would, in fact, be no proof at all, but itself a mystery requiring to be explained by the ordinary laws of physical causation? To demand a kind of proof which is irrelevant to the subject is a mark not of superior caution and judgment, but of ignorance and confusion of thought. The plain truth is, and the fact is abundantly illustrated by the teachings of the prophets and, above all, of our Divine Lord, that moral and spiritual truths are self-attesting to minds able to realise them: and they no more need supplementary corroboration than does the ultimate testimony of the senses of a sane person.

Now the Bible as a whole is an unique repertory of such truths; this is the secret of its age-long influence in the world. If a man does not care for the Bible, if he has not learned to appreciate this aspect of it, if he does not *love* it precisely on this account, I, in turn, care very little for his opinion about the Bible. There may be much in the Bible which is otherwise valuable, which is precious as history, as tradition, as bearing upon questions of interest to the ethnologist, the antiquarian, the man of letters. But these things are the shell, *that* is the kernel; these are the accidents, *that* is the substance; these are the bodily vesture, *that* is the immortal spirit. A man who has not felt this has yet to learn what the Bible is.

In his text as we now have it, Jeremiah proceeds to denounce punishment on the priests and prophets, whose fraudulent oracles and false interpretations of the Law ministered to their own greedy covetousness, and who smoothed over the alarming state of things by false assurances that all was well (vv. 10-12). The Septuagint, however, omits the whole passage after the words, "Therefore I will give their wives to others, their fields to conquerors!" and as these words are obviously an abridgment of the threat, vi. 12 (*cf.* Deut. xxviii. 30), while the rest of the passage agrees verbatim with vi. 13-15, it may be supposed that a later editor inserted it in the margin here, as generally apposite (*cf.* vi. 10 with ver. 9), whence it has crept into the text. It is true that Jeremiah himself is fond of repetition, but not so as to interrupt the context, as the "therefore" of ver. 10 seems to do. Besides, the "wise" of ver. 8 are the self-confident people; but if this passage be in place here, "the wise" of ver. 9 will have to be understood of their false guides, the prophets and priests. Whereas, if the passage be omitted, there is manifest continuity between the ninth verse and the thirteenth: "'I will sweep, sweep them away,' saith Iahvah; no grapes on the vine, and no figs on the fig tree, and the foliage is withered, and I have given them destruction" (or "blasting").

The opening threat is apparently quoted from the contemporary prophet Zephaniah (i. 2, 3). The point of the rest of the verse is not quite clear, owing to the fact that the last clause of the Hebrew text is undoubtedly corrupt. We might suppose that the term "laws" (חֻקִּים) had fallen out, and render, "and I gave them laws which they transgress" (*cf.* v. 22, xxxi. 35). The Vulgate has an almost literal translation, which gives the same sense: "et dedi eis quæ prætergressa sunt." * The Septuagint omits the clause, probably on the ground of its difficulty. It may be that bad crops and scarcity are threatened (*cf.* chap. xiv. v. 24, 25). In that case, we may correct the text in the manner suggested above שְׁבָרִים or בָּרוֹשָׁן xvii. 18, for יַעַבְרוּם ; or שִׁדָּפוֹן Amos iv. 9, for the יַעַבְדוּם of other MSS.). Others understand the verse in a metaphorical sense. The language seems to be coloured by a reminiscence of Micah vii. 1, 2; and the "grapes" and "figs" and "foliage" may be the fruits of righteousness, and the nation is like Isaiah's unfruitful vineyard (Isa. v.) or our Lord's barren fig tree (Matt. xxi. 19), fit only for destruction (*cf.* also vi. 9 and ver. 20). Another passage which resembles the present is Hab. iii. 17: "For the fig tree will not blossom, and there will be no yield on the vines; the produce of the olive will disappoint, and the fields will produce no food." It was natural that tillage should be neglected upon the rumour of invasion. The country-folk would crowd into the strong places, and leave their vineyards, orchards, and cornfields to their fate (ver. 14). This would, of course, lead to scarcity and want, and aggravate the horrors of war with those of dearth and famine. I think the passage of Habakkuk is a precise parallel to the one before us. Both contemplate a Chaldean invasion, and both anticipate its disastrous effects upon husbandry.

It is possible that the original text ran: "And I have given (will give) unto them their own work" (*i. e.*, the fruit of it, עֲבֹדָתָם : used of field-work, Ex. i. 14; of the earnings of labour, Isa. xxxii. 17). This, which is a frequent thought in Jeremiah, forms a very suitable close to the verse. The objection is that the prophet does not use this particular term for "work" elsewhere. But the fact of its only once occurring might have caused its corruption. (Another term, which would closely resemble the actual reading, and give much the same sense as this last, is צְבוּרָם "their produce." This, too, as a very rare expression, only known from Josh. v. 11, 12, might have been misunderstood and altered by an editor or copyist. It is akin to the Aramaic עִבּוּר, and there are other Aramaisms in our prophet.) One thing is certain; Jeremiah cannot have written what now appears in the Masoretic text.

It is now made clear what the threatened evil is, in a fine closing strophe, several expressions of which recall the prophet's magnificent alarm upon the coming of the Scythians (*cf.* iv. 5 with viii. 14; iv. 15 with viii. 16; iv. 19 with viii. 18). Here, however, the colouring is darker, and the prevailing gloom of the picture unrelieved by any ray of hope. The former piece belongs to the reign of Josiah, this to that of the worthless Jehoiakim. In the interval between the two, moral decline and social and political disintegration had advanced with fearfully accelerated speed, and Jeremiah knew that the end could not be far off.

The fatal news of invasion has come, and he sounds the alarm to his countrymen. "Why are we sitting still" (in silent stupefaction)? "assemble yourselves, that we may go into the defenced cities, and be silent" (or "amazed, stupefied," with terror) "there! for Iahvah our God hath silenced us" (with speechless terror) "and given us water of gall to drink; for we trespassed toward Iahvah. We looked for peace" (or, weal, prosperity, "and there is no good; for a time of healing, and behold panic fear!" So the prophet represents the effect of the evil tidings upon the rural population. At first they are taken by surprise; then they rouse themselves from their stupor to take refuge in the walled cities. They recognise in the trouble a sign of Iahvah's anger. Their fond hopes of returning prosperity are nipped in the bud; the wounds of the past are not to be healed; the country has hardly recovered from one shock, before another and more deadly blow falls upon it. The next verse describes more particularly the nature of the bad news; the enemy, it would seem, had actually entered the land, and given no uncertain indication of what the Judeans might expect, by his ravages on the northern frontier.

"From Dan was heard the snorting of his horses; at the sound of the neighings of his chargers all the land did quake: and they came in" (into the country) "and eat up the land and the fulness thereof, a city and them that dwelt therein." This was what the invaders did to city after city, once they had crossed the border; ravaging its domain, and sacking the place itself. Perhaps, however, it is better to take the perfects as prophetic, and to render: "From Dan shall be heard . . . shall quake: and they shall come and eat up the land," etc. This makes the connection easier with the next verse, which certainly has a future reference: "For behold I am about to send" (or simply, "I send") "against you serpents, basilisks" (Isa. xi. 8, the "çiſ'oni" was a small but very poisonous snake; Aquila βασιλίσκος, Vulg. regulus), "for whom there is no charm, and they will bite you! saith Iahvah." If the tenses be supposed to describe what has already happened, then the connection of thought may be expressed thus: all this evil that you have heard of has happened, not by mere ill fortune, but by the Divine will: Iahvah Himself has done it, and the evil will not stop there, *for*

* *Wa'etten lahem* can only mean "and I give (in prophetic idiom 'and I will give') unto them," and this, of course, requires an object. "I will give them to those who shall pass over them" is the rendering proposed by several scholars. But *lahem* does not mean "to those," and the thought does not harmonise with what precedes, and this use of עבר is doubtful, and the verb "to give" absolutely requires an object. The Vulgate rendering is really more in accordance with Hebrew syntax, as the masc. suffix of the verb might be used in less accurate writing. Targum: "because I gave them My law from Sinai, and they transgressed against it;" Peshito: "and I gave unto them, and they transgressed them." So also the Syro-Hexaplar of Milan (participle: "were transgressing") between asterisks.

He purposes to send these destroying serpents into your very midst (*cf.* Num. xxi. 6).

The eighteenth verse begins in the Hebrew with a highly anomalous word, which is generally supposed to mean "my source of comfort" (מבליגיתי). But both the strangeness of the form itself, which can hardly be paralleled in the language, and the indifferent sense which it yields, and the uncertainty of the Hebrew MSS., and the variations of the old versions, indicate that we have here another corruption of the text. Some Hebrew copies divide the word, and this is supported by the Septuagint and the Syro-Hexaplar version, which treat the verse as the conclusion of ver. 17, and render "and they shall bite you 'incurably, with pain of your perplexed heart'" (Syro-Hex. "without cure"). But if the first part of the word is "without" (מִבְּלִי? "for lack of" . . .), what is the second? No such root as the existing letters imply is found in Hebrew or the cognate languages. The Targum does not help us: "Because they were scoffing" (מלעינין) "against the prophets who prophesied unto them, sorrow and sighing will I bring" (איתי) "upon them on account of their sins: upon them, saith the prophet, my heart is faint." It is evident that this is no better than a kind of punning upon the words of the Masoretic text.* I incline to read "How shall I cheer myself? Upon me is sorrow; upon me my heart is sick." (The prophet would write עַל not עָלַי for "against," without a suffix. Read מַה אַבְלִיגָה עָלַי יָגוֹן Job ix. 27, x. 20; Ps. xxxix. 14.) The passage is much like iv. 19.

Another possible emendation is: "Iahvah causeth sorrow to flash forth upon me" (יהוה מבליג: after the archetype of Amos v. 9); but I prefer the former.

Jeremiah closes the section with an outpouring of his own overwhelming sorrow at the heart-rending spectacle of the national calamities. No reader endued with any degree of feeling can doubt the sincerity of the prophet's patriotism, or the willingness with which he would have given his own life for the salvation of his country. This one passage alone says enough to exonerate its author from the charge of indifference, much more of treachery to his fatherland. He imagines himself to hear the cry of the captive people, who have been carried away by the victorious invader into a distant land: "Hark! the sound of the imploring cry of the daughter of my people from a land far away! 'Is Iahvah not in Sion? or is not her King in her?'" (*cf.* Mic. iv. 9). Such will be the despairing utterance of the exiles of Judah and Jerusalem; and the prophet hastens to answer it with another question, which accounts for their ruin by their disloyalty to that heavenly King; "O why did they vex Me with their graven images, with alien vanities?" Compare a similar question and answer in an earlier discourse (v. 19). It may be doubted whether the pathetic words which follow —"The harvest is past, the fruit-gathering is finished, but as for us, we are not delivered!"—are to be taken as a further complaint of the captives, or as a reference by the prophet himself to hopes of deliverance which had been cherished in vain, month after month, until the season of campaigns was over. In Palestine, the grain crops are harvested in April and May, the ingathering of the fruit falls in August. During all the summer months, Jehoiakim, as a vassal of Egypt, may have been eagerly hoping for some decisive interference from that quarter. That he was on friendly terms with that power at the time appears from the fact that he was allowed to fetch back refugees from its territory (xxvi. 22 *sq.*). A provision for the extradition of offenders is found in the far more ancient treaty between Ramses II. and the king of the Syrian Chetta (fourteenth cent. B. C.). But perhaps the prophet is alluding to one of those frequent failures of the crops, which inflicted so much misery upon his people (*cf.* vers. 13, iii. 3, v. 24, 25), and which were a natural incident of times of political unsettlement and danger. In that case, he says, the harvest has come and gone, and left us unhelped and disappointed. I prefer the political reference, though our knowledge of the history of the period is so scanty that the particulars cannot be determined.

It is clear enough from the lyrical utterance which follows (vv. 21-23), that heavy disasters had already befallen Judah: "For the shattering of the daughter of my people am I shattered; I am a mourner; astonishment hath seized me!" This can hardly be pure anticipation. The next two verses may be a fragment of one of the prophet's elegies (*qinoth*). At all events, they recall the metre of Lam. iv. and v.:

> "Doth balm in Gilead fail?
> Fails the healer there?
> Why is not bound up
> My people's deadly wound?
>
> "Oh that my head were springs,
> Mine eye a fount of tears!
> To weep both day and night
> Over my people's slain."

It is not impossible that these two quatrains are cited from the prophet's elegy upon the last battle of Megiddo and the death of Josiah. Similar fragments seem to occur below (ix. 17, 18, 20) in the instructions to the mourning-women, the professional singers of dirges over the dead.

The beauty of the entire strophe, as an outpouring of inexpressible grief, is too obvious to require much comment. The striking question "Is there no balm in Gilead, is there no physician there?" has passed into the common dialect of religious aphorism; and the same may be said of the despairing cry, "The harvest is past, the summer is ended, and we are not saved!"

The wounds of the state are past healing; but how, it is asked, can this be? Does nature yield a balm which is sovereign for bodily hurts, and is there nowhere a remedy for those of the social organism? Surely that were something anomalous, strange, and unnatural (*cf.* viii. 7). "Is there no balm in Gilead?" Yes, it is found nowhere else (*cf.* Plin., "Hist. Nat.," xii. 25 *ad init.* "Sed omnibus odoribus præfertur balsamum, *uni terrarum Judææ concessum*"). Then has Iahvah mocked us, by providing a remedy for the lesser evil, and leaving us a hopeless prey to the greater? The question goes deep down to the roots of faith. Not only is there an analogy between the two realms of nature and spirit; in a sense, the whole physical world is an adumbration of things unseen, a manifestation of the spiritual. Is it conceivable that order should reign everywhere in the lower sphere, and chaos be the normal state of the higher? If our baser

* It seems to take the עלי each time as עליהון = 'עלי and to read מלעינים איתי for מבלגיתי: thus getting "Scoffers! I will bring upon them sorrow; upon them my heart is faint."

wants are met by provisions adapted in the most wonderful way to their satisfaction, can we suppose that the nobler—those cravings by which we are distinguished from irrational creatures—have not also their satisfactions included in the scheme of the world? To suppose it is evidence either of capricious unreason, or of a criminal want of confidence in the Author of our being.

"Is there no balm in Gilead? Is there no healer there?" There is a panacea for Israel's woes—the "law" or teaching of Iahvah; there is a Healer in Israel, Iahvah Himself (iii. 22, xvii. 14), who has declared of Himself, "I wound and I heal" (Deut. xxxii. 39; xxx. 17, xxxiii. 6). "Why then is no bandage applied to the daughter of my people?" This is like the cry of the captives; "Is Iahvah not in Sion, is not her King in her?" (ver. 19). The answer there is, Yes! it is not that Iahvah is wanting; it is that the national guilt is working out its own retribution. He leaves this to be understood here; having framed his question so as to compel people, if it might be, to the right inference and answer.

The precious balsam is the distinctive glory of the mountain land of Gilead, and the knowledge of Iahvah is the distinctive glory of His people Israel. Will no one, then, apply the true remedy to the hurt of the state? No, for priests and prophets and people "know not—they have refused to know" Iahvah (ver. 5). The nation will not look to the Healer and live. It is their misfortunes that they hate, not their sins. There is nothing left for Jeremiah but to sing the funeral song of his fatherland.

While weeping over their inevitable doom, the prophet abhors with his whole soul his people's wickedness, and longs to fly from the dreary scene of treachery and deceit. "O that I had in the wilderness a lodging-place of wayfaring men"—some lonely khan on a caravan track, whose bare, unfurnished walls, and blank almost oppressive stillness, would be a grateful exchange for the luxury and the noisy riot of Judah's capital—"that I might leave my people and go away from among them!" The same feeling finds expression in the sigh of the psalmist, who is perhaps Jeremiah himself: "O for the wings of a dove!" (Ps. lv. 6 *sqq.*). The same feeling has often issued in actual withdrawal from the world. And under certain circumstances, in certain states of religion and society, the solitary life has its peculiar advantages. The life of towns is doubtless busy, practical, intensely real; but its business is not always of the ennobling sort, its practice in the strain and struggle of selfish competition is often distinctly hostile to the growth and play of the best instincts of human nature; its intensity is often the mere result of confining the manifold energies of the mind to one narrow channel, of concentrating the whole complex of human powers and forces upon the single aim of self-advancement and self-glorification; and its reality is consequently an illusion, phenomenal and transitory as the unsubstantial prizes which absorb all its interest, engross its entire devotion, and exhaust its whole activity. It is not upon the broad sea, nor in the lone wilderness, that men learn to question the goodness, the justice, the very being of their Maker. Atheism is born in the populous wastes of cities, where human beings crowd together, not to bless, but to prey upon each other; where rich and poor dwell side by side, but are separated by the gulf of cynical indifference and social disdain; where selfishness in its ugliest forms is rampant, and is the rule of life with multitudes:—the selfishness which grasps at personal advantage and is deaf to the cries of human pain; the selfishness which calls all manner of fraud and trickery lawful means for the achievement of its sordid ends; and the selfishness of flagrant vice, whose activity is not only earthly and sensual, but also devilish, as directly involving the degradation and ruin of human souls. No wonder that they whose eyes have been blinded by the god of this world, fail to see evidence of any other God; no wonder that they in whose hearts a coarse or a subtle self-worship has dried the springs of pity and love can scoff at the very idea of a compassionate God; no wonder that a soul, shaken to its depths by the contemplation of this bewildering medley of heartlessness and misery, should be tempted to doubt whether there is indeed a Judge of all the earth, who doeth right.

There is no truth, no honour in their dealings with one another; falsehood is the dominant note of their social existence: "They are all adulterers, a throng of traitors!" The charge of adultery is no metaphor (v. 7, 8). Where the sense of religious sanctions is weakened or wanting, the marriage tie is no longer respected; and that which perhaps lust began, is ended by lust, and man and woman are faithless to each other, because they are faithless to God.

"And they bend their tongue, their bow, falsely." * The tongue is as a bow of which words are the arrows. Evildoers "stretch their arrow, the bitter word, to shoot in ambush at the blameless man" (Ps. lxiv. 4; *cf.* Ps. xi. 2). The metaphor is common in the language of poetry; we have an instance in Longfellow's "I shot an arrow into the air," and Homer's familiar ἔπεα πτερόεντα, "winged words," is a kindred expression. (Others render, "and they bend their tongue as their bow of falsehood," as though the term "sheqer, mendacium" were an epithet qualifying the term for "bow." I have taken it adverbially, a use justified by Pss. xxxviii. 20, lxix. 5, cxix. 78, 86.) In colloquial English a man who exaggerates a story is said to "draw the long bow."

Their tongue is a bow with which they shoot lies at their neighbours, "and it is not by truth"—faithfulness, honour, integrity—"that they wax mighty in the land;" their riches and power are the fruit of craft and fraud and overreaching. As was said in a former discourse, "their houses are full of deceit, therefore they become great, and amass wealth" (v. 27). "By truth," or more literally "unto truth, according to the rule or standard of truth" (*cf.* Isa. xxxii. 1, "according to right;" Gen. i. 11, "according to its kind"). With the idea of the verb, we may compare Ps. cxii. 2: "Mighty in the land shall his seed become" (*cf.* also Gen. vii. 18, 19). The passage chap. v. 2, 3, is essentially similar to the present, and is the only one besides where we find the term "by truth" לאמונה "le'emunah"). The idiom seems certain, and the parallel passages, especially v. 27, appear to establish the

* The irregular *Hiphil* form of the verb—*cf.* 1 Sam. xiv. 22; Job xix. 4—may be justified by Job xxviii. 8; we are not, therefore, bound to render the Masoretic text: "and they make their tongue bend their lying bow." Probably, however, *Qal* is right, the *Hiphil* being due to a misunderstanding, like that of the Targum, "And they taught their tongue words of lying."

translation above given; otherwise one might be tempted to render: "they stretch their tongue, their bow, for lying" (לשקר, v. 2), "and it is not for truth that they are strong in the land." "Noblesse oblige" is no maxim of theirs; they use their rank and riches for unworthy ends.

"For out of evil unto evil they go forth"—they go from one wickedness to another, adding sin to sin. Apparently, a military metaphor. What they have and are is evil, and they go forth to secure fresh conquests of the same kind. Neither good nor evil is stationary; progress is the law of each—"and Me they know not, saith Iahvah"—they know not that I am truth itself, and therefore irreconcilably opposed to all this fraud and falsehood.

"Beware ye, every one of his companion, and in no brother confide ye; for every brother will surely play the Jacob,—and every companion will go about slandering. And they deceive each his neighbour, and truth they speak not: they have trained their tongue to speak falsehood, to pervert" (their way, iii. 21) "they toil" (xx. 9; *cf.* Gen. xix. 11). "Thine inhabiting is in the midst of deceit; through deceit they refuse to know Me, saith Iahvah" (3-5).* As Micah had complained before him (Mic. vii. 5), and as bitter experience had taught our prophet (xi. 18 *sqq.*, xii. 6), neither friend nor brother was to be trusted; and that this was not merely the melancholy characteristic of a degenerate age, is suggested by the reference to the unbrotherly intrigues of the far-off ancestor of the Jewish people, in the traditional portrait of whom the best and the worst features of the national character are reflected with wonderful truth and liveliness.† "Every brother will not fail to play the Jacob" (Gen. xxv. 29 *sqq.*, xxvii. 36; Hos. xii. 4), to outwit, defraud, supplant; cunning and trickery will subserve acquisitiveness. But though an inordinate love of acquisition may still seem to be specially characteristic of the Jewish race, as in ancient times it distinguished the Canaanite and Semitic nations in general, the tendency to cozen and overreach one's neighbour is so far from being confined to it that some modern ethical speculators have not hesitated to assume this tendency to be an original and natural instinct of humanity. The fact, however, for which those who would account for human nature upon purely "natural" grounds are bound to supply some rational explanation, is not so much that aspect of it which has been well-known to resemble the instincts of the lower animals ever since observation began, but the aspect of revolt and protest against those lower impulses which we find reflected so powerfully in the documents of the higher religion, and which makes thousands of lives a perpetual warfare.

Jeremiah presents his picture of the universal deceit and dissimulation of his own time as something peculiarly shocking and startling to the common sense of right, and unspeakably revolting in the sight of God, the Judge of all. And yet the difficulty to the modern reader is to detect any essential difference between human nature then and human nature now—between those times and these. It is still true that avarice and lust destroy natural affection; that the ties of blood and friendship are no protection against a godless love of self. The work of slander and misrepresentation is not left to avowed enemies; your own acquaintance will ratify their envy, spite, or mere ill-will in this unworthy way. A simple child may tell the truth; but tongues have to be trained to expertness in lying, whether in commerce or in diplomacy, in politics or in the newspaper press, in the art of the salesman or in that of the agitator and the demagogue. Men still make a toil of perverting their way, and spend as much pains in becoming accomplished villains as honest folk take to excel in virtue. Deceit is still the social atmosphere and environment, and "through deceit" men "refuse to know Iahvah." The knowledge, the recognition, the steady recollection of what Iahvah is, and what His law requires, does not suit the man of lies; his objects oblige him to shut his eyes to the truth. Men "do not will" and "will not," to know the moral impediments that lie in the way of self-seeking and self-pleasing. Sinning is always a matter of choice, not of nature, nor of circumstances alone. To desire to be delivered from moral evil is, so far, a desire to know God.

"Thine inhabiting is in the midst of deceit:" who that ever lifts an eye above the things of time has not at times felt thus? "This is a Christian country." Why? Because the majority are as bent on self-pleasing, as careless of God, as heartlessly and systematically forgetful of the rights and claims of others, as they would have been had Christ never been heard of? A Christian country? Why? Is it because we can boast of some two hundred forms or fashions of supposed Christian belief, differentiated from each other by heaven knows what obscure shibboleths, which in the lapse of time have become meaningless and obsolete; while the old ill-will survives, and the old dividing lines remain, and Christians stand apart from Christians in a state of dissension and disunion that does despite and dishonour to Christ, and must be very dear to the devil? Some people are bold enough to defend this horrible condition of things by raising a cry of Free Trade in Religion. But religion is not a trade, not a thing to make a profit of, except with Simon Magus and his numerous followers both inside and outside of the Church.

A Christian country! But the rage of avarice, the worship of Mammon, is not less rampant in London than in old Jerusalem. If the more violent forms of oppression and extortion are restrained among us by the more complete organisation of public justice, the fact has only developed new and more insidious modes of attack upon the weak and the unwary. Deceit and fraud have been put upon their mettle by the challenge of the law, and thousands of people are robbed and plundered by devices which the law can hardly reach or restrain. Look where the human spider sits, weaving his web of guile, that he may catch and devour men! Look at the wonderful baits which the company-monger throws out day by day to human weakness and cupidity! Do you call him shrewd and clever and enterprising? It is a sorry part to play in life, that of Satan's decoy, tempting one's fellow-creatures to their ruin. Look at the lying advertisements, which meet your eyes wherever you

* Ewald prefers the reading of the LXX., which divides the words differently. If we suppose their version correct, they must have read: "They have trained their tongue to speak falsehood, to distort. They are weary of returning. Oppression is oppression, deceit in deceit! They refuse to know Me, saith Iahvah." But I do not think this an improvement on the present Masoretic text.

† If Jeremiah wrote Ps. lv., as Hitzig supposes, he may be alluding to the treachery of a particular friend; *cf.* Ps. lv. 13, 14.

turn, and make the streets of this great city almost as hideous from the point of view of taste as from that of morality! What a degrading resource! To get on by the industrious dissemination of lies, by false pretences, which one knows to be false! And to trade upon human misery—to raise hopes that can never be fulfilled—to add to the pangs of disease the smart of disappointment and the woe of a deeper despair, as countless quacks in this Christian country do!

A Christian country: where God is denied on the platform and through the press; where a novel is certain of widespread popularity if its aim be to undermine the foundations of the Christian faith; where atheism is mistaken for intelligence, and an inconsistent Agnosticism for the loftiest outcome of logic and reason; where flagrant lust walks the streets unrebuked, unabashed; where every other person you meet is a gambler in one form or another, and shopmen and labourers and loafers and errand boys are all eager about the result of races, and all agog to know the forecasts of some wily tipster, some wiseacre of the halfpenny press!

A Christian country: where the rich and noble have no better use for profuse wealth than horse-training, and no more elevating mode of recreation than hunting and shooting down innumerable birds and beasts; where some must rot in fever-dens, clothed in rags, pining for food, stifling for lack of air and room; while others spend thousands of pounds upon a whim, a banquet, a party, a toy for a fair woman. I am not a Socialist, I do not deny a man's right to do what he will with his own, and I believe that state interference would be in the last degree disastrous to the country. But I affirm the responsibility before God of the rich and great; and I deny that they who live and spend for themselves alone are worthy of the name of Christian.

A Christian country: where human beings die, year after year, in the unspeakable, unimaginable agonies of canine madness, and dogs are kept by the thousand in crowded cities, that the sacrifice to the fiend of selfishness and the mocking devil of vanity may never lack its victims! There is a more than Egyptian worship of Anubis, in the silly infatuation which lavishes tenderness upon an unclean brute, and credulously invests instinct with the highest attributes of reason; and there is a worse than heathenish besottedness in the heart that can pamper a dog, and be utterly indifferent to the helplessness and the sufferings of the children of the poor. And people will go to church, and hear what the preacher has to say, and "think he said what he ought to have said," or not, as the case may be, and return to their own settled habits of worldly living, as a matter of course. Oh yes! it is a Christian country—the name of Christ has been named in it for fifteen centuries past; and for that reason Christ will judge it.

"Therefore, thus said Iahvah Sabaoth: Lo, I am about to melt them and put them to proof" (Job xii. 11; Judg. xvii. 4; vi. 25); "for how am I to deal in face of" ("the wickedness of," LXX: the term has fallen out of the Heb. text: *cf.* iv. 4, vii. 12) "the daughter of My people?" This is the meaning of the disasters that have fallen and are even now falling upon the country. Iahvah will melt and assay this rough, intractable human ore in the fiery furnace of affliction; the strain of insincerity that runs through it, the base earthy nature, can only thus be separated and purged away (Isa. xlviii. 10). "A deadly arrow" (LXX. a "wounding" one, *i. e.*, one which does not miss, but hits and kills) "is their tongue; deceit it spake: with his mouth peace with his companion he speaketh, and inwardly he layeth his ambush" (Ps. lv. 22). The verse again specifies the wickedness complained of, and justifies our restoration of that word in the previous verse.

Perhaps, with the Peshito Syriac and the Targum, we ought rather to render: "a sharp arrow is their tongue." There is an Arabic saying quoted by Lane, "Thou didst sharpen thy tongue against us," which seems to present a kindred root * (*cf.* Ps. lii. 3, lvii. 4; Prov. xxv. 18). The Septuagint may be right, with its probable reading: "deceit are the words of his mouth." This certainly improves the symmetry of the verse.

"For such things" (emphatic) "shall I not"—or "should I not," with an implied "ought—shall I not punish them, saith Iahvah, or on such a nation shall not My soul avenge herself?" (v. 9, 29, after which the LXX. omits "them" here). These questions, like the previous one, "How am I to deal"—or, "how could I act—in face of the wickedness of the daughter of My people?" imply the moral necessity of the threatened evils. If Iahweh be what He has taught man's conscience that He is, national sin must involve national suffering, and national persistence in sin must involve national ruin. Therefore He will "melt and try" this people, both for their punishment and their reformation, if it may be so. For punishment is properly retributive, whatever may be alleged to the contrary. Conscience tells us that we *deserve* to suffer for ill-doing, and conscience is a better guide than ethical or sociological speculators who have lost faith in God. But God's chastisements as known to our experience, that is to say, in the present life, are reformatory as well as retributive; they compel us to recollect, they bring us, like the Prodigal, back to ourselves, out of the distractions of a sinful career, they humble us with the discovery that we have a Master, that there is a Power above ourselves and our apparently unlimited capacity to choose evil and to do it: and so by Divine grace we may become contrite and be healed and restored.

The prophet thus, perhaps, discerns a faint glimmer of hope, but his sky darkens again immediately. The land is already to a great extent desolate, through the ravages of the invaders, or through severe droughts (*cf.* iv. 25, viii. 20(?), xii. 4). "Upon the mountains will I lift up weeping and wailing, and upon the pastures of the prairie a lamentation, for they have been burnt up" (ii. 15; 2 Kings xxii. 13), "so that no man passeth over them, and they have not heard the cry of the cattle: from the birds of the air to the beasts, they are fled, are gone" (iv. 25). The perfects may be prophetic and announce what is certain to happen hereafter. The next verse, at all events, is unambiguous in this respect: "And I will make Jerusalem into heaps, a haunt of jackals; and the cities of Judah will I make a desolation without inhabitant." Not only the country districts, but the fortified towns, and Jerusalem itself, the heart and centre of the nation, will be desolated. Sennacherib boasts that he took forty-six strong cities, and "little

* *Shahadhta 'lisânaka alaina.* In this case, we should follow the Heb. margin or *Q'rê.*

towns without number," and carried off 200,150 male and female captives, and an immense booty in cattle, before proceeding to invest Jerusalem itself; a statement which shows how severe the sufferings of Judah might be, before the enemy struck at its vitals.

In the words "I will make Jerusalem heaps," there is not necessarily a change of subject. Jeremiah was authorised to "root up and pull down and destroy" in the name of Iahvah.

He now challenges the popular wise men (viii. 8, 9) to account for what, on their principles, must appear an inexplicable phenomenon. "Who is the (true) wise man, so that he understands this" (Hos. xiv. 9), "and who is he to whom the mouth of Iahvah hath spoken, so that he can explain it" ("unto you?" LXX.). "Why is the land undone, burnt up like the prairie, without a passer by?" Both to Jeremiah and to his adversaries the land was Iahvah's land; what befell it must have happened by His will, or at least with His consent. Why had He suffered the repeated ravages of foreign invaders to desolate His own portion, where, if anywhere on earth, He must display His power and the proof of His deity? Not for lack of sacrifices, for these were not neglected. Only one answer was possible, to those who recognised the validity of the Book of the Law, and the binding character of the covenant which it embodied. The people and their wise men cannot account for the national calamities; Jeremiah himself can only do so, because he is inwardly taught by Iahvah himself (ver. 12): "And Iahvah said." It may be supposed that ver. 11 states the popular dilemma, the anxious question which they put to the official prophets, whose guidance they accepted. The prophets could give no reasonable or satisfying answer, because their teaching hitherto had been that Iahvah could be appeased "with thousands of rams, and ten thousand torrents of oil" (Mic. vi. 7). On such conditions they had promised peace, and their teaching had been falsified by events. Therefore Jeremiah gives the true answer for Iahvah. But why did not the people cease to believe those whose word was thus falsified? Perhaps the false prophets would reply to objectors, as the refugees in Egypt answered Jeremiah's reproof of their renewed worship of the Queen of Heaven: "It was in the years that followed the abolition of this worship that our national disasters began" (xliv. 18). It is never difficult to delude those whose evil and corrupt hearts make them desire nothing so much as to be deluded.

"And Iahvah said: Because they forsook" (lit. "upon" = on account of "their forsaking") "'My Law which I set before them'" (Deut. iv. 18), "and they hearkened not unto My voice" (Deut. xxviii. 15), "and walked not therein" (in My Law; LXX. omits the clause); "and walked after the obstinacy of their own" ("evil:" LXX.) "heart, and after the Baals" (Deut. iv. 3) "which their fathers taught them"—instead of teaching them the laws of Iahvah (Deut. xi. 19). Such were, and had always been, the terms of the answer of Iahvah's true prophets. Do you ask "upon what ground" ("'al mah") misfortune has overtaken you? Upon the ground of your having forsaken Iahvah's "law" or instruction, His doctrine concerning Himself and your consequent obligations towards Him. They had this teaching in the Book of the Law, and had solemnly undertaken to observe it, in that great national assembly of the eighteenth year of Josiah. And they had had it from the first in the living utterances of the prophets.

This, then, is the reason why the land is waste and deserted. And *therefore*—because past and present experience is an index of the future, for Iahvah's character and purpose are constant—therefore the desolation of the cities of Judah and of Jerusalem itself, will ere long be accomplished. "Therefore thus said Iahvah Sabaoth," the God of Armies and "the God of Israel; Lo, I am about to feed them"—or, "I continue to feed them"—to wit, "this people" (an epexegetical gloss omitted by the LXX.) "with wormwood, and I will give them to drink waters of gall" (Deut. xxix. 17. An Israelite inclining to foreign gods is "a root bearing wormwood and gall"—bearing a bitter harvest of defeat, a cup of deadly disaster for his people; *cf.* Am. vi. 12); "and I will 'scatter them among the nations,' 'whom they and their fathers knew not'" (Deut. xxviii. 36, 64). The last phrase is remarkable as evidence of the isolation of Israel, whose country lay off the beaten track between the Trans-Euphratean empires and Egypt, which ran along the sea-coast. They knew not Assyria, until Tiglath Pileser's intervention (*circ.* 734), nor Babylon till the times of the New Empire. In Hezekiah's day, Babylon is still "a far country" (2 Kings xx. 14). Israel was in fact an agricultural people, trading directly with Phœnicia and Egypt, but not with the lands beyond the Great River. The prophets heighten the horror of exile by the strangeness of the land whither Israel is to be banished.

"And I will send after them the sword, until I have consumed them." The survivors are to be cut off (*cf.* viii. 3); there is no reserve, as in iv. 27, v. 10, 18; a "full end" is announced; which, again, corresponds to the aggravation of social and private evils in the time of Jehoiakim, and the prophet's despair of reform.

The judgment of Judah is the ruin of her cities, the dispersion of her people in foreign lands, and extermination by the sword. Nothing is left for this doomed nation but to sing its funeral song; to send for the professional wailing women, that they may come and chant their dirges, not over the dead, but over the living who are condemned to die: "Thus said Iahvah Sabaoth" (here as in ver. 6, LXX. omits the expressive "Sabaoth"), "Mark ye well" the present crisis, and what it implies (*cf.* ii. 10; LXX. wrongly omits this emphatic term), "and summon the women that sing dirges, that they come, and unto the skilful women send ye, that they come" (LXX. omits), "and hasten" (LXX. "and speak and") "to life up the death-wail over us, that our eyes may run down with tears, and our eyelids pour down waters." The "singing women" of 2 Chron. xxxv. 25, or the "minstrels" of St. Matt. ix. 23, are intended. The reason assigned for thus inviting them assumes that the prophet's forecast is already fulfilled. Already, as in viii. 19, Jeremiah hears the loud wailing of the captives as they are driven away from their ruined homes: "For the sound of the death-wail is heard from Sion, 'How are we undone! We are sore ashamed'"—of our false confidence and foolish security and deceitful hopes—"'for,'" after all, "'we have left the land, for our dwellings have cast (us) out!'" The last two lines appear to be parallels, which is against the rendering, "For men have cast down our dwellings." (*Cf.* Lev. xviii. 25;

xxii. 28.) From the wailing women, the address now seems to turn to the Judean women generally; but perhaps the former are still intended, as their peculiar calling was probably hereditary and passed on from mother to daughter: "For hear, ye women, the word of Iahvah, and let your ear take in the word of His mouth! and teach ye your daughters the death-wail, and each her companion the lamentation; for

> "Death scales our lattices,
> Enters our palaces,
> To cut off boy without,
> The young men from the streets."

"And the corpses of men will fall"—the tense certifies the future reference of the others—"like dung" (viii. 2) "on the face of the field" (2 Kings ix. 37, of Jezebel's corpse)—left without burial rites to rot and fatten the soil—"and like the corn-swath behind the reaper, and none shall gather (them)." The quatrain (ver. 20) is possibly quoted from some familiar elegy; and the allusion seems to be to a mysterious visitation like the plague, which used to be known in Europe as "the Black Death" (*cf.* xv. 2, xviii. 21, xliii. 11). In this time of closed gates and barred doors, death is represented as entering the house, not by the door, but "climbing up some other way" like a thief (Joel ii. 9; St. John x. 1). Bars and bolts will be futile against such an invader. The figure is not continued in the second half of the stanza.* The point of the closing comparison seems to be that whereas the corn-swaths are gathered up in sheaves and taken home, the bodies will lie where the reaper Death cuts them down.

"Thus said Iahvah: Let not a wise man glory in his wisdom, and let not the mighty man glory in his might! Let not a rich man glory in his riches, but in this let him glory that glorieth, in being prudent and knowing Me" (LXX. omits pronoun, *cf.* Gen. i. 4), "that I, Iahvah, do lovingkindness" ("and:" LXX. and Orientals), "justice and righteousness upon the earth: for in these I delight, saith Iahvah."

It is not easy, at first sight, to see the connection of this, one of the finest and deepest of Jeremiah's oracles, with the sentence of destruction which precedes it. It is not satisfactory to regard it as stating "the only means of escape and the reason why it is not used" (the latter being set forth in vv. 24, 25); for the leading idea of the whole composition, from vii. 13 to ix 22, is that retribution is coming, and no escape, not even that of a remnant, is contemplated. The passage looks like an appendix to the previous pieces, such as the prophet might have added at a later period when the crisis was over, and the country had begun to breathe again, after the shock of invasion had rolled away. And this impression is confirmed by its contents. We have no details about the first interference of the new Chaldean power in Judah; we only read that in Jehoiakim's days "Nebuchadrezzar the king of Babylon came up, and Jehoiakim became his servant three years: then he turned and rebelled against him" (2 Kings xxiv. 1). But before this, for some two or three years, Jehoiakim was the vassal of the king of Egypt to whom he owed his crown, and Nebuchadrezzar had to reduce Necho before he could attend to Jehoiakim. It may be, therefore, that the worst apprehensions of the time not having been realised, in the year or two of lull which followed, the politicians of Judah began to boast of their foresight and the caution and sagacity of their measures for the public safety, instead of ascribing the respite to God; the warrior class might vaunt the bravery which it had exhibited or intended to exhibit in the service of the country; and the rich nobles might exult in the apparent security of their treasures and the new lease of enjoyment accorded to themselves. To these various classes, who would not be slow to ridicule his dark forebodings as those of a moody and unpatriotic pessimist (xx. 7, xxvi. 11, xxix. 26, xxxvii. 13), Jeremiah now speaks, to remind them that if the danger is over for the present, it is the lovingkindness and the righteous government of Iahvah which has removed it, and to declare that it is only suspended and postponed, not abolished for ever: "Behold, days are coming, saith Iahvah, when I will visit" (his guilt) "upon every one that is circumcised in foreskin" (only, and not "in heart" also): "upon Egypt and upon Judah, and upon Edom and upon the benê Ammon and upon Moab, and upon all the tonsured folk that dwell in the wilderness: For all the nations are uncircumcised, and all the house of Israel are uncircumcised in heart." Egypt is mentioned first, as the leading nation, to which at the time the petty states of the west looked for help in their struggle against Babylon (*cf.* xxvii. 3). The prophet numbers Judah with the rest, not only as a member of the same political group, but as standing upon the same level of unspiritual life. Like Israel, Egypt also practised circumcision, and both the context here requires and their kinship with the Hebrews makes it probable that the other peoples mentioned observed the same custom (Herod., ii. 36, 104), which is actually portrayed in a wall-painting at Karnak. The "tonsured folk" or "cropt-heads" of the wilderness are north Arabian nomads like the Kedarenes (xlix. 28, 32), and the tribes of Dedan, Tema, and Buz (xxv. 23), whose ancestor was the circumcised Ishmael (Gen. xxv. 13 *sqq.*, xvii. 23). Herodotus records their custom of shaving the temples all round, and leaving a tuft of hair on the top of the head (Herod., iii. 8), which practice, like circumcision, had a religious significance, and was forbidden to the Israelites (Lev. xix. 27, xxi. 5).

Now why does Jeremiah mention circumcision at all? The case is, I think, parallel to his mention of another external distinction of the popular religion, the Ark of the Covenant (iii. 15). Just as in that place God promises "shepherds according to Mine heart which shall shepherd" the restored Israel "with knowledge and prudence," and then directly adds that, in the light and truth of those days, the ark will be forgotten (iii. 15, 16); so here, he bids the ruling classes, the actual shepherds of the nation, not to trust in their own wisdom or valour or wealth (*cf.* xvii. 5 *sqq.*), but in "being prudent and knowing Iahvah," and then adds that the outward sign of circumcision, upon which the people prided themselves as the mark of their dedication to Iahvah, was in itself of no value, apart from a "circumcised heart," *i. e.*, a heart purified of selfish aims and devoted to the will and glory of God (iv. 4). So far as Iahvah is concerned, all Judah's heathen neighbours are uncircumcised, in spite of their observance of the outward rite.

* "Speak thou, Thus saith Iahweh," is undoubtedly a spurious addition, and does not appear in the LXX. Jeremiah never says *Koh ne'um Iahvah*, and never uses the imperative *dabber!*

The Jews themselves would hardly admit the validity of heathen circumcision, because the manner of it was different, just as at this day the Muhammadan method differs from the Jewish. But Jeremiah puts "all the house of Israel," who were circumcised in the orthodox manner, on a level with the imperfectly circumcised heathen peoples around them. All alike are uncircumcised before God; those who have the orthodox rite, and those who have but an inferior semblance of it; and all alike will in the day of judgment be visited for their sins (*cf.* Amos i.).

With the increasing carelessness of moral obligations, an increasing importance would be attached to the observance of such a rite as circumcision, which was popularly supposed to devote a man to Iahvah in such sense that the tie was indissoluble. Jeremiah says plainly that this is a mistaken view. The outward sign must have an inward and spiritual grace corresponding thereto; else the Judeans are no better than those whose circumcision they despise as defective. His meaning is that of the Apostle, "Circumcision verily profiteth, *if thou keep the law;* but if thou be a breaker of law, thy circumcision hath become uncircumcision" (Rom. ii. 25). "Circumcision is nothing, and uncircumcision is nothing, *but the keeping of the commandments of God," scil.*, is everything (1 Cor. vii. 19). It is "faith working by love," it is the "new creature" that is essential in spiritual religion (Gal. v. 6, vi. 15).

Hæc dicit Dominus: Non glorietur sapiens in sapientia sua. Glancing back over the whole passage, we discern an inward relation between these verses and the preceding discourse. It is not the outward props of state-craft, and strong battalions, and inexhaustible wealth, that really and permanently uphold a nation; not these, but the knowledge of Iahvah, a just insight into the true nature of God, and a national life regulated in all its departments by that insight. At the outset of this third section of his discourse (ix. 3-6), Jeremiah declared that corrupt Israel "knew not" and "refused to know" its God. At the beginning of the entire piece (vii. 3 *sq.*), he urged his countrymen to "amend their ways and their doings," and not go on trusting in "lying words" and doing the opposite of "lovingkindness and justice and righteousness," which alone are pleasing to Iahvah (Mic. vi. 8), Who "delighteth in lovingkindness and not sacrifice, and in the knowledge of God more than in burnt-offerings" (Hos. vi. 6). And just as in the opening section the sacrificial worship was disparaged, taken as an "opus operatum," so here at the close circumcision is declared to have no independent value as a means of securing Divine favour (ix. 25). Thus the entire discourse is rounded off by the return of the end to the beginning; and the main thought of the whole, which Jeremiah has developed and enforced with so much variety of feeling and oratorical and poetical ornament, is the eternally true thought that a service of God which is purely external is no service at all, and that rites without a loving obedience are an insult to the Majesty of Heaven.

x. 17-25. The latter part of chap. x. resumes the subject suspended at ix. 22. It evidently contemplates the speedy departure of the people into banishment. "Away out of the land with thy pack" (or "thy goods"; LXX. ὑπόστασις, "property," Targ. "merchandise," the Heb. term, which is related to "Canaan," occurs here only), "O thou that sittest in distress!" (or "abidest in the siege": lii. 5; 2 Kings xxiv. 10). Sion is addressed, and bidden to prepare her scanty bundle of bare necessaries for the march into exile. So Egypt is bidden to "make for herself vessels of exile," xlvi. 19. Some think that Sion is warned to withdraw her goods from the open country to the protection of her strong walls, before the siege begins, as in viii. 14; but we have passed that stage in the development of the piece, and the next verse seems to show the meaning: "For thus hath Iahvah said, Lo, I am about to sling forth the inhabitants of the land this time"—as opposed to former occasions, when the enemy retired unsuccessful (2 Kings xvi. 5, xix. 36), or went off satisfied with plunder or an indemnity, like the Scythians (see also 2 Kings xiv. 14)—"and I will distress them that they may find out" the truth, which now they refuse to see. The aposiopesis "that they may find out!" is very striking. The Vulgate renders the verb in the passive: *Tribulabo eos ita ut inveniantur.* This, however, does not give so good a sense as the Masoretic pointing, and Ewald's reference of the term to the goods of the panic-stricken fugitives seems flat and tasteless ("the inhabitants of the land will this time . . . not be able to hide their goods from the enemy!"). The best comment on the phrase is supplied by a later oracle: "Lo, I am about to make them know this time—I will make them know My hand and My might; that they may know that My name is Iahvah" (xvi. 21). *Cf.* also xvii. 9; Eccles. viii. 17.

The last verse (17) resembles a poetical quotation; and this one looks like the explication of it. There the population is personified as a woman; here we have instead the plain prose expression, "inhabitants of the land." The figurative, "I will sling them forth" or "cast them out," explains the bidding of Sion to "pack up her bundle" or "belongings"—there seems to be a touch of contempt in this isolated word, as much as to signify that the people must go forth into exile with no more of their possessions than they can carry like a beggar in a bundle. The expression, "I will distress them," seems to show that "thou that sittest in the distress" is proleptic, or to be rendered "thou that art to sit in distress," which comes to the same thing.

And now the prophet imagines the distress and the remorse of this forlorn mother, as it will manifest itself when her house is ruined and her children are gone and she realises the folly of the past (*cf.* iv. 31):—

"Woe's me for my wound!
Fatal is my stroke!"

(perhaps quoted from a familiar elegy). "And yet I—I thought" (chap. xxii. 21; Ps. xxx. 7), "Only this"—no more than this—"is my sickness: I can bear it!" (חליי אשאנ אך וה; LXX. σου, Vulg. "mea"). The people had never fully realised the threatenings of the prophets, until they began to be accomplished. When they heard them, they had said, half-incredulously, half-mockingly, Is that all? Their false guides, too, had treated apparent danger as a thing of little moment, assuring them that their half reforms, and zealous outward worship, were sufficient to turn away the Divine displeasure (vi. 14). And so they said to themselves, as sinners are still in the habit of saying, "If the worst come to the worst, I can bear it. Besides, God is merciful, and things may turn out better for frail humanity than your preachers of wrath and woe predict. Meanwhile—I shall do as I please, and take my chance of the issue."

The lament of the mourning mother continues: "My tent is laid waste and all my cords are broken; My sons went forth of me" (to battle) "and are not; There is none to spread my tent any more, And to set up my curtains (*cf.* Amos ix. 11). Overhearing, as it were, this sorrowful lamentation ("qinah"), the prophet interposes with the reason of the calamity: "For the shepherds became brutish" or "behaved foolishly," *stulte egerunt* (Vulg.)—the leaders of the nation showed themselves as insensate and silly as cattle—"and Iahvah they sought not" (ii. 8); "Therefore"—as they had no regard for Divine counsel—"they dealt not wisely" (iii. 15, ix. 23, xx. 11), "and all their flock was scattered abroad."

Once more, and for the last time, the prophet sounds the alarm: "Hark! a rumour! lo, it cometh! and a great uproar from the land of the north; to make the cities of Judah a desolation, a haunt of jackals!" It is not likely that the verse is to be regarded as spoken by the mourning country; she contemplates the evil as already done, whereas here it is only imminent (*cf.* iv. 6, vi. 22, i. 15). The piece concludes with a prayer (vv. 23-25), which may be considered either as an intercession by the prophet on behalf of the nation (*cf.* xviii. 20), or as a form of supplication which he suggests as suitable to the existing crisis. "I know, Iahvah, that man's way is not his own; That it pertaineth not to a man to walk and direct his own steps: Correct me, Iahvah, but with justice; Not in Thine anger, lest Thou make me small!" Partly quoted, Ps. vi. 1, xxxviii. 1) "Pour out Thy fury upon the nations that know Thee not, And upon tribes that have not called upon Thy name; For they have devoured Jacob" ("and will devour him") ("and consumed him"), "and his pasture they have desolated!" (Ps. lxxix. 6, 7, quoted from this place. In Jer. the LXX. omits "and will devour him;" while the psalm omits both of the bracketed expressions.)

The Vulgate renders ver. 23: "Scio, Domine, quia non est hominis via ejus; nec viri est ut ambulet, et dirigat gressus suos." I think this indicates the correct reading of the Hebrew text הָלֹךְ וְהָכֵין; *cf.* ix. 23, where two infinitives absolute are used in a similar way). The Septuagint also must have had the same text, for it translates, "nor will (= can) a man walk and direct his own walking." The Masoretic punctuation is certainly incorrect; and the best that can be made of it is Hitzig's version, which, however, disregards the accents, although their authority is the same as that of the vowel points: "I know Iahvah that not to man belongeth his way, not to a perishing" (lit. "going," "departing") "man—and to direct his steps." Any reader of Hebrew may see at once that this is a very unusual form of expression. (For the thought, *cf.* Prov. xvi. 9, xix. 21; Ps. xxxvii. 23.)

The words express humble submission to the impending chastisement. The penitent people does not deprecate the penalty of its sins, but only prays that the measure of it may be determined by right rather than by wrath (*cf.* xlvi. 27, 28). The very idea of right and justice implies a limit, whereas wrath, like all passions, is without limit, blind and insatiable. "In the Old Testament, justice is opposed, not to mercy, but to high-handed violence and oppression, which recognise no law but subjective appetite and desire. The just man owns the claims of an objective law of right."

Non est hominis via ejus. Neither individuals nor nations are masters of their own fortunes in this world. Man has not his fate in his own hands; it is controlled and directed by a higher Power. By sincere submission, by a glad, unswerving loyalty, which honours himself as well as its Object, man may co-operate with that Power, to the furtherance of ends which are of all possible ends the wisest, the loftiest, the most beneficial to his kind. Self-will may oppose those ends, it cannot thwart them; at the most it can but momentarily retard their accomplishment, and exclude itself from a share in the universal blessing.

Israel now confesses, by the mouth of his best and truest representative, that he has hitherto loved to choose his own path, and to walk in his own strength, without reference to the will and way of God. Now, the overwhelming shock of irresistible calamity has brought him to his senses, has revealed to him his powerlessness in the hands of the Unseen Arbiter of events, has made him see, as he never saw, that mortal man can determine neither the vicissitudes nor the goal of his journey. Now he sees the folly of the mighty man glorying in his might, and the rich man glorying in his riches; now he sees that the *how* and the *whither* of his earthly course are not matters within his own control; that all human resources are nothing *against* God, and are only helpful when used *for* and *with* God. Now he sees that the path of life is not one which we enter upon and traverse of our own motion, but a path along which we are led; and so, resigning his former pride of independent choice, he humbly prays, "Lead Thou me on!" Lead me whither Thou wilt, in the way of trouble and disaster and chastisement for my sins; but remember my human frailty and weakness, and let not Thy wrath destroy me! Finally, the suppliant ventures to remind God that others are guilty as well as he, and that the ruthless destroyers of Israel are themselves fitted to be objects as well as instruments of Divine justice. They are such (i) because they have not "known" nor "called upon" Iahvah; and (ii) because they have "devoured Jacob" who was a thing consecrated to Iahvah (ii. 3), and therefore are guilty of sacrilege (*cf.* l. 28, 29).

It has never been our lot to see our own land overrun by a barbarous invader, our villages burnt, our peasantry slaughtered, our towns taken and sacked with all the horrors permitted or enjoined by a non-Christian religion. We read of but hardly realise the atrocities of ancient warfare. If we did realise them, we might even think a saint justified in praying for vengeance upon the merciless destroyers of his country. But apart from this, I see a deeper meaning in this prayer. The justice of this terrible visitation upon Judah is admitted by the prophet. Yet in Judah many righteous were involved in the general calamity. On the other hand, Jeremiah knew something of the vices of the Babylonians, against which his contemporary Habakkuk inveighs so bitterly. They "knew not" nor "called upon" Iahvah; but a base polytheism reflected and sanctioned the corruption of their lives. A kind of moral dilemma, therefore, is proposed here. If the purpose of this outpouring of Divine wrath be to bring Israel to "find out" (ver. 18) and to acknowledge the truth of God and his own guiltiness, can wrath persist, when that result is attained? Does not justice demand that the torrent of destruction be diverted upon the proud oppressor? So prayer, the forlorn hope of poor humanity, strives to overcome and compel and prevail with God, and to wrest a blessing even from the hand of Eternal Justice.

CHAPTER VI.

THE IDOLS OF THE HEATHEN AND THE GOD OF ISRAEL.

JEREMIAH x. 1-16.

THIS fine piece is altogether isolated from the surrounding context, which it interrupts in a very surprising manner. Neither the style nor the subject, neither the idioms nor the thoughts expressed in them, agree with what we easily recognise as Jeremiah's work. A stronger contrast can hardly be imagined than that which exists between the leading motive of this oracle as it stands, and that of the long discourse in which it is embedded with as little regard for continuity as an aerolite exhibits when it buries itself in a plain. In what precedes, the prophet's fellow-countrymen have been accused of flagrant and defiant idolatry (vii. 17 *sqq.*, 30 *sqq.*); the opening words of this piece imply a totally different situation. "To the way of the nations become not accustomed, and of the signs of heaven be not afraid; for the nations are afraid of them." * Jeremiah would not be likely to warn inveterate apostates not to "accustom themselves" to idolatry. The words presuppose, not a nation whose idolatry was notorious, and had just been the subject of unsparing rebuke and threats of imminent destruction; they presuppose a nation free from idolatry, but exposed to temptation from surrounding heathenism. The entire piece contains no syllable of reference to past or present unfaithfulness on the part of Israel. Here at the outset, and throughout, Israel is implicitly contrasted with "the nations" (τὰ ἔθνη) as the servant of Iahvah with the foolish worshippers of lifeless gods. There is a tone of contempt in the use of the term "goyim"—"To the way of the 'goyim' accustom not yourselves . . . for the 'goyim' are afraid of them" (of the signs of heaven); or as the Septuagint puts it yet more strongly, "for *they*" (the besotted "goyim") "are afraid" (*i. e.*, worship) "before them;" as though that alone—the sense of Israel's superiority—should be sufficient to deter Israelites from any bowings in the house of Rimmon.† Neither this contemptuous use of the term "goyim," "Gentiles," nor the scathing ridicule of the false gods and their devotees, is in the manner of Jeremiah. Both are characteristic of a later period. The biting scorn of image-worship, the intensely vivid perception of the utter incommensurableness of Iahvah, the Creator of all things, with the handiwork of the carpenter and the silversmith, are well-known and distinctive features of the great prophets of the Exile (see especially Isaiah xl.-lxvi.). There are plenty of allusions to idolatry in Jeremiah; but they are expressed in a tone of fervid indignation, not of ridicule. It was the initial offence, which issued in a hopeless degradation of public and private morality, and would have for its certain consequence the rejection and ruin of the nation (ii. 5-13, 20-28, iii. 1-9, 23 *sqq.*). All the disasters, past and present, which had befallen the country, were due to it (vii. 9, 17 *sqq.*, 30 *sqq.*, viii. 2, etc.). The people are urged to repent and return to Iahvah with their whole heart (iii. 12 *sqq.*, iv. 3 *sqq.*, v. 21 *sqq.*, vi. 8), as the only means of escape from deadly peril. The Baals are things that cannot help or save (ii. 8, 11); but the prophet does not say, as here (x. 5), "Fear them not; they cannot harm you!" The piece before us breathes not one word about Israel's apostasy, the urgent need of repentance, the impending ruin. Taken as a whole, it neither harmonises with Jeremiah's usual method of argument, nor does it suit the juncture of affairs implied by the language which precedes and follows (vii. 1-ix. 26, x. 17-25). For let us suppose that this oracle occupies its proper place here, and was actually written by Jeremiah at the crisis which called forth the preceding and following utterances. Then the warning cry, "Be not afraid of the signs of heaven!" can only mean "Be not afraid of the Powers under whose auspices the Chaldeans are invading your country; Iahvah, the true and living God, will protect you!" But consolation of this kind would be diametrically opposed to the doctrine which Jeremiah shares with all his predecessors; the doctrine that Iahvah Himself is the prime cause of the coming trouble, and that the heathen invaders are His instruments of wrath (v. 9 *sq.*, vi. 6); it would imply assent to that fallacious confidence in Iahvah, which the prophet has already done his utmost to dissipate (vi. 14, vii. 4 *sq.*).

The details of the idolatry satirised in the piece before us point to Chaldea rather than to Canaan. We have here a zealous worship of wooden images overlaid and otherwise adorned with silver and gold, and robed in rich garments of violet and purple (*cf.* Josh. vii. 21). This does not agree with what we know of Judean practice in Jeremiah's time, when, besides the worship of the Queen of Heaven, the people adored "stocks and stones;" probably the wooden symbols of the goddess Asherah and rude sun-pillars, but hardly works of the costly kind described in the text, which indicate a wealthy people whose religion reflected an advanced condition of the arts and commerce. The designation of the objects of heathen worship as "the signs of heaven," and the gibe at the custom of carrying the idol-statues in procession (Isa. xlvi. 1, 7), also point us to Babylon, "the land of graven images" (l. 38), and the home of star-worship and astrological superstition (Isa. xlvii. 13).

From all these considerations it would appear that not Israel in Canaan but Israel in Chaldea is addressed in this piece by some unknown prophet, whose leaflet has been inserted among the works of Jeremiah. In that case, the much disputed eleventh verse, written in Aramaic, and as such unique in the volume of the prophets proper, may really have belonged to the original piece. Aramaic was the common language of intercourse between East and West both be-

* LXX. "for *they* are afraid before them," :חמה לפניהם כי ירתו.

† This is the most natural interpretation of the passage according to the Hebrew punctuation. Another is given below

fore and during the captivity (*cf.* 2 Kings xviii. 26); and the suggestion that the tempted exiles should answer in this dialect the heathen who pressed them to join in their worship, seems suitable enough. The verse becomes very suspicious, if we suppose that the whole piece is really part and parcel of Jeremiah's discourse, and as such addressed to the Judeans in the reign of Jehoiakim. Ewald, who maintains this view upon grounds that cannot be called convincing, thinks the Aramaic verse was originally a marginal annotation on verse 15, and suggests that it is a quotation from some early book similar to the Book of Daniel. At all events, it is improbable that the verse proceeded from the pen of Jeremiah, who writes Aramaic nowhere else, not even in the letter to the exiles of the first Judean captivity (chap. xxix.).

But might not the piece be an address which Jeremiah sent to the exiles of the Ten Tribes, who were settled in Assyria, and with whom it is otherwise probable that he cultivated some intercourse? The expression "House of Israel" (ver. 1) has been supposed to indicate this. That expression, however, occurs in the immediately preceding context (ix. 26), as does also that of "the nations"; facts which may partially explain why the passage we are discussing occupies its present position. The unknown author of the Apocryphal Letter of Jeremiah and the Chaldee Targumist appear to have held the opinion that Jeremiah wrote the piece for the benefit of the exiles carried away with Jehoiachin in the first Judean captivity. The Targum introduces the eleventh verse thus: "This is a copy of the letter which Jeremiah the prophet sent to the remnant of the elders of the captivity which was in Babylon. And if the peoples among whom ye are shall say unto you, Fear the Errors, O house of Israel! thus shall ye answer and thus shall ye say unto them: The Errors whom ye fear are (but) errors, in which there is no profit: they from the heavens are not able to bring down rain, and from the earth they cannot make fruits to spring: they and those who fear them will perish from the earth, and will be brought to an end from under these heavens. And thus shall ye say unto them: We fear Him that maketh the earth by His power," etc. (ver. 12). The phrase "the remnant of the elders of the captivity which was" (or "who were") "in Babylon" is derived from Jer. xxix. 1. But how utterly different are the tone and substance of that message from those of the one before us! Far from warning his captive countrymen against the state-worship of Babylon, far from satirising its absurdity, Jeremiah bids the exiles be contented with their new home, and to pray for the peace of the city. The false prophets who appear at Babylon prophesy in Iahvah's name (vv. 15, 21), and in denouncing them Jeremiah says not a word about idolatry. It is evident from the whole context that he did not fear it in the case of the exiles of Jehoiachin's captivity. (See also the simile of the Good and Bad Figs, chap. xxiv., which further illustrates the prophet's estimation of the earlier body of exiles.)

The Greek Epistle of Jeremiah, which in MSS. is sometimes appended to Baruch, and which Fritzsche refers to the Maccabean times, appear to be partially based upon the passage we are considering. Its heading is: "Copy of a letter which Jeremiah sent unto those who were about to be carried away captives to Babylon, by the king of the Babylonians; to announce to them as was enjoined him by God." It then begins thus: "On account of your sins which ye have sinned before God ye will be carried away to Babylon as captives by Nabuchodonosor king of the Babylonians. Having come, then, into Babylon, ye will be there many years, and a long time, until seven generations; but after this I will bring you forth from thence in peace. But now ye will see in Babylon gods, silvern and golden and wooden, borne upon shoulders, showing fear" (an object of fear) "to the nations. Beware then, lest ye also become like unto the nations, and fear take you at them, when ye see a multitude before and behind them worshipping them. But say ye in the mind: Thee it behoveth us to worship, O Lord! For Mine angel is with you, and He is requiring your lives." The whole epistle is well worth reading as a kind of paraphrase of our passage. "For their tongue is carven" (or polished) "by a carpenter, and themselves are overlaid with gold and silver, but lies they are and they cannot speak." "They being cast about with purple apparel have their face wiped on account of the dust from the house, which is plentiful upon them" (13). "But he holds a dagger with right hand and an axe, but himself from war and robbers he will not" (cannot) "deliver" (15, *cf.* Jer. x. 15). "He is like one of the housebeams" (20, *cf.* Jer. x. 8, and perhaps 5). "Upon their body and upon their head alight bats, swallows, and the birds, likewise also the cats; whence ye will know that they are not gods; therefore fear them not" (*cf.* Jer. x. 5). "At all cost are they purchased, in which there is no spirit" (25; *cf.* Jer. x. 9-14). "Footless, upon shoulders they are carried, displaying their own dishonour to men" (26). "Neither if they suffer evil from any one, nor if good, will they be able to recompense" (34; *cf.* ver. 5). "But they that serve them will be ashamed" (39; *cf.* ver. 14). "By carpenters and goldsmiths are they prepared; they become nothing but what the craftsmen wish them to become. And the very men that prepare them cannot last long; how then are the things prepared by them likely to do so? for they left lies and a reproach to them that come after. For whenever war and evils come upon them, the priests consult together where to hide them. How then is it possible not to perceive that they are not gods, who neither save themselves from war nor from evils? For being of wood and overlaid with gold and silver they will be known hereafter, that they are lies. To all the nations and to the kings it will be manifest that they are not gods but works of men's hands, and no work of God is in them" (45-51; *cf.* Jer. x. 14-15). "A wooden pillar in a palace is more useful than the false gods" (59). "Signs among nations they will not show in heaven, nor yet will they shine like the sun, nor give light as the moon" (67). "For as a scarecrow in a cucumber-bed guarding nothing, so their gods are wooden and overlaid with gold and silver" (70 *cf.* Jer. x. 5). The mention of the sun, moon, and stars, the lightning, the wind, the clouds, and fire "sent forth from above," as totally unlike the idols in "forms and powers." seems to show that the author had verses 12, 13 before him.

When we turn to the Septuagint, we are immediately struck by its remarkable omissions. The four verses 6-8, and 10 do not appear at all in this oldest of the versions: while the ninth is inserted between the first clause and the remainder of the fifth verse. Now, on the one hand, it is just the verses which the LXX. translates, which both in style and matter contrast so strongly with Jeremiah's authentic work, and are plainly incongruous with the context and occasion; while, on the other hand, the omitted verses contain nothing which points positively to another author than Jeremiah, and, taken by themselves, harmonise very well with what may be supposed to have been the prophet's feeling at the actual juncture of affairs.

"There is none at all like Thee, O Iahvah!
Great art Thou, and great is Thy Name in might!
Who should not fear Thee, O King of the nations? for 'tis Thy due,
For among all the wise of the nations and in all their kingdom there is none at all like Thee.
And in one thing they are brute-like and dull;
In the doctrine of Vanities, which are wood!
But Iahvah Elohim is truth;
He is a living God, and an eternal King:
At His wrath the earth quaketh,
And nations abide not His indignation."

As Hitzig has observed, it is natural that now, as the terrible decision approaches, the prophet should seek and find comfort in the thought of the all-overshadowing greatness of the God of Israel. If, however, we suppose these verses to be Jeremiah's, we can hardly extend the same assumption to verses 12-16, in spite of one or two expressions of his which occur in them; and, upon the whole, the linguistic argument seems to weigh decisively against Jeremiah's authorship of this piece (see Naegelsbach).

It may be true enough that "the basis and possibility of the true prosperity and the hope of the genuine community are unfolded in these strophes" (Ewald); but that does not prove that they belong to Jeremiah. Nor can I see much force in the remark that "didactic language is of another kind than that of pure prophecy." But when the same critic affirms that "the description of the folly of idolatry . . . . is also quite new, and clearly serves as a model for the much more elaborate ones, Isa. xl. 19-24 (20), xli. 7, xliv. 8-20, xlvi. 5-7;" he is really giving up the point in dispute. Verses 12-16 are repeated in the prophecy against Babylon (li. 15-19); but this hardly proves that "the later prophet, chap. l. li., found *all these words* in our piece;" it is only evidence, so far as it goes, for those verses themselves.

The internal connection which Ewald assumes, is not self-evident. There is no proof that "the thought that the gods of the heathen might again rule" occurred for one moment to Jeremiah on this occasion; nor the thought that "the maintenance of the ancient true religion in conflict with the heathen must produce the regeneration of Israel." There is no reference throughout the disputed passage to the spiritual condition of the people, which is, in fact, presupposed to be good; and the return in verses 17-25 "to the main subject of the discourse" is inexplicable on Ewald's theory that the whole chapter, omitting verse 11, is one homogeneous structure.

"Hear ye the word that Iahvah spake upon you, O house of Israel! Thus said Iahvah." The terms imply a particular crisis in the history of Israel, when a Divine pronouncement was necessary to the guidance of the people. Iahvah speaks indeed in all existence and in all events, but His voice becomes audible, is recognised as His, only when human need asserts itself in some particular juncture of affairs. Then, in view of the actual emergency, the mind of Iahweh declares itself by the mouth of His proper spokesmen; and the prophetic "Thus said Iahvah" contrasts the higher point of view with the lower, the heavenly and spiritual with the earthly and the carnal; it sets forth the aspect of things as they appear to God, in the sharpest antithesis to the aspect of things as they appear to the natural unilluminated man. "Thus said Iahvah:" This is the thought of the Eternal, this is His judgment upon present conditions and passing events, whatever *your* thought and your judgment may happen or incline to be! Such, I think, is the essential import of this *vox solennis*, this customary formula of the dialect of prophecy.

On the present occasion, the crisis, in view of which a prophet declares the mind of Iahvah, is not a political emergency but a religious temptation. The day for the former has long since passed away, and the depressed and scattered communities of exiled Israelites are exposed among other trials to the constant temptation to sacrifice to present expediency the only treasure which they have saved from the wreck of their country, the faith of their fathers, the religion of the prophets. The uncompromising tone of this isolated oracle, the abruptness with which the writer at once enters *in medias res*, the solemn emphasis of his opening imperatives, proves that this danger pressed at the time with peculiar intensity. "Thus said Iahvah: Unto the way of the nations use not yourselves, And of the signs of heaven stand not in awe, for that the nations stand in awe of them!" (*cf.* Lev. xviii. 3; Ezek. xx. 18). The "way" of the nations is their religion, the mode and manner of their worship (v. 4, 5); and the exiles are warned not to suffer themselves to be led astray by example, as they had been in the land of Canaan; they are not to adore the signs of heaven, simply because they see their conquerors adoring them. The "signs of heaven" would seem to be the sun, moon, and stars, which were the objects of Babylonian worship; although the passage is unhappily not free from ambiguity. Some expositors have preferred to think of celestial phenomena such as eclipses and particular conjunctions of the heavenly bodies, which in those days were looked upon as portents, foreshadowing the course of national and individual fortunes. That there is really a reference to the astrological observation of the stars, is a view which finds considerable support in the words addressed to Babylon on the eve of her fall, by a prophet, who, if not identical was at least contemporary with him whose message we are discussing. In the forty-seventh chapter of the Book of Isaiah, it is said to Babylon: "Let now them that parcel out the heavens, that gaze at the stars, arise and save thee, prognosticating month by month the things that will come upon thee" (Isa. xlvii. 13). The "signs of heaven" are, in this case, the supposed indications of coming events furnished by the varying appearances of the heavenly bodies; and one might even suppose that the immediate occasion of our prophecy was some eclipse of the sun or moon, or some remarkable conjunction of the planets which at the time was exciting general anxiety among the motley populations of Babylonia. The prophecy then becomes a remarkable instance of the manner in which an elevated spiritual faith, free from all the contaminating and blinding influences of selfish motives and desires, may rise superior to universal superstition, and boldly contradict the suggestions of what is accounted the highest wisdom of the time, anticipating the results though not the methods nor the evidence of science, at an epoch when science is as yet in the mythological stage. And the prophet might well exclaim in a tone of triumph, "Among all the wise of the nations none at all is like unto Thee, O Lord, as a source of true wisdom and understanding for the guidance of life" (ver. 7).

The inclusion of eclipses and comets among the signs of heaven here spoken of has been thought to be barred by the considerations that these are sometimes alleged by the prophets themselves as signs of coming judgment exhibited by the God of Israel; that, as a matter of fact, they were as mysterious and awful to the Jews as to their heathen neighbours; and that what is here contemplated is not the terror inspired by rare occasional phenomena of this kind, but an habitual superstition in relation to some ever-present causes. It is certain that in another prophecy against Babylon, preserved in the Book of Isaiah, it is declared that, as a token of the impending destruction, "the stars of heaven and the Orions thereof shall not give their light: the sun shall be darkened in his going forth, and the moon shall not cause his light to shine" (Isa. xiii. 10); and the similar language of the prophet Joel is well known (Joel ii. 2, 10, 30, 31, iii. 15). But these objections are not conclusive, for what our author is denouncing is the heathen association of "the signs of the heavens," whatever may be intended by that expression, with a false system of religious belief. It is a special kind of idolatry that he contemplates, as is clear from the immediate context. Not only does the parallel clause "Unto the way of the nations use not yourselves" imply a gradual conformity to a heathen religion; not only is it the fact that the Hebrew phrase rendered in our versions "Be not dismayed!" may imply religious awe or worship (Mal. ii. 5), as indeed terms denoting fear or dread are used by the Semitic languages in general; but the prophet at once proceeds to an exposure of the absurdity of image-worship: "For the ordinances" (established modes of worship; 2 Kings xvii. 8; here, established objects of worship) "of the peoples are a mere breath" (*i. e.*, naught)! "for it" (the idol) "is a tree, which out of the forest one felled" (so the accents); "the handiwork of the carpenter with the bill. With silver and with gold one adorneth it" (or, "maketh it bright"); "with nails and with hammers they make them fast, that one sway not" (or, "that there be no shaking"). "Like the scarecrow of a garden of gourds are they, and they cannot speak; they are carried and carried, for they cannot take a step" (or, "march"): "be not afraid of them, for they cannot hurt, neither is it in their power to benefit!" "Be not afraid of them!" returns to the opening charge: "Of the signs of heaven stand not in awe!" (*cf.* Gen. xxxi. 42, 53; Isa. viii. 12, 13). Clearly, then, the *signa cœli* are the idols against whose worship the prophet warns his people; and they denote "the sun, the moon, the constellations" (of the Zodiac), "and all the host of heaven" (2 Kings xxiii. 5). We know that the kings of Judah, from Ahaz onwards, derived this worship from Assyria, and that its original home was Babylon, where in every temple the exiles would see images of the deities presiding over the heavenly bodies, such as Samas (the sun) and his consort Aa (the moon) at Sippara, Merodach (Jupiter) and his son Nebo (Mercurius) at Babylon and Borsippa, Nergal (Mars) at Cutha, daily served with a splendid and attractive ritual, and honoured with festivals and processions on the most costly and magnificent scale. The prophet looks through all this outward display to the void within, he draws no subtle distinction between the symbol and the thing symbolised; he accepts the popular confusion of the god with his image, and identifies all the deities of the heathen with the materials out of which their statues are made by the hands of men. And he is justified in doing this, because there can be but one god in his sense of the word; a multitude of *gods* is a contradiction in terms. From this point of view, he exposes the absurdity of the splendid idolatry which his captive countrymen see all around them. Behold that thing, he cries, which they call a god, and before which they tremble with religious fear! It is nothing but a tree trunk hewn in the forest, and trimmed into shape by the carpenter, and plated with silver and gold, and fixed on its pedestal with hammer and nails, for fear it should fall! Its terrors are empty terrors, like those of the palm-trunk, rough-hewn into human shape, and set up among the melons to frighten the birds away.

> "Olim truncus eram ficulnus, inutile lignum,
> Cum faber, incertus scamnum faceretne Priapum,
> Maluit esse deum. Deus inde ego, furum aviumque
> Maxima formido." (Hor., "Sat." i. 8, 1, *sqq.*)

Though the idol has the outward semblance of a man, it lacks his distinguishing faculty of speech; it is as dumb as the scarecrow, and as powerless to move from its place; so it has to be borne about on men's shoulders (a mocking allusion to the grand processions of the gods, which distinguished the Babylonian festivals). Will you then be afraid of things that can do neither good nor harm? asks the prophet: in terms that recall the challenge of another, or perchance of himself, to the idols of Babylon: "Do good or do evil, that we may look at each other and see it together" (Isa. xli. 23).

In utter contrast with the impotence, the nothingness of all the gods of the nations, whether Israel's neighbours or his invaders, stands for ever the God of Israel. "There is none at all like Thee, O Iahweh! great art Thou, and great is Thy Name in might!" With different vowel points, we might render, "Whence (cometh) Thy like, O Iahvah?" This has been supported by reference to chap. xxx. 7: "Alas! for great is that day. Whence" (is one) "like it?" (me'ayin?); but there too, as here, we may equally well translate, "there is none like it." The interrogative, in fact, presupposes a negative answer; and the Hebrew particle usually rendered "there is not, are not" ("'ayin, 'ên") has been explained as originally identical with the interrogative "where?" ("'ayin," implied in "me'ayin," "from where?" "whence?" *cf.* Job xiv. 10: "where is he?" = "he is not"). The idiom of the text expresses a more emphatic negation than the ordinary form would do; and, though rare, is by no means altogether unparalleled (see Isa. xl. 17, xli. 24; and other references in Gesenius). "Great art Thou and great is Thy Name in might;" that is to say, Thou art great in Thyself, and great in repute or manifestation among men, in respect of "might," virile strength or prowess (Ps. xxi. 14). Unlike the do-nothing idols, Iahvah reveals His strength in deeds of strength (*cf.* Exod. xv. 3 *sqq.*). "Who should not fear Thee, Thou King of the nations?" (*cf.* v. 22) "for Thee it beseemeth" (= it is Thy due, and Thine only): "for among all the wise of the nations and in all their realm, there is none at all" (as in ver. 6) "like Thee." Religious fear is instinctive in man; but, whereas the various nations lavish reverence upon innumerable objects utterly unworthy of the name of deity, rational religion sees clearly that there can be but One God, working His supreme will in heaven and earth; and that this Almighty being is the true "King of the nations," and disposes their destinies as well as that of His people Israel, although they know Him not, but call other imaginary beings their "kings" (a common Semitic designation of a national god: Ps. xx. 9; Isa. vi. 5, viii. 21). He, then, is the proper object of the instinct of religious awe; all the peoples of the earth owe Him adoration, even though they be ignorant of their obligation; worship is His unshared prerogative.

"Among all the wise of the nations and in all their realm, not one is like Thee!" Who are the wise thus contrasted with the Supreme God? Are the false gods the reputed wise ones, giving pretended counsel to their deluded worshippers through the priestly oracle? The term "kingdom" seems to indicate this view, if we take "their kingdom" to mean the kingdom of the wise ones of the nations, that is, the countries whose "kings" they are, where they are worshipped as such. The heathen in general, and the Babylonians in particular, ascribed wisdom to their gods. But there is no impropriety from an Old Testament point of view in comparing Iahvah's wisdom with the wisdom of man. The meaning of the prophet may be simply this, that no earthly wisdom, craft, or political sagacity, not even in the most powerful empires such as Babylon, can be a match for Iahvah the All-wise, or avail to thwart His purposes (Isa. xxxi. 1, 2). "Wise" and "sagacious" are titles which the kings of Babylon continually assert for themselves in their extant inscriptions; and the wisdom and learning of the Chaldeans were famous in the ancient world. Either view will agree with what follows: "But in one thing they"—the nations, or their wise men—"will turn out brutish and besotted:" (in) "the teaching of Vanities which are wood." The verse is difficult; but the expression "the teaching (or doctrine) of Vanities" may perhaps be regarded as equivalent to "the idols taught of;" and then the second half of the verse is constructed like the first member of ver. 3: "The ordinances of the peoples are Vanity," and may be rendered, "the idols taught of are mere wood" (*cf.* ver. 3 *b*, ii. 27, iii. 9). It is possible also that the right reading is "foundation" ("mûsad") not "doctrine" ("mûsar"): "the foundation" (basis, substratum, substance) "of idols is wood." (The term "Vanities —"habalim"—is used for "idols," viii. 19, xiv. 22; Ps. xxxi. 7). And, lastly, I think, the clause might be rendered: "a doctrine of Vanities, of mere wood, it"—their religion—"is!" * This supreme folly is the "one thing" that discredits all the boasted wisdom of the Chaldeans; and their folly will hereafter be demonstrated by events (ver. 14).

The body of the idol is wood, and outwardly it is decorated with silver and gold and costly apparel; but the whole and every part of it is the work of man. "Silver plate" (lit. "beaten out") "from Tarshish"—from far away Tartessus in Spain—"is brought, and gold from Uphaz" (Dan. x. 5), "the work of the smith, and of the hands of the founder"—who have beaten out the silver and smelted the gold: "blue and purple is their clothing" (Ex. xxvi. 31, xxviii. 8): "the work of the wise"—of skilled artists (Isa. xl. 20)—"is every part of them." Possibly the verse might better be translated: "Silver to be beaten out"—*argentum malleo diducendum*—"which is brought from Tarshish, and gold" which is brought "from Uphaz," are "the work of the smith and of the hands of the smelter; the blue and purple" which are "their clothing," are "the work of the wise all of them." At all events, the point of the verse seems to be that, whether you look at the inside or the outside of the idol, his heart of wood or his casing of gold and silver and his gorgeous robes, the whole and every bit of him as he stands before you is a manufactured article, the work of men's hands. The supernatural comes in nowhere. In sharpest contrast with this lifeless fetish, "Iahvah is a God that is truth," *i. e.*, a true God (*cf.* Prov. xxii. 21), or "Iahvah is God in truth"—is really God—"He is a living God, and an eternal King;" the sovereign whose rule is independent of the vicissitudes of time, and the caprices of temporal creatures: "at His wrath the earth quaketh, and nations cannot abide His indignation:" the world of nature and the world of man are alike dependent upon His Will, and He exhibits His power and his righteous anger in the disturbances of the one and the disasters of the other.

According to the Hebrew punctuation, we should rather translate: "But Iahvah Elohim" (the designation of God in the second account of creation, Gen. ii. 4-iii. 24) "is truth," *i. e.*, reality; as opposed to the falsity and nothingness of the idols; or "permanence," "lastingness" (Ps. xix. 10), as opposed to their transitoriness (vv. 11-15).

The statement of the tenth verse respecting the eternal power and godhead of Iahvah is confirmed in the twelfth and thirteenth by instances of His creative energy and continual activity as exhibited in the world of nature. "The Maker of the earth by His power, Establishing the habitable world by His wisdom, And by His insight He did stretch out the heavens: At the sound of His giving voice" (Ps. lxxvii. 18; *i. e.*, thundering) "there is an uproar of waters in the heavens, And He causeth the vapours to rise from the end of the earth; Lightnings for the rain He maketh, And causeth the wind to go forth out of His treasuries." There is no break in the sense between these sentences and the tenth verse. The construction resembles that of Amos v. 8, ix. 5, 6, and is interrupted by the eleventh verse, which in all probability was, to begin with, a marginal annotation.

The solid earth is itself a natural symbol of strength and stability. The original creation of this mighty and enduring structure argues the omnipotence of the Creator; while the "establishing" or "founding" of it upon the **waters**

* It is against usage to divide the clause as Naegelsbach does, "Vain instruction! It is wood!" or to render with Ewald "Simply vain doctrine is the wood!" which would require the article (*ha'eç*).

of the great deep is a proof of supreme wisdom (Ps. xxiv. 2; cxxxvi. 6), and the "spreading out" of the visible heavens or atmosphere like a vast canopy or tent over the earth (Ps. civ. 2; Isa. xl. 22), is evidence of a perfect insight into the conditions essential to the existence and well-being of man.

It is, of course, clear enough that physical facts and phenomena are here described in popular language as they appear to the eye, and by no means with the severe precision of a scientific treatise. It is not to be supposed that this prophet knew more about the actual constitution of the physical universe than the wise men of his time could impart. But such knowledge was not necessary to the enforcement of the spiritual truths which it was his mission to proclaim; and the fact that his brief oracle presents those truths in a garb which we can only regard as poetical, and which it would argue a want of judgment to treat as scientific prose, does not affect their eternal validity, nor at all impair their universal importance. The passage refers us to God as the ultimate source of the world of nature. It teaches us that the stability of things is a reflection of His eternal being; that the persistence of matter is an embodiment of His strength; that the indestructibility which science ascribes to the materials of the physical universe is the seal which authenticates their Divine original. Persistence, permanence, indestructibleness, are properly sole attributes of the eternal Creator, which He communicates to His creation. Things are indestructible as regards man, not as regards the Author of their being.

Thus the wisdom enshrined in the laws of the visible world, all its strength and all its stability, is a manifestation of the Unseen God. Invisible in themselves, the eternal power and godhead of Iahvah become visible in His creation. And, as the Hebrew mode of expression indicates, His activity is never suspended, nor His presence withdrawn. The conflict of the elements, the roar of the thunder, the flash of the lightning, the downpour of waters, the rush of the storm-wind, are His work; and not less His work, because we have found out the "natural" causes, that is, the established conditions of their occurrence; not less His work, because we have, in the exercise of faculties really though remotely akin to the Divine Nature, discovered how to imitate, or rather mimic, even the more awful of these marvellous phenomena. Mimicry it cannot but appear, when we compare the overwhelming forces that rage in a tropical storm with our electric toys. The lightnings in their glory and terror are still God's arrows, and man cannot rob His quiver.

Nowadays more is known about the machinery of the world, but hardly more of the Intelligence that contrived it, and keeps it continually in working order, nay, lends it its very existence. More is known about means and methods, but hardly more about aims and purposes. The reflection, how few are the master-conceptions which modern speculation has added to the treasury of thought, should suggest humility to the vainest and most self-confident of physical inquirers. In the very dawn of philosophy the human mind appears to have anticipated as it were by sudden flashes of insight some of the boldest hypotheses of modern science, including that of Evolution itself.

The unchangeable or invariable laws of nature, that is to say, the uniformity of sequence which we observe in physical phenomena, is not to be regarded as a thing that explains itself. It is only intelligible as the expression of the unchanging will of God. The prophet's word is still true. It is God who "causes the vapours to rise from the end of the earth," drawing them up into the air from oceans and lakes by the simple yet beautiful and efficient action of the solar heat; it is God who "makes lightnings for the rain," charging the clouds with the electric fluid, to burst forth in blinding flashes when the opposing currents meet. It is God who "brings the wind out of His treasuries." In the prophet's time the winds were as great a mystery as the thunder and lightning; it was not known whence they came nor whither they went. But the knowledge that they are but currents of air due to variations of temperature does not really deprive them of their wonder. Not only is it impossible, in the last resort, to comprehend what heat is, what motion is, what the thing moved is. A far greater marvel remains, which cries aloud of God's wisdom and presence and sovereignty over all; and that is the wonderful consilience of all the various powers and forces of the natural world in making a home for man, and enabling so apparently feeble a creature as he to live and thrive amidst the perpetual interaction and collision of the manifold and mighty elements of the universe.

The true author of all this magnificent system of objects and forces, to the wonder and the glory of which only custom can blind us, is the God of the prophet. This sublime, this just conception of God was possible, for it was actually realised, altogether apart from the influence of Hellenic philosophy and modern European science. But it was by no means as common to the Semitic peoples. In Babylon, which was at the time the focus of all earthly wisdom and power, in Babylon the ancient mother of sciences and arts, a crude polytheism stultified all the wisdom of the wise, and lent its sanction to a profound moral corruption. Rapid and universal conquests, enormous wealth accruing from the spoils and tributes of all nations, only subserved the luxury and riotous living which issued in a general effeminacy and social enervation; until the great fabric of empire, which Nabopalassar and Nebuchadrezzar had reared by their military and political genius, sank under the weight of its own vices.

Looking round upon this spectacle of superstitious folly, the prophet declares that "all men are become too brute-like for knowledge;" too degraded to appreciate the truth, the simplicity of a higher faith; too besotted with the worship of a hundred vain idols, which were the outward reflection of their own diseased imaginations, to receive the wisdom of the true religion, and to perceive especially the truth just enunciated, that it is Iahvah who gives the rain and upon whom all atmospheric changes depend (*cf.* xiv. 22): and thus, in the hour of need, "every founder blushes for the image, because his molten figure is a lie, and there is no breath in them;" because the lifeless idol, the work of his hands, can lend no help. Perhaps both clauses of the verse rather express a prophecy: "All men will be proven brutish, destitute of knowledge; every founder will blush for the graven image." Wise and strong as the Babylonians supposed themselves to be, the logic of events would undeceive them. They were doomed to a rude awakening; to discover in the hour of defeat and surrender that the molten idol was a delusion, that the work of their hands was an embodied lie, void of life, powerless to save. "Vanity"—a mere breath, naught—"are they, a work of knaveries" (a term recurring only in li. 18; the root seems to mean "to stammer," "to imitate"); "in the time of their visitation they will perish!" or simply "they perish!"—in the burning temples, in the crash of falling shrines.

It has happened so. At this day the temples of cedar and marble, with their woodwork overlaid with bronze and silver and gold, of whose glories the Babylonian sovereigns so proudly boast in their still existing records, as "shining like the sun, and like the stars of heaven," are shapeless heaps or rather mountains of rubbish, where Arabs dig for building materials and treasure trove, and European explorers for the relics of a civilisation and a superstition which have passed away for ever. *Vana sunt, et opus risu dignum.* In the revolutions of time, which are the outward measures of the eternally self-unfolding purposes of God, the word of the Judean prophets has been amply fulfilled. Babylon and her idols are no more.

All other idols, too, must perish in like manner. "Thus shall ye say of them: The gods who the" heavens "and earth did not make, perish from the earth and from under the heavens shall these!" The assertion that the idols of Babylon were doomed to destruction, was not the whole of the prophetic message. It is connected with and founded upon the antithetic assertion of the eternity of Iahvah. They will perish, but He endures. The one eternal is El Elyon, the Most High God, the Maker of heaven and earth. But heaven and earth and whatever partakes only of their material nature are also doomed to pass away. And in that day of the Lord, when the elements melt with fervent heat, and the earth and the works that are therein shall be burnt up (2 Pet. iii. 10), not only will the idols of the heathen world, and the tawdry dolls which a degenerate church suffers to be adored as a kind of magical embodiment of the Mother of God, but all other idols which the sensebound heart of man makes to itself, vanish into nothingness before that overwhelming revelation of the supremacy of God.

There is something amazing in the folly of worshipping man, whether in the abstract form of the cultus of "Humanity," or in any of the various forms of what is called "Hero-worship," or in the vulgar form of self-worship, which is the religion of the selfish and the worldly. To ascribe infallibility to any mortal, whether Pope or politician, is to sin in the spirit of idolatry. The Maker of heaven and earth, and He alone, is worthy of worship. "Where wast thou when I laid the foundations of the earth? declare, if thou hast understanding" (Job xxxviii. 4). No human wisdom nor power presided there; and to produce the smallest of asteroids is still a task which lies infinitely beyond the combined resources of modern science. Man and all that man has created is naught in the scale of God's creation. He and all the mighty works with which he amazes, overshadows, enslaves his little world, will perish and pass away; only that will survive which he builds of materials which are imperishable, fabrics of spiritual worth and excellence and glory (1 Cor. iii. 13). A Nineveh, a Babylon, a London, a Paris, may disappear; "but he that doeth the will of God abideth for ever" (1 John ii. 17). "Not like these" (*cf.* verse 11 *ad fin.*) "is Jacob's Portion, but the Maker and Moulder of the All—He is his heritage; Iahvah Sabaoth is His name!" (Both here and at li. 19 = xxviii. 19 the LXX. omits: "and Israel is the tribe," which seems to have been derived from Deut. xxxii. 9. Israel is elsewhere called "Iahvah's heritage," Ps. xxxiii. 12, and "portion," Deut. xxxii. 9; but that thought hardly suits the connection here.)

"Not like these:" for He is the Divine Potter who moulded all things, including the signs of heaven, and the idols of wood and metal, and their foolish worshippers. And he is "Jacob's portion"; for the knowledge and worship of Him were, in the Divine counsels, originally assigned to Israel (*cf.* Deut. iv. 19; and xxxii. 8, according to the true reading, preserved in the LXX.); and therefore Israel alone knows Him and His glorious attributes. "Iahvah Sabaoth is His name:" the Eternal, the Maker and Master of the hosts of heaven and earth, is the aspect under which He has revealed Himself to the true representatives of Israel, His servants the prophets.

The portion of Israel is his God—his abiding portion; of which neither the changes of time nor the misconceptions of man can avail to rob him. When all that is accidental and transitory is taken away, this distinction remains: Israel's portion is his God. Iahvah was indeed the national God of the Jews, argue some of our modern wise ones; and therefore He cannot be identified with the universal Deity. He has been developed, expanded, into this vast conception; but originally He was but the private god of a petty tribe, the Lar of a wandering household. Now herein is a marvellous thing. How was it that this particular household god thus grew to infinite proportions, like the genius emerging from the unsealed jar of Arab fable, until, from His prime foothold on the tent-floor of a nomad family, He towered above the stars and His form overshadowed the universe? How did it come to pass that His prophet could ask in a tone of indisputable truth, recognised alike by friend and foe, "Do not I fill heaven and earth, saith Iahvah"? (Jer. xxiii. 24). How, that this immense, this immeasurable expansion took place in this instance, and not in that of any one of the thousand rival deities of surrounding and more powerful tribes and nations? How comes it that we to-day are met to adore Iahvah, and not rather one of the forgotten gods of Canaan or Egypt or Babylon? Merodach and Nebo have vanished, but Iahvah is the Father of our Lord Jesus Christ. It certainly looks very much as if the Hebrew prophets were right; as if Iahvah were really the God of the creation as well as the Portion of Jacob.

"The portion of Jacob." Is His relation to that one people a stumbling-block? Can we see no eternal truth in the statement of the Psalmist that "the Lord's portion is His people?" Who can find fault with the enthusiastic faith of holy men thus exulting in the knowledge and love of God? It is a characteristic of all genuine religion, this sweet, this elevating consciousness that God is *our* God; this profound sense that He has revealed Himself to us in a special and peculiar and individual manner. But the actual historical results, as well as the sacred books, prove that the sense of possessing God and being possessed by Him was purer, stronger, deeper, more effectual, more abiding, in Israel than in any other race of the ancient world.

One must tread warily upon slippery ground; but I cannot help thinking that many of the arguments alleged against the probability of God revealing Himself to man at all or to a single nation in particular, are sufficiently met by the simple consideration that He has actually done so. Any event whatever may be very improbable until it has happened; and assuming that God has *not* revealed Himself, it may perhaps be shown to be highly improbable that He would reveal Himself. But, meanwhile, all religions and all faith and the phenomena of conscience and the highest intuitions of reason presuppose this improbable event as the fact apart from which they are insoluble riddles. This is not to say that the precise manner of revelation—the contact of the Infinite with the Finite Spirit—is definable. There are many less lofty experiences of man which also are indefinable and mysterious, but none the less actual and certain. Facts are not explained by denial, which is about the most barren and feeble attitude a man can take up in the presence of a baffling mystery. Nor is it for man to prescribe conditions to God. He who made us and knows us far better than we know ourselves, knows also how best to reveal Himself to His creatures.

The special illumination of Israel, however, does not imply that no light was vouchsafed elsewhere. The religious systems of other nations furnish abundant evidence to the contrary. God "left not Himself without witness," the silent witness of that beneficent order of the natural world, which makes it possible for man to live, and to live happily. St. Paul did not scruple to compliment even the degenerate Athenians of his own day on the ground of their attention to religious matters, and he could cite a Greek poet in support of his doctrine that man is the offspring of the one God and Father of all.

We may see in the fact a sufficient indication of what St. Paul would have said, had the nobler non-Christian systems fallen under his cognisance; had heathenism become known to him not in the heterogeneous polytheism of Hellas, which in his time had long since lost what little moral influence it had ever possessed, nor in the wild orgiastic nature worships of the Lesser Asia, which in their thoroughly sensuous basis did dishonour alike to God and to man; but in the sublime tenets of Zarathustra, with their noble morality and deep reverence for the One God, the spirit of all goodness and truth, or in the reformed Brahmanism of Gautama the Buddha, with its grand principle of self-renunciation and universal charity.

The peculiar glories of Bible religion are not dimmed in presence of these other lights. Allowing for whatever is valuable in these systems of belief, we may still allege that Bible religion comprises all that is good in them, and has, besides, many precious features peculiar to itself; we may still maintain that their excellences are rather testimonies to the truth of the biblical teachings about God than difficulties in the way of a rational faith; that it would be far more difficult to a thoughtful mind to accept the revelation of God conveyed in the Bible, if it were the fact that no rays of Divine light had cheered the darkness of the millions of struggling mortals beyond the pale of Judaism, than it is under the actual circumstances of the case: in short, that the truths implicated in imperfect religions, isolated from all contact with Hebrew or Christian belief, are a witness to and a foreshadowing of the truths of the gospel.

Our prophet declares that Jacob's portion—the God of Israel—is not like the gods of contemporary peoples. How, then, does he conceive of Him? Not as a metaphysical entity—a naked, perhaps empty abstraction of the understanding. Not as the Absolute and Infinite Being, who is out of all relation to space and time. His language—the language of the Old Testament—possesses no adjectives like "Infinite," "Absolute," "Eternal," "Omniscient," "Omnipresent," nor even "Almighty," although that word so often appears in our venerable Authorised Version. It is difficult for us, who are the heirs of ages of thought and intellectual toil, and whose thinking is almost wholly carried on by means of abstract ideas, to realise a state of mind and a habit of thought so largely different from our own as that of the Hebrew people and even of the Hebrew prophets. Yet unless we make an effort to realise it, however inadequately, unless we exert ourselves, and strive manfully to enter through the gate of an instructed imagination into that far-off stage of life and thought which presents so many problems to the historical student, and hides in its obscurity so many precious truths; we must inevitably fail to appreciate the full significance, and consequently fail of appropriating the full blessing of those wonderful prophecies of ancient Israel, which are not for an age but for all time.

Let us, then, try to apprehend the actual point of view from which the inspired Israelite regarded his God. In the first place, that point of view was eminently practical. As a recent writer has forcibly remarked, "The primitive mind does not occupy itself with things of no practical importance, and it is only in the later stages of society that we meet with traditional beliefs nominally accepted by every one but practically regarded by none; or with theological speculations which have an interest for the curious, but are not felt to have a direct bearing on the concerns of life."

The pious Israelite could not indulge a morbidly acute and restlessly speculative intellect with philosophical or scientific theories about the Deity, His nature in Himself, His essential and accidental attributes, His relation to the visible world. Neither did such theories then exist ready made to his hand, nor did his inward impulses and the natural course of thought urge him to pry into such abstruse matters, and with cold irreverence to subject his idea of God to critical analysis. Could he have been made to understand the attitude and the demands of some modern disputants, he would have been apt to exclaim, "Canst thou by searching find out God? Canst thou find out Shaddai unto perfection? It is as high as heaven, what canst thou do? deeper than hell, what canst thou know?" To find out and to know God as the understanding finds out and knows, how can that ever become possible to man? Such knowledge depends entirely upon processes of comparison; upon the perception of similarity between the object investigated and other known objects: upon accurate naming and classification. But who can dream of successfully referring the Deity to a class? "To what will ye liken God, or what likeness will ye compare unto Him?" In the brief prophecy before us, as in the fortieth chapter of Isaiah, with which it presents so many points of contact, we have a splendid protest against all attempts at bringing the Most High within the limitations of human cognition, and reducing God to the category of things known and understood. Directed in the first instance against idolatry—against vain efforts to find an adequate likeness of the Supreme in some one of the numberless creations of His hand, and so to compare and gauge and comprehend Himself,—that protest is still applicable, and with even greater force, against the idolatrous tendencies of the present age: when one school of devotees loudly declares,

> "Thou, Nature, art our goddess; to thy law
> Our services are bound: wherefore should we
> Stand in the plague of custom?"

and another is equally loud in asserting that it has found the true god in man himself; and another proclaims the divinity of brute force, and feels no shame in advocating the sovereignty of those gross instincts and passions which man shares with the beasts that perish. It is an unworthy and an inadequate conception of God, which identifies Him with Nature; it is a deplorably impoverished idea, the mere outcome of philosophic despair, which identifies him with Humanity; but what language can describe the grovelling baseness of that habit of thought which knows of nothing higher than the sensual appetite, and seeks nothing better than its continual indulgence; which sees the native impress of sovereignty on the brow of passing pleasure, and recognises the image and likeness of God in a temporary association of depraved instincts?

It is to this last form of idolatry, this utter heathenism in the moral life, that all other forms really converge, as St. Paul has shown in the introduction of his Epistle to the Romans, where, in view of the unutterable iniquities which were familiar occurrences in the world of his contemporaries, he affirms that moral decadence of the most appalling character is ultimately traceable to a voluntary indulgence of those idolatrous tendencies which ignore God's revelation of Himself to the heart and reason, and prefer to find their deity in something less awful in purity and holiness, less averse to the defilements of sin, less conversant with the secrets of the soul; and so, not liking to retain the true and only God in knowledge, change His truth into a lie, and worship and serve the creature more than the Creator: changing the glory of the incorruptible God into an image made like unto corruptible man, or even to birds and fourfooted beasts and creeping things.

CHAPTER VII.

THE BROKEN COVENANT.

JEREMIAH xi., xii.

THERE is no visible break between these two chapters. They seem to summarise the history of a particular episode in the prophet's career. At the same time, the style is so peculiar that it is not so easy as it might appear at a first glance to determine exactly what it is that the section has to tell us. When we come to take a closer look at it, we find a thoroughly characteristic mixture of direct narrative and soliloquy, of statement of facts and reflection upon those facts, of aspiration and prayer and prophecy, of self-communing and communing with God. Careful analysis may perhaps furnish us with a clue to the disentanglement of the general sense and drift of this characteristic medley. We may thus hope to get a clearer insight into the bearing of this old-world oracle upon our own needs and perplexities, our sins and the fruit of our sins, what we have done and what we may expect as the consequence of our doings. For the Word of God is "quick and powerful." Its outward form and vesture may change with the passing of time; but its substance never changes. The old interpreters die, but the Word lives, and its life is a life of power. By that Word men live in their successive generations; it is at once creative and regulative; it is the seed of life in man, and it is the law of that life. Apart from the Divine Word, man would be no more than a brute gifted with understanding, but denied all answer to the higher cravings of soul and spirit; a being whose conscious life was a mere mockery; a self-tormentor, tantalised with vain surmises, tortured with ever-recurring problems; longing for light, and beset with never-lifting clouds of impenetrable darkness; the one sole instance, among the myriads of sentient beings, of a creature whose wants Nature refuses to satisfy, and whose lot it is to consume for ever in the fires of hopeless desire.

The sovran Lord, who is the Eternal Wisdom, has not made such a mistake. He provides satisfaction for all His creatures, according to the varying degrees of their capacity, according to their rank in the scale of being, so that all may rejoice in the fulness and the freedom of a happy life for their allotted time. Man is no exception to the universal rule. His whole constitution, as God has fashioned it, is such that he can find his perfect satisfaction in the Word of the Lord. And the depth of his dissatisfaction, the poignancy and the bitterness of his disappointment and disgust at himself and at the world in which he finds himself, are the strongest evidence that he has sought satisfaction in things that cannot satisfy; that he has foolishly endeavoured to feed his soul upon ashes, to still the cravings of his spirit with something other than that Word of God which is the Bread of Life.

You will observe that the discourse we are to consider, is headed: "The word that fell to Jeremiah from Iahvah" (lit. "from with," that is, "from the presence of" the Eternal), "saying." I think that expression "saying" covers all that follows, to the end of the discourse. The prophet's preaching the Law, and the consequences of that preaching as regarded himself; his experience of the stubbornness and treachery of the people; the varying moods of his own mind under that bitter experience; his reflections upon the condition of Judah, and the condition of Judah's ill-minded neighbours; his forecasts of the after-course of events as determined by the unchanging will of a righteous God; all these things seem to be included in the scope of that "Word from the presence of Iahvah," which the prophet is about to put on record. You will see that it is not a single utterance of a precise and definite message, which he might have delivered in a few moments of time before a single audience of his countrymen. The Word of the Lord is progressively revealed; it begins with a thought in the prophet's mind, but its entire content is unfolded gradually, as he proceeds to act upon that thought or Divine impulse; it is, as it were, evolved as the result of collision between the prophet and his hearers; it emerges into clear light out of the darkness of storm and conflict; a conflict both internal and external; a conflict within, between his own contending emotions and impulses and sympathies; and a conflict without, between an unpopular teacher, and a wayward and corrupt and incorrigible people. "From with Iahvah." There may be strife and tumult and the darkness of ignorance and passion upon earth; but the star of truth shines in the firmament of heaven, and the eye of the inspired man sees it. This is his difference from his fellows.

"Hear ye the words of this covenant, and speak ye unto the men of Judah, and upon the dwellers in Jerusalem! And say thou unto them, Thus saith Iahvah, the God of Israel, Accursed are the men that hear not the words of this covenant, which I lay on your fathers, in the day that I brought them forth from the land of Egypt, from the furnace of iron, saying, Hearken unto My voice, and do these things, according to all that I shall charge you: that ye may become for Me a people, and that I Myself may become for you a God. That I may make good" (להקים *vid. infra*) "the oath which I sware to your forefathers, that I would give them a land flowing with milk and honey, as it now is" (or simply, "to-day"). "And I answered and said, Amen, Iahvah!" (xi. 1-5). "Hear ye . . . speak ye unto the men of Judah!" The occasion referred to is that memorable crisis in the eighteenth year of king Josiah, when Hilkiah the high priest had "found the book of the law in the house of the Lord" (2 Kings xxii. 8 *sqq.*), and the pious king had read in the hearing of the assembled people those fervid exhortations to obedience, those promises fraught with all manner of blessing, those terrible denunciations of wrath and ruin reserved for rebellion and apostasy, which we may still read in the closing chapters of the book of Deuteronomy (Deut. xxvii. *sq.*). Jeremiah is recalling the events of his own ministry, and passes in rapid review from the time of his preaching upon the Book of the Law, to the Chaldean invasion in the reign of Jehoiachin (xiii. 18 *sqq.*). He recalls the solemn occasion when the king and people bound themselves by oath to observe the law of their God; when "the king stood upon the platform, and made the covenant before Iahvah, that he would follow Iahvah, and keep his commandments, and his laws and his statutes, with whole heart and with whole soul; to make good (להקים) the words of this covenant that were written upon this roll; and all the people stood to the covenant" (2 Kings xxiii. 3). At or soon after this great meeting, the prophet gives, in the name of Iahvah, an emphatic approval to the public undertaking; and bids the leaders in the movement not to rest contented with this good beginning, but to impress the obligation more deeply upon the community at large, by sending a mission of properly qualified persons, including himself, which should at once enforce the reforms necessitated by the covenant of strict obedience to the Law, and reconcile the people both of the capital and of the rural towns and hamlets to the sudden and sweeping changes demanded of them, by showing their entire consonance with the Divine precepts. "Hear *ye*"—princes and priests—"the words of this covenant; and speak *ye* unto the men of Judah!" Then follows, in brief, the prophet's own commission, which is to reiterate, with all the force of his impassioned rhetoric, the awful menaces of the Sacred Book: "Cursed be the men that hear not the words of this covenant!" Now again, in these last years of their national existence, the chosen people are to hear an authoritative proclamation of that Divine Law upon which all their weal depends; the Law given them at the outset of their history, when the memory of the great deliverance was yet fresh in their minds; the Law which was the condition of their peculiar relation to the Universal God. At Sinai they had solemnly undertaken to observe that Law: and Iahweh had fulfilled His promise to their "fathers"—to Abraham, Isaac, and Jacob—and had given them a goodly land, in which they had now been established for at least six hundred years. The Divine truth and righteousness were manifest upon a retrospect of this long period of eventful history; and Jeremiah could not withhold his inward assent, in the formula prescribed by the Book of the Law (Deut. xxvii. 15 *sqq.*), to the perfect justice of the sentence: "Cursed be the men that hear not the words of this covenant." "And I answered and said, Amen, Iahvah!"* So to this true Israelite, thus deeply communing with his own spirit, two things had become clear as day. The one was the absolute righteousness of God's entire dealing with Israel, from first to last; the righteousness of disaster and overthrow as well as of victory and prosperity: the other was his own present duty to bring this truth home to the hearts and consciences of his fellow-countrymen. This is how he states the fact: "And Iahvah said unto me, Proclaim thou all these words in the cities of Judah and in the streets of Jerusalem, saying, Hear ye the words of this covenant and do them. For I earnestly adjured your fathers, when I brought them up from the land of Egypt" ("and I have done so continually") "even unto this very day, saying, Obey ye My voice! And they obeyed not, nor inclined their ear; and they walked, each and all, in the hardness of their wicked heart. So I brought upon them all the threats" (lit., "words") "of this covenant, which I had charged them to keep, and they kept it not" (xi. 6-8). God is always self-consistent; man is often inconsistent with himself; God is eternally true, man is ever giving fresh proofs of his natural faithlessness. God is not only just in keeping His promises; He is also merciful, in labouring ever to induce man to be self-consistent, and true to moral obligations. And Divine mercy is revealed alike in the pleadings of the Holy Spirit by the mouth of prophets, by the voice of conscience, and in the retribution that overtakes persistence in evil. The Divine Law is life and health to them that keep it; it is death to them that break it. "Thou, Lord, art merciful; for thou rewardest every man according to his works."

The relation of the One God to this one people was neither accidental nor arbitrary. It is sometimes spoken of as a thing glaringly unjust to the other nations of the ancient world, that the Father of all should have chosen Israel only to be the recipient of His special favours. Sometimes it is demanded, as an unanswerable

* But perhaps it is rather the prophet's love for his people, which fervently prays that the oath of blessing may be observed, and Judah maintained in the goodly land.

dilemma, How *could* the Universal God be the God of the Jews, in the restricted sense implied by the Old Testament histories? But difficulties of this kind rest upon misunderstanding, due to a slavishly literal interpretation of certain passages, and inability to take a comprehensive view of the general drift and tenor of the Old Testament writings as they bear upon this subject. God's choice of Israel was proof of His love for mankind. He did not select one people because He was indifferent or hostile to all other peoples; but because He wished to bring all the nations of the earth to the knowledge of Himself, and the observance of His law. The words of our prophet show that he was profoundly convinced that the favour of Iahvah had from the outset depended upon the obedience of Israel: "Hearken unto My voice, and do these things . . . that ye may become for Me a people, and that I Myself may become for you a God." How strangely must such words have sounded in the ears of people who believed, as the masses both in town and country appear for the most part to have done, that Iahvah as the ancestral god was bound by an indissoluble tie to Israel, and that He could not suffer the nation to perish without incurring irreparable loss, if not extinction, for Himself! It is as if the prophet had said: You call yourselves the people of God; but it is not so much that you *are* His people, as that you may become such by doing His will. You suppose that Iahvah, the Eternal, the Creator, is to you what Chemosh is to Moab, or Molech to Ammon, or Baal to Tyre; but that is just what He is not. If you entertain such ideas of Iahvah, you are worshipping a figment of your own carnal imaginations; your god is not the universal God, but a gross unspiritual idol. It is only upon your fulfilment of His conditions, only upon your yielding an inward assent to His law, a hearty acceptance to His rule of life, that He Himself—the One only God—can truly become your God. In accepting His law, you accept Him, and in rejecting His law, you reject Him; for His law is a reflection of Himself; a revelation, so far as such can be made to a creature like man, of His essential being and character. Therefore think not that you can worship Him by mere external rites; for the true worship is "righteousness, and holiness of life."

The progress of the reforming movement, which was doubtless powerfully stimulated by the preaching of Jeremiah, is briefly sketched in the chapter of the book of Kings, to which I have already referred (2 Kings xxiii.). That summary of the good deeds of king Josiah records apparently a very complete extirpation of the various forms of idolatry, and even a slaughter of the idol-priests upon their own altars. Heathenism, it would seem, could hardly have been practised again, at least openly, during the twelve remaining years of Josiah. But although a zealous king might enforce outward conformity to the Law, and although the earnest preaching of prophets like Zephaniah and Jeremiah might have considerable effect with the better part of the people, the fact remained that those whose hearts were really open to the word of the Lord were still, as always, a small minority; and the tendency to apostasy, though checked, was far from being rooted up. Here and there the forbidden rites were secretly observed; and the harsh measures which had accompanied their public suppression may very probably have intensified the attachment of many to the local forms of worship. Sincere conversions are not effected by violence; and the martyrdom of devotees may give new life even to degraded and utterly immoral superstitions. The transient nature of Josiah's reformation, radical as it may have appeared at the time to the principal agents engaged in it, is evident from the testimony of Jeremiah himself. "And Iahvah said unto me, There exists a conspiracy among the men of Judah, and among the inhabitants of Jerusalem. They have returned to the old sins of their fathers, who refused to hear My words; and they too have gone away after other gods, to serve them: the house of Israel and the house of Judah have broken My covenant, which I made with their forefathers. Therefore thus saith Iahvah, Behold I am about to bring unto them an evil from which they cannot get forth; and they will cry unto Me, and I will not listen unto them. And the cities of Judah and the inhabitants of Jerusalem will go and cry unto the gods to whom they burn incense" (*i. e.*, now; ptcp.); "and they will yield them no help at all in the time of their evil. For many as thy cities are thy gods become, O Judah! and many as the streets of Jerusalem have ye appointed altars to the Shame, altars for burning incense to the Baal. And as for thee, intercede thou not for this people, nor lift up for them outcry" (*i. e.*, mourning) "and intercession; for I intend not to hearken, in the time when they call unto Me, in the time of their evil" (so read: *cf.* vers. 12, בעת instead of בעד) (vv. 9-14). All this appears to indicate the course of the prophet's reflection, after it had become clear to him that the reformation was illusory, and that his own labours had failed of their purpose. He calls the relapse of the people a plot or conspiracy; thereby sugesting, perhaps, the secrecy with which the prohibited worships were at first revived, and the intrigues of the unfaithful nobles and priests and prophets, in order to bring about a reversal of the policy of reform, and a return to the old system; and certainly suggesting that the heart of the nation, as a whole, was disloyal to its Heavenly King, and that its renewed apostasy was a wicked disavowal of lawful allegiance, and an act of unpardonable treason against God.

But the word further signifies that a *bond* has been entered into, a bond which is the exact antithesis of the covenant with Iahvah; and it implies that this bond has about it a fatal strength and permanence, involving as its necessary consequence the ruin of the nation. Breaking covenant with Iahvah meant making a covenant with other gods; it was impossible to do the one thing without the other. And that is as true now, under totally different conditions, as it was in the land of Judah, twenty-four centuries ago. If you have broken faith with God in Christ it is because you have entered into an agreement with another; it is because you have foolishly taken the tempter at his word, and accepted his conditions, and surrendered to his proposals, and preferred his promises to the promises of God. It is because, against all reason, against conscience, against the Holy Spirit, against the witness of God's Word, against the witness of His Saints and Confessors in all ages, you have believed that a Being less than the Eternal God could ensure your weal and make you happy. And now your heart is no longer at unity in itself, and your allegiance is no longer single and undivided. "Many as thy cities are thy gods become, O Judah!" The soul that is not unified and harmonised by the fear of the One God, is torn and distracted by a thousand contending passions: and vainly seeks peace and deliverance by worship at a thousand unholy shrines. But Mammon and Belial and Ashtaroth and the whole rout of unclean spirits, whose seductions have lured you astray, will fail you at last; and in the hour of bitter need, you will learn too late that there is no god but God, and no peace nor safety nor joy but in Him.

It is futile to pray for those who have deliberately cast off the covenant of Iahvah, and made a covenant with His adversary. "Intercede not for this people, nor lift up outcry and intercession for them!" Prayer cannot save, nothing can save, the impenitent; and there is a state of mind in which one's own prayer is turned into sin; the state of mind in which a man prays, merely to appease God, and escape the fire, but without a thought of forsaking sin, without the faintest aspiration after holiness. There is a degree of guilt upon which sentence is already passed, which is "unto death," and for which intercession is interdicted alike by the Apostle of the New as to the prophet of the Old Covenant.

"What availeth it My beloved, that she fulfilleth her intent in Mine house? Can vows and hallowed flesh make thine evil to pass from thee? Then mightest thou indeed rejoice"* (ver. 15). Such appears to be the true sense of this verse, the only difficult one in the chapter. The prophet had evidently the same thought in his mind as in ver. 11: "I will bring unto them an evil, from which they cannot get forth; and they will cry unto Me, and I will not hearken unto them." The words also recall those of Isaiah (Isa. i. 11 *sqq.*): "For what to Me are your many sacrifices, saith Iahvah? When ye enter in to see My face, who hath sought this at your hand, to trample My courts? Bring no more a vain oblation; loathly incense it is to Me!" The term which I have rendered "intent," usually denotes an evil intention; so that, like Isaiah, our prophet implies that the popular worship is not only futile but sinful. So true it is that "He that turneth away his ear from hearing the law, even his prayer is an abomination" (Prov. xxviii. 9); or, as the Psalmist puts the same truth, "If I incline unto wickedness with my heart, the Lord will not hear me."

* Hitzig supposed that the "vows" and "hallowed flesh" were thank-offerings for the departure of the Scythians. "It is plain that the people are really present in the temple; they bring, presumably after the retreat of the Scythians, the offerings vowed at that time." But, considering the context, the reference appears to be more general. I have partly followed the LXX. in emending an obviously corrupt verse; the only one in the chapter which presents any textual difficulty. Read: זי : מה לידידי בביתי עֲשׂוֹתָהּ הַמְזִמָּתָה הַנְּדָרִים ובשר קדש יַעֲבִרוּ מֵעָלַיִכי רָעָתֵכִי אָז תַּעֲלֹזִי. The article with a noun with suffix, and the peculiar form of the 2 pers. pron. f., are found elsewhere in Jer. But I incline to correct further thus: "What avail to My beloved is her dealing (or sacrificing: עשה 2 Kings xvii. 32) in My house? וגו הַמִּזְבְּחוֹת הָרַבִּים ובשר קדש. "Can the many altars (ver. 13) and hallowed flesh cause thine evil to pass away from thee (or pass thee by)?" This seems very apposite to what precedes. The Hebrew, as it stands, cannot possibly mean what we read both in the A. V. and R. V., nor indeed anything else.

"A flourishing olive, fair with shapely fruit, did Iahvah call thy name. To the sound of a great uproar will He set her on fire; and his hanging boughs will crackle" ("in the flames"). "And Iahvah Sabaoth, that planted thee, Himself hath pronounced evil upon thee; because of the evil of the house of Israel and the house of Judah, which they have done to themselves" (iv. 18, vii. 19) "in provoking Me, in burning incense to the Baal" (vers. 16-17). The figure of the olive seems a very natural one (*cf.* Rom. xi. 17), when we remember the beauty and the utility for which that tree is famous in Eastern lands. "Iahvah called thy name;" that is, called thee into determinate being; endowed thee at thine origin with certain characteristic qualities. Thine original constitution, as thou didst leave thy Maker's hand, was fair and good. Israel among the nations was as beautiful to the eye as the olive among trees; and his "fruit," his doings, were a glory to God and a blessing to men, like that precious oil, for "which God and man honour" the olive (Judg. ix. 9; Zech. iv. 3; Hos. xiv. 7; Ps. lii. 10.) But now the noble stock had degenerated; the "green olive tree," planted in the very court of Iahvah's house, had become no better than a barren wilding, fit only for the fire. The thought is essentially similar to that of an earlier discourse: "I planted thee a noble vine, wholly a right seed; how then hast thou turned into the degenerate plant of a strange vine unto Me?" (ii. 21). Here, there is an abrupt transition, which forcibly expresses the *suddenness* of the destruction that must devour this degenerate people: "To the sound of a great uproar"—the din of invading armies—"he will set her" (the beloved, symbolised by the tree) "on fire; and his" (the olive's) "hanging boughs will crackle in the flames." And this fierce work of a barbarous soldiery is no chance calamity; it is the execution of a Divine judgment: "Iahvah Sabaoth . . . . Himself hath pronounced evil upon thee." And yet further, it is the nation's own doing; the two houses of Israel have persistently laboured for their own ruin; they have brought it upon themselves. Man is himself the author of his own weal and woe; and they who are not "working out their own salvation," are working out their own destruction.

"And it was Iahvah that gave me knowledge, so that I well knew; at that time, Thou didst show me their doings. But, for myself, like a favourite" (lit. tame, friendly, gentle: iii. 4) "lamb that is led to the slaughter, I wist not that against me they had laid a plot. 'Let us fell the tree in its prime,* and let us cut him off out of the land of the living, that his name be remembered no more.' Yea, but Iahvah† Sabaoth judgeth righteously, trieth reins and heart. I shall see Thy vengeance on them; for unto Thee have I laid bare my cause. Therefore thus said Iahvah: Upon the men of Anathoth that were seeking thy life, saying, Thou shalt not prophesy in the name of Iahvah, that thou die not by our hand:—therefore thus said Iahvah Sabaoth, Behold I am about to visit it upon them: the young men will die by the sword; their sons and their

* Reading בְּלֵחוֹ, with Hitzig, instead of בְּלַחְמוֹ which is meaningless. Deut. xxxiv. 7; Ezek. xxi. 3. Perhaps it would be better to keep *all* the letters, and point בְּלֵחָמוֹ, understanding עֵץ as collective, "the trees."

† Not a vocative: xx. 12, xvii. 10.

daughters will die by the famine. And a remnant they shall not have: for I will bring an evil unto the men of Anathoth, the year of their visitation" (vv. 18-23).

The prophet, it would seem, had made the round of the country places, and come to Anathoth, on his return journey to Jerusalem. Here, in his native town, he proclaimed to his own people that same solemn message which he had delivered to the country at large. It is very probable that the preceding verses (9-17) contain the substance of his address to his kinsfolk and acquaintance; an address which stirred them, not to repentance towards God, but to murderous wrath against His prophet. A plot was laid for Jeremiah's life by his own neighbours and even his own family (xii. 6); and he owed his escape to some providential circumstance, some "lucky accident," as men might say, which revealed to him their unsuspected perfidy. What the event was which thus suddenly disclosed the hidden danger, is not recorded; and the whole episode is rather alluded to than described. But it is clear that the prophet knew nothing about the plot, until it was ripe for execution. He was as wholly unconscious of the death prepared for him, as a petted lamb on the way to the altar. "Then"—when his fate seemed sure—then it was that something happened by which "Iahvah gave him knowledge," and "showed him their doings." The thought or saying attributed to his enemies, "Let us fell the tree(s) in the prime thereof!" may contain a sarcastic allusion really made to the prophet's own warning (ver. 16): "A flourishing olive, fair with shapely fruit, did Iahvah call thy name: to the noise of a great uproar will He set it on fire, and the branches thereof shall crackle in the flames." The words that follow (ver. 20), "yea, but" (or, and yet) "Iahvah Sabaoth judgeth righteously; trieth reins and heart" (*cf.* xx. 12), is the prophet's reply, in the form of an unexpressed thought, or a hurried ejaculation upon discovering their deadly malice. The timely warning which he had received, was fresh proof to him of the truth that human designs are, after all that their authors can do, dependent on the will of an Unseen Arbiter of events; and the Divine justice, thus manifested towards himself, inspired a conviction that those hardened and bloodthirsty sinners would, sooner or later, experience in their own destruction that display of the same Divine attribute which was necessary to its complete manifestation. It was this conviction, rather than personal resentment, however excusable under the circumstances that feeling would have been, which led Jeremiah to exclaim: "I shall see Thy vengeance on them, for unto Thee have I laid bare my cause."

He had appealed to the Judge of all the earth, that doeth right; and he knew the innocency of his own heart in the quarrel. He was certain, therefore, that his cause would one day be vindicated, when that ruin overtook his enemies, of which he had warned them in vain. Looked at in this light, his words are a confident assertion of the Divine justice, not a cry for vengeance. They reveal what we may perhaps call the ***human*** basis of the formal prophecy which follows; they show by what steps the prophet's mind was led on to the utterance of a sentence of destruction upon the men of Anathoth. That Jeremiah's invectives and threatenings of wrath and ruin should provoke hatred and opposition was perhaps not wonderful. Men in general are slow to recognise their own moral shortcomings, to believe evil of themselves; and they are apt to prefer advisers whose optimism, though ill-founded and misleading, is pleasant and reassuring and confirmatory of their own prejudices. But it does seem strange that it should have been reserved for the men of his own birthplace, his own "brethren and his father's house," to carry opposition to the point of meditated murder. Once more Jeremiah stands before us, a visible type of Him whose Divine wisdom declared that a prophet finds no honour in his own country, and whose life was attempted on that Sabbath day at Nazareth (St. Luke iv. 24 *sqq.*).

The sentence was pronounced, but the cloud of dejection was not at once lifted from the soul of the seer. He knew that justice must in the end overtake the guilty; but, in the meantime, "his enemies lived and were mighty," and their criminal designs against himself remained unnoticed and unpunished. The more he brooded over it, the more difficult it seemed to reconcile their prosperous immunity with the justice of God. He has given us the course of his reflections upon this painful question, ever suggested anew by the facts of life, never sufficiently answered by toiling reason. "Too righteous art Thou, Iahvah, for me to contend with Thee: I will but lay arguments before Thee" (*i. e.*, argue the case forensically). "Wherefore doth the way of the wicked prosper? Wherefore are they undisturbed, all that deal very treacherously? Thou plantest them, yea, they take root; they grow ever, yea, they bear fruit: Thou art nigh in their mouth, and far from their reins. And Thou, Iahvah, knowest me; Thou seest me, and triest mine heart in Thy mind. Separate them like sheep for the slaughter, and consecrate them for the day of killing! How long shall the land mourn, and the herbage of all the country wither? From the evil of the dwellers therein, beasts and birds perish: for they have said" (or, thought), He cannot see our end" (xii. 1-4). It is not merely that his would-be murderers thrive; it is that they take the holy Name upon their unclean lips; it is that they are hypocrites combining a pretended respect for God, with an inward and thorough indifference to God. He is nigh in their mouth and far from their reins. They "honour Him with their lips, but have removed their heart far from Him; and their worship of Him is a mere human commandment, learned by rote" (Isa. xxix. 13). They swear by His Name, when they are bent on deception (chap. v. 2). It is all this which especially rouses the prophet's indignation; and contrasting therewith his own conscious integrity and faithfulness to the Divine law, he calls upon Divine justice to judge between himself and them: "Pull them out like sheep for slaughter, and consecrate them" (set them apart—from the rest of the flock) "for the day of killing!" It has been said that Jeremiah throughout this whole paragraph speaks not as a prophet, but as a private individual; and that in this verse especially he "gives way to the natural man, and asks the life of his enemies" (1 Kings iii. 11; Job xxxi. 30). This is perhaps a tenable opinion. We have to bear in mind the difference of standpoint between the writers of the Old Covenant and those of the New. Not much is said by the former about the forgiveness of injuries, about withholding the hand from vengeance. The most ancient law, indeed, contained a noble precept, which pointed in this direction: "If thou meet thine enemy's ox or his ass going astray, thou shalt surely bring it back to him again. If thou see the ass of him that hateth thee lying under his burden, and wouldest forbear to help him, thou shalt surely help with him" (Ex. xxiii. 4, 5). And in the Book of Proverbs we read: "Rejoice not when thine enemy falleth, And let not thine heart be glad when he is overthrown." But the impression of magnanimity thus produced is somewhat diminished by the reason which is added immediately: "Lest the Lord see it and it displease Him, and He turn away His wrath from him:" a motive of which the best that can be said is that it is characteristic of the imperfect morality of the time (Prov. xxiv. 17 *sq.*). The same objection may be taken to that other famous passage of the same book: "If thine enemy be hungry, give him bread to eat; And if he be thirsty, give him water to drink: For thou shalt heap coals of fire upon his head, And the Lord shall reward thee" (Prov. xxv. 21 *sq.*). The reflection that the relief of his necessities will mortify and humiliate an enemy to the utmost, which is what seems to have been originally meant by "heaping coals of fire upon his head," however practically useful in checking the wild impulses of a hot-blooded and vindictive race, such as the Hebrews were, and such as their kindred the Bedawi Arabs have remained to this day under a system of faith which has not said, "Love your enemies"; and however capable of a new application in the more enlightened spirit of Christianity (Rom. xii. 19 *sqq.*); is undoubtedly a motive marked by the limitations of Old Testament ethical thought. And edifying as they may prove to be, when understood in that purely spiritual and universal sense, to which the Church has lent her authority, how many of the psalms were, in their primary intention, agonising cries for vengeance; prayers that the human victim of oppression and wrong might "see his desire upon his enemies"? All this must be borne in mind; but there are other considerations also which must not be omitted, if we would get at the exact sense of our prophet in the passage before us.

We must remember that he is laying a case before God. He has admitted at the outset that God is absolutely just, in spite of and in view of the fact that his murderous enemies are prosperous and unpunished. When he pleads his own sincerity and purity of heart, in contrast with the lip-service of his adversaries, it is perhaps that God may grant, not so much *their* perdition, as the salvation of the country from the evils they have brought and are bringing upon it. Ascribing the troubles already present and those which are yet to come, the desolations which he sees and those which he foresees, to their steady persistence in wickedness, he asks, How long must this continue? Would it not be better, would it not be more consonant with Divine wisdom and righteousness to purify the land of its fatal taint by the sudden destruction of those heinous and hardened offenders, who scoff at the very idea of a true forecast of their "end" (ver. 4)? But this is not all. There would be more apparent force in the allegation we are discussing if it were. The cry to heaven for an immediate act of retributive justice is not the last thing recorded of the prophet's experience on this occasion. He goes on to relate, for our satisfaction, the Divine answer to his questionings, which seems to have satisfied his own troubled mind. "If thou hast run with but footracers, and they have wearied thee, how then wilt thou compete with the coursers? And if thy confidence be in a land of peace" (or, "a quiet land"), "how then wilt thou do in the thickets" (jungles) "of Jordan?* For even thine own brethren and thy father's house, even they will deal treacherously with thee; even they will cry aloud after thee: trust thou not in them, though they speak thee fair!" (xii. 5, 6). The metaphors convey a rebuke of impatience and premature discouragement. Hitzig aptly quotes Demosthenes: "If they cannot face the candle, what will they do when they see the sun?" (*Plut. de vitioso pudore, c.* 5.) It is "the voice of the prophet's better feeling, and of victorious self-possession," adds the critic; and we, who earnestly believe that, of the two voices which plead against each other in the heart of man, the voice that whispers good is the voice of God, find it not hard to accept this statement in that sense. The prophet is giving us the upshot of his reflection upon the terrible danger from which he had been mercifully preserved; and we see that his thoughts were guided to the conclusion that, having once accepted the Divine Call, it would be unworthy to abdicate his mission on the first signal of danger. Great as that danger had been, he now, in his calmer hour, perceives that, if he is to fulfil his high vocation, he must be prepared to face even worse things. With serious irony he asks himself, if a runner who is overcome with a footrace can hope to outstrip horses? or how a man, who is only bold where no danger is, will face the perils that lurk in the jungles of the Jordan? He remembers that he has to fight a more arduous battle and on a greater scene. Jerusalem is more than Anathoth; and "the kings of Judah and the princes thereof" are mightier adversaries than the conspirators of a country town. And his present escape is an earnest of deliverance on the wider field: "They shall fight against thee, but they shall not prevail against thee: for I am with thee, said Iahvah, to deliver thee" (see i. 17-19). But to a deeply affectionate and sensitive nature like Jeremiah's, the thought of being forsaken by his own kindred might well appear as a trial worse than death. This is the "contending with horses," the struggle that is almost beyond the powers of man to endure; this is the deadly peril, like that of venturing into the lion-haunted thickets of Jordan, which he clearly foresees as awaiting him: "For even thine own brethren and thy father's house, even they will deal treacherously with thee."† It would seem that the prophet, with whose "timidity" some critics have not hesitated to find fault, had to renounce all that man holds dear, as a condition of faithfulness to his call. Again we are reminded of One, of whom it is

* That "the swelling" or "the pride of Jordan" should rather be read "the wilds" or "jungles of Jordan," is clear from xlix. 19. Zech xi. 3; quoted by Hitzig. נאון means "growth," "overgrowth," among other things; and the Heb. phrase coincides with the Ἰάρδην δρυμός of Josephus ("Bell. Jud.," vii. 6, 5).

† The form of the Heb. verbs implies the *certainty* of the event. Hitzig supposes that ver. 6 simply explains the expression "land of peace" in ver. 5. At Anathoth the prophet was at home; if he "ran away" (reading בורח "fleest" for בוטח "art confident") there, what would he do, when he had gone forth as a "sheep among wolves" (St. Luke x. 3)? But I think it is much better to regard ver. 6 as explaining the *whole* of ver. 5 in the manner suggested above.

recorded that "Neither did His brethren believe in Him" (St. John vii. 5), and that "His friends went out to lay hold on Him, for they said, He is beside Himself" (St. Mark iii. 21). The closeness of the parallel between type and antitype, between the sorrowful prophet and the Man of Sorrows, is seen yet further in the words, "Even they will cry aloud after thee" (lit. "with full cry"). The meaning may be: They will join in the hue and cry of thy pursuers, the mad shouts of "Stop him!" or "Strike him down!" such as may perhaps have rung in the prophet's ears as he fled from Anathoth. But we may also understand a metaphorical description of the efforts of his family to recall him from the unpopular path on which he had entered; and this perhaps agrees better with the warning: "Trust them not, though they speak thee fair." And understood in this sense, the words coincide with what is told us in the Gospel of the attempt of our Lord's nearest kin to arrest the progress of His Divine mission, when His mother and His brethren "standing without, sent unto Him, calling Him" (St. Mark iii. 31).

The lesson for ourselves is plain. The man who listens to the Divine call, and makes God his portion, must be prepared to surrender everything else. He must be prepared, not only to renounce much which the world accounts good; he must be prepared for all kinds of opposition passive and active, tacit and avowed; he may even find, like Jeremiah, that his foes are the members of his own household (St. Matt. x. 36). And, like the prophet, his acceptance of the Divine call binds him to close his ears against entreaties and flatteries, against mockery and menace; and to act upon his Master's word: "If any man would come after Me, let him deny himself, and take up his cross, and follow Me. For whosoever would save his life shall lose it; and whosoever shall lose his life for My sake and the gospel's shall save it" (St. Mark viii. 34 *sq.*). "If any man come unto Me, and hate not his father and mother and wife and children and brethren and sisters, yea and his own life also, he cannot be My disciple" (St. Luke xiv. 26). A great prize is worth a great risk; and eternal life is a prize infinitely great. It is therefore worth the hazard and the sacrifice of all (St. Luke xviii. 29 *sq.*).

The section which follows (vv. 7-17) has been supposed to belong to the time of Jehoiakim, and consequently to be out of place here, having been transposed from its original context, because the peculiar Hebrew term which is rendered "dearly beloved" (ver. 7), is akin to the term rendered "My beloved," chap. xi. 15. But this supposition depends on the assumption that the "historical basis of the section" is to be found in the passage 2 Kings xxiv. 2, which relates briefly that in Jehoiakim's time plundering bands of Chaldeans, Syrians, Moabites, and Ammonites overran the country. The prophecy concerning Iahvah's "evil neighbours" is understood to refer to these marauding inroads, and is accordingly supposed to have been uttered between the eighth and eleventh years of Jehoiakim (Hitzig). It has, however, been pointed out (Naegelsbach) that the prophet does not once name the Chaldeans in the present discourse; which "he invariably does in all discourses subsequent to the decisive battle of Carchemish in the fourth year of Jehoiakim," which gave the Chaldeans the sovereignty of Western Asia. This discourse must, therefore, be of earlier date, and belong either to the first years of Jehoiakim, or to the time immediately subsequent to the eighteenth of Josiah. The history as preserved in Kings and Chronicles is so incomplete that we are not bound to connect the reference to "evil neighbours" with what is so summarily told in 2 Kings xxiv. 2. There may have been other occasions when Judah's jealous and watchful enemies profited by her internal weakness and dissensions to invade and ravage the land; and throughout the whole period the country was exposed to the danger of plundering raids by the wild nomads of the eastern and southern borders. It is possible, however, that vv. 14-17 are a later postscript, added by the prophet when he wrote his book in the fifth or sixth year of Jehoiakim (xxxvi. 9, 32).

There is, in reality, a close connection of thought between ver. 7 *sqq.* and what precedes. The relations of the prophet to his own family are made to symbolise the relations of Iahvah to His rebellious people; just as a former prophet finds in his own merciful treatment of a faithless wife a parable of Iahvah's dealings with faithless Israel. "I have forsaken My house, I have cast away My domain; I have given My soul's love into the grasp of her foes. My domain hath become to Me like the lion in the wood; she hath given utterance with her voice against Me; therefore I hate her." It is Iahvah who still speaks, as in ver. 6; the "house" is His holy house,* the temple; the land is His domain, the land of Judah; His "soul's love," is the Jewish people. Yet the expressions, "my house," "my domain," "my soul's love," equally suit the prophet's own family and their estate; the mention of the "lion in the wood" and its threatening roar, and the enmity provoked thereby, recalls what was said about the "wilds of the Jordan" in ver. 5, and the full outcry of his kindred after the prophet in ver. 6; and the solemn words "I have forsaken Mine house, I have cast away My domain . . . . I hate her," clearly correspond with the sentence of destruction upon Anathoth, chap. xi. 21 *sqq.* The double reference of the language becomes intelligible when we remember that in rejecting His messengers, Israel, nay mankind, rejects God; and that words and deeds done and uttered by Divine authority may be ascribed directly to God Himself. And regarded in the light of the prophet's commission "to pluck up and to break down, and to destroy and to overthrow, to build and to plant" nations and kingdoms (i. 10), all that is here said may be taken to be the prophet's own deliverance concerning his country. This, at all events, is the case with verses 12, 13.

"What! do I see my domain (all) vultures (and) hyenas?† Are the vultures all around her? Go ye, assemble all the beasts of the field! Bring them to devour" (ver. 9). The questions express astonishment at an unlooked-for and unwelcome spectacle. The loss of Divine favour has exposed Judah to the active hostility of man; and her neighbours eagerly fall upon her, like birds and beasts of prey, swarming over a helpless quarry. It is—so the prophet puts it—it is

* Or perhaps rather the holy land itself, as Hitzig suggested: Hos. ix. 15.

† Lit. "Is my domain vultures, hyenas, to me?" The dative expresses the interest of the speaker in the fact (dat. ethic.). The Heb. term צבוע only occurs here. It is the Arabic *dhabu'*, "hyena" (so Sept.), St. Jerome renders *avis discolor*. So the Targum: "a strewn" "sprinkled," or "spotted fowl."

as if a proclamation had gone forth to the wolves and jackals of the desert, bidding them come and devour the fallen carcase.* In another oracle he speaks of the heathen as "devouring Jacob" (x. 25). The people of Iahvah are their natural prey (Ps. xiv. 4: "who eat up My people as they eat bread"); but they are not suffered to devour them, until they have forfeited His protection.

The image is now exchanged for another, which approximates more nearly to the fact portrayed. "Many shepherds have marred My vineyard; they have trodden down My portion; they have turned My pleasant portion into a desolate wilderness. He" (the foe, the instrument of this ruin) "hath made it a desolation; it mourneth against Me, being desolate; desolated is all the land, for there is no man that giveth heed" (vv. 10, 11). As in an earlier discourse, chap. vi. 3, the invaders are now compared to hordes of nomad shepherds, who enter the land with their flocks and herds, and make havoc of the crops and pastures. From time immemorial the wandering Bedawis have been a terror to the settled peasantry of the East, whose way of life they despise as ignoble and unworthy of free men. Of this traditional enmity we perhaps hear a far-off echo in the story of Cain the tiller of the ground and Abel the keeper of sheep; and certainly in the statement that "every shepherd was an abomination unto the Egyptians" (Gen. xlvi. 34). The picture of utter desolateness, which the prophet suggests by a four-fold repetition, is probably sketched from a scene which he had himself witnessed; if it be not rather a representation of the actual condition of the country at the time of his writing. That the latter is the case might naturally be inferred from a consideration of the whole passage; and the twelfth verse seems to lend much support to this view: "Over all bare hills in the wilderness have come ravagers; for Iahvah hath a devouring sword: from land's end to land's end no flesh hath peace." † The language indeed recalls that of chap. iv. 10, 11; and the entire description might be taken as an ideal picture of the ruin that must ensue upon Iahvah's rejection of the land and people, especially if the closing verses (14-17) be considered as a later addition to the prophecy, made in the light of accomplished facts. But, upon the whole, it would seem to be more probable that the prophet is here reading the moral of present or recent experience. He affirms (ver. 11) that the affliction of the country is really a punishment for the religious blindness of the nation: "there is no man that layeth to heart" the Divine teaching of events as interpreted by himself (*cf.* ver. 4). The fact that we are unable, in the scantiness of the records of the time, to specify the particular troubles to which allusion is made, is no great objection to this view, which is at least effectively illustrated by the brief statement of 2 Kings xxiv. 2. The reflection appended in ver. 13 points in the same direction: "They have sown wheat, and have reaped thorns; they have put themselves to pain" (or, "exhausted themselves") "without profit," (or, "made themselves sick with unprofitable toil"); "and they are ashamed of their* produce" (ingatherings), "through the heat of the wrath of Iahvah." When the enemy had ravaged the crops, thorns would naturally spring up on the wasted lands; and "the heat of the wrath of Iahvah" appears to have been further manifested in a parching drought, which ruined what the enemy had left untouched (ver. 4, chap. xiv.).

Thus, then, Jeremiah receives the answer to his doubts in a painfully visible demonstration of what the wrath of Iahvah means. It means drought and famine; it means the exposure of the country, naked and defenceless, to the will of rapacious and vindictive enemies. For Iahvah's wrongs are far deeper and more bitter than the prophet's. The misdeeds of individuals are lighter in the balance than the sins of a nation; the treachery of a few persons on a particular occasion is as nothing beside the faithlessness of many generations. The partial evils, therefore, under which the country groans, can only be taken as indications of a far more complete and terrible destruction reserved for final impenitence. The perception of this truth, we may suppose, sufficed for the time to silence the prophet's complaints; and in the revulsion of feeling inspired by the awful vision of the unimpeded outbreak of Divine wrath, he utters an oracle concerning his country's destroyers, in which retributive justice is tempered by compassion and mercy. "Thus hath Jehovah said, Upon all Mine evil neighbours, who touch the heritage which I caused My people Israel to inherit: Lo I am about to uproot" (i. 10) "them from off their own land, and the house of Judah will I uproot from their midst. And after I have uprooted them, I will have compassion on them again, and will restore them each to their own heritage and their own land. And if they truly learn the ways of My people, to swear by My name, 'as Iahvah liveth!' even as they taught My people to swear by the Baal; they shall be rebuilt in the midst of My people. And if they will not hear, I will uproot that nation, utterly and fatally; it is an oracle of Iahvah" (14-17). The preceding section (vv. 7-14), as we have seen, rapidly yet vividly sketches the calamities which have ensued and must further ensue upon the Divine desertion of the country. Iahvah has forsaken the land, left her naked to her enemies, for her causeless, capricious, thankless revolt against her Divine Lord. In this forlorn, defenceless condition, all manner of evils befall her; the vineyards and cornfields are ravaged, the goodly land is desolated, by hordes of savage freebooters pouring in from the eastern deserts. These invaders are called Iahvah's "evil neighbours;" an expression which implies, not individuals banded together for purposes of brigandage, but hostile nations.† Upon these nations also will the justice of God be vindicated; for that justice is universal in its operation, and cannot therefore be restricted to Israel. Judgment must "begin at the house of God;" but it will not end there. The "evil neighbours," the surrounding heathen kingdoms, have been Iahvah's instruments for the chastisement of His rebellious people; but they are not on that account exempted from recompense. They too must reap

* The references to "birds of prey," "beasts of the field," and "spoilers" (ver. 12), are interpreted by the phrase "mine evil neighbours" (ver. 14); and this constitutes a link between vv. 7-14 and 14-17.

† Such seems to be the best punctuation of the sentence. It involves the transfer of *Athnach* to אכלה.

* So the LXX. This agrees better with the context than "So be ye ashamed of *your* fruits."

† As Hitzig has observed, only a people, or a king, or a national god, could be spoken of as a "neighbour" to the God of Israel.

what they have sown. They have insulted Iahvah, by violating His territory; they have indulged their malice and treachery and rapacity, in utter disregard of the rights of neighbours, and the moral claims of kindred peoples. As they have done, so shall it be done unto them: Δράσαντι παθεῖν. They have laid hands on the possessions of their neighbour, and their own shall be taken from them; "I am about to uproot them from off their own land" (*cf.* Amos i. 3-ii. 3). And not only so, but "the house of Judah will I pluck up from their midst." The Lord's people shall be no more exposed to their unneighbourly ill-will; the butt of their ridicule, the victim of their malice will be removed to a foreign soil as well as they; but oppressed and oppressors will no longer be together; their new settlements will lie far apart; under the altered state of things, under the shadow of the great conqueror of the future, there will be no opportunity for the old injurious dealings. All alike, Judah and the enemies of Judah, will be subject to the will of the foreign lord. But that is not the end. The Judge of all the earth is merciful as well as just. He is loath to blot whole peoples out of existence, even though they have merited destruction by grievous and prolonged transgression of His laws. Therefore banishment will be followed by restoration, not in the case of Judah only, but of all the expatriated peoples. After enduring the Divine probation of adversity, they will be brought again, by the Divine compassion, "each to their own heritage and their own land." And then, if they will profit by the teaching of Iahvah's prophets, and "learn the ways," that is, the religion of His people, making their supreme appeal to Iahvah, as the fountain of all truth and the sovran vindicator of right and justice, as hitherto they have appealed to the Baal, and misled Israel into the same profane and futile course; then "they shall be built up," or rebuilt, or brought to great and evergrowing prosperity, "in the midst of My people." Such is to be the blessing of the Gentiles; they shall share in the glorious future that awaits repentant Israel. The present condition of things is to be completely reversed: now Judah sojourns in *their* midst; then *they* will be surrounded on every side by the emancipated and triumphant people of God; now *they* beset Judah with jealousies, suspicions, enmities; then Judah will embrace them all with the arms of an unselfish and protecting love. A last word of warning is added. The doom of the nation that will not accept the Divine teaching will be utter and absolute extermination.

The forecast is plainly of a Messianic nature; it recognises in Iahvah the Saviour, not of a nation, but of the world. It perceives that the disunion and mutual hatred of peoples, as of individuals, is a breach of Divine law; and it proclaims a general return to God, and submission to His guidance in all political as well as private affairs, as the sole cure for the numberless evils that flow from that hatred and disunion. It is only when men have learnt that God is their common Father and Lord that they come to see with the clearness and force of practical conviction that they themselves are all members of one family, bound as such to mutual offices of kindness and charity; it is only when there is a conscious identity of interest with all our fellows, based upon the recognition that all alike are children of God and heirs of eternal life, that true freedom and universal brotherhood become possible for man.

CHAPTER VIII.

THE FALL OF PRIDE.

JEREMIAH xiii.

THIS discourse is a sort of appendix to the preceding; as is indicated by its abrupt and brief beginning with the words "Thus said Iahvah unto me," without the addition of any mark of time, or other determining circumstance. It predicts captivity, in retribution for the pride and ingratitude of the people; and thus suitably follows the closing section of the last address, which announces the coming deportation of Judah and her evil neighbours. The recurrence here (ver. 9) of the peculiar term rendered "swelling" or "pride" in our English versions (chap. xii. 5), points to the same conclusion. We may subdivide it thus: It presents us with (i) a symbolical action, or acted parable, with its moral and application (vv. 1-11); (ii) a parabolic saying and its interpretation, which leads up to a pathetic appeal for penitence (vv. 12-17); (iii) a message to the sovereigns (vv. 18, 19); and (iv) a closing apostrophe to Jerusalem—the gay and guilty capital, so soon to be made desolate for her abounding sins (vv. 20-27).

In the first of these four sections, we are told how the prophet was bidden of God to buy a linen girdle, and after wearing it for a time, to bury it in a cleft of the rock at a place whose very name might be taken to symbolise the doom awaiting his people. A long while afterwards he was ordered to go and dig it up again, and found it altogether spoiled and useless. The significance of these proceedings is clearly enough explained. The relation between Israel and the God of Israel had been of the closest kind. Iahvah had chosen this people, and bound it to Himself by a covenant, as a man might bind a girdle about his body; and as the girdle is an ornament of dress, so had the Lord intended Israel to display His glory among men (ver. 11). But now the girdle is rotten; and like that rotten girdle will He cause the pride of Judah to rot and perish (vv. 9, 10).

It is natural to ask whether Jeremiah really did as he relates; or whether the narrative about the girdle be simply a literary device intended to carry a lesson home to the dullest apprehension. If the prophet's activity had been confined to the pen; if he had not been wont to labour by word and deed for the attainment of his purposes; the latter alternative might be accepted. For mere readers, a parabolic narrative might suffice to enforce his meaning. But Jeremiah, who was all his life a man of action, probably did the thing he professes to have done, not in thought nor in word only, but in deed and to the knowledge of certain competent witnesses. There was nothing novel in this method of attracting attention, and giving greater force and impressiveness to his prediction. The older prophets had often done the same kind of things, on the principle that deeds may be more effective than words. What could have conveyed a more vivid sense of the Divine intention, than the simple act of Ahijah the Shilonite, when he suddenly caught away the new mantle of Solomon's officer, and rent it into twelve pieces, and said to the astonished courtier, "Take thee ten pieces! for thus saith Iahvah, the God of Israel, Behold I am about to rend the kingdom out of the hand of Solomon, and will give the ten tribes to thee"? (1 Kings xi. 29 *sqq.*). In like manner when Ahab and Jehoshaphat, dressed in their robes of state, sat enthroned in the gateway of Samaria, and "all the prophets were prophesying before them" about the issue of their joint expedition to Ramoth-gilead, Zedekiah, the son of a Canaanitess—as the writer is careful to add of this false prophet—"made him horns of iron, and said, Thus said Iahvah, With these shalt thou butt the Arameans, until thou make an end of them" (1 Kings xxii. 11). Isaiah, Hosea, and Ezekiel, record similar actions of symbolical import. Isaiah for a time walked half-clad and bare-foot, as a sign that the Egyptians and Ethiopians, upon whom Judah was inclined to lean, would be led away captive, in this comfortless guise, by the king of Assyria (Isa. xx.). Such actions may be regarded as a further development of those significant gestures, with which men in what is called a state of nature are wont to give emphasis and precision to their spoken ideas. They may also be compared with the symbolism of ancient law. "An ancient conveyance," we are told, "was not written but acted. Gestures and words took the place of written technical phraseology, and any formula mispronounced, or symbolical act omitted, would have vitiated the proceeding as fatally as a material mistake in stating the uses or setting out the remainders would, two hundred years ago, have vitiated an English deed" (Maine, "Ancient Law," p. 276.) Actions of a purely symbolical nature surprise us, when we first encounter them in Religion or Law, but that is only because they are survivals. In the ages when they originated, they were familiar occurrences in all transactions between man and man. And this general consideration tends to prove that those expositors are wrong who maintain that the prophets did not really perform the symbolical actions of which they speak. Just as it is argued that the visions which they describe are merely a literary device; so the reality of these symbolical actions has needlessly enough been called in question. The learned Jews Abenezra and Maimonides in the twelfth century, and David Kimchi in the thirteenth, were the first to affirm this opinion. Maimonides held that all such actions passed in vision before the prophets; a view which has found a modern advocate in Hengstenberg: and Stäudlin, in the last century, affirmed that they had neither an objective nor a subjective reality, but were simply a "literary device." This, however, is only true, if true at all, of the declining period of prophecy, as in the case of the visions. In the earlier period, while the prophets were still accustomed to an oral delivery of their discourses, we may be quite sure that they suited the action to the word in the way that they have themselves recorded; in order to stir the popular imagination, and to create a more vivid and lasting impression. The narratives of the historical books leave no doubt about the matter. But in later times, when spoken addresses had for the most part become a thing of the past, and when prophets published their convictions in manuscript, it is possible that they were content with the description of symbolical doings, as a sort of parable, without any actual performance of them. Jeremiah's hiding his girdle in a cleft of the rock at "Euphrates" has been regarded by some writers as an instance of such purely ideal symbolism. And certainly it is difficult to suppose that the prophet made the long and arduous journey from Jerusalem to the Great River for such a purpose. It is, however, a highly probable conjecture that the place whither he was directed to repair was much nearer home; the addition of a single letter to the name rendered "Euphrates" gives the far preferable reading "Ephrath," that is to say, Bethlehem in Judah (Gen. xlviii. 7). Jeremiah may very well have buried his girdle at Bethlehem, a place only five miles or so to the south of Jerusalem; a place, moreover, where he would have no trouble in finding a "cleft of the rock," which would hardly be the case upon the alluvial banks of the Euphrates. If not accidental, the difference may be due to the intentional employment of an unusual form of the name, by way of hinting at the source whence the ruin of Judah was to flow. The enemy "from the north" (ver. 20) is of course the Chaldeans.

The mention of the queen-mother (ver. 18) along with the king appears to point unmistakably to the reign of Jehoiachin or Jechoniah. The allusion is compared with the threat of ch. xxii. 26: "I will cast thee out, and thy mother that bare thee into another country." Like Josiah, this king was but eight years old when he began to reign (2 Chron. xxxvi. 9, after which 2 Kings xxiv. 8 must be corrected); and he had enjoyed the name of king only for the brief period of three months, when the thunderbolt fell, and Nebuchadrezzar began his first siege of Jerusalem. The boy-king can hardly have had much to do with the issue of affairs, when "he and his mother and his servants and his princes and his eunuchs" surrendered the city, and were deported to Babylon, with ten thousand of the principal inhabitants (2 Kings xxiv. 12 *sqq.*). The date of our discourse will thus be the beginning of the year B. C. 599, which was the eighth year of Nebuchadrezzar (2 Kings xxiv. 12).

It is asserted, indeed, that the difficult verse 21 refers to the revolt from Babylon as an accomplished fact; but this is by no means clear from the verse itself. "What wilt thou say (demands the prophet) when He shall appoint over thee—albeit, thou thyself hast instructed them against thyself;—lovers to be thy head?" The term "lovers" or "lemans" applies best to the foreign idols, who will one day repay the foolish attachment of Iahvah's people by enslaving it (*cf.* ch. iii. 4, where Iahvah Himself is called the "lover" of Judah's youthful days); and this question might as well have been asked in the days of Josiah, as at any later period. At various times in the past Israel and Judah had courted the favour of foreign deities. Ahaz had introduced Aramean and Assyrian novelties; Manasseh and Amon had revived and aggravated his apostasy. Even Hezekiah had had friendly dealings with Babylon, and we must remember that in those times friendly intercourse with a foreign people implied some recognition of their gods, which is probably the true account of Solomon's chapels for Tyrian and other deities.

The queen of ver. 18 might conceivably be Jedidah, the mother of Josiah, for that king was only eight at his accession, and only thirty-nine at his death (2 Kings xxii. 1). And the message to the sovereigns (ver. 18) is not couched in terms of disrespect nor of reproach: it simply declares the imminence of overwhelming disaster, and bids them lay aside their royal pomp, and behave as mourners for the coming woe. Such words might perhaps have been addressed to Josiah and his mother, by way of deepening the impression produced by the Book of the Law, and the rumoured invasion of the Scythians. But the threat against "the kings that sit on David's throne" (ver. 13) is hardly suitable on this supposition; and the ruthless tone of this part of the address—"I will dash them in pieces, one against another, both the fathers and the sons together: I will not pity, nor spare, nor relent from destroying them"—considered along with the emphatic prediction of an utter and entire captivity (ver. 19), seems to indicate a later period of the prophet's ministry, when the obduracy of the people had revealed more fully the hopelessness of his enterprise for their salvation. The mention of the enemy "from the north" will then be a reference to present circumstances of peril, as triumphantly vindicating the prophet's former menaces of destruction from that quarter. The carnage of conquest and the certainty of exile are here threatened in the plainest and most direct style; but nothing is said by way of heightening the popular terror of the coming destroyer. The prophet seems to take it for granted that the **nature** of the evil which hangs over their heads is well known to the people, and does not need to be dwelt upon or amplified with the lyric fervour of former utterances (see ch. iv., v. 15 *sqq.*, vi. 22 *sqq.*). This appears quite natural, if we suppose that the first invasion of the Chaldeans was now a thing of the past; and that the nation was awaiting in trembling uncertainty the consequences of Jehoiakim's breach of faith with his Babylonian suzerain (2 Kings xxiv. 10). The prophecy may therefore be assigned with some confidence to the short reign of Jehoiachin, to which perhaps the short section, ch. x. 17-25, also belongs; a date which harmonises better than any other with the play on the name Euphrates in the opening of the chapter. It agrees, too, with the emphatic "Iahvah hath spoken!" (ver. 15), which seems to be more than a mere assertion of the speaker's veracity, and to point rather to the fact that the course of events had reached a crisis; that something had occurred in the political world which suggested imminent danger; that a black cloud was looming up on the national horizon, and signalling most unmistakably to the prophet's eye the intention of Iahvah. What other view so well explains the solemn tone of warning, the vivid apprehension of danger, the beseeching tenderness, that give so peculiar a stamp to the three verses in which the address passes from narrative and parable to direct appeal? "Hear ye and give ear: be not proud: for Iahvah hath spoken! Give glory to Iahvah your God"—the glory of confession, of avowing your own guilt and His perfect righteousness (Josh. vii. 19; St. John ix. 24); of recognising the due reward of your deeds in the destruction that threatens you; the glory involved in the cry, "God be merciful to me a sinner!"—Give glory to Iahvah your God, before the darkness fall, and before your feet stumble upon the twilight mountains; and ye wait for dawn, and He make it deepest gloom, He turn it to utter darkness." The day was declining; the evening shadows were descending and deepening; soon the hapless people would be wandering bewildered in the twilight, and lost in the darkness, unless, ere it had become too late, they would yield their pride, and throw themselves upon the pity of Him who "maketh the seven stars and Orion, and turneth the deepest gloom into morning" (Amos v. 8).

The verbal allusiveness of the opening section does not, according to Oriental taste, diminish the solemnity of the speaker; on the contrary, it tends to deepen the impression produced by his words. And perhaps there is a psychological reason for the fact, beyond the peculiar partiality of Oriental peoples for such displays of ingenuity. It is, at all events, remarkable that the greatest of all masters of human feeling has not hesitated to make a dying prince express his bitter and desponding thoughts in what may seem an artificial toying and trifling with the suggestiveness of his own familiar name: and when the king asks: "Can sick men play so nicely with their names?" the answer is: "No, misery makes sport to mock itself" (Rich. II., Act. 2, Sc. i. 72 *sqq.*). The Greek tragedian, too, in the earnestness of bitter sport, can find a prophecy in a name. "*Who* was for naming her thus, with truth so entire? (Was it One whom we see not, wielding tongue happily with full foresight of what was to be?) the Bride of Battles, fiercely contested *Helen:* seeing that, in full accord with her name, *haler* of ships, *haler* of men, *haler* of cities, forth of the soft and precious tapestries away she sailed, under the gale of the giant West" (Æsch., "Ag.," 68, *sqq.*). And so, to Jeremiah's ear, Ephrath is prophetic of Euphrates, upon whose distant banks the glory of his people is to languish and decay. "I to Ephrath, and you to Phrath!" is his melancholy cry. Their doom is as certain as if it were the mere fulfilment of an old-world prophecy, crystallised long ages ago in a familiar name; a word of destiny fixed in this strange form, and bearing its solemn witness from the outset of their history until now concerning the inevitable goal.

There is nothing so very surprising, as Ewald seems to have thought, in the suggestion that the *Perath* of the Hebrew text may be the same as Ephrath. But perhaps the valley and spring now called *Furāh* (or *Furāt*) which lies at about the same distance N. E. of Jerusalem, is the place intended by the prophet. The name, which means *fresh* or *sweet water*, is identical with the Arabic name of the Euphrates, which again is philologically identical with the Hebrew Perath. It is obvious that this place would suit the requirements of the text quite as well as the other, while the coincidence of name enables us to dispense with the supposition of an unusual form or even a corruption of the original; but *Furāt* or *Forāh* is not mentioned elsewhere in the Old Testament. The old versions send the prophet to the river Euphrates, which Jeremiah calls simply "The River" in one place (ii. 18), and "*The river* of Perath" in three others (xlvi. 2, 6, 10); while the rare "Perath," without any addition, is only found in the second account of the Creation (Gen. ii. 14), in 2 Chron. xxxv. 20, and in a passage of this book which does not belong, nor profess to belong, to Jeremiah (li. 63). We may, therefore, conclude that "Perath" in the present passage means not the great river of that name, but a place near Jerusalem, although that place was probably chosen with the intention, as above explained, of alluding to the Euphrates.

I cannot assent to the opinion which regards this narrative of the spoiled girdle as founded upon some accidental experience of the prophet's life, in which he afterwards recognised a Divine lesson. The precision of statement, and the nice adaptation of the details of the story to the moral which the prophet wished to convey, rather indicate a symbolical course of action, or what may be called an acted parable. The whole proceeding appears to have been carefully thought out beforehand. The intimate connection between Iahvah and Israel is well symbolised by a girdle—that part of an Easter dress which "cleaves to the loins of a man," that is, fits closest to the body, and is most securely attached thereto. And if the nations be represented by the rest of the apparel, as the girdle secures and keeps that in its place, we may see an implication that Israel was intended to be the chain that bound mankind to God. The girdle was of *linen*, the material of the priestly dress, not only because Jeremiah was a priest, but because Israel was called to be "a kingdom of priests," or the Priest among nations (Ex. xix. 6). The significance of the command to wear the girdle, but not to put it into water, seems to be clear enough. The unwashed garment which the prophet continues to wear for a time represents the foulness of Israel; just as the order to bury it at Perath indicates what Iahvah is about to do with His polluted people.

1. The exposition begins with the words, "Thus will I mar the great pride of Judah and of Jerusalem!" The spiritual uncleanness of the nation consisted in the proud selfwill which turned a deaf ear to the warnings of Iahvah's prophets, and obstinately persisted in idolatry (ver. 10). It continues: "For as the girdle cleaveth to the loins of a man, so made I the whole house of Israel and the whole house of Judah to cleave unto Me, saith Iahvah; that they might become to Me for a people, and for a name, and for a praise, and for an ornament" (Ex. xxviii. 2). Then their becoming morally unclean, through the defilements of sin, is briefly implied in the words, "And they obeyed not" (ver. 11).

It is not the pride of the tyrant king Jehoiakim that is here threatened with destruction. It is the *national* pride which had all along evinced itself in rebellion against its heavenly King—"the great pride of Judah and Jerusalem;" and this pride, inasmuch as it "trusted in man and made flesh its arm" (xvii. 5), and boasted in a carnal wisdom, and material strength and riches (ix. 23, xxi. 13), was to be brought low by the complete extinction of the national autonomy, and the reduction of a high-spirited and haughty race to the status of humble dependents upon a heathen power.

2. A parabolic saying follows, with its interpretation. "And say thou unto them this word: Thus saith Iahvah, the God of Israel: Every jar is wont to be filled (or shall be filled) with wine. And if they say unto thee, Are we really not aware that every jar is wont to be filled with wine? say thou unto them, Thus saith Iahvah, Lo, I am about to fill all the inhabitants of this land, and the kings that sit for David upon his throne, and the priests and the prophets, and all the inhabitants of Jerusalem, with drunkenness; and I will dash them in pieces against one another, and the fathers and the sons together, saith Iahvah: I will not forbear nor spare nor pity, so as not to mar them" (*cf.* vv. 7, 9).

The individual members of the nation, of all ranks and classes, are compared to earthenware jars, not "skins," as the LXX. gives it, for they are to be "dashed in pieces," "like a potter's vessel" (Ps. ii. 9; *cf.* ver. 14).* Regarding them all as ripe for destruction, Jeremiah exclaims, "Every jar is filled with wine," in the ordinary course of things; that is its destiny. His hearers answer with the mocking question, "Do you suppose that we don't know that?" They would, of course, be aware that a prophet's figure, however homely, covered an inner meaning of serious import; but derision was their favourite retort against unpopular truths (xvii. 15, xx. 7, 8). They would take it for granted that the thing suggested was unfavourable, from their past experience of Jeremiah. Their ill-timed banter is met by the instant application of the figure. They, and *the kings* then sitting on David's throne, *i. e.*, the young Jehoiachin and the queen-mother Nehushta (who probably had all the authority if not the title of a regent), and the priests and prophets who fatally misled them by false teachings and false counsels, are the wine-jars intended, and the wine that is to fill them is the wine of the wrath of God (Ps. lxxv. 8; Jer. xxv. 15; *cf.* li. 7; Rev. xvi. 19; Isa. xix. 14, 15). The effect is intoxication—a fatal bewilderment, a helpless lack of decision, an utter confusion and stupefaction of the faculties of wisdom and foresight, in the very moment of supreme peril (*cf.* Isa. xxviii. 7; Ps. lx. 5). Like drunkards, they will reel against and overthrow each other. The strong term, "I will dash them in pieces," is used to indicate the deadly nature of their fall, and because the prophet has still in his mind the figure of the wine-jars, which were probably amphoræ, pointed at the end, like those depicted in Egyptian mural paintings so that they could not stand upright without support. By their fall they are to be utterly "marred" (the term used of the girdle, ver. 9).

But even yet one way of escape lies open. It is to sacrifice their pride, and yield to the will of Iahvah. "Hear ye and give ear, be not haughty! for Iahvah hath spoken: give ye to Iahvah your God the glory, before it grow dark (or He cause darkness), and before your feet stumble upon mountains of twilight; and ye wait for the dawn, and He make it gloom, turning it to cloudiness!" (Isa. v. 30, viii. 20, 22; Amos viii. 9). It is very remarkable that even now, when the Chaldeans are actually in the country, and blockading the strong places of southern Judah (ver. 19), which was the usual preliminary to an advance upon Jerusalem itself (2 Chron. xii. 4, xxxii. 9; Isa. xxxvi. 1, 2), Jeremiah should still speak thus; assuring his fellow-citizens that confession and self-humiliation before their offended God might yet deliver them from the bitterest consequences of past misdoing. Iahvah had indeed spoken audibly enough, as it seemed to the prophet, in the calamities that had already befallen the country; these were an indication of more and worse to follow, unless they should prove efficacious in leading the people to repentance. If they failed, nothing would be left for the prophet but to mourn in solitude over his country's ruin (ver. 17). But Jeremiah was

* Also xlviii. 12; Lam. iv. 2; Isa. xxx. 14.

fully persuaded that the Hand that had stricken could heal; the Power that had brought the invaders into Judah, could cause them to "return by the way that they had come" (Isa. xxxvii. 34). Of course such a view was unintelligible from the standpoint of unbelief; but then the standpoint of the prophets is faith.

3. After this general appeal for penitence, the discourse turns to the two exalted persons whose position and interest in the country were the highest of all: the youthful king, and the empress or queen-mother. They are addressed in a tone which, though not disrespectful, is certainly despairing. They are called upon, not so much to set the example of penitence (*cf.* Jonah iii. 6), as to take up the attitude of mourners (Job ii. 13; Isa. iii. 26; Lam. ii. 10; Ezek. xxvi. 16) in presence of the public disasters. "Say thou to the king and to the empress, Sit ye low on the ground! (lit. make low your seat; *cf.* Isa. vii. for the construction) for it is fallen from your heads *—your beautiful crown! (Lam. v. 16). The cities of the south are shut fast, and there is none that openeth (Josh. vi. 1): Judah is carried away captive all of her, she is wholly carried away." There is no hope; it is in vain to expect help; nothing is left but to bemoan the irreparable. The siege of the great fortresses of the south country and the sweeping away of the rural population were sure signs of what was coming upon Jerusalem. The embattled cities themselves may be suggested by the fallen crown of beauty; Isaiah calls Samaria "the proud crown of the drunkards of Ephraim" (Isa. xxviii. 1), and cities are commonly represented in ancient art by female figures wearing mural crowns. In that case, both verses are addressed to the sovereigns, and the second is exegetical of the first.

As already observed, there is here no censure, but only sorrowful despair over the dark outlook. In the same way, Jeremiah's utterance (xxii. 20 *sqq.*) about the fate of Jehoiachin is less a malediction than a lament. And when we further consider his favourable judgment of the first body of exiles, who were carried away with this monarch soon after the time of the present oracle (chap. xxiv.), we may perhaps see reason to conclude that the surrender of Jerusalem to the Chaldeans on this occasion was partly due to his advice. The narrative of Kings, however, is too brief to enable us to come to any certain decision about the circumstances of Jehoiachin's submission (2 Kings xxiv. 10-12).

4. From the sovereigns the prophet turns to Jerusalem. "Lift up thine eyes (O Jerusalem †), and behold them that came from the north! Where is the flock that was given to thee, thy beautiful sheep? What wilt thou say when He shall appoint over thee—nay, thou thyself hast spurred them against thyself!—lovers (iii. 4, xi. 19) for head? Will not pangs take thee, as a woman in travail?" Jerusalem sits upon her hills, as a beautiful shepherdess. The country towns and unwalled villages lay about her, like a fair flock of sheep and goats entrusted to her care and keeping. But now these have been destroyed and their pastures are made a silent solitude, and the destroyer is advancing against herself. What pangs of shame and terror will be hers, when she recognises in the enemy triumphing over her grievous downfall the heathen "friends" whose love she had courted so long! Her sin is to be her scourge. She shall be made the thrall of her foreign lovers. Iahvah will "appoint them over her" (xv. 3, li. 27); they will become the "head," and she the "tail" (Lam. i. 5; Deut. xxviii. 44). Yet this will, in truth, be her own doing, not Iahvah's; she has herself "accustomed them to herself" (x. 2), or "instructed" or "spurred them on" against herself (ii. 33, iv. 18). The revolt of Jehoiakim, his wicked breach of faith with Nebuchadrezzar, had turned friends to enemies (iv. 30). But the chief reference seems to be more general—the continual craving of Judah for foreign alliances and foreign worships. "And if thou say in thine heart, 'Wherefore did these things befall me?' through the greatness of thy guilt were thy skirts uncovered, thine heels violated (Nah. iii. 5) or exposed. Will a Cushite change his skin, or a leopard his spots? ye, too, are ye able to do good, O ye that are wont to do evil? If, amid the sharp throes of suffering, Jerusalem should still fail to recognise the moral cause of them (v. 19), she may be assured beforehand that her unspeakable dishonour is the reward of her sins; *that* is why "the virgin daughter of Sion" is surprised and ravished by the foe (a common figure: Isa. xlvii. 1-3). Sin has become so ingrained in her that it can no more be eradicated than the blackness of an African skin, or the spots of a leopard's hide. The habit of sinning has become "a second nature," and, like nature, is not to be expelled (*cf.* viii. 4-7).

The effect of use and wont in the moral sphere could hardly be expressed more forcibly, and Jeremiah's comparison has become a proverb. Custom binds us all in every department of life; it is only by enlisting this strange influence upon the side of virtue, that we become virtuous. Neither virtue nor vice can be pronounced perfect, until the habit of either has become fixed and invariable. It is the tendency of habitual action of any kind to become automatic, and it is certain that sin may attain such a mastery over the active powers of a man that its indulgence may become almost an unconscious exercise of his will, and quite a matter of course. But this fearful result of evil habits does not excuse them at the bar of common sense, much less at the tribunal of God. The inveterate sinner, the man totally devoid of scruple, whose conscience is, as it were, "seared with a hot iron," is not on that account excused by the common judgment of his kind; the feeling he excites is not forbearance, but abhorrence; he is regarded not as a poor victim of circumstances over which he has no control, but as a monster of iniquity. And justly so; for if he has lost control of his passions, if he is no longer master of himself, but the slave of vice, he is responsible for the long course of self-indulgence which has made him what he is. The prophet's comparison cannot be applied in sup-

*LXX. ἀπὸ κεφαλῆς ὑμῶν. Read מְרַאֲשֹׁתֵיכֶם=מְרַאֲשֵׁיכֶם; and *cf.* Assyrian *resu*, plur. *resêtu* (= ראשות).

† For עיניכם we might read, with LXX., Vat., (ירושל(ם עיניך. The Arabic has Israel. But Vulg. and Targ, agree with the Q'rê, and take the verbs as plur.: "Lift ye up your eyes and see who are coming from the north." The sing. fem. is to be preferred as the more difficult reading, and on account of ver. 21, where it recurs. Jerusalem is addressed (ver. 27), and "*your* eyes," plur. masc. pron., may be justified as indicating the *collective* sense of the fem. sing. The population of the capital is meant. *Cf.* Mic. i. 11; Jer. xxi. 13, 14. In ver. 23, the masc. plur. appears again, the figure for a moment being dropped.

port of a doctrine of immoral fatalism. The very fact that he makes use of it, implies that he did not intend to be understood in such a sense. "Will a Cushite change his skin, or a leopard his spots? Ye also (supposing such a change as that) will be able to do good, O ye that are taught (trained, accustomed) to do evil!" (perhaps the preferable rendering).

Not only must we abstain from treating a rhetorical figure as a colourless and rigorous proposition of mathematical science; not only must we allow for the irony and the exaggeration of the preacher: we must also remember his object, which is, if possible, to shock his hearers into a sense of their condition, and to awaken remorse and repentance even at the eleventh hour. His last words (ver. 27) prove that he did not believe this result, improbable as it was, to be altogether impossible. Unless some sense of sin had survived in their hearts, unless the terms "good" and "evil," had still retained a meaning for his countrymen, Jeremiah would hardly have laboured still so strenuously to convince them of their sins.

For the present, when retribution is already at the doors, when already the Divine wrath has visibly broken forth, his prevailing purpose is not so much to suggest a way of escape as to bring home to the heart and conscience of the nation the true meaning of the public calamities. They are the consequence of habitual rebellion against God. "And I will scatter them like stubble passing away to (=before: *cf.* xix. 10) the wind of the wilderness. This is thy lot (fem. thine, O Jerusalem), the portion of thy measures (others: lap) from Me, saith Iahvah; because thou forgattest Me, and didst trust in the Lie. And I also—I will surely strip thy skirts to thy face, and thy shame shall be seen! (Nah. iii. 5). Thine adulteries and thy neighings, the foulness of thy fornications upon the hills in the field (iii. 2-6)—I have seen thine abominations. (For the construction, compare Isa. i. 13.) Woe unto thee, O Jerusalem! After how long yet wilt thou not become clean?" (2 Kings v. 12, 13). That which lies before the citizens in the near future is not deliverance, but dispersion in foreign lands. The onset of the foe will sweep them away, as the blast from the desert drives before it the dry stubble of the corn-fields (*cf.* iv. 11, 12). This is no chance calamity, but a recompense allotted and meted out by Iahvah to the city that forgot Him and "trusted in the Lie" of Baal-worship and the associated superstitions. The city that dealt shamefully in departing from her God, and dallying with foul idols, shall be put to shame by Him before all the world (ver. 26 recurring to the thought of ver. 22, but ascribing the exposure directly to Iahvah). Woe—certain woe—awaits Jerusalem; and it is but a faint and far-off glimmer of hope that is reflected in the final question, which is like a weary sigh: "After how long yet wilt thou not become clean?" How long must the fiery process of cleansing go on, ere thou be purged of thine inveterate sins? It is a recognition that the punishment will not be exterminative; that God's chastisements of His people can no more fail at last than His promises; that the triumph of a heathen power and the disappearance of Iahvah's Israel from under His heaven cannot be the final phase of that long eventful history which begins with the call of Abraham.

CHAPTER IX.

THE DROUGHT AND ITS MORAL IMPLICATIONS.

JEREMIAH xiv., xv. (xvii.?).

VARIOUS opinions have been expressed about the division of these chapters. They have been cut up into short sections, supposed to be more or less independent of each other; * and they have been regarded as constituting a well-organised whole, at least so far as the eighteenth verse of chap. xvii. The truth may lie between these extremes. Chapters xiv., xv. certainly hang together; for in them the prophet represents himself as twice interceding with Iahvah on behalf of the people, and twice receiving a refusal of his petition (xiv. 1-xv. 4), the latter reply being sterner and more decisive than the first. The occasion was a long period of drought, involving much privation for man and beast. The connection between the parts of this first portion of the discourse is clear enough. The prophet prays for his people, and God answers that He has rejected them, and that intercession is futile. Thereupon, Jeremiah throws the blame of the national sins upon the false prophets; and the answer is that both the people and their false guides will perish. The prophet then soliloquises upon his own hard fate as a herald of evil tidings, and receives directions for his own personal guidance in this crisis of affairs (xv. 10-xvi. 9). There is a pause, but no real break, at the end of chap. xv. The next chapter resumes the subject of directions personally affecting the prophet himself; and the discourse is then continuous so far as xvii. 18, although, naturally enough, it is broken here and there by pauses of considerable duration, marking transitions of thought, and progress in the argument.

The heading of the entire piece is marked in the original by a peculiar inversion of terms, which meets us again, chap. xlvi. 1, xlvii. 1,

* HITZIG: (1) xiv. 1-9, 19-22: "Lament and Prayer on occasion of a Drought." (2) xiv. 10-18. "Oracle against the false Prophets and the misguided People." (Hitzig mistakes the import of the phrase כן אהבו לנוע, "*Thus* have they loved to wander," ver. 10: supposing that the "thus" refers to xiii. 27, and that xiv. 1-9 is misplaced). (3) xv. 1-9. "The incorrrigible People will be punished mercilessly." Hitzig thinks C. B. Michaelis wrong in asserting close connection with the end of the preceding chapter, because the intercession, vv. 2-9, does not agree with the prohibition, xiv. 11; and because xiv. 19-22, merely prays for cessation of the Drought; while the rejection of "the hypothetical intercession," xv. 1 delivers the people over to all the horrors which follow in the train of war. xv. 1-9 may originally have followed xiv. 18. But this is far from cogent reasoning. There is nothing surprising in the renewal of the prophet's intercession, except on a theory of strictly verbal inspiration; and xv. 1 *sqq.* in refusing deliverance from the Drought, or rather in answer to the prayer imploring it, announces further and worse evils to follow. (4) "Complaint of the Seer against Iahvah, and Soothing of his Dejection," xv, 10-21. Hitzig thinks internal evidence here points to the fourth year of Jehoiakim; and that xvii. 1-4 originally preceded this section, especially as ch. xvi. connects closely with xv. 9. (5) xvi. 1-20. "Prediction of an imminent general judgment by Plague and Captivity." Written immediately after xv. 1-9, and falls with that in the short reign of Jehoiachin. (6) xvii. 1-4. "Judah's unforgotten Guilt will be punished by Captivity." Wanting in LXX. (as early as Jerome), but contains original of xv. 13, 14, and must therefore be genuine. Belongs 602 B. C., year of Jehoiakim's revolt. (7) xvii. 5-18. "The Vindication of Trust in God on Despisers and Believers. Prayers for its Vindication." Date immediately after death of Jehoiakim. (8) 19-27. "Warning to keep the Sabbath." Time of Jehoiachin.

xlix. 34, but which, in spite of this recurrence, wears a rather suspicious look. We might render it thus: "What fell as a word of Iahvah to Jeremiah, on account of the droughts" (the plural is intensive, or it signifies the long continuance of the trouble—as if one rainless period followed upon another). Whether or not the singular order of the words be authentic, the recurrence at chap. xvii. 8 of the remarkable term for "drought" (Heb. *baccoreth* of which *baccaróth* here is plur.) favours the view that that chapter is an integral portion of the present discourse. The exordium (xiv. 1-9) is a poetical sketch of the miseries of man and beast, closing with a beautiful prayer. It has been said that this is not "a word of Iahvah to Jeremiah," but rather the reverse. If we stick to the letter, this no doubt is the case; but, as we have seen in former discourses, the phrase "Iahvah's word" meant in prophetic use very much more than a direct message from God, or a prediction uttered at the Divine instigation. Here, as elsewhere, the prophet evidently regards the course of his own religious reflection as guided by Him who "fashioneth the hearts of men," and "knoweth their thoughts long before;" and if the question had suggested itself, he would certainly have referred his own poetic powers—the tenderness of his pity, the vividness of his apprehension, the force of his passion,—to the inspiration of the Lord who had called and consecrated him from the birth, to speak in His Name.

There lies at the heart of many of us a feeling, which has lurked there, more or less without our cognisance, ever since the childish days when the Old Testament was read at the mother's knee, and explained and understood in a manner proportioned to the faculties of childhood. When we hear the phrase "The Lord spake," we instinctively think, if we think at all, of an actual voice knocking sensibly at the door of the outward ear. It was not so; nor did the sacred writer mean it so. A knowledge of Hebrew idiom—the modes of expression usual and possible in that ancient speech—assures us that this statement, so startlingly direct in its unadorned simplicity, was the accepted mode of conveying a meaning which we, in our more complex and artificial idioms, would convey by the use of a multitude of words, in terms far more abstract, in language destitute of all that colour of life and reality which stamps the idiom of the Bible. It is as though the Divine lay farther off from us moderns; as though the marvellous progress of all that new knowledge of the measureless magnitude of the world, of the power and complexity of its machinery, of the surpassing subtlety and the matchless perfection of its laws and processes, had become an impassable barrier, at least an impenetrable veil, between our minds and God. We have lost the sense of His nearness, of His immediacy, so to speak; because we have gained, and are ever intensifying, a sense of the nearness of the world with which He environs us. Hence, when we speak of Him, we naturally cast about either for poetical phrases and figures, which must always be more or less vague and undefined, or for highly abstract expressions, which may suggest scientific exactness, but are, in truth, scholastic formulæ, dry as the dust of the desert, untouched by the breath of life; and even if they affirm a Person, destitute of all those living characters by which we instinctively and without effort recognise Personality. We make only a conventional use of the language of the sacred writers, of the prophets and prophetic historians, of the psalmists, and the legalists, of the Old Testament; the language which is the native expression of a peculiar intensity of religious faith, realising the Unseen as the Actual and, in truth, the only Real.

"Judah mourneth and the gates thereof languish,
They are clad in black down to the ground;
And the cry of Jerusalem hath gone up.
And their nobles have sent their lesser folk for water;
They have been to the pits, and found no water:
Their vessels have come back empty;
Ashamed and confounded, they have covered their heads.

"Because the ground is chapt, for there hath not been rain in the land,
The ploughmen are ashamed, they have covered their heads.

"For even the hind in the field hath yeaned and forsaken her fawn,
For there is no grass.
And the wild asses stand on the bare fells;
They snuff the wind like jackals;
Their eyes fail, for there is no pasturage.

"If our sins have answered against us,
Iahweh, act for Thine own Name sake;
For our relapses are many:
Against Thee have we trespassed.

"Hope of Israel, that savest him in time of trouble,
Wherefore wilt Thou be as a stranger in the land,
And as a traveller that leaveth the road but for the night?
Wherefore wilt Thou be as a man o'erpowered with sleep,
As a warrior that cannot rescue?

"Sith Thou art in our midst, O Iahvah,
And Thy Name upon us hath been called;
Cast us not down!"

How beautiful both plaint and prayer! The simple description of the effects of the drought is as lifelike and impressive as a good picture. The whole country is stricken; the city-gates, the place of common resort, where the citizens meet for business and for conversation, are gloomy with knots of mourners robed in black from head to foot, or, as the Hebrew may also imply, sitting on the ground, in the garb and posture of desolation (Lam. ii. 10, iii. 28). The magnates of Jerusalem send out their retainers to find water; and we see them returning with empty vessels, their heads muffled in their cloaks, in sign of grief at the failure of their errand (*cf.* 1 Kings xviii. 5, 6). The parched ground everywhere gapes with fissures;* the yeomen go about with covered heads in deepest dejection. The distress is universal, and affects not man only, but the brute creation. Even the gentle hind, that proverb of maternal tenderness, is driven by sorest need to forsake the fruit of her hard travail; her starved dugs are dry, and she flies from her helpless offspring. The wild asses of the desert, fleet, beautiful, and keen-eyed creatures, scan the withered landscape from the naked cliffs, and snuff the wind, like jackals scenting prey; but neither sight nor smell suggests relief. There is no moisture in the air, no glimpse of pasture in the wide sultry land.

The prayer is a humble confession of sin, an unreserved admission that the woes of man evince the righteousness of God. Unlike cer-

* The Heb. verb חַתָּה "is broken" may probably have this meaning. "Dismayed" is not nearly so suitable, though it is the usual meaning of the term. *Cf.* Isa. vii. 8.

tain modern poets, who bewail the sorrows of the world as the mere infliction of a harsh and arbitrary and inevitable Destiny, Jeremiah makes no doubt that human sufferings are due to the working of Divine justice. "Our sins have answered against our pleas at Thy judgment seat; our relapses are many; against Thee have we trespassed," against Thee, the sovereign Disposer of events, the Source of all that happens and all that is. If this be so, what plea is left? None, but that appeal to the *Name* of Iahvah, with which the prayer begins and ends. "Act for Thine own Name sake." . . . "Thy Name upon us hath been called." Act for Thine own honour, that is, for the honour of Mercy, Compassion, Truth, Goodness; which Thou hast revealed Thyself to be, and which are parts of Thy glorious Name (Ex. xxxiv. 6). Pity the wretched, and pardon the guilty: for so will Thy glory increase amongst men; so will man learn that the relentings of love are diviner affections than the ruthlessness of wrath and the cravings of vengeance.

There is also a touching appeal to the past. The very name by which Israel was sometimes designated as "the people of Iahvah," just as Moab was known by the name of its god as "the people of Chemosh" (Num. xxi. 29), is alleged as proof that the nation has an interest in the compassion of Him whose name it bears; and it is implied that, since the world knows Israel as Iahvah's people, it will not be for Iahvah's honour that this people should be suffered to perish in their sins. Israel had thus, from the outset of its history, been associated and identified with Iahvah; however ill the true nature of the tie has been understood, however unworthily the relation has been conceived by the popular mind, however little the obligations involved in the call of their fathers have been recognised and appreciated. God must be true, though man be false. There is no weakness, no caprice, no vacillation in God. In bygone "times of trouble" the "Hope of Israel" had saved Israel over and over again; it was a truth admitted by all—even by the prophet's enemies. Surely then He will save His people once again, and vindicate His Name of Saviour. Surely He who has dwelt in their midst so many changeful centuries, will not now behold their trouble with the lukewarm feeling of an alien dwelling amongst them for a time, but unconnected with them by ties of blood and kin and common country; or with the indifference of the traveller who is but coldly affected by the calamities of a place where he has only lodged one night. Surely the entire past shows that it would be utterly inconsistent for Iahvah to appear now as a man so buried in sleep that He cannot be roused to save His friends from imminent destruction (*cf.* 1 Kings xviii. 27, St. Mark iv. 38). He who had borne Israel and carried him as a tender nursling all the days of old (Isa. lxiii. 9) could hardly without changing His own unchangeable Name, His character and purposes, cast down His people and forsake them at last.

Such is the drift of the prophet's first prayer. To this apparently unanswerable argument his religious meditation upon the present distress has brought him. But presently the thought returns with added force, with a sense of utmost certitude, with a conviction that it is Iahvah's Word, that the people have wrought out their own affliction, that misery is the hire of sin.

"Thus hath Iahvah said of this people:
Even so have they loved to wander,
Their feet they have not refrained;
And as for Iahvah, He accepteth them not;

"He now remembereth their guilt,
And visiteth their trespasses.
And Iahvah said unto me,
Intercede thou not for this people for good!
If they fast, I will not hearken unto their cry;
And if they offer whole-offering and oblation,
I will not accept their persons;
But by the sword, the famine, and the plague, will I
consume them.

"And I said, Ah, Lord Iahvah!
Behold the prophets say to them, Ye shall not see
sword,
And famine shall not befall you;
For peace and permanence will I give you in this place.

"And Iahvah said unto me:
Falsehood it is that the prophets prophesy in My Name.
I sent them not, and I charged them not, and I spake
not unto them.
A vision of falsehood and jugglery and nothingness,
and the guile of their own heart,
They, for their part, prophesy you.

"Therefore thus said Iahvah:
Concerning the prophets who prophesy in My Name,
albeit I sent them not,
And of themselves say, Sword and famine there shall
not be in this land;
By the sword and by the famine shall those prophets be
fordone.
And the people to whom they prophesy shall lie thrown
out in the streets of Jerusalem,
Because of the famine and the sword,
With none to bury them,—
Themselves, their wives, and their sons and their
daughters:
And I will pour upon them their own evil.
And thou shalt say unto them this word:
Let mine eyes run down with tears, night and day,
And let them not tire;
For with mighty breach is broken
The virgin daughter of my people—
With a very grievous blow.
If I go forth into the field,
Then behold! the slain of the sword;
And if I enter the city,
Then behold! the pinings of famine:
For both prophet and priest go trafficking about the
land,
And understand not." *

It has been supposed that this whole section is misplaced, and that it would properly follow the close of chap. xiii. The supposition is due to a misapprehension of the force of the pregnant particle which introduces the reply of Iahvah to the prophet's intercession. "*Even so* have they loved to wander;" *even so,* as is naturally implied by the severity of the punishment of which thou complainest. The dearth is prolonged; the distress is widespread and grievous. *So* prolonged, *so* grievous, *so* universal, has been their rebellion against Me. The penalty corresponds to the offence. It is really "their own evil" that is being poured out upon their guilty heads (ver. 16; *cf.* iv. 18). Iahvah cannot accept them in their sin; the long drought is a token that their guilt is before His mind, unrepented, unatoned. Neither the supplications of another, nor their own fasts and sacrifices, avail to avert the visitation. So long as the disposition of the heart remains unaltered; so long as man hates, not his darling sins, but the penalties they entail, it is idle to seek to propitiate Heaven by such means as these. And not only so. The droughts are but a foretaste of worse evils to come; "by the sword, the famine, and the plague will I consume them." The condition is understood, If they repent and amend not. This is implied by the prophet's seeking to palliate the national guilt, as he proceeds to do, by the suggestion that the

* *Cf.* viii. 9. "And no wisdom is in them."

people are more sinned against than sinning, deluded as they are by false prophets; as also by the renewal of his intercession (ver. 19). Had he been aware in his inmost heart that an irreversible sentence had gone forth against his people, would he have been likely to think either excuses or intercessions availing? Indeed, however absolute the threats of the prophetic preachers may sound, they must, as a rule, be qualified by this limitation, which, whether expressed or not, is inseparable from the object of their discourses, which was the moral amendment of those who heard them.

Of the "false," that is, the common run of prophets, who were in league with the venal priesthood of the time, and no less worldly and self-seeking than their allies, we note that, as usual, they foretell what the people wishes to hear; "Peace (Prosperity), and Permanence," is the burden of their oracles. They knew that invectives against prevailing vices, and denunciations of national follies, and forecasts of approaching ruin, were unlikely means of winning popularity and a substantial harvest of offerings. At the same time, like other false teachers, they knew how to veil their errors under the mask of truth; or rather, they were themselves deluded by their own greed, and blinded by their covetousness to the plain teaching of events. They might base their doctrine of "Peace and Permanence in this place!" upon those utterances of the great Isaiah, which had been so signally verified in the lifetime of the seer himself; but their keen pursuit of selfish ends, their moral degradation, caused them to shut their eyes to everything else in his teachings, and, like his contemporaries, they "regarded not the work of Iahvah, nor the operation of His hand." Jeremiah accuses them of "lying visions;" visions, as he explains, which were the outcome of magical ceremonies, by aid of which, perhaps, they partially deluded themselves, before deluding others, but which were none the less, "things of naught," devoid of all substance, and mere fictions of a deceitful and self-deceiving mind (ver. 14). He expressly declares that they have no mission; in other words, their action is not due to the overpowering sense of a higher call, but is inspired by purely ulterior considerations of worldly gain and policy. They prophesy to order; to the order of man, not of God. If they visit the country districts, it is with no spiritual end in view; priest and prophet alike make a trade of their sacred profession, and, immersed in their sordid pursuits, have no eye for truth, and no perception of the dangers hovering over their country. Their misconduct and misdirection of affairs are certain to bring destruction upon themselves and upon those whom they mislead. War and its attendant famine will devour them all.

But the day of grace being past, nothing is left for the prophet himself but to bewail the ruin of his people (ver. 17). He will betake himself to weeping, since praying and preaching are vain. The words which announce this resolve may portray a sorrowful experience, or they may depict the future as though it were already present (vv. 17, 18). The latter interpretation would suit ver. 17, but hardly the following verse, with its references to "going forth into the field," and "entering into the city." The way in which these specific actions are mentioned seems to imply some present or recent calamity; and there is apparently no reason why we may not suppose that the passage was written at the disastrous close of the reign of Josiah, in the troublous interval of three months, when Jehoahaz was nominal king in Jerusalem, but the Egyptian arms were probably ravaging the country, and striking terror into the hearts of the people. In such a time of confusion and bloodshed, tillage would be neglected, and famine would naturally follow; and these evils would be greatly aggravated by drought. The only other period which suits is the beginning of the reign of Jehoiakim;* but the former seems rather to be indicated by chap. xv. 6-9.

Heartbroken at the sight of the miseries of his country, the prophet once more approaches the eternal throne. His despairing mood is not so deep and dark as to drown his faith in God. He refuses to believe the utter rejection of Judah, the revocation of the covenant. (The measure is Pentameter).

"Hast Thou indeed cast off Judah?
Hath Thy soul revolted from Sion?
Why hast Thou smitten us, past healing?
Waiting for peace, and no good came,
For a time of healing, and behold terror!

"We know, Iahvah, our wickedness, our fathers' guilt;
For we have trespassed toward Thee.
Scorn Thou not, for Thy Name sake,
Disgrace not Thy glorious throne!
Remember, break not, Thy covenant with us!

"Are there, in sooth, among the Nothings of the nation senders of rain?
And is it the heavens that bestow the showers?
Is it not Thou, Iahvah our God?
And we wait for Thee,
For Thou it was that madest the world."†

To all this the Divine answer is stern and decisive. "And Iahvah said unto me: If Moses and Samuel were to stand" (pleading) "before Me, My mind would not be towards this people: send them away from before Me" (dismiss them from My Presence), "that they may go forth!" After ages remembered Jeremiah as a mighty intercessor, and the brave Maccabeus could see him in his dream as a grey-haired man "exceeding glorious" and "of a wonderful and excellent majesty," who "prayed much for the people and for the holy city" (2 Macc. xv. 14). And the beauty of the prayers which lie like scattered pearls of faith and love among the prophet's soliloquies is evident at a glance. But here Jeremiah himself is conscious that his prayers are unavailing; and that the office to which God has called him is rather that of pronouncing judgment than of interceding for mercy. Even a Moses or a Samuel, the mighty intercessors of the old heroic times, whose pleadings had been irresistible with God, would now plead in vain (Ex. xvii. 11 *sqq.*, xxxii. 11 *sqq.*; Num. xiv. 13 *sqq.* for Moses; 1 Sam. vii. 9 *sqq.*, xii. 16 *sqq.*; Ps. xcix. 6; Ecclus. xlvi. 16 *sqq.* for Samuel). The day of grace has gone, and the day of doom is come. His sad function is to "send them away" or "let them go" from Iahvah's Presence; to pronounce the decree of their banishment from the holy land where His temple is, and where they have been wont to "see His face." The main part of his commission was "to root out, and to pull down, and to destroy, and to

* So Dathe, Naegelsbach.

† Lit. "all these things," *i. e.*, this visible world. There is no Heb. special term for the "universe" or "world." "The all" or "heaven and earth," or the phrase in the text, are used in this sense.

overthrow" (i. 10). "And if they say unto thee, Whither are we to go forth? Thou shalt say unto them, thus hath Iahvah said: They that belong to the Death" (*i. e.*, the Plague; as the Black Death was spoken of in mediæval Europe) "to death; and they that belong to the Sword, to the sword; and they that belong to the Famine, to famine; and they that belong to Captivity, to captivity!" The people were to "go forth" out of their own land, which was, as it were, the Presence-chamber of Iahvah, just as they had at the outset of their history gone forth out of Egypt, to take possession of it. The words convey a sentence of exile, though they do not indicate the place of banishment. The menace of woe is as general in its terms as that lurid passage of the Book of the Law upon which it appears to be founded (Deut. xxviii. 21-26). The time for the accomplishment of those terrible threatenings "is nigh, even at the doors." On the other hand, Ezekiel's "four sore judgments" (Ezek. xiv. 21) were suggested by this passage of Jeremiah.

The prophet avoids naming the actual destination of the captive people, because captivity is only one element in their punishment. The horrors of war—sieges and slaughters and pestilence and famine—must come first. In what follows, the intensity of these horrors is realised in a single touch. The slain are left unburied, a prey to the birds and beasts. The elaborate care of the ancients in the provision of honourable resting-places for the dead is a measure of the extremity thus indicated. In accordance with the feeling of his age, the prophet ranks the dogs and vultures and hyenas that drag and disfigure and devour the corpses of the slain, as three "kinds" of evil equally appalling with the sword that slays. The same feeling led our Spenser to write:

"To spoil the dead of weed
Is sacrilege, and doth all sins exceed."

And the destruction of Moab is decreed by the earlier prophet Amos, "because he burned the bones of the king of Edom into lime," thus violating a law universally recognised as binding upon the conscience of nations (Amos ii. 1). *Cf.* also Gen. xxiii.

Thus death itself was not to be a sufficient expiation for the inveterate guilt of the nation. Judgment was to pursue them even after death. But the prophet's vision does not penetrate beyond this present scene. With the visible world, so far as he is aware, the punishment terminates. He gives no hint here, nor elsewhere, of any further penalties awaiting individual sinners in the unseen world. The scope of his prophecy indeed is almost purely national, and limited to the present life. It is one of the recognised conditions of Old Testament religious thought.

And the ruin of the people is the retribution reserved for what Manasseh did in Jerusalem. To the prophet, as to the author of the book of Kings, who wrote doubtless under the influence of his words, the guilt contracted by Judah under that wicked king was unpardonable. But it would convey a false impression if we left the matter here; for the whole course of his after-preaching—his exhortations and promises, as well as his threats—prove that Jeremiah did not suppose that the nation could not be saved by genuine repentance and permanent amendment. What he intends rather to affirm is that the sins of the fathers will be visited upon children who are partakers of their sins. It is the doctrine of St. Matt. xxiii. 29 *sqq.*; a doctrine which is not merely a theological opinion, but a matter of historical observation.

"And I will set over them four kinds—It is an oracle of Iahvah—the sword to slay, and the dogs to hale, and the fowls of the air, and the beasts of the earth, to devour and to destroy. And I will make them a sport for all the realms of earth; on account of Manasseh ben Hezekiah king of Judah, for what he did in Jerusalem."

Jerusalem!—the mention of that magical name touches another chord in the prophet's soul; and the fierce tones of his oracle of doom change into a dirge-like strain of pity without hope.

"For who will have compassion on Thee, O Jerusalem?
And who will yield thee comfort?
And who will turn aside to ask of thy welfare?
'Twas thou that rejectedst Me (it is Iahvah's word);
Backward wouldst thou wend:
So I stretched forth My hand against thee and destroyed thee;
I wearied of relenting.
And I winnowed them with a fan in the gates of the land;
I bereaved, I undid My people:
Yet they returned not from their own ways.
His widows outnumbered before Me the sand of seas:
I brought them against the Mother of Warriors a harrier at high noon;
I threw upon her suddenly anguish and horrors.
She that had borne seven sons did pine away;
She breathèd out her soul.
Her sun did set, while it yet was day;
He blushed and paled.
But their remnant will I give to the sword
Before their foes: (It is Iahvah's word)."

The fate of Jerusalem would strike the nations dumb with horror; it would not inspire pity, for man would recognise that it was absolutely just. Or perhaps the thought rather is, In proving false to Me, thou wert false to thine only friend: Me thou hast estranged by thy faithlessness; and from the envious rivals, who beset thee on every side, thou canst expect nothing but rejoicing at thy downfall (Ps. cxxxvi.; Lam. ii. 15-17; Obad. 10 *sqq.*). The peculiar solitariness of Israel among the nations (Num. xxiii. 9) aggravated the anguish of her overthrow.

In what follows, the dreadful past appears as a prophecy of the yet more terrible future. The poetseer's pathetic monody moralises the lost battle of Megiddo—that fatal day when the sun of Judah set in what seemed the high day of her prosperity, and all the glory and the promise of good king Josiah vanished like a dream in sudden darkness. Men might think—doubtless Jeremiah thought, in the first moments of despair, when the news of that overwhelming disaster was brought to Jerusalem, with the corpse of the good king, the dead hope of the nation—that this crushing blow was proof that Iahvah had rejected His people, in the exercise of a sovereign caprice, and without reference to their own attitude towards Him. But, says or chants the prophet, in solemn rhythmic utterance,

"'Twas thou that rejectedst Me;
Backward wouldst thou wend:
So I stretched forth My hand against thee, and wrought thee hurt;
I wearied of relenting."

The cup of national iniquity was full, and its baleful contents overflowed in a devastating flood. "In the gates of the land"—the point on the northwest frontier where the armies met—Iahvah "winnowed His people with a fan," separating those who were doomed to fall from those who were to survive, as the winnowing fan separates the chaff from the wheat in the threshing-floor. There He "bereaved" the nation of their dearest hope, "the breath of their nostrils, the Lord's Anointed" (Lam. iv. 20); there He multiplied their widows. And after the lost battle He brought the victor in hot haste against the "Mother" of the fallen warriors, the ill-fated city, Jerusalem, to wreak vengeance upon her for her ill-timed opposition. But, for all this bitter fruit of their evil doings, the people "turned not back from their own ways"; and therefore the strophe of lamentation closes with a threat of utter extermination: "Their remnant"—the poor survival of these fierce storms—"Their remnant will I give to the sword before their foes." *

If the thirteenth and fourteenth verses be not a mere interpolation in this chapter (see xvii. 3, 4), their proper place would seem to be here, as continuing and amplifying the sentence upon the residue of the people. The text is unquestionably corrupt, and must be amended by help of the other passage, where it is partially repeated. The twelfth verse may be read thus:

"Thy wealth and thy treasures will I make a prey,
For the sin of thine high places in all thy borders." †

Then the fourteenth verse follows, naturally enough, with an announcement of the Exile:

"And I will enthral thee to thy foes
In a land thou knowest not:
'For a fire is kindled in Mine anger,
That shall burn for evermore!'" ‡

The prophet has now fulfilled his function of judge by pronouncing upon his people the extreme penalty of the law. His strong perception of the national guilt and of the righteousness of God has left him no choice in the matter. But how little this duty of condemnation accorded with his own individual feeling as a man and a citizen is clear from the passionate outbreak of the succeeding strophe.

"Woe's me, my mother," he exclaims, "that thou barest me,
A man of strife and a man of contention to all the country!
Neither lender nor borrower have I been;
Yet all of them do curse me."

A desperately bitter tone, evincing the anguish of a man wounded to the heart by the sense of fruitless endeavour and unjust hatred. He had done his utmost to save his country, and his reward was universal detestation. His innocence and integrity were requited with the odium of the pitiless creditor who enslaves his helpless victim, and appropriates his all; or the fraudulent borrower who repays a too ready confidence with ruin.§

* The reference to an eclipse of the sun in the words

"Her sun went down, while it yet was day;
He blushed and paled,"

appears fairly certain. Such an event is said have occurred in that part of the world, Sept. 30, B.C. 610.

† 13. Read כמתיך "Thine high places" for לא במחיר "without price"; and transpose בחטאת (xvii. 3).

‡ 14. Read והעבדתיך "and I will make thee serve" (xvii. 4) for והעברתי "and I will make to pass through. . ."

The third member is a quotation from Deut. xxxii. 22. In the fourth, read על-עולם "for ever" (xvii. 4) instead of עליכם "upon you."

§ The tone of all this indicates that the prophet was no novice in his office. It does not suit the time of Josiah; but agrees very well with the time of confusion and popular dismay which followed his death. That event must have brought great discredit upon Jeremiah and upon all who had been instrumental in the religious changes of his reign.

The next two verses answer this burst of grief and despair:

"Said Iahvah, Thine oppression shall be for good;
I will make the foe thy suppliant in time of evil and in time of distress.
Can one break iron,
Iron from the north, and brass?"

In other words, faith counsels patience, and assures the prophet that all things work together for good to them that love God. The wrongs and bitter treatment which he now endures will only enchance his triumph when the truth of his testimony is at last confirmed by events, and they who now scoff at his message come humbly to beseech his prayers. The closing lines refer, with grave irony, to that unflinching firmness, that inflexible resolution, which, as a messenger of God, he was called upon to maintain. He is reminded of what he had undertaken at the outset of his career, and of the Divine Word which made him "a pillar of iron and walls of brass against all the land" (i. 18). Is it possible that the pillar of iron can be broken, and the walls of brass beaten down by the present assault?

There is a pause, and then the prophet vehemently pleads his own cause with Iahvah. Smarting with the sense of personal wrong, he urges that his suffering is for the Lord's own sake; that consciousness of the Divine calling has dominated his entire life, ever since his dedication to the prophetic office; and that the honour of Iahvah requires his vindication upon his heartless and hardened adversaries.

"*Thou* knowest, Iahvah!
Remember me, and visit me, and avenge me on my persecutors.
Take me not away in thy longsuffering;
Regard my bearing of reproach for Thee.

"Thy words were found, and I did eat them,
And it became to me a joy and mine heart's gladness;
For I was called by Thy Name, O Iahvah, God of Sabaoth!

"I sate not in the gathering of the mirthful, nor rejoiced;
Because of Thine hand I sate solitary,
For with indignation Thou didst fill me.

"Why hath my pain become perpetual,
And my stroke malignant, incurable?
Wilt Thou indeed become to me like a delusive stream,
Like waters which are not lasting?"

The pregnant expression, "*Thou* knowest, Iahvah!" does not refer specially to anything that has been already said; but rather lays the whole case before God in a single word. The *Thou* is emphatic; Thou, Who knowest all things, knowest my heinous wrongs: Thou knowest and seest it all, though the whole world beside be blind with passion and self-regard and sin (Ps. x. 11-14). Thou knowest how pressing is my need; therefore "Take me not away in Thy longsuffering:" sacrifice not the life of Thy servant to the claims of forbearance with his enemies and Thine. The petition shows how great was the peril in which the prophet perceived himself to stand: he believes that if God delay to strike down his adversaries, that longsuffering will be fatal to his own life.

The strength of his case is that he is persecuted because he is faithful; he bears reproach for God. He has not abused his high calling for the sake of worldly advantage: he has not prostituted the name of prophet to the vile ends of pleasing the people, and satisfying personal covetousness. He has not feigned smooth prophecies, misleading his hearers with flattering falsehood; but he has considered the privilege of being called a prophet of Iahvah as in itself an all-sufficient reward; and when the Divine Word came to him, he has eagerly received, and fed his inmost soul upon that spiritual aliment, which was at once his sustenance and his deepest joy. Other joys, for the Lord's sake, he has abjured. He has withdrawn himself even from harmless mirth, that in silence and solitude he might listen intently to the inward Voice, and reflect with indignant sorrow upon the revelation of his people's corruption. "Because of Thine Hand"—under Thy influence; conscious of the impulse and operation of thy informing Spirit;—"I sate solitary; for with indignation Thou didst fill me." The man whose eye has caught a glimpse of eternal Truth, is apt to be dissatisfied with the shows of things; and the lighthearted merriment of the world rings hollow upon the ear that listens for the Voice of God. And the revelation of sin—the discovery of all that ghastly evil which lurks beneath the surface of smooth society—the appalling vision of the grim skeleton hiding its noisome decay behind the mask of smiles and gaiety; the perception of the hideous incongruity of revelling over a grave; has driven others, besides Jeremiah, to retire into themselves, and to avoid a world from whose evil they revolted, and whose foreseen destruction they deplored.

The whole passage is an assertion of the prophet's integrity and consistency, with which, it is suggested, that the failure which has attended his efforts, and the serious peril in which he stands, are morally inconsistent, and paradoxical in view of the Divine disposal of events. Here, in fact, as elsewhere, Jeremiah has freely opened his heart, and allowed us to see the whole process of his spiritual conflict in the agony of his moments of doubt and despair. It is an argument of his own perfect sincerity; and, at the same time, it enables us to assimilate the lesson of his experience, and to profit by the heavenly guidance he received, far more effectually than if he had left us ignorant of the painful struggles at the cost of which that guidance was won.

The seeming injustice or indifference of Providence is a problem which recurs to thoughtful minds in all generations of men.

> "O, goddes cruel, that govérne
> This world with byndyng of youre word eterne . . .
> What governance is in youre prescience
> That gilteles tormenteth innocence? . . . .
> Alas! I see a serpent or a theif,
> That many a trewé man hath doon mescheif,
> Gon at his large, and wher him luste may turne;
> But I moste be in prisoun."

That such apparent anomalies are but a passing trial, from which persistent faith will emerge victorious in the present life, is the general answer of the Old Testament to the doubts which they suggest. The only sufficient explanation was reserved, to be revealed by Him, who, in the fulness of time, "brought life and immortality to light."

The thought which restored the failing confidence and courage of Jeremiah was the reflection that such complaints were unworthy of one called to be a spokesman for the Highest; that the supposition of the possibility of the Fountain of Living Waters failing like a winter torrent, that runs dry in the summer heats, was an act of unfaithfulness that merited reproof; and that the true God could not fail to protect His messenger, and to secure the triumph of truth in the end.

> "*To this Iahvah said thus:*
> If thou come again,
> I will make thee again to stand before Me;
> And if thou utter that is precious rather than that is vile,
> As My mouth shalt thou become:
> They shall return unto thee,
> But Thou shalt not return unto them.
>
> "And I will make thee to this people an embattled wall of brass;
> And they shall fight against thee, but not overcome thee,
> For I will be with thee to help thee and to save thee;
> It is Iahvah's word.
> And I will save thee out of the grasp of the wicked,
> And will ransom thee out of the hand of the terrible."

In the former strophe, the inspired poet set forth the claims of the psychic man, and poured out his heart before God. Now he recognises a Word of God in the protest of his better feeling. He sees that where he remains true to himself, he will also stand near to his God. Hence springs the hope, which he cannot renounce, that God will protect His accepted servant in the execution of the Divine commands. Thus the discords are resolved; and the prophet's spirit attains to peace, after struggling through the storm.

It was an outcome of earnest prayer, of an unreserved exposure of his inmost heart before God. What a marvel it is—that instinct of prayer! To think that a being whose visible life has its beginning and its end, a being who manifestly shares possession of this earth with the brute creation, and breathes the same air, and partakes of the same elements with them for the sustenance of his body; who is organised upon the same general plan as they, has the same principal members discharging the same essential functions in the economy of his bodily system; a being who is born and eats and drinks and sleeps and dies like all other animals;—that this being and this being only of all the multitudinous kinds of animated creatures, should have and exercise a faculty of looking off and above the visible which appears to be the sole realm of actual existence, and of holding communion with the Unseen! That, following what seems to be an original impulse of his nature, he should stand in greater awe of this Invisible than any power that is palpable to sense; should seek to win its favour, crave its help in times of pain and conflict and peril; should professedly live, not according to the bent of common nature and the appetites inseparable from his bodily structure, but according to the will and guidance of that Unseen Power! Surely there is here a consummate marvel. And the wonder of it does not diminish when it is remembered that this instinct of turning to an unseen Guide and Arbiter of events is not peculiar to any particular section of the human race. Wide and manifold as are the differences which characterise and divide the families of man, all races possess in common the apprehension of the Unseen and the instinct of prayer. The oldest records of humanity bear witness to its primitive activity, and whatever is known of human history combines with what is known of the character and workings of the human mind to teach us that as prayer has never been unknown, so it is never likely to become obsolete.

May we not recognise in this great fact of

human nature a sure index of a great corresponding truth? Can we avoid taking it as a clear token of the reality of revelation; as a kind of immediate and spontaneous evidence on the part of nature that there is and always has been in this lower world some positive knowledge of that which far transcends it, some real apprehension of the mystery that enfolds the universe? a knowledge and an apprehension which, however imperfect and fragmentary, however fitful and fluctuating, however blurred in outline and lost in infinite shadow, is yet incomparably more and better than none at all. Are we not, in short, morally driven upon the conviction that this powerful instinct of our nature is neither blind nor aimless; that its Object is a true, substantive Being; and that this Being has discovered, and yet discovers, some precious glimpses of Himself and His essential character to the spirit of mortal man? It must be so, unless we admit that the soul's dearest desires are a mocking illusion, that her aspirations towards a truth and a goodness of superhuman perfection are moonshine and madness. It cannot be nothingness that avails to evoke the deepest and purest emotions of our nature; not mere vacuity and chaos, wearing the semblance of an azure heaven. It is not into a measureless waste of outer darkness that we reach forth trembling hands.

Surely the spirit of denial is the spirit that fell from heaven, and the best and highest of man's thoughts aim at and affirm something positive, something that is, and the soul thirsts after God, the Living God.

We hear much in these days of our physical nature. The microscopic investigations of science leave nothing unexamined, nothing unexplored, so far as the visible organism is concerned. Rays from many distinct sources converge to throw an ever-increasing light upon the mysteries of our bodily constitution. In all this, science presents to the devout mind a valuable subsidiary revelation of the power and goodness of the Creator. But science cannot advance alone one step beyond the things of time and sense; her facts belong exclusively to the material order of existence; her cognition is limited to the various modes and conditions of force that constitute the realm of sight and touch; she cannot climb above these to a higher plane of being. And small blame it is to science that she thus lacks the power of overstepping her natural boundaries. The evil begins when the men of science venture, in her much-abused name, to ignore and deny realities not amenable to scientific tests, and immeasurably transcending all merely physical standards and methods.

Neither the natural history nor the physiology of man, nor both together, are competent to give a complete account of his marvellous and many-sided being. Yet some thinkers appear to imagine that when a place has been assigned him in the animal kingdom, and his close relationship to forms below him in the scale of life has been demonstrated; when every tissue and structure has been analysed, and every organ described and its function ascertained; then the last word has been spoken, and the subject exhausted. Those unique and distinguishing faculties by which all this amazing work of observation, comparison, reasoning, has been accomplished, appear either to be left out of the account altogether, or to be handled with a meagre inadequacy of treatment that contrasts in the strongest manner with the fulness and the elaboration which mark the other discussion. And the more this physical aspect of our composite nature is emphasised; the more urgently it is insisted that, somehow or other, all that is in man and all that comes of man may be explained on the assumption that he is the natural climax of the animal creation, a kind of educated and glorified brute —that and nothing more;—the harder it becomes to give any rational account of those facts of his nature which are commonly recognised as spiritual, and among them of this instinct of prayer and its Object.

Under these discouraging circumstances, men are fatally prone to seek escape from their self-involved dilemma by a hardy denial of what their methods have failed to discover and their favourite theories to explain. The soul and God are treated as mere metaphysical expressions, or as popular designations of the unknown causes of phenomena; and prayer is declared to be an act of foolish superstition which persons of culture have long since outgrown. Sad and strange this result is; but it is also the natural outcome of an initial error, which is none the less real because unperceived. Men "seek the living among the dead"; they expect to find the soul by *post mortem* examination, or to see God by help of an improved telescope. They fail and are disappointed, though they have little right to be so, for "spiritual things are discerned spiritually," and not otherwise.

In speculating on the reason of this lamentable issue, we must not forget that there is such a thing as an unpurified intellect as well as a corrupt and unregenerate heart. Sin is not restricted to the affections of the lower nature; it has also invaded the realm of thought and reason. The very pursuit of knowledge, noble and elevating as it is commonly esteemed, is not without its dangers of self-delusion and sin. Wherever the love of self is paramount, wherever the object really sought is the delight, the satisfaction, the indulgence of self, no matter in which of the many departments of human life and action, there is sin. It is certain that the intellectual consciousness has its own peculiar pleasures, and those of the keenest and most transporting character; certain that the incessant pursuit of such pleasures may come to absorb the entire energies of a man, so that no room is left for the culture of humility or love or worship. Everything is sacrificed to what is called the pursuit of truth, but is in sober fact a passionate prosecution of private pleasure. It is not truth that is so highly valued; it is the keen excitement of the race, and not seldom the plaudits of the spectators when the goal is won. Such a career may be as thoroughly selfish and sinful and alienated from God as a career of common wickedness. And thus employed or enthralled, no intellectual gifts, however splendid, can bring a man to the discernment of spiritual truth. Not self-pleasing and foolish vanity and arrogant self-assertion, but a self-renouncing humility, an inward purity from idols of every kind, a reverence of truth as divine, are indispensable conditions of the perception of things spiritual.

The representation which is often given is a mere travesty. Believers in God do *not* want to alter His laws by their prayers—neither His laws physical, nor His laws moral and spiritual. It is their chief desire to be brought into submission or perfect obedience to the sum of His laws. They ask their Father in heaven to lead and teach them, to supply their wants in His own way, because He *is* their Father; because "It is He that made us, and His we are." Surely, a reasonable request, and grounded in reason.

To a plain man, seeking for arguments to justify prayer may well seem like seeking a justification of breathing or eating and drinking and sleeping, or any other natural function. Our Lord never does anything of the kind, because His teaching takes for granted the ultimate prevalence of common sense, in spite of all the subtleties and airspun perplexities in which a speculative mind delights to lose itself. So long as man has other wants than those which he can himself supply, prayer will be their natural expression.

If there be a spiritual as distinct from a material world, the difficulty to the ordinary mind is not to conceive of their contact but of their absolute isolation from each other. This is surely the inevitable result of our own individual experience, of the intimate though not indissoluble union of body and spirit in every living person.

How, it may be asked, can we really think of his Maker being cut off from man, or man from his Maker? God were not God, if He left man to himself. But not only are His wisdom, justice, and love manifested forth in the beneficent arrangements of the world in which we find ourselves; not only is He "kind to the unjust and the unthankful." In pain and loss He quickens our sense of Himself (*cf.* xiv. 19-22). Even in the first moments of angry surprise and revolt, that sense is quickened; we rebel, not against an inanimate world or an impersonal law, but against a Living and Personal Being, whom we acknowledge as the Arbiter of our destinies, and whose wisdom and love and power we affect for the time to question, but cannot really gainsay. The whole of our experience tends to this end—to the continual rousing of our spiritual consciousness. There is no interference, no isolated and capricious interposition or interruption of order within or without us. Within and without us, His Will is always energising, always manifesting forth His Being, encouraging our confidence, demanding our obedience and homage.

Thus prayer has its Divine as well as its human side; it is the Holy Spirit drawing the soul, as well as the soul drawing nigh unto God. The case is like the action and reaction of the magnet and the steel. And so prayer is not a foolish act of unauthorised presumption, not a rash effort to approach unapproachable and absolutely isolated Majesty. Whenever man truly prays, his Divine King has already extended the sceptre of His mercy, and bidden him speak.

xvi.-xvii. After the renewal of the promise there is a natural pause, marked by the formula with which the present section opens. When the prophet had recovered his firmness, through the inspired and inspiring reflections which took possession of his soul after he had laid bare his inmost heart before God (xv. 20, 21), he was in a position to receive further guidance from above. What now lies before us is the direction, which came to him as certainly Divine, for the regulation of his own future behaviour as the chosen minister of Iahvah at this crisis in the history of his people. "And there fell a word of Iahvah unto me, saying: Thou shalt not take thee a wife; that thou get not sons and daughters in this place." Such a prohibition reveals, with the utmost possible clearness and emphasis, the gravity of the existing situation. It implies that the "peace and permanence," so glibly predicted by Jeremiah's opponents, will never more be known by that sinful generation. "This place," the holy place which Iahvah had "chosen, to establish His name there," as the Book of the Law so often describes it; "this place," which had been inviolable to the fierce hosts of the Assyrian in the time of Isaiah (Isa. xxxvii. 33), was now no more a sure refuge, but doomed to utter and speedy destruction. To beget sons and daughters there was to prepare more victims for the tooth of famine, and the pangs of pestilence, and the devouring sword of a merciless conqueror. It was to fatten the soil with unburied carcases, and to spread a hideous banquet for birds and beasts of prey. Children and parents were doomed to perish together; and Iahvah's witness was to keep himself unencumbered by the sweet cares of husband and father, that he might be wholly free for his solemn duties of menace and warning, and be ready for every emergency.

"For thus hath Iahvah said:
Concerning the sons and concerning the daughters that are born in this place,
And concerning their mothers that bear them,
And concerning their fathers that beget them, in this land:
By deaths of agony shall they die;
They shall not be mourned nor buried;
For dung on the face of the ground shall they serve;
And by the sword and by the famine shall they be fordone:
And their carcase shall serve for food
To the fowls of the air and to the beasts of the earth" (xvi. 3-4).

The "deaths of agony" seem to indicate the pestilence, which always ensued upon the scarcity and vile quality of food, and the confinement of multitudes within the narrow bounds of a besieged city (see Josephus' well-known account of the last siege of Jerusalem).

The attitude of solitary watchfulness and strict separation, which the prophet thus perceived to be required by circumstances, was calculated to be a warning of the utmost significance, among a people who attached the highest importance to marriage and the permanence of the family.

It proclaimed more loudly than words could do, the prophet's absolute conviction that offspring was no pledge of permanence; that universal death was hanging over a condemned nation. But not only this. It marks a point of progress in the prophet's spiritual life. The crisis, through which we have seen him pass, has purged his mental vision. He no longer repines at his dark lot; no longer half envies the false prophets, who may win the popular love by pleasing oracles of peace and well-being; no longer complains of the Divine Will, which has laid such a burden upon him. He sees now that his part is to refuse even natural and innocent pleasures for the Lord's sake; to foresee calamity and ruin; to denounce unceasingly the sin he sees around him; to sacrifice a tender and affectionate heart to a life of rigid asceticism; and he manfully accepts his part. He knows that he stands alone—the last fortress of truth in a world of falsehood; and that for truth it becomes a man to surrender his all.

That which follows tends to complete the prophet's social isolation. He is to give no sign of sympathy in the common joys and sorrows of his kind.

"For thus hath Iahvah said:
Enter thou not into the house of mourning,
Nor go to lament, nor comfort thou them:
For I have taken away My friendship from this people
('Tis Iahvah's utterance!)
The lovingkindness and the compassion;
And old and young shall die in this land,
They shall not be buried, and men shall not wail for them;
Nor shall a man cut himself, nor make himself bald, for them:
Neither shall men deal out bread to them in mourning,
To comfort a man over the dead;
Nor shall they give them to drink the cup of consolation,
Over a man's father and over his mother.

"And the house of feasting thou shalt not enter,
To sit with them to eat and to drink.
For thus hath Iahvah Sabaoth, the God of Israel, said:
Lo, I am about to make to cease from this place,
Before your own eyes and in your own days,
Voice of mirth and voice of gladness,
The voice of the bridegroom and the voice of the bride."

Acting as prophet, that is, as one whose public actions were symbolical of a Divine intent, Jeremiah is henceforth to stand aloof, on occasions when natural feeling would suggest participation in the outward life of his friends and acquaintance. He is to quell the inward stirrings of affection and sympathy, and to abstain from playing his part in those demonstrative lamentations over the dead, which the immemorial custom and sentiment of his country regarded as obligatory; and this, in order to signify unmistakably that what thus appeared to be the state of his own feelings, was really the aspect under which God would shortly appear to a nation perishing in its guilt. "Enter not into the house of mourning . . . *for* I have taken away My friendship from this people, the lovingkindness and the compassion." An estranged and alienated God would view the coming catastrophe with the cold indifference of exact justice. And the consequence of the Divine aversion would be a calamity so overwhelming that the dead would be left without those rites of burial which the feeling and conscience of all races of mankind have always been careful to perform. There should be no burial, much less ceremonial lamentation, and those more serious modes of evincing grief by disfigurement of the person,* which, like tearing the hair and rending the garments, are natural tokens of the first distraction of bereavement. Not for wife or child (מֵת: see Gen. xxiii. 3), nor for father or mother should the funeral feast be held; for men's hearts would grow hard at the daily spectacle of death, and at last there would be no survivors.

In like manner, the prophet is forbidden to enter as guest "the house of feasting." He is not to be seen at the marriage-feast,—that occasion of highest rejoicing, the very type and example of innocent and holy mirth; to testify by his abstention that the day of judgment was swiftly approaching, which would desolate all homes, and silence for evermore all sounds of joy and gladness in the ruined city. And it is expressly added that the blow will fall "before your own eyes and in your own days;" showing that the hour of doom was very near, and would no more be delayed.

In all this, it is noticeable that the Divine answer appears to bear special reference to the peculiar terms of the prophet's complaint. In depairing tones he had cried (xv. 10), "Woe's me, my mother, that thou didst bear me!" and now he is himself warned not to take a wife and seek the blessing of children. The outward connection here may be: "Let it not be that thy children speak of thee, as thou hast spoken of thy mother!" * But the inner link of thought may rather be this, that the prophet's temporary unfaithfulness evinced in his outcry against God and his lament that ever he was born is punished by the denial to him of the joys of fatherhood—a penalty which would be severe to a loving, yearning nature like his, but which was doubtless necessary to the purification of his spirit from all worldly taint, and to the discipline of his natural impatience and tendency to repine under the hand of God. His punishment, like that of Moses, may appear disproportionate to his offence; but God's dealings with man are not regulated by any mechanical calculation of less and more, but by His perfect knowledge of the needs of the case; and it is often in truest mercy that His hand strike hard. "As gold in the furnace doth He try them"; and the purest metal comes out of the hottest fire.

Further, it is not the least prominent, but the leading part of a man's nature that most requires this heavenly discipline, if the best is to be made of it that can be made. The strongest element, that which is most characteristic of the person, that which constitutes his individuality, is the chosen field of Divine influence and operation; for here lies the greatest need. In Jeremiah this master element was an almost feminine tenderness; a warmly affectionate disposition, craving the love and sympathy of his fellows, and recoiling almost in agony from the spectacle of pain and suffering. And therefore it was that the Divine discipline was specially applied to this element in the prophet's personality. In him, as in all other men, the good was mingled with evil, which, if not purged away, might spread until it spoiled his whole nature. It is not virtue to indulge our own bent, merely because it pleases us to do so; nor is the exercise of affection any great matter to an affectionate nature. The involved strain of selfishness must be separated, if any naturally good gift is to be elevated to moral worth, to become acceptable in the sight of God. And so it was precisely here, in his most susceptible point, that the sword of trial pierced the prophet through. He was saved from all hazard of becoming satisfied with the love of wife and children, and forgetting in that earthly satisfaction the love of his God. He was saved from absorption in the pleasures of friendly intercourse with neighbours, from passing his days in an agreeable round of social amenities; at a time when ruin was impending over his country, and well-nigh ready to fall. And the means which God chose for the accomplishment of this result were precisely those of which the prophet had complained (xv. 17); his social isolation, which though in part a matter of choice, was partly forced upon him by the irritation and ill-will of his acquaintance. It is now declared that this trial is to continue. The Lord does not necessarily remove a trouble when entreated to do it. He manifests His love by giving strength to bear it, until the work of chastening be perfected.

An interruption is now supposed, such as may

* Practices forbidden, Lev. xxi. 5; Deut. xiv. 1. Jeremiah mentions them as ordinary signs of mourning, and doubtless they were general in his time. An ancient usage, having its root in natural feeling, is not easily extirpated.

* Naegelsbach.

often have occurred in the course of Jeremiah's public utterances. The audience demands to know why all this evil is ordained to fall upon them. "What is our guilt and what our trespass, that we have trespassed against Iahvah our God?" The answer is a twofold accusation. Their fathers were faithless to Iahvah, and they have outdone their fathers' sin; and the penalty will be expulsion and a foreign servitude.

"Because your fathers forsook Me (It is Iahvah's word!)
And went after other gods, and served them, and bowed down to them,
And Me they forsook, and My teaching they observed not:
And ye yourselves (or, as for you) have done worse than your fathers;
And lo, ye walk each after the stubbornness of his evil heart,
So as not to hearken unto Me.
Therefore will I hurl you from off this land,
On to the land that ye and your fathers knew not;
And ye may serve there other gods, day and night,
Since I will not grant you grace."

The damning sin laid to Israel's charge is idolatry, with all the moral consequences involved in that prime transgression. That is to say, the offence consisted not barely in recognising and honouring the gods of the nations along with their own God, though that were fault enough, as an act of treason against the sole majesty of Heaven; but it was aggravated enormously by the moral declension and depravity which accompanied this apostasy. They and their fathers forsook Iahvah "and kept not His teaching;" a reference to the Book of the Law, considered not only as a collection of ritual and ceremonial precepts for the regulation of external religion, but as a guide of life and conduct. And there had been a progress in evil; the nation had gone from bad to worse with fearful rapidity: so that now it could be said of the existing generation that it paid no heed at all to the monitions which Iahvah uttered by the mouth of His prophet, but walked simply in stubborn self-will and the indulgence of every corrupt inclination. And here too, as in so many other cases, the sin is to be its own punishment. The Book of the Law had declared that revolt from Iahvah should be punished by enforced service of strange gods in a strange land (Deut. iv. 28, xxviii. 36, 64); and Jeremiah repeats this threat, with the addition of a tone of ironical concesson: there, in your bitter banishment, you may have your wish to the full; you may serve the foreign gods, and that without intermission (implying that the service would be a slavery).

The whole theory of Divine punishment is implicit in these few words of the prophet. They who sin persistently against light and knowledge are at last given over to their own hearts' lust, to do as they please, without the gracious check of God's inward voice. And then there comes a strong delusion, so that they believe a lie, and take evil for good and good for evil, and hold themselves innocent before God, when their guilt has reached its climax; so that, like Jeremiah's hearers, if their evil be denounced, they can ask in astonishment: "What is our iniquity? or what is our trespass?"

They are so ripe in sin that they retain no knowledge of it as sin, but hold it virtue.

"And they, so perfect is their misery,
Not once perceive their foul disfigurement,
But boast themselves more comely than before."

And not only do we find in this passage a striking instance of judicial blindness as the penalty of sin. We may see also in the penalty predicted for the Jews a plain analogy to the doctrine that the permanence of the sinful state in a life to come is the penalty of sin in the present life. "He that is unjust, let him be unjust still; and he that is filthy, let him be filthy still!" and know himself to be what he is.

The prophet's dark horizon is here apparently lit up for a moment by a gleam of hope. The fourteenth and fifteenth verses, however, with their beautiful promise of restoration, really belong to another oracle, whose prevailing tones are quite different from the present gloomy forecast of retribution (xxiii. 7 *sqq.*). Here they interrupt the sense, and make a cleavage in the connection of thought, which can only be bridged over artificially, by the suggestion that the import of the two verses is primarily not consolatory but minatory; that is to say, that they threaten Exile rather than promise Return; a mode of understanding the two verses which does manifest violence to the whole form of expression, and, above all, to their obvious force in the original passage from which they have been transferred hither. Probably some transcriber of the text wrote them in the margin of his copy, by way of palliating the otherwise unbroken gloom of this oracle of coming woe. Then, at some later time, another copyist, supposing the marginal note indicated an omission, incorporated the two verses in his transcription of the text, where they have remained ever since. (See on xxiii. 7, 8.)

After plainly announcing in the language of Deuteronomy the expulsion of Judah from the land which they had desecrated by idolatry, the prophet develops the idea in his own poetic fashion; representing the punishment as universal, and insisting that it *is* a punishment, and not an unmerited misfortune.

"Lo, I am about to send many fishers (It is Iahvah's word!)
And they shall fish them;
And afterwards will I send many hunters,
And they shall hunt them,
From off every mountain,
And from off every hill,
And out of the clefts of the rocks."

Like silly fish, crowding helplessly one over another into the net,* when the fated moment arrives, Judah will fall an easy prey to the destroyer. And "afterwards," to ensure completeness, those who have survived this first disaster will be hunted like wild beasts, out of all the dens and caves in the mountains, the Adullams and Engedis, where they have found a refuge from the invader.

There is clearly reference to two distinct visitations of wrath, the latter more deadly than the former; else why the use of the emphatic note of time "afterwards"? If we understand by the "fishing" of the country the so-called first captivity, the carrying away of the boy-king Jehoiachin and his mother and his nobles and ten thousand principal citizens, by Nebuchadrezzar to Babylon (2 Kings xxiv. 10 *sqq.*); and by the "hunting" the final catastrophe in the time of Zedekiah; we get, as we shall see, a probable explanation of a difficult expression in the eighteenth verse, which cannot otherwise be sat-

* The figure recalls the Persian custom of sweeping off the whole population of an island, by forming a line and marching over it, a process of extermination called by the Greek writers *σαγηνεύειν*, "fishing with a seine or dragnet" (Herod., iii. 149, iv. 9, vi. 31).

isfactorily accounted for. The next words (ver. 17) refute an assumption, implied in the popular demand to know wherein the guilt of the nation consists, that Iahvah is not really cognisant of their acts of apostasy.

"For Mine eyes are upon all their ways,
They are not hidden away from before My face;
Nor is their guilt kept secret from before Mine eyes."

The verse is thus an indirect reply to the questions of verse 10; questions which in some mouths might indicate that unconsciousness of guilt which is the token of sin finished and perfected; in others, the presence of that unbelief which doubts whether God can, or at least whether He does regard human conduct. But "He that planted the ear, can He not hear? He that formed the eye, can He not see?" (Ps. xciv. 9). It is really an utterly irrational thought, that sight, and hearing, and the higher faculties of reflection and consciousness, had their origin in a blind and deaf, a senseless and unconscious source such as inorganic matter, whether we consider it in the atom or in the enormous mass of an embryo system of stars.

The measure of the penalty is now assigned.

"And I will repay first the double of their guilt and their trespass
For that they profaned My land with the carcases of their loathly offerings,
And their abominations filled Mine heritage." *

"I will repay *first.*" The term "first," which has occasioned much perplexity to expositors, means "the first time" (Gen. xxxviii. 28; Dan. xi. 29), and refers, if I am not mistaken, to the first great blow, the captivity of Jehoiachin, of which I spoke just now; an occasion which is designated again (ver. 21), by the expression "this once" or rather "at this time." And when it is said "I will repay the double of their guilt and of their trespass," we are to understand that the Divine justice is not satisfied with half measures; the punishment of sin is proportioned to the offence, and the cup of self-entailed misery has to be drained to the dregs. Even penitence does not abolish the physical and temporal consequences of sin; in ourselves and in others whom we have influenced they continue—a terrible and ineffaceable record of the past. The ancient law required that the man who had wronged his neighbour by theft or fraud should restore double (Ex. xxii. 4, 7, 9); and thus this expression would appear to denote that the impending chastisement would be in strict accordance with the recognised rule of law and justice, and that Judah must repay to the Lord in suffering the legal equivalent for her offence. In a like strain, towards the end of the Exile, the great prophet of the captivity comforts Jerusalem with the announcement that "her hard service is accomplished, her punishment is held sufficient; for she hath received of Iahvah's hand twofold for all her trespasses" (Isa. xl. 2). The Divine severity is, in fact, truest mercy. Only thus does mankind learn to realise "the exceeding sinfulness of sin," only as Judah learned the heinousness of desecrating the Holy Land with "loathly offerings" to the vile Nature-gods, and with the symbols in wood and stone of the cruel and obscene deities of Canaan; viz. by the fearful issue of transgression, the lesson of a calamitous experience, confirming the forecasts of its inspired prophets.

"Iahvah my strength and my stronghold and my refuge in the day of distress!
Unto Thee the very heathen will come from the ends of the earth, and will say:
'Mere fraud did our fathers receive as their own,
Mere breath, and beings among whom is no helper.
Should man make him gods,
When such things are not gods?'

"Therefore, behold I am about to let them know—
And this time will I let them know My hand and My might,
And they shall know that my name is Iahvah!"

In the opening words Jeremiah passionately recoils from the very mention of the hateful idols, the loathly creations, the lifeless "carcases," which his people have put in the place of the Living God. An overmastering access of faith lifts him off the low ground where these dead things lie in their helplessness, and bears him in spirit to Iahvah, the really and eternally existing, Who is his "strength and stronghold and refuge in the day of distress." From this height he takes an eagle glance into the dim future, and discerns—O marvel of victorious faith!—that the very heathen, who have never so much as known the Name of Iahvah, must one day be brought to acknowledge the impotence of their hereditary gods, and the sole deity of the Mighty One of Jacob. He enjoys a glimpse of Isaiah's and Micah's glorious vision of the latter days, when "the mountain of the Lord's House shall be exalted as chief of mountains, and all nations shall flow unto it."

In the light of this revelation, the sin and folly of Israel in dishonouring the One only God, by associating Him with idols and their symbols, becomes glaringly visible. The very heathen (the term is emphatic by position), will at last grope their way out of the night of traditional ignorance, and will own the absurdity of manufactured gods. Israel, on the other hand, has for centuries sinned against knowledge and reason. They had "Moses and the prophets"; yet they hated warning and despised reproof. They resisted the Divine teachings, because they loved to walk in their own ways, after the imaginings of their own evil hearts. And so they soon fell into that strange blindness, which suffered them to see no sin in giving companions to Iahvah, and neglecting His severer worship for the sensuous rites of Canaan.

A rude awakening awaits them. Once more will Iahvah interpose to save them from their infatuation. "This time" they shall be taught to know the nothingness of idols, not by the voice of prophetic pleadings, not by the fervid teachings of the Book of the Law, but by the sword of the enemy, by the rapine and ruin, in which the resistless might of Iahvah will be manifested against His rebellious people. Then, when the warnings which they have ridiculed find fearful accomplishment, then will they know that the name of the One God is Iahvah—He Who alone was and is and shall be for evermore. In the shock of overthrow, in the sorrows of captivity, they will realise the enormity of assimilating the Supreme Source of events, the Fountain of all being and power, to the miserable phantoms of a darkened and perverted imagination.

xvii. 1-18. Jeremiah, speaking for God, returns to the affirmation of Judah's guiltiness. He has answered the popular question (xvi. 10),

* For the construction, *cf.* Gen. i. 22; Jer. li. 11. Or "With their abominations they filled, etc.," a double accusative.

so far as it implied that it was no mortal sin to associate the worship of alien gods with the worship of Iahvah. He now proceeds to answer it with an indignant contradiction, so far as it suggested that Judah was no longer guilty of the grossest forms of idolatry.

1 "The trespass of Judah," he affirms, "is written with pen of iron, with point of adamant;
Graven upon the tablet of their heart,
And upon the horns of their altars:
Even as their sons remember their altars,
And their sacred poles by the evergreen trees,
Upon the high hills.

2 "O My mountain in the field!
Thy wealth and all thy treasures will I give for a spoil,
For the trespass of thine high-places in all thy borders.
And thou shalt drop thine hand * from thy demesne which I gave thee;
And I will enslave thee to thine enemies,
In the land that thou knowest not;

"For a fire have ye kindled in Mine anger;
It shall burn for evermore."

It is clear from the first strophe that the outward forms of idolatry were no longer openly practised in the country. Where otherwise would be the point of affirming that the national sin was "written with pen of iron, and point of adamant"—that it was "graven upon the tablet of the people's heart?" Where would be the point of alluding to the children's *memory* of the altars and sacred poles, which were the visible adjuncts of idolatry? Plainly it is implied that the hideous rites, which sometimes involved the sacrifice of children, are a thing of the past; yet not of the distant past, for the young of the present generation remember them; those terrible scenes are burnt in upon their memories, as a haunting recollection which can no more be effaced, than the guilt contracted by their parents as agents in those abhorrent rites can be done away. The indelible characters of sin are graven deeply upon their hearts; no need for a prophet to remind them of facts to which their own consciences, their own inward sense of outraged affections, and of nature sacrificed to a dark and bloody superstition, bears irrefragable witness. Rivers of water cannot cleanse the stain of innocent blood from their polluted altars. The crimes of the past are unatoned for, and beyond reach of atonement; they cry to heaven for vengeance, and the vengeance will surely fall (xv. 4).

Hitzig rather prosaically remarks that Josiah had destroyed the altars. But the stains of which the poet-seer speaks are not palpable to sense; he contemplates unseen realities.

"Will all great Neptune's ocean wash this blood
Clean from my hand? No, this my hand will rather
The multitudinous seas incarnadine,
Making the green one red."

The second strophe declares the nature of the punishment. The tender, yearning, hopeless love of the cry with which Iahvah resigns His earthly seat to profanation and plunder and red-handed ruin, enhances the awful impression wrought by the slow, deliberate enunciation of the details of the sentence—the utter spoliation of temple and palaces; the accumulated hordes of generations—all that represented the wealth and culture and glory of the time—carried away for ever; the enforced surrender of home and country; the harsh servitude to strangers in a far-off land.

It is difficult to fix the date of this short lyrical outpouring, if it be assumed, with Hitzig, that it is an independent whole. He refers it to the year B. C. 602, after Jehoiakim had revolted from Babylon—"a proceeding which made a future captivity well-nigh certain, and made it plain that the sin of Judah remained still to be punished." Moreover, the preceding year (B. C. 603) was what was known to the Law as a Year of Release or Remission (*shenath shemittah*); and the phrase "thou shalt drop thine hand," *i. e.*, "loose thine hold of" the land (xvii. 4), appears to allude to the peculiar usages of that year, in which the debtor was released from his obligations, and the corn-lands and vineyards were allowed to lie fallow. The Year of Release was also called the Year of Rest (*shenath shabbathon*, Lev. xxv. 5); and both in the present passage of Jeremiah, and in the book of Leviticus, the time to be spent by the Jews in exile is regarded as a period of rest for the desolate land, which would then "make good her sabbaths" (Lev. xxvi. 34, 35, 43). The Chronicler indeed seems to refer to this very phrase of Jeremiah; at all events, nothing else is to be found in the extant works of the prophet with which his language corresponds (2 Chron. xxxvi. 21).

If the rendering of the second verse, which we find in both our English versions, and which I have adopted above, be correct, there arises an obvious objection to the date assigned by Hitzig; and the same objection lies against the view of Naegelsbach, who translates:

"As their children remember their altars,
And their images of Baal *by* (*i. e.*, at the sight of) the green trees, by the high hills."

For in what sense could this have been written "not long before the fourth year of Jehoiakim," which is the date suggested by this commentator for the whole group of chapters, xiv.-xvii. 18? The entire reign of Josiah had intervened between the atrocities of Manasseh and this period; and it is not easy to suppose that any sacrifice of children had occurred in the three months' reign of Jehoahaz, or in the early years of Jehoiakim. Had it been so, Jeremiah, who denounces the latter king severely enough, would certainly have placed the horrible fact in the forefront of his invective; and instead of specifying Manasseh as the king whose offences Iahvah would not pardon, would have thus branded Jehoiakim, his own contemporary. This difficulty appears to be avoided by Hitzig, who explains the passage thus: "When they (the Jews) think of their children, they remember, and cannot but remember, the altars to whose horns the blood of their immolated children cleaves. In the same way, by a green tree on the hills, *i. e.*, when they come upon any such, their Asherim are brought to mind, which were trees of that sort." And since it is perhaps possible to translate the Hebrew as this suggests, "When they remember their sons, their altars, and their sacred poles, by" (*i. e.*, by means of) "the evergreen trees" (collective term) "upon the high hills," and this translation agrees well with the statement that the sin of Judah is "graven upon the tablet of their heart," his view deserves further consideration. The same objection, however, presses again, though with

* *i. e.*, Loose thine hold of . . . let go . . . release. Read ידך for ובך. The uses of שָׁמַט "to throw down," let fall," resemble those of the Greek ἵημι and its compounds. I corrected the passage thus, to find afterwards that I had been anticipated by J. D. Michaelis, Graf, and others.

somewhat diminished force. For if the date of the section be 602, the eighth year of Jehoiakim, more than forty years must have elapsed between the time of Manasseh's bloody rites and the utterance of this oracle. Would many who were parents then, and surrendered their children for sacrifice, be still living at the supposed date? And if not, where is the appropriateness of the words "When they remember their sons, their altars, and their Asherim?"

There seems no way out of the difficulty, but either to date the piece much earlier, assigning it, *e. g.*, to the time of the prophet's earnest preaching in connection with the reforming movement of Josiah, when the living generation would certainly remember the human sacrifices under Manasseh; or else to construe the passage in a very different sense, as follows. The first verse declares that the sin of *Judah* is graven upon the tablet of *their heart,* and upon the horns of *their* altars. The pronouns evidently show that it is the guilt of *the nation,* not of a particular generation, that is asserted. The subsequent words agree with this view. The expression, "*Their* sons" is to be understood in the same way as the expressions "*their* heart," "*their* altars." It is equivalent to the "sons of Judah" (*benê Jehudah*), and means simply the people of Judah, as now existing, the present generation. Now it does not appear that image-worship and the cultus of the high places revived after their abolition by Josiah. Accordingly, the symbols of impure worship mentioned in this passage are not high places and images, but altars and Asherim, *i. e.*, the wooden poles which were the emblems of the reproductive principle of Nature. What the passage therefore intends to say would seem to be this: "The guilt of the nation remains, so long as its children are mindful of their altars and Asherim erected beside * the evergreen trees on the high hills"; *i. e.*, so long as they remain attached to the modified idolatry of the day.

The general force of the words remains the same, whether they accuse the existing generation of serving sun-pillars (*maççeboth*) and sacred poles (*asherim*), or merely of hankering after the old, forbidden rites. For so long as the popular heart was wedded to the former superstitions, it could not be said that any external abolition of idolatry was a sufficient proof of national repentance. The longing to indulge in sin is sin; and sinful it is not to hate sin. The guilt of the nation remained, therefore, and would remain, until blotted out by the tears of a genuine repentance towards Iahvah.

But understood thus, the passage suits the time of Jehoiachin, as well as any other period.

"Why," asks Naegelsbach, "should not Moloch have been the terror of the Israelitish children, when there was such real and sad ground for it, as is wanting in other bugbears which terrify the children of the present day?" To this we may reply, (1) Moloch is not mentioned at all, but simply altars and *asherim;* (2) would the word "remember" be appropriate in this case?

The beautiful strophes which follow (5-13) are not obviously connected with the preceding text. They wear a look of self-completeness, which suggests that here and in many other places Jeremiah has left us, not whole discourses, written down substantially in the form in which they were delivered, but rather his more finished fragments; pieces which being more rhythmical in form, and more striking in thought, had imprinted themselves more deeply upon his memory.

"Thus hath Iahvah said:
Cursed is the man that trusteth in human kind,
And maketh flesh his arm,
And whose heart swerveth from Iahvah!
And he shall become like a leafless tree in the desert,
And shall not see when good cometh;
And shall dwell in parched places in the steppe,
A salt land and uninhabited.

"Blessed is the man that trusteth in Iahvah,
And whose trust Iahvah becometh!
And he shall become like a tree planted by water,
That spreadeth its roots by a stream,
And is not afraid when heat cometh,
And its leaf is evergreen;
And in the year of drought it feareth not,
Nor leaveth off from making fruit."

The form of the thought expressed in these two octostichs, the curse and the blessing, may have been suggested by the curses and blessings of that Book of the Law of which Jeremiah had been so faithful an interpreter (Deut. xxvii. 15-xxviii. 20); while both the thought and the form of the second stanza are imitated by the anonymous poet of the first psalm. The mention of "the year of drought" in the penultimate line may be taken, perhaps, as a link of connection between this brief section and the whole of what precedes it so far as chap. xiv., which is headed "Concerning the droughts." If, however, the group of chapters thus marked out really constitute a single discourse, as Naegelsbach assumes, one can only say that the style is episodical rather than continuous; that the prophet has often recorded detached thoughts, worked up to a certain degree of literary form, but hanging together as loosely as pearls on a string. Indeed, unless we suppose that he had kept full notes of his discourses and soliloquies, or that, like certain professional lecturers of our own day, he had been in the habit of indefinitely repeating to different audiences the same carefully elaborated compositions, it is difficult to understand how he would be able without the aid of a special miracle, to write down in the fourth year of Jehoiakim the numerous utterances of the previous three and twenty years. Neither of these suppositions appears probable. But if the prophet wrote from memory, so long after the original delivery of many of his utterances, the looseness of internal connection, which marks so much of his book, is readily understood.

The internal evidence of the fragment before us, so far as any such is traceable, appears to point to the same period as what precedes, the time immediately subsequent to the death of Jehoiakim. The curse pronounced upon trusting in man may be an allusion to that king's confidence in the Egyptian alliance, which probably

* There is something strange about the phrase "by (upon, *'al*) the evergreen tree." Twenty-five Heb. MSS., the Targ., and the Syriac, read "every" (*kol*) for "upon" (*'al*). We still feel the want of a preposition, and may confidently restore "under" (*tahath*), from the nine other passages in which "evergreen tree" (*'ec ra'anan*) occurs in connection with idolatrous worship. In all these instances the expression is "under every evergreen tree" (*tahath kol 'ec ra'anan*); from the Book of the Law (Deut. xii. 2), whence Jeremiah probably drew the phrase, to 2 Chron. xxviii. 4. Jeremiah has already used the phrase thrice (ii. 20, iii. 6, 13), in exactly the same form. The other passages are Ezek. vi. 13; Isa. lvii. 5; 2 Kings xvi. 4, xvii. 10. The corruption of *kol* into *'al* is found elsewhere. Probably *tahath* had dropped out of the text, before the change took place here.

induced him to revolt from Nebuchadrezzar, and so precipitate the final catastrophe of his country. He owed his throne to the Pharaoh's appointment (2 Kings xxiii. 34), and may perhaps have regarded this as an additional reason for defection from Babylon. But the chastisement of Egypt preceded that of Judah; and when the day came for the latter, the king of Egypt durst no longer go to the help of his too trustful allies (2 Kings xxiv. 7). Jehoiakim had died, but his son and successor was carried captive to Babylon. In the brief interval between those two events, the prophet may have penned these two stanzas, contrasting the issues of confidence in man and confidence in God. On the other hand, they may also be referred to some time not long before the fourth year of Jehoiakim, when that king, egged on by Egypt, was meditating rebellion against his suzerain; an act of which the fatal consequences might easily be foreseen by any thoughtful observer, who was not blinded by fanatical passion and prejudice, and which might itself be regarded as an index of the kindling of Divine wrath against the country.

"Deep is the heart above all things else:
And sore-diseased it is: who can know it?
I, Iahvah, search the heart, I try the reins,
And that, to give to a man according to his own ways,
According to the fruit of his own doings.

"A partridge that gathereth young which are not hers,
Is he that maketh wealth not by right.
In the middle of his days it will leave him,
And in his end he shall prove a fool.

"A throne of glory, a high seat from of old,
Is the place of our sanctuary.
Hope of Israel, Iahvah!
All that leave Thee shall be ashamed;
Mine apostates shall be written in earth;
For they left the Well of Living Waters, even Iahvah.

"Heal Thou me, Iahvah, and I shall be healed,
Save Thou me, and I shall be saved,
For Thou art my praise.

"Lo, *they* say unto me,
Where is the Word of Iahvah? Prithee, let it come!
Yet I, I hasted not from being a shepherd after Thee,
And woeful day I desired not—*Thou* knowest;
The issue of my lips, before Thy face it fell.

"Become not a terror to me!
Thou art my refuge in the day of evil.
Let my pursuers be ashamed, and let not me be ashamed!
Let *them* be dismayed, and let not me be dismayed;
Let Thou come upon them a day of evil,
And doubly with breaking break Thou them!"

In the first of these stanzas, the word "heart" is the connecting link with the previous reflections. The curse and the blessing had there been pronounced not upon any outward and visible distinctions, but upon a certain inward bent and spirit. He is called accursed, whose confidence is placed in changeable, perishable man, and "whose heart swerveth from Iahvah." And he is blessed, who pins his faith to nothing visible; who looks for help and stay not to the seen, which is temporal, but to the Unseen, which is eternal.

The thought now occurs that this matter of inward trust, being a matter of the heart, and not merely of the outward bearing, is a hidden matter, a secret which baffles all ordinary judgment. Who shall take upon him to say whether this or that man, this or that prince confided or not confided in Iahvah? The human heart is a sea, whose depths are beyond human search; or it is a shifty Proteus, transforming itself from moment to moment under the pressure of changing circumstances, at the magic touch of impulse, under the spell of new perceptions and new phases of its world. And besides, its very life is tainted with a subtle disease, whose hereditary influence is ever interfering with the will and affections, ever tampering with the conscience and the judgment, and making difficult a clear perception, much more a wise decision. Nay, where so many motives press, so many plausible suggestions of good, so many palliations of evil, present themselves upon the eve of action; when the colours of good and evil mingle and gleam together in such rich profusion before the dazzled sight that the mind is bewildered by the confused medley of appearances, and wholly at a loss to discern and disentangle them one from another; is it wonderful, if in such a case the heart should take refuge in the comfortable illusion of self-deceit, and seek, with too great success, to persuade itself into contentment with something which it calls not positive evil but merely a less sublime good?

It is not for man, who cannot see the heart, to pronounce upon the degree of his fellow's guilt. All sins, all crimes, are in this respect relative to the intensity of passion, the force of circumstances, the nature of surroundings, the comparative stress of temptation. Murder and adultery are absolute crimes in the eye of human law, and subject as such to fixed penalties; but the Unseen Judge takes cognisance of a thousand considerations, which, though they abolish not the exceeding sinfulness of these hideous results of a depraved nature, yet modify to a vast extent the degree of guilt evinced in particular cases by the same outward acts. In the sight of God a life socially correct may be stained with a deeper dye than that of profligacy or bloodshed; and nothing so glaringly shows the folly of inquiring what is the unpardonable sin as the reflection that any sin whatever may become such in an individual case.

Before God, human justice is often the liveliest injustice. And how many flagrant wrongs, how many monstrous acts of cruelty and oppression, how many wicked frauds and perjuries, how many of those vile deeds of seduction and corruption, which are, in truth, the murder of immortal souls; how many of those fearful sins, which make a sorrow-laden hell beneath the smiling surface of this pleasure-wooing world, are left unheeded, unavenged by any earthly tribunal! But all these things are noted in the eternal record of Him who searches the heart, and penetrates man's inmost being, not from a motive of mere curiosity, but with fixed intent to award a righteous recompense for all choice and all conduct.

The calamities which marked the last years of Jehoiakim, and his ignominious end, were a signal instance of Divine retribution. Here that king's lawless avarice is branded as not only wicked, but foolish. He is compared to the partridge, which gathers and hatches the eggs of other birds, only to be deserted at once by her stolen brood.* "In the middle of his days, it shall leave him" (or "it may leave him," for in Hebrew one form has to do duty for both shades of meaning). The uncertainty of possession, the certainty of absolute surrender within a few short years, this is the point which demonstrates the unreason of making riches the chief end of one's earthly activity. "Truly man walketh in a vain shadow, and disquieteth him-

* A popular opinion of the time.

self in vain: he heapeth up riches, and cannot tell who shall gather them." It is the point which is put with such terrible force in the parable of the Rich Fool. "Soul, thou hast much goods laid up for thyself for many years; take thine ease, eat, drink, and be merry." "And the Lord said unto him, Thou fool! this night shall thy soul be required of thee."

The covetousness, oppression, and bloodthirstiness of Jehoiakim are condemned in a striking prophecy (xxii. 13-19), which we shall have to consider hereafter. A vivid light is thrown upon the words, "In the middle of his days it shall leave him," by the fact recorded in Kings (2 Kings xxiii. 36), that he died in the thirty-sixth year of his age; when, that is, he had fulfilled but half of the threescore years and ten allotted to the ordinary life of man. We are reminded of that other psalm which declares that "bloody and deceitful men shall not live out half their days" (lv. 23).

Apart indeed from all consideration of the future, and apart from all reference to that loyalty to the Unseen Ruler which is man's inevitable duty, a life devoted to Mammon is essentially irrational. The man is mostly a "fool"—that is, one who fails to understand his own nature, one who has not attained to even a tolerable working hypothesis as to the needs of life, and the way to win a due share of happiness;—who has not discovered that

> "riches have their proper stint
> In the contented mind, not mint;"

and that

> "those who have the itch
> Of craving more, are never rich;"

and who has missed all apprehension of the grand secret that

> "Wealth cannot make a *life*, but love."

From the vanity of earthly thrones, whether of Egypt or of Judah, thrones whose glory is transitory, and whose power to help and succour is so ill-assured, the prophet lifts his eyes to the one throne whose glory is everlasting, and whose power and permanence are an eternal refuge.

> "Thou Throne of Glory, High Seat from of old,
> Place of our Sanctuary, Hope of Israel, Iahvah!
> All who leave Thee blush for shame:
> Mine apostates are written in earth;
> For they have forsaken the Well of Living Water, even Iahvah!"

It is his concluding reflection upon the unblest, unhonoured end of the apostate Jehoiakim. If Isaiah could speak of Shebna as a "throne of glory," * *i. e.*, the honoured support and mainstay of his family, there seems no reason why Iahvah might not be so addressed, as the supporting power and sovereign of the world.

The terms "Throne of Glory" . . . "Place of our Sanctuary" seem to be used much as we use the expressions, "the Crown," "the Court," "the Throne," when we mean the actual ruler with whom these things are associated. And when the prophet declares "Mine † apostates are written in earth," he asserts that oblivion is the portion of those of his people, high or low, who forsake Iahvah for another god. Their names are not written in the Book of Life (Ex. xxxii. 32; Ps. lxix. 28), but in the sand whence they are soon effaced. The prophets do not attempt to expose

> "The sweet strange mystery
> Of what beyond these things may lie."

They do not in express terms promise eternal life to the individual believer.

But how often do their words imply that comfortable doctrine! They who forsake Iahvah must perish, for there is neither permanence nor stay apart from IAHVAH, whose very Name denotes "He who Is," the sole Principle of Being and Fountain of Life. If they—nations and persons—who revolt from Him must die, the implication, the truth necessary to complete this affirmation, is that they who trust in Him, and make Him their arm, will live; for union with Him is eternal life.

In this Fountain of Living Water Jeremiah now seeks healing for himself. The malady that afflicts him is the apparent failure of his oracles. He suffers as a prophet whose word seems idle to the multitude. He is hurt with their scorn, and wounded to the heart with their scoffing. On all sides men press the mocking question, "Where is the word of Iahvah? Prithee, let it come to pass!" His threats of national overthrow had not been speedily realised; and men made a mock of the delays of Divine mercy. Conscious of his own integrity, and keenly sensitive to the ridicule of his triumphant adversaries, and scarcely able to endure longer his intolerable position, he pours out a prayer for healing and help. "Heal me," he cries, "and I shall be healed, Save me and I shall be saved" (really and truly saved, as the form of the Hebrew verb implies); "for Thou art my praise," my boast and my glory, as the Book of the Law affirms (Deut. x. 21). I have not trusted in man, but in God; and if this my sole glory be taken away, if events prove me a false prophet, as my friends allege, applying the very test of the sacred Law (Deut. xviii. 21 *sq.*), then shall I be of all men most forsaken and forlorn. The bitterness of his woe is intensified by the consciousness that he has not thrust himself without call into the prophetic office, like the false prophets whose aim was to traffic in sacred things (xiv. 14, 15); for then the consciousness of guilt might have made the punishment more tolerable, and the facts would have justified the jeers of his persecutors. But the case was far otherwise. He had been most unwilling to assume the function of prophet; and it was only in obedience to the stress of repeated calls that he had yielded. "But as for me," he protests, "I hasted not from being a shepherd to follow Thee." It would seem, if this be the correct, as it certainly is the simplest rendering of his words, that, at the time when he first became aware of his true vocation, the young prophet was engaged in tending the flocks that grazed in the priestly pasture-grounds of Anathoth. In that case, we are reminded of David, who was summoned from the sheepfold to camp and court, and of Amos, the prophet-herdsman of Tekoa. But the Hebrew term translated "from being a shepherd" is probably a disguise of some other original expression; and it would involve no very violent change to read "I made no haste to follow after

* Isa. xxii. 23.

† The Heb. term is probably written with omission of the final *mem*, a common abbreviation; and the right reading may be וסורים "and apostates."

Thee fully" or "entirely" * (Deut. i. 36); a reading which is partially supported by the oldest version. Or it may have been better, as involving a mere change in the punctuation,† to amend the text thus: "But as for me, I made no haste, in following Thee," more literally, "in accompanying Thee" (Judg. xiv. 20). This, however, is a point of textual criticism, which leaves the general sense the same in any case.

When the prophet adds: "and the ill day I desired not," some think that he means the day when he surrendered to the Divine calling, and accepted his mission. But it seems to suit the context better, if we understand by the "ill day" the day of wrath whose coming was the burden of his preaching; the day referred to in the taunts of his enemies, when they asked, "Where is the word of Iahvah?" adding with biting sarcasm: "Prithee, let it come to pass." They sneered at Jeremiah as one who seized every occasion to predict evil, as one who longed to witness the ruin of his country. The utter injustice of the charge, in view of the frequent cries of anguish which interrupt his melancholy forecasts, is no proof that it was not made. In all ages, God's representatives have been called upon to endure false accusations. Hence the prophet appeals from man's unrighteous judgment to God the Searcher of hearts. "*Thou* knowest; the utterance of my lips" (Deut. xxiii. 24) "before Thy face it fell": as if to say, No word of mine, spoken in Thy name, was a figment of my own fancy, uttered for my own purposes, without regard of Thee. I have always spoken as in Thy presence, or rather, in Thy presence. Thou, who hearest all, didst hear each utterance of mine; and therefore knowest that all I said was truthful and honest and in perfect accord with my commission.

If only we who, like Jeremiah, are called upon to speak for God, could always remember that every word we say is uttered in that Presence, what a sense of responsibility would lie upon us; with what labour and prayers should we not make our preparation! Too often alas! it is to be feared that our perception of the presence of man banishes all sense of any higher presence; and the anticipation of a fallible and frivolous criticism makes us forget for the time the judgment of God. And yet "by our words we shall be justified, and by our words we shall be condemned."

In continuing his prayer, Jeremiah adds the remarkable petition, "Become not Thou to me a cause of dismay!" He prays to be delivered from that overwhelming perplexity, which threatens to swallow him up, unless God should verify by events that which His own Spirit has prompted him to utter. He prays that Iahvah, his only "refuge in the day of evil," will not bemock him with vain expectations; will not falsify His own guidance; will not suffer His messenger to be "ashamed," disappointed and put to the blush by the failure of his predictions. And then once again, in the spirit of his time, he implores vengeance upon his unbelieving and cruel persecutors: "Let them be ashamed," disappointed in their expectation of immunity, "let *them* be dismayed," crushed in spirit and utterly overcome by the fulfilment of his dark presages of evil. "Let Thou come upon them a day of evil, And doubly with breaking break Thou them!" This indeed asks no more than that what has been spoken before in the way of prophecy—"I will repay the double of their guilt and their trespass" (xvi. 18)—may be forthwith accomplished. And the provocation was, beyond all question, immense. The hatred that burned in the taunt "where is the word of Iahvah? Prithee, let it come to pass!" was doubtless of like kind with that which at a later stage of Jewish history expressed itself in the words "He trusted in God, let Him deliver Him!" "If He be the Son of God, let Him now come down from the cross, and we will believe on Him!"

And how much fierce hostility that one term "my pursuers" may cover, it is easy to infer from the narratives of the prophet's evil experience in chaps. xx., xxvi., and xxxviii. But allowing for all this, we can at best only affirm that the prophet's imprecations on his foes are natural and human; we cannot pretend that they are evangelical and Christ-like.* Besides, the latter would be a gratuitous anachronism, which no intelligent interpreter of Scripture is called upon to perpetrate. It is neither necessary to the proper vindication of the prophet's writings as truly inspired of God, nor helpful to a right conception of the method of revelation.

CHAPTER X.

THE SABBATH—A WARNING.

JEREMIAH xvii. 19-27.

"THUS said Iahvah unto me: Go and stand in the gate of Benjamin, whereby the kings of Judah come in, and whereby they go out; and in all the gates of Jerusalem. And say unto them, Hear ye the word of Iahvah, O kings of Judah, and all Judah, and all inhabitants of Jerusalem, who come in by these gates!

"Thus said Iahvah: Beware, on your lives, and bear ye not a burden on the Day of Rest, nor bring it in by the gates of Jerusalem! Nor shall ye bring a burden forth out of your houses on the Day of Rest, nor shall ye do any work; but ye shall hallow the Day of Rest, as I commanded your fathers. (Albeit, they hearkened not, nor inclined their ear, but stiffened their neck against hearkening, and against receiving instruction.)

"And it shall come to pass, if ye will indeed hearken unto Me, saith Iahvah, not to bring a burden in by the gates of this city on the Day of Rest, but to hallow the Day of Rest, not to do therein any work; then there shall come in by the gates of this city kings (and princes) sitting upon the throne of David, riding on the chariots and on the horses, they and their princes, O men of Judah and inhabitants of Jerusalem! and this city shall be inhabited for ever. And people shall come in from the cities of Judah and from the places round Jerusalem, and from the land of Benjamin, and from the lowlands, and from the hill-country, and

* מלא for מרעה.

† מְרָעֶה for מֵרֹעֶה.

* I have left this paragraph as I wrote it, although I feel great doubts upon the subject. What I have remarked elsewhere on similar passages should be considered along with the present suggestions. We have especially to remember, (i) the peculiar status of the speaker as a true prophet; and (ii) the terrible invectives of Christ Himself on certain occasions (St. Matt. xxiii. 33-35; St. Luke x. 15; St. John viii. 44).

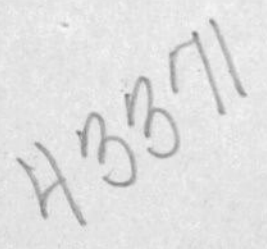

from the south, bringing in burnt-offering and thank-offering, and oblation and incense; and bringing a thanksgiving into the house of Iahvah.

"And if ye hearken not unto Me to hallow the Day of Rest, and not to bear a burden and come in by the gates of Jerusalem on the Day of Rest: I will kindle a fire in her gates, and it shall devour the palaces of Jerusalem, and shall not be quenched."

The matter and manner of this brief oracle mark it off from those which precede it as an independent utterance, and a whole complete in itself. Its position may be accounted for by its probable date, which may be fixed a little after the previous chapters, in the three-months' reign of the ill-starred Jehoiachin; and by the writer's or his editor's desire to break the monotony of commination by an occasional gleam of hope and promise. At the same time, the introductory formula with which it opens is so similar to that of the following oracles (chaps. xviii., xix.), as to suggest the idea of a connection in time between the members of the group. Further, there is an obvious connection of thought between chaps. xviii., xix. In the former, the house of Israel is represented as clay in the hand of the Divine Potter; in the latter, Judah is a potter's vessel, destined to be broken in pieces. And if we assume the priority of the piece before us, a logical progress is observable, from the alternative here presented for the people's choice, to their decision for the worst part (xviii. 12 *sqq.*), and then to the corresponding decision on the part of Iahvah (xix.). Or, as Hitzig puts it otherwise, in the piece before us the scales are still in equipoise; in chap. xviii. one goes down; Iahvah intends mischief (ver. 11), and the people are invited to appease His anger. But the warning is fruitless; and therefore the prophet announces their destruction, depicting it in the darkest colours (chap. xix.). The immediate consequence to Jeremiah himself is related in chap. xx. 1-6; and it is highly probable that the section, chap. xxi. 11-xxii. 9, is the continuation of the oracle addressed to Pashchur: so that we have before us a whole group of prophecies belonging to the same eventful period of the prophet's activity (xvii. 20 agrees closely with xxii. 2, and xvii. 25 with xxii. 4).

The circumstances of the present oracle are these. Jeremiah is inwardly bidden to station himself first in "the gate of the sons of the people"—a gate of Jerusalem which we cannot further determine, as it is not mentioned elsewhere under this designation, but which appears to have been a special resort of the masses of the population, because it was the one by which the kings were wont to enter and leave the city, and where they doubtless were accustomed to hear petitions and to administer justice; and afterwards, he is to take his stand in all the gates in turn, so as not to miss the chance of delivering his message to any of his countrymen. He is there to address the "kings of Judah" (ver. 20); an expression which may denote the young king Jehoiachin and his mother (xiii. 18), or the king and the princes of the blood, the "House of David" of chap. xxi. 12. The promise "kings shall come in by the gates of this city . . . and this city shall be inhabited for ever," and the threat "I will kindle a fire in her gates, and it shall devour the palaces of Jerusalem," may be taken to imply a time when the public danger was generally recognised. The first part of the promise may be intended to meet an apprehension, such as might naturally be felt after the death of Jehoiakim, that the incensed Chaldeans would come and take away the Jewish place and nation. In raising the boy Jehoiachin to the throne of his fathers, men may have sorrowfully foreboded that, as the event proved, he would never keep his crown till manhood, nor beget a race of future kings.*

The matter of the charge to rulers and people is the due observance of the fourth commandment: "ye shall hallow the Day of Rest, as I commanded your fathers" (see Ex. xx. 8, "Remember the Day of Rest, to hallow it"—which is probably the original form of the precept. Jeremiah, however, probably had in mind the form of the precept as it appears in Deuteronomy: "Observe the Day of Rest to hallow it, as Iahvah thy God commanded thee:" Deut. v. 12). The Hebrew term for "hallow" means *to separate* a thing from common things, and devote it to God.

To hallow the Day of Rest, therefore, is to make a marked distinction between it and ordinary days, and to connect it in some way with religion. What is here commanded is to abstain from "bearing burdens," and doing any kind of work (*melakah*, Gen. ii. 2, 3; Ex. xx. 9, 10, xxxi. 14, 15; Gen. xxxix. 11, "appointed task," "duty," "business"). The bearing of burdens into the gates and out of the houses clearly describes the ordinary commerce between town and country. The country folk are forbidden to bring their farm produce to the market in the city gates, and the townspeople to convey thither from their houses and shops the manufactured goods which they were accustomed to barter for these. Nehemiah's memoirs furnish a good illustration of the general sense of the passage (Neh. xiii. 15), relating how he suppressed this Sabbath traffic between town and country. Dr. Kuenen has observed that "Jeremiah is the first of the prophets who stands up for a stricter sanctification of the seventh day, treating it, however, merely as a day of rest. . . . What was traditional appears to have been only abstinence from field-work, and perhaps also from professional pursuits." In like manner, he had before stated that "tendencies to such an exaggeration of the Sabbath rest as would make it absolute, are found from the Chaldean period. Isaiah (i. 13) regards the Sabbath purely as a sacrificial day." The last statement here is hardly a fair inference. In the passage referred to Isaiah is inveighing against the futile worship of his contemporaries; and he only mentions the Sabbath in this connection. And that "tradition" required more than "abstinence from field-work" is evident from words of the prophet Amos, written at least a century and a half before the present oracle, and implying that very abstinence from trading which Jeremiah prescribes. Amos makes the grasping dealers of his time cry impatiently, "When will the new moon be gone,

* The context is against supposing, with Graf, that the prophet's call "hear ye!" extends also to princes yet unborn (*cf.* xiii. 13; xxv. 18 is different). If, however, it be thought that Jeremiah addressed not the sovereigns personally, but only the people passing in and out of the gates; then the expression becomes intelligible as a generalised plural, like the parallels in 2 Chron. xxviii. 3 ("his children"), *ibid.* 16 ("the kings of Assyria"=Tiglath-pileser II). The prophet might naturally avoid the singular as too personal, in affirming an obligation which lay upon the Judean kings in general.

that we may sell corn? and the sabbath, that we may set out wheat for sale?" (Amos viii. 5); a clear proof that buying and selling were suspended on the Sabbath festival in the eighth century B. C.

It is hardly likely that, when law or custom compelled covetous dealers to cease operations on the Sabbath, and buying and selling, the principal business of the time, were suspended, the artisans of town or country would be allowed by public opinion to ply their everyday tasks. Accordingly, when Jeremiah adds to his prohibition of Sabbath trading, a veto upon any kind of "work"—a term which includes this trafficking, but also covers the labour of handicraftsmen (*cf.* 1 Kings v. 30; 2 Kings xii. 12; Ex. xxxv. 35)—he is not really increasing the stringency of the traditional rule about Sabbath observance.

Further, it is difficult to understand how Dr. Kuenen could gather from this passage that Jeremiah treats the Sabbath "merely as a day of rest." This negative character of mere cessation from work, of enforced idleness, is far from being the sole feature of the Sabbath, either in Jeremiah's view of it, or as other more ancient authorities represent it. The testimony of the passage before us proves, if proof were needed, that the Sabbath was a day of worship. This is implied both by the phrase "ye shall hallow the Day of Rest," that is, consecrate it to Iahvah; and by the promise that if the precept be observed faithfully, abundant offerings shall flow into the temple from all parts of the country, that is, as the context seems to require, for the due celebration of the Sabbath festival. There is an intentional contrast between the bringing of innumerable victims, and "bearing burdens" of flour and oil and incense on the Sabbath, for the joyful service of the temple, including the festal meal of the worshippers, and that other carriage of goods for merely secular objects. And as the wealth of the Jerusalem priesthood chiefly depended upon the abundance of the sacrifices, it may be supposed that Jeremiah thus gives them a hint that it is really their interest to encourage the observance of the law of the Sabbath. For if men were busy with their buying and selling, their making and mending, upon the seventh as on other days, they would have no more time or inclination for religious duties than the Sunday traders of our large towns have under the vastly changed conditions of the present day. Moreover, the teaching of our prophet in this matter takes for granted that of his predecessors, with whose writings he was thoroughly acquainted. If in this passage he does not expressly designate the Sabbath as a religious festival, it is because it seemed needless to state a thing so obvious, so generally recognised in theory, however loosely observed in practice. The elder prophets Hosea, Amos, Isaiah, associate Sabbath and new moon together as days of festal rejoicing, when men appeared before Iahvah, that is, repaired to the sanctuary for worship and sacrifice (Hos. ii. 11; Isa. i. 11-14), and when all ordinary business was consequently suspended (Amos viii. 5).

It is clear, then, from this important passage of Jeremiah that in his time and by himself the Sabbath was still regarded under the double aspect of a religious feast and a day of cessation from labour, the latter being, as in the ancient world generally, a natural consequence of the former characteristic. Whether the abolition of the local sanctuaries in the eighteenth year of Josiah resulted in any practical modification of the conception of the Sabbath, so that, in the words of Professor Robertson Smith, "it became for most Israelites an institution of humanity divorced from ritual," is rendered doubtful by the following considerations. The period between the reform of Josiah and the fall of Jerusalem was very brief, including not more than about thirty-five years (621-586, according to Wellhausen). But that a reaction followed the disastrous end of the royal Reformer is both likely under the circumstances, and implied by the express assertions of the author of Kings, who declares of the succeeding monarchs that they "did evil in the sight of the Lord according to all that their fathers had done." As Wellhausen writes: "the battle of Megiddo had shown that in spite of the covenant with Jehovah the possibilities of non-success in war remained the same as before": so at least it would appear to the unspiritual mind of a populace, still hankering after the old forms of local worship, with their careless connivance at riot and disorder. It is not probable that a rapacious and bloody tyrant, like Jehoiakim, would evince more tenderness for the ritual laws than for the moral precepts of Deuteronomy. It is likely, then, that the worship at the local high places revived during this and the following reigns, just as it had revived after its temporary abolition by Hezekiah (2 Kings xviii. 22). Moreover, it is with Judah, not ruined and depopulated Israel, that we have to deal; and even in Judah the people must by this time have been greatly reduced by war and its attendant evils, so that Jerusalem itself and its immediate neighbourhood probably comprised the main part of the population to which Jeremiah addressed his discourses during this period. The bulk of the little nation would, in fact, naturally concentrate upon Jerusalem, in the troublous times that followed the death of Josiah. If so, it is superfluous to assume that "most men could only visit the central altar at rare intervals" during these last decades of the national existence.* The change of view belongs rather to the sixth than the seventh century, to Babylonia rather than to Judea.

The Sabbath observance prescribed by the old Law, and recommended by Jeremiah, was indeed a very different thing from the pedantic and burdensome obligation which it afterwards became in the hands of scribes and Pharisees. These, with their long catalogue of prohibited works, and their grotesque methods of evading the rigour of their own rules, had succeeded in making what was originally a joyous festival and day of rest for the weary, into an intolerable interlude of joyless restraint; when our Lord reminded them that the Sabbath was made for man, and not man for the Sabbath (St. Mark ii. 27). Treating the strict observance of the day as an end in itself, they forgot or ignored the fact that the oldest forms of the sacred Law agreed in justifying the institution by religious and humanitarian considerations (Ex. xx. 8, 10; Deut. v. 12). The difference in the grounds assigned by the different legislations—Deuteronomy alleging neither the Divine Rest of Exodus xx., nor the sign of Exodus xxxi. 13, but the enlightened and enduring motive "that thy bondman and thine handmaid may rest as well as thou," coupled with the feeling injunction, "Remember that thou wast a bondman in the land of Egypt" (Deut.

* "Encycl. Britann.," *s. v.* Sabbath, p. 125.

v. 14, 15)—need not here be discussed; for in any case, the different motives thus suggested were enough to make it clear to those who had eyes to see, that the Sabbath was not anciently conceived as an arbitrary institution established purely for its own sake, and without reference to ulterior considerations of public benefit. The Book of the Covenant affirmed the principle of Sabbath rest in these unmistakable terms: "Six days thou mayst do thy works, and on the seventh day thou shalt leave off, that thine ox and thine ass may rest, and the son of thine handmaid"—the home-born slave—"and the alien may be refreshed" (Ex. xxiii. 12), lit. recover breath, have respite. The humane care of the lawgiver for the dumb toilers and slaves requires no comment; and we have already noticed the same spirit of humanity in the later precept of the Book of the Law (Deut. v. 14, 15). These older rules, it will be observed, are perfectly general in their scope, and forbid not particular actions (Ex. xvi. 23, xxxv. 3; Num. xv. 32), but the continuance of ordinary labour; prescribing a merciful intermission alike for the cattle employed in husbandry and as beasts of burden, and for all classes of dependents.

The origin of the Sabbath festival is lost in obscurity. When the unknown writer of Gen. i. so beautifully connects it with the creation of the world, he betrays not only the belief of his contemporaries in its immemorial antiquity, but also a true perception of the utility of the institution, its perfect adaptation to the wants of humanity. He expresses his sense of the fact in the most emphatic way possible, by affirming the Divine origin of an institution whose value to man is divinely great; and by carrying back that origin to the very beginning, he implies that the Sabbath was made for mankind and not merely for Israel. To whom indeed could an ancient Jewish writer refer as the original source of this unique blessing of a Day of Rest and drawing near to God, if not to Iahvah, the fountain of all things good?

That Moses, the founder of the nation, gave Israel the Sabbath, is as likely as anything can be. Whether, in doing so, he simply sanctioned an ancient and salutary custom (investing it perhaps with new and better associations), dating from the tribal existence of the fathers in Chaldea, or ordered the matter so in purposeful contrast to the Egyptian week of ten days, cannot at present be determined. The Sabbath of Israel, both that of the prophets and that of the scribes, was an institution which distinguished the nation from all others in the period open to historical scrutiny; and with this knowledge we may rest content. That which made Israel what it was, and what it became to the world; the total of the good which this people realised, and left as a priceless heritage to mankind for ever, was the outcome, not of what it had in common with heathen antiquity, but of what was peculiar to itself in ideas and institutions. We cannot be too strongly on our guard against assuming external, superficial, and often accidental resemblances, to be an index of inward and essential likeness and unity. Whatever approximations may be established by modern archæology between Israel and kindred peoples, it will still be true that those points of contact do not explain, though to the apprehension of individuals they may obscure, what is truly characteristic of Israel, and what alone gives that nation its imperishable significance in the history of the world. After all deductions made upon such grounds, nothing can abolish the force of the fact that Moses and the prophets do not belong to Moab, Ammon, or Edom; that the Old Testament, though written in the language of Canaan, is not a monument of Canaanite, but of Israelite faith; that the Christ did not spring out of Babylon or Egypt, and that Christianity is not explicable as the last development of Accadian magic or Egyptian animal worship.

To those who believe that the prophets enjoyed a higher and less fallible guidance than human fancy, reflection, experience; who recognise in the general aim and effect of their teaching, as contrasted with that of other teachers, the best proof that their minds were subject to an influence and a spirit transcending the common limits of humanity; the prominence given by Jeremiah to the law of the Sabbath will be sufficient evidence of the importance of that law to the welfare of his contemporaries, if not of all subsequent generations. If we have rightly assigned the piece to the reign of Jehoiachin, we may suppose that among the contrary currents which agitated the national life at that crisis, there were indications of repentance and remorse at the misdoings of the late reign. The present utterance of the prophet might then be regarded as a test of the degree and worth of the revulsion of popular feeling towards the God of the Fathers. The nation was trembling for its existence, and Jeremiah met its fears by pointing out the path of safety. Here was one special precept hitherto but little observed. Would they keep it now and henceforth, in token of a genuine obedience? Repentance in general terms is never difficult. The rub is *conduct*. Recognition of the Divine Law is easy, so long as life is not submitted to its control. The prophet thus proposes, in a single familiar instance, a plain test of sincerity, which is perhaps not less applicable in our own day than it was then.

The wording of the final threat suggests a thought of solemn consequence for ourselves. "I will kindle a fire in her gates, and it shall devour the castles of Jerusalem—and shall not be quenched!" The gates were the scene of Judah's sinful breach of the Sabbath law, and in them her punishment is to begin. So in the after life of the lost those parts of the physical and mental organism which have been the principal seats of sin, the means and instruments of man's misdoing, will also be the seat of keenest suffering, the source and abode of the most poignant misery. "The fire that never shall be quenched"—Jesus has spoken of that awful mystery, as well as Jeremiah. It is the ever-kindling, never-dying fire of hopeless and insatiable desire; it is the withering flame of hatred of self, when the castaway sees with open eyes what that self has become; it is the burning pain of a sleepless memory of the unalterable past; it is the piercing sense of a life flung recklessly to ruin; it is the scorching shame, the scathing self-contempt, the quenchless, raging thirst for deliverance from ourselves; it is the fearful consciousness of self-destruction, branded upon the soul for ever and ever!

CHAPTER XI.

THE DIVINE POTTER.

JEREMIAH xviii.

JEREMIAH goes down into the Lower Town, or the valley between the upper and lower city; and there his attention is arrested by a potter sitting at work before his wheel. As the prophet watches, a vessel is spoiled in the making under the craftsman's hand; so the process begins afresh, and out of the same lump of clay another vessel is moulded, according to the potter's fancy.

Reflecting upon what he had seen, Jeremiah recognised a Divine Word alike in the impulse which led him thither, and in the familiar actions of the potter. Perhaps as he sat meditating at home, or praying in the court of the temple, the thought had crossed his mind that Iahvah was the Potter, and mankind the clay in His hands; a thought which recurs so often in the eloquent pages of the second Isaiah, who was doubtless indebted to the present oracle for the suggestion of it. Musing upon this thought, Jeremiah wanered half-unconsciously down to the workshop of the potter; and there, under the influence of the Divine Spirit, his thought developed itself into a lesson for his people and for us.

"Cannot I do unto you like this potter, O house of Israel? saith Iahvah; Behold, as the clay in the potter's hand, so are ye in My hand, O house of Israel." Iahvah has an absolute control over His people and over all peoples, to shape their condition and to alter their destiny; a control as absolute as that of the potter over the clay between his hands, which he moulds and remoulds at will. Men are wholly malleable in the hands of their Maker; incapable, by the nature of things, of any real resistance to His purpose. If the first intention of the potter fail in the execution, he does not fail to realise his plan on a second trial. And if man's nature and circumstances appear for a time to thwart the Maker's design; if the unyielding pride and intractable temper of a nation mar its beauty and worth in the eyes of its Creator, and render it unfit for its destined uses and functions; He can take away the form He has given, and reduce His work to shapelessness, and remodel the ruined mass into accordance with His sovereign design. Iahvah, the supreme Author of all existence, can do this. It is evident that the Creator can do as He will with His creature. But all His dealings with man are conditioned by moral considerations. He meddles with no nation capriciously, and irrespective of its attitude towards His laws. "At one moment I threaten a nation and a kingdom that I will uproot and pull down and destroy. And that nation which I threatened returneth from its evil, and I repent of the evil that I purposed to do it. And at another moment, I promise a nation and a kingdom that I will build and plant. And it doeth the Evil in Mine eyes, in not hearkening unto My voice; and I repent of the good that I said I would do it" (vv. 7-10).

This is a bold affirmation, impressive in its naked simplicity and directness of statement, of a truth which in all ages has taken possession of minds at all capable of a comprehensive survey of national experience; the truth that there is a power revealing itself in the changes and chances of human history, shaping its course, and giving it a certain definite direction, not without regard to the eternal principles of morality. When in some unexpected calamity which strikes down an individual sinner, men recognise a "judgment" or an instance of "the visitation of God," they infringe the rule of Christian charity, which forbids us to judge our brethren. Yet such judgment, liable as it is to be too readily suggested by private ill-will, envy, and other evil passions, which warp the even justice that should guide our decisions, and blind the mind to its own lack of impartiality, is in general the perversion of a true instinct which persists in spite of all scientific sophistries and philosophic fallacies. For it is an irrepressible instinct rather than a reasoned opinion which makes us all believe, however inconsistently and vaguely, that God rules; that Providence asserts itself in the stream of circumstance, in the current of human affairs. The native strength of this instinctive belief is shown by its survival in minds that have long since cast off allegiance to religious creeds. It only needs a sudden sense of personal danger, the sharp shock of a serious accident, the foreboding of bitter loss, the unexpected but utter overthrow of some well-laid scheme that seemed assured of success, to stir the faith that is latent in the depths of the most callous and worldly heart, and to force the acknowledgment of a righteous Judge enthroned above.

Compared with the mysterious Power which evinces itself continuously in the apparent chaos of conflicting events, man's free will is like the eddy whirling round upon the bosom of a majestic river as it floats irresistibly onward to its goal, bearing the tiny vortex along with it. Man's power of self-determination no more interferes with the counsels of Providence than the diurnal revolution of the earth on its axis interferes with its annual revolution round the sun. The greater comprises the less; and God includes the world.

The Creator has implanted in the creature a power of choice between good and evil, which is a pale reflection of His own tremendous Being. But how can we even imagine the dependent, the limited, the finite, acting independently of the will of the Absolute and Infinite? The fish may swim against the ocean current; but can it swim at all out of the ocean? Its entire activity depends upon the medium in which it lives and moves and has its being.

But Jeremiah exposes the secret of Providence to the eyes of his fellow-countrymen for a particular purpose. His aim is to eradicate certain prevalent misconceptions, so as to enable them to rightly apprehend the meaning of God's present dealings with themselves. The popular belief was that Zion was an inviolable sanctuary; that whatever disasters might have befallen the nation in the past, or might be imminent in the future, Iahvah could not, for His own sake, permit the extinction of Judah as a nation. For then His worship, the worship of the temple, the sacrifices of the one altar, would be abolished; and His honour and His Name would be forgotten among men. These were the thoughts which comforted them in the trying time when a thousand rumours of the coming of the Chaldeans to punish their revolt were flying about the land; and from day to day men lived in trembling expectation of impending siege and slaughter.

These were the beliefs which the popular prophets, themselves probably in most cases fanatical believers in their own doctrine, vehemently maintained in opposition to Jeremiah. Above all, there was the covenant between Iahvah and His people, admitted as a fact both by Jeremiah and his opponents. Was it conceivable that the God of the Fathers, who had chosen them and their posterity to be His people for ever, would turn from His purpose, and reject His chosen utterly?

Jeremiah meets these popular illusions by applying his analogy of the potter. The potter fashions a mass of clay into a vessel; and Iahvah had fashioned Israel into a nation. But as though the mass of inert matter had proven unwieldy or stubborn to the touches of his plastic hands; as the wheel revolved, a misshapen product resulted, which the artist broke up again, and moulded afresh on his wheel, till it emerged a fair copy of his ideal. And so, in the revolutions of time, Israel had failed of realising the design of his Maker, and had become a vessel of wrath, fitted to destruction. But as the rebellious lump was fashioned again by the deft hand of the master, so might this refractory people be broken and built up anew by the Divine master hand.

In the light of this analogy, the prophet interprets the existing complications of the political world. The serious dangers impending over the nation are a sure symptom that the Divine Potter is at work, "moulding" an evil fate for Judah and Jerusalem. "And now prithee say unto the men of Judah and the inhabitants of Jerusalem:

"Thus hath Iahvah said,
Behold I am moulding evil against you,
And devising a device against you!"

But Iahvah's menaces are not the mere vent of a tyrant's caprice or causeless anger: they are a deliberate effort to break the hard heart, to reduce it to contrition, to prepare it for a new creation in a more glorious likeness. Therefore the threat closes with an entreaty:

"Return ye, I pray you, each from his evil way,
And make good your ways and your doings!"

If the prophetic warning fulfil its purpose, and the nation repent, then as in the case of Nineveh, which repented at the preaching of Jonah, the sentence of destruction is revoked, and the doomed nation is granted a new lease of life. The same truth holds good reversely. God's promises are as conditional as His threats. If a nation lapse from original righteousness, the sure consequence is the withdrawal of Divine favour, and all of blessing and permanence that it confers. It is evident that the prophet directly contradicts the popular persuasion, which was also the current teaching of his professional opponents, that Iahvah's promises to Israel are absolute, that is, irrespective of moral considerations. Jeremiah is revealing, in terms suited to the intelligence of his time, the true law of the Divine dealings with Israel and with man. And what he has here written, it is important to bear in mind, when we are studying other passages of his writings and those of his predecessors, which foreshow judgments and mercies to individual peoples. However absolute the language of prediction, the qualification here supplied must usually be understood; so that it is not too much to say that this remarkable utterance is one of the keys to the comprehension of Hebrew prophecy.

But now, allowing for antique phraseology, and for the immense difference between ancient and modern modes of thought and expression; allowing also for the new light shed upon the problems of life and history by the teaching of Him who has supplemented all that was incomplete in the doctrine of the prophets and the revelation granted to the men of the elder dispensation; must we pronounce this oracle of Jeremiah's substantially true or the contrary? Is the view thus formulated an obsolete opinion, excusable in days when scientific thinking was unknown; useful indeed for the furtherance of the immediate aims of its authors, but now to be rejected wholly as a profound mistake, which modern enlightenment has at once exposed and rendered superfluous to an intelligent faith in the God of the prophets?

Here and everywhere else, Jeremiah's language is in form highly anthropomorphic. If it was to arrest the attention of the multitude, it could not well have been otherwise. He seems to say that God changes His intentions, according as a nation changes its behaviour. Something must be allowed for style, in a writer whose very prose is more than half poetry, and whose utterances are so often lyrical in form as well as matter. The Israelite thinkers, however, were also well aware that the Eternal is superior to change; as is clear from that striking word of Samuel: "The Glory of Israel lieth not nor repenteth; for He is not man, that He should repent" (1 Sam. xv. 29). And prophetic passages like that in Kings, which so nobly declares that the heaven and the heaven of heavens cannot contain God (*cf.* Jer. xxiii. 24), or that of the second Isaiah which affirms that the Divine ways and purposes are as much higher than those of His people, as the heavens are higher than the earth (Isa. lv. 9), prove that the vivid anthropomorphic expressions of the popular teaching of the prophets ought in mere justice to be limited by these wider conceptions of the Divine Nature and attributes. These passages are quite enough to clear the prophets of the accusation of entertaining such gross and crude ideas of Deity as those which Xenophanes ridiculed, and which find their embodiment in most mythologies.

There is indeed a sense in which all thinking, not only thought about God, but about the natural world, must be anthropomorphic. Man is unquestionably "the measure of all things," and he measures by a human standard. He interprets the world without in terms of his own consciousness; he imposes the forms and moulds of his own mind upon the universal mass of things. Time, space, matter, motion, number, weight, organ, function,—what are all these but inward conceptions by which the mind reduces a chaos of conflicting impressions to order and harmony? What the external world may be, apart from our ideas of it, no philosopher pretends to be able to say; and an equal difficulty embarrasses those who would define what the Deity is, apart from His relations to man. But then it is only those relations that really concern us; everything else is idle speculation, little becoming to creatures so frail and ephemeral as we.

From this point of view, we may fairly ask, what difference it makes whether the prophet affirm that Iahvah repents of retributive designs, when a nation repents of its sins, or that a nation's repentance will be followed by the restoration of temporal prosperity. It is a mere matter of statement; and the former way of putting the truth was the more intelligible way to his contemporaries, and has, besides, the advantage of implying the further truth that the fortunes of nations do not depend upon a blind and inexorable fate, but upon the Will and Law of a holy God. It affirms a Lawmaker as well as a Law, a Providence as well as an uniform sequence of events.

The prophet asserts, then, that nations reap what they have sown; that their history is, in general, a record of God's judgments upon their ways and doings. This is, of course, a matter of faith, as are all beliefs about the Unseen; but it is a faith which has its root in an apparently ineradicable instinct of humanity. Δράσαντι παθεῖν, "The doer must suffer," is not a conviction of Hebrew religion only; it belongs to the universal religious consciousness. Some critics are fond of pronouncing the "policy" of the prophets a mistaken one. They commend the high tone of their moral teachings, but consider their forecasts of the future and interpretations of passing events, as erroneous deductions from their general views of the Divine nature. We are not well acquainted with the times and circumstances under which the prophets wrote and spoke. This is true even in the case of Jeremiah; the history of the time exists only in the barest outline. But the writings of an Isaiah or an Amos make it difficult to suppose that their authors would not have occupied a leading position in any age and nation; their thought is the highest product of the Hebrew mind; and the policy of Isaiah at least, during the Assyrian crisis, was gloriously justified by the event.

We need not, however, stop here in attempting to vindicate the attitude and aims of the prophets. Without claiming infallibility for every individual utterance of theirs—without displaying the bad taste and entire lack of literary tact which would be implied by insisting upon the minute accuracy and close correspondence to fact, of all that the prophets forboded, all that they suggested as possible or probable, and by turning all their poetical figures and similes into bald assertions of literal fact; we may, I think, steadfastly affirm that the great principles of revealed religion, which it was their mission to enunciate and impress by all the resources of a fervid oratory and a high-wrought poetical imagination, are absolutely and eternally true. Man does reap as he sows; all history records it. The present welfare and future permanence of a nation do depend, and have always depended, upon the strength of its adhesion to religious and moral convictions. What was it that enabled Israel to gain a footing in Canaan, and to reduce, one after another, nations and communities far more advanced in the arts of civilisation than they? What but the physical and moral force generated by the hardy and simple life of the desert, and disciplined by wise obedience to the laws of their Invisible King? What but a burning faith in the Lord of Hosts, Iahvah Sabaoth, the true Leader of the armies of Israel? Had they only remained uncontaminated by the luxuries and vices of the conquered races; had they not yielded to the soft seduction of sensuous forms of worship; had they continued faithful to the God who had brought them out of Egypt, and lived, on the whole, by the teaching of the true prophets; who can say that they might not have successfully withstood the brunt of Assyrian or Chaldean invasion?

The disruption of the kingdom, the internecine conflicts, the dynastic revolutions, the entanglements with foreign powers which mark the progressive decline of the empire of David and Solomon, would hardly have found place in a nation that steadily lived by the rule of the prophets, clinging to Iahvah and Iahvah only, and "doing justice and loving mercy" in all the relations of life. The gradual differentiation of the idea of Iahvah into a multitude of Baals at the local sanctuaries must have powerfully tended to disintegrate the national unity. Solomon's temple and the recognition of the one God of all the tribes of Israel as supreme, which that religious centre implied, was, on the other hand, a real bond of union for the nation. We cannot forget that, at the outset of the whole history, Moses created or resuscitated the sense of national unity in the hearts of the Egyptian serfs, by proclaiming to them Iahvah, the God of their fathers. It is a one-sided representation which treats the policy of the prophets as purely negative; as confined to the prohibition of leagues with the foreigner, and the condemnation of walls and battlements, chariots and horses, and all the elements of social strength and display. The prophets condemn these things, regarded as substitutes for trust in the One God, and faithful obedience to His laws. They condemn the man who puts his confidence in man, and makes flesh his arm, and forgets the only true source of strength and protection. To those who allege that the policy of the prophets was a failure, we may reply that it never had a full and fair trial.

And they will say, Hopeless! for we will follow after our own devices, and will each practise the stubbornness of his own evil heart. Therefore thus hath Iahvah said:

1. "Ask ye now among the heathen,
Who hath heard the like?
The virgin (daughter) of Israel
Hath done a very horrible thing.

2. "Doth the snow of Lebanon cease
From overflowing the field?
Do the running waters dry up,
The icy streams?*

3. "For My people have forgotten me,
To vain things they burn incense:
And they have made them stumble in their ways,
the ancient paths,
To walk in bypaths, a way not cast up:

4. "To make their land a desolation,
Perpetual hissings;
Every one that passeth her by shall be amazed,
And shall shake his head.

5. "Like an east wind will I scatter them
In the face of the foe;
The back and not the face will I show them,
In the day of their overthrow."

God foresees that His gracious warning will be rejected as heretofore; the prophet's hearers will cry "It is hopeless!" thy appeal is in vain, thine enterprise desperate; "for after our own devices" or thoughts "will we walk," not after thine, though thou urge them as Iahvah's; "and we will each practise the stubbornness of his own

*Instead of מצור שדי "from the rock of the field," I have ventured to read מצוק שדי (Lam. iii. 54; Deut. xi. 4; 2 Kings vi. 6). For ינתשו "plucked up" "uprooted," which is inappropriate in connection with water, Schnurrer's ינשתו "dried up" (Isa. xix. 5; Jer. li. 30), is probably right. In the second couplet, I read זבים for זרים, which is meaningless, and transpose קרים with נוזלים.

evil heart"—this last in a tone of irony, as if to say, Very well; we accept thy description of us; our ways are stubborn, and our hearts evil: we will abide by our character, and stand true to your unflattering portrait. Otherwise, the words may be regarded as giving the substance of the popular reply, in terms which at the same time convey the Divine condemnation of it; but the former view seems preferable.

God foresees the obstinacy of the people, and yet the prophet does not cease his preaching. A cynical assent to his invective only provokes him to more strenuous endeavours to convince them that they are in the wrong; that their behaviour is against reason and nature. Once more (ii. 10 *sqq.*) he strives to shame them into remorse by contrasting their conduct with that of other nations. These were faithful to their own gods; among *them* such a crime as national apostasy was unheard of and unknown. It was reserved for Israel to give the first example of this abnormal offence; a fact as strange and fearful in the moral world as some unnatural revolution in the physical sphere. That Israel should forget his duty to Iahvah was as great and inexplicable a portent as if the perennial snows of the Lebanon should cease to supply the rivers of the land; or as if the ice-cold streams of its glens and gorges should suddenly cease to flow. And certainly, when we look at the matter with the eye of calm reason, the prophet cannot be said to have here exaggerated the mystery of sin. For, however strong the temptation that lures man from the path of duty, however occasion may suggest, and passion urge, and desire yearn, these influences cannot of themselves silence conscience, and obliterate experience, and overpower judgment, and defeat reason. As surely as it is possible to know anything, man knows that his vital interests coincide with duty; and that it is not only weak but absolutely irrational to sacrifice duty to the importunities of appetite.

When man forsakes the true God, it is to "burn incense to vain gods" or things of naught. He who worships what is less than God, worships nothing. No being below God can yield any true satisfaction to that human nature which was made for God. The man who fixes his hope upon things that perish in the using, the man who seeks happiness in things material, the man whose affections have sole regard to the joys of sense, and whose devotion is given wholly to worldly objects, is the man who will at the last cry out, in hopeless disappointment and bitterness of spirit, vanity of vanities! all is vanity! "For what shall it profit a man, if he shall gain the whole world, and lose his own soul? Or what shall a man give in exchange for his soul?" The soul's salvation consists in devotion to its Lord and Maker; its eternal loss and ruin, in alienation from Him who is its true and only life. The false gods are naught as regards help and profit; they are powerless to bless, but they are potent to hurt and betray. They "make men stumble out of their ways, out of the ancient paths, to walk in bypaths, in a way not cast up." So it was of old; so it is now. When the heart is estranged from God, and devoted to some meaner pursuit than the advancement of His glory, it soon deserts the straight road of virtue, the highway of honour, and falls into the crooked and uneven paths of fraud and hypocrisy, of oppression and vice. The end appears to sanctify the means, or at least to make them tolerable; and, once the ancient path of the Law is forsaken, men will follow the most tortuous, and often thorny and painful courses, to the goal of their choice. The path which leads away from God leads both individuals and nations to final ruin. Degraded ideas of the Deity, false ideas of happiness, a criminal indifference to the welfare of others, a base devotion to private and wholly selfish ends, must in the long run sap the vigour of a nation, and render it incapable of any effectual resistance to its enemies. Moral declension is a sure symptom of approaching political dissolution; so sure, that if a nation chooses and persists in evil, in the face of all dissuasion, it may be assumed to be bent on suicide Like Israel, it may be said to do thus, "in order to make its land an astonishment, perpetual hissings." Men will be surprised at the greatness of its fall, and at the same time will acknowledge by voice and gesture that its doom is absolutely just.

So far as his immediate hearers were concerned, the effect of the prophet's words was exactly what had been anticipated (ver. 18; *cf.* ver. 12). Jeremiah's preaching was a ministry of hardening, in a far more complete sense than Isaiah's had been. On the present occasion, the popular obduracy and unbelief evinced itself in a conspiracy to destroy the prophet by false accusation. They would doubtless find it not difficult to construe his words as blasphemy against Iahvah, and treason against the state. And they said: "Come and let us devise devices"—lay a plot—"against Jeremiah." Dispassionate wisdom, mere worldly prudence, would have said, Let us weigh well the probability or even possibility of the truth of his message. Moral earnestness, a sincere love of God and goodness, would have recognised in the prophet's fearful earnest a proof of good faith, a claim to consideration. Unbiassed common sense would have asked, What has Jeremiah to gain by persistence in unpopular teaching? What will be his reward, supposing his words come true? Is it to be supposed that a man whose woeful tidings are uttered in a voice broken with sobs, and interrupted by bursts of wild lamentation, will look with glad eyes upon destruction when it comes, if it come after all? But habitual sin blinds as well as pollutes the soul. And when admonition is unacceptable, it breeds hatred. The heart that is not touched by appeal becomes harder than it was before. The ice of indifference becomes the adamant of malignant opposition. The populace of Jerusalem, like that of more modern capitals, was enervated by ease and luxury, altogether given over to the pursuit of wealth and pleasure as the end of life. They hated the man who rebuked in the gate, and abhorred him that spoke uprightly (Amos v. 10). They could not abide one whose life and labours were a continual protest against their own. And now he had done his best to rob them of their pleasant confidence, to destroy the delusion of their fool's paradise. He had burst into the heathenish sanctuary where they offered a worship congenial to their hearts, and done his best to wreck their idols, and dash their altars to the ground. He had affirmed that the accredited oracles were all a lie, that the guides whom they blindly followed were leading them to ruin. So the passive dislike of good blazes out into murderous fury against the good man who dares to be good alone in the face of a sinful multitude. That they are made thoroughly uneasy by his message of judgment, that they are more than half convinced that he is right, is plain from the frantic passion with which they repeat and deny his words. "Law shall not perish from the priest, nor counsel from the wise, nor the word from the prophet:" these things cannot, "shall not" be. When people have pinned their faith to a false system—a system which accords with their worldly prejudices, and flatters their ungodly pride, and winks at or even sanctions their vices; when they have anchored their entire confidence upon certain men and certain teachings which are in perfect harmony with their own aims in life and their own selfish predilections, they are not only disturbed and distressed, but often enraged by a demonstration that they are lulled in a false security. And anger of this kind is apt to be so irrational that they may think to escape from the threatened evil by silencing its prophet. "Come and let us smite him with the tongue, and let us not hearken to any of his words!" They will first get rid of him, and then forget his words of warning. Their policy is no better than that of the bird which buries its head in the sand, when its pursuers have run it down; an infatuated Out of sight, out of mind. And Jeremiah's recompense for his disinterested zeal is another conspiracy against his life.

Once more he lays his cause before the one impartial Judge; the one Being who is exalted above all passion, and therefore sees the truth as it is.

"Hearken Thou, O Iahvah, unto me,
And hear Thou the voice of mine adversaries.
Should evil be recompensed for good?
For they have digged a pit for my life.
Remember my standing before Thee to speak good about them,
To turn back Thy wrath from them."

Hearken Thou, since *they* refuse to hearken; hear both sides, and pronounce for the right. Behold the glaring contrast between my innocence of all hurtful intent, and their clamorous injustice, between my truth and their falsehood, my prayers for their salvation and their outcry for my blood.

As we read this prayer of Jeremiah's, we are reminded of the very similar language of the thirty-fifth and hundred and ninth psalms, of which he was himself perhaps the author (see especially Ps. xxxv. 1, 4, 5, 7, 11, 12; cix. 2, 5). We have already partially considered the moral aspect of such petitions. It is necessary to bear in mind that the prophet is speaking of persons who have persistently rejected warning, and ridiculed reproof; and now, in return for his intercessions on their behalf, are attempting his life, not in a sudden outbreak of uncontrollable fury, but with craft and deliberate malice, after seeking, apparently, like their spiritual successors in a later age, to entrap him into admissions that might be construed as treason or blasphemy (Ps. xxxv. 19-21).

"Therefore give their sons to the famine,
And pour them into the hands of the sword;
And let their wives be bereaved and widows,
And let their husbands be slain of Death;
Let their young men be stricken down of the sword in the battle!

"Let a cry be heard from their houses,
When Thou bringest a troop upon them suddenly;
For they digged a pit to catch me,
And snares they hid for my feet.

"But of Thyself, Iahvah, Thou knowest all their plan against me for death;
Pardon Thou not their iniquity,
And blot not out their trespass from before Thee;
But let them be made to stumble before Thee,
In the time of Thine anger deal Thou with them!"

The passage is lyrical in form and expression, and something must be allowed for the fact in estimating its precise significance. Jeremiah had entreated God and man that all these things might not come to pass. Now, when the attitude of the people towards his message and himself at last leaves no doubt that their obduracy is invincible, in his despair and distraction he cries, Be it so, then! They are bent on destruction; let them have their will! Let the doom overtake them, that I have laboured in vain to avert! With a weary sigh, and a profound sense of the ripeness of his country for ruin, he gives up the struggle to save it. The passage thus becomes a rhetorical or poetical expression of the prophet's despairing recognition of the inevitable.

How vivid are the touches with which he brings out upon his canvas the horrors of war! In language lurid with all the colours of destruction, he sets before us the city taken by storm, he makes us hear the cry of the victims, as house after house is visited by pillage and slaughter. But stripped of its poetical form, all this is no more than a concentrated repetition of the sentence which he has over and over again pronounced against Jerusalem in the name of Iahvah. The imprecatory manner of it may be considered to be simply a solemn signification of the speaker's own assent and approval. He recalls the sentence, and he affirms its perfect consonance with his own sense of justice. Moreover all these terrible things actually happened in the sequel. The prophet's imprecations received the Divine seal of accomplishment. This fact alone seems to me to distinguish his prayer from a merely human cry for vengeance. So far as his feelings as a man and a patriot were concerned, we cannot doubt that he would have averted the catastrophe, had that been possible, by the sacrifice of his own life. That indeed was the object of his entire ministry. We may call the passage an emotional prediction; and it was probably the predictive character of it which led the prophet to put it on record.

While we admit that no Christian may ordinarily pray for the annihilation of any but spiritual enemies, we must remember that no Christian can possibly occupy the same peculiar position as a prophet of the Old Covenant; and we may fairly ask whether any who may incline to judge harshly of Jeremiah on the ground of passages like this, have fully realised the appalling circumstances which wrung these prayers from his cruelly tortured heart? *We* find it hard to forgive small personal slights, often less real than imaginary; how should we comport ourselves to persons whose shameless ingratitude rewarded evil for good to the extent of seeking our lives? Few would be content, as Jeremiah was, with putting the cause in the hand of God, and abstaining from all attempts at personal vindication of wrongs. It surely betrays a failure of imaginative power to realise the terrible difficulties which beset the path of one who, in a far truer sense than Elijah, was left alone to uphold the cause of true religion in Israel, and not less, a very inadequate knowledge of our own spiritual weakness, when we are bold to censure or even to apologise for the utterances of Jeremiah.

The whole question assumes a different aspect, when it is noticed that the brief "Thus said

Iahvah!" of the next chapter (xix.) virtually introduces the Divine reply to the prophet's prayer. He is now bidden to foreshow the utter destruction of the Jewish polity by a symbolic act which is even more unambiguous than the language of the prayer. He is to take a common earthenware bottle (*baqbûq*, as if "pour-pour"; from *baqaq*, "to pour out"), and, accompanied by some of the leading personages of the capital, heads of families and priests, to go out of the city to the valley of ben Hinnom, and there, after a solemn rehearsal of the crimes perpetrated on that very spot in the name of religion, and after predicting the consequent retribution which will shortly overtake the nation, he is to dash the vessel in pieces before his companions' eyes, in token of the utter and irreparable ruin which awaits their city and people.

Having enacted his part in this striking scene, Jeremiah returns to the courts of the temple, and there repeats the same terrible message in briefer terms before all the people; adding expressly that it is the reward of their stubborn obstinacy and deafness to the Divine voice.

The prophet's imprecations of evil thus appear to have been ratified at the time of their conception by the Divine voice, which spoke in the stillness of his after reflection.

CHAPTER XII.

THE BROKEN VESSEL—A SYMBOL OF JUDGMENT.

JEREMIAH xix.

THE result of his former address, founded upon the procedure of the potter, had only been to bring out into clearer distinctness the appalling extent of the national corruption. It was evident that Judah was incorrigible, and the Potter's vessel must be broken in pieces by its Maker.

"Thus said Iahvah: Go and buy a bottle" (*baqbûq*, as if "a pour-pour"; the meaning is alluded to in the first word of ver. 7: *ubaqqothi*, "and I will pour out") "of a moulder of pottery" (so the accents; but perhaps the Vulgate is right: "lagunculam figuli testeam," "a potter's earthen vessel," A. V.; lit. *a potter's bottle*, viz., *earthenware*), "and" (*take:* LXX. rightly adds) "some of the elders of the people and of the elders of the priests, and go out into the valley of ben Hinnom at the entry of the Pottery Gate" (a postern, where broken earthenware and rubbish were shot forth into the valley: the term is connected with that for "pottery," ver. 1, which is the same as that in Job ii. 8), "and cry there the words that I shall speak unto thee,"—Jeremiah does not pause here, to relate how he followed the Divine impulse, but goes on at once to communicate the tenor of the Divine "words"; a circumstance which points to the fact that this narrative was only written some time after the symbolical action which it records; "and say thou, Hear ye Iahvah's word, O kings of Judah and inhabitants of Jerusalem! Thus said Iahvah Sabaoth, the God of Israel: Lo, I am about to bring an evil upon this place, such that, whoever heareth it, his ears shall tingle!" If we suppose, as seems likely, that this series of oracles (xviii.-xx.) belongs to the reign of Jehoiachin, the expression "kings of Judah" may denote that king and the queen-mother. Another view is that the kings of Judah in general are addressed "as an indefinite class of persons," here and elsewhere (xvii. 20, xxii. 4), because the prophet did not write the main portion of his book until after the siege of Jerusalem (Ewald). The announcement of this verse is quoted by the compiler of Kings in relation to the crimes of king Manasseh (2 Kings xxi. 12).

"Because that they forsook Me, and made this place strange"—alienated it from Iahvah by consecrating it to "strange gods"; or, as the Targum and Syriac, "polluted" it—"and burnt incense therein to other gods, whom neither they nor their fathers knew" (xvi. 13); "and the kings of Judah did fill this place with blood of innocents" (so the LXX. "Nor the kings of Judah" gives a poor sense; they are included in the preceding phrase), "and built the bamoth Baal" (High places of Baal; a proper name, Josh. xiii. 17), "to burn their sons in the fire," ("as burnt-offerings to the Baal;" LXX. omits, and it is wanting, vii. 31, xxxii. 35. It may be a gloss, but is probably genuine, as there are slight variations in each passage), "which I commanded not" ("nor spake:" LXX. omits), "neither came it into My mind: therefore, behold days are coming, saith Iahvah, when this place will no more be called the Tophet and valley of ben Hinnom but the Valley of Slaughter!" ("and in Tophet shall they bury, so that there be"—remain—"no room to bury!" This clause, preserved at the end of ver. 11, but omitted there by the LXX., probably belongs here: see vii. 42). "And I will pour out" (ver. 1; Isa. xix. 3) "the counsel of Judah and Jerusalem in this place"—that is, I will *empty* the land of all wisdom and resourcefulness, as one empties a bottle of its water, so that the heads of the state shall be powerless to devise any effectual scheme of defence in the face of calamity (*cf.* xiii. 13)—"and I will cause them to fall by the sword 'before their enemies'" (Deut. xxviii. 25), "and by the hand of them that seek their life; and I will make 'their carcases food unto the birds of the air and the beasts of the earth'" (Deut. xxviii. 26; chap. vii. 33, xvi. 4). "And I will set this city 'for an astonishment'" (Deut. xxviii. 37) "and a hissing" (xviii. 16); "every one that passeth by her shall be astonished and hiss at all her 'strokes'" (xlix. 17, l. 13) or "plagues" (Deut. xxviii. 59). "And I will cause them to 'eat the flesh of their sons and the flesh of their daughters,' and each the flesh of his fellow shall they eat—'in the stress and the straitness wherewith their enemies' and they that seek their life 'shall straiten them.'" It will be seen from the references that the Deuteronomic colouring of these closing threats (vv. 7-9) is very strong, the last verse being practically a quotation (Deut. xxviii. 53). The effect of the whole oracle would thus be to suggest that the terrible sanctions of the sacred Law would not remain inoperative; but that the shameless violation of the solemn covenant under Josiah, by which the nation undertook to observe the code of Deuteronomy, would soon be visited with the retributive calamities so vividly foreshadowed in that book.

"And break thou the bottle, to the eyes of the men that go with thee, and say unto them: Thus said Iahvah Sabaoth; So will I break this people and this city, as one breaketh the potter's vessel so that it cannot be mended again! Thus will I do to this place, saith Iahvah, and to the inhabitants thereof, and make" (infin. constr. as in xvii. 10, continuing the mood and person of the preceding verb; which is properly a function of the infin. absol., as in ver. 13) "this city like a Tophet"—make it one huge altar of human sacrifice, a burning-place for thousands of human victims. "And the houses of Jerusalem, and the houses of the kings of Judah"—the palace of David and Solomon, in which king after king had reigned, and "done the evil in Iahvah's eyes,"—"shall become like the place of the Tophet, the defiled ones! even all the houses upon the roofs of which they burnt incense unto all the host of heaven, and poured outpourings" (libations of wine and honey) "unto other gods." (So the Heb. punctuation, which seems to give a very good sense. The principal houses, those of the kings and grandees, are called "the defiled," because their roofs especially have been polluted with idolatrous rites. The last clause of the verse explains the epithet, which might have been referred to "the kings of Judah," had it preceded "like the place of the Tophet." The houses were not to become "defiled"; they were already so, past all cleansing; they were to be destroyed with fire, and in their destruction to become the Tophet or sacrificial pyre of their inhabitants. We need not, therefore, read "Tophteh," after Isa. xxx. 33, as I at first thought of doing, to find afterwards that Ewald had already suggested it. The term rendered "even all," is lit. "unto all," that is, "including all"; *cf.* Ezek. xliv. 9).*

The command "and break thou the bottle . . . and say unto them . . ." compared with that of ver. 2, "and cry there the words that I shall speak unto thee!" seems to indicate the proper point of view from which the whole piece is to be regarded. Jeremiah is recalling and describing a particular episode in his past ministry; and he includes the whole of it, with the attendant circumstances and all that he said, first to the elders in the vale of ben Hinnom, and then to the people assembled in the temple, under the comprehensive "Thus said Iahvah!" with which he begins his narrative. In other words, he affirms that he was throughout the entire occurrence guided by the impulses of the Spirit of God. It is very possible that the longer first address (vv. 2-9) really gives the substance of what he said to the people in the temple on his return from the valley, which is merely summarised in verse 15.

"And Jeremiah came in"—into the temple—"from the Tophet, whither Iahvah had sent him to prophesy, and took his stand in the court of Iahvah's House, and said unto all the people: Thus said Iahvah Sabaoth Israel's God; Lo, I am about to bring upon" (ver. 3) "this city and upon all her cities" ("and upon her villages:" LXX. adds) "all the evil that I have spoken concerning her; because they stiffened their neck" (vii. 26), "not to hear My words!" In this apparent epitome of His discourse to the people in the temple, the prophet seems to sum up all his past labours, in view of an impending crisis. "All the evil" spoken hitherto concerning Jerusalem is upon the point of being accomplished (*cf.* xxv. 3).

In reviewing the entire oracle, we may note as in former instances, the care with which all the circumstances of the symbolical action are chosen, in order to enhance the effect of it upon the minds of the witnesses. The Oriental mind delights in everything that partakes of the nature of an enigma; it loves to be called upon to unravel the meaning of dark sentences, and to disentangle the wisdom wrapped up in riddling words and significant actions. It would have found eloquence in Tarquin's unspoken answer to his son's messenger. "Rex velut deliberabundus in hortum ædium transit, sequente nuncio filii: ibi inambulans tacitus summa papaverum capita dicitur baculo decussisse" (Liv. i. 54). No doubt Jeremiah's companions would watch his every step, and would not miss the fact that he carried his earthenware vessel out of the city by the "Sherd Gate." Here was a vessel yet whole, treated as though it were already a shattered heap of fragments! They would be prepared for the oracle in the valley.

It is worth while, by the way, to notice who those companions were. They were certain of "the elders of the people" and of "the elders of the priests." Jeremiah, it seems, was no wild revolutionary dreamer and schemer, whose hand and voice were against all established authority in Church and State. This was not the character of the Hebrew prophets in general, though some writers have conceived thus of them. There is no evidence that Jeremiah ever sought to divest himself of the duties and privileges of his hereditary priesthood; or that he looked upon the monarchy and the priestly guilds and the entire social organisation of Israel, as other than institutions divinely originated and divinely preserved through all the ages of the national history. He did not believe that man created these institutions, though experience taught him that man might abuse and pervert them from their lawful uses. His aim was always to reform, to restore, to lead the people back to "the old paths" of primitive simplicity and rectitude; not to abolish hereditary institutions, and substitute for the order which had become an integral part of the national life, some brand-new constitution which had never been tried, and would be no more likely to fit the body corporate than the armour of Saul fitted the free limbs of the young shepherd who was to slay Goliath.

The prophets never called for the abolition of those laws and customs, civil and ecclesiastical, which were the very framework of the state, and the pillars of the social edifice. They did not cry, "Down with kings and priests!" but to both kings and priests they cried, "Hear ye Iahvah's word!" And all experience proves that they were right. Paper constitutions have never yet redeemed a nation from its vices, nor delivered a community from the impotence and the decay which are the inevitable fruits of moral corruption. Arbitrary legislative changes will not alter the inward condition of a people; covetousness and hypocrisy, pride and selfishness, intemperance and uncleanness and cruelty, may be as rampant in a commonwealth as in a kingdom.

The contents of the oracle are much what we have had many times already. The chief difference lies in a calm definiteness of assurance, a tone of distinct certitude, as though the end were so near at hand as to leave no room for doubt or hesitation. And this difference is fittingly and impressively suggested by the particular symbol chosen—the shattering of an earthenware vessel, beyond the possibility of repair. The

* LXX. *ἀπὸ τῶν ἀκαθαρσιῶν αὐτων* makes it possible that they ead מטמאים which would represent מְטַמְּאִים "defiled."

direct mention of the king of Babylon and the Babylonian captivity, in the sequel (chap. xx.), points to the presence of a Babylonian invasion, probably that which ended with the exile of Jeconiah and the chief citizens of Jerusalem.

The fatal sin, from which the oracle starts and to which it returns, is forsaking Iahvah, and making the city of His choice "strange" to Him, that is, hateful and unclean, by contact with foreign and bloody superstitions, which were even falsely declared by their promoters to be pleasing to Iahvah, the Avenger of innocent blood! (chap. vii. 31). The punishment corresponds to the offence. The sacrifices of blood will be requited with blood, shed in torrents on the very spot which had been so foully polluted; they who had not scrupled to slay their children for the sacrifice, were to slay them again for food under the stress of siege and famine; the city and its houses, defiled with the foreign worships, will become one vast Molech-fire (xxxii. 35), in which all will perish together.

It may strike a modern reader that there is something repulsive and cold-blooded in this detailed enumeration of appalling horrors. But not only is it the case that Jeremiah is quoting from the Book of the Law, at a time when, to an unprejudiced eye, there was every likelihood that the course of events would verify his dark forebodings; in the dreadful experience of those times such incidents as those mentioned (ver. 9) were familiar occurrences in the obstinate defence and protracted sufferings of beleaguered cities. The prophet, therefore, simply affirms that obstinate persistence in following their own counsels and rejecting the higher guidance will bring upon the nation its irretrievable ruin. We know that in the last siege he did his utmost to prevent the occurrence of these unnatural horrors by urging surrender; but then, as always, the people "stiffened their neck, not to hear Iahvah's words."

Jeremiah knew his countrymen well. No phrase could have better described the resolute obstinacy of the national character. How were the headstrong self-will, the inveterate sensuality, the blind tenacity of fanatical and non-moral conceptions which characterised this people, to be purified and made serviceable in the interests of true religion, except by means of the fiery ordeal which all the prophets foresaw and foretold? As we have seen, polytheism exercised upon the popular mind a spell which we can hardly comprehend from our modern point of view; a polytheism foul and murderous, which violated the tenderest affections of our nature by demanding of the father the sacrifice of his child, and violated the very instinct of natural purity by the shameless indulgence of its worship. It was a consecration of lust and cruelty, —that worship of Molech, those rites of the Baals and Asheras. Meagre and monotonous as the sacred records may on these heads appear to be, their witness is supplemented by other sources, by the monuments of Babylon and Phœnicia.

It is hard to see how the religious instinct of men in this peculiar stage of belief and practice was to be enlightened and purified in any other way than the actual course of Providence. What arguments can be imagined that would have appealed to minds which found a fatal fascination, nay, we must suppose an intense satisfaction, in rites so hideous that one durst not even describe them; minds to which the lofty monotheism of Amos, the splendid eloquence of an Isaiah, the plaintive lyrical strain of a Jeremiah, appealed in vain? Appeals to the order of the world, to the wonders of organic life, were lost upon minds which made gods of the most obvious subjects of that order, the sun, moon, and stars; which even personified and adored the physical principle whereby the succession of life after life is perpetuated.

Nothing short of the perception "that the word of the prophets had come to pass," the recognition, therefore, that the prophetic idea of God was the true idea, could have succeeded in keeping the remnant of Judah safe from the contagion of surrounding heathenism in the land of their exile, and in radically transforming once for all the religious tendencies of the Jewish race.

In Jeremiah's view, the heinousness of Judah's idolatry is heightened by the consideration that the gods of their choice are gods "whom neither they nor their fathers knew" (ver. 4). The kings Ahaz, Manasseh, Amon, had introduced novel rites, and departed from "the old paths" more decidedly than any of their predecessors. In this connection, we may remember that, while modern Romish controversialists do not scruple to accuse the Church of this country with having unlawfully innovated at the Reformation, the Anglican appeal has always been to Scripture and primitive antiquity. Such, too, was the appeal of the prophets (Hos. vi. 1, 7, xi. 1; Jer. ii. 2, vi. 16, xi. 3). It is the glory of our Church, a glory of which neither the lies of Jesuits nor the envy of the sectaries can rob her, that she returned to "the old paths," boldly overleaping the dark ages of mediæval ignorance, imposture, and corruption, and planting her foot firmly on the rock of apostolic practice and the consent of the undivided Church.

Disunion among Christians is a sore evil, but union in the maintenance and propaganda of falsehood is a worse; and the guilt of disunion lies at the door of that system which abused its authority to crush out legitimate freedom of thought, to retard the advancement of learning, and to establish those monstrous innovations in doctrine and worship, which subtle dialecticians may prove to their own satisfaction to be innocent and non-idolatrous in essence and intention, though all the world can see that in practice they are grossly idolatrous. God preserve England from that toleration of serious error, which is so easy to sceptical indifference! God preserve her from lending an ear to the siren voices that would seduce her to yield her hard-won independence, her noble freedom, her manly rational piety, to the unhistorical and unscriptural claims of the Papacy!

If we reverence those Scriptures of the Old Testament to which our Lord and His Apostles made their constant appeal, we shall keep steadily before our minds the fact that, in the estimation of a prophet like Jeremiah, the sin of sins, the sin that involved the ruin of Israel and Judah, was the sin of associating other objects of worship with the One Only God. The temptation is peculiarly strong to some natures. The continual relapse of ancient Israel is not so great a wonder to those of us who have any knowledge of mankind, and who can observe what is passing around them at the present day. It is the severe demand of God's holy law, which makes men cast about for some plausible compromise—it is that demand which also makes them yearn after some intermediary power, whose compassion will be less subject to considerations of justice, whom prayers and entreaties and presents may overcome, and induce to wink at unrepented sin. In an age of unsettlement, the more daring spirits will be prone to silence their inconvenient scruples by rushing into atheism, while the more timid may take refuge in Popery. "For to disown a Moral Governour, or to admit that any observances of superstition can release men from the duty of obeying Him, equally serves the purpose of those, who resolve to be as wicked as they dare, or as little virtuous as they can" (Bp. Hurd).

Then too there is the glory of the saints and angels of God. How can frail man refuse to bow before the vision of their power and splendour, as they stand, the royal children of the King of kings, around the heavenly throne, deathless, radiant with love and joy and purity, exalted far above all human weakness and human sorrows? If the holy angels are "ministering spirits," why not the entire community of the Blessed? And what is to hinder us from casting ourselves at the feet of saint or angel, one's own appointed guardian, or chosen helper? Let good George Herbert answer for us all.

"Oh glorious spirits, who after all your bands
See the smooth face of God, without a frown,
Or strict commands;
Where every one is king, and hath his crown,
If not upon his head, yet in his hands:

"Not out of envy or maliciousness
Do I forbear to crave your special aid.
I would address
My vows to thee most gladly, blessed Maid,
And Mother of my God, in my distress:

. . . .

"But now, (alas!) I dare not; for our King,
Whom we do all jointly adore and praise,
Bids no such thing:
And where His pleasure no injunction lays,
('Tis your own case) ye never move a wing.

"All worship is prerogative, and a flower
Of His rich crown, from whom lies no appeal
At the last hour:
Therefore we dare not from His garland steal,
To make a posy for inferior power."

In this sense also, as in many others, the warning of St. John applies:

LITTLE CHILDREN, KEEP YOURSELVES FROM IDOLS!

CHAPTER XIII.

JEREMIAH UNDER PERSECUTION.

JEREMIAH XX.

THE prophet has now to endure something more than a scornful rejection of his message. "And Pashchur ben Immer the priest" (he was chief officer in the house of Iahvah) "heard Jeremiah prophesying these words. And Pashchur smote Jeremiah the prophet and put him in the stocks, which were in the upper gate of Benjamin in the house of Iahvah." Like the priest of Bethel, who abruptly put an end to the preaching of Amos in the royal sanctuary, Pashchur suddenly interferes, apparently before Jeremiah has finished his address to the people; and enraged at the tenour of his words, he causes him—"Jeremiah the prophet," as it is significantly added, to indicate the sacrilege of the act—to be beaten in the cruel Eastern manner on the soles of the feet, inflicting probably the full number of forty blows permitted by the Law (Deut.), and then leaving him in his agony of mind and body, fast bound in "the stocks." For the remainder of that day and all night long the prophet sat there in the gate, at first exposed to the taunts and jeers of his adversaries and the rabble of their followers, and as the weary hours slowly crept on, becoming painfully cramped in his limbs by the barbarous machine which held his hands and feet near together, and bent his body double. This cruel punishment seems to have been the customary mode of dealing with such as were accounted false prophets by the authorities. It was the treatment which Hanani endured in return for his warning to king Asa (2 Chron. xvi. 10), some three centuries earlier than Jeremiah's time; and a few years later in our prophet's history, an attempt was made to enforce it again in his case (Jer. xxix. 26). Thus, like the holy apostles of our Lord, was Jeremiah "counted worthy to suffer shame" for the **Name** in which he spoke (Acts v. 40, 41); and like Paul and Silas at Philippi, after enduring "many stripes" his feet were "made fast in the stocks" (Acts xvi. 23, 24). The message of Jeremiah was a message of judgment, that of the apostles was a message of forgiveness; and both met with the same response from a world whose heart was estranged from God. The heart that loves its own way is only at ease when it can forget God. Any reminder of His Presence, of His perpetual activity in mercy and judgment, is unwelcome, and makes its authors odious. From the outset, transgressors of the Divine law have sought to hide "among the trees of the garden"—in the engrossing pursuits and pleasures of life—from the Presence of God.

Pashchur's object was not to destroy Jeremiah, but to break his spirit, and discredit him with the multitude, and so silence him for ever. But in this expectation he was as signally disappointed as his successor was in the case of St. Peter (Acts v. 24, 29). Now as then, God's messenger could not be turned from his conviction that "we ought to obey God rather than men." And as he sat alone in his intolerable anguish, brooding over his shameful wrongs, and despairing of redress, a Divine Word came in the stillness of night to this victim of human tyranny. For it "came to pass on the morrow that Pashchur brought Jeremiah forth out of the stocks; and Jeremiah said unto him, Not Pashchur (as if "Glad and free")—but Magor-missabib —("Fear on every side") "hath Jehovah called thy name!" Sharpened with misery, the seer's eye pierces through the shows of life, and discerns the grim contrast of truth and appearance. Before him stands this great man, clothed with all the dignity of high office, and able to destroy him with a word; but Iahvah's prophet does not quail before abused authority. He sees the sword suspended by a hair over the head of this haughty and supercilious official; and he realises the solemn irony of circumstance, which has connected a name suggestive of gladness and freedom with a man destined to become the thrall of perpetual terrors. "For thus hath Iahvah said: Lo, I am about to make thee a Fear to thyself and to all thy lovers; and they will fall by the sword of their foes, while thine eyes look on!" This "glad and free" persecutor, wantoning in the abuse of power, blindly fearless of the future, is not doomed to be slain out of hand; a heavier fate is in store for him, a fate prefigured and foreshadowed by his present sins. His proud confidence is to give place to a haunting sense of danger and insecurity; he is to see his followers perish one after another, and evermore to be expecting the same end for himself: while the freedom which he has enjoyed and abused so long, is to be exchanged for a lifelong captivity in a foreign land. "And all Judah will I give into the hand of the king of Babylon, and he will transport them to Babylon, and smite them with the sword. And I will give all the store of this city" (the hoarded wealth of all sorts, which constitutes its strength and reserve force) "and all the gain thereof" (the produce of labour) "and all the value thereof" (things rare and precious of every kind, works of the carver's and the goldsmith's and the potter's and the weaver's art); "and all the treasures of the kings of Judah will I give into the hand of their foes, that they may spoil them and take them and bring them to Babylon.

"And for thyself, Pashchur, and all that dwell in thine house, ye shall depart among the captives; and to Babylon thou shalt come, and there thou shalt die, and there be buried, thyself and all thy lovers, to whom thou hast prophesied with untruth," or rather "by the Lie," *i. e.*, "by the Baal" (ii. 8, xxiii. 13, *cf.* xii. 16).

The play on the name of Pashchur is like that on Perath (ch. xiii.), and the change to Magor-missabib is like the change of Tophet into "Valley of Slaughter" (ch. xix.). Like Amos (vii. 16), Jeremiah repeats his obnoxious prophecy, with a special application to his cruel persecutor, and with the added detail that all the wealth of Jerusalem wil be carried as spoil to Babylon; a detail in which there may lie an oblique reference to the covetous worldliness and the interested opposition of such men as Pashchur. Riches and ease and popularity were the things for which he and those like him had bargained away their integrity, prophesying with conscious falsehood to the deluded people. His "lovers" are his partisans, who eagerly welcomed his presages of peace and prosperity, and doubtless actively opposed Jeremiah with ridicule and threats. The last detail is remarkable, for we do not otherwise know that Pashchur affected to prophesy. If it be not meant simply that Pashchur accepted and lent the weight of his official sanction to the false prophets, and especially those who uttered their divinations in the name of "the Baal," that is to say, either Molech, or the popular and delusive conception of the God of Israel, we see in this man one who combined a steady professional opposition to Jeremiah with power to enforce his hostility by legalised acts of violence. The conduct of Hananiah on a later occasion (xxviii. 10), clearly proves that, where the power was present, the will for such acts was not wanting in Jeremiah's professional adversaries.

It is generally taken for granted that the name of "Pashchur" has been substituted for that of "Malchijah" in the list of the priestly families which returned with Zerubbabel from the Babylonian captivity (Ezra ii. 38; Neh. vii. 41; *cf.* 1 Chron. xxiv. 9); but it seems quite possible that "the sons of Pashchur" were a subdivision of the family of Immer, which had increased largely during the Exile. In that case, the list affords evidence of the fulfilment of Jeremiah's prediction to Pashchur. The prophet elsewhere mentions another Pashchur, who was also a priest, of the course or guild of Malchijah (xxi. 1, xxxviii. 1), which was the designation of the fifth class of the priests, as "Immer" was that of the sixteenth (1 Chron. xxiv. 9, 14). The prince Gedaliah, who was hostile to Jeremiah, was apparently a son of the present Pashchur (Jer. xxxviii. 1).

It is not easy to determine the relation of the lyrical section which immediately follows the doom of Pashchur, to the preceding account (vv. 7-8). If the seventh verse be in its original place, it would seem that the prophet's word had failed of accomplishment, with the result of intensifying the unbelief and the ridicule which his teachings encountered. There is also something very strange in the sequence of the thirteenth and fourteenth verses, where, as the text now stands, the prophet passes at once, in the most abrupt fashion imaginable, from a fervid ascription of praise, a heartfelt cry of thanksgiving for deliverance either actual or contemplated as such, to utterances of unrelieved despair. I do not think that this is in the manner of Jeremiah; nor do I see how the violent contrast of the two sections (7-13 and 14-18) can fairly be accounted for, except by supposing either that we have here two unconnected fragments, placed in juxtaposition with each other because they belong to the same general period of the prophet's ministry; or that the two passages have by some accident of transcription been transposed, which is by no means an uncommon occurrence in the MSS. of the Biblical writers. Assuming this latter as the more probable alternative, we see in the entire passage a powerful representation of the mental conflict into which Jeremiah was thrown by Pashchur's high-handed violence and the seeming triumph of his enemies. Smarting with the sense of utter injustice, humiliated in his inmost soul by shameful indignities, crushed to the earth with the bitter consciousness of defeat and failure, the prophet, like Job, opens his mouth and curses his day.

1. "Cursed be the day wherein I was born!
The day that my mother bare me,
Let it not be blest!

2. "Cursed be the man who told the glad tidings to my father,
'There is born to thee a male child';
Who made him rejoice greatly.

3. "And let that man become like the cities that Iahweh overthrew, without relenting,
And let him hear a cry in the morning,
And an alarm at the hour of noon!

4. "For that he slew me not in the womb,
That my mother might have become my grave,
And her womb have been laden evermore!

5. "O why from the womb came I forth
To see labour and sorrow,
And my days foredone with shame?"

These five triplets afford a glimpse of the lively grief, the passionate despair, which agitated the prophet's heart as the first effect of the shame and the torture to which he had been so wickedly and wantonly subjected. The elegy, of which they constitute the proem, or opening strophe, is not introduced by any formula ascribing it to Divine inspiration; it is simply written down as a faithful record of Jeremiah's own feelings and reflections and self-communings, at this painful crisis in his career. The poet of the book of Job has apparently taken the hint supplied by these opening verses, and has elaborated the idea of cursing the day of birth through seven highly wrought and imaginative stanzas. The higher finish and somewhat artificial expansion of that passage leave little doubt that it was modelled upon the one before us. But the point to remember here is that both are lyrical effusions, expressed in language conditioned by Oriental rather than European standards of taste and usage. As the prophets were not inspired to express their thoughts and feelings in modern English dress, it is superfluous to inquire whether Jeremiah was morally justified in using these poetic formulas of imprecation. To insist on applying the doctrine of verbal inspiration to such a passage is to evince an utter want of literary tact and insight, as well as adhesion to an exploded and pernicious relic of sectarian theology. The prophet's curses are simply a highly effective form of poetical rhetoric, and are in perfect harmony with the immemorial modes of Oriental expression; and the underlying thought, so equivocally expressed, according to our ways of looking at things, is simply that his life has been a failure, and therefore it would have been better not to have been born. Who that is at all earnest for God's truth, nay, for far lower objects of human interest and pursuit, has not in moments of despondency and discouragement been overwhelmed for a time by the like feeling? Can we blame Jeremiah for allowing us to see in this faithful transcript of his inner life how intensely human, how entirely natural the spiritual experience of the prophets really was? Besides, the revelation does not end with this initial outburst of instinctive astonishment, indignation, and despair. The proem is succeeded by a psalm in seven stanzas of regular poetical form—six quatrains rounded off with a final couplet—in which the prophet's thought rises above the level of nature, and finds in an overruling Providence both the source and the justification of the enigma of his life.

1. "Thou enticedst me, Iahvah, and I was enticed,
Thou urgedst * me, and didst prevail!
I am become a derision all the day long.
Every one mocketh at me.

2. "For as oft as I speak, I cry alarm,
Violence and havoc do I proclaim;
For Iahvah's word is become to me a reproach,
And a scoff all the day long.

3. "And if I say, I will not mind it,
Nor speak any more in His Name;
Then it becometh in my heart like a burning fire prisoned in my bones.
And I weary of holding it in † and am not able.

4. "For I have heard the defaming of many, the terror on every side! ‡
All the men of my friendship are watching for my fall;
'Perchance he will be enticed, and we shall prevail over him,
And take our revenge of him.'

* Ex. xii. 33; Isa. viii. 11; Ezek. iii. 14; Jer. xv. 17.
† vi. 11 (or, of enduring, Mal. iii. 2).
‡ "Denounce ye, and we will denounce him!"

5. "Yet Iahvah is with me as a dread warrior,
Therefore my pursuers shall stumble and not prevail;
They shall be greatly ashamed, for that they have not prospered,
With eternal dishonour that shall not be forgotten.

6. "And Iahvah Sabaoth trieth the righteous,
Seeth the reins and the heart;
I shall see Thy revenge of them,
For unto Thee have I committed my quarrel.

7. "Sing ye to Iahvah, acclaim ye Iahvah!
For He hath snatched the poor man's life out of the hand of evildoers."

The cause was of God. "Thou didst lure me, Iahvah, and I let myself be lured; Thou urgedst me and wert victorious." He had not rashly and presumptuously taken upon himself this office of prophet; he had been called, and had resisted the call, until his scruples and his pleadings were overcome, as was only natural, by a Will more powerful than his own (chap. i. 6). In speaking of the inward persuasions which determined the course of his life, he uses the very terms which are used by the author of Kings in connection with the spirit that misled the prophets of Ahab before the fatal expedition to Ramoth Gilead. "And he said, Thou shalt entice, and also be victorious" (1 Kings xxii. 22). Iahvah, therefore, has treated him as an enemy rather than a friend, for He has lured him to his own destruction. Half in irony, half in bitter complaint, the prophet declares that Iahvah has succeeded only too well in His malign purpose: "I am become a derision all the day long; Every one mocketh at me."

In the second stanza, the thought appears to be continued thus: "Thou overcamest me; for as often as I speak," I am a prophet of evil, "I cry alarm" (*'ez' aq*; *cf.* *zĕ' aqah*, ver. 16); I proclaim the imminence of invasion, the "violence and havoc" of a ruthless conqueror. "Thou overcamest me" also, in Thy purpose of making me a laughing-stock to my adversaries: "for Iahvah's word is become to me a reproach, and a scoff all the day long" (the relation between the two halves of the stanza is that of coördination; each gives the reason of the corresponding couplet in the first stanza). His continual threats of a judgment that was still delayed, brought upon him the merciless ridicule of his opponents.

Or the prophet may mean to complain that the monotony of his message, his ever-recurring denunciation of prevalent injustice, is made a reproach against him. "For as often as I speak I make an outcry" of indignation at foul wrongdoing (Gen. iv. 10, xviii. 21, xix. 13); "wrong and robbery do I proclaim" (Hab. i. 2, 3)—the oppression of the poor by the covetous and luxurious ruling classes. A third view is that Jeremiah complains of the frequent attacks upon himself: "For as often as I speak I have to exclaim; Of assault and violence do I cry;" but the first suggestion appears to suit best, as giving a reason for the ridicule which the prophet finds so intolerable (*cf.* xvii. 15).

The third stanza carries this plea for justice a step further. Not only was the prophet's overwhelming trouble due to his having yielded to the persuasions and promises of Iahvah; not only has he been rewarded with scorn and the scourge and the stocks for his compliance with a Divine call. He has been in a manner forced and driven into his intolerable position by the coercive power of Iahvah, which left him no choice but to utter the word that burnt like a fire within him. Sometimes his fears of perfidy and betrayal suggested the thought of succumbing to the insuperable obstacles which seemed to block his path; of giving up once for all a thankless and fruitless and dangerous enterprise: but then the inward flame burnt so fiercely that he could find no relief for his anguish but by giving it vent in words (*cf.* Ps. xxxix. 1-3).

The verse finely illustrates that vivid sense of a Divine constraint which distinguishes the true prophet from pretenders to the office. Jeremiah does not protest the purity of his motives; indirectly and unconsciously he expresses it with a simplicity and a strength which leave no room for suspicion. He has himself no doubt at all that what he speaks is "Iahvah's word." The inward impulse is overpowering; he has striven in vain against its urgency; like Jacob at Peniel, he has wrestled with One stronger than himself. He is no vulgar fanatic or enthusiast, in whom rooted prejudices and irrational frenzies overbalance the judgment, making him incapable of estimating the hazards and the chances of his enterprise; he is as well aware of the perils that beset his path as the coolest and craftiest of his worldly adversaries. Thanks to his natural quickness of perception, his developed faculty of reflection, he is fully alive to the probable consequences of perpetually thwarting the popular will, of taking up a position of permanent resistance to the policy and the aims and the interests of the ruling classes. But while he has his mortal hopes and fears, his human capacity for anxiety and pain; while his heart bleeds at the sight of suffering, and aches for the woes that thickly crowd the field of his prophetic vision; his speech and his behaviour are dominated, upon the whole, by an altogether higher consciousness. His emotions may have their moments of mastery; at times they may overpower his fortitude, and lay him prostrate in an agony of lamentation and mourning and woe; at times they may even interpose clouds and darkness between the prophet and his vision of the Eternal; but these effects of mortality do not last: they shake but cannot loosen his grasp of spiritual realities; they cannot free him from the constraining influence of the Word of Iahvah. That word possesses, leads him captive, "triumphs over him," over all the natural resistance of flesh and blood; for he is "not as the many" (the false prophets) "who corrupt the Word of God; but as of sincerity, but as of God, in the sight of God, he speaks" (2 Cor. ii. 14, 17).

And still, unless a man be thus impelled by the Spirit; unless he have counted the cost and is prepared to risk all for God; unless he be ready to face unpopularity and social contempt and persecution; unless he knows what it is to suffer for and with Jesus Christ; I doubt if he has any moral right to speak in that most holy Name. For if the all-mastering motive be absent, if the love of Christ constrain him not, how can his desires and his doings be such as the Unseen Judge will either approve or bless?

The fourth stanza explains why the prophet laboured, though vainly, to keep silence. It was because of the malicious reports of his utterances, which were carefully circulated by his watchful antagonists. They beset him on every side; like Pashchur, they were to him a "magormissabib," an environing terror (*cf.* vi. 25), as they listened to his harangues, and eagerly invited each other to inform against him as a traitor (The words "Inform ye, and let us inform against him!" or "Denounce ye, and let us denounce him!" may be an ancient gloss upon the term *dibbah,* "ill report," "calumny;" Gen. xxxvii. 2; Num. xiii. 32; Job xvii. 5. For the construction, *cf.* Job xxxi. 37. They spoil the symmetry of the line. That *dibbah* really means "defaming," or "slander," appears not only from the passages in which it occurs, but also from the Arabic *dabûb,* "one who creeps about with slander," from *dabba,* "to move gently or slowly about." The Heb. *ragal, riggel,* "to go about slandering," and *rakîl,* "slander," are analogous).

And not only open enemies thus conspired for the prophet's destruction. Even professed friends (for the phrase, *cf.* xxxviii. 22; Ps. xli. 10) were treacherously watchful to catch him tripping (*cf.* ix. 2, xii. 6). Those on whom he had a natural claim for sympathy and protection, bore a secret and determined grudge against him. His unpopularity was complete, and his position full of peril. We have in the thirty-first and several of the following psalms outpourings of feeling under circumstances very similar to those of Jeremiah on the present occasion, even if they were not actually written by him at the same crisis in his career, as certain striking coincidences of expression seem to suggest (ver. 10; *cf.* Ps. xxxi. 13, xxxv. 15, xxxviii. 17, xli. 9; ver. 13 with Ps. xxxv. 9, 10).

The prophet closes his psalm-like monologue with an act of faith. He remembers that he has a Champion who is mightier than a thousand enemies. Iahvah is with him, not with them (*cf.* 2 Kings vi. 16); their plots, therefore, are foredoomed to failure, and themselves to the vengeance of a righteous God (xi. 20). The last words are an exultant anticipation of deliverance.

We thus see that the whole piece, like a previous one (xv. 10-21), begins with cursing and ends with an assurance of blessing.

THE BOOK OF JEREMIAH.

PREFACE.

The present work deals primarily with Jeremiah xxi.–lii., thus forming a supplement to the volume of the "Expositor's Bible" on Jeremiah by the Rev. C. J. Ball, M. A. References to the earlier chapters are only introduced where they are necessary to illustrate and explain the later sections.

I regret that two important works, Professor Skinner's "Ezekiel" in this series, and Cornill's "Jeremiah" in Dr. Haupt's "Sacred Books of the Old Testament," were published too late to be used in the preparation of this volume.

I have again to acknowledge my indebtedness to the Rev. T. H. Darlow, M. A., for a careful reading and much valuable criticism of my MS.

CONTENTS.

BOOK I.

PERSONAL UTTERANCES AND NARRATIVES.

BOOK II.

PROPHECIES CONCERNING FOREIGN NATIONS.

BOOK III.

JEREMIAH'S TEACHING CONCERNING ISRAEL AND JUDAH.

EPILOGUE.

CHRONOLOGICAL TABLE

In the present stage of investigation of Old Testament Chronology, absolute accuracy cannot be claimed for such a table as the following. Hardly any, if any, of these dates are supported by a general consensus of opinion. On the other hand, the range of variation is, for the most part, not more than three or four years, and the table will furnish an approximately accurate idea of sequences and synchronisms. In other respects also the data admit of alternative interpretations, and the course of events is partly matter of theory—hence the occasional insertion of (?).

CLASSICAL SYNCHRONISMS	JUDAH AND JEREMIAH	ASSYRIA	EGYPT
Traditional date of foundation of Rome, 753	MANASSEH (?)	**Esarhaddon**, 681 **Assurbanipal**, 668	XXVIth Dynasty **Psammetichus I.**, 666
	Jeremiah born, probably between 655 and 645 AMON, 640 JOSIAH, 638		
	Jeremiah's call in the 13th year of Josiah, 626 Habakkuk Zephaniah Scythian inroad into Western Asia	Last kings of Assyria, number and names uncertain, 626–607–6	Psammetichus besieges Ashdod for twenty-nine years
	Publication of Deuteronomy, 621	BABYLON **Nabopolassar**, 626	
	Josiah slain at Megiddo, 608 JEHOAHAZ, 608 (xxii. 10–12, Ch. I.) **Deposed by Necho, who appoints** JEHOIAKIM, 608 (xxii. 13–19, xxxvi. 30, 31, VI.)	*FALL OF NINEVEH*, 607–6	**Necho**, 612
	Jeremiah predicts ruin of Judah and is tried for blasphemy (xxvi., II.)	*BATTLE OF CARCHEMISH* (xlvi., XVII.)	
	FOURTH YEAR OF JEHOIAKIM, 605–4 Nebuchadnezzar* advances into Syria, is suddenly recalled to Babylon—*before* subduing Judah (?) Baruch writes Jeremiah's prophecies in a roll, which is read successively to the people, the nobles, and Jehoiakim, and destroyed by the king (xxxvi., III.; xlv., V.) Nebuchadnezzar invades Judah (?), the Rechabites take refuge in Jerusalem (?), the Jews rebuked by their example (xxxv., IV.) Jehoiakim submits to Nebuchadnezzar, revolts after three years, is attacked by various "bands," but dies before Nebuchadnezzar arrives	**Nebuchadnezzar**, 604	
	JEHOIACHIN, 597 (xxii. 20–30, VII.) Continues revolt, but surrenders to Nebuchadnezzar on his arrival; is deposed and carried to Babylon with many of his subjects. Nebuchadnezzar appoints		
	ZEDEKIAH, 596 Jeremiah attempts to keep Zedekiah loyal to Nebuchadnezzar, and contends with priests and prophets who support Egyptian party (xxiii., xxiv., VIII.)		**Psammetichus II.**, 596
Solon's legislation, 594	Proposed confederation against Nebuchadnezzar denounced by Jeremiah, but supported by Hananiah; proposal abandoned; Hananiah dies (xxvii., xxviii., IX.), 593–2	Ezekiel	**Hophra**, 591
	Controversy by letter with hostile prophets at Babylon (xxix., X.) Judah revolts, encouraged by Hophra. Jerusalem is besieged by Chaldeans. There being no prospect of relief by Egypt, Jeremiah regains his influence and pledges the people by covenant to release their slaves On the news of Hophra's advance, the Chaldeans raise the siege; the Egyptian party again become supreme and annul the covenant (xxi. 1–10, xxxiv., xxxvii. 1–10, XI.) Jeremiah attempts to leave the city, is arrested and imprisoned Hophra retreats into Egypt and the Chaldeans renew the siege (xxxvii. 11–21, xxxviii., xxxix., 15–18, XII.) While imprisoned Jeremiah buys his kinsman's inheritance (xxii., XXX.)		
	DESTRUCTION OF JERUSALEM, 586 Jeremiah remains for a month a prisoner amongst the other captives. Nebuzaradan arrives; arranges for deportation of bulk of population; appoints Gedaliah governor of residue; releases Jeremiah, who elects to join Gedaliah at Mizpah. Gedaliah murdered. Jeremiah carried off, but rescued by Johanan (xxxix.–xli., lii., XIII.) Johanan, in spite of Jeremiah's protest, goes down to Egypt and takes Jeremiah with him (xlii., xliii., XIV.) Jews in Egypt hold festival in honour of Queen of Heaven. Ineffectual protest of Jeremiah (xliv., XV.)	Siege of Tyre	**Amasis**, 570
		Nebuchadnezzar invades Egypt, (?) 568	
Pisistratus, 560–527	Release of Jehoiachin	**Evil-Merodach**, 561	
	CYRUS CONQUERS BABYLON AND GIVES THE JEWS PERMISSION TO RETURN, 538		

*For spelling, see note, page 123.

THE BOOK OF JEREMIAH.

BY THE REV. W. H. BENNETT, M. A.

BOOK I.

PERSONAL UTTERANCES AND NARRATIVES.

CHAPTER I.

INTRODUCTORY: * *JEHOAHAZ.*

JEREMIAH xxii. 10-12.

"Weep ye not for the dead, neither bemoan him: but weep sore for him that goeth away: for he shall return no more."—JER. xxii. 10.

As the prophecies of Jeremiah are not arranged in the order in which they were delivered, there is no absolute chronological division between the first twenty chapters and those which follow. For the most part, however, chaps. xxi-lii. fall in or after the fourth year of Jehoiakim (B. C. 605). We will therefore briefly consider the situation at Jerusalem in this crisis. The period immediately preceding B. C. 605 somewhat resembles the era of the dissolution of the Roman Empire or of the Wars of the French Revolution. An old-established international system was breaking in pieces, and men were quite uncertain what form the new order would take. For centuries the futile assaults of the Pharaohs had only served to illustrate the stability of the Assyrian supremacy in Western Asia. Then in the last two decades of the seventh century B. C. the Assyrian Empire collapsed, like the Roman Empire under Honorius and his successors. It was as if by some swift succession of disasters modern France or Germany were to become suddenly and permanently annihilated as a military power. For the moment, all the traditions and principles of European statesmanship would lose their meaning, and the shrewdest diplomatist would be entirely at fault. Men's reason would totter, their minds would lose their balance at the stupendous spectacle of so unparalleled a catastrophe. The wildest hopes would alternate with the extremity of fear; everything would seem possible to the conqueror.

Such was the situation in B. C. 605, to which our first great group of prophecies belongs. Two oppressors of Israel—Assyria and Egypt—had been struck down in rapid succession. When Nebuchadnezzar † was suddenly recalled to Babylon by the death of his father, the Jews would readily imagine that the Divine judgment had fallen upon Chaldea and its king. Sanguine prophets announced that Jehovah was about to deliver His people from all foreign dominion, and establish the supremacy of the Kingdom of God. Court and people would be equally possessed with patriotic hope and enthusiasm. Jehoiakim, it is true, was a nominee of Pharaoh Necho; but his gratitude would be far too slight to override the hopes and aspirations natural to a Prince of the House of David.

In Hezekiah's time, there had been an Egyptian and an Assyrian party at the court of Judah; the recent supremacy of Egypt had probably increased the number of her partisans. Assyria had disappeared, but her former adherents would retain their antipathy to Egypt, and their personal feuds with Jews of the opposite faction; they were as tools lying ready to any hand that cared to use them. When Babylon succeeded Assyria in the overlordship of Asia, she doubtless inherited the allegiance of the anti-Egyptian party in the various Syrian states. Jeremiah, like Isaiah, steadily opposed any dependence upon Egypt; it was probably by his advice that Josiah undertook his ill-fated expedition against Pharaoh Necho. The partisans of Egypt would be the prophet's enemies; and though Jeremiah never became a mere dependent and agent of Nebuchadnezzar, yet the friends of Babylon would be his friends, if only because her enemies were his enemies.

We are told in 2 Kings xxiii. 37 that Jehoiakim did evil in the sight of Jehovah according to all that his father had done. Whatever other sins may be implied by this condemnation, we certainly learn that the king favoured a corrupt form of the religion of Jehovah in opposition to the purer teaching which Jeremiah inherited from Isaiah.

When we turn to Jeremiah himself, the date "the fourth year of Jehoiakim" reminds us that by this time the prophet could look back upon a long and sad experience; he had been called in the thirteenth year of Josiah, some twenty-four years before. With what sometimes seems to our limited intelligence the strange irony of Providence, this lover of peace and quietness was called to deliver a message of ruin and condemnation, a message that could not fail to be extremely offensive to most of his hearers, and to make him the object of bitter hostility.

Much of this Jeremiah must have anticipated, but there were some from whose position and character the prophet expected acceptance, even of the most unpalatable teaching of the Spirit of Jehovah. The personal vindictiveness with which priests and prophets repaid his loyalty to the Divine mission and his zeal for truth came to him with a shock of surprise and bewilderment, which was all the greater because his most determined persecutors were his sacerdotal kinsmen and neighbours at Anathoth. "Let us destroy the tree," they said, "with the fruit thereof, and let us cut him off from the land of the living, that his name may be no more remembered." *

He was not only repudiated by his clan, but

Cf. Preface.

† We know little of Nebuchadnezzar's campaigns. In 2 Kings xxiv. 1 we are told that Nebuchadnezzar "came up" in the days of Jehoiakim, and Jehoiakim became his servant three years. It is not clear whether Nebuchadnezzar "came up" immediately after the battle of Carchemish, or at a later time after his return to Babylon. In either case the impression made by his hasty departure from Syria would be the same. *Cf.* Cheyne, "Jeremiah" (Men of the Bible), p. 132. I call the Chaldean king Nebuchadnezzar—not Nebuchadrezzar—because the former has been an English household word for centuries.

* xi. 19.

also forbidden by Jehovah to seek consolation and sympathy in the closer ties of family life: "Thou shalt not take a wife, thou shalt have no sons or daughters." * Like Paul, it was good for Jeremiah "by reason of the present distress" to deny himself these blessings. He found some compensation in the fellowship of kindred souls at Jerusalem. We can well believe that, in those early days, he was acquainted with Zephaniah, and that they were associated with Hilkiah and Shaphan and King Josiah in the publication of Deuteronomy and its recognition as the law of Israel. Later on Shaphan's son Ahikam protected Jeremiah when his life was in imminent danger.

The twelve years that intervened between Josiah's Reformation and his defeat at Megiddo were the happiest part of Jeremiah's ministry. It is not certain that any of the extant prophecies belong to this period. With Josiah on the throne and Deuteronomy accepted as the standard of the national life, the prophet felt absolved for a season from his mission to pluck up and break down, and perhaps began to indulge in hopes that the time had come to build and to plant. Yet it is difficult to believe that he had implicit confidence in the permanence of the Reformation or the influence of Deuteronomy. The silence of Isaiah and Jeremiah as to the ecclesiastical reforms of Hezekiah and Josiah stands in glaring contrast to the great importance attached to them by the Books of Kings and Chronicles. But, in any case, Jeremiah must have found life brighter and easier than in the reigns that followed. Probably, in these happier days, he was encouraged by the sympathy and devotion of disciples like Baruch and Ezekiel.

But Josiah's attempt to realise a Kingdom of God was short-lived; and, in a few months, Jeremiah saw the whole fabric swept away The king was defeated and slain; and his religious policy was at once reversed either by a popular revolution or a court intrigue. The people of the land made Josiah's son Shallum king, under the name of Jehoahaz. This young prince of twenty-three only reigned three months, and was then deposed and carried into captivity by Pharaoh Necho; yet it is recorded of him, that he did evil in the sight of Jehovah, according to all that his fathers had done.† He—or, more probably, his ministers, especially the queen-mother ‡ must have been in a hurry to undo Josiah's work. Jeremiah utters no condemnation of Jehoahaz; he merely declares that the young king will never return from his exile, and bids the people lament over his captivity as a more grievous fate than the death of Josiah:—

"Weep not for the dead,
Neither lament over him:
But weep sore for him that goeth into captivity;
For he shall return no more,
Neither shall he behold his native land." §

Ezekiel adds admiration to sympathy: Jehoahaz was a young lion skilled to catch the prey, he devoured men, the nations heard of him, he was taken in their pit, and they brought him with hooks into the land of Egypt.|| Jeremiah and Ezekiel could not but feel some tenderness towards the son of Josiah: and probably they had faith in his personal character, and believed that in time he would shake off the yoke of evil counsellors and follow in his father's footsteps. But any such hopes were promptly disappointed by Pharaoh Necho, and Jeremiah's spirits bowed beneath a new burden as he saw his country completely subservient to the dreaded influence of Egypt.

Thus, at the time when we take up the narrative, the government was in the hands of the party hostile to Jeremiah, and the king, Jehoiakim, seems to have been his personal enemy. Jeremiah himself was somewhere between forty and fifty years old, a solitary man without wife or child. His awful mission as the herald of ruin clouded his spirit with inevitable gloom. Men resented the stern sadness of his words and looks, and turned from him with aversion and dislike. His unpopularity had made him somewhat harsh; for intolerance is twice curst, in that it inoculates its victims with the virus of its own bitterness. His hopes and illusions lay behind him; he could only watch with melancholy pity the eager excitement of these stirring times. If he came across some group busily discussing the rout of the Egyptians at Carchemish, or the report that Nebuchadnezzar was posting in hot haste to Babylon, and wondering as to all that this might mean for Judah, his countrymen would turn to look with contemptuous curiosity at the bitter, disappointed man who had had his chance and failed, and now grudged them their prospect of renewed happiness and prosperity. Nevertheless Jeremiah's greatest work still lay before him. Jerusalem was past saving; but more was at stake than the existence of Judah and its capital. But for Jeremiah the religion of Jehovah might have perished with His Chosen People. It was his mission to save Revelation from the wreck of Israel. Humanly speaking, the religious future of the world depended upon this stern solitary prophet.

CHAPTER II.

A TRIAL FOR HERESY.

JEREMIAH xxvi.: *cf.* vii.-x.

"When Jeremiah had made an end of speaking all that Jehovah had commanded him to speak unto all the people, the priests and the prophets and all the people laid hold on him, saying, Thou shalt surely die."—JER. xxvi. 8.

THE date of this incident is given, somewhat vaguely, as the beginning of the reign of Jehoiakim. It was, therefore, earlier than B. C. 605, the point reached in the previous chapter. Jeremiah could offer no political resistance to Jehoiakim and his Egyptian suzerain; yet it was impossible for him to allow Josiah's policy to be reversed without a protest. Moreover, something, perhaps much, might yet be saved for Jehovah. The king, with his court and prophets and priests, was not everything. Jeremiah was only concerned with sanctuaries, ritual, and priesthoods as means to an end. For him the most important result of the work he had shared with Josiah was a pure and holy life for the nation and individuals. Renan—in some passages, for he is not always consistent—is inclined to minimise the significance of the change from Josiah to Jehoiakim; in fact, he writes very much as a cavalier might have done of the change from Cromwell to Charles II. Both the Jewish kings worshipped Jehovah, each in his own fashion:

* xvi. 2. † 2 Kings xxiii. 30–32. ‡ *Cf.* xxii. 26.
§ xxii. 10-12. || Ezek. xix. 3, 4.

Josiah was inclined to a narrow puritan severity of life; Jehoiakim was a liberal, practical man of the world. Probably this is a fair modern equivalent of the current estimate of the kings and their policy, especially on the part of Jehoiakim's friends; but then, as unhappily still in some quarters, "narrow puritan severity" was a convenient designation for a decent and honourable life, for a scrupulous and self-denying care for the welfare of others. Jeremiah dreaded a relapse into the old half-heathen ideas that Jehovah would be pleased with homage and service that satisfied Baal, Moloch, and Chemosh. Such a relapse would lower the ethical standard, and corrupt or even destroy any beginnings of spiritual life. Our English Restoration is an object-lesson as to the immoral effects of political and ecclesiastical reaction; if such things were done in sober England, what must have been possible to hot Eastern blood! In protesting against the attitude of Jehoiakim, Jeremiah would also seek to save the people from the evil effects of the king's policy. He knew from his own experience that a subject might trust and serve God with his whole heart, even when the king was false to Jehovah. What was possible for him was possible for others. He understood his countrymen too well to expect that the nation would continue to advance in paths of righteousness which its leaders and teachers had forsaken; but, scattered here and there through the mass of the people, was Isaiah's remnant, the seed of the New Israel, men and women to whom the Revelation of Jehovah had been the beginning of a higher life. He would not leave them without a word of counsel and encouragement.

At the command of Jehovah, Jeremiah appeared before the concourse of Jews, assembled at the Temple for some great fast or festival. No feast is expressly mentioned, but he is charged to address "all the cities of Judah"; * *all* the outlying population would only meet at the Temple on some specially holy day. Such an occasion would naturally be chosen by Jeremiah for his deliverance, just as Christ availed Himself of the opportunities offered by the Passover and the Feast of Tabernacles, just as modern philanthropists seek to find a place for their favourite topics on the platform of May Meetings.

The prophet was to stand in the court of the Temple and repeat once more to the Jews his message of warning and judgment, "all that I have charged thee to speak unto them, thou shalt not keep back a single word." The substance of this address is found in the various prophecies which expose the sin and predict the ruin of Judah. They have been dealt with in the Prophecies of Jeremiah,† and are also referred to in Book III. under our present head.

According to the universal principle of Hebrew prophecy, the predictions of ruin were conditional; they were still coupled with the offer of pardon to repentance, and Jehovah did not forbid his prophet to cherish a lingering hope that "perchance they may hearken and turn every one from his evil way, so that I may repent Me of the evil I purpose to inflict upon them because of the evil of their doings." Probably the phrase "every one from his evil way" is primarily collective rather than individual, and is intended to describe a national reformation, which would embrace all the individual citizens; but the actual words suggest another truth, which must also have been in Jeremiah's mind. The nation is, after all, an aggregate of men and women; there can be no national reformation except through the repentance and amendment of individuals.

Jeremiah's audience, it must be observed, consisted of worshippers on the way to the Temple, and would correspond to an ordinary congregation of churchgoers, rather than to the casual crowd gathered round a street preacher, or to the throngs of miners and labourers who listened to Whitefield and Wesley. As an acknowledged prophet, he was well within his rights in expecting a hearer from the attendants at the feast, and men would be curious to see and hear one who had been the dominant influence in Judah during the reign of Josiah. Moreover, in the absence of evening newspapers and shop-windows, a prophet was too exciting a distraction to be lightly neglected. From Jehovah's charge to speak all that He had commanded him to speak and not to keep back a word, we may assume that Jeremiah's discourse was long: it was also avowedly an old sermon; * most of his audience had heard it before, all of them were quite familiar with its main topics. They listened in the various moods of a modern congregation "sitting under" a distinguished preacher. Jeremiah's friends and disciples welcomed the ideas and phrases that had become part of their spiritual life. Many enjoyed the speaker's earnestness and eloquence, without troubling themselves about the ideas at all. There was nothing specially startling about the well-known threats and warnings; they had become

> "A tale of little meaning tho' the words were strong."

Men hardened their hearts against inspired prophets as easily as they do against the most pathetic appeals of modern evangelists. Mingled with the crowd were Jeremiah's professional rivals, who detested both him and his teaching—priests who regarded him as a traitor to his own caste, prophets who envied his superior gifts and his force of passionate feeling. To these almost every word he uttered was offensive, but for a while there was nothing that roused them to very vehement anger. He was allowed to finish what he had to say, "to make an end of speaking all that Jehovah had commanded him." But in this peroration he had insisted on a subject that stung the indifferent into resentment and roused the priests and prophets to fury.

"Go ye now unto My place which was in Shiloh, where I caused My name to dwell at the first, and see what I did to it for the wickedness of My people Israel. And now, because ye have done all these works, saith Jehovah, and I spake unto you, rising up early and speaking, but ye heard not; and I called you, but ye answered not: therefore will I do unto the house, that is called by My name, wherein ye trust, and unto the place which I gave to you and to your fathers, as I have done to Shiloh."†

* The expression is curious; it usually means all the cities of Judah, except Jerusalem; the LXX. reading varies between "all the Jews" and "all Judah."

† See especially the exposition of chaps. vii.–x., which are often supposed to be a reproduction of Jeremiah's utterance on this occasion.

* The Hebrew apparently implies that the discourse was a repetition of former prophecies.

† vii. 12–14. Even if chaps. vii.–x. are not a report of Jeremiah's discourse on this occasion, the few lines in xxvi. are evidently a mere summary, and vii. will best

The Ephraimite sanctuary of Shiloh, long the home of the Ark and its priesthood, had been overthrown in some national catastrophe. Apparently when it was destroyed it was no mere tent, but a substantial building of stone, and its ruins remained as a permanent monument of the fugitive glory of even the most sacred shrine.

The very presence of his audience in the place where they were met showed their reverence for the Temple: the priests were naturally devotees of their own shrine; of the prophets Jeremiah himself had said, "The prophets prophesy falsely, and the priests rule in accordance with their teaching." * Can we wonder that "the priests and the prophets and all the people laid hold on him, saying, Thou shalt surely die"? For the moment there was an appearance of religious unity in Jerusalem; the priests, the prophets, and the pious laity on one side, and only the solitary heretic on the other. It was, though on a small scale, as if the obnoxious teaching of some nineteenth-century prophet of God had given an unexpected stimulus to the movement for Christian reunion; as if cardinals and bishops, chairmen of unions, presidents of conferences, moderators of assemblies, with great preachers and distinguished laymen, united to hold monster meetings and denounce the Divine message as heresy and blasphemy. In like manner Pharisees, Sadducees, and Herodians found a basis of common action in their hatred of Christ, and Pilate and Herod were reconciled by His cross.

Meanwhile the crowd was increasing; new worshippers were arriving, and others as they left the Temple were attracted to the scene of the disturbance. Doubtless too the mob, always at the service of persecutors, hurried up in hope of finding opportunities for mischief and violence. Some six and a half centuries later, history repeated itself on the same spot, when the Asiatic Jews saw Paul in the Temple and "laid hands on him, crying out, Men of Israel, help: This is the man, that teacheth all men everywhere against the people and the law and this place, . . . and all the city was moved, and the people ran together and laid hold on Paul." †

Our narrative, as it stands, is apparently incomplete: we find Jeremiah before the tribunal of the princes, but we are not told how he came there; whether the civil authorities intervened to protect him, as Claudius Lysias came down with his soldiers and centurions and rescued Paul, or whether Jeremiah's enemies observed legal forms, as Annas and Caiaphas did when they arrested Christ. But, in any case, "the princes of Judah, when they heard these things, came up from the palace into the Temple, and took their seats as judges at the entry of the new gate of the Temple." The "princes of Judah" play a conspicuous part in the last period of the Jewish monarchy: we have little definite information about them, and are left to conjecture that they were an aristocratic oligarchy or an official clique, or both; but it is clear that they were a dominant force in the state, with recognised constitutional status, and that they often controlled the king himself. We are also ignorant as to the "new gate"; it may possibly be the upper gate built by Jotham * about a hundred and fifty years earlier.

indicate the substance of his utterance. The verses quoted occur towards the beginning of vii.-x., but from the emphatic reference to Shiloh in the brief abstract in xxvi., Jeremiah must have dwelt on this topic, and the fact that the outburst followed his conclusion suggests that he reserved this subject for his peroration.

* v. 31.

† Acts xxi. 27-30.

Before these judges, Jeremiah's ecclesiastical accusers brought a formal charge; they said, almost in the very words which the high priest and the Sanhedrin used of Christ, "This man is worthy of death, for he hath prophesied against this city, as ye have heard with your ears"—*i. e.*, when he said, "This house shall be like Shiloh, and this city shall be desolate without inhabitant." Such accusations have been always on the lips of those who have denounced Christ and His disciples as heretics. One charge against Himself was that He said, "I will destroy this Temple that is made with hands, and in three days I will build another that is made without hands." † Stephen was accused of speaking incessantly against the Temple and the Law, and teaching that Jesus of Nazareth would destroy the Temple and change the customs handed down from Moses. When he asserted that "the Most High dwelleth not in temples made with hands," the impatience of his audience compelled him to bring his defence to an abrupt conclusion.‡ Of Paul we have already spoken.

How was it that these priests and prophets thought that their princes might be induced to condemn Jeremiah to death for predicting the destruction of the Temple? A prophet would not run much risk nowadays by announcing that St. Paul's should be made like Stonehenge, or St. Peter's like the Parthenon. Expositors of Daniel and the Apocalypse habitually fix the end of the world a few years in advance of the date at which they write, and yet they do not incur any appreciable unpopularity. It is true that Jeremiah's accusers were a little afraid that his predictions might be fulfilled, and the most bitter persecutors are those who have a lurking dread that their victims are right, while they themselves are wrong. But such fears could not very well be evidence or argument against Jeremiah before any court of law.

In order to realise the situation we must consider the place which the Temple held in the hopes and affections of the Jews. They had always been proud of their royal sanctuary at Jerusalem, but within the last hundred and fifty years it had acquired a unique importance for the religion of Israel. First Hezekiah, and then Josiah, had taken away the other high places and altars at which Jehovah was worshipped, and had said to Judah and Jerusalem, "Ye shall worship before this altar." § Doubtless the kings were following the advice of Isaiah and Jeremiah. These prophets were anxious to abolish the abuses of the local sanctuaries, which were a continual incentive to an extravagant and corrupt ritual. Yet they did not intend to assign any supreme importance to a priestly caste or a consecrated building. Certainly for them the hope of Israel and the assurance of its salvation did not consist in cedar and hewn stones, in silver and gold. And yet the unique position given to the Temple inevitably became the starting-point for fresh superstition. Once Jehovah could be worshipped not only at Jerusalem, but at Beersheba and Bethel and many other places where He had chosen to set His name. Even then, it was felt that the Divine Presence must

* 2 Kings xv. 35.

† Mark xiv. 58.

‡ Acts vi. 13, 14, vii. 48.

§ 2 Kings xviii. 4, xxiii.; Isa. xxxvi. 7.

afford some protection for His dwelling-places. But now that Jehovah dwelt nowhere else but at Jerusalem, and only accepted the worship of His people at this single shrine, how could any one doubt that He would protect His Temple and His Holy City against all enemies, even the most formidable? Had He not done so already?

When Hezekiah abolished the high places, did not Jehovah set the seal of approval upon his policy by destroying the army of Sennacherib? Was not this great deliverance wrought to guard the Temple against desecration and destruction, and would not Jehovah work out a like salvation in any future time of danger? The destruction of Sennacherib was essential to the religious future of Israel and of mankind; but it had a very mingled influence upon the generations immediately following. They were like a man who has won a great prize in a lottery, or who has, quite unexpectedly, come into an immense inheritance. They ignored the unwelcome thought that the Divine protection depended on spiritual and moral conditions, and they clung to the superstitious faith that at any moment, even in the last extremity of danger and at the eleventh hour, Jehovah might, nay, even *must*, intervene. The priests and the inhabitants of Jerusalem could look on with comparative composure while the country was ravaged, and the outlying towns were taken and pillaged; Jerusalem itself might seem on the verge of falling into the hands of the enemy, but they still trusted in their Palladium. Jerusalem could not perish, because it contained the one sanctuary of Jehovah; they sought to silence their own fears and to drown the warning voice of the prophet by vociferating their watchword: "The Temple of Jehovah! the Temple of Jehovah! The Temple of Jehovah is in our midst!" *

In prosperous times a nation may forget its Palladium, and may tolerate doubts as to its efficacy; but the strength of the Jews was broken, their resources were exhausted, and they were clinging in an agony of conflicting hopes and fears to their faith in the inviolability of the Temple. To destroy their confidence was like snatching away a plank from a drowning man. When Jeremiah made the attempt, they struck back with the fierce energy of despair. It does not seem that at this time the city was in any immediate danger; the incident rather falls in the period of quiet submission to Pharaoh Necho that preceded the battle of Carchemish. But the disaster of Megiddo was fresh in men's memories, and in the unsettled state of Eastern Asia no one knew how soon some other invader might advance against the city. On the other hand, in the quiet interval, hopes began to revive, and men were incensed when the prophet made haste to nip these hopes in the bud, all the more so because their excited anticipations of future glory had so little solid basis. Jeremiah's appeal to the ill-omened precedent of Shiloh naturally roused the sanguine and despondent alike into frenzy.

Jeremiah's defence was simple and direct: "Jehovah sent me to prophesy all that ye have heard against this house and against this city. Now therefore amend your ways and your doings, and hearken unto the voice of Jehovah your God, that He may repent Him of the evil that He hath spoken against you. As for me, behold, I am in your hands: do unto me as it seems good and right unto you. Only know assuredly that, if ye put me to death, ye will bring the guilt of innocent blood upon yourselves, and upon this city and its inhabitants: for of a truth Jehovah sent me unto you to speak all these words in your ears." There is one curious feature in this defence. Jeremiah contemplates the possibility of two distinct acts of wickedness on the part of his persecutors: they may turn a deaf ear to his appeal that they should repent and reform, and their obstinacy will incur all the chastisements which Jeremiah had threatened; they may also put him to death and incur additional guilt. Scoffers might reply that his previous threats were so awful and comprehensive that they left no room for any addition to the punishment of the impenitent. Sinners sometimes find a grim comfort in the depth of their wickedness; their case is so bad that it cannot be made worse, they may now indulge their evil propensities with a kind of impunity. But Jeremiah's prophetic insight made him anxious to save his countrymen from further sin, even in their impenitence; the Divine discrimination is not taxed beyond its capabilities even by the extremity of human wickedness.

But to return to the main feature in Jeremiah's defence. His accusers' contention was that his teaching was so utterly blasphemous, so entirely opposed to every tradition and principle of true religion—or, as we should say, so much at variance with all orthodoxy—that it could not be a word of Jehovah. Jeremiah does not attempt to discuss the relation of his teaching to the possible limits of Jewish orthodoxy. He bases his defence on the bare assertion of his prophetic mission—Jehovah had sent him. He assumes that there is no room for evidence or discussion; it is a question of the relative authority of Jeremiah and his accusers, whether he or they had the better right to speak for God. The immediate result seemed to justify him in this attitude. He was no obscure novice, seeking for the first time to establish his right to speak in the Divine name. The princes and people had been accustomed for twenty years to listen to him, as to the most fully acknowledged mouthpiece of Heaven; they could not shake off their accustomed feeling of deference, and once more succumbed to the spell of his fervid and commanding personality. "Then said the princes and all the people unto the priests and the prophets, This man is not worthy of death; for he hath spoken to us in the name of Jehovah our God." For the moment the people were won over and the princes convinced; but priests and prophets were not so easily influenced by inspired utterances: some of these probably thought that they had an inspiration of their own, and their professional experience made them callous.

At this point again the sequence of events is not clear; possibly the account was compiled from the imperfect recollections of more than one of the spectators. The pronouncement of the princes and the people seems, at first sight, a formal acquittal that should have ended the trial, and left no room for the subsequent intervention of "certain of the elders," otherwise the trial seems to have come to no definite conclusion and the incident simply terminated in the personal protection given to Jeremiah by Ahikam ben Shaphan. Possibly, however, the tribunal of the princes was not governed by any

* vii. 4.

strict rules of procedure; and the force of the argument used by the elders does not depend on the exact stage of the trial at which it was introduced.

Either Jeremiah was not entirely successful in his attempt to get the matter disposed of on the sole ground of his own prophetic authority, or else the elders were anxious to secure weight and finality for the acquittal, by bringing forward arguments in its support. The elders were an ancient Israelite institution, and probably still represented the patriarchal side of the national life; nothing is said as to their relation to the princes, and this might not be very clearly defined. The elders appealed, by way of precedent, to an otherwise unrecorded incident of the reign of Hezekiah. Micah the Morasthite had uttered similar threats against Jerusalem and the Temple: "Zion shall be ploughed as a field, and Jerusalem shall become heaps, and the mountain of the house as the high places of the forest." * But Hezekiah and his people, instead of slaying Micah, had repented, and the city had been spared. They evidently wished that the precedent could be wholly followed in the present instance; but, at any rate, it was clear that one of the most honoured and successful of the kings of Judah had accepted a threat against the Temple as a message from Jehovah. Therefore the mere fact that Jeremiah had uttered such a threat was certainly not *primâ facie* evidence that he was a false prophet. We are not told how this argument was received, but the writer of the chapter, possibly Baruch, does not attribute Jeremiah's escape either to his acquittal by the princes or to the reasoning of the elders. The people apparently changed sides once more, like the common people in the New Testament, who heard Christ gladly and with equal enthusiasm clamoured for His crucifixion. At the end of the chapter we find them eager to have the prophet delivered into their hands that they may put him to death. Apparently the prophets and priests, having brought matters into this satisfactory position, had retired from the scene of action; the heretic was to be delivered over to the secular arm. The princes, like Pilate, seemed inclined to yield to popular pressure; but Ahikam, a son of the Shaphan who had to do with the finding of Deuteronomy, stood by Jeremiah, as John of Gaunt stood by Wyclif, and the Protestant Princes by Luther, and the magistrates of Geneva by Calvin; and Jeremiah could say with the Psalmist:—

"I have heard the defaming of many,
Terror on every side:
While they took counsel together against me,
They devised to take away my life.
But I trusted in Thee, O Jehovah:
I said, Thou art my God.
My times are in Thy hand:
Deliver me from the hand of mine enemies, and from them that persecute me.

. . . . . .

Let the lying lips be dumb,
Which speak against the righteous insolently.
With pride and contempt.
Oh, how great is Thy goodness, which Thou hast laid up for them that fear Thee,
Which Thou hast wrought for them that put their trust in Thee, before the sons of men." †

* Micah iii. 12. As the quotation exactly agrees with the verse in our extant Book of Micah, we may suppose that the elders were acquainted with his prophecies in writing.

† Psalm xxxi. 13–15, 18, 19. The Psalm is sometimes ascribed to Jeremiah, because it can be so readily applied to this incident. The reader will recognise his characteristic phrase "Terror on every side" (Magor-missabib).

We have here an early and rudimentary example of religious toleration, of the willingness, however reluctant, to hear as a possible Divine message unpalatable teaching, at variance with current theology; we see too the fountain-head of that freedom which since has "broadened down from precedent to precedent."

But unfortunately no precedent can bind succeeding generations, and both Judaism and Christianity have sinned grievously against the lesson of this chapter. Jehoiakim himself soon broke through the feeble restraint of this new-born tolerance. The writer adds an incident that must have happened somewhat later,* to show how real was Jeremiah's danger, and how transient was the liberal mood of the authorities. A certain Uriah ben Shemaiah of Kirjath Jearim had the courage to follow in Jeremiah's footsteps and speak against the city "according to all that Jeremiah had said." With the usual meanness of persecutors, Jehoiakim and his captains and princes vented upon this obscure prophet the ill-will which they had not dared to indulge in the case of Jeremiah, with his commanding personality and influential friends. Uriah fled into Egypt, but was brought back and slain, and his body cast out unburied into the common cemetery. We can understand Jeremiah's fierce and bitter indignation against the city where such things were possible.

This chapter is so full of suggestive teaching that we can only touch upon two or three of its more obvious lessons. The dogma which shaped the charge against Jeremiah and caused the martyrdom of Uriah was the inviolability of the Temple and the Holy City. This dogma was a perversion of the teaching of Isaiah, and especially of Jeremiah himself,† which assigned a unique position to the Temple in the religion of Israel. The carnal man shows a fatal ingenuity in sucking poison out of the most wholesome truth. He is always eager to discover that something external, material, physical, concrete—some building, organisation, ceremony, or form of words—is a fundamental basis of the faith and essential to salvation. If Jeremiah had died with Josiah, the "priests and prophets" would doubtless have quoted his authority against Uriah. The teaching of Christ and His apostles, of Luther and Calvin and their fellow-reformers, has often been twisted and forged into weapons to be used against their true followers. We are often tempted in the interest of our favourite views to lay undue stress on secondary and accidental statements of great teachers. We fail to keep the due proportion of truth which they themselves observed, and in applying their precepts to new problems we sacrifice the kernel and save the husk. The warning of Jeremiah's persecutors might often "give us pause." We need not be surprised at finding priests and prophets eager and interested champions of a perversion of revealed truth. Ecclesiastical office does not necessarily confer any inspiration from above. The hereditary priest follows the traditions of his caste, and even the prophet may become the mouthpiece of the passions and prejudices of

* This incident cannot be part of the speech of the elders; it would only have told against the point they were trying to make. The various phases—prophecy, persecution, flight, capture, and execution—must have taken some time, and can scarcely have preceded Jeremiah's utterance "at the beginning of the reign of King Jehoiakim."

† Assuming his sympathy with Deuteronomy.

those who accept and applaud him. When men will not endure sound doctrine, they heap to themselves teachers after their own lusts; having itching ears, they turn away their ears from the truth and turn unto fables.* Jeremiah's experience shows that even an apparent consensus of clerical opinion is not always to be trusted. The history of councils and synods is stained by many foul and shameful blots; it was the Œcumenical Council at Constance that burnt Huss, and most Churches have found themselves, at some time or other, engaged in building the tombs of the prophets whom their own officials had stoned in days gone by. We forget that "Athanasius contra mundum" implies also "Athanasius contra ecclesiam."

CHAPTER III.

THE ROLL.

JEREMIAH xxxvi.

"Take thee a roll of a book, and write therein all the words that I have spoken unto thee."—JER. xxxvi. 2.

THE incidents which form so large a proportion of the contents of our book do not make up a connected narrative; they are merely a series of detached pictures: we can only conjecture the doings and experiences of Jeremiah during the intervals. Chapter xxvi. leaves him still exposed to the persistent hostility of the priests and prophets, who had apparently succeeded in once more directing popular feeling against their antagonist. At the same time, though the princes were not ill-disposed towards him, they were not inclined to resist the strong pressure brought to bear upon them. Probably the attitude of the populace varied from time to time, according to the presence among them of the friends or enemies of the prophet; and, in the same way, we cannot think of "the princes" as a united body, governed by a single impulse. The action of this group of notables might be determined by the accidental preponderance of one or other of two opposing parties. Jeremiah's only real assurance of safety lay in the personal protection extended to him by Ahikam ben Shaphan. Doubtless other princes associated themselves with Ahikam in his friendly action on behalf of the prophet.

Under these circumstances, Jeremiah would find it necessary to restrict his activity. Utter indifference to danger was one of the most ordinary characteristics of Hebrew prophets, and Jeremiah was certainly not wanting in the desperate courage which may be found in any Mohammedan dervish. At the same time he was far too practical, too free from morbid self-consciousness, to court martyrdom for its own sake. If he had presented himself again in the Temple when it was crowded with worshippers, his life might have been taken in a popular tumult, while his mission was still only half accomplished. Possibly his priestly enemies had found means to exclude him from the sacred precincts.

Man's extremity was God's opportunity; this temporary and partial silencing of Jeremiah led to a new departure, which made the influence of his teaching more extensive and permanent. He was commanded to commit his prophecies to writing. The restriction of his active ministry was to bear rich fruit, like Paul's imprisonment, and Athanasius' exile, and Luther's sojourn in the Wartburg. A short time since there was great danger that Jeremiah and the Divine message entrusted to him would perish together. He did not know how soon he might become once more the mark of popular fury, nor whether Ahikam would still be able to protect him. The roll of the book could speak even if he were put to death.

But Jeremiah was not thinking chiefly about what would become of his teaching if he himself perished. He had an immediate and particular end in view. His tenacious persistence was not to be baffled by the prospect of mob violence, or by exclusion from the most favourable vantage-ground. Renan is fond of comparing the prophets to modern journalists; and this incident is an early and striking instance of the substitution of pen, ink, and paper for the orator's tribune. Perhaps the closest modern parallel is that of the speaker who is howled down at a public meeting and hands his manuscript to the reporters.

In the record of the Divine command to Jeremiah, there is no express statement as to what was to be done with the roll; but as the object of writing it was that "perchance the house of Judah might hear and repent," it is evident that from the first it was intended to be read to the people.

There is considerable difference of opinion* as to the contents of the roll. They are described as: "All that I have spoken unto thee concerning† Jerusalem‡ and Judah, and all the nations, since I (first) spake unto thee, from the time of Josiah until now." At first sight this would seem to include all previous utterances, and therefore all the extant prophecies of a date earlier than B. C. 605, *i. e.*, those contained in chapters i.-xii. and some portions of xiv.-xx. (we cannot determine which with any exactness), and probably most of those dated in the fourth year of Jehoiakim, *i. e.*, xxv. and parts of xlv.-xlix. Cheyne,§ however, holds that the roll simply contained the striking and comprehensive prophecy in chapter xxv. The whole series of chapters might very well be described as dealing with Jerusalem, Judah, and the nations; but at the same time xxv. might be considered equivalent, by way of summary, to all that had been spoken on these subjects. From various considerations which will appear as we proceed with the narrative, it seems probable that the larger estimate is the more correct, *i. e.*, that the roll contained a large fraction of our Book of Jeremiah, and not merely one or two chapters. We need not, however, suppose that every previous utterance of the prophet, even though still extant, must have been included in the roll; the "all" would of course be understood to be conditioned by relevancy; and the narratives of various incidents are obviously not part of what Jehovah had spoken.

Jeremiah dictated his prophecies, as St. Paul did his epistles, to an amanuensis; he called his disciple Baruch‖ ben Neriah, and dictated to

* 2 Tim. iv. 3.

* See Cheyne, Giesebrecht, Orelli, etc.

† R. V. "against." The Hebrew is ambiguous.

‡ So Septuagint. The Hebrew text has Israel, which is a less accurate description of the prophecies, and is less relevant to this particular occasion.

§ "Jeremiah" (Men of the Bible), p. 132.

‖ *Cf.* chap. v. on "Baruch."

him "all that Jehovah had spoken, upon a book, in the form of a roll."

It seems clear that, as in xxvi., the narrative does not exactly follow the order of events,* and that verse 9, which records the proclamation of a fast in the ninth month of Jehoiakim's fifth year, should be read before verse 5, which begins the account of the circumstances leading up to the actual reading of the roll. We are not told in what month of Jehoiakim's fourth year Jeremiah received this command to write his prophecies in a roll, but as they were not read till the ninth month of the fifth year, there must have been an interval of at least ten months or a year between the Divine command and the reading by Baruch. We can scarcely suppose that all or nearly all this delay was caused by Jeremiah and Baruch's waiting for a suitable occasion. The long interval suggests that the dictation took some time, and that therefore the roll was somewhat voluminous in its contents, and that it was carefully compiled, not without a certain amount of revision.

When the manuscript was ready, its authors had to determine the right time at which to read it; they found their desired opportunity in the fast proclaimed in the ninth month. This was evidently an extraordinary fast, appointed in view of some pressing danger; and, in the year following the battle of Carchemish, this would naturally be the advance of Nebuchadnezzar. As our incident took place in the depth of winter, the months must be reckoned according to the Babylonian year, which began in April; and the ninth month, Kisleu, would roughly correspond to our December. The dreaded invasion would be looked for early in the following spring, "at the time when kings go out to battle."†

Jeremiah does not seem to have absolutely determined from the first that the reading of the roll by Baruch was to be a substitute for his own presence. He had probably hoped that some change for the better in the situation might justify his appearance before a great gathering in the Temple. But when the time came he was "hindered"‡ —we are not told how—and could not go into the Temple. He may have been restrained by his own prudence, or dissuaded by his friends, like Paul when he would have faced the mob in the theatre at Ephesus; the hindrance may have been some ban under which he had been placed by the priesthood, or it may have been some unexpected illness, or legal uncleanness, or some other passing accident, such as Providence often uses to protect its soldiers till their warfare is accomplished.

Accordingly it was Baruch who went up to the Temple. Though he is said to have read the book "in the ears of all the people," he does not seem to have challenged universal attention as openly as Jeremiah had done; he did not stand forth in the court of the Temple,§ but betook himself to the "chamber" of the scribe,‖ or secretary of state, Gemariah ben Shaphan, the brother of Jeremiah's protector Ahikam. This chamber would be one of the cells built round the upper court, from which the "new gate"* led into an inner court of the Temple. Thus Baruch placed himself formally under the protection of the owner of the apartment, and any violence offered to him would have been resented and avenged by this powerful noble with his kinsmen and allies. Jeremiah's disciple and representative took his seat at the door of the chamber, and, in full view of the crowds who passed and repassed through the new gate, opened his roll and began to read aloud from its contents. His reading was yet another repetition of the exhortations, warnings, and threats which Jeremiah had rehearsed on the feast day when he spake to the people "all that Jehovah had commanded him"; and still both Jehovah and His prophet promised deliverance as the reward of repentance. Evidently the head and front of the nation's offence had been no open desertion of Jehovah for idols, else His servants would not have selected for their audience His enthusiastic worshippers as they thronged to His Temple. The fast itself might have seemed a token of penitence, but it was not accepted by Jeremiah, or put forward by the people, as a reason why the prophecies of ruin should not be fulfilled. No one offers the very natural plea: "In this fast we are humbling ourselves under the mighty hand of God, we are confessing our sins, and consecrating ourselves afresh to service of Jehovah. What more does He expect of us? Why does He still withhold His mercy and forgiveness? Wherefore have we fasted, and Thou seest not? Wherefore have we afflicted our soul, and Thou takest no knowledge?" Such a plea would probably have received an answer similar to that given by one of Jeremiah's successors: "Behold, in the day of your fast ye find your own pleasure, and oppress all your labourers. Behold, ye fast for strife and contention, and to smite with the fist of wickedness: ye fast not this day so as to make your voice to be heard on high. Is such the fast that I have chosen? the day for a man to afflict his soul? Is it to bow down his head as a rush, and to spread sackcloth and ashes under him? wilt thou call this a fast, and a day acceptable to Jehovah?

"Is not this the fast that I have chosen? to loose the bonds of wickedness, to undo the bands of the yoke, and to let the oppressed go free, and that ye break every yoke? Is it not to deal thy bread to the hungry, and that thou bring the poor that are cast out to thy house? when thou seest the naked, that thou cover him; and that thou hide not thyself from thine own flesh? Then shall thy light break forth as the morning, and thy healing shall spring forth speedily: and thy righteousness shall go before thee; the glory of Jehovah shall be thy rearward."†

Jeremiah's opponents did not grudge Jehovah His burnt-offerings and calves of a year old; He was welcome to thousands of rams, and ten thousands of rivers of oil. They were even willing to give their firstborn for their transgression, the

* Verses 5-8 seem to be a brief alternative account to 9-26.

† 1 Chron. xx. i.

‡ 'ĀCÛR: A. V., R. V., "shut up"; R. V. margin, "restrained." The term is used in xxxiii. 1, xxxix. 15, in the sense of "imprisoned," but here Jeremiah appears to be at liberty. The phrase 'ĀÇÛR W ĀZÛBH, A. V. "shut up or left" (Deut. xxxii. 36, etc.), has been understood, those under the restraints imposed upon ceremonial uncleanness and those free from these restraints, *i. e.*, everybody; the same meaning has been given to 'ĀÇÛR here.

§ xxvi. 2.

‖ So Cheyne; the Hebrew does not make it clear whether the title "scribe" refers to the father or the son. Giesebrecht understands it of Shaphan, who appears as scribe in 2 Kings xxii. 8. He points out that in verse 20 Elishama is called the scribe, but we cannot assume that the title was limited to a single officer of state.

* *Cf.* xxvi. 10.

† Isa. lviii. 3-8.

fruit of their body for the sin of their soul; but they were not prepared "to do justly, and to love mercy, and to walk humbly with their God."*

We are not told how Jeremiah and the priests and prophets formulated the points at issue between them, which were so thoroughly and universally understood that the record takes them for granted. Possibly Jeremiah contended for the recognition of Deuteronomy, with its lofty ideals of pure religion and a humanitarian order of society. But, in any case, these incidents were an early phase of the age-long struggle of the prophets of God against the popular attempt to make ritual and sensuous emotion into excuses for ignoring morality, and to offer the cheap sacrifice of a few unforbidden pleasures, rather than surrender the greed of gain, the lust of power, and the sweetness of revenge.

When the multitudes caught the sound of Baruch's voice and saw him sitting in the doorway of Gemariah's chamber, they knew exactly what they would hear. To them he was almost as antagonistic as a Protestant evangelist would be to the worshippers at some great Romanist feast; or perhaps we might find a closer parallel in a Low Church bishop addressing a ritualistic audience. For the hearts of these hearers were not steeled by the consciousness of any formal schism. Baruch and the great prophet whom he represented did not stand outside the recognised limits of Divine inspiration. While the priests and prophets and their adherents repudiated his teaching as heretical, they were still haunted by the fear that, at any rate, his threats might have some Divine authority. Apart from all theology, the prophet of evil always finds an ally in the nervous fears and guilty conscience of his hearer.

The feelings of the people would be similar to those with which they had heard the same threats against Judah, the city and the Temple, from Jeremiah himself. But the excitement aroused by the defeat of Pharaoh and the hasty return of Nebuchadnezzar to Babylon had died away. The imminence of a new invasion made it evident that this had not been the Divine deliverance of Judah. The people were cowed by what must have seemed to many the approaching fulfilments of former threatenings; the ritual of a fast was in itself depressing; so that they had little spirit to resent the message of doom. Perhaps too there was less to resent: the prophecies were the same, but Baruch may have been less unpopular than Jeremiah, and his reading would be tame and ineffective compared to the fiery eloquence of his master. Moreover the powerful protection which shielded him was indicated not only by the place he occupied, but also by the presence of Gemariah's son, Micaiah.

The reading passed off without any hostile demonstration on the part of the people, and Micaiah went in search of his father to describe to him the scene he had just witnessed. He found him in the palace, in the chamber of the secretary of state, Elishama, attending a council of the princes. There were present, amongst others, Elnathan ben Achbor, who brought Uriah back from Egypt, Delaiah ben Shemaiah, and Zedekiah ben Hananiah. Micaiah told them what he had heard. They at once sent for Baruch and the roll. Their messenger, Jehudi ben Nethaniah, seems to have been a kind of court-usher. His name signifies "the Jew," and as

* Micah vi. 6–8.

his great-grandfather was Cushi, "the Ethiopian," it has been suggested that he came of a family of Ethiopian descent, which had only attained in his generation to Jewish citizenship.*

When Baruch arrived, the princes greeted him with the courtesy and even deference due to the favourite disciple of a distinguished prophet. They invited him to sit down and read them the roll. Baruch obeyed; the method of reading suited the enclosed room and the quiet, interested audience of responsible men, better than the swaying crowd gathered round the door of Gemariah's chamber. Baruch now had before him ministers of state who knew from their official information and experience how extremely probable it was that the words to which they were listening would find a speedy and complete fulfilment. Baruch must almost have seemed to them like a doomster who announces to a condemned criminal the ghastly details of his coming execution. They exchanged looks of dismay and horror, and when the reading was over, they said to one another,† "We must tell the king of all these words." First, however, they inquired concerning the exact circumstances under which the roll had been written, that they might know how far responsibility in this matter was to be divided between the prophet and his disciple, and also whether all the contents rested upon the full authority of Jeremiah. Baruch assured them that it was simply a case of dictation: Jeremiah had uttered every word with his own mouth, and he had faithfully written it down; everything was Jeremiah's own.‡

The princes were well aware that the prophet's action would probably be resented and punished by Jehoiakim. They said to Baruch: "Do you and Jeremiah go and hide yourselves, and let no one know where you are." They kept the roll and laid it up in Elishama's room; then they went to the king. They found him in his winter room, in the inner court of the palace, sitting in front of a brasier of burning charcoal. On this fast-day the king's mind might well be careful and troubled, as he meditated on the kind of treatment that he, the nominee of Pharaoh Necho, was likely to receive from Nebuchadnezzar. We cannot tell whether he contemplated resistance or had already resolved to submit to the conqueror. In either case he would wish to act on his own initiative, and might be anxious lest a Chaldean party should get the upper hand in Jerusalem and surrender him and the city to the invader.

When the princes entered, their number and their manner would at once indicate to him that their errand was both serious and disagreeable. He seems to have listened in silence while they made their report of the incident at the door of Gemariah's chamber and their own interview with Baruch.§ The king sent for the roll by Jehudi, who had accompanied the princes into the presence chamber; and on his return the same serviceable official read its contents before Jehoiakim and the princes, whose number was now augmented by the nobles in attendance upon the king. Jehudi had had the advantage of hearing Baruch

* So Orelli, *in loco*.

† Hebrew text "to Baruch," which LXX. omits.

‡ In verse 18 the word "with ink" is not in the LXX., and may be an accidental repetition of the similar word for "his mouth."

§ The A. V. and R. V. "all the words" is misleading: it should rather be "everything"; the princes did not recite all the contents of the roll.

read the roll, but ancient Hebrew manuscripts were not easy to decipher, and probably Jehudi stumbled somewhat; altogether the reading of prophecies by a court-usher would not be a very edifying performance, or very gratifying to Jeremiah's friends. Jehoiakim treated the matter with deliberate and ostentatious contempt. At the end of every three or four columns,* he put out his hand for the roll, cut away the portion that had been read, and threw it on the fire; then he handed the remainder back to Jehudi, and the reading was resumed till the king thought fit to repeat the process. It at once appeared that the audience was divided into two parties. When Gemariah's father, Shaphan, had read Deuteronomy to Josiah, the king rent his clothes; but, now the writer tells us, half aghast, that neither Jehoiakim nor any of his servants were afraid or rent their clothes, but the audience, including doubtless both court officials and some of the princes, looked on with calm indifference. Not so the princes who had been present at Baruch's reading: they had probably induced him to leave the roll with them, by promising that it should be kept safely; they had tried to keep it out of the king's hands by leaving it in Elishama's room, and now they made another attempt to save it from destruction. They entreated Jehoiakim to refrain from open and insolent defiance of a prophet who might after all be speaking in the name of Jehovah. But the king persevered. The alternate reading and burning went on; the unfortunate usher's fluency and clearness would not be improved by the extraordinary conditions under which he had to read; and we may well suppose that the concluding columns were hurried over in a somewhat perfunctory fashion, if they were read at all. As soon as the last shred of parchment was shrivelling on the charcoal, Jehoiakim commanded three of his officers † to arrest Jeremiah and Baruch. But they had taken the advice of the princes and were not to be found: "Jehovah hid them."

Thus the career of Baruch's roll was summarily cut short. But it had done its work; it had been read on three separate occasions, first before the people, then before the princes, and last of all before the king and his court. If Jeremiah had appeared in person, he might have been at once arrested, and put to death like Uriah. No doubt this threefold recital was, on the whole, a failure; Jeremiah's party among the princes had listened with anxious deference, but the appeal had been received by the people with indifference and by the king with contempt. Nevertheless it must have strengthened individuals in the true faith, and it had proclaimed afresh that the religion of Jehovah gave no sanction to the policy of Jehoiakim: the ruin of Judah would be a proof of the sovereignty of Jehovah and not of His impotence. But probably this incident had more immediate influence over the king than we might at first sight suppose. When Nebuchadnezzar arrived in Palestine, Jehoiakim submitted to him a policy entirely in accordance with the views of Jeremiah. We may well believe that the experiences of this fast day had strengthened the hands of the prophet's friends, and cooled the enthusiasm of the court for more desperate and adventurous courses. Every year's respite for Judah fostered the growth of the true religion of Jehovah.

The sequel showed how much more prudent it was to risk the existence of a roll rather than the life of a prophet. Jeremiah was only encouraged to persevere. By the Divine command, he dictated his prophecies afresh to Baruch, adding besides unto them many like words. Possibly other copies were made of the whole or parts of this roll, and were secretly circulated, read, and talked about. We are not told whether Jehoiakim ever heard this new roll; but, as one of the many like things added to the older prophecies was a terrible personal condemnation of the king,* we may be sure that he was not allowed to remain in ignorance, at any rate, of this portion of it.

The second roll was, doubtless, one of the main sources of our present Book of Jeremiah, and the narrative of this chapter is of considerable importance for Old Testament criticism. It shows that a prophetic book may not go back to any prophetic autograph at all; its most original sources may be manuscripts written at the prophet's dictation, and liable to all the errors which are apt to creep into the most faithful work of an amanuensis. It shows further that, even when a prophet's utterances were written down during his lifetime, the manuscript may contain only his recollections† of what he said years before, and that these might be either expanded or abbreviated, sometimes even unconsciously modified, in the light of subsequent events. Verse 32 shows that Jeremiah did not hesitate to add to the record of his former prophecies "many like words": there is no reason to suppose that these were all contained in an appendix; they would often take the form of annotations.

The important part played by Baruch as Jeremiah's secretary and representative must have invested him with full authority to speak for his master and expound his views; such authority points to Baruch as the natural editor of our present book, which is virtually the "Life and Writings" of the prophet. The last words of our chapter are ambiguous, perhaps intentionally. They simply state that many like words were added, and do not say by whom; they might even include additions made later on by Baruch from his own reminiscences.

In conclusion, we may notice that both the first and second copies of the roll were written by the direct Divine command, just as in the Hexateuch and the Book of Samuel we read of Moses, Joshua, and Samuel committing certain matters to writing at the bidding of Jehovah. We have here the recognition of the inspiration of the scribe, as ancillary to that of the prophet. Jehovah not only gives His word to His servants, but watches over its preservation and transmission.‡ But there is no inspiration to *write* any new revelation: the spoken word, the consecrated life, are inspired; the book is only a record of inspired speech and action.

* The English tenses "cut," "cast," are ambiguous, but the Hebrew implies that the "cutting" and "casting on the fire" were repeated again and again.

† One is called Jerahmeel the son of Hammelech (A. V.), or "the king's son" (R. V.); if the latter is correct we must understand merely a prince of the blood-royal and not a son of Jehoiakim, who was only thirty.

* For verses 29-31 see chap. vi., where they are dealt with in connection with xxii. 13-19.

† The supposition that Jeremiah had written notes of previous prophecies is not an impossible one, but it is a pure conjecture.

‡ *Cf.* Orelli, *in loco.*

CHAPTER IV.

THE RECHABITES.

JEREMIAH XXXV.

"Jonadab the son of Rechab shall not want a man to stand before Me for ever."—JER. XXXV. 19.

THIS incident is dated "in the days of Jehoiakim." We learn from verse 11 that it happened at a time when the open country of Judah was threatened by the advance of Nebuchadnezzar with a Chaldean and Syrian army. If Nebuchadnezzar marched into the south of Palestine immediately after the battle of Carchemish, the incident may have happened, as some suggest, in the eventful fourth year of Jehoiakim; or if he did not appear in the neighbourhood of Jerusalem till after he had taken over the royal authority at Babylon, Jeremiah's interview with the Rechabites may have followed pretty closely upon the destruction of Baruch's roll. But we need not press the words "Nebuchadnezzar . . . came up into the land"; they may only mean that Judah was invaded by an army acting under his orders. The mention of Chaldeans and Assyrians suggests that this invasion is the same as that mentioned in 2 Kings xxiv. 1, 2, where we are told that Jehoiakim served Nebuchadnezzar three years and then rebelled against him, whereupon Jehovah sent against him bands of Chaldeans, Syrians, Moabites, and Ammonites, and sent them against Judah to destroy it. If this is the invasion referred to in our chapter it falls towards the end of Jehoiakim's reign, and sufficient time had elapsed to allow the king's anger against Jeremiah to cool, so that the prophet could venture out of his hiding-place.

The marauding bands of Chaldeans and their allies had driven the country people in crowds into Jerusalem, and among them the nomad clan of the Rechabites. According to 1 Chron. ii. 55, the Rechabites traced their descent to a certain Hemath, and were a branch of the Kenites, an Edomite tribe dwelling for the most part in the south of Palestine. These Kenites had maintained an ancient and intimate alliance with Judah, and in time the allies virtually became a single people, so that after the Return from the Captivity all distinction of race between Kenites and Jews was forgotten, and the Kenites were reckoned among the families of Israel. In this fusion of their tribe with Judah, the Rechabite clan would be included. It is clear from all the references both to Kenites and to Rechabites that they had adopted the religion of Israel and worshipped Jehovah. We know nothing else of the early history of the Rechabites. The statement in Chronicles that the father of the house of Rechab was Hemath perhaps points to their having been at one time settled at some place called Hemath near Jabez in Judah. Possibly too Rechab, which means "rider," is not a personal name, but a designation of the clan as horsemen of the desert.

These Rechabites were conspicuous among the Jewish farmers and townsfolk by their rigid adherence to the habits of nomad life; and it was this peculiarity that attracted the notice of Jeremiah, and made them a suitable object-lesson to the recreant Jews. The traditional customs of the clan had been formulated into positive commands by Jonadab, the son of Rechab, *i. e.*, the Rechabite. This must be the same Jonadab who co-operated with Jehu in overthrowing the house of Omri and suppressing the worship of Baal. Jehu's reforms concluded the long struggle of Elijah and Elisha against the house of Omri and its half-heathen religion. Hence we may infer that Jonadab and his Rechabites had come under the influence of these great prophets, and that their social and religious condition was one result of Elijah's work. Jeremiah stood in the true line of succession from the northern prophets in his attitude towards religion and politics; so that there would be bonds of sympathy between him and these nomad refugees.

The laws or customs of Jonadab, like the Ten Commandments, were chiefly negative: "Ye shall drink no wine, neither ye nor your sons for ever: neither shall ye build houses, nor sow seed, nor plant vineyards, nor have any: but all your days ye shall dwell in tents; that ye may live many days in the land wherein ye are strangers."

Various parallels have been found to the customs of the Rechabites. The Hebrew Nazarites abstained from wine and strong drink, from grapes and grape juice and everything made of the vine, "from the kernels even to the husk." * Mohammed forbade his followers to drink any sort of wine or strong drink. But the closest parallel is one often quoted from Diodorus Siculus,† who, writing about B. C. 8, tells us that the Nabatean Arabs were prohibited under the penalty of death from sowing corn or planting fruit trees, using wine, or building houses. Such abstinence is not primarily ascetic; it expresses the universal contempt of the wandering hunter and herdsman for tillers of the ground, who are tied to one small spot of earth, and for burghers, who further imprison themselves in narrow houses and behind city walls. The nomad has a not altogether unfounded instinct that such acceptance of material restraints emasculates both soul and body. A remarkable parallel to the laws of Jonadab ben Rechab is found in the injunctions of the dying highlander, Ranald of the Mist, to his heir: "Son of the Mist, be free as thy forefathers. Own no lord—receive no law—take no hire—give no stipend—build no hut—enclose no pasture—sow no grain." ‡ The Rechabite faith in the higher moral value of their primitive habits had survived their alliance with Israel, and Jonadab did his best to protect his clan from the taint of city life and settled civilisation. Abstinence from wine was not enjoined chiefly, if at all, to guard against intoxication, but because the fascinations of the grape might tempt the clan to plant vineyards, or, at any rate, would make them dangerously dependent upon vine-dressers and wine-merchants.

Till this recent invasion, the Rechabites had faithfully observed their ancestral laws, but the stress of circumstances had now driven them into a fortified city, possibly even into houses, though it is more probable that they were encamped in some open space within the walls.§ Jeremiah was commanded to go and bring them

* Num. vi. 2.

† xix. 94.

‡ Scott, "Legend of Montrose,' chap. xxii.

§ The term "house of the Rechabites" in verse 2 means "family" or "clan," and does not refer to a building.

into the Temple, that is, into one of the rooms in the Temple buildings, and offer them wine. The narrative proceeds in the first person, "I took Jaazaniah," so that the chapter will have been composed by the prophet himself. In somewhat legal fashion he tells us how he took "Jaazaniah ben Jeremiah, ben Habaziniah, and his brethren, and all his sons, and all the clan of the Rechabites." All three names are compounded of the Divine name Iah, Jehovah, and serve to emphasise the devotion of the clan to the God of Israel. It is a curious coincidence that the somewhat rare name Jeremiah * should occur twice in this connection. The room to which the prophet took his friends is described as the chamber of the disciples of the man of God† Hanan ben Igdaliah, which was by the chamber of the princes, which was above the chamber of the keeper of the threshold, Maaseiah ben Shallum. Such minute details probably indicate that this chapter was committed to writing while these buildings were still standing and still had the same occupants as at the time of this incident, but to us the topography is unintelligible. The "man of God" or prophet Hanan was evidently in sympathy with Jeremiah, and had a following of disciples who formed a sort of school of the prophets, and were a sufficiently permanent body to have a chamber assigned to them in the Temple buildings. The keepers of the threshold were Temple officials of high standing. The "princes" may have been the princes of Judah, who might very well have a chamber in the Temple courts; but the term is general, and may simply refer to other Temple officials. Hanan's disciples seem to have been in good company.

These exact specifications of person and place are probably designed to give a certain legal solemnity and importance to the incident, and seem to warrant us in rejecting Reuss' suggestion that our narrative is simply an elaborate prophetic figure.‡

After these details Jeremiah next tells us how he set before his guests bowls of wine and cups, and invited them to drink. Probably Jaazaniah and his clansmen were aware that the scene was intended to have symbolic religious significance. They would not suppose that the prophet had invited them all, in this solemn fashion, merely to take a cup of wine; and they would welcome an opportunity of showing their loyalty to their own peculiar customs. They said: "We will drink no wine: for our father Jonadab the son of Rechab commanded us, saying, Ye shall drink no wine, neither ye nor your sons for ever." They further recounted Jonadab's other commands and their own scrupulous obedience in every point, except that now they had been compelled to seek refuge in a walled city.

Then the word of Jehovah came unto Jeremiah; he was commanded to make yet another appeal to the Jews, by contrasting their disobedience with the fidelity of the Rechabites. The Divine King and Father of Israel had been untiring in His instruction and admonitions: "I have spoken unto you, rising up early and speaking." He had addressed them in familiar fashion through their fellow-countrymen: "I have sent also unto you all My servants the prophets, rising up early and sending them." Yet they had not hearkened unto the God of Israel or His prophets. The Rechabites had received no special revelation; they had not been appealed to by numerous prophets. Their Torah had been simply given them by their father Jonadab; nevertheless the commands of Jonadab had been regarded and those of Jehovah had been treated with contempt.

Obedience and disobedience would bring forth their natural fruit. "I will bring upon Judah, and upon all the inhabitants of Jerusalem, all the evil that I have pronounced against them: because I have spoken unto them, but they have not heard; and I have called unto them, but they have not answered." But because the Rechabites obeyed the commandment of their father Jonadab, "Therefore thus saith Jehovah Sabaoth, Jonadab the son of Rechab shall not want a man to stand before Me for ever."

Jehovah's approval of the obedience of the Rechabites is quite independent of the specific commands which they obeyed. It does not bind us to abstain from wine any more than from building houses and sowing seed. Jeremiah himself, for instance, would have had no more hesitation in drinking wine than in sowing his field at Anathoth. The tribal customs of the Rechabites had no authority whatever over him. Nor is it exactly his object to set forth their merit of obedience and its certain and great reward. These truths are rather touched upon incidentally. What Jeremiah seeks to emphasise is the gross, extreme, unique wickedness of Israel's disobedience. Jehovah had not looked for any special virtue in His people. His Torah was not made up of counsels of perfection. He had only expected the loyalty that Moab paid to Chemosh, and Tyre and Sidon to Baal. He would have been satisfied if Israel had observed His laws as faithfully as the nomads of the desert kept up their ancestral habits. Jehovah had spoken through Jeremiah long ago and said: "Pass over the isles of Chittim, and see; and send unto Kedar, and consider diligently, and see if there be any such thing. Hath a nation changed their gods, which are yet no gods? but My people have changed their glory for that which doth not profit." * Centuries later Christ found Himself constrained to upbraid the cities of Israel, "wherein most of His mighty works were done" "Woe unto thee, Chorazin! woe unto thee, Bethsaida! for if the mighty works which were done in you had been done in Tyre and Sidon, they would have repented long ago in sackcloth and ashes. . . . It shall be more tolerable for Tyre and Sidon at the day of judgment than for you."† And again and again in the history of the Church the Holy Spirit has been grieved because those who profess and call themselves Christians, and claim to prophesy and do many mighty works in the name of Christ, are less loyal to the gospel than the heathen to their own superstitions.

Buddhists and Mohammedans have been held up as modern examples to rebuke the Church, though as a rule with scant justification. Perhaps material for a more relevant contrast may be found nearer home. Christian societies have been charged with conducting their affairs by methods to which a respectable business firm would not stoop; they are said to be less scrupu-

* Eight Jeremiahs occur in O. T.
† Literally "sons of Hanan."
‡ Jeremiah, according to this view, had no interview with the Rechabites, but made an imaginary incident a text for his discourse.

* ii. 10, 11. † Matt. xi. 21, 22.

lous in their dealings and less chivalrous in their honour than the devotees of pleasure; at their gatherings they are sometimes supposed to lack the mutual courtesy of members of a Legislature or a Chamber of Commerce. The history of councils and synods and Church meetings gives colour to such charges, which could never have been made if Christians had been as jealous for the Name of Christ as a merchant is for his credit or a soldier for his honour.

And yet these contrasts do not argue any real moral and religious superiority of the Rechabites over the Jews or of unbelievers over professing Christians. It was comparatively easy to abstain from wine and to wander over wide pasture lands instead of living cooped up in cities—far easier than to attain to the great ideals of Deuteronomy and the prophets. It is always easier to conform to the code of business and society than to live according to the Spirit of Christ. The fatal sin of Judah was not that it fell so far short of the ideals, but that it repudiated them. So long as we lament our own failures and still cling to the Name and Faith of Christ, we are not shut out from mercy; our supreme sin is to crucify Christ afresh, by denying the power of His gospel, while we retain its empty form.

The reward promised to the Rechabites for their obedience was that "Jonadab the son of Rechab shall not want a man to stand before Me for ever"; to stand before Jehovah is often used to describe the exercise of priestly or prophetic ministry. It has been suggested that the Rechabites were hereby promoted to the status of the true Israel, "a kingdom of priests"; but this phrase may merely mean that their clan should continue in existence. Loyal observance of national law, the subordination of individual caprice and selfishness to the interests of the community, make up a large part of that righteousness that establisheth a nation.

Here, as elsewhere, students of prophecy have been anxious to discover some literal fulfilment; and have searched curiously for any trace of the continued existence of the Rechabites. The notice in Chronicles implies that they formed part of the Jewish community of the Restoration. Apparently Alexandrian Jews were acquainted with Rechabites at a still later date. Psalm lxxi. is ascribed by the Septuagint to "the sons of Jonadab." Eusebius * mentions "priests of the sons of Rechab," and Benjamin of Tudela, a Jewish traveller of the twelfth century, states that he met with them in Arabia. More recent travellers have thought that they discovered the descendants of Rechab amongst the nomads in Arabia or the Peninsula of Sinai that still practised the old ancestral customs.

But the fidelity of Jehovah to his promises does not depend upon our unearthing obscure tribes in distant deserts. The gifts of God are without repentance, but they have their inexorable conditions; no nation can flourish for centuries on the virtues of its ancestors. The Rechabites may have vanished in the ordinary stream of history, and yet we can hold that Jeremiah's prediction has been fulfilled and is still being fulfilled. No scriptural prophecy is limited in its application to an individual or a race, and every nation possessed by the spirit of true patriotism shall "stand before Jehovah for ever."

* "Ch. Hist.," ii. 23.

CHAPTER V.

BARUCH.

JEREMIAH xlv.

"Thy life will I give unto thee for a prey."—JER. xlv. 5.

THE editors of the versions and of the Hebrew text of the Old Testament have assigned a separate chapter to this short utterance concerning Baruch; thus paying an unconscious tribute to the worth and importance of Jeremiah's disciple and secretary, who was the first to bear the familiar Jewish name, which in its Latinised form of Benedict has been a favourite with saints and popes. Probably few who read of these great ascetics and ecclesiastics give a thought to the earliest recorded Baruch, nor can we suppose that Christian Benedicts have been named after him. One thing they may all have in common: either their own faith or that of their parents ventured to bestow upon a "man born unto trouble as the sparks fly upward" the epithet "Blessed." We can scarcely suppose that the life of any Baruch or Benedict has run so smoothly as to prevent him or his friends from feeling that such faith has not been outwardly justified and that the name suggested an unkind satire. Certainly Jeremiah's disciple, like his namesake Baruch Spinoza, had to recognise his blessings disguised as distress and persecution.

Baruch ben Neriah is said by Josephus * to have belonged to a most distinguished family, and to have been exceedingly well educated in his native language. These statements are perhaps legitimate deductions from the information supplied by our book. His title "scribe"† and his position as Jeremiah's secretary imply that he possessed the best culture of his time; and we are told in li. 59 that Seraiah ben Neriah, who must be Baruch's brother, was chief chamberlain (R. V.) to Zedekiah. According to the Old Latin Version of the Apocryphal Book of Baruch (i. 1) he was of the tribe of Simeon, a statement by no means improbable in view of the close connection between Judah and Simeon, but needing the support of some better authority.

Baruch's relation to Jeremiah is not expressly defined, but it is clearly indicated in the various narratives in which he is referred to. We find him in constant attendance upon the prophet, acting both as his "scribe," or secretary, and as his mouthpiece. The relation was that of Joshua to Moses, of Elisha to Elijah, of Gehazi to Elisha, of Mark to Paul and Barnabas, and of Timothy to Paul. It is described in the case of Joshua and Mark by the term "minister," while Elisha is characterised as having "poured water on the hands of Elijah." The "minister" was at once personal attendant, disciple, representative, and possible successor of the prophet. The poition has its analogue in the service of the squire to the mediæval knight, and in that of an unpaid private secretary to a modern cabinet minister. Squires expected to become knights, and private secretaries hope for a seat in future cabinets. Another less perfect parallel is the relation of the members of a German theological "seminar" to their professor.

Baruch is first‡ introduced to us in the narra-

* "Antt.," x. 9, 1. † xxxvi. 26, 32.
‡ In order of time, ch. xxxvi.

tive concerning the roll. He appears as Jeremiah's amanuensis and representative, and is entrusted with the dangerous and honourable task of publishing his prophecies to the people in the Temple. Not long before, similar utterances had almost cost the master his life, so that the disciple showed high courage and devotion in undertaking such a commission. He was called to share with his master at once the same cup of persecution—and the same Divine protection.

We next hear of Baruch in connection with the symbolic purchase of the field at Anathoth.* He seems to have been attending on Jeremiah during his imprisonment in the court of the guard, and the documents containing the evidence of the purchase were entrusted to his care. Baruch's presence in the court of the guard does not necessarily imply that he was himself a prisoner. The whole incident shows that Jeremiah's friends had free access to him; and Baruch probably not only attended to his master's wants in prison, but also was his channel of communication with the outside world.

We are nowhere told that Baruch himself was either beaten or imprisoned, but it is not improbable that he shared Jeremiah's fortunes even to these extremities. We next hear of him as carried down to Egypt† with Jeremiah, when the Jewish refugees fled thither after the murder of Gedaliah. Apparently he had remained with Jeremiah throughout the whole interval, had continued to minister to him during his imprisonment, and had been among the crowd of Jewish captives whom Nebuchadnezzar found at Ramah. Josephus probably makes a similar conjecture‡ in telling us that, when Jeremiah was released and placed under the protection of Gedaliah at Mizpah, he asked and obtained from Nebuzaradan the liberty of his disciple Baruch. At any rate Baruch shared with his master the transient hope and bitter disappointment of this period; he supported him in dissuading the remnant of Jews from fleeing into Egypt, and was also compelled to share their flight. According to a tradition recorded by Jerome, Baruch and Jeremiah died in Egypt. But the Apocryphal Book of Baruch places him at Babylon, whither another tradition takes him after the death of Jeremiah in Egypt.§ These legends are probably mere attempts of wistful imagination to supply unwelcome blanks in history.

It has often been supposed that our present Book of Jeremiah, in some stage of its formation, was edited or compiled by Baruch, and that this book may be ranked with biographies—like Stanley's Life of Arnold—of great teachers by their old disciples. He was certainly the amanuensis of the roll, which must have been the most valuable authority for any editor of Jeremiah's prophecies. And the amanuensis might very easily become the editor. If an edition of the book was compiled in Jeremiah's lifetime, we should naturally expect him to use Baruch's assistance; if it first took shape after the prophet's death, and if Baruch survived, no one would be better able to compile the "Life and Works of Jeremiah" than his favourite and faithful disciple. The personal prophecy about Baruch does not occur in its proper place in connection with the episode of the roll, but is appended at the end of the prophecies,‖ possibly as a kind of subscription on the part of the editor. These data do not constitute absolute proof, but they afford strong probability that Baruch compiled a book, which was substantially our Jeremiah. The evidence is similar in character to, but much more conclusive than, that adduced for the authorship of the Epistle to the Hebrews by Apollos.

* xxxii. † xliii. ‡ "Ant.," x. 9, 1.

§ Bissell's Introduction to Baruch in Lange's Commentary.

‖ So LXX., which here probably gives the true order.

Almost the final reference to Baruch suggests another aspect of his relation to Jeremiah. The Jewish captains accused him of unduly influencing his master against Egypt and in favour of Chaldea. Whatever truth there may have been in this particular charge, we gather that popular opinion credited Baruch with considerable influence over Jeremiah, and probably popular opinion was not far wrong. Nothing said about Baruch suggests any vein of weakness in his character, such as Paul evidently recognised in Timothy. His few appearances upon the scene rather leave the impression of strength and self-reliance, perhaps even self-assertion. If we knew more about him, possibly indeed if any one else had compiled these "Memorabilia," we might discover that much in Jeremiah's policy and teaching was due to Baruch, and that the master leaned somewhat heavily upon the sympathy of the disciple. The qualities that make a successful man of action do not always exempt their possessor from being directed or even controlled by his followers. It would be interesting to discover how much of Luther is Melanchthon. Of many a great minister, his secretaries and subordinates might say safely, in private, *Cujus pars magna fuimus.*

The short prophecy which has furnished a text for this chapter shows that Jeremiah was not unaware of Baruch's tendency to self-assertion, and even felt that sometimes it required a check. Apparently chapter xlv. once formed the immediate continuation of chapter xxxvi., the narrative of the incident of the roll. It was "the word spoken by Jeremiah the prophet to Baruch ben Neriah, when he wrote these words in a book at the dictation of Jeremiah in the fourth year of Jehoiakim." The reference evidently is to xxxvi. 32, where we are told that Baruch wrote at Jeremiah's dictation all the words of the book that had been burnt, and many like words.

Clearly Baruch had not received Jeremiah's message as to the sin and ruin of Judah without strong protest. It was as distasteful to him as to all patriotic Jews and even to Jeremiah himself. Baruch had not yet been able to accept this heavy burden or to look beyond to the brighter promise of the future. He broke out into bitter complaint: "Woe is me now! for Jehovah hath added sorrow to my pain; I am weary with my groaning, and find no rest."* Strong as these words are, they are surpassed by many of Jeremiah's complaints to Jehovah, and doubtless even now they found an echo in the prophet's heart. Human impatience of suffering revolts desperately against the conviction that calamity is inevitable; hope whispers that some unforeseen Providence will yet disperse the storm-clouds, and the portents of ruin will dissolve like some evil dream. Jeremiah had, now as always, the harsh, unwelcome task of compelling himself and his fellows to face the sad and appalling reality. "Thus saith Jehovah, Behold, I am breaking down that which I built, I am pluck-

*The clause "I am weary with my groaning" also occurs in Psalm vi. 6.

ing up that which I planted." * This was his familiar message concerning Judah, but he had also a special word for Baruch: "And as for thee, dost thou seek great things for thyself?" What "great things" could a devout and patriotic Jew, a disciple of Jeremiah, seek for himself in those disastrous times? The answer is at once suggested by the renewed prediction of doom. Baruch, in spite of his master's teaching, had still ventured to look for better things, and had perhaps fancied that he might succeed where Jeremiah had failed and might become the mediator who should reconcile Israel to Jehovah. He may have thought that Jeremiah's threats and entreaties had prepared the way for some message of reconcilation. Gemariah ben Shaphan and other princes had been greatly moved when Baruch read the roll. Might not their emotion be an earnest of the repentance of the people? If he could carry on his master's work to a more blessed issue than the master himself had dared to hope, would not this be a "great thing" indeed? We gather from the tone of the chapter that Baruch's aspirations were unduly tinged with personal ambition. While kings, priests, and prophets were sinking into a common ruin from which even the most devoted servants of Jehovah would not escape, Baruch was indulging himself in visions of the honour to be obtained from a glorious mission, successfully accomplished. Jeremiah reminds him that he will have to take his share in the common misery. Instead of setting his heart upon "great things" which are not according to the Divine purpose, he must be prepared to endure with resignation the evil which Jehovah "is bringing upon all flesh." Yet there is a word of comfort and promise: "I will give thee thy life for a prey in all places whither thou goest." Baruch was to be protected from violent or premature death.

According to Renan,† this boon was flung to Baruch half-contemptuously, in order to silence his unworthy and unseasonable importunity:—

"Dans une catastrophe qui va englober l'humanité tout entière, il est beau de venir réclamer de petites faveurs d'exception! Baruch aura la vie sauve partout où il ira; qu'il s'en contente!"

We prefer a more generous interpretation. To a selfish man, unless indeed he clung to bare life in craven terror or mere animal tenacity, such an existence as Baruch was promised would have seemed no boon at all. Imprisonment in a besieged and starving city, captivity and exile, his fellow-countrymen's ill-will and resentment from first to last—these experiences would be hard to recognise as privileges bestowed by Jehovah. Had Baruch been wholly self-centred, he might well have craved death instead, like Job, nay, like Jeremiah himself. But life meant for him continued ministry to his master, the high privilege of supporting him in his witness to Jehovah. If, as seems almost certain, we owe to Baruch the preservation of Jeremiah's prophecies, then indeed the life that was given him for a prey must have been precious to him as the devoted servant of God. Humanly speaking, the future of revealed religion and of Christianity depended on the survival of Jeremiah's teaching, and this hung upon the frail thread of Baruch's life. After all, Baruch was destined to achieve "great things," even though not those which he sought after; and as no editor's name is prefixed to our book, he cannot be accused of self-seeking. So too for every faithful disciple, his life, even if given for a prey, even if spent in sorrow, poverty, and pain, is still a Divine gift, because nothing can spoil its opportunity of ministering to men and glorifying God, even if only by patient endurance of suffering.

We may venture on a wider application of the promise, "Thy life shall be given thee for a prey." Life is not merely continued existence in the body: life has come to mean spirit and character, so that Christ could say, "He that loseth his life for My sake shall find it." In this sense the loyal servant of God wins as his prey, out of all painful experiences, a fuller and nobler life. Other rewards may come in due season, but this is the most certain and the most sufficient. For Baruch, constant devotion to a hated and persecuted master, uncompromising utterance of unpopular truth, had their chief issue in the redemption of his own inward life.

* The concluding clause of the verse is omitted by LXX., and is probably a gloss added to indicate that the ruin would not be confined to Judah, but would extend "over the whole earth." *Cf.* Kautzsch.

† "History of Israel," iii. 293.

CHAPTER VI.

THE JUDGMENT ON JEHOIAKIM.

JEREMIAH xxii. 13-19, xxxvi. 30, 31.

"Jehoiakim . . . slew him (Uriah) with the sword, and cast his dead body into the graves of the common people."—JER. xxvi. 23.

"Therefore thus saith Jehovah concerning Jehoiakim, . . . He shall be buried with the burial of an ass, drawn and cast forth beyond the gates of Jerusalem."—JER. xxii. 18, 19.

"Jehoiakim . . . did that which was evil in the sight of Jehovah, according to all that his fathers had done."—2 KINGS xxiii. 36, 37.

OUR last four chapters have been occupied with the history of Jeremiah during the reign of Jehoiakim, and therefore necessarily with the relations of the prophet to the king and his government. Before we pass on to the reigns of Jehoiachin and Zedekiah, we must consider certain utterances which deal with the personal character and career of Jehoiakim. We are helped to appreciate these passages by what we here read, and by the brief paragraph concerning this reign in the Second Book of Kings. In Jeremiah the king's policy and conduct are especially illustrated by two incidents, the murder of the prophet Uriah and the destruction of the roll. The historian states his judgment of the reign, but his brief record * adds little to our knowledge of the sovereign.

Jehoiakim was placed upon the throne as the nominee and tributary of Pharaoh Necho; but he had the address or good fortune to retain his authority under Nebuchadnezzar, by transferring his allegiance to the new suzerain of Western Asia. When a suitable opportunity offered, the unwilling and discontented vassal naturally "turned and rebelled against" his lord. Even then his good fortune did not forsake him; although in his latter days Judah was harried by predatory bands of Chaldeans, Syrians, Moabites, and Ammonites, yet Jehoiakim "slept with his fathers" before Nebuchadnezzar had set to work in earnest to chastise his refractory subject.

* 2 Kings xxiii. 34-xxiv. 7.

He was not reserved, like Zedekiah, to endure agonies of mental and physical torture, and to rot in a Babylonian dungeon.

Jeremiah's judgment upon Jehoiakim and his doings is contained in the two passages which form the subject of this chapter. The utterance in xxxvi. 30, 31, was evoked by the destruction of the roll, and we may fairly assume that xxii. 13-19 was also delivered after that incident. The immediate context of the latter paragraph throws no light on the date of its origin. Chapter xxii. is a series of judgments on the successors of Josiah, and was certainly composed after the deposition of Jehoiachin, probably during the reign of Zedekiah; but the section on Jehoiakim must have been uttered at an earlier period. Renan indeed imagines * that Jeremiah delivered this discourse at the gate of the royal palace at the very beginning of the new reign. The nominee of Egypt was scarcely seated on the throne, his "new name" Jehoiakim—"He whom Jehovah establisheth"—still sounded strange in his ears, when the prophet of Jehovah publicly menaced the king with condign punishment. Renan is naturally surprised that Jehoiakim tolerated Jeremiah even for a moment. But, here as often elsewhere, the French critic's dramatic instinct has warped his estimate of evidence. We need not accept the somewhat unkind saying that picturesque anecdotes are never true, but, at the same time, we have always to guard against the temptation to accept the most dramatic interpretation of history as the most accurate. The contents of this passage, the references to robbery, oppression, and violence, clearly imply that Jehoiakim had reigned long enough for his government to reveal itself as hopelessly corrupt. The final breach between the king and the prophet was marked by the destruction of the roll, and xxii. 13-19, like xxxvi. 30, 31, may be considered a consequence of this breach.

Let us now consider these utterances. In xxxvi. 30*a* we read, "Therefore thus saith Jehovah concerning Jehoiakim king of Judah, He shall have none to sit upon the throne of David." Later on,* a like judgment was pronounced upon Jehoiakim's son and successor Jehoiachin. The absence of this threat from xxii. 13-19 is doubtless due to the fact that the chapter was compiled when the letter of the prediction seemed to have been proved to be false by the accession of Jehoiachin. Its spirit and substance were amply satisfied by the latter's deposition and captivity after a brief reign of a hundred days.

The next clause in the sentence on Jehoiakim runs: "His dead body shall be cast out in the day to the heat, and in the night to the frost." The same doom is repeated in the later prophecy:—

"They shall not lament for him,
 Alas my brother! Alas my brother!
They shall not lament for him,
 Alas lord! Alas lord! ‡
He shall be buried with the burial of an ass,
 Dragged forth and cast away without the gates of
  Jerusalem."

Jeremiah did not need to draw upon his imagination for this vision of judgment. When the words were uttered, his memory called up the

* iii. 274.
† xxii. 30.
‡ R. V., "Ah my brother! or Ah sister! . . . Ah lord! or Ah his glory!" The text is based on an emendation of Graetz, following the Syriac. (Giesebrecht.)

murder of Uriah ben Shemaiah and the dishonour done to his corpse. Uriah's only guilt had been his zeal for the truth that Jeremiah had proclaimed. Though Jehoiakim and his party had not dared to touch Jeremiah or had not been able to reach him, they had struck his influence by killing Uriah. But for their hatred of the master, the disciple might have been spared. And Jeremiah had neither been able to protect him, nor allowed to share his fate. Any generous spirit will understand how Jeremiah's whole nature was possessed and agitated by a tempest of righteous indignation, how utterly humiliated he felt to be compelled to stand by in helpless impotence. And now, when the tyrant had filled up the measure of his iniquity, when the imperious impulse of the Divine Spirit bade the prophet speak the doom of his king, there breaks forth at last the long-pent-up cry for vengeance: "Avenge, O Lord, Thy slaughtered saint"—let the persecutor suffer the agony and shame which he inflicted on God's martyr, fling out the murderer's corpse unburied, let it lie and rot upon the dishonoured grave of his victim.

Can we say, Amen? Not perhaps without some hesitation. Yet surely, if our veins run blood and not water, our feelings, had we been in Jeremiah's place, would have been as bitter and our words as fierce. Jehoiakim was more guilty than our Queen Mary, but the memory of the grimmest of the Tudors still stinks in English nostrils. In our own days, we have not had time to forget how men received the news of Hannington's murder at Uganda, and we can imagine what European Christians would say and feel if their missionaries were massacred in China.

And yet, when we read such a treatise as Lactantius wrote "Concerning the Deaths of Persecutors," we cannot but recoil. We are shocked at the stern satisfaction he evinces in the miserable ends of Maximin and Galerius, and other enemies of the true faith. Discreet historians have made large use of this work, without thinking it desirable to give an explicit account of its character and spirit. Biographers of Lactantius feel constrained to offer a half-hearted apology for the "De Morte Persecutorum." Similarly we find ourselves of one mind with Gibbon,* in refusing to derive edification from a sermon in which Constantine the Great, or the bishop who composed it for him, affected to relate the miserable end of all the persecutors of the Church. Nor can we share the exultation of the Covenanters in the Divine judgment which they saw in the death of Claverhouse; and we are not moved to any hearty sympathy with more recent writers, who have tried to illustrate from history the danger of touching the rights and privileges of the Church. Doubtless God will avenge His own elect; nevertheless *Nemo me impune lacessit* is no seemly motto for the Kingdom of God. Even Greek mythologists taught that it was perilous for men to wield the thunderbolts of Zeus. Still less is the Divine wrath a weapon for men to grasp in their differences and dissensions, even about the things of God. Michael the Archangel, even when contending with the devil he disputed about the body of Moses, durst not bring against him a railing judgment, but said, The Lord rebuke thee.†

How far Jeremiah would have shared such modern sentiment, it is hard to say. At any

* Chap. xiii. † Jude 9.

rate his personal feeling is kept in the background; it is postponed to the more patient and deliberate judgment of the Divine Spirit, and subordinated to broad considerations of public morality. We have no right to contrast Jeremiah with our Lord and His proto-martyr Stephen, because we have no prayer of the ancient prophet to rank with, "Father, forgive them; for they know not what they do," or again with, "Lord, lay not this sin to their charge." Christ and His disciple forgave wrongs done to themselves: they did not condone the murder of their brethren. In the Apocalypse, which concludes the English Bible, and was long regarded as God's final revelation, His last word to man, the souls of the martyrs cry out from beneath the altar: "How long, O Master, the holy and true, dost Thou not judge and avenge our blood on them that dwell on the earth?" *

Doubtless God will avenge His own elect, and the appeal for justice may be neither ignoble nor vindictive. But such prayers, beyond all others, must be offered in humble submission to the Judge of all. When our righteous indignation claims to pass its own sentence, we do well to remember that our halting intellect and our purblind conscience are ill qualified to sit as assessors of the Eternal Justice.

When Saul set out for Damascus, "breathing out threatening and slaughter against the disciples of the Lord," the survivors of his victims cried out for a swift punishment of the persecutor, and believed that their prayers were echoed by martyred souls in the heavenly Temple. If that ninth chapter of the Acts had recorded how Saul of Tarsus was struck dead by the lightnings of the wrath of God, preachers down all the Christian centuries would have moralised on the righteous Divine judgment. Saul would have found his place in the homiletic Chamber of Horrors with Ananias and Sapphira, Herod and Pilate, Nero and Diocletian. Yet the Captain of our salvation, choosing His lieutenants, passes over many a man with blameless record, and allots the highest post to this blood-stained persecutor. No wonder that Paul, if only in utter self-contempt, emphasised the doctrine of Divine election. Verily God's ways are not our ways and His thoughts are not our thoughts.

Still, however, we easily see that Paul and Jehoiakim belong to two different classes. The persecutor who attempts in honest but misguided zeal to make others endorse his own prejudices, and turn a deaf ear with him to the teaching of the Holy Spirit, must not be ranked with politicians who sacrifice to their own private interests the Revelation and the Prophets of God.

This prediction which we have been discussing of Jehoiakim's shameful end is followed in the passage in chapter xxxvi. by a general announcement of universal judgment, couched in Jeremiah's usual comprehensive style:—

"I will visit their sin upon him and upon his children and upon his servants, and I will bring upon them and the inhabitants of Jerusalem and the men of Judah all the evil which I spake unto them and they did not hearken."

In chapter xxii. the sentence upon Jehoiakim is prefaced by a statement of the crimes for which he was punished. His eyes and his heart were wholly possessed by avarice and cruelty; as an administrator he was active in oppression and violence.* But Jeremiah does not confine himself to these general charges; he specifies and emphasises one particular form of Jehoiakim's wrong-doing, the tyrannous exaction of forced labour for his buildings. To the sovereigns of petty Syrian states, old Memphis and Babylon were then what London and Paris are to modern Ameers, Khedives, and Sultans. Circumstances, indeed, did not permit a Syrian prince to visit the Egyptian or Chaldean capital with perfect comfort and unrestrained enjoyment. Ancient Eastern potentates, like mediæval suzerains, did not always distinguish between a guest and a hostage. But the Jewish kings would not be debarred from importing the luxuries and imitating the vices of their conquerors.

Renan says† of this period: "L'Egypte était, à cette époque, le pays où les industries de luxe étaient le plus développées. Tout le monde raffolaient, en particulier, de sa carrosserie et de ses meubles ouvragés. Joiaquin et la noblesse de Jérusalem ne songeaient qu'à se procurer ces beaux objets, qui réalisaient ce qu'on avait vu de plus exquis en fait de goût jusque-là."

The supreme luxury of vulgar minds is the use of wealth as a means of display, and monarchs have always delighted in the erection of vast and ostentatious buildings. At this time Egypt and Babylon vied with one another in pretentious architecture. In addition to much useful engineering work, Psammetichus I. made large additions to the temples and public edifices at Memphis, Thebes, Sais, and elsewhere, so that "the entire valley of the Nile became little more than one huge workshop, where stone-cutters and masons, bricklayers and carpenters, laboured incessantly." ‡ This activity in building continued even after the disaster to the Egyptian arms at Carchemish.

Nebuchadnezzar had an absolute mania for architecture. His numerous inscriptions are mere catalogues of his achievements in building. His home administration and even his extensive conquests are scarcely noticed; he held them of little account compared with his temples and palaces—"this great Babylon, which I have built for the royal dwelling-place, by the might of my power and for the glory of my majesty." § Nebuchadnezzar created most of the magnificence that excited the wonder and admiration of Herodotus a century later.

Jehoiakim had been moved to follow the notable example of Chaldea and Egypt. By a strange irony of fortune, Egypt, once the cynosure of nations, has become in our own time the humble imitator of Western civilisation, and now boulevards have rendered the suburbs of Cairo "a shabby reproduction of modern Paris." Possibly in the eyes of Egyptians and Chaldeans Jehoiakim's efforts only resulted in a "shabby reproduction" of Memphis or Babylon. Nevertheless these foreign luxuries are always expensive; and minor states had not then learnt the art of trading on the resources of their powerful neighbours by means of foreign loans. Moreover Judah had to pay tribute first to Pharaoh Necho, and then to Nebuchadnezzar. The times were bad, and additional taxes for

* Apc. vi. 10.

* xxii. 17. The exact meaning of the word translated "violence" (so A. V., R. V.,) is very doubtful.

† "Hist.," etc., iii. 266.

‡ Rawlinson, "Ancient Egypt" (Story of the Nations).

§ Dan. iv. 30.

building purposes must have been felt as an intolerable oppression. Naturally the king did not pay for his labour; like Solomon and all other great Eastern despots, he had recourse to the *corvée*, and for this in particular Jeremiah denounced him.

"Woe unto him that buildeth his house by unrighteousness
And his chambers by injustice;
That maketh his neighbour toil without wages,
And giveth him no hire;
That saith, 'I will build me a wide house
And spacious chambers,'
And openeth out broad windows, with woodwork of cedar
And vermilion painting."

Then the denunciation passes into biting sarcasm:—

"Art thou indeed a king,
Because thou strivest to excel in cedar?"*

Poor imitations of Nebuchadnezzar's magnificent structures could not conceal the impotence and dependence of the Jewish king. The pretentiousness of Jehoiakim's buildings challenged a comparison which only reminded men that he was a mere puppet, with its strings pulled now by Egypt and now by Babylon. At best he was only reigning on sufferance.

Jeremiah contrasts Jehoiakim's government both as to justice and dignity with that of Josiah:—

"Did not thy father eat and drink?"†

(He was no ascetic, but, like the Son of Man, lived a full, natural, human life.)

"And do judgment and justice?
Then did he prosper.
He judged the cause of the poor and needy,
Then was there prosperity.
Is not this to know Me?
Jehovah hath spoken it."

Probably Jehoiakim claimed by some external observance, or through some subservient priest or prophet, to "know Jehovah"; and Jeremiah repudiates the claim.

Josiah had reigned in the period when the decay of Assyria left Judah dominant in Palestine, until Egypt or Chaldea could find time to gather up the outlying fragments of the shattered empire. The wisdom and justice of the Jewish king had used this breathing space for the advantage and happiness of his people; and during part of his reign Josiah's power seems to have been as extensive as that of any of his predecessors on the throne of Judah. And yet, according to current theology, Jeremiah's appeal to the prosperity of Josiah as a proof of God's approbation was a startling anomaly. Josiah had been defeated and slain at Megiddo in the prime of his manhood, at the age of thirty-nine. None but the most independent and enlightened spirits could believe that the Reformer's premature death, at the moment when his policy had resulted in national disaster, was not an emphatic declaration of Divine displeasure. Jeremiah's contrary belief might be explained and justified. Some such justification is suggested by the prophet's utterance concerning Jehoahaz: "Weep not for the dead, neither bemoan him: but weep sore for him that goeth away." Josiah had reigned with real authority, he died when independence was no longer possible; and therein he was happier and more honourable than his successors, who held a vassal throne by the uncertain tenure of time-serving duplicity, and were for the most part carried into captivity. "The righteous was taken away from the evil to come."*

The warlike spirit of classical antiquity and of Teutonic chivalry welcomed a glorious death upon the field of battle:—

"And how can man die better
Than facing fearful odds,
For the ashes of his fathers,
And the temples of his Gods?"

No one spoke of Leonidas as a victim of Divine wrath. Later Judaism caught something of the same temper. Judas Maccabæus, when in extreme danger, said, "It is better for us to die in battle, than to look upon the evils of our people and our sanctuary"; and later on, when he refused to flee from inevitable death, he claimed that he would leave behind him no stain upon his honour.† Islam also is prodigal in its promises of future bliss to those soldiers who fall fighting for its sake.

But the dim and dreary Sheôl of the ancient Hebrews was no glorious Valhalla or houri-peopled Paradise. The renown of the battle-field was poor compensation for the warm, full-blooded life of the upper air. When David sang his dirge for Saul and Jonathan, he found no comfort in the thought that they had died fighting for Israel. Moreover the warrior's self-sacrifice for his country seems futile and inglorious, when it neither secures victory nor postpones defeat. And at Megiddo Josiah and his army perished in a vain attempt to come

"Between the pass and fell incensed points
Of mighty opposites."

We can hardly justify to ourselves Jeremiah's use of Josiah's reign as an example of prosperity as the reward of righteousness; his contemporaries must have been still more difficult to convince. We cannot understand how the words of this prophecy were left without any attempt at justification, or why Jeremiah did not meet by anticipation the obvious and apparently crushing rejoinder that the reign terminated in disgrace and disaster.

Nevertheless these difficulties do not affect the terms of the sentence upon Jehoiakim, or the ground upon which he was condemned. We shall be better able to appreciate Jeremiah's attitude and to discover its lessons if we venture to reconsider his decisions. We cannot forget that there was, as Cheyne puts it, a duel between Jeremiah and Jehoiakim; and we should hesitate to accept the verdict of Hildebrand upon Henry IV. of Germany, or of Thomas à Becket on Henry II. of England. Moreover the data upon which we have to base our judgment, including the unfavourable estimate in the Book of Kings, come to us from Jeremiah or his disciples. Our ideas about Queen Elizabeth would be more striking than accurate if our only authorities for her reign were Jesuit historians of

*I have followed R. V., but the text is probably corrupt. Cheyne follows LXX. (A) in reading "because thou viest with Ahab": LXX. (B) has "Ahaz" (so Ewald). Giesebrecht proposes to neglect the accents and translate, "viest in cedar buildings with thy father" (*i. e.*, Solomon).

†According to Giesebrecht (*cf.*, however, the last note) this clause is an objection which the prophet puts into the mouth of the king. "My father enjoyed the good things of life—why should not I?" The prophet rejoins, "Nay, but he did judgment," etc.

*Isa. lvii. (English Versions).

†Macc. ii. 59, ix. 10

England. But Jeremiah is absorbed in lofty moral and spiritual issues; his testimony is not tainted with that sectarian and sacerdotal casuistry which is always so ready to subordinate truth to the interests of "the Church." He speaks of facts with a simple directness which leaves us in no doubt as to their reality; his picture of Jehoiakim may be one-sided, but it owes nothing to an inventive imagination.

Even Renan, who, in Ophite fashion, holds a brief for the bad characters of the Old Testament, does not seriously challenge Jeremiah's statements of fact. But the judgment of the modern critic seems at first sight more lenient than that of the Hebrew prophet: the former sees in Jehoiakim "un prince libéral et modéré," * but when this favourable estimate is coupled with an apparent comparison with Louis Philippe, we must leave students of modern history to decide whether Renan is really less severe than Jeremiah. Cheyne, on the other hand, holds† that "we have no reason to question Jeremiah's verdict upon Jehoiakim, who, alike from a religious and a political point of view, appears to have been unequal to the crisis in the fortunes of Israel." No doubt this is true; and yet perhaps Renan is so far right that Jehoiakim's failure was rather his misfortune than his fault. We may doubt whether any king of Israel or Judah would have been equal to the supreme crisis which Jehoiakim had to face. Our scanty information seems to indicate a man of strong will, determined character, and able statesmanship. Though the nominee of Pharaoh Necho, he retained his sceptre under Nebuchadnezzar, and held his own against Jeremiah and the powerful party by which the prophet was supported. Under more favourable conditions he might have rivalled Uzziah or Jeroboam II. In the time of Jehoiakim, a supreme political and military genius would have been as helpless on the throne of Judah as were the Palæologi in the last days of the Empire at Constantinople. Something may be said to extenuate his religious attitude. In opposing Jeremiah he was not defying clear and acknowledged truth. Like the Pharisees in their conflict with Christ, the persecuting king had popular religious sentiment on his side. According to that current theology which had been endorsed in some measure even by Isaiah and Jeremiah, the defeat at Megiddo proved that Jehovah repudiated the religious policy of Josiah and his advisers. The inspiration of the Holy Spirit enabled Jeremiah to resist this shallow conclusion, and to maintain through every crisis his unshaken faith in the profounder truth. Jehoiakim was too conservative to surrender at the prophet's bidding the long-accepted and fundamental doctrine of retribution, and to follow the forward leading of Revelation. He "stood by the old truth" as did Charles V. at the Reformation. "Let him that is without sin" in this matter "first cast a stone at" him.

Though we extenuate Jehoiakim's conduct, we are still bound to condemn it; not, however, because he was exceptionally wicked, but because he failed to rise above a low spiritual average: yet in this judgment we also condemn ourselves for our own intolerance, and for the prejudice and self-will which have often blinded our eyes to the teachings of our Lord and Master.

But Jeremiah emphasises one special charge against the king—his exaction of forced and unpaid labour. This form of taxation was in itself so universal that the censure can scarcely be directed against its ordinary and moderate exercise. If Jeremiah had intended to inaugurate a new departure, he would have approached the subject in a more formal and less casual fashion. It was a time of national danger and distress, when all moral and material resources were needed to avert the ruin of the state, or at any rate to mitigate the sufferings of the people; and at such a time Jehoiakim exhausted and embittered his subjects—that he might dwell in spacious halls with woodwork of cedar. The Temple and palaces of Solomon had been built at the expense of a popular resentment, which survived for centuries, and with which, as their silence seems to show, the prophets fully sympathised. If even Solomon's exactions were culpable, Jehoiakim was altogether without excuse.

His sin was that common to all governments, the use of the authority of the state for private ends. This sin is possible not only to sovereigns and secretaries of state, but to every town councillor and every one who has a friend on a town council, nay, to every clerk in a public office and to every workman in a government dockyard. A king squandering public revenues on private pleasures, and an artisan pilfering nails and iron with an easy conscience because they only belong to the state, are guilty of crimes essentially the same. On the one hand, Jehoiakim as the head of the state was oppressing individuals; and although modern states have grown comparatively tender as to the rights of the individual, yet even now their action is often cruelly oppressive to insignificant minorities. But, on the other hand, the right of exacting labour was only vested in the king as a public trust; its abuse was as much an injury to the community as to individuals. If Jeremiah had to deal with modern civilisation, we might, perchance, be startled by his passing lightly over our religious and political controversies to denounce the squandering of public resources in the interests of individuals and classes, sects and parties.

CHAPTER VII.

*JEHOIACHIN.**

JEREMIAH xxii. 20-30.

"A despised broken vessel."—JER. xxii. 28.

"A young lion. And he went up and down among the lions, he became a young lion and he learned to catch the prey, he devoured men."—EZEK. xix. 5, 6.

"Jehoiachin . . . did evil in the sight of Jehovah, according to all that his father had done."—2 KINGS xxiv. 8, 9.

WE have seen that our book does not furnish a consecutive biography of Jeremiah; we are not even certain as to the chronological order of the incidents narrated. Yet these chapters are clear and full enough to give us an accurate idea of what Jeremiah did and suffered during the eleven years of Jehoiakim's reign. He was forced to stand by while the king lent the weight of his authority to the ancient corruptions of the national religion, and conducted his home and foreign policy without any regard to the will of Jehovah, as expressed by His prophet.

* iii. 269. † P. 142.

* Also called Coniah and Jeconiah.

His position was analogous to that of a Romanist priest under Elizabeth or a Protestant divine in the reign of James II. According to some critics, Nebuchadnezzar was to Jeremiah what Philip of Spain was to the priest and William of Orange to the Puritan.

During all these long and weary years, the prophet watched the ever multiplying tokens of approaching ruin. He was no passive spectator, but a faithful watchman to the house of Israel; again and again he risked his life in a vain attempt to make his fellow-countrymen aware of their danger.* The vision of the coming sword was ever before his eyes, and he blew the trumpet and warned the people; but they would not be warned, and the prophet knew that the sword would come and take them away in their iniquity. He paid the penalty of his faithfulness; at one time or another he was beaten, imprisoned, proscribed, and driven to hide himself; still he persevered in his mission, as time and occasion served. Yet he survived Jehoiakim, partly because he was more anxious to serve Jehovah than to gain the glorious deliverance of martyrdom; partly because his royal enemy feared to proceed to extremities against a prophet of Jehovah, who was befriended by powerful nobles, and might possibly have relations with Nebuchadnezzar himself. Jehoiakim's religion—for like the Athenians he was probably "very religious"—was saturated with superstition, and it was only when deeply moved that he lost the sense of an external sanctity attaching to Jeremiah's person. In Israel prophets were hedged by a more potent divinity than kings.

Meanwhile Jeremiah was growing old in years and older in experience. When Jehoiakim died, it was nearly forty years since the young priest had first been called "to pluck up and to break down, and to destroy and to overthrow; to build and to plant"; it was more than eleven since his brighter hopes were buried in Josiah's grave. Jehovah had promised that He would make His servant into "an iron pillar and brasen walls." † The iron was tempered and hammered into shape during these days of conflict and endurance, like—

> " . . . iron dug from central gloom,
> And heated hot with burning fears
> And dipt in baths of hissing tears,
> And battered with the shocks of doom,
> To shape and use."

He had long lost all trace of that sanguine youthful enthusiasm which promises to carry all before it. His opening manhood had felt its happy illusions, but they did not dominate his soul and they soon passed away. At the Divine bidding, he had surrendered his most ingrained prejudices, his dearest desires. He had consented to be alienated from his brethren at Anathoth, and to live without home or family; although a patriot, he accepted the inevitable ruin of his nation as the just judgment of Jehovah; he was a priest, imbued by heredity and education with the religious traditions of Israel, yet he had yielded himself to Jehovah, to announce, as His herald, the destruction of the Temple, and the devastation of the Holy Land. He had submitted his shrinking flesh and reluctant spirit to God's most unsparing demands, and had dared the worst that man could inflict. Such surrender and such experiences wrought in him a certain stern and terrible strength, and made his life still more remote from the hopes and fears, the joys and sorrows of common men. In his isolation and his inspired self-sufficiency he had become an "iron pillar." Doubtless he seemed to many as hard and cold as iron; but this pillar of the faith could still glow with white heat of indignant passion, and within the shelter of the "brasen walls" there still beat a human heart, touched with tender sympathy for those less disciplined to endure.

* Considerable portions of chaps. i.-xx. are referred to the reigns of Jehoiakim and Jehoiachin: see Prophecies of Jeremiah, *antea*.

† i. 18.

We have thus tried to estimate the development of Jeremiah's character during the second period of his ministry, which began with the death of Josiah and terminated with the brief reign of Jehoiachin. Before considering Jeremiah's judgment upon this prince we will review the scanty data at our disposal to enable us to appreciate the prophet's verdict.

Jehoiakim died while Nebuchadnezzar was on the march to punish his rebellion. His son Jehoiachin, a youth of eighteen,* succeeded his father and continued his policy. Thus the accession of the new king was no new departure, but merely a continuance of the old order; the government was still in the hands of the party attached to Egypt, and opposed to Babylon and hostile to Jeremiah. Under these circumstances we are bound to accept the statement of Kings that Jehoiakim "slept with his fathers," *i. e.*, was buried in the royal sepulchre.† There was no literal fulfilment of the prediction that he should "be buried with the burial of an ass." Jeremiah had also declared concerning Jehoiakim: "He shall have none to sit upon the throne of David."‡ According to popular superstition, the honourable burial of Jehoiakim and the succession of his son to the throne further discredited Jeremiah and his teaching. Men read happy omens in the mere observance of ordinary constitutional routine. The curse upon Jehoiakim seemed so much spent breath: why should not Jeremiah's other predictions of ruin and exile also prove a mere *vox et præterea nihil?* In spite of a thousand disappointments, men's hopes still turned to Egypt; and if earthly resources failed they trusted to Jehovah Himself to intervene, and deliver Jerusalem from the advancing hosts of Nebuchadnezzar, as from the army of Sennacherib.

Ezekiel's elegy over Jehoiachin suggests that the young king displayed energy and courage worthy of a better fortune:—

> "He walked up and down among the lions,
> He became a young lion;
> He learned to catch the prey,
> He devoured men.
> He broke down § their palaces,
> He wasted their cities;
> The land was desolate, and the fulness thereof,
> At the noise of his roaring." ‖

* The Chronicler's account of Jehoiakim's end (2 Chron. xxviii. 6-8) is due to a misunderstanding of the older records. According to Chronicles Jehoiachin was only eight, but all our data indicate that Kings is right.

† In LXX. of 2 Chron. xxxvi. 8, Jehoiakim, like Manasseh and Amon, was "buried in the garden of Uzza": B, Ganozæ; A, Ganozan. Cheyne is inclined to accept this statement, which he regards as derived from tradition.

‡ xxxvi. 30.

§ So A. B. Davidson in Cambridge Bible, etc., by a slight conjectural emendation; there have been many other suggested corrections of the text. The Hebrew text as it stands would mean literally "he knew their widows" (R. V. margin); A. V., R. V., by a slight change, "he knew their (A. V. desolate) palaces."

‖ Ezek. xix. 5-7.

However figurative these lines may be, the hyperbole must have had some basis in fact. Probably before the regular Babylonian army entered Judah, Jehoiachin distinguished himself by brilliant but useless successes against the marauding bands of Chaldeans, Syrians, Moabites, and Ammonites, who had been sent to prepare the way for the main body. He may even have carried his victorious arms into the territory of Moab or Ammon. But his career was speedily cut short: "The servants of Nebuchadnezzar king of Babylon came up to Jerusalem and besieged the city." Pharaoh Necho made no sign, and Jehoiachin was forced to retire before the regular forces of Babylon, and soon found himself shut up in Jerusalem. Still for a time he held out, but when it was known in the beleaguered city that Nebuchadnezzar was present in person in the camp of the besiegers, the Jewish captains lost heart. Perhaps too they hoped for better treatment, if they appealed to the conqueror's vanity by offering him an immediate submission which they had refused to his lieutenants. The gates were thrown open; Jehoiachin and the Queen Mother, Nehushta, with his ministers and princes and the officers of his household, passed out in suppliant procession, and placed themselves and their city at the disposal of the conqueror. In pursuance of the policy which Nebuchadnezzar had inherited from the Assyrians, the king and his court and eight thousand picked men were carried away captive to Babylon.* For thirty-seven years Jehoiachin languished in a Chaldean prison, till at last his sufferings were mitigated by an act of grace, which signalised the accession of a new king of Babylon. Nebuchadnezzar's successor Evil Merodach, "in the year when he began to reign, lifted up the head of Jehoiachin king of Judah out of prison, and spake kindly to him, and set his throne above the throne of the kings that were with him in Babylon. And Jehoiachin changed his prison garments, and ate at the royal table continually all the days of his life, and had a regular allowance given him by the king, a daily portion, all the days of his life."† At the age of fifty-five, the last survivor of the reigning princes of the house of David emerges from his dungeon, broken in mind and body by his long captivity, to be a grateful dependent upon the charity of Evil Merodach, just as the survivor of the house of Saul had sat at David's table. The young lion that devoured the prey and caught men and wasted cities was thankful to be allowed to creep out of his cage and die in comfort—"a despised broken vessel."

We feel a shock of surprise and repulsion as we turn from this pathetic story to Jeremiah's fierce invectives against the unhappy king. But we wrong the prophet and misunderstand his utterance if we forget that it was delivered during that brief frenzy in which the young king and his advisers threw away the last chance of safety for Judah. Jehoiachin might have repudiated his father's rebellion against Babylon; Jehoiakim's death had removed the chief offender, no personal blame attached to his successor, and a prompt submission might have appeased Nebuchadnezzar's wrath against Judah and obtained his favour for the new king. If a hot-headed young rajah of some protected Indian state revolted against the English suzerainty

* 2 Kings xxiv. 8-17.
† 2 Kings xxv. 27-30; Jer. lii. 31-34.

and exposed his country to the misery of a hopeless war, we should sympathise with any of his counsellors who condemned such wilful folly; we have no right to find fault with Jeremiah for his severe censure of the reckless vanity which precipitated his country's fate.

Jeremiah's deep and absorbing interest in Judah and Jerusalem is indicated by the form of this utterance; it is addressed to the "Daughter of Zion"*:—

"Go up to Lebanon, and lament,
And lift up thy voice in Bashan,
And lament from Abarim,†
For thy lovers are all destroyed!"

Her "lovers," her heathen allies, whether gods or men, are impotent, and Judah is as forlorn and helpless as a lonely and unfriended woman; let her bewail her fate upon the mountains of Israel, like Jephthah's daughter in ancient days.

"I spake unto thee in thy prosperity;
Thou saidst, I will not hearken.
This hath been thy way from thy youth,
That thou hast not obeyed My voice.
The tempest shall be the shepherd to all thy shepherds."

Kings and nobles, priests and prophets, shall be carried off by the Chaldean invaders, as trees and houses are swept away by a hurricane. These shepherds who had spoiled and betrayed their flock would themselves be as silly sheep in the hands of robbers.

"Thy lovers shall go into captivity.
Then, verily, shalt thou be ashamed and confounded
Because of all thy wickedness.
O thou that dwellest in Lebanon!
O thou that hast made thy nest in the cedar!"

The former mention of Lebanon reminded Jeremiah of Jehoiakim's halls of cedar. With grim irony he links together the royal magnificence of the palace and the wild abandonment of the people's lamentation.

"How wilt thou groan ‡ when pangs come upon thee,
Anguish as of a woman in travail!"

The nation is involved in the punishment inflicted upon her rulers. In such passages the prophets largely identify the nation with the governing classes—not without justification. No government, whatever the constitution may be, can ignore a strong popular demand for righteous policy, at home and abroad. A special responsibility of course rests on those who actually wield the authority of the state, but the policy of rulers seldom succeeds in effecting much either for good or evil without some sanction of public feeling. Our revolution which replaced the Puritan Protectorate by the restored Monarchy was rendered possible by the change of popular sentiment. Yet even under the purest democracy men imagine that they divest themselves of civic responsibility by neglecting their civic duties; they stand aloof, and blame officials and professional politicians for the injustice and crime wrought by the state. National guilt seems happily disposed of when laid on the shoulders of that convenient abstraction "the government"; but neither the prophets nor the Providence which they interpret recognise this convenient theory of vicarious atone-

* The Hebrew verbs are in 2 s. fem.; the person addressed is not named, but from analogy she can only be the "Daughter of Zion," *i. e.*, Jerusalem personified.
† Identified with the mountains of Moab.
‡ R. V. margin, with LXX., Vulg., and Syr.

ment: the king sins, but the prophet's condemnation is uttered against and executed upon the nation.

Nevertheless a special responsibility rests upon the ruler, and now Jeremiah turns from the nation to its king.

"As I live—Jehovah hath spoken it—
Though Coniah ben Jehoiakim king of Judah were a signet ring upon My right hand——"

By a forcible Hebrew idiom Jehovah, as it were, turns and confronts the king and specially addresses him:—

"Yet I would pluck thee thence."

A signet ring was valuable in itself, and, as far as an inanimate object could be, was an "altar ego" of the sovereign; it scarcely ever left his finger, and when it did, it carried with it the authority of its owner. A signet ring could not be lost or even cast away without some reflection upon the majesty of the king. Jehoiachin's character was by no means worthless; he had courage, energy, and patriotism. The heir of David and Solomon, the patron and champion of the Temple, dwelt, as it were, under the very shadow of the Almighty. Men generally believed that Jehovah's honour was engaged to defend Jerusalem and the house of David. He Himself would be discredited by the fall of the elect dynasty and the captivity of the chosen people. Yet everything must be sacrificed—the career of a gallant young prince, the ancient association of the sacred Name with David and Zion, even the superstitious awe with which the heathen regarded the God of the Exodus and of the deliverance from Sennacherib. Nothing will be allowed to stand in the way of the Divine judgment. And yet we still sometimes dream that the working out of the Divine righteousness will be postponed in the interests of ecclesiastical traditions and in deference to the criticisms of ungodly men!

"And I will give thee into the hand of them that seek thy life,
Into the hand of them of whom thou art afraid,
Into the hand of Nebuchadnezzar king of Babylon and the Chaldeans.
And I will hurl thee and the mother that bare thee into another land, where ye were not born:
There shall ye die.
And unto the land whereunto their soul longeth to return,
Thither they shall not return."

Again the sudden change in the person addressed emphasises the scope of the Divine proclamation; the doom of the royal house is not only announced to them, but also to the world at large. The mention of the Queen Mother, Nehushta, reveals what we should in any case have conjectured, that the policy of the young prince was largely determined by his mother. Her importance is also indicated by xiii. 18, usually suposed to be addressed to Jehoiachin and Nehushta:—

"Say unto the king and the queen mother,
Leave your thrones and sit in the dust,
For your glorious diadems are fallen."

The Queen Mother is a characteristic figure of polygamous Eastern dynasties, but we may be helped to understand what Nehushta was to Jehoiachin if we remember the influence of Eleanor of Poitou over Richard I. and John, and the determined struggle which Margaret of Anjou made on behalf of her ill-starred son.

The next verse of our prophecy seems to be a protest against the severe sentence pronounced in the preceding clauses:—

"Is then this man Coniah a despised vessel, only fit to be broken?
Is he a tool, that no one wants?"

Thus Jeremiah imagines the citizens and warriors of Jerusalem crying out against him, for his sentence of doom against their darling prince and captain. The prophetic utterance seemed to them monstrous and incredible, only worthy to be met with impatient scorn We may find a mediæval analogy to the situation at Jerusalem in the relations of Clement IV. to Conradin, the last heir of the house of Hohenstaufen. When this youth of sixteen was in the full career of victory, the Pope predicted that his army would be scattered like smoke, and pointed out the prince and his allies as victims for the sacrifice. When Conradin was executed after his defeat at Tagliacozzo, Christendom was filled with abhorrence at the suspicion that Clement had countenanced the doing to death of the hereditary enemy of the Papal See. Jehoiachin's friends felt towards Jeremiah somewhat as these thirteenth-century Ghibellines towards Clement.

Moreover the charge against Clement was probably unfounded; Milman * says of him, "He was doubtless moved with inner remorse at the cruelties of 'his champion' Charles of Anjou." Jeremiah too would lament the doom he was constrained to utter. Nevertheless he could not permit Judah to be deluded to its ruin by empty dreams of glory:—

"O land, land, land,
Hear the word of Jehovah."

Isaiah had called all Nature, heaven and earth to bear witness against Israel, but now Jeremiah is appealing with urgent importunity to Judah. "O Chosen Land of Jehovah, so richly blessed by His favour, so sternly chastised by His discipline, Land of prophetic Revelation, now at last, after so many warnings, believe the word of thy God and submit to His judgment. Hasten not thy unhappy fate by shallow confidence in the genius and daring of Jehoiachin: he is no true Messiah."

"For saith Jehovah,
Write this man childless,
A man whose life shall not know prosperity:
For none of his seed shall prosper;
None shall sit upon the throne of David,
Nor rule any more over Judah."

Thus, by Divine decree, the descendants of Jehoiakim were disinherited; Jehoiachin was to be recorded in the genealogies of Israel as having no heir. He might have offspring,† but the Messiah, the Son of David, would not come of his line.

Two points suggest themselves in connection with this utterance of Jeremiah; first as to the circumstances under which it was uttered, then as to its application to Jehoiachin.

A moment's reflection will show that this prophecy implied great courage and presence of mind on the part of Jeremiah—his enemies might even have spoken of his barefaced audacity. He had predicted that Jehoiakim's corpse should be

* Milman's "Latin Christianity," vi. 392.

† 1 Chron. iii. 17 mentions the "sons" of Jeconiah, and in Matt. i. 12 Shealtiel is called his "son," but in Luke iii. 27 Shealtiel is called the son of Neri.

cast forth without any rites of honourable sepulture; and no son of his should sit upon the throne. Jehoiakim had been buried like other kings, he slept with his fathers, and Jehoiachin his son reigned in his stead. The prophet should have felt himself utterly discredited; and yet here was Jeremiah coming forward unabashed with new prophecies against the king whose very existence was a glaring disproof of his prophetic inspiration. Thus the friends of Jehoiachin. They would affect towards Jeremiah's message the same indifference which the present generation feels for the expositors of Daniel and the Apocalypse, who confidently announce the end of the world for 1866, and in 1867 fix a new date with cheerful and undiminished assurance. But these students of sacred records can always save the authority of Scripture by acknowledging the fallibility of their calculations. When their predictions fail, they confess that they have done their sum wrong and start it afresh. But Jeremiah's utterances were not published as human deductions from inspired data; he himself claimed to be inspired. He did not ask his hearers to verify and acknowledge the accuracy of his arithmetic or his logic, but to submit to the Divine message from his lips. And yet it is clear that he did not stake the authority of Jehovah or even his own prophetic status upon the accurate and detailed fulfilment of his predictions. Nor does he suggest that, in announcing a doom which was not literally accomplished, he had misunderstood or misinterpreted his message. The details which both Jeremiah and those who edited and transmitted his words knew to be unfulfilled were allowed to remain in the record of Divine Revelation—not, surely, to illustrate the fallibility of prophets, but to show that an accurate forecast of details is not of the essence of prophecy; such details belong to its form and not to its substance. Ancient Hebrew prophecy clothed its ideas in concrete images; its messages of doom were made definite and intelligible in a glowing series of definite pictures. The prophets were realists and not impressionists. But they were also spiritual men, concerned with the great issues of history and religion. Their message had to do with *these:* they were little interested in minor matters; and they used detailed imagery as a mere instrument of exposition. Popular scepticism exulted when subsequent facts did not exactly correspond to Jeremiah's images, but the prophet himself was unconscious of either failure or mistake. Jehoiakim might be magnificently buried, but his name was branded with eternal dishonour; Jehoiachin might reign for a hundred days, but the doom of Judah was not averted, and the house of David ceased for ever to rule in Jerusalem.

Our second point is the application of this prophecy to Jehoiachin. How far did the king deserve his sentence? Jeremiah indeed does not explicitly blame Jehoiachin, does not specify his sins as he did those of his royal sire. The estimate recorded in the Book of Kings doubtless expresses the judgment of Jeremiah, but it may be directed not so much against the young king as against his ministers. Yet the king cannot have been entirely innocent of the guilt of his policy and government. In chap. xxiv., however, Jeremiah speaks of the captives at Babylon, those carried away with Jehoiachin, as "good figs"; but we scarcely suppose he meant to include the king himself in this favourable estimate, otherwise we should discern some note of sympathy in the personal sentence upon him. We are left, therefore, to conclude that Jeremiah's judgment was unfavourable; although, in view of the prince's youth and limited opportunities, his guilt must have been slight, compared to that of his father.

And, on the other hand, we have the manifest sympathy and even admiration of Ezekiel. The two estimates stand side by side in the sacred record to remind us that God neither tolerates man's sins because there is a better side to his nature, nor yet ignores his virtues on account of his vices. For ourselves we may be content to leave the last word on this matter with Jeremiah. When he declares God's sentence on Jehoiachin, he does not suggest that it was undeserved, but he refrains from any explicit reproach. Probably if he had known how entirely his prediction would be fulfilled, if he had foreseen the seven-and-thirty weary years which the young lion was to spend in his Babylonian cage, Jeremiah would have spoken more tenderly and pitifully even of the son of Jehoiakim.

CHAPTER VIII.

BAD SHEPHERDS AND FALSE PROPHETS.

JEREMIAH xxiii., xxiv.

"Woe unto the shepherds that destroy and scatter the sheep of My pasture!"—JER. xxiii. 1.

"Of what avail is straw instead of grain? . . . Is not My word like fire, . . . like a hammer that shattereth the rocks?"—JER. xxiii. 28, 29.

THE captivity of Jehoiachin and the deportation of the flower of the people marked the opening of the last scene in the tragedy of Judah and of a new period in the ministry of Jeremiah. These events, together with the accession of Zedekiah as Nebuchadnezzar's nominee, very largely altered the state of affairs in Jerusalem. And yet the two main features of the situation were unchanged—the people and the government persistently disregarded Jeremiah's exhortations. "Neither Zedekiah, nor his servants, nor the people of the land, did hearken unto the words of Jehovah which He spake by the prophet Jeremiah." * They would not obey the will of Jehovah as to their life and worship, and they would not submit to Nebuchadnezzar. "Zedekiah . . . did evil in the sight of Jehovah, according to all that Jehoiakim had done; . . . and Zedekiah rebelled against the king of Babylon." †

It is remarkable that though Jeremiah consistently urged submission to Babylon, the various arrangements made by Nebuchadnezzar did very little to improve the prophet's position or increase his influence. The Chaldean king may have seemed ungrateful only because he was ignorant of the services rendered to him—Jeremiah would not enter into direct and personal cooperation with the enemy of his country, even with him whom Jehovah had appointed to be the scourge of His disobedient people—but the Chaldean policy served Nebuchadnezzar as little as it profited Jeremiah. Jehoiakim, in spite of

* xxxvii. 2. † 2 Kings xxiv. 18–20.

his forced submission, remained the able and determined foe of his suzerain, and Zedekiah, to the best of his very limited ability, followed his predecessor's example.

Zedekiah was uncle * of Jehoiachin, half-brother of Jehoiakim, and own brother to Jehoahaz. Possibly the two brothers owed their bias against Jeremiah and his teaching to their mother, Josiah's wife Hamutal, the daughter of another Jeremiah, the Libnite. Ezekiel thus describes the appointment of the new king: "The king of Babylon . . . took one of the seed royal, and made a covenant with him; he also put him under an oath, and took away the mighty of the land: that the kingdom might be base, that it might not lift itself up, but that by keeping of his covenant it might stand." † Apparently Nebuchadnezzar was careful to choose a feeble prince for his "base kingdom"; all that we read of Zedekiah suggests that he was weak and incapable. Henceforth the sovereign counted for little in the internal struggles of the tottering state. Josiah had firmly maintained the religious policy of Jeremiah, and Jehoiakim, as firmly, the opposite policy; but Zedekiah had neither the strength nor the firmness to enforce a consistent policy and to make one party permanently dominant. Jeremiah and his enemies were left to fight it out amongst themselves, so that now their antagonism grew more bitter and pronounced than during any other reign.

But whatever advantage the prophet might derive from the weakness of the sovereign was more than counterbalanced by the recent deportation. In selecting the captives Nebuchadnezzar had sought merely to weaken Judah by carrying away every one who would have been an element of strength to the "base kingdom." Perhaps he rightly believed that neither the prudence of the wise nor the honour of the virtuous would overcome their patriotic hatred of subjection; weakness alone would guarantee the obedience of Judah. He forgot that even weakness is apt to be foolhardy—when there is no immediate prospect of penalty.

One result of his policy was that the enemies and friends of Jeremiah were carried away indiscriminately; there was no attempt to leave behind those who might have counselled submission to Babylon as the acceptance of a Divine judgment, and thus have helped to keep Judah loyal to its foreign master. On the contrary Jeremiah's disciples were chiefly thoughtful and honourable men, and Nebuchadnezzar's policy in taking away "the mighty of the land" bereft the prophet of many friends and supporters, amongst them his disciple Ezekiel and doubtless a large class of whom Daniel and his three friends might be taken as types. When Jeremiah characterises the captives as "good figs," and those left behind as "bad figs,"‡ and the judgment is confirmed and amplified by Ezekiel,§ we may be sure that most of the prophet's adherents were in exile.

We have already had occasion to compare the changes in the religious policy of the Jewish government to the alternations of Protestant and Romanist sovereigns among the Tudors; but no Tudor was as feeble as Zedekiah. He may rather be compared to Charles IX. of France, helpless between the Huguenots and the League. Only the Jewish factions were less numerous, less evenly balanced; and by the speedy advance of Nebuchadnezzar civil dissensions were merged in national ruin.

The opening years of the new reign passed in nominal allegiance to Babylon. Jeremiah's influence would be used to induce the vassal king to observe the covenant he had entered into and to be faithful to his oath to Nebuchadnezzar. On the other hand a crowd of "patriotic" prophets urged Zedekiah to set up once more the standard of national independence, to "come to the help of the Lord against the mighty." Let us then briefly consider Jeremiah's polemic against the princes, prophets, and priests of his people. While Ezekiel in a celebrated chapter * denounces the idolatry of the princes, priests, and women of Judah, their worship of creeping things and abominable beasts, their weeping for Tammuz, their adoration of the sun, Jeremiah is chiefly concerned with the perverse policy of the government and the support it receives from priests and prophets, who profess to speak in the name of Jehovah. Jeremiah does not utter against Zedekiah any formal judgment like those on his three predecessors. Perhaps the prophet did not regard this impotent sovereign as the responsible representative of the state, and when the long-expected catastrophe at last befell the doomed people, neither Zedekiah nor his doings distracted men's attention from their own personal sufferings and patriotic regrets. At the point where a paragraph on Zedekiah would naturally have followed that on Jehoiachin, we have by way of summary and conclusion to the previous sections a brief denunciation of the shepherds of Israel.

"Woe unto the shepherds that destroy and scatter the sheep of My pasture! . . . Ye have scattered My flock, and driven them away, and have not cared for them; behold, I will visit upon you the evil of your doings."

These "shepherds" are primarily the kings, Jehoahaz, Jehoiakim, and Jehoiachin, who have been condemned by name in the previous chapter, together with the unhappy Zedekiah, who is too insignificant to be mentioned. But the term shepherds will also include the ruling and influential classes of which the king was the leading representative.

The image is a familiar one in the Old Testament and is found in the oldest literature of Israel,† but the denunciation of the rulers of Judah as unfaithful shepherds is characteristic of Jeremiah, Ezekiel, and one of the prophecies appended to the Book of Zechariah.‡ Ezekiel xxxiv. expands this figure and enforces its lessons:—

"Woe unto the shepherds of Israel that do feed themselves!
Should not the shepherds feed the sheep? Ye eat the fat, and ye clothe you with the wool.
Ye kill the fatlings: but ye feed not the sheep.
The diseased have ye not strengthened,
Neither have ye healed the sick,
Neither have ye bound up the bruised,
Neither have ye brought back again that which was driven away,

* 2 Chron. xxxvi. 10 makes Zedekiah the brother of Jehoiachin, possibly using the word in the general sense of "relation." Zedekiah's age shows that he cannot have been the son of Jehoiakim.

† Ezek. xvii. 13, 14.

‡ xxiv.

§ vii.-xi.

* viii.

† Gen. xlix. 24, J. from older source. Micah v 5

‡ ix.-xi., xiii. 7-9.

> Neither have ye sought for that which was lost,
> But your rule over them has been harsh and violent,
> And for want of a shepherd, they were scattered,
> And became food for every beast of the field."*

So in Zechariah ix., etc., Jehovah's anger is kindled against the shepherds, because they do not pity His flock.† Elsewhere‡ Jeremiah speaks of the kings of all nations as shepherds, and pronounces against them also a like doom. All these passages illustrate the concern of the prophets for good government. They were neither Pharisees nor formalists; their religious ideals were broad and wholesome. Doubtless the elect remnant will endure through all conditions of society; but the Kingdom of God was not meant to be a pure Church in a rotten state. This present evil world is no manure heap to fatten the growth of holiness: it is rather a mass for the saints to leaven.

Both Jeremiah and Ezekiel turn from the unfaithful shepherds whose "hungry sheep look up and are not fed" to the true King of Israel, the "Shepherd of Israel that led Joseph like a flock, and dwelt between the Cherubim." In the days of the Restoration He will raise up faithful shepherds, and over them a righteous Branch, the real Jehovah Zidqenu, instead of the sapless twig who disgraced the name "Zedekiah." Similarly Ezekiel promises that God will set up one shepherd over His people, "even My servant David." The pastoral care of Jehovah for His people is most tenderly and beautifully set forth in the twenty-third Psalm. Our Lord, the root and the offspring of David, claims to be the fulfilment of ancient prophecy when He calls Himself "the Good Shepherd." The words of Christ and of the Psalmist receive new force and fuller meaning when we contrast their pictures of the true Shepherd with the portraits of the Jewish kings drawn by the prophets. Moreover the history of this metaphor warns us against ignoring the organic life of the Christian society, the Church, in our concern for the spiritual life of the individual. As Sir Thomas More said, in applying this figure to Henry VIII., "Of the multitude of sheep cometh the name of a shepherd."§ A shepherd implies not merely a sheep, but a flock; His relation to each member is tender and personal, but He bestows blessings and requires service in fellowship with the Family of God.

By a natural sequence the denunciation of the unfaithful shepherds is followed by a similar utterance "concerning the prophets." It is true that the prophets are not spoken of as shepherds; and Milton's use of the figure in "Lycidas" suggests the New Testament rather than the Old. Yet the prophets had a large share in guiding the destinies of Israel in politics as well as in religion, and having passed sentence on the shepherds—the kings and princes—Jeremiah turns to the ecclesiastics, chiefly, as the heading implies, to the prophets. The priests indeed do not escape, but Jeremiah seems to feel that they are adequately dealt with in two or three casual references. We use the term "ecclesiastics" advisedly; the prophets were now a large professional class, more important and even more clerical than the priests. The prophets and priests together were the clergy of Israel. They claimed to be devoted servants of Jehovah, and for the most part the claim was made in all sincerity; but they misunderstood His character, and mistook for Divine inspiration the suggestions of their own prejudice and self-will.

Jeremiah's indictment against them has various counts. He accuses them of speaking without authority, and also of time-serving, plagiarism, and cant.

First, then, as to their unauthorised utterances: Jeremiah finds them guilty of an unholy license in prophesying, a distorted caricature of that "liberty of prophesying" which is the prerogative of God's accredited ambassadors.

> "Hearken not unto the words of the prophets that prophesy unto you.
> They make fools of you:
> The visions which they declare are from their own hearts,
> And not from the mouth of Jehovah.
>
> . . . .
>
> Who hath stood in the council of Jehovah,
> To perceive and hear His word?
> Who hath marked His word and heard it?
> I sent not the prophets—yet they ran;
> I spake not unto them—yet they prophesied."

The evils which Jeremiah describes are such as will always be found in any large professional class. To use modern terms—in the Church, as in every profession, there will be men who are not qualified for the vocation which they follow. They are indeed not called to their vocation; they "follow," but do not overtake it. They are not sent of God, yet they run; they have no Divine message, yet they preach. They have never stood in the council of Jehovah; they might perhaps have gathered up scraps of the King's purposes from His true councillors; but when they had opportunity they neither "marked nor heard"; and yet they discourse concerning heavenly things with much importance and assurance. But their inspiration, at its best, has no deeper or richer source than their own shallow selves; their visions are the mere product of their own imaginations. Strangers to the true fellowship, their spirit is not "a well of water springing up unto eternal life," but a stagnant pool. And, unless the judgment and mercy of God intervene, that pool will in the end be fed from a fountain whose bitter waters are earthly, sensual, devilish.

We are always reluctant to speak of ancient prophecy or modern preaching as a "profession." We may gladly dispense with the word, if we do not thereby ignore the truth which it inaccurately expresses. Men lived by prophecy, as, with Apostolic sanction, men live by "the gospel." They were expected, as ministers are now, though in a less degree, to justify their claims to an income and an official status, by discharging religious functions so as to secure the approval of the people or the authorities. Then, as now, the prophet's reputation, influence, and social standing, probably even his income, depended upon the amount of visible success that he could achieve.

In view of such facts, it is futile to ask men of the world not to speak of the clerical life as a profession. They discern no ethical difference between a curate's dreams of a bishopric and the aspirations of a junior barrister to the woolsack. Probably a refusal to recognise the element common to the ministry with law, medicine, and other professions, injures both the Church and its servants. One peculiar difficulty and most insidious temptation of the Christian ministry consists in its mingled resemblances to and dif-

* Ezek. xxxiv. 2–5
† Zech. x. 3, xi [illegible]
‡ xxv. 34–38.
§ Froude, i. 205.

ferences from the other professions. The minister has to work under similar worldly conditions, and yet to control those conditions by the indwelling power of the Spirit. He has to "run," it may be twice or even three times a week, whether he be sent or no: how can he always preach only that which God has taught him? He is consciously dependent upon the exercise of his memory, his intellect, his fancy: how can he avoid speaking "the visions of his own heart"? The Church can never allow its ministers to regard themselves as mere professional teachers and lecturers, and yet if they claim to be more, must they not often fall under Jeremiah's condemnation?

It is one of those practical dilemmas which delight casuists and distress honest and earnest servants of God. In the early Christian centuries similar difficulties peopled the Egyptian and Syrian deserts with ascetics, who had given up the world as a hopeless riddle. A full discussion of the problem would lead us too far away from the exposition of Jeremiah, and we will only venture to make two suggestions.

The necessity, which most ministers are under, of "living by the gospel," may promote their own spiritual life and add to their usefulness. It corrects and reduces spiritual pride, and helps them to understand and sympathise with their lay brethren, most of whom are subject to a similar trial.

Secondly, as a minister feels the ceaseless pressure of strong temptation to speak from and live for himself—his lower, egotistic self—he will be correspondingly driven to a more entire and persistent surrender to God. The infinite fulness and variety of Revelation is expressed by the manifold gifts and experience of the prophets. If only the prophet be surrendered to the Spirit, then what is most characteristic of himself may become the most forcible expression of his message. His constant prayer will be that he may have the child's heart and may never resist the Holy Ghost, that no personal interest or prejudice, no bias of training or tradition or current opinion, may dull his hearing when he stands in the council of the Lord, or betray him into uttering for Christ's gospel the suggestions of his own self-will or the mere watchwords of his ecclesiastical faction.

But to return to the ecclesiastics who had stirred Jeremiah's wrath. The professional prophets naturally adapted their words to the itching ears of their clients. They were not only officious, but also time-serving. Had they been true prophets, they would have dealt faithfully with Judah; they would have sought to convince the people of sin, and to lead them to repentance; they would thus have given them yet another opportunity of salvation.

"If they had stood in My council,
They would have caused My people to hear My words;
They would have turned them from their evil way,
And from the evil of their doings."

But now:—

"They walk in lies and strengthen the hands of evildoers,
That no one may turn away from his sin.
. . . .
They say continually unto them that despise the word of Jehovah,*
Ye shall have peace;
And unto every one that walketh in the stubbornness of his heart they say,
No evil shall come upon you."

* LXX. See R. V. margin.

Unfortunately, when prophecy becomes professional in the lowest sense of the word, it is governed by commercial principles. A sufficiently imperious demand calls forth an abundant supply. A sovereign can "tune the pulpits"; and a ruling race can obtain from its clergy formal ecclesiastical sanction for such "domestic institutions" as slavery. When evildoers grow numerous and powerful, there will always be prophets to strengthen their hands and encourage them not to turn away from their sin. But to give the lie to these false prophets God sends Jeremiahs, who are often branded as heretics and schismatics, turbulent fellows who turn the world upside-down.

The self-important, self-seeking spirit leads further to the sin of plagiarism:—

"Therefore I am against the prophets, is the utterance of Jehovah,
Who steal My word from one another."

The sin of plagiarism is impossible to the true prophet, partly because there are no rights of private property in the word of Jehovah. The Old Testament writers make free use of the works of their predecessors. For instance, Isaiah ii. 2-4 is almost identical with Micah iv. 1-3; yet neither author acknowledges his indebtedness to the other or to any third prophet.* Uriah ben Shemaiah prophesied acording to all the words of Jeremiah,† who himself owes much to Hosea, whom he never mentions. Yet he was not conscious of stealing from his predecessor, and he would have brought no such charge against Isaiah or Micah or Uriah. In the New Testament 2 Peter and Jude have so much in common that one must have used the other without acknowledgment. Yet the Church has not, on that ground, excluded either Epistle from the Canon. In the goodly fellowship of the prophets and the glorious company of the apostles no man says that the things which he utters are his own. But the mere hireling has no part in the spiritual communism wherein each may possess all things because he claims nothing. When a prophet ceases to be the messenger of God, and sinks into the mercenary purveyor of his own clever sayings and brilliant fancies, then he is tempted to become a clerical Autolycus, "a snapper-up of unconsidered trifles." Modern ideas furnish a curious parallel to Jeremiah's indifference to the borrowings of the true prophet, and his scorn of the literary pilferings of the false. We hear only too often of stolen sermons, but no one complains of plagiarism in prayers. Doubtless among these false prophets charges of plagiarism were bandied to and fro with much personal acrimony. But it is interesting to notice that Jeremiah is not denouncing an injury done to himself; he does not accuse them of thieving from him, but from one another. Probably assurance and lust of praise and power would have overcome any awe they felt for Jeremiah. He was only free from their depredations, because—from their point of view—his words were not worth stealing. There was nothing to be gained by repeating his stern denunciations, and even his promises were not exactly suited to the popular taste.

* Possibly, however, the insertion of this passage in one of the books may have been the work of an editor, and we cannot be sure that, in Jeremiah's time, collections entitled Isaiah and Micah both included this section.

† xxvi. 20.

These prophets were prepared to cater for the average religious appetite in the most approved fashion—in other words, they were masters of cant. Their office had been consecrated by the work of true men of God like Elijah and Isaiah. They themselves claimed to stand in the genuine prophetic succession, and to inherit the reverence felt for their great predecessors, quoting their inspired utterances and adopting their weighty phrases. As Jeremiah's contemporaries listened to one of their favourite orators, they were soothed by his assurances of Divine favour and protection, and their confidence in the speaker was confirmed by the frequent sound of familiar formulæ in his unctuous sentences. These had the true ring; they were redolent of sound doctrine, of what popular tradition regarded as orthodox.

The solemn attestation NE'UM YAHWE, "It is the utterance of Jehovah," is continually appended to prophecies, almost as if it were the sign-manual of the Almighty. Isaiah and other prophets frequently use the term MASSA (A. V., R. V., "burden") as a title, especially for prophecies concerning neighbouring nations. The ancient records loved to tell how Jehovah revealed Himself to the patriarchs in dreams. Jeremiah's rivals included dreams in their clerical apparatus:—

"Behold, I am against them that prophesy lying dreams
—*Ne'um Yahwe*—
And tell them, and lead astray My people
By their lies and their rodomontade;
It was not I who sent or commanded them,
Neither shall they profit this people at all,
Ne'um Yahwe."

These prophets "thought to cause the Lord's people to forget His name, as their fathers forgot His name for Baal, by their dreams which they told one another."

Moreover they could glibly repeat the sacred phrases as part of their professional jargon:—

"Behold, I am against the prophets,
It is the utterance of Jehovah (*Ne'um Yahwe*),
That use their tongues
To utter utterances (*Wayyin'amu Ne'um.*)"

"To utter utterances"—the prophets uttered them, not Jehovah. These sham oracles were due to no Diviner source than the imagination of foolish hearts. But for Jeremiah's grim earnestness, the last clause would be almost blasphemous. It is virtually a caricature of the most solemn formula of ancient Hebrew religion. But this was really degraded when it was used to obtain credence for the lies which men prophesied out of the deceit of their own heart. Jeremiah's seeming irreverence was the most forcible way of bringing this home to his hearers. There are profanations of the most sacred things which can scarcely be spoken of without an apparent breach of the Third Commandment. The most awful taking in vain of the name of the Lord God is not heard among the publicans and sinners, but in pulpits and on the platforms of religious meetings.

But these prophets and their clients had a special fondness for the phrase "The burden of Jehovah," and their unctuous use of it most especially provoked Jeremiah's indignation:—

"When this people, priest, or prophet shall ask thee,
What is the burden of Jehovah?
Then say unto them, Ye are the burden.*
But I will cast you off, *Ne'um Yahwe.*
If priest or prophet or people shall say, The burden of Jehovah,
I will punish that man and his house.
And ye shall say to one another,
What hath Jehovah answered? and, What hath Jehovah spoken?
And ye shall no more make mention of the burden of Jehovah:
For (if ye do) men's words shall become a burden to themselves.
. . . . . .
Thus shall ye inquire of a prophet,
What hath Jehovah answered thee?
What hath Jehovah spoken unto thee?
But if ye say, The burden of Jehovah,
Thus saith Jehovah: Because ye say this word, The burden of Jehovah,
When I have sent unto you the command,
Ye shall not say, The burden of Jehovah,
Therefore I will assuredly take you up,
And will cast away from before Me both you and the city which I gave to you and to your fathers.
I will bring upon you everlasting reproach
And everlasting shame, that shall not be forgotten."

Jeremiah's insistence and vehemence speak for themselves. Their moral is obvious, though for the most part unheeded. The most solemn formulæ, hallowed by ancient and sacred associations, used by inspired teachers as the vehicle of revealed truths, may be debased till they become the very legend of Antichrist, blazoned on the *Vexilla Regis Inferni.* They are like a motto of one of Charles' Paladins flaunted by his unworthy descendants to give distinction to cruelty and vice. The Church's line of march is strewn with such dishonoured relics of her noblest champions. Even our Lord's own words have not escaped. There is a fashion of discoursing upon "the gospel" which almost tempts reverent Christians to wish they might never hear that word again. Neither is this debasing of the moral currency confined to religious phrases; almost every political and social watchword has been similarly abused. One of the vilest tyrannies the world has ever seen—the Reign of Terror—claimed to be an incarnation of "Liberty, Equality, and Fraternity."

Yet the Bible, with that marvellous catholicity which lifts it so high above the level of all other religious literature, not only records Jeremiah's prohibition to use the term "Burden," but also tells us that centuries later Malachi could still speak of "the burden of the word of Jehovah." A great phrase that has been discredited by misuse may yet recover itself; the tarnished and dishonoured sword of faith may be baptised and burnished anew, and flame in the forefront of the holy war.

Jeremiah does not stand alone in his unfavourable estimate of the professional prophets of Judah; a similar depreciation seems to be implied by the words of Amos: "I am neither a prophet nor of the sons of prophets." * One of the unknown authors whose writings have been included in the Book of Zechariah takes up the teaching of Amos and Jeremiah and carries it a stage further:—

"In that day (it is the utterance of Jehovah Sabaoth) I will cut off the names of the idols from the land,
They shall not be remembered any more;
Also the prophets and the spirit of uncleanness
Will I expel from the land.
When any shall yet prophesy,
His father and mother that begat him shall say unto him,
Thou shalt not live, for thou speakest lies in the name of Jehovah:
And his father and mother that begat him shall thrust him through when he prophesieth.

* So LXX. and modern editors: see Giesebrecht, *in loco.* R. V. "What burden?"

* vii. 14; but *cf.* R. V., "I was," etc.

In that day every prophet when he prophesieth shall be ashamed of his vision ;
Neither shall any wear a hairy mantle to deceive :
He shall say, I am no prophet ;
I am a tiller of the ground,
I was sold for a slave in my youth." *

No man with any self-respect would allow his fellows to dub him prophet; slave was a less humiliating name. No family would endure the disgrace of having a member who belonged to this despised caste; parents would rather put their son to death than see him a prophet. To such extremities may the spirit of time-serving and cant reduce a national clergy. We are reminded of Latimer's words in his famous sermon to Convocation in 1536: "All good men, in all places accuse your avarice, your exactions, your tyranny. I commanded you that ye should feed my sheep, and ye earnestly feed yourselves from day to day, wallowing in delights and idleness. I commanded you to teach my law; you teach your own traditions, and seek your own glory." †

Over against their fluent and unctuous cant Jeremiah sets the terrible reality of his Divine message. Compared to this, their sayings are like chaff to the wheat; nay, this is too tame a figure—Jehovah's word is like fire, like a hammer that shatters rocks. He says of himself:—

"My heart within me is broken ; all my bones shake :
I am like a drunken man, like a man whom wine hath overcome,
Because of Jehovah and His holy words."

Thus we have in chapter xxiii. a full and formal statement of the controversy between Jeremiah and his brother-prophets. On the one hand, self-seeking and self-assurance winning popularity by orthodox phrases, traditional doctrine, and the prophesying of smooth things; on the other hand, a man to whom the word of the Lord was like a fire in his bones, who had surrendered prejudice and predilection that he might himself become a hammer to shatter the Lord's enemies, a man through whom God wrought so mightily that he himself reeled and staggered with the blows of which he was the instrument.

The relation of the two parties was not unlike that of St. Paul and his Corinthian adversaries: the prophet, like the Apostle, spoke "in demonstration of the Spirit of power" ; he considered "not the word of them which are puffed up, but the power. For the kingdom of God is not in word, but in power." In our next chapter we shall see the practical working of this antagonism which we have here set forth.

CHAPTER IX.

HANANIAH.

JEREMIAH xxvii., xxviii.

"Hear now, Hananiah ; Jehovah hath not sent thee, but thou makest this people to trust in a lie."—JER. xxviii. 15.

THE most conspicuous point at issue between Jeremiah and his opponents was political rather than ecclesiastical. Jeremiah was anxious that Zedekiah should keep faith with Nebuchadnezzar, and not involve Judah in useless misery by another hopeless revolt. The prophets preached the popular doctrine of an imminent Divine intervention to deliver Judah from her oppressors. They devoted themselves to the easy task of fanning patriotic enthusiasm, till the Jews were ready for any enterprise, however reckless.

During the opening years of the new reign, Nebuchadnezzar's recent capture of Jerusalem and the consequent wholesale deportation were fresh in men's minds; fear of the Chaldeans together with the influence of Jeremiah kept the government from any overt act of rebellion. According to li. 59, the king even paid a visit to Babylon, to do homage to his suzerain.

It was probably in the fourth year of his reign * that the tributary Syrian states began to prepare for a united revolt against Babylon. The Assyrian and Chaldean annals constantly mention such combinations, which were formed and broken up and reformed with as much ease and variety as patterns in a kaleidoscope. On the present occasion the kings of Edom, Moab, Ammon, Tyre, and Zidon sent their ambassadors to Jerusalem to arange with Zedekiah for concerted action. But there were more important persons to deal with in that city than Zedekiah. Doubtless the princes of Judah welcomed the opportunity for a new revolt. But before the negotiations were very far advanced, Jeremiah heard what was going on. By Divine command, he made "bands and bars," *i. e.*, yokes, for himself and for the ambassadors of the allies, or possibly for them to carry home to their masters. They received their answer not from Zedekiah, but from the true King of Israel, Jehovah Himself. They had come to solicit armed assistance to deliver them from Babylon; they were sent back with yokes to wear as a symbol of their entire and helpless subjection to Nebuchadnezzar. This was the word of Jehovah:—

"The nation and the kingdom that will not put its neck beneath the yoke of the king of Babylon,
That nation will I visit with sword and famine and pestilence until I consume them by his hand."

The allied kings had been encouraged to revolt by oracles similar to those uttered by the Jewish prophets in the name of Jehovah; but:—

"As for you, hearken not to your prophets, diviners, dreams, soothsayers and sorcerers,
When they speak unto you, saying, Ye shall not serve the king of Babylon.
They prophesy a lie unto you, to remove you far from your land ;
That I should drive you out, and that you should perish.
But the nation that shall bring their neck under the yoke of the king of Babylon, and serve him,
That nation will I maintain in their own land (it is the utterance of Jehovah), and they shall till it and dwell in it."

When he had sent his message to the foreign envoys, Jeremiah addressed an almost identical admonition to his own king. He bids him submit to the Chaldean yoke, under the same penalties for disobedience—sword, pestilence, and famine for himself and his people. He warns him also against delusive promises of the prophets, especially in the matter of the sacred vessels.

The popular doctrine of the inviolable sanctity of the Temple had sustained a severe shock when Nebuchadnezzar carried off the sacred vessels to Babylon. It was inconceivable that Jehovah would patiently submit to so gross an indignity.

* Zech. xiii. 2-5. Post-exilic, according to most critics (Driver's "Introduction," *in loco*).

† Froude, ii. 474.

* The close connection between xxvii. and xxviii. shows that the date in xxviii. 1, "the fourth year of Zedekiah," covers both chapters. "Jehoiakim" in xxvii. 1 is a misreading for "Zedekiah" : see R. V. margin.

In ancient days the Ark had plagued its Philistine captors till they were only too thankful to be rid of it. Later on a graphic narrative in the Book of Daniel told with what swift vengeance God punished Belshazzar for his profane use of these very vessels. So now patriotic prophets were convinced that the golden candlestick, the bowls and chargers of gold and silver, would soon return in triumph, like the Ark of old; and their return would be the symbol of the final deliverance of Judah from Babylon. Naturally the priests above all others would welcome such a prophecy, and would industriously disseminate it. But Jeremiah "spake to the priests and all this people, saying, Thus saith Jehovah:—

"Hearken not unto the words of your prophets, which prophesy unto you.
Behold, the vessels of the house of Jehovah shall be brought back from Babylon now speedily:
For they prophesy a lie unto you."

How could Jehovah grant triumphant deliverance to a carnally minded people who would not understand His Revelation, and did not discern any essential difference between Him and Moloch and Baal?

"Hearken not unto them; serve the king of Babylon and live.
Why should this city become a desolation?"

Possibly, however, even now, the Divine compassion might have spared Jerusalem the agony and shame of her final siege and captivity. God would not at once restore what was lost, but He might spare what was still left. Jeremiah could not endorse the glowing promises of the prophets, but he would unite with them to intercede for mercy upon the remnant of Israel.

"If they are prophets and the word of Jehovah is with them,
Let them intercede with Jehovah Sabaoth, that the rest of the vessels of the Temple, the Palace, and the City may not go to Babylon."

The God of Israel was yet ready to welcome any beginning of true repentance. Like the father of the Prodigal Son, He would meet His people when they were on the way back to Him. Any stirring of filial penitence would win an instant and gracious response.

We can scarcely suppose that this appeal by Jeremiah to his brother-prophets was merely sarcastic and denunciatory. Passing circumstances may have brought Jeremiah into friendly intercourse with some of his opponents; personal contact may have begotten something of mutual kindliness; and hence there arose a transient gleam of hope that reconciliation and co-operation might still be possible. But it was soon evident that the "patriotic" party would not renounce their vain dreams: Judah must drink the cup of wrath to the dregs: the pillars, the sea, the bases, the rest of the vessels left in Jerusalem must also be carried to Babylon, and remain there till Jehovah should visit the Jews and bring them back and restore them to their own land.

Thus did Jeremiah meet the attempt of the government to organise a Syrian revolt against Babylon, and thus did he give the lie to the promises of Divine blessing made by the prophets. In the face of his utterances, it was difficult to maintain the popular enthusiasm necessary to a successful revolt. In order to neutralise, if possible, the impression made by Jeremiah, the government put forward one of their prophetic supporters to deliver a counter-blast. The place and the occasion were similar to those chosen by Jeremiah for his own address to the people and for Baruch's reading of the roll—the court of the Temple where the priests and "all the people" were assembled. Jeremiah himself was there. Possibly it was a feast-day. The incident came to be regarded as of special importance, and a distinct heading is attached to it, specifying its exact date, "in the same year"—as the incidents of the previous chapter—"in the beginning of the reign of Zedekiah, in the fourth year, in the fifth month."

On such an occasion, Jeremiah's opponents would select as their representative some striking personality, a man of high reputation for ability and personal character. Such a man, apparently, they found in Hananiah ben Azzur of Gibeon. Let us consider for a moment this mouthpiece and champion of a great political and ecclesiastical party, we might almost say of a National government and a National Church. He is never mentioned except in chapter xxviii., but what we read here is sufficiently characteristic, and receives much light from the other literature of the period. As Gibeon is assigned to the priests in Joshua xxi. 17, it has been conjectured that, like Jeremiah himself, Hananiah was a priest. The special stress laid on the sacred vessels would be in accordance with this theory.

In our last chapter we expounded Jeremiah's description of his prophetic contemporaries, as self-important and time-serving, guilty of plagiarism and cant. Now from this dim, inarticulate crowd of professional prophets an individual steps for a moment into the light of history and speaks with clearness and emphasis. Let us gaze at him, and hear what he has to say.

If we could have been present at this scene immediately after a careful study of chapter xxvii. even the appearance of Hananiah would have caused us a shock of surprise—such as is sometimes experienced by a devout student of Protestant literature on being introduced to a live Jesuit, or by some budding secularist when he first makes the personal acquaintance of a curate. We might possibly have discerned something commonplace, some lack of depth and force in the man whose faith was merely conventional; but we should have expected to read, "liar and hypocrite" in every line of his countenance, and we should have seen nothing of the sort. Conscious of the enthusiastic support of his fellow-countrymen and especially of his own order, charged—as he believed—with a message of promise for Jerusalem, Hananiah's face and bearing, as he came forward to address his sympathetic audience, betrayed nothing unworthy of the high calling of a prophet. His words had the true prophetic ring, he spoke with assured authority:—

"Thus saith Jehovah Sabaoth, the God of Israel,
I have broken the yoke of the king of Babylon."

His special object was to remove the unfavourable impression caused by Jeremiah's contradiction of the promise concerning the sacred vessels. Like Jeremiah, he meets this denial in the strongest and most convincing fashion. He does not argue—he reiterates the promise in a more definite form and with more emphatic asseveration. Like Jonah at Nineveh, he ventures to fix an exact date in the immediate future for the fulfilment of the prophecy. "Yet forty days," said Jonah, but the next day he had to swallow his own words; and Hananiah's prophetic chronology met with no better fate:—

"Within two full years will I bring again to this place all the vessels of the Temple, that Nebuchadnezzar king of Babylon took away."

The full significance of this promise is shown by the further addition:—

"And I will bring again to this place the king of Judah, Jeconiah ben Jehoiakim, and all the captives of Judah that went to Babylon (it is the utterance of Jehovah); for I will break the yoke of the king of Babylon."

This bold challenge was promptly met:—

"The prophet Jeremiah said unto the prophet Hananiah before the priests and all the people that stood in the Temple." Not "the true prophet" and "the false prophet," not "the man of God" and "the impostor," but simply "the prophet Jeremiah" and "the prophet Hananiah." The audience discerned no obvious difference of status or authority between the two—if anything the advantage lay with Hananiah; they watched the scene as a modern churchman might regard a discussion between ritualistic and evangelical bishops at a Church Congress, only Hananiah was their ideal of a "good churchman." The true parallel is not debates between atheists and the Christian Evidence Society, or between missionaries and Brahmins, but controversies like those between Arius and Athanasius, Jerome and Rufinus, Cyril and Chrysostom.

These prophets, however, display a courtesy and self-restraint that have, for the most part, been absent from Christian polemics.

"Jeremiah the prophet said, Amen: may Jehovah bring it to pass; may He establish the words of thy prophecy, by bringing back again from Babylon unto this place both the vessels of the Temple and all the captives."

With that entire sincerity which is the most consummate tact, Jeremiah avows his sympathy with his opponent's patriotic aspirations, and recognises that they were worthy of Hebrew prophets. But patriotic aspirations were not a sufficient reason for claiming Divine authority for a cheap optimism. Jeremiah's reflection upon the past had led him to an entirely opposite philosophy of history. Behind Hananiah's words lay the claim that the religious traditions of Israel and the teaching of former prophets guaranteed the inviolability of the Temple and the Holy City. Jeremiah appealed to their authority for his message of doom:—

"The ancient prophets who were our predecessors prophesied war and calamity and pestilence against many countries and great kingdoms."

It was also a mark of the true prophet that he should be the herald of disaster. The prophetical books of the Old Testament Canon fully confirm this startling and unwelcome statement. Their main burden is the ruin and misery that await Israel and its neighbours. The presumption therefore was in favour of the prophet of evil, and against the prophet of good. Jeremiah does not, of course, deny that there had been, and might yet be, prophets of good. Indeed every prophet, he himself included, announced some Divine promise, but:—

"The prophet which prophesieth of peace shall be known as truly sent of Jehovah when his prophecy is fulfilled."

It seemed a fair reply to Hananiah's challenge. His prophecy of the return of the sacred vessels and the exiles within two years was intended to encourage Judah and its allies to persist in revolt. They would be at once victorious, and recover all and more than all which they had lost. Under such circumstances Jeremiah's criterion of "prophecies of peace" was eminently practical. "You are promised these blessings within two years: very well, do not run the terrible risks of a rebellion; keep quiet and see if the two years bring the fulfilment of this prophecy—it is not long to wait." Hananiah might fairly have replied that this fulfilment depended on Judah's faith and loyalty to the Divine promise; and their faith and loyalty would be best shown by rebelling against their oppressors. Jehovah promised Canaan to the Hebrews of the Exodus, but their carcases mouldered in the desert because they had not courage enough to attack formidable enemies. "Let us not," Hananiah might have said, "imitate their cowardice, and thus share alike their unbelief and its penalty."

Neither Jeremiah's premises nor his conclusions would commend his words to the audience, and he probably weakened his position by leaving the high ground of authority and descending to argument. Hananiah at any rate did not follow his example: he adheres to his former method, and reiterates with renewed emphasis the promise which his adversary has contradicted. Following Jeremiah in his use of the parable in action, so common with Hebrew prophets, he turned the symbol of the yoke against its author. As Zedekiah ben Chenaanah made him horns of iron and prophesied to Ahab and Jehoshaphat, "Thus saith Jehovah, With these shalt thou push the Syrians until thou have consumed them," * so now Hananiah took the yoke off Jeremiah's neck and broke it before the assembled people and said:—

"Thus saith Jehovah, Even so will I break the yoke of Nebuchadnezzar king of Babylon from the neck of all nations within two full years."

Naturally the promise is "for all nations"—not for Judah only, but for the other allies.

"And the prophet Jeremiah went his way." For the moment Hananiah had triumphed; he had had the last word, and Jeremiah was silenced. A public debate before a partisan audience was not likely to issue in victory for the truth. The situation may have even shaken his faith in himself and his message; he may have been staggered for a moment by Hananiah's apparent earnestness and conviction. He could not but remember that the gloomy predictions of Isaiah's earlier ministry had been followed by the glorious deliverance from Sennacherib. Possibly some similar sequel was to follow his own denunciations. He betook himself anew to fellowship with God, and awaited a fresh mandate from Jehovah.

"Then the word of Jehovah came unto Jeremiah, ... Go and tell Hananiah: Thou hast broken wooden yokes; thou shalt make iron yokes in their stead. For thus saith Jehovah Sabaoth, the God of Israel: I have put a yoke of iron upon the necks of all these nations, that they may serve Nebuchadnezzar king of Babylon." †

* 1 Kings xxii. 11.

† The rest of this verse has apparently been inserted from xxvii. 6 by a scribe. It is omitted by the LXX.

We are not told how long Jeremiah had to wait for this new message, or under what circumstances it was delivered to Hananiah. Its symbolism is obvious. When Jeremiah sent the yokes to the ambassadors of the allies and exhorted Zedekiah to bring his neck under the yoke of Nebuchadnezzar, they were required to accept the comparatively tolerable servitude of tributaries. Their impatience of this minor evil would expose them to the iron yoke of ruin and captivity.

Thus the prophet of evil received new Divine assurance of the abiding truth of his message and of the reality of his own inspiration. The same revelation convinced him that his opponent was either an impostor or woefully deluded:—

"Then said the prophet Jeremiah unto the prophet Hananiah, Hear now, Hananiah; Jehovah hath not sent thee, but thou makest this people to trust in a lie. Therefore thus saith Jehovah: I will cast thee away from off the face of the earth; this year thou shalt die, because thou hast preached rebellion against Jehovah."

By a judgment not unmixed with mercy, Hananiah was not left to be convicted of error or imposture, when the "two full years" should have elapsed, and his glowing promises be seen to utterly fail. He also was "taken away from the evil to come."

"So Hananiah the prophet died in the same year in the seventh month"—*i. e.*, about two months after this incident. Such personal judgments were most frequent in the case of kings, but were not confined to them. Isaiah * left on record prophecies concerning the appointment to the treasurership of Shebna and Eliakim; and elsewhere Jeremiah himself pronounces the doom of Pashhur ben Immer, the governor of the Temple; but the conclusion of this incident reminds us most forcibly of the speedy execution of the apostolic sentence upon Ananias and Sapphira.

The subjects of this and the preceding chapter raise some of the most important questions as to authority in religion. On the one hand, on the subjective side, how may a man be assured of the truth of his own religious convictions; on the other hand, on the objective side, how is the hearer to decide between conflicting claims on his faith and obedience?

The former question is raised as to the personal convictions of the two prophets. We have ventured to assume that, however erring and culpable Hananiah may have been, he yet had an honest faith in his own inspiration and in the truth of his own prophecies. The conscious impostor, unhappily, is not unknown either in ancient or modern Churches; but we should not look for edification from the study of this branch of morbid spiritual pathology. There were doubtless Jewish counterparts to "Mr. Sludge the Medium" and to the more subtle and plausible "Bishop Blougram"; but Hananiah was of a different type. The evident respect felt for him by the people, Jeremiah's almost deferential courtesy and temporary hesitation as to his rival's Divine mission, do not suggest deliberate hypocrisy. Hananiah's "lie" was a falsehood in fact but not in intention. The Divine message "Jehovah hath not sent thee" was felt by Jeremiah to be no mere exposure of what Hananiah had known all along, but to be a revelation to his adversary as well as to himself.

* xxii. 15–25.

The sweeping condemnation of the prophets in chapter xxiii. does not exclude the possibility of Hananiah's honesty, any more than our Lord's denunciation of the Pharisees as "devourers of widows' houses" necessarily includes Gamaliel. In critical times, upright, earnest men do not always espouse what subsequent ages hold to have been the cause of truth. Sir Thomas More and Erasmus remained in the communion which Luther renounced: Hampden and Falkland found themselves in opposite camps. If such men erred in their choice between right and wrong, we may often feel anxious as to our own decisions. When we find ourselves in opposition to earnest and devoted men, we may well pause to consider which is Jeremiah and which Hananiah.

The point at issue between these two prophets was exceedingly simple and practical—whether Jehovah approved of the proposed revolt and would reward it with success. Theological questions were only indirectly and remotely involved. Yet, in face of his opponent's persistent asseverations, Jeremiah—perhaps the greatest of the prophets—went his way in silence to obtain fresh Divine confirmation of his message. And the man who hesitated was right.

Two lessons immediately follow: one as to practice; the other as to principle. It often happens that earnest servants of God find themselves at variance, not on simple practical questions, but on the history and criticism of the remote past, or on abstruse points of transcendental theology. Before any one ventures to denounce his adversary as a teacher of deadly error, let him, like Jeremiah, seek, in humble and prayerful submission to the Holy Spirit, a Divine mandate for such denunciation.

But again Jeremiah was willing to reconsider his position, not merely because he himself might have been mistaken, but because altered circumstances might have opened the way for a change in God's dealings. It was a bare possibility, but we have seen elsewhere that Jeremiah represents God as willing to make a gracious response to the first movement of compunction. Prophecy was the declaration of His will, and that will was not arbitrary, but at every moment and at every point exactly adapted to conditions with which it had to deal. Its principles were unchangeable and eternal; but prophecy was chiefly an application of these principles to existing circumstances. The true prophet always realised that his words were for men as they were when he addressed them. Any moment might bring a change which would abrogate or modify the old teaching, and require and receive a new message. Like Jonah, he might have to proclaim ruin one day and deliverance the next. A physician, even after the most careful diagnosis, may have to recognise unsuspected symptoms which lead him to cancel his prescription and write a new one. The sickening and healing of the soul involve changes equally unexpected. The Bible does not teach that inspiration, any more than science, has only one treatment for each and every spiritual condition and contingency. The true prophet's message is always a word in season.

We turn next to the objective question: How is the hearer to decide between conflicting claims on his faith and obedience? We say the right was with Jeremiah; but how were the Jews to know that? They were addressed by two prophets, or, as we might say, two accredited ecclesiastics of the national Church; each with apparent earnestness and sincerity claimed to speak in the name of Jehovah and of the ancient faith of Israel, and each flatly contradicted the other on an immediate practical question, on which hung their individual fortunes and the destinies of their country. What were the Jews to do? Which were they to believe? It is the standing difficulty of all appeals to external authority. You inquire of this supposed Divine oracle and there issues from it a babel of discordant voices, and each demands that you shall unhesitatingly submit to its dictate on peril of eternal damnation; and some have the audacity to claim obedience, because their teaching is "*quod semper, quod ubique, quod ab omnibus.*"

One simple and practical test is indeed suggested—the prophet of evil is more likely to be truly inspired than the prophet of good; but Jeremiah naturally does not claim that this is an invariable test. Nor can he have meant that you can always believe prophecies of evil without any hesitation, but that you are to put no faith in promises until they are fulfilled. Yet it is not difficult to discern the truth underlying Jeremiah's words. The prophet whose words are unpalatable to his hearers is more likely to have a true inspiration than the man who kindles their fancy with glowing pictures of an imminent millennium. The divine message to a congregation of country squires is more likely to be an exhortation to be just to their tenants than a sermon on the duty of the labourer to his betters. A true prophet addressing an audience of working men would perhaps deal with the abuses of trades unions rather than with the sins of capitalists.

But this principle, which is necessarily of limited application, does not go far to solve the great question of authority in religion, on which Jeremiah gives us no further help.

There is, however, one obvious moral. No system of external authority, whatever pains may be taken to secure authentic legitimacy, can altogether release the individual from the responsibility of private judgment. Unreserved faith in the idea of a Catholic Church is quite consistent with much hesitation between the Anglican, Roman, and Greek communions; and the most devoted Catholic may be called upon to choose between rival antipopes.

Ultimately the inspired teacher is only discerned by the inspired hearer: it is the answer of the conscience that authenticates the divine message.

CHAPTER X.

CORRESPONDENCE WITH THE EXILES.

JEREMIAH xxix.

"Jehovah make thee like Zedekiah and Ahab, whom the king of Babylon roasted in the fire."—JER. xxix. 32.

NOTHING further is said about the proposed revolt, so that Jeremiah's vigorous protest seems to have been successful. In any case, unless irrevocable steps had been taken, the enterprise could hardly have survived the death of its advocate, Hananiah. Accordingly Zedekiah sent an embassy to Babylon, charged doubtless with plausible explanations and profuse professions of loyalty and devotion. The envoys were Elasah ben Shaphan and Gemariah ben Hilkiah. Shaphan and Hilkiah were almost certainly the scribe and high priest who discovered Deuteronomy in the eighteenth year of Josiah, and Elasah was the brother of Ahikam ben Shaphan, who protected Jeremiah in the fourth year of Jehoiakim, and of Gemariah ben Shaphan, in whose chamber Baruch read the roll, and who protested against its destruction. Probably Elasah and Gemariah were adherents of Jeremiah, and the fact of the embassy, as well as the choice of ambassadors, suggests that, for the moment, Zedekiah was acting under the influence of the prophet. Jeremiah took the opportunity of sending a letter to the exiles at Babylon. Hananiah had his allies in Chaldea: Ahab ben Kolaiah, Zedekiah ben Maaseiah, and Shemaiah the Nehelamite, with other prophets, diviners, and dreamers, had imitated their brethren in Judah; they had prophesied without being sent and had caused the people to believe a lie. We are not expressly told what they prophesied, but the narrative takes for granted that they, like Hananiah, promised the exiles a speedy return to their native land. Such teaching naturally met with much acceptance, the people congratulating themselves because, as they supposed, "Jehovah hath raised us up prophets in Babylon." The presence of prophets among them was received as a welcome proof that Jehovah had not deserted His people in their house of bondage.

Thus when Jeremiah had confounded his opponents in Jerusalem he had still to deal with their friends in Babylon. Here again the issue was one of immediate practical importance. In Chaldea as at Jerusalem the prediction that the exiles would immediately return was intended to kindle the proposed revolt. The Jews at Babylon were virtually warned to hold themselves in readiness to take advantage of any success of the Syrian rebels, and, if opportunity offered, to render them assistance. In those days information travelled slowly, and there was some danger lest the captives should be betrayed into acts of disloyalty, even after the Jewish government had given up any present intention of revolting against Nebuchadnezzar. Such disloyalty might have involved their entire destruction. Both Zedekiah and Jeremiah would be anxious to inform them at once that they must refrain from any plots against their Chaldean masters. Moreover the prospect of an immediate return had very much the same effect upon these Jews as the expectation of Christ's Second Coming had upon the primitive Church at Thessalonica. It made them restless and disorderly. They could not settle to any regular work, but became busybodies—wasting their time over the glowing promises of their popular preachers, and whispering to one another wild rumours of successful revolts in Syria; or were even more dangerously occupied in planning conspiracies against their conquerors.

Jeremiah's letter sought to bring about a better state of mind. It is addressed to the elders, priests, prophets, and people of the Captivity. The enumeration reminds us how thoroughly the exiled community reproduced the society of the ancient Jewish state—there was already a miniature Judah in Chaldea, the first of those Israels of the Dispersion which have since covered the face of the earth.

This is Jehovah's message by His prophet:—

"Build houses and dwell in them;
Plant gardens and eat the fruit thereof;
Marry and beget sons and daughters;
Marry your sons and daughters,
That they may bear sons and daughters,
That ye may multiply there and not grow few.
Seek the peace of the city whither I have sent you into captivity:
Pray for it unto Jehovah;
For in its peace, ye shall have peace."

There was to be no immediate return; their captivity would last long enough to make it worth their while to build houses and plant gardens. For the present they were to regard Babylon as their home. The prospect of restoration to Judah was too distant to make any practical difference to their conduct of ordinary business. The concluding command to "seek the peace of Babylon" is a distinct warning against engaging in plots, which could only ruin the conspirators. There is an interesting difference between these exhortations and those addressed by Paul to his converts in the first century. He never counsels them to marry, but rather recommends celibacy as more expedient for the present necessity. Apparently life was more anxious and harassed for the early Christians than for the Jews in Babylon. The return to Canaan was to these exiles what the millennium and the Second Advent were to the primitive Church. Jeremiah having bidden his fellow-countrymen not to be agitated by supposing that this much-longed-for event might come at any moment, fortifies their faith and patience by a promise that it should not be delayed indefinitely.

"When ye have fulfilled seventy years in Babylon I will visit you,
And will perform for you My gracious promise to bring you back to this place."*

Seventy is obviously a round number. Moreover the constant use of seven and its multiples in sacred symbolism forbids us to understand the prophecy as an exact chronological statement.

We should adequately express the prophet's meaning by translating "in about two generations." We need not waste time and trouble in discovering or inventing two dates exactly separated by seventy years, one of which will serve for the beginning and the other for the end of the Captivity. The interval between the destruction of Jerusalem and the Return was fifty years (B. C. 586-536), but as our passage refers more immediately to the prospects of those already in exile, we should obtain an interval of sixty-five years from the deportation of Jehoiachin and his companions in B. C. 601. But there can be no question of approximation, however close. Either the "seventy years" merely stands for a comparatively long period, or it is exact. We do not save the inspiration of a date by showing that it is only five years wrong, and not twenty. For an inspired date must be absolutely accurate; a mistake of a second in such a case would be as fatal as a mistake of a century.

Israel's hope is guaranteed by God's self-knowledge of His gracious counsel:—

"I know the purposes which I purpose concerning you, is the utterance of Jehovah,
Purposes of peace and not of evil, to give you hope for the days to come."

In the former clause "I" is emphatic in both places, and the phrase is parallel to the familiar formula "by Myself have I sworn, saith Jehovah." The future of Israel was guaranteed by the divine consistency. Jehovah, to use a colloquial phrase, knew His own mind. His everlasting purpose for the Chosen People could not be set aside. "Did God cast off His People? God forbid."

Yet this persistent purpose is not fulfilled without reference to character and conduct:—

"Ye shall call upon Me, and come and pray unto Me,
And I will hearken unto you.
Ye shall seek Me, and find Me,
Because ye seek Me with all your heart.
I will be found of you—it is the utterance of Jehovah.
I will bring back your captivity, and will gather you from all nations and places whither I have scattered you—it is the utterance of Jehovah.
I will bring you back to this place whence I sent you away to captivity."*

As in the previous chapter, Jeremiah concludes with a personal judgment upon those prophets who had been so acceptable to the exiles. If verse 23 is to be understood literally, Ahab and Zedekiah had not only spoken without authority in the name of Jehovah, but had also been guilty of gross immorality. Their punishment was to be more terrible than that of Hananiah. They had incited the exiles to revolt by predicting the imminent ruin of Nebuchadnezzar. Possibly the Jewish king proposed to make his own peace by betraying his agents, after the manner of our own Elizabeth and other sovereigns.

They were to be given over to the terrible vengeance which a Chaldean king would naturally take on such offenders, and would be publicly roasted alive, so that the malice of him who desired to curse his enemy might find vent in such words as:—

"Jehovah make thee like Zedekiah and Ahab, whom the king of Babylon roasted alive."

We are not told whether this prophecy was fulfilled, but it is by no means unlikely. The Assyrian king Assurbanipal says, in one of his inscriptions concerning a viceroy of Babylon who had revolted, that Assur and the other gods "in the fierce burning fire they threw him and destroyed his life"—possibly through the agency of Assurbanipal's servants.† One of the seven brethren who were tortured to death in the persecutions of Antiochus Epiphanes is said to have been "fried in the pan."‡ Christian hagiology commemorates St. Lawrence and many other martyrs, who suffered similar torments. Such punishments remained part of criminal procedure until a comparatively recent date; they are still sometimes inflicted by lynch law in the United States, and have been defended even by Christian ministers.

Jeremiah's letter caused great excitement and indignation among the exiles. We have no rejoinder from Ahab and Zedekiah; probably they were not in a position to make any. But Shemaiah the Nehelamite tried to make trouble for Jeremiah at Jerusalem. He, in his turn, wrote letters to "all the people at Jerusalem and to the

* Doubts have been expressed as to whether this verse originally formed part of Jeremiah's letter, or was ever written by him; but in view of his numerous references to a coming restoration those doubts are unnecessary.

* The Hebrew Text inserts a paragraph (vv. 16-20) substantially identical with other portions of the book, especially xxiv. 8-10, announcing the approaching ruin and captivity of Zedekiah and the Jews still remaining in Judah. This section is omitted by the LXX., and breaks the obvious connection between verses 15 and 21.

† Smith's "Assurbanipal," p. 163.

‡ 2 Macc. vii. 5.

priest Zephaniah ben Maaseiah and to all the priests" to this effect:—

"Jehovah hath made thee priest in the room of Jehoiada the priest, to exercise supervision over the Temple, and to deal with any mad fanatic who puts himself forward to prophesy, by placing him in the stocks and the collar. Why then hast thou not rebuked Jeremiah of Anathoth, who puts himself forward to prophesy unto you? Consequently he has sent unto us at Babylon: It (your captivity) will be long; build houses and dwell in them, plant gardens and eat the fruit thereof."

Confidence in a speedy return had already been exalted into a cardinal article of the exiles' faith, and Shemaiah claims that any one who denied this comfortable doctrine must be *ipso facto* a dangerous and deluded fanatic, needing to be placed under strict restraint. This letter travelled to Jerusalem with the returning embassy, and was duly delivered to Zephaniah. Zephaniah is spoken of in the historical section common to Kings and Jeremiah as "the second priest," * Seraiah being the High Priest; like Pashhur ben Immer, he seems to have been the governor of the Temple. He was evidently well disposed to Jeremiah, to whom Zedekiah twice sent him on important missions. On the present occasion, instead of acting upon the suggestions made by Shemaiah, he read the letter to Jeremiah, in order that the latter might have an opportunity of dealing with it.

Jeremiah was divinely instructed to reply to Shemaiah, charging him, in his turn, with being a man who put himself forward to prophesy without any commission from Jehovah, and who thus deluded his hearers into belief in falsehoods. Personal sentence is passed upon him, as upon Hananiah, Ahab, and Zedekiah; no son of his shall be reckoned amongst God's people or see the prosperity which they shall hereafter enjoy. The words are obscure: it is said that Jehovah will "visit Shemaiah and his seed," so that it cannot mean that he will be childless; but it is further said that "he shall not have a man to abide amongst this people." It is apparently a sentence of excommunication against Shemaiah and his family.

Here the episode abruptly ends. We are not told whether the letter was sent, or how it was received, or whether it was answered. We gather that, here also, the last word rested with Jeremiah, and that at this point his influence became dominant both at Jerusalem and at Babylon, and that King Zedekiah himself submitted to his guidance.

Chapters xxviii., xxix., deepen the impression made by other sections of Jeremiah's intolerance and personal bitterness towards his opponents. He seems to speak of the roasting alive of the prophets at Babylon with something like grim satisfaction, and we are tempted to think of Torquemada and Bishop Bonner. But we must remember that the stake, as we have already said, has scarcely yet ceased to be an ordinary criminal punishment, and that, after centuries of Christianity, More and Cranmer, Luther and Calvin, had hardly any more tenderness for their ecclesiastical opponents than Jeremiah.

Indeed the Church is only beginning to be ashamed of the complacency with which she has contemplated the fiery torments of hell as the eternal destiny of unrepentant sinners. One of the most tolerant and catholic of our religious teachers has written: "If the unlucky malefactor, who in mere brutality of ignorance or narrowness of nature or of culture has wronged his neighbour, excite our anger, how much deeper should be our indignation when intellect and eloquence are abused to selfish purposes, when studious leisure and learning and thought turn traitors to the cause of human well-being and the wells of a nation's moral life are poisoned." * The deduction is obvious: society feels constrained to hang or burn "the unlucky malefactor"; consequently such punishments are, if anything, too merciful for the false prophet. Moreover the teaching which Jeremiah denounced was no mere dogmatism about abstruse philosophical and theological abstractions. Like the Jesuit propaganda under Elizabeth, it was more immediately concerned with politics than with religion. We are bound to be indignant with a man, gifted in exploiting the emotions of his docile audience, who wins the confidence and arouses the enthusiasm of his hearers, only to entice them into hopeless and foolhardy ventures.

And yet we are brought back to the old difficulty, how are we to know the false prophet? He has neither horns nor hoofs, his tie may be as white and his coat as long as those of the true messenger of God. Again, Jeremiah's method affords us some practical guidance. He does not himself order and superintend the punishment of false prophets: he merely announces a Divine judgment, which Jehovah Himself is to execute. He does not condemn men by the code of any Church, but each sentence is a direct and special revelation from Jehovah. How many sentences would have been passed upon heretics, if their accusers and judges had waited for a similar sanction?

CHAPTER XI.

A BROKEN COVENANT.

JEREMIAH xxi. 1-10, xxxiv., xxxvii. 1-10.

"All the princes and people . . . changed their minds and reduced to bondage again all the slaves whom they had set free."—JER. xxxiv. 10, 11.

IN our previous chapter we saw that, at the point where the fragmentary record of the abortive conspiracy in the fourth year of Zedekiah came to an abrupt conclusion, Jeremiah seemed to have regained the ascendency he enjoyed under Josiah. The Jewish government had relinquished their schemes of rebellion and acquiesced once more in the supremacy of Babylon. We may possibly gather from a later chapter† that Zedekiah himself paid a visit to Nebuchadnezzar to assure him of his loyalty. If so, the embassy of Elasah ben Shaphan and Gemariah ben Hilkiah was intended to assure a favourable reception for their master.

The history of the next few years is lost in obscurity, but when the curtain again rises everything is changed and Judah is once more in revolt against the Chaldeans. No doubt one cause of this fresh change of policy was the re-

* lii. 24; 2 Kings xxv. 18.

* "Ecce Homo," xxi.

† li. 59, Hebrew Text. According to the LXX., Zedekiah sent another embassy and did not go himself to Babylon. The section is apparently a late addition.

newed activity of Egypt. In the account of the conspiracy in Zedekiah's fourth year, there is a significant absence of any reference to Egypt. Jeremiah succeeded in baffling his opponents partly because their fears of Babylon were not quieted by any assurance of Egyptian support. Now there seemed a better prospect of a successful insurrection.

About the seventh year of Zedekiah, Psammetichus II. of Egypt was succeeded by his brother Pharaoh Hophra, the son of Josiah's conqueror, Pharaoh Necho. When Hophra—the Apries of Herodotus—had completed the reconquest of Ethiopia, he made a fresh attempt to carry out his father's policy and to re-establish the ancient Egyptian supremacy in Western Asia; and, as of old, Egypt began by tampering with the allegiance of the Syrian vassals of Babylon. According to Ezekiel,* Zedekiah took the initiative: "he rebelled against him (Nebuchadnezzar) by sending his ambassadors into Egypt, that they might give him horses and much people."

The knowledge that an able and victorious general was seated on the Egyptian throne, along with the secret intrigues of his agents and partisans, was too much for Zedekiah's discretion. Jeremiah's advice was disregarded. The king surrendered himself to the guidance—we might almost say, the control—of the Egyptian party in Jerusalem; he violated his oath of allegiance to his suzerain, and the frail and battered ship of state was once more embarked on the stormy waters of rebellion. Nebuchadnezzar promptly prepared to grapple with the reviving strength of Egypt in a renewed contest for the lordship of Syria. Probably Egypt and Judah had other allies, but they are not expressly mentioned. A little later Tyre was besieged by Nebuchadnezzar; but as Ezekiel† represents Tyre as exulting over the fall of Jerusalem, she can hardly have been a benevolent neutral, much less a faithful ally. Moreover, when Nebuchadnezzar began his march into Syria, he hesitated whether he should first attack Jerusalem or Rabbath Ammon:—

"The king of Babylon stood at the parting of the way, . . . to use divination: he shook the arrows to and fro, he consulted the teraphim, he looked in the liver."‡

Later on Baalis, king of Ammon, received the Jewish refugees and supported those who were most irreconcilable in their hostility to Nebuchadnezzar. Nevertheless the Ammonites were denounced by Jeremiah for occupying the territory of Gad, and by Ezekiel§ for sharing the exultation of Tyre over the ruin of Judah. Probably Baalis played a double part. He may have promised support to Zedekiah, and then purchased his own pardon by betraying his ally.

Nevertheless the hearty support of Egypt was worth more than the alliance of any number of the petty neighbouring states, and Nebuchadnezzar levied a great army to meet this ancient and formidable enemy of Assyria and Babylon. He marched into Judah with "all his army, and all the kingdoms of the earth that were under his dominion, and all the peoples," and "fought against Jerusalem and all the cities thereof."‖

* xvii. 15.
† xxvi. 2.
‡ Ezek. xxi. 21.
§ xxv. 1–7.
‖ xxi. 1–10. The exact date of this section is not given, but it is closely parallel to xxxiv. 1–7, and seems to belong to the same period.

At the beginning of the siege Zedekiah's heart began to fail him. The course of events seemed to confirm Jeremiah's threats, and the king, with pathetic inconsistency, sought to be reassured by the prophet himself. He sent Pashhur ben Malchiah and Zephaniah ben Maaseiah to Jeremiah with the message:—

"Inquire, I pray thee, of Jehovah for us, for Nebuchadnezzar king of Babylon maketh war against us: peradventure Jehovah will deal with us according to all His wondrous works, that he may go up from us."

The memories of the great deliverance from Sennacherib were fresh and vivid in men's minds. Isaiah's denunciations had been as uncompromising as Jeremiah's, and yet Hezekiah had been spared. "Peradventure," thought his anxious descendant, "the prophet may yet be charged with gracious messages that Jehovah repents Him of the evil and will even now rescue His Holy City." But the timid appeal only called forth a yet sterner sentence of doom. Formidable as were the enemies against whom Zedekiah craved protection, they were to be reinforced by more terrible allies; man and beast should die of a great pestilence, and Jehovah Himself should be their enemy:—

"I will turn back the weapons of war that are in your hands, wherewith ye fight against the king of Babylon and the Chaldeans. . . . I Myself will fight against you with an outstretched hand and a strong arm, in anger and fury and great wrath."

The city should be taken and burnt with fire, and the king and all others who survived should be carried away captive. Only on one condition might better terms be obtained:—

"Behold, I set before you the way of life and the way of death. He that abideth in this city shall die by the sword, the famine, and the pestilence; but he that goeth out, and falleth to the besieging Chaldeans, shall live, and his life shall be unto him for a prey."*

On another occasion Zephaniah ben Maaseiah with a certain Tehucal ben Shelemiah was sent by the king to the prophet with the entreaty, "Pray now unto Jehovah our God for us." We are not told the sequel to this mission, but it is probably represented by the opening verses of chap. xxxiv. This section has the direct and personal note which characterises the dealings of Hebrew prophets with their sovereigns. Doubtless the partisans of Egypt had had a severe struggle with Jeremiah before they captured the ear of the Jewish king, and Zedekiah was possessed to the very last with a half-superstitious anxiety to keep on good terms with the prophet. Jehovah's "iron pillar and brasen wall" would make no concession to these royal blandishments: his message had been rejected, his Master had been slighted and defied, the Chosen People and the Holy City were being betrayed to their ruin; Jeremiah would not refrain from denouncing this iniquity because the king who had sanctioned it tried to flatter his vanity by sending deferential deputations of important notables. This is the Divine sentence:—

"I will give this city into the hand of the king of Babylon,
And he shall burn it with fire.
Thou shalt not escape out of his hand;
Thou shalt assuredly be taken prisoner;
Thou shalt be delivered into his hand.

* xxi. 1–10.

Thou shalt see the king of Babylon, face to face ;
He shall speak to thee, mouth to mouth,
And thou shalt go to Babylon."

Yet there should be one doubtful mitigation of his punishment:—

" Thou shalt not die by the sword ;
Thou shalt die in peace :
With the burnings of thy fathers, the former kings that were before thee,
So shall they make a burning for thee ;
And they shall lament thee, saying, Alas lord !
For it is I that have spoken the word—it is the utterance of Jehovah."

King and people were not proof against the combined terrors of the prophetic rebukes and the besieging enemy. Jeremiah regained his influence, and Jerusalem gave an earnest of the sincerity of her repentance by entering into a covenant for the emancipation of all Hebrew slaves. Deuteronomy had re-enacted the ancient law that their bondage should terminate at the end of six years,* but this had not been observed: "Your fathers hearkened not unto Me, neither inclined their ear."† A large proportion of those then in slavery must have served more than six years;‡ and partly because of the difficulty of discrimination at such a crisis, partly by way of atonement, the Jews undertook to liberate all their slaves. This solemn reparation was made because the limitation of servitude was part of the national Torah, "the covenant that Jehovah made with their fathers in the day that He brought them forth out of the land of Egypt"—*i. e.*, the Deuteronomic Code. Hence it implied the renewed recognition of Deuteronomy, and the restoration of the ecclesiastical order established by Josiah's reforms.

Even Josiah's methods were imitated. He had assembled the people at the Temple and made them enter into "a covenant before Jehovah, to walk after Jehovah, to keep His commandments and testimonies and statutes with all their heart and soul, to perform the words of this covenant that were written in this book. And all the people entered into the covenant."§ So now Zedekiah in turn caused the people to make a covenant before Jehovah, "in the house which was called by His name,"‖ "that every one should release his Hebrew slaves, male and female, and that no one should enslave a brother Jew."¶ A further sanction had been given to this vow by the observance of an ancient and significant rite. When Jehovah promised to Abraham a seed countless as the stars of heaven, He condescended to ratify His promise by causing the symbols of His presence—a smoking furnace and a burning lamp—to pass between the divided halves of a heifer, a she-goat, a ram, and between a turtle-dove and a young pigeon.** Now, in like manner, a calf was cut in twain, the two halves laid opposite each other, and "the princes of Judah and Jerusalem, the eunuchs, the priests, and all the people of the land, . . . passed between the parts of the calf."†† Similarly, after the death of Alexander the Great, the contending factions in the Macedonian army ratified a compromise by passing between the two halves of a dog. Such symbols spoke for themselves: those who used them laid themselves under a curse; they prayed that if they violated the covenant they might be slain and mutilated like the divided animals.

This covenant was forthwith carried into effect, the princes and people liberating their Hebrew slaves according to their vow. We cannot, however, compare this event with the abolition of slavery in British colonies or with Abraham Lincoln's Decree of Emancipation. The scale is altogether different: Hebrew bondage had no horrors to compare with those of the American plantations; and moreover, even at the moment, the practical results cannot have been great. Shut up in a beleaguered city, harassed by the miseries and terrors of a siege, the freedmen would see little to rejoice over in their new-found freedom. Unless their friends were in Jerusalem they could not rejoin them, and in most cases they could only obtain sustenance by remaining in the households of their former masters, or by serving in the defending army. Probably this special ordinance of Deuteronomy was selected as the subject of a solemn covenant, because it not only afforded an opportunity of atoning for past sin, but also provided the means of strengthening the national defence. Such expedients were common in ancient states in moments of extreme peril.

In view of Jeremiah's persistent efforts, both before and after this incident, to make his countrymen loyally accept the Chaldean supremacy, we cannot doubt that he hoped to make terms between Zedekiah and Nebuchadnezzar. Apparently no tidings of Pharaoh Hophra's advance had reached Jerusalem; and the non-appearance of his "horses and much people" had discredited the Egyptian party, and enabled Jeremiah to overthrow their influence with the king and people. Egypt, after all her promises, had once more proved herself a broken reed; there was nothing left but to throw themselves on Nebuchadnezzar's mercy.

But the situation was once more entirely changed by the news that Pharaoh Hophra had come forth out of Egypt "with a mighty army and a great company."* The sentinels on the walls of Jerusalem saw the besiegers break up their encampment, and march away to meet the relieving army. All thought of submitting to Babylon was given up. Indeed, if Pharaoh Hophra were to be victorious, the Jews must of necessity accept his supremacy. Meanwhile they revelled in their respite from present distress and imminent danger. Surely the new covenant was bearing fruit. Jehovah had been propitiated by their promise to observe the Torah; Pharaoh was the instrument by which God would deliver His people; or even if the Egyptians were defeated, the Divine resources were not exhausted. When Tirhakah advanced to the relief of Hezekiah, he was defeated at Eltekeh, yet Sennacherib had returned home baffled and disgraced. Naturally the partisans of Egypt, the opponents of Jeremiah, recovered their control of the king and the government. The king sent, perhaps at the first news of the Egyptian advance, to inquire of Jeremiah concerning their prospects of success. What seemed to every one else a Divine deliverance was to him a national misfortune; the hopes he had once more indulged of averting the ruin of Judah were again dashed to the ground. His answer is bitter and gloomy:—

* Deut. xv. 12. *Cf.* Exod. xxi. 2, xxiii. 10.
† xxxiv. 14.
‡ xxxiv. 13.
§ 2 Kings xxiii. 3.
‖ xxxiv. 15.
¶ xxxiv. 9.
** Gen. xv.
†† xxxiv. 19.

* Ezek. xvii. 17.

Behold, Pharaoh's army, which is come forth to help you,
Shall return to Egypt into their own land.
The Chaldeans shall come again, and fight against this city;
They shall take it, and burn it with fire.
Thus saith Jehovah:
Do not deceive yourselves, saying,
The Chaldeans shall surely depart from us:
They shall not depart.
Though ye had smitten the whole army of the Chaldeans that fight against you,
And there remained none but wounded men among them,
Yet should they rise up every man in his tent,
And burn this city with fire."

Jeremiah's protest was unavailing, and only confirmed the king and princes in their adherence to Egypt. Moreover Jeremiah had now formally disclaimed any sympathy with this great deliverance, which Pharaoh—and presumably Jehovah—had wrought for Judah. Hence it was clear that the people did not owe this blessing to the covenant to which they had submitted themselves by Jeremiah's guidance. As at Megiddo, Jehovah had shown once more that He was with Pharaoh and against Jeremiah. Probably they would best please God by renouncing Jeremiah and all his works—the covenant included. Moreover they could take back their slaves with a clear conscience, to their own great comfort and satisfaction. True, they had sworn in the Temple with solemn and striking ceremonies, but then Jehovah Himself had manifestly released them from their oath. "All the princes and people changed their mind, and reduced to bondage again all the slaves whom they had set free." The freedmen had been rejoicing with their former masters in the prospect of national deliverance; the date of their emancipation was to mark the beginning of a new era of Jewish happiness and prosperity. When the siege was raised and the Chaldeans driven away, they could use their freedom in rebuilding the ruined cities and cultivating the wasted lands. To all such dreams there came a sudden and rough awakening: they were dragged back to their former hopeless bondage—a happy augury for the new dispensation of Divine protection and blessing!

Jeremiah turned upon them in fierce wrath, like that of Elijah against Ahab when he met him taking possession of Naboth's vineyard. They had profaned the name of Jehovah, and—

"Therefore thus saith Jehovah:
Ye have not hearkened unto Me to proclaim a release every one to his brother and his neighbour:
Behold, I proclaim a release for you—it is the utterance of Jehovah—unto the sword, the pestilence, and the famine;
And I will make you a terror among all the kingdoms of the earth."

The prophet plays upon the word "release" with grim irony. The Jews had repudiated the "release" which they had promised under solemn oath to their brethren, but Jehovah would not allow them to be so easily quit of their covenant. There should be a "release" after all, and they themselves should have the benefit of it—a "release" from happiness and prosperity, from the sacred bounds of the Temple, the Holy City, and the Land of Promise—a "release" unto "the sword, the pestilence, and the famine."

"I will give the men that have transgressed My covenant into the hands of their enemies. . . .
Their dead bodies shall be meat for the fowls of heaven and for the beasts of the earth.
Zedekiah king of Judah and his princes will I give into the hand of . . . the host of the king of Babylon, which are gone up from you.
Behold, I will command—it is the utterance of Jehovah—and will bring them back unto this city:
They shall fight against it, and take it, and burn it with fire.
I will lay the cities of Judah waste, without inhabitant."

Another broken covenant was added to the list of Judah's sins, another promise of amendment speedily lost in disappointment and condemnation. Jeremiah might well say with his favourite Hosea:—

"Oh Judah, what shall I do unto thee?
Your goodness is as a morning cloud,
And as the dew that goeth early away."*

This incident has many morals; one of the most obvious is the futility of the most stringent oaths and the most solemn symbolic ritual. Whatever influence oaths may have in causing a would-be liar to speak the truth, they are very poor guarantees for the performance of contracts. William the Conqueror profited little by Harold's oath to help him to the crown of England, though it was sworn over the relics of holy saints. Wulfnoth's whisper in Tennyson's drama—

"Swear thou to-day, to-morrow is thine own"—

states the principle on which many oaths have been taken. The famous "blush of Sigismund" over the violation of his safe-conduct to Huss was rather a token of unusual sensitiveness than a confession of exceptional guilt. The Christian Church has exalted perfidy into a sacred obligation. As Milman says†:—

"The fatal doctrine, confirmed by long usage, by the decrees of Pontiffs, by the assent of all ecclesiastics, and the acquiescence of the Christian world, that no promise, no oath, was binding to a heretic, had hardly been questioned, never repudiated."

At first sight an oath seems to give firm assurance to a promise; what was merely a promise to man is made into a promise to God. What can be more binding upon the conscience than a promise to God? True; but He to whom the promise is made may always release from its performance. To persist in what God neither requires nor desires because of a promise to God seems absurd and even wicked. It has been said that men "have a way of calling everything they want to do a dispensation of Providence." Similarly, there are many ways by which a man may persuade himself that God has cancelled his vows, especially if he belongs to an infallible Church with a Divine commission to grant dispensations. No doubt these Jewish slaveholders had full sacerdotal absolution from their pledge. The priests had slaves of their own. Failing ecclesiastical aid, Satan himself will play the casuist—it is one of his favourite parts—and will find the traitor full justification for breaking the most solemn contract with Heaven. If a man's whole soul and purpose go with his promise, oaths are superfluous; otherwise, they are useless.

However, the main lesson of the incident lies in its added testimony to the supreme importance which the prophets attached to social righteousness. When Jeremiah wished to knit together again the bonds of fellowship between

* Hosea vi. 4.

† Milman's "Latin Christianity," viii. 255.

Judah and its God, he did not make them enter into a covenant to observe ritual or to cultivate pious sentiments, but to release their slaves. It has been said that a gentleman may be known by the way in which he treats his servants; a man's religion is better tested by his behaviour to his helpless dependents than by his attendance on the means of grace or his predilection for pious conversation. If we were right in supposing that the government supported Jeremiah because the act of emancipation would furnish recruits to man the walls, this illustrates the ultimate dependence of society upon the working classes. In emergencies, desperate efforts are made to coerce or cajole them into supporting governments by which they have been neglected or oppressed. The sequel to this covenant shows how barren and transient are concessions begotten by the terror of imminent ruin. The social covenant between all classes of the community needs to be woven strand by strand through long years of mutual helpfulness and goodwill, of peace and prosperity, if it is to endure the strain of national peril and disaster.

CHAPTER XII.

JEREMIAH'S IMPRISONMENT.

JEREMIAH xxxvii. 11-21, xxxviii., xxxix. 15-18.

"Jeremiah abode in the court of the guard until the day that Jerusalem was taken."—JER. xxxviii. 28.

"WHEN the Chaldean army was broken up from Jerusalem for fear of Pharaoh's army, Jeremiah went forth out of Jerusalem to go into the land of Benjamin" to transact certain family business at Anathoth.*

He had announced that all who remained in the city should perish, and that only those who deserted to the Chaldeans should escape. In these troubled times all who sought to enter or leave Jerusalem were subjected to close scrutiny, and when Jeremiah wished to pass through the gate of Benjamin he was stopped by the officer in charge—Irijah ben Shelemiah ben Hananiah—and accused of being about to practise himself what he had preached to the people: "Thou fallest away to the Chaldeans." The suspicion was natural enough; for, although the Chaldeans had raised the siege and marched away to the southwest, while the gate of Benjamin was on the north of the city, Irijah might reasonably suppose that they had left detachments in the neighbourhood, and that this zealous advocate of submission to Babylon had special information on the subject. Jeremiah indeed had the strongest motives for seeking safety in flight. The party whom he had consistently denounced had full control of the government, and even if they spared him for the present any decisive victory over the enemy would be the signal for his execution. When once Pharaoh Hophra was in full march upon Jerusalem at the head of a victorious army, his friends would show no mercy to Jeremiah. Probably Irijah was eager to believe in the prophet's treachery, and ready to snatch at any pretext for arresting him. The name of the captain's grandfather—Hananiah—is too common to suggest any connection with the prophet who withstood Jeremiah; but we may be sure that at this crisis the gates were in charge of trusty adherents of the princes of the Egyptian party. Jeremiah would be suspected and detested by such men as these. His vehement denial of the charge was received with real or feigned incredulity; Irijah "hearkened not unto him."

The arrest took place "in the midst of the people." * The gate was crowded with other Jews hurrying out of Jerusalem: citizens eager to breathe more freely after being cooped up in the overcrowded city; countrymen anxious to find out what their farms and homesteads had suffered at the hands of the invaders; not a few, perhaps, bound on the very errand of which Jeremiah was accused, friends of Babylon, convinced that Nebuchadnezzar would ultimately triumph, and hoping to find favour and security in his camp. Critical events of Jeremiah's life had often been transacted before a great assembly; for instance, his own address and trial in the Temple, and the reading of the roll. He knew the practical value of a dramatic situation. This time he had sought the crowd, rather to avoid than attract attention; but when he was challenged by Irijah, the accusation and denial must have been heard by all around. The soldiers of the guard, necessarily hostile to the man who had counselled submission, gathered round to secure their prisoner; for a time the gate was blocked by the guards and spectators. The latter do not seem to have interfered. Formerly the priests and prophets and all the people had laid hold on Jeremiah, and afterwards all the people had acquitted him by acclamation. Now his enemies were content to leave him in the hands of the soldiers, and his friends, if he had any, were afraid to attempt a rescue. Moreover men's minds were not at leisure and craving for new excitement, as at Temple festivals; they were preoccupied, and eager to get out of the city. While the news quickly spread that Jeremiah had been arrested as he was trying to desert, his guards cleared a way through the crowd, and brought the prisoner before the princes. The latter seem to have acted as a Committee of National Defence; they may either have been sitting at the time, or a meeting, as on a previous occasion,† may have been called when it was known that Jeremiah had been arrested. Among them were probably those enumerated later on:‡ Shephatiah ben Mattan, Gedaliah ben Pashhur, Jucal ben Shelemiah, and Pashhur ben Malchiah. Shephatiah and Gedaliah are named only here; possibly Gedaliah's father was Pashhur ben Immer, who beat Jeremiah and put him in the stocks. Both Jucal and Pashhur ben Malchiah had been sent by the king to consult Jeremiah. Jucal may have been the son of the Shelemiah who was sent to arrest Jeremiah and Baruch after the reading of the roll. We note the absence of the princes who then formed Baruch's audience, some of whom tried to dissuade Jehoiakim from burning the roll; and we especially miss the prophet's former friend and protector, Ahikam ben Shaphan. Fifteen or sixteen years had elapsed since these earlier events; some of Jeremiah's adherents were dead, others in exile, others powerless to help him. We may safely conclude that his judges were his personal and political enemies. Jere-

* *Cf.* xxxii. 6-8.

* xxxvii. 12; so R. V., Streane (Camb. Bible), Kautzsch, etc.

† xxvi. 10.

‡ xxxviii. 1.

miah was now their discomfited rival. A few weeks before he had been master of the city and the court. Pharaoh Hophra's advance had enabled them to overthrow him. We can understand that they would at once take Irijah's view of the case. They treated their fallen antagonist as a criminal taken in the act: "they were wroth with him," *i. e.*, they overwhelmed him with a torrent of abuse; "they beat him, and put him in prison in the house of Jonathan the secretary." But this imprisonment in a private house was not mild and honourable confinement under the care of a distinguished noble, who was rather courteous host than harsh gaoler. "They had made that the prison," duly provided with a dungeon and cells, to which Jeremiah was consigned and where he remained "many days." Prison accommodation at Jerusalem was limited; the Jewish government preferred more summary methods of dealing with malefactors. The revolution which had placed the present government in power had given them special occasion for a prison. They had defeated rivals whom they did not venture to execute publicly, but who might be more safely starved and tortured to death in secret. For such a fate they destined Jeremiah. We shall not do injustice to Jonathan the secretary if we compare the hospitality which he extended to his unwilling guests with the treatment of modern Armenians in Turkish prisons. Yet the prophet remained alive "for many days"; probably his enemies reflected that even if he did not succumb earlier to the hardships of his imprisonment, his execution would suitably adorn the looked-for triumph of Pharaoh Hophra.

Few however of the "many days" had passed before men's exultant anticipations of victory and deliverance began to give place to anxious forebodings. They had hoped to hear that Nebuchadnezzar had been defeated and was in headlong retreat to Chaldea; they had been prepared to join in the pursuit of the routed army, to gratify their revenge by massacring the fugitives, and to share the plunder with their Egyptian allies. The fortunes of war belied their hopes: Pharaoh retreated, either after a battle or perhaps even without fighting. The return of the enemy was announced by the renewed influx of the country people to seek the shelter of the fortifications, and soon the Jews crowded to the walls as Nebuchadnezzar's vanguard appeared in sight and the Chaldeans occupied their old lines and re-formed the siege of the doomed city.

There was no longer any doubt that prudence dictated immediate surrender. It was the only course by which the people might be spared some of the horrors of a prolonged siege, followed by the sack of the city. But the princes who controlled the government were too deeply compromised with Egypt to dare to hope for mercy. With Jeremiah out of the way, they were able to induce the king and the people to maintain their resistance, and the siege went on.

But though Zedekiah was, for the most part, powerless in the hands of the princes, he ventured now and then to assert himself in minor matters, and, like other feeble sovereigns, derived some consolation amidst his many troubles from intriguing with the opposition against his own ministers. His feeling and behaviour towards Jeremiah were similar to those of Charles IX. towards Coligny, only circumstances made the Jewish king a more efficient protector of Jeremiah.

At this new and disastrous turn of affairs, which was an exact fulfilment of Jeremiah's warnings, the king was naturally inclined to revert to his former faith in the prophet—if indeed he had ever really been able to shake himself free from his influence. Left to himself he would have done his best to make terms with Nebuchadnezzar, as Jehoiakim and Jehoiachin had done before him. The only trustworthy channel of help, human or divine, was Jeremiah. Accordingly he sent secretly to the prison and had the prophet brought into the palace. There in some inner chamber, carefully guarded from intrusion by the slaves of the palace, Zedekiah received the man who now for more than forty years had been the chief counsellor of the kings of Judah, often in spite of themselves. Like Saul on the eve of Gilboa, he was too impatient to let disaster be its own herald; the silence of Heaven seemed more terrible than any spoken doom, and again like Saul he turned in his perplexity and despair to the prophet who had rebuked and condemned him. "Is there any word from Jehovah? And Jeremiah said, There is: . . . thou shalt be delivered into the hand of the king of Babylon."

The Church is rightly proud of Ambrose rebuking Theodosius at the height of his power and glory, and of Thomas à Becket, unarmed and yet defiant before his murderers; but the Jewish prophet showed himself capable of a simpler and grander heroism. For "many days" he had endured squalor, confinement, and semi-starvation. His body must have been enfeebled and his spirit depressed. Weak and contemptible as Zedekiah was, yet he was the prophet's only earthly protector from the malice of his enemies. He intended to utilise this interview for an appeal for release from his present prison. Thus he had every motive for conciliating the man who asked him for a word from Jehovah. He was probably alone with Zedekiah, and was not nerved to self-sacrifice by any opportunity of making public testimony to the truth, and yet he was faithful alike to God and to the poor helpless king—"Thou shalt be delivered into the hand of the king of Babylon."

And then he proceeds, with what seems to us inconsequent audacity, to ask a favour. Did ever petitioner to a king preface his supplication with so strange a preamble? This was the request:—

"Now hear, I pray thee, O my lord the king: let my supplication, I pray thee, be accepted before thee; that thou do not cause me to return to the house of Jonathan the secretary, lest I die there.

"Then Zedekiah the king commanded, and they committed Jeremiah into the court of the guard, and they gave him daily a loaf of bread out of the bakers' street."

A loaf of bread is not sumptuous fare, but it is evidently mentioned as an improvement upon his prison diet: it is not difficult to understand why Jeremiah was afraid he would die in the house of Jonathan.

During this milder imprisonment in the court of the guard occurred the incident of the purchase of the field of Anathoth, which we have dealt with in another chapter. This low ebb of the prophet's fortunes was the occasion of Divine revelation of a glorious future in store for Judah. But this future was still remote, and does not seem to have been conspicuous in his public teaching. On the contrary Jeremiah availed himself of the comparative publicity of his new place of detention to reiterate in the ears of all the people the gloomy predictions with which they had so long been familiar: "This city shall assuredly be given into the hand of the army of the king of Babylon." He again urged his hearers to desert to the enemy: "He that abideth in this city shall die by the sword, the famine, and the pestilence; but he that goeth forth to the Chaldeans shall live." We cannot but admire the splendid courage of the solitary prisoner, helpless in the hands of his enemies and yet openly defying them. He left his opponents only two alternatives, either to give up the government into his hands or else to silence him. Jeremiah in the court of the guard was really carrying on a struggle in which neither side either would or could give quarter. He was trying to revive the energies of the partisans of Babylon, that they might overpower the government and surrender the city to Nebuchadnezzar. If he had succeeded, the princes would have had a short shrift. They struck back with the prompt energy of men fighting for their lives. No government conducting the defence of a besieged fortress could have tolerated Jeremiah for a moment. What would have been the fate of a French politician who should have urged Parisians to desert to the Germans during the siege of 1870? * The princes' former attempt to deal with Jeremiah had been thwarted by the king; this time they tried to provide beforehand against any officious intermeddling on the part of Zedekiah. They extorted from him a sanction of their proceedings.

"Then the princes said unto the king, Let this man, we pray thee, be put to death: for he weakeneth the hands of the soldiers that are left in this city, and of all the people, by speaking such words unto them: for this man seeketh not the welfare of this people, but the hurt." Certainly Jeremiah's word was enough to take the heart out of the bravest soldiers; his preaching would soon have rendered further resistance impossible. But the concluding sentence about the "welfare of the people" was merely cheap cant, not without parallel in the sayings of many "princes" in later times. "The welfare of the people" would have been best promoted by the surrender which Jeremiah advocated. The king does not pretend to sympathise with the princes; he acknowledges himself a mere tool in their hands. "Behold," he answers, "he is in your power, for the king can do nothing against you."

"Then they took Jeremiah, and cast him into the cistern of Malchiah ben Hammelech, that was in the court of the guard; and they let Jeremiah down with cords. And there was no water in the cistern, only mud, and Jeremiah sank in the mud."

The depth of this improvised oubliette is shown by the use of cords to let the prisoner down into it. How was it, however, that, after the release of Jeremiah from the cells in the house of Jonathan, the princes did not at once execute him? Probably, in spite of all that had happened, they still felt a superstitious dread of actually shedding the blood of a prophet. In some mysterious way they felt that they would be less guilty if they left him in the empty cistern to starve to death or be suffocated in the mud, than if they had his head cut off. They acted in the spirit of Reuben's advice concerning Joseph, who also was cast into an empty pit, with no water in it: "Shed no blood, but cast him into this pit in the wilderness, and lay no hand upon him." * By a similar blending of hypocrisy and superstition, the mediæval Church thought to keep herself unstained by the blood of heretics, by handing them over to the secular arm; and Macbeth, having hired some one else to kill Banquo, was emboldened to confront his ghost with the words:—

"Thou canst not say I did it. Never shake
Thy gory locks at me."

But the princes were again baffled; the prophet had friends in the royal household who were bolder than their master: Ebed-melech the Ethiopian, an eunuch, heard that they had put Jeremiah in the cistern. He went to the king, who was then sitting in the gate of Benjamin, where he would be accessible to any petitioner for favour or justice, and interceded for the prisoner:—

"My lord the king, these men have done evil in all that they have done to Jeremiah the prophet, whom they have cast into the cistern; and he is like to die in the place where he is because of the famine, for there is no more bread in the city."

Apparently the princes, busied with the defence of the city and in their pride "too much despising" their royal master, had left him for a while to himself. Emboldened by this public appeal to act according to the dictates of his own heart and conscience, and possibly by the presence of other friends of Jeremiah, the king acts with unwonted courage and decision.

"The king commanded Ebed-melech the Ethiopian, saying, Take with thee hence thirty men, and draw up Jeremiah the prophet out of the cistern, before he die. So Ebed-melech took the men with him, and went into the palace under the treasury, and took thence old cast clouts and rotten rags, and let them down by cords into the cistern to Jeremiah. And he said to Jeremiah, Put these old cast clouts and rotten rags under thine armholes under the cords. And Jeremiah did so. So they drew him up with the cords, and took him up out of the cistern: and he remained in the court of the guard."

Jeremiah's gratitude to his deliverer is recorded in a short paragraph in which Ebed-melech, like Baruch, is promised that "his life shall be given him for a prey." He should escape with his life from the sack of the city—"because he trusted" in Jehovah. As of the ten lepers whom Jesus cleansed only the Samaritan returned to give glory to God, so when none of God's people were found to rescue His prophet, the dangerous honour was accepted by an Ethiopian proselyte.†

Meanwhile the king was craving for yet another "word with Jehovah." True, the last "word" given him by the prophet had been, "Thou shalt be delivered into the hand of the king of Babylon." But now that he had just rescued Jehovah's prophet from a miserable death (he forgot that Jeremiah had been consigned to the cistern by his own authority), possibly there might be some more encouraging

* *Cf.* Renan, iii. 333.

* Gen. xxxvii. 22-24. † xxxix. 15-18.

message from God. Accordingly he sent and took Jeremiah unto him for another secret interview, this time in the "corridor of the body-guard," * a passage between the palace and the Temple.

Here he implored the prophet to give him a faithful answer to his questions concerning his own fate and that of the city: "Hide nothing from me." But Jeremiah did not respond with his former prompt frankness. He had had too recent a warning not to put his trust in princes. "If I declare it unto thee," said he, "wilt thou not surely put me to death? and if I give thee counsel, thou wilt not hearken unto me. So Zedekiah the king sware secretly to Jeremiah, As Jehovah liveth, who is the source and giver of our life, I will not put thee to death, neither will I give thee into the hand of these men that seek thy life.

"Then said Jeremiah unto Zedekiah, Thus saith Jehovah, the God of hosts, the God of Israel: If thou wilt go forth unto the king of Babylon's princes, thy life shall be spared, and this city shall not be burned, and thou and thine house shall live; but if thou wilt not go forth, then shall this city be given into the hand of the Chaldeans, and they shall burn it, and thou shalt not escape out of their hand.

"Zedekiah said unto Jeremiah, I am afraid of the Jews that have deserted to the Chaldeans, lest they deliver me into their hand, and they mock me."

He does not, however, urge that the princes will hinder any such surrender; he believed himself sufficiently master of his own actions to be able to escape to the Chaldeans if he chose.

But evidently, when he first revolted against Babylon, and more recently when the siege was raised, he had been induced to behave harshly towards her partisans: they had taken refuge in considerable numbers in the enemy's camp, and now he was afraid of their vengeance. Similarly, in "Quentin Durward," Scott represents Louis XI. on his visit to Charles the Bold as startled by the sight of the banners of some of his own vassals, who had taken service with Burgundy, and as seeking protection from Charles against the rebel subjects of France.

Zedekiah is a perfect monument of the miseries that wait upon weakness: he was everybody's friend in turn—now a docile pupil of Jeremiah and gratifying the Chaldean party by his professions of loyalty to Nebuchadnezzar, and now a pliant tool in the hands of the Egyptian party, persecuting his former friends. At the last he was afraid alike of the princes in the city, of the exiles in the enemy's camp, and of the Chaldeans. The mariner who had to pass between Scylla and Charybdis was fortunate compared to Zedekiah. To the end he clung with a pathetic blending of trust and fearfulness to Jeremiah. He believed him, and yet he seldom had courage to act according to his counsel.

Jeremiah made a final effort to induce this timid soul to act with firmness and decision. He tried to reassure him: "They shall not deliver thee into the hands of thy revolted subjects. Obey, I beseech thee, the voice of Jehovah, in that which I speak unto thee: so it shall be well with thee, and thy life shall be spared." He appealed to that very dread of ridicule which the king had just betrayed. If he refused to surrender, he would be taunted for his weakness and folly by the women of his own harem:—

"If thou refuse to go forth, this is the word that Jehovah hath showed me: Behold, all the women left in the palace shall be brought forth to the king of Babylon's princes, and those women shall say, Thy familiar friends have duped thee and got the better of thee; thy feet are sunk in the mire, and they have left thee in the lurch." He would be in worse plight than that from which Jeremiah had only just been rescued, and there would be no Ebed-melech to draw him out. He would be humiliated by the suffering and shame of his own family: "They shall bring out all thy wives and children to the Chaldeans." He himself would share with them the last extremity of suffering: "Thou shalt not escape out of their hand, but shalt be taken by the hand of the king of Babylon."

And as Tennyson makes it the climax of Geraint's degeneracy that he was not only—

> "Forgetful of his glory and his name,"

but also—

> "Forgetful of his princedom and its cares,"

so Jeremiah appeals last of all to the king's sense of responsibility for his people: "Thou wilt be the cause of the burning of the city."

In spite of the dominance of the Egyptian party, and their desperate determination, not only to sell their own lives dearly, but also to involve king and people, city and temple, in their own ruin, the power of decisive action still rested with Zedekiah; if he failed to use it, he would be responsible for the consequences.

Thus Jeremiah strove to possess the king with some breath of his own dauntless spirit and iron will.

Zedekiah paused irresolute. A vision of possible deliverance passed through his mind. His guards and the domestics of the palace were within call. The princes were unprepared; they would never dream that he was capable of anything so bold. It would be easy to seize the nearest gate, and hold it long enough to admit the Chaldeans. But no! he had not nerve enough. Then his predecessors Joash, Amaziah, and Amon had been assassinated, and for the moment the daggers of the princes and their followers seemed more terrible than Chaldean instruments of torture. He lost all thought of his own honour and his duty to his people in his anxiety to provide against this more immediate danger. Never was the fate of a nation decided by a meaner utterance. "Then said Zedekiah to Jeremiah, No one must know about our meeting, and thou shalt not die. If the princes hear that I have talked with thee, and come and say unto thee, Declare unto us now what thou hast said unto the king; hide it not from us, and we will not put thee to death: declare unto us what the king said unto thee: then thou shalt say unto them, I presented my supplication unto the king, that he would not cause me to return to Jonathan's house, to die there.

"Then all the princes came to Jeremiah, and asked him; and he told them just what the king had commanded. So they let him alone, for no report of the matter had got abroad." We are a little surprised that the princes so easily abandoned their purpose of putting Jeremiah to

* So Giesebrecht, *in loco*; A. V., R. V., "third entry." In any case it will naturally be a passage from the palace to the Temple.

death, and did not at once consign him afresh to the empty cistern. Probably they were too disheartened for vigorous action; the garrison were starving, and it was clear that the city could not hold out much longer. Moreover the superstition that had shrunk from using actual violence to the prophet would suspect a token of Divine displeasure in his release.

Another question raised by this incident is that of the prophet's veracity, which, at first sight, does not seem superior to that of the patriarchs. It is very probable that the prophet, as at the earlier interview, had entreated the king not to allow him to be confined in the cells in Jonathan's house, but the narrative rather suggests that the king constructed this pretext on the basis of the former interview. Moreover, if the princes let Jeremiah escape with nothing less innocent than a *suppressio veri*, if they were satisfied with anything less than an explicit statement that the place of the prophet's confinement was the sole topic of conversation, they must have been more guileless than we can easily imagine. But, at any rate, if Jeremiah did stoop to dissimulation, it was to protect Zedekiah, not to save himself.

Zedekiah is a conspicuous example of the strange irony with which Providence entrusts incapable persons with the decision of most momentous issues; It sets Laud and Charles I. to adjust the Tudor Monarchy to the sturdy self-assertion of Puritan England, and Louis XVI. to cope with the French Revolution. Such histories are after all calculated to increase the self-respect of those who are weak and timid. Moments come, even to the feeblest, when their action must have the most serious results for all connected with them. It is one of the crowning glories of Christianity that it preaches a strength that is made perfect in weakness.

Perhaps the most significant feature in this narrative is the conclusion of Jeremiah's first interview with the king. Almost in the same breath the prophet announces to Zedekiah his approaching ruin and begs from him a favour. He thus defines the true attitude of the believer towards the prophet.

Unwelcome teaching must not be allowed to interfere with wonted respect and deference, or to provoke resentment. Possibly, if this truth were less obvious men would be more willing to give it a hearing and it might be less persistently ignored. But the prophet's behaviour is even more striking and interesting as a revelation of his own character and of the true prophetic spirit. His faithful answer to the king involved much courage, but that he should proceed from such an answer to such a petition shows a simple and sober dignity not always associated with courage. When men are wrought up to the pitch of uttering disagreeable truths at the risk of their lives, they often develop a spirit of defiance, which causes personal bitterness and animosity between themselves and their hearers, and renders impossible any asking or granting of favours. Many men would have felt that a petition compromised their own dignity and weakened the authority of the divine message. The exaltation of self-sacrifice which inspired them would have suggested that they ought not to risk the crown of martyrdom by any such appeal, but rather welcome torture and death. Thus some amongst the early Christians would present themselves before the Roman tribunals and try to provoke the magistrates into condemning them. But Jeremiah, like Polycarp and Cyprian, neither courted nor shunned martyrdom; he was as incapable of bravado as he was of fear. He was too intent upon serving his country and glorifying God, too possessed with his mission and his message, to fall a prey to the self-consciousness which betrays men, sometimes even martyrs, into theatrical ostentation.

CHAPTER XIII.

GEDALIAH.

JEREMIAH xxxix.-xli., lii.*

"Then arose Ishmael ben Nethaniah, and the ten men that were with him, and smote with the sword and slew Gedaliah ben Ahikam ben Shaphan, whom the king of Babylon had made king over the land."—JER. xli. 2.

WE now pass to the concluding period of Jeremiah's ministry. His last interview with Zedekiah was speedily followed by the capture of Jerusalem. With that catastrophe the curtain falls upon another act in the tragedy of the prophet's life. Most of the chief *dramatis personæ* make their final exit; only Jeremiah and Baruch remain. King and princes, priests and prophets, pass to death or captivity, and new characters appear to play their part for a while upon the vacant stage.

We would gladly know how Jeremiah fared on that night when the city was stormed, and Zedekiah and his army stole out in a vain attempt to escape beyond Jordan. Our book preserves two brief but inconsistent narratives of his fortunes.

One is contained in xxxix. 11-14. Nebuchadnezzar, we must remember, was not present in person with the besieging army. His headquarters were at Riblah, far away in the north. He had, however, given special instructions concerning Jeremiah to Nebuzaradan, the general commanding the forces before Jerusalem: "Take him, and look well to him, and do him no harm; but do with him even as he shall say unto thee."

Accordingly Nebuzaradan and all the king of Babylon's princes sent and took Jeremiah out of the court of the guard, and committed him to Gedaliah ben Ahikam ben Shaphan, to take him to his house.† And Jeremiah dwelt among the people.

This account is not only inconsistent with that given in the next chapter, but it also represents Nebuzaradan as present when the city was taken, whereas, later on,‡ we are told that he did not come upon the scene till a month later. For these and similar reasons, this version of the story is generally considered the less trustworthy. It apparently grew up at a time when the other characters and interests of the period had been thrown into the shade by the reverent recollection of Jeremiah and his ministry. It seemed natural to suppose that Nebuchadnezzar was equally preoccupied with the fortunes of the great prophet who had consistently preached

*Chapter lii. = 2 Kings xxiv. 18—xxv. 30, and xxxix. 1-10 = lii. 4-16, in each case with minor variations which do not specially bear upon our subject. *Cf.* Driver, "Introduction," *in loco*. The detailed treatment of this section belongs to the exposition of the Book of Kings.

†Literally "the house"—either Jeremiah's or Gedaliah's, or possibly the royal palace.

‡lii. 6, 12.

obedience to his authority. The section records the intense reverence which the Jews of the Captivity felt for Jeremiah. We are more likely, however, to get a true idea of what happened by following the narrative in chap. xl.

According to this account, Jeremiah was not at once singled out for any exceptionally favourable treatment. When Zedekiah and the soldiers had left the city, there can have been no question of further resistance. The history does not mention any massacre by the conquerors, but we may probably accept Lamentations ii. 20, 21, as a description of the sack of Jerusalem:—

"Shall the priest and the prophet be slain in the sanctuary of the Lord?
The youth and the old man lie on the ground in the streets;
My virgins and my young men are fallen by the sword:
Thou hast slain them in the day of Thine anger;
Thou hast slaughtered, and not pitied."

Yet the silence of Kings and Jeremiah as to all this, combined with their express statements as to captives, indicates that the Chaldean generals did not order a massacre, but rather sought to take prisoners. The soldiers would not be restrained from a certain slaughter in the heat of their first breaking into the city; but prisoners had a market value, and were provided for by the practice of deportation which Babylon had inherited from Nineveh. Accordingly the soldiers' lust for blood was satiated or bridled before they reached Jeremiah's prison. The court of the guard probably formed part of the precincts of the palace, and the Chaldean commanders would at once secure its occupants for Nebuchadnezzar. Jeremiah was taken with other captives and put in chains. If the dates in lii. 6, 12, be correct, he must have remained a prisoner till the arrival of Nebuzaradan, a month later on. He was then a witness of the burning of the city and the destruction of the fortifications, and was carried with the other captives to Ramah. Here the Chaldean general found leisure to inquire into the deserts of individual prisoners and to decide how they should be treated. He would be aided in this task by the Jewish refugees from whose ridicule Zedekiah had shrunk, and they would at once inform him of the distinguished sanctity of the prophet and of the conspicuous services he had rendered to the Chaldean cause.

Nebuzaradan at once acted upon their representations. He ordered Jeremiah's chains to be removed, gave him full liberty to go where he pleased, and assured him of the favour and protection of the Chaldean government:—

"If it seem good unto thee to come with me into Babylon, come, and I will look well unto thee; but if it seem ill unto thee to come with me into Babylon, forbear: behold, all the land is before thee; go whithersoever it seemeth to thee good and right."

These words are, however, preceded by two remarkable verses. For the nonce, the prophet's mantle seems to have fallen upon the Chaldean soldier. He speaks to his auditor just as Jeremiah himself had been wont to address his erring fellow-countrymen:—

"Thy God Jehovah pronounced this evil upon this place: and Jehovah hath brought it, and done according as He spake; because ye have sinned against Jehovah, and have not obeyed His voice, therefore this thing is come unto you."

Possibly Nebuzaradan did not include Jeremiah personally in the "ye" and "you"; and yet a prophet's message is often turned upon himself in this fashion. Even in our day outsiders will not be at the trouble to distinguish between one Christian and another, and will often denounce a man for his supposed share in Church abuses he has strenuously combated.

We need not be surprised that a heathen noble can talk like a pious Jew. The Chaldeans were eminently religious, and their worship of Bel and Merodach may often have been as spiritual and sincere as the homage paid by most Jews to Jehovah. The Babylonian creed could recognise that a foreign state might have its own legitimate deity and would suffer for disloyalty to him. Assyrian and Chaldean kings were quite willing to accept the prophetic doctrine that Jehovah had commissioned them to punish this disobedient people. Still Jeremiah must have been a little taken aback when one of the cardinal points of his own teaching was expounded to him by so strange a preacher; but he was too prudent to raise any discussion on the matter, and too chivalrous to wish to establish his own rectitude at the expense of his brethren. Moreover he had to decide between the two alternatives offered him by Nebuzaradan. Should he go to Babylon or remain in Judah?

According to a suggestion of Gratz, accepted by Cheyne,* xv. 10-21 is a record of the inner struggle through which Jeremiah came to a decision on this matter. The section is not very clear, but it suggests that at one time it seemed Jehovah's will that he should go to Babylon, and that it was only after much hesitation that he was convinced that God required him to remain in Judah. Powerful motives drew him in either direction. At Babylon he would reap the full advantage of Nebuchadnezzar's favour, and would enjoy the order and culture of a great capital. He would meet with old friends and disciples, amongst the rest Ezekiel. He would find an important sphere for ministry amongst the large Jewish community in Chaldea, where the flower of the whole nation was now in exile. In Judah he would have to share the fortunes of a feeble and suffering remnant, and would be exposed to all the dangers and disorder consequent on the break-up of the national government—brigandage on the part of native guerilla bands and raids by the neighbouring tribes. These guerilla bands were the final effort of Jewish resistance, and would seek to punish as traitors those who accepted the dominion of Babylon.

On the other hand, Jeremiah's surviving enemies, priests, prophets, and princes, had been taken *en masse* to Babylon. On his arrival he would find himself again plunged into the old controversies. Many, if not the majority, of his countrymen there would regard him as a traitor. The *protégé* of Nebuchadnezzar was sure to be disliked and distrusted by his less fortunate brethren. And Jeremiah was not a born courtier like Josephus. In Judah, moreover, he would be amongst friends of his own way of thinking; the remnant left behind had been placed under the authority of his friend Geda-

* "Pulpit Commentary," *in loco*. *Cf.* the Prophecies of Jeremiah, *antea*.

liah, the son of his former protector Ahikam, the grandson of his ancient ally Shaphan. He would be free from the anathemas of corrupt priests and the contradiction of false prophets. The advocacy of true religion amongst the exiles might safely be left to Ezekiel and his school.

But probably the motives that decided Jeremiah's course of action were, firstly, that devoted attachment to the sacred soil which was a passion with every earnest Jew; and, secondly, the inspired conviction that Palestine was to be the scene of the future development of revealed religion. This conviction was coupled with the hope that the scattered refugees who were rapidly gathering at Mizpah under Gedaliah might lay the foundations of a new community, which should become the instrument of the divine purpose. Jeremiah was no deluded visionary, who would suppose that the destruction of Jerusalem had exhausted God's judgments, and that the millennium would forthwith begin for the special and exclusive benefit of his surviving companions in Judah. Nevertheless, while there was an organised Jewish community left on native soil, it would be regarded as the heir of the national religious hopes and aspirations, and a prophet, with liberty of choice, would feel it his duty to remain.

Accordingly Jeremiah decided to join Gedaliah.* Nebuzaradan gave him food and a present, and let him go.

Gedaliah's headquarters were at Mizpah, a town not certainly identified, but lying somewhere to the northwest of Jerusalem, and playing an important part in the history of Samuel and Saul. Men would remember the ancient record which told how the first Hebrew king had been divinely appointed at Mizpah, and might regard the coincidence as a happy omen that Gedaliah would found a kingdom more prosperous and permanent than that which traced its origin to Saul.

Nebuzaradan had left with the new governor "men, women, and children, ... of them that were not carried away captive to Babylon." These were chiefly of the poorer sort, but not altogether, for among them were "royal princesses" and doubtless others belonging to the ruling classes. Apparently after these arrangements had been made the Chaldean forces were almost entirely withdrawn, and Gedaliah was left to cope with the many difficulties of the situation by his own unaided resources. For a time all went well. It seemed at first as if the scattered bands of Jewish soldiers still in the field would submit to the Chaldean government and acknowledge Gedaliah's authority. Various captains with their bands came to him at Mizpah, amongst them Ishmael ben Nethaniah, Johanan ben Kareah and his brother Jonathan. Gedaliah swore to them that they should be pardoned and protected by the Chaldeans. He confirmed them in their possession of the towns and districts they had occupied after the departure of the enemy. They accepted his assurance, and their alliance with him seemed to guarantee the safety and prosperity of the settlement. Refugees from Moab, the Ammonites, Edom, and all the neighbouring countries flocked to Mizpah, and busied themselves in gathering in the produce of the oliveyards and vineyards which had been left ownerless when the nobles were slain or carried away captive. Many of the poorer Jews revelled in such unwonted plenty, and felt that even national ruin had its compensations.

Tradition has supplemented what the sacred record tells us of this period in Jeremiah's history. We are told* that "it is also found in the records that the prophet Jeremiah" commanded the exiles to take with them fire from the altar of the Temple, and further exhorted them to observe the law and to abstain from idolatry; and that "it was also contained in the same writing, that the prophet, being warned of God, commanded the tabernacle and the ark to go with him, as he went forth unto the mountain, where Moses climbed up, and saw the heritage of God. And when Jeremiah came thither, he found an hollow cave, wherein he laid the tabernacle and the ark and the altar of incense, and so stopped the door. And some of those that followed him came to mark the way, but they could not find it: which when Jeremiah perceived he blamed them, saying, As for that place, it shall be unknown until the time that God gather His people again together and receive them to His mercy."

A less improbable tradition is that which narrates that Jeremiah composed the Book of Lamentations shortly after the capture of the city. This is first stated by the Septuagint; it has been adopted by the Vulgate and various Rabbinical authorities, and has received considerable support from Christian scholars.† Moreover, as the traveller leaves Jerusalem by the Damascus Gate, he passes great stone quarries, where Jeremiah's Grotto is still pointed out as the place where the prophet composed his elegy.

Without entering into the general question of the authorship of Lamentations, we may venture to doubt whether it can be referred to any period of Jeremiah's life which is dealt with in our book; and even whether it accurately represents his feelings at any such period. During the first month that followed the capture of Jerusalem the Chaldean generals held the city and its inhabitants at the disposal of their king. His decision was uncertain; it was by no means a matter of course that he would destroy the city. Jerusalem had been spared by Pharaoh Necho after the defeat of Josiah, and by Nebuchadnezzar after the revolt of Jehoiakim. Jeremiah and the other Jews must have been in a state of extreme suspense as to their own fate and that of their city, very different from the attitude of Lamentations. This suspense was ended when Nebuzaradan arrived and proceeded to burn the city. Jeremiah witnessed the fulfilment of his own prophecies when Jerusalem was thus overtaken by the ruin he had so often predicted. As he stood there chained amongst the other captives, many of his neighbours must have felt towards him as we should feel towards an anarchist gloating over the spectacle of a successful dynamite explosion; and Jeremiah could not be ignorant of their sentiments. His own emotions would be sufficiently vivid, but they would not be so simple as those of the great elegy. Probably they were too poignant to be capable of

* The sequence of verses 4 and 5 has been spoilt by some corruption of the text. The versions diverge variously from the Hebrew. Possibly the original text told how Jeremiah found himself unable to give an immediate answer, and Nebuzaradan, observing his hesitation, bade him return to Gedaliah and decide at his leisure.

* 2 Macc. ii. 1-8.

† *Cf.* Professor Adeney's "Canticles and Lamentations."

articulate expression; and the occasion was not likely to be fertile in acrostics.

Doubtless when the venerable priest and prophet looked from Ramah or Mizpah towards the blackened ruins of the Temple and the Holy City, he was possessed by something of the spirit of Lamentations. But from the moment when he went to Mizpah he would be busily occupied in assisting Gedaliah in his gallant effort to gather the nucleus of a new Israel out of the flotsam and jetsam of the shipwreck of Judah. Busy with this work of practical beneficence, his unconquerable spirit already possessed with visions of a brighter future, Jeremiah could not lose himself in mere regrets for the past.

He was doomed to experience yet another disappointment. Gedaliah had only held his office for about two months,* when he was warned by Johanan ben Kareah and the other captains that Ishmael ben Nethaniah had been sent by Baalis, king of the Ammonites, to assassinate him. Gedaliah refused to believe them. Johanan, perhaps surmising that the governor's incredulity was assumed, came to him privately and proposed to anticipate Ishmael: "Let me go, I pray thee, and slay Ishmael ben Nethaniah, and no one shall know it: wherefore should he slay thee, that all the Jews which are gathered unto thee should be scattered, and the remnant of Judah perish? But Gedaliah ben Ahikam said unto Johanan ben Kareah, Thou shalt not do this thing: for thou speakest falsely of Ishmael."

Gedaliah's misplaced confidence soon had fatal consequences. In the second month, about October, the Jews in the ordinary course of events would have celebrated the Feast of Tabernacles, to return thanks for their plentiful ingathering of grapes, olives, and summer fruit. Possibly this occasion gave Ishmael a pretext for visiting Mizpah. He came thither with ten nobles who, like himself, were connected with the royal family and probably were among the princes who persecuted Jeremiah. This small and distinguished company could not be suspected of intending to use violence. Ishmael seemed to be reciprocating Gedaliah's confidence by putting himself in the governor's power. Gedaliah feasted his guests. Johanan and the other captains were not present; they had done what they could to save him, but they did not wait to share the fate which he was bringing on himself.

"Then arose Ishmael ben Nethaniah and his ten companions and smote Gedaliah ben Ahikam . . . and all the Jewish and Chaldean soldiers that were with him at Mizpah."

Probably the eleven assassins were supported by a larger body of followers, who waited outside the city and made their way in amidst the confusion consequent on the murder; doubtless, too, they had friends amongst Gedaliah's *entourage*. These accomplices had first lulled any suspicions that he might feel as to Ishmael, and had then helped to betray their master.

Not contented with the slaughter which he had already perpetrated, Ishmael took measures to prevent the news getting abroad, and lay in wait for any other adherents of Gedaliah who might come to visit him. He succeeded in entrapping a company of eighty men from Northern Israel: ten were allowed to purchase their lives by revealing hidden stores of wheat, barley, oil, and honey; the rest were slain and thrown into an ancient pit, "which King Asa had made for fear of Baasha king of Israel."

These men were pilgrims, who came with shaven chins and torn clothes, "and having cut themselves, bringing meal offerings and frankincense to the house of Jehovah." The pilgrims were doubtless on their way to celebrate the Feast of Tabernacles: with the destruction of Jerusalem and the Temple, all the joy of their festival would be changed to mourning and its songs to wailing. Possibly they were going to lament on the site of the ruined temple. But Mizpah itself had an ancient sanctuary. Hosea speaks of the priests, princes, and people of Israel as having been "a snare on Mizpah." Jeremiah may have sanctioned the use of this local temple, thinking that Jehovah would "set His name there" till Jerusalem was restored, even as He had dwelt at Shiloh before He chose the City of David. But to whatever shrine these pilgrims were journeying, their errand should have made them sacrosanct to all Jews. Ishmael's hypocrisy, treachery, and cruelty in this matter go far to justify Jeremiah's bitterest invectives against the princes of Judah.

But after this bloody deed it was high time for Ishmael to be gone and betake himself back to his heathen patron, Baalis the Ammonite. These massacres could not long be kept a secret. And yet Ishmael seems to have made a final effort to suppress the evidence of his crimes. In his retreat he carried with him all the people left in Mizpah, "soldiers, women, children, and eunuchs," including the royal princesses, and apparently Jeremiah and Baruch. No doubt he hoped to make money out of his prisoners by selling them as slaves or holding them to ransom. He had not ventured to slay Jeremiah: the prophet had not been present at the banquet and had thus escaped the first fierce slaughter, and Ishmael shrank from killing in cold blood the man whose predictions of ruin had been so exactly and awfully fulfilled by the recent destruction of Jerusalem.

When Johanan ben Kareah and the other captains heard how entirely Ishmael had justified their warning, they assembled their forces and started in pursuit. Ishmael's band seems to have been comparatively small, and was moreover encumbered by the disproportionate number of captives with which they had burdened themselves. They were overtaken "by the great waters that are in Gibeon," only a very short distance from Mizpah.

However Ishmael's original following of ten may have been reinforced, his band cannot have been very numerous and was manifestly inferior to Johanan's forces. In face of an enemy of superior strength, Ishmael's only chance of escape was to leave his prisoners to their own devices —he had not even time for another massacre. The captives at once turned round and made their way to their deliverer. Ishmael's followers seem to have been scattered, taken captive, or slain, but he himself escaped with eight men —possibly eight of the original ten—and found refuge with the Ammonites.

Johanan and his companions with the recovered captives made no attempt to return to Mizpah. The Chaldeans would exact a severe penalty for the murder of their governor Gedaliah,

* *Cf.* lii. 12, "fifth month," and xli. 1, "seventh month." Cheyne, however, points out that no year is specified in xli. 1, and holds that Gedaliah's governorship lasted for over four years, and that the deportation four years (lii. 30) after the destruction of the city was the prompt punishment of his murder.

and their own fellow-countrymen: their vengeance was not likely to be scrupulously discriminating. The massacre would be regarded as an act of rebellion on the part of the Jewish community in Judah, and the community would be punished accordingly. Johanan and his whole company determined that when the day of retribution came the Chaldeans should find no one to punish. They set out for Egypt, the natural asylum of the enemies of Babylon. On the way they halted in the neighbourhood of Bethlehem at a caravanserai * which bore the name of Chimham,† the son of David's generous friend Barzillai. So far the fugitives had acted on their first impulse of dismay; now they paused to take breath, to make a more deliberate survey of their situation, and to mature their plans for the future.

CHAPTER XIV.

THE DESCENT INTO EGYPT.

JEREMIAH xlii., xliii.

"They came into the land of Egypt, for they obeyed not the voice of Jehovah."—JER. xliii. 7.

THUS within a few days Jeremiah had experienced one of those sudden and extreme changes of fortune which are as common in his career as in a sensational novel. Yesterday the guide, philosopher, and friend of the governor of Judah, to-day sees him once more a helpless prisoner in the hands of his old enemies. Tomorrow he is restored to liberty and authority, and appealed to by the remnant of Israel as the mouthpiece of Jehovah. Johanan ben Kareah and all the captains of the forces, "from the least even unto the greatest, came near" and besought Jeremiah to pray unto "Jehovah thy God," "that Jehovah thy God may show us the way wherein we may walk, and the thing we may do." Jeremiah promised to make intercession and to declare faithfully unto them whatsoever Jehovah should reveal unto him.

And they on their part said unto Jeremiah: "Jehovah be a true and faithful witness against us, if we do not according to every word that Jehovah thy God shall send unto us by thee. We will obey the voice of Jehovah our God, to whom we send thee, whether it be good or evil, that it may be well with us, when we obey the voice of Jehovah our God."

The prophet returned no hasty answer to this solemn appeal. As in his controversy with Hananiah, he refrained from at once announcing his own judgment as the Divine decision, but waited for the express confirmation of the Spirit. For ten days prophet and people were alike kept in suspense. The patience of Johanan and his followers is striking testimony to their sincere reverence for Jeremiah.

On the tenth day the message came, and Jeremiah called the people together to hear God's answer to their question, and to learn that Divine will to which they had promised unreserved obedience. It ran thus:—

"If you will still abide in this land,
I will build you and not pull you down,
I will plant you and not pluck you up."

* The reading is doubtful; possibly the word (geruth) translated "caravanserai," or some similar word to be read instead of it, merely forms a compound proper name with Chimham.

† 2 Sam. xix. 31-40.

The words of Jeremiah's original commission seem ever present to his mind:—

"For I repent Me of the evil I have done unto you."

They need not flee from Judah as an accursed land; Jehovah had a new and gracious purpose concerning them, and therefore:—

"Be not afraid of the king of Babylon,
Of whom ye are afraid;
Be not afraid of him—it is the utterance of Jehovah—
For I am with you,
To save you and deliver you out of his hand.
I will put kindness in his heart toward you,
And he shall deal kindly with you,
And restore you to your lands."

It was premature to conclude that Ishmael's crime finally disposed of the attempt to shape the remnant into the nucleus of a new Israel. Hitherto Nebuchadnezzar had shown himself willing to discriminate; when he condemned the princes, he spared and honoured Jeremiah, and the Chaldeans might still be trusted to deal fairly and generously with the prophet's friends and deliverers. Moreover the heart of Nebuchadnezzar, like that of all earthly potentates, was in the hands of the King of Kings.

But Jeremiah knew too well what mingled hopes and fears drew his hearers towards the fertile valley and rich cities of the Nile. He sets before them the reverse of the picture: they might refuse to obey God's command to remain in Judah; they might say, "No, we will go into the land of Egypt, where we shall see no war, nor hear the sound of the trumpet, nor hunger for bread, and there will we dwell." As of old, they craved for the flesh-pots of Egypt; and with more excuse than their forefathers. They were worn out with suffering and toil, some of them had wives and children; the childless prophet was inviting them to make sacrifices and incur risks which he could neither share nor understand. Can we wonder if they fell short of his inspired heroism, and hesitated to forego the ease and plenty of Egypt in order to try social experiments in Judah?

"Let what is broken so remain.
The Gods are hard to reconcile:
'Tis hard to settle order once again.
. . .
Sore task to hearts worn out by many wars."

But Jeremiah had neither sympathy nor patience with such weakness. Moreover, now as often, valour was the better part of discretion, and the boldest course was the safest. The peace and security of Egypt had been broken in upon again and again by Asiatic invaders; only recently it had been tributary to Nineveh, till the failing strength of Assyria enabled the Pharaohs to recover their independence. Now that Palestine had ceased to be the seat of war the sound of Chaldean trumpets would soon be heard in the valley of the Nile. By going down into Egypt, they were leaving Judah where they might be safe under the broad shield of Babylonian power, for a country that would soon be afflicted by the very evils they sought to escape:—

"If ye finally determine to go to Egypt to sojourn there,
The sword, which ye fear, shall overtake you there in the land of Egypt.
The famine whereof ye are afraid, shall follow hard after you there in Egypt,
And there shall ye die."

The old familiar curses, so often uttered against Jerusalem and its inhabitants, are pronounced against any of his hearers who should take refuge in Egypt:—

"As Mine anger and fury hath been poured forth upon the inhabitants of Jerusalem,
So shall My fury be poured forth upon you, when ye shall enter in Egypt."

They would die "by the sword, the famine, and the pestilence"; they would be "an execration and an astonishment, a curse and a reproach."

He had set before them two alternative courses, and the Divine judgment upon each: he had known beforehand that, contrary to his own choice and judgment, their hearts were set upon going down into Egypt; hence, as when confronted and contradicted by Hananiah, he had been careful to secure divine confirmation before he gave his decision. Already he could see the faces of his hearers hardening into obstinate resistance or kindling into hot defiance; probably they broke out into interruptions which left no doubt as to their purpose. With his usual promptness, he turned upon them with fierce reproof and denunciation:—

"Ye have been traitors to yourselves.
Ye sent me unto Jehovah your God, saying,
Pray for us unto Jehovah our God;
According unto all that Jehovah our God shall say,
Declare unto us, and we will do it.
I have this day declared it unto you,
But ye have in no wise obeyed the voice of Jehovah your God.

. . . . .

Ye shall die by the sword, the famine, and the pestilence,
In the place whither ye desire to go to sojourn."

His hearers were equally prompt with their rejoinder; Johanan ben Kereah and "all the proud men" answered him:—

"Thou liest! It is not Jehovah our God who hath sent thee to say, Ye shall not go into Egypt to sojourn there; but Baruch ben Neriah setteth thee on against us, to deliver us into the hand of the Chaldeans, that they may slay us or carry us away captive to Babylon."

Jeremiah had experienced many strange vicissitudes, but this was not the least striking. Ten days ago the people and their leaders had approached him in reverent submission, and had solemnly promised to accept and obey his decision as the word of God. Now they called him a liar; they asserted that he did not speak by any Divine inspiration, but was a feeble impostor, an oracular puppet, whose strings were pulled by his own disciple.*

Such scenes are, unfortunately, only too common in Church history. Religious professors are still ready to abuse and to impute unworthy motives to prophets whose messages they dislike, in a spirit not less secular than that which is shown when some modern football team tries to mob the referee who has given a decision against its hopes.

Moreover we must not unduly emphasise the solemn engagement given by the Jews to abide Jeremiah's decision. They were probably sincere, but not very much in earnest. The proceedings and the strong formulæ used were largely conventional. Ancient kings and generals regularly sought the approval of their prophets or augurs before taking any important step, but they did not always act upon their advice. The final breach between Saul and the prophet Samuel seems to have been due to the fact that the king did not wait for his presence and counsel before engaging the Philistines.* Before the disastrous expedition to Ramoth Gilead, Jehoshaphat insisted on consulting a prophet of Jehovah, and then acted in the teeth of his inspired warning.†

Johanan and his company felt it essential to consult some divine oracle; and Jeremiah was not only the greatest prophet of Jehovah, he was also the only prophet available. They must have known from his consistent denunciation of all alliance with Egypt that his views were likely to be at variance with their own. But they were consulting Jehovah—Jeremiah was only His mouthpiece; hitherto He had set His face against any dealings with Egypt, but circumstances were entirely changed, and Jehovah's purpose might change with them, He might "repent." They promised to obey, because there was at any rate a chance that God's commands would coincide with their own intentions. Butler's remark that men may be expected to act "not only upon an even chance, but upon much less," specially applies to such promises as the Jews made to Jeremiah. Certain tacit conditions may always be considered attached to a profession of willingness to be guided by a friend's advice. Our newspapers frequently record breaches of engagements that should be as binding as that entered into by Johanan and his friends, and they do so without any special comment. For instance, the verdicts of arbitrators in trade disputes have been too often ignored by the unsuccessful parties; and—to take a very different illustration—the most unlimited professions of faith in the infallibility of the Bible have sometimes gone along with a denial of its plain teaching and a disregard of its imperative commands. While Shylock expected a favorable decision, Portia was "a Daniel come to judgment": his subsequent opinion of her judicial qualities has not been recorded. Those who have never refused or evaded unwelcome demands made by an authority whom they have promised to obey may cast the first stone at Johanan.

After the scene we have been describing, the refugees set out for Egypt, carrying with them the princesses and Jeremiah and Baruch. They were following in the footsteps of Abraham, Isaac, and Jacob, of Jeroboam, and many another Jew who had sought protection under the shadow of Pharaoh. They were the forerunners of that later Israel in Egypt which, through Philo and his disciples, exercised so powerful an influence on the doctrine, criticism, and exegesis of the early Christian Church.

Yet this exodus in the wrong direction was by no means complete. Four years later Nebuzaradan could still find seven hundred and forty-five Jews to carry away to Babylon.‡ Johanan's movements had been too hurried to admit of his gathering in the inhabitants of outlying districts.

When Johanan's company reached the frontier, they would find the Egyptian officials prepared to receive them. During the last few months there must have been constant arrivals of Jewish refugees, and rumour must have announced the approach of so large a company, consisting of almost all the Jews left in Palestine.

* *Cf.* chapter on "Baruch."

* Sam. xiii. † 1 Kings xxii. ‡ lii. 30.

The very circumstances that made them dread the vengeance of Nebuchadnezzar would ensure them a hearty welcome in Egypt. Their presence was an unmistakable proof of the entire failure of the attempt to create in Judah a docile and contented dependency and outpost of the Chaldean Empire. They were accordingly settled at Tahpanhes and in the surrounding district.

But no welcome could conciliate Jeremiah's implacable temper, nor could all the splendour of Egypt tame his indomitable spirit. Amongst his fellow-countrymen at Bethlehem, he had foretold the coming tribulations of Egypt. He now renewed his predictions within the very precincts of Pharaoh's palace, and enforced them by a striking symbol. At Tahpanhes—the modern Tell Defenneh—which was the ancient Egyptian frontier fortress and settlement on the more westerly route from Syria, "the word of Jehovah came to Jeremiah, saying Take great stones in thine hand, and hide them in mortar in the brick pavement, at the entry of Pharaoh's palace in Tahpanhes, in the presence of the men of Judah; and say unto them, Thus saith Jehovah Sabaoth, the God of Israel:

"Behold, I will send and take My servant Nebuchadnezzar king of Babylon:
I will set his throne upon these stones which I have hid,
And he shall spread his state pavilion over them."

He would set up his royal tribunal, and decide the fate of the conquered city and its inhabitants.

"He shall come and smite the land of Egypt;
Such as are for death shall be put to death,
Such as are for captivity shall be sent into captivity,
Such as are for the sword shall be slain by the sword.
I will kindle a fire in the temples of the gods of Egypt;
He shall burn their temples, and carry them away captive:
He shall array himself with the land of Egypt,
As a shepherd putteth on his garment."

The whole country would become a mere mantle for his dignity, a comparatively insignificant part of his vast possessions.

"He shall go forth from thence in peace."

A campaign that promised well at the beginning has often ended in despair, like Sennacherib's attack on Judah, and Pharaoh Necho's expedition to Carchemish. The invading army has been exhausted by its victories, or wasted by disease and compelled to beat an inglorious retreat. No such misfortune should overtake the Chaldean king. He would depart with all his spoil, leaving Egypt behind him subdued into a loyal province of his empire.

Then the prophet adds, apparently as a kind of afterthought:—

"He also shall break the obelisks of Heliopolis, in the land of Egypt"

(so styled to distinguish this Beth-Shemesh from Beth-Shemesh in Palestine),

"And shall burn with fire the temples of the gods of Egypt."

The performance of this symbolic act and the delivery of its accompanying message are not recorded, but Jeremiah would not fail to make known the Divine word to his fellow-countrymen. It is difficult to understand how the exiled prophet would be allowed to assemble the Jews in front of the main entrance of the palace, and hide "great stones" in the pavement. Possibly the palace was being repaired,* or the stones might be inserted under the front or side of a raised platform, or possibly the symbolic act was only to be described and not performed. Mr. Flinders Petrie recently discovered at Tell Defenneh a large brickwork pavement, with great stones buried underneath, which he supposed might be those mentioned in our narrative. He also found there another possible relic of these Jewish *émigrés* in the shape of the ruins of a large brick building of the twenty-sixth dynasty—to which Pharaoh Hophra belonged—still known as the "Palace of the Jew's Daughter." It is a natural and attractive conjecture that this was the residence assigned to the Jewish princesses whom Johanan carried with him into Egypt.

But while the ruined palace may testify to Pharaoh's generosity to the Royal House that had suffered through its alliance with him, the "great stones" remind us that, after a brief interval of sympathy and co-operation, Jeremiah again found himself in bitter antagonism to his fellow-countrymen. In our next chapter we shall describe one final scene of mutual recrimination.†

CHAPTER XV.

THE QUEEN OF HEAVEN.

JEREMIAH xliv.

"Since we left off burning incense and offering libations to the Queen of Heaven, we have been in want of everything, and have been consumed by the sword and the famine."—JER. xliv. 18.

THE Jewish exiles in Egypt still retained a semblance of national life, and were bound together by old religious ties. Accordingly we read that they came together from their different settlements—from Migdol and Tahpanhes on the northeastern frontier, from Noph or Memphis on the Nile south of the site of Cairo, and from Pathros or Upper Egypt—to a "great assembly," no doubt a religious festival. The list of cities shows how widely the Jews were scattered throughout Egypt.

Nothing is said as to where and when this "great assembly" met; but for Jeremiah, such a gathering at all times and anywhere, in Egypt as at Jerusalem, became an opportunity for fulfilling his Divine commission. He once again confronted his fellow-countrymen with the familiar threats and exhortations. A new climate had not created in them either clean hearts or a right spirit.

Recent history had added force to his warnings. He begins therefore by appealing to the direful consequences which had come upon the Holy Land, through the sins of its inhabitants:—

"Ye have seen all the evil that I have brought upon Jerusalem and upon all the cities of Judah.
Behold, this day they are an uninhabited waste,
Because of their wickedness which they wrought to provoke Me to anger,
By going to burn incense and to serve other gods whom neither they nor their fathers knew."

The Israelites had enjoyed for centuries intimate personal relations with Jehovah, and knew

* So Orelli, *in loco*.

† For the prophecy against Egypt and its fulfilment see further chapter xvii.

Him by this ancient and close fellowship and by all His dealings with them. They had no such knowledge of the gods of surrounding nations. They were like foolish children who prefer the enticing blandishments of a stranger to the affection and discipline of their home. Such children do not intend to forsake their home or to break the bonds of filial affection, and yet the new friendship may wean their hearts from their father. So these exiles still considered themselves worshippers of Jehovah, and yet their superstition led them to disobey and dishonour Him.

Before its ruin Judah had sinned against light and leading:—

"Howbeit I sent unto you all My servants the prophets,
Rising up early and sending them, saying,
Oh do not this abominable thing that I hate.
But they hearkened not, nor inclined their ears, so as to turn from their evil,
That they should not burn incense to other gods.
Wherefore My fury and my anger was poured forth."

Political and social questions, the controversies with the prophets who contradicted Jeremiah in the name of Jehovah, have fallen into the background; the poor pretence of loyalty to Jehovah which permitted His worshippers to degrade Him to the level of Baal and Moloch is ignored as worthless: and Jeremiah, like Ezekiel, finds the root of the people's sin in their desertion of Jehovah. Their real religion was revealed by their heathenish superstitions. Every religious life is woven of many diverse strands; if the web as a whole is rotten, the Great Taskmaster can take no account of a few threads that have a form and profession of soundness. Our Lord declared that He would utterly ignore and repudiate men upon whose lips His name was a too familiar word, who had preached and cast out devils and done many mighty works in that Holy Name. These were men who had worked iniquity, who had combined promising externals with the worship of "other gods," Mammon or Belial or some other of those evil powers, who place

"Within His sanctuary itself their shrines,
Abominations; and with cursed things
His holy rites and solemn feasts profane;
And with their darkness dare affront His light."

This profuse blending of idolatry with a profession of zeal for Jehovah had provoked the Divine wrath against Judah: and yet the exiles had not profited by their terrible experience of the consequences of sin; they still burnt incense unto other gods. Therefore Jeremiah remonstrates with them afresh, and sets before their eyes the utter ruin which will punish persistent sin. This discourse repeats and enlarges the threats uttered at Bethlehem. The penalties then denounced on disobedience are now attributed to idolatry. We have here yet another example of the tacit understanding attaching to all the prophet's predictions. The most positive declarations of doom are often warnings and not final sentences. Jehovah does not turn a deaf ear to the penitent, and the doom is executed not because He exacts the uttermost farthing, but because the culprit perseveres in his uttermost wrong. Lack of faith and loyalty at Bethlehem and idolatry in Egypt were both symptoms of the same deep-rooted disease.

On this occasion there was no rival prophet to beard Jeremiah and relieve his hearers from their fears and scruples. Probably indeed no professed prophet of Jehovah would have cared to defend the worship of other gods. But, as at Bethlehem, the people themselves ventured to defy their aged mentor. They seem to have been provoked to such hardihood by a stimulus which often prompts timorous men to bold words. Their wives were specially devoted to the superstitious burning of incense, and these women were present in large numbers. Probably, like Lady Macbeth, they had already in private

"Poured their spirits in their husbands' ears,
And chastised, with the valour of their tongues,
All that impeded."

those husbands from speaking their minds to Jeremiah. In their presence, the men dared not shirk an obvious duty, for fear of more domestic chastisement. The prophet's reproaches would be less intolerable than such inflictions. Moreover the fair devotees did not hesitate to mingle their own shrill voices in the wordy strife.

These idolatrous Jews—male and female—carried things with a very high hand indeed:—

"We will not obey thee in that which thou hast spoken to us in the name of Jehovah. We are determined to perform all the vows we have made to burn incense and offer libations to the Queen of Heaven, exactly as we have said and as we and our fathers and kings and princes did in the cities of Judah and in the streets of Jerusalem." *

Moreover they were quite prepared to meet Jeremiah on his own ground and argue with him according to his own principles and methods. He had appealed to the ruin of Judah as a proof of Jehovah's condemnation of their idolatry and of His power to punish: they argued that these misfortunes were a Divine *spretæ injuria formæ*, the vengeance of the Queen of Heaven, whose worship they had neglected. When they duly honoured her,—

"Then had we plenty of victuals, and were prosperous and saw no evil; but since we left off burning incense and offering libations to the Queen of Heaven, we have been in want of everything, and have been consumed by the sword and the famine."

Moreover the women had a special plea of their own:—

"When we burned incense and offered libations to the Queen of Heaven, did we not make cakes to symbolise her and offer libations to her with our husbands' permission?"

A wife's vows were not valid without her husband's sanction, and the women avail themselves of this principle to shift the responsibility for their superstition on the men's shoulders. Possibly too the unfortunate Benedicts were not displaying sufficient zeal in the good cause, and these words were intended to goad them into greater energy. Doubtless they cannot be entirely exonerated of blame for tolerating their wives' sins, probably they were guilty of participation as well as connivance. Nothing, however, but the utmost determination and moral courage would have curbed the exuberant religiosity of these devout ladies. The prompt suggestion that, if they had done wrong, their husbands are to blame for letting them have their own way, is an instance of the meanness which results from the worship of "other gods."

But these defiant speeches raise a more impor-

* Combined from verses, 16, 17, and 25.

tant question. There is an essential difference between regarding a national catastrophe as a Divine judgment and the crude superstition to which an eclipse expresses the resentment of an angry god. But both involve the same practical uncertainty. The sufferers or the spectators ask what god wrought these marvels and what sins they are intended to punish, and to these questions neither catastrophe nor eclipse gives any certain answer.

Doubtless the altars of the Queen of Heaven had been destroyed by Josiah in his crusade against heathen cults; but her outraged majesty had been speedily avenged by the defeat and death of the iconoclast, and since then the history of Judah had been one long series of disasters. Jeremiah declared that these were the just retribution inflicted by Jehovah because Judah had been disloyal to Him; in the reign of Manasseh their sin had reached its climax:—

"I will cause them to be tossed to and fro among all the nations of the earth, because of Manasseh ben Hezekiah, king of Judah, for that which he did in Jerusalem." *

His audience were equally positive that the national ruin was the vengeance of the Queen of Heaven. Josiah had destroyed her altars, and now the worshippers of Istar had retaliated by razing the Temple to the ground. A Jew, with the vague impression that Istar was as real as Jehovah, might find it difficult to decide between these conflicting theories.

To us, as to Jeremiah, it seems sheer nonsense to speak of the vengeance of the Queen of Heaven, not because of what we deduce from the circumstances of the fall of Jerusalem, but because we do not believe in any such deity. But the fallacy is repeated when, in somewhat similar fashion, Protestants find proof of the superiority of their faith in the contrast between England and Catholic Spain, while Romanists draw the opposite conclusion from a comparison of Holland and Belgium. In all such cases the assured truth of the disputant's doctrine, which is set forth as the result of his argument, is in reality the premiss upon which his reasoning rests. Faith is not deduced from, but dictates an interpretation of history. In an individual the material penalties of sin may arouse a sleeping conscience, but they cannot create a moral sense: apart from a moral sense the discipline of rewards and punishments would be futile:—

"Were no inner eye in us to tell,
Instructed by no inner sense,
The light of heaven from the dark of hell,
That light would want its evidence."

Jeremiah, therefore, is quite consistent in refraining from argument and replying to his opponents by reiterating his former statements that sin against Jehovah had ruined Judah and would yet ruin the exiles. He spoke on the authority of the "inner sense," itself instructed by Revelation. But, after the manner of the prophets, he gave them a sign—Pharaoh Hophra should be delivered into the hand of his enemies as Zedekiah had been. Such an event would indeed be an unmistakable sign of imminent calamity to the fugitives who had sought the protection of the Egyptian king against Nebuchadnezzar.†

We have reserved for separate treatment the question suggested by the referencs to the Queen

* xv. 4.

† As to the fulfilment of this prophecy see chap. xvii.

of Heaven.* This divine name only occurs again in the Old Testament in vii. 18, and we are startled, at first sight, to discover that a cult about which all other historians and prophets have been entirely silent is described in these passages as an ancient and national worship. It is even possible that the "great assembly" was a festival in her honour. We have again to remind ourselves that the Old Testament is an account of the progress of Revelation and not a history of Israel. Probably the true explanation is that given by Kuenen. The prophets do not, as a rule, speak of the details of false worship; they use the generic "Baal" and the collective "other gods." Even in this chapter Jeremiah begins by speaking of "other gods," and only uses the term "Queen of Heaven" when he quotes the reply made to him by the Jews. Similarly when Ezekiel goes into detail concerning idolatry† he mentions cults and ritual‡ which do not occur elsewhere in the Old Testament. The prophets were little inclined to discriminate between different forms of idolatry, just as the average churchman is quite indifferent to the distinctions of the various Nonconformist bodies, which are to him simply "dissenters." One might read many volumes of Anglican sermons and even some English Church History without meeting with the term Unitarian.

It is easy to find modern parallels—Christian and heathen—to the name of this goddess. The Virgin Mary is honoured with the title *Regina Cœli*, and at Mukden, the Sacred City of China, there is a temple to the Queen of Heaven. But it is not easy to identify the ancient deity who bore this name. The Jews are accused elsewhere of worshipping "the sun and the moon and all the host of heaven," and one or other of these heavenly bodies—mostly either the moon or the planet Venus—has been supposed to have been the Queen of Heaven.

Neither do the symbolic cakes help us. Such emblems are found in the ritual of many ancient cults: at Athens cakes called σελῆναι and shaped like a full-moon were offered to the moon-goddess Artemis; a similar usage seems to have prevailed in the worship of the Arabian goddess Al-Uzza, whose star was Venus, and also in connection with the worship of the sun.§

Moreover we do not find the title "Queen of Heaven" as an ordinary and well-established name of any neighbouring divinity. "Queen" is a natural title for any goddess, and was actually given to many ancient deities. Schrader ‖ finds our goddess in the Atar-samain (Athar-Astarte) who is mentioned in the Assyrian descriptions as worshipped by a North Arabian tribe of Kedarenes. Possibly too the Assyrian Istar is called Queen of Heaven.¶

Istar, however, is connected with the moon as well as with the planet Venus.** For the present,

* MELEKHETH HASHSHAMAYIM. The Masoretic pointing seems to indicate a rendering "service" or work of heaven, probably in the sense of "host of heaven," *i. e.* the stars, מְלֶכֶת being written defectively for מְלָאכֶת, but this translation is now pretty generally abandoned. *Cf.* C. J. Ball, Giesebrecht, Orelli, Cheyne, etc., on vii. 18, and especially Kuenen's treatise on the Queen of Heaven—in the "Gesammelte Abhandlungen," translated by Budde—to which this section is largely indebted.

† Ezek. viii.

‡ The worship of Tammuz and of "creeping things and abominable beasts," etc.

§ Kuenen, 208.

‖ Schrader (Whitehouse's translation), ii. 207.

¶ Kuenen, 206.

** Sayce, "Higher Criticism," etc., 80.

therefore we must be content to leave the matter an open question,* but any day some new discovery may solve the problem. Meanwhile it is interesting to notice how little religious ideas and practices are affected by differences in profession. St. Isaac the Great, of Antioch, who died about A. D. 460, tells us that the Christian ladies of Syria—whom he speaks of very ungallantly as "fools"—used to worship the planet Venus from the roofs of their houses, in the hope that she would bestow upon them some portion of her own brightness and beauty. This experience naturally led St. Isaac to interpret the Queen of Heaven as the luminary which his countrywomen venerated.†

The episode of the "great assembly" closes the history of Jeremiah's life. We leave him (as we so often met with him before) hurling ineffective denunciations at a recalcitrant audience. Vagrant fancy, holding this to be a lame and impotent conclusion, has woven romantic stories to continue and complete the narrative. There are traditions that he was stoned to death at Tahpanhes, and that his bones were removed to Alexandria by Alexander the Great; that he and Baruch returned to Judea or went to Babylon and died in peace; that he returned to Jerusalem and lived there three hundred years,—and other such legends. As has been said concerning the Apocryphal Gospels, these narratives serve as a foil to the history they are meant to supplement: they remind us of the sequels of great novels written by inferior pens, or of attempts made by clumsy mechanics to convert a bust by some inspired sculptor into a full-length statue.

For this story of Jeremiah's life is not a torso. Sacred biography constantly disappoints our curiosity as to the last days of holy men. We are scarcely ever told how prophets and apostles died. It is curious too that the great exceptions—Elijah in his chariot of fire and Elisha dying quietly in his bed—occur before the period of written prophecy. The deaths of Isaiah, Jeremiah, and Ezekiel, Peter, Paul, and John, are passed over in the Sacred Record, and when we seek to follow them beyond its pages, we are taught afresh the unique wisdom of inspiration. If we may understand Deuteronomy xxxiv. to imply that no eye was permitted to behold Moses in the hour of death, we have in this incident a type of the reticence of Scripture on such matters. Moreover a moment's reflection reminds us that the inspired method is in accordance with the better instincts of our nature. A death in opening manhood, or the death of a soldier in battle or of a martyr at the stake, rivets our attention; but when men die in a good old age, we dwell less on their declining years than on the achievements of their prime. We all remember the martyrdoms of Huss and Latimer, but how many of those in whose mouths Calvin and Luther are familiar as household words know how those great Reformers died?

There comes a time when we may apply to the aged saint the words of Browning's "Death in the Desert":—

"So is myself withdrawn into my depths,
The soul retreated from the perished brain
Whence it was wont to feel and use the world
Through these dull members, done with long ago."

And the poet's comparison of his soul to

"A stick once fire from end to end
Now, ashes save the tip that holds a spark"

Love craves to watch to the last, because the spark may

"Run back, spread itself
A little where the fire was. . . .
And we would not lose
The last of what might happen on his face."

Such privileges may be granted to a few chosen disciples, probably they were in this case granted to Baruch; but they are mostly withheld from the world, lest blind irreverence should see in the aged saint nothing but

"Second childishness, and mere oblivion;
Sans teeth, sans eyes, sans taste, sans everything."

BOOK II.

PROPHECIES CONCERNING FOREIGN NATIONS.

CHAPTER XVI.

JEHOVAH AND THE NATIONS.

JEREMIAH xxv. 15-38.

"Jehovah hath a controversy with the nations."—JER. xxv. 31.

As the son of a king only learns very gradually that his father's authority and activity extend beyond the family and the household, so Israel in its childhood thought of Jehovah as exclusively concerned with itself.

Such ideas as omnipotence and universal Providence did not exist; therefore they could not be denied; and the limitations of the national faith were not essentially inconsistent with later Revelation. But when we reach the period of recorded prophecy we find that, under the guidance of the Holy Spirit, the prophets had begun to recognise Jehovah's dominion over surrounding peoples. There was, as yet, no deliberate and formal doctrine of omnipotence, but, as Israel became involved in the fortunes first of one foreign power and then of another, the prophets asserted that the doings of these heathen states were overruled by the God of Israel. The idea of Jehovah's Lordship of the Nations enlarged with the extension of international relations, as our conception of the God of Nature has expanded with the successive discoveries of science. Hence, for the most part, the prophets devote special attention to the concerns of Gentile peoples. Hosea, Micah, Haggai, Zechariah, and Malachi are partial exceptions. Some of the minor prophets have for their main subject the doom of a heathen empire. Jonah and Nahum deal with Nineveh, Habakkuk with Chaldea, and Edom is specially honoured by being almost the sole object of the denunciations of Obadiah. Daniel also deals with the fate of the kingdoms of the world, but in the Apocalyptic fashion of the Pseudepigrapha. Jewish criticism rightly declined to recognise this book as prophetic, and

* So Giesebrecht on vii. 18. Kuenen argues for the identification of the Queen of Heaven with the planet Venus.

† Kuenen, 211.

relegated it to the latest collection of canonical scriptures.

Each of the other prophetical books contains a longer or shorter series of utterances concerning the neighbours of Israel, its friends and foes, its enemies and allies. The fashion was apparently set by Amos, who shows God's judgment upon Damascus, the Philistines, Tyre, Edom, Ammon, and Moab. This list suggests the range of the prophet's religious interest in the Gentiles. Assyria and Egypt were, for the present, beyond the sphere of Revelation, just as China and India were to the average Protestant of the seventeenth century. When we come to the Book of Isaiah, the horizon widens in every direction. Jehovah is concerned with Egypt and Ethiopia, Assyria and Babylon.* In very short books like Joel and Zephaniah we could not expect exhaustive treatment of this subject. Yet even these prophets deal with the fortunes of the Gentiles: Joel, variously held one of the latest or one of the earliest of canonical books, pronounces a Divine judgment on Tyre and Sidon and the Philistines, on Egypt and Edom; and Zephaniah, an elder contemporary of Jeremiah, devotes sections to the Philistines, Moab and Ammon, Ethiopia and Assyria.

The fall of Nineveh revolutionised the international system of the East. The judgment on Asshur was accomplished, and her name disappears from these catalogues of doom. In other particulars Jeremiah, as well as Ezekiel, follows closely in the footsteps of his predecessors. He deals, like them, with the group of Syrian and Palestinian states—Philistines, Moab, Ammon, Edom, and Damascus † He dwells with repeated emphasis on Egypt, and Arabia is represented by Kedar and Hazor. In one section the prophet travels into what must have seemed to his contemporaries the very far East, as far as Elam. On the other hand, he is comparatively silent about Tyre, in which Joel, Amos, the Book of Isaiah,‡ and above all Ezekiel display a lively interest. Nebuchadnezzar's campaigns were directed against Tyre as much as against Jerusalem; and Ezekiel, living in Chaldea, would have attention forcibly directed to the Phœnician capital, at a time when Jeremiah was absorbed in the fortunes of Zion.

But in the passage which we have chosen as the subject for this introduction to the prophecies of the nations, Jeremiah takes a somewhat wider range:—

"Thus saith unto me Jehovah, the God of Israel:
Take at My hand this cup of the wine of fury,
And make all the nations, to whom I send thee, drink it.
They shall drink, and reel to and fro, and be mad,
Because of the sword that I will send among them."

First and foremost of these nations, pre-eminent in punishment as in privilege, stand "Jerusalem and the cities of Judah, with its kings and princes."

This bad eminence is a necessary application of the principle laid down by Amos § :—

"You only have I known of all the families of the earth:
Therefore I will visit upon you all your iniquities."

* Doubts, however, have been raised as to whether any of the sections about Babylon are by Isaiah himself.

† Doubts have been expressed as to the genuineness of the Damascus prophecy.

‡ The Isaianic authorship of this prophecy (Isa. xxiii.) is rejected by very many critics.

§ Amos iii. 2.

But as Jeremiah says later on, addressing the Gentile nations,—

"I begin to work evil at the city which is called by My name.
Should ye go scot-free? Ye shall not go scot-free."

And the prophet puts the cup of God's fury to their lips also, and amongst them, Egypt, the *bête noir* of Hebrew seers, is most conspicuously marked out for destruction: "Pharaoh king of Egypt, and his servants and princes and all his people, and all the mixed population of Egypt." * Then follows, in epic fashion, a catalogue of "all the nations" as Jeremiah knew them: "All the kings of the land of Uz, all the kings of the land of the Philistines; Ashkelon, Gaza, Ekron, and the remnant of Ashdod; † Edom, Moab, and the Ammonites; all the kings ‡ of Tyre, all the kings of Zidon, and the kings of their colonies § beyond the sea; Dedan and Tema and Buz, and all that have the corners of their hair polled,‖ and all the kings of Arabia, and all the kings of the mixed populations that dwell in the desert; all the kings of Zimri, all the kings of Elam, and all the kings of the Medes." Jeremiah's definite geographical information is apparently exhausted, but he adds by way of summary and conclusion: "And all the kings of the north, far and near, one after the other; and all the kingdoms of the world, which are on the face of the earth."

There is one notable omission in the list. Nebuchadnezzar, the servant of Jehovah,¶ was the Divinely appointed scourge of Judah and its neighbours and allies. Elsewhere ** the nations are exhorted to submit to him, and here apparently Chaldea is exempted from the general doom, just as Ezekiel passes no formal sentence on Babylon. It is true that "all the kingdoms of the earth" would naturally include Babylon, possibly were even intended to do so. But the Jews were not long content with so veiled a reference to their conquerors and oppressors. Some patriotic scribe added the explanatory note, "And the king of Sheshach (*i. e.*, Babylon) shall drink after them." †† Sheshach is obtained from Babel by the cipher 'Athbash, according to which an alphabet is written out and a reversed alphabet written out underneath it, and the letters of the lower row used for those of the upper and *vice versâ*. Thus:

Aleph	B	.	.	.	.	K	L
T	SH	.	.	.	.	L	K

The use of cypher seems to indicate that the note was added in Chaldea during the Exile, when it was not safe to circulate documents which openly denounced Babylon. Jeremiah's enumeration of the peoples and rulers of his world is naturally more detailed and more exhaustive than the list of the nations against which he prophesied. It includes the Phœnician states, details the Philistine cities, associates with Elam the neighbouring nations of Zimri and the Medes, and substitutes for Kedar and Hazor

* So Giesebrecht, Orelli, etc.

† Psammetichus had recently taken Ashdod, after a continuous siege of twenty-nine years.

‡ The plural may refer to dependent chiefs or may be used for the sake of symmetry.

§ Lit. "the coasts" (*i. e.*, islands and coastland) where the Phœnicians had planted their colonies.

‖ See on xlix. 28-32.

¶ xxv. 9.

** xxvii. 8.

†† Sheshach (Sheshakh) for Babel also occurs in li. 41. This explanatory note is omitted by LXX.

Arabia and a number of semi-Arab states, Uz, Dedan, Tema, and Buz.* Thus Jeremiah's world is the district constantly shown in Scripture atlases in a map comprising the scenes of Old Testament history, Egypt, Arabia, and Western Asia, south of a line from the northeast corner of the Mediterranean to the southern end of the Caspian Sea, and west of a line from the latter point to the northern end of the Persian Gulf. How much of history has been crowded into this narrow area! Here science, art, and literature won those primitive triumphs which no subsequent achievements could surpass or even equal. Here, perhaps for the first time, men tasted the Dead Sea apples of civilisation, and learnt how little accumulated wealth and national splendour can do for the welfare of the masses. Here was Eden, where God walked in the cool of the day to commune with man; and here also were many Mount Moriahs, where man gave his firstborn for his transgression, the fruit of his body for the sin of his soul, and no angel voice stayed his hand.

And now glance at any modern map and see for how little Jeremiah's world counts among the great Powers of the nineteenth century. Egypt indeed is a bone of contention between European states, but how often does a daily paper remind its readers of the existence of Syria or Mesopotamia? We may apply to this ancient world the title that Byron gave to Rome, "Lone mother of dead empires," and call it:—

> "The desert, where we steer
> Stumbling o'er recollections."

It is said that Scipio's exultation over the fall of Carthage was marred by forebodings that Time had a like destiny in store for Rome. Where Cromwell might have quoted a text from the Bible, the Roman soldier applied to his native city the Homeric lines:—

> "Troy shall sink in fire,
> And Priam's city with himself expire."

The epitaphs of ancient civilisations are no mere matters of archæology; like the inscriptions on common graves, they carry a *Memento mori* for their successors.

But to return from epitaphs to prophecy: in the list which we have just given, the kings of many of the nations are required to drink the cup of wrath, and the section concludes with a universal judgment upon the princes and rulers of this ancient world under the familiar figure of shepherds, supplemented here by another, that of the "principal of the flock," or, as we should say, "bell-wethers." Jehovah would break out upon them to rend and scatter like a lion from his covert. Therefore:—

> "Howl, ye shepherds, and cry!
> Roll yourselves in the dust, ye bell-wethers!
> The time has fully come for you to be slaughtered.
> I will cast you down with a crash, like a vase of porcelain.†
> Ruin hath overtaken the refuge of the shepherds,
> And the way of escape of the bell-wethers."

Thus Jeremiah announces the coming ruin of an ancient world, with all its states and sovereigns, and we have seen that the prediction has been amply fulfilled. We can only notice two other points with regard to this section.

First, then, we have no right to accuse the prophet of speaking from a narrow national standpoint. His words are not the expression of the Jewish *adversus omnes alios hostile odium;*§ if they were, we should not hear so much of Judah's sin and Judah's punishment. He applied to heathen states as he did to his own the divine standard of national righteousness, and they too were found wanting. All history confirms Jeremiah's judgment. This brings us to our second point. Christian thinkers have been engrossed in the evidential aspect of these national catastrophes. They served to fulfil prophecy, and therefore the squalor of Egypt and the ruins of Assyria to-day have seemed to make our way of salvation more safe and certain. But God did not merely sacrifice these holocausts of men and nations to the perennial craving of feeble faith for signs. Their fate must of necessity illustrate His justice and wisdom and love. Jeremiah tells us plainly that Judah and its neighbours had filled up the measure of their iniquity before they were called upon to drink the cup of wrath; national sin justifies God's judgments. Yet these very facts of the moral failure and decadence of human societies perplex and startle us. Individuals grow old and feeble and die, but saints and heroes do not become slaves of vice and sin in their last days. The glory of their prime is not buried in a dishonoured grave. Nay rather, when all else fails, the beauty of holiness grows more pure and radiant. But of what nation could we say:—

> "Let me die the death of the righteous,
> Let my last end be like his"?

Apparently the collective conscience is a plant of very slow growth; and hitherto no society has been worthy to endure honourably or even to perish nobly. In Christendom itself the ideals of common action are still avowedly meaner than those of individual conduct. International and collective morality is still in its infancy, and as a matter of habit and system modern states are often wantonly cruel and unjust towards obscure individuals and helpless minorities. Yet surely it shall not always be so; the daily prayer of countless millions for the coming of the Kingdom of God cannot remain unanswered.

CHAPTER XVII

EGYPT.

Jeremiah xliii. 8-13, xliv. 30, xlvi.

"I will visit Amon of No, and Pharaoh, and Egypt, with their gods and their kings: even Pharaoh and all them that trust in him."—Jer. xlvi. 25.

The kings of Egypt with whom Jeremiah was contemporary—Psammetichus II., Pharaoh Necho, and Pharaoh Hophra—belonged to the twenty-sixth dynasty. When growing distress at home compelled Assyria to loose her hold on her distant dependencies, Egypt still retained something of her former vigorous elasticity. In the rebound from subjection under the heavy hand of Sennacherib, she resumed her ancient forms of life and government. She regained her unity and independence, and posed afresh as an

* As to Damascus *cf.* note on p. 174.

† This line is somewhat paraphrased. Lit. "I will shatter you, and ye shall fall like an ornamental vessel" (KELI HEMDA).

§ Tacitus, "History," v. 5.

equal rival with Chaldea for the supremacy of Western Asia. At home there was a renascence of art and literature, and, as of old, the wealth and devotion of powerful monarchs restored the ancient temples and erected new shrines of their own.

But this revival was no new growth springing up with a fresh and original life from the seeds of the past; it cannot rank with the European Renascence of the fifteenth century. It is rather to be compared with the reorganisations by which Diocletian and Constantine prolonged the decline of the Roman Empire, the rally of a strong constitution in the grip of mortal disease. These latter-day Pharaohs failed ignominiously in their attempts to recover the Syrian dominion of the Thothmes and Rameses; and, like the Roman Empire in its last centuries, the Egypt of the twenty-sixth dynasty surrendered itself to Greek influence and hired foreign mercenaries to fight its battles. The new art and literature were tainted by pedantic archaism. According to Brugsch,* "Even to the newly created dignities and titles, the return to ancient times had become the general watchword. . . . . The stone door-posts of this age reveal the old Memphian style of art, mirrored in its modern reflection after the lapse of four thousand years." Similarly Meyer† tells us that apparently the Egyptian state was reconstituted on the basis of a religious revival, somewhat in the fashion of the establishment of Deuteronomy by Josiah.

Inscriptions after the time of Psammetichus are written in archaic Egyptian of a very ancient past; it is often difficult to determine at first sight whether inscriptions belong to the earliest or latest period of Egyptian history.

The superstition that sought safety in an exact reproduction of a remote antiquity could not, however, resist the fascination of Eastern demonology. According to Brugsch,‡ in the age called the Egyptian Renascence the old Egyptian theology was adulterated with Græco-Asiatic elements—demons and genii of whom the older faith and its purer doctrine had scarcely an idea; exorcisms became a special science, and are favourite themes for the inscriptions of this period. Thus, amid many differences, there are also to be found striking resemblances between the religious movements of the period in Egypt and amongst the Jews, and corresponding difficulties in determining the dates of Egyptian inscriptions and of sections of the Old Testament.

This enthusiasm for ancient custom and tradition was not likely to commend the Egypt of Jeremiah's age to any student of Hebrew history. He would be reminded that the dealings of the Pharaohs with Israel had almost always been to its hurt; he would remember the Oppression and the Exodus—how, in the time of Solomon, friendly intercourse with Egypt taught that monarch lessons in magnificent tyranny, how Shishak plundered the Temple, how Isaiah had denounced the Egyptian alliance as a continual snare to Judah. A Jewish prophet would be prompt to discern the omens of coming ruin in the midst of renewed prosperity on the Nile.

Accordingly at the first great crisis of the new international system, in the fourth year of Jehoiakim, either just before or just after the battle of Carchemish—it matters little which—Jeremiah takes up his prophecy against Egypt. First of all, with an ostensible friendliness which only masks his bitter sarcasm, he invites the Egyptians to take the field:—

"Prepare buckler and shield, and draw near to battle.
Harness the horses to the chariots, mount the chargers
stand forth armed cap-à-pie for battle;
Furbish the spears, put on the coats of mail."

This great host with its splendid equipment must surely conquer. The prophet professes to await its triumphant return; but he sees instead a breathless mob of panic-stricken fugitives, and pours upon them the torrent of his irony:—

"How is it that I behold this? These heroes are dismayed
and have turned their backs;
Their warriors have been beaten down;
They flee apace, and do not look behind them:
Terror on every side—is the utterance of Jehovah."

Then irony passes into explicit malediction:—

"Let not the swift flee away, nor the warrior escape;
Away northward, they stumble and fall by the river
Euphrates."

Then, in a new strophe, Jeremiah again recurs in imagination to the proud march of the countless hosts of Egypt:—

"Who is this that riseth up like the Nile,
Whose waters toss themselves like the rivers?
Egypt riseth up like the Nile,
His waters toss themselves like the rivers.
And he saith, I will go up and cover the land"

(like the Nile in flood);

"I will destroy the cities and their inhabitants"

(and, above all other cities, Babylon).

Again the prophet urges them on with ironical encouragement:—

"Go up, ye horses; rage, ye chariots;
Ethiopians and Libyans that handle the shield,
Lydians that handle and bend the bow"

(the tributaries and mercenaries of Egypt).

Then, as before, he speaks plainly of coming disaster:

"That day is a day of vengeance for the Lord Jehovah
Sabaoth, whereon He will avenge Him of His adversaries"

(a day of vengeance upon Pharaoh Necho for Megiddo and Josiah).

"The sword shall devour and be sated, and drink its fill
of their blood:
For the Lord Jehovah Sabaoth hath a sacrifice in the
northern land, by the river Euphrates."

In a final strophe, the prophet turns to the land left bereaved and defenceless by the defeat at Carchemish:—

"Go up to Gilead and get thee balm, O virgin daughter of
Egypt:
In vain dost thou multiply medicines; thou canst not be
healed.
The nations have heard of thy shame, the earth is full of
thy cry:
For warrior stumbles against warrior; they fall both
together."

Nevertheless the end was not yet. Egypt was wounded to death, but she was to linger on for many a long year to be a snare to Judah and to vex the righteous soul of Jeremiah. The reed was broken, but it still retained an appearance of soundness, which more than once tempted the Jewish princes to lean upon it and find their hands pierced for their pains. Hence, as we

* Second edition, ii. 291, 292.
† Meyer, "Geschichte des alten Agypten," 371, 373.
‡ ii. 293.

have seen already, Jeremiah repeatedly found occasion to reiterate the doom of Egypt, of Necho's successor, Pharaoh Hophra, and of the Jewish refugees who had sought safety under his protection. In the concluding part of chap. xlvi., a prophecy of uncertain date sets forth the ruin of Egypt with rather more literary finish than in the parallel passages.

This word of Jehovah was to be proclaimed in Egypt, and especially in the frontier cities, which would have to bear the first brunt of invasion:—

"Declare in Egypt, proclaim in Migdol, proclaim in Noph and Tahpanhes:
Say ye, Take thy stand and be ready, for the sword hath devoured round about thee.
Why hath Apis* fled and thy calf not stood? Because Jehovah overthrew it."

Memphis was devoted to the worship of Apis, incarnate in the sacred bull; but now Apis must succumb to the mightier divinity of Jehovah, and his sacred city become a prey to the invaders.

"He maketh many to stumble; they fall one against another.
Then they say, Arise, and let us return to our own people
And to our native land, before the oppressing sword."

We must remember that the Egyptian armies were largely composed of foreign mercenaries. In the hour of disaster and defeat these hirelings would desert their employers and go home.

"Give unto Pharaoh king of Egypt the name † Crash; he hath let the appointed time pass by."

The form of this enigmatic sentence is probably due to a play upon Egyptian names and titles. When the allusions are forgotten, such paronomasia naturally results in hopeless obscurity. The "appointed time" has been explained as the period during which Jehovah gave Pharaoh the opportunity of repentance, or as that within which he might have submitted to Nebuchadnezzar on favourable terms.

"As I live, is the utterance of the King, whose name is Jehovah Sabaoth,
One shall come like Tabor among the mountains and like Carmel by the sea."

It was not necessary to name this terrible invader; it could be no other than Nebuchadnezzar.

"Get thee gear for captivity, O daughter of Egypt, that dwellest in thine own land:
For Noph shall become a desolation, and shall be burnt up and left without inhabitants.
Egypt is a very fair heifer, but destruction is come upon her from the north."

This tempest shattered the Greek phalanx in which Pharaoh trusted:—

"Even her mercenaries in the midst of her are like calves of the stall;
Even they have turned and fled together, they have not stood:
For their day of calamity hath come upon them, their day of reckoning."

We do not look for chronological sequence in such a poem, so that this picture of the flight and destruction of the mercenaries is not necessarily later in time than their overthrow and contemplated desertion in verse 15. The prophet is depicting a scene of bewildered confusion; the disasters that fell thick upon Egypt crowd into his vision without order or even coherence. Now he turns again to Egypt herself:—

"Her voice goeth forth like the (low hissing of) the serpent;
For they come upon her with a mighty army, and with axes like woodcutters."

A like fate is predicted in Isaiah xxix. 4 for "Ariel, the city where David dwelt":—

"Thou shalt be brought low and speak from the ground;
Thou shalt speak with a low voice out of the dust;
Thy voice shall come from the ground, like that of a familiar spirit,
And thou shalt speak in a whisper from the dust."

Thus too Egypt would seek to writhe herself from under the heel of the invader; hissing out the while her impotent fury, she would seek to glide away into some safe refuge amongst the underwood. Her dominions, stretching far up the Nile, were surely vast enough to afford her shelter somewhere; but no! the "woodcutters" are too many and too mighty for her:—

"They cut down her forest—it is the utterance of Jehovah—for it is impenetrable;
For they are more than the locusts, and are innumerable."

The whole of Egypt is overrun and subjugated; no district holds out against the invader, and remains unsubjugated to form the nucleus of a new and independent empire.

"The daughter of Egypt is put to shame; she is delivered into the hand of the northern people."

Her gods share her fate; Apis had succumbed at Memphis, but Egypt had countless other stately shrines whose denizens must own the overmastering might of Jehovah:—

"Thus saith Jehovah Sabaoth, the God of Israel:
Behold, I will visit Amon of No,
And Pharaoh, and Egypt, and all her gods and kings,
Even Pharaoh and all who trust in him."

Amon of No, or Thebes, known to the Greeks as Ammon and called by his own worshippers Amen, or "the hidden one," is apparently mentioned with Apis as sharing the primacy of the Egyptian divine hierarchy. On the fall of the twentieth dynasty, the high priest of the Theban Amen became king of Egypt, and centuries afterwards Alexander the Great made a special pilgrimage to the temple in the oasis of Ammon and was much gratified at being there hailed son of the deity.

Probably the prophecy originally ended with this general threat of "visitation" of Egypt and its human and divine rulers. An editor, however, has added,* from parallel passages, the more definite but sufficiently obvious statement that Nebuchadnezzar and his servants were to be the instruments of the Divine visitation.

A further addition is in striking contrast to the sweeping statements of Jeremiah:—

"Afterward it shall be inhabited, as in the days of old."

Similarly, Ezekiel foretold a restoration for Egypt:—

"At the end of forty years, I will gather the Egyptians, and will cause them to return . . . to their native land; and they shall be there a base kingdom: it shall be the basest of the kingdoms." †

And elsewhere we read yet more gracious promises to Egypt:—

* Giesebrecht, with LXX.

† Giesebrecht, Orelli, Kautzsch, with LXX., Syr., and Vulg., by an alteration of the pointing.

* LXX. omits verse 26. Verses 27, 28 = xxx. 10, 11, and probably are an insertion here.

§ Ezek. xxix. 13-15.

"Israel shall be a third with Egypt and Assyria, a blessing in the midst of the land: whom Jehovah Sabaoth shall bless, saying, Blessed be Egypt My people, and Assyria the work of My hands, and Israel Mine inheritance." *

Probably few would claim to discover in history any literal fulfilment of this last prophecy. Perhaps it might have been appropriated for the Christian Church in the days of Clement and Origen. We may take Egypt and Assyria as types of heathendom, which shall one day receive the blessings of the Lord's people and of the work of His hands. Of political revivals and restorations Egypt has had her share. But less interest attaches to these general prophecies than to more definite and detailed predictions; and there is much curiosity as to any evidence which monuments and other profane witnesses may furnish as to a conquest of Egypt and capture of Pharaoh Hophra by Nebuchadnezzar.

According to Herodotus,† Apries (Hophra) was defeated and imprisoned by his successor Amasis, afterwards delivered up by him to the people of Egypt, who forthwith strangled their former king. This event would be an exact fulfilment of the words, "I will give Pharaoh Hophra king of Egypt into the hand of his enemies, and into the hand of them that seek his life,"‡ if it were not evident from parallel passages§ that the Book of Jeremiah intends Nebuchadnezzar to be the enemy into whose hands Pharaoh is to be delivered. But Herodotus is entirely silent as to the relations of Egypt and Babylon during this period; for instance, he mentions the victory of Pharaoh Necho at Megiddo—which he miscalls Magdolium—but not his defeat at Carchemish. Hence his silence as to Chaldean conquests in Egypt has little weight. Even the historian's explicit statement as to the death of Apries might be reconciled with his defeat and capture by Nebuchadnezzar, if we knew all the facts. At present, however, the inscriptions do little to fill the gap left by the Greek historian; there are, however, references which seem to establish two invasions of Egypt by the Chaldean king, one of which fell in the reign of Pharaoh Hophra. But the spiritual lessons of this and the following prophecies concerning the nations are not dependent on the spade of the excavator or the skill of the decipherers of hieroglyphics and cuneiform script; whatever their relation may be to the details of subsequent historical events, they remain as monuments of the inspired insight of the prophet into the character and destiny alike of great empires and petty states. They assert the Divine government of the nations, and the subordination of all history to the coming of the Kingdom of God.

* Isa. xix. 25.
† Herodotus, II. clxix.
‡ xliv. 30.
§ xlvi. 25.

CHAPTER XVIII.

THE PHILISTINES.

JEREMIAH xlvii.

"O sword of Jehovah, how long will it be ere thou be quiet? put up thyself into thy scabbard; rest, and be still."—JER. xlvii. 6.

ACCORDING to the title placed at the head of this prophecy, it was uttered "before Pharaoh smote Gaza." The Pharaoh is evidently Pharaoh Necho, and this capture of Gaza was one of the incidents of the campaign which opened with the victory at Megiddo and concluded so disastrously at Carchemish. Our first impulse is to look for some connection between this incident and the contents of the prophecy: possibly the editor who prefixed the heading may have understood by the northern enemy Pharaoh Necho on his return from Carchemish; but would Jeremiah have described a defeated army thus?

"Behold, waters rise out of the north, and become an overflowing torrent;
They overflow the land, and all that is therein, the city and its inhabitants.
Men cry out, and all the inhabitants of the land howl,
At the sound of the stamping of the hoofs of his stallions,
At the rattling of his chariots and the rumbling of his wheels."

Here as elsewhere the enemy from the north is Nebuchadnezzar. Pharaohs might come and go, winning victories and taking cities, but these broken reeds count for little; not they, but the king of Babylon is the instrument of Jehovah's supreme purpose. The utter terror caused by the Chaldean advance is expressed by a striking figure:—

"The fathers look not back to their children for slackness of hands."

Their very bodies are possessed and crippled with fear, their palsied muscles cannot respond to the impulses of natural affection; they can do nothing but hurry on in headlong flight, unable to look round or stretch out a helping hand to their children:—

"Because of the day that cometh for the spoiling of all the Philistines,
For cutting off every ally that remaineth unto Tyre and Zidon:
For Jehovah spoileth the Philistines, the remnant of the coast of Caphtor.*
Baldness cometh upon Gaza; Ashkelon is destroyed:
O remnant of the Anakim,† how long wilt thou cut thyself?"

This list is remarkable both for what it includes and what it omits. In order to understand the reference to Tyre and Zidon, we must remember that Nebuchadnezzar's expedition was partly directed against these cities, with which the Philistines had evidently been allied. The Chaldean king would hasten the submission of the Phœnicians, by cutting off all hope of succour from without. There are various possible reasons why out of the five Philistine cities only two—Ashkelon and Gaza—are mentioned; Ekron, Gath, and Ashdod may have been reduced to comparative insignificance. Ashdod had recently been taken by Psammetichus after a twenty-nine years' siege. Or the names of two of these cities may be given by way of paronomasia in the text: Ashdod may be suggested by the double reference to the *spoiling* and the *spoiler*, *Shdod* and *Shoded;* Gath may be hinted at by the word used for the mutilation practised by mourners, *Tithgoddadi*, and by the mention of the Anakim, who are connected with Gath, Ashdod, and Gaza in Joshua xi. 22.

As Jeremiah contemplates this fresh array of victims of Chaldean cruelty, he is moved to protest against the weary monotony of ruin:—

"O sword of Jehovah, how long will it be ere thou be quiet?
Put up thyself into thy scabbard; rest, and be still."

* Referring to their ancient immigration from Caphtor, probably Crete.

† Kautzsch, Giesebrecht, with LXX., reading 'Nqm for the Masoretic 'Mqm; Eng. Vers., "their valley."

The prophet ceases to be the mouthpiece of God, and breaks out into the cry of human anguish. How often since, amid the barbarian inroads that overwhelmed the Roman Empire, amid the prolonged horrors of the Thirty Years' War, amid the carnage of the French Revolution, men have uttered a like appeal to an unanswering and relentless Providence! Indeed, not in war only, but even in peace, the tide of human misery and sin often seems to flow, century after century, with undiminished volume, and ever and again a vain "How long" is wrung from pallid and despairing lips. For the Divine purpose may not be hindered, and the sword of Jehovah must still strike home.

"How can it be quiet, seeing that Jehovah hath given it a charge?
Against Ashkelon and against the sea-shore, there hath He appointed it."

Yet Ashkelon survived to be a stronghold of the Crusaders, and Gaza to be captured by Alexander and even by Napoleon. Jehovah has other instruments besides His devastating sword; the victorious endurance and recuperative vitality of men and nations also come from Him.

"Come and let us return unto Jehovah:
For He hath torn, and He will heal us;
He hath smitten, and He will bind us up." *

CHAPTER XIX.

MOAB.

JEREMIAH xlviii.

"Moab shall be destroyed from being a people, because he hath magnified himself against Jehovah."—JER. xlviii. 42.

"Chemosh said to me, Go, take Nebo against Israel . . . and I took it . . . and I took from it the vessels of Jehovah, and offered them before Chemosh."—MOABITE STONE.

"Yet will I bring again the captivity of Moab in the latter days."—JER. xlviii. 47.

THE prophets show a very keen interest in Moab. With the exception of the very short Book of Joel, all the prophets who deal in detail with foreign nations devote sections to Moab. The unusual length of such sections in Isaiah and Jeremiah is not the only resemblance between the utterances of these two prophets concerning Moab. There are many parallels † of idea and expression, which probably indicate the influence of the elder prophet upon his successor; unless indeed both of them adapted some popular poem which was early current in Judah. ‡

It is easy to understand why the Jewish Scriptures should have much to say about Moab, just as the sole surviving fragment of Moabite literature is chiefly occupied with Israel. These two Terahite tribes—the children of Jacob and the children of Lot—had dwelt side by side for centuries, like the Scotch and English borderers before the accession of James I. They had experienced many alternations of enmity and friendship, and had shared complex interests, common and conflicting, after the manner of neighbours who are also kinsmen. Each in its turn had oppressed the other; and Moab had been the tributary of the Israelite monarchy till the victorious arms of Mesha had achieved independence for his people and firmly established their dominion over the debatable frontier lands. There are traces, too, of more kindly relations: the House of David reckoned Ruth the Moabitess amongst its ancestors, and Jesse, like Elimelech and Naomi, had taken refuge in Moab.

Accordingly this prophecy concerning Moab, in both its editions, frequently strikes a note of sympathetic lamentation and almost becomes a dirge.

"Therefore will I howl for Moab;
Yea, for all Moab will I cry out.
For the men of Kir-heres shall they mourn.
With more than the weeping of Jazer
Will I weep for thee, O vine of Sibmah.
. . . .
Therefore mine heart soundeth like pipes for Moab,
Mine heart soundeth like pipes for the men of Kir-heres."

But this pity could not avail to avert the doom of Moab; it only enabled the Jewish prophet to fully appreciate its terrors. The picture of coming ruin is drawn with the colouring and outlines familiar to us in the utterances of Jeremiah—spoiling and destruction, fire and sword and captivity, dismay and wild abandonment of wailing.

"Chemosh shall go forth into captivity, his priests and his princes together.
Every head is bald, and every beard clipped;
Upon all the hands are cuttings, and upon the loins sackcloth.
On all the housetops and in all the streets of Moab there is everywhere lamentation;
For I have broken Moab like a useless vessel—it is the utterance of Jehovah.
How is it broken down! Howl ye! Be thou ashamed!
How hath Moab turned the back!
All the neighbours shall laugh and shudder at Moab.
. . . .
The heart of the mighty men of Moab at that day
Shall be like the heart of a woman in her pangs."

This section of Jeremiah illustrates the dramatic versatility of the prophet's method. He identifies himself now with the blood-thirsty invader, now with his wretched victims, and now with the terror-stricken spectators; and sets forth the emotions of each in turn with vivid realism. Hence at one moment we have the pathos and pity of such verses as we have just quoted, and at another such stern and savage words as these:—

"Cursed be he that doeth the work of Jehovah negligently,
Cursed be he that stinteth his sword of blood."

These lines might have served as a motto for Cromwell at the massacre of Drogheda, for Tilly's army at the sack of Magdeburg, or for Danton and Robespierre during the Reign of Terror. Jeremiah's words were the more terrible because they were uttered with the full consciousness that in the dread Chaldean king * a servant of Jehovah was at hand who would be careful not to incur any curse for stinting his sword of blood. We shrink from what seems to us the prophet's brutal assertion that relentless and indiscriminate slaughter is sometimes the service which man is called upon to render to

* Hosea vi. 1.

† *E.g.*, xlviii. 5, "For by the ascent of Luhith with continual weeping shall they go up; for in going down of Horonaim they have heard the distress of the cry of destruction," is almost identical with Isa. xv. 5. *Cf.* also xlviii. 29–34 with Isa. xv. 4, xvi. 6–11.

‡ Verse 47 with the subscription, "Thus far is the judgment of Moab," is wanting in the LXX.

* The exact date of the prophecy is uncertain, but it must have been written during the reign of Nebuchadnezzar.

God. Such sentiment is for the most part worthless and unreal; it does not save us from epidemics of war fever, and is at once ignored under the stress of horrors like the Indian Mutiny. There is no true comfort in trying to persuade ourselves that the most awful events of history lie outside of the Divine purpose, or in forgetting that the human scourges of their kind do the work that God has assigned to them.

In this inventory, as it were, of the ruin of Moab our attention is arrested by the constant and detailed references to the cities. This feature is partly borrowed from Isaiah. Ezekiel too speaks of the Moabite cities which are the glory of the country; * but Jeremiah's prophecy is a veritable Domesday Book of Moab. With his epic fondness for lists of sonorous names—after the manner of Homer's catalogue of the ships—he enumerates Nebo, Kiriathaim, Heshbon, and Horonaim, city after city, till he completes a tale of no fewer than twenty-six,† and then summarises the rest as "all the cities of the land of Moab, far and near." Eight of these cities are mentioned in Joshua‡ as part of the inheritance of Reuben and Gad. Another, Bozrah, is usually spoken of as a city of Edom.§

The Moabite Stone explains the occurrence of Reubenite cities in these lists. It tells us how Mesha took Nebo, Jahaz, and Horonaim from Israel. Possibly in this period of conquest Bozrah became tributary to Moab, without ceasing to be an Edomite city. This extension of territory and multiplication of towns points to an era of power and prosperity, of which there are other indications in this chapter. "We are mighty and valiant for war," said the Moabites. When Moab fell "there was broken a mighty sceptre and a glorious staff." Other verses imply the fertility of the land and the abundance of its vintage.

Moab in fact had profited by the misfortunes of its more powerful and ambitious neighbours. The pressure of Damascus, Assyria, and Chaldea prevented Israel and Judah from maintaining their dominion over their ancient tributary. Moab lay less directly in the track of the invaders; it was too insignificant to attract their special attention, perhaps too prudent to provoke a contest with the lords of the East. Hence, while Judah was declining, Moab had enlarged her borders and grown in wealth and power.

And even as Jeshurun kicked, when he was waxen fat,‖ so Moab in its prosperity was puffed up with unholy pride. Even in Isaiah's time this was the besetting sin of Moab; he says in an indictment which Jeremiah repeats almost word for word:—

"We have heard of the pride of Moab, that he is very proud,
Even of his arrogancy and his pride and his wrath."¶

This verse is a striking example of the Hebrew method of gaining emphasis by accumulating derivatives of the same and similar roots. The verse in Jeremiah runs thus: "We have heard of the pride (Ge'ON) of Moab, that he is very proud (GE'EH); his loftiness (GABHeHO), and his pride (Ge'ONO), and his proudfulness (GA'aWATHO)."

Jeremiah dwells upon this theme:—

"Moab shall be destroyed from being a people,
Because he hath magnified himself against Jehovah."

Zephaniah bears like testimony *:—

"This shall they have for their pride,
Because they have been insolent, and have magnified themselves
Against the people of Jehovah Sabaoth."

Here again the Moabite Stone bears abundant testimony to the justice of the prophet's accusations; for there Mesha tells how in the name and by the grace of Chemosh he conquered the cities of Israel; and how, anticipating Belshazzar's sacrilege, he took the sacred vessels of Jehovah from His temple at Nebo and consecrated them to Chemosh. Truly Moab had "magnified himself against Jehovah."

Prosperity had produced other baleful effects beside a haughty spirit, and pride was not the only cause of the ruin of Moab. Jeremiah applies to nations the dictum of Polonius—

"Home-keeping youths have ever homely wits,"

and apparently suggests that ruin and captivity were necessary elements in the national discipline of Moab:—

"Moab hath been undisturbed from his youth;
He hath settled on his lees;
He hath not been emptied from vessel to vessel;
He hath not gone into captivity:
Therefore his taste remaineth in him,
His scent is not changed.
Wherefore, behold, the days come—it is the utterance of Jehovah—
That I will send men unto him that shall tilt him up;
They shall empty his vessels and break his† bottles."

As the chapter, in its present form, concludes with a note—

"I will bring again the captivity of Moab in the latter days—it is the utterance of Jehovah"—

we gather that even this rough handling was disciplinary; at any rate, the former lack of such vicissitudes had been to the serious detriment of Moab. It is strange that Jeremiah did not apply this principle to Judah. For, indeed, the religion of Israel and of mankind owes an incalculable debt to the captivity of Judah, a debt which later writers are not slow to recognise. "Behold," says the prophet of the Exile,—

"I have refined thee, but not as silver;
I have chosen thee in the furnace of affliction." ‡

History constantly illustrates how when Christians were undisturbed and prosperous the wine of truth settled on the lees and came to taste of the cask; and—to change the figure—how affliction and persecution proved most effectual tonics for a debilitated Church. Continental critics of modern England speak severely of the ill-effects which our prolonged freedom from invasion and civil war, and the unbroken continuity of our social life have had on our national character and manners. In their eyes England is a perfect Moab, concerning which they are ever ready to prophesy after the manner of Jeremiah. The Hebrew Chronicler blamed Josiah because he would not listen to the advice and

* Ezek. xxv. 9.
† Some of the names, however, may be variants.
‡ Josh. xiii. 15–28 (possibly on JE. basis).
§ xlix. 13, possibly this is not the Edomite Bozrah.
‖ Deut. xxxii. 15.
¶ Isa. xvi. 6.

* ii. 10.
† Kautzsch, Giesebrecht, with LXX.; A. V., R. V., with Hebrew Text, "their bottles."
‡ Isa. xlviii. 10.

criticism of Pharaoh Necho. There may be warnings which we should do well to heed, even in the acrimony of foreign journalists.

But any such suggestion raises wider and more difficult issues; for ordinary individuals and nations the discipline of calamity seems necessary. What degree of moral development exempts from such discipline, and how may it be attained? Christians cannot seek to compound for such discipline by self-inflicted loss or pain, like Polycrates casting away his ring or Browning's Caliban, who in his hour of terror,

> "Lo! 'Lieth flat and loveth Setebos!
> 'Maketh his teeth meet through his upper lip.
> Will let those quails fly, will not eat this month
> One little mess of whelks, so he may 'scape."

But though it is easy to counsel resignation and the recognition of a wise, loving Providence in national as in personal suffering, yet mankind longs for an end to the period of pupilage and chastisement and would fain know how it may be hastened.

CHAPTER XX.

AMMON.

JEREMIAH xlix. 1-6.

"Hath Israel no sons? hath he no heir? why then doth Moloch possess Gad, and his people dwell in the cities thereof?"—JER. xlix. 1.

THE relations of Israel with Ammon were similar but less intimate than they were with his twin-brother Moab. Hence this prophecy is, *mutatis mutandis*, an abridgment of that concerning Moab. As Moab was charged with magnifying himself against Jehovah, and was found to be occupying cities which Reuben claimed as its inheritance, so Ammon had presumed to take possession of the Gadite cities, whose inhabitants had been carried away captive by the Assyrians. Here again the prophet enumerates Heshbon, Ai, Rabbah, and the dependent towns, "the daughters of Rabbah." Only in the territory of this half-nomadic people the cities are naturally not so numerous as in Moab; and Jeremiah mentions also the fertile valleys wherein the Ammonites gloried. The familiar doom of ruin and captivity is pronounced against city and country and all the treasures of Ammon; Moloch,* like Chemosh, must go into captivity with his priests and princes. This prophecy also concludes with a promise of restoration:—

"Afterward I will bring again the captivity of the children of Ammon—it is the utterance of Jehovah."

CHAPTER XXI.

EDOM.

JEREMIAH xlix. 7-22.

"Bozrah shall become an astonishment, a reproach, a waste, and a curse."—JER. xlix. 13.

THE prophecy concerning Edom is not formulated along the same line as those which deal with the twin children of Lot, Moab and Ammon. Edom was not merely the cousin, but the brother of Israel. His history, his character and conduct, had marked peculiarities, which received special treatment. Edom had not only intimate relations with Israel as a whole, but was also bound by exceptionally close ties to the Southern Kingdom. The Edomite clan Kenaz had been incorporated in the tribe of Judah;* and when Israel broke up into two states, Edom was the one tributary which was retained or reconquered by the House of David, and continued subject to Judah till the reign of Jehoram ben Jehoshaphat.†

Much virtuous indignation is often expressed at the wickedness of Irishmen in contemplating rebellion against England: we cannot therefore be surprised that the Jews resented the successful revolt of Edom, and regarded the hostility of Mount Seir to its former masters as ingratitude and treachery. In moments of hot indignation against the manifold sins of Judah Jeremiah might have announced with great vehemence that Judah should be made a "reproach and a proverb"; but when, as Obadiah tells us, the Edomites stood gazing with eager curiosity on the destruction of Jerusalem, and rejoiced and exulted in the distress of the Jews, and even laid hands on their substance in the day of their calamity, and occupied the roads to catch fugitives and deliver them up to the Chaldeans,‡ then the patriotic fervour of the prophet broke out against Edom. Like Moab and Ammon, he was puffed up with pride, and deluded by baseless confidence into a false security. These hardy mountaineers trusted in their reckless courage and in the strength of their inaccessible mountain fastnesses.

> "Men shall shudder at thy fate,§ the pride of thy heart hath deceived thee,
> O thou that dwellest in the clefts of the rock, that holdest the height of the hill:
> Though thou shouldest make thy nest as high as the eagle,‖
> I will bring thee down from thence—it is the utterance of Jehovah."

Pliny speaks of the Edomite capital as "oppidum circumdatum montibus inaccessis,"¶ and doubtless the children of Esau had often watched from their eyrie Assyrian and Chaldean armies on the march to plunder more defenceless victims, and trusted that their strength, their good fortune, and their ancient and proverbial wisdom would still hold them scatheless. Their neighbours—the Jews amongst the rest—might be plundered, massacred, and carried away captive, but Edom could look on in careless security, and find its account in the calamities of kindred tribes. If

* xlix. 3: A. V., "their king"; R. V., "Malcam," which here and in verse 1 is a form of Moloch.

* *Cf.* the designation of Caleb "ben Jephunneh the Kenizzite," Num. xxxii. 12., etc., with the genealogies which trace the descent of Kenaz to Esau, Gen. xxxvi. 11, etc. *Cf.* also "Expositor's Bible, Chronicles."

† *Cf.* 1 Kings xxii. 47 with 2 Kings viii. 20.

‡ Obadiah 11-15. The difference between A. V. and R. V. is more apparent than real. The prohibition which R. V. gives must have been based on experience. The short prophecy of Obadiah has very much in common with this section of Jeremiah: Obad. 1-6, 8, are almost identical with Jer. xlix. 14-16, 9, 10*a*, 7. The relation of the two passages is matter of controversy, but probably both use a common original. *Cf.* Driver's "Introduction" on Obadiah.

§ Lit. "thy terror," *i. e.*, the terror inspired by thy fate. A. V., R. V., "thy terribleness," suggests that Edom trusted in the terror felt for him by his enemies, but we can scarcely suppose that even the fiercest highlanders eqpected Nebuchadnezzar to be terrified at them.

‖ Obad. 4: "Though thou set thy nest among the stars."

¶ "Hist. Nat.," vi. 28. Orelli.

Jerusalem was shattered by the Chaldean tempest, the Edomites would play the part of wreckers. But all this shrewdness was mere folly: how could these Solons of Mount Seir prove so unworthy of their reputation?

> "Is wisdom no more in Teman?
> Has counsel perished from the prudent?
> Has their wisdom vanished?"

They thought that Jehovah would punish Jacob whom He loved, and yet spare Esau whom He hated. But:—

> "Thus saith Jehovah:
> Behold, they to whom it pertained not to drink of the cup shall assuredly drink.
> Art thou he that shall go altogether unpunished?
> Thou shalt not go unpunished, but thou shalt assuredly drink" (12).

Aye, and drink to the dregs:—

> "If grape-gatherers come to thee, would they not leave gleanings?
> If thieves came by night, they would only destroy till they had enough.
> But I have made Esau bare, I have stripped him stark naked; he shall not be able to hide himself.
> His children, and his brethren, and his neighbours are given up to plunder, and there is an end of him" (9, 10).
> "I have sworn by Myself—is the utterance of Jehovah—
> That Bozrah shall become an astonishment, a reproach, a desolation, and a curse;
> All her cities shall become perpetual wastes.
> I have heard tidings from Jehovah, and an ambassador is sent among the nations, saying,
> Gather yourselves together and come against her, arise to battle" (13, 14).

There was obviously but one leader who could lead the nations to achieve the overthrow of Edom and lead her little ones away captive, who could come up like a lion from the thickets of Jordan, or "flying like an eagle and spreading his wings against Bozrah" (22)—Nebuchadnezzar, king of Babylon, who had come up against Judah with all the kingdoms and peoples of his dominions.*

In this picture of chastisement and calamity, there is one apparent touch of pitifulness:—

> "Leave thine orphans, I will preserve their lives;
> Let thy widows put their trust in Me" (11).

At first sight, at any rate, these seem to be the words of Jehovah. All the adult males of Edom would perish, yet the helpless widows and orphans would not be without a protector. The God of Israel would watch over the lambs of Edom,† when they were dragged away into captivity. We are reluctant to surrender this beautiful and touching description of a God, who, though he may visit the iniquity of the fathers upon the children unto the third and fourth generation, yet even in such judgment ever remembers mercy. It is impossible, however, to ignore the fact that such ideas are widely different from the tone and sentiment of the rest of the section. These words may be an immediate sequel to the previous verse, "No Edomite survives to say to his dying brethren, Leave thine orphans to me," or possibly they may be quoted, in bitter irony, from some message from Edom to Jerusalem, inviting the Jews to send their wives and children for safety to Mount Seir. Edom, ungrateful and treacherous Edom, shall utterly perish—Edom that offered an asylum to Jewish refugees, and yet shared the plunder of Jerusalem and betrayed her fugitives to the Chaldeans.

* xxxiv. 1. † Verse 20.

There is no word of restoration. Moab and Ammon and Elam might revive and flourish again, but for Esau, as of old, there should be no place of repentance. For Edom, in the days of the Captivity, trespassed upon the inheritance of Israel more grievously than Ammon and Moab upon Reuben and Gad. The Edomites possessed themselves of the rich pastures of the south of Judah, and the land was thenceforth called Idumea. Thus they earned the undying hatred of the Jews, in whose mouths Edom became a curse and a reproach, a term of opprobrium. Like Babylon, Edom was used as a secret name for Rome, and later on for the Christian Church.

Nevertheless, even in this prophecy, there is a hint that these predictions of utter ruin must not be taken too literally:—

> "For, behold, I will make thee small among the nations,
> Despised among men" (15).

These words are scarcely consistent with the other verses, which imply that, as a people, Edom would utterly perish from off the face of the earth. As a matter of fact, Edom flourished in her new territory till the time of the Maccabees, and when the Messiah came to establish the kingdom of God, instead of "saviours standing on Mount Zion to judge the Mount of Esau,"* an Edomite dynasty was reigning in Jerusalem.

CHAPTER XXII.

DAMASCUS.

JEREMIAH xlix. 23-27.

"I will kindle a fire in the wall of Damascus, and it shall devour the palaces of Benhadad."—JER. xlix. 27.

WE are a little surprised to meet with a prophecy of Jeremiah concerning Damascus and the palaces of Benhadad. The names carry our minds back for more than a couple of centuries. During Elisha's ministry Damascus and Samaria were engaged in their long, fierce duel for the supremacy over Syria and Palestine. In the reign of Ahaz these ancient rivals combined to attack Judah, so that Isaiah is keenly interested in Damascus and its fortunes. But about B. C. 745, about a hundred and fifty years before Jeremiah's time, the Assyrian king Tiglath-Pileser† overthrew the Syrian kingdom and carried its people into captivity. We know from Ezekiel,‡ what we might have surmised from the position and later history of Damascus, that this ancient city continued a wealthy commercial centre; but Ezekiel has no oracle concerning Damascus, and the other documents of the period and of later times do not mention the capital of Benhadad. Its name does not even occur in Jeremiah's exhaustive list of the countries of his world in xxv. 15-26. Religious interest in alien races depended on their political relations with Israel; when the latter ceased, the prophets had no word from Jehovah concerning foreign nations. Such considerations have suggested doubts as to the authenticity of this section, and it has been supposed that it may be a late echo of Isaiah's utterances concerning Damascus.

We know, however, too little of the history

* Obadiah 21. † 2 Kings xvi. 9. ‡ Ezek. xxvii. 18.

of the period to warrant such a conclusion. Damascus would continue to exist as a tributary state, and might furnish auxiliary forces to the enemies of Judah or join with her to conspire against Babylon, and would in either case attract Jeremiah's attention. Moreover, in ancient as in modern times, commerce played its part in international politics. Doubtless slaves were part of the merchandise of Damascus, just as they were among the wares of the Apocalyptic Babylon. Joel * denounces Tyre and Zidon for selling Jews to the Greeks, and the Damascenes may have served as slave-agents to Nebuchadnezzar and his captains, and thus provoked the resentment of patriot Jews. So many picturesque and romantic associations cluster around Damascus, that this section of Jeremiah almost strikes a jarring note. We love to think of this fairest of Oriental cities, "half as old as time," as the "Eye of the East" which Mohammed refused to enter—because "Man," he said, "can have but one paradise, and my paradise is fixed above"—and as the capital of Noureddin and his still more famous successor Saladin. And so we regret that, when it emerges from the obscurity of centuries into the light of Biblical narrative, the brief reference should suggest a disaster such as it endured in later days at the hands of the treacherous and ruthless Tamerlane.

"Damascus hath grown feeble :
She turneth herself to flee :
Trembling hath seized on her.
. . . . .
How is the city of praise forsaken,†
The city of joy !
Her young men shall fall in the streets,
All the warriors shall be put to silence in that day."

We are moved to sympathy with the feelings of Hamath and Arpad, when they heard the evil tidings, and were filled with sorrow, "like the sea that cannot rest."

Yet even here this most uncompromising of prophets may teach us, after his fashion, wholesome though perhaps unwelcome truths. We are reminded how often the mystic glamour of romance has served to veil cruelty and corruption, and how little picturesque scenery and interesting associations can do of themselves to promote a noble life. Feudal castles, with their massive grandeur, were the strongholds of avarice and cruelty; and ancient abbeys which, even in decay, are like a dream of fairyland, were sometimes the home of abominable corruption.

CHAPTER XXIII.

KEDAR AND HAZOR.

JEREMIAH xlix. 28-33.

"Concerning Kedar, and the kingdoms of Hazor which Nebuchadnezzar king of Babylon smote."—JER. xlix. 28.

FROM an immemorial seat of human culture, an "eternal city" which antedates Rome by centuries, if not millenniums, we turn to those Arab tribes whose national life and habits were as ancient and have been as persistent as the streets of Damascus. While Damascus has almost always been in the forefront of history, the Arab tribes—except in the time of Mohammed and the early Caliphs—have seldom played a more important part than that of frontier marauders. Hence, apart from a few casual references, the only other passage in the Old Testament which deals, at any length, with Kedar is the parallel prophecy of Isaiah. And yet Kedar was the great northern tribe, which ranged the deserts between Palestine and the Euphrates, and which must have had closer relations with Judah than most Arab peoples.

"The kingdoms of Hazor" are still more unknown to history. There were several "Hazors" in Palestine, besides sundry towns whose names are also derived from *Hāçēr*, a village; and some of these are on or beyond the southern frontier of Judah, in the wilderness of the Exodus, where we might expect to find nomad Arabs. But even these latter cities can scarcely be the "Hazor" of Jeremiah, and the more northern are quite out of the question. It is generally supposed that Hazor here is either some Arabian town, or, more probably, a collective term used for the district inhabited by Arabs, who lived not in tents, but in *Hāçērîm*, or villages. This district would be in Arabia itself, and more distant from Palestine than the deserts over which Kedar roamed. Possibly Isaiah's "villages (*Hāçērîm*) that Kedar doth inhabit" were to be found in the Hazor of Jeremiah, and the same people were called Kedar and Hazor respectively according as they lived a nomad life or settled in more permanent dwellings.

The great warlike enterprises of Egypt, Assyria, and Chaldea during the last centuries of the Jewish monarchy would bring these desert horsemen into special prominence. They could either further or hinder the advance of armies marching westward from Mesopotamia, and could command their lines of communication. Kedar, and possibly Hazor too, would not be slack to use the opportunities of plunder presented by the calamities of the Palestinian states. Hence their conspicuous position in the pages of Isaiah and Jeremiah.

As the Assyrians, when their power was at its height, had chastised the aggressions of the Arabs, so now Nebuchadnezzar "smote Kedar and the kingdoms of Hazor." Even the wandering nomads and dwellers by distant oases in trackless deserts could not escape the sweeping activity of this scourge of God. Doubtless the ravages of Chaldean armies might serve to punish many sins besides the wrongs they were sent to revenge. The Bedouin always had their virtues, but the wild liberty of the desert easily degenerated into unbridled license. Judah and every state bordering on the wilderness knew by painful experience how large a measure of rapine and cruelty might coexist with primitive customs, and the Jewish prophet gives Nebuchadnezzar a Divine commission as for a holy war:—

"Arise, go up to Kedar ;
Spoil the men of the east.
They (the Chaldeans) shall take away their tents and flocks ;
They shall take for themselves their tent-coverings,
And all their gear and their camels :
Men shall cry concerning them,
Terror on every side." *

Then the prophet turns to the more distant Hazor with words of warning:—

* Joel iii. 4.

† So Giesebrecht, with most of the ancient versions. A. V., R. V., with Masoretic Text, "not forsaken . . . my joy," possibly meaning, "Why did not the inhabitants forsake the doomed city?"

* Magor-missabib : *cf.* xlvi. 5.

"Flee, get you far off, dwell in hidden recesses of the land,
O inhabitants of Hazor—
It is the utterance of Jehovah—
For Nebuchadnezzar king of Babylon hath counselled a counsel and purposed a purpose against you."

But then, as if this warning were a mere taunt, he renews his address to the Chaldeans and directs their attack against Hazor:—

"Arise, go up against a nation that is at ease, that dwelleth without fear—it is the utterance of Jehovah—
Which abide alone, without gates or bars"—

like the people of Laish before the Danites came, and like Sparta before the days of Epaminondas.

Possibly we are to combine these successive "utterances," and to understand that it was alike Jehovah's will that the Chaldeans should invade and lay waste Hazor, and that the unfortunate inhabitants should escape—but escape plundered and impoverished: for

"Their camels shall become a spoil,
The multitude of their cattle a prey:
I will scatter to every wind them that have the corners of their hair polled;*
I will bring their calamity upon them from all sides.
Hazor shall be a haunt of jackals, a desolation for ever:
No one shall dwell there,
No soul shall sojourn therein."

CHAPTER XXIV.

ELAM.

JEREMIAH xlix. 34-39.

"I will break the bow of Elam, the chief of their might."—JER. xlix. 35.

WE do not know what principle or absence of principle determined the arrangement of these prophecies; but, in any case, these studies in ancient geography and politics present a series of dramatic contrasts. From two ancient and enduring types of Eastern life, the city of Damascus and the Bedouin of the desert, we pass to a state of an entirely different order, only slightly connected with the international system of Western Asia. Elam contended for the palm of supremacy with Assyria and Babylon in the farther east, as Egypt did to the southwest. Before the time of Abraham Elamite kings ruled over Chaldea, and Genesis xiv. tells us how Chedorlaomer with his subject-allies collected his tribute in Palestine. Many centuries later, the Assyrian king Ashur-bani-pal (B. C. 668-626) conquered Elam, sacked the capital Shushan, and carried away many of the inhabitants into captivity. According to Ezra iv. 9, 10, Elamites were among the mingled population whom "the great and noble Asnapper" (probably Ashur-bani-pal) settled in Samaria.

When we begin to recall even a few of the striking facts concerning Elam discovered in the last fifty years, and remember that for millenniums Elam had played the part of a first-class Asiatic power, we are tempted to wonder that Jeremiah only devotes a few conventional sentences to this great nation. But the prophet's interest was simply determined by the relations of Elam with Judah; and, from this point of view, an opposite difficulty arises. How came the Jews in Palestine in the time of Jeremiah to have any concern with a people dwelling beyond the Euphrates and Tigris, on the farther side of the Chaldean dominions? One answer to this question has already been suggested: the Jews may have learnt from the Elamite colonists in Samaria something concerning their native country; it is also probable that Elamite auxiliaries served in the Chaldean armies that invaded Judah.

Accordingly the prophet sets forth, in terms already familiar to us, how Elamite fugitives should be scattered to the four quarters of the earth and be found in every nation under heaven, how the sword should follow them into their distant places of refuge and utterly consume them.

"I will set My throne in Elam;
I will destroy out of it both king and princes—
It is the utterance of Jehovah;"

In the prophecy concerning Egypt, Nebuchadnezzar was to set his throne at Tahpanhes to decide the fate of the captives; but here Jehovah Himself is pictured as the triumphant and inexorable conqueror, holding His court as the arbiter of life and death. The vision of the "great white throne" was not first accorded to John in his Apocalypse. Jeremiah's eyes were opened to see beside the tribunals of heathen conquerors the judgment-seat of a mightier Potentate; and his inspired utterances remind the believer that every battle may be an Armageddon, and that at every congress there is set a mystic throne from which the Eternal King overrules the decisions of plenipotentiaries.

But this sentence of condemnation was not to be the final "utterance of Jehovah" with regard to Elam. A day of renewed prosperity was to dawn for Elam, as well as for Moab, Ammon, Egypt, and Judah:—

"In the latter days I will bring again the captivity of Ealm—
It is the utterance of Jehovah."

The Apostle Peter * tells us that the prophets "sought and searched diligently" concerning the application of their words, "searching what time and what manner of time the Spirit of Christ which was in them did point unto." We gather from these verses that, as Newton could not have foreseen all that was contained in the law of gravitation, so the prophets often understood little of what was involved in their own inspiration. We could scarcely have a better example than this prophecy affords of the knowledge of the principles of God's future action combined with ignorance of its circumstances and details. If we may credit the current theory, Cyrus, the servant of Jehovah, the deliverer of Judah, was a king of Elam. If Jeremiah had foreseen how his prophecies of the restoration of Elam and of Judah would be fulfilled, we may be sure that this utterance would not have been so brief, its hostile tone would have been mitigated, and the concluding sentence would not have been so cold and conventional.

CHAPTER XXV.

BABYLON.

JEREMIAH l., li.

"Babylon is taken, Bel is confounded, Merodach is broken in pieces."—JER. l. 2.

THESE chapters present phenomena analogous to those of Isaiah xl.-lxvi., and have been very commonly ascribed to an author writing at

* *I. e.*, cut off.

* 1 Peter i. 10, 11.

Babylon towards the close of the Exile, or even at some later date. The conclusion has been arrived at in both cases by the application of the same critical principles to similar data. In the present case the argument is complicated by the concluding paragraph of chapter li., which states that "Jeremiah wrote in a book all the evil that should come upon Babylon, even all these words that are written against Babylon," in the fourth year of Zedekiah, and gave the book to Seraiah ben Neriah to take to Babylon and tie a stone to it and throw it into the Euphrates.

Such a statement, however, cuts both ways. On the one hand, we seem to have—what is wanting in the case of Isaiah xl.-lxvi.—a definite and circumstantial testimony as to authorship. But, on the other hand, this very testimony raises new difficulties. If l. and li. had been simply assigned to Jeremiah, without any specification of date, we might possibly have accepted the tradition according to which he spent his last years at Babylon, and have supposed that altered circumstances and novel experiences account for the differences between these chapters and the rest of the book. But Zedekiah's fourth year is a point in the prophet's ministry at which it is extremely difficult to account for his having composed such a prophecy. If, however, li. 59-64 is mistaken in its exact and circumstantial account of the origin of the preceding section, we must hesitate to recognise its authority as to that section's authorship.

A detailed discussion of the question would be out of place here,* but we may notice a few passages which illustrate the arguments for an exilic date. We learn from Jeremiah xxvii.-xxix. that, in the fourth year of Zedekiah,† the prophet was denouncing as false teachers those who predicted that the Jewish captives in Babylon would speedily return to their native land. He himself asserted that judgment would not be inflicted upon Babylon for seventy years, and exhorted the exiles to build houses and marry, and plant gardens, and to pray for the peace of Babylon.‡ We can hardly imagine that, in the same breath almost, he called upon these exiles to flee from the city of their captivity, and summoned the neighbouring nations to execute Jehovah's judgment against the oppressors of His people. And yet we read:—

"There shall come the Israelites, they and the Jews together:
They shall weep continually, as they go to seek Jehovah their God;
They shall ask their way to Zion, with their faces hitherward" § (l. 4, 5).

. . . . .

"Remove from the midst of Babylon, and be ye as he-goats before the flock" (l. 8).

These verses imply that the Jews were already in Babylon, and throughout the author assumes the circumstances of the Exile. "The vengeance of the Temple," *i. e.*, vengeance for the destruction of the Temple at the final capture of Jerusalem, is twice threatened.‖ The ruin of Babylon is described as imminent·

"Set up a standard on the earth,
Blow the trumpet among the nations,
Prepare the nations against her."

If these words were written by Jeremiah in the fourth year of Zedekiah, he certainly was not practising his own precept to pray for the peace of Babylon.

Various theories have been advanced to meet the difficulties which are raised by the ascription of this prophecy to Jeremiah. It may have been expanded from an authentic original. Or again, li. 59-64 may not really refer to l. 1-li. 58; the two sections may once have existed separately, and may owe their connection to an editor, who met with l. 1-li. 58 as an anonymous document, and thought he recognised in it the "book" referred to in li. 59-64. Or again, l. 1-li. 58 may be a hypothetical reconstruction of a lost prophecy of Jeremiah; li. 59-64 mentioned such a prophecy and none was extant, and some student and disciple of Jeremiah's school utilised the material and ideas of extant writings to supply the gap. In any case, it must have been edited more than once, and each time with modifications. Some support might be obtained for any one of these theories from the fact that l. 1-li. 58 is *prima facie* partly a cento of passages from the rest of the book and from the Book of Isaiah.*

In view of the great uncertainty as to the origin and history of this prophecy, we do not intend to attempt any detailed exposition. Elsewhere whatever non-Jeremianic matter occurs in the book is mostly by way of expansion and interpretation, and thus lies in the direct line of the prophet's teaching. But the section on Babylon attaches itself to the new departure in religious thought that is more fully expressed in Isaiah xl.-lxvi. Chaps. l., li., may possibly be Jeremiah's swan-song, called forth by one of those Pisgah visions of a new dispensation sometimes granted to aged seers; but such visions of a new era and a new order can scarcely be combined with earlier teaching. We will therefore only briefly indicate the character and contents of this section.

It is apparently a mosaic, compiled from lost as well as extant sources; and dwells upon a few themes with a persistent iteration of ideas and phrases hardly to be paralleled elsewhere, even in the Book of Jeremiah. It has been reckoned † that the imminence of the attack on Babylon is introduced afresh eleven times, and its conquest and destruction nine times. The advent of an enemy from the north is announced four times.‡

The main theme is naturally that dwelt upon most frequently, the imminent invasion of Chaldea by victorious enemies who shall capture and destroy Babylon. Hereafter the great city and its territory will be a waste, howling wilderness:—

"Your mother shall be sore ashamed,
She that bare you shall be confounded;
Behold, she shall be the hindmost of the nations,
A wilderness, a parched land, and a desert.
Because of the wrath of Jehovah, it shall be uninhabited;
The whole land shall be a desolation.
Every one that goeth by Babylon
Shall hiss with astonishment because of all her plagues." §

* See against the authenticity Driver's "Introduction," *in loco*; and in support of it "Speaker's Commentary," Streane (C. B. S.). *Cf.* also Sayce, "Higher Criticism," etc., pp. 484-486.

† In xxvii. 1 we must read, "In the beginning of the reign of *Zedekiah*," not Jehoiakim.

‡ xxix. 4-14.

§ "Hitherward" seems to indicate that the writer's local standpoint is that of Palestine.

‖ l. 28, li. 11.

* *Cf.* l. 8, li. 6, with Isa. xlviii. 20; l. 13 with xlix. 17; l. 41-43 with vi. 22-24; l. 44-46 with xlix. 19-21; li. 15-19 with x. 12-16.

† Budde ap. Giesebrecht, *in loco*.

‡ l. 3, 9, li. 41, 48.

§ l. 12, 13: *cf.* l. 39, 40, li. 26, 29, 37, 41-43.

The gods of Babylon, Bel and Merodach, and all her idols, are involved in her ruin, and reference is made to the vanity and folly of idolatry.* But the wrath of Jehovah has been chiefly excited, not by false religion, but by the wrongs inflicted by the Chaldeans on His Chosen People. He is moved to avenge His Temple †:—

"I will recompense unto Babylon
And all the inhabitants of Chaldea
All the evil which they wrought in Zion,
And ye shall see it—it is the utterance of Jehovah" (li. 24).

Though He thus avenge Judah, yet its former sins are not yet blotted out of the book of His remembrance:—

"Their adversaries said, We incur no guilt.
Because they have sinned against Jehovah, the Pasture of Justice,
Against the Hope of their fathers, even Jehovah" (l. 7).

Yet now there is forgiveness:—

"The iniquity of Israel shall be sought for, and there shall be none;
And the sins of Judah, and they shall not be found:
For I will pardon the remnant that I preserve" (l. 20).

The Jews are urged to flee from Babylon, lest they should be involved in its punishment, and are encouraged to return to Jerusalem and enter afresh into an everlasting covenant with Jehovah. As in Jeremiah xxxi., Israel is to be restored as well as Judah:—

"I will bring Israel again to his Pasture:
He shall feed on Carmel and Bashan;
His desires shall be satisfied on the hills of Ephraim and in Gilead" (l. 19).

BOOK III.

JEREMIAH'S TEACHING CONCERNING ISRAEL AND JUDAH.

CHAPTER XXVI.

INTRODUCTORY.

"I will be the God of all the families of Israel, and they shall be My people."—JER. xxxi. 1.

IN this third book an attempt is made to present a general view of Jeremiah's teaching on the subject with which he was most preoccupied—the political and religious fortunes of Judah. Certain ‡ chapters detach themselves from the rest, and stand in no obvious connection with any special incident of the prophet's life. These are the main theme of this book, and have been dealt with in the ordinary method of detailed exposition. They have been treated separately, and not woven into the continuous narrative, partly because we thus obtain a more adequate emphasis upon important aspects of their teaching, but chiefly because their date and occasion cannot be certainly determined. With them other sections have been associated, on account of the connection of subject. Further material for a synopsis of Jeremiah's teaching has been collected from chapters xxi.-xlix. generally, supplemented by brief * references to the previous chapters. Inasmuch as the prophecies of our book do not form an ordered treatise on dogmatic theology, but were uttered with regard to individual conduct and critical events, topics are not exclusively dealt with in a single section, but are referred to at intervals throughout. Moreover, as both the individuals and the crises were very much alike, ideas and phrases are constantly reappearing, so that there is an exceptionally large amount of repetition in the Book of Jeremiah. The method we have adopted avoids some of the difficulties which would arise if we attempted to deal with these doctrines in our continuous exposition.

Our general sketch of the prophet's teaching is naturally arranged under categories suggested by the book itself, and not according to the sections of a modern treatise on Systematic Theology. No doubt much may legitimately be extracted or deduced concerning Anthropology, Soteriology, and the like; but true proportion is as important in exposition as accurate interpretation. If we wish to understand Jeremiah, we must be content to dwell longest upon what he emphasised most, and to adopt the standpoint of time and race which was his own. Accordingly in our treatment we have followed the cycle of sin, punishment, and restoration, so familiar to students of Hebrew prophecy.

* li. 17, 18.
† l. 28.
‡ xxx., xxxi., and, in part, xxxiii.

NOTE.

SOME CHARACTERISTIC EXPRESSIONS OF JEREMIAH.

This note is added partly for convenience of reference, and partly to illustrate the repetition just mentioned as characteristic of Jeremiah. The instances are chosen from expressions occurring in chapters xxi.-lii. The reader will find fuller lists dealing with the whole book in the "Speaker's Commentary" and the "Cambridge Bible for Schools and Colleges." The Hebrew student is referred to the list in Driver's "Introduction," upon which the following is partly based.

1. "Rising up early": vii. 13, 25; xi. 7; xxv. 3, 4; xxvi. 5; xxix. 19; xxxii. 33; xxxv. 14, 15; xliv. 4. This phrase, familiar to us in the narratives of Genesis and in the historical books, is used here, as in 2 Chron. xxxvi. 15, of God addressing His people on sending the prophets.

2. "Stubbornness of heart" (A. V. imagination of heart): iii. 17; vii. 24; ix. 14; xi. 8; xiii. 10; xvi. 12; xviii. 12: xxiii. 17; also found Deut. xxix. 19 and Ps. lxxxi. 15.

3. "The evil of your doings": iv. 4; xxi. 12: xxiii. 2, 22; xxv. 5; xxvi. 3; xliv. 22; also Deut. xxviii. 20: 1 Sam. xxv. 3; Isa. i. 16; Hos. ix. 15; Ps. xxviii. 4; and in slightly different form in xi. 18 and Zech. i. 4.

"The fruit of your doings": xvii. 10; xxi. 14; xxxii. 19; also found in Micah vii. 13.

"Doings, your doings," etc., are also found in Jeremiah and elsewhere.

4. "The sword, the pestilence, and the famine," in various orders, and either as a phrase or each word ocurring in one of three successive clauses: xiv. 12; xv. 2; xxi. 7, 9; xxiv. 10; xxvii. 8, 13; xxix. 17, 18; xxxii. 24, 36; xxxiv. 17; xxxviii. 2; xlii. 17, 22; xliv. 13.

"The sword and the famime," with similar variations: v. 12; xi. 22; xiv. 13, 15, 16, 18; xvi. 4; xviii. 21; xlii. 16; xliv. 12, 18, 27.

Cf. similar lists, etc., "death . . . sword . . . captivity," in xliii. 11: "war . . . evil . . . pestilence," xxviii. 8.

5. "Kings . . . princes . . . priests . . . prophets," in various orders and combinations: ii. 26; iv. 9; viii. 1; xiii. 13; xxiv. 8; xxxii. 32.

Cf. "Prophet . . . priest . . . people," xxiii. 33, 34. "Prophets . . . diviners . . . dreamers . . . enchanters . . . sorcerers," xxvii. 9.

* Brief, in order not to trespass more than is absolutely necessary upon the ground covered by the "Prophecies of Jeremiah," *antea*.

CHAPTER XXVII.

SOCIAL AND RELIGIOUS CORRUPTION.

"Very bad figs. . . . too bad to be eaten."—JER. xxiv. 2, 8, xxix. 17.

PROPHETS and preachers have taken the Israelites for God's helots, as if the Chosen People had been made drunk with the cup of the Lord's indignation, in order that they might be held up as a warning to His more favoured children throughout after ages. They seemed depicted as "sinners above all men," that by this supreme warning the heirs of a better covenant may be kept in the path of righteousness. Their sin is no mere inference from the long tragedy of their national history, "because they have suffered such things"; their own prophets and their own Messiah testify continually against them. Religious thought has always singled out Jeremiah as the most conspicuous and uncompromising witness to the sins of his people. One chief feature of his mission was to declare God's condemnation of ancient Judah. Jeremiah watched and shared the prolonged agony and overwhelming catastrophes of the last days of the Jewish monarchy, and ever and anon raised his voice to declare that his fellow-countrymen suffered, not as martyrs, but as criminals. He was like the herald who accompanies a condemned man on the way to execution, and proclaims his crime to the spectators.

What were these crimes? How was Jerusalem a sink of iniquity, an Augean stable, only to be cleansed by turning through it the floods of Divine chastisement? The annalists of Egypt and Chaldea show no interest in the morality of Judah; but there is no reason to believe that they regarded Jerusalem as more depraved than Tyre, or Babylon, or Memphis. If a citizen of one of these capitals of the East visited the city of David he might miss something of accustomed culture, and might have occasion to complain of the inferiority of local police arrangements, but he would be as little conscious of any extraordinary wickedness in the city as a Parisian would in London. Indeed, if an English Christian familiar with the East of the nineteenth century could be transported to Jerusalem under King Zedekiah, in all probability its moral condition would not affect him very differently from that of Cabul or Ispahan.

When we seek to learn from Jeremiah wherein the guilt of Judah lay, his answer is neither clear nor full: he does not gather up her sins into any complete and detailed indictment; we are obliged to avail ourselves of casual references scattered through his prophecies. For the most part Jeremiah speaks in general terms; a precise and exhaustive catalogue of current vices would have seemed too familiar and commonplace for the written record.

The corruption of Judah is summed up by Jeremiah in the phrase "the evil of your doings,"* and her punishment is described in a corresponding phrase as "the fruit of your doings," or as coming upon her "because of the evil of your doings." The original of "doings" is a peculiar word† occurring most frequently in Jeremiah, and the phrases are very common in Jeremiah, and hardly occur at all elsewhere. The constant reiteration of this melancholy refrain is an eloquent symbol of Jehovah's sweeping condemnation. In the total depravity of Judah, no special sin, no one group of sins, stood out from the rest. Their "doings" were evil altogether.

The picture suggested by the scattered hints as to the character of these evil doings is such as might be drawn of almost any Eastern state in its darker days. The arbitrary hand of the government is illustrated by Jeremiah's own experience of the bastinado * and the dungeon,† and by the execution of Uriah ben Shemaiah.‡ The rights of less important personages were not likely to be more scrupulously respected. The reproach of shedding innocent blood is more than once made against the people and their rulers;§ and the more general charge of oppression occurs still more frequently.‖

The motive for both these crimes was naturally covetousness;¶ as usual, they were specially directed against the helpless, "the poor," ** "the stranger, the fatherless, and the widow"; and the machinery of oppression was ready to hand in venal judges and rulers. Upon occasion, however, recourse was had to open violence—men could "steal and murder," as well as "swear falsely"; †† they lived in an atmosphere of falsehood, they "walked in a lie." ‡‡ Indeed the word "lie" is one of the keynotes of these prophecies.§§ The last days of the monarchy offered special temptations to such vices. Social wreckers reaped an unhallowed harvest in these stormy times. Revolutions were frequent, and each in its turn meant fresh plunder for unscrupulous partisans. Flattery and treachery could always find a market in the court of the suzerain or the camp of the invader. Naturally, amidst this general demoralization, the life of the family did not remain untouched: "the land was full of adulterers." ‖‖ Zedekiah and Ahab, the false prophets at Babylon are accused of having committed adultery with their neighbours' wives.¶¶ In these passages "adultery" can scarcely be a figure for idolatry; and even if it is, idolatry always involved immoral ritual.

In accordance with the general teaching of the Old Testament, Jeremiah traces the roots of the people's depravity to a certain moral stupidity; they are "a foolish people, without understanding," who, like the idols in Psalm cxv. 5, 6, "have eyes and see not" and "have ears and hear not." *** In keeping with their stupidity was an unconsciousness of guilt which even rose into proud self-righteousness. They could still come with pious fervour to worship in the temple of Jehovah and to claim the protection of its inviolable sanctity. They could still assail Jeremiah with righteous indignation because he announced the coming destruction of the place where Jehovah had chosen to set His name.††† They said that they had no sin, and met the prophet's rebukes with protests of conscious innocence: "Wherefore hath Jehovah pronounced

* "Characteristic Expressions" (1), p. 269.
† מעלל.

* xx. 2, xxxvii. 15.
† xxxvii., xxxviii.
‡ xxvi. 20–24.
§ ii. 34, xix. 4, xxii. 17.
‖ v. 25, vi. 6, vii. 5.
¶ vi. 13.
** ii. 34.
†† vii. 5–9.
‡‡ xxiii. 14.
§§ "Characteristic Expressions" (2), p. 269.
‖‖ xxiii. 10, 14.
¶¶ xxix. 23.
*** v. 21, quoted by Ezekiel, xii. 2. The verse is also the foundation of the description of Israel as "the blind people that have eyes, and the deaf that have ears," in Isa. xlii. 18 ff., xliii. 8. *Cf.* Giesebrecht on Jer. v. 21.
††† vii., xxvi.

all this great evil against us? or what is our iniquity? or what is our sin that we have committed against Jehovah our God?" *

When the public conscience condoned alike the abuse of the forms of law and its direct violation, actual legal rights would be strained to the utmost against debtors, hired labourers, and slaves. In their extremity, the princes and people of Judah sought to propitiate the anger of Jehovah by emancipating their Hebrew slaves; when the immediate danger had passed away for a time, they revoked the emancipation.† The form of their submission to Jehovah reveals their consciousness that their deepest sin lay in their behaviour to their helpless dependents. This prompt repudiation of a most solemn covenant illustrated afresh their callous indifference to the well-being of their inferiors.

The depravity of Judah was not only total, it was also universal. In the older histories we read how Achan's single act of covetousness involved the whole people in misfortune, and how the treachery of the bloody house of Saul brought three years' famine upon the land; but now the sins of individuals and classes were merged in the general corruption. Jeremiah dwells with characteristic reiteration of idea and phrase upon this melancholy truth. Again and again he enumerates the different classes of the community: "kings, princes, priests, prophets, men of Judah and inhabitants of Jerusalem." They had all done evil and provoked Jehovah to anger; they were all to share the same punishment.‡ They were all arch-rebels, given to slander; nothing but base metal;§ corrupters, every one of them.‖ The universal extent of total depravity is most forcibly expressed when Zedekiah with his court and people are summarily described as a basket of "very bad figs, too bad to be eaten."

The dark picture of Israel's corruption is not yet complete—Israel's corruption, for now the prophet is no longer exclusively concerned with Judah. The sin of these last days is no new thing; it is as old as the Israelite occupation of Jerusalem. "This city hath been to Me a provocation of My anger and of My fury from the day that they built it even unto this day"; from the earliest days of Israel's national existence, from the time of Moses and the Exodus, the people have been given over to iniquity. "The children of Israel and the children of Judah have done nothing but evil before Me from their youth up."¶ Thus we see at last that Jeremiah's teaching concerning the sin of Judah can be summed up in one brief and comprehensive proposition. Throughout their whole history all classes of the community have been wholly given over to every kind of wickedness.

This gloomy estimate of God's Chosen People is substantially confirmed by the prophets of the later monarchy, from Amos and Hosea onwards. Hosea speaks of Israel in terms as sweeping as those of Jeremiah. "Hear the word of Jehovah, ye children of Israel; for Jehovah hath a controversy with the inhabitants of the land, because there is no truth, nor mercy, nor knowledge of God in the land. Swearing and lying and killing and stealing and committing

* xvi. 10.
† xxxiv.
‡ xxxii. 26-35: *cf.* p. 269, "Characteristic Expressions" (3).
§ Literally "copper and iron."
‖ vi. 28.
¶ xxxii. 26-35.

adultery, they cast off all restraint, and blood toucheth blood." * As a prophet of the Northern Kingdom, Hosea is mainly concerned with his own country, but his casual references to Judah include her in the same condemnation.† Amos again condemns both Israel and Judah: Judah, "because they have despised the law of Jehovah, and have not kept His commandments, and their lies caused them to err, after the which their fathers walked"; Israel, "because they sold the righteous for silver and the poor for a pair of shoes, and pant after the dust of the earth on the head of the poor and turn aside the way of the meek." ‡ The first chapter of Isaiah is in a similar strain: Israel is "a sinful nation, a people laden with iniquity, a seed of evil-doers"; "the whole head is sick, the whole heart faint. From the sole of the foot even unto the head there is no soundness in it, but wounds and bruises and putrefying sores." According to Micah, "Zion is built up with blood and Jerusalem with iniquity. The heads thereof judge for reward, and the priests thereof teach for hire, and the prophets thereof divine for money." §

Jeremiah's older and younger contemporaries, Zephaniah and Ezekiel, alike confirm his testimony. In the spirit and even the style afterwards used by Jeremiah, Zephaniah enumerates the sins of the nobles and teachers of Jerusalem. "Her princes within her are roaring lions; her judges are evening wolves. . . . Her prophets are light and treacherous persons: her priests have polluted the sanctuary, they have done violence to the law." ‖ Ezekiel xx. traces the defections of Israel from the sojourn in Egypt to the Captivity. Elsewhere Ezekiel says that "the land is full of bloody crimes, and the city is full of violence";¶ and in xxii. 23-31 he catalogues the sins of priests, princes, prophets, and people, and proclaims that Jehovah "sought for a man among them that should make up the hedge, and stand in the gap before Me for the land, that I should not destroy it: but I found none."

We have now fairly before us the teaching of Jeremiah and the other prophets as to the condition of Judah: the passages quoted or referred to represent its general tone and attitude; it remains to estimate its significance. We should naturally suppose that such sweeping statements as to the total depravity of the whole people throughout all their history were not intended to be interpreted as exact mathematical formulæ. And the prophets themselves state or imply qualifications. Isaiah insists upon the existence of a righteous remnant. When Jeremiah speaks of Zedekiah and his subjects as a basket of very bad figs, he also speaks of the Jews who had already gone into captivity as a basket of very good figs. The mere fact of going into captivity can hardly have accomplished an immediate and wholesale conversion. The "good figs" among the captives were presumably good before they went into exile. Jeremiah's general statements that "they were all arch-rebels" do not therefore preclude the existence of righteous men in the community. Similarly, when he tells us that the city and people have always been given over to

* Hosea iv. 1, 2; also Hosea's general picture of the kingdom of Samaria.
† The A. V. translation of xi. 12 ("Judah yet ruleth with God, and is faithful with the saints") must be set aside. The sense is obscure and the text doubtful.
‡ Amos ii. 4-8.
§ Micah iii. 10, 11.
‖ Zeph. iii. 3, 4.
¶ Ezek. vii. 23: *cf.* vii. 9, xxii. 1-12.

iniquity, Jeremiah is not ignorant of Moses and Joshua, David and Solomon, and the kings "who did right in the eyes of Jehovah"; nor does he intend to contradict the familiar accounts of ancient history. On the other hand, the universality which the prophets ascribe to the corruption of their people is no mere figure of rhetoric, and yet it is by no means incompatible with the view that Jerusalem, in its worst days, was not more conspicuously wicked than Babylon or Tyre; or even, allowing for the altered circumstances of the times, than London or Paris. It would never have occurred to Jeremiah to apply the average morality of Gentile cities as a standard by which to judge Jerusalem; and Christian readers of the Old Testament have caught something of the old prophetic spirit. The very introduction into the present context of any comparison between Jerusalem and Babylon may seem to have a certain flavour of irreverence. We perceive with the prophets that the City of Jehovah and the cities of the Gentiles must be placed in different categories. The popular modern explanation is that heathenism was so utterly abominable that Jerusalem at its worst was still vastly superior to Nineveh or Tyre. However exaggerated such views may be, they still contain an element of truth; but Jeremiah's estimate of the moral condition of Judah was based on entirely different ideas. His standards were not relative, but absolute; not practical, but ideal. His principles were the very antithesis of the tacit ignoring of difficult and unusual duties, the convenient and somewhat shabby compromise represented by the modern word "respectable." Israel was to be judged by its relation to Jehovah's purpose for His people. Jehovah had called them out of Egypt, and delivered them from a thousand dangers. He had raised up for them judges and kings, Moses, David, and Isaiah. He had spoken to them by Torah and by prophecy. This peculiar munificence of Providence and Revelation was not meant to produce a people only better by some small percentage than their heathen neighbours.

The comparison between Israel and its neighbours would no doubt be much more favourable under David than under Zedekiah, but even then the outcome of Mosaic religion as practically embodied in the national life was utterly unworthy of the Divine ideal; to have described the Israel of David or the Judah of Hezekiah as Jehovah's specially cherished possession, a kingdom of priests and a holy nation,* would have seemed a ghastly irony even to the sons of Zeruiah, far more to Nathan, Gad, or Isaiah. Nor had any class, as a class, been wholly true to Jehovah at any period of the history. If for any considerable time the numerous order of professional prophets had had a single eye to the glory of Jehovah, the fortunes of Israel would have been altogether different, and where prophets failed, priests and princes and common people were not likely to succeed.

Hence, judged as citizens of God's Kingdom on earth, the Israelites were corrupt in every faculty of their nature: as masters and servants, as rulers and subjects, as priests, prophets, and worshippers of Jehovah, they succumbed to selfishness and cowardice, and perpetrated the ordinary crimes and vices of ancient Eastern life.

The reader is perhaps tempted to ask: Is this all that is meant by the fierce and impassioned denunciations of Jeremiah? Not quite all. Jeremiah had had the mortification of seeing the great religious revival under Josiah spend itself, apparently in vain, against the ingrained corruption of the people. The reaction, as under Manasseh, had accentuated the worst features of the national life. At the same time the constant distress and dismay caused by disastrous invasions tended to general license and anarchy. A long period of decadence reached its nadir.

But these are mere matters of degree and detail; the main thing for Jeremiah was not that Judah had become worse, but that it had failed to become better. One great period of Israel's probation was finally closed. The kingdom had served its purpose in the Divine Providence; but it was impossible to hope any longer that the Jewish monarchy was to prove the earthly embodiment of the Kingdom of God. There was no prospect of Judah attaining a social order appreciably better than that of the surrounding nations. Jehovah and His Revelation would be disgraced by any further association with the Jewish state.

Certain schools of socialists bring a similar charge against the modern social order; that it is not a Kingdom of God upon earth is sufficiently obvious; and they assert that our social system has become stereotyped on lines that exclude and resist progress towards any higher ideal. Now it is certainly true that every great civilisation hitherto has grown old and obsolete; if Christian society is to establish its right to abide permanently, it must show itself something more than an improved edition of the Athens of Pericles or the Empire of the Antonines.

All will agree that Christendom falls sadly short of its ideal, and therefore we may seek to gather instruction from Jeremiah's judgment on the shortcomings of Judah. Jeremiah specially emphasises the universality of corruption in individual character, in all classes of society and throughout the whole duration of history. Similarly we have to recognise that prevalent social and moral evils lower the general tone of individual character. Moral faculties are not set apart in watertight compartments. "Whosoever shall keep the whole law, and yet offend in one point, is guilty of all," is no mere forensic principle. The one offence impairs the earnestness and sincerity with which a man keeps the rest of the law, even though there may be no obvious lapse. There are moral surrenders made to the practical exigencies of commercial, social, political, and ecclesiastical life. Probably we should be startled and dismayed if we understood the consequent sacrifice of individual character.

We might also learn from the prophet that the responsibility for our social evils rests with all classes. Time was when the lower classes were plentifully lectured as the chief authors of public troubles; now it is the turn of the capitalist, the parson, and the landlord. The former policy had no very marked success, possibly the new method may not fare better.

Wealth and influence imply opportunity and responsibility which do not belong to the poor and feeble; but power is by no means confined to the privileged classes; and the energy, ability, and self-denial embodied in the great Trades Unions have sometimes shown themselves as cruel and selfish towards the weak and destitute as any association of capitalists. A necessary

* Exod. xix. 6.

preliminary to social amendment is a General Confession by each class of its own sins.

Finally, the Divine Spirit had taught Jeremiah that Israel had always been sadly imperfect. He did not deny Divine Providence and human hope by teaching that the Golden Age lay in the past, that the Kingdom of God had been realised and allowed to perish. He was under no foolish delusion as to "the good old times"; in his most despondent moods he was not given over to wistful reminiscence. His example may help us not to become discouraged through exaggerated ideas about the attainments of past generations.

In considering modern life it may seem that we pass to an altogether different quality of evil to that denounced by Jeremiah, that we have lost sight of anything that could justify his fierce indignation, and thus that we fail in appreciating his character and message. Any such illusion may be corrected by a glance at the statistics of congested town districts, sweated industries, and prostitution. A social reformer, living in contact with these evils, may be apt to think Jeremiah's denunciations specially adapted to the society which tolerates them with almost unruffled complacency.

CHAPTER XXVIII.

PERSISTENT APOSTASY.

"They have forsaken the covenant of Jehovah their God, and worshipped other gods, and served them."—JER. xxii. 9.

"Every one that walketh in the stubbornness of his heart."—JER. xxiii. 17.

THE previous chapter has been intentionally confined, as far as possible, to Jeremiah's teaching upon the moral condition of Judah. Religion, in the narrower sense, was kept in the background, and mainly referred to as a social and political influence. In the same way the priests and prophets were mentioned chiefly as classes of notables—estates of the realm. This method corresponds with a stage in the process of Revelation; it is that of the older prophets. Hosea, as a native of the Northern Kingdom, may have had a fuller experience and clearer understanding of religious corruption than his contemporaries in Judah. But, in spite of the stress that he lays upon idolatry and the various corruptions of worship, many sections of his book simply deal with social evils. We are not explicitly told why the prophet was "a fool" and "a snare of a fowler," but the immediate context refers to the abominable immorality of Gibeah.* The priests are not reproached with incorrect ritual, but with conspiracy to murder.† In Amos, the land is not so much punished on account of corrupt worship, as the sanctuaries are destroyed because the people are given over to murder, oppression, and every form of vice. In Isaiah again the main stress is constantly upon international policies and public and private morality.‡ For instance, none of the woes in v. 8-24 are directed against idolatry or corrupt worship, and in xxviii. 7 the charge brought against Ephraim does not refer to ecclesiastical matters; they have erred through strong drink.

In Jeremiah's treatment of the ruin of Judah, he insists, as Hosea had done as regards Israel, on the fatal consequences of apostasy from Jehovah to other gods. This very phrase "other gods" is one of Jeremiah's favourite expressions, and in the writings of the other prophets only occurs in Hosea iii. 1. On the other hand, references to idols are extremely rare in Jeremiah. These facts suggest a special difficulty in discussing the apostasy of Judah. The Jews often combined the worship of other gods with that of Jehovah. According to the analogy of other nations, it was quite possible to worship Baal and Ashtaroth, and the whole heathen Pantheon, without intending to show any special disrespect to the national Deity. Even devout worshippers, who confined their adorations to the one true God, sometimes thought they did honour to Him by introducing into His services the images and all the paraphernalia of the splendid cults of the great heathen empires. It is not always easy to determine whether statements about idolatry imply formal apostasy from Jehovah, or merely a debased worship. When the early Mohammedans spoke with lofty contempt of image-worshippers, they were referring to the Eastern Christians; the iconoclast heretics denounced the idolatry of the Orthodox Church, and the Covenanters used similar terms as to prelacy. Ignorant modern Jews are sometimes taught that Christians worship idols.

Hence when we read of the Jews, "They set their abominations in the house which is called by My name, to defile it," we are not to understand that the Temple was transferred from Jehovah to some other deities, but that the corrupt practices and symbols of heathen worship were combined with the Mosaic ritual. Even the high places of Baal, in the Valley of Ben-Hinnom, where children were passed through the fire unto Moloch, professed to offer an opportunity of supreme devotion to the God of Israel. Baal and Melech, Lord and King, had in ancient times been amongst His titles; and when they became associated with the more heathenish modes of worship, their misguided devotees still claimed that they were doing homage to the national Deity. The inhuman sacrifices to Moloch were offered in obedience to sacred tradition and Divine oracles, which were supposed to emanate from Jehovah. In three different places, Jeremiah explicitly and emphatically denies that Jehovah had required or sanctioned these sacrifices: "I commanded them not, neither came it into My mind, that they should do this abomination, to cause Judah to sin." * The Pentateuch preserves an ancient ordinance which the Moloch-worshippers probably interpreted in support of their unholy rites, and Jeremiah's protests are partly directed against the misinterpretation of the command "the first-born of thy sons shalt thou give Me." The immediate context also commanded that the firstlings of sheep and oxen should be given to Jehovah. The beasts were killed; must it not be intended that the children should be killed too? † A similar blind literalism has been responsible for many of the follies and crimes perpetrated in the name of Christ. The Church is apt to justify its most flagrant enormities by appealing to a misused and misinterpreted Old

* Hosea ix. 7-9: *cf.* Judges xix. 22.
† Hosea vi. 9.
‡ Isaiah xl.-lxvi. is excluded from this statement.

* xxxii. 34, 35, repeating vii. 30, 31, with slight variations. A similar statement occurs in xix. 4, 5. *Cf.* 2 Kings xvi. 3. xxi. 6, xxiii. 10; also Giesebrecht and Orelli *in loco*.
† Exod. xxii. 29 (JE.). Exod. xxxiv. 20 is probably a later interpretation intended to guard against misunderstandings.

Testament. "Thou shalt not suffer a witch to live" and "Cursed be Canaan" have been proof-texts for witch-hunting and negro-slavery; and the Book of Joshua has been regarded as a Divine charter, authorising the unrestrained indulgence of the passion for revenge and blood.

When it was thus necessary to put on record reiterated denials that inhuman rites of Baal and Moloch were a divinely sanctioned adoration of Jehovah, we can understand that the Baal-worship constantly referred to by Hosea, Jeremiah, and Zephaniah * was not generally understood to be apostasy. The worship of "other gods," "the sun, the moon, and all the host of heaven," † and of the "Queen of Heaven," would be more difficult to explain as mere syncretism, but the assimilation of Jewish worship to heathen ritual and the confusion of the Divine Name with the titles of heathen deities masked the transition from the religion of Moses and Isaiah to utter apostasy.

Such assimilation and confusion perplexed and baffled the prophets.‡ Social and moral wrong-doing were easily exposed and denounced; and the evils thus brought to light were obvious symptoms of serious spiritual disease. The Divine Spirit taught the prophets that sin was often most rampant in those who professed the greatest devotion to Jehovah and were most punctual and munificent in the discharge of external religious duties. When the prophecy in Isaiah i. was uttered it almost seemed as if the whole system of Mosaic ritual would have to be sacrificed, in order to preserve the religion of Jehovah. But the further development of the disease suggested a less heroic remedy. The passion for external rites did not confine itself to the traditional forms of ancient Israelite worship. The practices of unspiritual and immoral ritualism were associated specially with the names of Baal and Moloch and with the adoration of the host of heaven; and the departure from the true worship became obvious when the deities of foreign nations were openly worshipped.

Jeremiah clearly and constantly insisted on the distinction between the true and the corrupt worship. The worship paid to Baal and Moloch was altogether unacceptable to Jehovah. These and other objects of adoration were not to be regarded as forms, titles, or manifestations of the one God, but were "other gods," distinct and opposed in nature and attributes; in serving them the Jews were forsaking Him. So far from recognising such rites as homage paid to Jehovah, Jeremiah follows Hosea in calling them "backsliding,"§ a falling away from true loyalty. When they addressed themselves to their idols, even if they consecrated them in the Temple and to the glory of the Most High, they were not really looking to Him in reverent supplication, but with impious profanity were turning their backs upon Him: "They have turned unto Me the back, and not the face." ‖ These proceedings were a violation of the covenant between Jehovah and Israel.¶

The same anxiety to discriminate the true religion from spurious imitations and adulterations

* Baal is not mentioned in the other prophetical books.

† vii 2.

‡ Here and elsewhere, "prophet," unless specially qualified by the context, is used of the true prophet, the messenger of Divine Revelation, and does not include the mere professional prophets. *Cf.* chap. viii.

§ ii. 19, etc.

‖ xxxii. 33, etc.

¶ xxii. 9: *cf.* xi. 10, xxxi. 32, and Hosea vi. 7, viii. 1.

underlies the stress which Jeremiah lays upon the Divine Name. His favourite formula, "Jehovah Sabaoth is His name," * may be borrowed from Amos, or may be an ancient liturgical sentence; in any case, its use would be a convenient protest against the doctrine that Jehovah could be worshipped under the names of and after the manner of Baal and Moloch. When Jehovah speaks of the people forgetting "My name," He does not mean either that the people would forget all about Him, or would cease to use the name Jehovah; but that they would forget the character and attributes, the purposes and ordinances, which were properly expressed by His Name. The prophets who "prophesy lies in My name" "cause My people to forget My name." † Baal and Moloch had sunk into fit titles for a god who could be worshipped with cruel, obscene, and idolatrous rites, but the religion of Revelation had been for ever associated with the one sacred Name, when "Elohim said unto Moses, Thou shalt say unto the Israelites: Jehovah, the God of your fathers, the God of Abraham, the God of Isaac, and the God of Jacob, hath sent me unto you: this is My name for ever, and this is My memorial unto all generations." All religious life and practice inconsistent with this Revelation given through Moses and the prophets—all such worship, even if offered to beings which, as Jehovah, sat in the Temple of Jehovah, professing to be Jehovah—were nevertheless service and obedience paid to other and false gods. Jeremiah's mission was to hammer these truths into dull and unwilling minds.

His work seems to have been successful. Ezekiel, who is in a measure his disciple,‡ drops the phrase "other gods," and mentions "idols" very frequently.§ Argument and explanation were no longer necessary to show that idolatry was sin against Jehovah; the word "idol" could be freely used and universally understood as indicating what was wholly alien to the religion of Israel.‖ Jeremiah was too anxious to convince the Jews that all syncretism was apostasy to distinguish it carefully from the avowed neglect of Jehovah for other gods. It is not even clear that such neglect existed in his day. In chap. xliv. we have one detailed account of false worship to the Queen of Heaven. It was offered by the Jewish refugees in Egypt; shortly before, these refugees had unanimously entreated Jeremiah to pray for them to Jehovah, and had promised to obey His commands. The punishment of their false worship was that they should no longer be permitted to name the Holy Name. Clearly, therefore, they had supposed that offering incense to the Queen of Heaven was not inconsistent with worshipping Jehovah. We need not dwell on a distinction which is largely ignored by Jeremiah; the apostasy of Judah was real and widespread, it matters little how far the delinquents ventured to throw off the cloak of orthodox profession.¶ The most lapsed masses in a Christian country do not utterly break their connection with the Church; they consider themselves legitimate recipients of its alms,

* x. 16: *cf.* Amos iv. 13.

† xxiii. 25–27: *cf.* Giesebrecht, *in loco*.

‡ Cheyne, "Jeremiah: Life and Times," p. 150.

§ Jeremiah hardly mentions idols.

‖ *Cf.*, on this whole subject, Cheyne, "Jeremiah: Life and Times," p. 319.

¶ The strongest expressions are in chap. ii., for which see previous volume on Jeremiah.

and dimly contemplate as a vague and distant possibility the reformation of their life and character through Christianity. So the blindest worshippers of stocks and stones claimed a vested interest in the national Deity, and in the time of their trouble they turned to Jehovah with the appeal "Arise and save us." *

Jeremiah also dwells on the deliberate and persistent character of the apostasy of Judah. Nations have often experienced a sort of satanic revival when the fountains of the nether deep seemed broken up, and flood-tides of evil influence swept all before them. Such, in a measure, was the reaction from the Puritan Commonwealth, when so much of English society lapsed into reckless dissipation. Such too was the carnival of wickedness into which the First French Republic was plunged in the Reign of Terror. But these periods were transient, and the domination of lust and cruelty soon broke down before the reassertion of an outraged national conscience. But we noticed, in the previous chapter, that Israel and Judah alike steadily failed to attain the high social ideal of the Mosaic dispensation. Naturally, this continuous failure is associated with persistent apostasy from the religious teaching of the Mosaic and prophetic Revelation. Exodus, Deuteronomy, and the Chronicler agree with Jeremiah that the Israelites were a stiff-necked people; † and, in the Chronicler's time at any rate, Israel had played a part in the world long enough for its character to be accurately ascertained; and subsequent history has shown that, for good or for evil, the Jews have never lacked tenacity. Syncretism, the tendency to adulterate true teaching and worship with elements from heathen sources, had been all along a morbid affection of Israelite religion. The Pentateuch and the historical books are full of rebukes of the Israelite passion for idolatry, which must for the most part be understood as introduced into or associated with the worship of Jehovah. Jeremiah constantly refers to "the stubbornness of their evil heart": ‡ "they . . . have walked after the stubbornness of their own heart and after the Baalim." This stubbornness was shown in their resistance to all the means which Jehovah employed to wean them from their sin. Again and again, in our book, Jehovah speaks of Himself as "rising up early" § to speak to the Jews, to teach them, to send prophets to them, to solemnly adjure them to submit themselves to Him; but they would not hearken either to Jehovah or to His prophets, they would not accept His teaching or obey His commands, they made themselves stiff-necked and would not bow to His will. He had subjected them to the discipline of affliction, instruction had become correction; Jehovah had wounded them "with the wound of an enemy, with the chastisement of a cruel one"; but as they had been deaf to exhortation, so they were proof against chastisement—"they refused to receive correction." Only the ruin of the state and the captivity of the people could purge out this evil leaven.

Apostasy from the Mosaic and prophetic religion was naturally accompanied by social corruption. It has recently been maintained that the universal instinct which inclines man to be religious is not necessarily moral, and that it is the distinguishing note of the true faith, or of religion proper, that it enlists this somewhat neutral instinct in the cause of a pure morality. The Phœnician and Syrian cults, with which Israel was most closely in contact, sufficiently illustrated the combination of fanatical religious feeling with gross impurity. On the other hand, the teaching of Revelation to Israel consistently inculcated a high morality and an unselfish benevolence. The prophets vehemently affirmed the worthlessness of religious observances by men who oppressed the poor and helpless. Apostasy from Jehovah to Baal and Moloch involved the same moral lapse as a change from loyal service to Christ to a pietistic antinomianism. Widespread apostasy meant general social corruption. The most insidious form of apostasy was that specially denounced by Jeremiah, in which the authority of Jehovah was more or less explicitly claimed for practices and principles which defied His law. The Reformer loves a clear issue, and it was more difficult to come to close quarters with the enemy when both sides professed to be fighting in the King's name. Moreover the syncretism which still recognised Jehovah was able without any violent revolution to control the established institutions and orders of the state—palace and temple, king and princes, priests and prophets. For a moment the Reformation of Josiah, and the covenant entered into by the king and people to observe the law as laid down in the newly discovered Book of Deuteronomy, seemed to have raised Judah from its low estate. But the defeat and death of Josiah and the deposition of Jehoahaz followed, to discredit Jeremiah and his friends. In the consequent reaction it seemed as if the religion of Jehovah and the life of His people had become hopelessly corrupt.

We are too much accustomed to think of the idolatry of Israel as something openly and avowedly distinct from and opposed to the worship of Jehovah. Modern Christians often suppose that the true worshipper and the ancient idolater were as contrasted as a pious Englishman and a devotee of one of the hideous images seen on missionary platforms; or, at any rate, that they were as easily distinguishable as a native Indian evangelist from his unconverted fellow-countrymen.

This mistake deprives us of the most instructive lessons to be derived from the record. The sin which Jeremiah denounced is by no means outside Christian experience; it is much nearer to us than conversion to Buddhism—it is possible to the Church in every stage of its history. The missionary finds that the lives of his converts continually threaten to revert to a nominal profession which cloaks the immorality and superstition of their old heathenism. The Church of the Roman Empire gave the sanction of Christ's name and authority to many of the most unchristian features of Judaism and Paganism; once more the rites of strange gods were associated with the worship of Jehovah, and a new Queen of Heaven was honoured with unlimited incense. The Reformed Churches in their turn, after the first "kindness of their youth," the first "love of their espousals," have often fallen into the very abuses against which their great leaders protested; they have given way to the ritualistic spirit, have put the Church in the place

* ii. 27.

† xvii. 23: *cf.* Exod. xxxii. 9, etc. (JE.); Deut. ix. 6; 2 Chron. xxx. 8.

‡ "Characteristic Expressions," p. 269.

§ *Ibid.*, p. 269.

of Christ, and have claimed for human formulæ the authority that can only belong to the inspired Word of God. They have immolated their victims to the Baals and Molochs of creeds and confessions, and thought that they were doing honour to Jehovah thereby.

Moreover we have still to contend like Jeremiah with the continual struggle of corrupt human nature to indulge in the luxury of religious sentiment and emotion without submitting to the moral demands of Christ. The Church suffers far less by losing the allegiance of the lapsed masses than it does by those who associate with the service of Christ those malignant and selfish vices which are often canonised as Respectability and Convention.

CHAPTER XXIX.

RUIN.

JEREMIAH xxii. 1-9, xxvi. 14.

"The sword, the pestilence, and the famine,"—JER. xxi. 9 *and passim.**

"Terror on every side."—JER. vi. 25, xx. 10, xlvi. 5, xlix. 29; *also as proper name,* MAGOR-MISSABIB, xx. 3.

WE have seen, in the two previous chapters, that the moral and religious state of Judah not only excluded any hope of further progress towards the realisation of the Kingdom of God, but also threatened to involve Revelation itself in the corruption of His people. The Spirit that opened Jeremiah's eyes to the fatal degradation of his country showed him that ruin must follow as its swift result. He was elect from the first to be a herald of doom, to be set "over the nations and over the kingdoms, to pluck up and to break down, and to destroy and to overthrow."† In his earliest vision he saw the thrones of the northern conquerors set over against the walls of Jerusalem and the cities of Judah.‡

But Jeremiah was called in the full vigor of early manhood; § he combined with the uncompromising severity of youth its ardent affection and irrepressible hope. The most unqualified threats of Divine wrath always carried the implied condition that repentance might avert the coming judgment; ‖ and Jeremiah recurred again and again to the possibility that, even in these last days, amendment might win pardon. Like Moses at Sinai and Samuel at Ebenezer, he poured out his whole soul in intercession for Judah, only to receive the answer, "Though Moses and Samuel stood before Me, yet My mind could not be toward this people: cast them out of My sight and let them go forth." ¶ The record of these early hopes and prayers is chiefly found in chapters i.-xx., and is dealt with in "The Prophecies of Jeremiah," preceding. The prophecies in xiv. 1-xvii. 18 seem to recognise the destiny of Judah as finally decided, and to belong to the latter part of the reign of Jehoiakim,** and there is little in the later chapters of an earlier date. In xxii. 1-5 the king of Judah is promised that if he and his ministers and officers will refrain from oppression, faithfully administer justice, and protect the helpless, kings of the elect dynasty shall still pass with magnificent retinues in chariots and on horses through the palace gates to sit upon the throne of David. Possibly this section belongs to the earlier part of Jeremiah's career. But there were pauses and recoils in the advancing tide of ruin, alternations of hope and despair; and these varying experiences were reflected in the changing moods of the court, the people, and the prophet himself. We may well believe that Jeremiah hastened to greet any apparent zeal for reformation with a renewed declaration that sincere and radical amendment would be accepted by Jehovah. The proffer of mercy did not avert the ruin of the state, but it compelled the people to recognise that Jehovah was neither harsh nor vindictive. His sentence was only irrevocable because the obduracy of Israel left no other way open for the progress of Revelation, except that which led through fire and blood. The Holy Spirit has taught mankind in many ways that when any government or church, any school of thought or doctrine, ossifies so as to limit the expansion of the soul, that society or system must be shattered by the forces it seeks to restrain. The decadence of Spain and the distractions of France sufficiently illustrate the fruits of persistent refusal to abide in the liberty of the Spirit.

But, until the catastrophe is clearly inevitable, the Christian, both as patriot and as churchman,* will be quick to cherish all those symptoms of higher life which indicate that society is still a living organism. He will zealously believe and teach that even a small leaven may leaven the whole mass. He will remember that ten righteous men might have saved Sodom; that, so long as it is possible, God will work by encouraging and rewarding willing obedience rather than by chastising and coercing sin.

Thus Jeremiah, even when he teaches that the day of grace is over, recurs wistfully to the possibilities of salvation once offered to repentance.† Was not this the message of all the prophets: "Return ye now every one from his evil way, and from the evil of your doings, and dwell in the land that Jehovah hath given unto your fathers"?‡ Even at the beginning of Jehoiakim's reign Jehovah entrusted Jeremiah with a message of mercy, saying: "It may be they will hearken, and turn every man from his evil way; that I may repent Me of the evil, which I purpose to do unto them because of the evil of their doings." § When the prophet multiplied the dark and lurid features of his picture, he was not gloating with morbid enjoyment over the national misery, but rather hoped that the awful vision of judgment might lead them to pause, and reflect, and repent. In his age history had not accumulated her now abundant proofs that the guilty conscience is panoplied in triple brass against most visions of judgment. The sequel of Jeremiah's own mission was added evidence for this truth.

Yet it dawned but slowly on the prophet's

* "Characteristic Expressions," p. 269.
† i. 10.
‡ i. 15.
§ i. 7. The word for "child" (na'ar) is an elastic term, equalling "boy" or "young man," with all the range of meaning possible in English to the latter phrase.
‖ *Cf.* the Book of Jonah.
¶ xv. 1.
** Driver, "Introduction," p. 242.

* "Church" is used, in the true Catholic sense, to embrace all Christians.
† xxvii. 18.
‡ xxv. 5, xxxv. 15.
§ xxvi. 3, xxxvi. 2.

mind. The covenant of emancipation * in the last days of Zedekiah was doubtless proposed by Jeremiah as a possible beginning of better things, an omen of salvation, even at the eleventh hour. To the very last the prophet offered the king his life and promised that Jerusalem should not be burnt, if only he would submit to the Chaldeans, and thus accept the Divine judgment and acknowledge its justice.

Faithful friends have sometimes stood by the drunkard or the gambler, and striven for his deliverance through all the vicissitudes of his downward career; to the very last they have hoped against hope, have welcomed and encouraged every feeble stand against evil habit, every transient flash of high resolve. But, long before the end, they have owned, with sinking heart, that the only way to salvation lay through the ruin of health, fortune, and reputation. So, when the edge of youthful hopefulness had quickly worn itself away, Jeremiah knew in his inmost heart that, in spite of prayers and promises and exhortations, the fate of Judah was sealed. Let us therefore try to reproduce the picture of coming ruin which Jeremiah kept persistently before the eyes of his fellow-countrymen. The pith and power of his prophecies lay in the prospect of their speedy fulfilment. With him, as with Savonarola, a cardinal doctrine was that "before the regeneration must come the scourge," and that "these things will come quickly." Here, again, Jeremiah took up the burden of Hosea's utterances. The elder prophet said of Israel, "The days of visitation are come";† and his successor announced to Judah the coming of "the year of visitation."‡ The long-deferred assize was at hand, when the Judge would reckon with Judah for her manifold infidelities, would pronounce sentence and execute judgment.

If the hour of doom had struck, it was not difficult to surmise whence destruction would come or the man who would prove its instrument. The North (named in Hebrew the hidden quarter) was to the Jews the mother of things unforeseen and terrible. Isaiah menaced the Philistines with "a smoke out of the north," § *i. e.*, the Assyrians. Jeremiah and Ezekiel both speak very frequently of the destroyers of Judah as coming from the north. Probably the early references in our book to northern enemies denote the Scythians, who invaded Syria towards the beginning of Josiah's reign; but later on the danger from the north is the restored Chaldean Empire under its king Nebuchadnezzar. "North" is even less accurate geographically for Chaldea than for Assyria. Probably it was accepted in a somewhat symbolic sense for Assyria, and then transferred to Chaldea as her successor in the hegemony of Western Asia.

Nebuchadnezzar is first ‖ introduced in the fourth year of Jehoiakim; after the decisive defeat of Pharaoh Necho by Nebuchadnezzar at Carchemish, Jeremiah prophesied the devastation of Judah by the victor; it is also prophesied that he is to carry Jehoiachin away captive, ¶

* Chap. xi.
† Hosea ix. 7.
‡ xxiii. 12.
§ Isa. xiv. 31.
‖ xxv. 1–14: "first," *i. e.*, in time, not in the order of chapters in our Book of Jeremiah.
¶ xxii. 25. Jehoiachin (Kings, Chronicles, and Jer. lii. 31) is also called Coniah (Jer. xxii. 24, 28, xxxvii. 1) and Jeconiah (Chronicles, Esther, Jer. xxiv. 1, xxvii. 20, xxviii. 4. xxix. 2). They are virtually forms of the same name, the "Yah" of the Divine Name being prefixed in the first and affixed in the last two.

and similar prophecies were repeated during the reign of Zedekiah.* Nebuchadnezzar and his Chaldeans very closely resembled the Assyrians, with whose invasions the Jews had long been only too familiar; indeed, as Chaldea had long been tributary to Assyria, it is morally certain that Chaldean princes must have been present with auxiliary forces at more than one of the many Assyrian invasions of Palestine. Under Hezekiah, on the other hand, Judah had been allied with Merodach-baladan of Babylon against his Assyrian suzerain. So that the circumstances of Chaldean invasions and conquests were familiar to the Jews before the forces of the restored empire first attacked them; their imagination could readily picture the horrors of such experiences.

But Jeremiah does not leave them to their unaided imagination, which they might preferably have employed upon more agreeable subjects. He makes them see the future reign of teror, as Jehovah had revealed it to his shuddering and reluctant vision. With his usual frequency of iteration, he keeps the phrase "the sword, the famine, and the pestilence" ringing in their ears. The sword was the symbol of the invading hosts, "the splendid and awful military parade" of the "bitter and hasty nation" that was "dreadful and terrible."† "The famine" inevitably followed from the ravages of the invaders, and the impossibility of ploughing, sowing, and reaping. It became most gruesome in the last desperate agonies of besieged garrisons, when, as in Elisha's time and the last siege of Jerusalem, "men ate the flesh of their sons and the flesh of their daughters, and ate every one the flesh of his friend." ‡ Among such miseries and horrors, the stench of unburied corpses naturally bred a pestilence, which raged amongst the multitudes of refugees huddled together in Jerusalem and the fortified towns. We are reminded how the great plague of Athens struck down its victims from among the crowds driven within its walls during the long siege of the Peloponnesian war.

An ordinary Englishman can scarcely do justice to such prophecies; his comprehension is limited by a happy inexperience. The constant repetition of general phrases seems meagre and cold, because they carry few associations and awaken no memories. Those who have studied French and Russian realistic art, and have read Erckmann-Chatrain, Zola, and Tolstoï, may be stirred somewhat more by Jeremiah's grim rhetoric. It will not be wanting in suggestiveness to those who have known battles and sieges. For students of missionary literature we may roughly compare the Jews, when exposed to the full fury of a Chaldean attack, to the inhabitants of African villages raided by slave-hunters.

The Jews, therefore, with their extensive, first-hand knowledge of the miseries denounced against them, could not help filling in for themselves the rough outline drawn by Jeremiah. Very probably, too, his speeches were more detailed and realistic than the written reports. As time went on, the inroads of the Chaldeans and their allies provided graphic and ghastly illustrations of the prophecies that Jeremiah still reiterated. In a prophecy, possibly originally referring to the Scythian inroads and afterwards adapted to the Chaldean invasions, Jeremiah

* xxi. 7, xxviii. 14. † Habakkuk i. 6, 7. ‡ xix. 9.

speaks of himself: "I am pained at my very heart; my heart is disquieted in me; I cannot hold my peace; for my soul heareth * the sound of the trumpet, the alarm of war. . . . How long shall I see the standard, and hear the sound of the trumpet?" † Here, for once, Jeremiah expressed emotions that throbbed in every heart. There was "terror on every hand"; men seemed to be walking "through slippery places in darkness," ‡ or to stumble along rough paths in a dreary twilight. Wormwood was their daily food, and their drink maddening draughts of poison.§

Jeremiah and his prophecies were no mean part of the terror. To the devotees of Baal and Moloch Jeremiah must have appeared in much the same light as the fanatic whose ravings added to the horrors of the Plague of London, while the very sanity and sobriety of his utterances carried a conviction of their fatal truth.

When the people and their leaders succeeded in collecting any force of soldiers or store of military equipment, and ventured on a sally, Jeremiah was at once at hand to quench any reviving hope of effective resistance. How could soldiers and weapons preserve the city which Jehovah had abandoned to its fate? "Thus saith Jehovah, the God of Israel: Behold I will turn back the weapons in your hands, with which ye fight without the walls against your besiegers, the king of Babylon and the Chaldeans, and will gather them into the midst of this city. I Myself will fight against you in furious anger and in great wrath, with outstretched hand and strong arm. I will smite the inhabitants of this city, both man and beast: they shall die of a great pestilence." ‖

When Jerusalem was relieved for a time by the advance of an Egyptian army, and the people allowed themselves to dream of another deliverance like that from Sennacherib, the relentless prophet only turned upon them with renewed scorn: "Though ye had smitten the whole hostile army of the Chaldeans, and all that were left of them were desperately wounded, yet should they rise up every man in his tent and burn this city." ¶ Not even the most complete victory could avail to save the city.

The final result of invasions and sieges was to be the overthrow of the Jewish state, the capture and destruction of Jerusalem, and the captivity of the people. This unhappy generation were to reap the harvest of centuries of sin and failure. As in the last siege of Jerusalem there came upon the Jews "all the righteous blood shed on the earth, from the blood of righteous Abel unto the blood of Zachariah son of Barachiah," ** so now Jehovah was about to bring upon His Chosen people all the evil that He had spoken against them ††—all that had been threatened by Isaiah and his brother-prophets, all the curses written in Deuteronomy. But these threats were to be fully carried out, not because predictions must be fulfilled, nor even merely because Jehovah had spoken and His word must not return to Him void, but because the people had not hearkened and obeyed. His threats were never meant to exclude the penitent from the possibility of pardon.

As Jeremiah had insisted upon the guilt of every class of the community, so he is also careful to enumerate all the classes as about to suffer from the coming judgment: "Zedekiah king of Judah and his princes"; * "the people, the prophet, and the priest." † This last judgment of Judah, as it took the form of the complete overthrow of the State, necessarily included all under its sentence of doom. One of the mysteries of Providence is that those who are most responsible for national sins seem to suffer least by public misfortunes. Ambitious statesmen and bellicose journalists do not generally fall in battle and leave destitute widows and children. When the captains of commerce and manufacture err in their industrial policy, one great result is the pauperism of hundreds of families who had no voice in the matter. A spendthrift landlord may cripple the agriculture of half a county. And yet, when factories are closed and farmers ruined, the manufacturer and the landlord are the last to see want. In former invasions of Judah, the princes and priests had some share of suffering; but wealthy nobles might incur losses and yet weather the storm by which poorer men were overwhelmed. Fines and tribute levied by the invaders would, after the manner of the East, be wrung from the weak and helpless. But now ruin was to fall on all alike. The nobles had been flagrant in sin, they were now to be marked out for most condign punishment—"To whomsoever much is given, of him shall much be required."

Part of the burden of Jeremiah's prophecy, one of the sayings constantly on his lips, was that the city would be taken and destroyed by fire. ‡ The Temple would be laid in ruins like the ancient sanctuary of Israel at Shiloh.§ The palaces ‖ of the king and princes would be special marks for the destructive fury of the enemy, and their treasures and all the wealth of the city would be for a spoil; those who survived the sack of the city would be carried captive to Babylon.¶

In this general ruin the miseries of the people would not end with death. All nations have attached much importance to the burial of the dead and the due performance of funeral rites. In the touching Greek story Antigone sacrificed her life in order to bury the remains of her brother. Later Judaism attached exceptional importance to the burial of the dead, and the Book of Tobit lays great stress on this sacred duty. The angel Raphael declares that one special reason why the Lord had been merciful to Tobias was that he had buried dead bodies, and had not delayed to rise up and leave his meal to go and bury the corpse of a murdered Jew, at the risk of his own life.**

Jeremiah prophesied of the slain in this last overthrow: "They shall not be lamented, neither shall they be buried; they shall be as dung on the face of the ground; . . . their carcases shall be meat for the fowls of the heaven, and for the beasts of the earth."

When these last had done their ghastly work, the site of the Temple, the city, the whole land would be left silent and desolate. The stranger, wandering amidst the ruins, would hear no cheerful domestic sounds; when night fell, no light gleaming through chink or lattice would

* R. V. margin.
† iv. 21.
‡ xxiii. 12.
§ xxiii. 15.
‖ xxi. 3–6.
¶ xxxvii. 10.
** Matt. xxiii. 35.
†† xxxv. 17: *cf.* xix. 15, xxxvi. 31.

* xxxiv. 21.
† xxiii. 33, 34.
‡ xxxiv. 2, 22, xxxvii. 8.
§ vii. and xxvi.
‖ vi. 5.
¶ xx. 5.
** Tobit xii. 13: *cf.* ii.

give the sense of human neighbourhood. Jehovah "would take away the sound of the millstones and the light of the candle." * The only sign of life amidst the desolate ruins of Jerusalem and the cities of Judah would be the melancholy cry of the jackals round the traveller's tent.†

The Hebrew prophets and our Lord Himself often borrowed their symbols from the scenes of common life, as they passed before their eyes. As in the days of Noah, as in the days of Lot, as in the days of the Son of Man, so in the last agony of Judah there was marrying and giving in marriage. Some such festive occasion suggested to Jeremiah one of his favourite formulæ; it occurs four times in the Book of Jeremiah, and was probably uttered much oftener. Again and again it may have happened that, as a marriage procession passed through the streets, the gay company were startled by the grim presence of the prophet, and shrank back in dismay as they found themselves made the text for a stern homily of ruin: "Thus saith Jehovah Sabaoth, I will take away from them the voice of mirth and the voice of gladness, the voice of the bridegroom and the voice of the bride." At any rate, however, and whenever used, the figure could not fail to arrest attention, and to serve as an emphatic declaration that the ordinary social routine would be broken up and lost in the coming calamity.

Henceforth the land would be as some guilty habitation of sinners, devoted to eternal destruction, an astonishment and a hissing and a perpetual desolation.‡ When the heathen sought some curse to express the extreme of malignant hatred, they would use the formula, "God make thee like Jerusalem."§ Jehovah's Chosen People would become an everlasting reproach, a perpetual shame, which should not be forgotten. ‖ The wrath of Jehovah pursued even captives and fugitives. In chapter xxix. Jeremiah predicts the punishment of the Jewish prophets at Babylon. When we last hear of him, in Egypt, he is denouncing ruin against "the remnant of Judah that have set their faces to go into the land of Egypt to sojourn there." He still reiterates the same familiar phrases: "Ye shall die by the sword, by the famine, and by the pestilence"; they shall be "an execration, an astonishment, and a curse, and a reproach."

We have now traced the details of the prophet's message of doom. Fulfilment followed fast upon the heels of prediction, till Jeremiah rather interpreted than foretold the thick-coming disasters. When his book was compiled, the prophecies were already, as they are now, part of the history of the last days of Judah. The book became the record of this great tragedy, in which these prophecies take the place of the choric odes in a Greek drama.

CHAPTER XXX.

RESTORATION—I. THE SYMBOL.

JEREMIAH xxxii.

"And I bought the field of Hanameel."—JER. xxxii. 9.

WHEN Jeremiah was first called to his prophetic mission, after the charge "to pluck up and to break down, and to destroy and to overthrow," there were added—almost as if they were an afterthought—the words "to build and to plant." * Throughout a large part of the book little or nothing is said about building and planting; but, at last, four consecutive chapters, xxx.-xxxiii., are almost entirely devoted to this subject. Jeremiah's characteristic phrases are not all denunciatory; we owe to him the description of Jehovah as "the Hope of Israel."† Sin and ruin, guilt and punishment, could not quench the hope that centred in Him. Though the day of Jehovah might be darkness and not light,‡ yet, through the blackness of this day turned into night, the prophets beheld a radiant dawn. When all other building and planting were over for Jeremiah, when it might seem that much that he had planted was being rooted up again in the overthrow of Judah, he was yet permitted to plant shoots in the garden of the Lord, which have since become trees whose leaves are for the healing of the nations.

The symbolic act dealt with in this chapter is a convenient introduction to the prophecies of restoration, especially as chapters xxx., xxxi., have no title and are of uncertain date.

The incident of the purchase of Hanameel's field is referred by the title to the year 587 B. C., when Jeremiah was in prison and the capture of the city was imminent. Verses 2-6 are an introduction by some editor, who was anxious that his readers should fully understand the narrative that follows. They are compiled from the rest of the book, and contain nothing that need detain us.

When Jeremiah was arrested and thrown into prison, he was on his way to Anathoth "to receive his portion there,"§ *i. e.*, as we gather from this chapter to take possession of an inheritance that devolved upon him. As he was now unable to attend to his business at Anathoth, his cousin Hanameel came to him in the prison, to give him the opportunity of observing the necessary formalities. In his enforced leisure Jeremiah would often recur to the matter on which he had been engaged when he was arrested. An interrupted piece of work is apt to intrude itself upon the mind with tiresome importunity; moreover his dismal surroundings would remind him of his business—it had been the cause of his imprisonment. The bond between an Israelite and the family inheritance was almost as close and sacred as that between Jehovah and the Land of Promise. Naboth had died a martyr to the duty he owed to the land. "Jehovah forbid that I should give thee the inheritance of my fathers," ‖ said he to Ahab. And now, in the final crisis of the fortunes of Judah, the prophet whose heart was crushed by the awful task laid upon him had done what he could to secure the rights of his family in the "field" at Anathoth.

Apparently he had failed. The oppression of his spirits would suggest that Jehovah had disapproved and frustrated his purpose. His failure was another sign of the utter ruin of the nation. The solemn grant of the Land of Promise to the Chosen People was finally revoked; and Jehovah no longer sanctioned the ancient ceremonies which bound the households and clans of Israel to the soil of their inheritance.

In some such mood, Jeremiah received the intimation that his cousin Hanameel was on his

* xxv. 10. † ix. 11, x. 22. ‡ xxv. 9, 10. § xxvi. 6. ‖ xxiii. 40.

* i. 10. † xiv. 8, xvii. 13. ‡ Amos v. 18, 20. § xxxvii. 12 (R. V.). ‖ 1 Kings xxi. 3.

way to see him about this very business. "The word of Jehovah came unto him: Behold, thine uncle Shallum's son Hanameel is coming to thee, to say unto thee, Buy my field in Anathoth, for it is thy duty to buy it by way of redemption." The prophet was roused to fresh perplexity. The opportunity might be a Divine command to proceed with the redemption. And yet he was a childless man doomed to die in exile. What had he to do with a field at Anathoth in that great and terrible day of the Lord? Death or captivity was staring every one in the face; land was worthless. The transaction would put money into Hanameel's pocket. The eagerness of a Jew to make sure of a good bargain seemed no very safe indication of the will of Jehovah.

In this uncertain frame of mind Hanameel found his cousin, when he came to demand that Jeremiah should buy his field. Perhaps the prisoner found his kinsman's presence a temporary mitigation of his gloomy surroundings, and was inspired with more cheerful and kindly feelings. The solemn and formal appeal to fulfil a kinsman's duty towards the family inheritance came to him as a Divine command: "I knew that this was the word of Jehovah."

The cousins proceeded with their business, which was in no way hindered by the arrangements of the prison. We must be careful to dismiss from our minds all the associations of the routine and discipline of a modern English gaol. The "court of the guard" in which they were was not properly a prison; it was a place of detention, not of punishment. The prisoners may have been fettered, but they were together and could communicate with each other and with their friends. The conditions were not unlike those of a debtors' prison such as the old Marshalsea, as described in "Little Dorrit."

Our information as to this right or duty of the next-of-kin to buy or buy back land is of the scantiest.* The leading case is that in the Book of Ruth, where, however, the purchase of land is altogether secondary to the levirate marriage. The land custom assumes that an Israelite will only part with his land in case of absolute necessity, and it was evidently supposed that some member of the clan would feel bound to purchase. On the other hand, in Ruth, the next-of-kin is readily allowed to transfer the obligation to Boaz. Why Hanameel sold his field we cannot tell; in these days of constant invasion, most of the small landowners must have been reduced to great distress, and would gladly have found purchasers for their property. The kinsman to whom land was offered would pretty generally refuse to pay anything but a nominal price. Formerly the demand that the next-of-kin should buy an inheritance was seldom made, but the exceptional feature in this case was Jeremiah's willingness to conform to ancient custom.

The price paid for the field was seventeen shekels of silver, but, however precise this information may seem, it really tells us very little. A curious illustration is furnished by modern currency difficulties. The shekel, in the time of the Maccabees, when we are first able to determine its value with some certainty, contained about half an ounce of silver, *i. e.*, about the amount of metal in an English half-crown. The commentaries accordingly continue to reckon the shekel as worth half-a-crown, whereas its value by weight according to the present price of silver

* Lev. xxv. 25, Law of Holiness; Ruth iv.

would be about fourteenpence. Probably the purchasing power of silver was not more stable in ancient Palestine than it is now. Fifty shekels seemed to David and Araunah a liberal price for a threshing-floor and its oxen, but the Chronicler thought it quite inadequate.* We know neither the size of Hanameel's field nor the quality of the land, nor yet the value of the shekels;† but the symbolic use made of the incident implies that Jeremiah paid a fair and not a panic price.

The silver was duly weighed in the presence of witnesses and of all the Jews that were in the court of the guard, apparently including the prisoners; their position as respectable members of society was not affected by their imprisonment. A deed or deeds were drawn up, signed by Jeremiah and the witnesses, and publicly delivered to Baruch to be kept safely in an earthen vessel. The legal formalities are described with some detail; possibly they were observed with exceptional punctiliousness; at any rate, great stress is laid upon the exact fulfilment of all that law and custom demanded. Unfortunately, in the course of so many centuries, much of the detail has become unintelligible. For instance, Jeremiah the purchaser signs the record of the purchase, but nothing is said about Hanameel signing. When Abraham bought the field of Machpelah of Ephron the Hittite there was no written deed, the land was simply transferred in public at the gate of the city.‡ Here the written record becomes valid by being publicly delivered to Baruch in the presence of Hanameel and the witnesses. The details with regard to the deeds are very obscure, and the text is doubtful. The Hebrew apparently refers to two deeds, but the Septuagint for the most part to one only. The R. V. of verse 11 runs: "So I took the deed of the purchase, both that which was sealed, according to the law and the custom, and that which was open." The Septuagint omits everything after "that which was sealed"; and, in any case, the words "the law and the custom"—better, as R. V. margin, "*containing* the terms and the conditions"—are a gloss. In verse 14 the R. V. has: "Take these deeds, this deed of the purchase, both that which is sealed, and this deed which is open, and put *them* in an earthen vessel." The Septuagint reads: "Take this book of the purchase and this book that has been read,§ and thou shalt put *it* in an earthen vessel."‖ It is possible that, as has been suggested, the reference to two deeds has arisen out of a misunderstanding of the description of a single deed. Scribes may have altered or added to the text in order to make it state explicitly what they supposed to be implied. No reason is given for having two deeds. We could have understood the double record if each party had retained one of the documents, or if one had been buried in the earthen vessel and the other kept for reference, but both are put into the earthen vessel. The terms "that which is sealed" and "that which is open" may, however, be explained of either of one or two documents¶ somewhat as follows: the record was written, signed, and wit-

* 2 Sam. xxiv. 24: *cf.* 1 Chron. xxi. 25, where the price is six hundred shekels of *gold*. It is scarcely necessary to point out that "threshing-floor" (Sam.) and "place of the threshing-floor" (Chron.) are synonymous.

† By *value* here is meant purchasing power, to which the weight denoted by the term shekel is now no clue.

‡ Gen. xxiii (*P.*).

§ ἀνεγνωσμένον probably a corruption of ἀνεωγμένον.

‖ The text varies in different MSS. of the LXX.

¶ *Cf.* Cheyne, etc., *in loco*.

nessed; it was then folded up and sealed; part or the whole of the contents of this sealed-up record was then written again on the outside or on a separate parchment, so that the purport of the deed could easily be ascertained without exposing the original record. The Assyrian and Chaldean contract-tables were constructed on this principle; the contract was first written on a clay tablet, which was further enclosed in an envelope of clay, and on the outside was engraved an exact copy of the writing within. If the outer writing became indistinct or was tampered with, the envelope could be broken and the exact terms of the contract ascertained from the first tablet. Numerous examples of this method can be seen in the British Museum. The Jews had been vassals of Assyria and Babylon for about a century, and thus must have had ample opportunity to become acquainted with their legal procedure; and, in this instance, Jeremiah and his friends may have imitated the Chaldeans. Such an imitation would be specially significant in what was intended to symbolise the transitoriness of the Chaldean conquest.

The earthen vessel would preserve the record from being spoilt by the damp; similarly bottles are used nowadays to preserve the documents that are built up into the memorial stones of public buildings. In both cases the object is that "they may continue many days."

So far the prophet had proceeded in simple obedience to a Divine command to fulfil an obligation which otherwise might excusably have been neglected. He felt that his action was a parable which suggested that Judah might retain its ancient inheritance,* but Jeremiah hesitated to accept an interpretation seemingly at variance with the judgments he had pronounced upon the guilty people. When he had handed over the deed to Baruch, and his mind was no longer occupied with legal minutiæ, he could ponder at leisure on the significance of his purchase. The prophet's meditations naturally shaped themselves into a prayer; he laid his perplexity before Jehovah.† Possibly, even from the court of the guard, he could see something of the works of the besiegers; and certainly men would talk constantly of the progress of the siege. Outside the Chaldeans were pushing their mounds and engines nearer and nearer to the walls, within famine and pestilence decimated and enfeebled the defenders; the city was virtually in the enemy's hands. All this was in accordance with the will of Jehovah and the mission entrusted to His prophet. "What thou hast spoken of is come to pass, and, behold, thou seest it." And yet, in spite of all this, "Thou hast said unto me, O Lord Jehovah, Buy the field for money and take witnesses—and the city is in the hands of the Chaldeans!"

Jeremiah had already predicted the ruin of Babylon and the return of the captives at the end of seventy years.‡ It is clear, therefore, that he did not at first understand the sign of the purchase as referring to restoration from the Captivity. His mind, at the moment, was preoccupied with the approaching capture of Jerusalem; apparently his first thought was that his prophecies of doom were to be set aside, and at the last moment some wonderful deliverance might be wrought out for Zion. In the Book of Jonah, Nineveh is spared in spite of the prophet's unconditional and vehement declaration: "Yet forty days and Nineveh shall be overthrown." Was it possible, thought Jeremiah, that after all that had been said and done, buying and selling, building and planting, marrying and giving in marriage, were to go on as if nothing had happened? He was bewildered and confounded by the idea of such a revolution in the Divine purposes.

Jehovah in His answer at once repudiates this idea. He asserts His universal sovereignty and omnipotence; these are to be manifested, first in judgment and then in mercy. He declares afresh that all the judgments predicted by Jeremiah shall speedily come to pass. Then He unfolds His gracious purpose of redemption and deliverance. He will gather the exiles from all lands and bring them back to Judah, and they shall dwell there securely. They shall be His people and He will be their God. Henceforth He will make an everlasting covenant with them, that He will never again abandon them to misery and destruction, but will always do them good. By Divine grace they shall be united in purpose and action to serve Jehovah; He Himself will put His fear in their hearts.

And then returning to the symbol of the purchased field, Jehovah declares that fields shall be bought, with all the legal formalities usual in settled and orderly societies, deeds shall be signed, sealed, and delivered in the presence of witnesses. This restored social order shall extend throughout the territory of the Southern Kingdom, Benjamin, the environs of Jerusalem, the cities of Judah, of the hill country, of the Shephelah and the Negeb. The exhaustive enumeration partakes of the legal character of the purchase of Hanameel's field.

Thus the symbol is expounded: Israel's tenure of the Promised Land will survive the Captivity; the Jews will return to resume their inheritance, and will again deal with the old fields and vineyards and oliveyards, according to the solemn forms of ancient custom.

The familiar classical parallel to this incident is found in Livy, xxvi. 11, where we are told that when Hannibal was encamped three miles from Rome, the ground he occupied was sold in the Forum by public auction, and fetched a good price.

Both at Rome and at Jerusalem the sale of land was a symbol that the control of the land would remain with or return to its original inhabitants. The symbol recognised that access to land is essential to all industry, and that whoever controls this access can determine the conditions of national life. This obvious and often forgotten truth was constantly present to the minds of the inspired writers: to them the Holy Land was almost as sacred as the Chosen People; its right use was a matter of religious obligation, and the prophets and legislators always sought to secure for every Israelite family some rights in their native soil.

The selection of a legal ceremony and the

* Verse 15 anticipates by way of summary verses 42-44, and is apparently ignored in verse 25. It probably represents Jeremiah's interpretation of God's command at the time when he wrote the chapter. In the actual development of the incident, the conviction of the Divine promise of restoration came to him somewhat later.

† What was said of verse 15 partly applies to verses 17-23 (with the exception of the introductory words: "Ah, Lord Jehovah!"). These verses are not dealt with in the text, because they largely anticipate the ideas and language of the following Divine utterance. Kautzsch and Cornill, following Stade, mark these verses as a later addition; Giesebrecht is doubtful. *Cf.* v. 20 ff. and xxvii. 5 f.

‡ xxv. 12, xxix. 10.

stress laid upon its forms emphasise the truth that social order is the necessary basis of morality and religion. The opportunity to live healthily, honestly, and purely is an antecedent condition of the spiritual life. This opportunity was denied to slaves in the great heathen empires, just as it is denied to the children in our slums. Both here and more fully in the sections we shall deal with in the following chapters, Jeremiah shows that he was chiefly interested in the restoration of the Jews because they could only fulfil the Divine purpo e as a separate community in Judah.

Moreover, to use a modern term, he was no anarchist; spiritual regeneration might come through material ruin, but the prophet did not look for salvation either in anarchy or through anarchy. While any fragment of the State held together, its laws were to be observed; as soon as the exiles were re-established in Judah they would resume the forms and habits of an organised community. The discipline of society, like that of an army, is most necessary in times of difficulty and danger, and, above all, in the crisis of defeat.

CHAPTER XXXI.

RESTORATION—II. THE NEW ISRAEL.

JEREMIAH xxiii. 3-8, xxiv. 6, 7, xxx., xxxi., xxxiii.*

"In those days shall Judah be saved, and Jerusalem shall dwell safely: and this is the name whereby she shall be called."—JER. xxxiii. 16.

THE Divine utterances in chapter xxxiii. were given to Jeremiah when he was shut up in the "court of the guard" during the last days of the siege. They may, however, have been committed to writing at a later date, possibly in connection with chapters xxx. and xxxi., when the destruction of Jerusalem was already past. It is in accordance with all analogy that the final record of a "word of Jehovah" should include any further light which had come to the prophet through his inspired meditations on the original message. Chapters xxx., xxxi., and xxxiii. mostly expound and enforce leading ideas contained in xxxii. 37-44 and in earlier utterances of Jeremiah. They have much in common with II. Isaiah. The ruin of Judah and the captivity of the people were accomplished facts to both writers, and they were both looking forward to the return of the exiles and the restoration of the kingdom of Jehovah. We shall have occasion to notice individual points of resemblance later on.

In xxx. 2 Jeremiah is commanded to write in a book all that Jehovah has spoken to him; and according to the present context the "all," in this case, refers merely to the following four chapters. These prophecies of restoration would be specially precious to the exiles; and now that the Jews were scattered through many distant lands, they could only be transmitted and preserved in writing. After the command "to write in a book" there follows, by way of title, a repetition of the statement that Jehovah would bring back His people to their fatherland. Here, in the very forefront of the Book of Promise, Israel and Judah are named as being recalled together from exile. As we read twice * elsewhere in Jeremiah, the promised deliverance from Assyria and Babylon was to surpass all other manifestations of the Divine power and mercy. The Exodus would not be named in the same breath with it: "Behold, the days come, saith Jehovah, that it shall no more be said, As Jehovah liveth, that brought up the Israelites out of the land of Egypt: but, As Jehovah liveth, that brought up the Israelites from the land of the north, and from all the countries whither He had driven them." This prediction has waited for fulfilment to our own times: hitherto the Exodus has occupied men's minds much more than the Return; we are now coming to estimate the supreme religious importance of the latter event.

Elsewhere again Jeremiah connects his promise with the clause in his original commission "to build and to plant":† "I will set My eyes upon them" (the captives) "for good, and I will bring them again to this land; and I will build them, and not pull them down; and I will plant them, and not pluck them up." ‡ As in xxxii. 28-35, the picture of restoration is rendered more vivid by contrast with Judah's present state of wretchedness; the marvellousness of Jehovah's mercy is made apparent by reminding Israel of the multitude of its iniquities. The agony of Jacob is like that of a woman in travail. But travail shall be followed by deliverance and triumph. In the second Psalm the subject nations took counsel against Jehovah and against His Anointed:—

"Let us break their bands asunder,
And cast away their cords from us";

but now this is the counsel of Jehovah concerning His people and their Babylonian conqueror:—

"I will break his yoke from off thy neck,
And break thy bands asunder." §

Judah's lovers, her foreign allies, Assyria, Babylon, Egypt, and all the other states with whom she had intrigued, had betrayed her; they had cruelly chastised her, so that her wounds were grievous and her bruises incurable. She was left without a champion to plead her cause, without a friend to bind up her wounds, without balm to allay the pain of her bruises. "Because thy sins were increased, I have done these things unto thee, saith Jehovah." Jerusalem was an outcast, of whom men said contemptuously: "This is Zion, whom no man seeketh after." ‖ But man's extremity is God's opportunity; because Judah was helpless and despised, therefore Jehovah said, "I will restore health unto thee, and I will heal thee of thy wounds." ¶

* Vatke and Stade reject chapters xxx., xxxi., xxxiii., but they are accepted by Driver, Cornill Kautzsch (for the most part). Giesebrecht assigns them, partly to Baruch and partly to a later editor. It is on this account that the full exposition of certain points in xxxii. and elsewhere has been reserved for the present chapter. Moreover, if the cardinal ideas come from Jeremiah, we need not be over-anxious to decide whether the expansion, illustration, and enforcing of them are due to the prophet himself, or to his disciple Baruch, or to some other editor. The question is somewhat parallel to that relating to the discourses of our Lord in the Fourth Gospel.

* xvi. 14, 15, xxiii. 7, 8.
† i. 10.
‡ xxiv. 6.
§ xxx. 5-8.
‖ xxx. 12-17.
¶ The two verses xxx. 10, 11, present some difficulty here. According to Kautzsch, and of course Giesebrecht, they are a later addition. The ideas can mostly be paralleled

While Jeremiah was still watching from his prison the progress of the siege, he had seen the houses and palaces beyond the walls destroyed by the Chaldeans to be used for their mounds; and had known that every sally of the besieged was but another opportunity for the enemy to satiate themselves with slaughter, as they executed Jehovah's judgments upon the guilty city. Even at this extremity He announced solemnly and emphatically the restoration and pardon of His people. "Thus saith Jehovah, who established the earth, when He made and fashioned it—Jehovah is His name: Call upon Me, and I will answer thee, and will show thee great mysteries, which thou knowest not."*

"I will bring to this city healing and cure, and will cause them to know all the fulness of steadfast peace. . . . I will cleanse them from all their iniquities, and will pardon all their iniquities, whereby they have sinned and transgressed against Me."†

The healing of Zion naturally involved the punishment of her cruel and treacherous lovers.‡ The Return, like other revolutions, was not wrought by rose-water; the yokes were broken and the bands rent asunder by main force. Jehovah would make a full end of all the nations whither He had scattered them. Their devourers should be devoured, all their adversaries should go into captivity, those who had spoiled and preyed upon them should become a spoil and a prey. Jeremiah had been commissioned from the beginning to pull down foreign nations and kingdoms as well as his native Judah.§ Judah was only one of Israel's evil neighbours who were to be plucked up out of their land.‖ And at the Return, as at the Exodus, the waves at one and the same time opened a path of safety for Israel and overwhelmed her oppressors.

Israel, pardoned and restored, would again be governed by legitimate kings of the House of David. In the dying days of the monarchy Israel and Judah had received their rulers from the hands of foreigners. Menahem and Hoshea bought the confirmation of their usurped authority from Assyria. Jehoiakim was appointed by Pharaoh Necho, and Zedekiah by Nebuchadnezzar. We cannot doubt that the kings of Egypt and Babylon were also careful to surround their nominees with ministers who were devoted to the interests of their suzerains. But now "their nobles were to be of themselves, and their ruler was to proceed out of their midst,"¶ *i. e.*, nobles and rulers were to hold their offices according to national custom and tradition.

elsewhere in Jeremiah. Verse 11 *b*, "I will correct thee with judgment, and will in no wise leave thee unpunished," seems inconsistent with the context, which represents the punishment as actually inflicted. Still, the verses might be a genuine fragment misplaced. Driver ("Introduction," 246) says: "The title of honour 'My servant' . . . appears to have formed the basis upon which II. Isaiah constructs his great conception of Jehovah's ideal Servant."

* xxxiii. 2, 3; "earth" is inserted with the LXX. Many regard these verses as a later addition, based on II. Isaiah: *cf.* Isa. xlviii. 6. The phrase "Jehovah is His name" and the terms "make" and "fashion" are specially common in II. Isaiah. xxxiii. so largely repeats the ideas of xxx. that it is most convenient to deal with them together.

† xxxiii. 6-8, slightly paraphrased and condensed.

‡ xxx. 8, 11, 16, 20. *Cf.* also the chapters on the prophecies concerning foreign nations.

§ i. 10.

‖ xii. 14. xxx. 23, 24, is apparently a gloss, added as a suitable illustration of this chapter, from xxii. 19, 20, which are almost identical with these two verses.

¶ xxx. 21.

Jeremiah was fond of speaking of the leaders of Judah as shepherds. We have had occasion already* to consider his controversy with the "shepherds" of his own time. In his picture of the New Israel he uses the same figure. In denouncing the evil shepherds he predicts that, when the remnant of Jehovah's flock is brought again to their folds, He will set up shepherds over them which shall feed them,† shepherds according to Jehovah's own heart, who should feed them with knowledge and understanding.‡

Over them Jehovah would establish as Chief Shepherd a Prince of the House of David. Isaiah had already included in his picture of Messianic times the fertility of Palestine; its vegetation,§ by the blessing of Jehovah, should be beautiful and glorious: he had also described the Messianic King as a fruitful Branch‖ out of the root of Jesse. Jeremiah takes the idea of the latter passage, but uses the language of the former. For him the King of the New Israel is, as it were, a Growth (çemaḥ) out of the sacred soil, or perhaps more definitely from the roots of the House of David, that ancient tree whose trunk had been hewn down and burnt. Both the Growth (çemaḥ) and the Branch (neçer) had the same vital connection with the soil of Palestine and the root of David. Our English versions exercised a wise discretion when they sacrificed literal accuracy and indicated the identity of idea by translating both "çemaḥ" and "neçer" by "Branch."

"Behold, the days come, saith Jehovah, that I will raise up unto David a righteous Branch; and He shall be a wise and prudent King, and He shall execute justice and maintain the right. In His days Judah shall be saved and Israel shall dwell securely, and his name shall be Jehovah 'Çidqenu,' Jehovah is our righteousness."¶ Jehovah Çidqenu might very well be the personal name of a Jewish king, though the form would be unusual; but what is chiefly intended is that His character shall be such as the "name" describes. The "name" is a brief and pointed censure upon a king whose character was the opposite of that described in these verses, yet who bore a name of almost identical meaning—Zedekiah, Jehovah is my righteousness. The name of the last reigning Prince of the House of David had been a standing condemnation of his unworthy life, but the King of the New Israel, Jehovah's true Messiah, would realise in His administration all that such a name promised. Sovereigns delight to accumulate sonorous epithets in their official designations—Highness, High and Mighty, Majesty, Serene, Gracious. The glaring contrast between character and titles often only serves to advertise the worthlessness of those who are labelled with such epithets: the Majesty of James I., the Graciousness of Richard III. Yet these titles point to a standard of true royalty, whether the sovereign be an individual or a class or the people; they describe that Divine Sovereignty which will be realised in the Kingdom of God.**

* *Cf.* chap. viii.

† xxiii. 3, 4.

‡ iii. 15.

§ Isa. iv. 2, çemah; A. V. and R. V. Branch, R. V. margin Shoot or Bud.

‖ Isa. bi. 1.

¶ xxv. 5, 6; repeated in xxxiii. 15, 16, with slight variations.

** In xxxiii. 14–26 the permanence of the Davidic dynasty, the Levitical priests, and the people of Israel is solemnly

The material prosperity of the restored community is set forth with wealth of glowing imagery. Cities and palaces are to be rebuilt on their former sites with more than their ancient splendour. "Out of them shall proceed thanksgiving, and the voice of them that make merry: and I will multiply them, and they shall not be few; I will also glorify them, and they shall not be small. And the children of Jacob shall be as of old, and their assembly shall be established before Me." * The figure often used of the utter desolation of the deserted country is now used to illustrate its complete restoration: "Yet again shall there be heard in this place . . . the voice of joy and the voice of gladness, the voice of the bridegroom and the voice of the bride." Throughout all the land "which is waste, without man and without beast, and in all the cities thereof," shepherds shall dwell and pasture and fold their flocks; and in the cities of all the districts of the Southern Kingdom (enumerated as exhaustively as in xxxii. 44) shall the flocks again pass under the shepherd's hands to be told.†

Jehovah's own peculiar flock, His Chosen People, shall be fruitful and multiply according to the primæval blessing; under their new shepherds they shall no more fear nor be dismayed, neither shall any be lacking.‡ Jeremiah recurs again and again to the quiet, the restfulness, the freedom from fear and dismay of the restored Israel. In this, as in all else, the New Dispensation was to be an entire contrast to those long weary years of alternate suspense and panic, when men's hearts were shaken by the sound of the trumpet and the alarm of war.§ Israel is to dwell securely at rest from fear of harm.‖ When Jacob returns he "shall be quiet and at ease, and none shall make him afraid."¶ Egyptian, Assyrian, and Chaldean shall all cease from troubling; the memory of past misery shall become dim and shadowy.

The finest expansion of this idea is a passage which always fills the soul with a sense of utter rest. "He shall dwell on high: his refuge shall be the inaccessible rocks: his bread shall be given him; his waters shall be sure. Thine eyes shall see the king in his beauty: they shall behold a far-stretching land. Thine heart shall muse on the terror: where is he that counted, where is he that weighed the tribute? where is he that counted the towers? Thou shalt not see the fierce people, a people of a deep speech that thou canst not perceive; of a strange tongue that thou canst not understand. Look upon Zion, the city of our solemnities: thine eyes shall see Jerusalem a quiet habitation, a tent that shall not be removed, the stakes whereof shall never be plucked up, neither shall any of the cords thereof be broken. There Jehovah will be with us in majesty, a place of broad rivers and streams; wherein shall go no galley with oars, neither shall gallant ship pass thereby." *

For Jeremiah too the presence of Jehovah in majesty was the only possible guarantee of the peace and prosperity of Israel. The voices of joy and gladness in the New Jerusalem were not only those of bride and bridegroom, but also of those that said, "Give thanks to Jehovah Sabaoth, for Jehovah is good, for His mercy endureth for ever," and of those that "came to offer sacrifices of thanksgiving in the house of Jehovah."† This new David, as the Messianic King is called,‡ is to have the priestly right of immediate access to God: "I will cause Him to draw near, and He shall approach unto Me: for else who would risk his life by daring to approach Me?"§ Israel is liberated from foreign conquerors to serve Jehovah their God and David their King; and the Lord Himself rejoices in His restored and ransomed people.

The city that was once a desolation, an astonishment, a hissing, and a curse among all nations shall now be to Jehovah "a name of joy, a praise and a glory, before all the nations of the earth, which shall hear all the good that I do unto them, and shall tremble with fear for all the good and all the peace that I procure unto it."‖

assured by a Divine promise. These verses are not found in the LXX., and are considered by many to be a later addition; see Kautzsch, Giesebrecht, Cheyne, etc. They are mostly of a secondary character—15, 16, = xxiii. 5, 6; here Jerusalem and not its king is called Jehovah Çidqenu, possibly because the addition was made when there was no visible prospect of the restoration of the Davidic dynasty. Verse 17 is based on the original promise in 2 Sam. vii. 14–16, and is equivalent to Jer. xxii. 4, 30. The form and substance of the Divine promise imitate xxxi. 35–37.

* xxx. 18–20.
† xxxiii. 10–13.
‡ xxiii. 3, 4.
§ iv. 19.
‖ xxiii. 6.
¶ xxx. 10.

CHAPTER XXXII.

RESTORATION—III. REUNION.

JEREMIAH xxxi.

"I will sow the house of Israel and the house of Judah with the seed of man, and with the seed of beast."—Jer. xxxi. 27.

IN his prophecies of restoration, Jeremiah continually couples together Judah and Israel.¶ Israel, it is true, often stands for the whole elect nation, and is so used by Jeremiah. After the disappearance of the Ten Tribes, the Jewish community is spoken of as Israel. But Israel, in contrast to Judah, will naturally mean the Northern Kingdom or its exiled inhabitants. In this chapter Jeremiah clearly refers to this Israel; he speaks of it under its distinctive title of Ephraim, and promises that vineyards shall again be planted on the mountains of Samaria. Jehovah had declared that He would cast Judah out of His sight, as He had cast out the whole seed of Ephraim.** In the days to come Jehovah would make His new covenant with the House of Israel, as well as with the House of Judah. Amos,†† who was sent to declare the captivity of Israel, also prophesied its return; and similar promises are found in Micah and Isaiah.‡‡ But, in his attitude towards Ephraim, Jeremiah, as in so much else, is a disciple of Hosea. Both prophets have the same tender, affectionate interest in this wayward child of God. Hosea mourns over Ephraim's sin and punishment: "How shall I give thee up, Ephraim? how shall I deliver thee to thine enemies, O Israel? How shall I make thee as Admah? how shall I set thee as Zeboim?"§§

* Isa. xxxiii. 16–21: *cf.* xxxii. 15–18.
† xxxiii. 11.
‡ xxx. 9.
§ xxx. 21, as Kautzsch.
‖ xxxiii. 9.
¶ xxxiii. 7, etc.
** vii. 15.
†† Amos ix. 14.
‡‡ Micah ii. 12; Isa. xi. 10–16.
§§ Hosea xi. 8.

Jeremiah exults in the glory of Ephraim's restoration. Hosea barely attains to the hope that Israel will return from captivity, or possibly that its doom may yet be averted. "Mine heart is turned within Me, My compassions are kindled together. I will not execute the fierceness of Mine anger, I will not again any more destroy Ephraim: for I am God, and not man; the Holy One of Israel in the midst of thee." * But Jehovah rather longs to pardon than finds any sign of the repentance that makes pardon possible; and similarly the promise—"I will be as the dew unto Israel: he shall blossom as the lily, and cast forth his roots as Lebanon. His branches shall spread, and his beauty shall be as the olive tree, and his smell as Lebanon"—is conditioned upon the very doubtful response to the appeal "O Israel, return unto Jehovah thy God." † But Jeremiah's confidence in the glorious future of Ephraim is dimmed by no shade of misgiving. "They shall be My people, and I will be their God," is the refrain of Jeremiah's prophecies of restoration; this chapter opens with a special modification of the formula, which emphatically and expressly includes both Ephraim and Judah—"I will be the God of all the clans of Israel, and they shall be My people."

The Assyrian and Chaldean captivities carried men's thoughts back to the bondage in Egypt; and the experiences of the Exodus provided phrases and figures to describe the expected Return. The judges had delivered individual tribes or groups of tribes. Jeroboam II. had been the saviour of Samaria; and the overthrow of Sennacherib had rescued Jerusalem. But the Exodus stood out from all later deliverances as the birth of the whole people. Hence the prophets often speak of the Return as a New Exodus.

This prophecy takes the form of a dialogue between Jehovah and the Virgin of Israel, *i. e.*, the nation personified. Jehovah announces that the Israelite exiles, the remnant left by the sword of Shalmaneser and Sargon, were to be more highly favoured than the fugitives from the sword of Pharaoh, of whom Jehovah sware in His wrath "that they should not enter into My rest; whose carcases fell in the wilderness." "A people that hath survived the sword hath found favour in the wilderness; Israel hath entered into his rest," ‡—*hath* found favour—*hath* entered—because Jehovah regards His purpose as already accomplished.

Jehovah speaks from His ancient dwelling-place in Jerusalem, and, when the Virgin of Israel hears Him in her distant exile, she answers:—

"From afar hath Jehovah appeared unto me (saying),
With My ancient love do I love thee;
Therefore My lovingkindness is enduring toward thee." §

His love is as old as the Exodus, His mercy has endured all through the long, weary ages of Israel's sin and suffering.

* Hosea xi. 9.

† Hosea xiv.

‡ So Giesebrecht, reading with Jerome and Targum *l'margô'ô* for the obscure and obviously corrupt *l'hargî'ô*. The other versions vary widely in their readings.

§ R. V. "with lovingkindness have I drawn thee," R. V. margin "have I continued lovingkindness unto thee"; the word for "drawn" occurs also in Hosea xi. 4, "I drew them . . . with bands of love."

Then Jehovah replies:—

"Again will I build thee, and thou shalt be built, O Virgin of Israel;
Again shalt thou take thy tabrets, and go forth in the dances of them that make merry;
Again shalt thou plant vineyards on the mountains of Samaria, while they that plant shall enjoy the fruit."

This contrasts with the times of invasion when the vintage was destroyed or carried off by the enemy. Then follows the Divine purpose, the crowning mercy of Israel's renewed prosperity:—

"For the day cometh when the vintagers * shall cry in the hill-country of Ephraim,
Arise, let us go up to Zion, to Jehovah our God."

Israel will no longer keep her vintage feasts in schism at Samaria and Bethel and her countless high places, but will join with Judah in the worship of the Temple, which Josiah's covenant had accepted as the one sanctuary of Jehovah.

The exultant strain continues, stanza after stanza:—

"Thus saith Jehovah:
Exult joyously for Jacob, and shout for the chief of the nations;
Make your praises heard, and say, Jehovah hath saved His people, † even the remnant of Israel.
Behold, I bring them from the land of the north, and gather them from the uttermost ends of the earth;
Among them blind and lame, pregnant women and women in travail together."

None are left behind, not even those least fit for the journey.

"A great company shall return hither.
They shall come with weeping, and with supplications will I lead them."

Of old, weeping and supplication had been heard upon the heights of Israel because of her waywardness and apostasy; ‡ but now the returning exiles offer prayers and thanksgiving mingled with tears, weeping partly for joy, partly for pathetic memories.

"I will bring them to streams of water, by a plain path, wherein they cannot stumble:
For I am become once more a father to Israel, and Ephraim is My first-born son."

Of the two Israelite states, Ephraim, the Northern Kingdom, had long been superior in power, wealth, and religion. Judah was often little more than a vassal of Samaria, and owed her prosperity and even her existence to the barrier which Samaria interposed between Jerusalem and invaders from Assyria or Damascus. Until the latter days of Samaria, Judah had no prophets that could compare with Elijah and Elisha. The Jewish prophet is tenacious of the rights of Zion, but he does not base any claim for the ascendency of Judah on the geographical position of the Temple; he does not even mention the sacerdotal tribe of Levi. Jew and priest as he was, he acknowledges the political and religious hegemony of Ephraim. The fact is a striking illustration of the stress laid by

* So Giesebrecht's conjecture of *bocerim* (vintagers), for the *nocerim* (watchmen, R. V.). The latter is usually explained of the watcher who looked for the appearance of the new moon, in order to determine the time of the feasts. The practice is stated on negative grounds to be post-exilic, but seems likely to be ancient. On the other hand "vintagers" seems a natural sequel to the preceding clauses.

† According to the reading of the LXX. and the Targum. the Hebrew Text has (as R. V.) "O Jehovah, save Thy people."

‡ iii. 21.

the prophets on the unity of Israel, to which all sectional interests were to be sacrificed. If Ephraim was required to forsake his ancient shrines, Jeremiah was equally ready to forego any pride of tribe or caste. Did we, in all our different Churches, possess the same generous spirit, Christian reunion would no longer be a vain and distant dream. But, passing on to the next stanza,—

"Hear the word of Jehovah, O ye nations, and make it known in the distant islands.
Say, He that scattered Israel doth gather him, and watcheth over him as a shepherd over his flock.
For Jehovah hath ransomed Jacob and redeemed him from the hand of him that was too strong for him.
They shall come and sing for joy in the height of Zion;
They shall come in streams to the bounty of Jehovah, for corn and new wine and oil and lambs and calves."

Jeremiah does not dwell, in any grasping sacerdotal spirit, on the contributions which these reconciled schismatics would pay to the Temple revenues, but rather delights to make mention of their share in the common blessings of God's obedient children.

"They shall be like a well-watered garden; they shall no more be faint and weary:
Then shall they rejoice—the damsels in the dance—the young men and the old together.
I will turn their mourning into gladness, and will comfort them, and will bring joy out of their wretchedness.
I will fill the priests with plenty, and My people shall be satisfied with My bounty—
It is the utterance of Jehovah."

It is not quite clear how far, in this chapter, Israel is to be understood exclusively of Ephraim. If the foregoing stanza is, as it seems, perfectly general, the priests are simply those of the restored community, ministering at the Temple; but if the reference is specially to Ephraim, the priests belong to families involved in the captivity of the ten tribes, and we have further evidence of the catholic spirit of the Jewish prophet.

Another stanza:—

"Thus saith Jehovah:
A voice is heard in Ramah, lamentation and bitter weeping, Rachel weeping for her children.
She refuseth to be comforted for her children, for they are not."

Rachel, as the mother of Benjamin and Joseph, claimed an interest in both the Israelite kingdoms. Jeremiah shows special concern for Benjamin, in whose territory his native Anathoth was situated.*

"Her children" would be chiefly the Ephraimites and Manassites, who formed the bulk of the Northern Kingdom; but the phrase was doubtless intended to include other Jews, that Rachel might be a symbol of national unity.

The connection of Rachel with Ramah is not obvious; there is no precedent for it. Possibly Ramah is not intended for a proper name, and we might translate "A voice is heard upon the heights." In Gen. xxxv. 19, Rachel's grave is placed between Bethel and Ephrath,† and in 1 Sam. x. 2, in the border of Benjamin at Zelzah; only here has Rachel anything to do with Ramah. The name, however, in its various forms, was not uncommon. Ramah, to the north of Jerusalem, seems to have been a frontier town, and debatable territory‡ between the two kingdoms; and Rachel's appearance there might symbolise her relation to both. This Ramah was also a slave depôt for the Chaldeans* after the fall of Jerusalem, and Rachel might well revisit the glimpses of the moon at a spot where her descendants had drunk the first bitter draught of the cup of exile. In any case, the lines are a fresh appeal to the spirit of national unity. The prophet seems to say: "Children of the same mother, sharers in the same fate, whether of ruin or restoration, remember the ties that bind you, and forget your ancient feuds." Rachel, wailing in ghostly fashion, was yet a name to conjure with, and the prophet hoped that her symbolic tears could water the renewed growth of Israel's national life. Christ, present in His living Spirit, lacerated at heart by the bitter feuds of those who call Him Lord, should temper the harsh judgments that Christians pass on servants of their One Master. The Jewish prophet lamenting the miseries of schismatic Israel contrasts with the Pope singing *Te Deums* over the massacre of St. Bartholomew.

Then comes the answer:—

"Thus saith Jehovah:
Refrain thy voice from weeping, and thine eyes from tears.
Thou shalt have wages for thy labour—it is the utterance of Jehovah—they shall return from the enemy's land.
There is hope for thee in the days to come—it is the utterance of Jehovah—thy children shall return to their own border." †

The Niobe of the nation is comforted, but now is heard another voice:—

"Surely I hear Ephraim bemoaning himself: Thou hast chastised me; I am chastised like a calf not yet broken to the yoke.
Restore me to Thy favour, that I may return unto Thee, for Thou art Jehovah my God.
In returning unto Thee, I repent; when I come to myself, I smite upon my thigh in penitence." ‡

The image of the calf is another reminiscence of Hosea, with whom Israel figures as a "backsliding heifer" and Ephraim as a "heifer that has been broken in and loveth to tread out the corn"; though apparently in Hosea Ephraim is broken in to wickedness. Possibly this figure was suggested by the calves at Bethel and Dan.

The moaning of Ephraim, like the wailing of Rachel, is met and answered by the Divine compassion. By a bold and touching figure, Jehovah is represented as surprised at the depth of His passionate affection for His prodigal son:—

"Can it be that Ephraim is indeed a son that is precious to Me? is he indeed a darling child?
As often as I speak against him, I cannot cease to remember him,§
Wherefore My tender compassion is moved towards him: verily I will have mercy on him—
It is the utterance of Jehovah."

As with Hosea, Israel is still the child whom Jehovah loved, the son whom He called out of Egypt. But now Israel is called with a more effectual calling:—

"Set thee up pillars of stone,‖ to mark the way; make thee guideposts: set thy heart toward the highway whereby thou wentest.
Return, O Virgin of Israel, return unto these thy cities."

* Isaiah does not mention Benjamin.
† "Which is Bethlehem," in Genesis, is probably a later explanatory addition; and the explanation is not necessarily a mistake. *Cf.* Matt. ii. 18.
‡ 1 Kings xv. 17.

* xl. 1.
† LXX. omits verse 17 *b*, *i. e.*, from "Jehovah" to "border."
‡ Slightly paraphrased.
§ More literally as R. V., "I do earnestly remember him still."
‖ The Hebrew Text has the same word, "tamrurim," here that is used in verse 15 in the phrase "bekhi tam-

The following verse strikes a note of discord, that suggests the revulsion of feeling, the sudden access of doubt, that sometimes follows the most ecstatic moods:—

> "How long wilt thou wander to and fro, O backsliding daughter?
> Jehovah hath created a new thing in the earth—a woman shall compass a man."

It is just possible that this verse is not intended to express doubt of Israel's cordial response, but is merely an affectionate urgency that presses the immediate appropriation of the promised blessings. But such an exegesis seems forced, and the verse is a strange termination to the glowing stanzas that precede. It may have been added when all hope of the return of the ten tribes was over.*

The meaning of the concluding enigma is as profound a mystery as the fate of the lost tribes, and the solutions rather more unsatisfactory. The words apparently denote that the male and the female shall interchange functions, and an explanation often given is that, in the profound peace of the New Dispensation, the women will protect the men. This portent seems to be the sign which is to win the Virgin of Israel from her vacillation and induce her to return at once to Palestine.

In Isaiah xliii. 19 the "new thing" which Jehovah does is to make a way in the untrodden desert and rivers in the parched wilderness. A parallel interpretation, suggested for our passage, is that women should develop manly strength and courage, as abnormal to them as roads and rivers to a wilderness. When women were thus endowed, men could not for shame shrink from the perils of the Return.

In Isaiah iv. 1 seven women court one man, and it has been suggested† that the sense here is "women shall court men," but it is difficult to see how this would be relevant. Another parallel has been sought for in the Immanuel and other prophecies of Isaiah, in which the birth of a child is set forth as a sign. Our passage would then assume a Messianic character; the return of the Virgin of Israel would be postponed till her doubts and difficulties should be solved by the appearance of a new Moses.‡ This view has much to commend it, but does not very readily follow from the usage of the word translated "compass." Still less can we regard these words as a prediction of the miraculous conception of our Lord.

The next stanza connects the restoration of Judah with that of Ephraim, and, for the most part, goes over ground already traversed in our previous chapters; one or two points only need be noticed here. It is in accordance with the catholic and gracious spirit which characterises this chapter that the restoration of Judah is expressly connected with that of Ephraim. The combination of the future fortunes of both in a single prophecy emphasises their reunion. The heading of this stanza, "Thus saith Jehovah Sabaoth, the God of Israel," is different from that hitherto used, and has a special significance in its present context. It is "the God of Israel" to whom Ephraim is a darling child and a first-born son, the God of that Israel which for centuries stood before the world as Ephraim; it is this God who blesses and redeems Judah. Her faint and weary soul is also to be satisfied with His plenty; Zion is to be honoured as the habitation of justice and the mountain of holiness.

"Hereupon," saith the prophet, "I awaked and looked about me, and felt that my sleep had been pleasant to me." The vision had come to him, in some sense, as a dream. Zechariah* had to be aroused, like a man wakened out of his sleep, in order to receive the Divine message; and possibly Zechariah's sleep was the ecstatic trance in which he had beheld previous visions. Jeremiah, however, shows scant confidence† in the inspiration of those who dream dreams, and it does not seem likely that this is a unique exception to his ordinary experience. Perhaps we may say with Orelli that the prophet had become lost in the vision of future blessedness as in some sweet dream.

In the following stanza Jehovah promises to recruit the dwindled numbers of Israel and Judah; with a sowing more gracious and fortunate than that of Cadmus, He will scatter‡ over the land, not dragons' teeth, but the seed of man and beast. Recurring§ to Jeremiah's original commission, He promises that as He watched over Judah to pluck up and to break down, to overthrow and to destroy and to afflict, so now He will watch over them to build and to plant.

The next verse is directed against a lingering dread, by which men's minds were still possessed. More than half a century elapsed between the death of Manasseh and the fall of Jerusalem. He was succeeded by Josiah, who "turned to Jehovah with all his heart, and with all his soul, and with all his might."‖ Yet Jehovah declared to Jeremiah that Manasseh's sins had irrevocably fixed the doom of Judah, so that not even the intercession of Moses and Samuel could procure her pardon.¶ Men might well doubt whether the guilt of that wicked reign was even yet fully expiated, whether their teeth might not still be set on edge because of the sour grapes which Manasseh had eaten. Therefore the prophet continues: "In those days men shall no longer say, The fathers have eaten sour grapes, and the children's teeth are set on edge; but every man shall die for his own transgression, all who eat sour grapes shall have their own teeth set on edge." Or to use the explicit words of Ezekiel, in the great chapter in which he discusses this permanent theological difficulty: "The soul that sinneth, it shall die. The son shall not bear the iniquity of the father, neither shall the father bear the iniquity of the son; the righteousness of the righteous shall be upon him, and the wickedness of the wicked

rurim," "weeping of bitternesses" or "bitter weeping." It is difficult to believe that the coincidence is accidental, and Hebrew literature is given to paronomasia; at the same time the distance of the words and the complete absence of point in this particular instance are remarkable. The LXX., not understanding the word, represented it *more suo* by the similar Greek word τιμορίαν which may indicate that the original reading was "timorim," and the assimilation to "tamrurim" may be a scribe's caprice. In any case, the word here connects with "tamar," a palm, the post being made of or like a palm tree. *Cf.* Giesbrecht, Orelli, Cheyne, etc.

* Giesbrecht treats verses 21–26 as a later addition, but this seems unnecessary.

† So Kautzsch.

‡ *Cf.* Streane, Cambridge Bible.

* Zech. iv. 1.

† xxiii. 25–32, xxvii. 9, xxix. 8: *cf.* Deut. xiii. 1–5.

‡ *Cf.* Hosea ii. 23, "I will sow her unto Me in the earth" (or land), in reference to *Jezreel*, understood as "Whom God soweth" (R. V. margin).

§ i. 10–12.

‖ 2 Kings xxiii. 25.

¶ xv. 1–4.

shall be upon him." * With the fall of Jerusalem, a chapter in the history of Israel was concluded for ever; Jehovah blotted out the damning record of the past, and turned over a new leaf in the annals of His people. The account between Jehovah and the Israel of the monarchy was finally closed, and no penal balance was carried over to stand against the restored community.

The last portion of this chapter is so important that we must reserve it for separate treatment, but we may pause for a moment to consider the prophecy of the restoration of Ephraim from two points of view—the unity of Israel and the return of the ten tribes.

In the first place, this chapter is an eirenicon, intended to consign to oblivion the divisions and feuds of the Chosen People. After the fall of Samaria, the remnant of Israel had naturally looked to Judah for support and protection, and the growing weakness of Assyria had allowed the Jewish kings to exercise a certain authority over the territory of northern tribes. The same fate—the sack of the capital and the deportation of most of the inhabitants—had successively befallen Ephraim and Judah. His sense of the unity of the race was too strong to allow the prophet to be satisfied with the return of Judah and Benjamin, apart from the other tribes. Yet it would have been monstrous to suppose that Jehovah would bring back Ephraim from Assyria, and Judah from Babylon, only that they might resume their mutual hatred and suspicion. Even wild beasts are said not to rend one another when they are driven by floods to the same hill-top.

Thus various causes contributed to produce a kindlier feeling between the survivors of the catastrophes of Samaria and Jerusalem; and from henceforth those of the ten tribes who found their way back to Palestine lived in brotherly union with the other Jews. And, on the whole, the Jews have since remained united both as a race and a religious community. It is true that the relations of the later Jews to Samaria were somewhat at variance both with the letter and spirit of this prophecy, but that Samaria had only the slightest claim to be included in Israel. Otherwise the divisions between Hillel and Shammai, Sadducees and Pharisees, Karaites, Sephardim and Ashkenazim, Reformed and Unreformed Jews, have rather been legitimate varieties of opinion and practice within Judaism than a rendering asunder of the Israel of God.

Matters stand very differently with regard to the restoration of Ephraim. We know that individual members and families of the ten tribes were included in the new Jewish community, and that the Jews reoccupied Galilee and portions of Eastern Palestine. But the husbandmen who had planted vineyards on the hills of Samaria were violently repulsed by Ezra and Nehemiah, and were denied any part or lot in the restored Israel. The tribal inheritance of Ephraim and Manasseh was never reoccupied by Ephraimites and Manassites who came to worship Jehovah in His Temple at Jerusalem. There was no return of the ten tribes that in any way corresponded to the terms of this prophecy or that could rank with the return of their brethren. Our growing acquaintance with the races of the world seems likely to exclude even the possibility of any such restoration of Ephraim. Of the two divisions of Israel, so long united in common experiences of grace and chastisement, the one has been taken and the other left.

Christendom is the true heir of the ideals of Israel, but she is mostly content to inherit them as counsels of perfection. Isaiah † struck the keynote of this chapter when he prophesied that Ephraim should not envy Judah, nor Judah vex Ephraim. Our prophet, in the same generous spirit, propounds a programme of reconciliation. It might serve for a model to those who construct schemes for Christian Reunion. When two denominations are able to unite on such terms that the one admits the other to be the first-born of God, His darling child and precious in His sight, and the latter is willing to accept the former's central sanctuary as the headquarters of the united body, we shall have come some way towards realising this ancient Jewish ideal. Meanwhile Ephraim remains consumed with envy of Judah; and Judah apparently considers it her most sacred duty to vex Ephraim.

Moreover the disappearance of what was at one time the most flourishing branch of the Hebrew Church has many parallels in Church History. Again and again religious dissension has been one of the causes of political ruin, and the overthrow of a Christian state has sometimes involved the extinction of its religion. Christian thought and doctrine owe an immense debt to the great Churches of Northern Africa and Egypt. But these provinces were torn by the dissensions of ecclesiastical parties; and the quarrels of Donatists, Arians, and Catholics in North Africa, the endless controversies over the Person of Christ in Egypt, left them helpless before the Saracen invader. To-day the Church of Tertullian and Augustine is blotted out, and the Church of Origen and Clement is a miserable remnant. Similarly the ecclesiastical strife between Rome and Constantinople lost to Christendom some of the fairest provinces of Europe and Asia, and placed Christian races under the rule of the Turk.

Even now the cause of Christians in heathen and Mohammedan countries suffers from the jealousy of Christian states, and modern Churches sometimes avail themselves of this jealousy to try and oust their rivals from promising fields for mission work.

It is a melancholy reflection that Jeremiah's effort at reconciliation came too late, when the tribes whom it sought to reunite were hopelessly set asunder. Reconciliation, which involves a kind of mutual repentance, can ill afford to be deferred to the eleventh hour. In the last agonies of the Greek Empire, there was more than one formal reconciliation between the Eastern and Western Churches; but they also came too late, and could not survive the Empire which they failed to preserve.

* Ezek. xviii. 20: *cf.* Cheyne "Jeremiah" (Men of the Bible), x. 150.

† Isa. xi. 13.

CHAPTER XXXIII.

RESTORATION—IV. THE NEW COVENANT.

JEREMIAH xxxi. 31-38: *cf.* Hebrews viii.

"I will make a new covenant with the house of Israel and the house of Judah."—JER. xxxi. 31.

THE religious history of Israel in the Old Testament has for its epochs a series of covenants: Jehovah declared His gracious purposes towards His people, and made known the conditions upon which they were to enjoy His promised blessings; they, on their part, undertook to observe faithfully all that Jehovah commanded. We are told that covenants were made with Noah, after the Flood; with Abraham, when he was assured that his descendants should inherit the land of Canaan; at Sinai, when Israel first became a nation; with Joshua, after the Promised Land was conquered; and, at the close of Old Testament history, when Ezra and Nehemiah established the Pentateuch as the Code and Canon of Judaism.

One of the oldest sections of the Pentateuch, Exodus xx. 20-xxiii. 33, is called the "Book of the Covenant," * and Ewald named the Priestly Code the "Book of the Four Covenants." Judges and Samuel record no covenants between Jehovah and Israel; but the promise of permanence to the Davidic dynasty is spoken of as an everlasting covenant. Isaiah,† Amos, and Micah make no mention of the Divine covenants. Jeremiah, however, imitates Hosea‡ in emphasising this aspect of Jehovah's relation to Israel, and is followed in his turn by Ezekiel and II. Isaiah.

Jeremiah had played his part in establishing covenants between Israel and its God. He is not, indeed, even so much as mentioned in the account of Josiah's reformation; and it is not clear that he himself makes any express reference to it; so that some doubt must still be felt as to his share in that great movement. At the same time indirect evidence seems to afford proof of the common opinion that Jeremiah was active in the proceedings which resulted in the solemn engagement to observe the code of Deuteronomy. But yet another covenant occupies a chapter§ in the Book of Jeremiah, and in this case there is no doubt that the prophet was the prime mover in inducing the Jews to release their Hebrew slaves. This act of emancipation was adopted in obedience to an ordinance of Deuteronomy,‖ so that Jeremiah's experience of former covenants was chiefly connected with the code of Deuteronomy and the older Book of the Covenant upon which it was based.

The Restoration to which Jeremiah looked forward was to throw the Exodus into the shade, and to constitute a new epoch in the history of Israel more remarkable than the first settlement in Canaan. The nation was to be founded anew, and its regeneration would necessarily rest upon a New Covenant, which would supersede the Covenant of Sinai.

"Behold, the days come—it is the utterance of Jehovah—when I will enter into a new covenant with the House of Israel and the House of Judah: not according to the covenant into which I entered with your fathers, when I took them by the hand to bring them out of the land of Egypt."

The Book of the Covenant and Deuteronomy had both been editions of the Mosaic Covenant, and had neither been intended nor regarded as anything new. Whatever was fresh in them, either in form or substance, was merely the adaptation of existing ordinances to altered circumstances. But now the Mosaic Covenant was declared obsolete, the New Covenant was not to be, like Deuteronomy, merely a fresh edition of the earliest code. The Return from Babylon, like the primitive Migration from Ur and like the Exodus from Egypt, was to be the occasion of a new Revelation, placing the relations of Jehovah and His people on a new footing.

When Ezra and Nehemiah established, as the Covenant of the Restoration, yet another edition of the Mosaic ordinances, they were acting in the teeth of this prophecy—not because Jehovah had changed His purpose, but because the time of fulfilment had not yet come.*

The rendering of the next clause is uncertain, and, in any case, the reason given for setting aside the old covenant is not quite what might have been expected. The Authorised and Revised Versions translate: "Which My covenant they brake, although I was an husband unto them";† thus introducing that Old Testament figure of marriage between Jehovah and Israel which is transferred in Ephesians and the Apocalypse to Christ and the Church. The margin of the Revised Version has: "Forasmuch as they brake My covenant, although I was lord over them." There is little difference between these two translations, both of which imply that in breaking the covenant Israel was setting aside Jehovah's legitimate claim to obedience. A third translation, on much the same lines, would be "although I was Baal unto *or* over them";‡ Baal or ba'al being found for lord, husband, in ancient times as a name of Jehovah, and in Jeremiah's time as a name of heathen gods. Jeremiah is fond of paronomasia, and frequently refers to Baal, so that he may have been here deliberately ambiguous. The phrase might suggest to the Hebrew reader that Jehovah was the true lord or husband of Israel, and the true Baal or God, but that Israel had come to regard Him as a mere Baal, like one of the Baals of the heathen. "Forasmuch as they, on their part, set at nought My covenant; so that I, their true Lord, became to them as a mere heathen Baal." The covenant and the God who gave it were alike treated with contempt.

The Septuagint, which is quoted in Hebrews viii. 9, has another translation: "And I regarded them not."§ Unless this represents a different reading,‖ it is probably due to a feeling that the form of the Hebrew sentence required a close parallelism. Israel neglected to observe the covenant, and Jehovah ceased to feel any interest in Israel. But the idea of the latter clause seems alien to the context.

* Exod. xxiv. 7.
† *I. e.*, in the sections generally acknowledged.
‡ Hosea ii. 18, vi. 7, viii. 1.
§ xxxiv.
‖ *Cf.* xxxiv. 14 with Deut. xv. 12 and Exod. xxi. 2.

* *Cf.* Prof. Adeney's "Ezra, Nehemiah," etc., in Vol. III.
† So also Kautzsch, Reuss, Sugfried, and Stade. The same phrase is thus translated in iii. 14.
‡ "I was Baal" = "ba'alti."
§ ἠμέλησα.
‖ געלתי; געל occurs in xiv. 19, and is trarslated by A. and R. V. "loathed."

In any case, the new and better covenant is offered to Israel, after it has failed to observe the first covenant. This Divine procedure is not quite according to many of our theories. The law of ordinances is often spoken of as adapted to the childhood of the race. We set children easy tasks, and when these are successfully performed we require of them something more difficult. We grant them limited privileges, and if they make a good use of them the children are promoted to higher opportunities. We might perhaps have expected that when the Israelites failed to observe the Mosaic ordinances, they would have been placed under a narrower and harsher dispensation; yet their very failure leads to the promise of a better covenant still. Subsequent history, indeed, qualifies the strangeness of the Divine dealing. Only a remnant of Israel survived as the people of God. The Covenant of Ezra was very different from the New Covenant of Jeremiah; and the later Jews, as a community,* did not accept that dispensation of grace which ultimately realised Jeremiah's prophecy. In a narrow and unspiritual fashion the Jews of the Restoration observed the covenant of external ordinances; so that, in a certain sense, the Law was fulfilled before the new Kingdom of God was inaugurated. But if Isaiah and Jeremiah had reviewed the history of the restored community, they would have declined to receive it as, in any sense, the fulfilling of a Divine covenant. The Law of Moses was not fulfilled, but made void, by the traditions of the Pharisees. The fact therefore remains, that failure in the lower forms, so to speak, of God's school is still followed by promotion to higher privileges. However little we may be able to reconcile this truth with *a priori* views of Providence, it has analogies in nature, and reveals new depths of Divine love and greater resourcefulness of Divine grace. Boys whose early life is unsatisfactory nevertheless grow up into the responsibilities and privileges of manhood; and the wilful, disobedient child does not always make a bad man. We are apt to think that the highest form of development is steady, continuous, and serene, from good to better, from better to best. The real order is more awful and stupendous, combining good and evil, success and failure, victory and defeat, in its continuous advance through the ages. The wrath of man is not the only evil passion that praises God by its ultimate subservience to His purpose. We need not fear lest such Divine overruling of sin should prove any temptation to wrongdoing, seeing that it works, as in the exile of Israel, through the anguish and humiliation of the sinner.

The next verse explains the character of the New Covenant; once Jehovah wrote His law on tables of stone, but now:—

"This is the covenant which I will conclude with the House of Israel after those days—it is the utterance of Jehovah—
I will put My law within them, and will write it upon their heart;
And I will be their God, and they shall be My people."

These last words were an ancient formula for the immemorial relation of Jehovah and Israel, but they were to receive new fulness of meaning. The inner law, written on the heart, is in contrast to Mosaic ordinances. It has, therefore, two essential characteristics: first, it governs life, not by fixed external regulations, but by the continual control of heart and conscience by the Divine Spirit; secondly, obedience is rendered to the Divine Will, not from external compulsion, but because man's inmost nature is possessed by entire loyalty to God. The new law involves no alteration of the standards of morality or of theological doctrine, but it lays stress on the spiritual character of man's relation to God, and therefore on the fact that God is a spiritual and moral being. When man's obedience is claimed on the ground of God's irresistible power, and appeal is made to material rewards and punishments, God's personality is obscured and the way is opened for the deification of political or material Force. This doctrine of setting aside of ancient codes by the authority of the Inner Law is implied in many passages of our book. The superseding of the Mosaic Law is set forth by a most expressive symbol,* "When ye are multiplied and increased in the land, 'The Ark of the Covenant of Jehovah' shall no longer be the watchword of Israel: men shall neither think of the ark nor remember it; they shall neither miss the ark nor make another in its place." The Ark and the Mosaic Torah were inseparably connected; if the Ark was to perish and be forgotten, the Law must also be annulled.

Jeremiah moreover discerned with Paul that there was a law in the members warring against the Law of Jehovah: "The sin of Judah is written with a pen of iron, and with the point of a diamond: it is graven upon the table of their heart, and upon the horns of their altars." †

Hence the heart of the people had to be changed before they could enter into the blessings of the Restoration: "I will give them an heart to know Me, that I am Jehovah: and they shall be My people, and I will be their God: for they shall return unto Me with their whole heart." ‡ In the exposition of the symbolic purchase of Hanameel's field, Jehovah promises to make an everlasting covenant with His people, that He will always do them good and never forsake them. Such continual blessings imply that Israel will always be faithful. Jehovah no longer seeks to ensure their fidelity by an external law, with its alternate threats and promises: He will rather control the inner life by His grace. "I will give them one heart and one way, that they may fear Me for ever; . . . I will put My fear in their hearts, that they may not depart from Me." §

We must not, of course, suppose that these principles—of obedience from loyal enthusiasm, and of the guidance of heart and conscience by the Spirit of Jehovah—were new to the religion of Israel. They are implied in the idea of prophetic inspiration. When Saul went home to Gibeah, "there went with him a band of men, whose hearts God had touched." ‖ In Deuteronomy, Israel is commanded to "love Jehovah thy God with all thine heart, and with all thy soul, and with all thy might. And these words, which I command thee this day, shall be in thine heart." ¶

The novelty of Jeremiah's teaching is that these principles are made central in the New

* We usually underrate the proportion of Jews who embraced Christianity. Hellenistic Judaism disappeared as Christianity became widely diffused, and was probably for the most part absorbed into the new faith.

* iii. 14, slightly paraphrased.
† xvii. 1.
‡ xxxiv. 7.
§ xxxii. 39, 40.
‖ 1 Sam. x. 26.
¶ Deut. vi. 5, 6.

Covenant. Even Deuteronomy, which approaches so closely to the teaching of Jeremiah, was a new edition of the Covenant of the Exodus, an attempt to secure a righteous life by exhaustive rules and by external sanctions. Jeremiah had witnessed and probably assisted the effort to reform Judah by the enforcement of the Deuteronomic Code. But when Josiah's religious policy collapsed after his defeat and death at Megiddo, Jeremiah lost faith in elaborate codes, and turned from the letter to the spirit.

The next feature of the New Covenant naturally follows from its being written upon men's hearts by the finger of Jehovah:—

"Men shall no longer teach one another and teach each other, saying, Know ye Jehovah!
For all shall know Me, from the least to the greatest—it is the utterance of Jehovah."

In ancient times men could only "know Jehovah" and ascertain His will by resorting to some sanctuary, where the priests preserved and transmitted the sacred tradition and delivered the Divine oracles. Written codes scarcely altered the situation; copies would be few and far between, and still mostly in the custody of the priests. Whatever drawbacks arise from attaching supreme religious authority to a printed book were multiplied a thousandfold when codes could only be copied. But, in the New Israel, men's spiritual life would not be at the mercy of pen, ink, and paper, of scribe and priest. The man who had a book and could read would no longer be able, with the self-importance of exclusive knowledge, to bid his less fortunate brethren to know Jehovah. He Himself would be the one teacher, and His instruction would fall, like the sunshine and the rain, upon all hearts alike.

And yet again Israel is assured that past sin shall not hinder the fulfilment of this glorious vision:—

"For I will forgive their iniquity, and their sin will I remember no more."

Recurring to the general topic of the Restoration of Israel, the prophet affixes the double seal of two solemn Divine asseverations. Of old, Jehovah had promised Noah: "While the earth remaineth, seedtime and harvest, cold and heat, summer and winter, day and night, shall not cease." * Now He promises that while sun and moon and stars and sea continue in their appointed order, Israel shall not cease from being a nation. And, again, Jehovah will not cast off Israel on account of its sin till the height of heaven can be measured and the foundations of the earth searched out.†

* Gen. viii. 22 (J.).

† Verses 35-37 occur in the LXX. in the order 37, 35, 36. They are considered by many critics to be a later addition. The most remarkable feature of the paragraph is the clause translated by the Authorised Version "which divideth [Revised Version, text "stirreth up," margin "stilleth"] the sea when the waves thereof roar; The Lord of Hosts is His name." This whole clause is taken word for word from Isa. li. 15, "I am Jehovah thy God, which stirreth up," etc. It seems clear that either this clause or 35-37 as a whole were added by an editor acquainted with II. Isaiah. The prophecy, as it stands in the Masoretic text, is concluded by a detailed description of the site of the restored Jerusalem. The contrast between the glorious vision of the New Israel and these architectural specifications is almost grotesque. Verses 38-40 are regarded by many as a later addition; and even if they are by Jeremiah, they form an independent prophecy and have no connection with the rest of the chapter. Our knowledge of the geographical points mentioned is not sufficient to enable us to define the site assigned to the restored city. The point of verse 40 is that the most unclean districts of the ancient city shall partake of the sanctity of the New Jerusalem.

CHAPTER XXXIV.

RESTORATION—V. REVIEW.

JEREMIAH xxx.-xxxiii.

In reviewing these chapters we must be careful not to suppose that Jeremiah knew all that would ultimately result from his teaching. When he declared that the conditions of the New Covenant would be written, not in a few parchments, but on every heart, he laid down a principle which involved the most characteristic teaching of the New Testament and the Reformers, and which might seem to justify extreme mysticism. When we read these prophecies in the light of history, they seem to lead by a short and direct path to the Pauline doctrines of Faith and Grace. Constraining grace is described in the words: "I will put My fear in their hearts, that they shall not depart from Me." * Justification by faith instead of works substitutes the response of the soul to the Spirit of God for conformity to a set of external regulations—the writing on the heart for the carving of ordinances on stone. Yet, as Newton's discovery of the law of gravitation did not make him aware of all that later astronomers have discovered, so Jeremiah did not anticipate Paul and Augustine, Luther and Calvin: he was only their forerunner. Still less did he intend to affirm all that has been taught by the Brothers of the Common Life or the Society of Friends. We have followed the Epistle to the Hebrews in interpreting his prophecy of the New Covenant as abrogating the Mosaic code and inaugurating a new departure upon entirely different lines. This view is supported by his attitude towards the Temple, and especially the Ark. At the same time we must not suppose that Jeremiah contemplated the summary and entire abolition of the previous dispensation. He simply delivers his latest message from Jehovah, without bringing its contents into relation with earlier truth, without indeed waiting to ascertain for himself how the old and the new were to be combined. But we may be sure that the Divine writing on the heart would have included much that was already written in Deuteronomy, and that both books and teachers would have had their place in helping men to recognise and interpret the inner leadings of the Spirit.

In rising from the perusal of these chapters the reader is tempted to use the prophet's words with a somewhat different meaning: "I awaked and looked about me, and felt that I had had a pleasant dream." † Renan, with cynical frankness, heads a chapter on such prophecies with the title "Pious Dreams." While Jeremiah's glowing utterances rivet our attention, the gracious words fall like balm upon our aching hearts, and we seem, like the Apostle, caught up into Paradise. But as soon as we try to connect our visions with any realities, past, present, or in prospect, there comes a rude awakening. The restored community attained to no New Covenant, but was only found worthy of a fresh edition of the written code. Instead of being

* xxxii. 40.

† xxxi. 26.

committed to the guidance of the ever-present Spirit of Jehovah, they were placed under a rigid and elaborate system of externals—"carnal ordinances, concerned with meats and drinks and divers washings, imposed until a time of reformation." * They still remained under the covenant "from Mount Sinai, bearing children unto bondage, which is Hagar. Now this Hagar is Mount Sinai in Arabia, and answereth to the Jerusalem that now is: for she is in bondage with her children." †

For these bondservants of the letter, there arose no David, no glorious Scion of the ancient stock. For a moment the hopes of Zechariah rested on Zerubbabel, but this Branch quickly withered away and was forgotten. We need not underrate the merits and services of Ezra and Nehemiah, of Simon the Just and Judas Maccabæus; and yet we cannot find any one of them who answers to the Priestly King of Jeremiah's visions. The new growth of Jewish royalty came to an ignominious end in Aristobulus, Hyrcanus, and the Herods, Antichrists rather than Messiahs.

The Reunion of long-divided Israel is for the most part a misnomer; there was no healing of the wound, and the offending member was cut off.

Even now, when the leaven of the Kingdom has been working in the lump of humanity for nearly two thousand years, any suggestion that these chapters are realised in Modern Christianity would seem cruel irony. Renan accuses Christianity of having quickly forgotten the programme which its Founder borrowed from the prophets, and of having become a religion like other religions, a religion of priests and sacrifices, of external observances and superstitions.‡ It is sometimes asserted that Protestants lack faith and courage to trust to any law written on the heart, and cling to a printed book, as if there were no Holy Spirit—as if the Branch of David had borne fruit once for all, and Christ were dead. The movement for Christian Reunion seems thus far chiefly to emphasise the feuds that make the Church a kingdom divided against itself.

But we must not allow the obvious shortcomings of Christendom to blind us to brighter aspects of truth. Both in the Jews of the Restoration and in the Church of Christ we have a real fulfilment of Jeremiah's prophecies. The fulfilment is no less real because it is utterly inadequate. Prophecy is a guide-post and not a milestone; it shows the way to be trodden, not the duration of the journey. Jews and Christians have fulfilled Jeremiah's prophecies because they have advanced by the road along which he pointed towards the spiritual city of his vision. The "pious dreams" of a little group of enthusiasts have become the ideals and hopes of humanity. Even Renan ranks himself among the disciples of Jeremiah: "The seed sown in religious tradition by inspired Israelites will not perish; all of us who seek a God without priests, a revelation without prophets, a covenant written in the heart, are in many respects the disciples of these ancient fanatics (*ces vieux égarés*)." §

The Judaism of the Return, with all its faults and shortcomings, was still an advance in the direction Jeremiah had indicated. However ritualistic the Pentateuch may seem to us, it was far removed from exclusive trust in ritual. Where the ancient Israelite had relied upon correct observance of the forms of his sanctuary, the Torah of Ezra introduced a large moral and spiritual element, which served to bring the soul into direct fellowship with Jehovah. "Pity and humanity are pushed to their utmost limits, always of course in the bosom of the family of Israel." * The Torah moreover included the great commands to love God and man, which once for all placed the religion of Israel on a spiritual basis. If the Jews often attached more importance to the letter and form of Revelation than to its substance, and were more careful for ritual and external observances than for inner righteousness, we have no right to cast a stone at them.

It is a curious phenomenon that after the time of Ezra the further developments of the Torah were written no longer on parchment, but, in a certain sense on the heart. The decisions of the rabbis interpreting the Pentateuch, "the fence which they made round the law," were not committed to writing, but learnt by heart and handed down by oral tradition. Possibly this custom was partly due to Jeremiah's prophecy. It is a strange illustration of the way in which theology sometimes wrests the Scriptures to its own destruction, that the very prophecy of the triumph of the spirit over the letter was made of none effect by a literal interpretation.

Nevertheless, though Judaism moved only a very little way towards Jeremiah's ideal, yet it did move, its religion was distinctly more spiritual than that of ancient Israel. Although Judaism claimed finality and did its best to secure that no future generation should make further progress, yet in spite of, nay, even by means of, Pharisee and Sadducee, the Jews were prepared to receive and transmit that great resurrection of prophetic teaching which came through Christ.

If even Judaism did not altogether fail to conform itself to Jeremiah's picture of the New Israel, clearly Christianity must have shaped itself still more fully according to his pattern. In the Old Testament both the idea and the name of a "New Covenant," † superseding that of Moses, are peculiar to Jeremiah, and the New Testament consistently represents the Christian dispensation as a fulfilment of Jeremiah's prophecy. Besides the express and detailed application in the Epistle to the Hebrews, Christ instituted the Lord's Supper as the Sacrament of His New Covenant—"This cup is the New Covenant in My Blood"; ‡ and St. Paul speaks of himself as "a minister of the New Covenant." § Christianity has not been unworthy of the claim made on its behalf by its Founder, but has realised, at any rate in some measure, the visible peace, prosperity, and unity of Jeremiah's New Israel,

* Heb. ix. 10.
† Gal. iv. 24, 25.
‡ "Histoire du Peuple d'Israel," iii. 340.
§ Renan, iii. 340.

* Renan, iii. 425.
† We have the idea of a spiritual covenant in Isa. lix. 21, "This is My covenant with them: . . . My spirit that is upon thee, and My words which I have put in thy mouth, shall not depart out of thy mouth, nor out of the mouth of thy seed, nor out of the mouth of thy seed's seed, . . . from henceforth and for ever"; but nothing is said as to a *new* covenant.
‡ Luke xxii. 20; 1 Cor. xi. 25. The word "new" is omitted by Codd. Sin. and Vat. and the R. V. in Matt. xxvi. 28 and Mark xiv. 24.
§ 2 Cor. iii. 6.

as well as the spirituality of his New Covenant. Christendom has its hideous blots of misery and sin, but, on the whole, the standard of material comfort and intellectual culture has been raised to a high average throughout the bulk of a vast population. Internal order and international concord have made enormous strides since the time of Jeremiah. If an ancient Israelite could witness the happy security of a large proportion of English workmen and French peasants, he would think that many of the predictions of his prophets had been fulfilled. But the advance of large classes to a prosperity once beyond the dreams of the most sanguine only brings out in darker relief the wretchedness of their less fortunate brethren. In view of the growing knowledge and enormous resources of modern society, any toleration of its cruel wrongs is an unpardonable sin. Social problems are doubtless urgent because a large minority are miserable, but they are rendered still more urgent by the luxury of many and the comfort of most. The high average of prosperity shows that we fail to right our social evils, not for want of power, but for want of devotion. Our civilisation is a Dives, at whose gate Lazarus often finds no crumbs.

Again Christ's Kingdom of the New Covenant has brought about a larger unity. We have said enough elsewhere on the divisions of the Church. Doubtless we are still far from realising the ideals of chapter xxxi., but, at any rate, they have been recognised as supreme, and have worked for harmony and fellowship in the world. Ephraim and Judah are forgotten, but the New Covenant has united into brotherhood a worldwide array of races and nations. There are still divisions in the Church, and a common religion will not always do away with national enmities; but in spite of all, the influence of our common Christianity has done much to knit the nations together and promote mutual amity and goodwill. The vanguard of the modern world has accepted Christ as its standard and ideal, and has thus attained an essential unity, which is not destroyed by minor differences and external divisions.

And, finally, the promise that the New Covenant should be written on the heart is far on the way towards fulfilment. If Roman and Greek orthodoxy interposes the Church between the soul and Christ, yet the inspiration claimed for the Church to-day is, at any rate in some measure, that of the living Spirit of Christ speaking to the souls of living men. On the other hand, a predilection for Rabbinical methods of exegesis sometimes interferes with the influence and authority of the Bible. Yet in reality there is no serious attempt to take away the key of knowledge or to forbid the individual soul to receive the direct teaching of the Holy Ghost. The Reformers established the right of private judgment in the interpretation of the Scriptures; and the interpretation of the Library of Sacred Literature, the spiritual harvest of a thousand years, affords ample scope for reverent development of our knowledge of God.

One group of Jeremiah's prophecies has indeed been entirely fulfilled. In Christ God has raised up a Branch of Righteousness unto David, and through Him judgment and righteousness are wrought in the earth.*

* xxxiii. 15.

EPILOGUE.

CHAPTER XXXV.

JEREMIAH AND CHRIST.

"Jehovah thy God will raise up unto thee a prophet from amongst thee, of thy brethren, like unto me; unto him shall ye hearken."—DEUT. xviii. 15.

"Jesus . . . asked His disciples, saying Who do men say that the Son of Man is? And they said, Some say John the Baptist; some, Elijah: and others, Jeremiah, or one of the prophets."—MATT. xvi. 13, 14.

ENGLISH feeling about Jeremiah has long ago been summed up and stereotyped in the single word "jeremiad." The contempt and dislike which this word implies are partly due to his supposed authorship of Lamentations; but, to say the least, the Book of Jeremiah is not sufficiently cheerful to remove the impression created by the linked wailing, long drawn out, which has been commonly regarded as an appendix to its prophecies. We can easily understand the unpopularity of the prophet of doom in modern Christendom. Such prophets are seldom acceptable, except to the enemies of the people whom they denounce; and even ardent modern advocates of Jew-baiting would not be entirely satisfied with Jeremiah—they would resent his patriotic sympathy with sinful and suffering Judah. Most modern Christians have ceased to regard the Jews as monsters of iniquity, whose chastisement should give profound satisfaction to every sincere believer. History has recorded but few of the crimes which provoked and justified our prophet's fierce indignation, and those of which we do read repel our interest by a certain lack of the picturesque, so that we do not take the trouble to realise their actual and intense wickedness. Ahab is a by-word, but how many people know anything about Ishmael ben Nethaniah? The cruelty of the nobles and the unctuous cant of their prophetic allies are forgotten in—nay, they seem almost atoned for by—the awful calamities that befell Judah and Jerusalem. Jeremiah's memory may even be said to have suffered from the speedy and complete fulfilment of his prophecies. The national ruin was a triumphant vindication of his teaching, and his disciples were eager to record every utterance in which he had foretold the coming doom. Probably the book, in its present form, gives an exaggerated impression of the stress which Jeremiah laid upon this topic.

Moreover, while the prophet's life is essentially tragic, its drama lacks an artistic close and climax. Again and again Jeremiah took his life in his hand, but the good confession which he witnessed for so long does not culminate in the crown of martyrdom. A final scene like the death of John the Baptist would have won our sympathy and conciliated our criticism.

We thus gather that the popular attitude towards Jeremiah rests on a superficial appreciation of his character and work; it is not difficult to discern that a careful examination of his history establishes important claims on the veneration and gratitude of the Christian Church.

For Judaism was not slow to pay her tribute of admiration and reverence to Jeremiah as to a Patron Saint and Confessor. His prophecy of the Restoration of Israel is appealed to in Ezra and Daniel; and the Hebrew Chronicler, who says as little as he can of Isaiah, adds to the references made by the Book of Kings to Jeremiah. We have already seen that apocryphal legends clustered round his honoured name. He was credited with having concealed the Tabernacle and the Ark in the caves of Sinai.* On the eve of a great victory he appeared to Judas Maccabæus, in a vision, as "a man distinguished by grey hairs, and a majestic appearance; but something wonderful and exceedingly magnificent was the grandeur about him," and was made known to Judas as a "lover of the brethren, who prayeth much for the people and for the holy city, to wit, Jeremiah the prophet of God. And Jeremiah stretching forth his right hand delivered over to Judas a sword of gold."† The Son of Sirach does not fail to include Jeremiah in his praise of famous men;‡ and there is an apocryphal epistle purporting to be written by our prophet.§ It is noteworthy that in the New Testament Jeremiah is only mentioned by name in the Judaistic Gospel of St. Matthew.

In the Christian Church, notwithstanding the lack of popular sympathy, earnest students of the prophet's life and words have ranked him with some of the noblest characters of history. A modern writer enumerates as amongst those with whom he has been compared Cassandra, Phocion, Demosthenes, Dante, Milton, and Savonarola.‖ The list might easily be enlarged, but another parallel has been drawn which has supreme claims on our consideration. The Jews in New Testament times looked for the return of Elijah or Jeremiah to usher in Messiah's reign; and it seemed to some among them that the character and teaching of Jesus of Nazareth identified him with the ancient prophet who had been commissioned "to root out, pull down, destroy and throw down, to build and to plant." The suggested comparison has often been developed, but undue stress has been laid on such accidental and external circumstances as the prophet's celibacy and the statement that he was "sanctified from the womb." The discussion of such details does not greatly lend itself to edification. But it has also been pointed out that there is an essential resemblance between the circumstances and mission of Jeremiah and his Divine Successor, and to this some little space may be devoted.

Jeremiah and our Lord appeared at similar crises in the history of Israel and of revealed religion. The prophet foretold the end of the Jewish monarchy, the destruction of the First Temple and of ancient Jerusalem; Christ, in like manner, announced the end of the restored Israel, the destruction of the Second Temple and of the newer Jerusalem. In both cases the doom of the city was followed by the dispersion and captivity of the people. At both eras the religion of Jehovah was supposed to be indissolubly bound up with the Temple and its ritual; and, as we have seen, Jeremiah, like Stephen and Paul and our Lord Himself, was charged with blasphemy because he predicted its coming ruin. The prophet, like Christ, was at variance with the prevalent religious sentiment of his time and with what claimed to be orthodoxy. Both were regarded and treated by the great body of contemporary religious teachers as dangerous and intolerable heretics; and their heresy, as we have said, was practically one and the same. To the champions of the Temple their teaching seemed purely destructive, an irreverent attack upon fundamental doctrines and indispensable institutions. But the very opposite was the truth; they destroyed nothing but what deserved to perish. Both in Jeremiah's time and in our Lord's, men tried to assure themselves of the permanence of erroneous dogmas and obsolete rites by proclaiming that these were of the essence of Divine Revelation. In either age to succeed in this effort would have been to plunge the world into spiritual darkness: the light of Hebrew prophecy would have been extinguished by the Captivity, or, again, the hope of the Messiah would have melted away like a mirage, when the legions of Titus and Hadrian dispelled so many Jewish dreams. But before the catastrophe came, Jeremiah had taught men that Jehovah's Temple and city were destroyed of His own set purpose, because of the sins of His people; there was no excuse for supposing that He was discredited by the ruin of the place where He had once chosen to set His Name. Thus the Captivity was not the final page in the history of Hebrew religion, but the opening of a new chapter. In like manner Christ and His Apostles, more especially Paul, finally dissociated Revelation from the Temple and its ritual, so that the light of Divine truth was not hidden under the bushel of Judaism, but shone forth upon the whole world from the many-branched candle-stick of the Universal Church.

Again, in both cases, not only was ancient faith rescued from the ruin of human corruption and commentary, but the purging away of the old leaven made room for a positive statement of new teaching. Jeremiah announced a new covenant—that is, a formal and complete change in the conditions and method of man's service to God and God's beneficence to men. The ancient Church, with its sanctuary, its clergy, and its ritual, was to be superseded by a new order, without sanctuary, clergy, or ritual, wherein every man would enjoy immediate fellowship with his God. This great idea was virtually ignored by the Jews of the Restoration, but it was set forth afresh by Christ and His Apostles. The "New Covenant" was declared to be ratified by His sacrifice, and was confirmed anew at every commemoration of His death. We read in John iv. 21-23: "The hour cometh, when neither in this mountain, nor in Jerusalem, shall ye worship the Father. . . . The hour cometh, and now is, when the true worshippers shall worship the Father in spirit and truth."

Thus when we confess that the Church is built upon the foundation of the Prophets and Apostles, we have to recognise that to this foundation Jeremiah's ministry supplied indispensable elements, alike by its positive and in its negative parts. This fact was manifest even to Renan, who fully shared the popular prejudices against Jeremiah. Nothing short of Christianity, according to him, is the realisation of the prophet's dream: "Il ajoute un facteur essentiel à l'œuvre humaine; Jérémie est, avant Jean-Baptiste, l'homme qui a le plus contribué à la fondation du Christianisme; il doit compter, malgré la distance des siècles, entre les précurseurs immédiats de Jésus." *

* 2 Macc. ii. 1-8. † 2 Macc. xv. 12-16. ‡ Ecclus. xlix. 6, 7.
§ Sometimes appended to the Book of Baruch as a sixth chapter.
‖ Smith's "Dictionary of the Bible," art. "Jeremiah."

* "Hist.," iii. 251, 305.

THE BOOK OF EZEKIEL.

PREFACE.

In this volume I have endeavoured to present the substance of Ezekiel's prophecies in a form intelligible to students of the English Bible. I have tried to make the exposition a fairly adequate guide to the sense of the text, and to supply such information as seemed necessary to elucidate the historical importance of the prophet's teaching. Where I have departed from the received text I have usually indicated in a note the nature of the change introduced. Whilst I have sought to exercise an independent judgment on all the questions touched upon, the book has no pretensions to rank as a contribution to Old Testament scholarship.

The works on Ezekiel to which I am chiefly indebted are: Ewald's "Propheten des Alten Bundes" (vol. ii.); Smend's "Der Prophet Ezechiel erklärt" ("Kurzgefasstes Exegetisches Handbuch zum A. T."); Cornill's "Das Buch des Proph. Ezechiel"; and, above all, Dr. A. B. Davidson's commentary in the "Cambridge Bible for Schools," my obligations to which are almost continuous. In a less degree I have been helped by the commentaries of Hävernick and Orelli, by Valeton's "Viertal Voorlezingen" (iii.), and by Gautier's "La Mission du Prophète Ezechiel." Amongst works of a more general character special acknowledgment is due to "The Old Testament in the Jewish Church" and "The Religion of the Semites" by the late Dr. Robertson Smith.

I wish also to express my gratitude to two friends—the Rev. A. Alexander, Dundee, and the Rev. G. Steven, Edinburgh—who have read most of the work in manuscript or in proof, and made many valuable suggestions.

CONTENTS.

PART I.

THE PREPARATION AND CALL OF THE PROPHET.

PART II.

PROPHECIES RELATING MAINLY TO THE DESTRUCTION OF JERUSALEM.

PART III.

PROPHECIES AGAINST FOREIGN NATIONS.

PART IV.

THE FORMATION OF THE NEW ISRAEL.

PART V.

THE IDEAL THEOCRACY.

THE BOOK OF EZEKIEL.

BY THE REV. JOHN SKINNER, M. A.

PART I.

THE PREPARATION AND CALL OF THE PROPHET.

CHAPTER I.

DECLINE AND FALL OF THE JEWISH STATE.

EZEKIEL is a prophet of the Exile. He was one of the priests who went into captivity with King Jehoiachin in the year 597, and the whole of his prophetic career falls after that event. Of his previous life and circumstances we have no direct information, beyond the facts that he was a priest and that his father's name was Buzi. One or two inferences, however, may be regarded as reasonably certain. We know that the first deportation of Judæans to Babylon was confined to the nobility, the men of war, and the craftsmen (2 Kings xxiv. 14-16); and since Ezekiel was neither a soldier nor an artisan, his place in the train of captives must have been due to his social position. He must have belonged to the upper ranks of the priesthood, who formed part of the aristocracy of Jerusalem. He was thus a member of the house of Zadok; and his familiarity with the details of the Temple ritual makes it probable that he had actually officiated as a priest in the national sanctuary. Moreover, a careful study of the book gives the impression that he was no longer a young man at the time when he received his call to the prophetic office. He appears as one whose views of life are already matured, who has outlived the buoyancy and enthusiasm of youth, and learned to estimate the moral possibilities of life with the sobriety that comes through experience. This impression is confirmed by the fact that he was married and had a house of his own from the commencement of his work, and probably at the time of his captivity. But the most important fact of all is that Ezekiel had lived through a period of unprecedented public calamity, and one fraught with the most momentous consequences for the future of religion. Moving in the highest circles of society, in the centre of the national life, he must have been fully cognisant of the grave events in which no thoughtful observer could fail to recognise the tokens of the approaching dissolution of the Hebrew state. Amongst the influences that prepared him for his prophetic mission, a leading place must therefore be assigned to the teaching of history; and we cannot commence our study of his prophecies better than by a brief survey of the course of events that led up to the turning-point of his own career, and at the same time helped to form his conception of God's providential dealings with His people Israel.

At the time of the prophet's birth the kingdom of Judah was still a nominal dependency of the great Assyrian empire. From about the middle of the seventh century, however, the power of Nineveh had been on the wane. Her energies had been exhausted in the suppression of a determined revolt in Babylonia. Media and Egypt had recovered their independence, and there were many signs that a new crisis in the affairs of nations was at hand.

The first historic event which has left discernible traces in the writings of Ezekiel is an irruption of Scythian barbarians, which took place in the reign of Josiah (*cir.* 626). Strangely enough, the historical books of the Old Testament contain no record of this remarkable invasion, although its effects on the political situation of Judah were important and far-reaching. According to Herodotus, Assyria was already hard pressed by the Medes, when suddenly the Scythians burst through the passes of the Caucasus, defeated the Medes, and committed extensive ravages throughout Western Asia for a period of twenty-eight years. They are said to have contemplated the invasion of Egypt, and to have actually reached the Philistine territory, when by some means they were induced to withdraw.* Judah therefore was in imminent danger, and the terror inspired by these destructive hordes is reflected in the prophecies of Zephaniah and Jeremiah, who saw in the northern invaders the heralds of the great day of Jehovah. The force of the storm, however, was probably spent before it reached Palestine, and it seems to have swept past along the coast, leaving the mountain land of Israel untouched. Although Ezekiel was not old enough to have remembered the panic caused by these movements, the report of them would be one of the earliest memories of his childhood, and it made a lasting impression on his mind. One of his later prophecies, that against Gog, is coloured by such reminiscences, the last judgment on the heathen being represented under forms suggested by a Scythian invasion (chaps. xxxviii., xxxix.). We may note also that in chap. xxxii. the names of Meshech and Tubal occur in the list of conquering nations who have already gone down to the under-world. These northern peoples formed the kernel of the army of Gog, and the only occasion on which they can be supposed to have played the part of great conquerors in the past is in connection with the Scythian devastations, in which they probably had a share.

The withdrawal of the Scythians from the neighbourhood of Palestine was followed by the great reformation which made the eighteenth year of Josiah an epoch in the history of Israel. The conscience of the nation had been quickened by its escape from so great a peril, and the time was favourable for carrying out the changes which were necessary in order to bring the religious practice of the country into conformity with the requirements of the Law. The outstanding feature of the movement was the discovery of the book of Deuteronomy in the Temple, and the ratification of a solemn league and covenant, by which the king, princes, and people pledged themselves to carry out its demands. This took place in the year 621, some-

* Herodotus, i. 103-106.

where near the time of Ezekiel's birth.* The prophet's youth was therefore spent in the wake of the reformation; and although the first hopes cherished by its promoters may have died away before he was able to appreciate its tendencies, we may be sure that he received from it impulses which continued with him to the end of his life. We may perhaps allow ourselves to conjecture that his father belonged to that section of the priesthood which, under Hilkiah its head, co-operated with the king in the task of reform, and desired to see a pure worship established in the Temple. If so, we can readily understand how the reforming spirit passed into the very fibre of Ezekiel's mind. To how great an extent his thinking was influenced by the ideas of Deuteronomy appears from almost every page of his prophecies.

There was yet another way in which the Scythian invasion influenced the prospects of the Hebrew kingdom. Although the Scythians appear to have rendered an immediate service to Assyria by saving Nineveh from the first attack of the Medes, there is little doubt that their ravages throughout the northern and western parts of the empire prepared the way for its ultimate collapse, and weakened its hold on the outlying provinces. Accordingly we find that Josiah, in pursuance of his scheme of reformation, exercised a freedom of action beyond the boundaries of his own land which would not have been tolerated if Assyria had retained her old vigour. Patriotic visions of an independent Hebrew monarchy seem to have combined with new-born zeal for a pure national religion to make the latter part of Josiah's reign the short "Indian summer" of Israel's national existence.

The period of partial independence was brought to an end about 607 by the fall of Nineveh before the united forces of the Medes and Babylonians. In itself this event was of less consequence to the history of Judah than might be supposed. The Assyrian empire vanished from the earth with a completeness which is one of the surprises of history; but its place was taken by the new Babylonian empire, which inherited its policy, its administration, and the best part of its provinces. The seat of empire was transferred from Nineveh to Babylon; but any other change which was felt at Jerusalem was due solely to the exceptional vigour and ability of its first monarch, Nebuchadnezzar.

The real turning-point in the destinies of Israel came a year or two earlier with the defeat and death of Josiah at Megiddo. About the year 608, while the fate of Nineveh still hung in the balance, Pharaoh Necho prepared an expedition to the Euphrates, with the object of securing himself in the possession of Syria. It was assuredly no feeling of loyalty to his Assyrian suzerain which prompted Josiah to throw himself across Necho's path. He acted as an independent monarch, and his motives were no doubt the loftiest that ever urged a king to a dangerous, not to say foolhardy, enterprise. The zeal with which the crusade against idolatry and false worship had been prosecuted seems to have begotten a confidence on the part of the king's advisers that the hand of Jehovah was with them, and that His help might be reckoned on in any undertaking entered upon in His name. One would like to know what the prophet Jeremiah said about the venture; but probably the defence of Jehovah's land seemed so obvious a duty of the Davidic king that he was not even consulted. It was the determination to maintain the inviolability of the land which was Jehovah's sanctuary that encouraged Josiah, in defiance of every prudential consideration, to endeavour by force to intercept the passage of the Egyptian army. The disaster that followed gave the death-blow to this illusion and the shallow optimism which sprang from it. There was an end of idealism in politics; and the ruling class in Jerusalem fell back on the old policy of vacillation between Egypt and her eastern rival which had always been the snare of Jewish statesmanship. And with Josiah's political ideal the faith on which it was based also gave way. It seemed that the experiment of exclusive reliance on Jehovah as the guardian of the nation's interests had been tried and had failed, and so the death of the last good king of Judah was a signal for a great outburst of idolatry, in which every divine power was invoked and every form of worship sedulously practised, in order to sustain the courage of men who were resolved to fight to the death for their national existence.

By the time of Josiah's death Ezekiel was able to take an intelligent interest in public affairs. He lived through the troubled period that ensued in the full consciousness of its disastrous import for the fortunes of his people, and occasional references to it are to be found in his writings. He remembers and commiserates the sad fate of Jehoahaz, the king of the people's choice, who was dethroned and imprisoned by Pharaoh Necho during the short interval of Egyptian supremacy. The next king, Jehoiakim, received the throne as a vassal of Egypt, on the condition of paying a heavy annual tribute. After the battle of Carchemish, in which Necho was defeated by Nebuchadnezzar and driven out of Syria, Jehoiakim transferred his allegiance to the Babylonian monarch; but after three years' service he revolted, encouraged no doubt by the usual promises of support from Egypt. The incursions of marauding bands of Chaldæans, Syrians, Moabites, and Ammonites, instigated doubtless from Babylon, kept him in play until Nebuchadnezzar was free to devote his attention to the western part of his empire. Before that time arrived, however, Jehoiakim had died, and was followed by his son Jehoiachin. This prince was hardly seated on the throne, when a Babylonian army, with Nebuchadnezzar at its head, appeared before the gates of Jerusalem. The siege ended in a capitulation, and the king, the queen-mother, the army and nobility, a section of the priests and the prophets, and all the skilled artisans were transported to Babylonia (597).

With this event the history of Ezekiel may be said to begin. But in order to understand the conditions under which his ministry was exercised, we must try to realise the situation created by this first removal of Judæan captives. From this time to the final capture of Jerusalem, a period of eleven years, the national life was broken into two streams, which ran in parallel channels, one in Judah and the other in Babylon. The object of the captivity was of course to deprive the nation of its natural leaders, its

* If the "thirtieth year" of chap. i. 1 could refer to the prophet's age at the time of his call, his birth would fall in the very year in which the Law Book was found. Although that interpretation is extremely improbable, he can hardly have been much more, or less, than thirty years old at the time.

head and its hands, and leave it incapable of organised resistance to the Chaldæans. In this respect Nebuchadnezzar simply adopted the traditional policy of the later Assyrian kings, only he applied it with much less rigour than they were accustomed to display. Instead of making nearly a clean sweep of the conquered population, and filling the gap by colonists from a distant part of his empire, as had been done in the case of Samaria, he contented himself with removing the more dangerous elements of the state, and making a native prince responsible for the government of the country. The result showed how greatly he had underrated the fierce and fanatical determination which was already a part of the Jewish character. Nothing in the whole story is more wonderful than the rapidity with which the enfeebled remnant in Jerusalem recovered their military efficiency, and prepared a more resolute defence than the unbroken nation had been able to offer.

The exiles, on the other hand, succeeded in preserving most of their national peculiarities under the very eyes of their conquerors. Of their temporal condition very little is known beyond the fact that they found themselves in tolerably easy circumstances, with the opportunity to acquire property and amass wealth. The advice which Jeremiah sent them from Jerusalem, that they should identify themselves with the interests of Babylon, and live settled and orderly lives in peaceful industry and domestic happiness (Jer. xxix. 5-7), shows that they were not treated as prisoners or as slaves. They appear to have been distributed in villages in the fertile territory of Babylon, and to have formed themselves into separate communities under the elders, who were the natural authorities in a simple Semitic society. The colony in which Ezekiel lived was located in Tel Abib, near the *Nahr* (river or canal) Kebar, but neither the river nor the settlement can now be identified. The Kebar, if not the name of an arm of the Euphrates itself, was probably one of the numerous irrigating canals which intersected in all parts the great alluvial plain of the Euphrates and Tigris.* In this settlement the prophet had his own house, where the people were free to visit him, and social life in all probability differed little from that in a small provincial town in Palestine. That, to be sure, was a great change for the quondam aristocrats of Jerusalem, but it was not a change to which they could not readily adapt themselves.

Of much greater importance, however, is the state of mind which prevailed amongst these exiles. And here again the remarkable thing is their intense preoccupation with matters national and Israelitic. A lively intercourse with the mother country was kept up, and the exiles were perfectly informed of all that was going on in Jerusalem. There were, no doubt, personal and selfish reasons for their keen interest in the doings of their countrymen at home. The antipathy which existed between the two branches of the Jewish people was extreme. The exiles had left their children behind them (xxiv. 21, 25) to suffer under the reproach of their fathers' misfortunes. They appear also to have been compelled to sell their estates hurriedly on the eve of their departure, and such transactions, necessarily turning to the advantage of the purchasers, left a deep grudge in the breasts of the sellers. Those who remained in the land exulted in the calamity which had brought so much profit to themselves, and thought themselves perfectly secure in so doing because they regarded their brethren as men driven out for their sins from Jehovah's heritage. The exiles on their part affected the utmost contempt for the pretensions of the upstart plebeians who were carrying things with a high hand in Jerusalem. Like the French *Emigrés* in the time of the Revolution, they no doubt felt that their country was being ruined for want of proper guidance and experienced statesmanship. Nor was it altogether patrician prejudice that gave them this feeling of their own superiority. Both Jeremiah and Ezekiel regard the exiles as the better part of the nation, and the nucleus of the Messianic community of the future. For the present, indeed, there does not seem to have been much to choose, in point of religious belief and practice, between the two sections of the people. In both places the majority were steeped in idolatrous and superstitious notions; some appear even to have entertained the purpose of assimilating themselves to the heathen around, and only a small minority were steadfast in their allegiance to the national religion. Yet the exiles could not, any more than the remnant in Judah, abandon the hope that Jehovah would save His sanctuary from desecration. The Temple was "the excellency of their strength, the desire of their eyes, and that which their soul pitied" (xxiv. 21). False prophets appeared in Babylon to prophesy smooth things, and assure the exiles of a speedy restoration to their place in the people of God. It was not till Jerusalem was laid in ruins, and the Jewish state had disappeared from the earth, that the Israelites were in a mood to understand the meaning of God's judgment, or to learn the lessons which the prophecy of nearly two centuries had vainly striven to inculcate.

We have now reached the point at which the Book of Ezekiel opens, and what remains to be told of the history of the time will be given in connection with the prophecies on which it is fitted to throw light. But before proceeding to consider his entrance on the prophetic office, it will be useful to dwell for a little on what was probably the most fruitful influence of Ezekiel's youth—the personal influence of his contemporary and predecessor Jeremiah. This will form the subject of the next chapter.

CHAPTER II.

JEREMIAH AND EZEKIEL.

Each of the communities described in the last chapter was the theatre of the activity of a great prophet. When Ezekiel began to prophesy at Tel Abib, Jeremiah was approaching the end of his great and tragic career. For five-and-thirty years he had been known as a prophet, and during the latter part of that time had been the most prominent figure in Jerusalem. For the next five years their ministries were contemporaneous, and it is somewhat remarkable that they ignore each other in their writings so completely as they do. We would give a good deal to have some reference by Ezekiel to Jeremiah or by

* The opinion, once prevalent, that it was the Chaboras in Northern Mesopotamia, where colonies of Northern Israelites had been settled a century and a half before, has nothing to justify it, and is now universally abandoned.

Jeremiah to Ezekiel, but we find none. Scripture does not often favour us with those cross-lights which prove so instructive in the hands of a modern historian. While Jeremiah knows of the rise of false prophets in Babylonia, and Ezekiel denounces those he had left behind in Jerusalem, neither of these great men betrays the slightest consciousness of the existence of the other. This silence is specially noticeable on Ezekiel's part, because his frequent descriptions of the state of society in Jerusalem give him abundant opportunity to express his sympathy with the position of Jeremiah. When we read in the twenty-second chapter that there was not found a man to make up the fence and stand in the breach before God, we might be tempted to conclude that he really was not aware of Jeremiah's noble stand for righteousness in the corrupt and doomed city. And yet the points of contact between the two prophets are so numerous and so obvious that they cannot fairly be explained by the common operation of the Spirit of God on the minds of both. There is nothing in the nature of prophecy to forbid the view that one prophet learned from another, and built on the foundation which his predecessors had laid; and when we find a parallelism so close as that between Jeremiah and Ezekiel we are driven to the conclusion that the influence was unusually direct, and that the whole thinking of the younger writer had been moulded by the teaching and example of the older.

In what way this influence was communicated is a question on which some difference of opinion may exist. Some writers, such as Kuenen, think that the indebtedness of Ezekiel to Jeremiah was mainly literary. That is to say, they hold that it must be accounted for by prolonged study on Ezekiel's part of the written prophecies of him who was his teacher. Kuenen surmises that this happened after the destruction of Jerusalem, when some friends of Jeremiah arrived in Babylon, bringing with them the completed volume of his prophecies. Before Ezekiel proceeded to write his own prophecies, his mind is supposed to have been so saturated with the ideas and language of Jeremiah that every part of his book bears the impress and betrays the influence of his predecessor. In this fact, of course, Kuenen finds an argument for the view that Ezekiel's prophecies were written at a comparatively late period of his life. It is difficult to speak with confidence on some of the points raised by this hypothesis. That the influence of Jeremiah can be traced in all parts of the book of Ezekiel is undoubtedly true; but it is not so clear that it can be assigned equally to all periods of Jeremiah's activity. Many of the prophecies of Jeremiah cannot be referred to a definite date: and we do not know what means Ezekiel had of obtaining copies of those which belong to the period after the two prophets were separated. We know, however, that a great part of the book of Jeremiah was in writing several years before Ezekiel was carried away to Babylon; and we may safely assume that amongst the treasures which he took with him into exile was the roll written by Baruch to the dictation of Jeremiah in the fourth year of Jehoiakim (Jer. xxxvi.). Even later oracles may have reached Ezekiel either before or during his prophetic career through the active correspondence maintained between the exiles and Jerusalem. It is possible, therefore, that even the literary dependence of Ezekiel on Jeremiah may belong to a much earlier time than the final issue of the book of Ezekiel; and if it should be found that ideas in the earlier part of the book suggest acquaintance with a later utterance of Jeremiah, the fact need not surprise us. It is certainly no sufficient reason for concluding that the whole substance of Ezekiel's prophecy had been recast under the influence of a late perusal of the work of Jeremiah.

But, setting aside verbal coincidences and other phenomena which suggest literary dependence, there remains an affinity of a much deeper kind between the teaching of the two prophets, which can only be explained, if it is to be explained at all, by the personal influence of the older upon the younger. And it is these more fundamental resemblances which are of most interest for our present purpose, because they may enable us to understand something of the settled convictions with which Ezekiel entered on the prophet's calling. Moreover, a comparison of the two prophets will bring out more clearly than anything else certain aspects of the character of Ezekiel which it is important to bear in mind. Both are men of strongly marked individuality, and no conception of the age in which they lived can safely be formed from the writings of either, taken alone.

It has been already remarked that Jeremiah was the most conspicuous public character of his day. If it be the case that he threw his spell over the youthful mind of Ezekiel, the fact is the most striking tribute to his influence that could be conceived. No two men could differ more widely in natural temperament and character. Jeremiah is the prophet of a dying nation, and the agony of Judah's prolonged death-struggle is reproduced with tenfold intensity in the inward conflict which rends the heart of the prophet. Inexorable in his prediction of the coming doom, he confesses that this is because he is over-mastered by the Divine power which urges him into a path from which his nature recoiled. He deplores the isolation which is forced upon him, the alienation of friends and kinsmen, and the constant strife of which he is the reluctant cause. He feels as if he could gladly shake off the burden of prophetic responsibility and become a man amongst common men. His human sympathies go forth towards his unhappy country, and his heart bleeds for the misery which he sees hanging over the misguided people, for whom he is forbidden even to pray. The tragic conflict of his life reaches its height in those expostulations with Jehovah which are amongst the most remarkable passages of the Old Testament. They express the shrinking of a sensitive nature from the inward necessity in which he was compelled to recognise the higher truth; and the wrestling of an earnest spirit for the assurance of his personal standing with God, when all the outward institutions of religion were being dissolved.

To such mental conflicts Ezekiel was a stranger, or if he ever passed through them the traces of them have almost vanished from his written words. He can hardly be said to be more severe than Jeremiah; but his severity seems more a part of himself, and more in keeping with the bent of his disposition. He is wholly on the side of the divine sovereignty; there is no reaction of the human sympathies against the imperative dictates of the prophetic inspiration; he is one in whom every thought seems brought into captivity to the word of Jehovah. It is possible that the completeness with which Ezekiel surrendered himself to the judicial aspect of his message may be partly due to the fact that he had been familiar with its leading conceptions from the teaching of Jeremiah; but it must also be due to a certain austerity natural to him. Less emotional than Jeremiah, his mind was more readily taken possession of by the convictions that formed the substance of his prophetic message. He was evidently a man of profoundly ethical habits of thought, stern and uncompromising in his judgments, both on himself and other men, and gifted with a strong sense of human responsibility. As his captivity cut him off from living contact with the national life, and enabled him to survey his country's condition with something of the dispassionate scrutiny of a spectator, so his natural disposition enabled him to realise in his own person that breach with the past which was essential to the purification of religion. He had the qualities which marked him out for the prophet of the new order that was to be, as clearly as Jeremiah had those which fitted him to be the prophet of a nation's dissolution.

In social standing, also, and professional training, the men were far removed from each other. Both were priests, but Ezekiel belonged to the house of Zadok, who officiated in the central sanctuary, while Jeremiah's family may have been attached to one of the provincial sanctuaries.* The interests of the two classes of priests came into sharp collision as a consequence of Josiah's reformation. The law provided that the rural priesthood should be admitted to the service of the Temple on equal terms with their brethren of the sons of Zadok; but we are expressly informed that the Temple priests successfully resisted this encroachment on their peculiar privileges. It has been adduced by several expositors as a proof of Ezekiel's freedom from caste prejudice, that he was willing to learn from a man who was socially his inferior, and who belonged to an order which he himself was to declare unworthy of full priestly rights in the restored theocracy. But it must be said that there was little in Jeremiah's public work to call attention to the fact that he was by birth a priest. In the profound spiritual sense of the Epistle to the Hebrews we may indeed say that he was at heart a priest, "having compassion on the ignorant and them that are out of the way, forasmuch as he himself was compassed with infirmity." But this quality of spiritual sympathy sprang from his calling as a prophet rather than from his priestly training. One of the contrasts between him and Ezekiel lies just in the respective estimates of the worth of ritual which underlie their teaching. Jeremiah is distinguished even among the prophets by his indifference to the outward institutions and symbols of religion which it is the priest's function to conserve. He stands in the succession of Amos and Isaiah as an upholder of the purely ethical character of the service of God. Ritual forms no essential element of Jehovah's covenant with Israel, and it is doubtful if his prophecies of the future contain any reference to a priestly class or priestly ordinances.* In the present he repudiates the actual popular worship as offensive to Jehovah, and, except in so far as he may have given his support to Josiah's reforms, he does not concern himself to put anything better in its place. To Ezekiel, on the contrary, a pure worship is a primary condition of Israel's enjoyment of the fellowship of Jehovah. All through his teaching we detect his deep sense of the religious value of priestly ceremonies, and in the concluding vision that underlying thought comes out clearly as a fundamental principle of the new religious constitution. Here again we can see how each prophet was providentially fitted for the special work assigned him to do. To Jeremiah it was given, amidst the wreck of all the material embodiments in which faith had clothed itself in the past, to realise the essential truth of religion as personal communion with God, and so to rise to the conception of a purely spiritual religion, in which the will of God should be written in the heart of every believer. To Ezekiel was committed the different, but not less necessary, task of organising the religion of the immediate future, and providing the forms which were to enshrine the truths of revelation until the coming of Christ. And that task could not, humanly speaking, have been performed but by one whose training and inclination taught him to appreciate the value of those rules of ceremonial sanctity which were the tradition of the Hebrew priesthood.

Very closely connected with this is the attitude of the two prophets to what we may call the legal aspect of religion. Jeremiah seems to have become convinced at a very early date of the insufficiency and shallowness of the revival of religion which was expressed in the establishment of the national covenant in the reign of Josiah. He seems also to have discerned some of the evils which are inseparable from a religion of the letter, in which the claims of God are presented in the form of external laws and ordinances. And these convictions led him to the conception of a far higher manifestation of God's redeeming grace to be realised in the future, in the form of a new covenant, based on God's forgiving love, and operative through a personal knowledge of God, and the law written on the heart and mind of each member of the covenant people. That is to say, the living principle of religion must be implanted in the heart of each true Israelite, and his obedience must be what we call evangelical obedience, springing from the free impulse of a nature renewed by the knowledge of God. Ezekiel is also impressed by the failure of the Deuteronomic covenant and the need of a new heart before Israel is able to comply with the high requirements of the holy law of God. But he does not appear to have been led to connect the failure of the past with the inherent imperfection of a legal dispensation as such. Although his teaching is full of evangelical truths, amongst which the doctrine of regeneration holds a conspicuous place, we yet observe that with him a man's righteousness before God consists in acts of obedience to the objective precepts of the divine law. This of course does not mean that Ezekiel was concerned only about the outward act and indifferent

* This, however, is not certain. Although Jeremiah's property and residence were in Anathoth, his official connection may have been with the Temple in Jerusalem.

* The passage xxxiii. 14-26 is wanting in the LXX., and may possibly be a later insertion. Even if genuine it would hardly alter the general estimate of the prophet's teaching expressed above.

to the spirit in which the law was observed. But it does mean that the end of God's dealings with His people was to bring them into a condition for fulfilling His law, and that the great aim of the new Israel was the faithful observance of the law which expressed the conditions on which they could remain in communion with God. Accordingly Ezekiel's final ideal is on a lower plane, and therefore more immediately practicable, than that of Jeremiah. Instead of a purely spiritual anticipation expressing the essential nature of the perfect relation between God and man, Ezekiel presents us with a definite, clearly conceived vision of a new theocracy—a state which is to be the outward embodiment of Jehovah's will and in which life is minutely regulated by His law.

If in spite of such wide differences of temperament, of education, and of religious experience, we find nevertheless a substantial agreement in the teaching of the two prophets, we must certainly recognise in this a striking evidence of the stability of that conception of God and His providence which was in the main a product of Hebrew prophecy. It is not necessary here to enumerate all the points of coincidence between Jeremiah and Ezekiel; but it will be of advantage to indicate a few salient features which they have in common. Of these one of the most important is their conception of the prophetic office. It can hardly be doubted that on this subject Ezekiel had learned much both from observation of Jeremiah's career and from the study of his writings. He knew something of what it meant to be a prophet to Israel before he himself received the prophet's commission; and after he had received it his experience ran closely parallel with that of his master. The idea of the prophet as a man standing alone for God amidst a hostile world, surrounded on every side by threats and opposition, was impressed on each of them from the outset of his ministry. To be a true prophet one must know how to confront men with an inflexibility equal to theirs, sustained only by a divine power which assures him of ultimate victory. He is cut off, not only from the currents of opinion which play around him, but from all share in common joys and sorrows, living a solitary life in sympathy with a God justly alienated from His people. This attitude of antagonism to the people, as Jeremiah well knew, had been the common fate of all true prophets. What is characteristic of him and Ezekiel is that they both enter on their work in the full consciousness of the stern and hopeless nature of their task. Isaiah knew from the day he became a prophet that the effect of his teaching would be to harden the people in unbelief; but he says nothing of personal enmity and persecution to be faced from the outset. But now the crisis of the people's fate has arrived, and the relations between the prophet and his age become more and more strained as the great controversy approaches its decision.

Another point of agreement which may be here mentioned is the estimate of Israel's sin. Ezekiel goes further than Jeremiah in the way of condemnation, regarding the whole history of Israel as an unbroken record of apostasy and rebellion, while Jeremiah at least looks back to the desert wandering as a time when the ideal relation between Israel and Jehovah was maintained. But on the whole, and especially with respect to the present state of the nation, their judgment is substantially one. The source of all the religious and moral disorders of the nation is infidelity to Jehovah, which is manifested in the worship of false gods and reliance on the help of foreign nations. Specially noteworthy is the frequent recurrence in Jeremiah and Ezekiel of the figure of "whoredom," an idea introduced into prophecy by Hosea to describe these two sins. The extension of the figure to the false worship of Jehovah by images and other idolatrous emblems can also be traced to Hosea; and in Ezekiel it is sometimes difficult to say which species of idolatry he has in view, whether it be the actual worship of other gods or the unlawful worship of the true God. His position is that an unspiritual worship implies an unspiritual deity, and that such service as was performed at the ordinary sanctuaries could by no possibility be regarded as rendered to the true God who spoke through the prophets. From this fountain-head of a corrupted religious sense proceed all those immoral practices which both prophets stigmatise as "abominations" and as a defilement of the land of Jehovah. Of these the most startling is the prevalent sacrifice of children to which they both bear witness, although, as we shall afterwards see, with a characteristic difference in their point of view.

The whole picture, indeed, which Jeremiah and Ezekiel present of contemporary society is appalling in the extreme. Making all allowance for the practical motive of the prophetic invective, which always aims at conviction of sin, we cannot doubt that the state of things was sufficiently serious to mark Judah as ripe for judgment. The very foundations of society were sapped by the spread of license and high-handed violence through all classes of the community. The restraints of religion had been loosened by the feeling that Jehovah had forsaken the land, and nobles, priests, and prophets plunged into a career of wickedness and oppression which made salvation of the existing nation impossible. The guilt of Jerusalem is symbolised to both prophets in the innocent blood which stains her skirts and cries to heaven for vengeance. The tendencies which are uppermost are the evil legacy of the days of Manasseh, when, in the judgment of Jeremiah and the historian of the books of Kings,* the nation sinned beyond hope of mercy. In painting his lurid pictures of social degeneracy Ezekiel is no doubt drawing on his own memory and information; nevertheless the forms in which his indictment is cast show that even in this matter he has learned to look on things with the eyes of his great teacher.

It is scarcely necessary to add that both prophets anticipate a speedy downfall of the state and its restoration in a more glorious form after a short interval, fixed by Jeremiah at seventy years and by Ezekiel at forty years. The restoration is regarded as final, and as embracing both branches of the Hebrew nation, the kingdom of the ten tribes as well as the house of Judah. The Messianic hope in Ezekiel appears in a form similar to that in which it is presented by Jeremiah; in neither prophet is the figure of the ideal King so prominent as in the prophecies of Isaiah. The similarity between the two is all the more noteworthy as an evidence of dependence, because Ezekiel's final outlook is towards a state of things in which the Prince has a somewhat subordinate position assigned to Him.

* Jer. xv. 4; 2 Kings xxiii. 26.

Both prophets, again following Hosea, regard the spiritual renewal of the people as the effect of chastisement in exile. Those parts of the nation which go first into banishment are the first to be brought under the salutary influences of God's providential discipline; and hence we find that Jeremiah adopts a more hopeful tone in speaking of Samaria and the captives of 597 than in his utterances to those who remained in the land. This conviction was shared by Ezekiel, in spite of his daily contact with abominations from which his whole nature revolted. It has been supposed that Ezekiel lived long enough to see that no such spiritual transformation was to be wrought by the mere fact of captivity, and that, despairing of a general and spontaneous conversion, he put his hand to the work of practical reform as if he would secure by legislation the results which he had once expected as fruits of repentance. If the prophet had ever expected that punishment of itself would work a change in the religious condition of his countrymen, there might have been room for such a disenchantment as is here assumed. But there is no evidence that he ever looked for anything else than a regeneration of the people in captivity by the supernatural working of the divine Spirit; and that the final vision is meant to help out the divine plan by human policy is a suggestion negatived by the whole scope of the book. It may be true that his practical activity in the present was directed to preparing individual men for the coming salvation; but that was no more than any spiritual teacher must have done in a time recognised as a period of transition. The vision of the restored theocracy presupposes a national resurrection and a national repentance. And on the face of it it is such that man can take no step towards its accomplishment until God has prepared the way by creating the conditions of a perfect religious community, both the moral conditions in the mind of the people and the outward conditions in the miraculous transformation of the land in which they are to dwell.

Most of the points here touched upon will have to be more fully treated in the course of our exposition, and other affinities between the two great prophets will have to be noticed as we proceed. Enough has perhaps been said to show that Ezekiel's thinking has been profoundly influenced by Jeremiah, that the influence extends not only to the form but also to the substance of his teaching, and can therefore only be explained by early impressions received by the younger prophet in the days before the word of the Lord had come to him.

CHAPTER III.

THE VISION OF THE GLORY OF GOD.

EZEKIEL i.

IT might be hazardous to attempt, from the general considerations advanced in the last two chapters, to form a conception of Ezekiel's state of mind during the first few years of his captivity. If, as we have found reason to believe, he had already come under the influence of Jeremiah, he must have been in some measure prepared for the blow which had descended on him. Torn from the duties of the office which he loved, and driven in upon himself, Ezekiel must no doubt have meditated deeply on the sin and the prospects of his people. From the first he must have stood aloof from his fellow-exiles, who, led by their false prophets, began to dream of the fall of Babylon and a speedy return to their own land. He knew that the calamity which had befallen them was but the first instalment of a sweeping judgment before which the old Israel must utterly perish. Those who remained in Jerusalem were reserved for a worse fate than those who had been carried away; but so long as the latter remained impenitent there was no hope even for them of an alleviation of the bitterness of their lot. Such thoughts, working in a mind naturally severe in its judgments, may have already produced that attitude of alienation from the whole life of his companions in misfortune which dominates the first period of his prophetic career. But these convictions did not make Ezekiel a prophet. He had as yet no independent message from God, no sure perception of the issue of events, or the path which Israel must follow in order to reach the blessedness of the future. It was not till the fifth year of his captivity * that the inward change took place which brought him into Jehovah's counsel, and disclosed to him the outlines of all his future work, and endowed him with the courage to stand forth amongst his people as the spokesman of Jehovah.

Like other great prophets whose personal experience is recorded, Ezekiel became conscious of his prophetic vocation through a vision of God. The form in which Jehovah first appeared to him is described with great minuteness of detail in the first chapter of his book. It would seem that in some hour of solitary meditation by the river Kebar his attention was attracted to a storm-cloud forming in the north and advancing toward him across the plain. The cloud may have been an actual phenomenon, the natural basis of the theophany which follows. Falling into a state of ecstasy, the prophet sees the cloud grow luminous with an unearthly splendour. From the midst of it there shines a brightness which he compares to the lustre of electron.† Looking more closely, he discerns four living creatures, of strange composite form,—human in general appearance, but winged; and each having four heads combining the highest types of animal life—man, lion, ox, and eagle. These are afterwards identified with the cherubim of the Temple symbolism (x. 20); but some features of the conception may have been suggested by the composite animal figures of Babylonian art, with which the prophet must have been already familiar. The interior space is occupied by a

* In the superscription of the book (i. 1–3) a double date is given for this occurrence. In ver. 1 it is said to have taken place "in the thirtieth year"; but this expression has never been satisfactorily explained. The principal suggestions are: (1) that it is the year of Ezekiel's life; (2) that the reckoning is from the year of Josiah's reformation; and (3) that it is according to some Babylonian era. But none of these has much probability, unless, with Klostermann, we go further and assume that the explanation was given in an earlier part of the prophet's autobiography now lost—a view which is supported by no evidence and is contrary to all analogy. Cornill proposes to omit ver. 1 entirely, chiefly on the ground that the use of the first person before the writer's name has been mentioned is unnatural. That the superscription does not read smoothly as it stands has been felt by many critics; but the rejection of the verse is perhaps a too facile solution.

† Not "amber," but a natural alloy of silver and gold, highly esteemed in antiquity.

hearth of glowing coals, from which lightning-flashes constantly dart to and fro between the cherubim. Beside each cherub is a wheel, formed apparently of two wheels intersecting each other at right angles. The appearance of the wheels is like "chrysolite," and their rims are filled with eyes, denoting the intelligence by which their motions are directed. The wheels and the cherubim together embody the spontaneous energy by which the throne of God is transported whither He wills; although there is no mechanical connection between them, they are represented as animated by a common spirit, directing all their motions in perfect harmony. Over the heads and outstretched wings of the cherubim is a rigid pavement or "firmament," like crystal; and above this a sapphire stone * supporting the throne of Jehovah. The divine Being is seen in the likeness of a man; and around Him, as if to temper the fierceness of the light in which He dwells, is a radiance like that of the rainbow. It will be noticed that while Ezekiel's imagination dwells on what we must consider the accessories of the vision—the fire, the cherubim, the wheels—he hardly dares to lift his eyes to the person of Jehovah Himself The full meaning of what he is passing through only dawns on him when he realises that he is in the presence of the Almighty. Then he falls on his face, overpowered by the sense of his own insignificance.

There is no reason to doubt that what is thus described represents an actual experience on the part of the prophet. It is not to be regarded merely as a conscious clothing of spiritual truths in symbolic imagery. The *description* of a vision is of course a conscious exercise of literary faculty; and in all such cases it must be difficult to distinguish what a prophet actually saw and heard in the moment of inspiration from the details which he was compelled to add in order to convey an intelligible picture to the minds of his readers. It is probable that in the case of Ezekiel the element of free invention has a larger range than in the less elaborate descriptions which other prophets give in their visions. But this does not detract from the force of the prophet's own assertion that what he relates was based on a real and definite experience when in a state of prophetic ecstasy. This is expressed by the words "the hand of Jehovah was upon him" (ver. 3)—a phrase which is invariably used throughout the book to denote the prophet's peculiar mental condition when the communication of divine truth was accompanied by experiences of a visionary order. Moreover, the account given of the state in which this vision left him shows that his natural consciousness had been overpowered by the pressure of supersensible realities on his spirit. He tells us that he went "in bitterness, in the heat of his spirit, the hand of the Lord being heavy upon him; and came to the exiles at Tel-abib, . . . and sat there seven days stupefied in their midst" (iii. 14, 15).

Now whatever be the ultimate nature of the prophetic vision, its significance for us would appear to lie in the untrammelled working of the prophet's imagination under the influence of spiritual perceptions which are too profound to be expressed as abstract ideas. The prophet's consciousness is not suspended, for he remembers his vision and reflects on its meaning afterwards; but his intercourse with the outer world through the senses is interrupted, so that his mind moves freely amongst images stored in his memory, and new combinations are formed which embody a truth not previously apprehended. The *tableau* of the vision is therefore always capable to some extent of a psychological explanation. The elements of which it is composed must have been already present in the mind of the prophet, and in so far as these can be traced to their sources we are enabled to understand their symbolic import in the novel combination in which they appear. But the real significance of the vision lies in the immediate impression left on the mind of the prophet by the divine realities which govern his life, and this is especially true of the vision of God Himself which accompanies the call to the prophetic office. Although no vision can express the whole of a prophet's conception of God, yet it represents to the imagination certain fundamental aspects of the divine nature and of God's relation to the world and to men; and through all his subsequent career the prophet will be influenced by the form in which he once beheld the great Being whose words come to him from time to time. To his later reflection the vision becomes a symbol of certain truths about God, although in the first instance the symbol was created for him by a mysterious operation of the divine Spirit in a process over which he had no control. In one respect Ezekiel's inaugural vision seems to possess a greater importance for his theology than is the case with any other prophet. With the other prophets the vision is a momentary experience, of which the spiritual meaning passes into the thinking of the prophet, but which does not recur again in the visionary form. With Ezekiel, on the other hand, the vision becomes a fixed and permanent symbol of Jehovah, appearing again and again in precisely the same form as often as the reality of God's presence is impressed on his mind.

The essential question, then, with regard to Ezekiel's vision is, What revelation of God or what ideas respecting God did it serve to impress on the mind of the prophet? It may help us to answer that question if we begin by considering certain affinities which it presents to the great vision which opened the ministry of Isaiah. It must be admitted that Ezekiel's experience is much less intelligible as well as less impressive than Isaiah's. In Isaiah's delineation we recognise the presence of qualities which belong to genius of the highest order. The perfect balance of form and idea, the reticence which suggests without exhausting the significance of what is seen, the fine artistic sense which makes every touch in the picture contribute to the rendering of the emotion which fills the prophet's soul, combine to make the sixth chapter of Isaiah one of the most sublime passages in literature. No sympathetic reader can fail to catch the impression which the passage is intended to convey of the awful majesty of the God of Israel, and the effect produced on a frail and sinful mortal ushered into that holy Presence. We are made to feel how inevitably such a vision gives birth to the prophetic impulse, and how both vision and impulse inform the mind of the seer with the clear and definite purpose which rules all his subsequent work.

The point in which Ezekiel's vision differs most strikingly from Isaiah's is the almost entire

* *Cf.* Exod. xxiv. 10: "like the very heavens for pureness."

suppression of his subjectivity. This is so complete that it becomes difficult to apprehend the meaning of the vision in relation to his thought and activity. Spiritual realities are so overlaid with symbolism that the narrative almost fails to reflect the mental state in which he was consecrated for the work of his life. Isaiah's vision is a drama, Ezekiel's is a spectacle; in the one religious truth is expressed in a series of significant actions and words, in the other it is embodied in forms and splendours that appeal only to the eye. One fact may be noted in illustration of the diversity between the two representations. The scenery of Isaiah's vision is interpreted and spiritualised by the medium of language. The seraphs' hymn of adoration strikes the note which is the central thought of the vision, and the exclamation which breaks from the prophet's lips reveals the impact of that great truth on a human spirit. The whole scene is thus lifted out of the region of mere symbolism into that of pure religious ideas. Ezekiel's, on the other hand, is like a song without words. His cherubim are speechless. While the rustling of their wings and the thunder of the revolving wheels break on his ear like the sound of mighty waters, no articulate voice bears home to the mind the inner meaning of what he beholds. Probably he himself felt no need of it. The pictorial character of his thinking appears in many features of his work; and it is not surprising to find that the import of the revelation is expressed mainly in visual images.

Now these differences are in their own place very instructive, because they show how intimately the vision is related to the individuality of him who receives it, and how even in the most exalted moments of inspiration the mind displays the same tendencies which characterise its ordinary operations. Yet Ezekiel's vision represents a spiritual experience not less real than Isaiah's. His mental endowments are of a different order, of a lower order if you will, than those of Isaiah; but the essential fact that he too saw the glory of God and in that vision obtained the insight of the true prophet is not to be explained away by analysis of his literary talent or of the sources from which his images are derived. It is allowable to write worse Greek than Plato; and it is no disqualification for a Hebrew prophet to lack the grandeur of imagination and the mastery of style which are the notes of Isaiah's genius.

In spite of their obvious dissimilarities the two visions have enough in common to show that Ezekiel's thoughts concerning God had been largely influenced by the study of Isaiah. Truths that had perhaps long been latent in his mind now emerge into clear consciousness, clothed in forms which bear the impress of the mind in which they were first conceived. The fundamental idea is the same in each vision: the absolute and universal sovereignty of God. "Mine eyes have seen the King, Jehovah of hosts." Jehovah appears in human form, seated on a throne and attended by ministering creatures which serve to show forth some part of His glory. In the one case they are seraphim, in the other cherubim; and the functions imposed on them by the structure of the vision are very diverse in the two cases. But the points in which they agree are more significant than those in which they differ. They are the agents through whom Jehovah exercises His sovereign authority, beings full of life and intelligence and moving in swift response to His will. Although free from earthly imperfection they cover themselves with their wings before His majesty, in token of the reverence which is due from the creature in presence of the Creator. For the rest they are symbolic figures embodying in themselves certain attributes of the Deity, or certain aspects of His kingship. Nor can Ezekiel any more than Isaiah think of Jehovah as the King apart from the emblems associated with the worship of His earthly sanctuary. The cherubim themselves are borrowed from the imagery of the Temple, although their forms are different from those which stood in the Holy of Holies. So again the altar, which was naturally suggested to Isaiah by the scene of his vision being laid in the Temple, appears in Ezekiel's vision in the form of the hearth of glowing coals which is under the divine throne. It is true that the fire symbolises destructive might rather than purifying energy (see x. 2), but it can hardly be doubted that the origin of the symbol is the altar-hearth of the sanctuary and of Isaiah's vision. It is as if the essence of the Temple and its worship were transferred to the sphere of heavenly realities where Jehovah's glory is fully manifested. All this, therefore, is nothing more than the embodiment of the fundamental truth of the Old Testament religion—that Jehovah is the almighty King of heaven and earth, that He executes His sovereign purposes with irresistible power, and that it is the highest privilege of men on earth to render to Him the homage and adoration which the sight of His glory draws forth from heavenly beings.

The idea of Jehovah's kingship, however, is presented in the Old Testament under two aspects. On the one hand, it denotes the moral sovereignty of God over the people whom He had chosen as His own and to whom His will was continuously revealed as the guide of their national and social life. On the other hand, it denotes God's absolute dominion over the forces of nature and the events of history, in virtue of which all things are the unconscious instruments of His purposes. These two truths can never be separated, although the emphasis is laid sometimes on the one and sometimes on the other. Thus in Isaiah's vision the emphasis lies perhaps more on the doctrine of Jehovah's kingship over Israel. It is true that He is at the same time represented as One whose glory is the "fulness of the whole earth," and who therefore manifests His power and presence in every part of His world-wide dominions. But the fact that Jehovah's palace is the idealised Temple of Jerusalem suggests at once, what all the teaching of the prophet confirms, that the nation of Israel is the special sphere within which His kingly authority is to obtain practical recognition. While no man had a firmer grasp of the truth that God wields all natural forces and overrules the actions of men in carrying out His providential designs, yet the leading ideas of His ministry are those which spring from the thought of Jehovah's presence in the midst of His people and the obligation that lies on Israel to recognise His sovereignty. He is, to use Isaiah's own expression, the "Holy One of Israel."

This aspect of the divine kingship is undoubtedly represented in the vision of Ezekiel. We have remarked that the imagery of the vision is to some extent moulded on the idea of the sanctuary as the seat of Jehovah's government, and we shall find later on that the final resting-place of this emblem of His presence is a restored sanctuary in the land of Canaan. But the circumstances under which Ezekiel was called to be a prophet required that prominence should be given to the complementary truth that the kingship of Jehovah was independent of His special relation to Israel. For the present the tie between Jehovah and His land was dissolved. Israel had disowned her divine King, and was left to suffer the consequences of her disloyalty. Hence it is that the vision appears, not from the direction of Jerusalem, but "out of the north," in token that God has departed from His Temple and abandoned it to its enemies. In this way the vision granted to the exiled prophet on the plain of Babylonia embodied a truth opposed to the religious prejudices of his time, but reassuring to himself—that the fall of Israel leaves the essential sovereignty of Jehovah untouched; that He still lives and reigns, although His people are trodden underfoot by worshippers of other gods. But more than this, we can see that on the whole the tendency of Ezekiel's vision, as distinguished from that of Isaiah, is to emphasise the universality of Jehovah's relations to the world of nature and of mankind. His throne rests here on a sapphire stone, the symbol of heavenly purity, to signify that His true dwelling-place is above the firmament, in the heavens, which are equally near to every region of the earth. Moreover, it is mounted on a chariot, by which it is moved from place to place with a velocity which suggests ubiquity, and the chariot is borne by "living creatures" whose forms unite all that is symbolical of power and dignity in the living world. Further, the shape of the chariot, which is foursquare, and the disposition of the wheels and cherubim, which is such that there is no before or behind, but the same front presented to each of the four quarters of the globe, indicate that all parts of the universe are alike accessible to the presence of God. Finally, the wheels and the cherubim are covered with eyes, to denote that all things are open to the view of Him who sits on the throne. The attributes of God here symbolised are those which express His relations to created existence as a whole—omnipresence, omnipotence, omniscience. These ideas are obviously incapable of adequate representation by any sensuous image—they can only be suggested to the mind; and it is just the effort to suggest such transcendental attributes that imparts to the vision the character of obscurity which attaches to so many of its details.

Another point of comparison between Isaiah and Ezekiel is suggested by the name which the latter constantly uses for the appearance which he sees, or rather perhaps for that part of it which represents the personal appearance of God. He calls it the "glory of Jehovah," or "glory of the God of Israel." The word for glory (*kābôd*) is used in a variety of senses in the Old Testament. Etymologically it comes from a root expressing the idea of heaviness. When used, as here, concretely, it signifies that which is the outward manifestation of power or worth or dignity. In human affairs it may be used of a man's wealth, or the pomp and circumstance of military array, or the splendour and pageantry of a royal court—those things which oppress the minds of common men with a sense of magnificence. In like manner, when applied to God, it denotes some reflection in the outer world of His majesty, something that at once reveals and conceals His essential Godhead. Now we remember that the second line of the seraphs' hymn conveyed to Isaiah's mind this thought, that "that which fills the whole earth is His glory." What is this "filling of the whole earth" in which the prophet sees the effulgence of the divine glory? Is his feeling akin to Wordsworth's

> "sense sublime
> Of something far more deeply interfused,
> Whose dwelling is the light of setting suns,
> And the round ocean, and the living air,
> And the blue sky, and in the mind of man"?

At least the words must surely mean that all through nature Isaiah recognised that which declares the glory of God, and therefore in some sense reveals Him. Although they do not teach a doctrine of the divine immanence, they contain all that is religiously valuable in that doctrine. In Ezekiel, however, we find nothing that looks in this direction. It is characteristic of his thoughts about God that the very word "glory" which Isaiah uses of something diffused through the earth is here employed to express the concentration of all divine qualities in a single image of dazzling splendour, but belonging to heaven rather than to earth. Glory is here equivalent to brightness, as in the ancient conception of the bright cloud which led the people through the desert and that which filled the Temple with overpowering light when Jehovah took possession of it (2 Chron. vii. 1-3). In a striking passage of his last vision Ezekiel describes how this scene will be repeated when Jehovah returns to take up His abode amongst His people and the earth will be lighted up with His glory (xliii. 2). But meanwhile it may seem to us that earth is left poorer by the loss of that aspect of nature in which Isaiah discovered a revelation of the divine.

Ezekiel is conscious that what he has seen is after all but an imperfect semblance of the essential glory of God on which no mortal eye can gaze. All that he describes is expressly said to be an "appearance" and a "likeness." When he comes to speak of the divine form in which the whole revelation culminates he can say no more than that it is the "appearance of the likeness of the glory of Jehovah." The prophet appears to realise his inability to penetrate behind the appearance to the reality which it shadows forth. The clearest vision of God which the mind of man can receive is an after-look like that which was vouchsafed to Moses when the divine presence had passed by (Exod. xxxiii. 23). So it was with Ezekiel. The true revelation that came to him was not in what he saw with his eyes in the moment of his initiation, but in the intuitive knowledge of God which from that hour he possessed, and which enabled him to interpret more fully than he could have done at the time the significance of his first memorable meeting with the God of Israel. What he retained in his waking hours was first of all a vivid sense of the reality of God's being, and then a mental picture suggesting those attributes which lay at the foundation of his prophetic ministry.

It is easy to see how this vision dominates all Ezekiel's thinking about the divine nature. The God whom he saw was in the form of a man, and so the God of his conscience is a moral person to whom he fearlessly ascribes the parts and even the passions of humanity. He speaks through the prophet in the language of royal authority, as a king who will brook no rival in the affections of his people. As King of Israel He asserts His determination to reign over them with a mighty hand, and by mingled goodness and severity to break their stubborn heart and bend them to His purpose. There are perhaps other and more subtle affinities between the symbol of the vision and the prophet's inner consciousness of God. Just as the vision gathers up all in nature that suggests divinity into one resplendent image, so it is also with the moral action of God as conceived by Ezekiel. His government of the world is self-centred; all the ends which He pursues in His providence lie within Himself. His dealings with the nations, and with Israel in particular, are dictated by regard for His own glory, or, as Ezekiel expresses it, by pity for His great name. "Not for your sake do I act, O house of Israel, but for My holy name, which ye have profaned among the heathen whither ye went" (xxxvi. 22). The relations into which He enters with men are all subordinate to the supreme purpose of "sanctifying" Himself in the eyes of the world or manifesting Himself as He truly is. It is no doubt possible to exaggerate this feature of Ezekiel's theology in a way that would be unjust to the prophet. After all, Jehovah's desire to be known as He is implies a regard for His creatures which includes the ultimate intention to bless them. It is but an extreme expression in the form necessary for that time of the truth to which all the prophets bear witness, that the knowledge of God is the indispensable condition of true blessedness to men. Still, the difference is marked between the "not for your sake" of Ezekiel and the "human bands, the cords of love" of which Hosea speaks, the yearning and compassionate affection that binds Jehovah to His erring people.

In another respect the symbolism of the vision may be taken as an emblem of the Hebrew conception of the universe. The Bible has no scientific theory of God's relation to the world; but it is full of the practical conviction that all nature responds to His behests, that all occurrences are indications of His mind, the whole realm of nature and history being governed by one Will which works for moral ends. That conviction is as deeply rooted in the thinking of Ezekiel as in that of any other prophet, and, consciously or unconsciously, it is reflected in the structure of the *merkābā*, or heavenly chariot, which has no mechanical connection between its different parts, and yet is animated by one spirit and moves altogether at the impulse of Jehovah's will.

It will be seen that the general tendency of Ezekiel's conception of God is what might be described in modern language as "transcendental." In this, however, the prophet does not stand alone, and the difference between him and earlier prophets is not so great as is sometimes represented. Indeed, the contrast between transcendent and immanent is hardly applicable in the Old Testament religion. If by transcendence it is meant that God is a being distinct from the world, not losing Himself in the life of nature, but ruling over it and controlling it as His instrument, then all the inspired writers of the Old Testament are transcendentalists. But this does not mean that God is separated from the human spirit by a dead, mechanical universe which owes nothing to its Creator but its initial impulse and its governing laws. The idea that a world could come between man and God is one that would never have occurred to a prophet. Just because God is above the world He can reveal Himself directly to the spirit of man, speaking to His servants face to face as a man speaketh to his friend.

But frequently in the prophets the thought is expressed that Jehovah is "far off" or "comes from far" in the crises of His people's history. "Am I a God at hand, saith Jehovah, and not a God afar off?" is Jeremiah's question to the false prophets of his day; and the answer is, "Do not I fill heaven and earth? saith Jehovah." On this subject we may quote the suggestive remarks of a recent commentator on Isaiah: "The local deities, the gods of the tribal religions, are near; Jehovah is far, but at the same time everywhere present. The remoteness of Jehovah in space represented to the prophets better than our transcendental abstractions Jehovah's absolute ascendency. This 'far off' is spoken with enthusiasm. Everywhere and nowhere, Jehovah comes when His hour is come." * That is the idea of Ezekiel's vision. God comes to him "from far," but He comes very near. Our difficulty may be to realise the nearness of God. Scientific discovery has so enlarged our view of the material universe that we feel the need of every consideration that can bring home to us a sense of the divine condescension and interest in man's earthly history and his spiritual welfare. But the difficulty which beset the ordinary Israelite even so late as the Exile was as nearly as possible the opposite of ours. His temptation was to think of God as only a God "at hand," a local deity, whose range of influence was limited to a particular spot, and whose power was measured by the fortunes of His own people. Above all things he needed to learn that God was "afar off," filling heaven and earth, that His power was exerted everywhere, and that there was no place where either a man could hide himself from God or God was hidden from man. When we bear in mind these circumstances we can see how needful was the revelation of the divine omnipresence as a step towards the perfect knowledge of God which comes to us through Jesus Christ.

CHAPTER IV.

EZEKIEL'S PROPHETIC COMMISSION.

EZEKIEL ii., iii.

THE call of a prophet and the vision of God which sometimes accompanied it are the two sides of one complex experience. The man who has truly seen God necessarily has a message to men. Not only are his spiritual perceptions quickened and all the powers of his being stirred to the highest activity, but there is laid on his conscience the burden of a sacred duty and a lifelong vocation to the service of God and man. The true prophet therefore is one who can say with Paul, "I was not disobedient to the heavenly vision," for that cannot be a real

* Duhm on Isa. xxx. 27.

vision of God which does not demand obedience. And of the two elements the call is the one that is indispensable to the idea of a prophet. We can conceive a prophet without an ecstatic vision, but not without a consciousness of being chosen by God for a special work or a sense of moral responsibility for the faithful declaration of His truth. Whether, as with Isaiah and Ezekiel, the call springs out of the vision of God, or whether, as with Jeremiah, the call comes first and is supplemented by experiences of a visionary kind, the essential fact in the prophet's initiation always is the conviction that from a certain period in his life the word of Jehovah came to him, and along with it the feeling of personal obligation to God for the discharge of a mission entrusted to him. While the vision merely serves to impress on the imagination by means of symbols a certain conception of God's being, and may be dispensed with when symbols are no longer the necessary vehicle of spiritual truth, the call, as conveying a sense of one's true place in the kingdom of God, can never be wanting to any man who has a prophetic work to do for God amongst his fellow-men.

It has been already hinted that in the case of Ezekiel the connection between the call and the vision is less obvious than in that of Isaiah. The character of the narrative undergoes a change at the beginning of chap. ii. The first part is moulded, as we have seen, very largely on the inaugural vision of Isaiah; the second betrays with equal clearness the influence of Jeremiah. The appearance of a break between the first chapter and the second is partly due to the prophet's laborious manner of describing what he had passed through. It is altogether unfair to represent him as having first curiously inspected the mechanism of the *merkābā*, and then bethought himself that it was a fitting thing to fall on his face before it. The experience of an ecstasy is one thing, the relating of it is another. In much less time than it takes us to master the details of the picture, Ezekiel had seen and been overpowered by the glory of Jehovah, and had become aware of the purpose for which it had been revealed to him. He knew that God had come to him in order to send him as a prophet to his fellow-exiles. And just as the description of the vision draws out in detail those features which were significant of God's nature and attributes, so in what follows he becomes conscious step by step of certain aspects of the work to which he is called. In the form of a series of addresses of the Almighty there are presented to his mind the outlines of his prophetic career—its conditions, its hardships, its encouragements, and above all its binding and peremptory obligation. Some of the facts now set before him, such as the spiritual condition of his audience, had long been familiar to his thoughts—others were new; but now they all take their proper place in the scheme of his life; he is made to know their bearing on his work, and what attitude he is to adopt in face of them. All this takes place in the prophetic trance; but the ideas remain with him as the sustaining principles of his subsequent work.

1. Of the truths thus presented to the mind of Ezekiel the first, and the one that directly arises out of the impression which the vision made on him, is his personal insignificance. As he lies prostrate before the glory of Jehovah he hears for the first time the name which ever afterwards signalises his relation to the God who speaks through him. It hardly needs to be said that the term "son of man" in the Book of Ezekiel is no title of honour or of distinction. It is precisely the opposite of this. It denotes the absence of distinction in the person of the prophet. It signifies no more than "member of the human race"; its sense might almost be conveyed if we were to render it by the word "mortal." It expresses the infinite contrast between the heavenly and the earthly, between the glorious Being who speaks from the throne and the frail creature who needs to be supernaturally strengthened before he can stand upright in the attitude of service (ii. 1). He felt that there was no reason in himself for the choice which God made of him to be a prophet. He is conscious only of the attributes which he has in common with the race—of human weakness and insignificance; all that distinguishes him from other men belongs to his office, and is conferred on him by God in the act of his consecration. There is no trace of the generous impulse that prompted Isaiah to offer himself as a servant of the great King as soon as he realised that there was work to be done. He is equally a stranger to the shrinking of Jeremiah's sensitive spirit from the responsibilities of the prophet's charge. To Ezekiel the Divine Presence is so overpowering, the command is so definite and exacting, that no room is left for the play of personal feeling; the hand of the Lord is heavy on him, and he can do nothing but stand still and hear.

2. The next thought that occupies the attention of the prophet is the painful spiritual condition of those to whom he is sent. It is to be noted that his mission presents itself to him from the outset in two aspects. In the first place, he is a prophet to the whole house of Israel, including the lost kingdom of the ten tribes, as well as the two sections of the kingdom of Judah, those now in exile and those still remaining in their own land. This is his ideal audience; the sweep of his prophecy is to embrace the destinies of the nation as a whole, although but a small part be within the reach of his spoken words. But in literal fact he is to be the prophet of the exiles (iii. 11); that is the sphere in which he has to make proof of his ministry. These two audiences are for the most part not distinguished in the mind of Ezekiel; he sees the ideal in the real, regarding the little colony in which he lives as an epitome of the national life. But in both aspects of his work the outlook is equally dispiriting. If he looks forward to an active career amongst his fellow-captives, he is given to know that "thorns and thistles" are with him and that his dwelling is among scorpions (ii. 6). Petty persecution and rancorous opposition are the inevitable lot of a prophet there. And if he extends his thoughts to the idealised nation he has to think of a people whose character is revealed in a long history of rebellion and apostasy: they are "the rebels who have rebelled against Me, they and their fathers to this very day" (ii. 3). The greatest difficulty he will have to contend with is the impenetrability of the minds of his hearers to the truths of his message. The barrier of a strange language suggests an illustration of the impossibility of communicating spiritual ideas to such men as he is sent to. But it is a far more hopeless barrier that separates him from his people. "Not to a people of deep speech

and heavy tongue art thou sent; and not to many peoples whose language thou canst not understand: if I had sent thee to *them, they* would hear thee. But the house of Israel will refuse to hear thee; for they refuse to hear Me: for the whole house of Israel are hard of forehead and stout of heart" (iii. 5-7). The meaning is that the incapacity of the people is not intellectual, but moral and spiritual. They can understand the prophet's words, but they will not hear them because they dislike the truth which he utters and have rebelled against the God who sent him. The hardening of the national conscience which Isaiah foresaw as the inevitable result of his own ministry is already accomplished, and Ezekiel traces it to its source in a defect of the will, an aversion to the truths which express the character of Jehovah.

This fixed judgment on his contemporaries with which Ezekiel enters on his work is condensed into one of those stereotyped expressions which abound in his writings: "house of disobedience"*—a phrase which is afterwards amplified in more than one elaborate review of the nation's past. It no doubt sums up the result of much previous meditation on the state of Israel and the possibility of a national reformation. If any hope had hitherto lingered in Ezekiel's mind that the exiles might now respond to a true word from Jehovah, it disappears in the clear insight which he obtains into the state of their hearts. He sees that the time has not yet come to win the people back to God by assurances of His compassion and the nearness of His salvation. The breach between Jehovah and Israel was not begun to be healed, and the prophet who stands on the side of God must look for no sympathy from men. In the very act of his consecration his mind is thus set in the attitude of uncompromising severity towards the obdurate house of Israel: "Behold, I make thy face hard like their faces, and thy forehead hard like theirs, like adamant harder than flint. Thou shalt not fear them nor be dismayed at their countenance, for a disobedient house are they" (iii. 8, 9).

3. The significance of the transaction in which he takes part is still further impressed on the mind of the prophet by a symbolic act in which he is made to signify his acceptance of the commission entrusted to him (ii. 8-iii. 3). He sees a hand extended to him holding the roll of a book, and when the roll is spread out before him it is found to be written on both sides with "lamentations and mourning and woe." In obedience to the Divine command he opens his mouth and eats the scroll, and finds to his surprise that in spite of its contents its taste is "like honey for sweetness."

The meaning of this strange symbol appears to include two things. In the first place it denotes the removal of the inward hindrance of which every man must be conscious when he receives the call to be a prophet. Something similar occurs in the inaugural vision of Isaiah and Jeremiah. The impediment of which Isaiah was conscious was the uncleanness of his lips; and this being removed by the touch of the hot coal from the altar, he is filled with a new feeling of freedom and eagerness to engage in the service of God. In the case of Jeremiah the hindrance was a sense of his own weakness and unfitness for the arduous duties which were imposed on him; and this again was taken away by the consecrating touch of Jehovah's hand on his lips. The part of Ezekiel's experience with which we are dealing is obviously parallel to these, although it is not possible to say what feeling of incapacity was uppermost in his mind. Perhaps it was the dread lest in him there should lurk something of that rebellious spirit which was the characteristic of the race to which he belonged. He who had been led to form so hard a judgment of his people could not but look with a jealous eye on his own heart, and could not forget that he shared the same sinful nature which made their rebellion possible. Accordingly the book is presented to him in the first instance as a test of his obedience. "But *thou*, son of man, hear what I say to thee; Be not disobedient like the disobedient house: open thy mouth, and eat what I give thee" (ii. 8). When the book proves sweet to his taste, he has the assurance that he has been endowed with such sympathy with the thoughts of God that things which to the natural mind are unwelcome become the source of a spiritual satisfaction. Jeremiah had expressed the same strange delight in his work in a striking passage which was doubtless familiar to Ezekiel: "When Thy words were found I did eat them; and Thy word was to me the joy and rejoicing of my heart: for I was called by Thy name, O Jehovah God of hosts" (Jer. xv. 16). We have a still higher illustration of the same fact in the life of our Lord, to whom it was meat and drink to do the will of His Father, and who experienced a joy in the doing of it which was peculiarly His own. It is the reward of the true service of God that amidst all the hardships and discouragements which have to be endured the heart is sustained by an inward joy springing from the consciousness of working in fellowship with God.

But in the second place the eating of the book undoubtedly signifies the bestowal on the prophet of the gift of inspiration—that is, the power to speak the words of Jehovah. "Son of man, eat this roll, and go speak to the children of Israel. . . . Go, get thee to the house of Israel, and speak with My words to them" (iii. 1, 4). Now the call of a prophet does not mean that his mind is charged with a certain body of doctrine, which he is to deliver from time to time as circumstances require. All that can safely be said about the prophetic inspiration is that it implies the faculty of distinguishing the truth of God from the thoughts that naturally arise in the prophet's own mind. Nor is there anything in Ezekiel's experience which necessarily goes beyond this conception; although the incident of the book has been interpreted in ways that burden him with a very crude and mechanical theory of inspiration. Some critics have believed that the book which he swallowed is the book he was afterwards to write, as if he had reproduced in instalments what was delivered to him at this time. Others, without going so far as this, find it at least significant that one who was to be pre-eminently a literary prophet should conceive of the word of the Lord as communicated to him in the form of a book. When one writer speaks of "eigenthümliche Empfindungen im Schlunde"* as the basis of the figure, he seems to come perilously near to resolving in-

* *Bêth mĕrî*, or simply *mĕrî*, occurring about fifteen times in the first half of the book, but only once after chap. xxiv.

* Klostermann.

spiration into a nervous disease. All these representations go beyond a fair construction of the prophet's meaning. The act is purely symbolic. The book has nothing to do with the subject-matter of his prophecy, nor does the eating of it mean anything more than the self-surrender of the prophet to his vocation as a vehicle of the word of Jehovah. The idea that the word of God becomes a living power in the inner being of the prophet is also expressed by Jeremiah when he speaks of it as a "burning fire shut up in his bones" (Jer. xx. 9); and Ezekiel's conception is similar. Although he speaks as if he had once for all assimilated the word of God, although he was conscious of a new power working within him, there is no proof that he thought of the word of the Lord as dwelling in him otherwise than as a spiritual impulse to utter the truth revealed to him from time to time. That is the inspiration which all the prophets possess: "Jehovah God hath spoken, who can but prophesy?" (Amos iii. 8).

4. It was not to be expected that a prophet so practical in his aims as Ezekiel should be left altogether without some indication of the end to be accomplished by his work. The ordinary incentives to an arduous public career have indeed been denied to him. He knows that his mission contains no promise of a striking or an immediate success, that he will be misjudged and opposed by nearly all who hear him, and that he will have to pursue his course without appreciation or sympathy. It has been impressed on him that to declare God's message is an end in itself, a duty to be discharged with no regard to its issues, "whether men hear or whether they forbear." Like Paul he recognises that "necessity is laid upon him" to preach the word of God. But there is one word which reveals to him the way in which his ministry is to be made effective in the working out of Jehovah's purpose with Israel. "Whether they hear or whether they forbear, they shall know that a prophet hath been among them" (ii. 5). The reference is mainly to the destruction of the nation which Ezekiel well knew must form the chief burden of any true prophetic message delivered at that time. He will be approved as a prophet, and recognised as what he is, when his words are verified by the event. Does it seem a poor reward for years of incessant contention with prejudice and unbelief? It was at all events the only reward that was possible, but it was also to be the beginning of better days. For these words have a wider significance than their bearing on the prophet's personal position.

It has been truly said that the preservation of the true religion after the downfall of the nation depended on the fact that the event had been clearly foretold. Two religions and two conceptions of God were then struggling for the mastery in Israel. One was the religion of the prophets, who set the moral holiness of Jehovah above every other consideration, and affirmed that His righteousness must be vindicated even at the cost of His people's destruction. The other was the popular religion which clung to the belief that Jehovah could not for any reason abandon His people without ceasing to be God. This conflict of principles reached its climax in the time of Ezekiel, and it also found its solution. The destruction of Jerusalem cleared the issues. It was then seen that the teaching of the prophets afforded the only possible explanation of the course of events. The Jehovah of the opposite religion was proved to be a figment of the popular imagination; and there was no alternative between accepting the prophetic interpretation of history and resigning all faith in the destiny of Israel. Hence the recognition of Ezekiel, the last of the old order of prophets, who had carried their threatenings on to the eve of their accomplishment, was really a great crisis of religion. It meant the triumph of the only conception of God on which the hope of a better future could be built. Although the people might still be far from the state of heart in which Jehovah could remove His chastening hand, the first condition of national repentance was given as soon as it was perceived that there had been prophets among them who had declared the purpose of Jehovah. The foundation was also laid for a more fruitful development of Ezekiel's activity. The word of the Lord had been in his hands a power "to pluck up and to break down and to destroy" the old Israel that would not know Jehovah; henceforward it was destined to "build and plant" a new Israel inspired by a new ideal of holiness and a whole-hearted repugnance to every form of idolatry.

5. These then are the chief elements which enter into the remarkable experience that made Ezekiel a prophet. Further disclosures of the nature of his office were, however, necessary before he could translate his vocation into a conscious plan of work. The departure of the theophany appears to have left him in a state of mental prostration.* In "bitterness and heat of spirit" he resumes his place amongst his fellow-captives at Tel-abib, and sits among them like a man bewildered for seven days. At the end of that time the effects of the ecstasy seem to pass away, and more light breaks on him with regard to his mission. He realises that it is to be largely a mission to individuals. He is appointed as a watchman to the house of Israel, to warn the wicked from his way; and as such he is held accountable for the fate of any soul that might miss the way of life through failure of duty on his part.

It has been supposed that this passage (iii. 16-21) describes the character of a short period of public activity, in which Ezekiel endeavoured to act the part of a "reprover" (ver. 26) among the exiles. This is considered to have been his first attempt to act on his commission, and to have been continued until the prophet was convinced of its hopelessness and in obedience to the divine command shut himself up in his own house. But this view does not seem to be sufficiently borne out by the terms of the narrative. The words rather represent a point of view from which his whole ministry is surveyed, or an aspect of it which possessed peculiar importance from the circumstances in which he was placed. The idea of his position as a watchman responsible for individuals may have been present to the prophet's mind from the time of his call; but the practical development of that idea was not possible until the destruction of Jerusalem had prepared men's minds to give heed to his admonitions. Accordingly the second period of Ezekiel's work opens with a fuller statement of the principles indicated in this section (chap. xxxiii.).

* In iii. 12 read "As the glory of Jehovah arose from its place" instead of "Blessed be the glory," etc. (ברום for ברוך).

We shall therefore defer the consideration of these principles till we reach the stage of the prophet's ministry at which their practical significance emerges.

6. The last six verses of the third chapter may be regarded either as closing the account of Ezekiel's consecration or as the introduction to the first part of his ministry, that which preceded the fall of Jerusalem. They contain the description of a second trance, which appears to have happened seven days after the first. The prophet seemed to himself to be carried out in spirit to a certain plain near his residence in Tel-abib. There the glory of Jehovah appears to him precisely as he had seen it in his former vision by the river Kebar. He then receives the command to shut himself up within his house. He is to be like a man bound with ropes, unable to move about among his fellow-exiles. Moreover, the free use of speech is to be interdicted; his tongue will be made to cleave to his palate, so that he is as one "dumb." But as often as he receives a message from Jehovah his mouth will be opened that he may declare it to the rebellious house of Israel.

Now if we compare ver. 26 with xxiv. 27 and xxxiii. 22, we find that this state of intermittent dumbness continued till the day when the siege of Jerusalem began, and was not finally removed till tidings were brought of the capture of the city. The verses before us therefore throw light on the prophet's demeanour during the first half of his ministry. What they signify is his almost entire withdrawal from public life. Instead of being like his great predecessors, a man living full in the public view, and thrusting himself on men's notice when they least desired him, he is to lead an isolated and a solitary life, a sign to the people rather than a living voice.* From the sequel we gather that he excited sufficient interest to induce the elders and others to visit him in his house to inquire of Jehovah. We must also suppose that from time to time he emerged from his retirement with a message for the whole community. It cannot, indeed, be assumed that the chaps. iv.–xxiv. contain an exact reproduction of the addresses delivered on these occasions. Few of them profess to have been uttered in public, and for the most part they give the impression of having been intended for patient study on the written page rather than for immediate oratorical effect. There is no reason to doubt that in the main they embody the results of Ezekiel's prophetic experiences during the period to which they are referred, although it may be impossible to determine how far they were actually spoken at the time, and how far they are merely written for the instruction of a wider audience.

The strong figures used here to describe this state of seclusion appear to reflect the prophet's consciousness of the restraints providentially imposed on the exercise of his office. These restraints, however, were moral, and not, as has sometimes been maintained, physical. The chief element was the pronounced hostility and incredulity of the people. This, combined with the sense of doom hanging over the nation, seems to have weighed on the spirit of Ezekiel, and in the ecstatic state the incubus lying upon him and paralysing his activity presents itself to his imagination as if he were bound with ropes and afflicted with dumbness. The representation finds a partial parallel in a later passage in the prophet's history. From xxix. 21 (which is the latest prophecy in the whole book) we learn that the apparent non-fulfilment of his predictions against Tyre had caused a similar hindrance to his public work, depriving him of the boldness of speech characteristic of a prophet. And the opening of the mouth given to him on that occasion by the vindication of his words is clearly analogous to the removal of his silence by the news that Jerusalem had fallen.*

* A somewhat similar episode seems to have occurred in the life of Isaiah. See the commentaries on Isa. viii 16–18.

* These verses (iii. 22–27) furnish one of the chief supports of Klostermann's peculiar theory of Ezekiel's condition during the first period of his career. Taking the word "dumb" in its literal sense, he considers that the prophet was afflicted with the malady known as *alalia*, that this was intermittent down to the date of chap. xxiv. and then became chronic till the fugitive arrived from Jerusalem (xxxiii. 21), when it finally disappeared. This is connected with the remarkable series of symbolic actions related in chap. iv., which are regarded as exhibiting all the symptoms of catalepsy and hemiplegia. These facts, together with the prophet's liability to ecstatic visions, justify, in Klostermann's view, the hypothesis that for seven years Ezekiel laboured under serious nervous disorders. The partiality shown by a few writers to this view probably springs from a desire to maintain the literal accuracy of the prophet's descriptions. But in that aspect the theory breaks down. Even Klostermann admits that the binding with ropes had no existence save in Ezekiel's imagination. But if we are obliged to take into account what *seemed* to the prophet, it is better to explain the whole phenomena on the same principle. There can be no good grounds for taking the dumbness as real and the ropes as imaginary. Besides, it is surely a questionable expedient to vindicate a prophet's literalism at the expense of his sanity. In the hands of Klostermann and Orelli the hypothesis assumes a stupendous miracle; but it is obvious that a critic of another school might readily "wear his rue with a difference," and treat the whole of Ezekiel's prophetic experiences as hallucinations of a deranged intellect.

PART II.

PROPHECIES RELATING MAINLY TO THE DESTRUCTION OF JERUSALEM.

CHAPTER V.

THE END FORETOLD.

Ezekiel iv.–vii.

With the fourth chapter we enter on the exposition of the first great division of Ezekiel's prophecies. The chaps. iv.–xxiv. cover a period of about four and a half years, extending from the time of the prophet's call to the commencement of the siege of Jerusalem. During this time Ezekiel's thoughts revolved round one great theme—the approaching judgment on the city and the nation. Through contemplation of this fact there was disclosed to him the outline of a comprehensive theory of divine providence, in which the destruction of Israel was seen to be the necessary consequence of her past history and a necessary preliminary to her future restoration. The prophecies may be classified roughly under three heads. In the first class are those which exhibit the judgment itself in ways fitted to impress the prophet and his hearers with a conviction of its certainty; a second class is intended to demolish the illusions and false ideals which possessed the minds of the Israelites and made the announcement of disaster incredible;

and a third and very important class expounds the moral principles which were illustrated by the judgment, and which show it to be a divine necessity. In the passage which forms the subject of the present lecture the bare fact and certainty of the judgment are set forth in word and symbol and with a minimum of commentary, although even here the conception which Ezekiel had formed of the moral situation is clearly discernible.

I.

The certainty of the national judgment seems to have been first impressed on Ezekiel's mind in the form of a singular series of symbolic acts which he conceived himself to be commanded to perform. The peculiarity of these signs is that they represent simultaneously two distinct aspects of the nation's fate—on the one hand the horrors of the siege of Jerusalem, and on the other hand the state of exile which was to follow.*

That the destruction of Jerusalem should occupy the first place in the prophet's picture of national calamity requires no explanation. Jerusalem was the heart and brain of the nation, the centre of its life and its religion, and in the eyes of the prophets the fountain-head of its sin. The strength of her natural situation, the patriotic and religious associations which had gathered round her, and the smallness of her subject province gave to Jerusalem a unique position among the mother-cities of antiquity. And Ezekiel's hearers knew what he meant when he employed the picture of a beleaguered city to set forth the judgment that was to overtake them. That crowning horror of ancient warfare, the siege of a fortified town, meant in this case something more appalling to the imagination than the ravages of pestilence and famine and sword. The fate of Jerusalem represented the disappearance of everything that had constituted the glory and excellence of Israel's national existence. That the light of Israel should be extinguished amidst the anguish and bloodshed which must accompany an unsuccessful defence of the capital was the most terrible element in Ezekiel's message, and here he sets it in the forefront of his prophecy.

The manner in which the prophet seeks to impress this fact on his countrymen illustrates a peculiar vein of realism which runs through all his thinking (iv. 1-3). Being at a distance from Jerusalem, he seems to feel the need of some visible emblem of the doomed city before he can adequately represent the import of his prediction. He is commanded to take a brick and portray upon it a walled city, surrounded by the towers, mounds, and battering-rams which marked the usual operations of a besieging army. Then he is to erect a plate of iron between him and the city, and from behind this, with menacing gestures, he is as it were to press on the siege. The meaning of the symbols is obvious. As the engines of destruction appear on Ezekiel's diagram, at the bidding of Jehovah, so in due time the Chaldæan army will be seen from the walls of Jerusalem, led by the same unseen Power which now controls the acts of the prophet. In the last act Ezekiel exhibits the attitude of Jehovah Himself, cut off from His people by the iron wall of an inexorable purpose which no prayer could penetrate.

Thus far the prophet's actions, however strange they may appear to us, have been simple and intelligible. But at this point a second sign is as it were superimposed on the first, in order to symbolise an entirely different set of facts—the hardship and duration of the Exile (vv. 4-8). While still engaged in prosecuting the siege of the city, the prophet is supposed to become at the same time the representative of the guilty people and the victim of the divine judgment. He is to "bear their iniquity"—that is, the punishment due to their sin. This is represented by his lying bound on his left side for a number of days equal to the years of Ephraim's banishment, and then on his right side for a time proportionate to the captivity of Judah. Now the time of Judah's exile is fixed at forty years, dating of course from the fall of the city. The captivity of North Israel exceeds that of Judah by the interval between the destruction of Samaria (722) and the fall of Jerusalem, a period which actually measured about a hundred and thirty-five years. In the Hebrew text, however, the length of Israel's captivity is given as three hundred and ninety years—that is, it must have lasted for three hundred and fifty years before that of Judah begins. This is obviously quite irreconcilable with the facts of history, and also with the prophet's intention. He cannot mean that the banishment of the northern tribes was to be protracted for two centuries after that of Judah had come to an end, for he uniformly speaks of the restoration of the two branches of the nation as simultaneous. The text of the Greek translation helps us past this difficulty. The Hebrew manuscript from which that version was made had the reading a "hundred and ninety" instead of "three hundred and ninety" in ver. 5. This alone yields a satisfactory sense, and the reading of the Septuagint is now generally accepted as representing what Ezekiel actually wrote. There is still a slight discrepancy between the hundred and thirty-five years of the actual history and the hundred and fifty years expressed by the symbol; but we must remember that Ezekiel is using round numbers throughout, and moreover he has not as yet fixed the precise date of the capture of Jerusalem when the last forty years are to commence.*

In the third symbol (vv. 9-17) the two aspects of the judgment are again presented in the closest possible combination. The prophet's food and drink during the days when he is imagined to be lying on his side represents on the one hand, by its being small in quantity and carefully weighed and measured, the rigours of famine in Jerusalem during the siege—"Behold, I will break the staff of bread in Jerusalem: and they shall eat bread by weight, and with anxiety; and drink water by measure, and with horror" (ver. 16); on the other hand, by its mixed ingredients and by the fuel used in its preparation, it typifies the unclean religious condition of the people when in exile—"Even so shall the chil-

*An ingenious attempt has been made by Professor Cornill to rearrange the verses so as to bring out two separate series of actions, one referring exclusively to the exile and the other to the siege. But the proposed reading requires a somewhat violent handling of the text, and does not seem to have met with much acceptance. The blending of diverse elements in a single image appears also in xii. 3-16.

*The correspondence would be almost exact if we date the commencement of the northern captivity from 734, when Tiglath-pileser carried away the inhabitants of the northern and eastern parts of the country. This is a possible view, although hardly necessary.

dren of Israel eat their food unclean among the heathen" (ver. 13). The meaning of this threat is best explained by a passage in the book of Hosea. Speaking of the Exile, Hosea says: "They shall not remain in the land of Jehovah; but the children of Ephraim shall return to Egypt, and shall eat unclean food in Assyria. They shall pour out no wine to Jehovah, nor shall they lay out their sacrifices for Him: like the food of mourners shall their food be; all that eat thereof shall be defiled: for their bread shall only satisfy their hunger; it shall not come into the house of Jehovah" (Hos. ix. 3, 4). The idea is that all food which has not been consecrated by being presented to Jehovah in the sanctuary is necessarily unclean, and those who eat of it contract ceremonial defilement. In the very act of satisfying his natural appetite a man forfeits his religious standing. This was the peculiar hardship of the state of exile, that a man must become unclean, he must eat unconsecrated food unless he renounced his religion and served the gods of the land in which he dwelt. Between the time of Hosea and Ezekiel these ideas may have been somewhat modified by the introduction of the Deuteronomic law, which expressly permits secular slaughter at a distance from the sanctuary. But this did not lessen the importance of a legal sanctuary for the common life of an Israelite. The whole of a man's flocks and herds, the whole produce of his fields, had to be sanctified by the presentation of firstlings and firstfruits at the Temple before he could enjoy the reward of his industry with the sense of standing in Jehovah's favour. Hence the destruction of the sanctuary or the permanent exclusion of the worshippers from it reduced the whole life of the people to a condition of uncleanness which was felt to be as great a calamity as was a papal interdict in the Middle Ages. This is the fact which is expressed in the part of Ezekiel's symbolism now before us. What it meant for his fellow-exiles was that the religious disability under which they laboured was to be continued for a generation. The whole life of Israel was to become unclean until its inward state was made worthy of the religious privileges now to be withdrawn. At the same time no one could have felt the penalty more severely than Ezekiel himself, in whom habits of ceremonial purity had become a second nature. The repugnance which he feels at the loathsome manner in which he was at first directed to prepare his food, and the profession of his own practice in exile, as well as the concession made to his scrupulous sense of propriety (vv. 14-16), are all characteristic of one whose priestly training had made a defect of ceremonial cleanness almost equivalent to a moral delinquency.

The last of the symbols (v. 1-4) represents the fate of the population of Jerusalem when the city is taken. The shaving of the prophet's head and beard is a figure for the depopulation of the city and country. By a further series of acts, whose meaning is obvious, he shows how a third of the inhabitants shall die of famine and pestilence during the siege, a third shall be slain by the enemy when the city is captured, while the remaining third shall be dispersed among the nations. Even these shall be pursued by the sword of vengeance until but a few numbered individuals survive, and of them again a part passes through the fire. The passage reminds us of the last verse of the sixth chapter of Isaiah, which was perhaps in Ezekiel's mind when he wrote: "And if a tenth still remain in it [the land], it shall again pass through the fire: as a terebinth or an oak whose stump is left at their felling: a holy seed shall be the stock thereof" (Isa. vi. 13). At least the conception of a succession of sifting judgments, leaving only a remnant to inherit the promise of the future, is common to both prophets, and the symbol in Ezekiel is noteworthy as the first expression of his steadfast conviction that further punishments were in store for the exiles after the destruction of Jerusalem.

It is clear that these signs could never have been enacted, either in view of the people or in solitude, as they are here described. It may be doubted whether the whole description is not purely ideal, representing a process which passed through the prophet's mind, or was suggested to him in the visionary state but never actually performed. That will always remain a tenable view. An imaginary symbolic act is as legitimate a literary device as an imaginary conversation. It is absurd to mix up the question of the prophet's truthfulness with the question whether he did or did not actually do what he conceives himself as doing. The attempt to explain his action by catalepsy would take us but a little way, even if the arguments adduced in favour of it were stronger than they are. Since even a cataleptic patient could not have tied himself down on his side or prepared and eaten his food in that posture, it is necessary in any case to admit that there must be a considerable, though indeterminate, element of literary imagination in the account given of the symbols. It is not impossible that some symbolic representation of the siege of Jerusalem may have actually been the first act in Ezekiel's ministry. In the interpretation of the vision which immediately follows we shall find that no notice is taken of the features which refer to exile, but only of those which announce the siege of Jerusalem. It may therefore be the case that Ezekiel did some such action as is here described, pointing to the fall of Jerusalem, but that the whole was taken up afterwards in his imagination and made into an ideal representation of the two great facts which formed the burden of his earlier prophecy.

II.

It is a relief to turn from this somewhat fantastic, though for its own purpose effective, exhibition of prophetic ideas to the impassioned oracles in which the doom of the city and the nation is pronounced. The first of these (vv. 5-17) is introduced here as the explanation of the signs that have been described, in so far as they bear on the fate of Jerusalem; but it has a unity of its own, and is a characteristic specimen of Ezekiel's oratorical style. It consists of two parts: the first (vv. 5-10) deals chiefly with the reasons for the judgment on Jerusalem, and the second (vv. 11-17) with the nature of the judgment itself. The chief thought of the passage is the unexampled severity of the punishment which is in store for Israel, as represented by the fate of the capital. A calamity so unprecedented demands an explanation as unique as itself. Ezekiel finds the ground of it in the signal honour conferred on Jerusalem in her being set in the midst of the nations, in the possession of a religion which expressed the will of the one God, and in the fact that she had proved herself unworthy of her distinction and privileges and tried to live as the nations around. "This is Jerusalem which I have set in the midst of the nations, with the lands round about her. But she rebelled against My judgments wickedly * more than the nations, and My statutes more than [other] lands round about her: for they rejected My judgments, and in My statutes they did not walk. . . . Therefore thus saith the Lord Jehovah: Behold, even I am against you; and I will execute in thy midst judgments before the nations, and will do in thy case what I have not done [heretofore], and what I shall not do the like of any more, according to all thy abominations" (vv. 5-9). The central position of Jerusalem is evidently no figure of speech in the mouth of Ezekiel. It means that she is so situated as to fulfil her destiny in the view of all the nations of the world, who can read in her wonderful history the character of the God who is above all gods. Nor can the prophet be fairly accused of provincialism in thus speaking of Jerusalem's unrivalled physical and moral advantages. The mountain ridge on which she stood lay almost across the great highways of communication between the East and the West, between the hoary seats of civilisation and the lands whither the course of empire took its way. Ezekiel knew that Tyre was the centre of the old world's commerce,† but he also knew that Jerusalem occupied a central situation in the civilised world, and in that fact he rightly saw a providential mark of the grandeur and universality of her religious mission. Her calamities, too, were probably such as no other city experienced. The terrible prediction of ver. 10, "Fathers shall eat sons in the midst of thee, and sons shall eat fathers," seems to have been literally fulfilled. "The hands of the pitiful women have sodden their own children: they were their meat in the destruction of the daughter of My people" (Lam. iv. 10). It is likely enough that the annals of Assyrian conquest cover many a tale of woe which in point of mere physical suffering paralleled the atrocities of the siege of Jerusalem. But no other nation had a conscience so sensitive as Israel, or lost so much by its political annihilation. The humanising influences of a pure religion had made Israel susceptible of a kind of anguish which ruder communities were spared.

The sin of Jerusalem is represented after Ezekiel's manner as on the one hand transgression of the divine commandments, and on the other defilement of the Temple through false worship. These are ideas which we shall frequently meet in the course of the book, and they need not detain us here. The prophet proceeds (vv. 11-17) to describe in detail the relentless punishment which the divine vengeance is to inflict on the inhabitants and the city. The jealousy, the wrath, the indignation of Jehovah, which are represented as "satisfied" by the complete destruction of the people, belong to the limitations of the conception of God which Ezekiel had. It was impossible at that time to interpret such an event as the fall of Jerusalem in a religious sense otherwise than as a vehement outburst of Jehovah's anger, expressing the reaction of His holy nature against the sin of idolatry. There is indeed a great distance between the attitude of Ezekiel towards the hapless city and the yearning pity of Christ's lament over the sinful Jerusalem of His time. Yet the first was a step towards the second. Ezekiel realised intensely that part of God's character which it was needful to enforce in order to beget in his countrymen the deep horror at the sin of idolatry which characterised the later Judaism. The best commentary on the latter part of this chapter is found in those parts of the book of Lamentations which speak of the state of the city and the survivors after its overthrow. There we see how quickly the stern judgment produced a more chastened and beautiful type of piety than had ever been prevalent before. Those pathetic utterances, in which patriotism and religion are so finely blended, are like the timid and tentative advances of a child's heart towards a parent who has ceased to punish but has not begun to caress. This, and much else that is true and ennobling in the later religion of Israel, is rooted in the terrifying sense of the divine anger against sin so powerfully represented in the preaching of Ezekiel.

* Or, with a different pointing, "She changed my judgments to wickedness."

† See chap. xxvii.

III.

The next two chapters may be regarded as pendants to the theme which is dealt with in this opening section of the book of Ezekiel. In the fourth and fifth chapters the prophet had mainly the city in his eye as the focus of the nation's life; in the sixth he turns his eye to the land which had shared the sin, and must suffer the punishment, of the capital. It is, in its first part (vv. 2-10), an apostrophe to the mountain land of Israel, which seems to stand out before the exile's mind with its mountains and hills, its ravines and valleys, in contrast to the monotonous plain of Babylonia which stretched around him. But these mountains were familiar to the prophet as the seats of the rural idolatry in Israel. The word ***bāmāh***, which means properly "the height," had come to be used as the name of an idolatrous sanctuary. These sanctuaries were probably Canaanitish in origin; and although by Israel they had been consecrated to the worship of Jehovah, yet He was worshipped there in ways which the prophets pronounced hateful to Him. They had been destroyed by Josiah, but must have been restored to their former use during the revival of heathenism which followed his death. It is a lurid picture which rises before the prophet's imagination as he contemplates the judgment of this provincial idolatry: the altars laid waste, the "sun-pillars" * broken, and the idols surrounded by the corpses of men who had fled to their shrines for protection and perished at their feet. This demonstration of the helplessness of the rustic divinities to save their sanctuaries and their worshippers will be the means of breaking the rebellious heart and the whorish eyes that had led Israel so far astray from her true Lord, and will produce in exile the self-loathing which Ezekiel always regards as the beginning of penitence.

But the prophet's passion rises to a higher pitch, and he hears the command "Clap thy hands, and stamp with thy foot, and say, Aha for the abominations of the house of Israel!" These

* *Hammânîm*—a word of doubtful meaning, however The word for idols, *gillûlîm*, is all but peculiar to Ezekiel It is variously explained as *block-gods* or *dung-gods*—in any case an epithet of contempt. The *ashērah*, or sacred pole, is never referred to by Ezekiel.

are gestures and exclamations, not of indignation, but of contempt and triumphant scorn. The same feeling and even the same gestures are ascribed to Jehovah Himself in another passage of highly charged emotion (xxi. 17). And it is only fair to remember that it is the anticipation of the victory of Jehovah's cause that fills the mind of the prophet at such moments and seems to deaden the sense of human sympathy within him. At the same time the victory of Jehovah was the victory of prophecy, and in so far Smend may be right in regarding the words as throwing light on the intensity of the antagonism in which prophecy and the popular religion then stood. The devastation of the land is to be effected by the same instruments as were at work in the destruction of the city: first the sword of the Chaldæans, then famine and pestilence among those who escape, until the whole of Israel's ancient territory lies desolate from the southern steppes to Riblah in the north.*

Chap. vii. is one of those singled out by Ewald as preserving most faithfully the spirit and language of Ezekiel's earlier utterances. Both in thought and expression it exhibits a freedom and animation seldom attained in Ezekiel's writings, and it is evident that it must have been composed under keen emotion. It is comparatively free from those stereotyped phrases which are elsewhere so common, and the style falls at times into the rhythm which is characteristic of Hebrew poetry. Ezekiel hardly perhaps attains to perfect mastery of poetic form, and even here we may be sensible of a lack of power to blend a series of impressions and images into an artistic unity. The vehemence of his feeling hurries him from one conception to another, without giving full expression to any, or indicating clearly the connection that leads from one to the other. This circumstance, and the corrupt condition of the text together, make the chapter in some parts unintelligible, and as a whole one of the most difficult in the book. In its present position it forms a fitting conclusion to the opening section of the book. All the elements of the judgment which have just been foretold are gathered up in one outburst of emotion, producing a song of triumph in which the prophet seems to stand in the uproar of the final catastrophe and exult amid the crash and wreck of the old order which is passing away.

The passage is divided into five stanzas, which may originally have been approximately equal in length, although the first is now nearly twice as long as any of the others.†

i. 2-9.—The first verse strikes the keynote of the whole poem; it is the inevitableness and the finality of the approaching dissolution. A striking phrase of Amos ‡ is first taken up and expanded in accordance with the anticipations with which the previous chapters have now familiarised us: "An end is come, the end is come on the four skirts of the land." The poet already hears the tumult and confusion of the battle; the vintage songs of the Judæan peasant are silenced, and with the din and fury of war the day of the Lord draws near.

ii. 10-13.—The prophet's thoughts here revert to the present, and he notes the eager interest with which men both in Judah and Babylon are pursuing the ordinary business of life and the vain dreams of political greatness. "The diadem flourishes, the sceptre blossoms, arrogance shoots up." These expressions must refer to the efforts of the new rulers of Jerusalem to restore the fortunes of the nation and the glories of the old kingdom which had been so greatly tarnished by the recent captivity. Things are going bravely, they think; they are surprised at their own success; they hope that the day of small things will grow into the day of things greater than those which are past. The following verse is untranslatable; probably the original words, if we could recover them, would contain some pointed and scornful antithesis to these futile and vain-glorious anticipations. The allusion to "buyers and sellers" (ver. 12) may possibly be quite general, referring only to the absorbing interest which men continue to take in their possessions, heedless of the impending judgment.* But the facts that the advantage is assumed to be on the side of the buyer and that the seller expects to return to his heritage make it probable that the prophet is thinking of the forced sales by the expatriated nobles of their estates in Palestine, and to their deeply cherished resolve to right themselves when the time of their exile is over. All such ambitions, says the prophet, are vain—"the seller shall not return to what he sold, and a man shall not by wrong preserve his living." In any case Ezekiel evinces here, as elsewhere, a certain sympathy with the exiled aristocracy, in opposition to the pretensions of the new men who had succeeded to their honours.

iii. 14-18.—The next scene that rises before the prophet's vision is the collapse of Judah's military preparations in the hour of danger. Their army exists but on paper. There is much blowing of trumpets and much organising, but no men to go forth to battle. A blight rests on all their efforts; their hands are paralysed and their hearts unnerved by the sense that "wrath rests on all their pomp." Sword, famine, and pestilence, the ministers of Jehovah's vengeance, shall devour the inhabitants of the city and the country, until but a few survivors on the tops of the mountains remain to mourn over the universal desolation.

iv. 19-22.—At present the inhabitants of Jerusalem are proud of the ill-gotten and ill-used wealth stored up within her, and doubtless the exiles cast covetous eyes on the luxury which may still have prevailed amongst the upper classes in the capital. But of what avail will all this treasure be in the evil day now so near at hand? It will but add mockery to their sufferings to be surrounded by gold and silver which can do nothing to allay the pangs of hunger. It will be cast in the streets as refuse, for it cannot save them in the day of Jehovah's anger. Nay, more, it will become the prize of the most ruthless of the heathen (the Chaldæans); and when in the eagerness of their lust for gold they ransack the Temple treasury and so desecrate the Holy Place, Jehovah will avert His face and suffer them to work their will. The curse of Jehovah rests on the silver and gold of Jerusalem, which has been used for the making of idolatrous images, and now is made to them an unclean thing.

v. 23-27.—The closing strophe contains a powerful description of the dismay and despair that

* In ver. 14 the true sense has been lost by the corruption of the word Riblah into Diblah.

† The reason may be that two different recensions of the text have been combined and mixed up. So Hitzig and Cornill.

‡ Amos viii. 2.

* *Cf.* Luke xvii. 26-30.

will seize all classes in the state as the day of wrath draws near. Calamity after calamity comes, rumour follows hard on rumour, and the heads of the nation are distracted and cease to exercise the functions of leadership. The recognised guides of the people—the prophets, the priests, and the wise men—have no word of counsel or direction to offer; the prophet's vision, the priest's traditional lore, and the wise man's sagacity are alike at fault. So the king and the grandees are filled with stupefaction; and the common people, deprived of their natural leaders, sit down in helpless dejection. Thus shall Jerusalem be recompensed according to her doings. "The land is full of bloodshed, and the city of violence"; and in the correspondence between desert and retribution men shall be made to acknowledge the operation of the divine righteousness. "They shall know that I am Jehovah."

IV.

It may be useful at this point to note certain theological principles which already begin to appear in this earliest of Ezekiel's prophecies. Reflection on the nature and purpose of the divine dealings we have seen to be a characteristic of his work; and even those passages which we have considered, although chiefly devoted to an enforcement of the fact of judgment, present some features of the conception of Israel's history which had been formed in his mind.

1. We observe in the first place that the prophet lays great stress on the world-wide significance of the events which are to befall Israel. This thought is not as yet developed, but it is clearly present. The relation between Jehovah and Israel is so peculiar that He is known to the nations in the first instance only as Israel's God, and thus His being and character have to be learned from His dealings with His own people. And since Jehovah is the only true God and must be worshipped as such everywhere, the history of Israel has an interest for the world such as that of no other nation has. She was placed in the centre of the nations in order that the knowledge of God might radiate from her through all the world; and now that she has proved unfaithful to her mission, Jehovah must manifest His power and His character by an unexampled work of judgment. Even the destruction of Israel is a demonstration to the universal conscience of mankind of what true divinity is.

2. But the judgment has of course a purpose and a meaning for Israel herself, and both purposes are summed up in the recurring formula "Ye [they] shall know that I am Jehovah," or "that I, Jehovah, have spoken." These two phrases express precisely the same idea, although from slightly different starting-points. It is assumed that Jehovah's personality is to be identified by His word spoken through the prophets. He is known to men through the revelation of Himself in the prophet's utterances. "Ye shall know that I, Jehovah, have spoken" means therefore, Ye shall know that it is I, the God of Israel and the Ruler of the universe, who speak these things. In other words, the harmony between prophecy and providence guarantees the source of the prophet's message. The shorter phrase "Ye shall know that I am Jehovah" may mean Ye shall know that I who now speak am truly Jehovah, the God of Israel. The prejudices of the people would have led them to deny that the power which dictated Ezekiel's prophecy could be their God; but this denial, together with the false idea of Jehovah on which it rests, shall be destroyed for ever when the prophet's words come true.

There is of course no doubt that Ezekiel conceived Jehovah as endowed with the plenitude of deity, or that in his view the name expressed all that we mean by the word God. Nevertheless, historically the name Jehovah is a proper name, denoting the God who is the God of Israel. Renan has ventured on the assertion that a deity with a proper name is necessarily a false god. The statement perhaps measures the difference between the God of revealed religion and the god who is an abstraction, an expression of the order of the universe, who exists only in the mind of the man who names him. The God of revelation is a living person, with a character and will of His own, capable of being known by man. It is the distinction of revelation that it dares to regard God as an individual with an inner life and nature of His own, independent of the conception men may form of Him. Applied to such a Being, a personal name may be as true and significant as the name which expresses the character and individuality of a man. Only thus can we understand the historical process by which the God who was first manifested as the deity of a particular nation preserves His personal identity with the God who in Christ is at last revealed as the God of the spirits of all flesh. The knowledge of Jehovah of which Ezekiel speaks is therefore at once a knowledge of the character of the God whom Israel professed to serve, and a knowledge of that which constitutes true and essential divinity.*

3. The prophet, in vi. 8-10, proceeds one step further in delineating the effect of the judgment on the minds of the survivors. The fascination of idolatry for the Israelites is conceived as produced by that radical perversion of the religious sense which the prophets call "whoredom"—a sensuous delight in the blessings of nature, and an indifference to the moral element which can alone preserve either religion or human love from corruption. The spell shall at last be broken in the new knowledge of Jehovah which is produced by calamity; and the heart of the people, purified from its delusions, shall turn to Him who has smitten them, as the only true God. "When your fugitives from the sword are among the nations, when they are scattered through the lands, then shall your fugitives remember Me amongst the nations whither they have been carried captive, when I break their heart that goes awhoring from Me, and their whorish eyes which went after their idols." When the idolatrous propensity is thus eradicated, the conscience of Israel will turn inwards on itself, and in the light of its new knowledge of God will for the first time read its own history aright. The beginnings of a new spiritual

* Ezekiel's use of the divine names would hardly be satisfactory to Renan. Outside of the prophecies addressed to heathen nations the generic name אלהים is never used absolutely, except in the phrases "visions of God" (three times) and "spirit of God" (once, in chap. xi. 24, where the text may be doubtful). Elsewhere it is used only of God in His relation to men, as, *e. g.*, in the expression "be to you for a God." שדי occurs once (chap. x. 5) and אל alone three times in chap. xxviii. (addressed to the prince of Tyre). The prophet's word, when he wishes to express absolute divinity, is just the "proper" name יהוה, in accordance no doubt with the interpretation given in Exod. iii. 13, 14.

life will be made in the bitter self-condemnation which is one side of the national repentance. "They shall loathe themselves for all the evil that they have committed in all their abominations."

CHAPTER VI.

YOUR HOUSE IS LEFT UNTO YOU DESOLATE.

EZEKIEL viii.-xi.

ONE of the most instructive phases of religious belief among the Israelites of the seventh century was the superstitious regard in which the Temple at Jerusalem was held. Its prestige as the metropolitan sanctuary had no doubt steadily increased from the time when it was built. But it was in the crisis of the Assyrian invasion that the popular sentiment in favour of its peculiar sanctity was transmuted into a fanatical faith in its inherent inviolability. It is well known that during the whole course of this invasion the prophet Isaiah had consistently taught that the enemy should never set foot within the precincts of the Holy City—that, on the contrary, the attempt to seize it would prove to be the signal for his annihilation. The striking fulfilment of this prediction in the sudden destruction of Sennacherib's army had an immense effect on the religion of the time. It restored the faith in Jehovah's omnipotence which was already giving way, and it granted a new lease of life to the very errors which it ought to have extinguished. For here, as in so many other cases, what was a spiritual faith in one generation became a superstition in the next. Indifferent to the divine truths which gave meaning to Isaiah's prophecy, the people changed his sublime faith in the living God working in history into a crass confidence in the material symbol which had been the means of expressing it to their minds. Henceforth it became a fundamental tenet of the current creed that the Temple and the city which guarded it could never fall into the hands of an enemy; and any teaching which assailed that belief was felt to undermine confidence in the national deity. In the time of Jeremiah and Ezekiel this superstition existed in unabated vigour, and formed one of the greatest hindrances to the acceptance of their teaching. "The Temple of the Lord, the Temple of the Lord, the Temple of the Lord are these!" was the cry of the benighted worshippers as they thronged to its courts to seek the favour of Jehovah (Jer. vii. 4). The same state of feeling must have prevailed among Ezekiel's fellow-exiles. To the prophet himself, attached as he was to the worship of the Temple, it may have been a thought almost too hard to bear that Jehovah should abandon the only place of His legitimate worship. Amongst the rest of the captives the faith in its infallibility was one of the illusions which must be overthrown before their minds could perceive the true drift of his teaching. In his first prophecy the fact had just been touched on, but merely as an incident in the fall of Jerusalem. About a year later, however, he received a new revelation, in which he learned that the destruction of the Temple was no mere incidental consequence of the capture of the city, but a main object of the calamity. The time was come when judgment must begin at the house of God.

The weird vision in which this truth was conveyed to the prophet is said to have occurred during a visit of the elders to Ezekiel in his own house. In their presence he fell into a trance, in which the events now to be considered passed before him; and after the trance was removed he recounted the substance of the vision to the exiles. This statement has been somewhat needlessly called in question, on the ground that after so protracted an ecstasy the prophet would not be likely to find his visitors still in their places. But this matter-of-fact criticism overreaches itself. We have no means of determining how long it would take for this series of events to be realised. If we may trust anything to the analogy of dreams—and of all conditions to which ordinary men are subject the dream is surely the closest analogy to the prophetic ecstasy—the whole may have passed in an incredibly short space of time. If the statement were untrue, it is difficult to see what Ezekiel would have gained by making it. If the whole vision were a fiction, this must of course be fictitious too; but even so it seems a very superfluous piece of invention.

We prefer, therefore, to regard the vision as real, and the assigned situation as historical; and the fact that it is recorded suggests that there must be some connection between the object of the visit and the burden of the revelation which was then communicated. It is not difficult to imagine points of contact between them. Ewald has conjectured that the occasion of the visit may have been some recent tidings from Jerusalem which had opened the eyes of the "elders" to the real relation that existed between them and their brethren at home. If they had ever cherished any illusions on the point, they had certainly been disabused of them before Ezekiel had this vision. They were aware, whether the information was recent or not, that they were absolutely disowned by the new authorities in Jerusalem, and that it was impossible that they should ever come back peaceably to their old place in the state. This created a problem which they could not solve, and the fact that Ezekiel had announced the fall of Jerusalem may have formed a bond of sympathy between him and his brethren in exile which drew them to him in their perplexity. Some such hypothesis gives at all events a fuller significance to the closing part of the vision, where the attitude of the men in Jerusalem is described, and where the exiles are taught that the hope of Israel's future lies with them. It is the first time that Ezekiel has distinguished between the fates in store for the two sections of the people, and it would almost appear as if the promotion of the exiles to the first place in the true Israel was a new revelation to him. Twice during this vision he is moved to intercede for the "remnant of Israel," as if the only hope of a new people of God lay in sparing at least some of those who were left in the land. But the burden of the message that now comes to him is that in the spiritual sense the true remnant of Israel is not in Judæa, but among the exiles in Babylon. It was there that the new Israel was to be formed, and the land was to be the heritage, not of those who clung to it and exulted in the misfortunes of their banished brethren, but of those who under the discipline of exile were first prepared to use the land as Jehovah's holiness demanded.

The vision is interesting, in the first place, on account of the glimpse it affords of the state of mind prevailing in influential circles in Jerusalem at this time. There is no reason whatever to doubt that here in the form of a vision we have reliable information regarding the actual state of matters when Ezekiel wrote. It has been supposed by some critics that the description of the idolatries in the Temple does not refer to contemporary practices, but to abuses that had been rife in the days of Manasseh and had been put a stop to by Josiah's reformation. But the vision loses half its meaning if it is taken as merely an idealised representation of all the sins that had polluted the Temple in the course of its history. The names of those who are seen must be names of living men known to Ezekiel and his contemporaries, and the sentiments put in their mouth, especially in the latter part of the vision, are suitable only to the age in which he lived. It is very probable that the description in its general features would *also* apply to the days of Manasseh; but the revival of idolatry which followed the death of Josiah would naturally take the form of a restoration of the illegal cults which had flourished unchecked under his grandfather. Ezekiel's own experience before his captivity, and the steady intercourse which had been maintained since, would supply him with the material which in the ecstatic condition is wrought up into this powerful picture.

The thing that surprises us most is the prevailing conviction amongst the ruling classes that "Jehovah had forsaken the land." These men seem to have partly emancipated themselves, as politicians in Israel were apt to do, from the restraints and narrowness of the popular religion. To them it was a conceivable thing that Jehovah should abandon His people. And yet life was worth living and fighting for apart from Jehovah. It was of course a merely selfish life, not inspired by national ideals, but simply a clinging to place and power. The wish was father to the thought; men who so readily yielded to the belief in Jehovah's absence were very willing to be persuaded of its truth. The religion of Jehovah had always imposed a check on social and civic wrong, and men whose power rested on violence and oppression could not but rejoice to be rid of it. So they seem to have acquiesced readily enough in the conclusion to which so many circumstances seemed to point, that Jehovah had ceased to interest Himself either for good or evil in them and their affairs. Still, the wide acceptance of a belief like this, so repugnant to all the religious ideas of the ancient world, seems to require for its explanation some fact of contemporary history. It has been thought that it arose from the disappearance of the ark of Jehovah from the Temple. It seems from the third chapter of Jeremiah that the ark was no longer in existence in Josiah's reign, and that the want of it was felt as a grave religious loss. It is not improbable that this circumstance, in connection with the disasters which had marked the last days of the kingdom, led in many minds to the fear and in some to the hope that along with His most venerable symbol Jehovah Himself had vanished from their midst.

It should be noticed that the feeling described was only one of several currents that ran in the divided society of Jerusalem. It is quite a different point of view that is presented in the taunt quoted in chap. xi. 15, that the exiles were far from Jehovah, and had therefore lost their right to their possessions. But the religious despair is not only the most startling fact that we have to look at; it is also the one that is made most prominent in the vision. And the Divine answer to it given through Ezekiel is that the conviction is true; Jehovah *has* forsaken the land. But in the first place the cause of His departure is found in those very practices for which it was made the excuse; and in the second, although He has ceased to dwell in the midst of His people, He has lost neither the power nor the will to punish their iniquities. To impress these truths first on his fellow-exiles and then on the whole nation is the chief object of the chapter before us.

Now we find that the general sense of God-forsakenness expressed itself principally in two directions. On the one hand it led to the multiplication of false objects of worship to supply the place of Him who was regarded as the proper tutelary Divinity of Israel; on the other hand, it produced a reckless, devil-may-care spirit of resistance against any odds, such as was natural to men who had only material interests to fight for, and nothing to trust in but their own right hand. Syncretism in religion and fatalism in politics—these were the twin symptoms of the decay of faith among the upper classes in Jerusalem. But these belong to two different parts of the vision which we must now distinguish.

I.

The first part deals with the departure of Jehovah as caused by religious offences perpetrated in the Temple, and with the return of Jehovah to destroy the city on account of these offences. The prophet is transported in "visions of God" to Jerusalem and placed in the outer court near the northern gate, outside of which was the site where the "image of Jealousy" had stood in the time of Manasseh. Near him stands the appearance which he had learned to recognise as the glory of Jehovah, signifying that Jehovah has, for a purpose not yet disclosed, revisited His Temple. But first Ezekiel must be made to see the state of things which exists in this Temple which had once been the seat of God's presence. Looking through the gate to the north, he discovers that the image of Jealousy * has been restored to its old place. This is the first and apparently the least heinous of the abominations that defiled the sanctuary.

The second scene is the only one of the four which represents a secret cult. Partly perhaps for that reason it strikes our minds as the most repulsive of all; but that was obviously not Ezekiel's estimate of it. There are greater abominations to follow. It is difficult to understand the particulars of Ezekiel's description, especially in the Hebrew text (the LXX. is simpler); but it seems impossible to escape the impression that there was something obscene in a worship where idolatry appears as ashamed of itself. The essential fact, however, is that the very highest and

* Of what nature this idolatrous symbol was we cannot certainly determine. The word used for "image" (*semel*) occurs in only two other passages. The writer of the books of Chronicles uses it of the *asherah* which was set up by Manasseh in the Temple, and it is possible that he means thus to identify that object with what Ezekiel saw (*cf.* 2 Chron. xxxiii. 7, and 2 Kings xxi. 7). This interpretation is as satisfactory as any that has been proposed.

most influential men in the land were addicted to a form of heathenism, whose objects of worship were pictures of "horrid creeping things, and cattle, and all the gods of the house of Israel." The name of one of these men, the leader in this superstition, is given, and is significant of the state of life in Jerusalem shortly before its fall. Jaazaniah was the son of Shaphan, who is probably identical with the chancellor of Josiah's reign whose sympathy with the prophetic teaching was evinced by his zeal in the cause of reform. We read of other members of the family who were faithful to the national religion, such as his son Ahikam, also a zealous reformer, and his grandson Gedaliah, Jeremiah's friend and patron, and the governor appointed over Judah by Nebuchadnezzar after the taking of the city. The family was thus divided both in religion and politics. While one branch was devoted to the worship of Jehovah and favoured submission to the king of Babylon, Jaazaniah belonged to the opposite party and was the ringleader in a peculiarly obnoxious form of idolatry.*

The third "abomination" is a form of idolatry widely diffused over Western Asia—the annual mourning for Tammuz. Tammuz was originally a Babylonian deity (Dumuzi), but his worship is specially identified with Phœnicia, whence under the name Adonis it was introduced into Greece. The mourning celebrates the death of the god, which is an emblem of the decay of the earth's productive powers, whether due to the scorching heat of the sun or to the cold of winter. It seems to have been a comparatively harmless rite of nature-religion, and its popularity among the women of Jerusalem at this time may be due to the prevailing mood of despondency which found vent in the sympathetic contemplation of that aspect of nature which most suggests decay and death.

The last and greatest of the abominations practised in and near the Temple is the worship of the sun. The peculiar enormity of this species of idolatry can hardly lie in the object of adoration; it is to be sought rather in the place where it was practised, and in the rank of those who took part in it, who were probably priests. Standing between the porch and the altar, with their backs to the Temple, these men unconsciously expressed the deliberate rejection of Jehovah which was involved in their idolatry. The worship of the heavenly bodies was probably imported into Israel from Assyria and Babylon, and its prevalence in the later years of the monarchy was due to political rather than religious influences. The gods of these imperial nations were esteemed more potent than those of the states which succumbed to their power, and hence men who were losing confidence in their national deity naturally sought to imitate the religions of the most powerful peoples known to them.†

In the arrangement of the four specimens of the religious practices which prevailed in Jerusalem, Ezekiel seems to proceed from the most familiar and explicable to the more outlandish defections from the purity of the national faith. At the same time his description shows how different classes of society were implicated in the sin of idolatry—the elders, the women, and the priests. During all this time the glory of Jehovah has stood in the court, and there is something very impressive in the picture of these infatuated men and women preoccupied with their unholy devotions and all unconscious of the presence of Him whom they deemed to have forsaken the land. To the open eye of the prophet the meaning of the vision must be already clear, but the sentence comes from the mouth of Jehovah Himself: "Hast thou seen, Son of man? Is it too small a thing for the house of Judah to practise the abominations which they have here practised, that they must also fill the land with violence, and (so) provoke Me again to anger? So will I act towards them in anger: My eye shall not pity, nor will I spare" (viii. 17, 18).

The last words introduce the account of the punishment of Jerusalem, which is given of course in the symbolic form suggested by the scenery of the vision. Jehovah has meanwhile risen from His throne near the cherubim, and stands on the threshold of the Temple. There He summons to His side the destroyers who are to execute His purpose—six angels, each with a weapon of destruction in his hand. A seventh of higher rank clothed in linen appears with the implements of a scribe in his girdle. These stand "beside the brasen altar," and await the commands of Jehovah. The first act of the judgment is a massacre of the inhabitants of the city, without distinction of age or rank or sex. But, in accordance with his strict view of the Divine righteousness, Ezekiel is led to conceive of this last judgment as discriminating carefully between the righteous and the wicked. All those who have inwardly separated themselves from the guilt of the city by hearty detestation of the iniquities perpetrated in its midst are distinguished by a mark on their foreheads before the work of slaughter begins. What became of this faithful remnant it does not belong to the vision to declare. Beginning with the twenty men before the porch, the destroying angels follow the man with the inkhorn through the streets of the city, and slay all on whom he has not set his mark. When the messengers have gone out on their dread errand, Ezekiel, realising the full horror of a scene which he dare not describe, falls prostrate before Jehovah, deprecating the outbreak of indignation which threatened to extinguish "the remnant of Israel." He is reassured by the declaration that the guilt of Judah and Israel demands no less a punishment than this, because the notion that Jehovah had forsaken the land had opened the floodgates of iniquity, and filled the land with bloodshed and the city with oppression. Then the man in the linen robes returns and announces, "It is done as Thou hast commanded."

* The nature of the cults is best explained by Professor Robertson Smith, who supposes that they are a survival of aboriginal totemistic superstitions which had been preserved in secret circles till now, but suddenly assumed a new importance with the collapse of the national religion and the belief that Jehovah had left the land. Others, however, have thought that it is Egyptian rites which are referred to. This view might best explain its prevalence among the elders, but it has little positive support.

† It has been supposed, however, that the sun-worship referred to here is of Persian origin, chiefly because of the obscure expression in ver. 17: "Behold they put the twig to their nose." This has been explained by a Persian custom of holding up a branch before the face, lest the breath of the worshipper should contaminate the purity of the deity. But Persia had not yet played any great part in history, and it is hardly credible that a distinctively Persian custom should have found its way into the ritual of Jerusalem. Moreover, the words do not occur in the description of the sun-worshippers, nor do they refer particularly to them.

The second act of the judgment is the destruction of Jerusalem by fire. This is symbolised by the scattering over the city of burning coals taken from the altar-hearth under the throne of God. The man with the linen garments is directed to step between the wheels and take out fire for this purpose. The description of the execution of this order is again carried no further than what actually takes place before the prophet's eyes: the man took the fire and went out. In the place where we might have expected to have an account of the destruction of the city, we have a second description of the appearance and motions of the *merkaba*, the purpose of which it is difficult to divine. Although it deviates slightly from the account in chap. i., the differences appear to have no significance, and indeed it is expressly said to be the same phenomenon. The whole passage is certainly superfluous, and might be omitted but for the difficulty of imagining any motive that would have tempted a scribe to insert it. We must keep in mind the possibility that this part of the book had been committed to writing before the final redaction of Ezekiel's prophecies, and the description in vv. 8-17 may have served a purpose there which is superseded by the fuller narrative which we now possess in chap. i.

In this way Ezekiel penetrates more deeply into the inner meaning of the judgment on city and people whose external form he had announced in his earlier prophecy. It must be admitted that Jehovah's strange work bears to our minds a more appalling aspect when thus presented in symbols than the actual calamity would bear when effected through the agency of second causes. Whether it had the same effect on the mind of a Hebrew, who hardly believed in second causes, is another question. In any case it gives no ground for the charge made against Ezekiel of dwelling with a malignant satisfaction on the most repulsive features of a terrible picture. He is indeed capable of a rigorous logic in exhibiting the incidence of the law of retribution which was to him the necessary expression of the Divine righteousness. That it included the death of every sinner and the overthrow of a city that had become a scene of violence and cruelty was to him a self-evident truth, and more than this the vision does not teach. On the contrary, it contains traits which tend to moderate the inevitable harshness of the truth conveyed. With great reticence it allows the execution of the judgment to take place behind the scenes, giving only those details which were necessary to suggest its nature. While it is being carried out the attention of the reader is engaged in the presence of Jehovah, or his mind is occupied with the principles which made the punishment a moral necessity. The prophet's expostulations with Jehovah show that he was not insensible to the miseries of his people, although he saw them to be inevitable. Further, this vision shows as clearly as any passage in his writings the injustice of the view which represents him as more concerned for petty details of ceremonial than for the great moral interests of a nation. If any feeling expressed in the vision is to be regarded as Ezekiel's own, then indignation against outrages on human life and liberty must be allowed to weigh more with him than offences against ritual purity. And, finally, it is clearly one object of the vision to show that in the destruction of Jerusalem no individual shall be involved who is not also implicated in the guilt which calls down wrath upon her.

II.

The second part of the vision (chap. xi.) is but loosely connected with the first. Here Jerusalem still exists, and men are alive who must certainly have perished in the "visitation of the city" if the writer had still kept himself within the limits of his previous conception. But in truth the two have little in common, except the Temple, which is the scene of both, and the cherubim, whose movements mark the transition from the one to the other. The glory of Jehovah is already departing from the house when it is stayed at the entrance of the east gate, to give the prophet his special message to the exiles.

Here we are introduced to the more political aspect of the situation in Jerusalem. The twenty-five men who are gathered in the east gate of the Temple are clearly the leading statesmen in the city; and two of them, whose names are given, are expressly designated as "princes of the people." They are apparently met in conclave to deliberate on public matters, and a word from Jehovah lays open to the prophet the nature of their projects. "These are the men that plan ruin, and hold evil counsel in this city." The evil counsel is undoubtedly the project of rebellion against the king of Babylon which must have been hatched at this time and which broke out into open revolt about three years later. The counsel was evil because directly opposed to that which Jeremiah was giving at the time in the name of Jehovah. But Ezekiel also throws invaluable light on the mood of the men who were urging the king along the path which led to ruin. "Are not the houses recently built?" * they say, congratulating themselves on their success in repairing the damage done to the city in the time of Jehoiachin. The image of the pot and the flesh is generally taken to express the feeling of easy security in the fortifications of Jerusalem with which these light-hearted politicians embarked on a contest with Nebuchadnezzar. But their mood must be a gloomier one than that if there is any appropriateness in the language they use. To stew in their own juice, and over a fire of their own kindling, could hardly seem a desirable policy to sane men, however strong the pot might be. These councillors are well aware of the dangers they incur, and of the misery which their purpose must necessarily bring on the people. But they are determined to hazard everything and endure everything on the chance that the city may prove strong enough to baffle the resources of the king of Babylon. Once the fire is kindled, it will certainly be better to be in the pot than in the fire; and so long as Jerusalem holds out they will remain behind her walls. The answer which is put into the prophet's mouth is that the issue will not be such as they hope for. The only "flesh" that will be left in the city will be the dead bodies of those who have been slain within her walls by the very men who hope that their lives will be given them for a prey. They themselves shall be dragged forth to meet their fate far away from Jerusalem on the "borders of Israel." It is not unlikely that these conspirators kept their word. Although the king and all the men of war fled from the city as soon

* Following the LXX.

as a breach was made, we read of certain high officials who allowed themselves to be taken in the city (Jer. lii. 7). Ezekiel's prophecy was in their case literally fulfilled; for these men and many others were brought to the king of Babylon at Riblah, "and he smote them and put them to death at Riblah in the land of Hamath."

While Ezekiel was uttering this prophecy one of the councillors, named Pelatiah, suddenly fell down dead. Whether a man of this name had suddenly died in Jerusalem under circumstances that had deeply impressed the prophet's mind, or whether the death belongs to the vision, it is impossible for us to tell. To Ezekiel the occurrence seemed an earnest of the complete destruction of the remnant of Israel by the wrath of God, and, as before, he fell on his face to intercede for them. It is then that he receives the message which seems to form the Divine answer to the perplexities which haunted the minds of the exiles in Babylon.

In their attitude towards the exiles the new leaders in Jerusalem took up a position as highly privileged religious persons, quite at variance with the scepticism which governed their conduct at home. When they were following the bent of their natural inclinations by practising idolatry and perpetrating judicial murders in the city, their cry was, "Jehovah hath forsaken the land; Jehovah seeth it not." When they were eager to justify their claim to the places and possessions left vacant by their banished countrymen, they said, "They are far from Jehovah: to us the land is given in possession." They were probably equally sincere and equally insincere in both professions. They had simply learned the art which comes easily to men of the world of using religion as a cloak for greed, and throwing it off when greed could be best gratified without it. The idea which lay under their religious attitude was that the exiles had gone into captivity because their sins had incurred Jehovah's anger, and that now His wrath was exhausted and the blessing of His favour would rest on those who had been left in the land. There was sufficient plausibility in the taunt to make it peculiarly galling to the mind of the exiles, who had hoped to exercise some influence over the government in Jerusalem, and to find their places kept for them when they should be permitted to return. It may well have been the resentment produced by tidings of this hostility towards them in Jerusalem that brought their elders to the house of Ezekiel to see if he had not some message from Jehovah to reassure them.

In the mind of Ezekiel, however, the problem took another form. To him a return to the old Jerusalem had no meaning; neither buyer nor seller should have cause to congratulate himself on his position. The possession of the land of Israel belonged to those in whom Jehovah's ideal of the new Israel was realised, and the only question of religious importance was, Where is the germ of this new Israel to be found? Amongst those who survive the judgment in the old land, or amongst those who have experienced it in the form of banishment? On this point the prophet receives an explicit revelation in answer to his intercession for "the remnant of Israel." "Son of man, thy brethren, thy brethren, thy fellow-captives, and the whole house of Israel of whom the inhabitants of Jerusalem have said, They are far from Jehovah: to us it is given—the land for an inheritance! . . . . Because I have removed them far among the nations, and have scattered them among the lands, and have been to them but little of a sanctuary in the lands where they have gone, therefore say, Thus saith Jehovah, so will I gather you from the peoples, and bring you from the lands where ye have been scattered, and will give you the land of Israel." The difficult expression "I have been but little of a sanctuary" refers to the curtailment of religious privileges and means of access to Jehovah which was a necessary consequence of exile. It implies, however, that Israel in banishment had learned in some measure to preserve that separation from other peoples and that peculiar relation to Jehovah which constituted its national holiness. Religion perhaps perishes sooner from the overgrowth of ritual than from its deficiency. It is an historical fact that the very meagreness of the religion which could be practised in exile was the means of strengthening the more spiritual and permanent elements which constitute the essence of religion. The observances which could be maintained apart from the Temple acquired an importance which they never afterwards lost; and although some of these, such as circumcision, the Passover, the abstinence from forbidden food, were purely ceremonial, others, such as prayer, reading of the Scriptures, and the common worship of the synagogue, represent the purest and most indispensable forms in which communion with God can find expression. That Jehovah Himself became even in small measure what the word "sanctuary" denotes indicates an enrichment of the religious consciousness of which perhaps Ezekiel himself did not perceive the full import.

The great lesson which Ezekiel's message seeks to impress on his hearers is that the tenure of the land of Israel depends on religious conditions. The land is Jehovah's, and He bestows it on those who are prepared to use it as His holiness demands. A pure land inhabited by a pure people is the ideal that underlies all Ezekiel's visions of the future. It is evident that in such a conception of the relation between God and His people ceremonial conditions must occupy a conspicuous place. The sanctity of the land is necessarily of a ceremonial order, and so the sanctity of the people must consist partly in a scrupulous regard for ceremonial requirements. But after all the condition of the land with respect to purity or uncleanness only reflects the character of the nation whose home it is. The things that defile a land are such things as idols and other emblems of heathenism, innocent blood unavenged, and unnatural crimes of various kinds. These things derive their whole significance from the state of mind and heart which they embody; they are the plain and palpable emblems of human sin. It is conceivable that to some minds the outward emblems may have seemed the true seat of evil, and their removal an end in itself apart from the direction of the will by which it was brought about. But it would be a mistake to charge Ezekiel with any such obliquity of moral vision. Although he conceives sin as a defilement that leaves its mark on the material world, he clearly teaches that its essence lies in the opposition of the human will to the will of God. The ceremonial purity required of every Israelite is only the expression of certain aspects of Jehovah's holy nature, the bearing of which on man's spiritual life may have been obscure to the prophet, and is still more obscure to us. And the truly valuable element in compliance with such rules was the obedience to Jehovah's expressed will which flowed from a nature in sympathy with His. Hence in this chapter, while the first thing that the restored exiles have to do is to cleanse the land of its abominations, this act will be the expression of a nature radically changed, doing the will of God from the heart. As the emblems of idolatry that defile the land were the outcome of an irresistible national tendency to evil, so the new and sensitive spirit, taking on the impress of Jehovah's holiness through the law, shall lead to the purification of the land from those things that had provoked the eyes of His glory. "They shall come thither, and remove thence all its detestable things and all its abominations. And I will give them another heart, and put a new spirit within them. I will take away the stony heart from their flesh, and give them a heart of flesh: that they may walk in My statutes, and keep My judgments, and do them: and so shall they be My people, and I will be their God" (xi. 18-20).

Thus in the mind of the prophet Jerusalem and its Temple are already virtually destroyed. He seemed to linger in the Temple court until he saw the chariot of Jehovah withdrawn from the city as a token that the glory had departed from Israel. Then the ecstasy passed away, and he found himself in the presence of the men to whom the hope of the future had been offered, but who were as yet unworthy to receive it.

CHAPTER VII.

THE END OF THE MONARCHY.

EZEKIEL xii. 1-15, xvii., xix.

IN spite of the interest excited by Ezekiel's prophetic appearances, the exiles still received his prediction of the fall of Jerusalem with the most stolid incredulity. It proved to be an impossible task to disabuse their minds of the prepossessions which made such an event absolutely incredible. True to their character as a disobedient house, they had "eyes to see, and saw not; and ears to hear, but heard not" (xii. 2). They were intensely interested in the strange signs he performed, and listened with pleasure to his fervid oratory; but the inner meaning of it all never sank into their minds. Ezekiel was well aware that the cause of this obtuseness lay in the false ideals which nourished an overweening confidence in the destiny of their nation. And these ideals were the more difficult to destroy because they each contained an element of truth, so interwoven with the falsehood that to the mind of the people the true and the false stood and fell together. If the great vision of chaps. viii.-xi. had accomplished its purpose, it would doubtless have taken away the main support of these delusive imaginations. But the belief in the indestructibility of the Temple was only one of a number of roots through which the vain confidence of the nation was fed; and so long as any of these remained the people's sense of security was likely to remain. These spurious ideals, therefore, Ezekiel sets himself with characteristic thoroughness to demolish, one after another.

This appears to be in the main the purpose of the third subdivision of his prophecies on which we now enter. It extends from chap. xii. to chap. xix.; and in so far as it can be taken to represent a phase of his actual spoken ministry, it must be assigned to the fifth year before the capture of Jerusalem (August, 591-August, 590 B. C.). But since the passage is an exposition of ideas more than a narrative of experiences, we may expect to find that chronological consistency has been even less observed than in the earlier part of the book. Each idea is presented in the completeness which it finally possessed in the prophet's mind, and his allusions may anticipate a state of things which had not actually arisen till a somewhat later date. Beginning with a description and interpretation of two symbolic actions intended to impress more vividly on the people the certainty of the impending catastrophe, the prophet proceeds in a series of set discourses to expose the hollowness of the illusions which his fellow-exiles cherished, such as disbelief in prophecies of evil, faith in the destiny of Israel, veneration for the Davidic kingdom, and reliance on the solidarity of the nation in sin and in judgment. These are the principal topics which the course of exposition will bring before us, and in dealing with them it will be convenient to depart from the order in which they stand in the book and adopt an arrangement according to subject. By so doing we run the risk of missing the order of the ideas as it presented itself to the prophet's mind, and of ignoring the remarkable skill with which the transition from one theme to another is frequently effected. But if we have rightly understood the scope of the passage as a whole, this will not prevent us from grasping the substance of his teaching or its bearing on the final message which he had to deliver. In the present chapter we shall accordingly group together three passages which deal with the fate of the monarchy, and especially of Zedekiah, the last king of Judah.

That reverence for the royal house would form an obstacle to the acceptance of such teaching as Ezekiel's was to be expected from all we know of the popular feeling on this subject. The fact that a few royal assassinations which stain the annals of Judah were sooner or later avenged by the people shows that the monarchy was regarded as a pillar of the state, and that great importance was attached to the possession of a dynasty which perpetuated the glories of David's reign. And there is one verse in the Book of Lamentations which expresses the anguish which the fall of the kingdom caused to godly men in Israel, although its representatives were so unworthy of his office as Zedekiah: "The breath of our nostrils, the anointed of Jehovah, was taken in their pits, of whom we said, Under his shadow shall we live among the nations" (Lam. iv. 20). So long therefore as a descendant of David sat on the throne of Jerusalem it would seem the duty of every patriotic Israelite to remain true to him. The continuance of the monarchy would seem to guarantee the existence of the state; the prestige of Zedekiah's position as the anointed of Jehovah, and the heir of David's covenant, would warrant the hope that even yet Jehovah would intervene to save an institution of His own creating. Indeed, we can see from Ezekiel's own pages that the historic monarchy in Israel was to him an object of the highest veneration and regard. He speaks of its dignity in terms whose very exaggeration shows how largely the fact bulked in his imagination. He compares it to the noblest of the wild beasts of the earth and the most lordly tree of the forest. But his contention is that this monarchy no longer exists. Except in one doubtful passage, he never applies the title king (*melek*) to Zedekiah. The kingdom came to an end with the deportation of Jehoiachin, the last king who ascended the throne in legitimate succession. The present holder of the office is in no sense king by Divine right; he is a creature and vassal of Nebuchadnezzar, and has no rights against his suzerain.* His very name has been changed by the caprice of his master. As a religious symbol, therefore, the royal power is defunct; the glory has departed from it as surely as from the Temple. The makeshift administration organised under Zedekiah had a peaceful if inglorious future before it, if it were content to recognise facts and adapt itself to its humble position. But if it should attempt to raise its head and assert itself as an independent kingdom, it would only seal its own doom. And for men in Chaldea to transfer to this shadow of kingly dignity the allegiance due to the heir of David's house was a waste of devotion as little demanded by patriotism as by prudence.

I.

The first of the passages in which the fate of the monarchy is foretold requires little to be said by way of explanation. It is a symbolic action of the kind with which we are now familiar, exhibiting the certainty of the fate in store both for the people and the king. The prophet again becomes a "sign" or portent to the people—this time in a character which every one of his audience understood from recent experience. He is seen by daylight collecting "articles of captivity"—*i. e.*, such necessary articles as a person going into exile would try to take with him—and bringing them out to the door of his house. Then at dusk he breaks through the wall with his goods on his shoulder; and, with face muffled, he removes "to another place." In this sign we have again two different facts indicated by a series of not entirely congruous actions. The mere act of carrying out his most necessary furniture and removing from one place to another suggests quite unambiguously the captivity that awaits the inhabitants of Jerusalem. But the accessories of the action, such as breaking through the wall, the muffling of the face, and the doing of all this by night, point to quite a different event—viz., Zedekiah's attempt to break through the Chaldæan lines by night, his capture, his blindness, and his imprisonment in Babylon. The most remarkable thing in the sign is the circumstantial manner in which the details of the king's flight and capture are anticipated so long before the event. Zedekiah, as we read in the Second Book of Kings, as soon as a breach was made in the walls by the Chaldæans, broke out with a small party of horsemen, and succeeded in reaching the plain of Jordan. There he was overtaken and caught, and sent before Nebuchadnezzar's presence at **Riblah.** The Babylonian king punished his perfidy with a cruelty common enough amongst the Assyrian kings: he caused his eyes to be put out, and sent him thus to end his days in prison at Babylon. All this is so clearly hinted at in the signs that the whole representation is often set aside as a prophecy after the event. That is hardly probable, because the sign does not bear the marks of having been originally conceived with the view of exhibiting the details of Zedekiah's punishment. But since we know that the book was written after the event, it is a perfectly fair question whether in the interpretation of the symbols Ezekiel may not have read into it a fuller meaning than was present to his own mind at the time. Thus the covering of his head does not necessarily suggest anything more than the king's attempt to disguise his person.* Possibly this was all that Ezekiel originally meant by it. When the event took place he perceived a further meaning in it as an allusion to the blindness inflicted on the king, and introduced this into the explanation given of the symbol. The point of it lies in the degradation of the king through his being reduced to such an ignominious method of securing his personal safety. "The prince that is among them shall bear upon his shoulder in the darkness, and shall go forth: they shall dig through the wall to carry out thereby: he shall cover his face, that he may not be seen by any eye, and he himself shall not see the earth" (xii. 12).

II.

In chap. xvii. the fate of the monarchy is dealt with at greater length under the form of an allegory. The kingdom of Judah is represented as a cedar in Lebanon—a comparison which shows how exalted were Ezekiel's conceptions of the dignity of the old regime which had now passed away. But the leading shoot of the tree has been cropped off by a great, broad-winged, speckled eagle, the king of Babylon, and carried away to a "land of traffic, a city of merchants."† The insignificance of Zedekiah's government is indicated by a harsh contrast which almost breaks the consistency of the figure. In place of the cedar which he has spoiled the eagle plants a low vine trailing on the ground, such as may be seen in Palestine at the present day. His intention was that "its branches should extend towards him and its roots be under him"—*i. e.*, that the new principality should derive all its strength from Babylon and yield all its produce to the power which nourished it. For a time all went well. The vine answered the expectations of its owner, and prospered under the favourable conditions which he had provided for it. But another great eagle appeared on the scene, the king of Egypt, and the ungrateful vine began to send out its roots and turn its branches in his direction. The meaning is obvious: Zedekiah had sent presents to Egypt and sought its help, and by so doing had violated the conditions of his tenure of royal power. Such a policy could not prosper. "The bed where it was planted" was in possession of Nebuchadnezzar, and he could not tolerate there a state, however feeble, which employed the resources with which he had endowed

* It is noteworthy that in the dirge of chap. xix. Ezekiel ignores the reign of Jehoiakim. Is this because he too owed his elevation to the intervention of a foreign power?

* Especially if we read ver. 12, as in LXX., "That he may not be seen by any eye, and he shall not see the earth."

† By this name for Chaldæa Ezekiel seems to express his contempt for the commercial activity which formed so large an element in the greatness of Babylon (chap. xvi. 29 R. V.), perhaps also his sense of the uncongenial environment in which the disinherited king and the nobility of Judah now found themselves.

it to further the interests of his rival, Hophra, the king of Egypt. Its destruction shall come from the quarter whence it derived its origin: "when the east wind smites it, it shall wither in the furrow where it grew."

Throughout this passage Ezekiel shows that he possessed in full measure that penetration and detachment from local prejudices which all the prophets exhibit when dealing with political affairs. The interpretation of the riddle contains a statement of Nebuchadnezzar's policy in his dealings with Judah, whose impartial accuracy could not be improved on by the most disinterested historian. The carrying away of the Judæan king and aristocracy was a heavy blow to religious susceptibilities which Ezekiel fully shared, and its severity was not mitigated by the arrogant assumptions by which it was explained in Jerusalem. Yet here he shows himself capable of contemplating it as a measure of Babylonian statesmanship and of doing absolute justice to the motives by which it was dictated. Nebuchadnezzar's purpose was to establish a petty state unable to raise itself to independence, and one on whose fidelity to his empire he could rely. Ezekiel lays great stress on the solemn formalities by which the great king had bound his vassal to his allegiance: "He took of the royal seed, and made a covenant with him, and brought him under a curse; and the strong ones of the land he took away: that it might be a lowly kingdom, not able to lift itself up, to keep his covenant that it might stand" (vv. 13, 14). In all this Nebuchadnezzar is conceived as acting within his rights; and here lay the difference between the clear vision of the prophet and the infatuated policy of his contemporaries. The politicians of Jerusalem were incapable of thus discerning the signs of the times. They fell back on the time-honoured plan of checkmating Babylon by means of an Egyptian alliance—a policy which had been disastrous when attempted against the ruthless tyrants of Assyria, and which was doubly imbecile when it brought down on them the wrath of a monarch who showed every desire to deal fairly with his subject provinces.

The period of intrigue with Egypt had already begun when this prophecy was written. We have no means of knowing how long the negotiations went on before the overt act of rebellion; and hence we cannot say with certainty that the appearance of the chapter in this part of the book is an anachronism. It is possible that Ezekiel may have known of a secret mission which was not discovered by the spies of the Babylonian court; and there is no difficulty in supposing that such a step may have been taken as early as two and a half years before the outbreak of hostilities. At whatever time it took place, Ezekiel saw that it sealed the doom of the nation. He knew that Nebuchadnezzar could not overlook such flagrant perfidy as Zedekiah and his councillors had been guilty of; he knew also that Egypt could render no effectual help to Jerusalem in her death-struggle. "Not with a strong army and a great host will Pharaoh act for him in the war, when mounds are thrown up, and the towers are built, to cut off many lives" (ver. 17). The writer of the Lamentations again shows us how sadly the prophet's anticipation was verified: "As for us, our eyes as yet failed for our vain help: in our watching we have watched for a nation that could not save us" (Lam. iv. 17).

But Ezekiel will not allow it to be supposed that the fate of Jerusalem is merely the result of a mistaken forecast of political probabilities. Such a mistake had been made by Zedekiah's advisers when they trusted to Egypt to deliver them from Babylon, and ordinary prudence might have warned them against it. But that was the most excusable part of their folly. The thing that branded their policy as infamous and put them absolutely in the wrong before God and man alike was their violation of the solemn oath by which they had bound themselves to serve the king of Babylon. The prophet seizes on this act of perjury as the determining fact of the situation, and charges it home on the king as the cause of the ruin that is to overtake him: "Thus saith Jehovah, As I live, surely *My* oath which he hath despised, and *My* covenant which he has broken, I will return on his head; and I will spread My net over him, and in My snare shall he be taken, . . . and ye shall know that I Jehovah have spoken it" (vv. 19-21).

In the last three verses of the chapter the prophet returns to the allegory with which he commenced, and completes his oracle with a beautiful picture of the ideal monarchy of the future. The ideas on which the picture is framed are few and simple; but they are those which distinguished the Messianic hope as cherished by the prophets from the crude form which it assumed in the popular imagination. In contrast to Zedekiah's kingdom, which was a human institution without ideal significance, that of the Messianic age will be a fresh creation of Jehovah's power. A tender shoot shall be planted in the mountain land of Israel, where it shall flourish and increase until it overshadow the whole earth. Further, this shoot is taken from the "top of the cedar"—that is, the section of the royal house which had been carried away to Babylon—indicating that the hope of the future lay not with the king *de facto* Zedekiah, but with Jehoiachin and those who shared his banishment. The passage leaves no doubt that Ezekiel conceived the Israel of the future as a state with a monarch at its head, although it may be doubtful whether the shoot refers to a personal Messiah or to the aristocracy, who, along with the king, formed the governing body in an Eastern kingdom. This question, however, can be better considered when we have to deal with Ezekiel's Messianic conceptions in their fully developed form in chap. xxxiv.

III.

Of the last four kings of Judah there were two whose melancholy fate seems to have excited a profound feeling of pity amongst their countrymen. Jehoahaz or Shallum, according to the Chronicler the youngest of Josiah's sons, appears to have been even during his father's lifetime a popular favourite. It was he who after the fatal day of Megiddo was raised to the throne by the "people of the land" at the age of twenty-three years. He is said by the historian of the books of Kings to have done "that which was evil in the sight of the Lord"; but he had hardly time to display his qualities as a ruler when he was deposed and carried to Egypt by Pharaoh Necho, having worn the crown for only three months (608 B. C.). The deep attachment felt for him seems to have given rise to an expectation that he would be restored to his kingdom, a delusion against which the prophet Jeremiah found it necessary to protest (Jer. xxii. 10-12). He was succeeded by his elder brother, Eliakim,* the headstrong and selfish tyrant, whose character stands revealed in some passages of the books of Jeremiah and Habakkuk. His reign of nine years gave little occasion to his subjects to cherish a grateful memory of his administration. He died in the crisis of the conflict he had provoked with the king of Babylon, leaving his youthful son Jehoiachin to expiate the folly of his rebellion. Jehoiachin is the second idol of the populace to whom we have referred. He was only eighteen years old when he was called to the throne, and within three months he was doomed to exile in Babylon. In his room Nebuchadnezzar appointed a third son of Josiah—Mattaniah—whose name he changed to Zedekiah. He was apparently a man of weak and vacillating character; but he fell ultimately into the hands of the Egyptian and anti-prophetic party, and so was the means of involving his country in the hopeless struggle in which it perished.

The fact that two of their native princes were languishing, perhaps simultaneously, in foreign confinement, one in Egypt and the other in Babylon, was fitted to evoke in Judah a sympathy with the misfortunes of royalty something like the feeling embalmed in the Jacobite songs of Scotland. It seems to be an echo of this sentiment that we find in the first part of the lament with which Ezekiel closes his references to the fall of the monarchy (chap. xix.). Many critics have indeed found it impossible to suppose that Ezekiel should in any sense have yielded to sympathy with the fate of two princes who are both branded in the historical books as idolaters, and whose calamities on Ezekiel's own view of individual retribution proved them to be sinners against Jehovah. Yet it is certainly unnatural to read the dirge in any other sense than as an expression of genuine pity for the woes that the nation suffered in the fate of her two exiled kings. If Jeremiah, in pronouncing the doom of Shallum or Jehoahaz, could say, "Weep ye sore for him that goeth away; for he shall not return any more, nor see his native country," there is no reason why Ezekiel should not have given lyrical expression to the universal feeling of sadness which the blighted career of these two youths naturally produced. The whole passage is highly poetical, and represents a side of Ezekiel's nature which we have not hitherto been led to study. But it is too much to expect of even the most logical of prophets that he should experience no personal emotion but what fitted into his system, or that his poetic gift should be chained to the wheels of his theological convictions. The dirge expresses no moral judgment on the character or deserts of the two kings to which it refers: it has but one theme—the sorrow and disappointment of the "mother" who nurtured and lost them, that is, the nation of Israel, personified according to a usual Hebrew figure of speech. All attempts to go beyond this and to find in the poem an allegorical portrait of Jehoahaz and Jehoiachin are irrelevant. The mother is a lioness, the princes are young lions and behave as stalwart young lions do, but whether their exploits are praiseworthy or the reverse is a question that was not present to the writer's mind.

* Jehoiakim.

The chapter is entitled "A Dirge on the Princes of Israel," and embraces not only the fate of Jehoahaz and Jehoiachin, but also of Zedekiah, with whom the old monarchy expired. Strictly speaking, however, the name *qînah*, or dirge, is applicable only to the first part of the chapter (vv. 2-9), where the rhythm characteristic of the Hebrew elegy is clearly traceable.* With a few slight changes of the text † the passage may be translated thus:—

i. *Jehoahaz.*

"How was thy mother a lioness!—
Among the lions,
In the midst of young lions she couched—
She reared her cubs;
And she brought up one of her cubs—
A young lion he became,
And he learned to catch the prey—
He ate men.

"And nations raised a cry against him—
In their pit he was caught;
And they brought him with hooks—
To the land of Egypt (vv. 2-4).

ii. *Jehoiachin.*

"And when she saw that she was disappointed ‡—
Her hope was lost.
She took another of her cubs—
A young lion she made him;
And he walked in the midst of lions—
A young lion he became;
And he learned to catch prey—
He ate men.

"And he lurked in his lair—
The forests he ravaged:
Till the land was laid waste and its fulness—
With the noise of his roar.

"The nations arrayed themselves against him—
From the countries around;
"And spread over him their net—
In their pit he was caught.
And they brought him with hooks—
To the king of Babylon;
And he put him in a cage, . . .
That his voice might no more be heard—
On the mountains of Israel" (vv. 5-9).

The poetry here is simple and sincere. The mournful cadence of the elegiac measure, which is maintained throughout, is adapted to the tone of melancholy which pervades the passage and culminates in the last beautiful line. The dirge is a form of composition often employed in songs of triumph over the calamities of enemies; but there is no reason to doubt that here it is true to its original purpose, and expresses genuine sorrow for the accumulated misfortunes of the royal house of Israel.

The closing part of the "dirge" dealing with Zedekiah is of a somewhat different character. The theme is similar, but the figure is abruptly changed, and the elegiac rhythm is abandoned. The nation, the mother of the monarchy, is here compared to a luxuriant vine planted beside great waters; and the royal house is likened to a branch towering above the rest and bearing rods which were kingly sceptres. But she has been plucked up by the roots, withered, scorched by the fire, and finally planted in an arid region where she cannot thrive. The application of the metaphor to the ruin of the nation is very obvious. Israel, once a prosperous nation, richly

* The long line is divided into two unequal parts by a cæsura over the end.

† Mostly adopted from Cornill. The English reader may refer to Dr. Davidson's commentary.

‡ This word is uncertain.

endowed with all the conditions of a vigorous national life, and glorying in her race of native kings, is now humbled to the dust. Misfortune after misfortune has destroyed her power and blighted her prospects, till at last she has been removed from her own land to a place where national life cannot be maintained. But the point of the passage lies in the closing words: fire went out from one of her twigs and consumed her branches, so that she has no longer a proud rod to be a ruler's sceptre (ver. 14). The monarchy, once the glory and strength of Israel, has in its last degenerate representative involved the nation in ruin.

Such is Ezekiel's final answer to those of his hearers who clung to the old Davidic kingdom as their hope in the crisis of the people's fate.

CHAPTER VIII.

PROPHECY AND ITS ABUSES.

EZEKIEL xii. 21-xiv. 11.

THERE is perhaps nothing more perplexing to the student of Old Testament history than the complicated phenomena which may be classed under the general name of "prophecy." In Israel, as in every ancient state, there was a body of men who sought to influence public opinion by prognostications of the future. As a rule the repute of all kinds of divination declined with the advance of civilisation and general intelligence, so that in the more enlightened communities matters of importance came to be decided on broad grounds of reason and political expediency. The peculiarity in the case of Israel was that the very highest direction in politics, as well as religion and morals, was given in a form capable of being confounded with superstitious practices which flourished alongside of it. The true prophets were not merely profound moral thinkers, who announced a certain issue as the probable result of a certain line of conduct. In many cases their predictions are absolute, and their political programme is an appeal to the nation to accept the situation which they foresee, as the basis of its public action. For this reason prophecy was readily brought into competition with practices with which it had really nothing in common. The ordinary individual who cared little for principles and only wished to know what was likely to happen might readily think that one way of arriving at knowledge of the future was as good as another, and when the spiritual prophet's anticipations displeased him he was apt to try his luck with the sorcerer. It is not improbable that in the last days of the monarchy spurious prophecy of various kinds gained an additional vitality from its rivalry with the great spiritual teachers who in the name of Jehovah foretold the ruin of the state.

This is not the place for an exhaustive account of the varied developments in Israel of what may be broadly termed prophetic manifestations. For the understanding of the section of Ezekiel now before us it will be enough to distinguish three classes of phenomena. At the lowest end of the scale there was a rank growth of pure magic or sorcery, the ruling idea of which is the attempt to control or forecast the future by occult arts which are believed to influence the supernatural powers which govern human destiny. In the second place we have prophecy in a stricter sense—that is, the supposed revelation of the will of the deity in dreams or "visions" or half-articulate words uttered in a state of frenzy. Last of all there is the true prophet, who, though subject to extraordinary mental experiences, yet had always a clear and conscious grasp of moral principles, and possessed an incommunicable certainty that what he spoke was not his own word but the word of Jehovah.

It is obvious that a people subjected to such influences as these was exposed to temptations both intellectual and moral from which modern life is exempt. One thing is certain—the existence of prophecy did not tend to simplify the problems of national life or individual conduct. We are apt to think of the great prophets as men so signally marked out by God as His witnesses that it must have been impossible for any one with a shred of sincerity to question their authority. In reality it was quite otherwise. It was no more an easy thing then than now to distinguish between truth and error, between the voice of God and the speculations of men. Then, as now, divine truth had no available credentials at the moment of its utterance except its self-evidencing power on hearts that were sincere in their desire to know it. The fact that truth came in the guise of prophecy only stimulated the growth of counterfeit prophecy, so that only those who were "of the truth" could discern the spirits whether they were of God.

The passage which forms the subject of this chapter is one of the most important passages of the Old Testament in its treatment of the errors and abuses incident to a dispensation of prophecy. It consists of three parts: the first deals with difficulties occasioned by the apparent failure of prophecy (xii. 21-28); the second with the character and doom of the false prophets (chap. xiii.); and the third with the state of mind which made a right use of prophecy impossible (xiv. 1-11).

I.

It is one of Ezekiel's peculiarities that he pays close attention to the proverbial sayings which indicated the drift of the national mind. Such sayings were like straws, showing how the stream flowed, and had a special significance for Ezekiel, inasmuch as he was not in the stream himself, but only observed its motions from a distance. Here he quotes a current proverb, giving expression to a sense of the futility of all prophetic warnings: "The days are drawn out, and every vision faileth" (xii. 22). It is difficult to say what the feeling is that lies behind it, whether it is one of disappointment or of relief. If, as seems probable, ver. 27 is the application of the general principle to the particular case of Ezekiel, the proverb need not indicate absolute disbelief in the truth of prophecy. "The vision which he sees is for many days, and remote times does he prophesy"—that is to say. The prophet's words are no doubt perfectly true, and come from God; but no man can ever tell when they are to be fulfilled: all experience shows that they relate to a remote future which we are not likely to see. For men whose concern was to find direction in the present emerency, that was no doubt equivalent to a renunciation of the guidance of prophecy.

There are several things which may have tended to give currency to this view and make it plausible. First of all, of course, the fact that many of the "visions" that were published had nothing in them; they were false in their origin, and were bound to fail. Accordingly one thing necessary to rescue prophecy from the discredit into which it had fallen was the removal of those who uttered false predictions in the name of Jehovah: "There shall no more be any false vision or flattering divination in the midst of the house of Israel" (ver. 24). But besides the prevalence of false prophecy there were features of true prophecy which partly explained the common misgiving as to its trustworthiness. Even in true prophecy there is an element of idealism, the future being depicted in forms derived from the prophet's circumstances, and represented as the immediate continuation of the events of his own time. In support of the proverb it might have been equally apt to instance the Messianic oracles of Isaiah, or the confident predictions of Hananiah, the opponent of Jeremiah. Further, there is a contingent element in prophecy: the fulfilment of a threat or promise is conditional on the moral effect of the prophecy itself on the people. These things were perfectly understood by thoughtful men in Israel. The principle of contingency is clearly expounded in the eighteenth chapter of Jeremiah, and it was acted on by the princes who on a memorable occasion saved him from the doom of a false prophet (Jer. xxvi.). Those who used prophecy to determine their practical attitude towards Jehovah's purposes found it to be an unerring guide to right thinking and action. But those who only took a curious interest in questions of external fulfilment found much to disconcert them; and it is hardly surprising that many of them became utterly sceptical of its divine origin. It must have been to this turn of mind that the proverb with which Ezekiel is dealing owed its origin.

It is not on these lines, however, that Ezekiel vindicates the truth of the prophetic word, but on lines adapted to the needs of his own generation. After all prophecy is not wholly contingent. The bent of the popular character is one of the elements which it takes into account, and it foresees an issue which is not dependent on anything that Israel might do. The prophets rise to a point of view from which the destruction of the sinful people and the establishment of a perfect kingdom of God are seen to be facts unalterably decreed by Jehovah. And the point of Ezekiel's answer to his contemporaries seems to be that a final demonstration of the truth of prophecy was at hand. As the fulfilment drew near prophecy would increase in distinctness and precision, so that when the catastrophe came it would be impossible for any man to deny the inspiration of those who had announced it: "Thus saith Jehovah, I will suppress this proverb, and it shall no more circulate in Israel; but say unto them, The days are near, and the content [literally *word* or *matter*] of every vision" (ver. 23). After the extinction of every form of lying prophecy, Jehovah's words shall still be heard, and the proclamation of them shall be immediately followed by their accomplishment: "For I Jehovah will speak My words; I will speak and perform, it shall not be deferred any more: in your days, O house of rebellion, I will speak a word and perform it, saith Jehovah" (ver. 25). The immediate reference is to the destruction of Jerusalem which the prophet saw to be one of those events which were unconditionally decreed, and an event which must bulk more and more largely in the vision of the true prophet until it was accomplished.

II.

The thirteenth chapter deals with what was undoubtedly the greatest obstacle to the influence of prophecy—viz., the existence of a division in the ranks of the prophets themselves. That division had been of long standing. The earliest indication of it is the story of the contest between Micaiah and four hundred prophets of Jehovah, in presence of Ahab and Jehoshaphat (1 Kings xxii. 5-28). All the canonical prophets show in their writings that they had to contend against the mass of the prophetic order—men who claimed an authority equal to theirs, but used it for diametrically opposite interests. It is not, however, till we come to Jeremiah and Ezekiel that we find a formal apologetic of true prophecy against false. The problem was serious: where two sets of prophets systematically and fundamentally contradicted each other, both might be false, but both could not be true. The prophet who was convinced of the truth of his own visions must be prepared to account for the rise of false visions, and to lay down some criterion by which men might discriminate between the one and the other. Jeremiah's treatment of the question is of the two perhaps the more profound and interesting. It is thus summarised by Professor Davidson: "In his encounters with the prophets of his day Jeremiah opposes them in three spheres—that of policy, that of morals, and that of personal experience. In policy the genuine prophets had some fixed principles, all arising out of the idea that the kingdom of the Lord was not a kingdom of this world. Hence they opposed military preparation, riding on horses, and building of fenced cities, and counselled trust in Jehovah. . . . The false prophets, on the other hand, desired their country to be a military power among the powers around, they advocated alliance with the eastern empires and with Egypt, and relied on their national strength. Again, the true prophets had a stringent personal and state morality. In their view the true cause of the destruction of the state was its immoralities. But the false prophets had no such deep moral convictions, and seeing nothing unwonted or alarming in the condition of things prophesied of 'peace.' They were not necessarily irreligious men; but their religion had no truer insight into the nature of the God of Israel than that of the common people. . . . And finally Jeremiah expresses his conviction that the prophets whom he opposed did not stand in the same relation to the Lord as he did: they had not his experiences of the word of the Lord, into whose counsel they had not been admitted; and they were without that fellowship of mind with the mind of Jehovah which was the true source of prophecy. Hence he satirises their pretended supernatural 'dreams,' and charges them from conscious want of any true prophetic word with stealing words from one another." *

* "Ezekiel," p. 85

The passages in Jeremiah on which this statement is mainly founded may have been known to Ezekiel, who in this matter, as in so many others, follows the lines laid down by the elder prophet.

The first thing, then, that deserves attention in Ezekiel's judgment on false prophecy is his assertion of its purely subjective or human origin. In the opening sentence he pronounces a woe upon the prophets "who prophesy *from their own mind* without having seen"* (ver. 3). The words put in italics sum up Ezekiel's theory of the genesis of false prophecy. The visions these men see and the oracles they utter simply reproduce the thoughts, the emotions, the aspirations, natural to their own minds. That the ideas came to them in a peculiar form, which was mistaken for the direct action of Jehovah, Ezekiel does not deny. He admits that the men were sincere in their professions, for he describes them as "waiting for the fulfilment of the word" (ver. 6). But in this belief they were the victims of a delusion. Whatever there might be in their prophetic experiences that resembled those of a true prophet, there was nothing in their oracles that did not belong to the sphere of worldly interests and human speculation.

If we ask how Ezekiel knew this, the only possible answer is that he knew it because he was sure of the source of his own inspiration. He possessed an inward experience which certified to him the genuineness of the communications which came to him, and he necessarily inferred that those who held different beliefs about God must lack that experience. Thus far his criticism of false prophecy is purely subjective. The true prophet knew that he had that within him which authenticated his inspiration, but the false prophet could not know that he wanted it. The difficulty is not peculiar to prophecy, but arises in connection with religious belief as a whole. It is an interesting question whether the assent to a truth is accompanied by a feeling of certitude differing in quality from the confidence which a man may have in giving assent to a delusion. But it is not possible to elevate this internal criterion to an objective test of truth. A man who is awake may be quite sure he is not dreaming, but a man in a dream may readily enough fancy himself awake.

But there were other and more obvious tests which could be applied to the professional prophets, and which at least showed them to be men of a different spirit from the few who were "full of power by the spirit of the Lord, and of judgment, and of might, to declare to Israel his sin" (Mic. iii. 8). In two graphic figures Ezkeiel sums up the character and policy of these parasites who disgraced the order to which they belonged. In the first place he compares them to jackals burrowing in ruins and undermining the fabric which it was their professed function to uphold (vv. 4, 5). The existence of such a class of men is at once a symptom of advanced social degeneration and a cause of greater ruin to follow. A true prophet fearlessly speaking the words of God is a defence to the state; he is like a man who stands in the breach or builds a wall to ward off the danger which he foresees. Such were all genuine prophets whose names were held in honour in Israel—men of moral courage, never hesitating to incur personal risk for the welfare of the nation they loved. If Israel now was like a heap of ruins, the fault lay with the selfish crowd of hireling prophets who had cared more to find a hole in which they could shelter themselves than to build up a stable and righteous polity.

The prophet's simile calls to mind the type of churchman represented by Bishop Blougram in Browning's powerful satire. He is one who is content if the corporation to which he belongs can provide him with a comfortable and dignified position in which he can spend good days; he is triumphant if, in addition to this, he can defy any one to prove him more of a fool or a hypocrite than an average man of the world. Such utter abnegation of intellectual sincerity may not be common in any Church; but the temptation which leads to it is one to which ecclesiastics are exposed in every age and every communion. The tendency to shirk difficult problems, to shut one's eyes to grave evils, to acquiesce in things as they are, and calculate that the ruin will last one's own time, is what Ezekiel calls playing the jackal; and it hardly needs a prophet to tell us that there could not be a more fatal symptom of the decay of religion than the prevalence of such a spirit in its official representatives.

The second image is equally suggestive. It exhibits the false prophets as following where they pretended to lead, as aiding and abetting the men into whose hands the reins of government had fallen. The people build a wall and the prophets cover it with plaster (ver. 10)—that is to say, when any project or scheme of policy is being promoted they stand by, glozing it over with fine words, flattering its promoters, and uttering profuse assurances of its success. The uselessness of the whole activity of these prophets could not be more vividly described. The white-washing of the wall may hide its defects, but will not prevent its destruction; and when the wall of Jerusalem's shaky prosperity tumbles down, those who did so little to build and so much to deceive shall be overwhelmed with confusion. "Behold, when the wall is fallen, shall it not be said to them, Where is the plaster which ye plastered?" (ver. 12).

This will be the beginning of the judgment on false prophets in Israel. The overthrow of their vaticinations, the collapse of the hopes they fostered, and the demolition of the edifice in which they found a refuge shall leave them no more a name or a place in the people of God. "I will stretch out My hand against the prophets that see vanity and divine falsely: in the council of My people they shall not be, and in the register of the house of Israel they shall not be written, and into the land of Israel they shall not come" (ver. 9).

There was, however, a still more degraded type of prophecy, practised chiefly by women, which must have been exceedingly prevalent in Ezekiel's time. The prophets spoken of in the first sixteen verses were public functionaries who exerted their evil influence in the arena of politics. The prophetesses spoken of in the latter part of the chapter are private fortune-tellers who practised on the credulity of individuals who consulted them. Their art was evidently magical in the strict sense, a trafficking with the dark powers which were supposed to enter into alliance with men irrespective of moral considerations. Then, as now, such courses were followed for gain, and doubtless proved a lucrative means of livelihood. The "fillets" and "veils"

* Translating with LXX.

mentioned in ver. 18 are either a professional garb worn by the women, or else implements of divination whose precise significance cannot now be ascertained. To the imagination of the prophet they appear as the snares and weapons with which these wretched creatures "hunted souls"; and the extent of the evil which he attacks is indicated by his speaking of the whole people as being entangled in their meshes. Ezekiel naturally bestows special attention on a class of practitioners whose whole influence tended to efface moral landmarks and to deal out to men weal or woe without regard to character. "They slew souls that should not die, and saved alive souls that should not live; they made sad the heart of the righteous, and strengthened the hands of the wicked, that he should not return from his wicked way and be saved alive" (ver. 22). That is to say, while Ezekiel and all true prophets were exhorting men to live resolutely in the light of clear ethical conceptions of providence, the votaries of occult superstitions seduced the ignorant into making private compacts with the powers of darkness in order to secure their personal safety. If the prevalence of sorcery and witchcraft was at all times dangerous to the religion and public order of the state, it was doubly so at a time when, as Ezekiel perceived, everything depended on maintaining the strict rectitude of God in His dealings with individual men.

III.

Having thus disposed of the external manifestations of false prophecy, Ezekiel proceeds in the fourteenth chapter to deal with the state of mind amongst the people at large which rendered such a condition of things possible. The general import of the passage is clear, although the precise connection of ideas is somewhat difficult to explain. The following observations may suffice to bring out all that is essential to the understanding of the section.

The oracle was occasioned by a particular incident, undoubtedly historical—namely, a visit, such as was perhaps now common, from the elders to inquire of the Lord through Ezekiel. As they sit before him it is revealed to the prophet that the minds of these men are preoccupied with idolatry, and therefore it is not fitting that any answer should be given to them by a prophet of Jehovah. Apparently no answer *was* given by Ezekiel to the particular question they had asked, whatever it may have been. Generalising from the incident, however, he is led to enunciate a principle regulating the intercourse between Jehovah and Israel through the medium of a prophet: "Whatever man of the house of Israel sets his thoughts upon his idols, and puts his guilty stumbling-block before him, and comes to the prophet, I Jehovah will make Myself intelligible to him; * that I may take the house of Israel in their own heart, because they are all estranged from Me by their idols" (vv. 4, 5). It seems clear that one part of the threat here uttered is that the very withholding of the answer will unmask the hypocrisy of men who pretend to be worshippers of Jehovah, but in heart are unfaithful to Him and servants of false gods. The moral principle involved in the prophet's dictum is clear and of lasting value. It is that for a false heart there can be no fellowship with Jehovah, and therefore no true and sure knowledge of His will. The prophet occupies the point of view of Jehovah, and when consulted by an idolater he finds it impossible to enter into the point of view from which the question is put, and therefore cannot answer it.* Ezekiel assumes for the most part that the prophet consulted is a true prophet of Jehovah like himself, who will give no answer to such questions as he has before him. He must, however, allow for the possibility that men of this stamp may receive answers in the name of Jehovah from those reputed to be His true prophets. In that case, says Ezekiel, the prophet is "deceived" by God; he is allowed to give a response which is not a true response at all, but only confirms the people in their delusions and unbelief. But this deception does not take place until the prophet has incurred the guilt of deceiving himself in the first instance. It is his fault that he has not perceived the bent of his questioners' minds, that he has accommodated himself to their ways of thought, has consented to occupy their standpoint in order to be able to say something coinciding with the drift of their wishes. Prophet and inquirers are involved in a common guilt and share a common fate, both being sentenced to exclusion from the commonwealth of Israel.

The purification of the institution of prophecy necessarily appeared to Ezekiel as an indispensable feature in the restoration of the theocracy. The ideal of Israel's relation to Jehovah is "that they may be My people, and that I may be their God" (ver. 11). That implies that Jehovah shall be the source of infallible guidance in all things needful for the religious life of the individual and the guidance of the state. But it was impossible for Jehovah to be to Israel all that a God should be, so long as the regular channels of communication between Him and the nation were choked by false conceptions in the minds of the people and false men in the position of prophets. Hence the constitution of a new Israel demands such special judgments on false prophecy and the false use of true prophecy as have been denounced in these chapters. When these judgments have been executed, the ideal will have become possible which is described in the words of another prophet: "Thine eyes shall see thy teachers: and thine ears shall hear a word behind thee, saying, This is the way, walk ye in it" (Isa. xxx. 20, 21).

CHAPTER IX.

JERUSALEM—AN IDEAL HISTORY.

EZEKIEL xvi.

In order to understand the place which the sixteenth chapter occupies in this section† of the book, we must remember that a chief source of the antagonism between Ezekiel and his hearers was the proud national consciousness which sustained the courage of the people through all their humiliations. There were, perhaps, few

* The exact force of the reflexive form used (*na'ănêthi*, niphal) is doubtful. The translation given is that of Cornill, which is certainly forcible.

* The same rule is applied to direct communion with God in prayer in Psalm lxvi. 18: "If I regard iniquity in my heart, the Lord will not hear."

† See above, p. 244 f.

nations of antiquity in which the flame of patriotic feeling burned more brightly than in Israel. No people with a past such as theirs could be indifferent to the many elements of greatness embalmed in their history. The beauty and fertility of their land, the martial exploits and signal deliverances of the nation, the great kings and heroes she had reared, her prophets and lawgivers—these and many other stirring memories were witnesses to Jehovah's peculiar love for Israel and His power to exalt and bless His people. To cherish a deep sense of the unique privileges which Jehovah had conferred on her in giving her a distinct place among the nations of the earth was thus a religious duty often insisted on in the Old Testament. But in order that this sense might work for good it was necessary that it should take the form of grateful recognition of Jehovah as the source of the nation's greatness, and be accompanied by a true knowledge of His character. When allied with false conceptions of Jehovah's nature, or entirely divorced from religion, patriotism degenerated into racial prejudice and became a serious moral and political danger. That this had actually taken place is a common complaint of the prophets. They feel that national vanity is a great obstacle to the acceptance of their message, and pour forth bitter and scornful words intended to humble the pride of Israel to the dust. No prophet addresses himself to the task so remorselessly as Ezekiel. The utter worthlessness of Israel, both absolutely in the eyes of Jehovah and relatively in comparison with other nations, is asserted by him with a boldness and emphasis which at first startle us. From a different point of view prophecy and its results might have been regarded as fruits of the national life, under the divine education vouchsafed to that people. But that is not Ezekiel's standpoint. He seizes on the fact that prophecy was in opposition to the natural genius of the people, and was not to be regarded as in any sense an expression of it. Accepting the final attitude of Israel toward the word of Jehovah as the genuine outcome of her natural proclivities, he reads her past as an unbroken record of ingratitude and infidelity. All that was good in Israel was Jehovah's gift, freely bestowed and justly withdrawn; all that was Israel's own was her weakness and her sin. It was reserved for a later prophet to reconcile the condemnation of Israel's actual history with the recognition of the divine power working there and moulding a spiritual kernel of the nation into a true "servant of the Lord" (Isa. xl. ff.).

In chaps. xv. and xvi., therefore, the prophet exposes the hollowness of Israel's confidence in her national destiny. The first of these appears to be directed against the vain hopes cherished in Jerusalem at the time. It is not necessary to dwell on it at length. The image is simple and its application to Jerusalem obvious. Earlier prophets had compared Israel to a vine, partly to set forth the exceptional privileges she enjoyed, but chiefly to emphasise the degeneration she had undergone, as shown by the bad moral fruits which she had borne (*cf.* Isa. v. 1 ff.; Jer. ii. 21; Hos. x. 1). The popular imagination had laid hold of the thought that Israel was the vine of God's planting, ignoring the question of the fruit. But Ezekiel reminds his hearers that apart from its fruit the vine is the most worthless of trees. Even at the best its wood can be employed for no useful purpose; it is fit only for fuel. Such was the people of Israel, considered simply as a state among other states, without regard to its religious vocation. Even in its pristine vigour, when the national energies were fresh and unimpaired, it was but a weak nation, incapable of attaining the dignity of a great power. But now the strength of the nation has been worn away by a long succession of disasters, until only a shadow of her former glory remains. Israel is no longer like a green and living vine, but like a branch burned at both ends and charred in the middle, and therefore doubly unfit for any worthy function in the affairs of the world. By the help of this illustration men may read in the present state of the nation the irrevocable sentence of rejection which Jehovah has passed on His people.

We now turn to the striking allegory of chap. xvi., where the same subject is treated with far greater penetration and depth of feeling. There is no passage in the book of Ezekiel at once so powerful and so full of religious significance as the picture of Jerusalem, the foundling child, the unfaithful spouse, and the abandoned prostitute, which is here presented. The general conception is one that might have been presented in a form as beautiful as it is spiritually true. But the features which offend our sense of propriety are perhaps introduced with a stern purpose. It is the deliberate intention of Ezekiel to present Jerusalem's wickedness in the most repulsive light, in order that, if possible, he might startle men into abhorrence of their national sin. In his own mind the feelings of moral indignation and physical disgust were very close together, and here he seems to work on the minds of his readers, so that the feeling excited by the image may call forth the feeling appropriate to the reality.

The allegory is a highly idealised history of the city of Jerusalem from its origin to its destruction, and then onward to its future restoration. It falls naturally into four divisions:—

i. Vv. 1-14.—The first emergence of Jerusalem into civic life is compared to a new-born female infant, exposed to perish, after a cruel custom which is known to have prevailed among some Semitic tribes. None of the offices customary on the birth of a child were performed in her case, whether those necessary to preserve life or those which had a merely ceremonial significance. Unblessed and unpitied she lay in the open field, weltering in blood, exciting only repugnance in all who passed by, until Jehovah Himself passed by, and pronounced over her the decree that she should live. Thus saved from death, she grew up and reached maturity, but still "naked and bare," destitute of wealth and the refinements of civilisation. These were bestowed on her when a second time Jehovah passed by and spread His skirt over her, and claimed her for His own. Not till then had she been treated as a human being, with the possibilities of honourable life before her. But now she becomes the bride of her protector, and is provided for as a high-born maiden might be, with all the ornaments and luxuries befitting her new rank. Lifted from the lowest depth of degradation, she is now transcendently beautiful, and has "attained to royal estate." The fame of her loveliness went abroad among the nations: "for it was perfect through My glory, which I put upon thee, saith Jehovah" (ver. 14).

It will be seen that the points of contact with actual history are here extremely few as well as vague. It is indeed doubtful whether the subject of the allegory be the city of Jerusalem conceived as one through all its changes of population, or the Hebrew nation of which Jerusalem ultimately became the capital. The latter interpretation is certainly favoured by chap. xxiii., where both Jerusalem and Samaria are represented as having spent their youth in Egypt. That parallel may not be decisive as to the meaning of chap. xvi.; and the statement "thy father was the Amorite and thy mother an Hittite" may be thought to support the other alternative. Amorite and Hittite are general names for the pre-Israelite population of Canaan, and it is a well-known fact that Jerusalem was originally a Canaanitish city. It is not necessary to suppose that the prophet has any information about the early fortunes of Jerusalem when he describes the stages of the process by which she was raised to royal magnificence. The chief question is whether these details can be fairly applied to the history of the nation before it had Jerusalem as its metropolis. It is usually held that the first "passing by" of Jehovah refers to the preservation of the people in the patriarchal period, and the second to the events of the Exodus and the Sinaitic covenant. Against this it may be urged that Ezekiel would hardly have presented the patriarchal period in a hateful light, although he does go further in discrediting antiquity than any other prophet. Besides, the description of Jerusalem's betrothal to Jehovah contains points which are more naturally understood of the glories of the age of David and Solomon than of the events of Sinai, which were not accompanied by an access of material prosperity such as is suggested. It may be necessary to leave the matter in the vagueness with which the prophet has surrounded it, and accept as the teaching of the allegory the simple truth that Jerusalem in herself was nothing, but had been preserved in existence by Jehovah's will, and owed all her splendour to her association with His cause and His kingdom.

ii. Vv. 15-34.—The dainties and rich attire enjoyed by the highly favoured bride become a snare to her. These represent blessings of a material order bestowed by Jehovah on Jerusalem. Throughout the chapter nothing is said of the imparting of spiritual privileges, or of a moral change wrought in the heart of Jerusalem. The gifts of Jehovah are conferred on one incapable of responding to the care and affection that had been lavished on her. The inborn taint of her nature, the hereditary immorality of her heathen ancestors, breaks out in a career of licentiousness in which all the advantages of her proud position are prostituted to the vilest ends. "As is the mother, so is her daughter" (ver. 44); and Jerusalem betrayed her true origin by the readiness with which she took to evil courses as soon as she had the opportunity. The "whoredom" in which the prophet sums up his indictment against his people is chiefly the sin of idolatry. The figure may have been suggested by the fact that actual lewdness of the most flagrant kind was a conspicuous element in the form of idolatry to which Israel first succumbed—the worship of the Canaanite Baals. But in the hands of the prophets it has a deeper and more spiritual import than this. It signified the violation of all the sacred moral obligations which are enshrined in human marriage, or, in other words, the abandonment of an ethical religion for one in which the powers of nature were regarded as the highest revelation of the divine. To the mind of the prophet it made no difference whether the object of worship was called by the name of Jehovah or of Baal: the character of the worship determined the quality of the religion; and in the one case, as in the other, it was idolatry, or "whoredom."

Two stages in the idolatry of Israel appear to be distinguished in this part of the chapter. The first is the naïve, half-conscious heathenism which crept in insensibly through contact with Phœnician and Canaanite neighbours (vv. 15-25). The tokens of Jerusalem's implication in this sin were everywhere. The "high places" with their tents and clothed images (ver. 17), and the offerings set forth before these objects of adoration, were undoubtedly of Canaanitish origin, and their preservation to the fall of the kingdom was a standing witness to the source to which Israel owed her earliest and dearest "abominations." We learn that this phase of idolatry culminated in the atrocious rite of human sacrifice (vv. 20, 21). The immolation of children to Baal or Molech was a common practice amongst the nations surrounding Israel, and when introduced there seems to have been regarded as part of the worship of Jehovah.* What Ezekiel here asserts is that the practice came through Israel's illicit commerce with the gods of Canaan, and there is no question that this is historically true. The allegory exhibits the sin in its unnatural heinousness. The idealised city is the mother of her citizens, the children are Jehovah's children and her own, yet she has taken them and offered them up to the false lovers she so madly pursued. Such was her feverish passion for idolatry that the dearest and most sacred ties of nature were ruthlessly severed at the bidding of a perverted religious sense.

The second form of idolatry in Israel was of a more deliberate and politic kind (vv. 23-34). It consisted in the introduction of the deities and religious practices of the great world-powers —Egypt, Assyria, and Chaldæa. The attraction of these foreign rites did not lie in the fascination of a sensuous type of religion, but rather in the impression of power produced by the gods of the conquering peoples. The foreign gods came in mostly in consequence of a political alliance with the nations whose patrons they were; in other cases a god was worshipped simply because he had shown himself able to do great things for his servants. Jerusalem as Ezekiel knew it was full of monuments of this comparatively recent type of idolatry. In every street and at the head of every way there were erections (here called "arches" or "heights") which, from the connection in which they are mentioned, must have been shrines devoted to the strange gods from abroad. It is characteristic of the political idolatry here referred to that its monuments were found in the capital, while the more ancient and rustic worship was typified by the "high places" throughout the provinces. It is probable that the description applies mainly to the later period of the monarchy, when Israel, and especially Judah, began to lean for support on one or other of the great

* See below, pp. 266 f.

empires on either side of her. At the same time it must be remembered that Ezekiel elsewhere teaches distinctly that the influence of Egyptian religion had been continuous from the days of the Exodus (chap. xxiii.). There may, however, have been a revival of Egyptian influence, due to the political exigencies which arose in the eighth century.

Thus Jerusalem has "played the harlot"; nay, she has done worse—"she has been as a wife that committeth adultery, who though under her husband taketh strangers." * And the result has been simply the impoverishment of the land. The heavy exactions levied on the country by Egypt and Assyria were the hire she had paid to her lovers to come to her. If false religion had resulted in an increase of wealth or material prosperity, there might have been some excuse for the eagerness with which she plunged into it. But certainly Israel's history bore the lesson that false religion means waste and ruin. Strangers had devoured her strength from her youth, yet she never would heed the voice of her prophets when they sought to guide her into the ways of peace. Her infatuation was unnatural; it goes almost beyond the bounds of the allegory to exhibit it: "The contrary is in thee from other women, in that thou committest whoredoms, and none goeth awhoring after thee: and in that thou givest hire, and no hire is given to thee, therefore thou art contrary" (ver. 34).

iii. Vv. 35-58.—Having thus made Jerusalem to "know her abominations" (ver. 2), the prophet proceeds to announce the doom which must inevitably follow such a career of wickedness. The figures under which the judgment is set forth appear to be taken from the punishment meted out to profligate women in ancient Israel. The public exposure of the adulteress and her death by stoning in the presence of "many women" supply images terribly appropriate of the fate in store for Jerusalem.† Her punishment is to be a warning to all surrounding nations, and an exhibition of the jealous wrath of Jehovah against her infidelity. These nations, some of them hereditary enemies, others old allies, are represented as assembled to witness and to execute the judgment of the city. The remorseless realism of the prophet spares no detail which could enhance the horror of the situation. Abandoned to the ruthless violence of her former lovers, Jerusalem is stripped of her royal attire, the emblems of her idolatry are destroyed, and so, left naked to her enemies, she suffers the ignominious death of a city that has been false to her religion. The root of her sin had been the forgetfulness of what she owed to the goodness of Jehovah, and the essence of her punishment lies in the withdrawal of the gifts He had lavished upon her and the protection which, amid all her apostasies, she had never ceased to expect.

At this point (ver. 44 ff.) the allegory takes a new turn through the introduction of the sister cities of Samaria and Sodom. Samaria, although as a city much younger than Jerusalem, is considered the elder sister because she had once been the centre of a greater political power than Jerusalem, and Sodom, which was probably older than either, is treated as the youngest because of her relative insignificance. The order, however, is of no importance. The point of the comparison is that all three had manifested in different degrees the same hereditary tendency to immorality (ver. 45). All three were of heathen origin—their mother a Hittite and their father an Amorite—a description which it is even more difficult to understand in the case of Samaria than in that of Jerusalem. But Ezekiel is not concerned about history. What is prominent in his mind is the family likeness observed in their characters, which gave point to the proverb "Like mother, like daughter" when applied to Jerusalem. The prophet affirms that the wickedness of Jerusalem had so far exceeded that of Samaria and Sodom that she had "justified" her sisters—*i. e.*, she had made their moral condition appear pardonable by comparison with hers. He knows that he is saying a bold thing in ranking the iniquity of Jerusalem as greater than that of Sodom, and so he explains his judgment on Sodom by an analysis of the cause of her notorious corruptness. The name of Sodom lived in tradition as that of the foulest city of the old world, a *ne plus ultra* of wickedness. Yet Ezekiel dares to raise the question, What *was* the sin of Sodom? "This was the sin of Sodom thy sister, pride, superabundance of food, and careless ease was the lot of her and her daughters, but they did not succour the poor and needy. But they became proud, and committed abominations before Me: therefore I took them away as thou hast seen" (vv. 49, 50). The meaning seems to be that the corruptions of Sodom were the natural outcome of the evil principle in the Canaanitish nature, favoured by easy circumstances and unchecked by the saving influences of a pure religion. Ezekiel's judgment is like an anticipation of the more solemn sentence uttered by One who knew what was in man when He said, "If the mighty works which have been done in you had been done in Sodom and Gomorrha, they would have remained until this day."

It is remarkable to observe how some of the profoundest ideas in this chapter attach themselves to the strange conception of these two vanished cities as still capable of being restored to their place in the world. In the ideal future of the prophet's vision Sodom and Samaria shall rise from their ruins through the same power which restores Jerusalem to her ancient glory. The promise of a renewed existence to Sodom and Samaria is perhaps connected with the fact that they lay within the sacred territory of which Jerusalem is the centre. Hence Sodom and Samaria are no longer sisters, but daughters of Jerusalem, receiving through her the blessings of the true religion. And it is her relation to these her sisters that opens the eyes of Jerusalem to the true nature of her own relation to Jehovah. Formerly she had been proud and self-sufficient, and counted her exceptional prerogatives the natural reward of some excellence to which she could lay claim. The name of Sodom, the disgraced sister of the family, was not heard in her mouth in the days of her pride, when her wickedness had not been disclosed as it is now (ver. 57). But when she realises that her conduct has justified and comforted her sister, and when she has to take guilty Sodom to her heart as a daughter, she will understand that she owes

* Ver. 33 may, however, be an interpolation (Cornill).

† In ver. 41 the Syriac Version reads, with a slight alteration of the text, "they shall burn thee in the midst of the fire." The reading has something to recommend it. Death by burning was an ancient punishment of harlotry (Gen. xxxviii. 24), although it is not likely that it was still inflicted in the time of Ezekiel.

all her greatness to the same sovereign grace of Jehovah which is manifested in the restoration of the most abandoned community known to history. And out of this new consciousness of grace will spring the chastened and penitent temper of mind which makes possible the continuance of the bond which unites her to Jehovah.

iv. Vv. 59-63.—The way is thus prepared for the final promise of forgiveness with which the chapter closes. The reconciliation between Jehovah and Jerusalem will be effected by an act of recollection on both sides: "*I* will remember My covenant with thee. . . . *Thou* shalt remember thy ways" (vv. 60, 61). The mind of Jehovah and the mind of Jerusalem both go back on the past; but while Jehovah thinks only of the purpose of love which he had entertained towards Jerusalem in the days of her youth and the indissoluble bond between them, Jerusalem retains the memory of her own sinful history, and finds in the remembrance the source of abiding contrition and shame. It does not fall within the scope of the prophet's purpose to set forth in this place the blessed consequences which flow from this renewal of loving intercourse between Israel and her God. He has accomplished his object when he has shown how the electing love of Jehovah reaches its end in spite of human sin and rebellion, and how through the crushing power of divine grace the failures and transgressions of the past are made to issue in a relation of perfect harmony between Jehovah and His people. The permanence of that relation is expressed by an idea borrowed from Jeremiah—the idea of an everlasting covenant, which cannot be broken because based on the forgiveness of sin and a renewal of heart. The prophet knows that when once the power of evil has been broken by a full disclosure of redeeming love it cannot resume its old ascendency in human life. So he leaves us on the threshold of the new dispensation with the picture of Jerusalem humbled and bearing her shame, yet in the abjectness of her self-accusation realising the end towards which the love of Jehovah had guided her from the beginning: "I will establish My covenant with thee; and thou shalt know that I am Jehovah: that thou mayest remember, and be ashamed, and not open thy mouth any more for very shame, when I expiate for thee all that thou hast done, saith the Lord Jehovah" (vv. 62, 63).

Throughout this chapter we see that the prophet moves in the region of national religious ideas which are distinctive of the Old Testament. Of the influences that formed his conceptions that of Hosea is perhaps most discernible. The fundamental thoughts embodied in the allegory are the same as those by which the older prophet learned to interpret the nature of God and the sin of Israel through the bitter experiences of his family life. These thoughts are developed by Ezekiel with a fertility of imagination and a grasp of theological principles which were adapted to the more complex situation with which he had to deal. But the conception of Israel as the unfaithful wife of Jehovah, of the false gods and the world-powers as her lovers, of her conversion through affliction, and her final restoration by a new betrothal which is eternal, are all expressed in the first three chapters of Hosea. And the freedom with which Ezekiel handles and expands these conceptions shows how thoroughly he was at home in that national view of religion which he did much to break through. In the next chapter we shall have occasion to examine his treatment of the problem of the individual's relation to God, and we cannot fail to be struck by the contrast. The analysis of individual religion may seem meagre by the side of this most profound and suggestive chapter. This arises from the fact that the full meaning of religion could not then be expressed as an experience of the individual soul. The subject of religion being the nation of Israel, the human side of it could only be unfolded in terms of what we should call the national consciousness. The time was not yet come when the great truths which the prophets and psalmists saw embodied in the history of their people could be translated in terms of individual fellowship with God. Yet the God who spake to the fathers by the prophets is the same who has spoken to us in His Son; and when from the standpoint of a higher revelation we turn back to the Old Testament, it is to find in the form of a nation's history the very same truths which we realise as matters of personal experience.

From this point of view the chapter we have considered is one of the most evangelical passages in the writings of Ezekiel. The prophet's conception of sin, for example, is singularly profound and true. He has been charged with a somewhat superficial conception of sin, as if he saw nothing more in it than the transgression of a law arbitrarily imposed by divine authority. There are aspects of Ezekiel's teaching which give some plausibility to that charge, especially those which deal with the duties of the individual. But we see that to Ezekiel the real nature of sin could not possibly be manifested except as a factor in the national life. Now in this allegory it is obvious that he sees something far deeper in it than the mere transgression of positive commandments. Behind all the outward offences of which Israel had been guilty there plainly lies the spiritual fact of national selfishness, unfaithfulness to Jehovah, insensibility to His love, and ingratitude for His benefits. Moreover, the prophet, like Jeremiah before him, has a strong sense of sin as a tendency in human life, a power which is ineradicable save by the mingled severity and goodness of God. Through the whole history of Israel it is one evil disposition which he sees asserting itself, breaking out now in one form and then in another, but continually gaining strength, until at last the spirit of repentance is created by the experience of God's forgiveness. It is not the case, therefore, that Ezekiel failed to comprehend the nature of sin, or that in this respect he falls below the most spiritual of the prophets who had gone before him.

In order that this tendency to sin may be destroyed, Ezekiel sees that the consciousness of guilt must take its place. In the same way the apostle Paul teaches that "every mouth must be stopped, and all the world become guilty before God." Whether the subject be a nation or an individual, the dominion of sin is not broken till the sinner has taken home to himself the full responsibility for his acts and felt himself to be "without excuse." But the most striking thing in Ezekiel's representation of the process of conversion is the thought that this saving sense of sin is produced less by judgment than by free and undeserved forgiveness. Punishment he conceives to be necessary, being demanded alike by the righteousness of God and the good of the sinful people. But the heart of Jerusalem is not changed till she finds herself restored to her former relation to God, with all the sin of her past blotted out and a new life before her. It is through the grace of forgiveness that she is overwhelmed with shame and sorrow for sin, and learns the humility which is the germ of a new hope towards God. Here the prophet strikes one of the deepest notes of evangelical doctrine. All experience confirms the lesson that true repentance is not produced by the terrors of the law, but by the view of God's love in Christ going forth to meet the sinner and bring him back to the Father's heart and home.

Another question of great interest and difficulty is the attitude towards the heathen world assumed by Ezekiel. The prophecy of the restoration of Sodom is certainly one of the most remarkable things in the book. It is true that Ezekiel as a rule concerns himself very little with the religious state of the outlying world under the Messianic dispensation. Where he speaks of foreign nations it is only to announce the manifestation of Jehovah's glory in the judgments He executes upon them. The effect of these judgments is that "they shall know that I am Jehovah"; but how much is included in the expression as applied to the heathen it is impossible to say. This, however, may be due to the peculiar limitation of view which leads him to concentrate his attention on the Holy Land in his visions of the perfect kingdom of God. We can hardly suppose that he conceived all the rest of the world as a blank or filled with a seething mass of humanity outside the government of the true God. It is rather to be supposed that Canaan itself appeared to his mind as an epitome of the world such as it must be when the latter-day glory was ushered in. And in Canaan he finds room for Sodom, but Sodom turned to the knowledge of the true God and sharing in the blessings bestowed on Jerusalem. It is surely allowable to see in this the symptom of a more hopeful view of the future of the world at large than we should gather from the rest of the prophecy. If Ezekiel could think of Sodom as raised from the dead and sharing the glories of the people of God, the idea of the conversion of heathen nations could not have been altogether foreign to his mind. It is at all events significant that when he meditates most profoundly on the nature of sin and God's method of dealing with it, he is led to the thought of a divine mercy which embraces in its sweep those communities which had reached the lowest depths of moral corruption.

CHAPTER X.

THE RELIGION OF THE INDIVIDUAL.

EZEKIEL xviii.

IN the sixteenth chapter, as we have seen, Ezekiel has asserted in the most unqualified terms the validity of the principle of national retribution. The nation is dealt with as a moral unit, and the catastrophe which closes its history is the punishment for the accumulated guilt incurred by the past generations. In the eighteenth chapter he teaches still more explicitly the freedom and the independent responsibility of each individual before God. No attempt is made to reconcile the two principles as methods of the divine government; from the prophet's standpoint they do not require to be reconciled. They belong to different dispensations. So long as the Jewish state existed the principle of solidarity remained in force. Men suffered for the sins of their ancestors; individuals shared the punishment incurred by the nation as a whole. But as soon as the nation is dead, when the bonds that unite men in the organism of national life are dissolved, then the idea of individual responsibility comes into immediate operation. Each Israelite stands isolated before Jehovah, the burden of hereditary guilt falls away from him, and he is free to determine his own relation to God. He need not fear that the iniquity of his fathers will be reckoned against him; he is held accountable only for his own sins, and these can be forgiven on the condition of his own repentance.

The doctrine of this chapter is generally regarded as Ezekiel's most characteristic contribution to theology. It might be nearer the truth to say that he is dealing with one of the great religious problems of the age in which he lived. The difficulty was perceived by Jeremiah, and treated in a manner which shows that his thoughts were being led in the same direction as those of Ezekiel (Jer. xxxi. 29, 30). If in any respect the teaching of Ezekiel makes an advance on that of Jeremiah, it is in his application of the new truth to the duty of the present: and even here the difference is more apparent than real. Jeremiah postpones the introduction of personal religion to the future, regarding it as an ideal to be realised in the Messianic age. His own life and that of his contemporaries was bound up with the old dispensation which was passing away, and he knew that he was destined to share the fate of his people. Ezekiel, on the other hand, lives already under the powers of the world to come. The one hindrance to the perfect manifestation of Jehovah's righteousness has been removed by the destruction of Jerusalem, and henceforward it will be made apparent in the correspondence between the desert and the fate of each individual. The new Israel must be organised on the basis of personal religion, and the time has already come when the task of preparing the religious community of the future must be earnestly taken up. Hence the doctrine of individual responsibility has a peculiar and practical importance in the mission of Ezekiel. The call to repentance, which is the keynote of his ministry, is addressed to individual men, and in order that it may take effect their minds must be disabused of all fatalistic preconceptions which would induce paralysis of the moral faculties. It was necessary to affirm in all their breadth and fulness the two fundamental truths of personal religion—the absolute righteousness of God's dealings with individual men, and His readiness to welcome and pardon the penitent.

The eighteenth chapter falls accordingly into two divisions. In the first the prophet sets the individual's immediate relation to God against the idea that guilt is transmitted from father to children (vv. 2-20). In the second he tries to dispel the notion that a man's fate is so determined by his own past life as to make a change of moral condition impossible (vv. 21-32).

I.

It is noteworthy that both Jeremiah and Ezekiel, in dealing with the question of retribution, start from a popular proverb which had gained currency in the later years of the kingdom of Judah: "The fathers have eaten sour grapes, and the children's teeth are set on edge." In whatever spirit this saying may have been first coined, there is no doubt that it had come to be used as a witticism at the expense of Providence. It indicates that influences were at work besides the word of prophecy which tended to undermine men's faith in the current conception of the divine government. The doctrine of transmitted guilt was accepted as a fact of experience, but it no longer satisfied the deeper moral instincts of men. In early Israel it was otherwise. There the idea that the son should bear the iniquity of the father was received without challenge and applied without misgiving in judicial procedure. The whole family of Achan perished for the sin of their father; the sons of Saul expiated their father's crime long after he was dead. These are indeed but isolated facts, yet they are sufficient to prove the ascendency of the antique conception of the tribe or family as a unit whose individual members are involved in the guilt of the head. With the spread of purer ethical ideas among the people there came a deeper sense of the value of the individual life, and at a later time the principle of vicarious punishment was banished from the administration of human justice (*cf.* 2 Kings xiv. 6 with Deut. xxiv. 16). Within that sphere the principle was firmly established that each man shall be put to death for his own sin. But the motives which made this change intelligible and necessary in purely human relations could not be brought to bear immediately on the question of divine retribution. The righteousness of God was thought to act on different lines from the righteousness of man. The experience of the last generation of the state seemed to furnish fresh evidence of the operation of a law of providence by which men were made to inherit the iniquity of their fathers. The literature of the period is filled with the conviction that it was the sins of Manasseh that had sealed the doom of the nation. These sins had never been adequately punished, and subsequent events showed that they were not forgiven. The reforming zeal of Josiah had postponed for a time the final visitation of Jehovah's anger; but no reformation and no repentance could avail to roll back the flood of judgment that had been set in motion by the crimes of the reign of Manasseh. "Notwithstanding Jehovah turned not from the fierceness of His great wrath, wherewith His anger was kindled against Judah, because of all the provocations that Manasseh had provoked Him withal" (2 Kings xxiii. 26).

The proverb about the sour grapes shows the effect of this interpretation of providence on a large section of the people. It means no doubt that there is an irrational element in God's method of dealing with men, something not in harmony with natural laws. In the natural sphere if a man eats sour grapes his own teeth are blunted or set on edge; the consequences are immediate, and they are transitory. But in the moral sphere a man may eat sour grapes all his life and suffer no evil consequences whatever; the consequences, however, appear in his children who have committed no such indiscretion. There is nothing there which answers to the ordinary sense of justice. Yet the proverb appears to be less an arraignment of the divine righteousness than a mode of self-exculpation on the part of the people. It expresses the fatalism and despair which settled down on the minds of that generation when they realised the full extent of the calamity that had overtaken them: "If our transgressions and our sins be upon us, and we pine away in them, how then should we live?" (xxxiii. 10). So the exiles reasoned in Babylon, where they were in no mood for quoting facetious proverbs about the ways of Providence; but they accurately expressed the sense of the adage that had been current in Jerusalem before its fall. The sins for which they suffered were not their own, and the judgment that lay on them was no summons to repentance, for it was caused by sins of which they were not guilty and for which they could not in any real sense repent.

Ezekiel attacks this popular theory of retribution at what must have been regarded as its strongest point—the relation between the father and son. "Why should the son *not* bear the iniquity of his father?" the people asked in astonishment (ver. 19). "It is good traditional theology, and it has been confirmed by our own experience." Now Ezekiel would probably not have admitted that in any circumstances a son suffers because his father has sinned. With that notion he appears to have absolutely broken. He did not deny that the Exile was the punishment for all the sins of the past as well as for those of the present; but that was because the nation was treated as a moral unit, and not because of any law of heredity which bound up the fate of the child with that of the father. It was essential to his purpose to show that the principle of social guilt or collective retribution came to an end with the fall of the state; whereas in the form in which the people held to it, it could never come to an end so long as there are parents to sin and children to suffer. But the important point in the prophet's teaching is that, whether in one form or in another, the principle of solidarity is now superseded. God will no longer deal with men in the mass, but as individuals; and facts which gave plausibility and a relative justification to cynical views of God's providence shall no more occur. There will be no more occasion to use that objectionable proverb in Israel. On the contrary, it will be manifest in the case of each separate individual that God's righteousness is discriminating, and that each man's destiny corresponds with his own character. And the new principle is embodied in words which may be called the charter of the individual soul—words whose significance is fully revealed only in Christianity: "All souls are Mine. . . . The soul that sinneth, it shall die."

What is here asserted is of course not a distinction between the soul or spiritual part of a man's being and another part of his being which is subject to physical necessity, but one between the individual and his moral environment. The former distinction is real, and it may be necessary for us in our day to insist on it, but it was certainly not thought of by Ezekiel or perhaps by any other Old Testament writer. The word "soul" denotes simply the principle of individual life. "All persons are Mine" expresses the whole meaning which Ezekiel meant to convey. Consequently the death threatened to the sinner is not what we call spiritual death, but death in the literal sense—the death of the individual. The truth taught is the independence and freedom of the individual, or his moral personality. And that truth involves two things. First, each individual belongs to God, stands in immediate personal relation to Him. In the old economy the individual belonged to the nation or the family, and was related to God only as a member of a larger whole. Now he has to deal with God directly—possesses independent personal worth in the eye of God. Secondly, as a result of this, each man is responsible for his own acts, and for these alone. So long as his religious relations are determined by circumstances outside of his own life his personality is incomplete. The ideal relation to God must be one in which the destiny of every man depends on his own free actions. These are the fundamental postulates of personal religion as formulated by Ezekiel.

The first part of the chapter is nothing more than an illustration of the second of these truths in a sufficient number of instances to show both sides of its operation. There is first the case of a man perfectly righteous, who as a matter of course lives by his righteousness, the state of his father not being taken into account. Then this good man is supposed to have a son who is in all respects the opposite of his father, who answers none of the tests of a righteous man; he must die for his own sins, and his father's righteousness avails him nothing. Lastly, if the son of this wicked man takes warning by his father's fate and leads a good life, he lives just as the first man did because of his own righteousness, and suffers no diminution of his reward because his father was a sinner. In all this argument there is a tacit appeal to the conscience of the hearers, as if the case only required to be put clearly before them to command their assent. This is what shall be, the prophet says; and it is what ought to be. It is contrary to the idea of perfect justice to conceive of Jehovah as acting otherwise than as here represented. To cling to the idea of collective retribution as a permanent truth of religion, as the exiles were disposed to do, destroys belief in the Divine righteousness by making it different from the righteousness which expresses itself in the moral judgments of men.

Before we pass from this part of the chapter we may take note of some characteristics of the moral ideal by which Ezekiel tests the conduct of the individual man. It is given in the form of a catalogue of virtues, the presence or absence of which determines a man's fitness or unfitness to enter the future kingdom of God. Most of these virtues are defined negatively; the code specifies sins to be avoided rather than duties to be performed or graces to be cultivated. Nevertheless they are such as to cover a large section of human life, and the arrangement of them embodies distinctions of permanent ethical significance. They may be classed under the three heads of piety, chastity, and beneficence. Under the first head, that of directly religious duties, two offences are mentioned which are closely connected with each other, although to our minds they may seem to involve different degrees of guilt (ver. 6). One is the acknowledgment of other gods than Jehovah, and the other is participation in ceremonies which denoted fellowship with idols.* To us who "know that an idol is nothing in the world" the mere act of eating with the blood has no religious significance. But in Ezekiel's time it was impossible to divest it of heathen associations, and the man who performed it stood convicted of a sin against Jehovah. Similarly the idea of sexual purity is illustrated by two outstanding and prevalent offences (ver. 6). The third head, which includes by far the greater number of particulars, deals with the duties which we regard as moral in a stricter sense. They are embodiments of the love which "worketh no ill to his neighbour," and is therefore "the fulfilling of the law." It is manifest that the list is not meant to be an exhaustive enumeration of all the virtues that a good man must practise, or all the vices he must shun. The prophet has before his mind two broad classes of men—those who feared God, and those who did not; and what he does is to lay down outward marks which were practically sufficient to discriminate between the one class and the other.

The supreme moral category is Righteousness, and this includes the two ideas of right character and a right relation to God. The distinction between an active righteousness manifested in the life and a "righteousness which is by faith" is not explicitly drawn in the Old Testament. Hence the passage contains no teaching on the question whether a man's relation to God is determined by his good works, or whether good works are the fruit and outcome of a right relation to God. The essence of morality, according to the Old Testament, is loyalty to God, expressed by obedience to His will; and from that point of view it is self-evident that the man who is loyal to Jehovah stands accepted in His sight. In other connections Ezekiel makes it abundantly clear that the state of grace does not depend on any merit which man can have towards God.

The fact that Ezekiel defines righteousness in terms of outward conduct has led to his being accused of the error of legalism in his moral conceptions. He has been charged with resolving righteousness into "a sum of separate *tzedāqôth*," or virtues. But this view strains his language unduly, and seems moreover to be negatived by the presuppositions of his argument. As a man must either live or die at the day of judgment, so he must at any moment be either righteous or wicked. The problematic case of a man who should conscientiously observe some of these requirements and deliberately violate others would have been dismissed by Ezekiel as an idle speculation: "Whosoever shall keep the whole law, and yet offend in one point, he is guilty of all" (James ii. 10). The very fact that former good deeds are not remembered to a man in the day when he turns from his righteousness shows that the state of righteousness is something different from an average

* "To eat upon the mountains" (if that reading can be retained) must mean to take part in the sacrificial feasts which were held on the high places in honour of idols. But if with W. R. Smith and others we substitute the phrase "eat with the blood," assimilating the reading to that of ch. xxxiii. 25, the offence is still of the same nature. In the time of Ezekiel to eat with the blood probably meant not merely to eat that which had not been sacrificed to Jehovah, but to engage in a rite of distinctly heathenish character. *Cf.* Lev. xix. 20, and see the note in Smith's "Kinship and Marriage in Early Arabia," p. 310.

struck from the statistics of his moral career. The bent of the character towards or away from goodness is no doubt spoken of as subject to sudden fluctuations, but for the time being each man is conceived as dominated by the one tendency or the other; and it is the bent of the whole nature towards the good that constitutes the righteousness by which a man shall live. It is at all events a mistake to suppose that the prophet is concerned only about the external act and indifferent to the state of heart from which it proceeds. It is true that he does not attempt to penetrate beneath the surface of the outward life. He does not analyse motives. But this is because he assumes that if a man keeps God's law he does it from a sincere desire to please God and with a sense of the rightness of the law to which he subjects his life. When we recognise this the charge of externalism amounts to very little. We can never get behind the principle that "he that doeth righteousness is righteous" (1 John iii. 7), and that principle covers all that Ezekiel really teaches. Compared with the more spiritual teaching of the New Testament his moral ideal is no doubt defective in many directions, but his insistence on action as a test of character is hardly one of them. We must remember that the New Testament itself contains as many warnings against a false spirituality as it does against the opposite error of reliance on good works.

II.

The second great truth of personal religion is the moral freedom of the individual to determine his own destiny in the day of judgment. This is illustrated in the latter part of the chapter by the two opposite cases of a wicked man turning from his wickedness (vv. 21, 22) and a righteous man turning from his righteousness (ver. 24). And the teaching of the passage is that the effect of such a change of mind, as regards a man's relation to God, is absolute. The good life subsequent to conversion is not weighed against the sins of past years; it is the index of a new state of heart in which the guilt of the former transgressions is entirely blotted out: "All his transgressions that he hath committed shall not be remembered in regard to him; in his righteousness that he hath done he shall live." But in like manner the act of apostasy effaces the remembrance of good deeds done in an earlier period of the man's life. The standing of each soul before God, its righteousness or its wickedness, is thus wholly determined by its final choice of good or evil, and is revealed by the conduct which follows that great moral decision. There can be no doubt that Ezekiel regards these two possibilities as equally real, falling away from righteousness being as much a fact of experience as repentance. In the light of the New Testament we should perhaps interpret both cases somewhat differently. In genuine conversion we must recognise the imparting of a new spiritual principle which is ineradicable, containing the pledge of perseverance in the state of grace to the end. In the case of final apostasy we are compelled to judge that the righteousness which is renounced was only apparent, that it was no true indication of the man's character or of his condition in the sight of God. But these are not the questions with which the prophet is directly dealing. The essential truth which he inculcates is the emancipation of the individual, through repentance, from his own past. In virtue of his immediate personal relation to God each man has the power to accept the offer of salvation, to break away from his sinful life and escape the doom which hangs over the impenitent. To this one point the whole argument of the chapter tends. It is a demonstration of the possibility and efficacy of individual repentance, culminating in the declaration which lies at the very foundation of evangelical religion, that God has no pleasure in the death of him that dieth, but will have all men to repent and live (ver. 32).

It is not easy for us to conceive the effect of this revelation on the minds of people so utterly unprepared for it as the generation in which Ezekiel lived. Accustomed as they were to think of their individual fate as bound up in that of their nation, they could not at once adjust themselves to a doctrine which had never previously been enunciated with such incisive clearness. And it is not surprising that one effect of Ezekiel's teaching was to create fresh doubts of the rectitude of the Divine government. "The way of the Lord is not equal," it was said (vv. 25, 29). So long as it was admitted that men suffered for the sins of their ancestors or that God dealt with them in the mass, there was at least an appearance of consistency in the methods of Providence. The justice of God might not be visible in the life of the individual, but it could be roughly traced in the history of the nation as a whole. But when that principle was discarded, then the question of the Divine righteousness was raised in the case of each separate Israelite, and there immediately appeared all those perplexities about the lot of the individual which so sorely exercised the faith of Old Testament believers. Experience did not show that correspondence between a man's attitude towards God and his earthly fortunes which the doctrine of individual freedom seemed to imply; and even in Ezekiel's time it must have been evident that the calamities which overtook the state fell indiscriminately on the righteous and the wicked. The prophet's purpose, however, is a practical one, and he does not attempt to offer a theoretical solution of the difficulties which thus arose. There were several considerations in his mind which turned aside the edge of the people's complaint against the righteousness of Jehovah. One was the imminence of the final judgment, in which the absolute rectitude of the Divine procedure would be clearly manifested. Another seems to be the irresolute and unstable attitude of the people themselves towards the great moral issues which were set before them. While they professed to be more righteous than their fathers, they showed no settled purpose of amendment in their lives. A man might be apparently righteous to-day and a sinner to-morrow: the "inequality" of which they complained was in their own ways, and not in the way of the Lord (vv. 25, 29). But the most important element in the case was the prophet's conception of the character of God as one who, though strictly just, yet desired that men should live. The Lord is long-suffering, not willing that any should perish; and He postpones the day of decision that His goodness may lead men to repentance. "Have I any pleasure in the death of the wicked? saith the Lord: and not that he should turn from his ways, and live?" (ver. 23). And all these considerations lead up to the urgent call to repentance with which the chapter closes.

The importance of the questions dealt with in this eighteenth chapter is shown clearly enough by the hold which they have over the minds of men in the present day. The very same difficulties which Ezekiel had to encounter in his time confront us still in a somewhat altered form, and are often keenly felt as obstacles to faith in God. The scientific doctrine of heredity, for example, seems to be but a more precise modern rendering of the old proverb about the eating of sour grapes. The biological controversy over the possibility of the transmission of acquired characteristics scarcely touches the moral problem. In whatever way that controversy may be ultimately settled, it is certain that in all cases a man's life is affected both for good and evil by influences which descend upon him from his ancestry. Similarly within the sphere of the individual life the law of habit seems to exclude the possibility of complete emancipation from the penalty due to past transgressions. Hardly anything, in short, is better established by experience than that the consequences of past actions persist through all changes of spiritual condition, and, further, that children do suffer from the consequences of their parents' sin.

Do not these facts, it may be asked, amount practically to a vindication of the theory of retribution against which the prophet's argument is directed? How can we reconcile them with the great principles enunciated in this chapter? Dictates of morality, fundamental truths of religion, these may be: but can we say in the face of experience that they are true?

It must be admitted that a complete answer to these questions is not given in the chapter before us, nor perhaps anywhere in the Old Testament. So long as God dealt with men mainly by temporal rewards and punishments, it was impossible to realise fully the separateness of the soul in its spiritual relations to God; the fate of the individual is necessarily merged in that of the community, and Ezekiel's doctrine remains a prophecy of better things to be revealed. This indeed is the light in which he himself teaches us to regard it; although he applies it in all its strictness to the men of his own generation, it is nevertheless essentially a feature of the ideal kingdom of God, and is to be exhibited in the judgment by which that kingdom is introduced. The great value of his teaching therefore lies in his having formulated with unrivalled clearness principles which are eternally true of the spiritual life, although the perfect manifestation of these principles in the experience of believers was reserved for the final revelation of salvation in Christ.

The solution of the contradiction referred to lies in the separation between the natural and the penal consequences of sin. There is a sphere within which natural laws have their course, modified, it may be, but not wholly suspended by the law of the spirit of life in Christ. The physical effects of vicious indulgence are not turned aside by repentance, and a man may carry the scars of sin upon him to the grave. But there is also a sphere into which natural law does not enter. In his immediate personal relation to God a believer is raised above the evil consequences which flow from his past life, so that they have no power to separate him from the love of God. And within that sphere his moral freedom and independence are as much matter of experience as is his subjection to law in another sphere. He knows that all things work together for his good, and that tribulation itself is a means of bringing him nearer to God. Amongst those tribulations which work out his salvation there may be the evil conditions imposed on him by the sin of others, or even the natural consequences of his own former transgressions. But tribulations no longer bear the aspect of penalty, and are no longer a token of the wrath of God. They are transformed into chastisements by which the Father of spirits makes His children perfect in holiness. The hardest cross to bear will always be that which is the result of one's own sin; but He who has borne the guilt of it can strengthen us to bear even this and follow Him.*

CHAPTER XI.

THE SWORD UNSHEATHED.

EZEKIEL xxi.

THE date at the beginning of chap. xx. introduces the fourth and last section of the prophecies delivered before the destruction of Jerusalem. It also divides the first period of Ezekiel's ministry into two equal parts. The time is the month of August, 590 B. C., two years after his prophetic inauguration and two years before the investment of Jerusalem. It follows that if the Book of Ezekiel presents anything like a faithful picture of his actual work, by far his most productive year was that which had just closed. It embraces the long and varied series of discourses from chap. viii. to chap. xix.; whereas five chapters are all that remain as a record of his activity during the next two years. This result is not so improbable as at first sight it might appear. From the character of Ezekiel's prophecy, which consists largely of homiletic amplifications of one great theme, it is quite intelligible that the main lines of his teaching should have taken shape in his mind at an early period of his ministry. The discourses in the earlier part of the book may have been expanded in the act of committing them to writing; but there is no reason to doubt that the ideas they contain were present to the prophet's mind and were actually delivered by him within the period to which they

* In the striking passage ch. xiv. 12–23 the application of the doctrine of individual retribution to the destruction of Jerusalem is discussed. It is treated as "an exception to the rule" (Smend)—perhaps the exception which proves the rule. The rule is that in a national judgment the most eminent saints save neither son nor daughter by their righteousness, but only their own lives (vv. 13–20). At the fall of Jerusalem, however, a remnant escapes and goes into captivity with sons and daughters, in order that their corrupt lives may prove to the earlier exiles how necessary the destruction of the city was (vv. 21–23). The argument is an admission that the judgment on Israel was not carried out in accordance with the strict principle laid down in ch. xviii. It is difficult, indeed, to reconcile the various utterances of Ezekiel on this subject. In ch. xxi. 3, 4, he expressly announces that in the downfall of the state righteous and wicked shall perish together. In the vision of ch. ix., on the other hand, the righteous are marked for exemption from the fate of the city. The truth appears to be that the prophet is conscious of standing between two dispensations, and does not hold a consistent view regarding the time when the law proper to the perfect dispensation comes into operation. The point on which there is no ambiguity is that in the final judgment which ushers in the Messianic age the principle of individual retribution shall be fully manifested.

are assigned. We may therefore suppose that Ezekiel's public exhortations became less frequent during the two years that preceded the siege, just as we know that for two years after that event they were altogether discontinued.

In this last division of the prophecies relating to the destruction of Jerusalem we can easily distinguish two different classes of oracles. On the one hand we have two chapters dealing with contemporary incidents—the march of Nebuchadnezzar's army against Jerusalem (chap. xxi.), and the commencement of the siege of the city (chap. xxiv.). In spite of the confident opinion of some critics that these prophecies could not have been composed till after the fall of Jerusalem, they seem to me to bear the marks of having been written under the immediate influence of the events they describe. It is difficult otherwise to account for the excitement under which the prophet labours, especially in chap. xxi., which stands by the side of chap. vii. as the most agitated utterance in the whole book. On the other hand, we have three discourses of the nature of formal indictments—one directed against the exiles (chap. xx.), one against Jerusalem (chap. xxii.), and one against the whole nation of Israel (chap. xxiii.). It is impossible in these chapters to discover any advance in thought upon similar passages that have already been before us. Two of them (chaps. xx. and xxiii.) are historical retrospects after the manner of chap. xvi., and there is no obvious reason why they should be placed in a different section of the book. The key to the unity of the section must therefore be sought in the two historical prophecies and in the situation created by the events they describe.* It will therefore help to clear the ground if we commence with the oracle which throws most light on the historical background of this group of prophecies—the oracle of Jehovah's sword against Jerusalem in chap. xxi.†

The long-projected rebellion has at length broken out. Zedekiah has renounced his allegiance to the king of Babylon, and the army of the Chaldeans is on its way to suppress the insurrection. The precise date of these events is not known. For some reason the conspiracy of the Palestinian states had hung fire; many years had been allowed to slip away since the time when their envoys had met in Jerusalem to concert measures of united resistance (Jer. xxvii.). This procrastination was, as usual, a sure presage of disaster. In the interval the league had dissolved. Some of its members had made terms with Nebuchadnezzar; and it would appear that only Tyre, Judah, and Ammon ventured on open defiance of his power. The hope was cherished in Jerusalem, and probably also among the Jews in Babylon, that the first assault of the Chaldeans would be directed against the Ammonites, and that time would thus be gained to complete the defences of Jerusalem. To dispel this illusion is one obvious purpose of the prophecy before us. The movements of Nebuchadnezzar's army are directed by a wisdom higher than his own; he is the unconscious instrument by which Jehovah is executing His own purpose. The real object of his expedition is not to punish a few refractory tribes for an act of disloyalty, but to vindicate the righteousness of Jehovah in the destruction of the city which had profaned his holiness. No human calculations will be allowed even for a moment to turn aside the blow which is aimed directly at Jerusalem's sins, or to obscure the lesson taught by its sure and unerring aim.

We can imagine the restless suspense and anxiety with which the final struggle for the national cause was watched by the exiles in Babylon. In imagination they would follow the long march of the Chaldean hosts by the Euphrates and their descent by the valleys of the Orontes and Leontes upon the city. Eagerly would they wait for some tidings of a reverse which would revive their drooping hope of a speedy collapse of the great world-empire and a restoration of Israel to its ancient freedom. And when at length they heard that Jerusalem was enclosed in the iron grip of these victorious legions, from which no human deliverance was possible, their mood would harden into one in which fanatical hope and sullen despair contended for the mastery. Into an atmosphere charged with such excitement Ezekiel hurls the series of predictions comprised in chaps. xxi. and xxiv. With far other feelings than his fellows, but with as keen an interest as theirs, he follows the development of what he knows to be the last act in the long controversy between Jehovah and Israel. It is his duty to repeat once more the irrevocable decree—the Divine *delenda est* against the guilty Jerusalem. But he does so in this instance in language whose vehemence betrays the agitation of his mind, and perhaps also the restlessness of the society in which he lived. The twenty-first chapter is a series of rhapsodies, the product of a state bordering on ecstasy, where different aspects of the impending judgment are set forth by the help of vivid images which pass in quick succession through the prophet's mind.

I.

The first vision which the prophet sees of the approaching catastrophe (vv. 1-4) is that of a forest conflagration, an occurrence which must have been as frequent in Palestine as a prairie fire in America. He sees a fire break out in the "forest of the south," and rage with such fierceness that "every green tree and every dry tree" is burned up; the faces of all who are near it are scorched, and all men are convinced that so terrible a calamity must be the work of Jehovah Himself. This we may suppose to have been the form in which the truth first laid hold of Ezekiel's imagination; but he appears to have hesitated to proclaim his message in this form. His figurative manner of speech had become notorious among the exiles (ver. 5), and he was conscious that a "parable" so vague and general as this would be dismissed as an ingenious riddle which might mean anything or nothing. What

* This is true whether (as some expositors think) the date in ch. xx. is merely an external mark introducing a new division of the book, or whether (as seems more natural) it is due to the fact that here Ezekiel recognised a turning-point of his ministry. Such visits of the elders as that here recorded must have been of frequent occurrence. Two others are mentioned, and of these one is undated (ch. xiv. 1); the other at least admits the supposition that it was connected with a very definite change of opinion among the exiles (ch. viii. 1: see above, p. 239). We may therefore reasonably suppose that the precise note of time here introduced marks this particular incident as having possessed a peculiar significance in the relations between the prophet and his fellow-exiles. What its significance may have been we shall consider in the next chapter, see p. 264.

† The verses xx. 45-49 of the English Version really belong to ch. xxi. and are so placed in the Hebrew. In what follows the verses will be numbered according to the Hebrew text.

follows (vv. 7-10) gives the key to the original vision. Although it is in form an independent oracle, it is closely parallel to the preceding and elucidates each feature in detail. The "forest of the south" is explained to mean the land of Israel; and the mention of the sword of Jehovah instead of the fire intimates less obscurely that the instrument of the threatened calamity is the Babylonian army. It is interesting to observe that Ezekiel expressly admits that there were righteous men even in the doomed Israel. Contrary to his conception of the normal methods of the Divine righteousness, he conceives of *this* judgment as one which involves righteous and wicked in a common ruin. Not that God is less than righteous in this crowning act of vengeance, but His justice is not brought to bear on the fate of individuals. He is dealing with the nation as a whole, and in the exterminating judgment of the nation good men will no more be spared than the green tree of the forest escapes the fate of the dry. It was the fact that righteous men perished in the fall of Jerusalem; and Ezekiel does not shut his eyes to it, firmly as he believed that the time was come when God would reward every man according to his own character. The indiscriminateness of the judgment in its bearing on different classes of persons is obviously a feature which Ezekiel here seeks to emphasise.

But the idea of the sword of Jehovah drawn from its scabbard, to return no more till it has accomplished its mission, is the one that has fixed itself most deeply in the prophet's imagination, and forms the connecting link between this vision and the other amplifications of the same theme which follow.

II.

Passing over the symbolic action of vv. 11-13, representing the horror and astonishment with which the dire tidings of Jerusalem's fall will be received, we come to the point where the prophet breaks into the wild strain of dithyrambic poetry, which has been called the "Song of the Sword" (vv. 14-22). The following translation, although necessarily imperfect and in some places uncertain, may convey some idea both of the structure and the rugged vigour of the original. It will be seen that there is a clear division into four stanzas: *—

(i) Vv. 14-16.

"A sword, a sword! It is sharpened and burnished withal.
For a work of slaughter is it sharpened!
To gleam like lightning burnished!
. . . .
And 'twas given to be smoothed for the grip of the hand,
—Sharpened is it, and furbished—
To put in the hand of the slayer."

(ii) Vv. 17, 18.

"Cry and howl, son of man!
For it has come among my people;
Come among all the princes of Israel!
Victims of the sword are they, they and my people;
Therefore smite upon thy thigh!
. . . .
It shall not be, saith Jehovah the Lord."

(iii) Vv. 19, 20.

"But, thou son of man, prophesy, and smite hand on hand;
Let the sword be doubled and tripled (?).
A sword of the slain is it, the great sword of the slain whirling around them,—
That hearts may fail, and many be the fallen in all their gates.
. . . .
It is made like lightning, furbished for slaughter!"

(iv) Vv. 21, 22.

"Gather thee together! Smite to the right, to the left,
Whithersoever thine edge is appointed!
And I also will smite hand on hand,
And appease My wrath:
I Jehovah have spoken it."

* At three places the meaning is entirely lost, through corruption of the text.

In spite of its obscurity, its abrupt transitions, and its strange blending of the divine with the human personality, the ode exhibits a definite poetic form and a real progress of thought from the beginning to the close. Throughout the passage we observe that the prophet's gaze is fascinated by the glittering sword which symbolised the instrument of Jehovah's vengeance. In the opening stanza (i) he describes the *preparation* of the sword; he notes the keenness of its edge and its glittering sheen with an awful presentiment that an implement so elaborately fashioned is destined for some terrible day of slaughter. Then (ii) he announces the *purpose* for which the sword is prepared, and breaks into loud lamentation as he realises that its doomed victims are his own people and the princes of Israel. In the next stanza (iii) he sees the sword *in action;* wielded by an invisible hand, it flashes hither and thither, circling round its hapless victims as if two or three swords were at work instead of one. All hearts are paralysed with fear, but the sword does not cease its ravages until it has filled the ground with slain. Then at length the sword is *at rest* (iv), having accomplished its work. The divine Speaker calls on it in a closing apostrophe "to gather itself together" as if for a final sweep to right and left, indicating the thoroughness with which the judgment has been executed. In the last verse the vision of the sword fades away, and the poem closes with an announcement, in the usual prophetic manner, of Jehovah's fixed purpose to "assuage" His wrath against Israel by the crowning act of retribution.

III.

If any doubt still remained as to what the sword of Jehovah meant, it is removed in the next section (vv. 23-32), where the prophet indicates the way by which the sword is to come on the kingdom of Judah. The Chaldæan monarch is represented as pausing on his march, perhaps at Riblah or some place to the north of Palestine, and deliberating whether he shall advance first against Judah or the Ammonites. He stands at the parting of the ways —on the left hand is the road to Rabbath-ammon, on the right that to Jerusalem. In his perplexity he invokes supernatural guidance, resorting to various expedients then in use for ascertaining the will of the gods and the path of good fortune. He "rattles the arrows" (two of them in some kind of vessel, one for Jerusalem and the other for Riblah); he consults the teraphim and inspects the entrails of a sacrificial victim. This consulting of the omens was no doubt an invariable preliminary to every campaign, and was resorted to whenever an important military decision had to be made. It might seem a matter of indifference to a powerful monarch like Nebuchadnezzar which of two petty opponents he determined to crush first. But the kings of Babylon were religious men in their way, and never doubted that success depended on their following the indications that were given by the higher powers. In this case Nebuchadnezzar gets a true answer, but not from the deities whose aid he had invoked. In his right hand he finds the arrow marked "Jerusalem." The die is cast, his resolution is taken, but it is Jehovah's sentence sealing the fate of Jerusalem that has been uttered.

Such is the situation which Ezekiel in Babylon is directed to represent through a piece of obvious symbolism. A road diverging into two is drawn on the ground, and at the meeting-point a sign-post is erected, indicating that the one leads to Ammon and the other to Judah. It is of course not necessary to suppose that the incident so graphically described actually occurred. The divination scene may only be imaginary, although it is certainly a true reflection of Babylonian ideas and customs. The truth conveyed is that the Babylonian army is moving under the immediate guidance of Jehovah, and that not only the political projects of the king, but his secret thoughts and even his superstitious reliance on signs and omens, are all overruled for the furtherance of the one purpose for which Jehovah has raised him up.

Meanwhile Ezekiel is well aware that in Jerusalem a very different interpretation is put on the course of events. When the news of the great king's decision reaches the men at the head of affairs they are not dismayed. They view the decision as the result of "false divination"; they laugh to scorn the superstitious rites which have determined the course of the campaign,—not that they suppose the king will not act on his omens, but they do not believe they are an augury of success. They had hoped for a short breathing space while Nebuchadnezzar was engaged on the east of the Jordan, but they will not shrink from the conflict whether it be today or to-morrow. Addressing himself to this state of mind, Ezekiel once more * reminds those who hear him that these men are fighting against the moral laws of the universe. The existing kingdom of Judah occupies a false position before God and in the eyes of just men. It has no religious foundation; for the hope of the Messiah does not lie with that wearer of a dishonoured crown, the king Zedekiah, but with the legitimate heir of David now in exile. The state has no right to be except as part of the Chaldæan empire, and this right it has forfeited by renouncing its allegiance to its earthly superior. These men forget that in this quarrel the just cause is that of Nebuchadnezzar, whose enterprise only seems to "call to mind their iniquity" (ver. 28)—*i. e.*, their political crime. In provoking this conflict, therefore, they have put themselves in the wrong; they shall be caught in the toils of their own villainy.

The heaviest censure is reserved for Zedekiah, the "wicked one, the prince of Israel, whose day is coming in the time of final retribution." This part of the prophecy has a close resemblance to the latter part of chap. xvii. The prophet's sympathies are still with the exiled king, or at least with that branch of the royal family which he represents. And the sentence of rejection on Zedekiah is again accompanied by a promise of the restoration of the kingdom in the person of the Messiah. The crown which has been dishonoured by the last king of Judah shall be taken from his head; that which is low shall be exalted (the exiled branch of the Davidic house), and that which is high shall be abased (the reigning king); the whole existing order of things shall be overturned "until *He* comes who has the right." *

* *Cf.* ch. xvii.

IV.

The last oracle is directed against the children of Ammon. By Nebuchadnezzar's decision to subdue Jerusalem first the Ammonites had gained a short respite. They even exulted in the humiliation of their former ally, and had apparently drawn the sword in order to seize part of the land of Judah. Misled by false diviners, they had dared to seek their own advantage in the calamities which Jehovah had brought on His own people. The prophet threatens the complete annihilation of Ammon, even in its own land, and the blotting out of its remembrance among the nations. That is the substance of the prophecy; but its form presents several points of difficulty. It begins with what appears to be an echo of the "Song of the Sword" in the earlier part of the chapter:—

> "A sword! a sword!
> It is drawn for slaughter; it is furbished to shine like lightning" (ver. 33).

But as we proceed we find that it is the sword of the Ammonites that is meant, and they are ordered to return it to its sheath. If this be so, the tone of the passage must be ironical. It is in mockery that the prophet uses such magnificent language of the puny pretensions of Ammon to take a share in the work for which Jehovah has fashioned the mighty weapon of the Chaldæan army. There are other reminiscences of the earlier part of the chapter, such as the "lying divination" of ver. 34, and the "time of final retribution" in the same verse. The allusion to the "reproach" of Ammon and its aggressive attitude seems to point to the time after the destruction of Jerusalem and the withdrawal of the army of Nebuchadnezzar. Whether the Ammonites had previously made their submission or not we cannot tell; but the fortieth and forty-first chapters of Jeremiah show that Ammon was still a hotbed of conspiracy against the Babylonian interest in the days after the fall of Jerusalem. These appearances make it probable that this part of the chapter is an appendix, added at a later time, and dealing with a situation which was developed after the destruction of the city. Its insertion in its present place is easily accounted for by the circumstance that the fate of Ammon had been linked with that of Jerusalem in the previous part of the chapter. The vindictive little nationality had used its respite to gratify its hereditary hatred of Israel, and now the judgment, suspended for a time, shall return with redoubled fury and sweep it from the earth.

Looking back over this series of prophecies, there seems reason to believe that, with the exception of the last, they are really contemporaneous with the events they deal with. It is true that they do not illuminate the historical situ-

* The reference is to the Messiah, and seems to be based on the ancient prophecy of Gen. xlix. 10, reading there שֶׁלֹּה instead of שִׁלֹה.

ation to the same degree as those in which Isaiah depicts the advance of another invader and the development of another crisis in the people's history. This is due partly to the bent of Ezekiel's genius, but partly also to the very peculiar circumstances in which he was placed. The events which form the theme of his prophecy were transacted on a distant stage; neither he nor his immediate hearers were actors in the drama. He addresses himself to an audience wrought to the highest pitch of excitement, but swayed by hopes and rumours and vague surmises as to the probable issue of events. It was inevitable in these circumstances that his prophecy, even in those passages which deal with contemporary facts, should present but a pale reflection of the actual situation. In the case before us the one historical event which stands out clearly is the departure of Nebuchadnezzar with his army to Jerusalem. But what we read is genuine prophecy; not the artifice of a man using prophetic speech as a literary form, but the utterance of one who discerns the finger of God in the present, and interprets His purpose beforehand to the men of his day.

CHAPTER XII.

JEHOVAH'S CONTROVERSY WITH ISRAEL.

Ezekiel xx.

By far the hardest trial of Ezekiel's faith must have been the conduct of his fellow-exiles. It was amongst them that he looked for the great spiritual change which must precede the establishment of the kingdom of God; and he had already addressed to them words of consolation based on the knowledge that the hope of the future was theirs (xi. 18). Yet the time passed on without bringing any indications that the promise was about to be fulfilled. There were no symptoms of national repentance; there was nothing even to show that the lessons of the Exile as interpreted by the prophet were beginning to be laid to heart. For these men, among whom he lived, were still inveterately addicted to idolatry. Strange as it must seem to us, the very men who cherished a fanatical faith in Jehovah's power to save His people were assiduously practising the worship of other gods. It is too readily assumed by some writers that the idolatry of the exiles was of the ambiguous kind which had prevailed so long in the land of Israel, that it was the worship of Jehovah under the form of images—a breach of the second commandment, but not of the first. The people who carried Jeremiah down to Egypt were as eager as Ezekiel's companions to hear a word from Jehovah; yet they were devoted to the worship of the "Queen of Heaven," and dated all their misfortunes from the time when their women had ceased to pay court to her. There is no reason to believe that the Jews in Babylon were less catholic in their superstitions than those of Judæa; and indeed the whole drift of Ezekiel's expostulations goes to show that he has the worship of false gods in view. The ancient belief, that the worship of Jehovah was specially associated with the land of Canaan, is not likely to have been without influence on the minds of those who felt the fascination of idolatry, and must have strengthened the tendency to seek the aid of foreign gods in a foreign land.

The twentieth chapter deals with this matter of idolatry; and the fact that this important discourse was called forth by a visit from the elders of Israel shows how heavily the subject weighed on the prophet's mind. Whatever the purpose of the deputation may have been (and of that we have no information), it was certainly not to consult Ezekiel about the propriety of worshipping false gods. It is only because this great question dominates all his thoughts concerning them and their destiny that he connects the warning against idolatry with a casual inquiry addressed to him by the elders. The circumstances are so similar to those of chap xiv. that Ewald was led to conjecture that both oracles originated in one and the same incident, and were separated from each other in writing because of the difference of their subjects. Chap. xiv. on that view justifies the refusal of an answer from a consideration of the true function of prophecy, while chap. xx. expands the admonition of the sixth verse of chap. xiv. into an elaborate review of the religious history of Israel. But there is really no good reason for identifying the two incidents. In neither passage does the prophet think it worth while to record the object of the inquiry addressed to him, and therefore conjecture is useless.

But the very fact that a definite date is given for this visit leads us to consider whether it had not some peculiar significance to lodge it so firmly in Ezekiel's mind. Now the most suggestive hint which the chapter affords is the idea put into the lips of the exiles in ver. 32: "And as for the thought which arises in your mind, it shall not be, in that ye are thinking, We will become like the heathen, like the families of the lands, in worshipping wood and stone." These words contain the key to the whole discourse. It is difficult, no doubt, to decide how much exactly is implied in them. They may mean no more than the determination to keep up the external conformity to heathen customs which already existed in matters of worship—as, for example, in the use of images. But the form of expression used, "that which is coming up in your mind," almost suggests that the prophet was face to face with an incipient tendency among the exiles, a deliberate resolve to apostatise and assimilate themselves for all religious purposes to the surrounding heathen. It is by no means improbable that, amidst the many conflicting tendencies that distracted the exiled community, this idea of a complete abandonment of the national religion should have crystallised into a settled purpose in the event of their last hope being disappointed. If this was the situation with which Ezekiel had to deal, we should be able to understand how his denunciation takes the precise form which it assumes in this chapter.

For what is, in the main, the purport of the chapter? Briefly stated the argument is as follows. The religion of Jehovah had never been the true expression of the national genius of Israel. Not now for the first time has the purpose of Israel come into conflict with the immutable purpose of Jehovah; but from the very beginning the history had been one long struggle between the natural inclinations of the people and the destiny which was forced on it by the will of God. The love of idols had been the distinguishing feature of the national character from the beginning; and if it had been suffered to prevail, Israel would never have been known as Jehovah's people. Why had it not been suffered to prevail? Because of Jehovah's regard for the honour of His name; because in the eyes of the heathen His glory was identified with the fortunes of this particular people, to whom He had once revealed Himself. And as it has been in the past, so it will be in the future. The time has come for the age-long controversy to be brought to an issue, and it cannot be doubtful what the issue will be. "That which comes up in their mind"—this new resolve to live like the heathen—cannot turn aside the purpose of Jehovah to make of Israel a people for His own glory. Whatever further judgments may be necessary for that end, the land of Israel shall yet be the seat of a pure and acceptable worship of the true God, and the people shall recognise with shame and contrition that the goal of all its history has been accomplished in spite of its perversity by the "irresistible grace" of its divine King.

I.

The Lesson of History (vv. 5-29).—It is a magnificent conception of national election which the prophet here unfolds. It takes the form of a parallel between two desert scenes, one at the beginning and the other at the close of Israel's history. The first part of the chapter deals with the religious significance of the transactions in the wilderness of Sinai and the events in Egypt which were introductory to them. It starts from Jehovah's free choice of the people while they were still living as idolaters in Egypt. Jehovah there revealed Himself to them as their God, and entered into a covenant * with them; and the covenant included on the one hand the promise of the land of Canaan, and on the other hand a requirement that the people should separate themselves from all forms of idolatry whether native or Egyptian. "In the day that I chose Israel, . . . and made Myself known to them in the land of Egypt, . . . saying, I am Jehovah your God; in that day I lifted up My hand to them, to bring them out of the land of Egypt, into a land which I had sought out for them. And I said to them, Cast away each man the abomination of his eyes, and defile not yourselves with the block-gods of Egypt. I am Jehovah your God" (vv. 5-7). The point which Ezekiel specially emphasises is that this vocation to be the people of the true God was thrust on Israel without its consent, and that the revelation of Jehovah's purpose evoked no response in the heart of the people. By persistence in idolatry they had virtually renounced the kingship of Jehovah and forfeited their right to the fulfilment of the promise He had given them. And only from regard to His name, that it might not be profaned in the sight of the nations, before whose eyes He had made Himself known to them, did He turn from the purpose He had formed to destroy them in the land of Egypt.

In several respects this account of the occurrences in Egypt goes beyond what we learn from any other source. The historical books contain no reference to the prevalence of specifically Egyptian forms of idolatry among the Hebrews, nor do they mention any threat to exterminate the people for their rebellion. It is not to be supposed, however, that Ezekiel possessed other records of the period before the Exodus than those preserved in the Pentateuch. The fundamental conceptions are those attested by the history, that God first revealed Himself to Israel by the name Jehovah through Moses, and that the revelation was accompanied by a promise of deliverance from Egypt. That the people in spite of this revelation continued to worship idols is an inference from the whole of their subsequent history. And the conflict in the mind of Jehovah between anger against the people's sin and jealousy for His own name is not a matter of history at all, but is an inspired interpretation of the history in the light of the divine holiness, which embraces both these elements.

In the wilderness Israel entered on the second and decisive stage of its probation which falls into two acts, and whose determining factor was the legislation. To the generation of the Exodus Jehovah made known the way of life in a code of law which on its own intrinsic merits ought to have commended itself to their moral sense. The statutes and judgments that were then given were such that "if a man do them he shall live by them" (ver. 11). This thought of the essential goodness of the law as originally given reveals Ezekiel's view of God's relation to men. It derives its significance no doubt from the contrast with legislation of an opposite character afterward mentioned. Yet even that contrast expresses a conviction in the prophet's mind that morality is not constituted by arbitrary enactments on the part of God, but that there are eternal conditions of ethical fellowship between God and man, and that the law first offered for Israel's acceptance was the embodiment of those ethical relations which flow from the nature of Jehovah. It is probable that Ezekiel has in view the moral precepts of the Decalogue. If so, it is instructive to notice that the Sabbath law is separately mentioned, not as one of the laws by which a man lives, but as a sign of the covenant between Jehovah and Israel. The divine purpose was again defeated by the idolatrous proclivities of the people: "They despised My judgments, and they did not walk in My statutes, and they profaned My Sabbaths, *because* their heart went after their idols" (ver. 16).

To the second generation in the wilderness the offer of the covenant was renewed, with the same result (vv. 18-24). It should be observed that in both cases the disobedience of the people is answered by two distinct utterances of Jehovah's wrath. The first is a threat of immediate extermination, which is expressed as a momentary purpose of Jehovah, no sooner formed than withdrawn for the sake of His honour (vv. 14, 21). The other is a judgment of a more limited character, uttered in the form of an oath, and in the first case at least actually carried out. For the threat of exclusion from the Promised Land (ver. 15) was enforced so far as the first generation was concerned. Now the parallelism between the two sections leads us to expect that the similar threat of dispersion in ver. 23 is meant to be understood of a judgment actually inflicted. We may conclude, therefore, that ver. 23 refers to the Babylonian exile and the dispersion among the nations, which hung like a doom over the nation during its whole history

* The word "covenant" is not here used.

in Canaan, and is represented as a direct consequence of their transgressions in the wilderness. There seems reason to believe that the particular allusion is to the twenty-eighth chapter of Deuteronomy, where the threat of a dispersion among the nations concludes the long list of curses which will follow disobedience to the law (Deut. xxviii. 64-68). It is true that in that chapter the threat is only conditional; but in the time of Ezekiel it had already been fulfilled, and it is in accordance with his whole conception of the history to read the final issue back into the early period when the national character was determined.

But in addition to this, as if effectually to "conclude them under sin," Jehovah met the hardness of their hearts by imposing on them laws of an opposite character to those first given, and laws which accorded only too well with their baser inclinations: "And I also gave them statutes that were not good, and judgments by which they should not live; and I rendered them unclean in their offerings, by making over all that opened the womb, that I might horrify them" (vv. 25, 26).

This division of the wilderness legislation into two kinds, one good and life-giving and the other not good, presents difficulties both moral and critical which cannot perhaps be altogether removed. The general direction in which the solution must be sought is indeed tolerably clear. The reference is to the law which required the consecration of the firstborn of all animals to Jehovah. This was interpreted in the most rigorous sense as dedication in sacrifice; and then the principle was extended to the case of human beings. The divine purpose in appearing to sanction this atrocious practice was to "horrify" the people—that is to say, the punishment of their idolatry consisted in the shock to their natural instincts and affections caused by the worst development of the idolatrous spirit to which they were delivered. We are not to infer from this that human sacrifice was an element of the original Hebrew religion, and that it was actually based on legislative enactment. The truth appears to be that the sacrifice of children was originally a feature of Canaanitish worship, particularly of the god Melek or Molech, and was only introduced into the religion of Israel in the evil days which preceded the fall of the state.* The idea took hold of men's minds that this terrible rite alone revealed the full potency of the sacrificial act; and when the ordinary means of propitiation seemed to fail, it was resorted to as the last desperate expedient for appeasing an offended deity. All that Ezekiel's words warrant us in assuming is that when once the practice was established it was defended by an appeal to the ancient law of the firstborn, the principle of which was held to cover the case of human sacrifices. These laws, relating to the consecration of firstborn animals, are therefore the statutes referred to by Ezekiel; and their defect lies in their being open to such an immoral misinterpretation. This view is in accordance with the probabilities of the case. When we consider the tendency of the Old Testament writers to refer all actual events immediately to the will of God, we can partly understand the form in which Ezekiel expresses the facts; and this is perhaps all that can be said on the moral aspect of the difficulty. It is but an application of the principle that sin is punished by moral obliquity, and precepts which are accommodated to the hardness of men's hearts are by that same hardness perverted to fatal issues. It cannot even be said that there is a radical divergence of view between Ezekiel and Jeremiah on this subject. For when the older prophet, speaking of child-sacrifice, says that "Jehovah commanded it not, neither came it into His mind" (vii. 31 and xix. 5), he must have in view men who justified the custom by an appeal to ancient legislation. And although Jeremiah indignantly repudiates the suggestion that such horrors were contemplated by the law of Jehovah, he hardly in this goes beyond Ezekiel, who declares that the ordinance in question does not represent the true mind of Jehovah, but belongs to a part of the law which was intended to punish sin by delusion.*

In consequence of these transactions in the desert Israel entered the land of Canaan under the threat of eventual exile and under the curse of a polluted worship. The subsequent history has little significance from the point of view occupied throughout this discourse; and accordingly Ezekiel disposes of it in three verses (27-29). The entrance on the Promised Land, he says, furnished the opportunity for a new manifestation of disloyalty to Jehovah. He refers to the multiplication of heathen or semi-

* Apart from the case of Jephthah, which is entirely exceptional, the first historical instance is that of Ahaz (2 Kings xvi. 3).

* There still remain the critical difficulties. What are the ambiguous laws to which the prophet refers? It is of course not to be assumed as certain that they are to be found in the Pentateuch, at least in the exact form which Ezekiel has in view. There may have been at that time a considerable amount of uncodified legislative material which passed vaguely as the law of Jehovah. The "lying pen of the scribes" seems to have been busy in the multiplication of such enactments (Jer. viii. 8). Still, it is a legitimate inquiry whether any of the extant laws of the Pentateuch are open to the interpretation which Ezekiel seems to have in view. The parts of the Pentateuch in which the regulation about the dedication of the firstborn occurs are the so-called Book of the Covenant (Exod. xxii. 29, 30), the short code of Exod. xxxiv. 17-26 (vv. 19 f.), the enactment connected with the institution of the Passover (Exod. xiii. 12 f.), and the priestly ordinance (Numb. xviii. 15). Now, in three of these four passages, the inference to which Ezekiel refers is expressly excluded by the provision that the firstborn of men shall be redeemed. The only one which bears the appearance of ambiguity is that in the Book of the Covenant, where we read: "The firstborn of thy sons shalt thou give unto Me; likewise shalt thou do with thine oxen and thy sheep: seven days it shall be with its dam, on the eighth day thou shalt give it to Me." Here the firstborn children and the firstlings of animals are put on a level; and if any passage in our present Pentateuch would lend itself to the false construction which the later Israelites favoured, it would be this. On the other hand this passage does not contain the particular technical word (*he'ebîr*) used by Ezekiel. The word probably means simply "dedicate," although this was understood in the sense of dedication by sacrifice. The only passage of the four where the verb occurs is Exod. xiii. 12; and this accordingly is the one generally fixed on by critics as having sanctioned the abuse in question. But apart from its eqpress eqemption of firstborn children from the rule, the passage fails in another respect to meet the requirements of the case. The prophet appears to speak here of legislation addressed to the second generation in the wilderness, and this could not refer to the Passover ordinance in its present setting. On the whole, we seem to be driven to the conclusion that Ezekiel is not thinking of any part of our present Pentateuch, but to some other law similar in its terms to that of Exod. xiii. 12 f., although equivocal in the same way as Exod. xxii. 29 f.

In the text above I have given what appears to me the most natural interpretation of the passage, without referring to the numerous other views which have been put forward. Van Hoonacker, in *Le Museon* (1893), subjects the various theories to a searching criticism, and arrives himself at the nebulous conclusion that the "statutes which were not good" are not statutes at all, but providential chastisements. That cuts the knot; it does not untie it.

heathen sanctuaries throughout the land. Wherever they saw a high hill or a leafy tree, they made it a place of sacrifice, and there they practised the impure rites which were the outcome of their false conception of the Deity. To the mind of Ezekiel the unity of Jehovah and the unity of the sanctuary were inseparable ideas: the offence here alluded to is therefore of the same kind as the abominations practised in Egypt and the desert; it is a violation of the holiness of Jehovah. The prophet condenses his scorn for the whole system of religion which led to a multiplication of sanctuaries into a play on the etymology of the word *bāmah* (high places), the point of which, however, is obscure.*

II.

The Application (vv. 30-44).—Having thus described the origin of idolatry in Israel, and having shown that the destiny of the nation had been determined neither by its deserts nor by its inclinations, but by Jehovah's consistent regard for the honour of His name, the prophet proceeds to bring the lesson of the history to bear on his contemporaries. The Captivity has as yet produced no change in their spiritual condition; in Babylon they still defile themselves with the same abominations as their ancestors, even to the crowning atrocity of child-sacrifice. Their idolatry is if anything more conscious than before, for it takes the shape of a deliberate intention to be as other nations, worshipping wood and stone. It is necessary therefore that once for all Jehovah should assert His sovereignty over Israel, and bend their stubborn will to the accomplishment of His purpose. "As I live, saith the Lord Jehovah, surely with a strong hand, and with an outstretched arm, and wrath poured out, will I be king over you" (ver. 33). But how was this to be done? A heavier chastisement than that which had been inflicted on the exiles could hardly be conceived, yet it had effected nothing for the regeneration of Israel. Surely the time is come when the divine method must be changed, when those who have hardened themselves against the severity of God must be won by His goodness? Such, however, is not the thought expressed in Ezekiel's delineation of the future. It is possible that the description which follows (vv. 34-38) may only be meant as an ideal picture of spiritual processes to be effected by ordinary providential agencies. But certain it is that what Ezekiel is chiefly convinced of is the necessity for further acts of judgment—judgment which shall be decisive, because discriminating, and issuing in the annihilation of all who cling to the evil traditions of the past. This idea, indeed, of further chastisement in store for the exiles is a fixed element of Ezekiel's prophecy. It appears in his earliest public utterance (chap. v.), although it is perhaps only in this chapter that we perceive its full significance.

The scene of God's final dealings with Israel's sin is to be the "desert of the nations." That great barren plateau which stretches between the Jordan and the Euphrates valley, round which lay the nations chiefly concerned in Israel's history, occupies a place in the restoration analogous to that of the wilderness of Sinai (here called the "wilderness of Egypt") at the time of the Exodus. Into that vast solitude Jehovah will gather His people from the lands of their exile, and there He will once more judge them face to face. This judgment will be conducted on the principle laid down in chap. xviii. Each individual shall be dealt with according to his own character as a righteous man or a wicked. They shall be made to "pass under the rod," like sheep when they are counted by the shepherd.* The rebels and transgressors shall perish in the wilderness; for "out of the land of their sojournings will I bring them, and into the land of Israel they shall not come" (ver. 38). Those that emerge from the trial are the righteous remnant, who are to be brought into the land by number: † these constitute the new Israel, for whom is reserved the glory of the latter days.

The idea that the spiritual transformation of Israel was to be effected *during a second sojourn in the wilderness*, although a very striking one, occurs only here in the book of Ezekiel, and it can hardly be considered as one of the cardinal ideas of his eschatology. It is in all probability derived from the prophecies of Hosea, although it is modified in accordance with the very different estimate of the nation's history represented by Ezekiel. It is instructive to compare the teaching of these two prophets on this point. To Hosea the idea of a return to the desert presents itself naturally as an element of the process by which Israel is to be brought back to its allegiance to Jehovah. The return to the desert restores the conditions under which the nation had first known and followed Jehovah. He looks back to the sojourn in the wilderness of Sinai as the time of uninterrupted communion between Jehovah and Israel—a time of youthful innocence, when the sinful tendencies which may have been latent in the nation had not developed into actual infidelity. The decay of religion and morality dates from the possession of the land of Canaan, and is traced to the corrupting influence of Canaanitish idolatry and civilisation. It was at Baal-peor that they first succumbed to the attractions of a false religion and became contaminated with the spirit of heathenism. Then the rich produce of the land came to be regarded as the gift of the deities who were worshipped at the local sanctuaries, and this worship with its sensuous accompaniments was the means of estranging the people more and more from the knowledge of Jehovah. Hence the first step towards a renewal of the relation between God and Israel is the withdrawal of the gifts of nature, the suppression of religious ordinances and political institutions; and this is represented as effected by a return to the primitive life of the desert. Then in her desolation and affliction the heart of Israel shall respond once more to the love of Jehovah, who has never ceased to yearn after His unfaithful people. "I will allure her, and bring her into the wilderness, and speak to her heart: . . . and she shall make answer there, as in the days of her youth, and as in the day when she came up out of the land of Egypt" (Hos. ii. 14, 15). Here there may be a doubt whether the wilderness is to be taken literally or as a figure for exile, but in either case

* None of the interpretations of ver. 29 gives a satisfactory sense. Cornill rejects it as "absonderlich und aus dem Tenor des ganzen Cap. herausfallend."

* See Dillmann's note on Lev. xxvii. 32, quoted by Davidson.

† Reading במספר for במסרת with the LXX.

the image naturally arises out of Hosea's profoundly simple conception of religion.

To Ezekiel, on the other hand, the "wilderness" is a synonym for contention and judgment. It is the scene where the meanness and perversity of man stand out in unrelieved contrast with the majesty and purity of God. He recognises no glad springtime of promise and hope in the history of Israel, no "kindness of her youth" or "love of her espousals" when she went after Jehovah in the land that was not sown (Jer. ii. 2). The difference between Hosea's conception and Ezekiel's is that in the view of the exilic prophet there never has been any true response on the part of Israel to the call of God. Hence a return to the desert can only mean a repetition of the judgments that had marked the first sojourn of the people in the wilderness of Sinai, and the carrying of them to the point of a final decision between the claims of Jehovah and the stubbornness of His people.

If it be asked which of these representations of the past is the true one, the only answer possible is that from the standpoint from which the prophets viewed history both are true. Israel did follow Jehovah through the wilderness, and took possession of the land of Canaan animated by an ardent faith in His power. It is equally true that the religious condition of the people had its dark side, and that they were far from understanding the nature of the God whose name they bore. And a prophet might emphasise the one truth or the other according to the idea of God which it was given him to teach. Hosea, reading the religious symptoms of his own time, sees in it a contrast to the happier period when life was simple and religion comparatively pure, and finds in the desert sojourn an image of the purifying process by which the national life must be renewed. Ezekiel had to do with a more difficult problem. He saw that there was a power of evil which could not be eradicated merely by banishment from the land of Israel—a hard bed-rock of unbelief and superstition in the national character which had never yielded to the influence of revelation; and he dwells on all the manifestations of this which he read in the past. His hope for the future of the cause of God rests no longer on the moral influence of the divine love on the heart of man, but on the power of Jehovah to accomplish his purpose in spite of the resistance of human sin. That was not the whole truth about God's relation to Israel, but it was the truth that needed to be impressed on the generation of the Exile.

Of the final issue at all events Ezekiel is not doubtful. He is a man who is "very sure of God" and sure of nothing else. In man he finds nothing to inspire him with confidence in the ultimate victory of the true religion over polytheism and superstition. His own generation has shown itself fit only to perpetuate the evils of the past—the love of sensuous worship, the insensibility to the claims and nature of Jehovah, which had marked the whole history of Israel. He is compelled for the present to abandon them to their corrupt inclinations,* expecting no signs of amendment until his appeal is enforced by signal acts of judgment.

But all this does not shake his sublime faith in the fulfilment of Israel's destiny. Despairing of men, he falls back on what St. Paul calls the "purpose of God according to election" (Rom. ix. 11). And with an insight akin to that of the apostle of the Gentiles, he discerns through all Jehovah's dealing with Israel a principle and an ideal which must in the end prevail over the sin of men. The goal to which the history points stands out clear before the mind of the prophet; and already he sees in vision the restored Israel—a holy people in a renovated land—rendering acceptable worship to the one God of heaven and earth. "For in My holy mountain, in the mountain heights of Israel, saith the Lord Jehovah, *there* shall serve Me the whole house of Israel: there will I be gracious to them, and there will I require your oblations, and the first-fruits of your offerings, in all your holy things" (ver. 40).

There we have the thought which is expanded in the vision of the purified theocracy which occupies the closing chapters of the book. And it is important to notice this indication that the idea of that vision was present to Ezekiel during the earlier part of his ministry.

CHAPTER XIII.

OHOLA AND OHOLIBAH.

EZEKIEL xxiii.

THE allegory of chap. xxiii. adds hardly any new thought to those which have already been expounded in connection with chap. xvi. and chap. xx. The ideas which enter into it are all such as we are now familiar with. They are: the idolatry of Israel, learned in Egypt and persisted in to the end of her history; her fondness for alliances with the great Oriental empires, which was the occasion of new developments of idolatry; the corruption of religion by the introduction of human sacrifice into the service of Jehovah; and, finally, the destruction of Israel by the hands of the nations whose friendship she had so eagerly courted. The figure under which these facts are presented is the same as in chap. xvi., and many of the details of the earlier prophecy are reproduced here with little variation. But along with these resemblances we find certain characteristic features in this chapter which require attention, and perhaps some explanation.

In its treatment of the history this passage is distinguished from the other two by the recognition of the separate existence of the northern and southern kingdoms. In the previous retrospects Israel has either been treated as a unit (as in chap. xx.), or attention has been wholly concentrated on the fortunes of Judah, Samaria being regarded as on a level with a purely heathen city like Sodom (chap. xvi.). Ezekiel may have felt that he has not yet done justice to the truth that the history of Israel ran in two parallel lines, and that the full significance

* The transition ver. 39 is, however, very difficult. As it stands in the Hebrew text it contains an ironical concession (a good-natured one, Smend thinks) to the persistent advocates of idolatry, the only tolerable translation being, "So serve ye every man his idols, but hereafter ye shall surely hearken to Me, and My holy name ye shall no longer profane with your gifts and your idols." But this sense is not in itself very natural, and the Hebrew construction by which it is expressed would be somewhat strained. The most satisfactory rendering is perhaps that given in the Syriac Version, where two clauses of our Hebrew text are transposed: "But as for you, O house of Israel, if ye will not hearken to Me, go serve every man his idols! Yet hereafter ye shall no more profane My holy name in you," etc.

of God's dealings with the nation can only be understood when the fate of Samaria is placed alongside of that of Jerusalem. He did not forget that he was sent as a prophet to the "whole house of Israel," and indeed all the great pre-exilic prophets realised that their message concerned "the whole family which Jehovah had brought up out of Egypt" (Amos iii. 1). Besides this the chapter affords in many ways an interesting illustration of the workings of the prophet's mind in the effort to realise vividly the nature of his people's sin and the meaning of its fate. In this respect it is perhaps the most finished and comprehensive product of his imagination, although it may not reveal the depth of religious insight exhibited in the sixteenth chapter.

The main idea of the allegory is no doubt borrowed from a prophecy of Jeremiah belonging to the earlier part of his ministry (Jer. iii. 6-13). The fall of Samaria was even then a somewhat distant memory, but the use which Jeremiah makes of it seems to show that the lesson of it had not altogether ceased to impress the mind of the southern kingdom. In the third chapter he reproaches Judah the "treacherous" for not having taken warning from the fate of her sister the "apostate" Israel, who has long since received the reward of her infidelities. The same lesson is implied in the representation of Ezekiel (ver. 11); but, as is usual with our prophet, the simple image suggested by Jeremiah is drawn out in an elaborate allegory, into which as many details are crowded as it will bear. In place of the epithets by which Jeremiah characterises the moral condition of Israel and Judah, Ezekiel coins two new and somewhat obscure names—*Ohola* for Samaria, and *Oholibah* for Jerusalem.*

These women are children of one mother, and afterwards become wives of one husband—Jehovah. This need occasion no surprise in an allegorical representation, although it is contrary to a law which Ezekiel doubtless knew (Lev. xviii. 18). Nor is it strange, considering the freedom with which he handles the facts of history, that the division between Israel and Judah is carried back to the time of the oppression in Egypt. We have indeed no certainty that this view is not historical. The cleavage between the north and the south did not originate with the revolt of Jeroboam. That great schism only brought out elements of antagonism which were latent in the relations of the tribe of Judah to the northern tribes. Of this there are many indications in the earlier history, and for what we know the separation might have existed among the Hebrews in Goshen. Still, it is not probable that Ezekiel was thinking of any such thing. He is bound by the limits of his allegory; and there was no other way by which he could combine the presentation of the two essential elements of his conception—that Samaria and Jerusalem were branches of the one people of Jehovah, and that the idolatry which marked their history had been learned in the youth of the nation in the land of Egypt.

That neither Israel nor Judah ever shook off the spell of their adulterous connection with Egypt, but returned to it again and again down to the close of their history, is certainly one point which the prophet means to impress on the minds of his readers (vv. 8, 19, 27). With this exception the earlier part of the chapter (to ver. 35) deals exclusively with the later developments of idolatry from the eighth century and onwards. And one of the most remarkable things in it is the description of the manner in which first Israel and then Judah was entangled in political relations with the Oriental empires. There seems to be a vein of sarcasm in the sketch of the gallant Assyrian officers who turned the heads of the giddy and frivolous sisters and seduced them from their allegiance to Jehovah: "Ohola doted on her lovers, on the Assyrian warriors * clad in purple, governors and satraps, charming youths all of them, horsemen riding on horses; and she lavished on them her fornications, the *élite* of the sons of Asshur all of them, and with all the idols of all on whom she doted she defiled herself" (vv. 6, 7). The first intimate contact of North Israel with Assyria was in the reign of Menahem (2 Kings xv. 19), and the explanation of it given in these words of Ezekiel must be historically true. It was the magnificent equipment of the Assyrian armies, the imposing display of military power which their appearance suggested, that impressed the politicians of Samaria with a sense of the value of their alliance. The passage therefore throws light on what Ezekiel and the prophets generally mean by the figure of "whoredom." What he chiefly deplores is the introduction of Assyrian idolatry, which was the inevitable sequel to a political union. But that was a secondary consideration in the intention of those who were responsible for the alliance. The real motive of their policy was undoubtedly the desire of one party in the state to secure the powerful aid of the king of Assyria against the rival party. None the less it was an act of infidelity and rebellion against Jehovah.

Still more striking is the account of the first approaches of the southern kingdom to Babylon. After Samaria had been destroyed by the lovers whom she had gathered to her side, Jerusalem still kept up the illicit connection with the Assyrian empire. After Assyria had vanished from the stage of history, she eagerly sought an opportunity to enter into friendly relations with the new Babylonian empire. She did not even wait till she had made their acquaintance, but "when she saw men portrayed on the wall, pictures of Chaldæans portrayed in vermilion, girt with waist-cloths on their loins, with flowing

* It is not certain what is the exact meaning wrapped up in these designations. A very slight change in the pointing of the Hebrew would give the sense "*her* tent" for Ohola and "*my* tent in her" for Oholibah. This is the interpretation adopted by most commentators, the idea being that while the tent or temple of Jehovah was in Judah, Samaria's "tent" (religious system) was of her own making. It is not likely, however, that Ezekiel has any such sharp contrast in his mind, since the whole of the argument proceeds on the similarity of the course pursued by the two kingdoms. It is simpler to take the word Ohola as meaning "tent," and Oholibah as "tent in her," the signification of the names being practically identical. The allusion is supposed to be to the tents of the high places which formed a marked feature of the idolatrous worship practised in both divisions of the country (*cf.* ch. xvi. 16). This is better, though not entirely convincing, since it does not explain how Ezekiel came to fix on this particular emblem as a mark of the religious condition of Israel. It may be worth noting that the word אהלח contains the same number of consonants as שמרן (= Samaria, although the word is always written שטרון in the Old Testament), and אהליבה the same number as ירושלם. The Eastern custom of giving similar names to children of the same family (like Hasan and Husein) is aptly instanced by Smend and Davidson.

* This word is of doubtful meaning.

turbans on their heads, all of them champions to look upon, the likeness of the sons of Babel whose native land is Chaldæa—then she doted upon them when she saw them with her eyes, and sent messengers to them to Chaldæa" (vv. 14-16). The brilliant pictures referred to are those with which Ezekiel must have been familiar on the walls of the temples and palaces of Babylon. The representation, however, cannot be understood literally, since the Jews could have had no opportunity of even seeing the Babylonian pictures "on the wall" until they had sent ambassadors there.*

The meaning of the prophet is clear. The mere report of the greatness of Babylon was sufficient to excite the passions of Oholibah, and she began with blind infatuation to court the advances of the distant strangers who were to be her ruin. The exact historic reference, however, is uncertain. It cannot be to the compact between Merodach-baladan and Hezekiah, since at that time the initiative seems to have been taken by the rebel prince, whose sovereignty over Babylon proved to be of short duration. It may rather be some transaction about the time of the battle of Carchemish (604) that Ezekiel is thinking of; but we have not as yet sufficient knowledge of the circumstances to clear up the allusion.

Before the end came the soul of Jerusalem was alienated from her latest lovers—another touch of fidelity to the historical situation. But it was now too late. The soul of Jehovah is alienated from Oholibah (vv. 17, 18), and she is already handed over to the fate which had overtaken her less guilty sister Ohola. The principal agents of her punishment are the Babylonians and all the Chaldæans; but under their banner marches a host of other nations—Pekod and Shoa and Koa,† and, somewhat strangely, the sons of Asshur. In the pomp and circumstance of war which had formerly fascinated her imagination, they shall come against her, and after their cruel manner execute upon her the judgment meted out to adulterous women: "Thou hast walked in the way of thy sister, and I will put her cup into thy hand. Thus saith the Lord Jehovah, The cup of thy sister shalt thou drink,—deep and wide, and of large content,—filled with drunkenness and anguish—the cup of horror and desolation, the cup of thy sister Samaria. And thou shalt drink it and drain it out,‡ . . . for I have spoken it, saith the Lord Jehovah" (vv. 31-34).

Up to this point the allegory has closely followed the actual history of the two kingdoms. The remainder of the chapter (vv. 36-49) forms a pendant to the principal picture, and works out the central theme from a different point of view. Here Samaria and Jerusalem are regarded as still existent, and judgment is pronounced on both as if it were still future. This is thoroughly in keeping with Ezekiel's ideal delineations. The limitations of space and time are alike transcended. The image, once clearly conceived, fixes itself in the writer's mind, and must be allowed to exhaust its meaning before it is finally dismissed. The distinctions of far and near, of past and present and future, are apt to disappear in the intensity of his reverie. It is so here. The figures of Ohola and Oholibah are so real to the prophet that they are summoned once more to the tribunal to hear the recital of their "abominations" and receive the sentence which has in fact been already partly executed. Whether he is thinking at all of the ten tribes then in exile and awaiting further punishment it would be difficult to say. We see, however, that the picture is enriched with many features for which there was no room in the more historic form of the allegory, and perhaps the desire for completeness was the chief motive for thus amplifying the figure. The description of the conduct of the two harlots (vv. 40-44) is exceedingly graphic,* and is no doubt a piece of realism drawn from life. Otherwise the section contains nothing that calls for elucidation. The ideas are those which we have already met with in other connections, and even the setting in which they are placed presents no element of novelty.

Thus with words of judgment, and without a ray of hope to lighten the darkness of the picture, the prophet closes this last survey of his people's history.

CHAPTER XIV.

FINAL ORACLES AGAINST JERUSALEM.

EZEKIEL xxii., xxiv.

THE close of the first period of Ezekiel's work was marked by two dramatic incidents, which made the day memorable both in the private life of the prophet and in the history of the nation. In the first place it coincided exactly with the commencement of the siege of Jerusalem. The prophet's mysterious knowledge of what was happening at a distance was duly recorded, in order that its subsequent confirmation through the ordinary channels of intelligence might prove the divine origin of his message (xxiv. 1, 2). That Ezekiel actually did this we have no reason to doubt. Then the sudden death of his wife on the evening of the same day, and his unusual behaviour under the bereavement, caused a sensation among the exiles which the prophet was instructed to utilise as a means of driving home the appeal just made to them. These transactions must have had a profound effect on Ezekiel's fellow-captives. They made his personality the centre of absorbing interest to the Jews in Babylon; and the two years of silence on his part which ensued were to them years of anxious foreboding about the result of the siege.

At this juncture the prophet's thoughts naturally are occupied with the subject which hitherto formed the principal burden of his prophecy. The first part of his career accordingly closes, as it had begun, with a symbol of the fall of Jerusalem. Before this, however, he had drawn out the solemn indictment against Jerusalem which is given in chap. xxii., although the fin-

* Smend thinks that the illustration is explained by the secluded life of females in the East, which makes it quite intelligible that a woman might be captivated by the picture of a man she had never seen, and try to induce him to visit her.

† On these names of nations see Davidson's Commentary, p. 168, and the reference there to Delitzsch.

‡ The words rendered in E. V., "thou shalt be laughed to scorn and had in derision" (ver. 32), "and pluck off thy own breasts" (ver. 34), are wanting in the LXX. The passage gains in force by the omission. The words translated "break the sherds thereof" (ver. 34) are unintelligible.

* Although the text in parts of vv. 42, 43 is very imper fect.

ishing touches were probably added after the destruction of the city. The substance of that chapter is so closely related to the symbolic representation in the first part of chap. xxiv. that it will be convenient to consider it here as an introduction to the concluding oracles addressed more directly to the exiles of Tel-abib.

I.

The purpose of this arraignment—the most stately of Ezekiel's orations—is to exhibit Jerusalem in her true character as a city whose social condition is incurably corrupt. It begins with an enumeration of the prevalent sins of the capital (vv. 2-16); it ends with a denunciation of the various classes into which society was divided (vv. 23-31); while the short intervening passage is a figurative description of the judgment which is now inevitable (vv. 17-22).

1. The first part of the chapter, then, is a catalogue of the "abominations" which called down the vengeance of heaven upon the city of Jerusalem. The offences enumerated are nearly the same as those mentioned in the definitions of personal righteousness and wickedness given in chap. xviii. It is not necessary to repeat what was there said about the characteristics of the moral ideal which had been formed in the mind of Ezekiel. Although he is dealing now with a society, his point of view is quite different from that represented by purely allegorical passages like chaps. xvi. and xxiii. The city is not idealised and treated as a moral individual, whose relations with Jehovah have to be set forth in symbolic and figurative language. It is conceived as an aggregate of individuals bound together in social relations; and the sins charged against it are the actual transgressions of the men who are members of the community. Hence the standard of public morality is precisely the same as that which is elsewhere applied to the individual in his personal relation to God; and the sins enumerated are attributed to the city merely because they are tolerated and encouraged in individuals by laxity of public opinion and the force of evil example. Jerusalem is a community in which these different crimes are perpetrated: "Father and mother are despised *in thee;* the stranger is oppressed *in the midst of thee;* orphan and widow are wronged *in thee;* slanderous men seeking blood have been *in thee;* flesh with the blood is eaten *in thee;* lewdness is committed *in the midst of thee;* the father's shame is uncovered *in thee;* she that was unclean in her separation hath been humbled *in thee.*" So the grave and measured indictment runs on. It is because of these things that Jerusalem as a whole is "guilty" and "unclean" and has brought near her day of retribution (ver. 4). Such a conception of corporate guilt undoubtedly appeals more directly to our ordinary conscience of public morality than the more poetic representations where Jerusalem is compared to a faithless and treacherous woman. We have no difficulty in judging of any modern city in the very same way as Ezekiel here judges Jerusalem; and in this respect it is interesting to notice the social evils which he regards as marking out that city as ripe for destruction.

There are three features of the state of things in Jerusalem in which the prophet recognises the symptoms of an incurable social condition. The first is the loss of a true conception of God. In ancient Israel this defect necessarily assumed the form of idolatry. Hence the multiplication of idols appropriately finds a place among the marks of the "uncleanness" which made Jerusalem hateful in the eyes of Jehovah (ver. 3). But the root of idolatry in Israel was the incapacity or the unwillingness of the people to live up to the lofty conception of the Divine nature which was taught by the prophets. Throughout the ancient world religion was felt to be the indispensable bond of society, and the gods that were worshipped reflected more or less fully the ideals that swayed the life of the community. To Israel the religion of Jehovah represented the highest social ideal that was then known on earth. It meant righteousness, and purity, and brotherhood, and compassion for the poor and distressed. When these virtues decayed she forgot Jehovah (ver. 12)—forgot His character even if she remembered His name—and the service of false gods was the natural and obvious expression of the fact. There is therefore a profound truth in Ezekiel's mind when he numbers the idols of Jerusalem amongst the indications of a degenerate society. They were the evidence that she had lost the sense of God as a holy and righteous spiritual presence in her midst, and that loss was at once the source and symptom of widespread moral declension. It is one of the chief lessons of the Old Testament that a religion which was neither the product of national genius nor the embodiment of national aspiration, but was based on supernatural revelation, proved itself in the history of Israel to be the only possible safeguard against the tendencies which made for social disintegration.

A second mark of depravity which Ezekiel discovers in the capital is the perversion of certain moral **instincts** which are just as essential to the preservation of society as a true conception of God. For if society rests at one end on religion, it rests at the other on instinct. The closest and most fundamental of human relations depend on innate perceptions which may be easily destroyed, but which when destroyed can scarcely be recovered. The sanctities of marriage and the family will hardly bear the coarse scrutiny of utilitarian ethics; yet they are the foundation on which the whole social fabric is built. And there is no part of Ezekiel's indictment of Jerusalem which conveys to our minds a more vivid sense of utter corruption than where he speaks of the loss of filial piety and revolting forms of sexual impurity as prevalent sins in the city. Here at least he carries the conviction of every moralist with him. He instances no offence of this kind which would not be branded as unnatural by any system of ethics as heartily as it is by the Old Testament. It is possible, on the other hand, that he ranks on the same level with these sins ceremonial impurities appealing to feelings of a different order, to which no permanent moral value can be attached. When, for example, he instances eating with the blood* as an "abomination," he appeals to a law which is no longer binding on us. But even that regulation was not so worthless, from a moral point of view, at that time as we are apt to suppose. The abhorrence of eating blood was connected with certain sacrificial ideas which attributed a mystic significance to the blood as the seat of animal life. So long as these ideas existed no man could commit this offence

* On the reading here see above, p. 258.

without injuring his moral nature and loosening the Divine sanctions of morality as a whole. It is a false illuminism which seeks to disparage the moral insight of the prophet on the ground that he did not teach an abstract system of ethics in which ceremonial precepts were sharply distinguished from duties which we consider moral.*

The third feature of Jerusalem's guilty condition is lawless violation of human rights. Neither life nor property was secure. Judicial murders were frequent in the city, and minor forms of oppression, such as usury, spoliation of the unprotected, and robbery, were of daily occurrence. The administration of justice was corrupted by systematic bribery and perjury, and the lives of innocent men were ruthlessly sacrificed under the forms of law. This after all is the aspect of things which bulks most largely in the prophet's indictment. Jerusalem is addressed as a "city shedding blood in her midst," and throughout the accusation the charge of bloodshed is that which constantly recurs. Misgovernment and party strife, and perhaps religious persecution, had converted the city into a vast human shambles, and the blood of the innocent slain cried aloud to heaven for vengeance. "Of what avail," asks the prophet, "are the stores of wealth piled up in the hands of a few against this damning witness of blood? Jehovah smites His hand [in derision] against her gains that she has made, and against her blood which is in her midst. How can her heart stand or her hands be strong in the days when He deals with her?" (vv. 13, 14). Drained of her best blood, given over to internecine strife, and stricken with the cowardice of conscious guilt, Jerusalem, already disgraced among the nations, must fall an easy victim to the Chaldæan invaders, who are the agents of Jehovah's judgments.

2. But the most serious aspect of the situation is that which is dealt with in the peroration of the chapter (vv. 23-31). Outbursts of vice and lawlessness such as has been described may occur in any society, but they are not necessarily fatal to a community so long as it possesses a conscience which can be roused to effective protest against them. Now the worst thing about Jerusalem was that she lacked this indispensable condition of recovery. No voice was raised on the side of righteousness, no man dared to stem the tide of wickedness that swept through her streets. Not merely that she harboured within her walls men guilty of incest and robbery and murder, but that her leading classes were demoralised, that public spirit had decayed among her citizens, marked her as incapable of reformation. She was "a land not watered,"† "and not rained upon in a day of indignation" (ver. 24); the springs of her civic virtue were dried up, and a blight spread through all sections of her population.‡ Ezekiel's impeachment of different classes of society brings out this fact with great force. First of all the ancient institutions of social order, government, priesthood, and prophecy were in the hands of men who had lost the spirit of their office and abused their position for the advancement of private interests. Her princes * have been, instead of humane rulers and examples of noble living, cruel and rapacious tyrants, enriching themselves at the cost of their subjects (ver. 25). The priests, whose function was to maintain the outward ordinances of religion and foster the spirit of reverence, have done their utmost, by falsification of the *Torah*, to bring religion into contempt and obliterate the distinction between the holy and the profane (ver. 26). The nobles had been a pack of ravening wolves, imitating the rapacity of the court, and hunting down prey which the royal lion would have disdained to touch (ver. 27). As for the professional prophets—those degenerate representatives of the old champions of truth and mercy—we have already seen what they were worth (chap. xiii.). They who should have been foremost to denounce civil wrong are fit for nothing but to stand by and bolster up with lying oracles in the name of Jehovah a constitution which sheltered crimes like these (ver. 28).

From the ruling classes the prophet's glance turns for a moment to the "people of the land," the dim common population, where virtue might have been expected to find its last retreat. It is characteristic of the age of Ezekiel that the prophets begin to deal more particularly with the sins of the masses as distinct from the classes. This was due partly perhaps to a real increase of ungodliness in the body of the people, but partly also to a deeper sense of the importance of the individual apart from his position in the state. These prophets seem to feel that if there had been anywhere among rich or poor an honest response to the will of Jehovah it would have been a token that God had not altogether rejected Israel. Jeremiah puts this view very strongly when in the fifth chapter he says that if one man could be found in Jerusalem who did justice and sought truth the Lord would pardon her; and his vain search for that one man begins among the poor. It is this same motive that leads Ezekiel to include the humble citizen in his survey of the moral condition of Jerusalem. It is little wonder that under such leaders they had cast off the restraints of humanity, and oppressed those who were still more defenceless than themselves. But it showed nevertheless that real religion had no longer a foothold in the city. It proved that the greed of gain had eaten into the very heart of the people and destroyed the ties of kindred and mutual sympathy, through which alone the will of Jehovah could be realised. No matter although they were obscure householders, without political power or responsibility; if they had been good men in their private relations, Jerusalem would have been a better place to live in. Ezekiel indeed does not go so far as to say that a single good life would have saved the city. He expects of a good man that he be a man in the full sense—a man who speaks boldly on behalf of righteousness and resists the prevalent evils with all his strength: "I sought among them a man to build up a fence, and to stand in the breach before Me on

* The eighth verse, referring to the Sabbath and the sanctuary, is rejected by Cornill on internal grounds, but for that there is no justification. If the verse is retained, it will be seen that the enumeration of sins corresponds pretty closely in substance, though not in arrangement, with the precepts of the Decalogue.

† Read with the LXX. מטרה, instead of מטהרה, "purified."

‡ This appears to be the meaning of the simile in ver. 24; the judgment is conceived as a parching drought, and the point of the comparison is that its severity is not tempered by the fertilising streams which should have descended on the people in the shape of sound political and religious guidance.

* Following the LXX. we should read "whose princes" (אשר נשיאיה) for "the conspiracy of her prophets" (קשר נביאיה) in ver. 25.

behalf of the land, that it might not be destroyed; and I found none. So I poured out My indignation upon them; with the fire of My wrath I consumed them: I have returned their way upon their head, saith the Lord Jehovah" (vv. 30, 31).

3. But we should misunderstand Ezekiel's position if we supposed that his prediction of the speedy destruction of Jerusalem was merely an inference from his clear insight into the necessary conditions of social welfare which were being violated by her rulers and her citizens. That is one part of his message, but it could not stand alone. The purpose of the indictment we have considered is simply to explain the moral reasonableness of Jehovah's action in the great act of judgment which the prophet knows to be approaching. It is no doubt a general law of history that moribund communities are not allowed to die a natural death. Their usual fate is to perish in the struggle for existence before some other and sounder nation. But no human sagacity can foresee how that law will be verified in any particular case. It may seem clear to us now that Israel must have fallen sooner or later before the advance of the great Eastern empires, but an ordinary observer could not have foretold with the confidence and precision which mark the predictions of Ezekiel in what manner and within what time the end would come. Of that aspect of the prophet's mind no explanation can be given save that God revealed His secret to His servants the prophets.

Now this element of the prophecy seems to be brought out by the image of Jerusalem's fate which occupies the middle verses of the chapter (vv. 17-22). The city is compared to the crucible in which all the refuse of Israel's national life is to undergo its final trial by fire. The prophet sees in imagination the terror-stricken provincial population swept into the capital before the approach of the Chaldeans: and he says, "Thus doth Jehovah cast His ore into the furnace—the silver, the brass, the iron, the lead, and the tin; and He will kindle the fire with His anger, and blow upon it till He have consumed the impurities of the land." The image of the smelting-pot had been used by Isaiah as an emblem of purifying judgment, the object of which was the removal of injustice and the restoration of the state to its former splendour: "I will again bring My hand upon thee, smelting out thy dross with lye and taking away all thine alloy; and I will make thy judges to be again as aforetime, and thy counsellors as at the beginning: thereafter thou shalt be called the city of righteousness, the faithful city" (Isa. i. 25, 26). Ezekiel, however, can hardly have contemplated such a happy result of the operation. The whole house of Israel has become dross, from which no precious metal can be extracted; and the object of the smelting is only the demonstration of the utter worthlessness of the people for the ends of God's kingdom. The more refractory the material to be dealt with the fiercer must be the fire that tests it; and the severity of the exterminating judgment is the only thing symbolised by the metaphor as used by Ezekiel. In this he follows Jeremiah, who applies the figure in precisely the same sense: "The bellows snort, the lead is consumed of the fire; in vain he smelts and smelts: but the wicked are not taken away. Refuse silver shall men call them, for the Lord hath rejected them" (Jer. vi. 29, 30). In this way the section supplements the teaching of the rest of the chapter. Jerusalem is full of dross—that has been proved by the enumeration of her crimes and the estimate of her social condition. But the fire which consumes the dross represents a special providential intervention bringing the history of the state to a summary and decisive conclusion. And the Refiner who superintends the process is Jehovah, the Holy One of Israel, whose righteous will is executed by the march of conquering hosts, and revealed to men in His dealings with the people whom He had known of all the families of the earth.

II.

The chapter we have just studied was evidently not composed with a view to immediate publication. It records the view of Jerusalem's guilt and punishment which was borne in upon the mind of the prophet in the solitude of his chamber, but it was not destined to see the light until the whole of his teaching could be submitted in its final form to a wider and more receptive audience. It is equally obvious that the scenes described in chap. xxiv. were really enacted in the full view of the exiled community. We have reached the crisis of Ezekiel's ministry. For the last time until his warnings of doom shall be fulfilled he emerges from his partial seclusion, and in symbolism whose vivid force could not have failed to impress the most listless hearer he announces once more the destruction of the Hebrew nation. The burden of his mesage is that that day—the tenth day of the tenth month of the ninth year—marked the beginning of the end. "On that very day"—a day to be commemorated for seventy long years by a national fast (Zech. viii. 19: *cf.* vii. 5)—Nebuchadnezzar was drawing his lines around Jerusalem. The bare announcement to men who knew what a Chaldæan siege meant must have sent a thrill of consternation through their minds. If this vision of what was happening in a distant land should prove true, they must have felt that all hope of deliverance was now cut off. Sceptical as they may have been of the moral principles that lay behind Ezekiel's prediction, they could not deny that the issue he foresaw was only the natural sequel to the fact he so confidently announced.

The image here used of the fate of Jerusalem would recall to the minds of the exiles the ill-omened saying which expressed the reckless spirit prevalent in the city: "This city is the pot, and we are the flesh" (xi. 3). It was well understood in Babylon that these men were playing a desperate game, and did not shrink from the horrors of a siege. "Set on the pot," then, cries the prophet to his listeners, "set it on, and pour in water also, and gather the pieces into it, every good joint, leg, and shoulder; fill it with the choicest bones. Take them from the best of the flock, and then pile up the wood * under it; let its pieces be boiled and its bones cooked within it" (vv. 3-5). This part of the parable required no explanation; it simply represents the terrible miseries endured by the population of Jerusalem during the siege now commencing. But then by a sudden transition the speaker turns the thoughts of his hearers to another aspect of the judgment (vv. 6-8). The

* Read עצים, "wood," instead of עצמים, "bones" (Boettcher and others).

city itself is like a rusty caldron, unfit for any useful purpose until by some means it has been cleansed from its impurity. It is as if the crimes that had been perpetrated in Jerusalem had stained her very stones with blood. She had not even taken steps to conceal the traces of her wickedness; they lie like blood on the bare rock, an open witness to her guilt. Often Jehovah had sought to purify her by more measured chastisements, but it has now been proved that "her much rust will not go from her except by fire" * (ver. 12). Hence the end of the siege will be twofold. First of all the contents of the caldron will be indiscriminately thrown out—a figure for the dispersion and captivity of the inhabitants; and then the pot must be set empty on the glowing coals till its rust is thoroughly burned out—a symbol of the burning of the city and its subsequent desolation (ver. 11). The idea that the material world may contract defilement through the sins of those who live in it is one that is hard for us to realise, but it is in keeping with the view of sin presented by Ezekiel, and indeed by the Old Testament generally. There are certain natural emblems of sin, such as uncleanness or disease or uncovered blood, etc., which had to be largely used in order to educate men's moral perceptions. Partly these rest on the analogy between physical defect and moral evil; but partly, as here, they result from a strong sense of association between human deeds and their effects or circumstances. Jerusalem is unclean as a place where wicked deeds have been done, and even the destruction of the sinners cannot, in the mind of Ezekiel, clear her from the unhallowed associations of her history. She must lie empty and dreary for a generation, swept by the winds of heaven, before devout Israelites can again twine their affections round the hope of her glorious future.†

Even while delivering this message of doom to the people the prophet's heart was burdened by the presentiment of a great personal sorrow. He had received an intimation that his wife was to be taken from him by a sudden stroke, and along with the intimation a command to refrain from all the usual signs of mourning. "So I spake to the people" (as recorded in vv. 1-14) "in the morning, and my wife died in the evening" (ver. 18). Just one touch of tenderness escapes him in relating this mysterious occurrence. She was the "delight of his eyes": that phrase alone reveals that there was a fountain of tears sealed up within the breast of this stern preacher. How the course of his life may have been influenced by a bereavement so strangely coincident with a change in his whole attitude to his people, we cannot even surmise. Nor is it possible to say how far he merely used the incident to convey a lesson to the exiles, or how far his private grief was really swallowed up in concern for the calamity of his country. All we are told is that "in the morning he did as he was commanded." He neither uttered loud lamentations, nor disarranged his raiment, nor covered his head, nor ate the "bread of men," ‡ nor adopted any of the customary signs of mourning for the dead. When the astonished neighbours inquire the meaning of his strange demeanour, he assures them that his conduct *now* is a sign of what theirs will be when his words have come true. When the tidings reach them that Jerusalem has actually fallen, when they realise how many interests dear to them have perished—the desolation of the sanctuary, the loss of their own sons and daughters—they will experience a sense of calamity which will instinctively discard all the conventional and even the natural expressions of grief. They shall neither mourn nor weep, but sit in dumb bewilderment, haunted by a dull consciousness of guilt which yet is far removed from genuine contrition of heart. They shall pine away in their iniquities. For while their sorrow will be too deep for words, it will not yet be the godly sorrow that worketh repentance. It will be the sullen despair and apathy of men disenchanted of the illusions on which their national life was based, of men left without hope and without God in the world.

Here the curtain falls on the first act of Ezekiel's ministry. He appears to have retired for the space of two years into complete privacy, ceasing entirely his public appeals to the people, and waiting for the time of his vindication as a prophet. The sense of restraint under which he has hitherto exercised the function of a public teacher cannot be removed until the tidings have reached Babylon that the city has fallen. Meanwhile, with the delivery of this message, his contest with the unbelief of his fellow-captives comes to an end. But when that day arrives "his mouth shall be open, and he shall be no more dumb." A new career will open out before him, in which he can devote all his powers of mind and heart to the inspiring work of reviving faith in the promises of God, and so building up a new Israel out of the ruins of the old.

PART III.

PROPHECIES AGAINST FOREIGN NATIONS.

CHAPTER XV.

AMMON, MOAB, EDOM, AND PHILISTIA.

EZEKIEL XXV.

THE next eight chapters (xxv.-xxxii.) form an intermezzo in the Book of Ezekiel. They are inserted in this place with the obvious intention of separating the two sharply contrasted situations in which our prophet found himself before and after the siege of Jerusalem. The subject with which they deal is indeed an essential part of the prophet's message to his time, but it is separate from the central interest of the narrative, which lies in the conflict between the word of Jehovah in the hands of Ezekiel and the unbelief of the exiles among whom he lived. The perusal of this group of chapters is intended to prepare the reader for the completely altered conditions under which Ezekiel was to resume

* The words "except by fire" represent an emendation proposed by Cornill, which may be somewhat bold, but certainly expresses an idea in the passage.

† *Cf.* Jer. xiii. 27: "Thou shalt not be pronounced clean, for how long a time yet!"

‡ *I. e.*, as generally explained, bread brought by sympathising friends, to be shared with the mourning household: *cf.* Jer. xvi. 7; 2 Sam. iii. 35. Wellhausen, however, proposes to read "bread of mourners" (אֲנֹשִׁים for אֲנָשִׁים).

his public ministrations. The cycle of prophecies on foreign peoples is thus a sort of literary analogue of the period of suspense which interrupted the continuity of Ezekiel's work in the way we have seen. It marks the shifting of the scenes behind the curtain before the principal actors again step on the stage.

It is natural enough to suppose that the prophet's mind was really occupied during this time with the fate of Israel's heathen neighbours; but that alone does not account for the grouping of the oracles before us in this particular section of the book. Not only do some of the chronological notices carry us far past the limit of the time of silence referred to, but it will be found that nearly all the prophecies assume that the fall of Jerusalem is already known to the nations addressed. It is therefore a mistaken view which holds that in these chapters we have simply the result of Ezekiel's meditations during his period of enforced seclusion from public duty. Whatever the nature of his activity at this time may have been, the principle of arrangement here is not chronological, but literary; and no better motive for it can be suggested than the writer's sense of dramatic propriety in unfolding the significance of his prophetic life.

In uttering a series of oracles against heathen nations, Ezekiel follows the example set by some of his greatest predecessors. The Book of Amos, for example, opens with an impressive chapter of judgments on the peoples lying immediately round the borders of Palestine. The thundercloud of Jehovah's anger is represented as moving over the petty states of Syria before it finally breaks in all its fury over the two kingdoms of Judah and Israel. Similarly the Books of Isaiah and Jeremiah contain continuous sections dealing with various heathen powers, while the Book of Nahum is wholly occupied with a prediction of the ruin of the Assyrian empire. And these are but a few of the more striking instances of a phenomenon which is apt to cause perplexity to close and earnest students of the Old Testament. We have here to do, therefore, with a standing theme of Hebrew prophecy; and it may help us better to understand the attitude of Ezekiel if we consider for a moment some of the principles involved in this constant pre-occupation of the prophets with the affairs of the outer world.

At the outset it must be understood that prophecies of this kind form part of Jehovah's message to Israel. Although they are usually cast in the form of direct address to foreign peoples, this must not lead us to imagine that they were intended for actual publication in the countries to which they refer. A prophet's real audience always consisted of his own countrymen, whether his discourse was about themselves or about their neighbours. And it is easy to see that it was impossible to declare the purpose of God concerning Israel in words that came home to men's business and bosoms, without taking account of the state and destiny of other nations. Just as it would not be possible nowadays to forecast the future of Egypt without alluding to the fate of the Ottoman empire, so it was not possible then to describe the future of Israel in the concrete manner characteristic of the prophets without indicating the place reserved for those peoples with whom it had close intercourse. Besides this, a large part of the national consciousness of Israel was made up of interests, friendly or the reverse, in neighbouring states. The Hebrews had a keen eye for national idiosyncrasies, and the simple international relations of those days were almost as vivid and personal as of neighbours living in the same village. To be an Israelite was to be something characteristically different from a Moabite, and that again from an Edomite or a Philistine, and every patriotic Israelite had a shrewd sense of what the difference was. We cannot read the utterances of the prophets with regard to any of these nationalities without seeing that they often appeal to perceptions deeply lodged in the popular mind, which could be utilised to convey the spiritual lessons which the prophets desired to teach.

It must not be supposed, however, that such prophecies are in any degree the expression of national vanity or jealousy. What the prophets aim at is to elevate the thoughts of Israel to the sphere of eternal truths of the kingdom of God; and it is only in so far as these can be made to touch the conscience of the nation at this point that they appeal to what we may call its international sentiments. Now the question we have to ask is, What spiritual purpose for Israel is served by the announcements of the destiny of the outlying heathen populations? There are of course special interests attaching to each particular prophecy which it would be difficult to classify. But, speaking generally, prophecies of this class had a moral value for two reasons. In the first place, they re-echo and confirm the sentence of judgment passed on Israel herself. They do this in two ways: they illustrate the principle on which Jehovah deals with His own people, and His character as the righteous judge of men. Israel was to be destroyed for her national sins, her contempt of Jehovah, and her breaches of the moral law. But other nations, though more excusable, were not less guilty than Israel. The same spirit of ungodliness, in different forms, was manifested by Tyre, by Egypt, by Assyria, and by the petty states of Syria. Hence, if Jehovah was really the righteous ruler of the world, He must visit upon these nations their iniquities. Wherever a "sinful kingdom" was found, whether in Israel or elsewhere, that kingdom must be removed from its place among the nations. This appears most clearly in the Book of Amos, who, though he enunciates the paradoxical truth that Israel's sin must be punished just because it was the only people that Jehovah had known, nevertheless, as we have seen, thundered forth similar judgments on other nations for their flagrant violation of the universal law written in the human heart. In this way therefore the prophets enforced on their contemporaries the fundamental lesson of their teaching that the disasters which were coming on them were not the result of the caprice or impotence of their Deity, but the execution of His moral purpose, to which all men everywhere are subject. But again, not only was the principle of the judgment emphasised, but the manner in which it was to be carried out was more clearly exhibited. In all cases the pre-exilic prophets announce that the overthrow of the Hebrew states was to be effected either by the Assyrians or the Babylonians. These great world-powers were in succession the instruments fashioned and used by Jehovah for the performance of His great work in the earth. Now it was manifest that if this anticipation was well founded it involved the overthrow of all the nations in immediate contact with Israel. The policy of the

Mesopotamian monarchs was well understood; and if their wonderful successes were the revelation of the Divine purpose, then Israel would not be judged alone. Accordingly we find in most instances that the chastisement of the heathen is either ascribed directly to the invaders or else to other agencies set in motion by their approach. The people of Israel or Judah were thus taught to look on their fate as involved in a great scheme of Divine providence, overturning all the existing relations which gave them a place among the nations of the world and preparing for a new development of the purpose of Jehovah in the future.

When we turn to that ideal future we find a second and more suggestive aspect of these prophecies against the heathen. All the prophets teach that the destiny of Israel is inseparably bound up with the future of God's kingdom on earth. The Old Testament never wholly shakes off the idea that the preservation and ultimate victory of the true religion demands the continued existence of the one people to whom the revelation of the true God had been committed. The indestructibility of Israel's national life depends on its unique position in relation to the purposes of Jehovah, and it is for this reason that the prophets look forward with unwavering confidence to a time when the knowledge of Jehovah shall go forth from Israel to all the nations of mankind. And this point of view we must try to enter into if we are to understand the meaning of their declarations concerning the fate of the surrounding nations. If we ask whether an independent future is reserved in the new dispensation for the peoples with whom Israel had dealings in the past, we find that different and sometimes conflicting answers are given. Thus Isaiah predicts a restoration of Tyre after the lapse of seventy years, while Ezekiel announces its complete and final destruction. It is only when we consider these utterances in the light of the prophets' general conception of the kingdom of God that we discern the spiritual truth that gives them an abiding significance for the instruction of all ages. It was not a matter of supreme religious importance to know whether Phœnicia or Egypt or Assyria would retain their old place in the world, and share indirectly in the blessings of the Messianic age. What men needed to be taught then, and what we need to remember still, is that each nation holds its position in subordination to the ends of God's government, and no power or wisdom or refinement will save a state from destruction when it ceases to serve the interests of His kingdom. The foreign peoples that come under the survey of the prophets are as yet strangers to the true God, and are therefore destitute of that which could secure them a place in the reconstruction of political relationships of which Israel is to be the religious centre. Sometimes they are represented as having by their hostility to Israel or their pride of heart so encroached on the sovereignty of Jehovah that their doom is already sealed. At other times they are conceived as converted to the knowledge of the true God, and as gladly accepting the place assigned to them in the humanity of the future by consecrating their wealth and power to the service of His people Israel. In all cases it is their attitude to Israel and the God of Israel that determines their destiny: that is the great truth which the prophets design to impress on their countrymen. So long as the cause of religion was identified with the fortunes of the people of Israel no higher conception of the redemption of mankind could be formed than that of a willing subjection of the nations of the earth to the word of Jehovah which went forth from Jerusalem (*cf.* Isa. ii. 2-4). And whether any particular nation should survive to participate in the glories of that latter day depends on the view taken of its present condition and its fitness for incorporation in the universal empire of Jehovah soon to be established.

We now know that this was not the form in which Jehovah's purpose of salvation was destined to be realised in the history of the world. Since the coming of Christ the people of Israel has lost its distinctive and central position as the bearer of the hopes and promises of the true religion. In its place we have a spiritual kingdom of men united by faith in Jesus Christ, and in the worship of one Father in spirit and in truth—a kingdom which from its very nature can have no local centre or political organisation. Hence the conversion of the heathen can no longer be conceived as national homage paid to the seat of Jehovah's sovereignty on Zion; nor is the unfolding of the Divine plan of universal salvation bound up with the extinction of the nationalities which once symbolised the hostility of the world to the kingdom of God. This fact has an important bearing on the question of the fulfilment of the foreign prophecies of the Old Testament. Literal fulfilment is not to be looked for in this case any more than in the delineations of Israel's future, which are after all the predominant element of Messianic prediction. It is true that the nations passed under review have now vanished from history, and in so far as their fall was brought about by causes operating in the world in which the prophets moved, it must be recognised as a partial but real vindication of the truth of their words. But the details of the prophecies have not been historically verified. All attempts to trace their accomplishment in events that took place long afterwards and in circumstances which the prophets themselves never contemplated only lead us astray from the real interest which belongs to them. As concrete embodiments of the eternal principles exhibited in the rise and fall of nations they have an abiding significance for the Church in all ages; but the actual working out of these principles in history could not in the nature of things be complete within the limits of the world known to the inhabitants of Judæa. If we are to look for their ideal fulfilment, we shall only find it in the progressive victory of Christianity over all forms of error and superstition, and in the dedication of all the resources of human civilisation —its wealth, its commercial enterprise, its political power—to the advancement of the kingdom of our God and His Christ.

It was natural from the special circumstances in which he wrote, as well as from the general character of his teaching, that Ezekiel, in his oracles against the heathen powers, should present only the dark side of God's providence. Except in the case of Egypt, the nations addressed are threatened with annihilation, and even Egypt is to be reduced to a condition of utter impotence and humiliation. Very characteristic also is his representation of the purpose which comes to light in this series of judgments. It is to be a great demonstration to all the earth of the absolute sovereignty of Jehovah. "Ye shall know that I am Jehovah" is the formula that sums up the lesson of each nation's fall. We observe that the prophet starts from the situation created by the fall of Jerusalem. That great calamity bore in the first instance the appearance of a triumph of heathenism over Jehovah the God of Israel. It was, as the prophet elsewhere expresses it, a profanation of His holy name in the eyes of the nations. And in this light it was undoubtedly regarded by the petty principalities around Palestine, and perhaps also by the more distant and powerful spectators, such as Tyre and Egypt. From the standpoint of heathenism the downfall of Israel meant the defeat of its tutelary Deity; and the neighbouring nations, in exulting over the tidings of Jerusalem's fate, had in their minds the idea of the prostrate Jehovah unable to save His people in their hour of need. It is not necessary to suppose that Ezekiel attributes to them any consciousness of Jehovah's claim to be the only living and true God. It is the paradox of revelation that He who is the Eternal and Infinite first revealed Himself to the world as the God of Israel; and all the misconceptions that sprang out of that fact had to be cleared away by His self-manifestation in historical acts that appealed to the world at large. Amongst these acts the judgment of the heathen nations holds the first place in the mind of Ezekiel. A crisis has been reached at which it becomes necessary for Jehovah to vindicate His divinity by the destruction of those who have exalted themselves against Him. The world must learn once for all that Jehovah is no mere tribal god, but the omnipotent ruler of the universe. And this is the preparation for the final disclosure of His power and Godhead in the restoration of Israel to its own land, which will speedily follow the overthrow of its ancient foes. This series of prophecies forms thus an appropriate introduction to the third division of the book, which deals with the formation of the new people of Jehovah.

It is somewhat remarkable that Ezekiel's survey of the heathen nations is restricted to those in the immediate vicinity of the land of Canaan. Although he had unrivalled opportunities of becoming acquainted with the remote countries of the East, he confines his attention to the Mediterranean states which had long played a part in Hebrew history. The peoples dealt with are seven in number—Ammon, Moab, Edom, the Philistines, Tyre, Sidon, and Egypt. The order of the enumeration is geographical: first the inner circle of Israel's immediate neighbours, from Ammon on the east round to Sidon in the extreme north; then outside the circle the preponderating world-power of Egypt. It is not altogether an accidental circumstance that five of these nations are named in the twenty-seventh chapter of Jeremiah as concerned in the project of rebellion against Nebuchadnezzar in the early part of Zedekiah's reign. Egypt and Philistia are not mentioned there, but we may surmise at least that Egyptian diplomacy was secretly at work pulling the wires which set the puppets in motion. This fact, together with the omission of Babylon from the list of threatened nations, shows that Ezekiel regards the judgment as falling within the period of Chaldean supremacy, which he appears to have estimated at forty years. What is to be the fate of Babylon itself he nowhere intimates, a conflict between that great world-power and Jehovah's purpose being no part of his system. That Nebuchadnezzar is to be the agent of the overthrow of Tyre and the humiliation of Egypt is expressly stated; and although the crushing of the smaller states is ascribed to other agencies, we can hardly doubt that these were conceived as indirect consequences of the upheaval caused by the Babylonian invasion.

Chap. xxv., then, consists of four brief prophecies addressed respectively to Ammon, Moab, Edom, and the Philistines. A few words on the fate prefigured for each of these countries will suffice for the explanation of the chapter.

1. Ammon (vv. 2-7) lay on the edge of the desert, between the upper waters of the Jabbok and the Arnon, separated from the Jordan by a strip of Israelitish territory from twenty to thirty miles wide. Its capital, Rabbah, mentioned here (ver. 5), was situated on a southern tributary of the Jabbok, and its ruins still bear amongst the Arabs the ancient national name *'Ammân*. Although their country was pastoral (milk is referred to in ver. 4 as one of its chief products), the Ammonites seem to have made some progress in civilisation. Jeremiah (xlix. 4) speaks of them as trusting in their treasures: and in this chapter Ezekiel announces that they shall be for a spoil to the nations (ver. 7). After the deportation of the transjordanic tribes by Tiglath-pileser, Ammon seized the country that had belonged to the tribe of Gad, its nearest neighbour on the west. This encroachment is denounced by the prophet Jeremiah in the opening words of his oracle against Ammon: "Hath Israel no children? or has he no heir? why doth Milcom" (the national deity of the Ammonites) "inherit Gad, why hath his" (Milcom's) "folk settled in his" (Gad's) "cities" (Jer. xlix. 1). We have already seen (chap. xxi.) that the Ammonites took part in the rebellion against Nebuchadnezzar, and stood out after the other members of the league had gone back from their purpose. But this temporary union with Jerusalem did nothing to abate the old national animosity, and the disaster of Judah was a signal for an exhibition of malignant satisfaction on the part of Ammon. "Because thou hast said, Aha, against My sanctuary when it was profaned, and the land of Israel when it was laid waste, and the house of Judah when it went into captivity," etc. (ver. 3)—for this crowning offence against the majesty of Jehovah, Ezekiel denounces an exterminating judgment on Ammon. The land shall be given up to the "children of the East"—*i. e.*, the Bedouin Arabs—who shall pitch their tent encampments in it, eating its fruits and drinking its milk, and turning the "great city" Rabbah itself into a resting-place for camels (vv. 4, 5). It is not quite clear (though it is commonly assumed) that the children of the East are regarded as the actual conquerors of Ammon. Their possession of the country may be the consequence rather than the cause of the destruction of civilisation, the encroachment of the nomads being as inevitable under these circumstances as the extension of the desert itself where water fails.

2. Moab * (vv. 8-11) comes next in order. Its proper territory, since the settlement of Israel in Canaan, was the elevated tableland south of the Arnon, along the lower part of the Dead Sea.

* The words "and Seir" in ver. 8 are wanting in the true text of the LXX., and should probably be omitted.

But the tribe of Reuben, which bordered it on the north, was never able to hold its ground against the superior strength of Moab, and hence the latter nation is found in possession of the lower and more fertile district stretching northwards from the Arnon, now called the Belka. All the cities, indeed, which are mentioned in this chapter as belonging to Moab—Bethjeshimoth, Baal-meon, and Kirjathaim—were situated in this northern and properly Israelite region. These were the "glory of the land," which were now to be taken away from Moab (ver. 9). In Israel Moab appears to have been regarded as the incarnation of a peculiarly offensive form of national pride,* of which we happen to have a monument in the famous Moabite Stone, which was erected by the Mesha in the ninth century B. C. to commemorate the victories of Chemosh over Jehovah and Israel. The inscription shows, moreover, that in the arts of civilised life Moab was at that early time no unworthy rival of Israel itself. It is for a special manifestation of this haughty and arrogant spirit in the day of Jerusalem's calamity that Ezekiel pronounces Jehovah's judgment on Moab: "Because Moab hath said, Behold, the house of Judah is like all the nations" (ver. 8). These words no doubt reflect accurately the sentiment of Moab towards Israel, and they presuppose a consciousness on the part of Moab of some unique distinction pertaining to Israel in spite of all the humiliations it had undergone since the time of David. And the thought of Moab may have been more widely disseminated among the nations than we are apt to suppose: "The kings of the earth believed not, neither all the inhabitants of the world, that the adversary and the enemy should enter into the gates of Jerusalem" (Lam. iv. 12). The Moabites at all events breathed a sigh of relief when Israel's pretensions to religious ascendency seemed to be confuted, and thereby they sealed their own doom. They share the fate of the Ammonites, their land being handed over for a possession to the sons of the East (ver. 10).

Both these nations, Ammon and Moab, were absorbed by the Arabs, as Ezekiel had foretold; but Ammon at least preserved its separate name and nationality through many changes of fortune down to the second century after Christ.

3. Edom (vv. 12-14), famous in the Old Testament for its wisdom (Jer. xlix. 7; Obad. 8), occupied the country to the south of Moab from the Dead Sea to the head of the Gulf of Akaba. In Old Testament times the centre of its power was in the region to the east of the Arabah Valley, a position of great commercial importance, as commanding the caravan route from the Red Sea port of Elath to Northern Syria. From this district the Edomites were afterwards driven (about 300 B. C.) by the Arabian tribe of the Nabatæans, when they took up their abode in the south of Judah. None of the surrounding nations were so closely akin to Israel as Edom, and with none were its relations more embittered and hostile. The Edomites had been subjugated and nearly exterminated by David, had been again subdued by Amaziah and Uzziah, but finally recovered their independence during the attack of the Syrians and Ephraimites on Judah in the reign of Ahaz. The memory of this long struggle produced in Edom a "perpetual enmity," an undying hereditary hatred towards the kingdom of Judah. But that which made the name of Edom to be execrated by the later Jews was its conduct after the fall of Jerusalem. The prophet Obadiah represents it as sharing in the spoil of Jerusalem (ver. 10), and as "standing in the crossway to cut off those that escaped" (ver. 14). Ezekiel also alludes to this in the thirty-fifth chapter (ver. 5), and tells us further that in the time of the captivity the Edomites seized part of the territory of Israel (vv. 10-12), from which indeed the Jews were never able altogether to dislodge them. For the guilt they thus incurred by taking advantage of the humiliation of Jehovah's people, Ezekiel here threatens them with extinction; and the execution of the divine vengeance is in their case entrusted to the children of Israel themselves (vv. 13, 14). They were, in fact, finally subdued by John Hyrcanus in 126 B. C., and compelled to adopt the Jewish religion. But long before then they had lost their prestige and influence, their ancient seats having passed under the dominion of the Arabs in common with all the neighbouring countries.

4. The Philistines (vv. 15-17)—the "immigrants" who had settled along the Mediterranean coast, and who were destined to leave their name to the whole country—had evidently played a part very similar to the Edomites at the time of the destruction of Jerusalem; but of this nothing is known beyond what is here said by Ezekiel. They were at this time a mere "remnant" (ver. 16), having been exhausted by the Assyrian and Egyptian wars. Their fate is not precisely indicated in the prophecy. They were in point of fact gradually extinguished by the revival of Jewish domination under the Asmonean dynasty.

One other remark may here be made, as showing the discrimination which Ezekiel brought to bear in estimating the characteristics of each separate nation. He does not ascribe to the greater powers, Tyre, Sidon, and Egypt, the same petty and vindictive jealousy of Israel which actuated the diminutive nationalities dealt with in this chapter. These great heathen states, which played so imposing a part in ancient civilisation, had a wide outlook over the affairs of the world; and the injuries they inflicted on Israel were due less to the blind instinct of national hatred than to the pursuit of far-reaching schemes of selfish interest and aggrandisement. If Tyre rejoices over the fall of Jerusalem, it is because of the removal of an obstacle to the expansion of her commercial enterprise. When Egypt is described as having been an occasion of sin to the people of God, what is meant is that she had drawn Israel into the net of her ambitious foreign policy, and led her away from the path of safety pointed out by Jehovah's will through the prophets. Ezekiel pays a tribute to the grandeur of their position by the care he bestows on the description of their fate. The smaller nations embodying nothing of permanent value for the advancement of humanity, he dismisses each with a short and pregnant oracle announcing its doom. But when he comes to the fall of Tyre and of Egypt his imagination is evidently impressed; he lingers over all the details of the picture, he returns to it again and again, as if he would penetrate the secret of their greatness and understand the potent fascination which their names exercised throughout the world. It would be entirely erroneous to

* Isa. xvi. 6, xxv. 11; Jer. xlviii. 29, 42.

suppose that he sympathises with them in their calamity, but certainly he is conscious of the blank which will be caused by their disappearance from history; he feels that something will have vanished from the earth whose loss will be mourned by the nations far and near. This is most apparent in the prophecy on Tyre, to which we now proceed.

CHAPTER XVI.

TYRE.

EZEKIEL xxvi., xxix. 17-21.

IN the time of Ezekiel Tyre was still at the height of her commercial prosperity. Although not the oldest of the Phœnician cities, she held a supremacy among them which dated from the thirteenth century B. C.,* and she had long been regarded as the typical embodiment of the genius of the remarkable race to which she belonged. The Phœnicians were renowned in antiquity for a combination of all the qualities on which commercial greatness depends. Their absorbing devotion to the material interests of civilisation, their amazing industry and perseverance, their resourcefulness in assimilating and improving the inventions of other peoples, the technical skill of their artists and craftsmen, but above all their adventurous and daring seamanship, conspired to give them a position in the old world such as has never been quite rivalled by any other nation of ancient or modern times. In the grey dawn of European history we find them acting as pioneers of art and culture along the shores of the Mediterranean, although even then they had been displaced from their earliest settlements in the Ægean and the coast of Asia Minor by the rising commerce of Greece. Matthew Arnold has drawn a brilliant imaginative picture of this collision between the two races, and the effect it had on the dauntless and enterprising spirit of Phœnicia:—

" As some grave Tyrian trader, from the sea,
Descried at sunrise an emerging prow
Lifting the cool-hair'd creepers stealthily,
The fringes of a southward-facing brow
Among the Ægæan isles;
And saw the merry Grecian coaster come,
Freighted with amber grapes, and Chian wine,
Green, bursting figs, and tunnies steep'd in brine—
And knew the intruders on his ancient home,
The young light-hearted masters of the waves—
And snatch'd his rudder and shook out more sail;
And day and night held on indignantly
O'er the blue Midland waters with the gale,
Betwixt the Syrtes and soft Sicily,
To where the Atlantic raves
Outside the western straits; and unbent sails
There, where down cloudy cliffs, through sheets of foam,
Shy traffickers, the dark Iberians, come;
And on the beach undid his corded bales."†

It is that spirit of masterful and untiring ambition kept up for so many centuries that throws a halo of romance round the story of Tyre.

In the oldest Greek literature, however, Tyre is not mentioned, the place which she afterwards held being then occupied by Sidon. But after the decay of Sidon the rich harvest of her labours fell into the lap of Tyre, which thenceforth stands out as the foremost city of Phœnicia. She owed her pre-eminence partly to the wisdom and energy with which her affairs were administered, but partly also to the strength of her natural situation. The city was built both on the mainland and on a row of islets about half a mile from the shore. This latter portion contained the principal buildings (temples and palaces), the open place where business was transacted, and the two harbours. It was no doubt from it that the city derived its name (צוֹר =Rock); and it always was looked on as the central part of Tyre. There was something in the appearance of the island city—the Venice of antiquity, rising from mid-ocean with her " tiara of proud towers "—which seemed to mark her out as destined to be mistress of the sea. It also made a siege of Tyre an arduous and a tedious undertaking, as many a conqueror found to his cost. Favoured then by these advantages, Tyre speedily gathered the traffic of Phœnicia into her own hands, and her wealth and luxury were the wonder of the nations. She was known as " the crowning city, whose merchants were princes, and her traffickers the honourable of the earth " (Isa. xxiii. 8). She became the great commercial emporium of the world. Her colonies were planted all over the islands and coasts of the Mediterranean, and the one most frequently mentioned in the Bible, Tarshish, was in Spain, beyond Gibraltar. Her seamen had ventured beyond the Pillars of Hercules, and undertook distant Atlantic voyages to the Canary Islands on the south and the coasts of Britain on the north. The most barbarous and inhospitable regions were ransacked for the metals and other products needed to supply the requirements of civilisation, and everywhere she found a market for her own wares and manufactures. The carrying trade of the Mediterranean was almost entirely conducted in her ships, while her richly laden caravans traversed all the great routes that led into the heart of Asia and Africa.

It so happens that the twenty-seventh chapter of Ezekiel is one of the best sources of information we possess as to the varied and extensive commercial relations of Tyre in the sixth century B. C.* It will therefore be better to glance shortly at its contents here rather than in its proper connection in the development of the prophet's thought. It will easily be seen that the description is somewhat idealised; no details are given of the commodities which Tyre *sold* to the nations—only as an afterthought (ver. 33) is it intimated that by sending forth her wares she has enriched and satisfied many nations. So the goods she *bought* of them are not represented as given in exchange for anything else; Tyre is poetically conceived as an empress ruling the peoples by the potent spell of her influence, compelling them to drudge for her and bring to her feet the gains they have acquired by their heavy labour. Nor can the list of nations† or their gifts be meant as exhaustive; it only includes such things as served to exhibit the immense variety of useful and costly articles which ministered to the wealth and luxury of Tyre. But making allowance for this, and for the numerous difficulties which the text presents, the passage has evidently been compiled with great

* Rawlinson, " History of Phœnicia."
† Closing stanzas of " The Scholar Gipsy."

* Both Movers and Rawlinson make it the basis of their survey of Tyrian commerce.
† Babylon and Egypt are probably omitted because of the peculiar point of view assumed by the prophet. They were too powerful to be represented as slaves of Tyre, even in poetry.

care; it shows a minuteness of detail and fulness of knowledge which could not have been got from books, but displays a lively personal interest in the affairs of the world which is surprising in a man like Ezekiel.

The order followed in the enumeration of nations is not quite clear, but is on the whole geographical. Starting from Tarshish in the extreme west (ver. 12), the prophet mentions in succession Javan (Ionia), Tubal, and Meshech (two tribes to the southeast of the Black Sea), and Togarmah (usually identified with Armenia) (vv. 13, 14). These represent the northern limit of the Phœnician markets. The reference in the next verse (15) is doubtful, on account of a difference between the Septuagint and the Hebrew text. If with the former we read "Rhodes" instead of "Dedan," it embraces the nearer coasts and islands of the Mediterranean, and this is perhaps on the whole the more natural sense. In this case it is possible that up to this point the description has been confined to the sea trade of Phœnicia, if we may suppose that the products of Armenia reached Tyre by way of the Black Sea. At all events the overland traffic occupies a space in the list out of proportion to its actual importance, a fact which is easily explained from the prophet's standpoint. First, in a line from south to north, we have the nearer neighbours of Phœnicia—Edom, Judah, Israel, and Damascus (vv. 16-18). Then the remoter tribes and districts of Arabia—Uzal * (the chief city of Yemen), Dedan (on the eastern side of the Gulf of Akaba), Arabia and Kedar (nomads of the eastern desert), Havilah,† Sheba, and Raamah (in the extreme south of the Arabian peninsula) (vv. 19-22). Finally the countries tapped by the eastern caravan route—Haran (the great trade centre in Mesopotamia), Canneh (? Calneh, unknown), Eden (differently spelt from the garden of Eden, also unknown), Assyria, and Chilmad (unknown) (ver. 23). These were the "merchants" and "traders" of Tyre, who are represented as thronging her market-place with the produce of their respective countries.

The imports, so far as we can follow the prophet's enumeration, are in nearly all cases characteristic products of the regions to which they are assigned. Spain is known to have furnished all the metals here mentioned—silver, iron, lead, and tin. Greece and Asia Minor were centres of the slave traffic (one of the darkest blots on the commerce of Phœnicia), and also supplied hardware. Armenia was famous as a horse-breeding country, and thence Tyre procured her supply of horses and mules. The ebony and tusks of ivory must have come from Africa; and if the Septuagint is right in reading "Rhodes" in ver. 15, these articles can only have been collected there for shipment to Tyre.‡ Through Edom come pearls and precious stones.§ Judah and Israel furnished Tyre with agricultural and natural produce, as they had done from the days of David and Solomon —wheat and oil, wax and honey, balm and spices. Damascus yields the famous "wine of Helbon"—said to be the only vintage that the Persian kings would drink—perhaps also other choice wines.* A rich variety of miscellaneous articles, both natural and manufactured, is contributed by Arabia,—wrought iron (perhaps sword-blades) from Yemen; saddle-cloths from Dedan; sheep and goats from the Bedouin tribes; gold, precious stones, and aromatic spices from the caravans of Sheba. Lastly, the Mesopotamian countries provide the costly textile fabrics from the looms of Babylon so highly prized in antiquity—"costly garments, mantles of blue, purple, and broidered work," "many-coloured carpets," and "cords twisted and durable."†

This survey of the ramifications of Tyrian commerce will have served its purpose if it enables us to realise in some measure the conception which Ezekiel had formed of the power and prestige of the maritime city, whose destruction he so confidently announced. He knew, as did Isaiah before him, how deeply Tyre had struck her roots in the life of the old world, how indispensable her existence seemed to be to the whole fabric of civilisation as then constituted. Both prophets represent the nations as lamenting the downfall of the city which had so long ministered to their material welfare. The overthrow of Tyre would be felt as a world-wide calamity; it could hardly be contemplated except as part of a radical subversion of the established order of things. This is what Ezekiel has in view, and his attitude towards Tyre is governed by his expectation of a great shaking of the nations which is to usher in the perfect kingdom of God. In the new world to which he looks forward no place will be found for Tyre, not even the subordinate position of a handmaid to the people of God which Isaiah's vision of the future had assigned to her. Beneath all her opulence and refinement the prophet's eye detected that which was opposed to the mind of Jehovah—the irreligious spirit which is the temptation of a mercantile community, manifesting itself in overweening pride and self-exaltation, and in sordid devotion to gain as the highest end of a nation's existence.

The twenty-sixth chapter is in the main a literal prediction of the siege and destruction of Tyre by Nebuchadnezzar. It is dated from the year in which Jerusalem was captured, and was certainly written after that event. The number of the month has accidentally dropped out of the text, so that we cannot tell whether at the time of writing the prophet had received actual intelligence of the fall of the city. At all events it is assumed that the fate of Jerusalem is already known in Tyre, and the manner in which the tidings were sure to have been received there is the immediate occasion of the prophecy. Like many other peoples, Tyre had rejoiced over the disaster which had befallen the Jewish state; but her exultation had a peculiar note of selfish calculation, which did not escape the

* E. V., "going to and fro."

† So Cornill, חוילה for רכלי (= merchants).

‡ See ch. xxvii. 6, where ivory is said to come from Chittim or Cyprus.

§ The Hebrew text adds "purple, embroidered work, and byssus"; but most of these things are omitted in the LXX.

* The text of vv. 18, 19 is in confusion, and Cornill, from a comparison with a contemporary wine-list of Nebuchadnezzar, and also an Assyrian one from the library of Asshurbanipal, makes it read thus: "Wine of Helbon and Zimin and Arnaban they furnished in thy markets. From Uzal," etc. Both lists are quoted in Schrader's "Cuneiform Inscriptions and the Old Testament," under this verse.

† The latter half of this verse, however, is of very uncertain interpretation. For full explanation of the archæological details in this chapter it will be necessary to consult the commentaries and the lexicon. See also Rawlinson's "History of Phœnicia," pp. 285 ff.

notice of the prophet. Ever mindful of her own interest, she sees that a barrier to the free development of her commerce has been removed, and she congratulates herself on the fortunate turn which events have taken: "Aha! the door of the peoples is broken, it is turned towards me; she that was full hath been laid waste!"* (ver. 2). Although the relations of the two countries had often been friendly and sometimes highly advantageous to Tyre, she had evidently felt herself hampered by the existence of an independent state on the mountain ridge of Palestine. The kingdom of Judah, especially in days when it was strong enough to hold Edom in subjection, commanded the caravan routes to the Red Sea, and doubtless prevented the Phœnician merchants from reaping the full profit of their ventures in that direction. It is probable that at all times a certain proportion of the revenue of the kings of Judah was derived from toll levied on the Tyrian merchandise that passed through their territory; and what they thus gained represented so much loss to Tyre. It was, to be sure, a small item in the mass of business transacted on the exchange of Tyre. But nothing is too trivial to enter into the calculations of a community given over to the pursuit of gain; and the satisfaction with which the fall of Jerusalem was regarded in Tyre showed how completely she was debased by her selfish commercial policy, how oblivious she was to the spiritual interests bound up with the future of Israel.

Having thus exposed the sinful cupidity and insensibility of Tyre, the prophet proceeds to describe in general terms the punishment that is to overtake her. Many nations shall be brought up against her, irresistible as the sea when it comes up with its waves; her walls and fortifications shall be rased; the very dust shall be scraped from her site, so that she is left "a naked rock" rising out of the sea, a place where fishermen spread their nets to dry, as in the days before the city was built.

Then follows (vv. 7-14) a specific announcement of the manner in which judgment shall be executed on Tyre. The recent political attitude of the city left no doubt as to the quarter from which immediate danger was to be apprehended. The Phœnician states had been the most powerful members of the confederacy that was formed about 596 to throw off the yoke of the Chaldæans, and they were in open revolt at the time when Ezekiel wrote. They had apparently thrown in their lot with Egypt, and a conflict with Nebuchadnezzar was therefore to be expected. Tyre had every reason to avoid a war with a first-rate power, which could not fail to be disastrous to her commercial interests. But her inhabitants were not destitute of martial spirit; they trusted in the strength of their position and their command of the sea, and they were in the mood to risk everything rather than again renounce their independence and their freedom. But all this avails nothing against the purpose which Jehovah has purposed concerning Tyre. It is He who brings Nebuchadnezzar, the king of kings, from the north with his army and his siege-train, and Tyre shall fall before his assault, as Jerusalem has already fallen. First of all, the Phœnician cities on the mainland shall be ravaged and laid waste, and then operations commence against the mother-city herself. The description of the siege and capture of the island fortress is given with an abundance of graphic details, although, strangely enough, without calling attention to the peculiar method of attack that was necessary for the reduction of Tyre. The great feature of the siege would be the construction of a huge mole between the shore and the island; once the wall was reached the attack would proceed precisely as in the case of an inland town, in the manner depicted on Assyrian monuments. When the breach is made in the fortifications the whole army pours into the city, and for the first time in her history the walls of Tyre shake with the rumbling of chariots in her streets. The conquered city is then given up to slaughter and pillage, her songs and her music are stilled for ever, her stones and timber and dust are cast into the sea, and not a trace remains of the proud mistress of the waves.

In the third strophe (vv. 15-21) the prophet describes the dismay which will be caused when the crash of the destruction of Tyre resounds along the coasts of the sea. All the "princes of the sea" (perhaps the rulers of the Phœnician colonies in the Mediterranean) are represented as rising from their thrones, and putting off their stately raiment, and sitting in the dust bewailing the fate of the city. The dirge in which they lift up their voices (vv. 17, 18) is given by the Septuagint in a form which preserves more nearly than the Hebrew the structure as well as the beauty which we should expect in the original:—

"How is perished from the sea—
The city renowned!
She that laid her terror—
On all its inhabitants!
[Now] are the isles affrighted—
In the day of thy falling!"

But this beautiful image is not strong enough to express the prophet's sense of the irretrievable ruin that hangs over Tyre. By a bold flight of imagination he turns from the mourners on earth to follow in thought the descent of the city into the under-world (vv. 19-21). The idea that Tyre might rise from her ruins after a temporary eclipse and recover her old place in the world was one that would readily suggest itself to any one who understood the real secret of her greatness. To the mind of Ezekiel the impossibility of her restoration lies in the fixed purpose of Jehovah, which includes, not only her destruction, but her perpetual desolation. "When I make thee a desolate city, like the cities that are not inhabited; when I bring up against thee the deep, and the great waters cover thee; then I will bring thee down with them that go down to the pit, with the people of old time, and I will make thee dwell in the lowest parts of the earth, like the immemorial waste places, with them that go down to the pit, that thou be not inhabited nor establish thyself in the land of the living." The whole passage is steeped in weird poetic imagery. The "deep"* suggests something more than the blue waters of the Mediterranean; it is the name of the great primeval Ocean, out of which the habitable world was fashioned, and which is used as an emblem of the irresist-

* With a change of one letter in the Hebrew text, המלאה for אמלאה, as in the LXX. and Targum.

* Hebrew, *Tĕhôm*; Babylonian, *Tiamat*.

ible judgments of God.* The "pit" is the realm of the dead, Sheôl, conceived as situated under the earth, where the shades of the departed drag out a feeble existence from which there is no deliverance. The idea of Sheôl is a frequent subject of poetical embellishment in the later books of the Old Testament; and of this we have an example here when the prophet represents the once populous and thriving city as now a denizen of that dreary place. But the essential meaning he wishes to convey is that Tyre is numbered among the things that were. She "shall be sought, and shall not be found any more for ever," because she has entered the dismal abode of the dead, whence there is no return to the joys and activities of the upper world.

Such then is the anticipation which Ezekiel in the year 586 had formed of the fate of Tyre. No candid reader will suppose that the prophecy is anything but what it professes to be—a *bonâ fide* prediction of the total destruction of the city in the immediate future and by the hands of Nebuchadnezzar. When Ezekiel wrote, the siege of Tyre had not begun; and however clear it may have been to observant men that the next stage in the campaign would be the reduction of the Phœnician cities, the prophet is at least free from the suspicion of having prophesied after the event. The remarkable absence of characteristic and special details from the account of the siege is the best proof that he is dealing with the future from the true prophetic standpoint and clothing a divinely imparted conviction in images supplied by a definite historical situation. Nor is there any reason to doubt that in some form the prophecy was actually published among his fellow-exiles at the date to which it is assigned. On this point critical opinion is fairly unanimous. But when we come to the question of the fulfilment of the prediction we find ourselves in the region of controversy, and, it must be admitted, of uncertainty. Some expositors, determined at all hazards to vindicate Ezekiel's prophetic authority, maintain that Tyre was actually devastated by Nebuchadnezzar in the manner described by the prophet, and seek for confirmations of their view in the few historical notices we possess of this period of Nebuchadnezzar's reign. Others, reading the history differently, arrive at the conclusion that Ezekiel's calculations were entirely at fault, that Tyre was not captured by the Babylonians at all, and that his oracle against Tyre must be reckoned amongst the unfulfilled prophecies of the Old Testament. Others again seek to reconcile an impartial historical judgment with a high conception of the function of prophecy, and find in the undoubted course of events a real though not an exact verification of the words uttered by Ezekiel. It is indeed almost by accident that we have any independent corroboration of Ezekiel's anticipation with regard to the immediate future of Tyre. Oriental discoveries have as yet brought to light no important historical monuments of the reign of Nebuchadnezzar; and outside the book of Ezekiel itself we have nothing to guide us except the statement of Josephus, based on Phœnician and Greek authorities,† that Tyre underwent a thirteen years' siege by the Babylonian conqueror. There is no reason whatever to call in question the reliability of this important information, although the accompanying statement that the siege began in the seventh year of Nebuchadnezzar is certainly erroneous. But unfortunately we are not told how the siege ended. Whether it was successful or unsuccessful, whether Tyre was reduced or capitulated, or was evacuated or beat off her assailants, is nowhere indicated. To argue from the silence of the historians is impossible; for if one man argues that a catastrophe that took place "before the eyes of all Asia" would not have passed unrecorded in historical books, another might urge with equal force that a repulse of Nebuchadnezzar was too uncommon an event to be ignored in the Phœnician annals.* On the whole the most reasonable hypothesis is perhaps that after the thirteen years the city surrendered on not unfavourable terms; but this conclusion is based on other considerations than the data or the silence of Josephus.

The chief reason for believing that Nebuchadnezzar was not altogether successful in his attack on Tyre is found in a supplementary prophecy of Ezekiel's, given in the end of the twenty-ninth chapter (vv. 17-21). It was evidently written after the siege of Tyre was concluded, and so far as it goes it confirms the accuracy of Josephus' sources. It is dated from the year 570, sixteen years after the fall of Jerusalem; and it is, in fact, the latest oracle in the whole book. The siege of Tyre, therefore, which had not commenced in 586, when chap. xxvi. was written, was finished before 570; and between these terminal dates there is just room for the thirteen years of Josephus. The invasion of Phœnicia must have been the next great enterprise of the Babylonian army in Western Asia after the destruction of Judah, and it was only the extraordinary strength of Tyre that enabled it to protract the struggle so long. Now what light does Ezekiel throw on the issue of the siege? His words are: "Nebuchadnezzar, king of Babylon, has made his army to serve a great service against Tyre; every head made bald and every shoulder peeled, yet *he and his army got no wages out of Tyre* for the service which he served against her." The prophet then goes on to announce that the spoils of Egypt should be the recompense to the army for their unrequited labour against Tyre, inasmuch as it was work done for Jehovah. Here then, we have evidence first of all that the long siege of Tyre had taxed the resources of the besiegers to the utmost. The "peeled shoulders" and the "heads made bald" is a graphic detail which alludes not obscurely to the monotonous navvy work of carrying loads of stones and earth to fill up the narrow channel between the mainland and the island,† so as to allow the engines to be brought up to the walls. Ezekiel was well aware of the arduous nature of the undertaking, the expenditure of human effort and life which was involved, in the struggle with natural obstacles; and his striking conception of these obscure and toiling soldiers as unconscious servants of the Almighty shows how

* Psalm xxxvi. 6 *cf.* Gen. vii. 11.
† *Contra* "Ap.," I. 21; "Ant.," X. qi. 1.

* *Cf.* Hävernick against Hitzig and Winer, "Ezekiel," pp. 436 f.
† The same engineering feat was accomplished by Alexander the Great in seven months, but the Greek general probably adopted more scientific methods (such as pile-driving) than the Babylonians: and, besides, it is possible that the remains of Nebuchadnezzar's embankment may have facilitated the operation.

steadfast was his faith in the word he proclaimed against Tyre. But the important point is that they obtained from Tyre no reward—at least no adequate reward—for their herculean labours. The expression used is no doubt capable of various interpretations. It might mean that the siege had to be abandoned, or that the city was able to make extremely easy terms of capitulation, or, as Jerome suggests, that the Tyrians had carried off their treasures by sea and escaped to one of their colonies. In any case it shows that the historical event was not in accordance with the details of the earlier prophecy. That the wealth of Tyre would fall to the conquerors is there assumed as a natural consequence of the capture of the city. But whether the city was actually captured or not, the victors were somehow disappointed in their expectation of plunder. The rich spoil of Tyre, which was the legitimate reward of their exhausting toil, had slipped from their eager grasp; to this extent at least the reality fell short of the prediction, and Nebuchadnezzar had to be compensated for his losses at Tyre by the promise of an easy conquest of Egypt.

But if this had been all it is not probable that Ezekiel would have deemed it necessary to supplement his earlier prediction in the way we have seen after an interval of sixteen years. The mere circumstance that the sack of Tyre had failed to yield the booty that the besiegers counted on was not of a nature to attract attention amongst the prophet's auditors, or to throw doubt on the genuineness of his inspiration. And we know that there was a much more serious difference between the prophecy and the event than this. It is, from what has just been said, extremely doubtful whether Nebuchadnezzar actually destroyed Tyre, but even if he did she very quickly recovered much of her former prosperity and glory. That her commerce was seriously crippled during the struggle with Babylonia we may well believe, and it is possible that she never again was what she had been before this humiliation came upon her. But for all that the enterprise and prosperity of Tyre continued for many ages to excite the admiration of the most enlightened nations of antiquity. The destruction of the city, therefore, if it took place, had not the finality which Ezekiel had anticipated. Not till after the lapse of eighteen centuries could it be said with approximate truth that she was like "a bare rock in the midst of the sea."

The most instructive fact for us, however, is that Ezekiel reissued his original prophecy, knowing that it had not been literally fulfilled. In the minds of his hearers the apparent falsification of his predictions had revived old prejudices against him, which interfered with the prosecution of his work. They reasoned that a prophecy so much out of joint with the reality was sufficient to discredit his claim to be an authoritative exponent of the mind of Jehovah; and so the prophet found himself embarrassed by a recurrence of the old unbelieving attitude which had hindered his public activity before the destruction of Jerusalem. He has not for the present "an open mouth" amongst them, and he feels that his words will not be fully received until they are verified by the restoration of Israel to its own land. But it is evident that he himself did not share the view of his audience, otherwise he would certainly have suppressed a prophecy which lacked the mark of authenticity. On the contrary he published it for the perusal of a wider circle of readers, in the conviction that what he had spoken was a true word of God, and that its essential truth did not depend on its exact correspondence with the facts of history. In other words, he believed in it as a true reading of the principles revealed in God's moral government of the world—a reading which had received a partial verification in the blow which had been dealt at the pride of Tyre, and which would receive a still more signal fulfilment in the final convulsions which were to introduce the day of Israel's restoration and glory. Only we must remember that the prophet's horizon was necessarily limited; and as he did not contemplate the slow development and extension of the kingdom of God through long ages, so he could not have taken into account the secular operation of historic causes which eventually brought about the ruin of Tyre.

CHAPTER XVII.

TYRE (CONTINUED): SIDON.

EZEKIEL xxvii., xxviii.

THE remaining oracles on Tyre (chaps. xxvii., xxviii. 1-19) are somewhat different both in subject and mode of treatment from the chapter we have just finished. Chap. xxvi. is in the main a direct announcement of the fall of Tyre, delivered in the oratorical style which is the usual vehicle of prophetic address. She is regarded as a state occupying a definite place among the other states of the world, and sharing the fate of other peoples who by their conduct towards Israel or their ungodliness and arrogance have incurred the anger of Jehovah. The two great odes which follow are purely ideal delineations of what Tyre is in herself; her destruction is assumed as certain rather than directly predicted, and the prophet gives free play to his imagination in the effort to set forth the conception of the city which was impressed on his mind. In chap. xxvii. he dwells on the external greatness and magnificence of Tyre, her architectural splendour, her political and military power, and above all her amazing commercial enterprise. Chap. xxviii., on the other hand, is a meditation on the peculiar genius of Tyre, her inner spirit of pride and self-sufficiency, as embodied in the person of her king. From a literary point of view the two chapters are amongst the most beautiful in the whole book. In the twenty-seventh chapter the fiery indignation of the prophet almost disappears, giving place to the play of poetic fancy and a flow of lyric emotion more perfectly rendered than in any other part of Ezekiel's writings. The distinctive feature of each passage is the elegy pronounced over the fall of Tyre; and although the elegy seems just on the point of passing into the taunt-song, yet the accent of triumph is never suffered to overwhelm the note of sadness to which these poems owe their special charm.

I.

Chap. xxvii. is described as a dirge over Tyre. In the previous chapter the nations were represented as bewailing her fall, but here the prophet himself takes up a lamentation for her; and, as may have been usual in real funeral dirges, he commences by celebrating the might and riches of the doomed city. The fine image which is maintained throughout the chapter was probably suggested to Ezekiel by the picturesque situation of Tyre on her sea-girt rock at "the entries of the sea." He compares her to a stately vessel riding at anchor* near the shore, taking on board her cargo of precious merchandise, and ready to start on the perilous voyage from which she is destined never to return. Meanwhile the gallant ship sits proudly in the water, tight and seaworthy and sumptuously furnished; and the prophet's eye runs rapidly over the chief points of her elaborate construction and equipment (vv. 3-11). Her timbers are fashioned of cypress from Hermon,† her mast is a cedar of Lebanon, her oars are made of the oak of Bashan, her deck of sherbîn-wood‡ (a variety of cedar) inlaid with ivory imported from Cyprus. Her canvas fittings are still more exquisite and costly. The sail is of Egyptian byssus with embroidered work, and the awning over the deck was of cloth resplendent in the two purple dyes procured from the coasts of Elishah.§ The ship is fitted up for pleasure and luxury as well as for traffic, the fact symbolised being obviously the architectural and other splendours which justified the city's boast that she was "the perfection of beauty."

But Tyre was wise and powerful as well as beautiful; and so the prophet, still keeping up the metaphor, proceeds to describe how the great ship is manned. Her steersmen are the experienced statesmen whom she herself has bred and raised to power; her rowers are the men of Sidon and Aradus, who spend their strength in her service. The elders and wise men of Gebal are her shipwrights (literally "stoppers of leaks"); and so great is her influence that all the naval resources of the world are subject to her control. Besides this Tyre employs an army of mercenaries drawn from the remotest quarters of the earth—from Persia and North Africa, as well as the subordinate towns of Phœnicia; and these, represented as hanging their shields and helmets on her sides, make her beauty complete.‖ In these verses the prophet pays a tribute of admiration to the astuteness with which the rulers of Tyre used their resources to strengthen her position as the head of the Phœnician confederacy. Three of the cities mentioned—Sidon, Aradus, and Gebal or Byblus—were the most important in Phœnicia; two of them at least had a longer history than herself, yet they are here truly represented as performing the rough menial labour which brought wealth and renown to Tyre. It required no ordinary statecraft to preserve the balance of so many complex and conflicting interests, and make them all co-operate for the advancement of the glory of Tyre; but hitherto her "wise men" had proved equal to the task.

The second strophe (vv. 12-25) contains the survey of Tyrian commerce, which has already been analysed in another connection.* At first sight it appears as if the allegory were here abandoned, and the impression is partly correct. In reality the city, although personified, is regarded as the emporium of the world's commerce, to which all the nations stream with their produce. But at the end it appears that the various commodities enumerated represent the cargo with which the ship is laden. Ships of Tarshish—*i. e.*, the largest class of merchant vessels then afloat, used for the long Atlantic voyage—wait upon her, and fill her with all sorts of precious things (ver. 25). Then in the last strophe (vv. 26-36), which speaks of the destruction of Tyre, the figure of the ship is boldly resumed. The heavily freighted vessel is rowed into the open sea; there she is struck by an east wind and founders in deep water. The image suggests two ideas, which must not be pressed, although they may have an element of historic truth in them: one is that Tyre perished under the weight of her own commercial greatness, and the other that her ruin was hastened through the folly of her rulers. But the main idea is that the destruction of the city was wrought by the power of God, which suddenly overwhelmed her at the height of her prosperity and activity. As the waves close over the doomed vessel the cry of anguish that goes up from the drowning mariners and passengers strikes terror into the hearts of all seafaring men. They forsake their ships, and having reached the safety of the shore abandon themselves to frantic demonstrations of grief, joining their voices in a lamentation over the fate of the goodly ship which symbolised the mistress of the sea (vv. 32-36)†:—

"Who was like Tyre [so glorious]—
In the midst of the sea?
When thy wares went forth from the seas—
Thou filledst the peoples;
With thy wealth and thy merchandise—
Thou enrichedst the earth.
Now art thou broken from the seas—
In depths of the waters;
Thy merchandise and all thy multitude—
Are fallen therein.
All the inhabitants of the islands—
Are shocked at thee,
And their kings shudder greatly—
With tearful countenances.
They that trade among the peoples . . .—
Hiss over thee;
Thou art become a terror—
And art no more for ever."

Such is the end of Tyre. She has vanished utterly from the earth; the imposing fabric of her greatness is like an unsubstantial pageant faded; and nothing remains to tell of her former

* For the word גבוליך rendered "thy borders," Cornill proposes to read זבולך, which he thinks might mean "thine anchorage." The translation is doubtful, but the sense is certainly appropriate.

† Senir was the Amorite name of Mount Hermon, the Phœnician name being Sirion (Deut. iii. 9). Senir, however, occurs on the Assyrian monuments, and was probably widely known.

‡ "Teasshur" (read בִּתְאַשֻּׁרִים instead of בַּת־אֲשֻׁרִים) a kind of tree mentioned several times in the Old Testament, is generally identified with the sherbîn tree.

§ Elishah is one of the sons of Javan (Ionia) (Gen. x. 4), and must have been some part of the Mediterranean coast, subject to the influence of Greece. Italy, Sicily, and the Peloponnesus have been suggested.

‖ The details of the description are nearly all illustrated in pictures of Phœnician war-galleys found on Assyrian monuments. They show the single mast with its square sail, the double row of oars, the fighting men on the deck, and the row of shields along the bulwarks. In an Egyptian picture we have a representation of the embroidered *sail* (ancient ships are said not to have carried a *flag*). The canvas is richly ornamented with various devices over its whole surface, and beneath the sail we see the cabin or awning of coloured stuff mentioned in the text.

* See above, pp. 279 ff.

† It is not clear whether the dirge is continued to the end of the chapter, or whether vv. 33 ff. are spoken by the prophet in explanation of the distress of the nations. The proper elegiac measures cannot be made out without some alteration of the text.

glory but the mourning of the nations who were once enriched by her commerce.

II.

Chap. xxviii. 1-19.—Here the prophet turns to the prince of Tyre, who is addressed throughout as the impersonation of the consciousness of a great commercial community. We happen to know from Josephus that the name of the reigning king at this time was Ithobaal or Ethbaal II. But it is manifest that the terms of Ezekiel's message have no reference to the individuality of this or any other prince of Tyre. It is not likely that the king could have exercised any great political influence in a city "whose merchants were all princes"; indeed, we learn from Josephus that the monarchy was abolished in favour of some sort of elective constitution not long after the death of Ithobaal. Nor is there any reason to suppose that Ezekiel has in view any special manifestation of arrogance on the part of the royal house, such as a pretension to be descended from the gods. The king here is simply the representative of the genius of the community, the sins of heart charged against him are the expression of the sinful principle which the prophet detected beneath the refinement and luxury of Tyre, and his shameful death only symbolises the downfall of the city. The prophecy consists of two parts: first, an accusation against the prince of Tyre, ending with a threat of destruction (vv. 2-10); and second, a lament over his fall (vv. 11-19). The point of view is very different in these two sections. In the first the prince is still conceived as a man, and the language put into his mouth, although extravagant, does not exceed the limits of purely human arrogance. In the second, however, the king appears as an angelic being, an inhabitant of Eden and a companion of the cherub, sinless at first, and falling from his high estate through his own transgression. It almost seems as if the prophet had in his mind the idea of a tutelary spirit or genius of Tyre, like the angelic princes in the book of Daniel who preside over the destinies of different nations.* But in spite of its enhanced idealism, the passage only clothes in forms drawn from Babylonian mythology the boundless self-glorification of Tyre, and the expulsion of the prince from paradise is merely the ideal counterpart of the overthrow of the city which is his earthly abode.

The sin of Tyre is an overweening pride, which culminated in an attitude of self-deification on the part of its king. Surrounded on every hand by the evidences of man's mastery over the world, by the achievements of human art and industry and enterprise, the king feels as if his throne on the sea-girt island were a veritable seat of the gods, and as if he himself were a being truly divine. His heart is lifted up; and, forgetful of the limits of his mortality, he "sets his mind like the mind of a god." The godlike quality on which he specially prides himself is the superhuman wisdom evinced by the extraordinary prosperity of the city with which he identifies himself. Wiser than Daniel! the prophet ironically exclaims; "no secret thing is too dark for thee!" "By thy wisdom and thine insight thou hast gotten thee wealth, and hast gathered gold and silver into thy treasuries: by thy great wisdom in thy commerce thou hast multiplied thy wealth, and thy heart is lifted up because of thy riches." The prince sees in the vast accumulation of material resources in Tyre nothing but the reflection of the genius of her inhabitants; and being himself the incarnation of the spirit of the city, he takes the glory of it to himself and esteems himself a god. Such impious self-exaltation must inevitably call down the vengeance of Him who is the only living God; and Ezekiel proceeds to announce the humiliation of the prince by the "most ruthless of the nations"—*i. e.*, the Chaldæans. He shall then know how much of divinity doth hedge a king. In face of them that seek his life he shall learn that he is man and not God, and that there are forces in the world against which the vaunted wisdom of Tyre is of no avail. An ignominious death * at the hand of strangers is the fate reserved for the mortal who so proudly exalted himself against all that is called God.

The thought thus expressed, when disengaged from its peculiar setting, is one of permanent importance. To Ezekiel, as to the prophets generally, Tyre is the representative of commercial greatness, and the truth which he here seeks to illustrate is that the abnormal development of the mercantile spirit had in her case destroyed the capacity of faith in that which is truly divine. Tyre no doubt, like every other ancient state, still maintained a public religion of the type common to Semitic paganism. She was the sacred seat of a special cult, and the temple of Melkarth was considered the chief glory of the city. But the public and perfunctory worship which was there celebrated had long ceased to express the highest consciousness of the community. The real god of Tyre was not Baal nor Melkarth, but the king, or any other object that might serve as a symbol of her civic greatness. Her religion was one that embodied itself in no outward ritual; it was the enthusiasm which was kindled in the heart of every citizen of Tyre by the magnificence of the imperial city to which he belonged. The state of mind which Ezekiel regards as characteristic of Tyre was perhaps the inevitable outcome of a high civilisation informed by no loftier religious conceptions than those common to heathenism. It is the idea which afterwards found expression in the deification of the Roman emperors—the idea that the state is the only power higher than the individual to which he can look for the furtherance of his material and spiritual interests, the only power, therefore, which rightly claims his homage and his reverence. None the less it is a state of mind which is destructive of all that is essential to living religion; and Tyre in her proud self-sufficiency was perhaps further from a true knowledge of God than the barbarous tribes who in all sincerity worshipped the rude idols which represented the invisible power that ruled their destinies. And in exposing the irreligious spirit which lay at the heart of the Tyrian civilisation the prophet lays his finger on the spiritual danger which attends the successful pursuit of the finite interests of human life. The thought of God, the sense of an immediate relation of the spirit of man to the Eternal and the Infinite, are easily displaced from men's minds by undue admiration for the achievements of a culture based

* Dan x. 20, 21, xii. 1.

* "The death of the uncircumcised"—*i. e.*, a death which involves exclusion from the rites of honourable burial; like burial in unconsecrated ground among Christian nations.

on material progress, and supplying every need of human nature except the very deepest, the need of God. "For that is truly a man's religion, the object of which fills and holds captive his soul and heart and mind, in which he trusts above all things, which above all things he longs for and hopes for." * The commercial spirit is indeed but one of the forms in which men devote themselves to the service of this present world; but in any community where it reigns supreme we may confidently look for the same signs of religious decay which Ezekiel detected in Tyre in his own day. At all events his message is not superfluous in an age and country where energies are well-nigh exhausted in the accumulation of the means of living, and whose social problems all run up into the great question of the distribution of wealth. It is essentially the same truth which Ruskin, with something of the power and insight of a Hebrew prophet, has so eloquently enforced on the men who make modern England—that the true religion of a community does not live in the venerable institutions to which it yields a formal and conventional deference, but in the objects which inspire its most eager ambitions, the ideals which govern its standard of worth, in those things wherein it finds the ultimate ground of its confidence and the reward of its work.†

The lamentation over the fall of the prince of Tyre (vv. 11-19) reiterates the same lesson with a boldness and freedom of imagination not usual with this prophet. The passage is full of obscurities and difficulties which cannot be adequately discussed here, but the main lines of the conception are easily grasped. It describes the original state of the prince as a semi-divine being, and his fall from that state on account of sin that was found in him. The picture is no doubt ironical; Ezekiel actually means nothing more than that the soaring pride of Tyre enthroned its king or its presiding genius in the seat of the gods, and endowed him with attributes more than mortal. The prophet accepts the idea, and shows that there was sin in Tyre enough to hurl the most radiant of celestial creatures from heaven to hell. The passage presents certain obvious affinities with the account of the Fall in the second and third chapters of Genesis; but it also contains reminiscences of a mythology the key to which is now lost. It can hardly be supposed that the vivid details of the imagery, such as the "mountain of God," the "stones of fire," "the precious gems," are altogether due to the prophet's imagination. The mountain of the gods is now known to have been a prominent idea of the Babylonian religion; and there appears to have been a widespread notion that in the abode of the gods were treasures of gold and precious stones, jealously guarded by griffins, of which small quantities found their way into the possession of men. It is possible that fragments of these mythical notions may have reached the knowledge of Ezekiel during his sojourn in Babylon and been used by him to fill up his picture of the glories which surrounded the first estate of the king of Tyre. It should be observed, however, that the prince is not to be identified with the cherub or one of the cherubim. The words "Thou art the anointed cherub that covereth, and I have set thee so" (ver. 14) may be translated "With the . . . cherub I set thee"; and similarly the words of ver. 16, "I will destroy thee, O covering cherub," should probably be rendered "And the cherub hath destroyed thee." The whole conception is greatly simplified by these changes, and the principal features of it, so far as they can be made out with clearness, are as follows: The cherub is the warden of the "holy mountain of God," and no doubt also (as in chap. i.) the symbol and bearer of the divine glory. When it is said that the prince of Tyre was placed with the cherub, the meaning is that he had his place in the abode of God, or was admitted to the presence of God, so long as he preserved the perfection in which he was created (ver. 15). The other allusions to his original glory, such as the "covering" of precious stones and the "walking amidst fiery stones," cannot be explained with any degree of certainty.* When iniquity is found in him so that he must be banished from the presence of God, the cherub is said to destroy him from the midst of the stones of fire—*i. e.*, is the agent of the divine judgment which descends on the prince. It is thus doubtful whether the prince is conceived as a perfect human being, like Adam before his fall, or as an angelic, superhuman creature; but the point is of little importance in ideal delineation such as we have here. It will be seen that even on the first supposition there is no very close correspondence with the story of Eden in the book of Genesis, for there the cherubim are placed to guard the way of the tree of life only after man has been expelled from the garden.

But what is the sin that tarnished the sanctity of this exalted personage and cost him his place among the immortals? Ideally, it was an access of pride that caused his ruin, a spiritual sin, such as might originate in the heart of an angelic being.

> "By that sin fell the angels: how can man, then,
> The image of his Maker, hope to win by it?"

His heart was lifted up because of his beauty, and he forfeited his godlike wisdom over his brilliance (ver. 17). But really, this change passing over the spirit of the prince in the seat

* Dean Church, "Cathedral and University Sermons," p. 150.

† "We have, indeed, a nominal religion, to which we pay tithes of property and sevenths of time; but we have also a practical and earnest religion, to which we devote nine-tenths of our property, and six-sevenths of our time. And we dispute a great deal about the nominal religion: but we are all unanimous about this practical one; of which I think you will admit that the ruling goddess may be best generally described as the 'Goddess of Getting-on,' or 'Britannia of the Market.' The Athenians had an 'Athena Agoraia,' or Athena of the Market; but she was a subordinate type of their goddess, while our Britannia Agoraia is the principal type of ours. And all your great architectural works are, of course, built to her. It is long since you built a great cathedral; and how you would laugh at me if I proposed building a cathedral on the top of one of these hills of yours, to make it an Acropolis! But your railroad mound, vaster than the walls of Babylon; your railroad stations, vaster than the temple of Ephesus, and innumerable; your chimneys, how much more mighty and costly than cathedral spires! your harbour-piers; your warehouses; your exchanges!—all these are built to your great Goddess of 'Getting-on'; and she has formed, and will continue to form, your architecture, as long as you worship her; and it is quite vain to ask me to tell you how to build to *her*; you know far better than I."—"The Crown of Wild Olive."

* The "fiery stones" may represent the thunderbolts, which were harmless to the prince in virtue of his innocence. It may be noted that the "precious stones" that were his covering (ver. 13) correspond with nine out of twelve jewels that covered the high-priestly breast-plate (Exod. xxviii. 17-19), the stones of the third row being those not here represented. This suggests that the allusion is rather to bejewelled garments than to the plumage of the wings of the cherub with whom the prince has been wrongly identified.

of God is only the reflection of what is done on earth in Tyre. As her commerce increased, the proofs of her unjust and unscrupulous use of wealth were accumulated against her, and her midst was filled with violence (ver. 16). This is the only allusion in the three chapters to the wrong and oppression and the outrages on humanity which were the inevitable accompaniments of that greed of gain which had taken possession of the Tyrian community. And these sins are regarded as a demoralisation taking place in the nature of the prince, who is the representative of the city; by the "iniquity of his traffic he has profaned his holiness," and is cast down from his lofty seat to the earth, a spectacle of abject humiliation for kings to gloat over. By a sudden change of metaphor the destruction of the city is also represented as a fire breaking out in the vitals of the prince, and reducing his body to ashes—a conception which has not unnaturally suggested to some commentators the fable of the phœnix which was supposed periodically to immolate herself in a fire of her own kindling.

III.

A short oracle on Sidon completes the series of prophecies dealing with the future of Israel's immediate neighbours (vv. 20-23). Sidon lay about twenty miles farther north than Tyre, and was, as we have seen, at this time subject to the authority of the younger and more vigorous city. From the book of Jeremiah,* however, we see that Sidon was an autonomous state, and preserved a measure of independence even in matters of foreign policy. There is therefore nothing arbitrary in assigning a separate oracle to this most northerly of the states in immediate contact with the people of Israel, although it must be admitted that Ezekiel has nothing distinctive to say of Sidon. Phœnicia was in truth so overshadowed by Tyre that all the characteristics of the people have been amply illustrated in the chapters that have dealt with the latter city. The prophecy is accordingly delivered in the most general terms, and indicates rather the purpose and effect of the judgment than the manner in which it is to come or the character of the people against whom it is directed. It passes insensibly into a prediction of the glorious future of Israel, which is important as revealing the underlying motive of all the preceding utterances against the heathen nations. The restoration of Israel and the destruction of her old neighbours are both parts of one comprehensive scheme of divine providence, the ultimate object of which is a demonstration before the eyes of the world of the holiness of Jehovah. That men might know that He is Jehovah, God alone, is the end alike of His dealings with the heathen and with His own people. And the two parts of God's plan are in the mind of Ezekiel intimately related to each other; the one is merely a condition of the realisation of the other. The crowning proof of Jehovah's holiness will be seen in His faithfulness to the promise made to the patriarchs of the possession of the land of Canaan, and in the security and prosperity enjoyed by Israel when brought back to their land a purified nation. Now in the past Israel had been constantly interfered with, crippled, humiliated, and seduced by the petty heathen powers around her borders. These had been a pricking brier and a stinging thorn (ver. 24), constantly annoying and harassing her and impeding the free development of her national life. Hence the judgments here denounced against them are no doubt in the first instance a punishment for what they had been and done in the past; but they are also a clearing of the stage that Israel might be isolated from the rest of the world, and be free to mould her national life and her religious institutions in accordance with the will of her God. That is the substance of the last three verses of the chapter; and while they exhibit the peculiar limitations of the prophet's thinking, they enable us at the same time to do justice to the singular unity and consistency of aim which guided him in his great forecast of the future of the kingdom of God. There remains now the case of Egypt to be dealt with; but Egypt's relations to Israel and her position in the world were so unique that Ezekiel reserves consideration of her future for a separate group of oracles longer than those on all the other nations put together.

* Jer. xxv. 22, xxvii. 3.

CHAPTER XVIII.

EGYPT.

EZEKIEL xxix.-xxxii.

EGYPT figures in the prophecies of Ezekiel as a great world-power cherishing projects of universal dominion. Once more, as in the age of Isaiah, the ruling factor in Asiatic politics was the duel for the mastery of the world between the rival empires of the Nile and the Euphrates. The influence of Egypt was perhaps even greater in the beginning of the sixth century than it had been in the end of the eighth, although in the interval it had suffered a signal eclipse. Isaiah (chap. xix.) had predicted a subjugation of Egypt by the Assyrians, and this prophecy had been fulfilled in the year 672, when Esarhaddon invaded the country and incorporated it in the Assyrian empire. He divided its territory into twenty petty principalities governed by Assyrian or native rulers, and this state of things had lasted with little change for a generation. During the reign of Asshurbanipal Egypt was frequently overrun by Assyrian armies, and the repeated attempts of the Ethiopian monarchs, aided by revolts among the native princes, to reassert their sovereignty over the Nile Valley were all foiled by the energy of the Assyrian king or the vigilance of his generals. At last, however, a new era of prosperity dawned for Egypt about the year 645. Psammetichus, the ruler of Saïs, with the help of foreign mercenaries, succeeded in uniting the whole land under his sway; he expelled the Assyrian garrison, and became the founder of the brilliant twenty-sixth (Saïte) dynasty. From this time Egypt possessed in a strong central administration the one indispensable condition of her material prosperity. Her power was consolidated by a succession of vigorous rulers, and she immediately began to play a leading part in the affairs of Asia. The most distinguished king of the dynasty was Necho II., the son and successor of Psammetichus. Two striking facts mentioned by Herodotus are worthy of mention, as showing the originality and vigour with which the Egyptian administration was at this time conducted. One is the project of cutting a canal between the Nile and the Red Sea, an undertaking which was abandoned by Necho in consequence of an oracle warning him that he was only working for the advantage of foreigners—meaning no doubt the Phœnicians. Necho, however, knew how to turn the Phœnician seamanship to good account, as is proved by the other great stroke of genius with which he is credited—the circumnavigation of Africa. It was a Phœnician fleet, despatched from Suez by his orders, which first rounded the Cape of Good Hope, returning to Egypt by the straits of Gibraltar after a three years' voyage. And if Necho was less successful in war than in the arts of peace, it was not from want of activity. He was the Pharaoh who defeated Josiah in the plain of Megiddo, and afterwards contested the lorship of Syria with Nebuchadnezzar. His defeat at Carchemish in 604 compelled him to retire to his own land; but the power of Egypt was still unbroken, and the Chaldæan king knew that he would yet have to reckon with her in his schemes for the conquest of Palestine.

At the time to which these prophecies belong the king of Egypt was Pharaoh Hophra (in Greek, Apries), the grandson of Necho II. Ascending the throne in 588 B. C., he found it necessary for the protection of his own interests to take an active part in the politics of Syria. He is said to have attacked Phœnicia by sea and land, capturing Sidon and defeating a Tyrian fleet in a naval engagement. His object must have been to secure the ascendency of the Egyptian party in the Phœnician cities; and the stubborn resistance which Nebuchadnezzar encountered from Tyre was no doubt the result of the political arrangements made by Hophra after his victory. No armed intervention was needed to ensure a spirited defence of Jerusalem; and it was only after the Babylonians were encamped around the city that Hophra sent an Egyptian army to its relief. He was unable, however, to effect more than a temporary suspension of the siege, and returned to Egypt, leaving Judah to its fate, apparently without venturing on a battle (Jer. xxxvii. 5-7). No further hostilities between Egypt and Babylon are recorded during the lifetime of Hophra. He continued to reign with vigour and success till 571, when he was dethroned by Amasis, one of his own generals.

These circumstances show a remarkable parallel to the political situation with which Isaiah had to deal at the time of Sennacherib's invasion. Judah was again in the position of the "earthen pipkin between two iron pots." It is certain that neither Jehoiakim nor Zedekiah, any more than the advisers of Hezekiah in the earlier period, would have embarked on a conflict with the Mesopotamian empire but for delusive promises of Egyptian support. There was the same vacillation and division of counsels in Jerusalem, the same dilatoriness on the part of Egypt, and the same futile effort to retrieve a desperate situation after the favourable moment had been allowed to slip. In both cases the conflict was precipitated by the triumph of an Egyptian party in the Judæan court; and it is probable that in both cases the king was coerced into a policy of which his judgment did not approve. And the prophets of the later period, Jeremiah and Ezekiel, adhere closely to the lines laid down by Isaiah in the time of Sennacherib, warning the people against putting their trust in the vain help of Egypt, and counselling passive submission to the course of events which expressed the unalterable judgment of the Almighty. Ezekiel indeed borrows an image that had been current in the days of Isaiah in order to set forth the utter untrustworthiness and dishonesty of Egypt towards the nations who were induced to rely on her power. He compares her to a staff of reed, which breaks when one grasps it, piercing the hand and making the loins to totter when it is leant upon.* Such had Egypt been to Israel through all her history, and such she will again prove herself to be in her last attempt to use Israel as the tool of her selfish designs. The great difference between Ezekiel and Isaiah is that, whereas Isaiah had access to the councils of Hezekiah and could bring his influence to bear on the inception of schemes of state, not without hope of averting what he saw to be a disastrous decision, Ezekiel could only watch the development of events from afar, and throw his warnings into the form of predictions of the fate in store for Egypt.

The oracles against Egypt are seven in number: (i) xxix. 1-16; (ii) 17-21; (iii) xxx. 1-19; (iv) 20-26; (v) xxxi.; (vi) xxxii. 1-16; (vii) 17-32. They are all variations of one theme, the annihilation of the power of Egypt by Nebuchadnezzar, and little progress of thought can be traced from the first to the last. Excluding the supplementary prophecy of xxix. 17-21, which is a later addition, the order appears to be strictly chronological.† The series begins seven months before the capture of Jerusalem (xxix. 1), and ends about eight months after that event.‡ How far the dates refer to actual occurrences coming to the knowledge of the prophet it is impossible for us to say. It is clear that his interest is centred on the fate of Jerusalem then hanging in the balance; and it is possible that the first oracles (xxix. 1-16, xxx. 1-19) may be called forth by the appearance of Hophra's army on the scene, while the next (xxx. 20-26) plainly alludes to the repulse of the Egyptians by the Chaldæans. But no attempt can be made to connect the prophecies with incidents of the campaign; the prophet's thoughts are wholly occupied with the moral and religious issues involved in the contest, the vindication of Jehovah's holiness in the overthrow of the great world-power which sought to thwart His purposes.

Chap. xxix. 1-16 is an introduction to all that follows, presenting a general outline of the prophet's conceptions of the fate of Egypt. It describes the sin of which she has been guilty, and indicates the nature of the judgment that is to overtake her and her future place among the nations of the world. The Pharaoh is compared to a "great dragon," wallowing in his native waters, and deeming himself secure from molestation in his reedy haunts. The crocodile was a natural symbol of Egypt, and the image conveys accurately the impression of sluggish

* Ezek. xxix. 6, 7: *cf.* Isa. xxxvi. 6 (the words of Rabshakeh). In ver. 7 read כַּף "hand," for כָּתֵף, "shoulder," and הַמְעַדְתָּ, "madest to totter," for הַעֲמַדְתָּ, "madest to stand."

† This is probable according to the Hebrew text, which, however, omits the number of the *month* in ch. xxxii. 17. The Septuagint reads "in the *first* month"; if this is accepted, it would be better to read the *eleventh* year instead of the twelfth in ch. xxxii. 1, as is done by some ancient versions and Hebrew codices. The change involves a difference of only one letter in Hebrew.

‡ Ch. xxxii. 17, following the LXX. reading.

and unwieldy strength which Egypt in the days of Ezekiel had long produced on shrewd observers of her policy. Pharaoh is the incarnate genius of the country; and as the Nile was the strength and glory of Egypt, he is here represented as arrogating to himself the ownership and even the creation of the wonderful river. "My river is mine, and I have made it" is the proud and blasphemous thought which expresses his consciousness of a power that owns no superior in earth or heaven. That the Nile was worshipped by the Egyptians with divine honours did not alter the fact that beneath all their ostentatious religious observances there was an immoral sense of irresponsible power in the use of the natural resources to which the land owed its prosperity. For this spirit of ungodly self-exaltation the king and people of Egypt are to be visited with a signal judgment, from which they shall learn who it is that is God over all. The monster of the Nile shall be drawn from his waters with hooks, with all his fishes sticking to his scales, and left to perish ignominiously on the desert sands. The rest of the prophecy (vv. 8-16) gives the explanation of the allegory in literal, though still general, terms. The meaning is that Egypt shall be laid waste by the sword, its teeming population led into captivity, and the land shall lie desolate, untrodden by the foot of man or beast for the space of forty years. "From Migdol to Syene"* —the extreme limits of the country—the rich valley of the Nile shall be uncultivated and uninhabited for that period of time.

The most interesting feature of the prophecy is the view which is given of the final condition of the Egyptian empire (vv. 13-16). In all cases the prophetic delineations of the future of different nations are coloured by the present circumstances of those nations as known to the writers. Ezekiel knew that the fertile soil of Egypt would always be capable of supporting an industrious peasantry, and that her existence did not depend on her continuing to play the *rôle* of a great power. Tyre depended on her commerce, and apart from that which was the root of her sin could never be anything but the resort of poor fishermen, who would not even make their dwelling on the barren rock in the midst of the sea. But Egypt could still be a country, though shorn of the glory and power which had made her a snare to the people of God. On the other hand the geographical isolation of the land made it impossible that she should lose her individuality amongst the nations of the world. Unlike the small states, such as Edom and Ammon, which were obviously doomed to be swallowed up by the surrounding population as soon as their power was broken, Egypt would retain her distinct and characteristic life as long as the physical condition of the world remained what it was. Accordingly the prophet does not contemplate an utter annihilation of Egypt, but only a temporary chastisement, succeeded by her permanent degradation to the lowest rank among the kingdoms. The forty years of her desolation represent in round numbers the period of Chaldean supremacy during which Jerusalem lies in ruins. Ezekiel at this time expected the invasion of Egypt to follow soon after the capture of Jerusalem, so that the restoration of the two peoples would be simultaneous. At the end of forty years the whole world will be reorganised on a new basis, Israel occupying the central position as the people of God, and in that new world Egypt shall have a separate but subordinate place. Jehovah will bring back the Egyptians from their captivity, and cause them to return to "Pathros,* the land of their origin," and there make them a "lowly state," no longer an imperial power, but humbler than the surrounding kingdoms. The righteousness of Jehovah and the interest of Israel alike demand that Egypt should be thus reduced from her former greatness. In the old days her vast and imposing power had been a constant temptation to the Israelites, "a confidence, a reminder of iniquity," leading them to put their trust in human power and luring them into paths of danger by deceitful promises (vv. 6-7). In the final dispensation of history this shall no longer be the case: Israel shall then know Jehovah, and no form of human power shall be suffered to lead their hearts astray from Him who is the rock of their salvation.

Chap. xxx. 1-19.—The judgment on Egypt spreads terror and dismay among all the neighbouring nations. It signalises the advent of the great day of Jehovah, the day of His final reckoning with the powers of evil everywhere. It is the "time of the heathen" that has come (ver. 3). Egypt being the chief embodiment of secular power on the basis of pagan religion, the sudden collapse of her might is equivalent to a judgment on heathenism in general, and the moral effect of it conveys to the world a demonstration of the omnipotence of the one true God whom she had ignored and defied. The nations immediately involved in the fall of Egypt are the allies and mercenaries whom she has called to her aid in the time of her calamity. Ethiopians, and Lydians, and Libyans, and Arabs, and Cretans,† the "helpers of Egypt," who have furnished contingents to her motley army, fall by the sword along with her, and their countries share the desolation that overtakes the land of Egypt. Swift messengers are then seen speeding up the Nile in ships to convey to the careless Ethiopians the alarming tidings of the overthrow of Egypt (ver. 9). From this point the prophet confines his attention to the fate of Egypt, which he describes with a fulness of detail that implies a certain acquaintance both with the topography and the social circumstances of the country. In ver. 10 Nebuchadnezzar and the Chaldæans are for the first time mentioned by name as the human instruments employed by Jehovah to execute His judgments on Egypt. After the slaughter of the inhabi-

* Migdol was on the northeast border of Egypt, twelve miles south of Pelusium (Sin), at the mouth of the eastern arm of the Nile. Syene is the modern Assouan, at the first cataract of the Nile, and has always been the boundary between Egypt proper and Ethiopia.

* Pathros is the name of Upper Egypt, the narrow valley of the Nile above the Delta. In the Egyptian tradition it was regarded as the original home of the nation and the seat of the oldest dynasties. Whether Ezekiel means that the Egyptians shall recover *only* Pathros, while the Delta is allowed to remain uncultivated, is a question that must be left undecided.

† Hebrew, "Cush, and Put, and Lud, and all the mixed multitude, and Chub, and the sons of the land of the covenant." Cornill reads, "Cush, and Put, and Lud, and Lub, and all Arabia, and the sons of Crete." The emendations are partly based on somewhat intricate reasoning from the text of the Greek and Ethiopic versions; but they have the advantage of yielding a series of proper names, as the context seems to demand. Put and Lud are tribes lying to the west of Egypt, and so also is Lub, which may be safely substituted for the otherwise unknown Chub of the Hebrew text.

tants the next consequence of the invasion is the destruction of the canals and reservoirs and the decay of the system of irrigation on which the productiveness of the country depended. "The rivers" (canals) "are dried up, and the land is made waste, and the fulness thereof, by the hand of strangers" (ver. 12). And with the material fabric of her prosperity the complicated system of religious and civil institutions which was entwined with the hoary civilisation of Egypt vanishes for ever. "The idols are destroyed; the potentates * are made to cease from Memphis, and princes from the land of Egypt, so that they shall be no more" (ver. 13). Faith in the native gods shall be extinguished, and a trembling fear of Jehovah shall fill the whole land. The passage ends with an enumeration of various centres of the national life, which formed, as it were, the sensitive ganglia where the universal calamity was most acutely felt. On these cities,† each of which was identified with the worship of a particular deity, Jehovah executes the judgments, in which He makes known to the Egyptian His sole divinity and destroys their confidence in false gods. They also possessed some special military or political importance, so that with their destruction the sceptres of Egypt were broken and the pride of her strength was laid low (ver. 18).

Chap. xxx. 20-26.—A new oracle dated three months later than the preceding. Pharaoh is represented as a combatant, already disabled in one arm and sore pressed by his powerful antagonist, the king of Babylon. Jehovah announces that the wounded arm cannot be healed, although Pharaoh has retired from the contest for that purpose. On the contrary, both his arms shall be broken and the sword struck from his grasp, while the arms of Nebuchadnezzar are strengthened by Jehovah, who puts His own sword into his hand. The land of Egypt, thus rendered defenceless, falls an easy prey to the Chaldæans, and its people are dispersed among the nations. The occasion of the prophecy is the repulse of Hophra's expedition for the relief of Jerusalem, which is referred to as a past event. The date may either mark the actual time of the occurrence (as in xxiv. 1), or the time when it came to the knowledge of Ezekiel. The prophet at all events accepts this reverse to the Egyptian arms as an earnest of the speedy realisation of his predictions in the total submission of the proud empire of the Nile.

Chap. xxxi. occupies the same position in the prophecies against Egypt as the allegory of the richly laden ship in those against Tyre (chap. xxvii.). The incomparable majesty and overshadowing power of Egypt are set forth under the image of a lordly cedar in Lebanon, whose top reaches to the clouds and whose branches afford shelter to all the beasts of the earth. The exact force of the allegory is somewhat obscured by a slight error of the text, which must have crept in at a very early period. As it stands in the Hebrew and in all the ancient versions the whole chapter is a description of the greatness not of Egypt but of Assyria. "To whom art thou like in thy greatness?" asks the prophet (ver. 2); and the answer is, "Assyria was great as thou art, yet Assyria fell and is no more." There is thus a double comparison: Assyria is compared to a cedar, and then Egypt is tacitly compared to Assyria. This interpretation may not be altogether indefensible. That the fate of Assyria contained a warning against the pride of Pharaoh is a thought in itself intelligible, and such as Ezekiel might very well have expressed. But if he had wished to express it he would not have done it so awkwardly as this interpretation supposes. When we follow the connection of ideas we cannot fail to see that Assyria is not in the prophet's thoughts at all. The image is consistently pursued without a break to the end of the chapter, and then we learn that the subject of the description is "Pharaoh and all his multitude" (ver. 18). But if the writer is thinking of Egypt at the end, he must have been thinking of it from the beginning, and the mention of Assyria is out of place and misleading. The confusion has been caused by the substitution of the word "Asshur" (in ver. 3) for "T'asshur," the name of the sherbin tree, itself a species of cedar. We should therefore read, "Behold a T'asshur, a cedar in Lebanon," etc.; * and the answer to the question of ver. 2 is that the position of Egypt is as unrivalled among the kingdoms of the world as this stately tree among the trees of the forest.

With this alteration the course of thought is perfectly clear, although incongruous elements are combined in the representation. The towering height of the cedar with its top in the clouds symbolises the imposing might of Egypt and its ungodly pride (*cf.* vv. 10, 14). The waters of the flood which nourish its roots are those of the Nile, the source of Egypt's wealth and greatness. The birds that build their nests in its branches and the beasts that bring forth their young under its shadow are the smaller nations that looked to Egypt for protection and support. Finally, the trees in the garden of God who envy the luxuriant pride of this monarch of the forest represent the other great empires of the earth who vainly aspired to emulate the prosperity and magnificence of Egypt (vv. 3-9).

In the next strophe (vv. 10-14) we see the great trunk lying prone across mountain and valley, while its branches lie broken in all the water-courses. A "mighty one of the nations" (Nebuchadnezzar) has gone up against it, and felled it to the earth. The nations have been scared from under its shadow; and the tree which "but yesterday might have stood against the world" now lies prostrate and dishonoured —"none so poor as do it reverence." And the fall of the cedar reveals a moral principle and conveys a moral lesson to all other proud and stately trees. Its purpose is to remind the other

* Reading אֵלִים, "strong ones," instead of אֱלִילִים, "not gods," as in the LXX. The latter term is common in Isaiah, but does not occur elsewhere in Ezekiel, although he had constant occasion to use it.

† The cities are not mentioned in any geographical order. Memphis (Noph) and Thebes (No) are the ancient and populous capitals of Lower and Upper Egypt respectively; Tanis (Zoan) was the city of the Hyksos, and subsequently a royal seat; Pelusium (Sin), "the bulwark of Egypt," and Daphne (Tahpanhes) guarded the approach to the Delta from the East: Heliopolis (On, wrongly pointed Aven) was the famous centre of Egyptian wisdom, and the chief seat of the worship of the sun-god Ra; and Bubastis (Pi-beseth), besides being a celebrated religious centre, was one of the possessions of the Egyptian military caste.

* It is only fair to say that the construction "a T'asshur, a cedar," or, still more, "a T'asshur of a cedar," is somewhat harsh. It is not unlikely that the word "cedar" may have been added after the reading "Assyrian" had been established, in order to complete the sense.

great empires that they too are mortal, and to warn them against the soaring ambition and lifting up of the heart which had brought about the humiliation of Egypt: "that none of the trees by the water should exalt themselves in stature or shoot their tops between the clouds, and that their mighty ones should not stand proudly in their loftiness (all who are fed by water); for they are all delivered to death, to the underworld with the children of men, to those that go down to the pit." In reality there is no more impressive intimation of the vanity of earthly glory than the decay of those mighty empires and civilisations which once stood in the van of human progress; nor is there a fitter emblem of their fate than the sudden crash of some great forest tree before the woodman's axe.

The development of the prophet's thought, however, here reaches a point where it breaks through the allegory, which has been hitherto consistently maintained. All nature shudders in sympathy with the fallen cedar: the deep mourns and withholds her screams from the earth; Lebanon is clothed with blackness, and all the trees languish. Egypt was so much a part of the established order that the world does not know itself when she has vanished. While this takes place on earth, the cedar itself has gone down to Sheôl, where the other shades of vanished dynasties are comforted because this mightiest of them all has become like to the rest. This is the answer to the question that introduced the allegory. To whom art thou like? None is fit to be compared to thee; yet "thou shalt be brought down with the trees of Eden to the lower parts of the earth, thou shalt lie in the midst of the uncircumcised, with them that are slain of the sword." It is needless to enlarge on this idea, which is out of keeping here, and is more adequately treated in the next chapter.

Chap. xxxii. consists of two lamentations to be chanted over the fall of Egypt by the prophet and the daughters of the nations (vv. 16, 18). The first (vv. 1-16) describes the destruction of Pharaoh, and the effect which is produced on earth; while the second (vv. 17-32) follows his shade into the abode of the dead, and expatiates on the welcome that awaits him there. Both express the spirit of exultation over a fallen foe, which was one of the uses to which elegiac poetry was turned amongst the Hebrews. The first passage, however, can hardly be considered a dirge in any proper sense of the word. It is essential to a true elegy that the subject of it should be conceived as dead, and that whether serious or ironical it should celebrate a glory that has passed away. In this case the elegiac note (of the elegiac "measure" there is hardly a trace) is just struck in the opening line: "O young lion of the nations!" (How) "art thou undone!" But this is not sustained: the passage immediately falls into the style of direct prediction and threatening, and is indeed closely parallel to the opening prophecy of the series (chap. xxix.). The fundamental image is the same: that of a great Nile monster spouting from his nostrils and fouling the waters with his feet (ver. 2). His capture by many nations and his lingering death on the open field are described with the realistic and ghastly details naturally suggested by the figure (vv. 3-6). The image is then abruptly changed in order to set forth the effect of so great a calamity on the world of nature and of mankind. Pharaoh is compared to a brilliant luminary, whose sudden extinction is followed by a darkening of all the lights of heaven and by consternation amongst the nations and kings of earth (vv. 7-10). It is thought by some that the violence of the transition is to be explained by the idea of the heavenly constellation of the dragon, answering to the dragon of the Nile, to which Egypt has just been likened.* Finally all metaphors are abandoned, and the desolation of Egypt is announced in literal terms as accomplished by the sword of the king of Babylon and the "most terrible of the nations" (vv. 11-16).

But all the foregoing oracles are surpassed in grandeur of conception by the remarkable Vision of Hades which concludes the series—"one of the most weird passages in literature" (Davidson). In form it is a dirge supposed to be sung at the burial of Pharaoh and his host by the prophet along with the daughters of famous nations (ver. 18). But the theme, as has been already observed, is the entrance of the deceased warriors into the under-world, and their reception by the shades that have gone down thither before them. In order to understand it we must bear in mind some features of the conception of the under-world, which it is difficult for the modern mind to realise distinctly. First of all, Sheôl, or the "pit," the realm of the dead, is pictured to the imagination as an adumbration of the grave or sepulchre, in which the body finds its last resting-place; or rather it is the aggregate of all the burying-grounds scattered over the earth's surface. There the shades are grouped according to their clans and nationalities, just as on earth the members of the same family would usually be interred in one burying-place. The grave of the chief or king, the representative of the nation, is surrounded by those of his vassals and subjects, earthly distinctions being thus far preserved. The condition of the dead appears to be one of rest or sleep; yet they retain some consciousness of their state, and are visited at least by transient gleams of human emotion, as when in this chapter the heroes rouse themselves to address the Pharaoh when he comes among them. The most material point is that the state of the soul in Hades reflects the fate of the body after death. Those who have received the honour of decent burial on earth enjoy a corresponding honour among the shades below. They have, as it were, a definite status and individuality in their eternal abode, whilst the spirits of the unburied slain are laid in the lowest recesses of the pit, in the limbo of the uncircumcised. On this distinction the whole significance of the passage before us seems to depend. The dead are divided into two great classes: on the one hand the "mighty ones," who lie in state with their weapons of war around them; and on the other hand the multitude of "the uncircumcised,† slain by the sword"—*i. e.*, those who have perished on the field of battle and been

* See Smend on the passage. Dr. Davidson, however, doubts the possibility of this: see his commentary.

† This use of the word "uncircumcised" is peculiar. The idea seems to be that circumcision, among nations which like the Israelites practised the rite, was an indispensable mark of membership in the community: and those who lacked this mark were treated as social outcasts

buried promiscuously without due funeral rites.* There is, however, no moral distinction between the two classes. The heroes are not in a state of blessedness; nor is the condition of the uncircumcised one of acute suffering. The whole of existence in Sheôl is essentially of one character; it is on the whole a pitiable existence, destitute of joy and of all that makes up the fulness of life on earth. Only there is "within that deep a lower deep," and it is reserved for those who in the manner of their death have experienced the penalty of great wickedness. The moral truth of Ezekiel's representation lies here. The real judgment of Egypt was enacted in the historical scene of its final overthrow; and it is the consciousness of this tremendous visitation of divine justice, perpetuated amongst the shades to all eternity, that gives ethical significance to the lot assigned to the nation in the other world. At the same time it should not be overlooked that the passage is in the highest degree poetical, and cannot be taken as an exact statement of what was known or believed about the state after death in Old Testament times. It deals only with the fate of armies and nationalities and great warriors who filled the earth with their renown. These, having vanished from history, preserve through all time in the underworld the memory of Jehovah's mighty acts of judgment; but it is impossible to determine whether this sublime vision implies a real belief in the persistence of national identities in the region of the dead.

These, then, are the principal ideas on which the ode is based, and the course of thought is as follows. Ver. 18 briefly announces the occasion for which the dirge is composed; it is to celebrate the passage of Pharaoh and his host to the lower world, and consign him to his appointed place there. Then follows a scene which has a certain resemblance to a well-known representation in the fourteenth chapter of Isaiah (vv. 9-11). The heroes who occupy the place of honour among the dead are supposed to rouse themselves at the approach of this great multitude, and hailing them from the midst of Sheôl, direct them to their proper place amongst the dishonoured slain. "The mighty ones speak to him: 'Be thou in the recesses of the pit: whom dost thou excel in beauty? Go down and be laid to rest with the uncircumcised, in the midst of them that are slain with the sword.'"† Thither Pharaoh has been preceded by other great conquerors who once set their terror in the earth, but now bear their shame amongst those that go down to the pit. For there is Asshur and all his company; there too are Elam and Meshech and Tubal, each occupying its own allotment amongst nations that have perished by the sword (vv. 22-26). Not theirs is the enviable lot of the heroes of old time‡ who went down to Sheôl in their panoply of war, and rest with their swords under their heads and their shields* covering their bones. And so Egypt, which has perished like these other nations, must be banished with them to the bottom of the pit (vv. 27, 28). The enumeration of the nations of the uncircumcised is then resumed; Israel's immediate neighbours are amongst them—Edom and the dynasties of the north (the Syrians), and the Phœnicians, inferior states which played no great part as conquerors, but nevertheless perished in battle and bear their humiliation along with the others (vv. 29, 30). These are to be Pharaoh's companions in his last resting-place, and at the sight of them he will lay aside his presumptuous thoughts and comfort himself over the loss of his mighty army (vv. 31 f.).

It is necessary to say a few words in conclusion about the historical evidence for the fulfilment of these prophecies on Egypt. The supplementary oracle of chap. xxix. 17-21 shows us that the threatened invasion by Nebuchadnezzar had not taken place sixteen years after the fall of Jerusalem. Did it ever take place at all? Ezekiel was at that time confident that his words were on the point of being fulfilled, and indeed he seems to stake his credit with his hearers on their verification. Can we suppose that he was entirely mistaken? Is it likely that the remarkably definite predictions uttered both by him and Jeremiah† failed of even the partial fulfilment which that on Tyre received? A number of critics have strongly maintained that we are shut up by the historical evidence to this conclusion. They rely chiefly on the silence of Herodotus, and on the unsatisfactory character of the statement of Josephus. The latter writer is indeed sufficiently explicit in his affirmations. He tells us‡ that five years after the capture of Jerusalem Nebuchadnezzar invaded Egypt, put to death the reigning king, appointed another in his stead, and carried the Jewish refugees in Egypt captive to Babylon. But it is pointed out that the date is impossible, being inconsistent with Ezekiel's own testimony, that the account of the death of Hophra is contradicted by what we know of the matter from other sources (Herodotus and Diodorus), and that the whole passage bears the appearance of a translation into history of the prophecies of Jeremiah which it professes to substantiate. That is vigorous criticism, but the vigour is perhaps not altogether unwarrantable, especially as Josephus does not mention any authority. Other allusions by secular writers hardly count for much, and the state of the question is such that historians would probably have been content to confess their ignorance if the credit of a prophet had not been mixed up with it.

Within the last seventeen years, however, a new turn has been given to the discussion through the discovery of monumental evidence which was thought to have an important bearing on the point in dispute. In the same volume of an Egyptological magazine§ Wiedemann directed the attention of scholars to two inscriptions, one in the Louvre and the other in the British Museum, both of which he considered to furnish proof of an occupation of Egypt by

not entitled to honourable sepulture. Hence the word could be used, as here, in the sense of unhallowed.

* *Cf.* Isa. xiv. 18-20: "All of the kings of the nations, all of them, sleep in glory, every one in his own house. But thou art cast forth away from thy sepulchre, like an abominable branch, clothed, with the slain, that are thrust through with the sword, that go down to the stones of the pit; as a carcase trodden underfoot. Thou shalt not be joined with them in burial," etc.

† The text of these verses (19-21) is in some confusion. The above is a translation of the reading proposed by Cornill, who in the main follows the LXX.

‡ LXX. מעולם for מערלם = "of the uncircumcised."

* "Shields," a conjecture of Cornill, seems to be demanded by the parallelism.

† Jer. xliii 8-13; xliv. 12-14, 27-30; xlvi. 13-26.

‡ "Antt.," X. ix. 7.

§ *Zeitschrift für Aegyptische Sprache*, 1878, pp. 2 ff. and pp. 87 ff.

Nebuchadnezzar. The first was an Egyptian inscription of the reign of Hophra. It was written by an official of the highest rank, named "Nes-hor," to whom was entrusted the responsible task of defending Egypt on its southern or Ethiopian frontier. According to Wiedemann's translation, it relates among other things an irruption of Asiatic bands (Syrians, people of the north, Asiatics), which penetrated as far as the first cataract, and did some damage to the temple of Chnum in Elephantine. There they were checked by Nes-hor, and afterwards they were crushed or repelled by Hophra himself. Now the most natural explanation of this incident, in connection with the circumstances of the time, would seem to be that Nebuchadnezzar, finding himself fully occupied for the present with the siege of Tyre, incited roving bands of Arabs and Syrians to plunder Egypt, and that they succeeded so far as to penetrate to the extreme south of the country. But a more recent examination of the text, by Maspero and Brugsch,* reduces the incident to much smaller dimensions. They find that it refers to a mutiny of Egyptian mercenaries (Syrians, Ionians, and Bedouins) stationed on the southern frontier. The governor, Nes-hor, congratulates himself on a successful stratagem by which he got the rebels into a position where they were cut down by the king's troops. In any case it is evident that it falls very far short of a confirmation of Ezekiel's prophecy. Not only is there no mention of Nebuchadnezzar or a regular Babylonian army, but the invaders or mutineers are actually said to have been annihilated by Hophra. It may be said, no doubt, that an Egyptian governor was likely to be silent about an event which cast discredit on his country's arms, and would be tempted to magnify some temporary success into a decisive victory. But still the inscription must be taken for what it is worth, and the story it tells is certainly not the story of a Chaldean supremacy in the valley of the Nile. The only thing that suggests a connection between the two is the general probability that a campaign against Egypt must have been contemplated by Nebuchadnezzar about that time.

The second and more important document is a cuneiform fragment of the annals of Nebuchadnezzar. It is unfortunately in a very mutilated condition, and all that the Assyriologists have made out is that in the thirty-seventh year of his reign Nebuchadnezzar fought a battle with the king of Egypt. As the words of the inscription are those of Nebuchadnezzar himself, we may presume that the battle ended in a victory for him, and a few disconnected words in the latter part are thought to refer to the tribute or booty which he acquired.† The thirty-seventh year of Nebuchadnezzar is the year 568 B. C., about two years after the date of Ezekiel's last utterance against Egypt. The Egyptian king at this time was Amasis, whose name (only the last syllable of which is legible) is supposed to be that mentioned in the inscription.‡ What the ulterior consequences of this victory were on Egyptian history, or how long the Babylonian domination lasted, we cannot at present say. These are questions on which we may reasonably look for further light from the researches of Assyriology. In the meantime it appears to be established beyond reasonable doubt that Nebuchadnezzar did attack Egypt, and the probable issue of his expedition was in accordance with Ezekiel's last prediction: "Behold, I give to Nebuchadnezzar, king of Babylon, the land of Egypt; and he shall spoil her spoil, and plunder her plunder, and it shall be the wages for his army" (xxix. 19). There can of course be no question of a fulfilment of the earlier prophecies in their literal terms. History knows nothing of a total captivity of the population of Egypt, or a blank of forty years in her annals when her land was untrodden by the foot of man or of beast. These are details belonging to the dramatic form in which the prophet clothed the spiritual lesson which it was necessary to impress on his countrymen—the inherent weakness of the Egyptian empire as a power based on material resources and rearing itself in opposition to the great ends of God's kingdom. And it may well have been that for the illustration of that truth the humiliation that Egypt endured at the hands of Nebuchadnezzar was as effective as her total destruction would have been.

* *Zeitschrift für Aegyptische Sprache*, 1884, pp. 87 ff., 93 ff.

† See Schrader, "Keilinschriftliche Bibliothek," III. ii., pp. 140 f.

‡ The hypothesis of a joint reign of Hophra and Amasis from 570 to 564 (Wiedemann) may or may not be necessary to establish a connection between the Babylonian inscription and that of Nes-hor; it is certain that Amasis began to reign in 570, and that Hophra is *not* the Pharaoh mentioned by Nebuchadnezzar.

PART IV.

THE FORMATION OF THE NEW ISRAEL.

CHAPTER XIX.

THE PROPHET A WATCHMAN.

EZEKIEL xxxiii.

ONE day in January of the year 586 the tidings circulated through the Jewish colony at Tel-abib that "the city was smitten." The rapidity with which in the East intelligence is transmitted through secret channels has often excited the surprise of European observers. In this case there is no extraordinary rapidity to note, for the fate of Jerusalem had been decided nearly six months before it was known in Babylon.* But it is remarkable that the first intimation of the issue of the siege was brought to the exiles by one of their own countrymen, who had escaped at the capture of the city. It is probable that the messenger did not set out at once, but waited until he could bring some information as to how matters were settling down after the war. Or he may have been a captive who had trudged the weary road to Babylon in chains under the escort of Nebuzaradan, captain of the guard,†

* Jerusalem was taken in the fourth month of the eleventh year of Zedekiah or of Ezekiel's captivity. The announcement reached Ezekiel, according to the reading of the Hebrew text, in the tenth month of the twelfth year (ch. xxxiii. 21)—that is, about eighteen months after the event. It is hardly credible that the transmission of the news should have been delayed so long as this; and therefore the reading "eleventh year," found in some manuscripts and in the Syriac Version, is now generally regarded as correct.

† Jer. xxxix. 9.

and afterwards succeeded in making his escape to the older settlement where Ezekiel lived. All we know is that his message was not delivered with the despatch which would have been possible if his journey had been unimpeded, and that in the meantime the official intelligence which must have already reached Babylon had not transpired among the exiles who were waiting so anxiously for tidings of the fate of Jerusalem.*

The immediate effect of the announcement on the mind of the exiles is not recorded. It was doubtless received with all the signs of public mourning which Ezekiel had anticipated and foretold.† They would require some time to adjust themselves to a situation for which, in spite of all the warnings that had been sent them, they were utterly unprepared; and it must have been uncertain at first what direction their thoughts would take. Would they carry out their half-formed intention of abandoning their national faith and assimilating themselves to the surrounding heathenism? Would they sink into the lethargy of despair, and pine away under a confused consciousness of guilt? Or would they repent of their unbelief, and turn to embrace the hope which God's mercy held out to them in the teaching of the prophet whom they had despised? All this was for the moment uncertain; but one thing was certain—they could no more return to the attitude of complacent indifference and incredulity in which they had hitherto resisted the word of Jehovah. The day on which the tidings of the city's destruction fell like a thunderbolt in the community of Tel-abib was the turning-point of Ezekiel's ministry. In the arrival of the "fugitive" he recognises the sign which was to break the spell of silence which had lain so long upon him, and set him free for the ministry of consolation and upbuilding which was henceforth to be his chief vocation. A presentiment of what was coming had visited him the evening before his interview with the messenger, and from that time "his mouth was opened, and he was no more dumb" (ver. 22). Hitherto he had preached to deaf ears, and the echo of his ineffectual appeals had come back in a deadening sense of failure which had paralysed his activity. But now in one moment the veil of prejudice and vain self-confidence is torn from the heart of his hearers, and gradually but surely the whole burden of his message must disclose itself to their intelligence. The time has come to work for the formation of a new Israel, and a new spirit of hopefulness stimulates the prophet to throw himself eagerly into the career which is thus opened up before him.

It may be well at this point to try to realise the state of mind which emerged amongst Ezekiel's hearers after the first shock of consternation had passed away. The seven chapters (xxxiii.-xxxix.) with which we are to be occupied in this section all belong to the second period of the prophet's work, and in all probability to the earlier part of that period. It is obvious, however, that they were not written under the first impulse of the tidings of the fall of Jerusalem. They contain allusions to certain changes which must have occupied some time; and simultaneously a change took place in the temper of the people resulting ultimately in a definite spiritual situation to which the prophet had to address himself. It is this situation which we have to try to understand. It supplies the external conditions of Ezekiel's ministry, and unless we can in some measure interpret it we shall lose the full meaning of his teaching in this important period of his ministry.

At the outset we may glance at the state of those who were left in the land of Israel, who in a sense formed part of Ezekiel's audience. The very first oracle uttered by him after he had received his emancipation was a threat of judgment against these survivors of the nation's calamity (vv. 23-29). The fact that this is recorded in connection with the interview with the "fugitive" may mean that the information on which it is based was obtained from that somewhat shadowy personage. Whether in this way or through some later channel, Ezekiel had apparently some knowledge of the disastrous feuds which had followed the destruction of Jerusalem. These events are minutely described in the end of the book of Jeremiah (chaps. xl.-xliv.). With a clemency which in the circumstances is surprising the king of Babylon had allowed a small remnant of the people to settle in the land, and had appointed over them a native governor, Gedaliah, the son of Ahikam, who fixed his residence at Mizpah. The prophet Jeremiah elected to throw in his lot with this remnant, and for a time it seemed as if through peaceful submission to the Chaldæan supremacy all might go well with the survivors. The chiefs who had conducted the guerilla warfare in the open against the Babylonian army came in and placed themselves under the protection of Gedaliah, and there was every prospect that by refraining from projects of rebellion they might be left to enjoy the fruits of the land without disturbance. But this was not to be. Certain turbulent spirits under Ishmael, a member of the royal family, entered into a conspiracy with the king of Ammon to destroy this last refuge of peace-loving Israelites. Gedaliah was treacherously murdered; and although the murder was partially avenged, Ishmael succeeded in making his escape to the Ammonites, while the remains of the party of order, dreading the vengeance of Nebuchadnezzar, took their departure for Egypt and carried Jeremiah forcibly with them. What happened after this we do not know; but it is not improbable that Ishmael and his followers may have held possession of the land by force for some years. We read of a fresh deportation of Judæan captives to Babylon five years after the capture of Jerusalem (Jer. lii. 30); and this may have been the result of an expedition to suppress the depredations of the robber band that Ishmael had gathered round him. How much of this story had reached the ears of Ezekiel we do not know; but there is one allusion in his oracle which makes it probable that he had at least heard of the assassination of Gedaliah. Those he addresses are men who "stand upon their sword"—that is to say, they hold that might is right, and glory in deeds of blood and violence that gratify their passionate desire for revenge. Such language could hardly be used of any section of the remaining population of Judæa except the lawless banditti that enrolled themselves under the banner of Ishmael, the son of Nethaniah.

* It is possible, however, that the word *happālīt*, "the fugitive," may be used in a collective sense, of the whole body of captives carried away after the destruction of the city.

† Ch. xxiv. 21-24.

What Ezekiel is mainly concerned with, however, is the moral and religious condition of those to whom he speaks. Strange to say, they were animated by a species of religious fanaticism, which led them to regard themselves as the legitimate heirs to whom the reversion of the land of Israel belonged. "Abraham was one," so reasoned these desperadoes, "and yet he inherited the land: but we are many; to us the land is given for a possession" (ver. 24). Their meaning is that the smallness of their number is no argument against the validity of their claim to the heritage of the land. They are still many in comparison with the solitary patriarch to whom it was first promised; and if he was multiplied so as to take possession of it, why should they hesitate to claim the mastery of it? This thought of the wonderful multiplication of Abraham's seed after he had received the promise seems to have laid fast hold of the men of that generation. It is applied by the great teacher who stands next to Ezekiel in the prophetic succession to comfort the little flock who followed after righteousness and could hardly believe that it was God's good pleasure to give them the kingdom. "Look unto Abraham your father, and unto Sarah that bare you: for I called him alone, and blessed him, and increased him" (Isa. li. 2). The words of the infatuated men who exulted in the havoc they were making on the mountains of Judæa may sound to us like a blasphemous travesty of this argument; but they were no doubt seriously meant. They afford one more instance of the boundless capacity of the Jewish race for religious self-delusion, and their no less remarkable insensibility to that in which the essence of religion lay. The men who uttered this proud boast were the precursors of those who in the days of the Baptist thought to say within themselves, "We have Abraham to our father," not understanding that God was able "of these stones to raise up children to Abraham" (Matt. iii. 9). All the while they were perpetuating the evils for which the judgment of God had descended on the city and the Hebrew state. Idolatry, ceremonial impurity, bloodshed, and adultery were rife amongst them (vv. 25, 26); and no misgiving seems to have entered their minds that because of these things the wrath of God comes on the children of disobedience. And therefore the prophet repudiates their pretensions with indignation. "Shall ye possess the land?" Their conduct simply showed that judgment had not had its perfect work, and that Jehovah's purpose would not be accomplished until "the land was laid waste and desolate, and the pomp of her strength should cease, and the mountains of Israel be desolate, so that none passed through" (ver. 28). We have seen that in all likelihood this prediction was fulfilled by a punitive expedition from Babylonia in the twenty-third year of Nebuchadnezzar.

But we knew before that Ezekiel expected no good thing to come of the survivors of the judgment in Judæa. His hope was in those who had passed through the fires of banishment, the men amongst whom his own work lay, and amongst whom he looked for the first signs of the outpouring of the divine Spirit. We must now return to the inner circle of Ezekiel's immediate hearers, and consider the change which the calamity had produced on them. The chapter now before us yields two glimpses into the inner life of the people which help us to realise the kind of men with whom the prophet had to do.

In the first place it is interesting to learn that in his more frequent public appearances the prophet rapidly acquired a considerable reputation as a popular preacher (vv. 30-33). It is true that the interest which he excited was not of the most wholesome kind. It became a favourite amusement of the people hanging about the walls and doors to come and listen to the fervid oratory of their one remaining prophet as he declared to them "the word that came forth from Jehovah." It is to be feared that the substance of his message counted for little in their appreciative and critical listening. He was to them "as a very lovely song of one that hath a pleasant voice, and can play well on an instrument": "they heard his words, but did them not." It was pleasant to subject oneself now and then to the influence of this powerful and heart-searching preacher; but somehow the heart was never searched, the conscience was never stirred, and the hearing never ripened into serious conviction and settled purpose of amendment. The people were thoroughly respectful in their demeanour and apparently devout, coming in crowds and sitting before him as God's people should. But they were preoccupied: "their heart went after their gain" (ver. 31) or their advantage. Self-interest prevented them from receiving the word of God in honest and good hearts, and no change was visible in their conduct. Hence the prophet is not disposed to regard the evidences of his newly acquired popularity with much satisfaction. It presents itself to his mind as a danger against which he has to be on his guard. He has been tried by opposition and apparent failure; now he is exposed to the more insidious temptation of a flattering reception and superficial success. It is a tribute to his power, and an opportunity such as he had never before enjoyed. Whatever may have been the case heretofore, he is now sure of an audience, and his position has suddenly become one of great influence in the community. But the same resolute confidence in the truth of his message which sustained Ezekiel amidst the discouragements of his earlier career saves him now from the fatal attractions of popularity to which many men in similar circumstances have yielded. He is not deceived by the favourable disposition of the people towards himself, nor is he tempted to cultivate his oratorical gifts with a view to sustaining their admiration. His one concern is to utter the word that shall come to pass, and so to declare the counsel of God that men shall be compelled in the end to acknowledge that he has been "a prophet among them" (ver. 33). We may be thankful to the prophet for this little glimpse from a vanished past—one of those touches of nature that make the whole world kin. But we ought not to miss its obvious moral. Ezekiel is the prototype of all popular preachers, and he knew their peculiar trials. He was perhaps the first man who ministered regularly to an attached congregation, who came to hear him because they liked it and because they had nothing better to do. If he passed unscathed through the dangers of the position, it was through his overpowering sense of the reality of divine things and the importance of men's spiritual destiny; and also we may add through his fidelity in a department of ministerial duty which popular preachers are sometimes apt to neglect—the duty of close personal dealing with individual men about their sins and their state before God. To this subject we shall revert by-and-by.

This passage reveals to us the people in their lighter moods, when they are able to cast off the awful burden of life and destiny and take advantage of such sources of enjoyment as their circumstances afforded. Mental dejection in a community, from whatever cause it originates, is rarely continuous. The natural elasticity of the mind asserts itself in the most depressing circumstances; and the tension of almost unendurable sorrow is relieved by outbursts of unnatural gaiety. Hence we need not be surprised to find that beneath the surface levity of these exiles there lurked the feeling of despair expressed in the words of ver. 10 and more fully in those of xxxvii. 11: "Our transgressions and our sins are upon us, and we waste away in them: how should we then live?" "Our bones are dried, and our hope is lost: we are cut off." These accents of despondency reflect the new mood into which the more serious-minded portion of the community had been plunged by the calamities that had befallen them. The bitterness of unavailing remorse, the consciousness of national death, had laid fast hold of their spirits and deprived them of the power of hope. In sober truth the nation was dead beyond apparent hope of revival; and to an Israelite, whose spiritual interests were all identified with those of his nation, religion had no power of consolation apart from a national future. The people therefore abandoned themselves to despair, and hardened themselves against the appeals which the prophet addressed to them in the name of Jehovah. They looked on themselves as the victims of an inexorable fate, and were disposed perhaps to resent the call to repentance as a trifling with the misery of the unfortunate.

And yet, although this state of mind was as far removed as possible from the godly sorrow that worketh repentance, it was a step towards the accomplishment of the promise of redemption. For the present, indeed, it rendered the people more impenetrable than ever to the word of God. But it meant that they had accepted in principle the prophetic interpretation of their history. It was no longer possible to deny that Jehovah the God of Israel had revealed His secret to His servants the prophets. He was not such a Being as the popular imagination had figured. Israel had not known Him; only the prophets had spoken of Him the thing that was right. Thus for the first time a general conviction of sin, a sense of being in the wrong, was produced in Israel. That this conviction should at first lead to the verge of despair was perhaps inevitable. The people were not familiar with the idea of the divine righteousness, and could not at once perceive that anger against sin was consistent in God with pity for the sinner and mercy towards the contrite. The chief task that now lay before the prophet was to transform their attitude of sullen impenitence into one of submission and hope by teaching them the efficacy of repentance. They have learned the meaning of judgment; they have now to learn the possibility and the conditions of forgiveness. And this can only be taught to them through a revelation of the free and infinite grace of God, who has "no pleasure in the death of the wicked, but that the wicked should turn from his way and live" (ver. 11). Only thus can the hard and stony heart be taken away from their flesh and a heart of flesh given to them.

We can now understand the significance of the striking passage which stands as the introduction to this whole section of the book (xxxiii. 1-20). At this juncture of his ministry Ezekiel's thoughts went back on an aspect of his prophetic vocation which had hitherto been in abeyance. From the first he had been conscious of a certain responsibility for the fate of each individual within reach of his words (iii. 16-21). This truth had been one of the keynotes of his ministry; but the practical developments which it suggested had been hindered by the solidarity of the opposition which he had encountered. As long as Jerusalem stood the exiles had been swayed by one common current of feeling—their thoughts were wholly occupied by the expectation of an issue that would annul the gloomy predictions of Ezekiel; and no man dared to break away from the general sentiment and range himself on the side of God's prophet. In these circumstances anything of the nature of pastoral activity was obviously out of the question. But now that this great obstacle to faith was removed there was a prospect that the solidity of popular opinion would be broken up, so that the word of God might find an entrance here and there into susceptible hearts. The time was come to call for personal decisions, to appeal to each man to embrace for himself the offer of pardon and salvation. Its watchword might have been found in words uttered in another great crisis of religious destiny: "The kingdom of heaven suffereth violence, and the violent take it by force." Out of such "violent men," who act for themselves and have the courage of their convictions, the new people of God must be formed; and the mission of the prophet is to gather round him all those who are warned by his words to "flee from the wrath to come."

Let us look a little more closely at the teaching of these verses. We find that Ezekiel restates in the most emphatic manner the theological principles which underlie this new development of his prophetic duties (vv. 10-20). These principles have been considered already in the exposition of chap. xviii.; and it is not necessary to do more than refer to them here. They are such as these: the exact and absolute righteousness of God in His dealings with individuals; His unwillingness that any should perish, and His desire that all should be saved and live; the necessity of personal repentance; the freedom and independence of the individual soul through its immediate relation to God. On this closely connected body of evangelical doctrine Ezekiel bases the appeal which he now makes to his hearers. What we are specially concerned with here, however, is the direction which they imparted to his activity. We may study in the light of Ezekiel's example the manner in which these fundamental truths of personal religion are to be made effective in the ministry of the gospel for the building up of the Church of Christ.

The general conception is clearly set forth in the figure of the watchman, with which the chapter opens (vv. 1-9). The duties of the watchman are simple, but responsible. He is set apart in a time of public danger to warn the city of the approach of an enemy. The citizens trust him and go about their ordinary occupations in security so long as the trumpet is not sounded. Should he sleep at his post or neglect to give the signal, men are caught unprepared and lives are lost through his fault. Their blood is required at the watchman's hand. If, on the other hand, he gives the alarm as soon as he sees the sword coming, and any man disregards the warning and is cut down in his iniquity, his blood is upon his own head. Nothing could be clearer than this. Office always involves responsibility, and no responsibility could be greater than that of a watchman in time of invasion. Those who suffer are in either case the citizens whom the sword cuts off; but it makes all the difference in the world whether the blame of their death rests on themselves for their foolhardiness or on the watchman for his unfaithfulness. Such, then, as Ezekiel goes on to explain, is his own position as a prophet. The prophet is one who sees further into the spiritual issues of things than other men, and discovers the coming calamity which is to them invisible. We must notice that a background of danger is presupposed. In what form it was to come is not indicated; but Ezekiel knows that judgment follows hard at the heels of sin, and seeing sin in his fellow-men he knows that their state is one of spiritual peril. The prophet's course therefore is clear. His business is to announce as in trumpet tones the doom that hangs over every man who persists in his wickedness, to re-echo the divine sentence which he alone may have heard, "O wicked man, thou shalt surely die." And again the main question is one of responsibility. The watchman cannot ensure the safety of every citizen, because any man may refuse to take the warning he gives. No more can the prophet ensure the salvation of all his hearers, for each one is free to accept or despise the message. But whether men hear or whether they forbear, it is of the utmost moment for himself that that warning be faithfully proclaimed and that he should thus "deliver his soul." Ezekiel seems to feel that it is only by frankly accepting the responsibility which thus devolves on himself that he can hope to impress on his hearers the responsibility that rests on them for the use they make of his message.

These thoughts appear to have occupied the mind of Ezekiel on the eve of his emancipation, and must have influenced his subsequent action to an extent which we can but vaguely estimate. It is generally considered that this description of the prophet's functions covers a whole department of work of which no express account is given. Ezekiel writes no "Pastor's Sketches," and records no instances of individual conversion through his ministry. The unwritten history of the Babylonian captivity must have been rich in such instances of spiritual experience, and nothing could have been more instructive to us than the study of a few typical cases had it been possible. One of the most interesting features of the early history of Mohammedanism is found in the narratives of personal adhesion to the new religion; and the formation of the new Israel in the age of the Exile is a process of infinitely greater importance for humanity at large than the genesis of Islam. But neither in this book nor elsewhere are we permitted to follow that process in its details. Ezekiel may have witnessed the beginnings of it, but he was not called upon to be its historian. Still, the inference is probably correct that a conception of the prophet's office which holds him accountable to God for the fate of individuals led to something more than mere general exhortations to repentance. The preacher must have taken a personal interest in his hearers; he must have watched for the first signs of a response to his message, and been ready to advise and encourage those who turned to him for guidance in their perplexities. And since the sphere of his influence and responsibility included the whole Hebrew community in which he lived, he must have been eager to seize every opportunity to warn individual sinners of the error of their ways, lest their blood should be required at his hand. To this extent we may say that Ezekiel held a position amongst the exiles somewhat analogous to that of a spiritual director in the Catholic Church or the pastor of a Protestant congregation. But the analogy must not be pressed too far. The nurture of the spiritual life of individuals could not have presented itself to him as the chief end of his ministrations. His business was first to lay down the conditions of entrance into the new kingdom of God, and then out of the ruins of the old Israel to make ready a people prepared for the Lord. Perhaps the nearest parallel to this department of his work which history affords is the mission of the Baptist. The keynote of Ezekiel's preaching was the same as that of John: "Repent, for the kingdom of heaven is at hand." Both prophets were alike animated by a sense of crisis and urgency, based on the conviction that the impending Messianic age would be ushered in by a searching judgment in which the chaff would be separated from the wheat. Both laboured for the same end—the formation of a new circle of religious fellowship, in anticipation of the advent of the Messianic kingdom. And as John, by an inevitable spiritual selection, gathered round him a band of disciples, amongst whom our Lord found some of His most devoted followers, so we may believe that Ezekiel, by a similar process, became the acknowledged leader of those whom he taught to wait for the hope of Israel's restoration.

There is nothing in Ezekiel's ministry that appeals more directly to the Christian conscience than the serious and profound sense of pastoral responsibility to which this passage bears witness. It is a feeling which would seem to be inseparable from the right discharge of the ministerial office. In this, as in many other respects, Ezekiel's experience is repeated, on a higher level, in that of the apostle of the Gentiles, who could take his hearers to record that he was "pure from the blood of all men," inasmuch as he had "taught them publicly and from house to house," and "ceased not to warn every one night and day with tears" (Acts xx. 17-35). That does not mean, of course, that a preacher is to occupy himself with nothing else than the personal salvation of his hearers. St. Paul would have been the last to agree to such a limitation of the range of his teaching. But it does mean that the salvation of men and women is the supreme end which the minister of Christ is to set before him, and that to which all other instruction is subordinated. And unless a man realises that the truth he utters is of tremendous importance on the destiny of those to whom he speaks, he can hardly hope to approve himself as an ambassador for Christ. There are doubtless temptations, not in themselves ignoble, to use the pulpit for other purposes than this. The desire for public influence may be one of them, or the desire to utter one's mind on burning questions of the day. To say that these are temptations is not to say that matters of public interest are to be rigorously excluded from treatment in the pulpit. There are many questions of this kind on which the will of God is as clear and imperative as it can possibly be on any point of private conduct; and even in matters as to which there is legitimate difference of opinion amongst Christian men there are underlying principles of righteousness which may need to be fearlessly enunciated at the risk of obloquy and misunderstanding. Nevertheless it remains true that the great end of the gospel ministry is to reconcile men to God and to cultivate in individual lives the fruits of the Spirit, so as at the last to present every man perfect in Christ. And the preacher who may be most safely entrusted with the handling of all other questions is he who is most intent on the formation of Christian character and most deeply conscious of his responsibility for the effect of his teaching on the eternal destiny of those to whom he ministers. What is called preaching to the age may certainly become a very poor and empty thing if it is forgotten that the age is made up of individuals each of whom has a soul to save or lose. What shall it profit a man if the preacher teaches him how to win the whole world and lose his own life? It is fashionable to hold up the prophets of Israel as models of all that a Christian minister ought to be. If that is true, prophecy must at least be allowed to speak its whole lesson; and amongst other elements Ezekiel's consciousness of responsibility for the individual life must receive due recognition.

CHAPTER XX.

THE MESSIANIC KINGDOM

EZEKIEL xxxiv.

THE term "Messianic" as commonly applied to Old Testament prophecy bears two different senses, a wider and a narrower. In its wider use it is almost equivalent to the modern word "eschatological." It denotes that unquenchable hope of a glorious future for Israel and the world which is an all but omnipresent feature of the prophetic writings, and includes all predictions of the kingdom of God in its final and perfect manifestation. In its stricter sense it is applied only to the promise of the ideal king of the house of David, which, although a very conspicuous element of prophecy, is by no means universal, and perhaps does not bulk quite so largely in the Old Testament as is generally supposed. The later Jews were guided by a true instinct when they seized on this figure of the ideal ruler as the centre of the nation's hope; and to them we owe this special application of the name "Messiah," the "Anointed," which is never used of the Son of David in the Old Testament itself. To a certain extent we follow in their steps when we enlarge the meaning of the word "Messianic" so as to embrace the whole prophetic delineation of the future glories of the kingdom of God.

This distinction may be illustrated from the prophecies of Ezekiel. If we take the word in its more general sense we may say that all the chapters from the thirty-fourth to the end of the book are Messianic in character. That is to say, they describe under various aspects the final condition of things which is introduced by the restoration of Israel to its own land. Let us glance for a moment at the elements which enter into this general conception of the last things as they are set forth in the section of the book with which we are now dealing. We exclude from view for the present the last nine chapters, because there the prophet's point of view is somewhat different, and it is better to reserve them for separate treatment.

The chapters from the thirty-fourth to the thirty-seventh are the necessary complement of the call to repentance in the first part of chap. xxxiii. Ezekiel has enunciated the conditions of entrance to the new kingdom of God, and has urged his hearers to prepare for its appearing. He now proceeds to unfold the nature of that kingdom, and the process by which Jehovah is to bring it to pass. As has been said, the central fact is the restoration of Israel to the land of Canaan. Here the prophet found a point of contact with the natural aspirations of his fellow-exiles. There was no prospect to which they had clung with more eager longing than that of a return to national independence in their own land; and the feeling that this was no longer possible was the source of the abject despair from which the prophet sought to rouse them. How was this to be done? Not simply by asserting in the face of all human probability that the restoration would take place, but by presenting it to their minds in its religious aspects as an object worthy of the exercise of almighty power, and an object in which Jehovah was interested for the glory of His great name. Only by being brought round to Ezekiel's faith in God could the exiles recover their lost hope in the future of the nation. Thus the return to which Ezekiel looks forward has a Messianic significance; it is the establishment of the kingdom of God, a symbol of the final and perfect union betwen Jehovah and Israel.

Now in the chapters before us this general conception is exhibited in three separate pictures of the Restoration, the leading ideas being the Monarchy (chap. xxxiv.), the Land (chap. xxxv., xxxvi.), and the Nation (chap. xxxvii.). The order in which they are arranged is not that which might seem most natural. We should have expected the prophet to deal first with the revival of the nation, then with its settlement on the soil of Palestine, and last of all with its political organisation under a Davidic king. Ezekiel follows the reverse order. He begins with the kingdom, as the most complete embodiment of the Messianic salvation, and then falls back on its two presuppositions—the recovery and purification of the land on the one hand, and the restitution of the nation on the other. It is doubtful, indeed, whether any logical connection between the three pictures is intended. It is perhaps better to regard them as expressing three distinct and collateral aspects of the idea of redemption, to each of which a certain permanent religious significance is attached. They are at all events the outstanding elements of Ezekiel's eschatology so far as it is expounded in this section of his prophecies.

We thus see that the promise of the perfect king—the Messianic idea in its more restricted signification—holds a distinct but not a supreme place in Ezekiel's vision of the future. It appears for the first time in chap. xvii. at the end of an oracle denouncing the perfidy of Zedekiah and foretelling the overthrow of his kingdom; and again, in a similar connection, in an obscure verse of chap. xxi.* Both these prophecies belong to the time before the fall of the state, when the prophet's thoughts were not continuously occupied with the hope of the future. The former is remarkable, nevertheless, for the glowing terms in which the greatness of the future kingdom is depicted. From the top of the lofty cedar which the great eagle had carried away to Babylon Jehovah will take a tender shoot and plant it in the mountain height of Israel. There it will strike root and grow up into a lordly cedar, under whose branches all the birds of the air find refuge. The terms of the allegory have been explained in the proper place.† The great cedar is the house of David; the topmost bough which was taken to Babylon is the family of Jehoiachin, the direct heirs to the throne. The planting of the tender shoot in the land of Israel represents the founding of the Messiah's kingdom, which is thus proclaimed to be of transcendent earthly magnificence, overshadowing all the other kingdoms of the world, and convincing the nations that its foundation is the work of Jehovah Himself. In this short passage we have the Messianic idea in its simplest and most characteristic expression. The hope of the future is bound up with the destiny of the house of David; and the re-establishment of the kingdom in more than its ancient splendour is the great divine act to which all the blessings of the final dispensation are attached.

But it is in the thirty-fourth chapter that we find the most comprehensive exposition of Ezekiel's teaching on the subject of the monarchy and the Messianic kingdom. It is perhaps the most political of all his prophecies. It is pervaded by a spirit of genuine sympathy with the sufferings of the common people, and indignation against the tyranny practised and tolerated by the ruling classes. The disasters that have befallen the nation down to its final dispersion among the heathen are all traced to the misgovernment and anarchy for which the monarchy was primarily responsible. In like manner the blessings of the coming age are summed up in the promise of a perfect king, ruling in the name of Jehovah and maintaining order and righteousness throughout his realm. Nowhere else does Ezekiel approach so nearly to the political ideal foreshadowed by the statesman-prophet Isaiah of a "king reigning in righteousness and princes ruling in judgment" (Isa. xxxii. 1) securing the enjoyment of universal prosperity and peace to the redeemed people of God. It must be remembered of course that this is only a partial expression of Ezekiel's conception both of the past condition of the nation and of its future salvation. We have had abundant evidence‡ to show that he considered all classes of the community to be corrupt, and the people as a whole implicated in the guilt of rebellion against Jehovah. The statement that the kings have brought about the dispersion of the nation must not therefore be pressed to the conclusion that civic injustice was the sole cause of Israel's calamities. Similarly we shall find that the redemption of the people depends on other and more fundamental conditions than the establishment of good government under a righteous king. But that is no reason for minimising the significance of the passage before us as an utterance of Ezekiel's profound interest in social order and the welfare of the poor. It shows moreover that the prophet at this time attached real importance to the promise of the Messiah as the organ of Jehovah's rule over His people. If civil wrongs and legalised tyranny were not the only sins which had brought about the destruction of the state, they were at least serious evils, which could not be tolerated in the new Israel; and the chief safeguard against their recurrence is found in the character of the ideal ruler whom Jehovah will raise up from the seed of David. How far this high conception of the functions of the monarchy was modified in Ezekiel's subsequent teaching we shall see when we come to consider the position assigned to the prince in the great vision at the end of the book.*

In the meantime let us examine somewhat more closely the contents of chap. xxxiv. Its leading ideas seem to have been suggested by a Messianic prophecy of Jeremiah's with which Ezekiel was no doubt acquainted: "Woe to the shepherds that destroy and scatter the flock of My pasture! saith Jehovah. Therefore thus saith Jehovah, the God of Israel, against the shepherds that tend My people, Ye have scattered My flock, and dispersed them, and have not visited them: behold, I will visit upon you the evil of your doings, saith Jehovah. And I will gather the remnant of My flock from all the lands whither I have dispersed them, and will restore them to their folds; and they shall be fruitful and multiply. And I will set shepherds over them who shall feed them: and they shall not fear any more, nor be frightened, nor be lacking, saith Jehovah" (Jer. xxiii. 1-4). Here we have the simple image of the flock and its shepherds, which Ezekiel, as his manner is, expands into an allegory of the past history and future prospects of the nation. How closely he follows the guidance of his predecessor will be seen from the analysis of the chapter. It may be divided into four parts.

I. The first ten verses are a strongly worded denunciation of the misgovernment to which the people of Jehovah had been subjected in the past. The prophet goes straight to the root of the evil when he indignantly asks, "Should not the shepherds feed the flock?" (ver. 2). The first principle of all true government is that it must be in the interest of the governed. But the universal vice of Oriental despotism, as we see in the case of the Turkish empire at the present day, or Egypt before the English occupation, is that the rulers rule for their own advantage, and treat the people as their lawful spoil. So it had been in Israel: the shepherds had fed themselves, and not the flock. Instead of carefully tending the sick and the maimed, and searching out the strayed and the lost, they had been concerned only to eat the milk† and

* Chs. xvii. 22–24, xxi. 26, 27. † See xx. 245 ff.
‡ *Cf.* especially ch. xxii.

* See below, pp. 318 f., and ch. xxviii.
† Pointing the Hebrew text in accordance with the rendering of the LXX.

clothe themselves with the wool and slaughter the fat; they had ruled with "violence and rigour." That is to say, instead of healing the sores of the body politic, they had sought to enrich themselves at the expense of the people. Such misconduct in the name of government always brings its own penalty; it kills the goose that lays the golden eggs. The flock which is spoiled by its own shepherds is scattered on the mountain and becomes the prey of wild beasts; and so the nation that is weakened by internal misrule loses its powers of defence and succumbs to the attacks of some foreign invader. But the shepherds of Israel have to reckon with Him who is the owner of the flock, whose affection still watches over them, and whose compassion is stirred by the hapless condition of His people. "Therefore, O ye shepherds, hear the word of Jehovah; . . . Behold, I am against the shepherds; and I will require My flock at their hand; and I will make them to cease from feeding [My] flock, that they who feed themselves may no longer shepherd them; and I will deliver My flock from their mouth, that they be not food for them" (vv. 9, 10).

II. But Jehovah not only removes the unworthy shepherds; He Himself takes on Him the office of shepherd to the flock that has been so mishandled (vv. 11-16). As the shepherd goes out after the thunderstorm to call in his frightened sheep, so will Jehovah after the storm of judgment is over go forth to "gather together the outcasts of Israel" (Psalm cxlvii. 2). He will seek them out and deliver them from all places whither they were scattered in the day of clouds and darkness; then He will lead them back to the mountain height of Israel, where they shall enjoy abundant prosperity and security under His just and beneficent rule. By what agencies this deliverance is to be accomplished is nowhere indicated. It is the unanimous teaching of the prophets that the final salvation of Israel will be effected in a "day of Jehovah"—*i. e.*, a day in which Jehovah's own power will be specially manifested. Hence there is no need to describe the process by which the Almighty works out His purpose of salvation; it is indescribable: the results are certain, but the intermediate agencies are supernatural, and the precise method of Jehovah's intervention is, as a rule, left indefinite. It is particularly to be noted that the Messiah plays no part in the actual work of deliverance. He is not the hero of a national struggle for independence, but comes on the scene and assumes the reins of government after Jehovah has gotten the victory and restored peace to Israel.*

III. The next six verses (17-22) add a feature to the allegory which is not found in the corresponding passage in Jeremiah. Jehovah will judge between one sheep and another, especially between the rams and he-goats on the one hand and the weaker animals on the other. The strong cattle had monopolised the fat meadows and clear settled waters, and as if this were not enough, they had trampled down the residue of the pastures and fouled the waters with their feet. Those addressed are the wealthy and powerful upper class, whose luxury and wanton extravagance had consumed the resources of the country, and left no sustenance for the poorer members of the community. Allusions to this kind of selfish tyranny are frequent in the older prophets. Amos speaks of the nobles as panting after the dust on the head of the poor, and of the luxurious dames of Samaria as oppressing the poor and crushing the needy, and saying to their lords, "Bring us to drink" (Amos ii. 7, iv. 1). Micah says of the same class in the southern kingdom that they cast out the women of Jehovah's people from their pleasant houses, and robbed their children of His glory for ever (Micah ii. 9). And Isaiah, to take one other example, denounces those who "take away the right from the poor of My people, that widows may be their prey, and that they may rob the orphans" (Isa. x. 2). Under the corrupt administration of justice which the kings had tolerated for their own convenience litigation had been a farce; the rich man had always the ear of the judge, and the poor found no redress. But in Israel the true fountain of justice could not be polluted; it was only its channels that were obstructed. For Jehovah Himself was the supreme judge of His people; and in the restored commonwealth to which Ezekiel looks forward all civil relations will be regulated by a regard to His righteous will. He will "save His flock that they be no more a prey, and will judge between cattle and cattle."

IV. Then follows in the last section (vv. 23-31) the promise of the Messianic king, and a description of the blessings that accompany his reign: "I will set up one shepherd over them, and he shall feed them—My servant David: he shall feed them, and he shall be their shepherd. And I Jehovah will be their God, and My servant David shall be a prince in their midst: I Jehovah have spoken it." There are one or two difficulties connected with the interpretation of this passage, the consideration of which may be postponed till we have finished our analysis of the chapter. It is sufficient in the meantime to notice that a Davidic kingdom in some sense is to be the foundation of social order in the new Israel. A prince will arise, endowed with the spirit of his exalted office, to discharge perfectly the royal functions in which the former kings had so lamentably failed. Through him the divine government of Israel will become a reality in the national life. The Godhead of Jehovah and the kingship of the Messiah will be inseparably associated in the faith of the people: "Jehovah their God, and David their king" (Hosea iii. 5) is the expression of the ground of Israel's confidence in the latter days. And this kingdom is the pledge of the fulness of divine blessing descending on the land and the people. The people shall dwell in safety, none making them afraid, because of the covenant of peace which Jehovah will make for them, securing them against the assaults of other nations.* The heavens shall pour forth fertilising "showers of blessing"; and the land shall be clothed with a luxuriant vegetation which shall

* This seems to me to be the clear meaning of Isaiah's prophecy of the Messiah in the beginning of the ninth chapter, although the contrary is often asserted. Micah v. 1-6 may, however, be an exception to the rule stated above.

* Ver. 25. The idea is based on Hosea ii. 18, where God promises to make a covenant for Israel "with the beasts of the field, and the birds of heaven, and the creeping things of the ground." This is to be understood quite literally: it means immunity from the ravages of wild beasts and other noxious creatures. Ezekiel's promise, however, is probably to be explained in accordance with the terms of the allegory: the "evil beasts" are the foreign nations from whom Israel had suffered so severely in the past.

be the admiration of the whole earth.* Thus happily situated Israel shall shake off the reproach of the heathen, which they had formerly to endure because of the poverty of their land and their unfortunate history. In the plenitude of material prosperity they shall recognise that Jehovah their God is with them, and they shall know what it is to be His people and the flock of His pasture.†

We have now before us the salient features of the Messianic hope, as it is presented in the pages of Ezekiel. We see that the idèa is developed in contrast with the abuses that had characterised the historic monarchy in Israel. It represents the ideal of the kingdom as it exists in the mind of Jehovah, an ideal which no actual king had fully realised, and which most of them had shamefully violated. The Messiah is the vicegerent of Jehovah on earth, and the representative of His kingly authority and righteous government over Israel. We see further that the promise is based on the "sure mercies of David," the covenant which secured the throne to David's descendants for ever. Messianic prophecy is legitimist, the ideal king being regarded as standing in the direct line of succession to the crown. And to these features we may add another which is explicitly developed in chap. xxxvii. 22-26, although it is implied in the expression "one shepherd" in the passage with which we have been dealing. The Messianic kingdom represents the unity of all Israel, and particularly the reunion of the two kingdoms under one sceptre. The prophets attach great importance to this idea.‡ The existence of two rival monarchies, divided in interest and often at war with each other, although it had never effaced the consciousness of the original unity of the nation, was felt by the prophets to be an anomalous state of things, and seriously detrimental to the national religion. The ideal relation of Jehovah to Israel was as incompatible with two kingdoms as the ideal of marriage is incompatible with two wives to one husband. Hence in the glorious future of the Messianic age the schism must be healed, and the Davidic dynasty restored to its original position at the head of an undivided empire. The prominence given to this thought in the teaching of Hosea shows that even in the northern kingdom devout Israelites cherished the hope of reunion with their brethren under the house of David as the only form in which the redemption of the nation could be achieved. And although, long before Ezekiel's day, the kingdom of Samaria had disappeared from history, he too looks forward to a restoration of the ten tribes as an essential element of the Messianic salvation.

In these respects the teaching of Ezekiel reflects the general tenor of the Messianic prophecy of the Old Testament. There are just two questions on which some obscurity and uncertainty must be felt to rest. In the first place, what is the precise meaning of the expression "My servant David"? It will not be supposed that the prophet expected David, the founder of the Hebrew monarchy, to reappear in person and inaugurate the new dispensation. Such an interpretation would be utterly false to Eastern modes of thought and expression, besides being opposed to every indication we have of the prophetic conception of the Messiah. Even in popular language the name of David was current, after he had been long dead, as the name of the dynasty which he had founded. When the ten tribes revolted from Rehoboam they said, exactly as they had said in David's lifetime, "What portion have we in David? neither have we inheritance in the son of Jesse: to your tents, O Israel; now see to thine own house, David."* If the name of David could thus be invoked in popular speech at a time of great political excitement, we need not be surprised to find it used in a similar sense in the figurative style of the prophets. All that the word means is that the Messiah will be one who comes in the spirit and power of David, a representative of the ancient family who carries to completion the work so nobly begun by his great ancestor.

The real difficulty is whether the title "David" denotes a unique individual or a line of Davidic kings. To that question it is hardly possible to return a decided answer. That the idea of a succession of sovereigns is a possible form of the Messianic hope is shown by a passage in the thirty-third chapter of Jeremiah. There the promise of the righteous sprout of the house of David is supplemented by the assurance that David shall never want a man to sit on the throne of Israel:† the allusion therefore appears to be to the dynasty, and not to a single person. And this view finds some support in the case of Ezekiel from the fact that in the later vision of chaps. xl.-xlviii. the prophet undoubtedly anticipates a perpetuation of the dynasty through successive generations.‡ On the other hand it is difficult to reconcile this view with the expressions used in this and the thirty-seventh chapters. When we read that "My servant David shall be their prince for ever,"§ we can scarcely escape the impression that the prophet is thinking of a personal Messiah reigning eternally. If it were necessary to decide between these two alternatives, it might be safest to adhere to the idea of a personal Messiah, as conveying the fullest rendering of the prophet's thought. There is reason to think that in the interval between this prophecy and his final vision Ezekiel's conception of the Messiah underwent a certain modification, and therefore the teaching of the later passage cannot be used to control the explanation of this. But the obscurity is of such a nature that we cannot hope to remove it. In the prophet's delineations of the future there are many points on which the light of revelation had not been fully cast; for they, like the Christian apostle, "knew in part and prophesied in part." And the question of the way in which the Messiah's office is to be prolonged is precisely one of those which did not greatly occupy the mind of the prophets. There is no perspective in Messianic

* This is the sense of the expression מטע לשם in ver. 29 (literally "a plantation for a name"). The LXX., however, read מטע שלם, which may be translated "a perfect vegetation." At all events the phrase is not a title of the Messiah.

† The word "men" in ver. 31 should be omitted, as in the LXX.

‡ *Cf.* Amos ix. 11 f.; Hosea ii. 2, iii. 5; Isa. xi. 13; Micah ii. 12 f., v. 3.

* 1 Kings xii. 16 (*cf.* 2 Sam. xx. 1). It should be mentioned, however, that the last clause in the LXX. is replaced by a more prosaic sentence: "for this man is not fit to be a ruler nor a prince."

† Jer. xxxiii. 15-17.

‡ *Cf.* ch. xliii. 7, xlv. 8, xlvi. 16 ff.

§ Ch. xxxvii. 25.

prophecy: the future kingdom of God is seen, as it were, in one plane, and how it is to be transmitted from one age to another is never thought of. Thus it may become difficult to say whether a particular prophet, in speaking of the Messiah, has a single individual in view or whether he is thinking of a dynasty or a succession. To Ezekiel the Messiah was a divinely revealed ideal, which was to be fulfilled in a person; whether the prophet himself distinctly understood this is a matter of inferior importance.

The second question is one that perhaps would not readily occur to a plain man. It relates to the meaning of the word "prince" as applied to the Messiah. It has been thought by some critics that Ezekiel had a special reason for avoiding the title "king"; and from this supposed reason a somewhat sweeping conclusion has been deduced. We are asked to believe that Ezekiel had in principle abandoned the Messianic hope of his earlier prophecies—*i. e.*, the hope of a restoration of the Davidic kingdom in its ancient splendour. What he really contemplates is the abolition of the Hebrew monarchy, and the institution of a new political system entirely different from anything that had existed in the past. Although the Davidic prince will hold the first place in the restored community, his dignity will be less than royal; he will only be a titular monarch, his power being overshadowed by the presence of Jehovah, the true king of Israel. Now so far as this view is suggested by the use of the word "prince" (literally "leader" or "president") in preference to "king," * it is sufficiently answered by pointing to the Messianic passage in chap. xxxvii., where the name "king" is used three times and in a peculiarly emphatic manner of the Messianic prince.† There is no reason to suppose that Ezekiel drew a distinction between "princely" and "kingly" rank, and deliberately withheld the higher dignity from the Messiah. Whatever may be the exact relation of the Messiah to Jehovah, there is no doubt that he is conceived as a king in the full sense of the term, possessed of all regal qualities, and shepherding his people with the authority which belonged to a true son of David.

But there is another consideration which weighs more seriously with the writers referred to. There is reason to believe that Ezekiel's conception of the final kingdom of God underwent a change which might not unfairly be described as an abandonment of the Messianic expectation in its more restricted sense. In his latest vision the functions of the prince are defined in such a way that his position is shorn of the ideal significance which properly invests the office of the Messiah. The change does not indeed affect his merely political status. He is still the son of David and the king of Israel, and all that is here said about his duty towards his subjects is there presupposed. But his character seems to be no longer regarded as thoroughly reliable, or equal to all the temptations that arise wherever absolute power is lodged in human hands. The possibility that the king may abuse his authority for his private advantage is distinctly contemplated, and provision is made against it in the statutory constitution to which the king himself is subject. Such precautions are obviously inconsistent with the ideal of the Messianic kingdom which we find, for example, in the prophecy of Isaiah. The important question therefore comes to be, whether this lower view of the monarchy is anticipated in the thirty-fourth and thirty-seventh chapters. This does not appear to be the case. The prophet still occupies the same standpoint as in chap. xvii., regarding the Davidic monarchy as the central religious institution of the restored state. The Messiah of these chapters is a perfect king, endowed with the spirit of God for the discharge of his great office, one whose personal character affords an absolute security for the maintenance of public righteousness, and who is the medium of communication between God and the nation. In other words, what we have to do with is a Messianic prediction in the fullest sense of the term.

In concluding our study of Ezekiel's Messianic teaching, we may make one remark bearing on its typological interpretation. The attempt is sometimes made to trace a gradual development and enrichment of the Messianic idea in the hands of successive prophets. From that point of view Ezekiel's contribution to the doctrine of the Messiah must be felt to be disappointing. No one can imagine that his portrait of the coming king possesses anything like the suggestiveness and religious meaning conveyed by the ideal which stands out so clearly from the pages of Isaiah. And, indeed, no subsequent prophet excels or even equals Isaiah in the clearness and profundity of his directly Messianic conceptions. This fact shows us that the endeavour to find in the Old Testament a regular progress along one particular line proceeds on too narrow a view of the scope of prophecy. The truth is that the figure of the king is only one of many types of the Christian dispensation which the religious institutions of Israel supplied to the prophets. It is the most perfect of all types, partly because it is personal, and partly because the idea of kingship is the most comprehensive of the offices which Christ executes as our Redeemer. But, after all, it expresses only one aspect of the glorious future of the kingdom of God towards which prophecy steadily points. We must remember also that the order in which these types emerge is determined not altogether by their intrinsic importance, but partly by their adaptation to the needs of the age in which the prophet lived. The main function of prophecy was to furnish present and practical direction to the people of God; and the form under which the ideal was presented to any particular generation was always that best fitted to help it onwards, one stage nearer to the great consummation. Thus while Isaiah idealises the figure of the king, Jeremiah grasps the conception of a new religion under the form of a covenant, the second Isaiah unfolds the idea of the prophetic servant of Jehovah, Zechariah and the writer of the 110th Psalm idealise the priesthood. All these are Messianic prophecies, if we take the word in its widest acceptation; but they are not all cast in one mould, and the attempt to arrange them in a single series is obviously misleading. So

* "Das Königthum wird diese [the Davidic] Familie nicht wieder erhalten, denn Ezechiel fährt fort: 'Ich Iahwe werde ihnen Gott sein und mein Knecht David wird *nâsî* d. h. Fürst in ihrer Mitte sein.' Also *nur ein Fürstenthum* wird der Familie Davids in der besseren Zukunft Israel's zu Theil."—STADE, "Geschichte des Volkes Israel," vol. ii. p. 39.

† Ch. xxxvii. 22–24.

with regard to Ezekiel we may say that his chief Messianic ideal (still using the expression in a general sense) is the sanctuary, the symbol of Jehovah's presence in the midst of His people. At the end of chap. xxxvii. the kingdom and the sanctuary are mentioned together as pledges of the glory of the latter days. But while the idea of the Messianic monarchy was a legacy inherited from his prophetic precursors, the Temple was an institution whose typical significance Ezekiel was the first to unfold. It was moreover the one that met the religious requirements of the age in which Ezekiel lived. Ultimately the hope of the personal Messiah loses the importance which it still has in the present section of the book; and the prophet's vision of the future concentrates itself on the sanctuary as the centre of the restored theocracy, and the source from which the regenerating influences of the divine grace flow forth to Israel and the world.

CHAPTER XXI.

JEHOVAH'S LAND.

EZEKIEL xxxv., xxxvi

THE teaching of this important passage turns on certain ideas regarding the land of Canaan which enter very deeply into the religion of Israel. These ideas are no doubt familiar in a general way to all thoughtful readers of the Old Testament; but their full import is scarcely realised until we understand that they are not peculiar to the Bible, but form part of the stock of religious conceptions common to Israel and its heathen neighbours.* In the more advanced Semitic religions of antiquity each nation had its own god as well as its own land, and the bond between the god and the land was supposed to be quite as strong as that between the god and the nation. The god, the land, and the people formed a triad of religious relationship, and so closely were these three elements associated that the expulsion of a people from its land was held to dissolve the bond between it and the god. Thus while in practice the land of a god was coextensive with the territory inhabited by his worshippers, yet in theory the relation of the god to his land is independent of his relation to the inhabitants; it was *his* land whether the people in it were his worshippers or not. The peculiar confusion of ideas that arose when the people of one god came to reside permanently in the territory of another is well illustrated by the case of the heathen colony which the king of Assyria planted in Samaria after the exile of the ten tribes. These settlers brought their own gods with them; but when some of them were slain by lions, they perceived that they were making a mistake in ignoring the rights of the god of the land. They sent accordingly for a priest to instruct them in the religion of the god of the land; and the result was that they "feared Jehovah and served their own gods" (2 Kings xvii. 24-41). It was expected no doubt that in course of time the foreign deities would be acclimatised.

In the Old Testament we find many traces of the influence of this conception on the Hebrew religion. Canaan was the land of Jehovah (Hosea ix. 3) apart altogether from its possession by Israel, the people of Jehovah. It was Jehovah's land before Israel entered it, the inheritance which He had selected for His people out of all the countries of the world, the Land of Promise, given to the patriarchs while as yet they were but strangers and sojourners in it. Although the Israelites took possession of it as a nation of conquerors, they did so in the consciousness that they were expelling from Jehovah's dwelling-place a population which had polluted it by their abominations. From that time onwards the tenure of the soil of Palestine was regarded as an essential factor of the national religion. The idea that Jehovah could not be rightly worshipped outside of Hebrew territory was firmly rooted in the minds of the people, and was accepted by the prophets as a principle involved in the special relations that Jehovah maintained with the people of Israel.* Hence no threat could be more terrible in the ears of the Israelites than that of expatriation from their native soil; for it meant nothing less than the dissolution of the tie that subsisted between them and their God. When that threat was actually fulfilled there was no reproach harder to bear than the taunt which Ezekiel here puts into the mouth of the heathen: "These are Jehovah's people—and yet they are gone forth out of His land" (xxxvi. 20). They felt all that was implied in that utterance of malicious satisfaction over the collapse of a religion and the downfall of a deity.

There is another way in which the thought of Canaan as Jehovah's land enters into the religious conceptions of the Old Testament, and very markedly into those of Ezekiel. As the God of the land Jehovah is the source of its productiveness and the author of all the natural blessings enjoyed by its inhabitants. It is He who gives the rain in its season or else withholds it in token of His displeasure; it is He who multiplies or diminishes the flocks and herds which feed on its pastures, as well as the human population sustained by its produce. This view of things was a primary factor in the religious education of an agricultural people, as the ancient Hebrews mainly were. They felt their dependence on God most directly in the influences of their uncertain climate on the fertility of their land, with its great possibilities of abundant provision for man and beast, and on the other hand its extreme risk of famine and all the hardships that follow in its train. In the changeful aspects of nature they thus read instinctively the disposition of Jehovah towards themselves. Fruitful seasons and golden harvests, diffusing comfort and affluence through the community, were regarded as proofs that all was well between them and their God; while times of barrenness and scarcity brought home to them the conviction that Jehovah was alienated. From the allusions in the prophets to droughts and famines, to blastings and mildew, to the scourge of locusts, we seem to gather that, on the whole, the later history of Israel had been marked by agricultural distress. The impression is confirmed by a hint of Ezekiel's in the passage now before us. The land of Canaan had apparently acquired an unenviable reputation for barrenness. The reproach of the heathen lay upon it as a land

* On the whole subject of the relation of the gods to the land see Robertson Smith, "Religion of the Semites," pp. 91 ff.

* Josh. xxii. 19; 1 Sam. xxvi. 19; Hosea ix. 3-5.

that "devoured men and bereaved its population."* The reference may be partly (as Smend thinks) to the ravages of war, to which Palestine was peculiarly exposed on account of its important strategic situation. But the "reproach of famine"† was certainly one point in its ill fame among the surrounding nations, and it is quite sufficient to explain the strong language in which they expressed their contempt. Now this state of things was plainly inconsistent with the amicable relations between the nation and its God. It was evidence that the land lay under the blight of Jehovah's displeasure, and the ground of that displeasure lay in the sin of the people. Where the land counted for so much as an index to the mind of God, it was a postulate of faith that in the ideal future when God and Israel were perfectly reconciled the physical condition of Canaan should be worthy of Him whose land it was. And we have already seen that amongst the glories of the Messianic age the preternatural fertility of the Holy Land holds a prominent place.

This conception of Canaan as the Land of Jehovah undoubtedly has its natural affinities with religious notions of a somewhat primitive kind. It belongs to the stage of thought at which the power of a god is habitually regarded as subject to local limitations, and in which accordingly a particular territory is assigned to every deity as the sphere of his influence. It is probable that the great mass of the Hebrew people had never risen above this idea, but continued to think of their country as Jehovah's land in precisely the same way as Assyria was Asshur's land and Moab the land of Chemosh. The monotheism of the Old Testament revelation breaks through this system of ideas, and interprets Jehovah's relation to the land in an entirely different sense. It is not as the exclusive sphere of His influence that Canaan is peculiarly associated with Jehovah's presence, but mainly because it is the scene of His historical manifestation of Himself, and the stage on which events were transacted which revealed His Godhead to all the world. No prophet has a clearer perception of the universal sweep of the divine government than Ezekiel, and yet no prophet insists more strongly than he on the possession of the land of Canaan as an indispensable symbol of communion between God and His people. He has met with God in the "unclean land" of his exile, and he knows that the moral government of the universe is not suspended by the departure of Jehovah from His earthly sanctuary. Nevertheless he cannot think of this separation as other than temporary. The final reconciliation must take place on the soil of Palestine. The kingdom of God can only be established by the return both of Israel and Jehovah to their own land; and their joint possession of that land is the seal of the everlasting covenant of peace that subsists between them.

We must now proceed to study the way in which these conceptions influenced the Messianic expectations of Ezekiel at this period of his life. The passage we are to consider consists of three sections. The thirty-fifth chapter is a prophecy of judgment on Edom. The first fifteen verses of chap. xxxvi. contain a promise of the restoration of the land of Israel to its rightful owner. And the remainder of that chapter presents a comprehensive view of the divine necessity for the restoration and the power by which the redemption of the people is to be accomplished.

* Ch. xxxvi. 13. † Ch. xxxvi. 30: *cf.* xxxiv. 29.

I.

At the time when these prophecies were written the land of Israel was in the possession of the Edomites. By what means they had succeeded in effecting a lodgment in the country we do not know. It is not unlikely that Nebuchadnezzar may have granted them this extension of their territory as a reward for their services to his army during the last siege of Jerusalem. At all events their presence there was an accomplished fact, and it appeals to the mind of the prophet in two aspects. In the first place it was an outrage on the majesty of Jehovah which filled the cup of Edom's iniquity to the brim. In the second place it was an obstacle to the restoration of Israel which had to be removed by the direct intervention of the Almighty. These are the two themes which occupy the thoughts of Ezekiel, the one in chap. xxxv. and the other in chap. xxxvi. Hitherto he had spoken of the return to the land of Canaan as a matter of course, as a thing necessary and self-evident and not needing to be discussed in detail. But as the time draws near he is led to think more clearly of the historical circumstances of the return, and especially of the hindrances arising from the actual situation of affairs.

But besides this one cannot fail to be struck by the effective contrast which the two pictures—one of the mountain land of Israel, and the other of the mountain land of Seir—present to the imagination. It is like a prophetic amplification of the blessing and curse which Isaac pronounced on the progenitors of these two nations. Of the one it is said:—

"God give thee of the dew of heaven, and of the fatness of the earth,
And abundance of corn and wine."

And of the other:—

"Surely far from the fatness of the earth shall thy dwelling be,
And far from the dew of heaven from above.*"

In that forecast of the destiny of the two brothers the actual characteristics of their respective countries are tersely and accurately expressed. But now, when the history of both nations is about to be brought to an issue, the contrast is emphasised and perpetuated. The blessing of Jacob is confirmed and expanded into a promise of unimagined felicity, and the equivocal blessing on Esau is changed into an unqualified and permanent curse. Thus, when the mountains of Israel break forth into singing, and are clothed with all the luxuriance of vegetation in which the Oriental imagination revels, and cultivated by a happy and contented people, those of Seir are doomed to perpetual sterility and become a horror and desolation to all that pass by.

Confining ourselves, however, to the thirty-fifth chapter, what we have first to notice is the sins by which the Edomites had incurred this judgment. These may be summed up under three heads: first, their unrelenting hatred of Israel, which in the day of Judah's calamity

* Gen. xxvii. 28, 39.

had broken out in savage acts of revenge (ver. 5); second, their rejoicing over the misfortunes of Israel and the desolation of its land (ver. 15); and third, their eagerness to seize the land as soon as it was vacant (ver. 10). The first and second of these have been already spoken of under the prophecies on foreign nations; it is only the last that is of special interest in the present connection. Of course the motive that prompted Edom was natural, and it may be difficult to say how far real moral guilt was involved in it. The annexation of vacant territory, as the land of Israel practically was at this time, would be regarded according to modern ideas as not only justifiable but praiseworthy. Edom had the excuse of seeking to better its condition by the possession of a more fertile country than its own, and perhaps also the still stronger plea of pressure by the Arabs from behind. But in the consciousness of an ancient people there was always another thought present; and it is here if anywhere that the sin of Edom lies. The invasion of Israel did not cease to be an act of aggression because there were no human defenders to bar the way. It was still Jehovah's land, although it was unoccupied; and to intrude upon it was a conscious defiance of His power. The arguments by which the Edomites justified their seizure of it were none of those which a modern state might use in similar circumstances, but were based on the religious ideas which were common to all the world in those days. They were aware that by the unwritten law which then prevailed the step they meditated was sacrilege; and the spirit that animated them was arrogant exultation over what was esteemed the humiliation of Israel's national deity: "The two nations and the two countries shall be mine, and I will possess them, although Jehovah was there" (ver. 10: *cf.* vv. 12, 13). That is to say, the defeat and captivity of Israel had proved the impotence of Jehovah to guard His land; His power is broken, and the two countries called by His name lie open to the invasion of any people that dares to trample religious scruples underfoot. This was the way in which the action of Edom would be interpreted by universal consent; and the prophet is only reflecting the general sense of the age when he charges them with this impiety. Now it is true that the Edomites could not be expected to understand all that was involved in a defiance of the God of Israel. To them He was only one among many national gods, and their religion did not teach them to reverence the gods of a foreign state. But though they were not fully conscious of the degree of guilt they incurred, they nevertheless sinned against the light they had; and the consequences of transgression are never measured by the sinner's own estimate of his culpability. There was enough in the history of Israel to have impressed the neighbouring peoples with a sense of the superiority of its religion and the difference in character between Jehovah and all other gods. If the Edomites had utterly failed to learn that lesson, they were themselves partly to blame; and the spiritual insensibility and dulness of conscience which everywhere suppressed the knowledge of Jehovah's name is the very thing which in the view of Ezekiel needs to be removed by signal and exemplary acts of judgment.

It is not necessary to enter minutely into the details of the judgment threatened against Edom. We may simply note that it corresponds point for point with the demeanour exhibited by the Edomites in the time of Israel's final retribution. The "perpetual hatred" is rewarded by perpetual desolation (ver. 9); their seizure of Jehovah's land is punished by their annihilation in the land that was their own (vv. 6-8); and their malicious satisfaction over the depopulation of Palestine recoils on their own heads when their mountain land is made desolate "to the rejoicing of the whole earth" (vv. 14, 15). And the lesson that will be taught to the world by the contrast between the renewed Israel and the barren mountain of Seir will be the power and holiness of the one true God: "they shall know that I am Jehovah."

II.

The prophet's mind is still occupied with the sin of Edom as he turns in the thirty-sixth chapter to depict the future of the land of Israel. The opening verses of the chapter (vv. 1-7) betray an intensity of patriotic feeling not often expressed by Ezekiel. The utterance of the single idea which he wishes to express seems to be impeded by the multitude of reflections that throng upon him as he apostrophises "the mountains and the hills, the watercourses and the valleys, the desolate ruins and deserted cities" of his native country (ver. 4). The land is conceived as conscious of the shame and reproach that rest upon it; and all the elements that might be supposed to make up the consciousness of the land—its naked desolation, the tread of alien feet, the ravages of war, and the derisive talk of the surrounding heathen (Edom being specially in view)—present themselves to the mind of the prophet before he can utter the message with which he is charged: "Thus saith the Lord Jehovah; Behold, I speak in My jealousy and My anger, because ye have borne the shame of the heathen: therefore . . . I lift up My hand, Surely the nations that are round about you—even they shall bear their shame" (vv. 6, 7).

The jealousy of Jehovah is here His holy resentment against indignities done to Himself, and this attribute of the divine nature is now enlisted on the side of Israel because of the despite which the heathen had heaped on His land. But it is noteworthy that it is through the land and not the people that this feeling is first called into operation. Israel is still sinful and alienated from God; but the honour of Jehovah is bound up with the land not less than with the nation, and it is in reference to it that the necessity of vindicating His holy name first becomes apparent. There is what we might almost venture to call a divine patriotism, which is stirred into activity by the desolate condition of the land where the worship of the true God should be celebrated. On this feature of Jehovah's character Ezekiel builds the assurance of his people's redemption. The idea expressed by the verses is simply the certainty that Canaan shall be recovered from the heathen dominion for the purposes of the kingdom of God.

The following verses (8-15) speak of the positive aspects of the approaching deliverance. Continuing his apostrophe to the mountains of Israel, the prophet describes the transformation which is to pass over them in view of the return of the exiled nation, which is now on the eve of accomplishment (ver. 8). It might almost seem as if the return of the inhabitants were here treated as a mere incident of the rehabilitation of the land. That of course is only an appearance caused by the peculiar standpoint assumed throughout these chapters. Ezekiel was not one who could look on complacently

'Where wealth accumulates and men decay;"

nor was he indifferent to the social welfare of his people. On the contrary we have seen from chap. xxxiv. that he regards that as a supreme interest in the future kingdom of God. And even in this passage he does not make the interests of humanity subservient to those of nature. His leading idea is a reunion of land and people under happier auspices than had obtained of old. Formerly the land, in mysterious sympathy with the mind of Jehovah, had seemed to be animated by a hostile disposition towards its inhabitants. The reluctant and niggardly subsistence that had been wrung from the soil justified the evil report which the spies had brought up of it at the first as a "land that eateth up the inhabitants thereof." * Its inhospitable character was known among the heathen, so that it bore the reproach of being a land that "devoured men and bereaved its nation." But in the glorious future all this will be changed in harmony with Jehovah's altered relations with His people. In the language of a later prophet,† the land shall be "married" to Jehovah, and endowed with exuberant fertility. Yielding its fruits freely and generously, it will wipe off the reproach of the heathen; its cities shall be inhabited, its ruins rebuilt, and man and beast multiplied on its surface, so that its last state shall be better than its first (ver. 11). And those who till it and enjoy the benefits of its wonderful transformation shall be none other than the house of Israel, for whose sins it had borne the reproach of barrenness in the past (vv. 12-15).

III.

The next passage (vv. 16-38) deals more with the renewal of the nation than with that of the land; and thus forms a link of connection between the main theme of this chapter and that of chap. xxxvii. It contains the clearest and most comprehensive statement of the process of redemption to be found in the whole book, exhibiting as it does in logical order all the elements which enter into the divine scheme of salvation. The fact that it is inserted just at this point affords a fresh illustration of the importance attached by the prophet to the religious associations which gathered round the Holy Land. The land indeed is still the pivot on which his thoughts turn; he starts from it in his short review of God's past judgments on His people, and finally returns to it in summing up the world-wide effects of His gracious dealings with them in the immediate future. Although the connection of ideas is singularly clear, the passage throws so much light on the deepest theological conceptions of Ezekiel that it will be well to recapitulate the principal steps of the argument.

We need not linger on the cause of the rejection of Israel, for here the prophet only repeats the main lesson which we have found so often enforced in the first part of his book. Israel went into exile because its manner of life as a nation had been abhorrent to Jehovah, and it had defiled the land which was Jehovah's house. As in chap. xxii. and elsewhere, bloodshed and idols are the chief emblems of the people's sinful condition; these constitute a real physical defilement of the land, which must be punished by the eviction of its inhabitants: "So I poured out My wrath upon them [on account of the blood which they had shed upon the land, and the idols wherewith they had polluted it]: and I scattered them among the nations, and they were dispersed through the countries." *

Thus the Exile was necessary for the vindication of Jehovah's holiness as reflected in the sanctity of His land. But the effect of the dispersion on other nations was such as to compromise the honour of Israel's God in another direction. Knowing Jehovah only as a tribal god, the heathen naturally concluded that He had been too feeble to protect His land from invasion and His people from captivity. They could not penetrate to the moral reasons which rendered the chastisement inevitable; they only saw that these were Jehovah's people, and yet they were gone forth out of His land (ver. 20), and drew the natural inference. The impression thus produced by the presence of Israelites amongst the heathen was derogatory to the majesty of Jehovah, and obscured the knowledge of the true principles of His government which was destined to extend to all the earth. This is all that seems to be meant by the expression "profaned My holy name." † It is not implied that the exiles scandalised the heathen by their vicious lives, and so brought disgrace on "that glorious name by which they were called," ‡ although that idea is implied in chap. xii. 16. The profanation spoken of here was caused directly not by the sin but by the calamities of Israel. Yet it was their sins which brought down judgment upon them, and so indirectly gave occasion to the enemies of the Lord to blaspheme. There were probably already some of Ezekiel's compatriots who realised the bitterness of the thought that their fate was the means of bringing discredit on their God. Their experience would be similar to that of the lonely exile who composed the forty-second psalm:—

"As with a sword in my bones, mine enemies reproach me; While they say daily unto me, Where is thy God? §"

Now in this fact the prophet recognises an absolute ground of confidence in Israel's restoration. Jehovah cannot endure that His name should thus be held up to derision before the eyes of mankind. To allow this would be to frustrate the end of His government of the world, which is to manifest His Godhead in such a way that all men shall be brought to acknowledge it. Although He is known as yet only as the national God of a particular people, He must be disclosed to the world as all that the inspired teachers of Israel know Him to be—the one Being worthy of the homage of the human heart. There must be some way by which His name can be sanctified before the

* Numb. xiii. 32. † Isa. lxii. 4.

* Vv. 18, 19. The words in brackets are wanting in the LXX.
† Vv. 20, 22, 23. ‡ James ii. 7. § Psalm xlii. 10.

heathen, some means of reconciling the partial revelation of His holiness in Israel's dispersion with the complete manifestation of His power to the world at large. And this reconciliation can only be effected through the redemption of Israel. God cannot disown His ancient people, for that would be to stultify the whole past revelation of His character and leave the name by which He had made Himself known to contempt. That is divinely impossible; and therefore Jehovah must carry through His purpose by sanctifying Himself in the salvation of Israel. The outward token of salvation will be their restoration to their own land (ver. 24); but the inward reality of it will be a change in the national character which will make their dwelling in the land consistent with the revelation of Jehovah's holiness already given by their banishment from it.

At this point accordingly (ver. 25) Ezekiel passes to speak of the spiritual process of regeneration by which Israel is to be transformed into a true people of God. This is a necessary part of the sanctification of the divine name before the world. The new life of the people will reveal the character of the God whom they serve, and the change will explain the calamities that had befallen them in the past. The world will thus see "that the house of Israel went into captivity for their iniquity,"* and will understand the holiness which the true God requires in His worshippers. But for the present the prophet's thoughts are concentrated on the operations of the divine grace by which the renewal is effected. His analysis of the process of conversion is profoundly instructive, and anticipates to a remarkable degree the teaching of the Old Testament. We shall content ourselves at present with merely enumerating the different parts of the process. The first step is the removal of the impurities contracted by past transgressions. This is represented under the figure of sprinkling with clean water, suggested by the ablutions or lustrations which are so common a feature of the Levitical ritual (ver. 25). The truth symbolised is the forgiveness of sins, the act of grace which takes away the effect of moral uncleanness as a barrier to fellowship with God. The second point is what is properly called regeneration, the giving of a new heart and spirit (ver. 26). The stony heart of the old nation, whose obduracy had dismayed so many prophets, making them feel that they had spent their labour for nought and in vain, shall be taken away, and instead of it they shall receive a heart of flesh, sensitive to spiritual influences and responsive to the divine will. And to this is added in the third place the promise of the Spirit of God to be in them as the ruling principle of a new life of obedience to the law of God (ver. 27). The law, both moral and ceremonial, is the expression of Jehovah's holy nature, and both the will and the power to keep it perfectly must proceed from the indwelling of His Holy Spirit in the people.† It is thus Jehovah Himself who "saves" the people "out of all their uncleanness" (ver. 29), caused by the depravity and infirmity of their natural hearts. When these conditions are realised the harmony between Jehovah and Israel will be completely restored: He will be their God, and they shall be His people. They shall dwell for ever in the land promised to their fathers; and the blessing of God resting on land and people will multiply the fruit of the tree and the produce of the field, so that they receive no more the reproach of famine among the nations (vv. 28-30).

Having thus described the process of salvation as from first to last the work of Jehovah, the prophet proceeds to consider the impression which it will produce first on Israel and then on the surrounding nations (vv. 31-36). On Israel the effect of the goodness of God will be to lead them to repentance. Remembering what their past history has been, and contrasting it with the blessedness they now enjoy, they shall be filled with shame and self-contempt, loathing themselves for their iniquities and their abominations. It is not meant that all feelings of joy and gratitude will be swallowed up in the consciousness of unworthiness; but this is the feeling that will be called forth by the memory of their past transgressions. Their horror of sin will be such that they cannot think of what they have been without the deepest compunction and self-abasement. And this sense of the exceeding sinfulness of sin, reacting on their consciousness of themselves, will be the best moral guarantee against their relapse into the uncleanness from which they have been delivered.

To the heathen, on the other hand, the state of Israel will be a convincing demonstration of the power and godhead of Jehovah. Men will say, "Yonder land, which was desolate, has become like the garden of Eden; and the cities that were ruined and waste and destroyed are fenced and inhabited" (ver. 35). They will know that it is Jehovah's doing, and it will be marvellous in their eyes.

The last two verses seem to be an appendix. They deal with a special feature of the restoration, about which the minds of the exiles may have been exercised in thinking of the possibility of their deliverance. Where was the population of the new Israel to come from? The population of Judah must have been terribly reduced by the disastrous wars that had desolated the country since the time of Hezekiah. How was it possible, with a few thousands in exile, and a miserable remnant left in the land, to build up a strong and prosperous nation? This thought of theirs is met by the announcement of a great increase of the inhabitants of the land. Jehovah is ready to meet the questionings of human anxiety on this point: He will "let Himself be inquired of" for this.* The remembrance of the sacrificial flocks that used to throng the streets leading to the Temple at the time of the great festivals supplies Ezekiel with an image of the teeming population that shall be in all the cities of Canaan when this prophecy is fulfilled.

Such is in outline the scheme of redemption which Ezekiel presents to the minds of his readers. We shall reserve a fuller consideration of

* Ch. xxxix. 23.

† The phrase "cause you to walk" (ver. 27) is very strong in the Hebrew, almost "I will bring it about that ye walk."

* The thirty-seventh verse hardly bears the sense which is sometimes put upon it: "I am ready to do this for the house of Israel, yet I will not do it until they have learned to pray for it." That is true of spiritual blessings generally; but Ezekiel's idea is simpler. The particle "yet" is not adversative but temporal, and the "this" refers to what follows, and not to what precedes. The meaning is, "The time shall come when I will answer the prayer of the house of Israel," etc.

its more important doctrines for a separate chapter.* One general application of its teaching, however, may be pointed out before leaving the subject. We see that for Ezekiel the mysteries and perplexities of the divine government find their solution in the idea of redemption. He is aware of the false impression necessarily produced on the heathen mind by God's dealings with His people, as long as the process is incomplete. On account of Israel's sin the revelation of God in providence is gradual and fragmentary, and seems even for a time to defeat its own end. The omnipotence of God was obscured by the very act of vindicating His holiness; and what was in itself a great step towards the complete revelation of His character came on the world in the first instance as an evidence of His impotence. But the prophet, looking beyond this to the final effect of God's work upon the world, sees that Jehovah can be truly known only in the manifestation of His redeeming grace. All the enigmas and contradictions that arise from imperfect comprehension of His purpose find their answer in this truth, that God will yet redeem Israel from its iniquities. God is His own interpreter, and when His work of salvation is finished the result will be a conclusive demonstration of that lofty conception of God to which the prophet had attained.

Now this argument of Ezekiel's illustrates a principle of wide application. Many objections that are advanced against the theistic view of the universe seem to proceed on the assumption that the actual state of the world adequately represents the mind of its Creator. The heathen of Ezekiel's day have their modern representatives amongst dispassionate critics of Providence like J. S. Mill, who prove to their own satisfaction that the world cannot be the work of a being answering to the Christian idea of God. Do what you will, they say, to minimise the evils of existence, there is still an amount of undeniable pain and misery in the world which is fatal to your doctrine of an all-powerful and perfectly good Creator. Omnipotence could, and benevolence would find a remedy; the Author of the universe, therefore, cannot possess both. God, in short, if there be a God, may be benevolent, or He may be omnipotent; but if benevolent He is not omnipotent, and if omnipotent He cannot be benevolent. How very convincing this is—from the standpoint of the neutral, non-Christian observer! And how poor a defence is sometimes made by the optimism which tries to make out that most evils are blessings in disguise, and the rest not worth minding! The Christian religion rises superior to such criticism mainly in virtue of its living faith in redemption. It does not explain away evil, nor does it profess to account for its origin. It speaks of the whole creation groaning and travailing in pain together even until now. But it also describes the creation as waiting for the manifestation of the sons of God. It teaches us to discover in history the unfolding of a purpose of redemption the end of which will be the deliverance of mankind from the dominion of sin and their eternal blessedness in the kingdom of our God and His Christ. What Ezekiel foresaw in the form of a national restoration will be accomplished in a world-wide salvation, in a new heavens and a new earth, where there shall be no more curse. But meanwhile to judge of God from what is, apart from what is yet to be revealed, is to repeat the mistake of those who judge Jehovah to be an effete tribal deity because He had suffered His people to go forth out of their land. Those who have been brought into sympathy with the divine purpose, and have experienced the power of the Spirit of God in subduing the evil of their own hearts, can hold with unwavering confidence the hope of a universal victory of good over evil; and in the light of that hope the mysteries that surround the moral government of God cease to disturb their faith in the eternal Love which labours patiently and unceasingly for the redemption of man.

* Chapter xxiii. below.

CHAPTER XXII.

LIFE FROM THE DEAD.

EZEKIEL xxxvii.

THE most formidable obstacle to faith on the part of the exiles in the possibility of a national redemption was the complete disintegration of the ancient people of Israel. Hard as it was to realise that Jehovah still lived and reigned in spite of the cessation of His worship, and hard to hope for a recovery of the land of Canaan from the dominion of the heathen, these things were still conceivable. What almost surpassed conception was the restoration of national life to the feeble and demoralised remnant who had survived the fall of the state. It was no mere figure of speech that these exiles employed when they thought of their nation as dead. Cast off by its God, driven from its land, dismembered and deprived of its political organisation, Israel as a people had ceased to exist. Not only were the outward symbols of national unity destroyed, but the national spirit was extinct. Just as the destruction of the bodily organism implies the death of each separate member and organ and cell, so the individual Israelites felt themselves to be as dead men, dragging out an aimless existence without hope in the world. While Israel was alive they had lived in her and for her; all the best part of their life, religion, duty, liberty, and loyalty had been bound up with the consciousness of belonging to a nation with a proud history behind them and a brilliant future for their posterity. Now that Israel had perished all spiritual and ideal significance had gone out of their lives; there remained but a selfish and sordid struggle for existence, and this they felt was not life, but death in life. And thus a promise of deliverance which appealed to them as members of a nation seemed to them a mockery, because they felt in themselves that the bond of national life was irrevocably broken.

The hardest part of Ezekiel's task at this time was therefore to revive the national sentiment, so as to meet the obvious objection that even if Jehovah were able to drive the heathen from His land there was still no people of Israel to whom He could give it. If only the exiles could be brought to believe that Israel had a future, that although now dead it could be raised from the dead, the spiritual meaning of their life would be given back to them in the form of hope, and faith in God would be possible. Accordingly the prophet's thoughts are now directed to the idea of the nation as the third factor of the Messianic hope. He has spoken of the kingdom and the land, and each of these ideas has led him on to the contemplation of the final condition of the world, in which Jehovah's purpose is fully manifested. So in this chapter he finds in the idea of the nation a new point of departure, from which he proceeds to delineate once more the Messianic salvation in its completeness.

I.

The vision of the valley of dry bones described in the first part of the chapter contains the answer to the desponding thoughts of the exiles, and seems indeed to be directly suggested by the figure in which the popular feeling was currently expressed: "Our bones are dried; our hope is lost: we feel ourselves cut off" (ver. 11). The fact that the answer came to the prophet in a state of trance may perhaps indicate that his mind had brooded over these words of the people for some time before the moment of inspiration. Recognising how faithfully they represented the actual situation, he was yet unable to suggest an adequate solution of the difficulty by means of the prophetic conceptions hitherto revealed to him. Such a vision as this seems to presuppose a period of intense mental activity on the part of Ezekiel, during which the despairing utterance of his compatriots sounded in his ears; and the image of the dried bones of the house of Israel so fixed itself in his mind that he could not escape its gloomy associations except by a direct communication from above. When at last the hand of the Lord came upon him, the revelation clothed itself in a form corresponding to his previous meditations; the emblem of death and despair is transformed into a symbol of assured hope through the astounding vision which unfolds itself before his inner eye.

In the ecstasy he feels himself led out in spirit to the plain which had been the scene of former appearances of God to His prophet. But on this occasion he sees it covered with bones—"very many on the surface of the valley, and very dry." He is made to pass round about them, in order that the full impression of this spectacle of desolation might sink into his mind. His attention is engrossed by two facts—their exceeding great number, and their parched appearance, as if they had lain there long. In other circumstances the question might have suggested itself, How came these bones there? What countless host has perished here, leaving its unburied bones to bleach and wither on the open plain? But the prophet has no need to think of this. They are the bones which had been familiar to his waking thoughts, the dry bones of the house of Israel. The question he hears addressed to him is not, Whence are these bones? but, Can these bones live? It is the problem which had exercised his faith in thinking of a national restoration which thus comes back to him in vision, to receive its final solution from Him who alone can give it.

The prophet's hesitating answer probably reveals the struggle between faith and sight, between hope and fear, which was latent in his mind. He dare not say No, for that would be to limit the power of Him whom he knows to be omnipotent, and also to shut out the last gleam of hope from his own mind. Yet in presence of that appalling scene of hopeless decay and death he cannot of his own initiative assert the possibility of resurrection. In the abstract all things are possible with God; but whether this particular thing, so inconceivable to men, is within the active purpose of God, is a question which none can answer save God Himself. Ezekiel does what man must always do in such a case—he throws himself back on God, and reverently awaits the disclosure of His will, saying, "O Jehovah God, Thou Knowest."

It is instructive to notice that the divine answer comes through the consciousness of a duty. Ezekiel is commanded first of all to prophesy over these dry bones; and in the words given him to utter the solution of his own inward perplexity is wrapped up. "Say unto them, O ye dry bones, hear the word of Jehovah. . . . Behold, I will cause breath to enter into you, and ye shall live" (vv. 4, 5). In this way he is not only taught that the agency by which Jehovah will effect His purpose is the prophetic word, but he is also reminded that the truth now revealed to him is to be the guide of his practical ministry, and that only in the steadfast discharge of his prophetic duty can he hold fast the hope of Israel's resurrection. The problem that has exercised him is not one that can be settled in retirement and inaction. What he receives is not a mere answer, but a message, and the delivery of the message is the only way in which he can realise the truth of it: his activity as a prophet being indeed a necessary element in the fulfilment of his words. Let him preach the word of God to these dry bones, and he will know that they can live; but if he fails to do this, he will sink back into the unbelief to which all things are impossible. Faith comes in the act of prophesying.

Ezekiel did as he was commanded; he prophesied over the dry bones, and immediately he was sensible of the effect of his words. He heard a rustling, and looking he saw that the bones were coming together, bone to his bone. He does not need to tell us how his heart rejoiced at this first sign of life returning to these dead bones, and as he watched the whole process by which they were built up into the semblance of men. It is described in minute detail, so that no feature of the impression produced by the stupendous miracle may be lost. It is divided into two stages, the restoration of the bodily frame and the imparting of the principle of life. This division cannot have any special significance when applied to the actual nation, such as that the outward order of the state must be first established, and then the national consciousness renewed. It belongs to the imagery of the vision and follows the order observed in the original creation of man as described in the second chapter of Genesis. God first formed man of the dust of the ground, and afterwards breathed into his nostrils the breath of life, so that he became a living soul. So here we have first a description of the process by which the bodies were built up, the skeletons being formed from the scattered bones, and then clothed successively with sinews and flesh and skin. The reanimation of these still lifeless bodies is a separate act of creative energy, in which, however, the agency is still the word of God in the mouth of the prophet. He is bidden call for the breath to "come from the four winds of heaven, and breathe upon these slain that they may live." In Hebrew the words for wind, breath, and spirit are identical; and thus the wind becomes a symbol of the universal divine Spirit which is the source of all life, while the breath is a symbol of that Spirit as, so to speak, specialised in the individual man, or in other words of his personal life. In the case of the first man Jehovah breathed into his nostrils the breath of life, and the idea here is precisely the same. The wind from the four quarters of heaven which becomes the breath of this vast assemblage of men is conceived as the breath of God, and symbolises the life-giving Spirit which makes each of them a living person. The resurrection is complete. The men live, and stand up upon their feet, an exceeding great army.

This is the simplest, as well as the most suggestive, of Ezekiel's visions, and carries its interpretation on the face of it. The single idea which it expresses is the restoration of the Hebrew nationality through the quickening influence of the Spirit of Jehovah on the surviving members of the old house of Israel. It is not a prophecy of the resurrection of individual Israelites who have perished. The bones are "the whole house of Israel" now in exile; they are alive as individuals, but as members of a nation they are dead and hopeless of revival. This is made clear by the explanation of the vision given in vv. 11-14. It is addressed to those who think of themselves as cut off from the higher interests and activities of the national life. By a slight change of figure they are conceived as dead and buried; and the resurrection is represented as an opening of their graves. But the grave is no more to be understood literally than the dry bones of the vision itself; both are symbols of the gloomy and despairing view which the exiles take of their own condition. The substance of the prophet's message is that the God who raises the dead and calls the things that are not as though they were is able to bring together the scattered members of the house of Israel and form them into a new people through the operation of His life-giving Spirit.

It has often been supposed that, although the passage may not directly teach the resurrection of the body, it nevertheless implies a certain familiarity with that doctrine on the part of Ezekiel, if not of his hearers likewise. If the raising of dead men to life could be used as an analogy of a national restoration, the former conception must have been at least more obvious than the latter, otherwise the prophet would be explaining *obscurum per obscurius*. This argument, however, has only a superficial plausibility. It confounds two things which are distinct—the mere conception of resurrection, which is all that was necessary to make the vision intelligible, and settled faith in it as an element of the Messianic expectation. That God by a miracle could restore the dead to life no devout Israelite ever doubted.* But it is to be noted that the recorded instances of such miracles are all of those recently dead; and there is no evidence of a general belief in the possibility of resurrection for those whose bones were scattered and dry. It is this very impossibility, indeed, that gives point to the metaphor under which the people here express their sense of hopelessness. Moreover, if the prophet had presupposed the doctrine of individual resurrection, he could hardly have used it as an illustration in the way he does. The mere prospect of a resuscitation of the multitudes of Israelites who had perished would of itself have been a sufficient answer to the despondency of the exiles; and it would have been an anti-climax to use it as an argument for something much less wonderful. We must also bear in mind that while the resurrection of a nation may be to us little more than a figure of speech, to the Hebrew mind it was an object of thought more real and tangible than the idea of personal immortality.

* *Cf.* 1 Kings xvii.; 2 Kings iv. 13 ff., xiii. 21.

It would appear therefore that in the order of revelation the hope of the resurrection is first presented in the promise of a resurrection of the dead nation of Israel, and only in the second instance as the resurrection of individual Israelites who should have passed away without sharing in the glory of the latter days. Like the early converts to Christianity, the Old Testament believers sorrowed for those who fell asleep when the Messiah's kingdom was supposed to be just at hand, until they found consolation in the blessed hope of a resurrection with which Paul comforted the Church at Thessalonica.* In Ezekiel we find that doctrine as yet only in its more general form of a national resurrection; but it can hardly be doubted that the form in which he expressed it prepared the way for the fuller revelation of a resurrection of the individual. In two later passages of the prophetic Scriptures we seem to find clear indications of progress in this direction. One is a difficult verse in the twenty-sixth chapter of Isaiah—part of a prophecy usually assigned to a period later than Ezekiel—where the writer, after a lamentation over the disappointments and wasted efforts of the present, suddenly breaks into a rapture of hope as he thinks of a time when departed Israelites shall be restored to life to join the ranks of the ransomed people of God: "Let thy dead live again! Let my dead bodies arise! Awake and rejoice, ye that dwell in the dust, for thy dew is a dew of light, and the earth shall yield up [her] shades."† There does not seem to be any doubt that what is here predicted is the actual resurrection of individual members of the people of Israel to share in the blessings of the kingdom of God. The other passage referred to is in the book of Daniel, where we have the first explicit prediction of a resurrection both of the just and the unjust. In the time of trouble, when the people is delivered "many of them that sleep in the dust of the earth shall awake, some to everlasting life, and some to shame and everlasting contempt." ‡

These remarks are made merely to show in what sense Ezekiel's vision may be regarded as a contribution to the Old Testament doctrine of personal immortality. It is so not by its direct teaching, nor yet by its presuppositions, but by the suggestiveness of its imagery; opening out a line of thought which under the guidance of the Spirit of truth led to a fuller disclosure of the care of God for the individual life, and His purpose to redeem from the power of the grave those who had departed this life in His faith and fear.

But this line of inquiry lies somewhat apart from the main teaching of the passage before us as a message for the Church in all ages. The passage teaches with striking clearness the continuity of God's redeeming work in the world, in spite of hindrances which to human eyes seem insurmountable. The gravest hindrance, both

* 1 Thess. iv. 13 ff. † Isa. xxvi. 19. ‡ Dan. xii. 2.

in appearance and in reality, is the decay of faith and vital religion in the Church itself. There are times when earnest men are tempted to say that the Church's hope is lost and her bones are dried—when laxity of life and lukewarmness in devotion pervade all her members, and she ceases to influence the world for good. And yet when we consider that the whole history of God's cause is one long process of raising dead souls to spiritual life and building up a kingdom of God out of fallen humanity, we see that the true hope of the Church can never be lost. It lies in the life-giving, regenerating power of the divine Spirit, and the promise that the word of God does not return to Him void but prospers in the thing whereto He sends it. That is the great lesson of Ezekiel's vision, and although its immediate application may be limited to the occasion that called it forth, yet the analogy on which it is founded is taken up by our Lord Himself and extended to the proclamation of His truth to the world at large: "The hour is coming, and now is, when the dead shall hear the voice of the Son of God; and they that hear shall live." * We perhaps too readily empty these strong terms of their meaning. The Spirit of God is apt to become a mere expression for the religious and moral influences lodged in a Christian society, and we come to rely on these agencies for the dissemination of Christian principles and the formation of Christian character. We forget that behind all this there is something which is compared to the imparting of life where there was none, something which is the work of the Spirit of which we cannot tell whence it cometh and whither it goeth. But in times of low spirituality, when the love of many waxes cold, and there are few signs of zeal and activity in the service of Christ, men learn to fall back in faith on the invisible power of God to make His word effectual for the revival of His cause among men. And this happens constantly in narrow spheres which may never attract the notice of the world. There are positions in the Church still where Christ's servants are called to labour in the faith of Ezekiel, with appearances all against them, and nothing to inspire them but the conviction that the word they preach is the power of God and able even to bring life to the dead.

II.

The second half of the chapter speaks of a special feature of the national restoration, the reunion of the kingdoms of Judah and Israel under one sceptre. This is represented first of all by a symbolic action. The prophet is directed to take two pieces of wood, apparently in the form of sceptres, and to write upon them inscriptions dedicating them respectively to Judah and Joseph, the heads of the two confederacies out of which the rival monarchies were formed. The "companions" (ver. 16)—*i. e.*, allies—of Judah are the two tribes of Benjamin and Simeon; those of Joseph are all the other tribes, who stood under the hegemony of Ephraim. If the second inscription is rather more complicated than the first, it is because of the fact that there was no actual tribe of Joseph. It therefore runs thus: "For Joseph, the staff of Ephraim, and all the house of Israel his confederates." These two staves then he is to put together so that they become one sceptre in his hand. It is a little difficult to decide whether this was a sign that was actually performed before the people, or one that is only imagined. It depends partly on what we take to be meant by the joining of the two pieces. If Ezekiel merely took two sticks, put them end to end, and made them look like one, then no doubt he did this in public, for otherwise there would be no use in mentioning the circumstance at all. But if the meaning is, as seems more probable, that when the rods are put together they miraculously grow into one, then we see that such a sign has a value for the prophet's own mind as a symbol of the truth revealed to him, and it is no longer necessary to assume that the action was really performed. The purpose of the sign is not merely to suggest the idea of political unity, which is too simple to require any such illustration, but rather to indicate the completeness of the union and the divine force needed to bring it about. The difficulty of conceiving a perfect fusion of the two parts of the nation was really very great, the cleavage between Judah and the North being much older than the monarchy, and having been accentuated by centuries of political separation and rivalry.

To us the most noteworthy fact is the steadfastness with which the prophets of this period cling to the hope of a restoration of the northern tribes, although nearly a century and a half had now elapsed since "Ephraim was broken from being a people." * Ezekiel, like Jeremiah, is unable to think of an Israel which does not include the representatives of the ten northern tribes. Whether any communication was kept up with the colonies of Israelites that had been transported from Samaria to Assyria we do not know, but they are regarded as still existing, and still remembered by Jehovah. The resurrection of the nation which Ezekiel has just predicted is expressly said to apply to the whole house of Israel, and now he goes on to announce that this "exceeding great army" shall march to its land not under two banners, but under one.

We have touched already, in speaking of the Messianic idea, on the reasons which led the prophets to put so much emphasis on this union. They felt as strongly on the point as a High Churchman does about the sin of schism, and it would not be difficult for the latter to show that his point of view and his ideals closely resemble those of the prophets. The rending of the body of Christ which is supposed to be involved in a breach of external unity is paralleled by the disruption of the Hebrew state, which violates the unity of the one people of Jehovah. The idea of the Church as the bride of Christ is the same idea under which Hosea expresses the relations between Jehovah and Israel, and it necessarily carries with it the unity of the people of Israel in the one case and of the Church in the other. It must be admitted also that the evils resulting from the division between Judah and Israel have been reproduced, with consequences a thousand times more disastrous to religion, in the strife and uncharitableness, the party spirit and jealousies and animosities, which different denominations of Christians have invariably exhibited towards each other when they were close enough for mutual interest. But granting all this, and granting that what is called schism is essentially

* John v. 25: *cf.* vv. 28, 29.

* Isa. vii. 8.

the same thing that the prophets desired to see removed, it does not at once follow that dissent is in itself sinful, and still less that the sin is necessarily on the side of the Dissenter. The question is whether the national standpoint of the prophets is altogether applicable to the communion of saints in Christ, whether the body of Christ is really torn asunder by differences in organisation and opinion, whether, in short, anything is necessary to avoid the guilt of schism beyond keeping the unity of the Spirit in the bond of peace. The Old Testament dealt with men in the mass, as members of a nation, and its standards can hardly be adequate to the polity of a religion which has to provide for the freedom of the individual conscience before God. At the worst the Dissenter may point out that the Old Testament schism was necessary as a protest against tyranny and despotism, that in this aspect it was sanctioned by the inspired prophets of the age, that its undoubted evils were partly compensated by a freer expansion of religious life, and finally that even the prophets did not expect it to be healed before the millennium.

From the idea of the reunited nation Ezekiel returns easily to the promise of the Davidic king and the blessings of the Messianic dispensation. The one people implies one shepherd, and also one land, and one spirit to walk in Jehovah's judgments and to observe His statutes to do them. The various elements which enter into the conception of national salvation are thus gathered up and combined in one picture of the people's everlasting felicity. And the whole is crowned by the promise of Jehovah's presence with the people, sanctifyng and protecting them from His sanctuary. This final condition of things is permanent and eternal. The sources of internal dispeace are removed by the washing away of Israel's iniquities, and the impossibility of any disturbance from without is illustrated by the onslaught of the heathen nations described in the following chapters.

CHAPTER XXIII.

THE CONVERSION OF ISRAEL.

In one of our earlier chapters* we had occasion to notice some theological principles which appear to have guided the prophet's thinking from the beginning. It was evident even then that these principles pointed towards a definite theory of the conversion of Israel and the process by which it was to be effected. In subsequent prophecies we have seen how constantly Ezekiel's thoughts revert to this theme, as now one aspect of it and then another is disclosed to him. We have also glanced at one passage † which seemed to be a connected statement of the divine procedure as bearing on the restoration of Israel. But we have now reached a stage in the exposition where all this lies behind us. In the chapters that remain to be considered the regeneration of the people is assumed to have taken place; their religion and their morality are regarded as established on a stable and permanent basis, and all that has to be done is to describe the institutions by which the benefits of salvation may be conserved and handed down from age to age of the Messianic dispensation.

*Chapter v., above. † Ch. xxxvi. 16–38.

The present is therefore a fitting opportunity for an attempt to describe Ezekiel's doctrine of conversion as a whole. It is all the more desirable that the attempt should be made because the national salvation is the central interest of the whole book; and if we can understand the prophet's teaching on this subject, we shall have the key to his whole system of theology.

1. The first point to be noticed, and the one most characteristic of Ezekiel, is the divine motive for the redemption of Israel—Jehovah's regard for His own name. This thought finds expression in many parts of the book, but nowhere more clearly than in the twenty-second verse of the thirty-sixth chapter: "Not for your sakes do I act, O house of Israel, but for My holy name, which ye have profaned among the heathen, whither ye went." Similarly in the thirty-second verse: "Not for your sakes do I act, saith the Lord Jehovah, be it known unto you: be ashamed and confounded for your own ways, O house of Israel." There is an apparent harshness in these declarations which makes it easy to present them in a repellent light. They have been taken to mean that Jehovah is absolutely indifferent to the weal or woe of the people except in so far as it reflects on His own credit with the world; that He accepts the relationship between Him and Israel, but does so in the spirit of a selfish parent who exerts himself to save his child from disgrace merely in order to prevent his own name from being dragged in the mire. It would be difficult to explain how such a Being should be at all concerned about what men think of Him. If Jehovah has no interest in Israel, it is hard to see why He should be sensitive to the opinion of the rest of mankind. That is an idea of God which no man can seriously hold, and we may be certain that it is a perversion of Ezekiel's meaning. Everything depends on how much is included in the "name" of Jehovah. If it denotes mere arbitrary power, delighting in its own exercise and the awe which it excites, then we might conceive of the divine action as ruled by a boundless egotism, to which all human interests are alike indifferent. But that is not the conception of God which Ezekiel has. He is a moral Being, one who has compassion on other things besides His own name,* one who has no pleasure in the death of the wicked, but that he should turn from his way and live.† But when this aspect of His character is included in the name of God, we see that regard for His name cannot mean mere regard for His own interests, as if these were opposed to the interests of His creatures; but means the desire to be known as He is, as a God of mercy and righteousness as well as of infinite power.

The name of God is that by which He is known amongst men. It is more than His honour or reputation, although that is included in it according to Hebrew idiom; it is the expression of His character or His personality. To act for His name's sake, therefore, is to act so that His true character may be more fully revealed, and so that men's thoughts of Him may more truly correspond to that which in Himself He is. There is plainly nothing in this inconsistent with the deepest interest in men's spiritual well-being. Jehovah is the God of salvation, and desires to reveal Himself as such: and whether we say that He saves men in order

* Ch. xxxvi. 21. † Chs. xviii. 23, xxxiii. 11.

that He may be known as a Saviour, or that He makes Himself known in order to save them, does not make any real difference. Revelation and redemption are one thing. And when Ezekiel says that regard for His own name is the supreme motive of Jehovah's action, he does not teach that Jehovah is uninfluenced by care for man; if the question had been put to him, he would have said that care for man is one of the attributes included in the Name which Jehovah is concerned to reveal.

The real meaning of Ezekiel's doctrine will perhaps be best understood from its negative statement. What is meant to be excluded by the expression "not for your sakes"? It *might* no doubt mean, "not because I care at all for you"; but that we have seen to be inconsistent with other aspects of Ezekiel's teaching about the divine character. All that it necessarily implies is "not for any good that I find in you." It is a protest against the idea of Pharisaic self-righteousness that a man may have a legal claim upon God through his own merits. It is true that that was not a prevalent notion amongst the people in the time of Ezekiel. But their state of mind was one in which such a thought might easily arise. They were convinced of having been entirely in the wrong in their conceptions of the relation between them and Jehovah. The pagan notion that the people is indispensable to the god on account of a physical bond between them had broken down in the recent experience of Israel, and with it had vanished every natural ground for the hope of salvation. In such circumstances the promise of deliverance would naturally raise the thought that there must after all be something in Israel that was pleasing to Jehovah, and that the prophet's denunciations of their past sins were overdone. In order to guard against that error Ezekiel explicitly asserts, what was involved in the whole of his teaching, that the mercy of God was not called forth by any good in Israel, but that nevertheless there are immutable reasons in the divine nature on which the certainty of Israel's redemption may be built.

The truth here taught is therefore, in theological language, the sovereignty of the divine grace. Ezekiel's statement of it is liable to all the distortions and misrepresentations to which that doctrine has been subjected at the hands both of its friends and its enemies; but when fairly treated it is no more objectionable than any other expression of the same truth to be found in Scripture. In Ezekiel's case it was the result of a penetrating analysis of the moral condition of his people which led him to see that there was nothing in them to suggest the possibility of their being restored. It is only when he falls back on the thought of what God is, on the divine necessity of vindicating His holiness in the salvation of His people, that his faith in Israel's future finds a sure point of support. And so in general a profound sense of human sinfulness will always throw the mind back on the idea of God as the one immovable ground of confidence in the ultimate redemption of the individual and the world. When the doctrine is pressed to the conclusion that God saves men in spite of themselves, and merely to display His power over them, it becomes false and pernicious, and indeed self-contradictory. But so long as we hold fast to the truth that God is love, and that the glory of God is the manifestation of His love, the doctrine of the divine sovereignty only expresses the unchangeableness of that love and its final victory over the sin of the world.

2. The intellectual side of the conversion of Israel is the acceptance of that idea of God which to the prophet is summed up in the name of Jehovah. This is expressed in the standing formula which denotes the effect of all God's dealings with men, "They shall know that I am Jehovah." We need not, however, repeat what has been already said as to the meaning of these words.* Nor shall we dwell on the effect of the national judgment as a means towards producing a right impression of Jehovah's nature. It is possible that as time went on Ezekiel came to see that chastisement alone would not effect the moral change in the exiles which was necessary to bring them into sympathy with the divine purposes. In the early prophecy of chap. vi. the knowledge of Jehovah and the self-condemnation which accompanies it are spoken of as the direct result of His judgment on sin,† and this undoubtedly was one element in the conversion of the people to right thoughts about God. But in all other passages this feeling of self-loathing is not the beginning but the end of conversion; it is caused by the experience of pardon and redemption following upon punishment.‡ There is also another aspect of judgment which may be mentioned in passing for the sake of completeness. It is that which is expounded in the end of the twentieth chapter. There the judgment which still stands between the exiles and the return to their own land is represented as a sifting process, in which those who have undergone a spiritual change are finally separated from those who perish in their impenitence. This idea does not occur in the prophecies subsequent to the fall of Jerusalem, and it may be doubtful how it fits into the scheme of redemption there unfolded. The prophet here regards conversion as a process wholly carried through by the operation of Jehovah on the mind of the people; and what we have next to consider is the steps by which this great end is accomplished. They are these two—forgiveness and regeneration.

3. The forgiveness of sins is denoted in the thirty-sixth chapter, as we have already seen, by the symbol of sprinkling with clean water. But it must not be supposed that this isolated figure is the only form in which the doctrine appears in Ezekiel's exposition of the process of salvation. On the contrary forgiveness is the fundamental assumption of the whole argument, and is present in every promise of future blessedness to the people. For the Old Testament idea of forgiveness is extremely simple, resting as it does on the analogy of forgiveness in human life. The spiritual fact which constitutes the essence of forgiveness is the change in Jehovah's disposition towards His people which is manifested by the renewal of those indispensable conditions of national well-being which in His anger He had taken away. The restoration of Israel to its own land is thus not simply a token of forgiveness, but the act of forgiveness itself, and the only form in which the fact could be realised in the experience of the nation. In this sense the whole of Ezekiel's predictions of the Messianic deliverance and the glories that follow it are one continuous promise of forgive-

* See pp. 238 f. above. † Ch. vi. 8–10.
‡ Chs. xvi. 61–63, xx. 43, 44, xxxvi. 31, 32.

ness, setting forth the truth that Jehovah's love to His people persists in spite of their sin, and works victoriously for their redemption and restoration to the full enjoyment of His favour. There is perhaps one point in which we discover a difference between Ezekiel's conception and that of his predecessors. According to the common prophetic doctrine penitence, including amendment, is the moral effect of Jehovah's chastisement, and is the necessary condition of pardon. We have seen that there is some doubt whether Ezekiel regarded repentance as the result of judgment, and the same doubt exists as to whether in the order of salvation repentance is a preliminary or a consequence of forgiveness. The truth is that the prophet appears to combine both conceptions. In urging individuals to prepare for the coming of the kingdom of God he makes repentance a necessary condition of entering it; but in describing the whole process of salvation as the work of God he makes contrition for sin the result of reflection on the goodness of Jehovah already experienced in the peaceful occupation of the land of Canaan.

4. The idea of regeneration is very prominent in Ezekiel's teaching. The need for a radical change in the national character was impressed on him by the spectacle which he witnessed daily of evil tendencies and practices persisted in, in spite of the clearest demonstration that they were hateful to Jehovah and had been the cause of the nation's calamities. And he does not ascribe this state of things merely to the influence of tradition and public opinion and evil example, but traces it to its source in the hardness and corruption of the individual nature. It was evident that no mere change of intellectual conviction would avail to alter the currents of life among the exiles; the heart must be renewed, out of which are the issues both of personal and national life. Hence the promise of regeneration is expressed as a taking away of the stony, unimpressible heart that was in them, and putting within them a heart of flesh, a new heart and a new spirit. In exhorting individuals to repentance Ezekiel calls on them to make themselves a new heart and a new spirit,* meaning that their repentance must be genuine, extending to the inner motives and springs of action, and not be confined to outward signs of mourning.† But in other connections the new heart and spirit are represented as a gift, the result of the operation of the divine grace.‡

Closely connected with this, perhaps only the same truth in another form, is the promise of the outpouring of the Spirit of God.§ The general expectation of a new supernatural power infused into the national life in the latter days is common in the prophets. It appears in Hosea under the beautiful image of the dew,‖ and in Isaiah it is expressed in the consciousness that the desolation of the land must continue "until spirit be poured upon us from on high."¶ But no earlier prophet presents the idea of the Spirit as a principle of regeneration with the precision and clearness which the doctrine assumes in the hands of Ezekiel. What in Hosea and Isaiah may be only a divine influence, quickening and developing the flagging spiritual energies of the people, is here revealed as a creative power, the source of a new life, and the beginning of all that possesses moral or spiritual worth in the people of God.

5. It only remains for us now to note the twofold effect of these operations of Jehovah's grace in the religious and moral condition of the nation. There will be produced, in the first place, a new readiness and power of obedience to the divine commandments.* Like the apostle, they will not only "consent unto the law that it is good";† but in virtue of the new "Spirit of life" given to them, they will be in a real sense "free from the law,"‡ because the inward impulse of their own regenerate nature will lead them to fulfil it perfectly. The inefficiency of law as a mere external authority, acting on men by hope of reward and fear of punishment, was perceived both by Jeremiah and Ezekiel almost as clearly as by Paul, although this conviction on the part of the prophets was based on observation of national depravity rather than on their personal experience. It led Jeremiah to the conception of a new covenant under which Jehovah will write His law on men's hearts;§ and Ezekiel expresses the same truth in the promise of a new Spirit inclining the people to walk in Jehovah's statutes and to keep His judgments.

The second inward result of salvation is shame and self-loathing on account of past transgressions.‖ It seems strange that the prophet should dwell so much on this as a mark of Israel's saved condition. His strong protest against the doctrine of inherited guilt in the eighteenth chapter would have led us to expect that the members of the new Israel would not be conscious of any responsibility for the sins of the old. But here, as in other instances, the conception of the personified nation proves itself a better vehicle of religious truth from the Old Testament standpoint than the religious relations of the individual. The continuity of the national consciousness sustains that profound sense of unworthiness which is an essential element of true reconciliation to God, although each individual Israelite in the kingdom of God knows that he is not accountable for the iniquity of his fathers.

This outline of the prophet's conception of salvation illustrates the truth of the remark that Ezekiel is the first dogmatic theologian. In so far as it is the business of a theologian to exhibit the logical connection of the ideas which express man's relation to God, Ezekiel more than any other prophet may claim the title. Truths which are the presuppositions of all prophecy are to him objects of conscious reflection, and emerge from his hands in the shape of clearly formulated doctrines. There is probably no single element of his teaching which may not be traced in the writings of his predecessors, but there is none which has not gained from him a more distinct intellectual expression. And what is specially remarkable is the manner in which the doctrines are bound together in the unity of a system. In grounding the necessity of redemption in the divine nature, Ezekiel may be said to foreshadow the theology which is often called Calvinistic or Augustinian, but which might more truly be called Pauline. Al-

* Ch. xviii. 31.
† *Cf.* Joel's "Rend your heart, and not your garments" (Joel ii. 13).
‡ Chs. xi. 19, xxxvi. 26, 27.
§ Chs. xxxvi. 27, xxxvii. 14.
‖ Hosea xiv. 5.
¶ Isa. xxxii. 15.

* Chs. xi. 20, xxxvi. 27.
† Rom. vii. 16.
‡ Rom. viii. 2.
§ Jer. xxxi. 33.
‖ Chs. vi. 9, xvi. 63, xx. 43, xxxvi. 31, 32.

though the final remedy for the sin of the world had not yet been revealed, the scheme of redemption disclosed to Ezekiel agrees with much of the teaching of the New Testament regarding the effects of the work of Christ on the individual. Speaking of the passage xxxvi. 16-38 Dr. Davidson writes as follows:—

"Probably no passage in the Old Testament of the same extent offers so complete a parallel to New Testament doctrine, particularly to that of St. Paul. It is doubtful if the apostle quotes Ezekiel anywhere, but his line of thought entirely coincides with his. The same conceptions and in the same order belonging to both,—forgiveness (ver. 25); regeneration, a new heart and spirit (ver. 26); the Spirit of God as the ruling power in the new life (ver. 27); the issue of this, the keeping of the requirements of God's law (ver. 27; Rom. viii. 4); the effect of being 'under grace' in softening the human heart and leading to obedience (ver. 31; Rom. vi., vii.); and the organic connection of Israel's history with Jehovah's revelation of Himself to the nations (vv. 33-36; Rom. xi.)."

CHAPTER XXIV.

JEHOVAH'S FINAL VICTORY.

EZEKIEL xxxviii., xxxix.

THESE chapters give the impression of having been intended to stand at the close of the book of Ezekiel. Their present position is best explained on the supposition that the original collection of Ezekiel's prophecies actually ended here, and that the remaining chapters (xl.-xlviii.) form an appendix, added at a later period without disturbing the plan on which the book had been arranged. In chronological order, at all events, the oracle on Gog comes after the vision of the last nine chapters. It marks the utmost limit of Ezekiel's vision of the future of the kingdom of God. It represents the *dénouement* of the great drama of Jehovah's self-manifestation to the nations of the world. It describes an event which is to take place in the far-distant future, long after the Messianic age has begun and after Israel has long been settled peacefully in its own land. Certain considerations, which we shall notice at the end of this lecture, brought home to the prophet's mind the conviction that the lessons of Israel's restoration did not afford a sufficient illustration of Jehovah's glory or of the meaning of His past dealings with His people. The conclusive demonstration of this is therefore to be furnished by the destruction of Gog and his myrmidons when in the latter days they make an onslaught on the Holy Land.

The idea of a great world-catastrophe, following after a long interval the establishment of the kingdom of God, is peculiar to Ezekiel amongst the prophets of the Old Testament. According to other prophets the judgment of the nations takes place in a "day of Jehovah" which is the crisis of history; and the Messianic era which follows is a period of undisturbed tranquillity in which the knowledge of the true God penetrates to the remotest regions of the earth. In Ezekiel, on the other hand, the judgment of the world is divided into two acts. The nearer nations which have played a part in the history of Israel in the past form a group by themselves; their punishment is a preliminary to the restoration of Israel, and the impression produced by that restoration is for them a signal, though not perhaps a complete,* vindication of the Godhead of Jehovah. But the outlying barbarians, who hover on the outskirts of civilisation, are not touched by this revelation of the divine power and goodness; they seem to be represented as utterly ignorant of the marvellous course of events by which Israel has been brought to dwell securely in the midst of the nations.† These, accordingly, are reserved for a final reckoning, in which the power of Jehovah will be displayed with the terrible physical convulsions which mark the great day of the Lord.‡ Only then will the full meaning of Israel's history be disclosed to the world; in particular it will be seen that it was for their sin that they had fallen under the power of the heathen, and not because of Jehovah's inability to protect them.§

These are some general features of the prophecy which at once attract attention. We shall now examine the details of the picture, and then proceed to consider its significance in relation to other elements of Ezekiel's teaching.

I.

The thirty-eighth chapter may be divided into three sections of seven verses each.

i. Vv. 3-9.—The prophet having been commanded to direct his face towards Gog in the land of Magog, is commissioned to announce the fate that is in store for him and his hosts in the latter days. The name of this mysterious and formidable personage was evidently familiar to the Jewish world of Ezekiel's time, although to us its origin is altogether obscure. The most plausible suggestion, on the whole, is perhaps that which identifies it with the name of the Lydian monarch Gyges, which appears on the Assyrian monuments in the form of *Gugu*, corresponding as closely as is possible to the Hebrew Gog.‖ But in the mind of Ezekiel Gog is hardly an historical figure. He is but the impersonation of the dreaded power of the northern barbarians, already recognised as a serious danger to the peace of the world. His designation as prince of Rosh, Meshech, and Tubal points to the region east of the Black Sea as the seat of his power.¶ He is the captain of a vast multitude of horsemen, gorgeously arrayed, and armed with shield, helmet, and sword. But although Gog himself belongs to the "uttermost north," he gathers under his banner all the most distant nations both of the north and the south. Not only northern peoples like the Cimmerians and Armenians,** but Persians and Africans,†† all of them with shield and helmet, swell the ranks of his motley army. The name of Gog is thus on the way to become a symbol of the implacable enmity of this world to the kingdom of God; as in the book of the Revela-

* *Cf.* ch. xxxix. 23.
‡ Ch. xxxviii. 19-23.
† See ch. xxxviii. 11, 12.
§ Ch. xxxix. 23.
‖ See E. Meyer, "Geschichte des Alterthums," p. 558; Schrader, "Cuneiform Inscriptions," etc., on this passage.
¶ Meshech and Tubal are the Moschi and Tibareni of the Greek geographers, lying southeast of the Black Sea. A country or tribe Rosh has not been found.
** Gomer (according to others, however, Cappadocia) and Togarmah (ver. 6).
†† Cush and Put (ver. 5).

tion it appears as the designation of the ungodly world-power which perishes in conflict with the saints of God (Rev. xx. 7 ff.).

Gog therefore is summoned to hold himself in readiness, as Jehovah's reserve,* against the last days, when the purpose for which he has been raised up will be made manifest. After many days he shall receive his marching orders; Jehovah Himself will lead forth his squadrons and the innumerable hosts of nations that follow in his train,† and bring them up against the mountains of Israel, now reclaimed from desolation, and against a nation gathered from among many peoples, dwelling in peace and security. The advance of these destructive hordes is likened to a tempest, and their innumerable multitude is pictured as a cloud covering all the land (ver. 9).

ii. Vv. 10-16.—But like the Assyrian in the time of Isaiah, Gog "meaneth not so"; he is not aware that he is Jehovah's instrument, his purpose being to "destroy and cut off nations not a few."‡ Hence the prophet proceeds to a new description of the enterprise of Gog, laying stress on the "evil thought" that will arise in his heart and lure him to his doom. What urges him on is the lust of plunder. The report of the people of Israel as a people that has amassed wealth and substance, and is at the same time defenceless, dwelling in a land without walls or bolts or gates, will have reached him. These two verses (11, 12) are interesting as giving a picture of Ezekiel's conception of the final state of the people of God. They dwell in the "navel of the world"; they are rich and prosperous, so that the fame of them has gone forth through all lands; they are destitute of military resources, yet are unmolested in the enjoyment of their favoured lot because of the moral effect of Jehovah's name on all nations that know their history. To Gog, however, who knows nothing of Jehovah, they will seem an easy conquest, and he will come up confident of victory to seize spoil and take booty and lay his hand on waste places reinhabited and a people gathered out of the heathen. The news of the great expedition and the certainty of its success will rouse the cupidity of the trading communities from all the ends of the earth, and they will attach themselves as camp-followers to the army of Gog. In historic times this *rôle* would naturally have fallen to the Phœnicians, who had a keen eye for business of this description.§ But Ezekiel is thinking of a time when Tyre shall be no more; and its place is taken by the mercantile tribes of Arabia and the ancient Phœnician colony of Tarshish. The whole world will then resound with the fame of Gog's expedition, and the most distant nations will await its issue with eager expectation. This then is the meaning of Gog's destiny. In the time when Israel dwells peacefully he will be restless and eager for spoil;* his multitudes will be set in motion, and throw themselves on the land, covering it like a cloud. But this is Jehovah's doing, and the purpose of it is that the nations may know Him and that He may be sanctified in Gog before their eyes.

iii. Vv. 17-23.—These verses are in the main a description of the annihilation of Gog's host by the fierce wrath of Jehovah; but this is introduced by a reference to unfulfilled prophecies which are to receive their accomplishment in this great catastrophe. It is difficult to say what particular prophecies are meant. Those which most readily suggest themselves are perhaps the fourth chapter of Joel and the twelfth and fourteenth of Zechariah; but these probably belong to a later date than Ezekiel. The prophecies of Zephaniah and Jeremiah, called forth by the Scythian invasion,† have also been thought of, although the point of view there is different from that of Ezekiel. In Jeremiah and Zephaniah the Scythians are the scourge of God, appointed for the chastisement of the sinful nation; whereas Gog is brought up against a holy people, and for the express purpose of having judgment executed on himself. On the supposition that Ezekiel's vision was coloured by his recollection of the Scythians, this view has no doubt the greatest likelihood. It is possible, however, that the allusion is not to any particular group of prophecies, but to a general idea which pervades prophecy—the expectation of a great conflict in which the power of the world shall be arrayed against Jehovah and Israel, and the issue of which shall exhibit the sole sovereignty of the true God to all mankind.‡ It is of course unnecessary to suppose that any prophet had mentioned Gog by name in a prediction of the future. All that is meant is that Gog is the person in whom the substance of previous oracles is to be accomplished.

The question of ver. 17 leads thus to the announcement of the outpouring of Jehovah's indignation on the violators of His territory. As soon as Gog sets foot on the soil of Israel, Jehovah's wrath is kindled against him. A mighty earthquake shall shatter the mountains and level every wall to the ground and strike terror into the hearts of all creatures. The host of Gog shall be panic-stricken,§ each man turning his sword against his fellow; while Jehovah completes the slaughter by pestilence and blood, rain and hailstones, fire and brimstone. The deliverance of Israel is effected without the help of any human arm; it is the doing of Jehovah, who thus magnifies and sanctifies Himself and makes Himself known before the eyes of many peoples, so that they may know Him to be Jehovah.

iv. Chap. xxxix. 1-8.—Commencing afresh with a new apostrophe to Gog, Ezekiel here recapitulates the substance of the previous chapter—the bringing up of Gog from the farthest north, his destruction on the mountains of Israel, and the effect of this on the surrounding nations. Mention is expressly made of the bow and arrows which were the distinctive weapons of the Scythian horsemen.‖ These are struck

* Ver. 7. The LXX. reads "for me" instead of "unto them," giving to the word *mishmar* the sense of "reserve force."

† The words of ver. 4, "I will turn thee back, and put hooks into thy jaws," are wanting in the best manuscripts of the LXX., and are perhaps better omitted. Gog does not need to be dragged forth with hooks; he comes up willingly enough, as soon as the opportunity presents itself (vv. 11, 12.)

‡ Isa. x. 7.

§ An actual parallel is furnished by the crowds of slave-dealers who followed the army of Antiochus Epiphanes when it set out to crush the Maccabæan insurrection in 166 B. C.

* In ver. 14 the LXX. has "he stirred up" instead of "know," and gives a more forcible sense.

† Zeph. i.-iii. 8; Jer. iv.-vi.

‡ *Cf.*, besides the passages already cited, Isa. x. 5-34, xvii. 12-14; Micah iv. 11-13.

§ Ver. 21. LXX.: "I will summon against him every terror."

‖ ἱπποτοξόται (mounted archers) is the term applied to them by Herodotus (iv. 46).

from the grasp of Gog, and the mighty host falls on the open field to be devoured by wild beasts and by ravenous birds of every feather. But the judgment is universal in its extent; it reaches to Magog, the distant abode of Gog, and all the remote lands whence his auxiliaries were drawn. This is the day whereof Jehovah has spoken by His servants the prophets of Israel, the day which finally manifests His glory to all the ends of the earth.

v. Vv. 9-16.—Here the prophet falls into a more prosaic strain, as he proceeds to describe with characteristic fulness of detail the sequel of the great invasion. As the English story of the Invincible Armada would be incomplete without a reference to the treasures cast ashore from the wrecked galleons on the Orkneys and the Hebrides, so the fate of Gog's ill-starred enterprise is vividly set forth by the minute description of the traces it left behind in the peaceful life of Israel. The irony of the situation is unmistakable, and perhaps a touch of conscious exaggeration is permissible in such a picture. In the first place the weapons of the slain warriors furnish wood enough to serve for fuel to the Israelites for the space of seven years. Then follows a picture of the process of cleansing the land from the corpses of the fallen enemy. A burying-place is assigned to them in the valley of Abarim * on the eastern side of the Dead Sea, outside of the sacred territory. The whole people of Israel will be engaged for seven months in the operation of burying them; after this the mouth of the valley will be sealed,† and it will be known ever afterwards as the Valley of the Host of Gog. But even after the seven months have expired the scrupulous care of the people for the purity of their land will be shown by the precautions they take against its continued defilement by any fragment of a skeleton that may have been overlooked. They will appoint permanent officials, whose business will be to search for and remove relics of the dead bodies, that the land may be restored to its purity. Whenever any passer-by lights on a bone he will set up a mark beside it to attract the attention of the buriers. "Thus" (in course of time) "they shall cleanse the land."

vi. Vv. 17-24.—The overwhelming magnitude of the catastrophe is once more set forth under the image of a sacrificial feast, to which Jehovah summons all the birds of the air and every beast of the field (vv. 17-20). The feast is represented as a sacrifice not in any religious sense, but simply in accordance with ancient usage, in which the slaughtering of animals was invariably a sacrificial act. The only idea expressed by the figure is that Jehovah has decreed this slaughter of Gog and his host, and that it will be so great that all ravenous beasts and birds will eat flesh to the full and drink the blood of princes of the earth to intoxication. But we turn with relief from these images of carnage and death to the moral purpose which they conceal (vv. 21-24). This is stated more distinctly here than in earlier passages of this prophecy. It will teach Israel that Jehovah is indeed their God; the lingering sense of insecurity caused by the remembrance of their former rejection will be finally taken away by this signal deliverance. And through Israel it will teach a lesson to the heathen. They will learn something of the principles on which Jehovah has dealt with His people when they contrast this great salvation with His former desertion of them. It will then fully appear that it was for their sins that they went into captivity; and so the knowledge of God's holiness and His displeasure against sin will be extended to the nations of the world.

vii. Vv. 25-29.—The closing verses do not strictly belong to the oracle on Gog. The prophet returns to the standpoint of the present, and predicts once more the restoration of Israel, which has heretofore been assumed as an accomplished fact. The connection with what precedes is, however, very close. The divine attributes, whose final manifestation to the world is reserved for the far-off day of Gog's defeat, are already about to be revealed to Israel. Jehovah's compassion for His people and His jealousy for His own name will speedily be shown in "turning the fortunes" of Israel, bringing them back from the peoples, and gathering them from the land of their enemies. The consequences of this upon the nation itself are described in more gracious terms than in any other passage. They shall forget their shame and all their trespasses when they dwell securely in their own land, none making them afraid.* The saving knowledge of Jehovah as their God, who led them into captivity and brought them back again, will as far as Israel is concerned be complete; and the gracious relation thus established shall no more be interrupted, because of the divine Spirit which has been poured out on the house of Israel.

II.

It will be seen from this summary of the contents of the prophecy that, while it presents many features peculiar to itself, it also contains much in common with the general drift of the prophet's thinking. We must now try to form an estimate of its significance as an episode in the great drama of Providence which unfolded itself before his inspired imagination.

The ideas peculiar to the passage are for the most part such as might have been suggested to the mind of Ezekiel by the remembrance of the great Scythian invasion in the reign of Josiah. Although it is not likely that he had himself lived through that time of terror, he must have grown up whilst it was still fresh in the public recollection, and the rumour of it had apparently left upon him impressions never afterwards effaced. Several circumstances, none of them perhaps decisive by itself, conspire to show that at least in its imagery the oracle on Gog is based on the conception of

* This translation, which is given by Hitzig and Cornill, is obtained by a change in the punctuation of the word rendered "passengers" in ver. 11: *cf.* the "mountains of Abarim," Numb. xxxiii. 47, 48; Deut. xxxii. 49.

† "It shall stop the noses of the passengers" (ver. 11) gives no sense; and the text, as it stands, is almost untranslatable. The LXX. reads "and they shall seal up the valley," which gives a good enough meaning, so far as it goes.

* Ver. 26. The choice between the rendering "forget" and that of the English Version, "bear," depends on the position of a single dot in the Hebrew. In the former case "shame" must be taken in the sense of reproach (*schande*); in the latter it means the inward feeling of self-abasement (*schaam*). The forgetting of past trespasses, if that is the right reading, can only mean that they are entirely broken off and dismissed from mind; there is nothing inconsistent with passages like ch. xxxvi. 31. It must be understood that in any event the reference is to the future; *after that* "they have borne" is altogether wrong.

an irruption of Scythian barbarians. The name of Gog may be too obscure to serve as an indication; but his location in the extreme north, the description of his army as composed mainly of cavalry armed with bows and arrows, their innumerable multitude, and the love of pillage and destruction by which they are animated, all point to the Scythians as the originals from whom the picture of Gog's host is drawn. Besides the light which it casts on the genesis of the prophecy, this fact has a certain biographical interest for the reader of Ezekiel. That the prophet's furthest vista into the future should be a reflection of his earliest memory reminds us of a common human experience. "The thoughts of youth are long, long thoughts," reaching far into manhood and old age; and the mind as it turns back upon them may often discover in them that which carries it furthest in reading the divine mysteries of life and destiny.

"Thus while the Sun sinks down to rest
Far in the regions of the west,
Though to the vale no parting beam
Be given, not one memorial gleam,
A lingering light he fondly throws
On the dear hills where first he rose."

For it is not merely the imagery of the prophecy that reveals the influence of these early associations; the thoughts which it embodies are themselves partly the result of the prophet's meditation on questions suggested by the invasion. His youthful impressions of the descent of the northern hordes were afterwards illuminated, as we see from his own words, by the study of contemporary prophecies of Jeremiah and Zephaniah called forth by the event. From these and other predictions he learned that Jehovah had a purpose with regard to the remotest nations of the earth which yet awaited its accomplishment. That purpose, in accordance with his general conception of the ends of the divine government, could be nothing else than the manifestation of Jehovah's glory before the eyes of the world. That this involved an act of judgment was only too certain from the universal hostility of the heathen to the kingdom of God. Hence the prophet's reflections would lead directly to the expectation of a final onslaught of the powers of this world on the people of Israel, which would give occasion for a display of Jehovah's might on a grander scale than had yet been seen. And this presentiment of an impending conflict between Jehovah and the pagan world headed by the Scythian barbarians forms the kernel of the oracle against Gog.

But we must further observe that this idea, from Ezekiel's point of view, necessarily presupposes the restoration of Israel to its own land. The peoples assembled under the standard of Gog are those which have never as yet come in contact with the true God, and consequently have had no opportunity of manifesting their disposition towards Him. They have not sinned as Edom and Tyre, as Egypt and Assyria have sinned, by injuries done to Jehovah through His people. Even the Scythians themselves, although they had approached the confines of the sacred territory, do not seem to have invaded it. Nor could the opportunity present itself so long as Israel was in Exile. While Jehovah was without an earthly sanctuary or a visible emblem of His government, there was no possibility of such an infringement of His holiness on the part of the heathen as would arrest the attention of the world. The judgment of Gog, therefore, could not be conceived as a preliminary to the restoration of Israel, like that on Egypt and the nations immediately surrounding Palestine. It could only take place under a state of things in which Israel was once more "holiness to the Lord, and the firstfruits of His increase," so that "all that devoured him were counted guilty" (Jer. ii. 3). This enables us partly to understand what appears to us the most singular feature of the prophecy, the projection of the final manifestation of Jehovah into the remote future, when Israel is already in possession of all the blessings of the Messianic dispensation. It is a consequence of the extension of the prophetic horizon, so as to embrace the distant peoples that had hitherto been beyond the pale of civilisation.

There are other aspects of Ezekiel's teaching on which light is thrown by this anticipation of a world-judgment as the final scene of history. The prophet was evidently conscious of a certain inconclusiveness and want of finality in the prospect of the restoration as a justification of the ways of God to men. Although all the forces of the world's salvation were wrapped up in it, its effects were still limited and measurable, both as to their range of influence and their inherent significance. Not only did it fail to impress the more distant nations, but its own lessons were incompletely taught. He felt that it had not been made clear to the dull perceptions of the heathen why the God of Israel had ever suffered His land to be desecrated and His people to be led into captivity. Even Israel itself will not fully know all that is meant by having Jehovah for its God until the history of revelation is finished. Only in the summing up of the ages, and in the light of the last judgment, will men truly realise all that is implied in the terms God and sin and redemption. The end is needed to interpret the process; and all religious conceptions await their fulfilment in the light of eternity which is yet to break on the issues of human history.

PART V:

THE IDEAL THEOCRACY.

CHAPTER XXV.

THE IMPORT OF THE VISION.

We have now reached the last and in every way the most important section of the book of Ezekiel. The nine concluding chapters record what was evidently the crowning experience of the prophet's life. His ministry began with a vision of God; it culminates in a vision of the people of God; or rather of God in the midst of His people, reconciled to them, ruling over them, and imparting the blessings and glories of the final dispensation. Into that vision are thrown the ideals which had been gradually matured through twenty years of strenuous action and intense meditation. We have traced some of the steps by which the prophet was led towards this consummation of his work. We have seen how, under the idea of God which had been revealed to him, he was constrained to announce the destruction of that which called itself the people of Jehovah, but was in reality the means of obscuring His character and profaning His holiness (chaps. iv.-xxiv.). We have seen further how the same fundamental conception led him on in his prophecies against foreign nations to predict a great clearing of the stage of history for the manifestation of Jehovah (chaps. xxv.-xxxii.). And we have seen from the preceding section what are the processes by which the divine Spirit breathes new life into a dead nation and creates out of its scattered members a people worthy of the God whom the prophet has seen.

But there is still something more to accomplish before his task is finished. All through, Ezekiel holds fast the truth that Jehovah and Israel are necessarily related to each other, and that Israel is to be the medium through which alone the nature of Jehovah can be fully disclosed to mankind. It remains, therefore, to sketch the outline of a perfect theocracy—in other words, to describe the permanent forms and institutions which shall express the ideal relation between God and men. To this task the prophet addresses himself in the chapters now before us. That great New Year's Vision may be regarded as the ripe fruit of all God's training of His prophet, as it is also the part of Ezekiel's work which most directly influenced the subsequent development of religion in Israel.

It cannot be doubted, then, that these chapters are an integral part of the book, considered as a record of Ezekiel's work. But it is certainly a significant circumstance that they are separated from the body of the prophecies by an interval of thirteen years. For the greater part of that time Ezekiel's literary activity was suspended. It is probable, at all events, that the first thirty-nine chapters had been committed to writing soon after the latest date they mentioned, and that the oracle on Gog, which marks the extreme limit of Ezekiel's prophetic vision, was really the conclusion of an earlier form of the book. And we may be certain that, since the eventful period that followed the arrival of the fugitive from Jerusalem, no new divine communication had visited the prophet's mind. But at last, in the twenty-fifth year of the captivity, and on the first day of a new year,* he falls into a trance more prolonged than any he had yet passed through, and he emerged from it with a new message for his people.

In what direction were the prophet's thoughts moving as Israel passed into the midnight of her exile? That they have moved in the interval—that his standpoint is no longer quite identical with that represented in his earlier prophecies—seems to be shown by one slight modification of his previous conceptions, which has been already mentioned.† I refer to the position of the prince in the theocratic state. We find that the king is still the civil head of the commonwealth, but that his position is hardly reconcilable with the exalted functions assigned to the Messianic king in chap. xxxiv. The inference seems irresistible that Ezekiel's point of view has somewhat changed, so that the objects in his picture present themselves in a different perspective.

It is true that this change was effected by a vision, and it may be said that that fact forbids our regarding it as indicating a progress in Ezekiel's thoughts. But the vision of a prophet is never out of relation to his previous thinking. The prophet is always prepared for his vision; it comes to him as the answer to questions, as the solution of difficulties, whose force he has felt, and apart from which it would convey no revelation of God to his mind. It marks the point at which reflection gives place to inspiration, where the incommunicable certainty of the divine word lifts the soul into the region of spiritual and eternal truth. And hence it may help us, from our human point of view, to understand the true import of this vision, if from the answer we try to discover the questions which were of pressing interest to Ezekiel in the later part of his career.

Speaking generally, we may say that the problem that occupied the mind of Ezekiel at this time was the problem of a religious constitution. How to secure for religion its true place in public life, how to embody it in institutions which shall conserve its essential ideas and transmit them from one generation to another, how a people may best express its national responsibility to God—these and many kindred questions are real and vital to-day amongst the nations of Christendom, and they were far more vital in the age of Ezekiel. The conception of religion as an inward spiritual power, moulding the life of the nation and of each individual member, was at least as strong in him as in any other prophet; and it had been adequately expressed in the section of his book dealing with the formation of the new Israel. But he saw that this was not for that time sufficient. The mass of the community were dependent on the educative influence of the institutions under which they lived, and there was no way of impressing on a whole people the character of Jehovah except through a system of laws and observances which should constantly exhibit it to their minds. The time was not yet come when religion could be trusted to work as a hidden leaven, transforming life from within and bringing in the kingdom of God silently by the operation of spiritual forces. Thus, while the last section insists on the moral change that must pass over Israel, and the need of a direct influence from God on the heart of the people, that which now lies before us is devoted to the religious and political arrangements by which the sanctity of the nation must be preserved.

Starting from this general notion of what the prophet sought, we can see, in the next place, that his attention must be mainly concentrated on matters belonging to public worship and ritual. Worship is the direct expression in word and act of man's attitude to God, and no public religion can maintain a higher level of spirituality than the symbolism which gives it a place in the life of the people. That fact had been abundantly illustrated by the experience of centuries before the Exile. The popular worship had always been a stronghold of false religion in Israel. The high places were the nurseries of all the corruptions against which the prophets had to contend, not simply because of the immoral

* The beginning of the year is that referred to in Lev. xxv. 9, the tenth day of the seventh month (September-October). From the Exile downwards two calendars were in use, the beginning of the sacred year falling in the seventh month of the civil year. It was not necessary for Ezekiel to mention the number of the month.

† See pp. 302 f.

elements that mingled with their worship, but because the worship itself was regulated by conceptions of the deity which were opposed to the religion of revelation. Now the idea of using ritual as a vehicle of the highest spiritual truth is certainly not peculiar to Ezekiel's vision. But it is there carried through with a thoroughness which has no parallel elsewhere except in the priestly legislation of the Pentateuch. And this bears witness to a clear perception on the part of the prophet of the value of that whole side of things for the future development of religion in Israel. No one was more deeply impressed with the evils that had flowed from a corrupt ritual in the past, and he conceives the final form of the kingdom of God to be one in which the blessings of salvation are safeguarded by a carefully regulated system of religious ordinances. It will become manifest as we proceed that he regards the Temple ritual as the very centre of theocratic life, and the highest function of the community of the true religion.

But Ezekiel was prepared for the reception of this vision, not only by the practical reforming bent of his mind, but also by a combination in his own experience of the two elements which must always enter into a conception of this nature. If we may employ philosophical language to express a very obvious distinction, we have to recognise in the vision a material and a formal element. The matter of the vision is derived from the ancient religious and political constitution of the Hebrew state. All true and lasting reformations are conservative at heart; their object never is to make a clean sweep of the past, but so to modify what is traditional as to adapt it to the needs of a new era. Now Ezekiel was a priest, and possessed all a priest's reverence for antiquity, as well as a priest's professional knowledge of ceremonial and of consuetudinary law. No man could have been better fitted than he to secure the continuity of Israel's religious life along the particular line on which it was destined to move. Accordingly we find that the new theocracy is modelled from beginning to end after the pattern of the ancient institutions which had been destroyed by the Exile. If we ask, for example, what is the meaning of some detail of the Temple building, such as the cells surrounding the main sanctuary, the obvious and sufficient answer is that these things existed in Solomon's Temple, and there was no reason for altering them. On the other hand, whenever we find the vision departing from what had been traditionally established, we may be sure that there is a reason for it, and in most cases we can see what that reason was. In such departures we recognise the working of what we have called the formal element of the vision, the moulding influence of the ideas which the system was intended to express. What these ideas were we shall consider in subsequent chapters; here it is enough to say that they were the fundamental ideas which had been communicated to Ezekiel in the course of his prophetic work, and which have found expression in various forms in other parts of his writings. That they are not peculiar to Ezekiel, but are shared by other prophets, is true, just as it is true on the other hand that the priestly conceptions which occupy so large a place in his mind were an inheritance from the whole past history of the nation. Nor was this the first time when an alliance between the ceremonialism of the priesthood and the more ethical and spiritual teaching of prophecy had proved of the utmost advantage to the religious life of Israel.* The unique importance of Ezekiel's vision lies in the fact that the great development of prophecy was now almost complete, and that the time was come for its results to be embodied in institutions which were in the main of a priestly character. And it was fitting that this new era of religion should be inaugurated through the agency of one who combined in his own person the conservative instincts of the priest with the originality and the spiritual intuition of the prophet.

It is not suggested for a moment that these considerations account for the inception of the vision in the prophet's mind. We are not to regard it as merely the brilliant device of an ingenious man, who was exceptionally qualified to read the signs of the times, and to discover a solution for a pressing religious problem. In order that it might accomplish the end in view, it was absolutely necessary that it should be invested with a supernatural sanction and bear the stamp of divine authority. Ezekiel himself was well aware of this, and would never have ventured to publish his vision if he had thought it all out for himself. He had to wait for the time when "the hand of the Lord was upon him," and he saw in vision the new Temple and the river of life proceeding from it, and the renovated land, and the glory of God taking up its everlasting abode in the midst of His people. Until that moment arrived he was without a message as to the form which the life of the restored Israel must assume. Nevertheless the psychological conditions of the vision were contained in those parts of the prophet's experience which have just been indicated. Processes of thought which had long occupied his mind suddenly crystallised at the touch of the divine hand, and the result was the marvellous conception of a theocratic state which was Ezekiel's greatest legacy to the faith and hopes of his countrymen.

That this vision of Ezekiel's profoundly influenced the development of post-exilic Judaism may be inferred from the fact that all the best tendencies of the restoration period were towards the realisation of the ideals which the vision sets forth with surpassing clearness. It is impossible, indeed, to say precisely how far Ezekiel's influence extended, or how far the returning exiles consciously aimed at carrying out the ideas contained in his sketch of a theocratic constitution. That they did so to some extent is inferred from a consideration of some of the arrangements established in Jerusalem soon after the return from Babylon.† But it is certain that from the nature of the case the actual institutions of the restored community must have differed very widely in many points from those described in the last nine chapters of Ezekiel. When we look more closely at the composition of this vision, we see that it contains features which neither then nor at any subsequent time have been historically fulfilled. The most remarkable thing about it is that it unites in one picture two characteristics which seem at first sight difficult to combine. On the one hand it bears the aspect of a rigid legislative system intended to regulate human conduct in all matters of vital moment to the religious standing of the com-

* *Cf.* Davidson, "Ezekiel," pp. liv. f.

† See Prof. W. R. Smith, "The Old Testament in the Jewish Church," pp. 442 f.

munity; on the other hand it assumes a miraculous transformation of the physical aspect of the country, a restoration of all the twelve tribes of Israel under a native king, and a return of Jehovah in visible glory to dwell in the midst of the children of Israel for ever. Now these supernatural conditions of the perfect theocracy could not be realised by any effort on the part of the people, and as a matter of fact were never literally fulfilled at all. It must have been plain to the leaders of the Return that for this reason alone the details of Ezekiel's legislation were not binding for them in the actual circumstances in which they were placed. Even in matters clearly within the province of human administration we know that they considered themselves free to modify his regulations in accordance with the requirements of the situation in which they found themselves. It does not follow from this, however, that they were ignorant of the book of Ezekiel, or that it gave them no help in the difficult task to which they addressed themselves. It furnished them with an ideal of national holiness, and the general outline of a constitution in which that ideal should be embodied; and this outline they seem to have striven to fill up in the way best adapted to the straitened and discouraging circumstances of the time.

But this throws us back on some questions of fundamental importance for the right understanding of Ezekiel's vision. Taking the vision as a whole, we have to ask whether a fulfilment of the kind just indicated was the fulfilment that the prophet himself anticipated. Did he lay stress on the legislative or the supernatural aspect of the vision—on man's agency or on God's? In other words, does he issue it as a programme to be carried out by the people as soon as the opportunity is presented by their return to the land of Canaan? or does he mean that Jehovah Himself must take the initiative by miraculously preparing the land for their reception, and taking up His abode in the finished Temple, the "place of His throne, and the place of the soles of His feet"? The answer to that question is not difficult, if only we are careful to look at things from the prophet's point of view, and disregard the historical events in which his predictions were partly realised. It is frequently assumed that the elaborate description of the Temple buildings in chaps. xl.-xlii. is intended as a guide to the builders of the second Temple, who are to make it after the fashion of that which the prophet saw on the mount. It is quite probable that in some degree it may have served that purpose; but it seems to me that this view is not in keeping with the fundamental idea of the vision. The Temple that Ezekiel saw, and the only one of which he speaks, is a house not made with hands; it is as much a part of the supernatural preparation for the future theocracy as the "very high mountain" on which it stands, or the river that flows from it to sweeten the waters of the Dead Sea. In the important passage where the prophet is commanded to exhibit the plan of the house to the children of Israel (xliii. 10, 11), there is unfortunately a discrepancy between the Hebrew and Greek texts which throws some obscurity on this particular point. According to the Hebrew there can hardly be a doubt that a sketch is shown to them which is to be used as a builder's plan at the time of the Restoration.* But in the Septuagint, which seems on the whole to give a more correct text, the passage runs thus: "And, thou son of man, describe the house to the house of Israel (and let them be ashamed of their iniquities), and its form, and its construction: and they shall be ashamed of all that they have done. And do thou sketch the house, and its exits, and its outline; and all its ordinances and all its laws make known to them; and write it before them, that they may keep all its commandments and all its ordinances, and do them." There is nothing here to suggest that the construction of the Temple was left for human workmanship. The outline of it is shown to the people only that they may be ashamed of all their iniquities. When the arrangements of the ideal Temple are explained to them, they will see how far those of the first Temple transgressed the requirements of Jehovah's holiness, and this knowledge will produce a sense of shame for the dulness of heart which tolerated so many abuses in connection with His worship. No doubt that impression sank deep into the minds of Ezekiel's hearers, and led to certain important modifications in the structure of the Temple when it had to be built; but that is not what the prophet is thinking of. At the same time we see clearly that he is very much in earnest with the legislative part of his vision. Its laws are real laws, and are given that they may be obeyed—only they do not come into force until all the institutions of the theocracy, natural and supernatural alike, are in full working order. And apart from the doubtful question as to the erection of the Temple, that general conclusion holds good for the vision as a whole. Whilst it is pervaded throughout by the legislative spirit, the miraculous features are after all its central and essential elements. When these conditions are realised, it will be the duty of Israel to guard her sacred institutions by the most scrupulous and devoted obedience; but till then there is no kingdom of God established on earth, and therefore no system of laws to conserve a state of salvation, which can only be brought about by the direct and visible interposition of the Almighty in the sphere of nature and history.

This blending of seemingly incongruous elements reveals to us the true character of the vision with which we have to deal. It is in the strictest sense a Messianic prophecy—that is, a picture of the kingdom of God in its final state as the prophet was led to conceive it. It is common to all such representations that the human authors of them have no idea of a long historical development gradually leading up to the perfect manifestation of God's purpose with the world. The impending crisis in the affairs of the people of Israel is always regarded as the consummation of human history and the establishment of God's kingdom in the plenitude of its power and glory. In the time of Ezekiel the next step in the unfolding of the divine plan of redemption was the restoration of Israel to its own land; and in so far as his vision is a prophecy of that event, it was realised in the return of the exiles with Zerubbabel in the first year of Cyrus. But to the mind of Ezekiel this did not present itself as a mere step towards something immeasurably higher in the remote future. It is to include everything necessary for the complete and final inbringing of the Messianic dispensation, and all the powers of the world to come are to be dis-

*See ver. 10, "let them measure the pattern"; ver. 11, "that they may keep the whole form thereof."

played in the acts by which Jehovah brings back the scattered members of Israel to the enjoyment of blessedness in His own presence.

The thing that misleads us as to the real nature of the vision is the emphasis laid on matters which seem to us of merely temporal and earthly significance. We are apt to think that what we have before us can be nothing else than a legislative scheme to be carried out more or less fully in the new state that should arise after the Exile. The miraculous features in the vision are apt to be dismissed as mere symbolisms to which no great significance attaches. Legislating for the millennium seems to us a strange occupation for a prophet, and we are hardly prepared to credit even Ezekiel with so bold a conception. But that depends entirely on his idea of what the millennium will be. If it is to be a state of things in which religious institutions are of vital importance for the maintenance of the spiritual interests of the community of the people of God, then legislation is the natural expression for the ideals which are to be realised in it. And we must remember, too, that what we have to do with is a vision. Ezekiel is not the ultimate source of this legislation, however much it may bear the impress of his individual experience. He has seen the city of God, and all the minute and elaborate regulations with which these nine chapters are filled are but the exposition of principles that determine the character of a people amongst whom Jehovah can dwell.

At the same time we see that a separation of different aspects of the vision was inevitably effected by the teaching of history. The return from Babylon was accomplished without any of those supernatural adjuncts with which it had been invested in the rapt imagination of the prophet. No transformation of the land preceded it; no visible presence of Jehovah welcomed the exiles back to their ancient abode. They found Jerusalem in ruins, the holy and beautiful house a desolation, the land occupied by aliens, the seasons unproductive as of old. Yet in the hearts of these men there was a vision even more impressive than that of Ezekiel in his solitude. To lay the foundations of a theocratic state in the dreary, discouraging daylight of the present was an act of faith as heroic as has ever been performed in the history of religion. The building of the Temple was undertaken amidst many difficulties, the ritual was organised, the rudiments of a religious constitution appeared, and in all this we see the influence of those principles of national holiness that had been formulated by Ezekiel. But the crowning manifestation of Jehovah's glory was deferred. Prophet after prophet appeared to keep alive the hope that this Temple, poor in outward appearance as it was, would yet be the centre of a new world, and the dwelling-place of the Eternal. Centuries rolled past, and still Jehovah did not come to His Temple, and the eschatological features which had bulked so largely in Ezekiel's vision remained an unfulfilled aspiration. And when at length in the fulness of time the complete revelation of God was given, it was in a form that superseded the old economy entirely, and transformed its most stable and cherished institutions into adumbrations of a spiritual kingdom which knew no earthly Temple and had need of none.

This brings us to the most difficult and most important of all the questions arising in connection with Ezekiel's vision—What is its relation to the Pentateuchal Legislation? It is obvious at once that the significance of this section of the book of Ezekiel is immensely enhanced if we accept the conclusion to which the critical study of the Old Testament has been steadily driven, that in the chapters before us we have the first outline of that great conception of a theocratic constitution which attained its finished expression in the priestly regulations of the middle books of the Pentateuch. The discussion of this subject is so intricate, so far-reaching in its consequences, and ranges over so wide an historical field, that one is tempted to leave it in the hands of those who have addressed themselves to its special treatment, and to try to get on as best one may without assuming a definite attitude on one side or the other. But the student of Ezekiel cannot altogether evade it. Again and again the question will force itself on him as he seeks to ascertain the meaning of the various details of Ezekiel's legislation, How does this stand related to corresponding requirements in the Mosaic law? It is necessary, therefore, in justice to the reader of the following pages, that an attempt should be made, however imperfectly, to indicate the position which the present phase of criticism assigns to Ezekiel in the history of the Old Testament legislation.

We may begin by pointing out the kind of difficulty that is felt to arise on the supposition that Ezekiel had before him the entire body of laws contained in our present Pentateuch. We should expect in that case that the prophet would contemplate a restoration of the divine institutions established under Moses, and that his vision would reproduce with substantial fidelity the minute provisions of the law by which these institutions were to be maintained. But this is very far from being the case. It is found that while Ezekiel deals to a large extent with the subjects for which provision is made by the law, there is in no instance perfect correspondence between the enactments of the vision and those of the Pentateuch, while on some points they differ very materially from one another. How are we to account for these numerous and, on the supposition, evidently designed divergencies? It has been suggested that the law was found to be in some respects unsuitable to the state of things that would arise after the Exile, and that Ezekiel in the exercise of his prophetic authority undertook to adapt it to the conditions of a late age. The suggestion is in itself plausible, but it is not confirmed by the history. For it is agreed on all hands that the law as a whole had never been put in force for any considerable period of Israel's history previous to the Exile. On the other hand, if we suppose that Ezekiel judged its provisions unsuitable for the circumstances that would emerge after the Exile, we are confronted by the fact that where Ezekiel's legislation differs from that of the Pentateuch it is the latter and not the former that regulated the practice of the post-exilic community. So far was the law from being out of date in the age of Ezekiel that the time was only approaching when the first effort would be made to accept it in all its length and breadth as the authoritative basis of an actual theocratic polity. Unless, therefore, we are to hold that the legislation of the vision is entirely in the air, and that it takes no account whatever of practical considerations. we must feel that a certain difficulty is presented by its unexplained deviations from the carefully drawn ordinances of the Pentateuch.

But this is not all. The Pentateuch itself is not a unity. It consists of different strata of legislation which, while irreconcilable in details, are held to exhibit a continuous progress towards a clearer definition of the duties that devolve on different classes in the community, and a fuller exposition of the principles that underlay the system from the beginning. The analysis of the Mosaic writings into different legislative codes has resulted in a scheme which in its main outlines is now accepted by critics of all shades of opinion. The three great codes which we have to distinguish are: (1) the so-called Book of the Covenant (Exod. xx. 24-xxiii., with which may be classed the closely allied code of Exod. xxxiv. 10-28); (2) the Book of Deuteronomy; and (3) the Priestly Code (found in Exod. xxv.-xxxi., xxxv.-xl., the whole book of Leviticus, and nearly the whole of the book of Numbers).* Now of course the mere separation of these different documents tells us nothing, or not much, as to their relative priority or antiquity. But we possess at least a certain amount of historical and independent evidence as to the times when some of them became operative in the actual life of the nation. We know, for example, that the Book of Deuteronomy attained the force of statute law under the most solemn circumstances by a national covenant in the eighteenth year of Josiah. The distinctive feature of that book is its impressive enforcement of the principle that there is but one sanctuary at which Jehovah can be legitimately worshipped. When we compare the list of reforms carried out by Josiah, as given in the twenty-third chapter of 2 Kings, with the provisions of Deuteronomy, we see that it must have been that book and it alone that had been found in the Temple and that governed the reforming policy of the king. Before that time the law of the one sanctuary, if it was known at all, was certainly more honoured in the breach than the observance. Sacrifices were freely offered at local altars throughout the country, not merely by the ignorant common people and idolatrous kings, but by men who were the inspired religious leaders and teachers of the nation. Not only so, but this practice is sanctioned by the Book of the Covenant, which permits the erection of an altar in every place where Jehovah causes His name to be remembered, and only lays down injunctions as to the kind of altar that might be used (Exod. xx. 24-26). The evidence is thus very strong that the Book of Deuteronomy, at whatever time it may have been written, had not the force of public law until the year 621 B. C., and that down to that time the accepted and authoritative expression of the divine will for Israel was the law embraced in the Book of the Covenant.

To find similar evidence of the practical adoption of the Priestly Code we have to come down to a much later period. It is not till the year 444 B. C., in the time of Ezra and Nehemiah, that we read of the people pledging themselves by a solemn covenant to the observance of regulations which are clearly those of the finished system of Pentateuchal law (Neh. viii.-x). It is there expressly stated that this law had not been observed in Israel up to that time (Neh. ix., 34), and in particular that the great Feast of Tabernacles had not been celebrated in accordance with the requirements of the law since the days of Joshua (Neh. viii. 17). This is quite conclusive as to actual practice in Israel; and the fact that the observance of the law was thus introduced by instalments, and on occasions of epoch-making importance in the history of the community, raises a strong presumption against the hypothesis that the Pentateuch was an inseparable literary unit, which must be known in its entirety where it was known at all.

Now the date of Ezekiel's vision (572) lies between these two historic transactions—the inauguration of the law of Deuteronomy in 621, and that of the Priestly Code in 444; and in spite of the ideal character which belongs to the vision as a whole, it contains a system of legislation which admits of being compared point by point with the provisions of the other two codes on a variety of subjects common to all three. Some of the results of this comparison will appear as we proceed with the exposition of the chapters before us. But it will be convenient to state here the important conclusion to which a number of critics have been led by discussion of this question. It is held that Ezekiel's legislation represents on the whole a transition from the law of Deuteronomy to the more complex system of the Priestly document. The three codes exhibit a regular progression, the determining factor of which is a growing sense of the importance of the Temple worship and of the necessity for a careful regulation of the acts which express the religious standing and privileges of the community. On such matters as the feasts, the sacrifices, the distinction between priests and Levites, the Temple dues, and the provision for the maintenance of ordinances, it is found that Ezekiel lays down enactments which go beyond those of Deuteronomy and anticipate a further development in the same direction in the Levitical legislation.* The legislation of Ezekiel is accordingly regarded as a first step towards the codification of the ritual laws which regulated the usage of the first Temple. It is not of material consequence to know how far these laws had been already committed to writing, or how far they had been transmitted by oral tradition. The important point is that down to the time of Ezekiel the great body of ritual law had been the possession of the priests, who communicated it to the people in the shape of particular decisions as occasion demanded. Even the book of Deuteronomy, except on one or two points, such as the law of leprosy and of clean and unclean animals, does not encroach on matters of ritual, which it was the special province of the priesthood to administer. But now that the time was drawing near when the Temple and its worship were to be the very centre of the religious life of the nation, it was necessary that the essential elements of the ceremonial law should be systematised and published in a form understanded of the people. The last nine chapters of Ezekiel, then, contain the first draft of such a scheme, drawn from an ancient priestly tradition which in its origin went back to the time of Moses.

* This last group is considered to be composed of several layers of legislation, and one of its sections is of particular interest for us because of its numerous affinities with the book of Ezekiel. It is the short code contained in Lev. xvii.-xxvi., now generally known as the Law of Holiness.

* This argument is most fully worked out by Wellhausen in the first division of his "Prolegomena zur Geschichte Israels": I., "Geschichte des Cultus."

It is true that this was not the precise form in which the law was destined to be put in practice in the post-exilic community. But Ezekiel's legislation served its purpose when it laid down clearly, with the authority of a prophet, the fundamental ideas that underlie the conception of ritual as an aid to spiritual religion. And these ideas were not lost sight of, though it was reserved for others, working under the impulse supplied by Ezekiel, to perfect the details of the system, and to adapt the principles of the vision to the actual circumstances of the second Temple. Through what subsequent stages the work was carried we can hardly hope to determine with exactitude; but it was finished in all essential respects before the great covenant of Ezra and Nehemiah in the year 444.*

Let us now consider the bearing of this theory on the interpretation of Ezekiel's vision. It enables us to do justice to the unmistakable practical purpose which pervades its legislation. It frees us from the grave difficulties involved in the assumption that Ezekiel wrote with the finished Pentateuch before him. It vindicates the prophet from the suspicion of arbitrary deviations from a standard of venerable antiquity and of divine authority, which was afterwards proved by experience to be suited to the requirements of that restored Israel in whose interest Ezekiel legislated. And in doing so it gives a new meaning to his claim to speak as a prophet ordaining a new system of laws with divine authority. Whilst perfectly consistent with the inspiration of the Mosaic books, it places that of Ezekiel on a surer footing than does the supposition that the whole Pentateuch was of Mosaic authorship. It involves, no doubt, that the details of the Priestly law were in a more or less fluid condition down to the time of the Exile; but it explains the otherwise unaccountable fact that the several parts of the law became operative at different times in Israel's history, and explains it in a manner that reveals the working of a divine purpose through all the ages of the national existence. It becomes possible to see that Ezekiel's legislation and that of the Levitical books are in their essence alike Mosaic, as being founded on the institutions and principles established by Moses at the beginning of the nation's history. And an altogether new interest is imparted to the former when we learn to regard it as an epoch-making contribution to the task which laid the foundation of the post-exilic theocracy—the task of codifying and consolidating the laws which expressed the character of the new nation as a holy people consecrated to the service of Jehovah, the Holy One of Israel.

*It should perhaps be stated, even in so incomplete a sketch as this, that there is still some difference of opinion among critics as to Ezekiel's relation to the so-called "Law of Holiness" in Lev. xvii.-xxvi. It is agreed that this short but extremely interesting code is the earliest complete, or nearly complete, document that has been incorporated in the body of the Levitical legislation. Its affinities with Ezekiel both in thought and style are so striking that Colenso and others have maintained the theory that the author of the Law of Holiness was no other than the prophet himself. This view is now seen to be untenable; but whether the code is older or more recent than the vision of Ezekiel is still a subject of discussion among scholars. Some consider that it is an advance upon Ezekiel in the direction of the Priests' Code; while others think that the book of Ezekiel furnishes evidence that the prophet was acquainted with the Law of Holiness, and had it before him as he wrote. That he was acquainted with its *laws* seems certain; the question is whether he had them before him in their present written form. For fuller information on this and other points touched on in the above pages, the reader may consult Driver's "Introduction" and Robertson Smith's "Old Testament in the Jewish Church."

CHAPTER XXVI.

THE SANCTUARY.

EZEKIEL xl.-xliii.

THE fundamental idea of the theocracy as conceived by Ezekiel is the literal dwelling of Jehovah in the midst of His people. The Temple is in the first instance Jehovah's palace, where He manifests His gracious presence by receiving the gifts and homage of His subjects. But the enjoyment of this privilege of access to the presence of God depends on the fulfilment of certain conditions which, in the prophet's view, had been systematically violated in the arrangements that prevailed under the first Temple. Hence the vision of Ezekiel is essentially the vision of a Temple corresponding in all respects to the requirements of Jehovah's holiness, and then of Jehovah's entrance into the house so prepared for His reception. And the first step towards the realisation of the great hope of the future was to lay before the exiles a full description of this building, so that they might understand the conditions on which alone Israel could be restored to its own land.

To this task the prophet addresses himself in the first four of the chapters before us, and he executes it in a manner which, considering the great technical difficulties to be surmounted, must excite our admiration. He tells us first in a brief introduction how he was transported in prophetic ecstasy to the land of Israel, and there on the site of the old Temple, now elevated into a "very high mountain," he sees before him an imposing pile of buildings like the building of a city (ver. 2). It is the future Temple, the city itself having been removed nearly two miles to the south. At the east gate he is met by an angel, who conducts him from point to point of the buildings, calling his attention to significant structural details, and measuring each part as he goes along with a measuring-line which he carries in his hand. It is probable that the whole description would be perfectly intelligible but for the state of the text, which is defective throughout and in some places hopelessly corrupt. This is hardly surprising when we consider the technical and unfamiliar nature of the terms employed; but it has been suspected that some parts have been deliberately tampered with in order to bring them into harmony with the actual construction of the second Temple. Whether that is so or not, the description as a whole remains in its way a masterpiece of literary exposition, and a remarkable proof of the versatility of Ezekiel's accomplishments. When it is necessary to turn himself into an architectural draughtsman he discharges the duty to perfection. No one can study the detailed measurements of the buildings without being convinced that the prophet is working from a ground plan which he has himself prepared; indeed his own words leave no doubt that this was the case (see xliii. 10, 11). And it is a convincing demonstration of his descriptive powers that we are able, after the labours of many generations of scholars, to reproduce this plan with a certainty which, except with regard to a few minor features, leaves little to be desired. It has been remarked as a curious fact that of the three temples mentioned in the Old Testament the only one of whose construction we can form a clear conception is the one that was never built; * and certainly the knowledge we have of Solomon's Temple from the first book of Kings is very incomplete compared with what we know of the Temple which Ezekiel saw only in vision.

It is impossible in this chapter to enter into all the minutiæ of the description, or even to discuss all the difficulties of interpretation which arise in connection with different parts. Full information of these points will be found in short compass in Dr. Davidson's commentary on the passage. All that can be attempted here is to convey a general idea of the arrangements of the various buildings and courts of the sanctuary, and the extreme care with which they have been thought out by the prophet. After this has been done we shall try to discover the meaning of these arrangements in so far as they differ from the model supplied by the first Temple.

I.

Let the reader, then, after the manner of Euclid, draw a straight line A B, and describe thereon a square A B C D. Let him divide two adjacent sides of the square (say A B and A D) into ten equal parts, and let lines be drawn from the points of section parallel to the sides of the square in both directions. Let a side of the small squares represent a length of fifty cubits, and the whole consequently a square of five hundred cubits.† It will now be found that the bounding lines of Ezekiel's plan run throughout on the lines of this diagram;‡ and this fact gives a better idea than anything else of the symmetrical structure of the Temple and of the absolute accuracy of the measurements.

The sides of the large square represent of course the outer boundary of the enclosure, which is formed by a wall six cubits thick and six high.§ Its sides are directed to the four points of the compass, and at the middle of the north, east, and south sides the wall is pierced by the three gates, each with an ascent of seven steps outside. The gates, however, are not mere openings in the wall furnished with doors, but covered gateways, similar to those that penetrate the thick wall of a fortified town. In this case they are large separate buildings projecting into the court to a distance of fifty cubits, and twenty-five cubits broad, exactly half the size of the Temple proper. On either side of the passage are three recesses in the wall six cubits square, which were to be used as guard-rooms by the Temple police. Each gateway terminates towards the court in a large hall called "the porch," eight cubits broad (along the line of entry) by twenty long (across): the porch of the east gate was reserved for the use of the prince; the purpose of the other two is nowhere specified.

Passing through the eastern gateway, the prophet stands in the outer court of the Temple, the place where the people assembled for worship. It seems to have been entirely destitute of buildings, with the exception of a row of thirty cells along the three walls in which the gates were. The outer margin of the court was paved with stone up to the line of the inside of the gateways (*i. e.*, fifty cubits, less the thickness of the outer wall); and on this pavement stood the cells, the dimensions of which, however, are not given. There were, moreover, in the four corners of the court rectangular enclosures forty cubits by thirty, where the Levites were to cook the sacrifices of the people (xlvi. 21-24). The purpose of the cells is nowhere specified; but there is little doubt that they were intended for those sacrificial feasts of a semi-private character which had always been a prominent feature of the Temple worship. From the edge of the pavement to the inner court was a distance of a hundred cubits; but this space was free only on three sides, the western side being occupied by buildings to be afterwards described.

The inner court was a terrace standing probably about five feet above the level of the outer, and approached by flights of eight steps at the three gates. It was reserved for the exclusive use of the priests. It had three gateways in a line with those of the outer court, and precisely similar to them, with the single exception that the porches were not, as we might have expected, towards the inside, but at the ends next to the outer court. The free space of the inner court, within the line of the gateways, was a square of a hundred cubits, corresponding to the four middle squares of the diagram. Right in the middle, so that it could be seen through the gates, was the great altar of burnt-offering, a huge stone structure rising in three terraces to a height apparently of twelve cubits and having a breadth and length of eighteen cubits at the base. That this, rather than the Temple, should be the centre of the sanctuary, corresponds to a consciousness in Israel that the altar was the one indispensable requisite for the performance of sacrificial worship acceptable to Jehovah. Accordingly, when the first exiles returned to Jerusalem, before they were in a position to set about the erection of the Temple, they reared the altar in its place, and at once instituted the daily sacrifice and the stated order of the festivals. And even in Ezekiel's vision we shall find that the sacrificial consecration of the altar is considered as equivalent to the dedication of the whole sanctuary to the chief purpose for which it was erected. Besides the altar there were in the inner court certain other objects of special significance for the priestly and sacrificial service. By the side of the north and south gates were

* Gautier, "La Mission du Prophète Ezekiel." p. 118.

† The cubit which is the unit of measurement is said to be a hand-breadth longer than the cubit in common use (ver. 5). The length of the larger cubit is variously estimated as from eighteen to twenty-two inches. If we adopt the smaller estimate, we have only to take the half of Ezekiel's dimensions to get the measurement in English yards. The other, however, is more probable. Both the Egyptians and Babylonians had a larger and a smaller cubit, their respective lengths being approximately as follows:—

	Egypt.	Babylon.
Common cubit, .	17.8 in. .	19.5 in.
Royal cubit, . .	20.7 in. .	21.9 in.

In Egypt the royal cubit exceeded the common by a handbreadth, just as in Ezekiel. It is probable in any case that the large cubit used by the angel was of the same order of magnitude as the royal cubit of Egypt and Babylon—*i. e.*, was between twenty and a half and twenty-two inches long. *Cf.* Benzinger, "Hebräische Archäologie," pp. 178 ff.

‡ See the plan in Benzinger "Archäologie," p. 394.

§ The outer court, however, is some feet higher than the level of the ground, being entered by an ascent of seven steps; the height of the wall inside must therefore be less by this amount than the six cubits, which is no doubt an outside measurement.

two cells or chambers opening towards the middle space. The purpose for which these cells were intended clearly points to a division of the priesthood (which, however, may have been temporary and not permanent) into two classes—one of which was entrusted with the service of the Temple, and the other with the service of the altar. The cell on the north, we are told, was for the priests engaged in the service of the house, and that on the south for those who officiated at the altar (xl. 45, 46). There is mention also of tables on which different classes of sacrificial victims were slaughtered, and of a chamber in which the burnt-offering was washed (xl. 38-43); but so obscure is the text of this passage that it cannot even be certainly determined whether these appliances were situated at the east gate or the north gate, or at each of the three gates.

The four small squares immediately adjoining the inner court on the west are occupied by the Temple proper and its adjuncts. The Temple itself stands on a solid basement six cubits above the level of the inner court, and is reached by a flight of ten steps. The breadth of the basement (north to south) is sixty cubits: this leaves a free space of twenty cubits on either side, which is really a continuation of the inner court, although it bears the special name of the *gizra* ("separate place"). In length the basement measures a hundred and five cubits, projecting, as we immediately see, five cubits into the inner court in front.* The inner space of the Temple was divided, as in Solomon's Temple, into three compartments, communicating with each other by folding-doors in the middle of the partitions that separated them. Entering by the outer door on the east, we come first to the vestibule, which is twenty cubits broad (north to south) by twelve cubits east to west. Next to this is the hall or "palace" (*hêkāl*), twenty cubits by forty. Beyond this again is the innermost shrine of the Temple, the Most Holy Place, where the glory of the God of Israel is to take the place occupied by the ark and cherubim of the first Temple. It is a square of twenty cubits; but Ezekiel, although himself a priest, is not allowed to enter this sacred space; the angel goes in alone, and announces the measurements to the prophet, who waits without in the great hall of the Temple. The only piece of furniture mentioned in the Temple is an altar or table in the hall, immediately in front of the Most Holy Place (xli. 22). The reference is no doubt to the table on which the shewbread was laid out before Jehovah (*cf.* Exod. xxv. 23-30). Some details are also given of the wood-carving with which the interior was decorated (xli. 16-20, 25), consisting apparently of cherubs and palm trees in alternate panels. This appears to be simply a reminiscence of the ornamentation of the old Temple, and to have no direct religious significance in the mind of the prophet.

The Temple was enclosed first by a wall six cubits thick, and then on each side except the east by an outer wall of five cubits, separated from the inner by an interval of four cubits. This intervening space was divided into three ranges of small cells rising in three stories one over another. The second and third stories were somewhat broader than the lowest, the inner wall of the house being contracted so as to allow the beams to be laid upon it without breaking into its surface. We must further suppose that the inner wall rose above the cells and the outer wall, so as to leave a clear space for the windows of the Temple. The entire length of the Temple on the outside is a hundred cubits, and the breadth fifty cubits. This leaves room for a passage of five cubits broad round the edge of the elevated platform on which the main building stood. The two doors which gave access to the cells opened on this passage, and were placed in the north and south sides of the outer wall. There was obviously no need to continue the passage round the west side of the house, and this does not appear to be contemplated.

It will be seen that there still remains a square of a hundred cubits behind the Temple, between it and the west wall. The greater part of this was taken up by a structure vaguely designated as the "building" (*binyā* or *binyan*), which is commonly supposed to have been a sort of lumber-room, although its function is not indicated. Nor does it appear whether it stood on the level of the inner court or of the outer. But while this building fills the whole breadth of the square from north to south (a hundred cubits), the other dimension (east to west) is curtailed by a space of twenty cubits left free between it and the Temple, the *gizra* (see *supra*) being thus continuous round three sides of the house.

The most troublesome part of the description is that of two blocks of cells * situated north and south of the Temple building (xlii. 1-14). It seems clear that they occupied the oblong spaces between the *gizra* north and south of the Temple and the walls of the inner court. Their length is said to be a hundred cubits, and their breadth fifty cubits. But room has to be found for a passage ten cubits broad and a hundred long, so that the measurements do not exhibit in this case Ezekiel's usual accuracy. Moreover, we are told that while their length facing the Temple was a hundred cubits, the length facing the outer court was only fifty cubits. It is extremely difficult to gain a clear idea of what the prophet meant. Smend and Davidson suppose that each block was divided longitudinally into two sections, and that the passage of ten cubits ran between them from east to west. The inner section would then be a hundred cubits in length and twenty in breadth. But the other section towards the outer court would have only half this length, the remaining fifty cubits along the edge of the inner court being protected by a wall. This is perhaps the best solution that has been proposed, but one can hardly help thinking that if Ezekiel had had such an arrangement in view he would have expressed himself more clearly. The one thing that is perfectly unambiguous is the purpose for which these cells were to be used. Certain sacrifices to which a high degree of sanctity attached were consumed by the priests, and being "most holy" things they had to be eaten in a holy place. These chambers, then, standing within the sacred enclosure of the inner court, were assigned to the priests

* Smend and Stade assume that it was a hundred and ten cubits long, and extended five cubits to the west beyond the line of the square to which it belongs. This was not necessary, and it would imply that the *binya* behind the Temple, to be afterwards described, was without a wall on its eastern side, which is extremely improbable. (So Davidson.)

* According to the Septuagint they were either five or fifteen in number in each block.

for this purpose.* In them also the priests were to deposit the sacred garments in which they ministered, before leaving the inner court to mingle with the people.

II.

Such, then, are the leading features presented by Ezekiel's description of an ideal sanctuary. What are the chief impressions suggested to the mind by its perusal? The fact no doubt that surprises us most is that our attention is almost exclusively directed to the ground-plan of the buildings. It is evident that the prophet is indifferent to what seems to us the noblest element of ecclesiastical architecture, the effect of lofty spaces on the imagination of the worshipper. It is no part of his purpose to inspire devotional feeling by the aid of purely æsthetic impressions. "The height, the span, the gloom, the glory" of some venerable Gothic cathedral do not enter into his conception of a place of worship. The impressions he wishes to convey, although religious, are intellectual rather than æsthetic, and are such as could be expressed by the sharp outlines and mathematical precision of a ground-plan. Now of course the sanctuary was, to begin with, a place of sacrifice, and to a large extent its arrangements were necessarily dictated by a regard for practical convenience and utility. But leaving this on one side, it is obvious enough that the design is influenced by certain ruling principles, of which the most conspicuous are these three: separation, gradation, and symmetry. And these again symbolise three aspects of the one great idea of holiness, which the prophet desired to see embodied in the whole constitution of the Hebrew state as the guarantee of lasting fellowship between Jehovah and Israel.

In Ezekiel's teaching on the subject of holiness there is nothing that is absolutely new or peculiar to himself. That Jehovah is the one truly holy Being is the common doctrine of the prophets, and it means that He alone unites in Himself all the attributes of true Godhead. The Hebrew language does not admit of the formation of an adjective from the name for God like our word "divine," or an abstract noun corresponding to "divinity." What we denote by these terms the Hebrews expressed by the words *qādôsh*, "holy," and *qōdesh*, "holiness." All that constitutes true divinity is therefore summed up in the Old Testament idea of the holiness of God. The fundamental thought expressed by the word when applied to God appears to be the separation or contrast between the divine and the human—that in God which inspires awe and reverence on the part of man, and forbids approach to Him save under restrictions which flow from the nature of the Deity. In the light of the New Testament revelation we see that the only barrier to communion with God is sin; and hence to us holiness, both in God and man, is a purely ethical idea denoting moral purity and perfectness. But under the Old Testament access to God was hindered not only by sin, but also by natural disabilities to which no moral guilt attaches. The idea of holiness is therefore partly ethical and partly ceremonial, physical uncleanness being as really a violation of the divine holiness as offences against the moral law. The consequences of this view appear nowhere more clearly than in the legislation of Ezekiel. His mind was penetrated with the prophetic idea of the unique divinity or holiness of Jehovah, and no one can doubt that the moral attributes of God occupied the supreme place in his conception of what true Godhead is. But along with this he has a profound sense of what the nature of Jehovah demands in the way of ceremonial purity. The divine holiness, in fact, contains a physical as well as an ethical element; and to guard against the intrusion of anything unclean into the sphere of Jehovah's worship is the chief design of the elaborate system of ritual laws laid down in the closing chapters of Ezekiel. Ultimately no doubt the whole system served a moral purpose by furnishing a safeguard against the introduction of heathen practices into the worship of Israel. But its immediate effect was to give prominence to that aspect of the idea of holiness which seems to us of least value, although it could not be dispensed with so long as the worship of God took the form of material offerings at a local sanctuary.

Now, in reducing this idea to practice, it is obvious that everything depends on the strict enforcement of the principle of separation that lies at the root of the Hebrew conception of holiness. The thought that underlies Ezekiel's legislation is that the holiness of Jehovah is communicated in different degrees to everything connected with His worship, and in the first instance to the Temple, which is sanctified by His presence. The sanctity of the place is of course not fully intelligible apart from the ceremonial rules which regulate the conduct of those who are permitted to enter it. Throughout the ancient world we find evidence of the existence of sacred enclosures which could only be entered by those who fulfilled certain conditions of physical purity. The conditions might be extremely simple, as when Moses was commanded to take his shoes off his feet as he stood within the holy ground on Mount Sinai. But obviously the first essential of a permanently sacred place was that it should be definitely marked off from common ground, as the sphere within which superior requirements of holiness became binding. A holy place is necessarily a place "cut off," separated from ordinary use and guarded from intrusion by supernatural sanctions. The idea of the sanctuary as a separate place was therefore perfectly familiar to the Israelites long before the time of Ezekiel, and had been exhibited in a lax and imperfect way in the construction of the first Temple. But what Ezekiel did was to carry out the idea with a thoroughness never before attempted, and in such a way as to make the whole arrangements of the sanctuary an impressive object lesson on the holiness of Jehovah.

How important this notion of separateness was to Ezekiel's conception of the sanctuary is best seen from the emphatic condemnation of the arrangement of the old Temple pronounced by Jehovah Himself on His entrance into the house: "Son of man, [hast thou seen] * the place of My throne, and the place of the soles of My feet, where I shall dwell in the midst of the children of Israel for ever? No longer shall the house

* From a later passage (ch. xlvi. 19, 20) we learn that in some recess to the west of the northern block of cells there was a place where these sacrifices (the sin-, guilt-, and meal-offerings) were cooked, so that the people in the outer court might not run any risk of being brought in contact with them.

* So in the LXX.

of Israel defile My holy name, they and their kings, by their whoredom [idolatry], and by the corpses of their kings in their death; by placing their threshold alongside of My threshold, and their post beside My post, with only the wall between Me and them, and defiling My holy name by their abominations which they committed; so that I consumed them in My anger. But now they must remove their whoredom and the corpses of their kings from Me, and I will dwell amongst them for ever" (xliii. 7-9). There is here a clear allusion to defects in the structure of the Temple which were inconsistent with a due recognition of the necessary separation between the holy and the profane (xlii. 20). It appears that the first Temple had only one court, corresponding to the inner court of Ezekiel's vision. What answered to the outer court was simply an enclosure surrounding, not only the Temple, but also the royal palace and the other buildings of state. Immediately adjoining the Temple area on the south was the court in which the palace stood, so that the only division between the dwelling-place of Jehovah and the residence of the kings of Judah was the single wall separating the two courts. This of itself was derogatory to the sanctity of the Temple, according to the enhanced idea of holiness which it was Ezekiel's mission to enforce. But the prophet touches on a still more flagrant transgression of the law of holiness when he speaks of the dead bodies of the kings as being interred in the neighbourhood of the Temple. Contact with a dead body produced under all circumstances the highest degree of ceremonial uncleanness, and nothing could have been more abhorrent to Ezekiel's priestly sense of propriety than the close proximity of dead men's bones to the house in which Jehovah was to dwell. In order to guard against the recurrence of these abuses in the future it was necessary that all secular buildings should be removed to a safe distance from the Temple precincts. The "law of the house" is that "upon the top of the mountain it shall stand, and all its precincts round about shall be most holy" (xliii. 12). And it is characteristic of Ezekiel that the separation is effected, not by changing the situation of the Temple, but by transporting the city bodily to the southward; so that the new sanctuary stood on the site of the old, but isolated from the contact of that in human life which was common and unclean.*

The effect of this teaching, however, is immensely enhanced by the principle of gradation, which is the second feature exhibited in Ezekiel's description of the sanctuary. Holiness, as a predicate of persons or things, is after all a relative idea. That which is "most holy" in relation to the profane every-day life of men may be less holy in comparison with something still more closely associated with the presence of God. Thus the whole land of Israel was holy in contrast with the world lying outside. But it was impossible to maintain the whole land in a state of ceremonial purity corresponding to the sanctity of Jehovah. The full compass of the idea could only be illustrated by a carefully graded series of sacred spaces, each of which entailed provisions of sanctity peculiar to itself. First of all an "oblation" is set apart in the middle of the tribes; and of this the central portion is assigned for the residence of the priestly families. In the midst of this, again, stands the sanctuary with its wall and precinct, dividing the holy from the profane (xlii. 20). Within the wall are the two courts, of which the outer could only be trodden by circumcised Israelites and the inner only by the priests. Behind the inner court stands the Temple house, cut off from the adjoining buildings by a "separate place," and elevated on a platform, which still further guards its sanctity from profane contact. And finally the interior of the house is divided into three compartments, increasing in holiness in the order of entrance—first the porch, then the main hall, and then the Most Holy Place, where Jehovah Himself dwells. It is impossible to mistake the meaning of all this. The practical object is to secure the presence of Jehovah against the possibility of contact with those sources of impurity which are inseparably bound up with the incidents of man's natural existence on earth.*

Before we pass on let us return for a moment to the primary notion of separation in space as an emblem of the Old Testament conception of holiness. What is the permanent religious truth underlying this representation? We may find it in the idea conveyed by the familiar phrase "draw near to God." What we have just seen reminds us that there was a stage in the history of religion when these words could be used in the most literal sense of every act of complete worship. The worshipper actually came to the place where God was; it was impossible to realise His presence in any other way. To us the expression has only a metaphorical value; yet the metaphor is one that we cannot dispense with, for it covers a fact of spiritual experience. It may be true that with God there is no far or near, that He is omnipresent, that His eyes are in every place beholding the evil and the good. But what does that mean? Not surely that all men everywhere and at all times are equally under the influence of the divine Spirit? No; but only that God *may* be found in any place by the soul that is open to receive His grace and truth, that place has nothing to do with the conditions of true fellowship with Him. Trans-

* The actual building of the second Temple had of course to be carried out irrespective of the bold idealism of Ezekiel's vision. The miraculous transformation of the land had not taken place, and it was altogether impossible to build a new metropolis in the region marked out for it by the vision. The Temple had to be erected on its old site, and in the immediate neighbourhood of the city. To a certain extent, however, the requirements of the ideal sanctuary could be complied with. Since the new community had no use for royal buildings, the whole of the old Temple plateau was available for the sanctuary, and was actually devoted to this purpose. The new Temple accordingly had two courts, set apart for sacred uses; and in all probability these were laid out in a manner closely corresponding to the plan prepared by Ezekiel.

* It is not necessary to dwell on the third feature of the Temple plan, its symmetry. Although this has not the same direct religious significance as the other two, it is nevertheless a point to which considerable importance is attached even in matters of minute detail. Solomon's Temple had, for example, only one door to the side chambers, in the wall facing the south, and this was sufficient for all practical purposes. But Ezekiel's plan provides for two such doors, one in the south and the other in the north, for no assignable reason but to make the two sides of the house exactly alike. There are just two slight deviations from a strictly symmetrical arrangement that can be discerned; one is the washing-chamber by the side of one of the gates of the inner court, and the other the space for cooking the most holy class of sacrifices near the block of cells on the north side of the Temple. With these insignificant exceptions, all the parts of the sanctuary are disposed with mathematical regularity; nothing is left to chance, regard for convenience is everywhere subordinated to the sense of proportion which expresses the ideal order and perfection of the whole.

lated into terms of the spiritual life, drawing near to God denotes the act of faith or prayer or consecration, through which we seek the manifestation of His love in our experience. Religion knows nothing of "action at a distance"; God is near in every place to the soul that knows Him, and distant in every place from the heart that loves darkness rather than light.

Now when the idea of access to God is thus spiritualised the conception of holiness is necessarily transformed, but it is not superseded. At every stage of revelation holiness is that "without which no man shall see the Lord."* In other words, it expresses the conditions that regulate all true fellowship with God. So long as worship was confined to an earthly sanctuary these conditions were, so to speak, materialised. They resolved themselves into a series of "carnal ordinances"—gifts and sacrifices, meats, drinks, and divers washings—that could never make the worshipper perfect as touching the conscience. These things were "imposed until a time of reformation," the "Holy Ghost this signifying, that the way into the holy place had not been made manifest while as the first tabernacle was yet standing."† And yet when we consider what it was that gave such vitality to that persistent sense of distance from God, of His unapproachableness, of danger in contact with Him, what it was that inspired such constant attention to ceremonial purity in all ancient religions, we cannot but see that it was the obscure workings of the conscience, the haunting sense of moral defect cleaving to a man's common life and all his common actions. In heathenism this feeling took an entirely wrong direction; in Israel it was gradually liberated from its material associations and stood forth as an ethical fact. And when at last Christ came to reveal God as He is, He taught men to call nothing common or unclean. But He taught them at the same time that true holiness can only be attained through His atoning sacrifice, and by the indwelling of that Spirit which is the source of moral purity and perfection in all His people. These are the abiding conditions of fellowship with the Father of our spirits; and under the influence of these great Christian facts it is our duty to perfect holiness in the fear of God.

III.

No sooner has the prophet completed his tour of inspection of the sacred buildings than he is conducted to the eastern gate to witness the theophany by which the Temple is consecrated to the service of the true God. "He (the angel) led me to the gate that looks eastward, and, lo, the glory of the God of Israel came from the east; its sound was as the sound of many waters, and the earth shone with its glory. The appearance which I saw was like that which I had seen when He came to destroy the city, and like the appearance which I saw by the river Kebar, and I fell on my face. And the glory of Jehovah entered the house by the gate that looks towards the east. The Spirit caught me up, and brought me to the inner court; and, behold, the glory of Jehovah filled the house. Then I heard a voice from the house speaking to me—the man was standing beside me—and saying, Son of man, hast thou seen the place of My throne, and the place of the soles of My feet, where I shall dwell in the midst of the children of Israel for ever?" (xliii. 1-7).

This great scene, so simply described, is really the culmination of Ezekiel's prophecy. Its spiritual meaning is suggested by the prophet himself when he recalls the terrible act of judgment which he had seen in vision on that very spot some twenty years before (ix.-xi.). The two episodes stand in clear and conscious parallelism with each other. They represent in dramatic form the sum of Ezekiel's teaching in the two periods into which his ministry was divided. On the former occasion he had witnessed the exit of Jehovah from a Temple polluted by heathen abominations and profaned by the presence of men who had disowned the knowledge of the Holy One of Israel. The prophet had read in this the death sentence of the old Hebrew state, and the truth of his vision had been established in the tale of horror and disaster which the subsequent years had unfolded. Now he has been privileged to see the return of Jehovah to a new Temple, corresponding in all respects to the requirements of His holiness; and he recognises it as the pledge of restoration and peace and all the blessings of the Messianic age. The future worshippers are still in exile bearing the chastisement of their former iniquities; but "the Lord is in His holy Temple," and the dispersed of Israel shall yet be gathered home to enter His courts with praise and thanksgiving.

To us this part of the vision symbolises, under forms derived from the Old Testament economy, the central truth of the Christian dispensation. We do no injustice to the historic import of Ezekiel's mission when we say that the dwelling of Jehovah in the midst of His people is an emblem of reconciliation between God and man, and that his elaborate system of ritual observances points towards the sanctification of human life in all its relations through spiritual communion with the Father revealed in our Lord Jesus Christ. Christian interpreters have differed widely as to the manner in which the vision is to be realised in the history of the Church; but on one point at least they are agreed, that through the veil of legal institutions the prophet saw the day of Christ. And although Ezekiel himself does not distinguish between the symbol and the reality, it is nevertheless possible for us to see, in the essential ideas of his vision, a prophecy of that eternal union between God and man which is brought to pass by the work of Christ.

CHAPTER XXVII.

THE PRIESTHOOD.

EZEKIEL xliv.

IN the last chapter we saw how the principle of holiness through separation was exhibited in the plan of a new Temple, round which the Theocracy of the future was to be constituted, We have now to consider the application of the same principle to the *personnel* of the Sanctuary, the priests and others who are to officiate within its courts. The connection between the two is obvious. As has been already remarked, the sanctity of the Temple is not intelligible apart from the ceremonial purity required of the persons who are permitted to enter it. The degrees of holiness pertaining to its different areas

* Heb. xii. 14. † Heb. ix. 8-10.

imply an ascending scale of restrictions on access to the more sacred parts. We may expect to find that in the observance of these conditions the usage of the first Temple left much to be desired from the point of view represented by Ezekiel's ideal. Where the very construction of the sanctuary involved so many departures from the strict idea of holiness it was inevitable that a corresponding laxity should prevail in the discharge of sacred functions. Temple and priesthood in fact are so related that a reform of the one implies of necessity a reform of the other. It is therefore not in itself surprising that Ezekiel's legislation should include a scheme for the reorganisation of the Temple priesthood. But these general considerations hardly prepare us for the sweeping and drastic changes contemplated in the forty-fourth chapter of the book. It requires an effort of imagination to realise the situation with which the prophet has to deal. The abuses for which he seeks a remedy and the measures which he adopts to counteract them are alike contrary to preconceived notions of the order of worship in an Israelite sanctuary. Yet there is no part of the prophet's programme which shows the character of the earnest practical reformer more clearly than this. If we might regard Ezekiel as a mere legislator we should say that the boldest task to which he set his hand was a reformation of the Temple ministry, involving the degradation of an influential class from the priestly status and privileges to which they aspired.

I.

The first and most noteworthy feature of the new scheme is the distinction between priests and Levites. The passage in which this instruction is given is so important that it may be quoted here at length. It is an oracle communicated to the prophet in a peculiarly impressive manner. He has been brought into the inner court in front of the Temple, and there, in full view of the glory of God, he falls on his face, when Jehovah speaks to him as follows:—

"Son of man, give heed and see with thine eyes and hear with thine ears all that I speak to thee concerning all the ordinances and all the laws of Jehovah's house. Mark well the [rule of] entrance into the house, and all the outgoings in the sanctuary. And say to the house of rebellion, the house of Israel: Thus saith the Lord Jehovah, It is high time to desist from all your abominations, O house of Israel, in that ye bring in aliens uncircumcised in heart and uncircumcised in flesh to be in My sanctuary, profaning it, while ye offer My bread, the fat and the blood; thus ye have broken My covenant, in addition to all your (other) abominations; and ye have not kept the charge of My holy things, but have appointed them as keepers of My charge in My sanctuary. Therefore thus saith the Lord Jehovah, No alien uncircumcised in heart and flesh shall enter into My sanctuary, of all the foreigners who are amongst the Israelites. But the Levites who departed from Me when Israel went astray from Me after their idols, *they* shall bear their guilt, and shall minister in My sanctuary in charge at the gates of the house and as ministers of the house; they shall slay the burnt offering and the sacrifice for the people, and stand before them to minister to them. Because they ministered to them before their idols, and were to the house of Israel an occasion of guilt, therefore I lift My hand against them, saith the Lord Jehovah, and they shall ' ear their guilt, and shall not draw near to Me to act as priests to Me or to touch any of My holy things, the most holy things, but shall bear their shame and the abominations which they have committed. I will make them keepers of the charge of the house, for all its servile work and all that has to be done in it. But the priest-Levites, the sons of Zadok, who kept the charge of My sanctuary when the Israelites strayed from Me—they shall draw near to Me to minister to Me, and shall stand before Me to present to Me the fat and the blood, saith the Lord Jehovah. They shall enter into My sanctuary, and they shall draw near to My table to minister to Me, and shall keep My charge" (xliv. 5-16).

Now the first thing to be noticed here is that the new law of the priesthood is aimed directly against a particular abuse in the practice of the first Temple. It appears that down to the time of the Exile uncircumcised aliens were not only admitted to the Temple, but were entrusted with certain important functions in maintaining order in the sanctuary (ver. 8). It is not expressly stated that they took any part in the performance of the worship, although this is suggested by the fact that the Levites who are installed in their place had to slay the sacrifices for the people and render other necessary services to the worshippers (ver. 11). In any case the mere presence of foreigners while sacrifice was being offered (ver. 7) was a profanation of the sanctity of the Temple which was intolerable to a strict conception of Jehovah's holiness. It is therefore of some consequence to discover who these aliens were, and how they came to be engaged in the Temple.

For a partial answer to this question, we may turn first to the memorable scene of the coronation of the young king Joash as described in the eleventh chapter of the Second Book of Kings (*cir.* B. C. 837). The moving spirit in that transaction was the chief priest Jehoiada, a man who was honourably distinguished by his zeal for the purity of the national religion. But although the priest's motives were pure he could only accomplish his object by a palace revolution, carried out with the assistance of the captains of the royal bodyguard. Now from the time of David the royal guard had contained a corps of foreign mercenaries recruited from the Philistine country; and on the occasion with which we are dealing we find mention of a body of Carians, showing that the custom was kept up in the end of the ninth century. During the coronation ceremony these guards were drawn up in the most sacred part of the inner court, the space between the Temple and the altar, with the new king in their midst (ver. 11). Moreover we learn incidentally that keeping watch in the Temple was part of the regular duty of the king's bodyguard, just as much as the custody of the palace (vv. 5-7). In order to understand the full significance of this arrangement, it must be borne in mind that the Temple was in the first instance the royal sanctuary, maintained at the king's expense and subject to his authority. Hence the duty of keeping order in the Temple courts naturally devolved on the troops that attended the king's person and acted as the palace guard. So at an earlier period of the history we read that as often as the king went into the house of Jehovah, he was accompanied by the guard that kept the door of the king's house (1 Kings xiv. 27, 28).

Here, then, we have historical evidence of the admission to the sanctuary of a class of foreigners answering in all respects to the uncircumcised aliens of Ezekiel's legislation. That the practice of enlisting foreign mercenaries for the guard continued till the reign of Josiah seems to be indicated by an allusion in the Book of Zephaniah, where the prophet denounces a body of men in the service of the king who observed the Philistine custom of "leaping over the threshold" (Zeph. i. 9: *cf.* 1 Sam. v. 5). We have only to suppose that this usage, along with the subordination of the Temple to the royal authority, persisted to the close of the monarchy, in order to explain fully the abuse which excited the indignation of our prophet. It is possible no doubt that he had in view other uncircumcised persons as well, such as the Gibeonites (Josh. ix. 27), who were employed in the menial service of the sanctuary. But we have seen enough to show at all events that pre-exilic usage tolerated a freedom of access to the sanctuary and a looseness of administration within it which would have been sacrilegious under the law of the second Temple. It need not be supposed that Ezekiel was the only one who felt this state of things to be a scandal and an injury to religion. We may believe that in this respect he only expressed the higher conscience of his order. Amongst the more devout circles of the Temple priesthood there was probably a growing conviction similar to that which animated the early Tractarian party in the Church of England, a conviction that the whole ecclesiastical system with which their spiritual interests were bound up fell short of the ideal of sanctity essential to it as a Divine institution. But no scheme of reform had any chance of success so long as the palace of the kings stood hard by the Temple, with only a wall between them. The opportunity for reconstruction came with the Exile, and one of the leading principles of the reformed Temple is that here enunciated by Ezekiel, that no "alien uncircumcised in heart and uncircumcised in flesh" shall henceforth enter the sanctuary.

In order to prevent a recurrence of these abuses Ezekiel ordains that for the future the functions of the Temple guard and other menial offices shall be discharged by the Levites who had hitherto acted as priests of the idolatrous shrines throughout the kingdom (vv. 11-14). This singular enactment becomes at once intelligible when we understand the peculiar circumstances brought about by the enforcement of the Deuteronomic Law in the reformation of the year 621. Let us once more recall the fact that the chief object of that reformation was to do away with all the provincial sanctuaries and to concentrate the worship of the nation in the Temple at Jerusalem. It is obvious that by this measure the priests of the local sanctuaries were deprived of their means of livelihood. The rule that they who serve the altar shall live by the altar applied equally to the priests of the high places and to those in the Temple at Jerusalem. All the priests indeed throughout the country were members of a landless caste or tribe; the Levites had no portion or inheritance like the other tribes, but subsisted on the offerings of the worshippers at the various shrines where they ministered. Now the law of Deuteronomy recognises the principle of compensation for the vested interests that were thus abolished. Two alternatives were offered to the Levites of the high places: they might either remain in the villages or townships where they were known, or they might proceed to the central sanctuary and obtain admission to the ranks of the priesthood there. In the former case, the Lawgiver commends them earnestly, along with other destitute members of the community, to the charity of their well-to-do fellow-townsmen and neighbours. If, on the other hand, they elected to try their fortunes in the Temple at Jerusalem, he secures their full priestly status and equal rights with their brethren who regularly officiated there. On this point the legislation is quite explicit. Any Levite from any district of Israel who came of his own free will to the place which Jehovah had chosen might minister in the name of Jehovah his God, as all his brethren the Levites did who stood there before Jehovah, and have like portions to eat (Deut. xviii. 6-8). In this matter, however, the humane intention of the law was partly frustrated by the exclusiveness of the priests who were already in possession of the sacred offices in the Temple. The Levites who were brought up from the provinces to Jerusalem were allowed their proper share of the priestly dues, but were not permitted to officiate at the altar.* It is not probable that a large number of the provincial Levites availed themselves of this grudging provision for their maintenance. In the idolatrous reaction which set in after the death of Josiah the worship of the high places was revived, and the great body of the Levites would naturally be favourable to the re-establishment of the old order of things with which their professional interests were identified. Still, there would be a certain number who for conscientious motives attached themselves to the movement for a purer and stricter conception of the worship of Jehovah, and were willing to submit to the irksome conditions which this movement imposed on them. They might hope for a time when the generous provisions of the Deuteronomic Code would be applied to them; but their position in the meantime was both precarious and humiliating. They had to bear the doom pronounced long ago on the sinful house of Eli: "Every one that is left in thine house shall come and bow down to him (the high priest of the line of Zadok) for a piece of silver and a loaf of bread, and shall say, Thrust me, I pray thee, into one of the priests' offices, that I may eat a morsel of bread."†

We see thus that Ezekiel's legislation on the subject of the Levites starts from a state of things created by Josiah's reformation, and, let us remember, a state of things with which the prophet was familiar in his earlier days when he was himself a priest in the Temple. On the whole he justifies the exclusive attitude of the Temple priesthood towards the new-comers, and carries forward the application of the idea of sanctity from the point where it had been left by the law of Deuteronomy. That law recognises no sacerdotal distinctions within the ranks of the priesthood. Its regular designation of the priests of

* 2 Kings xxiii. 9. The sense of the passage is undoubtedly that given above; but the expression "unleavened bread" as a general name for the priests' portion is peculiar. It has been proposed to read, with a change merely of the punctuation, instead of מַצּוֹת, מִצְוֹת = "statutory portions," as in Neh. xiii. 5.

† 1 Sam. ii. 36.

the Temple is "the priests, the Levites"; that of the provincial priests is simply "the Levites." All priests are brethren, all belong to the same tribe of Levi; and it is assumed, as we have seen, that any Levite, whatever his antecedents, is qualified for the full privileges of the priesthood in the central sanctuary if he choose to claim them. But we have also seen that the distinction emerged as a consequence of the enforcement of the fundamental law of the single sanctuary. There came to be a class of Levites in the Temple whose position was at first indeterminate. They themselves claimed the full standing of the priesthood, and they could appeal in support of their claim to the authority of the Deuteronomic legislation. But the claim was never conceded in practice, the influence of the legitimate Temple priests being strong enough to exclude them from the supreme privilege of ministering at the altar. This state of things could not continue. Either the disparity of the two orders must be effaced by the admission of the Levites to a footing of equality with the other priests, or else it must be emphasised and based on some higher principle than the jealousy of a close corporation for its traditional rights. Now such a principle is supplied by the section of Ezekiel's vision with which we are dealing. The permanent exclusion of the Levites from the priesthood is founded on the unassailable moral ground that they had forfeited their rights by their unfaithfulness to the fundamental truths of the national religion. They had been a "stumbling-block of iniquity" to the house of Israel through their disloyalty to Jehovah's cause during the long period of national apostasy, when they lent themselves to the popular inclination towards impure and idolatrous worship. For this great betrayal of their trust they must bear the guilt and shame in their degradation to the lowest offices in the service of the new sanctuary. They are to fill the place formerly occupied by uncircumcised foreigners, as keepers of the gates and servants of the house and the worshipping congregation; but they may not draw near to Jehovah in the exercise of priestly prerogatives, nor put their hands to the most holy things. The priesthood of the new Temple is finally vested in the "sons of Zadok"—*i. e.*, the body of Levitical priests who had ministered in the Temple since its foundation by Solomon. Whatever the faults of these Zadokites had been—and Ezekiel certainly does not judge them leniently *—they had at least steadfastly maintained the ideal of a central sanctuary, and in comparison with the rural clergy they were doubtless a purer and better-disciplined body. The judgment is only a relative one, as all class judgments necessarily are. There must have been individual Zadokites worse than an ordinary Levite from the country, as well as individual Levites who were superior to the average Temple priest. But if it was necessary that in the future the interest of religion should be mainly confided to a priesthood, there could be no question that as a class the old priestly aristocracy of the central sanctuary were those best qualified for spirituaul leadership.

In Ezekiel's vision we thus seem to find the beginning of a statutory and official distinction between priests and Levites. This fact forms one of the arguments chiefly relied on by those who hold that the book of Ezekiel precedes the

* *Cf.* ch. xxii. 26.

introduction of the Priestly Code of the Pentateuch. Two things, indeed, appear to be clearly established. In the first place the tendency and significance of Ezekiel's legislation are adequately explained by the historical situation that existed in the generation immediately preceding the Exile. In the second place the Mosaic books, apart from Deuteronomy, had no influence on the scheme propounded in the vision. It is felt that these results are difficult to reconcile with the view that the middle books of the Pentateuch were known to the prophet as part of a divinely ordained constitution for the Israelite theocracy. We should have expected in that case that the prophet would simply have fallen back on the provisions of the earlier legislation, where the division between priests and Levites is formulated with perfect clearness and precision. Or, looking at the matter from the divine point of view, we should have expected that the revelation given to Ezekiel would endorse the principles of the revelation that had already been given. It is equally hard to suppose that any existing law should have been unknown to Ezekiel, or to suggest a reason for his ignoring it if it was known. The facts that have come before us seem thus, so far as they go, to be in favour of the theory that Ezekiel stands midway between Deuteronomy and the Priestly Code, and that the final codification and promulgation of the latter took place after his time.

It is nearer our purpose, however, to note the probable effect of these regulations on the *personnel* of the second Temple. In the book of Ezra we are told that in the first colony of returning exiles there were four thousand two hundred and eighty-nine priests and only seventy-four Levites.* One man in every ten was a priest, and the total number was probably in excess of the requirements of a fully equipped Temple. The number of Levites, on the other hand, would have been quite insufficient for the duties required of them under the new arrangements, had there not been a contingent of nearly four hundred of the old Temple servants to supply their lack of service.† Again, when Ezra came up from Babylon in the year 458, we find that not a single Levite volunteered to accompany him. It was only after some negotiations that about forty Levites were induced to go up with him to Jerusalem; and again they were far outnumbered by the Nethinim or Temple slaves.‡ These figures cannot possibly represent the proportionate strength of the tribe of Levi under the old monarchy. They indicate unmistakably that there was a great reluctance on the part of the Levites to share the perils and glory of the founding of the new Jerusalem. Is it not probable that the new conditions laid down by Ezekiel's legislation were the cause of this reluctance? That, in short, the prospect of being servants in a Temple where they had once claimed to be priests was not sufficiently attractive to the majority to lead them to break up their comfortable homes in exile, and take their proper place in the ranks of those who were forming the new community of Israel? And ought we not to spare a moment's admiration even at this distance of time for the public-spirited few who in self-sacrificing devotion to the cause of God willingly accepted a position which was scorned by the great mass of their tribesmen? If this was their spirit, they had their reward. Although

* Ezra ii. 36-40. † Ezra ii. 58. ‡ Ezra viii. 15-20.

the position of a Levite was at first a symbol of inferiority and degradation, it ultimately became one of very great honour. When the Temple service was fully organised, the Levites were a large and important order, second in dignity in the community only to the priests. Their ranks were swelled by the incorporation of the Temple musicians, as well as other functionaries; and thus the Levites are for ever associated in our minds with the magnificent service of praise which was the chief glory of the second Temple.

II.

The remainder of the forty-fourth chapter lays down the rules of ceremonial holiness to be observed by the priests, the duties they have to perform towards the community, and the provision to be made for their maintenance. A few words must here suffice on each of these topics.

1. The sanctity of the priests is denoted, first of all, by the obligation to wear special linen garments when they enter the inner court, which is the sphere of their peculiar ministrations. Vestries were provided, as we have seen from the description of the Temple, between the inner and outer courts, where these garments were to be put on and off as the priests passed to and from the discharge of their sacred duties. The general idea underlying this regulation is too obvious to require explanation. It is but an application of the fundamental principle that approach to the Deity, or entrance into a place sanctified by His presence, demands a condition of ceremonial purity which cannot be maintained and must not be imitated by persons of a lower degree of religious privilege. A strange but very suggestive extension of the principle is found in the injunction to put off the garments before going into the outer court, lest the ordinary worshipper should be sanctified by chance contact with them. That both holiness and uncleanness are propagated by contagion is of the very essence of the ancient idea of sanctity; but the remarkable thing is that in some circumstances communicated holiness is as much to be dreaded as communicated uncleanness. It is not said what would be the fate of an Israelite who should by chance touch the sacred vestments, but evidently he must be disqualified for participation in worship until he had purged himself of his illegitimate sanctity.*

In the next place the priests are under certain permanent obligations with regard to signs of mourning, marriage, and contact with death, which again are the mark of the peculiar sanctity of their caste. The rules as to mourning—prohibition of shaving the head and letting the hair flow dishevelled †—have been thought to be directed against heathen customs arising out of the worship of the dead. In marriage the priest may only take a virgin of the house of Israel or the widow of a priest. And only in the case of his nearest relatives—parent, child, brother, and unmarried sister—may he defile himself by rendering the last offices to the departed, and even these exceptions involve exclusion from the sacred office for seven days.*

The relations of these requirements to the corresponding parts of the Levitical law are somewhat complicated. The great point of difference is that Ezekiel knows nothing of the unique privileges and sanctity of the high priest. It might seem at first sight as if this implied a deliberate departure from the known usage of the first Temple. It is certain that there were high priests under the monarchy, and indeed we can discover the rudiments of a hierarchy in a distribution of authority between the high priest, second priest, keepers of the threshold, and chief officers of the house.† But the silence of Ezekiel does not necessarily mean that he contemplated any innovation on the established order of things. The historical books afford no ground for supposing that the high priest in the old Temple had a religious standing distinguished from that of his colleagues. He was *primus inter pares*, the president of the priestly college and the supreme authority in the internal administration of the Temple affairs, but probably nothing more. Such an office was almost necessary in the interest of order and authority, and there is nothing in Ezekiel's regulations inconsistent with its continuance.‡ On the other hand, it must be admitted that his silence would be strange if he had in view the position assigned to the high priest under the law. For there the high priest is as far elevated above his colleagues as these are above the Levites. He is the concentration of all that is holy in Israel, and the sole mediator of the nearest approach to God which the symbolism of Temple worship permitted. He is bound by the strictest conditions of ceremonial sanctity, and any transgression on his part has to be atoned for by a rite similar to that required for a transgression of the whole congregation.§ The omission of this striking figure from the pages of Ezekiel makes a comparison between his enactments concerning the priesthood and those of the law difficult and in some degree uncertain. Nevertheless there are points both of likeness and contrast which cannot escape observation. Thus the laws of this chapter on defilement by a dead body are identical with those enjoined in Lev. xxi. 1-3 (the "Law of Holiness") for ordinary priests; while the high priest is there forbidden to touch any dead body whatsoever. On the other hand Ezekiel's regulations as to priestly marriages seem as it were to strike an average between the restrictions imposed in the law on ordinary priests and those binding on the high priest. The former may marry any woman that is not violated or a harlot or a divorced wife; but the high priest is forbidden to marry any one but a virgin of his own people. Again, the priestly garments, according to Exod. xxviii. 39-42, xxxix. 27, are made partly of linen and partly of byssus (? cotton), which certainly looks like a refinement on the simpler attire prescribed by Ezekiel. But it is impossible to pursue this subject further here.

2. The duties of the priests towards the people

* On this peculiar affinity between holiness and uncleanness see the interesting argument in Robertson Smith's "Religion of the Semites," pp. 427 ff. The passage Hag. ii. 12–14 does not appear to be inconsistent with what is there said. The meaning is that "very indirect contact with the holy does not make holy, but very direct contact with the unclean makes unclean" (Wellhausen, "Die Kleinen Propheten," p. 170).

† *Cf.* ch. xxiv. 17; Lev. x. 6, xxi. 5, 10.

* It is remarkable that neither here nor in Leviticus (ch. xxi. 1–3) is the priest's wife mentioned as one for whom he may defile himself at her death.

† *Cf.* 2 Kings xii. 11, xxiii. 14, xxv. 18; Jer. xx. 1.

‡ Hence it does not seem to me that any argument can be based on the fact that a high priest was at the head of the returning exiles either for or against the existence of the Priestly Code at that date.

§ Lev. iv. 3, 13: *cf.* Lev. xvi. 6.

are few, but exceedingly important. In the first place they have to instruct the people in the distinctions between the holy and the profane and between the clean and the unclean. It will not be supposed that this instruction took the form of set lectures or homilies on the principles of ceremonial religion. The verb translated "teach" in ver. 23 means to give an authoritative decision in a special case; and this had always been the form of priestly instruction in Israel. The subject of the teaching was of the utmost importance for a community whose whole life was regulated by the idea of holiness in the ceremonial sense. To preserve the land in a state of purity befitting the dwelling-place of Jehovah required the most scrupulous care on the part of all its inhabitants; and in practice difficult questions would constantly occur which could only be settled by an appeal to the superior knowledge of the priest. Hence Ezekiel contemplates a perpetuation of the old ritual Torah or direction of the priests even in the ideal state of things to which his vision looks forward. Although the people are assumed to be all righteous in heart and responsive to the will of Jehovah, yet they could not all have the professional knowledge of ritual laws which was necessary to guide them on all occasions, and errors of inadvertence were unavoidable. Jeremiah could look forward to a time when none should teach his neighbour or his brother, saying, Know Jehovah, because the religion which consists in spiritual emotions and affections becomes the independent possession of every one who is the subject of saving grace. But Ezekiel, from his point of view, could not anticipate a time when all the Lord's people should be priests; for ritual is essentially an affair of tradition and technique, and can only be maintained by a class of experts specially trained for their office. Ritualism and sacerdotalism are natural allies; and it is not wholly accidental that the great ritualistic Churches of Christendom are those organised on the sacerdotal principle.

But, secondly, the priests have to act as judges or arbitrators in cases of disagreement between man and man (ver. 24). This again was an important department of priestly Torah in ancient Israel, the origin of which went back to the personal legislation of Moses in the wilderness.* Cases too hard for human judgment were referred to the decision of God at the sanctuary, and the judgment was conveyed through the agency of the priest. It is impossible to overestimate the service thus rendered by the priesthood to the cause of religion in Israel; and Hosea bitterly complains of the defection of the priests from the Torah of their God as the source of the widespread moral corruption of his time.† In the book of Deuteronomy the Levitical priests of the central sanctuary are associated with the civil magistrate as a court of ultimate appeal in matters of controversy that arise within the community; and this is by no means a tribute to the superior legal acumen of the clerical mind, but a reassertion of the old principle that the priest is the mouthpiece of Jehovah's judgment.‡ That the priests should be the sole judges in Ezekiel's ideal polity was to be expected from the high position assigned to the order generally; but there is another reason for it. We have once more to keep in mind that we are dealing

* Exod. xviii. 25 ff. † Hosea iv. 6.
‡ *Cf.* Deut. i. 17: "judgment is God's."

with the Messianic community, when the people are anxious to do the right when they know it, and only cases of honest perplexity require to be resolved. The priests' decision had never been backed up by executive authority, and in the kingdom of God no such sanction will be necessary. By this simple judicial arrangement the ethical demands of Jehovah's holiness will be made effective in the ordinary life of the community.

Finally, the priests have complete control of public worship, and are responsible for the due observance of the festivals and for the sanctification of the Sabbath (ver. 24).

3. With regard to the provisions for the support of the priesthood, the old law continues in force that the priests can hold no landed property and have no possession like the other tribes of Israel (ver. 28). It is true that a strip of land, measuring about twenty-seven square miles, was set apart for their residence; * but this was probably not to be cultivated, and at all events it is not reckoned as a possession yielding revenue for their maintenance. The priests' inheritance is Jehovah Himself, which means that they are to live on the offerings of the community presented to Jehovah at the sanctuary. In the practice of the first Temple this ancient rule appears to have been interpreted in a broad and liberal spirit, greatly to the advantage of the Zadokite priests. The Temple dues consisted partly of money payments by the worshippers; and at least the fines for ceremonial trespasses which took the place of the sin- and guilt-offerings were counted the lawful perquisites of the priests.‡ Ezekiel knows nothing of this system; and if it remained in force down to his time, he undoubtedly meant to abolish it. The tribute of the sanctuary is to be paid wholly in kind, and out of this the priests are to receive a stated allowance. In the first place those sacrifices which are wholly made over to the Deity, and yet are not consumed on the altar, have to be eaten by the priests in a holy place. These are the meal-offering, the sin-offering, and the guilt-offering, of which more hereafter. For precisely the same reason all that is *ḥerem*—*i. e.*, "devoted" irrevocably to Jehovah—becomes the possession of the priests, His representatives, except in the cases where it had to be absolutely destroyed. Besides this they have a claim to the best (an indefinite portion) of the firstfruits and "oblations" (*terûmah*) brought to the sanctuary in accordance with ancient custom to be consumed by the worshipper and his friends.‡

These regulations are undoubtedly based on pre-exilic usages, and consequently leave much to be supplied from the people's knowledge of use and wont. They do not differ very greatly from the enumeration of the priestly dues in the eighteenth chapter of Deuteronomy. There, as in Ezekiel, we find that the two great sources from which the priests derive their maintenance are the sacrifices and the firstfruits. The Deuteronomic Code, however, knows nothing of the special class of sacrifices called sin- and guilt-offerings, but simply assigns to the priest certain portions of each victim,§ except of course

* See below, p. 348.
† 2 Kings xii. 4–16.
‡ They also receive the best of the *'arîsoth*, a word of uncertain meaning, probably either dough or coarse meal. This offering is said to bring a blessing on the household.
§ Deut. xviii. 3.

the burnt-offerings, which were consumed entire on the altar. The priest's share of natural produce is the "best" of corn, new wine, oil, and wool,* and would be selected as a matter of course from the tithe and *terûmah* brought to the sanctuary; so that on this point there is practically complete agreement between Ezekiel and Deuteronomy. On the other hand the differences of the Levitical legislation are considerable, and all in the direction of a fuller provision for the Temple establishment. Such an increased provision was called for by the peculiar circumstances of the second Temple. The revenue of the sanctuary obviously depended on the size and prosperity of the constituency to which it ministered. The stipulations of Deut. xviii. were no doubt sufficient for the maintenance of the priesthood in the old kingdom of Judah; and similarly those of Ezekiel's legislation would amply suffice in the ideal condition of the people and land presupposed by the vision. But neither could have been adequate for the support of a costly ritual in a small community like that which returned from Babylon, where one man in ten was a priest. Accordingly we find that the arrangements made under Nehemiah for the endowment of the Temple ministry are conformed to the extended provisions of the Priestly Code (Neh. x. 32-39).†

III.

In conclusion, let us briefly consider the significance of this great institution of the priesthood in Ezekiel's scheme of an ideal theocracy. It would of course be an utter mistake to suppose that the prophet is merely legislating in the interests of the sacerdotal order to which he himself belonged. It was necessary for him to insist on the peculiar sanctity and privileges of the priests, and to draw a sharp line of division between them and ordinary members of the community. But he does this, not in the interest of a privileged caste within the nation, but in the interest of a religious ideal which embraced priests and people alike and had to be realised in the life of the nation as a whole. That ideal is expressed by the word "holiness," and we have already seen how the idea of holiness demanded ceremonial conditions of immediate access to Jehovah's presence which the ordinary Israelite could not observe. But "exclusion" could not possibly be the last word of a religion which seeks to bring men into fellowship with God. Access to God might be hedged about by restrictions and conditions of the most onerous kind, but access there must be if worship was to have any meaning and value for the nation or the individual. Although the worshipper might not himself lay his victim on the altar, he must at least be permitted to offer his gift and receive the assurance that it was accepted. If the priest stood between him and God, it was not merely to separate but also to mediate between them, and through the fulfilment of superior conditions of holiness to establish a communication between him and the holy Being whose face he sought. Hence the great function of the priesthood in the theocracy is to maintain the intercourse between Jehovah and Israel which was exhibited in the Temple ritual by acts of sacrificial worship.

Now it is manifest that this system of ideas rests on the representative character of the priestly office. If the principal idea symbolised in the sanctuary is that of holiness through separation, the fundamental idea of priesthood is holiness through representation. It is the holiness of Israel, concentrated in the priesthood, which qualifies the latter for entrance within the inner circle of the divine presence. Or perhaps it would be more correct to say that the presence of Jehovah first sanctifies the priests in an eminent degree, and then through them, though in a less degree, the whole body of the people. The idea of national solidarity was too deeply rooted in the Hebrew consciousness to admit of any other interpretation of the priesthood than this. The Israelite did not need to be told that his standing before God was secured by his membership in the religious community on whose behalf the priests ministered at the altar and before the Temple. It would not occur to him to think of his personal exclusion from the most sacred offices as a religious disability; it was enough for him to know that the nation to which he belonged was admitted to the presence of Jehovah in the persons of its representatives, and that he as an individual shared in the blessings which accrued to Israel through the privileged ministry of the priests. Thus to a Temple poet of a later age than Ezekiel's the figure of the high priest supplies a striking image of the communion of saints and the blessing of Jehovah resting on the whole people:—

"Behold, how good and how pleasant it is
That they who are brethren should also dwell together!
Like the precious oil on the head,
That flows down on the beard,
The beard of Aaron,
That flows down on the hem of his garments—
Like the Hermon-dew that descends on the hills of Zion;
For there hath Jehovah ordained the blessing,
Life for evermore." *

* Deut. xviii. 4.

† The regulations of the Priests' Code with regard to the revenues of the Temple clergy are most comprehensively given in Numb. xviii. 8-32. The first thing that strikes us there is the distinction between the due of the priests and that of the Levites. The absence of any express provision for the latter is a somewhat remarkable feature in Ezekiel's legislation, when we consider the care with which he has defined the status and duties of the order. It is evident, however, that no complete arrangements could be made for the Temple service without some law on this point such as is contained in the passage Numb. xviii. and referred to in Neh. x. 37-39; and this is closely connected with a disposition of the tithes and firstlings different from the directions of Deuteronomy, and probably also from the tacit assumption of Ezekiel. The book of Deuteronomy leaves no doubt that both the tithes of natural produce and the firstlings of the flock and herd were intended to furnish the material for sacrificial feasts at the sanctuary (*cf.* chs. xii. 6, 7, 11, 12, xiv. 22-27). The priest received the usual portions of the firstlings (ch. xviii. 3), and also a share of the tithe; but the rest was eaten by the worshipper and his guests. In Numb. xviii., on the other hand, all the firstlings are the property of the priest (ver. 15), and the whole of the tithes is assigned to the Levites, who in turn are required to hand over a tenth of the tithe to the priests (vv. 24-32). The portion of the priests consists of the following items: (1) The meal-offering, sin-offering, and guilt-offering (as in Ezekiel); (2) the best of oil, new wine, and corn (as in Deuteronomy (ver. 12); (3) all the first fruits (an advance on Ezekiel) (ver. 14); (4) every devoted thing (Ezekiel) (ver. 14); (5) all the firstlings (vv. 15-18); (6) the breast and right thigh of all ordinary private sacrifices (ver. 18: *cf.* Lev. vii. 31-34) (like Deuteronomy but choicer portions); (7) the tenth of the Levites' tithe. It will be seen from this enumeration that the Temple tariff of the Priestly law includes, with some slight modification, all the requirements of Deuteronomy and Ezekiel, besides the two important additions referred to above.

* Psalm cxxxiii.

CHAPTER XXVIII.

PRINCE AND PEOPLE.

EZEKIEL xliv.-xlvi. *passim.*

IT was remarked in a previous chapter that the "prince" of the closing vision appears to occupy a less exalted position than the Messianic king of chap. xxxiv. or chap. xxxvii. The grounds on which this impression rests require, however, to be carefully considered, if we are not to carry away a thoroughly false conception of the theocratic state foreshadowed by Ezekiel. It must not be supposed that the prince is a personage of less than royal rank, or that his authority is overshadowed by that of a priestly caste. He is undoubtedly the civil head of the nation, owing no allegiance within his own province to any earthly superior. Nor is there any reason to doubt that he is the heir of the Davidic house and holds his office in virtue of the divine promise which secured the throne to David's descendants. It would therefore be a mistake to imagine that we have here an anticipation of the Romish theory of the subordination of the secular to the spiritual power. It may be true that in the state of things presupposed by the vision very little is left for the king to do, whilst a variety of important duties falls to the priesthood; but at all events the king is there and is supreme in his own sphere. Ezekiel does not show the road to Canossa. If the king is overshadowed, it is by the personal presence of Jehovah in the midst of His people; and that which limits his prerogative is not the sacerdotal power, but the divine constitution of the theocracy as revealed in the vision itself, under which both king and priests have their functions defined and regulated with a view to the religious ends for which the community as a whole exists.

Our purpose in the present chapter is to put together the scattered references to the duties of the prince which occur in chaps. xliv.-xlvi., so as to gain as clear a picture as possible of the position of the monarchy in the theocratic state. It must be remembered, however, that the picture will necessarily be incomplete. National life in its secular aspects, with which the king is chiefly concerned, is hardly touched on in the vision. Everything being looked upon from the point of view of the Temple and its worship, there are but few allusions in which we can detect anything of the nature of a civil constitution. And these few are introduced incidentally, not for their own sake, but to explain some arrangement for securing the sanctity of the land or the community. This fact must never be lost sight of in judging of Ezekiel's conception of the monarchy. From all that appears in these pages we might conclude that the prince is a mere ornamental figurehead of the constitution, and that the few real duties assigned to him could have been equally well performed by a committee of priests or laymen elected for the purpose. But this is to forget that outside the range of subjects here touched upon there is a whole world of secular interests, of political and social action, where the king has his part to play in accordance with the precedents furnished by the best days of the ancient monarchy.

Let us glance first of all at Ezekiel's institutes of the kingdom in its more political relations. The notices here are all in the form of constitutional checks and safeguards against an arbitrary and oppressive exercise of the royal authority. They are instructive, not only as showing the interest which the prophet had in good government and his care for the rights of the subject, but also for the light they cast on certain administrative methods in force previous to the Exile.

The first point that calls for attention is the provision made for the maintenance of the prince and his court. It would seem that the revenue of the prince was to be derived mainly, if not wholly, from a portion of territory reserved as his exclusive property in the division of the country among the tribes.* These crown lands are situated on either side of the sacred "oblation" around the sanctuary, set apart for the use of the priests and Levites; and they extend to the sea on the west and to the Jordan Valley on the east. Out of these he is at liberty to assign a possession to his sons in perpetuity, but any estate bestowed on his courtiers reverts to the prince in the "year of liberty." † The object of this last regulation apparently is to prevent the formation of a new hereditary aristocracy between the royal family and the peasantry. A life peerage, so to speak, or something less, is deemed a sufficient reward for the most devoted service to the king or the state. And no doubt the certainty of a revision of all royal grants every seventh year would tend to keep some persons mindful of their duty. The whole system of royal demesnes, which the king might dispose of as appanages for his younger children or his faithful retainers, presents a curious resemblance to a well-known feature of feudalism in the Middle Ages; but it was never practically enforced in Israel. Before the Exile it was evidently unknown, and after the Exile there was no king to provide for. But why does the prophet bestow so much care on a mere detail of a political system in which, as a whole, he takes so little interest? It is because of his concern for the rights of the common people against the high-handed tyranny of the king and his nobles. He recalls the bad times of the old monarchy when any man was liable to be ejected from his land for the benefit of some court favourite, or to provide a portion for a younger son of the king. The cruel evictions of the poorer peasant proprietors, which all the early prophets denounce as an outrage against humanity, and of which the story of Naboth furnished a typical example, must be rendered impossible in the new Israel; and as the king had no doubt been the principal offender in the past, the rule is firmly laid down in his case that on no pretext must he take the people's inheritance. And this, be it observed, is an application of the religious principle which underlies the constitution of the theocracy. The land is Jehovah's, and all interference with the ancient landmarks which guard the rights of private ownership is an offence against the holiness of the true divine King who has His abode amongst the tribes of Israel. This suggests developments of the idea of holiness which reach to the very foundations of social well-being. A conception of holiness which secures each man in the possession of his own vine and fig tree is

* Chs. xlv. 7, 8, xlviii. 21, 22.

† *I. e.*, either the seventh year, as in Jer. xxxiv. 14, or the year of Jubilee, the fiftieth year (Lev. xxv. 10); more probably the former.

at all events not open to the charge of ignoring the practical interests of common life for the sake of an unprofitable ceremonialism.

In the next place we come across a much more startling revelation of the injustice habitually practised by the Hebrew monarchs. Just as later sovereigns were wont to meet their deficits by debasing the currency, so the kings of Judah had learned to augment their revenue by a systematic falsification of weights and measures. We know from the prophet Amos * that this was a common trick of the wealthy landowners who sold grain at exorbitant prices to the poor whom they had driven from their possessions. They "made the ephah small and the shekel great, and dealt falsely with balances of deceit." But it was left for Ezekiel to tell us that the same fraud was a regular part of the fiscal system of the Judæan kingdom. There is no mistaking the meaning of his accusation: "Have done, O princes of Israel, with your violent and oppressive rule; execute judgment and justice, and take away your exactions from My people, saith Jehovah God. *Ye shall have just balances, and a just ephah, and a just bath.*" † That is to say, the taxes were surreptitiously increased by the use of a large shekel (for weighing out money payments) and a large bath and ephah (for measuring tribute paid in kind). And if it was impossible for the poor to protect themselves against the rapacity of private dealers, poor and rich alike were helpless when the fraud was openly practised in the king's name. This Ezekiel had seen with his own eyes, and the shameful injustice of it was so branded on his spirit that even in a vision of the late days it comes back to him as an evil to be sedulously guarded against. It was eminently a case for legislation. If there was to be such a thing as fair dealing and commercial probity in the community, the system of weights and measurement must be fixed beyond the power of the royal caprice to alter it. It was as sacred as any principle of the constitution. Accordingly he finds a place in his legislation for a corrected scale of weights and measures, restored no doubt to their original values. The ephah for dry measure and the bath or liquid measure are each fixed at the tenth part of a homer. "The shekel shall be twenty geras: ‡ five shekels shall be five, and ten shekels shall be ten, and fifty shekels shall be your maneh." §

These regulations extend far beyond the immediate object for which they are introduced, and have both a moral and a religious bearing. They express a truth often insisted on in the Old Testament, that commercial morality is a matter in which the holiness of Jehovah is involved: "A false balance is an abomination to Jehovah, but a just weight is His delight." ‖ In the Law of Holiness an ordinance very similar to Ezekiel's occurs amongst the conditions by which the precept is to be fulfilled: "Be ye holy, for I am holy." ¶ It is evident that the Israelites had learned to regard with a religious abhorrence all tampering with the fixed standards of value on which the purity of commercial life depended. To overreach by lying words was a sin; but to cheat by the use of a false balance was a species of profanity comparable to a false oath in the name of Jehovah.

These rules about weights and measures required, however, to be supplemented by a fixed tariff, regulating the taxes which the prince might impose on the people.* It is not quite clear whether any part of the prince's own income was to be derived from taxation. The tribute is called an "oblation," and there is no doubt that it was intended principally for the support of the Temple ritual, which in any case must have been the heaviest charge on the royal exchequer. But the oblation was rendered to the prince in the first instance; and the prophet's anxiety to prevent unjust exactions springs from a fear that the king might make the Temple tax a pretext for increasing his own revenue. At all events the people's duty to contribute to the support of public ordinances according to their ability is here explicitly recognised. Compared with the provision of the Levitical law the scale of charges here proposed must be pronounced extremely moderate. The contribution of each householder varies from one-sixtieth to one-two-hundredth of his income, and is wholly paid in kind.† The proper equivalent under the second Temple of Ezekiel's "oblation" was a poll-tax of one-third of a shekel, voluntarily undertaken at the time of Nehemiah's covenant "for the service of the house of our God; for the shewbread and for the continual meal-offering, and for the continual burnt-offering, of the Sabbaths, of the new moons, for the set feasts, and for the holy things, and for the sin-offerings to make atonement for Israel, and for all the work of the house of our God." ‡ In the Priestly Code this tax is fixed at half a shekel for each man.§ But in addition to this money payment the law required a tenth of all produce of the soil and the flock to be given to the priests and Levites. In Ezekiel's legislation the tithes and firstfruits are still left for the use of the owner, who is expected to consume them in sacrificial feasts at the sanctuary. The only charge, therefore, of the nature of a fixed tribute for religious purposes is the oblation here required for the regular sacrifices which represent the stated worship rendered on behalf of the community as a whole.

This brings us now to the more important aspect of the kingly office—its religious privileges and duties. Here there are three points which require to be noticed.

1. In the first place it is the duty of the prince to supply the material of the public sacrifices offered in the name of the people.‖ Out of the tribute levied on the people for this purpose he has to furnish the altar with the stated number of victims for the daily service, the Sabbaths, and

* Amos viii. 5.

† Ezek. xlv. 9, 10. In the translation of ver. 9 I have followed an emendation proposed by Cornill. The sense is not affected, but the grammatical construction seems to demand some alteration in the Massoretic text.

‡ In Exod. xxx. 13, Lev. xxvii. 25, Numb. iii. 47 (Priests' Code) the shekel of twenty geras is described as the "shekel of the sanctuary," or "sacred shekel," clearly implying that another shekel was in common use.

§ Ezek. xlv. 12, according to the LXX.

‖ Prov. xi. 1.

¶ Lev. xix. 35, 36.

* Ezek. xlv. 13–16.

† The exact figures, are, one part in sixty of cereal produce (wheat and barley), one share in a hundred of oil, and one animal out of every two hundred from the flock (ch. xlv. 13–15).

‡ Neh. x. 32, 33: *cf.* Ezek. xlv. 15.

§ Exod. xxx. 11–16. Whether the third of a shekel in the book of Nehemiah is a concession to the poverty of the people, or whether the law represents an increased charge found necessary for the full Temple service, is a question that need not be discussed here.

‖ Ch. xlv. 17.

new moons, and the great yearly festivals. It is clear that some one must be charged with the responsibility of this important part of the worship, and it is significant of Ezekiel's relations to the past that the duty does not yet devolve directly on the priests. They seem to exercise no authority outside of the Temple, the king standing between them and the community as a sort of patron of the sanctuary. But the position of the prince is not simply that of an official receiver, collecting the tribute and then handing it over to the Temple as it was required. He is the representative of the religious unity of the nation, and in this capacity he presents in person the regular sacrifices offered on behalf of the community. Thus on the day of the Passover he presents a sin-offering for himself and the people,* as the high priest does in the ceremonial of the Great Day of Atonement.† And so all the sacrifices of the stated ritual are his sacrifices, officiating as the head of the nation in its acts of common worship. In this respect the prince succeeds to the rights exercised by the kings of Judah in the ritual of the first Temple, although on a different footing. Before the Exile the king had a proprietary interest in the central sanctuary, and the expense of the stated service was defrayed as a matter of course out of the royal revenues. Part of this revenue, as we see in the case of Joash, was raised by a system of Temple dues paid by the worshippers and expended on the repairs of the house; but at a much later date than this we find Ahaz assuming absolute control over the daily sacrifices,‡ which were doubtless maintained at his expense.

Now the tendency of Ezekiel's legislation is to bring the whole community into a closer and more personal connection with the worship of the sanctuary, and to leave no part of it subject to the arbitrary will of the prince. But still the idea is preserved that the prince is the religious as well as the civil representative of the nation; and although he is deprived of all control over the performance of the ritual, he is still required to provide the public sacrifices and to offer them in the name of his people.

2. In virtue of his representative character the prince possesses certain privileges in his approaches to God in the sanctuary not accorded to ordinary worshippers. In this connection it is necessary to explain some details regulating the use of the sanctuary by the people. The outer court might be entered by prince or people either through the north or south gate, but not from the east. The eastern gate was that by which Jehovah had entered His dwelling-place, and the doors of it are for ever closed. No foot might cross its threshold. But the prince—and this is one of his peculiar rights—might enter the gateway from the court to eat his sacrificial meals.§ It seems therefore to have served the same purpose for the prince as the thirty cells along the wall did for common worshippers. The east gate of the inner court was also shut, as a rule, and was probably never used as a passage even by the priests. But on the Sabbaths and new moons it was thrown open to receive the sacrifices which the prince had to bring on these days, and it remained open till the evening. On days when the gate was open the worshipping congregation assembled at its door, while the prince entered as far as the threshold and looked on while the priests presented his offering; then he went out by the way he had entered. If on any other occasion he presented a voluntary sacrifice in his private capacity, the east gate was opened for him as before, but was shut as soon as the ceremony was over. On those occasions when the eastern gate was not opened, as at the great annual festivals, the people probably gathered round the north and south gates, from which they could see the altar; and at these seasons the prince enters and departs in the common throng of worshippers. A very peculiar regulation, for which no obvious reason appears, is that each man must leave the Temple by the gate opposite to that at which he entered; if he entered by the north, he must leave by the south, and *vice versa*.*

Many of these arrangements were no doubt suggested by Ezekiel's acquaintance with the practice in the first Temple, and their precise object is lost to us. But one or two facts stand out clearly enough, and are very instructive as to the whole conception of Temple worship. The chief thing to be noticed is that the principal sacrifices are representative. The people are merely spectators of a transaction with God on their behalf, the efficacy of which in no way depends on their co-operation. Standing at the gates of the inner court, they see the priests performing the sacred ministrations; they bow themselves in humble reverence before the presence of the Most High; and these acts of devotion may have been of the utmost importance for the religious life of the individual Israelite. But the congregation takes no real part in the worship; it is done for them, but not by them; it is on *opus operatum* performed by the prince and the priests for the good of the community, and is equally necessary and equally valid whether there is a congregation present to witness it or not. Those who attend are themselves but representatives of the nation of Israel, in whose interest the ritual is kept up. But the supreme representative of the people is the king, and we note how everything is done to emphasise his peculiar dignity within the sanctuary. It was necessary perhaps to do something to compensate for the loss of distinction caused by the exclusion of the royal body-guard from the Temple. The prince is still the one conspicuous figure in the outer court. Even his private sacrificial meals are eaten in solitary state, in the eastern gateway, which is used for no other purpose. And in the great functions where the prince appears in his representative character, he approaches nearer to the altar than is permitted to any other layman. He ascends the steps of the eastern gateway in the sight of the people, and passing through he presents his offerings on the verge of the inner court which none but the priests may enter. His whole position is thus one of great importance in the celebration of public ordinances. In detail his functions are no doubt determined by ancient prescriptive usages not known to us, but modified in accordance with the stricter ideal of

* Ch. xlv. 22.
† Lev. xvi. 11, 15.
‡ 2 Kings xvi. 15, 16.
§ Ch. xliv. 1–3.

* See ch. xlvi. 1–12. The Syriac Version indeed makes an exception to this rule in the case of the prince. Ver. 10 reads: "But the prince in their midst shall go out by the gate by which he entered." But why the prince more than any other body should go back by the road he came, or what particular honour there was in that, is a mystery; and it is probable that the reading is an error originating in repetition of ver. 8. The real meaning of the verse seems to be that the prince must go in and out without the retinue of foreigners who used to give *éclat* to royal visits to the sanctuary.

holiness which Ezekiel's vision was intended to enforce.

3. Finally, we have to observe that the prince is rigorously excluded from properly priestly offices. It is true that in some respects his position is analogous to that of the high priest under the law. But the analogy extends only to that aspect of the high priest's functions in which he appears as the head and representative of the religious community, and ceases the moment he enters upon priestly duties. So far as the special degree of sanctity which characterises the priesthood is concerned, the prince is a layman, and as such he is jealously debarred from aproaching the altar, and even from intruding into the sacred inner court where the priests minister. Now this fact has perhaps a deeper historical importance than we are apt to imagine. There is good reason to believe that in the old Temple the kings of Judah frequently officiated in person at the altar. At the time when the monarchy was established it was the rule that any man might sacrifice for himself and his household, and that the king as the representative of the nation should sacrifice on its behalf was an extension of the principle too obvious to require express sanction. Accordingly we find that both Saul and David on public occasions built altars and offered sacrifice to Jehovah. The older theory indeed seems to have been that priestly rights were inherent in the kingly office, and that the acting priests were the ministers to whom the king delegated the greater part of his priestly functions. Although the king might not appoint any one to this duty without respect to the Levitical qualification, he exercised within certain limits the right of deposing one family and installing another in the priesthood of the royal sanctuary. The house of Zadok itself owed its position to such an act of ecclesiastical authority on the part of David and Solomon.

The last occasion on which we read of a king of Judah officiating in person in the Temple is at the dedication of the new altar of Ahaz, when the king not only himself sacrificed, but gave directions to the priests as to the future observance of the ritual. The occasion was no doubt unusual, but there is not a word in the narrative to indicate that the king was committing an irregular action or exceeding the recognised prerogatives of his position. It would be unsafe, however, to conclude that this state of things continued unchanged till the close of the monarchy. After the time of Isaiah the Temple rose greatly in the religious estimation of the people, and a very probable result of this would be an increasing sense of the importance of the ministration of the official priesthood. The silence of the historical books and of Deuteronomy may not count for much in an argument on this question; but Ezekiel's own decisions lack the emphasis and solemnity with which he introduces an absolute innovation like the separation between priests and Levites in chap. xliv. It is at least possible that the later kings had gradually ceased to exercise the right of sacrifice, so that the privilege had lapsed through desuetude. Nevertheless it was a great step to have the principle affirmed as a fundamental law of the theocracy; and this Ezekiel undoubtedly does. If no other practical object were gained, it served at least to illustrate in the most emphatic way the idea of holiness, which demanded the exclusion of every layman from unhallowed contact with the most sacred emblems of Jehovah's presence.

It will be seen from all that has been said that the real interest of Ezekiel's treatment of the monarchy lies far apart from modern problems which might seem to have a superficial affinity with it. No lessons can fairly be deduced from it on the relations between Church and State, or the propriety of endowing and establishing the Christian religion, or the duty of rulers to maintain ordinances for the benefit of their subjects. Its importance lies in another direction. It shows the transition in Israel from a state of things in which the king is both *de jure* and *de facto* the source of power and the representative of the nation and where his religious status is the natural consequence of his civic dignity, to a very different state of things, where the forms of the ancient constitution are retained although the power has largely vanished from them. The prince now requires to have his religious duties imposed on him by an abstract political system whose sole sanction is the authority of the Deity. It is a transition which has no precise parallel anywhere else, although resemblances more or less instructive might doubtless be instanced from the history of Catholicism. Nowhere does Ezekiel's idealism appear more wonderfully blended with his equally characteristic conservatism than here. There is no real trace of the tendency attributed to the prophet to exalt the priesthood at the expense of the monarchy. The prince is after all a much more imposing personage even in the ceremonial worship than any priest. Although he lacks the priestly quality of holiness, his duties are quite as important as those of the priests, while his dignity is far greater than theirs. The considerations that enter in to limit his power and importance come from another quarter. They are such as these: first, the loss of military leadership, which is at least to be presumed in the circumstances of the Messianic kingdom; second, the welfare of the people at large; and third, the principle of holiness, whose supremacy has to be vindicated in the person of the king no less than in that of his meanest subject.

Perhaps the most remarkable thing is that the transition referred to was not actually accomplished even in the history of Israel itself. It was only in a vision that the monarchy was ever to be represented in the form which it bears here. From the time of Ezekiel no native king was ever to rule over Israel again save the priest-princes of the Asmonean dynasty, whose constitutional position was defined by their high-priestly dignity. Ezekiel's vision is therefore a preparation for the kingless state of post-exilic Judaism. The foreign potentates to whom the Jews were subject did in some instances provide materials for the Temple worship, but their local representatives were of course unqualified to fill the position assigned to the prince by the great prophet of the Exile. The community had to get along as best it could without a king, and the task was not difficult. The Temple dues were paid directly to the priests and Levites, and the function of representing the community before the altar was assigned to the High Priest. It was then indeed that the High Priesthood came to the front and blossomed out into all the magnificence of its legal position. It was not only the religious part of the prince's duties that fell to it, but a considerable share of his political importance as well. As the only hereditary institution that had survived the Exile, it naturally became the chief centre of social order in the community. By degrees the Persian and Greek kings found it expedient to deal with the Jews through the High Priest, whose authority they were bound to respect, and thus to leave him a free hand in the internal affairs of the commonwealth. The High Priesthood, in fact, was a civil as well as a priestly dignity. We can see that this great revolution would have broken the continuity of Hebrew history far more violently than it did but for the stepping-stone furnished by the ideal "prince" of Ezekiel's vision.

CHAPTER XXIX.

THE RITUAL.

EZEKIEL xlv., xlvi.

IT is difficult to go back in imagination to a time when sacrifice was the sole and sufficient form of every complete act of worship.* That the slaughter of an animal, or at least the presentation of a material offering of some sort, should ever have been considered of the essence of intercourse with the Deity may seem to us incredible in the light of the idea of God which we now possess. Yet there can be no doubt that there was a stage of religious development which recognised no true approach to God except as consummated in a sacrificial action. The word "sacrifice" itself preserves a memorial of this crude and early type of religious service. Etymologically it denotes nothing more than a sacred act. But amongst the Romans, as amongst ourselves, it was regularly applied to the offerings at the altar, which were thus marked out as *the* sacred actions *par excellence* of ancient religion. It would be impossible to explain the extraordinary persistence and vitality of the institution amongst races that had attained a relatively high degree of civilisation, unless we understand that the ideas connected with it go back to a time when sacrifice was the typical and fundamental form of primitive worship.

By the time of Ezekiel, however, the age of sacrifice in this strict and absolute sense may be said to have passed away, at least in principle. Devout Jews who had lived through the captivity in Babylon and found that Jehovah was there to them "a little of a sanctuary,"† could not possibly fall back into the belief that their God was only to be approached and found through the ritual of the altar. And long before the Exile, the ethical teaching of the prophets had led Israel to appreciate the external rites of sacrifice at their true value.

"Wherewithal shall I come before Jehovah,
Or bow myself before God on high?
Shall I come before Him with burnt-offerings,
With calves of a year old?
Is Jehovah pleased with thousands of rams,
With myriads of rivers of oil?
Shall I give my firstborn as an atonement for me,
The fruit of my body as a sin-offering for my life?
He hath showed thee, O man, what is good;
And what does Jehovah require of thee,
But to do justice and to love mercy,
And to walk humbly with thy God?" ‡

* Smith, "Religion of the Semites," pp. 196 f.
† Ch. xi. 16.
‡ Micah vi. 6-8.

This great word of spiritual religion had been uttered long before Ezekiel, as a protest against the senseless multiplication of sacrifices which came in in the reign of Manasseh. Nor can we suppose that Ezekiel, with all his engrossment in matters of ritual, was insensible to the lofty teaching of his predecessors, or that his conception of God was less spiritual than theirs. As a matter of fact the worship of Israel was never afterwards wholly absorbed in the routine of the Temple ceremonies. The institution of the synagogue, with its purely devotional exercises of prayer and reading of the Scriptures, must have been nearly coeval with the second Temple, and prepared the way far more than the latter for the spiritual worship of the New Testament. But even the Temple worship was spiritualised by the service of praise and the marvellous development of devotional poetry which it called forth. "The emotion with which the worshipper approaches the second Temple, as recorded in the Psalter, has little to do with sacrifice, but rests rather on the fact that the whole wondrous history of Jehovah's grace to Israel is vividly and personally realised as he stands amidst the festal crowd at the ancient seat of God's throne, and adds his voice to the swelling song of praise." *

How then, it may be asked, are we to account for the fact that the prophet shows such intense interest in the details of a system which was already losing its religious significance? If sacrifice was no longer of the essence of worship, why should he be so careful to legislate for a scheme of ritual in which sacrifice is the prominent feature, and say nothing of the inward state of heart which alone is an acceptable offering to God? The chief reason no doubt is that the ritual elements of religion were the only matters, apart from moral duties, which admitted of being reduced to a legal system, and that the formation of such a system was demanded by the circumstances with which the prophet had to deal. The time was not yet come when the principle of a central national sanctuary could be abandoned, and if such a sanctuary was to be maintained without danger to the highest interests of religion it was necessary that its service should be regulated with a view to preserve the deposit of revealed truth that had been committed to the nation through the prophets. The essential features of the sacrificial institutions were charged with a deep religious significance, and there existed in the popular mind a great mass of sound religious impression and sentiment clustering around that central rite. To dispense with the institution of sacrifice would have rendered worship entirely impossible for the great body of the people, while to leave it unregulated was to invite a recurrence of the abuses which had been so fruitful a source of corruption in the past. Hence the object of the ritual ordinances which we are about to consider is twofold: in the first place to provide an authorised code of ritual free from everything that savoured of pagan usages, and in the second to utilise the public worship as a means of deepening and purifying the religious conceptions of those who could be influenced in no other way. Ezekiel's legislation has a special regard for the wants of the "common rude man" whose religious life needs all the help it can get from external observances. Such persons form the majority of every religious society; and to train

* Smith, "Old Testament in Jewish Church," p. 379.

their minds to a deeper sense of sin and a more vivid apprehension of the divine holiness proved to be the only way in which the spiritual teaching of the prophets could be made a practical power in the community at large. It is true that the highest spiritual needs were not satisfied by the legal ritual. But the irrepressible longings of the soul for nearer fellowship with God cannot be dealt with by rigid formal enactments. Ezekiel is content to leave them to the guidance of that Spirit whose saving operations will have changed the heart of Israel and made it a true people of God. The system of external observances which he foreshadows in his vision was not meant to be the life of religion, but it was, so to speak, the trellis-work which was necessary to support the delicate tendrils of spiritual piety until the time when the spirit of filial worship should be the possession of every true member of the Church of God.

Bearing these facts in mind, we may now proceed to examine the scheme of sacrificial worship contained in chaps. xlv. and xlvi. Only its leading features can here be noticed, and the points most deserving of attention may be grouped under three heads: the Festivals, the Representative Service, and the Idea of Atonement.

I. The Yearly Feasts.—The most striking thing in Ezekiel's festal calendar * is the division of the ecclesiastical year into two precisely similar parts. Each half of the year commences with an atoning sacrifice for the purification of the sanctuary from defilement contracted during the previous half.† Each contains a great festival—in the one case the Passover, beginning on the fourteenth day of the first month and lasting seven days, and in the other the Feast of Tabernacles (simply called the Feast), beginning on the fifteenth day of the seventh month and also lasting for seven days.‡ The passage is chiefly devoted to a minute regulation of the public sacrifices to be offered on these occasions, other and more characteristic features of the celebration being assumed as well known from tradition.

It is difficult to see what is the precise meaning of the proposed rearrangement of the feasts in two parallel series. It may be due simply to the prophet's love of symmetry in all departments of public life, or it may have been suggested by the fact that at this time the Babylonian calendar, according to which the year begins in spring, was superimposed on the old Hebrew year commencing in the autumn.§ At all events it involved a breach with pre-exilic tradition, and was never carried out in practice. The earlier legislation of the Pentateuch recognises a cycle of three festivals—Passover and Unleavened Bread, the Feast of Harvest or of Weeks (Pentecost), and the Feast of Ingathering or of Tabernacles.‖ In order to carry through his symmetrical division of the sacred year Ezekiel has to ignore one of these, the Feast of Pentecost, which seems to have always been counted the least important of the three. It is not to be supposed that he contemplated its abolition, for he is careful not to alter in any particular the positive regulations of Deuteronomy; only it did not fall into his scheme, and so he does not think it of sufficient importance to prescribe regular public sacrifices for it. After the Exile, however, Jewish practice was regulated by the canons of the Priestly Code, in which, along with other festivals, the ancient threefold cycle is continued, and stated sacrifices are prescribed for Pentecost, just as for the other two.* Similarly, the two atoning ceremonies in the beginning of the first and seventh months,† which are not mentioned in the older legislation, are replaced in the Priests' Code by the single Day of Atonement on the tenth day of the seventh month, whilst the beginning of the year is celebrated by the Feast of Trumpets on the first day of the same month.‡

But although the details of Ezekiel's system thus proved to be impracticable in the circumstances of the restored Jewish community, it succeeded in the far more important object of infusing a new spirit into the celebration of the feasts, and impressing on them a different character. The ancient Hebrew festivals were all associated with joyous incidents of the agricultural year. The Feast of Unleavened Bread marked the beginning of harvest, when "the sickle first was put into the corn."§ At this time also the firstlings of the flock and herd were sacrificed. The seven weeks which elapse till Pentecost are the season of the cereal harvest, which is then brought to a close by the Feast of Harvest, when the goodness of Jehovah is acknowledged by the presentation of part of the produce at the sanctuary. Finally the Feast of Tabernacles celebrates the most joyous occasion of the year, the storing of the produce of the winepress and the threshing-floor.‖ The nature of the festivals is easily seen from the events with which they are thus associated. They are occasions of social mirth and festivity, and the religious rites observed are the expressions of the nation's heartfelt gratitude to Jehovah for the blessing that has rested on the labours of husbandman and shepherd throughout the year. The Passover with its memories of anxiety and escape was no doubt of a more sombre character than the others, but the joyous and festive nature of Pentecost and Tabernacles is strongly insisted on in the book of Deuteronomy. By these in-

* Ch. xlv. 18-25.

† Vv. 18-20. In ver. 20 we should read with the LXX. "in the seventh month, on the first day of the month," etc.

‡ Vv. 21-25. Some critics, as Smend and Cornill, think that in ver. 14 we should read fifteenth instead of fourteenth, to perfect the symmetry of the two halves of the year. There is no MS. authority for the proposed change.

§ Smend.

‖ Exod. xxiii. 14-17 (Book of the Covenant, with which the other code—Exod. xxxiv. 18-22—agrees); Deut. xvi. 1-17.

* *Cf.* Lev. xxiii. 4-44 (Law of Holiness); Numb. xxviii., xxix.

† It is usual to speak of these ceremonies in Ezekiel as festivals. But this seems to go beyond the prophet's meaning. Only a single sacrifice, a sin-offering, is mentioned; and there is no hint of any public assemblage of the people on these days. It was the priests' business to see that the sanctuary was purified, and there was no occasion for the people to be present at the ceremony. The congregation would be the ordinary congregation at the new moon feast, which of course did not represent the whole population of the country. No doubt, as we see from the references below, the ceremony developed into a special feast after the Exile.

‡ *Cf.* Lev. xxiii. 23-32; Numb. xxix. 1-11.

§ *Cf.* Deut. xvi. 9. with Lev. xxiii. 10 f., 15 f. In the one case the seven weeks to Pentecost are reckoned from the putting of the sickle into the corn, in the other from the presentation of a first sheaf of ripe corn in the Temple, which falls within the Passover week. The latter can only be regarded as a more precise determination of the former, and thus Unleavened Bread must have coincided with the beginning of barley harvest.

‖ Deut. xvi. 13.

stitutions religion was closely intertwined with the great interests of every-day life, and the fact that the sacred seasons of the Israelites' year were the occasions on which the natural joy of life was at its fullest, bears witness to the simple-minded piety which was fostered by the old Hebrew worship. There was, however, a danger that in such a state of things religion should be altogether lost sight of in the exuberance of natural hilarity and expressions of social good-will. And indeed no great height of spirituality could be nourished by a type of worship in which devotional feeling was concentrated on the expression of gratitude to God for the bountiful gifts of His providence. It was good for the childhood of the nation, but when the nation became a man it must put away childish things.

The tendency of the post-exilic ritual was to detach the sacred seasons more and more from the secular associations which had once been their chief significance. This was done partly by the addition of new festivals which had no such natural occasion, and partly by a change in the point of view from which the older celebrations were regarded. No attempt was made to obliterate the traces of the affinity with events of common life which endeared them to the hearts of the people, but increasing importance was attached to their historic significance as memorials of Jehovah's gracious dealings with the nation in the period of the Exodus. At the same time they take on more and more the character of religious symbols of the permanent relations between Jehovah and His people. The beginnings of this process can be clearly discerned in the legislation of Ezekiel. Not indeed in the direction of a historic interpretation of the feasts, for this is ignored even in the case of the Passover, where it was already firmly established in the national consciousness. But the institution of a special series of public sacrifices, which was the same for the Passover and the Feast of Tabernacles, and particularly the prominence given to the sin-offering, obviously tended to draw the mind of the people away from the passing interest of the occasion, and fix it on those standing obligations imposed by the holiness of Jehovah on which the continuance of all His bounties depended. We cannot be mistaken in thinking that one design of the new ritual was to correct the excesses of unrestrained animal enjoyment by deepening the sense of guilt and the fear of possible offences against the sanctity of the divine presence. For it was at these festivals that the prince was required to offer the atoning sacrifice for himself and the people.* Thus the effect of the whole system was to foster the sensitive and tremulous tone of piety which was characteristic of Judaism, in contrast to the hearty, if undisciplined, religion of the ancient Hebrew feasts.

* Ch. xlv. 22.

II. The Stated Service.—In the course of this chapter we have had occasion more than once to touch on the prominence given in Ezekiel's vision to sacrifices offered in accordance with a fixed rubric in the name of the whole community. The significance of this fact may best be seen from a comparison with the sacrificial regulations of the book of Deuteronomy. These are not numerous, but they deal exclusively with private sacrifices. The person addressed is the individual householder, and the sacrifices which he is enjoined to render are for himself and his family. There is no explicit allusion in the whole book to the official sacrifices which were offered by the regular priesthood and maintained at the king's expense. In Ezekiel's scheme of Temple worship the case is exactly the reverse. Here there is no mention of private sacrifice except in the incidental notices as to the free-will offerings and the sacrificial meal of the prince,* while on the other hand great attention is paid to the maintenance of the regular offerings provided by the prince for the congregation. This of course does not mean that there were no statutory sacrifices in the old Temple, or that Ezekiel contemplated the cessation of private sacrifice in the new. Deuteronomy passes over the public sacrifices because they were under the jurisdiction of the king, and the people at large were not directly responsible for them; and similarly Ezekiel is silent as to private offerings because their observance was assured by all the traditions of the sanctuary. Still it is a noteworthy fact that of two codes of Temple worship, separated by only half a century, each legislates exclusively for that element of the ritual which is taken for granted by the other.

What it indicates is nothing less than a change in the ruling conception of public worship. Before the Exile the idea that Jehovah could desert His sanctuary hardly entered into the mind of the people, and certainly did not in the least affect the confidence with which they availed themselves of the privileges of worship. The Temple was there and God was present within it, and all that was necessary was that the spontaneous devotion of the worshippers should be regulated by the essential conditions of ceremonial propriety. But the destruction of the Temple had proved that the mere existence of a sanctuary was no guarantee of the favour and protection of the God who was supposed to dwell within it. Jehovah might be driven from His Temple by the presence of sin among the people, or even by a neglect of the ceremonial precautions which were necessary to guard against the profanation of His holiness. On this idea the whole edifice of the later ritual is built up, and here as in other respects Ezekiel has shown the way. In his view the validity and efficiency of the whole Temple service hangs on the due performance of the public rites which preserve the nation in a condition of sanctity and continually represent it as a holy people before God. Under cover of this representative service the individual may draw near with confidence to seek the face of his God in acts of private homage, but apart from the regular official ceremonial his worship has no reality, because he can have no assurance that Jehovah will accept his offering. His right of access to God springs from his fellowship with the religious community of Israel, and hence the indispensable presupposition of every act of worship is that the standing of the community before Jehovah be preserved intact by the rites appointed for that purpose. And, as has been already said, these rites are representative in character. Being performed on behalf of the nation, the obligation of presenting them rests with the prince in his representative capacity, and the share of the people in them is indicated by the tribute which the prince is empowered to levy for this end. In this way the ideal unity of the nation

* Ch. xlvi. 12: *cf.* xliv. 3.

finds continual expression in the worship of the sanctuary, and the supreme interest of religion is transferred from the mere act of personal homage to the abiding conditions of acceptance with God symbolised by the stated service.

Let us now look at some details of the scheme in which this important idea is embodied. The foundation of the whole system is the daily burnt-offering—the *tāmîd.* Under the first Temple the daily offering seems to have been a burnt-offering in the morning and a meal-offering (*minhah*) in the evening,* and this practice seems to have continued down to the time of Ezra.† According to the Levitical law it consists of a lamb morning and evening, accompanied on each occasion by a minhah and a libation of wine.‡ Ezekiel's ordinance occupies a middle position between these two. Here the tāmîd is a lamb for a burnt-offering in the morning, along with a minhah of flour mingled with oil; and there is no provision for an evening sacrifice.§ The presentation of this sacrifice on the altar in the morning, as the basis on which all other offerings through the day were laid, may be taken to symbolise the truth that the acceptance of all ordinary acts of worship depended on the representation of the community before God in the regular service. To the spiritual perception of a Psalmist it may have suggested the duty of commencing each day's work with an act of devotion:—

"Jehovah, in the morning shalt Thou hear my voice;
In the morning will I set [my prayer] in order before Thee, and will look out."‖

The offerings for the Sabbaths and new moons may be considered as amplifications of the daily sacrifice. They consist exclusively of burnt-offerings. On the Sabbath six lambs are presented, perhaps one for each working-day of the week, together with a ram for the Sabbath itself (Smend). At the new moon feast this offering is repeated with the addition of a bullock. It may be noted here once for all that each burnt sacrifice is accompanied by a corresponding minhah, according to a fixed scale. For sin-offerings, on the other hand, no minhah seems to be appointed.

At the annual (or rather half-yearly) celebrations the sin-offering appears for the first time among the stated sacrifices. The sacrifice for the cleansing of the sanctuary at the beginning of each half of the year consists of a young bullock for a sin-offering, in addition of course to the burnt-offerings which were prescribed for the first day of the month. For the Passover and the Feast of Tabernacles the daily offering is a he-goat for a sin-offering, and seven bullocks and seven rams for a burnt-offering during the week covered by these festivals. Besides this, at Passover, and probably also at Tabernacles, the prince presents a bullock as a sin-offering for himself and the people. We have now to consider more particularly the place which this class of sacrifices occupies in the ritual.

III. Atoning Sacrifices.—It is evident, even from this short survey, that the idea of atonement holds a conspicuous place in the symbolism of Ezekiel's Temple. He is, indeed, the earliest writer (setting aside the Levitical Code) who mentions the special class of sacrifices known as sin- and guilt-offerings. Under the first Temple ceremonial offences were regularly atoned for at one time by money payments to the priests, and these fines were called by the names afterwards applied to the expiatory sacrifices.* It does not follow, of course, that such sacrifices were unknown before the time of Ezekiel, nor is such a conclusion probable in itself. The manner in which the prophet alludes to them rather shows that the idea was perfectly familiar to his contemporaries. But the prominence of the sin-offering in the public ritual may be safely set down as a new departure in the Temple service, as it is one of the most striking symptoms of the change that passed over the spirit of Israel's religion at the time of the Exile.

Of the elements that contributed to this change the most important was the deepened consciousness of sin that had been produced by the teaching of the prophets as verified in the terrible calamity of the Exile. We have seen how frequently Ezekiel insists on this effect of the Divine judgment; how, even in the time of her pardon and restoration, he represents Israel as ashamed and confounded, not opening her mouth any more for the remembrance of all that she had done. We are therefore prepared to find that full provision is made for the expression of this abiding sense of guilt in the revised scheme of worship. This was done not by new rites invented for the purpose, but by seizing on those elements of the old ritual which represented the wiping out of iniquity, and by so remodelling the whole sacrificial system as to place these prominently in the foreground. Such elements were found chiefly in the sin-offering and guilt-offering, which occupied a subsidiary position in the old Temple, but are elevated to a place of commanding importance in the new. The precise distinction between these two kinds of sacrifice is an obscure point of the Levitical ritual which has never been perfectly cleared up. In the system of Ezekiel, however, we observe that the guilt-offering plays no part in the stated service, and must therefore have been reserved for private transgressions of the law of holiness. And in general it may be remarked that the atoning sacrifices differ from others, not in their material, but in certain features of the sacred actions to be observed with regard to them. We cannot here enter upon the details of the symbolism, but the most important fact is that the flesh of the victims is neither offered on the altar as in the burnt-offering, nor eaten by the worshippers as in the peace-offering, but belongs to the category of most holy things, and must be consumed by the priests in a holy place. In certain extreme cases, however, it has to be burned without the sanctuary.†

Now in the chapters before us the idea of sacrificial atonement is chiefly developed in connection with the material fabric of the sanctuary. The sanctuary may contract defilement by involuntary lapses from the stringent rules of ceremonial purity on the part of those who use it, whether priests or laymen. Such errors of inadvertence were almost unavoidable under the complicated set of formal regulations into which the

* 2 Kings xvi. 15: *cf.* 1 Kings xviii. 29, 36.
† Ezra ix. 5.
‡ Numb. xxviii. 3-8; Exod. xxix. 38-42.
§ Ch. xlvi. 13-15.
‖ Psalm v. 3, probably used at the presentation of the morning tāmîd. A more distinct recognition of the spiritual significance of the *evening* sacrifice is found in Psalm cxli. 2.

* 2 Kings xii. 17.
† *Cf.* ch. xliii. 21.

fundamental idea of holiness branched out, yet they are regarded as endangering the sanctity of the Temple, and require to be carefully atoned for from time to time, lest by their accumulation the worship should be invalidated and Jehovah driven from His dwelling-place. But besides this the Temple (or at least the altar) is unfit for its sacred functions until it has undergone an initial process of purification. The principle involved still survives in the consecration of ecclesiastical buildings in Christendom, although its application had doubtless a much more serious import under the old dispensation than it can possibly have under the new.

A full account of this initial ceremony of purification is given in the end of the forty-third chapter, and a glance at the details of the ritual may be enough to impress on us the conceptions that underlie the process. It is a protracted operation, extending apparently over eight days.* The first and fundamental act is the offering of a sin-offering of the highest degree of sanctity, the victim being a bullock and the flesh being burned outside the sanctuary. The blood alone is sprinkled on the four horns of the altar, the four corners of the "settle," and the "border": this is the first stage in the dedication of the altar. Then for seven days a he-goat is offered for a sin-offering, the same rites being observed, and after it a burnt-offering consisting of a bullock and a ram. These sacrifices are intended only for the purification of the altar, and only on the day after their completion is the altar ready to receive ordinary public or private gifts—burnt-offerings and peace-offerings. Now four expressions are used to denote the effect of these ceremonies on the altar. The most general is "consecrate," literally "fill its hand"†—a phrase used originally of the installation of a priest into his office, and then applied metaphorically to consecration or initiation in general. The others are "purify,"‡ "unsin,"§ (the special effect of the sin-offering) and "expiate."‖ Of these the last is the most important. It is the technical priestly term for atonement for sin, the reference being of course generally to persons. As to the fundamental meaning of the word, there has been a great deal of discussion, which has not yet led to a decisive result. The choice seems to lie between two radical ideas, either to "wipe out" or to "cover," and so render inoperative.¶ But either etymology enables us to understand the use of the word in legal terminology. It means to undo the effect of a transgression on the religious status of the offender, or, as in the case before us, to remove natural or contracted impurity from a material object. And whether this is conceived as a covering up of the fault so as to conceal it from view, or a wiping out of it, amounts in the end to the same thing.

* Another explanation, however, is possible, and is adopted by Smend and Davidson. Assuming that a burnt-offering was offered on the first day, and holding the whole description to be somewhat elliptical, they bring the entire process within the limits of the week. This certainly looks more satisfactory in itself. But would Ezekiel be likely to admit an ellipsis in describing so important a function? I have taken for granted above that the seven days of the double sacrifice are counted from the "second day" of ver. 22.

† Ver. 26.

‡ טִהֵר (ver. 20).

§ חִטֵּא a denominative form from חֵטְא = sin (ver. 22).

‖ כִּפֵּר (ver. 26).

¶ See Smith, "Old Testament in Jewish Church," p. 381.

The significant fact is that the same word is applied both to persons and things. It furnishes another illustration of the intimate way in which the ideas of moral guilt and physical defect are blended in the ceremonial of the Old Testament.

The meaning of the two atoning services appointed for the beginning of the first and the seventh month is now clear. They are intended to renew periodically the holiness of the sanctuary established by the initiatory rites just described. For it is evident that no indelible character can attach to the kind of sanctity with which we are here dealing. It is apt to be lost, if not by mere lapse of time, at least by the repeated contact of frail men who with the best intentions are not always able to fulfil the conditions of a right use of sacred things. Every failure and mistake detract from the holiness of the Temple, and even unnoticed and altogether unconscious offences would in course of time profane it if not purged away. Hence "for every one that erreth and for him that is simple"* atonement has to be made for the house twice a year. The ritual to be observed on these occasions bears a general resemblance to that of the inaugural ceremony, but is simpler, only a single bullock being presented for a sin-offering. On the other hand, it expressly symbolises a purification of the Temple as well as of the altar. The blood is sprinkled not only on the "settle" of the altar, but also on the doorposts of the house, and the posts of the eastern gate of the inner court.

We may now pass on to the second application made by Ezekiel of the idea of sacrificial atonement. These purifications of the sanctuary, which bulk so largely in his system, have their counterpart in atonements made directly for the faults of the people. For this purpose, as we have already seen, a sin-offering was to be presented at each of the great annual festivals by the prince, for himself and the nation which he represented. But it is important to observe that the idea of atonement is not confined to one particular class of sacrifices. It lies at the foundation of the whole system of the stated service, the purpose of which is expressly said to be "to make atonement for the house of Israel."† Thus while the half-yearly sin-offering afforded a special opportunity for confession of sin on the part of the people, we are to understand that the holiness of the nation was secured by the observance of every part of the prescribed ritual which regulated its intercourse with God. And since the nation is in itself imperfectly holy and stands in constant need of forgiveness, the maintenance of its sanctity by sacrificial rites was equivalent to a perpetual act of atonement. Special offences of individuals had of course to be expiated by special sacrifices, but beneath all particular transgressions lay the broad fact of human impurity and infirmity; and in the constant "covering up" of this by a Divinely instituted system of religious ordinances we recognise an atoning element in the regular Temple service.

The sacrificial ritual may therefore be regarded as a barrier interposed between the natural uncleanness of the people and the awful holiness of Jehovah seated in His Temple. That men should be permitted to approach Him at all is an unspeakable privilege conferred on Israel in virtue of its covenant relation to God. But that the approach is surrounded by so many precau-

* Ch. xlv. 20.

† Ch. xlv. 15, 17.

tions and restrictions is a perpetual witness to the truth that God is of purer eyes than to behold iniquity and one with whom evil cannot dwell. If these precautions could have been always perfectly observed, it is probable that no periodical purification of the sanctuary would have been enjoined. The ordinary ritual would have sufficed to maintain the nation in a state of holiness corresponding with the requirements of Jehovah's nature. But this was impossible on account of the slowness of men's minds and their liability to err in their most sacred duties. Sin is so subtle and pervasive that it is conceived as penetrating the network of ordinances destined to intercept it, and reaching even to the dwelling-place of Jehovah Himself. It is to remove such accidental, though inevitable, violations of the majesty of God that the ritual edifice is crowned by ceremonies for the purification of the sanctuary. They are, so to speak, atonements in the second degree. Their object is to compensate for defects in the ordinary routine of worship, and to remove the arrears of guilt which had accumulated through neglect of some part of the ceremonial scheme. This idea appears quite clearly in Ezekiel's legislation, but it is far more impressively exhibited in the Levitical law, where different elements of Ezekiel's ritual are gathered up into one celebration in the Great Day of Atonement, the most solemn and imposing of the whole year.

Hence we see that the whole system of sacrificial worship is firmly knit together, being pervaded from end to end by the one principle of expiation, behind which lay the assurance of pardon and acceptance to all who approached God in the use of the appointed means of grace. Herein lay the chief value of the Temple ritual for the religious life of Israel. It served to impress on the mind of the people the great realities of sin and forgiveness, and so to create that profound consciousness of sin which has passed over, spiritualised but not weakened, into Christian experience. Thus the law proved itself a schoolmaster to bring men to Christ, in whose atoning death the evil of sin and the eternal conditions of forgiveness are once for all and perfectly revealed.

The positive truths taught or suggested by the ritual of atonement are too numerous to be considered here. It is a remarkable fact that neither in Ezekiel nor in any other part of the Old Testament is an authoritative interpretation given of the most essential features of the ritual. The people seem to have been left to explain the symbolism as best they could, and many points which are obscure and uncertain to us must have been perfectly intelligible to the least instructed amongst them. For us the only safe rule is to follow the guidance of the New Testament writers in their use of sacrificial institutions as types of the death of Christ. The investigation is too large and intricate to be attempted in this place. But it may be well in conclusion to point out one or two general principles, which ought never to be overlooked in the typical interpretation of the expiatory sacrifices of the Old Testament.

In the first place atonement is provided only for sins committed in ignorance; and moral and ceremonial offences stand precisely on the same footing in the eye of the law. In Ezekiel's system, indeed, it was only sins of inadvertence that needed to be considered. He has in view the final state of things in which the people, though not perfect nor exempt from liability to error, are wholly inclined to obey the law of Jehovah so far as their knowledge and ability extend. But even in the Levitical legislation there is no legal dispensation for guilt incurred through wanton and deliberate defiance of the law of Jehovah. To sin thus is to sin "with a high hand," * and such offences have to be expiated by the death of the sinner, or at least his exclusion from the religious community. And whether the precept belong to what we call the ceremonial or to the moral side of the law, the same principle holds good, although of course its application is one-sided; strictly moral transgressions being for the most part voluntary, while ritual offences may be either voluntary or inadvertent. But for wilful and high-handed departure from any precept, whether ethical or ceremonial, no atonement is provided by the law; the guilty person "falls into the hands of the living God," and forgiveness is possible only in the sphere of personal relations between man and God, into which the law does not enter.

This leads to a second consideration. Atoning sacrifices do not purchase forgiveness. That is to say, they are never regarded as exercising any influence on God, moving Him to Mercy towards the sinner. They are simply the forms to which, by Jehovah's own appointment, the promise of forgiveness is attached. Hence sacrifice has not the fundamental significance in Old Testament religion that the death of Christ has in the New. The whole sacrificial system, as we see quite clearly from Ezekiel's prophecy, presupposes redemption; the people are already restored to their land and sanctified by Jehovah's presence amongst them before these institutions come into operation. The only purpose that they serve in the system of religion to which they belong is to secure that the blessings of salvation shall not be lost. Both in this vision and throughout the Old Testament the ultimate ground of confidence in God lies in historic acts of redemption in which Jehovah's sovereign grace and love to Israel are revealed. Through the sacrifices the individual was enabled to assure himself of his interest in the covenant blessings promised to his nation. They were the sacraments of his personal acceptance with Jehovah, and as such were of the highest importance for his normal religious life. But they were not and could not be the basis of the forgiveness of sins, nor did later Judaism ever fall into the error of seeking to appease the Deity by a multiplication of sacrificial gifts. When the insufficiency of the ritual system to give true peace of conscience or to bring back the outward tokens of God's favour is dwelt upon, the ancient Church falls back on the spiritual conditions of forgiveness already enunciated by the prophets.

"Thou desirest not sacrifice that I should give it,
Thou delightest not in burnt-offering.
The sacrifices of God are a broken spirit:
A broken and a contrite heart, O God, Thou wilt not despise." †

Finally we have learned from Ezekiel that the idea of atonement is not lodged in any particular rite, but pervades the sacrificial system as a whole. Suggestive as the ritual of the sin-offer-

* As distinguished from sins, בִּשְׁגָגָה, or through inadvertence. See Numb. xv. 30, 31.

† Psalm li. 16, 17.

ing is to the Christian conscience, it must not be isolated from other developments of the sacrificial idea or taken to embody the whole permanent meaning of the institution. There are at least two other aspects of sacrifice which are clearly expressed in the ritual legislation of the Old Testament—that of homage, chiefly symbolised by the burnt-offering, and that of communion, symbolised by the peace-offering and the sacrificial feast observed in connection with it. And although, both in Ezekiel and the Levitical law, these two elements are thrown into the shade by the idea of expiation, yet there are subtle links of affinity between all three, which will have to be traced out before we are in a position to understand the first principles of sacrificial worship. The brilliant and learned researches of the late Professor Robertson Smith have thrown a flood of light on the original rite of sacrifice and the important place which it occupies in ancient religion.* He has sought to explain the intricate system of the Levitical legislation as an unfolding, under varied historical influences, of different aspects of the idea of communion between God and men, which is the essence of primitive sacrifice. In particular he has shown how special atoning sacrifices arise through emphasising by appropriate symbolism the element of reconciliation which is implicitly contained in every act of religious communion with God. This at least enables us to understand how the atoning ritual with all its distinctive features yet resembles so closely that which is common to all types of sacrifice, and how the idea of expiation, although concentrated in a particular class of sacrifices, is nevertheless spread over the whole surface of the sacrificial ritual. It would be premature as well as presumptuous to attempt here to estimate the consequences of this theory for Christian theology. But it certainly seems to open up the prospect of a wider and deeper apprehension of the religious truths which are differentiated and specialised in the Old Testament dispensation, to be reunited in that great Atoning Sacrifice, in which the blood of the new covenant has been shed for many for the remission of sins.

CHAPTER XXX.

RENEWAL AND ALLOTMENT OF THE LAND.

EZEKIEL xlvii., xlviii.

IN the first part of the forty-seventh chapter the visionary form of the revelation, which had been interrupted by the important series of communications on which we have been so long engaged, is again resumed. The prophet, once more under the direction of his angelic guide, sees a stream of water issuing from the Temple buildings and flowing eastward into the Dead Sea.† Afterwards he receives another series of directions relating to the boundaries of the land and its division among the twelve tribes.‡ With this the vision and the book find their appropriate close.

* See his Burnet Lectures on the "Religion of the Semites," to which, as well as to his "Old Testament in the Jewish Church," the present chapter is largely indebted.

† Ch. xlvii. 1-12.

‡ Chs. xlvii. 13-xlviii. 35.

I.

The Temple stream, to which Ezekiel's attention is now for the first time directed, is a symbol of the miraculous transformation which the land of Canaan is to undergo in order to fit it for the habitation of Jehovah's ransomed people. Anticipations of a renewal of the face of nature are a common feature of Messianic prophecy. They have their roots in the religious interpretation of the possession of the land as the chief token of the Divine blessing on the nation. In the vicissitudes of agricultural or pastoral life the Israelite read the reflection of Jehovah's attitude towards Himself and His people: fertile seasons and luxuriant harvests were the sign of His favour; drought and famine were the proof that He was offended. Even at the best of times, however, the condition of Palestine left much to be desired from the husbandman's point of view, especially in the kingdom of Judah. Nature was often stern and unpropitious, the cultivation of the soil was always attended with hardship and uncertainty, large tracts of the country were given over to irreclaimable barrenness. There was always a vision of better things possible, and in the last days the prophets cherished the expectation that that vision would be realised. When all causes of offence are removed from Israel and Jehovah smiles on His people, the land will blossom into supernatural fertility, the ploughman overtaking the reaper, and the treader of grapes him that soweth seed, the mountains dropping new wine and the hills melting.* Such idyllic pictures of universal plenty and comfort abound in the writings of the prophets, and are not wanting in the pages of Ezekiel. We have already had one in the description of the blessings of the Messianic kingdom;† and we shall see that in this closing vision a complete remodelling of the land is presupposed, rendering it all alike suitable for the habitation of the tribes of Israel.

The river of life is the most striking presentation of this general conception of Messianic felicity. It is one of those vivid images from Eastern life which, through the Apocalypse, have passed into the symbolism of Christian eschatology. "And He showed me a pure river of water of life, clear as crystal, proceeding out of the throne of God and of the Lamb. In the midst of the street of it, and on either side of the river, was there the tree of life, which bare twelve manner of fruits, and yielded her fruits every month: and the leaves of the tree were for the healing of the nations." ‡ So writes the seer of Patmos, in words whose music charms the ear even of those to whom running water means much less than it did to a native of thirsty Palestine. But John had read of the mystic river in the pages of his favourite prophet before he saw it in vision. The close resemblance between the two pictures leaves no doubt that the origin of the conception is to be sought in Ezekiel's vision. The underlying religious truth is the same in both representations, that the presence of God is the source from which the influences flow forth that renew and purify human existence. The tree of life on each bank of the river, which yields its fruit every month and whose leaves are for healing, is a detail transferred directly from Ezekiel's imagery to fill out the description of the glorious city of God into which

* Amos ix. 13. † Ch. xxxiv. 25-29. ‡ Rev. xxii. 1, 2.

the nations of them that are saved are gathered.

But with all its idealism, Ezekiel's conception presents many points of contact with the actual physiography of Palestine; it is less universal and abstract in its significance than that of the Apocalypse. The first thing that might have suggested the idea to the prophet is that the Temple mount had at least one small stream, whose "soft-flowing" waters were already regarded as a symbol of the silent and unobtrusive influence of the Divine presence in Israel.* The waters of this stream flowed eastward, but they were too scanty to have any appreciable effect on the fertility of the region through which they passed. Further, to the southeast of Jerusalem, between it and the Dead Sea, stretched the great wilderness of Judah, the most desolate and inhospitable tract in the whole country. There the steep declivity of the limestone range refuses to detain sufficient moisture to nourish the most meagre vegetation, although the few spots where wells are found, as at Engedi, are clothed with almost tropical luxuriance. To reclaim these barren slopes and render them fit for human industry, the Temple waters are sent eastward, making the desert to blossom as the rose. Lastly, there was the Dead Sea itself, in whose bitter waters no living thing can exist, the natural emblem of resistance to the purposes of Him who is the God of life. These different elements of the physical reality were familiar to Ezekiel, and come back to mind as he follows the course of the new Temple river, and observes the wonderful transformation which it is destined to effect. He first sees it breaking forth from the wall of the Temple at the right-hand side of the entrance, and flowing eastward through the courts by the south side of the altar. Then at the outer wall he meets it rushing from the south side of the eastern gate, and still pursuing its easterly course. At a thousand cubits from the sanctuary it is only ankle-deep, but at successive distances of a thousand cubits it reaches to the knees, to the loins, and becomes finally an impassable river. The stream is of course miraculous from source to mouth. Earthly rivers do not thus broaden and deepen as they flow, except by the accession of tributaries, and tributaries are out of the question here. Thus it flows on, with its swelling volume of water, through "the eastern circuit," "down to the Arabah" (the trough of the Jordan and the Dead Sea), and reaching the sea it sweetens its waters so that they teem with fishes of all kinds like those of the Mediterranean. Its uninviting shores become the scene of a busy and thriving industry; fishermen ply their craft from Engedi to Eneglaim,† and the food supply of the country is materially increased. The prophet may not have been greatly concerned about this, but one characteristic detail illustrates his careful forethought in matters of practical utility. It is from the Dead Sea that Jerusalem has always obtained its supply of salt. The purification of this lake might have its drawbacks if the production of this indispensable commodity should be interfered with. Salt, besides its culinary uses, played an important part in the Temple ritual, and Ezekiel was not likely to forget it. Hence the strange but eminently practical provision that the shallows and marshes at the south end of the lake shall be exempted from the influence of the healing waters. "They are given for salt." *

*Isa. viii. 6.

†Engedi, "well of the kid," is at the middle of the western shore; Eneglaim, "well of two calves," is unknown, but probably lay at the north end. The eastern side is left to the Arabian nomads.

We may venture to draw one lesson for our own instruction from this beautiful prophetic image of the blessings that flow from a pure religion. The river of God has its source high up in the mount where Jehovah dwells in inaccessible holiness, and where the white-robed priests minister ceaselessly before Him; but in its descent it seeks out the most desolate and unpromising region in the country and turns it into a garden of the Lord. Whlie the whole land of Israel is to be renewed and made to minister to the good of man in fellowship with God, the main stream of fertility is expended in the apparently hopeless task of reclaiming the Judean desert and purifying the Dead Sea. It is an emblem of the earthly ministry of Him who made Himself the friend of publicans and sinners, and lavished the resources of His grace and the wealth of His affection on those who were deemed beyond ordinary possibility of salvation. It is to be feared, however, that the practice of most Churches has been too much the reverse of this. They have been tempted to confine the water of life within fairly respectable channels, amongst the prosperous and contented, the occupants of happy homes, where the advantages of religion are most likely to be appreciated. That seems to have been found the line of least resistance, and in times when spiritual life has run low it has been counted enough to keep the old ruts filled and leave the waste places and stagnant waters of our civilisation ill provided with the means of grace. Nowadays we are sometimes reminded that the Dead Sea must be drained before the gospel can have a fair chance of influencing human lives, and there may be much wisdom in the suggestion. A vast deal of social drainage may have to be accomplished before the word of God has free course. Unhealthy and impure conditions of life may be mitigated by wise legislation, temptations to vice may be removed, and vested interests that thrive on the degradation of human lives may be crushed by the strong arm of the community. But the true spirit of Christianity can neither be confined to the watercourses of religious habit, nor wait for the schemes of the social reformer. Nor will it display its powers of social salvation until it carries the energies of the Church into the lowest haunts of vice and misery with an earnest desire to seek and to save that which is lost. Ezekiel had his vision, and he believed in it. He believed in the reality of God's presence in the sanctuary and in the stream of blessings that flowed from His throne, and he believed in the possibility of reclaiming the waste places of his country for the kingdom of God. When Christians are united in like faith in the power of Christ and the abiding presence of His Spirit, we may expect to see times of refreshing from the presence of God and the whole earth filled with the knowledge of the Lord as the waters cover the sea.

II.

Ezekiel's map of Palestine is marked by something of the same mathematical regularity which was exhibited in his plan of the Temple. His

*Ver. 11.

boundaries are like those we sometimes see on the map of a newly setttled country like America or Australia—that is to say, they largely follow the meridian lines and parallels of latitude, but take advantage here and there of natural frontiers supplied by rivers and mountain ranges. This is absolutely true of the internal divisions of the land between the tribes. Here the northern and southern boundaries are straight lines running east and west over hill and dale, and terminating at the Mediterranean Sea and the Jordan Valley, which form of course the western and eastern limits. As to the external delimitation of the country it is unfortunately not possible to speak with certainty. The eastern frontier is fixed by the Jordan and the Dead Sea so far as they go, and the western is the sea. But on the north and south the lines of demarcation cannot be traced, the places mentioned being nearly all unknown. The north frontier extends from the sea to a place called Hazar-enon, said to lie on the border of Hauran. It passes the "entrance to Hamath," and has to the north not only Hamath, but also the territory of Damascus. But none of the towns through which it passes—Hethlon, Berotha, Sibraim—can be identified, and even its general direction is altogether uncertain.*

From Hazar-enon the eastern border stretches southward till it reaches the Jordan, and is prolonged south of the Dead Sea to a place called Tamar, also unknown. From this we proceed westwards by Kadesh till we strike the river of Egypt, the Wady el-Arish, which carries the boundary to the sea. It will be seen that Ezekiel, for reasons on which it is idle to speculate, excludes the transjordanic territory from the Holy Land. Speaking broadly, we may say that he treats Palestine as a rectangular strip of country, which he divides into transverse sections of indeterminate breadth, and then proceeds to parcel out these amongst the twelve tribes.

A similar obscurity rests on the motives which determined the disposition of the different tribes within the sacred territory. We can understand, indeed, why seven tribes are placed to the north and only five to the south of the capital and the sanctuary. Jerusalem lay much nearer the south of the land, and in the original distribution all the tribes had their settlements to the north of it except Judah and Simeon. Ezekiel's arrangement seems thus to combine a desire for symmetry with a recognition of the claims of historical and geographic reality. We can also see that to a certain extent the relative positions of the tribes correspond with those they held before the Exile, although of course the system requires that they shall lie in a regular series from north to south. Dan, Asher, and Naphtali are left in the extreme north, Manasseh and Ephraim to the south of them, while Simeon lies as of old in the south with one tribe between it and the capital. But we cannot tell why Benjamin should be placed to the south and Judah to the north of Jerusalem, why Issachar and Zebulun are transferred from the far north to the south, or why Reuben and Gad are taken from the east of the Jordan to be settled one to the north and the other to the south of the city. Some principle of arrangement there must have been in the mind of the prophet, and several have been suggested; but it is perhaps better to confess that we have lost the key to his meaning.*

The prophet's interest is centred on the strip of land reserved for the sanctuary and public purposes, which is subdivided and measured out with the utmost precision. It is twenty-five thousand cubits (about eight and one-third miles) broad, and extends right across the country. The two extremities east and west are the crown lands assigned to the prince for the purposes we have already seen. In the middle a

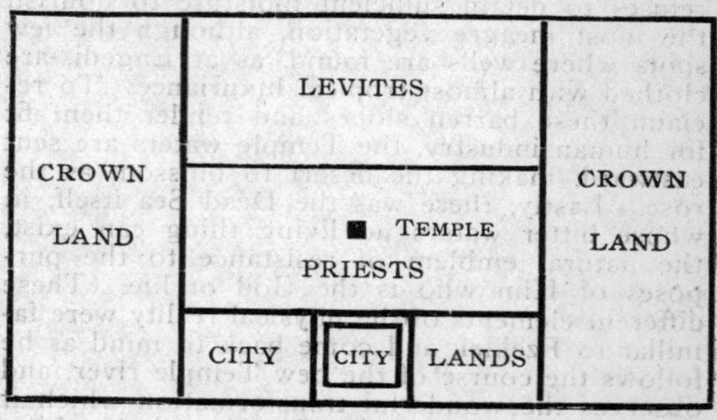

square of twenty-five thousand cubits is marked off; this is the "oblation" or sacred offering of land, in the middle of which the Temple stands. This again is subdivided into three parallel sections, as shown in the accompanying diagram. The most northerly, ten thousand cubits in breadth, is assigned to the Levites; the central portion, including the sanctuary, to the priests; and the remaining five thousand cubits is a "profane place" for the city and its common lands. The city itself is a square of four thousand five hundred cubits, situated in the middle of this southmost section of the oblation. With its free space of two hundred and fifty cubits in width belting the wall it fills the entire breadth of the section; the communal possessions flanking it on either hand, just as the prince's domain does the "oblation" as a whole. The produce of these lands is "for food to them that 'serve' (*i. e.*, inhabit) the city."† Residence in the capital, it appears, is to be regarded as a public service. The maintenance of the civic life of Jerusalem was an object in which the whole nation was interested, a truth symbolised by naming its twelve gates after the twelve sons of Jacob.‡ Hence, also, its population is to be representative of all the tribes of Israel, and who-

*I do not myself see much objection to supposing that it leaves the sea near Tyre and proceeds about due east to Hazar-enon, which may be near the foot of Hermon, where Robinson located it. In this case the "entrance to Hamath" would be the south end of the *Beka'*, where one strikes north to go to Hamath. This would correspond nearly to the extent of the country actually occupied by the Hebrews under the judges and the monarchy. The statement that the territory of Damascus lies to the north presents some difficulty on any theory. It may be added that Hazar-hattikon in ver. 16 is the same as Hazar-enon; it is probably, as Cornill suggests, a scribe's error for חצרה ענן (the locative ending being mistaken for the article).

*Smend, for example, points out that if we count the Levites' portion as a tribal inheritance, and include Manasseh and Ephraim under the house of Joseph (as is done in the naming of the gates of the city), we have the sons of Rachel and Leah evenly distributed on either side of the "oblation." Then at the farthest distance from the Temple are the sons of Jacob's handmaids, Gad in the extreme south, and Dan, Asher, and Naphtali in the north. This is ingenious, but not in the least convincing.

† Ver. 18.

‡ Vv. 31-34. It is difficult to trace a clear connection between the positions of the gates and the geographical distribution of the tribes in the country. The fact that

ever comes to dwell there is to have a share in the land belonging to the city.* But evidently the legislation on this point is incomplete. How were the inhabitants of the capital to be chosen out of all the tribes? Would its citizenship be regarded as a privilege or as an onerous responsibility? Would it be necessary to make a selection out of a host of applications, or would special inducements have to be offered to procure a sufficient population? To these questions the vision furnishes no answer, and there is nothing to show whether Ezekiel contemplated the possibility that residence in the new city might present few attractions and many disadvantages to an agricultural community such as he had in view. It is a curious incident of the return from the Exile that the problem of peopling Jerusalem emerged in a more serious form than Ezekiel from his ideal point of view could have foreseen. We read that "the rulers of the people dwelt at Jerusalem: the rest of the people also cast lots, to bring one of ten to dwell in Jerusalem, the holy city, and nine parts in [other] cities. And the people blessed all the men that willingly offered themselves to dwell at Jerusalem."† There may have been causes for this general reluctance which are unknown to us, but the principal reason was doubtless the one which has been hinted at, that the new colony lived mainly by agriculture, and the district in the immediate vicinity of the capital was not sufficiently fertile to support a large agricultural population. The new Jerusalem was at first a somewhat artificial foundation, and a city too largely developed for the resources of the community of which it was the centre. Its existence was necessary more for the protection and support of the Temple than for the ordinary ends of civilisation; and hence to dwell in it was for the majority an act of self-sacrifice by which a man was felt to deserve well of his country. And the only important difference between the actual reality and Ezekiel's ideal is that in the latter the supernatural fertility of the land and the reign of universal peace obviate the difficulties which the founders of the post-exilic theocracy had to encounter.

This seeming indifference of the prophet to the secular interests represented by the metropolis strikes us as a singular feature in his programme. It is strange that the man who was so thoughtful about the salt-pans of the Dead Sea should pass so lightly over the details of the reconstruction of a city. But we have had several intimations that this is not the department of things in which Ezekiel's hold on reality is most conspicuous. We have already remarked on the boldness of the conception which changes the site of the capital in order to guard the sanctity of the Temple. And now, when its situation and form are accurately defined, we have no sketch of municipal institutions, no hint of the purposes for which the city exists, and no glimpse of the busy and varied activities which we naturally connect with the name. If Ezekiel thought of it at all, except as existing on paper, he was probably interested in it as furnishing the representative congregation on minor occasions of public worship, such as the Sabbaths and new moons, when the whole people could not be expected to assemble. The truth is that the idea of the city in the vision is simply an abstract religious symbol, a sort of epitome and concentration of theocratic life. Like the figure of the prince in earlier chapters, it is taken from the national institutions which perished at the Exile; the outline is retained, the typical significance is enhanced, but the form is shadowy and indistinct, the colour and variety of concrete reality are absent. It was perhaps a stage through which political conceptions had to pass before their religious meaning could be apprehended. And yet the fact that the symbol of the Holy City is preserved is deeply suggestive and indeed scarcely less important in its own way than the retention of the type of the king. Ezekiel can no more think of the land without a capital than of the state without a prince. The word "city"—synonym of the fullest and most intense form of life, of life regulated by law and elevated by devotion to a common ideal, in which every worthy faculty of human nature is quickened by the close and varied intercourse of men with each other—has definitely taken its place in the vocabulary of religion. It is there, not to be superseded, but to be refined and spiritualised, until the city of God, glorified in the praises of Israel, becomes the inspiration of the loftiest thought and the most ardent longing of Christendom. And even for the perplexing problems that the Church has to face at this day there is hardly a more profitable exercise of the Christian imagination than to dream with practical intent of the consecration of civic life through the subjection of all its influences to the ends of the Redeemer's kingdom.

On the other hand we must surely recognise that this vision of a Temple and a city separated from each other—where religious and secular interests are as it were concentrated at different points, so that the one may be more effectually subordinated to the other—is not the final and perfect vision of the kingdom of God. That ideal has played a leading and influential part in the history of Christianity. It is essentially the ideal formulated in Augustine's great work on the city of God, which ruled the ecclesiastical polity of the mediæval Church. The State is an unholy institution; it is an embodiment of the power of this present evil world: the true city of God is the visible Catholic Church, and only by subjection to the Church can the State be redeemed from itself and be made a means of blessing. That theory served a providential purpose in preserving the traditions of Christianity through dark and troubled ages, and training the rude nations of Europe in purity and righteousness and reverence for that by which God makes Himself known. But the Reformation was, amongst other things, a protest against this conception of the relation of Church to State, of the sacred to the secular. By asserting the right of each believer to deal with Christ directly without the mediation of Church or priest it broke down the middle wall of partition between religion and every-day duty; it sanctified common life by showing how a man may serve God as a citizen in the family or the workshop better than in the cloister or at the altar. It made the kingdom of God to be a present power wherever there are lives transformed by love to Christ and serving their fellow-men for His sake. And if Catholicism may

here Levi is counted as a tribe and Ephraim and Manasseh are united under the name of Joseph indicates perhaps that none was intended.

* Ver 19.

† Neh. xi. 1, 2.

find some plausible support for its theory in Ezekiel and the Old Testament theocracy in general, Protestants may perhaps with better right appeal to the grander ideal represented by the new Jerusalem of the Apocalypse—the city that needs no Temple, because the Lord Himself is in her midst.

"And I John saw the holy city, new Jerusalem, coming down from God out of heaven, prepared as a bride adorned for her husband. And I heard a great voice out of heaven saying, Behold, the tabernacle of God is with men, and He will dwell with them, and they shall be His people, and God Himself shall be with them, and be their God. . . . And I saw no temple therein: for the Lord God Almighty and the Lamb are the temple of it. And the city had no need of the sun, neither of the moon, to shine in it: for the glory of God did lighten it, and the Lamb is the light thereof." *

It may be difficult for us amid the entanglements of the present to read that vision aright—difficult to say whether it is on earth or in heaven that we are to look for the city in which there is no Temple. Worship is an essential function of the Church of Christ; and so long as we are in our earthly abode worship will require external symbols and a visible organisation. But this at least we know, that the will of God must be done on earth as it is in heaven. The true kingdom of God is within us; and His presence with men is realised, not in special religious services which stand apart from our common life, but in the constant influence of His Spirit, forming our characters after the image of Christ, and permeating all the channels of social intercourse and public action, until everything done on earth is to the glory of our Father which is in heaven. That is the ideal set forth by the coming of the holy city of God, and only in this way can we look for the fulfilment of the promise embodied in the new name of Ezekiel's city, Jehovah-shammah,—

THE LORD IS THERE.

* Rev. xxi. 2, 3, 22, 23.

THE BOOK OF DANIEL.

CONTENTS.

PART I.

INTRODUCTION.

PART II.

COMMENTARY ON THE HISTORIC SECTION.

PART III.

THE PROPHETIC SECTION OF THE BOOK.

APPENDIX.

THE BOOK OF DANIEL.

BY THE REV. F. W. FARRAR, D. D., F. R. S.

PART I.

INTRODUCTION.

CHAPTER I.

THE HISTORIC EXISTENCE OF THE PROPHET DANIEL.

"Trothe is the hiest thinge a man may kepe."—CHAUCER.

WE propose in the following pages to examine the Book of the Prophet Daniel by the same general methods which have been adopted in other volumes of the Expositor's Bible. It may well happen that the conclusions adopted as regards its origin and its place in the Sacred Volume will not command the assent of all our readers. On the other hand, we may feel a reasonable confidence that, even if some are unable to accept the views at which we have arrived, and which we have here endeavoured to present with fairness, they will still read them with interest, as opinions which have been calmly and conscientiously formed, and to which the writer has been led by strong conviction.

All Christians will acknowledge the sacred and imperious duty of sacrificing every other consideration to the unbiased acceptance of that which we regard as truth. Further than this our readers will find much to elucidate the Book of Daniel chapter by chapter, apart from any questions which affect its authorship or age.

But I should like to say on the threshold that, though I am compelled to regard the Book of Daniel as a work which, in its present form, first saw the light in the days of Antiochus Epiphanes, and though I believe that its six magnificent opening chapters were never meant to be regarded in any other light than that of moral and religious Haggadoth, yet no words of mine can exaggerate the value which I attach to this part of our Canonical Scriptures. The Book, as we shall see, has exercised a powerful influence over Christian conduct and Christian thought. Its right to a place in the Canon is undisputed and indisputable, and there is scarcely a single book of the Old Testament which can be made more richly "profitable for teaching, for reproof, for correction, for instruction in righteousness, that the man of God may be complete, completely furnished unto every good work." Such religious lessons are eminently suitable for the aims of the Expositor's Bible. They are not in the slightest degree impaired by those results of archæological discovery and "criticism" which are now almost universally accepted by the scholars of the Continent, and by many of our chief English critics. Finally unfavourable to the authenticity, they are yet in no way derogatory to the preciousness of this Old Testament Apocalypse.

The first question which we must consider is, "What is known about the Prophet Daniel?"

I. If we accept as historical the particulars narrated of him in this Book, it is clear that few Jews have ever risen to so splendid an eminence. Under four powerful kings and conquerors, of three different nationalities and dynasties, he held a position of high authority among the haughtiest aristocracies of the ancient world. At a very early age he was not only a satrap, but the Prince and Prime Minister over *all* the satraps in Babylonia and Persia; not only a Magian, but the Head Magian, and Chief Governor over all the wise men of Babylon. Not even Joseph, as the chief ruler over all the house of Pharaoh, had anything like the extensive sway exercised by the Daniel of this Book. He was placed by Nebuchadrezzar "over the whole province of Babylon"; * under Darius he was President of the Board of Three to "whom all the satraps" sent their accounts; † and he was continued in office and prosperity under Cyrus the Persian. ‡

II. It is natural, then, that we should turn to the monuments and inscriptions of the Babylonian, Persian, and Median Empires to see if any mention can be found of so prominent a ruler. But hitherto neither has his name been discovered, nor the faintest trace of his existence.

III. If we next search other non-Biblical sources of information, we find much respecting him in the Apocrypha—"The Song of the Three Children," "The Story of Susanna," and "Bel and the Dragon." But these additions to the Canonical Books are avowedly valueless for any historic purpose. They are romances, in which the vehicle of fiction is used, in a manner which at all times was popular in Jewish literature, to teach lessons of faith and conduct by the example of eminent sages or saints.§ The few other fictitious fragments preserved by Fabricius have not the smallest importance.‖ Josephus, beyond mentioning that Daniel and his three companions were of the family of King Zedekiah,¶ adds nothing appreciable to our information. He narrates the story of the Book, and in doing so adopts a somewhat apologetic tone, as though he specially declined to vouch for its historic exactness. For he says: "Let no one blame me for writing down everything of this nature, as I find it in our ancient books: for as to that matter, I have plainly assured those that think me defective in any such point, or complain of my management, and have told

* Dan. ii. 48.

† Dan. v. 29, vi. 2.

‡ Dan. vi. 28. There is a Daniel of the sons of Ithamar in Ezra viii. 2, and among those who sealed the covenant in Neh. x. 6.

§ For a full account of the Agada (also called Agadtha and Haggada), I must refer the reader to Hamburger's "Real-Encyklopädie für Bibel und Talmud," ii. 19-27, 921-934. The first two forms of the words are Aramaic; the third was a Hebrew form in use among the Jews in Babylonia. The word is derived from נָגַד, "to say" or "explain." Halacha was the rule of religious praxis, a sort of Directorium Judaicum: Haggada was the result of free religious reflection. See further Strack, "Einl. in den Thalmud," iv. 122.

‖ Fabricius, "Cod. Pseudepigr. Vet. Test.," i. 1124.

¶ Jos., "Antt.," X. xi. 7. But Pseudo-Epiphanius ("De Vit. Dan.," x.) says: Γέγονε τῶν ἐξόχων τῆς βασιλικῆς ὑπηρεσίας. So to the "Midrash" on Ruth, 7.

them, in the beginning of this history, that I intended to do no more than to translate the Hebrew books into the Greek language, and promised them to explain these facts, without adding anything to them of my own, or taking anything away from them." *

IV. In the Talmud, again, we find nothing historical. Daniel is always mentioned as a champion against idolatry, and his wisdom is so highly esteemed, that, "if all the wise men of the heathen," we are told, "were on one side, and Daniel on the other, Daniel would still prevail." † He is spoken of as an example of God's protection of the innocent, and his three daily prayers are taken as our rule of life.‡ To him are applied the verses of Lam. iii. 55-57: "I called upon Thy name, O Lord, out of the lowest pit. . . . Thou drewest near in the day that I called: Thou saidst, Fear not. O Lord, Thou hast pleaded the causes of my soul; Thou hast redeemed my life." We are assured that he was of Davidic descent; obtained permission for the return of the exiles; survived till the rebuilding of the Temple; lived to a great age, and finally died in Palestine.§ Rav even went so far as to say, "If there be any like the Messiah among the living, it is our Rabbi the Holy: if among the dead, it is Daniel." ‖ In the "Avoth" of Rabbi Nathan it is stated that Daniel exercised himself in benevolence by endowing brides, following funerals, and giving alms. One of the Apocryphal legends respecting him has been widely spread. It tells us that, when he was a second time cast into the den of lions under Cyrus, and was fasting from lack of food, the Prophet Habakkuk was taken by a hair of his head and carried by the angel of the Lord to Babylon, to give to Daniel the dinner which he had prepared for his reapers.¶ It is with reference to this Haggada that in the catacombs Daniel is represented in the lions' den standing naked between two lions—an emblem of the soul between sin and death—and that a youth with a pot of food is by his side.

There is a Persian apocalypse of Daniel translated by Merx ("Archiv," i. 387), and there are a few worthless Mohammedan legends about him which are given in D'Herbelot's "Bibliothèque Orientale." They only serve to show how widely extended was the reputation which became the nucleus of strange and miraculous stories. As in the case of Pythagoras and Empedocles, they indicate the deep reverence which the ideal of his character inspired. They are as the fantastic clouds which gather about the loftiest mountain peaks. In later days he seems to have been comparatively forgotten.**

These references would not, however, suffice to prove Daniel's *historical* existence. They might merely result from the literal acceptance of the story narrated in the Book. From the name "Daniel," which is by no means a common one, and means "Judge of God," nothing can be learnt. It is only found in three other instances.*

Turning to the Old Testament itself, we have reason for surprise both in its allusions and its silences. One only of the sacred writers refers to Daniel, and that is Ezekiel. In one passage (xxviii. 3) the Prince of Tyrus is apostrophised in the words, "Behold, thou art wiser than Daniel; there is no secret that they can hide from thee." In the other (xiv. 14, 20) the word of the Lord declares to the guilty city, that "though these three men, Noah, Daniel, and Job, were in it, they should deliver but their own souls by their righteousness"; "they shall deliver neither son nor daughter."

The last words may be regarded as a general allusion, and therefore we may pass over the circumstance that Daniel—who was undoubtedly a eunuch in the palace of Babylon, and who is often pointed to as a fulfilment of the stern prophecy of Isaiah to Hezekiah †—could never have had either son or daughter.

But in other respects the allusion is surprising.

i. It was very unusual among the Jews to elevate their contemporaries to such a height of exaltation, and it is indeed startling that Ezekiel should thus place his youthful contemporary on such a pinnacle as to unite his name to those of Noah the antediluvian patriarch and the mysterious man of Uz.

ii. We might, with Theodoret, Jerome, and Kimchi, account for the mention of Daniel's name at all in this connection by the peculiar circumstances of his life; ‡ but there is little probability in the suggestions of bewildered commentators as to the reason why his name should be placed *between* those of Noah and Job. It is difficult, with Hävernick, to recognise any *climax* in the order; § nor can it be regarded as quite satisfactory to say, with Delitzsch, that the collocation is due to the fact that "as Noah was a righteous man of the old world, and Job of the ideal world, Daniel represented immediately the contemporaneous world." ‖ If Job was a purely ideal instance of exemplary goodness, why may not Daniel have been the same?

To some critics the allusion has appeared so strange that they have referred it to an imaginary Daniel who had lived at the Court of Nineveh during the Assyrian exile; ¶ or to some mythic hero who belonged to ancient days—perhaps, like Melchizedek, a contemporary of the ruin of the cities of the Plain.** Ewald tries to urge something for the former conjecture; yet neither for it nor for the latter is there any tittle of real evidence.†† This, however, would not be decisive against the hypothesis, since in 1 Kings iv. 31 we have references to men of pre-eminent

* Jos., "Antt.," X. x. 6.
† "Yoma," f. 77.
‡ "Berachôth," f. 31.
§ "Sanhedrin," f. 93. "Midrash Rabba" on Ruth, 7, etc., quoted by Hamburger, "Real-Encyclopädie," i. 225.
‖ "Kiddushin," f. 72, 6: Hershon, "Genesis acc. to the Talmud," p. 471.
¶ Bel and the Dragon, 33-39. It seems to be an old Midrashic legend. It is quoted by Dorotheus and Pseudo-Epiphanius, and referred to by some of the Fathers. Eusebius supposes another Habakkuk and another Daniel; but "anachronisms, literary extravagances, or legendary character are obvious on the face of such narratives. Such faults as these, though valid against any pretensions to the rank of authentic history, do not render the stories less effective as pieces of Haggadic satire, or less interesting as preserving vestiges of a cycle of popular legends relating to Daniel" (Rev. C. J. Ball, "Speaker's Commentary," on Apocrypha, ii. 350).
** Höttinger, "Hist. Orientalis," p. 92.

* Ezra viii. 2; Neh. x. 6. In 1 Chron. iii. 1 Daniel is an alternative name for David's son Chileab—perhaps a clerical error. If so, the names Daniel, Mishael, Azariah, and Hananiah are only found in the two post-exilic books, whence Kamphausen supposes them to have been borrowed by the writer.
† Isa. xxxix. 7.
‡ See Rosenmüller, "Scholia," *ad loc.*
§ "Ezek.," p., 207.
‖ Herzog, "R. E.," *s. v.*
¶ Ewald, "Proph. d. Alt. Bund.," ii. 560; De Wette, "Einleit.," § 253.
** So Von Lengerke, "Dan.," xciii. ff.; Hitzig, "Dan.," viii.
†† He is followed by Bunsen, "Gott in der Gesch," i. 514.

wisdom respecting whom no breath of tradition has come down to us.*

iii. But if we accept the Book of Daniel as literal history, the allusion of Ezekiel becomes still more difficult to explain; for Daniel must have been not only a contemporary of the prophet of the Exile, but a very youthful one. We are told—a difficulty to which we shall subsequently allude—that Daniel was taken captive in the third year of Jehoiakim (Dan. i. 1), about the year B. C. 606. Ignatius says that he was twelve years old when he foiled the elders; and the narrative shows that he could not have been much older when taken captive.† If Ezekiel's prophecy was uttered B. C. 584, Daniel at that time could only have been twenty-two; if it was uttered as late as B. C. 572,‡ Daniel would still have been only thirty-four, and therefore little more than a youth in Jewish eyes. It is undoubtedly surprising that among Orientals, who regard age as the chief passport to wisdom, a living youth should be thus canonised between the Patriarch of the Deluge and the Prince of Uz.

iv. Admitting that this pinnacle of eminence may have been due to the peculiar splendour of Daniel's career, it becomes the less easy to account for the total silence respecting him in the other books of the Old Testament—in the Prophets who were contemporaneous with the Exile and its close, like Haggai, Zechariah, and Malachi; and in the Books of Ezra and Nehemiah, which give us the details of the Return. No post-exilic prophets seem to know anything of the Book of Daniel.§ Their expectations of Israel's future are very different from his.‖ The silence of Ezra is specially astonishing. It has often been conjectured that it was Daniel who showed to Cyrus the prophecies of Isaiah.¶ Certainly it is stated that he held the very highest position in the Court of the Persian King; yet neither does Ezra mention his existence, nor does Nehemiah—himself a high functionary in the Court of Artaxerxes—refer to his illustrious predecessor. Daniel outlived the first return of the exiles under Zerubbabel, and he did not avail himself of this opportunity to revisit the land and desolate sanctuary of his fathers which he loved so well.** We might have assumed that patriotism so burning as his would not have preferred to stay at Babylon, or at Shushan, when the priests and princes of his people were returning to the Holy City. Others of great age faced the perils of the Restoration; and if he stayed behind to be of greater use to his countrymen, we cannot account for the fact that he is not distantly alluded to in the record which tells how "the chief of the fathers, with all those whose spirit God had raised, rose up to go to build the House of the Lord which is in Jerusalem." †† That the difficulty was felt is shown by the Mohammedan legend that Daniel *did* return with Ezra,‡‡ and that he received the office of Governor of Syria, from which country he went back to Susa, where his tomb is still yearly visited by crowds of adoring pilgrims.

v. If we turn to the New Testament, the name of Daniel only occurs in the reference to "the abomination of desolation, spoken of by Daniel the prophet."* The Book of Revelation does not name him, but is profoundly influenced by the Book of Daniel both in its form and in the symbols which it adopts.†

vi. In the Apocrypha Daniel is passed over in complete silence among the lists of Hebrew heroes enumerated by Jesus the son of Sirach. We are even told that "neither was there a man born like unto Joseph, a leader of his brethren, a stay of the people" (Ecclus. xlix. 15). This is the more singular because not only are the achievements of Daniel under four heathen potentates greater than those of Joseph under one Pharaoh, but also several of the stories of Daniel at once remind us of the story of Joseph, and even appear to have been written with silent reference to the youthful Hebrew and his fortunes as an Egyptian slave who was elevated to be governor of the land of his exile.

CHAPTER II.

GENERAL SURVEY OF THE BOOK.

I. The Language.

Unable to learn anything further respecting the professed author of the Book of Daniel, we now turn to the Book itself. In this section I shall merely give a general sketch of its main, external phenomena, and shall chiefly pass in review those characteristics which, though they have been used as arguments respecting the age in which it originated, are not absolutely irreconcilable with the supposition of *any* date between the termination of the Exile (B. C. 536) and the death of Antiochus Epiphanes (B. C. 164).

I. First we notice the fact that there is an interchange of the first and third person. In chapters i.-vi. Daniel is mainly spoken of in the third person; in chaps. vii.-xii. he speaks mainly in the first.

Kranichfeld tries to account for this by the supposition that in chaps. i.-vi. we practically have extracts from Daniel's diaries,‡ whereas in the remainder of the Book he describes his own visions. The point cannot be much insisted upon, but the mention of his own high praises (*e. g.*, in such passages as vi. 4) is perhaps hardly what we should have expected.

II. Next we observe that the Book of Daniel, like the Book of Ezra,§ is written partly in the sacred Hebrew, partly in the vernacular Aramaic, which is often, but erroneously, called Chaldee.‖

* Reuss, "Heil. Schrift.," p. 570.

† Ignat., "Ad Magnes," 3 (Long Revision: see Lightfoot, ii., § ii., p. 749). So too in "Ps. Mar. ad Ignat.," 3. Lightfoot thinks that this is a transference from Solomon (*l. c.*, p. 727).

‡ See Ezek. xxix. 17.

§ See Zech. ii. 6-10; Ezek. xxxvii. 9, etc.

‖ See Hag. ii. 6-9, 20-23; Zech. ii, 5-17, iii. 8-10; Mal. iii. 1.

¶ Ezra (i. 1) does not mention the striking prophecies of the later Isaiah (xliv. 28, xlv. 1), but refers to Jeremiah only (xxv. 12, xxix. 10).

** Dan. x. 1-18, vi. 10.

†† Ezra i. 5.

‡‡ D'Herbelot, *l. c.*

* Matt. xxiv. 15; Mark xiii. 14. There can be of course no certainty that the "spoken of by Daniel the prophet" is not the comment of the Evangelist.

† See Elliott, "Horæ Apocalypticæ," *passim*.

‡ Kranichfeld, "Das Buch Daniel," p. 4.

§ See Ezra iv. 7, vi. 18. vii. 12-26.

‖ "The term 'Chaldee' for the Aramaic of either the Bible or the Targums is a misnomer, the use of which is only a source of confusion" (Driver, p. 471). A single verse of Jeremiah (x. 11) is in Aramaic: "Thus shall ye say unto them, The gods who made not heaven and earth shall perish from the earth and from under heaven." Perhaps Jeremiah gave the verse "to the Jews as an answer to the heathen among whom they were" (Pusey, p. 11).

The first section (i. 1-ii. 4*a*) is in Hebrew. The language changes to Aramaic after the words, "Then spake the Chaldeans to the king *in Syriac*" (ii. 4*a*); and this is continued to vii. 28. The eighth chapter begins with the words, "In the third year of the reign of King Belshazzar a vision appeared unto me, even unto me Daniel"; and here the Hebrew is resumed, and is continued till the end of the Book.

The question at once arises why the two languages were used in the same Book.

It is easy to understand that, during the course of the seventy years' Exile, many of the Jews became practically bilingual, and would be able to write with equal facility in one language or in the other.

This circumstance, then, has no bearing on the date of the Book. Down to the Maccabean age some books continued to be written in Hebrew. These books must have found readers. Hence the knowledge of Hebrew cannot have died away so completely as has been supposed. The notion that after the return from the Exile Hebrew was at once superseded by Aramaic is untenable. Hebrew long continued to be the language normally spoken at Jerusalem (Neh. xiii. 24), and the Jews did not bring back Aramaic with them to Palestine, but found it there.*

But it is not clear why the linguistic *divisions* in the Book were adopted. Auberlen says that, after the introduction, the section ii. 4 *a*-vii. 28 was written in Chaldee, because it describes the development of the power of the world from a world-historic point of view; and that the remainder of the Book was written in Hebrew, because it deals with the development of the world-powers in their relation to Israel the people of God.† There is very little to be said in favour of a structure so little obvious and so highly artificial. A simpler solution of the difficulty would be that which accounts for the use of Chaldee by saying that it was adopted in those parts which involved the introduction of Aramaic documents. This, however, would not account for its use in chap. vii., which is a chapter of visions in which Hebrew might have been naturally expected as the vehicle of prophecy. Strack and Meinhold think that the Aramaic and Hebrew parts are of different origin. König supposes that the Aramaic sections were meant to indicate special reference to the Syrians and Antiochus.‡ Some critics have thought it possible that the Aramaic sections were once written in Hebrew. That the text of Daniel has not been very carefully kept becomes clear from the liberties to which it was subjected by the Septuagint translators. If the Hebrew of Jer. x. 11 (a verse which only exists in Aramaic) has been lost, it is not inconceivable that the same may have happened to the Hebrew of a section of Daniel.§

The Talmud throws no light on the question. It only says that—

i. "The men of the Great Synagogue wrote" ‖ —by which is perhaps meant that they "edited" —"the Book of Ezekiel, the Twelve Minor Prophets, the Book of Daniel, and the Book of Ezra"; * and that—

ii. "The Chaldee passages in the Book of Ezra and the Book of Daniel defile the hands." †

The first of these two passages is merely an assertion that the preservation, the arrangement, and the admission into the Canon of the books mentioned was due to the body of scribes and priests—a very shadowy and unhistorical body —known as the Great Synagogue.‡

The second passage sounds startling, but is nothing more than an authoritative declaration that the Chaldee sections of Daniel and Ezra are still parts of Holy Scripture, though not written in the sacred language.

It is a standing rule of the Talmudists that "All Holy Scripture defiles the hands"—even the long-disputed Books of Ecclesiastes and Canticles.§ Lest any should misdoubt the sacredness of the Chaldee sections, they are expressly included in the rule. It seems to have originated thus: The eatables of the heave offerings were kept in close proximity to the scroll of the Law, for both were considered equally sacred. If a mouse or rat happened to nibble either, the offerings and the books became defiled, and therefore defiled the hands that touched them.‖ To guard against this hypothetical defilement it was decided that *all* handling of the Scriptures should be followed by ceremonial ablutions. To say that the Chaldee chapters "defile the hands" is the Rabbinic way of declaring their Canonicity.

Perhaps nothing certain can be inferred from the philological examination either of the Hebrew or of the Chaldee portions of the Book; but they seem to indicate a date earlier than the age of Alexander (B. C. 333). On this part of the subject there has been a great deal of rash and incompetent assertion. It involves delicate problems on which an independent and a valuable opinion can only be offered by the merest handful of living scholars, and respecting which even these scholars sometimes disagree. In deciding upon such points ordinary students can only weigh the authority and the arguments of specialists who have devoted a minute and lifelong study to the grammar and history of the Semitic languages.

I know no higher contemporary authorities on the date of Hebrew writings than the late veteran scholar F. Delitzsch and Professor Driver.

1. Nothing was more beautiful and remarkable in Professor Delitzsch than the open-minded candour which compelled him to the last to advance with advancing thought; to admit all fresh elements of evidence; to continue his education as a Biblical inquirer to the latest days of his life; and without hesitation to correct, modify, or even reverse his previous conclusions in accordance with the results of deeper study and fresh discoveries. He wrote the article on Daniel in Herzog's "Real-Encyclopädie," and in the first edition of that work maintained its genuineness; but in the later editions (iii. 470) his

* Driver, p. 471; Nöldeke, "Enc. Brit.," xxi. 647; Wright, "Grammar," p. 16. Ad. Merx has a treatise on "Cur in lib. Dan. juxta Hebr. Aramaica sit adhibita dialectus," 1865; but his solution, "Scriptorem omnia quæ rudioribus vulgi ingeniis apta viderentur Aramaice præposuisse" is wholly untenable.

† Auberlen, "Dan.," pp. 28, 29 (E. Tr.)

‡ "Einleit.," § 383.

§ Cheyne, "Enc. Brit.," *s. v.* "Daniel."

‖ כתבו. See 2 Esdras xiv. 22-48: "In forty days they *wrote* two hundred and four books."

* "Baba-Bathra," f. 15, 6: comp. "Sanhedrin," f. 83, 6.

† "Yaddayim," iv.; "Mish.," 5.

‡ See Rau, "De Synag. Magna.," ii. 66 ff.; Kuenen, "Over de Mannen der Groote Synagoge," 1876; Ewald, "Hist. of Israel," v. 168-170 (E. Tr.): Westcott, *s. v.* "Canon" (Smith's "Dict.," i. 500).

§ "Yaddayim," iii.; "Mish.," 5; Hershon, "Treasures of the Talmud," pp. 41-43.

‖ Hershon (*l. c.*) refers to "Shabbath," f. 14, 1.

views approximate more and more to those of the Higher Criticism. Of the Hebrew of Daniel he says that "it attaches itself here and there to Ezekiel, and also to Habakkuk; in general character it resembles the Hebrew of the Chronicler who wrote shortly before the beginning of the Greek period (B. C. 332), and as compared either with the ancient Hebrew of the 'Mishnah' is full of singularities and harshnesses of style." *

So far, then, it is clear that, if the Hebrew mainly resembles that of B. C. 332, it is hardly likely that it should have been written *before* B. C. 536.

Professor Driver says, "The Hebrew of Daniel in all distinctive features resembles, not the Hebrew of Ezekiel, or even of Haggai and Zechariah, but that of the age subsequent to Nehemiah"—whose age forms the great turning-point in Hebrew style.

He proceeds to give a list of linguistic peculiarities in support of this view, and other specimens of sentences constructed, not in the style of classical Hebrew, but in "the later uncouth style" of the Book of Chronicles. He points out in a note that it is no explanation of these peculiarities to argue that, during his long exile, Daniel may have partially forgotten the language of his youth; "for this would not account for the resemblance of the new and decadent idioms to those which appeared in Palestine independently two hundred and fifty years afterwards." † Behrmann, in the latest commentary on Daniel, mentions, in proof of the late character of the Hebrew: (1) the introduction of Persian words which could not have been used in Babylonia before the conquest of Cyrus (as in i. 3, 5, xi. 45, etc.); (2) many Aramaic or Aramaising words, expressions and grammatical forms (as in i. 5, 10, 12, 16, viii. 18, 22, x. 17 21, etc.); (3) neglect of strict accuracy in the use of the Hebrew tenses (as in viii. 14, ix. 3 f., xi. 4 f., etc.); (4) the borrowing of archaic expressions from ancient sources (as in viii. 26, ix. 2, xi. 10, 40, etc.); (5) the use of technical terms and periphrases common in Jewish apocalypses (xi. 6, 13, 35, 40, etc.).‡

2. These views of the character of the Hebrew agree with those of previous scholars. Bertholdt and Kirms declare that its character differs *toto genere* from what might have been expected had the Book been genuine. Gesenius says that the language is even more corrupt than that of Ezra, Nehemiah, and Malachi. Professor Driver says the *Persian* words *presuppose* a period after the Persian empire had been well established; the *Greek* words *demand*, the *Hebrew supports*, and the *Aramaic permits* a date after the conquest of Palestine by Alexander the Great. De Wette and Ewald have pointed out the lack of the old passionate spontaniety of early prophecy; the absence of the numerous and profound paronomasiæ, or plays on words, which characterised the burning oratory of the prophets; and the peculiarities of the style—which is sometimes obscure and careless, sometimes pompous, iterative, and artificial.*

3. It is noteworthy that in this Book the name of the great Babylonian conqueror, with whom, in the narrative part, Daniel is thrown into such close connection, is invariably written in the absolutely erroneous form which his name assumed in later centuries—Nebuchad*n*ezzar. A contemporary, familiar with the Babylonian language, could not have been ignorant of the fact that the only correct form of the name is Nebuchad*r*ezzar—*i. e.*, *Nebu-kudurri-utsur*, "Nebo protect the throne." †

4. But the erroneous form Nebuchad*n*ezzar is not the only one which entirely militates against the notion of a contemporary writer. There seem to be other mistakes about Babylonian matters into which a person in Daniel's position could not have fallen. Thus the name Belteshazzar seems to be connected in the writer's mind with Bel, the favourite deity of Nebuchadrezzar; but it can only mean *Balatu-utsur*, "his life protect," which looks like a mutilation. Abed-*nego* is an astonishingly corrupt form of Abed-*nabu*, "the servant of Nebo." Hammelzar, Shadrach, Meshach, Ashpenaz, are declared by Assyriologists to be "out of keeping with Babylonian science." In ii. 48 *signîn* means a civil ruler;—does not imply Archimagus, as the context seems to require, but, according to Lenormant, a high civil officer.

5. The *Aramaic* of Daniel closely resembles that of Ezra. Nöldeke calls it a Palestinian or Western Aramaic dialect, later than that of the Book of Ezra.‡ It is of earlier type than that of the Targums of Jonathan and Onkelos; but that fact has very little bearing on the date of the Book, because the differences are slight, and the resemblances manifold, and the Targums did not appear till after the Christian Era, nor assume their present shape perhaps before the fourth century. Further, "recently discovered inscriptions have shown that many of the forms in which the Aramaic of Daniel differs from that of the Targums were actually in use in neighbouring countries down to the first century A. D." §

6. Two further philological considerations bear on the age of the Book.

i. One of these is the existence of no less than fifteen *Persian* words (according to Nöldeke and others), especially in the Aramaic part. These words, which would not be surprising after the complete establishment of the Persian empire, are surprising in passages which describe Babylonian institutions before the conquest of Cyrus. ‖ Various attempts have been made to account for this phenomenon. Professor Fuller attempts to

* Herzog, *l. c.*; so too König, "Einleit.," § 387: "Das Hebr. der B. Dan. ist nicht blos nachexilisch sondern auch nachchronistisch." He instances *ribbo* (Dan. xi. 12) for *rebaba*, "myriads" (Ezek. xvi. 7); and *tamîd*, "the daily burnt offering" (Dan. viii. 11), as post-Biblical Hebrew for *'olath hatamîd* (Neh. x. 34), etc. Margoliouth (*Expositor*, April, 1890) thinks that the Hebrew proves a date before B. C. 168; on which view see Driver, p. 483.

† "Lit. of Old Test.," pp. 473-476.

‡ "Das Buch Dan.," iii.

* See Glassius, "Philol. Sacr.," p. 931; Ewald, "Die Proph. d. A. Bundes," i. 48; De Wette, "Einleit.," § 347.

† Ezekiel always uses the correct form (xxvi. 7, xxix. 18, xxx. 10.) Jeremiah uses the correct form except in passages which properly belong to the Book of Kings.

‡ Nöldeke, "Semit. Spr.," p. 30; Driver, p. 472; König, p. 387.

§ Driver, p. 472, and the authorities there quoted; as against McGill and Pusey ("Daniel," pp. 45 ff., 602 ff.). Dr. Pusey's is the fullest repertory of arguments in favour of the authenticity of Daniel, many of which have become more and more obviously untenable as criticism advances. But he and Keil add little or nothing to what had been ingeniously elaborated by Hengstenberg and Hävernick. For a sketch of the peculiarities in the Aramaic see Behrmann, "Daniel," v.-x. Renan ("Hist. Gén. des Langues Sém.," p. 219) exaggerates when he says, "La langue des parties chaldénnes est beaucoup plus basse que celle des fragments chaldéens du Livre d'Esdras, et s'incline *beaucoup* vers la langue du Talmud."

‖ Meinhold, "Beiträge," pp. 30-32; Driver, p. 470.

show, but with little success, that some of them may be Semitic.* Others argue that they are amply accounted for by the Persian trade which, as may be seen from the "Records of the Past," † existed between Persia and Babylonia as early as the days of Belshazzar. To this it is replied that some of the words are not of a kind which one nation would at once borrow from another, and that "no Persian words have hitherto been found in Assyrian or Babylonian inscriptions prior to the conquest of Babylon by Cyrus, except the name of the god Mithra."

ii. But the linguistic evidence unfavourable to the genuineness of the Book of Daniel is far stronger than this, in the startling fact that it contains at least three Greek words. After giving the fullest consideration to all that has been urged in refutation of the conclusion, this circumstance has always been to me a strong confirmation of the view that the Book of Daniel in its present form is not older than the days of Antiochus Epiphanes.

Those three Greek words occur in the list of musical instruments mentioned in iii. 5, 7, 10, 15. They are קיתרס *kitharos*, κίθαρις, "harp"; פסנתרין, *psanterîn*, ψαλτήριον, "psaltery"; ‡ סומפניא, *sūmpōnyāh*, συμφωνία, A. V. "dulcimer," but perhaps "bagpipes." §

Be it remembered that these musical instruments are described as having been used at the great idol-festival of Nebuchadrezzar (B. C. 550). Now, this is the date at which Pisistratus was tyrant at Athens, in the days of Pythagoras and Polycrates, before Athens became a fixed democracy. It is just conceivable that in those days the Babylonians might have borrowed from Greece the word *kitharis*.‖ It is, indeed, supremely *unlikely*, because the harp had been known in the East from the earliest days; and it is at least as probable that Greece, which at this time was only beginning to sit as a learner at the feet of the immemorial East, borrowed the idea of the instrument from Asia. Let it, however, be admitted that such words as *yayîn*, "wine" (οἶνος), *lappid*, "a torch" (λαμπάς), and a few others, *may* indicate some early intercourse between Greece and the East, and that some commercial relations of a rudimentary kind were existent even in prehistoric days.¶

But what are we to say of the two other words? Both are derivatives. *Psalterion* does not occur in Greek before Aristotle (d. 322); nor *symphonia* before Plato (d. 347). In relation to music, and probably as the name of a musical instrument, *sumphonia* is first used by Polybius (xxvi. 10, § 5, xxxi. 4, § 8), and *in express connection* with the festivities of the very king with whom the apocalyptic section of Daniel is mainly occupied—Antiochus Epiphanes.** The attempts of Professor Fuller and others to derive these words from Semitic roots are a desperate resource, and cannot win the assent of a single trained philologist. "These words," says Professor Driver, "could not have been used in the Book of Daniel, unless it had been written after the dissemination of Greek influence in Asia through the conquest of Alexander the Great." *

2. The Unity of the Book.

The *Unity* of the Book of Daniel is now generally admitted. No one thought of questioning it in days before the dawn of criticism, but in 1772 Eichhorn and Corrodi doubted the genuineness of the Book. J. D. Michaelis endeavoured to prove that it was "a collection of fugitive pieces," consisting of six historic pictures, followed by four prophetic visions.† Bertholdt, followed the erroneous tendency of criticism which found a foremost exponent in Ewald, and imagined the possibility of detecting the work of many different hands. He divided the Book into fragments by nine different authors.

Zöckler, in Lange's "Bibelwerk," persuaded himself that the old "orthodox" views of Hengstenberg and Auberlen were right; but he could only do this by sacrificing the authenticity of part of the Book, and assuming more than one redaction. Thus he supposes that xi. 5-39 are an interpolation by a writer in the days of Antiochus Epiphanes. Similarly, Lenormant admits interpolations in the *first* half of the Book. But to concede this is practically to give up the Book of Daniel as it now stands.

The *unity* of the Book of Daniel is still admitted or assumed by most critics. It has only been recently questioned in two directions.

Meinhold thinks that the Aramaic and historic sections are older than the rest of the Book, and were written about B. C. 300 to convert the Gentiles to monotheism.‡ He argues that the apocalyptic section was written later, and was subsequently incorporated with the Book. A somewhat similar view is held by Zöckler,§ and some have thought that Daniel could never have written of himself in such highly favourable terms as, *e. g.*, in Dan. vi. 4.‖ The first chapter, which is essential as an introduction to the Book, and the seventh, which is apocalyptic, and is yet in Aramaic, create objections to the acceptance of this theory. Further, it is impossible not to observe a certain unity of style and parallelism of treatment between the two parts. Thus, if the prophetic section is mainly devoted to Antiochus Epiphanes, the historic section seems to have an allusive bearing on his impious madness. In

* "Speaker's Commentary," vi. 246–250.

† New Series, iii. 124.

‡ The change of *n* for *l* is not uncommon: comp. βέντιον, φίντατος, etc.

§ The word שַׂבְּכָא, *Sab'ka*, also bears a suspicious resemblance to σαμβύκη, but Athenæus says ("Deipnos.," iv. 173) that the instrument was invented by the Syrians. Some have seen in *kārôz* (iii. 4, "herald") the Greek κήρυξ, and in *hamnîk*, "chain," the Greek μαμιάκης; but these cannot be pressed.

‖ It is true that there was *some* small intercourse between even the Assyrians and Ionians (Ja-am-na-a) as far back as the days of Sargon (B. C. 722–705); but not enough to account for such words.

¶ Sayce, *Contemp. Rev.*, December, 1878.

** Some argue that in this passage συμφωνία means "a concert" (comp. Luke xv. 25); but Polybius mentions it with "a horn" (κεράτιον). Behrmann (p. ix.) connects it with σίφων, and makes it mean "a pipe."

* Pusey says all he can on the other side (pp. 23–28), and has not changed the opinion of scholars (pp. 27-33). Fabre d'Envieu (i. 101) also desperately denies the existence of any Greek words. On the other side see Derenbourg, "Les Mots grecs dans le Livre biblique de Daniel" (Mélanges Graux, 1884).

† "Orient. u. Exeg. Bibliothek," 1772, p. 141. This view was revived by Lagarde in the "Göttingen Gel. Anzeigen," 1891.

‡ "Beiträge," 1888. See too Kranichfeld, "Das Buch Daniel," p. 4. The view is refuted by Budde, *Theol. Lit. Zeitung*, 1888, No. 26. The conjecture has often occurred to critics. Thus Sir Isaac Newton, believing that Daniel wrote the last six chapters, thought that the six first "are a collection of historical papers written by others" ("Observations," i. 10).

§ "Einleit.," p. 6.

‖ Other critics who incline to one or other modification of this view of the *two* Daniels are Tholuck, "d. A. T. in N. T." 1872; C. v. Orelli, "Alttest. Weissag.," 1882; and Strack.

ii. 10, 11, and vi. 8, we have descriptions of daring Pagan edicts, which might be intended to furnish a contrast with the attempts of Antiochus to *suppress* the worship of God. The feast of Belshazzar may well be a "reference to the Syrian despot's revelries at Daphne." Again, in ii. 43 —where the mixture of iron and clay is explained by "they shall mingle themselves with the seed of men"—it seems far from improbable that there is a reference to the unhappy intermarriages of Ptolemies and Seleucidæ. Berenice, daughter of Ptolemy II. (Philadelphus), married Antiochus II. (Theos), and this is alluded to in this vision of xi. 6. Cleopatra, daughter of Antiochus III. (the Great), married Ptolemy V. (Epiphanes), which is alluded to in xi. 17.* The style seems to be stamped throughout with the characteristics of an individual mind, and the most cursory glance suffices to show that the historic and prophetic parts are united by many points of connection and resemblance. Meinhold is quite successful in the attempt to prove a sharp contrast of views between the sections. The interchange of persons—the *third* person being mainly used in the first seven chapters, and the first person in the last five—may be partly due to the final editor; but in any case it may easily be paralleled, and is found in other writers, as in Isaiah (vii. 3, xx. 2) and the Book of Enoch (xii.).

But it may be said in general that the authenticity of the Book is now rarely defended by any competent critic, except at the cost of abandoning certain sections of it as interpolated additions; and as Mr. Bevan somewhat caustically remarks, "the defenders of Daniel have, during the last few years, been employed chiefly in cutting Daniel to pieces."†

3. The General Tone of the Book.

The general tone of the Book marks an era in the education and progress of the Jews. The lessons of the Exile uplifted them from a too narrow and absorbing particularism to a wider interest in the destinies of humanity. They were led to recognise that God "has made of one every nation of men for to dwell on all the face of the earth, having determined their appointed seasons, and the bounds of their habitation; that they should seek God, if haply they might feel after Him, and find Him, though He is not far from each one of us."‡ The standpoint of the Book of Daniel is larger and more cosmopolitan in this respect than that of earlier prophecy. Israel had begun to mingle more closely with other nations, and to be a sharer in their destinies. Politically the Hebrew race no longer formed a small though independent kingdom, but was reduced to the position of an entirely insignificant sub-province in a mighty empire. The Messiah is no longer the Son of David, but the Son of Man; no longer only the King of Israel, but of the world. Mankind—not only the seed of Jacob—fills the field of prophetic vision. Amid widening horizons of thought the Jews turned their eyes upon a great past, rich in events, and crowded with the figures of heroes, saints, and sages. At the same time

*Hengstenberg also points to verbal resemblances between ii. 44 and vii. 14; iv. 5 and vii. 1; ii. 31 and vii. 2; ii. 38 and vii. 17. etc. ("Genuineness of Daniel," E. Tr., pp. 186 ff.).

† "A Short Commentary," p. 8.

‡ Acts xvii. 26, 27.

the world seemed to be growing old, and its ever-deepening wickedness seemed to call for some final judgment. We begin to trace in the Hebrew writings the colossal conceptions, the monstrous imagery, the daring conjectures, the more complex religious ideas, of an exotic fancy.*

> "The giant forms of Empires on their way
> To ruin, dim and vast,"

begin to fling their weird and sombre shadows over the page of sacred history and prophetic anticipation.

4. The Style of the Book.

The style of the Book of Daniel is new, and has very marked characteristics, indicating its late position in the Canon. It is rhetorical rather than poetic. "Totum Danielis librum," says Lowth, "e poetarum censu excludo."† How widely does the style differ from the rapt passion, and glowing picturesqueness of Isaiah, from the elegiac tenderness of Jeremiah, from the lyrical sweetness of many of the Psalms! How very little does it correspond to the three great requirements of poetry, that it should be, as Milton so finely said, "simple, sensuous, passionate"! A certain artificiality of diction, a sounding oratorical stateliness, enhanced by dignified periphrases and leisurely repetitions, must strike the most casual reader; and this is sometimes carried so far as to make the movement of the narrative heavy and pompous.‡ This peculiarity is not found to the same extent in any other book of the Old Testament Canon, but it recurs in the Jewish writings of a later age. From the apocryphal books, for instance, the poetical element is with trifling exceptions, such as the Song of the Three Children, entirely absent, while the taste for rhetorical ornamentation, set speeches, and dignified elaborateness is found in many of them.

This evanescence of the poetic and impassioned element separates Daniel from the Prophets, and marks the place of the Book among the Hagiographa, where it was placed by the Jews themselves. In all the great Hebrew seers we find something of the ecstatic transport, the fire shut up within the bones and breaking forth from the volcanic heart, the burning lips touched by the hands of the seraphim with a living coal from off the altar. The word for prophet (*nabî, Vates*) implies an inspired singer rather than a soothsayer or seer (*roeh, chozeh*). It is applied to Deborah and Miriam§ because they poured forth from exultant hearts the pæan of victory. Hence arose the close connection between music and poetry.‖ Elisha required the presence of a minstrel to soothe the agitation of a heart thrown into tumult by the near presence of a revealing Power.¶ Just as the Greek word μάντις, from μαίνομαι, implies a sort of madness, and recalls the foaming lip and streaming hair of the spirit-dilated messenger, so the Hebrew verb *naba* meant, not only to proclaim God's oracles, but

* See Hitzig, p. xii.; Auberlen, p. 41.

† Reuss says too severely, "Die Schilderungen aller dieser Vorgänge machen keinen gewinnenden Eindruck. . . . Der Stil ist unbeholfen, die Figuren grotesk, die Farben grell." He admits, however, the suitableness of the Book for the Maccabean epoch, and the deep impression it made ("Heil. Schrift. A. T.," p. 571).

‡ See iii. 2, 3, 5, 7; viii. 1, 10, 19; xi. 15, 22, 31, etc.

§ Exod. xv. 20; Judg. iv. 4.

‖ 1 Sam. x. 5; 1 Chron. xxv. 1, 2, 3.

¶ 2 Kings iii. 15.

to be inspired by His possession as with a Divine frenzy.* "Madman" seemed a natural term to apply to the messenger of Elisha.† It is easy therefore to see why the Book of Daniel was not placed among the prophetic rolls. This *vera passio*, this ecstatic elevation of thought and feeling, are wholly wanting in this earliest attempt at a philosophy of history. We trace in it none of that "blasting with excess of light," none of that shuddering sense of being uplifted out of self, which marks the higher and earlier forms of prophetic inspiration. Daniel is addressed through the less exalted medium of visions, and in his visions there is less of "the faculty Divine." The instinct—if instinct it were and not knowledge of the real origin of the Book—which led the "Men of the Great Synagogue" to place this Book among the *Ketubhîm*, not among the prophets was wise and sure.‡

5. The Standpoint of the Author.

"In Daniel öffnet sich eine ganz neue Welt."—Eichhorn, "Einleit.," iv. 472.

The author of the Book of Daniel seems naturally to place himself on a level lower than that of the prophets who had gone before him. He does not count himself among the prophets; on the contrary, he puts them far higher than himself, and refers to them as though they belonged to the dim and distant past (ix. 2, 6). In his prayer of penitence he confesses, "Neither have we hearkened unto thy servants the prophets, which spake in Thy Name to our kings, our princes, and our fathers"; "Neither have we obeyed the voice of the Lord our God, to walk in His laws, which He set before us by His servants the prophets." Not once does he use the mighty formula "Thus saith Jehovah"—not once does he assume, in his prophecies, a tone of high personal authority. He shares the view of the Maccabean age that prophecy is dead.§

In Dan. ix. 2 we find yet another decisive indication of the late age of this writing. He tells us that he "understood by books" (more correctly, as in the A. V., "by *the* books"‖) "the number of the years whereof the word of the Lord came to Jeremiah the prophet." The writer here represents himself as an humble student of previous prophets, and this necessarily marks a position of less freshness and independence. "To the old prophets," says Bishop Westcott, "Daniel stands in some sense as a commentator." No doubt the possession of those living oracles was an immense blessing, a rich inheritance; but it involved a danger. Truths established by writings and traditions, safe-guarded by schools and institutions, are too apt to come to men only as a power from without, and less as "a hidden and inly burning flame."*

By "*the* books" can hardly be meant anything but some approach to a definite Canon. If so, the Book of Daniel in its present form can only have been written subsequently to the days of Ezra. "The account which assigns a collection of books to Nehemiah (2 Macc. ii. 13)," says Bishop Westcott, "is in itself a confirmation of the general truth of the gradual formation of the Canon during the Persian period. The various classes of books were completed in succession; and this view harmonises with what must have been the natural development of the Jewish faith after the Return. The persecution of Antiochus (B. C. 168) was for the Old Testament what the persecution of Diocletian was for the New—the final crisis which stamped the sacred writings with their peculiar character. The king sought out the Books of the Law (1 Macc. i. 56) and burnt them; and the possession of a 'Book of the Covenant' was a capital crime. According to the common tradition, the proscription of the Law led to the public use of the writings of the prophets."†

The whole *method* of Daniel differs even from that of the later and inferior prophets of the Exile—Haggai, Malachi, and the second Zechariah. The Book is rather an apocalypse than a prophecy: "the eye and not the ear is the organ to which the chief appeal is made." Though symbolism in the form of visions is not unknown to Ezekiel and Zechariah, yet those prophets are far from being apocalyptic in character. On the other hand, the grotesque and gigantic emblems of Daniel—these animal combinations, these interventions of dazzling angels who float in the air or over the water, these descriptions of historical events under the veil of material types seen in dreams—are a frequent phenomenon in such late apocryphal writings as the Second Book of Esdras, the Book of Enoch, and the pre-Christian Sibylline oracles, in which talking lions and eagles, etc., are frequent. Indeed, this style of symbolism originated among the Jews from their contact with the graven mysteries and colossal images of Babylonian worship. The Babylonian Exile formed an epoch in the intellectual development of Israel fully as important as the sojourn in Egypt. It was a stage in their moral and religious education. It was the psychological preparation requisite for the moulding of the last phase of revelation—that apocalyptic form which succeeds to theophany and prophecy, and embodies the final results of national religious inspiration. That the apocalyptic method of dealing with history in a religious and an imaginative manner naturally arises towards the close of any great cycle of special revelation is illustrated by the flood of apocalypses which overflowed the early literature of the Christian Church. But the Jews clearly saw that, as a rule, an apocalypse is inherently inferior to a prophecy, even when it is made the vehicle of genuine prediction. In estimating the grades of inspiration the Jews placed highest the inward illumination of the Spirit, the Reason, and the Understanding; next to this

* Jer. xxix. 26; 1 Sam. xviii. 10, xix. 21–24.

† 2 Kings ix. 11. See Expositor's Bible, "Second Book of Kings," p. 113.

‡ On this subject see Ewald, "Proph. d. A. Bundes," i. 6; Novalis, "Schriften," ii. 472; Herder, "Geist der Ebr. Poesie," ii. 61; Knobel, "Prophetismus," i. 103. Even the Latin poëts were called *prophetæ*, "bards" (Varro, "De Ling. Lat.," vi. 3). Epimenides is called "a prophet" in Tit. i. 12. See Plato, "Tim.," 72, A.; "Phædr.," 262, D.; Pind., "Fr.," 118; and comp. Eph. iii. 5, iv. 11.

§ Dan. ix. 6, 10. So conscious was the Maccabean age of the absence of prophets, that just as after the Captivity a question is postponed "till there should arise a priest with the Urim and Thummim," so Judas postponed the decision about the stones of the desecrated altar "until there should come a prophet to show what should be done with them" (1 Macc. iv. 45, 46, ix. 27, xiv. 41). Comp. Song of the Three Children, 15; Psalm lxxiv. 9; "Sota," f. 48, 2. See *infra*, Introd., chap. viii.

‖ Dan. ix. 2, *hassepharîm*, τὰ βίβλια.

* Ewald, "Proph. d. A. B.," p. 10. Judas Maccabæus is also said to have "restored" (ἐπισυνήγαγε) the lost (διαπεπτωκότα) sacred writings (2 Macc. ii. 14).

† Smith's "Dict. of the Bible," i. 501. The daily lesson from the Prophets was called the *Haphtarah* (Hamburger, "Real-Encycl.," ii. 334).

they placed dreams and visions; and lowest of all they placed the accidental auguries derived from the *Bath Qôl*. An apocalypse may be of priceless value, like the Revelation of St. John; it may, like the Book of Daniel, abound in the noblest and most thrilling lessons; but in intrinsic dignity and worth it is always placed by the instinct and conscience of mankind on a lower grade than such outpourings of Divine teachings as breathe and burn through the pages of a David and an Isaiah.

6. The Moral Element.

Lastly, among these salient phenomena of the Book of Daniel we are compelled to notice the absence of the predominantly moral element from its prophetic portion. The author does not write in the tone of a preacher of repentance, or of one whose immediate object is to ameliorate the moral and spiritual condition of his people. His aims were different.* The older prophets were the ministers of dispensations between the Law and the Gospel. They were, in the beautiful language of Herder,—

"Die Saitenspiel in Gottes mächtigen Händen."

Doctrine, worship, and consolation were their proper sphere. They were "*oratores Legis, advocati patriæ.*" In them prediction is wholly subordinate to moral warning and instruction. They denounce, they inspire: they smite to the dust with terrible invective; they uplift once more into glowing hope. The announcement of events yet future is the smallest part of the prophet's office, and rather its sign than its substance. The highest mission of an Amos or an Isaiah is not to be a prognosticator, but to be a religious teacher. He makes his appeals to the conscience, not to the imagination—to the spirit, not to the sense. He deals with eternal principles, and is almost wholly indifferent to chronological verifications. To awaken the death-like slumber of sin, to fan the dying embers of faithfulness, to smite down the selfish oppressions of wealth and power, to startle the sensual apathy of greed, were the ordinary and the noblest aims of the greater and the minor prophets. It was their task far rather to *forth-tell* than to *fore-tell;* and if they announce, in general outline and uncertain perspective, things which shall be hereafter, it is only in subordination to high ethical purposes, or profound spiritual lessons. So it is also in the Revelation of St. John. But in the "prophetic" part of Daniel it is difficult for the keenest imagination to discern any deep moral, or any special doctrinal significance, in all the details of the obscure wars and petty diplomacy of the kings of the North and South.

In point of fact the Book of Daniel, even as an apocalypse, suffers severely by comparison with that latest canonical Apocalypse of the Beloved Disciple which it largely influenced. It is strange that Luther, who spoke so slightingly of the Revelation of St. John, should have placed the Book of Daniel so high in his estimation. It is indeed a noble book, full of glorious lessons. Yet surely it has but little of the sublime and mysterious beauty, little of the heart-shaking pathos, little of the tender sweetness of consolatory power, which fill the closing book of the New Testament. Its imagery is far less exalted, its hope of immortality far less distinct and unquenchable. Yet the Book of Daniel, while it is one of the earliest, still remains one of the greatest specimens of this form of sacred literature. It inaugurated the new epoch of "apocalyptic" which in later days was usually pseudepigraphic, and sheltered itself under the names of Enoch, Noah, Moses, Ezra, and even the heathen sibyls. These apocalypses are of very unequal value. "Some," as Kuenen says, "stand comparatively high; others are far below mediocrity." But the genus to which they belong has its own peculiar defect. They are works of art: they are not spontaneous; they smell of the lamp. A fruitless and an unpractical peering into the future was encouraged by these writings, and became predominant in some Jewish circles. But the Book of Daniel is incomparably superior in every possible respect to Baruch, or the Book of Enoch, or the Second Book of Esdras; and if we place it for a moment by the side of such books as those contained in the "Codex Pseudepigraphus" of Fabricius, its high worth and Canonical authority are vindicated with extraordinary force. How lofty and enduring are the lessons to be learnt alike from its historic and predictive sections we shall have abundant opportunities of seeing in the following pages. So far from undervaluing its teaching, I have always been strongly drawn to this Book of Scripture. It has never made the least difference in my reverent acceptance of it that I have, for many years, been convinced that it cannot be regarded as literal history or ancient prediction. Reading it as one of the noblest specimens of the Jewish Haggada or moral Ethiopœia, I find it full of instruction in righteousness, and rich in examples of life. That Daniel was a real person, that he lived in the days of the Exile, and that his life was distinguished by the splendour of its faithfulness I hold to be entirely possible. When we regard the stories here related of him as moral legends, possibly based on a groundwork of real tradition, we read the Book with a full sense of its value, and feel the power of the lessons which it was designed to teach, without being perplexed by its apparent improbabilities, or worried by its immense historic and other difficulties.

The Book is in all respects unique, a writing *sui generis;* for the many limitations to which it led are but imitations. But, as the Jewish writer Dr. Jöel truly says, the unveiling of the secret as to the real lateness of its date and origin, so far from causing any loss in its beauty and interest, enhance both in a remarkable degree. It is thus seen to be the work of a brave and gifted anonymous author about B. C. 167, who brought his piety and his patriotism to bear on the troubled fortunes of his people at an epoch in which such piety and patriotism were of priceless value. We have in its later sections no voice of enigmatic prediction, foretelling the minutest complications of a distant secular future, but mainly the review of contemporary events by a wise and an earnest writer, whose faith and hope remained unquenchable in the deepest night of persecution and apostasy.* Many passages of the Book are dark, and will remain dark, owing partly perhaps to corruptions and uncertainties of the text, and partly to imitation of a style which had become archaic,

* On this subject see Kuenen, "The Prophets," iii. 95 ff.; Davison, "On Prophecy," pp. 34-67; Herder, "Hebr. Poesie," ii. 64; De Wette, "Christl. Sittenlehre," ii. 1.

* Joël, "Notizen," p. 7.

as well as to the peculiarities of the apocalyptic form. But the general idea of the Book has now been thoroughly elucidated, and the interpretation of it in the following pages is accepted by the great majority of earnest and faithful students of the Scriptures.

CHAPTER III.

PECULIARITIES OF THE HISTORIC SECTION.

No one can have studied the Book of Daniel without seeing that, alike in the character of its miracles and the minuteness of its supposed predictions, it makes a more stupendous and a less substantiated claim upon our credence than any other book of the Bible, and a claim wholly different in character. It has over and over again been asserted by the uncharitableness of a merely traditional orthodoxy that inability to accept the historic verity and genuineness of the Book arises from secret faithlessness, and antagonism to the admission of the supernatural. No competent scholar will think it needful to refute such calumnies. It suffices us to know before God that we are actuated simply by the love of truth, by the abhorrence of anything which in us would be a pusillanimous spirit of falsity. We have too deep a belief in the God of the Amen, the God of eternal and essential verity, to offer to Him "the unclean sacrifice of a lie." An error is not sublimated into a truth even when that lie has acquired a quasi-consecration, from its supposed desirability for purposes of orthodox controversy, or from its innocent acceptance by generations of Jewish and Christian Churchmen through long ages of uncritical ignorance. Scholars, if they be Christians at all, can have no possible *a priori* objection to belief in the supernatural. If they believe, for instance, in the Incarnation of our Lord and Saviour Jesus Christ, they believe in the most mysterious and unsurpassable of all miracles, and beside that miracle all minor questions of God's power or willingness to manifest His immediate intervention in the affairs of men sink at once into absolute insignificance.

But our belief in the Incarnation, and in the miracles of Christ, rests on evidence which, after repeated examination, is to us overwhelming. Apart from all questions of personal verification, or the Inward Witness of the Spirit, we can show that this evidence is supported, not only by existing records, but by myriads of external and independent testimonies. The very same Spirit which makes men believe where the demonstration is decisive, compels them to refuse belief to the literal verity of unique miracles and unique predictions which come before them without any convincing evidence. The narratives and visions of this Book present difficulties on every page. They were in all probability never intended for anything but what they are—Haggadoth, which, like the parables of Christ, convey their own lessons without depending on the necessity for accordance with historic fact.

Had it been any part of the Divine will that we should accept these stories as pure history, and these visions as predictions of events which were not to take place till centuries afterwards, we should have been provided with some aids to such belief. On the contrary, in whatever light we examine the Book of Daniel, the evidence *in its favour* is weak, dubious, hypothetical, and *a priori;* while the evidence *against* it acquires increased intensity with every fresh aspect in which it is examined. The Book which would make the most extraordinary demands upon our credulity, if it were meant for history, is the very Book of which the genuineness and authenticity are decisively discredited by every fresh discovery and by each new examination. There is scarcely one learned European scholar by whom they are maintained, except with such concessions to the Higher Criticism as practically involve the abandonment of all that is essential in the traditional theory.

And we have come to a time when it will not avail to take refuge in such transferences of the discussions in *alteram materiam,* and such purely vulgar appeals *ad invidiam,* as are involved in saying, "Then the Book must be a forgery," and "an imposture," and "a gross lie." To assert that "to give up the Book of Daniel is to betray the cause of Christianity" is a coarse and dangerous misuse of the weapons of controversy. Such talk may still have been excusable even in the days of Dr. Pusey (with whom it was habitual); it is no longer excusable now. Now it can only prove the uncharitableness of the apologist, and the impotence of a defeated cause. Yet even this abandonment of the sphere of honourable argument is only one degree more painful than the tortuous subterfuges and wild assertions to which such apologists as Hengstenberg, Keil, and their followers were long compelled to have recourse. Anything can be proved about anything if we call to our aid indefinite suppositions of errors of transcription, interpolations, transpositions, extraordinary silences, still more extraordinary methods of presenting events, and (in general) the unconsciously disingenuous resourcefulness of traditional harmonics. To maintain that the Book of Daniel, as it now stands, was written by Daniel in the days of the Exile is to cherish a belief which can only, at the utmost, be extremely uncertain, and which must be maintained in defiance of masses of opposing evidence. There can be little intrinsic value in a determination to believe historical and literary assumptions which can no longer be maintained except by preferring the flimsiest hypotheses to the most certain facts.

My own conviction has long been that in these Haggadoth, in which Jewish literature delighted in the pre-Christian era, and which continued to be written even till the Middle Ages, there was not the least pretence or desire to deceive at all. I believe them to have been put forth as moral legends—as avowed fiction nobly used for the purposes of religious teaching and encouragement. In ages of ignorance, in which no such thing as literary criticism existed, a popular Haggada might soon come to be regarded as historical, just as the Homeric lays were among the Greeks, or just as Defoe's story of the Plague of London was taken for literal history by many readers even in the seventeenth century.

Ingenious attempts have been made to show that the author of this Book evinces an intimate familiarity with the circumstances of the Babylonian religion, society, and history. In many cases this is the reverse of the fact. The instances adduced in favour of any knowledge, except of the most general description, are entirely delusive. It is frivolous to maintain, with Lenormant, that an exceptional acquaintance with Babylonian custom was required to describe Nebuchadrezzar as consulting diviners for the interpretation of a dream! To say nothing of the fact that a similar custom has prevailed in all nations and all ages from the days of Samuel to those of Lobengula, the writer had the prototype of Pharaoh before him, and has evidently been influenced by the story of Joseph.* Again, so far from showing surprising acquaintance with the organisation of the caste of Babylonian diviners, the writer has made a mistake in their very name, as well as in the statement that a faithful Jew, like Daniel, was made the chief of their college!† Nor, again, was there anything so unusual in the presence of women at feasts —also recognised in the Haggada of Esther —as to render this a sign of extraordinary information. Once more, is it not futile to adduce the allusion to punishment by burning alive as a proof of insight into Babylonian peculiarities? This punishment had already been mentioned by Jeremiah in the case of Nebuchadrezzar. "Then shall be taken up a curse by all the captivity of Judah which are in Babylon, saying, The Lord make thee like Zedekiah and like Ahab" (two false prophets), "whom the King of Babylon roasted in the fire." ‡ Moreover, it occurs in the Jewish traditions which described a miraculous escape of exactly the same character in the legend of Abraham. He, too, had been supernaturally rescued from the burning fiery furnace of Nimrod, to which he had been consigned because he refused to worship idols in Ur of the Chaldees.§

When the instances *mainly* relied upon prove to be so evidentially valueless, it would be waste of time to follow Professor Fuller through the less important and more imaginary proofs of accuracy which his industry has amassed. Meanwhile the feeblest reasoner will see that while a writer may easily be accurate in general facts, and even in details, respecting an age long previous to that in which he wrote, the existence of violent errors as to matters with which a contemporary must have been familiar at once refutes all pretence of historic authenticity in a book professing to have been written by an author in the days and country which he describes.

Now such mistakes there seem to be, and not a few of them, in the pages of the Book of Daniel. One or two of them can perhaps be explained away by processes which would amply suffice to show that "yes" means "no," or that "black" is a description of "white"; but each repetition of such processes leaves us more and more incredulous. If errors be treated as corruptions of the text, or as later interpolations, such arbitrary methods of treating the Book are practically an admission that, as it stands, it cannot be regarded as historical.

I. We are, for instance, met by what seems to be a remarkable error in the very first verse of the Book, which tells us that "In the third year of Jehoiakim, King of Judah, came Nebuchad*nezzar*"—as in later days he was incorrectly called—"King of Babylon, unto Jerusalem, and besieged it."

It is easy to trace whence the error sprang. Its source lies in a book which is the latest in the whole Canon, and in many details difficult to reconcile with the Book of Kings—a book of which the Hebrew resembles that of Daniel—the Book of Chronicles. In 2 Chron. xxxvi. 6 we are told that Nebuchad*nezzar* came up against Jehoiakim, and "bound him in fetters to carry him to Babylon"; and also—to which the author of Daniel directly refers—that he carried off some of the vessels of the House of God, to put them in the treasure-house of his god. In this passage it is *not* said that this occurred "*in the third year* of Jehoiakim," who reigned eleven years; but in 2 Kings xxiv. 1 we are told that "in his days Nebuchad*nezzar* came up, and Jehoiakim *became his servant three years*." The passage in Daniel looks like a confused reminiscence of the "three years" with "the third year of Jehoiakim." The elder and better authority (the Book of Kings) is silent about any deportation having taken place in the reign of Jehoiakim, and so is the contemporary Prophet Jeremiah. But in any case it seems impossible that it should have taken place so early as the *third year* of Jehoiakim, for at that time he was a simple vassal of the King of Egypt. If this deportation took place in the reign of Jehoiakim, it would certainly be singular that Jeremiah, in enumerating three others, in the seventh, eighteenth, and twenty-third year of Nebuchadrezzar,* should make no allusion to it. But it is hard to see how it could have taken place before Egypt had been defeated in the Battle of Carchemish, and that was not till B. C. 597, the *fourth* year of Jehoiakim.† Not only does Jeremiah make no mention of so remarkable a deportation as this, which as the earliest would have caused the deepest anguish, but, in the *fourth* year of Jehoiakim (Jer. xxxvi. 1), he writes a roll to threaten evils which are still future, and in the *fifth* year proclaims a fast in the hope that the imminent peril may even yet be averted (Jer. xxxvi. 6-10). It is only after the violent obstinacy of the king that the destructive advance of Nebuchadrezzar is finally prophesied (Jer. xxxvi. 29) as something which has not yet occurred.‡

II. Nor are the names in this first chapter free from difficulty. Daniel is called Belteshazzar, and the remark of the King of Babylon—"whose name was Belteshazzar, according to the name of my god"—certainly suggests that the first syllable is (as the Massorets assume) connected with the god Bel. But the name has nothing to do with Bel. No contemporary could have fallen into such an error;§ still less

* Gen. xli.
† See Lenormant, "La Divination," p. 219.
‡ Jer. xxix. 22. The tenth verse of *this very chapter* is referred to in Dan. ix. 2. The custom continued in the East centuries afterwards. "And if it was known to a Roman writer (Quintus Curtius, v. 1) in the days of Vespasian, why" (Mr. Bevan pertinently asks) "should it not have been known to a Palestinian writer who lived centuries earlier?" (A. A. Bevan, "Short Commentary," p. 22).
§ "Avodah-Zarah," f. 3, 1; "Sanhedrin," f. 93, 1; "Pesachim," f. 118, 1; "Eiruvin," f. 53, 1.

* Jer. lii. 28-30. These were in the reign of Jehoiachin.
† Jer. xlvi. 2: comp. Jer. xxv. The passage of Berossus, quoted in Jos., "Antt.," X. xi. 1, is not trustworthy, and does not remove the difficulty.
‡ The attempts of Keil and Pusey to get over the difficulty, if they were valid, would reduce Scripture to a hopeless riddle. The reader will see all the latest efforts in this direction in the "Speaker's Commentary" and the work of Fabre d'Envieu. Even such "orthodox" writers as Dorner, Delitzsch, and Gess, not to mention hosts of other great critics, have long seen the desperate impossibility of these arguments.
§ *Balatsu-utsur*, "protect his life." The root *balâtu*, "life," is common in Assyrian names. The mistake comes

a king who spoke Babylonian. Shadrach *may* be "Shudur-aku," "command of Aku," the moon-god; but Meshach is inexplicable; and Abed-nego is a strange corruption for the obvious and common Abed-nebo, "servant of Nebo." Such a corruption could hardly have arisen till Nebo was practically forgotten. And what is the meaning of "the *Melzar*" (Dan. i. 11)? The A. V. takes it to be a proper name; the R. V. renders it "the steward." But the title is unique and obscure.* Nor can anything be made of the name of Ashpenaz, the prince of the eunuchs, whom, in one manuscript, the LXX. call Abiesdri.†

III. Similar difficulties and uncertainties meet us at every step. Thus, in the second chapter (ii. 1), the dream of Nebuchadrezzar is fixed in the *second* year of his reign. This does not seem to be in accord with i. 3, 18, which says that Daniel and his three companions were kept under the care of the prince of the eunuchs for three years. Nothing, of course, is easier than to invent harmonistic hypotheses, such as that of Rashi, that "the second year of the reign of Nebuchadrezzar" has the wholly different meaning of "the second year after the destruction of the Temple"; or as that of Hengstenberg, followed by many modern apologists, that Nebuchadrezzar had previously been associated in the kingdom with Nabopolassar, and that this was the second year of his independent reign. Or, again, we may, with Ewald, read "the twelfth year." But by these methods we are not taking the Book as it stands, but are supposing it to be a network of textual corruptions and conjectural combinations.

IV. In ii. 2 the king summons four classes of hierophants to disclose his dream and its interpretation. They are the magicians ("Chartummîm"), the enchanters ("Ashshaphim"), the sorcerers ("Mechashsh'phîm"), and the Chaldeans ("Kasdîm").‡ The "Chartummîm" occur in Gen. xli. 8 (which seems to be in the writer's mind); and the "Mechashsh'phîm" occur in Exod. vii. 11, xxii. 18; but the mention of *Kasdîm*, "Chaldeans," is, so far as we know, an immense anachronism. In much later ages the name was used, as it was among the Roman writers, for wandering astrologers and quacks.§ But this degenerate sense of the word was, so far as we can judge, wholly unknown to the age of Daniel. It never once occurs in this sense on any of the monuments. Unknown to the Assyrian-Babylonian language, and only acquired long after the end of the Babylonian Empire, such a usage of the word is, as Schrader says, "an indication of the post-exilic composition of the Book."‖ In the days of Daniel "Chaldeans" had no meaning resembling that of "magicians" or "astrologers." In every other writer of the Old Testament, and in all contemporary records, "Kasdîm" simply means the Chaldean nation and *never* a learned caste.¶

from the wrong vocalisation adopted by the Massorets (Meinhold, "Beiträge," p. 27).

* Schrader dubiously connects it with *matstsara*, "guardian."

† Lenormant, p. 182, regards it as a corruption of Ashbenazar, "the goddess has pruned the seed" (??); but assumed corruptions of the text are an uncertain expedient.

‡ On these see Rob. Smith, *Cambr. Journ. of Philol.*, No. 27, p. 125.

§ Juv., "Sat.," x. 96: "Cum grege Chaldæo": Val. Max., iii. 1; Cic., "De Div.," i. 1, etc.

‖ "Keilinschr.," p. 429; Meinhold, p. 28.

¶ Isa. xxiii. 13; Jer. xxv. 12; Ezek. xii. 13; Hab. i. 6.

This single circumstance has decisive weight in proving the late age of the Book of Daniel.

V. Again, we find in ii. 14, "Arioch, the chief of the executioners." Schrader precariously derives the name from "Eri-aku," "servant of the moon-god"; but, however that may be, we already find the name as that of a king Ellasar in Gen. xiv. 1, and we find it again for a king of the Elymæans in Judith i. 6. In ver. 16 Daniel "went in and desired of the king" a little respite; but in ver. 25 Arioch tells the king, as though it were a sudden discovery of his own, "I have found a man of the captives of Judah, that will make known unto the king the interpretation." This was a surprising form of introduction, after we have been told that the king himself had, by personal examination, found that Daniel and his young companions were "ten times better than all the magicians and astrologers that were in all his realm." It seems, however, as if each of these chapters were intended to be recited as a separate Haggada.

VI. In ii. 46, after the interpretation of the dream, "the King Nebuchadnezzar fell upon his face, and worshipped Daniel, and commanded that they should offer an oblation and sweet odours unto him." This is another of the immense surprises of the Book. It is exactly the kind of incident in which the haughty theocratic sentiment of the Jews found delight, and we find a similar spirit in the many Talmudic inventions in which Roman emperors, or other potentates, are represented as paying extravagant adulation to Rabbinic sages. There is (as we shall see) a similar story narrated by Josephus of Alexander the Great prostrating himself before the high priest Jaddua, but it has long been relegated to the realm of fable as an outcome of Jewish self-esteem.* It is probably meant as a concrete illustration of the glowing promises of Isaiah, that "kings and queens shall bow down to thee with their faces towards the earth, and lick up the dust of thy feet";† and "the sons of them that despised thee shall bow themselves down at the soles of thy feet."‡

VII. We further ask in astonishment whether Daniel could have accepted without indignant protest the offering of "an oblation and sweet odours." To say that they were only offered to God in the person of Daniel is the idle pretence of all idolatry. They are expressly said to be offered "to Daniel." A Herod could accept blasphemous adulations;§ but a Paul and a Barnabas deprecate such devotions with intense disapproval.‖

VIII. In ii. 48 Nebuchadrezzar appoints Daniel, as a reward for his wisdom, to rule over the whole province of Babylon, and to be *Rab-signîn*, "chief ruler," and to be over all the wise men ("Khakamîm") of Babylon. Lenormant treats this statement as an interpolation, because he regards it as "*evidently* impossible." We know that in the Babylonian priesthood, and especially among the sacred caste, there was a passionate religious intolerance. It is inconceivable that they should have accepted as their religious superior a monotheist who was the avowed and uncompromising enemy to their whole system of idolatry. It is equally inconceivable that Daniel should have accepted the position of a hierophant in a polytheistic cult.

* Jos., "Antt.," XI. viii. 5.

† Isa. xlix. 23.

‡ Isa. lx. 14.

§ Acts xii. 22, 23.

‖ Acts xiv. 11, 12, xxviii. 6.

In the next three chapters there is no allusion to Daniel's tenure of these strange and exalted offices, either civil or religious.*

IX. The third chapter contains another story, told in a style of wonderful stateliness and splendour, and full of glorious lessons; but here again we encounter linguistic and other difficulties. Thus in iii. 2, though "all the rulers of the provinces" and officers of all ranks are summoned to the dedication of Nebuchadrezzar's colossus, there is not an allusion to Daniel throughout the chapter. Four of the names of the officers in iii. 2, 3, appear, to our surprise, to be Persian;† and, of the six musical instruments, three—the lute, psaltery, and bagpipe ‡—have obvious Greek names, two of which (as already stated) are of late origin, while another, the "sab'ka," resembles the Greek σαμβύκη, but may have come to the Greeks from the Aramæans.§ The incidents of the chapter are such as find no analogy throughout the Old or New Testament, but exactly resemble those of Jewish moralising fiction, of which they furnish the most perfect specimen. It is exactly the kind of concrete comment which a Jewish writer of piety and genius, for the encouragement of his afflicted people, might have based upon such a passage as Isa. xliii. 2, 3: "When thou walkest through the fire, thou shalt not be burned; neither shall the flame kindle upon thee. For I am the Lord thy God, the Holy One of Israel, thy Saviour." Nebuchadrezzar's decree, "That every people, nation, and language, which speak anything amiss against the God of Shadrach, Meshach, and Abed-nego, shall be cut in pieces, and their houses shall be made a dunghill," can only be paralleled out of the later Jewish literature.‖

X. In chap. iv. we have another monotheistic decree of the King of Babylon, announcing to "all people, nations, and languages" what "the high God hath wrought towards me." It gives us a vision which recalls Ezek. xxxi. 3-18, and may possibly have been suggested by that fine chapter.¶ The language varies between the third and the first person. In iv. 13 Nebuchadrezzar speaks of "a watcher and a holy one." This is the first appearance in Jewish literature of the word *'îr*, "watcher," which is so common in the Book of Enoch.** In ver. 26 the expression "after thou shalt have known that *the heavens* do rule" is one which has no analogue in the Old Testament, though exceedingly common in the superstitious periphrases of the later Jewish literature. As to the story of the strange lycanthropy with which Nebuchadrezzar was afflicted, though it receives nothing but the faintest shadow of support from any historic record, it may be based on some fact preserved by tradition. It is probably meant to reflect on the mad ways of Antiochus. The general phrase of Berossus, which tells us that Nebuchadrezzar "fell into a sickness and died,"* has been pressed into an historical verification of this narrative! But the phrase might have been equally well used in the most ordinary case,† which shows what fancies have been adduced to prove that we are here dealing with history. The fragment of Abydenus in his "Assyriaca," preserved by Eusebius,‡ shows that there was *some* story about Nebuchadrezzar having uttered remarkable words upon his palace-roof. The announcement of a coming irrevocable calamity to the kingdom from a Persian mule, "the son of a Median woman," and the wish that "the alien conqueror" might be driven "through the desert where wild beasts seek their food, and birds fly hither and thither," has, however, very little to do with the story of Nebuchadrezzar's madness. Abydenus says that, "when he had thus prophesied, he suddenly vanished"; and he adds nothing about any restoration to health or to his kingdom. All that can be said is that there was current among the Babylonian Jews some popular legend of which the writer of the Book of Daniel availed himself for the purpose of his edifying "Midrash."

XI. When we reach the fifth chapter we are faced by a new king, Belshazzar, who is somewhat emphatically called the son of Nebuchadrezzar.§

History knows of no such king.‖ The prince of whom it *does* know was never king, and was a son, not of Nebuchadrezzar, but of the usurper Nabunaid; and between Nebuchadrezzar and Nabunaid there were three other kings.¶

There *was* a Belshazzar—"Bel-sar-utsur," "Bel protect the prince"—and we possess a clay cylinder of his father Nabunaid, the last king of Babylon, praying the moon-god that "my son, the offspring of my heart, might honour his godhead, and not give himself to sin."** But if we follow Herodotus, this Belshazzar never came to the throne; and according to Berossus he was conquered in Borsippa. Xenophon, indeed, speaks of "an impious king" as being slain in Babylon; but this is only in an avowed romance which has not the smallest historic validity.†† Schrader conjectures that Nabunaid may have

* See Jer. xxxix. 3. And if he held this position, how could he be absent in chap. iii.?

† Namely, the words for "satraps," "governors," "counsellors," and "judges," as well as the courtiers in iii. 24. Bleek thinks that to enhance the stateliness of the occasion the writer introduced as many official names as he knew.

‡ *Supra*, p. 360.

§ Athen., "Deipnos.," iv. 175.

‖ The Persian titles in iii. 24 alone suffice to indicate that this could not be Nebuchadrezzar's actual decree. See further, Meinhold, pp. 30, 31. We are evidently dealing with a writer who introduces many Persian words, with no consciousness that they could not have been used by Babylonian kings.

¶ The writer of Daniel was evidently acquainted with the Book of Ezekiel. See Delitzsch in Herzog, *s. v.* "Daniel," and Driver, p. 476.

** See iv. 16, 25-30.

* Preserved by Jos.: comp. "Ap.," I. 20.

† The phrase is common enough: *e. g.*, in Jos., "Antt.," X. xi. 1 (comp. "c. Ap.," I. 19); and a similar phrase, ἐμπεσὼν εἰς ἀρρωστίαν, *is used of Antiochus Epiphanes* in 1 Macc. vi. 8.

‡ "Præp. Ev.," ix. 41. Schrader ("K. A. T.," ii. 432) thinks that Berossus and the Book of Daniel may both point to the same tradition; but the Chaldee tradition quoted by the late writer Abydenus errs likewise in only recognising *two* Babylonish kings instead of *four*, exclusive of Belshazzar. See, too, Schrader, "Jahrb. für Prot. Theol.," 1881, p. 618.

§ Dan. v. 11. The emphasis seems to show that "son" is really meant—not grandson. This is a little strange, for Jeremiah (xxvii. 7) had said that the nations should serve Nebuchadrezzar, "and his son, *and his son's son*"; and in no case was Belshazzar Nebuchadrezzar's *son's son*, for his father Nabunaid was an usurping son of a Rab-mag.

‖ Schrader, p. 434 ff.; and in Riehm, "Handwörterb.," ii. 163; Pinches, in Smith's "Bibl. Dict.," i. 388. 2d ed. The contraction into Belshazzar from *Bel-sar-utsur* seems to show a late date.

¶ That the author of Daniel should have fallen into these errors is the more remarkable because Evil-merodach is mentioned in 2 Kings xxv. 27; and Jeremiah in his round number of seventy years includes *three* generations (Jer. xxvii. 7). Herodotus and Abydenus made the same mistake. See Kamphausen, pp. 30, 31.

** Herod., i. 191. See Rawlinson, "Herod.," i. 434.

†† Xen., "Cyrop.," VII. v. 3.

gone to take the field against Cyrus (who conquered and pardoned him, and allowed him to end his days as governor of Karamania), and that Belshazzar may have been killed in Babylon. These are mere hypotheses; as are those of Josephus,* who identifies Belshazzar with Nabunaid (whom he calls Naboandelon); and of Babelon, who tries to make him the same as Maruduk-shar-utsur (as though Bel was the same as Maruduk), which is impossible, as this king reigned *before* Nabunaid. No contemporary writer could have fallen into the error either of calling Belshazzar "king"; or of insisting on his being "the son" of Nebuchadrezzar; † or of representing him as Nebuchadrezzar's successor. Nebuchadrezzar was succeeded by—

	circ. B. C.
Evil-merodach, . .	561 (Avil-marduk).‡
Nergal-sharezer, . .	559 (Nergal-sar-utsur).
Lakhabbashi-marudu (Laborosoarchod) .	555 (an infant).
Nabunaid, . .	554.

Nabunaid reigned till about B. C. 538, when Babylon was taken by Cyrus.

The conduct of Belshazzar in the great feast of this chapter is probably meant as an allusive contrast to the revels and impieties of Antiochus Epiphanes, especially in his infamous festival at the grove of Daphne.

XII. "That night," we are told, "Belshazzar, the Chaldean king, was slain." It has always been supposed that this was an incident of the capture of Babylon by assault, in accordance with the story of Herodotus, repeated by so many subsequent writers. But on this point the inscriptions of Cyrus have "revolutionised" our knowledge. "There was no siege and capture of Babylon; the capital of the Babylonian Empire opened its gates to the general of Cyrus. Gobryas and his soldiers entered the city without fighting, and the daily services in the great temple of Bel-merodach suffered no interruption. Three months later Cyrus himself arrived, and made his peaceful entry into the new capital of his empire. We gather from the contract-tablets that even the ordinary business of the place had not been affected by the war. The siege and capture of Babylon by Cyrus is really a reflection into the past of the actual sieges undergone by the city in the reigns of Darius, son of Hystaspes and Xerxes. It is clear, then, that the editor of the fifth chapter of the Book of Daniel could have been as little a contemporary of the events he professes to record as Herodotus. For both alike, the true history of the Babylonian Empire has been overclouded and foreshortened by the lapse of time. The three kings who reigned between Nebuchadrezzar and Nabunaid have been forgotten, and the last king of the Babylonian Empire has become the son of its founder." §

Snatching at the merest straws, those who try to vindicate the accuracy of the writer—although he makes Belshazzar a king, which he never was; and the son of Nebuchadrezzar, which is not the case; or his grandson, of which there is no tittle of evidence; and his successor, whereas four kings intervened;—think that they improve the case by urging that Daniel was made "the third ruler in the kingdom"—Nabunaid being the first, and Belshazzar being the second! Unhappily for their very precarious hypothesis, the translation "third ruler" appears to be entirely untenable. It means "one of a board of three."

XIII. In the sixth chapter we are again met by difficulty after difficulty.

Who, for instance, was Darius the Mede? We are told (v. 30, 31) that, on the night of his impious banquet, "Belshazzar the king of the Chaldeans" was slain, "and Darius the Median took the kingdom, being about threescore and two years old." We are also told that Daniel "prospered in the reign of Darius, and in the reign of Cyrus the Persian" (vi. 28). But this Darius is not even noticed elsewhere. Cyrus was the conqueror of Babylon, and between B. C. 538-536 there is no room or possibility for a Median ruler.

The inference which we should naturally draw from these statements in the Book of Daniel, and which all readers have drawn, was that Babylon had been conquered by the Medes, and that only after the death of a Median king did Cyrus the Persian succeed.

But historic monuments and records entirely overthrow this supposition. Cyrus was the king of Babylon from the day that his troops entered it without a blow He had conquered the Medes and suppressed their royalty. "The numerous contract-tables of the ordinary daily business transactions of Babylon, dated as they are month by month, and almost day by day from the reign of Nebuchadrezzar to that of Xerxes, prove that between Nabonidus and Cyrus *there was no intermediate ruler*." The contemporary scribes and merchants of Babylon knew nothing of any King Belshazzar, and they knew even less of any King Darius the Mede. No contemporary writer could possibly have fallen into such an error.*

And against this obvious conclusion of what possible avail is it for Hengstenberg to quote a late Greek lexicographer (Harpocration, A. D. 170?), who says that the coin "a daric" was named after a Darius earlier than the father of Xerxes?—or for others to identify this shadowy Darius the Mede with Astyages? †—or with Cyaxares II. in the romance of Xenophon? ‡—or to say that Darius the Mede is Gobryas (Ugbaru) of Gutium §—a Persian, and not a king at

* "Antt.," X. xi. 2. In "c. Ap.," I. 20, he calls him Nabonnedus.

† This is now supposed to mean "grandson by marriage," by inventing the hypothesis that Nabunaid married a daughter of Nebuchadrezzar. But this does not accord with Dan. v. 2, 11, 22; and so in Baruch i. 11, 12.

‡ 2 Kings xxv. 27.

§ Sayce, "The Higher Criticism and the Monuments," p. 527.

* I need not enter here upon the confusion of the Manda with the Medes, on which see Sayce, "Higher Criticism and Monuments," p. 519 ff.

† Winer, "Realwörterb.," *s. v.* "Darius."

‡ So Bertholdt, Von Lengerke, Auberlen. It is decidedly rejected by Schrader (Riehm, "Handwörterb.," i. 259). Even Cicero said, "Cyrus ille a Xenophonte non ad historiæ fidem scriptus est" ("Ad Quint. Fratr.," Ep. i. 3). Niebuhr called the "Cyropædia" "einen *elenden* und läppischen Roman" ("Alt. Gesch.," i. 116). He classes it with "Télémaque" or "Rasselas." Xenophon was probably the ultimate authority for the statement of Josephus ("Antt.," X. xi. 4), which has no weight. Herodotus and Ktesias know nothing of the existence of any Cyaxares II., nor does the Second Isaiah (xlv.), who evidently contemplates Cyrus as the conqueror and the first king of Babylon. Are we to set a professed romancer like Xenophon, and a late compiler like Josephus, against these authorities?

§ T. W. Pinches, in Smith's "Bibl. Dict.," i. 716, 2d ed. Into this theory are pressed the general expressions that Darius "received the kingdom" and was "made king," which have not the least bearing on it. They may simply mean that he became king by conquest, and not in the ordinary course—so Rosenmüller, Hitzig, Von Lengerke.

all—who under no circumstances could have been called "the king" by a contemporary (vi. 12, ix. 1), and whom, apparently for three months only, Cyrus made governor of Babylon? How could a contemporary governor have appointed "one hundred and twenty princes which should be over the whole kingdom," * when, even in the days of Darius Hystaspis, there were only twenty or twenty-three satrapies in the Persian Empire? † And how could a mere provincial viceroy be approached by "'all the presidents of the kingdom,' the governors, and the princes, the counsellors, and the captains," to pass a decree that any one who for thirty days offered any prayer to God or man, except to him, should be cast into the den of lions? The fact that such a decree could only be made by "a king" is emphasised in the narrative itself (vi. 12: comp. iii. 29). The supposed analogies offered by Professor Fuller and others in favour of a decree so absurdly impossible—except in the admitted license and for the high moral purpose of a Jewish Haggada—are to the last degree futile. In any ordinary criticism they would be set down as idle special pleading. Yet this is only one of a multitude of wildly improbable incidents, which, from misunderstanding of the writer's age and purpose, have been taken for sober history, though they receive from historical records and monuments no shadow of confirmation, and are in not a few instances directly opposed to all that we now know to be certain history. Even if it were conceivable that this hypothetic "Darius the Mede" was Gobryas, or Astyages, or Cyaxares, it is plain that the author of Daniel gives him a name and national designation which lead to mere confusion, and speaks of him in a way which would have been surely avoided by any contemporary.

"Darius the Mede," says Professor Sayce, "is in fact a *reflection* into the past of 'Darius the son of Hystaspes,' ‡ just as the siege and capture of Babylon by Cyrus are a reflection into the past of its siege and capture by the same prince. The name of Darius and the story of the slaughter of the Chaldean king go together. They are alike derived from the unwritten history which, in the East of to-day, is still made by the people, and which blends together in a single picture the manifold events and personages of the past. It is a history which has no perspective, though it is based on actual facts; the accurate combinations of the chronologer have no meaning for it, and the events of a century are crowded into a few years. This is the kind of history which the Jewish mind in the age of the Talmud loved to adapt to moral and religious purposes. This kind of history then becomes as it were a parable, and under the name of Haggada serves to illustrate that teaching of the law." *

The favourable view given of the character of the imaginary Darius the Mede, and his regard for Daniel, may have been a confusion with the Jewish reminiscences of Darius, son of Hystaspes, who permitted the rebuilding of the Temple under Zerubbabel.†

If we look for the *source* of the confusion we see it perhaps in the prophecy of Isaiah (xiii. 17, xiv. 6-22), that the *Medes* should be the destroyers of Babylon; or in that of Jeremiah—a prophet of whom the author had made a special study (Dan. ix. 2)—to the same effect (Jer. li. 11-28); together with the tradition that *a* Darius—namely, the son of Hystaspes—*had* once conquered Babylon.

XIV. But to make confusion worse confounded, if these chapters were meant for history, the problematic "Darius the Mede" is in Dan. ix. 1 called "the son of Ahasuerus."

Now Ahasuerus (Achashverosh) is the same as Xerxes, and is the *Persian* name Khshyarsha; and Xerxes was the *son,* not the father, of Darius Hystaspis, who was a *Persian,* not a Mede. Before Darius Hystaspis could have been transformed into the son of his own son Xerxes, the reigns, not only of Darius, but also of Xerxes, must have long been past.

XV. There is yet another historic sign that this Book did not originate till the Persian Empire had long ceased to exist. In xi. 2 the writer only knows of *four* kings of Persia.‡ These are evidently Cyrus, Cambyses, Darius Hystaspis, and Xerxes—whom he describes as the richest of them. This king is destroyed by the kingdom of Grecia—an obvious confusion of popular tradition between the defeat inflicted on the Persians by the Republican Greeks in the days of Xerxes (B. C. 480), and the overthrow of the Persian kingdom under Darius Codomannus by Alexander the Great (B. C. 333).

These, then, are some of the apparent historic impossibilities by which we are confronted when we regard this Book as professed history. The doubts suggested by such seeming errors are not in the least removed by the acervation of endless conjectures. They are greatly increased by the fact that, so far from standing alone, they are intensified by other difficulties which arise under every fresh aspect under which the Book is studied. Behrmann, the latest editor, sums up his studies with the remark that "there is an almost universal agreement that the Book, in its present form and as a whole, had its origin in the Maccabean age; while there is a widening impression that in its purpose it is not an exclusive product of that period." No amount of casuistical ingenuity can long prevail to overthrow the spreading conviction that the views of Hengstenberg, Hävernick, Keil, Pusey, and their followers, have been refuted by the light of advancing knowledge—which is a light kindled for us by God Himself.

etc.; or perhaps the words show some sense of uncertainty as to the exact course of events. The sequence of Persian kings in "Seder Olam," 28-30, and in Rashi on Dan. v. 1, ix. 1, is equally unhistorical.

* This is supported by the remark that this three-months viceroy "appointed governors in Babylon"!

† Herod., iii. 89; "Records of the Past," viii. 88.

‡ See, too, Meinhold ("Beiträge," p. 46), who concludes his survey with the words, "Sprachliche wie sachliche Gründe machen es *nicht nur wahrscheinlich sondern gewiss* dass an danielsche Autorschaft von Dan. ii.-vi., überhaupt an die Entstehung zur Zeit der jüdischen Verbannung nicht zu denken ist." He adds that almost all scholars believe the chapters to be no older than the age of the Maccabees, and that even Kahnis ("Dogmatik," i. 376) and Delitzsch (Herzog, *s. v.* "Dan.") give up their genuineness. He himself believes that these Aramaic chapters were *incorporated* by a later writer, who wrote the introduction.

* Sayce, *l. c.*, p. 529.

† Kamphausen, p. 45.

‡ Sayce, *l. c.* The author of the Book of Daniel seems only to have known of *three* kings of Persia after Cyrus (xi. 2). But five are mentioned in the Old Testament—Cyrus, Darius, Artaxerxes, Xerxes, and Darius III. (Codomannus, Neh. xii. 22). There were three Dariuses and three Artaxerxes, but he only knows one of each name (Kamphausen, p. 32). He might easily have overlooked the fact that the Darius of Neh. xii. 22 was a wholly different person from the Darius of Ezra vi. 1.

CHAPTER IV.

GENERAL STRUCTURE OF THE BOOK.

In endeavouring to see the idea and construction of a book there is always much room for the play of subjective considerations. Meinhold has especially studied this subject, but we cannot be certain that his views are more than imaginative. He thinks that chap. ii., in which we are strongly reminded of the story of Joseph and of Pharaoh's dreams, is intended to set forth God as Omniscient, and chap. iii. as Omnipotent. To these conceptions is added in chap. iv. the insistence upon God's All-holiness. The fifth and sixth chapters form one conception. Since the death of Belshazzar is assigned to the night of his banquet no edict could be ascribed to him resembling those attributed to Nebuchadrezzar. The effect of Daniel's character and of the Divine protection accorded to him on the mind of Darius is expressed in the strong edict of the latter in vi. 26, 27. This is meant to illustrate that the All-wise, Almighty, All-holy God is the Only Living God. The consistent and homogeneous object of the whole historic section is to set forth the God of the Hebrews as exalting Himself in the midst of heathendom, and extorting submission by mighty portents from heathen potentates. In this the Book offers a general analogy to the section of the history of the Israelites in Egypt narrated in Exod. i. 12. The culmination of recognition as to the power of God is seen in the decree of Darius (vi. 26, 27), as compared with that of Nebuchadrezzar in iv. 33. According to this view, the meaning and essence of each separate chapter are given in its closing section, and there is artistic advance to the great climax, marked alike by the resemblances of these four paragraphs (ii. 47, iii. 28, 29, iv. 37, vi. 26, 27), and by their differences. To this main purpose all the other elements of these splendid pictures—the faithfulness of Hebrew worshippers, the abasement of blaspheming despots, the mission of Israel to the nations—are subordinated. The chief aim is to set forth the helpless humiliation of all false gods before the might of the God of Israel. It might be expressed in the words, "Of a truth, Lord, the kings of Assyria have laid waste all the nations, and cast their gods into the fire; for they were no gods, but the work of men's hands, wood and stone."

A closer glance at these chapters will show some grounds for these conclusions.

Thus, in the second chapter, the magicians and sorcerers repudiate all possibility of revealing the king's dream and its interpretation, because they are but men, and the gods have not their dwelling with mortal flesh (ii. 11); but Daniel can tell the dream because he stands near to his God, who, though He is in heaven, yet is All-wise, and revealeth secrets.

In the third chapter the destruction of the strongest soldiers of Nebuchadrezzar by fire, and the absolute deliverance of the three Jews whom they have flung into the furnace, convince Nebuchadrezzar that no god can deliver as the Almighty does, and that therefore it is blasphemy deserving of death to utter a word against Him.

In chap. iv. the supremacy of Daniel's wisdom as derived from God, the fulfilment of the threatened judgment, and the deliverance of the mighty King of Babylon from his degrading madness when he lifts up his eyes to heaven, convince Nebuchadrezzar still more deeply that God is not only a *Great* God, but that no other being, man or god, can even be compared to Him. He is the Only and the Eternal God, who "doeth according to His will in the army of heaven," as well as "among the inhabitants of the earth," and "none can stay His hand." This is the highest point of conviction. Nebuchadrezzar confesses that God is not only "Primus inter pares," but the Irresistible God, and his own God. And after this, in the fifth chapter, Daniel can speak to Belshazzar of "the Lord of heaven" (v. 23); and as the king's Creator; and of the nothingness of gods of silver, and gold, and brass, and wood, and stone;—as though those truths had already been decisively proved. And this belief finds open expression in the decree of Darius (vi. 26, 27), which concludes the historic section.

It is another indication of this main purpose of these histories that the plural form of the Name of God—"Elohîm"—does not once occur in chaps. ii.-vi. It is used in i. 2, 9, 17; but not again till the ninth chapter, where it occurs twelve times; once in the tenth (x. 12); and twice of God in the eleventh chapter (xi. 32, 37). In the prophetic section (vii. 18, 22, 25, 27) we have "Most High" in the plural ("'elionîn"); * but with reference only to the One God (see vii. 25). But in all cases where the heathen are addressed this plural becomes the singular ("ehlleh," אֱלָה), as throughout the first six chapters. This avoidance of so common a word as the plural "Elohîm" for God, because the plural form might conceivably have been misunderstood by the heathen, shows the elaborate construction of the Book.† God is called *Eloah* Shamaîn, "God of heaven," in the second and third chapters; but in later chapters we have the common post-exilic phrase in the plural.‡

In the fourth and fifth chapters we have God's Holiness first brought before us, chiefly on its avenging side; and it is not till we have witnessed the proof of His Unity, Wisdom, Omnipotence, and Justice, which it is the mission of Israel to make manifest among the heathen, that all is summed up in the edict of Darius to all people, nations, and languages.

The omission of any express recognition of God's tender compassion is due to the structure of these chapters; for it would hardly be possible for heathen potentates to recognise that attribute in the immediate presence of His judgments. It is somewhat remarkable that the name "Jehovah" is avoided.§ As the Jews purposely pronounced it with wrong vowels, and the LXX. render it by κύριος, the Samaritan by שימה, and the Rabbis by "the Name," so we find in the Book of Daniel a similar avoidance of the awful Tetragrammaton.

* Literally, as in margin, "*most high things*" or *places*."

† In iv. 5, 6; and *elohîn* means "gods" in the mouth of a heathen ("spirit of the holy gods").

‡ *Elohîn* occurs repeatedly in chap. ix., and in x. 12, xi. 32, 37.

§ It only occurs in Dan. ix.

CHAPTER V.

THE THEOLOGY OF THE BOOK OF DANIEL.

As regards the religious views of the Book of Daniel some of them at any rate are in full accordance with the belief in the late origin of the Book to which we are led by so many indications.*

I. Thus in Dan. xii. 2 (for we may here so far anticipate the examination of the second section of the Book) we meet, for the first time in Scripture, with a distinct recognition of the resurrection of the individual dead.† This, as all know, is a doctrine of which we only find the faintest indication in the earlier books of the Canon. Although the doctrine is still but dimly formulated, it is clearer in this respect than Isa. xxv. 8, xxvi. 19.

II. Still more remarkable is the special prominence of angels. It is not God who goes forth to war (Judg. v. 13, 23), or takes personal part in the deliverance or punishment of nations (Isa. v. 26, vii. 18). Throned in isolated and unapproachable transcendence, He uses the agency of intermediate beings (Dan. iv. 14).‡

In full accordance with late developments of Jewish opinion angels are mentioned by special names, and appear as Princes and Protectors of special lands.§ In no other book in the Old Testament have we any names given to angels, or any distinction between their dignities, or any trace of their being in mutual rivalry as Princes or Patrons of different nationalities. These remarkable features of angelology only occur in the later epoch, and in the apocalyptic literature to which this Book belongs. Thus they are found in the LXX. translations of Deut. xxxii. 8 and Isa. xxx. 4, and in such post-Maccabean books as those of Enoch and Esdras.‖

III. Again, we have the fixed custom of three daily formal prayers, uttered towards the Kibleh of Jerusalem. This may, possibly, have begun during the Exile. It became a normal rule for later ages.¶ The Book, however, like that of Jonah, is, as a whole, remarkably free from any extravagant estimate of Levitical minutiæ.

IV. Once more, for the first time in Jewish story, we find extreme importance attached to the Levitical distinction of clean and unclean meats, which also comes into prominence in the age of the Maccabees, as it afterwards constituted a most prominent element in the ideal of Talmudic religionism.** Daniel and the Three Children are vegetarians, like the Pharisees after the destruction of the Second Temple, mentioned in "Baba Bathra," f. 60, 2.

* The description of God as "the Ancient of Days" with garments white as snow, and of His throne of flames on burning wheels, is found again in the Book of Enoch, written about B. C. 141 (Enoch xiv.).

† See Dan. xii 2. Comp. Jos., "B. J.," II. viii. 14; Enoch xxii. 13, lx. 1-5, etc.

‡ Comp. Smend, "Alttest. Relig. Gesch.," p. 530. For references to angels in Old Testament see Job. i. 6, xxxviii. 7; Jer. xxiii. 18; Psalm lxxxix. 7; Josh. v. 13-15; Zech. i. 12, iii. 1. See further Behrmann, "Dan.," p. xxiii.

§ Dan. iv. 14, ix. 21, x. 13, 20.

‖ See Enoch lxxi. 17, lxviii. 10, and the six archangels Uriel, Raphael, Reguel, Michael, Saragael, and Gabriel in Enoch xx.-xxxvi. See "Rosh Hashanah," f. 56, 1; "Bereshîth Rabba," c. 48; Hamburger, i. 305-312.

¶ "Berachôth," f. 31; Dan. vi. 11. Comp. Psalm lv. 18; 1 Kings viii. 38-48.

** 1 Macc. i. 62: Dan. i. 8; 2 Macc. v. 27, vi. 18-vii. 42.

V. We have already noticed the avoidance of the sacred name "Jehovah" even in passages addressed to Jews (Dan. ii. 18), though we find "Jehovah" in 2 Chron. xxxvi. 7. Jehovah only occurs in reference to Jer. xxv. 8-11, and in the prayer of the ninth chapter, where we also find "Adonai" and "Elohîm."

Periphrases for God, like "the Ancient of Days," become normal in Talmudic literature.

VI. Again, the doctrine of the Messiah, like these other doctrines, is, as Professor Driver says, "taught with greater distinctness and in a more developed form than elsewhere in the Old Testament, and with features approximating to, though not identical with, those met with in the earlier parts of the Book of Enoch (B. C. 100). In one or two instances these developments may have been partially moulded by foreign influences." * They undoubtedly mark a later phase of revelation than that which is set before us in other books of the Old Testament. And the conclusion indicated by these *special* features in the Book is confirmed by the *general* atmosphere which we breathe throughout it. The atmosphere and tone are not those of any other writings belonging to the Jews of the Exile; it is rather that of the Maccabean "Chasidîm." How far the Messianic "Bar Enosh" (vii. 13) is meant to be *a person* will be considered in the comment on that passage.

We shall see in later pages that the supreme value and importance of the Book of Daniel, rightly understood, consists in this—that "it is the first attempt at a Philosophy, or rather at a Theology of History." † Its main object was to teach the crushed and afflicted to place unshaken confidence in God.

CHAPTER VI.

PECULIARITIES OF THE APOCALYPTIC AND PROPHETIC SECTION OF THE BOOK.

If we have found much to lead us to serious doubts as to the authenticity and genuineness—*i. e.*, as to the literal historicity and the real author—of the Book of Daniel in its historic section, we shall find still more in the prophetic section. If the phenomena already passed in review are more than enough to indicate the impossibility that the Book could have been written by the historic Daniel, the phenomena now to be considered are such as have sufficed to convince the immense majority of learned critics that, in its present form, the Book did not appear before the days of Antiochus Epiphanes.‡ The probable date is B. C. 164. As in the Book of Enoch xc. 15, 16, it contains history written under the form of prophecy.

Leaving minuter examinations to later chapters of commentary, we will now take a brief survey of this unique apocalypse.

I. As regards the style and method the only distant approach to it in the rest of the Old

* Introd., p. 477. Comp. 2 Esdras xiii. 31-45, and *passim*; Enoch xl., xlv., xlvi., xlix., and *passim*; Hamburger, "Real-Encycl.," ii. 267 ff. With "the time of the end" and the numerical calculations comp. 2 Esdras vi. 6, 7.

† Roszmann, "Die Makkabäische Erhebung," p. 45. See Wellhausen, "Die Pharis. u. d. Sadd.," 77 ff.

‡ Among these critics are Delitzsch, Riehm, Ewald, Bunsen, Hilgenfeld, Cornill, Lücke, Strack, Schürer, Kuenen, Meinhold, Orelli, Joël, Reuss, König, Kamphausen, Cheyne, Driver, Briggs, Bevan, Behrmann, etc.

Testament is in a few visions of Ezekiel and Zechariah, which differ greatly from the clear, and so to speak classic, style of the older prophets. But in Daniel we find visions far more enigmatical, and far less full of passion and poetry. Indeed, as regards style and intellectual force, the splendid historic scenes of chaps. i.-vi. far surpass the visions of vii.-xii., some of which have been described as "composite logographs," in which the ideas are forcibly juxtaposed without care for any coherence in the symbols—as, for instance, when *a horn* speaks and has eyes.*

Chap. vii. contains a vision of four different wild beasts rising from the sea: a lion, with eagle-wings, which afterwards becomes semi-human; a bear, leaning on one side, and having three ribs in its mouth; a four-winged, four-headed panther; and a still more terrible creature, with iron teeth, brazen claws, and ten horns, among which rises a little horn, which destroyed three of the others—it has man's eyes and a mouth speaking proud things.

There follows an epiphany of the Ancient of Days, who destroys the little horn, but prolongs for a time the existence of the other wild beasts. Then comes One in human semblance, who is brought before the Ancient of Days, and is clothed by Him with universal and eternal power.

We shall see reasons for the view that the four beasts—in accordance with the interpretation of the vision given to Daniel himself—represent the Babylonian, the Median, the Persian, and the Greek empires, issuing in the separate kingdoms of Alexander's successors; and that the little horn is Antiochus Epiphanes, whose overthrow is to be followed immediately by the Messianic Kingdom.†

The vision of the eighth chapter mainly pursues the history of the fourth of these kingdoms. Daniel sees a ram standing eastward of the river-basin of the Ulai, having two horns, of which one is higher than the other. It butts westward, northward, and southward, and seemed irresistible, until a he-goat from the West, with one horn between its eyes, confronted it, and stamped it to pieces. After this its one horn broke into four towards the four winds of heaven, and one of them shot forth a puny horn, which grew great towards the South and East, and acted tyrannously against the Holy People, and spoke blasphemously against God. Daniel hears the holy ones declaring that its powers shall only last two thousand three hundred evening-mornings. An angel bids Gabriel to explain the vision to Daniel; and Gabriel tells the seer that the ram represents the Medo-Persian and the he-goat the Greek Kingdom. Its great horn is Alexander; the four horns are the kingdoms of his successors, the Diadochi; the little horn is a king bold of vision and versed in enigmas, whom all agree to be Antiochus Epiphanes.

In the ninth chapter we are told that Daniel has been meditating on the prophecy of Jeremiah that Jerusalem should be rebuilt after seventy years, and as the seventy years seem to be drawing to a close he humbles himself with prayer and fasting. But Gabriel comes flying to him at the time of the evening sacrifice, and explains to him that the seventy years is to mean seventy *weeks* of years—*i. e.*, four hundred and ninety years, divided into three periods of $7 + 62 + 1$. At the end of seven (*i. e.*, forty-nine) years an anointed prince will order the restoration of Jerusalem. The city will continue, though in humiliation, for sixty-two (*i. e.*, four hundred and thirty-four) years, when "an anointed" will be cut off, and a prince will destroy it. During half a week (*i. e.*, for three and a half years) he will cause the sacrifice and oblation to cease; and he will make a covenant with many for one week, at the end of which he will be cut off.

Here, again, we shall have reason to see that the whole prophecy culminates in, and is mainly concerned with, Antiochus Epiphanes. In fact, it furnishes us with a sketch of his fortunes, which, in connection with the eleventh chapter, tells us more about him than we learn from any extant history.

In the tenth chapter Daniel, after a fast of twenty-one days, sees a vision of Gabriel, who explains to him why his coming has been delayed, soothes his fears, touches his lips, and prepares him for the vision of chapter eleven. That chapter is mainly occupied with a singularly minute and circumstantial history of the murders, intrigues, wars, and intermarriages of the Lagidæ and Seleucidæ. So detailed is it that in some cases the history has to be reconstructed out of it. This sketch is followed by the doings and final overthrow of Antiochus Epiphanes.

The twelfth chapter is the picture of a resurrection, and of words of consolation and exhortation addressed to Daniel.

Such in briefest outline are the contents of these chapters, and their peculiarities are very marked. Until the reader has studied the more detailed explanation of the chapters separately, and especially of the eleventh, he will be unable to estimate the enormous force of the arguments adduced to prove the impossibility of such "prophecies" having emanated from Babylon and Susa about B. C. 536. Long before the astonishing enlargement of our critical knowledge which has been the work of the last generation —nearly fifty years ago—the mere perusal of the Book as it stands produced on the manly and honest judgment of Dr. Arnold a strong impression of uncertainty. He said that the latter chapters of Daniel would, if genuine, be a clear exception to the canons of interpretation which he laid down in his "Sermons on Prophecy," since "there can be no reasonable spiritual meaning made out of the kings of the North and South." "But," he adds, "I have long thought that the greater part of the Book of Daniel is most certainly a very late work of the time of the Maccabees; and the pretended prophecies about the kings of Grecia and Persia, and of the North and South, are mere history, like the poetical prophecies in Virgil and elsewhere. In fact, you can trace distinctly the date when it was written, because the events up to that date are given with historical minuteness, totally unlike the character of real prophecy; and beyond that date all is imaginary." *

The Book is the earliest specimen of its kind known to us. It inaugurated a new and impor-

* Renan, "History of Israel," iv. 354. He adds, "L'essence du genre c'est le pseudonyme, ou si l'on veut l'apocryphisme" (p. 356).

† Lagarde, "Gott. Gel. Anzieg.," 1891, pp. 497-520, stands almost, if not quite, alone in arguing that Dan. vii. was not written till A. D. 69, and that the "little horn" is meant for Vespasian. The relation of the fourth empire of Dan. vii. to the iron part of the image in Dan. ii. refutes this view: both can only refer to the Greek Empire. Josephus ("Antt.," X. xi. 7) does not refer to Dan. vii.; but neither does he to ix.-xii., for reasons already mentioned. See Cornill, "Einleit," p. 262.

* Stanley, "Life of Arnold," p. 505.

tant branch of Jewish literature, which influenced many subsequent writers. An apocalypse, so far as its literary form is concerned, "claims throughout to be a supernatural revelation given to mankind by the mouth of those men in whose names the various writings appear." An apocalypse—such, for instance, as the Books of Enoch, the Assumption of Moses, Baruch, 1, 2 Esdras, and the Sibylline Oracles—is characterised by its enigmatic form, which shrouds its meaning in parables and symbols. It indicates persons without naming them, and shadows forth historic events under animal forms, or as operations of Nature. Even the explanations which follow, as in this Book, are still mysterious and indirect.

II. In the next place an apocalypse is literary, not oral. Schürer, who classes Daniel among the oldest and most original of "pseudepigraphic prophecies," etc., rightly says that "the old prophets in their teachings and exhortations addressed themselves directly to the people first and foremost through their oral utterances; and then, but only as subordinate to these, by written discourses as well. But now, when men felt themselves at any time compelled by their religious enthusiasm to influence their contemporaries, instead of directly addressing them in person like the prophets of old, they did so by a writing purporting to be the work of some one or other of the great names of the past, in the hope that in this way the effect would be all the surer and all the more powerful." * The Daniel of this Book represents himself, not as a prophet, but as a humble student of the prophets. He no longer claims, as Isaiah did, to speak in the Name of God Himself with a "Thus saith Jehovah."

III. Thirdly, it is impossible not to notice that Daniel differs from all other prophecies by its all-but-total indifference to the circumstances and surroundings in the midst of which the prediction is supposed to have originated. The Daniel of Babylon and Susa is represented as the writer; yet his whole interest is concentrated, not in the events which immediately interest the Jews of Babylon in the days of Cyrus, or of Jerusalem under Zerubbabel, but deals with a number of predictions which revolve almost exclusively about the reign of a very inferior king four centuries afterwards. And with this king the predictions abruptly stop short, and are followed by the very general promise of an immediate Messianic age.

We may notice further the constant use of round and cyclic numbers, such as three and its compounds (i. 5, iii. 1, vi. 7, 10, vii. 5, 8); four (ii., vii. 6, and viii. 8, xi. 12); seven and its compounds (iii. 19, iv. 16, 23, ix. 24, etc.). The apocalyptic symbols of Bears, Lions, Eagles, Horns, Wings, etc., abound in the contemporary and later Books of Enoch, Baruch, 4 Esdras, the Assumption of Moses, and the Sibyllines, as well as in the early Christian apocalypses, like that of Peter. The authors of the Sibyllines (B. C. 140) were acquainted with Daniel; the Book of Enoch breathes exactly the same spirit with this Book, in the transcendentalism which avoids the name Jehovah (vii. 13; Enoch xlvi. 1, xlvii. 3), in the number of angels (vii. 10; Enoch xl. 1, lx. 2), their names, the title of "watchers" given to them, and their guardianship of men (Enoch xx. 5). The Judgment and the Books (vii. 9, 10, xii. 1) occur again in Enoch xlvii. 3, lxxxi. 1, as in the Book of Jubilees, and the Testament of the Twelve Patriarchs.*

* Schürer. "Hist. of the Jew. People," iii. 24 (E. Tr.).

* On the close resemblance between Daniel and other apocryphal books see Behrmann, "Dan.," pp. 37-39; Dillmann, "Das Buch Henoch." For its relation to the Book of Baruch see Schrader, "Keilinschriften," 435 f. Philo does not allude to Daniel.

CHAPTER VII.

INTERNAL EVIDENCE.

I. Other prophets start from the ground of the *present*, and to exigencies of the present their prophecies were primarily directed. It is true that their lofty moral teaching, their rapt poetry, their impassioned feeling, had its inestimable value for all ages. But these elements scarcely exist in the Book of Daniel. Almost the whole of its prophecies bear on one short particular period *nearly four hundred years after* the supposed epoch of their delivery. What, then, is the phenomenon they present? Whereas other prophets, by studying the problems of the present in the light flung upon them by the past, are enabled, by combining the present with the past, to gain, with the aid of God's Holy Spirit, a vivid glimpse of the immediate future, for the instruction of the living generation, the reputed author of Daniel passes over the *immediate* future with a few words, and spends the main part of his revelations on a triad of years separated by centuries from contemporary history. Occupied as this description is with the wars and negotiations of empires which were yet unborn, it can have had little practical significance for Daniel's fellow-exiles. Nor could these "predictions" have been to prove the possibility of supernatural foreknowledge,† since, even after their supposed fulfilment, the interpretation of them is open to the greatest difficulties and the gravest doubts. If to a Babylonian exile was vouchsafed a gift of prevision so minute and so marvellous as enabled him to describe the intermarriages of Ptolemies and Seleucidæ four centuries later, surely the gift must have been granted for some decisive end. But these predictions are precisely the ones which seem to have the smallest significance. We must say, with Semler, that no such benefit seems likely to result from this predetermination of comparatively unimportant minutiæ as God must surely intend when He makes use of means of a very extraordinary character. It might perhaps be said that the Book was written, four hundred years before the crisis occurred, to console the Jews under their brief period of persecution by the Seleucidæ. It would be indeed extraordinary that so curious, distant, and roundabout a method should have been adopted for an end which, in accordance with the entire economy of God's dealings with men in revelation, could have been so much more easily and so much more effectually accomplished in simpler ways. Further, unless we accept an isolated allusion to Daniel in the imaginary speech of the dying Mattathias, there is no trace whatever that the Book had the smallest influence in inspiring the Jews in that terrible epoch. And the reference of Mattathias, if it was ever made at all, may be to old tradition, and does

† Any apparently requisite modification of these words will be considered hereafter.

not allude to the prophecies about Antiochus and his fate.

But, as Hengstenberg, the chief supporter of the authenticity of the Book of Daniel, well observes,* "Prophecy can never entirely separate itself from the ground of the present, to influence which is always its more immediate object, and to which therefore it must constantly construct a bridge.† On this also rests all certainty of exposition as to the future. And that the means should be provided for such a certainty is a necessary consequence of the Divine nature of prophecy. A truly Divine prophecy cannot possibly swim in the air; nor can the Church be left to mere guesses in the exposition of Scripture which has been given to her as a light amid the darkness."

II. And as it does not start from the ground of the present, so too the Book of Daniel reverses the method of prophecy with reference to the future.

For the genuine predictions of Scripture *advance* by slow and gradual degrees from the uncertain and the general to the definite and the special. Prophecy marches with history, and takes a step forward at each new period.‡ So far as we know there is not a single instance in which any prophet alludes to, much less dwells upon, any kingdom which had not then risen above the political horizon.§

In Daniel the case is reversed: the only kingdom which was looming into sight is dismissed with a few words, and the kingdom most dwelt upon is the most distant and quite the most insignificant of all, of the very existence of which neither Daniel nor his contemporaries had even remotely heard.‖

III. Then again, although the prophets, with their Divinely illuminated souls, reached far beyond intellectual sagacity and political foresight, yet their hints about the future never distantly approach to detailed history like that of Daniel. They do indeed so far lift the veil of the Unseen as to shadow forth the outline of the near future, but they do this only on general terms and on general principles.¶ Their object, as I have repeatedly observed, was mainly moral, and it was also confessedly conditional, even when no hint is given of the implied condition.** Nothing is more certain than the wisdom and beneficence of that Divine provision which has hidden the future from men's eyes, and even taught us to regard all prying into its minute events as vulgar and sinful.†† Stargazing and monthly prognostication were rather the characteristics of false religion and unhallowed divinations than of faithful and holy souls. Nitzsch ‡‡ most justly lays it down as an esential condition of prophecy that it "should not disturb man's relation to history." Anything like detailed description of the future would intolerably perplex and confuse our sense of human free-will. It would drive us to the inevitable conclusion that men are but puppets moved irresponsibly by the hand of inevitable fate. Not one such prophecy, unless this be one, occurs anywhere in the Bible. We do not think that (apart from Messianic prophecies) a single instance can be given in which any prophet distinctly and minutely predicts a future series of events of which the fulfilment was not *near* at hand. In the few cases when some event, already imminent, is predicted apparently with some detail, it is not certain whether some touches—names, for instance—may not have been added by editors living subsequently to the occurrence of the event.* That there has been at all times a gift of prescience, whereby the Spirit of God, "entering into holy souls, has made them sons of God and prophets," is indisputable. It is in virtue of this high foreknowledge † that the voice of the Hebrew Sibyl has

"Rolled sounding onwards through a thousand years
Her deep prophetic bodiments."

Even Demosthenes, by virtue of a statesman's thoughtful experience, can describe it as his office and duty "to see events in their beginnings, to discern their purport and tendencies from the first, and to forewarn his countrymen accordingly." Yet the power of Demosthenes was as nothing compared with that of an Isaiah or a Nahum; and we may safely say that the writings alike of the Greek orator and the Hebrew prophets would have been comparatively valueless had they merely contained anticipations of future history, instead of dealing with truths whose value is equal for all ages—truths and principles which give clearness to the past, security to the present, and guidance to the future. Had it been the function of prophecy to remove the veil of obs urity which God in His wisdom has hung over the destinies of men and kingdoms, it would never have attained, as it has done, to the love and reverence of mankind.

IV. Another unique and abnormal feature is found in the close and accurate *chronological calculations* in which the Book of Daniel abounds. We shall see later on that the dates of the Maccabean reconsecration of the Temple and the ruin of Antiochus Epiphanes are indicated *almost to the day.* The numbers of prophecy are in all other cases symbolical and general. They are intentional compounds of seven—the sum of three and four, which are the numbers that mystically shadow forth God and the world—a number which even Cicero calls "*rerum omnium fere modus*"; and of ten, the number of the world. ‡ If we except the prophecy of the seventy years' captivity—which was a round number, and is in no respect parallel to the periods of Daniel—there is no other instance in the Bible of a *chronological* prophecy. We say no other instance, because one of the commentators who, in writing upon Daniel, objects to the remark of Nitzsch that the numbers of prophecy are mystical, yet observes on the one thousand two hundred and sixty days of Rev. xii. that the number one thousand two hundred and sixty, or three and a half

* "On Revelations," vol. i. p. 408 (E. Tr.).

† "Dient bei ihnen die Zukunft der Gegenwart, und ist selbst fortgesetzte *Gegenwart*" (Behrmann, "Dan.," p. xi).

‡ See M. de Pressensé, "Hist. des Trois Prem. Siècles," p. 283.

§ See some admirable remarks on this subject in Éwald, "Die Proph. d. Alt. Bund.," i. 23, 24; Winer, "Realwörterb.," *s. v.* "Propheten" Stähelin, "Einleit," § 197.

‖ Comp. Enoch i. 2.

¶ Ewald, "Die Proph.," i. 27; Michel Nicolas, "Études sur la Bible," pp. 336 ff.

** Comp. Mic. iii. 12; Jer. xxvi. 1-19; Ezek. i. 21. Comp. xxix. 18, 19.

†† Deut. xviii. 10.

‡‡ "System der christlichen Lehre," p. 66.

* *E. g.*, in the case of Josiah (1 Kings xiii. 2).

† "De Corona," 73: ἰδεῖν τὰ πράγματα ἀρχόμενα καὶ προαισθέσθαι καὶ προειπεῖν τοῖς ἄλλοις.

‡ The symbolism of numbers is carefully and learnedly worked out in Bähr's "Symbolik": *cf.* Auberlen, p. 133. The *several* fulfilments of the prophesied seventy years' captivity illustrate this.

years, "has *no* historical signification whatever, and is only to be viewed in its relation to the number seven—viz., as symbolising the apparent victory of the world over the Church." *

V. Alike, then, in style, in matter, and in what has been called by V. Orelli its "exoteric" manner,—alike in its definiteness and its indefiniteness—in the point from which it starts and the period at which it terminates—in its minute details and its chronological indications—in the absence of the moral and the impassioned element, and in the sense of fatalism which it must have introduced into history had it been a genuine prophecy,—the Book of Daniel differs from all the other books which compose that prophetic canon. From that canon it was rightly and deliberately excluded by the Jews. Its worth and dignity can only be rationally vindicated or rightly understood by supposing it to have been the work of an unknown moralist and patriot of the Maccabean age.

And if anything further were wanting to complete the cogency of the internal evidence which forces this conclusion upon us, it is amply found in a study of those books, confessedly apocryphal, which, although far inferior to the Book before us, are yet of value, and which we believe to have emanated from the same era.

They resemble this book in their language, both Hebrew and Aramaic, as well as in certain recurring expressions and forms to be found in the Books of Maccabees and the Second Book of Esdras;—in their style—rhetorical rather than poetical, stately rather than ecstatic, diffuse rather than pointed, and wholly inferior to the prophets in depth and power;—in the use of an apocalyptic method, and the strange combination of dreams and symbols;—in the insertion, by way of embellishment, of speeches and formal documents which can at the best be only semi-historical;—finally, in the whole tone of thought, especially in the quite peculiar doctrine of archangels, of angels guarding kingdoms, and of opposing evil spirits. In short, the Book of Daniel may be illustrated by the Apocryphal books in every single particular. In the adoption of an illustrious name—which is the most marked characteristic of this period—it resembles the *additions* to the Book of Daniel, the Books of Esdras, the Letters of Baruch and Jeremiah, and the Wisdom of Solomon. In the imaginary and quasi-legendary treatment of history it finds a parallel in Wisdom xvi.-xix., and parts of the Second Book of Maccabees and the Second Book of Esdras. As an allusive narrative bearing on contemporaneous events under the guise of describing the past, it is closely parallel to the Book of Judith,† while the character of Daniel bears the same relation to that of Joseph as the representation of Judith does to that of Jael. As an ethical development of a few scattered historical data, tending to the mavellous and supernatural, but rising to the dignity of a very noble and important religious fiction, it is analogous, though incomparably superior, to Bel and the Dragon, and to the stories of Tobit and Susanna.‡

The conclusion is obvious; and it is equally obvious that, when we suppose the name of Daniel to have been assumed, and the assumption to have been supported by an antique colouring, we do not for a moment charge the unknown author—who may very well have been Onias IV.—with any dishonesty. Indeed, it appears to us that there are many traces in the Book—χωνâντα συνετοῖσιν—which exonerate the writer from any suspicion of *intentional* deception. They may have been meant to remove any tendency to error in understanding the artistic guise which was adopted for the better and more forcible inculcation of the lessons to be conveyed. That the stories of Daniel offered peculiar opportunities for this treatment is shown by the apocryphal additions to the Book; and that the practice was well understood even before the closing of the Canon is sufficiently shown by the Book of Ecclesiastes. The writer of that strange and fascinating book, with its alternating moods of cynicism and resignation, merely adopted the name of Solomon, and adopted it with no dishonourable purpose; for he could not have dreamed that utterances which in page after page betray to criticism their late origin would really be identified with the words of the son of David a thousand years before Christ. This may now be regarded as an indisputable, and is indeed a no longer disputed, result of all literary and philological inquiry.

It is to Porphyry, a Neoplatonist of the third century (born at Tyre, A. D. 233; died in Rome, A. D. 303), that we owe our ability to write a continuous historical commentary on the symbols of Daniel. That writer devoted the twelfth book of his Λόγοι κατὰ Χριστιανῶν to a proof that Daniel was not written till *after* the epoch which it so minutely described.* In order to do this he collected with great learning and industry a history of the obscure Antiochian epoch from authors most of whom have perished. Of these authors Jerome—the most valuable part of whose commentary is derived from Porphyry—gives a formidable list, mentioning among others Callinicus, Diodorus, Polybius, Posidonius, Claudius, Theo, and Andronicus. It is a strange fact that the exposition of a canonical book should have been mainly rendered possible by an avowed opponent of Christianity. It was the object of Porphyry to prove that the apocalyptic portion of the Book was not a prophecy at all.† It used to be a constant taunt against those who adopt his critical conclusions that their weapons are borrowed from the armoury of an infidel. The objection hardly seems worth answering. "*Fas est et ab hoste doceri.*" If the enemies of our religion have sometimes helped us the better to understand our sacred books, or to judge more correctly respecting them, we should be grateful that their assaults have been overruled to our instruction. The reproach is wholly beside the question. We may apply to it the manly words of Grotius: "*Neque me pudeat consentire Porphyrio, quando is*

* Hengstenberg, "On Revelations," p. 609.

† All these particulars may be found, without any allusion to the Book of Daniel, in the admirable article on the Apocrypha by Dean Plumptre in Dr. Smith's "Dict. of the Bible."

‡ Ewald, "Gesch. Isr.," iv. 541.

* "Et non tam Danielem *ventura dixisse* quam illum *narrasse præterita*" (Jer.).

† "Ad intelligendas autem extremas Danielis partes multiplex Græcorum historia necessaria est" (Jer., "Procem. Explan. in Dan. Proph.," *ad f.*). Among these Greek historians he mentions *eight* whom Porphyry had consulted, and adds, "Et si quando cogimur litterarum sæcularium recordari . . . non nostræ est voluntatis, sed ut dicam, *gravissimæ necessitatis.*" We know Porphyry's arguments mainly through the commentary of Jerome, who, indeed, derived from Porphyry the historic data without which the eleventh chapter, among others, would have been wholly unintelligible.

in veram sententiam incidit." Moreover, St. Jerome himself could not have written his commentary, as he himself admits, without availing himself of the aid of the erudition of the heathen philosopher, whom no less a person than St. Augustine called "*doctissimus philosophorum*," though unhappily he was "*acerrimus christianorum inimicus.*"

CHAPTER VIII.

EVIDENCE IN FAVOUR OF THE GENUINENESS UNCERTAIN AND INADEQUATE.

We have seen that there are many circumstances which force upon us the gravest doubts as to the authenticity of the Book of Daniel. We now proceed to examine the evidence urged in its favour, and deemed adequate to refute the conclusion that in its present form it did not see the light before the time of Antiochus IV.

Taking Hengstenberg as the most learned reasoner in favour of the genuineness of Daniel, we will pass in review all the positive arguments which he has adduced.* They occupy no less than one hundred and ten pages (pp. 182-291) of the English translation of his work on the genuineness of Daniel. Most of them are tortuous specimens of special pleading inadequate in themselves, or refuted by increased knowledge derived from the monuments and from further inquiry. To these arguments neither Dr. Pusey nor any subsequent writer has made any material addition. Some of them have been already answered, and many of them are so unsatisfactory that they may be dismissed at once.

I. Such, for instance, is *the testimony of the author himself*. In one of those slovenly treatises which only serve to throw dust in the eyes of the ignorant we find it stated that, "although the name of Daniel is not prefixed to his Book, the passages in which he speaks in the first person *sufficiently prove* that he was the author"! Such assertions deserve no answer. If the mere assumption of a name be a *sufficient proof* of the authorship of the book, we are rich indeed in Jewish authors—and, not to speak of others, our list includes works by Adam, Enoch, Eldad, Medad, and Elijah. "Pseudonymity," says Behrmann, "was a very common characteristic of the literature of that day, and the conception of literary property was alien to that epoch, and especially to the circle of writings of this class."

II. The character of the language, as we have seen already, proves nothing. Hebrew and Aramaic long continued in common use side by side, at least among the learned,† and the divergence of the Aramaic in Daniel from that of the Targums leads to no definite result, considering the late and uncertain age of those writings.

III. How any argument can be founded on the exact knowledge of history displayed by local colouring we cannot understand. Were the knowledge displayed ever so exact it would only prove that the author was a learned man, which is obvious already. But so far from any remarkable accuracy being shown by the author, it is, on the contrary, all but impossible to reconcile many of his statements with acknowledged facts. The elaborate and tortuous explanations, the frequent *subauditur*, the numerous assumptions required to force the text into accordance with the certain historic data of the Babylonian and Persian empires, tell far more against the Book than for it. The methods of accounting for these inaccuracies are mostly self-confuting, for they leave the subject in hopeless confusion, and each orthodox commentator shows how untenable are the views of others.

IV. Passing over other arguments of Keil, Hengstenberg, etc., which have been either refuted already, or which are too weak to deserve repetition, we proceed to examine one or two of a more serious character. Great stress, for instance, is laid on the reception of the Book into the Canon. We acknowledge the canonicity of the Book, its high value when rightly apprehended, and its rightful acceptance as a sacred book; but this in nowise proves its authenticity. The history of the Old Testament Canon is involved in the deepest obscurity. The belief that it was finally completed by Ezra and the Great Synagogue rests on no foundation; indeed, it is irreconcilable with later historic notices and other facts conected with the Books of Ezra, Nehemiah, Esther, and the two Books of Chronicles. The Christian Fathers in this, as in some other cases, implicitly believed what came to them from the most questionable sources, and was mixed up with mere Jewish fables. One of the oldest Talmudic books, the "Pirke Aboth," is entirely silent on the collection of the Old Testament, though in a vague way it connects the Great Synagogue with the preservation of the Law. The earliest mention of the legend about Ezra is the Second Book of Esdras (xiv. 29-48). This book does not possess the slightest claim to authority, as it was not completed till a century after the Christian era; and it mingles up with this very narrative a number of particulars thoroughly fabulous and characteristic of a period when the Jewish writers were always ready to subordinate history to imaginative fables. The account of the magic cup, the forty days' and forty nights' dictation, the ninety books of which seventy were secret and intended only for the learned, form part of the very passage from which we are asked to believe that Ezra established our existing Canon, though the genuine Book of Ezra is wholly silent about his having performed any such inestimable service. It adds nothing to the credit of this fable that it is echoed by Irenæus, Clemens Alexandrinus, and Tertullian.* Nor are there any external considerations which render it probable. The Talmudic tradition in the "Baba Bathra,"† which says (among other remarks in a passage of which "the notorious errors prove the unreliability of its testimony") that the "men of the Great Synagogue *wrote* the Books of Ezekiel, the Twelve Minor Prophets, *Daniel*, and Ezra." ‡ It is evident that, so far as this evidence is worth anything, it rather goes *against* the authenticity of Daniel than for it. The "Pirke Aboth" makes Simon the Just (about B. C. 290) a member of this Great Synagogue, of which the very existence is dubious.§

* Hävernick is another able and sincere supporter; but Droysen truly says ("Gesch. d. Hellenismus," ii. 211), "Die Hävernickschen Auffassung kann kein vernunftiger Mensch bestimmen."

† See Grimm, "Comment., zum I. Buch der Makk., Einleit.," xvii.; Mövers in *Bonner Zeitschr.*, Heft 13, pp. 31 ff.; Stähelin, "Einleit.," p. 356.

* Iren., "Adv. Hæres.," iv. 25; Clem., "Strom." i. 21, § 146; Tert., "De Cult. Fæm.," i. 3; Jerome, "Adv. Helv.," 7; Ps. August., "De Mirab.," ii. 32, etc.

† "Baba Bathra," f. 13 *b*. 14 *b*.

‡ See Oehler, *s. v.* "Kanon" (Herzog, "Encycl.").

§ Rau "De Synag. Magna," ii. 66.

Again, the author of the forged letter at the beginning of the Second Book of Maccabees—"the work" says Hengstenberg, "of an arrant impostor" *—attributes the connection of certain books first to Nehemiah, and then, when they had been lost, to Judas Maccabæus (2 Macc. ii. 13, 14). The canonicity of the Old Testament books does not rest on such evidence as this,† and it is hardly worth while to pursue it further. That the Book of Daniel was regarded as authentic by Josephus is clear; but this by no means decides its date or authorship. It is one of the very few books of which Philo makes no mention whatever.

V. Nor can the supposed traces of the early existence of the Book be considered adequate to prove its genuineness. With the most important of these, the story of Josephus ("Antt.," XI. viii. 5) that the high priest Jaddua showed to Alexander the Great the prophecies of Daniel respecting himself, we shall deal later. The alleged traces of the Book in Ecclesiasticus are very uncertain, or rather wholly questionable; and the allusion to Daniel in Macc. ii. 60 decides nothing, because there is nothing to prove that the speech of the dying Mattathias is authentic, and because we know nothing certain as to the date of the Greek translator of that book or of the Book of Daniel. The absence of all allusion to the *prophecies* of Daniel is, on the other hand, a far more cogent point against the authenticity. Whatever be the date of the Books of Maccabees, it is inconceivable that they should offer no vestige of proof that Judas and his brothers received any hope or comfort from such explicit predictions as Dan. xi., had the Book been in the hands of those pious and noble chiefs.

The First Book of Maccabees cannot be certainly dated more than a century before Christ, nor have we reason to believe that the Septuagint version of the Book is much older.‡

VI. The badness of the Alexandrian version, and the apocryphal additions to it, seem to be rather an argument for the late age and less established authority of the Book than for its genuineness.§ Nor can we attach much weight to the assertion (though it is endorsed by the high authority of Bishop Westcott) that "it is far more difficult to explain its composition in the Maccabean period than to meet the peculiarities which it exhibits with the exigencies of the Return." So far is this from being the case that, as we have seen already, it resembles in almost every particular the acknowledged productions of the age in which we believe it to have been written. Many of the statements made on this subject by those who defend the authenticity cannot be maintained. Thus Hengstenberg ‖ remarks that (1) "at this time the Messianic hopes are dead," and (2) "that no great literary work appeared between the Restoration from the Captivity and the time of Christ." Now the facts are *precisely the reverse in each instance.* For (i) the little book called the Psalms of Solomon,* which belongs to this period, contains *the strongest and clearest Messianic hopes,* and the Book of Enoch most closely resembles Daniel in its Messianic predictions. Thus it speaks of the pre-existence of the Messiah (xlviii. 6, lxii. 7), of His sitting on a throne of glory (lv. 4, lxi. 8), and receiving the power of rule.

(ii) Still less can we attach any force to Hengstenberg's argument that, in the Maccabean age, the gift of prophecy was believed to have departed for ever. Indeed, that is an argument in favour of the pseudonymity of the Book. For in the age at which—for purposes of literary form—it is represented as having appeared the spirit of prophecy was far from being dead. Ezekiel was still living, or had died but recently. Zechariah, Haggai, and long afterwards Malachi, were still to continue the succession of the mighty prophets of their race. Now, if prediction be an element in the prophet's work, no prophet, nor all the prophets together, ever distantly approached any such power of minutely foretelling the events of a distant future—even the half-meaningless and all-but-trivial events of four centuries later, in kingdoms which had not yet thrown their distant shadows on the horizon—as that which Daniel must have possessed, if he were indeed the author of this Book.† Yet, as we have seen, he never thinks of claiming the functions of the prophets, or speaking in the prophet's commanding voice, as the foreteller of the message of God. On the contrary, he adopts the comparatively feebler and more entangled methods of the literary composers in an age when men saw not their tokens and there was no prophet more.‡

We must postpone a closer examination of the questions as to the "four kingdoms" intended by the writer, and of his curious and enigmatic chronological calculations; but we must reject at once the monstrous assertion—excusable in the days of Sir Isaac Newton, but which has now become unwise and even portentous—that "to reject Daniel's prophecies would be to undermine the Christian religion, *which is all but founded on his prophecies respecting Christ*"! Happily the Christian religion is not built on such foundations of sand. Had it been so, it would long since have been swept away by the beating rain and the rushing floods. Here, again, the arguments urged by those who believe in the authenticity of Daniel recoil with tenfold force upon themselves. Sir Isaac Newton's observations on the prophecies of Daniel only show how little transcendent genius in one domain of inquiry can save a great thinker from absolute mistakes in another. In writing upon prophecy the great astronomer was writing on the assumption of baseless premisses which he had drawn from stereotyped tradition; and he was also writing at an epoch when the elements for the final solution of the problem had not as yet been discovered or elaborated. It is as certain that, had he been living now, he would have accepted the conclusion of all the ablest and most candid in-

* "On Daniel," p. 195.

† "Even after the Captivity," says Bishop Westcott, "the history of the Canon, like all Jewish history up to the date of the Maccabees, is wrapped in great obscurity. Faint traditions alone remain to interpret results which are found realised when the darkness is first cleared away" (*s. v.* "Canon," Smith's "Dict. of Bible").

‡ See König, "Einleit.," § 80, 2.

§ "In propheta Daniele Septuaginta interpretes multum ab Hebraica veritate discordant" (Jerome, ed. Vallarsi, v. 646). In the LXX. are first found the three apocryphal additions. For this reason the version of Theodotion was substituted for the LXX., which latter was only re-discovered in 1772 in a manuscript in the library of Cardinal Chigi.

‖ "On the Authenticity of Daniel," pp. 159, 290 (E. Tr.).

* Psalms of Sol., xvii. 36, xviii. 8, etc. See Fabric., "Cod. Pseudep.," i. 917-972; Ewald, "Gesch. d. Volkes Isr.," iv. 244.

† Even Auberlen says ("Dan.," p. 3, E. Tr.), "If prophecy is anywhere a history of the future, it is here."

‡ See Vitringa, "De defectu Prophetiæ post Malachiæ tempora Obss. Sacr.," ii. 336.

quirers, as it is certain that Bacon, had he now been living, would have accepted the Copernican theory. It is *absurdly* false to say that "the Christian religion is all but founded on Daniel's prophecies respecting Christ." If it were not absurdly false, we might well ask, How it came that neither Christ nor His Apostles ever once alluded to the existence of any such argument, or ever pointed to the Book of Daniel and the prophecy of the seventy weeks as containing the least germ of evidence in favour of Christ's mission or the Gospel teaching? No such argument is remotely alluded to till long afterwards by some of the Fathers.

But so far from finding any *agreement* in the opinions of the Christian Fathers and commentators on a subject which, in Newton's view, was so momentous, we only find ourselves weltering in a chaos of uncertainties and contradictions. Thus Eusebius records the attempt of some early Christian commentators to treat the *last* of the seventy weeks as representing, not, like all the rest, seven years, but seventy years, in order to bring down the prophecy to the days of Trajan! Neither Jewish nor Christian exegetes have ever been able to come to the least agreement between themselves or with one another as to the beginning or end—the *terminus a quo* or the *terminus ad quem*—with reference to which the seventy weeks are to be reckoned. The Christians naturally made great efforts to make the seventy weeks end with the Crucifixion. But Julius Africanus * (†A. D. 232), beginning with the twentieth year of Artaxerxes (Neh. ii. 1-9, B. C. 444), gets only four hundred and seventy-five to the Crucifixion, and to escape the difficulty makes the years *lunar* years.†

Hippolytus ‡ separates the last week from all the rest, and relegates it to the days of Antichrist and the end of the world. Eusebius himself refers "the anointed one" to the line of Jewish high priests, separates the last week from the others, ends it with the fourth year after the Crucifixion, and refers the ceasing of the sacrifice (Deut. ix. 27) to the rejection of Jewish sacrifices by God after the death of Christ. Apollinaris makes the seventy weeks begin with the birth of Christ, and argues that Elijah and Antichrist were to appear A. D. 490! None of these views found general acceptance.§ Not one of them was sanctioned by Church authority. Every one, as Jerome says, argued in this direction or that *pro captu ingenii sui*. The climax of arbitrariness is reached by Keil—the last prominent defender of the so-called "orthodoxy" of criticism—when he makes the weeks not such commonplace things as "earthly chronological weeks," but Divine, symbolic, and therefore unknown and unascertainable periods. And are we to be told that it is on such fantastic, self-contradictory, and mutually refuting calculations that "the Christian religion is all but founded"? Thank God, the assertion is entirely wild.

* "Demonstr. Evang.," viii.

† Of the Jews, the LXX. translators seem to make the seventy weeks end with Antiochus Epiphanes; but in Jerome's day they made the first year of "Darius the Mede" the *terminus a quo*, and brought down the *terminus ad quem* to Hadrian's description of the Temple. Saadia the Gaon and Rashi reckon the seventy weeks from Nebuchadrezzar to Titus, and make Cyrus the anointed one of ix. 25. Abn Ezra, on the other, takes Nehemiah for "the anointed one." What can be based on such varying and undemonstrable guesses? See Behrmann, "Dan.," p. xliii.

‡ Hippolytus, "Fragm. in Dan." (Migne, "Patr. Græc.," x.).

§ See Bevan, pp. 141-145.

CHAPTER IX.

EXTERNAL EVIDENCE AND RECEPTION INTO THE CANON.

THE reception of the Book of Daniel anywhere into the Canon might be regarded as an argument in favour of its authenticity, if the case of the Books of Jonah and Ecclesiastes did not sufficiently prove that canonicity, while it does constitute a proof of the value and sacred significance of a book, has no weight as to its traditional authorship. But in point of fact the position assigned by the Jews to the Book of Daniel—not among the Prophets, where, had the Book been genuine, it would have had a supreme right to stand, but only with the Book of Esther, among the latest of the Hagiographa *—is a strong argument for its late date. The division of the Old Testament into Law, Prophets, and Hagiographa first occurs in the Prologue to Ecclesiasticus (about B. C. 131)—"the Law, the Prophecies, and the rest of the books." † In spite of its peculiarities, its prophetic claims among those who accepted it as genuine were so strong that the LXX. and the later translations unhesitatingly reckon the author among the four greater prophets. If the Daniel of the Captivity had written this Book, he would have had a far greater claim to this position among the prophets than Haggai, Malachi, or the later Zechariah. Yet the Jews deliberately placed the Book among the *Kethubîm*, to the writers of which they indeed ascribe the Holy Spirit (*Ruach Hakkodesh*), but whom they did not credit with the higher degree of prophetic inspiration. Josephus expresses the Jewish conviction that, since the days of Artaxerxes onwards, the writings which had appeared had not been deemed worthy of the same reverence as those which had preceded them, because there had occurred no unquestionable succession of prophets.‡ The Jews who thus decided the true nature of the Book of Daniel must surely have been guided by strong traditional, critical, historical, or other grounds for denying (as they did) to the author the gift of prophecy. Theodoret denounces this as "shameless impudence" (ἀναισχυντίαν) on their part; § but may it not rather have been fuller knowledge or simple honesty? At any rate, on any other grounds it would have been strange indeed of the Talmudists to decide that the most minutely predictive of the prophets—if indeed this *were* a prophecy—wrote *without* the gift of prophecy.‖ It can only have been the late and suspected appearance of the Book, and its marked phenomena, which led to its relegation to the lowest place in the Jewish Canon. Already in 1 Macc. iv. 46 we find that the stones

* Jacob Perez of Valentia accounted for this by the hatred of the Jews for Christianity! (Diestel, "Gesch. d. A. T.," p. 211).

† Comp. Luke xxiv. 44; Acts xxviii. 23; Philo, "De Vit. Cont.," 3. See Oehler in Herzog, *s. v.* "Kanon."

‡ "Jos. c. Ap.," I. 8.

§ "Opp," ed. Migne, ii. 1260: Εἰς τοσαύτην ἀναισχυντίαν ἤλασαν ὡς καὶ τοῦ χόρου τῶν προφήτων τοῦτον ἀποσχοινίζειν. He may well add, on his view of the date, εἰ γὰρ ταῦτα τῆς προφητείας ἀλλότρια, τίνα προφητείας τὰ ἴδια;

‖ "Megilla," 3, 1. Josephus, indeed, regards apocalyptic visions as the highest form of prophecy ("Antt.," X. xi. 7); but the Rabbis Kimchi, Maimonides, Joseph Albo, etc., are strongly against him. See Behrmann, p. xxxix.

of the demolished pagan altar are kept "until there should arise a prophet to show what should be done with them"; and in 1 Macc. xiv. 41 we again meet the phrase "until there should arise a faithful prophet." Before this epoch there is no trace of the existence of the Book of Daniel, and not only so, but the prophecies of the post-exilic prophets as to the future contemplate a wholly different horizon and a wholly different order of events. Had Daniel existed before the Maccabean epoch, it is impossible that the rank of the Book should have been deliberately ignored. The Jewish Rabbis of the age in which it appeared saw, quite correctly, that it had points of affinity with other pseudepigraphic apocalypses which arose in the same epoch. The Hebrew scholar Dr. Joel has pointed out how, amid its immeasurable superiority to such a poem as the enigmatic "Cassandra" of the Alexandrian poet Lycophron,* it resembles that book in its *indirectness* of nomenclature. Lycophron is one of the pleiad of poets in the days of Ptolemy Philadelphus; but his writings, like the Book before us, have probably received interpolations from later hands. He never calls a god or a hero by his name, but always describes him by a periphrasis, just as here we have "the King of the North" and "the King of the South," though the name "Egypt" slips in (Dan. xi. 8). Thus Hercules is "a three-nights' lion" (τριέσπερος λέων), and Alexander the Great is "a wolf." A son is always "an off-shoot" (φίτυμα), or is designed by some other metaphor. When Lycophron wants to allude to Rome, the Greek Ῥωμή is used in its sense of "strength." The name Ptolemaios becomes by anagram ἀπὸ μέλιτος, "from honey"; and the name Arsinoë becomes ἴον Ἥρας, "the violet of Hera." We may find some resemblances to these procedures when we are considering the eleventh chapter of Daniel.

It is a serious abuse of argument to pretend, as is done by Hengstenberg, by Dr. Pusey, and by many of their feebler followers, that "there are few books whose Divine authority is so fully established by the testimony of the New Testament, and in particular by our Lord Himself, as the Book of Daniel."† It is to the last degree dangerous, irreverent, and unwise to stake the Divine authority of our Lord on the maintenance of those ecclesiastical traditions of which so many have been scattered to the winds for ever. Our Lord, on one occasion, in the discourse on the Mount of Olives, warned His disciples that, "when they should see the abomination of desolation, spoken of by Daniel the prophet, standing in the holy place, they should flee from Jerusalem into the mountain district." ‡ There is nothing to prove that He Himself uttered either the words "let him that readeth understand," or even "spoken of by Daniel the prophet." Both of those may belong to the explanatory narrative of the Evangelist, and the latter does not occur in St. Mark. Further, in St. Luke (xxi. 20) there is *no* specific allusion to Daniel at all; but instead of it we find, "When ye see Jerusalem being encircled by armies, then know that its desolation is near." We cannot be certain that the specific reference to Daniel may not be due to the Evangelist. But without so much as raising these questions, it is fully admitted that, whether exactly in its present form or not, the Book of Daniel formed part of the Canon in the days of Christ. If He directly refers to it as a book known to His hearers, His reference lies as wholly outside all questions of genuineness and authenticity as does St. Jude's quotation from the Book of Enoch, or St. Paul's (possible) allusions to the Assumption of Elijah,* or Christ's own passing reference to the Book of Jonah. Those who attempt to drag in these allusions as decisive critical dicta transfer them to a sphere wholly different from that of the moral application for which they were intended. They not only open vast and indistinct questions as to the self-imposed limitations of our Lord's human knowledge as part of His own voluntary "emptying Himself of His glory," but they also do a deadly disservice to the most essential cause of Christianity.† The only thing which is acceptable to the God of truth is truth; and since He has given us our reason and our conscience as lights which light every man who is born into the world, we must walk by these lights in all questions which belong to these domains. History, literature and criticism, and the interpretation of human language do belong to the domain of pure reason; and we must not be bribed by the misapplication of hypothetical exegesis to give them up for the support of traditional views which advancing knowledge no longer suffers us to maintain. It may be true or not that our Lord adopted the title "Son of Man" (*Bar Enosh*) from the Book of Daniel; but even if He did, which is at least disputable, that would only show, what we all already admit, that in His time the Book was an acknowledged part of the Canon. On the other hand, if our Lord and His Apostles regarded the Book of Daniel as containing the most explicit prophecies of Himself and of His kingdom, why did they never appeal or even allude to it to prove that He was the promised Messiah?

Again, Hengstenberg and his school try to prove that the Book of Daniel existed before the Maccabean age, because Josephus says that the high priest Jaddua showed to Alexander the Great, in the year B. C. 332, the prophecy of himself as the Grecian he-goat in the Book of Daniel; and that the leniency which Alexander showed towards the Jews was due to the favourable impression thus produced.‡

The story, which is a beautiful and an interesting one, runs as folllows:—

On his way from Tyre, after capturing Gaza, Alexander decided to advance to Jerusalem. The news threw Jaddua the high priest into an agony of alarm. He feared that the king was displeased with the Jews, and would inflict severe vengeance upon them. He ordered a general supplication with sacrifices, and was encouraged by God in a dream to decorate the city, throw open the gates, and go forth in procession at the head of priests and people to meet the dreaded conqueror. The procession, so unlike that of any other nation, went forth as soon as they heard that Alexander was approaching the city. They met the king on the summit of Scopas, the watch-tower—the height of Mizpah, from which the first glimpse of the city is obtained. It is the famous Blanca

* It has been described as "ein Versteck für Belesenheit, und ein grammatischer Monstrum."

† Hengstenberg, p. 209.

‡ Matt. xxiv. 15; Mark xiii. 14.

* 1 Cor. ii. 9; Eph. v. 11.

† Hengstenberg's reference to 1 Peter i. 10–12, 1 Thess. ii. 3, 1 Cor. vi. 2, Heb. xi. 12, deserve no further notice

‡ Jos., "Antt.," XI. viii. 5.

Guarda of the Crusaders, on the summit of which Richard I. turned away, and did not deem himself worthy to glance at the city which he was too weak to rescue from the infidel. The Phœnicians and Chaldeans in Alexander's army promised themselves that they would now be permitted to plunder the city and torment the high priest to death. But it happened far otherwise. For when the king saw the white-robed procession approaching, headed by Jaddua in his purple and golden array, and wearing on his head the golden *petalon*, with its inscription "Holiness to Jehovah," he advanced, saluted the priest, and adored the Divine Name. The Jews encircled and saluted him with unanimous greeting, while the King of Syria and his other followers fancied that he must be distraught. "How is it," asked Parmenio, "that you, whom all others adore, yourself adore the Jewish high priest?" "I did not adore the high priest," said Alexander, "but God, by whose priesthood He has been honoured. When I was at Dium in Macedonia, meditating on the conquest of Asia, I saw this very man in this same apparel, who invited me to march boldly and without delay, and that he would conduct me to the conquest of the Persians." Then he took Jaddua by the hand, and in the midst of the rejoicing priests entered Jerusalem, where he sacrificed to God.* Jaddua showed him the prediction about himself in the Book of Daniel, and in extreme satisfaction he granted to the Jews, at the high priest's request, all the petitions which they desired of him.

But this story, so grateful to Jewish vanity, is a transparent fiction. It does not find the least support from any other historic source, and is evidently one of the Jewish Haggadoth in which the intense national self-exaltation of that strange nation delighted to depict the homage which they, and their national religion, extorted from the supernaturally caused dread of the greatest heathen potentates. In this respect it resembles the earlier chapters of the Book of Daniel itself, and the numberless stories of the haughty superiority of great Rabbis to kings and emperors in which the Talmud delights. Roman Catholic historians, like Jahn and Hess, and older writers, like Prideaux,† accept the story, even when they reject the fable about Sanballat and the Temple on Gerizim which follows it. Stress is naturally laid upon it by apologists like Hengstenberg; but an historian like Grote does not vouchsafe to notice it by a single word, and most modern writers reject it. The Bishop of Bath and Wells thinks that these stories are "probably derived from some apocryphal book of Alexandrian growth, in which chronology and history gave way to romance and Jewish vanity."‡ All the historians except Josephus say that Alexander went straight from Gaza to Egypt, and make no mention of Jerusalem or Samaria; and Alexander was by no means "adored" by all men at that period of his career, for he never received προσκύνησις till after his conquest of Persia. Nor can we account for the presence of "Chaldeans" in his army at this time, for Chaldea was then under the rule of Babylon. Besides which, Daniel was expressly bidden, as Bleek observes, to "seal up his prophecy till the time of the end"; and the "time of the end" was certainly not the era of Alexander,—not to mention the circumstance that Alexander, if the prophecies were pointed out to him at all, would hardly have been content with the single verse or two about himself, and would have been anything but gratified by what immediately follows.*

I pass over as meaningless Hengstenberg's arguments in favour of the genuineness of the Book from the predominance of symbolism; from the moderation of tone towards Nebuchadrezzar; from the political gifts shown by the writer; and from his prediction that the Messianic Kingdom would at once appear after the death of Antiochus Epiphanes! When we are told that these circumstances "can only be explained on the assumption of a Babylonian origin"; that "they are directly opposed to the spirit of the Maccabean time"; that the artifice with which the writing is pervaded, supposing it to be a pseudepigraphic book, "far surpasses the powers of the most gifted poet"; and that "such a distinct expectation of the near advent of the Messianic Kingdom is utterly without analogy in the whole of prophetic literature,"—such arguments can only be regarded as appeals to ignorance. They are either assertions which float in the air, or are disproved at once alike by the canonical prophets and by the apocryphal literature of the Maccabean age. Symbolism is the distinguishing characteristic of apocalypses, and is found in those of the late post-exilic period. The views of the Jews about Nebuchadrezzar varied. Some writers were partially favourable to him, others were severe upon him. It does not in the least follow that a writer during the Antiochian persecution, who freely adapted traditional or imaginative elements, should necessarily represent the old potentates as irredeemably wicked, even if he meant to satirise Epiphanes in the story of their extravagances. It was necessary for his purpose to bring out the better features of their characters, in order to show the conviction wrought in them by Divine interpositions. The notion that the Book of Daniel could only have been written by a statesman or a consummate politician is mere fancy. And, lastly, in making the Messianic reign begin immediately at the close of the Seleucid persecution, the writer both expresses his own faith and hope, and follows the exact analogy of Isaiah and all the other Messianic prophets.

But though it is common with the prophets to pass at once from the warnings of destruction to the hopes of a Messianic Kingdom which is to arise immediately beyond the horizon which limits their vision, it is remarkable—and the consideration tells strongly against the authenticity of Daniel—that not one of them had the least glimpse of the four successive kingdoms or of the four hundred and ninety years;—not even those prophets "who, if the Book of Daniel were genuine, must have had it in their hands." To imagine that Daniel took means to have his Book left undiscovered for some four hundred years, and then brought to light during the Maccabean struggle, is a grotesque impossibility. In

* There is nothing to surprise us in this circumstance, for Ptolemy III. ("Jos. c. Ap.," II. 5) and Antiochus VII. (Sidetes, "Antt.," XIII. viii. 2), Marcus Agrippa (*id.*, XVI. ii. 1.), and Vitellius *id.*, XVIII. v. 3) are said to have done the same. Comp. Suet., "Aug.," 93; Tert., "Apolog.," 6; and other passages adduced by Schürer, i., § 24.

† Jahn, "Hebr. Commonwealth," 71; Hess, "Gesch.," ii. 37; Prideaux, "Connection," i. 540 ff.

‡ "Dict. of Bibl," *s. v.* "Jaddua." See Schürer, i. 187; **Van** Dale, "Dissert. de LXX. Interpr.," 68 ff.

* This part of the story is a mere doublet of that about Cyrus and the prophecies of Isaiah ("Antt.," XI. i. 2).

the Book existed, it must have been known. Yet not only is there no real trace of its existence before B. C. 167, but the post-exilic prophets pay no sort of regard to its detailed predictions, and were evidently unaware that any such predictions had ever been uttered. What room is there for Daniel's four empires and four hundred and ninety years in such a prophecy as Zech. ii. 6-13? The pseudepigraphic Daniel possibly took the symbolism of four horns from Zech. i. 18, 19; but there is not the slightest connection between Zechariah's symbol and that of the pseudo-Daniel. If the number four in Zechariah be not a mere number of completeness with reference to the four quarters of the world (comp. Zech. i. 18), the four horns symbolise either Assyria, Babylonia, Egypt, and Persia, or more generally the nations which had then scattered Israel (Zech. ii. 8, vi. 1-8; Ezek. xxxvii. 9); so that the following promise does not even contemplate a victorious succession of heathen powers. Again, what room is there for Daniel's four successive pagan empires in any natural interpretation of Haggai's "yet a little while and I will shake all nations" (Hag. ii. 7), and in the promise that this shaking shall take place in the lifetime of Zerubbabel (Hag. ii. 20-23)? And can we suppose that Malachi wrote that the messenger of the Lord should "suddenly" come to His Temple with such prophecies as those of Daniel before him? *

But if it be thought extraordinary that a pseudepigraphic prophecy should have been admitted into the Canon at all, even when placed low among the "Kethubîm," and if it be argued that the Jews would never have conferred such an honour on such a composition, the answer is that even when compared with such fine books as those of Wisdom and Jesus the Son of Sirach, the Book has a right to such a place by its intrinsic superiority. Taken as a whole it is far superior in moral and spiritual instructiveness to any of the books of the Apocrypha. It was profoundly adapted to meet the needs of the age in which it originated. It was in its favour that it was written partly in Hebrew as well as in Aramaic, and it came before the Jewish Church under the sanction of a famous ancient name which was partly at least traditional and historical. There is nothing astonishing in the fact that in an age in which literature was rare and criticism unknown it soon came to be accepted as genuine. Similar phenomena are quite common in much later and more comparatively learned ages. One or two instances will suffice. Few books have exercised a more powerful influence on Christian literature than the spurious letters of Ignatius and the pseudo-Clementines. They were accepted, and their genuineness was defended for centuries; yet in these days no sane critic would imperil his reputation by an attempt to defend their genuineness. The book of the pseudo-Dionysius the Areopagite was regarded as genuine and authoritative down to the days of the Reformation, and the author professes to have seen the supernatural darkness of the Crucifixion; yet "Dionysius the Areopagite" did not write before A. D. 532! The power of the Papal usurpation was mainly built on the Forged Decretals, and for centuries no one ventured to question the genuineness and authenticity of those gross forgeries, till Laurentius

* Mal. iii. 1. LXX., ἐξαίφνης; Vulg., *statim*; but it is rather "unawares" (*unversehens*).

Valla exposed the cheat and flung the tatters of the Decretals to the winds. In the eighteenth century Ireland could deceive even the acutest critics into the belief that his paltry "Vortigern" was a rediscovered play of Shakespeare; and a Cornish clergyman wrote a ballad which even Macaulay took for a genuine production of the reign of James II. Those who read the Book of Daniel in the light of Seleucid and Ptolemaic history saw that the writer was well acquainted with the events of those days, and that his words were full of hope, consolation, and instruction. After a certain lapse of time they were in no position to estimate the many indications that by no possibility could the Book have been written in the days of the Babylonian Exile; nor had it yet become manifest that all the detailed knowledge stops short with the close of the reign of Antiochus Epiphanes. The enigmatical character of the Book, and the varying elements of its calculations, led later commentators into the error that the fourth beast and the iron legs of the image stood for the Roman Empire, so that they did not expect the Messianic reign at the close of the Greek Empire, which, in the prediction, it immediately succeeds.*

How late was the date before the Jewish Canon was finally settled we see from the Talmudic stories that but for Hananiah ben-Hizkiah, with the help of his three hundred bottles of oil burnt in nightly studies, even the Book of Ezekiel would have been suppressed, as being contrary to the Law ("Shabbath," f. 13, 2); and that but for the mystic line of interpretation adopted by Rabbi Aqiba (A. B. 120) a similar fate might have befallen the Song of Songs ("Yaddayim," c. iii.; "Mish.," 5).

There is, then, the strongest reason to adopt the conclusion that the Book of Daniel was the production of one of the "Chasidim" towards the beginning of the Maccabean struggle, and that its immediate object was to warn the Jews against the apostasies of commencing Hellenism. It was meant to encourage the faithful, who were waging a fierce battle against Greek influences and against the mighty and persecuting heathen forces by which they were supported.† Although the writer's knowledge of history up to the time of Alexander the Great is vague and erroneous, and his knowledge of the period which followed Antiochus entirely nebulous, on the other hand his acquaintance with the period of Antiochus Epiphanes is so extraordinarily precise as to furnish our chief information on some points of that king's reign. Guided by these indications, it is perhaps possible to fix the exact year and month in which the Book saw the light—namely, about January, B. C. 164.‡

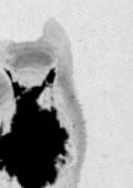

From Dan. viii. 14 it seems that the author had lived till the cleansing of the Temple after its pollution by the Seleucid King (1 Macc. iv.

* That the fourth empire could not be the Roman has *long* been seen by many critics, as far back as Grotius, L'Empereur, Chamier, J. Voss, Bodinus, Becmann, etc. (Diestel, "Gesch. A. T.," p. 523).

† See Hamburger, "Real-Encycl.," *s. v.* "Geheimlehre," ii. 265. The "Geheimlehre" (Heb. "Sithrî Thorah") embraces a whole region of Jewish literature, of which the Book of Daniel forms the earliest beginning. See Dan. xii. 4-9. The phrases of Dan. vii. 22 are common in the "Zohar."

‡ "Plötzlich bei Antiochus IV. angekommen hört alle seine Wissenschaft auf, so dass wir, den Kalendar in den Hand, *fast den Tag angeben konnen* wo dies oder jenes niedergeschrieben worden ist" (Reuss, "Gesch. d. Heil. Schrift.," § 464).

42-58). For though the Maccabean uprising is only called "a little help" (xi. 34), this is in comparison with the splendid future triumph and epiphany to which he looked forward. It is sufficiently clear from 1 Macc. v. 15, 16, that the Jews, even after the early victories of Judas, were in evil case, and that the nominal adhesion of many Hellenising Jews to the national cause was merely hypocritical (Dan. xi. 34).

Now the Temple was dedicated on December 25, B. C. 165; and the Book appeared before the death of Antiochus, which the writer expected to happen at the end of the seventy weeks, or, as he calculated them, in June, 164. The king did not actually die till the close of 164 or the beginning of 163 (1 Macc. vi. 1-16).*

CHAPTER X.

SUMMARY AND CONCLUSION.

THE contents of the previous sections may be briefly summarised.

I. The objections to the authenticity and genuineness of Daniel do not arise, as is falsely asserted, from any *a priori* objection to admit to the full the reality either of miracles or of genuine prediction. Hundreds of critics who have long abandoned the attempt to maintain the early date of Daniel believe both in miracles and prophecy.

II. The grounds for regarding the Book as a pseudepigraph are many and striking. The very Book which would most stand in need of overwhelming evidence in its favour is the one which furnishes the most decisive arguments against itself, and has the least external testimony in its support.

III. The historical errors in which it abounds tell overwhelmingly against it. There was no deportation in the third year of Jehoiakim; there was no King Belshazzar; the Belshazzar son of Nabunaid was not a son of Nebuchadrezzar; the names Nebuchad*n*ezzar and Abed-nego are erroneous in form; there was no "Darius the Mede" who preceded Cyrus as king and conqueror of Babylon, though there was a later Darius, the son of Hystaspes, who conquered Babylon; the demands and decrees of Nebuchadrezzar are unlike anything which we find in history, and show every characteristic of the Jewish Haggada; and the notion that a faithful Jew could become President of the Chaldean Magi is impossible. It is not true that there were only two Babylonian kings—there were five: nor were there only four Persian kings—there were twelve. Xerxes seems to be confounded alike with Darius Hystaspis and Darius Codomannus as the last king of Persia. All correct accounts of the reign, even of Antiochus Epiphanes, seem to end about B. C. 164, and the indications in vii. 11-14, viii. 25, xi. 40-45, do not seem to accord with the historic realities of the time indicated.

IV. The philological peculiarities of the Book are no less unfavourable to its genuineness. The Hebrew is pronounced by the majority of experts to be of a later character than the time assumed for it. The Aramaic is not the Babylonian East-Aramaic, but the later Palestinian West-Aramaic. The word "Kasdim" is used for "diviners," whereas at the period of the Exile it was a national name. Persian words and titles occur in the decrees attributed to Nebuchadrezzar. At least three Greek words occur, of which one is certainly of late origin, and is known to have been a favourite instrument with Antiochus Epiphanes.

V. There are no traces of the existence of the Book before the second century B. C.,* although there are abundant traces of the other books—Jeremiah, Ezekiel, the Second Isaiah—which belong to the period of the Exile. Even in Ecclesiasticus, while Isaiah, Jeremiah, Ezekiel, and the twelve Minor Prophets are mentioned (Ecclus. xlviii. 20-25, xlix. 6-10), not a syllable is said about Daniel, and that although the writer erroneously regards prophecy as mainly concerned with *prediction.* Jesus, son of Sirach, even goes out of his way to say that no man like Joseph had risen since Joseph's time, though the story of Daniel repeatedly recalls that of Joseph, and though, if Dan. i.-vi. had been authentic history, Daniel's work was far more marvellous and decisive, and his faithfulness more striking and continuous, than that of Joseph. The earliest trace of the Book is in an imaginary speech of a book written about B. C. 100 (1 Macc. ii. 59, 60).

VI. The Book was admitted by the Jews into the Canon; but so far from being placed where, if genuine, it would have had a right to stand—among the four Great Prophets—it does not even receive a place among the twelve Minor Prophets, such as is accorded to the much shorter and far inferior Book of Jonah. It is relegated to the "Kethubim," side by side with such a book as Esther. If it originated during the Babylonian Exile, Josephus might well speak of its "undeviating prophetic accuracy."† Yet this absolutely unparalleled and even unapproached foreteller of the minute future is not allowed by the Jews any place at all in their prophetic Canon! In the LXX. it is treated with remarkable freedom, and a number of other Haggadoth are made a part of it. It resembles Old Testament literature in very few respects, and all its peculiarities are such as abound in the later apocalypses and Apochrypha.‡ Philo, though he quotes so frequently both from the Prophets and the Hagiographa, does not even allude to the Book of Daniel.

VII. Its author seems to accept for himself the view of his age that the spirit of genuine prophecy had departed for evermore.§ He speaks of himself as a student of the older prophecies, and alludes to the Scriptures as an authoritative Canon—*Hassepharim,* "*the* books." His views and practices as regards three daily prayers towards Jerusalem (vi. 11); the importance attached to Levitical rules about food (i. 8-21); the expiatory and other value attached to alms and fasting (iv. 24, ix. 3, x. 3); the angelology involving even the names, distinctions, and rival offices of angels; the form taken by the Messianic hope; the twofold resurrection of good and evil,—are all in close accord with

* For arguments in favour of this view see Cornill, "Theol. Stud aus Ostpreussen," 1889, pp. 1-32, and "Einleit.," p. 261. He reckons twelve generations, sixty-nine "weeks," from the destruction of Jerusalem to the murder of the high priest Onias III.

* It is alluded to about B. C. 140 in the Sibylline Oracles (iii. 391-416), and in 1 Macc. ii. 59, 60.

† Jos., "Antt.," X. xi. 7.

‡ Ewald ("Hist. of Israel," v. 208) thinks that the author had read Baruch in Hebrew, because Dan. ix. 4-19 is an abbreviation of Baruch i. 15-ii. 17.

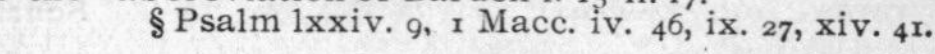

§ Psalm lxxiv. 9, 1 Macc. iv. 46, ix. 27, xiv. 41.

the standpoint of the second century before Christ as shown distinctly in its literature.*

VIII. When we have been led by decisive arguments to admit the real date of the Book of Daniel, its place among the Hagiographa confirms all our conclusions. The Law, the Prophets, and the Hagiographa represent, as Professor Sanday has pointed out, three layers or stages in the history of the collection of the Canon. If the Book of Chronicles was not accepted among the Histories (which were designated "The Former Prophets"), nor the Book of Daniel among the Greater or Lesser Prophets, the reason was that, at the date when the Prophets were formally collected into a division of the Canon, these books were not yet in existence, or at any rate had not been accepted on the same level with the other books.†

IX. All these circumstances, and others which have been mentioned, have come home to earnest, unprejudiced, and profoundly learned critics with so irresistible a force, and the counter-arguments which are adduced are so little valid that the defenders of the genuineness are now an ever-dwindling body, and many of them can only support their basis at all by the hypothesis of interpolations or twofold authorship. Thus C. v. Orelli ‡ can only accept a modified genuineness, for which he scarcely offers a single argument; but even he resorts to the hypothesis of a late editor in the Maccabean age who put together the traditions and general prophecies of the real Daniel. He admits that without such a supposition—by which it does not seem that we gain much—the Book of Daniel is wholly exceptional, and without a single analogy in the Old Testament. And he clearly sees that all the rays of the Book are focussed in the struggle against Antiochus as in their central point,§ and that the best commentary on the prophetic section of the Book is the First Book of Maccabees.‖

X. It may then be said with confidence that the critical view has finally won the day. The human mind will in the end accept that theory which covers the greatest number of facts, and harmonises best with the sum-total of knowledge. Now, in regard to the Book of Daniel, these conditions appear to be far better satisfied by the supposition that the Book was written in the second century than in the sixth. The history, imperfect as to the pseudepigraphic date, but very precise as it approaches B. C. 176-164, the late characteristics which mark the language, the notable silence respecting the Book from the sixth to the second century, and its subsequent prominence and the place which it occupies in the "Kethubîm," are arguments which few candid minds can resist. The critics of Germany, even the most moderate, such as Delitzsch, Cornill, Riehm, Strack, C. v. Orelli, Meinhold, are unanimous as to the late date of, and even in the far more conservative criticism of England there is no shadow of doubt on the subject left in the minds of such scholars as Driver, Cheyne, Sanday, Bevan, and Robertson Smith. Yet, so far from detracting from the value of the Book, we add to its real value and to its accurate apprehension when we regard it, not as the work of a prophet in the Exile, but of some faithful "Chasid" in the days of the Seleucid tyrant, anxious to inspire the courage and console the sufferings of his countrymen. Thus considered, the Book presents some analogy to St. Augustine's "City of God." It sets forth, in strong outlines, and with magnificent originality and faith, the contrast between the kingdoms of this world and the kingdoms of our God and of His Christ, to which the eternal victory has been foreordained from the foundation of the world. In this respect we must compare it with the Apocalypse. Antiochus Epiphanes was an anticipated Nero. And just as the agonies of the Neronian persecutions wrung from the impassioned spirit of St. John the Divine those visions of glory and that denunciation of doom, in order that the hearts of Christians in Rome and Asia might be encouraged to the endurance of martyrdom, and to the certain hope that the irresistible might of their weakness would ultimately shake the world, so the folly and fury of Antiochus led the holy and gifted Jew who wrote the Book of Daniel to set forth a similar faith, partly in Haggadoth, which may, to some extent, have been drawn from tradition, and partly in prophecies, of which the central conception was that which all history teaches us—namely, that "for every false word and unrighteous deed, for cruelty and oppression, for lust and vanity, the price has to be paid at last, not always by the chief offenders, but paid by some one. Justice and truth alone endure and live. Injustice and oppression may be long-lived, but doomsday comes to them at last." * And when that doom has been carried to its ultimate issues, then begins the Kingdom of the Son of Man, the reign of God's Anointed, and the inheritance of the earth by the Saints of God.

* See Cornill, "Einleit.," pp. 257-260.

† Sanday, "Inspiration," p. 101. The name of "Earlier Prophets" was given to the two Books of Samuel, of Kings, and of Isaiah, Jeremiah, and Ezekiel; and the twelve Minor Prophets (the latter regarded as one book) were called "The Later Prophets." Cornill places the collection of the Prophets into the Canon about B. C. 250.

‡ "Alttestament. Weissagung," pp. 513-530 (Vienna, 1882).

§ "Alle strahlen des Buches sich in dieser Epoche als in ihrem Brennpunkte vereinigen" (C. v. Orelli, p. 514).

‖ Compare the following passages: Unclean meats, 1 Macc. i. 62-64, "Many in Israel were fully resolved not to eat any unclean thing," etc.; 2 Macc. vi. 18-31, vii. 1-42. The decrees of Nebuchadrezzar (Dan. iii. 4-6) and Darius (Dan. vi. 6-9) with the proceedings of Antiochus (1 Macc. i. 47-51). Belshazzar's profane use of the Temple vessels (Dan. v. 2.) with 1 Macc. i. 23; 2 Macc. v. 16, etc.

PART II.

COMMENTARY ON THE HISTORIC SECTION.

CHAPTER XI.

THE PRELUDE.

"His loyalty he kept, his faith, his love."—MILTON.

THE first chapter of the Book of Daniel serves as a beautiful introduction to the whole, and strikes the keynote of faithfulness to the institutions of Judaism which of all others seemed most important to the mind of a pious Hebrew in the days of Antiochus Epiphanes. At a time when many were wavering, and many had lapsed into open apostasy, the writer wished to set before his countrymen in the most winning and vivid

* Froude, "Short Studies," i. 17.

manner the nobleness and the reward of obeying God rather than man.

He had read in 2 Kings xxiv. 1, 2, that Jehoiakim had been a vassal of Nebuchadrezzar for three years, which were not, however, the first three years of his reign, and then had rebelled, and been subdued by "bands of the Chaldeans" and their allies. In 2 Chron. xxxvi. 6 he read that Nebuchadrezzar had "bound Jehoiakim in fetters to carry him to Babylon."* Combining these two passages, he seems to have inferred, in the absence of more accurate historical indications, that the Chaldeans had besieged and captured Jerusalem in the third year of Jehoiakim. That the date is erroneous there can hardly be a question, for, as already stated,† neither Jeremiah, the contemporary of Jehoiakim, nor the Book of Kings, nor any other authority, knows anything of any siege of Jerusalem by the Babylonian King in the third year of Jehoiakim. The Chronicler, a very late writer, seems to have heard some tradition that Jehoiakim had been taken captive, but he does not date this capture; and in Jehoiakim's third year the king was a vassal, not of Babylon, but of Egypt. Nabopolassar, not Nebuchadrezzar, was then King of Babylon. It was not till the following year (B. C. 605), when Nebuchadrezzar, acting as his father's general, had defeated Egypt at the Battle of Carchemish, that any siege of Jerusalem would have been possible. Nor did Nebuchadrezzar advance against the Holy City even after the Battle of Carchemish, but dashed home across the desert to secure the crown of Babylon on hearing the news of his father's death. The only two considerable Babylonian deportations of which we know were apparently in the eighth and nineteenth years of Nebuchadrezzar's reign. In the former Jehoiachin was carried captive with ten thousand citizens (2 Kings xxiv. 14-16; Jer. xxvii. 20); in the latter Zedekiah was slain, and eight hundred and thirty-two persons carried to Babylon (Jer. lii. 29; 2 Kings xxv. 11).‡

There seems then to be, on the very threshold, every indication of an historic inaccuracy such as could not have been committed if the historic Daniel had been the true author of this Book; and we are able, with perfect clearness, to point to the passages by which the Maccabean writer was misled into a mistaken inference. To him, however, as to all Jewish writers, a mere variation in a date would have been regarded as a matter of the utmost insignificance. It in no way concerned the high purpose which he had in view, or weakened the force of his moral fiction. Nor does it in the smallest degree diminish from the instructiveness of the lessons which he has to teach to all men for all time. A fiction which is true to human experience may be as rich in spiritual meaning as a literal history. Do we degrade the majesty of the Book of Daniel if we regard it as a Haggada any more than we degrade the story of the Prodigal Son when we describe it as a Parable?

The writer proceeds to tell us that, after the siege, Nebuchadrezzar—whom the historic Daniel could never have called by the erroneous name Nebuchad*n*ezzar—took Jehoiakim (for this seems to be implied), with some of the sacred vessels of the Temple (comp. v. 2, 3), "into the land of Shinar,* to the house of his god." This god, as we learn from Babylonian inscription, was Bel or Bel-merodach, in whose temple, built by Nebuchadrezzar, was also "the treasure-house of his kingdom."†

Among the captives were certain "of the king's seed, and of the princes" ("Parthemîm").‡ They were chosen from among such boys as were pre-eminent for their beauty and intelligence, and the intention was to train them as pages in the royal service, and also in such a knowledge of the Chaldean language and literature as should enable them to take their places in the learned caste of priestly diviners. Their home was in the vast palace of the Babylonian King, of which the ruins are now called Kasr. Here they may have seen the hapless Jehoiachin still languishing in his long captivity.

They are called "children," and the word, together with the context, seems to imply that they were boys of the age of from twelve to fourteen. The king personally handed them over to the care of Ashpenaz,§ the Rabsaris, or "master of the eunuchs," who held the position of lord high chamberlain.‖ It is probably implied that the boys were themselves made eunuchs, for the incident seems to be based on the rebuke given by Isaiah to the vain ostentation of Hezekiah in showing the treasures of his temple and palace to Merodach-baladan: "Behold the days come, that all that is in thine house . . . shall be carried to Babylon: nothing shall be left, saith the Lord. And of thy sons that shall issue from thee, which thou shalt beget, shall they take away; and they shall be eunuchs in the palace of the King of Babylon."¶

They were to be trained in the learning (lit. "the book") and language of Chaldea for three years; at the end of which period they were to be admitted into the king's presence, that he might see how they looked and what progress they had made. During those three years he provided them with a daily maintenance of food and wine from his table. Those who were thus maintained in Eastern courts were to be counted by hundreds, and even by thousands, and their position was often supremely wretched and degraded, as it still is in such Eastern courts. The

*Comp. Jer. xxii. 18, 19, xxxvi. 30.

† See *supra*, p. 365.

‡ Jeremiah (lii. 28-30) mentions *three* deportations, in the seventh, eighteenth, and twenty-third year of Nebuchadrezzar; but there are great difficulties about the historic verification, and the paragraph (which is of doubtful genuineness) is omitted by the LXX.

*Shinar is an archaism, supposed by Schrader to be a corruption of Sumir, or Northern Chaldea ("Keilinschr.," p. 34): but see Hommel, "Gesch. Bab. u. Assyr.," 220; F. Delitzsch, "Assyr. Gram.," 115. The more common name in the exilic period was Babel (Jer. li. 9, etc.) or Eretz Kasdim (Ezek. xii. 13).

† On this god—Marduk or Maruduk (Jer. l. 2)—comp. 2 Chron. xxxvi. 7. See Schrader, "K. A. T.," pp. 273, 276; and Riehm, "Handwörterb.," ii. 982.

‡ This seems to be a Persian word, *fratama*, "first." It is only found in Esther. Josephus says that the four boys were connected with Zedekiah ("Antt.," X. x. 1). Comp. Jer. xli. 1.

§ Dan. i. 3; LXX., Ἀβιεσδρί. The name is of quite uncertain derivation. Lenormant connects it with Abai-Istar, "astronomer of the goddess Istar" ("La Divination," p. 182). Hitzig sees in this strange rendering Abiesdri the meaning "eunuch." A eunuch could have no son to help him, so that his father is his help (*'ezer*). Ephræm Syrus, in his Commentary, preserves both names (Schleusner, "Thesaurus," *s. v.* Ἀβιέσερ). We find the name Ash*k*enaz in Gen. x. 3. Theodot. has Ἀσφανέζ. Among other guesses Lenormant makes Ashpenaz = Assa-ibni-zir. Dr. Joel ("Notizen zum Buche Daniel," p. 17) says that since the Vulgate reads Ab*r*iesri, "ob nicht der Wort von rechts zu links gelesen müsste?"

‖ Called in i. 7-11 the Sar-hassarîsîm (comp. Jer. xxxix. 3; Gen. xxxvii. 36, *marg.*: 2 Kings xviii. 17; Esther ii. 3) This officer now bears the title of *Gyzlar Agha*.

¶ Isa. xxxix. 6, 7.

wine was probably imported. The food consisted of meat, game, fish, joints, and wheaten bread. The word used for "provision" is interesting. It is "path-bag," and seems to be a transliteration, or echo of a Persian word, "patibaga" (Greek ποτίβαζις), a name applied by the historian Deinon (B. C. 340) to barley bread and "mixed wine in a golden egg from which the king drinks."

But among these captives were four young Jews named Daniel, Hananiah, Mishael, and Azariah.

Their very names were a witness not only to their nationality, but to their religion. Daniel means "God is my judge"; Hananiah, "Jehovah is gracious"; Mishael (perhaps), "who is equal to God?" Azariah, "God is a helper."

It is hardly likely that the Chaldeans would have tolerated the use of such names among their young pupils, since every repetition of them would have sounded like a challenge to the supremacy of Bel, Merodach, and Nebo. It was a common thing to change names in heathen courts, as the name of Joseph had been changed by the Egyptians to Zaphnath-paaneah (Gen. xli. 45), and the Assyrians changed the name of Psammetichus II. into "Nebo-serib-ani," "Nebo save me." They therefore made the names of the boys echo the names of the Babylonian deities. Instead of "God is my judge," Daniel was called Belteshazzar, "protect Thou his life." Perhaps the prayer shows the tender regard in which he was held by Ashpenaz. Hananiah was called Shadrach, perhaps Shudur-aku, "command of Aku," the moon-deity; Mishael was called Meshach, a name which we cannot interpret; and Azariah, instead of "God is a help," was called Abed-nego, a mistaken form for Abed-nebo, or "servant of Nebo." Even in this slight incident there may be an allusion to Maccabean days. It appears that in that epoch the apostate Hellenising Jews were fond of changing their names into Gentile names, which had a somewhat similar sound. Thus Joshua was called "Jason," and Onias "Menelaus." This was done as part of the plan of Antiochus to force upon Palestine the Greek language. So far the writer may have thought the practice a harmless one, even though imposed by heathen potentates. Such certainly was the view of the later Jews, even of the strictest sect of the Pharisees. Not only did Saul freely adopt the name of Paul, but Silas felt no scruple in being called by the name Sylvanus, though that was the name of a heathen deity.

It was far otherwise with acquiescence in the eating of heathen meats, which, in the days of the Maccabees, was forced upon many of the Jews, and which, since the institution or reinstitution of Levitism after the return from the Exile, had come to be regarded as a deadly sin. It was during the Exile that such feelings had acquired fresh intensity. At first they do not seem to have prevailed. Jehoiachin was a hero among the Jews. They remembered him with intense love and pity, and it does not seem to have been regarded as any stain upon his memory that, for years together, he had, almost in the words of Dan. i. 5, received a daily allowance from the table of the King of Babylon.*

In the days of Antiochus Epiphanes the ordinary feeling on this subject was very different, for the religion and nationality of the Jews were at stake. Hence we read: "Howbeit many in Israel were fully resolved and confirmed in themselves not to eat any unclean thing. Wherefore they chose rather to die, that they might not be defiled with meats, that they might not profane the holy covenant: so then they died." *

And in the Second Book of Maccabees we are told that on the king's birthday Jews "were constrained by bitter constraint to eat of the sacrifices," and that Eleazar, one of the principal scribes, an aged and noble-looking man, preferred rather to be tortured to death, "leaving his death for an example of noble courage, and a memorial of value, not only unto young men, but unto all his nation." In the following chapter is the celebrated story of the constancy and cruel death of seven brethren and their mother, when they preferred martyrdom to tasting swine's flesh. The brave Judas Maccabæus, with some nine companions, withdrew himself into the wilderness, and "lived in the mountains after the manner of beasts with his company, who fed on herbs continually, lest they should be partakers of the pollution." The tone and object of these narratives are precisely the same as the tone and object of the stories in the Book of Daniel; and we can well imagine how the heroism of resistance would be encouraged in every Jew who read those narratives or traditions of former days of persecution and difficulty. "This Book," says Ewald, "fell like a glowing spark from a clear heaven upon a surface which was already intensely heated far and wide, and waiting to burst into flames."

It may be doubtful whether such views as to ceremonial defilement were already developed at the beginning of the Babylonian Captivity.† The Maccabean persecution left them ingrained in the habits of the people, and Josephus tells us a contemporary story which reminds us of that of Daniel and his companions. He says that certain priests, who were friends of his own, had been imprisoned in Rome, and that he endeavoured to procure their release, "especially because I was informed that they were not unmindful of piety towards God, but supported themselves with figs and nuts," because in such eating of dry food (ξηροφαγία, as it was called) there was no chance of heathen defilement.‡ It need hardly be added that when the time came to break down the partition-wall which separated Jewish particularism from the universal brotherhood of mankind redeemed in Christ, the Apostles—especially St. Paul—had to show the meaningless nature of many distinctions to which the Jews attached consummate importance. The Talmud abounds in stories intended to glorify the resoluteness with which the Jews maintained their stereotyped Levitism; but Christ taught, to the astonishment of the Pharisees and even of the disciples, that it is not what entereth into a man which makes him unclean, but the unclean thoughts which come from within, from

* See Ewald, "Gesch. Isr.," vi. 654. "They shall eat unclean things in Assyria" (Hosea ix. 3). "The children of Israel shall eat their defiled bread among the Gentiles" (Ezek. iv. 13, 14).

* Macc. i. 62, 63.

† Mr. Bevan says that the verb for "defile" (גאל), as a ritual term for the idea of ceremonial uncleanness, is post-exilic: the Pentateuch and Ezekiel used טמא ("Comment.," p. 61.) The idea intended is that the three boys avoided meat which might have been killed with the blood and offered to idols, and therefore was not "Kashar" (Exod. xxxiv. 15).

‡ Jos., "Vit.," iii. Comp. Isa. lii. 11.

the heart.* And this He said, *καθαρίζων πάντα τὰ βρώματα*—*i. e.*, abolishing thereby the Levitic Law, and "making all meats clean." Yet, even after this, it required nothing less than that Divine vision on the tanner's roof at Joppa to convince Peter that he was not to call "common" what God had cleansed,† and it required all the keen insight and fearless energy of St. Paul to prevent the Jews from keeping an intolerable yoke upon their own necks, and also laying it upon the necks of the Gentiles.‡

The four princely boys—they may have been from twelve to fourteen years old §—determined not to share in the royal dainties, and begged the Sar-hassarisîm to allow them to live on pulse and water, rather than on the luxuries in which—for them—lurked a heathen pollution. The eunuch not unnaturally demurred. The daily rations were provided from the royal table. He was responsible to the king for the beauty and health, as well as for the training, of his young scholars; and if Nebuchadrezzar saw them looking more meagre or haggard‖ than the rest of the captives and other pages, the chamberlain's head might pay the forfeit.¶ But Daniel, like Joseph in Egypt, had inspired affection among his captors; and since the prince of the eunuchs regarded him "with favour and tender love," he was the more willing to grant, or at least to connive at, the fulfilment of the boy's wish. So Daniel gained over the Melzar (or steward?),** who was in immediate charge of the boys, and begged him to try the experiment for ten days. If at the end of that time their health or beauty had suffered, the question might be reconsidered.

So for ten days the four faithful children were fed on water, and on the "seeds"—*i. e.*, vegetables, dates, raisins, and other fruits, which are here generally called "pulse." †† At the end of the ten days—a sort of mystic Persian week ‡‡—they were found to be fairer and fresher than all the other captives of the palace.§§ Thenceforth they were allowed without hindrance to keep the customs of their country.

Nor was this all. During the three probationary years they continued to flourish intellectually as well as physically. They attained to conspicuous excellence "in all kinds of books and wisdom," and Daniel also had understanding in all kinds of dreams and visions, to which the Chaldeans attached supreme importance.‖‖ The Jews exulted in these pictures of four youths of their own race who, though they were strangers in a strange land, excelled all their alien compeers in their own chosen fields of learning. There were already two such pictures in Jewish history,—that of the youthful Moses, learned in all the wisdom of the Egyptians, and a great man and a prince among the magicians of Pharaoh; and that of Joseph, who, though there were so many Egyptian diviners, alone could interpret dreams, whether in the dungeon or at the foot of the throne. A third picture, that of Daniel at the court of Babylon, is now added to them, and in all three cases the glory is given directly, not to them, but to the God of heaven, the God of their fathers.

At the close of the three years the prince of the eunuchs brought all his young pages into the presence of the King Nebuchadrezzar. He tested them by familiar conversation,* and found the four Jewish lads superior to all the rest. They were therefore chosen "to stand before the king"—in other words, to become his personal attendants. As this gave free access to his presence, it involved a position not only of high honour, but of great influence. And their superiority stood the test of time. Whenever the king consulted them on matters which required "wisdom of understanding," he found them not only better, but "ten times better," than all the "magicians" and "astrologers" that were in all his realm.†

The last verse of the chapter, "And Daniel continued even unto the first year of King Cyrus," is perhaps a later gloss, for it appears from x. 1 that Daniel lived, at any rate, till the *third* year of Cyrus. Abn Ezra adds the words "continued in *Babylon*," and Ewald "at the king's court." Some interpret "continued" to mean "remained alive." The reason for mentioning "the first year of Cyrus" may be to show that Daniel survived the return from the Exile,‡ and also to mark the fact that he attained a great age. For if he were about fourteen at the beginning of the narrative, he would be eighty-five in the first year of Cyrus. Dr. Pusey remarks: "Simple words, but what a volume of tried faithfulness is unrolled by them! Amid all the intrigues indigenous at all times in dynasties of Oriental despotism, amid all the envy towards a foreign captive in high office as a king's councillor, amid all the trouble incidental to the insanity of the king and the murder of two of his successors, in that whole critical period for his people, Daniel *continued*." §

But this was, so to speak, *extra fabulam*. It did not enter into the writer's scheme of moral edification. If, however, the story is meant to imply that these youths accepted the heathen training, though (as we know from tablets and inscriptions) the incantations, etc., in which it abounded were intimately connected with idolatry, and were entirely unharmed by it, this may indicate that the writer did not disapprove of the "Greek training" which Antiochus tried to introduce, so far as it merely involved an acquaintance with Greek learning and literature. This is the view of Grätz. If so, the writer belonged to the more liberal Jewish school which did not object to a study of the "Chokmath Javanîth," or "Wisdom of Javan" (Derenbourg, "Palestine, p. 361).

* Mark vii. 19 (according to the true reading and translation).

† Acts x. 14.

‡ 1 Cor. xi. 25. This rigorism was specially valued by the Essenes and Therapeutæ. See Derenbourg, "Palestine," note, vi.

§ Plato, "Alcib.," i. 37; Xen., "Cyrop.," i. 2. Youths entered the king's service at the age of seventeen.

‖ Lit. "sadder." LXX., *σκυθρωποί*.

¶ LXX., *κινδυνεύσω τῷ ἰδίῳ τραχήλῳ*.

** Perhaps the Assyrian *matstsara*, "guardian" (Delitzsch). There are various other guesses (Behrmann, p. 5).

†† Heb., זֵרֹעִים; LXX., *σπέρματα*; Vulg., *legumina*. Abn Ezra took the word to mean "rice." Com. Deut. xii. 15, 16; 1 Sam. xvii. 17, 18. Comp. Josephus ("Vit.," iii.), who tells us how the Jewish priests, prisoners in Rome, fed on *σύκοις καὶ καρύοις*.

‡‡ Ewald, "Antiquities," p. 131 f.

§§ Pusey (p. 17) quotes from Chardin's notes in Harmer ("Obs.," lix.): "I have remarked that the countenance of the Kechicks (monks) are, in fact, more rosy and smooth than those of others, and that those who fast much are, notwithstanding, very beautiful, sparkling with health, with a clear and lively countenance."

‖‖ The *Chartummîm* are like the Egyptian *ἱερογραμματεῖς*. It is difficult to conceive that there was less chance of pollution in being elaborately trained in heathen magic and dream-interpretation than in eating Babylonian food.

* LXX., *ἐλάλησε μετ' αὐτῶν*. Considering the normal degradation of pages at Oriental courts, of which Rycaut (referred to by Pusey, p. 18) "gives a horrible account," their escape from the corruption around them was a blessed reward of their faithfulness. They may now have been seventeen, the age for entering the king's service (Xen., "Cyrop.," I. ii. 8). On the ordinary curse of the rule of eunuchs at Eastern courts see an interesting note in Pusey, p. 21.

† On the names see Gesenius, "Isaiah," ii. 355.

‡ Alluded to in ix. 25.

§ "Daniel," pp. 20, 21.

The domestic anecdote of this chapter, like the other more splendid narratives which succeed it, has a value far beyond the circumstances in which it may have originated. It is a beautiful moral illustration of the blessings which attend on faithfulness and on temperance, and whether it be an Haggada or an historic tradition, it equally enshrines the same noble lesson as that which was taught to all time by the early stories of the Books of Genesis and Exodus.*

It teaches the crown and blessing of faithfulness. It was the highest glory of Israel "to uplift among the nations the banner of righteousness." It matters not that, in this particular instance, the Jewish boys were contending for a mere ceremonial rule which in itself was immaterial, or at any rate of no eternal significance. Suffice it that this rule presented itself to them in the guise of a *principle* and of a sacred duty, exactly as it did to Eleazar the Scribe, and Judas the Maccabee, and the Mother and her seven strong sons in the days of Antiochus Epiphanes. They regarded it as a duty to their laws, to their country, to their God; and therefore upon them it was sacredly incumbent. And they were faithful to it. Among the pampered minions and menials of the vast Babylonian palace—undazzled by the glitter of earthly magnificence, untempted by the allurements of pomp, pleasure, and sensuous indulgence—

> "Amid innumerable false, unmoved,
> Unshaken, unseduced, unterrified,
> Their loyalty they kept, their faith, their love."

And because God loves them for their constancy, because they remain pure and true, all the Babylonian varletry around them learns the lesson of simplicity, the beauty of holiness. Amid the outpourings of the Divine favour they flourish, and are advanced to the highest honours. This is one great lesson which dominates the historic section of this Book: "Them that honour Me I will honour, and they that despise Me shall be lightly esteemed." It is the lesson of Joseph's superiority to the glamour of temptation in the house of Potiphar; of the choice of Moses, preferring to suffer affliction with the people of God rather than all the treasures of Egypt and "to be called the son of Pharaoh's daughter"; of Samuel's stainless innocence beside the corrupting example of Eli's sons; of David's strong, pure, ruddy boyhood as a shepherd-lad on Bethlehem's hills. It is the anticipated story of that yet holier childhood of Him who—subject to His parents in the sweet vale of Nazareth—blossomed "like the flower of roses in the spring of the year, and as lilies by the water-courses." The young human being who grows up in innocence and self-control grows up also in grace and beauty, in wisdom and "in favour with God and man." The Jews specially delighted in these pictures of boyish continence and piety, and they lay at the basis of all that was greatest in their national character.

But there also lay incidentally in the story a warning against corrupting luxury, the lesson of the need for, and the healthfulness of,

> "The rule of not too much by temperance taught."

"The love of sumptuous food and delicious drinks is never good," says Ewald, "and with the use of the most temperate diet body and soul can flourish most admirably, as experience had at that time sufficiently taught."

To the value of this lesson the Nazarites among the Jews were a perpetual witness. Jeremiah seems to single them out for the special beauty which resulted from their youthful abstinence when he writes of Jerusalem, "Her Nazarites were purer than snow, they were whiter than milk, they were more ruddy in body than rubies, their polishing was of sapphires." *

It is the lesson which Milton reads in the story of Samson,—

> "O madness! to think use of strongest wines
> And strongest drinks our chief support of health,
> When God, with these forbidden, made choice to rear
> His mighty champion, strong above compare,
> Whose drink was only from the liquid brook!"

It is the lesson which Shakespeare inculcates when he makes the old man say in "As You Like It,"—

> "When I was young I never did apply
> Hot and rebellious liquors in my blood,
> Nor did not with unblushful forehead woo
> The means of weakness and debility;
> Therefore mine age is as a lusty winter,
> Frosty, yet kindly."

The writer of this Book connects intellectual advance as well as physical strength with this abstinence, and here he is supported even by ancient and pagan experience. Something of this kind may perhaps lurk in the ἄριστον μὲν ὕδωρ of Pindar; and certainly Horace saw that gluttony and repletion are foes to insight when he wrote,—

> "Nam corpus onustum
> Hesternis vitiis animum quoque prægravat una,
> Atque affigit humo divinæ particulam auræ." †

Pythagoras was not the only ancient philosopher who recommended and practised a vegetable diet, and even Epicurus, whom so many regard as

> "The soft garden's rose-encircled child.

placed over his garden door the inscription that those who came would only be regaled on barley-cakes and fresh water, to satisfy, but not to allure, the appetite.

But the grand lesson of the picture is meant to be that the fair Jewish boys were kept safe in the midst of every temptation to self-indulgence, because they lived as in God's sight: and "he that holds himself in reverence and due esteem for the dignity of God's image upon him, accounts himself both a fit person to do the noblest and godliest deeds, and much better worth than to deject and defile, with such debasement and pollution as Sin is, himself so highly ransomed and ennobled to a new friendship and filial relation with God." ‡

CHAPTER XII.

THE DREAM-IMAGE OF RUINED EMPIRES.

> "With thee will I break in pieces rulers and captains."
> —JER. li. 23.

THE Book of Daniel is constructed with consummate skill to teach the mighty lessons which it was designed to bring home to the minds of

* Comp. Gen. xxxix. 21; 1 Kings viii. 50; Neh. i. 1; Psalm cvi. 46.

* Lam. iv. 7. † Hor., "Sat.," II. ii. 77.

‡ Milton, "Reason of Church Government."

its readers, not only in the age of its first appearance, but for ever. It is a book which, so far from being regarded as unworthy of its place in the Canon by those who cannot accept it as either genuine or authentic, is valued by many such critics as a very noble work of inspired genius, from which all the difficulties are removed when it is considered in the light of its true date and origin. This second chapter belongs to all time. All that might be looked upon as involving harshnesses, difficulties, and glaring impossibilities, if it were meant for literal history and prediction, vanishes when we contemplate it in its real perspective as a lofty specimen of imaginative fiction, used, like the parables of our Blessed Lord, as the vehicle for the deepest truths. We shall see how the imagery of the chapter produced a deep impress on the imagination of the holiest thinkers—how magnificent a use is made of it fifteen centuries later by the great poet of mediæval Catholicism.* It contains the germs of the only philosophy of history which has stood the test of time. It symbolises that ultimate conviction of the Psalmist that "God is the Governor among the nations." No other conviction can suffice to give us consolation amid the perplexity which surrounds the passing phases of the destinies of empires.

The first chapter serves as a keynote of soft, simple, and delightful music by way of overture. It calms us for the contemplation of the awful and tumultuous scenes that are now in succession to be brought before us.

The model which the writer has had in view in this Haggadah is the forty-first chapter of the Book of Genesis. In both chapters we have magnificent heathen potentates—Pharaoh of Egypt, and Nebuchadrezzar of Babylon. In both chapters the kings dream dreams by which they are profoundly troubled. In both, their spirits are saddened. In both, they send for all the "Chakamîm" and all the "Chartummîm" of their kingdoms to interpret the dreams. In both, these professional magicians prove themselves entirely incompetent to furnish the interpretation. In both, the failure of the heathen oneirologists is emphasised by the immediate success of a Jewish captive. In both, the captives are described as young, gifted, and beautiful. In both, the interpretation of the King's dream is rewarded by the elevation to princely civil honours. In both, the immediate elevation to ruling position is followed by life-long faithfulness and prosperity. When we add that there are even close verbal resemblances between the chapters, it is difficult not to believe that the one has been influenced by the other.

The dream is placed "in the second year of the reign of Nebuchadrezzar." The date is surprising; for the first chapter has made Nebuchadrezzar a king of Babylon after the siege of Jerusalem "in the third year of Jehoiakim"; and setting aside the historic impossibilities involved in that date, this scene would then fall in the *second* year of the probation of Daniel and his companions, and at a time when Daniel could only have been a boy of fifteen.† The apologists get over the difficulty with the ease which suffices superficial readers who are already convinced. Thus Rashi says "the second year of Nebuchadnezzar," meaning "the second year after the destruction of the Temple," *i. e.*, his twentieth year! Josephus, no less arbitrarily, makes it mean "the second year after the devastation of Egypt."* By such devices anything may stand for anything. Hengstenberg and his school, after having made Nebuchadrezzar a king, conjointly with his father—a fact of which history knows nothing, and indeed seems to exclude—say that the second year of his reign does not mean the second year after he became king, but the second year of his independent rule after the death of Nabopolassar. This style of interpretation is very familiar among harmonists, and it makes the interpretation of Scripture perpetually dependent on pure fancy. It is perhaps sufficient to say that Jewish writers, in works meant for spiritual teaching, troubled themselves extremely little with minutiæ of this kind. Like the Greek dramatists, they were unconcerned with details, to which they attached no importance, which they regarded as lying outside the immediate purpose of their narrative. But if any explanation be needful, the simplest way is, with Ewald, Herzfeld, and Lenormant, to make a slight alteration in the text, and to read "in the *twelfth*" instead of "in the *second* year of the reign of Nebuchadnezzar."

There was nothing strange in the notion that God should have vouchsafed a prophetic dream to a heathen potentate. Such instances had already been recorded in the case of Pharaoh (Gen. xli.), as well as of his chief courtiers (Gen. xl.); and in the case of Abimelech (Gen. xx. 5-7). It was also a Jewish tradition that it was in consequence of a dream that Pharaoh Necho had sent a warning to Josiah not to advance against him to the Battle of Megiddo.† Such dreams are recorded in the cuneiform inscriptions as having occurred to Assyrian monarchs. Ishtar, the goddess of battles, had appeared to Assur-bani-pal, and promised him safety in his war against Teumman, King of Elam; and the dream of a seer had admonished him to take severe steps against his rebel brother, the Viceroy of Babylon. Gyges, King of Lydia, had been warned in a dream to make alliance with Assur-bani-pal. In Egypt Amên-meri-hout had been warned by a dream to unite Egypt against the Assyrians.‡ Similarly in Persian history Afrasiab has an ominous dream, and summons all the astrologers to interpret it; and some of them bid him pay no attention to it.§ Xerxes (Herod., iii. 19) and Astyages (Herod., i. 108) have dreams indicative of future prosperity or adversity. The fundamental conception of the chapter was therefore in accordance with history ‖—though to say, with the "Speaker's Commentary," that these parallels "*endorse the authenticity* of the Biblical narratives," is either to use inaccurate terms, or to lay the unhallowed fire of false argument on the sacred altar of truth. It is impossible to think without a sigh of the vast amount which would have to be extracted from so-called "orthodox" commentaries, if such pas-

* Dante, "Inferno," xiv. 94-120.

† The Assyrian and Babylonian kings, however, only dated their reigns from the first new year after their accession.

* "Antt.," X. x. 3.

† 2 Chron. xxxv. 21. See "The Second Book of Kings," p. 440 (Expositor's Bible).

‡ See Professor Fuller, "Speaker's Commentary," vi. 265.

§ Malcolm, "Hist. of Persia," i. 39.

‖ The belief that dreams come from God is not peculiar to the Jews, or to Egypt, or Assyria, or Greece (Hom., "Il.," i. 62: "Od.," iv. 841), or Rome (Cic., "De Div.," *passim*), but to every nation of mankind, even the most savage.

sages were rigidly reprobated as a dishonour to the cause of God.

Nebuchadrezzar then—in the second or twelfth year of his reign—dreamed a dream, by which (as in the case of Pharaoh) his spirit was troubled and his sleep interrupted.* His state of mind on waking is a psychological condition with which we are all familiar. We awake in a tremor. We have seen something which disquieted us, but we cannot recall what it was; we have had a frightful dream, but we can only remember the terrifying impression which it has left upon our minds.

Pharaoh, in the story of Joseph, remembered his dreams, and only asked the professors of necromancy to furnish him with its interpretation. But Nebuchadrezzar is here represented as a rasher and fiercer despot, not without a side-glance at the raging folly and tyranny of Antiochus Epiphanes. He has at his command an army of priestly prognosticators, whose main function it is to interpret the various omens of the future. Of what use were they, if they could not be relied upon in so serious an exigency? Were they to be maintained in opulence and dignity all their lives, only to fail him at a crisis? It was true that he had forgotten the dream, but it was obviously one of supreme importance; it was obviously an intimation from the gods: was it not clearly their duty to say what it meant?

So Nebuchadrezzar summoned together the whole class of Babylonian augurs in all their varieties—the *Chartummîm*, "magicians," or book-learned; † the *Ashshaphîm*, "enchanters"; ‡ the *Mekashaphîm*, "sorcerers"; § and the *Kasdîm*, to which the writer gives the long later sense of "dream-interpreters," which had become prevalent in his own day. ‖ In later verses he adds two further sections of the students—the *Khakhamîm*, "wise men," and the *Gazerîm*, or "sooth-sayers." Attempts have often been made, and most recently by Lenormant, to distinguish accurately between these classes of magi, but the attempts evaporate for the most part into shadowy etymologies.¶ It seems to have been a literary habit with the author to amass a number of names and titles together.** It is a part of the stateliness and leisureliness of style which he adopts, and he gives no indication of any sense of difference between the classes which he enumerates, either here or when he describes various ranks of Babylonian officials.

When they were assembled before him, the king informed them that he had dreamed an important dream, but that it produced such agitation of spirit as had caused him to forget its import.* He plainly expected them to supply the failure of his memory, for "a dream not interpreted," say the Rabbis, "is like a letter not read." †

Then spake the Chaldeans to the king, and their answer follows in Aramaic ("Aramîth"), a language which continues to be used till the end of chap. vii. The Western Aramaic, however, here employed could not have been the language in which they spoke, but their native Babylonian, a Semitic dialect more akin to Eastern Aramaic. The word "Aramîth" here, as in Ezra iv. 7, is probably a gloss or marginal note, to point out the sudden change in the language of the Book.

With the courtly phrase, "O king, live for ever," they promised to tell the king the interpretation, if he would tell them the dream.

"That I cannot do," said the king, "for it is gone from me. Nevertheless, if you do not tell me both the dream and its interpretation, you shall be hacked limb by limb, and your houses shall be made a dunghill." ‡

The language was that of brutal despotism such as had been customary for centuries among the ferocious tyrants of Assyria. The punishment of dismemberment, dichotomy, or death by mutilation was comm n among them, and had constantly been depicted on their monuments. It was doubtless known to the Babylonians also, being familiar to the apathetic cruelty of the East. Similarly the turning of the houses of criminals into draught-houses was a vengeance practised among other nations.§ On the other hand, if the "Chaldeans" arose to the occasion, the king would give them rewards and great honours. It is curious to observe that the Septuagint translators, with Antiochus in their mind, render the verse in a form which would more directly remind their readers of Seleucid methods. "If you fail," they make the king say, "you shall be made an example, and your goods shall be forfeited to the crown." ‖

With "nervous servility" the magi answer to the king's extravagantly unreasonable demand, that he must tell them the dream before they can tell him the interpretation. Ewald is probably not far wrong in thinking that a subtle element of irony and humour underlies this scene. It was partly intended as a satirical reflection on the mad vagaries of Epiphanes.

For the king at once breaks out into fury, and tells them that they only want to gain (lit. "buy") time; ¶ but that this should not avail them. The dream had evidently been of crucial significance and extreme urgency; something im-

* Dan. ii. 1: "His dreaming brake from him." Comp. vi. 18; Esther vi. 1: Jerome says, "Umbra quædam, et, ut ita dicam, aura somnii atque vestigium remansit in corde regis, ut, referentibus aliis posset reminisci eorum quæ viderat."

† Gen. xli. 8; Schrader, "K. A. T.," p. 26; "Records of the Past," i. 136.

‡ The word is peculiar to Daniel, both here in the Hebrew and in the Aramaic. Pusey calls it "a common Syriac term, representing some form of divination with which Daniel had become familiar in Babylonia" (p. 40.).

§ Exod. vii. 11; Deut. xviii. 10; Isa. xlvii. 9, 12. Assyrian *Kashshapu*.

‖ As in the rule, *Chaldæos ne consulito*. See *supra*, p. 366.

¶ The equivalents in the LXX., Vulgate, A. V.. and other versions are mostly based on uncertain guess-work. See E. Meyer, "Gesch. d. Alterth.," i. 185; Hommel, "Gesch. Bab. u. Assyr.," v. 386; Behrmann, p. 2.

** *E. g.*, iii. 2, 3, officers of state; iii. 4, 5, etc., instruments of music; iii. 21, clothes.

* ii. 5: "The dream is gone from me," as in ver. 8 (Theodotion, ἀπέστη). But the meaning may be the decree (or word) is "sure": for, according to Nöldeke, *azda* is a Persian word for "*certain*." Comp. Esther vii. 7; Isa. xlv. 23.

† "Berachôth," f. 10, 2. This book supplies a charm to be spoken by one who has forgotten his dream (f. 55, 2).

‡ Dan. ii. 5, iii. 29. Theodot., εἰς ἀπωλείαν ἔσεσθε. Lit. "ye shall be made into limbs." The LXX. render it by διαμελίζομαι, *membratim concidor, in frusta fio.* Comp. Matt. xxiv. 51; Smith's "Assur-bani-pal," p. 137. The word *haddam*, "a limb," seems to be of Persian origin—in modern Persian *andam*. Hence the verb *hadîm* in the Targum of 1 Kings xviii. 33. Comp. 2 Macc. i. 16, μέλη ποιεῖν.

§ Comp. Ezra vi. 11; 2 Kings x. 27: "Records of the Past," i. 27, 43.

‖ In iii. 96, καὶ ἡ οἰκία αὐτοῦ δημευθήσεται. Comp. 2 Macc. iii. 13: "But Heliodorus, because of the king's commandment, said, That in anywise it must be brought into the king's treasury."

¶ LXX. Theodot., καιρὸν ἐξαγοράζετε (not in a *good* sense, as in Eph. v. 16, Col. iv. 5).

portant, and perhaps even dreadful, must be in the air. The very *raison d'être* of these thaumaturgists and stargazers was to read the omens of the future. If the stars told of any human events, they could not fail to indicate something about the vast trouble which overshadowed the monarch's dream, even though he had forgotten its details. The king gave them to understand that he looked on them as a herd of impostors; that their plea for delay was due to mere tergiversation; * and that, in spite of the lying and corrupt words which they had prepared in order to gain respite "till the time be changed" †—that is, until they were saved by some "lucky day" or change of fortune ‡—there was but one sentence for them, which could only be averted by their vindicating their own immense pretensions, and telling him his dream.

The "Chaldeans" naturally answered that the king's request was impossible. The adoption of the Aramaic at this point may be partly due to the desire for local colouring.§ No king or ruler in the world had ever imposed such a test on any "Kartum" or "Ashshaph" in the world.‖ No living man could possibly achieve anything so difficult. There were some gods whose dwelling *is* with flesh; they tenant the souls of their servants. But it is not in the power of these genii to reveal what the king demands; they are limited by the weakness of the souls which they inhabit.¶ It can only be done by those highest divinities whose dwelling is not with flesh, but who

"haunt
The lucid interspace of world and world,"

and are too far above mankind to mingle with their thoughts.**

Thereupon the unreasonable king was angry and very furious, and the decree went forth that the magi were to be slain *en masse*.

How it was that Daniel and his companions were not summoned to help the king, although they had been already declared to be "ten times wiser" than all the rest of the astrologers and magicians put together, is a feature in the story with which the writer does not trouble himself, because it in no way concerned his main purpose. Now, however, since they were prominent members of the magian guild, they are doomed to death among their fellows. Thereupon Daniel sought an interview with Arioch, "the chief of the bodyguard," †† and asked with gentle prudence why the decree was so harshly urgent. By Arioch's intervention he gained an interview with Nebuchadrezzar, and promised to tell him the dream and its interpretation, if only the king would grant him a little time—perhaps but a single night.*

The delay was conceded, and Daniel went to his three companions, and urged them to join in prayer that God would make known the secret to them and spare their lives. Christ tells us that "if two shall agree on earth as touching anything that they ask, it shall be done for them." † The secret was revealed to Daniel in a vision of the night, and he blessed "the God of heaven." ‡ Wisdom and might are his. Not dependent on "lucky" or "unlucky" days, He changeth the times and seasons; § He setteth down one king and putteth up another. By His revelation of deep and sacred things—for the light dwelleth with Him—He had, in answer to their common prayer, made known the secret. ‖

Accordingly Daniel bids Arioch not to execute the magians, but to go and tell the king that he will reveal to him the interpretation of his dream.

Then, by an obvious verbal inconsistency in the story, Arioch is represented as going with haste to the king, with Daniel, and saying that *he* had found a captive Jew who would answer the king's demands. Arioch could never have claimed any such merit, seeing that Daniel had already given his promise to Nebuchadrezzar in person, and did not need to be described. The king formally puts to Daniel the question whether he could fulfil his pledge; and Daniel answers that, though none of the "Khakhamîm," "Ashshaphîm," "Chartummîm," or "Gazerîm" ¶ could tell the king his dream, yet there is a God in heaven—higher, it is implied, than either the genii or those whose dwelling is not with mortals—who reveals secrets, and has made known to the king what shall be in the latter days.**

The king, before he fell asleep, had been deeply pondering the issues of the future; and God, "the revealer of secrets," †† had revealed those issues to him, not because of any supreme wisdom possessed by Daniel, but simply that the interpretation might be made known.‡‡

The king had seen §§ a huge, gleaming, terrible colossus of many colours and of different metals, but otherwise not unlike the huge colossi which guarded the portals of his own palace. Its head was of fine gold; its torso of silver; its belly and thighs of brass; its legs of iron; its feet

* Theodot., συνέθεσθε. *Cf.* John ix. 22.

† Theodot., ἕως οὗ ὁ καιρὸς παρέλθῃ.

‡ Esther iii. 7.

§ The word *Aramîth* may be (as Lenormant thinks) a gloss, as in Ezra iv. 7.

‖ A curious parallel is adduced by Behrmann ("Daniel," p. 7). Rabia-ibn-nazr, King of Yemen, has a dream which he cannot recall, and acts precisely as Nebuchadrezzar does (Wüstenfeld, p. 9).

¶ See Lenormant, "La Magie," pp. 181–183.

** "LXX., ii. 11: εἰ μή τις ἄγγελος.

†† Lit. "chief of the slaughter-men" or "executioners." LXX., ἀρχιμάγειρος. The title is perhaps taken from the story, which in this chapter is so prominently in the writer's mind, where the same title is given to Potiphar (Gen. xxxvii. 36). Comp. 2 Kings xxv. 8; Jer. xxxix. 9. The name Arioch has been derived from "Erî-aku," "servant of the moon-god" (*supra*, p. 366), but is found in Gen. xiv. 1 as the name of "the King of Ellasar." It is also found in Judith i. 6, "Arioch, King of the Elymæans." An Erim-akû, King of Larsa, is found in cuneiform.

* If Daniel went (as the text says) *in person*, he must have been already a very high official. (Comp. Esther v. 1; Herod., i. 99.) If so, it would have been strange that he should not have been consulted among the magians. All these details are regarded as insignificant, being extraneous to the general purport of the story (Ewald, "Hist.," iii. 194).

† Matt. xviii. 19. The LXX. interpolate a ritual gloss: καὶ παρήγγειλε νηστείαν καὶ δέησιν καὶ τιμωρίαν ζητῆσαι παρὰ τοῦ Κυρίου.

‡ The title is found in Gen. xxiv. 7, but only became common after the Exile (Ezra i. 2, vi. 9, 10; Neh. i. 5, ii. 4).

§ Comp. Dan. vii. 12; Jer. xxvii. 7; Acts i. 7, χρόνοι ἢ καιροί; 1 Thess. v. 1; Acts xvii. 26, ὁρίσας προτεταγμένους καιρούς.

‖ With the phraseology of this prayer comp. Psalm xxxvi. 9, xli., cxxxix. 12; Neh. ix. 5; 1 Sam. ii. 8; Jer. xxxii. 19; Job xii. 22.

¶ Here the new title *Gazerîm*, "prognosticators," is added to the others, and is equally vague. It may be derived from "*Gazar*," "to cut"—that is, "to determine."

** Comp. Gen. xx. 3, xli. 25; Numb. xxii. 35.

†† Comp. Gen. xli. 45.

‡‡ Dan. ii. 30: "For *their* sakes that shall make known the interpretation to the king" (A. V.). But the phrase seems merely to be one of the vague forms for the impersonal which are common in the "Mishnah." The R. V. and Ewald rightly render it as in the text.

§§ Here we have (ver. 31) *aloo!* "behold!" as in iv. 7, 10, vii. 8; but in vii. 2, 5, 6, 7, 13, we have *aroo!*

partly of iron and partly of clay.* But while he gazed upon it as it reared into the sunlight, as though in mute defiance and insolent security, its grim metallic glare, a mysterious and unforeseen fate fell upon it.† The fragment of a rock broke itself loose, not with hands, smote the image upon its feet of iron and clay, and broke them to pieces. It had now nothing left to stand upon, and instantly the hollow multiform monster collapsed into promiscuous ruins.‡ Its shattered fragments became like the chaff of the summer threshing-floor, and the wind swept them away; § but the rock, unhewn by any earthly hands, grew over the fragments into a mountain that filled the earth.

That was the haunting and portentous dream; and this was its interpretation:—

The head of gold was Nebuchadrezzar himself, the king of what Isaiah had called "the golden city" ‖—a King of kings, ruler over the beasts of the field, and the fowls of heaven, and the children of men.¶

After him should come a second and an inferior kingdom, symbolised by the arms and heart of silver.

Then a third kingdom of brass.

Finally a fourth kingdom, strong and destructive as iron. But in this fourth kingdom was an element of weakness, symbolised by the fact that the feet are partly of iron and partly of weak clay. An attempt should be made, by intermarriages, to give greater coherency to these elements; but it should fail, because they could not intermix. In the days of these kings, indicated by the ten toes of the image, swift destruction should come upon the kingdoms from on high; for the King of heaven should set up a kingdom indestructible and eternal, which should utterly supersede all former kingdoms. "The intense nothingness and transitoriness of man's might in its highest estate, and the might of God's kingdom, are the chief subjects of this vision." **

Volumes have been written about the four empires indicated by the constituents of the colossus in this dream; but it is entirely needless to enter into them at length. The vast majority of the interpretations have been simply due to *a priori* prepossessions, which are arbitrary and baseless. The object has been to make the interpretations fit in with preconceived theories of prophecy, and with the traditional errors about the date and object of the Book of Daniel. If we first see the irresistible evidence that the Book appeared in the days of Antiochus Epiphanes, and then observe that all its earthly "predictions" culminate in a minute description of his epoch, the general explanation of the four empires, apart from an occasional and a subordinate detail, becomes perfectly clear. In the same way the progress of criticism has elucidated in its general outlines the interpretation of the Book which has been so largely influenced by the Book of Daniel—the Revelation of St. John. The all-but-unanimous consensus of the vast majority of the sanest and most competent exegetes now agrees in the view that the Apocalypse was written in the age of Nero, and that its tone and visions were predominantly influenced by his persecution of the early Christians, as the Book of Daniel was by the ferocities of Antiochus against the faithful Jews. Ages of persecution, in which plain-speaking was impossible to the oppressed, were naturally prolific of apocalyptic cryptographs. What has been called the "futurist" interpretation of these books—which, for instance, regards the fourth empire of Daniel as some kingdom of Antichrist as yet unmanifested—is now universally abandoned. It belongs to impossible forms of exegesis, which have long been discredited by the boundless variations of absurd conjectures, and by the repeated refutation of the predictions which many have ventured to base upon these erroneous methods. Even so elaborate a work as Elliott's "Horæ Apocalypticæ" would now be regarded as a curious anachronism.

That the first empire, represented by the head of gold, is the Babylonian, concentrated in Nebuchadrezzar himself, is undisputed, because it is expressly stated by the writer (ii. 37, 38).

Nor can there be any serious doubt, if the Book be one coherent whole, written by one author, that by the fourth empire is meant, as in later chapters, that of Alexander and his successors—"the Diadochi," as they are often called.

For it must be regarded as certain that the four elements of the colossus, which indicate the four empires as they are presented to the imagination of the heathen despot, are closely analogous to the same four empires which in the seventh chapter present themselves as wild beasts out of the sea to the imagination of the Hebrew seer. Since the fourth empire is there, beyond all question, that of Alexander and his successors, the symmetry and purpose of the Book prove conclusively that the fourth empire here is also the Græco-Macedonian, strongly and irresistibly founded by Alexander, but gradually sinking to utter weakness by its own divisions, in the persons of the kings who split his dominion into four parts. If this needed any confirmation, we find it in the eighth chapter, which is mainly concerned with Alexander the Great and Antiochus Epiphanes; and in the eleventh chapter, which enters with startling minuteness into the wars, diplomacy, and intermarriages of the Ptolemaic and Seleucid dynasties. In viii. 21 we are expressly told that the strong he-goat is "the King of Grecia," who puts an end to the kingdoms of Media and Persia. The arguments of Hengstenberg, Pusey, etc., that the Greek Empire was a civilising and an ameliorating power, apply at least as strongly to the Roman Empire. But when Alexander thundered his way across the dreamy East, he was looked upon as a sort of shattering levin-bolt. The intercon-

* In the four metals there is perhaps the same underlying thought as in the Hesiodic and ancient conceptions of the four ages of the world (Ewald, "Hist.," i. 368). Comp. the vision of Zoroaster quoted from Delitzsch by Pusey, p. 97. "Zoroaster saw a tree from whose roots sprang four trees of gold, silver, steel, and brass; and Ormuzd said to him, 'This is the world; and the four trees are the four "times" which are coming.' After the fourth comes, according to Persian doctrine, Sosiosh, the Saviour." Behrmann refers also to Bahman Yesht (Spiegel, "Eran. Alterth.," ii. 152); the Laws of Manu (Schroder, "Ind. Litt.," 448); and Roth ("Mythos von den Weltaltern," 1860).

† Much of the imagery seems to have been suggested by Jer. li.

‡ Comp. Rev. xx. 11: καὶ τόπος οὐχ εὑρέθη αὐτοῖς.

§ Psalm i. 4, ii. 9; Isa. xli. 15; Jer. li. 33, etc.

‖ Isa. xiv. 4.

¶ King of kings. Comp. Ezek. xxvi. 7: Ezra vii. 12; Isa. xxxvi. 4. It is the Babylonian *Shar-sharrâni*, or *Sharru-rabbu* (Behrmann). The Rabbis tried (impossibly) to construe this title, which they thought only suitable to God, with the following clause. But Nebuchadrezzar was so addressed (Ezek. xxvi. 7), as the Assyrian kings had been before him (Isa. x. 8), and the Persian kings were after him (Ezra vii.12). The expression seems strange, but comp. Jer. xxvii. 6, xxviii. 14. The LXX. and Theodotion mistakenly interpolate ἰχθύες τῆς θαλάσσης.

** Pusey, p. 63.

nection of these visions is clearly marked even here, for the juxtaposition of iron and miry clay is explained by the clause "they shall mingle themselves with the seed of men: * but they shall not cleave one to another, even as iron is not mixed with clay." This refers to the same attempts to consolidate the rival powers of the Kings of Egypt and Syria which are referred to in xi. 6, 7, and 17. It is a definite allusion which becomes meaningless in the hands of those interpreters who attempt to explain the iron empire to be that of the Romans. "That the *Greek* Empire is to be the last of the Gentile empires appears from viii. 17, where the vision is said to refer to 'the time of the end.' Moreover, in the last vision of all (x.-xii.), the rise and progress of the Greek Empire are related with many details, *but nothing whatever* is said of any subsequent empire. Thus to introduce the Roman Empire into the Book of Daniel is to set at naught the plainest rules of exegesis." †

The reason of the attempt is to make the termination of the prophecy coincide with the coming of Christ, which is then—quite unhistorically—regarded as followed by the destruction of the fourth and last empire. But the interpretation can only be thus arrived at by a falsification of facts. For the victory of Christianity over Paganism, so decisive and so Divine, was in no sense a destruction of the Roman Empire. In the first place that victory was not achieved til' three centuries after Christ's advent, and in the second place it was rather a continuation and defence of the Roman Empire than its destruction. The Roman Empire, in spite of Alaric and Genseric and Attila, and because of its alliance with Christianity, may be said to have practically continued down to modern times. So far from being regarded as the shatterers of the Roman Empire, the Christian popes and bishops were, and were often called, the "Defensores Civitatis." That many of the Fathers, following many of the Rabbis, regarded Rome as the iron empire, and the fourth wild beast, was due to the fact that until modern days the science of criticism was unknown, and exegesis was based on the shifting sand.‡ If we are to accept their authority on this question, we must accept it on many others, respecting views and methods which have now been unanimously abandoned by the deeper insight and advancing knowledge of mankind. The influence of Jewish exegesis over the Fathers—erroneous as were its principles and fluctuating as were its conclusions—was enormous. It was not unnatural for the later Jews, living under the hatred and oppression of Rome, and still yearning for the fulfilment of Messianic promises, to identify Rome with the fourth empire. And this seems to have been the opinion of Josephus, whatever that may be worth. But it is doubtful whether it corresponds to another and earlier Jewish tradition. For among the Fathers even Ephræm Syrus identifies the *Macedonian* Empire with the fourth empire, and he may have borrowed this from Jewish tradition. But of how little value were early conjectures may be seen in the fact that, for reasons analogous to those which had made earlier Rabbis regard Rome as the fourth empire, two mediæval exegetes so famous as Saadia the

* Comp. Jer. xxxi. 27.

† Bevan, p. 66.

‡ The interpretation is first found, amid a chaos of false exegesis, in the Epistle of Barnabas, iv. 4, § 6.

Gaon and Abn Ezra had come to the conclusion that the fourth empire was—the Mohammedan! *

Every detail of the vision as regards the fourth kingdom is minutely in accord with the kingdom of Alexander. It can only be applied to Rome by deplorable shifts and sophistries, the untenability of which we are now more able to estimate than was possible in earlier centuries. So far indeed as the *iron* is concerned, that might by itself stand equally well for Rome or for Macedon, if Dan. vii. 7, 8, viii. 3, 4, and xi. 3 did not definitely describe the conquests of Alexander. But all which follows is meaningless as applied to Rome, nor is there anything in Roman history to explain any division of the kingdom (ii. 41), or attempt to strengthen it by intermarriage with other kingdoms (ver. 43). In the divided Græco-Macedonian Empires of the Diadochi, the dismemberment of one mighty kingdom into the four much weaker ones of Cassander, Ptolemy, Lysimachus, and Seleucus began immediately after the death of Alexander (B. C. 323). It was completed as the result of twenty-two years of war after the Battle of Ipsus (B. C. 301). The marriage of Antiochus Theos to Berenice, daughter of Ptolemy Philadelphus (B. C. 249, Dan. xi. 6), was as ineffectual as the later marriage of Ptolemy V. (Epiphanes) to Cleopatra, the daughter of Antiochus the Great (B. C. 193), to introduce strength or unity into the distracted kingdoms (xi. 17, 18).

The two legs and feet are possibly meant to indicate the two most important kingdoms—that of the Seleucidæ in Asia, and that of the Ptolemies in Egypt. If we are to press the symbolism still more closely, the ten toes may shadow forth the ten kings who are indicated by the ten horns in vii. 7.

Since, then, we are told that the first empire represents Nebuchadrezzar by the head of gold, and since we have incontestably verified the fourth empire to be the Greek Empire of Alexander and his successors, it only remains to identify the intermediate empires of silver and brass. And it becomes obvious that they *can* only be the Median and the Persian. That the writer of Daniel regarded these empires as distinct is clear from v. 31 and vi.

It is obvious that the silver is meant for the Median Empire, because, closely as it was allied with the Persian in the view of the writer (vi. 9, 13, 16, viii. 7), he yet spoke of the two as separate. The rule of "Darius the Mede," not of "Cyrus the Persian," is, in his point of view, the "other smaller kingdom" which arose after that of Nebuchadrezzar (v. 31). Indeed, this is also indicated in the vision of the ram (viii. 3); for it has two horns, of which the higher and stronger (the Persian Empire) rose up after the other (the Median Empire); just as in this vision the Persian Empire represented by the thighs of brass is clearly stronger than the Median Empire, which, being wealthier, is represented as being of silver, but is smaller than the other.† Further, the second empire is represented later on by the second beast (vii. 5), and

* See Bevan. p. 65.

† On the distinction in the writer's mind between the Median and Persian Empires see v. 28, 31, vi, 8. 12, 15, ix. 1, xi. 1. compared with vi. 28, x. 1. In point of fact, the Persians and Medians were long spoken of as distinct, though they were closely allied; and to the Medes had been specially attributed the forthcoming overthrow of Babylon: Jer. li. 28, "Prepare against her the nations with the kings of the Medes." Comp. Jer. li. 11, and Isa. xiii. 17, xxi. 2, "Besiege, O Media."

the three ribs in its mouth may be meant for the three satrapies of vi. 2.

It may then be regarded as a certain result of exegesis that the four empires are—(1) the Babylonian; (2) the Median; (3) the Persian; (4) the Græco-Macedonian.

But what is the stone cut without hands which smote the image upon his feet? It brake them in pieces, and made the collapsing *débris* of the colossus like chaff scattered by the wind from the summer threshing-floor. It grew till it became a great mountain which filled the earth.

The meaning of the image being first smitten upon its *feet* is that the overthrow falls on the iron empire.

All alike are agreed that by the mysterious rock-fragment the writer meant the Messianic Kingdom. The "mountain" out of which (as is here first mentioned) the stone is cut is "the Mount Zion." * It commences "in the days of these kings." Its origin is not earthly, for it is "cut without hands." It represents "a kingdom" which "shall be set up by the God of heaven," and shall destroy and supersede all the kingdoms, and shall stand for ever.

Whether a personal Messiah was definitely prominent in the mind of the writer is a question which will come before us when we consider the seventh chapter. Here there is only a Divine Kingdom; and that this is the dominion of Israel seems to be marked by the expression, "the kingdom shall not be left to another people."

The prophecy probably indicates the glowing hopes which the writer conceived of the future of his nation, even in the days of its direst adversity, in accordance with the predictions of the mighty prophets his predecessors, whose writings he had recently studied. Very few of those predictions have as yet been literally fulfilled; not one of them was fulfilled with such immediateness as the prophets conceived, when they were "rapt into future times." To the prophetic vision was revealed the glory that should be hereafter, but not the times and seasons, which God hath kept in His own power, and which Jesus told His disciples were not even known to the Son of Man Himself in His human capacity.

Antiochus died, and his attempts to force Hellenism upon the Jews were so absolute a failure that, in point of fact, his persecution only served to stereotype the ceremonial institutions which —not entirely *proprio motu*, but misled by men like the false high priests Jason and Menelaus— he had attempted to obliterate. But the magnificent expectations of a golden age to follow were indefinitely delayed. Though Antiochus died and failed, the Jews became by no means unanimous in their religious policy. Even under the Hasmonæan princes fierce elements of discord were at work in the midst of them. Foreign usurpers adroitly used these dissensions for their own objects, and in B. C. 37 Judaism acquiesced in the national acceptance of a depraved Edomite usurper in the person of Herod, and a section of the Jews attempted to represent *him* as the promised Messiah! †

Not only was the Messianic prediction unfulfilled in its literal aspect "in the days of these kings," * but even yet it has by no means received its complete accomplishment. The "stone cut without hands" indicated the kingdom, not—as most of the prophets seem to have imagined when they uttered words which meant more than they themselves conceived—of the literal Israel, but of that ideal Israel which is composed, not of Jews, but of Gentiles. The divinest side of Messianic prophecy is the expression of that unquenchable hope and of that indomitable faith which are the most glorious outcome of all that is most Divine in the spirit of man. That faith and hope have never found even an ideal or approximate fulfilment save in Christ and in His kingdom, which is now, and shall be without end.

But apart from the Divine predictions of the eternal sunlight visible on the horizon over vast foreshortened ages of time which to God are but as one day, let us notice how profound is the symbolism of the vision—how well it expresses the surface glare, the inward hollowness, the inherent weakness, the varying successions, the predestined transience of overgrown empires. The great poet of Catholicism makes magnificent use of Daniel's image, and sees its deep significance. He too describes the ideal of all earthly empire as a colossus of gold, silver, brass, and iron, which yet mainly rests on its right foot of baked and brittle clay. But he tells us that every part of this image, except the gold, is crannied through and through by a fissure, down which there flows a constant stream of tears.† These effects of misery trickle downwards, working their way through the cavern in Mount Ida in which the image stands, till, descending from rock to rock, they form those four rivers of hell,—

> "Abhorrèd Styx, the flood of deadly hate;
> Sad Acheron of sorrow, black and deep;
> Cocytus, named of lamentation loud
> Heard on the rueful stream; fierce Phlegethon
> Whose waves of torrent fire inflame with rage." ‡

There is a terrible grandeur in the emblem. Splendid and venerable looks the idol of human empire in all its pomp and pricelessness. But underneath its cracked and fissured weakness drop and trickle and stream the salt and bitter runnels of misery and anguish, till the rivers of agony are swollen into overflow by their coagulated scum.

It was natural that Nebuchadrezzar should have felt deeply impressed when the vanished outlines of his dream were thus recalled to him and its awful interpretation revealed. The manner in which he expresses his amazed reverence may be historically improbable, but it is psychologically true. We are told that "he fell upon his face and worshipped Daniel," and the word "worshipped" implies genuine adoration. That so magnificent a potentate should have lain on his face before a captive Jewish youth and adored him is amazing.§ It is still more so that Daniel, without protest, should have accepted, not only his idolatrous homage, but also the

* See Isa. ii. 2, xxvii. 16; Matt. xxi. 42-44. "Le *mot* de Messie n'est pas dans Daniel. Le mot de *Meshiach*, ix. 26, désigne l'autorité (probablement sacerdotale) de la Judée" (Renan, "Hist.," iv. 358).

† See Kuenen, "The Prophets," iii.

* No kings have been mentioned, but the ten toes symbolise ten kings. Comp. vii. 24.

† Dante, "Inferno," xiv. 94-120.

‡ Milton, "Paradise Lost," ii. 575.

§ It may be paralleled by the legendary prostrations of Alexander the Great before the high priest Jaddua (Jos., "Antt.," XI. viii. 5), and of Edwin of Deira before Paulinus of York (Bæda, "Hist.," ii. 14-16).

offering of "an oblation and sweet incense." * That a Nebuchadrezzar should have been thus prostrate in the dust before their young countryman would no doubt be a delightful picture to the Jews, and if, as we believe, the story is an unconnected Haggada, it may well have been founded on such passages as Isa. xlix. 23, "Kings shall bow down to thee with their faces toward the earth, and lick up the dust of thy feet"; † together with Isa. lii. 15, "Kings shall shut their mouths at him: for that which had not been told them shall they see; and that which they had not heard shall they perceive."

But it is much more amazing that Daniel, who, as a boy, had been so scrupulous about the Levitic ordinance of unclean meats, in the scruple against which the *gravamen* lay in the possibility of their having been offered to idols, ‡ should, as a man, have allowed himself to be treated exactly as the king treated his idols! To say that he accepted this worship because the king was not adoring *him*, but the God whose power had been manifested in him, § is an idle subterfuge, for that excuse is offered by all idolaters in all ages. Very different was the conduct of Paul and Barnabas when the rude population of Lystra wished to worship them as incarnations of Hermes and Zeus. The moment they heard of it they rent their clothes in horror, and leapt at once among the people, crying out, "Sirs, why do ye such things? We also are men of like passions with you, and are preaching unto you that ye should turn from these vain ones unto the living God." ‖

That the King of Babylon should be represented as at once acknowledging the God ot Daniel as "a God of gods," though he was a fanatical votary of Bel-merodach, belongs to the general plan of the Book. Daniel received in reward many great gifts, and is made "ruler of all the wise men of Babylon, and chief of the governors (*signîn*) over all the wise men of Babylon." About his acceptance of the civil office there is no difficulty; but there is a quite insuperable historic difficulty in his becoming a chief magian. All the wise men of Babylon, whom the king had just threatened with dismemberment as a pack of impostors, were, at any rate, a highly sacerdotal and essentially idolatrous caste. That Daniel should have objected to particular kinds of food from peril of defilement, and yet that he should have consented to be chief hierarch of a heathen cult, would indeed have been to strain at gnats and to swallow camels!

And so great was the distinction which he earned by his interpretation of the dream, that, at his further request, satrapies were conferred on his three companions; but he himself, like Mordecai, afterwards "sat in the gate of the king." ¶

* Isa. xlvi. 6. The same verbs, "they fall down, yea they worship," are there used of idols.

† Comp. Isa. lx. 14: "The sons also of them that afflicted thee shall come bending unto thee; and all they that despised thee shall bow themselves down at the soles of thy feet."

‡ Comp. Rom. xiv. 23; Acts xv. 29: Heb. xiii. 9; 1 Cor. viii. 1; Rev. ii. 14, 20.

§ So Jerome: "Non tam Danielem quam in Daniele adorat Deum, qui mysteria revelavit." Comp. Jos., "Antt.," XI: viii. 5, where Alexander answers the taunt of Parmenio about his προσκύνησις of the high priest: *οὐ τοῦτον προσεκύνησα, τὸν δὲ Θεόν.*

‖ Acts xiv. 14, 15.

¶ Esther iii. 2. Comp. 1 Chron. xxvi. 30. This corresponds to what Xenophon calls αἱ ἐπὶ τὰς θύρας φοιτήσεις, and to our "right of *entrée*."

CHAPTER XIII.

THE IDOL OF GOLD, AND THE FAITHFUL THREE.

REGARDED as an instance of the use of historic fiction to inculcate the noblest truths, the third chapter of Daniel is not only superb in its imaginative grandeur, but still more in the manner in which it sets forth the piety of ultimate faithfulness, and of that

"Death-defying utterance of truth"

which is the essence of the most heroic and inspiring forms of martyrdom. So far from slighting it, because it does not come before us with adequate evidence to prove that it was even intended to be taken as literal history, I have always regarded it as one of the most precious among the narrative chapters of Scripture. It is of priceless value as illustrating the deliverance of undaunted faithfulness—as setting forth the truth that they who love God and trust in Him must love Him and trust in Him even till the end, in spite not only of the most overwhelming peril, but even when they are brought face to face with apparently hopeless defeat. Death itself, by torture or sword or flame, threatened by the priests and tyrants and multitudes of the earth set in open array against them, is impotent to shake the purpose of God's saints. When the servant of God can do nothing else against the banded forces of sin, the world, and the devil, he at least can die, and can say like the Maccabees, "Let us die in our simplicity!" He may be saved from death; but even if not, he must prefer death to apostasy, and will save his own soul. That the Jews were ever reduced to such a choice during the Babylonian exile there is no evidence; indeed, all evidence points the other way, and seems to show that they were allowed with perfect tolerance to hold and practise their own religion.* But in the days of Antiochus Epiphanes the question which to choose—martyrdom or apostasy—became a very burning one. Antiochus set up at Jerusalem "the abomination of desolation," and it is easy to understand what courage and conviction a tempted Jew might derive from the study of this splendid defiance. That the story is of a kind well fitted to haunt the imagination is shown by the fact that Firdausi tells a similar story from Persian tradition of "a martyr hero who came unhurt out of a fiery furnace." †

This immortal chapter breathes exactly the same spirit as the forty-fourth Psalm.

"Our heart is not turned back,
Neither our steps gone out of Thy way:
No, not when Thou hast smitten us into the place of dragons,
And covered us with the shadow of death.
If we have forgotten the Name of our God,
And holden up our hands to any strange god,
Shall not God search it out?
For He knoweth the very secrets of the heart."

* The false prophets Ahab and Zedekiah were "roasted in the fire" (Jer. xxix. 22), which may have suggested the idea of this punishment to the writer; but it was for committing "lewdness"—"folly," Judg. xx. 6—in Israel, and for adultery and lies, which were regarded as treasonable. In some traditions they are identified with the two elders of the Story of Susanna. Assur-bani-pal burnt Samas-sum-ucin, his brother, who was Viceroy of Babylon (about B. C. 648), and Te-Umman, who cursed his gods (Smith, "Assur-bani-pal," p. 138). Comp. Ewald, "Prophets," iii. 240. See *supra*, p. 365.

† Malcolm, "Persia," i. 29, 30.

"Nebuchadnezzar the king," we are told in one of the stately overtures in which this writer rejoices, "made an image of gold, whose height was threescore cubits, and the breadth thereof six cubits, and he set it up in the plains of Dura, in the province of Babylon."

No date is given, but the writer may well have supposed or have traditionally heard that some such event took place about the eighteenth year of Nebuchadrezzar's reign, when he had brought to conclusion a series of great victories and conquests.* Nor are we told whom the image represented. We may imagine that it was an idol of Bel-merodach, the patron deity of Babylon, to whom we know that he did erect an image; † or of Nebo, from whom the king derived his name. When it is said to be "of gold," the writer, in the grandiose character of his imaginative faculty, may have meant his words to be taken literally, or he may merely have meant that it was gilded, or overlaid with gold.‡ There were colossal images in Egypt and in Nineveh, but we never read in history of any other gilded image ninety feet high and nine feet broad.§ The name of the plain or valley in which it was erected—Dura—has been found in several Babylonian localities.

Then the king proclaimed a solemn dedicatory festival, to which he invited every sort of functionary, of which the writer, with his usual *πύργωσις* and rotundity of expression, accumulates the eight names. They were:—

1. The Princes, "satraps," or wardens of the realm.
2. The Governors (ii. 48).
3. The Captains.
4. The Judges.
5. The Treasurers or Controllers.
6. The Counsellors.
7. The Sheriffs.
8. All the Rulers of the Provinces.

Any attempts to attach specific values to these titles are failures. They seem to be a catalogue of Assyrian, Babylonian, and Persian titles, and may perhaps (as Ewald conjectured) be meant to represent the various grades of three classes of functionaries—civil, military, and legal.

Then all these officials, who with leisurely stateliness are named again, came to the festival, and stood before the image. It is not improbable that the writer may have been a witness of some such splendid ceremony to which the Jewish magnates were invited in the reign of Antiochus Epiphanes.

Then a herald (*kerooza*) cried aloud a proclamation "to all peoples, nations, and languages." Such a throng might easily have contained Greeks, Phœnicians, Jews, Arabs, and Assyrians, as well as Babylonians. At the outburst of a blast of "boisterous janizary-music" they are all to fall down and worship the golden image.

Of the six different kinds of musical instruments, which, in his usual style, the writer names and reiterates, and which it is neither possible nor very important to distinguish, three—the harp, psaltery, and bagpipe—are Greek; two, the horn and sackbut, have names derived from roots found in both Aryan and Semitic languages; and one, "the pipe," is Semitic. As to the list of officials, the writer had added "and all the rulers of the provinces"; so here he adds "and all kinds of music." *

Any one who refused to obey the order was to be flung, the same hour, into the burning furnace of fire. Professor Sayce, in his "Hibbert Lectures," connects the whole scene with an attempt, first by Nebuchadrezzar, then by Nabunaid, to make Merodach—who, to conciliate the prejudices of the worshippers of the older deity Bel, was called Bel-merodach—the chief deity of Babylon. He sees in the king's proclamation an underlying suspicion that some would be found to oppose his attempted centralisation of worship.†

The music burst forth, and the vast throng all prostrated themselves, except Daniel's three companions, Shadrach, Meshach, and Abednego.

We naturally pause to ask where then was Daniel? If the narrative be taken for literal history, it is easy to answer with the apologist that he was ill; or was absent; or was a person of too much importance to be required to prostrate himself; or that "the Chaldeans" were afraid to accuse him. "*Certainly,*" says Professor Fuller, "had this chapter been the composition of a pseudo-Daniel, or the record of a fictitious event, Daniel would have been introduced and his immunity explained." Apologetic literature abounds in such fanciful and valueless arguments. It would be just as true, and just as false, to say that "certainly," if the narrative were historic, his absence would have been explained; and all the more because he was expressly elected to be "in the gate of the king." But if we regard the chapter as a noble Haggada, there is not the least difficulty in accounting for Daniel's absence. The separate stories were meant to cohere to a certain extent; and though the writers of this kind of ancient imaginative literature, even in Greece, rarely trouble themselves with any questions which lie outside the immediate purpose, yet the introduction of Daniel into the story would have been to violate every vestige of verisimilitude. To represent Nebuchadrezzar worshipping Daniel as a god, and offering oblations to him on one page, and on the next to represent the king as throwing him into a furnace for refusing to worship an idol, would have involved an obvious incongruity. Daniel is represented in the other chapters as playing his part and bearing his testi-

* Both in Theodotion and the LXX. we have ἔτους ὀκτωκαιδεκάτου. The siege of Jerusalem was not, however, finished till the nineteenth year of Nebuchadrezzar (2 Kings xxv. 8). Others conjecture that the scene occurred in his thirty-first year, when he was "at rest in his house, and flourishing in his palace" (Dan. iv. 4).

† "Records of the Past." v. 113. The inscriptions of Nebuchadrezzar are full of glorification of Marduk (Merodach. *id.*, v. 115, 135, vii. 75.

‡ Comp. Isa. xliv. 9-20. Mr. Hormuzd Rassan discovered a colossal statue of Nebo at Nimroud in 1853. Shalmanezer III. says on his obelisk, "I made an image of my royalty; upon it I inscribed the praise of Asshur my master, and a true account of my exploits." Herodotus (i. 183) mentions a statue of Zeus in Babylon, on which was spent eight hundred talents of gold, and of another made of "solid gold" twelve ells high.

§ By the apologists the "image" or "statue" is easily toned down into a bust on a hollow pedestal (Archdeacon Rose, "Speaker's Commentary," p. 270). The colossus of Nero is said to have been a hundred and ten feet high, but was of marble. Nestle ("Marginalia," 35) quotes a passage from Ammianus Marcellinus, which mentions a colossal statue of Apollo reared by Antiochus Epiphanes, to which there may be a side-allusion here.

* See *supra*, p. 360. The *qar'na* (horn, κέρας) and *sab'ka* (σαμβύκη) are in root both Greek and Aramean. The "pipe" (*mash'rôkitha*) is Semitic. Brandig tries to prove that even in Nebuchadrezzar's time these three Greek names (even the *symphonia*) had been borrowed by the Babylonians from the Greeks; but the combined weight of philological authority is against him.

† See "Hibbert Lectures," chap. lxxxix., etc.

mony to the God of Israel; this chapter is separately devoted to the heroism and the testimony of his three friends.

Observing the defiance of the king's edict, certain Chaldeans, actuated by jealousy, came near to the king and "accused" the Jews.*

The word for "accused" is curious and interesting. It is literally "*ate the pieces of the Jews,*"† evidently involving a metaphor of fierce devouring malice.‡ Reminding the king of his decree, they inform him that three of the Jews to whom he has given such high promotion "thought well not to regard thee; thy god will they not serve, nor worship the golden image which thou hast set up."§

Nebuchadrezzar, like other despots who suffer from the vertigo of autocracy, was liable to sudden outbursts of almost spasmodic fury. We read of such storms of rage in the case of Antiochus Epiphanes, of Nero, of Valentinian I., and even of Theodosius. The double insult to himself and to his god on the part of men to whom he had shown such conspicuous favour transported him out of himself. For Bel-merodach, whom he had made the patron god of Babylon, was, as he says in one of his own inscriptions, "the lord, the joy of my heart in Babylon, which is the seat of my sovereignty and empire." It seemed to him too intolerable that this god, who had crowned him with glory and victory, and that he himself, arrayed in the plenitude of his imperial power, should be defied and set at naught by three miserable and ungrateful captives.

He puts it to them whether it was their set purpose‖ that they would not serve his gods or worship his image. Then he offers them a *locus pœnitentiæ*. The music should sound forth again. If they would then worship—but if not, they should be flung into the furnace,—"and who is that God that shall deliver you out of my hands?"

The question is a direct challenge and defiance of the God of Israel, like Pharaoh's "And who is Jehovah, that I shall obey His voice?" or like Sennacherib's "Who are they among all the gods that have delivered their land out of my hand?"¶ It is answered in each instance by a decisive interposition.

The answer of Shadrach, Meshach, and Abednego is truly magnificent in its unflinching courage. It is: "O Nebuchadnezzar, we have no need to answer thee a word concerning this.** If our God whom we serve be able to deliver us, He will deliver us from the burning fiery furnace, and out of thy hand, O king. But if not,†† be it known unto thee, O king,‡‡ that we will not serve thy gods, nor worship the golden image which thou hast set up."

By the phrase "if our God be able" no doubt as to God's *power* is expressed. The word "able" merely means "able in accordance with His own plans."* The three children knew well that God can deliver, and that He has repeatedly delivered His saints. Such deliverances abound on the sacred page, and are mentioned in the "Dream of Gerontius":—

"Rescue him, O Lord, in this his evil hour,
As of old so many by Thy mighty Power:
Enoch and Elias from the common doom;
Noe from the waters in a saving home;
Abraham from th' abounding guilt of Heathenesse,
Job from all his multiform and fell distress;
Isaac, when his father's knife was raised to slay;
Lot from burning Sodom on its judgment-day;
Moses from the land of bondage and despair;
Daniel from the hungry lions in their lair;
David from Golia, and the wrath of Saul;
And the two Apostles from their prison-thrall."

But the willing martyrs were also well aware that in many cases it has *not* been God's purpose to deliver His saints out of the peril of death; and that it has been far better for them that they should be carried heavenwards on the fiery chariot of martyrdom. They were therefore perfectly prepared to find that it was the will of God that they too should perish, as thousands of God's faithful ones had perished before them, from the tyrannous and cruel hands of man; and they were cheerfully willing to confront that awful extremity. Thus regarded, the three words "*And if not*" are among the sublimest words uttered in all Scripture. They represent the truth that the man who trusts in God will continue to say even to the end, "Though He slay me, yet will I trust in Him." They are the triumph of faith over all adverse circumstances. It has been the glorious achievement of man to have attained, by the inspiration of the breath of the Almighty, so clear an insight into the truth that the voice of duty must be obeyed to the very end, as to lead him to defy every combination of opposing forces. The gay lyrist of heathendom expressed it in his famous ode,—

"Justum et tenacem propositi virum
Non civium ardor prava jubentium,
Non vultus instantis tyranni,
Mente quatit solida"

It is man's testimony to his indomitable belief that the things of sense are not to be valued in comparison to that high happiness which arises from obedience to the law of conscience, and that no extremities of agony are commensurate with apostasy. This it is which, more than anything else, has, in spite of appearances, shown that the spirit of man is of heavenly birth, and has enabled him to unfold

"The wings within him wrapped, and proudly rise
Redeemed from earth, a creature of the skies."

For wherever there is left in man any true manhood, he has never shrunk from accepting death rather than the disgrace of compliance with what he despises and abhors. This it is which sends our soldiers on the forlorn hope, and makes them march with a smile upon the batteries which vomit their cross-fires upon them; "and so die by thousands the unnamed demigods." By virtue of this it has been that all the martyrs have, "with the irresistible might of their weakness," shaken the solid world.

On hearing the defiance of the faithful Jews—absolutely firm in its decisiveness, yet perfectly

* Comp. vi. 13, 14.

† "Akaloo Qar'tsîhîn."

‡ It is "found in the Targum rendering of Lev. xix. 16 for a tale-bearer, and is frequent as a Syriac and Arabic idiom" (Fuller).

§ Jerome emphasises the element of jealousy, "Quos prætulisti nobis et *captivos ac servos principes fecisti*, ii *elati in superbiam* tua præcepta contemnunt."

‖ The phrase is unique and of uncertain meaning.

¶ Exod. v. 2; Isa. xxxvi. 20; 2 Chron. xxxii. 13–17.

** Dan. iii. 16. LXX., *οὐ χρείαν ἔχομεν;* Vulg., *non oportet nos*. To soften the brusqueness of the address, in which the Rabbis (*e. g.*, Rashi) rejoice, the LXX. add another *βασιλεῦ*.

†† Jerome explains "But if not" by "Quodsi noluerit"; and Theodoret by *εἴτε οὖν ῥύεται εἴτε καὶ μή*.

‡‡ iii. 18. LXX., *καὶ τότε φανερόν σοι ἔσται.* Tert., from the Vet. Itala, "tunc manifestum erit tibi" ("Scorp.," 8).

* Comp. Gen. xix. 22: "*I cannot do anything* until thou be come thither."

respectful in its tone—the tyrant was so much beside himself, that, as he glared on Shadrach, Meshach, and Abed-nego, his very countenance was disfigured. The furnace was probably one used for the ordinary cremation of the dead.* He ordered that it should be heated seven times hotter than it was wont to be heated,† and certain men of mighty strength who were in his army were bidden to bind the three youths and fling them into the raging flames. So, bound in their hosen, their tunics, their long mantles, and their other garments, they were cast into the seven-times-heated furnace. The king's commandment was so urgent, and the "tongue of flame" was darting so fiercely from the horrible kiln, that the executioners perished in planting the ladders to throw them in, but they themselves fell into the midst of the furnace.

The death of the executioners seems to have attracted no special notice, but immediately afterwards Nebuchadrezzar started in amazement and terror from his throne, and asked his chamberlains, "Did we not cast *three* men *bound* into the midst of the fire?"

"True, O king," they answered.

"Behold," he said, "I see *four* men *loose*, walking in the midst of the fire, and they have no hurt, and the aspect of the fourth is like a son of the gods!" ‡

Then the king approached the door of the furnace of fire, and called, "Ye servants of the Most High God, come forth." Then Shadrach, Meshach, and Abed-nego came out of the midst of the fire; and all the satraps, prefects, presidents, and court chamberlains gathered round to stare on men who were so completely untouched by the fierceness of the flames that not a hair of their heads had been singed, nor their hosen shrivelled, nor was there even the smell of burning upon them.§ According to the version of Theodotion, the king worshipped the Lord before them, and he then published a decree in which, after blessing God for sending His angel to deliver His servants who trusted in Him, he somewhat incoherently ordained that "every *people, nation, or language* which spoke any blasphemy against the God of Shadrach, Meshach, and Abed-nego, should *be cut in pieces*, and *his house made a dunghill:* since there is no other god that can deliver after this sort."

Then the king—as he had done before—promoted Shadrach, Meshach, and Abed-nego in the province of Babylon.‖

Henceforth they disappear alike from history, tradition, and legend; but the whole magnificent Haggada is the most powerful possible commentary on the words of Isa. xliii. 2: "When thou walkest through the fire thou shalt not be burned, neither shall the flame kindle upon thee." *

How powerfully the story struck the imagination of the Jews is shown by the not very apposite Song of the Three Children, with the other apocryphal additions. Here we are told that the furnace was heated "with rosin, pitch, tow, and small wood; so that the flame streamed forth above the furnace forty and nine cubits. And it passed through and burned those Chaldeans it found about the furnace. But the angel of the Lord came down into the furnace together with Azarias and his fellows, and smote the flame of the fire out of the oven; and made the midst of the furnace as it had been a moist whistling wind, so that the fire touched them not at all, neither hurt nor troubled them." †

In the Talmud the majestic limitations of the Biblical story are sometimes enriched with touches of imagination, but more often coarsened by tasteless exhibitions of triviality and rancour. Thus in the "Vayyikra Rabba" Nebuchadrezzar tries to persuade the youths by fantastic misquotations of Isa. x. 10, Ezek. xxiii. 14, Deut. iv. 28, Jer. xxvii. 8; and they refute him and end with clumsy plays on his name, telling him that he should bark (*nabach*) like a dog, swell like a water-jar (*cod*), and chirp like a cricket (*tsirtsir*), which he immediately did—*i. e.*, he was smitten with lycanthropy.‡

In "Sanhedrin," f. 93, 1, the story is told of the adulterous false prophets Ahab and Zedekiah, and it is added that Nebuchadrezzar offered them the ordeal of fire from which the Three Children had escaped. They asked that Joshua the high priest might be with them, thinking that his sanctity would be their protection. When the king asked why Abraham, though alone, had been saved from the fire of Nimrod, and the Three Children from the burning furnace, and yet the high priest should have been singed (Zech. iii. 2), Joshua answered that the presence of two wicked men gave the fire power over him, and quoted the proverb, "Two dry sticks kindle one green one."

In "Pesachin," f. 118, 1, there is a fine imaginative passage on the subject, attributed to Rabbi Samuel of Shiloh:—

"In the hour when Nebuchadrezzar the wicked threw Hananiah, Mishrael, and Azariah into the midst of the furnace of fire, Gorgemi, the prince of the hail, stood before the Holy One (blessed be He!) and said, 'Lord of the world, let me go down and cool the furnace.' 'No,' answered Gabriel; 'all men know that hail quenches fire;§ but I, the prince of fire, will go down and make the furnace cool within and hot without, and thus work a miracle within a miracle.' The Holy One (blessed be He!) said unto him, 'Go down.' In the self-same hour

* Cremation prevailed among the Accadians, and was adopted by the Babylonians (G. Bertin, "Bab. and Orient. Records," i. 17-21). Fire was regarded as the great purifier. In the Catacombs the scene of the Three Children in the fire is common. They are painted walking in a sort of open cistern full of flames, with doors beneath. The Greek word is κάμινος (Matt. xiii. 42), "a calcining furnace."

† It seems very needless to introduce here, as Mr. Deane does in Bishop Ellicott's commentary, the notion of the seven *Maskim* or demons of Babylonian mythology. In the Song of the Three Children the flames stream out forty-nine (7 x 7) cubits. Comp. Isa. xxx. 26.

‡ The A. V., "like the Son of God," is quite untenable. The expression may mean a heavenly or an angelic being (Gen. vi. 2; Job i. 6). So ordinary an expression does not need to be superfluously illustrated by references to the Assyrian and Babylonian inscriptions, but they may be found in Sayce, "Hibbert Lectures," 128 and *passim*.

§ So in Persian history the Prince Siawash clears himself from a false accusation in the reign of his father Kai Kaoos by passing through the fire (Malcolm, "Hist. of Persia," i. 38).

‖ Comp. Psalm xvi. 12: "We went through fire and water, and Thou broughtest us out into a safe place."

* Comp. Gen. xxiv. 7; Exod. xxiii. 20; Deut. xxxvi. 1. The phrase applied to Joshua the high priest (Zech. iii. 2), "Is not this a brand plucked out of the burning?" originated the legend that, when the false prophets Ahab and Zedekiah had been burnt by Nebuchadrezzar (Jer. xxix 22), Joshua had been saved, though singed. This and other apocryphal stories illustrate the evolution of "Haggadoth" out of metaphoric allusions.

† Song of the Three Children, 23-27.

‡ "Vay. Rab.," xxv. 1 (Wünsche, "Bibliotheca Rabbinica").

§ Ecclus. xviii. 16: "Shall not the dew assuage the heat?"

Gabriel opened his mouth and said, 'And the truth of the Lord endureth for ever.'"

Mr. Ball, who quotes these passages from Wünsche's "Bibliotheca Rabbinica" in his Introduction to the Song of the Three Children,* very truly adds that many Scriptural commentators wholly lack the *orientation* derived from the study of Talmudic and Midrashic literature which is an indispensable preliminary to a right understanding of the treasures of Eastern thought. They do not grasp the inveterate tendency of Jewish teachers to convey doctrine by concrete stories and illustrations, and not in the form of abstract thought. "*The doctrine is everything; the mode of presentation has no independent value.*" To make the story the first consideration, and the doctrine it was intended to convey an after-thought, as we, with our dry Western literalness, are predisposed to do, is to reverse the Jewish order of thinking, and to inflict unconscious injustice on the authors of many edifying narratives of antiquity.

The part played by Daniel in the apocryphal Story of Susanna is probably suggested by the meaning of his name: "Judgment of God." Both that story and Bel and the Dragon are in their way effective fictions, though incomparably inferior to the canonical part of the Book of Daniel.

And the startling decree of Nebuchadrezzar finds its analogy in the decree published by Antiochus the Great to all his subjects in honour of the Temple at Jerusalem, in which he threatened the infliction of heavy fines on any foreigner who trespassed within the limits of the Holy Court.†

CHAPTER XIV.

THE BABYLONIAN CEDAR, AND THE STRICKEN DESPOT.

THRICE already, in these magnificent stories, had Nebuchadrezzar been taught to recognise the existence and to reverence the power of God. In this chapter he is represented as having been brought to a still more overwhelming conviction, and to an open acknowledgment of God's supremacy, by the lightning-stroke of terrible calamity.

The chapter is dramatically thrown into the form of a decree which, after his recovery and shortly before his death, the king is represented as having promulgated to "all people, nations, and languages that dwell in all the earth." ‡ But the literary form is so absolutely subordinated to the general purpose—which is to show that where God's "judgments are in the earth the inhabitants of the earth will learn righteousness," §—that the writer passes without any difficulty from the first to the third person (iv. 20-30). He does not hesitate to represent Nebuchadrezzar as addressing all the subject nations in favour of the God of Israel, even placing in his imperial decree a cento of Scriptural phraseology.

* "Speaker's Commentary," on the Apocrypha, ii. 305-307.

† Jos., "Antt.," XII. iii. 3; Jahn, "Hebr. Commonwealth," § xc.

‡ Comp. 1 Macc. i. 41, 42: "And the king [Antiochus Epiphanes] wrote to his whole kingdom, that all should be one people, and every one should leave his laws."

§ Isa. xxvi. 9.

Readers unbiassed by *a-priori* assumptions, which are broken to pieces at every step, will ask, "Is it even historically conceivable that Nebuchadrezzar (to whom the later Jews commonly gave the title of *Ha-Rashang*, 'the wicked') could ever have issued such a decree?" They will further ask, "Is there any shadow of evidence to show that the king's degrading madness and recovery rest upon any real tradition?"

As to the monuments and inscriptions, they are entirely silent upon the subject; nor is there any trace of these events in any historic record. Those who, with the school of Hengstenberg and Pusey, think that the narrative receives support from the phrase of Berossus that Nebuchadrezzar "fell sick and departed this life when he had reigned forty-three years," must be easily satisfied, since he says very nearly the same of Nabopolassar. Such writers too much assume that immemorial prejudices on the subject have so completely weakened the independent intelligence of their readers, that they may safely make assertions which, in matters of secular criticism, would be set aside as almost childishly nugatory.

It is different with the testimony of Abydenus, quoted by Eusebius.* Abydenus, in his book on the Assyrians, quoted from Megasthenes the story that, after great conquests, "Nebuchadrezzar" (as the Chaldean story goes), "*when he had ascended the roof of his palace, was inspired by some god or other,* and cried aloud, 'I, Nebuchadrezzar, announce to you the future calamity which neither Bel, my ancestor, nor our queen Beltis, can persuade the Fates to avert. There shall come a Persian, a mule, who shall have your own gods as his allies, and he shall make you slaves. Moreover, he who shall help to bring this about shall be the son of a Median woman, the boast of the Assyrian. Would that before his countrymen perish some whirlpool or flood might seize him and destroy him utterly;† or else would that he might betake himself to some other place, and *might be driven to the desert, where is no city nor track of men, where wild beasts seek their food and birds fly hither and thither! Would that among rocks and mountain clefts he might wander alone!* And as for me, may I, before he imagines this, meet with some happier end!' *When he had thus prophesied, he suddenly vanished.*"

I have italicised the passages which, amid immense differences, bear a remote analogy to the story of this chapter. To quote the passage as any proof that the writer of Daniel is narrating literal history is an extraordinary misuse of it.

Megasthenes flourished B. C. 323, and wrote a book which contained many fabulous stories, three centuries after the events to which he alludes. Abydenus, author of "Assyriaca," was a Greek historian of still later, and uncertain, date. The writer of Daniel may have met with their works, or, quite independently of them, he may have learned from the Babylonian Jews that there was *some* strange legend or other about the death of Nebuchadrezzar. The Jews in Babylonia were more numerous and more distinguished than those in Palestine, and kept up constant communication with them. So far

* "Præp. Ev.," lx. 41.

† I follow the better readings which Mr. Bevan adopts from Von Gutschmid and Toup.

from any historical accuracy about Babylon in a Palestinian Jew of the age of the Maccabees being strange, or furnishing any proof that he was a contemporary of Nebuchadrezzar, the only subject of astonishment would be that he should have fallen into so many mistakes and inaccuracies, were it not that the ancients in general, and the Jews particularly, paid little attention to such matters.

Aware, then, of some dim traditions that Nebuchadrezzar at the close of his life ascended his palace roof and there received some sort of inspiration, after which he mysteriously disappeared, the writer, giving free play to his imagination for didactic purposes, after the common fashion of his age and nation, worked up these slight elements into the stately and striking *Midrash* of this chapter. He too makes the king mount his palace roof and receive an inspiration; but in his pages the inspiration does not refer to the "mule" or half-breed, Cyrus, nor to Nabunaid, the son of a Median woman, nor to any imprecation pronounced upon them, but is an admonition to himself; and the imprecation which he denounced upon the future subverters of Babylon is dimly analogous to the fate which fell on his own head. Instead of making him "vanish" immediately afterwards, the writer makes him fall into a beast-madness for "seven times," after which he suddenly recovers and publishes a decree that all mankind should honour the true God.

Ewald thinks that a verse has been lost at the beginning of the chapter, indicating the nature of the document which follows; but it seems more probable that the author began this, as he begins other chapters, with the sort of imposing overture of the first verse.

Like Assur-bani-pal and the ancient despots, Nebuchadrezzar addresses himself to "all people in the earth," and after the salutation of peace * says that he thought it right to tell them "the signs and wonders that the High God hath wrought towards me. How great are His signs, and how mighty are His wonders! His kingdom is an everlasting kingdom, and His dominion is from generation to generation."†

He goes on to relate that, while he was at ease and secure in his palace,‡ he saw a dream which affrighted him, and left a train of gloomy forebodings. As usual he summoned the whole train of "Khakhamîm, Ashshaphîm, Mekashshaphîm, Kasdîm, Chartummîm," and "Gazerîm," to interpret his dream, and as usual they failed to do so. Then, lastly, Daniel, surnamed Belteshazzar, after Bel, Nebuchadrezzar's god,§ and "chief of the magicians,"‖ in whom was "the spirit of the holy gods," is summoned. To him the king tells his dream.

The writer probably derives the images of the dream from the magnificent description of the King of Assyria as a spreading cedar in Ezek. xxxi. 3-18:—

"Behold, the Assyrian was a cedar in Lebanon with fair branches, and with a shadowing shroud, and of an high stature; and his top was among the thick boughs. The waters nourished him, the deep made him to grow. . . . Therefore his stature was exalted above all the trees of the field; and his boughs were multiplied, and his branches became long by reason of many waters. All the fowls of the air made their nests in his boughs, and under his branches did all the beasts of the field bring forth their young, and under his shadow dwelt all great nations. . . . The cedars in the garden of God could not hide him . . . nor was any tree in the garden of God like him in his beauty. . . . Therefore thus saith the Lord God: Because thou art exalted in stature . . . I will deliver him into the hand of the mighty one of the nations. . . . And strangers, the terrible of the nations, have cut him off, and have left him. Upon the mountains and in all the valleys his branches are broken . . . and all the people of the earth are gone down from his shadow, and have left him. . . . I made the nations to shake at the sound of his fall."

We may also compare this dream with that of Cambyses narrated by Herodotus *: "He fancied that a vine grew from the womb of his daughter and overshadowed the whole of Asia. . . . The magian interpreter expounded the vision to foreshow that the offspring of his daughter would reign over Asia in his stead."

So too Nebuchadrezzar in his dream had seen a tree in the midst of the earth, of stately height, which reached to heaven and overshadowed the world, with fair leaves and abundant fruit, giving large nourishment to all mankind, and shade to the beasts of the field and fowls of the heaven. The LXX. adds with glowing exaggeration, "The sun and moon dwelled in it, and gave light to the whole earth. And, behold, a watcher (*'îr*) and a holy one (*qaddîsh*) came down from heaven, and bade, Hew down, and lop, and strip the tree, and scatter his fruit, and scare away the beasts and birds from it, but leave the stump in the greening turf bound by a band of brass and iron, and let it be wet with heaven's dews,"—and then, passing from the image to the thing signified, "and let his portion be with the beasts in the grass of the earth. Let his heart be changed from man's, and let a beast's heart be given unto him, and let seven times pass over him." We are not told to whom the mandate is given—that is left magnificently vague. The object of this "sentence of the watchers, and utterance of the holy ones," is that the living may know that the Most High is the Supreme King, and can, if He will, give rule even to the lowliest. Nebuchadrezzar, who tells us in his inscription that "he never forgave impiety," has to learn that he is nothing, and that God is all,—that "He pulleth down the mighty from their seat, and exalteth the humble and meek."

This dream Nebuchadrezzar bids Daniel to interpret, "because thou hast the spirit of a Holy God in thee."

Before we proceed let us pause for a moment to notice the agents of the doom. It is one of the never-sleeping ones—an *'îr* and a holy one —who flashes down from heaven with the mandate; and he is only the mouthpiece of the whole body of the watchers and holy ones.

Generally, no doubt, the phrase means an angelic denizen of heaven. The LXX. translates watcher by "angel." Theodotion, feeling that

* Comp. Ezra iv. 7, vii. 12.

† If Nebuchadrezzar wrote this edict, he must have been very familiar with the language of Scripture. See Deut. vi. 22; Isa. viii. 18; Psalm lxxviii. 12-16, cvi. 2; Mic. iv. 7, etc.

‡ *Heykal*, "palace"; Bab., *ikallu*. Comp. Amos viii. 3. See the palace described in Layard, "Nineveh and Babylon."

§ A mistake of the writer. See *supra*, p. 385.

‖ "Rab-chartummaya."

* Herod.," i. 108.

there is something technical in the word, which only occurs in this chapter, renders it by εἴρ. This is the first appearance of the term in Jewish literature, but it becomes extremely common in later Jewish writings—as, for instance, in the Book of Enoch. The term "a holy one"* connotes the dedicated separation of the angels; for in the Old Testament holiness is used to express consecration and setting apart, rather than moral stainlessness.† The "seven watchers" are alluded to in the post-exilic Zechariah (iv. 10): "They see with joy the plummet in the hand of Zerubbabel, even those seven, the *eyes* of the Lord; they run to and fro through the whole earth." In this verse Kohut‡ and Kuenen read "watchers" (*'îrîm*) for "eyes" (*'înîm*), and we find these seven watchers in the Book of Enoch (chap. xx.). We see as an historic fact that the familiarity of the Jews with Persian angelology and demonology seems to have developed their views on the subject. It is only after the Exile that we find angels and demons playing a more prominent part than before, divided into classes, and even marked out by special names. The Apocrypha becomes more precise than the canonical books, and the later pseudepigraphic books, which advance still further, are left behind by the Talmud. Some have supposed a connection between the seven watchers and the Persian "amschashpands."§ The "shedim," or evil spirits, are also seven in number,—

"Seven are they, seven are they!
In the channel of the deep seven are they,
In the radiance of heaven seven are they!"‖

It is true that in Enoch (xc. 91) the prophet sees "the first six white ones," and we find six also in Ezek. ix. 2. On the other hand, we find seven in Tobit: "I am Raphael, one of the seven holy angels which present the prayers of the saints, and which go in and out before the glory of the Holy One."¶ The names are variously given; but perhaps the commonest are Michael, Gabriel, Uriel, Raphael, and Raguel.** In the Babylonian mythology seven deities stood at the head of all Divine beings, and the seven planetary spirits watched the gates of Hades.††

To Daniel, when he had heard the dream, it seemed so full of portentous omen that "he was astonished for one hour."‡‡ Seeing his agitation, the king bids him take courage and fearlessly interpret the dream. But it is an augury of fearful visitation; so he begins with a formula intended as it were to avert the threatened consequences. "My Lord," he exclaimed, on recovering voice, "the dream be to them that hate thee, and the interpretation to thine enemies."§§

* Comp. Zech. xiv. 5; Psalm lxxxix. 6.
† See Job xv. 15.
‡ Dr. A. Kohut, "Die jüdische Angelologie," p. 6, n. 17.
§ For a full examination of the subject see Oehler, "Theol. of the O. T.," § 59, pp. 195 ff.; Schultz, "Alttest. Theol.," p. 555; Hamburger, "Real-Encycl.," i., *s. v.* "Engel"; Professor Fuller, "Speaker's Commentary" on the Apocrypha, Tobit, i., 171–183.
‖ Sayce, "Records of the Past," ix. 140.
¶ The number seven is not, however, found in all texts.
** The Jewish tradition admits that the names of the angels came from Persia ("Rosh Hashanah," f. 56, 1; "Bereshîth Rabba," c. 48; Riehm, "R. W. B.," i. 381).
†† Descent of Ishtar, "Records of the Past," i. 141. Botta found seven rude figures buried under the thresholds of doors.
‡‡ The Targum understands it "for a moment."
§§ The wish was quite natural. It is needless to follow Rashi, etc., in making this an address to God, as though it were a prayer to Him that ruin might fall on His enemy Nebuchadrezzar. Comp. Ov., "Fast.," iii. 494: "Eveniat nostris hostibus ille color."

The king would regard it as a sort of appeal to the averting deities (the Roman *Dî Averrunci*), and as analogous to the current formula of his hymns, "From the noxious spirit may the King of heaven and the king of earth preserve thee!"* He then proceeds to tell the king that the fair, stately, sheltering tree—"it is thou, O king"; and the interpretation of the doom pronounced upon it that he should be driven from men, and should dwell with the beasts of the field, and be reduced to eat grass like the oxen, and be wet with the dew of heaven, "and seven times shall pass over thee, till thou shalt know that the Most High ruleth in the kingdom of men, and giveth it to whomsoever He will." But as the stump of the tree was to be left in the fresh green grass, so the kingdom should be restored to him when he had learnt that the Heavens do rule.

The only feature of the dream which is left uninterpreted is the binding of the stump with bands of iron and brass. Most commentators follow Jerome in making it refer to the fetters with which maniacs are bound,† but there is no evidence that Nebuchadrezzar was so restrained, and the bands round the stump are for its protection from injury. This seems preferable to the view which explains them as "the stern and crushing sentence under which the king is to lie."‡ Josephus and the Jewish exegetes take the "seven times" to be "seven years"; but the phrase is vague, and the event is evidently represented as taking place at the close of the king's reign. Instead of using the awful name of Jehovah, the prophet uses the distant periphrases of "the Heavens." It was a phrase which became common in later Jewish literature, and a Babylonian king would be familiar with it; for in the inscriptions we find Maruduk addressed as the "great Heavens," the father of the gods.§

Having faithfully interpreted the fearful warning of the dream, Daniel points out that the menaces of doom are sometimes conditional, and may be averted or delayed. "Wherefore," he says, "O king, let my counsel be acceptable unto thee, and break off thy sins by righteousness, and thine iniquities by showing mercy to the poor; if so be there may be a healing of thy error."‖

This pious exhortation of Daniel has been severely criticised from opposite directions.

The Jewish Rabbis, in the very spirit of bigotry and false religion, said that Daniel was subsequently thrown into the den of lions to punish him for the crime of tendering good advice to Nebuchadrezzar;¶ and, moreover, the advice could not be of any real use; "for even if the nations of the world do righteousness and mercy to prolong their dominion, it is only sin to them."**

On the other hand, the Roman Catholics have made it their chief support for the doctrine of good works, which is so severely condemned in the twelfth of our Articles.

Probably no such theological questions re-

* "Records of the Past," i. 133.
† Mark v. 3.
‡ Bevan, p. 92.
§ In the "Mishnah" often *Shamayim*; N. T., ἡ βασίλεια τῶν οὐρανῶν.
‖ Or, as in A. V. and Hitzig, "if it may be a lengthening of thy tranquillity"; but Ewald reads *arukah*, "healing" (Isa. lviii. 8), for *ar'kah*.
¶ "Baba Bathra," f. 4, 1.
** "Berachôth," f. 10, 2: f. 57, 2.

motely entered into the mind of the writer. Perhaps the words should be rendered "break off thy sins by righteousness," rather than (as Theodotion renders them) "redeem thy sins by almsgiving." * It is, however, certain that among the Pharisees and the later Rabbis there was a grievous limitation of the sense of the word *tzedakah*, "righteousness," to mean merely almsgiving. In Matt. vi. 1 it is well known that the reading "alms" (ἐλεημοσύνην) has in the received text displaced the reading "righteousness" (δικαιοσύνην); and in the Talmud "righteousness"—like our shrunken misuse of the word "charity"—means almsgiving. The value of "alms" has often been extravagantly exalted. Thus we read: "Whoever shears his substance for the poor escapes the condemnation of hell" ("Nedarim," f. 22, 1).

In "Baba Bathra," f. 10, 1, and "Rosh Hashanah," f. 16, 2, we have "*alms* delivered from death," as a gloss on the meaning of Prov. xi. 4.†

We cannot tell that the writer shared these views. He probably meant no more than that cruelty and injustice were the chief vices of despots, and that the only way to avert a threatened calamity was by repenting of them. The necessity for compassion in the abstract was recognised even by the most brutal Assyrian kings.

We are next told the fulfilment of the dark dream. The interpretation had been meant to warn the king; but the warning was soon forgotten by one arrayed in such absolutism of imperial power. The intoxication of pride had become habitual in his heart, and twelve months sufficed to obliterate all solemn thoughts. The Septuagint adds that "he kept the words in his heart"; but the absence of any mention of rewards or honours paid to Daniel is perhaps a sign that he was rather offended that impressed.

A year later he was walking on the flat roof of the great palace of the kingdom of Babylon. The sight of that golden city in the zenith of its splendour may well have dazzled the soul of its founder. He tells us in an inscription that he regarded that city as the apple of his eye, and that the palace was its most glorious ornament.‡ It was in the centre of the whole country; it covered a vast space, and was visible far and wide. It was built of brick and bitumen, enriched with cedar and iron, decorated with inscriptions and paintings. The tower "contained the treasures of my imperishable royalty; and silver, gold, metals, gems, nameless and priceless, and immense treasures of rare value," had been lavished upon it. Begun "in a happy month, and on an auspicious day," it had been finished in fifteen days by armies of slaves. This palace and its celebrated hanging gardens were one of the wonders of the world.

Beyond this superb edifice, where now the hyena prowls amid miles of *débris* and mounds of ruin, and where the bittern builds amid pools of water, lay the unequalled city Its walls were three hundred and eighty feet high and eighty-five feet thick, and each side of the quadrilateral they enclosed was fifteen miles in length. The mighty Euphrates flowed through the midst of the city, which is said to have covered a space of two hundred square miles; and on its farther bank, terrace above terrace, up to its central altar, rose the huge Temple of Bel, with all its dependent temples and palaces.* The vast circuit of the walls enclosed no mere wilderness of houses, but there were interspaces of gardens, and palm-groves, and orchards, and corn-land, sufficient to maintain the whole population. Here and there rose the temples reared to Nebo, and Sin the moon-god, and Mylitta, and Nana, and Samas, and other deities; and there were aqueducts or conduits for water, and forts and palaces; and the walls were pierced with a hundred brazen gates. When Milton wanted to find some parallel to the city of Pandemonium in "Paradise Lost," he could only say,—

> "Not Babylon,
> Nor great Alcairo such magnificence
> Equall'd in all their glories, to enshrine
> Belus or Serapis their gods, or seat
> Their kings, when Egypt with Assyria strove
> In wealth and luxury."

Babylon, to use the phrase of Aristotle, included, not a city, but a nation.†

Enchanted by the glorious spectacle of this house of his royalty and abode of his majesty, the despot exclaimed almost in the words of some of his own inscriptions, "Is not this great Babylon, that I have built for the house of the kingdom by the might of my treasures and for the honour of my majesty?"

The Bible always represents to us that pride and arrogant self-confidence are an offence against God. The doom fell on Nebuchadrezzar "while the haughty boast was still in the king's mouth." The suddenness of the Nemesis of pride is closely paralleled by the scene in the Acts of the Apostles in which Herod Agrippa I. is represented as entering the theatre at Cæsarea to receive the deputies of Tyre and Sidon. He was clad, says Josephus, in a robe of intertissued silver, and when the sun shone upon it he was surrounded with a blaze of splendour. Struck by the scene, the people, when he had ended his harangue to them, shouted, "It is the voice of a god, and not of a man!" Herod, too, in the story of Josephus, had received, just before, an ominous warning; but it came to him in vain. He accepted the blasphemous adulation, and immediately, smitten by the angel of God, he was eaten of worms, and in three days was dead.‡

And something like this we see again and again in what the late Bishop Thirlwall called the "irony of history"—the very cases in which men seem to have been elevated to the very summit of power only to heighten the dreadful precipice over which they immediately fall. He mentions the cases of Persia, which was on the verge of ruin, when with lordly arrogance she dictated the Peace of Antalcidas; of Boniface VIII., in the Jubilee of 1300, immediately preceding his deadly overthrow; of Spain, under Philip II., struck down by the ruin of the Armada at the zenith of her wealth and pride. He might have added the instances of Ahab, Sennacherib, Nebu-

* Theodot., τὰς ἁμαρτίας σου ἐν ἐλεημοσύναις λύτρωσαι; Vulg., *peccata tua eleemosynis redime*. Comp. Psalm cxii. 9. This exaltation of almsgiving is a characteristic of later Judaism (Ecclus. iv. 5-10; Tobit iv. 11).

† Comp. Prov. x. 2, xvi. 6; "Sukka," f. 49, 2. The theological and ethical question involved is discussed by Calvin, "Instt.," iii. 4; Bellarmine, "De Pœnitent.," ii. 6 (Behrmann).

‡ It is now called Kasr, but the Arabs call it *Mujelibé*, "The Ruined."

* Birs-Nimrod (Grote, "Hist. of Greece," III., chap. xix.; Layard, "Nin. and Bab.," chap. ii.).

† Arist., "Polit.," III. i. 12. He says that three days after its capture some of its inhabitants were still unaware of the fact.

‡ Acts xii. 20-23; Jos., "Antt.," XIV. viii. 2.

chadrezzar, and Herod Antipas; of Alexander the Great, dying as the fool dieth, drunken and miserable, in the supreme hour of his conquests; of Napoleon, hurled into the dust, first by the retreat from Moscow, then by the overthrow at Waterloo.

"While the word was yet in the king's mouth, there fell a voice from heaven." It was what the Talmudists alluded to so frequently as the "Bath Qôl," or "daughter of a voice," which came sometimes for the consolation of suffering, sometimes for the admonition of overweening arrogance. It announced to him the fulfilment of the dream and its interpretation. As with one lightning-flash the glorious cedar was blasted, its leaves scattered, its fruits destroyed, its shelter reduced to burning and barrenness. Then somehow the man's heart was taken from him. He was driven forth to dwell among the beasts of the field, to eat grass like oxen. Taking himself for an animal in his degrading humiliation he lived in the open field. The dews of heaven fell upon him. His unkempt locks grew rough like eagles' feathers, his uncut nails like claws. In this condition he remained till "seven times"—some vague and sacred cycle of days—passed over him.

His penalty was nothing absolutely abnormal. His illness is well known to science and national tradition as that form of hypochondriasis in which a man takes himself for a wolf (lycanthropy), or a dog (kynanthropy), or some other animal.* Probably the fifth-century monks, who were known as "Boskoi," from feeding on grass, may have been, in many cases, half maniacs who in time took themselves for oxen. Cornill, so far as I know, is the first to point out the curious circumstance that a notion as to the points of analogy between Nebuchad*n*ezzar (thus spelt) and Antiochus Epiphanes may have been strengthened by the Jewish method of mystic commentary known in the Talmud as "Gematria," and in Greek as "Isopsephism." That such methods, in other forms, were known and practised in early times we find from the substitution of Sheshach for Babel in Jer. xxv. 26, li. 41, and of Tabeal (by some cryptogram) for Remaliah in Isa. vii. 6; and of *lebh kamai* ("them that dwell in the midst of them") for *Kasdîm* (Chaldeans) in Jer. li. 1. These forms are only explicable by the interchange of letters known as Athbash, Albam, etc. Now Nebuchadnezzar = 423:—

נ = 50; ב = 2; ו = 6; כ = 20; ד = 4;
נ = 50; א = 1; צ = 90; ר = 200 = 423.

And Antiochus Epiphanes = 423:—

א = 1; נ = 50; ט = 9; י = 10; ו = 6;
כ = 20; ו = 6; ס = 60 = . . 162 }
א = 1; פ = 70; י = 10; פ = 70; נ = 50; } = 423.
ס = 60 = ... 261 }

The madness of Antiochus was recognised in the popular change of his name from Epiphanes to Epimanes. But there were obvious points of resemblance between these potentates. Both of them conquered Jerusalem. Both of them robbed the Temple of its holy vessels. Both of them were liable to madness. Both of them tried to dictate the religion of their subjects.

* For further information on this subject I may refer to my paper on "Rabbinic Exegesis," *Expositor*, v. 362-378. The fact that there are slight variations in spelling Nebuchad*n*ezzar and Antiochus Epiphanes is of no importance.

What happened to the kingdom of Babylon during the interim is a point with which the writer does not trouble himself. It formed no part of his story or of his moral. There is, however, no difficulty in supposing that the chief mages and courtiers may have continued to rule in the king's name—a course rendered all the more easy by the extreme seclusion in which most Eastern monarchs pass their lives, often unseen by their subjects from one year's end to the other. Alike in ancient days as in modern—witness the cases of Charles VI. of France, Christian VII. of Denmark, George III. of England, and Otho of Bavaria—a king's madness is not allowed to interfere with the normal administration of the kingdom.

When the seven "times"—whether years or brief periods—were concluded, Nebuchadrezzar "lifted up his eyes to heaven," and his understanding returned to him. No further light is thrown on his recovery, which (as is not infrequently the case in madness) was as sudden as his aberration. Perhaps the calm of the infinite azure over his head flowed into his troubled soul, and reminded him that (as the inscriptions say) "the Heavens" are "the father of the gods." * At any rate, with that upward glance came the restoration of his reason.

He instantly blessed the Most High, "and praised and honoured Him who liveth for ever, whose dominion is an everlasting dominion, and His kingdom is from generation to generation.† And all the inhabitants of the earth are reputed as nothing; and He doeth according to His will ‡ in the army of heaven, and among the inhabitants of the earth;§ and none can stay His hand, or say unto Him, What doest Thou?" ‖

Then his lords and counsellors reinstated him in his former majesty; his honour and brightness returned to him; he was once more "that head of gold" in his kingdom.¶

He concludes the story with the words: "Now I Nebuchadnezzar praise and extol and honour the King of heaven, all whose works are truth and His ways judgment; ** and those that walk in pride He is able to abase."††

He died B. C. 561, and was deified, leaving behind him an invincible name.

CHAPTER XV.

THE FIERY INSCRIPTION.

In this chapter again we have another magnificent fresco-picture, intended, as was the last—but under circumstances of aggravated guilt and more terrible menace—to teach the lesson that "verily there is a God that judgeth the earth."

The truest way to enjoy the chapter, and to grasp the lessons which it is meant to inculcate in their proper force and vividness, is to consider it wholly apart from the difficulties as to

* Psalm cxxiii. 1. See Eurypides, "Bacchæ," 699.
† Exod. xvii. 16.
‡ Psalm cxlv. 13.
§ Isa. xxiv. 21, xl. 15, 17. For the "host of heaven" (στρατία οὐράνιος, Luke ii. 13) see Isa. xl. 26; Job xxxviii. 7; 1 Kings xxii. 19; Enoch xviii. 14-16; Matt. xi. 25.
‖ Isa. xliii. 13, xlv. 9; Psalm cxxxv. 6; Job ix. 12; Eccles. viii. 4. The phrase for "to reprove" is literally "to strike on the hand," and is common in later Jewish writers.
¶ Dan. ii. 38.
** Psalm xxxiii. 4.
†† Exod. xviii. 11.

its literal truth. To read it aright, and duly estimate its grandeur, we must relegate to the conclusion of the story all worrying questions, impossible of final solution, as to whom the writer intended by Belshazzar, or whom by Darius the Mede.* All such discussions are extraneous to edification, and in no way affect either the consummate skill of the picture or the eternal truths of which it is the symbolic expression. To those who, with the present writer, are convinced, by evidence from every quarter—from philology, history, the testimony of the inscriptions, and the manifold results obtained by the Higher Criticism—that the Book of Daniel is the work of some holy and highly gifted "Chasîd" in the days of Antiochus Epiphanes, it becomes clear that the story of Belshazzar, whatever dim fragments of Babylonian tradition it may enshrine, is really suggested by the profanity of Antiochus Epiphanes in carrying off, and doubtless subjecting to profane usage, many of the sacred vessels of the Temple of Jerusalem.† The retribution which awaited the wayward Seleucid tyrant is prophetically intimated by the menace of doom which received such immediate fulfilment in the case of the Babylonian King. The humiliation of the guilty conqueror, "Nebuchadrezzar the Wicked," who founded the Empire of Babylon, is followed by the overthrow of his dynasty in the person of his "son," and the capture of his vast capital.

"It is natural," says Ewald, "that thus the picture drawn in this narrative should become, under the hands of our author, a true night-piece, with all the colours of the dissolute, extravagant riot, of luxurious passion and growing madness, of ruinous bewilderment, and of the mysterious horror and terror of such a night of revelry and death."

The description of the scene begins with one of those crashing overtures of which the writer duly estimated the effect upon the imagination.

"Belshazzar the king made a great feast to a thousand of his lords, and drank wine before the thousand."‡ The banquet may have been intended as some propitiatory feast in honour of Bel-merodach. It was celebrated in that palace which was a wonder of the world, with its winged statues and splendid spacious halls. The walls were rich with images of the Chaldeans, painted in vermilion and exceeding in dyed attire—those images of goodly youths riding on goodly horses, as in the Panathenaic procession on the frieze of the Acropolis—the frescoed pictures, on which, in the prophet's vision, Aholah and Aholibah, gloated in the chambers of secret imagery.* Belshazzar's princes were there, and his wives, and his concubines, whose presence the Babylonian custom admitted, though the Persian regarded it as unseemly.† The Babylonian banquets, like those of the Greeks, usually ended by a "Kōmos" or revelry, in which intoxication was regarded as no disgrace. Wine flowed freely. Doubtless, as in the grandiose picture of Martin, there were brasiers of precious metal, which breathed forth the fumes of incense;‡ and doubtless, too, there were women and boys and girls with flutes and cymbals, to which the dancers danced in all the orgiastic abandonment of Eastern passion. All this was regarded as an element in the religious solemnity; and while the revellers drank their wine, hymns were being chanted, in which they praised "the gods of gold and silver, of brass, of iron, of wood, and of stone." That the king drank wine before the thousand is the more remarkable because usually the kings of the East banquet in solitary state in their own apartments.§

Then the wild king, with just such a burst of folly and irreverence as characterised the banquets of Antiochus Epiphanes, bethought him of yet another element of splendour with which he might make his banquet memorable, and prove the superiority of his own victorious gods over those of other nations. The Temple of Jerusalem was famous over all the world, and there were few monarchs who had not heard of the marvels and the majesty of the God of Israel. Belshazzar, as the "son" of Nebuchadrezzar, must—if there was any historic reality in the events narrated in the previous chapter—have heard of the "signs and wonders" displayed by the King of heaven, whose unparalleled awfulness his "father" had publicly attested in edicts addressed to all the world. He must have known of the Rab-mag Daniel, whose wisdom, even as a boy, had been found to be superior to that of all the "Chartummîm" and "Ashshaphîm"; and how his three companions had been elevated to supreme satrapies; and how they had been delivered unsinged from the seven-times-heated furnace, whose flames had killed his father's executioners. Under no conceivable circumstances could such marvels have been forgotten; under no circumstances could they have possibly failed to create an intense and profound impression. And Belshazzar could hardly fail to have heard

* The question has already been fully discussed (*supra*, pp. 367-368). The apologists say that—

1. Belshazzar was Evil-merodach (Niebuhr, Wolff, Bishop Westcott, Zöckler, Keil, etc.), as the son of Nebuchadrezzar (Dan. v. 2, 11, 18, 22), and his successor (Baruch i. 11, 12, where he is called Balthasar, as in the LXX.). The identification is impossible (see Dan. v. 28, 31); for Evil-merodach (B. C. 561) was murdered by his brother-in-law Neriglissar (B. C. 559). Besides, the Jews were well acquainted with Evil-merodach (2 Kings xxv. 27; Jer. lii. 31).

2. Belshazzar was Nabunaid (St. Jerome, Ewald, Winer, Herzfeld, Auberlen, etc.). But the usurper Nabunaid, son of a Rab-mag, was wholly unlike Belshazzar; and so far from being slain, he was pardoned, and sent by Cyrus to be Governor of Karmania, in which position he died.

3. Belshazzar was *the son of Nabunaid*. But though Nabunaid *had* a son of the name he was never king. We know nothing of any relationship between him and Nebuchadrezzar, nor does Cyrus in his records make the most distant allusion to him. The attempt to identify Nebuchadrezzar with an unknown Marduk-sar-utsur, mentioned in Babylonian tablets, breaks down; for Mr. Boscawen (*Soc. Bibl.*, in § vi., p. 108) finds that he reigned *before* Nabunaid. Further, the son of Nabunaid perished, not in Babylon, but in Accad.

† See 1 Macc. i. 21-24. He "entered proudly into the sanctuary, and took away the golden altar, and the candlestick of light, and all the vessels thereof, and the table of the showbread, and the pouring vessels, and the vials, and the censers of gold. . . He took also the silver and the gold, and the precious vessels: also he took the hidden treasures which he found," etc. Comp. 2 Macc. v. 11-14; Diod. Sic., XXXI. i. 48. The value of precious metals which he carried off was estimated at one thousand eight hundred silver talents—about £350,000 (2 Macc. v. 21).

‡ The LXX. says "two thousand." Comp. Esther i. 3, 4. Jerome adds, "Unusquisque secundum suam bibit ætatem."

* Ezek xxiii. 15.

† Herod., i. 191, v. 18; Xen., "Cyrop.," V. ii. 28; Q. Curt., V. i. 38. Theodotion, perhaps scandalised by the fact, omits the wives, and the LXX. omits both wives and concubines.

‡ Layard, "Nin. and Bab.," ii. 262-269.

§ Athen., "Deipnos," iv. 145. See the bas-relief in the British Museum of King Assur-bani-pal drinking wine with his queen, while the head of his vanquished enemy, Te-Umman, King of Elam, dangles from a palm-branch full in his view, so that he can feast his eyes upon it. None others are present except the attendant eunuchs.

of the dreams of the golden image and of the shattered cedar, and of Nebuchadrezzar's unspeakably degrading lycanthropy. His "father" had publicly acknowledged—in a decree published "to all peoples, nations, and languages that dwell in all the earth"—that humiliation had come upon him as a punishment for his overweening pride. In that same decree the mighty Nebuchadrezzar—only a year or two before, if Belshazzar succeeded him—had proclaimed his allegiance to the King of heaven; and in all previous decrees he had threatened "all people, nations, and languages" that, if they spake anything amiss against the God of Shadrach, Meshach, and Abed-nego, they should be cut in pieces, and their houses made a dunghill.* Yet now Belshazzar, in the flush of pride and drunkenness,† gives his order to insult this God with deadly impiety by publicly defiling the vessels of His awful Temple,‡ at a feast in honour of his own idol deities!

Similarly Antiochus Epiphanes, if he had not been half mad, might have taken warning, before he insulted the Temple and the sacred vessels of Jerusalem, from the fact that his father, Antiochus the Great, had met his death in attempting to plunder the Temple at Elymais (B. C. 187). He might also have recalled the celebrated discomfiture—however caused—of Heliodorus in the Temple of Jerusalem.§

Such insulting and reckless blasphemy could not go unpunished. It is fitting that the Divine retribution should overtake the king on the same night, and that the same lips which thus profaned with this wine the holiest things should sip the wine of the Divine poison-cup, whose fierce heat must in the same night prove fatal to himself. But even such sinners, drinking as it were over the pit of hell, "according to a metaphor used elsewhere,‖ must still at the last moment be warned by a suitable Divine sign, that it may be known whether they will honour the truth."¶ Nebuchadrezzar had received *his* warning, and in the end it had not been wholly in vain. Even for Belshazzar it might perhaps not prove to be too late.

For at this very moment,** when the revelry was at its zenith, when the whirl of excited self-exaltation was most intense, when Judah's gold was "treading heavy on the lips"—the profane lips—of satraps and concubines, there appeared a portent, which seems at first to have been visible to the king alone.

Seated on his lofty and jewelled throne, which

"Outshone the wealth of Ormuz or of Ind,
Or where the gorgeous East with richest hand
Showers on its kings barbaric pearl and gold,"

his eye caught *something* visible on the white stucco of the wall above the line of frescoes. He saw it over the lights which crowned the huge golden "Nebrashta," or chandelier. The fingers of a man's hand were writing letters on the wall, and the king saw the hollow of that gigantic supernatural palm.

The portent astounded and horrified him. The flush of youth and of wine faded from his cheek; —"his brightnesses were changed"; his thoughts troubled him; the bands of his loins were loosed, his knees smote one against another in his trembling attitude, as he stood arrested by the awful sight.

With a terrible cry he ordered that the whole familiar tribe of astrologers and soothsayers should be summoned. For though the hand had vanished, its trace was left on the wall of the banqueting-chamber in letters of fire. And the stricken king, anxious to know above all things the purport of that strange writing, proclaims that he who could interpret it should be clothed in scarlet, and have a chain of gold about his neck, and should be one of the triumvirs of the kingdom.*

It was the usual resource; and it failed as it had done in every previous instance. The Babylonian magi in the Book of Daniel prove themselves to be more futile even than Pharaoh's magicians with their enchantments.

The dream-interpreters in all their divisions entered the banquet-hall. The king was perturbed, the omen urgent, the reward magnificent. But it was all in vain. As usual they failed, as in very instance in which they are introduced in the Old Testament. And their failure added to the visible confusion of the king, whose livid countenance retained its pallor. The banquet, in all its royal magnificence, seemed likely to end in tumult and confusion; for the princes, and satraps, and wives, and concubines all shared in the agitation and bewilderment of their sovereign.

Meanwhile the tidings of the startling prodigy had reached the ears of the Gebirah—the queen-mother—who, as always in the East, held a higher rank than even the reigning sultana.† She had not been present at—perhaps had not approved of—the luxurious revel, held when the Persians were at the very gates. But now in her young son's extremity, she comes forward to help and advise him. Entering the hall with her attendant maidens, she bids the king to be no longer troubled, for there is a man of the highest rank—invariably, as would appear, overlooked and forgotten till the critical moment, in spite of his long series of triumphs and achievements—who was quite able to read the fearful augury, as he had often done before, when all others had been foiled by Him who "frustrateth the tokens of the liars and maketh diviners mad."‡ Strange that he should not have been thought of, though "the king thy father, the king, I say, thy father, made him master of the whole college of mages and astrologers. Let Belshazzar send for Belteshazzar, and he would untie the knot and read the awful enigma."§

* Dan. iii. 29.

† The Babylonians were notorious for drunken revels. Q. Curt., V. i., "Babylonii maxime in vinum et quæ ebrietatem sequuntur, effusi sunt."

‡ Dan. i. 2. Comp. 1 Macc. i. 21 ff.

§ 2 Macc. iii.

‖ Psalm lv. 15.

¶ Ewald.

** Comp. Dan. iii. 7.

* Doubtless suggested by Gen. xli. 42 (comp. Herod., iii. 20; Xen., "Anab.," I. ii. 27; "Cyrop." VIII. v. 18), as other parts of Daniel's story recall that of Joseph. Comp. Esther vi. 8, 9. The word for "scarlet" or red-purple is *argona*. The word for "chain" (*Q'rî. ham'nîka*) is in Theodotion rendered μανιάκης, and occurs in later Aramaic. The phrase rendered "third ruler" is very uncertain. The inference drawn from it in the "Speaker's Commentary," that Nabunaid was king, and Belshazzar second ruler—is purely nugatory. For the Hebrew word *taltî* cannot mean "third," which would be תְּלִיתַי. Ewald and most Hebraists take it to mean "rule, as one of the board of three." For "triumvir" comp. vi. 2.

† 1 Kings xv. 13. She is precariously identified by the apologists with the Nitocris of Herodotus; and it is imagined that she may have been a daughter of Nebuchadrezzar, married to Nabunaid before the murder of Neriglissar.

‡ Isa. xliv. 25.

§ The word *Qistrîn*, "knots," may mean "hard questions"; but Mr. Bevan (p. 104) thinks there may be an

Then Daniel was summoned; and since the king "has heard of him, that the spirit of the gods is in him, and that light and understanding and excellent wisdom is found in him," and that he is one who can interpret dreams, and unriddle hard sentences and untie knots, he shall have the scarlet robe, and the golden chain, and the seat among the triumvirs, if he will read and interpret the writing.

"Let thy gifts be thine, and thy rewards to another," * answered the seer, with fearless forthrightness: "yet, O king, I will read and interpret the writing." Then, after reminding him of the consummate power and majesty of his father Nebuchadrezzar; and how his mind had become indurated with pride; and how he had been stricken with lycanthropy, "till he knew that the Most High God ruled in the kingdom of men"; and that, in spite of all this, he, Belshazzar, in his infatuation, had insulted the Most High God by profaning the holy vessels of His Temple in a licentious revelry in honour of idols of gold, silver, brass, iron, and stone, which neither see, nor know, nor hear,—for this reason (said the seer) had the hollow hand been sent and the writing stamped upon the wall.

And now what was the writing? Daniel at the first glance had read that fiery quadrilateral of letters, looking like the twelve gems of the high priest's ephod with the mystic light gleaming upon them.

M.	N.	A.
M.	N.	A.
T.	Q.	L.
P.	R.	S.

Four names of weight.†

A Mina.
A Mina.
A Shekel.
A Half-mina.‡

What possible meaning could there be in that? Did it need an archangel's colossal hand, flashing forth upon a palace-wall to write the menace of doom, to have inscribed no more than the names of four coins or weights? No wonder that the Chaldeans could not interpret such writing!

It may be asked why they could not even *read* it, since the words are evidently Aramaic, and Aramaic was the common language of trade. The Rabbis say that the words, instead of being written from right to left, were written κιονηδόν, "pillar-wise," as the Greeks called it, from above downwards: thus—

פ	ת	מ	מ
ר	ק	נ	נ
ס	ל	א	א

Read from left to right, they would look like gibberish; read from above downwards, they became clear as far as the reading was concerned, though their interpretation might still be surpassingly enigmatic.

But words may stand for all sorts of mysterious meanings; and in the view of analogists—as those are called who not only believe in the mysterious force and fascination of words, but even in the physiological quality of sounds—they may hide awful indications under harmless vocables. Herein lay the secret.

A mina! a mina! Yes; but the names of the weights recall the word *m'nah*, "hath numbered": and "God hath numbered thy kingdom and finished it."

A shekel! Yes; *t'qilta:* "Thou hast been weighed in a balance and found wanting."

Peres—a half-mina! Yes; but *p'rîsath:* "Thy kingdom has been divided, and given to the Medes and Persians." *

allusion to knots used as magic spells. (Comp. Sen., "Œdip.," 101, "*Nodosa* sortis verba et *implexos* dolos.") He quotes Al-Baidawi on the Koran, lxiii. 4, who says that "a Jew casts a spell on Mohammed by tying knots in a cord, and hiding it in a well." But Gabriel told the prophet to send for the cord, and at each verse of the Koran recited over it a knot untied itself. See "Records of the Past," iii. 141; and Duke, "Rabb. Blumenlehre," 231.

* So Elisha, 2 Kings v. 16.

† The *Menê* is repeated for emphasis. In the *Upharsîn* (ver. 25) the *u* is merely the "and," and the word is slightly altered, perhaps to make the paronomasia with "Persians" more obvious. According to Buxtorf and Gesenius, *peras*, in the sense of "divide," is very rare in the Targums.

‡ *Journal Asiatique*, 1886. (Comp. Nöldeke, *Ztsch. für Assyriologie*, i. 414-418; Kamphausen, p. 46.) It is M. Clermont-Ganneau who has the credit of discovering what seems to be the true interpretation of these mysterious words. *M'nê* (Heb. *Maneh*) is the Greek μνâ, Lat. *mina*, which the Greeks borrowed from the Assyrians. "Tekel" (in the Targum of Onkelos *tîkla*) is the Hebrew *shekel*. In the "Mishnah" a half-mina is called *peras*, and an Assyrian weight in the British Museum bears the inscription *perash* in the Aramaic character. (See Bevan, p. 106; Schrader, *s. v.* "Mene" in Riehm, "R. W. B.") *Peres* is used for a half-mina in "Yoma," f. 4, 4; often in the Talmud; and in "Corp. Inscr. Sem.," ii. 10 (Behrmann).

* The word occurs in *Perez* Uzza. There still, however, remain some obviously unexplored mysteries about these words. Paronomasia, as I showed long ago in other works, plays a noble and profound part in the language of emotion; and that the interpretation should here be made to turn upon it is not surprising by any means. We find it in the older prophets. Thus in Jer. i. 11, 12: "What seest thou? And I said, I see a rod of *an almond tree*. Then said the Lord unto me, Thou hast well seen: for I will *hasten* My word to perform it." The meaning here depends on the resemblance in Hebrew between *shaqeed*, "an almond tree" ("a wakeful, or early tree"), and *shoqeed*, "I will hasten," or "am wakeful over."

And that the same use of plays on words was still common in the Maccabean epoch we see in the Story of Susanna. There Daniel plays on the resemblance between σχῖνος, "a mastick tree," and σχίσει, "shall cut thee in two"; and πρῖνος, "a holm oak," and πρίσαι, "to cut asunder." We may also point to the fine paronomasia in the Hebrew of Isa. v. 7, Mic. i. 10-15, and other passages. "Such a conceit," says Mr. Ball, "may seem to us farfetched and inappropriate; but the Oriental mind delights in such *lusus verborum*, and the peculiar force of

At this point the story is very swiftly brought to a conclusion, for its essence has been already given. Daniel is clothed in scarlet, and ornamented with the chain of gold, and proclaimed triumvir.*

But the king's doom is sealed! "That night was Belshazzar, king of the Chaldeans, slain." His name meant, "Bel! preserve thou the king!" But Bel bowed down, and Nebo stooped, and gave no help to their votary.

"Evil things in robes of sorrow
  Assailed the monarch's high estate;
Ah, woe is me! for never morrow
  Shall dawn upon him desolate!
And all about his throne the glory
  That blushed and bloomed
Is but an ill-remembered story
  Of the old time entombed."

"And Darius the Mede took the kingdom, being about sixty-two years old."

As there is no such person known as "Darius the Mede," the age assigned to him must be due either to some tradition about some other Darius, or to chronological calculations to which we no longer possess the key.†

He is called the son of *Achashverosh*, Ahasuerus (ix. 1), or Xerxes. The apologists have argued that—

1. Darius was Cyaxares II., father of Cyrus, on the authority of Xenaphon's romance,‡ and Josephus's echo of it.§ But the "Cyropædia" is no authority, being, as Cicero said, a non-historic fiction written to describe an ideal kingdom.‖ History knows nothing of a Cyaxares II.

2. Darius was Astyages.¶ Not to mention other impossibilities which attach to this view, Astyages would have been far older than sixty-two at the capture of Babylon by Cyrus. Cyrus had suppressed the Median dynasty altogether some years before he took Babylon.

3. Darius was the satrap Gobryas, who, so far as we know, only acted as governor for a few months. But he is represented on the contrary as an extremely absolute king, setting one hundred and twenty princes "over the whole kingdom," and issuing mandates to "all people, nations, and languages that dwell in all the earth." Even if such an identification were admissible, it would not in the least save the historic accuracy of the writer. This "Darius the Mede" is ignored by history, and Cyrus is represented by the ancient records as having been the sole and undisputed king of Babylon from the time of his conquest.** "Darius the Mede" probably owes his existence to a literal understanding of the prophecies of Isaiah (xiii. 17) and Jeremiah (li. 11, 28).

We can now proceed to the examination of the next chapter unimpeded by impossible and half-hearted hypotheses. We understand it, and it was meant to be understood, as a moral and spiritual parable, in which unverified historic names and traditions are utilised for the purpose of inculcating lessons of courage and faithfulness. The picture, however, falls far below those of the other chapters in power, finish, and even an approach to natural verisimiltude.

CHAPTER XVI.

STOPPING THE MOUTHS OF LIONS.

On the view which regards these pictures as powerful parables, rich in spiritual instructiveness, but not primarily concerned with historic accuracy, nor even necessarily with ancient tradition, we have seen how easily "the great strong fresco-strokes" which the narrator loves to use "may have been suggested to him by his diligent study of the Scriptures."

The first chapter is a beautiful picture which serves to set forth the glory of moderation and to furnish a vivid concrete illustration of such passages as those of Jeremiah: "Her Nazarites were purer than snow; they were whiter than milk; they were more ruddy in body than rubies; their polishing was of sapphire." *

The second chapter, closely reflecting in many of its details the story of Joseph, illustrated how God "frustrateth the tokens of the liars, and maketh diviners mad; turneth wise men backward, and maketh their knowledge foolish; confirmeth the word of His servant, and performeth the counsel of His messengers." †

The third chapter gives vividness to the promise, "When thou walkest through the fire, thou shalt not be burned, neither shall the flame kindle upon thee." ‡

The fourth chapter repeats the apologue of Ezekiel, in which he compares the King of Assyria to a cedar in Lebanon with fine branches, and with a shadowy shroud, and fair by the multitude of his branches, so that all the trees of Eden that were in the garden of God envied him, but whose boughs were "broken by all the watercourses until the peoples of the earth left his shadow." § It was also meant to show that "pride goeth before destruction, and a haughty spirit before a fall." ‖ It illustrates the words of Isaiah: "Behold, the Lord, the Lord of hosts, shall lop the bough with terror; and the high ones of stature shall be hewn down, and the haughty shall be humbled." ¶

The fifth chapter gives a vivid answer to Isaiah's challenge: "Let now the astrologers, the stargazers, the monthly prognosticators, stand up and save thee from these things which shall come upon thee." ** It describes a fulfilment of his vision: "A grievous vision is declared unto thee; the treacherous dealer dealeth treacherously, and the spoiler spoileth. Go up, O Elam:

all such passages in the Hebrew prophets is lost in our version because they have not been preserved in translation."

As regards the Medes, they are placed *after* the Persians in Isa xxi. 2, Esther i. 3, but generally *before* them.

* LXX., ἔδωκεν ἐξουσίαν αὐτῷ τοῦ τρίτου μέρους; Theodot., ἄρχοντα τρίτον. See *supra*, p. 404.

† The LXX. evidently felt some difficulty or followed some other text, for they render it. "And *Artaxerxes of the Medes* took the kingdom, and Darius full of *days and glorious in old age*." So, too, Josephus ("Antt.," X. xi. 4), who says that "he was called by another name among the Greeks."

‡ "Cyrop.," I. v. 2.

§ "Antt.," X. xi. 4. This was the view of Vitringa, Bertholdt, Gesenius, Winer, Keil, Hengstenberg, Hävernick, etc.

‖ "Ad. Q. Fratr.," i. 8.

¶ The view of Niebuhr and Westcott.

** See Herod., i. 109. The Median Empire fell B. C. 559; Babylon was taken about B. C. 539. It is regarded as "important" that a late Greek lexicographer, long after the Christian era, makes the vague and wholly unsupported assertion that the "Daric" was named after some Darius other than the father of Xerxes! See *supra*, pp. 368-369.

* Lam. iv. 7.
† Isa. xliv. 25, 26.
‡ Isa. xliii. 2.
§ Ezek. xxxi. 2-15.
‖ Prov. xvi. 18.
¶ Isa. x. 33.
** Isa. xlvii. 13.

besiege, O Media."* The more detailed prophecy of Jeremiah had said: "Prepare against Babylon the nations with the kings of the Medes. . . . The mighty men of Babylon have forborne to fight. . . . One post shall run to meet another, and one messenger to meet another, to show the King of Babylon that his city is taken at one end. . . . In their heat I will make their feasts, and I will make them drunken, that they shall rejoice, and sleep a perpetual sleep, and not wake, saith the Lord. . . . How is Sheshach taken! † and how is the praise of the whole earth surprised! . . . And I will make drunk her princes, and her wise men; her captains, and her rulers, and her mighty men; and they shall sleep a perpetual sleep, and not wake, saith the King, whose name is the Lord of hosts."‡

The sixth chapter puts into concrete form such passages of the Psalmist as: "My soul is among lions: and I lie even among them that are set on fire, even the sons of men, whose teeth are spears and arrows, and their tongue a sharp sword"; § and—"Break the jaw-bones of the lions, O Lord"; ‖ and—"They have cut off my life in the dungeon, and cast a stone upon me" ¶:—and more generally such promises as those in Isaiah. "No weapon that is formed against thee shall prosper; and every tongue that shall rise against thee in judgment thou shalt condemn. This is the heritage of the servants of the Lord, and their righteousness is of Me, saith the Lord."**

This genesis of Haggadoth is remarkably illustrated by the apocryphal additions to Daniel. Thus the History of Susanna was very probably suggested by Jeremiah's allusion (xxix. 22) to the two false prophets Ahab and Zedekiah, whom Nebuchadrezzar burnt.†† Similarly the story of Bel and the Dragon is a fiction which expounds Jer. li. 44: "And I will punish Bel in Babylon, and I will bring forth out of his mouth that which he hath swallowed up."‡‡

Hitherto the career of Daniel had been personally prosperous. We have seen him in perpetual honour and exaltation, and he had not even incurred—though he may now have been ninety years old—such early trials and privations in a heathen land as had fallen to the lot of Joseph, his youthful prototype. His three companions had been potential martyrs; he had not even been a confessor. Terrible as was the doom which he had twice been called upon to pronounce upon Nebuchadrezzar and upon his kingdom, the stern messages of prophecy, so far from involving him in ruin, had only helped to uplift him to the supremest honours. Not even the sternness of his bearing, and the terrible severity of his interpretations of the flaming message to Belshazzar, had prevented him from being proclaimed triumvir, and clothed in scarlet, and decorated with a chain of gold, on the last night of the Babylonian Empire. And now a new king of a new dynasty is represented as seated on the throne; and it might well have seemed that Daniel was destined to close his days, not only in peace, but in consummate outward felicity.

* Isa. xxi. 2.
† The word is a cabalistic cryptogram—an instance of *Gematria*—for Babel.
‡ Jer. li. 28-57.
§ Psalm lvii. 4.
‖ Psalm lviii. 6.
¶ Lam. iii. 53.
** Isa. liv. 17.
†† "Sanhedrin," f. 93, 1. See another story in "Vayyikra Rabba." c. xix.
‡‡ "Bereshîth Rabba," § 68.

Darius the Mede began his reign by appointing one hundred and twenty princes over the whole kingdom; * and over these he placed three presidents. Daniel is one of these "eyes" of the king.† "Because an excellent spirit was in him," he acquired preponderant influence among the presidents; and the king, considering that Daniel's integrity would secure him from damage in the royal accounts, designed to set him over the whole realm.

But assuming that the writer is dealing, not with the real, but with the ideal, something would be lacking to Daniel's eminent saintliness, if he were not set forth as no less capable of martyrdom on behalf of his convictions than his three companions had been. From the fiery trial in which their faithfulness had been proved like gold in the furnace, he had been exempt. His life thus far had been a course of unbroken prosperity. But the career of a pre-eminent prophet and saint hardly seems to have won its final crown, unless he also be called upon to mount his Calvary, and to share with all prophets and all saints the persecutions which are the invariable concomitants of the hundredfold reward.‡ Shadrach, Meshach, and Abed-nego had been tested in early youth: the trial of Daniel is reserved for his extreme old age. It is not, it could not be, a *severer* trial than that which his friends braved, nor could his deliverance be represented as more supernatural or more complete, unless it were that they endured only for a few moments the semblable violence of the fire, while he was shut up for all the long hours of night alone in the savage lions' den. There are, nevertheless, two respects in which this chapter serves as a climax to those which preceded it. On the one hand, the virtue of Daniel is of a marked character in that it is *positive*, and not negative—in that it consists, not in rejecting an overt sin of idolatry, but in continuing the private duty of prayer; on the other, the decree of Darius surpasses even those of Nebuchadrezzar in the intensity of its acknowledgment of the supremacy of Israel's God.

Daniel's age—for by this time he must have passed the allotted limit of man's threescore years and ten—might have exempted him from envy, even if, as the LXX. adds, "he was clad in purple." But jealous that a captive Jew should be exalted above all the native satraps and potentates by the king's favour, his colleagues the presidents (whom the LXX. calls "two young men") and the princes "*rushed*" before the king with a request which they thought would enable them to overthrow Daniel by subtlety. Faithfulness is required in stewards;§ and they knew that his faithfulness and wisdom were such that they would be unable to undermine him in any ordinary way. There was but one point at which they considered him to be vulnerable, and that was in any matter which affected his allegiance to an alien worship. But it was difficult to invent an incident which would give them the sought-for opportunity. All polytheisms are as tolerant as their priests will let them be. The worship of the Jews in the Exile was of a neces-

* The LXX. says 127, and Josephus ("Antt.," X xi. 4) says 360 (comp. Esther i. 1, viii. 9, ix. 3). Under Darius, son of Hystaspes, there were only twenty divisions of the empire (Herod., iii. 89).
† Dan. vi. 2: "Of whom Daniel was"—not "*first*," as in A. V, but "*one*," R. V.
‡ Matt. xix. 29.
§ 1 Cor. iv. 2.

sarily private nature. They had no Temple, and such religious gatherings as they held were in no sense unlawful. The problem of the writer was to manage his Haggada in such a way as to make private prayer an act of treason; and the difficulty is met—not, indeed, without violent improbability, for which, however, Jewish haggadists cared little, but with as much skill as the circumstances permitted.

The phrase that they "made a tumult" or "rushed"* before the king, which recurs in vi. 11 and 18, is singular, and looks as if it were *intentionally* grotesque by way of satire. The etiquette of Oriental courts is always most elaborately stately, and requires solemn obeisance. This is why Æschylus makes Agamemnon say, in answer to the too-obsequious fulsomeness of his false wife,—

> "*καί τἀλλα, μὴ γυναικὸς ἐν τρόποις ἐμὲ*
> *ἅβρυνε, μηδὲ βαρβάρου φωτὸς δίκην*
> *χαμαιπετὲς βόαμα προσχάνῃς ἐμοί.*"

> "Besides, prithee, use not too fond a care
> To me, as to some virgin whom thou strivest
> To deck with ornaments, whose softness looks
> Softer, hung round the softness of her youth;
> Ope not the mouth to me, nor cry amain
> As at the footstool of a man of the East
> Prone on the ground: so stoop not thou to me!"

That these "presidents and satraps," instead of trying to win the king by such flatteries and "gaping upon him an earth-grovelling howl," should on each occasion have "rushed" into his presence, must be regarded either as a touch of intentional sarcasm, or, at any rate, as being more in accord with the rude familiarities of license permitted to the courtiers of the half-mad Antiochus, than with the prostrations and solemn approaches which since the days of Deïoces would alone have been permitted by any conceivable "Darius the Mede."

However, after this tumultuous intrusion into the king's presence, "all the presidents, governors, chief chamberlains," present to him the monstrous but unanimous request that he would, by an irrevocable interdict, forbid that any man should, for thirty days, ask any petition of any god or man, on peril of being cast into the den of lions.†

Professor Fuller, in the "Speaker's Commentary," considers that "this chapter gives a valuable as well as an interesting insight into Median customs," because the king is represented as living a secluded life, and keeps lions, and is practically deified! The importance of the remark is far from obvious. The chapter presents no particular picture of a secluded life. On the contrary, the king moves about freely, and his courtiers seem to have free access to him whenever they choose. As for the semi-deification of kings, it was universal throughout the East, and even Antiochus II. had openly taken the surname of *Theos*, the "god." Again, every Jew throughout the world must have been very well aware, since the days of the Exile, that Assyrian and other monarchs kept dens of lions, and occasionally flung their enemies to them.‡ But so far as the decree of Darius is concerned, it may well be said that throughout all history no single parallel to it can be quoted. Kings have very often been deified in absolutism; but not even a mad Antiochus, a mad Caligula, a mad Elagabalus, or a mad Commodus ever dreamt of passing an interdict that no one was to prefer any petition either to God or man for thirty days, except to himself! A decree so preposterous, which might be violated by millions many times a day without the king being cognisant of it, would be a proof of positive imbecility in any king who should dream of making it. Strange, too—though a matter of indifference to the writer, because it did not affect his moral lesson—that Darius should not have noticed the absence of his chief official, and the one man in whom he placed the fullest and deepest confidence.

The king, without giving another thought to the matter, at once signs the irrevocable decree.

It naturally does not make the least difference to the practices or the purposes of Daniel. His duty towards God transcends his duty to man. He has been accustomed, thrice a day, to kneel and pray to God, with the window of his upper chamber open, looking towards the *Kibleh* of Jerusalem; and the king's decree makes no change in his manner of daily worship.

Then the princes "rushed" thither again, and found Daniel praying and asking petitions before his God.

Instantly they go before the king, and denounce Daniel for his triple daily defiance of the sacrosanct decree, showing that "he regardeth not thee, O king, nor the decree that thou hast signed."

Their denunciations produced an effect very different from what they had intended. They had hoped to raise the king's wrath and jealousy against Daniel, as one who lightly esteemed his divine autocracy. But so far from having any such ignoble feeling, the king only sees that he has been an utter fool, the dupe of the worthlessness of his designing courtiers. All his anger was against himself for his own folly; his sole desire was to save the man whom for his integrity and ability he valued more than the whole crew of base plotters who had entrapped him against his will into a stupid act of injustice. All day, till sunset, he laboured hard to deliver Daniel. The whole band of satraps and chamberlains feel that this will not do at all; so they again "rush" to the king to remind him of the Median and Persian law that no decree which the king has passed can be altered. To alter it would be a confession of fallibility, and therefore an abnegation of godhead! Yet the strenuous action which he afterwards adopted shows that he might, even then, have acted on the principle which the mages laid down to Cambyses, son of Cyrus, that "the king can do no wrong." There seems to be no reason why he should not have told these "tumultuous" princes that if they interfered with Daniel they should be flung into the lions' den. This would probably have altered their opinion as to pressing the royal infallibility of irreversible decrees.

But as this resource did not suggest itself to Darius, nothing could be done except to cast Daniel into the den or "pit" of lions; but in sentencing him the king offers the prayer, "May the God whom thou servest continually deliver thee!" Then a stone is laid over the mouth of

*Dan. vi. 6, *char'ggishoo;* Vulg., *surripuerunt regi;* A. V. marg., "came tumultuously." The word is found in the Targum in Ruth i. 19 (Bevan).

† The den (*goob* or *gubba*) seems to mean a vault. The Hebrew word for "pit" is *boor*.

‡ See Layard, "Nin. and Bab.," i. 335, 447, 475; Smith, "Hist. of Assur-bani-pal," xxiv.

the pit, and, for the sake of double security, that even the king may not have the power of tampering with it, it is sealed, not only with his own seal, but also with that of his lords.

From the lion-pit the king went back to his palace, but only to spend a miserable night. He could take no food. No dancing-women were summoned to his harem; no sleep visited his eyelids. At the first glimpse of morning he rose, and went with haste to the den—taking the satraps with him, adds the LXX.—and cried with a sorrowful voice, "O Daniel, servant of the living God, hath thy God whom thou servest continually been able to deliver thee from the lions?"

And the voice of the prophet answered, "O king, live for ever! My God sent His angel, and shut the mouths of the lions, that they should not destroy me; forasmuch as before Him innocency was found in me; and also before thee, O king, have I committed no offence."

Thereupon the happy king ordered that Daniel should be taken up out of the lion-pit; and he was found to be unhurt, because he believed in his God.

We would have gladly spared the touch of savagery with which the story ends. The deliverance of Daniel made no difference in the guilt of his accusers. What they had charged him with was a fact, and was a transgression of the ridiculous decree which they had caused the king to pass. But his deliverance was regarded as a Divine judgment upon them—as proof that vengeance should fall on them. Accordingly, not they only, but, with the brutal solidarity of revenge and punishment which, in savage and semi-civilised races, confounds the innocent with the guilty, their wives and even their children were also cast into the den of lions, and they did not reach the bottom of the pit before "the lions got hold of them and crushed all their bones." * They are devoured, or caught, by the hungry lions in mid-air.

"Then King Darius wrote to all the nations, communities, and tongues who dwell in the whole world, May your peace be multiplied! I make a decree, That in every dominion of my kingdom men tremble and fear before the God of Daniel: for He is the living God, and steadfast for ever, and His kingdom that which shall not be destroyed, and His dominion even unto the end. He delivereth and He rescueth, and He worketh signs and wonders in heaven and in earth, who delivered Daniel from the power of the lions."

The language, as in Nebuchadrezzar's decrees, is purely Scriptural.† What the Median mages and the Persian fire-worshippers would think of such a decree, and whether it produced the slightest effect before it vanished without leaving a trace behind, are questions with which the author of the story is not concerned.

He merely adds that Daniel prospered in the reign of Darius and of Cyrus the Persian.

* Comp. Esther ix. 13, 14; Josh. vii. 24; 2 Sam. xxi. 1-6. The LXX. modifies the savagery of the story by making the vengeance fall only on the *two* young men who were Daniel's fellow-presidents. But comp. Herod., iii. 119; Am. Marcell., xxiii. 6; and "Ob noxam unius omnis propinquitas perit," etc.

† Psalm xxix. 1, x. 16, etc. Professor Fuller calls it "a *Mazdean* colouring in the language"!

PART III.

THE PROPHETIC SECTION OF THE BOOK.

CHAPTER XVII.

VISION OF THE FOUR WILD BEASTS.

We now enter upon the second division of the Book of Daniel—the apocalyptic. It is unquestionably inferior to the first part in grandeur and importance as a whole, but it contains not a few great conceptions, and it was well adapted to inspire the hopes and arouse the heroic courage of the persecuted Jews in the terrible days of Antiochus Epiphanes. Daniel now speaks in the first person,* whereas throughout the historical section of the Book the third person has been used.

In the form of apocalypse which he adopts he had already had partial precursors in Ezekiel and Zechariah; but their symbolic visions were far less detailed and developed—it may be added far more poetic and classical—than his. And in later apocalypses, for which this served as a model, little regard is paid to the grotesqueness or incongruity of the symbols, if only the intended conception is conveyed. In no previous writer of the grander days of Hebrew literature would such symbols have been permitted as horns which have eyes and speak, or lions from which the wings are plucked, and which thereafter stand on their feet as a man, and have a man's heart given to them.

The vision is dated, "In the first year of Belshazzar, King of Babylon." It therefore comes chronologically between the fourth and fifth chapters. On the pseudepigraphic view of the Book we may suppose that this date is merely a touch of literary verisimilitude, designed to assimilate the prophecies to the form of those uttered by the ancient prophets; or perhaps it may be intended to indicate that with three of the four empires—the Babylonian, the Median, and the Persian—Daniel had a personal acquaintance. Beyond this we can see no significance in the date; for the predictions which are here recorded have none of that immediate relation to the year in which they originated which we see in the writings of Isaiah and Jeremiah. Perhaps the verse itself is a later guess or gloss, since there are slight variations in Theodotion and the LXX. Daniel, we are told, both saw and wrote and narrated the dream.†

In the vision of the night he had seen the four winds of heaven travelling, or bursting forth, on the great sea;‡ and from those tumultuous waves came four immense wild beasts, each unlike the other.

The first was a lion, with four eagles' wings. The wings were plucked off, and it then raised

* Except in the heading of chap. x.

† In the opinion of Lagarde and others this chapter—which is not noticed by Josephus, and which Meinhold thinks cannot have been written by the author of chap. ii., since it says nothing of the sufferings or deliverance of Israel—did not belong to the original form of the Book. Lagarde thinks that it was written A. D. 69, after the persecution of the Christians by Nero.

‡ St. Ephræm Syrus says, "The sea is the world." Isa. xvii. 12, xxvii. 1, xxxii. 2. But compare Dan. vii. 17; Ezek. xxix. 3; Rev. xiii. 1, xvii. 1-8, xxi. 1.

itself from the earth, stood on its feet like a man, and a man's heart was given to it.

The second was like a bear, raising itself on one side, and having three ribs between its teeth; and it is bidden to "arise and devour much flesh."

The third is a leopard, or panther, with four wings and four heads, to which dominion is given.

The fourth—a yet more terrible monster, which is left undescribed, as though indescribable—has great devouring teeth of iron, and feet that stamp and crush.* It has ten horns, and among them came up a little horn, before which three of the others are plucked up by the roots; and this horn has eyes, and a mouth speaking great things.

Then the thrones were set for the Divine judges,† and the Ancient of Days seats Himself —His raiment as white snow, His hair as bright wool, His throne of flames, His wheels of burning fire. A stream of dazzling fire goes out before Him. Thousand thousands stand before Him; ten thousand times ten thousand minister to Him. The judgment is set; the books are opened. The fourth monster is then slain and burned because of the blaspheming horn; the other beasts are suffered to live for a season and a time, but their dominion is taken away.‡

But then, in the night vision, there came "one even as a son of man" with the clouds of heaven, and is brought before the Ancient of Days, and receives from Him power and glory and a kingdom—an everlasting dominion, a kingdom that shall not be destroyed—over *all people*, nations, and languages.

Such is the vision, and its interpretation follows. The heart of Daniel "is pierced in the midst of its sheath" by what he has seen, and the visions of his head troubled him. Coming near to one of them that stood by—the angelic ministrants of the Ancient of Days—he begs for an interpretation of the vision.

It is given him with extreme brevity.

The four wild beasts represent four kings, the founders of four successive kingdoms. But the ultimate and eternal dominion is not to be with them. It is to be given, till the eternities of the eternities, to "the holy ones of the Lofty One."§

What follows is surely an indication of the date of the Book. Daniel is quite satisfied with this meagre interpretation, in which no single detail is given as regards the first three world-empires, which one would have supposed would chiefly interest the real Daniel. His whole curiosity is absorbed in *a detail* of the vision of the *fourth* monster. It is all but inconceivable that a contemporary prophet should have felt no further interest in the destinies which affected the great golden Empire of Babylon under which he lived, nor in those of Media and Persia, which were already beginning to loom large on the horizon, and should have cared only for an incident in the story of a fourth empire as yet unheard of, which was only to be fulfilled four centuries later. The interests of every other Hebrew prophet are always mainly absorbed, so far as earthly things are concerned, in the immediate or not-far-distant future. That is true also of the author of Daniel, if, as we have had reason to see, he wrote under the rule of the persecuting and blaspheming horn.

In his appeal for the interpretation of this symbol there are fresh particulars about this horn which had eyes and spake very great things. We are told that "his look was more stout than his fellows"; and that "he made war against the saints and prevailed against them, until the Ancient of Days came. Then judgment was given to the saints, and the time came that the saints possessed the kingdom."

The interpretation is that the fourth beast is an earth-devouring, trampling, shattering kingdom, diverse from all kingdoms; its ten horns are ten kings that shall arise from it.* Then another king shall arise, diverse from the first, who shall subdue three kings, shall speak blasphemies, shall wear out the saints, and will strive to change times and laws. But after "a time, two times, and a half,"† the judgment shall sit, and he will be annihilated, and his dominion shall be given for ever to the people of the saints of the Most High.

Such was the vision; such its interpretation; and there can be no difficulty as to its general significance.

I. That the four empires, and their founders, are not identical with the four empires of the metal colossus in Nebuchadrezzar's dream, is an inference which, apart from dogmatic bias, would scarcely have occurred to any unsophisticated reader. To the imagination of Nebuchadrezzar, the heathen potentate, they would naturally present themselves in their strength and towering grandeur, splendid and impassive and secure, till the mysterious destruction smites them. To the Jewish seer they present themselves in their cruel ferocity and headstrong ambition as destroying wild beasts. The symbolism would naturally occur to all who were familiar with the winged bulls and lions and other gigantic representations of monsters which decorated the palace-walls of Nineveh and Babylon. Indeed, similar imagery had already found a place on the prophetic page.‡

II. The turbulent sea, from which the immense beasts emerge after the struggling of the four winds of heaven upon its surface, is the sea of nations.§

III. The first great beast is Nebuchadrezzar and the Babylonian Empire.‖ There is nothing strange in the fact that there should be a certain transfusion or overlapping of the symbols, the object not being literary congruity, but the creation of a general impression. He is represented as a lion, because lions were prevalent in Babylonia, and were specially prominent in Babylonian decorations. His eagle-wings symbolise rapacity and swiftness.¶ But, according to the

* In the vision of the colossus in ii. 41-43 stress is laid on the division of the fourth empire into stronger and weaker elements (iron and clay). That point is here passed over.

† A. V., "the thrones were cast down."

‡ In ii. 35, 44, the four empires are represented as finally destroyed.

§ A. V. marg., "high ones"—*i. e.*, things or places.

* Not kingdoms, as in viii. 8.

† Comp. Rev. xii. 14; Luke iv. 25; James v. 17.

‡ Isa. xxvii 1, li. 9; Ezek. xxix. 3, xxxii. 2.

§ Comp. Job xxxviii. 16, 17; Isa. viii. 7, xvii. 12.

‖ Comp. Dan. ii. 38. Jeremiah had likened Nebuchadrezzar both to the lion (iv. 7, xlix. 19, etc.) and to the eagle (xlviii. 40, xlix. 22). Ezekiel had compared the king (xvii. 3), and Habakkuk his armies (i. 8), as also Jeremiah (iv. 13; Lam. iv. 19), to the eagle (Pusey, p. 690). See too Layard, "Nin. and Bab.," ii. 460. For other beast-symbols see Isa. xxvii. 1, li. 9; Ezek. xxix. 3; Psalm lxxiv. 13.

¶ Comp. Jer. iv. 7, 13, xlix. 16; Ezek. xvii. 3, 12; Hab. i. 8; Lam. iv. 19.

narrative already given, a change had come over the spirit of Nebuchadrezzar in his latter days. That subduing and softening by the influence of a Divine power is represented by the plucking off of the lion's eagle-wings, and its fall to earth. But it was not left to lie there in impotent degradation. It is lifted up from the earth, and humanised, and made to stand on its feet as a man, and a man's heart is given to it.*

IV. The bear, which places itself upon one side, is the Median Empire, smaller than the Chaldean, as the bear is smaller and less formidable than the lion. The crouching on one side is obscure. It is explained by some as implying that it was lower in exaltation than the Babylonian Empire; by others that "it gravitated, as regards its power, only towards the countries west of the Tigris and Euphrates."† The meaning of the "three ribs in its mouth" is also uncertain. Some regard the number three as a vague round number; others refer it to the three countries over which the Median dominion extended—Babylonia, Assyria, and Syria; others, less probably, to the three chief cities. The command, "Arise, devour much flesh," refers to the prophecies of Median conquest,‡ and perhaps to uncertain historical reminiscences which confused "Darius the Mede" with Darius the son of Hystaspes. Those who explain this monster as an emblem, not of the Median but of the Medo-Persian Empire, neglect the plain indications of the Book itself, for the author regards the Median and Persian Empires as distinct.§

V. The leopard or panther represents the Persian kingdom.‖ It has four wings on its back, to indicate how freely and swiftly it soared to the four quarters of the world. Its four heads indicate four kings. There were indeed twelve or thirteen kings of Persia between B. C. 536 and B. C. 333; but the author of the Book of Daniel, who of course had no books of history before him, only thinks of the four who were most prominent in popular tradition—namely (as it would seem), Cyrus, Darius, Artaxerxes, and Xerxes.¶ These are only four names which the writer knew, because they are the only ones which occur in Scripture. It is true that the Darius of Neh. xii. 22 is not the Great Darius, son of Hystaspes, but Darius Codomannus (B. C. 424-404). But this fact may most easily have been overlooked in uncritical and unhistoric times. And "power was given to it," for it was far stronger than the preceding kingdom of the Medes.

VI. The fourth monster won its chief aspect of terribleness from the conquest of Alexander, which blazed over the East with such irresistible force and suddenness.** The great Macedonian, after his massacres at Tyre, struck into the Eastern world the intense feeling of terror which we still can recognise in the narrative of Josephus. His rule is therefore symbolised by a monster diverse from all the beasts before it in its sudden leap out of obscurity, in the lightning-like rapidity of its flash from West to East, and in its instantaneous disintegration into four separate kingdoms. It is with one only of those four kingdoms of the Diadochi, the one which so terribly affected the fortunes of the Holy Land, that the writer is predominantly concerned—namely, the empire of the Seleucid kings. It is in that portion of the kingdom—namely, from the Euxine to the confines of Arabia—that the ten horns arise which, we are told, symbolise ten kings. It seems almost certain that these ten kings are intended for:—

	B. C.
1. Seleucus I. (Nicator) * .	312-280
2. Antiochus I. (Soter) . .	280-261
3. Antiochus II. (Theos) . .	261-246
4. Seleucus II. (Kallinikos) .	246-226
5. Seleucus III. (Keraunos) .	226-223
6. Antiochus III. (Megas) .	223-187
7. Seleucus IV. (Philopator) .	187-176

Then followed the three kings (actual or potential) who were plucked up before the little horn: namely—

	B. C.
8. Demetrius	175
9. Heliodorus	176
10. Ptolemy Philometor . .	181-146

Of these three who succumbed to the machinations of Antiochus Epiphanes, or the little horn,† the first, Demetrius, was the only son of Seleucus Philopator, and true heir to the crown. His father sent him to Rome as a hostage, and released his brother Antiochus. So far from showing gratitude for this generosity, Antiochus, on the murder of Seleucus IV. (B. C. 175), usurped the rights of his nephew (Dan. xi. 21).

The second, Heliodorus, seeing that Demetrius the heir was out of the way, poisoned Seleucus Philopator, and himself usurped the kingdom.

Ptolemy Philometor was the son of Cleopatra, the sister of Seleucus Philopator. A large party was in favour of uniting Egypt and Persia under his rule. But Antiochus Epiphanes ignored the compact which had made Cœle-Syria and Phœnicia the dower of Cleopatra, and not only kept Philometor from his rights, but would have deprived him of Egypt also but for the strenuous interposition of the Romans and their ambassador M. Popilius Lænas.

When the three horns had thus fallen before him, the little horn—Antiochus Epiphanes—sprang into prominence. The mention of his "eyes" seems to be a reference to his shrewdness, cunning, and vigilance. The "mouth that spoke very great things" alludes to the boastful arrogance which led him to assume the title of Epiphanes, or "the illustrious"—which his scornful subjects changed into Epimanes, "the mad"—and to his assumption even of the title Theos, "the god," on some of his coins. His look "was bigger than his fellows," for he inspired the kings of Egypt and other countries with terror. "He made war against the saints," with the aid of "Jason and Menelaus, those ungodly wretches," and "prevailed against them." He "wore out the saints of the Most

* The use of *enôsh*—not *eesh*—indicates chastening and weakness.

† Ewald.

‡ Isa. xiii. 17; Jer. li. 11, 28. Aristotle, "H. N.," viii. 5, calls the bear πάμφαγος, "all-devouring." A bear appears as a dream-symbol in an Assyrian book of auguries (Lenormant, "Magie," 492).

§ Dan. v. 28, 31, vi 8, 12, 15, 28, viii. 20, ix. 1, xi. 1.

‖ The composite beast of Rev. xiii. 2 combines leopard, bear, and lion.

¶ Comp. viii. 4-8.

** Battle of the Granicus, B. C. 334; Battle of Issus, 333; Siege of Tyre, 332; Battle of Arbela, 331; Death of Darius, 330. Alexander died B. C. 323.

* This was the interpretation given by the great father Ephræm Syrus in the first century. Hitzig, Kuenen, and others count from Alexander the Great, and omit Ptolemy Philometor.

† Dan. xi. 21

High," for he took Jerusalem by storm, plundered it, slew eighty thousand men, women, and children, took forty thousand prisoners, and sold as many into slavery (B. C. 170). "As he entered the sanctuary to plunder it, under the guidance of the apostate high priest Menelaus, he uttered words of blasphemy, and he carried off all the gold and silver he could find, including the golden table, altar of incense, candlesticks, and vessels, and even rifled the subterraneous vaults, so that he seized no less than eighteen hundred talents of gold." He then sacrificed swine upon the altar, and sprinkled the whole Temple with the broth.

Further than all this, "he thought to change times and laws"; and they were "given into his hand until a time, and two times, and a half." For he made a determined attempt to put down the Jewish feasts, the Sabbath, circumcision, and all the most distinctive Jewish ordinances. In B. C. 167, two years after his cruel devastation of the city, he sent Apollonius, his chief collector of tribute, against Jerusalem, with an army of twenty-two thousand men. On the first Sabbath after his arrival, Apollonius sent his soldiers to massacre all the men whom they met in the streets, and to seize the women and children as slaves. He occupied the castle on Mount Zion, and prevented the Jews from attending the public ordinances of their sanctuary. Hence in June B. C. 167 the daily sacrifice ceased, and the Jews fled for their lives from the Holy City. Antiochus then published an edict forbidding all his subjects in Syria and elsewhere—even the Zoroastrians in Armenia and Persia—to worship any gods, or acknowledge any religion but his.* The Jewish sacred books were burnt, and not only the Samaritans but many Jews apostatised, while others hid themselves in mountains and deserts.† He sent an old philosopher named Athenæus to instruct the Jews in the Greek religion, and to enforce its observance. He dedicated the Temple to Zeus Olympios, and built on the altar of Jehovah a smaller altar for sacrifice to Zeus, to whom he must also have erected a statue. This heathen altar was set up on Kisleu (December) 15, and the heathen sacrifice began on Kisleu 25. All observance of the Jewish Law was now treated as a capital crime. The Jews were forced to sacrifice in heathen groves at heathen altars, and to walk, crowned with ivy, in Bacchic processions. Two women who had braved the despot's wrath by circumcising their children were flung from the Temple battlements into the vale below.‡

The triumph of this blasphemous and despotic savagery was arrested, first by the irresistible force of determined martyrdom which preferred death to unfaithfulness, and next by the armed resistance evoked by the heroism of Mattathias, the priest at Modin. When Apelles visited the town, and ordered the Jews to sacrifice, Mattathias struck down with his own hand a Jew who was preparing to obey. Then, aided by his strong heroic sons, he attacked Apelles, slew him and his soldiers, tore down the idolatrous altar, and with his sons and adherents fled into the wilderness, where they were joined by many of the Jews.

The news of this revolt brought Antiochus to Palestine in B. C. 166, and among his other atrocities he ordered the execution by torture of the venerable scribe Eleazar, and of the pious mother with her seven sons. In spite of all his efforts the party of the *Chasidîm* grew in numbers and in strength. When Mattathias died, Judas the Maccabee became their leader, and his brother Simon their counsellor.* While Antiochus was celebrating his mad and licentious festival at Daphne, Judas inflicted a severe defeat on Apollonius, and won other battles, which made Antiochus vow in an access of fury that he would exterminate the nation (Dan. xi. 44). But he found himself bankrupt, and the Persians and Armenians were revolting from him in disgust. He therefore sent Lysias as his general to Judæa, and Lysias assembled an immense army of forty thousand foot and seven thousand horse, to whom Judas could only oppose six thousand men.† Lysias pitched his camp at Beth-shur, south of Jerusalem. There Judas attacked him with irresistible valour and confidence, slew five thousand of his soldiers, and drove the rest to flight.

Lysias retired to Antioch, intending to renew the invasion next year. Thereupon Judas and his army recaptured Jerusalem, and restored and cleansed and reconsecrated the dilapidated and desecrated sanctuary. He made a new shew-bread-table, incense-altar, and candlestick of gold in place of those which Antiochus had carried off, and new vessels of gold, and a new veil before the Holiest Place. All this was completed on Kisleu 25, B. C. 165, about the time of the winter solstice, "on the same day of the year on which, three years before, it had been profaned by Antiochus, and just three years and a half—'a time, two times, and half a time'—after the city and Temple had been desolated by Apollonius." ‡ They began the day by renewing the sacrifices, kindling the altar and the candlestick by pure fire struck by flints. The whole law of the Temple service continued thenceforward without interruption till the destruction of the Temple by the Romans. It was a feast in commemoration of this dedication—called the Encænia and "the Lights"—which Christ honoured by His presence at Jerusalem.§

The neighbouring nations, when they heard of this revolt of the Jews, and its splendid success, proposed to join with Antiochus for their extermination. But meanwhile the king, having been shamefully repulsed in his sacrilegious attack on the Temple of Artemis at Elymais, retired in deep chagrin to Ecbatana, in Media. It was there that he heard of the Jewish successes and set out to chastise the rebels. On his way he heard of the recovery of Jerusalem, the destruction of his heathen altars, and the purification of the Temple. The news flung him into one of those paroxysms of fury to which he was liable, and, breathing out threatenings and slaughter, he declared that he would turn Jerusalem into one vast cemetery for the whole Jewish race. Suddenly smitten with a violent

* 1 Macc. i. 29-40; 2 Macc. v. 24-26; Jos., "Antt.," XII. v. 4. Comp. Dan. xi. 30, 31. See Schürer, i. 155 ff.

† Jerome, "Comm. in Dan.," viii., ix.; Tac., "Hist.," v. 8; 1 Macc. i. 41-53, 2 Macc. v. 27, vi. 2; Jos., "Antt.," XII. v. 4.

‡ 1 Macc. ii. 41-64, iv. 54; 2 Macc. vi. 1-9, x. 5; Jos., "Antt.," XII. v. 4; Dan. xi. 31.

* Maccabee perhaps means "the Hammerer" (comp. the names Charles *Martel* and *Malleus hæreticorum*). Simeon was called *Tadshi*, "he increases" (? Gk., Θασσίς).

† The numbers vary in the records.

‡ Prideaux, "Connection," ii. 212. Comp. Rev. xii. 14, xi. 2, 3.

§ John x. 22.

internal malady, he would not stay his course, but still urged his charioteer to the utmost speed.* In consequence of this the chariot was overturned, and he was flung violently to the ground, receiving severe injuries. He was placed in a litter, but, unable to bear the agonies caused by its motion, he stopped at Tabæ, in the mountains of Parætacene, on the borders of Persia and Babylonia, where he died, B. C. 164, in very evil case, half mad with the furies of a remorseful conscience.† The Jewish historians say that, before his death, he repented, acknowledged the crimes he had committed against the Jews, and vowed that he would repair them if he survived. The stories of his death resemble those of the deaths of Herod, of Galerius, of Philip II., and of other bitter persecutors of the saints of God. Judas the Maccabee, who had overthrown his power in Palestine, died at Eleasa in B. C. 161, after a series of brilliant victories.

Such were the fortunes of the king whom the writer shadows forth under the emblem of the little horn with human eyes and a mouth which spake blasphemies, whose power was to be made transitory, and to be annihilated and destroyed unto the end.‡ And when this wild beast was slain, and its body given to the burning fire, the rest of the beasts were indeed to be deprived of their splendid dominions, but a respite of life is given them, and they are suffered to endure for a time and a period.§

But the eternal life, and the imperishable dominion, which were denied to them, are given to another in the epiphany of the Ancient of Days. The vision of the seer is one of a great scene of judgment. Thrones are set for the heavenly assessors, and the Almighty appears in snow-white raiment, and on His chariot-throne of burning flame which flashes round Him like a vast photosphere.‖ The books of everlasting record are opened before the glittering faces of the myriads of saints who accompany Him, and the fiery doom is passed on the monstrous world-powers who would fain usurp His authority.¶

But who is the "one even as a son of man," who "comes with the clouds of heaven," and who is brought before "the Ancient of Days," ** to whom is given the imperishable dominion? That he is not an angel appears from the fact that he seems to be separate from all the ten thousand times ten thousand who stand around the cherubic chariot. He is not a man, but something more. In this respect he resembles the angels described in Dan. viii. 15, x. 16-18. He has "the appearance of a man," and is "like the similitude of the sons of men."††

We should naturally answer, in accordance with the multitude of ancient and modern commentators both Jewish and Christian, that the Messiah is intended; * and, indeed, our Lord alludes to the prophecy in Matt. xxvi. 64. That the vision is meant to indicate the establishment of the Messianic theocracy cannot be doubted. But if we follow the interpretation given by the angel himself in answer to Daniel's entreaty, the personality of the Messiah seems to be at least somewhat subordinate or indistinct. For the interpretation, without mentioning any person, seems to point only to the saints of Israel who are to inherit and maintain that Divine kingdom which has been already thrice asserted and prophesied. It is the "holy ones" (*Qaddîshîn*), "the holy ones of the Most High" (*Qaddîshî Eloînîn*), upon whom the never-ending sovereignty is conferred;† and who these are cannot be misunderstood, for they are the very same as those against whom the little horn has been engaged in war.‡ The Messianic kingdom is here predominantly represented as the spiritual supremacy of the chosen people. Neither here, nor in ii. 44, nor in xii. 3, does the writer separately indicate any Davidic king, or priest upon his throne, as had been already done by so many previous prophets.§ This vision does not seem to have brought into prominence the rule of any Divinely Incarnate Christ over the kingdom of the Highest. In this respect the interpretation of the "one even as a son of man" comes upon us as a surprise, and seems to indicate that the true interpretation of that element of the vision is that the kingdom of the saints is there personified; so that as wild beasts were appropriate emblems of the world-powers, the reasonableness and sanctity of the saintly theocracy are indicated by a human form, which has its origin in the clouds of heaven, not in the miry and troubled sea. This is the view of the Christian father Ephræm Syrus, as well as of the Jewish exegete Abn Ezra; and it is supported by the fact that in other apocryphal books of the later epoch, as in the Assumption of Moses and the Book of Jubilees, the Messianic hope is concentrated in the conception that the holy nation is to have the dominance over the Gentiles. At any rate, it seems that, if truth is to guide us rather than theological prepossession, we must take the significance of the writer, not from the elements of the vision, but from the divinely imparted interpretation of it; and there the figure of "one as a son of man" is persistently (vv. 18, 22, 27) explained to stand, not for the Christ Himself, but for "the holy ones of the Most High,"‖ whose dominion Christ's coming should inaugurate and secure.

The chapter closes with the words: "Here is

*On the death of Antiochus see 1 Macc. vi. 8; 2 Macc. ix.; Polybius, xxxi. 11; Jos., "Antt.," XII. ix. 1, 2.

†Polybius, "De Virt. et Vit.," Exc. Vales, p. 144; Q. Curtius, v. 13; Strabo, xi. 522; Appian, "Syriaca," xlvi. 80; 1 Macc. vi.; 2 Macc. ix.; Jos., "Antt.," XII. ix. 1; Prideaux, ii. 217; Jahn, "Hebr. Commonwealth" § xcvi.

‡Dan. vii. 26.

§Dan. vii. 12. This is only explicable at all—and then not clearly—on the supposition that the fourth beast represents Alexander and the Diadochi. See even Pusey, p. 78.

‖Ezek. i. 26; Psalm l. 3. Comp. the adaptation of this vision in Enoch xlvi. 1-3.

¶Isa. l. 11. lx. 10-12, lxvi. 24, Joel iii. 1, 2. See Rev. i. 13. In the Gospels it is not "a son of man," but generally ὁ υἱὸς τοῦ ἀνθρώπου. Comp. Matt. xvi. 13, xxiv. 30; John xii. 34; Acts vii. 56; Justin, "Dial c. Tryph.," 31.

**Comp. Mark xiv. 62; Rev. i. 7; Hom., "Il.," v. 867, ὁμοῦ νεφέεσσιν.

††Comp. Ezek. i. 26.

*It is so understood by the Book of Enoch; the Talmud ("Sanhedrin," f. 98, 1); the early father Justin Martyr, "Dial. c. Tryph." 31, etc. Some of the Jewish commentators (*e. g.*, Abn Ezra) understood it of the people of God, and so Hofmann, Hitzig, Meinhold, etc. See Behrmann, "Dan.," p. 48.

†Dan. iv. 3, 34, vi. 26. See Schürer, ii. 247; Wellhausen, "Die Pharis. u. Sadd.," 24 ff.

‡Dan. vii. 16, 22, 23, 27.

§Zech. ix. 9.

‖See Schürer, ii. 138-187, "The Messianic Hope": he refers to Ecclus. xxxii. 18, 19, xxxiii. 1-11, xl. 13, l. 24; Judith xvi. 12; 2 Macc. ii. 18; Baruch ii. 27-35; Tobit xiii. 11-18; Wisdom iii. 8, v. 1, etc. The Messianic King appears more distinctly in "Orac. Sibyll.," iii.; in parts of the Book of Enoch (of which, however, xlv.-lvii. are of unknown date); and the Psalms of Solomon. In Philo we seem to have traces of the King as well as of the kingdom. See Drummond, "The Jewish Messiah," pp. 196 ff.; Stanton, "The Jewish and Christian Messiah," pp. 109-118.

the end of the matter. As for me, Daniel, my thoughts much troubled me, and my brightness was changed in me: but I kept the matter in my heart."

CHAPTER XVIII.

THE RAM AND THE HE-GOAT.

THIS vision is dated as having occurred in the third year of Belshazzar; but it is not easy to see the significance of the date, since it is almost exclusively occupied with the establishment of the Greek Empire, its dissolution into the kingdoms of the Diadochi, and the godless despotism of King Antiochus Epiphanes.

The seer imagines himself to be in the palace of Shushan: "As I beheld I was in the castle of Shushan." * It has been supposed by some that Daniel was really there upon some business connected with the kingdom of Babylon. But this view creates a needless difficulty. Shushan, which the Greeks called Susa, and the Persians Shush (now Shushter), "the city of the lily," was "the palace" or fortress (*bîrah* †) of the Achæmenid kings of Persia, and it is most unlikely that a chief officer of the kingdom of Babylon should have been there in the third year of the imaginary King Belshazzar, just when Cyrus was on the eve of capturing Babylon without a blow. If Belshazzar is some dim reflection of the son of Nabunaid (though he never reigned), Shushan was not then subject to the King of Babylonia. But the ideal presence of the prophet there, in vision, is analogous to the presence of the exile Ezekiel in Jerusalem (Ezek. xl. 1); and these transferences of the prophets to the scenes of their operation were sometimes even regarded as bodily, as in the legend of Habakkuk taken to the lions' den to support Daniel.

Shushan is described as being in the province of Elam or Elymais, which may be here used as a general designation of the district in which Susiana was included. The prophet imagines himself as standing by the river-basin (*oobâl*‡) of the Ulai, which shows that we must take the words "in the castle of Shushan" in an ideal sense; for, as Ewald says, "it is only in a dream that images and places are changed so rapidly." The Ulai is the river called by the Greeks the Eulæus, now the Karûn.§

Shushan is said by Pliny and Arrian to have been on the river Eulæus, and by Herodotus to have been on the banks of

"Choaspes, amber stream,
The drink of none but kings."

It seems now to have been proved that the Ulai was merely a branch of the Choaspes or Kerkhah.‖

* Ezra vi. 2; Neh. i. 1; Herod., v. 49; Polyb., v. 48. A supposed tomb of Daniel has long been revered at Shushan.

† Pers., *baru;* Skr., *bura;* Assyr., *birtu;* Gk., βάρις. Comp. Æsch., "Pers.," 554; Herod., ii. 96.

‡ Theodot., οὐβάλ: Ewald. *Stromgebiet*—a place where several rivers meet. The Jews prayed on river-banks (Acts xvi. 13), and Ezekiel had seen his vision on the Chebar (Ezek. i. 1, iii. 15, etc.); but this Ulai is here mentioned because the palace stood on its bank. Both the LXX. and Theodotion omit the word Ulai.

§ "Susianam ab Elymaide disterminat amnis Eulæus" (Plin., "H. N.," vi. 27).

‖ See Loftus, "Chaldæa," p. 346, who visited Shush in 1854; Herzog, "R. E.," *s. v.* "Susa." A tile was found by Layard at Kuyunjik representing a large city between two rivers. It probably represents Susa. Loftus says that the city stood between the Choaspes and the Kopratas (now the Dizful).

Lifting up his eyes, Daniel sees a ram standing eastward of the river-basin. It has two lofty horns, the loftier of the two being the later in origin. It butts westward, northward, and southward, and does great things.* But in the midst of its successes a he-goat, with a conspicuous horn between its eyes,† comes from the West so swiftly over the face of all the earth that it scarcely seems even to touch the ground,‡ and runs upon the ram in the fury of his strength,§ conquering and trampling upon him, and smashing in pieces his two horns. But his impetuosity was shortlived, for the great horn was speedily broken, and four others‖ rose in its place towards the four winds of heaven. Out of these four horns shot up a puny horn,¶ which grew exceedingly great towards the South, and towards the East, and towards the "Glory," *i. e.*, towards the Holy Land.** It became great even to the host of heaven, and cast down some of the host and of the stars to the ground, and trampled on them.†† He even behaved proudly against the prince of the host, took away from him ‡‡ "the daily" (sacrifice), polluted the dismantled sanctuary with sacrilegious arms,§§ and cast the truth to the ground and prospered. Then "one holy one called to another and asked, For how long is the vision of the daily [sacrifice], and the horrible sacrilege, that thus both the sanctuary and host are surrendered to be trampled underfoot?" ‖‖ And the answer is, "Until two thousand three hundred *'erebh-bôqer*, 'evening-morning'; then will the sanctuary be justified."

Daniel sought to understand the vision, and immediately there stood before him one in the semblance of a man, and he hears the distant voice of some one ¶¶ standing between the Ulai—*i. e.*, between its two banks,*** or perhaps between its two branches the Eulæus and the Choaspes—who called aloud to "Gabriel." The archangel Gabriel is here first mentioned in Scripture.†††

* The Latin word for "to butt" is *arietare*, from *aries*, "a ram." It butts in three directions (comp. Dan. vii. 5). Its conquests in the East were apart from the writer's purpose. Crœsus called the Persians ὑβρισταί, and Æschylus ὑπέρκομποι ἄγαν, "Pers." (Stuart). For horns as the symbol of strength see Amos vi. 13; Psalm lxxv. 5.

† Unicorns are often represented on Assyrio-Babylonian sculptures.

‡ 1 Macc. i. 3; Isa. xli. 2; Hosea xiii. 7, 8; Hab. i. 6.

§ Fury (*chemah*), "heat," "violence"—also of *deadly* venom (Deut. xxxii. 24).

‖ A. V., "four *notable* horns"; but the word *chazoth* means literally "a sight of four"—*i. e.*, "four *other* horns" (comp. ver. 8). Grätz reads *achëroth*; LXX., ἕτερα τέσσαρα (comp. xi. 4).

¶ Lit. "out of littleness."

** *Hatstsebî*. Comp. xi. 45; Ezek. xx. 6: Jer. iii. 19; Zech. vii. 14; Psalm cvi. 24. The Rabbis make the word mean "the gazelle" for fanciful reasons ("Taanîth," 69, *a*).

†† The physical image implies the war against the spiritual host of heaven, the holy people with their leaders. See 1 Macc. i. 24–30; 2 Macc. ix. 10. The *Tsebaoth* mean primarily the stars and angels, but next the Israelites (Exod. vii. 4).

‡‡ So in the Hebrew margin (*Q'rî*), followed by Theodoret and Ewald; but in the text (*Kethîbh*) it is, "by him the daily was abolished"; and with this reading the Peshito and Vulgate agree. *Hattamîd*, "the daily" sacrifice; LXX., ἐνδελεχισμός; Numb. xxviii. 3; 1 Macc. i. 39, 45, iii. 45.

§§ The Hebrew is here corrupt. The R. V. renders it, "And the host was given over *to it*, together with the continual *burnt offering* through transgression; and it cast down truth to the ground, and it did *its pleasure* and prospered."

‖‖ Dan. viii. 13. I follow Ewald in this difficult verse, and with him Von Lengerke and Hitzig substantially agree: but the text is again corrupt, as appears also in the LXX. It would be useless here to enter into minute philological criticism. "How long?" (comp. Isa. vi. 11).

¶¶ LXX., φελμωνί; *nescio quis* (Vulg., *viri*).

*** Comp. for the expression xii. 6.

††† We find no names in Gen. xxxii. 30; Judg. xiii. 18.

"Gabriel," cried the voice, "explain to him what he has seen." So Gabriel came and stood beside him; but he was terrified, and fell on his face. "Observe, thou son of man," * said the angel to him; "for unto the time of the end is the vision." But since Daniel still lay prostrate on his face, and sank into a swoon, the angel touched him, and raised him up, and said that the great wrath was only for a fixed time, and he would tell him what would happen at the end of it.

The two-horned ram, he said, the *Baalkeranaîm*, or "lord of two horns," represents the King of Media and Persia; the shaggy goat is the Empire of Greece; and the great horn is its first king—Alexander the Great.†

The four horns rising out of the broken great horn are four inferior kingdoms. In one of these, sacrilege would culminate in the person of a king of bold face,‡ and skilled in cunning, who would become powerful, though not by his own strength.§ He would prosper and destroy mighty men and the people of the holy ones,‖ and deceit would succeed by his double-dealing. He would contend against the Prince of princes,¶ and yet without a hand would he be broken in pieces.

Such is the vision and its interpretation; and though there is here and there a difficulty in the details and translation, and though there is a necessary crudeness in the emblematic imagery, the general significance of the whole is perfectly clear.

The scene of the vision is ideally placed in Shushan, because the Jews regarded it as the royal capital of the Persian dominion, and the dream begins with the overthrow of the Medo-Persian Empire.** The ram is a natural symbol of power and strength, as in Isa. lx. 7. The two horns represent the two divisions of the empire, of which the later—the Persian—is the loftier and the stronger. It is regarded as being already the lord of the East, but it extends its conquests by butting westward over the Tigris into Europe, and southwards to Egypt and Africa, and northwards towards Scythia, with magnificent success.

The he-goat is Greece.†† Its one great horn represents "the great Emathian conqueror." ‡‡ So swift was the career of Alexander's conquests, that the goat seems to speed along without so much as touching the ground.* With irresistible fury, in the great battles of the Granicus (B. C. 334), Issus (B. C. 333), and Arbela (B. C. 331, he stamps to pieces the power of Persia and of its king, Darius Codomannus.† In this short space of time Alexander conquers Syria, Phœnicia, Cyprus, Tyre, Gaza, Egypt, Babylonia, Persia, Media, Hyrcania, Aria, and Arachosia. In B. C. 330 Darius was murdered by Bessus, and Alexander became lord of his kingdom. In B. C. 329 the Greek King conquered Bactria, crossed the Oxus and Jaxartes, and defeated the Scythians. In B. C. 328 he conquered Sogdiana. In B. C. 327 and 326 he crossed the Indus, Hydaspes, and Akesines, subdued Northern and Western India, and—compelled by the discontent of his troops to pause in his career of victory—sailed down the Hydaspes and Indus to the Ocean. He then returned by land through Gedrosia, Karmania, Persia, and Susiana to Babylon.

There the great horn is suddenly broken without hand.‡ Alexander in B. C. 323, after a reign of twelve years and eight months, died as a fool dieth, of a fever brought on by fatigue, exposure, drunkenness, and debauchery. He was only thirty-two years old.

The dismemberment of his empire immediately followed. In B. C. 322 its vast extent was divided among his principal generals. Twenty-two years of war ensued; and in B. C. 301, after the defeat of Antigonus and his son Demetrius at the Battle of Ipsus, four horns are visible in the place of one. The battle was won by the confederacy of Cassander, Lysimachus, Ptolemy, and Seleucus, and they founded four kingdoms. Cassander ruled in Greece and Macedonia; Lysimachus in Asia Minor; Ptolemy in Egypt, Cœle-Syria, and Palestine; Seleucus in Upper Asia.

With one only of the four kingdoms, and with one only of its kings, is the vision further concerned—with the kingdom of the Seleucidæ, and with the eighth king of the Dynasty, Antiochus Epiphanes. In this chapter, however, a brief sketch only of him is furnished. Many details of the minutest kind are subsequently added.

He is called "a puny horn," because, in his youth, no one could have anticipated his future greatness. He was only a younger son of Antiochus III. (the Great). When Antiochus III. was defeated in the Battle of Magnesia under Mount Sipylus (B. C. 190), his loss was terrible. Fifty thousand foot and four thousand horse were slain on the battlefield, and fourteen hundred were taken prisoners. He was forced to make peace with the Romans, and to give them hostages, one of whom was Antiochus the Younger, brother of Seleucus, who was heir to the throne. Antiochus for thirteen years languished miserably as a hostage at Rome. His father, Antiochus the Great, was either slain in B. C. 187 by the people of Elymais, after his sacrilegious plundering of the Temple of Jupiter-Belus;§ or murdered by some of his own attendants whom he had beaten during a fit of drunkenness.‖ Seleucus Philopator succeeded him, and

For the presence of angels at the vision comp. Zech. i. 9, 13, etc. Gabriel means "man of God." In Tobit iii. 17 Raphael is mentioned; in 2 Esdras v. 20. Uriel. This is the first mention of any angel's name. Michael is the highest archangel (Weber, "System.," 162 ff.), and in Jewish angelology Gabriel is identified with the Holy Spirit (*Ruach Haqqodesh*). As such he appears in the Qurân, ii. 91 (Behrmann).

* Ben-Adam (Ezek. ii. 1).

† Comp. Isa. xiv. 9: "All the great goats of the earth." A ram is a natural symbol for a chieftain—Hom., "Il.," xiii. 491–493; Cic., "De Div.," i. 22; Plut., "Sulla," c. 27; Jer. l. 8; Ezek. xxxiv. 17; Zech. x. 3, etc. See Vaux, "Persia," p. 72.

‡ "Strength of face" (LXX., ἀναιδὴς προσώπῳ; Deut. xxviii. 50. etc.). "Understanding dark sentences" (Judg. xiv. 12; Ezek. xvii. 2: comp. v. 12).

§ The meaning is uncertain. It may mean (1) that he is only strong by God's permission; or (2) only by cunning, not by strength.

‖ Comp. 2 Macc. iv. 9-15: "The priests had no courage to serve any more at the altar, but despising the Temple, and neglecting the sacrifices, hastened to be partakers of the unlawful allowance in the place of exercise . . . not setting by the honours of their fathers, but liking the glory of the Grecians best of all."

¶ Not merely the angelic prince of the host (Josh. v. 14), but God—"Lord of lords."

** Comp. Esther i. 2. Though the vision took place under Babylon, the seer is strangely unconcerned with the present, or with the fate of the Babylonian Empire.

†† It is said to be the national emblem of Macedonia.

‡‡ He is called the "King of Javan"—*i. e.*, of the Ionians.

* Isa. v. 26–29. Comp. 1 Macc. i. 3.

† The *fury* of the he-goat represents the vengeance cherished by the Greeks against Persia since the old days of Marathon, Thermopylæ, Salamis, Platæa, and Mycale. Persia had invaded Greece under Mardonius (B. C. 492), under Datis and Artaphernes (B. C. 490), and under Xerxes (B. C. 480).

‡ 1 Macc. vi. 1-16; Macc. ix. 9; Job vii. 6, Prov. xxvi. 20.

§ So Diodorus Siculus (Exc. Vales., p. 293); Justin, xxxii. 2; Jer. "in Dan.," xi.; Strabo, xvi. 744.

‖ Aurel. Vict., "De Virr. Illustr.," c. liv.

after having reigned for thirteen years, wished to see his brother Antiochus again. He therefore sent his son Demetrius in exchange for him, perhaps desiring that the boy, who was then twelve years old, should enjoy the advantage of a Roman education, or thinking that Antiochus would be of more use to him in his designs against Ptolemy Philometor, the child-king of Egypt. When Demetrius was on his way to Rome, and Antiochus had not yet reached Antioch, Heliodorus, the treasurer, seized the opportunity to poison Seleucus and usurp the crown.

The chances, therefore, of Antiochus seemed very forlorn. But he was a man of ability, though with a taint of folly and madness in his veins. By allying himself with Eumenes, King of Pergamum, as we shall see hereafter, he suppressed Heliodorus, secured the kingdom, and "becoming very great," though only by fraud, cruelty, and stratagem, assumed the title of Epiphanes "the Illustrious." He extended his power "towards the South" by intriguing and warring against Egypt and his young nephew, Ptolemy Philometor; * and "towards the Sunrising" by his successes in the direction of Media and Persia; † and towards "the Glory" or "Ornament" (*hatstsebî*)—*i. e.*, the Holy Land.‡ Inflated with insolence, he now set himself against the stars, the host of heaven—*i. e.*, against the chosen people of God and their leaders. He cast down and trampled on them,§ and defined the Prince of the host; for he

"Not e'en against the Holy One of heaven
Refrained his tongue blasphémous."

His chief enormity was the abolition of "the daily" (*tamîd*)—*i. e.*, the sacrifice daily offered in the Temple; and the desecration of the sanctuary itself by violence and sacrilege, which will be more fully set forth in the next chapters. He also seized and destroyed the sacred books of the Jews. As he forbade the reading of the Law—of which the daily lesson was called the *Parashah*—there began from this time the custom of selecting a lesson from the Prophets, which was called the *Haphtarah.*||

It was natural to make one of the holy ones, who are supposed to witness this horrible iniquity,¶ inquire how long it was to be permitted. The enigmatic answer is, "Until an evening-morning two thousand three hundred."

In the further explanation given to Daniel by Gabriel a few more touches are added.

Antiochus Epiphanes is described as a king "bold of visage, and skilled in enigmas." His boldness is sufficiently illustrated by his many campaigns and battles, and his braggart insolence has been already alluded to in vii. 8. His skill in enigmas is illustrated by his dark and tortuous diplomacy, which was exhibited in all his proceedings,** and especially in the whole of his

* He conquered Egypt B. C. 170 (1 Macc. i. 17–20).

† See 1 Macc. iii. 29–37.

‡ Comp. Ezek. xx. 6, "which is the glory of all lands"; Psalm l. 2; Lam. ii. 15.

§ 1 Macc. i. 24–30. Dr. Pusey endeavours, without even the smallest success, to show that many things said of Antiochus in this book do not apply to him. The argument is based on the fact that the characteristics of Antiochus—who was a man of versatile impulses—are somewhat differently described by different authors; but here we have the aspect he presented to a few who regarded him as the deadliest of tyrants and persecutors.

|| See Hamburger, ii. 334 (*s. v.* "Haftara").

¶ Comp. ὀργὴ μεγάλη (1 Macc. i. 64; Isa. x. 5, 25, xxvi. 20; Jer. l. 5; Rom. ii. 5, etc.)

** Comp. xi. 21.

dealings with Egypt, in which country he desired to usurp the throne from his young nephew Ptolemy Philometor. The statement that "he will have mighty strength, but not by his own strength," may either mean that his transient prosperity was due only to the permission of God, or that his successes were won rather by cunning than by prowess. After an allusion to his cruel persecution of the holy people, Gabriel adds that "without a hand shall he be broken in pieces"; in other words, his retribution and destruction shall be due to no human intervention, but will come from God Himself.*

Daniel is bidden to hide the vision for many days—a sentence which is due to the literary plan of the Book; and he is assured that the vision concerning the "evening-morning" was true. He adds that the vision exhausted and almost annihilated him; but, afterwards, he arose and did the king's. business. He was silent about the vision, for neither he nor any one else understood it.† Of course, had the real date of the chapter been in the reign of Belshazzar, it was wholly impossible that either the seer or any one else should have been able to attach any significance to it.‡

Emphasis is evidently attached to the "two thousand three hundred evening-morning" during which the desolation of the sanctuary is to continue.

What does the phrase "evening-morning" (*'erebh-bôqer*) mean?

In ver. 26 it is called "the vision concerning the evening and the morning."

Does "evening-morning" mean a *whole* day, like the Greek νυχθήμερον, or *half* a day? The expression is doubly perplexing. If the writer meant "days," why does he not say "*days,*" as in xii. 11, 12? § And why, in any case, does he here use the solecism *'erebh-bôqer* (*Abendmorgen*), and not, as in ver. 26, "evening *and* morning"? Does the expression mean two thousand three hundred days? or eleven hundred and fifty days?

It is a natural supposition that the time is meant to correspond with the three years and a half ("a time, two times, and half a time") of vii. 25. But here again all certainty of detail is precluded by our ignorance as to the exact length of years by which the writer reckoned; and how he treated the month *Ve-adar*, a month of thirty days, which was intercalated once in every six years.

Supposing that he allowed an intercalary fifteen days for three and a half years, and took the Babylonian reckoning of twelve months of thirty days, then three and a half years gives us twelve hundred and seventy-five days, or, omitting any allowance for intercalation, twelve hundred and sixty days.

* Comp. ii. 34, xi. 45. Antiochus died of a long and terrible illness in Persia. Polybius (xxxi. 11) describes his sickness by the word δαιμονήσας. Arrian ("Syriaca," 66) says φθίνων ἐτελεύτησε. In 1 Macc. vi. 8–16 he dies confessing his sins against the Jews, but there is another story in 2 Macc. ix. 4–28.

† Ver. 27, "I was gone" (or, "came to an end") "whole days." With this ἔκστασις comp. ii. 1, vii. 28; Exod. xxxiii. 20; Isa. vi. 5; Luke ix. 32; Acts ix. 4, etc. Comp. xii. 8; Jer. xxxii. 14, and (*contra*) Rev. xxii. 10.

‡ In ver. 26 the R. V. renders "it belongeth to many days *to come.*"

§ Comp. Gen. i. 5; 2 Cor. xi. 25. The word *tamîd* includes both the morning and evening sacrifice (Exod. xxix. 41). Pusey says (p. 220), "The shift of halving the days is one of those monsters which have disgraced scientific expositions 'of Hebrew.'" Yet this is the view of such scholars as Ewald, Hitzig, Kuenen, Cornill, Behrmann. The latter quotes a parallel: "vgl. im Hildebrandsliede *sumaro ente wintro* sehstie = 30 Jahr."

If, then, "two thousand three hundred evening-morning" means two thousand three hundred *half* days, we have *one hundred and ten days too many* for the three and a half years.

And if the phrase means two thousand three hundred *full* days, that gives us (counting thirty intercalary days for *Ve-adar*) too little for seven years by two hundred and fifty days. Some see in this a mystic intimation that the period of chastisement shall for the elect's sake be shortened.* Some commentators reckon seven years roughly, from the elevation of Menelaus to the high-priesthood (Kisleu, B. C. 168: 2 Macc. v. 11) to the victory of Judas Maccabæus over Nicanor at Adasa, March, B. C. 161 (1 Macc. vii. 25-50; 2 Macc. xv. 20-35).

In neither case do the calculations agree with the twelve hundred and ninety or the thirteen hundred and thirty-five days of xii. 12, 13.

Entire volumes of tedious and wholly inconclusive comment have been written on these combinations, but by no reasonable supposition can we arrive at close accuracy. Strict chronological accuracy was difficult of attainment in those days, and was never a matter about which the Jews, in particular, greatly troubled themselves. We do not know either the *terminus a quo* from which or the *terminus ad quem* to which the writer reckoned. All that can be said is that it is perfectly impossible for us to identify or exactly equiparate the three and a half years (vii. 25), the "two thousand three hundred evening-morning" (viii. 14), the seventy-two weeks (ix. 26), and the twelve hundred and ninety days (xii. 11). Yet all those dates have this point of resemblance about them, that they very roughly indicate a space of *about* three and a half years (more or less) as the time during which the daily sacrifice should cease, and the Temple be polluted and desolate.†

Turning now to the dates, we know that Judas the Maccabee cleansed‡ ("justified" or "vindicated," viii. 14) the Temple on Kisleu 25 (December 25th, B. C. 165). If we reckon back two thousand three hundred *full* days from this date, it brings us to B. C. 171, in which Menelaus, who bribed Antiochus to appoint him high priest, robbed the Temple of some of its treasures, and procured the murder of the high priest Onias III. In this year Antiochus sacrificed a great sow on the altar of burnt offerings, and sprinkled its broth over the sacred building. These crimes provoked the revolt of the Jews in which they killed Lysimachus, governor of Syria, and brought on themselves a heavy retribution.§

If we reckon back two thousand three hundred *half*-days, eleven hundred and fifty *whole* days, we must go back three years and seventy days, but we cannot tell what exact event the writer had in mind as the starting-point of his calculations. The actual time which elapsed from the final defilement of the Temple by Apollonius, the general of Antiochus, in B. C. 168, till its repurification was roughly three years. Perhaps, however—for all is uncertain—the writer reckoned from the earliest steps taken, or contemplated, by Antiochus for the suppression of Judaism. The purification of the Temple did not end the time of persecution, which was to continue, first, for one hundred and forty days longer, and then forty-five days more (xii. 11, 12). It is clear from this that the writer reckoned the beginning and the end of troubles from different epochs which we have no longer sufficient data to discover.

It must, however, be borne in mind that no minute certainty about the exact dates is attainable. Many authorities, from Prideaux* down to Schürer,† place the desecration of the Temple towards the close of B. C. 168. Kuenen sees reason to place it a year later. Our authorities for this period of history are numerous, but they are fragmentary, abbreviated, and often inexact. Fortunately, so far as we are able to see, no very important lesson is lost by our inability to furnish an undoubted or a rigidly scientific explanation of the minuter details.

APPROXIMATE DATES AS INFERRED BY CORNILL AND OTHERS.‡

	B. C.
Jeremiah's prophecy in Jer. xxv. 12	605
Jeremiah's prophecy in Jer. xxix. 10	594
Destruction of the Temple	586 or 588
Return of the Jewish exiles	537
Decree of Artaxerxes Longimanus (Ezra vii. 1)	458
Second decree (Neh. ii. 1)	445
Accession of Antiochus Epiphanes (August, Clinton)	175
Usurpation of the high-priesthood by Jason	175
Jason displaced by Menelaus	172 (?)
Murder of Onias III. (June)	171
Apollonius defiles the Temple	168
War of Independence	166
Purification of the Temple by Judas the Maccabee (December)	165
Death of Antiochus	163

CHAPTER XIX.

THE SEVENTY WEEKS.

THIS chapter is occupied with the prayer of Daniel, and with the famous vision of the seventy weeks which has led to such interminable controversies, but of which the interpretation no longer admits of any certainty, because accurate data are not forthcoming.

The vision is dated in the first year of Darius, the son of Achashverosh, of the Median stock.§ We have seen already that such a person is unknown to history. The date, however, accords well in this instance with the literary standpoint of the writer. The vision is sent as a consolation of perplexities suggested by the writer's study of the Scriptures; and nothing is more naturally imagined than the fact that the overthrow of the Babylonian Empire should have sent a Jewish exile to the study of the rolls of his holy proph-

* Matt. xxiv. 22.
† These five passages agree in making the final distress last during three years and a fraction: the only difference lies in the magnitude of the fraction" (Bevan, p. 127.)
‡ 1 Macc. iv. 41-56; 2 Macc. x. 1-5.
§ See on this period Diod. Sic., "Fr.," xxvi. 79; Liv., xlii. 29; Polyb., "Legat.," 71; Justin, xxxiv. 2; Jer., "Comm. in Dan.," xi. 22; Jahn, "Hebr. Commonwealth," § xciv.; Prideaux, "Connection," ii. 146.

* "Connection," ii. 188.
† "Gesch. d. V. Isr.," i. 155.
‡ Some of these dates are *uncertain*, and are variously given by different authorities.
§ Achashverosh, Esther viii. 10; perhaps connected with "Kshajârsha, "eye of the kingdom" ("Corp. Inscr. Sem.," ii. 125).

ets, to see what light they threw on the exile of his people.

He understood from "the books" the number of the years "whereof the word of the Lord came to Jeremiah the prophet for the accomplishing of the desolation of Jerusalem, even seventy years." * Such is the rendering of our Revisers, who here follow the A. V. ("I understood by books"), except that they rightly use the definite article (LXX., ἐν τοῖς βίβλοις). Such too is the view of Hitzig. Mr. Bevan seems to have pointed out the real meaning of the passage, by referring not only to the Pentateuch generally, as helping to interpret the words of Jeremiah, but especially to Lev. xxvi. 18, 21, 24, 28.† It was there that the writer of Daniel discovered the method of interpreting the "seventy years" spoken of by Jeremiah. The Book of Leviticus had four times spoken of a sevenfold punishment—a punishment "seven times more" for the sins of Israel. Now this thought flashed upon the writer like a luminous principle. Daniel, in whose person he wrote, had arrived at the period at which the literal seventy years of Jeremiah were—on some methods of computation—upon the eve of completion; the writer himself is living in the dreary times of Antiochus. Jeremiah had prophesied that the nations should serve the King of Babylon seventy years (Jer. xxv. 11), after which time God's vengeance should fall on Babylon; and again (Jer. xxix. 10, 11), that after seventy years the exiles should return to Palestine, since the thoughts of Jehovah towards them were thoughts of peace and not of evil, to give them a future and a hope.

The writer of Daniel saw, nearly four centuries later, that after all only a mere handful of the exiles, whom the Jews themselves compared to the chaff in comparison with the wheat, had returned from exile; that the years which followed had been cramped, dismal, and distressful; that the splendid hopes of the Messianic kingdom, which had glowed so brightly on the foreshortened horizon of Isaiah and so many of the prophets, had never yet been fulfilled; and that these anticipations never showed fewer signs of fulfilment than in the midst of the persecuting furies of Antiochus, supported by the widespread apostasies of the Hellenising Jews, and the vile ambition of such renegade high priests as Jason and Menelaus.

That the difficulty was felt is shown by the fact that the Epistle of Jeremy (ver. 2) extends the epoch of captivity to two hundred and ten years (7 × 30), whereas in Jer. xxix. 10 "seventy years" are distinctly mentioned.‡

What was the explanation of this startling apparent discrepancy between "the sure word of prophecy" and the gloomy realities of history?

The writer saw it in a *mystic* or allegorical interpretation of Jeremiah's seventy years. The prophet could not (he thought) have meant seventy *literal* years. The number seven indeed played its usual mystic part in the epoch of punishment. Jerusalem had been taken B. C. 588; the first return of the exiles had been about B. C. 538. The Exile therefore had, from one point of view, lasted forty-nine years—*i. e.*, 7 × 7. But even if seventy years were reckoned from the fourth year of Jehoiakim (B. C. 606?) to the decree of Cyrus (B. C. 536), and if these seventy years could be made out, still the hopes of the Jews were on the whole miserably frustrated.*

Surely then—so thought the writer—the real meaning of Jeremiah must have been misunderstood; or, at any rate, only partially understood. He must have meant, not "years," but *weeks of years—Sabbatical* years. And that being so, the real Messianic fulfilments were not to come till *four hundred and ninety years* after the beginning of the Exile; and this clue he found in Leviticus. It was indeed a clue which lay ready to the hand of any one who was perplexed by Jeremiah's prophecy, for the word שָׁבוּעַ, ἑβδομάς, means, not only the week, but also "seven," and *the seventh year*;† and the Chronicler had already declared that the reason why the land was to lie waste for seventy years was that "the land" was "to enjoy her Sabbaths"; in other words, that, as seventy Sabbatical years had been wholly neglected (and indeed unheard of) during the period of the monarchy—which he reckoned at four hundred and ninety years—therefore it was to enjoy those Sabbatical years continuously while there was no nation in Palestine to cultivate the soil.‡

Another consideration may also have led the writer to his discovery. From the coronation of Saul to the captivity of Zachariah, reckoning the recorded length of each reign and giving seventeen years to Saul (since the "forty years" of Acts xiii. 21 is obviously untenable), gave four hundred and ninety years, or, as the Chronicler implies, seventy unkept Sabbatic years. The writer had no means for an accurate computation of the time which had elapsed since the destruction of the Temple. But as there were four hundred and eighty years and twelve high priests from Aaron to Ahimaaz, and four hundred and eighty years and twelve high priests from Azariah I. to Jozadak, who was priest at the beginning of the Captivity,—so there were twelve high priests from Jozadak to Onias III.; and this seemed to imply a lapse of some four hundred and ninety years in round numbers.§

The writer introduces what he thus regarded as a consoling and illuminating discovery in a striking manner. Daniel, coming to understand for the first time the real meaning of Jeremiah's "seventy years," "set his face unto the Lord

* By "the books" is here probably meant the Thorah or Pentateuch, in which the writer discovered the key to the mystic meaning of the seventy years. It was not in the two sections of Jeremiah himself (called, according to Kimchi, *Sepher Hamattanah* and *Sepher Hagalon*) that he found this key. Jeremiah is here *Yir'myah*, as in Jer. xxvii.–xxix. See Jer. xxv. 11; Ezek. xxxvii. 21; Zech. i. 12. In the Epistle of Jeremy (ver. 2.) the seventy years become seven generations (χρόνος μακρὸς ἕως ἑπτὰ γενεῶν). See too Dillmann's "Enoch," p. 293.

† "Dan.," p. 146. Comp. a similar usage in Aul Gell., "Noct. Att." iii. 10, "Se jam *undecimam annorum hebdomadem* ingressum esse"; and Arist., "Polit.," vii. 16.

‡ See Fritzsche *ad loc.*; Ewald, "Hist. of Isr.," v. 140.

* The writer of 2 Chron xxxv. 17, 18, xxxvi. 21, 22, evidently supposed that seventy years had elapsed between the destruction of Jerusalem and the decree of Cyrus—which is only a period of fifty years. The Jewish writers were wholly without means for forming an accurate chronology. For instance, the Prophet Zechariah (i. 12), writing in the second year of Darius, son of Hystaspes (B. C. 520), thinks that the seventy years were only then concluding. In fact, the seventy years may be dated from B. C. 606 (fourth year of Jehoiakim); or B. C. 598 (Jehoiachin); or from the destruction of the Temple (B. C. 588); and may be supposed to end at the decree of Cyrus (B. C. 536); or the days of Zerubbabel (Ezra v. 1); or the decree of Darius (B. C. 518, Ezra vi. 1–12).

† Lev. xxv. 2, 4.

‡ 2 Chron xxxvi. 21. See Bevan, p. 14.

§ See Cornill, "Die Siebzig Jahrwochen **Daniels," pp.** 14–18.

God, to seek prayer and supplication with fasting and sackcloth and ashes." *

His prayer is thus given:—

It falls into three strophes of equal length, and is "all alive and aglow with a pure fire of genuine repentance, humbly assured faith, and most intense petition." † At the same time it is the composition of a literary writer, for in phrase after phrase it recalls various passages of Scripture.‡ It closely resembles the prayers of Ezra and Nehemiah, and is so nearly parallel with the prayer of the apocryphal Baruch that Ewald regards it as an intentional abbreviation of Baruch ii. 1-iii. 39. Ezra, however, confesses the sins of his nation without asking for forgiveness; and Nehemiah likewise praises God for His mercies, but does not plead for pardon or deliverance; but Daniel entreats pardon for Israel and asks that his own prayer may be heard. The sins of Israel in vv. 5, 6, fall under the heads of wandering, lawlessness, rebellion, apostasy, and heedlessness. It is one of the marked tendencies of the later Jewish writings to degenerate into centos of phrases from the Law and the Prophets. It is noticeable that the name Jehovah occurs in this chapter of Daniel *alone* (in vv. 2, 4, 10, 13, 14, 20); and that he also addresses God as El, Elohim, and Adonai.

In the first division of the prayer (vv. 4-10) Daniel admits the faithfulness and mercy of God, and deplores the transgressions of his people from the highest to the lowest in all lands.

In the second part (vv. 11-14) he sees in these transgressions the fulfilment of "the curse and the oath" written in the Law of Moses, with special reference to Lev. xxvi. 14, 18, etc. In spite of all their sins and miseries they had not "stroked the face" of the Lord their God.

The third section (vv. 15-19) appeals to God by His past mercies and deliverances to turn away His wrath and to pity the reproach of His people. Daniel entreats Jehovah to hear his prayer, to make His face shine on His desolated sanctuary, and to behold the horrible condition of His people and of His holy city. Not for their sakes is He asked to show His great compassion, but because His Name is called upon His city and His people.

Such is the prayer; and while Daniel was still speaking, praying, confessing his own and Israel's sins, and interceding before Jehovah for the holy mountain—yea, even during the utterance of his prayer—the Gabriel of his former vision came speeding to him in full flight at the time of the evening sacrifice. The archangel tells him that no sooner had his supplication begun than he sped on his way, for Daniel is a dearly beloved one. Therefore he bids him take heed to the word and to the vision:—

1. Seventy weeks are decreed upon thy people, and upon thy holy city—

(α) to finish (or "restrain") the transgression;

(β) to make an end of (or "seal up," Theodot. σφραγίσαι) sins;

(γ) to make reconciliation for (or "to purge away") iniquity;

(δ) to bring in everlasting righteousness;

(ε) to seal up vision and prophet (Heb., *nābî* LXX., προφήτην); and

(ζ) to anoint the Most Holy (or "a Most Holy Place"; LXX., εὐφρᾶναι ἅγιον ἁγίων).

2. From the decree to restore Jerusalem unto the Anointed One (or "the Messiah"), the Prince, shall be seven weeks. For sixty-two weeks Jerusalem shall be built again with street and moat, though in troublous times.

3. After these sixty-two weeks—

(α) an Anointed One shall be cut off, and shall have no help (?) (or "there shall be none belonging to him"); *

(β) the people of the prince that shall come shall destroy the city and the sanctuary;

(γ) his end and the end shall be with a flood, and war, and desolation;

(δ) for one week this alien prince shall make a covenant with many;

(ε) for half of that week he shall cause the sacrifice and burnt offering to cease;

(ζ) and upon the wing of abominations [*shall come*] one that maketh desolate;

(η) and unto the destined consummation [*wrath*] shall be poured out upon a desolate one (?) (or "the horrible one").

Much is uncertain in the text, and much in the translation; but the general outline of the declaration is clear in many of the chief particulars, so far as they are capable of historic verification. Instead of being a mystical prophecy which floated purely in the air, and in which a week stands (as Keil supposes) for unknown, heavenly, and symbolic periods—in which case no real information would have been vouchsafed—we are expressly told that it was intended to give the seer a definite, and even a minutely detailed, indication of the course of events.

Let us now take the revelation which is sent to the perplexed mourner step by step.

1. Seventy weeks are to elapse before any perfect deliverance is to come. We are nowhere expressly told that *year-weeks* are meant, but this is implied throughout, as the only possible means of explaining either the vision or the history. The conception, as we have seen, would come to readers quite naturally, since *Shabbath* meant in Hebrew, not only the seventh day of the week, but the seventh year in each week of years. Hence "seventy weeks" means four hundred and ninety years.† Not until the four hundred

* The LXX. and Theodotion, with a later ritual bias, make the *fasting* a means towards the prayer: εὑρεῖν προσευχὴν καὶ ἔλεος ἐν νηστείαις.

† Ewald, p. 278. The first part (vv. 4-14) is mainly occupied with confessions and acknowledgment of God's justice; the last part (vv. 15-19) with entreaty for pardon: *confessio* (vv. 4-14); *consolatio* (vv. 15-19) (Melancthon).

‡ Besides the parallels which follow, it has phrases from Exod. xx. 6; Deut. vii. 21, x. 17; Jer. vii. 19; Psalm xliv. 16, cxxx. 4; 2 Chron. xxxvi. 15, 16. Mr. Deane (Bishop Ellicott's "Commentary," p. 407) thus exhibits the details of special resemblances:—

Dan. ix.	Ezra ix.	Neh. ix.	Baruch.
Verse.	Verse.	Verse.	
4	7	32	...
5	7	33, 34	i. 11
6	7	32, 33	...
7	6, 7	32, 33	i. 15-17
8	6, 7	33	...
9	...	17	...
13	...	...	ii. 7
14	15	33	...
15	...	10	ii. 11
18	...	...	ii. 19
19	...	...	ii. 15

* Perhaps because neither Jason nor Menelaus (being apostate) were regarded as genuine successors of Onias III.

† Numb. xiv. 34; Lev. xxvi. 34; Ezek. iv. 6.

and ninety *years*—the seventy *weeks of years*—are ended will the time have come to complete the prophecy which only had a sort of initial and imperfect fulfilment in seventy *actual* years.

The *precise* meaning attached in the writer's mind to the events which are to mark the close of the four hundred and ninety years—namely, (α) the ending of transgression; (β) the sealing up of sins; (γ) the atonement for iniquity; (δ) the bringing in of everlasting righteousness; and (ε) the sealing up of the vision and prophet (or prophecy *)—cannot be further defined by us. It belongs to the Messianic hope.† It is the prophecy of a time which may have had some dim and partial analogies at the end of Jeremiah's seventy years, but which the writer thought would be more richly and finally fulfilled at the close of the Antiochian persecution. At the actual time of his writing that era of restitution had not yet begun.

But (ϛ) another event, which would mark the close of the seventy year-weeks, was to be "the anointing of a Most Holy."

What does this mean?

Theodotion and the ancient translators render it "*a* Holy of Holies." But throughout the whole Old Testament "Holy of Holies" *is never once used of a person*, though it occurs forty-four times.‡ Keil and his school point to 1 Chron. xxiii. 13 as an exception; but "*Nil agit exemplum quod litem lite resolvit.*"

In that verse some propose the rendering, "to sanctify, as most holy, Aaron and his sons for ever"; but both the A. V. and the R. V. render it, "Aaron was separated that he should sanctify *the most holy things*, he and his sons for ever." If there be a doubt as to the rendering, it is perverse to adopt the one which makes the usage differ from that of every other passage in Holy Writ.

Now the phrase "most holy" is most frequently applied to the great altar of sacrifice.§ It is therefore natural to explain the present passage as a reference to the reanointing of the altar of sacrifice, primarily in the days of Zerubbabel, and secondarily by Judas Maccabæus after its profanation by Antiochus Epiphanes.‖

2. But in the more detailed explanation which follows, the seventy year-weeks are divided into $7 + 62 + 1$.

(α) At the end of the first seven week-years (after forty-nine years) Jerusalem should be restored, and there should be "an Anointed, a Prince."

Some ancient Jewish commentators, followed by many eminent and learned moderns, understand this Anointed One (*Mashiach*) and Prince (*Nagîd*) to be Cyrus; and that there can be no objection to conferring on him the exalted title of "Messiah" is amply proved by the fact that Isaiah himself bestows it upon him (Isa. xlv. 1).

Others, however, both ancient (like Eusebius) and modern (like Grätz), prefer to explain the term of the anointed Jewish high priest, Joshua, the son of Jozadak. For the term "Anointed" is given to the high priest in Lev. iv. 3, vi. 20; and Joshua's position among the exiles might well entitle him, as much as Zerubbabel himself, to the title of *Nagîd* or Prince.*

(β) After this restoration of Temple and priest, sixty-two weeks (*i. e.*, four hundred and thirty-four years) are to elapse, during which Jerusalem is indeed to exist "with street and trench"—but in the straitness of the times.†

This, too, is clear and easy of comprehension. It exactly corresponds with the depressed condition of Jewish life during the Persian and early Grecian epochs, from the restoration of the Temple, B. C. 538, to B. C. 171, when the false high priest Menelaus robbed the Temple of its best treasures. This is indeed, so far as accurate chronology is concerned, an unverifiable period, for it only gives us three hundred and sixty-seven years instead of four hundred and thirty-four:—but of that I will speak later on. The punctuation of the original is disputed. Theodotion, the Vulgate, and our A. V. punctuate in ver. 25, "From the going forth of the commandment" ("decree" or "word") "that Jerusalem should be restored and rebuilt, unto an Anointed, a Prince, are seven weeks, and sixty-two weeks." Accepting this view, Von Lengerke and Hitzig make the seven weeks run *parallel* with the first seven in the sixty-two. This indeed makes the chronology a little more accurate, but introduces an unexplained and a fantastic element. Consequently most modern scholars, including even such writers as Keil, and our Revisers follow the Masoretic punctuation, and put the stop after the seven weeks, separating them entirely from the following sixty-two.

3. After the sixty-two weeks is to follow a series of events, and all these point quite distinctly to the epoch of Antiochus Epiphanes.

(α) Ver. 26.—An Anointed One shall be cut off with all that belongs to him.

There can be no reasonable doubt that this is a reference to the deposition of the high priest Onias III., and his murder by Andronicus (B. C. 171). This startling event is mentioned in 2 Macc. iv. 34, and by Josephus ("Antt.," XII. v. 1), and in Dan. xi. 22. It is added, "*and no . . . to him.*" Perhaps the word "helper" (xi. 45) has fallen out of the text, as Grätz supposes; or the words may mean, "there is no [priest] for it [the people]." The A. V. renders it, "but not for himself"; and in the margin, "and shall have nothing"; or, "and they [the Jews] shall be no more his people." The R. V. renders it, "and shall have nothing." I believe, with Dr. Joël, that in the Hebrew words *veeyn lô* there may be a sort of cryptographic allusion to the name Onias.

(β) The people of the coming prince shall devastate the city and the sanctuary (translation uncertain).

This is an obvious allusion to the destruction and massacre inflicted on Jerusalem by Apollonius and the army of Antiochus Epiphanes (B. C. 167). Antiochus is called "the prince *that shall come*," because he was at Rome when Onias III. was murdered (B. C. 171).

(γ) "And until the end shall be a war, a sen-

* Comp. Jer. xxxii. 11, 44.

† See Isa. xlvi. 3, li. 5, liii. 11; Jer. xxiii. 6, etc.

‡ For the *anointing* of the altar see Exod. xxix. 36, xl. 10; Lev. viii. 11; Numb. vii. 1. It would make no difference in the *usus loquendi* if neither Zerubbabel's nor Judas's altar was *actually* anointed.

§ It is only used thirteen times of the *Debhîr*, or Holiest place.

‖ 1 Macc. iv. 54.

* Hag. i. 1; Zech. iii. 1; Ezra iii. 2. Comp. Ecclus. xlv. 24; Jos., "Antt.," XII. iv. 2, προστάτης; and see Bevan, p. 156.

† We see from Zech. i. 12, ii. 4, that even in the second year of Darius Hystaspis Jerusalem had neither walls nor gates; and even in the twentieth year of Artaxerxes the wall was still broken down and the gates burnt (Neh. 3).

tence of desolation" (Hitzig, etc.); or, as Ewald renders it, "Until the end of the war is the decision concerning the horrible thing."

This alludes to the troubles of Jerusalem until the heaven-sent Nemesis fell on the profane enemy of the saints in the miserable death of Antiochus in Persia.

(δ) But meanwhile he will have concluded a covenant with many for one week.

In any case, whatever be the exact reading or rendering, this seems to be an allusion to the fact that Antiochus was confirmed in his perversity and led on to extremes in the enforcement of his attempt to Hellenise the Jews and to abolish their national religion by the existence of a large party of flagrant apostates. These were headed by their godless and usurping high priests, Jason and Menelaus. All this is strongly emphasised in the narrative of the Book of Maccabees. This attempted apostasy lasted for one week—*i. e.*, for seven years; the years intended being probably the first seven of the reign of Antiochus, from B. C. 175 to B. C. 168. During this period he was aided by wicked men, who said, "Let us go and make a covenant with the heathen round about us; for since we departed from them we have had much sorrow." Antiochus "gave them license to do after the ordinances of the heathen," so that they built a gymnasium at Jerusalem, obliterated the marks of circumcision, and were joined to the heathen (1 Macc. i. 10-15).

(ε) For the half of this week (*i. e.*, for three and a half years) the king abolished the sacrifice and the oblation or meat offering.

This alludes to the suppression of the most distinctive ordinances of Jewish worship, and the general defilement of the Temple after the setting up of the heathen altar. The reckoning seems to be from the edict promulgated some months before December, 168, to December, 165, when Judas the Maccabee reconsecrated the Temple.

(ϛ) The sentence which follows is surrounded with every kind of uncertainty.

The R. V. renders it, "And upon the wing [or, pinnacle] of abominations shall come [or, be] one that maketh desolate."

The A. V. has, "And for the overspreading of abominations" (or *marg.*, "with the abominable armies") "he shall make it desolate."

It is from the LXX. that we derive the famous expression, "abomination of desolation," referred to by St. Matthew (xxiv. 15: *cf.* Luke xxi. 20) in the discourse of our Lord.

Other translations are as follows:—

Gesenius: "Desolation comes upon the horrible wing of a rebel's host."

Ewald: "And above will be the horrible wing of abominations."

Wieseler: "And a desolation shall arise against the wing of abominations."

Von Lengerke, Hengstenberg, Pusey: "And over the edge [or, pinnacle *] of abominations [cometh] the desolator";—which they understand to mean that Antiochus will rule over the Temple defiled by heathen rites.

Kranichfeld and Keil: "And a destroyer comes on the wings of idolatrous abominations."

Kuenen, followed by others, boldly alters the text from *ve'al k'naph*, "and upon the wing," into *ve'al kannô*, "and instead thereof." †

"And instead thereof" (*i. e.*, in the place of the sacrifice and meat offering) "there shall be abominations."

It is needless to weary the reader with further attempts at translation; but however uncertain may be the exact reading or rendering, few modern commentators doubt that the allusion is to the smaller heathen altar built by Antiochus above (*i. e.*, on the summit) of the "Most Holy" —*i. e.*, the great altar of burnt sacrifice—overshadowing it like "a wing" (*kanaph*), and causing desolations or abominations (*shiqqootsîm*) That this interpretation is the correct one can hardly be doubted in the light of the clearer references to "the abomination that maketh desolate" in xi. 31 and xii. 11. In favour of this we have the almost contemporary interpretation of the Book of Maccabees. The author of that history directly applies the phrase "the abomination of desolation" to the idol altar set up by Antiochus (1 Macc. i. 54, vi. 7).

(η) Lastly, the terrible drama shall end by an outpouring of wrath, and a sentence of judgment on "the desolation" (R. V.) or "the desolate" (A. V.).

This can only refer to the ultimate judgment with which Antiochus is menaced.

It will be seen then that, despite all uncertainties in the text, in the translation, and in the details, we have in these verses an unmistakably clear foreshadowing of the same persecuting king, and the same disastrous events, with which the mind of the writer is so predominantly haunted, and which are still more clearly indicated in the subsequent chapter.

Is it necessary, after an inquiry inevitably tedious, and of little or no apparent spiritual profit or significance, to enter further into the intolerably and interminably perplexed and voluminous discussions as to the beginning, the ending, and the exactitude of the seventy weeks? Even St. Jerome gives, by way of specimen, *nine* different interpretations in his time, and comes to no decision of his own. After confessing that all the interpretations were individual guesswork, he leaves every reader to his own judgment, and adds: "Dicam quid unusquisque senserit, lectoris arbitrio derelinquens cujus expositionem sequi debeat."

I cannot think that the least advantage can be derived from doing so.

For scarcely any two leading commentators agree as to details;—or even as to any fixed principles by which they profess to determine the date at which the period of seventy weeks is to begin or is to end;—or whether they are to be reckoned continuously, or with arbitrary misplacements or discontinuations;—or even whether they are not purely symbolical, so as to have no reference to any chronological indications;—or whether they are to be interpreted as referring to one special series of events, or to be regarded as having many fulfilments by "springing and germinal developments." The latter view is, however, distinctly tenable. It applies to all prophecies, inasmuch as history repeats itself; and our Lord referred to another "abomination of desolation" which in His days was yet to come.

There is not even an initial agreement—or even the data as to an agreement—whether the "years" to be counted are solar years of three hundred and forty-three days, or lunar years, or "mystic" years, or Sabbath years of forty-nine years, or "indefinite" years; or where they are to begin and end, or in what fashion they are

* Comp. πτερύγιον (Matt. iv. 5).

† Kuenen, "Hist. Crit. Onderzoek," ii. 472

to be divided. All is chaos in the existing commentaries.

As for any received or authorised interpretation, there not only is none, but never has been. The Jewish interpreters differ from one another as widely as the Christian. Even in the days of the Fathers, the early exegetes were so hopelessly at sea in their methods of application that St. Jerome contents himself, just as I have done, with giving no opinion of his own.

The attempt to refer the prophecy of the seventy weeks primarily or directly to the coming and death of Christ, or the desolation of the Temple by Titus, can only be supported by immense manipulations, and by hypotheses so crudely impossible that they would have made the prophecy practically meaningless both to Daniel and to any subsequent reader. The hopelessness of this attempt of the so-called "orthodox" interpreters is proved by their own fundamental disagreements. It is finally discredited by the fact that neither our Lord, nor His Apostles, nor any of the earliest Christian writers once appealed to the evidence of this prophecy, which, on the principles of Hengstenberg and Dr. Pusey, would have been so decisive! If such a proof lay ready to their hand—a proof definite and chronological—why should they have deliberately passed it over, while they referred to other prophecies so much more general, and so much less precise in dates?

Of course it is open to any reader to adopt the view of Keil and others, that the prophecy is Messianic, but only *typically* and *generally* so.

On the other hand, it may be objected that the Antiochian hypothesis breaks down, because—though it does not pretend to resort to any of the wild, arbitrary, and I had almost said preposterous, hypotheses invented by those who approach the interpretation of the Book with *a-priori* and *a-posteriori* * assumptions—it still does not accurately correspond to ascertainable dates.

But to those who are guided in their exegesis, not by unnatural inventions, but by the great guiding principles of history and literature, this consideration presents no difficulty. Any exact accuracy of chronology would have been far more surprising in a writer of the Maccabean era than round numbers and vague computations. Precise computation is nowhere prevalent in the sacred books. The object of those books always is the conveyance of eternal, moral, and spiritual instruction. To such purely mundane and secondary matters as close reckoning of dates the Jewish writers show themselves manifestly indifferent. It is possible that, if we were able to ascertain the data which lay before the writer, his calculations might seem less divergent from exact numbers than they now appear. More than this we cannot affirm.

What was the date from which the writer calculated his seventy weeks? Was it from the date of Jeremiah's first prophecy (xxv. 12), B. C. 605? or his second prophecy (xxix. 10), eleven years later, B. C. 594? or from the destruction of the first Temple, B. C. 586? or, as some Jews thought, from the first year of "Darius the Mede"? or from the decree of Artaxerxes in Neh. ii. 1-9? or from the birth of Christ—the date assumed by Apollinaris? All these views have been adopted by various Rabbis and Fathers; but it is obvious that not one of them accords with the allusions of the narrative and prayer, except that which makes the destruction of the Temple the *terminus a quo*. In the confusion of historic reminiscences and the rarity of written documents, the writer may not have consciously distinguished this date (B. C. 588) from the date of Jeremiah's prophecy (B. C. 594). That there were differences of computation as regards Jeremiah's seventy years, even in the age of the Exile, is sufficiently shown by the different views as to their termination taken by the Chronicler (2 Chron. xxxvi. 22), who fixes it B. C. 536, and by Zechariah (Zech. i. 12), who fixes it about B. C. 519.

As to the *terminus ad quem*, it is open to any commentator to say that the prediction may point to many subsequent and analogous fulfilments; but no competent and serious reader who judges of these chapters by the chapters themselves and by their own repeated indications can have one moment's hesitation in the conclusion that the writer is thinking mainly of the defilement of the Temple in the days of Antiochus Epiphanes, and its reconsecration (in round numbers) three and a half years later by Judas Maccabæus (December 25th, B. C. 164).

It is true that from B. C. 588 to B. C. 164 only gives us four hundred and twenty-four years, instead of four hundred and ninety years. How is this to be accounted for? Ewald supposes the loss of some passage in the text which would have explained the discrepancy; and that the text is in a somewhat chaotic condition is proved by its inherent philological difficulties, and by the appearance which it assumes in the Septuagint. The first seven weeks indeed, or forty-nine years, approximately correspond to the time between B. C. 588 (the destruction of the Temple) and B. C. 536 (the decree of Cyrus); but the following sixty-two weeks should give us four hundred and thirty-four years from the time of Cyrus to the cutting off of the Anointed One, by the murder of Onias III. in B. C. 171, whereas it only gives us three hundred and sixty-five. How are we to account for this miscalculation to the extent of at least sixty-five years?

Not one single suggestion has ever accounted for it, or has ever given exactitude to these computations on any tenable hypothesis.*

But Schürer has shown that *exactly similar mistakes of reckoning* are made even by so learned and industrious an historian as Josephus.

1. Thus in his "Jewish War" (VI. iv. 8) he says that there were six hundred and thirty-nine years between the second year of Cyrus and the destruction of the Temple by Titus (A. D. 70). Here is an error of more than thirty years.

2. In his "Antiquities" (XX. x.) he says that there were four hundred and thirty-four years between the Return from the Captivity (B. C. 536) and the reign of Antiochus Eupator (B. C. 164-162). Here is an error of more than sixty years.

3. In "Antt.," XIII. xi. 1, he reckons four hundred and eighty-one years between the Return from the Captivity and the time of Aristobulus (B. C. 105-104). Here is an error of some fifty years.

* Thus Eusebius, without a shadow of any pretence at argument, makes the *last week* mean *seventy years!* ("Dem. Evan.," viii.).

* Jost ("Gesch. d. Judenthums," i. 99) contents himself with speaking of "die Liebe zu prophetischer Auffassung der Vergangenheit, mit möglichst genauen Zahlenagaben, befriedigt, *die uns leider nicht mehr verständlich erscheinen*."

Again, the Jewish Hellenist Demetrius * reckons five hundred and seventy-three years from the Captivity of the Ten Tribes (B. C. 722) to the time of Ptolemy IV. (B. C. 222), which is seventy years too many. In other words, he makes as nearly as possible the same miscalculations as the writer of Daniel. This seems to show that there was some traditional error in the current chronology; and it cannot be overlooked that in ancient days the means for coming to accurate chronological conclusion were exceedingly imperfect. "Until the establishment of the Seleucid era (B. C. 312), the Jew had no fixed era whatsoever"; † and nothing is less astonishing than that an apocalyptic writer of the date of Epiphanes, basing his calculations on uncertain data to give an allegoric interpretation to an ancient prophecy, should have lacked the records which would alone have enabled him to calculate with exact precision.‡

And, for the rest, we must say with Grotius, "*Modicum nec prætor curat, nec propheta.*"

CHAPTER XX.

INTRODUCTION TO THE CONCLUDING VISION.

THE remaining section of the Book of Daniel forms but one vision, of which this chapter is the Introduction or Prologue.

Daniel is here spoken of in the third person.

It is dated in the third year of Cyrus (B. C. 535).§ We have already been told that Daniel lived to see the first year of Cyrus (i. 21). This verse, if accepted historically, would show that at any rate Daniel did not return to Palestine with the exiles. Age, high rank, and opportunities of usefulness in the Persian Court may have combined to render his return undesirable for the interests of his people. The date—the last given in the life of the real or ideal Daniel—is perhaps here mentioned to account for the allusions which follow to the kingdom of Persia. But with the great and moving fortunes of the Jews after the accession of Cyrus, and even with the beginning of their new national life in Jerusalem, the author is scarcely at all concerned. He makes no mention of Zerubbabel the prince, nor of Joshua the priest, nor of the decree of Cyrus, nor of the rebuilding of the Temple; his whole concern is with the petty wars and diplomacy of the reign of Antiochus Epiphanes, of which an account is given, so minute as either to furnish us with historical materials unknown to any other historian, or else is difficult to reconcile with the history of that king's reign as it has been hitherto understood.

In this chapter, as in the two preceding, there are great difficulties and uncertainties about the exact significance of some of the verses, and textual emendations have been suggested. The readers of the Expositor's Bible would not, however, be interested in the minute and dreary philological disquisitions, which have not the smallest moral significance, and lead to no certain result. The difficulties affect points of no doctrinal importance, and the greatest scholars have been unable to arrive at any agreement respecting them. Such difficulties will, therefore, merely be mentioned, and I shall content myself with furnishing what appears to be the best authenticated opinion.

The first and second verses are rendered partly by Ewald and partly by other scholars, "*Truth is the revelation, and distress is great; therefore understand thou the revelation, since there is understanding of it in the vision.*" The admonition calls attention to the importance of "the word," and the fact that reality lies beneath its enigmatic and apocalyptic form.

Daniel had been mourning for three full weeks, during which he ate no dainty bread, nor flesh, nor wine, nor did he anoint himself with oil. But in the Passover month of Abib or Nisan, the first month of the year, and on the twenty-fourth day of that month, he was seated on the bank of the great river, Hiddekel or Tigris, when, lifting up his eyes, he saw a certain man clothed in fine linen like a Jewish priest, and his loins girded with gold of Uphaz. His body was like chrysolite, his face flashed like lightning, his eyes were like torches of fire, his arms and feet gleamed like polished brass, and the sound of his words was as the sound of a deep murmur. Daniel had companions with him; they did not see the vision, but some supernatural terror fell upon them, and they fled to hide themselves.

At this great spectacle his strength departed, and his brightness was changed to corruption; and when the vision spoke he fell to the earth face downwards. A hand touched him, and partly raised him to the trembling support of his knees and the palms of his hands, and a voice said to him, "Daniel, thou greatly beloved, stand upright, and attend; for I am sent to thee." The seer was still trembling; but the voice bade him fear not, for his prayer had been heard, and for that reason this message had been sent to him. Gabriel's coming had, however, been delayed for three weeks, by his having to withstand for twenty days the prince of the kingdom of Persia. The necessity of continuing the struggle was only removed by the arrival of Michael, one of the chief princes, to help him, so that Gabriel was no longer needed to resist the kings of Persia. The vision was for many days, and he had come to enable Daniel to understand it.

Once more Daniel was terrified, remained silent, and fixed his eyes on the ground, until one like the sons of men touched his lips, and then he spoke to apologise for his timidity and faintheartedness.

A third time the vision touched, strengthened, blessed him, and bade him be strong. "Knowest thou," the angel asked, "why I am come to thee? I must return to fight against the Prince of Persia, and while I am gone the Prince of Greece (Javan) will come. I will, however, tell thee what is announced in the writing of truth, the book of the decrees of heaven, though there is no one to help me against these hostile princes of Persia and Javan, except Michael your prince."

The difficulties of the chapter are, as we have

* In Clem. Alex., "Strom.," i. 21.

† Cornill, p. 14; Bevan, p. 54.

‡ Schurer, "Hist. of Jewish People," iii. 53, 54 (E. Tr.). This is also the view of Graf, Nöldeke, Cornill, and many others. In any case we must not be misled into an impossible style of exegesis of which Bleek says that "bei ihr alles möglich ist und alles für erlaubt gilt."

§ The LXX. date it in "the *first* year of Cyrus," perhaps an intentional alteration (i. 21). We see from Ezra, Nehemiah, and the latest of the Minor Prophets that there was scarcely even an attempt to restore the ruined walls of Jerusalem before B. C. 444.

said, of a kind that the expositor cannot easily remove. I have given what appears to be the general sense. The questions which the vision raises bear on matters of angelology, as to which all is purposely left vague and indeterminate, or which lie in a sphere wholly beyond our cognisance.

It may first be asked whether the splendid angel of the opening vision is also the being in the similitude of a man who thrice touches, encourages, and strengthens Daniel. It is perhaps simplest to suppose that this is the case, and that the Great Prince tones down his overpowering glory to more familiar human semblance in order to dispel the terrors of the seer.

The general conception of the archangels as princes of the nations, and as contending with each other, belongs to the later developments of Hebrew opinion on such subjects. Some have supposed that the "princes" of Persia and Javan, to whom Gabriel and Michael are opposed, are not good angels, but demoniac powers,—"the world-rulers of this darkness"—subordinate to the evil spirit whom St. Paul does not hesitate to call "the god of this world," and "the prince of the powers of the air." This is how they acount for this "war in heaven," so that "the dragon and his angels" fight against "Michael and his angels." Be that as it may, this mode of presenting the guardians of the destinies of nations is one respecting which we have no further gleams of revelation to help us.

Ewald regards the two last verses of the chapter as a sort of soliloquy of the angel Gabriel with himself. He is pressed for time. His coming had already been delayed by the opposition of the guardian power of the destinies of Persia. If Michael, the great archangel of the Hebrews, had not come to his aid, and (so to speak) for a time relieved guard, he would have been unable to come. But even the respite leaves him anxious. He seems to feel it almost necessary that he should at once return to contend against the Prince of Persia, and against a new adversary, the Prince of Javan, who is on his way to do mischief. Yet on the whole he will stay and enlighten Daniel before he takes his flight, although there is no one but Michael who aids him against these menacing princes. It is difficult to know whether this is meant to be ideal or real—whether it represents a struggle of angels against demons, or is merely meant for a sort of parable which represents the to-and-fro conflicting impulses which sway the destinies of earthly kingdoms. In any case the representation is too unique and too remote from earth to enable us to understand its spiritual meaning, beyond the bare indication that God sitteth above the water-floods and God remaineth a king for ever. It is another way of showing us that the heathen rage, and the people imagine a vain thing; that the kings of the earth set themselves and the rulers take counsel together; but that they can only accomplish what God's hand and God's counsel have predetermined to be done; and that when they attempt to overthrow the destinies which God has foreordained, "He that sitteth in the heavens shall laugh them to scorn, the Lord shall have them in derision." These, apart from all complications or developments of angelology or demonology, are the continuous lesson of the Word of God, and are confirmed by all that we decipher of His providence in His ways of dealing with nations and with men.

CHAPTER XXI.

AN ENIGMATIC PROPHECY PASSING INTO DETAILS OF THE REIGN OF ANTIOCHUS EPIPHANES.

If this chapter were indeed the utterance of a prophet in the Babylonian Exile, nearly four hundred years before the events—events of which many are of small comparative importance in the world's history—which are here so enigmatically and yet so minutely depicted, the revelation would be the most unique and perplexing in the whole Scriptures. It would represent a sudden and total departure from every method of God's providence and of God's manifestation of His will to the minds of the prophets. It would stand absolutely and abnormally alone as an abandonment of the limitations of all else which has ever been foretold. And it would then be still more surprising that such a reversal of the entire economy of prophecy should not only be so widely separated in tone from the high moral and spiritual lessons which it was the special glory of prophecy to inculcate, but should come to us entirely devoid of those decisive credentials which could alone suffice to command our conviction of its genuineness and authenticity. "We find in this chapter," says Mr. Bevan, "a complete survey of the history from the beginning of the Persian period down to the time of the author. Here, even more than in the earlier vision, we are able to perceive how the account gradually becomes more definite as it approaches the latter part of the reign of Antiochus Epiphanes, and how it then passes suddenly from the domain of historical facts to that of ideal expectations."* In recent days, when the force of truth has compelled so many earnest and honest thinkers to the acceptance of historic and literary criticism, the few scholars who are still able to maintain the traditional views about the Book of Daniel find themselves driven, like Zöckler and others, to admit that even if the Book of Daniel as a whole can be regarded as a production of the exiled seer five and a half centuries before Christ, yet in this chapter at any rate there must be large interpolations.†

There is here an unfortunate division of the chapters. The first verse of chap. xi. clearly belongs to the last verses of chap. x. It seems to furnish the reason why Gabriel could rely on the help of Michael, and therefore may delay for a few moments his return to the scene of conflict with the Prince of Persia and the coming King of Javan. Michael will for that brief period undertake the sole responsibility of maintaining the struggle, because Gabriel has put him under a direct obligation by special assistance which he rendered to him only a little while previously in the first year of the Median Darius.‡ Now, therefore, Gabriel, though in haste, will announce to Daniel the truth.

The announcement occupies five sections.

* "Daniel," p. 162.

† On this chapter see Smend, "Zeitschr. für Alttest. Wissenschaft," v. 241.

‡ Ewald, "Prophets," v. 293 (E. Tr.).

First Section (xi. 2-9).—Events from the rise of Alexander the Great (B. C. 336) to the death of Seleucus Nicator (B. C. 280). There are to be three kings of Persia after Cyrus (who is then reigning), of whom the third is to be the richest; and "when he is waxed strong through his riches, he shall stir up the all against the realm of Javan."

There were of course many more than four kings of Persia: viz.—

	B. C.
Cyrus	536
Cambyses	529
Pseudo-Smerdis	522
Darius Hystaspis	521
Xerxes I.	485
Artaxerxes I. (Longimanus)	464
Xerxes II.	425
Sogdianus	425
Darius Nothus	424
Artaxerxes II. (Mnemon)	405
Artaxerxes III.	359
Darius Codomannus	336

But probably the writer had no historic sources to which to refer, and only four Persian kings are prominent in Scripture—Cyrus, Darius, Xerxes, and Artaxerxes. Darius Codomannus is indeed mentioned in Neh. xii. 22, but might have easily been overlooked, and even confounded with another Darius in uncritical and unhistorical times. The rich fourth king who "stirs up the all against the realm of Grecia" might be meant for Artaxerxes I., but more probably refers to Xerxes (Achashverosh, or Ahaseurus), and his immense and ostentatious invasion of Greece (B. C. 480). His enormous wealth is dwelt upon by Herodotus.

Ver. 3 (B. C. 336-323).—Then shall rise a mighty king (Alexander the Great), and shall rule with great dominion, and do according to his will. "Fortunam solus omnium mortalium in potestate habuit," says his historian, Quintus Curtius.

Ver. 4 (B. C. 323).—But when he is at the apparent zenith of his strength his kingdom shall be broken, and shall not descend to any of his posterity, but (B. C. 323-301) shall be for others, and shall ultimately (after the Battle of Ipsus, B. C. 301) be divided towards the four winds of heaven, into the kingdoms of Cassander (Greece and Macedonia), Ptolemy (Egypt, Cœle-Syria, and Palestine), Lysimachus (Asia Minor), and Seleucus (Upper Asia).

Ver. 5.—Of these four kingdoms and their kings the vision is only concerned with two—the kings of the South (*i. e.*, the Lagidæ, or Egyptian Ptolemies, who sprang from Ptolemy Lagos), and the kings of the North (*i. e.*, the Antiochian Seleucidæ). They alone are singled out because the Holy Land became a sphere of contentions between these rival dynasties.

B. C. 306.—The King of the South (Ptolemy Soter, son of Lagos) shall be strong, and shall ultimately assume the title of Ptolemy I., King of Egypt.

But one of his princes or generals (Seleucus Nicator) shall be stronger and, asserting his independence, shall establish a great dominion over Northern Syria and Babylonia.

Ver. 6 (B. C. 250).—The vision then passes over the reign of Antiochus II. (Soter), and proceeds to say that "at the end of years" (*i. e.*, some half-century later, B. C. 250) the kings of the North and South should form a matrimonial alliance. The daughter of the King of the South—the Egyptian Princess Berenice, daughter of Ptolemy II. (Philadelphus), should come to the King of the North (Antiochus Theos) to make an agreement. This agreement (*marg.*, "equitable conditions") was that Aniochus Theos should divorce his wife and half-sister Laodice, and disinherit her children, and bequeath the throne to any future child of Berenice, who would thus unite the empires of the Ptolemies and the Seleucidæ. Berenice took with her so vast a dowry that she was called "the dowry-bringer" (φερνόφορος). Antiochus himself accompanied her as far as Pelusium (B. C. 247). But the compact ended in nothing but calamity. For, two years after, Ptolemy II. died, leaving an infant child by Berenice. But Berenice did "*not retain the strength of her arm,*" since the military force which accompanied her proved powerless for her protection; nor did Ptolemy II. abide, nor any support which he could render. On the contrary, there was overwhelming disaster. Berenice's escort, her father, her husband, all perished, and she herself and her infant child were murdered by her rival Laodice (B. C. 246), in the sanctuary of Daphne, whither she had fled for refuge.

Ver. 7 (B. C. 285-247).—But the murder of Berenice shall be well avenged. For "out of a shoot from her roots" stood up one in his office, even her brother Ptolemy III. (Euergetes), who, unlike the effeminate Ptolemy II., did not entrust his wars to his generals, but came himself to his armies. He shall completely conquer the King of the North (Seleucus II., Kallinikos, son of Antiochus Theos and Laodice), shall seize his fortress (Seleucia, the port of Antioch).

Ver. 8 (B. C. 247).—In this campaign Ptolemy Euergetes, who earned the title of "Benefactor" by this vigorous invasion, shall not only win immense booty—four thousand talents of gold and many jewels, and forty thousand talents of silver—but shall also carry back with him to Egypt the two thousand five hundred molten images, and idolatrous vessels, which, two hundred and eighty years before (B. C. 527), Cambyses had carried away from Egypt.

After this success he will, for some years, refrain from attacking the Seleucid kings.

Ver. 9 (B. C. 240).—Seleucus Kallinikos makes an attempt to avenge the shame and loss of the invasion of Syria by invading Egypt, but he returns to his own land totally foiled and defeated, for his fleet was destroyed by a storm.

Second Section (vv. 10-19).—Events from the death of Ptolemy Euergetes (B. C. 247) to the death of Antiochus III. (the Great, B. C. 175). In the following verses, as Behrmann observes, there is a sort of dance of shadows, only fully intelligible to the initiated.

Ver. 10.—The sons of Seleucus Kallinikos were Seleucus III. (Keraunos, B. C. 227-224) and Antiochus the Great (B. C. 224-187). Keraunos only reigned two years, and in B. C. 224 his brother Antiochus III. succeeded him. Both kings assembled immense forces to avenge the insult of the Egyptian invasion, the defeat of their father, and the retention of their port and fortress of Seleucia. It was only sixteen miles from Antioch, and being still garrisoned by Egyptians, constituted a standing danger and insult to their capital city.

Ver. 11.—After twenty-seven years the port of Seleucia is wrested from the Egyptians by Antiochus the Great, and he so completely reverses the former successes of the King of the South as to conquer Syria as far as Gaza.

Ver. 12 (B. C. 217).—But at last the young Egyptian King, Ptolemy IV. (Philopator), is roused from his dissipation and effeminacy, advances to Raphia (southwest of Gaza) with a great army of twenty thousand foot, five thousand horse, and seventy-three elephants, and there, to his own immense self-exaltation, he inflicts a severe defeat on Antiochus, and "*casts down tens of thousands.*" Yet the victory is illusive, although it enables Ptolemy to annex Palestine to Egypt. For Ptolemy "*shall not show himself strong,*" but shall, by his supineness, and by making a speedy peace, throw away all the fruits of his victory, while he returns to his past dissipation (B. C. 217-204).

Ver. 13.—Twelve years later (B. C. 205) Ptolemy Philopator died, leaving an infant son, Ptolemy Epiphanes. Antiochus, smarting from his defeat at Raphia, again assembled an army, which was still greater than before (B. C. 203), and much war-material. In the intervening years he had won great victories in the East as far as India.

Ver. 14.—Antiochus shall be aided by the fact that many—including his ally Philip, King of Macedon, and various rebel-subjects of Ptolemy Epiphanes—stood up against the King of Egypt and wrested Phœnicia and Southern Syria from him. The Syrians were further strengthened by the assistance of the "children of the violent" among the Jews, "*who shall lift themselves up to fulfil the vision of the oracle; but they shall fall.*" We read in Josephus that many of the Jews helped Antiochus; but the allusion to "the vision" is entirely obscure. Ewald supposes a reference to some prophecy no longer extant. Dr. Joël thinks that the Hellenising Jews may have referred to Isa. xix. in favour of the plans of Antiochus against Egypt.

Vv. 15, 16.—But however much any of the Jews may have helped Antiochus under the hope of ultimately regaining their independence, their hopes were frustrated. The Syrian King came, besieged, and took a well-fenced city—perhaps an allusion to the fact that he wrested Sidon from the Egyptians. After his great victory over the Egyptian general Scopas at Mount Panium (B. C. 198), the routed Egyptian forces, to the number of ten thousand, flung themselves into that city. This campaign ruined the interests of Egypt in Palestine, "the glorious land." Palestine now passed to Antiochus, who took possession "with destruction in his hand."

Ver. 17 (B. C. 198-195).—After this there shall again be an attempt at "equitable negotiations"; by which, however, Antiochus hoped to get final possession of Egypt and destroy it. He arranged a marriage between "a daughter of women"—his daughter Cleopatra—and Ptolemy Epiphanes. But this attempt also entirely failed.

Ver. 18 (B. C. 190).—Antiochus therefore "sets his face in another direction," and tries to conquer the islands and coasts of Asia Minor. But a captain—the Roman general, Lucius Cornelius Scipio Asiaticus—puts an end to the insolent scorn with which he had spoken of the Romans, and pays him back with equal scorn, utterly defeating him in the great Battle of Magnesia (B. C. 190), and forcing him to ignominious terms.

Ver. 19 (B. C. 175).—Antiochus next turns his attention ("sets his face") to strengthen the fortress of his own land in the east and west; but making an attempt to recruit his dissipated wealth by the plunder of the Temple of Belus in Elymais, "stumbles and falls, and is not found."

THIRD SECTION (VV. 20-27).—Events under Seleucus Philopator down to the first attempts of Antiochus Epiphanes against Egypt (B. C. 170).

Ver. 20.—Seleucus Philopator (B. C. 187-176) had a character the reverse of his father's. He was no restless seeker for glory, but desired wealth and quietness. Among the Jews, however, he had a very evil reputation, for he sent an "exactor"—a mere tax-collector, Heliodorus—"to pass through the glory of the kingdom." He only reigned twelve years, and then was "broken"—*i. e.*, murdered by Heliodorus, neither in anger nor in battle, but by poison administered by this "tax-collector." The versions all vary, but I feel little doubt that Dr. Joël is right when he sees in the curious phrase "nogesh heder malkooth," "one that shall cause a raiser of taxes to pass over the kingdom"—of which neither Theodotion nor the Vulgate can make anything—a cryptographic allusion to the name "Heliodorus"; and possibly the predicted fate may (by a change of subject) also refer to the fact that Heliodorus was checked, not by force, but by the vision in the Temple (2 Macc. v. 18, iii. 24-29). We find from 2 Macc. iv. 1 that Simeon, the governor of the Temple, charged Onias with a trick to terrify Heliodorus. This is a very probable view of what occurred.

Ver. 21.—Seleucus Philopator died B. C. 175 without an heir. This made room for a contemptible person, a reprobate, who had no real claim to royal dignity, being only a younger son of Antiochus the Great. He came by surprise, "in time of security," and obtained the kingdom by flatteries.

Ver. 22.—Yet "the overflowing wings of Egypt" (or "the arms of a flood") "were swept away before him and broken; yea, and even a covenanted or allied prince." Some explain this of his nephew Ptolemy Philometor, others of Onias III., "the prince of the covenant"—*i. e.*, the princely high priest, whom Antiochus displaced in favour of his brother, the apostate Joshua, who Græcised his name into Jason, as his brother Onias did in calling himself Menelaus.

Ver. 23.—This mean king should prosper by deceit which he practised on all connected with him; and though at first he had but few adherents, he should creep into power.

Ver. 24.—"In time of security shall he come, even upon the fattest places of the province." By this may be meant his invasions of Galilee and Lower Egypt. Acting unlike any of his royal predecessors, he shall lavishly scatter his gains and his booty among needy followers, and shall plot to seize Pelusium, Naucratis, Alexandria, and other strongholds of Egypt for a time.

Ver. 25.—After this (B. C. 171) he shall, with a "great army," seriously undertake his first invasion of Egypt, and shall be met by his nephew Ptolemy Philometor with another immense army. In spite of this, the young Egyptian

King shall fail through the treachery of his own courtiers. He shall be outwitted and treacherously undermined by his uncle Antiochus. Yes! even while his army is fighting, and many are being slain, the very men who "eat of his dainties," even his favourite and trusted courtiers, Eulæus and Lenæus, will be devising his ruin, and his army shall be swept away.

Vv. 26, 27 (B. C. 174).—The Syrians and the Egyptian King, nephew and uncle, shall in nominal amity sit at one banquet, eating from one table; but all the while they will be distrustfully plotting against each other and "speaking lies" to each other. Antiochus will pretend to ally himself with the young Philometor against his brother Ptolemy Euergetes II.—generally known by his derisive nickname as Ptolemy Physkon—whom after eleven months the Alexandrians had proclaimed king. But all these plots and counter-plots should be of none effect, for the end was not yet.

FOURTH SECTION (vv. 28-35).—Events between the first attack of Antiochus on Jerusalem (B. C. 170) and his plunder of the Temple to the first revolt of the Maccabees (B. C. 167).

Ver. 28 (B. C. 168).—Returning from Egypt with great plunder, Antiochus shall set himself against the Holy Covenant. He put down the usurping high priest Jason, who, with much slaughter, had driven out his rival usurper and brother, Menelaus. He massacred many Jews, and returned to Antioch enriched with golden vessels seized from the Temple.

Ver. 29.—In B. C. 168 Antiochus again invaded Egypt, but with none of the former splendid results. For Ptolemy Philometor and Physkon had joined in sending an embassy to Rome to ask for help and protection. In consequence of this, "ships from Kittim"—namely, the Roman fleet—came against him, bringing the Roman commissioner, Gaius Popilius Lænas. When Popilius met Antiochus, the king put out his hand to embrace him; but the Roman merely held out his tablets, and bade Antiochus read the Roman demand that he and his army should at once evacuate Egypt. "I will consult my friends on the subject," said Antiochus. Popilius, with infinite haughtiness and audacity, simply drew a circle in the sand with his vine-stick round the spot on which the king stood, and said, "You must decide before you step out of that circle." Antiochus stood amazed and humiliated; but seeing that there was no help for it, promised in despair to do all that the Romans demanded.

Ver. 30.—Returning from Egypt in an indignant frame of mind, he turned his exasperation against the Jews and the Holy Covenant, especially extending his approval to those who apostatised from it.

Ver. 31.—Then (B. C. 168) shall come the climax of horror. Antiochus shall send troops to the Holy Land, who shall desecrate the sanctuary and fortress of the Temple, and abolish the daily sacrifice (Kisleu 15), and set up the abomination that maketh desolate.

Ver. 32.—To carry out these ends the better, and with the express purpose of putting an end to the Jewish religion, he shall pervert or "make profane" by flatteries the renegades who are ready to apostatise from the faith of their fathers. But there shall be a faithful remnant who will bravely resist him to the uttermost. "The people who know their God will be valiant, and do great deeds."

Ver. 33.—To keep alive the national faith "wise teachers of the people shall instruct many," and will draw upon their own heads the fury of persecution, so that many shall fall by sword, and by flame, and by captivity, and by spoliation for many days.

Ver. 34.—But in the midst of this fierce onslaught of cruelty they shall be "holpen with a little help." There shall arise the sect of the "Chasidim," or "the Pious," bound together by "Tugendbund" to maintain the Laws which Israel received from Moses of old. These good and faithful champions of a righteous cause will indeed be weakened by the false adherence of waverers and flatterers.

Ver. 35.—To purge the party from such spies and Laodiceans, the teachers, like the aged priest Mattathias at Modin, and the aged scribe Eleazar, will have to brave even martyrdom itself till the time of the end.

FIFTH SECTION (vv. 36-45, B. C. 147-164).—Events from the beginning of the Maccabean rising to the death of Antiochus Epiphanes.

Ver. 36.—Antiochus will grow more arbitrary, more insolent, more blasphemous, from day to day, calling himself "God" (Theos) on his coins, and requiring all his subjects to be of his religion, and so even more kindling against himself the wrath of the God of gods by his monstrous utterances, until the final doom has fallen.

Ver. 37.—He will, in fact, make himself his own god, paying no regard (by comparison) to his national or local god, the Olympian Zeus, nor to the Syrian deity, Tammuz-Adonis, "the desire of women."

"Tammuz came next behind,
Whose yearly wound in Lebanon allured
The Syrian damsels to lament his fate
In amorous ditties all a summer day.
While smooth Adonis from his native rock
Ran purple to the sea—supposed with blood
Of Tammuz yearly wounded. The love tale
Infected Zion's daughters with like heat."

Ver. 38.—The only God to whom he shall pay marked respect shall be the Roman Jupiter, the god of the Capitol. To this god, to Jupiter Capitolinus, not to his own Zeus Olympios, the god of his Greek fathers, he shall erect a temple in his capital city of Antioch, and adorn it with gold and silver and precious stones.

Ver. 39.—"And he shall deal with the strongest fortresses by the help of a strange god"—namely, the Capitoline Jupiter (Zeus Polieus)—and shall crowd the strongholds of Judæa with heathen colonists who worship the Tyrian Hercules (Melkart) and other idols; and to these heathen he shall give wealth and power.

Ver. 40.—But his evil career shall be cut short. Egypt, under the now-allied brothers Philometor and Physkon, shall unite to thrust at him. Antiochus will advance against them like a whirlwind, with many chariots and horsemen, and with the aid of a fleet.

Vv. 41-45.—In the course of his march he shall pass through Palestine, "the glorious land," with disastrous injury; but Edom, Moab, and the bloom of the kingdom of Ammon shall escape his hand. Egypt, however, shall not escape. By the aid of the Libyans and Ethiopians who are in his train he shall plunder Egypt of its treasures.

How far these events correspond to historic realities is uncertain. Jerome says that Antiochus invaded Egypt a third time in B. C. 165, the eleventh year of his reign; but there are no historic traces of such an invasion, and most certainly Antiochus towards the close of his reign, instead of being enriched with vast Egyptian spoils, was struggling with chronic lack of means. Some therefore suppose that the writer composed and published his enigmatic sketch of these events before the close of the reign of Antiochus, and that he is here passing from contemporary fact into a region of ideal anticipations which were never actually fulfilled.

Ver. 43 (B. C. 165).—In the midst of this devastating invasion of Egypt, Antiochus shall be troubled with disquieting rumours of troubles in Palestine and other realms of his kingdom. He will set out with utter fury to subjugate and to destroy, determining above all to suppress the heroic Maccabean revolt which had inflicted such humiliating disasters upon his generals, Seron, Apollonius, and Lysias.

Ver. 45 (B. C. 164).—He shall indeed advance so far as to pitch his palatial tent "between the sea and the mountain of the High Glory": but he will come to a disastrous and an unassisted end.

These latter events either do not correspond with the actual history, or cannot be verified. So far as we know Antiochus did not invade Egypt at all after B. C. 168. Still less did he advance from Egypt, or pitch his tent anywhere near Mount Zion. Nor did he die in Palestine, but in Persia (B. C. 165). The writer, indeed, strong in faith, anticipated, and rightly, that Antiochus would come to an ignominious and a sudden end—God shooting at him with a swift arrow, so that he should be wounded. But all accurate details seem suddenly to stop short with the doings in the fourth section, which may refer to the strange conduct of Antiochus in his great festival in honour of Jupiter at Daphne. Had the writer published his book *after* this date, he could not surely have failed to speak with triumphant gratitude and exultation of the heroic stand made by Judas Maccabæus and the splendid victories which restored hope and glory to the Holy Land. I therefore regard these verses as a description rather of ideal expectation than of historic facts.

We find notices of Antiochus in the Books of Maccabees, in Josephus, in St. Jerome's Commentary on Daniel, and in Appian's "Syriaca." We should know more of him and be better able to explain some of the allusions in this chapter if the writings of the secular historians had not come down to us in so fragmentary a condition. The relevant portions of Callinicus Sutoricus, Diodorus Siculus, Polybius, Posidonius, Claudius, Theon, Andronicus, Alypius, and others are all lost—except a few fragments which we have at second or third hand. Porphyry introduced quotations from these authors into the twelfth book of his "Arguments against the Christians"; but we only know his book from Jerome's *ex-parte* quotations. Other Christian treatises, written in answer to Porphyry by Apollinaris, Eusebius, and Methodius, are only preserved in a few sentences by Nicetas and John of Damascus. The loss of Porphyry and Apollinarius is especially to be regretted. Jerome says that it was the extraordinarily minute correspondence of this chapter of Daniel with the history of Antiochus Epiphanes that led Porphyry to the conviction that it only contained *vaticinia ex eventu*.*

* Jahn, § xcv.

Antiochus died at Tabæ in Paratacæne on the frontiers of Persia and Babylonia about B. C. 163. The Jewish account of his remorseful deathbed may be read in 1 Macc. vi. 1-16: "He laid him down upon his bed, and fell sick for grief; and there he continued many days, for his grief was ever more and more; and he made account that he should die." He left a son, Antiochus Eupator, aged nine, under the charge of his flatterer and foster-brother Philip. Recalling the wrongs he had inflicted on Judæa and Jerusalem, he said: "I perceive, therefore, that for this cause these troubles are come upon me; and, behold, I perish through great grief in a strange land."

CHAPTER XXII.

THE EPILOGUE.

The twelfth chapter of the Book of Daniel serves as a general epilogue to the Book, and is as little free from difficulties in the interpretation of the details as are the other apocalyptic chapters.

The keynote, however, to their right understanding must be given in the words "At that time," with which the first verse opens. The words can only mean "the time" spoken of at the end of the last chapter, the days of that final effort of Antiochus against the holy people which ended in his miserable death.

"At that time," then—*i. e.*, about the year B. C. 163—the guardian archangel of Israel, "Michael, the great prince which standeth for the children of thy people," shall stand up for their deliverance.

But this deliverance should resemble many similar crises in its general characteristics. It should not be immediate. On the contrary, it should be preceded by days of unparalleled disorder and catastrophe—"a time of trouble, such as never was since there was a nation even to that same time." We may, for instance, compare with this the similar prophecy of Jeremiah (xxx. 4-11): "And these are the words which the Lord spake concerning Israel and concerning Judah. For thus saith the Lord; We have heard a voice of trembling, of fear, and not of peace. . . . Alas! for that day is great, so that none is like it: it is even the time of Jacob's trouble; but he shall be saved out of it. And it shall come to pass in that day, saith the Lord, that I will burst thy bonds. . . . Therefore fear thou not, O Jacob, My servant, saith the Lord; neither be dismayed, O Israel. . . . For I am with thee, saith the Lord, to save thee. For I will make a full end of all the nations whither I have scattered thee, but I will not make a full end of thee: but I will correct thee with judgment, and will in nowise leave thee unpunished." *

The general conception is so common as even to have found expression in proverbs,—such as, "The night is darkest just before the dawn"; and, "When the tale of bricks is doubled, Moses comes." Some shadow of similar individual and historic experiences is found also among the Greek and Romans. It lies in the expression θεὸς ἀπὸ μηχανῆς, and also in the lines of Horace,—

> "Nec Deus intersit nisi *dignus vindice nodus*
> Intersit."

* See too Joel ii. 2.

We find the same expectation in the apocryphal Book of Enoch,* and we find it reflected in the Revelation of St. John,† where he describes the devil as let loose and the powers of evil as gathering themselves together for the great final battle of Armageddon before the eternal triumph of the Lamb and of His saints. In Rabbinic literature there was a fixed anticipation that the coming of the Messiah must inevitably be preceded by "pangs" or "birth-throes," of which they spoke as the חבלי משיח.‡ These views may partly have been founded on individual and national experience, but they were doubtless deepened by the vision of Zechariah (xii.).

"Behold, a day of the Lord cometh, when thy spoil shall be divided in the midst of thee. For I will gather all nations against Jerusalem to battle; and the city shall be taken, and the houses rifled, and the women ravished; and half of the people shall go forth into captivity, and the residue of the people shall not be cut off from the city. Then shall the Lord go forth, and fight against those nations, as when He fought in the day of battle. And His feet shall stand in that day upon the Mount of Olives. . . . And it shall come to pass in that day, that the light shall not be light, but cold and ice:§ but it shall be one day that is known unto the Lord, not day and not night: but it shall come to pass that at evening time there shall be light."‖

The anticipation of the saintly writer in the days of the early Maccabean uprising, while all the visible issues were still uncertain, and hopes as yet unaccomplished could only be read by the eyes of faith, were doubtless of a similar character. When he wrote Antiochus was already concentrating his powers to advance with the utmost wrath and fury against the Holy City. Humanly speaking, it was certain that the holy people could oppose no adequate resistance to his overwhelming forces, in which he would doubtless be able to enlist contingents from many allied nations. What could ensue but immeasurable calamity to the great majority? Michael indeed, their prince, should do his utmost for them; but it would not be in his power to avert the misery which should fall on the nation generally.

Nevertheless, they should not be given up to utter or to final destruction. As in the days of the Assyrians the name Shear-jashub, which Isaiah gave to one of his young sons, was a sign that "a remnant should be left," so now the seer is assured that "thy people shall be delivered"—at any rate "every one that shall be found written in the book."

"Written in the book"—for all true Israelites had ever believed that a book of record, a book of remembrance, lies ever open before the throne of God, in which are inscribed the names of God's faithful ones; as well as that awful book in which are written the evil deeds of men.¶ Thus in Exodus (xxxii. 33) we read, "Whosoever hath sinned against Me, him will I blot out of My book," which tells us of the records against the guilty. In Psalm lxix. 28 we read, "Let them be blotted out of the book of life, and not be written with the righteous." That book of the righteous is specially mentioned by Malachi: "Then they that feared the Lord spake one with another: and the Lord hearkened and heard, and a book of remembrance was written before him for them that feared the Lord and called upon His Name." * And St. John refers to these books at the close of the Apocalypse: "And I saw the dead, the great and the small, standing before the throne; and books were opened: and another book was opened, which is the book of life: and the dead were judged out of the things which were written in the books, according to their works. . . . And if any one was not found written in the book of life, he was cast in the lake of fire."

In the next verse the seer is told that "many of them that sleep in the dust of the earth shall awake, some to everlasting life, and some to shame and everlasting abhorrence."

It is easy to glide with insincere confidence over the difficulties of this verse, but they are many.

We should naturally connect it with what goes before as a reference to "that time"; and if so, it would seem as though—perhaps with reminiscences of the concluding prophecy of Isaiah—the writer contemplated the end of all things and the final resurrection. If so, we have here another instance to be added to the many in which this prophetic vision of the future passed from an immediate horizon to another infinitely distant. And if that be the correct interpretation, this is the earliest trace in Scripture of the doctrine of individual immortality. Of that doctrine there was no full knowledge—there were only dim prognostications or splendid hopes—until in the fulness of the times Christ brought life and immortality to light. For instance, the passage here seems to be doubly limited. It does not refer to mankind in general, but only to members of the chosen people; and it is not said that all men shall rise again and receive according to their works, but only that "many" shall rise to receive the reward of true life, while others shall live indeed, but only in everlasting shame.

To them that be wise—to "the teacher," and to those that turn the many to "righteousness"—there is a further promise of glory. They "shall shine as the brightness of the firmament, and as the stars for ever and ever." There is here, perhaps, a reminiscence of Prov. iv. 18, 19, which tells us that the way of the wicked is as darkness, whereas the path of the just is as the shining light that shineth more and more unto the perfect day. Our Lord uses a similar metaphor in his explanation of the Parable of the Tares: "Then shall the righteous shine forth as the sun in the kingdom of their Father." We find it once again in the last verse of the Epistle of St. James: "Let him know, that he who hath converted a sinner from the error of his way shall save a soul from death, and shall hide a multitude of sins."

But there is a further indication that the writer expected this final consummation to take place immediately after the troubles of the Antiochian assault; for he describes the angel Gabriel as bidding Daniel "to seal the Book even to the time of the end." Now as it is clear that the Book was, on any hypothesis, meant for the special consolation of the persecuted Jews under

* Enoch xc. 16.
† Rev. xvi. 14, xix. 19.
‡ Comp. Matt. xxiv. 6, 7, 21, 22.
§ Such is the reading of the LXX., Vulgate, Peshitta, Symmachus, etc.
‖ Zech. xiv. 1-7.
¶ Comp. vii. 10: "And the books were opened."

* Mal. iii. 16.

the cruel sway of the Seleucid King, and that then first could the Book be understood, the writer evidently looked for the fulfilment of his last prophecies at the termination of these troubles. This meaning is a little obscured by the rendering, "many *shall run to and fro*, and knowledge shall be increased." Ewald, Maurer, and Hitzig take the verse, which literally implies movement hither and thither, in the sense, "many shall *peruse* the Book." * Mr. Bevan, however, from a consideration of the Septuagint Version of the words, "and knowledge shall be increased"—for which they read, "and the land be filled with injustice"—thinks that the original rendering would be represented by, "many shall rush hither and thither, and many shall be the calamities." In other words, "the revelation must remain concealed, because there is to ensue a long period of commotion and distress."† If we have been convinced by the concurrence of many irresistible arguments that the Book of Daniel is the product of the epoch which it most minutely describes, we can only see in this verse a part of the literary form which the Book necessarily assumed as the vehicle for its lofty and encouraging messages.

The angel here ceases to speak, and Daniel, looking round him, becomes aware of the presence of two other celestial beings, one of whom stood on either bank of the river. "And one said to the man clothed in linen, which was above the waters of the river, How long to the end of these wonders?" There is a certain grandeur in the vagueness of description, but the speaker seems to be one of the two angels standing on either "lip" of the Tigris. "The man clothed in linen," who is hovering in the air above the waters of the river, is the same being who in viii. 16 wears "the appearance of a man," and calls "from between the banks of Ulai" to Gabriel that he is to make Daniel understand the vision. He is also, doubtless, the "one man clothed in linen, whose loins were girded with fine gold of Uphaz, his body like the beryl, his face as flashing lightning, his eyes as burning torches, and his voice like the deep murmur of a multitude," who strikes such terror into Daniel and his comrades in the vision of chap. x. 5, 6;—and though all is left uncertain, "the great prince Michael" may perhaps be intended.

The question how long these marvels were to last, and at what period the promised deliverance should be accomplished, was one which would naturally have the intensest interest to those Jews who—in the agonies of the Antiochian persecution and at the beginning of the "little help" caused by the Maccabean uprising—read for the first time the fearful yet consolatory and inspiring pages of this new apocalypse. The answer is uttered with the most solemn emphasis. The Vision of the priest-like and gold-girded angel, as he hovers above the river-flood, "held up both his hands to heaven," and swears by Him that liveth for ever and ever that the continuance of the affliction shall be "for a time, times, and a half." So Abraham, to emphasise his refusal of any gain from the King of Sodom, says that he has "lifted up his hand unto the Lord, the Most High God, that he would not take from a thread to a shoe-latchet." And in Exod. vi. 8, when Jehovah says "I did swear," the expression means literally, "I lifted up My hand." * It is the natural attitude of calling God to witness; and in Rev. x. 5, 6, with a reminiscence of this passage, the angel is described as standing on the sea, and lifting his right hand to heaven to swear a mighty oath that there should be no longer delay.

The "time, two times, and half a time" of course means three years and a half, as in vii. 25. There can be little doubt that their commencement is the *terminus a quo* which is expressly mentioned in ver. 11: "the time that the daily sacrifice shall be taken away." We have already had occasion to see that three years, with a margin which seems to have been variously computed, does roughly correspond to the continuance of that total desecration of the Temple, and extinction of the most characteristic rites of Judaism, which preceded the death of Antiochus and the triumph of the national cause.

Unhappily the reading, rendering, and interpretation of the next clause of the angel's oath are obscure and uncertain. It is rendered in the R. V., "and when they have made an end of breaking in pieces the power of the holy people, all these things shall be finished." As to the exact translation many scholars differ. Von Lengerke translates it, "and when the scattering of a part of the holy people should come to an end, all this should be ended." The Septuagint Version is wholly unintelligible. Mr. Bevan suggests an alteration of the text which would imply that, "when the power of the shatterer of the holy people [*i. e.*, Antiochus] should come to an end, all these things should be ended." This no doubt would not only give a very clear sense, but also one which would be identical with the prophecy of vii. 25, that "they [the times and the law] shall be given unto his hand until a time and times and half a time." † But if we stop short at the desperate and uncertain expedient of correcting the original Hebrew, we can only regard the words as implying (in the rendering of our A. V. and R. V.) that the persecution and suppression of Israel should proceed to their extremest limit, before the woe was ended; and of this we have already been assured.‡

The writer, in the person of Daniel, is perplexed by the angel's oath, and yearns for further enlightenment and certitude. He makes an appeal to the vision with the question, "O my lord, what shall be the issue [or, latter end] of these things?" In answer he is simply bidden to go his way—*i. e.*, to be at peace, and leave all these events to God, since the words are shut up and sealed till the time of the end. In other words, the Daniel of the Persian Court could not possibly have attached any sort of definite meaning to minutely detailed predictions affecting the existence of empires which would not so much as emerge on the horizon till centuries after his death. These later visions could only be apprehended by the contemporaries of the events which they shadowed forth.

"Many," continued the angel, "shall purify

* Comp. Zech. iv. 10. This sense cannot be rigidly established.

† He refers to 1 Macc. i. 9, which says of the successors of Alexander, καὶ ἐπλήθυναν κακὰ ἐν τῇ γῇ.

* Comp. Gen. xiv. 22; Deut. xxxii. 40, "For I lift up My hand unto heaven, and say, I live for ever"; Ezek. xx. 5, 6, etc.

† Those who can rest content with such exegesis may explain this to imply that "the reign of *antichrist* will be divided into three periods—the first long, the second longer, the third shortest of all," just as the seventy weeks of chap. ix. are composed of 7 x 62 x 1.

‡ By way of comment see 1 Macc. v.; 2 Macc. viii.

themselves, and make themselves white, and be refined; but the wicked shall do wickedly: and none of the wicked shall understand; the teachers shall understand."

The verse describes the deep divisions which should be cleft among the Jews by the intrigues and persecutions of Antiochus. Many would cling to their ancient and sacred institutions, and purified by pain, purged from all dross of worldliness and hypocrisy in the fires of affliction, like gold in the furnace, would form the new parties of the *Chasidîm* and the *Anavîm*, "the pious" and "the poor." They would be such men as the good high priest Onias, Mattathias of Modin and his glorious sons, the scribe Eleazar, and the seven dauntless martyrs, sons of the holy woman who unflinchingly watched their agonies and encouraged them to die rather than to apostatise. But the wicked would continue to be void of all understanding, and would go on still in their wickedness, like Jason and Menelaus, the renegade usurpers of the high-priesthood. These and the whole Hellenising party among the Jews, for the sake of gain, plunged into heathen practices, made abominable offerings to gods which were no gods, and in order to take part in the naked contests of the Greek gymnasium which they had set up in Jerusalem, deliberately attempted to obliterate the seal of circumcision which was the covenant pledge of their national consecration to the Jehovah of their fathers.

"And from the time that the continual burnt offering shall be taken away, and the abomination that maketh desolate set up, there shall be a thousand two hundred and ninety days."

If we suppose the year to consist of twelve months of thirty days, then (with the insertion of one intercalary month of thirty days) twelve hundred and ninety days is exactly three and a half years. We are, however, faced by the difficulty that the time from the desecration of the Temple till its reconsecration by Judas Maccabæus seems to have been exactly three years; * and if that view be founded on correct chronology we can give no exact interpretation of the very specific date here furnished.

Our difficulties are increased by the next clause: "Blessed is he that waiteth, and cometh to the thousand three hundred and five and thirty days."

All that we can conjecture from this is that, at the close of twelve hundred and ninety days, by the writer's reckoning from the cessation of the daily burnt offering, and the erection of the heathen abomination which drove all faithful Jews from the Temple, up to the date of some marked deliverance, would be three and a half years, but that this deliverance would be less complete and beatific than another and later deliverance which would not occur till forty-five days later.†

Reams of conjecture and dubious history and imaginative chronology have been expended upon the effort to give any interpretation of these precise data which can pretend to the dignity of firm or scientific exegesis. Some, for instance, like Keil, regard the numbers as *symbolical*, which is equivalent to the admission that they have little or no bearing on literal history; others suppose that they are *conjectural*, having been penned before the actual termination of the Seleucid troubles. Others regard them as only intended to represent *round numbers*. Others again attempt to give them historic accuracy by various manipulations of the dates and events in and after the reign of Antiochus. Others relegate the entire vision to periods separated from the Maccabean age by hundreds of years, or even into the remotest future. And none of these commentators, by their researches and combinations, have succeeded in establishing the smallest approach to conviction in the minds of those who take the other views. There can be little doubt that to the writer and his readers the passage pointed either to very confident expectations or very well-understood realities; but for us the exact clue to the meaning is lost. All that can be said is that we should probably understand the dates better if our knowledge of the history of B. C. 165-164 was more complete. We are forced to content ourselves with their general significance. It is easy to record and to multiply elaborate guesses, and to deceive ourselves with the merest pretence and semblance of certainty. For reverent and severely honest inquiries it seems safer and wiser to study and profit by the great lessons and examples clearly set before us in the Book of Daniel, but, as regards many of its unsolved difficulties, to obey the wise exhortation of the Rabbis,—

"Learn to say, 'I do not know.'"

APPROXIMATE CHRONOLOGICAL TABLES.

	B. C.		B. C.
Jehoiakim, . .	608-597	Malachi, ...	420
Zedekiah, . .	597-588	Alexander the Great invades Persia, . .	334
Jerusalem taken, . .	588	Battle of Granicus, .	334
Death of Nebuchadrezzar, ...	561	Battle of Issus, . .	333
Evil-merodach, . .	561	Battle of Arbela, . .	331
Neriglissar, . .	559	Death of Darius Codomannus, . . .	330
Laborosoarchod, . .	555	Death of Alexander, .	323
Nabunaid, ...	555	Ptolemy Soter captures Jerusalem, .	320
Capture of Babylon, .	538	Simon the Just high priest, ...	310
Decree of Cyrus, . .	536	Beginning of Septuagint translation. . .	284
Cambyses, ...	529	Antiochus the Great quers Palestine, . (?)	202
Darius, son of Hystaspes, ...	521		
Dedication of the Second Temple, ...	516		
Battle of Salamis, . .	480		
Ezra, ...	458		
Nehemiah, ...	444		
Nehemiah's reforms, .	428		

	B. C.	
Accession of Antiochus Epiphanes, ...	176	Dan. vii. 8, 20.
Joshua (Jason), brother of Onias III., gets the priesthood by bribery, and promotes Hellenism among the Jews, ...	174	Dan. xi. 22-24, ix. 26.

* The small heathen altar to Zeus was built by Antiochus upon the great altar of burnt offering on Kisleu 15, B. C. 168. The revolt of Mattathias and his seven sons began B. C. 167. Judas the Maccabee defeated the Syrian generals Apollonius, Seron, and Gorgias B. C. 166, and Lysias at Beth-sur in B. C. 165. He cleansed and rededicated the Temple on Kisleu 25, B. C. 165.

† The "time, times, and a half." The 1290 days, 1335 days, and the 1150 days, and the 2300 days of viii. 14 all agree in indicating three years with a shorter or longer fraction. It will be observed that in each case there is a certain reticence or vagueness as to the *terminus ad quem*. It is interesting to note that in Rev. xi. 2, 3, the period of 42 months = 1260 days = 3½ years of months of 30 days with no intercalary month.

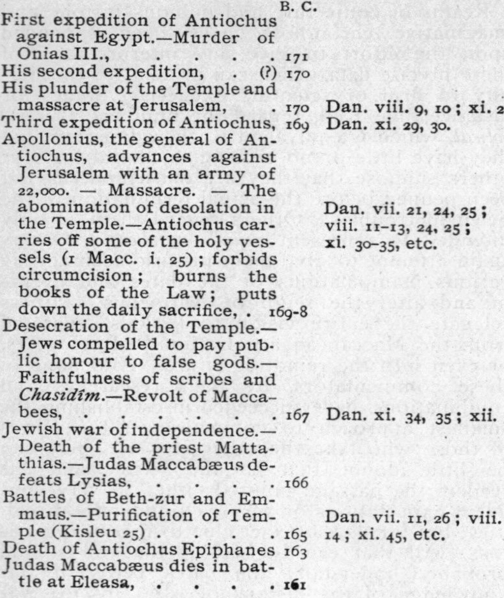

	B. C.	
First expedition of Antiochus against Egypt.—Murder of Onias III., . . .	171	
His second expedition, . . (?)	170	
His plunder of the Temple and massacre at Jerusalem, .	170	Dan. viii. 9, 10; xi. 28.
Third expedition of Antiochus,	169	Dan. xi. 29, 30.
Apollonius, the general of Antiochus, advances against Jerusalem with an army of 22,000. — Massacre. — The abomination of desolation in the Temple.—Antiochus carries off some of the holy vessels (1 Macc. i. 25); forbids circumcision; burns the books of the Law; puts down the daily sacrifice, .	169-8	Dan. vii. 21, 24, 25; viii. 11-13, 24, 25; xi. 30-35, etc.
Desecration of the Temple.—Jews compelled to pay public honour to false gods.—Faithfulness of scribes and *Chasidîm*.—Revolt of Maccabees, ...	167	Dan. xi. 34, 35; xii. 3.
Jewish war of independence.—Death of the priest Mattathias.—Judas Maccabæus defeats Lysias, ...	166	
Battles of Beth-zur and Emmaus.—Purification of Temple (Kisleu 25) . .	165	Dan. vii. 11, 26; viii. 14; xi. 45, etc.
Death of Antiochus Epiphanes	163	
Judas Maccabæus dies in battle at Eleasa, ...	161	

GENEALOGICAL TABLE OF THE LAGIDÆ, PTOLEMIES, AND SELEUCIDÆ.

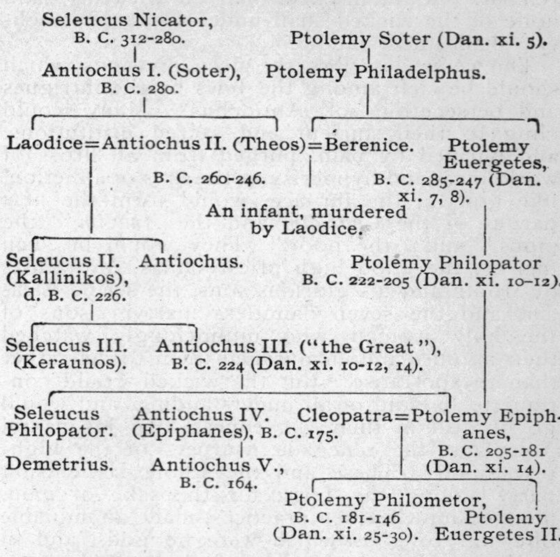

For a fuller list and further identifications see Driver, pp. 461, 462, and *supra*. For the genealogical table see Mr. Deane (Bishop Ellicott's "Commentary, v. 402).

THE BOOK OF THE TWELVE PROPHETS

PART I.

PREFACE.

THE Prophets, to whom this and a following Part are dedicated, have, to our loss, been haunted for centuries by a peddling and ambiguous title. Their Twelve Books are in size smaller than those of the great Three which precede them, and doubtless none of their chapters soar so high as the brilliant summits to which we are swept by Isaiah and the Prophet of the Exile. But in every other respect they are undeserving of the niggardly name of "Minor." Two of them, Amos and Hosea, were the first of all prophecy—rising cliff-like, with a sheer and magnificent originality, to a height and a mass sufficient to set after them the trend and slope of the whole prophetic range. The Twelve together cover the extent of that range, and illustrate the development of prophecy at almost every stage from the eighth century to the fourth. Yet even more than in the case of Isaiah or Jeremiah, the Church has been content to use a passage here and a passage there, leaving the rest of the books to absolute neglect or the almost equal oblivion of routine-reading. Among the causes of this disuse have been the more than usually corrupt state of the text; the consequent disorder and in parts unintelligibleness of all the versions; the ignorance of the various historical circumstances out of which the books arose; the absence of successful efforts to determine the periods and strophes, the dramatic dialogues (with the names of the speakers), the lyric effusions and the passages of argument, of all of which the books are composed.

The following exposition is an attempt to assist the bettering of all this. As the Twelve Prophets illustrate among them the whole history of written prophecy, I have thought it useful to prefix a historical sketch of the Prophet in early Israel, or as far as the appearance of Amos. The Twelve are then taken in chronological order. Under each of them a chapter is given of historical and critical introduction to his book; then some account of the prophet himself as a man and a seer; then a complete translation of the various prophecies handed down under his name, with textual footnotes, and an exposition and application to the present day in harmony with the aim of the series to which these volumes belong: finally, a discussion of the main doctrines the prophet has taught, if it has not been found possible to deal with these in the course of the exposition.

An exact critical study of the Twelve Prophets is rendered necessary by the state of the entire text. The present work is based on a thorough examination of this in the light of the ancient versions and of modern criticism. The emendations which I have proposed are few and insignificant, but I have examined and discussed in footnotes all that have been suggested, and in many cases my translation will be found to differ widely from that of the Revised Version. To questions of integrity and authenticity more space is devoted than may seem to many to be necessary. But it is certain that the criticism of the prophetic books has now entered on a period of the same analysis and discrimination which is almost exhausted in the case of the Pentateuch. Some hints were given of this in a previous book on Isaiah, chapters xl.–lxvi., which are evidently a composite work. Among the books now before us, the same fact has long been clear in the case of Obadiah and Zechariah, and also since Ewald's time with regard to Micah. But Duhm's "Theology of the Prophets," which appeared in 1875, suggested interpolations in Amos. Wellhausen (in 1873) and Stade (from 1883 onwards) carried the discussion further both on those, and others, of the Twelve; while a recent work by Andrée on Haggai proves that many similar questions may still be raised and have to be debated. The general fact must be admitted that hardly one book has escaped later additions—additions of an entirely justifiable nature, which supplement the point of view of a single prophet with the richer experience or the riper hopes of a later day, and thus afford to ourselves a more catholic presentment of the doctrines of prophecy and the Divine purposes for mankind. This general fact, I say, must be admitted. But the questions of detail are still in process of solution. It is obvious that settled results can be reached (as to some extent they have been already reached in the criticism of the Pentateuch) only after years of research and debate by all schools of critics. Meantime it is the duty of each of us to offer his own conclusions, with regard to every separate passage, on the understanding that, however final they may at present seem to him, the end is not yet. In previous criticism the defects, of which work in the same field has made me aware, are four: 1. A too rigid belief in the exact parallelism and symmetry of the prophetic style, which I feel has led, for instance, Wellhausen, to whom we otherwise owe so much on the Twelve Prophets, into many unnecessary emendations of the text, or, where some amendment is necessary, to absolutely unprovable changes. 2. In passages between which no connection exists, the forgetfulness of the principle that this fact may often be explained as justly by the hypothesis of the omission of some words, as by the favourite theory of the later intrusion of portions of the extant text. 3. Forgetfulness of the possibility, which in some cases amounts almost to certainty, of the incorporation, among the authentic words of a prophet, of passages of earlier as well as of later date. And, 4, depreciation of the spiritual insight and foresight of pre-exilic writers. These, I am persuaded, are defects in previous criticism of the prophets. Probably my own criticism will reveal many more. In the beginnings of such analysis as we are engaged on, we must be prepared for not a little arbitrariness and want of proportion; these are often necessary for insight and fresh points of view, but they are as easily eliminated by the progress of discussion.

All criticism, however, is preliminary to the real work which the immortal prophets demand from scholars and preachers in our age. In a review of a previous volume, I was blamed for applying a prophecy of Isaiah to a problem of our own day. This was called "prostituting prophecy." *The* prostitution of the prophets is their confinement to academic uses. One cannot conceive an ending, at once more pathetic and more ridiculous, to those great streams of living water, than to allow them to run out in the sands of criticism and exegesis, however golden these sands may be. The prophets spoke for a practical purpose; they aimed at the hearts of men; and everything that scholarship can do for their writings has surely for its final aim the illustration of their witness to the ways of God with men, and its application to living questions and duties and hopes. Besides, therefore, seeking to tell the story of that wonderful stage in the history of the human spirit—surely next in wonder to the story of Christ Himself—I have not feared at every suitable point to apply its truths to our lives to-day. The civilisation in which prophecy flourished was in its essentials marvellously like our own. To mark only one point, the rise of prophecy in Israel came fast upon the passage of the nation from an agricultural to a commercial basis of society, and upon the appearance of the very thing which gives its name to civilisation—city-life, with its unchanging sins, problems, and ideals.

A recent Dutch critic, whose exact scholarship is known to all readers of Stade's "Journal of Old Testament Science," has said of Amos and Hosea: "These prophecies have a word of God, as for all times, so also especially for our own. Before all it is relevant to 'the social question' of our day, to the relation of religion and morality. . . Often it has been hard for me to refrain from expressly pointing out the agreement between Then and To-day."* This feeling will be shared by all students of prophecy whose minds and consciences are quick; and I welcome the liberal plan of the series in which this book appears, because, while giving room for the adequate discussion of critical and historical questions, its chief design is to show the eternal validity of the Books of the Bible as the Word of God, and their meaning for ourselves to-day.

Previous works on the Minor Prophets are almost innumerable. Those to which I owe most will be found indicated in the footnotes. The translation has been executed upon the purpose, not to sacrifice the literal meaning or exact emphasis of the original to the frequent possibility of greater elegance. It reproduces every word, with the occasional exception of a copula. With some hesitation I have retained the traditional spelling of the Divine Name, Jehovah, instead of the more correct Jahve or Yahweh; but where the rhythm of certain familiar passages was disturbed by it, I have followed the English versions and written LORD. The reader will keep in mind that a line may be destroyed by substituting our pronunciation of proper names for the more musical accents of the original. Thus, for instance, we obliterate the music of "Isra'el" by making it two syllables and putting the accent on the first: it has three syllables with the accent on the last. We crush Yerushalayîḿ into Jerúsalem; we shred off Asshûr into Assyria, and dub Miṣraîḿ Egypt. Hebrew has too few of the combinations which sound most musical to our ears to afford the suppression of any one of them.

* J. J. P. Valeton, jun., "Amos en Hosea," 1894; quoted by Budde in the *Theologische Literaturzeitung*, September, 1894.

CONTENTS.

CHRONOLOGY OF THE DOUBLE KINGDOM OF ISRAEL, *c.* 940–639 B. C.

*** *c* = *circa:* it refers only to the accession of the kings of Judah and Israel; the years are exact so far as they concern the Assyrian data. A date opposite the mere name of a king signifies the year of his accession.

	JUDAH	ISRAEL	THE PROPHETS	SYRIA, ETC.	ASSYRIA	
940 *c*	Disruption of the	Kingdom				
	Rehoboam	**Jeroboam I**				
		Establishment of calf images in N. Israel				
923 *c*	**Abijam**					
920 *c*	**Asa**					
918 *c*		**Nadab**				
915		**Baasha**				
891 *c*		**Elah**				
888 *c*		**Zimri Omri**				
876 *c*		**Ahab**		Revolt of **Mesha** of Moab: the		
874 *c*	**Jehoshaphat**		**Elijah**	Moabite Stone (*circa* 860)		
854		First contact of Israel		and Syria with Assyria at the	Battle of **Karkar**	854
853 *c*		**Ahaziah**				
852 *c*		**Joram**				
		Invades Moab with Judah and Edom				
850				Campaigns in all these three	years by **Shalmaneser II** of	850
849 *c*	**Jehoram**			Assyria against **Dadidri** or	**Hadadezer** of Damascus	849
846				Revolt of Edom from Judah (2 Kings viii. 20 ff.)		846
844 *c*	**Ahaziah**					
842 *c*	**Athaliah**	**Jehu**	**Elisha**		Tribute from **Jehu**	842
				War of **Hazael** with	Assyria	
839				War of **Hazael** with	Assyria	839
836 *c*	**Joash**			**Hazael** subdues Gilead (Amos		836
814 *c*		**Jehoahaz**		i. 3); attacks Gath, but is bought off from Jerusalem		814
812					Accession of **Ramman-Nirari**	812
806				Arpad, campaign against, by	Assyria	806
803				Damascus, under **Meri**,	besieged and taken by Assyria	803
				A year of pestilence		
798 *c*		**Joash**				
797 *c*	**Amaziah**					
783 *c*		**Jeroboam II**			**Shalmaneser III**	783
778 *c*	**Uzziah (Azariah)**					
775					Expedition to Cedar Country	775
773		**Jeroboam** re-conquers		Damascus, campaign against,	by Assyria	773
772		Moab, Gilead, and		Hadrach, campaign against,	by Assyria	772
765		part of Aram		A pestilence	Accession of **Assur-dan-il**	765
				Hadrach, campaign against,	by Assyria	
763	Total eclipse of	the sun on June 15th,		visible in Syria and at	Nineveh	763
759				A pestilence in Western Asia		759
755				Hadrach suffers attack from	Assyria	755
754			**Amos**	Arpad suffers attack from	Assyria	754
753					Accession of **Assur-Nirari**	753
745					Accession of **Tiglath-Pileser III**	745
743		**Zechariah,** son of **Jeroboam** (6 months)				743
		Shallum (1 month)				
		Menahem		Arpad besieged, and after two	or three years taken by Assyria	
742						742
741			**Hosea**			741
740	"The year **King Uzziah** died"					
736 ?	**Jotham** sole ruler					
738		**Menahem** is		mentioned as tributary to	Assyria	738
737 *c*		**Pekahiah**				
736 *c*	**Ahaz**	**Pekah**, the Gileadite				
735	**Ahaz** is attacked	both by **Pekah** and		by **Rezin** of Damascus (Isa. vii.)		735
734		Captivity of **Gilead, Galilee,** etc.			by Assyria (Isa. viii., ix.),	734
733				Damascus besieged and taken	by Assyria	733
732	**Ahaz** pays homage			at Damascus to the King of	Assyria	732
731					**Tiglath-Pileser** becomes **King** of Babylon under the name **of Pul**	731
730 *c*		**Hoshea**				
727 *c*	**Hezekiah**				**Shalmaneser IV**	727
725		Siege of Samaria begins	**Isaiah**			
722 or 1		Fall of Samaria			**Sargon** takes Samaria	722 or 1
720 or 19				Gaza overthrown by	**Sargon** as he marches **past Judah** and defeats Egypt at **Raphia**	720 or 19
715		Samaria peopled			by subjugated tribes deported from Assyria	715
711				Ashdod taken by	**Sargon**	711
709					**Sargon** takes Babylon from **Merodach-Baladan**	709
705			**Micah**		Death of **Sargon**	705
					Accession of **Sennacherib**	
704					War with **Merodach-Baladan**	704
701	Invasion of Judah			and of all Syria	by **Sennacherib**	701
	Deliverance of **Jerusalem**			Siege of Ekron. Battle of Eltekeh		
695 *c**	**Manasseh**					
681					**Sennacherib** murdered. **Asarhaddon** succeeds	681
678				Phœnicia subdued by	**Asarhaddon**	678
676	**Manasseh,**	tributary to			Assyria	676
671				Tyre taken by	**Asarhaddon** on his march to Egypt, and conquest of **Memphis**	671
668					**Assurbanipal**	668
666	**Manasseh**	and the		other Syrian kings	tributary to Assyria	666
641 *c*	**Amon**			Tyre assists	**Assurbanipal** against	641
				the Phœnician Arvad		
639 *c*	**Josiah**					

* This date is very uncertain. It may have been 690, or according to some 685.

THE BOOK OF THE TWELVE PROPHETS.

BY GEORGE ADAM SMITH, D. D., LL. D.

PART I.

INTRODUCTION.

CHAPTER I.

THE BOOK OF THE TWELVE.

In the order of our English Bible the Minor Prophets, as they are usually called, form the last twelve books of the Old Testament. They are immediately preceded by Daniel, and before him by the three Major Prophets, Isaiah, Jeremiah (with Lamentations), and Ezekiel. Why all sixteen were thus gathered at the end of the other sacred books we do not know. Perhaps, because it was held fitting that prophecy should occupy the last outposts of the Old Testament towards the New.

In the Hebrew Bible, however, the order differs, and is much more significant. The Prophets * form the second division of the threefold Canon: Law, Prophets, and Writings; and Daniel is not among them. The Minor follow immediately after Ezekiel. Moreover, they are not twelve books, but one. They are gathered under the common title "Book of the Twelve;" † and although each of them has the usual colophon detailing the number of its own verses, there is also one colophon for all the twelve, placed at the end of Malachi and reckoning the sum of their verses from the first of Hosea onwards. This unity, which there is reason to suppose was given to them before their reception into the Canon,‡ they have never since lost. However much their place has changed in the order of the books of the Old Testament, however much their own internal arrangement has differed, the Twelve have always stood together. There has been every temptation to scatter them because of their various dates. Yet they never have been scattered; and in spite of the fact that they have not preserved their common title in any Bible outside the Hebrew, that title has lived on in literature and common talk. Thus the Greek Canon omits it; but Greek Jews and Christians always counted the books as one volume,§ calling them "The Twelve Prophets," or "The Twelve-Prophet" Book.‖ It was the Latins who designated them "The Minor Prophets": "on account of their brevity as compared with those who are called the Major because of their ampler volumes." * And this name has passed into most modern languages,† including our own. But surely it is better to revert to the original, canonical and unambiguous title of "The Twelve."

The collection and arrangement of "The Twelve" are matters of obscurity, from which, however, three or four facts emerge that are tolerably certain. The inseparableness of the books is a proof of the ancient date of their union. They must have been put together before they were received into the Canon. The Canon of the Prophets—Joshua to Second Kings and Isaiah to Malachi—was closed by 200 B. C. at the latest, and perhaps as early as 250; but if we have (as seems probable) portions of "The Twelve," ‡ which must be assigned to a little later than 300, this may be held to prove that the whole collection cannot have long preceded the fixing of the Canon of the Prophets. On the other hand, the fact that these latest pieces have not been placed under a title of their own, but are attached to the Book of Zechariah, is pretty sufficient evidence that they were added after the collection and fixture of twelve books—a round number which there would be every disposition not to disturb. That would give us for the date of the first edition (so to speak) of our Twelve some year before 300; and for the date of the second edition some year towards 250. This is a question, however, which may be reserved for final decision after we have examined the date of the separate books, and especially of Joel and the second half of Zechariah. That there was a previous collection, as early as the Exile, of the books written before then, may be regarded as more than probable. But we have no means of fixing its exact limits. Why the Twelve were all ultimately put together is reasonably suggested by Jewish writers. They are small, and, as separate rolls, might have been lost.§ It is possible that the desire of the round number twelve is responsible for the admission of Jonah, a book very different in form from all the others; just as we have hinted that the fact of there being already twelve may account for the attachment of the late fragments to the Book of Zechariah. But all this is only to guess, where we have no means of certain knowledge.

"The Book of the Twelve" has not always held the place which it now occupies in the Hebrew Canon, at the end of the Prophets. The rabbis taught that Hosea, but for the comparative smallness of his prophecy, should have stood first of all the writing prophets, of whom they regarded him as the oldest.‖ And doubtless it was for the same chronological reasons that early Christian catalogues of the Scriptures

* Including, of course, the historical books, Joshua to 2 Kings, which were known as "the Former Prophets"; while what we call the prophets, Isaiah to Malachi, were known as "the Latter."

† ספר תרי עשר, the Aramaic form of the Hebrew עשר שנים, which appears with the other in the colophon to the book. A later contraction is תריסר. This is the form transliterated in Epiphanius: δαθαριασαρα.

‡ See Ryle, "Canon of the O. T.," p. 105.

§ So Josephus, "Contra Apion," i. 8 (*circa* 90 A. D.), reckons the prophetical books as thirteen, of which the Minor Prophets could only have been counted as one—whatever the other twelve may have been. Melito of Sardis (*c.* 170), quoted by Eusebius ("Hist. Eccl.," iv. 26), speaks of τῶν δώδεκα ἐν μονοβίβλῳ. To Origen (*c.* 250: *apud Ibid.*, vi. 25) they could only have been one out of the twenty-two he gives for the O. T. *Cf.* Jerome ("Prolog. Galeatus"), "Liber duodecim Prophetarum."

‖ Οἱ Δώδεκα Προφῆται: Jesus son of Sirach xlix. 10; Τὸ δωδεκαπρόφητον.

* Augustine, "De Civ. Dei," xviii. 29: *cf.* Jerome, "Proem. in Esaiam."

† The German usage generally preserves the numeral, "Die zwölf kleinen Propheten."

‡ See Vol. II. on Zech. ix. ff.

§ "Talmud": Baba Bathra, 14*a*: *cf.* Rashi's Commentary.

‖ "Talmud," *ibid.*

and various editions of the Septuagint placed the whole of "The Twelve" in front of Isaiah.*

The internal arrangement of "The Twelve" in our English Bible is the same as that of the Hebrew Canon, and was probably determined by what the compilers thought to be the respective ages of the books. Thus, first we have six, all supposed to be of the earlier Assyrian period, before 700—Hosea, Joel, Amos, Obadiah, Jonah, and Micah; then three from the late Assyrian and the Babylonian periods—Nahum, Habakkuk, and Zephaniah; and then three from the Persian period after the Exile—Haggai, Zechariah, and Malachi. The Septuagint have altered the order of the first six, arranging Hosea, Amos, Micah, Joel, and Obadiah according to their size, and setting Jonah after them, probably because of his different form. The remaining six are left as in the Hebrew.

Recent criticism, however, has made it clear that the Biblical order of "The Twelve Prophets" is no more than a very rough approximation to the order of their real dates; and, as it is obviously best for us to follow in their historical succession prophecies which illustrate the whole history of prophecy from its rise with Amos to its fall with Malachi and his successors, I propose to do this. Detailed proofs of the separate dates must be left to each book. All that is needful here is a general statement of the order.

Of the first six prophets the dates of Amos, Hosea, and Micah (but of the latter's book in part only) are certain. The Jews have been able to defend Hosea's priority only on fanciful grounds.† Whether or not he quotes from Amos, his historical allusions are more recent. With the exception of a few fragments incorporated by later authors, the Book of Amos is thus the earliest example of prophetic literature, and we take it first. The date we shall see is about 755. Hosea begins five or ten years later, and Micah just before 722. The three are in every respect—originality, comprehensiveness, influence upon other prophets—the greatest of our Twelve, and will therefore be treated with most detail, occupying the whole of the first volume.

The rest of the first six are Obadiah, Joel, and Jonah. But the Book of Obadiah, although it opens with an early oracle against Edom, is in its present form from after the Exile. The Book of Joel is of uncertain date, but, as we shall see, the great probability is that it is late; and the Book of Jonah belongs to a form of literature so different from the others that we may, most conveniently, treat of it last.

This leaves us to follow Micah, at the end of the eighth century, with the group Zephaniah, Nahum, and Habakkuk from the second half of the seventh century; and finally to take in their order the post-exilic Haggai, Zechariah i.-ix., Malachi, and the other writings which we feel obliged to place about or even after that date.

One other word is needful. This assignment of the various books to different dates is not to be held as implying that the whole of a book belongs to such a date or to the author whose name it bears. We shall find that hands have been busy with the texts of the books long after the authors of these must have passed away; that besides early fragments incorporated by later writers, prophets of Israel's new dawn mitigated the judgments and enlightened the gloom of the watchmen of her night; that here and there are passages which are evidently intrusions, both because they interrupt the argument and because they reflect a much later historical environment than their context. This, of course, will require discussion in each case, and such discussion will be given. The text will be subjected to an independent examination. Some passages hitherto questioned we may find to be unjustly so; others not hitherto questioned we may see reason to suspect. But in any case we shall keep in mind that the results of an independent inquiry are uncertain; and that in this new criticism of the prophets, which is comparatively recent, we cannot hope to arrive for some time at so general a consensus as is being rapidly reached in the far older and more elaborated criticism of the Pentateuch.*

Such is the extent and order of the journey which lies before us. If it is not to the very summits of Israel's outlook that we climb—Isaiah, Jeremiah, and the great Prophet of the Exile—we are yet to traverse the range of prophecy from beginning to end. We start with its first abrupt elevations in Amos. We are carried by the side of Isaiah and Jeremiah, yet at a lower altitude, on to the Exile. With the returned Israel we pursue an almost immediate rise to vision, and then by Malachi and others are conveyed down dwindling slopes to the very end. Beyond the land is flat. Though Psalms are sung and brave deeds done, and faith is strong and bright, there is no height of outlook; "there is no more any prophet"† in Israel.

But our "Twelve" do more than thus carry us from beginning to end of the Prophetic Period. Of second rank as are most of the heights of this mountain range, they yet bring forth and speed on their way not a few of the streams of living water which have nourished later ages and are flowing to-day. Impetuous cataracts of righteousness—"let it roll on like water, and justice as an everlasting stream"; the irrepressible love of God to sinful men; the perseverance and pursuits of His grace; His mercies that follow the exile and the outcast; His truth that goes forth richly upon the heathen; the hope of the Saviour of mankind; the outpouring of the Spirit; counsels of patience; impulses of tenderness and of healing; melodies innumerable,—all sprang from these lower hills of prophecy, and sprang so strongly that the world hears and feels them still.

And from the heights of our present pilgrimage there are also clear those great visions of the Stars and the Dawn, of the Sea and the Storm, concerning which it is true that as long as men live they shall seek out the places whence they can be seen, and thank God for His prophets.

* So the Codices Vaticanus and Alexandrinus, but not Cod. Sin. So also Cyril of Jerusalem († 386), Athanasius (365), Gregory Naz. († 390), and the spurious Canon of the Council of Laodicea (*c.* 400) and Epiphanius (403). See Ryle, "Canon of the O. T.," 215 ff.

† By a forced interpretation of the phrase in chap. i. 2, "When the Lord spake at the first by Hosea" (R. V.) "Talmud": Baba Bathra, 14*a*.

* For further considerations on this point see pp. 477, 491, 493 ff., 497 ff., 518 ff., etc.

† Psalm lxxiv. 9.

CHAPTER II.

THE PROPHET IN EARLY ISRAEL.

OUR "Twelve Prophets" will carry us, as we have seen, across the whole extent of the Prophetical period—the period when prophecy became literature, assuming the form and rising to the intensity of an imperishable influence on the world. The earliest of the Twelve, Amos and Hosea, were the inaugurators of this period. They were not only the first (so far as we know) to commit prophecy to writing, but we find in them the germs of all its subsequent development. Yet Amos and Hosea were not unfathered. Behind them lay an older dispensation, and their own was partly a product of this, and partly a revolt against it. Amos says of himself: "The Lord hath spoken, who can but prophesy?"—but again: "No prophet I, nor prophet's son!" Who were those earlier prophets whose office Amos assumed while repudiating their spirit—whose name he abjured, yet could not escape from it? And, while we are about the matter, what do we mean by "prophet" in general?

In vulgar use the name "prophet" has degenerated to the meaning of "one who foretells the future." Of this meaning it is, perhaps, the first duty of every student of prophecy earnestly and stubbornly to rid himself. In its native Greek tongue "prophet" meant not "one who speaks before," but "one who speaks for, or on behalf of, another." At the Delphic oracle "The Prophêtês" was the title of the official who received the utterances of the frensied Pythoness and expounded them to the people; * but Plato says that this is a misuse of the word, and that the true prophet is the inspired person himself, he who is in communication with the Deity and who speaks directly for the Deity.† So Tiresias, the seer, is called by Pindar the "prophet" or "interpreter of Zeus," ‡ and Plato even styles poets "the prophets of the Muses." § It is in this sense that we must think of the "Prophet" of the Old Testament. He is a speaker for God. The sharer of God's counsels, as Amos calls him, he becomes the bearer and preacher of God's Word. Prediction of the future is only a part, and often a subordinate and accidental part, of an office whose full function is to declare the character and the will of God. But the prophet does this in no systematic or abstract form. He brings his revelation point by point, and in connection with some occasion in the history of his people, or some phase of their character. He is not a philosopher nor a theologian with a system of doctrine (at least before Ezekiel), but the messenger and herald of God at some crisis in the life or conduct of His people. His message is never out of touch with events. These form either the subject-matter or the proof or the execution of every oracle he utters. It is, therefore, God not merely as Truth, but far more as Providence, whom the prophet reveals. And although that Providence includes the full destiny of Israel and mankind, the prophet brings the news of it, for the most part, piece by piece, with reference to some present sin or duty, or some impending crisis or calamity. Yet he does all this, not merely because the word needed for the day has been committed to him by itself, and as if he were only its mechanical vehicle; but because he has come under the overwhelming conviction of God's presence and of His character, a conviction often so strong that God's word breaks through him and God speaks in the first person to the people.

I. FROM THE EARLIEST TIMES TILL SAMUEL.

There was no ancient people but believed in the power of certain personages to consult the Deity and to reveal His will. Every man could sacrifice; but not every man could render in return the oracle of God. This pertained to select individuals or orders. So the prophet seems to have been an older specialist than the priest, though in every tribe he frequently combined the latter's functions with his own.*

The matters on which ancient man consulted God were as wide as life. But naturally at first, in a rude state of society and at a low stage of mental development, it was in regard to the material defence and necessities of life, the bare law and order, that men almost exclusively sought the Divine will. And the whole history of prophecy is just the effort to substitute for these elementary provisions a more personal standard of the moral law, and more spiritual ideals of the Divine grace.

By the Semitic race—to which we may now confine ourselves, since Israel belonged to it—Deity was worshipped, in the main, as the god of a tribe. Every Semitic tribe had its own god; it would appear that there was no god without a tribe: † the traces of belief in a supreme and abstract Deity are few and ineffectual. The tribe was the medium by which the god made himself known, and became an effective power on earth: the god was the patron of the tribe, the supreme magistrate and the leader in war. The piety he demanded was little more than loyalty to ritual; the morality he enforced was only a matter of police. He took no cognisance of the character or inner thoughts of the individual. But the tribe believed him to stand in very close connection with all the practical interests of their common life. They asked of

* Herodotus, viii. 36, 37.

† "Timæus," 71, 72. The whole passage is worth transcribing:

"No man, when in his senses, attains prophetic truth and inspiration; but when he receives the inspired word either his intelligence is enthralled by sleep, or he is demented by some distemper or possession. And he who would understand what he remembers to have been said, whether in dream or when he was awake, by the prophetic and enthusiastic nature, or what he has seen, must recover his senses; and then he will be able to explain rationally what all such words and apparitions mean, and what indications they afford, to this man or that, of past, present, or future, good and evil. But, while he continues demented, he cannot judge of the visions which he sees or the words which he utters; the ancient saying is very true that 'only a man in his senses can act or judge about himself and his own affairs.' And for this reason it is customary to appoint diviners or interpreters as discerners of the oracles of the gods. Some persons call them prophets; they do not know that they are only repeaters of dark sayings and visions, and are not to be called prophets at all, but only interpreters of prophecy" (Jowett's "Translation").

‡ "Nik.," i. 91.

§ "Phædrus," 262 D.

* It is still a controversy whether the original meaning of the Semitic root KHN is prophet, as in the Arabic KâHiN, or priest, as in the Hebrew KôHeN.

† *Cf.* Jer. ii. 10: "For pass over to the isles of Chittim; and see; and send unto Kedar, and consider diligently, and see if there be such a thing. Hath a nation changed their gods?" From the isles of Chittim unto Kedar—the limits of the Semitic world.

him the detection of criminals, the discovery of lost property, the settlement of civil suits, sometimes when the crops should be sown, and always when war should be waged and by what tactics.

The means by which the prophet consulted the Deity on these subjects were for the most part primitive and rude. They may be summed up under two kinds: Visions either through falling into ecstasy or by dreaming in sleep, and Signs or Omens. Both kinds are instanced in Balaam.* Of the signs some were natural, like the whisper of trees, the flight of birds, the passage of clouds, the movement of stars. Others were artificial, like the casting or drawing of lots. Others were between these, like the shape assumed by the entrails of the sacrificed animals when thrown on the ground. Again, the prophet was often obliged to do something wonderful in the people's sight in order to convince them of his authority. In Biblical language he had to work a miracle or give a sign. One instance throws a flood of light on this habitual expectancy of the Semitic mind. There was once an Arab chief who wished to consult a distant soothsayer as to the guilt of a daughter. But before he would trust the seer to give him the right answer to such a question he made him discover a grain of corn which he had concealed about his horse.† He required the physical sign before he would accept the moral judgment.

Now, to us, the crudeness of the means employed, the opportunities of fraud, the inadequacy of the tests for spiritual ends, are very obvious. But do not let us, therefore, miss the numerous moral opportunities which lay before the prophet even at that early stage of his evolution. He was trusted to speak in the name of Deity. Through him men believed in God and in the possibility of a revelation. They sought from him the discrimination of evil from good. The highest possibilities of social ministry lay open to him: the tribal existence often hung on his word for peace or war; he was the mouth of justice, the rebuke of evil, the champion of the wronged. Where such opportunities were present, can we imagine the Spirit of God to have been absent—the Spirit Who seeks men more than they seek Him, and, as He condescends to use their poor language for religion, must also have stooped to the picture language, to the rude instruments, symbols and sacraments, of their early faith?

In an office of such mingled possibilities everything depended—as we shall find it depend to the very end of prophecy—on the moral insight and character of the prophet himself, on his conception of God and whether he was so true to this as to overcome his professional temptations to fraud and avarice, malice towards individuals, subservience to the powerful, or, worst snares of all, the slothfulness and insincerity of routine. We see this moral issue put very clearly in such a story as that of Balaam, or in such a career as that of Mohammed.

So much for the Semitic soothsayer in general. Now let us turn to Israel.

Among the Hebrews the "man of God,"‡ to use his widest designation, is at first called "Seer," § or "Gazer," * the word which Balaam uses of himself. In consulting the Divine will he employs the same external means, he offers the people for their evidence the same signs, as do the seers or soothsayers of other Semitic tribes. He gains influence by the miracles, "the wonderful things," which he does.† Moses himself is represented after this fashion. He meets the magicians of Egypt on their own level. His use of "rods"; the holding up of his hands that Israel may prevail against Amaleq; Joshua's casting of lots to discover a criminal; Samuel's dream in the sanctuary; his discovery for a fee of the lost asses of Saul; David and the images in his house, the ephod he consulted; the sign to go to battle "what time thou hearest the sound of a going in the tops of the mulberry trees"; Solomon's inducement of dreams by sleeping in the sanctuary at Gibeah,—these are a few of the many proofs that early prophecy in Israel employed not only the methods but even much of the furniture of the kindred Semitic religions. But then those tools and methods were at the same time accompanied by the noble opportunities of the prophetic office to which I have just alluded—opportunities of religious and social ministry—and still more, these opportunities were at the disposal of moral influences which, it is a matter of history, were not found in any other Semitic religion than Israel's. However you will explain it, that Divine Spirit, which we have felt unable to conceive as absent from any Semitic prophet who truly sought after God, that Light which lighteth every man who cometh into the world, was present to an unparalleled degree with the early prophets of Israel. He came to individuals, and to the nation as a whole, in events and in influences which may be summed up as the impression of the character of their national God, Jehovah: to use Biblical language, as "Jehovah's spirit" and "power." It is true that in many ways the Jehovah of early Israel reminds us of other Semitic deities. Like some of them He appears with thunder and lightning; like all of them He is the God of one tribe who are His peculiar people. He bears the same titles —Melek, Adon, Baal ("King," "Lord," "Possessor"). He is propitiated by the same offerings. To choose one striking instance, captives and spoil of war are sacrificed to Him with the same relentlessness, and by a process which has even the same names given to it, as in the votive inscriptions of Israel's heathen neighbours.‡ Yet, notwithstanding all these elements, the religion of Jehovah from the very first evinced, by the confession of all critics, an ethical force shared by no other Semitic creed. From the first there was in it the promise and the potency of that sublime monotheism, which in the period of our "Twelve" it afterwards reached.§ Its earliest effects of course were chiefly political: it welded the twelve tribes into the unity of a nation; it preserved them as one amid the many temptations to scatter along those divergent lines of culture and of faith

* Numbers xxiv. 4, "falling but having his eyes open." Ver. 1, *enchantments* ought to be *omens*.

† Instanced by Wellhausen, "Skizzen u. Vorarb.," No. v.

‡ איש אלהים

§ רֹאֶה

* חֹזֶה

† Deut. xiii. 1 ff. admits that heathen seers were able to work miracles and give signs, as well as the prophets of Jehovah.

‡ *Cf.* Mesha's account of himself and Chemosh on the Moabite Stone, with the narrative of the taking of Ai in the Book of Joshua.

§ *Cf.* Kuenen: "Gesammelte Abhandlungen" (trans. by Budde), p. 461.

which the geography of their country placed so attractively before them.* It taught them to prefer religious loyalty to material advantage, and so inspired them with high motives for self-sacrifice and every other duty of patriotism. But it did even better than thus teach them to bear one another's burdens. It inspired them to care for one another's sins. The last chapters of the Book of Judges prove how strong a national conscience there was in early Israel. Even then Israel was a moral, as well as a political, unity. Gradually there grew up, but still unwritten, a body of Torah, or revealed law, which, though its framework was the common custom of the Semitic race, was inspired by ideals of humanity and justice not elsewhere in that race discernible by us.

When we analyse this ethical distinction of early Israel, this indubitable progress which the nation were making while the rest of their world was morally stagnant, we find it to be due to their impressions of the character of their God. This character did not affect them as Righteousness only. At first it was even a more wonderful Grace. Jehovah had chosen them when they were no people, had redeemed them from servitude, had brought them to their land; had borne with their stubbornness, and had forgiven their infidelities. Such a Character was partly manifest in the great events of their history, and partly communicated itself to their finest personalities—as the Spirit of God does communicate with the spirit of man made in His image. Those personalities were the early prophets from Moses to Samuel. They inspired the nation to believe in God's purposes for itself; they rallied it to war for the common faith, and war was then the pitch of self-sacrifice; they gave justice to it in God's name, and rebuked its sinfulness without sparing. Criticism has proved that we do not know nearly so much about those first prophets as perhaps we thought we did. But under their God they made Israel. Out of their work grew the monotheism of their successors, whom we are now to study, and later the Christianity of the New Testament. For myself I cannot but believe that in the influence of Jehovah which Israel owned in those early times there was the authentic revelation of a real Being.

2. From Samuel to Elisha.

Of the oldest order of Hebrew prophecy, Samuel was the last representative. Till his time, we are told, the prophet in Israel was known as the Seer,† but now, with other tempers and other habits, a new order appears whose name —and that means to a certain extent their spirit —is to displace the older name and the older spirit.

When Samuel anointed Saul he bade him, for a sign that he was chosen of the Lord, go forth to meet "a company of prophets"—Nebi'im, the singular is Nabi'—coming down from the high place or sanctuary with viols, drums and pipes, and *prophesying*. "There," he added, "the spirit of Jehovah shall come upon thee, and thou shalt prophesy with them, and shalt be turned into another man." So it happened; and the people "said one to another, What is this that is come to the son of Kish? Is Saul also among the prophets?"* Another story, probably from another source, tells us that later, when Saul sent troops of messengers to the sanctuary at Ramah to take David, they saw "the company of prophets prophesying and Samuel standing appointed over them, and the spirit of God fell" upon one after another of the troops; as upon Saul himself when he followed them up. "And he stripped off his clothes also, and prophesied before Samuel in like manner, and lay down naked all that day and all that night. Wherefore they say, Is Saul also among the prophets?"†

All this is very different from the habits of the Seer, who had hitherto represented prophecy. He was solitary, but these went about in bands. They were filled with an infectious enthusiasm, by which they excited each other and all sensitive persons whom they touched. They stirred up this enthusiasm by singing, playing upon instruments, and dancing: its results were frensy, the tearing of their clothes, and prostration. The same phenomena have appeared in every religion—in Paganism often, and several times within Christianity. They may be watched to-day among the dervishes of Islam, who by singing (as one has seen them in Cairo), by swaying of their bodies, by repeating the Divine Name, and dwelling on the love and ineffable power of God, work themselves into an excitement which ends in prostration and often in insensibility.‡ The whole process is due to an overpowering sense of the Deity—crude and unintelligent if you will, but sincere and authentic —which seems to haunt the early stages of all religions, and to linger to the end with the stagnant and unprogressive. The appearance of this prophecy in Israel has given rise to a controversy as to whether it was purely a native product, or was induced by infection from the Canaanite tribes around. Such questions are of little interest in face of these facts: that the ecstasy sprang up in Israel at a time when the spirit of the people was stirred against the Philistines, and patriotism and religion were equally excited; that it is represented as due to the Spirit of Jehovah; and that the last of the old order of Jehovah's prophets recognised its harmony with his own dispensation, presided over it, and gave Israel's first king as one of his signs, that he should come under its power. These things being so, it is surprising that a recent critic§ should have seen in the dancing prophets nothing but eccentrics into whose company it was shame for so good a man as Saul to fall. He reaches this conclusion only by supposing that the reflexive verb used for their "prophesying" —*hithnabbē'*—had at this time that equivalence to mere madness to which it was reduced by the excesses of later generations of prophets. With Samuel we feel that the word had no reproach: the Nebi'îm were recognised by him as standing in the prophetical succession. They sprang up in sympathy with a national movement. The king who joined himself to them was the same who sternly banished from Israel all the baser

* So in Deborah's Song.

† 1 Sam. ix. 9.

* 1 Sam. x. 1–16, xi. 1–11, 15. Chap. x. 17–27, xi. 12–14, belong to other and later documents. *Cf.* Robertson Smith, "Old Testament in the Jewish Church," 135 ff.

† 1 Sam. xix. 20–24.

‡ What seemed most to induce the frensy of the dervishes whom I watched was the fixing of their attention upon, the yearning of their minds after, the love of God. "Ya habeebi!"—"O my beloved!"—they cried.

§ Cornill, in the first of his lectures on "Der Israelitische Prophetismus," one of the very best popular studies of prophecy, by a master on the subject. See p. 73 *n*.

forms of soothsaying and traffic with the dead. But, indeed, we need no other proof than this: the name Nebi'im so establishes itself in the popular regard that it displaces the older names of Seer and Gazer, and becomes the classical term for the whole body of prophets from Moses to Malachi.

There was one very remarkable change effected by this new order of prophets, probably the very greatest relief which prophecy experienced in the course of its evolution. This was separation from the ritual and from the implements of soothsaying. Samuel had been both priest and prophet. But after him the names and the duties were specialised, though the specialising was incomplete. While the new Nebi'im remained in connection with the ancient centres of religion, they do not appear to have exercised any part of the ritual. The priests, on the other hand, did not confine themselves to sacrifice, and other forms of public worship, but exercised many of the so-called prophetic functions. They also, as Hosea tells us, were expected to give Tôrôth—revelations of the Divine will on points of conduct and order. There remained with them the ancient forms of oracle—the Ephod, or plated image, the Teraphim, the lot, and the Urim and Thummim,* all of these apparently still regarded as indispensable elements of religion.† From such rude forms of ascertaining the Divine Will, prophecy in its new order was absolutely free. And it was free of the ritual of the sanctuaries. As has been justly remarked, the ritual of Israel always remained a peril to the people, the peril of relapsing into Paganism. Not only did it materialise faith and engross affections in the worshipper which were meant for moral objects, but very many of its forms were actually the same as those of the other Semitic religions, and it tempted its devotees to the confusion of their God with the gods of the heathen. Prophecy was now wholly independent of it, and we may see in such independence the possibility of all the subsequent career of prophecy along moral and spiritual lines. Amos absolutely condemns the ritual, and Hosea brings the message from God, "I will have mercy and not sacrifice." This is the distinctive glory of prophecy in that era in which we are to study it. But do not let us forget that it became possible through the ecstatic Nebi'im of Samuel's time, and through their separation from the national ritual and the material forms of soothsaying. It is the way of Providence to prepare for the revelation of great moral truths, by the enfranchisement, sometimes centuries before, of an order or a nation of men from political or professional interests which would have rendered it impossible for their descendants to appreciate those truths without prejudice or compromise.

We may conceive then of these Nebi'im, these prophets, as enthusiasts for Jehovah and for Israel. For Jehovah—if to-day we see men cast by the adoration of the despot-deity of Islam into transports so excessive that they lose all consciousness of earthly things and fall into a trance, can we not imagine a like effect produced on the same sensitive natures of the East by the contemplation of such a God as Jehovah, so mighty in earth and heaven, so faithful to His people, so full of grace? Was not such an ecstasy of worship most likely to be born of the individual's ardent devotion in the hour of the nation's despair? * Of course there would be swept up by such a movement all the more volatile and unbalanced minds of the day—as these always have been swept up by any powerful religious excitement—but that is not to discredit the sincerity of the main volume of the feeling nor its authenticity as a work of the Spirit of God, as the impression of the character and power of Jehovah.

But these ecstatics were also enthusiasts for Israel; and this saved the movement from morbidness. They worshipped God neither out of sheer physical sympathy with nature, like the Phœnician devotees of Adonis or the Greek Bacchantes; nor out of terror at the approaching end of all things, like some of the ecstatic sects of the Middle Ages; nor out of a selfish passion for their own salvation, like so many a modern Christian fanatic; but in sympathy with their nation's aspirations for freedom and her whole political life. They were enthusiasts for their people. The ecstatic prophet was not confined to his body nor to nature for the impulses of Deity. Israel was his body, his atmosphere, his universe. Through it all he felt the thrill of Deity. Confine religion to the personal, it grows rancid, morbid. Wed it to patriotism, it lives in the open air and its blood is pure. So in days of national danger the Nebi'im would be inspired like Saul to battle for their country's freedom; in more settled times they would be lifted to the responsibilities of educating the people, counselling the governors, and preserving the national traditions. This is what actually took place. After the critical period of Saul's time has passed, the prophets still remain enthusiasts; but they are enthusiasts for affairs. They counsel and they rebuke David.† They warn Rehoboam, and they excite Northern Israel to revolt.‡ They overthrow and they set up dynasties.§ They offer the king advice on campaigns.‖ Like Elijah, they take up against the throne the cause of the oppressed; ¶ like Elisha, they stand by the throne its most trusted counsellors in peace and war.** That all this is no new order of prophecy in Israel, but the developed form of the ecstacy of Samuel's day, is plain from the continuance of the name Nebi'im and from these two facts besides: that the ecstasy survives and that the prophets still live in communities. The greatest figures of the period, Elijah and Elisha, have upon them "the hand of the Lord," as the influence is now called: Elijah when he runs before Ahab's chariot across Esdraelon, Elisha when by music he induces upon himself the prophetic mood.†† Another ecstatic figure is the prophet who was sent to anoint Jehu; he swept in and he swept out again, and the soldiers called him "that mad fellow." ‡‡

* It is now past doubt that these were two sacred stones used for decision in the case of an alternative issue. This is plain from the amended reading of Saul's prayer in 1 Sam. xiv. 41, 42 (after the LXX.): "O Jehovah God of Israel, wherefore hast Thou not answered Thy servant this day? If the iniquity be in me or in Jonathan my son, O Jehovah God of Israel, give Urim: and if it be in Thy people Israel, give, I pray Thee, Thummim."

† Hosea iii. 4. See next chapter, p. 451.

* *Cf.* Deut. xxviii. 34.

† 2 Sam. xii. 1 ff.

‡ 1 Kings xi. 29; xii. 22.

§ 1 Kings xiv. 2, 7-11; xix. 15 f.; 2 Kings ix. 3 ff.

‖ 1 Kings xxii. 5 ff.; 2 Kings iii. 11 ff.

¶ 1 Kings xxi. 1 ff.

** 2 Kings vi.-viii., etc.

†† 1 Kings xviii. 46; 2 Kings iii. 15.

‡‡ 2 Kings ix. 11. *Mad fellow*, not necessarily a term of reproach.

But the roving bands had settled down into more or less stationary communities, who partly lived by agriculture and partly by the alms of the people or the endowments of the crown.* Their centres were either the centres of national worship, like Bethel and Gilgal, or the centres of government, like Samaria, where the dynasty of Omri supported prophets both of Baal and of Jehovah.† They were called prophets, but also "sons of the prophets," the latter name not because their office was hereditary, but by the Oriental fashion of designating every member of a guild as the son of the guild. In many cases the son may have succeeded his father; but the ranks could be recruited from outside, as we see in the case of the young farmer Elisha, whom Elijah anointed at the plough. They probably all wore the mantle which is distinctive of some of them, the mantle of hair, or skin of a beast.‡

The risks of degeneration, to which this order of prophecy was liable, arose both from its ecstatic temper and from its connection with public affairs.

Religious ecstasy is always dangerous to the moral and intellectual interests of religion. The largest prophetic figures of the period, though they feel the ecstasy, attain their greatness by rising superior to it. Elijah's raptures are impressive; but nobler are his defence of Naboth and his denunciation of Ahab. And so Elisha's inducement of the prophetic mood by music is the least attractive element in his career: his greatness lies in his combination of the care of souls with political insight and vigilance for the national interests. Doubtless there were many of the sons of the prophets who with smaller abilities cultivated a religion as rational and moral. But for the herd ecstasy would be everything. It was so easily induced or imitated that much of it cannot have been genuine. Even where the feeling was at first sincere we can understand how readily it became morbid; how fatally it might fall into sympathy with that drunkenness from wine and that sexual passion which Israel saw already cultivated as worship by the surrounding Canaanites. We must feel these dangers of ecstasy if we would understand why Amos cut himself off from the Nebi'im, and why Hosea laid such emphasis on the moral and intellectual sides of religion: "My people perish for lack of knowledge." Hosea indeed considered the degeneracy of ecstasy as a judgment: "the prophet is a fool, the man of the spirit is mad—for the multitude of thine iniquity."§ A later age derided the ecstatics, and took one of the forms of the verb "to prophesy" as equivalent to the verb "to be mad."‖

But temptations as gross beset the prophet from that which should have been the discipline of his ecstasy—his connection with public affairs. Only some prophets were brave rebukers of the king and the people. The herd which fed at the royal table—four hundred under Ahab—were flatterers, who could not tell the truth, who said Peace, peace, when there was no peace. These were false prophets. Yet it is curious that

* 1 Kings xviii. 4, *cf.* 19; 2 Kings ii. 3, 5; iv. 38-44; v. 20 ff.; vi. 1 ff.; viii. 8 f., etc.

† 1 Kings xviii. 19; xxii. 6.

‡ So Elijah, 2 Kings i. 8: *cf.* John the Baptist, Matt. iii. 4.

§ Hosea ix. 7.

‖ Jer. xxix. 26: "Every man that is mad, and worketh himself into prophecy" (מתנבא, the same form as is used without moral reproach in 1 Sam. x. 10 ff.).

the very early narrative which describes them* does not impute their falsehood to any base motives of their own, but to the direct inspiration of God, who sent forth a lying spirit upon them. So great was the reverence still for the "man of the spirit"! Rather than doubt his inspiration, they held his very lies to be inspired. One does not of course mean that these consenting prophets were conscious liars; but that their dependence on the king, their servile habits of speech, disabled them from seeing the truth. Subserviency to the powerful was their great temptation. In the story of Balaam we see confessed the base instinct that he who paid the prophet should have the word of the prophet in his favour. In Israel prophecy went through exactly the same struggle between the claims of its God and the claims of its patrons. Nor were those patrons always the rich. The bulk of the prophets were dependent on the charitable gifts of the common people, and in this we may find reason for that subjection of so many of them to the vulgar ideals of the national destiny, to signs of which we are pointed by Amos. The priest at Bethel only reflects public opinion when he takes for granted that the prophet is a thoroughly mercenary character: "Seer, get thee gone to the land of Judah: eat there thy bread, and play the prophet there!"† No wonder Amos separates himself from such hireling craftsmen!

Such was the course of prophecy up to Elisha, and the borders of the eighth century. We have seen how even for the ancient prophet, mere soothsayer though we might regard him in respect of the rude instruments of his office, there were present moral opportunities of the highest kind, from which, if he only proved true to them, we cannot conceive the Spirit of God to have been absent. In early Israel we are sure that the Spirit did meet such strong and pure characters, from Moses to Samuel, creating by their means the nation of Israel, welding it to a unity, which was not only political but moral—and moral to a degree not elsewhere realised in the Semitic world. We saw how a new race of prophets arose under Samuel, separate from the older forms of prophecy by lot and oracle, separate, too, from the ritual as a whole; and therefore free for a moral and spiritual advance of which the priesthood, still bound to images and the ancient rites, proved themselves incapable. But this new order of prophecy, besides its moral opportunities, had also its moral perils: its ecstasy was dangerous, its connection with public affairs was dangerous too. Again, the test was the personal character of the prophet himself. And so once more we see raised above the herd great personalities, who carry forward the work of their predecessors. The results are, besides the discipline of the monarchy and the defence of justice and the poor, the firm establishment of Jehovah as the one and only God of Israel, and the impression on Israel both of His omnipotent guidance of them in the past and of a worldwide destiny, still vague but brilliant, which He had prepared for them in the future.

This brings us to Elisha, and from Elisha there are but forty years to Amos. During those forty years, however, there arose within Israel a new civilisation; beyond her there opened up a new world; and with Assyria there entered the re-

* 1 Kings xxii. † Amos vii. 12.

sources of Providence, a new power. It was these three facts—the New Civilisation, the New World, and the New Power—which made the difference between Elisha and Amos, and raised prophecy from a national to a universal religion.

CHAPTER III.

THE EIGHTH CENTURY IN ISRAEL.

THE long life of Elisha fell to its rest on the margin of the eighth century.* He had seen much evil upon Israel. The people were smitten in all their coasts. None of their territory across Jordan was left to them; and not only Hazael and his Syrians, but bands of their own former subjects, the Moabites, periodically raided Western Palestine, up to the very gates of Samaria.† Such a state of affairs determined the activity of the last of the older prophets. Elisha spent his life in the duties of the national defence, and in keeping alive the spirit of Israel against her foes. When he died they called him "Israel's chariot and the horsemen thereof," ‡ so incessant had been both his military vigilance § and his political insight.|| But Elisha was able to leave behind him the promise of a new day of victory.¶ It was in the peace and liberty of this day that Israel rose a step in civilisation; that prophecy, released from the defence, became the criticism, of the national life; and that the people, no longer absorbed in their own borders, looked out, and for the first time realised the great world, of which they were only a part.

King Joash, whose arms the dying Elisha had blessed, won back in the sixteen years of his reign (798-783) the cities which the Syrians had taken from his father.** His successor, Jeroboam II., came in, therefore, with a flowing tide. He was a strong man, and he took advantage of it. During his long reign of about forty years (783-743) he restored the border of Israel from the Pass of Hamath between the Lebanons to the Dead Sea, and occupied at least part of the territory of Damascus.†† This means that the constant raids to which Israel had been subjected now ceased, and that by the time of Amos, about 755, a generation was grown up who had not known defeat, and the most of whom had perhaps no experience even of war.

Along the same length of years Uzziah (*circa* 778-740) had dealt similarly with Judah.‡‡ He had pushed south to the Red Sea, while Jeroboam pushed north to Hamath: and while Jeroboam had taken the Syrian towns he had crushed the Philistine. He had reorganised the army, and invented new engines of siege for casting stones. On such of his frontiers as were opposed to the desert he had built towers: there is no better means of keeping the nomads in subjection.

All this meant such security across broad Israel as had not been known since the glorious days of Solomon. Agriculture must everywhere have revived: Uzziah, the Chronicler tells us, "loved husbandry." But we hear most of Trade and Building. With quarters in Damascus and a port on the Red Sea, with allies in the Phœnician towns and tributaries in the Philistine, with command of all the main routes between Egypt and the North as between the Desert and the Levant, Israel, during those forty years of Jeroboam and Uzziah, must have become a busy and a wealthy commercial power. Hosea calls the Northern Kingdom a very Canaan *—Canaanite being the Hebrew term for trader—as we should say a very Jew; and Amos exposes all the restlessness, the greed, and the indifference to the poor of a community making haste to be rich. The first effect of this was a large increase of the towns and of town-life. Every document of the time—up to 720—speaks to us of its buildings.† In ordinary building houses of ashlar seem to be novel enough to be mentioned. Vast *palaces*—the name of them first heard of in Israel under Omri and his Phœnician alliance, and then only as that of the king's citadel ‡—are now built by wealthy grandees out of money extorted from the poor; they can have risen only since the Syrian wars. There are summer houses in addition to winter houses; and it is not only the king, as in the days of Ahab, who furnishes his buildings with ivory. When an earthquake comes and whole cities are overthrown, the vigour and wealth of the people are such that they build more strongly and lavishly than before.§ With all this we have the characteristic tempers and moods of city-life: the fickleness and liability to panic which are possible only where men are gathered in crowds; the luxury and false art which are engendered only by artificial conditions of life; the deep poverty which in all cities, from the beginning to the end of time, lurks by the side of the most brilliant wealth, its dark and inevitable shadow.

In short, in the half-century between Elisha and Amos, Israel rose from one to another of the great stages of culture. Till the eighth century they had been but a kingdom of fighting husbandmen. Under Jeroboam and Uzziah city-life was developed, and civilisation, in the proper sense of the word, appeared. Only once before had Israel taken so large a step: when they crossed Jordan, leaving the nomadic life for the agricultural; and that had been momentous for their religion. They came among new temptations: the use of wine, and the shrines of local gods who were believed to have more influence on the fertility of the land than Jehovah who had conquered it for His people. But now this further step, from the agricultural stage to the mercantile and civil, was equally fraught with danger. There was the closer intercourse with foreign nations and their cults. There were all the temptations of rapid wealth, all the dangers of an equally increasing poverty. The growth of comfort among the rulers meant the growth of thoughtlessness. Cruelty multiplied with refinement. The upper classes were lifted away from feeling the real woes of the people. There

* He died in 798 or 797.
† 2 Kings x. 32, xiii. 20, 22.
‡ 2 Kings xiii. 14.
§ vi. 12 ff., etc.
|| viii., etc.
¶ xiii. 17 ff.
** 2 Kings xiii. 23-25.
†† xiv. 28, if not Damascus itself.
‡‡ 2 Kings xv. : *cf.* 2 Chron. xxvi.

* xii. 7 (Heb. ver. 8). Trans., "As for Canaan, the balances," etc.
† Amos, *passim.* Hosea viii. 14, etc.; Micah iii. 12; Isa. ix. 10.
‡ ארמון, a word not found in the Pentateuch, Joshua, Judges, or Samuel, is used in 1 Kings xvi. 18, 2 Kings xv. 25, for a citadel within the palace of the king. Similarly in Isa. xxv. 2; Prov. xviii. 19. But in Amos generally of any large or grand house. That the name first appears in the time of Omri's alliance with Tyre, points to a Phœnician origin. Probably from root ארם, "to be high."
§ Isa. ix. 10.

was a well-fed and sanguine patriotism, but at the expense of indifference to social sin and want. Religious zeal and liberality increased, but they were coupled with all the proud's misunderstanding of God: an optimist faith without moral insight or sympathy.

It is all this which makes the prophets of the eighth century so modern, while Elisha's life is still so ancient. With him we are back in the times of our own border wars—of Wallace and Bruce, with their struggles for the freedom of the soil. With Amos we stand among the conditions of our own day. The City has arisen. For the development of the highest form of prophecy, the universal and permanent form, there was needed that marvellously unchanging mould of human life, whose needs and sorrows, whose sins and problems, are to-day the same as they were all those thousands of years ago.

With Civilisation came Literature. The long peace gave leisure for writing; and the just pride of the people in boundaries broad as Solomon's own, determined that this writing should take the form of heroic history. In the parallel reigns of Jeroboam and Uzziah many critics have placed the great epics of Israel: the earlier documents of our Pentateuch which trace God's purposes to mankind by Israel, from the creation of the world to the settlement of the Promised Land; the histories which make up our Books of Judges, Samuel, and Kings. But whether all these were composed now or at an earlier date, it is certain that the nation lived in the spirit of them, proud of its past, aware of its vocation, and confident that its God, who had created the world and so mightily led itself, would bring it from victory by victory to a complete triumph over the heathen. Israel of the eighth century were devoted to Jehovah; and although passion or self-interest might lead individuals or even communities to worship other gods, He had no possible rival upon the throne of the nation.

As they delighted to recount His deeds by their fathers, so they thronged the scenes of these with sacrifice and festival. Bethel and Beersheba, Dan and Gilgal, were the principal; * but Mizpeh, the top of Tabor,† and Carmel,‡ perhaps Penuel,§ were also conspicuous among the countless "high places" ‖ of the land. Of those in Northern Israel Bethel was the chief. It enjoyed the proper site for an ancient shrine, which was nearly always a market as well—near a frontier and where many roads converged; where traders from the East could meet halfway with traders from the West, the woolgrowers of Moab and the Judæan desert with the merchants of Phœnicia and the Philistine coast. Here, on the spot on which the father of the nation had seen heaven open,¶ a great temple was now built, with a priesthood endowed and directed by the crown,** but lavishly supported also by the tithes and free-will offerings of the people.* "It is a sanctuary of the king and a house of the kingdom."† Jeroboam had ordained Dan, at the other end of the kingdom, to be the fellow of Bethel;‡ but Dan was far away from the bulk of the people, and in the eighth century Bethel's real rival was Gilgal.§ Whether this was the Gilgal by Jericho, or the other Gilgal on the Samarian hills near Shiloh, is uncertain. The latter had been a sanctuary in Elijah's day, with a settlement of the prophets; but the former must have proved the greater attraction to a people so devoted to the sacred events of their past. Was it not the first resting-place of the Ark after the passage of Jordan, the scene of the reinstitution of circumcision, of the anointing of the first king, of Judah's second submission to David?‖ As there were many Gilgals in the land—literally "cromlechs," ancient "stone-circles" sacred to the Canaanites as well as to Israel—so there were many Mizpehs, "Watch-towers," "Seers' stations": the one mentioned by Hosea was probably in Gilead.¶ To the southern Beersheba, to which Elijah had fled from Jezebel, pilgrimages were made by northern Israelites traversing Judah. The sanctuary on Carmel was the ancient altar of Jehovah which Elijah had rebuilt; but Carmel seems at this time to have lain, as it did so often, in the power of the Phœnicians, for it is imagined by the prophets only as a hiding-place from the face of Jehovah.**

At all these sanctuaries it was Jehovah and no other who was sought: "thy God, O Israel, which brought thee up out of the land of Egypt." †† At Bethel and at Dan He was adored in the form of a calf; probably at Gilgal also, for there is a strong tradition to that effect; ‡‡ and elsewhere men still consulted the other images which had been used by Saul and by David, the Ephod and the Teraphim.§§ With these there was the old Semitic symbol of the Maççebah, or upright stone on which oil was poured.‖‖ All of them had been used in the worship of Jehovah by the great examples and leaders of the past; all of them had been spared by Elijah and Elisha: it was no wonder that the common people of the eighth century felt them to be indispensable elements of religion, the removal of which, like the removal of the monarchy or of sacrifice itself, would mean utter divorce from the nation's God.¶¶

* 1 Kings xii. 25 ff., and Amos and Hosea *passim*.
† Hosea v. 1.
‡ 1 Kings xviii. 30 ff.
§ 1 Kings xii. 25.
‖ Originally so called from their elevation (though oftener on the flank than on the summit of a hill); but like the name High Street or the Scottish High Kirk, the term came to be dissociated from physical height and was applied to any sanctuary, even in a hollow, like so many of the sacred wells.
¶ The sanctuary itself was probably on the present site of the Burj Beitin (with the ruins of an early Christian Church), some few minutes to the southeast of the present village of Beitin, which probably represents the city of Bethel that was called Luz at the first.
** 1 Kings xii. 25 ff.; Amos vii.

* Amos iv. 4.
† Amos. vii. 13.
‡ 1 Kings xii. 25 ff.
§ Curiously enough conceived by many of the early Christian Fathers as containing the second of the calves. Cyril, "Comm. in Hoseam," 5; Epiph., "De Vitis Proph.," 237; "Chron. Pasc.," 161.
‖ Josh. iv. 20 ff., v. 2 ff.; 1 Sam. xi. 14, 15, etc.; 2 Sam. xix. 15, 40. This Gilgal by Jericho fell to N. Israel after the Disruption; but there is nothing in Amos or Hosea to tell us whether it or the Gilgal near Shiloh, which seems to have absorbed the sanctity of the latter, is the shrine which they couple with Bethel—except that they never talk of "going up" to it. The passage from Epiphanius in previous note speaks of the Gilgal with the calf as the "Gilgal which is in Shiloh."
¶ Site uncertain. See "Hist. Geog.," pp. 579, 586.
** Amos ix. 3. But *cf.* i. 2.
†† 2 Kings xii. 28.
‡‡ See *antea*.
§§ The Ephod, *the plated thing;* presumably a wooden image covered either with a skin of metal or a cloak of metal. The Teraphim were images in human shape.
‖‖ The *menhir* of modern Palestine—not a hewn pillar, but oblong natural stone narrowing a little towards the top (*cf.* W. R. Smith, "Religion of the Semites," (183-188). From Hosea x. 1, 2, it would appear that the maççeboth of the eighth century were artificial. *They make good* maççeboth (A. V. wrongly *images*).
¶¶ So indeed Hosea iii. 4 implies. The Asherah, the pole

One great exception must be made. Compared with the sanctuaries we have mentioned, Zion itself was very modern. But it contained the main repository of Israel's religion, the Ark, and in connection with the Ark the worship of Jehovah was not a worship of images. It is significant that from this, the original sanctuary of Israel, with the pure worship, the new prophecy derived its first inspiration. But to that we shall return later with Amos.* Apart from the Ark, Jerusalem was not free from images, nor even from the altars of foreign deities.

Where the externals of the ritual were thus so much the same as those of the Canaanite cults, which were still practised in and around the land, it is not surprising that the worship of Jehovah should be further invaded by many pagan practices, nor that Jehovah Himself should be regarded with imaginations steeped in pagan ideas of the Godhead. That even the foulest tempers of the Canaanite ritual, those inspired by wine and the sexual passion, were licensed in the sanctuaries of Israel, both Amos and Hosea testify. But the worst of the evil was wrought in the popular conception of God. Let us remember again that Jehovah had no real rival at this time in the devotion of His people, and that their faith was expressed both by the legal forms of His religion and by a liberality which exceeded these. The tithes were paid to Him, and paid, it would appear, with more than legal frequency.† Sabbath and New Moon, as days of worship and rest from business, were observed with a Pharisaic scrupulousness for the letter if not for the spirit.‡ The prescribed festivals were held, and thronged by zealous devotees who rivalled each other in the amount of their free-will offerings.§ Pilgrimages were made to Bethel, to Gilgal, to far Beersheba, and the very way to the latter appeared as sacred to the Israelite as the way to Mecca does to a pious Moslem of to-day.‖ Yet, in spite of all this devotion to their God, Israel had no true ideas of Him. To quote Amos, they sought His sanctuaries, but Him they did not seek; in the words of Hosea's frequent plaint, they "did not know Him." To the mass of the people, to their governors, their priests, and the most of their prophets, Jehovah was but the characteristic Semitic deity—patron of His people, and caring for them alone—who had helped them in the past, and was bound to help them still—very jealous as to the correctness of His ritual and the amount of His sacrifices, but indifferent about real morality. Nay, there were still darker streaks in their views of Him. A god, figured as an ox, could not be adored by a cattle-breeding people without starting in their minds thoughts too much akin to the foul tempers of the Canaanite faiths. These things it is almost a shame to mention; but without knowing that they fermented in the life of that generation, we shall not appreciate the vehemence of Amos or of Hosea.

Such a religion had no discipline for the busy, mercenary life of the day. Injustice and fraud were rife in the very precincts of the sanctuary. Magistrates and priests alike were smitten with their generation's love of money, and did everything for reward. Again and again do the prophets speak of bribery. Judges took gifts and perverted the cause of the poor; priests drank the mulcted wine, and slept on the pledged garments of religious offenders. There was no disinterested service of God or of the commonweal. Mammon was supreme. The influence of the commercial character of the age appears in another very remarkable result. An agricultural community is always sensitive to the religion of nature. They are awed by its chastisements—droughts, famines, and earthquakes. They feel its majestic order in the course of the seasons, the procession of day and night, the march of the great stars, all the host of the Lord of hosts. But Amos seems to have had to break into passionate reminders of Him that maketh Orion and the Pleiades, and turneth the murk into morning.* Several physical calamities visited the land. The locusts are bad in Palestine every sixth or seventh year: one year before Amos began they had been very bad. There was a monstrous drought, followed by a famine. There was a long-remembered earthquake—"the earthquake in the days of Uzziah." With Egypt so near, the home of the plague, and with so much war afoot in Northern Syria, there were probably more pestilences in Western Asia than those recorded in 803, 765, and 759. There was a total eclipse of the sun in 763. But of all these, except perhaps the pestilence, a commercial people are independent as an agricultural are not. Israel speedily recovered from them, without any moral improvement. Even when the earthquake came "they said in pride and stoutness of heart, The bricks are fallen down, but we will build with hewn stones; the sycamores are cut down, but we will change to cedars." † It was a marvellous generation—so joyous, so energetic, so patriotic, so devout. But its strength was the strength of cruel wealth, its peace the peace of an immoral religion.

I have said that the age is very modern, and we shall indeed go to its prophets feeling that they speak to conditions of life extremely like our own. But if we wish a still closer analogy from our history, we must travel back to the fourteenth century in England—Langland's and Wyclif's century, which, like this one in Israel, saw both the first real attempts towards a national literature, and the first real attempts towards a moral and religious reform. Then as in Israel a long and victorious reign was drawing to a close, under the threat of disaster when it should have passed. Then as in Israel there had been droughts, earthquakes, and pestilences with no moral results upon the nation. Then also there was a city life developing at the expense of country life. Then also the wealthy began to draw aloof from the people. Then also there was a national religion, zealously cultivated and endowed by the liberality of the people, but superstitious, mercenary, and corrupted by sexual disorder. Then too there were many pilgrimages to popular shrines, and the land was strewn with mendicant priests and hireling preachers. And then too prophecy raised its voice, for the first time fearless in England. As we study the verses of Amos we shall find again and again the most exact parallels to them in

or symbolic tree of Canaanite worship, does not appear to have been used as a part of the ritual of Jehovah's worship. But, that there was constantly a temptation so to use it is clear from Deut. xvi. 21, 22. See Driver on that passage.

* See below, p. 466.

† Amos iv. 4 ff.

‡ Amos vii. 4: *cf.* 2 Kings v. 23.

§ Amos iv. 4 f.

‖ See below, p. 488.

* But whether these be by Amos see Chap. XI.

† Isa. ix. 10.

the verses of Langland's "Vision of Piers the Plowman," which denounce the same vices in Church and State, and enforce the same principles of religion and morality.

It was when the reign of Jeroboam was at its height of assured victory, when the nation's prosperity seemed impregnable after the survival of those physical calamities, when the worship and the commerce were in full course throughout the land, that the first of the new prophets broke out against Israel in the name of Jehovah, threatening judgment alike upon the new civilisation of which they were so proud and the old religion in which they were so confident. These prophets were inspired by feelings of the purest morality, by the passionate conviction that God could no longer bear such impurity and disorder. But, as we have seen, no prophet in Israel ever worked on the basis of principles only. He came always in alliance with events. These first appeared in the shape of the great physical disasters. But a more powerful instrument of Providence, in the service of judgment, was appearing on the horizon. This was the Assyrian Empire. So vast was its influence on prophecy that we must devote to it a separate chapter.

CHAPTER IV.

THE INFLUENCE OF ASSYRIA UPON PROPHECY.

By far the greatest event in the eighth century before Christ was the appearance of Assyria in Palestine. To Israel since the Exodus and Conquest, nothing had happened capable of so enormous an influence at once upon their national fortunes and their religious development. But while the Exodus and Conquest had advanced the political and spiritual progress of Israel in equal proportion, the effect of the Assyrian invasion was to divorce these two interests, and destroy the state while it refined and confirmed the religion. After permitting the Northern Kingdom to reach an extent and splendour unrivalled since the days of Solomon, Assyria overthrew it in 721, and left all Israel scarcely a third of their former magnitude. But while Assyria proved so disastrous to the state, her influence upon the prophecy of the period was little short of creative. Humanly speaking, this highest stage of Israel's religion could not have been achieved by the prophets except in alliance with the armies of that heathen empire. Before then we turn to their pages it may be well for us to make clear in what directions Assyria performed this spiritual service for Israel. While pursuing this inquiry we may be able to find answers to the scarcely less important questions: why the prophets were at first doubtful of the part Assyria was destined to play in the providence of the Almighty; and why, when the prophets were at last convinced of the certainty of Israel's overthrow, the statesmen of Israel and the bulk of the people still remained so unconcerned about her coming, or so sanguine of their power to resist her. This requires, to begin with, a summary of the details of the Assyrian advance upon Palestine.

In the far past Palestine had often been the hunting-ground of the Assyrian kings. But after 1100 B. C., and for nearly two centuries and a half, her states were left to themselves. Then Assyria resumed the task of breaking down that disbelief in her power with which her long withdrawal seems to have inspired their politics. In 870 Assurnasirpal reached the Levant, and took tribute from Tyre and Sidon. Omri was reigning in Samaria, and must have come into close relations with the Assyrians, for during more than a century and a half after his death they still called the land of Israel by his name.* In 854 Salmanassar II. defeated at Karkar the combined forces of Ahab and Benhadad. In 850, 849, and 846 he conducted campaigns against Damascus. In 842 he received tribute from Jehu,† and in 839 again fought Damascus under Hazael. After this there passed a whole generation during which Assyria came no farther south than Arpad, some sixty miles north of Damascus; and Hazael employed the respite in those campaigns which proved so disastrous for Israel, by robbing her of the provinces across Jordan, and ravaging the country about Samaria.‡ In 803 Assyria returned, and accomplished the siege and capture of Damascus. The first consequence to Israel was that restoration of her hopes under Joash, at which the aged Elisha was still spared to assist,§ and which reached its fulfilment in the recovery of all Eastern Palestine by Jeroboam II.‖ Jeroboam's own relations to Assyria have not been recorded either by the Bible or by the Assyrian monuments. It is hard to think that he paid no tribute to the "king of kings." At all events it is certain that, while Assyria again overthrew the Arameans of Damascus in 773 and their neighbours of Hadrach in 772 and 765, Jeroboam was himself invading Aramean land, and the Book of Kings even attributes to him an extension of territory, or at least of political influence, up to the northern mouth of the great pass between the Lebanons.¶ For the next twenty years Assyria only once came as far as Lebanon—to Hadrach in 759—and it may have been this long quiescence which enabled the rulers and people of Israel to forget, if indeed their religion and sanguine patriotism had ever allowed them to realise, how much the conquests and splendour of Jeroboam's reign were due, not to themselves, but to the heathen power which had maimed their oppressors. Their dreams were brief. Before Jeroboam himself was dead, a new king had usurped the Assyrian throne (745 B. C.) and inaugurated a more vigorous policy. Borrowing the name of the ancient Tiglath-Pileser, he followed that conqueror's path across the Euphrates. At first it seemed as if he was to suffer check. His forces were engrossed by the siege of Arpad for three years (*c.* 743), and this delay, along with that of two years more, during which he had to return to the conquest of Babylon, may well have given cause to the courts of Damascus and Samaria to believe that the Assyrian power had not really revived. Combining, they attacked Judah under Ahaz. But Ahaz appealed to Tiglath-Pileser, who within a year

* "The house of Omri": so even in Sargon's time, 722–705.

† The Black Obelisk of Salmanassar in the British Museum, on which the messengers of Jehu are portrayed.

‡ 2 Kings x. 32 f.; xiii. 3.

§ 2 Kings xiii. 14 ff.

‖ The phrase in 2 Kings xiii. 5, "Jehovah gave Israel a saviour," is interpreted by certain scholars as if the saviour were Assyria. In xiv. 27 he is plainly said to be Jeroboam.

¶ The entering in of Hamath (2 Kings xiv. 25).

(734-733) had overthrown Damascus and carried captive the populations of Gilead and Galilee. There could now be no doubt as to what the Assyrian power meant for the political fortunes of Israel. Before this resistless and inexorable empire the people of Jehovah were as the most frail of their neighbours—sure of defeat, and sure, too, of that terrible captivity in exile which formed the novel policy of the invaders against the tribes who withstood them. Israel dared to withstand. The vassal Hoshea, whom the Assyrians had placed on the throne of Samaria in 730, kept back his tribute. The people rallied to him; and for more than three years this little tribe of highlanders resisted in their capital the Assyrian siege. Then came the end. Samaria fell in 721, and Israel went into captivity beyond the Euphrates.

In following the course of this long tragedy, a man's heart cannot but feel that *all* the splendour and the glory did not lie with the prophets, in spite of their being the only actors in the drama who perceived its moral issues and predicted its actual end. For who can withhold admiration from those few tribesmen, who accepted no defeat as final, but so long as they were left to their fatherland rallied their ranks to its liberty and defied the huge empire. Nor was their courage always as blind, as in the time of Isaiah Samaria's so fatally became. For one cannot have failed to notice, how fitful and irregular was Assyria's advance, at least up to the reign of Tiglath-Pileser; nor how prolonged and doubtful were her sieges of some of the towns. The Assyrians themselves do not always record spoil or tribute after what they are pleased to call their victories over the cities of Palestine. To the same campaign they had often to return for several years in succession.* It took Tiglath-Pileser himself three years to reduce Arpad; Salmanassar IV. besieged Samaria for three years, and was slain before it yielded. These facts enable us to understand that, apart from the moral reasons which the prophets urged for the certainty of Israel's overthrow by Assyria, it was always within the range of political possibility that Assyria would not come back, and that while she was engaged with revolts of other portions of her huge and disorganised empire, a combined revolution on the part of her Syrian vassals would be successful. The prophets themselves felt the influence of these chances. They were not always confident, as we shall see, that Assyria was to be the means of Israel's overthrow. Amos, and in his earlier years Isaiah, describe her with a caution and a vagueness for which there is no other explanation than the political uncertainty that again and again hung over the future of her advance upon Syria. If, then, even in those high minds, to whom the moral issue was so clear, the political form that issue should assume was yet temporarily uncertain, what good reasons must the mere statesmen of Syria have often felt for the proud security which filled the intervals between the Assyrian invasions, or the sanguine hopes which inspired their resistance to the latter.

We must not cast over the whole Assyrian advance the triumphant air of the annals of such kings as Tiglath-Pileser or Sennacherib. Campaigning in Palestine was a dangerous business even to the Romans; and for the Assyrian armies there was always possible besides some sudden recall by the rumour of a revolt in a distant province. Their own annals supply us with good reasons for the sanguine resistance offered to them by the tribes of Palestine. No defeat, of course, is recorded; but the annals are full of delays and withdrawals. Then the Plague would break out; we know how in the last year of the century it turned Sennacherib, and saved Jerusalem.* In short, up almost to the end the Syrian chiefs had some fair political reasons for resistance to a power which had so often defeated them; while at the very end, when no such reason remained and our political sympathy is exhausted, we feel it replaced by an even warmer admiration for their desperate defence. Mere mountain-cats of tribes as some of them were, they held their poorly furnished rocks against one, two, or three years of cruel siege.

In Israel these political reasons for courage against Assyria were enforced by the whole instincts of the popular religion. The century had felt a new outburst of enthusiasm for Jehovah.† This was consequent, not only upon the victories He had granted over Aram, but upon the literature of the peace which followed those victories: the collection of the stories of the ancient miracles of Jehovah in the beginning of His people's history, and of the purpose He had even then announced of bringing Israel to supreme rank in the world. Such a God, so anciently manifested, so recently proved, could never surrender His own nation to a mere Goi ‡—a heathen and a barbarian people. Add this dogma of the popular religion of Israel to those substantial hopes of Assyria's withdrawal from Palestine, and you see cause, intelligible and adequate, for the complacency of Jeroboam and his people to the fact that Assyria had at last, by the fall of Damascus, reached their own borders, as well as for the courage with which Hoshea in 725 threw off the Assyrian yoke, and, with a willing people, for three years defended Samaria against the great king. Let us not think that the opponents of the prophets were utter fools or mere puppets of fate. They had reasons for their optimism; they fought for their hearths and altars with a valour and a patience which proves that the nation as a whole was not so corrupt as we are sometimes, by the language of the prophets, tempted to suppose.

But all this—the reasonableness of the hope of resisting Assyria, the valour which so stubbornly fought her, the religious faith which sanctioned both valour and hope—only the more vividly illustrates the singular independence of the prophets, who took an opposite view, who so consistently affirmed that Israel must fall, and so early foretold that she should fall to Assyria.

The reason of this conviction of the prophets was, of course, their fundamental faith in the righteousness of Jehovah. That was a belief quite independent of the course of events. As a matter of history the ethical reasons for Israel's doom were manifest to the prophets within Israel's own life, before the signs grew clear on the horizon that the doomster was to be Assyria.§ Nay, we may go further, and say

* Salmanassar II. in 850, 849, 846 to war against Dad'idri of Damascus, and in 842 and 839 against Hazael, his successor.

* See in this series "Isaiah," Vol. III. pp. 706 ff.

† See above, pp. 451 ff.

‡ To use the term which Amos adopts with such ironical force: vi. 14.

§ When we get down among the details we shall see clear evidence for this fact, for instance, that Amos

that it could not possibly have been otherwise. For except the prophets had been previously furnished with the ethical reasons for Assyria's resistless advance on Israel, to their sensitive minds that advance must have been a hopeless and a paralysing problem. But they nowhere treat it as a problem. By them Assyria is always either welcomed as a proof or summoned as a means—the proof of their conviction that Israel requires humbling, the means of carrying that humbling into effect. The faith of the prophets is ready for Assyria from the moment that she becomes ominous for Israel, and every footfall of her armies on Jehovah's soil becomes the corroboration of the purpose He has already declared to His servants in the terms of their moral consciousness. The spiritual service which Assyria rendered to Israel was therefore secondary to the prophets' native convictions of the righteousness of God, and could not have been performed without these. This will become even more clear if we look for a little at the exact nature of that service.

In its broadest effects, the Assyrian invasion meant for Israel a very considerable change in the intellectual outlook. Hitherto Israel's world had virtually lain between the borders promised of old to their ambition—"the river of Egypt,* and the great river, the River Euphrates." These had marked not merely the sphere of Israel's politics, but the horizon within which Israel had been accustomed to observe the action of their God and to prove His character, to feel the problems of their religion rise and to grapple with them. But now there burst from the outside of this little world that awful power, sovereign and inexorable, which effaced all distinctions and treated Israel in the same manner as her heathen neighbours. This was more than a widening of the world: it was a change of the very poles. At first sight it appeared merely to have increased the scale on which history was conducted; it was really an alteration of the whole character of history. Religion itself shrivelled up, before a force so much vaster than anything it had yet encountered, and so contemptuous of its claims. "What is Jehovah," said the Assyrian in his laughter, "more than the gods of Damascus, or of Hamath, or of the Philistines?" In fact, for the mind of Israel, the crisis, though less in degree, was in quality not unlike that produced in the religion of Europe by the revelation of the Copernican astronomy. As the earth, previously believed to be the centre of the universe, the stage on which the Son of God had achieved God's eternal purposes to mankind, was discovered to be but a satellite of one of innumerable suns, a mere ball swung beside millions of others by a force which betrayed no sign of sympathy with the great transactions which took place on it, and so faith in the Divine worth of these was rudely shaken—so Israel, who had believed themselves to be the peculiar people of the Creator, the solitary agents of the God of Righteousness to all mankind,† and who now felt themselves brought to an equality with other tribes by this sheer force, which, brutally indifferent to spiritual distinctions, swayed the fortunes of all alike, must have been tempted to unbelief in the spiritual facts of their history, in the power of their God and the destiny He had promised them. Nothing could have saved Israel, as nothing could have saved Europe, but a conception of God which rose to this new demand upon its powers—a faith which said, "Our God is sufficient for this greater world and its forces that so dwarf our own; the discovery of these only excites in us a more awful wonder of His power." The prophets had such a conception of God. To them He was absolute righteousness—righteousness wide as the widest world, stronger than the strongest force. To the prophets, therefore, the rise of Assyria only increased the possibilities of Providence. But it could not have done this had Providence not already been invested in a God capable by His character of rising to such possibilities.

Assyria, however, was not only Force: she was also the symbol of a great Idea—the Idea of Unity. We have just ventured on one historical analogy. We may try another and a more exact one. The Empire of Rome, grasping the whole world in its power and reducing all races of men to much the same level of political rights, powerfully assisted Christian theology in the task of imposing upon the human mind a clearer imagination of unity in the government of the world and of spiritual equality among men of all nations. A not dissimilar service to the faith of Israel was performed by the Empire of Assyria. History, that hitherto had been but a series of angry pools, became as the ocean swaying in tides to one almighty impulse. It was far easier to imagine a sovereign Providence when Assyria reduced history to a unity by overthrowing all the rulers and all their gods, than when history was broken up into the independent fortunes of many states, each with its own religion divinely valid in its own territory. By shattering the tribes Assyria shattered the tribal theory of religion, which we have seen to be the characteristic Semitic theory—a god for every tribe, a tribe for every god. The field was cleared of the many: there was room for the One. That He appeared, not as the God of the conquering race, but as the Deity of one of their many victims, was due to Jehovah's righteousness. At this juncture, when the world was suggested to have one throne and that throne was empty, there was a great chance, if we may so put it, for a god with a character. And the only God in all the Semitic world who had a character was Jehovah.

It is true that the Assyrian Empire was not constructive, like the Roman, and, therefore, could not assist the prophets to the idea of a Catholic Church. But there can be no doubt that it did assist them to a feeling of the moral unity of mankind. A great historian has made the just remark that, whatsoever widens the imagination, enabling it to realise the actual experience of other men, is a powerful agent of ethical advance.* Now Assyria widened the imagination and the sympathy of Israel in precisely this way. Consider the universal Pity of the Assyrian conquest: how state after state went down before it, how all things mortal yielded and were swept away. The mutual hatreds and ferocities

prophesied against Israel at a time when he thought that the Lord's anger was to be exhausted in purely natural chastisements of His people, and before it was revealed to him that Assyria was required to follow up these chastisements with a heavier blow. See Chap. VI., Section 2.

* That is, of course, not the Nile, but the great Wady, at present known as the Wady el 'Arish, which divides Palestine from Egypt.

† So already in the JE narratives of the Pentateuch.

* Lecky: "History of European Morals," I.

of men could not persist before a common Fate, so sublime, so tragic. And thus we understand how in Israel the old envies and rancours of that border warfare with her foes which had filled the last four centuries of her history is replaced by a new tenderness and compassion towards the national efforts, the achievements, and all the busy life of the Gentile peoples. Isaiah is especially distinguished by this in his treatment of Egypt and of Tyre; and even where he and others do not, as in these cases, appreciate the sadness of the destruction of so much brave beauty and serviceable wealth, their tone in speaking of the fall of the Assyrian on their neighbours is one of compassion and not of exultation.* As the rivalries and hatreds of individual lives are stilled in the presence of a common death, so even that factious, ferocious world of the Semites ceased to "fret its anger and watch it for ever" (to quote Amos' phrase) in face of the universal Assyrian Fate. But in that Fate there was more than Pity. On the data of the prophets Assyria was afflicting Israel for moral reasons: it could not be for other reasons that she was afflicting their neighbours. Israel and the heathen were suffering for the same righteousness' sake. What could have better illustrated the moral equality of all mankind! No doubt the prophets were already theoretically convinced† of this—for the righteousness they believed in was nothing if not universal. But it is one thing to hold a belief on principle and another to have practical experience of it in history. To a theory of the moral equality of mankind Assyria enabled the prophets to add sympathy and conscience. We shall see all this illustrated in the opening prophecies of Amos against the foreign nations.

But Assyria did not help to develop monotheism in Israel only by contributing to the doctrines of a moral Providence and of the equality of all men beneath it. The influence must have extended to Israel's conception of God in Nature. Here, of course, Israel was already possessed of great beliefs. Jehovah had created man; He had divided the Red Sea and Jordan. The desert, the storm, and the seasons were all subject to Him. But at a time when the superstitious mind of the people was still feeling after other Divine powers in the earth, the waters and the air of Canaan, it was a very valuable antidote to such dissipation of their faith to find one God swaying, through Assyria, all families of mankind. The Divine unity to which history was reduced must have reacted on Israel's views of Nature, and made it easier to feel one God also there. Now, as a matter of fact, the imagination of the unity of Nature, the belief in a reason and method pervading all things, was very powerfully advanced in Israel throughout the Assyrian period.

We may find an illustration of this in the greater, deeper meaning in which the prophets use the old national name of Israel's God—Jehovah Ṣeba'oth, "Jehovah of Hosts." This title, which came into frequent use under the early kings, when Israel's vocation was to win freedom by war, meant then (as far as we can gather) only "Jehovah of the armies of Israel"—the God of battles, the people's leader in war,* whose home was Jerusalem, the people's capital, and His sanctuary their battle emblem, the Ark. Now the prophets hear Jehovah go forth (as Amos does) from the same place, but to them the Name has a far deeper significance. They never define it, but they use it in associations where "hosts" must mean something different from the armies of Israel. To Amos the hosts of Jehovah are not the armies of Israel, but those of Assyria: they are also the nations whom He marshals and marches across the earth, Philistines from Caphtor, Aram from Qir, as well as Israel from Egypt. Nay, more; according to those Doxologies which either Amos or a kindred spirit has added to his lofty argument,† Jehovah sways and orders the powers of the heavens: Orion and Pleiades, the clouds from the sea to the mountain peaks where they break, day and night in constant processsion. It is in associations like these that the Name is used, either in its old form or slightly changed as "Jehovah God of hosts," or "the hosts": and we cannot but feel that the hosts of Jehovah are now looked upon as all the influences of earth and heaven—human armies, stars and powers of nature, which obey His word and work His will.

* The present writer has already pointed out this with regard to Egypt and Phœnicia in "Isaiah" (Expositor's Bible Series), Part I., chaps. xxii. and xxiii., and with regard to Philistia in "Hist. Geog.," p. 178.

† I put it this way only for the sake of making the logic clear; for it is a mistake to say that the prophets at any time held merely theoretic convictions. All their conviction was really experimental—never held apart from some illustration or proof of principle in actual history.

* יהוה צבאות: 1 Sam. i. 3; iv. 4; xvii. 45, where it is explained by the parallel phrase "God of the armies of Israel"; 2 Sam. vi. 2, where it is connected with Israel's battle emblem, the Ark (*cf.* Jer. xxii. 18); and so throughout Samuel and Kings, and also Chronicles, the Psalms, and most prophets. The plural צבאות is never used in the Old Testament except of human hosts, and generally of the armies or hosts of Israel. The theory therefore which sees the same meaning in the Divine title is probably the correct one. It was first put forward by Herder ("Geist der Eb. Poesie," ii. 84, 85), and after some neglect it has been revived by Kautzsch ("Z. A. T. W.," vi. ff.) and Stade ("Gesch.," i. 437, *n.* 3). The alternatives are that the hosts originally meant those of heaven, either the angels (so, among others, Ewald, "Hist.," Eng. Ed., iii. 62) or the stars (so Delitzsch, Kuenen, Baudissin, Cheyne, "Prophecies of Isaiah," i. 11). In the former of these two there is some force; but the reason given for the latter, that the name came to the front in Israel when the people were being drawn into connection with star-worshipping nations, especially Aram, seems to me baseless. Israel had not been long in touch with Aram in Saul's time, yet even then the name is accepted as if one of much earlier origin. A clear account of the argument on the other side to that taken in this note will be found in Smend "Alttestamentliche Religionsgeschichte," pp. 185 ff.

† See below, chap. xi.

AMOS.

"Towers in the distance, like an earth-born Atlas . . . such a man in such a historical position, standing on the confines of light and darkness, like day on the misty mountain-tops."

CHAPTER V.

THE BOOK OF AMOS.

THE genuineness of the bulk of the Book of Amos is not doubted by any critic. The only passages suspected as interpolations are the three references to Judah, the three famous outbreaks in praise of the might of Jehovah the Creator, the final prospect of a hope that does not gleam in any other part of the book, with a few clauses alleged to reflect a stage of history later than that in which Amos worked.* In all, these verses amount to only twenty-six or twenty-seven out of one hundred and forty-six. Each of them can be discussed separately as we reach it, and we may now pass to consider the general course of the prophecy which is independent of them.

The Book of Amos consists of Three Groups of Oracles, under one title, which is evidently meant to cover them all.

The title runs as follows:—

"Words of 'Amoṣ—who was of the herdsmen of Teḳôa'—which he saw concerning Israel in the days of 'Uzziah king of Judah, and in the days of Jarab'am son of Joash,† king of Israel: two years before the earthquake."

The Three Sections, with their contents, are as follows:—

First Section: Chaps. I., II. The Heathen's Crimes and Israel's.

A series of short oracles of the same form, directed impartially against the political crimes of all the states of Palestine, and culminating in a more detailed denunciation of the social evils of Israel, whose doom is foretold, beneath the same flood of war as shall overwhelm all her neighbours.

Second Section: Chaps. III.-VI. Israel's Crimes and Doom.

A series of various oracles of denunciation, which have no further logical connection than is supplied by a general sameness of subject, and a perceptible increase of detail and articulateness from beginning to end of the section. They are usually grouped according to the recurrence of the formula "Hear this word," which stands at the head of our present chaps. iii., iv., and v.; and by the two cries of "Woe" at v. 18 and vi. 1. But even more obvious than these commencements are the various climaxes to which they lead up. These are all threats of judgment, and each is more strenuous or explicit than the one that has preceded it. They close with iii. 15, iv. 3, iv. 12, v. 17, v. 27, and vi. 14; and according to them the oracles may be conveniently divided into six groups.

1. III. 1-15. After the main theme of judgment is stated in 1, 2, we have in 3-8 a parenthesis on the prophet's right to threaten doom; after which 9-15, following directly on 2, emphasise the social disorder, threaten the land with invasion, the people with extinction and the overthrow of their civilisation.

2. IV. 1-3, beginning with the formula "Hear this word," is directed against women and describes the siege of the capital and their captivity.

3. IV. 4-12, with no opening formula, contrasts the people's vain propitiation of God by ritual with His treatment of them by various physical chastisements—drought, blight, and locusts, pestilence, earthquake—and summons them to prepare for another, unnamed, visitation. "Jehovah God of Hosts is His Name."

4. V. 1-17, beginning with the formula "Hear this word," and a dirge over a vision of the nation's defeat, attacks, like the previous group, the lavish ritual, sets in contrast to it Jehovah's demands for justice and civic purity; and, offering a reprieve if Israel will repent, closes with the prospect of an universal mourning (vv. 16, 17), which, though introduced by a "therefore," has no logical connection with what precedes it.

5. V. 18-26 is the first of the two groups that open with "Woe." Affirming that the eagerly expected "Day of Jehovah" will be darkness and disaster on disaster inevitable (18-20), it again emphasises Jehovah's desire for righteousness rather than worship (21-26), and closes with the threat of captivity beyond Damascus. "Jehovah God of Hosts is His Name," as at the close of 3.

6. VI. 1-14. The second "Woe," on them "that are at ease in Zion" (1, 2): a satire on the luxuries of the rich and their indifference to the national suffering (3-6): captivity must come, with the desolation of the land (9, 10); and in a peroration the prophet reiterates a general downfall of the nation because of its perversity. "A Nation"—needless to name it!—will oppress Israel from Hamath to the River of the Arabah.

Third Section: Chaps. VII.-IX. Visions with Interludes.

The Visions betray traces of development; but they are interrupted by a piece of narrative and addresses on the same themes as chaps. iii.-vi. The First Two Visions (vii. 1-6) are of disasters —locusts and drought—in the realm of nature; they are averted by prayer from Amos. The Third (7-9) is in the sphere, not of nature, but history: Jehovah standing with a plumbline, as if to show the nation's fabric to be utterly twisted, announces that it shall be overthrown, and that the dynasty of Jeroboam must be put to the sword. Upon this mention of the king, the first in the book, there starts the narrative (10-17) of how Amaziah, priest at Bethel—obviously upon hearing the prophet's threat—sent word to Jeroboam; and then (whether before or after getting a reply) proceeded to silence Amos, who, however, reiterates his prediction of doom, again described as captivity in a foreign land, and adds a Fourth Vision (viii. 1-3), of the Kaits or "Summer Fruit," which suggests Kêts, or "End" of the Nation. Here it would seem Amos' discourses at Bethel take end. Then comes viii. 4-6, another exposure of the sins of the rich; followed by a triple pronouncement of doom (7), again in the terms of physical calamities—earthquake (8), eclipse (9, 10), and famine (11-14), in the last of which the public worship is again attacked. A Fifth Vision, of the Lord by the Altar commanding to smite (ix. 1), is followed by a powerful threat of the hopelessness of escape from God's punishment (ix. 1*b*-4); the third of the great apostrophes to the might of Jehovah (5, 6); another statement of the equality in judgment of Israel with other peoples, and of their utter destruction (7-8*a*). Then (8*b*) we meet the first qualification of the hitherto unrelieved sentence of death. Captivity is described, not as doom, but as discipline (9); the sinners of the people, scoffers at doom, shall die (10). And this seems to leave room for two final oracles

* The full list of suspected passages is this: (1) References to Judah—ii. 4, 5; vi. 1, "in Zion"; ix. 11, 12. (2) The three Outbreaks of Praise—iv. 13; v. 8, 9; ix. 5, 6. (3) The Final Hope—ix. 8-15, including vv. 11, 12, already mentioned. (4) Clauses alleged to reflect a later stage of history—i. 9-12; v. 1, 2, 15; vi. 2, 14. (5) Suspected for incompatibility—viii. 11-13.

† So designated to distinguish him from the first Jeroboam, the son of Nebat.

of restoration and glory, the only two in the book, which are couched in the exact terms of the promises of later prophecy (11-15) and are by many denied to Amos.

Such is the course of the prophesying of Amos. To have traced it must have made clear to us the unity of his book,* as well as the character of the period to which he belonged. But it also furnishes us with a good deal of evidence towards the answer of such necessary questions as these—whether we can fix an exact date for the whole or any part, and whether we can trace any logical or historical development through the chapters, either as these now stand, or in some such re-arrangement as we saw to be necessary for the authentic prophecies of Isaiah.

Let us take first the simplest of these tasks—to ascertain the general period of the book. Twice—by the title and by the portion of narrative †—we are pointed to the reign of Jeroboam II., *circa* 783-743; other historical allusions suit the same years. The principalities of Palestine are all standing, except Gath: ‡ but the great northern cloud which carries their doom has risen and is ready to burst. Now Assyria, we have seen, had become fatal to Palestine as early as 854. Infrequent invasions of Syria had followed, in one of which, in 803, Rimmon Nirari III. had subjected Tyre and Sidon, besieged Damascus, and received tribute from Israel. So far then as the Assyrian data are concerned, the Book of Amos might have been written early in the reign of Jeroboam. Even then was the storm lowering as he describes it. Even then had the lightning broken over Damascus. There are other symptoms, however, which demand a later date. They seem to imply, not only Uzziah's overthrow of Gath,§ and Jeroboam's conquest of Moab‖ and of Aram,¶ but that establishment of Israel's political influence from Lebanon to the Dead Sea, which must have taken Jeroboam several years to accomplish. With this agree other features of the prophecy—the sense of political security in Israel, the large increase of wealth, the ample and luxurious buildings, the gorgeous ritual, the easy ability to recover from physical calamities, the consequent carelessness and pride of the upper classes. All these things imply that the last Syrian invasions of Israel in the beginning of the century were at least a generation behind the men into whose careless faces the prophet hurled his words of doom. During this interval Assyria had again advanced—in 775, in 773, and in 772.** None of these expeditions, however, had come south of Damascus, and this, their invariable arrest at some distance from the proper territory of Israel, may have further flattered the people's sense of security, though probably the truth was that Jeroboam, like some of his predecessors, bought his peace by tribute to the emperor. In 765, when the Assyrians for the second time invaded Hadrach, in the neighbourhood of Damascus, their records mention a pestilence, which, both because their armies were then in Syria, and because the plague generally spreads over the whole of Western Asia, may well have been the pestilence mentioned by Amos. In 763 a total eclipse of the sun took place, and is perhaps implied by the ninth verse of his eighth chapter. If this double allusion to pestilence and eclipse be correct, it brings the book down to the middle of the century and the latter half of Jeroboam's long reign. In 755 the Assyrians came back to Hadrach; in 754 to Arpad: with these exceptions Syria was untroubled by them till after 745. It was probably these quiet years in which Amos found Israel "at ease in Zion." * If we went down further, within the more forward policy of Tiglath-Pileser, who ascended the throne in 745 and besieged Arpad from 743 to 740, we should find an occasion for the urgency with which Amos warns Israel that the invasion of her land and the overthrow of the dynasty of Jeroboam will be immediate.† But Amos might have spoken as urgently even before Tiglath-Pileser's accession; and the probability that Hosea, who prophesied within Jeroboam's reign, quotes from Amos seems to imply that the prophecies of the latter had been current for some time.

Towards the middle of the eighth century—is, therefore, the most definite date to which we are able to assign the Book of Amos. At so great a distance the difference of a few unmarked years is invisible. It is enough that we know the moral dates—the state of national feeling, the personages alive, the great events which are behind the prophet, and the still greater which are imminent. We can see that Amos wrote in the political pride of the latter years of Jeroboam's reign, after the pestilence and eclipse of the sixties, and before the advance of Tiglath-Pileser in the last forties of the eighth century.

A particular year is indeed offered by the title of the book, which, if not by Amos himself, must be from only a few years later:‡ "Words of Amos, which he saw in the days of Uzziah and of Jeroboam, two years before the earthquake." This was the great earthquake of which other prophets speak as having happened in the days of Uzziah.§ But we do not know where to place the year of the earthquake, and are as far as ever from a definite date.

The mention of the earthquake, however, introduces us to the answer of another of our questions—whether, with all its unity, the Book of Amos reveals any lines of progress, either of event or of idea, either historical or logical.

Granting the truth of the title, that Amos had his prophetic eyes opened two years before the earthquake, it will be a sign of historical progress if we find in the book itself any allusions to the earthquake. Now these are present. In the first division we find none, unless the threat

* Apart from the suspected parentheses already mentioned.

† Chap. vii.

‡ And, if vi. 2 be genuine, Hamath.

§ 2 Chron. xxvi. 6. In the list of the Philistine cities, Amos i. 6-8, Gath does not occur, and in harmony with this in vi. 2 it is said to be overthrown; see p. 485.

‖ 2 Kings. In Amos ii. 3 the ruler of Moab is called not king, but שופט, or regent, such as Jeroboam substituted for the king of Moab.

¶ According to Grätz's emendation of vi. 13: "we have taken Lo-Debar and Karnaim." Perhaps too in iii. 12, though the verse is very obscure, some settlement of Israelites in Damascus is implied. For Jeroboam's conquest of Aram (2 Kings xiv. 28), see p. 406.

** In 775 to Erini, "the country of the cedars"—that is, Mount Amanus, near the Gulf of Antioch; in 773 to Damascus; in 772 to Hadrach.

* vi. 1.

† vii. 9.

‡ Even König denies that the title is from Amos ("Einleitung," 307); yet the ground on which he does so, the awkwardness of the double relative, does not appear sufficient. One does not write a title in the same style as an ordinary sentence.

§ Zech. xiv. 5, and probably Isa. ix. 9, 10 (Eng.,

of God's visitation in the form of a shaking of the land be considered as a tremor communicated to the prophet's mind from the recent upheaval. But in the second division there is an obvious reference: the last of the unavailing chastisements with which Jehovah has chastised His people is described as a "great overturning." * And in the third division, in two passages, the judgment, which Amos has already stated will fall in the form of an invasion, is also figured in the terms of an earthquake. Nor does this exhaust the tremors which that awful convulsion had started; but throughout the second and third divisions there is a constant sense of instability, of the liftableness and breakableness of the very ground of life. Of course, as we shall see, this was due to the prophet's knowledge of the moral explosiveness of society in Israel; but he could hardly have described the results of that in the terms he has used, unless himself and his hearers had recently felt the ground quake under them, and seen whole cities topple over. If, then, Amos began to prophesy two years before the earthquake, the bulk of his book was spoken, or at least written down, after the earthquake had left all Israel trembling.†

This proof of progress in the book is confirmed by another feature. In the abstract given above it is easy to see that the judgments of the Lord upon Israel were of a twofold character. Some were physical—famine, drought, blight, locusts, earthquake; and some were political—battle, defeat, invasion, captivity. Now it is significant—and I do not think the point has been previously remarked—that not only are the physical represented as happening first, but that at one time the prophet seems to have understood that no others would be needed, that indeed God did not reveal to him the imminence of political disaster till He had exhausted the discipline of physical calamities. For this we have double evidence. In chapter iv. Amos reports that the Lord has sought to rouse Israel out of the moral lethargy into which their religious services have soothed them, by withholding bread and water; by blighting their orchards; by a pestilence, a thoroughly Egyptian one; and by an earthquake. But these having failed to produce repentance, God must visit the people once more: how, the prophet does not say, leaving the imminent terror unnamed, but we know that the Assyrian overthrow is meant. Now precisely parallel to this is the course of the Visions in chapter vii. The Lord caused Amos to see (whether in fancy or in fact we need not now stop to consider) the plague of locusts. It was so bad as to threaten Israel with destruction. But Amos interceded, and God answered, "It shall not be." Similarly with a plague of drought. But then the Vision shifts from the realm of nature to that of politics. The Lord sets the plumbline to the fabric of Israel's life: this is found hopelessly bent and unstable. It must be pulled down, and the pulling down shall be political: the family of Jeroboam is to be slain, the people are to go into captivity. The next Vision, therefore, is of the End—the Final Judgment of war and defeat, which is followed only by Silence.

Thus, by a double proof, we see not only that the Divine method in that age was to act first by physical chastisement, and only then by an inevitable, ultimate doom of war and captivity; but that the experience of Amos himself, his own intercourse with the Lord, passed through these two stages. The significance of this for the picture of the prophet's life we shall see in our next chapter. Here we are concerned to ask whether it gives us any clue as to the extant arrangement of his prophecies, or any justification for rearranging them, as the prophecies of Isaiah have to be re-arranged, according to the various stages of historical development at which they were uttered.

We have just seen that the progress from the physical chastisements to the political doom is reflected in both the last two sections of the book. But the same gradual, cumulative method is attributed to the Divine Providence by the First Section: "For three transgressions, yea, for four, I will not turn it back"; and then follow the same disasters of war and captivity as are threatened in Sections II. and III. But each section does not only thus end similarly; each also begins with the record of an immediate impression made on the prophet by Jehovah (chaps. i. 2; iii. 3-8; vii. 1-9).

To sum up:—The Book of Amos consists of three sections, which seem to have received their present form * towards the end of Jeroboam's reign; and which, after emphasising their origin as due to the immediate influence of Jehovah Himself on the prophet, follow pretty much the same course of the Divine dealings with that generation of Israel—a course which began with physical chastisements that failed to produce repentance, and ended with the irrevocable threat of the Assyrian invasion. Each section, that is to say, starts from the same point, follows much the same direction, and arrives at exactly the same conclusion. Chronologically you cannot put one of them before the other; but from each it is possible to learn the stages of experience through which Amos himself passed—to discover how God taught the prophet, not only by the original intuitions from which all prophecy starts, but by the gradual events of his day both at home and abroad.

This decides our plan for us. We shall first trace the life and experience of Amos, as his book enables us to do; and then we shall examine, in the order in which they lie, the three parallel forms in which, when he was silenced at Bethel, he collected the fruits of that experience, and gave them their final expression.

The style of the book is simple and terse. The fixity of the prophet's aim—upon a few moral principles and the doom they demand—keeps his sentences firm and sharp, and sends his para-

* iv. 11.

† Of course it is always possible to suspect—and let us by all means exhaust the possibilities of suspicion—that the title has been added by a scribe, who interpreted the forebodings of judgment which Amos expresses in the terms of earthquake as if they were the predictions of a real earthquake, and was anxious to show, by inserting the title, how they were fulfilled in the great convulsion of Uzziah's days. But to such a suspicion we have a complete answer. No later scribe, who understood the book he was dealing with, would have prefixed to it a title, with the motive just suspected, when in chap. iv. he read that an earthquake had just taken place. The very fact that such a title appears over a book, which speaks of the earthquake as past, surely attests the *bona fides* of the title. With that mention in chap. iv. of the earthquake as past, none would have ventured to say that Amos began to prophesy before the earthquake, unless they had known this to be the case.

* Except for the later additions, not by Amos, to be afterwards noted.

graphs rapidly to their climax. That he sees nature only under moral light renders his poetry austere and occasionally savage. His language is very pure. There is no ground for Jerome's charge that he was "imperitus sermone": we shall have to notice only a few irregularities in spelling, due perhaps to the dialect of the deserts in which he passed his life.*

The text of the book is for the most part well preserved; but there are a number of evident corruptions. Of the Greek Version the same holds good as we have said in more detail of the Greek of Hosea.† It is sometimes correct where the Hebrew text is not, sometimes suggestive of the emendations required, and sometimes hopelessly astray.

CHAPTER VI.

THE MAN AND THE PROPHET.

The Book of Amos opens one of the greatest stages in the religious development of mankind. Its originality is due to a few simple ideas, which it propels into religion with an almost unrelieved abruptness. But, like all ideas which ever broke upon the world, these also have flesh and blood behind them. Like every other Reformation this one in Israel began with the conscience and the protest of an individual. Our review of the book has made this plain. We have found in it, not only a personal adventure of a heroic kind, but a progressive series of visions, with some other proofs of a development both of facts and ideas. In short, behind the book there beats a life, and our first duty is to attempt to trace its spiritual history. The attempt is worth the greatest care. "Amos," says a very critical writer,‡ "is one of the most wonderful appearances in the history of the human spirit."

1. The Man and His Discipline.

Amos i. 1; iii. 3-8; vii. 14, 15.

When charged at the crisis of his career with being but a hireling-prophet, Amos disclaimed the official name and took his stand upon his work as a man: "No prophet I, nor prophet's son, but a herdsman and a dresser of sycamores. Jehovah took me from behind the flock." § We shall enhance our appreciation of this manhood, and of the new order of prophecy which it asserted, if we look for a little at the soil on which it was so bravely nourished.

Six miles south from Bethlehem, as Bethlehem is six from Jerusalem, there rises on the edge of the Judæan plateau, towards the desert, a commanding hill, the ruins on which are still known by the name of Tekôa'.‖

In the time of Amos Tekoa was a place without sanctity and almost without tradition. The name suggests that the site may at first have been that of a camp. Its fortification by Rehoboam, and the mission of its wise woman to David, are its only previous appearances in history. Nor had nature been less grudging to it than fame. The men of Tekoa looked out upon a desolate and haggard world. South, west, and north the view is barred by a range of limestone hills, on one of which directly north the grey towers of Jerusalem are hardly to be discerned from the grey mountain lines. Eastward the prospect is still more desolate, but it is open; the land slopes away for nearly eighteen miles to a depth of four thousand feet. Of this long descent the first step, lying immediately below the hill of Tekoa, is a shelf of stony moorland with the ruins of vineyards. It is the lowest ledge of the settled life of Judæa. The eastern edge drops suddenly by broken rocks to slopes spotted with bushes of "retem," the broom of the desert, and with patches of poor wheat. From the foot of the slopes the land rolls away in a maze of low hills and shallow dales that flush green in spring, but for the rest of the year are brown with withered grass and scrub. This is the "Wilderness" or "Pasture-land of Tekoa," * across which by night the wild beasts howl, and by day the blackened sites of deserted camps, with the loose cairns that mark the nomads' graves, reveal a human life almost as vagabond and nameless as that of the beasts. Beyond the rolling land is Jeshimon, or Devastation—a chaos of hills, none of whose ragged crests are tossed as high as the shelf of Tekoa, while their flanks shudder down some further thousands of feet, by crumbling precipices and corries choked with débris, to the coast of the Dead Sea. The northern half of this is visible, bright blue against the red wall of Moab, and the level top of the wall, broken only by the valley of the Arnon, constitutes the horizon. Except for the blue water—which shines in its gap between the torn hills like a bit of sky through rifted clouds—it is a very dreary world. Yet the sun breaks over it, perhaps all the more gloriously; mists, rising from the sea simmering in its great vat, drape the nakedness of the desert noon; and through the dry desert night the planets ride with a majesty they cannot assume in our more troubled atmospheres. It is also a very empty and a very silent world, yet every stir of life upon it excites, therefore, the greater vigilance, and man's faculties, relieved from the rush and confusion of events, form the instinct of marking, and reflecting upon, every single phenomenon. And it is a very savage world. Across it all the towers of Jerusalem give the only signal of the spirit, the one token that man has a history.

Upon this unmitigated wilderness, where life is reduced to poverty and danger; where nature starves the imagination, but excites the faculties of perception and curiosity; with the mountain tops and the sunrise in his face, but above all with Jerusalem so near,—Amos did the work which made him a man, heard the voice of God calling him to be a prophet, and gathered those symbols and figures in which his prophet's

* *Cf.* ii. 13; v. 11.; vi. 8, 10; vii. 9, 16; viii. 8 (?).

† See below, p. 497.

‡ Cornill: "Der Israelitische Prophetismus. Five Lectures for the Educated Laity." 1894.

§ Amos vii. 14. See further p. 461.

‖ Khurbet Takûa', Hebrew Tekôa', תְּקוֹעַ, from תקצ, *to blow a trumpet* (*cf.* Jer. vi. 1, "Blow the trumpet in Tekoa") or *to pitch a tent*. The latter seems the more probable derivation of the name, and suggests a nomadic origin, which agrees with the position of Tekoa on the borders of the desert. Tekoa does not occur in the list of the towns taken by Joshua. There are really no reasons for supposing that some other Tekoa is meant. The two that have been alleged are (1) that Amos exclusively refers to the Northern Kingdom, (2) that sycamores do not grow at such levels as Tekoa. These are dealt with on p. 461.

* 2 Chron. xx. 20.

message still reaches us with so fresh and so austere an air.

Amos was "among the shepherds of Tekoa." The word for "shepherd" is unusual, and means the herdsman of a peculiar breed of desert sheep, still under the same name prized in Arabia for the excellence of their wool.* And he was "a dresser of sycamores." The tree, which is not our sycamore, is very easily grown in sandy soil with a little water. It reaches a great height and mass of foliage. The fruit is like a small fig, with a sweet but watery taste, and is eaten only by the poor. Born not of the fresh twigs, but of the trunk and older branches, the sluggish lumps are provoked to ripen by pinching or bruising, which seems to be the literal meaning of the term that Amos uses of himself—"a pincher of sycamores."† The sycamore does not grow at so high a level as Tekoa;‡ and this fact, taken along with the limitation of the ministry of Amos to the Northern Kingdom, has been held to prove that he was originally an Ephraimite, a sycamore-dresser, who had migrated and settled down, as the peculiar phrase of the title says, "among the shepherds of Tekoa."§ We shall presently see, however, that his familiarity with life in Northern Israel may easily have been won in other ways than through citizenship in that kingdom; while the very general nature of the definition, "among the shepherds of Tekoa," does not oblige us to place either him or his sycamores so high as the village itself. The most easterly township of Judæa, Tekoa commanded the whole of the wilderness beyond, to which indeed it gave its name, "the wilderness of Tekoa." The shepherds of Tekoa were therefore, in all probability, scattered across the whole region down to the oases on the coast of the Dead Sea, which have generally been owned by one or other of the settled communities in the hill-country above, and may at that time have belonged to Tekoa, just as in Crusading times they belonged to the monks of Hebron, or are to-day cultivated by the Rushaideh Arabs, who pitch their camps not far from Tekoa itself. As you will still find everywhere on the borders of the Syrian desert shepherds nourishing a few fruit-trees round the chief well of their pasture, in order to vary their milk diet, so in some low oasis in the wilderness of Judæa Amos cultivated the poorest, but the most easily grown of fruits, the sycamore.* All this pushes Amos and his dwarf sheep deeper into the desert, and emphasises what has been said above, and still remains to be illustrated, of the desert's influence on his discipline as a man and on his speech as a prophet. We ought to remember that in the same desert another prophet was bred, who was also the pioneer of a new dispensation, and whose ministry, both in its strength and its limitations, is much recalled by the ministry of Amos. John the son of Zacharias "grew and waxed strong in spirit, and was in the deserts till the day of his showing unto Israel."† Here, too, our Lord was "with the wild beasts."‡ How much Amos had been with them may be seen from many of his metaphors. "The lion roareth, who shall not fear? . . . . As when the shepherd rescueth from the mouth of the lion two shinbones or a bit of an ear. . . . It shall be as when one is fleeing from a lion and a bear cometh upon him; and he entereth a house, and leaneth his hand on the wall, and a serpent biteth him."

As a wool-grower, however, Amos must have had his yearly journeys among the markets of the land; and to such were probably due his opportunities of familiarity with Northern Israel, the originals of his vivid pictures of her town-life, her commerce, and the worship at her great sanctuaries. One hour westward from Tekoa would bring him to the high-road between Hebron and the North, with its troops of pilgrims passing to Beersheba.§ It was but half-an-hour more to the watershed and an open view of the Philistine plain. Bethlehem was only six, Jerusalem twelve, miles from Tekoa. Ten miles farther, across the border of Israel, lay Bethel with its temple, seven miles farther Gilgal, and twenty miles farther still Samaria the capital, in all but two days' journey from Tekoa. These had markets as well as shrines;‖ their annual festivals would be also great fairs. It is certain that Amos visited them; it is even possible that he went to Damascus, in which the Israelites had at the time their own quarters for trading. By road and market he would meet with men of other lands. Phœnician pedlars, or Canaanites as they were called, came up to buy the homespun for which the housewives of Israel were famed ¶—hard-faced men who were also willing to purchase slaves, and haunted even the battle-fields of their neighbours for this sinister purpose. Men of Moab, at the time subject to Israel; Aramean hostages; Philistines who held the export trade to Egypt,—these Amos must have met and may have talked with; their dialects scarcely differed from his own. It is no distant, desert echo of life which we hear in his

* נֹקֵד, nôkêd, is doubtless the same as the Arabic "nakkâd," or keeper of the "nakad," defined by Freytag as a short-legged and deformed race of sheep in the Bahrein province of Arabia, from which comes the proverb "viler than a nakad"; yet the wool is very fine. The king of Moab is called נוֹקֵד in 2 Kings iii. 4 (A. V. *sheepmaster*). In vii. 14 Amos calls himself בּוֹקֵר, *cattle-man*, which there is no reason to alter, as some do, to נוֹקֵד.

† בּוֹלֵס, bôlês, probably from a root (found in Æthiopic) balas, *a fig;* hence one who *had to do with figs, handled them, ripened them.*

‡ The Egyptian sycamore, *Ficus sycomorus*, is not found in Syria above one thousand feet above the sea, while Tekoa is more than twice as high as that. *Cf.* 1 Kings x. 27, "the sycamores that are in the vale or valley land," עֵמֶק; 1 Chron. xxvii. 28, "the sycamores that are in the low plains." "The sycamore grows in sand on the edge of the desert as vigorously as in the midst of a well-watered country. Its roots go deep in search of water, which infiltrates as far as the gorges of the hills, and they absorb it freely even where drought seems to reign supreme" (Maspero on the Egyptian sycamore: "The Dawn of Civilization," translated by McClure, p. 26). "Everywhere on the confines of cultivated ground, and even at some distance from the valley, are fine single sycamores flourishing as though by miracle amid the sand. . . . They drink from water, which has infiltrated from the Nile, and whose existence is nowise betrayed upon the surface of the soil" (*ib.*, 121). Always and still reverenced by Moslem and Christian.

§ So practically Oort ("Th. Tjidsch.," 1891, 121 ff.), when compelled to abandon his previous conclusion (*ib.*, 1880, 122 ff.) that the Tekoa of Amos lay in Northern Israel.

* In 1891 we met the Rushaideh, who cultivate Engedi, encamped just below Tekoa. But at other parts of the borders between the hill-country of Judæa and the desert, and between Moab and the desert, we found round most of the herdsmen's central wells a few fig-trees or pomegranates, or even apricots occasionally.

† Luke i. 80.

‡ Mark i. 18.

§ v. 5; viii. 14.

‖ See p. 451.

¶ Prov. xxxi. 24.

pages, but the thick and noisy rumour of caravan and market-place: how the plague was marching up from Egypt; * ugly stories of the Phœnician slave-trade; † rumours of the advance of the awful Power, which men were hardly yet accustomed to name, but which had already twice broken from the North upon Damascus. Or it was the progress of some national mourning—how lamentation sprang up in the capital, rolled along the highways, and was re-echoed from the husbandmen and vinedressers on the hill-sides.‡ Or, at closer quarters, we see and hear the bustle of the great festivals and fairs—the "solemn assemblies," the reeking holocausts, the "noise of songs and viols:"§ the brutish religious zeal kindling into drunkenness and lust on the very steps of the altar; ‖ the embezzlement of pledges by the priests, the covetous restlessness of the traders, their false measures, their entanglement of the poor in debt; ¶ the careless luxury of the rich, their "banquets, buckets of wine, ivory couches," pretentious, preposterous music.** These things are described as by an eyewitness. Amos was not a citizen of the Northern Kingdom, to which he almost exclusively refers; but it was because he went up and down in it, using those eyes which the desert air had sharpened, that he so thoroughly learned the wickedness of its people, the corruption of Israel's life in every rank and class of society.††

But the convictions which he applied to this life Amos learned at home. They came to him over the desert, and without further material signal than was flashed to Tekoa from the towers of Jerusalem. This is placed beyond doubt by the figures in which he describes his call from Jehovah. Contrast his story, so far as he reveals it, with that of another. Some twenty years later, Isaiah of Jerusalem saw the Lord in the Temple, high and lifted up, and all the inaugural vision of this greatest of the prophets was conceived in the figures of the Temple—the altar, the smoke, the burning coals. But to his predecessor "among the shepherds of Tekoa," although revelation also starts from Jerusalem, it reaches him, not in the sacraments of her sanctuary, but across the bare pastures, and as it were in the roar of a lion. "Jehovah from Zion roareth, and uttereth His voice from Jerusalem." ‡‡ We read of no formal process of consecration for this first of the prophets. Through his clear desert air the word of God breaks upon him without medium or sacrament. And the native vigilance of the man is startled, is convinced by it, beyond all argument or question. "The lion hath roared, who shall not fear? Jehovah hath spoken, who can but prophesy?"

These words are taken from a passage in which Amos illustrates prophecy from other instances of his shepherd life. We have seen what a school of vigilance the desert is. Upon the bare surface all that stirs is ominous. Every shadow, every noise—the shepherd must know what is behind and be warned. Such a vigilance Amos would have Israel apply to his own message, and to the events of their history. Both of these he compares to certain facts of desert life, behind which his shepherdly instincts have taught him to feel an ominous cause. "Do two men walk together except they have trysted?"—except they have made an appointment. Hardly in the desert; for there men meet and take the same road by chance as seldom as ships at sea. "Doth a lion roar in the jungle and have no prey, or a young lion let out his voice in his den except he be taking something?" The hunting lion is silent till his quarry be in sight; when the lonely shepherd hears the roar across the desert he knows the lion leaps upon his prey, and he shudders as Israel ought to do when they hear God's voice by the prophet, for this also is never loosened but for some grim fact, some leap of doom. Or "doth a little bird fall on the snare earthwards and there be no noose upon her?" The reading may be doubtful, but the meaning is obvious: no one ever saw a bird pulled roughly down to earth when it tried to fly away without knowing there was the loop of a snare about her. Or "does the snare itself rise up from the ground, except indeed it be capturing something?"—except there be in the trap or net something to flutter, struggle, and so lift it up. Traps do not move without life in them. Or "is the alarum trumpet * blown in a city"—for instance, in high Tekoa up there, when some Arab raid sweeps from the desert on to the fields—"and do the people not tremble?" Or "shall calamity happen in a city and Jehovah not have done it? Yea, the Lord Jehovah doeth nothing but He has revealed His purpose to His servants the prophets." My voice of warning and these events of evil in your midst have the same cause—Jehovah—behind them. "The lion hath roared, who shall not fear? Jehovah hath spoken, who can but prophesy?" †

We cannot miss the personal note which rings through this triumph in the reality of things unseen. Not only does it proclaim a man of sincerity and conviction: it is resonant with the discipline by which that conviction was won—were won, too, the freedom from illusion and the power of looking at facts in the face, which Amos alone of his contemporaries possessed.

St. Bernard has described the first stage of the Vision of God as the Vision Distributive, in which the eager mind distributes her attention upon common things and common duties in themselves. It was in this elementary school that the earliest of the new prophets passed his apprenticeship and received his gifts. Others excel Amos in the powers of the imagination and the intellect. But by the incorrupt habits of his shepherd's life, by daily wakefulness to its alarms and daily faithfulness to its opportunities, he was trained in that simple power of appreciating facts and causes, which, applied to the great phenomena of the spirit and of history, forms his distinction among his peers. In this we find perhaps the reason why he records of himself no solemn hour of cleansing and initiation. "Jehovah took me from following the flock, and Jehovah said unto me, Go, prophesy unto My people Israel." Amos was of them of whom it is written, "Blessed are those servants whom the Lord when He cometh shall find watching." Through all his hard life this shepherd had kept his mind open and his conscience quick, so that when the word of God came to him he knew it, as fast as he knew the roar of the lion across the moor. Certainly there

* vi. 10.
† i. 9.
‡ v. 16.
§ v. 21 ff.
‖ ii. 7, 8.
¶ viii. 4 ff.
** vi. 1, 4-7.
†† See pp. 476 f.
‡‡ i. 2.

* שופר, as has been pointed out, means in early Israel always the trumpet blown as a summons to war; only in later Israel was the name given to the temple trumpet.

† See further on this important passage, p. 464.

is no habit which, so much as this of watching facts with a single eye and a responsible mind, is indispensable alike in the humblest duties and in the highest speculations of life. When Amos gives those naïve illustrations of how real the voice of God is to him, we receive them as the tokens of a man, honest and awake. Little wonder that he refuses to be reckoned among the professional prophets of his day who found their inspiration in excitement and trance. Upon him the impulses of the Deity come in no artificial and morbid ecstasy, removed as far as possible from real life. They come upon him, as it were, in the open air. They appeal to the senses of his healthy and expert manhood. They convince him of their reality with the same force as do the most startling events of his lonely shepherd watches. "The lion hath roared, who shall not fear? Jehovah hath spoken, who can but prophesy?"

The influence of the same discipline is still visible when Amos passes from the facts of his own consciousness to the facts of his people's life. His day in Israel sweltered with optimism. The glare of wealth, the fulsome love of country, the rank incense of a religion that was without morality—these thickened all the air, and neither the people nor their rulers had any vision. But Amos carried with him his clear desert atmosphere and his desert eyes. He saw the raw facts: the poverty, the cruel negligence of the rich, the injustice of the rulers, the immorality of the priests. The meaning of these things he questioned with as much persistence as he questioned every suspicious sound or sight upon those pastures of Tekoa. He had no illusions: he knew a mirage when he saw one. Neither the military pride of the people, fostered by recent successes over Syria, nor the dogmas of their religion, which asserted Jehovah's swift triumph upon the heathen, could prevent him from knowing that the immorality of Israel meant Israel's political downfall. He was one of those recruits from common life, by whom religion and the state have at all times been reformed. Springing from the laity and very often from among the working classes, their freedom from dogmas and routine, as well as from the compromising interests of wealth, rank, and party, renders them experts in life to a degree that almost no professional priest, statesman, or journalist, however honest or sympathetic, can hope to rival. Into politics they bring facts, but into religion they bring vision.

It is of the utmost significance that this reformer, this founder of the highest order of prophecy in Israel, should not only thus begin with facts, but to the very end be occupied with almost nothing else than the vision and record of them. In Amos there is but one prospect of the Ideal. It does not break till the close of his book, and then in such contrast to the plain and final indictments, which constitute nearly all the rest of his prophesying, that many have not unnaturally denied to him the verses which contain it. Throughout the other chapters we have but the exposure of present facts, material and moral, nor the sight of any future more distant than to-morrow and the immediate consequences of to-day's deeds. Let us mark this. The new prophecy which Amos started in Israel reached Divine heights of hope, unfolded infinite powers of moral and political regeneration—dared to blot out all the past, dared to believe all things possible in the future. But it started from the truth about the moral situation of the present. Its first prophet not only denied every popular dogma and ideal, but appears not to have substituted for them any others. He spent his gifts of vision on the discovery and appreciation of facts. Now this is necessary, not only in great reformations of religion, but at almost every stage in her development. We are constantly disposed to abuse even the most just and necessary of religious ideals as substitutes for experience or as escapes from duty, and to boast about the future before we have understood or mastered the present. Hence the need of realists like Amos. Though they are destitute of dogma, of comfort, of hope, of the ideal, let us not doubt that they also stand in the succession of the prophets of the Lord.

Nay, this is a stage of prophecy on which may be fulfilled the prayer of Moses: "Would to God that all the Lord's people were prophets!" To see the truth and tell it, to be accurate and brave about the moral facts of our day—to this extent the Vision and the Voice are possible for every one of us. Never for us may the doors of heaven open, as they did for him who stood on the threshold of the earthly temple, and he saw the Lord enthroned, while the Seraphim of the Presence sang the glory. Never for us may the skies fill with that tempest of life which Ezekiel beheld from Shinar, and above it the sapphire throne, and on the throne the likeness of a man, the likeness of the glory of the Lord. Yet let us remember that to see facts as they are and to tell the truth about them—this also is prophecy. We may inhabit a sphere which does not prompt the imagination, but is as destitute of the historic and traditional as was the wilderness of Tekoa. All the more may our unglamoured eyes be true to the facts about us. Every common day leads forth her duties as shining as every night leads forth her stars. The deeds and the fortunes of men are in our sight, and spell, to all who will honestly read, the very Word of the Lord. If only we be loyal, then by him who made the rude sounds and sights of the desert his sacraments, and whose vigilance of things seen and temporal became the vision of things unseen and eternal, we also shall see God, and be sure of His ways with men.

Before we pass from the desert discipline of the prophet we must notice one of its effects, which, while it greatly enhanced the clearness of his vision, undoubtedly disabled Amos for the highest prophetic rank. He who lives in the desert lives without patriotism—detached and aloof. He may see the throng of men more clearly than those who move among it. He cannot possibly so much feel for them. Unlike Hosea, Isaiah, and Jeremiah, Amos was not a citizen of the kingdom against which he prophesied, and indeed no proper citizen of any kingdom, but a nomad herdsman, hovering on the desert borders of Judæa. He saw Israel from the outside. His message to her is achieved with scarcely one sob in his voice. For the sake of the poor and the oppressed among the people he is indignant. But with the erring, staggering nation as a whole he has no real sympathy. His pity for her is exhausted in one elegy and two brief intercessions; hardly more than once does he even call her to repentance.

His sense of justice, in fact, had almost never to contend with his love. This made Amos the better witness, but the worse prophet. He did not rise so high as his great successors, because he did not so feel himself one with the people whom he was forced to condemn, because he did not bear their fate as his own nor travail for their new birth. "Ihm fehlt die Liebe." Love is the element lacking in his prophecy; and therefore the words are true of him which were uttered of his great follower across this same wilderness of Judæa, that mighty as were his voice and his message to prepare the way of the Lord, yet "the least in the Kingdom of Heaven is greater than he."

2. The Word and its Origins.

Amos i. 2; iii. 3-8; and *passim.*

We have seen the preparation of the Man for the Word. We are now to ask, Whence came the Word to the Man?—the Word that made him a prophet. What were its sources and sanctions outside himself? These involve other questions. How much of his message did Amos inherit from the previous religion of his people? And how much did he teach for the first time in Israel? And again, how much of this new element did he owe to the great events of his day? And how much demands some other source of inspiration?

To all these inquiries, outlines of the answers ought by this time to have become visible. We have seen that the contents of the Book of Amos consist almost entirely of two kinds: facts, actual or imminent, in the history of his people; and certain moral principles of the most elementary order. Amos appeals to no dogma nor form of law, nor to any religious or national institution. Still more remarkably, he does not rely upon miracle nor any so-called "supernatural sign." To employ the terms of Mazzini's famous formula, Amos draws his materials solely from "conscience and history." Within himself he hears certain moral principles speak in the voice of God, and certain events of his day he recognises as the judicial acts of God. The principles condemn the living generation of Israel as morally corrupt; the events threaten the people with political extinction. From this agreement between inward conviction and outward event Amos draws his full confidence as a prophet, and enforces on the people his message of doom as God's own word.

The passage in which Amos most explicitly illustrates this harmony between event and conviction is one whose metaphors we have already quoted in proof of the desert's influence upon the prophet's life. When Amos asks, "Can two walk together except they have made an appointment?" his figure is drawn, as we have seen, from the wilderness in which two men will hardly meet except they have arranged to do so; but the truth he would illustrate by the figure is that two sets of phenomena which coincide must have sprung from a common purpose. Their conjunction forbids mere chance. What kind of phenomena he means, he lets us see in his next instance: "Doth a lion roar in the jungle and have no prey? Doth a young lion let forth his voice from his den except he be catching something?" That is, those ominous sounds never happen without some fell and terrible deed happening along with them. Amos thus plainly hints that the two phenomena on whose coincidence he insists are an utterance on one side, and on the other side a deed fraught with destruction. The reading of the next metaphor about the bird and the snare is uncertain; at most what it means is that you never see signs of distress or a vain struggle to escape without there being, though out of sight, some real cause for them.* But from so general a principle he returns in his fourth metaphor to the special coincidence between utterance and deed. "Is the alarum-trumpet blown in a city and do the people not tremble?" Of course they do; they know such sound is never made without the approach of calamity. But who is the author of every calamity? God Himself: "Shall there be evil in a city and Jehovah not have done it?" Very well then; we have seen that common life has many instances in which, when an ominous sound is heard, it is because it is closely linked with a fatal deed. These happen together, not by mere chance, but because the one is the expression, the warning, or the explanation of the other. And we also know that fatal deeds which happen to any community in Israel are from Jehovah. He is behind them. But they, too, are accompanied by a warning voice from the same source as themselves. This is the voice which the prophet hears in his heart—the moral conviction which he feels as the Word of God. "The Lord Jehovah doeth nothing but He hath revealed His counsel to His servants the prophets." Mark the grammar: the revelation comes first to the prophet's heart; then he sees and recognises the event, and is confident to give his message about it. So Amos, repeating his metaphor, sums up his argument. "The Lion hath roared, who shall not fear?"—certain that there is more than sound to happen. "The Lord Jehovah hath spoken, who can but prophesy?"—certain that what Jehovah has spoken to him inwardly is likewise no mere sound, but that deeds of judgment are about to happen, as the ominous voice requires they should.†

The prophet then is made sure of his message by the agreement between the inward convictions of his soul and the outward events of the day. When these walk together, it proves that they have come of a common purpose. He who causes the events—it is Jehovah Himself, "for shall there be evil in a city and Jehovah not have done it?"—must be author also of the inner voice or conviction which agrees with them. "Who" then "can but prophesy?" Observe again that no support is here derived from miracle; nor is any claim made for the prophet on the ground of his ability to foretell the event. It is the agreement of the idea with the fact, their evident common origin in the purpose of Jehovah, which makes a man sure that he has in him the Word of God. Both are necessary, and together are enough. Are we then to leave the origin of the Word in this coincidence of fact and thought—as it were an electric flash produced by the contact of conviction with event?

* "Shall a little bird fall on the snare earthwards and there be no noose about her? Shall a snare rise from the ground and not be taking something?" On this see p. 462. Its meaning seems to be equivalent to the Scottish proverb: "There's aye some water whan the stirkie droons."

† There is thus no reason to alter the words "who shall not prophesy" to "who shall not tremble"—as Wellhausen does. To do so is to blunt the point of the argument.

Hardly: there are questions behind this coincidence. For instance, as to how the two react on each other—the event provoking the conviction, the conviction interpreting the event? The argument of Amos seems to imply that the ethical principles are experienced by the prophet prior to the events which justify them. Is this so, or was the shock of the events required to awaken the principles? And if the principles were prior, whence did Amos derive them? These are some questions that will lead us to the very origins of revelation.

The greatest of the events with which Amos and his contemporaries dealt was the Assyrian invasion. In a previous chapter we have tried to estimate the intellectual effects of Assyria on prophecy.* Assyria widened the horizon of Israel, put the world to Hebrew eyes into a new perspective, vastly increased the possibilities of history, and set to religion a novel order of problems. We can trace the effects upon Israel's conceptions of God, of man, and even of nature.† Now it might be plausibly argued that the new prophecy in Israel was first stirred and quickened by all this mental shock and strain, and that even the loftier ethics of the prophets were thus due to the advance of Assyria. For, as the most vigilant watchmen of their day, the prophets observed the rise of that empire, and felt its fatality for Israel. Turning then to inquire the Divine reasons for such a destruction, they found these in Israel's sinfulness, to the full extent of which their hearts were at last awakened. According to such a theory the prophets were politicians first and moralists afterwards: alarmists to begin with, and preachers of repentance only second. Or—to recur to the language employed above—the prophets' experience of the historical event preceded their conviction of the moral principle which agreed with it.

In support of such a theory it is pointed out that after all the most original element in the prophecy of the eighth century was the announcement of Israel's fall and exile. The Righteousness of Jehovah had often previously been enforced in Israel, but never had any voice drawn from it this awful conclusion that the nation must perish. The first in Israel to dare this was Amos, and surely what enabled him to do so was the imminence of Assyria upon his people. Again, such a theory might plausibly point to the opening verse of the Book of Amos, with its unprefaced, unexplained pronouncement of doom upon Israel:—

> "The Lord roareth from Zion,
> And giveth voice from Jerusalem;
> And the pastures of the shepherds mourn,
> And the summit of Carmel is withered!"

Here, it might be averred, is the earliest prophet's earliest utterance. Is it not audibly the voice of a man in a panic—such a panic as, ever on the eve of historic convulsions, seizes the more sensitive minds of a doomed people? The distant Assyrian thunder has reached Amos, on his pastures, unprepared—unable to articulate its exact meaning, and with only faith enough to hear in it the voice of his God. He needs reflection to unfold its contents; and the process of this reflection we find through the rest of his book. There he details for us, with increasing clearness, both the ethical reasons and the political results of that Assyrian terror, by which he was at first so wildly shocked into prophecy.

But the panic-born are always the still-born; and it is simply impossible that prophecy, in all her ethical and religious vigour, can have been the daughter of so fatal a birth. If we look again at the evidence which is quoted from Amos in favour of such a theory, we shall see how fully it is contradicted by other features of his book.

To begin with, we are not certain that the terror of the opening verse of Amos is the Assyrian terror. Even if it were, the opening of a book does not necessarily represent the writer's earliest feelings. The rest of the chapters contain visions and oracles which obviously date from a time when Amos was not yet startled by Assyria, but believed that the punishment which Israel required might be accomplished through a series of physical calamities—locusts, drought, and pestilence.* Nay, it was not even these earlier judgments, preceding the Assyrian, which stirred the word of God in the prophet. He introduces them with a "now" and a "therefore." That is to say, he treats them only as the consequence of certain facts, the conclusion of certain premises. These facts and premises are moral—they are exclusively moral. They are the sins of Israel's life, regarded without illusion and without pity. They are certain simple convictions, which fill the prophet's heart, about the impossibility of the survival of any state which is so perverse and so corrupt.

This origin of prophecy in moral facts and moral intuitions, which are in their beginning independent of political events, may be illustrated by several other points. For instance, the sins which Amos marked in Israel were such as required no "red dawn of judgment" to expose their flagrance and fatality. The abuse of justice, the cruelty of the rich, the shameless immorality of the priests, are not sins which we feel only in the cool of the day, when God Himself draws near to judgment. They are such things as make men shiver in the sunshine. And so the Book of Amos, and not less that of Hosea, tremble with the feeling that Israel's social corruption is great enough of itself, without the aid of natural convulsions, to shake the very basis of national life. "Shall not the land tremble for this," Amos says after reciting some sins, "and every one that dwelleth therein?"† Not drought nor pestilence nor invasion is needed for Israel's doom, but the elemental force of ruin which lies in the people's own wickedness. This is enough to create gloom long before the political skies be overcast—or, as Amos himself puts it, this is enough

> "To cause the sun to go down at noon,
> And to darken the earth in the clear day."‡

And once more—in spite of Assyria the ruin may be averted, if only the people will repent: "Seek good and not evil, and Jehovah of hosts will be with you, as you say."§ Assyria, however threatening, becomes irrelevant to Israel's future from the moment that Israel repents.

Such beliefs, then, are obviously not the results of experience, nor of a keen observation of history. They are the primal convictions of the heart, which are deeper than all experience, and themselves contain the sources of historical foresight. With Amos it was not the outward

* See chap. iv. † See pp. 455 ff.

* See p. 459. † viii. 8. ‡ viii. 9. § v. 14

event which inspired the inward conviction, but the conviction which anticipated and interpreted the event, though when the event came there can be no doubt that it confirmed, deepened, and articulated the conviction.*

But when we have thus tracked the stream of prophecy as far back as these elementary convictions we have not reached the fountain-head. Whence did Amos derive his simple and absolute ethics? Were they original to him? Were they new in Israel? Such questions start an argument which touches the very origins of revelation.

It is obvious that Amos not only takes for granted the laws of righteousness which he enforces: he takes for granted also the people's conscience of them. New, indeed, is the doom which sinful Israel deserves, and original to himself is the proclamation of it; but Amos appeals to the moral principles which justify the doom, as if they were not new, and as if Israel ought always to have known them. This attitude of the prophet to his principles has, in our time, suffered a curious judgment. It has been called an anachronism. So absolute a morality, some say, had never before been taught in Israel; nor had righteousness been so exclusively emphasised as the purpose of Jehovah. Amos and the other prophets of his century were the virtual "creators of ethical monotheism": it could only be by a prophetic license or prophetic fiction that he appealed to his people's conscience of the standards he promulgated, or condemned his generation to death for not having lived up to them.

Let us see how far this criticism is supported by the facts.

To no sane observer can the religious history of Israel appear as anything but a course of gradual development. Even in the moral standards, in respect to which it is confessedly often most difficult to prove growth, the signs of the nation's progress are very manifest. Practices come to be forbidden in Israel and tempers to be mitigated, which in earlier ages were sanctioned to their extreme by the explicit decrees of religion. In the nation's attitude to the outer world sympathies arise, along with ideals of spiritual service, where previously only war and extermination had been enforced in the name of the Deity. Now in such an evolution it is equally indubitable that the longest and most rapid stage was the prophecy of the eighth century. The prophets of that time condemn acts which had been inspired by their immediate predecessors;† they abjure, as impeding morality, a ceremonial which the spiritual leaders of earlier generations had felt to be indispensable to religion; and they unfold ideals of the nation's moral destiny, of which older writings give us only the faintest hints. Yet, while the fact of a religious evolution in Israel is thus certain, we must not fall into the vulgar error which interprets evolution as if it were mere addition, nor forget that even in the most creative periods of religion nothing is brought forth which has not already been promised, and, at some earlier stage, placed, so to speak, within reach of the human mind. After all it is the mind which grows; the moral ideals which become visible to its more matured vision are so Divine that, when they present themselves, the mind cannot but think they were always real and always imperative. If we remember these commonplaces we shall do justice both to Amos and to his critics.

In the first place it is clear that most of the morality which Amos enforced is of that fundamental order which can never have been recognised as the discovery or invention of any prophet. Whatever be their origin, the conscience of justice, the duty of kindness to the poor, the horror of wanton cruelty towards one's enemies, which form the chief principles of Amos, are discernible in man as far back as history allows us to search for them. Should a generation have lost them, they can be brought back to it, never with the thrill of a new lesson, but only with the shame of an old and an abused memory. To neither man nor people can the righteousness which Amos preached appear as a discovery, but always as a recollection and a remorse. And this is most emphatically true of the people of Moses and of Samuel, of Nathan, of Elijah, and of the Book of the Covenant. Ethical elements had been characteristic of Israel's religion from the very first. They were not due to a body of written law, but rather to the character of Israel's God, appreciated by the nation in all the great crises of their history.* Jehovah had won for Israel freedom and unity. He had been a spirit of justice to their lawgivers and magistrates.† He had raised up a succession of consecrated personalities,‡ who by life and word had purified the ideals of the whole people. The results had appeared in the creation of a strong national conscience, which avenged with horror, as "folly in Israel," the wanton crimes of any person or section of the commonwealth; in the gradual formation of a legal code, founded indeed in the common custom of the Semites, but greatly more moral than that; and even in the attainment of certain profoundly ethical beliefs about God and His relations, beyond Israel, to all mankind. Now, let us understand once for all, that in the ethics of Amos there is nothing which is not rooted in one or other of these achievements of the previous religion of his people. To this religion Amos felt himself attached in the closest possible way. The word of God comes to him across the desert, as we have seen, yet not out of the air. From the first he hears it rise from that one monument of his people's past which we have found visible on his physical horizon §—"from Zion, from Jerusalem," ‖ from the city of David, from the Ark, whose ministers were Moses and Samuel, from the repository of the main tradition of Israel's religion.¶ Amos felt himself in the sacred succession; and his feeling is confirmed by the contents of his book. The details of that civic justice which he demands from his generation are found in the Book of

* How far Assyria assisted the development of prophecy we have already seen. But we have been made aware, at the same time, that Assyria's service to Israel in this respect presupposed the possession by the prophets of certain beliefs in the character and will of their God, Jehovah. The prophets' faith could never have risen to the magnitude of the new problems set to it by Assyria if there had not been already inherent in it that belief in the sovereignty of a Righteousness of which all things material were but the instruments.

† Compare, for instance, Hosea's condemnation of Jehu's murder of Joram, with Elisha's command to do it; also 2 Kings iii. 19, 25, with Deut. xx. 19.

* See above, p. 444.

† Isa. xxviii.

‡ Amos ii.

§ *Ante* p. 460.

‖ i. 2.

¶ Therefore we see at a glance how utterly inadequate is Renan's brilliant comparison of Amos to a modern revolutionary journalist ("Histoire du Peuple Israel," II.). Journalist indeed! How all this would-be cosmopolitan and impartial critic's judgments smack of the boulevards!

the Covenant—the only one of Israel's great codes which appears by this time to have been in existence; * or in those popular proverbs which almost as certainly were found in early Israel.†

Nor does Amos go elsewhere for the religious sanctions of his ethics. It is by the ancient mercies of God towards Israel that he shames and convicts his generation—by the deeds of grace which made them a nation, by the organs of doctrine and reproof which have inspired them, unfailing from age to age. "I destroyed the Amorite before them. . . . Yea, I brought you up out of the land of Egypt, and I led you forty years in the wilderness, to possess the land of the Amorites. And I raised up of your sons for prophets, and of your young men for Nazarites. Was it not even thus, O ye children of Israel? saith Jehovah." ‡ We cannot even say that the belief which Amos expresses in Jehovah as the supreme Providence of the world § was a new thing in Israel, for a belief as universal inspires those portions of the Book of Genesis which, like the Book of the Covenant, were already extant.

We see, therefore, what right Amos had to present his ethical truths to Israel, as if they were not new, but had been within reach of his people from of old.

We could not, however, commit a greater mistake than to confine the inspiration of our prophet to the past, and interpret his doctrines as mere inferences from the earlier religious ideas of Israel—inferences forced by his own passionate logic, or more naturally ripened for him by the progress of events. A recent writer has thus summarised the work of the prophets of the eighth century: "In fact they laid hold upon that bias towards the ethical which dwelt in Jahwism from Moses onwards, and they allowed it alone to have value as corresponding to the true religion of Jehovah." ‖ But this is too abstract to be an adequate statement of the prophets' own consciousness. What overcame Amos was a Personal Influence—the Impression of a Character; and it was this not only as it was revealed in the past of his people. The God who stands behind Amos is indeed the ancient Deity of Israel, and the facts which prove Him God are those which made the nation—the Exodus, the guidance through the wilderness, the overthrow of the Amorites, the gift of the land. "Was it not even thus, O ye children of Israel?" But what beats and burns through the pages of Amos is not the memory of those wonderful works, so much as a fresh vision and understanding of the Living God who worked them. Amos has himself met with Jehovah on the conditions of his own time—on the moral situation provided by the living generation of Israel. By an intercourse conducted, not through the distant signals of the past, but here and now, through the events of the prophet's own day, Amos has received an original and overpowering conviction of his people's God as absolute righteousness. What prophecy had hitherto felt in part, and applied to one or other of the departments of Israel's life, Amos is the first to feel in its fulness, and to every extreme of its consequences upon the worship, the conduct, and the fortunes of the nation. To him Jehovah not only commands this and that righteous law, but Jehovah and righteousness are absolutely identical. "Seek Jehovah and ye shall live . . . seek good and ye shall live." * The absoluteness with which Amos conceived this principle, the courage with which he applied it, carry him along those two great lines upon which we most clearly trace his originality as a prophet. In the strength of this principle he does what is really new in Israel: he discards the two elements which had hitherto existed alongside the ethical, and had fettered and warped it.

Up till now the ethical spirit of the religion of Jehovah † had to struggle with two beliefs which we can trace back to the Semitic origins of the religion—the belief, namely, that, as the national God, Jehovah would always defend their political interests, irrespective of morality; and the belief that a ceremonial of rites and sacrifices was indispensable to religion. These principles were mutual: as the deity was bound to succour the people, so were the people bound to supply the deity with gifts, and the more of these they brought the more they made sure of his favours. Such views were not absolutely devoid of moral benefit. In the formative period of the nation they had contributed both discipline and hope. But of late they had between them engrossed men's hearts, and crushed out of religion both conscience and common-sense. By the first of them, the belief in Jehovah's predestined protection of Israel, the people's eyes were so holden they could not see how threatening were the times; by the other, the confidence in ceremonial, conscience was dulled, and that immorality permitted which they mingled so shamelessly with their religious zeal. Now the conscience of Amos did not merely protest against the predominance of the two, but was so exclusive, so spiritual, that it boldly banished both from religion. Amos denied that Jehovah was bound to save His people; he affirmed that ritual and sacrifice were no part of the service He demands from men. This is the measure of originality in our prophet. The two religious principles which were inherent in the very fibre of Semitic religion, and which till now had gone unchallenged in Israel, Amos cast forth from religion in the name of a pure and absolute righteousness. On the one hand, Jehovah's peculiar connection with Israel meant no more than jealousy for their holiness: "You only have I known of all the families of the earth, therefore will I visit upon you all your iniquities." ‡ And, on the other hand, all their ceremonial was abhorrent to Him: "I hate, I despise your festivals. . . . Though ye offer Me burnt offerings and your meal offerings, I will not accept them. . . . Take thou away from Me the noise of thy songs; I will not hear the music of thy viols. But let justice run down as waters, and righteousness as a perennial stream." §

It has just been said that emphasis upon morality as the sum of religion, to the exclusion of sacrifice, is the most original element in the prophecies of Amos. He himself, however, does

* Exod. xx.; incorporated in the JE book of history, and, according to nearly all critics, complete by 750; the contents must have been familiar in Israel long before that. There is no trace in Amos of any influence peculiar to either the Deuteronomic or the Levitical legislation.

† See especially Schultz, "O. T. Theol.," Eng. Trans. by Paterson, I. 214.

‡ ii. 9–11. On this passage see further p. 476.

§ If iv. 13, v. 8 and ix. 6 be genuine, this remark equally applies to belief in Jehovah as Creator.

‖ Kayser, "Old Testament Theology."

* v. 6, 14.

† See above, p. 446.

‡ iii. 2.

§ v. 21 ff.

not regard this as proclaimed for the first time in Israel, and the precedent he quotes is so illustrative of the sources of his inspiration that we do well to look at it for a little. In the verse next to the one last quoted he reports these words of God: "Did ye offer unto Me sacrifices and gifts in the wilderness, for forty years, O house of Israel?" An extraordinary challenge! From the present blind routine of sacrifice Jehovah appeals to the beginning of His relations with the nation: did they then perform such services to Him? Of course, a negative answer is expected. No other agrees with the main contention of the passage. In the wilderness Israel had not offered sacrifices and gifts to Jehovah. Jeremiah quotes a still more explicit word of Jehovah: "I spake not unto your fathers in the day that I brought them out of the land of Egypt concerning burnt offerings and sacrifices: but this thing I commanded them, saying, Obey My voice, and I will be your God, and ye shall be My people." *

To these Divine statements we shall not be able to do justice if we hold by the traditional view that the Levitical legislation was proclaimed in the wilderness. Discount that legislation, and the statements become clear. It is true, of course, that Israel must have had a ritual of some kind from the first; and that both in the wilderness and in Canaan their spiritual leaders must have performed sacrifices as if these were acceptable to Jehovah. But even so the Divine words which Amos and Jeremiah quote are historically correct; for while the ethical contents of the religion of Jehovah were its original and essential contents—"I commanded them, saying, Obey My voice"—the ritual was but a modification of the ritual common to all Semites; and ever since the occupation of the land, it had, through the infection of the Canaanite rites on the high places, grown more and more Pagan, both in its functions and in the ideas which these were supposed to express.† Amos was right. Sacrifice had never been the Divine, the revealed element in the religion of Jehovah. Nevertheless, before Amos no prophet in Israel appears to have said so. And what enabled this man in the eighth century to offer testimony, so novel but so true, about the far-away beginnings of his people's religion in the fourteenth, was plainly neither tradition nor historical research, but an overwhelming conviction of the spiritual and moral character of God—of Him who had been Israel's God both then and now, and whose righteousness had been, just as much then as now, exalted above all purely national interests and all susceptibility to ritual. When we thus see the prophet's knowledge of the Living God enabling him, not only to proclaim an ideal of religion more spiritual than Israel had yet dreamed, but to perceive that such an ideal had been the essence of the religion of Jehovah from the first, we understand how thoroughly Amos was mastered by that knowledge. If we need any further proof of his "possession" by the character of God, we find it in those phrases in which his own consciousness disappears, and we have no longer the herald's report of the Lord's words, but the very accents of the Lord Himself, fraught with personal feeling of the most intense quality. "I" Jehovah "hate, I despise your feast days. . . . Take thou away from Me the noise of thy songs; I will not hear the music of thy viols.* . . . I abhor the arrogance of Jacob, and hate his palaces.† . . . The eyes of the Lord Jehovah are upon the sinful kingdom.‡ . . . . Jehovah sweareth, I will never forget any of their works."§ Such sentences reveal a Deity who is not only manifest Character, but surgent and importunate Feeling. We have traced the prophet's word to its ultimate source. It springs from the righteousness, the vigilance, the urgency of the Eternal. The intellect, imagination, and heart of Amos—the convictions he has inherited from his people's past, his conscience of their evil life to-day, his impressions of current and coming history—are all enforced and illuminated, all made impetuous and radiant, by the Spirit, that is to say the Purpose and the Energy, of the Living God. Therefore, as he says in the title of his book, or as some one says for him, Amos *saw* his words. They stood out objective to himself. And they were not mere sound. They glowed and burned with God.

When we realise this, we feel how inadequate it is to express prophecy in the terms of evolution. No doubt, as we have seen, the ethics and religion of Amos represent a large and measurable advance upon those of earlier Israel. And yet with Amos we do not seem so much to have arrived at a new stage in a Process, as to have penetrated to the Idea which has been behind the Process from the beginning. The change and growth of Israel's religion are realities—their fruits can be seen, defined, catalogued—but a greater reality is the unseen Purpose which impels them. They have been expressed only now. He has been unchanging from old and for ever—from the first absolute righteousness in Himself, and absolute righteousness in His demands from men.

3. The Prophet and His Ministry.

Amos vii., viii. 1-4.

We have seen the preparation of the Man for the Word; we have sought to trace to its source the Word which came to the Man. It now remains for us to follow the Prophet, Man and Word combined, upon his Ministry to the people.

For reasons given in a previous chapter,‖ there must always be some doubt as to the actual course of the ministry of Amos before his appearance at Bethel. Most authorities, however, agree that the visions recounted in the beginning of the seventh chapter form the substance of his address at Bethel, which was interrupted by the priest Amaziah. These visions furnish a probable summary of the prophet's experience up to that point. While they follow the same course, which we trace in the two series of oracles that now precede them in the book, the ideas in them are less elaborate. At the same time it is evident that Amos must have already spoken upon other points than those which he puts into the first three visions. For instance, Amaziah reports to the king that Amos had explicitly predicted the exile of the whole people ¶—a conviction which, as we have seen, the prophet reached only after some length of experience. It is equally certain that Amos must have already exposed the

* Jer. vii. 22 f.

† See above, p. 448.

* v. 21-23.

† vi. 8.

‡ ix. 8.

§ viii. 7.

‖ Chap. v. p. 459.

¶ vii. 11.

sins of the people in the light of the Divine righteousness. Some of the sections of the book which deal with this subject appear to have been originally spoken; and it is unnatural to suppose that the prophet announced the chastisements of God without having previously justified these to the consciences of men.

If this view be correct, Amos, having preached for some time to Israel concerning the evil state of society, appeared at a great religious festival in Bethel, determined to bring matters to a crisis, and to announce the doom which his preaching threatened and the people's continued impenitence made inevitable. Mark his choice of place and of audience. It was no mere king he aimed at. Nathan had dealt with David, Gad with Solomon, Elijah with Ahab and Jezebel. But Amos sought the people, them with whom resided the real forces and responsibilities of life: the wealth, the social fashions, the treatment of the poor, the spirit of worship, the ideals of religion.* And Amos sought the people upon what was not only a great popular occasion, but one on which was arrayed, in all pomp and lavishness, the very system he essayed to overthrow. The religion of his time—religion as mere ritual and sacrifice—was what God had sent him to beat down, and he faced it at its headquarters, and upon one of its high days, in the royal and popular sanctuary where it enjoyed at once the patronage of the crown, the lavish gifts of the rich, and the thronged devotion of the multitude. As Savonarola at the Duomo in Florence, as Luther at the Diet of Worms, as our Lord Himself at the feast in Jerusalem, so was Amos at the feast in Bethel. Perhaps he was still more lonely. He speaks nowhere of having made a disciple, and in the sea of faces which turned on him when he spoke, it is probable that he could not welcome a single ally. They were officials, or interested traders, or devotees; he was a foreigner and a wild man, with a word that spared the popular dogma as little as the royal prerogative. Well for him was it that over all those serried ranks of authority, those fanatic crowds, that lavish splendour, another vision commanded his eyes. "I saw the Lord standing over the altar, and He said, Smite."

Amos told the pilgrims at Bethel that the first events of his time in which he felt a purpose of God in harmony with his convictions about Israel's need of punishment were certain calamities of a physical kind. Of these, which in chap. iv. he describes as successively drought, blasting, locusts, pestilence, and earthquake, he selected at Bethel only two—locusts and drought—and he began with the locusts. It may have been either the same visitation as he specifies in chap. iv., or a previous one; for of all the plagues of Palestine locusts have been the most frequent, occurring every six or seven years. "Thus the Lord Jehovah caused me to see: and, behold, a brood † of locusts at the beginning of the coming up of the spring crops." In the Syrian year there are practically two tides of verdure: one which starts after the early rains of October and continues through the winter, checked by the cold; and one which comes away with greater force under the influence of the latter rains and more genial airs of spring.* Of these it was the later and richer which the locusts had attacked. "And, behold, it was after the king's mowings." These seem to have been a tribute which the kings of Israel levied on the spring herbage, and which the Roman governors of Syria used annually to impose in the month Nisan.† "After the king's mowings" would be a phrase to mark the time when everybody else might turn to reap their green stuff. It was thus the very crisis of the year when the locusts appeared; the April crops devoured, there was no hope of further fodder till December. Still, the calamity had happened before, and had been survived; a nation so vigorous and wealthy as Israel was under Jeroboam II. need not have been frightened to death. But Amos felt it with a conscience. To him it was the beginning of that destruction of his people which the spirit within him knew that their sin had earned. So "it came to pass when" the locusts "had made an end of devouring the verdure of the earth, that I said, Remit, I pray Thee," or "pardon"—a proof that there already weighed on the prophet's spirit something more awful than loss of grass—"how shall Jacob rise again? for he is little." ‡ The prayer was heard. "Jehovah repented for this: It shall not be, said Jehovah." The unnameable "it" must be the same as in the frequent phrase of the first chapter: "I will not turn It back"—namely, the final execution of doom on the people's sin. The reserve with which this is mentioned, both while there is still chance for the people to repent and after it has become irrevocable, is very impressive.

The next example which Amos gave at Bethel of his permitted insight into God's purpose was a great drought. "Thus the Lord Jehovah made me to see: and, behold, the Lord Jehovah was calling fire into the quarrel." § There was, then, already a quarrel between Jehovah and His people—another sign that the prophet's moral conviction of Israel's sin preceded the rise of the events in which he recognised its punishment. "And" the fire "devoureth the Great Deep, yea, it was about to devour the land." ‖ Severe drought in Palestine might well be described as fire, even when it was not accompanied by the flame and smoke of those forest and prairie fires which Joel describes as its consequences.¶ But to have the full fear of such a drought, we should need to feel beneath us the curious world which the men of those days felt. To them the earth rested in a great deep, from whose stores all her springs and fountains burst. When these failed it meant that the unfathomed floods below were

* On the ministry of eighth-century prophets to the people see the author's "Isaiah," I. p. 119.

† So LXX., followed by Hitzig and Wellhausen, by reading יֵצֶר for יוֹצֵר.

* *Cf.* "Hist. Geography of the Holy Land," pp. 64 ff. The word translated "spring crop" above is לקשׁ, and from the same root as the name of the latter rain, מַלְקוֹשׁ, which falls in the end of March or beginning of April *Cf. Zeitschrift des deutschen Palästina-Vereins*, IV. 83; VIII. 62.

† *Cf.* 1 Kings xviii. 5 with 1 Sam. vii. 15, 17; 1 Kings iv. 7 ff. See Robertson Smith, "Religion of the Semites," 228.

‡ LXX.: "Who shall raise up Jacob again "

§ So Professor A. B. Davidson. But the grammar might equally well afford the rendering "one calling that the Lord will punish with the fire," the ל of לריב marking the introduction of indirect speech (*cf.* Ewald, § 338*a*). But Hitzig for קרא reads קרה (Deut. xxv. 18), "to occur," "happen." So similarly Wellhausen, "es nahte sich zu strafen mit Feuer der Herr Jahve". All these renderings yield practically the same meaning.

‖ A. B. Davidson, "Syntax," § 57, Rem. 1.

¶ i. 19 f.

burnt up. But how fierce the flame that could effect this! And how certainly able to devour next the solid land which rested above the deep —the very "Portion" * assigned by God to His people. Again Amos interceded: "Lord Jehovah, I pray Thee forbear: how shall Jacob rise? for he is little." And for the second time Jacob was reprieved. "Jehovah repented for this: It also shall not come to pass, said the Lord Jehovah."

We have treated these visions, not as the imagination or prospect of possible disasters,† but as insight into the meaning of actual plagues. Such a treatment is justified, not only by the invariable habit of Amos to deal with real facts, but also by the occurrence of these same plagues among the series by which, as we are told, God had already sought to move the people to repentance.‡ The general question of sympathy between such purely physical disasters and the moral evil of a people we may postpone to another chapter, confining ourselves here to the part played in the events by the prophet himself.

Surely there is something wonderful in the attitude of this shepherd to the fires and plagues that Nature sweeps upon his land. He is ready for them. And he is ready not only by the general feeling of his time that such things happen of the wrath of God. His sovereign and predictive conscience recognises them as her ministers. They are sent to punish a people whom she has already condemned. Yet, unlike Elijah, Amos does not summon the drought, nor even welcome its arrival. How far has prophecy travelled since the violent Tishbite! With all his conscience of Israel's sin, Amos yet prays that their doom may be turned. We have here some evidence of the struggle through which these later prophets passed, before they accepted their awful messages to men. Even Amos, desert-bred and living aloof from Israel, shrank from the judgment which it was his call to publish. For two moments—they would appear to be the only two in his ministry—his heart contended with his conscience, and twice he entreated God to forgive. At Bethel he told the people all this, in order to show how unwillingly he took up his duty against them, and how inevitable he found that duty to be. But still more shall we learn from his tale, if we feel in his words about the smallness of Jacob, not pity only, but sympathy. We shall learn that prophets are never made solely by the bare word of God, but that even the most objective and judicial of them has to earn his title to proclaim judgment by suffering with men the agony of the judgment he proclaims. Never to a people came there a true prophet who had not first prayed for them. To have entreated for men, to have represented them in the highest courts of Being, is to have deserved also supreme judicial rights upon them. And thus it is that our Judge at the Last Day shall be none other than our great Advocate who continually maketh intercession for us. It is prayer, let us repeat, which, while it gives us all power with God, endows us at the same time with moral rights over men. Upon his mission of judgment we shall follow Amos with the greater sympathy that he thus comes forth to it from the mercy-seat and the ministry of intercession.

The first two visions which Amos told at Bethel were of disasters in the sphere of nature, but his third lay in the sphere of politics. The two former were, in their completeness at least, averted; and the language Amos used of them seems to imply that he had not even then faced the possibility of a final overthrow. He took for granted *Jacob* was *to rise again:* he only feared as to *how* this should be. But the third vision is so final that the prophet does not even try to intercede. Israel is measured, found wanting, and doomed. Assyria is not named, but is obviously intended; and the fact that the prophet arrives at certainty with regard to the doom of Israel, just when he thus comes within sight of Assyria, is instructive as to the influence exerted on prophecy by the rise of that empire.*

"Thus He gave me to see: and, behold, the Lord had taken His station"—'tis a more solemn word than the "stood" of our versions—"upon a city wall" built to "the plummet,† and in His hand a plummet. And Jehovah said unto me, What art thou seeing, Amos?" The question surely betrays some astonishment shown by the prophet at the vision or some difficulty he felt in making it out. He evidently does not feel it at once, as the natural result of his own thinking: it is objective and strange to him; he needs time to see into it. "And I said, A plummet. And the Lord said, Behold, I am setting a plummet in the midst of My people Israel. I will not again pass them over." To set a measuring line or a line with weights attached to any building means to devote it to destruction;‡ but here it is uncertain whether the plummet threatens destruction, or means that Jehovah will at last clearly prove to the prophet the insufferable obliquity of the fabric of the nation's life, originally set straight by Himself—originally "a wall of a plummet." For God's judgments are never arbitrary: by a standard we men can read He shows us their necessity. Conscience itself is no mere voice of authority: it is a convincing plummet, and plainly lets us see *why* we should be punished. But whichever interpretation we choose, the result is the same. "The high places of Israel shall be desolate, and the sanctuaries of Isaac laid waste; and I will rise against the house of Jeroboam with the sword." A declaration of war! Israel is to be invaded, her dynasty overthrown. Every one who heard the prophet would know, though he named them not, that the Assyrians were meant.

It was apparently at this point that Amos was interrupted by Amaziah. The priest, who was conscious of no spiritual power with which to oppose the prophet, gladly grasped the oppor-

* *Cf.* Micah ii. 3. חֵלֶק is the word used, and according to the motive given above stands well for the climax of the fire's destructive work. This meets the objection of Wellhausen, who proposes to omit חֵלֶק, because the heat does not dry up first the great deep and then the fields (*Ackerflur*). This is to mistake the obvious point of the sentence. The drought was so great that, after the fountains were exhausted, it seemed as if the solid framework of the land, described with very apt pathos as the *Portion*, would be the next to disappear. Some take חלק as *divided*, therefore cultivated, ground.

† So for instance, Von Orelli.

‡ Chap. iv.

* See chap. iv. p. 454.

† Literally "of the plummet," an obscure expression. It cannot mean plumb-straight, for the wall is condemned.

‡ 2 Kings xxi. 13: "I will stretch over Jerusalem the line of Samaria and the plummet or weight (מִשְׁקֹלֶת) of the house of Ahab." Isa. xxxiv. 11: "He shall stretch over it the cord of confusion, and the weights [literally *stones*] of emptiness."

tunity afforded him by the mention of the king, and fell back on the invariable resource of a barren and envious sacerdotalism: "He speaketh against Cæsar." * There follows one of the great scenes of history—the scene which, however fast the ages and the languages, the ideals and the deities may change, repeats itself with the same two actors. Priest and Man face each other—Priest with King behind, Man with God—and wage that debate in which the whole warfare and progress of religion consist. But the story is only typical by being real. Many subtle traits of human nature prove that we have here an exact narrative of fact. Take Amaziah's report to Jeroboam. He gives to the words of the prophet just that exaggeration and innuendo which betray the wily courtier, who knows how to accentuate a general denunciation till it feels like a personal attack. And yet, like every Caiaphas of his tribe, the priest in his exaggerations expresses a deeper meaning than he is conscious of. "Amos"—note how the mere mention of the name without description proves that the prophet was already known in Israel, perhaps was one on whom the authorities had long kept their eye—"Amos hath conspired against thee"—yet God was his only fellow-conspirator! —"in the midst of the house of Israel"—this royal temple at Bethel. "The land is not able to hold his words"—it must burst; yes, but in another sense than thou meanest, O Caiaphas-Amaziah! "For thus hath Amos said, By the sword shall Jeroboam die"—Amos had spoken only of the dynasty, but the twist which Amaziah lends to the words is calculated—"and Israel going shall go into captivity from off his own land." This was the one unvarnished spot in the report.

Having fortified himself, as little men will do, by his duty to the powers that be, Amaziah dares to turn upon the prophet; and he does so, it is amusing to observe, with that tone of intellectual and moral superiority which it is extraordinary to see some men derive from a merely official station or touch with royalty. "Visionary,† begone! Get thee off to the land of Judah; and earn‡ thy bread there, and there play the prophet. But at Bethel"—mark the rising accent of the voice—"thou shalt not again prophesy. The King's Sanctuary it is, and the House of the Kingdom."§ With the official mind this is more conclusive than that it is the House of God! In fact the speech of Amaziah justifies the hardest terms which Amos uses of the religion of his day. In all this priest says there is no trace of the spiritual—only fear, pride, and privilege. Divine truth is challenged by human law, and the Word of God silenced in the name of the king.

We have here a conception of religion, which is not merely due to the unspiritual character of the priest who utters it, but has its roots in the far back origins of Israel's religion. The Pagan Semite identified absolutely State and Church; and on that identification was based the religious practice of early Israel. It had many healthy results: it kept religion in touch with public life; order, justice, patriotism, self-sacrifice for the common weal, were devoutly held to be matters of religion. So long, therefore, as the system was inspired by truly spiritual ideals, nothing for those times could be better. But we see in it an almost inevitable tendency to harden to the sheerest officialism. That it was more apt to do so in Israel than in Judah, is intelligible from the origin of the Northern Schism, and the erection of the national sanctuaries from motives of mere statecraft.* Erastianism could hardly be more flagrant or more ludicrous in its opposition to true religion than at Bethel. And yet how often have the ludicrousness and the flagrancy been repeated, with far less temptation! Ever since Christianity became a state religion, she that needed least to use the weapons of this world has done so again and again in a thoroughly Pagan fashion. The attempts of Churches by law established, to stamp out by law all religious dissent; or where such attempts were no longer possible, the charges now of fanaticism and now of sordidness and religious shopkeeping, which have been so frequently made against dissent by little men who fancied their state connection, or their higher social position to mean an intellectual and moral superiority; the absurd claims which many a minister of religion makes upon the homes and the souls of a parish, by virtue not of his calling in Christ, but of his position as official priest of the parish,—all these are the sins of Amaziah, priest of Bethel. But they are not confined to an established Church. The Amaziahs of dissent are also very many. Wherever the official masters the spiritual; wherever mere dogma or tradition is made the standard of preaching; wherever new doctrine is silenced, or programmes of reform condemned, as of late years in Free Churches they have sometimes been, not by spiritual argument, but by the *ipse dixit* of the dogmatist, or by ecclesiastical rule or expediency,—there you have the same spirit. The dissenter who checks the Word of God in the name of some denominational law or dogma is as Erastian as the churchman who would crush it, like Amaziah, by invoking the state. These things in all the Churches are the beggarly rudiments of Paganism; and religious reform is achieved, as it was that day at Bethel, by the adjuring of officialism.

"But Amos answered and said unto Amaziah, No prophet I, nor prophet's son. But a herdsman† I, and a dresser of sycamores; and Jehovah took me from behind the flock, and Jehovah said unto me, Go, prophesy unto My people Israel."

On such words we do not comment; we give them homage. The answer of this shepherd to this priest is no mere claim of personal disinterestedness. It is the protest of a new order of prophecy,‡ the charter of a spiritual religion. As we have seen, the "sons of the prophets" were guilds of men who had taken to prophesying because of certain gifts of temper and natural disposition, and they earned their bread by the ex-

* John xix. 12.

† The word "seer," is here used in a contemptuous sense and has therefore to be translated by some such word as "visionary."

‡ Literally "eat."

§ בֵּית מַמְלָכָה—that is, a "central" or "capital sanctuary." *Cf.* עִיר הַמַּמְלָכָה (1 Sam, xxvii. 5), "city of the kingdom" *i. e.*, chief or capital town.

* 1 Kings xii. 26, 27.

† "Prophet" and "prophet's son" are equivalent terms, the latter meaning one of the professional guilds of prophets. There is no need to change herdsman, בוקר, as Wellhausen does, into נוקד, shepherd, the word used in i. 1.

‡ *Cf.* Wellhausen, "Hist.," Eng. Ed., § 6: "Amos was the founder and the purest type of a new order of prophecy."

ercise of these. Among such abstract craftsmen Amos will not be reckoned. He is a prophet, but not of the kind with which his generation was familiar. An ordinary member of society, he has been suddenly called by Jehovah from his civil occupation for a special purpose and by a call which has not necessarily to do with either gifts or a profession. This was something new, not only in itself, but in its consequences upon the general relations of God to men. What we see in this dialogue at Bethel is, therefore, not merely the triumph of a character, however heroic, but rather a step forward—and that one of the greatest and most indispensable—in the history of religion.

There follows a denunciation of the man who sought to silence this fresh voice of God. "Now therefore hearken to the word of Jehovah thou that sayest, Prophesy not against Israel, nor let drop thy words against the house of Israel; therefore thus saith Jehovah. . . ." Thou hast presumed to say; "Hear what God will say." Thou hast dared to set thine office and system against His word and purpose. See how they must be swept away. In defiance of its own rules the grammar flings forward to the beginnings of its clauses, each detail of the priest's estate along with the scene of its desecration. "Thy wife in the city—shall play the harlot; and thy sons and thy daughters by the sword—shall fall; and thy land by the measuring rope—shall be divided; and thou in an unclean land—shalt die." Do not let us blame the prophet for a coarse cruelty in the first of these details. He did not invent it. With all the rest it formed an ordinary consequence of defeat in the warfare of the times—an inevitable item of that general overthrow which, with bitter emphasis, the prophet describes in Amaziah's own words: "Israel going shall go into captivity from off his own land."

There is added a vision in line with the three which preceded the priest's interruption. We are therefore justified in supposing that Amos spoke it also on this occasion, and in taking it as the close of his address at Bethel. "Then the Lord Jehovah gave me to see: and, behold, a basket of Kaits," that is, "summer fruit. And He said, What art thou seeing, Amos? And I said, A basket of Kaits. And Jehovah said unto me, The Kets—the End—has come upon My people Israel. I will not again pass them over." This does not carry the prospect beyond the third vision, but it stamps its finality, and there is therefore added a vivid realisation of the result. By four disjointed lamentations, "howls" the prophet calls them, we are made to feel the last shocks of the final collapse, and in the utter end an awful silence. "And the songs of the temple shall be changed into howls in that day, saith the Lord Jehovah. Multitude of corpses! In every place! He hath cast out! Hush!"

These then were probably the last words which Amos spoke to Israel. If so, they form a curious echo of what was enforced upon himself, and he may have meant them as such. He was "cast out"; he was "silenced." They might almost be the verbal repetition of the priest's orders. In any case the silence is appropriate. But Amaziah little knew what power he had given to prophecy the day he forbade it to speak. The gagged prophet began to write; and those accents which, humanly speaking, might have died out with the songs of the temple of Bethel were clothed upon with the immortality of literature. Amos silenced wrote a book—first of prophets to do so—and this is the book we have now to study.

CHAPTER VII.

ATROCITIES AND ATROCITIES.

AMOS i. 3-ii.

LIKE all the prophets of Israel, Amos receives oracles for foreign nations. Unlike them, however, he arranges these oracles not after, but before, his indictment of his own people, and so as to lead up to this. His reason is obvious and characteristic. If his aim be to enforce a religion independent of his people's interests and privileges, how can he better do so than by exhibiting its principles at work outside his people, and then, with the impetus drained from many areas, sweep in upon the vested iniquities of Israel herself? This is the course of the first section of his book—chaps. i. and ii. One by one the neighbours of Israel are cited and condemned in the name of Jehovah; one by one they are told they must fall before the still unnamed engine of the Divine Justice. But when Amos has stirred his people's conscience and imagination by his judgment of their neighbours' sins, he turns with the same formula on themselves. Are they morally better? Are they more likely to resist Assyria? With greater detail he shows them worse and their doom the heavier for all their privileges. Thus is achieved an oratorical triumph, by tactics in harmony with the principles of prophecy and remarkably suited to the tempers of that time.

But Amos achieves another feat, which extends far beyond his own day. The sins he condemns in the heathen are at first sight very different from those which he exposes within Israel. Not only are they sins of foreign relations, of treaty and war, while Israel's are all civic and domestic; but they are what we call the atrocities of Barbarism—wanton war, massacre, and sacrilege—while Israel's are rather the sins of Civilisation—the pressure of the rich upon the poor, the bribery of justice, the seduction of the innocent, personal impurity, and other evils of luxury. So great is this difference that a critic more gifted with ingenuity than with insight might plausibly distinguish in the section before us two prophets with two very different views of national sin—a ruder prophet, and of course an earlier, who judged nations only by the flagrant drunkenness of their war, and a more subtle prophet, and of course a later, who exposed the masked corruptions of their religion and their peace. Such a theory would be as false as it would be plausible. For not only is the diversity of the objects of the prophet's judgment explained by this, that Amos had no familiarity with the interior life of other nations, and could only arraign their conduct at those points where it broke into light in their foreign relations, while Israel's civic life he knew to the very core. But Amos had besides a strong and a deliberate aim in placing the sins of civilisation as the climax of a list of the atrocities of barbarism. He would recall what men are always forgetting, that the former are really more cruel and criminal than the latter; that luxury, bribery, and intolerance, the oppression of the poor, the corruption of the innocent and the silencing of the prophet—what Christ calls offences against His little ones—are even more awful atrocities than the wanton horrors of barbarian warfare. If we keep in mind this moral purpose, we shall study with more interest than we could otherwise do the somewhat foreign details of this section. Horrible as the outrages are which Amos describes, they were repeated only yesterday by Turkey: many of the crimes with which he charges Israel blacken the life of Turkey's chief accuser, Great Britain.

In his survey Amos includes all the six states of Palestine that bordered upon Israel, and lay in the way of the advance of Assyria—Aram of Damascus, Philistia, Tyre (or Phœnicia), Edom, Ammon, and Moab. They are not arranged in geographical order. The prophet begins with Aram in the northeast, then leaps to Philistia in the southwest, comes north again to Tyre, crosses to the southeast and Edom, leaps Moab to Ammon, and then comes back to Moab. Nor is any other explanation of his order visible. Damascus heads the list, no doubt, because her cruelties had been most felt by Israel, and perhaps too because she lay most open to Assyria. It was also natural to take next to Aram Philistia,* as Israel's other greatest foe; and nearest to Philistia lay Tyre. The three southeastern principalities come together. But there may have been a chronological reason now unknown to us.

The authenticity of the oracles on Tyre, Edom, and Judah has been questioned: it will be best to discuss each case as we come to it.

Each of the oracles is introduced by the formula: "Thus saith," or "hath said, Jehovah: Because of three crimes of . . . yea, because of four, I will not turn It back." In harmony with the rest of the book,† Jehovah is represented as moving to punishment, not for a single sin, but for repeated and cumulative guilt. The unnamed "It" which God will not recall is not the word of judgment, but the anger and the hand stretched forth to smite.‡ After the formula, an instance of the nation's guilt is given, and then in almost identical terms he decrees the destruction of all by war and captivity. Assyria is not mentioned, but it is the Assyrian fashion of dealing with conquered states which is described. Except in the case of Tyre and Edom, the oracles conclude as they have begun, by asserting themselves to be the "word of Jehovah," or of "Jehovah the Lord." It is no abstract righteousness which condemns these foreign peoples, but the God of Israel, and their evil deeds are described by the characteristic Hebrew word for sin—"crimes," "revolts," or "treasons" against Him.§

1. Aram of Damascus.—"Thus hath Jehovah said: Because of three crimes of Damascus, yea, because of four, I will not turn It back; for that they threshed Gilead with iron"—or "basalt threshing-sledges." The word is "iron," but the Arabs of to-day call basalt iron; and the threshing-sledges, curved slabs ¶ drawn rapidly by horses over the heaped corn, are studded with sharp basalt teeth that not only thresh out the grain, but chop the straw into little pieces. So cruelly had Gilead been chopped by Hazael and his son Ben-Hadad some fifty or forty years before Amos prophesied.* Strongholds were burned, soldiers slain without quarter, children dashed to pieces, and women with child put to a most atrocious end.† But "I shall send fire on the house of Hazael, and it shall devour the palaces of Ben-Hadad"—these names are chosen, not because they were typical of the Damascus dynasty, but because they were the very names of the two heaviest oppressors of Israel.‡ "And I will break the bolt § of Damascus, and cut off the inhabitant from Biḳ'ath-Aven"—the Valley of Idolatry, so called, perhaps, by a play upon Biḳ'ath On,‖ presumably the valley between the Lebanons, still called the Bek'a, in which lay Heliopolis ¶—"and him that holdeth the sceptre from Beth-Eden"—some royal Paradise in that region of Damascus which is still the Paradise of the Arab world—"and the people of Aram shall go captive to Kir"—Kir in the unknown north, from which they had come: ** "Jehovah hath said" it.

2. Philistia.—"Thus saith Jehovah: For three crimes of Gaza and for four I will not turn It back, because they led captive a whole captivity, in order to deliver them up to Edom." It is difficult to see what this means if not the wholesale depopulation of a district in contrast to the enslavement of a few captives of war. By all tribes of the ancient world, the captives of their bow and spear were regarded as legitimate property: it was no offence to the public conscience that they should be sold into slavery. But the Philistines seem, without excuse of war, to have descended upon certain districts and swept the whole of the population before them, for purely commercial purposes. It was professional slave-catching. The Philistines were exactly like the Arabs of to-day in Africa—not warriors who win their captives in honourable fight, but slave-traders, pure and simple. In warfare in Arabia itself it is still a matter of conscience with the wildest nomads not to extinguish a hostile tribe, however bitter one be against them.†† Gaza is chiefly blamed by Amos, for she was the emporium of the trade on the border of the desert, with roads and regular caravans to Petra and Elah on the Gulf of Akaba, both of them places in Edom and depots for the traffic with Arabia.‡‡ "But I will cut off the inhabitant from Ashdod, and the holder of the sceptre from Askalon, and I will turn My hand upon Ekron"—four of the five great Philistine towns, Gath being already destroyed, and never again to be mentioned with the others §§—"and the last of the Philistines shall perish: Jehovah hath said it."

* As is done in chap. vi. 2, ix. 7.
† So against Israel in chap. iv.
‡ So Isa. v. 25: לא שב אפו ועוד ידו נטויה *Cf.* Ezek. xx. 22 והשיבותי את ידי.
§ פשעים.
¶ Called *lûh*, *i. e.*, slab.

* These Syrian campaigns in Gilead must have taken place between 839 and 806, the long interval during which Damascus enjoyed freedom from Assyrian invasion.
† 2 Kings viii. 12; xiii. 7: *cf.* above, p. 450.
‡ "He delivered them into the hand of Hazael king of Aram, and into the hand of Ben-Hadad the son of Hazael, continually" (2 Kings xiii. 3).
§ No need here to render *prince*, as some do.
‖ So the LXX.
¶ The present Baalbek (Baal of the Bek'a ?). Wellhausen throws doubt on the idea that Heliopolis was at this time an Aramean town.
** ix. 7.
†† Doughty: "Arabia Deserta," I. 335.
‡‡ On the close connection of Edom and Gaza see "Hist. Geog.," pp. 182 ff.
§§ See "Hist. Geog.," pp. 194 ff. Wellhausen thinks Gath was not yet destroyed, and quotes vi. 2; Micah i. 10, 14. But we know that Hazael destroyed it, and that fact, taken in conjunction with its being the only omission

3. Tyre.—"Thus saith Jehovah: Because of three crimes of Tyre and because of four I will not turn It back; for that they gave up a whole captivity to Edom"—the same market as in the previous charge—"and did not remember the covenant of brethren." We do not know to what this refers. The alternatives are three: that the captives were Hebrews and the alliance one between Israel and Edom; that the captives were Hebrews and the alliance one between Israel and Tyre; * that the captives were Phœnicians and the alliance the natural brotherhood of Tyre and the other Phœnician towns.† But of these three alternatives the first is scarcely possible, for in such a case the blame would have been rather Edom's in buying than Tyre's in selling. The second is possible, for Israel and Tyre had lived in close alliance for more than two centuries; but the phrase "covenant of brethren" is not so well suited to a league between two tribes who felt themselves to belong to fundamentally different races,‡ as to the close kinship of the Phœnician communities. And although, in the scrappy records of Phœnician history before this time, we find no instance of so gross an outrage by Tyre on other Phœnicians, it is quite possible that such may have occurred. During next century Tyre twice over basely took sides with Assyria in suppressing the revolts of her sister cities.§ Besides, the other Phœnician towns are not included in the charge. We have every reason, therefore, to believe that Amos expresses here not resentment against a betrayal of Israel, but indignation at an outrage upon natural rights and feelings with which Israel's own interests were not in any way concerned. And this also suits the lofty spirit of the whole prophecy. "But I will send fire upon the wall of Tyre, and it shall devour her palaces. . . ."

This oracle against Tyre has been suspected by Wellhausen,‖ for the following reasons: that it is of Tyre alone, and silence is kept regarding the other Phœnician cities, while in the case of Philistia other towns than Gaza are condemned; that the charge is the same as against Gaza; and that the usual close to the formula is wanting. But it would have been strange if from a list of states threatened by the Assyrian doom we had missed Tyre, Tyre which lay in the avenger's very path. Again, that so acute a critic as Wellhausen should cite the absence of other Phœnician towns from the charge against Tyre is really amazing, when he has just allowed that it was probably against some or all of these cities that Tyre's crime was committed. How could they be included in the blame of an outrage done upon themselves? The absence of the usual formula at the close may perhaps be explained by omission, as indicated above.¶

4. Edom.—"Thus saith Jehovah: Because of three crimes of Edom and because of four I will not turn It back; for that he pursued with the sword his brother," who cannot be any other than Israel, "corrupted his natural feelings"—literally "his bowels of mercies"—"and kept aye fretting * his anger, and his passion he watched"—like a fire, or "paid heed" to it—"for ever."† "But I will send fire upon Teman"—the "South" Region belonging to Edom—"and it shall devour the palaces of Bosrah"—the Edomite Boṣrah, southeast of Petra.‡ The Assyrians had already compelled Edom to pay tribute.§

The objections to the authenticity of this oracle are more serious than those in the case of the oracle on Tyre. It has been remarked‖ that before the Jewish Exile so severe a tone could not have been adopted by a Jew against Edom, who had been mostly under the yoke of Judah, and not leniently treated. What were the facts? Joab subdued Edom for David with great cruelty.¶ Jewish governors were set over the conquered people, and this state of affairs seems to have lasted, in spite of an Edomite attempt against Solomon,** till 850. In Jehoshaphat's reign, 873-850, "there was no king of Edom, a deputy was king," who towards 850 joined the kings of Judah and Israel in an invasion of Moab through his territory.†† But, soon after this invasion and perhaps in consequence of its failure, Edom revolted from Joram of Judah (849-842), who unsuccessfully attempted to put down the revolt.‡‡ The Edomites appear to have remained independent for fifty years at least. Amaziah of Judah (797-779) smote them,§§ but not, it would seem, into subjection; for, according to the Chronicler, Uzziah had to win back Elath for the Jews after Amaziah's death.‖‖ The history, therefore, of the relations of Judah and Edom before the time of Amos was of such a kind as to make credible the existence in Judah at that time of the feeling about Edom which inspires this oracle. Edom had shown just the vigilant, implacable hatred here described. But was the right to blame them for it Judah's, who herself had so persistently waged war, with confessed cruelty, against Edom? Could a Judæan prophet be just in blaming Edom and saying nothing of Judah? It is true that in the fifty years of Edom's independence—the period, we must remember, from which Amos seems to draw the materials of all his other charges—there may have been events to justify this oracle as spoken by him; and our ignorance of that period is ample reason why we should pause before rejecting the oracle so dogmatically as Wellhausen does. But we have at least serious grounds for suspecting it. To charge Edom, whom Judah has conquered and treated cruelly, with restless hate towards Judah seems to fall below that high impartial tone which prevails in the other oracles of this section. The charge was much

here from the five Philistine towns, is evidence enough. In the passages quoted by Wellhausen there is nothing to the contrary: vi. 2 implies that Gath has fallen; Micah i. 10 is the repetition of an old proverb.

* Farrar, 53; Pusey on ver. 9; Pietschmann "Geschichte de Phönizier," 298.

† To which Wellhausen inclines.

‡ Gen. x.

§ Under Asarhaddon, 678-676 B. C., and later under Assurbanipal (Pietschmann, "Gesch.," pp. 302 f.).

‖ And he omits it from his translation.

¶ So far from such an omission proving that the oracle is an insertion, is it not more probable that an insertor would have taken care to make his insertion formally correct?

* There seems no occasion to amend with Olshausen to the "kept" of Psalm ciii. 9.

† Read with LXX. שׁמר לנצח, though throughout the verse the LXX. translation is very vile.

‡ In other two passages, Bosrah, the city, is placed in parallel not to another city, but just as here to a whole region: Isa. xxxiv. 6, where the parallel is the "land of Edom," and lxiii. 1, where it is "Edom." There is therefore no need to take Teman in our passage as a city, as which it does not appear before Eusebius.

§ Under Rimmân-nirari III. (812-783). See Buhl's "Gesch. der Edomiter," 65: this against Wellhausen.

‖ Wellhausen, *in loco*.

¶ 2 Sam. viii. 13, with 1 Kings xi. 16.

** 1 Kings xi. 14-25.

†† 2 Kings iii.

‡‡ 2 Kings viii. 20-22.

§§ 2 Kings xiv. 10.

‖‖ 2 Chron. xxvi. 2.

more justifiable at the time of the Exile, when Edom did behave shamefully towards Israel.* Wellhausen points out that Teman and Boṣrah are names which do not occur in the Old Testament before the Exile, but this is uncertain and inconclusive. The oracle wants the concluding formula of the rest.†

5. AMMON.—"Thus saith Jehovah: Because of three crimes of Ammon and because of four I will not turn It back; for that they ripped up Gilead's women with child—in order to enlarge their borders!" For such an end they committed such an atrocity! The crime is one that has been more or less frequent in Semitic warfare. Wellhausen cites several instances in the feuds of Arab tribes about their frontiers. The Turks have been guilty of it in our own day.‡ It is the same charge which the historian of Israel puts into the mouth of Elisha against Hazael of Aram,§ and probably the war was the same; when Gilead was simultaneously attacked by Arameans from the north and Ammonites from the south. "But I will set fire to the wall of Rabbah"—Rabbath-Ammon, literally "chief" or "capital" of Ammon—"and it shall devour her palaces, with clamour in the day of battle, with tempest in the day of storm." As we speak of "storming a city," Amos and Isaiah‖ use the tempest to describe the overwhelming invasion of Assyria. There follows the characteristic Assyrian conclusion: "And their king shall go into captivity, he and his princes¶ together, saith Jehovah."

6. MOAB.—"Thus saith Jehovah: Because of three crimes of Moab and because of four I will not turn It back; for that he burned the bones of the king of Edom to lime."** In the great invasion of Moab, about 850, by Israel, Judah, and Edom conjointly, the rage of Moab seems to have been directed chiefly against Edom.†† Whether opportunity to appease that rage occurred on the withdrawal of Israel we cannot say. But either then or afterwards, balked of their attempt to secure the king of Edom alive, Moab wreaked their vengeance on his corpse, and burnt his bones to lime. It was, in the religious belief of all antiquity, a sacrilege; yet it does not seem to have been the desecration of the tomb—or he would have mentioned it—but the wanton meanness of the deed, which Amos felt. "And I will send fire on Moab, and it shall devour the palaces of The-Cities"—Ḳerîoth,‡‡ perhaps the present Ḳureiyat,§§ on the Moab plateau where Chemosh had his shrine ‖‖—"and in tumult shall Moab die"—to Jeremiah ¶¶ the Moabites were the sons of tumult—"with clamour and with the noise of the war-trumpet. And I will cut off the ruler"—literally "judge," probably the vassal king placed by Jeroboam II.—"from her* midst, and all his† princes will I slay with him: Jehovah hath said" it.

* See, however, Buhl, *op. cit.*, 67.

† It is, however, no reason against the authenticity of the oracle to say that Edom lay outside the path of Assyria. In answer to that see the Assyrian inscriptions, *e. g.*, Asarhaddon's: *cf.* above, p. 474, *n.*

‡ Notably in the recent Armenian massacres.

§ 2 Kings viii. 12.

‖ xxviii. 2, xxvii. 7, 8, where the Assyrian and another invasion are both described in terms of tempest.

¶ The LXX. reading, "their priests and their princes," must be due to taking Malcam = "their king" as Milcom = the Ammonite god. See Jer. xlix. 3.

** "Great Cæsar dead and turned to clay
Might stop a hole to turn the wind away."

†† 2 Kings iii. 26. So rightly Pusey.

‡‡ Jer. xlviii. 24 without article, but in 41 with.

§§ Though this is claimed by most for Ḳiriathaim.

‖‖ Moabite Stone, l. 13.

¶¶ xlviii. 45.

These, then, are the charges which Amos brings against the heathen neighbours of Israel.

If we look as a whole across the details through which we have been working, what we see is a picture of the Semitic world so summary and so vivid that we get the like of it nowhere else—the Semitic world in its characteristic brokenness and turbulence; its factions and ferocities, its causeless raids and quarrels, tribal disputes about boundaries flaring up into the most terrible massacres, vengeance that wreaks itself alike on the embryo and the corpse—"cutting up women with child in Gilead," and "burning to lime the bones of the king of Edom." And the one commerce which binds these ferocious tribes together is the slave-trade in its wholesale and most odious form.

Amos treats none of the atrocities subjectively. It is not because they have been inflicted upon Israel that he feels or condemns them. The appeals of Israel against the tyrant become many as the centuries go on; the later parts of the Old Testament are full of the complaints of God's chosen people, conscious of their mission to the world against the heathen, who prevented them from it. Here we find none of these complaints, but a strictly objective and judicial indictment of the characteristic crimes of heathen men against each other; and though this is made in the name of Jehovah, it is not in the interests of His people or of any of His purposes through them, but solely by the standard of an impartial righteousness which, as we are soon to hear, must descend in equal judgment on Israel.

Again, for the moral principles which Amos enforces no originality can be claimed. He condemns neither war as a whole nor slavery as a whole, but limits his curse to wanton and deliberate aggravations of them: to the slave-trade in cold blood, in violation of treaties, and for purely commercial ends;‡ to war for trifling causes, and that wreaks itself on pregnant women and dead men; to national hatreds, that never will be still. Now against such things there has always been in mankind a strong conscience, of which the word "humanity" is in itself a sufficient proof. We need not here inquire into the origin of such a common sense—whether it be some native impulse of tenderness which asserts itself as soon as the duties of self-defence are exhausted, or some rational notion of the needlessness of excesses, or whether, in committing these, men are visited by fear of retaliation from the wrath they have unnecessarily exasperated. Certain it is that warriors of all races have hesitated to be wanton in their war, and have foreboded the special judgment of heaven upon every blind extravagance of hate or cruelty. It is well known how "fey" the Greeks felt the insolence of power and immoderate anger; they are the fatal element in many a Greek tragedy.§ But the Semites themselves, whose racial ferocity is so notorious, are not without the same feeling. "Even the Beduins' old cruel rancours are often less than the golden piety of the wilderness. The danger past, they can think of the defeated foemen with kindness, . . . putting only their

* The land's. † The king's. ‡ See above, p. 473.

§ δυσσεβίας μὲν ὕβρις τέκος (Æschylus, "Eumen.," 534): *cf.* "Odyssey," xiv. 262; xvii. 431.

trust in Ullah to obtain the like at need for themselves. It is contrary to the Arabian conscience to extinguish a Kabila." * Similarly in Israel some of the earliest ethical movements were revolts of the public conscience against horrible outrages, like that, for instance, done by the Benjamites of Gibeah.† Therefore in these oracles on his wild Semitic neighbours Amos discloses no new ideal for either tribe or individual. Our view is confirmed that he was intent only upon arousing the natural conscience of his Hebrew hearers in order to engage this upon other vices to which it was less impressionable—that he was describing those deeds of war and slavery, whose atrocity all men admitted, only that he might proceed to bring under the same condemnation the civic and domestic sins of Israel.

We turn with him, then, to Israel. But in his book as it now stands in our Bibles, Israel is not immediately reached. Between her and the foreign nations two verses are bestowed upon Judah: "Thus saith Jehovah: Because of three crimes of Judah and because of four I will not turn It back; for that they despised the Torah of Jehovah, and His statutes they did not observe, and their falsehoods"—false gods—"led them astray, after which their fathers walked. But I will send fire on Judah, and it shall devour the palaces of Jerusalem." These verses have been suspected as a later insertion,‡ on the ground that every reference to Judah in the Book of Amos must be late, that the language is very formal, and that the phrases in which the sin of Judah is described sound like echoes of Deuteronomy. The first of these reasons may be dismissed as absurd; it would have been far more strange if Amos had never at all referred to Judah.§ The charges, however, are not like those which Amos elsewhere makes, and though the phrases may be quite as early as his time,‖ the reader of the original, and even the reader of the English version, is aware of a certain tameness and vagueness of statement, which contrasts remarkably with the usual pungency of the prophet's style. We are forced to suspect the authenticity of these verses.

We ought to pass, then, straight from the third to the sixth verse of this chapter, from the oracles on foreign nations to that on Northern Israel. It is introduced with the same formula as they are: "Thus saith Jehovah: Because of three crimes of Israel and because of four I will not turn It back." But there follow a great number of details, for Amos has come among his own people whom he knows to the heart, and he applies to them a standard more exact and an obligation more heavy than any he could lay to the life of the heathen. Let us run quickly through the items of his charge. "For that they sell an honest man¶ for silver, and a needy man for a pair of shoes"—proverbial, as we should say "for an old song"—"who trample to the dust of the earth the head of the poor"—the least improbable rendering of a corrupt passage *—"and pervert the way of humble men. And a man and his father will go into the maid," the same maid,† "to desecrate My Holy Name"—without doubt some public form of unchastity introduced from the Canaanite worship into the very sanctuary of Jehovah, the holy place where He reveals His Name—"and on garments given in pledge they stretch themselves by every altar, and the wine of those who have been fined they drink in the house of their God." A riot of sin: the material of their revels is the miseries of the poor, its stage the house of God! Such is religion to the Israel of Amos' day—indoors, feverish, sensual. By one of the sudden contrasts he loves, Amos sweeps out of it into God's idea of religion—a great historical movement, told in the language of the open air: national deliverance, guidance on the highways of the world, the inspiration of prophecy, and the pure, ascetic life. "But I, I destroyed the Amorite‡ before you, whose height was as the cedars, and he was strong as oaks, and I destroyed his fruit from above and his roots from below." What a contrast to the previous picture of the temple filled with fumes of wine and hot with lust! We are out on open history; God's gales blow and the forests crash before them. "And I brought you up out of the land of Egypt, and led you through the wilderness forty years, to inherit the land of the Amorite." Religion is not chambering and wantonness; it is not selfish comfort or profiting by the miseries of the poor and the sins of the fallen. But religion is history—the freedom of the people and their education, the winning of the land and the defeat of the heathen foe; and then, when the land is firm and the home secure, it is the raising, upon that stage and shelter, of spiritual guides and examples. "And I raised up of your sons to be prophets, and of your young men to be Nazarites"—consecrated and ascetic lives. "Is it not so, O children of Israel? (oracle of Jehovah). But ye made the Nazarites drink wine, and the prophets ye charged, saying, Prophesy not!"

Luxury, then, and a very sensual conception of religion, with all their vicious offspring in the abuse of justice, the oppression of the poor, the corrupting of the innocent, and the intolerance of spiritual forces—these are the sins of an enlightened and civilised people, which Amos describes as worse than all the atrocities of barbarism, and as certain of Divine vengeance. How far beyond his own day are his words still warm! Here in the nineteenth century is Great Britain, destroyer of the slave-traffic, and champion of oppressed nationalities—yet this great and Christian people, at the very time they are abolishing slavery, suffer their own children to work in factories and clay-pits for sixteen hours

* *I. e.*, a tribe; Doughty, "Arabia Deserta," I. 335.

† Judges xix., xx.

‡ Duhm was the first to publish reasons for rejecting the passage ("Theol. der Propheten," 1875, p. 119), but Wellhausen had already reached the same conclusion ("Kleine Propheten," p. 71). Oort and Stade adhere. On the other side see Robertson Smith, "Prophets of Israel," 398, and Kuenen, who adheres to Smith's arguments ("Onderzoek").

§ "It is plain that Amos could not have excepted Judah from the universal ruin which he saw to threaten the whole land; or at all events such exception would have required to be expressly made on special grounds."—Robertson Smith, "Prophets," 398.

‖ *Ibid.*

¶ צדיק, *righteous*: hardly, as most commentators take it, the *legally* (as distinguished from the *morally*) *righteous*; the rich cruelly used their legal rights to sell respectable and honest members of society into slavery.

* By adapting the LXX. So far as we know, Wellhausen is right in saying that the Massoretic text, which our English version follows, gives no sense. LXX. reads, also without much sense as a whole, τὰ πατοῦντα ἐπὶ τὸν χοῦν τῆς γῆς, καὶ ἐκονδύλιζον εἰς κεφαλὰς πτώχων.

† So rightly the LXX. Or the definite article may be here used in conformity with the common Hebrew way of employing it to designate, not a definite individual, but a member of a definite, well-known genus.

‡ On the use of Amorite for all the inhabitants of Canaan see Driver's "Deut.," pp. 11 f.

a day, and in mines set women to a labour for which horses are deemed too valuable. Things improve after 1848, but how slowly, and against what callousness of Christians, Lord Shaftesbury's long and often disappointed labours painfully testify. Even yet our religious public, that curses the Turk, and in an indignation, which can never be too warm, cries out against the Armenian atrocities, is callous, nay, by the avarice of some, the haste and passion for enjoyment of many more, and the thoughtlessness of all, itself contributes, to conditions of life and fashions of society, which bear with cruelty upon our poor, taint our literature, needlessly increase the temptations of our large towns, and render pure child life impossible among masses of our population. Along some of the highways of our Christian civilisation we are just as cruel and just as lustful as Kurd or Turk.

Amos closes this prophecy with a vision of immediate judgment. "Behold, I am about to crush" or "squeeze down upon you, as a waggon crushes * that is full of sheaves." † An alternative reading supplies the same general impression of a crushing judgment: "I will make the ground quake under you, as a waggon makes it quake," or "as a waggon" itself "quakes under its load of sheaves." This shock is to be War. "Flight shall perish from the swift, and the strong shall not prove his power, nor the mighty man escape with his life. And he that graspeth the bow shall not stand, nor shall the swift of foot escape, nor the horseman escape with his life. And he that thinketh himself strong among the heroes shall flee away naked in that day—'tis the oracle of Jehovah."

* The verb עוק of the Massoretic text is not found elsewhere, and whether we retain it, or take it as a variant of, or mistake for, צוק, or adopt some other reading, the whole phrase is more or less uncertain, and the exact shade of meaning has to be guessed, though the general sense remains pretty much the same. The following is a complete note on the subject, with reasons for adopting the above conclusion.

(1) LXX.: "Behold, I roll (*κυλίω*) under you as a waggon full of straw is rolled." A. V.: "I am pressed under you as a cart is pressed." Pusey: "I straiten myself under you," etc. These versions take עוק in the sense of צוק, "to press," and תחת in its usual meaning of "beneath"; and the result is conformable to the well-known figure of the Old Testament by which God is said to be laden and weary with the transgressions of His people. But this does not mean an actual descent of judgment, and yet vv. 14–16 imply that such an intimation has been made in ver. 13; and besides מעיק and תעיק are both in the Hiphil, the active, "to press," or causative, "make to press." (2) Accordingly some, adopting this sense of the verb, take תחת in an unusual sense of "down upon." Ewald: "I press down upon you as a cart that is full of sheaves presseth." Guthe (in Kautzsch's "Bibel"): "Ich will euch quetschen." Rev. Eng. Ver.: "I will press you in your place."—But עוק has been taken in other senses. (3) Hoffmann ("Z. A. T. W.," III. 100) renders it "groan" in conformity with Arab 'îk. (4) Wetzstein (*ibid.*, 278 ff.) quotes Arab 'âk, to "stop, hinder," and suggests "I will bring to a stop." (5) Buhl (12th Ed. of Gesenius' "Handwört," sub עוק), in view of possibility of עגלה being threshing-roller, recalls Arab. 'aḳḳ, "to cut in pieces." (6) Hitzig ("Exeg. Handbuch") proposed to read מפיק and תפיק: "I will make it shake under you, as the laden waggon shakes" (the ground). So rather differently Wellhausen: "I will make the ground quake under you, as a waggon quakes under its load of sheaves."

I have only to add that, in the Alex. Cod. of LXX., which reads *κωλύω* for *κυλίω*, we have an interesting analogy to Wetzstein's proposal; and that in support of the rendering of Ewald, and its unusual interpretation of תחתיכם, which seems to me on the whole the most probable, we may compare Job xxxvi. 16, לא מוצק תחתיה. This, it is true, suggests rather the choking of a passage than the crushing of the ground; but, by the way, that sense is even more applicable to a harvest waggon laden with sheaves.

† "Waggon full of sheaves."—Wellhausen goes too far when he suggests that Amos would have to go outside Palestine to see such a waggon. That a people who already knew the use of chariots for travelling (*cf.* Gen. xlvi. 5, JE) and waggons for agricultural purposes (1 Sam. vi. 7 ff.) did not use them at least in the lowlands of their country is extremely improbable. *Cf.* "Hist. Geog.," Appendix on Roads and Wheeled Vehicles in Syria.

CHAPTER VIII.

CIVILISATION AND JUDGMENT.

AMOS iii.–iv. 3.

WE now enter the Second Section of the Book of Amos: chaps. iii.–vi. It is a collection of various oracles of denunciation, grouped partly by the recurrence of the formula "Hear this word," which stands at the head of our present chaps. iii., iv., and v., which are therefore probably due to it; partly by two cries of "Woe" at v. 18 and vi. 1; and also by the fact that each of the groups thus started leads up to an emphatic, though not at first detailed, prediction of the nation's doom (iii. 13–15; iv. 3; iv. 12; v. 16, 17; v. 26, 27; vi. 14). Within these divisions lie a number of short indictments, sentences of judgment, and the like, which have no further logical connection than is supplied by their general sameness of subject, and a perceptible increase of articulateness from beginning to end of the Section. The sins of Israel are more detailed, and the judgment of war, coming from the North, advances gradually till we discern the unmistakable ranks of Assyria. But there are various parentheses and interruptions, which cause the student of the text no little difficulty. Some of these, however, may be only apparent: it will always be a question whether their want of immediate connection with what precedes them is not due to the loss of several words from the text rather than to their own intrusion into it. Of others it is true that they are obviously out of place as they lie; their removal brings together verses which evidently belong to each other. Even such parentheses, however, may be from Amos himself. It is only where a verse, besides interrupting the argument, seems to reflect a historical situation later than the prophet's day, that we can be sure it is not his own. And in all this textual criticism we must keep in mind that the obscurity of the present text of a verse, so far from being an adequate proof of its subsequent insertion, may be the very token of its antiquity, scribes or translators of later date having been unable to understand it. To reject a verse, only because *we* do not see the connection, would surely be as arbitrary as the opposite habit of those who, missing a connection, invent one, and then exhibit their artificial joint as evidence of the integrity of the whole passage. In fact we must avoid all headstrong surgery, for to a great extent we work in the dark.

The general subject of the Section may be indicated by the title: Religion and Civilisation. A vigorous community, wealthy, cultured, and honestly religious, are, at a time of settled peace and growing power, threatened, in the name of the God of justice, with their complete political overthrow. Their civilisation is counted for nothing; their religion, on which they base their confidence, is denounced as false and unavailing. These two subjects are not, and could not have been, separated by the prophet in any one of his oracles. But in the first, the briefest, and most summary of these, chaps. iii.-iv. 3, it is mainly with the doom of the civil structure of Israel's life that Amos deals; and it will be more convenient for us to take them first, with all due reference to the echoes of them in later parts of the Section. From iv. 4-vi. it is the Religion and its false peace which he assaults; and we shall take that in the next chapter. *First,* then, Civilisation and Judgment (iii.-iv. 3); *second,* The False Peace of Ritual (iv. 4-vi.).

These few brief oracles open upon the same note as that in which the previous Section closed—that the crimes of Israel are greater than those of the heathen; and that the people's peculiar relation to God means, not their security, but their greater judgment. It is then affirmed that Israel's wealth and social life are so sapped by luxury and injustice that the nation must perish. And, as in every luxurious community the women deserve especial blame, the last of the group of oracles is reserved for them (iv. 1-3).

"Hear this word, which Jehovah hath spoken against you, O children of Israel, against the whole family which I brought up from the land of Egypt"—Judah as well as North Israel, so that we see the vanity of a criticism which would cast out of the Book of Amos as unauthentic every reference to Judah. "Only you have I known of all the families of the ground"—not world, but "ground," purposely chosen to stamp the meanness and mortality of them all—"therefore will I visit upon you all your iniquities."

This famous text has been called by various writers "the keynote," "the license," and "the charter" of prophecy. But the names are too petty for what is not less than the fulmination of an element. It is a peal of thunder we hear. It is, in a moment, the explosion and discharge of the full storm of prophecy. As when from a burst cloud the streams immediately below rise suddenly and all their banks are overflowed, so the prophecies that follow surge and rise clear of the old limits of Israel's faith by the unconfined, unmeasured flood of heaven's justice that breaks forth by this single verse. Now, once for all, are submerged the lines of custom and tradition within which the course of religion has hitherto flowed; and, as it were, the surface of the world is altered. It is a crisis which has happened more than once again in history: when helpless man has felt the absolute relentlessness of the moral issues of life; their renunciation of the past, however much they have helped to form it; their sacrifice of every development however costly, and of every hope however pure; their deafness to prayer, their indifference to penitence; when no faith saves a Church, no courage a people, no culture or prestige even the most exalted order of men; but at the bare hands of a judgment, uncouth of voice and often unconscious of a Divine mission, the results of a great civilisation are for its sins swept remorselessly away.

Before the storm bursts, we learn by its lightnings some truths from the old life that is to be destroyed. "You only have I known of all the families of the ground: therefore will I visit your iniquities upon you." Religion is no insurance against judgment, no mere atonement and escape from consequences. Escape! Religion is only opportunity—the greatest moral opportunity which men have, and which if they violate nothing remains for them but a certain fearful looking forward unto judgment. You only have I known; and because you did not take the moral advantage of My intercourse, because you felt it only as privilege and pride, pardon for the past and security for the future, therefore doom the more inexorable awaits you.

Then as if the people had interrupted him with the question, What sign do you give us that this judgment is near?—Amos goes aside into that noble digression (vv. 3-8) on the harmony between the prophet's word and the imminent events of the time, which we have already studied.* From this apologia, verse 9 returns to the note of verses 1 and 2 and develops it. Not only is Israel's responsibility greater than that of other people's. Her crimes themselves are more heinous. "Make proclamation over the palaces in Ashdod"—if we are not to read Assyria here,† then the name of Ashdod has perhaps been selected from all other heathen names because of its similarity to the Hebrew word for that "violence"‡ with which Amos is charging the people—"and over the palaces of the land of Egypt, and say, Gather upon the Mount§ of Samaria and see! Confusions manifold in the midst of her; violence to her very core! Yea, they know not how to do uprightness, saith Jehovah, who store up wrong and violence in their palaces."

"To their crimes," said the satirist of the Romans, "they owe their gardens, palaces, stables, and fine old plate."‖ And William Langland declared of the rich English of his day:—

> "For toke thei on trewly · they tymbred not so heigh,
> Ne boughte non burgages · be ye full certayne."¶

"Therefore thus saith the Lord Jehovah: Siege and Blockade of the Land.** And they shall bring down from off thee thy fortresses, and plundered shall be thy palaces." Yet this shall be no ordinary tide of Eastern war, to ebb like the Syrian as it flowed, and leave the nation to rally on their land again. For Assyria devours the peoples. "Thus saith Jehovah: As the shepherd saveth from the mouth of the lion a pair of shin-bones or a bit of an ear, so shall the children of Israel be saved—they who sit in Samaria in the corner of the diwan and . . . on a couch."†† The description, as will be seen from

* See above, pp. 462 ff. and pp. 464 ff.

† With the LXX. באשור for באשדוד.

‡ שד (ver. 10).

§ Singular as in LXX., and not plural as in the M. T. and English versions.

‖ Juvenal, "Satires," I.

¶ "Vision of Piers Plowman." Burgages = tenements.

** Or "The Enemy, and that right round the Land!"

†† "In Damascus on a couch:" "on a Damascus couch:" "on a Damascus-cloth couch:" or "Damascus-fashion on a couch"—alternatives all equally probable and equally beyond proof. The text is very difficult, nor do the versions give help. (1) The consonants of the word before "a couch" spell "in Damascus," and so the LXX. take it. This would be in exact parallel to the "in Samaria" of the previous half of the clause. But although Jeroboam II. is said to have recovered Damascus (2 Kings xiv. 28) this is not necessarily the town itself, of whose occupation by Israel we have no evidence, while Amos always assumes it to be Aramean, and here he is addressing Israelites. Still retaining the name of the city, we can take it with "couch" as parallel, not to "in Samaria," but to "on the side of a diwan;" in that case the meaning may have been "a Damascus couch" (though as the two words stand it is impossible to parse them, and Gen. xv.

the note below, is obscure. Some think it is intended to satirise a novel and affected fashion of sitting adopted by the rich. Much more probably it means that carnal security in the luxuries of civilisation which Amos threatens more than once in similar phrases.* The corner of the diwan is in Eastern houses the seat of honour.† To this desert shepherd, with only the hard ground to rest on, the couches and ivory-mounted diwans of the rich must have seemed the very symbols of extravagance. But the pampered bodies that loll their lazy lengths upon them shall be left like the crumbs of a lion's meal—"two shin-bones and the bit of an ear!" Their whole civilisation shall perish with them. "Hearken and testify against the house of Israel—oracle of the Lord Jehovah, God of Hosts" ‡—those addressed are still the heathen summoned in ver. 9. "For on the day when I visit the crimes of Israel upon him, I shall then make visitation upon the altars of Bethel, and the horns of the altar," which men grasp in their last despair, "shall be smitten and fall to the earth. And I will strike the winter-house upon the summer-house, and the ivory houses shall perish, yea, swept away shall be houses many —oracle of Jehovah."

But the luxury of no civilisation can be measured without its women, and to the women of Samaria Amos now turns with the most scornful of all his words. "Hear this word"—this for you—"kine of Bashan that are in the mount of Samaria, that oppress the poor, that crush the needy, that say to their lords, Bring, and let us drink. Sworn hath the Lord Jehovah by His holiness, lo, days are coming when there shall be a taking away of you with hooks, and of the last of you with fish-hooks." They put hooks§ in the nostrils of unruly cattle, and the figure is often applied to human captives;‖ but so many should these cattle of Samaria be that for the "last of them fish-hooks" must be used. "Yea, by the breaches" in the wall of the stormed city "shall ye go out, every one headlong, and ye shall be cast . .* oracle of Jehovah." It is a cowherd's rough picture of women: a troop of kine—heavy, heedless animals, trampling in their anxiety for food upon every frail and lowly object in the way. But there is a prophet's insight into character. Not of Jezebels, or Messalinas, or Lady-Macbeths is it spoken, but of the ordinary matrons of Samaria. Thoughtlessness and luxury are able to make brutes out of women of gentle nurture, with homes and a religion.†

Such are these three or four short oracles of Amos. They are probably among his earliest—the first peremptory challenges of prophecy to that great stronghold which before forty years she is to see thrown down in obedience to her word. As yet, however, there seems to be nothing to justify the menaces of Amos. Fair and stable rises the structure of Israel's life. A nation, who know themselves elect, who in politics are prosperous and in religion proof to every doubt, build high their palaces, see the skies above them unclouded, and bask in their pride, heaven's favourites without a fear. This man, solitary and sudden from his desert, springs upon them in the name of God and their poor. Straighter word never came from Deity: "Jehovah hath spoken, who can but prophesy?" The insight of it, the justice of it, are alike convincing. Yet at first it appears as if it were sped on the personal and very human passion of its herald. For Amos not only uses the desert's cruelties—the lion's to the sheep—to figure God's impending judgment upon His people, but he enforces the latter with all a desert-bred man's horror of cities and civilisation. It is their costly furniture, their lavish and complex building, on which he sees the storm break. We seem to hear again that frequent phrase of the previous section: "the fire shall devour the palaces thereof." The palaces, he says, are simply storehouses of oppression; the palaces will be plundered. Here, as throughout his book,‡ couches and diwans draw forth the scorn of a man accustomed to the simple furniture of the tent. But observe his especial hatred of houses. Four times in one verse he smites them: "winter-house on summer-house and the ivory houses shall perish—yea, houses manifold, saith the Lord." So in another oracle of the same section: "Houses of ashlar ye have built, and ye shall not inhabit them; vineyards of delight have ye planted, and ye shall not drink of their wine."§ And in another: "I loathe the pride of Jacob, and his palaces I hate; and I will give up a city and all that is in it. . . . For, lo, the Lord is about to command, and He will smite the great house into ruins and the small house into

2 cannot be quoted in support of this, for it is too uncertain itself, being possibly a gloss, though it is curious that as the two passages run the name Damascus should be in the same strange grammatical conjunction in each), or possibly "Damascus-fashion on a couch," which (if the first half of the clause, as some maintain, refers to some delicate or affected posture then come into fashion) is the most probable rendering. (2) The Massoretes have pointed, not "bedammeseq" = "in Damascus," but "bedemesheq," a form not found elsewhere, which some (Ges., Hitz., Ew., Rev. Eng. Ver., etc.) take to mean some Damascene stuff (as perhaps our Damask and the Arabic "dimshaq" originally meant, though this is not certain), *e. g.*, "silk" or "velvet" or "cushions." (3) Others rearrange the text. *E. g.*, Hoffman ("Z. A. T. W." III. 102) takes the whole clause away from ver. 12 and attaches it to ver. 13, reading "O those who sit in Samaria on the edge of the diwan, and in Damascus on a couch, hearken and testify against the house of Jacob." But, as Wellhausen points out, those addressed in ver. 13 are the same as those addressed in ver 9. Wellhausen prefers to believe that after the words "children of Israel," which end a sentence, something has fallen out. The LXX. translator, who makes several blunders in the course of this chapter, instead of translating עֶרֶשׂ couch, the last word of the verse, merely transliterates it into ἱερεῖς ! !

* *Cf.* vi. 4: "that lie on ivory diwans and sprawl on their couches."

† Van Lennep, "Bible Lands and Customs," p. 460.

‡ See p. 494. *n.*

§ The words for hook in Hebrew—the two used above, צִנּוֹת and סִירוֹת, and a third, חוֹחַ—all mean originally "thorns," doubtless the first hooks of primitive man; but by this time they would signify metal hooks—a change analogous to the English word "pen."

‖ *Cf.* Isa. xxxvii. 29; 2 Chron. xxxiii. 11. On the use of fish-hooks, Job xl. 26 (Heb.), xli. 2 (Eng.); Ezek. xxix. 4.

* The verb, which in the text is active, must be taken in the passive. The word not translated above is הַהַרְמוֹנָה, "unto the Harmôn," which name does not occur elsewhere. LXX. read εἰς τὸ ὄρος τὸ Ῥομμάν, which Ewald renders "ye shall cast the Rimmon to the mountain" (*cf.* Isa. ii. 20), and he takes Rimmon to be the Syrian goddess of love. Steiner (quoted by Wellhausen) renders "ye shall be cast out to Hadad Rimmon," that is, "violated as" קְדֵשׁוֹת. Hitzig separates ההר from מונה, which he takes as contracted from מענה, and renders "ye shall fling yourselves out on the mountains as a refuge." But none of these is satisfactory.

† I have already treated this passage in connection with Isaiah's prophecies on women in the Prophecies of Isaiah i.—xxxix. ("Expositor's Bible"), chap. xvi.

‡ *Cf.* chap. vi. 4.

§ v. 11.

splinters." * No wonder that such a prophet found war with its breached walls insufficient, and welcomed, as the full ally of his word, the earthquake itself. †

Yet all this is no mere desert *razzia* in the name of the Lord, a nomad's hatred of cities and the culture of settled men. It is not a temper; it is a vision of history. In the only argument which these early oracles contain, Amos claims to have events on the side of his word. "Shall the lion roar and not be catching" something? Neither does the prophet speak till he knows that God is ready to act. History accepted this claim. Amos spoke about 755. In 734 Tiglath-Pileser swept Gilead and Galilee; in 724 Shalmaneser overran the rest of Northern Israel: "siege and blockade of the whole land!" For three years the Mount of Samaria was invested, and then taken; the houses overthrown, the rich and the delicate led away captive. It happened as Amos foretold; for it was not the shepherd's rage within him that spoke. He had "seen the Lord standing, and He said, Smite."

But this assault of a desert nomad upon the structure of a nation's life raises many echoes in history and some questions in our own minds to-day. Again and again have civilisations far more powerful than Israel's been threatened by the desert in the name of God, and in good faith it has been proclaimed by the prophets of Christianity and other religions that God's kingdom cannot come on earth till the wealth, the culture, the civil order, which men have taken centuries to build, have been swept away by some great political convulsion. To-day Christianity herself suffers the same assaults, and is told by many, the high life and honest intention of whom cannot be doubted, that till the civilisation which she has so much helped to create is destroyed, there is no hope for the purity or the progress of the race. And Christianity, too, has doubts within herself. What is the world which our Master refused in the Mount of Temptation, and so often and so sternly told us that it must perish?—how much of our wealth, of our culture, of our politics, of the whole fabric of our society? No thoughtful and religious man, when confronted with civilisation, not in its ideal, but in one of those forms which give it its very name, the life of a large city, can fail to ask, How much of this deserves the judgment of God? How much must be overthrown, before His will is done on earth? All these questions rise in the ears and the heart of a generation, which more than any other has been brought face to face with the ruins of empires and civilisations, which have endured longer, and in their day seemed more stable, than her own.

In face of the confused thinking and fanatic speech which have risen on all such topics, it seems to me that the Hebrew prophets supply us with four cardinal rules.

First, of course, they insist that it is the moral question upon which the fate of a civilisation is decided. By what means has the system grown? Is justice observed in essence as well as form? Is there freedom, or is the prophet silenced? Does luxury or self-denial prevail? Do the rich make life hard for the poor? Is childhood sheltered and is innocence respected? By these, claim the prophets, a nation stands or falls; and history has proved the claim on wider worlds than they dreamt of.

But by themselves moral reasons are never enough to justify a prediction of speedy doom upon any system or society. None of the prophets began to foretell the fall of Israel till they read, with keener eyes than their contemporaries, the signs of it in current history. And this, I take it, was the point which made a notable difference between them, and one who like them scourged the social wrongs of his civilisation, yet never spoke a word of its fall. Juvenal nowhere calls down judgments, except upon individuals. In his time there were no signs of the decline of the empire, even though, as he marks, there was a flight from the capital of the virtue which was to keep the empire alive. But the prophets had political proof of the nearness of God's judgment, and they spoke in the power of its coincidence with the moral corruption of their people.

Again, if conscience and history (both of them, to the prophets, being witnesses of God) thus combine to announce the early doom of a civilisation, neither the religion that may have helped to build it, nor any remanent virtue in it, nor its ancient value to God, can avail to save. We are tempted to judge that the long and costly development of ages is cruelly thrown away by the convulsion and collapse of an empire; it feels impious to think that the patience, the providence, the millennial discipline of the Almighty are to be in a moment abandoned to some rude and savage force. But we are wrong. "You only have I known of all the families of the ground," yet I must "visit upon you your iniquities." Nothing is too costly for justice. And God finds some other way of conserving the real results of the past.

Again, it is a corollary of all this, that the sentence upon civilisation must often seem to come by voices that are insane, and its execution by means that are criminal. Of course, when civilisation is arraigned as a whole, and its overthrow demanded, there may be nothing behind the attack but jealousy or greed, the fanaticism of ignorant men or the madness of disordered lives. But this is not necessarily the case. For God has often in history chosen the outsider as the herald of doom, and sent the barbarian as its instrument. By the statesmen and patriots of Israel, Amos must have been regarded as a mere savage, with a savage's hate of civilisation. But we know what he answered when Amaziah called him rebel. And it was not only for its suddenness that the apostles said the "day of the Lord should come as a thief," but also because of its methods. For over and over again has doom been pronounced, and pronounced truly, by men who in the eyes of civilisation were criminals and monsters.

Now apply these four principles to the question of ourselves. It will scarcely be denied that our civilisation tolerates, and in part lives by, the existence of vices which, as we all admit, ruined the ancient empires. Are the political possibilities of overthrow also present? That there exist among us means of new historic convulsions is a thing hard for us to admit. But the signs cannot be hid. When we see the jealousies of the Christian peoples, and their enormous preparations for battle; the arsenals of Europe which a few sparks may blow up; the millions of soldiers one man's word may mobilise; when

* vi. 8, 11.

† *Cf.* what was said on building above, p. 450.

we imagine the opportunities which a general war would furnish to the discontented masses of the European proletariat—we must surely acknowledge the existence of forces capable of inflicting calamities, so severe as to affect not merely this nationality or that type of culture, but the very vigour and progress of civilisation herself; and all this without our looking beyond Christendom, or taking into account the rise of the yellow races to a consciousness of their aproach to equality with ourselves. If, then, in the eyes of the Divine justice Christendom merits judgment,—if life continue to be left so hard to the poor; if innocence be still an impossibility for so much of the childhood of the Christian nations; if with so many of the leaders of civilisation prurience be lifted to the level of an art, and licentiousness followed as a cult; if we continue to pour the evils of our civilisation upon the barbarian, and "the vices of our young nobles," to paraphrase Juvenal, "are aped in" Hindustan,—then let us know that the means of a judgment more awful than any which has yet scourged a delinquent civilisation are extant and actual among us. And if one should reply, that our Christianity makes all the difference, that God cannot undo the development of nineteen centuries, or cannot overthrow the peoples of His Son,—let us remember that God does justice at whatever cost; that as He did not spare Israel at the hands of Assyria, so He did not spare Christianity in the East when the barbarians of the desert found her careless and corrupt. "You only have I known of all the families of the ground, therefore will I visit upon you all your iniquities."

CHAPTER IX.

THE FALSE PEACE OF RITUAL.

AMOS iv. 4-vi.

THE next four groups of oracles *—iv. 4-13, v. 1-17, v. 18-27, and vi.—treat of many different details, and each of them has its own emphasis; but all are alike in this, that they vehemently attack the national worship and the sense of political security which it has engendered. Let us at once make clear that this worship is the worship of Jehovah. It is true that it is mixed with idolatry, but, except possibly in one obscure verse,† Amos does not concern himself with the idols. What he strikes at, what he would sweep away, is his people's form of devotion to their own God. The cult of the national God, at the national sanctuaries, in the national interest and by the whole body of the people, who practise it with a zeal unparalleled by their forefathers—this is what Amos condemns. And he does so absolutely. He has nothing but scorn for the temples and the feasts. The assiduity of attendance, the liberality of gifts, the employment of wealth and art and patriotism in worship—he tells his generation that God loathes it all. Like Jeremiah, he even seems to imply that God never instituted in Israel any sacrifice or offering.‡ It is all this which gives these oracles their interest for us; and that interest is not merely historical.

It is indeed historical to begin with. When we find, not idolatry, but all religious ceremonial —temples, public worship, tithes, sacrifice, the praise of God by music, in fact every material form in which man has ever been wont to express his devotion to God—scorned and condemned with the same uncompromising passion as idolatry itself, we receive a needed lesson in the history of religion. For when one is asked, What is the distinguishing characteristic of heathenism? one is always ready to say, Idolatry, which is not true. The distinguishing characteristic of heathenism is the stress which it lays upon ceremonial. To the pagan religions, both of the ancient and of the modern world, rites were the indispensable element in religion. The gifts of the gods, the abundance of fruits, the security of the state, depended upon the full and accurate performance of ritual. In Greek literature we have innumerable illustrations of this: the "Iliad" itself starts from a god's anger, roused by an insult to his priest, whose prayers for vengeance he hears because sacrifices have been assiduously offered to him. And so too with the systems of paganism from which the faith of Israel, though at first it had so much in common with them, broke away to its supreme religious distinction. The Semites laid the stress of their obedience to the gods upon traditional ceremonies; and no sin was held so heinous by them as the neglect or infringement of a religious rite. By the side of it offences against one's fellowmen or one's own character were deemed mere misdemeanours. In the day of Amos this pagan superstition thoroughly penetrated the religion of Jehovah, and so absorbed the attention of men, that without the indignant and complete repudiation of it prophecy could not have started on her task of identifying morality with religion, and of teaching men more spiritual views of God. But even when we are thus aware of ceremonialism as the characteristic quality of the pagan religions, we have not measured the full reason of that uncompromising attack on it, which is the chief feature of this part of the permanent canon of our religion. For idolatries die everywhere; but everywhere a superstitious ritualism survives. It continues with philosophies that have ceased to believe in the gods who enforced it. Upon ethical movements which have gained their freedom by breaking away from it, in the course of time it makes up, and lays its paralysing weight. With offers of help it flatters religions the most spiritual in theory and intention. The Pharisees, than whom few parties had at first purer ideals of morality, tithed mint, anise, and cummin, to the neglect of the essence of the Law; and even sound Christians, who have assimilated the Gospel of St. John, find it hard and sometimes impossible to believe in salvation apart from their own sacraments, or outside their own denominational forms. Now this is because ritual is a thing which appeals both to the baser and to the nobler instincts of man. To the baser it offers itself as a mechanical atonement for sin, and a substitute for all moral and intellectual effort in connection with faith; to the nobler it insists on a man's need in religion of order and routine, of sacrament and picture. Plainly then the words of Amos have significance for more than the immediate problems of his day. And if it seem to some that Amos goes too far with his cry to sweep away all ceremonial, let them remember, besides the crisis of his times, that the temper he exposes and seeks to dissipate is a rank

* See p. 477. † v. 26. ‡ v. 25.

and obdurate error of the human heart. Our Lord, who recognised the place of ritual in worship, who said, "Thus it behoveth us to fulfil all righteousness," which righteousness in the dialect of His day was not the moral law, but man's due of rite, sacrifice, tithe, and alms,* said also, "I will have mercy and not sacrifice." There is an irreducible minimum of rite and routine in worship; there is an invaluable loyalty to traditional habits; there are holy and spiritual uses in symbol and sacrament. But these are all dispensable; and because they are all constantly abused, the voice of the prophet is ever needed which tells us that God will have none of them; but let justice roll on like water, and righteousness like an unfailing stream.

For the superstition that ritual is the indispensable bond between God and man, Amos substitutes two other aspects of religion. They are history as God's discipline of man: and civic justice as man's duty to God. The first of them he contrasts with religious ceremonialism in chap. iv. 4-13, and the second in chap. v.; while in chap. vi. he assaults once more the false political peace which the ceremonialism engenders.

1. For Worship, Chastisement.

Amos iv. 4-13.

In chap. ii. Amos contrasted the popular conception of religion as worship with God's conception of it as history. He placed a picture of the sanctuary, hot with religious zeal, but hot too with passion and the fumes of wine, side by side with a great prospect of the national history: God's guidance of Israel from Egypt onwards. That is, as we said at the time, he placed an indoors picture of religion side by side with an open-air one. He repeats that arrangement here. The religious services he sketches are more pure, and the history he takes from his own day; but the contrast is the same. Again we have on the one side the temple worship—artificial, exaggerated, indoors, smoky; but on the other a few movements of God in Nature, which, though they all be calamities, have a great moral majesty upon them. The first opens with a scornful call to worship, which the prophet, letting out his whole heart at the beginning, shows to be equivalent to sin. Note next the impossible caricature of their exaggerated zeal: sacrifices every morning instead of once a year, tithes every three days instead of every three years.† To offer leavened bread was a departure from the older fashion of unleavened.‡ To publish their liberality was like the later Pharisees, who were not dissimilarly mocked by our Lord: "When thou doest alms, cause not a trumpet to be sounded before thee, as the hypocrites do in the synagogues and in the streets, that they may have glory of men." § There is a certain rhythm in the taunt; but the prose style seems to be resumed with fitness when the prophet describes the solemn approach of God in deeds of doom.

* Another proof of how the spirit of ritualism tends to absorb morality.

† Ver. 4: *cf.* 1 Sam. i.; Deut. xiv. 28. Wellhausen offers another exegesis: Amos is describing exactly what took place at Bethel—sacrifice on the morning, *i. e.*, next to the day of their arrival, tithes on the third day thereafter.

‡ See Wellhausen's note, and compare Lev. vii. 13.

§ Matt. vi. 2.

Come away to Bethel and transgress,
At Gilgal exaggerate your transgression!
And bring every morning your sacrifices,
Every three days your tithes!
And send up the savour of leavened bread as a thank-offering,
And call out *your* liberalities—make them to be heard!
For so ye love *to do*, O children of Israel:
Oracle of Jehovah.

"But I on My side have given you cleanness of teeth in all your cities, and want of bread in all your places—yet ye did not return to Me: oracle of Jehovah.

"But I on My side withheld from you the winter rain,* while it was still three months to the harvest: and I let it rain repeatedly on one city, and upon one city I did not let it rain: one lot was rained upon, and the lot that was not rained upon withered; and two or three cities kept straggling to one city to drink water, and were not satisfied—yet ye did not return to Me: oracle of Jehovah.

"I smote you with blasting and with mildew: many of your gardens and your vineyards and your figs and your olives the locust devoured—yet ye did not return to Me: oracle of Jehovah.

"I sent among you a pestilence by way of Egypt:† I slew with the sword your youths—besides the capture of your horses—and I brought up the stench of your camps to your nostrils—yet ye did not return to Me: oracle of Jehovah.

"I overturned among you, like God's own overturning of Sodom and Gomorrah, till ye became as a brand plucked from the burning—yet ye did not return to Me: oracle of Jehovah."

This recalls a passage in that English poem of which we are again and again reminded by the Book of Amos, "The Vision of Piers Plowman." It is the sermon of Reason in Passus V. (Skeat's edition):—

"He preved that thise pestilences · were for pure synne,
And the southwest wynde · in saterday et evene
Was pertliche ‡ for pure pride · and for no poynt elles.
Piries and plomtrees · were puffed to the erthe,
In ensample ze segges § · ze shulden do the bettere.
Beches and brode okes · were blowen to the grounde.
Torned upward her tailles · in tokenynge of drede,
That dedly synne at domesday · shal fordon ‖ hem alle."

In the ancient world it was a settled belief that natural calamities like these were the effects of the deity's wrath. When Israel suffers from them the prophets take for granted that they are for the people's punishment. I have elsewhere shown how the climate of Palestine lent itself to these convictions; in this respect the Book of Deuteronomy contrasts it with the climate of Egypt.¶ And although some, perhaps rightly, have scoffed at the exaggerated form of the belief, that God is angry with the sons of men every time drought or floods happen, yet the instinct is sound which in all ages has led re-

* גֶּשֶׁם: "Hist. Geog.," p. 64. It is interesting that this year (1895) the same thing was threatened, according to a report in the "Mittheilungen u. Nachrichten des D. P. V.," p. 44: "Nachdem es im December einigemal recht stark geregnet hatte besonders an der Meeresküste ist seit kurz vor Weihnachten das Wetter immer schön u. mild geblieben, u. wenn nicht weiterer Regen fällt, so wird grosser Wassermangel entstehen denn bis jetzt (16 Febr.) hat Niemand Cisterne voll." The harvest is in April-May.

† Or in the fashion of Egypt, *i. e.*, a thoroughly Egyptian plague; so called, not with reference to the plagues of Egypt, but because that country was always the nursery of the pestilence. See "Hist. Geog.," p. 157 ff. Note how it comes with war.

‡ Apertly, openly.

§ Men.

‖ Undo.

¶ "Hist. Geog." chap. iii. pp. 73 f.

ligious people to feel that such things are inflicted for moral purposes. In the economy of the universe there may be ends of a purely physical kind served by such disasters, apart altogether from their meaning to man. But man at least learns from them that nature does not exist solely for feeding, clothing, and keeping him wealthy; nor is it anything else than his monotheism, his faith in God as the Lord both of his moral life and of nature, which moves him to believe, as Hebrew prophets taught and as our early English seer heard Reason herself preach. Amos had the more need to explain those disasters as the work of the God of righteousness, because his contemporaries, while willing to grant Jehovah leadership in war, were tempted to attribute to the Canaanite gods of the land all power over the seasons.

What, however, more immediately concerns us in this passage is its very effective contrast between men's treatment of God and God's treatment of men. They lavish upon Him gifts and sacrifices. He—"on His side"—sends them cleanness of teeth, drought, blasting of their fruits, pestilence, war, and earthquake. That is to say, they regard Him as a being only to be flattered and fed. He regards them as creatures with characters to discipline, even at the expense of their material welfare. Their views of Him, if religious, are sensuous and gross; His views of them, if austere, are moral and ennobling. All this may be grim, but it is exceeding grand; and short as the efforts of Amos are, we begin to perceive in him something already of the greatness of an Isaiah.

And have not those who have believed as Amos believed ever been the strong spirits of our race, making the very disasters which crushed them to the earth the tokens that God has great views about them? Laugh not at the simple peoples, who have their days of humiliation, and their fast-days after floods and stunted harvests. For they take these, not like other men, as the signs of their frailty and helplessness; but as measures of the greatness God sees in them, His provocation of their souls to the infinite possibilities which He has prepared for them.

Israel, however, did not turn even at the fifth call to penitence, and so there remained nothing for her but a fearful looking forward to judgment, all the more terrible that the prophet does not define what the judgment shall be.

"Therefore thus shall I do to thee, O Israel: because I am going to do this to thee, prepare to meet thy God, O Israel. For, lo, He that formeth the mountains, and createth the wind, and declareth to man what His thought is, that maketh morning darkness, and marcheth on the high places of earth, Jehovah, God of Hosts, is His Name." *

2. For Worship, Justice.

Amos v.

In the next of these groups of oracles Amos continues his attack on the national ritual, and now contrasts it with the service of God in public life—the relief of the poor, the discharge of justice. But he does not begin with this. The group opens with an elegy, which bewails the nation as already fallen. It is always difficult to mark where the style of a prophet passes from rhythmical prose into what we may justly call a metrical form. But in this short wail, we catch the well-known measure of the Hebrew dirge; not so artistic as in later poems, yet with at least the characteristic couplet of a long and a short line.

"Hear this word which I lift up against you—a Dirge, O house of Israel:—

"Fallen, no more shall she rise,
Virgin of Israel!
Flung down on her own ground,
No one to raise her!"

The "Virgin," which with Isaiah is a standing title for Jerusalem and occasionally used of other cities, is here probably the whole nation of Northern Israel. The explanation follows. It is War. "For thus saith the Lord Jehovah: The city that goeth forth a thousand shall have an hundred left; and she that goeth forth an hundred shall have left ten for the house of Israel."

But judgment is not yet irrevocable. There break forthwith the only two promises which lighten the lowering darkness of the book. Let the people turn to Jehovah Himself—and that means let them turn from the ritual, and instead of it purge their civic life, restore justice in their courts, and help the poor. For God and moral good are one. It is "seek Me and ye shall live," and "seek good and ye shall live." Omitting for the present all argument as to whether the interruption of praise to the power of Jehovah be from Amos or another, we read the whole oracle as follows.

"Thus saith Jehovah to the house of Israel: Seek Me and live. But seek not Bethel, and come not to Gilgal, and to Beersheba pass not over"—to come to Beersheba one had to cross all Judah. "For Gilgal shall taste the gall of exile"—it is not possible except in this clumsy way to echo the prophet's play upon words, "Ha-Gilgal galoh yigleh"—"and Bethel," God's house, "shall become an idolatry." This rendering, however, scarcely gives the rude force of the original; for the word rendered idolatry, Aven, means also falsehood and perdition, so that we should not exaggerate the antithesis if we employed a phrase which once was not vulgar: "And Bethel, house of God, shall go to the devil!" * The epigram was the more natural that near Bethel, on a site now uncertain, but close to the edge of the desert to which it gave its name, there lay from ancient times a village actually called Beth-Aven, however the form may have risen. And we shall find Hosea stereotyping this epigram of Amos, and calling the sanctuary Beth-Aven oftener than he calls it Beth-el.† "Seek ye Jehovah and live," he begins again, "lest He break forth like fire, O house of Joseph, and it consume and there be none to quench at Bethel. ‡ . . . § He that made the

* This and similar passages are dealt with by themselves in chap. xi.

* *Cf.* LXX.: Βαιθὴλ ἔσται ὡς οὐχ ὑπάρχουσα.

† The name Bethel is always printed as one word in our Hebrew texts. See Baer on Gen. xii. 8.

‡ Wellhausen thinks *at Bethel* not genuine. But Bethel has been singled out as the place where the people put their false confidence, and is naturally named here. LXX.: τῷ οἴκῳ Ἰσραήλ.

§ Ver. 7 is plainly out of place here, as the LXX. perceived, and therefore tried to give it another rendering which would make it seem in place: ὁ ποιῶν εἰς ὕψος κρίμα, καὶ δικαιοσύνην εἰς γὴν ἔθηκεν. So Ewald removed it to between vv. 9 and 10. There it begins well another oracle; and it may be that we should insert before it הוי, as in vv. 18, vi. 1.

Seven Stars and Orion,* that turneth the murk,† into morning, and day He darkeneth to night, that calleth for the waters of the sea and poureth them out on the face of the earth—Jehovah His Name. He it is that flasheth out ruin‡ on strength, and bringeth down§ destruction on the fortified." This rendering of the last verse is uncertain, and rightly suspected, but there is no alternative so probable, and it returns to the keynote from which the passage started, that God should break forth like fire.

Ah, "they that turn justice to wormwood, and abase‖ righteousness to the earth! They hate him that reproveth in the gate"—in an Eastern city both the law-court and place of the popular council—"and him that speaketh sincerely they abhor." So in the English mystic's Vision Peace complains of Wrong:—

"I dar noughte for fere of hym : fyghte ne chyde."¶

"Wherefore, because ye trample on the weak and take from him a present of corn,** ye have built houses of ashlar,†† but ye shall not dwell in them; vineyards for pleasure have ye planted, but ye shall not drink of their wine. For I know how many are your crimes, and how forceful‡‡ your sins—ye that browbeat the righteous, take bribes, and bring down the poor in the gate! Therefore the prudent in such a time is dumb, for an evil time is it" indeed.

"Seek good and not evil, that ye may live, and Jehovah God of Hosts be with you, as ye say" He is. "Hate evil and love good; and in the gate set justice on her feet again—peradventure Jehovah God of Hosts may have pity on the remnant of Joseph." If in the Book of Amos there be any passages, which, to say the least, do not now lie in their proper places, this is one of them. For, firstly, while it regards the nation as still responsible for the duties of government, it recognises them as reduced to a remnant. To find such a state of affairs we have to come down to the years subsequent to 734, when Tiglath-Pileser swept into captivity all Gilead and Galilee—that is, two-thirds, in bulk, of the territory of Northern Israel—but left Ephraim untouched. In answer to this, it may, of course, be pointed out that in thus calling the people to repentance, so that a remnant might be saved, Amos may have been contemplating a disaster still future, from which, though it was inevitable, God might be moved to spare a remnant.* That is very true. But it does not meet this further difficulty, that the verses (14, 15) plainly make interruption between the end of ver. 13 and the beginning of ver. 16; and that the initial "therefore" of the latter verse, while it has no meaning in its present sequence, becomes natural and appropriate when made to follow immediately on ver. 13. For all these reasons, then, I take vv. 14 and 15 as a parenthesis, whether from Amos himself or from a later writer who can tell? But it ought to be kept in mind that in other prophetic writings where judgment is very severe, we have some proof of the later insertion of calls to repentance, by way of mitigation.

Ver. 13 had said the time was so evil that the prudent man kept silence. All the more must the Lord Himself speak, as ver. 16 now proclaims. "Therefore thus saith Jehovah, God of Hosts,† Lord: On all open ways lamentation, and in all streets they shall be saying, Ah woe! Ah woe! And in all vineyards lamentation,‡ and they shall call the ploughman to wailing and to lamentation them that are skilful in dirges"—town and country, rustic and artist alike—"for I shall pass through thy midst, saith Jehovah." It is the solemn formula of the Great Passover, when Egypt was filled with wailing and there were dead in every house.

The next verse starts another, but a kindred, theme. As blind as was Israel's confidence in ritual, so blind was their confidence in dogma, and the popular dogma was that of the "Day of Jehovah."

All popular hopes expect their victory to come in a single sharp crisis—a day. And again, the day of any one means either the day he has appointed, or the day of his display and triumph. So Jehovah's day meant to the people the day of His judgment, or of His triumph: His triumph in war over their enemies, His judgment upon the heathen. But Amos, whose keynote has been that judgment begins at home, cries woe upon such hopes, and tells his people that for them the day of Jehovah is not victory, but rather insidious, importunate, inevitable death. And this he describes as a man who has lived, alone with wild beasts, from the jungles of the Jordan, where the lions lurk, to the huts of the desert infested by snakes.

"Woe unto them that long for the day of Jehovah! What have you to do with the day of Jehovah? It is darkness, and not light. As when a man fleeth from the face of a lion, and a bear falls upon him; and he comes into his home,§ and," breathless, "leans his hand upon the wall, and a serpent bites him." And then, as if appealing to Heaven for confirmation: Is it not so? "Is it not darkness, the day of Jehovah, and not light? storm darkness, and not a ray of light upon it?"

Then Amos returns to the worship, that nurse of their vain hopes, that false prophet of peace, and he hears God speak more strongly than ever of its futility and hatefulness.

* Literally "the Group," and "the Giant." כימה, Kimah, signifies group, or little heap. Here it is rendered by Aq. and at Job ix. 9 by LXX. Ἀρκτοῦρος; and here by Theod. and in Job xxxviii. 31, the "chain," or "cluster," of the group" Πλειάδες. The Targ. and Pesh. always give it as Kima, *i e.*, Pleiades. And this is the rendering of most moderns. But Stern takes it for Sirius with its constellation of the Great Dog, for the reason that this is the brightest of all stars, and therefore a more suitable fellow for Orion than the dimmer Pleiades can be. כסיל, the Fool or Giant, is the Hebrew name of Ὠρίων, by which the LXX. render it. Targum נִיפלא. To the ancient world the constellation looked like the figure of a giant fettered in heaven, "a fool so far as he trusted in his bodily strength" (Dillmann). In later times he was called Nimrod. His early setting came at the time of the early rains. *Cf.* with the passage Job ix. 9 and xxxviii. 31.

† The abstract noun meaning "deep shadow," LXX. σκιά, and rendered "shadow of death" by many modern versions.

‡ So LXX., reading שֹׁבר for שֹׁד; it improves the rhythm, and escapes the awkward repetition of שֹׁד.

§ So LXX.

‖ Possible alternative : "make stagnant."

¶ "Vision of Piers Plowman," Passus IV. l. 52. *Cf.* the whole passage.

** Uncertain ; Hitzig takes it as the apodosis of the previous clause : "Ye shall have to take from him a present of corn," *i. e.*, as alms.

†† See above, p. 450.

‡‡ *Cf.* "Pecca fortiter."

* As, for instance, the prophet looks forward to in iii. 12.

† "God of Hosts," perhaps an intrusion (?) between אדני and יהוה.

‡ I have ventured to rearrange the order of the clauses, which in the original is evidently dislocated.

§ Lit. "the house."

"I hate, I loathe your feasts, and I will not smell the savour of your gatherings to sacrifice." For with pagan folly they still believed that the smoke of their burnt-offerings went up to heaven and flattered the nostrils of Deity. How ingrained was this belief may be judged by us from the fact that the terms of it had to be adopted by the apostles of a spiritual religion, if they would make themselves understood, and are now the metaphors of the sacrifices of the Christian heart.* "Though ye bring to Me burnt-offerings and your meal-offerings I will not be pleased, or your thank-offerings of fatted calves, I will not look at them. Let cease from Me the noise of thy songs; to the playing of thy viols I will not listen. But let justice roll on like water, and righteousness like an unfailing stream."

Then follows the remarkable appeal from the habits of this age to those of the times of Israel's simplicity. "Was it flesh- or meal-offerings that ye brought Me in the wilderness, forty years, O house of Israel?" † That is to say, at the very time when God made Israel His people, and led them safely to the promised land—the time when of all others He did most for them—He was not moved to such love and deliverance by the propitiatory bribes, which this generation imagine to be so availing and indispensable. Nay, those still shall not avail, for exile from the land shall now as surely come in spite of them, as the possession of the land in old times came without them. This at least seems to be the drift of the very obscure verse which follows, and is the unmistakable statement of the close of the oracle. "But ye shall lift up . . . your king and . . . your god, images which you have made for yourselves;‡ and

* Eph. v. 2, etc.

† No one doubts that this verse is interrogative. But the Authorised Eng. Ver. puts it in a form—"Have ye brought unto Me?" etc.—which implies blame that they did not do so. Ewald was the first to see that, as rendered above, an appeal to the forty years was the real intention of the verse. So after him nearly all critics, also the Revised Eng. Ver.: "Do ye bring unto Me?" On the whole question of the possibility of such an appeal see above, pp. 467 ff., and *cf.* Jer. vii. 22, which distinctly declares that in the wilderness God prescribed no ritual to Israel.

‡ Ver. 26 is very difficult, for both the text and the rendering of all the possible alternatives of it are quite uncertain. (1) As to the "text," the present division into words must be correct; at least no other is possible. But the present order of the words is obviously wrong. For "your images" is evidently described by the relative clause "which you have made," and ought to stand next it. What then is to be done with the two words that at present come between—"star of your god"? Are they both a mere gloss, as Robertson Smith holds, and therefore to be struck out? or should they precede the pair of words, כיון צלמיכם, which they now follow? This is the order of the text which the LXX. translator had before him, only for כון he misread רֵיפָן or רֵיוָן: *καὶ ἀνελάβετε τὴν σκηνὴν τοῦ Μωλὸχ καὶ τὸ ἄστρον τοῦ Θεοῦ ὑμῶν Ῥαιφάν* [*Ῥεφάν*, Q], *τοὺς τύπους αὐτῶν* [om. AQ] *οὓς ἐποιήσατε ἑαυτοῖς*. This arrangement has the further evidence in its favour, that it brings "your god" into proper parallel with "your king." The Hebrew text would then run thus:—

ונשאתם את סכות מלככם ואת (כוכב אלהיכם)
כיון צלמיכם אשר עשיתם לכם

(2) The translation of this text is equally difficult: not in the verb ונשאתם, for both the grammar and the argument oblige us to take it as future, "and ye shall lift up;" but in the two words סכות and כיון. Are these common nouns, or proper names of deities in apposition to "your king and your god"? The LXX. takes סכות as = "tabernacle," and כיון as a proper name (Theodotion takes both as proper names). The Auth. Eng. Ver. follows the LXX.

I will carry you away into exile far beyond Damascus, saith Jehovah—God of Hosts is His Name!" * So this chapter closes like the previous, with the marshalling of God's armies. But as there His hosts were the movements of Nature and the Great Stars, so here they are the nations of the world. By His rule of both He is the God of Hosts.

3. "At Ease in Zion."

Amos vi.

The evil of the national worship was the false political confidence which it engendered. Leaving the ritual alone, Amos now proceeds to assault this confidence. We are taken from the public worship of the people to the private banquets of the rich, but again only in order to have their security and extravagance contrasted with the pestilence, the war, and the captivity that are rapidly approaching.

"Woe unto them that are at ease in Zion" †—it is a proud and overweening ease which the word expresses—"and that trust in the mount of Samaria! Men of mark of the first of the peoples"—ironically, for that is Israel's opinion of itself—"and to them do the house of Israel resort! . . .‡ Ye that put off the day of calam-

(except that it takes "king" for the name "Moloch"). Schrader ("Stud. u. Krit.," 1874, 324; "K. A. T.," 442 f.) takes them as the consonants of Sakkut, a name of the Assyrian god Adar, and of Kewan, the Assyrian name for the planet Saturn: "Ye shall take up Sakkut your king and Kewan your star-god, your images which . . ." Baethgen goes further and takes both the מלך of מלכיכם and the צלם of צלמיכם as Moloch and Selam, proper names, in combination with Sakkut and Kewan ("Beitr. z. Sem. Rel.," 239). Now it is true that the Second Book of Kings implies that the worship of the host of heaven existed in Samaria before its fall (2 Kings xvii. 16), but the introduction into Samaria of Assyrian gods (among them Adar is placed by it after the fall (2 Kings xvii. 31), and besides, Amos does not elsewhere speak of the worship of foreign gods, nor is the mention of them in any way necessary to the argument here. On the contrary, even if Amos were to mention the worship of idols by Israel, would he have selected at this point the Assyrian ones? (See, however, Tiele, "Revue de l'Histoire des Religions," III. p. 211, who makes Koun and the planet Keiwan purely Phœnician deities.) Some critics take סכות and כיון as common nouns in the construct state. So Ewald, and so most recently Robertson Smith ("O. T. J. C.," 2): "the shrine of your king and the stand of your images." This is more in harmony with the absence from the rest of Amos of any hint as to the worship of idols, but an objection to it, and a very strong one, is that the alleged common nouns are not found elsewhere in Hebrew. In view of this conflicting evidence it is best therefore to leave the words untranslated, as in the text above. It is just possible that they may themselves be later insertions, for the verse would read very well without them: "And ye shall lift up your king and your images which you have made to yourselves."

* The last clause is peculiar. Two clauses seem to have run into one—"saith Jehovah, God of Hosts," and "God of Hosts is His Name." The word שמו = "His Name," may have been added to give the oracle the same conclusion as the oracle at the end of the preceding chapter; and it is not to be overlooked that שמו at the end of a clause does not occur elsewhere in the book outside the three questioned Doxologies iv. 13, v. 8, ix. 6. Further see below, pp. 493 f.

† "In Zion": "very suspicious," Cornill. But see pp. 476 f.

‡ I remove ver. 2 to a note, not that I am certain that it is not by Amos—who can be dogmatic on such a point?—but because the text of it, the place which it occupies, and its relation to the facts of current history, all raise doubts. Moreover, it is easily detached from the context, without disturbing the flow of the chapter, which indeed runs more equably without it. The Massoretic text gives: "Pass over to Calneh, and see; and go thence to Hamath Rabbah, and come down to Gath of the Philistines: are they better than these kingdoms, or is their territory

ity * and draw near the sessions of injustice" †—an epigram and proverb, for it is the universal way of men to wish and fancy far away the very crisis that their sins are hastening on. Isaiah described this same generation as drawing iniquity with cords of hypocrisy, and sin as it were with a cart-rope! "That lie on ivory diwans and sprawl on their couches"—another luxurious custom, which filled this rude shepherd with contempt—"and eat lambs from the flock and calves from the midst of the stall" ‡—that is, only the most delicate of meats—"who prate" or "purr" or "babble to the sound of the viol, and as if they were David" himself "invent for them instruments of song; § who drink wine by ewerfuls—waterpotfuls—and anoint with the finest of oil—yet never do they grieve at the havoc of Joseph!" The havoc is the moral havoc, for the social structure of Israel is obviously still secure.‖ The rich are indifferent to it; they have wealth, art, patriotism, religion, but neither heart for the poverty nor conscience for the sin of their people. We know their kind! They are always with us, who live well and imagine they are proportionally clever and refined. They have their political zeal, will rally to an election when the interests of their class or their trade is in danger. They have a robust and exuberant patriotism, talk grandly of commerce, empire, and the national destiny; but for the real woes and sores of the people, the poverty, the overwork, the drunkenness, the dissoluteness, which more affect a nation's life than anything else, they have no pity and no care.

"Therefore now"—the double initial of judgment—"shall they go into exile at the head of the exiles, and stilled shall be the revelry of the dissolute"—literally "the sprawlers," as in ver. 4, but used here rather in the moral than in the physical sense. "Sworn hath the Lord Jehovah by Himself—'tis the oracle of Jehovah God of Hosts: I am loathing * the pride of Jacob, and his palaces do I hate, and I will pack up a city and its fulness.† . . . For, behold, Jehovah is commanding, and He will smite the great house into ruins and the small house into splinters." The collapse must come, postpone it as their fancy will, for it has been worked for and is inevitable. How could it be otherwise? "Shall horses run on a cliff, or the sea be ploughed by oxen ‡—that ye should turn justice to poison and the fruit of righteousness to wormwood! Ye that exult in Lo-Debar and say, By our own strength have we taken to ourselves Karnaim." So Grätz rightly reads the verse. The Hebrew text and all the versions take these names as if they were common nouns—Lo-Debar, "a thing of naught"; Ḳarnaim, "a pair of horns"—and doubtless it was just because of this possible play upon their names, that Amos selected these two out of all the recent conquests of Israel. Karnaim, in full Ashteroth Karnaim, "Astarte of Horns," was that immemorial fortress and sanctuary which lay out upon the great plateau of Bashan towards Damascus; so obvious and cardinal a site that it appears in the sacred history both in the earliest recorded campaign in Abraham's time and in one of the latest under the Maccabees.§ Lo-Debar was of Gilead, and probably lay on that last rampart of the province northward, overlooking the Yarmuk, a strategical point which must have often been contested by Israel and Aram, and with which no other Old Testament name has been identified.‖ These two fortresses, with many others, Israel had lately taken from Aram; but not, as they boasted, "by their own strength." It was only Aram's pre-occupation with Assyria, now surgent on the n[illegible]hern flank, which allowed Israel these easy victories. And this same northern foe would soon overwhelm themselves. "For, behold, I am to raise up against you, O house of Israel—'tis the oracle of Jehovah God of the hosts ¶—a Nation, and they shall oppress you from the Entrance of Hamath to the Torrent of the 'Arabah." Every one knows the former, the Pass between the Lebanons, at whose mouth stands Dan, northern limit of Israel; but it is hard to identify the latter. If Amos means to include Judah, we should have expected the Torrent of Egypt, the present Wady el 'Arish; but the Wady of the 'Arabah may be a corresponding valley in the eastern watershed issuing in the 'Arabah. If Amos threatens only the Northern Kingdom, he intends some wady running down to that Sea of the 'Arabah, the Dead Sea, which is elsewhere given as the limit of Israel.**

larger than yours?" Presumably, "these kingdoms" are Judah and Israel. But that can only mean that Israel is the best of the peoples, a statement out of harmony with the irony of ver. 1, and impossible in the mouth of Amos. Geiger, therefore, proposes to read: "Are you better than these kingdoms—*i. e.*, Calneh, Hamath, Gath—or is your territory larger than theirs?" But this is also unlikely, for Israel's territory was much larger than Gath's. Besides, the question would have force only if Calneh, Hamath, and Gath had already fallen. Gath had, but it is at least very questionable whether Hamath had. Therefore Schrader ("K. A. T.," 444) rejects the whole verse; and Kuenen agrees that if we are to understand Assyrian conquests, it is hardly possible to retain the verses. Bickell's first argument against the verse, that it does not fit into the metrical system of Amos vi. 1–7, is precarious; his second, that it disturbs the grammar, which it makes to jump suddenly from the third person in ver. 1 to the second in ver. 2, and back to the third in ver. 3, is not worth anything, for such a jump occurs within ver. 3 itself.

* Davidson, "Syntax," § 100, R. 5.

† שבת חמס; LXX. *σαββάτων ψευδῶν*, on which hint Hoffmann renders the verse: "you that daily demanh the tribute of evil (*cf.* Ezek. xvi. 33), and every Sabbatd extort by violence." But this is both unnecessary and opposed to viii. 5, which tells us no trade was done on the Sabbath. שבת is to be taken in the common sense of sitting in judgment rather than (with Wellhausen) in the sense of the enthronement of wrong-doing.

‡ To this day, in some parts of Palestine, the general fold into which the cattle are shut contains a portion railed off for calves and lambs (*cf.* Dr. M. Blanckenhorn of Erlangen in the "Mittheilungen u. Nachrichten" of the D. P. V., 1895, p. 37, with a sketch). It must be this to which Amos refers.

§ Or perhaps "melodies, airs."

‖ Of course, it is possible that here again, as in v. 15 and 16, we have prophecy later than the disaster of 734, when Tiglath-Pileser made a great "breach" or "havoc" in the body politic of Israel by taking Gilead and Galilee captive. But this is scarcely probable, for Amos almost everywhere lays stress upon the moral corruption of Israel, as her real and essential danger.

* מתאב for מתעב.

† Some words must have dropped out here. For these and the following verses 9 and 10 on the pestilence see pp. 487 ff.

‡ So Michaelis, בְּבָקָר יָם for בַּבְּקָרִים.

§ Gen. xiv. 5; 1 Macc. v. In the days of Eusebius and Jerome (4th century) there were two places of the name: one of them doubtless the present Tell Ashtara south of El-Merkez, the other distant from that fourteen Roman miles.

‖ Along this ridge ran, and still runs, one of the most important highways to the East, that from Beth-Shan by Gadera to Edrei. About seven miles east from Gadera lies a village, Ibdar, "with a good spring and some ancient remains" (Schumacher, "N. Ajlun," 101). Lo-Debar is mentioned in 2 Sam. ix. 45; xvii. 27; and doubtless the Lidebir of Josh. xiii. 26 on the north border of Gilead is the same.

¶ With the article, an unusual form of the title. LXX. here *κύριος τῶν δυνάμεων*.

** 2 Kings xiv. 25. The Torrent of the 'Arabah can

The Assyrian flood, then, was about to break, and the oracles close with the hopeless prospect of the whole land submerged beneath it.

4. A Fragment from the Plague.

In the above exposition we have omitted two very curious verses, 9 and 10, which are held by some critics to interrupt the current of the chapter, and to reflect an entirely different kind of calamity from that which it predicts. I do not think these critics right, for reasons I am about to give; but the verses are so remarkable that it is most convenient to treat them by themselves apart from the rest of the chapter. Here they are, with the verse immediately in front of them.

"I am loathing the pride of Jacob, and his palaces I hate. And I will give up a city and its fulness" to . . . (perhaps "siege" or "pestilence"?). "And it shall come to pass, if there be left ten men in one house, and they die,* . . . that his cousin† and the man to burn him shall lift him to bring the body‡ out of the house, and they shall say to one who is in the recesses of the house,§ Are there any more with thee? And he shall say, Not one . . . and they shall say, Hush! (for one must not make mention of the name of Jehovah)."

This grim fragment is obscure in its relation to the context. But the death of even so large a household as ten—the funeral left to a distant relation—the disposal of the bodies by burning instead of the burial customary among the Hebrews ||—sufficiently reflect the kind of calamity. It is a weird little bit of memory, the recollection of an eye-witness, from one of those great pestilences which, during the first half of the eighth century, happened not seldom in Western Asia.¶ But what does it do here? Wellhausen says that there is nothing to lead up to the incident; that before it the chapter speaks, not of pestilence, but only of political destruction by an enemy. This is not accurate. The phrase immediately preceding may mean either "I will shut up a city and its fulness," in which case a siege is meant, and a siege was the possibility both of famine and pestilence; or "I will give up the city and its fulness . . .," in which case a word or two may have been dropped, as words have undoubtedly been dropped at the end of the next verse, and one ought perhaps to add "to the pestilence." ** The latter alternative is the more probable, and this may be one of the passages, already alluded to,* in which the want of connection with the preceding verses is to be explained, not upon the favourite theory that there has been a violent intrusion into the text, but upon the too much neglected hypothesis that some words have been lost.

The uncertainty of the text, however, does not weaken the impression of its ghastly realism: the unclean and haunted house; the kinsman and the body-burner afraid to search through the infected rooms, and calling in muffled voice to the single survivor crouching in some far corner of them, "Are there any more with thee?" his reply, "None"—himself the next! Yet these details are not the most weird. Over all hangs a terror darker than the pestilence. "Shall there be evil in a city and Jehovah not have done it?" Such, as we have heard from Amos, was the settled faith of the age. But in times of woe it was held with an awful and a craven superstition. The whole of life was believed to be overhung with loose accumulations of Divine anger. And as in some fatal hollow in the high Alps, where any noise may bring down the impending masses of snow, and the fearful traveller hurries along in silence, so the men of that superstitious age feared, when an evil like the plague was imminent, even to utter the Deity's name, lest it should loosen some avalanche of His wrath. "And he said, Hush! for," adds the comment, one "must not make mention of the name of Jehovah."

This reveals another side of the popular religion which Amos has been attacking. We have seen it as the sheer superstition of routine; but we now know that it was a routine broken by panic. The God who in times of peace was propitiated by regular supplies of savoury sacrifice and flattery, is conceived, when His wrath is roused and imminent, as kept quiet only by the silence of its miserable objects. The false peace of ritual is tempered by panic.

CHAPTER X.

DOOM OR DISCIPLINE?

Amos viii. 4-ix.

We now enter the Third Section of the Book of Amos: chaps. vii.-ix. As we have already treated the first part of it—the group of four visions, which probably formed the prophet's discourse at Bethel, with the interlude of his adventure there (vii.-viii. 3) †—we may pass at once to what remains: from viii. 4 to the end of the book. This portion consists of groups of oracles more obscure in their relations to each other than any we have yet studied, and probably containing a number of verses which are not from Amos himself. They open in a denunciation of the rich, which echoes previous oracles, and soon pass to judgments of a kind already threatened, but now with greater relentlessness. Then, just as all is at the darkest, lights break; exceptions are made; the inevitable captivity is described no more as doom, but as discipline; and, with only this preparation for a change, we are swept out on a scene, in which, although the land is strewn with the ruins that have been threatened, the sunshine of a new day floods them; the promise of restoration is given; Nature herself will be

scarcely be the Torrent of the 'Arabim of Isa. xv. 7, for the latter was outside Israel's territory, and the border between Moab and Edom. The LXX. render "Torrent of the West," τῶν δυσμῶν.

* Here there is evidently a gap in the text. The LXX. insert καὶ ὑπολειφθήσονται οἱ κατάλοιποι; perhaps therefore the text originally ran "and the survivors die."

† Or "uncle"—that is, a distant relative, presumably because all the near ones are dead.

‡ Literally "bones."

§ LXX. τοῖς προεστηκόσι: evidently in ignorance of the reading or the meaning.

|| The burning of a body was regarded, as we have seen (Amos ii. 1), as a great sacrilege; and was practised, outside times of pestilence, only in cases of great criminals: Lev. xx. 14; xxi. 9; Josh. vii. 25. Doughty ("Arabia Deserta," 68) mentions a case in which, in Medina, a Persian pilgrim was burned to death by an angry crowd for defiling Mohammed's tomb.

¶ The Assyrian inscriptions record at least three—in 803, 765, 759.

** As in Psalm lxxviii. 50. הִסְגִּיר, to give up, is so seldom used absolutely (Deut. xxxii. 30 is poetry and elliptic) that we may well believe it was followed by words signifying to what the city was to be given up.

* Pp. 477 f. † See chapter vi., section 3.

regenerated, and the whole life of Israel planted on its own ground again.

Whether it was given to Amos himself to behold this day—whether these last verses of the book were his "Nunc Dimittis," or the hope of a later generation, which found his book intolerably severe, and mingled with its judgments their own new mercies—we shall try to discover further on. Meanwhile there is no doubt that we start with the authentic oracles of the prophet. We know the ring of his voice. To the tyranny of the rich, which he has so often lashed, he now adds the greed and fraud of the traders; and he paints Israel's doom in those shapes of earthquake, eclipse, and famine with which his own generation had recently become familiar. Note that in this first group Amos employs only physical calamities, and says nothing of war and captivity. If the standard which we have already applied to the growth of his doctrine be correct, these ought therefore to be counted among his earlier utterances. War and captivity follow in chap. ix. That is to say, this Third Section follows the same line of development as both the First and the Second.

1. Earthquake, Eclipse, and Famine.

Amos viii. 4-14.

"Hear this, ye who trample the needy, and would put an end to * the lowly of the land, saying, When will the New-Moon be over, that we may sell grain, and the Sabbath, that we may open corn (by making small the measure, but large the weight, and falsifying the fraudulent balances; buying the wretched for silver, and the needy for a pair of shoes!), and that we may sell as grain the refuse of the corn!" The parenthesis puzzles, but is not impossible: in the speed of his scorn, Amos might well interrupt the speech of the merchants by these details of their fraud,† flinging these in their teeth as they spoke. The existence at this date of the New-Moon and Sabbath as days of rest from business is interesting; but even more interesting is the peril to which they lie open. As in the case of the Nazarites and the prophets, we see how the religious institutions and opportunities of the people are threatened by worldliness and greed. And, as in every other relevant passage of the Old Testament, we have the interests of the Sabbath bound up in the same cause with the interests of the poor. The Fourth Commandment enforces the day of rest on behalf of the servants and bondsmen. When a later prophet substitutes for religious fasts the ideals of social service, he weds with the latter the security of the Sabbath from all business.‡ So here Amos emphasises that the Sabbath is threatened by the same worldliness and love of money which tramples on the helpless. The interests of the Sabbath are the interests of the poor: the enemies of the Sabbath are the enemies of the poor. And all this illustrates our Saviour's saying, that "the Sabbath was made for man."

But, as in the rest of the book, judgment again follows hard on sin. "Sworn hath Jehovah by the pride of Jacob, Never shall I forget their deeds." It is as before. The chief spring of the prophet's inspiration is his burning sense of the personal indignation of God against crimes so abominable. God is the God of the poor, and His anger rises, as we see the anger of Christ arise, heavy against their tyrants and oppressors. Such sins are intolerable to Him. But the feeling of their intolerableness is shared by the land itself, the very fabric of nature; the earthquake is the proof of it. "For all this shall not the land tremble and her every inhabitant mourn? and she shall rise like the Nile in mass, and heave and sink like the Nile of Egypt."*

To the earthquake is added the eclipse: one had happened in 803, and another in 763, the memory of which probably inspired the form of this passage. "And it shall be in that day—'tis the oracle of the Lord Jehovah—that I shall bring down the sun at noon, and cast darkness on the earth in broad day.† And I will turn your festivals into mourning, and all your songs to a dirge. And I will bring up upon all loins sackcloth and on every head baldness, and I will make it like the mourning for an only son, and the end of it as a bitter day."

But the terrors of earthquake and eclipse are not sufficient for doom, and famine is drawn upon.

"Lo, days are coming—'tis the oracle of the Lord Jehovah—that I will send famine on the land, not a famine of bread nor a drouth of water, but of hearing the words of Jehovah. And they shall wander from sea to sea, and from the dark North to the Sunrise shall they run to and fro, to seek the word of Jehovah, and they shall not find it; . . . who swear by Samaria's Guilt"—the golden calf in the house of the kingdom at Bethel ‡—"and say, As liveth thy God, O Dan! and, As liveth the way to Beersheba! and they shall fall and not rise any more." I have omitted ver. 13: "in that day shall the fair maids faint and the youths for thirst"; and I append my reasons in a note. Some part of the received text must go, for while vv. 11 and 12 speak of a spiritual drought, the drought of 13 is physical. And ver. 14 follows 12 better than it follows 13. The oaths mentioned by Bethel, Dan, Beersheba, are not specially those of young men and maidens, but of the whole nation, that run from one end of the land to the other, Dan to Beersheba, seeking for some word of Jehovah.§ One of the oaths,

* The phrase is uncertain.

† Wellhausen thinks that the prophet could not have put the parenthesis in the mouth of the traders, and therefore regards it as an intrusion or gloss. But this is hypercriticism. The last clause, however, may be a mere clerical repetition of ii. 6.

‡ Isa. lviii. See the exposition of the passage in the writer's "Isaiah" xl.-lxvi. (Expositor's Bible Series): "Our prophet, while exalting the practical service of man at the expense of certain religious forms, equally exalts the observance of the Sabbath; . . . he places the keeping of the Sabbath on a level with the practice of love."

* "She shall rise," etc.—The clause is almost the same as in ix. 5*b*, and the text differs from the LXX., which omits "and heave." Is it an insertion?

† Literally "in the day of light."

‡ That is, Samaria is used in the wider sense of the kingdom, not the capital, and there is no need for Wellhausen's substitution of Bethel for it.

§ This in answer to Gunning ("De Godspraken van Amos," 1885), Wellh. *in loco*, and König ("Einleitung," p. 304, *d*), who reckon vv. 11 and 12 to be the insertion: the latter on the additional ground that the formula of ver. 13, "in that day," points back to ver. 9; but not to the "Lo, days are coming" of ver. 11. But thus to miss out vv. 11 and 12 leaves us with greater difficulties than before. For without them how are we to explain the "thirst" of ver. 13. It is left unintroduced; there is no hint of a drought in 9 and 10. It seems to me then that, since we must omit some verse, it ought to be ver. 13; and this the rather that if omitted it is not missed. It is just the kind of general statement that would be added by an unthinking scribe; and it does not readily connect with ver. 14, while ver. 12 does do so. For why should youths and

"As liveth the way to Beersheba," * is so curious that some have doubted if the text be correct. But strange as it may appear to us to speak of the life of the lifeless, this often happens among the Semites. To-day Arabs "swear *wa hyât*, 'by the life of,' even of things inanimate; 'By the life of this fire, or of this coffee.'" † And as Amos here tells us that the Israelite pilgrims swore by the way to Beersheba, so do the Moslems affirm their oaths by the sacred way to Mecca.

Thus Amos returns to the chief target of his shafts—the senseless, corrupt worship of the national sanctuaries. And this time—perhaps in remembrance of how they had silenced the word of God when he brought it home to them at Bethel—he tells Israel that, with all their running to and fro across the land, to shrine after shrine in search of the word, they shall suffer from a famine and drouth of it. Perhaps this is the most effective contrast in which Amos has yet placed the stupid ritualism of his people. With so many things to swear by; with so many holy places that once were the homes of Vision, Abraham's Beersheba, Jacob's Bethel, Joshua's Gilgal—nay, a whole land over which God's voice had broken in past ages, lavish as the rain; with, too, all their assiduity of sacrifice and prayer, they should nevertheless starve and pant for that living word of the Lord, which they had silenced in His prophet.

Thus, men may be devoted to religion, may be loyal to their sacred traditions and institutions, may haunt the holy associations of the past and be very assiduous with their ritual—and yet, because of their worldliness, pride, and disobedience, never feel that moral inspiration, that clear call to duty, that comfort in pain, that hope in adversity, that good conscience at all times, which spring up in the heart like living water. Where these be not experienced, orthodoxy, zeal, lavish ritual, are all in vain.

2. Nemesis.

Amos ix. 1-6.

There follows a Vision in Bethel, the opening of which, "I saw the Lord," immediately recalls the great inauguration of Isaiah. He also "saw the Lord"; but how different the Attitude, how other the Word! To the statesman-prophet the Lord is *enthroned*, surrounded by the court of heaven; and though the temple rocks to the intolerable thunder of their praise, they bring to the contrite man beneath the consciousness of a life-long mission. But to Amos the Lord is *standing* and alone—to this lonely prophet God is always alone—and His message may be summed up in its initial word, "Smite." There—Government: hierarchies of service, embassies, clemencies, healings, and though at first devastation, thereafter the indestructible hope of a future. Here—Judgment: that Figure of Fate which terror's fascinated eye ever sees alone; one final blow and irreparable ruin. And so, as with Isaiah we saw how constructive prophecy may be, with Amos we behold only the preparatory havoc, the levelling and clearing of the ground of the future.

"I have seen the Lord standing over the Altar, and He said, Smite the capital"—of the pillar—"that the" very "thresholds * quake, and break them on the head of all of them!" It is a shock that makes the temple reel from roof-tree to basement. The vision seems subsequent to the prophet's visit to Bethel; and it gathers his whole attack on the national worship into one decisive and irreparable blow. "The last of them will I slay with the sword: there shall not flee away of them one fugitive: there shall not escape of them a" single "survivor!" Neither hell nor heaven, mountain-top nor sea-bottom, shall harbour one of them. "If they break through to Sheol, thence shall My hand take them; and if they climb to heaven, thence shall I bring them down. If they hide in Carmel's top, thence will I find them out and fetch them; and if they conceal themselves from before Mine eyes in the bottom of the sea, thence shall I charge the Serpent and he shall bite them; and if they go into captivity before their foes"—to Israel as terrible a distance from God's face as Sheol itself!—"thence will I charge the sword and it shall slay them; and I will set Mine eye upon them for evil and not for good."

It is a ruder draft of the Hundred and Thirty-Ninth Psalm; but the Divine Pursuer is Nemesis, and not Conscience.

"And the Lord, Jehovah of the Hosts; Who toucheth the earth and it melteth, and all its inhabitants mourn, and it rises like the Nile, all of it" together, "and sinks like the Nile of Egypt; Who buildeth His stories in the heavens, and His vault on the earth He foundeth; Who calleth to the waters of the sea and poureth them forth on the face of the earth—Jehovah" of Hosts "is His Name." †

3. The Voices of Another Dawn.

Amos ix. 7-15.

And now we are come to the part where, as it seems, voices of another day mingle with that of Amos, and silence his judgments in the chorus of their unbroken hope. At first, however, it is himself without doubt who speaks. He takes up the now familiar truth, that when it comes to judgment for sin, Israel is no dearer to Jehovah than any other people of His equal Providence.

"Are ye not unto Me, O children of Israel—'tis the oracle of Jehovah—just like the children of Kushites?" mere black folk and far away! "Did I not bring up Israel from Egypt, and the Philistines from Caphtor, and Aram from Ḳir?" Mark again the universal Providence which Amos proclaims: it is the due concomitant of his universal morality. Once for all the religion of Israel breaks from the characteristic Semitic belief that gave a god to every people, and limited both his power and his interests to that people's territory and fortunes. And if we remember how everything spiritual in the reli-

maids be specially singled out as swearing by Samaria, Dan, and Beersheba? These were the oaths of the whole people, to whom vv. 11 and 12 refer. I see a very clear case, therefore, for omitting v. 13.

* LXX. here gives a mere repetition of the preceding oath.

† Doughty: "Arabia Deserta" I. 269.

* Since it is the capital that has been struck, and the command is given to break "the thresholds on the head of all of them," many translate "lintels" or "architraves" instead of "thresholds (*e. g.*, Hitzig, and Guthe in Kautzsch's "Bibel"). But the word ספים always means thresholds, and the blow here is fundamental.

† LXX. adds "of Hosts": on the whole passage see next chapter.

gion of Israel, everything in its significance for mankind, was rendered possible only because at this date it broke from and abjured the particularism in which it had been born, we shall feel some of the Titanic force of the prophet, in whom that break was achieved with an absoluteness which leaves nothing to be desired. But let us also emphasise that it was by no mere method of the intellect or observation of history that Amos was led to assert the unity of the Divine Providence. The inspiration in this was a moral one: Jehovah was ruler and guide of all the families of mankind, because He was exalted in righteousness; and the field in which that righteousness was proved and made manifest was the life and the fate of Israel. Therefore to this Amos now turns. "Lo, the eyes of the Lord Jehovah are on the sinful kingdom, and I will destroy it from the face of the ground." In other words, Jehovah's sovereignty over the world was not proved by Israel's conquest of the latter, but by His unflinching application of the principles of righteousness, at whatever cost, to Israel herself.

Up to this point, then, the voice of Amos is unmistakable, uttering the doctrine, so original to him, that in the judgment of God Israel shall not be specially favoured, and the sentence, we have heard so often from him, of her removal from her land. Remember, Amos has not yet said a word in mitigation of the sentence: up to this point of his book it has been presented as inexorable and final. But now to a statement of it as absolute as any that has gone before, there is suddenly added a qualification: "nevertheless I will not utterly destroy the house of Jacob—'tis the oracle of Jehovah." And then there is added a new picture of exile changed from doom to discipline, a process of sifting by which only the evil in Israel, "all the sinners of My people," shall perish, but not a grain of the good. "For, lo, I am giving command, and I will toss the house of Israel among all the nations, like" something "that is tossed in a sieve, but not a pebble * shall fall to earth. By the sword shall die all the sinners of My people, they who say, The calamity shall not reach nor anticipate us." †

Now as to these qualifications of the hitherto unmitigated judgments of the book, it is to be noted that there is nothing in their language to lead us to take them from Amos himself. On the contrary, the last clause describes what he has always called a characteristic sin of his day. Our only difficulties are that hitherto Amos has never qualified his sentences of doom, and that the change now appears so suddenly that the two halves of the verse in which it does so absolutely contradict each other. Read them again, ver. 8: "Lo, the eyes of the Lord Jehovah are on the sinful nation, and I will destroy it from off the face of the ground—nevertheless destroying I shall not destroy the house of Jacob: 'tis the oracle of Jehovah." Can we believe the same prophet to have uttered at the same time these two statements? And is it possible to believe that prophet to be the hitherto unwavering, unqualifying Amos? Noting these things, let us pass to the rest of the chapter. We break from all shadows; the verses are verses of pure hope. The judgment on Israel is not averted; but having taken place her ruin is regarded as not irreparable.

"In that day"—the day Amos has threatened of overthrow and ruin—"I will raise again the fallen hut of David and will close up its breaches, and his ruins I will raise, and I will build it up as in the days of old,* that they may possess the remnant of Edom and all the nations upon whom My Name has been called"—that is, as once their Possessor—"'tis the oracle of Jehovah, He who is about to do this."

The "fallen hut of David" undoubtedly means the fall of the kingdom of Judah. It is not language Amos uses, or, as it seems to me, could have used, of the fall of the Northern Kingdom only.† Again, it is undoubted that Amos contemplated the fall of Judah: this is implicit in such a phrase as "the whole family that I brought up from Egypt." ‡ He saw then "the day" and "the ruins" of which ver. 11 speaks. The only question is, can we attribute to him the prediction of a restoration of these ruins? And this is a question which must be answered in face of the facts that the rest of his book is unrelieved by a single gleam of hope, and that his threat of the nation's destruction is absolute and final. Now it is significant that in face of those facts Cornill (though he has changed his opinion) once believed it was "surely possible for Amos to include restoration in his prospect of ruin," as (he might have added) other prophets undoubtedly do. I confess I cannot so readily get over the rest of the book and its gloom; and am the less inclined to be sure about these verses being Amos' own that it seems to have been not unusual for later generations, for whom the daystar was beginning to rise, to add their own inspired hopes to the unrelieved threats of their predecessors of the midnight. The mention of Edom does not help us much: in the days of Amos after the partial conquest by Uzziah the promise of "the rest of Edom" was singularly appropriate. On the other hand, what interest had so purely ethical a prophet in the mere addition of territory? To this point we shall have to return for our final decision. We have still the closing oracle—a very pleasant piece of music, as if the birds had come out after the thunderstorm, and the wet hills were glistening in the sunshine.

"Lo, days are coming—'tis the oracle of Jehovah—when the ploughman shall catch up the reaper, and the grape-treader him that streweth the seed." The seasons shall jostle each other, harvest following hard upon seed-time, vintage

* We should have expected "a grain," but the word צְרוֹר only means small stone: *cf.* 2 Sam. xvii. 13. The LXX. has here *σύντριμμα*, fracture, ruin. *Cf.* "Z. A. T. W.," III. 125.

† The text has been disturbed here; the verbs are in forms not possible to the sense. For תַּגִּישׁ read either תַּשִּׂיג with Hitzig or תִּגַּשׁ with Wellhausen. תַּקְדִּים, Hiph., is not impossible in an intransitive sense, but probably Wellhausen is right in reading Pi, תְּקַדֵּם. The reading עדינו which the Greek suggests and Hoffmann and Wellhausen adopt is not so appropriate to the preceding verb as בצדינו of the text.

* The text reads "their breaches," and some accordingly point סֻכֹּת, "hut," as if it were the plural "huts" (Hoffmann, "Z. A. T. W.," 1883, 125; Schwally, *id.*, 1890, 226, n. 1; Guthe in Kautzsch's "Bibel"). The LXX. has the sing., and it is easy to see how the plur. fem. suffix may have risen from confusion with the following conjunction.

† This against Cornill, "Einleitung," 176.

‡ iii. 1.

upon spring. It is that "happy contention of seasons" which Josephus describes as the perpetual blessing of Galilee.* "And the mountains shall drip with new wine, and all the hills shall flow down. And I will bring back the captivity of My people Israel, and they shall build" the "waste cities and dwell" in them, "and plant vineyards and drink the wine thereof, and make gardens and eat their fruits. And I will plant them on their own ground; and they shall not be uprooted any more from their own ground which I have given to them, saith Jehovah thy God." † Again we meet the difficulty: does the voice that speaks here speak with captivity already realised? or is it the voice of one who projects himself forward to a day, which, by the oath of the Lord Himself, is certain to come?

We have now surveyed the whole of this much-doubted, much-defended passage. I have stated fully the arguments on both sides. On the one hand, we have the fact that nothing in the language of the verses, and nothing in their historical allusions, precludes their being by Amos; we have also to admit that, having threatened a day of ruin, it was possible for Amos to realise by his mind's eye its arrival, and standing at that point to see the sunshine flooding the ruins and to prophesy a restoration. In all this there is nothing impossible in itself or inconsistent with the rest of the book. On the other hand, we have the impressive and incommensurable facts: *first*, that this change to hope comes suddenly, without preparation and without statement of reasons, at the very end of a book whose characteristics are not only a final and absolute sentence of ruin upon the people, and an outlook of unrelieved darkness, but scornful discouragement of every popular vision of a prosperous future; and, *second*, that the prophetic books contain numerous signs that later generations wove their own brighter hopes into the abrupt and hopeless conclusions of prophecies of judgment.

To this balance of evidence is there anything to add? I think there is; and that it decides the question. All these prospects of the future restoration of Israel are absolutely without a moral feature. They speak of return from captivity, of political restoration, of supremacy over the Gentiles, and of a revived Nature, hanging with fruit, dripping with must. Such hopes are natural and legitimate to a people who were long separated from their devastated and neglected land, and whose punishment and penitence were accomplished. But they are not natural to a prophet like Amos. Imagine him predicting a future like this! Imagine him describing the consummation of his people's history, without mentioning one of those moral triumphs to rally his people to which his whole passion and energy had been devoted. To me it is impossible to hear the voice that cried, "Let justice roll on like waters and righteousness like a perennial stream," in a peroration which is content to tell of mountains dripping with must and of a people satisfied with vineyards and gardens. These are legitimate hopes; but they are the hopes of a generation of other conditions and of other deserts than the generation of Amos.

*III. "Wars," x. 8. With the above verses of the Book of Amos Lev. xxvi. 5 has been compared: "your threshing shall reach to the vintage and the vintage to the sowing time." But there is no reason to suppose that either of two so natural passages depends on the other.

† LXX. "God of Hosts."

If then the gloom of this great book is turned into light, such a change is not due to Amos.

CHAPTER XI.

COMMON-SENSE AND THE REIGN OF LAW.

AMOS iii. 3-8; iv. 6-13; v. 8, 9; vi. 12; viii. 8; ix. 5, 6.

FOOLS, when they face facts, which is seldom, face them one by one, and, as a consequence, either in ignorant contempt or in panic. With this inordinate folly Amos charged the religion of his day. The superstitious people, careful of every point of ritual and very greedy of omens, would not ponder real facts nor set cause to effect. Amos recalled them to common life. "Does a bird fall upon a snare, except there be a loop on her? Does the trap itself rise from the ground, except it be catching something"—something alive in it that struggles, and so lifts the trap? "Shall the alarum be blown in a city, and the people not tremble?" Daily life is impossible without putting two and two together. But this is just what Israel will not do with the sacred events of their time. To religion they will not add common-sense.

For Amos himself, all things which happen are in sequence and in sympathy. He has seen this in the simple life of the desert; he is sure of it throughout the tangle and hubbub of history. One thing explains another; one makes another inevitable. When he has illustrated the truth in common life, Amos claims it for especially four of the great facts of the time. The sins of society, of which society is careless; the physical calamities, which they survive and forget; the approach of Assyria, which they ignore; the word of the prophet, which they silence,—all these belong to each other. Drought, Pestilence, Earthquake, Invasion conspire—and the Prophet holds their secret.

Now it is true that for the most part Amos describes this sequence of events as the personal action of Jehovah. "Shall evil befall, and Jehovah not have done it? . . . I have smitten you. . . . I will raise up against you a Nation. . . . Prepare to meet thy God, O Israel!" * Yet even where the personal impulse of the Deity is thus emphasised, we feel equal stress laid upon the order and the inevitable certainty of the process. Amos nowhere uses Isaiah's great phrase: "a God of Mishpat," a "God of Order" or "Law." But he means almost the same thing: God works by methods which irresistibly fulfil themselves. Nay more. Sometimes this sequence sweeps upon the prophet's mind with such force as to overwhelm all his sense of the Personal within it. The Will and the Word of the God who causes the thing are crushed out by the "Must Be" of the thing itself. Take even the descriptions of those historical crises, which the prophet most explicitly proclaims as the visitations of the Almighty. In some of the verses all thought of God Himself is lost in the roar and foam with which that tide of necessity bursts up through them. The fountains of the great deep break loose, and while the universe trembles to the shock, it seems that even the voice of the Deity is overwhelmed. In one passage, immediately

* iii. 6 *b*; iv. 9; vi. 14; iv. 12 *b*.

after describing Israel's ruin as due to Jehovah's word, Amos asks how could it have happened otherwise:—

"Shall horses run up a cliff, or oxen plough the sea? that ye turn justice into poison, and the fruit of righteousness into wormwood."* A moral order exists, which it is as impossible to break without disaster as it would be to break the natural order by driving horses upon a precipice. There is an inherent necessity in the sinners' doom. Again, he says of Israel's sin: "Shall not the Land tremble for this? Yea, it shall rise up together like the Nile, and heave and sink like the Nile of Egypt."† The crimes of Israel are so intolerable, that in its own might the natural frame of things revolts against them. In these great crises, therefore, as in the simple instances adduced from everyday life, Amos had a sense of what we call law, distinct from, and for moments even overwhelming, that sense of the personal purpose of God, admission to the secrets of which had marked his call to be a prophet.‡

These instincts we must not exaggerate into a system. There is no philosophy in Amos, nor need we wish there were. Far more instructive is what we do find—a virgin sense of the sympathy of all things, the thrill rather than the theory of a universe. And this faith, which is not a philosophy, is especially instructive on these two points: that it springs from the moral sense; and that it embraces, not history only, but nature.

It springs from the moral sense. Other races have arrived at a conception of the universe along other lines: some by the observation of physical laws valid to the recesses of space; some by logic and the unity of Reason. But Israel found the universe through the conscience. It is a historical fact that the Unity of God, the Unity of History, and the Unity of the World, did, in this order, break upon Israel, through conviction and experience of the universal sovereignty of righteousness. We see the beginnings of the process in Amos. To him the sequences which work themselves out through history and across nature are moral. Righteousness is the hinge on which the world hangs; loosen it, and history and nature feel the shock. History punishes the sinful nation. But nature, too, groans beneath the guilt of man; and in the Drought, the Pestilence, and the Earthquake provides his scourges. It is a belief which has stamped itself upon the language of mankind. What else is "plague" than "blow" or "scourge"?

This brings us to the second point—our prophet's treatment of Nature.

Apart from the disputed passages (which we shall take afterwards by themselves) we have in the Book of Amos few glimpses of nature, and these always under a moral light. There is not in any chapter a landscape visible in its own beauty. Like all desert-dwellers, who when they would praise the works of God lift their eyes to the heavens, Amos gives us but the outlines of the earth—a mountain range,§ or the crest of a forest,‖ or the bare back of the land, bent from sea to sea.¶ Nearly all his figures are drawn from the desert—the torrent, the wild beasts, the wormwood.* If he visits the meadows of the shepherds, it is with the terror of the people's doom;† if the vineyards or orchards, it is with the mildew and the locust;‡ if the towns, it is with drought, eclipse, and earthquake.§ To him, unlike his fellows, unlike especially Hosea, the whole land is one theatre of judgment; but it is a theatre trembling to its foundations with the drama enacted upon it. Nay, land and nature are themselves actors in the drama. Physical forces are inspired with moral purpose, and become the ministers of righteousness. This is the converse of Elijah's vision. To the older prophet the message came that God was not in the fire nor in the earthquake nor in the tempest, but only in the still small voice. But to Amos the fire, the earthquake, and the tempest are all in alliance with the Voice, and execute the doom which it utters. The difference will be appreciated by us, if we remember the respective problems set to prophecy in those two periods. To Elijah, prophet of the elements, wild worker by fire and water, by life and death, the spiritual had to be asserted and enforced by itself. Ecstatic as he was, Elijah had to learn that the Word is more Divine than all physical violence and terror. But Amos understood that for his age the question was very different. Not only was the God of Israel dissociated from the powers of nature, which were assigned by the popular mind to the various Ba'alim of the land, so that there was a divorce between His government of the people and the influences that fed the people's life; but morality itself was conceived as provincial. It was narrowed to the national interests; it was summed up in mere rules of police, and these were looked upon as not so important as the observances of the ritual. Therefore Amos was driven to show that nature and morality are one. Morality is not a set of conventions. "Morality is the order of things." Righteousness is on the scale of the universe. All things tremble to the shock of sin; all things work together for good to them that fear God.

With this sense of law, of moral necessity, in Amos we must not fail to connect that absence of all appeal to miracle, which is also conspicuous in his book.

We come now to the three disputed passages:—

iv. 13:—"For, lo! He Who formed the hills,‖ and createth the wind,¶ and declareth to man what His ** mind is; Who maketh the dawn into darkness, and marcheth on the heights of the land—Jehovah, God of Hosts, is His Name."

v. 8, 9:—"Maker of the Pleiades and Orion,†† turning to morning the murk, and day into night He darkeneth; Who calleth for the waters of the sea, and poureth them forth on the face of the earth—Jehovah His Name; Who flasheth ruin on the strong, and destruction cometh down on the fortress."‡‡

ix. 5, 6:—"And the Lord Jehovah of the Hosts, Who toucheth the earth and it rocketh, and all mourn that dwell on it, and it riseth like the Nile together, and sinketh like the Nile of Egypt; Who hath builded in the heavens His ascents, and founded His vault upon the earth;

* vi. 12.
† viii. 8.
‡ iii. 7: "Jehovah God doeth nothing, but He hath revealed His secret to His servants the prophets."
§ i. 2; iii. 9; ix. 3. ‖ ii. 9. ¶ viii. 12.

* v. 24; 19, 20, etc.; 7; vi. 12.
† i. 2.
‡ iv. 9 ff.
§ iv. 6–11; vi. 11; viii. 8 ff.
‖ LXX. "the thunder."
¶ Or "spirit."
** *I. e.*, "God's;" a more natural rendering than to take "his" (as Hitzig does) as meaning "man's."
†† See above, pp. 484 f. *n.*
‡‡ Text of last clause uncertain; see above, p. 484.

Who calleth to the waters of the sea, and poureth them on the face of the earth—Jehovah * His Name."

These sublime passages it is natural to take as the triple climax of the doctrine we have traced through the Book of Amos. Are they not the natural leap of the soul to the stars? The same shepherd's eye which has marked sequence and effect unfailing on the desert soil, does it not now sweep the clear heavens above the desert, and find there also all things ordered and arrayed? The same mind which traced the Divine processes down history, which foresaw the hosts of Assyria marshalled for Israel's punishment, which felt the overthrow of justice shock the nation to their ruin, and read the disasters of the husbandman's year as the vindication of a law higher than the physical—does it not now naturally rise beyond such instances of the Divine order, round which the dust of history rolls, to the lofty, undimmed outlines of the Universe as a whole, and, in consummation of its message, declare that "all is Law," and Law intelligible to man?

But in the way of so attractive a conclusion the literary criticism of the book has interposed. It is maintained† that, while none of these sublime verses are indispensable to the argument of Amos, some of them actually interrupt it, so that when they are removed it becomes consistent; that such ejaculations in praise of Jehovah's creative power are not elsewhere met with in Hebrew prophecy before the time of the Exile; that they sound very like echoes of the Book of Job; and that in the Septuagint version of Hosea we actually find a similar doxology, wedged into the middle of an authentic verse of the prophet.‡ To these arguments against the genuineness of the three famous passages, other critics, not less able and not less free, like Robertson Smith and Kuenen,§ have replied that such ejaculations at critical points of the prophet's discourse "are not surprising under the general conditions of prophetic oratory"; and that, while one of the doxologies does appear to break the argument ‖ of the context, they are all of them thoroughly in the spirit and the style of Amos. To this point the discussion has been carried; it seems to need a closer examination.

We may at once dismiss the argument which has been drawn from that obvious intrusion into the Greek of Hosea xiii. 4. Not only is this verse not so suited to the doctrine of Hosea as the doxologies are to the doctrine of Amos; but while they are definite and sublime, it is formal and flat—"Who made firm the heavens and founded the earth, Whose hands founded all the host of heaven, and He did not display them that thou shouldest walk after them." The passages in Amos are vision; this is a piece of catechism crumbling into homily.

Again—an argument in favour of the authenticity of these passages may be drawn from the character of their subjects. We have seen the part which the desert played in shaping the temper and the style of Amos. But the works of the Creator, to which these passages lift their praise, are just those most fondly dwelt upon by all the poetry of the desert. The Arabian nomad, when he magnifies the power of God, finds his subjects not on the bare earth about him, but in the brilliant heavens and the heavenly processes.

Again, the critic who affirms that the passages in Amos "in every case sensibly disturb the connection," * exaggerates. In the case of the first of them, chap. iv. 13, the disturbance is not at all "sensible"; though it must be admitted that the oracle closes impressively enough without it. The last of them, chap. ix. 5, 6—which repeats a clause already found in the book †—is as much in sympathy with its context as most of the oracles in the somewhat scattered discourse of that last section of the book. The real difficulty is the second doxology, chap. v. 8, 9, which does break the connection, and in a sudden and violent way. Remove it, and the argument is consistent. We cannot read chap. v. without feeling that, whether Amos wrote these verses or not, they did not originally stand where they stand at present.

Now, taken with this dispensableness of two of the passages and this obvious intrusion of one of them, the following additional fact becomes ominous. "Jehovah is His Name" (which occurs in two of the passages),‡ or "Jehovah of Hosts is His Name" (which occurs at least in one),§ is a construction which does not happen elsewhere in the book, except in a verse where it is awkward and where we have already seen reason to doubt its genuineness.‖ But still more, the phrase does not occur in any other prophet, till we come down to the oracles which compose Isaiah xl.-lxvi. Here it happens thrice —twice in passages dating from the Exile,¶ and once in a passage suspected by some to be of still later date.** In the Book of Jeremiah the phrase is found eight times; but either in passages already on other grounds judged by many critics to be later than Jeremiah,†† or where by itself it is probably an intrusion into the text.‡‡ Now is it a mere coincidence that a phrase, which, outside the Book of Amos, occurs only in writing of the time of the Exile and in passages considered for other reasons to be post-exilic insertions—is it a mere coincidence that within the Book of Amos it should again be found only in suspected verses?

There appears to be in this more than a coincidence; and the present writer cannot but feel a very strong case against the traditional belief that these doxologies are original and integral portions of the Book of Amos. At the same time a case which has failed to convince critics like Robertson Smith and Kuenen cannot be considered conclusive, and we are so ignorant of many of the conditions of prophetic oratory at this period that dogmatism is impossible. For instance, the use by Amos of the Divine titles is a matter over which uncertainty still lingers;

* LXX. "Jehovah of Hosts."

† First in 1875 by Duhm, "Theol. der Proph.," p. 119; and after him by Oort, "Theol. Tjidschrift.," 1880, pp. 116 f.; Wellhausen, *in locis*: Stade "Gesch.," I. 571; Cornill, "Einletung," 176.

‡ Hosea xiii. 4.

§ Smith, "Prophets of Israel," p. 399; Kuenen, "Hist. Krit. Einl." (Germ. Ed.), II. 347.

‖ v. 8, 9.

* Cornill, "Einl.," 176.

† *Cf.* viii. 8.

‡ v. 8; ix. 6, though here LXX. read "Jehovah of Hosts is His Name."

§ iv. 13. See previous note.

‖ v. 27. See above, pp. 485 f. *n.*: *cf.* Hosea xii. 6.

¶ xlvii. 4 and liv. 5.

** xlviii. 2: *cf.* Duhm, *in loco*, and Cheyne, "Introduction to the Book of Isaiah," 301.

†† x. 16; xxxi. 35; xxxii. 18; l. 34 (perhaps a quotation from Isa. xlvii. 4); li. 19, 57.

‡‡ xlvi. 18, where the words צבאות שמו fail in LXX.; xlviii. 15 *b*, where the clause in which it occurs is wanting in the LXX.

and any further argument on the subject must include a fuller discussion than space here allows of the remarkable distribution of those titles throughout the various sections of the book.*

But if it be not given to us to prove this kind of authenticity—a question whose data are so obscure, yet whose answer frequently is of so little significance—let us gladly welcome that greater Authenticity whose undeniable proofs these verses so splendidly exhibit. No one questions their right to the place which some great spirit gave them in this book—their suitableness to its grand and ordered theme, their pure vision and their eternal truth. That common-sense, and that conscience, which, moving among the events of earth and all the tangled processes of history, find everywhere reason and righteousness at work, in these verses claim the Universe for the same powers, and see in stars and clouds and the procession of day and night the One Eternal God Who "declareth to man what His mind is."

HOSEA.

"For leal love have I desired and not sacrifice
And the knowledge of God rather than burnt-offerings."

CHAPTER XII.

THE BOOK OF HOSEA.

THE Book of Hosea consists of two unequal sections, chaps. i.-iii. and chaps. iv.-xiv., which differ in the dates of their standpoints, to a large extent also in the details of their common subjects, but still more largely in their form and style. The First Section is the main narrative; though the style rises to the pitch of passionate pleading and promise, it is fluent and equable. If one verse be omitted and three others transposed,* the argument is continuous. In the Second Section, on the contrary, we have a stream of addresses and reflections, appeals, upbraidings, sarcasms, recollections of earlier history, denunciations and promises, which, with little logical connection and almost no pauses or periods, start impulsively from each other, and for a large part are expressed in elliptic and ejaculatory phrases. In the present restlessness of Biblical Criticism it would have been surprising if this difference of style had not prompted some minds to a difference of authorship. Grätz† has distinguished two Hoseas, separated by a period of fifty years. But if, as we shall see, the First Section reflects the end of the reign of Jeroboam II., who died about 743, then the next few years, with their revolutionary changes in Israel, are sufficient to account for the altered outlook of the Second Section; while the altered style is fully explained by difference of occasion and motive. In both sections not only are the religious principles identical, and many of the characteristic expressions,‡ but there breathes throughout the same urgent and jealous temper which renders Hosea's personality so distinctive among the prophets. Within this unity, of course, we must not be surprised to find, as in the Book of Amos, verses which cannot well be authentic.

FIRST SECTION: HOSEA'S PROPHETIC LIFE.

With the removal of some of the verses the argument becomes clear and consecutive. After the story of the wife and children (i. 2-9), who are symbols of the land and people of Israel in their apostasy from God (2, 4, 6, 9), the Divine voice calls on the living generation to plead with their mother lest destruction come (ii. 2-5, Eng.; ii. 4-7, Heb.§), but then passes definite sentence of desolation on the land and of exile on the people (6-13, Eng.; 8-15, Heb.), which, however, is not final doom, but discipline,‖ with the ultimate promise of the return of the nation's youth, their renewed betrothal to Jehovah and the restoration of nature (14-23). Then follows the story of the prophet's restoration of his wife, also with discipline (chap. iii.).

Notice that, although the story of the wife's fall has preceded the declaration of Israel's apostasy, it is Israel's restoration which precedes the wife's. The ethical significance of this order we shall illustrate in the next chapter.

In this section the disturbing verses are i. 7

* But I have room at least for a bare statement of these remarkable facts:

The titles for the God of Israel used in the Book of Amos are these: (1) "Thy God, O Israel," אלהיך ישראל; (2) "Jehovah, יהוה; (3) "Lord Jehovah," אדני יהוה; (4) "Lord Jehovah of the Hosts," אדני יהוה צבאות; (5) "Jehovah God of Hosts" or "of the Hosts," יהוה אלהי צבאות or הצבאות.

Now in the First Section, chaps. i., ii., it is interesting that we find none of the variations which are compounded with "Hosts," צבאות. By itself יהוה (especially in the phrase "Thus saith Jehovah," כה אמר יהוה) is general; and once only (i. 8) is "Lord Jehovah" employed. The phrase, "oracle of Jehovah," נְאֻם יהוה, is also rare; it occurs only twice (ii. 11, 16), and then only in the passage dealing with Israel, and not at all in the oracles against foreign nations.

In Sections II. and III. the simple יהוה is again most frequently used. But we find also "Lord Jehovah," אדני יהוה (iii. 7, 8; iv. 2, 5; v. 3, with יהוה alone in the parallel ver 4; vi. 8; vii. 1, 2, 4 *bis*, 5, 6; viii. 1, 3, 9, 11), used either indifferently with יהוה; or in verses where it seems more natural to emphasise the sovereignty of Jehovah than His simple Name (as, *e. g.*, where "He swears," iv. 2, vi. 8, yet when the same phrase occurs in viii. 7 יהוה alone is used); or in the solemn Visions of the Third Section (but not in the Narrative); and sometimes we find in the Visions "Lord," אדני, alone without יהוה (vii. 7, 8; ix. 1). The titles containing צבאות or אלהי צבאות occur *nine* times. Of these *five* are in passages which we have seen other reasons to suppose are insertions: two of the Doxologies—iv. 13, יהוה אלהי צבאות, and ix. 5, אדני יהוה הצבאות (in addition the LXX. read in ix. 6 יהוה צבאות), and in v. 14, 15 (see p. 484) and 27 (see p. 485), in all three יהוה אלהי צבאות. The *four* genuine passages are iii. 13, where we find יהוה אלהי הצבאות preceded by אדני; v. 16, where we have יהוה אלהי צבאות followed by אדני; vi. 8, יהוה אלהי צבאות, and vi. 14, יהוה אלהי צבאות. Throughout the last two sections of the book נְאֻם is used with all these forms of the Divine title.

* See below, pp. 495 f.

† "Geschichte," pp. 93 ff., 214 ff., 439 f.

‡ A list of the more obvious is given by Kuenen, p. 324.

§ The first chapter in the Hebrew closes with ver. 9.

‖ *Cf.* this with Amos; above, pp. 490 ff.

and the group of three—i. 10, 11, ii. 1 (Eng.; but ii. 1-3 Heb.). Chap. i. 7 introduces Judah as excepted from the curse passed upon Israel; it is so obviously intrusive in a prophecy dealing only with Israel, and it so clearly reflects the deliverance of Judah from Sennacherib in 701, that we cannot hold it for anything but an insertion of a date subsequent to that deliverance, and introduced by a pious Jew to signalise Judah's fate in contrast with Israel's.*

The other three verses (i. 10, 11, ii. 1, Eng.; ii. 1-3, Heb.) introduce a promise of restoration before the sentence of judgment is detailed, or any ethical conditions of restoration are stated. That is, they break and tangle an argument otherwise consistent and progressive from beginning to end of the Section. Every careful reader must feel them out of place where they lie. Their awkwardness has been so much appreciated that, while in the Hebrew text they have been separated from chap. i., in the Greek they have been separated from chap. ii. That is to say, some have felt they have no connection with what precedes them, others none with what follows them; while our English version, by distributing them between the two chapters, only makes more sensible their superfluity. If they really belong to the prophecy, their proper place is after the last verse of chap. ii.† This is actually the order in which part of it and part of them are quoted by St. Paul.‡ At the same time, when so arranged, they repeat somewhat awkwardly the language of ii. 23, and scarcely form a climax to the chapter. There is nothing in their language to lead us to doubt that they are Hosea's own; and ver. 11 shows that they must have been written at least before the captivity of Northern Israel.§

The only other suspected clause in this section is that in iii. 5, "and David their king;" ‖ but if it be struck out the verse is rendered awkward, if not impossible, by the immediate repetition of the Divine name, which would not have been required in the absence of the suspected clause.¶

The text of the rest of the section is remarkably free from obscurities. The Greek version offers few variants, and most of these are due to mistranslation.** In iii. 1 for "loved of a husband" it reads "loving evil."

Evidently this section was written before the death of Jeroboam II. The house of Jehu still reigns; and as Hosea predicts its fall by war on the classic battle-ground of Jezreel, the prophecy must have been written before the actual fall, which took the form of an internal revolt against Zechariah, the son of Jeroboam. With this agrees the tone of the section. There are the same evils in Israel which Amos exposed in the prosperous years of the same reign; but Hosea appears to realise the threatened exile from a nearer standpoint. It is probable also that part of the reason of his ability to see his way through the captivity to the people's restoration is due to a longer familiarity with the approach of captivity than Amos experienced before he wrote. But, of course, for Hosea's promise of restoration there were, as we shall see, other and greater reasons of a religious kind.*

* König's arguments ("Einleitung," 309) in favour of the possibility of the genuineness of the verse do not seem to me to be conclusive. He thinks the verse admissible because Judah had sinned less than Israel; the threat in vv. 4-6 is limited to Israel; the phrase "Jehovah their God" is so peculiar that it is difficult to assign it to a mere expander of the text; and if it was a later hand that put in the verse, why did he not alter the judgments against Judæa, which occur further on in the book?

† So Cheyne and others, Kuenen adhering. König agrees that they have been removed from their proper place and the text corrupted.

‡ Rom. ix. 25, 26, which first give the end of Hosea ii. 23 (Heb. 25), and then the end of i. 10 (Heb. ii. 2). See below, p. 504, *n.*

§ 721 B. C.

‖ Stade, "Gesch.," I. 577; Cornill, "Einleitung," who also would exclude "no king and no prince," in iii. 4.

¶ This objection, however, does not hold against the removal of merely "and David," leaving "their king."

** ii. 7, 11, 14, 17 (Heb.). In i. 4 B-text reads Ἰούδα for יהוא while Qmq have Ἰηου.

* In determining the date of the Book of Hosea the title in chap. i. is of no use to us: "The Word of Jehovah which was to Hosea ben Be'eri in the days of Uzziah, Jotham, Ahaz, Hezekiah, kings of Judah, and in the days of Jeroboam ben Joash, king of Israel." This title is trebly suspicious. First: the given reigns of Judah and Israel do not correspond; Jeroboam was dead before Uzziah. Second: there is no proof either in the First or Second Section of the book that Hosea prophesied after the reign of Jotham. Third: it is curious that in the case of a prophet of Northern Israel kings of Judah should be stated first, and four of them be given while only one king of his own country is placed beside them. On these grounds critics are probably correct who take the title as it stands to be the work of some later Judæan scribe who sought to make it correspond to the titles of the Books of Isaiah and Micah. He may have been the same who added chap. i. 7. The original form of the title probably was "The Word of God which was to Hosea son of Be'erî in the days of Jeroboam ben Joash, king of Israel," and designed only for the First Section of the book, chaps. i.-iii.

Second Section: Chaps. IV.-XIV.

When we pass into these chapters we feel that the times are changed. The dynasty of Jehu has passed: kings are falling rapidly: Israel devours its rulers:† there is no loyalty to the king; he is suddenly cut off;‡ all the princes are revolters.§ Round so despised and so unstable a throne the nation tosses in disorder. Conspiracies are rife. It is not only, as in Amos, the sins of the luxurious, of them that are at ease in Zion, which are exposed; but also literal bloodshed: highway robbery with murder, abetted by the priests; ‖ the thief breaketh in and the robber-troop maketh a raid.¶ Amos looked out on foreign nations across a quiet Israel; his views of the world are wide and clear; but in the Book of Hosea the dust is up, and into what is happening beyond the frontier we get only glimpses. There is enough, however, to make visible another great change since the days of Jeroboam. Israel's self-reliance is gone. She is as fluttered as a startled bird: "They call unto Egypt, they go unto Assyria.** Their wealth is carried as a gift to King Jareb,†† and they evidently engage in intrigues with Egypt. But everything is hopeless: kings cannot save, for Ephraim is seized by the pangs of a fatal crisis.‡‡

This broken description reflects—and all the more faithfully because of its brokenness—the ten years which followed on the death of Jeroboam II. about 743.§§ His son Zechariah, who

† vii. 7. There are also other passages which, while they may be referred, as they stand, to the whole succession of illegitimate dynasties in Northern Israel from the beginning to the end of that kingdom, more probably reflect the same ten years of special anarchy and disorder after the death of Jeroboam II. See vii. 3 ff.; viii. 4, where the illegitimate king-making is coupled with the idolatry of the Northern Kingdom; xiii. 10, 11.

‡ x. 3, 7, 8, 15.

§ ix. 15.

‖ vi. 8, 9.

¶ vii. 1.

** vii. 11.

†† x. 6.

‡‡ xiii. 121.

§§ The chronology of these years is exceedingly uncertain. Jeroboam was dead about 743; in 738 Menahem gave tribute to Assyria; in 734 Tiglath-Pileser had conquered Aram, Gilead, and Galilee in response to King

succeeded him, was in six months assassinated by Shallum ben Jabesh, who within a month more was himself cut down by Menahem ben Gadi.* Menahem held the throne for six or seven years, but only by sending to the King of Assyria an enormous tribute which he exacted from the wealthy magnates of Israel.† Discontent must have followed these measures, such discontent with their rulers as Hosea describes. Pekahiah ben Menahem kept the throne for little over a year after his father's death, and was assassinated by his captain,‡ Pekah ben Remaliah, with fifty Gileadites, and Pekah took the throne about 736. This second and bloody usurpation may be one of those on which Hosea dwells; but if so it is the last historical allusion in his book. There is no reference to the war of Pekah and Rezin against Ahaz of Judah which Isaiah describes,§ and to which Hosea must have alluded had he been still prophesying.‖ There is no allusion to its consequence in Tiglath-Pileser's conquest of Gilead and Galilee in 734-733. On the contrary, these provinces are still regarded as part of the body politic of Israel.¶ Nor is there any sign that Israel have broken with Assyria; to the last the book represents them as fawning on the Northern Power.**

In all probability, then, the Book of Hosea was closed before 734 B. C. The Second Section dates from the years behind that and back to the death of Jeroboam II. about 743, while the First Section, as we saw, reflects the period immediately before the latter.

We come now to the general style of chaps. iv.-xiv. The period, as we have seen, was one of the most broken of all the history of Israel; the political outlook, the temper of the people, were constantly changing. Hosea, who watched these kaleidoscopes, had himself an extraordinarily mobile and vibrant mind. There could be no greater contrast to that fixture of conscience which renders the Book of Amos so simple in argument, so firm in style.†† It was a leaden plummet which Amos saw Jehovah setting to the structure of Israel's life.‡‡ But Hosea felt his own heart hanging at the end of the line; and this was a heart that could never be still. Amos is the prophet of law; he sees the Divine processes work themselves out, irrespective of the moods and intrigues of the people, with which, after all, he was little familiar. So each of his paragraphs moves steadily forward to a climax, and every climax is Doom—the captivity of the people to Assyria. You can divide his book by these things; it has its periods, strophes, and refrains. It marches like the hosts of the Lord of Hosts. But Hosea had no such unhampered vision of great laws. He was too familiar with the rapid changes of his fickle people; and his affection for them was too anxious. His style has all the restlessness and irritableness of hunger about it—the hunger of love. Hosea's eyes are never at rest. He seeks, he welcomes, for moments of extraordinary fondness he dwells upon every sign of his people's repentance. But a Divine jealousy succeeds, and he questions the motives of the change. You feel that his love has been overtaken and surprised by his knowledge; and in fact his whole style might be described as a race between the two—a race varying and uncertain up to almost the end. The transitions are very swift. You come upon a passage of exquisite tenderness: the prophet puts the people's penitence in his own words with a sympathy and poetry that are sublime and seem final. But suddenly he remembers how false they are, and there is another light in his eyes. The lustre of their tears dies from his verses, like the dews of a midsummer morning in Ephraim; and all is dry and hard again beneath the brazen sun of his amazement. "What shall I do unto thee, Ephraim? What shall I do unto thee, Judah?" Indeed, this figure of his own is insufficient to express the suddenness with which Hosea lights up some intrigue of the statesmen of the day, or some evil habit of the priests, or some hidden orgy of the common people. Rather than the sun it is the lightning—the lightning in pursuit of a serpent.

The elusiveness of the style is the greater that many passages do not seem to have been prepared for public delivery. They are more the play of the prophet's mind than his set speech. They are not formally addressed to an audience, and there is no trace in them of oratorical art.

Hence the language of this Second Section of the Book of Hosea is impulsive and abrupt beyond all comparison. There is little rhythm in it, and almost no argument. Few metaphors are elaborated. Even the brief parallelism of Hebrew poetry seems too long for the quick spasms of the writer's heart. "Osee," said Jerome,* "commaticus est, et quasi per sententias loquitur." He speaks in little clauses, often broken off; he is impatient even of copulas. And withal he uses a vocabulary full of strange words, which the paucity of parallelism makes much the more difficult.

To this original brokenness and obscurity of the language are due, *first*, the great corruption of the text; *second*, the difficulty of dividing it; *third*, the uncertainty of deciding its genuineness or authenticity.

1. The Text of Hosea is one of the most dilapidated in the Old Testament, and in parts beyond possibility of repair. It is probable that glosses were found necessary at an earlier period

Ahaz, who had a year or two before been attacked by Rezin of Aram and Pekah of Israel.

* 2 Kings xv. 8-16. It may be to this appearance of three kings within one month that there was originally an allusion in the now obscure verse of Hosea, v. 7.

† 2 Kings xv. 17-22.

‡ Or prince, שַׂר; *cf.* Hosea's denunciation of the שָׂרִים as rebels.

§ Isa. vii.; 2 Kings xv. 37, 38.

‖ Some have found a later allusion in chap. x, 14: "like unto the destruction" of (?) "Shalman (of?) "Beth' Arbe'l." Pusey, p. 5 *b*, and others take this to allude to a destruction of the Galilean Arbela, the modern Irbid, by Salmanassar IV., who ascended the Assyrian throne in 727 and besieged Samaria in 724 ff. But since the construction of the phrase leaves it doubtful whether the name Shalman is that of the agent or object of the destruction, and whether, if the agent, he be one of the Assyrian Salmanassars or a Moabite King Salman (*c.* 730 B. C.), it is impossible to make use of the verse in fixing the date of the Book of Hosea. See further, p. 514. Wellhausen omits.

¶ v. 1; vi. 8; xii. 12: *cf.* W. R. Smith, "Prophets," 156.

** *Cf.* W. R. Smith, *l. c.*

†† *Cf.* W. R. Smith, "Prophets," 157: Hosea's "language and the movement of his thoughts are far removed from the simplicity and self-control which characterise the prophecy of Amos. Indignation and sorrow, tenderness and severity, faith in the sovereignty of Jehovah's love, and a despairing sense of Israel's infidelity are woven together in a sequence which has no logical plan, but is determined by the battle and alternate victory of contending emotions; and the swift transitions, the fragmentary unbalanced utterance, the half-developed allusions, that make his prophecy so difficult to the commentator, express the agony of this inward conflict."

‡‡ See above, p. 470.

* "Præf. in Duod. Prophetas."

and to a larger extent than in most other books: there are evident traces of some; yet it is not always possible to disentangle them.* The value of the Greek version is curiously mixed. The authors had before them much the same difficulties as we have, and they made many more for themselves. Some of their mistranslations are outrageous: they occur not only in obscure passages, where they may be pardoned;† but even where there are parallel terms with which the translators show themselves familiar.‡ Sometimes they have translated word by word, without any attempt to give the general sense; and as a whole their version is devoid both of beauty and compactness. Yet not infrequently they supply us with a better reading than the Massoretic text. Occasionally they divide words properly which the latter misdivides.§ They often give more correctly the easily confused pronominal suffixes;‖ and the copula.¶ And they help us to the true readings of many other words.** Here and there an additional clause in the Greek is plethoric, perhaps copied by mistake from a similar verse in the context.†† All of these will be noticed separately as we reach them. But, even after these and other aids, we shall find that the text not infrequently remains impracticable.

2. As great as the difficulty of reaching a true text in this Second Section of the book is the difficulty of Dividing it. Here and there, it is true, the Greek helps us to improve upon the division into chapters and verses of the Hebrew text, which is that of our own English version. Chap. vi. 1-4 ought to follow immediately on to the end of chap. v., with the connecting word "saying." The last few words of chap. vi. go with the first two of chap. vii., but perhaps both are gloss. The openings of chaps. xi. and xii. are better arranged in the Hebrew than in the Greek. As regards verses we shall have to make several rearrangements.‡‡ But beyond this more or less conventional division into chapters and verses our confidence ceases. It is impossible to separate the section, long as it is, into subsections, or into oracles, strophes, or periods. The reason of this we have already seen, in the turbulence of the period reflected, in the divided interest and abrupt and emotional style of the author, and in the probability that part at least of the book was not prepared for public speaking. The periods and climaxes, the refrains, the catchwords by which we are helped to divide even the confused Second Section of the Book of Amos, are not found in Hosea. Only twice does the exordium of a spoken address occur: at the beginning of the section (chap. iv. 1), and at what is now the opening of the next chapter (v. 1). The phrase "'tis the oracle of Jehovah," which occurs so periodically in Amos, and thrice in the second chapter of Hosea, is found only once in chaps. iv.-xiv. Again, the obvious climaxes or perorations, of which we found so many in Amos, are very few,* and even when they occur the next verses start impulsively from them, without a pause.

In spite of these difficulties, since the section is so long, attempts at division have been made. Ewald distinguished three parts in three different tempers: *First*, iv.-vi. 11 *a*, God's Plaint against His people; *Second*, vi. 11 *b*-ix. 9, Their Punishment; *Third*, ix. 10-xiv. 10, Retrospect of the earlier history—warning and consolation. Driver also divides into three subsections, but differently: *First*, iv.-viii., in which Israel's Guilt predominates; *Second*, ix.-xi. 11, in which the prevailing thought is their Punishment; *Third*, xi. 12-xiv. 10, in which both lines of thought are continued, but followed by a glance at the brighter future.† What is common to both these arrangements is the recognition of a certain progress from feelings about Israel's guilt which prevail in the earlier chapters, to a clear vision of the political destruction awaiting them; and finally more hope of repentance in the people, with a vision of the blessed future that must follow upon it. It is, however, more accurate to say that the emphasis of Hosea's prophesying, instead of changing from the Guilt to the Punishment of Israel, changes about the middle of chap. vii. from their Moral Decay to their Political Decay, and that the description of the latter is modified or interrupted by Two Visions of better things: one of Jehovah's early guidance of the people, with a great outbreak of His Love upon them, in chap. xi.; and one of their future Return to Jehovah and restoration in chap. xiv. It is on these features that the division of the following Exposition is arranged.

3. It will be obvious that with a text so corrupt, with a style so broken and incapable of logical division, questions of Authenticity are raised to a pitch of the greatest difficulty. Allusion has been made to the number of glosses which must have been found necessary from even an early period, and of some of which we can discern the proofs.‡ We will deal with these as they occur. But we may here discuss, as a whole, another class of suspected passages—suspected for the same reason that we saw a number in Amos to be, because of their reference to Judah. In the Book of Hosea (chaps. iv.-xiv.) they are twelve in number. Only one of them is favourable (iv. 15): "Though Israel play the harlot, let not Judah sin." Kuenen§ argues that this is genuine, on the ground that the peculiar verb "to sin" or "take guilt to oneself" is used several other times in the book,‖ and that the wish expressed is in consonance with what he understands to be Hosea's favourable feeling towards Judah. Yet Hosea nowhere else makes any distinction between Ephraim and Judah in the matter of sin, but condemns both

* Especially in chap. vii.

† As in xi. 2 *b*.

‡ This is especially the case in x. 11-13, xi. 4; xiv. 5.

§ *E. g.* vi. 5 *b*: M. T. משפטיך אור יצא, which is nonsense; LXX. משפטי כאור, "My judgment shall go forth like light." xi. 2: M. T. מִפְּנֵיהֶם; LXX. מִפְּנֵי הֵם.

‖ iv. 4, עמי for עמך; 8, נפשם for נפ—perhaps; 13, צִלָּהּ for צִלָּה; v. 2; vi. 2 (possibly); viii. 4, read יכרתוּ; ix. 2; xi. 2, 3; xi. 5, 6, where for לא read לו; 10, read לְךָ; xii. 9; xiv. 9 *a*, לוֹ for לִי. On the other hand, they are either improbable or quite wrong, as in v. 2 *b*; xi. 2 (but the LXX. may be right here); vii. 1 *b*; xi. 1, 4; xii. 5; xiii. 14, 15 (ter.).

¶ v. 5 (so as to change the tense: "and Judah shall stumble"); xii. 3, etc.

** vi. 3; viii. 10, 13; ix. 2; x. 4, 13 *b*, 15 (probably); xii. 2 · xiii. 9; xiv. 3. Wrong tense, xii. 11. *Cf.* also vi. 3.

†† *E. g.*, viii. 13.

‡‡ *Cf.* the Hebrew and Greek, of *e. g.*, iv. 10, 11, 12; vi. 9, 10; viii. 5, 6; ix. 8, 9.

* viii. 13 (14 must be omitted); ix. 17.

† "Introd.," 284.

‡ *E. g.*, iv. 15 (?); vi. 11-vii. (?); vii. 4; viii. 2; xii. 6.

§ "Einl.," 323.

‖ אשם, v. 15; x. 2; xiii. 1; xiv. 1.

equally; and as iv. 15 f. are to be suspected on other grounds as well, I cannot hold this reference to Judah to be beyond doubt. Nor is the reference in viii. 14 genuine: "And Israel forgat her Maker and built temples, and Judah multiplied fenced cities, but I will send fire on his cities and it shall devour her palaces." Kuenen * refuses to reject the reference to Judah, on the ground that without it the rhythm of the verse is spoiled; but the fact is the whole verse must go. Chap. v. 13 forms a climax, which v. 14 only weakens; the style is not like Hosea's own, and indeed is but an echo of verses of Amos.† Nor can we be quite sure about v. 5: "Israel and Ephraim shall stumble by their iniquities, and" (LXX.) "stumble also shall Judah with them;" or vi. 10, 11: "In Bethel I have seen horrors: there playest thou the harlot, Ephraim; there Israel defiles himself; also Judah" . . . (the rest of the text is impracticable). In both these passages Judah is the awkward third of a parallelism, and is introduced by an "also," as if an afterthought. Yet the afterthought may be the prophet's own; for in other passages, to which no doubt attaches, he fully includes Judah in the sinfulness of Israel. Cornill rejects x. 11, "Judah must plough," but I cannot see on what grounds; as Kuenen says, it has no appearance of being an intrusion.‡ In xii. 3 Wellhausen reads "Israel" for "Judah," but the latter is justified if not rendered necessary by the reference to Judah in ver. 1, which Wellhausen admits. Against the other references—v. 10, "The princes of Judah are as removers of boundaries;" v. 12, "I shall be as the moth to Ephraim, and a worm to the house of Judah;" v. 13, "And Ephraim saw his disease, and Judah his sore;" v. 14, "For I am as a roaring lion to Ephraim, and as a young lion to the house of Judah;" vi. 4, "What shall I do to thee, Ephraim? what shall I do to thee, Judah?"—there are no apparent objections and they are generally admitted by critics. As Kuenen says, it would have been surprising if Hosea had made no reference to the sister kingdom. His judgment of her is amply justified by that of her own citizens, Isaiah and Micah.

Other short passages of doubtful authenticity will be treated as we come to them; but again it may be emphasised that, in a book of such a style as this, certainty on the subject is impossible.

Finally, there may be given here the only notable addition which the Septuagint makes to the Book of Hosea. It occurs in xiii. 4, after "I am Jehovah thy God:" "That made fast the heavens and founded the earth, whose hands founded all the host of the heaven, and I did not show them to thee that thou shouldest follow after them, and I led thee up"—"from the land of Egypt."

At first this recalls those apostrophes to Jehovah's power which break forth in the Book of Amos; and the resemblance has been taken to prove that they also are late intrusions. But this both obtrudes itself as they do not, and is manifestly of much lower poetical value. See page 493.

We have now our material clearly before us, and may proceed to the more welcome task of tracing our prophet's life, and expounding his teaching.

* P. 313.
† viii. 14 is also rejected by Wellhausen and Cornill.
‡ *Loc. cit.*

CHAPTER XIII.

THE PROBLEM THAT AMOS LEFT.

Amos was a preacher of righteousness almost wholly in its judicial and punitive offices. Exposing the moral conditions of society in his day, emphasising on the one hand its obduracy and on the other the intolerableness of it, he asserted that nothing could avert the inevitable doom—neither Israel's devotion to Jehovah nor Jehovah's interest in Israel. "You alone have I known of all the families of the ground: therefore will I visit upon you all your iniquities." The visitation was to take place in war and in the captivity of the people. This is practically the whole message of the prophet Amos.

That he added to it the promise of restoration which now closes his book, we have seen to be extremely improbable.* Yet even if that promise is his own, Amos does not tell us how the restoration is to be brought about. With wonderful insight and patience he has traced the captivity of Israel to moral causes. But he does not show what moral change in the exiles is to justify their restoration, or by what means such a moral change is to be effected. We are left to infer the conditions and the means of redemption from the principles which Amos enforced while there yet seemed time to pray for the doomed people: "Seek the Lord and ye shall live."† According to this, the moral renewal of Israel must precede their restoration; but the prophet seems to make no great effort to effect the renewal. In short Amos illustrates the easily-forgotten truth that a preacher to the conscience is not necessarily a preacher of repentance.

Of the great antitheses between which religion moves, Law and Love, Amos had therefore been the prophet of Law. But we must not imagine that the association of Love with the Deity was strange to him. This could not be to any Israelite who remembered the past of his people—the romance of their origins and early struggles for freedom. Israel had always felt the grace of their God; and unless we be wrong about the date of the great poem in the end of Deuteronomy, they had lately celebrated that grace in lines of exquisite beauty and tenderness:—

"He found him in a desert land,
In a waste and a howling wilderness.
He compassed him about, cared for him,
Kept him as the apple of His eye.
As an eagle stirreth up his nest,
Fluttereth over his young,
Spreadeth his wings, taketh them,
Beareth them up on his pinions—
So Jehovah alone led him." ‡

The patience of the Lord with their waywardness and their stubbornness had been the ethical influence on Israel's life at a time when they had probably neither code of law nor system of doctrine. "Thy gentleness," as an early Psalmist says for his people, "Thy gentleness hath made me great."§ Amos is not unaware of this ancient grace of Jehovah. But he speaks of it in a fashion which shows that he feels it to be exhausted and without hope for his generation.

* See above, pp. 490 ff.
† v. 4.
‡ Deut. xxxii. 10-12: a song probably earlier than the eighth century. But some put it later.
§ Psalm xviii.

"I brought you up out of the land of Egypt, and led you forty years in the wilderness, to possess the land of the Amorites. And I raised up of your sons for prophets and of your young men for Nazarites."* But this can now only fill the cup of the nation's sin. "You alone have I known of all the families of the earth: therefore will I visit upon you all your iniquities."† Jehovah's ancient Love but strengthens now the justice and the impetus of His Law.

We perceive, then, the problem which Amos left to prophecy. It was not to discover Love in the Deity whom he had so absolutely identified with Law. The Love of God needed no discovery among a people with the Deliverance, the Exodus, the Wilderness, and the Gift of the Land in their memories. But the problem was to prove in God so great and new a mercy as was capable of matching that Law, which the abuse of His millennial gentleness now only the more fully justified. There was needed a prophet to arise with as keen a conscience of Law as Amos himself, and yet affirm that Love was greater still; to admit that Israel were doomed, and yet promise their redemption by processes as reasonable and as ethical as those by which the doom had been rendered inevitable. The prophet of Conscience had to be followed by the prophet of Repentance.

Such an one was found in Hosea, the son of Be'eri, a citizen and probably a priest of Northern Israel, whose very name, *Salvation*, the synonym of Joshua and of Jesus, breathed the larger hope, which it was his glory to bear to his people. Before we see how for this task Hosea was equipped with the love and sympathy which Amos lacked, let us do two things. Let us appreciate the magnitude of the task itself, set to him first of prophets; and let us remind ourselves that, greatly as he achieved it, the task was not one which could be achieved even by him once for all, but that it presents itself to religion again and again in the course of her development.

For the first of these duties, it is enough to recall how much all subsequent prophecy derives from Hosea. We shall not exaggerate if we say that there is no truth uttered by later prophets about the Divine Grace, which we do not find in germ in him. Isaiah of Jerusalem was a greater statesman and a more powerful writer, but he had not Hosea's tenderness and insight into motive and character. Hosea's marvellous sympathy both with the people and with God is sufficient to foreshadow every grief, every hope, every gospel, which make the Books of Jeremiah and the great Prophet of the Exile exhaustless in their spiritual value for mankind. These others explored the kingdom of God: it was Hosea who took it by storm.‡ He is the first prophet of Grace, Israel's earliest Evangelist; yet with as keen a sense of law, and of the inevitableness of ethical discipline, as Amos himself.

But the task which Hosea accomplished was not one that could be accomplished once for all. The interest of his book is not merely historical. For so often as a generation is shocked out of its old religious ideals, as Amos shocked Israel, by a realism and a discovery of law, which have no respect for ideals, however ancient and however dear to the human heart, but work their own pitiless way to doom inevitable; so often must the Book of Hosea have a practical value for living men. At such a crisis we stand to-

*ii. 10 f. †iii. 2. ‡Matt. xi. 12.

day. The older Evangelical assurance, the older Evangelical ideals have to some extent been rendered impossible by the realism to which the sciences, both physical and historical, have most healthily recalled us, and by their wonderful revelation of Law working through nature and society without respect to our creeds and pious hopes. The question presses: Is it still possible to believe in repentance and conversion, still possible to preach the power of God to save, whether the individual or society, from the forces of heredity and of habit? We can at least learn how Hosea mastered the very similar problem which Amos left to him, and how, with a moral realism no less stern than his predecessor and a moral standard every whit as high, he proclaimed Love to be the ultimate element in religion; not only because it moves man to a repentance and God to a redemption more sovereign than any law; but because if neglected or abused, whether as love of man or love of God, it enforces a doom still more inexorable than that required by violated truth or by outraged justice. Love our Saviour, Love our almighty and unfailing Father, but, just because of this, Love our most awful Judge—we turn to the life and the message in which this eternal theme was first unfolded.

CHAPTER XIV.

THE STORY OF THE PRODIGAL WIFE.

HOSEA i.-iii.

IT has often been remarked that, unlike the first Doomster of Israel, Israel's first Evangelist was one of themselves, a native and citizen, perhaps even a priest, of the land to which he was sent. This appears even in his treatment of the stage and soil of his ministry. Contrast him in this respect with Amos.

In the Book of Amos we have few glimpses of the scenery of Israel, and these always by flashes of the lightnings of judgment: the towns in drought or earthquake or siege; the vineyards and orchards under locusts or mildew; Carmel itself desolate, or as a hiding-place from God's wrath.

But Hosea's love steals across his whole land like the dew, provoking every separate scent and colour, till all Galilee lies before us lustrous and fragrant as nowhere else outside the parables of Jesus. The Book of Amos, when it would praise God's works, looks to the stars. But the poetry of Hosea clings about his native soil like its trailing vines. If he appeals to the heavens, it is only that they may speak to the earth, and the earth to the corn and the wine, and the corn and the wine to Jezreel.* Even the wild beasts —and Hosea tells us of their cruelty almost as much as Amos—he cannot shut out of the hope of his love: "I will make a covenant for them with the beasts of the field, and with the fowls of heaven, and with the creeping things of the ground."† God's love-gifts to His people are corn and wool, flax and oil; while spiritual blessings are figured in the joys of them who sow and reap. With Hosea we feel all the seasons of the Syrian year: early rain and latter rain, the first flush of the young corn, the scent of the vine blossom, the "first ripe fig of the fig-tree in her first season," the bursting of the lily; the

*ii. 23, Heb. †ii. 20, Heb.

wild vine trailing on the hedge, the field of tares, the beauty of the full olive in sunshine and breeze; the mists and heavy dews of a summer morning in Ephraim, the night winds laden with the air of the mountains, "the scent of Lebanon." * Or it is the dearer human sights in valley and field: the smoke from the chimney, the chaff from the threshing-floor, the doves startled to their towers, the fowler and his net; the breaking up of the fallow ground, the harrowing of the clods, the reapers, the heifer that treadeth out the corn; the team of draught oxen surmounting the steep road, and at the top the kindly driver setting in food to their jaws.†

Where, I say, do we find anything like this save in the parables of Jesus? For the love of Hosea was as the love of that greater Galilean: however high, however lonely it soared, it was yet rooted in the common life below, and fed with the unfailing grace of a thousand homely sources.

But just as the Love which first showed itself in the sunny Parables of Galilee passed onward to Gethsemane and the Cross, so the love of Hosea, that had wakened with the spring lilies and dewy summer mornings of the North, had also, ere his youth was spent, to meet its agony and shame. These came upon the prophet in his home, and in her in whom so loyal and tender a heart had hoped to find his chiefest sanctuary next to God. There are, it is true, some of the ugliest facts of human life about this prophet's experience; but the message is one very suited to our own hearts and times. Let us read this story of the Prodigal Wife as we do that other Galilean tale of the Prodigal Son. There as well as here are harlots; but here as well as there is the clear mirror of the Divine Love. For the Bible never shuns realism when it would expose the exceeding hatefulness of sin or magnify the power of God's love to redeem. To an age which is always treating conjugal infidelity either as a matter of comedy or as a problem of despair, the tale of Hosea and his wife may still become, what it proved to his own generation, a gospel full of love and hope.

The story, and how it led Hosea to understand God's relations to sinful men, is told in the first three chapters of his book. It opens with the very startling sentence: "The beginning of the word of Jehovah to Hosea:—And Jehovah said to Hosea, Go, take thee a wife of harlotry and children of harlotry: for the Land hath committed great harlotry in departing from Jehovah." ‡

The command was obeyed. "And he went and took Gomer, daughter of Diblaim; § and she

* vi. 3, 4; vii. 8; ix. 10; xiv. 6, 7, 8.

† vii. 11, 12; x. 11; xi. 4, etc.

‡ Pregnant construction, "hath committed great harlotry from after Jehovah."

§ These personal names do not elsewhere occur. גֹּמֶר; Γομερ. דִּבְלַיִם; Δεβηλαιμ, B; Δεβηλαειμ, AQ. They have, of course, been interpreted allegorically in the interests of the theory discussed below. גמר has been taken to mean "completion," and interpreted as various derivatives of that root: Jerome, "the perfect one"; Raschi, "that fulfilled all evil"; Kimchi, "fulfilment of punishment"; Calvin, "consumptio," and so on. דבלים has been traced to דבלה, Pl. דְּבֵלִים. cakes of pressed figs, as if a name had been sought to connect the woman at once with the idol-worship and a rich sweetness; or to an Arabic root, דבל, to press, as if it referred either to the

conceived, and bare to him a son. And Jehovah said unto him, Call his name Jezreel; for yet a little and I shall visit the blood of Jezreel upon the house of Jehu, and will bring to an end the kingdom of the house of Israel; and it shall be on that day that I shall break the bow of Israel in the Vale of Jezreel"—the classic battle-field of Israel.* "And she conceived again, and bare a daughter; and He said to him, Call her name Un-Loved," or "That-never-knew-a-Father's-Pity; † for I will not again have pity" —such pity as a Father hath—" on the house of Israel, that I should fully forgive them.‡ And she weaned Un-Pitied, and conceived, and bare a son. And He said, Call his name Not-My-People; for ye are not My people, and I—I am not yours." §

It is not surprising that divers interpretations have been put upon this troubled tale. The words which introduce it are so startling that very many have held it to be an allegory, or parable, invented by the prophet to illustrate, by familiar human figures, what was at that period the still difficult conception of the Love of God for sinful men. But to this well-intended argument there are insuperable objections. It implies that Hosea had first awakened to the relations of Jehovah and Israel—He faithful and full of affection, she unfaithful and thankless—and that then, in order to illustrate the relations, he had invented the story. To that we have an adequate reply. In the first place, though it were possible, it is extremely improbable, that such a man should have invented such a tale about his wife, or, if he was unmarried, about himself. But, in the second place, he says expressly that his domestic experience was the "beginning of Jehovah's word to him." That is, he passed through it first, and only afterwards, with the sympathy and insight thus acquired, he came to appreciate Jehovah's relation to Israel. Finally, the style betrays narrative rather than parable. The simple facts are told; there is an absence of elaboration; there is no effort to make every detail symbolic; the names Gomer and Diblaim are apparently those of real persons; every attempt to attach a symbolic value to them has failed.

She was, therefore, no dream, this woman, but flesh and blood: the sorrow, the despair, the sphinx of the prophet's life; yet a sphinx who in the end yielded her riddle to love.

Accordingly a large number of other interpreters have taken the story throughout as the literal account of actual facts. This is the theory

plumpness of the body (*cf.* Ezek. xvi. 7; so Hitzig) or to the woman's habits. But all these are far-fetched and vain. There is no reason to suppose that either of the two names is symbolic. The alternative (allowed by the language) naturally suggests itself that דבלים is the name of Gomer's birthplace. But there is nothing to prove this. No such place-name occurs elsewhere: one cannot adduce the Diblathaim in Moab (Num. xxxiii. 46 ff.; Jer. xlviii. 2).

* "Hist. Geog.," chap. xviii.

† לֹא רֻחָמָה, probably 3d pers. sing. fem. Pual (in Pause *cf.* Prov. xxviii. 13); literally, "She is not loved or pitied." The word means love as pity: "such pity as a father hath unto his children dear" (Psalm ciii.), or God to a penitent man (Psalm xxviii. 13). The Greek versions alternate between love and pity. LXX. οὐκ ἠλεημένη διότι οὐ μὴ προσθήσω ἔτι ἠλεῆσαι, for which the Complutensian has ἀγαπῆσαι, the reading followed by Paul (Rom. ix. 25: *cf.* 1 Peter ii. 10).

‡ Here ver. 7 is to be omitted, as explained above, p. 495.

§ Do not belong to you; but the "I am," אהיה, recalls the "I am that I am" of Exodus.

of many of the Latin and Greek Fathers,* of many of the Puritans and of Dr. Pusey—by one of those agreements into which, from such opposite schools, all these commentators are not infrequently drawn by their common captivity to the letter of Scripture.† When you ask them, How then do you justify that first strange word of God to Hosea,‡ if you take it literally and believe that Hosea was charged to marry a woman of public shame? they answer either that such an evil may be justified by the bare word of God, or that it was well worth the end, the salvation of a lost soul.§ And indeed this tragedy would be invested with an even greater pathos if it were true that the human hero had passed through a self-sacrifice so unusual, had incurred such a shame for such an end. The interpretation, however, seems forbidden by the essence of the story. Had not Hosea's wife been pure when he married her she could not have served as a type of the Israel whose earliest relations to Jehovah he describes as innocent. And this is confirmed by other features of the book: by the high ideal which Hosea has of marriage, and by that sense of early goodness and early beauty passing away like morning mist, which is so often and so pathetically expressed that we cannot but catch in it the echo of his own experience. As one has said to whom we owe, more than to any other, the exposition of the gospel in Hosea,‖ "The struggle of Hosea's shame and grief when he found his wife unfaithful is altogether inconceivable unless his first love had been pure and full of trust in the purity of its object."

How then are we to reconcile with this the statement of that command to take a wife of the character so frankly described? In this way—and we owe the interpretation to the same lamented scholar.¶ When, some years after his marriage, Hosea at last began to be aware of the character of her whom he had taken to his home, and while he still brooded upon it, God revealed to him why He who knoweth all things from the beginning had suffered His servant to marry such a woman; and Hosea, by a very natural anticipation, in which he is imitated by other prophets,** pushed back his own knowledge of God's purpose to the date when that purpose began actually to be fulfilled, the day of his betrothal. This, though he was all unconscious of its fatal future, had been to Hosea the beginning of the word of the Lord. On that uncertain voyage he had sailed with sealed orders.

Now this is true to nature, and may be matched from our own experience. "The beginning of God's word" to any of us—where does it lie? Does it lie in the first time the meaning of our life became articulate, and we are able to utter it to others? Ah, no; it always lies far behind that, in facts and in relationships, of the Divine meaning of which we are at the time unconscious, though now we know. How familiar this is in respect to the sorrows and adversities of life: dumb, deadening things that fall on us at the time with no more voice than clods falling on coffins of dead men, we have been able to read them afterwards as the clear call of God to our souls. But what we thus so readily admit about the sorrows of life may be equally true of any of those relations which we enter with light and unawed hearts, conscious only of the novelty and the joy of them. It is most true of the love which meets a man as it met Hosea in his opening manhood.

How long Hosea took to discover his shame he indicates by a few hints which he suffers to break from the delicate reserve of his story. He calls the first child his own; and the boy's name, though ominous of the nation's fate, has no trace of shame upon it. Hosea's Jezreel was as Isaiah's Shear-Jashub or Maher-shalal-hash-baz. But Hosea does not claim the second child; and in the name of this little lass, Lo-Ruhamah, "she-that-never-knew-a-father's-love," orphan not by death but by her mother's sin, we find proof of the prophet's awakening to the tragedy of his home. Nor does he own the third child, named "Not-my-people," that could also mean "No-kin-of-mine." The three births must have taken at least six years;* and once at least, but probably oftener, Hosea had forgiven the woman, and till the sixth year she stayed in his house. Then either he put her from him, or she went her own way. She sold herself for money, and finally drifted, like all of her class, into slavery.†

Such were the facts of Hosea's grief, and we have now to attempt to understand how that grief became his gospel. We may regard the stages of the process as two: first, when he was led to feel that his sorrow was the sorrow of the whole nation; and, second, when he comprehended that it was of similar kind to the sorrow of God Himself.

While Hosea brooded upon his pain one of the first things he would remember would be the fact, which he so frequently illustrates, that the case of his home was not singular, but common and characteristic of his day. Take the evidence of his book, and there must have been in Israel many such wives as his own. He describes their sin as the besetting sin of the nation, and the plague of Israel's life. But to lose your own sorrow in the vaster sense of national trouble—that is the first consciousness of a duty and a mission. In the analogous vice of intemperance among ourselves we have seen the same experience operate again and again. How many a man has joined the public warfare against that sin, because he was aroused to its national consequences by the ruin it had brought to his own house! And one remembers from recent years a more illustrious instance, where a domestic grief—it is true of a very different kind—became not dissimilarly the opening of a great career of service to the people:—

"I was in Leamington, and Mr. Cobden called on me. I was then in the depths of grief—I

*Augustine, Ambrose, Theodoret, Cyril Alex., and Theodore of Mopsuestia.

†It is interesting to read in parallel the interpretations of Matthew Henry and Dr. Pusey. They are very alike, but the latter has the more delicate taste of his age.

‡i. 2.

§The former is Matthew Henry's; the latter seems to be implied by Pusey.

‖Robertson Smith, "Prophets of Israel."

¶Apparently it was W. R. Smith's interpretation which caused Kuenen to give up the allegorical theory.

**Two instances are usually quoted. The one is Isaiah vi., where most are agreed that what Isaiah has stated there as his inaugural vision is not only what happened in the earliest moments of his prophetic life, but this spelt out and emphasised by his experience since. See "Isaiah i.-xxxix." ("Exp. Bible"), pp. 630 f. The other instance is Jeremiah xxxii. 8, where the prophet tells us that he became convinced that the Lord spoke to him on a certain occasion only after a subsequent event proved this to be the case.

*An Eastern woman seldoms weans her child before the end of its second year.

†iii. 2.

may almost say of despair, for the light and sunshine of my house had been extinguished. All that was left on earth of my young wife, except the memory of a sainted life and a too brief happiness, was lying still and cold in the chamber above us. Mr. Cobden called on me as his friend, and addressed me, as you may suppose, with words of condolence. After a time he looked up and said: 'There are thousands and thousands of homes in England at this moment where wives and mothers and children are dying of hunger. Now, when the first paroxysm of your grief is passed, I would advise you to come with me, and we will never rest until the Corn Laws are repealed.' "*

Not dissimilarly was Hosea's pain overwhelmed by the pain of his people. He remembered that there were in Israel thousands of homes like his own. Anguish gave way to sympathy. The mystery became the stimulus to a mission.

But, again, Hosea traces this sin of his day to the worship of strange gods. He tells the fathers of Israel, for instance, that they need not be surprised at the corruption of their wives and daughters when they themselves bring home from the heathen rites the infection of light views of love.† That is to say, the many sins against human love in Israel, the wrong done to his own heart in his own home, Hosea connects with the wrong done to the Love of God, by His people's desertion of Him for foreign and impure rites. Hosea's own sorrow thus became a key to the sorrow of God. Had he loved this woman, cherished and honoured her, borne with and forgiven her, only to find at the last his love spurned and hers turned to sinful men: so also had the Love of God been treated by His chosen people, and they had fallen to the loose worship of idols.

Hosea was the more naturally led to compare his relations to his wife with Jehovah's to Israel, by certain religious beliefs current among the Semitic peoples. It was common to nearly all Semitic religions to express the union of a god with his land or with his people by the figure of marriage. The title which Hosea so often applies to the heathen deities, Ba'al, meant originally not "lord" of his worshippers, but "possessor" and endower of his land, its husband and fertiliser. A fertile land was "a land of Ba'al," or "Be'ulah," that is, "possessed" or "blessed by a Ba'al."‡ Under the fertility was counted not only the increase of field and flock, but the human increase as well; and thus a nation could speak of themselves as the children of the Land, their mother, and of her Ba'al, their father.§ When Hosea, then, called Jehovah the husband of Israel, it was not an entirely new symbol which he invented. Up to his time, however, the marriage of Heaven and Earth, of a god and his people, seems to have been conceived in a physical form which ever tended to become more gross; and was expressed, as Hosea points out, by rites of a sensual and debasing nature, with the most disastrous effects on the domestic morals of the people. By an inspiration, whose ethical character is very conspicuous, Hosea breaks the physical connection altogether. Jehovah's Bride is not the Land, but the People, and His marriage with her is conceived wholly as a moral relation. Not that He has no connection with the physical fruits of the land: corn, wine, oil, wool, and flax. But these are represented only as the signs and ornaments of the marriage, love-gifts from the husband to the wife.* The marriage itself is purely moral: "I will betroth her to Me in righteousness and justice, in leal love and tender mercies."† From her in return are demanded faithfulness and growing knowledge of her Lord.

It is the re-creation of an Idea. Slain and made carrion by the heathen religions, the figure is restored to life by Hosea. And this is a life everlasting. Prophet and apostle, the Israel of Jehovah, the Church of Christ, have alike found in Hosea's figure an unfailing significance and charm. Here we cannot trace the history of the figure; but at least we ought to emphasise the creative power which its recovery to life proves to have been inherent in prophecy. This is one of those triumphs of which the God of Israel said: "Behold, I make all things new."‡

Having dug his figure from the mire and set it upon the rock, Hosea sends it on its way with all boldness. If Jehovah be thus the husband of Israel, "her first husband, the husband of her youth," then all her pursuit of the Ba'alim is unfaithfulness to her marriage vows. But she is worse than an adulteress; she is a harlot. She has fallen for gifts. Here the historical facts wonderfully assisted the prophet's metaphor. It was a fact that Israel and Jehovah were first wedded in the wilderness upon conditions, which by the very circumstances of desert life could have little or no reference to the fertility of the earth, but were purely personal and moral. And it was also a fact that Israel's declension from Jehovah came after her settlement in Canaan, and was due to her discovery of other deities, in possession of the soil, and adored by the natives as the dispensers of its fertility. Israel fell under these superstitions, and, although she still formally acknowledged her bond to Jehovah, yet in order to get her fields blessed and her flocks made fertile, her orchards protected from blight and her fleeces from scab, she went after the local Ba'alim.§ With bitter scorn Hosea points out that there was no true love in this: it was the mercenariness of a harlot, selling herself for gifts.‖ And it had the usual results. The children whom Israel bore were not her husband's.¶ The new generation in Israel grew up in ignorance of Jehovah, with characters and lives strange to His Spirit. They were Lo-Ruhamah: He could not feel towards them such pity as a father hath.** They were Lo-Ammi: not at all His people. All was in exact parallel to Hosea's own experience with his wife; and only the real pain of that experience could have made the man brave enough to use it as a figure of his God's treatment by Israel.

Following out the human analogy, the next step should have been for Jehovah to divorce His

* From a speech by John Bright.

† iv. 13, 14.

‡ *Cf.* the spiritual use of the term, Isa. lxii. 4.

§ For proof and exposition of all this see Robertson Smith, "Religion of the Semites," 92 ff.

* ii. 8.

† So best is rendered חסד, ḥesedh, which means always not merely an affection, "lovingkindness," as our version puts it, but a relation loyally observed.

‡ An expansion of this will be found in the present writer's "Isaiah xl.-lxvi." (Expositor's Bible), pp. 828 ff.

§ ii. 13.

‖ ii. 5, 13.

¶ ii. 5.

** See above, p. 500.

erring spouse. But Jehovah reveals to the prophet that this is not His way. For He is "God and not man, the Holy One in the midst of thee. How shall I give thee up, Ephraim? How shall I surrender thee, O Israel? My heart is turned within Me, My compassions are kindled together!"

Jehovah will seek, find, and bring back the wanderer. Yet the process shall not be easy. The gospel which Hosea here preaches is matched in its great tenderness by its full recognition of the ethical requirements of the case. Israel may not be restored without repentance, and cannot repent without disillusion and chastisement. God will therefore show her that her lovers, the Ba'alim, are unable to assure to her the gifts for which she followed them. These are His corn, His wine, His wool, and His flax, and He will take them away for a time. Nay more, as if mere drought and blight might still be regarded as some Ba'al's work, He who has always manifested Himself by great historic deeds will do so again. He will remove herself from the land, and leave it a waste and a desolation. The whole passage runs as follows, introduced by the initial "Therefore" of judgment:—

"Therefore, behold, I am going to hedge * up her † way with thorns, and build her ‡ a wall, so that she find not her paths. And she shall pursue her paramours and shall not come upon them, seek them and shall not find them; and she shall say, Let me go and return to my first husband, for it was better for me then than now. She knew not, then, that it was I *who* gave her the corn and the wine and the oil; yea, silver I heaped upon her and gold—they worked it up for the Ba'al!" § Israel had deserted the religion that was historical and moral for the religion that was physical. But the historical religion was the physical one. Jehovah who had brought Israel to the land was also the God of the Land. He would prove this by taking away its blessings. "Therefore I will turn and take away My corn in its time and My wine in its season, and I will withdraw My wool and My flax that should have covered her nakedness. And now"—the other initial of judgment—"I will lay bare her shame to the eyes of her lovers, and no man shall rescue her from My hand. And I will make an end of all her joyaunce, her pilgrimages, her New-Moons and her Sabbaths, with every festival; and I will destroy her vines and her figs of which she said, 'They are a gift, mine own, which my lovers gave me,' and I will turn them to jungle and the wild beast shall devour them. So shall I visit upon her the days of the Ba'alim, when she used to offer incense to them, and decked herself with her rings and her jewels and went after her paramours, but Me she forgat—'tis the oracle of Jehovah." All this implies something more than such natural disasters as those in which Amos saw the first chastisements of the Lord. Each of the verses suggests, not only a devastation of the land by war,‖ but the removal of the people into captivity. Evidently, therefore, Hosea, writing about 745, had in view a speedy invasion by Assyria, an invasion which was always followed up by the exile of the people subdued.

This is next described, with all plainness, under the figure of Israel's early wanderings in the wilderness, but is emphasised as happening only for the end of the people's penitence and restoration. The new hope is so melodious that it carries the language into metre.

"Therefore, lo! I am to woo her, and I will bring her to the wilderness,
And I will speak home to her heart.
And from there I will give to her her vineyards,
And the Valley of Achor for a doorway of hope.
And there she shall answer Me as in the days of her youth,
And as the day when she came up from the land of Misraim."

To us the terms of this passage may seem formal and theological. But to every Israelite some of these terms must have brought back the days of his own wooing. "I will speak home to her heart" is a forcible expression, like the German "an das Herz" or the sweet Scottish "it cam' up roond my heart," and was used in Israel as from man to woman when he won her.* But the other terms have an equal charm. The prophet, of course, does not mean that Israel shall be literally taken back to the desert. But he describes her coming Exile under that ancient figure, in order to surround her penitence with the associations of her innocency and her youth. By the grace of God, everything shall begin again as at first. The old terms "wilderness," "the giving of vineyards," "Valley of Achor," are, as it were, the wedding ring restored.

As a result of all this (whether the words be by Hosea or another),†

"It shall b in that day—'tis Jehovah's oracle—that thou shalt call Me, My husband,
And thou shalt not again call Me, My Ba'al:
For I will take away the names of the Ba'alim from her mouth,
And they shall no more be remembered by their names."

There follows a picture of the ideal future, in which—how unlike the vision that now closes the Book of Amos!—moral and spiritual beauty, the peace of the land and the redemption of the people, are wonderfully mingled together, in a style so characteristic of Hosea's heart. It is hard to tell where the rhythmical prose passes into actual metre.

"And I will make for them a covenant in that day with the wild beasts, and with the birds of the heavens, and with the creeping things of the ground; and the bow and the sword and battle will I break from the land, and I will make you to dwell in safety. And I will betroth thee to Me for ever, and I will betroth thee to Me in righteousness and in justice, in leal love and in tender mercies; and I will betroth thee to Me in faithfulness, and thou shalt know Jehovah.

"And it shall be on that day I will speak—'tis the oracle of Jehovah—I will speak to the heavens, and they shall speak to the earth; and

* The participle Qal, used by God of Himself in His proclamations of grace or of punishment, has in this passage (*cf.* ver. 16) and elsewhere (especially in Deuteronomy) the force of an immediate future.

† So LXX.; Mass. Text, *thy*.

‡ The reading גְּדֵרָהּ is more probable than גְּדֵרָה.

§ Or "they made it into a Ba'al" image. So Ew., Hitz., Nowack. But Wellhausen omits the clause.

‖ Wellhausen thinks that up to ver. 14 only physical calamities are meant, but the הצלתו of ver. 11, as well as others of the terms used, imply not the blighting of crops before their season, but the carrying of them away in their season, when they had fully ripened, by invaders. The cessation of all worship points to the removal of the people from their land, which is also implied, of course, by the promise that they shall be sown again in ver. 23.

* *Cf.* Isa. xl. 1: which to the same exiled Israel is the fulfilment of the promise made by Hosea. See "Isaiah xl.-lxvi." ("Expositor's Bible"), pp. 749 ff.

† Wellhausen calls ver. 18 a gloss to ver 19.

the earth shall speak to the corn and the wine and the oil, and they shall speak to Jezreel," the "scattered like seed" across many lands; "but I will sow him * for Myself in the land: and I will have a father's pity upon Un-Pitied; and to Not-My-People" I will say, "My people thou art! and he shall say, My God!"†

The circle is thus completed on the terms from which we started. The three names which Hosea gave to the children, evil omens of Israel's fate, are reversed, and the people restored to the favour and love of their God.

We might expect this glory to form the culmination of the prophecy. What fuller prospect could be imagined than that we see in the close of the second chapter? With a wonderful grace, however, the prophecy turns back from this sure vision of the restoration of the people as a whole, to pick up again the individual from whom it had started, and whose unclean rag of a life had fluttered out of sight before the national fortunes sweeping in upon the scene. This was needed to crown the story—this return to the individual.

"And Jehovah said unto me, Once more go, love a wife that is loved of a paramour and is an adulteress,‡ as Jehovah loveth the children of Israel," the "while they are turning to other gods, and love raisin-cakes"—probably some element in the feasts of the gods of the land, the givers of the grape. "Then I bought her to me for fifteen" pieces "of silver and a homer of barley and a lethech of wine.§ And I said to her, For many days shalt thou abide for me alone; thou shalt not play the harlot, thou shalt not be for any husband; and I for my part also shall be so towards thee. For the days are many that the children of Israel shall abide without a king and without a prince, without sacrifice and without maççebah, and without ephod and teraphim.‖ Afterwards the children of Israel shall turn and seek Jehovah their God and David their king, and shall be in awe of Jehovah and towards His goodness in the end of the days."¶

Do not let us miss the fact that the story of the wife's restoration follows that of Israel's, although the story of the wife's unfaithfulness had come before that of Israel's apostasy. For this order means that, while the prophet's private pain preceded his sympathy with God's pain, it was not he who set God, but God who set him, the example of forgiveness. The man learned the God's sorrow out of his own sorrow; but conversely he was taught to forgive and redeem his wife only by seeing God forgive and redeem the people. In other words, the Divine was suggested by the human pain; yet the Divine Grace was not started by any previous human grace, but, on the contrary, was itself the precedent and origin of the latter. This is in harmony with all Hosea's teaching. God forgives because "He is God and not man."* Our pain with those we love helps us to understand God's pain; but it is not our love that leads us to believe in His love. On the contrary, all human grace is but the reflex of the Divine. So St. Paul: "Even as Christ forgave you, so also do ye." So St. John: "We love Him," and one another, "because He first loved us."

But this return from the nation to the individual has another interest. Gomer's redemption is not the mere formal completion of the parallel between her and her people. It is, as the story says, an impulse of the Divine Love, recognised even then in Israel as seeking the individual. He who followed Hagar into the wilderness, who met Jacob at Bethel and forgat not the slave Joseph in prison,† remembers also Hosea's wife. His love is not satisfied with His Nation-Bride: He remembers this single outcast. It is the Shepherd leaving the ninety-and-nine in the fold to seek the one lost sheep.

For Hosea himself his home could never be the same as it was at the first. "And I said to her, For many days shalt thou abide, as far as I am concerned, alone. Thou shalt not play the harlot. Thou shalt not be for a husband: and I on my side also shall be so towards thee." Discipline was needed there; and abroad the nation's troubles called the prophet to an anguish and a toil which left no room for the sweet love or hope of his youth. He steps at once to his hard warfare for his people; and through the rest of his book we never again hear him speak of home, or of children, or of wife. So Arthur passed from Guinevere to his last battle for his land:—

"Lo! I forgive thee, as Eternal God
Forgives: do thou for thine own soul the rest.
But how to take last leave of all I loved?
. . . .
I cannot touch thy lips, they are not mine; . . .
I cannot take thy hand; that too is flesh,
And in the flesh thou hast sinned; and mine own flesh,
Here looking down on thine polluted, cries
'I loathe thee'; yet not less, O Guinevere,
For I was ever virgin save for thee,
My love thro' flesh hath wrought into my life
So far, that my doom is, I love thee still.
Let no man dream but that I love thee still.
Perchance, and so thou purify thy soul,
And so thou lean on our fair father Christ,
Hereafter in that world where all are pure
We two may meet before high God, and thou
Wilt spring to me, and claim me thine, and know
I am thine husband, not a smaller soul. . . .
Leave me that,
I charge thee, my last hope. Now must I hence.
Thro' the thick night I hear the trumpet blow."

CHAPTER XV.

THE THICK NIGHT OF ISRAEL.

HOSEA iv.-xiv.

IT was indeed a "thick night" into which this Arthur of Israel stepped from his shattered home. The mists drive across Hosea's long agony with his people, and what we see, we see blurred and broken. There are stumbling and clashing; crowds in drift; confused rallies; gangs

* Massoretic Text, "her."

† It is at this point, if at any, that i. 10, 11, ii. 1 (Eng., but ii. 1-3 Heb.) ought to come in. It will be observed, however, that even here they are superfluous: "And the number of the children of Israel shall be as the sand of the sea, which cannot be measured nor counted; and it shall be in the place where it was said to them, No People of Mine are ye! it shall be said to them, Sons of the Living God! And the children of Judah and the children of Israel shall be gathered together, and they shall appoint themselves one head, and shall go up from the land: for great is the day of Jezreel. Say unto your brothers, My People, and to your sisters (LXX. sister), She-is-Pitied." On the whole passage see above, p. 494 f.

‡ Or "that is loved of her husband though an adulteress."

§ So LXX. The homer was eight bushels. The lethech is a measure not elsewhere mentioned.

‖ On these see above, Introduction, chap. iii., p. 451.

¶ On the text see above, p. 495.

* xi. 9.

† As the stories all written down before this had made familiar to Israel.

of assassins breaking across the highways; doors opening upon lurid interiors full of drunken riot. Voices, which other voices mock, cry for a dawn that never comes. God Himself is Laughter, Lightning, a Lion, a Gnawing Worm. Only one clear note breaks over the confusion—the trumpet summoning to war.

Take courage, O great heart! Not thus shall it always be! There wait thee, before the end, of open Visions at least two—one of Memory and one of Hope, one of Childhood and one of Spring. Past this night, past the swamp and jungle of these fetid years, thou shalt see thy land in her beauty, and God shall look on the face of His Bride.

Chaps. iv.-xiv. are almost indivisible. The two Visions just mentioned, chaps. xi. and xiv. 3-9, may be detached by virtue of contributing the only strains of gospel which rise victorious above the Lord's controversy with His people and the troubled story of their sins. All the rest is the noise of a nation falling to pieces, the crumbling of a splendid past. And as decay has no climax and ruin no rhythm, so we may understand why it is impossible to divide with any certainty Hosea's record of Israel's fall. Some arrangement we must attempt, but it is more or less artificial, and to be undertaken for the sake of our own minds, that cannot grasp so great a collapse all at once. Chap. iv. has a certain unity, and is followed by a new exordium, but as it forms only the theme of which the subsequent chapters are variations, we may take it with them as far as chap. vii., ver. 7; after which there is a slight transition from the moral signs of Israel's dissolution to the political—although Hosea still combines the religious offences of idolatry with the anarchy of the land. These form the chief interest to the end of chap. x. Then breaks the bright Vision of the Past, chap. xi., the temporary victory of the Gospel of the Prophet over his Curse. In chaps. xii.-xiv. 2 we are plunged into the latter once more, and reach in xiv. 3 ff. the second bright Vision, the Vision of the Future To each of these phases of Israel's Thick Night—we can hardly call them Sections—we may devote a chapter of simple exposition, adding three chapters more of detailed examination of the main doctrines we shall have encountered on our way—the Knowledge of God, Repentance, and the Sin against Love.

CHAPTER XVI.

A PEOPLE IN DECAY: I. MORALLY.

Hosea iv.-vii. 7.

Pursuing the plan laid down in the last chapter, we now take the section of Hosea's discourse which lies between chap. iv. 1 and chap. vii. 7. Chap. iv. is the only really separable bit of it; but there are also slight breaks at v. 15 and vii. 2. So we may attempt a division into four periods: 1. Chap. iv., which states God's general charge against the people; 2. Chap. v. 1-14, which discusses the priests and princes; 3. Chaps. v. 15-vii. 2, which abjures the people's attempts at repentance; and 4. Chap. vii. 3-7, which is a lurid spectacle of the drunken and profligate court. All these give symptoms of the moral decay of the people,—the family destroyed by impurity, and society by theft and murder; the corruption of the spiritual guides of the people; the debauchery of the nobles; the sympathy of the throne with evil,—with the despairing judgment that such a people are incapable even of repentance. The keynotes are these: "No troth, leal love, nor knowledge of God in the land. Priest and Prophet stumble. Ephraim and Judah stumble. I am as the moth to Ephraim. What can I make of thee, Ephraim? When I would heal them, their guilt is only the more exposed." Morally, Israel is rotten. The prophet, of course, cannot help adding signs of their political incoherence. But these he deals with more especially in the part of his discourse which follows chap. vii. 7.

1. The Lord's Quarrel with Israel.

Hosea iv.

"Hear the word of Jehovah, sons of Israel! * Jehovah hath a quarrel with the inhabitants of the land, for there is no troth nor leal love nor knowledge of God in the land. Perjury † and murder and theft and adultery! ‡ They break out, and blood strikes upon blood."

That stable and well-furnished life, across which, while it was still noon, Amos hurled his alarms—how quickly it has broken up! If there be still "ease in Zion," there is no more "security in Samaria." § The great Jeroboam is dead, and society, which in the East depends so much on the individual, is loose and falling to pieces. The sins which are exposed by Amos were those that lurked beneath a still strong government, but Hosea adds outbreaks which set all order at defiance. Later we shall find him describing housebreaking, highway robbery, and assassination. "Therefore doth the land wither, and every one of her denizens languisheth, even to the beast of the field and the fowl of the heaven; yea, even the fish of the sea are swept up" in the universal sickness of man and nature: for Hosea feels, like Amos, the liability of nature to the curse upon sin.

Yet the guilt is not that of the whole people, but of their religious guides. "Let none find fault and none upbraid, for My people are but as their priestlings.‖ O Priest, thou hast stumbled to-day: and stumble to-night shall the prophet with thee." One order of the nation's ministers goes staggering after the other! "And I will destroy thy Mother," presumably the nation herself. "Perished are My people for lack of knowledge." But how? By the sin of their teachers. "Because thou," O Priest, "hast rejected knowledge, I reject thee from being priest

* כי formally introduces the charge.

† Lit. "swearing and falsehood."

‡ Ninth, sixth, eighth, and seventh of the Decalogue.

§ Amos vi. 1.

‖ iv. 4. According to the excellent emendation of Beck (quoted by Wünsche, p. 142), who instead of ועמכככמריב proposes ועמי ככמריו, for the first word of which there is support in the LXX. ὁ λαός μου. The second word, כמר, is used for priest only in a bad sense by Hosea himself, x. 5, and in 2 Kings xxiii. 5 of the calf-worship and in Zech. i. 4 of the Baal priesthood. As Wellhausen remarks, this emendation restores sense to a passage that had none before. "Ver. 4 cannot be directed against the people, but must rather furnish the connection for ver. 5, and effect the transference from the reproof of the people (vv. 1-3) to the reproof of the priests (5 ff.)." The letters יכהן which are left over in ver. 4 by the emendation are then justly improved by Wellhausen (following Zunz) into the vocative הכהן and taken with the following verse.

to Me; and as thou hast forgotten the Torah of thy God, I forget thy children *—I on My side. As many as they be, so many have sinned against Me." Every jack-priest of them is culpable. "They have turned † their glory into shame. They feed on the sin of My people, and to the guilt of these lift up their appetite!" The more the people sin, the more merrily thrive the priests by fines and sin-offerings. They live upon the vice of the day, and have a vested interest in its crimes. English Langland said the same thing of the friars of his time. The contention is obvious. The priests have given themselves wholly to the ritual; they have forgotten that their office is an intellectual and moral one. We shall return to this when treating of Hosea's doctrine of knowledge and its responsibilities. Priesthood, let us only remember, priesthood is an intellectual trust.

"Thus it comes to be—like people like priest:" they also have fallen under the ritual, doing from lust what the priests do from greed. "But I will visit upon them their ways, and their deeds will I requite to them. For they" (those) "shall eat and not be satisfied," (these) "shall play the harlot and have no increase, because they have left off heeding Jehovah." This absorption in ritual at the expense of the moral and intellectual elements of religion has insensibly led them over into idolatry, with all its unchaste and drunken services. "Harlotry, wine, and new wine take away the brains!" ‡ The result is seen in the stupidity with which they consult their stocks for guidance. "My people! of its bit of wood it asketh counsel, and its staff telleth to it" the oracle! "For a spirit of harlotry hath led them astray, and they have played the harlot from their God. Upon the headlands of the hills they sacrifice, and on the heights offer incense, under oak or poplar or terebinth, for the shade of them is pleasant." On "headlands," not summits, for here no trees grow; and the altar was generally built under a tree and near water on some promontory, from which the flight of birds or of clouds might be watched. "Wherefore"—because of this your frequenting of the heathen shrines—"your daughters play the harlot and your daughters-in-law commit adultery. I will not come with punishment upon your daughters because they play the harlot, nor upon your daughters-in-law because they commit adultery." Why? For "they themselves," the fathers of Israel—or does he still mean the priests?—"go aside with the harlots and sacrifice with the common women of the shrines!" It is vain for the men of a nation to practise impurity and fancy that nevertheless they can keep their womankind chaste. "So the stupid people fall to ruin!"

("Though thou play the harlot, Israel, let not Judah bring guilt on herself. And come not to Gilgal, and go not up to Beth-Aven, and take not your oath" at the Well-of-the-Oath, Beer-Sheba,§ "By the life of Jehovah!" This obvious parenthesis may be either by Hosea or a later writer; the latter is more probable.*)

"Yea, like a wild heifer Israel has gone wild. How now can Jehovah feed them like a lamb in a broad meadow?" To treat this clause interrogatively is the only way to get sense out of it.† "Wedded to idols is Ephraim: leave him alone." The participle means "mated" or "leagued." The corresponding noun is used of a wife as the "mate" of her husband ‡ and of an idolater as the "mate" of his idols.§ The expression is doubly appropriate here, since Hosea used marriage as the figure of the relation of a deity to his worshippers. "Leave him alone"—he must go from bad to worse. "Their drunkenness over, they take to harlotry: her rulers have fallen in love with shame," or "they love shame more than their pride." ‖ But in spite of all their servile worship the Assyrian tempest shall sweep them away in its trail. "A wind hath wrapt them up in her skirts; and they shall be put to shame by their sacrifices."

This brings the passage to such a climax as Amos loved to crown his periods. And the opening of the next chapter offers a new exordium.

2. Priests and Princes Fail.

Hosea v. 1-14.

The line followed in this paragraph is almost parallel to that of chap. iv., running out to a prospect of invasion. But the charge is directed solely against the chiefs of the people, and the strictures of chap. vii. 7 ff. upon the political folly of the rulers are anticipated.

"Hear this, O Priests, and hearken, House of Israel, and House of the King, give ear. For on you is the sentence!" You who have hitherto been the judges, this time shall be judged.

"A snare have ye become at Mizpeh, and a net spread out upon Tabor, and a pit have they made deep upon Shittim;¶ but I shall be the scourge of them all. I know Ephraim, and Israel is not hid from me—for now hast thou played the harlot, Ephraim, Israel is defiled." The worship on the high places, whether nominally of Jehovah or not, was sheer service of Ba'alim. It was in the interest both of the priesthood and of the rulers to multiply these sanctuaries, but they were only traps for the people. "Their deeds will not let them return to their God; for a harlot spirit is in their midst, and Jehovah," for all their oaths by Him, "they have not known. But the pride of Israel shall testify to his face; and Israel and Ephraim shall stumble by their guilt—stumble also shall Judah with them." By Israel's pride many understand God. But the term is used too opprobriously by Amos to allow us to agree to this. The phrase must mean that Israel's arrogance, or her proud prosperity, by the wounds which it feels in this time of national decay, shall itself testify against the

* The application seems to swerve here. "Thy children" would seem to imply that, for this clause at least, the whole people, and not the priests only, were addressed. But Robertson Smith takes "thy mother" as equivalent, not to the nation, but to the priesthood.

† A reading current among Jewish writers and adopted by Geiger, "Urschrift," 316.

‡ Heb. "the heart," which ancient Israel conceived as the seat of the intellect.

§ Wellhausen thinks this third place-name (*cf.* Amos v. 5) has been dropped. It certainly seems to be understood.

* But see above, p. 497.

† So all critics since Hitzig.

‡ Mal. ii. 4.

§ Isa. xliv. 11.

‖ The verse is very uncertain. LXX. read a different and a fuller text from "Ephraim" in the previous verse to "harlotry" in this: "Ephraim hath set up for himself stumbling-blocks and chosen Canaanites." In the first of alternate readings of the latter half of the verse omit הבו as probably a repetition of the end of the preceding word; the second alternative is adapted from LXX., which for מגיניה must have read מגאונה.

¶ So by slightly altering the consonants. But the text is uncertain.

people—a profound ethical symptom to which we shall return when treating of Repentance.* Yet the verse may be rendered in harmony with the context: "the pride of Israel shall be humbled to his face. With their sheep and their cattle they go about to seek Jehovah, and shall not find" Him; "He hath drawn off from them. They have been unfaithful to Jehovah, for they have begotten strange children." A generation has grown up who are not His. "Now may a month devour them with their portions!" Any month may bring the swift invader. Hark! the alarum of war! How it reaches to the back of the land!

"Blow the trumpet in Gibeah, the clarion in Ramah;
Raise the slogan, Beth-Aven: 'After thee Benjamin!'" †

"Ephraim shall become desolation in the day of rebuke! Among the tribes of Israel I have made known what is certain!"

At this point (ver. 10) the discourse swerves from the religious to the political leaders of Israel; but as the princes were included with the priests in the exordium (ver. 1), we can hardly count this a new oracle.‡

"The princes of Judah are like landmark-removers"—commonest cheats in Israel—"upon them will I pour out My wrath like water. Ephraim is oppressed, crushed is" his "right, for he wilfully went after vanity.§ And I am as the moth to Ephraim, and as rottenness to the house of Judah." Both kingdoms have begun to fall to pieces, for by this time Uzziah of Judah also is dead, and the weak politicians are in charge whom Isaiah satirised. "And Ephraim saw his sickness, and Judah his sore; and Ephraim went to Asshur and‖ sent to King Jareb—King Combative, King Pick-Quarrel,"¶ a nickname for the Assyrian monarch. The verse probably refers to the tribute which Menahem sent to Assyria in 738. If so, then Israel has drifted full five years into her "thick night." "But he cannot heal you, nor dry up your sore. For I," Myself, "am like a lion to Ephraim, and like a young lion to the house of Judah. I, I rend and go My way; I carry off and there is none to deliver." It is the same truth which Isaiah expressed with even greater grimness.* God Himself is His people's sore; and not all their statecraft nor alliances may heal what He inflicts. Priests and Princes, then, have alike failed. A greater failure is to follow.

3. Repentance Fails.

Hosea v. 15-vii. 2.

Seeing that their leaders are so helpless, and feeling their wounds, the people may themselves turn to God for healing, but that will be with a repentance so shallow as also to be futile. They have no conviction of sin, nor appreciation of how deeply their evils have eaten.

This too facile repentance is expressed in a prayer which the Christian Church has paraphrased into one of its most beautiful hymns of conversion. Yet the introduction to this prayer, and its own easy assurance of how soon God will heal the wounds He has made, as well as the impatience with which God receives it, oblige us to take the prayer in another sense than the hymn which has been derived from it.† It offers but one more symptom of the optimism of this light-hearted people, whom no discipline and no judgment can impress with the reality of their incurable decay. They said of themselves, "The bricks are fallen, let us build with stones,"‡ and now they say just as easily and airily of their God, "He hath torn" only "that He may heal:" we are fallen, but "He will raise us up again in a day or two." At first it is still God who speaks.

"I am going My way, I am returning to My own place,§ until they feel their guilt and seek My face. When trouble comes upon them, they will soon" enough "seek Me, saying:‖—

"Come and let us return to Jehovah;
For He hath rent, that He may heal us,
And hath wounded,¶ that He may bind us up.
He will bring us to life in a couple of days;
On the third day He will raise us up *again*,
That we may live in His presence."

"Let us know, let us follow up ** to know, Jehovah:
As soon as we seek Him, we shall find Him ††
And He shall come to us like the winter-rain,
Like the spring-rain, pouring on the land!"

But how is this fair prayer received by God? With incredulity, with impatience. "What can I make of thee, Ephraim? what can I make

* *Note on the Pride of Israel.*—גאון means "grandeur," and is (1) so used of Jehovah's majesty (Micah v. 3; Isa. ii. 10, 19, 21; xxiv. 14), and (2) of the greatness of human powers (Zech. x. 11; Ezek. xxxii. 12). In Psalm xlvii. 5 it is parallel to the land of Israel (*cf.* Nahum ii. 3). (3) In a grosser sense the word is used of the rank vegetation of Jordan (Eng. wrongly "swelling") (Jer. xii. 5; Zech. xi. 3: *cf.* Job xxxviii. 11). It would appear to be this grosser sense of "rankness, arrogance," in which Amos vi. 8 takes it as parallel to "the palaces of Israel" which "Jehovah loathes and will destroy." In Amos viii. 7 the phrase may be used in scorn; yet some take it even there of God Himself (Buhl. last ed. of Gesenius' "Lexicon").

Now in Hosea it occurs twice in the phrase given above —גאון ישראל בפניו וענה (v. 5. vii. 10). LXX., Targum and some Jewish exegetes take ענה as a ל"ן verb, "to be humbled," and this suits both contexts. But the word בפניו, "to his face" almost compels us to take ענה as a ל"י verb, "to witness against" (*cf.* Job xvi. 8; Jer. xiv. 7). Hence Wellhausen renders "With his arrogance Israel witnesseth against himself," and confirms the plaint of Jehovah—the arrogance being the trust in the ritual and the feeling of no need to turn from that and repent (*cf.* vii. 10). Orelli quotes Amos vi. 8 and Nahum ii. 3, and says injustice cleaves to all Israel's splendour, so it testifies against him.

But the context, which in both cases speaks of Israel's gradual decay, demands rather the interpretation that Israel's material grandeur shows unmistakable signs of breaking down. For the ethical development of this interpretation, see below, pp. 641 f.

† Probably the ancient war-cry of the clan. *Cf.* Judg. v. 14.

‡ Yet ver. 9 goes with ver. 8 (so Wellhausen), and not with ver. 10 (so Ewald).

§ For צו read שׁוא.

‖ Wellhausen inserts "Judah," with that desire to complete a parallel which seems to me to be overdone by so many critics. If Judah be inserted we should need to bring the date of these verses down to the reign of Ahaz in 734.

¶ Guthe: "King Fighting-Cock."

* See "Isaiah i.-xxxix." ("Expositor's Bible"), pp. 677 ff.

† Cheyne indeed (Introduction to Robertson Smith's "Prophets of Israel") takes the prayer to be genuine, but an intrusion. His reasons do not persuade me. But at least it is clear that there is a want of connection between the prayer and what follows it, unless the prayer be understood in the sense explained above.

‡ Isaiah ix. 10.

§ *Cf.* Isaiah xviii. 4.

‖ *Saying:* so the LXX. adds and thereby connects chap. v. with chap. vi.

¶ Read וַיַּךְ.

** Literally "hunt, pursue." It is the same word as is used of the unfaithful Israel's pursuit of the Ba'alim, chap. ii. 9.

†† So by a rearrangement of consonants (כן נמצאהו

of thee, Judah? since your love is like the morning cloud and like the dew so early gone." Their shallow hearts need deepening. Have they not been deepened enough? "Wherefore I have hewn" them "by the prophets, I have slain them by the words of My mouth, and My judgment goeth forth like the lightning.* For leal love have I desired, and not sacrifice; and the knowledge of God more than burnt-offerings."

That the discourse comes back to the ritual is very intelligible. For what could make repentance seem so easy as the belief that forgiveness can be won by simply offering sacrifices? Then the prophet leaps upon what each new year of that anarchy revealed afresh—the profound sinfulness of the people.

"But they in human fashion† have transgressed the covenant! There"—he will now point out the very spots—"have they betrayed ‡ Me! Gilead is a city of evil-doers: stamped with the bloody footprints; assassins § in troops; a gang of priests murder on the way to Shechem. Yea, crime ‖ have they done. In the house of Israel I have seen horrors: there Ephraim hath played the harlot: Israel is defiled—Judah as well." ¶

Truly the sinfulness of Israel is endless. Every effort to redeem them only discovers more of it. "When I would turn, when I would heal Israel, then the guilt of Ephraim displays itself and the evils of Samaria," these namely: "that they work fraud and the thief cometh in"—evidently a technical term for housebreaking **—"while abroad a crew" of highwaymen "foray. And they never think in their hearts that all their evil is recorded by Me. Now have their deeds encompassed them: they are constantly before Me."

Evidently real repentance on the part of such a people is impossible. As Hosea said before, "Their deeds will not let them return." ††

4. Wickedness in High Places.

Hosea vii. 3-7.

There follows now a very difficult passage. The text is corrupt, and we have no means of determining what precise events are intended. The drift of meaning, however, is evident. The disorder and licentiousness of the people are favoured in high places; the throne itself is guilty.

"With their evil they make a king glad, and princes with their falsehoods: all of them are adulterers, like an oven heated by the baker, . . .‡‡

"On the day of our king"—some coronation or king's birthday—"the princes were sick with fever from wine. He stretched forth his hand with loose fellows," * presumably made them his associates. "Like an oven have they made† their hearts with their intriguing.‡ All night their anger sleepeth: § in the morning it blazes like a flame of fire. All of them glow like an oven, and devour their rulers: all their kings have fallen, without one of them calling on Me."

An obscure passage upon obscure events; yet so lurid with the passion of that fevered people in the flagrant years 743-735 that we can make out the kind of crimes described. A king surrounded by loose and unscrupulous nobles: adultery, drunkenness, conspiracies, assassination: every man striking for himself; none appealing to God.

From the court, then, downwards, by princes, priests, and prophets, to the common fathers of Israel and their households, immorality prevails. There is no redeeming feature, and no hope of better things. For repentance itself the capacity is gone.

In making so thorough an indictment of the moral condition of Israel, it would have been impossible for Hosea not to speak also of the political stupidity and restlessness which resulted from it. But he has largely reserved these for that part of his discourse which now follows, and which we will take in the next chapter.

CHAPTER XVII.

A PEOPLE IN DECAY: II. POLITICALLY.

Hosea vii. 8-x.

Moral decay means political decay. Sins like these are the gangrene of nations. It is part of Hosea's greatness to have traced this, a proof of that versatility which distinguishes him above other prophets. The most spiritual of them all, he is at the same time the most political. We owe him an analysis of repentance to which the New Testament has little to add; ‖ but he has also left us a criticism of society and of politics in Israel, unrivalled except by Isaiah. We owe him an intellectual conception of God,¶ which for the first time in Israel exploded idolatry; yet he also is the first to define Israel's position in the politics of Western Asia. With the single courage of conscience Amos had said to the people: You are bad, therefore you must perish. But Hosea's is the insight to follow the processes by which sin brings forth death—to trace, for instance, the effects of impurity upon a nation's powers of reproduction, as well as upon its intellectual vigour.

כשחרנו) and the help of the LXX. (*εὑρήσομεν αὐτόν*) Giesebrecht ("Beiträge," p. 208) proposes to read the clause, which in the traditional text runs, "like the morn His going forth shall be certain."

* Read מִשְׁפָּטִי כָאוֹר יֵצֵא.

† Or "like Adam," or (Guthe) "like the heathen."

‡ The verb means to prove false to any contract, but especially marriage.

§ Read מחכי.

‖ In several passages of the Old Testament the word means unchastity.

¶ Here the LXX. close chap. vi., taking 11 *b* along with chap. vii. Some think the whole of ver. 11 to be a Judæan gloss.

** *Cf.* Joel ii. 9, and the New Testament phrase "to come as a thief."

†† v. 4.

‡‡ The text is unsound. Heb.: "like an oven kindled by the baker, the stirrer (stoker or kneader?) resteth from kneading the dough until it be leavened." LXX.: *ὡς κλίβανος καιόμενος εἰς πέψιν κατακαύματος ἀπὸ τῆς φλογός ἀπὸ φυράσεως στέατος ἕως τοῦ ξυμωθῆναι αὐτό*—*i. e.*, for ישבת they read אש לחבת. Oort emends Heb to בוער הם אפהו, which gets rid of the difficulty of a feminine participle with תנור. Wellhausen omits whole clause as a gloss on ver. 6. But if there be a gloss it properly commences with ישבת.

* LXX. *μετατοιμῶν* ??

† LXX. "kindled," בָּעֲרוּ. So Vollers, "Z. A. T. W.," III. 250.

‡ Lit. "lurking."

§ Massoretic Text with different vowels reads "their baker." LXX. Εφραιμ !

‖ See below, chap. xxii.

¶ See chap. xxi.

So intimate are these two faculties of Hosea that in chapters devoted chiefly to the sins of Israel we have already seen him expose the political disasters that follow. But from the point we have now reached—chap. vii. 8—the proportion of his prophesying is reversed: he gives us less of the sin and more of the social decay and political folly of his age.

1. The Confusion of the Nation.

Hosea vii. 8–viii. 3.

Hosea begins by summing up the public aspect of Israel in two epigrams, short but of marvellous adequacy (vii. 8):—

> "Ephraim—among the nations he mixeth himself:
> Ephraim has become a cake not turned."

It is a great crisis for any nation to pass from the seclusion of its youth and become a factor in the main history of the world. But for Israel the crisis was trebly great. Their difference from all other tribes about them had struck the Canaanites on their first entry to the land:* their own earliest writers had emphasised their seclusion as their strength;† and their first prophets consistently deprecated every overture made by them either to Egypt or to Assyria. We feel the force of the prophets' policy when we remember what happened to the Philistines. These were a people as strong and as distinctive as Israel, with whom at one time they disputed possession of the whole land. But their position as traders in the main line of traffic between Asia and Africa rendered the Philistines peculiarly open to foreign influence. They were now Egyptian vassals, now Assyrian victims; and after the invasion of Alexander the Great their cities became centres of Hellenism, while the Jews upon their secluded hills still stubbornly held unmixed their race and their religion. This contrast, so remarkably developed in later centuries, has justified the prophets of the eighth in their anxiety that Israel should not annul the advantages of her geographical seclusion by trade or treaties with the Gentiles. But it was easier for Judæa to take heed to the warning than for Ephraim. The latter lies as open and fertile as her sister province is barren and aloof. She has many gates into the world, and they open upon many markets. Nobler opportunities there could not be for a nation in the maturity of its genius and loyal to its vocation:—

> "Rejoice, O Zebulun, in thine outgoings:
> They shall call the nations to the mountain;
> They shall suck of the abundance of the seas,
> And of the treasure that is stored in the sands." ‡

But in the time of his outgoings Ephraim was not sure of himself nor true to his God, the one secret and strength of the national distinctiveness. So he met the world weak and unformed, and, instead of impressing it, was by it dissipated and confused. The tides of a lavish commerce scattered abroad the faculties of the people, and swept back upon their life alien fashions and tempers, to subdue which there was neither native strength nor definiteness of national purpose. All this is what Hosea means by the first of his epigrams: "Ephraim—among the nations he lets himself be poured out," or "mixed up." The form of the verb does not elsewhere occur; but it is reflexive, and the meaning of the root is certain. "Balal" is to "pour out," or "mingle," as of oil in the sacrificial flour. Yet it is sometimes used of a mixing which is not sacred, but profane and hopeless. It is applied to the first great confusion of mankind, to which a popular etymology has traced the name Babel, as if for Balbel. Derivatives of the stem bear the additional ideas of staining and impurity. The alternative renderings which have been proposed, "lets himself be soaked" and "scatters himself" abroad like wheat among tares, are not so probable, yet hardly change the meaning.* Ephraim wastes and confuses himself among the Gentiles. The nation's character is so disguised that Hosea afterwards nicknames him Canaan;† their religion so filled with foreign influences that he calls the people the harlot of the Ba'alim.

If the first of Hosea's epigrams satirises Israel's foreign relations, the second, with equal brevity and wit, hits off the temper and constitution of society at home. For the metaphor of which this epigram is composed Hosea has gone to the baker. Among all classes in the East, especially under conditions requiring haste, there is in demand a round flat scone, which is baked by being laid on hot stones or attached to the wall of a heated oven. The whole art of baking consists in turning the scone over at the proper moment. If this be mismanaged it does not need a baker to tell us that one side may be burnt to a cinder, while the other remains raw. "Ephraim," says Hosea, "is an unturned cake."

By this he may mean one of several things, or all of them together, for they are infectious of each other. There was, for instance, the social conditions of the people. What can better be described as an unturned scone than a community one half of whose number are too rich, and the other too poor? Or Hosea may refer to that unequal distribution of religion through life with which in other parts of his prophecy he reproaches Israel. They keep their religion, as Amos more fully tells us, for their temples, and neglect to carry its spirit into their daily business. Or he may refer to Israel's politics, which were equally in want of thoroughness. They rushed hotly at an enterprise, but having expended so much fire in the beginning of it, they let the end drop cold and dead. Or he may wish to satirise, like Amos, Israel's imperfect culture—the pretentious and overdone arts, stuck excrescence-wise upon the unrefined bulk of the nation, just as in many German principalities last century society took on a few French fashions in rough and exaggerated forms, while at heart still brutal and coarse. Hosea may mean any one of

* Numb. xxiii. 9 *b*; Josh. ii. 8. † Deut. xxxiii. 27. ‡ Deut. xxxiii. 18, 19.

* יִתְבֹּלָל from בלל. In Phœn. בלל seems to have been used as in Israel of the sacrificial mingling of oil and flour (*cf.* Robertson Smith, "Religion of Semites," I. 203); in Arabic "ball" is to weaken a strong liquid with water, while "balbal" is to be confused, disordered. The Syriac "balal" is to mix. Some have taken Hosea's יתבלל as if from בליל (Isa. xxx. 24; Job vi. 5), usually understood as a mixed crop of wheat and inferior vegetables for fodder; but there is reason to believe בליל means rather fresh corn. The derivation from בלה, to grow old, does not seem probable.

† xii. 8.

these things, for the figure suits all, and all spring from the same defect. Want of thoroughness and equable effort was Israel's besetting sin, and it told on all sides of his life. How better describe a half-fed people, a half-cultured society, a half-lived religion, a half-hearted policy, than by a half-baked scone?

We who are so proud of our political bakers, we who scorn the rapid revolutions of our neighbours and complacently dwell upon our equable ovens, those slow and cautious centuries of political development which lie behind us—have we anything better than our neighbours, anything better than Israel, to show in our civilisation? Hosea's epigram fits us to the letter. After all those ages of baking, society is still with us "an unturned scone": one end of the nation with the strength burnt out of it by too much enjoyment of life, the other with not enough of warmth to be quickened into anything like adequate vitality. No man can deny that this is so; we are able to live only by shutting our hearts to the fact. Or is religion equally distributed through the lives of the religious portion of our nation? Of late years religion has spread, and spread wonderfully, but of how many Christians is it still true that they are but half-baked—living a life one side of which is reeking with the smoke of sacrifice, while the other is never warmed by one religious thought. We may have too much religion if we confine it to one day or one department of life: our worship overdone, with the sap and the freshness burnt out of it, cindry, dusty, unattractive, fit only for crumbling; our conduct cold, damp, and heavy, like dough the fire has never reached.

Upon the theme of these two epigrams the other verses of this chapter are variations. Has Ephraim mixed himself among the peoples? "Strangers have devoured his strength, and he knoweth it not," senselessly congratulating himself upon the increase of his trade and wealth, while he does not feel that these have sucked from him all his distinctive virtue. "Yea, grey hairs are sprinkled upon him, and he knoweth it not." He makes his energy the measure of his life, as Isaiah also marked,* but sees not that it all means waste and decay. "The pride of Israel testifieth to his face, yet"—even when the pride of the nation is touched to the quick by such humiliating overtures as they make to both Assyria and Egypt †—"they do not return to Jehovah their God, nor seek Him for all this."

With virtue and single-hearted faith have disappeared intellect and the capacity for affairs. "Ephraim is become like a silly dove—a dove without heart," to the Hebrews the organ of the wits of a man—"they cry to Egypt, they go off to Assyria." Poor pigeon of a people, fluttering from one refuge to another! But "as they go I will throw over them My net, like a bird of the air I will bring them down. I will punish them as their congregation have heard"—this text as it stands‡ can only mean "in the manner I have publicly proclaimed in Israel." "Woe to them that they have strayed from Me! Damnation to them that they have rebelled against Me! While I would have redeemed them they spoke lies about Me. And they have never cried unto Me with their heart, but they keep howling from their beds for corn and new wine." No real repentance theirs, but some fear of drought

* ix. 9 f. † See above, p. 507, and below, p. 641.
‡ But the reading is very doubtful.

and miscarriage of the harvests, a sensual and servile sorrow in which they wallow. They seek God with no heart, no true appreciation of what He is, but use the senseless means by which the heathen invoke their gods: "they cut themselves,* and" so "apostatise from Me! And yet it was I who disciplined them, I strengthened their arm, but with regard to Me they kept thinking" only "evil!" So fickle and sensitive to fear, "they turn" indeed "but not upwards;" no Godward conversion theirs. In their repentance "they are like a bow which swerves"—off upon some impulse of their ill-balanced natures. "Their princes must fall by the sword because of the bitterness"—we should have expected "falseness"—"of their tongue: this is their scorn in the land of Egypt!" To the allusion we have no key.

With so false a people nothing can be done. Their doom is inevitable. So

"Cry havoc and let slip the dogs of war."

"To thy mouth with the trumpet! The Eagle is down upon the house of Jehovah!" † Where the carcase is, there are the eagles gathered together. "For"—to sum up the whole crisis—"they have transgressed My covenant, and against My law have they rebelled. To Me they cry, My God, we know Thee, we Israel!" What does it matter? "Israel hath spurned the good:‡ the Foe must pursue him."

It is the same climax of inevitable war to which Amos led up his periods; and a new subject is now introduced.

2. Artificial Kings and Artificial Gods.

Hosea viii. 4-13.

The curse of such a state of dissipation as that to which Israel had fallen is that it produces no men. Had the people had in them "the root of the matter," had there been the stalk and the fibre of a national consciousness and purpose, it would have blossomed to a man. In the similar time of her outgoings upon the world Prussia had her Frederick the Great, and Israel, too, would have produced a leader, a heaven-sent king, if the national spirit had not been squandered on foreign trade and fashions. But after the death of Jeroboam every man who rose to eminence in Israel, rose, not on the nation, but only on the fevered and transient impulse of some faction; and through the broken years one party monarch was lifted after another to the brief tenancy of a blood-stained throne. They were not from God, these monarchs; but man-made, and sooner or later man-murdered. With his sharp insight Hosea likens these artificial kings to the artificial gods, also the work of men's hands; and till near the close of his

* For יתגררו read יתגדדו.

† Wellhausen's objection to the first clause, that one does not set a trumpet to one's "gums," which חֵךְ literally means, is beside the mark. חֵךְ is more than once used of the mouth as a whole (Job viii. 7; Prov. v. 3). The second clause gives the reason of the trumpet, the alarum trumpet, in the first. Read כי נשר (so also Wellhausen).

‡ *Cf.* Amos: "Seek Me = Seek the good;" and Jesus: "Not every one that saith unto Me, Lord, Lord; but he that doeth the will of My Father in heaven."

book the idols of the sanctuary and the puppets of the throne form the twin targets of his scorn. "They have made kings, but not from Me; they have made princes, but I knew not. With their silver and their gold they have manufactured themselves idols, only that they * may be cut off"—king after king, idol upon idol. "He loathes thy Calf, O Samaria," the thing of wood and gold which thou callest Jehovah. And God confirms this. "Kindled is Mine anger against them! How long will they be incapable of innocence?"—unable to clear themselves of guilt! The idol is still in his mind. "For from Israel is it also"—as much as the puppet-kings; "a workman made it, and no god is it. Yea, splinters shall the Calf of Samaria become." † Splinters shall everything in Israel become. "For they sow the wind, and the whirlwind shall they reap." Indeed like a storm Hosea's own language now sweeps along; and his metaphors are torn into shreds upon it. "Stalk it hath none: the sprout brings forth no grain: if it were to bring forth, strangers would swallow it." ‡ Nay, "Israel hath let herself be swallowed up! Already are they becoming among the nations like a vessel there is no more use for." Heathen empires have sucked them dry. "They have gone up to Assyria like a runaway wild-ass. Ephraim hath hired lovers." § It is again the note of their mad dissipation among the foreigners. "But if they" thus "give themselves away among the nations, I must gather them in, and" then "shall they have to cease a little from the anointing of a king and princes." ‖ This wilful roaming of theirs among the foreigners shall be followed by compulsory exile, and all their unholy artificial politics shall cease. The discourse turns to the other target. For Ephraim hath multiplied altars—to sin; altars are his own—to sin. Were I to write for him by myriads My laws,¶ as those of a stranger would they be accounted. They slay burnt-offerings for Me and eat flesh.** Jehovah hath no delight in them. Now must He remember their guilt and make visitation upon their sin. They—to Egypt—shall return. . . ." †† Back to their ancient servitude must they go, as formerly He said He would withdraw them to the wilderness.‡‡

3. The Effects of Exile.

Hosea ix. 1–9.

Hosea now turns to describe the effects of exile upon the social and religious habits of the people. It must break up at once the joy and the sacredness of their lives. Every pleasure will be removed, every taste offended. Indeed, even now, with their conscience of having deserted Jehovah, they cannot pretend to enjoy the feasts of the Ba'alim in the same hearty way as the heathen with whom they mix. But, whether or no, the time is near when nature-feasts and all other religious ceremonies—all that makes life glad and regular and solemn—shall be impossible.

"Rejoice not, O Israel, to" the pitch of "rapture like the heathen, for thou hast played the harlot from thy God; a harlot's hire hast thou loved on all threshing-floors.* Threshing-floor and wine-vat shall ignore † them, and the new wine shall play them false. They shall not abide in the land of Jehovah, but Ephraim shall return to Egypt, and in Assyria they shall eat what is unclean. They shall not pour libations to Jehovah, nor prepare ‡ for Him their sacrifices. Like the bread of sorrows shall their bread § be; all that eat of it shall be defiled:" yea, "their bread shall be" only "for their appetite; they shall not bring" it ‖ "to the temple of Jehovah." He cannot be worshipped off His own land. They will have to live like animals, divorced from religion, unable to hold communion with their God. "What shall ye do for days¶ of festival, or for a day of pilgrimage to Jehovah? For lo," they "shall be gone forth from destruction," ** the shock and invasion of their land, only "that Egypt may gather them in, Memphis give them sepulchre, nettles inherit their jewels of silver, thorns" come up "in their tents." The threat of exile still wavers between Assyria and Egypt. And in Egypt Memphis is chosen as the destined grave of Israel; for even then her Pyramids and mausoleums were ancient and renowned, her vaults and sepulchres were countless and spacious.

But what need is there to seek the future for Israel's doom, when already this is being fulfilled by the corruption of her spiritual leaders?

"The days of visitation have come, have come the days of requital. Israel" already "experiences†† them! A fool is the prophet, raving mad the man of the spirit." The old ecstasy of Saul's day has become delirium and fanaticism.‡‡ Why? "For the mass of thy guilt and the multiplied treachery! Ephraim acts the spy with My God." There is probably a play on the name, for with the meaning a "watchman" for God it is elsewhere used as an honourable title of the prophets. "The prophet is a fowler's snare upon all his ways. Treachery—they have made it profound in the" very "house of their God.§§ They have done corruptly, as in the days of Gibeah. Their iniquity is remembered; visitation is made on their sin."

These, then, were the symptoms of the profound political decay which followed on Israel's immorality. The national spirit and unity of the people had disappeared. Society—half of it was

* So LXX., but Hebrew *it*.
† Davidson's "Syntax," § 136, Rom. 1, and § 71, Rom. 4.
‡ So by the accents runs the verse, but, as Wellhausen has pointed out, both its sense and its assonance are better expressed by another arrangement: "Hath it grown up?" then "it hath no shoot, nor bringeth forth fruit."

ên lo ṣemach,
b'li ya'aṣeh qemach.

Yet to this there is a grammatical obstacle.
§ Wellhausen's reading "to Egypt with love gifts" scarcely suits the verb "go up." Notice the play upon P(h)ere', "wild-ass" and Ephra'[im].
‖ So LXX. reads. Heb.: "they shall involve themselves with tribute to the king of princes," presumably the Assyrian monarch.
¶ So LXX.
** Text obscure.
†† LXX. addition here is plainly borrowed from ix. 3. For the reasons for omitting ver. 14 see above, p. 497.
‡‡ ii. 16.

* On this verse see more particularly below, pp. 642 ff.
† So LXX.
‡ Read יערכו. *Cf.* with the whole passage iii. 4 f.
§ לחמם for להם.
‖ יָבִיאוּ.
¶ Plural: so LXX.
** Others read "they are gone to Assyria."
†† Literally "knows. See below, p. 522, *n*.
‡‡ See above, p. 449.
§§ So, after the LXX, by taking הצמיקו with this verse, 8, instead of with ver. 9.

raw, half of it was baked to a cinder. The nation, broken into fractions, produced no man to lead, no king with the stamp of God upon him. Anarchy prevailed; monarchs were made and murdered. There was no prestige abroad, nothing but contempt among the Gentiles for a people whom they had exhausted. Judgment was inevitable by exile—nay, it had come already in the corruption of the spiritual leaders of the nation.

Hosea now turns to probe a deeper corruption still.

4. "The Corruption that is Through Lust."

Hosea ix. 10-17: *cf.* iv. 11-14.

Those who at the present time are enforcing among us the revival of a Paganism—without the Pagan conscience—and exalting licentiousness to the level of an art, forget how frequently the human race has attempted their experiment, with far more sincerity than they themselves can put into it, and how invariably the result has been recorded by history to be weariness, decay, and death. On this occasion we have the story told to us by one who to the experience of the statesman adds the vision of the poet.

The generation to which Hosea belonged practised a periodical unchastity under the alleged sanctions of nature and religion. And, although their prophet told them that—like our own apostates from Christianity—they could never do so with the abandon of the Pagans, for they carried within them the conscience and the memory of a higher faith, it appears that even the fathers of Israel resorted openly and without shame to the licentious rites of the sanctuaries. In an earlier passage of his book Hosea insists that all this must impair the people's intellect. "Harlotry takes away the brains." * He has shown also how it confuses the family, and has exposed the old delusion that men may be impure and keep their womankind chaste.† But now he diagnoses another of the inevitable results of this sin. After tracing the sin and the theory of life which permitted it, to their historical beginnings at the entry of the people into Canaan, he describes how the long practice of it, no matter how pretentious its sanctions, inevitably leads not only to exterminating strifes, but to the decay of the vigour of the nation, to barrenness and a diminishing population.

"Like grapes in the wilderness I found Israel, like the first fruit on a fig-tree in her first season I saw your fathers." So had the lusty nation appeared to God in its youth; in that dry wilderness all the sap and promise of spring were in its eyes, because it was still pure. But "they—they came to Ba'al-Peor"—the first of the shrines of Canaan which they touched—"and dedicated themselves to the Shame, and became as abominable as the object of their love. Ephraim"—the "Fruitful" name is emphasised—"their glory is flown away like a bird. No more birth, no more motherhood, no more conception!‡ Blasted is Ephraim, withered the root of them, fruit they produce not: yea, even when they beget children I slay the darlings of their womb. Yea, though they bring up their sons I bereave them," till they are "poor in men. Yea, woe upon themselves also, when I look away from them! Ephraim"—again the "Fruitful" name is dragged to the front—"for prey, as I have seen, are his sons destined.* Ephraim"—he "must lead his sons to the slaughter."

And the prophet interrupts with his chorus: "Give them, O Lord—what wilt Thou give them? Give them a miscarrying womb and breasts that are dry!"

"All their mischief is in Gilgal"—again the Divine voice strikes the connection between the national worship and the national sin—"yea, there do I hate them: for the evil of their doings from My house I will drive them. I will love them no more: all their nobles are rebels."†

And again the prophet responds: "My God will cast them away, for they have not hearkened to Him, and they shall be vagabonds among the nations."

Some of the warnings which Hosea enforces with regard to this sin have been instinctively felt by mankind since the beginnings of civilisation, and are found expresed among the proverbs of nearly all the languages.‡ But I am unaware of any earlier moralist in any literature who traced the effects of national licentiousness in a diminishing population, or who exposed the persistent delusion of libertine men that they themselves may resort to vice, yet keep their womankind chaste. Hosea, so far as we know, was the first to do this. History in many periods has confirmed the justice of his observations, and by one strong voice after another enforced his terrible warnings. The experience of ancient Persia and Egypt; the languor of the Greek cities; the "deep weariness and sated lust" which in Imperial Rome "made human life a hell"; the decay which overtook Italy after the renascence of Paganism without the Pagan virtues; the strife and anarchy that have rent every court where, as in the case of Henri Quatre, the king set the example of libertinage; the incompetence, the poltroonery, the treachery, that have corrupted every camp where, as in French Metz in 1870, soldiers and officers gave way so openly to vice; the checks suffered by modern civilisation in face of barbarism because its pioneers mingled in vice with the savage races they were subduing; the number of great statesmen falling by their passions, and in their fall frustrating the hopes of nations; the great families worn out by indulgence; the homes broken up by infidelities; the tainting of the blood of a new generation by the poisonous practices of the old,—have not all these things been in every age, and do they not still happen near enough to ourselves to give us a great fear of the sin which causes them all? Alas! how slow men are to listen and to lay to heart! Is it possible that we can gild by the names of frivolity and piquancy habits the wages of which are death? Is it possible that we can enjoy comedies which make such things their

* iv. 12.
† iv. 13, 14.
‡ Here, between vv. 11 and 12, Wellhausen with justice proposes to insert ver. 16.

* So Wellhausen after LXX., ; probably correct.
† So we may attempt to echo the play on the words.
‡ *Cf.*, *e. g.*, the "Proverbs of Ptah-Hotep" the Egyptian, *circa* 2500 B. C. "There is no prudence in taking part in it, and thousands of men destroy themselves in order to enjoy a moment, brief as a dream, while they gain death so as to know it. It is a villainous . . . that of a man who excites himself (?); if he goes on to carry it out, his mind abandons him. For as for him who is without repugnance for such an [act], there is no good sense at all in him."—From the translation in "Records of the Past," Second Series, Vol. III., p. 24.

jest? We have among us many who find their business in the theatre, or in some of the periodical literature of our time, in writing and speaking and exhibiting as closely as they dare to limits of public decency. When will they learn that it is not upon the easy edge of mere conventions that they are capering, but upon the brink of those eternal laws whose further side is death and hell—that it is not the tolerance of their fellow-men they are testing, but the patience of God Himself? As for those loud few who claim license in the name of art and literature, let us not shrink from them as if they were strong or their high words true. They are not strong, they are only reckless; their claims are lies. All history, the poets and the prophets, whether Christian or Pagan, are against them. They are traitors alike to art, to love, and to every other high interest of mankind.

It may be said that a large part of the art of the day, which takes great license in dealing with these subjects, is exercised only by the ambition to expose that ruin and decay which Hosea himself affirms. This is true. Some of the ablest and most popular writers of our time have pictured the facts, which Hosea describes, with so vivid a realism that we cannot but judge them to be inspired to confirm his ancient warnings, and to excite a disgust of vice in a generation which otherwise treats vice so lightly. But if so, their ministry is exceeding narrow, and it is by their side that we best estimate the greatness of the ancient prophet. Their transcript of human life may be true to the facts it selects, but we find in it no trace of facts which are greater and more essential to humanity. They have nothing to tell us of forgiveness and repentance, and yet these are as real as the things they describe. Their pessimism is unrelieved. They see the "corruption that is in the world through lust;" they forget that there is an *escape* from it.* It is Hosea's greatness that, while he felt the vices of his day with all needed thoroughness and realism, he yet never allowed them to be inevitable or ultimate, but preached repentance and pardon, with the possibility of holiness even for his depraved generation. It is the littleness of the Art of our day that these great facts are forgotten by her, though once she was their interpreter to men. When she remembers them the greatness of her past will return.

5. Once More: Puppet-Kings and Puppet-Gods.

Hosea x.

For another section, the tenth chapter, the prophet returns to the twin targets of his scorn: the idols and the puppet-kings. But few notes are needed. Observe the reiterated connection between the fertility of the land and the idolatry of the people.

"A wanton vine is Israel; he lavishes his fruit;† the more his fruit, the more he made his altars; the goodlier his land, the more goodly he made his" maççeboth, or "sacred pillars. False is the heart of them: now must they atone for it. He shall break the neck of their altars; He shall ruin their pillars. For already they are saying, No king have we, for we have not feared Jehovah, and the king—what could he do for us? Speaking* of words, swearing of false oaths, making of bargains—till law† breaks out like weeds in the furrows of the field.

"For the Calf of Beth-Aven the inhabitants‡ of Samaria shall be anxious: yea, mourn for him shall his people, and his priestlings shall writhe for him—for his glory that it is banished from him." In these days of heavy tribute shall the gold of the golden calf be safe? "Yea, himself shall they pack§ to Assyria; he shall be offered as tribute to King Pick-Quarrel.‖ Ephraim shall take disgrace, and Israel be ashamed because of his counsel.¶ Undone Samaria! Her king like chip** on the face of the waters!" This may refer to one of the revolutions in which the king was murdered. But it seems more appropriate to the final catastrophe of 724-21: the fall of the kingdom, and the king's banishment to Assyria. If the latter, the verse has been inserted; but the following verse would lead us to take these disasters as still future. "And the high places of idolatry shall be destroyed, the sin of Israel; thorn and thistle shall come up on their altars. And they shall say to the mountains, Cover us, and to the hills, Fall on us." It cannot be too often repeated: these handmade gods, these chips of kings, shall be swept away together.

Once more the prophet returns to the ancient origins of Israel's present sins, and once more to their shirking of the discipline necessary for spiritual results, but only that he may lead up as before to the inevitable doom. "From†† the days of Gibeah thou hast sinned, O Israel. There have they remained"—never progressed beyond their position there—"and this without war overtaking them in Gibeah against the dastards.‡‡ As soon as I please, I can chastise them, and peoples shall be gathered against them in chastisement for their double sin." This can scarcely be, as some suggest, the two calves at Bethel and Dan. More probably it is still the idols and the man-made kings. Now he returns to the ambition of the people for spiritual results without a spiritual discipline.

"And Ephraim is a broken-in heifer, that loveth to thresh.§§ But I have come on her fair neck. I will yoke Ephraim; Judah must plough; Jacob must harrow for himself." It is all very well for the unmuzzled beast‖‖ to love the threshing, but harder and unrewarded labours of ploughing and

* 2 Peter i.

† Doubtful. The Heb. text gives an inappropriate if not impossible clause, even if ישוה be taken from a root שוה, to "set" or "produce" (Barth, "Etym. Stud." 66). LXX.: ὁ καρπὸς εὐθηνῶν αὐτῆς (A. Q. αὐτῆς εὐθηνῶν), "her [the vine's] fruit flourishing." Some parallel is required to בקק of the first clause; and it is possible that it may have been from a root שׂוּחַ or שִׂיח, corresponding to Arabic sâh, "to wander" in the sense of scattering or being scattered.

* After LXX.

† Doubtful. Lawsuits?

‡ Calf," "inhabitants"—so LXX.

§ LXX. supplies.

‖ See above, p. 507.

¶ Very uncertain. Wellhausen reads "from his idol," מעצבו.

** קצף: compare Arabic qṣf, "to break"; but there is also the assonant Arabic qṣb, "reed." The Rabbis translate "foam": *cf.* the other meaning of קצף = outbreak of anger, which suggests "bubble."

†† Rosenmüller: "more than in." These days are evidently not the beginning of the kingship under Saul (so Wellhausen), for with that Hosea has no quarrel, but either the idolatry of Micah (Judg. xvii. 3 ff.), or more probably the crime of Benjamin (Judg. xix. 22).

‡‡ Obscure; text corrupt, and in next verse uncertain.

§§ For the sense of the verse both participles are surely needed. Wellhausen thinks two redundant.

‖‖ Deut. xxv. 4; 1 Cor. ix. 9; 1 Tim. v. 18.

harrowing have to come before the floor be heaped with sheaves. Israel must not expect religious festival without religious discipline. "Sow for yourselves righteousness; then shall ye reap the fruit of God's leal love.* Break up your fallow ground, for it is time to seek Jehovah, till He come and shower salvation† upon you.‡ Ye have ploughed wickedness; disaster have ye reaped: ye have eaten the fruit of falsehood; for thou didst trust in thy chariots,§ in the multitude of thy warriors. For the tumult of war shall arise among thy tribes,‖ and all thy fenced cities shall be ruined, as Salman beat to ruin Beth-Arbel¶ in the day of war: the mother shall be broken on the children"—presumably the land shall fall with the falling of her cities. "Thus shall I do to you, O house of Israel,** because of the evil of your evil: soon shall the king of Israel be undone—undône."

The political decay of Israel, then, so deeply figured in all these chapters, must end in utter collapse. Let us sum up the gradual features of this decay: the substance of the people scattered abroad; the national spirit dissipated; the national prestige humbled; the kings mere puppets; the prophets corrupted; the national vigour sapped by impurity; the idolatry conscious of its impotence.

CHAPTER XVIII.

THE FATHERHOOD AND HUMANITY OF GOD.

HOSEA xi.

FROM the thick jungle of Hosea's travail, the eleventh chapter breaks like a high and open mound. The prophet enjoys the first of his two clear visions—that of the Past.†† Judgment continues to descend. Israel's Sun is near his setting, but before he sinks—

> "A lingering light he fondly throws
> On the dear hills, whence first he rose."

Across these confused and vicious years, through which he has painfully made his way, Hosea sees the tenderness and the romance of the early history of his people. And although he must strike the old despairing note—that, by the insincerity of the present generation, all the ancient guidance of their God must end in this!—yet for some moments the blessed memory shines by itself, and God's mercy appears to triumph over Israel's ingratitude. Surely their sun will not set; Love must prevail. To which assurance a later voice from the Exile has added, in verses 10 and 11, a confirmation suitable to its own circumstances.

> "When Israel was a child, then I loved him,
> And from Egypt I called *him* to be My son.

The early history was a romance. Think of it historically. Before the Most High there spread an array of kingdoms and peoples. At their head were three strong princes—sons indeed of God, if all the heritage of the past, the power of the present, and the promise of the future be tokens. Egypt, wrapt in the rich and jewelled web of centuries, basked by Nile and Pyramid, all the wonder of the world's art in his dreamy eyes. Opposite him Assyria, with barer but more massive limbs, stood erect upon his highlands, grasping in his sword the promise of the world's power. Between the two, and using both of them, yet with his eyes westward on an empire of which neither dreamed, the Phœnician on his sea-coast built his storehouses and sped his navies, the promise of the world's wealth. It must ever remain the supreme romance of history, that the true son of God, bearer of His love and righteousness to all mankind, should be found, not only outside this powerful trinity, but in the puny and despised captive of one of them—in a people that was not a state, that had not a country, that was without a history, and, if appearances be true, was as yet devoid of even the rudiments of civilisation—a child people and a slave.

That was the Romance, and Hosea gives us the Grace which made it. "When Israel was a child then I loved him." The verb is a distinct impulse: "I began, I learned, to love him." God's eyes, that passed unheeding the adult princes of the world, fell upon this little slave boy, and He loved him and gave him a career: "from Egypt I called" him "to be My son."

Now, historically, it was the persuasion of this which made Israel. All their distinctiveness and character, their progress from a level with other nomadic tribes to the rank of the greatest religious teachers of humanity, started from the memory of these two facts—that God loved them, and that God called them. This was an unfailing conscience—the obligation that they were not their own, the irresistible motive to repentance even in their utmost backsliding, the unquenchable hope of a destiny in their direst days of defeat and scattering.

Some, of course, may cavil at the narrow, national scale on which such a belief was held, but let them remember that it was held in trust for all mankind. To snarl that Israel felt this sonship to God only for themselves, is to forget that it is they who have persuaded humanity that this is the only kind of sonship worth claiming. Almost every other nation of antiquity imagined a filial relation to the deity, but it was either through some fabulous physical descent, and then often confined only to kings and heroes, or by some mystical mingling of the Divine with the human, which was just as gross and sensuous. Israel alone defined the connection as a historical and a moral one. "The sons of God are begotten not of blood, nor of the will of the flesh, nor of the will of man, but of God." * Sonship to God is something not physical, but moral and historical, into which men are carried by a supreme awakening to the Divine love and authority. Israel, it is true, felt this only in a general way for the nation as a whole;† but their conception of it embraced just those moral contents which form the glory of Christ's doctrine of the

* LXX.: "fruit of life."

† צדק surely in the sense in which we find it in Isa. xl. ff. LXX.: "the fruits of righteousness shall be yours."

‡ We shall return to this passage in dealing with Repentance; see p. 643.

§ So LXX. Wellhausen suspects authenticity of the whole clause.

‖ Wellhausen proposes to read בעריך for בעמיך, but there is no need.

¶ See above, p. 495, *n*.

** So LXX.

†† See above, p. 505.

* St. John's Gospel, i. 12, 13.

† Or occasionally for the king as the nation's representative.

Divine sonship of the individual. The belief that God is our Father does not come to us with our carnal birth—except in possibility: the persuasion of it is not conferred by our baptism except in so far as that is Christ's own seal to the fact that God Almighty loves us and has marked us for His own. To us sonship is a becoming, not a being—the awakening of our adult minds into the surprise of a Father's undeserved mercy, into the constraint of His authority and the assurance of the destiny He has laid up for us. It is conferred by love, and confirmed by duty. Neither has power brought it, nor wisdom, nor wealth, but it has come solely with the wonder of the knowledge that God loves us, and has always loved us, as well as in the sense, immediately following, of a true vocation to serve Him. Sonship which is less than this is no sonship at all. But so much as this is possible to every man through Jesus Christ. His constant message is that the Father loves every one of us, and that if we *know* * that love, we are God's sons indeed. To them who feel it, adoption into the number and privileges of the sons of God comes with the amazement and the romance which glorified God's choice of the child-slave Israel. "Behold," they cry, "what manner of love the Father hath bestowed upon us, that we should be called the sons of God." †

But we cannot be loved by God and left where we are. Beyond the grace there lie the long discipline and destiny. We are called from servitude to freedom, from the world of God—each of us to run a course, and do a work, which can be done by no one else. That Israel did not perceive this was God's sore sorrow with them.

"The more I ‡ called to them the farther they went from Me.§ They to the Ba'alim kept sacrificing, and to images offering incense." But God persevered with grace, and the story is at first continued in the figure of Fatherhood with which it commenced; then it changes to the metaphor of a humane man's goodness to his beasts. "Yet I taught Ephraim to walk, holding them on Mine arms,‖ but they knew not that I healed them"—presumably when they fell and hurt themselves. "With the cords of a man I would draw them, with bands of love; and I was to them as those who lift up the yoke on their jaws, and gently would I give them to eat."¶ It is the picture of a team of bullocks, in charge of a kind driver. Israel are no longer the wanton young cattle of the previous chapter, which need the yoke firmly fastened on their neck,** but a team of toiling oxen mounting some steep road. There is no use now for the rough ropes, by which frisky animals are kept to their work; but the driver, coming to his beasts' heads, by the gentle touch of his hand at their mouths and by words of sympathy *draws* them after him. "I drew them with cords of a man, and with bands of love." Yet there is the yoke, and it would seem that certain forms of this, when beasts were working upwards, as we should say "against the collar," pressed and rubbed upon them, so that the humane driver, when he came to their heads, eased the yoke with his hands. "I was as they that take the yoke off their jaws;" * and then, when they got to the top of the hill, he would rest and feed them. That is the picture, and however uncertain we may feel as to some of its details, it is obviously a passage —Ewald says "the earliest of all passages"—in which "humane means precisely the same as love." It ought to be taken along with that other passage in the great Prophecy of the Exile, where God is described as He that led them through "the deep, as an horse in the wilderness, that they should not stumble: as a beast goeth down into the valley, the Spirit of the Lord gave him rest." †

Thus then the figure of the fatherliness of God changes into that of His gentleness or humanity. Do not let us think that there is here either any descent of the poetry or want of connection between the two figures. The change is true, not only to Israel's, but to our own experience. Men are all either the eager children of happy, irresponsible days, or the bounden, plodding draught-cattle of life's serious burdens and charges. Hosea's double figure reflects human life in its whole range. Which of us has not known this fatherliness of the Most High, exercised upon us, as upon Israel, throughout our years of carelessness and disregard? It was God Himself who taught and trained us then;—

"When through the slippery paths of youth
With heedless steps I ran,
Thine arm unseen conveyed me safe,
And led me up to man."

Those speedy recoveries from the blunders of early wilfulness, those redemptions from the sins of youth—happy were we if we knew that it was "He who healed us." But there comes a time when men pass from leading-strings to harness—when we feel faith less and duty more—when our work touches us more closely than our God. Death must be a strange transformer of the spirit, yet surely not more strange than life, which out of the eager buoyant child makes in time the slow automaton of duty. It is such a stage which the fourth of these verses suits, when we look up, not so much for the fatherliness as for the gentleness and humanity of our God. A man has a mystic power of a very wonderful kind upon the animals over whom he is placed. On any of these wintry roads of ours we may see it, when a kind carter gets down at a hill, and, throwing the reins on his beast's back, will come to its head and touch it with his bare hands, and speak to it as if it were his fellow; till the deep eyes fill with light, and out of these things, so much weaker than itself, a touch, a glance, a word, there will come to it new strength to pull the stranded wagon onward. The man is as a god to the beast, coming down to help it, and it almost makes the beast human that he does so. Not otherwise does Hosea feel the help which God gives His own on the weary hills of life. We need not discipline, for our work is discipline enough, and the cares we carry of themselves keep us straight and steady. But we need sympathy and gentleness—this very humanity which the prophet attributes to our **God.**

* See below, pp. 321–3.
† 1 John iii.
‡ So rightly the LXX.
§ LXX., rightly separating מִפְּנֵיהֶם into מִפְּנֵי and הֵם, which latter is the nominative to the next clause.
‖ So again rightly the LXX.
¶ The reading is uncertain. The לֹא of the following verse (6) must be read **as the Greek reads it, as** לוֹ**, and** taken with ver. 5.
** x. 11.

* Or lifted forward from the neck to the **jaws.**
† Isa. lxiii. 13, 14.

God comes and takes us by the head; through the mystic power which is above us, but which makes us like itself, we are lifted to our task. Let no one judge this incredible. The incredible would be that our God should prove any less to us than the merciful man to his beast. But we are saved from argument by experience. When we remember how, as life has become steep and our strength exhausted, there has visited us a thought which has sharpened to a word, a word which has warmed to a touch, and we have drawn ourselves together and leapt up new men, can we feel that God was any less in these things, than in the voice of conscience or the message of forgiveness, or the restraints of His discipline? Nay, though the reins be no longer felt, God is at our head, that we should not stumble nor stand still.

Upon this gracious passage there follows one of those swift revulsions of feeling, which we have learned almost to expect in Hosea. His insight again overtakes his love. The people will not respond to the goodness of their God; it is impossible to work upon minds so fickle and insincere. Discipline is what they need. "He shall return to the land of Egypt, or Asshur shall be his king" (it is still an alternative), "for they have refused to return" to Me. . . .* 'Tis but one more instance of the age-long apostasy of the people. "My people have a bias † to turn from Me; and though they" (the prophets) "call them upwards, none of them can lift them." ‡

Yet God is God, and though prophecy fail He will attempt His love once more. There follows the greatest passage in Hosea—deepest if not highest of his book—the breaking forth of that exhaustless mercy of the Most High which no sin of man can bar back nor wear out.

> "How am I to give thee up, O Ephraim?
> How am I to let thee go, O Israel?
> How am I to give thee up?
> Am I to make an Admah of thee—a Ṣeboim?
> My heart is turned upon Me,
> My compassions begin to boil:
> I will not perform the fierceness of Mine anger,
> I will not turn to destroy Ephraim;
> For God am I and not man,
> The Holy One in the midst of thee, yet I come
> not to consume! §

Such a love has been the secret of Hosea's persistence through so many years with so faithless a people, and now, when he has failed, it takes voice to itself and in its irresistible fulness makes this last appeal. Once more before the end let Israel hear God in the utterness of His Love!

The verses are a climax, and obviously to be succeeded by a pause. On the brink of his doom, will Israel turn to such a God, at such a call? The next verse, though dependent for its promise on this same exhaustless Love, is from an entirely different circumstance, and cannot have been put by Hosea here.‖

CHAPTER XIX.

THE FINAL ARGUMENT.

Hosea xii.-xiv. 1.

The impassioned call with which the last chapter closed was by no means an assurance of salvation: "How am I to give thee up, Ephraim? how am I to let thee go, Israel?" On the contrary, it was the anguish of Love, when it hovers over its own on the brink of the destruction to which their wilfulness has led them, and before relinquishing them would seek, if possible, some last way to redeem. Surely that fatal morrow and the people's mad leap into it are not inevitable! At least, before they take the leap, let the prophet go back once more upon the moral situation of to-day, go back once more upon the past of the people, and see if he can find anything else to explain that bias to apostasy * which has brought them to this fatal brink—anything else which may move them to repentance even there. So in chaps. xii. and xiii. Hosea turns upon the now familiar trail of his argument, full of the Divine jealousy, determined to give the people one other chance to turn; but if they will not, he at least will justify God's relinquishment of them. The chapters throw even a brighter light upon the temper and habits of that generation. They again explore Israel's ancient history for causes of the present decline; and, in especial, they cite the spiritual experience of the Father of the Nation, as if to show that what of repentance was possible for him is possible for his posterity also. But once more all hope is seen to be in vain; and Hosea's last travail with his obstinate people closes in a doom even more awful than its predecessors.

The division into chapters is probably correct; but while chap. xiii. is well ordered and clear, the arrangement, and, in parts, the meaning of chap. xii. are very obscure.

1. The People and Their Father Jacob.

Hosea xii.

In no part even of the difficult Book of Hosea does the sacred text bristle with more problems. It may well be doubted whether the verses lie in their proper order, or, if they do, whether we have them entire as they came from the prophet, for the connection is not always perceptible.† We cannot believe, however, that the chapter is a bundle of isolated oracles, for the analogy between Jacob and his living posterity runs through the whole of it,‡ and the refrain that God must requite upon the nation their deeds is found both near the beginning and at the end

* Ver. 6 has an obviously corrupt text, and, weakening as it does the climax of ver. 5, may be an insertion.

† "Are hung or swung towards turning away from Me."

‡ This verse is also uncertain.

§ For בעיר, which makes nonsense, read לבעור, "to consume," or with Wellhausen amend further לבער לא אובה, "I am not willing to consume."

‖ "They will follow Jehovah; like a lion He will roar, and they shall hurry trembling from the west. Like birds shall they hurry trembling from Egypt, and like doves from the land of Assyria, and I will bring them to their homes—'tis the oracle of Jehovah." Not only does this verse contain expressions which are unusual to Hosea, and a very strange metaphor, but it is not connected either historically or logically with the previous verse. The latter deals with the people before God has scattered them—offers them one more chance before exile comes on them. But in this verse they are already scattered, and just about to be brought back. It is such a promise as both in language and metaphor was common among the prophets of the Exile. In the LXX. the verse is taken from chap. xi. and put with chap. xii.

* xi. 7.

† This is especially true of vv. 11 and 12.

‡ Even in the most detachable portion. vv. 8-10, where the און of ver. 9 seems to refer to the באונו of ver. 4.

of the chapter.* One is tempted to take the two fragments about the Patriarch (vv. 4, 5, and 13 f.) by themselves, and the more so that ver. 8 would follow so suitably on either ver. 2 or ver. 3. But this clue is not sufficient; and till one more evident is discovered, it is perhaps best to keep to the extant arrangement.†

As before, the argument starts from the falseness of Israel, which is illustrated in the faithlessness of their foreign relations. "Ephraim hath compassed Me with lies, and the house of Israel with deceit, and Judah . . .‡ Ephraim herds the wind,§ and hunts the sirocco. All day long they heap up falsehood and fraud: ‖ they strike a bargain with Assyria, and carry oil to Egypt," as Isaiah also complained.¶

"Jehovah hath a quarrel with Israel** and is about to visit upon Jacob his ways; according to his deeds will He requite them. In the womb he supplanted his brother, and in his man's strength he wrestled with God.†† Yea, he wrestled with *the* Angel and prevailed; he wept and besought of Him mercy. At Bethel he met with Him, and there he spake with Him," ‡‡ (or "with us"—that is, in the person of our father). . . . §§ "So that thou by thy God"—by His help,‖‖ for no other way is possible except, like thy father, through wrestling with Him—"shouldest return: keep leal love and justice, and wait on thy God without ceasing."¶¶ To this passage we shall return in dealing with Hosea's doctrine of Repentance.

In characteristic fashion the discourse now swerves from the ideal to the real state of the people.

* Viz. in. vv. 3 and 15.

† Beer indeed, at the close of a very ingenious analysis of the chapter ("Z. A. T. W.", 1893, pp. 281 ff.), claims to have proved that it contains "eine wohlgegliederte Rede des Propheten" (p. 292). But he reaches this conclusion only by several forced and precarious arguments. Especially unsound do his pleas appear that in 8*b* לעשק is a play upon the root-meaning of כנען, "lowly"; that כנען, in analogy to the בבטן of ver. 4, is the crude original, the raw material, of the Ephraim of ver. 9; and that כימי מועד is "the determined time" of the coming judgment on Israel.

‡ Something is written about Judah (remember what was said above about Hosea's treble parallels), but the text is too obscure for translation. The theory that it has been altered by a later Judæan writer in favour of his own people is probably correct: the Authorised Version translates in favour of Judah; so too Guthe in Kautzsch's "Bibel." But an adverse statement is required by the parallel clauses, and the Hebrew text allows this: "Judah is still wayward with God, and with the Holy One who is faithful." So virtually Ewald, Hitzig, Wünsche, Nowack, and Cheyne. But Cornill and Wellhausen read the second half of the clause as נצמד עם-קדשים, "profanes himself with Qedeshim" ("Z. A., T. W.", 1887, pp. 286 ff.).

§ Why should not Hosea, the master of many forced phrases, have also uttered this one? This in answer to Wellhausen.

‖ To LXX., reading שוא for שד.

¶ Isa. xxx. 6.

** Heb. "Judah," but surely Israel is required by the next verse, which is a play upon the two names Israel and Jacob.

†† "Supplanted" is ʿaqab, the presumable root of Jaʿaqab (Jacob). "Wrestled with God" is Sarah eth Elohim, the presumable origin of Yisraʿel (Israel).

‡‡ Heb. "us," LXX. "them."

§§ Ver. 6—"And Jehovah God of Hosts, Jehovah is His memorial," *i. e.*, name—is probably an insertion for the reasons mentioned above, pp. 493 f.

‖‖ This, the most natural rendering of the Hebrew phrase, has been curiously omitted by Beer, who says that באלהיך can only mean "to thy God." Hitzig: "durch deinen Gott."

¶¶ Some take these words as addressed by Jehovah at Bethel to the Patriarch.

"Canaan!" So the prophet nicknames his mercenary generation.* "With false balances in his hand, he loves to defraud. For Ephraim said," Ah, but "I have grown rich, I have won myself wealth.† None of my gains can touch me with guilt which is sin.‡ But I, Jehovah thy God from the land of Egypt—I could make thee dwell in tents again, as in the days of the Assembly" in Horeb—I could destroy all this commercial civilisation of thine, and reduce thee to thine ancient level of nomadic life—"and I spake to the prophets: it was I who multiplied vision, and by the hand of the prophets gave parables. If Gilead" be for "idolatry, then shall it become vanity!" If "in Gilgal"—Stone-Circle—"they sacrifice bullocks,§ stone heaps shall their altars become among the furrows of the field." One does not see the connection of these verses with the preceding. But now the discourse oscillates once more to the national father, and the parallel between his own and his people's experience.

"And Jacob fled to the land‖ of Aram, and Israel served for a wife, and for a wife he herded *sheep*. And by a prophet Jehovah brought Israel up from Egypt, and by a prophet he was shepherded. And Ephraim hath given bitter provocation; but his blood-guiltiness shall be upon him, and his Lord shall return it to him."

I cannot trace the argument here.

2. The Last Judgment.

Hosea xiii.-xiv. 1.

The crisis draws on. On the one hand Israel's sin, accumulating, bulks ripe for judgment. On the other the times grow more fatal, or the prophet more than ever feels them so. He will gather once again the old truths on the old lines—the great past when Jehovah was God alone, the descent to the idols and the mushroom monarchs of to-day, the people, who once had been strong, sapped by luxury, forgetful, stupid, not to be roused. The discourse has every mark of being Hosea's latest. There are clearness and definiteness beyond anything since chap. iv. There are ease and lightness of treatment, a playful sarcasm, as if the themes were now familiar both to the prophet and his audience. But, chiefly, there is the passion—so suitable to last words—of how different it all might have been, if to this crisis Israel had come with store of strength instead of guilt. How these years, with their opening into the great history of the world, might have meant a birth for the nation, which instead was lying upon them like a miscarried child in the mouth of the womb! It was a fatality God Himself could not help in. Only death and hell remained. Let them, then, have their way! Samaria must expiate her guilt in the worst horrors of war.

Instead of with one definite historical event,

* So nearly all interpreters. Hitzig aptly quotes Polybius, "De Virtute," L. ix.: διὰ τὴν ἔμφυτον Φοίνιξι πλεονεξίαν, κ. τ. λ. One might also refer to the Romans' idea of the "Punica fides."

† Or, full man's strength: *cf.* ver. 4.

‡ But the LXX. reads: "All his gains shall not be found of him because of the iniquity which he has sinned;" and Wellhausen emends this to: "All his gain sufficeth not for the guilt which it has incurred."

§ Others "to demons."

‖ Field, but here in sense of territory. See "Hist. Geog.", pp. 79 f.

this last effort of Hosea opens more naturally with a summary of all Ephraim's previous history. The tribe had been the first in Israel till they took to idols.

"Whenever Ephraim spake there was trembling.* Prince † was he in Israel; but he fell into guilt through the Ba'al, and so—died. Even now they continue to sin and make them a smelting of their silver, idols after their own model,‡ smith's work all of it. To them"—to such things —"they speak! Sacrificing men kiss calves!" In such unreason have they sunk. They cannot endure. "Therefore shall they be like the morning cloud and like the dew that early vanisheth, like chaff which whirleth up from the floor and like smoke from the window. And I was thy God § from the land of Egypt; and god besides Me thou knowest not, nor saviour has there been any but Myself. I shepherded ‖ thee in the wilderness, in the land of droughts"—long before they came among the gods of fertile Canaan. But once they came hither, "the more pasture they had, the more they ate themselves full, and the more they ate themselves full, the more was their heart uplifted, so they forgat Me. So that I must be ¶ to them like a lion, like a leopard in the way I must leap.** I will fall on them like a bear robbed of its young, and will tear the caul of their hearts, and will devour them like a lion—wild beasts shall rend them." ††

When "He hath destroyed thee, O Israel—who then may help thee? ‡‡ Where is thy king now? that he may save thee, or all thy princes? that they may rule thee; §§ those of whom thou hast said, Give me a king and princes." Aye, "I give thee a king in Mine anger, and I take him away in My wrath!" Fit summary of the short and bloody reigns of these last years.

"Gathered is Ephraim's guilt, stored up is his sin." The nation is pregnant—but with guilt! "Birth pangs seize him, but"—the figure changes, with Hosea's own swiftness, from mother to child—"he is an impracticable son; ‖‖ for *this* is no time to stand in the mouth of the womb." The years that might have been the nation's birth are by their own folly to prove their death. Israel lies in the way of its own redemption—how truly this has been forced home upon them in one chapter after another! Shall God then step in and work a deliverance on the brink of death? "From the hand of Sheol shall I deliver them? from death shall I redeem them?" Nay, let death and Sheol have their way. "Where are thy plagues, O death? where thy destruction, Sheol?" Here with them. "Compassion is hid from Mine eyes."

This great verse has been variously rendered. Some have taken it as a promise: "I will deliver . . . I will redeem . . ." So the Septuagint translated, and St. Paul borrowed, not the whole Greek verse, but its spirit and one or two of its terms, for his triumphant challenge to death in the power of the Resurrection of Christ.* As it stands in Hosea, however, the verse must be a threat. The last clause unambiguously abjures mercy, and the statement that His people will not be saved, for God cannot save them, is one in thorough harmony with all Hosea's teaching.†

An appendix follows with the illustration of the exact form which doom shall take. As so frequently with Hosea, it opens with a play upon the people's name, which at the same time faintly echoes the opening of the chapter.

"Although he among his brethren ‡ is the fruit-bearer"—yaphri', he Ephraim—"there shall come an east wind, a wind of Jehovah rising from the wilderness, so that his fountain dry up and his spring be parched." He—"himself," not the Assyrian, but Menahem, who had to send gold to the Assyrian—"shall strip the treasury of all its precious jewels. Samaria must bear her guilt: for she hath rebelled against her God." To this simple issue has the impenitence of the people finally reduced the many possibilities of those momentous years; and their last prophet leaves them looking forward to the crash which came some dozen years later in the invasion and captivity of the land. "They shall fall by the sword; their infants shall be dashed in pieces, and their women with child ripped up." Horrible details, but at that period certain to follow every defeat in war.

CHAPTER XX.

"I WILL BE AS THE DEW."

HOSEA xiv. 2-10.

LIKE the Book of Amos, the Book of Hosea, after proclaiming the people's inevitable doom, turns to a blessed prospect of their restoration to favour with God. It will be remembered that we decided against the authenticity of such an epilogue in the Book of Amos; and it may now be asked, how can we come to any other conclusion with regard to the similar peroration in the Book of Hosea? For the following reasons.

* Uncertain.

† נשיא for נשא.

‡ Read with Ewald כתבנתם. LXX. read כתמונת.

§ Here the LXX. makes the insertion noted on pp. 493, 498.

‖ So LXX., רעיתיך.

¶ Read וָאֱהִי.

** אָשׁוּר, usually taken as first fut. of שׁוּר, "to lurk." But there is a root of common use in Arabic, sar, "to spring up suddenly," of wine into the head or of a lion on its prey; sawâr, "the springer," is one of the Arabic names for lion.

†† We shall treat this passage later in connection with Hosea's doctrine of the knowledge of God: see pp. 524 f.

‡‡ After the LXX.

§§ Read with Houtsma וכל שריך וישפטוך.

‖‖ Literally a "son not wise," perhaps a name given to children whose birth was difficult.

* The LXX. reads: Ποῦ ἡ δίκη σου, θάνατε; ποῦ τὸ κέντρον σου, ᾅδη; But Paul says: Ποῦ σου, θάνατε, τὸ νῖκος; ποῦ σου, θάνατε, τὸ κέντρον; 1 Cor. xv. 55 (Westcott and Hort's Ed.).

† The following is a list of the interpretations of verse 14.

A. Taken as a threat. 1. "It is I who redeemed you from the grip of the grave, and who delivered you from death—but now I will call up the words (*sic*) of death against you; for repentance is hid from My eyes." So Raschi. 2. "I would have redeemed them from the grip of Sheol, etc., if they had been wise, but being foolish I will bring on them the plagues of death." So Kimchi, Eichhorn, Simson, etc. 3. "Should I" or "shall I deliver them from the hand of Sheol, redeem them from death?" etc., as in the text above. So Wünsche, Wellhausen, Guthe in Kautzsch's "Bibel," etc.

B. Taken as a promise. "From the hand of Sheol I will deliver them, from death redeem them," etc. So Umbreit, Ewald, Hitzig, and Authorised and Revised English Versions. In this case repentance in the last clause must be taken as "resentment" (Ewald). But, as Ewald sees, the whole verse must then be put in a parenthesis as an ejaculation of promise in the midst of a context that only threatens. Some without change of word render: "I will be thy plagues, O death! I will be thy sting, O hell." So the Authorised English Version.

‡ Text doubtful.

We decided against the genuineness of the closing verses of Amos, because their sanguine temper is opposed to the temper of the whole of the rest of the book, and because they neither propose any ethical conditions for the attainment of the blessed future, nor in their picture of the latter do they emphasise one single trace of the justice, or the purity, or the social kindliness, on which Amos has so exclusively insisted as the ideal relations of Israel to Jehovah. It seemed impossible to us that Amos could imagine the perfect restoration of his people in the terms only of requickened nature, and say nothing about righteousness, truth, and mercy towards the poor. The prospect which now closes his book is psychologically alien to him, and, being painted in the terms of later prophecy, may be judged to have been added by some prophet of the Exile, speaking from the standpoint, and with the legitimate desires, of his own day.

But the case is very different for this epilogue in Hosea. In the first place, Hosea has not only continually preached repentance, and been, from his whole affectionate temper of mind, unable to believe repentance impossible; but he has actually predicted the restoration of his people upon certain well-defined and ethical conditions. In chap. ii. he has drawn for us in detail the whole prospect of God's successful treatment of his erring spouse. Israel should be weaned from their sensuousness and its accompanying trust in idols by a severe discipline, which the prophet describes in terms of their ancient wanderings in the wilderness. They should be reduced as at the beginning of their history, to moral converse with their God; and abjuring the Ba'alim (later chapters imply also their foreign allies and foolish kings and princes) should return to Jehovah, when He, having proved that these could not give them the fruits of the land they sought after, should Himself quicken the whole course of nature to bless them with the fertility of the soil and the friendliness even of the wild beasts.

Now in the epilogue and its prospect of Israel's repentance we find no feature, physical or moral, which has not already been furnished by these previous promises of the book. All their ethical conditions are provided; nothing but what they have conceived of blessing is again conceived. Israel is to abjure senseless sacrifice and come to Jehovah with rational and contrite confession.* She is to abjure her foreign alliances. † She is to trust in the fatherly love of her God. ‡ He is to heal her,§ and His anger is to turn away.‖ He is to restore nature, just as described in chap. ii., and the scenery of the restoration is borrowed from Hosea's own Galilee. There is, in short, no phrase or allusion of which we can say that it is alien to the prophet's style or environment, while the very keynotes of his book —"return," "backsliding," "idols the work of our hands," "such pity as a father hath," and perhaps even the "answer" or "converse" of verse 9—are all struck once more.

The epilogue then is absolutely different from the epilogue to the Book of Amos, nor can the present expositor conceive of the possibility of a stronger case for the genuineness of any passage of Scripture. The sole difficulty seems to be the place in which we find it—a place where its contradiction to the immediately preceding sentence of doom is brought out into relief. We need not suppose, however, that it was uttered by Hosea in immediate proximity to the latter, nor even that it formed his last word to Israel. But granting only (as the above evidence obliges us to do) that it is the prophet's own, this fourteenth chapter may have been a discourse addressed by him at one of those many points when, as we know, he had some hope of the people's return. Personally, I should think it extremely likely that Hosea's ministry closed with that final, hopeless proclamation in chap. xiii.: no other conclusion was possible so near the fall of Samaria and the absolute destruction of the Northern Kingdom. But Hosea had already in chap. ii. painted the very opposite issue as a possible ideal for his people; and during some break in those years when their insincerity was less obtrusive, and the final doom still uncertain, the prophet's heart swung to its natural pole in the exhaustless and steadfast love of God, and he uttered his unmingled gospel. That either himself or the unknown editor of his prophecies should have placed it at the very end of his book is not less than what we might have expected. For if the book were to have validity beyond the circumstances of its origin, beyond the judgment which was so near and so inevitable, was it not right to let something else than the proclamation of this latter be its last word to men? was it not right to put as the conclusion of the whole matter the ideal eternity valid for Israel—the gospel which is ever God's last word to His people? *

At some point or other, then, in the course of his ministry, there was granted to Hosea an open vision like to the vision which he has recounted in the second chapter. He called on the people to repent. For once, and in the power of that Love to which he had already said all things are possible, it seemed to him as if repentance came. The tangle and intrigue of his generation fell away; fell away the reeking sacrifices and the vain show of worship. The people turned from their idols and puppet-kings, from Assyria and from Egypt, and with contrite hearts came to God Himself, who, healing and loving, opened to them wide the gates of the future. It is not strange that down this spiritual vista the prophet should see the same scenery as daily filled his bodily vision. Throughout Galilee Lebanon† dominates the landscape. You cannot

* *Cf.* vi. 6, etc. † *Cf.* xii. 2, etc. ‡ *Cf.* i. 7; ii. 22, 25. § *Cf.* xi. 4. ‖ *Cf.* xi. 8, 9.

* Since preparing the above for the press there has come into my hands Professor Cheyne's "Introduction" to the new edition of Robertson Smith's "The Prophets of Israel," in which (p. xix.) he reaches with regard to Hosea xiv. 2-10 conclusions entirely opposite to those reached above. Professor Cheyne denies the passage to Hosea on the grounds that it is akin in language and imagery and ideas to writings of the age which begins with Jeremiah, and which among other works includes the Song of Songs. But, as has been shown above, the "language, imagery, and ideas" are all akin to what Professor Cheyne admits to be genuine prophecies of Hosea; and the likeness to them of, *e. g.*, Jer. xxxi. 10-20, may be explained on the same ground as so much else in Jeremiah by the influence of Hosea. The allusion in ver. 3 suits Hosea's own day more than Jeremiah's. Nor can I understand what Professor Cheyne means by this: "The spirituality of the tone of vers. 1-3 is indeed surprising (contrast the picture in Hos. v. 6)." Spirituality surprising in the book that contains "I will have love and not sacrifice, and the knowledge of God rather than burnt-offerings"! The verse, v. 6, he would contrast with xiv. 1-3 is actually one in which Hosea says that when they go "with flocks and herds" Israel shall not find God! He says that "to understand Hosea aright we must omit it" (*i. e.*, the whole epilogue). But after the argument I have given above it will be plain that if we "understand Hosea aright" we have every reason "not" "to omit it." His last contention, that "to have added anything to the stern warning in xiii. 16 would have robbed it of half its force," is fully met by the considerations stated above on this page.

† By Lebanon in the fourteenth chapter, and almost

lift your eyes from any spot of Northern Israel without resting them upon the vast mountain. From the unhealthy jungles of the Upper Jordan, the pilgrim lifts his heart to the cool hill air above, to the ever-green cedars and firs, to the streams and waterfalls that drop like silver chains off the great breastplate of snow. From Esdraelon and every plain the peasants look to Lebanon to store the clouds and scatter the rain; it is not from heaven but from Hermon that they expect the dew, their only hope in the long drought of summer. Across Galilee and in Northern Ephraim, across Bashan and in Northern Gilead, across Hauran and on the borders of the desert, the mountain casts its spell of power, its lavish promise of life.* Lebanon is everywhere the summit of the land, and there are points from which it is as dominant as heaven.

No wonder then that our northern prophet painted the blessed future in the poetry of the Mountain—its air, its dew, and its trees. Other seers were to behold, in the same latter days, the mountain of the Lord above the tops of the mountains; the ordered city, her steadfast walls salvation, and her open gates praise; the wealth of the Gentiles flowing into her, profusion of flocks for sacrifice, profusion of pilgrims; the great Temple and its solemn services; and "the glory of Lebanon shall come unto thee, fir-tree and pine and box-tree together, to beautify the place of My Sanctuary." † But, with his home in the north, and weary of sacrifice and ritual, weary of everything artificial, whether it were idols or puppet-kings, Hosea turns to the "glory of Lebanon" as it lies, untouched by human tool or art, fresh and full of peace from God's own hand. Like that other seer of Galilee, Hosea in his vision of the future "saw no temple therein." ‡ His sacraments are the open air, the mountain breeze, the dew, the vine, the lilies, the pines; and what God asks of men are not rites nor sacrifices, but life and health, fragrance and fruitfulness, beneath the shadow and the Dew of His Presence.

"Return, O Israel, to Jehovah thy God, for thou hast stumbled by thine iniquity. Take with you words§ and return unto Jehovah. Say unto Him, Remove iniquity altogether, and take good, so will we render the calves‖ of our lips;" confessions, vows, these are the sacrificial offerings God delights in. Which vows are now registered:—

"Asshur shall not save us;
We shall not ride upon horses (from Egypt);
And we will say no more "O our God," to the work of our hands:
For in Thee the fatherless findeth a father's pity."

Alien help, whether in the protection of Assyria or the cavalry which Pharaoh sends in return for Israel's homage; alien gods, whose idols we have ourselves made,—we abjure them all, for we remember how Thou didst promise to show a father's love to the people whom Thou didst name, for their mother's sins, Lo-Ruhamah, the Unfathered. Then God replies:—

"I will heal their backsliding,
I will love them freely:
For Mine anger is turned away from them.
I will be as the dew unto Israel:
He shall blossom as the lily,
And strike his roots *deep* as Lebanon:
His branches shall spread,
And his beauty shall be as the olive-tree,
And his smell as Lebanon—

smell of clear mountain air with the scent of the pines upon it. The figure in the end of ver. 6 seems forced to some critics, who have proposed various emendations, such as "like the fast-rooted trees of Lebanon," * but any one who has seen how the mountain himself rises from great roots, cast out across the land like those of some giant oak, will not feel it necessary to mitigate the metaphor.

The prophet now speaks:—

"They shall return and dwell in His shadow.
They shall live well-watered as a garden,
Till they flourish like the vine,
And be fragrant like the wine of Lebanon." †

God speaks:—

"Ephraim, what has he ‡ to do any more with idols!
I have spoken *for him*, and I will look after him.
I am like an ever-green fir;
From Me is thy fruit found."

This version is not without its difficulties; but the alternative that God is addressed and Ephraim is the speaker—"Ephraim" says, "What have I to do any more with idols? I answer and look to Him: I am like a green fir-tree; from me is Thy fruit found"—has even greater difficulties,§ although it avoids the unusual comparison of the Deity with a tree. The difficulties of both

always in the Old Testament, we must understand not the western range now called Lebanon, for that makes no impression on the Holy Land, its bulk lying too far to the north, but Hermon, the southmost and highest summits of Anti-Lebanon. See "Hist. Geog.," pp. 417 f.

* Full sixty miles off, in the Jebel Druze, the ancient Greek amphitheatres were so arranged that Hermon might fill the horizon of the spectators.

† Isa. lx. 13.

‡ Revelation of St. John xxi. 22.

§ On all this exhortation see below, p. 527.

‖ LXX. "fruit, פרי for פרים; the whole verse is obscure.

* So Guthe; some other plant Wellhausen, who for ויך reads וילכו.

† Ver. 8 obviously needs emendation. The Hebrew text contains at least one questionable construction, and gives no sense: "They that dwell in his shadow shall turn, and revive corn and flourish like the vine, and his fame," etc. To cultivate corn and be themselves like a vine is somewhat mixed. The LXX. reads: *ἐπιστρέψουσιν καὶ καθιοῦνται ὑπὸ τὴν σκέπην αὐτοῦ, ζήσονται καὶ μεθυσθήσονται σίτῳ· καὶ ἐξανθήσει ἄμπελος μνημόσυνην αὐτοῦ ὡς οἶνος Λιβάνου.* It removes the grammatical difficulty from clause 1, which then reads בְּצִלּוֹ יָשְׁבוּ וְיָשְׁבוּ; the supplied *vau* may easily have dropped after the final *vau* of the previous word. In the second clause the LXX. takes יחיו as an intransitive, which is better suited to the other verbs, and adds *καὶ μεθυσθήσονται*, ורוין (a form that may have easily slipped from the Hebrew text, through its likeness to the preceding ויחיו). "And they shall be well-watered." After this it is probable that דגן should read כַּגַּן. In the third clause the Hebrew text may stand. In the fourth זכר may not, as many propose, be taken for זכרם and translated "their perfume;" but the parallelism makes it now probable that we have a verb here; and if זכר in the Hiph. has the sense "to make a perfume" (*cf.* Isa. lxvi. 3), there is no reason against the Kal being used in the intransitive sense here. In the LXX. for *μεθυσθήσονται* Qa reads *στηριχθήσονται.*

‡ LXX.

§ This alternative, which Robertson Smith adopted, "though not without some hesitation" ("Prophets," 413) is that which follows the Hebrew text, reading in the first clause לִי, and not, like LXX., לוֹ, and avoids the unusual figure of comparing Jehovah to a tree. But it does not account for the singular emphasis laid in the second clause on the first personal pronoun, and implies that God, whose name has not for several verses been mentioned, is meant by the mere personal suffix, "I will look to Him." Wellhausen suggests changing the second clause to "I am his Anat and his Aschera."

interpretations may be overcome by dividing the verse between God and the people:—

> "Ephraim! what has he to do any more with idols:
> I have spoken *for him*, and will look after him."

In this case the *speaking* would be intended in the same sense as the *speaking* in chap. ii. to the heavens and earth, that they might *speak* to the *corn and wine*.* Then Ephraim replies:—

> "I am like an ever-green fir-tree;
> From me is Thy fruit found."

But the division appears artificial, and the text does not suggest that the two I's belong to different speakers. The first version therefore is the preferable.

Some one has added a summons to later generations to lay this book to heart in face of their own problems and sins. May we do so for ourselves!

> "Who is wise, that he understands these things?
> Intelligent, that he knows them?
> Yea straight are the ways of Jehovah,
> And the righteous shall walk therein, but sinners shall stumble upon them."

CHAPTER XXI.

THE KNOWLEDGE OF GOD.

HOSEA *passim.*

WE have now finished the translation and detailed exposition of Hosea's prophecies. We have followed his minute examination of his people's character; his criticism of his fickle generation's attempts to repent; and his presentation of true religion in contrast to their shallow optimism and sensual superstitions. We have seen an inwardness and spirituality of the highest kind—a love not only warm and mobile, but nobly jealous, and in its jealousy assisted by an extraordinary insight and expertness in character. Why Hosea should be distinguished above all prophets for inwardness and spirituality must by this time be obvious to us. From his remote watchfulness, Amos had seen the nations move across the world as the stars across heaven; had seen, within Israel, class distinct from class, and given types of all: rich and poor; priest, merchant, and judge; the panic-stricken, the bully; the fraudulent and the unclean. The observatory of Amos was the world, and the nation. But Hosea's was the home; and there he had watched a human soul decay through every stage from innocence to corruption. It was a husband's study of a wife which made Hosea the most inward of all the prophets. This was "the beginning of God's word by him."†

Among the subjects in the subtle treatment of which Hosea's service to religion is most original and conspicuous, there are especially three that deserve a more detailed treatment than we have been able to give them. These are the Knowledge of God, Repentance, and the Sin against Love. We may devote a chapter to each of them, beginning in this with the most characteristic and fundamental truth Hosea gave to religion—the Knowledge of God.

If to the heart there be one pain more fatal than another, it is the pain of not being understood. That prevents argument: how can you reason with one who will not come to quarters with your real self? It paralyses influence: how can you do your best with one who is blind to your best? It stifles Love; for how dare she continue to speak when she is mistaken for something else? Here as elsewhere "against stupidity the gods themselves fight in vain."

This anguish Hosea had suffered. As closely as two souls may live on earth, he had lived with Gomer. Yet she had never wakened to his worth. She must have been a woman with a power of love, or such a heart had hardly wooed her. He was a man of deep tenderness and exquisite powers of expression. His tact, his delicacy, his enthusiasm are sensible in every chapter of his book. Gomer must have tasted them all before Israel did. Yet she never knew him. It was her curse that, being married, she was not awake to the meaning of marriage, and, being married to Hosea, she never appreciated the holy tenderness and heroic patience which were deemed by God not unworthy of becoming a parable of His own.

Now I think we do not go far wrong if we conclude that it was partly this long experience of a soul that loved, but had neither conscience nor ideal in her love, which made Hosea lay such frequent and pathetic emphasis upon Israel's *ignorance* of Jehovah. To have his character ignored, his purposes baffled, his gifts unappreciated, his patience mistaken—this was what drew Hosea into that wonderful sympathy with the heart of God towards Israel which comes out in such passionate words as these: "My people perish for lack of knowledge.* There is no troth, nor leal love, nor knowledge of God in the land.† They have not known the Lord.‡ She did not know that I gave her corn and wine.§ They knew not that I healed them.‖ For now, because thou hast rejected knowledge, I will reject thee.¶ I will have leal love and not sacrifice, and the knowledge of God rather than burnt-offerings."** Repentance consists in change of knowledge. And the climax of the new life which follows is again knowledge: "I will betroth thee to Me, and thou shalt know the Lord.†† Israel shall cry, My God, we know Thee."‡‡

To understand what Hosea meant by knowledge we must examine the singularly supple word which his language lent him to express it. The Hebrew root "Yadh'a," §§ almost exclusively rendered in the Old Testament by the English verb to know, is employed of the many processes of knowledge, for which richer languages have separate terms. It is by turns to perceive, be aware of, recognise, understand or conceive, experience, and be expert in.‖‖ But there is besides nearly always a practical effectiveness, and in connection with religious objects a moral consciousness.

The barest meaning is to be aware that something is present or has happened, and perhaps the root meant simply to see.¶¶ But it was the frequent duty of the prophets to mark the difference between perceiving a thing and laying it to

* ענה, ii. 23.

† i. 2.

* iv. 6.
† iv. 1.
‡ v. 4.
§ ii. 10.
‖ xi. 3.
¶ iv. 6.
** vi. 6.
†† ii, 22.
‡‡ viii. 2.
§§ ידע.

‖‖ The Latin "videre, scire, noscere, cognoscere, intelligere, sapere" and "peritus esse."

¶¶ *Cf.* the Greek οἶδα from εἴδειν.

heart. Isaiah speaks of the people "seeing," but not so as "to know;"* and Deuteronomy renders the latter sense by adding "with the heart," which to the Hebrews was the seat, not of the feeling, but of the practical intellect.† "And thou knowest with thy heart that as a man chastiseth his son, so the Lord your God chastiseth you."‡ Usually, however, the word "know" suffices by itself. This practical vigour naturally developed in such directions as "intimacy, conviction, experience," and "wisdom." Job calls his familiars "my knowers;"§ of a strong conviction he says, "I know that my Redeemer liveth,"‖ and referring to wisdom, "We are of yesterday and know not;"¶ while Ecclesiastes says, "Whoso keepeth the commandment shall know"—that is, "experience," or "suffer—no evil."** But the verb rises into a practical sense —to the knowledge that leads a man to regard or care for its object. Job uses the verb "know" when he would say, "I do not care for my life;" †† and in the description of the sons of Eli, that "they were sons of Belial, and did not know God," it means that they did not have any regard for Him.‡‡ Finally, there is a moral use of the word in which it approaches the meaning of conscience: "Their eyes were opened, and they knew that they were naked." §§ They were aware of this before, but they felt it now with a new sense. Also it is the mark of the awakened and the full-grown to know, or to feel, the difference between good and evil.‖‖

Here, then, we have a word for *knowing*, the utterance of which almost invariably starts a moral echo, whose very sound, as it were, is haunted by sympathy and by duty. It is knowledge, not as an effort of, so much as an effect upon, the mind. It is not *to know* so as to see the fact of, but *to know* so as to feel the force of; knowledge, not as acquisition and mastery, but as impression, passion. To quote Paul's distinction, it is not so much the apprehending as the being apprehended. It leads to a vivid result—either warm appreciation or change of mind or practical effort. It is sometimes the talent conceived as the trust, sometimes the enlistment of all the affections. It is knowledge that is followed by shame, or by love, or by reverence, or by the sense of a duty. One sees that it closely approaches the meaning of our "conscience," and understands how easily there was developed from it the evangelical name for repentance, Metanoia—that is, change of mind under a new impression of facts.

There are three writers who thus use knowledge as the key to the Divine life—in the Old Testament Hosea and the author of Deuteronomy, in the New Testament St. John. We likened Amos to St. John the Baptist: it is not only upon his similar temperament, but far more upon his use of the word knowledge for spiritual purposes, that we may compare Hosea to St. John the Evangelist.

Hosea's chief charge against the people is one of stupidity. High and low they are "a people without intelligence." * Once he defines this as want of political wisdom: "Ephraim is a silly dove without heart," or, as we should say, "without brains;"† and again, as insensibility to every ominous fact: "Strangers have devoured his strength, and he knoweth it not; yea, grey hairs are scattered upon him, and he knoweth it not," ‡ or, as we should say, "lays it not to heart."

But Israel's most fatal ignorance is of God Himself. This is the sign and the cause of every one of their defects. "There is no troth, nor leal love, nor knowledge of God in the land.§ They have not known the Lord.‖ They have not known Me."

With the causes of this ignorance the prophet has dealt most explicitly in the fourth chapter.¶ They are two: the people's own vice and the negligence of their priests. Habitual vice destroys a people's brains. "Harlotry, wine, and new wine take away the heart of My people." ** Lust, for instance, blinds them to the domestic consequences of their indulgence in the heathen worship, "and so the stupid people come to their end." †† Again, their want of political wisdom is due to their impurity, drunkenness, and greed to be rich.‡‡ Let those take heed who among ourselves insist that art is independent of moral conditions—that wit and fancy reach their best and bravest when breaking from any law of decency. They lie: such license corrupts the natural intelligence of a people, and robs them of insight and imagination.

Yet Hosea sees that all the fault does not lie with the common people. Their teachers are to blame, priest and prophet alike, for both "stumble," and it is true that a people shall be like its priests.§§ "The *priests* have rejected knowledge and forgotten the Torah" of their God; they think only of the ritual of sacrifice and the fines by which they fill their mouths. It was, as we have seen, *the* sin of Israel's religion in the eighth century. To the priests religion was a mass of ceremonies which satisfied the people's superstitions and kept themselves in bread. To the prophets it was an equally sensuous, an equally mercenary ecstasy. But to Hosea religion is above all a thing of the intellect and conscience: it is that *knowing* which is at once common-sense, plain morality, and the recognition by a pure heart of what God has done and is doing in history. Of such a knowledge the priests and prophets are the stewards, and it is because they have ignored their trust that the people have been provided with no antidote to the vices that corrupt their natural intelligence and make them incapable of seeing God.

In contrast to such ignorance Hosea describes

*vi. 9.
†See above, pp. 506, 510.
‡viii. 5: *cf.* xxix. 3 (Eng. 4), "Jehovah did not give you a heart to know."
§Job. xix. 13: still more close, of course, the intimacy between the sexes for which the verb is so often used in the Old Testament.
‖xix. 25: *cf.* Gen. xx. 6.
¶viii. 9.
**viii. 5: *cf.* Hosea ix. 7.
††ix. 21.
‡‡1 Sam. ii. 12. A similar meaning is probably to be attached to the word in Gen. xxxix. 6: Potiphar "had no thought or care for anything" that was in Joseph's hand. *Cf.* Prov. ix. 13; xxvii. 23; Job xxxv. 15.
§§Gen. iii. 7.
‖‖Gen. iii. 5; Isa. vii. 15, etc.

*iv. 14, עם לא־יבין: if the original meaning of בין be to "get between, see through" or "into," so "discriminate, understand," then intelligence is its etymological equivalent.
†vii. 11.
‡vii. 9.
§iv. 1.
‖v. 4.
¶For exposition of this chapter see above, pp. 505 ff.
**iv. 11, 12, LXX.
††iv. 14 f. See above, pp. 506 f.
‡‡vii. *passim*.
§§iv. 4-9. Above, pp. 505 f.

the essential temper and contents of a true understanding of God. Using the word *knowledge*, in the passive sense characteristic of his language, not so much the acquisition as the impression of facts, an impression which masters not only a man's thoughts but his heart and will, Hosea describes the *knowledge of God* as feeling, character, and conscience. Again and again he makes it parallel to loyalty, repentance, love, and service. Again and again he emphasises that it comes from God Himself. It is not something which men can reach by their own endeavours, or by the mere easy turning of their fickle hearts. For it requires God Himself to speak, and discipline to chasten. The only passage in which the knowledge of God is described as the immediate prize of man's own pursuit is that prayer of the people on whose facile religiousness Hosea pours his scorn.* "Let us know, let us follow on to know the Lord," he heard them say, and promise themselves, "As soon as we seek Him we shall find Him." But God replies that He can make nothing of such ambitions; they will pass away like the morning cloud and the early dew.† This discarded prayer, then, is the only passage in the book in which the knowledge of God is described as man's acquisition. Elsewhere, in strict conformity to the temper of the Hebrew word to know, Hosea presents the knowledge of the Most High, not as something man finds out for himself, but something which comes down on him from above.

The means which God took to impress Himself upon the heart of His people were, according to Hosea, the events of their history. Hosea, indeed, also points to another means. "The Torah of thy God," which in one passage‡ he makes parallel to "knowledge," is evidently the body of instruction, judicial, ceremonial, and social, which has come down by the tradition of the priests. This was not all oral; part of it at least was already codified in the form we now know as the Book of the Covenant.§ But Hosea treats of the Torah only in connection with the priests. And the far more frequent and direct means by which God has sought to reveal Himself to the people are the great events of their past. These Hoșea never tires of recalling. More than any other prophet, he recites the deeds done by God in the origins and making of Israel. So numerous are his references that from them alone we could almost rebuild the early history. Let us gather them together. The nation's father Jacob "in the womb overreached his brother, and in his manhood strove with God; yea, he strove with the Angel and he overcame,‖ he wept and supplicated Him; at Bethel he found Him, and there He spake with us—Jehovah God of Hosts, Jehovah is His name.¶ . . . And Jacob fled to the territory * of Aram, and he served for a wife, and for a wife he tended sheep. And by a prophet Jehovah brought Israel up out of Egypt, and by a prophet he was tended.† When Israel was young,‡ then I came to love him, and out of Egypt I called My son.§ As often as I called to them, so often did they go from me: ‖ they to the Ba'alim kept sacrificing, and to images offering incense. But I taught Ephraim to walk, taking him upon Mine¶ arms, and they did not know that I nursed them.** . . . Like grapes in the wilderness I found Israel, like the firstfruits on an early fig-tree I saw your fathers;" but "they went to Ba'al-Peor, and consecrated themselves to the Shame.†† . . . But I am Jehovah thy God from the land of Egypt, and gods besides Me thou knowest not, and Saviour there is none but Me. I knew thee in the wilderness, in the land of burning heats. But the more pasture they had, the more they fed themselves full; as they fed themselves full their heart was lifted up: therefore they forgat Me.‡‡ . . . I Jehovah thy God from the land of Egypt." §§ And all this revelation of God was not only in that marvellous history, but in the yearly gifts of nature and even in the success of the people's commerce: "She knew not that it was I who have given her the corn and the wine and the oil, and silver have I multiplied to her." ‖‖

This, then, is how God gave Israel knowledge of Himself. *First* it broke upon the Individual, the Nation's Father. And to him it had not come by miracle, but just in the same fashion as it has broken upon men from them until now. He woke to find God no tradition, but an experience. Amid the strife with others of which life for all so largely consists, Jacob became aware that God also has to be reckoned with, and that, hard as is the struggle for bread and love and justice with one's brethren and fellowmen, with the Esaus and with the Labans, a more inevitable wrestle awaits the soul when it is left alone in the darkness with the Unseen. Oh, this is our sympathy with those early patriarchs, not that they saw the sea dry up before them or the bush ablaze with God, but that upon some lonely battle-field of the heart they also endured those moments of agony, which imply a more real Foe than we ever met in flesh and blood, and which leave upon us marks deeper than the waste of toil or the rivalry of the world can inflict. So the Father of the Nation came to "find" God at Bethel, and there, adds Hosea, where the Nation still worship God "spake with us"¶¶ in the person of our Father.

The *second* stage of the knowledge of God was when the Nation awoke to His leading, and "through a prophet," Moses, were "brought up

* vi. 1 ff. See above, pp. 507 ff.

† vi. 4.

‡ iv. 6. See above, p. 506.

§ See above, pp. 466 f. On the other doubtful phrase, viii. 12—literally "I write multitudes of My Torah, as a stranger they have reckoned it"—no argument can be built; for even if we take the first clause as conditional and render, "Though I wrote multitudes of My Torôth, yet as those of a stranger they would regard them," that would not necessarily mean that no Torôth of Jehovah were yet written, but, on the contrary, might equally well imply that some at least had been written.

‖ Or "was overcome."

¶ xii. 4–6. See above, p. 517. LXX. reads "they supplicated Me . . they found Me . . . He spoke with them." Many propose to read the last clause "with him." The passage is obscure. Note the order of the events—the wrestling at Peniel, the revelation at Bethel, then in the subsequent passage the flight to Aram. This, however, does not prove that in Hosea's information the last happened after the two first.

* שדה, "field," here used in its political sense: *cf.* "Hist. Geog.," p. 79. Our word "country," now meaning territory and now the rural as opposed to the urban districts, is strictly analogous to the Hebrew "field."

† xii. 13, 14.

‡ "A youth."

§ LXX., followed by many critics, "his sons." But "My son" is a better parallel to "young" in the preceding clause. Or trans.: "to be My son."

‖ So LXX. See p. 515.

¶ So rightly LXX.

** xi. 1–3.

†† ix. 10.

‡‡ xiii. 4–6.

§§ xii. 10. Other references to the ancient history are the story of Gibeah and the Valley of Achor.

‖‖ ii. 10.

¶¶ See above, p. 517.

out of Egypt. Here again no miracle is adduced by Hosea, but with full heart he appeals to the grace and the tenderness of the whole story. To him it is a wonderful romance. Passing by all the empires of earth, the Almighty chose for Himself this people that was no people, this tribe that were the slaves of Egypt. And the choice was of love only: "When Israel was young I came to love him, and out of Egypt I called My son." It was the adoption of a little slave-boy, adoption by the heart; and the fatherly figure continues, "I taught Ephraim to walk, taking him upon Mine arms." It is just the same charm, seen from another point of view, when Hosea hears God say that He had "found Israel like grapes in the wilderness, like the firstfruits on an early fig-tree I saw your fathers."

Now these may seem very imperfect figures of the relation of God to this one people, and the ideas they present may be felt to start more difficulties than ever their poetry could soothe to rest: as, for instance, why Israel alone was chosen—why this of all tribes was given such an opportunity to know the Most High. With these questions prophecy does not deal, and for Israel's sake had no need to deal. What alone Hosea is concerned with is the Character discernible in the origin and the liberation of his people. He hears that Character speak for itself; and it speaks of a love and of a joy, to find figures for which it goes to childhood and to spring—to the love a man feels for a child, to the joy a man feels at the sight of the firstfruits of the year. As the human heart feels in those two great dawns, when nothing is yet impossible, but all is full of hope and promise, so humanly, so tenderly, so joyfully had God felt towards His people. Never again say that the gods of Greece were painted more living or more fair! The God of Israel is Love and Springtime to His people. Grace, patience, pure joy of hope and possibility—these are the Divine elements which this spiritual man, Hosea, sees in the early history of his people, and not the miraculous, about which, from end to end of his book, he is utterly silent.

It is ignorance, then, of such a Character, so evident in these facts of their history, with which Hosea charges his people—not ignorance of the facts themselves, not want of devotion to their memory, for they are a people who crowd the sacred scenes of the past, at Bethel, at Gilgal, at Beersheba, but ignorance of the Character which shines through the facts. Hosea also calls it forgetfulness, for the people once had knowledge.* The cause of their losing it has been their prosperity in Canaan: "As their pastures were increased they grew satisfied; as they grew satisfied their heart was lifted up, and therefore they forgat Me."†

Equally instructive is the method by which Hosea seeks to move Israel from this oblivion and bring them to a true knowledge of God. He insists that their recovery can only be the work of God Himself—the living God working in their lives to-day as He did in the past of the nation. To those past deeds it is useless for this generation to go back, and seek again the memory of which they have disinherited themselves. Let them rather realise that the same God still lives. The knowledge of Him may be recovered by appreciating His deeds in the life of to-day. And these deeds must first of all be violence and terror, if only to rouse them from their sensuous

* iv. 6.

† xiii. 5.

sloth. The last verse we have quoted, about Israel's complacency and pride, is followed by this terrible one: "I shall be* to them like a lion, like a leopard I shall leap† upon the way. I will meet them as a bear bereft" of her cubs, "that I may tear the caul of their heart, that I may devour them there like a lion: the wild beast shall rend them."‡ This means that into Israel's insensibility to Himself God must break with facts, with wounds, with horrors they cannot evade. Till He so acts, their own efforts, "then shall we know if we hunt up to know,"§ and their assurance, "My God, we do know Thee,"‖ are very vain. Hosea did not speak for nothing. Events were about to happen more momentous than even the Exodus and the Conquest of the Land. By 734 the Assyrians had depopulated Gilead and Galilee; in 725 the capital itself was invested, and by 721 the whole nation carried into captivity. God had made Himself known.

We are already aware, however, that Hosea did not count this as God's final revelation to His people. Doom is not doom to him, as it was to Amos, but discipline; and God withdraws His people from their fascinating land only that He may have them more closely to Himself. He will bring His Bride into the wilderness again, the wilderness where they first met, and there, when her soul is tender and her stupid heart broken, He will plant in her again the seeds of His knowledge and His love. The passages which describe this are among the most beautiful of the book. They tell us of no arbitrary conquest of Israel by Jehovah, of no magic and sudden transformation. They describe a process as natural and gentle as a human wooing; they use, as we have seen, the very terms of this: "I will woo her, bring her into the wilderness, and speak home to her heart. . . . And it shall be in that day that thou shalt call Me, My husband, . . . and I will betroth thee to Me for ever in righteousness and in justice, and in leal love and in mercies and in faithfulness; and thou shalt know Jehovah."¶

CHAPTER XXII.

REPENTANCE.

HOSEA *passim.*

IF we keep in mind what Hosea meant by knowledge—a new impression of facts implying a change both of temper and of conduct—we shall feel how natural it is to pass at once from his doctrine of knowledge to his doctrine of repentance. Hosea may be accurately styled the first preacher of repentance, yet so thoroughly did he deal with this subject of eternal interest to the human heart, that between him and ourselves almost no teacher has increased the insight with which it has been examined, or the passion with which it ought to be enforced.

One thing we must hold clear from the outset. To us repentance is intelligible only in the individual. There is no motion of the heart which more clearly derives its validity from its personal character. Repentance is the conscience, the

* With Wellhausen read אֶהְיֶה for וָאֱהִי.

† See above, p. 518, *n.*

‡ xiii. 7 ff.

§ vi. 3.

‖ viii. 2.

¶ i. 16, 18, 21, 22.

feeling, the resolution of a man by himself and for himself—"*I* will arise and go to my Father." Yet it is not to the individual that Hosea directs his passionate appeals. For him and his age the religious unit was not the Israelite but Israel. God had called and covenanted with the nation as a whole; He had revealed Himself through their historical fortunes and institutions. His grace was shown in their succour and guidance as a people; His last judgment was threatened in their destruction as a state. So similarly, when by Hosea God calls to repentance, it is the whole nation whom He addresses.

At the same time we must remember those qualifications which we adduce with regard to Hosea's doctrine of the nation's knowledge of God.* They affect also his doctrine of the national repentance. Hosea's experience of Israel had been preceded by his experience of an Israelite. For years the prophet had carried on his anxious heart a single human character—lived with her, travailed for her, pardoned and redeemed her. As we felt that this long cure of a soul must have helped Hosea to his very spiritual sense of the knowledge of God, so now we may justly assume that the same cannot have been without effect upon his very personal teaching about repentance. But with his experience of Gomer, there conspired also his intense love for Israel. A warm patriotism necessarily personifies its object. To the passionate lover of his people, their figure rises up one and individual—his mother, his lover, his wife. Now no man ever loved his people more intimately or more tenderly than Hosea loved Israel. The people were not only dear to him, because he was their son, but dear and vivid also for their loneliness and their distinction among the peoples of the earth, and for their long experience as the intimate of the God of grace and lovingkindness. God had chosen this Israel as His Bride; and the remembrance of the unique endowment and lonely destiny stimulated Hosea's imagination in the work of personifying and individualising his people. He treats Israel with the tenderness and particularity with which the Shepherd, leaving the ninety and nine in the wilderness, seeks till He find it the one lost lamb. His analysis of his fickle generation's efforts to repent, of their motives in turning to God, and of their failures, is as inward and definite as if it were a single heart he were dissecting. Centuries have passed; the individual has displaced the nation; the experience of the human heart has been infinitely increased, and prophecy and all preaching has grown more and more personal. Yet it has scarcely ever been found either necessary to add to the terms which Hosea used for repentance, or possible to go deeper in analysing the processes which these denote.

Hosea's most simple definition of repentance is that "of returning unto God." For "turning" and "re-turning" the Hebrew language has only one verb—shûbh. In the Book of Hosea there are instances in which it is employed in the former sense;† but, even apart from its use for repentance, the verb usually means to return. Thus the wandering wife in the second chapter says, "I will return to my former husband;"* and in the threat of judgment it is said, "Ephraim will return to Egypt."† Similar is the sense in the phrases "His deeds will I turn back upon him"‡ and "I will not turn back to destroy Ephraim."§ The usual meaning of the verb is therefore, not merely to turn or change, but to turn right round, to turn back and home.‖ This is obviously the force of its employment to express repentance. For this purpose Hosea very seldom uses it alone.¶ He generally adds either the name by which God had always been known, Jehovah,** or the designation of Him, as "their own God."††

We must emphasise this point if we would appreciate the thoroughness of our prophet's doctrine, and its harmony with the preaching of the New Testament. To Hosea repentance is no mere change in the direction of one's life. It is a turning back upon one's self, a retracing of one's footsteps, a confession and acknowledgment of what one has abandoned. It is a coming back and a coming home to God, exactly as Jesus Himself has described in the Parable of the Prodigal. As Hosea again and again affirms, the Return to God, like the New Testament Metanoia, is the effect of new knowledge; but the new knowledge is not of new facts—it is of facts which have been present for a long time and which ought to have been appreciated before.

Of these facts Hosea describes three kinds: the nation's misery, the unspeakable grace of their God, and their great guilt in turning from Him. Again it is as in the case of the prodigal: his hunger, his father, and his cry, "I have sinned against heaven and in thy sight."

We have already felt the pathos of those passages in which Hosea describes the misery and the decay of Israel, the unprofitableness and shame of all their restless traffic with other gods and alien empires. The state is rotten;‡‡ anarchy prevails.§§ The national vitality is lessened: "Ephraim hath grey hairs." ‖‖ Power of birth and begetting has gone; the universal unchastity causes the population to diminish: "their glory flieth away like a bird."¶¶ The presents to Egypt,*** the tribute to Assyria, drain the wealth of the people: "strangers devour his strength."††† The prodigal Israel has his far-off country where he spends his substance among strangers. It is in this connection that we must take the repeated verse: "the pride of Israel testifieth to his face."‡‡‡ We have seen §§§ the impossibility of the usual exegesis of these words, that by "the Pride of Israel" Hosea means Jehovah; the word "pride" is probably to be taken in the sense in

* See above, p. 521.

† vii. 16, "They turn, but not upwards;" xiv. 5, "Mine anger is turned away."

* ii. 9.

† viii. 13; ix. 3; xi. 5.

‡ iv. 9: *cf.* xii. 3, 15.

§ xi. 9: *cf.* ii. 11.

‖ This may be further seen in the very common phrase עמי שוב שבות. "*to turn again* the captivity of My people" (see Hosea vi. 11); or in the use of שוב in xiv. 8, where it has the force, auxiliary to the other verb in the clause, of repeating or coming back to do a thing. But the text here needs emendation: *cf.* above, p. 520. *Cf.* Amos' use of the Hiphil form to "draw back, withdraw." i. 3, 6, 9, 11, 13; ii. 1, 4, 6.

¶ *Cf.* xi. 5, "they refused to return."

** vi. 1, "Come and let us return to Jehovah;" vii. 10, "They did not return to Jehovah;" xiv. 2, 3, "Return, O Israel, to Jehovah."

†† iii. 5, "They shall return and seek Jehovah their God; v. 4, "Their deeds do not allow them to return to their God."

‡‡ v. 12, etc.

§§ iv. 2 ff.; vi. 7 ff., etc.

‖‖ vii. 7.

¶¶ ix. 11 ff.

*** xii. 2.

††† vii. 7.

‡‡‡ v. 5; vii. 10.

§§§ See above, p. 506.

which Amos employs it of the exuberance and arrogance of Israel's civilisation. If we are right then Hosea describes a very subtle symptom of the moral awakening whether of the individual or of a community. The conscience of many a man, of many a kingdom, has been reached only through their pride. Pride is the last nerve which comfort and habit leave quick; and when summons to a man's better nature fail, it is still possible in most cases to touch his pride with the presentation of the facts of his decadence. This is probably what Hosea means. Israel's prestige suffers. The civilisation of which they are proud has its open wounds. Their politicians are the sport of Egypt; * their wealth, the very gold of their Temple, is lifted by Assyria. † The nerve of pride was also touched in the prodigal: "How many hired servants of my father have enough and to spare, while I perish with hunger." Yet, unlike him, this prodigal son of God will not therefore return. ‡ Though there are grey hairs upon him, though strangers devour his strength, "he knoweth it not;" of him it cannot be said that "he has come to himself." And that is why the prophet threatens the further discipline of actual exile from the land and its fruits, § of bitter bread ‖ and poverty ¶ on an unclean soil. Israel must also eat husks and feed with swine before he arises and "returns to his God."

But misery alone never led either man or nation to repentance: the sorrow of this world worketh only death. Repentance is the return to God; and it is the awakening to the truth about God, to the facts of His nature and His grace, which alone makes repentance possible. No man's doctrine of repentance is intelligible without his doctrine of God; and it is because Hosea's doctrine of God is so rich, so fair, and so tender, that his doctrine of repentance is so full and gracious. Here we see the difference between him and Amos. Amos had also used the phrase with frequency; again and again he had appealed to the people to seek God and to return to God.** But from Amos it went forth only as a pursuing voice, a voice crying in the wilderness. Hosea lets loose behind it a heart, plies the people with gracious thoughts of God, and brings about them, not the voices only, but the atmosphere, of love. "I will be as the dew unto Israel," promises the Most High; but He is before His promise. The chapters of Hosea are drenched with the dew of God's mercy, of which no drop falls on those of Amos, but there God is rather the roar as of a lion, the flash as of lightning. Both prophets bid Israel turn to God; but Amos means by that, to justice, truth, and purity, while Hosea describes a husband, a father, long-suffering and full of mercy. "I bid you come back," cries Amos. But Hosea pleads, "If only you were aware of what God is, you would come back." "Come back to God and live," cries Amos; but Hosea, "Come back to God, for He is Love." Amos calls, "Come back at once, for there is but little time left till God must visit you in judgment"; but Hosea, "Come back at once, for God has loved you so long and so kindly." Amos cries, "Turn, for in front of you is destruction"; but Hosea, "Turn, for behind you is God." And that is why all Hosea's

* vii. 16.
† x. 5.
‡ vii. 10.
§ ii. 16, etc.; ix. 2 ff., etc.
‖ ix. 4.
¶ xii. 10.
** iv. 6, 8, 9, 10, 11.

preaching of repentance is so evangelical. "I will arise and go *to my Father*."

But the *third* element of the new knowledge which means repentance is the conscience of guilt. "My Father, I have sinned." On this point it might be averred that the teaching of Hosea is less spiritual than that of later prophets in Israel, and that here at last he comes short of the evangelical inwardness of the New Testament. There is truth in the charge; and here perhaps we feel most the defects of his standpoint as one who appeals, not to the individual, but to the nation as a whole. Hosea's treatment of the sense of guilt cannot be so spiritual as that, say, of the fifty-first Psalm. But, at least, he is not satisfied to exhaust it by the very thorough exposure which he gives us of the social sins of his day, and of their terrible results. He, too, understands what is meant by a conscience of sin. He has called Israel's iniquity harlotry, unfaithfulness to God; and in a passage of equal insight and beauty of expression he points out that in the service of the Ba'alim Jehovah's people can never feel anything but a harlot's shame and bitter memories of the better past.

"Rejoice not, O Israel, to the pitch of rapture like the heathen: for thou hast played the harlot from thine own God; 'tis hire thou hast loved on all threshing-floors. Floor and vat shall not acknowledge them; the new wine shall play them false." * Mere children of nature may abandon themselves to the riotous joy of harvest and vintage festivals, for they have never known other gods than are suitably worshipped by these orgies. But Israel has a past—the memory of a holier God, the conscience of having deserted Him for material gifts. With such a conscience she can never enjoy the latter; as Hosea puts it, they will not "acknowledge" or "take to" † her. Here there is an instinct of the profound truth, that even in the fulness of life conscience is punishment; by itself the sense of guilt is judgment.

But Hosea does not attack the service of strange gods only because it is unfaithfulness to Jehovah, but also because, as the worship of images, it is a senseless stupidity utterly inconsistent with that spiritual discernment of which repentance so largely consists. And with the worship of heathen idols Hosea equally condemns the worship of Jehovah under the form of images.

Hosea was the first in Israel to lead the attack upon the idols. Elijah had assaulted the worship of a foreign god, but neither he nor Elisha nor Amos condemned the worship of Israel's own God under the form of a calf. Indeed Amos, except in one doubtful passage, ‡ never at all attacks idols or false gods. The reason is very obvious. Amos and Elijah were concerned only with the proclamation of God as justice and purity; and to the moral aspects of religion the question of idolatry is not relevant; the two things do not come directly into collision. But Hosea had deeper and more wide views of God, with which idolatry came into conflict at a hundred points. We know what Hosea's "knowledge of God" was—how spiritual, how extensive—and we can appreciate how incongruous idolatry must have appeared against it. We are prepared to find him treating the images, whether of the Ba'alim or of Jehovah,

* ix. 1. See above, p. 511.
† See above, p. 511, *n*.
‡ v. 26.

with that fine scorn which a passionate monotheism, justly conscious of its intellectual superiority, has ever passed upon the idolatry even of civilisations in other respects higher than its own. To Hosea the idol is an "'eseb, a made thing." * It is made of the very silver and gold with which Jehovah Himself had endowed the people.† It is made only "to be cut off" ‡ by the first invader! Chiefly, however, does Hosea's scorn fall upon the image under which Jehovah Himself was worshipped. "Thy Calf, O Samaria!" § he contemptuously calls it. "From Israel is it also," as much as the Ba'alim. "A workman made it, and no god is it: chips shall the Calf of Samaria become!" In another place he mimics the "anxiety of Samaria for their Calf; his people mourn for him, and his priestlings writhe for his glory," why?—"because it is going into exile:" ‖ the gold that covers him shall be stripped for the tribute to Assyria. And once more: "They continue to sin; they make them a smelting of their silver, idols after their own modelling, smith's work all of it. To these things they speak! Sacrificing men" actually "kiss calves!" ¶ All this in the same vein of satire which we find grown to such brilliance in the great Prophet of the Exile.** Hosea was the first in whom it sparkled; and it was due to his conception of "the knowledge of God." Its relevancy to his doctrine of repentance is this, that so spiritual an apprehension of God as repentance implies, so complete a "metanoia" or "change of mind," is intellectually incompatible with idolatry. You cannot speak of repentance to men who "kiss calves" and worship blocks of wood. Hence he says: "Ephraim is wedded to idols: leave him alone." ††

There was more than idolatry, however, in the way of Israel's repentance. The whole of the national worship was an obstacle. Its formalism and its easy and mechanical methods of "turning to God" disguised the need of that moral discipline and change of heart, without which no repentance can be genuine. Amos had contrasted the ritualism of the time with the duty of civic justice and the service of the poor: ‡‡ Hosea opposes to it leal love and the knowledge of God. "I will have leal love and not sacrifice, and the knowledge of God rather than burnt-offerings." §§ It is characteristic of Hosea to class sacrifices with idols. Both are senseless and inarticulate, incapable of expressing or of answering the deep feelings of the heart. True repentance, on the contrary, is rational, articulate, definite. "Take with you words," says Hosea, "and so return to Jehovah." ‖‖

To us who, after twenty-five more centuries of talk, know painfully how words may be abused, it is strange to find them enforced as the tokens of sincerity. But let us consider against what the prophet enforces them. Against the "kissing of calves" and such mummery—worship of images that neither hear nor speak. Let us remember the inarticulateness of ritualism, how it stifles rather than utters the feelings of the heart. Let us imagine the dead routine of the legal sacrifices, their original symbolism worn bare, bringing forward to the young hearts of new generations no interpretation of their ancient and distorted details, reducing those who perform them to irrational machines like themselves. Then let us remember how our own Reformers had to grapple with the same hard mechanism in the worship of their time, and how they bade the heart of every worshipper "speak"—speak for itself to God with rational and sincere words. So in place of the frozen ritualism of the Church there broke forth from all lands of the Reformation, as though it were birds in springtime, a great burst of hymns and prayers, with the clear notes of the Gospel in the common tongue. So intolerable was the memory of what had been, that it was even enacted that henceforth no sacrament should be dispensed but the Word should be given to the people along with it. If we keep all these things in mind, we shall know what Hosea means when he says to Israel in their penitence, "Take with you words."

No one, however, was more conscious of the danger of words. Upon the lips of the people Hosea has placed a confession of repentance, which, so far as the words go, could not be more musical or pathetic.* In every Christian language it has been paraphrased to an exquisite confessional hymn. But Hosea describes it as rejected. Its words are too easy; its thoughts of God and of His power to save are too facile. Repentance, it is true, starts from faith in the mercy of God, for without this there were only despair. Nevertheless in all true penitence there is despair. Genuine sorrow for sin includes a feeling of the irreparableness of the past, and the true penitent, as he casts himself upon God, does not dare to feel that he ever can be the same again. "I am no more worthy to be called Thy son: make me as one of Thy hired servants." Such necessary thoughts as these Israel does not mingle with her prayer. "Come and let us return to Jehovah, for He hath torn" only "that He may heal, and smitten" only "that He may bind up. He will revive us again in a couple of days, on the third day raise us up, that we may live before Him. Then shall we know if we hunt up to know the Lord. As soon as we seek Him we shall find Him: and he shall come upon us like winter-rain, and like the spring-rain pouring on the land." This is too facile, too shallow. No wonder that God despairs of such a people. "What am I to make of thee, Ephraim?" †

Another familiar passage, the Parable of the Heifer, describes the same ambition to reach spiritual results without spiritual processes. "Ephraim is a broken-in heifer—one that loveth to tread" out the corn. "But I will pass upon her goodly neck. I will give Ephraim a yoke. Judah must plough. Jacob must harrow for himself." ‡ Cattle, being unmuzzled by law§ at threshing time, loved this best of all their year's work. Yet to reach it they must first go through the harder and unrewarded trials of ploughing and harrowing. Like a heifer, then, which loved harvest only, Israel

* עָצֵב from עָצַב, which in Job x. 8 is parallel to עשה.

† ii. 8.
‡ viii. 4.
§ viii. 5.
‖ x. 5.
¶ xiii. 2.
** Isa. xli. ff.
†† iv. 17.
‡‡ Amos v.
§§ vi. 6.
‖‖ xiv. 2. Perhaps the curious expression at the close of the verse, "so will we render the calves of our lips," or (as a variant reading gives) "fruit of our lips," has the same intention. Articulate confession (or vows), these are the sacrifices, "the calves," which are acceptable to God.

* vi. 1-4.
† For the reasons for this interpretation see above, pp. 507 ff.
‡ x. 11.
§ See above, p. 513.

would spring at the rewards of penitence, the peaceable fruits of righteousness, without going through the discipline and chastisement which alone yield them. Repentance is no mere turning or even re-turning. It is a deep and an ethical process—the breaking up of fallow ground, the labour and long expectation of the sower, the seeking and waiting for Jehovah till Himself send the rain. "Sow to yourselves in righteousness; reap in proportion to love" (the love you have sown), "break up your fallow ground: for it is time to seek Jehovah, until He come and rain righteousness upon us." *

A repentance so thorough as this cannot but result in the most clear and steadfast manner of life. Truly it is a returning not by oneself, but "a returning by God," and it leads to the "keeping of leal love and justice, and waiting upon God continually." †

CHAPTER XXIII.

THE SIN AGAINST LOVE.

HOSEA i.-iii.; iv. 11 ff.; ix. 10 ff.; xi. 8 f.

THE Love of God is a terrible thing—that is the last lesson of the Book of Hosea. "My God will cast them away." ‡

"My God"—let us remember the right which Hosea had to use these words. Of all the prophets he was the first to break into the full aspect of the Divine Mercy—to learn and to proclaim that God is Love. But he was worthy to do so, by the patient love of his own heart towards another who for years had outraged all his trust and tenderness. He had loved, believed and been betrayed; pardoned and waited and yearned, and sorrowed and pardoned again. It is in this long-suffering that his breast beats upon the breast of God with the cry "My God." As He had loved Gomer, so had God loved Israel, past hope, against hate, through ages of ingratitude and apostasy. Quivering with his own pain, Hosea has exhausted all human care and affection for figures to express the Divine tenderness, and he declares God's love to be deeper than all the passion of men, and broader than all their patience: "How can I give thee up, Ephraim? How can I let thee go, Israel? I will not execute the fierceness of Mine anger. For I am God, and not man." And yet, like poor human affection, this Love of God, too, confesses its failure—"My God shall cast them away." It is God's sentence of relinquishment upon those who sin against His Love, but the poor human lips which deliver it quiver with an agony of their own, and here, as more explicitly in twenty other passages of the book, declare it to be equally the doom of those who outrage the love of their fellow men and women.

We have heard it said: "The lives of men are never the same after they have loved; if they are not better, they must be worse." "Be afraid of the love that loves you: it is either your heaven or your hell." "All the discipline of men springs from their love—if they take it not so, then all their sorrow must spring from the same source." "There is a depth of sorrow, which can only be known to a soul that has loved the most perfect thing and beholds itself fallen." These things are true of the Love, both of our brother and of our God. And the eternal interest of the life of Hosea is that he learned how, for strength and weakness, for better or for worse, our human and our Divine loves are inseparably joined.

I.

Most men learn that love is inseparable from pain where Hosea learned it—at home. There it is that we are all reminded that when love is strongest she feels her weakness most. For the anguish which love must bear, as it were from the foundation of the world, is the contradiction at her heart between the largeness of her wishes and the littleness of her power to realise them. A mother feels it, bending over the bed of her child, when its body is racked with pain or its breath spent with coughing. So great is the feeling of her love that it ought to do something, that she will actually feel herself cruel because nothing can be done. Let the sick-bed become the beach of death, and she must feel the helplessness and the anguish still more as the dear life is now plucked from her and now tossed back by the mocking waves, and then drawn slowly out to sea upon the ebb from which there is no returning.

But the pain which disease and death thus cause to love is nothing to the agony that Sin inflicts when he takes the game into his unclean hands. We know what pain love brings, if our love be a fair face and a fresh body in which Death brands his sores while we stand by, as if with arms bound. But what if our love be a childlike heart, and a frank expression and honest eyes, and a clean and clever mind. Our powerlessness is just as great and infinitely more tormented when Sin comes by and casts his shadow over these. Ah, that is Love's greatest torment when her children, who have run from her to the bosom of sin, look back and their eyes are changed! That is the greatest torment of Love—to pour herself without avail into one of those careless natures which seem capacious and receptive, yet never fill with love, for there is a crack and a leak at the bottom of them. The fields where Love suffers her sorest defeats are not the sick-bed and not death's margin, not the cold lips and sealed eyes kissed without response; but the changed eyes of children, and the breaking of the "full-orbed face," and the darkening look of growing sons and daughters, and the home the first time the unclean laugh breaks across it. To watch, though unable to soothe, a dear body racked with pain, is peace beside the awful vigil of watching a soul shrink and blacken with vice, and your love unable to redeem it.

Such a clinical study Hosea endured for years. The prophet of God, we are told, brought a dead child to life by taking him in his arms and kissing him. But Hosea with all his love could not make Gomer a true, whole wife again. Love had no power on this woman—no power even at the merciful call to make all things new. Hosea, who had once placed all hope in tenderness, had to admit that Love's moral power is not absolute. Love may retire defeated from the highest issues of life. Sin may conquer Love.

Yet it is in this his triumph that Sin must feel the ultimate revenge. When a man has

*x. 12. †xii. 7. ‡x. 17.

conquered this weak thing, and beaten her down beneath his feet, God speaks the sentence of abandonment.

There is enough of the whipped dog in all of us to make us dread penalty when we come into conflict with the strong things of life. But it takes us all our days to learn that there is far more condemnation to them who offend the weak things of life, and particularly the weakest of all, its love. It was on sins against the weak that Christ passed His sternest judgments: "Woe unto him that offends one of these little ones; it were better for him that he had never been born." God's little ones are not only little children, but all things which, like little children, have only love for their strength. They are pure and loving men and women—men with no weapon but their love, women with no shield but their trust. They are the innocent affections of our own hearts—the memories of our childhood, the ideals of our youth, the prayers of our parents, the faith in us of our friends. These are the little ones of whom Christ spake, that he who sins against them had better never have been born. Often may the dear solicitudes of home, a father's counsels, a mother's prayers, seem foolish things against the challenges of a world calling us to play the man and do as it does; often may the vows and enthusiasms of boyhood seem impertinent against the temptations which are so necessary to manhood: yet let us be true to the weak, for if we betray them, we betray our own souls. We may sin against law and maim or mutilate ourselves, but to sin against love is to be cast out of life altogether. He who violates the purity of the love with which God has filled his heart, he who abuses the love God has sent to meet him in his opening manhood, he who slights any of the affections, whether they be of man or woman, of young or of old, which God lays upon us as the most powerful redemptive forces of our life, next to that of His dear Son—he sinneth against his own soul, and it is of such that Hosea spake: "My God will cast them away."

We talk of breaking law: we can only break ourselves against it. But if we sin against Love, we do destroy her: we take from her the power to redeem and sanctify us. Though in their youth men think Love a quick and careless thing—a servant always at their side, a winged messenger easy of despatch—let them know that every time they send her on an evil errand she returns with heavier feet and broken wings. When they make her a pander they kill her outright. When she is no more they waken to that which Gomer came to know, that love abused is love lost, and love lost means Hell.

II.

This, however, is only the margin from which Hosea beholds an abandonment still deeper. All that has been said of human love and the penalty of outraging it is equally true of the Divine love and the sin against that.

The love of God has the same weakness which we have seen in the love of man. It, too, may fail to redeem; it, too, has stood defeated on some of the highest moral battle-fields of life. God Himself has suffered anguish and rejection from sinful men. "Herein," says a theologian, "is the mystery of this love, . . . that God can never by His Almighty Power compel that which is the very highest gift in the life of His creatures—love to Himself, but that He receives it as the free gift of His creatures, and that He is only able to allow men to give it to Him in a free act of their own will." So Hosea also has told us how God does not compel, but allure or "woo," the sinful back to Himself. And it is the deepest anguish of the prophet's heart, that this free grace of God may fail through man's apathy or insincerity. The anguish appears in those frequent antitheses in which his torn heart reflects herself in the style of his discourse. "I have redeemed them—yet they have spoken lies against Me.* I found Israel like grapes in the wilderness—they went to Ba'al-Peor.† When Israel was a child, then I loved him . . . but they sacrificed to Ba'alim.‡ I taught Ephraïm to walk, but they knew not that I healed them.§ How can I give thee up, Ephraim? how can I let thee go, O Israel? . . . Ephraim compasseth Me with lies, and the house of Israel with deceit."‖

We fear to apply all that we know of the weakness of human love to the love of God. Yet though He be God and not man, it was as man He commended His love to us. He came nearest us, not in the thunders of Sinai, but in Him Who presented Himself to the world with the caresses of a little child; who met men with no angelic majesty or heavenly aureole, but whom when we saw we found nothing that we should desire Him, His visage was so marred more than any man, and his form than the sons of men; Who came to His own and His own received Him not; Who, having loved His own that were in the world, loved them up to the end, and yet at the end was by them deserted and betrayed,—it is of Him that Hosea prophetically says: "I drew them with cords of a man and with bands of love."

We are not bound to God by any unbreakable chain. The strands which draw us upwards to God, to holiness and everlasting life, have the weakness of those which bind us to the earthly souls we love. It is possible for us to break them. We love Christ, not because He has compelled us by any magic, irresistible influence to do so; but, as John in his great simplicity says, "We love Him because He first loved us."

Now this is surely the terror of God's love—that it can be resisted; that even as it is manifest in Jesus Christ we men have the power, not only to remain as so many do, outside its scope, feeling it to be far-off and vague, but having tasted it to fall away from it, having realised it to refuse it, having allowed it to begin its moral purposes in our lives to baffle and nullify these; to make the glory of Heaven absolutely ineffectual in our own characters; and to give our Saviour the anguish of rejection.

Give Him the anguish, yet pass upon ourselves the doom! For, as I read the New Testament, the one unpardonable sin is the sin against our Blessed Redeemer's Love as it is brought home to the heart by the power of the Holy Spirit. Every other sin is forgiven to men but to crucify afresh Him who loved us and gave Himself for us. The most terrible of His judgments is "the wail of a heart wounded because its love has been despised": "Jerusalem, Jerusalem! how often would I have gathered thy children as a hen gathereth her chick-

* vii. 13. † ix. 10. ‡ xi. 1, 2. § xi. 4. ‖ xi. 8; xii. 1.

ens, and ye would not. Behold your house is left unto you desolate!"

Men say they cannot believe in hell, because they cannot conceive how God may sentence men to misery for the breaking of laws they were born without power to keep. And one would agree with the inference if God had done any such thing. But for them which are under the law and the sentence of death, Christ died once for all, that He might redeem them. Yet this does not make a hell less believable. When we see how Almighty was that Love of God in Christ Jesus, lifting our whole race and sending them forward with a freedom and a power of growth nothing else in history has won for them; when we prove again how weak it is, so that it is possible for millions of characters that have felt it to refuse its eternal influence for the sake of some base and transient passion; nay, when *I myself* know this power and this weakness of Christ's love, so that one day being loyal I am raised beyond the reach of fear and of doubt, beyond the desire of sin and the habit of evil, and the next day finds me capable of putting it aside in preference for some slight enjoyment or ambition—then I know the peril and the terror of this love, that it may be to a man either Heaven or Hell.

Believe then in hell, because you believe in the Love of God—not in a hell to which God condemns men of His will and pleasure, but a hell into which men cast themselves from the very face of His love in Jesus Christ. The place has been painted as a place of fires. But when we contemplate that men come to it with the holiest flames in their nature quenched, we shall justly feel that it is rather a dreary waste of ash and cinder, strewn with snow—some ribbed and frosty Arctic zone, silent in death, for there is no life there, and there is no life there because there is no Love, and no Love because men, in rejecting or abusing her, have slain their own power ever again to feel her presence.

MICAH.

'But I am full of power by the Spirit of Jehovah
To declare to Jacob his transgressions, and to Israel his sin."

CHAPTER XXIV.

THE BOOK OF MICAH.

THE Book of Micah lies sixth of the Twelve Prophets in the Hebrew Canon, but in the order of the Septuagint third, following Amos and Hosea. The latter arrangement was doubtless directed by the size of the respective books; * in the case of Micah it has coincided with the prophet's proper chronological position. Though his exact date be not certain, he appears to have been a younger contemporary of Hosea, as Hosea was of Amos.

The book is not two-thirds the size of that of Amos, and about half that of Hosea. It has been arranged in seven chapters, which follow, more or less, a natural method of division.† They are usually grouped in three sections, distinguishable from each other by their subject-matter, by their temper and standpoint, and to a less degree by their literary form. They are A. Chaps. i.-iii.; B. Chaps. iv., v.; C. Chaps. vi., vii.

There is no book of the Bible, as to the date of whose different parts there has been more discussion, especially within recent years. The history of this is shortly as follows:—

Tradition and the criticism of the early years of this century accepted the statement of the title, that the book was composed in the reigns of Jotham, Ahaz, and Hezekiah—that is, between 740 and 700 B. C. It was generally agreed that there were in it only traces of the first two reigns, but that the whole was put together before the fall of Samaria in 721.* Then Hitzig and Steiner dated chaps. iii.-vi. after 721; and Ewald denied that Micah could have given us chaps. vi., vii., and placed them under King Manasseh, *circa* 690-640. Next Wellhausen† sought to prove that vii. 7-20 must be post-exilic. Stade‡ took a further step and, on the ground that Micah himself could not have blunted or annulled his sharp pronouncements of doom, by the promises which chaps. iv. and v. contain, he withdrew these from the prophet and assigned them to the time of the Exile.§ But the sufficiency of this argument was denied by Vatke.‖ Also in opposition to Stade, Kuenen¶ refused to believe that Micah could have been content with the announcement of the fall of Jerusalem as his last word, that therefore much of chaps. iv. and v. is probably from himself, but since their argument is obviously broken and confused, we must look in them for interpolations, and he decides that such are iv. 6-8, 11-13, and the working up of v. 9-14. The famous passage in iv. 1-4 may have been Micah's, but was probably added by another. Chaps. vi. and vii. were written under Manasseh by some of the persecuted adherents of Jehovah.

We may next notice two critics who adopt an extremely conservative position. Von Ryssel,** as the result of a very thorough examination, declared that all the chapters were Micah's, even the much doubted ii. 12, 13, which have been placed by an editor of the book in the wrong position, and chap. vii. 7-20, which, he agrees with Ewald, can only date from the reign of Manasseh, Micah himself having lived long enough into that reign to write them himself. Another careful analysis by Elhorst†† also reached the conclusion that the bulk of the book was authentic, but for his proof of this Elhorst requires a radical rearrangement of the verses, and that on grounds which do not always

* See above, pp. 443 f.

† Note that the Hebrew and English divisions do not coincide between chaps. iv. and v. In the Hebrew chap. iv. includes a fourteenth verse, which in the English stands as the first verse of chap. v. In this the English agrees with the Septuagint.

* Caspari.

† In the fourth edition of Bleek's "Introduction."

‡ "Z. A. T. W.," Vols. I., III., IV.

§ See also Cornill, "Einleitung," 183 f. Stade takes iv. 1-4, iv. 11-v. 3, v. 6-14, as originally one prophecy (distinguished by certain catch-words and an outlook similar to that of Ezekiel and the great Prophet of the Exile), in which the two pieces iv. 5-10 and v. 4, 5, were afterwards inserted by the author of ii. 12, 13.

‖ "Einleitung in das A. T.," pp. 690 ff.

¶ "Einleitung."

** "Untersuchungen über die Textgestalt u. die Echtheit des Buches Micha," 1887.

†† "De Profetie van Micha," 1891, which I have not seen. It is summarised in Wildeboer's "Litteratur des A. T.," 1895.

commend themselves. He holds chap. iv. 9-14 and v. 8 for post-exilic insertions. Driver * contributes a thorough examination of the book, and reaches the conclusions that ii. 12, 13, though obviously in their wrong place, need not be denied to Micah; that the difficulties of ascribing chaps. iv., v., to the prophet are not insuperable, nor is it even necessary to suppose in them interpolations. He agrees with Ewald as to the date of vi.-vii. 6, and, while holding that it is quite possible for Micah to have written them, thinks they are more probably due to another, though a confident conclusion is not to be achieved. As to vii. 7-20, he judges Wellhausen's inferences to be unnecessary. A prophet in Micah's or Manasseh's time may have thought destruction nearer than it actually proved to be, and, imagining it as already arrived, have put into the mouth of the people a confession suited to its circumstance. Wildeboer† goes further than Driver. He replies in detail to the arguments of Stade and Cornill, denies that the reasons for withdrawing so much from Micah are conclusive, and assigns to the prophet the whole book, with the exception of several interpolations.

We see, then, that all critics are practically agreed as to the presence of interpolations in the text, as well as to the occurrence of certain verses of the prophet out of their proper order. This indeed must be obvious to every careful reader as he notes the somewhat frequent breaks in the logical sequence, especially of chaps. iv. and v. All critics, too, admit the authenticity of chaps. i.-iii., with the possible exception of ii. 12, 13; while a majority hold that chaps. vi. and vii., whether by Micah or not, must be assigned to the reign of Manasseh. On the authenticity of chaps. iv. and v.—*minus* interpolations—and of chaps. vi. and vii., opinion is divided; but we ought not to overlook the remarkable fact that those who have recently written the fullest monographs of Micah ‡ incline to believe in the genuineness of the book as a whole.§ We may now enter for ourselves upon the discussion of the various sections, but before we do so let us note how much of the controversy turns upon the general question, whether after decisively predicting the overthrow of Jerusalem it was possible for Micah to add prophecies of her restoration. It will be remembered that we have had to discuss this same point with regard both to Amos and Hosea. In the case of the former we decided against the authenticity of visions of a blessed future which now close his book; in the case of the latter we decided for the authenticity. What were our reasons for this difference? They were, that the closing vision of the Book of Amos is not at all in harmony with the exclusively ethical spirit of the authentic prophecies; while the closing vision of the Book of Hosea is not only in language and in ethical temper thoroughly in harmony with the chapters which precede it, but in certain details has been actually anticipated by these. Hosea, therefore, furnishes us with the case of a prophet who, though he predicted the ruin of his impenitent people (and that ruin was verified by events), also spoke of the possibility of their restoration upon conditions in harmony with his reasons for the inevitableness of their fall. And we saw, too, that the hopeful visions of the future, though placed last in the collection of his prophecies, need not necessarily have been spoken last by the prophet, but stand where they do because they have an eternal spiritual validity for the remnant of Israel.* What was possible for Hosea is surely possible for Micah. That promises come in his book, and closely after the conclusive threats which he gave of the fall of Jerusalem, does not imply that originally he uttered them all in such close proximity. That indeed would have been impossible. But considering how often the political prospect in Israel changed during Micah's time, and how far the city was in his day from her actual destruction—more than a century distant—it seems to be improbable that he should not (in whatever order) have uttered both threat and promise. And naturally, when his prophecies were arranged in permanent order, the promises would be placed after the threats.†

First Section: Chaps. I.-III.

No critic doubts the authenticity of the bulk of these chapters. The sole question at issue is the date or (possibly) the dates of them. Only chap. ii. 12, 13, are generally regarded as out of place, where they now stand.

Chap. i. trembles with the destruction of both Northern Israel and Judah—a destruction either very imminent or actually in the process of happening. The verses which deal with Samaria, 6 ff., do not simply announce her inevitable ruin. They throb with the sense either that this is immediate, or that it is going on, or that it has just been accomplished. The verbs suit each of these alternatives: "And I shall set," or "am setting," or "have set, Samaria for a ruin of the field," and so on. We may assign them to any time between 725 B. C., the beginning of the siege of Samaria by Shalmaneser, and a year or two after its destruction by Sargon in 721. Their intense feeling seems to preclude the possibility of their having been written in the years to which some assign them, 705-700, or twenty years after Samaria was actually overthrown.

In the next verses the prophet goes on to mourn the fact that the affliction of Samaria reaches even to the gate of Jerusalem, and he especially singles out as partakers in the danger of Jerusalem a number of towns, most of which (so far as we can discern) lie not between Jerusalem and Samaria, but at the other corner of Judah, in the Shephelah or out upon the Philistine plain.‡ This was the region which Sennacherib invaded in 701, simultaneously with his detachment of a corps to attack the capital; and accordingly we might be shut up to affirm that this end of chap. i. dates from that invasion,

* "Introduction," 1892.
† "Litteratur des A. T.," pp. 148 ff.
‡ Wildeboer ("De Profet Micha"), Von Ryssel and Elhorst.
§ Cheyne, therefore, is not correct when he says ("Introduction" to second edition of Robertson Smith's "Prophets," p. xxiii.) that it is "becoming more and more doubtful whether more than two or three fragments of the heterogeneous collection of fragments in chaps. iv.-vii. can have come from that prophet."

* See above, p. 519.
† Wildeboer seems to me to have good grounds for his reply to Stade's assertion that the occurrence of promises after the threats only blunts and nullifies the latter. "These objections," says Wildeboer, "raise themselves only against *the spoken*, but not against the written word." See, too, the admirable remarks he quotes from De Goeje.
‡ See below, pp. 536 ff.

if no other explanation of the place-names were possible. But another is possible. Micah himself belonged to one of these Shephelah towns, Moresheth-Gath, and it is natural that, anticipating the invasion of all Judah, after the fall of Samaria (as Isaiah * also did), he should single out for mourning his own district of the country. This appears to be the most probable solution of a very doubtful problem, and accordingly we may date the whole of chap. i. somewhere between 725 and 720 or 718. Let us remember that in 719 Sargon marched past this very district of the Shephelah in his campaign against Egypt, whom he defeated at Raphia.†

Our conclusion is supported by chap. ii. Judah, though Jehovah be planning evil against her, is in the full course of her ordinary social activities. The rich are absorbing the lands of the poor (vv. i. ff.): note the phrase *upon their beds;* it alone signifies a time of security. The enemies of Israel are internal (8). The public peace is broken by the lords of the land, and men and women, disposed to live quietly, are robbed (8 ff.). The false prophets have sufficient signs of the times in their favour to regard Micah's threats of destruction as calumnies (6). And although he regards destruction as inevitable, it is not to be to-day; but *in that day* (4), viz., some still indefinite date in the future, the blow will fall and the nation's elegy be sung. On this chapter, then, there is no shadow of a foreign invader. We might assign it to the years of Jotham and Ahaz (under whose reigns the title of the book places part of the prophesying of Micah), but since there is no sense of a double kingdom, no distinction between Judah and Israel, it belongs more probably to the years when all immediate danger from Assyria had passed away, between Sargon's withdrawal from Raphia in 719 and his invasion of Ashdod in 710, or between the latter date and Sennacherib's accession in 705.

Chap. iii. contains three separate oracles, which exhibit a similar state of affairs: the abuse of the common people by their chiefs and rulers, who are implied to be in full sense of power and security. They have time to aggravate their doings (4); their doom is still future—*them at that time* (*ib.*). The bulk of the prophets determine their oracles by the amount men give them (5), another sign of security. Their doom is also future (6 f.). In the third of the oracles the authorities of the land are in the undisturbed exercise of their judicial offices (9 f.), and the priests and prophets of their oracles (10), though all these professions practise only for bribe and reward. Jerusalem is still being built and embellished (9). But the prophet not because there are political omens pointing to this, but simply in the force of his indignation at the sins of the upper classes, prophesies the destruction of the capital (10). It is possible that these oracles of chap. iii. may be later than those of the previous chapters.

* x. 18.

† Smend assigns the prophecy of the destruction of Jerusalem in iii. 14, along with Isaiah xxviii.–xxxii., to 704–701, and suggests that the end of chap. i. refers to Sennacherib's campaign in Philistia in 701 ("A. T. Religionsgeschichte," p. 225, *n.*). The former is possible, but the latter passage, following so closely on i. 6, which implies the fall of Samaria to be still recent, if not in actual course, is more suitably placed in the time of the campaign of Sargon over pretty much the same ground.

Second Section: Chaps. IV., V.

This section of the book opens with two passages, verses 1-5 and verses 6, 7, which there are serious objections against assigning to Micah.

1. The first of these, 1-5, is the famous prophecy of the Mountain of the Lord's House, which is repeated in Isaiah ii. 2-5. Probably the Book of Micah presents this to us in the more original form.* The alternatives therefore are four: Micah was the author, and Isaiah borrowed from him; or both borrowed from an earlier source; † or the oracle is authentic in Micah, and has been inserted by a later editor in Isaiah; or it has been inserted by later editors in both Micah and Isaiah.

The last of these conclusions is required by the arguments first stated by Stade and Hackmann, and then elaborated, in a very strong piece of reasoning, by Cheyne. Hackmann, after marking the want of connection with the previous chapter, alleges the keynotes of the passage to be three: that it is not the arbitration of Jehovah,‡ but His sovereignty over foreign nations, and their adoption of His law, which the passage predicts; that it is the Temple at Jerusalem whose future supremacy is affirmed; and that there is a strong feeling against war. These, Cheyne contends, are the doctrines of a much later age than that of Micah; he holds the passage to be the work of a post-exilic imitator of the prophets, which was first intruded into the Book of Micah and afterwards borrowed from this by an editor of Isaiah's prophecies. It is just here, however, that the theory of these critics loses its strength. Agreeing heartily as I do with recent critics that the genuine writings of the early prophets have received some, and perhaps considerable, additions from the Exile and later periods, it seems to me extremely improbable that the same post-exilic insertion should find its way into *two* separate books. And I think that the undoubted bias towards the post-exilic period of all Canon Cheyne's recent criticism, has in this case hurried him past due consideration of the possibility of a pre-exilic date. In fact, the gentle temper shown bv the passage towards foreign nations, the absence of hatred or of any ambition to subject the Gentiles to servitude to Israel, contrasts strongly with the temper of many exilic and post-exilic prophecies; § while the position which it demands for Jehovah and His religion is quite consistent with the fundamental principles of earlier prophecy. The passage really claims no more than a suzerainty of Jehovah over the heathen tribes, with the result only that their war with Israel and with one another shall cease, not that they shall become, as the great prophecy of the Exile demands, tributaries and servitors. Such a claim was no more than the natural deduction from the early prophet's belief of Jehovah's supremacy in righteousness. And although Amos had not driven the principle so far as to promise the absolute cessation of war, he also had recognised in the most unmistakable fashion the responsibility of the Gentiles to Jehovah, and His supreme

* So Hitzig ("ohne Zweifel"), and Cheyne, "Introduction to the Book of Isaiah"; Ryssel, *op. cit.*, pp. 218 f. Hackmann ("Die Zukunftserwartung des Jesaia," 127-8, *n.*) prefers the Greek of Micah. Ewald is doubtful. Duhm, however, inclines to authorship by Isaiah, and would assign the composition to Isaiah's old age.

† Hitzig; Ewald.

‡ As against Duhm.

§ So rightly Duhm on Isa. ii. 2-4.

arbitrament upon them.* And Isaiah himself, in his prophecy on Tyre, promised a still more complete subjection of the life of the heathen to the service of Jehovah.† Moreover the fifth verse of the passage in Micah (though it is true its connection with the previous four is not apparent) is much more in harmony with pre-exilic than with post-exilic prophecy: "All the nations shall walk each in the name of his god, and we shall walk in the name of Jehovah our God for ever and aye." This is consistent with more than one prophetic utterance before the Exile,‡ but it is not consistent with the beliefs of Judaism after the Exile. Finally, the great triumph achieved for Jerusalem in 701 is quite sufficient to have prompted the feelings expressed by this strange passage for the "mountain of the house of the Lord;" though if we are to bring it down to a date subsequent to 701, we must rearrange our views with regard to the date and meaning of the second chapter of Isaiah. In Micah the passage is obviously devoid of all connection, not only with the previous chapter, but with the subsequent verses of chap. iv. The possibility of a date in the eighth or beginning of the seventh century is all that we can determine with regard to it: the other questions must remain in obscurity.

2. Verses 6, 7, may refer to the Captivity of Northern Israel, the prophet adding that when it shall be restored the united kingdom shall be governed from Mount Zion; but a date during the Exile is, of course, equally probable.

3. Verses 8-13 contain a series of small pictures of Jerusalem in siege, from which, however, she issues triumphant.§ It is impossible to say whether such a siege is actually in course while the prophet writes, or is pictured by him as inevitable in the near future. The words "thou shalt go to Babylon" may be, but are not necessarily, a gloss.

4. Chap. iv. 14-v. 8 again pictures such a siege of Jerusalem, but promises a deliverer out of Bethlehem, the city of David.‖ Sufficient heroes will be raised up along with him to drive the Assyrians from the land, and what is left of Israel after all these disasters shall prove a powerful and sovereign influence upon the peoples. These verses were probably not all uttered at the same time.

5. Verses 9-14.—In prospect of such a deliverance the prophet returns to what chap. i. has already described and Isaiah frequently emphasises as the sin of Judah—her armaments and fortresses, her magic and idolatries, the things she trusted in instead of Jehovah. They will no more be necessary, and will disappear. The nations that serve not Jehovah will feel His wrath.

In all these oracles there is nothing inconsistent with the authorship in the eighth century: there is much that witnesses to this date. Everything that they threaten or promise is threatened or promised by Hosea and by Isaiah, with

* Amos i. and ii. See above, pp. 473, 475.

† Isa. xxiii. 17 f.

‡ Jer. xvii.

§ Wellhausen indeed thinks that ver. 8 presupposes that Jerusalem is already devastated, reduced to the state of a shepherd's tower in the wilderness. This, however, is incorrect. The verse implies only that the whole country is overrun by the foe, Jerusalem alone standing with the flock of God in it, like a fortified fold (*cf.* Isaiah i.).

‖ Roorda, reasoning from the Greek text, takes "House of Ephratha" as the original reading, with Bethlehem added later; and Hitzig properly reads Ephrath, giving its final letter to the next word, which improves the grammar, thus: אפרת הצעיר.

the exception of the destruction (in ver. 12) of the Maççeboth, or sacred pillars, against which we find no sentence going forth from Jehovah before the Book of Deuteronomy, while Isaiah distinctly promises the erection of a Maççebah to Jehovah in the land of Egypt.* But waiving for the present the possibility of a date for Deuteronomy, or for part of it, in the reign of Hezekiah, we must remember the destruction, which took place under this king, of idolatrous sanctuaries in Judah, and feel also that, in spite of such a reform, it was quite possible for Isaiah to introduce a Maççebah into his poetic vision of the worship of Jehovah in Egypt. For has he not also dared to say that the "harlot's hire" of the Phœnician commerce shall one day be consecrated to Jehovah?

Third Section: Chaps. VI., VII.

The style now changes. We have had hitherto a series of short oracles, as if delivered orally. These are succeeded by a series of conferences or arguments, by several speakers. Ewald accounts for the change by supposing that the latter date from a time of persecution, when the prophet, unable to speak in public, uttered himself in literature. But chap. i. is also dramatic.

1. Chap. vi. 1-8.—An argument in which the prophet as herald calls on the hills to listen to Jehovah's case against the people (1, 2). Jehovah Himself appeals to the latter, and in a style similar to Hosea's cites His deeds in their history, as evidence of what he seeks from them (3-5). The people, presumably penitent, ask how they shall come before Jehovah (6, 7). And the prophet tells them what Jehovah has declared in the matter (8). Opening very much like Micah's first oracle (chap. i. 1), this argument contains nothing strange either to Micah or the eighth century. Exception has been taken to the reference in ver. 7 to the sacrifice of the first-born, which appears to have been more common from the gloomy age of Manasseh onwards, and which, therefore, led Ewald to date all chaps. vi. and vii. from that king's reign. But child-sacrifice is stated simply as a possibility, and—occurring as it does at the climax of the sentence—as an extreme possibility.† I see no necessity, therefore, to deny the piece to Micah or the reign of Hezekiah. Of those who place it under Manasseh, some, like Driver, still reserve it to Micah himself, whom they suppose to have survived Hezekiah and seen the evil days which followed.

2. Verses 9-16.—Most expositors‡ take these verses along with the previous eight, as well as with the six which follow in chap. vii. But there is no connection between verses 8 and 9; and 9-16 are better taken by themselves. The prophet heralds, as before, the speech of Jehovah to *tribe and city* (9). Addressing Jerusalem, Jehovah asks how He can forgive such fraud and violence as those by which her wealth has been gathered (10-12). Then addressing the people (note the change from feminine to masculine in the second personal pronouns) He tells them He must smite; they shall not enjoy the fruit of their labours (14, 15). They have sinned the sins of Omri and the house of Ahab (query—should it not be of Ahab and the house of Omri?), so that they must be put to shame be-

* Isa. xix. 19. † So also Wellhausen.

‡ *E. g.*, Ewald and Driver.

fore the Gentiles * (16). In this section three or four words have been marked as of late Hebrew.† But this is uncertain, and the inference made from it precarious. The deeds of Omri and Ahab's house have been understood as the persecution of the adherents of Jehovah, and the passage has, therefore, been assigned by Ewald and others to the reign of the tyrant Manasseh. But such habits of persecution could hardly be imputed to the City or People as a whole; and we may conclude that the passage means some other of that notorious dynasty's sins. Among these, as is well known, it is possible to make a large selection—the favouring of idolatry, or the tyrannous absorption by the rich of the land of the poor (as in Naboth's case), a sin which Micah has already marked as that of his age. The whole treatment of the subject, too, whether under the head of the sin or its punishment, strongly resembles the style and temper of Amos. It is, therefore, by no means impossible for this passage also to have been Micah's, and we must accordingly leave the question of its date undecided. Certainly we are not shut up, as the majority of modern critics suppose, to a date under Manasseh or Amon.

3. Chap. vii. 1-6.—These verses are spoken by the prophet in his own name or that of the people's. The land is devastated; the righteous have disappeared; everybody is in ambush to commit deeds of violence and take his neighbour unawares. There is no justice: the great ones of the land are free to do what they like; they have intrigued with and bribed the authorities. Informers have crept in everywhere. Men must be silent, for the members of their own families are their foes. Some of these sins have already been marked by Micah as those of his age (chap. ii.), but the others point rather to a time of persecution, such as that under Manasseh. Wellhausen remarks the similarity of the state of affairs described in Mal. iii. 24 and in some Psalms. We cannot fix the date.

4. Verses 7-20.—This passage starts from a totally different temper of prophecy, and presumably, therefore, from very different circumstances. Israel, as a whole, speaks in penitence. She has sinned, and bows herself to the consequences, but in hope. A day shall come when her exiles shall return and the heathen acknowledge her God. The passage, and with it the Book of Micah, concludes by apostrophising Jehovah as the God of forgiveness and grace to His people. Ewald, and following him Driver, assign the passage, with those which precede it, to the times of Manasseh, in which of course it is possible that Micah was still active, though Ewald supposes a younger and anonymous prophet as the author. Wellhausen‡ goes further, and, while recognising that the situation and temper of the passage resemble those of Isaiah xl. ff., is inclined to bring it even further down to post-exilic times, because of the universal character of the Diaspora. Driver objects to these inferences, and maintains that a prophet in the time of Manasseh, thinking the destruction of Jerusalem to be nearer than it actually was, may easily have pictured it as having taken place, and put an ideal confession in the mouth of the people. It seems to me that all these critics have failed to appreciate a piece of evidence even more remarkable than any they have insisted on in their argument for a late date. This is, that the passage speaks of a restoration of the people only to Bashan and Gilead, the provinces overrun by Tiglath-Pileser III. in 734. It is not possible to explain such a limitation either by the circumstances of Manasseh's time or by those of the Exile. In the former surely Samaria would have been included; in the latter Zion and Judah would have been emphasised before any other region. It would be easy for the defenders of a post-exilic date, and especially of a date much subsequent to the Exile, to account for a longing after Bashan and Gilead, though they also would have to meet the objection that Samaria or Ephraim is not mentioned. But how natural it would be for a prophet writing soon after the captivity of Tiglath-Pileser III. to make this precise selection! And although there remain difficulties (arising from the temper and language of the passage) in the way of assigning all of it to Micah or his contemporaries, I feel that on the geographical allusions much can be said for the origin of this part of the passage in their age, or even in an age still earlier: that of the Syrian wars in the end of the ninth century, with which there is nothing inconsistent either in the spirit or the language of vv. 14-17. And I am sure that if the defenders of a late date had found a selection of districts as suitable to the post-exilic circumstances of Israel as the selection of Bashan and Gilead is to the circumstances of the eighth century, they would, instead of ignoring it, have emphasised it as a conclusive confirmation of their theory. On the other hand, ver. 11 can date only from the Exile, or the following years, before Jerusalem was rebuilt. Again, vv. 18-20 appear to stand by themselves.

It seems likely, therefore, that chap. vii. 7-20 is a Psalm composed of little pieces from various dates, which, combined, give us a picture of the secular sorrows of Israel, and of the conscience she ultimately felt in them, and conclude by a doxology to the everlasting mercies of her God.

* For עמי read עמים with the LXX.

† Wellhausen states four. But תושיה of ver. 9 is an uncertain reading. רמיה is found in Hosea vii. 16, though the text of this, it is true, is corrupt. זכה in another verbal form is found in Isa. i. 16. There only remains מטה, but again it is uncertain whether we should take this in its late sense of tribe.

‡ And also Giesebrecht, "Beiträge," p. 217.

CHAPTER XXV.

MICAH THE MORASTHITE.

MICAH i.

SOME time in the reign of Hezekiah, when the kingdom of Judah was still inviolate, but shivering to the shock of the fall of Samaria, and probably while Sargon the destroyer was pushing his way past Judah to meet Egypt at Raphia, a Judean prophet of the name of Micah, standing in sight of the Assyrian march, attacked the sins of his people and prophesied their speedy overthrow beneath the same flood of war. If we be correct in our surmise, the exact year was 720-719 B. C. Amos had been silent thirty years, Hosea hardly fifteen; Isaiah was in the midway of his career. The title of Micah's book asserts that he had previously prophesied under Jotham and Ahaz, and though we have seen it to be possible, it is by no means proved, that certain passages of the book date from these reigns.

Micah is called the Morasthite.* For this designation there appears to be no other meaning than that of a native of Moresheth-Gath, a village mentioned by himself.† It signifies *Property* or *Territory* of Gath, and after the fall of the latter, which from this time no more appears in history, Moresheth may have been used alone. Compare the analogous cases of Helkath (*portion of*—) Galilee, Ataroth, Chesulloth, and Iim.‡

In our ignorance of Gath's position, we should be equally at fault about Moresheth, for the name has vanished, were it not for one or two plausible pieces of evidence. Belonging to Gath, Moresheth must have lain near the Philistine border: the towns among which Micah includes it are situate in that region; and Jerome declares that the name—though the form, Morasthi, in which he cites it is suspicious—was in his time still extant in a small village to the east of Eleutheropolis or Beit-Jibrin. Jerome cites Morasthi as distinct from the neighbouring Mareshah, which is also quoted by Micah beside Moresheth-Gath.§

Moresheth was, therefore, a place in the Shephelah, or range of low hills which lie between the hill country of Judah and the Philistine plain. It is the opposite exposure from the wilderness of Tekoa,‖ some seventeen miles away across the watershed. As the home of Amos is bare and desert, so the home of Micah is fair and fertile. The irregular chalk hills are separated by broad glens, in which the soil is alluvial and red, with room for cornfields on either side of the perennial or almost perennial streams. The olive groves on the braes are finer than either those of the plain below or of the Judean tableland above. There is herbage for cattle. Bees murmur everywhere, larks are singing, and although to-day you may wander in the maze of hills for hours without meeting a man or seeing a house, you are never out of sight of the traces of ancient habitation, and seldom beyond sound of the human voice—shepherds and ploughmen calling to their flocks and to each other across the glens. There are none of the conditions or of the occasions of a large town. But, like the south of England, the country is one of villages and homesteads, breeding good yeomen—men satisfied and in love with their soil, yet borderers with a far outlook and a keen vigilance and sensibility. The Shephelah is sufficiently detached from the capital and body of the land to beget in her sons an independence of mind and feeling, but so much upon the edge of the open world as to endue them at the same time with that sense of the responsibilities of warfare, which the national statesmen, aloof and at ease in Zion, could not possibly have shared.

Upon one of the westmost terraces of this Shephelah, nearly a thousand feet above the sea, lay Moresheth itself. There is a great view across the undulating plain with its towns and fortresses, Lachish, Eglon, Shaphir, and others, beyond which runs the coast road, the famous war-path between Asia and Africa. Ashdod and Gaza are hardly discernible against the glitter of the sea, twenty-two miles away. Behind roll the round bush-covered hills of the Shephelah, with David's hold at Adullam,* the field where he fought Goliath, and many another scene of border warfare; while over them rises the high wall of the Judean plateau, with the defiles breaking through it to Hebron and Bethlehem.

The valley-mouth near which Moresheth stands has always formed the southwestern gateway of Judea, the Philistine or Egyptian gate, as it might be called, with its outpost at Lachish, twelve miles across the plain. Roads converge upon this valley-mouth from all points of the compass. Beit-Jibrin, which lies in it, is midway between Jerusalem and Gaza, about twenty-five miles from either, nineteen miles from Bethlehem, and thirteen from Hebron. Visit the place at any point of the long history of Palestine, and you find it either full of passengers or a centre of campaign. Asa defeated the Ethiopians here. The Maccabees and John Hyrcanus contested Mareshah, two miles off, with the Idumeans. Gabinius fortified Mareshah. Vespasian and Saladin both deemed the occupation of the valley necessary before they marched upon Jerusalem. Septimius Severus made Beit-Jibrin the capital of the Shephelah, and laid out military roads, whose pavements still radiate from it in all directions. The *Onomasticon* measures distances in the Shephelah from Beit-Jibrin. Most of the early pilgrims from Jerusalem by Gaza to Sinai or Egypt passed through it, and it was a centre of Crusading operations, whether against Egypt during the Latin kingdom or against Jerusalem during the Third Crusade. Not different was the place in the time of Micah. Micah must have seen pass by his door the frequent embassies which Isaiah tells us went down to Egypt from Hezekiah's court, and seen return those Egyptian subsidies in which a foolish people put their trust instead of in their God.

In touch, then, with the capital, feeling every throb of its folly and its panic, but standing on that border which must, as he believed, bear the brunt of the invasion that its crimes were attracting, Micah lifted up his voice. They were days of great excitement. The words of Amos and Hosea had been fulfilled upon Northern Israel. Should Judah escape, whose injustice and impurity were as flagrant as her sister's? It were vain to think so. The Assyrians had come up to her northern border. Isaiah was expecting their assault upon Mount Zion.† The Lord's Controversy was not closed. Micah will summon the whole earth to hear the old indictment and the still unexhausted sentence.

* Micah i.; Jer. xxvi. 18.

† i. 14.

‡ Ataroth (Numb. xxxii. 3) is Atroth-Shophan (*ib.* 35); Chesulloth (Josh. xix. 18) is Chisloth-Tabor (*ib.* 12); Iim (Numb. xxxiii. 45) is Iye-Abarim (*ib.* 44).

§ "Michæam de Morasthi qui usque hodie juxta Eleutheropolim, haud grandis est viculus."—Jerome, Preface to Micha. "Morasthi, unde fuit Micheas propheta, est autem vicus contra orientem Eleutheropoleos."—"Onomasticon," which also gives "Maresa, in tribu Juda; cujus nunc tantummodo sunt ruinæ in secundo lapide Eleutheropoleos." See, too, the "Epitaphium S. Paulæ:" "Videam Morasthim sepulchrum quondam Michææ, nunc ecclesiam, et ex latere derelinquam Choræos, et Gitthæos et Maresam." The occurrence of a place bearing the name Property-of-Gath so close to Beit-Jibrin certainly strengthens the claims of the latter to be Gath. See "Hist. Geog.," p. 196.

‖ See above, pp. 460 ff.

* For the situation of Adullam in the Shephelah see "Hist. Geog.," p. 229.

† Isa. x. 28 ff. This makes it quite conceivable that Micah i. 9, "it hath struck right up to the gate of Jerusalem," was composed immediately after the fall of Jerusalem, and not, as Smend imagines, during the campaign of Sennacherib. Against the latter date there is the objection that by then the fall of Samaria, which Micah i. 6 describes as present, was already nearly twenty years past.

The prophet speaks:—

"Hear ye, peoples* all;
Hearken, O Earth, and her fulness!
That Jehovah may be among you to testify,
The Lord from His holy temple!
For, lo! Jehovah goeth forth from His place;
He descendeth and marcheth on the heights of the earth.†
Molten are the mountains beneath Him,
And the valleys gape open,
Like wax in face of the fire,
Like water poured over a fall.

God speaks:—

"For the transgression of Jacob is all this,
And for the sins of the house of Israel.
What is the transgression of Jacob? is it not Samaria?
And what is the sin of the house ‡ of Judah? is it not Jerusalem?
Therefore do I turn Samaria into a ruin of the field,§
And into vineyard terraces;
And I pour down her stones to the glen,
And lay bare her foundations.‖
All her images are shattered,
And all her hires are being burned in the fire;
And all her idols I lay desolate,
For from the hire of a harlot they were gathered,¶
And to a harlot's hire they return.**

The prophet speaks:—

"For this let me mourn, let me wail,
Let me go barefoot and stripped (of my robe),
Let me make lamentations like the jackals,
And mourning like the daughters of the desert,††
For her stroke ‡‡ is desperate;
Yea, it hath come unto Judah!
It hath smitten right up to the gate of my people.
Up to Jerusalem."

Within the capital itself Isaiah was also recording the extension of the Assyrian invasion to its walls, but in a different temper.§§ He was full of the exulting assurance that, although at the very gate, the Assyrian could not harm the city of Jehovah, but must fall when he lifted his impious hand against it. Micah has no such hope: he is overwhelmed with the thought of Jerusalem's danger. Provincial though he be, and full of wrath at the danger into which the politicians of Jerusalem had dragged the whole country, he profoundly mourns the peril of the capital, "the gate of my people," as he fondly calls her. Therefore we must not exaggerate the frequently drawn contrast between Isaiah and himself.‖‖ To Micah also Jerusalem was dear, and his subsequent prediction of her overthrow* ought to be read with the accent of this previous mourning for her peril. Nevertheless his heart clings most to his own home, and while Isaiah pictures the Assyrian entering Judah from the north by Migron, Michmash, and Nob, Micah anticipates invasion by the opposite gateway of the land, at the door of his own village. His elegy sweeps across the landscape so dear to him. This obscure province was even more than Jerusalem his world, the world of his heart. It gives us a living interest in the man that the fate of these small villages, many of them vanished, should excite in him more passion than the fortunes of Zion herself. In such passion we can incarnate his spirit. Micah is no longer a book, or an oration, but flesh and blood upon a home and a countryside of his own. We see him on his housetop pouring forth his words before the hills and the far-stretching heathen land. In the name of every village within sight he reads a symbol of the curse that is coming upon his country, and of the sins that have earned the curse. So some of the greatest poets have caught their music from the nameless brooklets of their boyhood's fields; and many a prophet has learned to read the tragedy of man and God's verdict upon sin in his experience of village life. But there was more than feeling in Micah's choice of his own country as the scene of the Assyrian invasion. He had better reasons for his fears than Isaiah, who imagined the approach of the Assyrian from the north. For it is remarkable how invaders of Judea, from Sennacherib to Vespasian and from Vespasian to Saladin and Richard, have shunned the northern access to Jerusalem and endeavoured to reach her by the very gateway at which Micah stood mourning. He had, too, this greater motive for his fear, that Sargon, as we have seen, was actually in the neighbourhood, marching to the defeat of Judah's chosen patron, Egypt. Was it not probable that, when the latter was overthrown, Sargon would turn back upon Judah by Lachish and Mareshah? If we keep this in mind we shall appreciate, not only the fond anxiety, but the political foresight that inspires the following passage, which is to our Western taste so strangely cast in a series of plays upon place-names. The disappearance of many of these names, and our ignorance of the transactions to which the verses allude, often render both the text and the meaning very uncertain. Micah begins with the well-known play upon the name of Gath; the Acco which he couples with it is either the Phœnician port to the north of Carmel, the modern Acre, or some Philistine town, unknown to us, but in any case the line forms with the previous one an intelligible couplet: "Tell it not in Tell-town; Weep not in Weep-town." The following Beth-le-ʿAphrah, "House of Dust," must be taken with them, for in the phrase "roll thyself" there is a play upon the name Philistine. So, too, Shaphir, or Beauty, the modern Suafir, lay in the Philistine Region. Saʿanan and Beth-esel and Maroth are unknown; but if Micah, as is probable, begins his list far away on the western horizon and comes gradually inland, they also are to be sought for on the maritime plain. Then he draws nearer by Lachish, on the first hills, and in the leading pass towards Judah, to Moresheth-Gath, Achzib, Mareshah, and Adullam, which all lie within Israel's territory and about the

* The address is either to the tribes, in which case we must substitute "land" for "earth" in the next line; or much more probably it is to the Gentile "nations," but in this case we cannot translate (as all do) in the third line that the Lord will be a witness "against" them, for the charge is only against Israel. They are summoned in the same sense as Amos summons a few of the nations in chap. iii. 9 ff.—The opening words of Micah are original to this passage, and interpolated in the exordium of the other Micah, 1 Kings xxii. 28.

† Jehovah's "Temple" or "Place" is not, as in earlier poems, Sinai or Seir (*cf.* Deborah's song and Deut. xxxiii.), but Heaven (*cf.* Isaiah xix. or Psalm xxix.).

‡ So LXX. and other versions.

§ Wellhausen's objections to this phrase are arbitrary and incorrect. A ruin in the midst of soil gone out of cultivation, where before there had been a city among vineyards, is a striking figure of desolation.

‖ Which is precisely how Herod's Samaria lies at the present day.

¶ So Ewald.

** It must be kept in mind that all the verbs in the above passage may as correctly be given in the future tense; in that case the passage will be dated just before the fall of Samaria, in 722-1, instead of just after.

†† בנות יענה, that is, the ostriches: *cf.* Arab. waʿana, "white, barren ground." The Arabs call the ostrich "father of the desert: abu sahârâ."

‡‡ LXX.

§§ Isa. x. 28 ff.

‖‖ It is well put by Robertson Smith's "Prophets," pp. 289 ff.

* iii. 12.

prophet's own home. We understand the allusion, at least, to Lachish in ver. 13. As the last Judean outpost towards Egypt, and on a main road thither, Lachish would receive the Egyptian subsidies of horses and chariots, in which the politicians put their trust instead of in Jehovah. Therefore she "was the beginning of sin to the daughter of Zion." And if we can trust the text of ver. 14, Lachish would pass on the Egyptian ambassadors to Moresheth-Gath, the next stage of their approach to Jerusalem. But this is uncertain. With Moresheth-Gath is coupled Achzib, a town at some distance from Jerome's site for the former, to the neighbourhood of which, Mareshah, we are brought back again in ver. 15. Adullam, with which the list closes, lies some eight or ten miles to the northeast of Mareshah.

The prophet speaks:—

"Tell it not in Gath,
Weep not in Acco.*
In Beth-le-'Aphrah † roll thyself in dust.
Pass over, inhabitress of Shaphir,‡ thy shame uncovered!
The inhabitress of Ṣa'anan § shall not march forth;
The lamentation of Beth-esel ‖ taketh from you its standing.
The inhabitress of Maroth ¶ trembleth for good,
For evil hath come down from Jehovah to the gate of Jerusalem.
Harness the horse to the chariot, inhabitress of Lachish,**
That hast been the beginning of sin to the daughter of Zion;
Yea, in thee are found the transgressions of Israel.
Therefore thou givest . . †† to Moresheth-Gath: ‡‡
The houses of Achzib §§ *shall* deceive the kings of Israel.
Again shall I bring the Possessor [conqueror] to thee, inhabitress of Mareshah; ‖‖
To Adullam ¶¶ shall come the glory of Israel.
Make thee bald, and shave thee for thy darlings;
Make broad thy baldness like the vulture,
For they go into banishment from thee.

This was the terrible fate which the Assyrian kept before the peoples with whom he was at war. Other foes raided, burned, and slew: he carried off whole populations into exile.

Having thus pictured the doom which threatened his people, Micah turns to declare the sins for which it has been sent upon them.

* LXX. ἐν Ἀκειμ; Heb. "weep not at all."

† לְעַפְרָה cannot be the Ophrah, עָפְרָה, of Benjamin. It may be connected with עֹפֶר, a gazelle; and it is to be noted that S. of Beit-Jibrin there is a wady now called El-Ghufr, the corresponding Arabic word. But, as stated in the text above, the name ought to be one of a Philistine town.

‡ Beauty town. This is usually taken to be the modern Suafîr on the Philistine plain, 4½ miles S. E. of Ashdod, a site not unsuitable for identification with the Σαφειρ of the "Onom.," "between Eleutheropolis and Ascalon," except that Σαφειρ is also described as "in the hill country." Guérin found the name Safar a very little N. of Beit-Jibrin ("Judée," II. 317).

§ March-town: perhaps the same as Senan (צְנָן) of Josh. xv. 37; given along with Migdal-Gad and Hadashah; not identified.

‖ Unknown.

¶ "Bitternesses": unknown.

** Tell-el-Hesy.

†† "Ambassadors" or "letters of dismissal."

‡‡ See above, p. 535.

§§ Josh. xv. 44; mentioned with Keilah and Mareshah; perhaps the present Ain Kezbeh, 8 miles N. N. E., of Beit-Jibrin.

‖‖ מָרֵשָׁה, but in Josh, xv. 44 מראשה, which is identical with spelling of the present name of a ruin 1 mile S. of Beit-Jibrin. Μαρησα is placed by Eusebius ("Onom.") 2 Roman miles S. of Eleutheropolis (=Beit-Jibrin).

¶¶ 6 miles N. E. of Beit-Jibrin.

CHAPTER XXVI.

THE PROPHET OF THE POOR.

MICAH ii., iii.

WE have proved Micah's love for his country-side in the effusion of his heart upon her villages with a grief for their danger greater than his grief for Jerusalem. Now in his treatment of the sins which give that danger its fatal significance, he is inspired by the same partiality for the fields and the folk about him. While Isaiah chiefly satirises the fashions of the town and the intrigues of the court, Micah scourges the avarice of the landowner and the injustice which oppresses the peasant. He could not, of course, help sharing Isaiah's indignation for the fatal politics of the capital, any more than Isaiah could help sharing his sense of the economic dangers of the provinces; * but it is the latter with which Micah is most familiar and on which he spends his wrath. These so engross him, indeed, that he says almost nothing about the idolatry, or the luxury, or the hideous vice, which, according to Amos and Hosea, were now corrupting the nation.

Social wrongs are always felt most acutely, not in the town, but in the country. It was so in the days of Rome, whose earliest social revolts were agrarian.† It was so in the Middle Ages: the fourteenth century saw both the Jacquerie in France and the Peasants' Rising in England; Langland, who was equally familiar with town and country, expends nearly all his sympathy upon the poverty of the latter, "the poure folk in cotes." It was so after the Reformation, under the new spirit of which the first social revolt was the Peasants' War in Germany. It was so at the French Revolution, which began with the march of the starving peasants into Paris. And it is so still, for our new era of social legislation has been forced open, not by the poor of London and the large cities, but by the peasantry of Ireland and the crofters of the Scottish Highlands. Political discontent and religious heresy take their start among industrial and manufacturing centres, but the first springs of the social revolt are nearly always found among the rural populations.

Why the country should begin to feel the acuteness of social wrong before the town is sufficiently obvious. In the town there are mitigations, and there are escapes. If the conditions of one trade become oppressive, it is easier to pass to another. The workers are better educated and better organised; there is a middle class, and the tyrant dare not bring matters to so high a crisis. The might of the wealthy, too, is divided; the poor man's employer is seldom at the same time his landlord. But in the country power easily gathers into the hands of the few. The labourer's opportunities and means of work, his home, his very standing-ground, are often all of them the property of one man. In the country the rich have a real power of life and death, and are less hampered by competition with each other and by the force of public opinion. One man cannot hold a city in fee, but one man can

* Isa. v. 8.

† Mr. Congreve, in his Essay on Slavery appended to his edition of Aristotle's "Politics," p. 496, points out that all the servile wars from which Rome suffered arose, not in the capital, but in the provinces, notably in Sicily.

affect for evil or for good almost as large a population as a city's, when it is scattered across a countryside.

This is precisely the state of wrong which Micah attacks. The social changes of the eighth century in Israel were peculiarly favourable to its growth.* The enormous increase of money which had been produced by the trade of Uzziah's reign threatened to overwhelm the simple economy under which every family had its croft. As in many another land and period, the social problem was the descent of wealthy men, land-hungry, upon the rural districts. They made the poor their debtors, and bought out the peasant proprietors. They absorbed into their power numbers of homes, and had at their individual disposal the lives and the happiness of thousands of their fellow-countrymen. Isaiah had cried. "Woe upon them that join house to house, that lay field to field, till there be no room" for the common people, and the inhabitants of the rural districts grow fewer and fewer.† Micah pictures the recklessness of those plutocrats—the fatal ease with which their wealth enabled them to dispossess the yeomen of Judah.

The prophet speaks:—

"Woe to them that plan mischief,
And on their beds work out evil!
As *soon as* morning breaks they put it into execution,
For—it *lies* to the power of their hands!

They covet fields and—seize them,
Houses and—lift them up.
So they crush a good man and his home,
A man and his heritage."

This is the evil—the ease with which wrong is done in the country! "It lies to the power of their hands: they covet and seize." And what is it that they get so easily—not merely field and house, so much land and stone and lime: it is human life, with all that makes up personal independence, and the security of home and of the family. That these should be at the mercy of the passion or the caprice of one man—this is what stirs the prophet's indignation. We shall presently see how the tyranny of wealth was aided by the bribed and unjust judges of the country; and how, growing reckless, the rich betook themselves, as the lords of the feudal system in Europe continually did, to the basest of assaults upon the persons of peaceful men and women. But meantime Micah feels that by themselves the economic wrongs explain and justify the doom impending on the nation. When this doom falls, by the Divine irony of God it shall take the form of a conquest of the land by the heathen, and the disposal of these great estates to the foreigner.

The prophet speaks:—

"Therefore thus saith Jehovah:
Behold, I am planning evil against this race,
From which ye shall not withdraw your necks,
Nor walk upright:
For an evil time it is! ‡
In that day shall they raise a taunt-song against you
And wail out the wailing ("It is done"); § and say,
'We be utterly undone:
My people's estate is measured off! ‖
How they take it away from me! ¶
To the rebel our fields are allotted.'
So thou shalt have none to cast the line by lot
In the congregation of Jehovah."

No restoration at time of Jubilee for lands taken away in this fashion! There will be no congregation of Jehovah left!

At this point the prophet's pessimist discourse, that must have galled the rich, is interrupted by their clamour to him to stop.

The rich speak:—

"Prate not, they prate, let none prate of such things!
Revilings will never cease!
O thou that speakest *thus* to the house of Jacob,*
Is the spirit of Jehovah cut short?
Or are such His doings?
Shall not His words mean well with him that walketh uprightly?"

So the rich, in their immoral confidence that Jehovah was neither weakened nor could permit such a disaster to fall on His own people, tell the prophet that his sentence of doom on the nation, and especially on themselves, is absurd, impossible. They cry the eternal cry of Respectability: "God can mean no harm to the like of us! His words are good to them that walk uprightly—and we are conscious of being such. What you, prophet, have charged us with are nothing but natural transactions." The Lord Himself has His answer ready. Upright indeed! They have been unprovoked plunderers!

God speaks:—

"But ye are the foes of My people,
Rising against those that are peaceful;
The mantle ye strip from them that walk quietly by,
Averse to war! †
Women of My people ye tear from their happy homes, ‡
From their children ye take My glory for ever.
Rise and begone—for this is no resting-place!
Because of the uncleanness that bringeth destruction,
Destruction incurable."

Of the outrages on the goods of honest men, and the persons of women and children, which are possible in a time of peace, when the rich are tyrannous and abetted by mercenary judges and prophets, we have an illustration analogous to Micah's in the complaint of Peace in Langland's vision of English society in the fourteenth century. The parallel to our prophet's words is very striking:—

"And thanne come Pees into parlement · and put forth a bille,
How Wronge ageines his wille · had his wyf taken.
'Both my gees and my grys § · his gadelynges ‖ feccheth;
I dar noughte for fere of hym · fyghte ne chyde.
He borwed of me bayard ¶ · he broughte hym home nevre,
Ne no ferthynge ther-fore · for naughte I couthe plede.
He meynteneth his men · to marther myne hewen,**
Forstalleth my feyres †† · and fighteth in my chepynge,

* See above, pp. 450 ff.

† Isa. v. 8.

‡ *Cf.* Amos v. 13.

§ "Fuit." But whether this is a gloss, as of the name of the dirge or of the tune, or a part of the text, is uncertain. Query: ונחה ינהה ואמר.

‖ So LXX., and adds: "with the measuring rope."

¶ Or (after the LXX.) "there is none to give it back to me."

* Uncertain. "Is the house of Jacob . . .?" "Wellhausen). "What a saying, O house of Jacob?" (Ewald and Guthe). In the latter case the interruption of the rich ceases with the previous line, and this one is the beginning of the prophet's answer to them.

† So we may conjecture the very obscure details of a verse whose general meaning, however, is evident. For ואתמול read ואתם ל. The LXX. takes שלמה as "peace" and not as "cloak," for which there seems to be no place beside אדר (or אדרת). Wellhausen with further alterations renders: "But ye come forward as enemies against My people; from good friends ye rob their . . ., from peaceful wanderers war-booty."

‡ Wellhausen reads בני for ביה, "tenderly bred children," another of the many emendations which he proposes in the interests of complete parallelism. See the Preface, p. 435.

§ Little pigs.

‖ Fellows.

¶ A horse.

** Servants.

†† Fairs, markets.

And breketh up my bernes dore · and bereth aweye my whete,
And taketh me but a taile * · for ten quarters of otes,
And yet he bet me ther-to · and lyth bi my mayde,
I nam † noughte hardy for hym · uneth ‡ to loke.' "

They pride themselves that all is stable and God is with them. How can such a state of affairs be stable! They feel at ease, yet injustice can never mean rest. God has spoken the final sentence, but with a rare sarcasm the prophet adds his comment on the scene. These rich men had been flattered into their religious security by hireling prophets, who had opposed himself. As they leave the presence of God, having heard their sentence, Micah looks after them and muses in quiet prose.

The prophet speaks:—

"Yea, if one whose walk is wind and falsehood were to try to cozen" thee, saying, "I will babble to thee of wine and strong drink, then he might be the prophet of such a people."

At this point in chap. ii. there have somehow slipped into the text two verses (12, 13), which all are agreed do not belong to it, and for which we must find another place.§ They speak of a return from the Exile, and interrupt the connection between ver. 11 and the first verse of chap. iii. With the latter Micah begins a series of three oracles, which give the substance of his own prophesying in contrast to that of the false prophets whom he has just been satirising. He has told us what they say, and he now begins the first of his own oracles with the words, "But I said." It is an attack upon the authorities of the nation, whom the false prophets flatter. Micah speaks very plainly to them. Their business is to know justice, and yet they love wrong. They flay the people with their exactions; they cut up the people like meat.

The prophet speaks:—

"But I said,
Hear now, O chiefs of Jacob,
And rulers of the house of Israel:
Is it not yours to know justice?—
Haters of good and lovers of evil,
Tearing their hide from upon them

(he points to the people)

And their flesh from the bones of them;
And who devour the flesh of my people,
And their hide they have stripped from them
And their bones have they cleft,
And served it up as if from a pot,
Like meat from the thick of the caldron!
At that time shall they cry to Jehovah,
And He will not answer them;
But hide His face from them at that time,
Because they have aggravated their deeds."

These words of Micah are terribly strong, but there have been many other ages and civilisations than his own of which they have been no more than true. "They crop us," said a French peasant of the lords of the great Louis' time, "as the sheep crops grass." "They treat us like their food," said another on the eve of the Revolution.

Is there nothing of the same with ourselves? While Micah spoke he had wasted lives and bent backs before him. His speech is elliptic till you see his finger pointing at them. Pinched peasant faces peer between all his words and fill the ellipses. And among the living poor to-day are there not starved and bitten faces—bodies with the blood sucked from them, with the Divine image crushed out of them? Brothers, we cannot explain all of these by vice. Drunkenness and unthrift do account for much; but how much more is explicable only by the following facts! Many men among us are able to live in fashionable streets and keep their families comfortable only by paying their employes a wage upon which it is impossible for men to be strong or women to be virtuous. Are those not using these as their food? They tell us that if they are to give higher wages they must close their business, and cease paying wages at all; and they are right if they themselves continue to live on the scale they do. As long as many families are maintained in comfort by the profits of businesses in which some or all of the employes work for less than they can nourish and repair their bodies upon, the simple fact is that the one set are feeding upon the other set. It may be inevitable, it may be the fault of the system and not of the individual, it may be that to break up the system would mean to make things worse than ever—but all the same the truth is clear that many families of the middle class, and some of the very wealthiest of the land, are nourished by the waste of the lives of the poor. Now and again the fact is acknowledged with as much shamelessness as was shown by any tyrant in the days of Micah. To a large employer of labour who was complaining that his employes, by refusing to live at the low scale of Belgian workmen, were driving trade from this country, the present writer once said: "Would it not meet your wishes if, instead of your workmen being levelled down, the Belgians were levelled up? This would make the competition fair between you and the employers in Belgium." His answer was, "I care not so long as I get my profits." He was a religious man, a liberal giver to his Church, and he died leaving more than one hundred thousand pounds.

Micah's tyrants, too, had religion to support them. A number of the hireling prophets, whom we have seen both Amos and Hosea attack, gave their blessing to this social system, which crushed the poor, for they shared its profits. They lived upon the alms of the rich, and flattered according as they were fed. To them Micah devotes the second oracle of chap. iii., and we find confirmed by his words the principle we laid down before, that in that age the one great difference between the false and the true prophet was what it has been in every age since then till now—an ethical difference; and not a difference of dogma, or tradition, or ecclesiastical note. The false prophet spoke, consciously or unconsciously, for himself and his living. He sided with the rich; he shut his eyes to the social condition of the people; he did not attack the sins of the day. This made him *false*—robbed him of insight and the power of prediction. But the true prophet exposed the sins of his people. Ethical insight and courage, burning indignation of wrong, clear vision of the facts of the day—this was what Jehovah's spirit put into him, this was what Micah felt to be inspiration.

* A tally.
† Am not.
‡ Scarcely.
§ "I will gather, gather thee, O Jacob, in mass,
I will bring, bring together the Remnant of Israel!
I will set them like sheep in a fold,
Like a flock in the midst of the pasture.
They shall hum with men!
The breach-breaker hath gone up before them:
They have broken the breach, have carried the gate, and are gone out by it;
And their king hath passed on before them, and Jehovah at their head."

The prophet speaks:—

"Thus saith Jehovah against the prophets who lead my people astray,
Who while they have aught between their teeth proclaim peace,
But against him who will not lay to their mouths they sanctify war!
Wherefore night shall be yours without vision,
And yours shall be darkness without divination;
And the sun shall go down on the prophets,
And the day shall darken about them;
And the seers shall be put to the blush,
And the diviners be ashamed:
All of them shall cover the beard,
For there shall be no answer from God.
But I—I am full of power by the spirit of Jehovah, and justice and might,
To declare to Jacob his transgressions and to Israel his sin."

In the third oracle of this chapter rulers and prophets are combined—how close the conspiracy between them! It is remarkable that, in harmony with Isaiah, Micah speaks no word against the king. But evidently Hezekiah had not power to restrain the nobles and the rich. When this oracle was uttered it was a time of peace, and the lavish building, which we have seen to be so marked a characteristic of Israel in the eighth century,* was in process. Jerusalem was larger and finer than ever. Ah, it was a building of God's own city *in blood!* Judges, priests, and prophets were all alike mercenary, and the poor were oppressed for a reward. No walls, however sacred, could stand on such foundations. Did they say that they built her so grandly, for Jehovah's sake? Did they believe her to be inviolate because He was in her? They should see. Zion—yes, Zion—should be ploughed like a field, and the Mountain of the Lord's Temple become desolate.

The prophet speaks:—

"Hear now this, O chiefs of the house of Jacob,
And rulers of the house of Israel,
Who spurn justice and twist all that is straight,
Building Zion in blood, and Jerusalem with crime!
Her chiefs give judgment for a bribe,
And her priests oracles for a reward,
And her prophets divine for silver;
And on Jehovah they lean, saying:
'Is not Jehovah in the midst of us?
Evil cannot come at us.'
Therefore for your sakes shall Zion be ploughed like a field,
And Jerusalem become heaps,
And the Mount of the House mounds in a jungle."

It is extremely difficult for us to place ourselves in a state of society in which bribery is prevalent, and the fingers both of justice and of religion are gilded by their suitors. But this corruption has always been common in the East. "An Oriental state can never altogether prevent the abuse by which officials, small and great, enrich themselves in illicit ways."† The strongest government takes the bribery for granted, and periodically prunes the rank fortunes of its great officials. A weak government lets them alone. But in either case the poor suffer from unjust taxation and from laggard or perverted justice. Bribery has always been found, even in the more primitive and puritan forms of Semitic life. Mr. Doughty has borne testimony with regard to this among the austere Wahabees of Central Arabia. "When I asked if there were no handling of bribes at Hâyil by those who are nigh the prince's ear, it was answered, 'Nay.' The Byzantine corruption cannot enter into the eternal and noble simplicity of this people's (airy) life, in the poor nomad country; but (we have seen) the art is not unknown to the subtle-headed Shammar princes, who thereby help themselves with the neighbour Turkish governments."* The bribes of the ruler of Hâyil "are, according to the shifting weather of the world, to great Ottoman government men; and now on account of Kheybar, he was gilding some of their crooked fingers in Medina."† Nothing marks the difference of Western government more than the absence of all this, especially from our courts of justice. Yet the improvement has only come about within comparatively recent centuries. What a large space, for instance, does Langland give to the arraigning of "Mede," the corrupter of all authorities and influences in the society of his day! Let us quote his words, for again they provide a most exact parallel to Micah's, and may enable us to realise a state of life so contrary to our own. It is Conscience who arraigns Mede before the King:—

"By ihesus with here jeweles · youre justices she shendeth,‡
And lith § agein the lawe · and letteth hym the gate,
That feith may noughte have his forth ‖ · here floreines go so thikke,
She ledeth the lawe as hire list · and lovedays maketh
And doth men lese thorw hire love · that law myghte wynne,
The mase ¶ for a mene man · though he mote ** hir eure.
Law is so lordeliche · and loth to make ende,
Without presentz or pens †† · she pleseth wel fewe.

. . . .

For pore men mowe ‡‡ have no powere · to pleyne §§ hem though thei smerte;
Suche a maistre is Mede · amonge men of gode." ‖‖

* See above, p. 450.
† Nöldeke, "Sketches from Eastern History," translated by Black, pp. 134 f.

CHAPTER XXVII.

ON TIME'S HORIZON.

MICAH iv. 1-7.

THE immediate prospect of Zion's desolation which closes chap. iii. is followed in the opening of chap. iv. by an ideal picture of her exaltation and supremacy "in the issue of the days." We can hardly doubt that this arrangement has been made of purpose, nor can we deny that it is natural and artistic. Whether it be due to Micah himself, or whether he wrote the second passage, are questions we have already discussed.¶¶ Like so many others of their kind, they cannot be answered with certainty, far less with dogmatism. But I repeat, I see no conclusive reason for denying either to the circumstances of Micah's times or to the principles of their prophecy the possibility of such a hope as inspires chap. iv. 1-4. Remember how the prophets of the eighth century identified Jehovah with supreme and universal righteousness; remember how Amos explicitly condemned the aggravations of war and slavery among the heathen as sins against Him, and how Isaiah claimed the future gains of Tyrian commerce as gifts for His sanctuary; remember how Amos heard His voice come forth from Jerusalem, and Isaiah counted upon the eternal inviolateness of His shrine and city,—and you will not think it impossible for a third Judean prophet of that age, whether he was Micah or another, to have drawn the prospect of Jerusalem which now opens before us.

* "Arabia Deserta," I. 607.
† *Id.*, II. 20.
‡ Ruins.
§ Lieth.
‖ Course.
¶ Confusion.
** Summon.
†† Pence.
‡‡ May.
§§ Complain.
‖‖ Substance or property.
¶¶ See above, pp. 532 ff.

It is the far-off horizon of time, which, like the spatial horizon, always seems a fixed and eternal line, but as constantly shifts with the shifting of our standpoint or elevation. Every prophet has his own vision of "the latter days"; seldom is that prospect the same. Determined by the circumstances of the seer, by the desires these prompt or only partially fulfil, it changes from age to age. The ideal is always shaped by the real, and in this vision of the eighth century there is no exception. This is not any of the ideals of later ages, when the evil was the oppression of the Lord's people by foreign armies or their scattering in exile; it is not, in contrast to these, the spectacle of the armies of the Lord of Hosts imbrued in the blood of the heathen, or of the columns of returning captives filling all the narrow roads to Jerusalem, "like streams in the south"; nor, again, is it a nation of priests gathering about a rebuilt temple and a restored ritual. But because the pain of the greatest minds of the eighth century was the contradiction between faith in the God of Zion as Universal Righteousness and the experience that, nevertheless, Zion had absolutely no influence upon surrounding nations, this vision shows a day when Zion's influence will be as great as her right, and from far and wide the nations whom Amos has condemned for their transgressions against Jehovah will acknowledge His law, and be drawn to Jerusalem to learn of Him. Observe that nothing is said of Israel going forth to teach the nations the law of the Lord. That is the ideal of a later age, when Jews were scattered across the world. Here, in conformity with the experience of a still untravelled people, we see the Gentiles drawing in upon the Mountain of the House of the Lord. With the same lofty impartiality which distinguishes the oracles of Amos on the heathen, the prophet takes no account of their enmity to Israel; nor is there any talk—such as later generations were almost forced by the hostility of neighbouring tribes to indulge in—of politically subduing them to the king in Zion. Jehovah will arbitrate between them, and the result shall be the institution of a great peace, with no special political privilege to Israel, unless this be understood in ver. 5, which speaks of such security to life as was impossible, at that time at least, in all borderlands of Israel. But among the heathen themselves there will be a resting from war: the factions and ferocities of that wild Semitic world, which Amos so vividly characterised,* shall cease. In all this there is nothing beyond the possibility of suggestion by the circumstances of the eighth century or by the spirit of its prophecy.

A prophet speaks:—

"And it shall come to pass in the issue of the days,†
That the Mount of the House of Jehovah shall be
established on the tops ‡ of the mountains,
And lifted shall it be above the hills,
And peoples shall flow to it,

* See above, chap. vii.

† אחריה is the hindmost, furthest, ultimate, whether of space (Psalm cxxxix. 9: "the uttermost part of the sea"), or of time (Deut. xi. 12: "the end of the year"). It is the end as compared with the beginning, the sequel with the start, the future with the present (Job xlii. 12). In proverbs it is chiefly used in the moral sense of issue or result. But it chiefly occurs in the phrase used here, אחרית הימים, not "the latter days," as A. V., nor ultimate days, for in these phrases lurks the idea of time having an end, but the "after-days" (Cheyne), or, better still, the "the issue of the days."

‡ LXX.

And many nations shall go and say:
'Come, and let us up to the Mount of Jehovah,
And to the House of the God of Jacob,
That He may teach us of His ways,
And we will walk in His paths.'
For from Zion goeth forth the law,
And the word of Jehovah from out of Jerusalem!
And He shall judge between many peoples,
And decide * for strong nations far and wide;†
And they shall hammer their swords into ploughshares,
And their spears into pruning-hooks:
They shall not lift up, nation against nation, a sword,
And they shall not any more learn war.
Every man shall dwell under his vine
And under his fig-tree,
And none shall make afraid;
For the mouth of Jehovah of Hosts has spoken."

What connection this last verse is intended to have with the preceding is not quite obvious. It may mean that every family among the Gentiles shall dwell in peace; or, as suggested above, that with the voluntary disarming of the surrounding heathendom, Israel herself shall dwell secure, in no fear of border raids and slave-hunting expeditions, with which especially Micah's Shephelah and other borderlands were familiar. The verse does not occur in Isaiah's quotation of the three which precede it. We can scarcely suppose, fain though we may be to do so, that Micah added the verse in order to exhibit the future correction of the evils he has been deploring in chap. iii.: the insecurity of the householder in Israel before the unscrupulous land-grabbing of the wealthy. Such are not the evils from which this passage prophesies redemption. It deals only, like the first oracles of Amos, with the relentlessness and ferocity of the heathen: under Jehovah's arbitrament these shall be at peace, and whether among themselves or in Israel, hitherto so exposed to their raids, men shall dwell in unalarmed possession of their houses and fields. Security from war, not from social tyranny, is what is promised.

The following verse (5) gives in a curious way the contrast of the present to that future in which all men will own the sway of one God. "For" at the present time "all the nations are walking each in the name of his God, but we go in the name of Jehovah for ever and aye."

To which vision, complete in itself, there has been added by another hand, of what date we cannot tell, a further effect of God's blessed influence. To peace among men shall be added healing and redemption, the ingathering of the outcast and the care of the crippled.

"In that day—'tis the oracle of Jehovah—
I will gather the halt,
And the cast-off I will bring in, and *all* that I have
afflicted;
And I will make the halt for a Remnant,‡
And her that was weakened § into a strong people,
And Jehovah shall reign over them
In the Mount of Zion from now and for ever."

Whatever be the origin of the separate oracles which compose this passage (iv. 1-7), they form as they now stand a beautiful whole, rising from Peace through Freedom to Love. They begin with obedience to God and they culminate in the most glorious service which God or man may undertake, the service of saving the lost. See how the Divine spiral ascends. We have, first, Religion the centre and origin of all, compelling the attention of men by its historical evidence of justice and righteousness. We have the

* Or "arbitrate."

† Literally: "up to far away."

‡ That which shall abide and be the stock of the future.

§ LXX. "cast off."

world's willingness to learn of it. We have the results in the widening brotherhood of nations, in universal Peace, in Labour freed from War, and with none of her resources absorbed by the conscriptions and armaments which in our times are deemed necessary for enforcing peace. We have the universal diffusion and security of Property, the prosperity and safety of the humblest home. And, finally, we have this free strength and wealth inspired by the example of God Himself to nourish the broken and to gather in the forwandered.

Such is the ideal world, seen and promised two thousand five hundred years ago, out of as real an experience of human sin and failure as ever mankind awoke to. Are we nearer the Vision to-day, or does it still hang upon time's horizon, that line which seems so stable from every seer's point of view, but which moves from the generations as fast as they travel to it?

So far from this being so, there is much in the Vision that is not only nearer us than it was to the Hebrew prophets, and not only abreast of us, but actually achieved and behind us, as we live and strive still onward. Yes, brothers, actually behind us! History has in part fulfilled the promised influence of religion upon the nations. The Unity of God has been owned, and the civilised peoples bow to the standards of justice and of mercy first revealed from Mount Zion. "Many nations" and "powerful nations" acknowledge the arbitrament of the God of the Bible. We have had revealed that High Fatherhood of which every family in heaven and earth is named; and wherever that is believed the brotherhood of men is confessed. We have seen Sin, that profound discord in man and estrangement from God, of which all human hatreds and malices are the fruit, atoned for and reconciled by a Sacrifice in face of which human pride and passion stand abashed. The first part of the Vision is fulfilled. "The nations stream to the God of Jerusalem and His Christ." And though to-day our Peace be but a paradox, and the "Christian" nations stand still from war not in love, but in fear of one another, there are in every nation an increasing number of men and women, with growing influence, who, without being fanatics for peace, or blind to the fact that war may be a people's duty in fulfilment of its own destiny or in relief of the enslaved, do yet keep themselves from foolish forms of patriotism, and by their recognition of each other across all national differences make sudden and unconsidered war more and more of an impossibility. I write this in the sound of that call to stand upon arms which broke like thunder upon our Christmas peace; but, amid all the ignoble jealousies and hot rashness which prevail, how the air, burned clean by that first electric discharge, has filled with the determination that war shall not happen in the interests of mere wealth or at the caprice of a tyrant! God help us to use this peace for the last ideals of His prophet! May we see, not that of which our modern peace has been far too full, mere freedom for the wealth of the few to increase at the expense of the mass of mankind. May our Peace mean the gradual disarmament of the nations, the increase of labour, the diffusion of property, and, above all, the redemption of the waste of the people and the recovery of our outcasts. Without this, peace is no peace; and better were war to burn out by its fierce fires those evil humours of our secure comfort, which render us insensible to the needy and the fallen at our side. Without the redemptive forces at work which Christ brought to earth, peace is no peace; and the cruelties of war, that slay and mutilate so many, are as nothing to the cruelties of a peace which leaves us insensible to the outcasts and the perishing, of whom there are so many even in our civilisation.

One application of the prophecy may be made at this moment. We are told by those who know best and have most responsibility in the matter that an ancient Church and people of Christ are being left a prey to the wrath of an infidel tyrant, not because Christendom is without strength to compel him to deliver, but because to use the strength, would be to imperil the peace, of Christendom. It is an ignoble peace which cannot use the forces of redemption, and with the cry of Armenia in our ears the Unity of Europe is but a mockery.

CHAPTER XXVIII.

THE KING TO COME.

MICAH iv. 8-v.

WHEN a people has to be purged of long injustice, when some high aim of liberty or of order has to be won, it is remarkable how often the drama of revolution passes through three acts. There is first the period of criticism and of vision, in which men feel discontent, dream of new things, and put their hopes into systems: it seems then as if the future were to come of itself. But often a catastrophe, relevant or irrelevant, ensues: the visions pale before a vast conflagration, and poet, philosopher, and prophet disappear under the feet of a mad mob of wreckers. Yet this is often the greatest period of all, for somewhere in the midst of it a strong character is forming, and men, by the very anarchy, are being taught, in preparation for him, the indispensableness of obedience and loyalty. With their chastened minds he achieves the third act, and fulfils all of the early vision that God's ordeal by fire has proved worthy to survive. Thus history, when distraught, rallies again upon the Man.

To this law the prophets of Israel only gradually gave expression. We find no trace of it among the earliest of them; and in the essential faith of all there was much which predisposed them against the conviction of its necessity. For, on the one hand, the seers were so filled with the inherent truth and inevitableness of their visions, that they described these as if already realised; there was no room for a great figure to rise before the future, for with a rush the future was upon them. On the other hand, it was ever a principle of prophecy that God is able to dispense with human aid. "In presence of the Divine omnipotence all secondary causes, all interposition on the part of the creature, fall away." * The more striking is it that before long the prophets should have begun, not only to look for a Man, but to paint him as the central figure of their hopes. In Hosea, who has no such promise, we already see the instinct at work. The age of revolution which he describes is cursed by its want of men: there is no great

* Schultz, "A. T. Theol.," p. 722.

leader of the people sent from God; those who come to the front are the creatures of faction and party; there is no king from God.* How different it had been in the great days of old, when God had ever worked for Israel through some man—a Moses, a Gideon, a Samuel, but especially a David. Thus memory, equally with the present dearth of personalities, prompted to a great desire, and with passion Israel waited for a Man. The hope of the mother for her firstborn, the pride of the father in his son, the eagerness of the woman for her lover, the devotion of the slave to his liberator, the enthusiasm of soldiers for their captain—unite these noblest affections of the human heart, and you shall yet fail to reach the passion and the glory with which prophecy looked for the King to Come. Each age, of course, expected him in the qualities of power and character needed for its own troubles, and the ideal changed from glory unto glory. From valour and victory in war, it became peace and good government, care for the poor and the oppressed, sympathy with the sufferings of the whole people, but especially of the righteous among them, with fidelity to the truth delivered unto the fathers, and, finally, a conscience for the people's sin, a bearing of their punishment and a travail, for their spiritual redemption. But all these qualities and functions were gathered upon an individual—a Victor, a King, a Prophet, a Martyr, a Servant of the Lord.

Micah stands among the first, if he is not the very first, who thus focussed the hopes of Israel upon a great Redeemer; and his promise of Him shares all the characteristics just described. In his book it lies next a number of brief oracles with which we are unable to trace its immediate connection. They differ from it in style and rhythm: they are in verse, while it seems to be in prose. They do not appear to have been uttered along with it. But they reflect the troubles out of which the Hero is expected to emerge, and the deliverance which He shall accomplish, though at first they picture the latter without any hint of Himself. They apparently describe an invasion which is actually in course, rather than one which is near and inevitable; and if so they can only date from Sennacherib's campaign against Judah in 701 B. C. Jerusalem is in siege, standing alone in the land,† like one of those solitary towers with folds round them which were built here and there upon the border pastures of Israel for defence of the flock against the raiders of the desert.‡ The prophet sees the possibility of Zion's capitulation, but the people shall leave her only for their deliverance elsewhere. Many are gathered against her, but he sees them as sheaves upon the floor for Zion to thresh. This oracle (vv. 11-13) cannot, of course, have been uttered at the same time as the previous one, but there is no reason why the same prophet should not have uttered both at different periods. Isaiah had prospects of the fate of Jerusalem which differ quite as much.§ Once more (ver. 14) the blockade is established. Israel's ruler is helpless, "smitten on the cheek by the foe."* It is to this last picture that the promise of the Deliverer is attached.

The prophet speaks:—

"But thou, O Tower of the Flock,
Hill of the daughter of Zion,
To thee shall arrive the former rule,
And *the* kingdom shall come to the daughter of Zion.
Now wherefore criest thou *so* loud?
Is there no king in thee,† or is thy counsellor perished,
That throes have seized thee like a woman in childbirth?
Quiver and writhe, daughter of Zion, like one in childbirth:
For now must thou forth from the city,
And encamp on the field (and come unto Babel);‡
There shalt thou be rescued,
There shall Jehovah redeem thee from the hand of thy foes!

"And now gather against thee many nations, that say,
'Let her be violate, that our eyes may fasten on Zion!'
But they know not the plans of Jehovah,
Nor understand they His counsel,
For He hath gathered them in like sheaves to the floor
Up and thresh, O daughter of Zion!
For thy horns will I turn into iron,
And thy hoofs will I turn into brass;
And thou wilt beat down many nations,
And devote to Jehovah their spoil,
And their wealth to the Lord of all earth.

"Now press thyself together, thou daughter of pressure:§
The foe hath set a wall around us,
With a rod they smite on the cheek Israel's regent!
But thou, Beth-Ephrath,‖ smallest among the thousands¶ of Judah,
From thee unto Me shall come forth the Ruler to be in Israel!
Yea, of old are His goings forth, from the days of long ago!
Therefore shall He suffer them till the time that one bearing shall have born.**
(Then the rest of His brethren shall return with the children of Israel.)††
And He shall stand and shepherd His flock‡‡ in the strength of Jehovah,
In the pride of the name of His God.
And they shall abide!
For now is He great to the ends of the earth.
And Such an One shall be our Peace.§§

Bethlehem was the birthplace of David, but when Micah says that the Deliverer shall emerge from her he does not only mean what Isaiah affirms by his promise of a rod from the stock of Jesse, that the King to Come shall spring from the one great dynasty in Judah. Micah means rather to emphasise the rustic and popular origin of the Messiah, "too small to be among the thousands of Judah." David, the son of Jesse the Bethlehemite, was a dearer figure than Solomon son of David the King. He impressed the people's imagination, because he had sprung from themselves, and in his lifetime had been the popular rival of an unlovable despot. Micah himself was the prophet of the country as distinct from the capital, of the peasants as against the

* See above, pp. 510 ff.

† Wellhausen declares that this is unsuitable to the position of Jerusalem in the eighth century, and virtually implies her ruin and desolation. But, on the contrary, it is not so: Jerusalem is still standing, though alone (*cf.* the similar figure in Isa. i.). Consequently the contradiction which Wellhausen sees between this eighth verse and vv. 9, 10, does not exist. He grants that the latter may belong to the time of Sennacherib's invasion—unless it be a *vaticinium post eventum!*

‡ See above, p. 450.

§ This in answer to Wellhausen, who thinks the two oracles incompatible, and that the second one is similar to the eschatological prediction common from Ezekiel onwards. Jerusalem, however, is surely still standing.

* Even Wellhausen agrees that this verse is most suitably dated from the time of Micah.

† Those who maintain the exilic date understand by this Jehovah Himself. In any case it may be He who is meant.

‡ The words in parenthesis are perhaps a gloss.

§ Uncertain.

‖ The name Bethlehem is probably a later insertion. I read with Hitzig and others אפרת הצעיר, and omit להיות.

¶ Smallest form of district: *cf.* English "hundreds."

** *Cf.* the prophecy of Immanuel, Isa. vii.

†† This seems like a later insertion: it disturbs both sense and rhythm.

‡‡ So LXX.

§§ Take this clause from ver. 4 and the following oracle and put it with ver. 3.

rich who oppressed them. When, therefore, he fixed upon Bethlehem as the Messiah's birthplace, he doubtless desired, without departing from the orthodox hope in the Davidic dynasty, to throw round its new representative those associations which had so endeared to the people their father-monarch. The shepherds of Judah, that strong source of undefiled life from which the fortunes of the state and prophecy itself had ever been recuperated, should again send forth salvation. Had not Micah already declared that, after the overthrow of the capital and the rulers, the glory of Israel should come to Adullam, where of old David had gathered its soiled and scattered fragments?

We may conceive how such a promise would affect the crushed peasants for whom Micah wrote. A Saviour, who was one of themselves, not born up there in the capital, foster-brother of the very nobles who oppressed them, but born among the people, sharer of their toils and of their wrongs!—it would bring hope to every broken heart among the disinherited poor of Israel. Yet meantime, be it observed, this was a promise, not for the peasants only, but for the whole people. In the present danger of the nation the class disputes are forgotten, and the hopes of Israel gather upon their Hero for a common deliverance from the foreign foe. "Such an One shall be our peace." But in the peace He is "to stand and shepherd His flock," conspicuous and watchful. The country folk knew what such a figure meant to themselves for security and weal on the land of their fathers. Heretofore their rulers had not been shepherds, but thieves and robbers.

We can imagine the contrast which such a vision must have offered to the fancies of the false prophets. What were they beside this? Deity descending in fire and thunder, with all the other features of the ancient Theophanies that had now become so much cant in the mouths of mercenary traditionalists. Besides those, how sane was this, how footed upon the earth, how practical, how popular in the best sense!

We see, then, the value of Micah's prophecy for his own day. Has it also any value for ours—especially in that aspect of it which must have appealed to the hearts of those for whom chiefly Micah arose? "Is it wise to paint the Messiah, to paint Christ, so much a workingman? Is it not much more to our purpose to remember the general fact of His humanity, by which He is able to be Priest and Brother to all classes, high and low, rich and poor, the noble and the peasant alike? Is not the Man of Sorrows a much wider name than the Man of Labour?" Let us answer these questions.

The value of such a prophecy of Christ lies in the correctives which it supplies to the Christian apocalypse and theology. Both of these have raised Christ to a throne too far above the actual circumstance of His earthly ministry and the theatre of His eternal sympathies. Whether enthroned in the praises of Heaven, or by scholasticism relegated to an ideal and abstract humanity, Christ is lifted away from touch with the common people. But His lowly origin was a fact. He sprang from the most democratic of peoples. His ancestor was a shepherd, and His mother a peasant girl. He Himself was a carpenter: at home, as His parables show, in the fields and the folds and the barns of His country; with the servants of the great houses, with the unemployed in the market; with the woman in the hovel seeking one piece of silver, with the shepherd on the moors seeking the lost sheep. "The poor had the gospel preached to them; and the common people heard Him gladly." As the peasants of Judea must have listened to Micah's promise of His origin among themselves with new hope and patience, so in the Roman empire the religion of Jesus Christ was welcomed chiefly, as the Apostles and the Fathers bear witness, by the lowly and the labouring of every nation. In the great persecution which bears His name, the Emperor Domitian heard that there were two relatives alive of this Jesus whom so many acknowledged as their King, and he sent for them that he might put them to death. But when they came, he asked them to hold up their hands, and seeing these brown and chapped with toil, he dismissed the men, saying, "From such slaves we have nothing to fear." Ah but, Emperor! it is just the horny hands of this religion that thou and thy gods have to fear! Any cynic or satirist of thy literature, from Celsus onwards, could have told thee that it was by men who worked with their hands for their daily bread, by domestics, artisans, and all manner of slaves, that the power of this King should spread, which meant destruction to thee and thine empire! "From little Bethlehem came forth the Ruler," and "now He is great to the ends of the earth."

There follows upon this prophecy of the Shepherd a curious fragment which divides His office among a number of His order, though the grammar returns towards the end to One. The mention of Assyria stamps this oracle also as of the eighth century. Mark the refrain which opens and closes it.*

"When Asshûr cometh into our land,
And when he marcheth on our borders,†
Then shall we raise against him seven shepherds
And eight princes of men.
And they shall shepherd Asshûr with a sword,
And Nimrod's land with her own bare blades.
And He shall deliver from Asshûr,
When he cometh into our land,
And marcheth upon our borders."

There follows an oracle in which there is no evidence of Micah's hand or of his times; but if it carries any proof of a date, it seems a late one.

"And the remnant of Jacob shall be among many peoples
Like the dew from Jehovah,
Like showers upon grass,
Which wait not for a man,
Nor tarry for the children of men.
And the remnant of Jacob (among nations,) among many peoples,
Shall be like the lion among the beasts of the jungle,
Like a young lion among the sheepfolds,
Who, when he cometh by, treadeth and teareth,
And none may deliver.
Let thine hand be high on thine adversaries,
And all thine enemies be cut off!"

Finally in this section we have an oracle full of the notes we had from Micah in the first two chapters. It explains itself. Compare Micah ii. and Isaiah ii.

"And it shall be in that day—'tis the oracle of Jehovah—
That I will cut off thy horses from the midst of thee,
And I will destroy thy chariots;
That I will cut off the cities of thy land,
And tear down all thy fortresses,

* Wellhausen alleges in the numbers another trace of the late Apocalyptic writings—but this is not conclusive.

† So LXX. *Cf.* the refrain at the close.

And I will cut off thine enchantments from thy hand,
And thou shalt have no more soothsayers;
And I will cut off thine images and thy pillars from the midst of thee,
And thou shalt not bow down any more to the work of thy hands;
And I will uproot thine Asheras from the midst of thee,
And will destroy thine idols.
So shall I do, in My wrath and Mine anger,
Vengeance to the nations, who have not known Me."

CHAPTER XXIX.

THE REASONABLENESS OF TRUE RELIGION.

MICAH vi. 1-8.

WE have now reached a passage from which all obscurities of date and authorship * disappear before the transparence and splendour of its contents. "These few verses," says a great critic, "in which Micah sets forth the true essence of religion, may raise a well-founded title to be counted as the most important in the prophetic literature. Like almost no others, they afford us an insight into the innermost nature of the religion of Israel, as delivered by the prophets."

Usually it is only the last of the verses upon which the admiration of the reader is bestowed: "What doth the Lord require of thee, O man, but to do justice and love mercy and walk humbly with thy God?" But in truth the rest of the passage differeth not in glory; the wonder of it lies no more in its peroration than in its argument as a whole.

The passage is cast in the same form as the opening chapter of the book—that of the Argument or Debate between the God of Israel and His people, upon the great theatre of Nature. The heart must be dull that does not leap to the Presences before which the trial is enacted.

The prophet speaks:—

"Hear ye now that which Jehovah is saying;
Arise, contend before the mountains,
And let the hills hear thy voice!
Hear, O mountains, the Lord's Argument,
And ye, the everlasting foundations of earth!"

This is not mere scenery. In all the moral questions between God and man, the prophets feel that Nature is involved. Either she is called as a witness to the long history of their relations to each other, or as sharing God's feeling of the intolerableness of the evil which men have heaped upon her, or by her droughts and floods and earthquakes as the executioner of their doom. It is in the first of these capacities that the prophet in this passage appeals to the mountains and eternal foundations of earth. They are called, not because they are the biggest of existences, but because they are the most full of memories and associations with both parties to the Trial.

The main idea of the passage, however, is the Trial itself. We have seen more than once that the forms of religion which the prophets had to combat were those which expressed it mechanically in the form of ritual and sacrifice, and those which expressed it in mere enthusiasm and ecstasy. Between such extremes the prophets insisted that religion was knowledge and that it was conduct—rational intercourse and loving duty between God and man. This is what they figure in their favourite scene of a Debate which is now before us.

"Jehovah hath a Quarrel with His People,
And with Israel He cometh to argue."

To us, accustomed to communion with the Godhead, as with a Father, this may seem formal and legal. But if we so regard it we do it an injustice. The form sprang by revolt against mechanical and sensational ideas of religion. It emphasised religion as rational and moral, and at once preserved the reasonableness of God and the freedom of man. God spoke with the people whom He had educated: He plead with them, listened to their statements and questions, and produced His own evidences and reasons. Religion—such a passage as this asserts—religion is not a thing of authority nor of ceremonial nor of mere feeling, but of argument, reasonable presentation and debate. Reason is not put out of court: man's freedom is respected; and he is not taken by surprise through his fears or his feelings. This sublime and generous conception of religion, which we owe first of all to the prophets in their contest with superstitious and slothful theories of religion that unhappily survive among us, was carried to its climax in the Old Testament by another class of writers. We find it elaborated with great power and beauty in the Books of Wisdom. In these the Divine Reason has emerged from the legal forms now before us, and has become the Associate and Friend of Man. The Prologue to the Book of Proverbs tells how Wisdom, fellow of God from the foundation of the world, descends to dwell among men. She comes forth into their streets and markets, she argues and pleads there with an urgency which is equal to the urgency of temptation itself. But it is not till the earthly ministry of the Son of God, His arguments with the doctors, His parables to the common people, His gentle and prolonged education of His disciples, that we see the reasonableness of religion in all its strength and beauty.

In that free court of reason in which the prophets saw God and man plead together, the subjects were such as became them both. For God unfolds no mysteries, and pleads no power, but the debate proceeds upon the facts and evidences of life: the appearance of Character in history; whether the past be not full of the efforts of Love; whether God had not, as human wilfulness permitted Him, achieved the liberation and progress of His people.

God speaks:—

"My people, what have I done unto thee?
And how have I wearied thee—answer Me!
For I brought thee up from the land of Misraim,
And from the house of slavery I redeemed thee.
I sent before thee Moses, Aharon and Miriam.
My people, remember now what Balak king of Moab counselled,
And how he was answered by Bala'am, Be'or's son—
So that *thou* mayest know the righteous deeds of Jehovah." *

Always do the prophets go back to Egypt or the wilderness. There God made the people, there He redeemed them. In lawbook as in prophecy, it is the fact of redemption which forms the main ground of His appeal. Redeemed by Him, the people are not their own, but His. Treated with that wonderful love and patience, like patience and love they are called to bestow upon

* See above, pp. 533 ff.

* Omitted from the above is the strange clause "from Shittim to Gilgal," which appears to be a gloss.

the weak and miserable beneath them.* One of the greatest interpreters of the prophets to our own age, Frederick Denison Maurice, has said upon this passage: "We do not know God till we recognise Him as a Deliverer; we do not understand our own work in the world till we believe we are sent into it to carry out His designs for the deliverance of ourselves and the race. The bondage I groan under is a bondage of the will. God is emphatically the Redeemer of the will. It is in that character He reveals Himself to us. We could not think of God at all as the God, the living God, if we did not regard Him as such a Redeemer. But if of my will, then of all wills: sooner or later I am convinced He will be manifested as the Restorer, Regenerator—not of something else, but of this—of the fallen spirit that is within us."

In most of the controversies which the prophets open between God and man, the subject on the side of the latter is his sin. But that is not so here. In the controversy which opens the Book of Micah the argument falls upon the transgressions of the people, but here upon their sincere though mistaken methods of approaching God. There God deals with dull consciences, but here with darkened and imploring hearts. In that case we had rebels forsaking the true God for idols, but here are earnest seekers after God, who have lost their way and are weary. Accordingly, as indignation prevailed there, here prevails pity; and though formally this be a controversy under the same legal form as before, the passage breathes tenderness and gentleness from first to last. By this as well as by the recollections of the ancient history of Israel we are reminded of the style of Hosea. But there is no expostulation, as in his book, with the people's continued devotion to ritual. All that is past, and a new temper prevails. Israel have at last come to feel the vanity of the exaggerated zeal with which Amos pictures them exceeding the legal requirements of sacrifice;† and with a despair, sufficiently evident in the superlatives which they use, they confess the futility and weariness of the whole system, even in the most lavish and impossible forms of sacrifice. What then remains for them to do? The prophet answers with the beautiful words that express an ideal of religion to which no subsequent century has ever been able to add either grandeur or tenderness.

The people speak:—

"Wherewithal shall I come before Jehovah,
Shall I bow myself to God the Most High?
Shall I come before Him with burnt-offerings,
With calves of one year?
Will Jehovah be pleased with thousands of rams,
With myriads of rivers of oil?
Shall I give my firstborn for a guilt-offering,‡
The fruit of my body for the sin of my soul?"

The prophet answers:—

"He hath shown thee, O man, what is good;
And what is the Lord seeking from thee,
But to do justice and love mercy,
And humbly § to walk with thy God?"

This is the greatest saying of the Old Testament; and there is only one other in the New which excels it:—

"Come unto Me, all ye that labour and are heavy laden, and I will give you rest.

"Take My yoke upon you, and learn of Me; for I am meek and lowly in heart: and ye shall find rest unto your souls.

"For My yoke is easy, and My burden is light."

CHAPTER XXX.

THE SIN OF THE SCANT MEASURE.

MICAH vi. 9-vii. 6.

THE state of the text of Micah vi. 9-vii. 6 is as confused as the condition of society which it describes: it is difficult to get reason, and impossible to get rhyme, out of the separate clauses. We had best give it as it stands, and afterwards state the substance of its doctrine, which, in spite of the obscurity of details, is, as so often happens in similar cases, perfectly clear and forcible. The passage consists of two portions, which may not originally have belonged to each other, but which seem to reflect the same disorder of civic life, with the judgment that impends upon it.* In the first of them, vi. 9-16, the prophet calls for attention to the voice of God, which describes the fraudulent life of Jerusalem, and the evils He is bringing on her. In the second, vii. 1-6, Jerusalem bemoans her corrupt society; but perhaps we hear her voice only in ver. 1, and thereafter the prophet's.

The prophet speaks:—

"Hark! Jehovah crieth to the city!
('Tis salvation to fear Thy name!)†
"Hear ye, O tribe and council of the city!" (?).‡

God speaks:—

". . . *in* the house of the wicked treasures
of wickedness,
And the scant measure accursed?
Can she be pure with the evil balances,
And with the bag of false weights,
Whose rich men are full of violence,§

* See the passages on the subject in Professor Harper's work on Deuteronomy in this series.

† See above, p. 482.

‡ See above, p. 534, on the futility of the argument which because of this line would put the whole passage in Manasseh's reign.

§ This word הצנע is only once used again, in Prov. xi. 2, in another grammatical form, where also it might mean "humbly." But the root-meaning is evidently "in secret," or "secretly" (*cf.* the Aram. צנע, to be hidden; צניע, one who lives noiselessly, humble, pious; in the feminine of a bride who is modest); and it is uncertain whether we should not take that sense here.

* See above, pp. 534 ff.

† Probably a later parenthesis. The word תוּשיה is one which, unusual in the prophets, the Wisdom literature, has made its own, Prov. ii. 7, xviii. 1; Job v. 12, etc. For *Thy* LXX. read "His."

‡ Translation of LXX. emended by Wellhausen so as to read מועד העיר, the עיר being obtained by taking and transferring the עוד of the next verse, and relieving that verse of an unusual formation, viz., עוד before the interrogative האש. But for an instance of עוד preceding an interrogative see Gen. xix. 12.

§ The text of the two preceding verses, which is acknowledged to be corrupt, must be corrected by the undoubted 3d feminine suffix in this one—"*her* rich men." Throughout the reference must be to the city. We ought therefore to change האזכה of ver. 11 into התִזכה, which agrees with the LXX. δικαιωθήσεται. Ver. 10 is more uncertain, but for the same reason that "the city" is referred to throughout vv. 9-12, it is possible that it is the nominative to זעומה; translate "cursed with the short measure." Again for אצרות LXX. read אוֹצֶרֶת אֹצָרוֹת, to which also the city would be nominative. And this suggests the query whether in the letters האש בית, that make little sense as they stand in the Massoretic Text,

And her citizens speak falsehood,
And their tongue is deceit in their mouth?
But I on my part have begun to plague thee,
To lay *thee* in ruin because of thy sins.
Thou eatest and art not filled,
But thy famine * is in the very midst of thee!
And *but* try to remove,† thou canst not bring off:
And what thou bringest off, I give to the sword.
Thou sowest, but never reapest;
Treadest olives, but never anointest with oil,
And must, but not to drink wine!
So thou keepest the statutes of Omri,‡
And the habits of the house of Ahab,
And walkest in their principles,
Only that I may give thee to ruin,
And her inhabitants for sport—
Yea, the reproach of the Gentiles § shall ye bear!"

Jerusalem speaks:—

"Woe, woe is me, for I am become like sweepings of harvest,
Like gleanings of the vintage—
Not a cluster to eat, *not* a fig that my soul lusteth after.
Perished are the leal from the land,
Of the upright among men there is none:
All of them are lurking for blood;
Every man takes his brother in a net.
Their hands are on evil to do it thoroughly.‖
The prince makes requisition,
The judge *judgeth* for payment,
And the great man he speaketh his lust;
So *together* they weave it out.
The best of them is but a thorn thicket,¶
The most upright *worse* than a prickly hedge.**
The day that thy sentinels *saw*, thy visitation, draweth on;
Now is their havoc †† come!
Trust not any friend! Rely on no confidant!
From her that lies in thy bosom guard the gates of thy mouth.
For son insulteth father, daughter is risen against her mother, daughter-in-law against her mother-in-law;
And the enemies of a man are the men of his house.

Micah, though the prophet of the country and stern critic of its life, characterised Jerusalem herself as the centre of the nation's sins. He did not refer to idolatry alone, but also to the irreligion of the politicians, and the cruel injustice of the rich in the capital. The poison which weakened the nation's blood had found its entrance to their veins at the very heart. There had the evil gathered which was shaking the state to a rapid dissolution.

This section of the Book of Micah, whether it be by that prophet or not, describes no features of Jerusalem's life which were not present in the eighth century; and it may be considered as the more detailed picture of the evils he summarily denounced. It is one of the most poignant criticisms of a commercial community which have ever appeared in literature. In equal relief we see the meanest instruments and the most prominent agents of covetousness and cruelty—the scant measure, the false weights, the unscrupulous prince, and the venal judge. And although there are some sins denounced which are impossible in our civilisation, yet falsehood, squalid fraud, pitilessness of the everlasting struggle for life are exposed exactly as we see them about us to-day. Through the prophet's ancient and often obscure eloquence we feel just those shocks and sharp edges which still break everywhere through our Christian civilisation. Let us remember, too, that the community addressed by the prophet was, like our own, professedly religious.

The most widespread sin with which the prophet charges Jerusalem in these days of her commercial activity is falsehood: "Her inhabitants speak lies, and their tongue is deceit in their mouth." In Mr. Lecky's "History of European Morals" we find the opinion that "the one respect in which the growth of industrial life has exercised a favourable influence on morals has been in the promotion of truth." The tribute is just, but there is another side to it. The exigencies of commerce and industry are fatal to most of the conventional pretences, insincerities, and flatteries which tend to grow up in all kinds of society. In commercial life, more perhaps than in any other, a man is taken, and has to be taken, in his inherent worth. Business, the life which is called *par excellence* Busyness, wears off every mask, all false veneer and unction, and leaves no time for the cant and parade which are so prone to increase in all other professions. Moreover the soul of commerce is credit. Men have to show that they can be trusted before other men will traffic with them, at least upon that large and lavish scale on which alone the great undertakings of commerce can be conducted. When we look back upon the history of trade and industry, and see how they have created an atmosphere in which men must ultimately seem what they really are; how they have of their needs replaced the jealousies, subterfuges, intrigues which were once deemed indispensable to the relations of men of different peoples, by large international credit and trust; how they break through the false conventions that divide class from class, we must do homage to them, as among the greatest instruments of the truth which maketh free.

But to all this there is another side. If commerce has exploded so much conventional insincerity, it has developed a species of the genus which is quite its own. In our days nothing can lie like an advertisement. The saying, "the tricks of the trade" has become proverbial. Every one knows that the awful strain and harassing of commercial life are largely due to the very amount of falseness that exists. The haste to be rich, the pitiless rivalry and competition, have developed a carelessness of the rights of others to the truth from ourselves, with a capacity for subterfuge and intrigue, which reminds one of nothing so much as that state of barbarian war out of which it was the ancient glory of commerce to have assisted mankind to rise. Are the prophet's words about Jerusalem too strong for large portions of our own commercial communities? Men who know these best will not say that they are. But let us cherish rather the powers of commerce which make for truth. Let us tell men who engage in trade that there are none for whom it is more easy to be clean and straight; that lies, whether of action or of speech, only increase the mental

there was not originally another feminine participle. The recommendation of a transformation of this kind is that it removes the abruptness of the appearance of the 3d feminine suffix in ver. 12.

* The word is found only here. The stem יחש is no doubt the same as the Arabic verb waḥash, which in Form V. means "Inani ventre fuit præ fame; vacuum reliquit stomachum" (Freytag). In modern colloquial Arabic wahsha means a "longing for an absent friend."

† Jussive. The objects removed can hardly be goods, as Hitzig and others infer; for it is to "the sword" they afterwards fall. They must be persons.

‡ LXX. "Zimri."

§ So LXX.; but Heb. "My people."

‖ Uncertain.

¶ *Cf.* Prov. xv. 19.

** Roorda, by rearranging letters and clauses (some of them after LXX.), and by changing points, gets a reading which may be rendered: "For evil are their hands! To do good the prince demandeth a bribe, and the judge, for the reward of the great, speaketh what he desireth. And they entangle the good more than thorns, and the righteous more than a thorn hedge."

†† *Cf.* Isa. xxii. 5.

expense and the moral strain of life; and that the health, the capacity, the foresight, the opportunities of a great merchant depend ultimately on his resolve to be true and on the courage with which he sticks to the truth.

One habit of falseness on which the prophet dwells is the use of unjust scales and short measures. The "stores" or fortunes of his day are "stores of wickedness," because they have been accumulated by the use of the "lean ephah," the "balances of wrong," and "the bag of false weights." These are evils more common in the East than with us: modern government makes them almost impossible. But, all the same, ours is the sin of the scant measure, and the more so in proportion to the greater speed and rivalry of our commercial life. The prophet's name for it, "measure of leanness," of "consumption" or "shrinkage," is a proper symbol of all those duties and offices of man to man, the full and generous discharge of which is diminished by the haste and the grudge of a prevalent selfishness. The speed of modern life tends to shorten the time expended on every piece of work, and to turn it out untempered and incomplete. The struggle for life in commerce, the organised rivalry between labour and capital, not only puts every man on his guard against giving any other more than his due, but tempts him to use every opportunity to scamp and curtail his own service and output. You will hear men defend this parsimony as if it were a law. They say that business is impossible without the temper which they call "sharpness" or the habit which they call "cutting it fine." But such character and conduct are the very decay of society. The shrinkage of the units must always and everywhere mean the disintegration of the mass. A society whose members strive to keep within their duties is a society which cannot continue to cohere. Selfishness may be firmness, but it is the firmness of frost, the rigour of death. Only the unselfish excess of duty, only the generous loyalty to others, give to society the compactness and indissolubleness of life. Who is responsible for the enmity of classes, and the distrust which exists between capital and labour? It is the workman whose one aim is to secure the largest amount of wages for the smallest amount of work, and who will, in his blind pursuit of that, wreck the whole trade of a town or a district; it is the employer who believes he has no duties to his men beyond paying them for their work the least that he can induce them to take; it is the customer who only and ever looks to the cheapness of an article—procurer in that prostitution of talent to the work of scamping which is fast killing art, and joy, and all pity for the bodies and souls of our brothers. These are the true anarchists and breakers-up of society. On their methods social coherence and harmony are impossible. Life itself is impossible. No organism can thrive whose various limbs are ever shriking in upon themselves. There is no life except by living to others.

But the prophet covers the whole evil when he says that the "pious are perished out of the land." "Pious" is a translation of despair. The original means the man distinguished by "ḥesedh," that word which we have on several occasions translated "leal love," because it implies not only an affection but loyalty to a relation. And, as the use of the word frequently reminds us, "ḥesedh" is love and loyalty both to God and to our fellow-men. We need not dissociate these: they are one. But here it is the human direction in which the word looks. It means a character which fulfils all the relations of society with the fidelity, generosity, and grace which are the proper affections of man to man. Such a character, says the prophet, is perished from the land. Every man now lives for himself, and as a consequence preys upon his brother. "They all lie in wait for blood; they hunt every man his brother with a net." This is not murder which the prophet describes: it is the reckless, pitiless competition of the new conditions of life developed in Judah by the long peace and commerce of the eighth century. And he carries this selfishness into a very striking figure in ver. 4: "The best of them is as a thorn thicket, the most upright" worse "than a prickly hedge." He realises exactly what we mean by sharpness and sharp-dealing: bristling self-interest, all points; splendid in its own defence, but barren of fruit, and without nest or covert for any life.

CHAPTER XXXI.

OUR MOTHER OF SORROWS.

MICAH vii. 7-20.

AFTER so stern a charge, so condign a sentence, confession is natural, and, with prayer for forgiveness and praise to the mercy of God, it fitly closes the whole book. As we have seen,* the passage is a cento of several fragments, from periods far apart in the history of Israel. One historical allusion suits best the age of the Syrian wars; another can only refer to the day of Jerusalem's ruin. In spirit and language the Confessions resemble the prayers of the Exile. The Doxology has echoes of several Scriptures.†

But from these fragments, it may be of many centuries, there rises clear the One Essential Figure: Israel, all her secular woes upon her; our Mother of Sorrows, at whose knees we learned our first prayers of confession and penitence. Other nations have been our teachers in art and wisdom and government. But she is our mistress in pain and in patience, teaching men with what conscience they should bear the chastening of the Almighty, with what hope and humility they should wait for their God. Surely not less lovable, but only more human, that her pale cheeks flush for a moment with the hate of the enemy and the assurance of revenge. Her passion is soon gone, for she feels her guilt to be greater; and, seeking forgiveness, her last word is what man's must ever be, praise to the grace and mercy of God.

Israel speaks:—

"But I will look for the Lord,
I will wait for the God of my salvation:
My God will hear me!
Rejoice not, O mine enemy, at me:
If I be fallen, I rise;
If I sit in the darkness, the Lord is a light to me.

"The anger of the Lord will I bear—
For I have sinned against Him—
Until that He take up my quarrel,
And execute my right.
He will carry me forth to the light;

* Above, pp. 534 ff.

† *Cf.* with it Exod. xxxiv. 6, 7 (J); Jer. iii. 5, l. 20; Isa. lvii. 16; Psalms ciii. 9, cv. 9, 10.

I will look on His righteousness:
So shall mine enemy see, and shame cover her,
She that saith unto me, Where is Jehovah thy God?—
Mine eyes shall see her,
Now is she for trampling, like mire in the streets!

The prophet * responds:—

"A day for the building of thy walls shall that day be!
Broad shall thy border be † on that day!
. . . . . ‡ and shall come to thee
From Assyria unto Egypt, and from Egypt to the River,
And to Sea from Sea, and Mountain from Mountain; §
Though ‖ the land be waste on account of her inhabitants.
Because of the fruit of their doings."

An Ancient Prayer:—

"Shepherd Thy people with Thy staff,
The sheep of Thy heritage dwelling solitarily. . . .¶
May they pasture in Bashan and Gilead as in days of old!
As in the days when Thou wentest forth from the land of Misraim, give us wonders to see!
Nations shall see and despair of all their might;
Their hands to their mouths shall they put,
Their ears shall be deafened.
They shall lick the dust like serpents;
Like worms of the ground from their fastnesses,
To Jehovah our God they shall come trembling,
And in fear before Thee!"

A Doxology:—

"Who is a God like to Thee? Forgiving iniquity,
And passing by transgression, to the remnant of His heritage;
He keepeth not hold of His anger for ever,
But One who delighteth in mercy is He;
He will come back, He will pity us,
He will tread under foot our iniquities—
Yea, Thou wilt cast to the depths of the sea every one of our sins.
Thou wilt show faithfulness to Jacob, leal love to Abraham,
As Thou hast sworn to our fathers from the days of yore."

* It was a woman who spoke before, the People or the City. But the second personal pronouns to which this reply of the prophet is addressed are all masculine. Notice the same change in vi. 9-16 (above, p. 546).

† ירחק-חק, Ewald: "distant the date." Notice the assonance. It explains the use of the unusual word for "border." LXX. "thy border." The LXX. also takes into ver. 11 (as above) the יום הוא of ver. 12.

‡ Something has probably been lost here.

§ For ההר read מהר.

‖ It is difficult to get sense when translating the conjunction in any other way. But these two lines may belong to the following.

¶ The words omitted above are literally "jungle in the midst of gardenland" or "Carmel." Plausible as it would be to take the proper name Carmel here along with Bashan and Gilead (see "Hist. Geog.," 338), the connection prefers the common noun "garden" or "garden-land": translate "dwelling alone like a bit of jungle in the midst of cultivated land." Perhaps the clause needs rearrangement: יעדבתוככרמל, with a verb to introduce it. Yet compare יַעַר כַּרְמִלּוֹ, 2 Kings xix. 23; Isa. xxxvii. 24.

THE BOOK OF THE TWELVE PROPHETS.

PART II.

PREFACE.

THE first Part on the Twelve Prophets dealt with the three who belonged to the Eighth Century: Amos, Hosea, and Micah. This second Part includes the other nine books arranged in chronological order: Zephaniah, Nahum, and Habakkuk, of the Seventh Century; Obadiah, of the Exile; Haggai, Zechariah i.–viii., "Malachi," and Joel, of the Persian Period, 538–331; "Zechariah" ix.–xiv., and the Book of Jonah, of the Greek Period, which began in 332, the date of Alexander's Syrian campaign.

The same plan has been followed as in Part I. A historical introduction is offered to each period. To each prophet are given, first a chapter of critical introduction, and then one or more chapters of exposition. A complete translation has been furnished, with critical and explanatory notes. All questions of date and of text, and nearly all of interpretation, have been confined to the introductions and the notes, so that those who consult the book only for expository purposes will find the exposition unencumbered by the discussion of technical points.

The necessity of including within one volume so many prophets, scattered over more than three centuries, and each of them requiring a separate introduction, has reduced the space available for the practical application of their teaching to modern life. But this is the less to be regretted, that the contents of the nine books before us are not so applicable to our own day as we have found their greater predecessors to be. On the other hand, however, they form a more varied introduction to Old Testament Criticism, while, by the long range of time which they cover, and the many stages of religion to which they belong, they afford a wider view of the development of prophecy. Let us look for a little at these two points.

1. To Old Testament Criticism these books furnish valuable introduction—some of them, like Obadiah, Joel, and "Zechariah" ix.–xiv., by the great variety of opinion that has prevailed as to their dates or their relation to other prophets with whom they have passages in common; some, like Zechariah and "Malachi," by their relation to the Law, in the light of modern theories of the origin of the latter; and some, like Joel and Jonah, by the question whether we are to read them as history, or as allegories of history, or as apocalypse. That is to say, these nine books raise, besides the usual questions of genuineness and integrity, every other possible problem of Old Testament Criticism. It has, therefore, been necessary to make the critical introductions full and detailed. The enormous differences of opinion as to the dates of some must start the suspicion of arbitrariness, unless there be included in each case a history of the development of criticism, so as to exhibit to the English reader the principles and the evidence of fact upon which that criticism is based. I am convinced that what is chiefly required just now by the devout student of the Bible is the opportunity to judge for himself how far Old Testament Criticism is an adult science; with what amount of reasonableness it has been prosecuted; how gradually its conclusions have been reached, how jealously they have been contested; and how far, amid the many varieties of opinion which must always exist with refer-

ence to facts so ancient and questions so obscure, there has been progress towards agreement upon the leading problems. But, besides the accounts of past criticism given in this book, the reader will find in each case an independent attempt to arrive at a conclusion. This has not always been successful. A number of points have been left in doubt; and even where results have been stated with some degree of positiveness, the reader need scarcely be warned (after what was said in the Preface to Part I.) that many of these must necessarily be provisional. But, in looking back from the close of this work upon the discussions which it contains, I am more than ever convinced of the extreme probability of most of the conclusions. Among these are the following: that the correct interpretation of Habakkuk is to be found in the direction of the position to which Budde's ingenious proposal has been carried on pages 590 ff. with reference to Egypt; that the most of Obadiah is to be dated from the sixth century; that "Malachi" is an anonymous work from the eve of Ezra's reforms; that Joel follows "Malachi"; and that "Zechariah" ix.–xiv. has been rightly assigned by Stade to the early years of the Greek Period. I have ventured to contest Kosters' theory that there was no return of Jewish exiles under Cyrus, and am the more disposed to believe his strong argument inconclusive, not only upon a review of the reasons I have stated in chap. xvi., but on this ground also, that many of its chief adherents in this country and Germany have so modified it as virtually to give up its main contention. I think, too, there can be little doubt as to the substantial authenticity of Zephaniah ii. (except the verses on Moab and Ammon) and iii. 1–13, of Habakkuk ii. 5 ff., and of the whole of Haggai; or as to the ungenuine character of the lyric piece in Zechariah ii. and the intrusion of "Malachi" ii. 11–13*a*. On these and smaller points the reader will find full discussion at the proper places.

[I may here add a word or two upon some of the critical conclusions reached in Part I., which have been recently contested. The student will find strong grounds offered by Canon Driver in his "Joel and Amos"* for the authenticity of those passages in Amos which, following other critics, I regarded or suspected as not authentic. It makes one diffident in one's opinions when Canon Driver supports Professors Kuenen and Robertson Smith on the other side. But on a survey of the case I am unable to feel that even they have removed what they admit to be "forcible" objections to the authorship by Amos of the passages in question. They seem to me to have established not more than a possibility that the passages are authentic; and on the whole I still feel that the probability is in the other direction. If I am right, then I think that the date of the apostrophes to Jehovah's creative power which occur in the Book of Amos, and the reference to astral deities in chap. v. 27, may be that which I have suggested on page 562 of this Part. Some critics have charged me with inconsistency in denying the authenticity of the epilogue to Amos while defending that of the epilogue to Hosea. The two cases, as my arguments proved, are entirely different. Nor do I see any reason to change the conclusions of Part I. upon the questions of the authenticity of various parts of Micah.]

The text of the nine prophets treated in this book has presented even more difficulties than that of the three treated in Part I. And these difficulties must be my apology for the delay of this work.

2. But the critical and textual value of our nine books is far exceeded by the historical. Each exhibits a development of Hebrew prophecy of the greatest interest. From this point of view, indeed, the book might be entitled "The Passing of

* "Cambridge Bible for Schools," 1897.

the Prophet." For throughout our nine books we see the spirit and the style of the classic prophecy of Israel gradually dissolving into other forms of religious thought and feeling. The clear start from the facts of the prophet's day, the ancient truths about Jehovah and Israel, and the direct appeal to the conscience of the prophet's contemporaries, are not always given, or when given are mingled, coloured, and warped by other religious interests, both present and future, which are even powerful enough to shake the ethical absolutism of the older prophets. With Nahum and Obadiah the ethical is entirely missed in the presence of the claims—and we cannot deny that they were natural claims—of the long-suffering nation's hour of revenge upon her heathen tyrants. With Zephaniah prophecy, still austerely ethical, passes under the shadow of apocalypse; and the future is solved, not upon purely historical lines, but by the intervention of "supernatural" elements. With Habakkuk the ideals of the older prophets encounter the shock of the facts of experience: we have the prophet as sceptic. Upon the other margin of the Exile, Haggai and Zechariah (i.–viii.), although they are as practical as any of their predecessors, exhibit the influence of the exilic developments of ritual, angelology, and apocalypse. God appears further off from Zechariah than from the prophets of the eighth century, and in need of mediators, human and superhuman. With Zechariah the priest has displaced the prophet, and it is very remarkable that no place is found for the latter beside *the two sons of oil*, the political and priestly heads of the community, who, according to the Fifth Vision, stand in the presence of God and between them feed the religious life of Israel. Nearly sixty years later "Malachi" exhibits the working of Prophecy within the Law, and begins to employ the didactic style of the later Rabbinism. Joel starts, like any older prophet, from the facts of his own day, but these hurry him at once into apocalypse; he calls, as thoroughly as any of his predecessors, to repentance, but under the imminence of the Day of the Lord, with its "supernatural" terrors, he mentions no special sin and enforces no single virtue. The civic and personal ethics of the earlier prophets are absent. In the Greek Period, the oracles now numbered from the ninth to the fourteenth chapters of the Book of Zechariah repeat to aggravation the exulting revenge of Nahum and Obadiah, without the strong style or the hold upon history which the former exhibits, and show us prophecy still further enwrapped in apocalypse. But in the Book of Jonah, though it is parable and not history, we see a great recovery and expansion of the best elements of prophecy. God's character and Israel's true mission to the world are revealed in the spirit of Hosea and of the Seer of the Exile, with much of the tenderness, the insight, the analysis of character, and even the humour of classic prophecy. These qualities raise the Book of Jonah, though it is probably the latest of our Twelve, to the highest rank among them. No book is more worthy to stand by the side of Isaiah xl.–lv.; none is nearer in spirit to the New Testament.

All this gives unity to the study of prophets so far separate in time, and so very distinct in character, from each other. From Zephaniah to Jonah, or over a period of three centuries, they illustrate the dissolution of Prophecy and its passage into other forms of religion.

The scholars to whom every worker in this field is indebted are named throughout the book. I regret that Nowack's recent commentary on the Minor Prophets (Göttingen: Vandenhoeck & Ruprecht) reached me too late for use (except in footnotes) upon the earlier of the nine prophets.

GEORGE ADAM SMITH

CONTENTS.

CHRONOLOGICAL TABLE No. I.

FROM THE FALL OF SAMARIA TO THE FALL OF JERUSALEM.

*** *c.=circa:* it refers chiefly to the accession of the kings of Judah ; the years are exact so far as they concern nearly all the Assyrian data. A date opposite the mere name of a king signifies the year of his accession.

	EGYPT.	JUDAH.	THE PROPHETS.	PHILISTIA, PHŒNICIA, ARABIA, CYPRUS, ETC.	ASSYRIA.	
727 *c.*	**Shabaka.**	**Hezekiah.**	...	...	**Shalmaneser IV.**	727
725	...	(Siege of Samaria begins.)		.		
722 or 1	...	(Fall of Samaria.)	...	...	**Sargon** takes Samaria.	722 or 1
720 or 19	...	..	...	Gaza overthrown by . .	Sargon as he marches past Judah and defeats Egypt at Raphia.	720 or 19
715	...	(Samaria peopled . .	. . .	. . . . . .	by subjugated tribes deported from Assyria.)	715
			Isaiah.	Ashdod taken by . . .	Sargon.	711
709	...	...	...	...	Sargon takes Babylon from **Merodach-Baladan.**	709
705	...	...	Micah.	...	Death of Sargon. Accession of **Sennacherib.**	705
704	**Taharka.**	Events in Isaiah xxxix.?	...	...	War with Merodach-Baladan.	704
701	...	Invasion of Judah . . Deliverance of Jerusalem.	. . .	and all Palestine . . . Siege of Ekron.	by Sennacherib.	701
	Defeat of Egypt .	. . . .	. . .	at Battle of Eltekeh . . .	by Sennacherib.	
? 695 *c.*	...	**Manasseh.**				
692	...	...	...	...	Sennacherib destroys Babylon.	692
681	...	...	...	...	Sennacherib murdered. **Asarhaddon.**	681
678	...	...	...	Sidon subdued and Sidonians deported	by Asarhaddon.	678
676	...	Manasseh and . . .	. . . .	21 Palestine princes pay tribute to Assyria: also Greek princes of Cyprus.		676
675	...	...	...	Arabia invaded	by Asarhaddon.	675
674	...	...	...	Sinai invaded	by Asarhaddon.	674
671	...	...	...	Tyre besieged	by Asarhaddon.	671
670 *c*	Taharka defeated at Memphis .	. . . .	. . . .	. . . .	by Asarhaddon.	670 *c.*
668	Taharka regains Egypt.	...	...	...	**Assurbanipal.**	668
666	...	Manasseh and . . .	. . . .	21 Palestine princes pay tribute to Assyria.		666
664 *c.*	Taharka overthrown, Memphis taken, Dodekarchy established	. . . .	. . . . .	(Palestine princes aiding) . .	by Assurbanipal.	664 *c.*
663 *c.*	**Urdamman** overthrown and Thebes taken }	. . . . . .	. . . .	. . . .	{ 2nd Egyptian campaign of Assurbanipal.	663 *c.*
662	**Psamtik I.**	...	...	Tyre and Arvad taken . .	by Assurbanipal.	662
652	Psamtik I., . .	. . . . . .	. .	Palestine princes, Arabia, Lydia,	Elam and Babylon revolt from Assyria.	652
649	...	...	...	...	Assurbanipal reduces Elam and Babylon.	649
647	...	...	...	Hauran, N. Arabia and Edom }	{ reduced in two campaigns by	647
645	...	...	...	Ammon, Moab and Nabatea }	{ Assurbanipal.	645
				Usu "by the sea" and Akko .	punished by Assurbanipal.	
641 *c.*	...	**Amon.**	...	Tyre assists, against Arvad, .	Assurbanipal.	641
639 *c.*	...	**Josiah.**				
630 *c.*	...	...	...	...	Scythians invade Media and Western Asia.	630 *c.*
627	...	Jeremiah appears.				
626 *c.*	...	...	**Zephaniah.**	Western Palestine . . .	invaded by Scythians. **Assur-itil-ilani.**	626 *c.*
625	...	...	...	...	Niniveh attacked by Medes. Nabopolassar independent in Babylon.	625
621	...	Book of the Law (Deut. v.–xxvi., xxviii.) discovered. Josiah's reforms begin. Passover (2 Kings xxii., xxiii.).				
620 *c.*	...	...	**? Habakkuk.**	...	**Sin-sar-uskin.**	? 620 *c.*
610	**Necho II.**					
608	Necho defeats and slays Josiah at Megiddo .	Judah Egyptian vassal. **Jehoahaz** reigns three months: taken to Egypt. **Jehoiakim** succeeds.	. . . **? Nahum.**	. . . .	and Nebuchadrezzar on Euphrates	608
607-6	...	...	... **Jeremiah.**	...	Fall of Niniveh to Medes and Chaldeans under Nabopolassar.	607-6
605	Necho defeated .	. . . . . .	. . .	. . . .	by Nebuchadrezzar at Carchemish.	605
604	...	...	...	...	**Nebuchadrezzar.**	604
602 or 600	...	Judah vassal . . . but is subdued (2 Kings xxiv. 2 ff.).	. . .	. . . .	of Babylon (2 Kings xxiv. 1);	602 or 600
599 or 597	...	Judah withholds . .	. . .	. . . .	tribute from Babylon.	599 or 597
		Judah invaded . . .	. . .	by Moab, Ammon and Arameans	in alliance with Babylon.	
597	...	**Jehoiachin** yields . . Temple plundered.	. . .	. . . .	to Nebuchadrezzar.	597
		First Great Exile . .	. . .	. . . .	to Babylonia.	
		Zedekiah vassal . .	. . .	. . . .	of Babylon.	
594	**Psamtik II.**					
593	...	Jewish revolt . . . stayed by Jeremiah.	. . .	. . . .	against Babylon,	593
589	**Uah-ab-ra** (Hophra, Apries)	offers help to Zedekiah, who	. . .	. . . .	revolts from Babylon.	589
587-6	...	Jerusalem taken . .	. . .	. . . .	by Nebuchadrezzar.	587-6
		Second Great Exile . .	. . .	. . . .	to Babylonia.	

THE BOOK OF THE TWELVE PROPHETS.

BY GEORGE ADAM SMITH, D. D., LL. D.

PART II.

INTRODUCTION TO THE PROPHETS OF THE SEVENTH CENTURY.

CHAPTER I.

THE SEVENTH CENTURY BEFORE CHRIST.

THE three prophets who were treated in the first volume of this work belonged to the eighth century before Christ: if Micah lived into the seventh his labours were over by 675. The next group of our twelve, also three in number, Zephaniah, Nahum, and Habakkuk, did not appear till after 630. To make our study continuous * we must now sketch the course of Israel's history between.

In another volume of this series,† some account was given of the religious progress of Israel from Isaiah and the Deliverance of Jerusalem in 701 to Jeremiah and the Fall of Jerusalem in 587. Isaiah's strength was bent upon establishing the inviolableness of Zion. Zion, he said, should not be taken, and the people, though cut to their roots, should remain planted in their own land, the stock of a noble nation in the latter days. But Jeremiah predicted the ruin both of City and Temple, summoned Jerusalem's enemies against her in the name of Jehovah, and counselled his people to submit to them. This reversal of the prophetic ideal had a twofold reason. In the first place the moral condition of Israel was worse in 600 B. C. than it had been in 700; another century had shown how much the nation needed the penalty and purgation of exile. But secondly, however the inviolableness of Jerusalem had been required in the interests of pure religion in 701, religion had now to show that it was independent even of Zion and of Israel's political survival. Our three prophets of the eighth century (as well as Isaiah himself) had indeed preached a gospel which implied this, but it was reserved to Jeremiah to prove that the existence of state and temple was not indispensable to faith in God, and to explain the ruin of Jerusalem, not merely as a well-merited penance, but as the condition of a more spiritual intercourse between Jehovah and His people.

It is our duty to trace the course of events through the seventh century, which led to this change of the standpoint of prophecy, and which moulded the messages especially of Jeremiah's contemporaries, Zephaniah, Nahum, and Habakkuk. We may divide the century into three periods: *First*, that of the Reaction and Persecution under Manasseh and Amon, from 695 or 690 to 639, during which prophecy was silent or anonymous; *Second*, that of the Early Years of Josiah, 639 to 625, near the end of which we meet with the young Jeremiah and Zephaniah; *Third*, the Rest of the Century, 625 to 600, covering the Decline and Fall of Nineveh, and the prophets Nahum and Habakkuk, with an addition carrying on the history to the Fall of Jerusalem in 587-586.

* See p. 435.

† "Expositor's Bible," "Isaiah xl.-lxvi." chap. ii.

I. REACTION UNDER MANASSEH AND AMON (695?-639).

Jerusalem was delivered in 701, and the Assyrians kept away from Palestine for twenty-three years.* Judah had peace, and Hezekiah was free to devote his latter days to the work of purifying the worship of his people. What he exactly achieved is uncertain. The historian imputes to him the removal of the high places, the destruction of all Maççeboth and Asheras, and of the brazen serpent.† That his measures were drastic is probable from the opinions of Isaiah, who was their inspiration, and proved by the reaction which they provoked when Hezekiah died. The *removal* of the high places and the concentration of the national worship within the Temple would be the more easy that the provincial sanctuaries had been devastated by the Assyrian invasion, and that the shrine of Jehovah was glorified by the raising of the siege of 701.

While the first of Isaiah's great postulates for the future, the inviolableness of Zion, had been fulfilled, the second, the reign of a righteous prince in Israel, seemed doomed to disappointment. Hezekiah died early in the seventh century,‡ and was succeeded by his son Manasseh, a boy of twelve, who appears to have been captured by the party whom his father had opposed. The few years' peace—peace in Israel was always dangerous to the health of the higher religion—the interests of those who had suffered from the reforms, the inevitable reaction which a rigorous puritanism provokes—these swiftly reversed the religious fortunes of Israel. Isaiah's and Micah's predictions of the final overthrow of Assyria seemed falsified, when in 681 the more vigorous Asarhaddon succeeded Sennacherib, and in 678 swept the long absent armies back upon Syria. Sidon was destroyed, and twenty-two princes of Palestine immediately yielded their tribute to the conqueror. Manasseh was one of them, and his political homage may have brought him, as it brought Ahaz, within the infection of foreign idolatries.§ Everything, in short, worked for the revival of that eclectic paganism which Hezekiah had striven to stamp out. The high places were rebuilt; altars were erected to Baal, with the sacred pole of Asherah, as in the time of Ahab;‖ shrines to the "host

* It is uncertain whether Hezekiah was an Assyrian vassal during these years, as his successor Manasseh is recorded to have been in 676.

† 2 Kings xviii. 4.

‡ The exact date is quite uncertain; 695 is suggested on the chronological table prefixed to this volume, but it may have been 690 or 685.

§ *Cf.* McCurdy, "History, Prophecy and the Monuments," § 799.

‖ Stade ("Gesch. des Volkes Israel," I. pp. 627 f.) denies to Manasseh the reconstruction of the high places, the Baal altars, and the Asheras, for he does not believe that Hezekiah had succeeded in destroying these. He takes 2 Kings xxi. 3, which describes these reconstructions, as a late interpolation rendered necessary to reconcile the tradition that Hezekiah's reforms had been quite in the

of heaven" defiled the courts of Jehovah's house; there was recrudescence of sooth-saying, divination, and traffic with the dead.

But it was all very different from the secure and sunny temper which Amos had encountered in Northern Israel.* The terrible Assyrian invasions had come between. Life could never again feel so stable. Still more destructive had been the social poisons which our prophets described as sapping the constitution of Israel for nearly three generations. The rural simplicity was corrupted by those economic changes which Micah bewails. With the ousting of the old families from the soil, a thousand traditions, memories, and habits must have been broken, which had preserved the people's presence of mind in days of sudden disaster, and had carried them, for instance, through so long a trial as the Syrian wars. Nor could the blood of Israel have run so pure after the luxury and licentiousness described by Hosea and Isaiah. The novel obligations of commerce, the greed to be rich, the increasing distress among the poor, had strained the joyous temper of that nation of peasants' sons, whom we met with Amos, and shattered the nerves of their rulers. There is no word of fighting in Manasseh's days, no word of revolt against the tyrant. Perhaps also the intervening puritanism, which had failed to give the people a permanent faith, had at least awakened within them a new conscience.

At all events there is now no more "ease in Zion," but a restless fear, driving the people to excesses of religious zeal. We do not read of the happy country festivals of the previous century, nor of the careless pride of that sudden wealth which built vast palaces and loaded the altar of Jehovah with hecatombs. The full-blooded patriotism, which at least kept ritual in touch with clean national issues, has vanished. The popular religion is sullen and exasperated. It takes the form of sacrifices of frenzied cruelty and lust. Children are passed through the fire to Moloch, and the Temple is defiled by the orgies of those who abuse their bodies to propitiate a foreign and a brutal god.†

But the most certain consequence of a religion whose nerves are on edge is persecution, and this raged all the earlier years of Manasseh. The adherents of the purer faith were slaughtered, and Jerusalem drenched‡ with innocent blood. Her "own sword," says Jeremiah, "devoured the prophets like a destroying lion."§

It is significant that all that has come down to us from this "killing time" is anonymous; ‖ we do not meet with our next group of public prophets till Manasseh and his like-minded son have passed away. Yet prophecy was not wholly stifled. Voices were raised to predict the exile and destruction of the nation. "Jehovah spake by His servants";* while others wove into the prophecies of an Amos, a Hosea, or an Isaiah some application of the old principles to the new circumstances. It is probable, for instance, that the extremely doubtful passage in the Book of Amos, v. 26 f., which imputes to Israel as a whole the worship of astral deities from Assyria, is to be assigned to the reign of Manasseh. In its present position it looks very like an intrusion: nowhere else does Amos charge his generation with serving foreign gods; and certainly in all the history of Israel we could not find a more suitable period for so specific a charge than the days when into the central sanctuary of the national worship images were introduced of the host of heaven, and the nation was, in consequence, threatened with exile.†

In times of persecution the documents of the suffering faith have ever been reverenced and guarded with especial zeal. It is not improbable that the prophets, driven from public life, gave themselves to the arrangement of the national scriptures; and some critics date from Manasseh's reign the weaving of the two earliest documents of the Pentateuch into one continuous book of history.‡ The Book of Deuteronomy forms a problem by itself. The legislation which composes the bulk of it§ appears to have been found among the Temple archives at the end of our period, and presented to Josiah as an old and forgotten work.‖ There is no reason to charge with fraud those who made the presentation by affirming that they really invented the book. They were priests of Jerusalem, but the book is written by members of the prophetic party, and ostensibly in the interests of the priests of the country. It betrays no tremor of the awful persecutions of Manasseh's reign; it does not hint at the distinction, then for the first time apparent, between a false and a true Israel. But it does draw another distinction, familiar to the eighth century, between the true and the false prophets. The political and

spirit of Deuteronomy, with the fact that there were still high places in the land when Josiah began his reforms. Further, Stade takes the rest of 2 Kings xxi. 2 *b*–7 as also an interpolation, but unlike verse 3 an accurate account of Manasseh's idolatrous institutions, because it is corroborated by the account of Josiah's reforms, 2 Kings xxiii. Stade also discusses this passage in "Z. A. T. W.," 1886, pp. 186 ff.

* See p. 452. In addition to the reasons of the change given above, we must remember that we are now treating, not of Northern Israel, but of the more stern and sullen Judeans.

† 2 Kings xxi., xxiii.

‡ "Filled from mouth to mouth" (2 Kings xxi. 16).

§ Jer. ii. 30.

‖ We have already seen that there is no reason for that theory of so many critics which assigns to this period Micah. See p. 533.

* 2 Kings xxi. 10 ff.

† Whether the parenthetical apostrophes to Jehovah as Maker of the heavens, their hosts, and all the powers of nature (Amos iv. 13, v. 8, 9, ix. 5, 6), are also to be attributed to Manasseh's reign is more doubtful. Yet the following facts are to be observed: that these passages are also (though to a less degree than v. 26 f.) parenthetic, that their language seems of a later cast than that of the time of Amos (see p. 493: though here evidence is adduced to show that the late features are probably post-exilic); and that Jehovah is expressly named as the "Maker" of certain of the stars. Similarly when Mohammed seeks to condemn the worship of the heavenly bodies, he insists that God is their Maker. Koran, Sur. 41, 37: "To the signs of His Omnipotence belong night and day, sun and moon; but do not pray to sun or moon, for God hath created them." Sur. 53, 50: "Because He is the Lord of Sirius." On the other side see Driver's "Joel and Amos" Cambridge Bible for School Series), 1897, pp. 118 f., 189.

How deeply Manasseh had planted in Israel the worship of the heavenly host may be seen from the survival of the latter through all the reforms of Josiah and the destruction of Jerusalem (Jer. vii. 18, viii., xliv.; Ezek. viii., *Cf.* Stade, "Gesch. des V. Israel," I., pp. 629 ff.).

‡ The Jehovist and Elohist into the closely mortised JE. Stade indeed assigns to the period of Manasseh Israel's first acquaintance with the Babylonian cosmogonies and myths which led to that reconstruction of them in the spirit of her own religion which we find in the Jehovistic portions of the beginning of Genesis ("Gesch. des V. Isr.," I. pp. 630 ff.). But it may well be doubted (1) whether the reign of Manasseh affords time for this assimilation, and (2) whether it was likely that Assyrian and Babylonian theology could make so deep and lasting impression upon the purer faith of Israel at a time when the latter stood in such sharp hostility to all foreign influences and was so bitterly persecuted by the parties in Israel who had succumbed to these influences.

§ Chaps. v.–xxvi., xxviii.

‖ 621 B. C.

spiritual premisses of the doctrine of the book were all present by the end of the reign of Hezekiah, and it is extremely improbable that his reforms, which were in the main those of Deuteronomy, were not accompanied by some code, or by some appeal to the fountain of all law in Israel.

But whether the Book of Deuteronomy now existed or not, there were those in the nation who through all the dark days between Hezekiah and Josiah laid up its truth in their hearts and were ready to assist the latter monarch in his public enforcement of it.

While these things happened within Judah, very great events were taking place beyond her borders. Asarhaddon of Assyria (681-668) was a monarch of long purposes and thorough plans. Before he invaded Egypt, he spent a year (675) in subduing the restless tribes of Northern Arabia, and another (674) in conquering the peninsula of Sinai, an ancient appanage of Egypt. Tyre upon her island baffled his assaults, but the rest of Palestine remained subject to him. He received his reward in carrying the Assyrian arms farther into Egypt than any of his predecessors, and about 670 took Memphis from the Ethiopian Pharaoh Taharka. Then he died. Assurbanipal, who succeeded, lost Egypt for a few years, but about 665, with the help of his tributaries in Palestine, he overthrew Taharka, took Thebes, and established along the Nile a series of vassal states. He quelled a revolt there in 663 and overthrew Memphis for a second time. The fall of the Egyptian capital resounds through the rest of the century; we shall hear its echoes in Nahum. Tyre fell at last with Arvad in 662. But the Assyrian empire had grown too vast for human hands to grasp, and in 652 a general revolt took place in Egypt, Arabia, Palestine, Elam, Babylon, and Asia Minor. In 649 Assurbanipal reduced Elam and Babylon; and by two further campaigns (647 and 645) Hauran, Edom, Ammon, Moab, Nabatea, and all the northern Arabs. On his return from these he crossed Western Palestine to the sea and punished Usu and Akko. It is very remarkable that, while Assurbanipal, who thus fought the neighbours of Judah, makes no mention of her, nor numbers Manasseh among the rebels whom he chastised, the Book of Chronicles should contain the statement that "Jehovah sent upon Manasseh the captains of the host of the king of Assyria, who bound him with fetters and carried him to Babylon." * What grounds the Chronicler had for such a statement are quite unknown to us. He introduces Manasseh's captivity as the consequence of idolatry, and asserts that on his restoration Manasseh abolished in Judah all worship save that of Jehovah, but if this happened (and the Book of Kings has no trace of it) it was without result. Amon, son of Manasseh, continued to sacrifice to all the images which his father had introduced.

2. The Early Years of Josiah (639-625): Jeremiah and Zephaniah.

Amon had not reigned for two years when "his servants conspired against him, and he was slain in his own house." † But the "people of the land" rose against the court, slew the conspirators, and secured the throne for Amon's son, Josiah, a child of eight. It is difficult to know what we ought to understand by these movements. Amon, who was slain, was an idolater; the popular party, who slew his slayers, put his son on the throne, and that son, unlike both his father and grandfather, bore a name compounded with the name of Jehovah. Was Amon then slain for personal reasons? Did the people, in their rising, have a zeal for Jehovah? Was the crisis purely political, but usurped by some school or party of Jehovah who had been gathering strength through the later years of Manasseh, and waiting for some such unsettlement of affairs as now occurred? The meagre records of the Bible give us no help, and for suggestions towards an answer we must turn to the wider politics of the time.

* 2 Chron. xxxiii. 11 ff.

† 2 Kings xxi. 23.

Assurbanipal's campaigns of 647 and 645 were the last appearances of Assyria in Palestine. He had not attempted to reconquer Egypt,* and her king, Psamtik I., began to push his arms northward. Progress must have been slow, for the siege of Ashdod, which Psamtik probably began after 645, is said to have occupied him twenty-nine years. Still, he must have made his influence to be felt in Palestine, and in all probability there was once more, as in the days of Isaiah, an Egyptian party in Jerusalem. As the power of Assyria receded over the northern horizon, the fascination of her idolatries which Manasseh had established in Judah must have waned. The priests of Jehovah's house, jostled by their pagan rivals, would be inclined to make common cause with the prophets under a persecution which both had suffered. With the loosening of the Assyrian yoke the national spirit would revive, and it is easy to imagine prophets, priests, and people working together in the movement which placed the child Josiah on the throne. At his tender age, he must have been wholly in the care of the women of the royal house; and among these the influence of the prophets may have found adherents more readily than among the counsellors of an adult prince. Not only did the new monarch carry the name of Jehovah in his own; this was the case also with his mother's father.† In the revolt, therefore, which raised this unconscious child to the throne and in the circumstances which moulded his character, we may infer that there already existed the germs of the great work of reform which his manhood achieved.

For some time little change would be possible, but from the first facts were working for great issues. The Book of Kings, which places the destruction of the idols after the discovery of the law-book in the eighteenth year of Josiah's reign, records a previous cleansing and restoration of the house of Jehovah.‡ This points to the growing ascendency of the prophetic party during the first fifteen years of Josiah's reign. Of the first ten years we know nothing, except that the prestige of Assyria was waning; but this

* But in his conquests of Hauran, Northern Arabia, and the eastern neighbours of Judah, he had evidently sought to imitate the policy of Asarhaddon in 675 f., and secure firm ground in Palestine and Arabia for a subsequent attack upon Egypt. That this never came shows more than anything else could Assyria's consciousness of growing weakness.

† The name of Josiah's (יאשיהו) mother was Jedidah (ידידה), daughter of Adaiah (עדיה) of Boskath in the Shephelah of Judah.

‡ 2 Kings xxii., xxiii.

fact, along with the preaching of the prophets, who had neither a native tyrant nor the exigencies of a foreign alliance to silence them, must have weaned the people from the worship of the Assyrian idols. Unless these had been discredited, the repair of Jehovah's house could hardly have been attempted; and that this progressed means that part of Josiah's destruction of the heathen images took place before the discovery of the Book of the Law, which happened in consequence of the cleansing of the Temple.

But just as under the good Hezekiah the social condition of the people, and especially the behaviour of the upper classes, continued to be bad, so it was again in the early years of Josiah. There was a "remnant of Baal"* in the land. The shrines of "the host of heaven" might have been swept from the Temple, but they were still worshipped from the housetops.† Men swore by the Queen of Heaven, and by Moloch, the King. Some turned back from Jehovah; some, grown up in idolatry, had not yet sought Him. Idolatry may have been disestablished from the national sanctuary: its practices still lingered (how intelligibly to us!) in social and commercial life. Foreign fashions were affected by the court and nobility; trade, as always, was combined with the acknowledgment of foreign gods.‡ Moreover, the rich were fraudulent and cruel. The ministers of justice, and the great in the land, ravened among the poor. Jerusalem was full of oppression. These were the same disorders as Amos and Hosea exposed in Northern Israel, and as Micah exposed in Jerusalem. But one new trait of evil was added. In the eighth century, with all their ignorance of Jehovah's true character, men had yet believed in Him, gloried in His energy, and expected Him to act —were it only in accordance with their low ideals. They had been alive and bubbling with religion. But now they "had thickened on their lees." They had grown sceptical, dull, indifferent; they said in their hearts, "Jehovah will not do good, neither will He do evil!"

Now, just as in the eighth century there had risen, contemporaneous with Israel's social corruption, a cloud in the north, black and pregnant with destruction, so was it once more. But the cloud was not Assyria. From the hidden world beyond her, from the regions over Caucasus, vast, nameless hordes of men arose, and, sweeping past her unchecked, poured upon Palestine. This was the great Scythian invasion recorded by Herodotus.§ We have almost no other report than his few paragraphs, but we can realise the event from our knowledge of the Mongol and Tartar invasions which in later centuries pursued the same path southwards. Living in the saddle, and (it would seem) with no infantry nor chariots to delay them, these Centaurs swept on with a speed of invasion hitherto unknown. In 630 they had crossed the Caucasus, by 626 they were on the borders of Egypt. Psamtik I. succeeded in purchasing their retreat,‖ and they swept back again as swiftly as they came. They must have followed the old Assyrian war-paths of the eighth century, and, without foot-soldiers, had probably kept even more closely to the plains. In Palestine their way would lie, like Assyria's, across Hauran, through the plain of Esdraelon, and down the Philistine coast, and in fact it is only on this line that there exists any possible trace of them.* But they shook the whole of Palestine into consternation. Though Judah among her hills escaped them, as she escaped the earlier campaigns of Assyria, they showed her the penal resources of her offended God. Once again the dark, sacred North was seen to be full of the possibilities of doom.

Behold, therefore, exactly the two conditions, ethical and political, which, as we saw, called forth the sudden prophets of the eighth century, and made them so sure of their message of judgment: on the one side Judah, her sins calling aloud for punishment; on the other side, the forces of punishment swiftly drawing on. It was precisely at this juncture that prophecy again arose, and as Amos, Hosea, Micah, and Isaiah appeared in the end of the eighth century, Zephaniah, Habakkuk, Nahum, and Jeremiah appeared in the end of the seventh. The coincidence is exact, and a remarkable confirmation of the truth which we deduced from the experience of Amos, that the assurance of the prophet in Israel arose from the coincidence of his conscience with his political observation. The justice of Jehovah demands His people's chastisement, but see—the forces of chastisement are already upon the horizon. Zephaniah uses the same phrase as Amos: "the Day of Jehovah," he says, "is drawing near."

We are now in touch with Zephaniah, the first of our prophets, but, before listening to him, it will be well to complete our survey of those remaining years of the century in which he and his immediate successors laboured.

3. The Rest of the Century (625-586): the Fall of Nineveh; Nahum and Habakkuk.

Although the Scythians had vanished from the horizon of Palestine and the Assyrians came over it no more, the fateful North still lowered dark and turbulent. Yet the keen eyes of the watchman in Palestine perceived that, for a time at least, the storm must break where it had gathered. It is upon Nineveh, not upon Jerusalem, that the prophetic passion of Nahum and Habakkuk is concentrated; the new day of the Lord is filled with the fate, not of Israel, but of Assyria.

For nearly two centuries Nineveh had been the capital and cynosure of Western Asia; for more than one she had set the fashions, the art, and even, to some extent, the religion of all the Semitic nations. Of late years, too, she had drawn to herself the world's trade. Great roads from Egypt, from Persia, and from the Ægean converged upon her, till like Imperial Rome she was filled with a vast motley of peoples, and men went forth from her to the ends of the earth. Under Assurbanipal travel and research had increased, and the city acquired renown as the centre of the world's wisdom. Thus her size and glory, with all her details of rampart and tower, street, palace, and temple, grew everywhere familiar. But the peoples gazed at her as those who had been bled to build her. The most remote of them had seen face to face on their own fields, trampling, stripping, burning, the warriors who manned her walls. She had dashed their little ones against the rocks. Their

* Zeph. i. 4: the LXX. reads "names of Baal." See below, p. 570 *n.*

† *Ibid.*, 5.

‡ *Ibid.*, 8-12.

§ I. 102 ff.

‖ Herod., I. 105.

* The new name of Bethshan in the mouth of Esdraelon, viz., Scythopolis, is said to be derived from them (but see "Hist. Geog. of the Holy Land," pp. 633 f.); they conquered Askalon (Herod., I. 105).

kings had been dragged from them and hung in cages about her gates. Their gods had lined the temples of her gods. Year by year they sent her their heavy tribute, and the bearers came back with fresh tales of her rapacious insolence. So she stood, bitterly clear to all men, in her glory and her cruelty! Their hate haunted her every pinnacle; and at last, when about 625 the news came that her frontier fortresses had fallen and the great city herself was being besieged, we can understand how her victims gloated on each possible stage of her fall, and saw her yield to one after another of the cruelties of battle, siege, and storm, which for two hundred years she had inflicted on themselves. To such a vision the prophet Nahum gives voice, not on behalf of Israel alone, but of all the nations whom Nineveh had crushed.

It was obvious that the vengeance which Western Asia thus hailed upon Assyria must come from one or other of two groups of peoples, standing respectively to the north and to the south of her.

To the north, or northeast, between Mesopotamia and the Caspian, there were gathered a congeries of restless tribes known to the Assyrians as the Madai or Matai, the Medes. They are mentioned first by Shalmaneser II. in 840, and few of his successors do not record campaigns against them. The earliest notice of them in the Old Testament is in connection with the captives of Samaria, some of whom in 720 were settled among them.* These Medes were probably of Turanian stock, but by the end of the eighth century, if we are to judge from the names of some of their chiefs,† their most easterly tribes had already fallen under Aryan influence, spreading westward from Persia.‡ So led, they became united and formidable to Assyria. Herodotus relates that their King Phraortes, or Fravartis, actually attempted the siege of Nineveh, probably on the death of Assurbanipal in 625, but was slain.§ His son Kyaxares, Kastarit, or Uvakshathra, was forced by a Scythian invasion of his own country to withdraw his troops from Assyria; but having either bought off or assimilated the Scythian invaders, he returned in 608, with forces sufficient to overthrow the northern Assyrian fortresses and to invest Nineveh herself.

The other and southern group of peoples which threatened Assyria were Semitic. At their head were the Kasdim and Chaldeans.‖ This name appears for the first time in the Assyrian annals a little earlier than that of the Medes,¶ and from the middle of the ninth century onwards the people designated by it frequently engage the Assyrian arms. They were, to begin with, a few half-savage tribes to the south of Babylon, in the neighbourhood of the Persian Gulf; but they proved their vigour by the repeated lordship of all Babylonia and by inveterate rebellion against the monarchs of Nineveh. Before the end of the seventh century we find their names used by the prophets for the Babylonians as a whole. Assurbanipal, who was a patron of Babylonian culture, kept the country quiet during the last years of his reign, but his son Asshur-itil-ilani, upon his accession in 625, had to grant the viceroyalty to Nabopolassar the Chaldean with a considerable degree of independence. Asshur-itil-ilani was succeeded in a few years * by Sincuriskin, the Sarakos of the Greeks, who preserved at least a nominal sovereignty over Babylon,† but Nabopolassar must already have cherished ambitions of succeeding the Assyrian in the empire of the world. He enjoyed sufficient freedom to organise his forces to that end.

These were the two powers which from north and south watched with impatience the decay of Assyria. That they made no attempt upon her between 625 and 608 was probably due to several causes: their jealousy of each other, the Medes' trouble with the Scythians, Nabopolassar's genius for waiting till his forces were ready, and above all the still considerable vigour of the Assyrian himself. The Lion, though old,‡ was not broken. His power may have relaxed in the distant provinces of his empire, though, if Budde be right about the date of Habakkuk,§ the peoples of Syria still groaned under the thought of it; but his own land—his "lair," as the prophets call it—was still terrible. It is true that, as Nahum perceives, the capital was no longer native and patriotic as it had been; the trade fostered by Assurbanipal had filled Nineveh with a vast and mercenary population, ready to break and disperse at the first breach in her walls. Yet Assyria proper was covered with fortresses, and the tradition had long fastened upon the peoples that Nineveh was impregnable. Hence the tension of those years. The peoples of Western Asia looked eagerly for their revenge; but the two powers which alone could accomplish this stood waiting—afraid of each other perhaps, but more afraid of the object of their common ambition.

It is said that Kyaxares and Nabopolassar at last came to an agreement;‖ but more probably the crisis was hastened by the appearance of another claimant for the coveted spoil. In 608 Pharaoh Necho "went up against the king of Assyria towards the river Euphrates."¶ This Egyptian advance may have forced the hand of Kyaxares, who appears to have begun his investment of Nineveh a little after Necho defeated Josiah at Megiddo.** The siege is said to have

* 2 Kings xvii. 6: "and in the cities" (LXX. "mountains") of the Medes." The Heb. is מָדַי, Madai.

† Mentioned by Sargon.

‡ Sayce, "Empires of the East," 239: *cf.* McCurdy, § 823 f.

§ Herod., I. 103.

‖ Heb. Kasdîm, כַּשְׂדִּים; LXX. Χαλδαῖοι; Assyr. Kaldâa, Kaldu. The Hebrew form with *s* is regarded by many authorities as the original, from the Assyrian root "kashadu," to conquer, and the Assyrian form with *l* to have arisen by the common change of *sh* through *r* into *l*. The form with *s* does not occur, however, in Assyrian, which also possesses the root "kaladu," with the same meaning as "kashadu." See Mr. Pinches' articles on Chaldea and the Chaldeans in the new edition of Vol. I. of Smith's "Bible Dictionary."

¶ About 880 B. C. in the annals of Assurnatsirpal. See Chronological Table p. 441.

* No inscriptions of Asshur-itil-ilani have been found later than the first two years of his reign.

† Billerbeck-Jeremias, "Der Untergang Niniveh's," in Delitzsch and Haupt's "Beiträge zur Assyriologie," III., p. 113.

‡ Nahum ii.

§ See below, p. 589.

‖ Abydenus (*apud* Euseb., "Chron.," I. 9) reports a marriage between Nebuchadrezzar, Nabopolassar's son, and the daughter of the Median king.

¶ 2 Kings xxiii. 29. The history is here very obscure. Necho, met at Megiddo by Josiah, and having slain him, appears to have spent a year or two in subjugating, and arranging for the government of Syria (*ibid.*, verses 33–35), and only reached the Euphrates in 605, when Nebuchadrezzar defeated him.

** The reverse view is taken by Wellhausen, who says ("Israel u. Jüd. Gesch.," pp. 97 f.): "Der Pharaoh scheint

lasted two years. Whether this included the delays necessary for the reduction of fortresses upon the great roads of approach to the Assyrian capital we do not know; but Nineveh's own position, fortifications, and resources may well account for the whole of the time. Colonel Billerbeck, a military expert, has suggested * that the Medes found it possible to invest the city only upon the northern and eastern sides. Down the west flows the Tigris, and across this the besieged may have been able to bring in supplies and reinforcements from the fertile country beyond. Herodotus affirms that the Medes effected the capture of Nineveh by themselves, † and for this some recent evidence has been found, ‡ so that another tradition that the Chaldeans were also actively engaged, § which has nothing to support it, may be regarded as false. Nabopolassar may still have been in name an Assyrian viceroy; yet, as Colonel Billerbeck points out, he had it in his power to make Kyaxares' victory possible by holding the southern roads to Nineveh, detaching other viceroys of her provinces and so shutting her up to her own resources. But among other reasons which kept him away from the siege may have been the necessity of guarding against Egyptian designs on the moribund empire. Pharaoh Necho, as we know, was making for the Euphrates as early as 608. Now if Nabopolassar and Kyaxares had arranged to divide Assyria between them, then it is likely that they agreed also to share the work of making their inheritance sure, so that while Kyaxares overthrew Nineveh, Nabopolassar, or rather his son Nebuchadrezzar, ‖ waited for and overthrew Pharaoh by Carchemish on the Euphrates. Consequently Assyria was divided between the Medes and the Chaldeans; the latter, as her heirs in the south, took over her title to Syria and Palestine.

The two prophets with whom we have to deal at this time are almost entirely engrossed with the fall of Assyria. Nahum exults in the destruction of Nineveh; Habakkuk sees in the Chaldeans nothing but the avengers of the peoples whom Assyria ¶ had oppressed. For both these events are the close of an epoch: neither prophet looks beyond this. Nahum (not on behalf of Israel alone) gives expression to the epoch's long thirst for vengeance on the tyrant; Habakkuk (if Budde's reading of him be right *) states the problems with which its victorious cruelties had filled the pious mind—states the problem and beholds the solution in the Chaldeans. And, surely, the vengeance was so just and so ample, the solution so drastic and for the time complete, that we can well understand how two prophets should exhaust their office in describing such things, and feel no motive to look either deep into the moral condition of Israel, or far out into the future which God was preparing for His people. It might, of course, be said that the prophets' silence on the latter subjects was due to their positions immediately after the great Reform of 621, when the nation, having been roused to an honest striving after righteousness, did not require prophetic rebuke, and when the success of so godly a prince as Josiah left no spiritual ambitions unsatisfied. But this (even if the dates of the two prophets were certain) is hardly probable; and the other explanation is sufficient. Who can doubt this who has realised the long epoch which then reached a crisis, or has been thrilled by the crash of the crisis itself? The fall of Nineveh was deafening enough to drown for the moment, as it does in Nahum, even a Hebrew's clamant conscience of his country's sin. The problems, which the long success of Assyrian cruelty had started, were old and formidable enough to demand statement and answer before either the hopes or the responsibilities of the future could find voice. The past also requires its prophets. Feeling has to be satisfied, and experience balanced, before the heart is willing to turn the leaf and read the page of the future.

Yet, through all this time of Assyria's decline, Israel had her own sins, fears, and convictions of judgment to come. The disappearance of the Scythians did not leave Zephaniah's predictions of doom without means of fulfilment; nor did the great Reform of 621 remove the necessity of that doom. In the deepest hearts the assurance that Israel must be punished was by these things only confirmed. The prophetess Huldah, the first to speak in the name of the Lord after the Book of the Law was discovered, emphasised not the reforms which it enjoined but the judgments which it predicted. Josiah's righteousness could at most ensure for himself a peaceful death: his people were incorrigible and doomed. † The reforms indeed proceeded, there was public and widespread penitence, idolatry was abolished. But those were only shallow pedants who put their trust in the possession of a revealed Law and purged Temple, ‡ and who boasted that therefore Israel was secure. Jeremiah repeated the gloomy forecasts of Zephaniah and Huldah, and even before the wickedness of Jehoiakim's reign proved the obduracy of Israel's heart, he affirmed "the imminence of the evil out of the north and the great destruction." § Of our three prophets in this period Zephaniah, though

ausgezogen zu sein um sich seinen Teil an der Erbschaft Ninives vorwegzunehmen, während die Meder und Chaldäer die Stadt belagerten."

* See above, p. 565, *n.*

† I. 106.

‡ A stele of Nabonidus discovered at Hilleh and now in the museum at Constantinople relates that in his third year, 553, the king restored at Harran the temple of Sin, the moon-god, which the Medes had destroyed fifty-four years before, *i. e.*, 607. Whether the Medes did this before, during, or after the siege of Nineveh is uncertain, but the approximate date of the siege, 608–606, is thus marvellously confirmed. The stele affirms that the Medes alone took Nineveh, but that they were called in by Marduk, the Babylonian god, to assist Nabopolassar and avenge the deportation of his image by Sennacherib to Nineveh. Messerschmidt ("Mittheilungen der Vorderasiatischen Gesellschaft," I., 1896) argues that the Medes were summoned by the Babylonians while the latter were being sore pressed by the Assyrians. Winckler had already ("Untersuch," pp. 124 ff., 1889) urged that the Babylonians would refrain from taking an active part in the overthrow of Nineveh, in fear of incurring the guilt of sacrilege. Neither Messerschmidt's paper, nor Scheil's (who describes the stele in the *Recueil des Travaux*, XVIII., 1896), being accessible to me, I have written this note on the information supplied by Rev. C. H. W. Johns, of Cambridge, in the *Expository Times*, 1896, and by Prof. A. B. Davidson in App. I. to "Nah., Hab. and Zeph."

§ Berosus and Abydenus in Eusebius.

‖ This spelling (Jer. xlix. 28) is nearer the original than the alternative Hebrew Nebuchad*n*ezzar. But the LXX. Ναβουχοδονόσορ, and the Ναβουκοδρόσορος of Abydenus and Megasthenes and Ναβοκοδρόσορος of Strabo, have preserved the more correct vocalisation; for the original is Nabu-kudurri-usur = Nebo, defend the crown!

¶ But see below, p. 590.

* Below, p. 589.

† 2 Kings xxii. 11–20. The genuineness of this passage is proved (as against Stade, "Gesch. des Volkes Israel," I.) by the promise which it gives to Josiah of a peaceful death. Had it been written after the battle of Megiddo, in which Josiah was slain, it could not have contained such a promise.

‡ Jer. vii. 4, viii. 8.

§ vi. 1.

the earliest, had therefore the last word. While Nahum and Habakkuk were almost wholly absorbed with the epoch that is closing, he had a vision of the future. Is this why this book has been ranged among our Twelve after those of his slightly later contemporaries?

The precise course of events in Israel was this—and we must follow them, for among them we have to seek exact dates for Nahum and Habakkuk. In 621 the Book of the Law was discovered, and Josiah applied himself with thoroughness to the reforms which he had already begun. For thirteen years he seems to have had peace to carry them through. The heathen altars were thrown down, with all the high places in Judah and even some in Samaria. Images were abolished. The heathen priests were exterminated, with the wizards and soothsayers. The Levites, except the sons of Zadok, who alone were allowed to minister in the Temple, henceforth the only place of sacrifice, were debarred from priestly duties. A great passover was celebrated.* The king did justice and was the friend of the poor; † it went well with him and the people.‡ He extended his influence into Samaria; it is probable that he ventured to carry out the injunctions of Deuteronomy with regard to the neighbouring heathen.§ Literature flourished: though critics have not combined upon the works to be assigned to this reign, they agree that a great many were produced in it. Wealth must have accumulated: certainly the nation entered the troubles of the next reign with an arrogant confidence that argues under Josiah the rapid growth of prosperity in every direction. Then of a sudden came the fatal year of 608. Pharaoh Necho appeared in Palestine ‖ with an army destined for the Euphrates, and Josiah went up to meet him at Megiddo. His tactics are plain—it is the first strait on the land-road from Egypt to the Euphrates—but his motives are obscure. Assyria can hardly have been strong enough at this time to fling him as her vassal across the path of her ancient foe. He must have gone of himself. "His dream was probably to bring back the scattered remains of the northern kingdom to a pure worship, and to unite the whole people of Israel under the sceptre of the house of David; and he was not inclined to allow Egypt to cross his aspirations, and rob him of the inheritance which was falling to him from the dead hand of Assyria." ¶

Josiah fell, and with him not only the liberty of his people, but the chief support of their faith. That the righteous king was cut down in the midst of his days and in defence of the Holy Land—what could this mean? Was it, then, vain to serve the Lord? Could He not defend His own? With some the disaster was a cause of sore complaint, and with others, perhaps, of open desertion from Jehovah.

But the extraordinary thing is, how little effect Josiah's death seems to have had upon the people's self-confidence at large, or upon their adherence to Jehovah. They immediately placed Josiah's second son on the throne; but Necho, having got him by some means to his camp at Riblah between the Lebanons, sent him in fetters to Egypt, where he died, and established in his place Eliakim, his elder brother. On his accession Eliakim changed his name to Jehoiakim, a proof that Jehovah was still regarded as the sufficient patron of Israel; and the same blind belief that, for the sake of His Temple and of His Law, Jehovah would keep His people in security, continued to persevere in spite of Megiddo. It was a most immoral ease, and filled with injustice. Necho subjected the land to a fine. This was not heavy, but Jehoiakim, instead of paying it out of the royal treasures, exacted it from "the people of the land," * and then employed the peace which it purchased in erecting a costly palace for himself by the forced labour of his subjects.† He was covetous, unjust, and violently cruel. Like prince like people: social oppression prevailed, and there was a recrudescence of the idolatries of Manasseh's time,‡ especially (it may be inferred) after Necho's defeat at Carchemish in 605. That all this should exist along with a fanatic trust in Jehovah need not surprise us who remember the very similar state of the public mind in North Israel under Amos and Hosea. Jeremiah attacked it as they had done. Though Assyria was fallen, and Egypt was promising protection, Jeremiah predicted destruction from the north on Egypt **and** Israel alike. When at last the Egyptian defeat at Carchemish stirred some vague fears in the people's hearts, Jeremiah's conviction broke out into clear flame. For three-and-twenty years he had brought God's word in vain to his countrymen. Now God Himself would act: Nebuchadrezzar was but His servant to lead Israel into captivity.§

The same year, 605 or 604, Jeremiah wrote all these things in a volume; ‖ and a few months later, at a national fast, occasioned perhaps by the fear of the Chaldeans, Baruch, his secretary, read them in the house of the Lord, in the ears of all the people. The king was informed, the roll was brought to him, and as it was read, with his own hands he cut it up and burned it, three or four columns at a time. Jeremiah answered by calling down on Jehoiakim an ignominious death, and repeated the doom already uttered on the land. Another prophet, Urijah, had recently been executed for the same truth; but Jeremiah and Baruch escaped into hiding.

This was probably in 603, and for a little time Jehoiakim and the populace were restored to their false security by the delay of the Chaldeans to come south. Nebuchadrezzar was occupied in Babylon, securing his succession to his father. At last, either in 602 or more probably in 600, he marched into Syria, and Jehoiakim "became his servant for three years." ¶ In such a condi-

* All these reforms in 2 Kings xxiii.

† Jer. xxii. 15 f.

‡ *Ibid.*, ver. 16.

§ We have no record of this, but a prince who so rashly flung himself in the way of Egypt would not hesitate to claim authority over Moab and Ammon.

‖ 2 Kings xxiii. 24. The question whether Necho came by land from Egypt or brought his troops in his fleet to Acre is hardly answered by the fact that Josiah went to Megiddo to meet him. But Megiddo on the whole tells more for the land than the sea. It is not on the path from Acre to the Euphrates; it is the key of the land-road from Egypt to the Euphrates. Josiah could have no hope of stopping Pharaoh on the broad levels of Philistia; but at Megiddo there was a narrow pass, and the only chance of arresting so large an army as it moved in detachments. Josiah's tactics were therefore analogous to those of Saul, who also left his own territory and marched north to Esdraelon, to meet his foe—and death.

¶ A. B. Davidson, "The Exile and the Restoration," p. 8 (Bible Class Primers, ed. by Salmond; Edin., T. & T. Clark, 1897).

* 2 Kings xxiii. 33-35.

† Jer. xxii. 13-15.

‡ Jer. xi.

§ xxv. 1 ff.

‖ xxxvi.

¶ 2 Kings, xxiv. 1. In the chronological table appended to Kautzsch's "Bibel" this verse and Jehoiakim's sub-

tion the Jewish state might have survived for at least another generation,* but in 599 or 597 Jehoiakim, with the madness of the doomed, held back his tribute. The revolt was probably instigated by Egypt, which, however, did not dare to support it. As in Isaiah's time against Assyria, so now against Babylon, Egypt was a blusterer "who blustered and sat still." She still "helped in vain and to no purpose." † Nor could Judah count on the help of the other states of Palestine. They had joined Hezekiah against Sennacherib, but remembering perhaps how Manasseh had failed to help them against Assurbanipal, and that Josiah had carried things with a high hand towards them,‡ they obeyed Nebuchadrezzar's command and raided Judah till he himself should have time to arrive.§ Amid these raids the senseless Jehoiakim seems to have perished,‖ for when Nebuchadrezzar appeared before Jerusalem in 597, his son Jehoiachin, a youth of eighteen, had succeeded to the throne. The innocent reaped the harvest sown by the guilty. In the attempt (it would appear) to save his people from destruction,¶ Jehoiachin capitulated. But Nebuchadrezzar was not content with the person of the king: he deported to Babylon the court, a large number of influential persons, "the mighty men of the land," or what must have been nearly all the fighting men, with the necessary military artificers and swordsmiths. Priests also went, Ezekiel among them, and probably representatives of other classes not mentioned by the annalist. All these were the flower of the nation. Over what was left Nebuchadrezzar placed a son of Josiah on the throne who took the name of Zedekiah. Again with a little common-sense, the state might have survived; but it was a short respite. The new court began intrigues with Egypt, and Zedekiah, with the Ammonites and Tyre, ventured a revolt in 589. Jeremiah and Ezekiel knew it was in vain. Nebuchadrezzar marched on Jerusalem, and though for a time he had to raise the siege in order to defeat a force sent by Pharaoh Hophra, the Chaldean armies closed in again upon the doomed city. Her defence was stubborn; but famine and pestilence sapped it, and numbers fell away to the enemy. About the eighteenth month, the besiegers took the northern suburb and stormed the middle gate. Zedekiah and the army broke their lines, only to be captured at Jericho. In a few weeks more the city was taken and given over to fire. Zedekiah was blinded, and with a large number of his people carried to Babylon. It was the end; for although a small community of Jews was left at Mizpeh under a Jewish viceroy and with Jeremiah to guide them, they were soon broken up and fled to Egypt. Judah had perished. Her savage neighbours, who had gathered with glee to the day of Jerusalem's calamity, assisted the Chaldeans in capturing the fugitives, and Edomites came up from the south on the desolate land.

mission are assigned to 602. But this allows too little time for Nebuchadrezzar to confirm his throne in Babylon and march to Palestine, and it is not corroborated by the record in the Book of Jeremiah of events in Judah in 604–602.

* Nebuchadrezzar did not die till 562.

† See "Isaiah i.–xxxix." ("Expositor's Bible"), pp. 671 f.

‡ See above, p. 507, n.

§ 2 Kings xxiv. 2.

‖ Jer. xxxvii. 30, but see 2 Kings xxiv. 6.

¶ So Josephus puts it ("X. Antiq.," vii. 1). Jehoiachin was unusually bewailed (Lam. iv. 20; Ezek. xvii. 22 ff.). He survived in captivity till the death of Nebuchadrezzar, whose successor Evil-Merodach in 561 took him from prison and gave him a place in his palace (2 Kings xxv. 27 ff.).

It has been necessary to follow so far the course of events, because of our prophets Zephaniah is placed in each of the three sections of Josiah's reign, and by some even in Jehoiakim's; Nahum has been assigned to different points between the eve of the first and the eve of the second siege of Nineveh; and Habakkuk has been placed by different critics in almost every year from 621 to the reign of Jehoiakim; while Obadiah, whom we shall find reasons for dating during the Exile, describes the behaviour of Edom at the final siege of Jerusalem. The next of the Twelve, Haggai, may have been born before the Exile, but did not prophesy till 520. Zechariah appeared the same year, Malachi not for half a century after. These three are prophets of the Persian period. With the approach of the Greeks Joel appears, then comes the prophecy which we find in the end of Zechariah's book, and last of all the Book of Jonah. To all these post-exilic prophets we shall provide, later on, the necessary historical introductions

---

ZEPHANIAH.

CHAPTER II.

THE BOOK OF ZEPHANIAH.

Dies Iræ, Dies Illa!—ZEPH. i. 15.

"His book is the first tinging of prophecy with apocalypse: that is the moment which it supplies in the history of Israel's religion."

THE Book of Zephaniah is one of the most difficult in the prophetic canon. The title is very generally accepted; the period from which chap. i. dates is recognised by practically all critics to be the reign of Josiah, or at least the last third of the seventh century. But after that doubts start, and we find present nearly every other problem of introduction.

To begin with, the text is very damaged. In some passages we may be quite sure that we have not the true text;* in others we cannot be sure that we have it,† and there are several glosses.‡ The bulk of the second chapter was written in the Qinah, or elegiac measure, but as it now stands the rhythm is very much broken. It is difficult to say whether this is due to the dilapidation of the original text or to wilful insertion of glosses and other later passages. The Greek version of Zephaniah possesses the same general features as that of other difficult prophets. Occasionally it enables us to correct the text; but by the time it was made the text must already have contained the same corruptions which we encounter, and the translators were ignorant besides of the meaning of some phrases which to us are plain.§

The difficulties of textual criticism as well as of translation are aggravated by the large number of words, grammatical forms, and phrases

* i. 3*b*, 5*b*; ii. 2, 5, 6, 7, 8 last word, 14*b*; iii. 18, 19*a*, 20.

† i. 14*b*; ii. 1, 3; iii. 1, 5, 6, 7, 8, 10, 15, 17.

‡ i. 3*b*, 5*b*; ii. 2, 6; iii. 5 (?).

§ For details see translation below.

which either happen very seldom in the Old Testament,* or nowhere else in it at all.† Of the rare words and phrases, a very few (as will be seen from the appended notes) are found in earlier writings. Indeed all that are found are from the authentic prophecies of Isaiah, with whose style and doctrine Zephaniah's own exhibit most affinity. All the other rarities of vocabulary and grammar are shared only by *later* writers; and as a whole the language of Zephaniah exhibits symptoms which separate it by many years from the language of the prophets of the eighth century, and range it with that of Jeremiah, Ezekiel, the Second Isaiah, and still later literature. It may be useful to the student to collect in a note the most striking of these symptoms of the comparative lateness of Zephaniah's dialect.‡

We now come to the question of date, and we take, to begin with, the First Chapter. It was said above that critics agree as to the general period—between 639, when Josiah began to reign, and 600. But this period was divided into three very different sections, and each of these has received considerable support from modern criticism. The great majority of critics place the chapter in the early years of Josiah, before the enforcement of Deuteronomy and the great Reform in 621.§ Others have argued for the later years of Josiah, 621-608, on the ground that the chapter implies that the great Reform has already taken place, and otherwise shows knowledge of Deuteronomy;* while some prefer the days of reaction under Jehoiakim, 608 ff.,† and assume that the phrase in the title, " in the days of Josiah," is a late and erroneous inference from i. 4.

The evidence for the argument consists of the title and the condition of Judah reflected in the body of the chapter. The latter is a definite piece of oratory. Under the alarm of an immediate and general war, Zephaniah proclaims a vast destruction upon the earth. Judah must fall beneath it: the worshippers of Baal, of the host of heaven, and of Milcom, the apostates from Jehovah, the princes and house of the king, the imitators of foreign fashions, and the forceful and fraudulent, shall be cut off in a great slaughter. Those who have grown sceptical and indifferent to Jehovah shall be unsettled by invasion and war. This shall be the Day of Jehovah, near and immediate, a day of battle and disaster on the whole land.

The conditions reflected are thus twofold—the idolatrous and sceptical state of the people, and an impending invasion. But these suit, more or less exactly, each of the three sections of our period. For Jeremiah distinctly states that he had to attack idolatry in Judah for twenty-three years, 627 to 604;‡ he inveighs against the falseness and impurity of the people alike before the great Reform, and after it while Josiah was still alive, and still more fiercely under Jehoiakim. And, while before 621 the great Scythian invasion was sweeping upon Palestine from the north, after 621, and especially after 604, the Babylonians from the same quarter were visibly threatening the land. But when looked at more closely, the chapter shows several features which suit the second section of our period less than they do the other two. The worship of the host of heaven, probably introduced under Manasseh, was put down by Josiah in 621; it revived under Jehoiakim,§ but during the latter years of Josiah it cannot possibly have been so public as Zephaniah describes.‖ Other reasons which have been given for those years are inconclusive ¶—the chapter, for instance, makes no indubitable reference to Deuteronomy or the Covenant of 621—and on the whole we may leave the end of

* i. 3, מַכְשֵׁלוֹת, only in Isa. iii. 6; 15, משואה, only in Job xxx. 3, xxxviii. 27—*cf.* Psalms lxxiii. 18, lxxiv. 3; ii. 8, גדפים, Isa. xliii. 28—*cf.* li. 7; 9, חרול, Prov. xxiv. 31, Job xxx. 7; 15, עליזה, Isa. xxii. 2, xxiii. 7, xxxii. 13—*cf.* xiii. 3, xxiv. 8; iii. 1, נג לה, see next note but one; 3, זאבי ערב, Hab. i. 8; 11, עליזי גאותך, Isa. xiii. 3; 18, נוגי, Lam. i. 4, נוגות.

† i. 11, המכתש as the name of a part of Jerusalem, otherwise only Jer. xv. 19; נטילי כסף; 12, קפא, in pt. Qal, and otherwise only Exod. xv. 8, Zech. xiv. 6, Job x. 10; 14, מַהֵר (adj.), but the pointing may be wrong—*cf.* Maher-shalal-hash-baz, Isa. viii. 1, 3; צרח in Qal, elsewhere only once in Hi. Isa. xlii. 13; 17, לחום in sense of flesh, *cf.* Job xx. 23; 18, נבהלה if a noun (?); ii. 1. קשש, in Qal and Hithpo, elsewhere only in Polel; 9, ממשק, מכרה; 11, רזה, to make lean, otherwise only in Isa. xvii. 4, to be lean; 14, ארזה (?); iii. 1, מראה, pt. of מרה; יונה, pt. Qal, in Jer. xlvi. 16, l. 16, it may be a noun; 4, אנשי בגדות; 6, נצדו; 9, שכם אחד; 10, עתרי בת־פוצי (?); 15, פנה in sense to " turn away"; 18, ממך היו (?).

‡ i. 8, etc., פקד על, followed by person, but not by thing—*cf.* Jer. ix. 24, xxiii. 34, etc., Job xxxvi. 23, 2 Chron. xxxvi. 23, Ezek. i. 2; 13, משסה, only in Hab. ii. 7, Isa. xlii., Jer. xxx. 16, 2 Kings xxi. 14; 17, הֵצַר, Hi. of צרר, only in 1 Kings viii. 37, and Deut., 2 Chron., Jer., Neh., ii. 3, ענוה; 8, גדופים, Isa. xliii. 28, li. 7 (fem. pl.); 9, חרול, Prov. xxiv. 31, Job xxx. 7; iii. 1, נגאלה, Ni, pt. = impure, Isa. lix. 3, Lam. iv. 14; יונה, a pt. in Jer. xlvi. 16, l. 16; 3, זאבי ערב, Hab. i. 8—*cf.* Jer. v. 6, זאב ערבות; 9, ברור, Isa. xlix. 2, ברר, Ezek. xx. 38, 1 Chron. vii. 40, ix. 22, xvi. 41, Neh. v. 18, Job xxxiii. 3, Eccles. iii. 18, ix. 1; 11, גאות עליזי, Isa. xiii. 3; 18 נוּגֵי. Lam. i. 4 has נוּגות.

§ So Hitzig, Ewald, Pusey, Kuenen, Robertson Smith ("Encyc. Brit."), Driver, Wellhausen, Kirkpatrick, Budde, von Orelli, Cornill, Schwally, Davidson.

* So Delitzsch, Kleinert, and Schulz ("Commentar über den Proph. Zeph.," 1892, p. 7, quoted by König).

† So König.

‡ Jer. xxv.

§ Jer. vii. 18.

‖ i. 3.

¶ Kleinert in his Commentary in Lange's "Bibelwerk," and Delitzsch in his article in Herzog's "Real-Encyclopadie," both offer a number of inconclusive arguments. These are drawn from the position of Zephaniah after Habakkuk, but, as we have seen, the order of the Twelve is not always chronological; from the supposition that Zephaniah i. 7, "Silence before the Lord Jehovah," quotes Habakkuk ii. 20, "Keep silence before Him, all the earth," but the phrase common to both is too general to be decisive, and if borrowed by one or other may just as well have been Zephaniah's originally as Habakkuk's; from the phrase "remnant of Baal" (i. 4), as if this were appropriate only after the Reform of 621, but it was quite as appropriate after the beginnings of reform six years earlier; from the condemnation of "the sons of the king" (i. 8), whom Delitzsch takes as Josiah's sons, who before the great Reform were too young to be condemned, while later their characters did develop badly and judgment fell upon all of them, but "sons of the king," even if that be the correct reading (LXX. "house of the king"), does not necessarily mean the reigning monarch's children; and from the assertion that Deuteronomy is quoted in the first chapter of Zephaniah, and "so quoted as to show that the prophet needs only to put the people in mind of it as something supposed to be known," but the verses cited in support of this (viz. 13, 15, 17: *cf.* Deut. xxviii. 30 and 29) are too general in their character to prove the assertion. See translation below.

Josiah's reign out of account. Turning to the third section, Jehoiakim's reign, we find one feature of the prophecy which suits it admirably. The temper described in ver. 12—"men who are settled on their lees, who say in their heart, Jehovah doeth neither good nor evil"—is the kind of temper likely to have been produced among the less earnest adherents of Jehovah by the failure of the great Reform in 621 to effect either the purity or the prosperity of the nation. But this is more than counterbalanced by the significant exception of the king from the condemnation which ver. 8 passes on the "princes and the sons of the king." Such an exception could not have been made when Jehoiakim was on the throne; it points almost conclusively to the reign of the good Josiah. And with this agrees the title of the chapter—"in the days of Josiah." * We are, therefore, driven back to the years of Josiah before 621. In these we find no discrepancy either with the chapter itself, or with its title. The southward march of the Scythians, † between 630 and 625, accounts for Zephaniah's alarm of a general war, including the invasion of Judah; the idolatrous practices which he describes may well have been those surviving from the days of Manasseh, ‡ and not yet reached by the drastic measures of 621; the temper of scepticism and hopelessness condemned by ver. 12 was possible among those adherents of Jehovah who had hoped greater things from the overthrow of Amon than the slow and small reforms of the first fifteen years of Josiah's reign. Nor is a date before 621 made at all difficult by the genealogy of Zephaniah in the title. If, as is probable, § the Hezekiah given as his great-great-grandfather be Hezekiah the king, and if he died about 695, and Manasseh, his successor, who was then twelve, was his eldest son, then by 630 Zephaniah cannot have been much more than twenty years of age, and not more than twenty-five by the time the Scythian invasion had passed away. ‖ It is therefore by no means impossible to suppose that he prophesied before 625; and besides, the data of the genealogy in the title are too precarious to make them valid, as against an inference from the contents of the chapter itself.

The date, therefore, of the first chapter of Zephaniah may be given as about 625 B. C., and probably rather before than after that year, as the tide of Scythian invasion has apparently not yet ebbed.

The other two chapters have within recent years been almost wholly denied to Zephaniah. Kuenen doubted chap. ii. 9-20. Stade makes all chap. iii. post-exilic, and suspects ii. 1-3, 11. A very thorough examination of them has led Schwally ¶ to asign to exilic or post-exilic times the whole of the little sections comprising them, with the possible exceptions of chap. iii. 1-7, which "may be" Zephaniah's. His essay has been subjected to a searching and generally hostile criticism by a number of leading scholars; * and he has admitted the inconclusiveness of some of his reasons. †

Chap. ii. 1-4 is assigned by Schwally to a date later than Zephaniah's, principally because of the term *meekness* (ver. 3), which is a favourite one with post-exilic writers. He has been sufficiently answered; ‡ and the close connection of vv. 1-3 with chap. i. has been clearly proved. § Chap. ii. 4-15 is the passage in elegiac measure but broken, an argument for the theory that insertions have been made in it. The subject is a series of foreign nations—Philistia (5-7), Moab and Ammon (8-10), Egypt (11) and Assyria (13-15). The passage has given rise to many doubts; every one must admit the difficulty of coming to a conclusion as to its authenticity. On the one hand, the destruction just predicted is so universal that, as Professor Davidson says, we should expect Zephaniah to mention other nations than Judah. ‖ The concluding oracle on Nineveh must have been published before 608, and even Schwally admits that it may be Zephaniah's own. But if this be so, then we may infer that the first of the oracles on Philistia is also Zephaniah's, for both it and the oracle on Assyria are in the elegiac measure, a fact which makes it probable that the whole passage, however broken and intruded upon, was originally a unity. Nor is there anything in the oracle on Philistia incompatible with Zephaniah's date. Philistia lay on the path of the Scythian invasion; the phrase in ver. 7, "shall turn their captivity," is not necessarily exilic. As Cornill, too, points out, the expression in ver. 13, "He will stretch out His hand to the north," implies that the prophecy has already looked in other directions. There remains the passage between the oracles on Philistia and Assyria. This is not in the elegiac measure. Its subject is Moab and Ammon, who were not on the line of the Scythian invasion, and Wellhausen further objects to it, because the attitude to Israel of the two peoples whom it describes is that which is attributed to them only just before the Exile and surprises us in Josiah's reign. Dr. Davidson meets this objection by pointing out that, just as in Deuteronomy, so here, Moab and Ammon are denounced, while Edom, which in Deuteronomy is spoken of with kindness, is here not denounced at all. A stronger objection to the passage is that ver. 11 predicts the conversion of the nations, while ver. 12 makes them the prey of Jehovah's sword, and in this ver. 12 follows on naturally to ver. 7. On this ground, as well as on the absence of the elegiac measure, the oracle on Moab and Ammon is strongly to be suspected.

On the whole, then, the most probable conclusion is that chap. ii. 4-15 was originally an authentic oracle of Zephaniah's in the elegiac

* König has to deny the authenticity of this in order to make his case for the reign of Jehoiakim. But nearly all critics take the phrase as genuine.

† See above, p. 564. For inconclusive reasons Schwally, "Z. A. T. W.," 1890, pp. 215-217, prefers the Egyptians under Psamtik. See in answer Davidson, p. 98.

‡ Not much stress can be laid upon the phrase "I will cut off the remnant of Baal," ver. 4, for, if the reading be correct, it may only mean the destruction of Baal-worship, and not the uprooting of what has been left over.

§ See below, p. 571, *n*.

‖ If 695 be the date of the accession of Manasseh, being then twelve, Amariah, Zephaniah's great-grandfather, cannot have been more than ten, that is, born in 705. His son Gedaliah was probably not born before 689, his son Kushi probably not before 672, and his son Zephaniah probably not before 650.

¶ "Z. A. T. W.," 1890, Heft 1.

* Bacher, "Z. A. T. W.," 1891, 186; Cornill, "Einleitung," 1891; Budde, "Theol. Stud. u. Krit.," 1893, 393 ff.; Davidson, "Nah., Hab. and Zeph.," 100 ff.

† "Z. A. T. W." 1891, Heft 2.

‡ By especially Bacher, Cornill and Budde as above.

§ See Budde and Davidson.

‖ The ideal of chap. i.-ii. 3, of the final security of a poor and lowly remnant of Israel, "necessarily implies that they shall no longer be threatened by hostility from without, and this condition is satisfied by the prophet's view of the impending judgment on the ancient enemies of his nation," *i. e.*, those mentioned in ii. 4-15 (Robertson Smith, "Encyc. Brit.," art. "Zephaniah").

metre, uttered at the same date as chap. i.-ii. 3, the period of the Scythian invasion, though from a different standpoint; and that it has suffered considerable dilapidation (witness especially vv. 6 and 14), and probably one great intrusion, vv. 8-10.

There remains the Third Chapter. The authenticity has been denied by Schwally, who transfers the whole till after the Exile. But the chapter is not a unity.* In the first place, it falls into two sections, vv. 1-13 and 14-20. There is no reason to take away the bulk of the first section from Zephaniah. As Schwally admits, the argument here is parallel to that of chap. i.-ii. 3. It could hardly have been applied to Jerusalem during or after the Exile, but suits her conditions before her fall. Schwally's linguistic objections to a pre-exilic date have been answered by Budde.† He holds ver. 6 to be out of place and puts it after ver. 8, and this may be. But as it stands it appeals to the impenitent Jews of ver. 5 with the picture of the judgment God has already completed upon the nations, and contrasts with ver. 7, in which God says that He trusts Israel will repent. Vv. 9 and 10 are, we shall see, obviously an intrusion, as Budde maintains and Davidson admits to be possible.‡

We reach more certainty when we come to the second section of the chapter, vv. 14-20. Since Kuenen it has been recognised by the majority of critics that we have here a prophecy from the end of the Exile or after the Return. The temper has changed. Instead of the austere and sombre outlook of chap. i.-ii. 3 and chap. iii. 1-13, in which the sinful Israel is to be saved indeed, but only as by fire, we have a triumphant prophecy of her recovery from all affliction (nothing is said of her sin) and of her glory among the nations of the world. To put it otherwise, while the genuine prophecies of Zephaniah almost grudgingly allow a door of escape to a few righteous and humble Israelites from a judgment which is to fall alike on Israel and the Gentiles, chap. iii. 14-20 predicts Israel's deliverance from her Gentile oppressors, her return from captivity, and the establishment of her renown over the earth. The language, too, has many resemblances to that of Second Isaiah.§ Obviously therefore we have here, added to the severe prophecies of Zephaniah, such a more hopeful, peaceful epilogue as we saw was added, during the Exile, or immediately after it, to the despairing prophecies of Amos.

*See, however, Davidson for some linguistic reasons for taking the two sections as one. Robertson Smith, also in 1888 ("Encyc. Brit.," art. "Zephaniah"), assumed (though not without pointing out the possibility of the addition of other pieces to the genuine prophecies of Zephaniah) that "a single leading motive runs through the whole" book, and "the first two chapters would be incomplete without the third, which moreover is certainly pre-exilic (vv. 1-4) and presents specific points of contact with what precedes, as well as a general agreement in style and idea."

† Schwally (234) thinks that the epithet צדיק (ver. 5) was first applied to Jehovah by the Second Isaiah (xlv. 21, lxiv. 2, xlii. 21), and became frequent from his time on. In disproof Budde (3398) quotes Exod. ix. 27, Jer. xii. 1. Lam. i. 18. Schwally also points to נצדו as borrowed from Aramaic.

‡ Budde, p. 395; Davidson, 103. Schwally (230 ff.) seeks to prove the unity of 9 and 10 with the context, but he has apparently mistaken the meaning of ver. 8 (231). That surely does not mean that the nations are gathered in order to punish the godlessness of the Jews, but that they may themselves be punished.

§ See Davidson, 103.

CHAPTER III.

THE PROPHET AND THE REFORMERS.

ZEPHANIAH i.-ii. 3.

TOWARDS the year 625, when King Josiah had passed out of his minority,* and was making his first efforts at religious reform, prophecy, long slumbering, woke again in Israel.

Like the king himself, its first heralds were men in their early youth. In 627 Jeremiah calls himself but a boy, and Zephaniah can hardly have been out of his teens.† For the sudden outbreak of these young lives there must have been a large reservoir of patience and hope gathered in the generation behind them. So Scripture itself testifies. To Jeremiah it was said: "Before I formed thee in the belly I knew thee, and before thou camest forth out of the womb I consecrated thee."‡ In an age when names were bestowed only because of their significance,§ both prophets bore that of Jehovah in their own. So did Jeremiah's father, who was of the priests of Anathoth. Zephaniah's "forbears" are given for four generations, and with one exception they also are called after Jehovah: "The Word of Jehovah which came to Ṣephanyah, son of Kushi, son of Gedhalyah, son of Amaryah, son of Hizḳiyah, in the days of Joshiyahu,‖ Amon's son, king of Judah." Zephaniah's great-great-grandfather Hezekiah was in all probability the king.¶ His father's name Kushi, or *Ethiop*, is curious. If we are right, that Zephaniah was a young man towards 625, then Kushi must have been born towards 663, about the time of the conflicts between Assyria and Egypt, and it is possible that, as Manasseh and the predominant party in Judah so closely hung upon and imitated Assyria, the adherents of Jehovah put their hope in Egypt, whereof, it may be, this name Kushi is a token.** The name Zephaniah itself, meaning "Jehovah hath hidden," suggests the prophet's birth in the "killing-time" of Manasseh. There was at least one other contemporary of the same name—a priest executed by Nebuchadrezzar.††

Of the adherents of Jehovah, then, and probably of royal descent, Zephaniah lived in Jerusalem. We descry him against her, almost as clearly as we descry Isaiah. In the glare and smoke of the conflagration which his vision

* Josiah, born *c.* 648, succeeded *c.* 639, was about eighteen in 630, and then appears to have begun his reforms.

† See above, p. 570, n.

‡ Jer. i. 5.

§ See G. B. Gray, "Hebrew Proper Names."

‖ Josiah.

¶ It is not usual in the O. T. to carry a man's genealogy beyond his grandfather, except for some special purpose, or in order to include some ancestor of note. Also the name Hezekiah is very rare apart from the king. The number of names compounded with Jah or Jehovah is another proof that the line is a royal one. The omission of the phrase "king of Judah" after Hezekiah's name proves nothing; it may have been of purpose because the phrase has to occur immediately again.

** It was not until 652 that a league was made between the Palestine princes and Psamtik I. against Assyria. This certainly would have been the most natural year for a child to be named Kushi. But that would set the birth of Zephaniah as late as 632, and his prophecy towards the end of Josiah's reign, which we have seen to be improbable on other grounds.

†† Jer. xxi. 1, xxix. 25, 29, xxxvii. 3, lii. 24 ff.; 2 Kings xxv. 18. The analogous Phœnician name צפנבעל, Saphanba'al = "Baal protects or hides," is found in No. 207 of the Phœnician inscriptions in the "Corpus Inscr. Semiticarum."

sweeps across the world, only her features stand out definite and particular: the flat roofs with men and women bowing in the twilight to the host of heaven, the crowds of priests, the nobles and their foreign fashions: the *Fishgate*, the New or *Second* Town, where the rich lived, the *Heights* to which building had at last spread, and between them the hollow *Mortar*, with its markets, Phœnician merchants, and money-dealers. In the first few verses of Zephaniah we see almost as much of Jerusalem as in the whole book either of Isaiah or Jeremiah.

For so young a man the vision of Zephaniah may seem strangely dark and final. Yet not otherwise was Isaiah's inaugural vision, and as a rule it is the young and not the old whose indignation is ardent and unsparing. Zephaniah carries this temper to the extreme. There is no great hope in his book, hardly any tenderness, and never a glimpse of beauty. A townsman, Zephaniah has no eye for nature; not only is no fair prospect described by him, he has not even a single metaphor drawn from nature's loveliness or peace. He is pitilessly true to his great keynotes: "I will sweep, sweep from the face of the ground; He will burn," burn up everything. No hotter book lies in all the Old Testament. Neither dew nor grass nor tree nor any blossom lives in it, but it is everywhere fire, smoke, and darkness, drifting chaff, ruins, nettles, salt-pits, and owls and ravens looking from the windows of desolate palaces. Nor does Zephaniah foretell the restoration of nature in the end of the days. There is no prospect of a redeemed and fruitful land, but only of a group of battered and hardly saved characters: a few meek and righteous are hidden from the fire and creep forth when it is over. Israel is left "a poor and humble folk." No prophet is more true to the doctrine of the remnant, or more resolutely refuses to modify it. Perhaps he died young.

The full truth, however, is that Zephaniah, though he found his material in the events of his own day, tears himself loose from history altogether. To the earlier prophets the Day of the Lord, the crisis of the world, is a definite point in history: full of terrible, Divine events, yet "natural" ones—battle, siege, famine, massacre, and captivity. After it history is still to flow on, common days come back and Israel pursue their way as a nation. But to Zephaniah the Day of the Lord begins to assume what we call the "supernatural." The grim colours are still woven of war and siege, but mixed with vague and solemn terrors from another sphere, by which history appears to be swallowed up, and it is only with an effort that the prophet thinks of a rally of Israel beyond. In short, with Zephaniah the Day of the Lord tends to become the Last Day. His book is the first tinging of prophecy with apocalypse: that is the moment which it supplies in the history of Israel's religion. And, therefore, it was with a true instinct that the great Christian singer of the Last Day took from Zephaniah his keynote. The "Dies Iræ, Dies Illa" of Thomas of Celano is but the Vulgate translation of Zephaniah's "A day of wrath is that day." *

Nevertheless, though the first of apocalyptic writers, Zephaniah does not allow himself the license of apocalypse. As he refuses to imagine great glory for the righteous, so he does not dwell on the terrors of the wicked. He is sober and restrained, a matter-of-fact man, yet with power of imagination, who, amidst the vague horrors he summons, delights in giving a sharp realistic impression. The Day of the Lord, he says, what is it? "A strong man—there!—crying bitterly." *

It is to the fierce ardour, and to the elemental interests of the book, that we owe the absence of two features of prophecy which are so constant in the prophets of the eighth century. Firstly, Zephaniah betrays no interest in the practical reforms which (if we are right about the date) the young king, his contemporary, had already started.† There was a party of reform, the party had a programme, the programme was drawn from the main principles of prophecy and was designed to put these into practice. And Zephaniah was a prophet and ignored them. This forms the dramatic interest of his book. Here was a man of the same faith which kings, priests, and statesmen were trying to realise in public life, in the assured hope—as is plain from the temper of Deuteronomy—that the nation as a whole would be reformed and become a very great nation, righteous and victorious. All this he ignored, and gave his own vision of the future: Israel is a brand plucked from the burning; a very few meek and righteous are saved from the conflagration of a whole world. Why? Because for Zephaniah the elements were loose, and when the elements were loose what was the use of talking about reforms? The Scythians were sweeping down upon Palestine, with enough of God's wrath in them to destroy a people still so full of idolatry as Israel was; and if not the Scythians, then some other power in that dark, rumbling North which had ever been so full of doom. Let Josiah try to reform Israel, but it was neither Josiah's nor Israel's day that was falling. It was the Day of the Lord, and when He came it was neither to reform nor to build up Israel, but to make visitation and to punish in His wrath for the unbelief and wickedness of which the nation was still full.

An analogy to this dramatic opposition between prophet and reformer may be found in our own century. At its crisis, in 1848, there were many righteous men rich in hope and energy. The political institutions of Europe were being rebuilt. In our own land there were great measures for the relief of labouring children and women, the organisation of labour, and the just distribution of wealth. But Carlyle that year held apart from them all, and, though a personal friend of many of the reformers, counted their work hopeless: society was too corrupt, the rudest forces were loose, "Niagara" was near. Carlyle was proved wrong and the reformers right, but in the analogous situation of Israel the reformers were wrong and the prophet right. Josiah's hope and daring were overthrown at Megiddo, and, though the Scythians passed away, Zephaniah's conviction of the sin and doom of Israel was fulfilled, not forty years later, in the fall of Jerusalem and the great Exile.

Again, to the same elemental interests, as we

* Chap. i. 15. With the above paragraph *cf.* Robertson Smith, "Encyc. Brit.," art, "Zephaniah."

* Chap. i. 14 *b*.

† In fact this forms one difficulty about the conclusion which we have reached as to the date. We saw that one reason against putting the Book of Zephaniah after the great Reforms of 621 was that it betrayed no sign of their effects. But it might justly be answered that, if Zephaniah prophesied before 621, his book ought to betray some sign of the approach of reform. Still the explanation given above is satisfactory.

may call them, is due the absence from Zephaniah's pages of all the social and individual studies which form the charm of other prophets. With one exception, there is no analysis of character, no portrait, no satire. But the exception is worth dwelling upon: it describes the temper equally abhorred by both prophet and reformer—that of the indifferent and stagnant man. Here we have a subtle and memorable picture of character, which is not without its warnings for our own time.

Zephaniah heard God say: "And it shall be at that time that I will search out Jerusalem with lights, and I will make visitation upon the men who are become stagnant upon their lees, who say in their hearts, Jehovah doeth no good and doeth no evil." * The metaphor is clear. New wine was left upon its lees only long enough to fix its colour and body.† If not then drawn off it grew thick and syrupy—sweeter indeed than the strained wine, and to the taste of some more pleasant, but feeble and ready to decay. "To settle upon one's lees" became a proverb for sloth, indifference, and the muddy mind. "Moab hath been at ease from his youth and hath settled upon his lees, and hath not been emptied from vessel to vessel; therefore his taste stands in him and his scent is not changed." ‡ The characters stigmatised by Zephaniah are also obvious. They were a precipitate from the ferment of fifteen years back. Through the cruel days of Manasseh and Amon hope had been stirred and strained, emptied from vessel to vessel, and so had sprung, sparkling and keen, into the new days of Josiah. But no miracle came, only ten years of waiting for the king's majority and five more of small, tentative reforms. Nothing Divine happened. They were but the ambiguous successes of a small party who had secured the king for their principles. The court was still full of foreign fashions, and idolatry was rank upon the housetops. Of course disappointment ensued—disappointment and listlessness. The new security of life became a temptation; persecution ceased, and religious men lived again at ease. So numbers of eager and sparkling souls, who had been in the front of the movement, fell away into a selfish and idle obscurity. The prophet hears God say, "I must search Jerusalem with lights" in order to find them. They had "fallen from the van and the freemen"; they had "sunk to the rear and the slaves," where they wallowed in the excuse that "Jehovah" Himself "would do nothing—neither good," therefore it is useless to attempt reform like Josiah and his party, "nor evil," therefore Zephaniah's prophecy of destruction is also vain. Exactly the same temper was encountered by Mazzini in the second stage of his career. Many of those who with him had eagerly dreamt of a free Italy fell away when the first revolt failed—fell away not merely into weariness and fear, but, as he emphasises, into the very two tempers which are described by Zephaniah, scepticism and self-indulgence.

All this starts questions for ourselves. Here is evidently the same public temper, which at all periods provokes alike the despair of the reformer and the indignation of the prophet: the criminal apathy of the well-to-do classes sunk in ease and religious indifference. We have today the same mass of obscure, nameless persons, who oppose their almost unconquerable inertia to every movement of reform, and are the drag upon all vital and progressive religion. The great causes of God and Humanity are not defeated by the hot assaults of the Devil, but by the slow, crushing, glacier-like masses of thousands and thousands of indifferent nobodies. God's causes are never destroyed by being blown up, but by being sat upon. It is not the violent and anarchical whom we have to fear in the war for human progress, but the slow, the staid, the respectable. And the danger of these does not lie in their stupidity. Notwithstanding all their religious profession, it lies in their real scepticism. Respectability may be the precipitate of unbelief. Nay, it is that, however religious its mask, wherever it is mere comfort, decorousness, and conventionality; where, though it would abhor articulately confessing that God does nothing, it virtually means so—*says* so (as Zephaniah puts it) *in its heart*, by refusing to share manifest opportunities of serving Him, and covers its sloth and its fear by sneering that God is not with the great crusades of freedom and purity to which it is summoned. In these ways, Respectability is the precipitate which unbelief naturally forms in the selfish ease and stillness of so much of our middle-class life. And that is what makes mere respectability so dangerous. Like the unshaken, unstrained wine to which the prophet compares its obscure and muddy comfort, it tends to decay. To some extent our respectable classes are just the dregs and lees of our national life; like all dregs, they are subject to corruption. A great sermon could be preached on the putrescence of respectability—how the ignoble comfort of our respectable classes and their indifference to holy causes lead to sensuality, and poison the very institutions of the Home and the Family, on which they pride themselves. A large amount of the licentiousness of the present day is not that of outlaw and disordered lives, but is bred from the settled ease and indifference of many of our middle-class families.

It is perhaps the chief part of the sin of the obscure units, which form these great masses of indifference, that they think they escape notice and cover their individual responsibility. At all times many have sought obscurity, not because they are humble, but because they are slothful, cowardly, or indifferent. Obviously it is this temper which is met by the words, "I will search out Jerusalem with lights." None of us shall escape because we have said, "I will go with the crowd," or "I am a common man and have no right to thrust myself forward." We shall be followed and judged, each of us for his or her personal attitude to the great movements of our time. These things are not too high for us: they are *our* duty; and we cannot escape our duty by slinking into the shadow.

For all this wickedness and indifference Zephaniah sees prepared the Day of the Lord—near, hastening, and very terrible. It sweeps at first in vague desolation and ruin of all things, but then takes the outlines of a solemn slaughter-feast for which Jehovah has consecrated the guests, the dim unnamed armies from the north. Judah shall be invaded, and they that are at ease, who say "Jehovah does nothing" shall be unsettled and routed. One vivid trait comes in like a screech upon the hearts of a people unaccus-

* Chap. i. 12.
† So "wine upon the lees" is a generous wine, according to Isa. xxv. 6.
‡ Jer. xlviii. 11.

tomed for years to war. "Hark, Jehovah's Day!" cries the prophet. "A strong man—there!—crying bitterly." From this flash upon the concrete he returns to a great vague terror, in which earthly armies merge in heavenly; battle, siege, storm, and darkness are mingled, and destruction is spread abroad upon the whole earth. The first shades of Apocalypse are upon us.

We may now take the full text of this strong and significant prophecy. We have already given the title. Textual emendations and other points are explained in footnotes.

"I will sweep, sweep away everything from the face of the ground—oracle of Jehovah—sweep man and beast, sweep the fowl of the heaven and the fish of the sea, and I will bring to ruin * the wicked and cut off the men of wickedness from the ground—oracle of Jehovah. And I will stretch forth My hand upon Judah, and upon all the inhabitants of Jerusalem; and I will cut off from this place the remnant † of the Baal,‡ the names§ of the priestlings with the priests, and them who upon the housetops bow themselves to the host of heaven, and them who . . . . ‖ swear by their Melech,¶ and them who have turned from following Jehovah, and who do not seek Jehovah nor have inquired of Him.

"Silence for the Lord Jehovah! For near is Jehovah's Day. Jehovah has prepared a ** slaughter, He has consecrated His guests.

"And it shall be in Jehovah's day of slaughter that I will make visitation upon the princes and the house †† of the king, and upon all who array themselves in foreign raiment; and I will make visitation upon all who leap over the threshold ‡‡ on that day, who fill their lord's house full of violence and fraud.

"And on that day—oracle of Jehovah—there shall be a noise of crying from the Fishgate, and wailing from the Mishneh,* and great havoc on the Heights. Howl, O dwellers in the Mortar,† for undone are all the merchant folk,‡ cut off are all the money-dealers.§

"And in that time it shall be, that I will search Jerusalem with lanterns, and make visitation upon the men who are become stagnant upon their lees, who in their hearts say, Jehovah doeth no good and doeth no evil.‖ Their substance shall be for spoil, and their houses for wasting. . . . ¶

"Near is the great Day of Jehovah, near and very speedy.** Hark, the Day of Jehovah! A strong man—there!—crying bitterly.

"A Day of wrath is that Day! †† Day of siege and blockade, day of stress and distress,‡‡ day of darkness and murk, day of cloud and heavy mist, day of the war-horn and battle-roar, up against the fenced cities and against the highest turrets! And I will beleaguer men, and they shall walk like the blind, for they have sinned against Jehovah; and poured out shall their blood be like dust, and the flesh of them like dung. Even their silver, even their gold shall not avail to save them in the day of Jehovah's wrath,§§ and in the fire of His zeal shall all the earth be devoured, *for* destruction, yea,‖‖ sudden collapse shall He make of all the inhabitants of the earth."

Upon this vision of absolute doom there follows ¶¶ a qualification for the few meek and righteous. They may be hidden on the day of the Lord's anger; but even for them escape is only a possibility. Note the absence of all mention of the Divine mercy as the cause of deliverance. Zephaniah has no gospel of that kind. The conditions of escape are sternly ethical—meekness, the doing of justice and righteousness. So austere is our prophet.

* The text reads, "the ruins" (מַכְשֵׁלוֹת,) unless we prefer with Wellhausen מִכְשֹׁלִים, "the stumbling-blocks," *i. e.*, "idols") "with the wicked, and I will cut off man" (LXX. "the lawless") "from off the face of the ground." Some think the clause partly too redundant, partly too specific, to be original. But suppose we read וְהִכְשַׁלְתִּי (*cf.* Mal. ii. 8, Lam. i. 14 and *passim*; this is more probable than Schwally's כִּשַּׁלְתִּי, *op cit.*, p. 169), and for אדם the reading which probably the LXX. had before them, אדם רשע (Job xx. 29, xxvii. 13, Prov. xi. 7: *cf.* אדם בליעל, Prov. vi. 12) or אדם עַוָּל (*cf.* iii. 5), we get the rendering adopted in the translation above. Some think the whole passage an intrusion, yet it is surely probable that the earnest moral spirit of Zephaniah would aim at the wicked from the very outset of his prophecy.

† LXX. "names," held by some to be the original reading (Schwally, etc.). In that case the phrase might have some allusion to the well-known promise in Deut., "the place where I shall set My name." This is more natural than a reference to Hosea ii. 19, which is quoted by some.

‡ Some Greek codd. take Baal as fem., others as plur.

§ So LXX.

‖ Heb. reads "and them who bow themselves, who swear, by Jehovah." So LXX. B with "and" before "who swear." But LXX. A omits "and." LXX. Q omits "them who bow themselves." Wellhausen keeps the clause with the exception of "who swear," and so reads (to the end of verse) "them who bow themselves to Jehovah and swear by Milcom."

¶ Or Molech = king. LXX. "by their king." Other Greek versions: Moloch and Melchom. Vulg. Melchom.

** LXX. "His."

†† So LXX. Heb. "sons."

‡‡ Is this some superstitious rite of the idol-worshippers as described in the case of Dagon, 1 Sam. v. 5? Or is it a phrase for breaking into a house, and so parallel to the second clause of the verse? Most interpreters prefer the latter. The idolatrous rites have been left behind. Schwally suggests the original order may have been: "princes and sons of the king, who fill their lord's house full of violence and deceit; and I will visit upon every one that leapeth over the threshold on that day, and upon all that wear foreign raiment."

* The *Second* or New Town: *cf.* 2 Kings xxii. 14, 2 Chron. xxxiv. 22, which state that the prophetess Huldah lived there. *Cf.* Neh. iii. 9, 12, xi. 9.

† The hollow probably between the western and eastern hills, or the upper part of the Tyropœan (Orelli).

‡ Heb. "people of Canaan."

§ נְטִיל, found only here, from נטל, to lift up, and in Isa. xl. 15 to weigh. Still it may have a wider meaning, "all they that carry money" (Davidson).

‖ See above, p. 573.

¶ The Hebrew text and versions here add: "And they shall build houses and not inhabit" (Greek "in them") "and plant vineyards and not drink the wine thereof." But the phrase is a common one (Deut. xxviii. 30; Amos v. 11: *cf.* Micah vi. 15), and while likely to have been inserted by a later hand, is here superfluous, and mars the firmness and edge of Zephaniah's threat.

** For מהר Wellhausen reads ממהר, pt. Pi; but מהר may be a verbal adj.; compare the phrase מהר שלל, Isa. viii. 1.

†† "Dies Iræ, Dies Illa!"

‡‡ Heb. "sho'ah u-mesho'ah." Lit. ruin (or devastation) and destruction.

§§ Some take this first clause of ver. 18 as a gloss. See Schwally *in loco*.

‖‖ Read אף for אך. So LXX., Syr., Wellhausen, Schwally.

¶¶ In vv. 1-3 of chap. ii., wrongly separated from chap. i.: see Davidson.

. . . .* "O people unabashed!† before that ye become as the drifting chaff before the anger of Jehovah come upon you,‡ before there come upon you the day of Jehovah's wrath;§ seek Jehovah, all ye meek of the land who do His ordinance,‖ seek righteousness, seek meekness, peradventure ye may hide yourselves in the day of Jehovah's wrath."

CHAPTER IV.

NINIVE DELENDA.

ZEPHANIAH ii. 4-15.

THERE now come a series of articles on foreign nations, connected with the previous prophecy by the conjunction *for*, and detailing the worldwide judgment which it had proclaimed. But though dated from the same period as that prophecy, *circa* 626, these oracles are best treated by themselves.¶

These oracles originally formed one passage in the well-known Qinah or elegiac measure; but this has suffered sadly both by dilapidation and rebuilding. How mangled the text is may be seen especially from vv. 6 and 14, where the Greek gives us some help in restoring it. The verses (8-11) upon Moab and Ammon cannot be reduced to the metre which both precedes and follows them. Probably, therefore, they are a later addition: nor did Moab and Ammon lie upon the way of the Scythians, who are presumably the invaders pictured by the prophet.*

The poem begins with Philistia and the seacoast, the very path of the Scythian raid.† Evidently the latter is imminent, the Philistine cities are shortly to be taken and the whole land reduced to grass. Across the emptied strip the long hope of Israel springs seaward; but—mark!—not yet with a vision of the isles beyond. The prophet is satisfied with reaching the edge of the Promised Land: "by the sea shall they feed" ‡ their flocks.

> "For Gaza forsaken shall be,
> Ashk'lôn a desert.
> Ashdod—by noon shall they rout her,
> And Ekron be torn up! §
>
> "Ah! woe, dwellers of the sea-shore,
> Folk of Kerēthim.
> The word of Jehovah against thee, Kĕna'an,‖
> Land of the Philistines!"
>
> "And I destroy thee to the last inhabitant,¶
> And Kereth shall become shepherds' cots,**
> And folds for flocks.

*Heb. הִתְקוֹשְׁשׁוּ וָקוֹשׁוּ. A. V. "Gather yourselves together, yea, gather together (קוֹשֵׁשׁ is "to gather straw" or "sticks"—*cf.* Arab. "kash," to sweep up—and Nithp. of the Aram. is to assemble). Orelli: "Crowd and crouch down." Ewald compares Aram. "ḳash," late Heb. קְשַׁשׁ "to grow old," which he believes originally meant "to be withered, grey." Budde suggests בשו התבששו, but, as Davidson remarks, it is not easy to see how this, if once extant, was altered to the present reading.

† נִכְסָף is usually thought to have as its root meaning "to be pale" or "colourless," *i. e.*, either white or black (*Journal of Phil.*, 14, 125), whence כֶּסֶף, "silver" or "the pale metal": hence in the Qal to long for, Job xiv. 15, Ps. xvii. 12; so Ni, Gen. xxxi. 30, Ps. lxxxiv. 3; and here "to be ashamed." But the derivation of the name for silver is quite imaginary, and the colour of shame is red rather than white: *cf.* the mod. Arab, saying, "They are a people that cannot blush; they have no blood in their faces," *i. e.*, shameless. Indeed Schwally says (*in loco*), "Die Bedeutung fahl, blass ist unerweislich." Hence (in spite of the meanings of the Aram. כסף both to lose colour and to be ashamed) a derivation for the Hebrew is more probably to be found in the root "kasaf," to cut off. The Arabic verb which in the classic tongue means to cut a thread or eclipse the sun, is in colloquial Arabic to give a rebuff, refuse a favour, disappoint, shame. In the forms "inkasaf" and "itkasaf" it means to receive a rebuff, be disappointed, then shy or timid, and "kasûf" means shame, shyness (as well as eclipse of the sun), See Spiro's "Arabic-English Vocabulary." In Ps. lxxxiv. נכסף is evidently used of unsatisfied longing (but see Cheyne), which is also the proper meaning of the parallel כלה (*cf.* other passages where כלה is used of still unfulfilled or rebuffed hopes: Job xix. 27, Ps. lxix. 4, cxix. 81, cxliii. 7), So in Ps. xvii. 4 כסף is used of a lion who is longing for, *i. e.* still disappointed in, his prey, and so in Job xiv. 15.

‡ LXX. πρὸ τοῦ γένεσθαι ὑμᾶς ὡς ἄνθος (here in error reading נץ for מץ) παραπορευόμενον, πρὸ τοῦ ἐπελθεῖν ἐφ' ὑμᾶς ὀργὴν κυρίου (last clause omitted by אcl). According to this the Hebrew text, which is obviously disarranged, may be restored to הֲרוֹן יהוה בְּטֶרֶם לֹא־תִהיוּ כַּמֹּץ עֹבֵר בְּטֶרֶם לֹא־יָבֹא עֲלֵיכֶם.

§ This clause Wellhausen deletes. *Cf.* Hexaplar Syriac translation.

‖ LXX. take this also as imperative, "do judgment," and so co-ordinate to the other clauses.

¶ See above, pp. 570 ff.

* Some, however, think the prophet is speaking in prospect of the Chaldean invasion of a few years later. This is not so likely, because he pictures the overthrow of Nineveh as subsequent to the invasion of Philistia, while the Chaldeans accomplished the latter only after Nineveh had fallen.

† According to Herodotus.

‡ Ver. 7, LXX.

§ The measure, as said above, is elegiac: alternate lines long with a rising, and short with a falling, cadence. There is a play upon the names, at least on the first and last—"Gazzah" or "'Azzah 'Azubah"—which in English we might reproduce by the use of Spenser's word for "dreary": "For Gaza ghastful shall be." "Ekron te'aker." LXX. Ἀκκαρων ἐκριζωθήσεται (B), ἐκριφήσεται (A). In the second line we have a slighter assonance, 'Ashkelōn lishemamah. In the third the verb is יְגָרְשׁוּהָ; Bacher ("Z. A. T. W.," 1891, 185 ff.) points out that גרש is not used of cities, but of their populations or of individual men, and suggests (from Abulwalid) יירשוה, "shall possess her," as "a plausible emendation." Schwally (*ibid.*, 260) prefers to alter to יְשָׁרְשׁוּהָ; with the remark that this is not only a good parallel to תעקר, but suits the LXX. ἐκριφήσεται.—On the expression "by noon" see Davidson, "N. H. and Z.," Appendix, Note 2, where he quotes a parallel expression, in the Senjerli inscription, of Asarhaddon: that he took Memphis by midday or in half a day (Schrader). This suits the use of the phrase in Jer. xv. 8, where it is parallel to "suddenly."

‖ Canaan omitted by Wellhausen, who reads עליך for עליכם. But as the metre requires a larger number of syllables in the first line of each couplet than in the second, Kena'an should probably remain. The difficulty is the use of Canaan as synonymous with "Land of the Philistines." Nowhere else in the Old Testament is it expressly applied to the coast south of Carmel, though it is so used in the Egyptian inscriptions, and even in the Old Testament in a sense which covers this as well as other lowlying parts of Palestine.

¶ An odd long line, either the remains of two, or perhaps we should take the two previous lines as one, omitting Canaan.

** So LXX.: Hebrew text "and the sea-coast shall become dwellings, cots (כְּרֹת) of shepherds." But the pointing and meaning of כרת are both conjectural, and the "sea-coast" has probably fallen by mistake into this verse from the next. On Kereth and Kerethim as names for Philistia and the Philistines see "Hist. Geog.," p. 171.

And the coast * for the remnant of Judah's house ;
By the sea † shall they feed.
In Ashkelon's houses at even shall they couch ;
. . . ‡
For Jehovah their God shall visit them,
And turn their captivity.§

There comes now an oracle upon Moab and Ammon (vv. 8-11). As already said, it is not in the elegiac measure which precedes and follows it, while other features cast a doubt upon its authenticity. Like other oracles on the same peoples, this denounces the loud-mouthed arrogance of the sons of Moab and Ammon.

"I have heard‖ the reviling of Moab and the insults of the sons of Ammon, who have reviled My people and vaunted themselves upon their ¶ border. Wherefore as I live, saith Jehovah of Hosts, God of Israel, Moab shall become as Sodom, and Ammon's sons as Gomorrah—the possession ** of nettles, and saltpits,†† and a desolation forever; the remnant of My people shall spoil them, and the rest of My nation possess them. This to them for their arrogance, because they reviled, and vaunted themselves against, the people of ‡‡ Jehovah of Hosts. Jehovah showeth Himself terrible §§ against them, for He hath made lean ‖‖ all gods of earth, that all the coasts of the nations may worship Him, every man from his own place."¶¶

The next oracle is a very short one (ver. 12) upon Egypt, which after its long subjection to Ethiopic dynasties is called, not Misraim, but Kush, or Ethiopia. The verse follows on naturally to ver. 7, but is not reducible to the elegiac measure.

Also ye, O Kushites, are the slain of My sword.***

The Elegiac measure is now renewed ††† in an oracle against Assyria, the climax and front of heathendom (vv. 13-15). It must have been written before 608; there is no reason to doubt that it is Zephaniah's.

"And may He stretch out His hand against the North,
And destroy Asshur ;
And may He turn Nineveh to desolation,
Dry as the desert.

* LXX. adds "of the sea." So Wellhausen, but unnecessarily and improbably for phonetic reasons, as "sea" has to be read in the next line.

† So Wellhausen, reading for עֲל־הַיָּם עֲלֵיהֶם.

‡ Some words must have fallen out, for *first* a short line is required here by the metre, and *second* the LXX. have some additional words, which, however, give us no help to what the lost line was: ἀπὸ προσώπου υἱῶν Ἰούδα.

§ As stated above, there is no conclusive reason against the pre-exilic date of this expression.

‖ *Cf.* Isa. xvi. 6.

¶ LXX. "My."

** Doubtful word, not occurring elsewhere.

†† Heb. singular.

‡‡ LXX. omits "the people of."

§§ LXX. "maketh Himself manifest," נראה for נורא.

‖‖ ἅπαξ λεγόμενον. The passive of the verb means "to grow lean" (Isa. xvii. 4).

¶¶ מקום has probably here the sense which it has in a few other passages of the Old Testament, and in Arabic, of "sacred place."

Many will share Schwally's doubts (p. 192) about the authenticity of ver. 11; nor, as Wellhausen points out, does its prediction of the conversion of the heathen agree with ver. 12, which devotes them to destruction. Ver. 12 follows naturally on to ver. 7.

*** Wellhausen reads "His sword," to agree with the next verse. Perhaps חרבי is an abbreviation for יהוה חרב.

††† See Budde, "Z. A. T. W.," 1882, 25.

And herds shall couch in her midst,
Every beast of . . . .*
Yea, pelican and bittern † shall roost on the capitals,
The owl shall hoot in the window,
The raven on the doorstep.
. . . . . ‡

"Such is the City, the Jubilant,
She that sitteth at ease,
She that saith in her heart, I am
And there is none else!
How hath she become desolation!
A lair of beasts.
Everyone passing by her hisses,
Shakes his hand.

The essence of these oracles is their clear confidence in the fall of Nineveh. From 652, when Egypt revolted from Assyria, and, Assurbanipal notwithstanding, began to push northward, men must have felt, throughout all Western Asia, that the great empire upon the Tigris was beginning to totter. This feeling was strengthened by the Scythian invasion, and after 625 it became a moral certainty that Nineveh would fall §—which happened in 607-6. These are the feelings, 625 to 608, which Zephaniah's oracles reflect. We can hardly over-estimate what they meant. Not a man was then alive who had ever known anything else than the greatness and the glory of Assyria. It was two hundred and thirty years since Israel first felt the weight of her arms.‖ It was more than a hundred since her hosts had swept through Palestine,¶ and for at least fifty her supremacy had been accepted by Judah. Now the colossus began to totter. As she had menaced, so she was menaced. The ruins with which for nigh three centuries she had strewn Western Asia—to these were to be reduced her own impregnable and ancient glory. It was the close of an epoch.

CHAPTER V.

SO AS BY FIRE.

ZEPHANIAH iii.

THE third chapter of the Book of Zephaniah consists ** of two sections, of which only the first, vv. 1-13, is a genuine work of the prophet;

* Heb. reads "a nation," and Wellhausen translates "ein buntes Gemisch von Volk." LXX. "beasts of the earth."

† קאת, a water-bird according to Deut. xiv. 17, Lev. xi. 18, mostly taken as "pelican"; so R. V., A. V. "cormorant." קִפֹּד has usually been taken from קפד, to draw together, therefore "hedgehog" or "porcupine." But the other animals mentioned here are birds, and it is birds which would naturally roost on capitals. Therefore "bittern" is the better rendering (Hitzig, Cheyne). The name is onomatopœic. *Cf.* Eng. butter-dump. LXX. translates "chameleons and hedgehogs."

‡ Heb.: "a voice shall sing in the window, desolation on the threshold, for He shall uncover the cedar-work." LXX. καὶ θηρία φωνήσει ἐν τοῖς διορύγμασιν αὐτῆς, κόρακες ἐν τοῖς πυλῶσιν αὐτῆς, διότι κέδρος τὸ ἀνάστημα αὐτῆς: Wild beasts shall sound in her excavations, ravens in her porches, because (the) cedar is her height. For קול, "voice," Wellhausen reads כוס, "owl," and with the LXX. ערב, "raven," for חרב, "desolation." The last two words are left untranslated above. אַרְזָה occurs only here and is usually taken to mean cedar-work; but it might be pointed "her" cedar. ערה, "he," or "one, has stripped the cedar-work."

§ See above, p. 564.

‖ At the battle of Karkar, 854.

¶ Under Tiglath-Pileser in 734.

** See above, p. 571.

while the second, vv. 14-20, is a later epilogue such as we found added to the genuine prophecies of Amos. It is written in the large hope and brilliant temper of the Second Isaiah, saying no word of Judah's sin or judgment, but predicting her triumphant deliverance out of all her afflictions.

In a second address to his City (vv. 1-13) Zephaniah strikes the same notes as he did in his first. He spares the king, but denounces the ruling and teaching classes. Jerusalem's princes are lions, her judges wolves, her prophets braggarts, her priests pervert the law, her wicked have no shame. He repeats the proclamation of a universal doom. But the time is perhaps later. Judah has disregarded the many threats. She will not accept the Lord's discipline; and while in chap. i.-ii. 3 Zephaniah had said that the meek and righteous might escape the doom, he now emphatically affirms that all proud and impenitent men shall be removed from Jerusalem, and a humble people be left to her, righteous and secure. There is the same moral earnestness as before, the same absence of all other elements of prophecy than the ethical. Before we ask the reason and emphasise the beauty of this austere gospel, let us see the exact words of the address. There are the usual marks of poetic diction in it —elliptic phrases, the frequent absence of the definite article, archaic forms, and an order of the syntax different from that which obtains in prose. But the measure is difficult to determine, and must be printed as prose. The echo of the elegiac rhythm in the opening is more apparent than real: it is not sustained beyond the first verse. Verses 9 and 10 are relegated to a footnote, as very probably an intrusion, and disturbance of the argument.

"Woe, rebel and unclean, city of oppression! * She listens to no voice, she accepts no discipline, in Jehovah she trusts not, nor has drawn near to her God.

"Her princes in her midst are roaring lions; her judges evening wolves,† they . . . .‡ not till morning; her prophets are braggarts and traitors; her priests have profaned what is holy and done violence to the Law.§ Jehovah is righteous in the midst of her, He does no wrong. Morning by morning He brings His judgment to light: He does not let Himself fail *—but the wicked man knows no shame. I have cut off nations, their turrets are ruined; I have laid waste their broad streets, till no one passes upon them; destroyed are their cities, without a man, without a dweller.† I said, Surely she will fear Me, she will accept punishment,‡ and all that I have visited upon her§ shall never vanish from her eyes.‖ But *only* the more zealously have they corrupted all their doings.¶

"Wherefore wait ye for Me—oracle of Jehovah—*wait* for the day of My rising to testify, for 'tis My fixed purpose ** to sweep nations together, to collect kingdoms, to pour upon them . . .†† all the heat of My wrath—yea, with the fire of My jealousy shall the whole earth be consumed.‡‡

"In that day thou shalt not be ashamed §§ of all thy deeds, by which thou hast rebelled against Me: for then will I turn out of the midst of thee all who exult with *that* arrogance of thine,‖‖ and thou wilt not again vaunt thyself upon the Mount of My Holiness. But I will leave in thy midst a people humble and poor, and they shall trust in the name of Jehovah. The Remnant of Israel shall do no evil, and shall not speak falsehood, and no fraud shall be found in their mouth, but they shall pasture and they shall couch, with none to make them afraid."

Such is the simple and austere gospel of Zephaniah. It is not to be overlooked amid the lavish and gorgeous promises which other prophets have poured around it, and by ourselves, too, it is needed in our often unscrupulous enjoyment of the riches of grace that are in Christ Jesus. A thorough purgation, the re-

* Heb. "the city the oppressor." The two participles in the first clause are not predicates to the noun and adjective of the second (Schwally), but vocatives, though without the article, after הוֹי.

† LXX. "wolves of Arabia."

‡ The verb left untranslated, גרמו, is quite uncertain in meaning. גרם is a root common to the Semitic languages and seems to mean originally "to cut off," while the noun גרם is "a bone." In Num. xxiv. 8 the Piel of the verb used with another word for bone means "to gnaw, munch." (The only other passage where it is used, Ezek. xxiii. 34, is corrupt.) So some take it here: "they do not gnaw bones till morning," *i. e.*, devour all at once; but this is awkward, and Schwally (198) has proposed to omit the negative, "they do gnaw bones till morning," yet in that case surely the impf. and not the perf. tense would have been used. The LXX. render "they do not leave over," and it has been attempted, though inconclusively, to derive this meaning from that of "cutting off," *i. e.*, "laying aside" (the Arabic Form II. means, however, "to leave behind"). Another line of meaning perhaps promises more. In Aram. the verb means "to be the cause of anything, to bring about," and perhaps contains the idea of "deciding" (Levy *sub voce* compares κρίνω "cerno); in Arab. it means, among other things, "to commit a crime, be guilty," but in mod. Arabic "to fine." Now it is to be noticed that here the expression is used of "judges," and it may be there is an intentional play upon the double possibility of meaning in the root.

§ Ezek. xxii. 26: "Her priests have done violence to My Law and have profaned My holy things; they have put no difference between the holy and profane, between the clean and the unclean." *Cf.* Jer. ii. 8.

* Schwally by altering the accents: "morning by morning He giveth forth His judgment: no day does He fail.

† On this ver. 6 see above, p. 571. It is doubtful.

‡ Or "discipline.

§ Wellhausen: "that which I have commanded her." *Cf.* Job xxxvi. 23; 2 Chron. xxxvi. 23; Ezra i. 2.

‖ So LXX., reading מְעֵינֶיהָ for the Heb. מְעוֹנָהּ, "her dwelling."

¶ A frequent phrase of Jeremiah's.

** משפטי, decree, ordinance, decision.

†† Heb. "My anger." LXX. omits.

‡‡ That is to say, the prophet returns to that general judgment of the whole earth, with which in his first discourse he had already threatened Judah. He threatens her with it again in this eighth verse, because, as he has said in the preceding ones, all other warnings have failed. The eighth verse therefore follows naturally upon the seventh, just as naturally as in Amos iv. ver. 12, introduced by the same לָכֵן as here, follows its predecessors. The next two verses of the text, however, describe an opposite result: instead of the destruction of the heathen, they picture their conversion, and it is only in the eleventh verse that we return to the main subject of the passage, Judah herself, who is represented (in harmony with the close of Zephaniah's first discourse) as reduced to a righteous and pious remnant. Vv. 9 and 10 are therefore obviously a later insertion, and we pass to the eleventh verse. Vv. 9 and 10: "For then" (this has no meaning after ver. 8) "will I give to the peoples a pure lip" (elliptic phrase: "turn to the peoples a pure lip"—*i. e.*, "turn their" evil lip into "a pure lip": pure = "picked out, select, excellent," *cf.* Isa. xlix. 2), "that they may all of them call upon the name of the Lord, that they may serve Him with one consent" (Heb. "shoulder," LXX. "yoke"). From beyond the rivers of Ethiopia" —there follows a very obscure phrase, עֲתָרַי בַּת־פּוּצַי, "suppliants (?) of the daughter of My dispersed," but Ewald "of the daughter of Phut—they shall bring Mine offering."

§§ Wellhausen "despair."

‖‖ Heb. "the jubilant ones of thine arrogance."

moval of the wicked, the sparing of the honest and the meek; insistence only upon the rudiments of morality and religion; faith in its simplest form of trust in a righteous God, and character in its basal elements of meekness and truth,—these and these alone survive the judgment. Why does Zephaniah never talk of the Love of God, of the Divine Patience, of the Grace that has spared and will spare wicked hearts if only it can touch them to penitence? Why has he no call to repent, no appeal to the wicked to turn from the evil of their ways? We have already seen part of the answer. Zephaniah stands too near to judgment and the last things. Character is fixed, the time for pleading is past; there remains only the separation of bad men from the good. It is the same standpoint (at least ethically) as that of Christ's visions of the Judgment. Perhaps also an austere gospel was required by the fashionable temper of the day. The generation was loud and arrogant; it gilded the future to excess, and knew no shame.* The true prophet was forced to reticence; he must make his age feel the desperate earnestness of life, and that salvation is by fire. For the gorgeous future of its unsanctified hopes he must give it this severe, almost mean, picture of a poor and humble folk, hardly saved but at last at peace.

The permanent value of such a message is proved by the thirst which we feel even to-day for the clear, cold water of its simple promises. Where a glaring optimism prevails, and the future is preached with a loud assurance, where many find their only religious enthusiasm in the resurrection of mediæval ritual or the singing of stirring and gorgeous hymns of second-hand imagery, how needful to be recalled to the earnestness and severity of life, to the simplicity of the conditions of salvation, and to their ethical, not emotional, character! Where sensationalism has so invaded religion, how good to hear the sober insistence upon God's daily commonplaces—"morning by morning He bringeth forth His judgment to light"—and to know that the acceptance of discipline is what prevails with Him. Where national reform is vaunted and the progress of education, how well to go back to a prophet who ignored all the great reforms of his day that he might impress his people with the indispensableness of humility and faith. Where Churches have such large ambitions for themselves, how necessary to hear that the future is destined for "a poor folk," the meek and the honest. Where men boast that their religion—Bible, Creed, or Church—has undertaken to save them, "vaunting themselves on the Mount of My Holiness," how needful to hear salvation placed upon character and a very simple trust in God.

But, on the other hand, is any one in despair at the darkness and cruelty of this life, let him hear how Zephaniah proclaims that, though all else be fraud, "the Lord is righteous in the midst" of us, "He doth not let Himself fail," that the resigned heart and the humble, the just, and the pure heart, is imperishable, and in the end there is at least peace.

Epilogue.

Verses 14-20.

Zephaniah's prophecy was fulfilled. The Day of the Lord came, and the people met their judgment. The Remnant survived—"a folk poor and humble." To them, in the new estate and temper of their life, came a new song from God—perhaps it was nearly a hundred years after Zephaniah had spoken—and they added it to his prophecies. It came in with wonderful fitness, for it was the song of the redeemed, whom he had foreseen, and it tuned his book, severe and simple, to the full harmony of prophecy, so that his book might take a place in the great choir of Israel—the diapason of that full salvation which no one man, but only the experience of centuries, could achieve.

"Sing out, O daughter of Zion! shout aloud, O Israel! Rejoice and be jubilant with all thy* heart, daughter of Jerusalem! Jehovah hath set aside thy judgments,† He hath turned thy foes. King of Israel, Jehovah is in thy midst; thou shalt not see‡ evil any more.

"In that day it shall be said to Jerusalem, Fear not, O Zion, let not thy hands droop! Jehovah, thy God, in the midst of thee is mighty;§ He will save, He will rejoice over thee with joy, He will make new‖ His love, He will exult over thee with singing.

"The scattered of thy congregation¶ have I gathered—thine ** are they, . . .†† reproach upon her. Behold, I am about to do all for thy sake at that time,‡‡ and I will rescue the lame and the outcast will I bring in,§§ and I will make them for renown and fame whose shame is in the

* See vv. 4, 5, 11.

* Heb. "the."

† מִשְׁפָּטַיִךְ. But Wellhausen reads מְשׁוֹפְטַיִךְ, thine adversaries: *cf.* Job ix. 15.

‡ Reading תִּרְאִי (with LXX., Wellhausen and Schwally) for תִּירְאִי of the Hebrew text, "fear."

§ Lit. "hero, mighty man."

‖ Heb. "will be silent in, יַחֲרִישׁ, but not in harmony with the next clause. LXX. and Syr. render "will make new," which translates יְחַדֵּשׁ, a form that does not elsewhere occur, though that is no objection to finding it in Zephaniah, or יְחַדֵּשׁ. Hitzig: "He makes new things in His love." Buhl: "He renews His love." Schwally suggests יחדה, "He rejoices in His love.

¶ LXX. "In the days of thy festival," which it takes with the previous verse. The Heb. construction is ungrammatical, though not unprecedented—the construct state before a preposition. Besides נוגי is obscure in meaning. It is a Ni. pt. for נוגה from יגה, "to be sad": *cf.* the Pi. in Lam. iii. 33. But the Hiphil הוגה in 2 Sam. xx. 13, followed (as here) by מן, means "to thrust away from," and that is probably the sense here.

** LXX. "thine oppressed" in acc. governed by the preceding verb, which in LXX. begins the verse.

†† The Heb., מַשְׂאֵת, "burden of," is unintelligible. Wellhausen proposes מִשְׂאֵת עֲלֵיהֶם.

‡‡ This rendering is only a venture in the almost impossible task of restoring the text of the clause. As it stands the Heb. runs, "Behold, I am about to do," or "deal, with thine oppressors" (which Hitzig and Ewald accept). Schwally points מְעַנַּיִךְ (active) as a passive, מְעֻנַּיִךְ, "thine oppressed." LXX. has *ἰδοὺ ἐγὼ ποιῶ ἐν σοὶ ἕνεκεν σοῦ*, *i. e.*, it read לְמַעֲנֵךְ אִתָּךְ. Following its suggestion we might read אֶת־כֹּל לְמַעֲנֵךְ, and so get the above translation.

§§ Micah iv. 6.

whole earth.* In that time I will bring you in,† even in the time that I gather you.‡ For I will set you for fame and renown among all the peoples of the earth, when I turn again your captivity before your eyes, saith Jehovah."§

NAHUM.

"Woe to the City of Blood,
All of her guile, robbery-full, ceaseless rapine!

"Hark the whip,
And the rumbling of wheels!
Horses at the gallop,
And the rattling dance of the chariot!
Cavalry at the charge,
Flash of sabres, and lightning of lances!"

CHAPTER VI.

THE BOOK OF NAHUM.

THE Book of Nahum consists of a double title and three odes. The title runs "Oracle of Nineveh: Book of the Vision of Nahum the Elḳoshite." The three odes, eager and passionate pieces, are all of them apparently vibrant to the impending fall of Assyria. The first, chap. i. with the possible inclusion of chap. ii. 2,‖ is general and theological, affirming God's power of vengeance and the certainty of the overthrow of His enemies. The second, chap. ii. with the omission of ver. 2,¶ and the third, chap. iii., can hardly be disjoined; they both present a vivid picture of the siege, the storm, and the spoiling of Nineveh.

The introductory questions, which title and contents start, are in the main three: 1. The position of Elkôsh, to which the title assigns the prophet; 2. The authenticity of chap. i.; 3. The date of chaps. ii., iii.: to which siege of Nineveh do they refer?

1. THE POSITION OF ELḲÔSH.

The title calls Nahum the Elkôshite—that is, native or citizen of Elḳôsh.** Three positions have been claimed for this place, which is not mentioned elsewhere in the Bible.

The first we take is the modern Al-Ḳûsh, a town still flourishing about twenty-four miles to the north of the site of Nineveh,†† with "no

* This rendering (Ewald's) is doubtful. The verse concludes with "in the whole earth their shame." But בשתם may be a gloss. LXX. takes it as a verb with the next verse.

† LXX. "do good to you"; perhaps אטיב for אביא.

‡ So Heb. literally, but the construction is very awkward. Perhaps we should read "in that time I will gather you."

§ "Before your eyes," *i. e.*, in your lifetime. It is doubtful whether ver. 20 is original to the passage. For it is simply a variation on ver. 19, and it has more than one impossible reading: see previous note, and for שבותיכם for שבותכם.

‖ In the English version, but in the Hebrew chap. ii. vv, 1 and 3; for the Hebrew text divides chap. i. from chap. ii. differently from the English, which follows the Greek. The Hebrew begins chap. ii. with what in the English and Greek is the fifteenth verse of chap. i.: "Behold, upon the mountains," etc.

¶ In the English text, but in the Hebrew with the omission of vv. 1 and 3: see previous note.

** Other meanings have been suggested, but are impossible.

†† So it lies on Billerbeck's map in Delitzsch and Haupt's "Beiträge zur Assyr.," III. Smith's "Bible Dictionary" puts it at only 2 m. N. of Mosul.

fragments of antiquity" about it, but possessing a "simple plaster box," which Jews, Christians, and Mohammedans alike reverence as the tomb of Nahum.* There is no evidence that Al-Ḳûsh, a name of Arabic form, is older than the Arab period, while the tradition which locates the tomb there is not found before the sixteenth century of our era, but on the contrary Nahum's grave was pointed out to Benjamin of Tudela in 1165 at 'Ain Japhata, on the south of Babylon.† The tradition that the prophet lived and died at Al-Ḳûsh is therefore due to the similarity of the name to that of Nahum's Elḳôsh, as well as to the fact that Nineveh was the subject of his prophesying.‡ In his book there is no trace of proof for the assertion that Nahum was a descendant of the ten tribes exiled in 721 to the region to the north of Al-Ḳûsh. He prophesies for Judah alone. Nor does he show any more knowlege of Nineveh than her ancient fame must have scattered to the limits of the world.§ We might as well argue from chap. iii. 8-10 that Nahum had visited Thebes of Egypt.

The second tradition of the position of Elkôsh is older. In his commentary on Nahum Jerome says that in his day it still existed, a petty village of Galilee, under the name of Helkesei,‖ or Elkese, and apparently with an established reputation as the town of Nahum.¶ But the book itself bears no symptom of its author's connection with Galilee, and although it was quite possible for a prophet of that period to have lived there, it is not very probable.**

A third tradition places Elḳôsh in the south of Judah. A Syriac version of the accounts of the prophets, which are ascribed to Epiphanius,†† describes Nahum as "of Elkôsh beyond Bêt Gabrê, of the tribe of Simeon"; ‡‡ and it may be

* Layard, "Nineveh and its Remains," I. 233, 3d ed., 1849.

† Bohn's "Early Travels in Palestine," p. 102.

‡ Just as they show Jonah's tomb at Nineveh itself.

§ See above, p. 565.

‖ Just as in Micah's case Jerome calls his birthplace Moresheth by the adjective Morasthi, so with equal carelessness he calls Elkosh by the adjective with the article Ha-elḳoshi, the Elḳoshite. Jerome's words are: "Quum Elcese usque hodie in Galilea viculus sit, parvus quidem et vix ruinis veterum ædificiorum indicans vestigia, sed tamen notus Judæis et mihi quoque a circumducente monstratus" (in "Prol. ad Prophetiam Nachumi"). In the "Onomasticon" Jerome gives the name as Elcese, Eusebius as 'Ελκεσέ, but without defining the position.

¶ This Elkese has been identified, though not conclusively, with the modern El Kauze near Ramieh, some seven miles W. of Tibnin.

** *Cf.* Kuenen, § 75, n. 5; Davidson, p. 12 (2).

Capernaum, which the Textus Receptus gives as Καπερναούμ, but most authorities as Καφαρναούμ and the Peshitto as Kaphar Nahum, obviously means Village of Nahum, and both Hitzig and Knobel looked for Elḳosh in it. See "Hist. Geog.," p. 456.

Against the Galilean origin of Nahum it is usual to appeal to John vii. 52: "Search and see that out of Galilee ariseth no prophet;" but this is not decisive, for Jonah came out of Galilee.

†† Though perhaps falsely.

‡‡ This occurs in the Syriac translation of the Old Testament by Paul of Tella, 617 A. D., in which the notices of Epiphanius (Bishop of Constantia in Cyprus, A. D. 367) or Pseudepiphanius are attached to their respective prophets. It was first communicated to the "Z. D. P. V.," I. 122 ff., by Dr. Nestle: *cf.* "Hist. Geog.," p. 231, n. 1. The previously known readings of the passage were either geographically impossible, as "He came from Elkesei beyond Jordan, towards Begabar of the tribe of Simeon" (so in Paris edition, 1622, of the works of St. Epiphanius, Vol. II. p. 147: *cf.* Migne, "Patr. Gr.," XLIII. 409); or based on a misreading of the title of the book: "Nahum son of Elkesaios was of Jesbe of the tribe of Simeon"; or indefinable: "Nahum was of Elkesem beyond Betabarem of the tribe of Simeon"; these last two from recensions of Epiphanius published in 1855 by Tischendorf (quoted by Davidson, p. 13). In the Στιχηρὸν τῶν ΙΒ′ Προφητῶν καὶ 'Ισαιοῦ; attributed to Hesychius, Presbyter of Jerusalem, who died 428 or 433 (Migne, "Patrologia Gr.," XCIII.

noted that Cyril of Alexandria says * that Elkese was a village in the country of the Jews. This tradition is superior to the first in that there is no apparent motive for its fabrication, and to the second in so far as Judah was at the time of Nahum a much more probable home for a prophet than Galilee; nor does the book give any references except such as might be made by a Judean.† No modern place-name, however, can be suggested with any certainty as the echo of Elḳôsh. Umm Lâkis, which has been proved not to be Lachish, contains the same radicals, and some six and a quarter miles east from Beit-Jibrin, at the upper end of the Wady es Sur, there is an ancient well with the name Bir el Kûs.‡

2. THE AUTHENTICITY OF CHAP. I.

Till recently no one doubted that the three chapters formed a unity. "Nahum's prophecy," said Kuenen in 1889, "is a whole." In 1891 § Cornill affirmed that no questions of authenticity arose in regard to the book; and in 1892 Wellhausen saw in chap. i. an introduction leading "in no awkward way to the proper subject of the prophecy."

Meanwhile, however, Bickell,‖ discovering what he thought to be the remains of an alphabetic Psalm in chap. i. 1-7, attempted to reconstruct throughout chaps. i.-ii. 3 twenty-two verses, each beginning with a successive letter of the alphabet. And, following this, Gunkel in 1893 produced a more full and plausible reconstruction of the same scheme.¶ By radical emendations of the text, by excision of what he believes to be glosses, and by altering the order of many of the verses, Gunkel seeks to produce twenty-three distichs, twenty of which begin with the successive letters of the alphabet, two are wanting, while in the first three letters of the twenty-third, שבי, he finds very probably the name of the author, Shobai or Shobi.* He takes this ode, therefore, to be an eschatological Psalm of the later Judaism, which from its theological bearing has been thought suitable as an introduction to Nahum's genuine prophecies.

The text of chaps. i.-ii. 4 has been badly mauled and is clamant for reconstruction of some kind. As it lies, there are traces of an alphabetical arrangement as far as the beginning of ver. 9,† and so far Gunkel's changes are comparatively simple. Many of his emendations are in themselves, and apart from the alphabetic scheme, desirable. They get rid of difficulties and improve the poetry of the passage.‡ His reconstruction is always clever and as a whole forms a wonderfully spirited poem. But to have produced good or poetical Hebrew is not conclusive proof of having recovered the original, and there are obvious objections to the process. Several of the proposed changes are unnatural in themselves and unsupported by anything except the exigencies of the scheme; for example, *2b* and *3a* are dismissed as a gloss only because, if they be retained, the "Aleph" verse is two bars too long. The gloss, Gunkel thinks, was introduced to mitigate the absoluteness of the declaration that Jehovah is a God of wrath and vengeance; but this is not obvious and would hardly have been alleged apart from the needs of the alphabet scheme. In order to find a "Daleth," it is quite arbitrary to say that the first אמלל in *4b* is redundant in face of the second, and that a word beginning with "Daleth" originally filled its place, but was removed because it was a rare or difficult word! The re-arrangement of 7 and *8a* is very clever, and reads as if it were right; but the next effort, to get a verse beginning with "Lamed," is of the kind by which anything might be proved. These, however, are nothing to the difficulties which vv. 9-14 and chap. ii. 1, 3, present to an alphabetic scheme, or to the means which Gunkel takes to surmount them. He has to re-arrange the order of the verses,§ and of the words within the verses. The distichs beginning with "Nun" and "Ḳoph" are wanting, or at least undecipherable. To provide one with initial "Resh" the interjection has to be removed from the opening of chap. ii. 1, and the verse made to begin with רגלי and to run thus: "the feet of him that bringeth good news on the mountains; behold him that publisheth peace." Other unlikely changes will be noticed when we come to the translation. Here we may ask the question: if the passage was originally alphabetic, that is, furnished with so fixed and easily recognised a

1357), it is said that Nahum was ἀπὸ Ἐλκεσεὶν (Helcesin) πέραν τοῦ τηνβαρεὶν ἐκ φυλῆς Συμεών; to which has been added a note from Theophylact, Ἐλκασαῒ πέραν τοῦ Ἰορδάνου εἰς Βιγαβρὶ.

* Ad Nahum i. 1 (Migne, "Patr. Gr.," LXXI. 780): Κώμη δὲ αὕτη πάντως ποῦ τῆς Ἰουδαίων χώρας.

† The selection Bashan, Carmel, and Lebanon (i. 4), does not prove northern authorship.

‡ אֶלְקוֹשׁ may be (1) a theophoric name = Ḳosh is God; and Ḳosh might then be the Edomite deity קוס whose name is spelt with a Shin on the Assyrian monuments (Baethgen, "Beiträge z. Semit. Religionsgeschichte," p. 11; Schrader, "K. A. T." pp. 150, 613), and who is probably the same as the Arab deity Kais (Baethgen, *id.*, p. 108); and this would suit a position in the south of Judah, in which region we find the majority of place-names compounded with אל. Or else (2) the א is prosthetic, as in the place-names אכזיב on the Phœnician coast, אכשף in Southern Canaan, אשדוד, etc. In this case we might find its equivalent in the form לְקוֹשׁ (*cf.* כזיב אכזיב); but no such form is now extant or recorded at any previous period. The form Lâḳis would not suit. On Bir el Kûs see Robinson, "B. R.," III. p. 14, and Guérin, "Judée," III. p. 341. Bir el Ḳûs means Well of the Bow, or, according to Guérin, of the Arch, from ruins that stand by it. The position, *east* of Beit-Jibrin, is unsuitable; for the early Christian texts quoted in the previous note fix it *beyond*, presumably south or southwest of Beit-Jibrin, and in the tribe of Simeon. The error "tribe of Simeon" does not matter, for the same fathers place Bethzecharias, the alleged birthplace of Habakkuk, there.

§ "Einleitung," 1st ed.

‖ Who seems to have owed the hint to a quotation by Delitzsch on Psalm ix. from G. Frohnmeyer to the effect that there were traces of "alphabetic" verses in chap i., at least in vv. 3-7. See Bickell's "Beiträge zur Semit. Metrik," Separatabdruck, Wien, 1894.

¶ "Z. A. T. W.," 1893, pp. 223 ff.

* *Cf.* Ezra ii. 42; Neh. vii. 45; 2 Sam. xvii. 27.

† Ver. 1 is title; 2 begins with א; ב is found in בסופה, *3b*; ג in גוער, 4; ד is wanting—Bickell proposes to substitute a New-Hebrew word דצק, Gunkel דאב, for אמלל, *4b*: ה in הרים, *5a*; ו in ותשא, *5b*; ז by removing לפני of ver. *6a* to the end of the clause (and reading it there לפניו), and so leaving זעמו as the first word; ח in חמתו in *6b*; ט in טוב, *7a*; י by eliding ו from וידע, *7b*; כ in כלה, 8; ל is wanting, though Gunkel seeks to supply it by taking *9c*, beginning לא, with *9b*, before *9a*; מ begins *9a*.

‡ See below in the translation.

§ As thus: 9 *a*, 11 *b*, 12 (but unintelligible), 10, 13, 14, ii. 1, 3.

frame, why has it so fallen to pieces? And again, if it has so fallen to pieces, is it possible that it can be restored? The many arbitrarinesses of Gunkel's able essay would seem to imply that it is not. Dr. Davidson says: "Even if it should be assumed that an alphabetical poem lurks under chap. i., the attempt to restore it, just as in Psalm x., can never be more than an academic exercise."

Little is to be learned from the language. Wellhausen, who makes no objection to the genuineness of the passage, thinks that about ver. 7 we begin to catch the familiar dialect of the Psalms. Gunkel finds a want of originality in the language, with many touches that betray connection not only with the Psalms but with late eschatological literature. But when we take one by one the clauses of chap. i., we discover very few parallels with the Psalms, which are not at the same time parallels with Jeremiah's or some earlier writings. That the prophecy is vague, and with much of the air of the later eschatology about it, is no reason for removing it from an age in which we have already seen prophecy beginning to show the same apocalyptic temper.* Gunkel denies any reference in ver. 9*b* to the approaching fall of Nineveh, although that is seen by Kuenen, Wellhausen, König, and others, and he omits ver. 11*a*, in which most read an allusion to Sennacherib.

Therefore, while it is possible that a later poem has been prefixed to the genuine prophecies of Nahum, and the first chapter supplies many provocations to belief in such a theory, this has not been proved, and the able essays of proof have much against them. The question is open.†

3. The Date of Chaps. II. and III.

We turn now to the date of the Book, apart from this prologue. It was written after a great overthrow of the Egyptian Thebes ‡ and when the overthrow of Nineveh was imminent. Now Thebes had been devastated by Assurbanipal about 664 (we know of no later overthrow), and Nineveh fell finally about 607. Nahum flourished, then, somewhere between 664 and 607.§ Some critics, feeling in his description of the fall of Thebes the force of a recent impression, have placed his prophesying immediately after that, or about 660.‖ But this is too far away from the fall of Nineveh. In 660 the power of Assyria was unthreatened. Nor is 652, the year of the revolt of Babylon, Egypt, and the princes of Palestine, a more likely date.¶ For although in that year Assyrian supremacy ebbed from Egypt never to return, Assurbanipal quickly reduced Elam, Babylon, and all Syria. Nahum, on the other hand, represents the very centre of the empire as threatened. The land of Assyria is apparently already invaded (iii. 13, etc.). Nineveh, if not invested, must immediately be so, and that by forces too great for resistance. Her mixed populace already show signs of breaking up. Within, as without, her doom is sealed. All this implies not only the advance of an enormous force upon Nineveh, but the reduction of her people to the last stage of hopelessness. Now, as we have seen,* Assyria proper was thrice overrun. The Scythians poured across her about 626, but there is no proof that they threatened Nineveh.† A little after Assurbanipal's death in 625, the Medes under King Phraortes invaded Assyria, but Phraortes was slain and his son Kyaxares called away by an invasion of his own country. Herodotus says that this was after he had defeated the Assyrians in a battle and had begun the siege of Nineveh,‡ but before he had succeeded in reducing the city. After a time he subdued or assimilated the Scythians, and then investing Nineveh once more, about 607, in two years he took and destroyed her.

To which of these two sieges by Kyaxares are we to assign the Book of Nahum? Hitzig, Kuenen, Cornill, and others incline to the first on the ground that Nahum speaks of the yoke of Assyria as still heavy on Judah, though about to be lifted. They argue that by 608, when King Josiah had already felt himself free enough to extend his reforms into Northern Israel, and dared to dispute Necho's passage across Esdraelon, the Jews must have been conscious that they had nothing more to fear from Assyria, and Nahum could hardly have written as he does in i. 13, "I will break his yoke from off thee and burst thy bonds in sunder."§ But this is not conclusive, for *first*, as we have seen, it is not certain that i. 13 is from Nahum himself, and *second*, if it be from himself, he might as well have written it about 608 as about 625, for he speaks not from the feelings of any single year, but with the impression upon him of the whole epoch of Assyrian servitude then drawing to a close. The eve of the later siege as a date from the book is, as Davidson remarks,‖ "well within the verge of possibility," and some critics prefer it because in their opinion Nahum's descriptions thereby acquire greater reality and naturalness. But this is not convincing, for if Kyaxares actually began the siege of Nineveh about 625, Nahum's sense of the imminence of her fall is perfectly natural. Wellhausen indeed denies that earlier siege. "Apart from Herodotus," he says, "it would never have occurred to anybody to doubt that Nahum's prophecy coincided with the fall of Nineveh." ¶ This is true, for it is to Herodotus alone that we owe the tradition of the earlier siege. But what if we believe Herodotus? In that case, it is impossible to come to a decision as between the two sieges. With our present scanty knowledge of both, the prophecy of Nahum suits either equally well.**

* See above on Zephaniah, pp. 572 ff.

† Cornill, in the 2d ed. of his "Einleitung," has accepted Gunkel's and Bickell's main contentions.

‡ iii. 8–10.

§ The description of the fall of No-Amon precludes the older view almost universally held before the discovery of Assurbanipal's destruction of Thebes, viz., that Nahum prophesied in the days of Hezekiah or in the earlier years of Manasseh (Lightfoot, Pusey, Nägelsbach, etc.).

‖ So Schrader, Volck in Herz. "Real. Enc.," and others.

¶ It is favoured by Winckler, "A. T. Untersuch.," pp. 127 f.

* Above p. 564 ff.

† This in answer to Jeremias in Delitzsch's and Haupt's "Beiträge zur Assyriologie," III. 96.

‡ I. 103.

§ Hitzig's other reason, that the besiegers of Nineveh are described by Nahum in ii. 3 ff. as single, which was true of the siege in 625 *c.*, but not of that of 607–6, when the Chaldeans joined the Medes, is disposed of by the proof on p. 566 above, that even in 607–6 the Medes carried on the siege alone.

‖ Page 564.

¶ In commenting on chap. i. 9; p. 156 of "Kleine Propheten."

** The phrase which is so often appealed to by both sides, i. 9, "Jehovah maketh a complete end, not twice shall trouble arise," is really inconclusive. Hitzig maintains that if Nahum had written this after the first and

Fortunately it is not necessary to come to a decision. Nahum, we cannot too often insist, expresses the feelings neither of this nor of that decade in the reign of Josiah, but the whole volume of hope, wrath, and just passion of vengeance which had been gathering for more than a century and which at last broke into exultation when it became certain that Nineveh was falling. That suits the eve of either siege by Kyaxares. Till we learn a little more about the first siege and how far it proceeded towards a successful result, perhaps we ought to prefer the second. And of course those who feel that Nahum writes not in the future but the present tense of the details of Nineveh's overthrow, must prefer the second.

That the form as well as the spirit of the Book of Nahum is poetical is proved by the familiar marks of poetic measure—the unusual syntax, the frequent absence of the article and particles, the presence of elliptic forms and archaic and sonorous ones. In the two chapters on the siege of Nineveh the lines are short and quick, in harmony with the dashing action they echo.

As we have seen, the text of chap. i. is very uncertain. The subject of the other two chapters involves the use of a number of technical and some foreign terms, of the meaning of most of which we are ignorant.* There are apparently some glosses; here and there the text is obviously disordered. We get the usual help, and find the usual faults, in the Septuagint; they will be noticed in the course of the translation.

CHAPTER VII.

THE VENGEANCE OF THE LORD.

Nahum i.

The prophet Nahum, as we have seen,† arose probably in Judah, if not about the same time as Zephaniah and Jeremiah, then a few years later. Whether he prophesied before or after the great Reform of 621 we have no means of deciding. His book does not reflect the inner history, character, or merits of his generation. His sole interest is the fate of Nineveh. Zephaniah had also doomed the Assyrian capital, yet he was much more concerned with Israel's unworthiness of the opportunity presented to them. The yoke of Asshur, he saw, was to be broken, but the same cloud which was bursting from the north upon Nineveh must overwhelm the incorrigible people of Jehovah. For this Nahum has no thought. His heart, for all its bigness, holds room only for the bitter memories, the baffled hopes, the unappeased hatreds of a hundred years. And that is why we need not be anxious to fix his date upon one or other of the shifting phases of Israel's history during that last quarter of the seventh century. For he represents no single movement of his fickle people's progress, but the passion of the whole epoch then drawing to a close. Nahum's book is one great At Last!

And, therefore, while Nahum is a worse prophet than Zephaniah, with less conscience and less insight, he is a greater poet, pouring forth the exultation of a people long enslaved, who see their tyrant ready for destruction. His language is strong and brilliant; his rhythm rumbles and rolls, leaps and flashes, like the horsemen and chariots he describes. It is a great pity the text is so corrupt. If the original lay before us, and that full knowledge of the times which the excavation of ancient Assyria may still yield to us, we might judge Nahum to be an even greater poet than we do.

We have seen that there are some reasons for doubting whether he wrote the first chapter of the book,* but no one questions its fitness as an introduction to the exultation over Nineveh's fall in chaps. ii. and iii. The chapter is theological, affirming those general principles of Divine Providence, by which the overthrow of the tyrant is certain and God's own people are assured of deliverance. Let us place ourselves among the people, who for so long a time had been thwarted, crushed, and demoralised by the most brutal empire which was ever suffered to roll its force across the world, and we shall sympathise with the author, who for the moment will feel nothing about his God, save that He is a God of vengeance. Like the grief of a bereaved man, the vengeance of an enslaved people has hours sacred to itself. And this people had such a God! Jehovah must punish the tyrant, else were He untrue. He had been patient, and patient, as a verse seems to hint,† just because He was omnipotent, but in the end He must rise to judgment. He was God of heaven and earth, and it is the old physical proofs of His power, so often appealed to by the peoples of the East, for they feel them as we cannot, which this hymn calls up as Jehovah sweeps to the overthrow of the oppressor. "Before such power of wrath who may stand? What think ye of Jehovah?" The God who works with such ruthless, absolute force in nature will not relax in the fate He is preparing for Nineveh. "He is one who maketh utter destruction," not needing to raise up His forces a second time, and as stubble before fire so His foes go down before Him. No half-measures are His, Whose are the storm, the drought, and the earthquake.

Such is the sheer religion of the Proem to the Book of Nahum—thoroughly Oriental in its sense of God's method and resources of destruction; very Jewish, and very natural to that age of Jewish history, in the bursting of its long-pent hopes of revenge. We of the West might express these hopes differently. We should not attribute so much personal passion to the Avenger. With our keener sense of law, we should emphasise the slowness of the process, and select for its illustration the forces of decay

before the second siege of Nineveh he would have had to say, "not thrice *shall trouble arise*." This is not conclusive: the prophet is looking only at the future and thinking of it—"not twice *again* shall trouble rise"; and if there were really two sieges of Nineveh, would the words "not twice" have been suffered to remain, if they had been a confident prediction *before* the first siege? Besides, the meaning of the phrase is not certain; it may be only a general statement corresponding to what seems a general statement in the first clause of the verse. Kuenen and others refer the "trouble" not to that which is about to afflict Assyria, but to the long slavery and slaughter which Judah has suffered at Assyria's hands. Davidson leaves it ambiguous.

* Technical military terms: ii. 2, מצורה; 4, פלדת (?); 4, הרעלו; 6 הסכך; iii. 3, מעלה (?). Probably foreign terms: ii. 8, הצב; iii. 17, מנזריך. Certainly foreign: iii. 17, טפסריך.

† Above, pp. 579 ff., 581 ff.

* See above. pp. 580 ff.

† Ver. 3, if the reading be correct.

rather than those of sudden ruin. But we must remember the crashing times in which the Jews lived. The world was breaking up. The elements were loose, and all that God's own people could hope for was the bursting of their yoke, with a little shelter in the day of trouble. The elements were loose, but amidst the blind crash the little people knew that Jehovah knew them.

"A God jealous and avenging is Jehovah;
Jehovah is avenger and lord of wrath;
Vengeful is Jehovah towards His enemies,
And implacable He to His foes.

"Jehovah is long-suffering and great in might,*
Yet He will not absolve.
Jehovah! His way is in storm and in hurricane,
And clouds are the dust of His feet.†
He curbeth the sea, and drieth it up;
All the streams hath He parched.
Withered ‡ be Bashan and Carmel;
The bloom of Lebānon is withered.
Mountains have quaked before Him,
And the hills have rolled down.
Earth heaved at His presence,
The world and all its inhabitants.
Before His rage who may stand,
Or who abide in the glow of His anger?
His wrath pours forth like fire,
And rocks are rent before Him.

"Good is Jehovah to them that wait upon Him in the day of trouble,§
And He knoweth them that trust Him.
With an overwhelming flood He makes an end of His rebels,
And His foes He comes down on ‖ with darkness.

"What think ye of Jehovah?
He is one that makes utter destruction;
Not twice need trouble arise.
For though they be like plaited thorns,
And sodden as . . . ,¶
They shall be consumed like dry stubble.

"Came there not ** out of thee one to plan evil against Jehovah,
A counsellor of mischief?" ††

"Thus saith Jehovah, . . . many waters,‡‡ yet shall they be cut off and pass away, and I will so humble thee that I need humble thee §§ no more; ‖‖ and Jehovah hath ordered concerning thee, that no more of thy seed be sown: from the house of thy God, I will cut off graven and molten images. I will make thy sepulchre, . . ."*

Disentangled from the above verses are three which plainly refer not to Assyria but to Judah. How they came to be woven among the others we cannot tell. Some of them appear applicable to the days of Josiah after the great Reform.

"And now will I break his yoke from upon thee,
And burst thy bonds asunder.
Lo, upon the mountains the feet of Him that bringeth good tidings,
That publisheth peace!
Keep thy feasts, O Judah,
Fulfil thy vows:
For no more shall the wicked attempt to pass through thee;
Cut off is the whole of him.†
For Jehovah hath turned the pride of Jacob,
Like to the pride of Israēl: ‡
For the plunderers plundered them,
And destroyed their vinebranches."

CHAPTER VIII.

THE SIEGE AND FALL OF NINEVEH.

NAHUM ii., iii.

THE scene now changes from the presence and awful arsenal of the Almighty to the historical consummation of His vengeance. Nahum foresees the siege of Nineveh. Probably the Medes have already overrun Assyria.§ The "Old Lion" has withdrawn to his inner den, and is making his last stand. The suburbs are full of the enemy, and the great walls which made the inner city one vast fortress are invested. Nahum describes the details of the assault. Let us try, before we follow him through them, to form some picture of Assyria and her capital at this time.‖

As we have seen, ¶ the Assyrian Empire began

* Gunkel amends to "in mercy" to make the parallel exact. But see above, p. 580.

† Gunkel's emendation is quite unnnecessary here.

‡ See above, p. 580.

§ So LXX. Heb. = "for a stronghold in the day of trouble."

‖ "Thrusts into," Wellhausen, reading ינדף or ידף for ירדף. LXX. "darkness shall pursue."

¶ Heb. and R. V. "drenched as with their drink." LXX. "like a tangled yew." The text is corrupt.

** The superfluous word מלא at the end of ver. 10 Wellhausen reads as הלא at the beginning of ver. 11.

†† Usually taken as Sennacherib.

‡‡ The Hebrew is given by the R. V. "though they be in full strength and likewise many." LXX. "Thus saith Jehovah ruling over many waters," reading מים רבים משל and omitting the first וכן. Similarly Syr. "Thus saith Jehovah of the heads of many waters," מים רבים על משלי. Wellhausen, substituting מים for the first וכן. translates, "Let the great waters be ever so full, they will yet all" . . . ? (misprint here) "and vanish." For עבר read עברו with LXX., borrowing ו from next word.

§§ Lit. "and I will afflict thee, I will not afflict thee again." This rendering implies that Nineveh is the object. The A. V., "though I have afflicted thee I will afflict thee no more," refers to Israel.

‖‖ Omit ver. 13 and run 14 on to 12. For the curious alternation now occurs: Assyria in one verse, Judah in the other. Assyria: i. 12, 14, ii. 2 (Heb.; Eng. ii. 1) 4 ff. Judah: i. 13, ii, 1 (Heb.; Eng. i. 15,) 3 (Heb.; Eng. 2). Remove these latter, as Wellhausen does, and the verses on Assyria remain a connected and orderly whole. So in the text above.

* Syr. "make it thy sepulchre." The Hebrew left untranslated above might be rendered "for thou art vile." Bickell amends into "dunghills." Lightfoot, "Chron. Temp. et Ord. Text. V. T." in Collected Works, I. 109, takes this as a prediction of Sennacherib's murder in the temple, an interpretation which demands a date for Nahum under either Hezekiah or Manasseh. See Pusey also, p. 357.

† LXX. "destruction," כָּלָה for כלֻּה.

‡ Davidson: "restoreth the excellency of Jacob, as the excellency of Israel," but when was the latter restored?

§ See above, p. 566.

‖ The authorities are very full. First there is M. Botta's huge work "Monument de Ninive," Paris, 5 vols., 1845. Then must be mentioned the work of which we availed ourselves in describing Babylon in "Isaiah xl.-lxvi." (Expositor's Bible), pp. 744 ff.: "Memoirs by Commander James Felix Jones, I. N.," in "Selections from the Records of the Bombay Government." No. XLIII., New Series, 1857. It is good to find that the careful and able observations of Commander Jones, too much neglected in his own country, have had justice done them by the German Colonel Billerbeck in the work about to be cited. Then there is the invaluable "Nineveh and its Remains," by Layard. There are also the works of Rawlinson and George Smith. And recently Colonel Billerbeck, founding on these and other works, has published an admirable monograph (lavishly illustrated by maps and pictures), not only upon the military state of Assyria proper and of Nineveh at this period, but upon the whole subject of Assyrian fortification and art of besieging, as well as upon the course of the Median invasions. It forms the larger part of an article to which Dr. Alfred Jeremias contributes an introduction, and reconstruction with notes of chaps. ii. and iii. of the Book of Nahum: "Der Untergang Niniveh's und die Weissagungschrift des Nahum von Elkosh," in Vol. III. of "Beiträge zur Assyriologie und Semitischen Sprachwissenschaft," edited by Friedrich Delitzsch and Paul Haupt, with the support of Johns Hopkins University of Baltimore, U. S. A.: Leipzig, 1895.

¶ Pages 565 f.

about 625 to shrink to the limits of Assyria proper, or Upper Mesopotamia, within the Euphrates on the southwest, the mountain-range of Kurdistan on the northeast, the river Chabor on the northwest, and the Lesser Zab on the southeast.* This is a territory of nearly a hundred and fifty miles from north to south, and rather more than two hundred and fifty from east to west. To the south of it the Viceroy of Babylon, Nabopolassar, held practically independent sway over Lower Mesopotamia, if he did not command as well a large part of the Upper Euphrates Valley. On the north the Medes were urgent, holding at least the farther ends of the passes through the Kurdish mountains, if they had not already penetrated these to their southern issues.

The kernel of the Assyrian territory was the triangle, two of whose sides are represented by the Tigris and the Greater Zab, the third by the foot of the Kurdistan mountains. It is a fertile plain, with some low hills. To-day the level parts of it are covered by a large number of villages and well-cultivated fields. The more frequent mounds of ruin attest in ancient times a still greater population. At the period of which we are treating, the plains must have been covered by an almost continuous series of towns. At either end lay a group of fortresses. The southern was the ancient capital of Assyria, Kalchu, now Nimrud, about six miles to the north of the confluence of the Greater Zab and the Tigris. The northern, close by the present town of Khorsabad, was the great fortress and palace of Sargon, Dur-Sargina:† it covered the roads upon Nineveh from the north, and standing upon the upper reaches of the Choser protected Nineveh's water supply. But besides these there were scattered upon all the main roads and round the frontiers of the territory a number of other forts, towers, and posts, the ruins of many of which are still considerable, but others have perished without leaving any visible traces. The roads thus protected drew in upon Nineveh from all directions. The chief of those, along which the Medes and their allies would advance from the east and north, crossed the Greater Zam, or came down through the Kurdistan mountains upon the citadel of Sargon. Two of them were distant enough from the latter to relieve the invaders from the necessity of taking it, and Kalchu lay far to the south of all of them. The brunt of the first defence of the land would therefore fall upon the smaller fortresses.

Nineveh itself lay upon the Tigris between Kalchu and Sargon's city, just where the Tigris is met by the Choser. Low hills descend from the north upon the very site of the fortress, and then curve east and south, bow-shaped, to draw west again upon the Tigris at the south end of the city. To the east of the latter they leave a level plain, some two and a half miles by one and a half. These hills appear to have been covered by several forts. The city itself was four-sided, lying lengthwise to the Tigris and cut across its breadth by the Choser. The circumference was about seven and a half miles, enclosing the largest fortified space in Western Asia, and capable of holding a population of three hundred thousand. The western wall, rather over two and a half miles long, touched the Tigris at the other end, but between there lay a broad, bow-shaped stretch of land, probably in ancient times, as now, free of buildings. The northwestern wall ran up from the Tigris for a mile and a quarter to the low ridge which entered the city at its northern corner. From this the eastern wall, with a curve upon it, ran down in face of the eastern plain for a little more than three miles, and was joined to the western by the short southern wall of not quite half a mile. The ruins of the western wall stand from ten to twenty, those of the others from twenty-five to sixty, feet above the natural surface, with here and there the still higher remains of towers. There were several gates, of which the chief were one in the northern and two in the eastern wall. Round all the walls except the western ran moats about a hundred and fifty feet broad—not close up to the foot of the walls, but at a distance of some sixty feet. Water was supplied by the Choser to all the moats south of it; those to the north were fed from a canal which entered the city near its northern corner. At these and other points one can still trace the remains of huge dams, batardeaux, and sluices; and the moats might be emptied by opening at either end of the western wall other dams, which kept back the waters from the bed of the Tigris. Beyond its moat, the eastern wall was protected north of the Choser by a large outwork covering its gate, and south of the Choser by another outwork, in shape the segment of a circle, and consisting of a double line of fortification more than five hundred yards long, of which the inner wall was almost as high as the great wall itself, but the outer considerably lower. Again, in front of this and in face of the eastern plain was a third line of fortification, consisting of a low inner wall and a colossal outer wall still rising to a height of fifty feet, with a moat one hundred and fifty feet broad between them. On the south this third line was closed by a large fortress.

Upon the trebly fortified city the Medes drew in from east and north, far away from Kalchu and able to avoid even Dur-Sargina. The other fortresses on the frontier and the approaches fell into their hands, says Nahum, like "ripe fruit."* He cries to Nineveh to prepare for the siege.† Military authorities‡ suppose that the Medes directed their main attack upon the northern corner of the city. Here they would be upon a level with its highest point, and would command the waterworks by which most of the moats were fed. Their flank, too, would be protected by the ravines of the Choser. Nahum describes fighting in the suburbs before the assault of the walls, and it was just here, according to some authorities,§ that the famous suburbs of Nineveh lay, out upon the canal and the road to Khorsabad. All the open fighting which Nahum foresees would take place in these "out-places" and "broad streets"‖—the mustering of the "red" ranks,¶ the "prancing horses"**

* Colonel Billerbeck (p. 115) thinks that the southeast frontier at this time lay more to the north, near the Greater Zab.

† First excavated by M. Botta, 1842–1845. See also George Smith, "Assyr. Disc.," pp. 98 f.

* iii. 12.

† iii. 14.

‡ See Jones and Billerbeck.

§ Delitzsch places the עיר רחבות of Gen. x. 11, the "ribit Nina" of the inscriptions, on the northeast of Nineveh.

‖ ii. 4 Eng., 5 Heb.

¶ ii. 3 Eng., 4 Heb

** *Ibid.* LXX.

and "rattling chariots"* and "cavalry at the charge."† Beaten there the Assyrians would retire to the great walls, and the waterworks would fall into the hands of the besiegers. They would not immediately destroy these, but in order to bring their engines and battering-rams against the walls they would have to lay strong dams across the moats; the eastern moat has actually been found filled with rubbish in face of a great breach at the north end of its wall. This breach may have been effected not only by the rams but by directing upon the wall the waters of the canal; or farther south the Choser itself, in its spring floods, may have been confined by the besiegers and swept in upon the sluices which regulate its passage through the eastern wall into the city. To this means tradition has assigned the capture of Nineveh,‡ and Nahum perhaps foresees the possibility of it: "the gates of the rivers are opened, the palace is dissolved."§

Now of all this probable progress of the siege Nahum, of course, does not give us a narrative, for he is writing upon the eve of it, and probably, as we have seen, in Judah, with only such knowledge of the position and strength of Nineveh as her fame had scattered across the world. The military details, the muster, the fighting in the open, the investment, the assault, he did not need to go to Assyria or to wait for the fall of Nineveh to describe as he has done. Assyria herself (and herein lies much of the pathos of the poem) had made all Western Asia familiar with their horrors for the last two centuries. As we learn from the prophets and now still more from herself, Assyria was the great Besieger of Men. It is siege, siege, siege, which Amos, Hosea, and Isaiah tell their people they shall feel: "siege and blockade, and that right round the land!" It is siege, irresistible and full of cruelty, which Assyria records as her own glory. Miles of sculpture are covered with masses of troops marching upon some Syrian or Median fortress. Scaling ladders and enormous engines are pushed forward to the walls under cover of a shower of arrows. There are assaults and breaches, panic-stricken and suppliant defenders. Streets and places are strewn with corpses, men are impaled, women led away weeping, children dashed against the stones. The Jews had seen, had felt these horrors for a hundred years, and it is out of their experience of them that Nahum weaves his exultant predictions. The Besieger of the world is at last besieged; every cruelty he has inflicted upon men is now to be turned upon himself. Again and again does Nahum return to the vivid details,—he hears the very whips crack beneath the walls, and the rattle of the leaping chariots; the end is slaughter, dispersion, and a dead waste.‖

Two other points remain to be emphasised.

There is a striking absence from both chapters of any reference to Israel.* Jehovah of Hosts is mentioned twice in the same formula,† but otherwise the author does not obtrude his nationality. It is not in Judah's name he exults, but in that of all the peoples of Western Asia. Nineveh has sold "peoples" by her harlotries and "races" by her witchcraft; it is "peoples" that shall gaze upon her nakedness and "kingdoms" upon her shame. Nahum gives voice to no national passions, but to the outraged conscience of mankind. We see here another proof, not only of the large, human heart of prophecy, but of that which in the introduction to these Twelve Prophets we ventured to assign as one of its causes. By crushing all peoples to a common level of despair, by the universal pity which her cruelties excited, Assyria contributed to the development in Israel of the idea of a common humanity.‡

The other thing to be noticed is Nahum's feeling of the incoherence and mercenariness of the vast population of Nineveh. Nineveh's command of the world had turned her into a great trading power. Under Assurbanipal the lines of ancient commerce had been diverted so as to pass through her. The immediate result was an enormous increase of population, such as the world had never before seen within the limits of one city. But this had come out of all races and was held together only by the greed of gain. What had once been a firm and vigorous nation of warriors, irresistible in their united impact upon the world, was now a loose aggregate of many peoples, without patriotism, discipline, or sense of honour. Nahum likens it to a reservoir of waters,§ which as soon as it is breached must scatter, and leave the city bare. The Second Isaiah said the same of Babylon, to which the bulk of Nineveh's mercenary populace must have fled:—

"Thus are they grown to thee, they who did weary thee,
Traders of thine from thy youth up;
Each as he could escape have they fled!
None is thy helper.‖

The prophets saw the truth about both cities. Their vastness and their splendour were artificial. Neither of them, and Nineveh still less than Babylon, was a natural centre for the world's commerce. When their political power fell, the great lines of trade, which had been twisted to their feet, drew back to more natural courses, and Nineveh in especial became deserted. This is the explanation of the absolute collapse of that mighty city. Nahum's foresight, and the very metaphor in which he expressed it, were thoroughly sound. The population vanished like water. The site bears little trace of any disturbance since the ruin by the Medes, except such as has been inflicted by the weather and the wandering tribes around. Mosul, Nineveh's

* iii. 2.

† iii. 3.

‡ It is the waters of the Tigris that the tradition avers to have broken the wall; but the Tigris itself runs in a bed too low for this. It can only have been the Choser. See both Jones and Billerbeck.

§ ii. 6.

‖ If the above conception of chaps. ii. and iii. be correct, then there is no need for such a re-arrangement of these verses as has been proposed by Jeremias and Billerbeck. In order to produce a continuous narrative of the progress of the siege, they bring forward iii. 12–15 (describing the fall of the fortresses and gates of the land and the call to the defence of the city), and place it immediately after ii. 2, 4 (the description of the invader) and ii. 5–11 (the appearance of chariots in the suburbs of the city, the opening of the floodgates, the flight and the spoiling of the city). But if they believe that the original gave an orderly account of the progress of the siege, why do they not bring forward also iii. 2 f., which describe the arrival of the foe under the city walls? The truth appears to be as stated above. We have really two poems against Nineveh, chap. ii. and chap. iii. They do not give an orderly description of the siege, but exult over Nineveh's imminent downfall, with gleams scattered here and there of how this is to happen. Of these "impressions" of the coming siege there are three, and in the order in which we now have them they occur very naturally: ii. 5 ff., iii. 2 f., and iii. 12 ff.

* ii. 2 goes with the previous chapter. See above, pp. 583 f.

† ii. 13, iii. 5.

‡ See above, chap. iv., especially pp. 455 ff.

§ ii. 8.

‖ "Isaiah xl.-lxvi." (Expositor's Bible), pp. 779 ff.

representative to-day, is not built upon it, and is but a provincial town. The district was never meant for anything else.

The swift decay of these ancient empires from the climax of their commercial glory is often employed as a warning to ourselves. But the parallel, as the previous paragraphs suggest, is very far from exact. If we can lay aside for the moment the greatest difference of all, in religion and morals, there remain others almost of cardinal importance. Assyria and Babylonia were not filled, like Great Britain, with reproductive races, able to colonise distant lands, and carry everywhere the spirit which had made them strong at home. Still more, they did not continue at home to be homogeneous. Their native forces were exhausted by long and unceasing wars. Their populations, especially in their capitals, were very largely alien and distraught, with nothing to hold them together save their commercial interests. They were bound to break up at the first disaster. It is true that we are not without some risks of their peril. No patriot among us can observe without misgiving the large and growing proportion of foreigners in that department of our life from which the strength of our defence is largely drawn—our merchant navy. But such a fact is very far from bringing our empire and its chief cities into the fatal condition of Nineveh and Babylon. Our capitals, our commerce, our life as a whole are still British to the core. If we only be true to our ideals of righteousness and religion, if our patriotism continue moral and sincere, we shall have the power to absorb the foreign elements that throng to us in commerce, and stamp them with our own spirit.

We are now ready to follow Nahum's two great poems delivered on the eve of the Fall of Nineveh. Probably, as we have said, the first of them has lost its original opening. It wants some notice at the outset of the object to which it is addressed: this is indicated only by the second personal pronoun. Other needful comments will be given in footnotes.

I.

. . . . .

"The Hammer * is come up to thy face!
Hold the rampart! † Keep watch on the way!
Brace the loins! ‡ Pull thyself firmly together! §
The shields ‖ of his heroes are red,
The warriors are in scarlet; ¶
Like ** fire are the . . . †† of the chariots in the day
of his muster,
And the horsemen * are prancing.
Through the markets rage chariots,
They tear across the squares; †
The look of them is like torches,
Like lightnings they dart to and fro.
He musters his nobles. . . . ‡
They rush to the wall and the mantlet § is fixed!
The river-gates ‖ burst open, the palace dissolves. ¶
And Huṣṣab ** is stripped, is brought forth,
With her maids sobbing like doves,
Beating their breasts.
And Nineveh! she was like a reservoir of waters,
Her waters . . . ††
And now they flee. "Stand, stand!" but there is
none to rally.
Plunder silver, plunder gold!
Infinite treasures, mass of all precious things!
Void and devoid and desolate ‡‡ is she.
Melting hearts and shaking knees,
And anguish in all loins,
And nothing but faces full of black fear. §§

* Read מַפֵּץ with Wellhausen (*cf.* Siegfried-Stade's "Wörterbuch," sub פוץ) for מֵפִיץ "Breaker in pieces." In Jer. li. 20 Babylon is also called by Jehovah His מַפֵּץ, "Hammer" or "Maul."

† "Keep watch," Wellhausen.

‡ This may be a military call to attention, the converse of "Stand at ease!"

§ Heb. literally: "brace up thy power exceedingly."

‖ Heb. singular.

¶ Rev. ix. 17. Purple or red was the favourite colour of the Medes. The Assyrians also loved red.

** Read כאשׁ for באשׁ.

†† פלדות, the word omitted, is doubtful; it does not occur elsewhere. LXX. ἡνίαι; Vulg. "habenæ." Some have thought that it means "scythes"—*cf.* the Arabic "falad," "to cut"—but the earliest notice of chariots armed with scythes is at the battle of Cunaxa, and in Jewish literature they do not appear before 2 Macc. xiii. 2. *Cf.* Jeremias, *op. cit.* p. 97, where Billerbeck suggests that the words of Nahum are applicable to the covered siege-engines, pictured on the Assyrian monuments, from which the besiegers flung torches on the walls: *cf. ibid.*, p. 167, *n.* *** But from the parallelism of the verse it is more probable that ordinary chariots are meant. The leading chariots were covered with plates of metal (Billerbeck, p. 167).

* So LXX., reading פרשים for ברשים of Heb. text, that means "fir-trees." If the latter be correct, then we should need to suppose with Billerbeck that either the long lances of the Aryan Medes were meant, or the great, heavy spears which were thrust against the walls by engines. We are not, however, among these yet; it appears to be the cavalry and chariots in the open that are here described.

† Or "broad places," or "suburbs." See above, pp. 584 ff.

‡ Heb. "They stumble in their goings." Davidson holds this is more probably of the defenders. Wellhausen takes the verse as of the besiegers. See next note.

§ הַסֹּכֵךְ. Partic. of the verb "to cover," hence covering thing: whether "mantlet" (on the side of the besiegers) or "bulwark" (on the side of the besieged: *cf.* מָסָךְ, Isa. xxii. 8) is uncertain. Billerbeck says, if it be an article of defence, we can read ver. 5 as illustrating the vanity of the hurried defence, when the elements themselves break in vv. 6 and 7 (p. 101: *cf.* p. 176, *n.* *).

‖ "Sluices" (Jeremias) or "bridge-gates" (Wellhausen)?

¶ Or "breaks into motion," *i. e.*, "flight."

** הֻצַּב, if a Hebrew word, might be Hophal of נצב and has been taken to mean "it is determined, she (Nineveh) is taken captive." Volck (in Herzog), Kleinert, Orelli: "it is settled." LXX. ὑπόστασις = מצב. Vulg. "miles" (as if some form of צבא?)" Hitzig points it הַצָּב, "the lizard," Wellhausen "the toad." But this noun is masculine (Lev. xi. 29) and the verbs feminine. Davidson suggests the other הַצָּב, fem., the "litter" or "palanquin" (Isa. lxvi. 20): "in lieu of anything better one might be tempted to think that the litter might mean the woman or lady, just as in Arab. ḍḥa'inah means a woman's litter and then a woman." One is also tempted to think of הַצְּבִי, "the beauty." The Targ. has מלכתא, "the queen." From as early as at least 1527 ("Latina Interpretatio" Xantis Pagnini Lucensis revised and edited for the Plantin Bible, 1615) the word has been taken by a series of scholars as a proper name, Hussab. So Ewald and others. It may be an Assyrian word, like some others in Nahum. Perhaps, again, the text is corrupt.

Mr. Paul Ruben (*Academy*, March 7, 1896) has proposed instead of העלתה, "is brought forth," to read העתלה, and to translate it by analogy of the Assyrian "etellu," fem. "etellitu" = great or exalted, "The Lady." The line would then run "Huṣṣab, the lady, is stripped." (With העתלה Cheyne, *Academy*, June 21, 1896, compares עתליה, which, he suggests, is "Yahwe is great" or "is lord.")

†† Heb. מִימֵי הִיא for מימי אשר היא, "from days she was." A. V. "is of old." R. V. "hath been of old," and Marg. "from the days that she hath been." LXX. "her waters," מֵימֶיהָ. On waters fleeing, *cf.* Ps. civ. 7.

‡‡ Bukah, umebukah, umebullākah. Ewald: "desert and desolation and devastation." The adj. are feminine.

§§ Literally: "and the faces of all them gather lividness."

"Where is the Lion's den,
And the young lions' feeding ground *?
Whither the Lion retreated,†
The whelps of the Lion, with none to affray:
The Lion, who tore enough for his whelps,
And strangled for his lionesses.
And he filled his pits with prey,
And his dens with rapine.

"Lo, I am at thee (oracle of Jehovah of Hosts):
I will put up thy . . . ‡ in flames,
The sword shall devour thy young lions:
I will cut off from the earth thy rapine,
And the noise of thine envoys shall no more be heard.

2.

"Woe to the City of Blood,
All of her guile, robbery-full. ceaseless rapine!

"Hark the whip,
And the rumbling of the wheel,
And horses galloping,
And the rattling dance of the chariot! §
Cavalry at the charge,‖ and flash of sabres,
And lightning of lances,
Mass of slain and weight of corpses,
Endless dead bodies—
They stumble on their dead!
—For the manifold harlotries of the Harlot,
The well-favoured, mistress of charms,
She who sold nations with her harlotries
And races by her witchcrafts!

"Lo, I am at thee (oracle of Jehovah of Hosts):
I will uncover thy skirts to thy face; ¶
Give nations to look on thy nakedness,
And kingdoms upon thy shame;
Will have thee pelted with filth, and disgrace thee,
And set thee for a gazingstock;
So that every one seeing thee shall shrink from thee and say,
'Shattered is Nineveh—who will pity her?
Whence shall I seek for comforters to thee?'

"Shalt thou be better than No-Amon,**
Which sat upon the Nile streams ††—waters were round her—
Whose rampart was the sea,‡‡ and waters her wall? §§
Kush was her strength and Misraim without end;
Phut and the Lybians were there to assist her.‖‖
Even she was for exile. she went to captivity:
Even her children were dashed on every street corner;
For her nobles they cast lots.
And all her great men were fastened with fetters.

"Thou too shalt stagger,¶¶ shalt grow faint;
Thou too shalt seek help from *** the foe!

All thy fortresses are fig-trees with figs early-ripe:
Be they shaken they fall on the mouth of the eater.

* For מרעה Wellhausen reads מערה, "cave" or "hold."

† LXX., reading לבוא for לביא.

‡ Heb. "her chariots." LXX. and Syr. suggest "thy mass" or "multitude," רבכה. Davidson suggests "thy lair," רבצכה.

§ Literally "and the chariot dancing," but the word, merakedah, has a rattle in it.

‖ Doubtful, מַעֲלֶה. LXX. ἀναβαίνοντος.

¶ Jeremias (104) shows how the Assyrians did this to female captives.

** Jer. xlvi. 25: "I will punish Amon at No." Ezek. xxx. 14-16: ". . . judgments in No . . . . I will cut off No-Amon" (Heb. and A. V. "multitude of No," reading המון; so also LXX. τὸ πλῆθος for אמון) ". . . and No shall be broken up." It is Thebes, the Egyptian name of which was Nu-Amen. The god Amen had his temple there: Herod. I. 182, II. 42. Nahum refers to Assurbanipal's account of the fall of Thebes. See above, p. 563.

†† היארים. Pl. of the word for Nile.

‡‡ Arabs still call the Nile the sea.

§§ So LXX., reading מַיִם for Heb. מִיָּם.

‖‖ So LXX.; Heb. "thee."

¶¶ Heb. "be drunken."

*** *I. e.*, "against, because of."

Lo, thy folk are but women in thy midst: *
To thy foes the gates of thy land fly open;
Fire has devoured thy bars.

"Draw thee water for siege, strengthen thy forts!
Get thee down to the mud, and tramp in the clay!
Grip fast the brick-mould!
There fire consumes thee, the sword cuts thee off.†
Make thyself many as a locust swarm,
Many as grasshoppers,
Multiply thy traders more than heaven's stars,
—The locusts break off ‡ and fly away,
Thy . . . § are as locusts and thy . . . as grasshoppers,
That hive in the hedges in the cold of the day: ‖
The sun is risen, they are fled,
And one knows not the place where they be.

"Asleep are thy shepherds, O king of Assyria,
Thy nobles do slumber; ¶
Thy people are strewn on the mountains,
Without any to gather.
There is no healing of thy wreck,
Fatal thy wound!
All who hear the bruit of thee shall clap the hand at thee.
For upon whom hath not thy cruelty passed without ceasing?"

HABAKKUK.

"Upon my watch-tower will I stand,
And take up my post on the rampart.
I will watch to see what He will say to me,
And what answer I get back to my plea."
. . . . .
The righteous shall live by his faithfulness.

"The beginning of speculation in Israel.

CHAPTER IX.

THE BOOK OF HABAKKUK.

As it has reached us, the Book of Habakkuk under the title "The Oracle which Habakkuk the prophet received by vision," consists of three chapters, which fall into three sections. *First:* chap. i. 2-ii. 4 (or 8), a piece in dramatic form; the prophet lifts his voice to God against the wrong and violence of which his whole horizon is full, and God sends him answer. *Second:* chap. ii. 5 (or 9)-20, a taunt-song in a series of Woes upon the wrong-doer. *Third:* chap. iii., part psalm, part prayer, descriptive of a Theophany and expressive of Israel's faith in their

* Jer. l. 37, li. 30.

† Heb. and LXX. add "devour thee like the locust," probably a gloss.

‡ *Cf.* Jer. ix. 33. Some take it of the locusts stripping the skin which confines their wings: Davidson.

§ מנזריך. A. V. "thy crowned ones"; but perhaps like its neighbour an Assyrian word, meaning we know not what. Wellhausen reads ממזריך, LXX. ὁ συμμικτός σοῦ (applied in Deut. xxiii. 3 and Zech. ix. 6 to the offspring of a mixed marriage between an Israelite and a Gentile), deine Mischlinge: a term of contempt for the floating foreign or semi-foreign population which filled Nineveh and was ready to fly at sight of danger. Similarly Wellhausen takes the second term, טפסר. This, which occurs, also in Jer. li. 27, appears to be some kind of official. In Assyrian "dupsar" is scribe, which may, like Heb. שֹׁטר, have been applied to any high official. See Schrader, "K. A. T.," Eng. Tr., I. 141, II. 118. See also Fried. Delitzsch, "Wo lag Parad.," p. 142. The name and office were ancient. Such Babylonian officials are mentioned in the Tell el Amarna letters as present at the Egyptian court

‖ Heb. "day of cold."

¶ ישכנו, "dwell," is the Heb. reading. But LXX. ישנו, ἐκοίμισεν. Sleep must be taken in the sense of death: *cf.* Jer. li. 39, 57: Isa. xiv. 18.

God. Of these three sections no one doubts the authenticity of the *first;* opinion is divided about the *second;* about the *third* there is a growing agreement that it is not a genuine work of Habakkuk, but a poem from a period after the Exile.

1. Chap. I. 2-II. 4 (or 8).

Yet it is the first piece which raises the most difficult questions. All * admit that it is to be dated somewhere along the line of Jeremiah's long career, *c.* 627-586. There is no doubt about the general trend of the argument: it is a plaint to God on the sufferings of the righteous under tyranny, with God's answer. But the order and connection of the paragraphs of the argument are not clear. There is also difference of opinion as to who the tyrant is—native, Assyrian, or Chaldee; and this leads to a difference, of course, about the date, which ranges from the early years of Josiah to the end of Jehoiakim's reign, or from about 630 to 597.

As the verses lie, their argument is this. In chap. i. 2-4 Habakkuk asks the Lord how long the wicked are to oppress the righteous, to the paralysing of the Torah, or Revelation of His Law, and the making futile of judgment. For answer the Lord tells him, vv. 5-11, to look round among the heathen: He is about to raise up the Chaldees to do His work, a people swift, self-reliant, irresistible. Upon which Habakkuk resumes his question, vv. 12-17, how long will God suffer a tyrant who sweeps up the peoples into his net like fish? Is he to go on with this for ever? In ii. 1 Habakkuk prepares for an answer, which comes in ii. 2, 3, 4: let the prophet wait for the vision though it tarries; the proud oppressor cannot last, but the righteous shall live by his constancy, or faithfulness.

The difficulties are these. Who are the wicked oppressors in chap. i. 2-4? Are they Jews, or some heathen nation? And what is the connection between vv. 1-4 and vv. 5-11? Are the Chaldees, who are described in the latter, raised up to punish the tyrant complained against in the former? To these questions three different sets of answers have been given.

First: the great majority of critics take the wrong complained of in vv. 2-4 to be wrong done by unjust and cruel Jews to their countrymen, that is, civic disorder and violence, and believe that in vv. 5-11 Jehovah is represented as raising up the Chaldees to punish the sin of Judah—a message which is pretty much the same as Jeremiah's. But Habakkuk goes further: the Chaldees themselves with their cruelties aggravate his problem how God can suffer wrong, and he appeals again to God, vv. 12-17. Are the Chaldees to be allowed to devastate for ever? The answer is given, as above, in chap. ii. 1-4. Such is practically the view of Pusey, Delitzsch, Kleinert, Kuenen, Sinker,† Driver, Orelli, Kirkpatrick, Wildeboer, and Davidson, a formidable league, and Davidson says "this is the most natural sense of the verses and of the words used in them." But these scholars differ as to the date. Pusey, Delitzsch, and Volck take the whole passage from i. 5 as prediction, and date it from before the rise of the Chaldee power in 625, attributing the internal wrongs of Judah described in vv. 2-4 to Manasseh's reign or the early years of Josiah.* But the rest, on the grounds that the prophet shows some experience of the Chaldean methods of warfare, and that the account of the internal disorder in Judah does not suit Josiah's reign, bring the passage down to the reign of Jehoiakim, 608-598, or of Jehoiachin, 597. Kleinert and Von Orelli date it before the battle of Carchemish, 605, in which the Chaldean Nebuchadrezzar wrested from Egypt the Empire of the Western Asia, on the ground that after that Habakkuk could not have called a Chaldean invasion of Judah incredible (i. 5). But Kuenen, Driver, Kirkpatrick, Wildeboer, and Davidson date it after Carchemish. To Driver it must be immediately after, and before Judah became alarmed at the consequences to herself. To Davidson the description of the Chaldeans "is scarcely conceivable before the battle," "hardly one would think before the deportation of the people under Jehoiachin." † This also is Kuenen's view, who thinks that Judah must have suffered at least the first Chaldean raids, and he explains the use of an undoubted future in chap. i. 5, "Lo, I am about to raise up the Chaldeans," as due to the prophet's predilection for a dramatic style. "He sets himself in the past, and represents the already experienced chastisement [of Judah] as having been then announced by Jehovah. His contemporaries could not have mistaken his meaning."

Second: others, however, deny that chap. i. 2-4 refers to the internal disorder of Judah, except as the effect of foreign tyranny. The "righteous" mentioned there are Israel as a whole, "the wicked" their heathen oppressors. So Hitzig, Ewald, König, and practically Smend. Ewald is so clear that Habakkuk ascribes no sin to Judah, that he says we might be led by this to assign the prophecy to the reign of the righteous Josiah; but he prefers, because of the vivid sense which the prophet betrays of actual experience of the Chaldees, to date the passage from the reign of Jehoiakim, and to explain Habakkuk's silence about his people's sinfulness as due to his overwhelming impression of Chaldean cruelty. König‡ takes vv. 2-4 as a general complaint of the violence that fills the prophet's day, and vv. 5-11 as a detailed description of the Chaldeans, the instruments of this violence. Vv. 5-11, therefore, give not the judgment upon the wrongs described in vv. 2-4, but the explanation of them. Lebanon is already wasted by the Chaldeans (ii. 17); therefore the whole prophecy must be assigned to the days of Jehoiakim. Giesebrecht§ and Wellhausen adhere to the view that no sins of Judah are mentioned, but that the "righteous" and "wicked" of chap. i. 4 are the same as in

* Except one or two critics who place it in Manasseh's reign. See below.

† See next note.

* So Pusey. Delitzsch in his commentary on Habakkuk, 1843, preferred Josiah's reign, but in his "O. T. Hist of Redemption," 1881, p. 226, Manasseh's. Volck (in Herzog, "Real Encyc.," art. "Habakkuk," 1879,) assuming that Habakkuk is quoted both by Zephaniah (see above, p. 569, *n.*) and Jeremiah, places him before these. Sinker ("The Psalm of Habakkuk:" see below, p. 591, *n.*) deems "the prophecy, taken as a whole," to bring "before us the threat of the Chaldean invasion, the horrors that follow in its train," etc., with a vision of the day "when the Chaldean host itself, its work done, falls beneath a mightier foe." He fixes the date either in the concluding years of Manasseh's reign, or the opening years of that of Josiah (Preface, 1-4).

† Kirkpatrick (Smith's "Dict. of the Bible," art. "Habakkuk," 1893) puts it not later than the sixth year of Jehoiakim.

‡ "Einl. in das A. T."

§ "Beiträge zur Jesaiakritik," 1890, pp. 197 f.

ver. 13, viz., Israel and a heathen tyrant. But this leads them to dispute that the present order of the paragraphs of the prophecy is the right one. In chap. i. 5 the Chaldeans are represented as about to be raised up for the first time, although their violence has already been described in vv. 1-4, and in vv. 12-17 these are already in full career. Moreover ver. 12 follows on naturally to ver. 4. Accordingly these critics would remove the section vv. 5-11. Giesebrecht prefixes it to ver. 1, and dates the whole passage from the Exile. Wellhausen calls 5-11 an older passage than the rest of the prophecy, and removes it altogether as not Habakkuk's. To the latter he assigns what remains, i. 1-4, 12-17, ii. 1-5, and dates it from the reign of Jehoiakim.*

Third: from each of these groups of critics Budde of Strasburg borrows something, but so as to construct an arrangement of the verses, and to reach a date, for the whole, from which both differ.† With Hitzig, Ewald, König, Smend, Giesebrecht, and Wellhausen he agrees that the violence complained of in i. 2-4 is that inflicted by a heathen oppressor, "the wicked," on the Jewish nation, the "righteous." But with Kuenen and others he holds that the Chaldeans are raised up, according to i. 5-11, to punish the violence complained of in i. 2-4 and again in i. 12-17. In these verses it is the ravages of another heathen power than the Chaldeans which Budde describes. The Chaldeans are still to come, and cannot be the same as the devastator whose long continued tyranny is described in i. 12-17. They are rather the power which is to punish him. He can only be the Assyrian. But if that be so, the proper place for the passage, i. 5-11, which describes the rise of the Chaldeans must be after the description of the Assyrian ravages in i. 12-17, and in the body of God's answer to the prophet which we find in ii. 2 ff. Budde therefore places i. 5-11 after ii. 2-4. But if the Chaldeans are still to come, and Budde thinks that they are described vaguely and with a good deal of imagination, the prophecy thus arranged must fall somewhere between 625, when Nabopolassar the Chaldean made himself independent of Assyria and King of Babylon, and 607, when Assyria fell. That the prophet calls Judah "righteous" is proof that he wrote after the great Reform of 621; hence, too, his reference to Torah and Mishpat (i. 4), and his complaint of the obstacles which Assyrian supremacy presented to their free course. As the Assyrian yoke appears not to have been felt anywhere in Judah by 608, Budde would fix the exact date of Habakkuk's prophecy about 615. To these conclusions of Budde Cornill, who in 1891 had very confidently assigned the prophecy of Habakkuk to the reign of Jehoiakim, gave his adherence in 1896.‡

Budde's very able and ingenious argument has been subjected to a searching criticism by Professor Davidson, who emphasises first the difficulty of accounting for the transposition of chap. i. 5-11 from what Budde alleges to have been its original place after ii. 4 to its present position in chap. i.§ He points out that if chap. i. 2-4 and 12-17 and ii. 5 ff. refer to the Assyrian, it is strange the latter is not once mentioned. Again, by 615 we may infer (though we know little of Assyrian history at this time) that the Assyrian's hold on Judah was already too relaxed for the prophet to impute to him power to hinder the Law, especially as Josiah had begun to carry his reforms into the northern kingdom; and the knowledge of the Chaldeans displayed in i. 5-11 is too fresh and detailed * to suit so early a date: it was possible only after the battle of Carchemish. And again, it is improbable that we have two different nations, as Budde thinks, described by the very similar phrases in i. 11, "his own power becomes his god," and in i. 16, "he sacrifices to his net." Again, chap. i. 5-11 would not read quite naturally after chap. ii. 4. And in the woes pronounced on the oppressor it is not one nation, the Chaldeans, which are to spoil him, but all the remnant of the peoples (ii. 7, 8).

These objections are not inconsiderable. But are they conclusive? And if not, is any of the other theories of the prophecy less beset with difficulties?

The objections are scarcely conclusive. We have no proof that the power of Assyria was altogether removed from Judah by 615; on the contrary, even in 608 Assyria was still the power with which Egypt went forth to contend for the empire of the world. Seven years earlier her hand may well have been strong upon Palestine. Again, by 615 the Chaldeans, a people famous in Western Asia for a long time, had been ten years independent: men in Palestine may have been familiar with their methods of warfare; at least it is impossible to say they were not.† There is more weight in the objection drawn from the absence of the name of Assyria from all of the passages which Budde alleges describe it; nor do we get over all difficulties of text by inserting i. 5-11 between ii. 4 and 5. Besides, how does Budde explain i. 12*b* on the theory that it means Assyria? Is the clause not premature at that point? Does he propose to elide it, like Wellhausen? And in any case an erroneous transposition of the original is impossible to prove and difficult to account for.‡

But have not the other theories of the Book of Habakkuk equally great difficulties? Surely, we cannot say that the "righteous" and the "wicked" in i. 4 mean something different from what they do in i. 13? But if this is impossible the construction of the book supported by the great majority of critics § falls to the ground. Professor Davidson justly says that it has "something artificial in it" and "puts a strain on the natural sense." ‖ How can the Chaldeans be described in i. 5 as "just about to be raised up," and in 14-17 as already for a long time the devastators of earth? Ewald's, Hitzig's,

* See further note on p. 591.

† "Studien u. Kritiken" for 1893.

‡ *Cf.* the opening of § 30 in the first edition of his "Einleitung" with that of § 34 in the third and fourth editions.

§ Budde's explanation of this is, that to the later editors of the book, long after the Babylonian destruction of Jews, it was incredible that the Chaldean should be represented as the deliverer of Israel, and so the account of him was placed where, while his call to punish Israel for her sins was not emphasised, he should be pictured as destined to doom; and so the prophecy originally referring to the Assyrian was read of him. "This is possible," says Davidson. "If it be true, criticism is not without its romance."

* This in opposition to Budde's statement that the description of the Chaldeans in i. 5-11 "ist eine phantastische Schilderung" (p. 387).

† It is, however, a serious question whether it would be possible in 615 to describe the Chaldeans as "a nation that traversed the breadth of the earth to occupy dwelling-places that were not his own" (i, 6). This suits better after the battle of Carchemish.

‡ See above.

§ See above, pp. 587 ff.

‖ Page 572.

and König's views * are equally beset by these difficulties; König's exposition also "strains the natural sense." Everything, in fact, points to i. 5-11 being out of its proper place; it is no wonder that Giesebrecht, Wellhausen, and Budde independently arrived at this conclusion.† Whether Budde be right in inserting i. 5-11 after ii. 4, there can be little doubt of the correctness of his views that i. 12-17 describe a heathen oppressor who is not the Chaldeans. Budde says this oppressor is Assyria. Can he be any one else? From 608 to 605 Judah was sorely beset by Egypt, who had overrun all Syria up to the Euphrates. The Egyptians killed Josiah, deposed his successor, and put their own vassal under a very heavy tribute; "gold and silver were exacted of the people of the land:" the picture of distress in i. 1-4 might easily be that of Judah in these three terrible years. And if we assigned the prophecy to them, we should certainly give it a date at which the knowledge of the Chaldeans expressed in i. 5-11 was more probable than at Budde's date of 615. But then does the description in chap. i. 14-17 suit Egypt so well as it does Assyria? We can hardly affirm this, until we know more of what Egypt did in those days, but it is very probable.

Therefore, the theory supported by the majority of critics being unnatural, we are, with our present meagre knowledge of the time, flung back upon Budde's interpretation that the prophet in i. 2-ii. 4 appeals from oppression by a heathen power, which is not the Chaldean, but upon which the Chaldean shall bring the just vengeance of God. The tyrant is either Assyria up to about 615 or Eygpt from 608 to 605, and there is not a little to be said for the latter date.

In arriving at so uncertain a conclusion about i.-ii. 4, we have but these consolations, that no other is possible in our present knowledge, and that the uncertainty will not hamper us much in our appreciation of Habakkuk's spiritual attitude and poetic gifts.‡

2. Chap. II. 5-20.

The dramatic piece i. 2-ii. 4 is succeeded by a series of fine taunt-songs, starting after an introduction from *6b*, then 9, 11, 15, and (18) 19, and each opening with "Woe!" Their subject is, if we take Budde's interpretation of the dramatic piece, the Assyrian and not the Chaldean § tyrant. The text, as we shall see when we come to it, is corrupt. Some words are manifestly wrong, and the rhythm must have suffered beyond restoration. In all probability these fine lyric Woes, or at least as many of them as are authentic—for there is doubt about one or two—were of equal length. Whether they all originally had the refrain now attached to two is more doubtful.

Hitzig suspected the authenticity of some parts of this series of songs. Stade * and Kuenen have gone further and denied the genuineness of vv. 9-20. But this is with little reason. As Budde says, a series of Woes was to be expected here by a prophet who follows so much the example of Isaiah.† In spite of Kuenen's objection, vv. 9-11 would not be strange of the Chaldean, but they suit the Assyrian better. Vv. 12-14 are doubtful: 12 recalls Micah iii. 10; 13 is a repetition of Jer. li. 58; 14 is a variant of Isa. xi. 9. Very likely Jer. li. 58, a late passage, is borrowed from this passage; yet the addition used here, "Are not these things ‡ from the Lord of Hosts?" looks as if it noted a citation. Vv. 15-17 are very suitable to the Assyrian; there is no reason to take them from Habakkuk.§ The final song, vv. 18 and 19, has its Woe at the beginning of its second verse, and closely resembles the language of later prophets.‖ Moreover the refrain forms a suitable close at the end of ver. 17. Ver. 20 is a quotation from Zephaniah,¶ perhaps another sign of the composite character of the end of this chapter. Some take it to have been inserted as an introduction to the theophany in chap. iii.

Smend has drawn up a defence ** of the whole passage, ii. 9-20, which he deems not only to stand in a natural relation to vv. 4-8, but to be indispensable to them. That the passage quotes from other prophets, he holds to be no proof against its authenticity. If we break off with ver. 8, he thinks that we must impute to Habakkuk the opinion that the wrongs of the world are chiefly avenged by human means—a conclusion which is not to be expected after chap. i.-ii. 1 ff.

3. Chap. III.

The third chapter, an Ode or Rhapsody, is ascribed to Habakkuk by its title. This, however, does not prove its authenticity: the title is too like those assigned to the Psalms in the period of the Second Temple.†† On the contrary, the title itself, the occurrence of the musical sign Selah in the contents, and the colophon suggest for the chapter a liturgical origin after the Exile.‡‡ That this is more probable than the alternative opinion, that, being a genuine work of Habakkuk, the chapter was afterwards arranged as a Psalm for public worship, is confirmed by

* See above, pp. 588 f.

† Wellhausen in 1873 (see p. 661); Giesebrecht in 1890; Budde in 1892, before he had seen the opinions of either of the others (see "Stud. und Krit.," 1893, p. 386, *n.* 2).

‡ Cornill quotes a rearrangement of chaps. i., ii., by Rothstein, who takes i. 2-4, 12 *a*, 13, ii. 1-3, 4, 5 *a*, i. 6-10, 14, 15 *a*, ii. 6 *b*, 7, 9, 10 *a b β*, 11, 15, 16, 19, 18, as an oracle against Jehoiakim and the godless in Israel about 605, which during the Exile was worked up into the present oracle against Babylon. Cornill esteems it "too complicated." Budde ("Expositor," 1895, pp. 372 ff.) and Nowack hold it untenable.

§ As of course was universally supposed according to either of the other two interpretations given above.

* "Z. A. T. W.," 1884, p. 154.

† *Cf.* Isa. v. 8 ff (x. 1-4), etc.

‡ So LXX.

§ *Cf.* Davidson, p. 56, and Budde, p. 391, who allows 9-11 and 15-17.

‖ *E. g.*, Isa. xl. 18 ff., xliv. 9 ff., xlvi. 5 ff., etc. On this ground it is condemned by Stade, Kuenen, and Budde. Davidson finds this not a serious difficulty, for, he points out, Habakkuk anticipates several later lines of thought.

¶ See above, p. 569, *n.*

** "A. T. Religionsgeschichte," p. 229, *n.* 2.

†† *Cf.* the ascription by the LXX. of Psalms cxlvi.—cl. to the prophets Haggai and Zechariah.

‡‡ *Cf.* Kuenen, who conceives it to have been taken from a post-exilic collection of Psalms. See also Cheyne, "The Origin of the Psalter: "exilic or more probably post-exilic" (p. 125). "The most natural position for it is in the Persian period. It was doubtless appended to Habakkuk, for the same reason for which Isa. lxiii. 7-lxiv. was attached to the great prophecy of Restoration, viz., that the earlier national troubles seemed to the Jewish Church to be typical of its own sore troubles after the Return. . . . The lovely closing verses of Hab. iii. are also in a tone congenial to the later religion" (p. 156). Much less certain is the assertion that the language is imitative and artificial (*ibid.*); while the statement that in ver. 3—*cf.* with Deut. xxxiii. 2—we have an instance of the effort to avoid the personal name of the Deity (p. 287) is disproved by the use of the latter in ver. 2 and other verses.

the fact that no other work of the prophets has been treated in the same way. Nor do the contents support the authorship by Habakkuk. They reflect no definite historical situation like the preceding chapters. The style and temper are different. While in them the prophet speaks for himself, here it is the nation or congregation of Israel that addresses God. The language is not, as some have maintained, late;* but the designation of the people as "Thine anointed," a term which before the Exile was applied to the king, undoubtedly points to a post-exilic date. The figures, the theophany itself, are not necessarily archaic, but are more probably moulded on archaic models. There are many affinities with Psalms of a late date.

At the same time a number of critics† maintain the genuineness of the chapter, and they have some grounds for this. Habakkuk was, as we can see from chaps. i. and ii., a real poet. There was no need why a man of his temper should be bound down to reflecting only his own day. If so practical a prophet as Hosea, and one who has so closely identified himself with his times, was wont to escape from them to a retrospect of the dealings of God with Israel from of old, why should not the same be natural for a prophet who was much less practical and more literary and artistic? There are also many phrases in the Psalm which may be interpreted as reflecting the same situation as chaps. i., ii. All this, however, only proves possibility.

The Psalm has been adapted in Psalm lxxvii. 17-20.

Further Note on Chap. I.-II. 4.

Since this chapter was in print Nowack's "Die Kleinen Propheten" in the "Handkommentar z. A. T." has been published. He recognises emphatically that the disputed passage about the Chaldeans, chap. i. 5-11, is out of place where it lies (this against Kuenen and the other authorities cited above, p. 588), and admits that it follows on, with a natural connection, to chap. ii. 4, to which Budde proposes to attach it. Nevertheless, for other reasons, which he does not state, he regards Budde's proposal as untenable; and reckons the disputed passage to be by another hand than Habakkuk's, and intruded into the latter's argument. Habakkuk's argument he assigns to after 605; perhaps 590. The tyrant complained against would therefore be the Chaldean.—Driver in the 6th ed. of his "Introduction" (1897) deems Budde's argument "too ingenious," and holds by the older and most numerously supported argument (above, pp. 588 ff.).—On a review of the case in the light of these two discussions, the present writer holds to his opinion that Budde's rearrangement, which he has adopted, offers the fewest difficulties.

CHAPTER X.

THE PROPHET AS SCEPTIC.

Habakkuk i.-ii. 4.

Of the prophet Habaḳḳuk we know nothing that is personal save his name—to our ears his somewhat odd name. It is the intensive form of a root which means to caress or embrace. More probably it was given to him as a child, than afterwards assumed as a symbol of his clinging to God.‡

Tradition says that Habakkuk was a priest, the son of Joshua, of the tribe of Levi, but this is only an inference from the late liturgical notes to the Psalm which has been appended to his prophecy.* All that we know for certain is that he was a contemporary of Jeremiah, with a sensitiveness under wrong and impulses to question God which remind us of Jeremiah; but with a literary power which is quite his own. We may emphasise the latter, even though we recognise upon his writing the influence of Isaiah's.

Habakkuk's originality, however, is deeper than style. He is the earliest who is known to us of a new school of religion in Israel. He is called "prophet," but at first he does not adopt the attitude which is characteristic of the prophets. His face is set in an opposite direction to theirs. They address the nation Israel, on behalf of God: he rather speaks to God on behalf of Israel. Their task was Israel's sin, the proclamation of God's doom, and the offer of His grace to their penitence. Habakkuk's task is God Himself, the effort to find out what He means by permitting tyranny and wrong. They attack the sins, he is the first to state the problems, of life. To him the prophetic revelation, the Torah, is complete: it has been codified in Deuteronomy and enforced by Josiah. Habakkuk's business is not to add to it, but to ask why it does not work. Why does God suffer wrong to triumph, so that the Torah is paralysed, and Mishpat, the prophetic "justice" or "judgment," comes to naught? The prophets travailed for Israel's character—to get the people to love justice till justice prevailed among them: Habakkuk feels justice cannot prevail in Israel, because of the great disorder which God permits to fill the world. It is true that he arrives at a prophetic attitude, and before the end authoritatively declares God's will; but he begins by searching for the latter, with an appreciation of the great obscurity cast over it by the facts of life. He complains to God, asks questions, and expostulates. This is the beginning of speculation in Israel. It does not go far: it is satisfied with stating questions *to* God; it does not, directly at least, state questions *against* Him. But Habakkuk at least feels that revelation is baffled by experience, that the facts of life bewilder a man who believes in the God whom the prophets have declared to Israel. As in Zephaniah prophecy begins to exhibit traces

* ישע את, ver. 13, cannot be taken as a proof of lateness; read probably הושיע את.

† Pusey, Ewald, König, Sinker ("The Psalm of Habakkuk," Cambridge, 1890.) Kirkpatrick (Smith's "Bible Dict.," art. "Habakkuk"), Von Orelli.

‡ חֲבַקּוּק (the Greek Ἀμβακουμ, LXX. version of the title of this book, and again the inscription to "Bel and the Dragon," suggests the pointing חַבְּקוּק; Epiph., "De Vitis Proph."—see next note—spells it Ἀββακουμ), from חבק, "to embrace." Jerome: "He is called 'embrace' either because of his love to the Lord, or because he wrestles with God." Luther: "Habakkuk means one who comforts and holds up his people as one embraces a weeping person."

* See above, pp. 590 ff. The title to the Greek version of "Bel and the Dragon" bears that the latter was taken from the prophecy of Hambakoum, son of Jesus, of the tribe of Levi. Further details are offered in the "De Vitis Prophetarum" of (Pseud-) Epiphanius, "Epiph. Opera," ed. Paris, 1622, Vol. II. p. 147, according to which Habakkuk belonged to Βεθζοχηρ, which is probably Βεθζαχαριας of 1 Macc. vi. 32, the modern Beit-Zakaryeh, a little to the north of Hebron, and placed by this notice, as Nahum's Elkosh is placed, in the tribe of Simeon. His grave was shown in the neighbouring Keilah. The notice further alleges that when Nebuchadrezzar came up to Jerusalem Habakkuk fled to Ostracine, where he travelled in the country of the Ishmaelites; but he returned after the fall of Jerusalem, and died in 538, two years before the return of the exiles. "Bel and the Dragon" tells an extraordinary story of his miraculous carriage of food to Daniel in the lions' den soon after Cyrus had taken Babylon.

of apocalypse, so in Habakkuk we find it developing the first impulses of speculation.

We have seen that the course of events which troubles Habakkuk and renders the Torah ineffectual is somewhat obscure. On one interpretation of these two chapters, that which takes the present order of their verses as the original, Habakkuk asks why God is silent in face of the injustice which fills the whole horizon (chap. i. 1-4), is told to look round among the heathen and see how God is raising up the Chaldeans (i. 5-11), presumably to punish this injustice (if it be Israel's own) or to overthrow it (if vv. 1-4 mean that it is inflicted on Israel by a foreign power). But the Chaldeans only aggravate the prophet's problem; they themselves are a wicked and oppressive people: how can God suffer them? (i. 12-17). Then come the prophet's waiting for an answer (ii. 1) and the answer itself (ii. 2 ff.). Another interpretation takes the passage about the Chaldeans (i. 5-11) to be out of place where it now lies, removes it to after chap. ii. 4 as a part of God's answer to the prophet's problem, and leaves the remainder of chap. i. as the description of the Assyrian oppression of Israel, baffling the Torah and perplexing the prophet's faith in a Holy and Just God.* Of these two views the former is, we have seen, somewhat artificial, and though the latter is by no means proved, the arguments for it are sufficient to justify us in re-arranging the verses chap. i.-ii. 4 in accordance with its proposals.

"The Oracle which Habakkuk the Prophet
Received by Vision.†

How long, O Jehovah, have I called and Thou hearest not?
I cry to Thee, Wrong! and Thou sendest no help.
Why make me look upon sorrow,
And fill mine eyes with trouble?
Violence and wrong are before me,
Strife comes and quarrel arises.‡
So the Law is benumbed, and judgment never gets forth: §
For the wicked beleaguers the righteous,
So judgment comes forth perverted.

. . . . . . ‖

Art not Thou of old, Jehovah, my God, my Holy One? . . . ¶
Purer of eyes than to behold evil,
And that canst not gaze upon trouble!
Why gazest Thou upon traitors,**
Art dumb when the wicked swallows him that is more righteous than he? ††
Thou hast let men be made ‡‡ like fish of the sea,
Like worms that have no ruler! §§
He lifts the whole of it with his angle;
Draws it in with his net, sweeps it in his drag-net:
So rejoices and exults.
So he sacrifices to his net, and offers incense to his drag-net;
For by them is his portion fat, and his food rich.
Shall he for ever draw his sword,‖‖
And ceaselessly, ruthlessly massacre nations? ¶¶

* See above, pp. 589 ff.
† Heb. "saw."
‡ Text uncertain. Perhaps we should read, "Why make me look upon sorrow and trouble? why fill mine eyes with violence and wrong? Strife is come before me, and quarrel arises."
§ "Never gets away," to use a colloquial expression.
‖ Here vv. 5-11 come in the original.
¶ Ver. 12*b*: "We shall not die" (many Jewish authorities read "Thou shalt not die"). "O Jehovah, for judgment hast Thou set him, and, O my Rock, for punishment hast Thou appointed him."
** Wellhausen; "on the robbery of robbers."
†† LXX. "devoureth the righteous."
‡‡ Literally "Thou hast made men."
§§ Wellhausen: *cf.* Jer. xviii. 1, xix. 1.
‖‖ So Giesebrecht (see above, p. 588, *n.*), reading הרבו
העולם יריק for העל־כן יריק חרמו. "shall he therefore empty his net?"
¶¶ Wellhausen, reading יהרג for לַהרג: "should he therefore be emptying his net continually, and slaughtering the nations without pity?"

"Upon my watch-tower I will stand,
And take my post on the rampart.*
I will watch to see what He will say to me,
And what answer I † get back to my plea.

"And Jehovah answered me and said:
Write the vision, and make it plain upon tablets,
That he may run who reads it.

"For ‡ the vision is for a time yet to be fixed,
Yet it hurries § to the end, and shall not fail:
Though it linger, wait thou for it;
Coming it shall come, and shall not be behind.‖
Lo! swollen,¶ not level is his ** soul within him;
But the righteous shall live by his faithfulness.††

. . . .

Look ‡‡ round among the heathen, and look well,
Shudder and be shocked; §§
For I am ‖‖ about to do a work in your days,
Ye shall not believe it when told.
For, lo, I am about to raise up the Kasdim,¶¶
A people the most bitter and the most hasty,
That traverse the breadths of the earth,
To possess dwelling-places not their own.
Awful and terrible are they;
From themselves *** start their purpose and rising.

"Fleeter than leopards their steeds,
Swifter than night-wolves.
Their horsemen leap ††† from afar;
They swoop like the eagle a-haste to devour.
All for wrong do they ‡‡‡ come:
The set of their faces is forward,§§§
And they sweep up captives like sand.
They—at kings do they scoff,
And princes are sport to them.

* מצור. But Wellhausen takes it as from נצר and = "ward" or "watch-tower." So Nowack.
† So Heb. and LXX.; but Syr. "he": so Wellhausen, "what answer He returns to my plea."
‡ Bredenkamp ("Stud. u. Krit.," 1889, pp. 161 ff.) suggests that the writing on the tablets begins here and goes on to ver. 5*a*. Budde ("Z. A. T. W.," 1889, pp. 155 f.) takes the כי which opens it as simply equivalent to the Greek ὅτι, introducing, like our marks of quotation, the writing itself.
§ וְיָפֵחַ: *cf.* Psalm xxvii. 12. Bredenkamp emends to וְיִפְרַח.
‖ "Not be late," or past its fixed time.
¶ So literally the Heb. עֻפְּלָה, *i. e.*, "arrogant, false": *cf.* the colloquial expression "swollen-head" = conceit, as opposed to level-headed. Bredenkamp, "Stud. u. Krit.," 1889, 121, reads הַנֶּעְלָף for הִנֵּה עֻפְּלָה. Wellhausen suggests הִנֵּה הָעַוָּל, "Lo, the sinner," in contrast to צדיק of next clause. Nowack prefers this.
** LXX. wrongly "my."
†† LXX. πίστις "faith," and so in N. T.
‡‡ Chap. i. 5-11.
§§ So to bring out the assonance, reading וּתְמָהוּ
הִתְמַהְמְהוּ וּתְמָהוּ.
‖‖ So LXX.
¶¶ Or Chaldeans; on the name and people see above, p. 565.
*** Heb. singular.
††† Omit ופרשיו (evidently a dittography) and the lame יבאו which is omitted by LXX. and was probably inserted to afford a verb for the second פרשיו.
‡‡‡ Heb. sing., and so in all the clauses here except the next.
§§§ A problematical rendering. מגמה is found only here, and probably means "direction." Hitzig translates "desire, effort, striving." קדימה, "towards the front" or "forward"; but elsewhere it means only "eastward": קדים, "the east wind." *Cf.* Judg. v. 21, נהל קישון נהל קדומים, "a river of spates" or "rushes is the river Kishon" ("Hist. Geog.," p. 395). Perhaps we should change פניהים to a singular suffix as in the clauses before and after and this would leave מ to form with קדימה a participle from הקדים (*cf.* Amos ix. 10.)

They—they laugh at each fortress,
Heap dust up and take it!
Then the wind shifts * and they pass!
But doomed are those whose own strength is their god!" †

The difficulty of deciding between the various arrangements of the two chapters of Habakkuk does not, fortunately, prevent us from appreciating his argument. What he feels throughout (this is obvious, however you arrange his verses) is the tyranny of a great heathen power,‡ be it Assyrian, Egyptian, or Chaldean. The prophet's horizon is filled with wrong: § Israel thrown into disorder, revelation paralysed, justice perverted. ‖ But, like Nahum, Habakkuk feels not for Israel alone. The tyrant has outraged humanity.¶ He "sweeps peoples into his net," and as soon as he empties this, he fills it again "ceaselessly," as if there were no just God above. He exults in his vast cruelty, and has success so unbroken that he worships the very means of it. In itself such impiety is gross enough, but to a heart that believes in God it is a problem of exquisite pain. Habakkuk's is the burden of the finest faith. He illustrates the great commonplace of religious doubt, that problems arise and become rigorous in proportion to the purity and tenderness of man's conception of God. It is not the coarsest but the finest temperaments which are exposed to scepticism. Every advance in assurance of God or in appreciation of His character develops new perplexities in face of the facts of experience, and faith becomes her own most cruel troubler. Habakkuk's questions are not due to any cooling of the religious temper in Israel, but are begotten of the very heat and ardour of prophecy in its encounter with experience. His tremulousness, for instance, is impossible without the high knowledge of God's purity and faithfulness, which older prophets had achieved in Israel:—

"Art not Thou of old, O Lord, my God, my Holy One,
Purer of eyes than to behold evil,
And incapable of looking upon wrong?"

His despair is that which comes only from eager and persevering habits of prayer:—

"How long, O Lord, have I called and Thou hearest not!
I cry to Thee of wrong and Thou givest no help!"

His questions, too, are bold with that sense of God's absolute power, which flashed so bright in Israel as to blind men's eyes to all secondary and intermediate causes. "Thou," he says,—

"Thou hast made men like fishes of the sea,
Like worms that have no ruler,"

boldly charging the Almighty, in almost the temper of Job himself, with being the cause of the cruelty inflicted by the unchecked tyrant upon the nations; "for shall evil happen, and Jehovah not have done it?" ** Thus all through we perceive that Habakkuk's trouble springs from the central founts of prophecy. This scepticism—if we may venture to give the name to the first motions in Israel's mind of that temper which undoubtedly became scepticism—this scepticism was the inevitable heritage of prophecy: the stress and pain to which prophecy was forced by its own strong convictions in face of the facts of experience. Habakkuk, "the prophet," as he is called, stood in the direct line of his order, but just because of that he was the father also of Israel's religious doubt.

But a discontent springing from sources so pure was surely the preparation of its own healing. In a verse of exquisite beauty the prophet describes the temper in which he trusted for an answer to all his doubts:—

"On my watch-tower will I stand,
And take up my post on the rampart;
I will watch to see what He says to me,
And what answer I get back to my plea."

This verse is not to be passed over, as if its metaphors were merely for literary effect. They express rather the moral temper in which the prophet carries his doubt, or, to use New Testament language, "the good conscience, which some having put away, concerning faith have made shipwreck." Nor is this temper patience only and a certain elevation of mind, nor only a fixed attention and sincere willingness to be answered. Through the chosen words there breathes a noble sense of responsibility. The prophet feels he has a post to hold, a rampart to guard. He knows the heritage of truth, won by the great minds of the past; and in a world seething with disorder, he will take his stand upon that and see what more his God will send him. At the very least, he will not indolently drift, but feel that he has a standpoint, however narrow, and bravely hold it. Such has ever been the attitude of the greatest sceptics—not only, let us repeat, earnestness and sincerity, but the recognition of duty towards the truth: the conviction that even the most tossed and troubled minds have somewhere a ποῦ στῶ appointed of God, and upon it interests human and Divine to defend. Without such a conscience, scepticism, however intellectually gifted, will avail nothing. Men who drift never discover, never grasp aught. They are only dazzled by shifting gleams of the truth, only fretted and broken by experience.

Taking then his stand within the patient temper, but especially upon the conscience of his great order, the prophet waits for his answer and the healing of his trouble. The answer comes to him in the promise of "a Vision," which, though it seem to linger, will not be later than the time fixed by God. "A Vision" is something realised, experienced—something that will be as actual and present to the waiting prophet as the cruelty which now fills his sight. Obviously some series of historical events is meant, by which, in the course of time, the unjust oppressor of the nations shall be overthrown and the righteous vindicated. Upon the re-arrangement of the text proposed by Budde,* this series of events is the rise of the Chaldeans, and it is an argument in favour of his proposal that the promise of "a Vision" requires some such historical picture to follow it as we find in the description of the Chaldeans

*Or "their spirit changes," or "they change like the wind" (Wellhausen suggests כרוח). Grätz reads כֹּה and יַחֲלִיף, 'he renews his strength."

† Von Orelli For אשם Wellhausen proposes וַיָּשֶׂם, "and sets."

‡ "The wicked" of chap. i. 4 must, as we have seen, be the same as "the wicked" of chap. i. 13—a heathen oppressor of "the righteous," *i. e.*, the people of God.

§ i. 3.

‖ i. 4.

¶ i. 13–17.

** Amos iii. 6. See p. 464.

*See above, pp. 589 ff.

—chap. i. 5-11. This, too, is explicitly introduced by terms of vision: "See among the nations and look round . . . . Yea, behold I am about to raise up the Kasdim." But before this vision is given,* and for the uncertain interval of waiting ere the facts come to pass, the Lord enforces upon His watching servant the great moral principle that arrogance and tyranny cannot, from the nature of them, last, and that if the righteous be only patient he will survive them:—

"Lo, swollen, not level, is his soul within him;
But the righteous shall live by his faithfulness."

We have already seen † that the text of the first line of this couplet is uncertain. Yet the meaning is obvious, partly in the words themselves, and partly by their implied contrast with the second line. The soul of the wicked is a radically morbid thing: *inflated, swollen* (unless we should read *perverted*, which more plainly means the same thing ‡), not *level*, not natural and normal. In the nature of things it cannot endure. "But the righteous shall live by his faithfulness." This word, wrongly translated *faith* by the Greek and other versions, is concentrated by Paul in his repeated quotation from the Greek§ upon that single act of faith by which the sinner secures forgiveness and justification. With Habakkuk it is a wider term. *'Emunah,*‖ from a verb meaning originally to be firm, is used in the Old Testament in the physical sense of steadfastness. So it is applied to the arms of Moses held up by Aaron and Hur over the battle with Amalek: "they were steadiness till the going down of the sun."¶ It is also used of the faithful discharge of public office,** and of fidelity as between man and wife.†† It is also faithful testimony,‡‡ equity in judgment,§§ truth in speech,‖‖ and sincerity or honest dealing.¶¶ Of course it has faith in God as its secret—the verb from which it is derived is the regular Hebrew term to believe—but it is rather the temper which faith produces of endurance, steadfastness, integrity. Let the righteous, however baffled his faith be by experience, hold on in loyalty to God and duty, and he shall live. Though St. Paul, as we have said, used the Greek rendering of "faith" for the enforcement of trust in God's mercy through Jesus Christ as the secret of forgiveness and life, it is rather to Habakkuk's wider intention of patience and fidelity that the author of the Epistle to the Hebrews returns in his fuller quotation of the verse: "For yet a little while and He that shall come will come and will not tarry; now the just shall live by faith, but if he draw back My soul shall have no pleasure in him."***

Such, then, is the tenor of the passage. In face of experience that baffles faith, the duty of Israel is patience in loyalty to God. In this the nascent scepticism of Israel received its first great commandment, and this it never forsook. Intellectual questions arose, of which Habakkuk's were but the faintest foreboding—questions concerning not only the mission and destiny of the nation, but the very foundation of justice and the character of God Himself. Yet did no sceptic, however bold and however provoked, forsake his *faithfulness*. Even Job, when most audaciously arraigning the God of his experience, turned from Him to God as in his heart of hearts he believed He must be, experience notwithstanding. Even the Preacher, amid the aimless flux and drift which he finds in the universe, holds to the conclusion of the whole matter in a command, which better than any other defines the contents of the *faithfulness* enforced by Habakkuk: "Fear God and keep His commandments, for this is the whole of man." It has been the same with the great mass of the race. Repeatedly disappointed of their hopes, and crushed for ages beneath an intolerable tyranny, have they not exhibited the same heroic temper with which their first great questioner was endowed? Endurance—this above all others has been the quality of Israel: "though He slay me, yet will I trust Him." And, therefore, as Paul's adaptation, "The just shall live by faith," has become the motto of evangelical Christianity, so we may say that Habakkuk's original of it has been the motto and the fame of Judaism: "The righteous shall live by His faithfulness."

CHAPTER XI.

TYRANNY IS SUICIDE.

HABAKKUK ii. 5-20.

IN the style of his master Isaiah, Habakkuk follows up his "Vision" with a series of lyrics on the same subject: chap. ii. 5-20. They are taunt-songs, the most of them beginning with "Woe unto," addressed to the heathen oppressor. Perhaps they were all at first of equal length, and it has been suggested that the striking refrain in which two of them close:—

"For men's blood, and earth's waste,
Cities and their inhabitants—"

was once attached to each of the others as well. But the text has been too much altered, besides suffering several interpolations,* to permit of its restoration, and we can only reproduce these taunts as they now run in the Hebrew text. There are several quotations (not necessarily an argument against Habakkuk's authorship); but, as a whole, the expression is original, and there are some lines of especial force and freshness. Verses 5-6*a* are properly an introduction, the first Woe commencing with 6*b*.

The belief which inspires these songs is very simple. Tyranny is intolerable. In the nature of things it cannot endure, but works out its own penalties. By oppressing so many nations, the tyrant is preparing the instruments of his own destruction. As he treats them, so in time shall they treat him. He is like a debtor who increases the number of his creditors. Some day they shall rise up and exact from him the last penny. So that in cutting off others he is "but forfeiting his own life." The very violence done to nature, the deforesting of Lebanon for instance, and the vast hunting of wild beasts, shall recoil on him. This line of thought is exceedingly in-

*Its proper place in Budde's re-arrangement is after chap. ii. 4.
† Above, p. 592, *n.*
‡ עֻקְּלָה instead of עֻפְּלָה.
§ Rom. i. 17; Gal. iii. 11.
‖ אֱמוּנָה.
¶ Exod. xvii. 12.
** 2 Chron. xix. 9.
†† Hosea ii. 22 (Heb.).
‡‡ Prov. xiv. 5.
§§ Isa. xi. 5.
‖‖ Prov. xii. 17: *cf.* Jer. ix. 2.
¶¶ Prov. xii. 22, xxviii. 30.
*** Heb. x. 37, 38.

* See above, p. 590.

teresting. We have already seen in prophecy, and especially in Isaiah, the beginnings of Hebrew Wisdom—the attempt to uncover the moral processes of life and express a philosophy of history. But hardly anywhere have we found so complete an absence of all reference to the direct interference of God Himself in the punishment of the tyrant; for "the cup of Jehovah's right hand" in ver. 16 is simply the survival of an ancient metaphor. These "proverbs" or "taunt-songs," in conformity with the proverbs of the later Wisdom, dwell only upon the inherent tendency to decay of all injustice. Tyranny, they assert, and history ever since has affirmed their truthfulness—tyranny is suicide.

The last of the taunt-songs, which treats of the different subject of idolatry, is probably, as we have seen, not from Habakkuk's hand, but of a later date.*

INTRODUCTION TO THE TAUNT-SONGS (ii. 5-6*a*).

"For . . . † treacherous,
An arrogant fellow, and is not . . ‡
Who opens his desire wide as Sheol;
He is like death, unsatisfied;
And hath swept to himself all the nations,
And gathered to him all peoples.
Shall not these, all of them, take up a proverb upon him,
And a taunt-song against him? and say:—

FIRST TAUNT-SONG (ii. 6*b*-8).

"Woe unto him who multiplies what is not his own,—
How long?—
And loads him with debts! §
Shall not thy creditors ‖ rise up,
And thy troublers awake,
And thou be for spoil ¶ to them?
Because thou hast spoiled many nations,
All the rest of the peoples shall spoil thee.
For men's blood, and earth's waste,
Cities and all their inhabitants." **

SECOND TAUNT-SONG (ii. 9-11).

"Woe unto him that gains evil gain for his house, ††
To set high his nest, to save him from the grasp of calamity!

* See above, p. 590. Nowack (1897) agrees that Cornill's and others' conclusion that vv. 9-20 are not Habakkuk's is too sweeping. He takes the first, second, and fourth of the taunt-songs as authentic, but assigns the third (vv. 12-14) and the fifth (18-20) to another hand. He deems the refrain, 8*b* and 17*b*, to be a gloss, and puts 19 before 18. Driver, "Introd.," 6th ed., holds to the authenticity of all the verses.

† The text reads, "For also wine is treacherous," under which we might be tempted to suspect some such original as, "As wine is treacherous, so" (next line) "the proud fellow," etc. (or, as Davidson suggests, "Like wine is the treacherous dealer"), were it not that the word "wine" appears neither in the Greek nor in the Syrian version. Wellhausen suggests that היין, "wine," is a corruption of הוי, with which the verse, like vv. 6*b*, 9, 12, 15, 19, may have originally begun, but according to 6*a* the taunt-songs, opening with הוי, start first in 6*b*. Bredenkamp proposes וְאֶפֶס כְּאַיִן.

‡ The text is ינוה, a verb not elsewhere found in the Old Testament, and conjectured by our translators to mean "keepeth at home," because the noun allied to it means "homestead" or "resting-place." The Syriac gives "is not satisfied," and Wellhausen proposes to read ירוה with that sense. See Davidson's note on the verse.

§ A. V. "thick clay," which is reached by breaking up the word עבטיט, "pledge" or "debt," into עב, "thick cloud," and טיט, "clay."

‖ Literally "thy biters," נשכיך, but נשך, "biting," is "interest" or "usury," and the Hiphil of נשך is "to exact interest."

¶ LXX. sing., Heb. pl.

** These words occur again in ver 17. Wellhausen thinks they suit neither here nor there. But they suit all the taunt-songs, and some suppose that they formed the refrain to each of these.

†† Dynasty or people?

Thou hast planned shame for thy house;
Thou hast cut off * many people,
While forfeiting thine own life. †
For the stone shall cry out from the wall,
And the lath ‡ from the timber answer it.

THIRD TAUNT-SONG (ii. 12-14).

"Woe unto him that builds a city in blood, §
And stablishes a town in iniquity! ‖
Lo, is it not from Jehovah of hosts,
That the nations shall toil for smoke, ¶
And the peoples shall wear themselves out for nought?
But earth shall be filled with the knowledge of the glory of Jehovah, **
Like the waters that cover the sea.

FOURTH TAUNT-SONG (ii. 15-17).

"Woe unto him that gives his neighbour to drink,
From the cup of his wrath †† till he be drunken,
That he may gloat on his ‡‡ nakedness!
Thou art sated with shame—not with glory;
Drink also thou, and stagger. §§
Comes round to thee the cup of Jehovah's right hand,
And foul shame ‖‖ on thy glory.
For the violence to Lebánon shall cover thee,
The destruction of the beasts shall affray thee. ¶¶
For men's blood, and earth's waste,
Cities and all their inhabitants. ***

FIFTH TAUNT-SONG (ii. 18-20).

"What boots an image, when its artist has graven it,
A cast-image and lie-oracle, that its moulder has trusted upon it,
Making dumb idols?
Woe to him that saith to a block, Awake!
To a dumb stone, Arise!
Can it teach?
Lo, it . . . ††† with gold and silver;
There is no breath at all in the heart of it.
But Jehovah is in His Holy Temple:
Silence before Him, all the earth!"

CHAPTER XII.

"IN THE MIDST OF THE YEARS."

HABAKKUK iii.

WE have seen the impossibility of deciding the age of the ode which is attributed to Habakkuk in the third chapter of his book. ‡‡‡ But this is only one of the many problems raised by that

* So LXX.; Heb. "cutting off."

† The grammatical construction is obscure, if the text be correct. There is no mistaking the meaning.

‡ כפים, not elsewhere found in the O. T., is in Rabbinic Hebrew both "cross-beam" and "lath."

§ Micah iii. 10.

‖ Jer. xxii. 13.

¶ Literally "fire."

** Jer. li. 58: which original?

†† After Wellhausen's suggestion to read מסף חמתו instead of the text מספח חמתך, "adding," or "mixing, thy wrath."

‡‡ So LXX. Q.; Heb. "their."

§§ Read הרעל (*cf.* Nahum ii. 4; Zech. xii. 2). The text is הערל, not found elsewhere, which has been conjectured to mean "uncover the foreskin." And there is some ground for this, as parallel to "his nakedness" in the previous clause. Wellhausen also removes the first clause to the end of the verse: "Drink also thou and reel; there comes to thee the cup in Jehovah's right hand, and thou wilt glut thyself with shame instead of honour."

‖‖ So R. V. for קיקלון, which A. V. has taken as two words—קי, for which *cf.* Jer. xxv. 27, where, however, the text is probably corrupt, and קלון. With this confusion *cf.* above, ver. 6, עבטיט.

¶¶ Read with LXX. יחתך for יחיתן of the text.

*** See above, ver. 8.

††† תְּפוּשׂ?

‡‡‡ Above, pp. 590 ff.

brilliant poem. Much of its text is corrupt, and the meaning of many single words is uncertain. As in most Hebrew poems of description, the tenses of the verbs puzzle us; we cannot always determine whether the poet is singing of that which is past or present or future, and this difficulty is increased by his subject, a revelation of God in nature for the deliverance of Israel. Is this the deliverance from Egypt, with the terrible tempests which accompanied it? Or have the features of the Exodus been borrowed to describe some other deliverance, or to sum up the constant manifestation of Jehovah for His people's help?

The introduction, in ver. 2, is clear. The singer has heard what is to be heard of Jehovah, and His great deeds in the past. He prays for a revival of these "in the midst of the years." The times are full of trouble and turmoil. Would that God, in the present confusion of baffled hopes and broken issues, made Himself manifest by power and brilliance, as of old! "In turmoil remember mercy!" To render "turmoil" by "wrath," as if it were God's anger against which the singer's heart appealed, is not true to the original word itself,* affords no parallel to "the midst of the years," and misses the situation. Israel cries from a state of life in which the obscure years are huddled together and full of turmoil. We need not wish to fix the date more precisely than the writer himself does, but may leave it with him "in the midst of the years."

There follows the description of the Great Theophany, of which, in his own poor times, the singer has heard. It is probable that he has in his memory the events of the Exodus and Sinai. On this point his few geographical allusions agree with his descriptions of nature. He draws all the latter from the desert, or Arabian, side of Israel's history. He introduces none of the sea-monsters, or imputations of arrogance and rebellion to the sea itself, which the influence of Babylonian mythology so thickly scattered through the later sea-poetry of the Hebrews. The Theophany takes place in a violent tempest of thunder and rain, the only process of nature upon which the desert poets of Arabia dwell with any detail. In harmony with this, God appears from the southern desert, from Teman and Paran, as in the theophanies in Deuteronomy xxxiii. and in the Song of Deborah; † a few lines recall the Song of the Exodus,‡ and there are many resemblances to the phraseology of the Sixty-eighth Psalm. The poet sees under trouble the tents of Kushan and of Midian, tribes of Sinai. And though the Theophany is with floods of rain and lightning, and foaming of great waters, it is not with hills, rivers, or sea that God is angry, but with the *nations*, the oppressors of His poor people, and in order that He may deliver the latter. All this, taken with the fact that no mention is made of Egypt, proves that, while the singer draws chiefly upon the marvellous events of the Exodus and Sinai for his description, he celebrates not them alone but all the ancient triumphs of God over the heathen oppressors of Israel. Compare the obscure line—these be "His goings of old."

The report of it all fills the prophet with trembling (ver. 16 returns upon ver. 26), and although his language is too obscure to permit us to follow with certainty the course of his feeling, he appears to await in confidence the issue of Israel's present troubles. His argument seems to be, that such a God may be trusted still, in face of approaching invasion (ver. 16). The next verse, however, does not express the experience of trouble from human foes; but figuring the extreme affliction of drought, barrenness, and poverty, the poet speaking in the name of Israel declares that, in spite of them, he will still rejoice in the God of their salvation (ver. 17). So sudden is this change from human foes to natural plagues that some scholars have here felt a passage to another poem describing a different situation. But the last lines with their confidence in the "God of salvation," a term always used of deliverance from enemies, and the boast, borrowed from the Eighteenth Psalm, "He maketh my feet like to hinds' feet, and gives me to march on my heights," reflect the same circumstances as the bulk of the Psalm, and offer no grounds to doubt the unity of the whole.*

PSALM † OF HABAKKUK THE PROPHET.

"Lord, I have heard the report of Thee ;
I stand in awe ! ‡
Lord, revive Thy work in the midst of the years,
In the midst of the years make Thee known ; §
In turmoil ‖ remember mercy !
God comes from Teman,¶
The Holy from Mount Paran.**
He covers the heavens with His glory.
And filled with His praise is the earth.
The flash is like lightning ;
He has rays from each hand of Him,
Therein †† is the ambush of His might.

Pestilence travels before Him,
The plague-fire breaks forth at His feet.
He stands and earth shakes, ‡‡

* רֹגֶז nowhere in the Old Testament means "wrath," but either roar and noise of thunder (Job xxxvii. 2) and of horsehoofs (xxxix. 24), or the raging of the wicked (iii. 17) or the commotion of fear (iii. 26 ; Isa. xiv. 3).

† "Jehovah from Sinai hath come,
And risen from Se'ir upon them ;
He shone from Mount Paran,
And broke from Meribah of Kadesh :
From the South fire . . . to them."

Deut. xxxiii. 2, slightly altered after the LXX. "South :" some form of ימין must be read to bring the line into parallel with the others ; תימן, Teman, is from the same root.

"Jehovah, in Thy going forth from Se'ir,
In Thy marching from Edom's field,
Earth shook, yea, heaven dropped,
Yea, the clouds dropped water.
Mountains flowed down before Jehovah,
Yon Sinai at the face of the God of Israel."
—Judges v. 4, 5.

‡ Exod. xv.

* In this case ver. 17 would be the only one that offered any reason for suspicion that it was an intrusion.

† תפלה, lit. Prayer, but used for Psalm : *cf.* Psalm cii. 1.

‡ Sinker takes with this the first two words of next line : "I have trembled, O Lord, at Thy work."

§ תודע, Imp. Niph., after LXX. γνωσθήσῃ. The Hebrew has תּוֹדִיעַ, Hi., "make known." The LXX. had a text of these verses which reduplicated them, and it has translated them very badly.

‖ רֹגֶז, "turmoil, noise," as in Job : a meaning that offers a better parallel to "in the midst of the years" than "wrath," which the word also means. Davidson, however, thinks it more natural to understand the "wrath" manifest at the coming of Jehovah to judgment. So Sinker.

¶ Vulg. *ab. Austro*, "from the South."

** LXX. adds κατασκίου δασέος, which seems the translation of a clause, perhaps a gloss, containing the name of Mount Se'ir, as in the parallel descriptions of a theophany. Deut. xxiii. 2, Judg. v. 4. See Sinker, p. 45.

†† Wellhausen, reading שָׂם for שָׁם, translates "He made them," etc.

‡‡ So LXX. Heb. "and measures the earth."

He looks and drives nations asunder;
And the ancient mountains are cloven,
The hills everlasting sink down.
These be His ways from of old.*

"Under trouble I see the tents of Kûshān,†,
The curtains of Midian's land are quivering.
Is it with hils‡ Jehovah is wroth?
Is Thine anger with rivers?
Or against the sea is Thy wrath,
That Thou ridest *it* with horses,
Thy chariots of victory?
Thy bow is stripped bare; §
Thou gluttest (?) *Thy* shafts.‖
Into rivers Thou cleavest the earth; ¶
Mountains see Thee and writhe;
The rainstorm sweeps on: **
The Deep utters his voice,
He lifts up his roar upon high.††
Sun and moon stand still in their dwelling,
At the flash of Thy shafts as they speed,
At the sheen of the lightning, Thy lance.
In wrath Thou stridest the earth,
In anger Thou threshest the nations!
Thou art forth to the help of Thy people,
To save Thine anointed.§§

Thou hast shattered the head from the house of the wicked,
Laying bare *from* . . . * to the neck.
Thou hast pierced with Thy spears the head of his princes.†
They stormed forth to crush me;
Their triumph was as to devour the poor in secret.‡
Thou hast marched on the sea with Thy horses;
Foamed § the great waters.

I have heard, and my heart ‖ shakes;
At the sound my lips tremble,¶
Rottenness enters my bones,**
My steps shake under me.††
I will . . . ‡‡ for the day of trouble
That pours in on the people.§§

Though the fig-tree do not blossom,‖‖
And no fruit be on the vines,
Fail the produce of the olive,
And the fields yield no meat,
Cut off ¶¶ be the flock from the fold,
And no cattle in the stalls,
Yet in the Lord will I exult,
I will rejoice in the God of my salvation.
Jehovah, the Lord, is my might;
He hath made my feet like the hinds',
And on my heights He gives me to march."

This Psalm, whose musical signs prove it to have been employed in the liturgy of the Jewish Temple, has also largely entered into the use of the Christian Church. The vivid style, the sweep of vision, the exultation in the extreme of adversity with which it closes, have made it a frequent theme of preachers and of poets. St. Augustine's exposition of the Septuagint version spiritualises almost every clause into a description of the first and second advents of Christ.*** Calvin's more sober and accurate learning interpreted it of God's guidance of Israel from the time of the Egyptian plagues to the days of Joshua and Gideon, and made it enforce the lesson that He who so wonderfully delivered His people in their youth will not forsake them in the midway of

* This is the only way of rendering the verse so as not to make it seem superfluous: so rendered it sums up and clenches the theophany from ver. 3 onwards; and a new strophe now begins. There is, therefore, no need to omit the verse as Wellhausen does.

† LXX. Αἰθιοπες; but these are Kush, and the parallelism requires a tribe in Arabia. Calvin rejects the meaning "Ethiopian" on the same ground, but takes the reference as to King Kushan in Judg. iii. 8, 10, on account of the parallelism with Midian. The Midianite wife whom Moses married is called the Kushite (Num. xii. 1). Hommel (" Anc. Hebrew Tradition as illustrated by the Monuments," p. 315 and *n*. 1) appears to take Zerah the Kushite of 2 Chron. xiv. 9 ff. as a prince of Kush in Central Arabia. But the narrative which makes him deliver his invasion of Judah at Mareshah surely confirms the usual opinion that he and his host were Ethiopians coming up from Egypt.

‡ For הבנהרים, "is it with streams," read הבהרים, "is it with hills:" because hills have already been mentioned, and rivers occur in the next clause, and are separated by the same disjunctive particle, אִם, which separates "the sea" in the third clause from them. The whole phrase might be rendered, "Is it with hills" Thou art "angry, O Jehovah?"

§ Questionable: the verb תֵּעוֹר, Ni. of a supposed עוּר, does not elsewhere occur, and is only conjectured from the noun עֶרְוָה, "nakedness," and עֶרְיָה, "stripping." LXX. has ἐντείνων ἐνέτεινας, and Wellhausen reads, after 2 Sam. xxiii. 18, עוֹרֵר תְּעוֹרֵר, "Thou bringest into action Thy bow."

‖ שְׁבֻעוֹת מַטּוֹת אֹמֶר, literally "sworn are staves" or "rods of speech." A. V.: according "to the oaths of the tribes," even Thy "word." LXX. (omitting שְׁבֻעוֹת and adding יהוה) ἐπὶ σκῆπτρα, λέγει κύριος. These words "form a riddle which all the ingenuity of scholars has not been able to solve. Delitzsch calculates that a hundred translations of them have been offered" (Davidson). In parallel to previous clause about a "bow," we ought to expect מטות, "staves," though it is not elsewhere used for "shafts" or "arrows." שבעות may have been שִׂבַּעְתָּ, "Thou satest." The Cod. Barb. reads: ἐχόρτασας βολίδας τῆς φαρέτρης αὐτοῦ, "Thou hast satiated the shafts of his quiver." Sinker: "sworn are the punishments of the solemn decree," and relevantly compares Isa. xi. 4; "the rod of His mouth;" xxx. 32, "rod of doom." Ewald: "sevenfold shafts of war." But *cf*. Psalm cxviii. 12.

¶ Uncertain, but a more natural result of cleaving than "the rivers Thou cleavest into dry land" (Davidson and Wellhausen).

** But Ewald takes this as of the Red Sea floods sweeping on the Egyptians.

†† רום ידיהו נשא = "he lifts up his hands on high." But the LXX. read מריהו, φαντασίας αὐτῆς, and took נשא with the next verse. The reading מריהו (for מראיהו) is indeed nonsense, but suggests an emendation to מזרהו, "his shout" or "wail:" *cf*. Amos vi. 7, Jer. xvi. 5.

§§ Reading for הושיע ישע, required by the acc. following. "Thine anointed," lit. "Thy Messiah," according to Isa. xl. ff. the whole people.

* Heb. יסוד, "foundation." LXX. "bonds." Some suggest laying bare from the foundation to the neck, but this is mixed unless "neck" happened to be a technical name for a part of a building: *cf*. Isa. viii. 8, xxx. 28.

† Heb. "his spears" or "staves; his own" (Von Orelli). LXX. ἐν ἐκστάσει; see Sinker, pp. 56 ff. "Princes:" פְּרָזָו only here. Hitzig: "his brave ones." Ewald, Wellhausen, Davidson: "his princes." Delitzsch: "his hosts." LXX. κεφαλὰς δυναστῶν.

‡ So Heb. literally. A very difficult line. On LXX. see Sinker, pp. 60 f.

§ For חֹמֶר, "heap" (so A. V.), read some part of חמר, "to foam." LXX. ταράσσοντας: *cf*. Psalm xlvi. 4.

‖ So LXX. א (some codd.), softening the original "belly."

¶ Or "my lips quiver aloud" לקול, "vocally" (Von Orelli).

** By the Hebrew the bones were felt, as a modern man feels his nerves: Psalms xxxii., li.; Job.

†† For אשר, for which LXX. gives ἡ ἕξις μου, read אשרי, "my steps"; and for ארגז. LXX. ἐταράχθη, ירגזו.

‡‡ אָנוּחַ. LXX. ἀναπαύσομαι, "I will rest." A. V.: "that I might rest in the day of trouble." Others: "I will wait for." Wellhausen suggests אֶנָּחֵם (Isa. l. 24), "I will take comfort." Sinker takes אשר as the simple relative: "I who will wait patiently for the day of doom." Von Orelli takes it as the conjunction "because."

§§ יְגוּדֶנּוּ, "it invades, brings up troops on them," only in Gen. xlix. 19 and here. Wellhausen: "which invades us." Sinker; "for the coming up against the people of him who shall assail it."

‖‖ תפרח; but LXX. תפרה οὐ καρποφορήσει, "bear no fruit."

¶¶ For נזר Wellhausen reads נגזר. LXX. ἐξέλιπεν.

*** "De Civitate Dei," XVIII. 32.

their career.* The closing verses have been torn from the rest to form the essence of a large number of hymns in many languages.

For ourselves, it is perhaps most useful to fasten upon the poet's description of his own position in the midst of the years, and like him to take heart, amid our very similar circumstances, from the glorious story of God's ancient revelation, in the faith that He is still the same in might and in purpose of grace to His people. We, too, live among the nameless years. We feel them about us, undistinguished by the manifest workings of God, slow and petty, or, at the most, full of inarticulate turmoil. At this very moment we suffer from the frustration of a great cause, on which believing men had set their hearts as God's cause; Christendom has received from the infidel no greater reverse since the days of the Crusades. Or, lifting our eyes to a larger horizon, we are tempted to see about us a wide, flat waste of years. It is nearly nineteen centuries since the great revelation of God in Christ, the redemption of mankind, and all the wonders of the Early Church. We are far, far away from that, and unstirred by the expectation of any crisis in the near future. We stand "in the midst of the years," equally distant from beginning and from end. It is the situation which Jesus Himself likened to the long double watch in the middle of the night—"if he come in the second watch or in the third watch"—against whose dulness He warned His disciples. How much need is there at such a time to recall, like this poet, what God has done—how often He has shaken the world and overturned the nations, for the sake of His people and the Divine causes they represent. "His ways are everlasting." As He then worked, so He will work now for the same ends of redemption. Our prayer for "a revival of His work" will be answered before it is spoken.

It is probable that much of our sense of the staleness of the years comes from their prosperity. The dull feeling that time is mere routine is fastened upon our hearts by nothing more firmly than by the constant round of fruitful seasons—that fortification of comfort, that regularity of material supplies, which modern life assures to so many. Adversity would brace us to a new expectation of the near and strong action of our God. This is perhaps the meaning of the sudden mention of natural plagues in the seventeenth verse of our Psalm. Not in spite of the extremes of misfortune, but just because of them, should we exult in "the God of our salvation;" and realise that it is by discipline He makes His Church to feel that she is not marching over the dreary levels of nameless years, but "on our high places He makes us to march."

"Grant, Almighty God, as the dulness and hardness of our flesh is so great that it is needful for us to be in various ways afflicted—oh, grant that we patiently bear Thy chastisement and under a deep feeling of sorrow flee to Thy mercy displayed to us in Christ, so that we depend not on the earthly blessings of this perishable life, but relying on Thy word go forward in the course of our calling, until at length we be gathered to that blessed rest which is laid up for us in heaven, through Christ our Lord. Amen." †

* So he paraphrases "in the midst of the years."

† From the prayer with which Calvin concludes his exposition of Habakkuk.

OBADIAH.

"And Saviours shall come up on Mount Zion to judge Mount Esau, and the kingdom shall be Jehovah's."

CHAPTER XIII.

THE BOOK OF OBADIAH.

THE Book of Obadiah is the smallest among the prophets, and the smallest in all the Old Testament. Yet there is none which better illustrates many of the main problems of Old Testament criticism. It raises, indeed, no doctrinal issue nor any question of historical accuracy. All that it claims to be is "The Vision of Obadiah"; * and this vague name, with no date or dwelling-place to challenge comparison with the contents of the book, introduces us without prejudice to the criticism of the latter. Nor is the book involved in the central controversy of Old Testament scholarship, the date of the Law. It has no reference to the Law. Nor is it made use of in the New Testament. The more freely, therefore, may we study the literary and historical questions started by the twenty-one verses which compose the book. Their brief course is broken by differences of style, and by sudden changes of outlook from the past to the future. Some of them present a close parallel to another passage of prophecy, a feature which when present offers a difficult problem to the critic. Hardly any of the historical allusions are free from ambiguity, for although the book refers throughout to a single nation—and so vividly that even if Edom were not named we might still discern the character and crimes of that bitter brother of Israel—yet the conflict of Israel and Edom was so prolonged and so monotonous in its cruelties, that there are few of its many centuries to which some scholar has not felt himself able to assign, in part or whole, Obadiah's indignant oration. The little book has been tossed out of one century into another by successive critics, till there exists in their es-

* עֹבַדְיָה, 'Obadyah, the later form of עֹבַדְיָהוּ, 'Obadyahu (a name occurring thrice before the Exile: Ahab's steward who hid the prophets of the Lord, 1 Kings xviii. 3–7, 16, of a man in David house, 1 Chron. xxvii. 19; a Levite in Josiah's reign, 2 Chron. xxxiv. 12), is the name of several of the Jews who returned from exile; Ezra viii. 9, the son of Jehi'el (in 1 Esdras viii. 'Αβαδιας); Neh. x. 6, a priest, probably the same as the Obadiah in xii. 25, a porter, and the עַבְדָּא, the singer, in xi. 17, who is called עֹבַדְיָה in 1 Chron. ix. 16. Another 'Obadyah is given in the eleventh generation from Saul, 1 Chron. viii. 38, ix. 44; another in the royal line in the time of the Exile, iii. 21: a man of Issachar, vii. 3; a Gadite under David, xii. 9; a "prince" under Jehoshaphat sent "to teach in the cities of Judah," 2 Chron. xvii. 7. With the Massoretic points עֹבַדְיָה means worshipper of Jehovah: *cf.* Obed-Edom, and so in the Greek form, 'Οβδειου, of Cod. B. But other Codd., A. θ and א give 'Αβδιου or 'Αβδειου, and this, with the alternative Hebrew form אַבְדָּא of Neh. xi. 17, suggests rather עֶבֶד יָהּ, "servant of Jehovah." The name as given in the title is probably intended to be that of an historical individual, as in the titles of all the other books; but which, or if any, of the above mentioned it is impossible to say. Note, however, that it is the later post-exilic form of the name that is used, in spite of the book occurring among the pre-exilic prophets. Some, less probably, take the name Obadyah to be symbolic of the prophetic character of the writer.

timates of its date a difference of nearly six hundred years.* Such a fact seems, at first sight, to convict criticism either of arbitrariness or helplessness; † yet a little consideration of details is enough to lead us to an appreciation of the reasonable methods of Old Testament criticism, and of its indubitable progress towards certainty, in spite of our ignorance of large stretches of the history of Israel. To the student of the Old Testament nothing could be more profitable than to master the historical and literary questions raised by the Book of Obadiah, before following them out among the more complicated problems which are started by other prophetical books in their relation to the Law of Israel, or to their own titles, or to claims made for them in the New Testament.

The Book of Obadiah contains a number of verbal parallels to another prophecy against Edom which appears in Jeremiah xlix. 7-22. Most critics have regarded this prophecy of Jeremiah as genuine, and have assigned it to the year 604 B. C. The question is whether Obadiah or Jeremiah is the earlier. Hitzig and Vatke ‡ answered in favour of Jeremiah; and as the Book of Obadiah also contains a description of Edom's conduct in the day of Jerusalem's overthrow by Nebuchadrezzar, in 586, they brought the whole book down to post-exilic times. Very forcible arguments, however, have been offered for Obadiah's priority.§ Upon this priority, as well as on the facts that Joel, whom they take to be early, quotes from Obadiah, and that Obadiah's book occurs among the first six—presumably the pre-exilic members—of the Twelve, a number of scholars have assigned all of it to an early period in Israel's history. Some fix upon the reign of Jehoshaphat, when Judah was invaded by Edom and his allies Moab and Ammon, but saved from disaster through Moab and Ammon turning upon the Edomites and slaughtering them.‖ To this they refer the phrase in Obadiah 9, "the men of thy covenant have betrayed thee." Others place the whole book in the reign of Joram of Judah (849-842 B. C.), when, according to the Chronicles,¶ Judah was invaded and Jerusalem partly sacked by Philistines and Arabs.** But in the story of this invasion there is no mention of Edomites, and the argument which is drawn from Joel's quotation of Obadiah fails if Joel, as we shall see, be of late date. With greater prudence Pusey declines to fix a period.

The supporters of a pre-exilic origin for the *whole* book of Obadiah have to explain vv. 11-14, which appear to reflect Edom's conduct at the sack of Jerusalem by Nebuchadrezzar in 586, and they do so in two ways. Pusey takes the verses as predictive of Nebuchadrezzar's siege. Orelli and others believe that they suit better the conquest and plunder of the city in the time of Jehoram. But, as Calvin has said, "they seem to be mistaken who think that Obadiah lived before the time of Isaiah."

The question, however, very early arose, whether it was possible to take Obadiah as a unity. Vv. 1-9 are more vigorous and firm than vv. 10-21. In vv. 1-9 Edom is destroyed by nations who are its allies; in vv. 10-21 it is still to fall, along with other Gentiles in the general judgment of the Lord.* Vv. 10-21 admittedly describe the conduct of the Edomites at the overthrow of Jerusalem in 586; but vv. 1-9 probably reflect earlier events; and it is significant that in them alone occur the parallels to Jeremiah's prophecy against Edom in 604. On some of these grounds Ewald regarded the little book as consisting of two pieces, both of which refer to Edom, but the first of which was written before Jeremiah, and the second is post-exilic. As Jeremiah's prophecy has some features more original than Obadiah's,† he traced both prophecies to an original oracle against Edom, of which Obadiah on the whole renders an exact version. He fixed the date of this oracle in the earlier days of Isaiah, when Rezin of Syria enabled Edom to assert again its independence of Judah, and Edom won back Elath, which Uzziah had taken.‡ Driver, Wildeboer and Cornill§ adopt this theory, with the exception of the period to which Ewald refers the original oracle. According to them, the Book of Obadiah consists of two pieces, vv. 1-9 pre-exilic, and vv. 10-21 post-exilic and descriptive in 11-14 of Nebuchadrezzar's sack of Jerusalem.

This latter point need not be contested.‖ But is it clear that 1-9 are so different from 10-21 that they must be assigned to another period? Are they necessarily pre-exilic? Wellhausen thinks not, and has constructed still another theory of the origin of the book, which, like Vatke's brings it all down to the period after the Exile.

There is no mention in the book either of Assyria or of Babylonia.¶ The allies who have

* 889 B. C. Hofmann, Keil, etc.; and soon after 312, Hitzig.

† *Cf.* the extraordinary tirade of Pusey in his Introd. to Obadiah.

‡ The first in his Commentary on "Die Zwölf Kleine Propheten"; the other in his "Einleitung."

§ Caspari ("Der. Proph. Ob. ausgelegt," 1842), Ewald Graf, Pusey, Driver, Giesebrecht, Wildeboer, and König. *Cf.* Jer. xlix. 9 with Ob. 5; Jer. xlix. 14 ff. with Ob. 1-4. The opening of Ob. 1 ff. is held to be more in its place than where it occurs in the middle of Jeremiah's passage. The language of Obadiah is "terser and more forcible. Jeremiah seems to expand Obadiah, and parts of Jeremiah which have no parallel in Obadiah are like Obadiah's own style" (Driver). This strong argument is enforced in detail by Pusey: "Out of the sixteen verses of which the prophecy of Jeremiah against Edom consists, four are identical with those of Obadiah; a fifth embodies a verse of Obadiah's; of the eleven which remain ten have some turns of expression or idioms, more or fewer, which occur in Jeremiah, either in these prophecies against foreign nations, or in his prophecies generally. Now it would be wholly improbable that a prophet, selecting verses out of the prophecy of Jeremiah, should have selected precisely those which contain none of Jeremiah's characteristic expressions; whereas it perfectly fits in with the supposition that Jeremiah interwove verses of Obadiah with his own prophecy, that in verses so interwoven there is not one expression which occurs elsewhere in Jeremiah." Similarly Nowack, "Comm.," 1897.

‖ 2 Chron. xx.

¶ 2 Chron. xxi. 14-17.

** So Delitzsch, Keil, Volck in Herzog's "Real. Ency." II., Orelli, and Kirkpatrick. Delitzsch indeed suggests that the prophet may have been "Obadiah the prince" appointed by Jehoshaphat "to teach in the cities of Judah." See above, p. 598, *n.*

* Driver, "Introd."

† Jer. xlix. 9 and 16 appear to be more original than Ob. 3 and 2*b*. Notice the presence in Jer. xlix. 16 of תפלצתך, which Obadiah omits.

‡ 2 Kings xiv. 22; xvi. 6, Revised Version margin.

§ "Einl." pp. 185 f.: "In any case Obadiah 1-9 are older than the fourth year of Jehoiakim."

‖ "That the verses Obadiah 10 ff. refer to this event [the sack of Jerusalem] will always remain the most natural supposition, for the description which they give so completely suits that time that it is not possible to take any other explanation into consideration."

¶ Edom paid tribute to Sennacherib in 701, and to Asarhaddon (681-669). According to 2 Kings xxiv. 2 Nebuchadrezzar sent Ammonites, Moabites and Edomites [for ארם read אדם] against Jehoiakim, who had broken his oath to Babylonia.

betrayed Edom (ver. 7) are therefore probably those Arabian tribes who surrounded it and were its frequent confederates.* They are described as "sending" Edom "to the border" (*ib.*). Wellhausen thinks that this can only refer to the great northward movement of Arabs which began to press upon the fertile lands to the southeast of Israel during the time of the Captivity. Ezekiel† prophesies that Ammon and Moab will disappear before the Arabs, and we know that by the year 312 the latter were firmly settled in the territories of Edom.‡ Shortly before this the Hagarenes appear in Chronicles, and Se'ir is called by the Arabic name Gebal,§ while as early as the fifth century Malachi ‖ records the desolation of Edom's territory by the "jackals of the wilderness," and the expulsion of the Edomites, who will not return. The Edomites were pushed up into the Negeb of Israel, and occupied the territory round, and to the south of, Hebron till their conquest by John Hyrcanus about 130; even after that it was called Idumæa.¶ Wellhausen would assign Obadiah 1-7 to the same stage of this movement as is reflected in Malachi i. 1-5; and, apart from certain parentheses, would therefore take the whole of Obadiah as a unity from the end of the fifth century before Christ. In that case Giesebrecht argues that the parallel prophecy, Jeremiah xlix. 7-22, must be reckoned as one of the passages of the Book of Jeremiah in which post-exilic additions have been inserted.**

Our criticism of this theory may start from the seventh verse of Obadiah: "To the border they have sent thee, all the men of thy covenant have betrayed thee, they have overpowered thee, the men of thy peace." On our present knowledge of the history of Edom it is impossible to assign the first of these clauses to any period before the Exile. No doubt in earlier days Edom was more than once subjected to Arab *razzias.* But up to the Jewish Exile the Edomites were still in possession of their own land. So the Deuteronomist †† implies, and so Ezekiel ‡‡ and perhaps the author of Lamentations. §§ Wellhausen's claim, therefore, that the seventh verse of Obadiah refers to the expulsion of Edomites by Arabs in the sixth or fifth century B. C. may be granted. ‖‖ But does this mean that verses 1-6 belong, as he maintains, to the same period? A negative answer seems required by the following facts. To begin with, the seventh verse is not found in the parallel prophecy in Jeremiah. There is no reason why it should not have been used there, if that prophecy had been compiled at a time when the expulsion of the Edomites was already an accomplished fact. But both by this omission and by all its other features, that prophecy suits the time of Jeremiah, and we may leave it, therefore, where it was left till the appearance of Wellhausen's theory—namely, with Jeremiah himself.* Moreover Jeremiah xlix. 9 seems to have been adapted in Obadiah 5 in order to suit verse 6. But again, Obadiah 1-6, which contains so many parallels to Jeremiah's prophecy, also seems to imply that the Edomites are still in possession of their land. "The nations" (we may understand by this the Arab tribes) are risen against Edom, and Edom is already despicable in face of them (vv. 1-2); but he has not yet fallen, any more than, to the writer of Isaiah xlv.-xlvii., who uses analogous language, Babylon is already fallen. Edom is weak and cannot resist the Arab *razzias.* But he still makes his eyrie on high and says: "Who will bring me down?" To which challenge Jehovah replies, not "I have brought thee down," but "I will bring thee down." The post-exilic portion of Obadiah, then, I take to begin with verse 7; and the author of this prophecy has begun by incorporating in vv. 1-6 a pre-exilic prophecy against Edom, which had been already, and with more freedom, used by Jeremiah. Verses 8-9 form a difficulty. They return to the future tense, as if the Edomites were still to be cut off from Mount Esau. But verse 10, as Wellhausen points out, follows on naturally to verse 7, and, with its successors, clearly points to a period subsequent to Nebuchadrezzar's overthrow of Jerusalem. The change from the past tense in vv. 10-11 to the imperatives of 12-14 need cause, in spite of what Pusey says, no difficulty, but may be accounted for by the excited feelings of the prophet. The suggestion has been made, and it is plausible, that Obadiah speaks as an eye-witness of that awful time. Certainly there is nothing in the rest of the prophecy (vv. 15-21) to lead us to bring it further down than the years following the destruction of Jerusalem. Everything points to the Jews being still in exile. The verbs which describe the inviolateness of Jerusalem (17), and the reinstatement of Israel in their heritage (17, 19), and their conquest of Edom (18), are all in the future. The prophet himself appears to write in exile (20). The captivity of Jerusalem is in Sepharad (*ib.*) and the "saviours" have to "come up" to Mount Zion; that is to say, they are still beyond the Holy Land (21).†

The one difficulty in assigning this date to the prophecy is that nothing is said in the Hebrew of ver. 19 about the re-occupation of the hill-country of Judæa itself, but here the Greek may help us. ‡ Certainly every other feature suits the early days of the Exile.

The result of our inquiry is that the Book of Obadiah was written at that time by a prophet in exile, who was filled by the same hatred of Edom as filled another exile, who in Babylon wrote Psalm cxxxvii.; and that, like so many of the exilic writers, he started from an earlier prophecy against Edom, already used by Jeremiah.§ [Nowack ("Comm.," 1897) takes vv. 1-14

*For Edom's alliances with Arab tribes *cf.* Gen. xxv. 13 with xxxvi. 3, 12, etc.

† Ezek. xxv. 4, 5, 10.

‡ Diod. Sic. XIX. 94. A little earlier they are described as in possession of Iturea, on the southeast slopes of Anti-Lebanon (Arrian II. 20, 4).

§ Psalm lxxxiii. 8.

‖ i. 1-5.

¶ *E.g.* in the New Testament: Mark iii. 8.

** So too Nowack, 1897.

†† Deut. ii. 5, 8, 12.

‡‡ Ezek. xxxv., esp. 2 and 15.

§§ iv. 21: yet "Uz" fails in LXX., and some take ארץ to refer to the Holy Land itself. Buhl, "Gesch. der Edomiter," 73.

‖‖ It can hardly be supposed that Edom's treacherous allies were Assyrians or Babylonians, for even if the phrase "men of thy covenant" could be applied to those to whom Edom was tributary, the Assyrian or Babylonian method of dealing with conquered peoples is described by saying that they took them off into captivity, not that they "sent them to the border."

* So even Cornill, "Einl."

† This in answer to Wellhausen on the verse.

‡ See below, p. 175, *n.*

§ Calvin, while refusing in his introduction to Obadiah to fix a date (except in so far as he thinks it impossible for the book to be earlier than Isaiah), implies throughout his commentary on the book that it was addressed to Edom while the Jews were in exile. See his remarks on vv. 18-20.

(with additions in vv. 1, 5, 6, 8 f. and 12) to be from a date not long after the Fall of Jerusalem, alluded to in vv. 11-14; and vv. 15-21 to belong to a later period, which it is impossible to fix exactly.]

There is nothing in the language of the book to disturb this conclusion. The Hebrew of Obadiah is pure; unlike its neighbour, the Book of Jonah, it contains neither Aramaisms nor other symptoms of decadence. The text is very sound. The Septuagint Version enables us to correct vv. 7 and 17, offers the true division between vv. 9 and 10, but makes an omission which leaves no sense in ver. 17.* It will be best to give all the twenty-one verses together before commenting on their spirit.

The Vision of Obadiah.

Thus hath the Lord Jehovah spoken concerning Edom. †

"A report have we heard from Jehovah, and a messenger has been sent through the nations, 'Up and let us rise against her to battle.' Lo, I have made thee small among the nations, thou art very despised! The arrogance of thy heart hath misled thee, dweller in clefts of the Rock; ‡ the height is his dwelling, that saith in his heart 'Who shall bring me down to earth!' Though thou build high as the eagle, though between the stars thou set thy nest, thence will I bring thee down—oracle of Jehovah. If thieves had come into thee by night (how art thou humbled!),§ would they not steal *just* what they wanted? If vine-croppers had come into thee, would they not leave *some* gleanings? (How searched out is Esau, how rifled his treasures!)" *But now* to *thy very* border have they sent thee, all the men of thy covenant‖ have betrayed thee, the men of thy peace have overpowered thee ¶; they kept setting traps for thee—there is no understanding in him! "** Shall it not be in that day—oracle of Jehovah—that I will cause the wise men to perish from Edom, and understanding from Mount Esau? And thy heroes, O Teman, shall be dismayed, till †† every man be cut off from Mount Esau." For the slaughter, ‡‡ for the outraging of thy brother Jacob, shame doth cover thee, and thou art cut off for ever. In the day of thy standing aloof,§§ in the day when strangers took captive his substance, and aliens came into his gates, ‖‖ and they cast lots on Jerusalem, even thou wert as one of them! *Ah,* gloat not * upon the day of thy brother,† the day of his misfortune ‡; exult not over the sons of Judah in the day of their destruction, and make not thy mouth large§ in the day of distress. Come not up into the gate of My people in the day of their disaster. Gloat not thou, yea thou, upon his ills, in the day of his disaster, nor put forth thy hand to his substance in the day of his disaster, nor stand at the parting‖ *of the ways* (?) to cut off his fugitives; not arrest his escaped ones in the day of distress.

For near is the day of Jehovah, upon all the nations—as thou hast done, so shall it be done to thee: thy deed shall come back on thine own head.¶

For as ye ** have drunk on my holy mount, all the nations shall drink continuously, drink and reel, and be as though they had not been. †† But on Mount Zion shall be refuge, and it shall be inviolate, and the house of Jacob shall inherit those who have disinherited them. ‡‡ For the house of Jacob shall be fire, and the house of Joseph a flame, but the house of Esau shall become stubble, and they shall kindle upon them and devour them, and there shall not one escape of the house of Esau—for Jehovah hath spoken.

And the Negeb shall possess Mount Esau, and the Shephelah the Philistines, §§ and the Mountain ‖‖ shall possess Ephraim and the field of Samaria, ¶¶ and Benjamin shall possess Gilead. And the exiles of this host *** of the children of Israel shall possess (?) the land ††† of the Canaanites unto Sarephath, and the exiles of Jerusalem who are in Sepharad ‡‡‡ shall inherit the cities of

* There is a mistranslation in ver. 18: שׂריד is rendered by πυρόφορος.

† This is no doubt from the later writer, who before he gives the new word of Jehovah with regard to Edom, quotes the earlier prophecy, marked above by quotation marks. In no other way can we explain the immediate following of the words "Thus hath the Lord spoken" with "*We* have heard a report," etc.

‡ "Sela," the name of the Edomite capital, Petra.

§ The parenthesis is not in Jer. xlix. 9; Nowack omits it. "If spoilers" occur in Heb. before "by night": delete.

‖ Antithetic to "thieves" and "spoilers by night," as the sending of the people to their border is antithetic to the thieves taking only what they wanted.

¶ לחמך, "thy bread," which here follows, is not found in the LXX., and is probably an error due to a mechanical repetition of the letters of the previous word.

** Again perhaps a quotation from an earlier prophecy: Nowack counts it from another hand. Mark the sudden change to the future.

†† Heb. "so that."

‡‡ With LXX. transfer this expression from the end of the ninth to the beginning of the tenth verse.

§§ "When thou didst stand on the opposite side."—Calvin.

‖‖ Plural; LXX. and Qeri.

* Sudden change to imperative. The English versions render, "Thou shouldest not have looked on," etc.

† *Cf.* Ps. cxxxvii. 7, "the day of Jerusalem."

‡ The day of his strangeness = "aliena fortuna."

§ With laughter. Wellhausen and Nowack suspect ver. 13 as an intrusion.

‖ פֶּרֶק does not elsewhere occur. It means cleaving, and the LXX. render it by διεκβολή, *i. e.*, pass between mountains. The Arabic forms from the same root suggest the sense of a band of men standing apart from the main body, on the watch for stragglers *cf.* נגר, in ver. 11). Calvin, "the going forth"; Grätz, פרץ, "breach," but see Nowack.

¶ Wellhausen proposes to put the last two clauses immediately after ver. 14.

** The prophet seems here to turn to address his own countrymen: the drinking will therefore take the meaning of suffering God's chastising wrath. Others, like Calvin, take it in the opposite sense, and apply it to Edom: "as ye have exulted," etc.

†† "Reel"—for לעו we ought (with Wellhausen) probably to read נעו: *cf.* Lam. iv. 2. Some codd. of LXX. omit "all the nations . . . continuously, drink and reel." But א c. a A and Q have "all the nations shall drink wine."

‡‡ So LXX. Heb. "their heritages."

§§ That is the reverse of the conditions after the Jews went into exile, for then the Edomites came up on the Negeb and the Philistines on the Shephelah.

‖‖ *I. e.*, of Judah, the rest of the country outside the Negeb and Shephelah. The reading is after the LXX.

¶¶ Whereas the pagan inhabitants of these places came upon the hill-country of Judea during the Exile.

*** An unusual form of the word. Ewald would read "coast." The verse is obscure.

††† So LXX.

‡‡‡ The Jews themselves thought this to be Spain: so Onkelos, who translates ספרד by אַסְפַּמְיָא = Hispania. Hence the origin of the name Sephardim Jews. The supposition that it is Sparta need hardly be noticed. Our decision must lie between two other regions—the one in Asia Minor, the other in S. W. Media. *First* in the ancient Persian inscriptions there thrice occurs (great Behistun inscription, I. 15; inscription of Darius, ll. 12, 13; and inscription of Darius from Naksh-i-Rustam) Çparda. It is connected with Janua or Ionia and Katapatuka or Cappadocia (Schrader, "Cun. Inscr. and O. T.," Germ. ed.,

the Negeb. And saviours shall come up on Mount Zion to judge Mount Esau, and the kingdom shall be Jehovah's.

CHAPTER XIV.

EDOM AND ISRAEL.

OBADIAH 1-21.

IF the Book of Obadiah presents us with some of the most difficult questions of criticism, it raises besides one of the hardest ethical problems in all the vexed history of Israel.

Israel's fate has been to work out their calling in the world through antipathies rather than by sympathies, but of all the antipathies which the nation experienced none was more bitter and more constant than that towards Edom. The rest of Israel's enemies rose and fell like waves: Canaanites were succeeded by Philistines, Philistines by Syrians, Syrians by Greeks. Tyrant relinquished his grasp of God's people to tyrant: Egyptian, Assyrian, Babylonian, Persian; the Seleucids, the Ptolemies. But Edom was always there, "and fretted his anger for ever." * From that far back day when their ancestors wrestled in the womb of Rebekah to the very eve of the Christian era, when a Jewish king† dragged the Idumeans beneath the yoke of the Law, the two peoples scorned, hated, and scourged each other, with a relentlessness that finds no analogy, between kindred and neighbour nations, anywhere else in history. About 1030 David, about 130 the Hasmoneans, were equally at war with Edom; and few are the prophets between those distant dates who do not cry for vengeance against him or exult in his overthrow. The Book of Obadiah is singular in this, that it contains nothing else than such feelings and such cries. It brings no spiritual message. It speaks no word of sin, or of righteousness, or of mercy, but only doom upon Edom in bitter resentment at his cruelties, and in exultation that, as he has helped to disinherit Israel, Israel shall disinherit him. Such a book among the prophets surprises us. It seems but a dark surge staining the stream of revelation, as if to exhibit through what a muddy channel these sacred waters have been poured upon the world. Is the book only an outbreak of Israel's selfish patriotism? This is the question we have to discuss in the present chapter.

Reasons for the hostility of Edom and Israel are not far to seek. The two nations were neighbours with bitter memories and rival interests. Each of them was possessed by a strong sense of distinction from the rest of mankind, which goes far to justify the story of their common descent. But while in Israel this pride was chiefly due to the consciousness of a peculiar destiny not yet realised—a pride painful and hungry—in Edom it took the complacent form of satisfaction in a territory of remarkable isolation and self-sufficiency, in large stores of wealth, and in a reputation for worldly wisdom—a fulness that recked little of the future, and felt no need of the Divine.

The purple mountains, into which the wild sons of Esau clambered, run out from Syria upon the desert, some hundred miles by twenty of porphyry and red sandstone. They are said to be the finest rock scenery in the world. "Salvator Rosa never conceived so savage and so suitable a haunt for banditti." * From Mount Hor, which is their summit, you look down upon a maze of mountains, cliffs, chasms, rocky shelves and strips of valley. On the east the range is but the crested edge of a high, cold plateau, covered for the most part by stones, but with stretches of corn land and scattered woods. The western walls, on the contrary, spring steep and bare, black and red, from the yellow of the desert 'Arabah. The interior is reached by defiles, so narrow that two horsemen may scarcely ride abreast, and the sun is shut out by the overhanging rocks. Eagles, hawks, and other mountain birds fly screaming round the traveller. Little else than wild-fowls' nests are the villages; human eyries perched on high shelves or hidden away in caves at the ends of the deep gorges. There is abundance of water. The gorges are filled with tamarisks, oleanders, and wild figs. Besides the wheat lands on the eastern plateau, the wider defiles hold fertile fields and terraces for the vine. Mount Esau is, therefore, no mere citadel with supplies for a limited siege, but a well-stocked, well-watered country, full of food and lusty men, yet lifted so high, and locked so fast by precipice and slippery mountain, that it calls for little trouble of defence. "Dweller in the clefts of the rock, the height is his habitation, that saith in his heart: Who shall bring me down to earth?" †

On this rich fortress-land the Edomites enjoyed a civilisation far above that of the tribes who swarmed upon the surrounding deserts; and at the same time they were cut off from the lands of those Syrian nations who were their equals in culture and descent. When Edom looked out of himself, he looked "down" and "across"—down upon the Arabs, whom his position enabled him to rule with a loose, rough hand, and across at his brothers in Palestine, forced by their more open territories to make alliances with and against each other, from all of which he could afford to hold himself free. That alone was bound to exasperate them. In Edom himself it appears to have bred a want of sympathy, a habit of keeping to himself and ignoring the claims both of pity and of kinship—with which

p. 446: Eng., Vol. II., p. 145); and Sayce shows that, called Shaparda on a late cuneiform inscription of 275 B. C., it must have lain in Bithynia or Galatia ("Higher Criticism and Monuments," p. 483). Darius made it a satrapy. It is clear, as Cheyne says ("Founders of O. T. Criticism," p. 312), that those who on other grounds are convinced of the post-exilic origin of this part of Obadiah, of its origin in the Persian period, will identify Sepharad with this Çparda, which both he and Sayce do. But to those of us who hold that this part of Obadiah is from the time of the Babylonian exile, as we have sought to prove above on pp. 600 f., then Sepharad cannot be Çparda, for Nebuchadrezzar did not subdue Asia Minor and cannot have transported Jews there. Are we then forced to give up our theory of the date of Obadiah 10–21 in the Babylonian exile? By no means. For, *second*, the inscriptions of Sargon, king of Assyria, (721–705 B. C.), mention a Shaparda, in S. W. Media towards Babylonia, a name phonetically correspondent to ספרד (Schrader, *l. c.*), and the identification of the two is regarded as "exceedingly probable" by Fried. Delitzsch "Wo lag das Paradies?" p. 249). But even if this should be shown to be impossible, and if the identification Sepharad = Çparda be proved, that would not oblige us to alter our opinion as to the date of the whole of Obadiah 10–21, for it is possible that later additions, including Sepharad, have been made to the passage.

* Amos i. 11. See p. 474.

† John Hyrcanus, about 130 B. C.

* Irby and Mangles' "Travels": *cf.* Burckhardt, "Travels in Syria," and Doughty, "Arabia Deserta," I.

† Obadiah 3.

he is charged by all the prophets. "He corrupted his natural feelings, and watched his passion for ever.* Thou stoodest aloof!"†

This self-sufficiency was aggravated by the position of the country among several of the main routes of ancient trade. The masters of Mount Se'ir held the harbours of 'Akaba, into which the gold ships came from Ophir. They intercepted the Arabian caravans and cut the roads to Gaza and Damascus. Petra, in the very heart of Edom, was in later times the capital of the Nabatean kingdom, whose commerce rivalled that of Phœnicia, scattering its inscriptions from Teyma in Central Arabia up to the very gates of Rome.‡ The earlier Edomites were also traders, middlemen between Arabia and the Phœnicians; and they filled their caverns with the wealth both of East and West.§ There can be little doubt that it was this which first drew the envious hand of Israel upon a land so cut off from their own and so difficult of invasion. Hear the exultation of the ancient prophet whose words Obadiah has borrowed: "How searched out is Esau, and his hidden treasures rifled!"‖ But the same is clear from the history. Solomon, Jehoshaphat, Amaziah, Uzziah, and other Jewish invaders of Edom were all ambitious to command the Eastern trade through Elath and Ezion-geber. For this it was necessary to subdue Edom; and the frequent reduction of the country to a vassal state, with the revolts in which it broke free, were accompanied by terrible cruelties upon both sides.¶ Every century increased the tale of bitter memories between the brothers, and added the horrors of a war of revenge to those of a war for gold.

The deepest springs of their hate, however, bubbled in their blood. In genius, temper, and ambition, the two peoples were of opposite extremes. It is very singular that we never hear in the Old Testament of the Edomite gods. Israel fell under the fascination of every neighbouring idolatry, but does not even mention that Edom had a religion. Such a silence cannot be accidental, and the inference which it suggests is confirmed by the picture drawn of Esau himself. Esau is a "profane person"**; with no conscience of a birthright, no faith in the future, no capacity for visions; dead to the unseen, and clamouring only for the satisfaction of his appetites. The same was probably the character of his descendants; who had, of course, their own gods, like every other people in that Semitic world,†† but were essentially irreligious, living for food, spoil, and vengeance, with no national conscience or ideals—a kind of people who deserve even more than the Philistines to have their name descend to our times as a symbol of hardness and obscurantism. It is no contradiction to all this that the one intellectual quality imputed to the Edomites should be that of shrewdness and a wisdom which was obviously worldly. "The wise men of Edom, the cleverness of Mount Esau"* were notorious. It is the race which has given to history only the Herods—clever, scheming, ruthless statesmen, as able as they were false and bitter, as shrewd in policy as they were destitute of ideals. "That fox," cried Christ, and, crying, stamped the race.

But of such a national character Israel was in all points, save that of cunning, essentially the reverse. Who had such a passion for the ideal? Who such a hunger for the future, such hopes or such visions? Never more than in the day of their prostration, when Jerusalem and the sanctuary fell in ruins, did they feel and hate the hardness of the brother, who "stood aloof" and "made large his mouth."†

It is, therefore, no mere passion for revenge, which inspires these few, hot verses of Obadiah. No doubt, bitter memories rankle in his heart. He eagerly repeats‡ the voices of a day when Israel matched Edom in cruelty and was cruel for the sake of gold, when Judah's kings coveted Esau's treasures and were foiled. No doubt there is exultation in the news he hears, that these treasures have been rifled by others; that all the cleverness of this proud people has not availed against its treacherous allies; and that it has been sent packing to its borders.§ But beneath such savage tempers, there beats the heart which has fought and suffered for the highest things, and now in its martyrdom sees them baffled and mocked by a people without vision and without feeling. Justice, mercy, and truth; the education of humanity in the law of God, the establishment of His will upon earth—these things, it is true, are not mentioned in the Book of Obadiah, but it is for the sake of some dim instinct of them that its wrath is poured upon foes whose treachery and malice seek to make them impossible by destroying the one people on earth who then believed and lived for them. Consider the situation. It was the darkest hour of Israel's history. City and Temple had fallen, the people had been carried away. Up over the empty land the waves of mocking heathen had flowed, there was none to beat them back. A Jew who had lived through these things, who had seen‖ the day of Jerusalem's fall and passed from her ruins under the mocking of her foes, dared to cry back into the large mouths they made: Our day is not spent; we shall return with the things we live for; the land shall yet be ours, and the kingdom our God's.

Brave, hot heart! It shall be as thou sayest; it shall be for a brief season. But in exile thy people and thou have first to learn many more things about the heathen than you can now feel. Mix with them on that far-off coast, from which thou criest. Learn what the world is, and that more beautiful and more possible than the narrow rule which thou hast promised to Israel over her neighbours shall be that worldwide service of man, of which, in fifty years, all the best of thy people shall be dreaming.

The Book of Obadiah at the beginning of the Exile, and the great prophecy of the Servant at the end of it—how true was his word who said: "He that goeth forth and weepeth, bearing precious seed, shall doubtless come again with rejoicing, bringing his sheaves with him."

* Amos i. : *cf*. Ezek. xxxv. 5.
† Obadiah 10.
‡ "C. I. S.," II. i. 183 ff.
§ Obadiah 6.
‖ Verse 6.
¶ See the details in pp. 591 f.
** Heb. xii. 16.
†† We even know the names of some of these deities from the theophorous names of Edomites: *e. g.*, Baal-chanan (Gen. xxxvi. 38), Hadad (*ib*. 35; 1 Kings xi. 14 ff.); Malikram, Kausmalaka, Kausgabri (on Assyrian inscriptions: Schrader, "K. A. T." 150, 613); Κοσαδαρος, Κοσβανος, Κοσγηρος, Κοσνατανος (*Rev. archéol.*, 1870, I. pp. 109 ff., 170 ff.), Κοστοβαρος (Jos. XV. "Ant." vii. 9). See Baethgen, "Beiträge zur Semit. Rel. Gesch.," pp. 10 ff.

* Obabiah 8: *cf*. Jer. xlix. 7.
† Obadiah 11, 12: *cf*. Ezek. xxxv. 12 f.
‡ 1-5 or 6. See above, pp. 599, 600 f.
§ Verse 7.
‖ See above, p. 600.

The subsequent history of Israel and Edom may be quickly traced. When the Jews returned from exile they found the Edomites in possession of all the Negeb, and of the Mountain of Judah far north of Hebron. The old warfare was resumed, and not till 130 B. C. (as has been already said) did a Jewish king bring the old enemies of his people beneath the Law of Jehovah. The Jewish scribes transferred the name of Edom to Rome, as if it were the perpetual symbol of that hostility of the heathen world, against which Israel had to work out her calling as the peculiar people of God. Yet Israel had not done with the Edomites themselves. Never did she encounter foes more dangerous to her higher interests than in her Idumean dynasty of the Herods; while the savage relentlessness of certain Edomites in the last struggles against Rome proved that the fire which had scorched her borders for a thousand years, now burned a still more fatal flame within her. More than anything else, this Edomite fanaticism provoked the splendid suicide of Israel, which, beginning in Galilee, was consummated upon the rocks of Masada, half-way between Jerusalem and Mount Esau.

INTRODUCTION TO THE PROPHETS OF THE PERSIAN PERIOD.

(539-331 B. C.)

"The exiles returned from Babylon to found not a kingdom, but a church."—KIRKPATRICK.

"Israel is no longer a kingdom, but a colony."

CHAPTER XV.

ISRAEL UNDER THE PERSIANS.

THE next group of the Twelve Prophets—Haggai, Zechariah, Malachi, and perhaps Joel—fall within the period of the Persian Empire. The Persian Empire was founded on the conquest of Babylon by Cyrus in 539 B. C., and it fell in the defeat of Darius III. by Alexander the Great at the battle of Gaugamela, or Arbela, in 331. The period is thus one of a little more than two centuries.

During all this time Israel were the subjects of the Persian monarchs, and bound to them and their civilisation by the closest of ties. They owed them their liberty and revival as a separate community upon its own land. The Jewish State—if we may give that title to what is perhaps more truly described as a Congregation or Commune—was part of an empire which stretched from the Ægean to the Indus, and the provinces of which were held in close intercourse by the first system of roads and posts that ever brought different races together. Jews were scattered almost everywhere across this empire. A vast number still remained in Babylon, and there were many at Susa and Ecbatana, two of the royal capitals. Most of these were subject to the full influence of Aryan manners and religion; some were even members of the Persian Court and had access to the Royal Presence. In the Delta of Egypt there were Jewish settlements, and Jews were found also throughout Syria and along the coast, at least, of Asia Minor. Here they touched another civilisation, destined to impress them in the future even more deeply than the Persian. It is the period of the struggle between Asia and Europe, between Persia and Greece: the period of Marathon and Thermopylæ, of Salamis and Platæa, of Xenophon and the Ten Thousand. Greek fleets occupied Cyprus and visited the Delta. Greek armies—in the pay of Persia—trod for the first time the soil of Syria.*

In such a world, dominated for the first time by the Aryan, Jews returned from exile, rebuilt their Temple and resumed its ritual, revived Prophecy and codified the Law: in short, restored and organised Israel as the people of God, and developed their religion to those ultimate forms in which it has accomplished its supreme service to the world.

In this period Prophecy does not maintain that lofty position which it has hitherto held in the life of Israel, and the reasons for its decline are obvious. To begin with, the national life, from which it springs, is of a far poorer quality. Israel is no longer a kingdom, but a colony. The state is not independent: there is virtually no state. The community is poor and feeble, cut off from all the habit and prestige of their past, and beginning the rudiments of life again in hard struggle with nature and hostile tribes. To this level Prophecy has to descend, and occupy itself with these rudiments. We miss the civic atmosphere, the great spaces of public life, the large ethical issues. Instead we have tearful questions, raised by a grudging soil and bad seasons, with all the petty selfishness of hunger-bitten peasants. The religious duties of the colony are mainly ecclesiastical: the building of a temple, the arrangement of ritual, and the ceremonial discipline of the people in separation from their heathen neighbours. We miss, too, the clear outlook of the earlier prophets upon the history of the world, and their calm, rational grasp of its forces. The world is still seen, and even to further distances than before. The people abate no whit of their ideal to be the teachers of mankind. But it is all through another medium. The lurid air of Apocalypse envelops the future, and in their weakness to grapple either politically or philosophically with the problems which history offers, the prophets resort to the expectation of physical catastrophes and of the intervention of supernatural armies. Such an atmosphere is not the native air of Prophecy, and Prophecy yields its supreme office in Israel to other forms of religious development. On one side the ecclesiastic comes to the front—the legalist, the organiser of ritual, the priest; on

* The chief authorities for this period are as follows: A. Ancient: the inscriptions of Nabonidus, last native King of Babylon, Cyrus, and Darius I.; the Hebrew writings which were composed in, or record the history of, the period; the Greek historians Herodotus, fragments of Ctesias in Diodorus Sic., etc; of Abydenus in Eusebius, Berosus. B. Modern: Meyer's and Duncker's Histories of Antiquity; art. "Ancient Persia" in "Encycl. Brit." by Nöldeke and Gutschmid; Sayce, "Anc. Empires"; the works of Kuenen, Van Hoonacker, and Kosters given on p. 192; recent histories of Israel, *e. g.*, Stade's, Wellhausen's, and Klostermann's; P. Hay Hunter, "After the Exile, a Hundred Years of Jewish History and Literature," 2 Vols., Edin., 1890; W. Fairweather, "From the Exile to the Advent," Edin., 1895. On Ezra and Nehemiah see especially Ryle's "Commentary" in the "Cambridge Bible for Schools," and Bertheau-Ryssel's in "Kurzgefasstes Exegetisches Handbuch": *cf.* also Charles C. Torrey, "The Composition and Historical Value of Ezra-Nehemiah," in the "Beihefte zur Z. A. T. W.," II., 1896.

another, the teacher, the moralist, the thinker, and the speculator. At the same time personal religion is perhaps more deeply cultivated than at any other stage of the people's history. A large number of lyrical pieces bear proof to the existence of a very genuine and beautiful piety throughout the period.

Unfortunately the Jewish records for this time are both fragmentary and confused; they touch the general history of the world only at intervals, and give rise to a number of difficult questions, some of which are insoluble. The clearest and only consecutive line of data through the period is the list of the Persian monarchs. The Persian Empire, 539-331, was sustained through eleven reigns and two usurpations, of which the following is a chronological table:—

	B. C.
Cyrus (Kurush) the Great . .	539-529
Cambyses (Kambujiya) . .	529-522
Pseudo-Smerdis, or Baradis .	522
Darius (Darayahush) I., Hystaspis	521-485
Xerxes (Kshayarsha) I. . .	485-464
Artaxerxes (Artakshathra) I., Longimanus	464-424
Xerxes II.	424-423
Sogdianus	423
Darius II., Nothus . . .	423-404
Artaxerxes II., Mnemon . .	404-358
Artaxerxes III., Ochus . . .	358-338
Arses	338-335
Darius III., Codomannus . .	335-331

Of these royal names, Cyrus, Darius, Xerxes (Ahasuerus), and Artaxerxes are given among the Biblical data; but the fact that there are three Darius', two Xerxes' and three Artaxerxes' makes possible more than one set of identifications, and has suggested different chronological schemes of Jewish history during this period. The simplest and most generally accepted identification of the Darius, Xerxes (Ahasuerus), and Artaxerxes of the Biblical history,* is that they were the first Persian monarchs of these names; and after needful rearrangement of the somewhat confused order of events in the narrative of the Book of Ezra, it was held as settled that, while the exiles returned under Cyrus about 537, Haggai and Zechariah prophesied and the Temple was built under Darius I. between the second and the sixth year of his reign, or from 520 to 516; that attempts were made to build the walls of Jerusalem under Xerxes I. (485-464), but especially under Artaxerxes I. (464-424), under whom first Ezra in 458 and then Nehemiah in 445 arrived at Jerusalem, promulgated the Law, and reorganised Israel.

But this has by no means satisfied all modern critics. Some in the interest of the authenticity and correct order of the Book of Ezra, and some for other reasons, argue that the Darius under whom the Temple was built was Darius II., or Nothus, 423-404, and thus bring down the building of the Temple and the prophets Haggai and Zechariah a whole century later than the accepted theory;† and that therefore the Artaxerxes under whom Ezra and Nehemiah laboured was not the first Artaxerxes, or Longimanus (464-424), but the second, or Mnemon (404-358).* This arrangement of the history finds some support in the data, and especially in the *order* of the data, furnished by the Book of Ezra, which describes the building of the Temple under Darius *after* its record of events under Xerxes I. (Ahasuerus) and Artaxerxes I.† But, as we shall see in the next chapter, the Compiler of the Book of Ezra has seen fit, for some reason, to violate the chronological order of the data at his disposal, and nothing reliable can be built upon his arrangement. Unravel his somewhat confused history, take the contemporary data supplied in Haggai and Zechariah, add to them the historical probabilities of the time, and you will find, as the three Dutch scholars Kuenen, Van Hoonacker and Kosters have done,‡ that the rebuilding of the Temple cannot possibly be dated so late as the reign of the second Darius (423-404), but must be left, according to the usual acceptation, under Darius I. (521-485). Haggai, for instance, plainly implies that among those who saw the Temple rising were men who had seen its predecessor destroyed in 586,§ and Zechariah declares that God's wrath on Jerusalem has just lasted seventy years.‖ Nor (however much his confusion may give grounds to the contrary) can the Compiler of the Book of Ezra have meant any other reign for the building of the Temple than that of Darius I. He mentions that nothing was done to the Temple "all the days of Cyrus and up to the reign of Darius:" ¶ by this he cannot intend to pass over the first Darius and leap on three more reigns, or a century, to Darius II. He mentions Zerubbabel and Jeshua both as at the head of the exiles who returned under Cyrus, and as presiding at the building of the Temple under Darius. ** If alive in 536, they may well have been alive in 521, but cannot have survived till 423. †† These data are fully supported by the historical probabilities. It is inconceivable that the Jews should have delayed the building of the Temple for more than a century from the time of Cyrus. That the Temple was built by Zerubbabel and Jeshua in the beginning of the reign of Darius I. may be considered as one of the unquestionable data of our period.

But if this be so, then there falls away a great part of the argument for placing the building of the walls of Jerusalem and the labours of Ezra and Nehemiah under Artaxerxes II. (404-358) instead of Artaxerxes I. It is true that some who accept the building of the Temple under Darius I. nevertheless put Ezra and Nehemiah under Artaxerxes II. The weakness of their case, however, has been clearly exposed by

* Ezra iv. 5-7, etc.; vi. 1-14, etc.

† Havet, *Revue des Deux Mondes* XCIV. 799 ff. (art. "La Modernité des Prophètes"); Imbert (in defence of the historical character of the Book of Ezra), "Le Temple Reconstruit par Zorobabel," extrait du *Muséon*, 1888-9 (this I have not seen); Sir Henry Howorth in the *Academy* for 1893—see especially pp. 326 ff.

* Another French writer, Bellangé, in the *Muséon* for 1890, quoted by Kuenen ("Ges. Abhandl.," p. 213), goes further, and places Ezra and Nehemiah under the *third* Artaxerxes, Ochus (358-338).

† Ezra iv. 6-v.

‡ Kuenen, "De Chronologie van het Perzische Tijdvak der Joodsche Geschiedems," 1890, translated by Budde in Kuenen's "Gesammelte Abhandlungen," pp. 212 ff.; Van Hoonacker, "Zorobabel et le Second Temple" (1892); Kosters, "Het Herstel van Israel," in "Het Perzische Tijdvak," 1894, translated by Basedow, "Die Wiederherstellung Israels im Persischen Zeitalter," 1896.

§ Hag. ii. 3.

‖ Zech. i. 12.

¶ Ezra iv. 5.

** Ezra ii. 2, iv. 1 ff., v. 2.

†† As Kuenen shows, p. 226, nothing can be deduced from Ezra vi. 14.

Kuenen,* who proves that Nehemiah's mission to Jerusalem must have fallen in the twentieth year of Artaxerxes I., or 445.† "On this fact there can be no further difference of opinion." ‡

These two dates then are fixed: the beginning of the Temple in 520 by Zerubbabel and Jeshua, and the arrival of Nehemiah at Jerusalem in 445. Other points are more difficult to establish, and in particular there rests a great obscurity on the date of the two visits of Ezra to Jerusalem. According to the Book of Ezra§ he went there first in the seventh year of Artaxerxes I., or 458 B. C., thirteen years before the arrival of Nehemiah. He found many Jews married to heathen wives, laid it to heart, and called a general assembly of the people to drive the latter out of the community. Then we hear no more of him: neither in the negotiations with Artaxerxes about the building of the walls, nor upon the arrival of Nehemiah, nor in Nehemiah's treatment of the mixed marriages. He is absent from everything, till suddenly he appears again at the dedication of the walls by Nehemiah and at the reading of the Law.‖ This "eclipse of Ezra," as Kuenen well calls it, taken with the mixed character of all the records left of him, has moved some to deny to him and his reforms and his promulgation of the Law any historical reality whatever;¶ while others, with a more sober and rational criticism, have sought to solve the difficulties by another arrangement of the events than that usually accepted. Van Hoonacker makes Ezra's *first* appearance in Jerusalem to be at the dedication of the walls and promulgation of the Law in 445, and refers his arrival described in Ezra vii. and his attempts to abolish the mixed marriages to a second visit to Jerusalem in the twentieth year, not of Artaxerxes I., but of Artaxerxes II., or 398 B. C. Kuenen has exposed the extreme unlikelihood, if not impossibility, of so late a date for Ezra, and in this Kosters holds with him. ** But Kosters agrees with Van Hoonacker in placing Ezra's activity subsequent to Nehemiah''s and to the dedication of the walls.

These questions about Ezra have little bearing on our present study of the prophets, and it is not our duty to discuss them. But Kuenen, in answer to Van Hoonacker, has shown very strong reasons †† for holding in the main to the generally accepted theory of Ezra's arrival in Jerusalem in 458, the seventh year of Artaxerxes I.; and though there are great difficulties about the narrative which follows, and especially about Ezra's sudden disappearance from the scene till after Nehemiah's arrival, reasons may be found for this.*

We are therefore justified in holding, in the meantime, to the traditional arrangement of the great events in Israel in the fifth century before Christ. We may divide the whole Persian period by the two points we have found to be certain, the beginning of the Temple under Darius I. in 520 and the mission of Nehemiah to Jerusalem in 445, and by the other that we have found to be probable, Ezra's arrival in 458.

On these data the Persian period may be arranged under the following four sections, among which we place those prophets who respectively belong to them:—

1. From the Taking of Babylon by Cyrus to the Completion of the Temple in the sixth year of Darius I., 538-516: Haggai and Zechariah in 520 ff.

2. From the Completion of the Temple under Darius I. to the arrival of Ezra in the seventh year of Artaxerxes I., 516-458: sometimes called the period of silence, but probably yielding the Book of Malachi.

3. The Work of Ezra and Nehemiah under Artaxerxes I., Longimanus, 458-425.

4. The Rest of the Period, Xerxes II. to Darius III., 425-331: the prophet Joel and perhaps several other anonymous fragments of prophecy.

Of these four sections we must now examine the first, for it forms the necessary introduction to our study of Haggai and Zechariah, and above all it raises a question almost greater than any of those we have just been discussing. The fact recorded by the Book of Ezra, and till a few years ago accepted without doubt by tradition and modern criticism, the first Return of Exiles from Babylon under Cyrus, has lately been altogether denied; and the builders of the Temple in 520 have been asserted to be, not returned exiles, but the remnant of Jews left in Judah by Nebuchadrezzar in 586. The importance of this for our interpretation of Haggai and Zechariah, who instigated the building of the Temple, is obvious: we must discuss the question in detail.

CHAPTER XVI.

FROM THE RETURN FROM BABYLON TO THE BUILDING OF THE TEMPLE.

(536-516 B. C.).

CYRUS the Great took Babylon and the Babylonian Empire in 539. Upon the eve of his conquest the Second Isaiah had hailed him as the Liberator of the people of God and the builder of their Temple. The Return of the Exiles and the Restoration both of Temple and City were predicted by the Second Isaiah for the immediate future; and a Jewish historian, the Compiler of the books of Ezra and Nehemiah, who lived about 300 B. C., has taken up the story of how these events came to pass from the very first year of Cyrus onward. Before discussing the dates and proper order of these events, it will

* P. 227; in answer to De Saulcy, "Étude Chronologique des Livres d'Esdras et de Nehémie" (1868), "Sept Siècles de l'Histoire Judaïque" (1874). De Saulcy's case rests on the account of Josephus (XI. "Ant." vii. 2-8: *cf.* ix. 1), the untrustworthy character of which and its confusion of two distant eras Kuenen has no difficulty in showing.

† When Nehemiah came to Jerusalem Eliyashib was high priest, and he was a grandson of Jeshua, who was high priest in 520, or seventy-five years before; but between 520 and the twentieth year of Artaxerxes II. lie one hundred and thirty-six years. And again, the Artaxerxes of Ezra iv. 8-23, under whom the walls of Jerusalem were begun, was the immediate follower of Xerxes (Ahasuerus), and therefore Artaxerxes I., and Van Hoonacker has shown that he must be the same as the Artaxerxes of Nehemiah.

‡ Kosters, p. 43.

§ vii. 1-8.

‖ Neh. xii. 36, viii., x.

¶ Vernes, "Précis d'Histoire Juive depuis les Origines jusqu'à l'Époque Persane" (1889), pp. 579 ff. (not seen); more recently also Charles C. Torrey of Andover, "The Composition and Historical Value of Ezra-Nehemiah," in the "Beihefte zur Z. A. T. W.," II., 1896.

** Pages 113 ff.

†† Page 237.

* The failure of his too hasty and impetuous attempts at so wholesale a measure as the banishment of the heathen wives; or his return to Babylon, having accomplished his end. See Ryle, "Ezra and Nehemiah," in the "Cambridge Bible for Schools," Introd., pp. xl. f.

be well to have this Chronicler's narrative before us. It lies in the first and following chapters of our Book of Ezra.

According to this, Cyrus, soon after his conquest of Babylon, gave permission to the Jewish exiles to return to Palestine, and between forty and fifty thousand * did so return, bearing the vessels of Jehovah's house which the Chaldeans had taken away in 586. These Cyrus delivered "to Sheshbazzar, prince of Judah" † (who is further described in an Aramaic document incorporated by the Compiler of the Book of Ezra as "Pehah," or "provincial governor," ‡ and as laying the foundation of the Temple §), and there is also mentioned in command of the people a Tirshatha, probably the Persian Tarsâta,‖ which also means "provincial governor." Upon their arrival at Jerusalem, the date of which will be immediately discussed, the people are said to be under Jeshu'a ben Jōsadak ¶ and Zerubbabel ben She'alti'el ** who had already been mentioned as the head of the returning exiles, †† and who is called by his contemporary Haggai Pehah, or "governor, of Judah." ‡‡ Are we to understand by Sheshbazzar and Zerubbabel one and the same person? Most critics have answered in the affirmative, believing that Sheshbazzar is but the Babylonian or Persian name by which the Jew Zerubbabel was known at court; §§ and this view is supported by the facts that Zerubbabel was of the house of David and is called Peḥah by Haggai, and by the argument that the command given by the Tirshatha to the Jews to abstain from "eating the most holy things" ‖‖ could only have been given by a native Jew. ¶¶ But others, arguing that Ezra v. 1, compared with vv. 14 and 16, implies that Zerubbabel and Sheshbazzar were two different persons, take the former to have been the most prominent of the Jews themselves, but the latter an official, Persian or Babylonian, appointed by Cyrus to carry out such business in connection with the Return as could only be discharged by an imperial officer.*** This is, on the whole, the more probable theory.

If it is right, Sheshbazzar, who superintended the Return, had disappeared from Jerusalem by 521, when Haggai commenced to prophesy, and had been succeeded as Peḥah, or governor, by Zerubbabel. But in that case the Compiler has been in error in calling Sheshbazzar "a prince of Judah." †††

The next point to fix is what the Compiler considers to have been the date of the Return. He names no year, but he recounts that the same people, whom he has just described as receiving the command of Cyrus to return, did immediately leave Babylon,* and he says that they arrived at Jerusalem in "the seventh month," but again without stating a year.† In any case, he obviously intends to imply that the Return followed immediately on reception of the permission to return, and that this was given by Cyrus very soon after his occupation of Babylon in 539-8. We may take it that the Compiler understood the year to be that we know as 537 B. C. He adds that, on the arrival of the caravans from Babylon, the Jews set up the altar on its old site and restored the morning and evening sacrifices; that they kept also the Feast of Tabernacles, and thereafter all the rest of the feasts of Jehovah; and further, that they engaged masons and carpenters for building the Temple, and Phœnicians to bring them cedar-wood from Lebanon.‡

Another section from the Compiler's hand states that the returned Jews set to work upon the Temple "in the second month of the second year" of their Return, presumably 536 B. C., laying the foundation-stone with due pomp, and amid the excitement of the whole people.§ Whereupon certain "adversaries," by whom the Compiler means Samaritans, demanded a share in the building of the Temple, and when Joshua and Zerubbabel refused this, "the people of the land" frustrated the building of the Temple even until the reign of Darius, 521 ff.

This—the second year of Darius—is the point to which contemporary documents, the prophecies of Haggai and Zechariah, assign the beginning of new measures to build the Temple. Of these the Compiler of the Book of Ezra says in the meantime nothing, but after barely mentioning the reign of Darius leaps at once ‖ to further Samaritan obstructions—though not of the building of the Temple (be it noted), but of the building of the city walls—in the reigns of Ahasuerus, that is Xerxes, presumably Xerxes I., the successor of Darius, 485-464, and of his successor Artaxerxes I., 464-424; ¶ the account of the latter of which he gives not in his own language, but in that of an Aramaic document, Ezra iv. 8 ff. And this document, after recounting how Artaxerxes empowered the Samaritans to stop the building of the walls of Jerusalem, records ** that the building ceased "till the second year of the reign of Darius," when the prophets Haggai and Zechariah stirred up Zerubbabel and Joshua to rebuild, not the city walls, be it observed, but the Temple, and with the permission of Darius this building was at last completed in his sixth year. †† That is to say, this Aramaic document brings us back, with the frustrated building of the walls under Xerxes I. and Artaxerxes I. (485-424), to the same date under their predecessor Darius I., viz. 520, to which the Compiler had brought

* 42,360, "besides their servants," is the total sum given in Ezra ii. 64; but the detailed figures in Ezra amount only to 29,818, those in Nehemiah to 31,089, and those in 1 Esdras to 30,143 (other MSS. 30,678). See Ryle on Ezra ii. 64.

† Ezra i. 8.

‡ Ezra v. 14.

§ *Ib.* 16.

‖ Ezra ii. 63.

¶ יֵשׁוּעַ בֶּן־יוֹצָדָק: Ezra iii. 2, like Ezra i. 1-8, from the Compiler of Ezra-Nehemiah.

** זְרֻבָּבֶל בֶּן־שְׁאַלְתִּיאֵל.

†† Ezra ii. 2.

‡‡ Hag. i. 14, ii. 2, 21, and perhaps by Nehemiah (vii. 65-70). Nehemiah himself is styled both Peḥah (xiv. 20) and Tirshatha (viii. 9, x. 1).

§§ As Daniel and his three friends had also Babylonian names.

‖‖ Ezra ii. 63.

¶¶ *Cf.* Ryle, xxxi. ff.; and on Ezra i. 8, ii. 63.

*** Stade, "Gesch. des Volkes Israel," II. 98 ff.: *cf.* Kuenen "Gessammelte Abhandl.," 220.

††† Ezra i. 8.

* Ezra i. compared with ii. 1.

† Some think to find this in 1 Esdras v. 1-6, where it is said that Darius, a name they take to be an error for that of Cyrus, brought up the exiles with an escort of a thousand cavalry, starting in the first month of the second year of the king's reign. This passage, however, is not beyond suspicion as a gloss (see Ryle on Ezra i. 11), and even if genuine may be intended to describe a second contingent of exiles despatched by Darius I. in his second year, 520. The names given include that of Jesua, son of Josedec, and instead of Zerubbabel, that of his son Joacim.

‡ Ezra iii. 3-7.

§ *Ib.* 8-13.

‖ Ezra iv. 7.

¶ See above, p. 605.

** iv. 24.

†† Ezra iv. 24-vi. 15.

down the *frustrated building of the Temple!* The most reasonable explanation of this confusion, not only of chronology, but of two distinct processes—the erection of the Temple and the fortification of the city—is that the Compiler was misled by his desire to give as strong an impression as possible of the Samaritan obstructions by placing them all together. Attempts to harmonise the order of his narrative with the ascertained sequence of the Persian reigns have failed.*

Such then is the character of the compilation known to us as the Book of Ezra. If we add that in its present form it cannot be of earlier date than 300 B. C., or two hundred and thirty-six years after the Return, and that the Aramaic document which it incorporates is probably not earlier than 430, or one hundred years after the Return, while the List of Exiles which it gives (in chap. ii.) also contains elements that cannot be earlier than 430, we shall not wonder that grave doubts should have been raised concerning its trustworthiness as a narrative.

These doubts affect, with one exception, all the great facts which it professes to record. The exception is the building of the Temple between the second and sixth years of Darius I., 520-516, which we have already seen to be past doubt.† But all that the Book of Ezra relates before this has been called in question, and it has been successively alleged: (1) that there was no such attempt as the book describes to build the Temple before 520, (2) that there was no Return of Exiles at all under Cyrus, and that the Temple was not built by Jews who had come from Babylon, but by Jews who had never left Judah.

These conclusions, if justified, would have the most important bearing upon our interpretation of Haggai and Zechariah. It is therefore necessary to examine them with care. They were reached by critics in the order just stated, but as the second is the more sweeping and to some extent involves the other, we may take it first.

1. Is the Book of Ezra, then, right or wrong in asserting that there was a great return of Jews, headed by Zerubbabel and Jeshua, about the year 536, and that it was they who in 520-516 rebuilt the Temple?

The argument that in recounting these events the Book of Ezra is unhistorical has been fully stated by Professor Kosters of Leiden.‡ He reaches his conclusion along three lines of evidence: the Books of Haggai and Zechariah, the sources from which he believes the Aramaic narrative Ezra v. 1-vi. 18 to have been compiled, and the list of names in Ezra ii. In the Books of Haggai and Zechariah, he points out that the inhabitants of Jerusalem whom the prophets summon to build the Temple are not called by any name which implies that they are returned exiles; that nothing in the description of them would lead us to suppose this; that God's anger against Israel is represented as still unbroken; that neither prophet speaks of a Return as past, but that Zechariah seems to look for it as still to come.* The second line of evidence is an analysis of the Aramaic document, Ezra v. 6 ff., into two sources, neither of which implies a Return under Cyrus. But these two lines of proof cannot avail against the List of Returned Exiles offered us in Ezra ii. and Nehemiah vii., if the latter be genuine. On his third line of evidence, Dr. Kosters, therefore, disputes the genuineness of this List, and further denies that it even gives itself out as a List of Exiles returned under Cyrus. So he arrives at the conclusion that there was no Return from Babylon under Cyrus, nor any before the Temple was built in 520 ff., but that the builders were "people of the land," Jews who had never gone into exile.

The evidence which Dr. Kosters draws from the Book of Ezra least concerns us. Both because of this and because it is the weakest part of his case, we may take it first.

Dr. Kosters analyses the bulk of the Aramaic document, Ezra v.-vi. 18, into two constituents. His arguments for this are very precarious.† The first document, which he takes to consist of chap. v. 1-5 and 10, with perhaps vi. 6-15 (except a few phrases), relates that Thathnai, Satrap of the West of the Euphrates, asked Darius whether he might allow the Jews to proceed with the building of the Temple, and received command not only to allow, but to help them, on the ground that Cyrus had already given them permission. The second, chap. v. 11-17, vi. 1-3, affirms that the building had actually begun under Cyrus, who had sent Sheshbazzar, the Satrap, to see it carried out. Neither of these documents says a word about any order from Cyrus to the Jews to return: and the implication of the second, that the building had gone on uninterruptedly from the time of Cyrus' order to the second year of Darius,‡ is not in harmony with the evidence of the Compiler of the Book of Ezra, who, as we have seen,§ states that Samaritan obstruction stayed the building till the second year of Darius.

But suppose we accept Koster's premisses and agree that these two documents really exist within Ezra v.-vi. 18. Their evidence is not irreconcilable. Both imply that Cyrus gave command to rebuild the Temple; if they were originally independent that would but strengthen

* There are in the main two classes of such attempts. (*a*) Some have suggested that the Ahasuerus (Xerxes) and Artaxerxes mentioned in Ezra iv. 6 and 7 ff. are not the successors of Darius I. who bore these names, but titles of his predecessors Cambyses and the Pseudo-Smerdis (see above, p. 605). This view has been disposed of by Kuenen, "Ges. Abhandl.," pp. 224 ff.. and by Ryle, pp. 65 ff. (*b*) The attempt to prove that the Darius under whom the Temple was built was not Darius I. (521-485), the predecessor of Xerxes I. and Artaxerxes I. (485-424), but their successor once removed, Darius II., Nothus (423-404). So, in defence of the Book of Ezra, Imbert. For his theory and the answer to it see above pp. 605 f.

† See above, pp. 605 ff.

‡ For his work see above, p. 605, *n*. I regret that neither Wellhausen's answer to it, nor Kosters' reply to Wellhausen, was accessible to me in preparing this chapter. Nor did I read Mr. Torry's *résumé* of Wellhausen's answer, or Wellhausen's notes to the second edition of his "Isr. u. Jud. Geschichte," till the chapter was written. Previous to Kosters, the Return under Cyrus had been called in question only by the very arbitrary French scholar, M. Vernes, in 1889-90.

* ii. 6. ff. Eng., 10 ff. Heb.

† His chief grounds for this analysis are (1) that in v. 1-5 the Jews are said to have *begun* to build the Temple in the second year of Darius, while in v. 16 the foundation-stone is said to have been laid under Cyrus; (2) the frequent want of connection throughout the passage; (3) an alleged doublet: in v. 17-vi. 1 search is said to have been made for the edict of Cyrus "in Babylon," while in vi. 2 the edict is said to have been found "in Ecbatana." But (1) and (3) are capable of very obvious explanations, and (2) is far from conclusive.—The remainder of the Aramaic text, iv. 8-24, Kosters seeks to prove is by the Chronicler or Compiler himself. As Torrey (*op. cit.*, p. 11) has shown, this "is as unlikely as possible." At the most he may have made additions to the Aramaic document.

‡ Ezra v. 16.

§ Above, pp. 607 f.

the tradition of such a command, and render a little weaker Dr. Kosters' contention that the tradition arose merely from a desire to find a fulfilment of the Second Isaiah's predictions * that Cyrus would be the Temple's builder. That neither of the supposed documents mentions the Return itself is very natural, because both are concerned with the building of the Temple. For the Compiler of the Book of Ezra, who on Kosters' argument put them together, the interest of the Return is over; he has already sufficiently dealt with it. But more—Kosters' second document, which ascribes the building of the Temple to Cyrus, surely by that very statement implies a Return of Exiles during his reign. For is it at all probable that Cyrus would have committed the rebuilding of the Temple to a Persian magnate like Sheshbazzar, without sending with him a large number of those Babylonian Jews who must have instigated the king to give his order for rebuilding? We may conclude then that Ezra v.-vi. 18, whatever be its value and its date, contains no evidence, positive or negative, against a Return of the Jews under Cyrus, but, on the contrary, takes this for granted.

We turn now to Dr. Kosters' treatment of the so-called List of the Returned Exiles. He holds this List to have been, not only borrowed for its place in Ezra ii. from Nehemiah vii., † but even interpolated in the latter. His reasons for this latter conclusion are very improbable, as will be seen from the appended note, and really weaken his otherwise strong case. ‡ As to the contents of the List, there are, it is true, many elements which date from Nehemiah's own time and even later. But these are not sufficient to prove that the List was not originally a List of Exiles returned under Cyrus. The verses in which this is asserted—Ezra ii. 1, 2; Nehemiah vii. 6, 7—plainly intimate that those Jews who came up out of the Exile were the same who built the Temple under Darius. Dr. Kosters endeavours to destroy the force of this statement (if true so destructive of his theory) by pointing to the number of the leaders which the List assigns to the returning exiles. In fixing this number as twelve, the author, Kosters maintains, intended to make the leaders representative of the twelve tribes and the body of returned exiles as equivalent to All-Israel. But, he argues, neither Haggai nor Zechariah considers the builders of the Temple to be equivalent to All-Israel, nor was this conception realised in Judah till after the arrival of Ezra with his bands. The force of this argument is greatly weakened by remembering how natural it would have been for men, who felt the Return under Cyrus, however small, to be the fulfilment of the Second Isaiah's glorious predictions of the restoration of All-Israel, to appoint twelve leaders, and to make them representative of the nation as a whole. Kosters' argument against the naturalness of such an appointment in 537, and therefore against the truth of the statement of the List about it, falls to the ground.

But in the Books of Haggai and Zechariah Dr. Kosters finds much more formidable witnesses for his thesis that there was no Return of Exiles from Babylon before the building of the Temple under Darius. These books nowhere speak of a Return under Cyrus, nor do they call the community who built the Temple by the names of Gôlah or B'ne ha-Gôlah, "Captivity" or "Sons of the Captivity," which are given after the Return of Ezra's bands; but they simply name them "this people" * or "remnant of the people," † "people of the land," ‡ "Judah" or "House of Judah," § names perfectly suitable to Jews who had never left the neighbourhood of Jerusalem. Even if we except from this list the phrase "the remnant of the people," as intended by Haggai and Zechariah in the numerical sense of "the rest" or "all the others," ‖ we have still to deal with the other titles, with the absence from them of any symptom descriptive of return from exile, and with the whole silence of our two prophets concerning such a return. These are very striking phenomena, and they undoubtedly afford considerable evidence for Dr. Kosters' thesis. ¶ But it cannot escape notice that the evidence they afford is mainly negative, and this raises two questions: (1) Can the phenomena in Haggai and Zechariah be accounted for? and (2) whether accounted for or not, can they be held to prevail against the mass of positive evidence in favour of a Return under Cyrus?

An explanation of the absence of all allusion in Haggai and Zechariah to the Return is certainly possible.

No one can fail to be struck with the spirituality of the teaching of Haggai and Zechariah. Their one ambition is to put courage from God

* Isa. xliv. 28, xlv. 1. According to Kosters, the statement of the Aramaic document about the rebuilding of the Temple is therefore a pious invention of a literal fulfilment of prophecy. To this opinion Cheyne adheres ("Introd. to the Book of Isaiah," 1895, xxxviii.), and adds the further assumption that the Chronicler, being "shocked at the ascription to Cyrus (for the Judæan builders have no credit given them) of what must, he thought, have been at least equally due to the zeal of the exiles," invented his story in the earlier chapters of Ezra as to the part the exiles themselves took in the rebuilding. It will be noticed that these assumptions have precisely the value of such. They are merely the imputation of motives, more or less probable to the writers of certain statements, and may therefore be fairly met by probabilities from the other side. But of this more later on.

† This is the usual opinion of critics, who yet hold it to be genuine—*e. g.*, Ryle.

‡ He seeks to argue that a List of Exiles returned under Cyrus in 536 could be of no use for Nehemiah's purpose to obtain in 445 a census of the inhabitants of Jerusalem; but surely, if in his efforts to make a census Nehemiah discovered the existence of such a List, it was natural for him to give it as the basis of his inquiry, or (because the List—see above, p. 608—contains elements from Nehemiah's own time) to enlarge it and bring it down to date. But Dr. Kosters thinks also that as Nehemiah would never have broken the connection of his memoirs with such a List, the latter must have been inserted by the Compiler, who at this point grew weary of the discursiveness of the memoirs, broke from them, and then—inserted this lengthy List! This is simply incredible—that he should seek to atone for the diffuseness of Nehemiah's memoirs by the intrusion of a very long catalogue which had no relevance to the point at which he broke them off.

* Hag. i. 2, 12; ii. 14.

† Hag. i. 12, 14; ii. 2; Zech. viii. 6, 11, 12.

‡ Hag. ii. 4; Zech. vii. 5.

§ Zech. ii. 16; viii. 13, 15.

‖ It is used in Hag. i. 12, 14, ii. 2, only after the mention of the leaders; see, however, Pusey's note 9 to Hag. i. 12; while in Zech. viii. 6, 11, 18, it might be argued that it was employed in such a way as to cover not only Jews who had never left their land, but all Jews as well who were left of ancient Israel.

¶ Compare Cheyne, "Introduction to the Book of Isaiah," 1895, xxxv. ff., who says that in the main points Kosters' conclusions "appear so inevitable" that he has "constantly presupposed them" in dealing with chaps. lvi.-lxvi. of Isaiah; and Torrey, *op. cit.*, 1896, p. 53; "Kosters has demonstrated, from the testimony of Haggai and Zechariah, that Zerubbabel and Jeshua were not returned exiles; and furthermore that the prophets Haggai and Zechariah knew nothing of an important return of exiles from Babylonia." *Cf.* also Wildeboer, "Litteratur des A. T.," pp. 291 ff.

into the poor hearts before them, that these out of their own resources may rebuild their Temple. As Zechariah puts it, "Not by might, nor by power, but by My Spirit, saith Jehovah of Hosts." * It is obvious why men of this temper should refrain from appealing to the Return, or to the royal power of Persia by which it had been achieved. We can understand why, while the annals employed in the Book of Ezra record the appeal of the political leaders of the Jews to Darius upon the strength of the edict of Cyrus, the prophets, in their effort to encourage the people to make the most of what they themselves were and to enforce the omnipotence of God's Spirit apart from all human aids, should be silent about the latter. We must also remember that Haggai and Zechariah were addressing a people to whom (whatever view we take of the transactions under Cyrus) the favour of Cyrus had been one vast disillusion in the light of the predictions of Second Isaiah.† The Persian magnate Sheshbazzar himself, invested with full power, had been unable to build the Temple for them, and had apparently disappeared from Judah, leaving his powers as Peḥah, or governor, to Zerubbabel. Was it not, then, as suitable to these circumstances, as it was essential to the prophets' own religious temper, that Haggai and Zechariah should refrain from alluding to any of the political advantages to which their countrymen had hitherto trusted in vain?‡

Another fact should be marked. If Haggai is silent about any return from exile in the past, he is equally silent about any in the future. If for him no return had yet taken place, would he not have been likely to predict it as certain to happen?§ At least his silence on the subject proves how absolutely he confined his thoughts to the circumstances before him, and to the needs of his people at the moment he addressed them. Kosters, indeed, alleges that Zechariah describes the Return from Exile as still future —viz., in the lyric piece appended to his Third Vision.‖ But, as we shall see when we come to it, this lyric piece is most probably an intrusion among the Visions, and is not to be assigned to Zechariah himself. Even, however, if it were from the same date and author as the Visions, it would not prove that no return from Babylon had taken place, but only that numbers of Jews still remained in Babylon.

But we may now take a further step. If there were these natural reasons for the silence of Haggai and Zechariah about a return of exiles under Cyrus, can that silence be allowed to prevail against the mass of testimony which we have that such a return took place? It is true that, while the Books of Haggai and Zechariah are contemporary with the period in question, some of the evidence for the Return, Ezra i. and iii.-iv. 7, is at least two centuries later, and upon the date of the rest, the List in Ezra ii. and the Aramaic document in Ezra iv. 8 ff., we have no certain information. But that the List is from a date very soon after Cyrus is allowed by a large number of the most advanced critics,* and even if we ignore it, we still have the Aramaic document, which agrees with Haggai and Zechariah in assigning the real, effectual beginning of the Temple-building to the second year of Darius and to the leadership of Zerubbabel and Jeshua at the instigation of the two prophets. May we not trust the same document in its relation of the main facts concerning Cyrus? Again, in his memoirs Ezra† speaks of the transgressions of the Gôlah or B'ne ha-Gôlah in effecting marriages with the mixed people of the land, in a way which shows that he means by the name, not the Jews who had just come up with himself from Babylon, but the older community whom he found in Judah, and who had had time, as his own bands had not, to scatter over the land and enter into social relations with the heathen.

But, as Kuenen points out,‡ we have yet further evidence for the probability of a Return under Cyrus in the explicit predictions of the Second Isaiah that Cyrus would be the builder of Jerusalem and the Temple. "If they express the expectation, nourished by the prophet and his contemporaries, then it is clear from their preservation for future generations that Cyrus did not disappoint the hope of the exiles, from whose midst this voice pealed forth to him." And this leads to other considerations. Whether was it more probable for the poverty-stricken "people of the land," the dregs which Nebuchadrezzar had left behind, or for the body and flower of Israel in Babylon to rebuild the Temple? Surely for the latter.§ Among them had risen, as Cyrus drew near to Babylon, the hopes and the motives, nay, the glorious assurance of the Return and the Rebuilding; and with them was all the material for the latter. Is it credible that they took no advantage of their opportunity under Cyrus? Is it credible that they waited nearly a century before seeking to return to Jerusalem, and that the building of the Temple was left to people who were half-heathen, and, in the eyes of the exiles, despicable and unholy? This would be credible only upon one condition, that Cyrus and his immediate successors disappointed the predictions of the Second Isaiah and refused to allow the exiles to leave Babylon. But the little we know of these Persian monarchs points all the other way: nothing is more probable, for nothing is more in harmony with

* iv. 4.

† Of course it is always possible that, if there had been no great Return from Babylon under Cyrus, the community at Jerusalem in 520 had not heard of the Prophecies of the Second Isaiah.

‡ This argument, it is true, does not fully account for the curious fact that Haggai and Zechariah never call the Jewish community at Jerusalem by a name significant of their return from exile. But in reference to this it ought to be noted that even the Aramaic document in the Book of Ezra which records the Return under Cyrus does not call the builders of the Temple by any name which implies that they have come up from exile, but styles them simply "the Jews who were in Judah and Jerusalem" (Ezra v. 1), in contrast to the Jews who were in foreign lands.

§ Indeed, why does he ignore the whole Exile if no return from it has taken place?

‖ Zech. ii. 10-17 Heb., 6-13 Eng.

* *E.g.*, Stade, Kuenen (*op. cit.*, p. 216). So, too, Klostermann, "Gesch. des Volkes Israel," München, 1896. Wellhausen, in the second edition of his "Gesch.," does not admit that the List is one of exiles returned under Cyrus (p. 155, n.).

† ix. 4; x. 6. 7.

‡ *Op. cit.*, p. 216, where he also quotes the testimony of the Book of Daniel (ix. 25).

§ Since writing the above I have seen the relevant notes to the second edition of Wellhausen's "Gesch.," pp. 155 and 160. "The refounding of Jerusalem and the Temple cannot have started from the Jews left behind in Palestine." "The remnant left in the land would have restored the old popular cultus of the high places. Instead of that we find even before Ezra the legitimate cultus and the hierocracy in Jerusalem: in the Temple-service proper Ezra discovers nothing to reform. Without the leaven of the Gôlah the Judaism of Palestine is in its origin incomprehensible."

Persian policy, than that Cyrus should permit the captives of the Babylon which he conquered to return to their own lands.*

Moreover, we have another, and to the mind of the present writer an almost conclusive argument, that the Jews addressed by Haggai and Zechariah were Jews returned from Babylon. Neither prophet ever charges his people with idolatry; neither prophet so much as mentions idols. This is natural if the congregation addressed was composed of such pious and ardent adherents of Jehovah as His word had brought back to Judah, when His servant Cyrus opened the way. But had Haggai and Zechariah been addressing "the people of the land," who had never left the land, they could not have helped speaking of idolatry.

Such considerations may very justly be used against an argument which seeks to prove that the narratives of a Return under Cyrus were due to the pious invention of a Jewish writer who wished to record that the predictions of the Second Isaiah were fulfilled by Cyrus, their designated trustee.† They certainly possess a far higher degree of probability than that argument does.

Finally there is this consideration. If there was no return from Babylon under Cyrus, and the Temple, as Dr. Kosters alleges, was built by the poor people of the land, is it likely that the latter should have been regarded with such contempt as they were by the exiles who returned under Ezra and Nehemiah? Theirs would have been the glory of reconstituting Israel, and their position very different from what we find it.

On all these grounds, therefore, we must hold that the attempt to discredit the tradition of an important return of exiles under Cyrus has not been successful; that such a return remains the more probable solution of an obscure and difficult problem; and that therefore the Jews who with Zerubbabel and Jeshua are represented in Haggai and Zechariah as building the Temple in the second year of Darius, 520, had come up from Babylon about 537.‡ Such a conclusion, of course, need not commit us to the various data offered by the Chronicler in his story of the Return, such as the Edict of Cyrus, nor to all of his details.

2. Many, however, who grant the correctness of the tradition that a large number of Jewish exiles returned under Cyrus to Jerusalem, deny the statement of the Compiler of the Book of Ezra that the returned exiles immediately prepared to build the Temple and laid the foundation-stone with solemn festival, but were hindered from proceeding with the building till the second year of Darius.§ They maintain that this late narrative is contradicted by the contemporary statements of Haggai and Zechariah, who, according to them, imply that no foundation-stone was laid till 520 B. C.* For the interpretation of our prophets this is not a question of cardinal importance. But for clearness' sake we do well to lay it open.

We may at once concede that in Haggai and Zechariah there is nothing which necessarily implies that the Jews had made any beginning to build the Temple before the start recorded by Haggai in the year 520. The one passage, Haggai ii. 18, which is cited to prove this† is at the best ambiguous, and many scholars claim it as a fixture of that date for the twenty-fourth day of the ninth month of 520.‡ At the same time, and even granting that the latter interpretation of Haggai ii. 18 is correct, there is nothing in either Haggai or Zechariah to make it impossible that a foundation-stone had been laid some years before, but abandoned in consequence of the Samaritan obstruction, as alleged in Ezra iii. 8-11. If we keep in mind Haggai's and Zechariah's silence about the Return from Babylon, and their very natural concentration upon their own circumstances,§ we shall not be able to reckon their silence about previous attempts to build the Temple as a conclusive proof that these attempts never took place. Moreover, the Aramaic document, which agrees with our two prophets in assigning the only effective start of the work on the Temple to 520‖ does not deem it inconsistent with this to record that the Persian Satrap of the West of the Euphrates¶ reported to Darius that, when he asked the Jews why they were rebuilding the Temple, they replied not only that a decree of Cyrus had granted them permission,** but that his legate Sheshbazzar had actually laid the foundation-stone upon his arrival at Jerusalem, and that the building had gone on without interruption from that time to 520.†† This last assertion, which of course was false, may have been due either to a misunderstanding of the Jewish elders by the reporting Satrap, or else to the Jews themselves, anxious to make their case as strong as possible. The latter is the more probable alternative. As even Stade admits, it was a very natural assertion for the Jews to make, and so conceal that their effort of 520 was due to the instigation of their own prophets. But in any case the Aramaic document corroborates the statement of the Compiler that there was a foundation-stone laid in the early years of Cyrus, and does not conceive this to be inconsistent with its own narrative of a stone being laid in 520, and an effective start at last made upon the Temple works. So much does Stade feel the force of this that he concedes not only that Sheshbazzar may have started some preparation for building the Temple, but that he may even have laid the stone with ceremony.‡‡

* The inscription of Cyrus is sometimes quoted to this effect: *cf.* P. Hay Hunter, *op. cit.*, I. 35. But it would seem that the statement of Cyrus is limited to the restoration of Assyrian idols and their worshippers to Assur and Akkad. Still, what he did in this case furnishes a strong argument for the probability of his having done the same in the case of the Jews.

† See above, p. 609, and especially *n.*

‡ Even Cheyne, after accepting Kosters' conclusions as in the main points inevitable (*op. cit.*, p. xxxv.), considers (p. xxxviii.) that "the earnestness of Haggai and Zechariah (who cannot have stood alone) implies the existence of a higher religious element at Jerusalem long before 432 B. C. Whence came this higher element but from its natural home among the more cultured Jews in Babylonia?"

§ Ezra iii. 8-13.

* Schrader, "Ueber die Dauer des Tempelbaues," in "Stud. u. Krit.," 1879, 460 ff.; Stade "Gesch. des Volkes Israel," II. 115 ff.; Kuenen, *op. cit.*, p. 222; Kosters, *op. cit.*, chap. i. § 1. To this opinion others have adhered: König ("Einleit. in das A. T."), Ryssel (*op. cit.*), and Marti (2d edition of Kaysers' "Theol. des A. T.") p. 200. Schrader (p. 563) argues that Ezra iii. 8-13 was not founded on a historical document, but is an imitation of Neh. vii. 73-viii.; and Stade that the Aramaic document in Ezra which ascribes the laying of the foundation-stone to Sheshbazzar, the legate of Cyrus, was not earlier than 430.

† Ryle, *op. cit.*, p. xxx.

‡ Stade, Wellhausen, etc. See below, chap. **xviii.** on Hag. ii. 18.

§ See above, pp. 610 f.

‖ Ezra iv. 24, v. 1.

¶ Ezra v. 6.

** *Ib.* 13.

†† *Ib.* 16.

‡‡ "Gesch.," **II. p. 123.**

And indeed, is it not in itself very probable that some early attempt was made by the exiles returned under Cyrus to rebuild the house of Jehovah? Cyrus had been predicted by the Second Isaiah not only as the redeemer of God's people, but with equal explicitness as the builder of the Temple; and all the argument which Kuenen draws from the Second Isaiah for the fact of the Return from Babylon * tells with almost equal force for the fact of some efforts to raise the fallen sanctuary of Israel immediately after the Return. Among the returned were many priests, and many no doubt of the most sanguine spirits in Israel. They came straight from the heart of Jewry, though that heart was in Babylon; they came with the impetus and obligation of the great Deliverance upon them; they were the representatives of a community which we know to have been comparatively wealthy. Is it credible that they should not have begun the Temple at the earliest possible moment?

Nor is the story of their frustration by the Samaritans any less natural.† It is true that there were not any adversaries likely to dispute with the colonists the land in the immediate neighbourhood of Jerusalem. The Edomites had overrun the fruitful country about Hebron, and part of the Shephelah. The Samaritans held the rich valleys of Ephraim, and probably the plain of Ajalon. But if any peasants struggled with the stony plateaus of Benjamin and Northern Judah, such must have been of the remnants of the Jewish population who were left behind by Nebuchadrezzar, and who clung to the sacred soil from habit or from motives of religion. Jerusalem was never a site to attract men, either for agriculture, or, now that its shrine was desolate and its population scattered, for the command of trade.‡ The returned exiles must have been at first undisturbed by the envy of their neighbours. The tale is, therefore, probable which attributes the hostility of the latter to purely religious causes—the refusal of the Jews to allow the half-heathen Samaritans to share in the construction of the Temple.§ Now the Samaritans could prevent the building. While stones were to be had by the builders in profusion from the ruins of the city and the great quarry to the north of it, ordinary timber did not grow in their neighbourhood, and though the story be true that a contract was already made with Phœnicians to bring cedar to Joppa, it had to be carried thence for thirty-six miles. Here, then, was the opportunity of the Samaritans. They could obstruct the carriage both of the ordinary timber and of the cedar. To this state of affairs the present writer found an analogy in 1891 among the Circassian colonies settled by the Turkish Government a few years earlier in the vicinity of Gerasa and Rabbath-Ammon. The colonists had built their houses from the numerous ruins of these cities, but at Rabbath-Ammon they said their great difficulty had been about timber. And we could well understand how the Beduin, who resented the settlement of Circassians on lands they had used for ages, and with whom the Circassians were nearly always at variance,* did what they could to make the carriage of timber impossible. Similarly with the Jews and their Samaritan adversaries. The site might be cleared and the stone of the Temple laid, but if the timber was stopped there was little use in raising the walls, and the Jews, further discouraged by the failure of their impetuous hopes of what the Return would bring them, found cause for desisting from their efforts. Bad seasons followed, the labours for their own sustenance exhausted their strength, and in the sordid toil their hearts grew hard to higher interests. Cyrus died in 529, and his legate Sheshbazzar, having done nothing but lay the stone, appears to have left Judea. † Cambyses marched more than once through Palestine, and his army garrisoned Gaza, but he was not a monarch to have any consideration for Jewish ambitions. Therefore—although Samaritan opposition ceased on the stoppage of the Temple works and the Jews procured timber enough for their private dwellings ‡—is it wonderful that the site of the Temple should be neglected and the stone laid by Sheshbazzar forgotten, or that the disappointed Jews should seek to explain the disillusions of the Return by arguing that God's time for the restoration of His house had not yet come?

The death of a cruel monarch is always in the East an occasion for the revival of shattered hopes, and the events which accompanied the suicide of Cambyses in 522 were particularly fraught with the possibilities of political change. Cambyses' throne had been usurped by one Gaumata, who pretended to be Smerdis or Barada, a son of Cyrus. In a few months Gaumata was slain by a conspiracy of seven Persian nobles, of whom Darius, the son of Hystaspes both by virtue of his royal descent and his own great ability, was raised to the throne in 521. The empire had been too profoundly shocked by the revolt of Gaumata to settle at once under the new king, and Darius found himself engaged by insurrections in all his provinces except Syria and Asia Minor.§ The colonists in Jerusalem, like all their Syrian neighbours, remained loyal to the new king; so loyal that their Peḥah or Satrap was allowed to be one of themselves—Zerubbabel, son of She'altî'el,‖ a son of their royal house. Yet though they were quiet, the nations were rising against each other and the world was shaken. It was just such a crisis as had often before in Israel reawakened prophecy. Nor did it fail now; and when prophecy was roused what duty lay more clamant for its inspiration than the duty of building the Temple?

We are in touch with the first of our post-exilic prophets, Haggai and Zechariah.

* See above, p. 610.

† Ezra iv. 1–4. "That the relation of Ezra iv. 1–4 is historical seems to be established against objections which have been taken to it by the reference to Esarhaddon, which A. v. Gutschmidt has vindicated by an ingenious historical combination with the aid of the Assyrian monuments" ('Neue Beiträge,' p. 145)."—Robertson Smith, art. "Haggai," "Encyc. Brit."

‡ *Cf.* "Hist. Geog.," pp. 317 ff.

§ Ezra iv.

* There was a sharp skirmish at Rabbath-Ammon the night we spent there, and at least one Circassian was shot.

† "Sheshbazzar presumably having taken up his task with the usual conscientiousness of an Oriental governor, that is, having done nothing, though the work was nominally in hand all along (Ezra v. 16)."—Robertson Smith, art. "Haggai," "Encyc. Brit."

‡ See below, chap. xviii.

§ Herod., I. 130, III. 127.

‖ 1 Chron. iii. 19 makes him a son of Pedaiah, brother of She'altî'el, son of Jehoiachin, the king who was carried away by Nebuchadrezzar in 597 and remained captive till 561, when King Evil-Merodach set him in honour. It has been supposed that, She'altî'el dying childish, Pedaiah by levirate marriage with his widow became father of Zerubbabel.

HAGGAI.

"Go up into the mountain, and fetch wood, and build the House."

CHAPTER XVII.

THE BOOK OF HAGGAI.

THE Book of Haggai contains thirty-eight verses, which have been divided between two chapters.* The text is, for the prophets, a comparatively sound one. The Greek version affords a number of corrections, but has also the usual amount of misunderstandings, and, as in the case of other prophets, a few additions to the Hebrew text.† These and the variations in the other ancient versions will be noted in the translation below.‡

The book consists of four sections, each recounting a message from Jehovah to the Jews in Jerusalem in 520 B. C., "the second year of Darius" (Hystaspis), "by the hand of the prophet Haggai."

The *first*, chap. i., dated the first day of the sixth month, during our September, reproves the Jews for building their own "ceiled houses," while they say that "the time for building Jehovah's house has not yet come"; affirms that this is the reason of their poverty and of a great drought which has afflicted them. A piece of narrative is added recounting how Zerubbabel and Jeshua, the heads of the community, were stirred by this word to lead the people to begin work on the Temple, on the twenty-fourth day of the same month.

The *second* section, chap. ii. 1-9, contains a message, dated the twenty-first day of the seventh month, during our October, in which the builders are encouraged for their work. Jehovah is about to shake all nations, these shall contribute of their wealth, and the latter glory of the Temple be greater than the former.

The *third* section, chap. ii. 10-19, contains a word of Jehovah which came to Haggai on the twenty-fourth day of the ninth month, during our December. It is in the form of a parable based on certain ceremonial laws, according to which the touch of a holy thing does not sanctify so much as the touch of an unholy pollutes. Thus is the people polluted, and thus every work of their hands. Their sacrifices avail nought, and adversity has persisted: small increase of fruits, blasting, mildew and hail. But from this day God will bless.

The *fourth* section, chap. ii. 20-23, is a second word from the Lord to Haggai on the twenty-fourth day of the ninth month. It is for Zerubbabel, and declares that God will overthrow the thrones of kingdoms and destroy the forces of many of the Gentiles by war. In that day Zerubbabel, the Lord's elect servant, shall be as a signet to the Lord.

* In the English Bible the division corresponds to that of the Hebrew, which gives fifteen verses to chap i. The LXX. takes the fifteenth verse along with ver. 1 of chap. ii.

† ii. 9, 14: see on these passages, pp. 617, *n.* 618, *n.*

‡ Besides the general works on the text of the Twelve Prophets, already cited, M. Tony Andrée has published "État Critique du Texte d'Aggée: Quatre Tableaux Comparatifs," (Paris, 1893), which is also included in his general introduction and commentary on the prophet, quoted below.

The authenticity of all these four sections was doubted by no one,* till ten years ago W. Böhme, besides pointing out some useless repetitions of single words and phrases cast suspicion on chap. i. 13, and questioned the whole of the *fourth* section, chap. ii. 20-23.† With regard to chap. i. 13, it is indeed curious that Haggai should be described as "the messenger of Jehovah"; while the message itself, "I am with you," seems superfluous here, and if the verse be omitted, ver. 14 runs on naturally to ver. 12.‡ Böhme's reasons for disputing the authenticity of chap. ii. 20-23 are much less sufficient. He thinks he sees the hand of an editor in the phrase "for a second time" in ver. 20; notes the omission of the title "prophet"§ after Haggai's name, and the difference of the formula "the word came to Haggai" from that employed in the previous sections, "by the hand of Haggai," and the repetition of ver. 6*b* in ver. 21; and otherwise concludes that the section is an insertion from a later hand. But the formula "the word came to Haggai" occurs also in ii. 10:‖ the other points are trivial, and while it was most natural for Haggai the contemporary of Zerubbabel to entertain of the latter such hopes as the passage expresses, it is inconceivable that a later writer, who knew how they had not been fulfilled in Zerubbabel, should have invented them.¶

Recently M. Tony Andrée, *privat-docent* in the University of Geneva, has issued a large work on Haggai,** in which he has sought to prove that the *third* section of the book, chap. ii. (10) 11-19, is from the hand of another writer than the rest. He admits †† that in neither form, nor style, nor language is there anything to prove this distinction, and that the ideas of all the sections suit perfectly the condition of the Jews in the time soon after the Return. But he considers that chap. ii. (10) 11-19 interrupts the connection between the sections upon either side of it; that the author is a legalist or casuist, while the author of the other sections is a man whose only ecclesiastical interest is the rebuilding of the Temple; that there are obvious contradictions between chap. ii. (10) 11-19 and the rest of the book; and that there is a difference of vocabulary. Let us consider each of these reasons.

The first, that chap. ii. (10) 11-19 interrupts the connection between the sections on either side of it, is true only in so far as it has a different subject from that which the latter have more or less in common. But the second of the latter, chap. ii. 20-23, treats only of a corollary of the first, chap. ii. 1-9, and that corollary may well have formed the subject of a separate oracle. Besides, as we shall see, chap. ii. 10-19 is a natural development of chap. i.‡‡ The contradictions alleged by M. Andrée are two. He points out that while chap. i. speaks only of a

* Robertson Smith ("Encyc. Brit.," art. "Haggai," 1880) does not even mention authenticity. "Without doubt from Haggai himself" (Kuenen). "The Book of Haggai is without doubt to be dated, according to its whole extant contents, from the prophet Haggai, whose work fell in the year 520" (König). So Driver, Kirkpatrick, Cornill, etc.

† "Z. A. T. W.," 1887, 215 f.

‡ So also Wellhausen.

§ Which occurs only in the LXX.

‖ See note on that verse.

¶ *Cf.* Wildeboer, "Litter. des A. T.," 294.

** "Le Prophète Aggée, Introduction Critique et Commentaire." Paris, Fischbacher, 1893.

†† Page 151.

‡‡ Below, p. 619.

"drought,"* chap. ii. (10) 11-19 mentions† as the plagues on the crops shiddāphôn and yērākôn, generally rendered *blasting* and *mildew* in our English Bible, and bārād, or *hail;* and these he reckons to be plagues due not to drought but to excessive moisture. But shiddāphôn and yērākôn, which are always connected in the Old Testament and are words of doubtful meaning, are not referred to damp in any of the passages in which they occur, but, on the contrary, appear to be the consequences of drought.‡ The other contradiction alleged refers to the ambiguous verse ii. 18, on which we have already seen it difficult to base any conclusion, and which will be treated when we come to it in the course of translation.§ Finally, the differences in language which M. Andrée cites are largely imaginary, and it is hard to understand how a responsible critic has come to cite, far more to emphasise them, as he has done. We may relegate the discussion of them to a note,‖ and need here only remark that there is among them but one of any significance: while the rest of the book calls the Temple "the House" or "the House of Jehovah" (or "of Jehovah of Hosts"), chap. ii. (10) 11-19 styles it "palace," or temple, of Jehovah.¶ On such a difference between two comparatively brief passages it would be unreasonable to decide for a distinction of authorship.

There is, therefore, no reason to disagree with the consensus of all other critics in the integrity of the Book of Haggai. The four sections are either from himself or from a contemporary of his. They probably represent,* not the full addresses given by him on the occasions stated, but abstracts or summaries of these. "It is never an easy task to persuade a whole population to make pecuniary sacrifices, or to postpone private to public interest; and the probability is, that in these brief remains of the prophet Haggai we have but one or two specimens of a ceaseless diligence and persistent determination, which upheld and animated the whole people till the work was accomplished." † At the same time it must be noticed that the style of the book is not wholly of the bare, jejune prose which it is sometimes described to be. The passages of Haggai's own exhortation are in the well-known parallel rhythm of prophetic discourse: see especially chap. i., ver. 6.

The only other matter of Introduction to the prophet Haggai is his name. The precise form ‡ is not elsewhere found in the Old Testament; but one of the clans of the tribe of Gad is called Haggai,§ and the letters H G I occur as the consonants of a name on a Phœnician inscription.‖ Some¶ have taken Haggai to be a contraction of Haggiyah, the name of a Levitical family, ** but although the final *yod* of some proper names stands for Jehovah, we cannot certainly conclude that it is so in this case. Others †† see in Haggai a probable contraction of Hagariah,‡‡ as Zaccai, the original of Zacchæus, is a contraction of Zechariah.§§ A more general opinion‖‖ takes the termination as adjectival, ¶¶ and the root to be "hag," *feast* or *festival.**** In that case Haggai would mean *festal*, and it has been supposed that the name would be given to him from his birth on the day of some feast. It is impossible to decide with certainty among these alternatives. M. Andrée,††† who accepts the meaning *festal*, ventures the hypothesis that, like "Malachi," Haggai is a symbolic title given by a later hand to the anonymous writer of the book, because of the coincidence of his various prophecies with solemn festivals.‡‡‡ But the name is too often and too naturally introduced into the book to present any analogy to that of "Malachi"; and

*i. 10, 11.

† ii. 17.

‡ They follow drought in Amos iv. 9; and in the other passages where they occur—Deut. xxviii. 22; 1 Kings viii. 37, 2 Chron. vi. 28—they are mentioned in a list of possible plagues after famine, or pestilence, or fevers, all of which with the doubtful exception of fevers, followed drought.

§ Above, p. 611; below, p. **619** ***n.***

‖ Some of M. Andrée's alleged differences need not be discussed at all, *e. g.*, that between מפני and לפני. But here are the others. He asserts that while chap. i. calls "oil and wine" "yishar and tîrôsh," chap. ii. (10) 11-19 call them "yayin and shemen." But he overlooks the fact that the former pair of names, meaning the newly pressed oil and wine, suit their connection, in which the fruits of the earth are being catalogued, i. 11, while the latter pair, meaning the finished wine and oil, equally suit their connection, in which articles of food are being catalogued, ii. 12. Equally futile is the distinction drawn between i. 9, which speaks of bringing the crops "to the house," or as we should say "home," and ii. 19, which speaks of seed being "in the barn." Again, what is to be said of a critic who adduces in evidence of distinction of authorship the fact that i. 6 employs the verb labhash, "to clothe," while ii. 12 uses beged for "garment," and who actually puts in brackets the root bagad, as if it anywhere in the Old Testament meant "to clothe"! Again, Andrée remarks that while ii. (10) 11-19 does not employ the epithet "Jehovah of Hosts," but only "Jehovah," the rest of the book frequently uses the former; but he omits to observe that the rest of the book, besides using "Jehovah of Hosts," often uses the name Jehovah alone [the phrase in ii. (10) 11-19 is נאם יהוה, and occurs twice, ii. 14, 17; but the rest of the book has also נאם יהוה, ii. 4; and besides דבר יהוה, i. 1, ii. 1, ii. 20; אמר יהוה, i. 8; and יהוה אלהים and מפני יהוה, i. 12]. Again, Andrée observes that while the rest of the book designates Israel always by עם and the heathen by גוי, chap. ii. (10) 11-19, in ver. 14, uses both terms of Israel. Yet in this latter case גוי is used only in parallel to עם, as frequently in other parts of the Old Testament. Again, that while in the rest of the book Haggai is called the prophet (the doubtful i. 13 may be omitted), he is simply named in ii. (10) 11-19, means nothing, for the name here occurs only in introducing his contribution to a conversation, in recording which it was natural to omit titles. Similarly insignificant is the fact that while the rest of the book mentions only "the High Priest," chap. ii. (10) 11-19 talks only of "the priests": because here again each is suitable to the connection.—Two or three of Andrée's alleged grounds (such as that from the names for wine and oil and that from labhash and beged) are enough to discredit his whole case.

¶ ii. 15, 18.

* In this opinion, stated first by Eichhorn, most critics agree.

† Marcus Dods, "Haggai, Zechariah and Malachi," 1879 in Handbooks for Bible Classes: Edin., T. & T. Clark.

‡ חַגַּי, Greek 'Ἀγγαῖος.

§ חַגִּי, Gen. xlvi. 16, Num. xxvi. 15; Greek 'Αγγει, 'Αγγεις. The feminine חַגִּית, Haggith, was the name of one of David's wives: 2 Sam. iii. 4.

‖ No. 67 of the Phœnician inscriptions in "C. I. S."

¶ Hiller, "Onom. Sacrum," Tüb., 1706 (quoted by Andrée), and Pusey.

** חַגִּיָּה, 1 Chron. vi. 15; Greek 'Αγγια, Lu. 'Ανaια.

†† Köhler, "Nachexil. Proph.," I. 2; Wellhausen in fourth edition of Bleek's "Einleitung;" Robertson Smith, "Encyc. Brit.," art. "Haggai."

‡‡ חגריה = "Jehovah hath girded."

§§ Derenbourg, "Hist. de la Palestine," pp. 95, 150.

‖‖ Jerome, Gesenius, and most moderns.

¶¶ As in the names בַּרְזִלַּי, כְּלוּבַי, לַלַּי, etc.

*** The radical double *g* of which appears in composition.

††† *Op cit.*, p. 8.

‡‡‡ i. 1, the new moon; ii. 1, the seventh day of the Feast of Tabernacles; ii. 18, the foundation of the Temple (?).

the hypothesis may be dismissed as improbable and unnatural.

Nothing more is known of Haggai than his name and the facts given in his book. But as with the other prophets whom we have treated, so with this one, Jewish and Christian legends have been very busy. Other functions have been ascribed to him; a sketch of his biography has been invented. According to the Rabbis he was one of the men of the Great Synagogue, and with Zechariah and "Malachi" transmitted to that mythical body the tradition of the older prophets.* He was the author of several ceremonial regulations, and with Zechariah and "Malachi" introduced into the alphabet the terminal forms of the five elongated letters.† The Christian Fathers narrate that he was of the tribe of Levi,‡ that with Zachariah he prophesied in exile of the Return,§ and was still young when he arrived in Jerusalem,‖ where he died and was buried. A strange legend, founded on the doubtful verse which styles him "the messenger of Jehovah," gave out that Haggai, as well as for similar reasons "Malachi" and John the Baptist, were not men, but angels in human shape.¶ With Zechariah Haggai appears on the titles of Psalms cxxxvii., cxlv.-cxlviii. in the Septuagint; cxi., cxlv., cxlvi. in the Vulgate; and cxxv., cxxvi., and cxlv.-cxlviii. in the Peshitto.** "In the Temple at Jerusalem he was the first who chanted the Hallelujah, . . . wherefore we say: Hallelujah, which is the hymn of Haggai and Zechariah." †† All these testimonies are, of course, devoid of value.

Finally, the modern inference from chap. ii. 3, that Haggai in his youth had seen the former Temple, had gone into exile, and was now returned a very old man,‡‡ may be probable, but is not certain. We are quite ignorant of his age at the time the word of Jehovah came to him.

CHAPTER XVIII.

HAGGAI AND THE BUILDING OF THE TEMPLE.

HAGGAI i., ii.

WE have seen that the most probable solution of the problems presented to us by the inadequate and confused records of the time is that a considerable number of Jewish exiles returned from Jerusalem to Babylon about 537, upon the permission of Cyrus, and that the Satrap whom he sent with them not only allowed them to raise the altar on its ancient site, but himself laid for them the foundation-stone of the Temple.§§

We have seen, too, why this attempt led to nothing, and we have followed the Samaritan obstructions, the failure of the Persian patronage, the drought and bad harvests, and all the disillusion of the fifteen years which succeeded the Return.* The hostility of the Samaritans was entirely due to the refusal of the Jews to give them a share in the construction of the Temple, and its virulence, probably shown by preventing the Jews from procuring timber, seems to have ceased when the Temple works were stopped. At least we find no mention of it in our prophets; and the Jews are furnished with enough of timber to panel and ceil their own houses.† But the Jews must have feared a renewal of Samaritan attacks if they resumed work on the Temple, and for the rest they were too sodden with adversity, and too weighted with the care of their own sustenance, to spring at higher interests. What immediately precedes our prophets is a miserable story of barren seasons and little income, money leaking fast away, and every man's sordid heart engrossed with his own household. Little wonder that critics have been led to deny the great Return of sixteen years back, with its grand ambitions for the Temple and glorious future of Israel. But the like collapse has often been experienced in history when bands of religious men, going forth, as they thought, to freedom and the immediate erection of a holy commonwealth, have found their unity wrecked and their enthusiasm dissipated by a few inclement seasons on a barren and a hostile shore. Nature and their barbarous fellow-men have frustrated what God had promised. Themselves, accustomed from a high stage of civilisation to plan still higher social structures, are suddenly reduced to the primitive necessities of tillage and defence against a savage foe. Statesmen, poets, and idealists of sorts have to hoe the ground, quarry stones, and stay up of nights to watch as sentinels. Destitute of the comforts and resources with which they have grown up, they live in constant battle with their bare and unsympathetic environs. It is a familiar tale in history, and we read it with ease in the case of Israel. The Jews enjoyed this advantage, that they came not to a strange land, but to one crowded with inspiring memories, and they had behind them the most glorious impetus of prophecy which ever sent a people forward to the future. Yet the very ardours of this hurried them past a due appreciation of the difficulties they would have to encounter, and when they found themselves on the stony soil of Judah, which they had been idealising for fifty years, and were further afflicted by barren seasons, their hearts must have suffered an even more bitter disillusion than has so frequently fallen to the lot of religious emigrants to an absolutely new coast.

1. THE CALL TO BUILD (Chap. i).

It was to this situation, upon an autumn day, when the colonists felt another year of beggarly effort behind them and their wretched harvest had been brought home, that the prophet Haggai addressed himself. With rare sense he confined his efforts to the practical needs of the moment. The sneers of modern writers have not been spared upon a style that is crabbed and jejune, and they have esteemed this to be a collapse of the prophetic spirit, in which Haggai ignored all the achievements of prophecy and interpreted

* Baba-bathra, 15*a*, etc.
† Megilla, 2*b*.
‡ Hesychius; see above, p. 579, *n*.
§ Augustine, "Enarratio in Psalm cxlvii."
‖ Pseud-Epiphanius, "De Vitis Prophetarum."
¶ Jerome on Hag. i. 13.
** Eusebius did not find these titles in the Hexaplar Septuagint. See Field's "Hexaplar" on Psalm cxlv. 1. The titles are of course wholly without authority.
†† Pseud-Epiphanius, as above.
‡‡ So Ewald, Wildeboer (p. 295), and others.
§§ See above, pp. 610-612, and emphasise specially the facts that the most pronounced adherents of Kosters' theory seek to qualify his absolute negation of a Return under Cyrus, by the admission that some Jews did return; and that even Stade, who agrees in the main with Schrader that no attempt was made by the Jews to begin building the Temple till 520, admits the probability of a stone being laid by Sheshbazzar about 536.

* See above, pp. 612 ff. † Hag. i. 4.

the word of God as only a call to hew wood and lay stone upon stone. But the man felt what the moment needed, and that is the supreme mark of the prophet. Set a prophet there, and what else could a prophet have done? It would have been futile to rewaken those most splendid voices of the past, which had in part been the reason of the people's disappointment, and equally futile to interpret the mission of the great world powers towards God's people. What God's people themselves could do for themselves—that was what needed telling at the moment; and if Haggai told it with a meagre and starved style, this also was in harmony with the occasion. One does not expect it otherwise when hungry men speak to each other of their duty.

Nor does Haggai deserve blame that he interpreted the duty as the material building of the Temple. This was no mere ecclesiastical function. Without the Temple the continuity of Israel's religion could not be maintained. An independent state, with the full courses of civic life, was then impossible. The ethical spirit, the regard for each other and God, could prevail over their material interests in no other way than by common devotion to the worship of the God of their fathers. In urging them to build the Temple from their own unaided resources, in abstaining from all hopes of imperial patronage, in making the business one, not of sentiment nor of comfortable assurance derived from the past promises of God, but of plain and hard duty—Haggai illustrated at once the sanity and the spiritual essence of prophecy in Israel.

Professor Robertson Smith has contrasted the central importance which Haggai attached to the Temple with the attitude of Isaiah and Jeremiah, to whom "the religion of Israel and the holiness of Jerusalem have little to do with the edifice of the Temple. The city is holy because it is the seat of Jehovah's sovereignty on earth, exerted in His dealings with and for the state of Judah and the kingdom of David." * At the same time it ought to be pointed out that even to Isaiah the Temple was the dwelling-place of Jehovah, and if it had been lying in ruins at his feet, as it was at Haggai's, there is little doubt he would have been as earnest as Haggai in urging its reconstruction. Nor did the Second Isaiah, who has as lofty an idea of the spiritual destiny of the people as any other prophet, lay less emphasis upon the cardinal importance of the Temple to their life, and upon the certainty of its future glory.

"In the second year of Darius† the king, in the sixth month and the first day of the month"—that is, on the feast of the new moon—"the word of Jehovah came by‡ Haggai the prophet to Zerubbabel, son of She'altî'el, § Satrap of Judah, and to Jehoshua', son of Jehoṣadaḳ,‖ the high priest"—the civil and religious heads of the community—"as follows ¶ :—

"Thus hath Jehovah of Hosts spoken, saying: This people have said, Not yet ** is come the time for the building of Jehovah's House. Therefore Jehovah's word is come by Haggai the prophet, saying: Is it a time for you—you *—to be dwelling in houses ceiled with planks,† while this House is waste? And now thus saith Jehovah of Hosts: Lay to heart how things have gone with you.‡ Ye sowed much but had little income, ate and were not satisfied, drank and were not full, put on clothing and there was no warmth, while he that earned wages has earned them into a bag with holes.

"Thus saith Jehovah of Hosts:§ Go up into the mountain"—the hill-country of Judah—"and bring in timber, and build the House, that I may take pleasure in it, and show My glory, saith Jehovah. Ye looked for much and it has turned out little,‖ and what ye brought home I puffed at. On account of what?—oracle of Jehovah of Hosts—on account of My House which is waste, while ye are hurrying every man after his own house. Therefore ¶ hath heaven shut off the dew,** and earth shut off her increase. And I have called drought upon the earth, both upon the mountains,†† and upon the corn, and upon the wine, and upon the oil, and upon what the ground brings forth, and upon man, and upon beast, and upon all the labour of the hands."

For ourselves, Haggai's appeal to the barren seasons and poverty of the people as proof of God's anger with their selfishness must raise questions. But we have already seen, not only that natural calamities were by the ancient world interpreted as the penal instruments of the Deity, but that all through history they have had a wonderful influence on the spirits of men, forcing them to search their own hearts and to believe that Providence is conducted for other ends than those of our physical prosperity. "Have not those who have believed as Amos believed ever been the strong spirits of our race, making the very disasters which crushed them to the earth the tokens that God has great views about them?" ‡‡ Haggai, therefore, takes no sordid view of Providence when he interprets the seasons, from which his countrymen had suffered, as God's anger upon their selfishness and delay in building His House.

The straight appeal to the conscience of the Jews had an immediate effect. Within three weeks they began work on the Temple.

"And Zerubbabel, son of She'altî'el, and Jehoshua', son of Jehoṣadak, the high priest, and all the rest of the people, hearkened to the voice

*Art. "Haggai," "Encyc. Brit." †Heb. Daryavesh.
‡Heb. "by the hand of."
§See pp. 607 f. and 612.
‖See below, pp. 621, 626, 630 ff. ¶Heb. "saying."

** For לֹא עֶת־בֹּא = "not the time of coming" read with Hitzig and Wellhausen לֹא עַתָּ בָא, "not now is come;" for עַתָּ cf. Ezek. xxiii. 4, Psalm lxxiv. 6.

* The emphasis may be due only to the awkward grammatical construction.

† ספונים, from ספן, "to cover" with planks of cedar, 2 Kings vi. 9: *cf.* iii. 7.

‡ Heb. "set your hearts" (see pp. 506, 510, 522) "upon your ways;" but "your ways" cannot mean here, as elsewhere, "your conduct," but obviously from what follows "the ways" you have been led, "the way" things have gone with you—the barren seasons and little income.

§ The Hebrew and Versions here insert "set your hearts upon your ways," obviously a mere clerical repetition from ver. 5.

‖ For והנה למעט read with the LXX. והיה למעט or ויהי.

¶ The עליכם here inserted in the Hebrew text is unparsable, not found in the LXX. and probably a clerical error by dittography from the preceding על־כן.

** Heb. "heavens are shut from dew." But perhaps the מ of מטל should be deleted. So Wellhausen. There is no instance of an intransitive Qal of כלא.

†† Query?

‡‡ Pages 482 ff.

of Jehovah their God, and to the words of Haggai the prophet, as Jehovah their God had sent him; and the people feared before the face of Jehovah. (And Haggai, the messenger of Jehovah, in Jehovah's mission to the people, spake, saying, I am with you—oracle of Jehovah.) * And Jehovah stirred the spirit of Zerubbabel, son of She'alti'el, Satrap of Judah, and the spirit of Jehoshua', son of Jehoṣadaḳ, the high priest, and the spirit of all the rest of the people; and they went and did work in the House of Jehovah of Hosts, their God, on the twenty-fourth day of the sixth month, in the second year of Darius the king." †

Note how the narrative emphasises that the new energy was, as it could not but be from Haggai's unflattering words, a purely spiritual result. It was the *spirit* of Zerubbabel, and the *spirit* of Jehoshua, and the *spirit* of all the rest of the people, which was stirred—their conscience and radical force of character. Not in vain had the people suffered their great disillusion under Cyrus, if now their history was to start again from sources so inward and so pure.

2. Courage, Zerubbabel! Courage, Jehoshua and all the People! (Chap. ii. 1-9).

The second occasion on which Haggai spoke to the people was another feast the same autumn, the seventh day of the Feast of Tabernacles, ‡ the twenty-first of the seventh month. For nearly four weeks the work on the Temple had proceeded. Some progress must have been made, for comparisons became possible between the old Temple and the state of this one. Probably the outline and size of the building were visible. In any case it was enough to discourage the builders with their efforts and the means at their disposal. Haggai's new word is a very simple one of encouragement. The people's conscience had been stirred by his first; they need now some hope. Consequently he appeals to what he had ignored before, the political possibilities which the present state of the world afforded—always a source of prophetic promise. But again he makes his former call upon their own courage and resources. The Hebrew text contains a reference to the Exodus which would be appropriate to a discourse delivered during the Feast of Tabernacles, but it is not found in the Septuagint, and is so impossible to construe that it has been justly suspected as a gloss, inserted by some later hand, only because the passage had to do with the Feast of Tabernacles.

"In the seventh" month, "on the twenty-first day of the month, the word of Jehovah came by§ Haggai the prophet, saying:—

"Speak now to Zerubbabel, son of She'alti'el, Satrap of Judah, and to Johoshua', son of Jehoṣadaḳ, the high priest, and to the rest of the people, saying: Who among you is left that saw this House in its former glory, and how do ye see it now? Is it not as nothing in your eyes? ‖

* See above, p. 613.

† The LXX. wrongly takes this last verse of chap. i. as the first half of the first verse of chap. ii.

‡ Lev. xxiii. 34, 36, 40-42.

§ "By the hand of."

‖ הֲלֹא כָמֹהוּ כְּאַיִן בְּעֵינֵיכֶם. Literally, "is not the like of it as nothing in your eyes?" But that can hardly be the meaning. It might be equivalent to "is it not, as it stands, as nothing in your eyes?" But the fact is that in Hebrew construction of a simple, unemphasised comparison, the comparing particle כ stands before *both*

And now courage,* O Zerubbabel—oracle of Jehovah—and courage, Jehoshua', son of Jehoṣadaḳ, O high priest;† and courage, all people of the land!—oracle of Jehovah; and get to work, for I am with you—oracle of Jehovah of Hosts ‡—and My Spirit is standing in your midst. Fear not! For thus saith Jehovah of Hosts: It is but a little while, and I will shake the heavens, and the earth and the sea and the dry land; and I will shake all nations, and the costly things§ of all nations shall come in, and I will fill this House with glory, saith Jehovah of Hosts. Mine is the silver and Mine the gold—oracle of Jehovah of Hosts. Greater shall the latter glory of this House be than the former, saith Jehovah of Hosts, and in this place will I give peace ‖—oracle of Jehovah of Hosts."

From the earliest times this passage, by the majority of the Christian Church, has been interpreted of the coming of Christ. The Vulgate renders ver. *7b*, "Et veniet Desideratus cunctis gentibus," and so a large number of the Latin Fathers, who are followed by Luther, "Der Trost aller Heiden," and by our own Authorised Version, "And the Desire of all nations shall come." This was not contrary to Jewish tradition, for Rabbi Akiba had defined the clause of the Messiah, and Jerome received the interpretation from his Jewish instructors. In itself the noun, as pointed in the Massoretic text, means "longing" or "object of longing."¶ But the verb which goes with it is in the plural, and by a change of points the noun itself may be read as a plural.** That this was the original reading is made extremely probable by the fact that it lay before the translators of the Septuagint, who render: "the picked," or "chosen, things of the nations." †† So the old Italic version: "Et venient omnia electa gentium." ‡‡ Moreover this meaning suits the context, as the other does not. The next verse mentions silver

objects compared: as, for instance, in the phrase (Gen. xliv. 18) כִּי כָמוֹךָ כְּפַרְעֹה, "thou art as Pharaoh."

* Literally: "be strong."

† It is difficult to say whether "high priest" belongs to the text or not.

‡ Here occurs the anacolouthic clause, introduced by an acc. without a verb, which is not found in the LXX. and is probably a gloss: "The promise which I made with you in your going forth from Egypt."

§ Hebrew has singular, "costly thing" or "desirableness," חֶמְדַּת (fem. for neut.), but the verb "shall come" is in the plural, and the LXX. has τὰ ἐκλεκτά, "the choice things."

‖ The LXX. add a parallel clause, καὶ εἰρήνην ψυχῆς εἰς περιποίησιν παντὶ τῷ κτίζοντι τοῦ ἀναστῆσαι τὸν ναὸν τοῦτον, which would read in Hebrew כָּל־הַהוֹסֵד לְקוֹמֵם הַהֵיכָל הַזֶּה וּשְׁלַוַת נֶפֶשׁ לְחַיּוֹת. On היות Wellhausen cites 1 Chron. xi. 8, = "restore" or "revive."

¶ חֶמְדַּת = "longing," 2 Chron. xxi. 2, and "object of longing," Dan. xi. 37. It is the feminine or neuter, and might be rendered as a collective, "desirable things." Pusey cites Cicero's address to his wife: "Valete, mea desideria, valete" ("Ep. ad Famil.," xiv. 2 fin.).

** חֲמֻדֹת, plural feminine of pass. part., as in Gen. xxvii. 15, where it is an adjective, but used as a noun = "precious things," Dan. xi. 38, 43, which use meets the objection of Pusey, *in loco*, where he wrongly maintains that "precious things," if intended, must have been expressed by מַחֲמַדֵּי.

†† ἥξει τὰ ἐκλεκτὰ πάντων τῶν ἐθνῶν. Theodore of Mopsuestia takes it as "elect persons of all nations," to which a few moderns adhere.

‡‡ Augustini "Contra Donatistas post Collationem," cap. xx. 30 (Migne, "Latin Patrology," XLIII., p. 671).

and gold. "We may understand what he says," writes Calvin, "of Christ; we indeed know that Christ was the expectation of the whole world; . . . but as it immediately follows, 'Mine is the silver and Mine is the gold,' the more simple meaning is that which I first stated: that the nations would come, bringing with them all their riches, that they might offer themselves and all their possessions a sacrifice to God." *

3. The Power of the Unclean (Chap. ii. 10-19).

Haggai's third address to the people is based on a deliverance which he seeks from the priests. The Book of Deuteronomy had provided that, in all difficult cases not settled by its own code, the people shall seek a "deliverance" or "Torah" from the priests, "and shall observe to do according to the deliverance which the priests deliver to thee." † Both noun and verb, which may be thus literally translated, are also used for the completed and canonical Law in Israel, and they signify that in the time of the composition of the Book of Deuteronomy that Law was still regarded as in process of growth. So it is also in the time of Haggai: he does not consult a code of laws, nor asks the priests what the canon says, as, for instance, our Lord does with the question, "how readest thou?" But he begs them to give him *a* Torah or *deliverance*, ‡ based of course upon existing custom, but not yet committed to writing.§ For the history of the Law in Israel this is, therefore, a passage of great interest.

"On the twenty-fourth of the ninth month, in the second year of Darius, the word of Jehovah came to ‖ Haggai the prophet, saying: Thus saith Jehovah of Hosts, Ask, I pray, of the priests a deliverance,¶ saying:—

"If a man be carrying flesh that is holy in the skirt of his robe, and with his skirt touch bread or pottage or wine or oil or any food, shall *the latter* become holy? And the priests gave answer and said, No! And Haggai said, If one unclean by a corpse ** touch any of these, shall *the latter* become unclean? And the priests gave answer and said, It shall." That is to say, holiness which passed from the source to an object immediately in touch with the latter did not spread further; but pollution infected not only the person who came into contact with it, but whatever he touched.* "The flesh of the sacrifice hallowed whatever it should touch, but not further; but the human being who was defiled by touching a dead body, defiled all he might touch." † "And Haggai answered and said: So is this people, and so is this nation before Me—oracle of Jehovah—and so is all the work of their hands, and what they offer there"—at the altar erected on its old site—"is unclean." ‡ That is to say, while the Jews had expected their restored ritual to make them holy to the Lord, this had not been effective, while, on the contrary, their contact with sources of pollution had thoroughly polluted both themselves and their labour and their sacrifices. What these sources of pollution are is not explicitly stated, but Haggai, from his other messages, can only mean, either the people's want of energy in building the Temple, or the unbuilt Temple itself. Andrée goes so far as to compare the latter with the corpse, whose touch, according to the priests, spreads infection through more than one degree. In any case Haggai means to illustrate and enforce the building of the Temple without delay; and meantime he takes one instance of the effect he has already spoken of, "the work of their hands," and shows how it has been spoilt by their neglect and delay. "And now, I pray, set your hearts backward from to-day,§ before stone was laid upon stone in the Temple of Jehovah: . . . ‖ when one came to a heap of grain of twenty measures, and it had become ten, or went to the winevat to draw fifty measures,¶ and it had become twenty. I smote you with blasting and with withering,** and with hail all the work of

* Calvin, "Comm. in Haggai," ii. 6-9.

† Deut. xii. 8 ff.: עַל־פִּי הַתּוֹרָה אֲשֶׁר יוֹרוּךָ. Compare the expression כֹּהֵן מוֹרֶה, 2 Chron. xv. 3, and the duties of the teaching priests assigned by the Chronicler (2 Chron. xvii. 7-9) to the days of Jehoshaphat.

‡ Note that it is not "the Torah," but "a Torah."

§ The nearest passage to the "deliverance" of the priests to Haggai is Lev. vi. 20, 21 (Heb.), 27, 28 (Eng.). This is part of the Priestly Code not promulgated till 445 B. C., but based, of course, on long extant custom, some of it very ancient. "Everything that touches the flesh" (of the sin-offering, which is holy) "shall be holy"—יִקְדָּשׁ, the verb used by the priests in their answer to Haggai—"and when any of its blood has been sprinkled on a garment, that whereon it was sprinkled shall be washed in a holy place. The earthen vessel wherein it has been boiled shall be broken, and if it has been boiled in a brazen vessel, this shall be scoured and rinsed with water."

‖ So several old edd. and many codd., and adopted by Baer (see his note *in loco*) in his text. But most of the edd. of the Massoretic text read ביד after Cod. Hill. For the importance of the question see above, p. 613.

¶ Torah.

** טְמֵא נֶפֶשׁ.

* There does not appear to be the contrast between indirect contact with a holy thing and direct contact with a polluted which Wellhausen says there is. In either case the articles whose character is in question stand second from the source of holiness and pollution—the holy flesh and the corpse.

† Pusey, *in loco*.

‡ The LXX. have here found inserted three other clauses: *ἕνεκεν τῶν λημμάτων αὐτῶν τῶν ὀρθρινῶν, ὀδυνηθήσονται ἀπὸ προσώπου πόνων αὐτῶν, καὶ ἐμισεῖτε ἐν πύλαις ἐλέγχοντας.* The first clause is a misreading (Wellhausen), לְקָחְתָּם שֹׁחַד יַעַן for יַעַן לְקַחְתֶּם שֹׁחַד, "because ye take a bribe," and goes well with the third clause, modified from Amos v. 10: שָׂנְאוּ בַשַּׁעַר מוֹכִיחַ, "they hate him who reproves in the gate." These may have been inserted into the Hebrew text by some one puzzled to know what the source of the people's pollution was, and who absurdly found it in sins which in Haggai's time it was impossible to impute to them. The middle clause, יִתְעַנּוּ מִפְּנֵי עַצְּבֵיהֶם, "they vex themselves with their labours," is suitable to the sense of the Hebrew text of the verse, as Wellhausen points out, but besides gives a connection with what follows.

§ From this day and onward.

‖ Heb. literally "since they were." A. V. "since those days were."

¶ Winevat, יֶקֶב, is distinguished from winepress, גַּת, in Josh. ix. 13, and is translated by the Greek *ὑπολήνιον* (Mark xii. 1), *ληνόν*, (Matt. xxi. 33), "dug a pit for the winepress"; but the name is applied sometimes to the whole winepress—Hosea ix. 2 etc., Job xxiv. 11, "to tread the winepress." The word translated "measures," as in LXX. *μετρητάς*. is פּוּרָה, and that is properly the vat in which the grapes were trodden (Isa. lxiii. 3), but here it can scarcely mean fifty "vatfuls," but must refer to some smaller measure—cask?

** See above, pp. 613 f., *n*.

your hands, and . . . *—oracle of Jehovah. Lay now your hearts" on the time "before to-day † (the twenty-fourth day of the ninth month ‡), before the day of the foundation of the Temple of Jehovah §—lay your hearts" to that time! "Is there yet *any* seed in the barn? ‖ And

* The words omitted cannot be construed in the Hebrew, וְאֵין־אֶתְכֶם אֵלַי, literally "and not you (acc.) to Me." Hitzig, etc, propose to read אִתְּכֶם and render "there was none with you" who turned "to Me." Others propose אֵינְכֶם, "as if none of you" turned "to Me." Others retain אֶתְכֶם and render "as for you." The versions LYY. Syr., Vulg. "ye will not return" or "did not return to Me," reading perhaps for לֹא שַׁבְתֶּם ,אֵין אֶתְכֶם, which is found in Amos iv. 9, of which the rest of the verse is an echo. Wellhausen deletes the whole verse as a gloss. It is certainly suspicious, and remarkable in that the LXX. text has already introduced two citations from Amos. See above on ver. 14.

† Heb. "from this day backwards."

‡ The date Wellhausen thinks was added by a latter hand.

§ This is the ambiguous clause on different interpretations of which so much has been founded: הֵיכַל־יְהוָֹה לְמִן־הַיּוֹם אֲשֶׁר־יֻסַּד. Does this clause, in simple parallel to the previous one, describe the day on which the prophet was speaking, *the twenty-fourth of the ninth month*, the *terminus a quo* of the people's retrospect? In that case Haggai regards the foundation-stone of the Temple as laid on the twenty-fourth day of the ninth month 520 B. C., and does not know, or at least ignores, any previous laying of the foundation stone. So Kuenen, Kosters, Andrée, etc. Or does למן *signify up to the time the foundation-stone was laid* and state a *terminus ad quem* for the people's retrospect? So Ewald and others, who therefore find in the verse a proof that Haggai knew of an earlier laying of the foundation-stone. But that למן is ever used for ועד cannot be proved, and indeed is disproved by Jer. vii. 7, where it occurs in contrast to ועד. Van Hoonacker finds the same, but in a more subtle translation of למן. מן, he says, is never used except of a date distant from the speaker or writer of it; למן (if I understand him aright) refers therefore to a date previous to Haggai to which the people's thoughts are directed by the ל and then brought back from it to the date at which he was speaking by means of the מן: "la preposition ל signifie la direction de l'esprit vers une époque du passé d'où il est ramené par la preposition מן." But surely מן can be used (as indeed Haggai has just used it) to signify extension backwards from the standpoint of the speaker; and although in the passages cited by Van Hoonacker of the use of למן it always refers to a past date—Deut. ix. 7, Judg. xix. 30, 2 Sam. vi. 11, Jer. vii. 7 and 25—still, as it is there nothing but a pleonastic form for מן, it surely might be employed as מן is sometimes employed for departure from the present backwards. Nor in any case is it used to express what Van Hoonacker seeks to draw from it here, the idea of direction of the mind to a past event and then an immediate return from that. Had Haggai wished to express that idea he would have phrased it thus: היום אשר יסד היכל יהוה ועד היום הזה למן (as Kosters remarks). Besides, as Kosters has pointed out (pp. 7 ff. of the Germ. trans. of "Het Herstel," etc.), even if Van Hoonacker's translation of למן were correct, the context would show that it might refer only to a laying of the foundation-stone since Haggai's first address to the people, and therefore the question of an earlier foundation-stone under Cyrus would remain unsolved. Consequently Haggai ii. 18 cannot be quoted as a proof of the latter. See above, p. 611.

‖ Meaning "there is none"

as yet * the vine, the fig-tree, the pomegranate and the olive have not borne *fruit*. From this day I will bless thee."

This then is the substance of the whole message. On the twenty-fourth day of the ninth month, somewhere in our December, the Jews had been discouraged that their attempts to build the Temple, begun three months before,† had not turned the tide of their misfortunes and produced prosperity in their agriculture. Haggai tells them, there is not yet time for the change to work. If contact with a holy thing has only a slight effect, but contact with an unclean thing has a much greater effect (verses 11-13), then their attempts to build the Temple must have less good influence upon their condition than the bad influence of all their past devotion to themselves and their secular labours. That is why adversity still continues, but courage! from this day on God will bless. The whole message is, therefore, opportune to the date at which it was delivered, and comes naturally on the back of Haggai's previous oracles. Andrée's reason for assigning it to another writer, on the ground of its breaking the connection, does not exist.‡

These poor colonists, in their hope deferred, were learning the old lesson, which humanity finds so hard to understand, that repentance and new-born zeal do not immediately work a change upon our material condition; but the natural consequences of sin often outweigh the influence of conversion, and though devoted to God and very industrious we may still be punished for a sinful past. Evil has an infectious power greater than that of holiness. Its effects are more extensive and lasting.§ It was no bit of casuistry which Haggai sought to illustrate by his appeal to the priests on the ceremonial law, but an ethical truth deeply embedded in human experience.

4. THE REINVESTMENT OF ISRAEL'S HOPE (Chap. ii. 20-23).

On the same day Haggai published another oracle, in which he put the climax to his own message by reinvesting in Zerubbabel the ancient hopes of his people. When the monarchy fell the Messianic hopes were naturally no longer concentrated in the person of a king; and the great evangelist of the Exile found the elect and anointed Servant of Jehovah in the people as a whole, or in at least the pious part of them, with functions not of political government but of moral influence and instruction towards all the peoples of the earth. Yet in the Exile Ezekiel still predicted an individual Messiah, a son of the house of David; only it is significant that, in his latest prophecies delivered after the overthrow of Jerusalem, Ezekiel calls him not *king*‖ any more, but *prince*.¶

* ועוד or וְעֹד for וְצַד, after LXX. καὶ εἰ ἔτι.

† The twenty-fourth day of the sixth month, according to chap. i. 15.

‡ See above, p. 613.

§ "For I believe the devil's voice
Sinks deeper in our ear,
Than any whisper sent from heaven,
However sweet and clear."

‖ Only in xxxiv. 24, xxxvii. 22, 24.

¶ נשׂא: *cf.* Skinner, "Ezekiel" pp. 336 ff., *antea*, who, however, attributes the diminution of the importance of the civil head in Israel, not to the feeling that he would henceforth always be subject to a foreign emperor, but to the conviction that in the future he will be "overshadowed by the personal presence of Jehovah in the midst of His people."

After the return of Sheshbazzar to Babylon this position was virtually filled by Zerubbabel, a grandson of Jehoiakin, the second last king of Judah, and appointed by the Persian king Pehah or Satrap of Judah. Him Haggai now formally names the elect servant of Jehovah. In that overturning of the kingdoms of the world which Haggai had predicted two months before, and which he now explains as their mutual destruction by war, Jehovah of Hosts will make Zerubbabel His signet-ring, inseparable from Himself and the symbol of His authority.

"And the word of Jehovah came a second time to* Haggai on the twenty-fourth day of the *ninth* month, saying: Speak to Zerubbabel, Satrap of Judah, saying: I am about to shake the heavens and the earth,† and I will overturn the thrones‡ of kingdoms, and will shatter the power of the kingdoms of the Gentiles, and will overturn chariots§ and their riders, and horses and their riders will come down, every man by the sword of his brother. In that day—oracle of Jehovah of Hosts—I will take Zerubbabel, son of She'alti'el, My servant—oracle of Jehovah—and will make him like a signet-ring; for thee have I chosen—oracle of Jehovah of Hosts."

The wars and mutual destruction of the Gentiles, of which Haggai speaks, are doubtless those revolts of races and provinces which threatened to disrupt the Persian Empire upon the accession of Darius in 521. Persians, Babylonians, Medes, Armenians, the Sacæ and others rose together or in succession. In four years Darius quelled them all, and reorganised his empire before the Jews finished their Temple. Like all the Syrian governors, Zerubbabel remained his poor lieutenant and submissive tributary. History rolled westward into Europe. Greek and Persian began their struggle for the control of its future, and the Jews fell into an obscurity and oblivion unbroken for centuries. The "signet-ring of Jehovah" was not acknowledged by the world—does not seem even to have challenged its briefest attention. But Haggai had at least succeeded in asserting the Messianic hope of Israel, always baffled, never quenched, in this re-opening of her life. He had delivered the ancient heritage of Israel to the care of the new Judaism.

Haggai's place in the succession of prophecy ought now to be clear to us. The meagreness of his words and their crabbed style, his occupation with the construction of the Temple, his unfulfilled hope in Zerubbabel, his silence on the great inheritance of truth delivered by his predecessors, and the absence from his prophesying of all visions of God's character and all emphasis upon the ethical elements of religion—these have moved some to depress his value as a prophet almost to the vanishing point. Nothing could be more unjust. In his opening message Haggai evinced the first indispensable power of the prophet: to speak to the situation of the moment, and to succeed in getting men to take up the duty at their feet; in another message he announced a great ethical principle; in his last he conserved the Messianic traditions of his religion, and though not less disappointed than Isaiah in the personality to whom he looked for their fulfilment, he succeeded in passing on their hope undiminished to future ages.

* See above, p. 613.
† LXX. enlarges: "and the sea and the dry land."
‡ Heb. sing. collect. LXX. plural.
§ Again a sing. coll.

ZECHARIAH.

(i-viii.)

"Not by might, and not by force, but by My Spirit, saith Jehovah of Hosts.

"Be not afraid, strengthen your hands! Speak truth every man to his neighbour; truth and wholesome judgment judge ye in your gates, and in your hearts plan no evil for each other, nor take pleasure in false swearing, for all these things do I hate—oracle of Jehovah."

CHAPTER XIX.

THE BOOK OF ZECHARIAH (I.—VIII.).

THE Book of Zechariah, consisting of fourteen chapters, falls clearly into two divisions: *First*, chaps. i.-viii., ascribed to Zechariah himself and full of evidence for their authenticity; *Second*, chaps. ix.-xiv., which are not ascribed to Zechariah, and deal with conditions different from those upon which he worked. The full discussion of the date and character of this second section we shall reserve till we reach the period at which we believe it to have been written. Here an introduction is necessary only to chaps. i.-viii.

These chapters may be divided into five sections.

I. Chap. i. 1-6.—A Word of Jehovah which came to Zechariah in the eighth month of the second year of Darius, that is in November, 520 B. C., or between the second and the third oracles of Haggai.* In this the prophet's place is affirmed in the succession of the prophets of Israel. The ancient prophets are gone, but their predictions have been fulfilled in the calamities of the Exile, and God's Word abides for ever.

II. Chap. i. 7-vi. 9.—A Word of Jehovah which came to Zechariah on the twenty-fourth of the eleventh month of the same year, that is January or February, 519, and which he reproduces in the form of eight Visions by night. (1) The Vision of the Four Horsemen: God's new mercies to Jerusalem (chap. i. 7-17). (2) The Vision of the Four Horns, or Powers of the World, and the Four Smiths, who smite them down (ii. 1-4 Heb., but in the Septuagint and in the English Version i. 18-21). (3) The Vision of the Man with the Measuring Rope: Jerusalem shall be rebuilt, no longer as a narrow fortress, but spread abroad for the multitude of her population (chap. ii. 5-9 Heb., ii. 1-5 LXX. and Eng.). To this Vision is appended a lyric piece of probably older date calling upon the Jews in Babylon to return, and celebrating the joining of many peoples to Jehovah, now that He takes up again His habitation in Jerusalem (chap. ii. 10-17 Heb., ii. 6-13 LXX. and Eng.). (4) The Vision of Joshua, the High Priest, and the Satan or Accuser: the Satan is rebuked, and Joshua is cleansed from his foul garments and clothed with a new turban and festal apparel; the land is purged and secure

* See above, pp. 613 ff.

(chap. iii.). (5) The Vision of the Seven-Branched Lamp and the Two Olive-Trees (chap. iv. 1-6*a*, 10*b*-14): into the centre of this has been inserted a Word of Jehovah to Zerubbabel (vv. 6*b*-10*a*), which interrupts the Vision and ought probably to come at the close of it. (6) The Vision of the Flying Book: it is the curse of the land, which is being removed, but after destroying the houses of the wicked (chap. v. 1-4). (7) The Vision of the Bushel and the Woman: that is the guilt of the land and its wickedness; they are carried off and planted in the land of Shinar (v. 5-11). (8) The Vision of the Four Chariots: they go forth from the Lord of all the earth, to traverse the earth and bring His Spirit, or anger, to bear on the North country (chap. vi. 1-8)).

III. Chap. vi. 9-15.—A Word of Jehovah, undated (unless it is to be taken as of the same date as the Visions to which it is attached), giving directions as to the gifts sent to the community at Jerusalem from the Babylonian Jews. A crown is to be made from the silver and gold, and, according to the text, placed upon the head of Joshua. But, as we shall see,* the text gives evident signs of having been altered in the interest of the High Priest; and probably the crown was meant for Zerubbabel, at whose right hand the priest is to stand, and there shall be a counsel of peace between the two of them. The far-away shall come and assist at the building of the Temple. This section breaks off in the middle of a sentence.

IV. Chap. vii.—The Word of Jehovah which came to Zechariah on the fourth of the ninth month of the fourth year of Darius, that is nearly two years after the date of the Visions. The Temple was approaching completion; and an inquiry was addressed to the priests who were in it and to the prophets concerning the Fasts, which had been maintained during the Exile, while the Temple lay desolate (chap. vii. 1-3). This inquiry drew from Zechariah a historical explanation of how the Fasts arose (chap. vii. 4-14).

V. Chap. viii.—Ten short undated oracles, each introduced by the same formula, "Thus saith Jehovah of Hosts," and summarising all Zechariah's teaching since before the Temple began up to the question of the cessation of the Fasts upon its completion—with promises for the future. (1) A Word affirming Jehovah's new zeal for Jerusalem and His Return to her (vv. 1, 2). (2) Another of the same (ver. 3). (3) A Word promising fulness of old folk and children in her streets (vv. 4, 5). (4) A Word affirming that nothing is too wonderful for Jehovah (ver. 6). (5) A Word promising the return of the people from east and west (vv. 7, 8). (6 and 7) Two Words contrasting, in terms similar to Haggai i., the poverty of the people before the foundation of the Temple with their new prosperity: from a curse Israel shall become a blessing. This is due to God's anger having changed into a purpose of grace to Jerusalem. But the people themselves must do truth and justice, ceasing from perjury and thoughts of evil against each other (vv. 9-17). (8) A Word which recurs to the question of Fasting, and commands that the four great Fasts, instituted to commemorate the siege and overthrow of Jerusalem, and the murder of Gedaliah, be changed to joy and gladness (vv. 18, 19). (9) A Word predicting the coming of the Gentiles to the worship of Jehovah at Jerusalem (vv. 20-22). (10) Another of the same (ver. 23).

* Below, p. 634.

There can be little doubt that, apart from the few interpolations noted, these eight chapters are genuine prophecies of Zechariah, who is mentioned in the Book of Ezra as the colleague of Haggai, and contemporary of Zerubbabel and Joshua at the time of the rebuilding of the Temple.* Like the oracles of Haggai, these prophecies are dated according to the years of Darius the king, from his second year to his fourth. Although they may contain some of the exhortations to build the Temple, which the Book of Ezra informs us that Zechariah made along with Haggai, the most of them presuppose progress in the work, and seek to assist it by historical retrospect and by glowing hopes of the Messianic effects of its completion. Their allusions suit exactly the years to which they are assigned. Darius is king. The Exile has lasted about seventy years.† Numbers of Jews remain in Babylon,‡ and are scattered over the rest of the world.§ The community at Jerusalem is small and weak: it is the mere colony of young men and men in middle life who came to it from Babylon; there are few children and old folk.‖ Joshua and Zerubbabel are the heads of the community, and the pledges for its future.¶ The exact conditions are recalled as recent which Haggai spoke of a few years before.** Moreover, there is a steady and orderly progress throughout the prophecies, in harmony with the successive dates at which they were delivered. In November, 520, they begin with a cry to repentance and lessons drawn from the past of prophecy.†† In January, 519, Temple and city are still to be built.‡‡ Zerubbabel has laid the foundation; the completion is yet future.§§ The prophet's duty is to quiet the people's apprehensions about the state of the world,‖‖ to provoke their zeal,¶¶ give them confidence in their great men,*** and, above all, assure them that God is returned to them††† and their sin pardoned.‡‡‡ But in December, 518, the Temple is so far built that the priests are said to belong to it;§§§ there is no occasion for continuing the fasts of the Exile,‖‖‖ the future has opened and the horizon is bright with the Messianic hopes.¶¶¶ Most of all, it is felt that the hard struggle with the forces of nature is over, and the people are exhorted to the virtues of the civic life.**** They have time to lift their eyes from their work and see the nations coming from afar to Jerusalem.††††

These features leave no room for doubt that the great bulk of the first eight chapters of the Book of Zechariah are by the prophet himself, and from the years to which he assigns them, November, 520, to December, 518. The point requires no argument.

* Ezra v. 1, vi. 14.

† i. 12, vii. 5: reckoning in round numbers from 590, midway between the two Exiles of 597 and 586, that brings us to about 520, the second year of Darius.

‡ ii. 6 (Eng., Heb. 10). On the question whether the Book of Zechariah gives no evidence of a previous Return from Babylon see above, pp. 609 ff.

§ viii. 7, etc.

‖ viii. 4, 5.

¶ iii. 1–10, iv. 6–10, vi. 11 ff.

** viii. 9, 10.

†† i. 1–6.

‡‡ i. 7–17.

§§ iv. 6–10.

‖‖ i. 7-21 (Eng., Heb. i. 7—ii. 4).

¶¶ iv. 6 ff.

*** iii., iv.

††† i. 16.

‡‡‡ v.

§§§ vii. 3.

‖‖‖ vii. 1–7, viii. 18, 19.

¶¶¶ viii. 20-23.

**** viii. 16, 17.

†††† viii. 20–23.

There are, however, three passages which provoke further examination—two of them because of the signs they bear of an earlier date, and one because of the alteration it has suffered in the interests of a later day in Israel's history.

The lyric passage which is appended to the Second Vision (chap. ii. 10-17 Heb., 6-13 LXX. and Eng.) suggests questions by its singularity: there is no other such among the Visions. But in addition to this it speaks not only of the Return from Babylon as still future *—this might still be said after the First Return of the exiles in 536 †—but it differs from the language of all the Visions proper in describing the return of Jehovah Himself to Zion as still future. The whole, too, has the ring of the great odes in Isaiah xl.-lv., and seems to reflect the same situation, upon the eve of Cyrus' conquest of Babylon. There can be little doubt that we have here inserted in Zechariah's Visions a song of twenty years earlier, but we must confess inability to decide whether it was adopted by Zechariah himself or added by a later hand.‡

Again, there are the two passages called the Word of Jehovah to Zerubbabel, chap. iv. 6*b*-10*a*; and the Word of Jehovah concerning the gifts which came to Jerusalem from the Jews in Babylon, chap. vi. 9-15. The first, as Wellhausen has shown,§ is clearly out of place; it disturbs the narrative of the Vision, and is to be put at the end of the latter. The second is undated, and separate from the Visions. The second plainly affirms that the building of the Temple is still future. The man whose name is Branch or Shoot is designated: "and he shall build the Temple of Jehovah." The first is in the same temper as the first two oracles of Haggai. It is possible then that these two passages are not, like the Visions with which they are taken, to be dated from 519, but represent that still earlier prophesying of Zechariah with which we are told he assisted Haggai in instigating the people to begin to build the Temple.

The style of the prophet Zechariah betrays special features almost only in the narrative of the Visions. Outside these his language is simple, direct, and pure, as it could not but be, considering how much of it is drawn from, or modelled upon, the older prophets,‖ and chiefly Hosea and Jeremiah. Only one or two lapses into a careless and degenerate dialect show us how the prophet might have written had he not been sustained by the music of the classical periods of the language.¶

This directness and pith is not shared by the language in which the Visions are narrated* Here the style is involved and redundant. The syntax is loose; there is a frequent omission of the copula, and of other means by which, in better Hebrew, connection and conciseness are sustained. The formulas, "thus saith" and "saying," are repeated to weariness. At the same time it is fair to ask how much of this redundancy was due to Zechariah himself? Take the Septuagint version. The Hebrew text, which it followed, not only included a number of repetitions of the formulas, and of the designations of the personages introduced into the Visions, which do not occur in the Massoretic text,† but omitted some which are found in the Massoretic text.‡ These two sets of phenomena prove that from an early date the copiers of the original text of Zechariah must have been busy in increasing its redundancies. Further, there are still earlier intrusions and expansions, for these are shared by both the Hebrew and the Greek texts: some of them very natural efforts to clear up the personages and conversations recorded in the dreams,§ some of them stupid mistakes in understanding the drift of the argument.‖ There must of course have been a certain amount of redundancy in the original to provoke such aggravations of it, and of obscurity or tortuousness of style to cause them to be deemed necessary. But it would be very unjust to charge all the faults of our present text to Zechariah himself, especially when we find such force and simplicity in the passages outside the Visions. Of course the involved and misty subjects of the latter naturally forced upon the description of them a laboriousness of art, to which there was no provocation in directly exhorting the people to a pure life, or in straightforward predictions of the Messianic era.

Beyond the corruptions due to these causes, the text of Zechariah i.-viii. has not suffered more than that of our other prophets. There are one or two clerical errors;¶ an occasional preposition or person of a verb needs to be amended. Here and there the text has been disarranged;** and as already noticed, there has been one serious alteration of the original.††

From the foregoing paragraphs it must be apparent what help and hindrance in the reconstruction of the text is furnished by the Septuagint. A list of its variant readings and of its mistranslations is appended.‡‡

* ii. 10 f. Heb., 6 f., LXX., and Eng.

† Though the expression "I have scattered you to the four winds of heaven" seems to imply the Exile before any return.

‡ For the bearing of this on Kosters' theory of the Return see pp. 610 f.

§ See below, p. 632.

‖ Outside the Visions the prophecies contain these echoes or repetitions of earlier writers: chap. i. 1-6 quotes the constant refrain of prophetic preaching before the Exile, and in chap. vii. 7-14 (ver. 8 must be deleted) is given a summary of that preaching; in chap. viii. ver. 3 echoes Isa. i. 21, 26, "city of troth," and Jer. xxxi. 23, "mountain of holiness" (there is really no connection, as Kuenen holds, between ver. 4 and Isa. lxv. 20; it would create more interesting questions as to the date of the latter if there were); ver. 8 is based on Hosea ii. 15 Heb., 19 Eng., and Jer. xxxi. 33; ver. 12 is based on Hosea ii. 21 f. (Heb. 23 f.); with ver. 13 compare Jer. xlii. 18, "a curse"; vv. 21 ff. with Isa. ii. 3 and Micah iv. 2.

¶ *E. g.*, vii. 5, צַמְתֻּנִי אָנִי for צַמְתֶּם לִי: *cf.* Ewald, "Syntax," § 315*b*. The curious use of the acc. in the following verse is perhaps only apparent; part of the text may have fallen out.

* Though there are not wanting, of course, echoes here as in the other prophecies of older writings, *e. g.*, i. 12, 17.

† לאמר, "saying," ii. 8 (Gr. ii. 4); iv. 5, "And the angel who spoke with me said;" i. 17, *cf.* vi. 5. "All" is inserted in i. 11, iii. 9; "lord" in ii. 2; "of hosts" (after "Jehovah") viii. 17; and there are other instances of palpable expansion, *e. g.*, i. 6, 8, ii. 4 bis, 6, viii. 19.

‡ *E. g.*, ii. 2, iv. 2, 13, v. 9, vi. 12 bis, vii. 8: *cf.* also vi. 13.

§ i. 8 ff., iii. 4 ff.: *cf.* also vi. 3 with vv. 6 f.

‖ *E. g.* (but this is outside the Visions), the very flagrant misunderstanding to which the insertion of vii. 8 is due.

¶ v. 6, עינם for עונם as in LXX., and the last words of v. 11; perhaps vi. 10; and almost certainly vii. 2*a*.

** Chap. iv. On 6*a*, 10*b*-14 should immediately follow, and 6*b*-10*a* come after 14.

†† vi. 11 ff. See below, pp. 634 f.

‡‡ Chief variants: i. 8, 10: ii. 15; iii. 4; iv. 7, 12; v. 1, 3, 4, 9; vi. 10, 13; vii. 3; viii. 8, 9, 12, 20. Obvious mistranslations or misreadings: ii. 9, 10, 15, 17; iii. 4; iv. 7, 10; v. 1, 4, 9; vi. 10 *cf.* 14; vii. 3.

CHAPTER XX.

ZECHARIAH THE PROPHET.

ZECHARIAH i. 1-6, etc.; EZRA v. 1, vi. 14.

ZECHARIAH is one of the prophets whose personality as distinguished from their message exerts some degree of fascination on the student. This is not due, however, as in the case of Hosea or Jeremiah, to the facts of his life, for of these we know extremely little; but to certain conflicting symptoms of character which appear through his prophecies.

His name was a very common one in Israel, Zekher-Yah, "Jehovah remembers." * In his own book he is described as "the son of Berekh-Yah, the son of Iddo," † and in the Aramaic document of the Book of Ezra as "the son of Iddo." ‡ Some have explained this difference by supposing that Berekhyah was the actual father of the prophet, but that either he died early, leaving Zechariah to the care of the grandfather, or else that he was a man of no note, and Iddo was more naturally mentioned as the head of the family. There are several instances in the Old Testament of men being called the sons of their grandfathers: § as in these cases the grandfather was the reputed founder of the house, so in that of Zechariah Iddo was the head of his family when it came out of Babylon and was anew planted in Jerusalem. Others, however, have contested the genuineness of the words "son of Berekh-Yah," and have traced their insertion to a confusion of the prophet with Zechariah son of Yĕbherekh-Yahu, the contemporary of Isaiah.‖ This is precarious, while the other hypothesis is a very natural one.¶ Whichever be correct, the prophet Zechariah was a member of the priestly family of Iddo, that came up to Jerusalem from Babylon under Cyrus.** The Book of Nehemiah adds that in the high-priesthood of Yoyakim, the son of Joshua, the head of the house of Iddo was a Zechariah.†† If this be our prophet, then he was probably a young man in 520,‡‡ and had come up as a child in the caravans from Babylon. The Aramaic document of the Book of Ezra §§ assigns to Zechariah a share with Haggai in the work of instigating Zerubbabel and Jeshua to begin the Temple. None of his oracles is dated previous to the beginning of the work in August, 520, but we have seen * that among those undated there are one or two which by referring to the building of the Temple as still future may contain some relics of that first stage of his ministry. From November, 520, we have the first of his dated oracles; his Visions followed in January, 519, and his last recorded prophesying in December, 518.†

These are all the certain events of Zechariah's history. But in the well-attested prophecies he has left we discover, besides some obvious traits of character, certain problems of style and expression which suggest a personality of more than usual interest. Loyalty to the great voices of old, the temper which appeals to the experience, rather than to the dogmas, of the past, the gift of plain speech to his own times, a wistful anxiety about his reception as a prophet,‡ combined with the absence of all ambition to be original or anything but the clear voice of the lessons of the past and of the conscience of to-day—these are the qualities which characterise Zechariah's orations to the people. But how to reconcile them with the strained art and obscure truths of the Visions—it is this which invests with interest the study of his personality. We have proved that the obscurity and redundancy of the Visions cannot all have been due to himself. Later hands have exaggerated the repetitions and ravelled the processes of the original. But these gradual blemishes have not grown from nothing: the original style must have been sufficiently involved to provoke the interpolations of the scribes, and it certainly contained all the weird and shifting apparitions which we find so hard to make clear to ourselves. The problem, therefore, remains—how one who had gift of speech, so straight and clear, came to torture and tangle his style; how one who presented with all plainness the main issues of his people's history found it laid upon him to invent, for the further expression of these, symbols so laboured and intricate.

We begin with the oracle which opens his book and illustrates those simple characteristics of the man that contrast so sharply with the temper of his Visions.

"In the eighth month, in the second year of

* זְכַרְיָה ; LXX. Ζαχαρίας.

† i. 1 : בֶּן־בֶּרֶכְיָה בֶּן־עִדּוֹ. In i. 7: בֶּרֶכְיָהוּ בֶּן־עִדּוֹא.

‡ Ezra v. 1, vi. 14 : בַּר־עִדּוֹא.

§ Gen. xxiv. 47, *cf.* xxix. 5 ; 1 Kings xix. 16, *cf.* 2 Kings ix. 14, 20.

‖ Isa. viii. 2 : בֶּן־יְבֶרֶכְיָהוּ. This confusion, which existed in early Jewish and Christian times, Knobel, Von Ortenberg, Bleek, Wellhausen, and others take to be due to the effort to find a second Zechariah for the authorship of chaps. ix. ff.

¶ So Vatke, König, and many othors. Marti prefers it ("Der Prophet Sacharja," p. 58). See also Ryle on Ezra v. 1.

** Neh. xii. 4.

†† *Ib.* 16.

‡‡ This is not proved, as Pusey, König ("Einl.," p. 364) and others think, by נַעַר, or young man, of the Third Vision (ii. 8. Heb., ii. 4 LXX. and Eng.). *Cf.* Wright, "Zechariah and his Prophecies," p. xvi.

§§ v. 1, vi. 14.

* Above, p. 622.

† More than this we do not know of Zechariah. The Jewish and Christian traditions of him are as unfounded as those of other prophets. According to the Jews he was, of course, a member of the mythical Great Synagogue. See above on Haggai, pp. 615 f. As in the case of the prophets we have already treated, the Christian traditions of Zechariah are found in (Pseud-) Epiphanius, "De Vitis Prophetarum," Dorotheus, and Hesychius, as quoted above, p. 580. They amount to this, that Zechariah, after predicting in Babylon the birth of Zerubbabel, and to Cyrus his victory over Crœsus and his treatment of the Jews, came in his old age to Jerusalem, prophesied, died, and was buried near Beit-Jibrin—another instance of the curious relegation by Christian tradition of the birth and burial places of so many of the prophets to that neighbourhood. Compare Beit-Zakharya, 12 miles from Beit-Jibrin. Hesychius says he was born in Gilead. Dorotheus confuses him, as the Jews did, with Zechariah of Isa. viii 1.

Zechariah was certainly not the Zechariah whom our Lord describes as slain between the Temple and the Altar (Matt. xxiii. 35 ; Luke xi. 51). In the former passage alone is this Zechariah called the son of Barachiah. In the "Evang. Nazar." Jerome read "the son of Yehoyada." Both readings may be insertions. According to 2 Chron., xxiv. 21, in the reign of Joash, Zechariah, the son of Yehoyada the priest, was stoned in the court of the Temple, and according to Josephus (IV. "Wars," v. 4), in the year 68 A. D. Zechariah son of Baruch was assassinated in the Temple by two zealots. The latter murder may, as Marti remarks (pp. 58 f.), have led to the insertion of Barachiah into Matt. xxiii. 35.

‡ ii. 13, 15 ; iv. 9 ; vi. 15.

Darius, the word of Jehovah came to the prophet Zechariah, son of Berekhyah, son of Iddo,* saying: Jehovah was very wroth† with your fathers. And thou shalt say unto them: Thus saith Jehovah of Hosts: Turn ye to Me—oracle of Jehovah of Hosts—that I may turn to you, saith Jehovah of Hosts! Be not like your fathers, to whom the former prophets preached, saying: 'Thus saith Jehovah of Hosts, Turn now from your evil ways and from‡ your evil deeds,' but they hearkened not, and paid no attention to Me—oracle of Jehovah. Your fathers, where are they? And the prophets, do they live for ever? But§ My words and My statutes, with which I charged My servants the prophets, did they not overtake your fathers? till these turned and said, As Jehovah of Hosts did purpose to do unto us, according to our deeds and according to our ways, so hath He dealt with us."

It is a sign of the new age which we have reached, that its prophet should appeal to the older prophets with as much solemnity as they did to Moses himself. The history which led to the Exile has become to Israel as classic and sacred as her great days of deliverance from Egypt and of conquest in Canaan. But still more significant is what Zechariah seeks from that past; this we must carefully discover, if we would appreciate with exactness his rank as a prophet.

The development of religion may be said to consist of a struggle between two tempers, both of which indeed appeal to the past, but from very opposite motives. The one proves its devotion to the older prophets by adopting the exact formulas of their doctrine, counts these sacred to the letter, and would enforce them in detail upon the minds and circumstances of the new generation. It conceives that truth has been promulgated once for all in forms as enduring as the principles they contain. It fences ancient rites, cherishes old customs and institutions, and when these are questioned it becomes alarmed and even savage. The other temper is no whit behind this one in its devotion to the past, but it seeks the ancient prophets not so much for what they have said as for what they have been, not for what they enforced but for what they encountered, suffered, and confessed. It asks not for dogmas, but for experience and testimony. He who can thus read the past and interpret it to his own day—he is the prophet. In his reading he finds nothing so clear, nothing so tragic, nothing so convincing as the working of the Word of God. He beholds how this came to men, haunted them, and was entreated by them. He sees that it was their great opportunity, which being rejected became their judgment. He finds abused justice vindicated, proud wrong punished, and all God's neglected commonplaces achieving in time their triumph. He reads how men came to see this, and to confess their guilt. He is haunted by the remorse of generations who know how they might have obeyed the Divine call, but wilfully did not. And though they have perished, and the prophets have died and their formulas are no more applicable, the victorious Word itself still lives and cries to men with the terrible emphasis of their fathers' experience. All this is the vision of the true prophet, and it was the vision of Zechariah.

His generation was one whose chief temptation was to adopt towards the past the other attitude we have described. In their feebleness what could the poor remnant of Israel do but cling servilely to the former greatness? The vindication of the Exile had stamped the Divine authority of the earlier prophets. The habits, which the life in Babylon had perfected, of arranging and codifying the literature of the past, and of employing it, in place of altar and ritual, in the stated service of God, had canonised Scripture and provoked men to the worship of its very letter. Had the real prophet not again been raised, these habits might have too early produced the belief that the Word of God was exhausted, and must have fastened upon the feeble life of Israel that mass of stiff and stark dogmas, the literal application of which Christ afterwards found crushing the liberty and the force of religion. Zechariah prevented this—for a time. He himself was mighty in the Scriptures of the past: no man in Israel makes larger use of them. But he employs them as witnesses, not as dogmas; he finds in them not authority, but experience.* He reads their testimony to the ever-living presence of God's Word with men. And seeing that, though the old forms and figures have perished with the hearts which shaped them, the Word itself in its bare truth has vindicated its life by fulfilment in history, he knows that it lives still, and hurls it upon his people, not in the forms published by this or that prophet of long ago, but in its essence and direct from God Himself, as His Word for to-day and now. "The fathers, where are they? And the prophets, do they live for ever? But My words and My statutes, with which I charged My servants the prophets, have they not overtaken your fathers? Thus saith Jehovah of Hosts, Be ye not like your fathers, but turn ye to Me that I may turn to you."

The argument of this oracle might very naturally have been narrowed into a credential for the prophet himself as sent from God. About his reception as Jehovah's messenger Zechariah shows a repeated anxiety. Four times he concludes a prediction with the words. "And ye shall know that Jehovah hath sent me,"† as if after his first utterances he had encountered that suspicion and unbelief which a prophet never failed to suffer from his contemporaries. But in this oracle there is no trace of such personal anxiety. The oracle is pervaded only with the desire to prove the ancient Word of God as still alive, and to drive it home in its own sheer force. Like the greatest of his order Zechariah appears with the call to repent: "Turn ye to Me—oracle of Jehovah of Hosts—that I may turn to you." This is the pivot on which history has turned, the one condition on which God has been able to help men. Wherever it is read as the conclusion of all the past, wherever it is proclaimed as the conscience of the present, there the true prophet is found and the Word of God has been spoken.

This same possession by the ethical spirit reappears, as we shall see, in Zechariah's orations

* LXX. 'Αδδω. See above, p. 264.
† Heb "angered with anger;" Gr. "with great anger."
‡ As in LXX.
§ LXX. has misunderstood and expanded this verse.

* It is to be noticed that Zechariah appeals to the Torah of the prophets, and does not mention any Torah of the priests. *Cf.* Smend, "A. T. Rel. Gesch.," pp. 176 f.
† Page 623 *n.*

to the people after the anxieties of building are over and the completion of the Temple is in sight. In these he affirms again that the whole essence of God's Word by the older prophets has been moral—to judge true judgment, to practise mercy, to defend the widow and orphan, the stranger and poor, and to think no evil of one another. For the sad fasts of the Exile Zechariah enjoins gladness, with the duty of truth and the hope of peace. Again and again he enforces sincerity and the love without dissimulation. His ideals for Jerusalem are very high, including the conversion of the nations to her God. But warlike ambitions have vanished from them, and his pictures of her future condition are homely and practical. Jerusalem shall be no more a fortress, but spread village-wise without walls.* Full families, unlike the present colony with its few children and its men worn out in middle life by harassing warfare with enemies and a sullen nature; streets rife with children playing and old folk sitting in the sun; the return of the exiles; happy harvests and springtimes of peace; solid gain of labour for every man, with no raiding neighbours to harass, nor the mutual envies of peasants in their selfish struggle with famine.

It is a simple, hearty, practical man whom such prophesying reveals, the spirit of him bent on justice and love, and yearning for the unharassed labour of the field and for happy homes. No prophet has more beautiful sympathies, a more direct word of righteousness, or a braver heart. "Fast not, but love truth and peace. Truth and wholesome justice set ye up in your gates. Be not afraid; strengthen your hands! Old men and women shall yet sit in the streets of Jerusalem, each with staff in hand for the fulness of their years; the city's streets shall be rife with boys and girls at play."

CHAPTER XXI.

THE VISIONS OF ZECHARIAH.

ZECHARIAH i. 7–vi.

THE Visions of Zechariah do not lack those large and simple views of religion which we have just seen to be the charm of his other prophecies. Indeed it is among the Visions that we find the most spiritual of all his utterances: † "Not by might, and not by force, but by My Spirit, saith Jehovah of Hosts." The Visions express the need of the Divine forgiveness, emphasise the reality of sin, as a principle deeper than the civic crimes in which it is manifested, and declare the power of God to banish it from His people. The Visions also contain the remarkable prospect of Jerusalem as the City of Peace, her only wall the Lord Himself.‡ The overthrow of the heathen empires is predicted by the Lord's own hand, and from all the Visions there are absent both the turmoil and the glory of war.

We must also be struck by the absence of another element, which is a cause of complexity in the writings of many prophets—the polemic against idolatry. Zechariah nowhere mentions the idols. We have already seen what proof this silence bears for the fact that the community to which he spoke was not that half-heathen remnant of Israel which had remained in the land, but was composed of worshippers of Jehovah who at His word had returned from Babylon.* Here we have only to do with the bearing of the fact upon Zechariah's style. That bewildering confusion of the heathen pantheon and its rites, which forms so much of our difficulty in interpreting some of the prophecies of Ezekiel and the closing chapters of the Book of Isaiah, is not to blame for any of the complexity of Zechariah's Visions.

Nor can we attribute the latter to the fact that the Visions are dreams, and therefore bound to be more involved and obscure than the words of Jehovah which came to Zechariah in the open daylight of his people's public life. In chaps. i. 7–vi. we have not the narrative of actual dreams, but a series of conscious and artistic allegories—the deliberate translation into a carefully constructed symbolism of the Divine truths with which the prophet was entrusted by his God. Yet this only increases our problem—why a man with such gifts of direct speech, and such clear views of his people's character and history, should choose to express the latter by an imagery so artificial and involved? In his orations Zechariah is very like the prophets whom we have known before the Exile, thoroughly ethical and intent upon the public conscience of his time. He appreciates what they were, feels himself standing in their succession, and is endowed both with their spirit and their style. But none of them constructs the elaborate allegories which he does, or insists upon the religious symbolism which he enforces as indispensable to the standing of Israel with God. Not only are their visions few and simple, but they look down upon the visionary temper as a rude stage of prophecy and inferior to their own, in which the Word of God is received by personal communion with Himself, and conveyed to His people by straight and plain words. Some of the earlier prophets even condemn all priesthood and ritual; none of them regards these as indispensable to Israel's right relations with Jehovah; and none employs those superhuman mediators of the Divine truth by whom Zechariah is instructed in his Visions.

I. THE INFLUENCES WHICH MOULDED THE VISIONS.

The explanation of this change that has come over prophecy must be sought for in certain habits which the people formed in exile. During the Exile several causes conspired to develop among Hebrew writers the tempers both of symbolism and apocalypse. The chief of these was their separation from the realities of civic life, with the opportunity their political leisure afforded them of brooding and dreaming. Facts and Divine promises, which had previously to be dealt with by the conscience of the moment, were left to be worked out by the imagination. The exiles were not responsible citizens or statesmen, but dreamers. They were inspired by mighty hopes for the future, and not fettered by the practical necessities of a definite historical

* This picture is given in one of the Visions: the Third.
† iv. 6. Unless this be taken as an earlier prophecy. See above, p. 622.
‡ ii. 9, 10 Heb., 5, 6 LXX. and Eng.

* See above, pp. 610 ff., where this is stated as an argumet against Kosters' theory that there was no Return from Babylon in the reign of Cyrus.

situation upon which these hopes had to be immediately realised. They had a far-off horizon to build upon, and they occupied the whole breadth of it. They had a long time to build, and they elaborated the minutest details of their architecture. Consequently their construction of the future of Israel, and their description of the processes by which it was to be reached, became colossal, ornate, and lavishly symbolic. Nor could the exiles fail to receive stimulus for all this from the rich imagery of Babylonian art by which they were surrounded.

Under these influences there were three strong developments in Israel. One was that development of Apocalypse the first beginnings of which we traced in Zephaniah—the representation of God's providence of the world and of His people, not by the ordinary political and military processes of history, but by awful convulsions and catastrophes, both in nature and in politics, in which God Himself appeared, either alone in sudden glory or by the mediation of heavenly armies. The second—and it was but a part of the first—was the development of a belief in Angels: superhuman beings who had not only a part to play in the apocalyptic wars and revolutions; but, in the growing sense, which characterises the period, of God's distance and awfulness, were believed to act as His agents in the communication of His Word to men. And, thirdly, there was the development of the Ritual. To some minds this may appear the strangest of all the effects of the Exile. The fall of the Temple, its hierarchy and sacrifices, might be supposed to enforce more spiritual conceptions of God and of His communion with His people. And no doubt it did. The impossibility of the legal sacrifices in exile opened the mind of Israel to the belief that God was satisfied with the sacrifices of the broken heart, and drew near, without mediation, to all who were humble and pure of heart. But no one in Israel therefore understood that these sacrifices were for ever abolished. Their interruption was regarded as merely temporary even by the most spiritual of Jewish writers. The Fifty-first Psalm, for instance, which declares that "the sacrifices of God are a broken spirit; a broken and a contrite heart, O Lord, Thou wilt not despise," immediately follows this declaration by the assurance that "when God builds again the walls of Jerusalem," He will once more take delight in "the legal sacrifices: burnt offering and whole burnt offering, the oblation of bullocks upon Thine altar." * For men of such views the ruin of the Temple was not its abolition with the whole dispensation which it represented, but rather the occasion for its reconstruction upon wider lines and a more detailed system, for the planning of which the nation's exile afforded the leisure and the carefulness of art described above. The ancient liturgy, too, was insufficient for the stronger convictions of guilt and need of purgation, which sore punishment had impressed upon the people. Then, scattered among the heathen as they were, they learned to require stricter laws and more drastic ceremonies to restore and preserve their holiness. Their ritual, therefore, had to be expanded and detailed to a degree far beyond what we find in Israel's earlier systems of worship. With the fall of the monarchy and the absence of civic life the importance of the priesthood was proportionately enhanced; and the growing sense of God's aloofness from the world, already alluded to, made the more indispensable human, as well as superhuman, mediators between Himself and His people. Consider these things, and it will be clear why prophecy, which with Amos had begun a war against all ritual, and with Jeremiah had achieved a religion absolutely independent of priesthood and Temple, should reappear after the Exile, insistent upon the building of the Temple, enforcing the need both of the priesthood and sacrifice, and while it proclaimed the Messianic King and the High Priest as the great feeders of the national life and worship, finding no place beside them for the Prophet himself.*

* Vv. 17 and 19.

The force of these developments of Apocalypse, Angelology, and the Ritual appears both in Ezekiel and in the exilic codification of the ritual which forms so large a part of the Pentateuch. Ezekiel carries Apocalypse far beyond the beginnings started by Zephaniah. He introduces, though not under the name of angels, superhuman mediators between himself and God. The Priestly Code does not mention angels, and has no Apocalypse; but like Ezekiel it develops, to an extraordinary degree, the ritual of Israel. Both its author and Ezekiel base on the older forms, but build as men who are not confined by the lines of an actually existing system. The changes they make, the innovations they introduce, are too numerous to mention here. To illustrate their influence upon Zechariah, it is enough to emphasise the large place they give in the ritual to the processes of propitiation and cleansing from sin, and the increased authority with which they invest the priesthood. In Ezekiel Israel has still a Prince, though he is not called King. He arranges the cultus,† and sacrifices are offered for him and the people,‡ but the priests teach and judge the people.§ In the Priestly Code‖ the priesthood is more rigorously fenced than by Ezekiel from the laity, and more regularly graded. At its head appears a High Priest (as he does not in Ezekiel), and by his side the civil rulers are portrayed in lesser dignity and power. Sacrifices are made, no longer as with Ezekiel for Prince and People, but for Aaron and the congregation; and throughout the narrative of ancient history, into the form of which this Code projects its legislation, the High Priest stands above the captain of the host, even when the latter is Joshua himself. God's enemies are defeated not so much by the wisdom and valour of the secular powers, as by the miracles of Jehovah Himself, mediated through the priesthood. Ezekiel and the Priestly Code both elaborate the sacrifices of atonement and sanctification beyond all the earlier uses.

2. General Features of the Visions.

It was beneath these influences that Zechariah grew up, and to them we may trace, not only numerous details of his Visions, but the whole of their involved symbolism. He was himself a priest and the son of a priest, born and bred in the very order to which we owe the codifi-

* See Zechariah's Fifth Vision.
† xliv. 1 ff.
‡ xlv. 22.
§ xliv. 23, 24.
‖ Its origin was the Exile, whether its date be before or after the First Return under Cyrus in 537 B. C.

cation of the ritual, and the development of those ideas of guilt and uncleanness that led to its expansion and specialisation. The Visions in which he deals with these are the Third to the Seventh. As with Haggai there is a High Priest, in advance upon Ezekiel and in agreement with the Priestly Code. As in the latter the High Priest represents the people and carries their guilt before God.* He and his colleagues are pledges and portents of the coming Messiah. But the civil power is not yet diminished before the sacerdotal, as in the Priestly Code. We shall find indeed that a remarkable attempt has been made to alter the original text of a prophecy appended to the Visions,† in order to divert to the High Priest the coronation and Messianic rank there described. But any one who reads the passage carefully can see for himself that the crown (a single crown, as the verb which it governs proves ‡) which Zechariah was ordered to make was designed for Another than the priest, that the priest was but to stand at this Other's right hand, and that there was to be concord between the two of them. This Other can only have been the Messianic King, Zerubbabel, as was already proclaimed by Haggai.§ The altered text is due to a later period, when the High Priest became the civil as well as the religious head of the community. To Zechariah he was still only the right hand of the monarch in government; but, as we have seen, the religious life of the people was already gathered up and concentrated in him. It is the priests, too, who by their perpetual service and holy life bring on the Messianic era.‖ Men come to the Temple to propitiate Jehovah, for which Zechariah uses the anthropomorphic expression "to make smooth" or "placid His face."¶ No more than this is made of the sacrificial system, which was not in full course when the Visions were announced. But the symbolism of the Fourth Vision is drawn from the furniture of the Temple. It is interesting that the great candelabrum seen by the prophet should be like, not the ten lights of the old Temple of Solomon, but the seven-branched candlestick described in the Priestly Code. In the Sixth and Seventh Visions the strong convictions of guilt and uncleanness, which were engendered in Israel by the Exile, are not removed by the sacrificial means enforced in the Priestly Code, but by symbolic processes in the style of the Visions of Ezekiel.

The Visions in which Zechariah treats of the outer history of the world are the first two and the last, and in these we notice the influence of the Apocalypse developed during the Exile. In Zechariah's day Israel had no stage for their history save the site of Jerusalem and its immediate neighbourhood. So long as he keeps to this Zechariah is as practical and matter-of-fact as any of the prophets, but when he has to go beyond it to describe the general overthrow of the heathen, he is unable to project that, as Amos or Isaiah did, in terms of historic battle, and has to call in the apocalyptic. A people such as that poor colony of exiles, with no issue upon history, is forced to take refuge in Apocalypse, and carries with it even those of its prophets whose conscience, like Zechariah's, is most strongly bent upon the practical present. Consequently these three historical Visions are the most vague of the eight. They reveal the whole earth under the care of Jehovah and the patrol of His angels. They definitely predict the overthrow of the heathen empires. But, unlike Amos or Isaiah, the prophet does not see by what political movements this is to be effected. The world "is *still* quiet and at peace."* The time is hidden in the Divine counsels; the means, though clearly symbolised in "four smiths" who come forward to smite the horns of the heathen,† and in a chariot which carries God's wrath to the North,‡ are obscure. The prophet appears to have intended, not any definite individuals or political movements of the immediate future, but God's own supernatural forces. In other words, the Smiths and Chariots are not an allegory of history, but powers apocalyptic. The forms of the symbols were derived by Zechariah from different sources. Perhaps that of the "smiths" who destroy the horns in the Second Vision was suggested by "the smiths of destruction" threatened upon Ammon by Ezekiel.§ In the horsemen of the First Vision and the chariots of the Eighth, Ewald sees a reflection of the couriers and posts which Darius organised throughout the empire; they are more probably, as we shall see, a reflection of the military bands and patrols of the Persians. But from whatever quarter Zechariah derived the exact aspect of these Divine messengers, he found many precedents for them in the native beliefs of Israel. They are, in short, angels incarnate as Hebrew angels always were, and in fashion like men. But this brings up the whole subject of the angels, whom he also sees employed as the mediators of God's Word to him; and that is large enough to be left to a chapter by itself.‖

We have now before us all the influences which led Zechariah to the main form and chief features of his Visions.

3. Exposition of the Several Visions.

For all the Visions there is one date, "in the twenty-fourth day of the eleventh month, the month Shebat, in the second year of Darius," that is, January or February, 519; and one Divine impulse, "the Word of Jehovah came to the prophet Zekharyah, son of Berekhyahu, son of Iddo, as follows."

The First Vision: The Angel-Horsemen.

(i. 7–17).

The seventy years which Jeremiah had fixed for the duration of the Babylonian servitude were drawing to a close. Four months had elapsed since Haggai promised that in a little while God would shake all nations.¶ But the world was not shaken: there was no political movement which promised to restore her glory to Jerusalem. A very natural disappointment

* Fourth Vision, chap. iii.
† vi. 9–15.
‡ See ver. 11.
§ ii. 20–23.
‖ iii. 8.
¶ חִלָּה אֶת־פְּנֵי יהוה. The verb (Piel) originally means "to make weak or flaccid" (the Kal means "to be sick,") and so "to soften" or "weaken by flattery." 1 Sam. xiii. 12: 1 Kings xiii. 6, etc.

* First Vision, chap. i. 11.
† Second Vision, ii. 1–4 Heb., i. 18–21 LXX. and Eng.
‡ Eighth Vision, chap. vi. 1–8.
§ xxi. 36 Heb., 31 Eng.: "skilful to destroy."
‖ See next chapter.
¶ Jer. xxv. 12; Hag. ii. 7.

must have been the result among the Jews. In this situation of affairs the Word came to Zechariah, and both situation and Word he expressed by his First Vision.

It was one of the myrtle-covered glens in the neighbourhood of Jerusalem:* Zechariah calls it *the* Glen or Valley-Bottom, either because it was known under that name to the Jews, or because he was himself wont to frequent it for prayer. He discovers in it what seems to be a rendezvous of Persian cavalry-scouts,† the leader of the troop in front, and the rest behind him, having just come in with their reports. Soon, however, he is made aware that they are angels, and with that quick, dissolving change both of function and figure, which marks all angelic apparitions,‡ they explain to him their mission. Now it is an angel-interpreter at his side who speaks, and now the angel on the front horse. They are scouts of God come in from their survey of the whole earth. The world lies quiet. Whereupon "the angel of Jehovah" asks Him how long His anger must rest on Jerusalem and nothing be done to restore her; and the prophet hears a kind and comforting answer. The nations have done more evil to Israel than God empowered them to do. Their aggravations have changed His wrath against her to pity, and in pity He is come back to her. She shall soon be rebuilt and overflow with prosperity.

The only perplexity in all this is the angels' report that the whole earth lies quiet. How this could have been in 519 is difficult to understand. The great revolts against Darius were then in active progress, the result was uncertain, and he took at least three more years to put them all down. They were confined, it is true, to the east and northeast of the empire, but some of them threatened Babylon, and we can hardly ascribe the report of the angels to such a limitation of the Jews' horizon at this time as shut out Mesopotamia or the lands to the north of her. There remain two alternatives. Either these far-away revolts made only more impressive the stagnancy of the tribes of the rest of the empire, and the helplessness of the Jews and their Syrian neighbours was convincingly shown by their inability to take advantage even of the desperate straits to which Darius was reduced; or else in that month of vision Darius had quelled one of the rebellions against him, and for the moment there was quiet in the world.

"By night I had a vision, and behold! a man riding a brown horse,§ and he was standing between the myrtles that are in the Glen;‖ and behind him horses brown, bay* and white. And I said, What are these, my lord? And the angel who talked with me said; I will show you what these are. And the man who was standing among the myrtles answered and said, These are they whom Jehovah hath sent to go to and fro through the earth. And they answered the angel of Jehovah who stood among the myrtles,† and said, We have gone up and down through the earth, and lo! the whole earth is still and at peace.‡ And the angel of Jehovah answered and said, Jehovah of Hosts, how long hast Thou no pity for Jerusalem and the cities of Judah, with which§ Thou hast been wroth these seventy years? And Jehovah answered the angel who talked with me,‖ kind words and comforting. And the angel who talked with me said to me, Proclaim now as follows: Thus saith Jehovah of Hosts, I am zealous for Jerusalem and for Zion, with a great zeal; but with great wrath am I wroth against the arrogant Gentiles. For I was but a little angry *with Israel*, but they aggravated the evil.¶ Therefore thus saith Jehovah, I am returned to Jerusalem with mercies. My house shall be built in her—oracle of Jehovah of Hosts—and the measuring line shall be drawn over Jerusalem. Proclaim yet again, saying: Thus saith Jehovah of Hosts, My cities shall yet overflow with prosperity, and Jehovah shall again comfort Zion, and again make choice of Jerusalem."

Two things are to be noted in this oracle. No political movement is indicated as the means of Jerusalem's restoration: this is to be the effect of God's free grace in returning to dwell in Jerusalem, which is the reward of the building of the Temple. And there is an interesting explanation of the motive for God's new grace: in executing His sentence upon Israel, the heathen had far exceeded their commission, and now themselves deserved punishment. That is to say, the restoration of Jerusalem and the resumption of the worship are not enough for the future of Israel. The heathen must be chastised. But Zechariah does not predict any overthrow of the world's power, either by earthly or by heavenly forces. This is entirely in harmony with the insistence upon peace which distinguishes him from other prophets.

The Second Vision: The Four Horns and the Four Smiths (ii. 1-4 Heb., i. 18-21 Eng.).

The Second Vision supplies what is lacking in the First, the destruction of the tyrants who have oppressed Israel. The prophet sees four horns, which, he is told by his interpreting angel, are the powers that have scattered Judah. The many attempts to identify these with four heathen nations are ingenious but futile. "*Four* horns were seen as representing the totality of Israel's enemies—her enemies from all

* Myrtles were once common in the Holy Land, and have been recently found (Hasselquist, "Travels"). For their prevalence near Jerusalem see Neh. viii. 15. They do not appear to have any symbolic value in the Vision.

† For a less probable explanation see above, p. 627.

‡ See p. 635.

§ Ewald omits "riding a brown horse," as "marring the lucidity of the description, and added from a misconception by an early hand." But we must not expect lucidity in a phantasmagoria like this.

‖ מְצֻלָּה, Mesullah, either "shadow" from צלל, or for מְצוּלָה, "ravine," or else a proper name. The LXX., which uniformly for הֲדַסִּים, "myrtles," reads הרים, "mountains," renders אשר במצלה by τῶν κατασκίων. Ewald and Hitzig read מְצִלָּה, Arab. mizhallah, "shadowing" or "tent."

* Heb. שרקים, only here. For this LXX. gives two kinds, καὶ ψαροὶ καὶ ποικίλοι, "and dappled and piebald." Wright gives a full treatment of the question, pp. 531 ff. He points out that the cognate word in Arabic means sorrel, or yellowish red.

† "Who stood among the myrtles" omitted by Nowack.

‡ Isa. xxxvii. 29; Jer. xlviii. 11; Psalm cxxiii. 4; Zeph. i. 12.

§ Or "for."

‖ "Who talked with me" omitted by Nowack.

¶ Heb. "helped for evil," or "till it became a calamity."

quarters." * And to destroy these horns four smiths appear. Because in the Vision the horns are of iron, in Israel an old symbol of power, the first verb used of the action can hardly be, as in the Hebrew text, to terrify. The Greek reads "sharpen," and probably some verb meaning "to cut" or "chisel" stood in the original.†

"And I lifted mine eyes and looked, and lo! four horns. And I said to the angel who spoke with me, What are these? And he said to me, These are the horns which scattered Judah, Israel and Jerusalem.‡ And Jehovah showed me four smiths. And I said, What are these coming to do? And he spake, saying, These are the horns which scattered Judah, so that none lifted up his head;§ and these are come to . . .‖ them, to strike down the horns of the nations, that lifted the horn against the land of Judah to scatter it."

The Third Vision: The City of Peace.
(ii. 5-9 Heb., ii. 1-5 Eng.).

Like the Second Vision, the Third follows from the First, another, but a still more significant, supplement. The First had promised the rebuilding of Jerusalem, and now the prophet beholds "a young man"—by this term he probably means "a servant" or "apprentice"—who is attempting to define the limits of the new city. In the light of what this attempt encounters, there can be little doubt that the prophet means to symbolise by it the intention of building the walls upon the old lines, so as to make Jerusalem again the mountain fortress she had previously been. Some have considered that the young man goes forth only to see, or to show, the extent of the city in the approaching future. But if this had been his motive there would have been no reason in interrupting him with other orders. The point is that he has narrow ideas of what the city should be, and is prepared to define it upon its old lines of a fortress. For the interpreting angel who "comes forward"¶ is told by another angel to run and tell the young man that in the future Jerusalem shall be a large unwalled town, and this, not only because of the multitude of its population, for even then it might still have been fortified like Nineveh, but because Jehovah Himself shall be its wall. The young man is prevented, not merely from making it small, but from making it a citadel. And this is in conformity with all the singular absence of war from Zechariah's Visions, both of the future deliverance of Jehovah's people and of their future duties before Him. It is indeed remarkable how Zechariah not only develops none of the warlike elements of earlier Messianic prophecies, but tells us here of how God Himself actually prevented their repetition, and insists again and again only on those elements of ancient prediction which had filled the future of Israel with peace.

"And I lifted mine eyes and looked, and lo! a man with a measuring rope in his hand. So I said, Whither art thou going? And he said to me, To measure Jerusalem: to see how much its breadth and how much its length should be. And lo! the angel who talked with me came forward,* and another angel came forward to meet him. And he said to him, Run and speak to yonder young man thus: *Like* a number of open villages shall Jerusalem remain, because of the multitude of men and cattle in the midst of her. And I Myself will be to her—oracle of Jehovah—a wall of fire round about, and for glory will I be in her midst."

In this Vision Zechariah gives us, with his prophecy, a lesson in the interpretation of prophecy. His contemporaries believed God's promise to rebuild Jerusalem, but they defined its limits by the conditions of an older and a narrower day. They brought forth their measuring rods to measure the future by the sacred attainments of the past. Such literal fulfilment of His Word God prevented by that ministry of angels which Zechariah beheld. He would not be bound by those forms which His Word had assumed in suitableness to the needs of ruder generations. The ideal of many of the returned exiles must have been that frowning citadel, those gates of everlastingness,† which some of them celebrated in Psalms, and from which the hosts of Sennacherib had been broken and swept back as the angry sea is swept from the fixed line of Canaan's coast.‡ What had been enough for David and Isaiah was enough for them, especially as so many prophets of the Lord had foretold a Messianic Jerusalem that should be a counterpart of the historical. But God breaks the letter of His Word to give its spirit a more glorious fulfilment. Jerusalem shall not "be builded as a city that is compact together,"§ but open and spread abroad villagewise upon her high mountains, and God Himself her only wall.

The interest of this Vision is therefore not only historical. For ourselves it has an abiding doctrinal value. It is a lesson in the method of applying prophecy to the future. How much it is needed we must feel as we remember the readiness of men among ourselves to construct the Church of God upon the lines His own hand drew for our fathers, and to raise again the bulwarks behind which they sufficiently sheltered His shrine. Whether these ancient and sacred defences be dogmas or institutions we have no right, God tells us, to cramp behind them His powers for the future. And the great men whom He raises to remind us of this, and to prevent by their ministry the timid measurements of the zealous but servile spirits who would confine every thing to the exact letter of ancient Scripture—are they any less His angels to us than those ministering spirits whom Zechariah beheld preventing the narrow measures of the poor apprentice of his dream?

To the Third Vision there has been appended

* Marcus Dods, "Hag., Zech. and Mal.," p. 71. Orelli: "In distinction from Daniel, Zechariah is fond of a simultaneous survey, not the presenting of a succession."

† For the symbolism of iron horns see Micah iv. 13, and compare Orelli's note, in which it is pointed out that the destroyers must be smiths as in Isa. xliv. 12, "workmen of iron," and not as in LXX. "carpenters"

‡ Wellhausen and Nowack delete "Israel and Jerusalem;" the latter does not occur in Codd. A. Q, of Septuagint.

§ Wellhausen reads, after Mal. ii. 9, כפי אשר, "so that it lifted not its head"; but in that case we should not find ראשו, but ראשה.

‖ החריד, but LXX. read החריד, and either that or some verb of cutting must be read.

¶ The Hebrew, literally "comes forth," is the technical term throughout the Visions for the entrance of the figures upon the stage of vision.

* LXX. ἵστηκει, "stood up:" adopted by Nowack.

† Psalm xxiv.

‡ Isa. xvii. 12-14.

§ Psalm cxxii. 3.

the only lyrical piece which breaks the prose narrative of the Visions. We have already seen that it is a piece of earlier date. Israel is addressed as still scattered to the four winds of heaven, and still inhabiting Babylon. While in Zechariah's own oracles and visions Jehovah has returned to Jerusalem, His return according to this piece is still future. There is nothing about the Temple: God's holy dwelling from which He has roused Himself is Heaven. The piece was probably inserted by Zechariah himself: its lines are broken by what seem to be a piece of prose, in which the prophet asserts his mission in words he twice uses elsewhere. But this is uncertain.

"Ho, ho! Flee from the Land of the North (oracle of Jehovah);
For as the four winds have I spread you abroad * (oracle of Jehovah).
Ho! to Zion escape, thou inhabitress of Babel.†
For thus saith Jehovah of Hosts ‡ to the nations that plunder you (for he that toucheth you toucheth the apple of His eye), that, lo! I am about to wave My hand over them, and they shall be plunder to their own servants, and ye shall know that Jehovah of Hosts hath sent me.
Sing out and rejoice, O daughter of Zion;
For, lo! I come, and will dwell in thy midst (oracle of Jehovah).
And many nations shall join themselves to Jehovah in that day.
And shall be to Him § a people.
And I will dwell in thy midst
(And thou shalt know that Jehovah of Hosts hath sent me to thee).
And Jehovah will make Judah His heritage,
His portion shall be upon holy soil,
And make choice once more of Jerusalem.
Silence, all flesh, before Jehovah; ‖
For He hath roused Himself up from His holy dwelling."

The Fourth Vision: The High Priest and the Satan (Chap. iii.).

The next Visions deal with the moral condition of Israel and their standing before God. The Fourth is a judgment scene. The Angel of Jehovah, who is not to be distinguished from Jehovah Himself,¶ stands for judgment, and there appear before him Joshua the High Priest and the Satan or Adversary who has come to accuse him. Now those who are accused by the Satan—see next chapter of this volume upon the Angels of the Visions—are, according to Jewish belief, those who have been overtaken by misfortune. The people who are standing at God's bar in the person of their High Priest still suffer from the adversity in which Haggai found them, and the continuance of which so disheartened them after the Temple had begun. The evil seasons and poor harvests tormented their hearts with the thought that the Satan still

* Some codd. read "with the four winds." LXX. "from the four winds will I gather you" (συνάξω ὑμᾶς), and this is adopted by Wellhausen and Nowack. But it is probably a later change intended to adapt the poem to its new context.

† "Dweller of the daughter of Babel." But בת, "daughter," is mere dittography of the termination of the preceding word.

‡ A curious phrase here occurs in the Heb. and versions, "After glory hath He sent me," which we are probably right in omitting. In any case it is a parenthesis, and ought to go not with "sent me" but with "saith Jehovah of Hosts."

§ So LXX. Heb. "to me."

‖ *Cf.* Zeph. i. 7; Hab. ii. 20. "Among the Arabians, after the slaughter of the sacrificial victim, the participants stood for some time in silence about the altar. That was the moment in which the Deity approached in order to take His share in the sacrifice" (Smend, "A. T. Rel. Gesch.," p. 124).

¶ *Cf.* vv. 1 and 2.

slandered them in the court of God. But Zechariah comforts them with the vision of the Satan rebuked. Israel has indeed been sorely beset by calamity, a brand much burned, but now of God's grace plucked from the fire. The Satan's rôle is closed, and he disappears from the Vision.* Yet something remains: Israel is rescued, but not sanctified. The nation's troubles are over: their uncleanness has still to be removed. Zechariah sees that the High Priest is clothed in filthy garments while he stands before the Angel of Judgment. The Angel orders his servants, those "that stand before him," † to give him clean festal robes. And the prophet, breaking out in sympathy with what he sees, for the first time takes part in the Visions. "Then I said, Let them also put a clean turban on his head"—the turban being the headdress, in Ezekiel of the Prince of Israel, and in the Priestly Code of the High Priest.‡ This is done, and the national effect of his cleansing is explained to the High Priest. If he remains loyal to the law of Jehovah, he, the representative of Israel, shall have right of entry to Jehovah's presence among the angels who stand there. But more, he and his colleagues the priests are a portent of the coming of the Messiah—"the Servant of Jehovah, the Branch," as he has been called by many prophets.§ A stone has already been set before Joshua, with seven eyes upon it. God will engrave it with inscriptions, and on the same day take away the guilt of the land. Then shall be the peace upon which Zechariah loves to dwell.

"And he showed me Joshua, the high priest, standing before the Angel of Jehovah, and the Satan ‖ standing at his right hand to accuse him.¶ And Jehovah ** said to the Satan: Jehovah rebuke thee, O Satan! Jehovah who makes choice of Jerusalem rebuke thee! Is not this a brand saved from the fire? But Joshua was clothed in foul garments while he stood before the Angel. And he"—the Angel—"answered and said to those who stood in his presence, Take the foul garments from off him (and he said to him, See, I have made thy guilt to pass away from thee),†† and clothe him ‡‡ in fresh clothing. And I said,§§ Let them put a clean

* See below, p. 637.

† In this Vision the verb "to stand before" is used in two technical senses: (*a*) of the appearance of plaintiff and defendant before their judge (vv. 1 and 3); (*b*) of servants before their masters (vv. 4 and 7).

‡ See below, p. 631, *n.*

§ Isa. iv. 2, xi. 1; Jer. xxiii. 5, xxxiii. 15; Isa. liii. 2. Stade ("Gesch. des Volkes Isr.," II. 125), followed by Marti ("Der Proph. Zach.," 85 n.), suspects the clause "I will bring in My Servant the Branch" as a later interpolation, entangling the construction and finding in this section no further justification.

‖ Or "Adversary;" see p. 637.

¶ "To Satan him": "slander," or "accuse, him."

** That is "the Angel of Jehovah," which Wellhausen and Nowack read; but see below, p. 636.

†† This clause interrupts the Angel's speech to the servants. Wellh. and Nowack omit it. העביר: *cf.* 2 Sam. xii. 13; Job vii. 21.

‡‡ So LXX. Heb. has a degraded grammatical form, "clothe thyself" which has obviously been made to suit the intrusion of the previous clause, and is therefore an argument against the authenticity of the latter.

§§ LXX. omits "I said" and reads "Let them put" as another imperative, "Do ye put," following on the two of the previous verse. Wellhausen adopts this (reading שימו for ישימו). Though it is difficult to see how ואמר dropped out of the text if once there, it is equally so to understand why, if not original, it was inserted. The whole passage has been tampered with. If we accept the Massoretic text, then we have a sympathetic interference in the vision of the dreamer himself which is very

turban* on his head. And they put the clean turban upon his head, and clothed him with garments, the Angel of Jehovah standing up" the while.† "And the Angel of Jehovah certified unto Joshua, saying: Thus saith Jehovah of Hosts, If in My ways thou walkest, and if My charges thou keepest in charge, then thou also shalt judge my house, and have charge of My courts, and I will give thee entry‡ among these who stand in My presence. Hearken now, O Joshua, high priest, thou and thy fellows who sit before thee are men of omen, that, lo! I am about to bring My servant, Branch. For see the stone which I have set before Joshua, one stone with seven eyes.§ Lo, I will etch the engraving upon it (oracle of Jehovah), and I will wash away the guilt of that land in one day. In that day (oracle of Jehovah of Hosts) ye will invite one another in under vine and under fig-tree."

The theological significance of the Vision is as clear as its consequences in the subsequent theology and symbolism of Judaism. The uncleanness of Israel which infests their representative before God is not defined. Some‖ hold that it includes the guilt of Israel's idolatry. But they have to go back to Ezekiel for this, and we have seen that Zechariah nowhere mentions or feels the presence of idols among his people. The Vision itself supplies a better explanation. Joshua's filthy garments are replaced by festal and official robes. He is warned to walk in the whole law of the Lord, ruling the Temple and guarding Jehovah's court. The uncleanness was the opposite of all this. It was not ethical failure: covetousness, greed, immorality. It was, as Haggai protested, the neglect of the Temple, and of the whole worship of Jehovah. If this be now removed, in all fidelity to the law, the High Priest shall have access to God, and the Messiah will come. The High Priest himself shall not be the Messiah—this dogma is left to a later age to frame. But before God he will be as one of the angels, and himself and his faithful priesthood omens of the Messiah. We need not linger on the significance of this for the place of the priesthood in later Judaism. Note how the High Priest is already the religious representative of his people; their uncleanness is his; when he is pardoned and cleansed, "the uncleanness of the land" is purged away. In such a High Priest Christian theology has seen the prototype of Christ.

The stone is very difficult to explain. Some have thought of it as the foundation-stone of the Temple, which had already been employed as a symbol of the Messiah and which played so important a part in later Jewish symbolism.* Others prefer the top-stone of the Temple, mentioned in chap. iv. 7,† and others an altar or substitute for the ark.‡ Again, some take it to be a jewel, either on the breastplate of the High Priest,§ or upon the crown afterwards prepared for Zerubbabel.‖ To all of these there are objections. It is difficult to connect with the foundation-stone an engraving still to be made; neither the top-stone of the Temple, nor a jewel on the breastplate of the priest, nor a jewel on the king's crown, could properly be said to be set *before* the High Priest. We must rather suppose that the stone is symbolic of the finished Temple.¶ The Temple is the full expression of God's providence and care—His "seven eyes." Upon it shall His will be engraved, and by its sacrifices the uncleanness of the land shall be taken away.

The Fifth Vision: The Temple Candlestick and the Two Olive Trees (Chap. iv.).

As the Fourth Vision unfolded the dignity and significance of the High Priest, so in the Fifth we find discovered the joint glory of himself and Zerubbabel, the civil head of Israel. And to this is appended a Word for Zerubbabel himself. In our present text this Word has become inserted in the middle of the Vision, vv. 6*b*-10*a*; in the translation which follows it has been removed to the end of the Vision, and the reasons for this will be found in the notes.

The Vision is of the great golden lamp which stood in the Temple. In the former Temple light was supplied by ten several candlesticks.** But the Levitical Code ordained one seven-branched lamp, and such appears to have stood in the Temple built while Zechariah was prophesying.†† The lamp Zechariah sees has also seven branches, but differs in other respects, and especially in some curious fantastic details only possible in dream and symbol. Its seven lights were fed by seven pipes from a bowl or reservoir of oil which stood higher than themselves, and this was fed, either directly from two olive-trees which stood to the right and left of it, or, if ver. 12 be genuine, by two tubes which brought the oil from the trees. The seven lights are the seven eyes of Jehovah—if, as we ought, we run the second half of ver. 10 on to the first half of ver. 6. The pipes and reservoir are given no symbolic force; but the olive-trees which feed them are called "the two sons of oil which stand before the Lord of all the earth." These can only be the two anointed heads of the community—Zerubbabel, the civil head, and Joshua, the religious head. Theirs was the equal and

natural; and he speaks, as is proper, not in the direct, but indirect, imperative, "Let them put."

* צָנִיף, the headdress of rich women (Isa. iii. 23), as of eminent men (Job xxix. 14), means something wound round and round the head—*cf.* the use of צנף (to form like a ball) in Isa. xxii. 18, and the use of חבשׁ (to wind) to express the putting on of the headdress (Ezek. xvi. 10, etc.). Hence "turban" seems to be the proper rendering. Another form from the same root, מצנפת, is the name of the headdress of the Prince of Israel (Ezek. xxi. 31); and in the Priestly Codex of the Pentateuch the headdress of the high priest (Exod. xxviii. 37, etc.).

† Wellhausen takes the last words of ver. 5 with ver. 6, reads עָמַד and renders "And the Angel of Jehovah stood up" or "stepped forward." But even if עָמַד be read, the order of the words would require translation in the pluperfect, which would come to the same as the original text. And if Wellhausen's proposal were correct the words "Angel of Jehovah" in ver. 6 would be superfluous.

‡ Read מַהְלְכִים (Smend, "A. T. Rel. Gesch.," p. 324, n. 2).

§ Or "facets."

‖ *E. g.*, Marti, "Der Prophet Sacharja," p. 83.

* Hitzig, Wright, and many others. On the place of this stone in the legends of Judaism see Wright, pp. 75 f.

† Ewald, Marcus Dods.

‡ Von Orelli, Volck.

§ Bredenkamp.

‖ Wellhausen, *in loco*, and Smend, "A. T. Rel. Gesch," 345.

¶ So Marti, p. 88.

** 1 Kings vii. 49.

†† 1 Macc. i. 21; iv. 49, 50. Josephus, XIV. *Ant.* iv. 4.

co-ordinate duty of sustaining the Temple, figured by the whole candelabrum, and ensuring the brightness of the sevenfold revelation. The Temple, that is to say, is nothing without the monarchy and the priesthood behind it; and these stand in the immediate presence of God. Therefore this Vision, which to the superficial eye might seem to be a glorification of the mere machinery of the Temple and its ritual, is rather to prove that the latter derive all their power from the national institutions which are behind them, from the two representatives of the people who in their turn stand before God Himself. The Temple so near completion will not of itself reveal God: let not the Jews put their trust in it, but in the life behind it. And for ourselves the lesson of the Vision is that which Christian theology has been so slow to learn, that God's revelation under the old covenant shone not directly through the material framework, but was mediated by the national life, whose chief men stood and grew fruitful in His presence.

One thing is very remarkable. The two sources of revelation are the King and the Priest. The Prophet is not mentioned beside them. Nothing could prove more emphatically the sense in Israel that prophecy was exhausted.

The appointment of so responsible a position for Zerubbabel demanded for him a special promise of grace. And therefore, as Joshua had his promise in the Fourth Vision, we find Zerubbabel's appended to the Fifth. It is one of the great sayings of the Old Testament: there is none more spiritual and more comforting. Zerubbabel shall complete the Temple, and those who scoffed at its small beginnings in the day of small things shall frankly rejoice when they see him set the top-stone by plummet in its place. As the moral obstacles to the future were removed in the Fourth Vision by the vindication of Joshua and by his cleansing, so the political obstacles, all the hindrances described by the Book of Ezra in the building of the Temple, shall disappear. "Before Zerubbabel the great mountain shall become a plain." And this, because he shall not work by his own strength, but the Spirit of Jehovah of Hosts shall do everything. Again we find that absence of expectation in human means, and that full trust in God's own direct action, which characterise all the prophesying of Zechariah.

"Then the angel who talked with me returned and roused me like a man roused out of his sleep. And he said to me, What seest thou? And I said, I see, and lo! a candlestick all of gold, and its bowl upon the top of it, and its seven lamps on it, and seven* pipes to the lamps which are upon it. And two olive-trees stood over against it, one on the right of the bowl,† and one on the left. And I began‡ and said to the angel who talked with me,§ What be these, my lord? And the angel who talked with me answered and said, Knowest thou not what these be? And I said, No, my lord! And he answered and said to me,‖ These seven are the eyes of Jehovah which sweep through the whole earth. And I asked and said to him, What are these two olive-trees on the right of the candlestick and on its left? And again I asked and said to him, What are the two olive-branches which are beside the two golden tubes that pour forth the oil* from them?† And he said to me, Knowest thou not what these be? And I said, No, my lord! And he said, These are the two sons of oil which stand before the Lord of all the earth.

"This is Jehovah's Word to Zerubbabel, and it says:‡ Not by might, and not by force, but by My Spirit, saith Jehovah of Hosts. What art thou, O great mountain? Before Zerubbabel be thou level! And he§ shall bring forth the top-stone with shoutings, Grace, grace to it!‖ And the Word of Jehovah came to me, saying, The hands of Zerubbabel have founded this house, and his hands shall complete it, and thou shalt know that Jehovah of Hosts hath sent me to you. For whoever hath despised the day of small things, they shall rejoice when they see the plummet¶ in the hand of Zerubbabel."

THE SIXTH VISION: THE WINGED VOLUME (Chap. v. 1-4).

The religious and political obstacles being now removed from the future of Israel, Zechariah in the next two Visions beholds the land purged of its crime and wickedness. These Visions are very simple, if somewhat after the ponderous fashion of Ezekiel.

The first of them is the Vision of the removal of the curse brought upon the land by its civic criminals, especially thieves and perjurers—the two forms which crime takes in a poor and rude community like the colony of the returned exiles. The prophet tells us he beheld a roll flying. He uses the ordinary Hebrew name for the rolls of skin or parchment upon which writing was set down. But the proportions of its colossal size—twenty cubits by ten—prove that it was not a cylindrical but an oblong shape which he saw. It consisted, therefore, of sheets laid on each other like our books, and as our word "volume," which originally meant, like his own term, a roll, means now an oblong article, we may use this in our translation. The volume is the record of the crime of the land, and Zechariah sees it flying from the land. But it is also the curse upon this crime, and so again he beholds it entering every thief's and perjurer's house and destroying it. Smend gives a possible explanation of this: "It appears that in ancient times curses were written on pieces of paper and sent down the wind into the houses"**

* LXX. Heb. has "seven sevens" of pipes.

† Wellhausen reads "its right" and deletes "the bowl."

‡ ואען. ענה is not only "to answer," but to take part in a conversation, whether by starting or continuing it. LXX. rightly ἐπηρώτησα.

§ Heb. "saying."

‖ In the Hebrew text, followed by the ancient and modern versions, including the English Bible, there here follows *6b*-10*a*, the Word to Zerubbabel. They obviously disturb the narrative of the Vision, and Wellhausen has rightly transferred them to the end of it, where they come in as naturally as the word of hope to Joshua comes in at the end of the preceding Vision. Take them away, and, as can be seen above, ver. 10*b* follows quite naturally upon *6a*.

* Heb. "gold." So LXX.

† Wellhausen omits the whole of this second question (ver. 12) as intruded and unnecessary. So also Smend as a doublet on ver. 11 ("A. T. Rel. Gesch.," 343 n.). So also Nowack.

‡ Heb. "saying."

§ LXX. "I."

‖ Or "Fair, fair is it!" Nowack.

¶ "The stone, the leaden." Marti, "St. u. Kr.," 1892, p. 213 n., takes "the leaden" for a gloss, and reads simply "the stone," *i. e.*, the top-stone; but the plummet is the last thing laid to the building to test the straightness of the top-stone.

** "A. T. Rel. Gesch.," 312 n.

of those against whom they were directed. But the figure seems rather to be of birds of prey.

"And I turned and lifted my eyes and looked, and lo! a volume * flying. And he said unto me, What dost thou see? And I said, I see a volume flying, its length twenty cubits and its breadth ten. And he said unto me, This is the curse that is going out upon the face of all the land. For every thief is hereby purged away from hence,† and every perjurer is hereby purged away from hence. I have sent it forth—oracle of Jehovah of Hosts—and it shall enter the thief's house, and the house of him that hath sworn falsely by My name, and it shall roost‡ in the midst of his house and consume it, with its beams and its stones." §

The Seventh Vision: The Woman in the Barrel (Chap. v. 5-11).

It is not enough that the curse fly from the land after destroying every criminal. The living principle of sin, the power of temptation, must be covered up and removed. This is the subject of the Seventh Vision.

The prophet sees an ephah, the largest vessel in use among the Jews, of more than seven gallons capacity, and round‖ like a barrel. Presently the leaden top is lifted, and the prophet sees a woman inside. This is Wickedness, feminine because she figures the power of temptation. She is thrust back into the barrel, the leaden lid is pushed down, and the whole carried off by two other female figures, winged like the strong, far-flying stork, into the land of Shin'ar, "which at that time had the general significance of the counterpart of the Holy Land," ¶ and was the proper home of all that was evil.

"And the angel of Jehovah who spake with me came forward ** and said to me, Lift now thine eyes and see what this is that comes forth. And I said, What is it? And he said, This is a bushel coming forth. And he said, This is their transgression* in all the land.† And behold! the round leaden *top* was lifted up, and lo!‡ a woman sitting inside the bushel. And he said, This is the Wickedness, and he thrust her back into the bushel, and thrust the leaden disc upon the mouth of it. And I lifted mine eyes and looked, and lo! two women came forth with the wind in their wings, for they had wings like storks' wings, and they bore the bushel betwixt earth and heaven. And I said to the angel that talked with me, Whither do they carry the bushel? And he said to me, To build it a house in the land of Shin'ar, that it may be fixed and brought to rest there on a place of its own." §

We must not allow this curious imagery to hide from us its very spiritual teaching. If Zechariah is weighted in these Visions by the ponderous fashion of Ezekiel, he has also that prophet's truly moral spirit. He is not contented with the ritual atonement for sin, nor with the legal punishment of crime. The living power of sin must be banished from Israel; and this cannot be done by any efforts of men themselves, but by God's action only, which is thorough and effectual. If the figures by which this is illustrated appear to us grotesque and heavy, let us remember how they would suit the imagination of the prophet's own day. Let us lay to heart their eternally valid doctrine, that sin is not a formal curse, nor only expressed in certain social crimes, nor exhausted by the punishment of these, but, as a power of attraction and temptation to all men, it must be banished from the heart, and can be banished only by God.

The Eighth Vision: The Chariots of the Four Winds (Chap. vi. 1-8).

As the series of Visions opened with one of the universal providences of God, so they close with another of the same. The First Vision had postponed God's overthrow of the nations till His own time, and this the Last Vision now describes as begun, the religious and moral needs of Israel having meanwhile been met by the Visions which come between, and every obstacle to God's action for the deliverance of His people being removed.

The prophet sees four chariots, with horses of different colour in each, coming out from between two mountains of brass. The horsemen of

* מגלהט, "roll" or "volume." LXX. δρέπανον, "sickle," מַגָּל.

† A group of difficult expressions. The verb נִקָּה is Ni. of a root which originally had the physical meaning to "clean out of a place," and this Ni. is so used of a plundered town in Isa. iii. 26. But its more usual meaning is to be spoken free from guilt (Psalm xix. 14, etc.). Most commentators take it here in the physical sense, Hitzig quoting the use of καθαρίζω in Mark vii. 19. מִזֶּה כָּמוֹהָ are variously rendered. מזה is mostly understood as locative, "hence," *i.e.*, from the land just mentioned, but some take it with "steal" (Hitzig), some with "cleaned out" (Ewald, Orelli, etc.). כָּמוֹהָ is rendered "like it"—the flying roll (Ewald, Orelli), which cannot be, since the roll flies upon the face of the land, and the sinner is to be purged out of it; or in accordance with the roll or its curse (Jerome, Köhler). But Wellhausen reads כַּמֶּה מִזֶּה, and takes נִקָּה in its usual meaning and in the past tense, and renders "Every thief has for long remained unpunished"; and so in the next clause. So, too, Nowack, LXX. "Every thief shall be condemned to death," ἕως θανάτου ἐκδιϑήσεται.

‡ Heb. "lodge, pass the night": *cf.* Zeph. ii. 14 (above, p. 65), "pelican and bittern shall roost upon the capitals."

§ Smend sees a continuation of Ezekiel's idea of the guilt of man overtaking him (iii. 20, xxxiv.). Here God's curse does all.

‖ This follows from the shape of the disc that fits into it. Seven gallons are seven-eighths of the English bushel: that in use in Canada and the United States is somewhat smaller.

¶ Ewald.

** Upon the stage of vision.

* For Heb. עֵינָם read עֲוֹנָם with LXX.

† By inserting איפה after מה in ver. 5, and deleting ויאמר . . . היוצאת in verse 6, Wellhausen secures the more concise text: "And see what this bushel is that comes forth. And I said, What is it? And he said, That is the evil of the people in the whole land." But to reduce the redundancies of the Visions is to delete the most characteristic feature of their style. Besides, Wellhausen's result gives no sense. The prophet would not be asked to see what a bushel is: the angel is there to tell him this. So Wellhausen in his translation has to omit the מה of ver. 5, while telling us in his note to replace האיפה after it. His emendation is, therefore, to be rejected. Nowack, however, accepts it.

‡ LXX. Heb. "this."

§ In the last clause the verbal forms are obscure if not corrupt. LXX. καὶ ἕτοιμασαι καὶ ϑήσουσιν αὐτο ἐκεῖ = שָׁם לְהָכִין וְהִנִּיחָה; but see Ewald, "Syntax," 131 *d*.

the First Vision were bringing in reports: these chariots are coming forth with their commissions from the presence of the Lord of all the earth. They are the four winds of heaven, servants of Him who maketh the winds His angels. They are destined for different quarters of the world. The prophet has not been admitted to the Presence, and does not know what exactly they have been commissioned to do; that is to say, Zechariah is ignorant of the actual political processes by which the nations are to be overthrown and Israel glorified before them. But his Angel-interpreter tells him that the black horses go north, the white west, and the dappled south, while the horses of the fourth chariot, impatient because no direction is assigned to them, are ordered to roam up and down through the earth. It is striking that none are sent eastward.* This appears to mean that, in Zechariah's day, no power oppressed or threatened Israel from that direction; but in the north there was the centre of the Persian empire, to the south Egypt, still a possible master of the world, and to the west the new forces of Europe that in less than a generation were to prove themselves a match for Persia. The horses of the fourth chariot are therefore given the charge to exercise supervision upon the whole earth—unless in ver. 7 we should translate, not "earth," but "land," and understand a commission to patrol the land of Israel. The centre of the world's power is in the north, and therefore the black horses, which are despatched in that direction, are explicitly described as charged to bring God's spirit, that is His anger or His power, to bear on that quarter of the world.

"And once more† I lifted mine eyes and looked, and lo! four chariots coming forward from between two mountains, and the mountains were mountains of brass. In the first chariot were brown horses, and in the second chariot black horses, and in the third chariot white horses, and in the fourth chariot dappled . . .‡ horses. And I broke in and said to the angel who talked with me, What are these, my lord? And the angel answered and said to me, These be the four winds of heaven that come forth from presenting themselves before the Lord of all the earth.§ *That* with the black horses goes forth to the land of the north, while the white go out west‖ (?), and the dappled go to the land of the south. And the . . .¶ go forth and seek to go, to march up and down on the earth. And he said, Go, march up and down on the earth; and they marched up and down on the earth. And he called me and spake to me, saying, See they that go forth to the land of the north have brought my spirit to bear * on the land of the north."

THE RESULT OF THE VISIONS: THE CROWNING OF THE KING OF ISRAEL (Chap. vi. 9-15).

The heathen being overthrown, Israel is free, and may have her king again. Therefore Zechariah is ordered—it would appear on the same day as that on which he received the Visions—to visit a certain deputation from the captivity in Babylon, Heldai, Tobiyah and Yedayah, at the house of Josiah the son of Zephaniah, where they have just arrived; and to select from the gifts they have brought enough silver and gold to make circlets for a crown. The present text assigns this crown to Joshua, the high priest, but as we have already remarked, and will presently prove in the notes to the translation, the original text assigned it to Zerubbabel, the civil head of the community, and gave Joshua, the priest, a place at his right hand—the two to act in perfect concord with each other. The text has suffered some other injuries, which it is easy to amend; and the end of it has been broken off in the middle of a sentence.

"And the Word of Jehovah came to me, saying: Take from the Gôlah,† from Heldai‡ and from Tobiyah and from Yeda'yah; and do thou go on the same day, yea, go thou to the house of Yosiyahu, son of Sephanyah, whither they have arrived from Babylon.§ And thou shalt take silver and gold, and make a crown, and set it on the head of . . .‖ And say to him: Thus saith Jehovah of Hosts, Lo! a man called Branch; from his roots shall a branch come, and he shall build the Temple of Jehovah. Yea, he shall build Jehovah's Temple,¶ and he shall wear the royal majesty and sit and rule upon his throne, and *Joshua* shall be priest on his right hand,†† and there will be a counsel of peace between the two of them.‡‡ And the crown

* Wellhausen suggests that in the direction assigned to the white horses, אחרהים (ver. 6), which we have rendered "westward," we might read ארע הקדם, "land of the east;" and that from ver. 7 "the west" has probably fallen out after "they go forth."

† Heb. "I turned again and."

‡ Hebrew reads אֲמֻצִּים, "strong;" LXX. ψαροί, "dappled," and for the previous בְּרֻדִּים, "spotted" or "dappled," it reads ποικίλοι, "piebald." Perhaps we should read חמצים (*cf.* Isa. lxiii. 1), "dark red" or "sorrel," with "grey spots." So Ewald and Orelli. Wright keeps "strong."

§ Wellhausen, supplying ל before ארבע, renders "These go forth to the four winds of heaven after they have presented themselves," etc.

‖ Heb. "behind them."

¶ אמצים, the second epithet of the horses of the fourth chariot, ver. 3. See note there.

* Or "anger to bear," Heb. "rest."

† The collective name for the Jews in exile.

‡ LXX. παρὰ τῶν ἀρχόντων, מֵחָרִים; but since an accusative is wanted to express the articles taken, Hitzig proposes to read מַחֲמַדַּי, "My precious things." The LXX. reads the other two names καὶ παρὰ τῶν χρησίμων αὐτῆς καὶ παρὰ τῶν ἐπεγνωκότων αὐτήν.

§ The construction of ver. 10 is very clumsy; above it is rendered literally. Wellhausen proposes to delete "and do thou go . . . to the house of," and take Yosiyahu's name as simply a fourth with the others, reading the last clause "who have come from Babylon." This is to cut, not disentangle, the knot.

‖ The Hebrew text here has "Joshua son of Jehosadak, the high priest," but there is good reason to suppose that the crown was meant for Zerubbabel, but that the name of Joshua was inserted instead in a later age, when the high priest was also the king—see below, note. For these reasons Ewald had previously supposed that the whole verse was genuine, but that there had fallen out of it the words "and on the head of Zerubbabel." Ewald found a proof of this in the plural form עטרות, which he rendered "crowns." (So also Wildeboer, "A. T. Litteratur," p. 297.) But עטרות is to be rendered "crown"; see ver. 11, where it is followed by a singular verb. The plural form refers to the several circlets of which it was woven.

¶ Some critics omit the repetition.

** So Wellhausen proposes to insert. The name was at least understood in the original text.

†† So LXX. Heb. "on his throne."

‡‡ With this phrase, vouched for by both the Heb. and the Sept., the rest of the received text cannot be harmonised. There were two: one is the priest just mentioned who is to be at the right hand of the crowned. The received text makes this crowned one to be the high priest Joshua. But if there are two and the priest is only sec-

shall be for Heldai * and Tobiyah and Yeda'yah, and for the courtesy † of the son of Ṣephanyah, for a memorial in the Temple of Jehovah. And the far-away shall come and build at the Temple of Jehovah, and ye shall know that Jehovah of Hosts hath sent me to you; and it shall be if ye hearken to the voice of Jehovah your God . . ." ‡

CHAPTER XXII.

THE ANGELS OF THE VISIONS.

ZECHARIAH i. 7-vi. 8.

AMONG the influences of the Exile which contributed the material of Zechariah's Visions we included a considerable development of Israel's belief in Angels. The general subject is in itself so large, and the Angels play so many parts in the Visions, that it is necessary to devote to them a separate chapter.

From the earliest times the Hebrews had conceived their Divine King to be surrounded by a court of ministers, who besides celebrating His glory went forth from His presence to execute His will upon earth. In this latter capacity they were called Messengers, Malĕ'akim, which the Greeks translated Angeloi, and so gave us our Angels. The origin of this conception is wrapped in obscurity. It may have been partly due to a belief, shared by all early peoples, in the existence of superhuman beings inferior to the gods,§ but even without this it must have sprung up in the natural tendency to provide the royal deity of a people with a court, an army and servants. In the pious minds of early Israel there must have been a kind of necessity to believe and develop this—a necessity imposed *firstly* by the belief in Jehovah's residence as confined to one spot, Sinai or Jerusalem, from which He Himself went forth only upon great occasions to the deliverance of His people as a whole; and *secondly* by the unwillingness to conceive of His personal appearance in missions of a menial nature, or to represent Him in the human form in which, according to primitive ideas, He could alone hold converse with men.

It can easily be understood how a religion, which was above all a religion of revelation, should accept such popular conceptions in its constant record of the appearance of God and His Word in human life. Accordingly, in the earliest documents of the Hebrews, we find angels who bring to Israel the blessings, curses, and commands of Jehovah.* Apart from this duty and their human appearance, these beings are not conceived to be endowed either with character or, if we may judge by their namelessness† with individuality. They are the Word of God personified. Acting as God's mouthpiece, they are merged in Him, and so completely that they often speak of themselves by the Divine *I*.‡ "The *function* of an Angel so overshadows his *personality* that the Old Testament does not ask who or what this Angel is, but what he does. And the answer to the last question is that he represents God to man so directly and fully that when he speaks or acts God Himself is felt to speak or act." § Besides the carriage of the Divine Word, angels bring back to their Lord report of all that happens: kings are said, in popular language, to be "as wise as the wisdom of an angel of God, to know all the things that are in the earth." ‖ They are also employed in the deliverance and discipline of His people.¶ By them come the pestilence,** and the restraint of those who set themselves against God's will.††

Now the prophets before the Exile had so spiritual a conception of God, worked so immediately from His presence, and above all were so convinced of His personal and practical interest in the affairs of His people, that they felt no room for Angels between Him and their hearts, and they do not employ Angels, except when Isaiah in his inaugural vision penetrates to the heavenly palace and court of the Most High.‡‡ Even when Amos sees a plummet laid to the walls of Jerusalem, it is by the hands of Jehovah himself,§§ and we have not encountered an Angel in the mediation of the Word to any of the prophets whom we have already studied. But Angels reappear, though not under the name, in the visions of Ezekiel, the first prophet of the Exile. They are in human form, and he calls them "Men." Some execute God's wrath upon Jerusalem,‖‖ and one, whose appearance is as the appearance of brass, acts as the interpreter of God's will to the prophet, and instructs him in the details of the building of City and Temple.¶¶ When the glory of Jehovah appears and Jehovah Himself speaks to the prophet out of the Temple, this "Man" stands by the prophet,*** distinct from the Deity, and afterwards continues his work of explanation. "Therefore," as Dr. Davidson remarks, "it is not the sense of distance to which God is removed that causes Ezekiel to create these intermediaries." The necessity for them rather arises from the same natural feeling which we have suggested as giving rise to the earliest conceptions of Angels: the unwillingness, namely, to engage the Person of God Himself in the subordinate task of explaining the details of the Temple. Note,

ondary, the crowned one must be Zerubbabel, whom Haggai has already designated as Messiah. Nor is it difficult to see why, in a later age, when the high priest was sovereign in Israel, Joshua's name should have been inserted in place of Zerubbabel's, and at the same time the phrase "priest at his right hand," to which the LXX. testifies in harmony with "the two of them," should have been altered to the reading of the received text, "priest upon his throne." With the above agree Smend, "A. T. Rel. Gesh.," 343 n., and Nowack.

* Heb. חֵלֶם, Hĕlem, but the reading Heldai, חלדי, is proved by the previous occurrence of the name and by the LXX. reading here, *τοῖς ὑπομένουσιν*, *i. e.*, from root חלד. "to last."

† הן, but Wellhausen and others take it as abbreviation or misreading for the name of Yosiyahu (see ver. 10).

‡ Here the verse and paragraph break suddenly off in the middle of a sentence. On the passage see Smend, 343 and 345.

§ So Robertson Smith, art. "Angels" in the "Encyc. Brit.," 9th ed.

* So already in Deborah's Song, Judg. v. 23, and throughout both J and E.

† *Cf.* especially Gen. xxxii. 29.

‡ Judg. vi. 12 ff.

§ Robertson Smith, as above.

‖ 2 Sam. xiv. 20.

¶ Exod. xiv. 19 (?), xxiii. 20, etc.; Josh. v. 13.

** 2 Sam. xxiv 16, 17; 2 Kings xix. 35; Exod. xii. 23. In Eccles. v. 6 this destroying angel is the minister of God: *cf.* Psalm lxxviii. 49*b*, "hurtful angels"—Cheyne, "Origin of Psalter," p. 157.

†† Balaam: Num. xxii. 23, 31.

‡‡ vi. 2-6.

§§ Page 470.

‖‖ ix.

¶¶ xl. 3 ff.

*** xliii. 6.

too, how the Divine Voice, which speaks to Ezekiel out of the Temple, blends and becomes one with the "Man" standing at his side. Ezekiel's Angel-interpreter is simply one function of the Word of God.

Many of the features of Ezekiel's Angels appear in those of Zechariah. "The four smiths" or smiters of the four horns recall the six executioners of the wicked in Jerusalem.* Like Ezekiel's Interpreter, they are called "Men," † and like him one appears as Zechariah's instructor and guide: "he who talked with me." ‡ But while Zechariah calls these beings "Men," he also gives them the ancient name, which Ezekiel had not used, of Male'akim, "messengers, angels." The Instructor is "the Angel who talked with me." In the First Vision, "the Man riding the brown horse, the Man that stood among the myrtles, *is* the Angel of Jehovah that stood among the myrtles."§ The Interpreter is also called "the Angel of Jehovah," and if our text of the First Vision be correct, the two of them are curiously mingled, as if both were functions of the same Word of God, and in personality not to be distinguished from each other. The Reporting Angel among the myrtles takes up the duty of the Interpreting Angel and explains the Vision to the prophet. In the Fourth Vision this dissolving view is carried further, and the Angel of Jehovah is interchangeable with Jehovah Himself;‖ just as in the Vision of Ezekiel the Divine Voice from the Glory and the Man standing beside the prophet are curiously mingled. Again in the Fourth Vision we hear of those "who stand in the presence of Jehovah,"¶ and in the Eighth of executant angels coming out from His presence with commissions upon the whole earth.**

In the Visions of Zechariah, then, as in the earlier books, we see the Lord of all the earth, surrounded by a court of angels, whom He sends forth in human form to interpret His Word and execute His will, and in their doing of this there is the same indistinctness of individuality, the same predominance of function over personality. As with Ezekiel, one stands out more clearly than the rest, to be the prophet's interpreter, whom, as in the earlier visions of angels, Zechariah calls "my lord," †† but even he melts into the figures of the rest. These are the old and borrowed elements in Zechariah's doctrine of Angels. But he has added to them in several important particulars, which make his Visions an intermediate stage between the Book of Ezekiel and the very intricate angelology of later Judaism.

In the first place Zechariah is the earliest prophet who introduces orders and ranks among the angels. In his Fourth Vision the Angel of Jehovah is the Divine Judge "before whom" ‡‡ Joshua appears with the Adversary. He also has others standing "before him" §§ to execute his sentences. In the Third Vision, again, the Interpreting Angel does not communicate directly with Jehovah, but receives his words from another Angel who has come forth.* All these are symptoms, that even with a prophet, who so keenly felt as Zechariah did the ethical directness of God's word and its pervasiveness through public life, there had yet begun to increase those feelings of God's sublimity and awfulness, which in the later thought of Israel lifted Him to so far a distance from men, and created so complex a host of intermediaries, human and superhuman, between the worshipping heart and the Throne of Grace. We can best estimate the difference in this respect between Zechariah and the earlier prophets whom we have studied by remarking that his characteristic phrase "talked with me," literally "spake in" or "by me," which he uses of the Interpreting Angel, is used by Habakkuk of God Himself.† To the same awful impressions of the Godhead is perhaps due the first appearance of the Angel as intercessor. Amos, Isaiah, and Jeremiah themselves directly interceded with God for the people; but with Zechariah it is the Interpreting Angel who intercedes, and who in return receives the Divine comfort.‡ In this angelic function, the first of its kind in Scripture, we see the small and explicable beginnings of a belief destined to assume enormous dimensions in the development of the Church's worship. The supplication of Angels, the faith in their intercession and in the prevailing prayers of the righteous dead, which has been so egregiously multiplied in certain sections of Christendom, may be traced to the same increasing sense of the distance and awfulness of God, but is to be corrected by the faith Christ has taught us of the nearness of our Father in Heaven, and of His immediate care of His every human child.

The intercession of the Angel in the First Vision is also a step towards that identification of special Angels with different peoples which we find in the Book of Daniel. This tells us of heavenly princes not only for Israel—"Michael, your prince, the great prince which standeth up for the children of thy people" §—but for the heathen nations, a conception the first beginnings of which we see in a prophecy that was perhaps not far from being contemporaneous with Zechariah.‖ Zechariah's Vision of a hierarchy among the angels was also destined to further development. The head of the patrol among the myrtles, and the Judge-Angel before whom Joshua appears, are the first Archangels. We know how these were further specialised, and had even personalities and names given them by both Jewish and Christian writers.¶

Among the Angels described in the Old Testament, we have seen some charged with powers of hindrance and destruction—"a troop of angels of evil." ** They too are the servants of God, who is the author of all evil as well as good, †† and the instruments of His wrath. But the temptation of men is also part of His Provi-

* Zech. i. 18 ff.; Ezek. ix. 1 ff.
† Zech. i. 8: so even in the Book of Daniel we have "the man" Gabriel—ix. 21.
‡ i. 9, 19; ii. 3; iv. 1, 4, 5; v. 5, 10; vi. 4. But see above, pp. 622 f.
§ i. 8, 10, 11.
‖ iii. 1 compared with 2.
¶ iii. 6, 7.
** vi. 5.
†† i. 9, etc.
‡‡ iii. 1. "Stand before" is here used forensically: *cf.* the N. T. phrases to "stand before God," Rev. xx. 12; "before the judgment-seat of Christ," Rom. xiv. 10; and "be acquitted," Luke xxi. 36.
§§ iii. 4. Here the phrase is used domestically of servants in the presence of their master. See above, p. 630, *n.*

* ii. 3, 4.
† Hab. ii. 1: *cf.* also Num. xii. 6-9.
‡ First Vision, i. 12.
§ x. 21, xii. 1.
‖ Isa. xxiv. 21.
¶ Book of Daniel x., xii.; Tobit xii. 15; Book of Enoch *passim;* Jude 9; Rev. viii. 2, etc.
** Psalm lxxviii. 49. See above, p. 635, *n.*
†† Amos iii. 6.

dence. Where wilful souls have to be misled, the *spirit* who does so, as in Ahab's case, comes from Jehovah's presence.* All these spirits are just as devoid of character and personality as the rest of the angelic host. They work evil as mere instruments: neither malice nor falseness is attributed to themselves. They are not rebel nor fallen angels, but obedient to Jehovah. Nay, like Ezekiel's and Zechariah's Angels of the Word, the Angel who tempts David to number the people is interchangeable with God Himself.† Kindred to the duty of tempting men is that of discipline, in its forms both of restraining or accusing the guilty, and of vexing the righteous in order to test them. For both of these the same verb is used, "to satan,"‡ in the general sense of "withstanding," or antagonising. The Angel of Jehovah stood in Balaam's way "to satan him."§ The noun, "the Satan," is used repeatedly of a human foe.‖ But in two passages, of which Zechariah's Fourth Vision is one, and the other the Prologue to Job,¶ the name is given to an Angel, one of "the sons of Elohim," or Divine powers who receive their commission from Jehovah. The noun is not yet, what it afterwards became,** a proper name; but has the definite article, "the Adversary" or "Accuser"—that is, the Angel to whom that function was assigned. With Zechariah his business is the official one of prosecutor in the supreme court of Jehovah, and when his work is done he disappears. Yet, before he does so, we see for the first time in connection with any angel a gleam of character. This is revealed by the Lord's rebuke of him. There is something blameworthy in the accusation of Joshua: not indeed false witness, for Israel's guilt is patent in the foul garments of their High Priest, but hardness or malice, that would seek to prevent the Divine grace. In the Book of Job "the Satan" is also a function, even here not a fallen or rebel angel, but one of God's court, †† the instrument of discipline or chastisement. Yet, in that he himself suggests his cruelties and is represented as forward and officious in their infliction, a character is imputed to him even more clearly than in Zechariah's Vision. But the Satan still shares that identification with his function which we have seen to characterise all the angels of the Old Testament, and therefore he disappears from the drama so soon as his place in its high argument is over.‡‡

In this description of the development of Israel's doctrine of Angels, and of Zechariah's contributions to it, we have not touched upon the question whether the development was assisted by Israel's contact with the Persian religion and with the system of Angels which the latter contains. For several reasons the question is a difficult one. But so far as present evidence goes, it makes for a negative answer. Scholars who are in no way prejudiced against the theory of a large Persian influence upon Israel declare that the religion of Persia affected the Jewish doctrine of Angels "only in secondary points," such as their "number and personality, and the existence of demons and evil spirits."* Our own discussion has shown us that Zechariah's Angels, in spite of the new features they introduce, are in substance one with the Angels of pre-exilic Israel. Even the Satan is primarily a function, and one of the servants of God. If he has developed an immoral character, this cannot be attributed to the influence of Persian belief in a Spirit of evil opposed to the Spirit of good in the universe, but may be explained by the native, or selfish, resentment of Israel against their prosecutor before the bar of Jehovah. Nor can we fail to remark that this character of evil appears in the Satan, not, as in the Persian religion, in general opposition to goodness, but as thwarting that saving grace which was so peculiarly Jehovah's own. And Jehovah said to the Satan, "Jehovah rebuke thee, O Satan, yea, Jehovah who hath chosen Jerusalem rebuke thee! Is not this a brand plucked from the burning?"

* 1 Kings xxii. 20 ff.

† 2 Sam. xxiv. 1; 1 Chron. xxi. 1. Though here difference of age between the two documents may have caused the difference of view.

‡ There are two forms of the verb, שׂטן, satan, and שׂטם, satam, the latter apparently the older.

§ Num. xxii. 22, 32.

‖ 1 Sam. xxix. 4; 2 Sam. xix. 23 Heb., 22 Eng.; 1 Kings v. 18, xi. 14, etc.

¶ Zech. iii. 1 ff.; Job i. 6 ff.

** 1 Chron. xxi. 1.

†† i. 6*b*.

‡‡ See Davidson in "Cambridge Bible for Schools" on Job i. 6-12, especially on ver. 9: "The Satan of this book may show the beginnings of a personal malevolence against man, but he is still rigidly subordinated to Heaven, and in all he does subserves its interests. His function is as the minister of God to try the sincerity of man; hence when his work of trial is over he is no more found, and no place is given him among the *dramatis personæ* of the poem."

* Cheyne, "The Origin of the Psalter," p. 272. Read carefully on this point the very important remarks on pp. 270 ff. and 281 f.

CHAPTER XXIII.

"THE SEED OF PEACE."

ZECHARIAH vii., viii.

THE Visions have revealed the removal of the guilt of the land, the restoration of Israel to their standing before God, the revival of the great national institutions, and God's will to destroy the heathen forces of the world. With the Temple built, Israel should be again in the position which she enjoyed before the Exile. Zechariah, therefore, proceeds to exhort his people to put away the fasts which the Exile had made necessary, and address themselves, as of old, to the virtues and duties of the civic life. And he introduces his orations to this end by a natural appeal to the experience of the former days.

The occasion came to him when the Temple had been building for two years, and when some of its services were probably resumed.† A deputation of Jews appeared in Jerusalem and raised the question of the continuance of the great Fasts of the Exile. Who the deputation were is not certain: probably we ought to delete "Bethel" from the second verse, and read either "El-sar'eser sent Regem-Melekh and his men to the house of Jehovah to propitiate Jehovah," or else "the house of El-sar'eser sent Regem-Melekh and his men to propitiate Jehovah." It has been thought that they came from the Jews in Babylon: this would agree with their arrival in the ninth month to inquire about a fast in the fifth month. But Zechariah's answer is addressed to Jews in Judea. The deputation limited their inquiry to the fast of the fifth month, which commemorated the

† *Cf.* chap. vii. 3: "the priests which were of the house of Jehovah."

burning of the Temple and the City, now practically restored. But with a breadth of view which reveals the prophet rather than the priest, Zechariah replies, in the following chapter, upon all the fasts by which Israel for seventy years had bewailed her ruin and exile. He instances two, that of the fifth month, and that of the seventh month, the date of the murder of Gedaliah, when the last poor remnant of a Jewish state was swept away.* With a boldness which recalls Amos to the very letter, Zechariah asks his people whether in those fasts they fasted at all to their God. Jehovah had not charged them, and in fasting they had fasted for themselves, just as in eating and drinking they had eaten and drunken to themselves. They should rather hearken to the words He really sent them. In a passage, the meaning of which has been perverted by the intrusion of the eighth verse, that therefore ought to be deleted, Zechariah recalls what those words of Jehovah had been in the former times when the land was inhabited and the national life in full course. They were not ceremonial; they were ethical: they commanded justice, kindness, and the care of the helpless and the poor. And it was in consequence of the people's disobedience to those words that all the ruin came upon them for which they now annually mourned. The moral is obvious if unexpressed. Let them drop their fasts, and practise the virtues the neglect of which had made their fasts a necessity. It is a sane and practical word, and makes us feel how much Zechariah has inherited of the temper of Amos and Isaiah. He rests, as before, upon the letter of the ancient oracles, but only so as to bring out their spirit. With such an example of the use of ancient Scripture, it is deplorable that so many men, both among the Jews and the Christians, should have devoted themselves to the letter at the expense of the spirit.

"And it came to pass in the fourth year of Darius the king, that the Word of Jehovah came to Zechariah on the fourth of the ninth month, Kislev. For there sent to *the* house *of Jehovah*, El-sar'eser and Regem-Melekh and his men,† to propitiate ‡ Jehovah, to ask of the priests which were in the house of Jehovah of Hosts and of the prophets as follows: Shall I weep in the fifth month with fasting as I have now done so many years? And the Word of Jehovah of Hosts came to me: Speak now to all the people of the land, and to the priests, saying: When ye fasted and mourned in the fifth and in the seventh month,§ and this for seventy years, did ye fast at all to Me? And when ye eat and when ye drink, are not ye the eaters and ye the drinkers? Are not these‖ the words which Jehovah proclaimed by the hand of the former prophets, when Jerusalem was inhabited and at peace, with her cities round about her, and the Negeb and the Shephelah were inhabited?

*"Thus spake Jehovah of Hosts: Judge true judgment, and practise towards each other kindness and mercy; oppress neither widow nor orphan, stranger nor poor, and think not evil in your hearts towards one another. But they refused to hearken, and turned a rebellious shoulder,† and their ears they dulled from listening. And their heart they made adamant, so as not to hear the Torah and the words which Jehovah of Hosts sent through His Spirit by the hand of the former prophets; and there was great wrath from Jehovah of Hosts. And it came to pass that, as He had called and they heard not, so they shall call and I will not hear, said Jehovah of Hosts, but I will whirl ‡ them away among nations whom they know not. And the land was laid waste behind them, without any to pass to and fro, and they made the pleasant land desolate."

There follow upon this deliverance ten other short oracles: chap. viii. Whether all of this decalogue are to be dated from the same time as the answer to the deputation about the fasts is uncertain. Some of them appear rather to belong to an earlier date, for they reflect the situation, and even the words, of Haggai's oracles, and represent the advent of Jehovah to Jerusalem as still future. But they return to the question of the fasts, treating it still more comprehensively than before, and they close with a promise, fitly spoken as the Temple grew to completion, of the coming of the heathen to worship at Jerusalem.

We have already noticed the tender charm and strong simplicity of these prophecies,§ and there is little now to add except the translation of them. As with the older prophets, and especially the great Evangelist of the Exile, they start from the glowing love of Jehovah for His people, to which nothing is impossible;‖ they promise a complete return of the scattered Jews to their land, and are not content except with the assurance of a world converted to the faith of their God. With Haggai Zechariah promises the speedy end of the poverty of the little colony; and he adds his own characteristic notes of a reign of peace to be used for hearty labour, bringing forth a great prosperity. Only let men be true and just and kind, thinking no evil of each other, as in those hard days when hunger and the fierce rivalry for sustenance made every one's neighbour his enemy, and the petty life, devoid of large interests for the commonweal, filled their hearts with envy and malice. For ourselves the chief profit of these beautiful oracles is their lesson that the remedy for the sordid tempers and cruel hatreds, engendered by the fierce struggle for existence, is found in civic and religious hopes, in a noble ideal for the national life, and in the assurance that God's Love is at the back of all, with nothing impossible to it. Amid these glories, however, the heart will probably thank Zechariah most for his immortal picture of the streets of the new Je-

* Jer. xli. 2; 2 Kings xxv. 25.

† The Hebrew text is difficult if not impossible to construe: "For Bethel sent Sar'eser" (without sign of accusative) "and Regem-Melekh and his men." Wellhausen points out that Sar'eser is a defective name, requiring the name or title of deity in front of it, and Marti proposes to find this in the last syllable of Bethel, and to read 'El-sar'eser. It is tempting to find in the first syllable of Bethel the remnant of the phrase "to the house of Jehovah."

‡ To stroke the face of.

§ The fifth month Jerusalem fell, the seventh month Gedaliah was murdered: Jer. lii. 12 f.; 2 Kings xxv. 8 f., 25.

‖ So LXX. Heb. has acc. sign before "words," perhaps implying "Is it not rather necessary to do the words?" etc.

* Omit here ver. 8, "And the Word of Jehovah came to Zechariah, saying." It is obviously a gloss by a scribe who did not notice that the כה אמר of ver. 9 is God's statement by the former prophets.

† *Cf.* the phrase "with one shoulder," *i. e.*, unanimously.

‡ So Heb. and LXX.; but perhaps we ought to point "and I whirled them away," taking the clause with the next.

§ See above, pp. 625 ff.

‖ *Cf.* especially Isa. xl. ff.

rusalem: old men and women sitting in the sun, boys and girls playing in all the open places. The motive of it, as we have seen, was found in the circumstances of his own day. Like many another emigration for religion's sake, from the heart of civilisation to a barren coast, the poor colony of Jerusalem consisted chiefly of men, young and in middle life. The barren years gave no encouragement to marriage. The constant warfare with neighbouring tribes allowed few to reach grey hairs. It was a rough and a hard society, unblessed by the two great benedictions of life, childhood and old age. But this should all be changed, and Jerusalem filled with placid old men and women, and with joyous boys and girls. The oracle, we say, had its motive in Zechariah's day. But what an oracle for these times of ours! Whether in the large cities of the old world, where so few of the workers may hope for a quiet old age sitting in the sun, and the children's days of play are shortened by premature toil and knowledge of evil; or in the newest fringes of the new world, where men's hardness and coarseness are, in the struggle for gold, unawed by reverence for age and unsoftened by the fellowship of childhood,—Zechariah's great promise is equally needed. Even there shall it be fulfilled if men will remember his conditions—that the first regard of a community, however straitened in means, be the provision of religion, that truth and whole-hearted justice abound in the gates, with love and loyalty in every heart towards every other.

"And the Word of Jehovah of Hosts came, saying:—

1. "Thus saith Jehovah of Hosts: I am jealous for Zion with a great jealousy, and with great anger am I jealous for her.

2. "Thus saith Jehovah: I am returned to Zion, and I dwell in the midst of Jerusalem, and Jerusalem shall be called the City of Troth,* and the mountain of Jehovah of Hosts the Holy Mountain.

3. "Thus saith Jehovah of Hosts: Old men and old women shall yet sit in the streets of Jerusalem, each with staff in hand, for fulness of days; and the streets of the city shall be full of boys and girls playing in her streets.

4. "Thus saith Jehovah of Hosts: Because it seems too wonderful to the remnant of this people in those days, shall it also seem too wonderful to Me?—oracle of Jehovah of Hosts.

5. "Thus saith Jehovah of Hosts: Lo! I am about to save My people out of the land of the rising and out of the land of the setting of the sun; and I will bring them home, and they shall dwell in the midst of Jerusalem, and they shall be to Me for a people,† and I will be to them for God, in troth and in righteousness.

6. "Thus saith Jehovah of Hosts: Strengthen your hands, O ye who have heard in such days such words from the mouth of the prophets, since* the day when the House of Jehovah of Hosts was founded: the sanctuary was to be built! For before those days there was no gain for man, † and none to be *made* by cattle; and neither for him that went out nor for him that came in was there any peace from the adversary, and I set every man's hand against his neighbour. But not now as in the past days am I towards the remnant of this people—oracle of Jehovah of Hosts. For I am sowing the seed of peace.‡ The vine shall yield her fruit, and the land yield her increase, and the heavens yield their dew, and I will give them all for a heritage to the remnant of this people. And it shall come to pass, that as ye have been a curse among the nations, O house of Judah and house of Israel, so will I save you and ye shall be a blessing! Be not afraid, strengthen your hands!

7. "For thus saith Jehovah of Hosts: As I have planned to do evil to you, for the provocation your fathers gave Me, saith Jehovah of Hosts, and did not relent, so have I turned and planned in these days to do good to Jerusalem and the house of Judah. Be not afraid! These are the things which ye shall do: Speak truth to one another; truth and wholesome judgment decree ye in your gates; and plan no evil to each other in your hearts, nor take pleasure in false swearing: for it is all these that I hate—oracle of Jehovah.

"And the Word of Jehovah of Hosts came to me, saying:—

8. "Thus saith Jehovah of Hosts: The fast of the fourth *month*, and the fast of the fifth, and the fast of the seventh, and the fast of the tenth, shall become to the house of Judah joy and gladness and happy feasts.§ But love ye truth and peace.

9. "Thus saith Jehovah of Hosts: There shall yet come peoples and citizens of great cities; and the citizens of one city ‖ will go to another city, saying: 'Let us go to propitiate Jehovah, and to seek Jehovah of Hosts!' 'I will go too!' And many peoples and strong nations shall come to seek Jehovah of Hosts in Jerusalem and to propitiate Jehovah.

10. "Thus saith Jehovah of Hosts: In those days ten men, of all languages of the nations, shall take hold of the skirt of a Jew and say, We will go with you, for we have heard that God is with you."

* Isa. i. 26.

† Not merely "My people" (Wellhausen), but their return shall constitute them a people once more. The quotation is from Hosea ii. 25.

* So LXX.

† "But he that made wages made them to put them into a bag with holes," Haggai i. 6.

‡ Read כי אזרעה השלום for כי זרע השלום of the text, "for the seed of peace." The LXX. makes זרע a verb. *Cf.* Hosea ii. 23 ff., which the next clauses show to be in the mind of our prophet. Klostermann and Nowack prefer זַרְעָהּ שָׁלוֹם, "her" (the remnant's) "seed shall be peace."

§ In the tenth month the siege of Jerusalem had begun (2 Kings xxv. 1); on the ninth of the fourth month Jerusalem was taken (Jer. xxxix. 2); on the seventh of the fifth City and Temple were burnt down (2 Kings xxv. 8); in the seventh month Gedaliah was assassinated and the poor relics of a Jewish state swept from the land (Jer. xli.). See above, pp. 568 ff.

‖ LXX. "the citizens of five cities will go to one."

"MALACHI."

"Have we not all One Father? Why then are we unfaithful to each other?"

"The lips of a Priest guard knowledge, and men seek instruction from his mouth, for he is the Angel of Jehovah of Hosts."

CHAPTER XXIV.

THE BOOK OF "MALACHI."

THIS book, the last in the arrangement of the prophetic canon, bears the title: "Burden" or "Oracle of the Word of Jehovah to Israel by the hand of male'akhi." Since at least the second century of our era the word has been understood as a proper name, Malachi, or Malachias. But there are strong objections to this, as well as to the genuineness of the whole title, and critics now almost universally agree that the book was originally anonymous.

It is true that neither in form nor in meaning is there any insuperable obstacle to our understanding "malĕ'akhi" as the name of a person. If so, however, it cannot have been, as some have suggested, an abbreviation of Malĕ'akhiyah, for, according to the analogy of other names of such formation, this could only express the impossible meaning "Jehovah is Angel."* But, as it stands, it might have meant "My Angel" or "Messenger," or it may be taken as an adjective, "Angelicus."† Either of these meanings would form a natural name for a Jewish child, and a very suitable one for a prophet. There is evidence, however, that some of the earliest Jewish interpreters did not think of the title as containing the name of a person. The Septuagint read "by the hand of His messenger,"‡ "malĕ'akho"; and the Targum of Jonathan, while retaining "malĕ'akhi," rendered it "My messenger," adding that it was Ezra the Scribe who was thus designated.§ This opinion was adopted by Calvin.

Recent criticism has shown that, whether the word was originally intended as a personal name or not, it was a purely artificial one borrowed from chap. iii. 1, "Behold, I send My messenger," "malĕ'akhi," for the title, which itself has been added by the editor of the Twelve Prophets in the form in which we now have them. The peculiar words of the title, "Burden" or "Oracle of the Word of Jehovah," occur nowhere else than in the titles of the two prophecies which have been appended to the Book of Zechariah, chap. ix. 1 and chap. xii. 1, and immediately precede this book of "Malachi." In chap. ix. 1 "the Word of Jehovah" belongs to the text; "Burden" or "Oracle" has been inserted before it as a title; then the whole phrase has been inserted as a title in chap. xii. 1. These two pieces are anonymous, and nothing is more likely than that another anonymous prophecy should have received, when attached to them, the same heading.* The argument is not final, but it is the most probable explanation of the data, and agrees with the other facts. The cumulative force of all that we have stated—the improbability of malĕ'akhi being a personal name, the fact that the earliest versions do not treat it as such, the obvious suggestion for its invention in the malĕ'akhi of chap. iii. 1, the absence of a father's name and place of residence, and the character of the whole title—is enough for the opinion rapidly spreading among critics that our book was, like so much more in the Old Testament, originally anonymous.† The author attacks the religious authorities of his day; he belongs to a pious remnant of his people, who are overborne and perhaps oppressed by the majority.‡ In these facts, which are all we know of his personality, he found sufficient reason for not attaching his name to his prophecy.

The book is also undated, but it reflects its period almost as clearly as do the dated Books of Haggai and Zechariah. The conquest of Edom by the Nabateans, which took place during the Exile,§ is already past.‖ The Jews are under a Persian viceroy.¶ They are in touch with a heathen power, which does not tyrannise over them, for this book is the first to predict no judgment upon the heathen, and the first, moreover, to acknowledge that among the heathen the true God is worshipped "from the rising to the setting of the sun." ** The only judgment predicted is one upon the false and disobedient portion of Israel, whose arrogance and success have cast true Israelites into de-

* מלאכיה or מלאכיהו. To judge from the analogy of other cases of the same formation (*e. g.*, Abiyah = Jehovah is Father, and not Father of Jehovah), this name, if ever extant, could not have borne the meaning, which Robertson Smith, Cornill, Kirkpatrick, etc., suppose it must have done, of "Angel of Jehovah." These scholars, it should be added, oppose, for various reasons, the theory that it is a proper name.

† *Cf.* the suggested meaning of Haggai, Festus. Above, p. 614.

‡ And added the words, "lay *it* to your hearts": ἐν χειρὶ ἀγγέλου αὐτοῦ· θέσθε δὴ ἐπὶ τὰς καρδίας ὑμῶν. Bachmann ("A. T. Untersuch.," Berlin, 1894, pp. 109 ff.) takes this added clause as a translation of וְשִׂימוּ בָלֵב, and suggests that it may be a corruption of an original וּשְׁמוֹ כָלֵב. "and his name was Kaleb." But the reading וְשִׂימוּ בָלֵב is not the exact equivalent of the Greek phrase.

§ מַלְאָכִי דִיתְקְרֵי שְׁמֵיהּ עֶזְרָא סָפְרָא.

* See Stade, "Z. A. T. W.," 1881, p. 14; 1882, p. 308; Cornill, "Einleitung," 4th ed., pp. 207 f.

† So (besides Calvin, who takes it as a title) even Hengstenberg in his "Christology of the O. T.," Ewald, Kuenen, Reuss, Stade, Rob. Smith, Cornill, Wellhausen, Kirkpatrick (probably), Wildeboer, Nowack. On the other side Hitzig, Vatke, Nägelsbach and Volck (in Herzog) Von Orelli, Pusey, and Robertson hold it to be a personal name—Pusey with this qualification, "that the prophet may have framed it for himself," similarly Orelli. They support their opinion by the fact that even the LXX. entitle the book Μαλαχιας; that the word was regarded as a proper name in the early Church, and that it is a possible name for a Hebrew. In opposition to the hypothesis that it was borrowed from chap. iii. 1, Hitzig suggests the converse that in the latter the prophet plays upon his own name. None of these critics, however, meets the objections to the name drawn from the peculiar character of the title and its relations to Zech. ix. 1, xii. 1. The supposed name of the prophet gave rise to the legend supported by many of the Fathers that Malachi, like Haggai and John the Baptist, was an incarnate angel. This is stated and condemned by Jerome, "Comm. ad Hag." i. 13, but held by Origen, Tertullian, and others. The existence of such an opinion is itself proof for the impersonal character of the name. As in the case of the rest of the prophets, Christian tradition furnishes the prophet with the outline of a biography. See (Pseud-) Epiphanius and other writers quoted above, p. 615.

‡ iii. 16 ff.

§ See above on Obadiah, p. 600, and below on the passage itself.

‖ i. 2–5.

¶ i. 8.

** i. 11: the verbs here are to be taken in the present, not as in A. V. in the future, tense.

spair.* All this reveals a time when the Jews were favourably treated by their Persian lords. The reign must be that of Artaxerxes Longhand, 464-424.

The Temple has been finished,† and years enough have elapsed to disappoint those fervid hopes with which about 518 Zechariah expected its completion. The congregation has grown worldly and careless. In particular the priests are corrupt and partial in the administration of the Law.‡ There have been many marriages with the heathen women of the land;§ and the laity have failed to pay the tithes and other dues to the Temple.‖ These are the evils against which we find strenuous measures directed by Ezra, who returned from Babylon in 458,¶ and by Nehemiah, who visited Jerusalem as its governor for the first time in 445 and for the second time in 433. Besides, "the religious spirit of the book is that of the prayers of Ezra and Nehemiah. A strong sense of the unique privileges of the children of Jacob, the objects of electing love,** the children of the Divine Father, †† is combined with an equally strong assurance of Jehovah's righteousness amidst the many miseries that pressed on the unhappy inhabitants of Judea. . . . Obedience to the law is the sure path to blessedness." ‡‡ But the question still remains whether the Book of "Malachi" prepared for, assisted, or followed up the reforms of Ezra and Nehemiah. An ancient tradition already alluded to §§ assigned the authorship to Ezra himself.

Recent criticism has been divided among the years immediately before Ezra's arrival in 458, those immediately before Nehemiah's first visit in 445, those between his first government and his second, and those after Nehemiah's disappearance from Jerusalem. But the years in which Nehemiah held office may be excluded, because the Jews are represented as bringing gifts to the governor, which Nehemiah tells us he did not allow to be brought to him.‖‖ The whole question depends upon what Law was in practice in Israel when the book was written. In 445 Ezra and Nehemiah, by solemn covenant between the people and Jehovah, instituted the code which we now know as the Priestly Code of the Pentateuch. Before that year the ritual and social life of the Jews appear to have been directed by the Deuteronomic Code. Now the Book of "Malachi" enforces a practice with regard to the tithes, which agrees more closely with the Priestly Code than it does with Deuteronomy. Deuteronomy commands that every third year the whole tithe is to be given to the Levites and the poor who reside "within the gates" of the giver, and is there to be eaten by them. "Malachi" commands that the whole tithe be brought into the storehouse of the Temple for the Levites in service there; and so does the Priestly Code.¶¶ On this ground many date the Book of "Malachi" after 445.*** But "Malachi's" divergence from Deuteronomy on this point may be explained by the fact that in his time there were practically no Levites outside Jerusalem; and it is to be noticed that he joins the tithe with the terûmah or heave-offering exactly as Deuteronomy does.* On other points of the Law he agrees rather with Deuteronomy than with the Priestly Code. He follows Deuteronomy in calling the priests "sons of Levi," † while the Priestly Code limits the priesthood to the sons of Aaron. He seems to quote Deuteronomy when forbidding the oblation of blind, lame, and sick beasts; ‡ appears to differ from the Priestly Code which allows the sacrificial beast to be male or female, when he assumes that it is a male; § follows the expressions of Deuteronmy and not those of the Priestly Code in detailing the sins of the people; ‖ and uses the Deuteronomic phrases "the Law of Moses," "My servant Moses," "statutes and judgments," and "Horeb" for the Mount of the Law.¶ For the rest, he echoes or implies only Ezekiel and that part of the Priestly Code ** which is regarded as earlier than the rest, and probably from the first years of exile. Moreover he describes the Torah as not yet fully codified. †† The priests still deliver it in a way improbable after 445. The trouble of the heathen marriages with which he deals (if indeed the verses on this subject be authentic and not a later intrusion ‡‡) was that which engaged Ezra's attention on his arrival in 458, but Ezra found that it had already for some time been vexing the heads of the community. While, therefore, we are obliged to date the Book of "Malachi" before 445 B. C., it is uncertain whether it preceded or followed Ezra's attempts at reform in 458. Most critics now think that it preceded them. §§

The Book of "Malachi" is an argument with the prophet's contemporaries, not only with the wicked among them, who, in forgetfulness of what Jehovah is, corrupt the ritual, fail to give the Temple its dues, abuse justice, marry foreign wives, ‖‖ divorce their own, and commit various other sins; but also with the pious, who, equally

* *Passim:* especially iii. 13 ff., 24.

† i. 10; iii. 1, 10.

‡ ii. 1-9.

§ ii. 10-16.

‖ iii. 7-12.

¶ See above, pp. 606 f.

** i. 2.

†† ii. 10.

‡‡ ii. 17-iii. 12; iii. 22 f., Eng. iv. The above sentences are from Robertson Smith, art. "Malachi," "Encyc. Brit.," 9th ed.

§§ Above, p. 640, *n.*

‖‖ "Mal." i. 8; Neh. v.

¶¶ Deut. xii. 11, xxvi. 12; "Mal." iii. 8, 10; Num. xviii. 21 f. (P).

*** Vatke (contemporaneous with Nehemiah), Schrader, Keil, Kuenen (perhaps in second governorship of Nehemiah, but see above for a decisive reason against this), Köhler, Driver, Von Orelli (between Nehemiah's first and second visit), Kirkpatrick, Robertson.

* Deut. xii. 11. In P terûmah is a due paid to priests as distinct from Levites.

† ii. 4-8: *cf.* Deut. xxxiii. 8.

‡ i. 8; Deut. xv. 21.

§ i. 14; Lev. iii. 1, 6.

‖ iii. 5; Deut. v. 11 ff., xviii. 10, xxiv. 17 ff.; Lev. xix. 31, 33 f., xx. 6.

¶ iii. 22 Heb., iv. 4 Eng. "Law of Moses" and "Moses My servant" are found only in the Deuteronomistic portions of the Hexateuch and historical books and here. In P Sinai is the Mount of the Law. To the above may be added "segullah," iii. 17, which is found in the Pentateuch only outside P and in Psalm cxxxv. 4. All these resemblances between "Malachi" and Deuteronomy and "Malachi's" divergences from P are given in Robertson Smith's "Old Test. in the Jewish Church," 2d ed., 425 ff.: *cf.* 444 ff.

** Lev. xvii.-xxvi. From this and Ezekiel he received the conception of the profanation of the sanctuary by the sins of the people—ii. 11: *cf.* also ii. 2, iii. 3, 4, for traces of Ezekiel's influence.

†† ii. 6 ff.

‡‡ See below, pp. 642, 648, 649.

§§ Herzfeld, Bleek, Stade, Kautzsch (probably), Wellhausen ("Gesch." p. 125), Nowack before the arrival of Ezra, Cornill either soon before or soon after 458, Robertson Smith either before or soon after 445. Hitzig at first put it before 458, but was afterwards moved to date it after 358, as he took the overthrow of the Edomites described in chap. i. 2-5 to be due to a campaign in that year by Artaxerxes Ochus (*cf.* Euseb., "Chron." II. 221).

‖‖ But see below, pp. 642, 649.

forgetful of God's character, are driven by the arrogance of the wicked to ask, whether He loves Israel, whether He is a God of justice, and to murmur that it is vain to serve Him. To these two classes of his contemporaries the prophet has the following answers. God does love Israel. He is worshipped everywhere among the heathen. He is the Father of all Israel. He will bless His people when they put away all abuses from their midst and pay their religious dues; and His Day of Judgment is coming, when the good shall be separated from the wicked. But before it come, Elijah the prophet will be sent to attempt the conversion of the wicked, or at least to call the nation to decide for Jehovah. This argument is pursued in seven or perhaps eight paragraphs, which do not show much consecutiveness, but are addressed, some to the wicked, and some to the despairing adherents of Jehovah.

1. Chap. i. 2-5.—To those who ask how God loves Israel, the proof of Jehovah's election of Israel is shown in the fall of the Edomites.

2. Chap. i. 6-14.—Charge against the people of dishonouring their God, whom even the heathen reverence.

3. Chap. ii. 1-9.—Charge against the priests, who have broken the covenant God made of old with Levi, and debased their high office by not reverencing Jehovah, by misleading the people, and by perverting justice. A curse is therefore fallen on them—they are contemptible in the people's eyes.

4. Chap. ii. 10-16.—A charge against the people for their treachery to each other; instanced in the heathen marriages, if the two verses, 11 and 12, upon this be authentic, and in their divorce of their wives.

5. Chap. ii. 17-iii. 5 or 6.—Against those who in the midst of such evils grow sceptical about Jehovah. His Angel, or Himself, will come *first* to purge the priesthood and ritual that there may be pure sacrifices, and *second* to rid the land of its criminals and sinners.

6. Chap. iii. 6 or 7-12.—A charge against the people of neglecting tithes. Let these be paid, disasters shall cease and the land be blessed.

7. Chap. iii. 13-21 Heb., Chap. iii. 13-iv. 2 LXX. and Eng.—Another charge against the pious for saying it is vain to serve God. God will rise to action and separate between the good and bad in the terrible Day of His coming.

8. To this, Chap. iii. 22-24 Heb., Chap. iv. 3-5 Eng., adds a call to keep the Law, and a promise that Elijah will be sent to see whether he may not convert the people before the Day of the Lord comes upon them with its curse.

The authenticity of no part of the book has been till now in serious question. Böhme,* indeed, took the last three verses for a later addition, on account of their Deuteronomic character, but, as Kuenen points out, this is in agreement with other parts of the book. Sufficient attention has not yet been paid to the question of the integrity of the text. The Septuagint offers a few emendations.† There are other passages obviously or probably corrupt.‡ The text of the title, as we have seen, is uncertain, and probably a later addition. Professor Robertson Smith has called attention to chap. ii. 16, where the Massoretic punctuation seems to have been determined with the desire to support the rendering of the Targum "if thou hatest her put her away," and so pervert into a permission to divorce a passage which forbids divorce almost as clearly as Christ Himself did. But in truth the whole of this passage, chap. ii. 10-16, is in such a curious state that we can hardly believe in its integrity. It opens with the statement that God is the Father of all us Israelites, and with the challenge, why then are we faithless to each other?—ver. 10. But vv. 11 and 12 do not give an instance of this: they describe the marriages with the heathen women of the land, which is not a proof of faithlessness between Israelites. Such a proof is furnished only by vv. 13-16, with their condemnation of those who divorce the wives of their youth. The verses, therefore, cannot lie in their proper order, and vv. 13-16 ought to follow immediately upon ver. 10. This raises the question of the authenticity of vv. 11 and 12, against the heathen marriages. If they bear such plain marks of having been intruded into their position, we can understand the possibility of such an intrusion in subsequent days, when the question of the heathen marriages came to the front with Ezra and Nehemiah. Besides, these verses 11 and 12 lack the characteristic mark of all the other oracles of the book: they do not state a general charge against the people, and then introduce the people's question as to the particulars of the charge. On the whole, therefore, these verses are suspicious. If not a later intrusion, they are at least out of place where they now lie. The peculiar remark in ver. 13, "and this secondly ye do," must have been added by the editor to whom we owe the present arrangement.

CHAPTER XXV.

FROM ZECHARIAH TO "MALACHI."

BETWEEN the completion of the Temple in 516 and the arrival of Ezra in 458, we have almost no record of the little colony round Mount Zion. The Jewish chronicles devote to the period but a few verses of unsupported tradition.* After 517 we have nothing from Zechariah himself; and if any other prophet appeared during the next half-century, his words have not survived. We are left to infer what was the true condition of affairs, not less from this ominous silence than from the hints which are given to us in the writings of "Malachi," Ezra, and Nehemiah after the period was over. Beyond a partial attempt to rebuild the walls of the city in the reign of Artaxerxes I.,† there seems to have been nothing

* "Z. A. T. W.," 1887, 210 ff.

† i. 11, for גדול, δεδόξασται; perhaps ii. 12, עד for ער; perhaps iii. 8 ff., for עקב קבע; 16, for אז, ταῦτα.

‡ i. 11 ff.; ii. 3, and perhaps 12, 15.

* Ezra iv. 6-23.

† This is recorded in the Aramean document which has been incorporated in our Book of Ezra, and there is no reason to doubt its reality. In that document we have already found, in spite of its comparatively late date, much that is accurate history. See above, p. 610. And it is clear that, the Temple being finished, the Jews must have drawn upon themselves the same religious envy of the Samaritans which had previously delayed the construction of the Temple. To meet it, what more natural than that the Jews should have attempted to raise the walls of their city? It is almost impossible to believe that they who had achieved the construction of the Temple in 516 should not, in the next fifty years, make some effort to raise their fallen walls. And indeed Nehemiah's account of his own work almost necessarily im-

to record. It was a period of disillusion, disheartening, and decay. The completion of the Temple did not bring in the Messianic era. Zerubbabel, whom Haggai and Zechariah had crowned as the promised King of Israel, died without reaching higher rank than a minor satrapy in the Persian Empire, and even in that he appears to have been succeeded by a Persian official.* The re-migrations from Babylon and elsewhere, which Zechariah predicted, did not take place. The small population of Jerusalem were still harassed by the hostility, and their morale sapped by the insidiousness, of their Samaritan neighbours: they were denied the stimulus, the purgation, the glory of a great persecution. Their Persian tyrants for the most part left them alone. The world left them alone. Nothing stirred in Palestine except the Samaritan intrigues. History rolled away westward, and destiny seemed to be settling on the Greeks. In 490 Miltiades defeated the Persians at Marathon. In 480 Thermopylæ was fought and the Persian fleet broken at Salamis. In 479 a Persian army was destroyed at Platæa, and Xerxes lost Europe and most of the Ionian coast. In 460 Athens sent an expedition to Egypt to assist the Egyptian revolt against Persia, and in 457 "her slain fell in Cyprus, in Egypt, in Phœnicia, at Haliæ, in Ægina, and in Megara in the same year."

Thus severely left to themselves and to the petty hostilities of their neighbours, the Jews appear to have sunk into a careless and sordid manner of life. They entered the period, it is true, with some sense of their distinction.† In exile they had suffered God's anger,‡ and had been purged by it. But out of discipline often springs pride, and there is no subtler temptation of the human heart. The returned Israel felt this to the quick, and it sorely unfitted them for encountering the disappointment and hardship which followed upon the completion of the Temple. The tide of hope, which rose to flood with that consummation, ebbed rapidly away, and left God's people struggling, like any ordinary tribe of peasants, with bad seasons and the cruelty of their envious neighbours. Their pride was set on edge, and they fell, not as at other periods of disappointment into despair, but into a bitter carelessness and a contempt of their duty to God. This was a curious temper, and, so far as we know, new in Israel. It led them to despise both His love and His holiness.§ They neglected their Temple dues, and impudently presented to their God polluted bread and blemished beasts which they would not have dared to offer to their Persian governor.‖ Like people like priest: the priesthood lost not reverence only, but decency and all conscience of their office.¶ They "despised the Table of the Lord," ceased to instruct the people, and grew partial in judgment. As a consequence they became contemptible in the eyes of the community. Immorality prevailed among all classes: "every man dealt treacherously with his brother." **

plies that they had done so, for what he did after 445 was not to build new walls, but rather to repair shattered ones.

* See above, p. 641, *n.*, and below, p. 646, on "Mal." i. 8.

† *Cf.* Stade, "Gesch. des Volkes Israel," II., pp. 128-138, the best accour[illegible] of this period.

‡ "Mal." iii. 14.

§ "Mal." i. 2, 6; ii[illegible]

‖ *Id.* i. 7 f., 12-[illegible]

¶ *Id.* i. 6f., ii.

** *Id.* ii. 10.

Adultery, perjury, fraud, and the oppression of the poor were very rife.

One particular fashion, in which the people's wounded pride spited itself, was the custom of marriage which even the best families contracted with the half-heathen "people of the land." Across Judah there were scattered the descendants of those Jews whom Nebuchadrezzar had not deemed worth removing to Babylon. Whether regarded from a social or a religious point of view, their fathers had been the dregs of the old community. Their own religion, cut off as they were from the main body of Israel and scattered among the old heathen shrines of the land, must have deteriorated still further; but in all probability they had secured for themselves the best portions of the vacant soil, and now enjoyed a comfort and a stability of welfare far beyond that which was yet attainable by the majority of the returned exiles. More numerous than these dregs of ancient Jewry were the very mixed race of the Samaritans. They possessed a rich land, which they had cultivated long enough for many of their families to be settled in comparative wealth. With all these half-pagan Jews and Samaritans, the families of the true Israel, as they regarded themselves, did not hesitate to form alliances, for in the precarious position of the colony, such alliances were the surest way both to wealth and to political influence. How much the Jews were mastered by their desire for them is seen from the fact that, when the relatives of their half-heathen brides made it a condition of the marriages that they should first put away their old wives, they readily did so. Divorce became very frequent, and great suffering was inflicted on the native Jewish women.*

So the religious condition of Israel declined for nearly two generations, and then about 460 the Word of God, after long silence, broke once more through a prophet's lips.

We call this prophet "Malachi," following the error of an editor of his book, who, finding it nameless, inferred or invented that name from its description of the priest as the "Malĕ'ach," or "messenger, of the Lord of Hosts." † But the prophet gave himself no name. Writing from the midst of a poor and persecuted group of the people, and attacking the authorities both of church and state, he preferred to publish his charge anonymously. His name was in "the Lord's own book of remembrance." ‡

The unknown prophet addressed himself both to the sinners of his people and to those querulous adherents of Jehovah whom the success of the sinners had tempted to despair in their service of God. His style shares the practical directness of his predecessors among the returned exiles. He takes up one point after another, and drives them home in a series of strong, plain paragraphs of prose. But it is sixty years since Haggai and Zechariah, and in the circumstances we have described, a prophet could no longer come forward as a public inspirer of his nation. Prophecy seems to have been driven from public life, from the sudden enforcement of truth in the face of the people to the more deliberate and ordered argument which marks the teacher who works in private. In the Book of "Malachi" there are many of

* "Mal." ii. 10-16.

† For proof of this see above, pp. 640 f.

‡ "Mal." iii. 16.

the principles and much of the enthusiasm of the ancient Hebrew seer. But the discourse is broken up into formal paragraphs, each upon the same academic model. First a truth is pronounced, or a charge made against the people; then with the words "but ye will say" the prophet states some possible objection of his hearers, proceeds to answer it by detailed evidence, and only then drives home his truth, or his charge, in genuine prophetic fashion. To the student of prophecy this peculiarity of the book is of the greatest interest, for it is no merely personal idiosyncrasy. We rather feel that prophecy is now assuming the temper of the teacher. The method is the commencement of that which later on becomes the prevailing habit in Jewish literature. Just as with Zephaniah we saw prophecy passing into Apocalypse, and with Habakkuk into the speculation of the schools of Wisdom, so now in "Malachi" we perceive its transformation into the scholasticism of the Rabbis.

But the interest of this change of style must not prevent us from appreciating the genuine prophetic spirit of our book. Far more fully than, for instance, that of Haggai, to the style of which its practical sympathy is so akin, it enumerates the prophetic principles: the everlasting Love of Jehovah for Israel, the Fatherhood of Jehovah and His Holiness, His ancient Ideals for Priesthood and People, the need of a Repentance proved by deeds, the consequent Promise of Prosperity, the Day of the Lord, and Judgment between the evil and the righteous. Upon the last of these the book affords a striking proof of the delinquency of the people during the last half-century, and in connection with it the prophet introduces certain novel features. To Haggai and Zechariah the great Tribulation had closed with the Exile and the rebuilding of the Temple: Israel stood on the margin of the Messianic age. But the Book of "Malachi" proclaims the need of another judgment as emphatically as the older prophets had predicted the Babylonian doom. "Malachi" repeats their name for it, "the great and terrible Day of Jehovah." But he does not foresee it, as they did, in the shape of a historical process. His description of it is pure Apocalypse—"the fire of the smelter and the fuller's acid: the day that burns like a furnace," when all wickedness is as stubble, and all evil men are devoured, but to the righteous "the Sun of Righteousness shall arise with healing in His wings," and they shall tread the wicked under foot.* To this the prophet adds a novel promise. God is so much the God of Love,† that before the Day comes He will give His people an opportunity of conversion. He will send them Elijah the prophet to change their hearts, that He may be prevented from striking the land with His Ban.

In one other point the book is original, and that is in its attitude towards the heathen. Among the heathen, it boldly says, Jehovah is held in higher reverence than among His own people.‡ In such a statement we can hardly fail to feel the influence upon Israel of their contact, often close and personal, with their wise and mild tyrants the Persians. We may emphasise the verse as the first note of that recognition of the real religiousness of the heathen, which we shall find swelling to such fulness and tenderness in the Book of Jonah.

* iii. 2, 19 ff. Heb., iv. 1 ff. Eng. † iii. 6. ‡ i. 11.

Such are in brief the style and the principles of the Book of "Malachi," whose separate prophecies we may now proceed to take up in detail.

CHAPTER XXVI.

PROPHECY WITHIN THE LAW.

"Malachi" i.-iv.

Beneath this title we may gather all the eight sections of the Book of "Malachi." They contain many things of perennial interest and validity: their truth is applicable, their music is still musical, to ourselves. But their chief significance is historical. They illustrate the development of prophecy *within* the Law. Not *under* the Law, be it observed. For if one thing be more clear than another about "Malachi's" teaching, it is that the spirit of prophecy is not yet crushed by the legalism which finally killed it within Israel. "Malachi" observes and enforces the demands of the Deuteronomic law under which his people had lived since the Return from Exile. But he traces each of these to some spiritual principle, to some essential of religion in the character of Israel's God, which is either doubted or neglected by his contemporaries in their lax performance of the Law. That is why we may entitle his book Prophecy within the Law.

The essential principles of the religion of Israel which had been shaken or obscured by the delinquency of the people during the half-century after the rebuilding of the Temple were three—the distinctive Love of Jehovah for His people, His Holiness, and His Righteousness. The Book of "Malachi" takes up each of these in turn, and proves or enforces it according as the people have formally doubted it or in their carelessness done it despite.

1. God's Love for Israel and Hatred of Edom (Chap. i. 2-5).

He begins with God's Love, and in answer to the disappointed* people's cry, "Wherein hast Thou loved us?" he does not, as the older prophets did, sweep the whole history of Israel, and gather proofs of Jehovah's grace and unfailing guidance in all the great events from the deliverance from Egypt to the deliverance from Babylon. But he confines himself to a comparison of Israel with the Gentile nation which was most akin to Israel according to the flesh, their own brother Edom. It is possible, of course, to see in this a proof of our prophet's narrowness, as contrasted with Amos or Hosea or the great Evangelist of the Exile. But we must remember that out of all the history of Israel "Malachi" could not have chosen an instance which would more strongly appeal to the heart of his contemporaries. We have seen from the Book of Obadiah how ever since the beginning of the Exile Edom had come to be regarded by Israel as their great antithesis.† If

* See above, p. 643.
† See above, chapter xiv. on "Edom and Israel."

we needed further proof of this we should find it in many Psalms of the Exile, which like the Book of Obadiah remember with bitterness the hostile part that Edom played in the day of Israel's calamity. The two nations were utterly opposed in genius and character. Edom was a people of as unspiritual and self-sufficient a temper as ever cursed any of God's human creatures. Like their ancestor they were "profane," * without repentance, humility, or ideals, and almost without religion. Apart, therefore, from the long history of war between the two peoples, it was a true instinct which led Israel to regard their brother as representative of that heathendom against which they had to realise their destiny in the world as God's own nation. In choosing the contrast of Edom's fate to illustrate Jehovah's love for Israel, "Malachi" was not only choosing what would appeal to the passions of his contemporaries, but what is the most striking and constant antithesis in the whole history of Israel: the absolutely diverse genius and destiny of these two Semitic nations who were nearest neighbours and, according to their traditions, twin-brethren after the flesh. If we keep this in mind we shall understand Paul's use of the antithesis in the passage in which he clenches it by a quotation from "Malachi": "as it is written, Jacob have I loved, but Esau have I hated." † In these words the doctrine of the Divine election of individuals appears to be expressed as absolutely as possible. But it would be unfair to read the passage except in the light of Israel's history. In the Old Testament it is a matter of fact that the doctrine of the Divine preference of Israel to Esau appeared only after the respective characters of the nations were manifested in history, and that it grew more defined and absolute only as history discovered more of the fundamental contrast between the two in genius and destiny.‡ In the Old Testament, therefore, the doctrine is the result, not of an arbitrary belief in God's bare fiat, but of historical experience; although, of course, the distinction which experience proves is traced back, with everything else of good or evil that happens, to the sovereign will and purpose of God. Nor let us forget that the Old Testament doctrine of election is of election to service only. That is to say, the Divine intention in electing covers not the elect individual or nation only, but the whole world and its needs of God and His truth.

The event to which "Malachi" appeals as evidence for God's rejection of Edom is "the desolation of" the latter's ancient "heritage, and" the abandonment of it to the "jackals of the desert." Scholars used to think that these vague phrases referred to some act of the Persian kings: some removal of the Edomites from the lands of the Jews in order to make room for the returned exiles.§ But "Malachi" says expressly that it was Edom's own "heritage" which was laid desolate. This can only be Mount Esau or Se'ir, and the statement that it was delivered "to the jackals of the desert" proves that the reference is to that same expulsion of Edom from their territory by the Nabatean Arabs which we have already seen the Book of Obadiah relate about the beginning of the Exile.*

But it is now time to give in full the opening passage of "Malachi," in which he appeals to this important event as proof of God's distinctive love for Israel, and, "Malachi" adds, of His power beyond Israel's border ("Mal." chap. i. 2-5).

"I have loved you, saith Jehovah. But ye say, 'Wherein hast Thou loved us?' Is not Esau brother to Jacob?—oracle of Jehovah—and I have loved Jacob and Esau have I hated. I have made his mountains desolate, and given his heritage to the jackals of the desert. Should *the people of* Edom say, † 'We are destroyed, but we will rebuild the waste places,' thus saith Jehovah of Hosts, They may build, but I will pull down: men shall call them 'The Border of Wickedness' and 'The People with whom Jehovah is wroth for ever.' And your eyes shall see it, and yourselves shall say, 'Great is Jehovah beyond Israel's border.'"

2. "Honour Thy Father" (Chap. i. 6-14).

From God's Love, which Israel have doubted, the prophet passes to His Majesty or Holiness, which they have wronged. Now it is very remarkable that the relation of God to the Jews in which the prophet should see His Majesty illustrated is not only His lordship over them but His Fatherhood: "A son honours a father, and a servant his lord; but if I be Father, where is My honour? and if I be Lord, where is there reverence for Me? saith Jehovah of Hosts."‡ We are so accustomed to associate with the Divine Fatherhood only ideas of love and pity that the use of the relation to illustrate not love but Majesty, and the setting of it in parallel to the Divine Kingship, may seem to us strange. Yet this was very natural to Israel. In the old Semitic world, even to the human parent, honour was due before love. "Honour thy father and thy mother," said the Fifth Commandment; and when, after long shyness to do so, Israel at last ventured to claim Jehovah as the Father of His people, it was at first rather with the view of increasing their sense of His authority and their duty of reverencing Him, than with the view of bringing Him near to their hearts and assuring them of His tenderness. The latter elements, it is true, were not absent from the conception. But even in the Psalter, in which we find the most intimate and tender fellowship of the believer with God, there is only one passage in which His love for His own is compared to the love of a human father.§ And in the other very few passages of the Old Testament where He is revealed or appealed to as the Father of the na-

* Heb. xii. 16.

† Romans ix. 13. The citation is from the LXX.: τὸν Ἰακὼβ ἠγάπησα, τὸν δὲ Ἠσαῦ ἐμίσησα.

‡ This was mainly "after" the beginning of exile. Shortly before that Deut. xxiii. 7 says: "Thou shalt not abhor an Edomite, for he is thy brother."

§ So even so recently as 1888, Stade, "Gesch. des Volkes Israel," II. p. 112.

* See above, p. 600. This interpretation is there said to be Wellhausen's; but Cheyne, in a note contributed to the "Z. A. T. W.," 1894, p. 142, points out that Grätz, in an article "Die Anfänge der Nabatäer-Herrschaft" in the "Monatschrift für Wissenschaft u. Geschichte des Judenthums," 1875, pp. 60-66, had already explained "Mal." i. 1-5 as describing the conquest of Edom by the Nabateans. This is adopted by Buhl in his "Gesch. der Edomiter," p. 79.

† The verb in the feminine indicates that the population of Edom is meant.

‡ i. 6.

§ Psalm ciii. 9. In Psalm lxxiii. 15 believers are called "His children"; but elsewhere sonship is claimed only for the king—ii. 7, lxxxix. 27 f.

tion, it is, with two exceptions,* in order either to emphasise His creation of Israel or His discipline. So in Jeremiah,† and in an anonymous prophet of the same period perhaps as "Malachi."‡ This hesitation to ascribe to God the name of Father, and this severe conception of what Fatherhood meant, was perhaps needful for Israel in face of the sensuous ideas of the Divine Fatherhood cherished by their heathen neighbours.§ But, however this may be, the infrequency and austerity of Israel's conception of God's Fatherhood, in contrast with that of Christianity, enables us to understand why "Malachi" should employ the relation as proof, not of the Love, but of the Majesty and Holiness of Jehovah.

This Majesty and this Holiness have been wronged, he says, by low thoughts of God's altar, and by offering upon it, with untroubled conscience, cheap and blemished sacrifices. The people would have been ashamed to present such to their Persian governor: how can God be pleased with them? Better that sacrifice should cease than that such offerings should be presented in such a spirit! "Is there no one," cries the prophet, "to close the doors" of the Temple altogether, so that "the altar" smoke not "in vain?"

The passage shows us what a change has passed over the spirit of Israel since prophecy first attacked the sacrificial ritual. We remember how Amos would have swept it all away as an abomination to God.‖ So, too, Isaiah and Jeremiah. But their reason for this was very different from "Malachi's." Their contemporaries were assiduous and lavish in sacrificing, and were devoted to the Temple and the ritual with a fanaticism which made them forget that Jehovah's demands upon His people were righteousness and the service of the weak. But "Malachi" condemns his generation for depreciating the Temple, and for being stingy and fraudulent in their offerings. Certainly the post-exilic prophet assumes a different attitude to the ritual from that of his predecessors in ancient Israel. They wished it all abolished, and placed the chief duties of Israel towards God in civic justice and mercy. But he emphasises it as the first duty of the people towards God, and sees in their neglect the reason of their misfortunes and the cause of their coming doom. In this change which has come over prophecy we must admit the growing influence of the Law. From Ezekiel onwards the prophets become more ecclesiastical and legal. And though at first they do not become less ethical, yet the influence which was at work upon them was of such a character as was bound in time to engross their interest, and lead them to remit the ethical elements of their religion to a place secondary to the ceremonial. We see symptoms of this even in "Malachi," we shall find more in Joel, and we know how aggravated these symptoms afterwards became in all the leaders of Jewish religion. At the same time we ought to remember that this change of emphasis, which many will think to be for the worse, was largely rendered necessary by the change of temper in the people to whom the prophets ministered. "Malachi" found among his contemporaries a habit of religious performance which was not only slovenly and indecent, but mean and fraudulent, and it became his first practical duty to attack this. Moreover the neglect of the Temple was not due to those spiritual conceptions of Jehovah and those moral duties He demanded, in the interests of which the older prophets had condemned the ritual. At bottom the neglect of the Temple was due to the very same reasons as the superstitious zeal and fanaticism in sacrificing which the older prophets had attacked —false ideas, namely, of God Himself, and of what was due to Him from His people. And on these grounds, therefore, we may say that "Malachi" was performing for his generation as needful and as Divine a work as Amos and Isaiah had performed for theirs. Only, be it admitted, the direction of "Malachi's" emphasis was more dangerous for religion than that of the emphasis of Amos or Isaiah. How liable the practice he inculcated was to exaggeration and abuse is sadly proved in the later history of his people: it was against that exaggeration, grown great and obdurate through three centuries, that Jesus delivered His most unsparing words.

"A son honours a father, and a servant his lord. But if I am Father, where is My honour? and if I am Lord, where is reverence for Me? saith Jehovah of Hosts to you, O priests, who despise My Name. Ye say, 'How' *then* 'have we despised Thy Name?' Ye are bringing polluted food to Mine Altar. Ye say, 'How have we polluted Thee?'* By saying,† 'The Table of Jehovah may be despised'; and when ye bring a blind *beast* to sacrifice, 'No harm!'‡ Pray, take it to thy Satrap: will he be pleased with thee, or accept thy person? saith Jehovah of Hosts. But now, propitiate§ God, that He may be gracious to us. When *things like* this come from your hands can He accept your persons? saith Jehovah of Hosts. Who is there among you to close the doors" of the Temple altogether, "that ye kindle not Mine Altar in vain? I have no pleasure in you, saith Jehovah of Hosts, and I will not accept an offering from your hands. For from the rising of the sun and to its setting My Name is glorified ‖ among the nations; and in every sacred place ¶ incense is offered to My Name, and a pure offering: ** for great is My Name among the nations, saith Jehovah of Hosts. But ye

* Hosea xi. 1 ff. (though even here the idea of discipline is present) and Isa. lxiii. 16.

† iii. 4.

‡ Isa. lxiv. 8, *cf.* Deut. xxxii. 11 where the discipline of Israel by Jehovah, shaking them out of their desert circumstance and tempting them to their great career in Palestine, is likened to the father-eagle's training of his new-fledged brood to fly: A. V. mother-eagle.

§ *Cf.* Cheyne, "Origin of the Psalter," p. 305, n. O.

‖ Page 481 ff.

* Or used polluted things with respect to Thee. For similar construction see Zech. vii. 5: צמתוני. This in answer to Wellhausen, who, on the ground that the phrase gives גאל a wrong object and destroys the connection, deletes it. Further he takes מגאל, not in the sense of pollution, but as equivalent to נבזה, "despised."

† Obviously "in their hearts = thinking."

‡ LXX. "is there no harm?"

§ "Pacify the face of," as in Zechariah.

‖ So LXX. Heb. "is great," but the phrase is probably written by mistake from the instance further on: "is glorified" could scarcely have been used in the very literal version of the LXX. unless it had been found in the original.

¶ מקום, here to be taken in the sense it bears in Arabic of "sacred place." See on Zeph. ii. 11: above, 576, *n.*

** Wellhausen deletes מגש as a gloss on מקטר, and the vau before מנחה.

are profaning it, in that ye think * that the Table of the Lord is polluted, and † its food contemptible. And ye say, What a weariness! and ye sniff at it,‡ saith Jehovah of Hosts. *When* ye bring what has been plundered,§ and the lame and the diseased, yea, *when* ye *so* bring an offering, can I accept it with grace from your hands? saith Jehovah. Cursed be the cheat in whose flock is a male *beast* and he vows it,‖ and slays for the Lord a miserable beast.¶ For a great King am I, saith Jehovah of **Hosts,** and My Name is reverenced among the nations."

Before we pass from this passage we must notice in it one very remarkable feature—perhaps the most original contribution which the Book of "Malachi" makes to the development of prophecy. In contrast to the irreverence of Israel and the wrong they do to Jehovah's Holiness, He Himself asserts that not only is "His Name great and glorified among the heathen, from the rising to the setting of the sun," but that "in every sacred place incense and a pure offering are offered to His Name." This is so novel a statement, and, we may truly say, so startling, that it is not wonderful that the attempt should have been made to interpret it, not of the prophet's own day, but of the Messianic age and the kingdom of Christ. So, many of the Christian Fathers, from Justin and Irenæus to Theodoret and Augustine; ** so, our own Authorised Version, which boldly throws the verbs into the future; and so, many modern interpreters like Pusey, who declares that the style is "a vivid present such as is often used to describe the future; but the things spoken of show it to be future." All these take the passage to be an anticipation of Christ's parables declaring the rejection of the Jews and ingathering of the Gentiles to the kingdom of heaven, and of the argument of the Epistle to the Hebrews, that the bleeding and defective offerings of the Jews were abrogated by the sacrifice of the Cross. But such an exegesis is only possible by perverting the text and misreading the whole argument of the prophet. Not only are the verbs of the original in the present tense—so also in the early versions—but the prophet is obviously contrasting the contempt of God's own people for Himself and His institutions with the reverence paid to His Name among the heathen. It is not the mere question of there being righteous people in every nation, well-pleasing to Jehovah because of their lives. The very sacrifices of the heathen are pure and acceptable to Him. Never have we had in prophecy, even the most far-seeing and evangelical, a statement so generous and so catholic as this. Why it should appear only now in the history of prophecy is a question we are unable to answer with certainty. Many have seen in it the result of Israel's intercourse with their tolerant and religious masters the Persians. None of the Persian kings had up to this time persecuted the Jews, and numbers of pious and large-minded Israelites must have had opportunity of acquaintance with the very pure doctrines of the Persian religion, among which it is said that there was already numbered the recognition of true piety in men of all religions.* If Paul derived from his Hellenic culture the knowledge which made it possible for him to speak as he did in Athens of the religiousness of the Gentiles, it was just as probable that Jews who had come within the experience of a still purer Aryan faith should utter an even more emphatic acknowledgment that the One True God had those who served Him in spirit and in truth all over the world. But, whatever foreign influences may have ripened such a faith in Israel, we must not forget that its roots were struck deep in the native soil of their religion. From the first they had known their God as a God of grace so infinite that it was impossible it should be exhausted on themselves. If His righteousness, as Amos showed, was over all the Syrian states, and His pity and His power to convert, as Isaiah showed, covered even the cities of Phœnicia, the great Evangelist of the Exile could declare that He quenched not the smoking wicks of the dim heathen faiths.

As interesting, however, as the origin of "Malachi's" attitude to the heathen, are two other points about it. In the first place, it is remarkable that it should occur, especially in the form of emphasising the purity of heathen sacrifices, in a book which lays such heavy stress upon the Jewish Temple and ritual. This is a warning to us not to judge harshly the so-called legal age of Jewish religion, nor to despise the prophets who have come under the influence of the Law. And in the second place, we perceive in this statement a step towards the fuller acknowledgment of Gentile religiousness which we find in the Book of Jonah. It is strange that none of the post-exilic Psalms strike the same note. They often predict the conversion of the heathen; but they do not recognise their native reverence and piety. Perhaps the reason is that in a body of song, collected for the national service, such a feature would be out of place.

3. The Priesthood of Knowledge (Chap. ii. 1-9).

In the third section of his book "Malachi" addresses himself to the priests. He charges them not only with irreverence and slovenliness in their discharge of the Temple service—for this he appears to intend by the phrase "filth of your feasts"—but with the neglect of their intellectual duties to the people. "The lips of a priest guard knowledge, and men seek instruction from his mouth, for he is the Angel"—the revealing Angel—"of Jehovah of Hosts." Once more, what a remarkable saying to come from the legal age of Israel's religion, and from a writer who so emphasises the ceremonial law! In all the range of prophecy there is not any more in harmony with the prophetic ideal. How needed it is in our own age!—needed against those two extremes of religion from which we suffer, the limitation of the ideal of priesthood

* Heb. "say."

† Heb. also has ניבו, found besides only in Keri of Isa. lvii. 19. But Robertson Smith ("O. T. J. C.," 2, p. 444) is probably right in considering this an error for נבזה, which has kept its place after the correction was inserted.

‡ This clause is obscure, and comes in awkwardly before that which follows it. Wellhausen omits.

§ גָּזוּל. Wellhausen emends אֶת־הָעִוֵּר, borrowing the first three letters from the previous word. LXX. ἁρπάγματα.

‖ LXX.

¶ *Cf.* Lev. iii. 1, 6.

** Quoted by Pusey, *in loco.*

* See Cheyne, "Origin of the Psalter," 292 and 305 f.

to the communication of a magic grace, and its evaporation in a vague religiosity from which the intellect is excluded as if it were perilous, worldly, and devilish.* "Surrender of the intellect" indeed! This is the burial of the talent in the napkin, and, as in the parable of Christ, it is still in our day preached and practised by the men of one talent. Religion needs all the brains we poor mortals can put into it. There is a priesthood of knowledge, a priesthood of the intellect, says "Malachi," and he makes this a large part of God's covenant with Levi. Every priest of God is a priest of truth; and it is very largely by the Christian ministry's neglect of their intellectual duties that so much irreligion prevails. As in "Malachi's" day, so now, "the laity take hurt and hindrance by our negligence."† And just as he points out, so with ourselves, the consequence is the growing indifference with which large bodies of the Christian ministry are regarded by the thoughtful portions both of our labouring and professional classes. Were the ministers of all the Churches to awake to their ideal in this matter, there would surely come a very great revival of religion among us.

"And now this Charge for you, O priests: If ye hear not, and lay not to heart to give glory to My Name, saith Jehovah of Hosts, I will send upon you the curse, and will curse your blessings—yea, I have cursed them ‡—for none of you layeth it to heart. Behold, I . . . you . . .§ and I will scatter filth in your faces, the filth of your feasts. . . .‖ And ye shall know that I have sent to you this Charge, to be My covenant with Levi,¶ saith Jehovah of Hosts. My covenant was with him life and peace** and I gave them to him, fear and he feared Me, and humbled himself before My Name.†† The revelation of truth was in his mouth, and wickedness was not found upon his lips. In wholeheartedness ‡‡ and integrity he walked with Me, and turned many from iniquity. For the lips of a priest guard knowledge, and men seek instruction * from his mouth, for he is the Angel of Jehovah of Hosts. But ye have turned from the way, ye have tripped up many by the Torah, ye have spoiled the covenant of Levi, saith Jehovah of Hosts. And I on My part† have made you contemptible to all the people, and abased in proportion as ye kept not My ways and had respect of persons in *delivering your* Torah."

* "Isaiah i.-xxxix." (Expositor's Bible): p. 664.

† See most admirable remarks on this subject in Archdeacon Wilson's "Essays and Addresses," No. III. "The Need of giving Higher Biblical Teaching, and Instruction on the Fundamental Questions of Religion and Christianity." London: Macmillan, 1887.

‡ Doubtful. LXX. adds *καὶ διεσκεδάσω τὴν εὐλόγιαν ὑμῶν καὶ οὐκ ἔσται ἐν ὑμῖν*: obvious redundancy, if not mere dittography.

§ An obscure phrase, הִנְנִי גֹּעֵר לָכֶם אֶת־הַזֶּרַע, "Behold, I rebuke you the seed." LXX. "Behold, I separate from you the arm" or "shoulder," reading זְרֹעַ for זֶרַע and perhaps גֹּדֵעַ for גֹּעֵר, both of which readings Wellhausen adopts, and Ewald the former. The reference may be to the arm of the priest raised in blessing. Orelli reads "seed" = "posterity." It may mean the whole "seed" or "class" or "kind" of the priests. The next clause tempts one to suppose that את־הזרע contains the verb of this one, as if scattering something.

‖ Heb. וְנָשָׂא אֶתְכֶם אֵלָיו, "and one shall bear you to it" Hitzig · filth shall be cast on them, and they on the filth.

¶ Others would render "My covenant being with Levi." Wellhausen: "for My covenant was with Levi." But this new Charge or covenant seems contrasted with a former covenant in the next verse.

** Num. xxv. 12.

†† This sentence is a literal translation of the Hebrew. With other punctuation Wellhausen renders "My covenant was with him, life and peace I gave them to him, fear . . ."

‡‡ Or peace' שָׁלוֹם.

4. The Cruelty of Divorce (Chap. ii. 10-17).

In his fourth section, upon his countrymen's frequent divorce of their native wives in order to marry into the influential families of their half-heathen neighbours,‡ "Malachi" makes another of those wide and spiritual utterances which so distinguish his prophecy and redeem his age from the charge of legalism that is so often brought against it. To him the Fatherhood of God is not merely a relation of power and authority, requiring reverence from the nation. It constitutes the members of the nation one close brotherhood, and against this divorce is a crime and unnatural cruelty. Jehovah makes the "wife of a man's youth his mate" for life "and his wife by covenant." He "hates divorce," and His altar is so wetted by the tears of the wronged women of Israel that the gifts upon it are no more acceptable in His sight. No higher word on marriage was spoken except by Christ Himself. It breathes the spirit of our Lord's utterance: if we were sure of the text of ver. 15, we might almost say that it anticipated the letter. Certain verses, 11-13*a*, which disturb the argument by bringing in the marriages with heathen wives, are omitted in the following translation, and will be given separately.

"Have we not all One Father? Hath not One God created us? Why then are we unfaithful to one another, profaning the covenant of our fathers? . . .§ Ye cover with tears the altar of Jehovah, with weeping and with groaning, because respect is no longer had to the offering, and acceptable gifts are not taken from your hands. And ye say, 'Why?' Because Jehovah has been witness between thee and the wife of thy youth, with whom thou hast broken faith, though she is thy mate‖ and thy wife by covenant. And . . .¶ And what is the one

* Or "revelation," Torah.

† וְגַם־אֲנִי: *cf.* Amos iv.

‡ See above, p. 643.

§ Here occur the two verses and a clause, 11-13*a*, upon the foreign marriages, which seem to be an intrusion.

‖ See p. 506.

¶ Heb. literally: "And not one did, and a remnant of spirit was his"; which (1) A. V. renders: "And did not he make one? Yet he had the residue of the spirit." which Pusey accepts and applies to Adam and Eve, interpreting the second clause as "the breath of life," by which Adam "became a living soul" (Gen. ii. 7). In Gen. i. 27 Adam and Eve are called one. In that case the meaning would be that the law of marriage was prior to that of divorce, as in the words of our Lord, Matt. xix. 4-6. (2) The Hebrew might be rendered, "Not one has done this who had any spirit left in him." So Hitzig and Orelli. In that case the following clauses of the verse are referred to Abraham. "But what about the One"? (LXX. insert "ye say" after "But")—the one who did put away his wife. Answer: "He was seeking a Divine seed." The objection to this interpretation is that Abraham did not cast off the wife of his youth, Sarah, but the foreigner Hagar. (3) Ewald made a very different proposal: "And has not One created them, and all the Spirit" (*cf.* Zeph. i. 4) "is His? And what doth the One seek? A Divine seed." So Reinke. Similarly Kirk-

seeking? A Divine Seed. Take heed, then, to your spirit, and be not unfaithful to the wife of thy youth.* For I hate divorce, saith Jehovah, God of Israel, and that a man cover his clothing† with cruelty, saith Jehovah of Hosts. So take heed to your spirit, and deal not faithlessly."

The verses omitted in the above translation treat of the foreign marriages, which led to this frequent divorce by the Jews of their native wives. So far, of course, they are relevant to the subject of the passage. But they obviously disturb its argument, as already pointed out.‡ They have nothing to do with the principle from which it starts that Jehovah is the Father of the whole of Israel. Remove them and the awkward clause in ver. 13*a*, by which some editor has tried to connect them with the rest of the paragraph, and the latter runs smoothly. The motive of their later addition is apparent, if not justifiable. Here they are by themselves:—

"Judah was fruitless, and abomination was practised in Israel § and in Jerusalem, for Judah hath defiled the sanctuary of Jehovah, which was dear to Him, and hath married the daughter of a strange god. May Jehovah cut off from the man who doeth this witness and champion ‖ from the tents of Jacob, and offerer of sacrifices to Jehovah of Hosts."¶

5. "Where is the God of Judgment?" (Chap. ii. 17-iii. 5).

In this section "Malachi" turns from the sinners of his people to those who weary Jehovah with the complaint that sin is successful, or, as they put it, "Every one that does evil is good in the eyes of Jehovah, and He delighteth in them"; and again, "Where is the God of Judgment?" The answer is, The Lord Himself shall come. His Angel shall prepare His way before Him, and suddenly shall the Lord come to His Temple. His coming shall be for judgment, terrible and searching. Its first object (note the order) shall be the cleansing of the priesthood, that proper sacrifices may be established, and its second the purging of the immorality of the people. Mark that although the coming of the Angel is said to precede that of Jehovah Himself, there is the same blending of the two as we have seen in previous accounts of angels.** It is uncertain whether this section closes with ver. 5 or 6: the latter goes equally well with it and with the following section.

"Ye have wearied Jehovah with your words; and ye say, 'In what have we wearied *Him?*' In that ye say, 'Every one that does evil is good in the eyes of Jehovah, and He delighteth in them'; or else, 'Where is the God of Judgment?' Behold, I will send My Angel, to prepare the way before Me, and suddenly shall come to His Temple the Lord whom ye seek and the Angel of the Covenant whom ye desire. Behold, He comes! saith Jehovah of Hosts. But who may bear the day of His coming, and who stand when He appears? For He is like the fire of the smelter and the acid of the fullers. He takes His seat to smelt and to purge; * and He will purge the sons of Levi, and wash them out like gold or silver, and they shall be to Jehovah bringers of an offering in righteousness. And the offering of Judah and Jerusalem shall be pleasing to Jehovah, as in the days of old and as in long past years. And I will come near you to judgment, and I will be a swift witness against the sorcerers and the adulterers and the perjurers, and against those who wrong the hireling in his wage, and the widow and the orphan, and oppress the stranger, and fear not Me, saith Jehovah of Hosts."

6. Repentance by Tithes (Chap. iii. 6-12).

This section ought perhaps to follow on to the preceding. Those whom it blames for not paying the Temple tithes may be the sceptics addressed in the previous section, who have stopped their dues to Jehovah out of sheer disappointment that He does nothing. And ver. 6, which goes well with either section, may be the joint between the two. However this be, the new section enforces the need of the people's repentance and return to God, if He is to return to them. And when they ask, how are they to return, "Malachi" plainly answers, By the payment of the tithes they have not paid. In withholding these they robbed God, and to this, their crime, are due the locusts and bad seasons which have afflicted them. In our temptation to see in this a purely legal spirit, let us remember that the neglect to pay the tithes was due to a religious cause, unbelief in Jehovah, and that the return to belief in Him could not therefore be shown in a more practical way than by the payment of tithes. This is not prophecy subject to the Law, but prophecy employing the means and vehicles of grace with which the Law at that time provided the people.

"For I Jehovah have not changed, but ye sons of Jacob have not done with(?).† In the days of your fathers ye turned from My statutes and did not keep *them.* Return to Me, and I will return to you, saith Jehovah of Hosts. But you say, 'How then shall we return?' Can a man rob‡ God? yet ye are robbing Me. But ye say, 'In what have we robbed Thee?' In

patrick ("Doct. of the Proph.," p. 502): "And did not One make" [you both]? 'And why" [did] "the One" [do so]? "Seeking a goodly seed." (4) Wellhausen goes further along the same line. Reading הלא for ולא, and וישאר for ושאר, and לנו for לו, he translates: "Hath not the same God created and sustained your" (? "our") "breath? And what does He desire? A seed of God."

* Literally: "let none be unfaithful to the wife of thy youth," a curious instance of the Hebrew habit of mixing the pronominal references. Wellhausen's emendation is unnecessary.

† See Gesenius and Ewald for Arabic analogies for the use of clothing = wife.

‡ See above, p. 642.

§ Wellhausen omits.

‖ Heb. עֵר וְעֹנֶה, "caller and answerer." But LXX. read עד, "witness" (see iii. 5), though it pointed it differently.

¶ 13*a*, "But secondly ye do this," is the obvious addition of the editor in order to connect his intrusion with what follows.

** See above, pp. 631 652 f.

* Delete "silver": the longer LXX. text shows how easily it was added.

† "Made an end of," reading the verb as Piel (Orelli). LXX. "refrain from." "Your sins" are understood, the sins which have always characterised the people. LXX. connects the opening of the next verse with this, and with a different reading of the first word translates "from the sins of your fathers."

‡ Heb. קבע, only here and Prov. xxii. 32. LXX. read צקב, "supplant, cheat," which Wellhausen adopts.

the tithe and the tribute.* With the curse are ye cursed, and yet Me ye are robbing, the whole people of you. Bring in the whole tithe to the storehouse, that there may be provision† in My House, and pray, prove Me in this, saith Jehovah of Hosts—whether I will not open to you the windows of heaven, and pour blessing upon you till there is no more need. And I will check for you the devourer,‡ and he shall not destroy for you the fruit of the ground, nor the vine in the field miscarry, saith Jehovah of Hosts. And all nations shall call you happy, for ye shall be a land of delight, saith Jehovah of Hosts."

7. The Judgment to Come (Chap. iii. 13-21 Heb., iii. 13-iv. 2 Eng.).

This is another charge to the doubters among the pious remnant of Israel, who, seeing the success of the wicked, said it is vain to serve God. Deuteronomy was their Canon, and Deuteronomy said that if men sinned they decayed, if they were righteous they prospered. How different were the facts of experience! The evil men succeeded: the good won no gain by their goodness, nor did their mourning for the sins of their people work any effect. Bitterest of all, they had to congratulate wickedness in high places, and Jehovah Himself suffered it to go unpunished. "Such things," says "Malachi," "spake they that feared God to each other"—tempted thereto by the dogmatic form of their religion, and forgetful of all that Jeremiah and the Evangelist of the Exile had taught them of the value of righteous sufferings. Nor does "Malachi" remind them of this. His message is that the Lord remembers them, has their names written before Him, and when the day of His action comes they shall be separated from the wicked and spared. This is simply to transfer the fulfilment of the promise of Deuteronomy to the future and to another dispensation. Prophecy still works within the Law.

The Apocalypse of this last judgment is one of the grandest in all Scripture. To the wicked it shall be a terrible fire, root and branch shall they be burned out, but to the righteous a fair morning of God, as when dawn comes to those who have been sick and sleepless through the black night, and its beams bring healing, even as to the popular belief of Israel it was the rays of the morning sun which distilled the dew.§ They break into life and energy, like young calves leaping from the dark pen into the early sunshine. To this morning landscape a grim figure is added. They shall tread down the wicked and the arrogant like ashes beneath their feet.

"Your words are hard upon Me, saith Jehovah. Ye say, 'What have we said against Thee?' Ye have said, 'It is vain to serve God,' and 'What gain is it to us to have kept His charge, or to have walked in funeral garb before Jehovah of Hosts? Even now we have got to congratulate the arrogant; yea, the workers of wickedness are fortified; yea, they tempt God and escape!' Such things* spake they that fear Jehovah to each other. But Jehovah gave ear and heard, and a book of remembrance† was written before Him about those who fear Jehovah, and those who keep in mind‡ His Name. And they shall be Mine own property, saith Jehovah of Hosts, in the day when I rise to action,§ and I will spare them even as a man spares his son that serves him. And ye shall once more see *the difference* between righteous and wicked, between him that serves God and him that does not serve Him.

"For, lo! the day is coming that shall burn like a furnace, and all the overweening and every one that works wickedness shall be as stubble, and the day that is coming shall devour them, saith Jehovah of Hosts, so that there be left them neither root nor branch. But to you that fear My Name the Sun of Righteousness shall rise with healing in His wings, and ye shall go forth and leap‖ like calves of the stall.¶ And ye shall tread down the wicked, for they shall be as ashes** beneath the soles of your feet, in the day that I *begin to* do, saith Jehovah of Hosts.

8. The Return of Elijah (Chap. iii. 22-24 Heb., iv. 3-5 Eng.).

With his last word the prophet significantly calls upon the people to remember the Law. This is their one hope before the coming of the great and terrible day of the Lord. But, in order that the Law may have full effect, Prophecy will be sent to bring it home to the hearts of the people—Prophecy in the person of her founder and most drastic representative. Nothing could better gather up than this conjunction does that mingling of Law and of Prophecy which we have seen to be so characteristic of the work of "Malachi." Only we must not overlook the fact that "Malachi" expects this prophecy, which with the Law is to work the conversion of the people, not in the continuance of the prophetic succession by the appearance of original personalities, developing further the great principles of their order, but in the return of the first prophet Elijah. This is surely the confession of Prophecy that the number of her servants is exhausted and her message to Israel fulfilled. She can now do no more for the people than she has done. But she will summon up her old energy and fire in the return of her most powerful personality, and make one grand effort to convert the nation before the Lord come and strike it with judgment.

"Remember the Torah of Moses, My servant, with which I charged him in Horeb for all

* תְּרוּמָה, "the heave offering," the tax or tribute given to the sanctuary or priests and associates with the tithes, as here in Deut. xii. 11, to be eaten by the offerer (*ib.* 17) but in Ezekiel by the priests (xliv. 30); taken by the people and the Levites to the Temple treasury for the priests (Neh. x. 38, xii. 44): corn, wine, and oil. In the Priestly Writing it signifies the part of each sacrifice which was the priest's due. Ezekiel also uses it of the part of the Holy Land that fell to the prince and priests.

† טֶרֶף in its later meaning: *cf.* Job xxiv. 5; Prov. xxxi. 15.

‡ *I. e.*, locust.

§ "A dew of lights."

* So LXX.; Heb. "then."

† Ezek. xiii. 9.

‡ חשב, "to think, plan," has much the same meaning as here in Isa. xiii. 17, xxxiii. 8, liii. 3.

§ Heb. "when I am doing;" but in the sense in which the word is used of Jehovah's decisive and final doing, Psalms xx., xxxii., etc.

‖ Hab. i. 8.

¶ See note to Amos vi. 4: p. 486, *n.*

** Or "dust."

Israel: statutes and judgments. Lo! I am sending to you Elijah the prophet, before the coming of the great and terrible day of Jehovah. And he shall turn the heart of the fathers to the sons, and the heart of the sons to their fathers, ere I come and strike the land with the Ban."

"Malachi" makes this promise of the Law in the dialect of Deuteronomy: "statutes and judgments with which Jehovah charged Moses for Israel." But the Law he enforces is not that which God delivered to Moses on the plains of Shittim, but that which He gave him in Mount Horeb. And so it came to pass. In a very few years after "Malachi" prophesied Ezra the Scribe brought from Babylon the great Levitical Code, which appears to have been arranged there, while the colony in Jerusalem were still organising their life under Deuteronomic legislation. In 444 B. C. this Levitical Code, along with Deuteronomy, became by covenant between the people and their God their Canon and Law. And in the next of our prophets, Joel, we shall find its full influence at work.

JOEL.

"The Day of Jehovah is great and very awful, and who may abide it?

"But now the oracle of Jehovah—Turn ye to Me with all your heart, and with fasting and with weeping and with mourning. And rend your hearts and not your garments, and turn to Jehovah your God, for gracious and merciful is He, long-suffering and abounding in love."

CHAPTER XXVII.

THE BOOK OF JOEL.

In the criticism of the Book of Joel there exist differences of opinion—upon its date, the exact reference of its statements and its relation to parallel passages in other prophets—as wide as even those by which the Book of Obadiah has been assigned to every century between the tenth and the fourth before Christ.* As in the case of Obadiah, the problem is not entangled with any doctrinal issue or question of accuracy; but while we saw that Obadiah was not involved in the central controversy of the Old Testament, the date of the Law, not a little in Joel turns upon the latter. And besides, certain descriptions raise the large question between a literal and an allegorical interpretation. Thus the Book of Joel carries the student further into the problems of Old Testament Criticism, and forms an even more excellent introduction to the latter, than does the Book of Obadiah.

1. The Date of the Book.

In the history of prophecy the Book of Joel must be either very early or very late, and with few exceptions the leading critics place it either before 800 B. C. or after 500. So great a difference is due to most substantial reasons. Unlike every other prophet, except Haggai, "Malachi" and "Zechariah" ix.-xiv., Joel mentions neither Assyria, which emerged upon the prophetic horizon about 760,* nor the Babylonian Empire, which had fallen by 537. The presumption is that he wrote before 760 or after 537. Unlike all the prophets, too,† Joel does not charge his people with civic or national sins; nor does his book bear any trace of the struggle between the righteous and unrighteous in Israel nor of that between the spiritual worshippers of Jehovah and the idolaters. The book addresses an undivided nation, who know no God but Jehovah; and again the presumption is that Joel wrote before Amos and his successors had started the spiritual antagonisms which rent Israel in twain, or after the Law had been accepted by the whole people under Nehemiah.‡ The same wide alternative is suggested by the style and phraseology. Joel's Hebrew is simple and direct. Either he is an early writer, or imitates early writers. His book contains a number of phrases and verses identical, or nearly identical, with those of prophets from Amos to "Malachi." Either they all borrowed from Joel, or he borrowed from them.§

Of this alternative modern criticism at first preferred the earlier solution, and dated Joel before Amos. So Credner in his Commentary in 1831, and following him Hitzig, Bleek, Ewald, Delitzsch, Keil, Kuenen (up to 1864),‖ Pusey and others. So, too, at first some living critics of the first rank, who, like Kuenen, have since changed their opinion. And so, even still, Kirkpatrick (on the whole), Von Orelli, Robertson,¶ Stanley Leathes and Sinker.‡‡ The reasons which these scholars have given for the early date of Joel are roughly as follows.†† His book occurs among the earliest of the Twelve: while it is recognised that the order of these is not strictly chronological, it is alleged that there is a division between the pre-exilic and post-exilic prophets, and that Joel is found among the former. The vagueness of his representations in general, and of his pictures of the Day of Jehovah in particular, is attributed to the simplicity of the earlier religion of Israel, and to the want of that analysis of its leading conceptions which was the work of later prophets.‡‡ His horror of the interruption of the daily offerings in the Temple, caused by the plague of locusts,§§ is ascribed to a fear which pervaded the primitive ages of all peoples.‖‖ In Joel's attitude towards other nations, whom he condemns to judgment, Ewald saw "the old unsubdued warlike spirit of the times of Deborah and David." The prophet's absorption in the ravages of the locusts is held to reflect the feeling of a purely agricultural community, such as Israel was before the eighth century. The absence of the name of Assyria from the book is assigned to the same unwillingness to give

* See above, chap. xiii.

* The Assyria of "Zech." x. 11 is Syria. See below.

† The two exceptions, Nahum and Habakkuk, are not relevant to this question. Their dates are fixed by their references to Assyria and Babylon.

‡ See Rob. Smith, art. "Joel," "Encyc. Brit."

§ So obvious is this alternative that all critics may be said to grant it, except König ("Einl."), on whose reasons for placing Joel in the end of the seventh century see below, p. 654, *n.* Kessner ("Das Zeitalter der Proph. Joel" (1888) deems the date unprovable.

‖ See "The Religion of Israel," Vol. I., pp. 86 f.

¶ The "O. T. and its Contents," p. 105.

** "Lex Mosaica," pp. 422, 450.

†† See especially Ewald on Joel in his "Prophets of the O. T.," and Kirkpatrick's very fair argument in "Doctrine of the Prophets," pp. 57 ff.

‡‡ On Joel's picture of the Day of Jehovah Ewald says: "We have it here in its first simple and clear form, nor has it become a subject of ridicule as in Amos."

§§ i. 9, 13, 16, ii. 14.

‖‖ So Ewald.

the name as we see in Amos and the earlier prophecies of Isaiah, and it is thought by some that, though not named, the Assyrians are symbolised by the locusts. The absence of all mention of the Law is also held by some to prove an early date: though other critics, who believe that the Levitical legislation was extant in Israel from the earliest times, find proof of this in Joel's insistence upon the daily offering. The absence of all mention of a king and the prominence given to the priests are explained by assigning the prophecy to the minority of King Joash of Judah, when Jehoyada the priest was regent; * the charge against Egypt and Edom of spilling innocent blood by Shishak's invasion of Judah,† and by the revolt of the Edomites under Jehoram;‡ the charge against the Philistines and Phœnicians by the Chronicler's account of Philistine raids§ in the reign of Jehoram of Judah, and by the oracles of Amos against both nations;‖ and the mention of the Vale of Jehoshaphat by that king's defeat of Moab, Ammon, and Edom in the Vale of Berakhah.¶ These allusions being recognised, it was deduced from them that the parallels between Joel and Amos were due to Amos having quoted from Joel.**

These reasons are not all equally cogent,†† and even the strongest of them do not prove more than the possibility of an early date for Joel.‡‡ Nor do they meet every historical difficulty. The minority of Joash, upon which they converge, fell at a time when Aram was not only prominent to the thoughts of Israel, but had already been felt to be an enemy as powerful as the Philistines or Edomites. But the Book of Joel does not mention Aram. It mentions the Greeks,§§ and, although we have no right to say that such a notice was impossible in Israel in the ninth century, it was not only improbable, but no other Hebrew document from before the Exile speaks of Greece, and in particular Amos does not when describing the Phœnicians as slave-traders.‖‖ The argument that the Book of Joel must be early because it was placed among the first six of the Twelve Prophets by the arrangers of the Prophetic Canon, who could not have forgotten Joel's date had he lived after 450, loses all force from the fact that in the same group of pre-exilic prophets we find the exilic Obadiah and the post-exilic Jonah, both of them in precedence to Micah.

The argument for the early date of Joel is, therefore, not conclusive. But there are besides serious objections to it, which make for the other solution of the alternative we started from, and lead us to place Joel after the establishment of the Law by Ezra and Nehemiah in 444 B. C.

A post-exilic date was first proposed by Vatke,¶¶ and then defended by Hilgenfeld,*** and by Duhm in 1875.* From this time the theory made rapid way, winning over many who had previously held the early date of Joel, like Oort,† Kuenen,‡ A. B. Davidson,§ Driver and Cheyne,‖ perhaps also Wellhausen,¶ and finding acceptance and new proofs from a gradually increasing majority of younger critics, Merx,** Robertson Smith,†† Stade,‡‡ Matthes and Scholz,§§ Holzinger,‖‖ Farrar,¶¶ Kautzsch,*** Cornill,††† Wildeboer,‡‡‡ G. B. Gray §§§ and Nowack.‖‖‖ The reasons which have led to this formidable change of opinion in favour of the late date of the Book of Joel are as follows.

In the first place, the Exile of Judah appears in it as already past. This is proved, not by the ambiguous phrase, "when I shall bring again the captivity of Judah and Jerusalem," ¶¶¶ but by the plain statement that "the heathen have scattered Israel among the nations and divided their land. **** The plunder of the Temple seems also to be implied. †††† Moreover, no great world-power is pictured as either threatening or actually persecuting God's people; but Israel's active enemies and enslavers are represented as her own neighbours, Edomites, Philistines and Phœnicians, and the last are represented as selling Jewish captives to the Greeks. All this suits, if it does not absolutely prove, the Persian age, before the reign of Artaxerxes Ochus, who was the first Persian king to treat the Jews with cruelty.‡‡‡‡ The Greeks, Javan, do not appear in any Hebrew writer before the Exile;§§§§ the form in which their name is given by Joel, B'ne ha-Jevanim, has admittedly a late sound about it, ‖‖‖‖ and we know from other sources that it was in the fifth and fourth centuries that Syrian slaves were in demand in Greece. ¶¶¶¶ Similarly with the internal condition of the Jews as reflected in Joel. No

* 2 Kings xi. 4-21.

† 1 Kings xiv. 25, f.: *cf.* Joel iii. 17*b*, 19.

‡ 2 Kings viii. 20-22 : *cf.* Joel iii. 19.

§ 2 Chron. xxi. 16, 17, xxii. 1 : *cf.* Joel iii. 4-6.

‖ Amos i.: *cf.* Joel iii. 4-6.

¶ 2 Chron. xx., especially 26 : *cf.* Joel iii. 2.

** Joel iii. (Eng.; iv. Heb.) 16 ; Amos i. 2. For a list of the various periods to which Joel has been assigned by supporters of this early date see Kuenen, § 68.

†† The reference of Egypt in iii. 19 to Shishak's invasion appears particularly weak.

‡‡ *Cf.* Robertson, "O. T. and its Contents," 105, and Kirkpatrick's cautious, though convinced, statement of the reasons for an early date.

§§ iii. 6 (Heb. iv. 6).

‖‖ Amos i. 9.

¶¶ "Bibl. Theol.," I. p. 462 ; "Einl.," pp. 675 ff.

*** "Zeitschr. f. wissensch. Theol.," X., Heft 4.

* "Theol. der Proph.," pp. 275 ff.

† "Theol. Tijd.," 1876, pp. 362 ff. (not seen).

‡ "Onderz.," § 68.

§ *Expositor*, 1888, Jan.-June, pp. 198 ff.

‖ See Cheyne, "Origin of Psalter," xx.; Driver, "Introd.," in the sixth edition of which, 1897, he supports the late date of Joel more strongly than in the first edition, 1892.

¶ Wellhausen allowed the theory of the early date of Joel to stand in his edition of Bleek's "Einleitung," but adopts the late date in his own "Kleine Propheten."

** "Die Prophetie des Joels u. ihre Ausleger," 1879.

†† "Encyc. Brit.," art. "Joel," 1881.

‡‡ "Gesch.," II. 207.

§§ "Theol. Tijdschr.," 1885, p. 151 ; "Comm.," 1885 (neither seen).

‖‖ "Sprachcharakter u. Abfassungszeit des B. Joels" in "Z. A. T. W.," 1889, pp. 89 ff.

¶¶ "Minor Prophets."

*** "Bibel."

††† "Einleit."

‡‡‡ "Litteratur des A. T."

§§§ *Expositor*, September, 1893.

‖‖‖ "Comm.," 1897.

¶¶¶ iv. (Heb.; iii. Eng.) 1. For this may only mean "turn again the fortunes of Judah and Jerusalem."

**** iv. (Heb.; iii. Eng.) 2. The supporters of a pre-exilic date either passed this over or understood it of incursions by the heathen into Israel's territories in the ninth century. It is, however, too universal to suit these.

†††† iv. (Heb.; iii. Eng.) 5.

‡‡‡‡ Kautzsch dates after Artaxerxes Ochus, and *c.* 350.

§§§§ Ezekiel (xxvii. 13, 19) is the first to give the name Javan, *i. e.*, ΙαϝωνPor Ionian (earlier writers name Egypt, Edom, Arabia, and Phœnicia as the great slave-markets: Amos i.; Isa. xi. 11; Deut. xxviii. 68) ; and Greeks are also mentioned in Isa. lxvi. 19 (a post-exilic passage); Zech. ix. 13 ; Dan. viii. 21, x. 20, xi. 2 ; 1 Chron. i. 5, 7, and Gen. x. 2. See below, chap. xxxi.

‖‖‖‖ בני היונים instead of בני יון, just as the Chronicler gives בני הקרחים for בני קרח : see Wildeboer, p. 348, and Matthes, quoted by Holzinger, p. 94.

¶¶¶¶ Movers, "Phön. Alterthum.," II. 1, pp. 70 *sqq.*: which reference I owe to R. Smith's art. in the "Encyc. Brit."

king is mentioned; but the priests are prominent, and the elders are introduced at least once.* It is an agricultural calamity, and that alone, unmixed with any political alarm, which is the omen of the coming Day of the Lord. All this suits the state of Jerusalem under the Persians. Take again the religious temper and emphasis of the book. The latter is laid, as we have seen, very remarkably upon the horror of the interruption by the plague of locusts of the daily meal and drink offerings, and in the later history of Israel the proofs are many of the exceeding importance with which the regularity of this was regarded.† This, says Professor A. B. Davidson, "is very unlike the way in which all other prophets down to Jeremiah speak of the sacrificial service." The priests, too, are called to take the initiative; and the summons to a solemn and formal fast, without any notice of the particular sins of the people or exhortations to distinct virtues, contrasts with the attitude to fasts of the earlier prophets, and with their insistence upon a change of life as the only acceptable form of penitence.‡ And another contrast with the earliest prophets is seen in the general apocalyptic atmosphere and colouring of the Book of Joel, as well as in some of the particular figures in which this is expressed, and which are derived from later prophets like Zephaniah and Ezekiel.§

These evidences for a late date are supported, on the whole, by the language of the book. Of this Merx furnishes many details, and by a careful examination, which makes due allowance for the poetic form of the book and for possible glosses, Holzinger has shown that there are symptoms in vocabulary, grammar, and syntax which at least are more reconcilable with a late than with an early date.‖ There are a number of Aramaic words, of Hebrew words used in the sense in which they are used by Aramaic, but by no other Hebrew, writers, and several terms and constructions which appear only in the later books of the Old Testament or very seldom in the early ones.¶ It is true that these do not stand in a large proportion to the rest of Joel's vocabulary and grammar, which is classic and suitable to an early period of the literature; but this may be accounted for by the large use which the prophet makes of the very words of earlier writers. Take this large use into account, and the unmistakable Aramaisms of the book become even more emphatic in their proof of a late date.

The literary parallels between Joel and other writers are unusually many for so small a book. They number at least twenty in seventy-two verses. The other books of the Old Testament in which they occur are about twelve. Where one writer has parallels with many, we do not necessarily conclude that he is the borrower, unless we find that some of the phrases common to both are characteristic of the other writers, or that, in his text of them, there are differences from theirs which may reasonably be reckoned to be of a later origin. But that both of these conditions are found in the parallels between Joel and other prophets has been shown by Prof. Driver and Mr. G. B. Gray. "Several of the parallels—either in their entirety or by virtue of certain words which they contain—have their affinities solely or chiefly in the later writings. But the significance [of this] is increased when the very difference between a passage in Joel and its parallel in another book consists in a word or phrase characteristic of the later centuries. That a passage in a writer of the ninth century should differ from its parallel in a subsequent writer by the presence of a word elsewhere confined to the later literature would be strange; a single instance would not, indeed, be inexplicable in view of the scantiness of extant writings; but every additional instance—though itself not very convincing—renders the strangeness greater." And again, "the variations in some of the parallels as found in Joel have other common peculiarities. This also finds its natural explanation in the fact that Joel quotes: for that the *same* author even when quoting from different sources should quote with variations of the same character is natural, but that *different* authors quoting from a common source should follow the same method of quotation is improbable." * "While in some of the parallels a comparison discloses indications that the phrase in Joel is probably the later, in other cases, even though the expression may in itself be met with earlier, it becomes frequent only in a later age, and the use of it by Joel increases the presump-

* With these might be taken the use of קהל (ii. 16) in its sense of a gathering for public worship. The word itself was old in Hebrew, but as time went on it came more and more to mean the convocation of the nation for worship or deliberation. Holzinger, pp. 105 f.

† *Cf.* Neh. x. 33; Dan. viii. 11, xi. 31, xii. 11. Also Acts xxvi. 7: τὸ δωδεκάφυλον ἡμῶν ἐν ἐκτενεία νύκτα καὶ ἡμέραν λατρεύον. Also the passages in Jos., XIV. "Ant." iv. 3, xvi. 2, in which Josephus mentions the horror caused by the interruption of the daily sacrifice by famine in the last siege of Jerusalem, and adds that it had happened in no previous siege of the city.

‡ *Cf.* Jer. xiv. 12; Isa. lviii. 6; Zech. vii. 5, vi. 11, 19, with Neh. i. 4, ix. 1; Ezra viii. 21; Jonah iii. 5, 7; Esther iv. 3, 16, ix. 31; Dan. ix. 3.

§ The gathering of the Gentiles to judgment, Zeph. iii. 8 (see above, p. 577) and Ezek. xxxviii. 22; the steam issuing from the Temple to fill the Wady ha-Shittim, Ezek. xlvii. 1 ff., *cf.* Zech. xiv. 8; the outpouring of the Spirit, Ezek. xxxix. 29.

‖ "Z. A. T. W.," 1889, pp. 89–136. Holzinger's own conclusion is stated more emphatically than above.

¶ For an exhaustive list the reader must be referred to Holzinger's article (*cf.* Driver, "Introd.," sixth edition; "Joel and Amos," p. 24; G. B. Gray, *Expositor*, September, 1893, p. 212). But the following (a few of which are not given by Holzinger) are sufficient to prove the conclusion come to above: i. 2, iv. 4, הֲ . . . וְאִם—this is the form of the disjunctive interrogative in later O. T. writings, replacing the earlier הֲ . . . אִם; i. 8, אלי only here in O. T., but frequent in Aram.; 13, נמנע in Ni. only from Jeremiah onwards, Qal only in two passages before Jeremiah and in a number after him; 18, נאנחה, if the correct reading occurs only in the latest O. T. writings, the Qal only in these and Aram.; ii. 2, iv. (Heb.; iii. Eng.) 20, דור ודור first in Deut. xxxii. 7, and then exilic and post-exilic frequently; 8, שלח, a late word, only in Job xxxiii. 18, xxxvi. 12, 2 Chron. xxiii. 10, xxxii. 5, Neh. iii. 15, iv. 11, 17; 20, סוֹף, "end," only in 2 Chron. xx. 16 and Eccles., Aram. of Daniel, and post Bibl. Aram. and Heb.; iv. (Heb.; iii. Eng.) 4, גמל על, *cf.* 2 Chron. xx. 11; 10, רמח, see below on this verse; 11, הנחת, Aram.; 13 בשל, in Hebrew to cook (*cf.* Ezek. xxiv. 5), and in other forms always with that meaning down to the Priestly Writing and "Zech." ix.–xiv., is used here in the sense of "ripen," which is frequent in Aram., but does not occur elsewhere in O. T. Besides, Joel uses for the first personal pronoun אני—ii. 27 (*bis*), iv. 10, 17—which is by far the most usual form with later writers, and not אנכי, preferred by pre-exilic writers. (See below on the language of Jonah.)

* G. B. Gray, *Expositor*, September, 1893, pp. 213 f. For the above conclusions ample proof is given in Mr. Gray's detailed examination of the parallels: pp. 214 ff.

tion that he stands by the side of the later writers." *

In face of so many converging lines of evidence, we shall not wonder that there should have come about so great a change in the opinion of the majority of critics on the date of Joel, and that it should now be assigned by them to a post-exilic date. Some place it in the sixth century before Christ,† some in the first half of the fifth before "Malachi" and Nehemiah,‡ but the most after the full establishment of the Law by Ezra and Nehemiah in 444 B. C.§ It is difficult, perhaps impossible, to decide. Nothing certain can be deduced from the mention of the "city wall" in chap. ii. 9, from which Robertson Smith and Cornill infer that Nehemiah's walls were already built. Nor can we be sure that Joel quotes the phrase, "before the great and terrible day of Jehovah come," from "Malachi,"‖ although this is rendered probable by the character of Joel's other parallels. But the absence of all reference to the prophets as a class, the promise of the rigorous exclusion of foreigners from Jerusalem,¶ the condemnation to judgment of all the heathen, and the strong apocalyptic character of the book, would incline us to place it after Ezra rather than before. How far after, it is impossible to say, but the absence of feeling against Persia requires a date before the cruelties inflicted by Artaxerxes about 360.**

One solution, which has lately been offered for the problems of date presented by the Book of Joel, deserves some notice. In his German translation of Driver's "Introduction to the Old Testament," †† Rothstein questions the integrity of the prophecy, and alleges reasons for dividing it into two sections. Chaps. i. and ii. (Heb.; i.-ii. 27 Eng.) he assigns to an early author, writing in the minority of King Joash, but chaps. iii. and iv. (Heb.; ii. 28-iii. Eng.) to a

* Driver, "Joel and Amos," p. 27.

† Scholz and Rosenzweig (not seen).

‡ Hilgenfeld, Duhm, Oort. Driver puts it "most safely shortly after Haggai and Zechariah i.-viii., *c.* 500 B. C."

§ Vernes, Robertson Smith, Kuenen, Matthes, Cornill, Nowack, etc.

‖ Joel iii. 4 (Heb.; Eng. ii. 31); "Mal." iv. 5.

¶ iii. (Eng.; iv. Heb.) 17.

** Perhaps this is the most convenient place to refer to König's proposal to place Joel in the last years of Josiah. Some of his arguments (*e. g.*, that Joel is placed among the first of the Twelve) we have already answered. He thinks that i. 17-20 suit the great drought in Josiah's reign (Jer. xiv. 2-6), that the nâme given to the locusts, הצפוני, ii. 20, is due to Jeremiah's enemy "from the north," and that the phrases "return with all your heart," ii. 12, and "return to Jehovah your God," 13, imply a period of apostasy. None of these conclusions is necessary. The absence of reference to the "high places" finds an analogy in Isa. i. 13; the מנחה is mentioned in Isa. i. 13: if Amos viii. 5 testifies to observance of the Sabbath, and Nahum ii. 1 to other festivals, who can say a pre-exilic prophet would not be interested in the meal and drink offerings? But surely no pre-exilic prophet would have so emphasised these as Joel has done. Nor is König's explanation of iv. 2 as of the Assyrian and Egyptian invasion of Judah so probable as that which refers the verse to the Babylonian exile. Nor are König's objections to a date after "Malachi" convincing. They are that a prophet near "Malachi's" time must have specified as "Malachi" did the reasons for the repentance to which he summoned the people, while Joel gives none, but is quite general (ii. 13*a*). But the change of attitude may be accounted for by the covenant and Law of 444. "Malachi" i. 11 speaks of the Gentiles worshipping Jehovah, but not even in Jonah iii. 5 is any relation of the Gentiles to Jehovah predicated. Again, the greater exclusiveness of Ezra and his Law may be the cause. Joel, it is true, as König says, does not mention the Law, while "Malachi" does (ii. 8, etc.); but this was not necessary if the people had accepted it in 444. Professor Ryle (Canon of O. T., 106 n.) leaves the question of Joel's date open.

†† Pages 640 f. *n*.

date after the Exile, while ii. 20, which, it will be remembered, Robertson Smith takes as a gloss, he attributes to the editor who has joined the two sections together. His reasons are that chaps. i. and ii. are entirely taken up with the physical plague of locusts, and no troubles from heathen are mentioned; while chaps. iii. and iv. say nothing of a physical plague, but the evils they deplore for Israel are entirely political, the assaults of enemies. Now it is quite within the bounds of possibility that chaps. iii. and iv. are from another hand than chaps. i. and ii.: we have nothing to disprove that. But, on the other hand, there is nothing to prove it. On the contrary, the possibility of all four chapters being from the same hand is very obvious. Joel mentions no heathen in the first chapter, because he is engrossed with the plague of locusts. But when this has passed, it is quite natural that he should take up the standing problem of Israel's history—their relation to heathen peoples. There is no discrepancy between the two different subjects, nor between the styles in which they are respectively treated. Rothstein's arguments for an early date for chaps. i. and ii. have been already answered, and when we come to the exposition of them we shall find still stronger reasons for assigning them to the end of the fifth century before Christ. The assault on the integrity of the prophecy may therefore be said to have failed, though no one who remembers the composite character of the prophetical books can deny that the question is still open.*

2. The Interpretation of the Book: Is it Description, Allegory, or Apocalypse?

Another question to which we must address ourselves before we can pass to the exposition of Joel's prophecies is of the attitude and intention of the prophet. Does he describe or predict? Does he give history or allegory?

Joel starts from a great plague of locusts, which he describes not only in the ravages they commit upon the land, but in their ominous foreshadowing of the Day of the Lord. They are the heralds of God's near judgment upon the nation. Let the latter repent instantly with a day of fasting and prayer. Peradventure Jehovah will relent, and spare His people. So far chap. i. 2-ii. 17. Then comes a break. An uncertain interval appears to elapse; and in chap. ii. 18 we are told that Jehovah's zeal for Israel has been stirred, and He has had pity on His folk. Promises follow, *first*, of deliverance from the plague and of restoration of the harvests it has consumed, and *second*, of the outpouring of the Spirit on all classes of the community: chap. ii. 17-32 (Eng.; ii. 17-iii. Heb.). Chap. iii. (Eng.; iv. Heb.) gives another picture of the Day of Jehovah, this time described as a judgment upon the heathen enemies of Israel. They shall be brought together, condemned judicially by Him, and slain by His hosts, His "supernatural" hosts. Jerusalem shall be freed from

* Vernes, "Histoire des Idées Messianiques depuis Alexandre," pp. 13 ff., had already asserted that chaps. i. and ii. must be by a different author from chaps. iii and iv., because the former has to do wholly with the writer's present, with which the latter has no connection whatever, but it is entirely eschatological. But in his "Mélanges de Crit. Relig., pp. 218 ff., Vernes allows that his arguments are not conclusive, and that all four chapters may have come from the same hand.

the feet of strangers, and the fertility of the land restored.

These are the contents of the book. Do they describe an actual plague of locusts, already experienced by the people? Or do they predict this as still to come? And again, are the locusts which they describe real locusts, or a symbol and allegory of the human foes of Israel? To these two questions, which in a measure cross and involve each other, three kinds of answer have been given.

A large and growing majority of critics of all schools * hold that Joel starts, like other prophets, from the facts of experience. His locusts, though described with poetic hyperbole—for are they not the vanguard of the awful Day of God's judgment?—are real locusts; their plague has just been felt by his contemporaries, whom he summons to repent, and to whom, when they have repented, he brings promises of the restoration of their ruined harvests, the outpouring of the Spirit, and judgment upon their foes. Prediction is therefore found only in the second half of the book (ii. 18 onwards): it rests upon a basis of narrative and exhortation which fills the first half.

But a number of other critics have argued (and with great force) that the prophet's language about the locusts is too aggravated and too ominous to be limited to the natural plague which these insects periodically inflicted upon Palestine. Joel (they reason) would hardly have connected so common an adversity with so singular and ultimate a crisis as the Day of the Lord. Under the figure of locusts he must be describing some more fateful agency of God's wrath upon Israel. More than one trait of his description appears to imply a human army. It can only be one or other, or all, of those heathen powers whom at different periods God raised up to chastise His delinquent people; and this opinion is held to be supported by the facts that chap. ii. 20 speaks of them as the Northern and chap. iii. (Eng.; iv. Heb.) deals with the heathen. The locusts of chaps. i. and ii. are the same as the heathen of chap. iii. In chaps. i. and ii. they are described as threatening Israel, but on condition of Israel repenting (chap. ii. 18 ff.) the Day of the Lord which they herald shall be their destruction and not Israel's (chap. iii.).†

The supporters of this allegorical interpretation of Joel are, however, divided among themselves as to whether the heathen powers symbolised by the locusts are described as having already afflicted Israel or are predicted as still to come. Hilgenfeld,‡ for instance, says that the prophet in chaps. i. and ii. speaks of their ravages as already past. To him their fourfold plague described in chap. i. 4 symbolises four Persian assaults upon Palestine, after the last of which in 358 the prophecy must therefore have been written.§ Others read them as still to come. In our own country Pusey has been the strongest supporter of this theory.‖ To him the whole book, written before Amos, is prediction. "It extends from the prophet's own day to the end of time." Joel calls the scourge the Northern: he directs the priests to pray for its removal, that "the heathen may not rule over" God's heritage; * he describes the agent as a responsible one; † his imagery goes far beyond the effects of locusts, and threatens drought, fire, and plague, ‡ the assault of cities and the terrifying of peoples.§ The scourge is to be destroyed in a way physically inapplicable to locusts; ‖ and the promises of its removal include the remedy of ravages which mere locusts could not inflict: the captivity of Judah is to be turned, and the land recovered from foreigners who are to be banished from it.¶ Pusey thus reckons as future the relenting of God, consequent upon the people's penitence: chap. ii. 18 ff. The past tenses in which it is related, he takes as instances of the well-known prophetic perfect, according to which the prophets express their assurance of things to come by describing them as if they had already happened.

This is undoubtedly a strong case for the predictive and allegorical character of the Book of Joel; but a little consideration will show us that the facts on which it is grounded are capable of a different explanation than that which it assumes, and that Pusey has overlooked a number of other facts which force us to a literal interpretation of the locusts as a plague already past, even though we feel they are described in the language of poetical hyperbole.

For, in the first place, Pusey's theory implies that the prophecy is addressed to a future generation, who shall be alive when the predicted invasions of heathen come upon the land. Whereas Joel obviously addresses his own contemporaries. The prophet and his hearers are one. "Before our eyes," he says, "the food has been cut off." ** As obviously, he speaks of the plague of locusts as of something that has just happened. His hearers can compare its effects with past disasters, which it has far exceeded;†† and it is their duty to hand down the story of it to future generations.‡‡ Again, his description is that of a physical, not of a political, plague. Fields and gardens, vines and figs, are devastated by being stripped and gnawed. Drought accompanies the locusts, the seed shrivels beneath the clods, the trees languish, the cattle pant for want of water.§§ These are not the trail which an invading army leave behind them. In support of his theory that human hosts are meant, Pusey points to the verses which bid the people pray "that the heathen rule not over them," and which describe the invaders as attacking cities.‖‖ But the former phrase may be rendered with equal propriety, "that the heathen make not satirical songs about them"; ¶¶ and as to the latter, not only do locusts invade towns exactly as Joel describes, but his words that the invader steals into houses like "a thief" are far more applicable to the insidious entrance of locusts than to the bold and noisy assault of a storming party. Moreover Pusey and the other allegorical interpreters of the book overlook the fact that Joel never so much as hints at the invariable

* *I. e.*, Hitzig, Vatke, Ewald, Robertson Smith, Kuenen, Kirkpatrick, Driver, Davidson, Nowack, etc.

† This allegorical interpretation was a favourite one with the early Christian Fathers: *cf.* Jerome.

‡ "Zeitschr. für wissensch. Theologie," 1860, pp. 412 ff.

§ Cambyses 525, Xerxes 484, Artaxerxes Ochus 460 and 458.

‖ In Germany, among other representatives of this opinion, are Bertholdt ("Einl.") and Hengstenberg ("Christol." III. 352 ff.) the latter of whom saw in the four kinds of locusts the Assyrian-Babylonian, the Persian, the Greek, and the Roman tyrants of Israel.

* ii. 17.

† ii. 20.

‡ i. 19, 20.

§ Plur. ii. 6.

‖ ii. 20.

¶ iii. (Heb. iv.) 1 f., 17.

** i. 16.

†† i. 2 f.

‡‡ i. 3.

§§ i. 17.

‖‖ ii. 17, ii. 9 ff.

¶¶ למשל בם.

effects of a human invasion, massacre, and plunder. He describes no slaying and no looting; but when he comes to the promise that Jehovah will restore the losses which have been sustained by His people, he defines them as the years which His army has *eaten.** But all this proof is clenched by the fact that Joel compares the locusts to actual soldiers.† They are *like* horsemen, the sound of them is *like* chariots, they run *like* horses, and *like* men of war they leap upon the wall. Joel could never have compared a real army to itself!

The allegorical interpretation is therefore untenable. But some critics, while admitting this, are yet not disposed to take the first part of the book for narrative. They admit that the prophet means a plague of locusts, but they deny that he is speaking of a plague already past, and hold that his locusts are still to come, that they are as much a part of the future as the pouring out of the Spirit‡ and the judgment of the heathen in the Valley of Jehoshaphat.§ All alike, they are signs or accompaniments of the Day of Jehovah, and that Day has still to break. The prophet's scenery is apocalyptic; the locusts are "eschatological locusts," not historical ones. This interpretation of Joel has been elaborated by Dr. Adalbert Merx, and the following is a summary of his opinions.‖

After examining the book along all the lines of exposition which have been proposed, Merx finds himself unable to trace any plan or even sign of a plan; and his only escape from perplexity is the belief that no plan can ever have been meant by the author. Joel weaves in one past, present, and future, paints situations only to blot them out and put others in their place, starts many processes but develops none. His book shows no insight into God's plan with Israel, but is purely external; the bearing and the end of it is the material prosperity of the little land of Judah. From this Merx concludes that the book is not an original work, but a mere summary of passages from previous prophets, that with a few reflections of the life of the Jews after the Return lead us to assign it to that period of literary culture which Nehemiah inaugurated by the collection of national writings and which was favoured by the cessation of all political disturbance. Joel gathered up the pictures of the Messianic age in the older prophets, and welded them together in one long prayer by the fervid belief that that age was near. But while the older prophets spoke upon the ground of actual fact and rose from this to a majestic picture of the last punishment, the still life of Joel's time had nothing such to offer him and he had to seek another basis for his prophetic flight. It is probable that he sought this in the relation of Type and Antitype. The Antitype he found in the liberation from Egypt, the darkness and the locusts of which he transferred to his canvas from Exod. x. 4-6. The locusts, therefore, are neither real nor symbolic, but ideal. This is the method of the Midrash and Haggada in Jewish literature, which constantly placed over against each other the deliverance from Egypt and the last judgment. It is a method that is already found in such portions of the Old Testament as Ezek. xxxvii. and Psalm lxxviii. Joel's locusts are borrowed from the Egyptian plagues, but are presented as the signs of the Last Day. They will bring it near to Israel by famine, drought, and the interruption of worship described in chap. i. Chap. ii., which Merx keeps distinct from chap. i., is based on a study of Ezekiel, from whom Joel has borrowed, among other things, the expressions "the garden of Eden" and "the Northerner." The two verses generally held to be historic, 18 and 19, Merx takes to be the continuation of the prayer of the priests, pointing the verbs so as to turn them from perfects into futures.* The rest of the book, Merx strives to show, is pieced together from many prophets, chiefly Isaiah and Ezekiel, but without the tender spiritual feeling of the one, or the colossal magnificence of the other. Special nations are mentioned, but in this portion of the work we have to do not with events already past, but with general views, and these not original, but conditioned by the expressions of earlier writers. There is no history in the book: it is all ideal, mystical, apocalyptic. That is to say, according to Merx, there is no real prophet or prophetic fire, only an old man warming his feeble hands over a few embers that he has scraped together from the ashes of ancient fires, now nearly wholly dead.

Merx has traced Joel's relations to other prophets, and reflection of a late date in Israel's history, with care and ingenuity; but his treatment of the text and exegesis of the prophet's meaning are alike forced and fanciful. In face of the support which the Massoretic reading of the hinge of the book, chap. ii. 18 ff., receives from the ancient versions, and of its inherent probability and harmony with the context, Merx's textual emendation is unnecessary, besides being in itself unnatural.† While the very same objections which we have already found valid against the allegorical interpretation equally dispose of this mystical one. Merx outrages the evident features of the book almost as much as Hengstenberg and Pusey have done. He has lifted out of time altogether that which plainly purports to be historical. His literary criticism is as unsound as his textual. It is only by ignoring the beautiful poetry of chap. i. that he transplants it to the future. Joel's figures are too vivid, too actual, to be predictive or mystical. And the whole interpretation wrecks itself in the same verse as the allegorical, the verse, viz., in which Joel plainly speaks of himself as having suffered with his hearers the plague he describes.‡

We may, therefore, with confidence conclude that the allegorical and mystical interpretations of Joel are impossible; and that the only reasonable view of our prophet is that which regards him as calling, in chap. i. 2-ii. 17, upon his contemporaries to repent in face of a plague of locusts, so unusually severe that he has felt it to be ominous of even the Day of the Lord; and in the rest of his book, as promising material,

* A. B. Davidson, *Expos.*, 1888, pp. 200 f.
† ii. 4 ff.
‡ Eng. ii. 28 ff., Heb. iii.
§ Eng. iii. Heb. iv.
‖ "Die Prophetie des Joel u. ihre Ausleger," 1879. The following summary and criticism of Merx's views I take from an (unpublished) review of his work which I wrote in 1881.

* For וַיְקַנֵּא, etc., he reads וִיקַנֵּא, etc.

† "The proposal of Merx, to change the pointing so as to transform the perfects into futures, . . . is an exegetical monstrosity."—Robertson Smith, art. "Joel," "Encyc. Brit."
‡ i. 16.

political and spiritual triumphs to Israel in consequence of their repentance, either already consummated, or anticipated by the prophet as certain.

It is true that the account of the locusts appears to bear features which conflict with the literal interpretation. Some of these, however, vanish upon a fuller knowlege of the awful degree which such a plague has been testified to reach by competent observers within our own era.* Those that remain may be attributed partly to the poetic hyperbole of Joel's style, and partly to the fact that he sees in the plague far more than itself. The locusts are signs of the Day of Jehovah. Joel treats them as we found Zephaniah treating the Scythian hordes of his day. They are as real as the latter, but on them as on the latter the lurid glare of Apocalypse has fallen, magnifying them and investing them with that air of ominousness which is the sole justification of the allegorical and mystic interpretation of their appearance.

To the same sense of their office as heralds of the last day, we owe the description of the locusts as "the Northerner."† The North is not the quarter from which locusts usually reach Palestine, nor is there any reason to suppose that by naming the North Joel meant only to emphasise the unusual character of these swarms. Rather he takes a name employed in Israel since Jeremiah's time to express the instruments of Jehovah's wrath in the day of His judgment of Israel. The name is typical of Doom, and therefore Joel applies it to his fateful locusts.

3. State of the Text and the Style of the Book.

Joel's style is fluent and clear, both when he is describing the locusts, in which part of his book he is most original, and when he is predicting, in apocalyptic language largely borrowed from earlier prophets, the Day of Jehovah. To the ease of understandng him we may attribute the sound state of the text and its freedom from glosses. In this, like most of the books of the post-exilic prophets, especially the Books of Haggai, "Malachi" and Jonah, Joel's book contrasts very favourably with those of the older prophets; and that also, to some degree, is proof of the lateness of his date. The Greek translators have, on the whole, understood Joel easily and with little error. In their version there are the usual differences of grammatical construction, especially in the pronominal suffixes and verbs, and of punctuation; but very few bits of expansion and no real additions. These are all noted in the translation below.

CHAPTER XXVIII.

THE LOCUSTS AND THE DAY OF THE LORD.

Joel i.-ii. 17.

Joel, as we have seen, found the motive of his prophecy in a recent plague of locusts, the appearance of which and the havoc they worked are described by him in full detail. Writing not only as a poet but as a seer, who reads in the locusts signs of the great Day of the Lord, Joel has necessarily put into his picture several features which carry the imagination beyond the limits of experience. And yet, if we ourselves had lived through such a plague, we should be able to recognise how little license the poet has taken, and that the seer, so far from unduly mixing with his facts the colours of Apocalypse, must have experienced in the terrible plague itself enough to provoke all the religious and monitory use which he makes of it.

The present writer has seen but one swarm of locusts, in which, though it was small and soon swept away by the wind, he felt not only many of the features that Joel describes, but even some degree of that singular helplessness before a calamity of portent far beyond itself, something of that supernatural edge and accent, which, by the confession of so many observers, characterise the locust-plague and the earthquake above all other physical disasters. One summer afternoon, upon the plain of Hauran, a long bank of mist grew rapidly from the western horizon. The day was dull, and as the mist rose athwart the sunbeams, struggling through clouds, it gleamed cold and white, like the front of a distant snow-storm. When it came near, it seemed to be more than a mile broad, and was dense enough to turn the atmosphere raw and dirty, with a chill as of a summer sea-fog, only that this was not due to any fall in the temperature. Nor was there the silence of a mist. We were enveloped by a noise, less like the whirring of wings than the rattle of hail or the crackling of bush on fire. Myriads upon myriads of locusts were about us, covering the ground, and shutting out the view in all directions. Though they drifted before the wind, there was no confusion in their ranks. They sailed in unbroken lines, sometimes straight, sometimes wavy; and when they passed pushing through our caravan, they left almost no stragglers, except from the last battalion, and only the few dead which we had caught in our hands. After several minutes they were again but a lustre on the air, and so melted away into some heavy clouds in the east.

Modern travellers furnish us with terrible impressions of the innumerable multitudes of a locust-plague, the succession of their swarms through days and weeks, and the utter desolation they leave behind them. Mr. Doughty writes: * "There hopped before our feet a minute brood of second locusts, of a leaden colour, with budding wings like the spring leaves, and born of those gay swarms which a few weeks before had passed over and despoiled the desert. After forty days these also would fly as a pestilence, yet more hungry than the former, and fill the atmosphere." And later: "The clouds of the second locust brood which the Aarab call 'Am'dan, 'pillars,' flew over us for some days, invaded the booths and for blind hunger even bit our shins."† It was "a storm of rustling wings."‡ "This year was remembered for the locust swarms and great summer heat."§ A traveller in South Africa‖ says: "For the space of ten miles on each side of the Sea-Cow river

* Even the comparison of the ravages of the locusts to burning by fire. But probably also Joel means that they were accompanied by drought and forest fires. See below.

† ii. 20.

* "Arabia Deserta," p. 307.

† "*Id.*," p. 355.

‡ *Id.*, 396.

§ *Id.*, 335.

‖ Barrow, "South Africa," p. 257, quoted by Pusey.

and eighty or ninety miles in length, an area of sixteen or eighteen hundred square miles, the whole surface might literally be said to be covered with them." In his recently published book on South Africa, Mr. Bryce writes:—*

"It is a strange sight, beautiful if you can forget the destruction it brings with it. The whole air, to twelve or even eighteen feet above the ground, is filled with the insects, reddish brown in body, with bright gauzy wings. When the sun's rays catch them it is like the sea sparkling with light. When you see them against a cloud they are like the dense flakes of a driving snow-storm. You feel as if you had never before realised immensity in number. Vast crowds of men gathered at a festival, countless tree-tops rising along the slope of a forest ridge, the chimneys of London houses from the top of St. Paul's—all are as nothing to the myriads of insects that blot out the sun above and cover the ground beneath and fill the air whichever way one looks. The breeze carries them swiftly past, but they come on in fresh clouds, a host of which there is no end, each of them a harmless creature which you can catch and crush in your hand, but appalling in their power of collective devastation."

And take three testimonies from Syria: "The quantity of these insects is a thing incredible to any one who has not seen it himself; the ground is covered by them for several leagues." † "The whole face of the mountain ‡ was black with them. On they came like a living deluge. We dug trenches and kindled fires, and beat and burnt to death heaps upon heaps, but the effort was utterly useless. They rolled up the mountain-side, and poured over rocks, walls, ditches, and hedges, those behind covering up and passing over the masses already killed. For some days they continued to pass. The noise made by them in marching and foraging was like that of a heavy shower falling upon a distant forest." § "The roads were covered with them, all marching and in regular lines, like armies of soldiers, with their leaders in front; and all the opposition of man to resist their progress was in vain." Having consumed the plantations in the country, they entered the towns and villages. "When they approached our garden all the farm servants were employed to keep them off, but to no avail; though our men broke their ranks for a moment, no sooner had they passed the men than they closed again, and marched forward through hedges and ditches as before. Our garden finished, they continued their march toward the town, devastating one garden after another. They have also penetrated into most of our rooms: whatever one is doing one hears their noise from without, like the noise of armed hosts, or the running of many waters. When in an erect position their appearance at a little distance is like that of a well-armed horseman." ‖

Locusts are notoriously adapted for a plague, "since to strength incredible for so small a creature, they add saw-like teeth, admirably calculated to eat up all the herbs in the land." * They are the incarnation of hunger. No voracity is like theirs, the voracity of little creatures, whose million separate appetites nothing is too minute to escape. They devour first grass and leaves, fruit and foliage, everything that is green and juicy. Then they attack the young branches of trees, and then the hard bark of the trunks. † "After eating up the corn, they fell upon the vines, the pulse, the willows, and even the hemp, notwithstanding its great bitterness." ‡ "The bark of figs, pomegranates, and oranges, bitter, hard, and corrosive, escaped not their voracity." § "They are particularly injurious to the palm-trees; these they strip of every leaf and green particle, the trees remaining like skeletons with bare branches." ‖ "For eighty or ninety miles they devoured every green herb and every blade of grass." ¶ "The gardens outside Jaffa are now completely stripped, even the bark of the young trees having been devoured, and look like a birch-tree forest in winter." ** "The bushes were eaten quite bare, though the animals could not have been long on the spot. They sat by hundreds on a bush gnawing the rind and the woody fibres." †† "Bamboo groves have been stripped of their leaves and left standing like saplings after a rapid bush fire, and grass has been devoured so that the bare ground appeared as if burned." ‡‡ "The country did not seem to be burnt, but to be much covered with snow through the whiteness of the trees and the dryness of the herbs." §§ The fields finished, they invade towns and houses, in search of stores. Victual of all kinds, hay, straw, and even linen and woollen clothes and leather bottles, they consume or tear in pieces.‖‖ They flood through the open, unglazed windows and lattices: nothing can keep them out.

These extracts prove to us what little need Joel had of hyperbole in order to read his locusts as signs of the Day of Jehovah; especially if we keep in mind that locusts are worst in very hot summers, and often accompany an absolute drought along with its consequence of prairie and forest fires. Some have thought that, in introducing the effects of fire, Joel only means to paint the burnt look of a land after locusts have ravaged it. But locusts do not drink up the streams, nor cause the seed to shrivel in the earth.¶¶ By these the prophet must mean drought, and by "the flame that has burned all the trees of the field," *** the forest fire, finding an easy prey in the trees which have been reduced to firewood by the locusts' teeth.

Even in the great passage in which he passes from history to Apocalypse, from the gloom and terror of the locusts to the lurid dawn of Je-

* "Impressions of South Africa," by James Bryce: Macmillans, 1897.

† Volney, "Voyage en Syrie," I. 277, quoted by Pusey.

‡ Lebanon.

§ Abridged from Thomson's "The Land and the Book," ed. 1877, Northern Palestine, pp. 416 ff.

‖ From Driver's abridgment ("Joel and Amos," p. 90) of an account in the *Journ. of Sac. Lit.*, October, 1865, pp. 235 f.

* Morier, "A Second Journey through Persia," p. 99, quoted by Pusey, from whose notes and Driver's excursus upon locusts in "Joel and Amos" the following quotations have been borrowed.

† Shaw's "Travels in Barbary," 1738, pp. 236–8; Jackson's "Travels to Morocco."

‡ Adansson, "Voyage au Senegal," p. 88.

§ Chénier, "Recherches Historiques sur les Maures," III. p. 496.

‖ Burckhardt, "Notes," II. 90.

¶ Barrow, "South Africa," p. 257.

** *Journ. of Sac. Lit.*, October, 1865.

†† Lichtenstein, "Travels in South Africa."

‡‡ *Standard*, December 25, 1896.

§§ Fr. Alvarez.

‖‖ Barheb., "Chron. Syr.," p. 784; Burckhardt, "Notes," II. 90.

¶¶ i. 20, 17.

*** i. 19.

hovah's Day, Joel keeps within the actual facts of experience:—

> "Day of darkness and murk,
> Day of cloud and heavy mist,
> Like dawn scattered on the mountains,
> A people many and powerful."

No one who has seen a cloud of locusts can question the realism even of this picture: the heavy gloom of the immeasurable mass of them, shot by gleams of light where a few of the sun's imprisoned beams have broken through or across the storm of lustrous wings. This is like dawn beaten down upon the hilltops, and crushed by rolling masses of cloud, in conspiracy to prolong the night. No: the only point at which Joel leaves absolute fact for the wilder combinations of Apocalypse is at the very close of his description, chap. ii. 10 and 11, and just before his call to repentance. Here we find, mixed with the locusts, earthquake and thunderstorm; and Joel has borrowed these from the classic pictures of the Day of the Lord, using some of the very phrases of the latter:—

> "Earth trembles before them,
> Heaven quakes,
> Sun and moon become black,
> The stars withdraw their shining,
> And Jehovah utters His voice before His army."

Joel, then, describes, and does not unduly enhance, the terrors of an actual plague. At first his whole strength is so bent to make his people feel these, that, though about to call to repentance, he does not detail the national sins which require it. In his opening verses he summons the drunkards,* but that is merely to lend vividness to his picture of facts, because men of such habits will be the first to feel a plague of this kind. Nor does Joel yet ask his hearers what the calamity portends. At first he only demands that they shall feel it, in its uniqueness and its own sheer force.

Hence the peculiar style of the passage. Letter for letter, this is one of the heaviest passages in prophecy. The proportion in Hebrew of liquids to the other letters is not large; but here it is smaller than ever. The explosives and dentals are very numerous. There are several key-words, with hard consonants and long vowels, used again and again: Shuddadh, 'ābhlah, 'umlal, hôbhish. The longer lines into which Hebrew parallelism tends to run are replaced by a rapid series of short, heavy phrases, falling like blows. Critics have called it rhetoric. But it is rhetoric of a very high order and perfectly suited to the prophet's purpose. Look at chap. i. 10: Shuddadh sadheh, 'ābhlah 'adhamah, shuddadh daghan, hôbhish tîrôsh, 'umlal yiṣhar.† Joel loads his clauses with the most leaden letters he can find, and drops them in quick succession, repeating the same heavy word again and again, as if he would stun the careless people into some sense of the bare, brutal weight of the calamity which has befallen them.

Now Joel does this because he believes that, if his people feel the plague in its proper violence, they must be convinced that it comes from Jehovah. The keynote of this part of the prophecy is found in chap. i. 15: "Keshôdh mishshaddhai," "like violence from the All-violent doth it come." "If you feel this as it is, you will feel Jehovah Himself in it. By these very blows, He and His Day are near. We had been forgetting how near." Joel mentions no crime, nor enforces any virtue: how could he have done so in so strong a sense that "the Judge was at the door"? To make men feel that they had forgotten they were in reach of that Almighty Hand, which could strike so suddenly and so hard—Joel had time only to make men feel that, and to call them to repentance. In this we probably see some reflection of the age: an age when men's thoughts were thrusting the Deity further and further from their life; when they put His Law and Temple between Him and themselves; and when their religion, devoid of the sense of His Presence, had become a set of formal observances, the rending of garments and not of hearts. But He, whom His own ordinances had hidden from His people, has burst forth through nature and in sheer force of calamity. He has revealed Himself, El-Shaddhai, "God All-violent," as He was known to their fathers, who had no elaborate law or ritual to put between their fearful hearts and His terrible strength, but cowered before Him, helpless on the stripped soil, and naked beneath His thunder. By just these means did Elijah and Amos bring God home to the hearts of ancient Israel. In Joel we see the revival of the old nature-religion, and the revenge that it was bound to take upon the elaborate systems which had displaced it, but which by their formalism and their artificial completeness had made men forget that near presence and direct action of the Almighty which it is nature's own office to enforce upon the heart.

The thing is true, and permanently valid. Only the great natural processes can break up the systems of dogma and ritual in which we make ourselves comfortable and formal, and drive us out into God's open air of reality. In the crash of nature's forces even our particular sins are forgotten, and we feel, as in the immediate presence of God, our whole, deep need of repentance. So far from blaming the absence of special ethics in Joel's sermon, we accept it as natural and proper to the occasion.

Such, then, appears to be the explanation of the first part of the prophecy, and its development towards the call to repentance, which follows it. If we are correct, the assertion * is false that no plan was meant by the prophet. For not only is there a plan, but the plan is most suitable to the requirements of Israel, after their adoption of the whole Law in 445, and forms one of the most necessary and interesting developments of all religion: the revival, in an artificial period, of those primitive forces of religion which nature alone supplies, and which are needed to correct formalism and the forgetfulness of the near presence of the Almighty. We see in this, too, the reason of Joel's archaic style, both of conception and expression: that likeness of his to early prophets which has led so many to place him between Elijah and Amos.† They are wrong. Joel's simplicity is that not of early prophecy, but of the austere forces of this revived and applied to the artificiality of a later age.

One other proof of Joel's conviction of the religious meaning of the plague might also have been pled by the earlier prophets, but certainly not in the terms in which Joel expresses it. Amos and Hosea had both described the de-

* i. 5. † *Cf.* i. 12, 13, and many verses in chap. ii.

* On Merx and others: see above, p. 656.
† See above, p. 651.

struction of the country's fertility in their day as God's displeasure on His people and (as Hosea puts it) His divorce of His Bride from Himself.* But by them the physical calamities were not threatened alone: banishment from the land and from enjoyment of its fruits was to follow upon drought, locusts, and famine. In threatening no captivity Joel differs entirely from the early prophets. It is a mark of his late date. And he also describes the divorce between Jehovah and Israel, through the interruption of the ritual by the plague, in terms and with an accent which could hardly have been employed in Israel before the Exile. After the rebuilding of the Temple and restoration of the daily sacrifices morning and evening, the regular performance of the latter was regarded by the Jews with a most superstitious sense of its indispensableness to the national life. Before the Exile, Jeremiah, for instance, attaches no importance to it, in circumstances in which it would have been not unnatural for him, priest as he was, to do so.† But after the Exile, the greater scrupulousness of the religious life, and its absorption in ritual, laid extraordinary emphasis upon the daily offering, which increased to a most painful degree of anxiety as the centuries went on.‡ The New Testament speaks of "the Twelve Tribes constantly serving God day and night"; § and Josephus, while declaring that in no siege of Jerusalem before the last did the interruption ever take place in spite of the stress of famine and war combined, records the awful impression made alike on Jew and heathen by the giving up of the daily sacrifice on the 17th of July, A. D. 70, during the investment of the city by Titus.‖ This disaster, which Judaism so painfully feared at every crisis in its history, actually happened, Joel tells us, during the famine caused by the locusts. "Cut off are the meal and the drink offerings from the house of Jehovah.¶ Is not food cut off from our eyes, joy and gladness from the house of our God? ** Perhaps He will turn and relent, and leave a blessing behind Him, meal and drink offering for Jehovah our God." †† The break "of the continual symbol of gracious intercourse between Jehovah and His people, and the main office of religion," means divorce between Jehovah and Israel. "Wail like a bride girt in sackcloth for the husband of her youth! Wail, O ministers of the altar, O ministers of God!" ‡‡ This then was another reason for reading in the plague of locusts more than a physical meaning. This was another proof, only too intelligible to scrupulous Jews, that the great and terrible Day of the Lord was at hand.

Thus Joel reaches the climax of his argument. Jehovah is near, His Day is about to break. From this it is impossible to escape on the narrow path of disaster by which the prophet has led up to it. But beneath that path the prophet passes the ground of a broad truth, and on that truth, while judgment remains still as real, there is room for the people to turn from it. If experience has shown that God is in the present, near and inevitable, faith remembers that He is there not willingly for judgment, but with all His ancient feeling for Israel and His zeal to save her. If the people choose to turn, Jehovah, as their God and as one who works for their sake, will save them. Of this God assures them by His own word. For the first time in the prophecy He speaks for Himself. Hitherto the prophet has been describing the plague and summoning to penitence. "But now oracle of Jehovah of Hosts." * The great covenant name, "Jehovah your God," is solemnly repeated as if symbolic of the historic origin and age-long endurance of Jehovah's relation to Israel; and the very words of blessing are repeated which were given when Israel was called at Sinai and the covenant ratified:—

"For He is gracious and merciful,
Long-suffering and plenteous in leal love.
And relents Him of the evil"

He has threatened upon you. Once more the nation is summoned to try Him by prayer: the solemn prayer of all Israel, pleading that He should not give His people to reproach.

"The Word of Jehovah
which came to Jo'el the son of Pethû'el.†
Hear this, ye old men,
And give ear, all inhabitants of the land!
Has the like been in your days,
Or in the days of your fathers?
Tell it to your children,
And your children to their children,
And their children to the generation that follows.
That which the Shearer left the Swarmer hath eaten,
And that which the Swarmer left the Lapper hath eaten,
And that which the Lapper left the Devourer hath eaten."

These are four different names for locusts, which it is best to translate by their literal meaning. Some think that they represent one swarm of locusts in four stages of development, but this cannot be, because the same swarm never returns upon its path, to complete the work of destruction which it had begun in an earlier stage of its growth. Nor can the first-named be the adult brood from whose eggs the others spring, as Doughty has described,‡ for that would account only for two of the four names. Joel rather describes successive swarms of the insect, without reference to the stages of its growth, and he does so as a poet, using, in order to bring out the full force of its devastation, several of the Hebrew names that were given to the locust as epithets of various aspects of its destructive power. The names, it is true, cannot be said to rise in climax, but at least the most sinister is reserved to the last.§

"Rouse ye, drunkards, and weep,
And wail, all ye bibbers of wine!
The new wine is cut off from your month!
For a nation is come up on My land,
Powerful and numberless;
His teeth are the teeth of the lion,
And the fangs ‖ of the lioness his.
My vine he has turned to waste,
And My fig-tree to splinters;
He hath peeled it and strawed it,
Bleached are its branches!

* See pp. 502, 503 f.
† Jer. xiv.
‡ *Cf.* Ezek. xlvi. 15 on the Thamid, and Neh. x. 33; Dan. viii. 11, xi. 31, xii. 11: *cf.* p. 653.
§ Acts xxvi. 7.
‖ XIV. "Antt." iv. 3, xvi. 2; VI. "Wars" ii. 1.
¶ i. 9, 13.
** i. 16.
†† ii. 14.
‡‡ i. 8, 13.

* ii. 12.
† LXX. Βαθουήλ.
‡ See above, pp. 657 f.
§ חסיל from חסל, used in the O. T. only in Deut. xxviii. 38, "to devour"; but in post-biblical Hebrew "to utterly destroy, bring to an end." "Talmud Jerus.": Taanith III. 66*d*, "Why is the locust called חסיל? Because it brings everything to an end."
‖ A. V. "cheek-teeth," R. V. "jaw-teeth," or "eye-teeth." "Possibly (from the Arabic) 'projectors'" Driver.

"Wail as a bride girt in sackcloth for the spouse of her youth.
Cut off are the meal and drink offerings from the house of Jehovah!
In grief are the priests, the ministers of Jehovah.
The fields are blasted, the ground is in grief,
Blasted is the corn, abashed is the new wine, the oil pines away.
Be ye abashed, O ploughmen!
Wail, O vine-dressers,
For the wheat and the barley;
The harvest is lost from the field!
The vine is abashed, and the fig-tree is drooping;
Pomegranate, palm too and apple,
All trees of the field are dried up:
Yea, joy is abashed *and* away from the children of men."

In this passage the same feeling is attributed to men and to the fruits of the land: "In grief are the priests, the ground is in grief." And it is repeatedly said that all alike are "abashed." By this heavy word we have sought to render the effect of the similarly sounding "hôbhisha," that our English version renders "ashamed." It signifies to be frustrated, and so "disheartened," "put out": "soured" would be an equivalent, applicable to the vine and to joy and to men's hearts.

"Put on *mourning*, O priests, beat the breast;
Wail, ye ministers of the altar;
Come, lie down in sackcloth, O ministers of my God:
For meal-offering and drink-offering are cut off from the house of your God.

"Hallow a fast, summon an assembly,
Gather * all the inhabitants of the land to the house of your God;
And cry to Jehovah:
'Alas for the Day! At hand is the Day of Jehovah!
And as vehemence from the Vehement † doth it come.'
Is not food cut off from before us,
Gladness and joy from the house of our God?
The grains shrivel under their hoes,‡
The garners are desolate, the barns broken down,
For the corn is withered—what shall we put in them? §
The herds of cattle huddle together,‖ for they have no pasture;
Yea, the flocks of sheep are forlorn.¶
To Thee, Jehovah, do I cry:
For fire has devoured the pastures of the steppes,**
Tnd the flame hath scorched all the trees of the field.
Ahe wild beasts pant up to Thee:
For the watercourses are dry,
And fire has devoured the pastures of the steppes."

Here, with the close of chap. i., Joel's discourse takes pause, and in chap. ii. he begins a second with another call to repentance in face of the same plague. But the plague has progressed. The locusts are described now in their invasion not of the country but of the towns, to which they pass after the country is stripped. For illustration of the latter see above, p. 658.

* Heb. text inserts "elders," which may be taken as vocative, or with the LXX. as accusative, but after the latter we should expect "and." Wellhausen suggests its deletion, and Nowack regards it as an intrusion. For אספו Wellhausen reads האספו, "be ye gathered."

† Keshödh mishshaddhai (Isa. xiii. 6); Driver, "as overpowering from the Overpowerer."

‡ A. V. "clods." מגרפותיהם: the meaning is doubtful, but the corresponding Arabic word means "besom" or "shovel" or ("P. E. F. Q.," 1891, p. 111, with plate) "hoe," and the Aram. "shovel." See Driver's note.

§ Reading, after the LXX. τί ἀποθήσομεν ἑαυτοῖς (probably an error for ἐν αὐτοῖς) מה נניחה בהם for the Massoretic מה נאנחה בהמה "How the beasts sob!" to which A. V. and Driver adhere.

‖ Lit. "press themselves" in perplexity.

¶ Reading with Wellhausen and Nowack ("perhaps rightly," Driver) נשמו for נאשמו "are guilty" or "punished."

** מדבר, usually rendered "wilderness" or "desert," but literally "place where the sheep are driven," land not cultivated. See "Hist. Geog.," p. 656.

The "horn" which is to be blown, ver. 1, is an "alarm horn," * to warn the people of the approach of the Day of the Lord, and not the Shophar which called the people to a general assembly, as in ver. 15.

"Blow a horn in Zion,
Sound the alarm in My holy mountain!
Let all inhabitants of the land tremble,
For the Day of Jehovah comes—it is near!
Day of darkness and murk, day of cloud and heavy mist.†
Like dawn scattered ‡ on the mountains,
A people many and powerful;
Its like has not been from of old,
And shall not again be for years of generation upon generation.
Before it the fire devours,§
And behind the flame consumes.
Like the garden of Eden ‖ is the land in front,
And behind it a desolate desert;
Yea, it lets nothing escape.
Their visage is the visage of horses,
And like horsemen they run.
They rattle like chariots over the tops of the hills,
Like the crackle of flames devouring stubble,
Like a powerful people prepared for battle.
Peoples are writhing before them,
Every face gathers blackness.

"Like warriors they run,
Like fighting men they come up the wall;
They march every man by himself,¶
And they ravel ** not their paths.
None jostles his comrade,
They march every man on his track,††
And plunge through the missiles unbroken.‡‡
They scour the city, run upon the walls,
Climb into the houses, and enter the windows like a thief,
Earth trembles before them,
Heaven quakes,
Sun and moon become black,
The stars withdraw their shining.
And Jehovah utters His voice before His army:
For very great is His host;
Yea, powerful is He that performeth His word,
Great is the Day of Jehovah, and very awful:
Who may abide it? §§

"But now *hear* the oracle of Jehovah:
Turn ye to Me with all your heart,
And with fasting and weeping and mourning,
Rend ye your hearts and not your garments,
And turn to Jehovah your God:
For He is gracious and merciful,
Long-suffering and plenteous in love,
And relents of the evil.
Who knows but He will turn and relent,
And leave behind Him a blessing,
Meal-offering and drink-offering to Jehovah your God?

"Blow a horn in Zion,
Hallow a fast, summon the assembly!
Gather the people, hallow the congregation,
Assemble the old men,‖‖ gather the children, and infants at the breast;
Let the bridegroom come forth from his chamber,
And the bride from her bower.¶¶

* See on Amos iii. 6; p. 462.

† Zeph. i. 15. See above, p. 574.

‡ פרש in Qal to spread abroad, but the passive is here to be taken in the same sense as the Ni. in Ezek. xvii. 21, "dispersed." The figure is of dawn crushed by and struggling with a mass of cloud and mist, and expresses the gleams of white which so often break through a locust cloud. See above, p. 659.

§ So travellers have described the effect of locusts. See above, p. 658.

‖ Ezek. xxxvi. 35.

¶ Heb. "in his own ways."

** יעבטון, an impossible metaphor, so that most read יעבתון, a root found only in Micah vii. 3 (see p. 547), "to twist" or "tangle;" but Wellhausen reads יְעַוְּתוּן, "twist," Eccles. vii. 13.

†† Heb. "highroad," as if defined and heaped up for him alone.

‡‡ See above, p. 658.

§§ Zeph. i. 14; "Mal." iii. 2.

‖‖ So (and not "elders") in contrast to children.

¶¶ "Canopy" or "pavilion," bridal tent.

Let the priests, the ministers of Jehovah, weep between porch and altar;
Let them say, Spare, O Jehovah, Thy people,
And give not Thine heritage to dishonour, for the heathen to mock them:*
Why should it be said among the nations, Where is their God?"

CHAPTER XXIX.

PROSPERITY AND THE SPIRIT.

JOEL ii. 18-32 (Eng.; ii. 18-iii. Heb.).

"THEN did Jehovah become jealous for His land, and took pity upon His people"—with these words Joel opens the second half of his book. Our Authorised Version renders them in the future tense, as the continuation of the prophet's discourse, which had threatened the Day of the Lord, urged the people to penitence, and now promises that their penitence shall be followed by the Lord's mercy. But such a rendering forces the grammar;† and the Revised English Version is right in taking the verbs, as the vast majority of critics do, in the past. Joel's call to repentance has closed, and has been successful. The fast has been hallowed, the prayers are heard. Probably an interval has elapsed between vv. 17 and 18, but, in any case, the people having repented, nothing more is said of their need of doing so, and instead we have from God Himself a series of promises, vv. 19-27, in answer to their cry for mercy. These promises relate to the physical calamity which has been suffered. God will destroy the locusts, still impending on the land, and restore the years which His great army has eaten. There follows in vv. 28-32 (Eng.; Heb., chap. iii.) the promise of a great outpouring of the Spirit on all Israel, amid terrible manifestations in heaven and earth.

I. THE RETURN OF PROSPERITY (ii. 19-27).

"And Jehovah answered and said to His people:
Lo, I will send you corn and wine and oil,
And your fill shall ye have of them;
And I will not again make you a reproach among the heathen.
And the Northern *Foe*‡ will I remove far from you;
And I will push him into a land barren and waste,
His van to the eastern sea and his rear to the western,*
Till the stench of him rises,†
Because he hath done greatly."

Locusts disappear with the same suddenness as they arrive. A wind springs up and they are gone.‡ Dead Sea and Mediterranean are at the extremes of the compass, but there is no reason to suppose that the prophet has abandoned the realism which has hitherto distinguished his treatment of the locusts. The plague covered the whole land, on whose high watershed the winds suddenly veer and change. The dispersion of the locusts upon the deserts and the opposite seas was therefore possible at one and the same time. Jerome vouches for an instance in his own day. The other detail is also true to life. Jerome says that the beaches of the two seas were strewn with putrefying locusts, and Augustine§ quotes heathen writers in evidence of large masses of locusts, driven from Africa upon the sea, and then cast up on the shore, which gave rise to a pestilence. "The south and east winds," says Volney of Syria, "drive the clouds of locusts with violence into the Mediterranean, and drown them in such quantities that when their dead are cast on the shore they infect the air to a great distance."‖ The prophet continues, celebrating this destruction of the locusts as if it were already realised—"the Lord hath done greatly," ver. 21. That among the blessings he mentions a full supply of rain proves that we were right in interpreting him to have spoken of drought as accompanying the locusts.¶

"Fear not, O Land! Rejoice and be glad,
For Jehovah hath done greatly.**
Fear not, O beasts of the field!
For the pastures of the steppes are springing with new grass,
The trees bear their fruit,
Fig-tree and vine yield their substance.
O sons of Zion, be glad,
And rejoice in Jehovah your God:
For He hath given you the early rain in normal measure,††

* למשל בם, which may mean either "rule over them" or "mock them," but the parallelism decides for the latter.

† A. V., adhering to the Massoretic text, in which the verbs are pointed for the past, has evidently understood them as instances of the prophetic perfect. But "this is grammatically indefensible": Driver, *in loco;* see his "Heb. Tenses," § 82, Obs. Calvin and others, who take the verbs of ver. 18 as future, accept those of the next verse as past and with it begin the narrative. But if God's answer to His people's prayer be in the past, so must His jealousy and pity. All these verbs are in the same sequence of time. Merx proposes to change the vowel-points of the verbs and turn them into futures. But see above, p. 656. Ver. 21 shows that Jehovah's action is past, and Nowack points out the very unusual character of the construction that would follow from Merx's emendation. Ewald, Hitzig, Kuenen, Robertson Smith, Davidson, Robertson, Steiner, Wellhausen, Driver, Nowack, etc., all take the verbs in the past.

‡ This is scarcely a name for the locusts, who, though they might reach Palestine from the N. E. under certain circumstances, came generally from E. and S. E. But see above, p. 657: so Kuenen, Wellhausen, Nowack. W. R. Smith suggests the whole verse as an allegorising gloss. Hitzig thought of the locusts only, and rendered הצפוני, ὁ τυφωνικός, Acts xxvi. 14; but this is not proved.

* *I. e.*, the Dead Sea (Ezek. xlvii. 18; Zech. xiv. 8) and the Mediterranean.

† The construction shows that the clause preceding this, ועלה באשו, is a gloss. So Driver. But Nowack gives the other clause as the gloss.

‡ Nah. iii. 17; Exod. x. 19.

§ "De Civitate Dei," III. 31.

‖ I. 278, quoted by Pusey.

¶ i. 17-20: see above, p. 658.

** Prophetic past: Driver.

†† Opinion is divided as to the meaning of this phrase: לצדקה = "for righteousness." A. There are those who take it as having a *moral* reference; and (1) this is so emphatic to some that they render the word for "early rain," מורה, which also means "teacher" or "revealer," in the latter significance. So (some of them applying it to the Messiah) Targum, Symmachus, the Vulgate, *doctorem justitiæ*, some Jews, *e. g.*, Rashi and Abarbanel, and some moderns, *e. g.* (at opposite extremes), Pusey and Merx. But, as Calvin points out (this is another instance of his sanity as an exegete, and refusal to be led by theological presuppositions: he says, "I do not love strained expositions"), this does not agree with the context, which speaks not of spiritual, but wholly of physical blessings.

(2) Some, who take מורה as "early rain," give לצדקה the meaning "for righteousness," *ad justitiam*, either in the sense that God will give the rain as a token of His own righteousness, or in order to restore or vindicate the people's righteousness (so Davidson, *Expositor*, 1888. I. p. 203 n.), in the frequent sense in which צדקה is employed in Isa. xl. ff. (see "Isaiah xl.-lxvi.," Expositor's Bible, pp. 785 ff.). *Cf.* Hosea x. 13. צדק; above, p. 514, *n.* This of course is possible, especially in view of Israel having been made by their plagues a reproach among the heathen. Still, if Joel had intended this meaning, he would have applied the phrase, not to the "early rain" only, but to the whole series of blessings by which the people were restored to their standing before God.

And poured * on you winter rain † and latter rain as
before.‡
And the threshing-floors shall be full of wheat,
And the vats stream over with new wine and oil.
And I will restore to you the years which the Swarmer
has eaten,
The Lapper, the Devourer and the Shearer,
My great army whom I sent among you.
And ye shall eat your food and be full,
And praise the Name of Jehovah your God,
Who hath dealt so wondrously with you;
And My people shall be abashed nevermore.
Ye shall know I am in the midst of Israel,
That I am Jehovah your God and none else;
And nevermore shall My people be abashed."

2. The Outpouring of the Spirit (ii. 28-32 Eng.; iii. Heb.).

Upon these promises of physical blessing there follows another of the pouring forth of the Spirit: the prophecy by which Joel became the Prophet of Pentecost, and through which his book is best known among Christians.

When fertility has been restored to the land, the seasons again run their normal courses, and the people eat their food and be full—"It shall come to pass after these things, I will pour out My Spirit upon all flesh." The order of events makes us pause to question: does Joel mean to imply that physical prosperity must precede spiritual fulness? It would be unfair to assert that he does, without remembering what he understands by the physical blessings. To Joel these are the token that God has returned to His people. The drought and the famine produced by the locusts were signs of His anger and of His divorce of the land. The proofs that He has relented, and taken Israel back into a spiritual relation to Himself, can, therefore, from Joel's point of view, only be given by the healing of the people's wounds. In plenteous rains and full harvests God sets His seal to man's penitence. Rain and harvest are not merely physical benefits, but religious sacraments: signs that God has returned to His people, and that His zeal is again stirred on their behalf.§ This has to be made clear before there can be talk of any higher blessing. God has to return to His people and to show His love for them before He pours forth His Spirit upon them. That is what Joel intends by the order he pursues, and not that a certain stage of physical comfort is indispensable to a high degree of spiritual feeling and experience. The early and latter rains, the fulness of corn, wine, and oil, are as purely religious to Joel, though not so highly religious, as the phenomena of the Spirit in men.

But though that be an adequate answer to our question so far as Joel himself is concerned, it does not exhaust the question with regard to history in general. From Joel's own standpoint physical blessings may have been as religious as spiritual; but we must go further, and assert that for Joel's anticipation of the baptism of the Spirit by a return of prosperity there is an ethical reason and one which is permanently valid in history. A certain degree of prosperity, and even of comfort, is an indispensable condition of that universal and lavish exercise of the religious faculties which Joel pictures under the pouring forth of God's Spirit.

The history of prophecy itself furnishes us with proofs of this. When did prophecy most flourish in Israel? When had the Spirit of God most freedom in developing the intellectual and moral nature of Israel? Not when the nation was struggling with the conquest and settlement of the land, not when it was engaged with the embarrassments and privations of the Syrian wars; but an Amos, a Hosea, an Isaiah came forth at the end of the long, peaceful, and prosperous reigns of Jeroboam II. and Uzziah. The intellectual strength and liberty of the great Prophet of the Exile, his deep insight into God's purposes and his large view of the future, had not been possible without the security and comparative prosperity of the Jews in Babylon, from among whom he wrote. In Haggai and Zechariah, on the other hand, who worked in the hunger-bitten colony of returned exiles, there was no such fulness of the Spirit. Prophecy, we saw,* was then starved by the poverty and meanness of the national life from which it rose. All this is very explicable. When men are stunned by such a calamity as Joel describes, or when they are engrossed by the daily struggle with bitter enemies and a succession of bad seasons, they may feel the need of penitence and be able to speak with decision upon the practical duty of the moment, to a degree not attainable in better days, but they lack the leisure, the freedom, and the resources amid which their various faculties of mind and soul can alone respond to the Spirit's influence.

Has it been otherwise in the history of Christianity? Our Lord Himself found His first disciples, not in a hungry and ragged community, but amid the prosperity and opulence of Galilee. They left all to follow Him and achieved their ministry in poverty and persecution, but they brought to that ministry the force of minds and bodies trained in a very fertile land and by a prosperous commerce.† Paul, in his apostolate, sustained himself by the labour of his hands, but he was the child of a rich civilisation and the citizen of a great empire. The Reformation was preceded by the Renaissance, and on the Continent of Europe drew its forces, not from the enslaved and impoverished populations of Italy and Southern Austria, but from the large civic and commercial centres of Germany. An acute historian, in his recent lectures on the "Economic Interpretation of History,"‡ observes that every religious revival in England has happened upon a basis of comparative prosperity. He has proved "the opulence of Norfolk during the epoch of Lollardy," and pointed out that "the Puritan movement was essentially and originally one of the middle classes, of the traders in towns and of the farmers in the country"; that the religious state of the Church of England was

B. It seems, therefore, right to take לצדקה in a purely physical sense, of the measure or quality of the "early rain." So even Calvin, "rain according to what is just or fit"; A. V. "moderately" (inexact); R. V. "in just measure"; Siegfried-Stade "sufficient." The root-meaning of צדק is probably "according to norm," *cf.* "Isaiah xl.-lxvi.," p. 784), and in that case the meaning would be "rain of normal quantity." This too suits the parallel in the next clause: "as formerly." In Himyaritic the word is applied to good harvests. A man prays to God for צדקם אפקל ואתמר, "full" or "good harvests and fruits": "Corp. Inscr. Sem.," Pars Quarta, Tomus I., No. 2, lin. 1-5; *cf.* the note.

* Driver *in loco*.

† Heb. also repeats here "early rain," but redundantly.

‡ בראשון, "in the first." A. V. adds "month." But LXX. and Syr. read כבראשנה, which is probably the correct reading, "as before" or "formerly."

§ i. 18.

* Above, p. 604.

† *Cf.* "Hist. Geog.," chap. xxi., especially p. 463.

‡ By Thorold Rogers, pp. 80 ff.

never so low as among the servile and beggarly clergy of the seventeenth and part of the eighteenth centuries; that the Nonconformist bodies who kept religion alive during this period were closely identified with the leading movements of trade and finance; * and that even Wesley's great revival of religion among the labouring classes of England took place at a time when prices were far lower than in the previous century, wages had slightly risen and "most labourers were small occupiers; there was therefore in the comparative plenty of the time an opening for a religious movement among the poor, and Wesley was equal to the occasion." He might have added that the great missionary movement of the nineteenth century is contemporaneous with the enormous advance of our commerce and our empire.

On the whole, then, the witness of history is uniform. Poverty and persecution, "famine, nakedness, peril, and sword," put a keenness upon the spirit of religion, while luxury rots its very fibres; but a stable basis of prosperity is indispensable to every social and religious reform, and God's Spirit finds fullest course in communities of a certain degree of civilisation and of freedom from sordidness.

We may draw from this an impressive lesson for our own day. Joel predicts that, upon the new prosperity of his land, the lowest classes of society shall be permeated by the spirit of prophecy. Is it not part of the secret of the failure of Christianity to enlist large portions of our population, that the basis of their life is so sordid and insecure? Have we not yet to learn from the Hebrew prophets that some amount of freedom in a people and some amount of health are indispensable to a revival of religion? Lives which are strained and starved, lives which are passed in rank discomfort and under grinding poverty, without the possibility of the independence of the individual or of the sacredness of the home, cannot be religious except in the most rudimentary sense of the word. For the revival of energetic religion among such lives we must wait for a better distribution, not of wealth, but of the bare means of comfort, leisure, and security. When, to our penitence and our striving, God restores the years which the locust has eaten, when the social plagues of rich men's selfishness and the poverty of the very poor are lifted from us, then may we look for the fulfilment of Joel's prediction—"even upon all the slaves and upon the handmaidens will I pour out My Spirit in those days."

The economic problem, therefore, has also its place in the warfare for the kingdom of God.

"And it shall be that after such things, I will pour out
 My Spirit on all flesh;
And your sons and your daughters shall prophesy,
Your old men shall dream dreams,
Your young men shall see visions:
And even upon all the slaves and the handmaidens in
 those days will I pour out My Spirit.
And I will set signs in heaven and on earth,
Blood and fire and pillars of smoke.
The sun shall be turned to darkness,
And the moon to blood,
Before the coming of the Day of Jehovah, the great and
 the awful.
And it shall be that every one who calls on the name of
 Jehovah shall be saved:
For in Mount Zion and in Jerusalem shall be a remnant,
 as Jehovah hath spoken,
And among the fugitives *those* whom Jehovah calleth."

* *E. g.*, the Quakers and the Independents. The Independents of the seventeenth century "were the founders of the Bank of England."

This prophecy divides into two parts—the outpouring of the Spirit, and the appearance of the terrible Day of the Lord.

The Spirit of God is to be poured "on all flesh," says the prophet. By this term, which is sometimes applied to all things that breathe, and sometimes to mankind as a whole,* Joel means Israel only: the heathen are to be destroyed.† Nor did Peter, when he quoted the passage at the Day of Pentecost, mean anything more. He spoke to Jews and proselytes: "for the promise is to you and your children, and to them that are afar off": it was not till afterwards that he discovered that the Holy Ghost was granted to the Gentiles, and then he was unready for the revelation and surprised by it.‡ But within Joel's Israel the operation of the Spirit was to be at once thorough and universal. All classes would be affected, and affected so that the simplest and rudest would become prophets.

The limitation was therefore not without its advantages. In the earlier stages of all religions it is impossible to be both extensive and intensive. With a few exceptions, the Israel of Joel's time was a narrow and exclusive body, hating and hated by other peoples. Behind the Law it kept itself strictly aloof. But without doing so, Israel could hardly have survived or prepared itself at that time for its influence on the world. Heathenism threatened it from all sides with the most insidious of infections; and there awaited it in the near future a still more subtle and powerful means of disintegration. In the wake of Alexander's expeditions, Hellenism poured across all the East. There was not a community nor a religion, save Israel's, which was not Hellenised. That Israel remained Israel, in spite of Greek arms and the Greek mind, was due to the legalism of Ezra and Nehemiah, and to what we call the narrow enthusiasm of Joel. The hearts which kept their passion so confined felt all the deeper for its limits. They would be satisfied with nothing less than the inspiration of every Israelite, the fulfilment of the prayer of Moses: "Would to God that all Jehovah's people were prophets!" And of itself this carries Joel's prediction to a wider fulfilment. A nation of prophets is meant for the world. But even the best of men do not see the full force of the truth God gives to them, nor follow it even to its immediate consequences. Few of the prophets did so, and at first none of the apostles. Joel does not hesitate to say that the heathen shall be destroyed. He does not think of Israel's mission as foretold by the Second Isaiah; nor of "Malachi's" vision of the heathen waiting upon Jehovah. But in the near future of Israel there was waiting another prophet to carry Joel's doctrine to its full effect upon the world, to rescue the gospel of God's grace from the narrowness of legalism and the awful pressure of Apocalypse, and by the parable of Jonah, the type of the prophet nation, to show to Israel that God had granted to the Gentiles also repentance unto life.

That it was the lurid clouds of Apocalypse which thus hemmed in our prophet's view, is clear from the next verses. They bring the terrible manifestations of God's wrath in nature very closely upon the lavish outpouring of the Spirit: "the sun turned to darkness and the

* All living things, Gen. vi. 17, 19, etc.; mankind, Isa. xl. 5, xlix. 26. See Driver's note.

† Next chapter.

‡ Acts. x. 45.

moon to blood, the great and terrible Day of the Lord." Apocalypse must always paralyse the missionary energies of religion. Who can think of converting the world when the world is about to be convulsed? There is only time for a remnant to be saved.

But when we get rid of Apocalypse, as the Book of Jonah does, then we have time and space opened up again, and the essential forces of such a prophecy of the Spirit as Joel has given us burst their national and temporary confines, and are seen to be applicable to all mankind.

CHAPTER XXX.

THE JUDGMENT OF THE HEATHEN.

JOEL iii. (Eng.; iv. Heb.).

HITHERTO Joel has spoken no syllable of the heathen, except to pray that God by His plagues will not give Israel to be mocked by them. But in the last chapter of the Book we have Israel's captivity to the heathen taken for granted, a promise made that it will be removed and their land set free from the foreigner. Certain nations are singled out for judgment, which is described in the terms of Apocalypse; and the Book closes with the vision, already familiar in prophecy, of a supernatural fertility for the land.

It is quite another horizon and far different interests from those of the preceding chapter. Here for the first time we may suspect the unity of the Book, and listen to suggestions of another authorship than Joel's. But these can scarcely be regarded as conclusive. Every prophet, however national his interests, feels it his duty to express himself upon the subject of foreign peoples, and Joel may well have done so. Only, in that case, his last chapter was delivered by him at another time and in different circumstances from the rest of his prophecies. Chaps. i.-ii. (Eng.; i.-iii. Heb.) are complete in themselves. Chap. iii. (Eng.; iv. Heb.) opens without any connection of time or subject with those that precede it.*

The time of the prophecy is a time when Israel's fortunes are at low ebb,† her sons scattered among the heathen, her land, in part at least, held by foreigners. But it would appear (though this is not expressly said, and must rather be inferred from the general proofs of a post-exilic date) that Jerusalem is inhabited. Nothing is said to imply that the city needs to be restored.‡

All the heathen nations are to be brought together for judgment into a certain valley, which the prophet calls first the Vale of Jehoshaphat and then the Vale of Decision. The second name leads us to infer that the first, which means "Jehovah-judges," is also symbolic. That is to say, the prophet does not single out a definite valley already called Jehoshaphat. In all probability, however, he has in his mind's eye some vale in the neighbourhood of Jerusalem, for since Ezekiel * the judgment of the heathen in face of Jerusalem has been a standing feature in Israel's vision of the last things; and as no valley about that city lends itself to the picture of judgment so well as the valley of the Kedron with the slopes of Olivet, the name Jehoshaphat has naturally been applied to it.† Certain nations are singled out by name. These are not Assyria and Babylon, which had long ago perished, nor the Samaritans, Moab and Ammon, which harassed the Jews in the early days of the Return from Babylon, but Tyre, Sidon, Philistia, Edom, and Egypt. The crime of the first three is the robbery of Jewish treasures, not necessarily those of the Temple, and the selling into slavery of many Jews. The crime of Edom and Egypt is that they have shed the innocent blood of Jews. To what precise events these charges refer we have no means of knowing in our present ignorance of Syrian history after Nehemiah. That the chapter has no explicit reference to the cruelties of Artaxerxes Ochus in 360 would seem to imply for it a date earlier than that year. But it is possible that ver. 17 refers to that, the prophet refraining from accusing the Persians for the very good reason that Israel was still under their rule.

Another feature worthy of notice is that the Phœnicians are accused of selling Jews to the sons of the Jevanim, Ionians or Greeks.‡ The latter lie on the far horizon of the prophet,§ and we know from classical writers that from the fifth century onward numbers of Syrian slaves were brought to Greece. The other features of the chapter are borrowed from earlier prophets.

"For, behold, in those days and in that time,
When I bring again the captivity ‖ of Judah and Jerusalem,
I will also gather all the nations,
And bring them down to the Vale of Jehoshaphat; ¶
And I will enter into judgment with them there,
For My people and for My heritage Israel,
Whom they have scattered among the heathen,
And My land have they divided.
And they have cast lots for My people: **
They have given a boy for a harlot,††
And a girl have they sold for wine and drunk it.
And again, what are ye to Me, Tyre and Sidon and all circuits of Philistia? ‡‡
Is it any deed of Mine ye are repaying?
Or are ye doing anything to Me? §§
Swiftly, speedily will I return your deed on your head,
Who have taken My silver and My gold,
And My goodly jewels ye have brought into your palaces.
The sons of Judah and the sons of Jerusalem have ye sold to the sons of the Greeks,
In order that ye might set them as far *as possible* from their own border.
Lo! I will stir them up from the place to which ye have sold them,
And I will return your deed upon your head.
I will sell your sons and your daughters into the hands of the sons of Judah,
And they shall sell them to the Shebans,‖‖
To a nation far off; for Jehovah hath spoken.

* I am unable to feel Driver's and Nowack's arguments for a connection conclusive. The only reason Davidson gives is (p. 204) that the judgment of the heathen is an essential element in the Day of Jehovah, a reason which does not make Joel's authorship of the last chapter certain, but only possible.

† The phrase of ver. 1, "when I turn again the captivity of Judah and Jerusalem," may be rendered "when I restore the fortunes of Israel."

‡ See above, p. 654, especially *n*.

* xxxviii.

† Some have unnecessarily thought of the Vale of Berakhah, in which Jehoshaphat defeated Moab, Ammon, and Edom (2 Chron. xx.).

‡ See above, p. 652, *nn*.

§ Ver. 6*b*.

‖ Or "turn again the fortunes."

¶ "Jehovah-judges." See above, p. 665.

** See above, Obadiah 11 and Nahum iii. 10.

†† בזונה. Oort suggests במזון, "for food."

‡‡ Gelîlôth, the plural feminine of Galilee—the "circuit" (of the Gentiles). "Hist. Geog.," p. 413.

§§ Scil. "that I must repay."

‖‖ LXX. "they shall give them into captivity."

Proclaim this among the heathen, hallow a war,
Wake up the warriors, let all the fighting-men muster and go up.*
Beat your ploughshares into swords,
And your pruning-hooks into lances.
Let the weakling say, I am strong.
. . . †and come, all ye nations round about,
And gather yourselves together.
Thither bring down Thy warriors, Jehovah,
Let the heathen be roused,
And come up to the Vale of Jehoshaphat,
For there will I sit to judge all the nations round about.
Put in the sickle,‡ for ripe is the harvest.
Come, get you down; for the press is full,
The vats overflow, great is their wickedness.
Multitudes, multitudes in the Vale of Decision!
For near is Jehovah's day in the Vale of Decision.
Sun and moon have turned black,
And the stars withdrawn their shining.
Jehovah thunders from Zion,
And from Jerusalem gives § forth His voice
Heaven and earth do quake.
But Jehovah is a refuge to His people,
And for a fortress to the sons of Israel.
And ye shall know that I am Jehovah your God,
Who dwell in Zion, the mount of My holiness;
And Jerusalem shall be holy,
Strangers shall not pass through her again.
And it shall be on that day
The mountains shall drop sweet wine,
And the hills be liquid with milk,
And all the channels of Judah flow with water;
A fountain shall spring from the house of Jehovah,
And shall water the Wady of Shittim.‖
Egypt shall be desolation,
And Edom desert-land,
For the outrage *done* to the children of Judah,
Because they shed innocent blood in their land.
Judah shall abide *peopled* for ever,
And Jerusalem for generation upon generation.
And I will declare innocent their blood,¶ which I have not declared innocent,
By ** Jehovah who dwelleth in Zion."

INTRODUCTION TO THE PROPHETS OF THE GRECIAN PERIOD.

331 B. C.

CHAPTER XXXI.

ISRAEL AND THE GREEKS.

APART from the author of the tenth chapter of Genesis, who defines Javan or Greece as the father of Elishah and Tarshish, of Kittim or Cyprus and Rodanim or Rhodes,†† the first Hebrew writer who mentions the Greeks is Ezekiel,* *c.* 580 B. C. He describes them as engaged in commerce with the Phœnicians, who bought slaves from them. Even while Ezekiel wrote in Babylonia, the Babylonians were in touch with the Ionian Greeks through the Lydians.† The latter were overthrown by Cyrus about 545, and by the beginning of the next century the Persian lords of Israel were in close struggle with the Greeks for the supremacy of the world, and had virtually been defeated so far as concerned Europe, the west of Asia Minor, and the sovereignty of the Mediterranean and Black Seas. In 460 Athens sent an expedition to Egypt to assist a revolt against Persia, and even before that Greek fleets had scoured the Levant and Greek soldiers, though in the pay of Persia, had trodden the soil of Syria. Still Joel, writing towards 400 B. C., mentions Greece ‡ only as a market to which the Phœnicians carried Jewish slaves; and in a prophecy which some take to be contemporary with Joel, Isaiah lxvi., the coasts of Greece are among the most distant of Gentile lands.§ In 401 the younger Cyrus brought to the Euphrates to fight against Artaxerxes Mnemon the ten thousand Greeks whom, after the battle of Cunaxa, Xenophon led north to the Black Sea. For nearly seventy years thereafter Athenian trade slowly spread eastward, but nothing was yet done by Greece to advertise her to the peoples of Asia as a claimant for the world's throne. Then suddenly in 334 Alexander of Macedon crossed the Hellespont, spent a year in the conquest of Asia Minor, defeated Darius at Issus in 332, took Damascus, Tyre, and Gaza, overran the Delta and founded Alexandria. In 331 he marched back over Syria, crossed the Euphrates, overthrew the Persian Empire on the field of Arbela, and for the next seven years till his death in 324 extended his conquests to the Oxus and the Indus. The story that on his second passage of Syria Alexander visited Jerusalem ‖ is probably false. But he must have encamped repeatedly within forty miles of it, and he visited Samaria. ¶ It is impossible that he received no embassy from a people who had not known political independence for centuries and must have been only too ready to come to terms with the new lord of the world. Alexander left behind him colonies of his veterans, both to the east and west of the Jordan, and in his wake there poured into all the cities of the Syrian seaboard a considerable volume of Greek immigration.** It is from this time

* Technical use of עלה, to go up to war.

† עושו, not found elsewhere, but supposed to mean "gather." *Cf.* Zeph. ii. 1. Others read חושו, "hasten" (Driver); Wellhausen עורו.

‡ מגל, only here and in Jer. l. 16: other Heb. word for sickle hermesh (Deut. xvi. 9, xxiii. 26).

§ Driver, future.

‖ Not the well-known scene of early Israel's camp across Jordan, but it must be some dry and desert valley near Jerusalem (so most comm.) Nowack thinks of the Wadi el Sant on the way to Askalon, but this did not need watering and is called the Vale of Elah.

¶ Merx applies this to the Jews of the Messianic era. LXX. read ἐκζητήσω = ונקמתי. So Syr. *Cf.* 2 Kings ix. 7. Steiner: "Shall I leave their blood unpunished? I will not leave it unpunished." Nowack deems this to be unlikely, and suggests, "I will avenge their blood; I will not leave unpunished" the shedders of it.

** Heb. construction is found also in Hosea xii. 5.

†† Gen. x. 2, 4. יון, Javan, is ΙαϜων or Ιαων, the older form of the name of the Ionians, the first of the Greek race with whom Eastern peoples came into contact. They are perhaps named on the Tell-el-Amarna tablets as "Yivana," serving "in the country of Tyre" (*c.* 1400 B. C.); and on an inscription of Sargon (*c.* 709) Cyprus is called Yâvanu.

* xxvii. 13.

† "Isaiah xl.-lxvi." (Expositor's Bible), 757 f.

‡ iii. 6 (Eng.; iv. 6 Heb.).

§ The sense of distance between the two peoples was mutual. Writing in the middle of the fifth century B. C., Herodotus has heard of the Jews only as a people that practise circumcision and were defeated by Pharaoh Necho at Megiddo (II. 104, 159; on the latter passage see "Hist. Geog.," p. 405, n.). He does not even know them by name. The fragment of Chœrilos of Samos, from the end of the fifth century, which Josephus cites ("Contra Apionem," I. 22) as a reference to the Jews, is probably of a people in Asia Minor. Even in the last half of the fourth century and before Alexander's campaigns, Aristotle knows of the Dead Sea only by a vague report ("Meteor.," II. iii. 39). His pupil Theophrastus (*d.* 287) names and describes the Jews (Porphyr. "de Abstinentia," II. 26: Eusebius, "Prepar. Evang.," IX. 2: *cf.* Josephus, "C. Apion.," I. 22); and another pupil, Clearchus of Soli, records the mention by Aristotle of a travelled Jew of Cœla-Syria, but "Greek in soul as in tongue," whom the great philosopher had met, and learned from him that the Jews were descended from the philosophers of India (quoted by Josephus, "C. Apion.," I. 22).

‖ Jos., XI. "Antt." iv. 5.

¶ "Hist. Geog.," p. 347.

** "Hist. Geog.," pp. 593 f.

onward that we find in Greek writers the earliest mention of the Jews by name. Theophrastus and Clearchus of Soli, disciples of Aristotle, both speak of them; but while the former gives evidence of some knowledge of their habits, the latter reports that in the perspective of his great master they had been so distant and vague as to be confounded with the Brahmins of India, a confusion which long survived among the Greeks.*

Alexander's death delivered his empire to the ambitions of his generals, of whom four contested for the mastery of Asia and Egypt—Antigonus, Ptolemy, Lysimachus, and Seleucus. Of these Ptolemy and Seleucus emerged victorious, the one in possession of Egypt, the other of Northern Syria and the rest of Asia. Palestine lay between them, and both in the wars which led to the establishment of the two kingdoms and in those which for centuries followed Palestine became the battle-field of the Greeks.

Ptolemy gained Egypt within two years of Alexander's death, and from its definite and strongly entrenched territory he had by 320 conquered Syria and Cyprus. In 315 or 314 Syria was taken from him by Antigonus, who also expelled Seleucus from Babylon. Seleucus fled to Egypt and stirred up Ptolemy to the reconquest of Syria. In 312 Ptolemy defeated Demetrius, the general of Antigonus, at Gaza, but the next year was driven back into Egypt by Antigonus himself. Meanwhile Seleucus regained Babylon.† In 311 the three made peace with each other, but Antigonus retained Syria. In 306 they assumed the title of kings, and in the same year renewed their quarrel. After a naval battle Antigonus wrested Cyprus from Ptolemy, but in 301 he was defeated and slain by Seleucus and Lysimachus at the battle of Ipsus in Phrygia. His son Demetrius retained Cyprus and part of the Phœnician coast till 287, when he was forced to yield them to Seleucus, who had moved the centre of his power from Babylon to the new Antioch on the Orontes, with a seaport at Seleucia. Meanwhile in 301 Ptolemy had regained what the Greeks then knew as Cœle-Syria, that is all Syria to the south of Lebanon except the Phœnician coast.‡ Damascus belonged to Seleucus. But Ptolemy was not allowed to retain Palestine in peace, for in 297 Demetrius appears to have invaded it, and Seleucus, especially after his marriage with Stratonike, the daughter of Demetrius, never wholly resigned his claims to it.§ Ptolemy, however, established a hold upon the land which continued practically unbroken for a century, and yet during all that time had to be maintained by frequent wars, in the course of which the land itself must have severely suffered (264-248).

Therefore, as in the days of their earliest prophets, the people of Israel once more lay between two rival empires. And as Hosea and Isaiah pictured them in the eighth century, the possible prey either of Egypt or Assyria, so now in these last years of the fourth they were tossed between Ptolemy and Antigonus, and in the opening years of the third were equally wooed by Ptolemy and Seleucus. Upon this new alternative of tyranny the Jews appear to have bestowed the actual names of their old oppressors. Ptolemy was Egypt to them; Seleucus, with one of his capitals at Babylon, was still Assyria, from which came in time the abbreviated Greek form of Syria.* But, unlike the ancient empires, these new rival lords were of one race. Whether the tyranny came from Asia or Africa, its quality was Greek; and in the sons of Javan the Jews saw the successors of those world-powers of Egypt, Assyria, and Babylonia, in which had been concentrated against themselves the whole force of the heathen world. Our records of the times are fragmentary, but though Alexander spared the Jews it appears that they had not long to wait before feeling the force of Greek arms. Josephus quotes† from Agatharchides of Cnidos (180-145 B. C.) to the effect that Ptolemy I. surprised Jerusalem on a Sabbath day and easily took it; and he adds that at the same time he took a great many captives from the hill-country of Judea, from Jerusalem and from Samaria, and led them into Egypt. Whether this was in 320 or 312 or 301‡ we cannot tell. It is possible that the Jews suffered in each of these Egyptian invasions of Syria, as well as during the southward marches of Demetrius and Antigonus. The later policy, both of the Ptolemies, who were their lords, and of the Seleucids, was for a long time exceedingly friendly to Israel. Their sufferings from the Greeks were therefore probably over by 280, although they cannot have remained unscathed by the wars between 264 and 248.

The Greek invasion, however, was not like the Assyrian and Babylonian, of arms alone; but of a force of intellect and culture far surpassing even the influences which the Persians had impressed upon the religion and mental attitude of Israel. The ancient empires had transplanted the nations of Palestine to Assyria and Babylonia. The Greeks did not need to remove them to Greece; for they brought Greece to Palestine. "The Orient," says Wellhausen, "became their America." They poured into Syria, infecting, exploiting, assimilating its peoples. With dismay the Jews must have seen themselves surrounded by new Greek colonies, and still more by the old Palestinian cities Hellenised in polity and religion. The Greek translator of Isaiah ix. 12 renders Philistines by Hellenes. Israel were compassed and penetrated by influences as subtle as the atmosphere: not as of old uprooted from their fatherland, but with their fatherland itself infected and altered beyond all powers of resistance. The full alarm of this, however, was not felt for many years to come. It was at first the policy both of the Seleucids and the Ptolemies to flatter and foster the Jews. They en-

*See above, p. 666, *n.*
†Hence the Seleucid era dates from 312.
‡"Hist. Geog.," 538.
§*Cf.* Ewald, "Hist." (Eng. Ed.), V. 226 f

* Asshur or Assyria fell in 607 (as we have seen), but her name was transferred to her successor Babylon (2 Kings xxiii. 29; Jer. ii. 18; Lam. v. 6), and even to Babylon's successor Persia (Ezra vi. 22). When Seleucus secured what was virtually the old Assyrian Empire with large extensions to Phrygia on the west and the Punjaub on the east, the name would naturally be continued to his dominion, especially as his first capital was Babylon, from his capture of which in 312 the Seleucid era took its start. There is actual record of this. Brugsch ("Gesch. Aeg.," p. 218) states that in the hieroglyphic inscriptions of the Ptolemæan period the kingdom of the Seleucids is called Asharu (*cf.* Stade, "Z. A. T. W.," 1882, p. 292, and Cheyne, "Book of Psalms," p. 253, and "Introd. to Book of Isaiah" p. 107, n. 3). As the Seleucid kingdom shrank to this side of the Euphrates, it drew the name Assyria with it. But in Greek mouths this had long ago (*cf.* Herod.) been shortened to Syria: Herodotus also appears to have applied it only to the west of the Euphrates. *Cf.* "Hist. Geog.," pp. 3 f.
†XII. "Antt." 1.: *cf.* "Con. Apion.," I. 22.
‡See above, Eusebius, "Chron. Arm.," II. 225, assigns it to 320.

couraged them to feel that their religion had its own place beside the forces of Greece, and was worth interpreting to the world. Seleucus I. gave to Jews the rights of citizenship in Asia Minor and Northern Syria; and Ptolemy I. atoned for his previous violence by granting them the same in Alexandria. In the matter of the consequent tribute Seleucus respected their religious scruples: and it was under Ptolemy Philadelphus (283-247), if not at his instigation, that the Law was first translated into Greek.

To prophecy, before it finally expired, there was granted the opportunity to assert itself, upon at least the threshold of this new era of Israel's history.

We have from the first half-century of the era perhaps three or four, but certainly two, prophetic pieces. By many critics Isaiah xxiv.-xxvii. are assigned to the years immediately following Alexander's campaigns. Others assign Isaiah xix. 16-25 to the last years of Ptolemy I.* And of our Book of the Twelve Prophets, the chapters attached to the genuine prophecies of Zechariah, or chaps. ix.-xiv. of his book, most probably fall to be dated from the contests of Syria and Egypt for the possession of Palestine; while somewhere about 300 is the most likely date for the Book of Jonah.

In "Zech." ix.-xiv. we see prophecy perhaps at its lowest ebb. The clash with the new foes produces a really terrible thirst for the blood of the heathen: there are schisms and intrigues within Israel which in our ignorance of her history during this time it is not possible for us to to follow: the brighter gleams, which contrast so forcibly with the rest, may be more ancient oracles that the writer has incorporated with his own stern and dark Apocalypse.

In the Book of Jonah, on the other hand, we find a spirit and a style in which prophecy may not unjustly be said to have given its highest utterance. And this alone suffices, in our uncertainty as to the exact date of the book, to take it last of all our Twelve. For "in this book," as Cornill has finely said, "the prophecy of Israel quits the scene of battle as victor, and as victor in its severest struggle—that against self."

* Cheyne, "Introd. to Book of Isaiah," p. 105.

"ZECHARIAH."

(ix.-xiv.)

"Lo, thy King cometh to thee, vindicated and victorious, meek and riding on an ass, and on a colt, the foal of an ass.

"Up, Sword, against My Shepherd! . . . Smite the Shepherd, that the sheep may be scattered!

"And I will pour upon the house of David and upon all the inhabitants of Jerusalem the spirit of grace and of supplication, and they shall look to Him whom they have pierced; and they shall lament for Him, as with lamentation for an only son, and bitterly grieve for Him, as with grief for a first-born."

CHAPTER XXXII.

CHAPTERS IX.-XIV. OF "ZECHARIAH."

We saw that the first eight chapters of the Book of Zechariah were, with the exception of a few verses, from the prophet himself. No one has ever doubted this. No one could doubt it: they are obviously from the years of the building of the Temple, 520-516 B. C. They hang together with a consistency exhibited by few other groups of chapters in the Old Testament.

But when we pass into chap. ix. we find ourselves in circumstances and an atmosphere altogether different. Israel is upon a new situation of history, and the words addressed to her breathe another spirit. There is not the faintest allusion to the building of the Temple—the subject from which all the first eight chapters depend. There is not a single certain reflection of the Persian period, under the shadow of which the first eight chapter were all evidently written. We have names of heathen powers mentioned which not only do not occur in the first eight chapters, but of which it is not possible to think that they had any interest whatever for Israel between 520 and 516: Damascus, Hadrach, Hamath, Assyria, Egypt, and Greece. The peace, and the love of peace, in which Zechariah wrote, has disappeared.* Nearly everything breathes of war actual or imminent. The heathen are spoken of with a ferocity which finds few parallels in the Old Testament. There is a revelling in their blood of which the student of the authentic prophecies of Zechariah will at once perceive that gentle lover of peace could not have been capable. And one passage figures the imminence of a thorough judgment upon Jerusalem, very different from Zechariah's outlook upon his people's future from the eve of the completion of the Temple. It is not surprising, therefore, that one of the earliest efforts of Old Testament criticism should have been to prove another author than Zechariah for chaps. ix.-xiv. of the book called by his name.

The very first attempt of this kind was made so far back as 1632 by the Cambridge theologian Joseph Mede,† who was moved thereto by the desire to vindicate the correctness of St. Matthew's ascription‡ of "Zech." xi. 13 to the prophet Jeremiah. Mede's effort was developed by other English exegetes. Hammond assigned chaps. x.-xii., Bishop Kidder§ and William Whiston, the translator of Josephus, chaps. ix.-xiv., to Jeremiah. Archbishop Newcome‖ divided them, and sought to prove that while chaps. ix.-xi. must have been written before 721, or a century earlier than Jeremiah, because of the heathen powers they name, and the divisions between Judah and Israel, chaps. xii.-xiv. reflect the imminence of the Fall of Jerusalem. In 1784 Flügge¶ offered independent proof that chaps. ix.-xiv. were by Jeremiah; and in 1814 Bertholdt** suggested that chaps. ix.-xi. might be by Zechariah the contemporary of Isaiah,†† and on that account attached to the prophecies of his younger namesake. These opinions gave the trend to the main volume of criticism, which, till fifteen years ago, deemed "Zech." ix.-xiv. to be pre-exilic. So Hitzig, who at first took the

* Except in the passage ix. 10-12, which seems strangely out of place in the rest of ix.-xiv.

† "Works," 4th ed. 1677, pp. 786 ff. (1632), 834. Mede died 1638.

‡ Matt. xxvii. 9.

§ "Demonstration of the Messias," 1700.

‖ "An Attempt towards an Improved Version of the Twelve Minor Prophets," 1785 (not seen). See also Wright on Archbishop Secker.

¶ "Die Weissagungen, welche bei den Schriften des Proph. Sacharja beygebogen sind, übersetzt," etc., Hamburg (not seen).

** "Einleitung in A. u. N. T." (not seen).

†† Isa. viii. 2. See above, p. 623.

whole to be from one hand, but afterwards placed xii.-xiv. by a different author under Manasseh. So Ewald, Bleek, Kuenen (at first), Samuel Davidson, Schrader, Duhm (in 1875), and more recently König and Orelli, who assign chaps. ix.-xi. to the reign of Ahaz, but xii.-xiv. to the eve of the Fall of Jerusalem, or even a little later.

Some critics, however, remained unmoved by the evidence offered for a pre-exilic date. They pointed out in particular that the geographical references were equally suitable to the centuries after the Exile. Damascus, Hadrach, and Hamath,* though politically obsolete by 720, entered history again with the campaigns of Alexander the Great in 332-331, and the establishment of the Seleucid kingdom in Northern Syria.† Egypt and Assyria‡ were names used after the Exile for the kingdom of the Ptolemies, and for those powers which still threatened Israel from the north or Assyrian quarter Judah and Joseph or Ephraim § were names still used after the Exile to express the whole of God's Israel; and in chaps. ix.-xiv. they are presented, not divided as before 721, but united. None of the chapters give a hint of any king in Jerusalem; and all of them, while representing the great Exile of Judah as already begun, show a certain dependence in style and even in language upon Jeremiah, Ezekiel, and Isaiah xl.-lxvi. Moreover, the language is post-exilic, sprinkled with Aramaisms and with other words and phrases used only, or mainly, by Hebrew writers from Jeremiah onwards.

But though many critics judged these grounds to be sufficient to prove the post-exilic origin of "Zech." ix.-xiv., they differed as to the author and exact date of these chapters. Conservatives like Hengstenberg,‖ Delitzsch, Keil, Köhler, and Pusey used the evidence to prove the authorship of Zechariah himself after 516, and interpreted the references to the Greek period as pure prediction. Pusey says¶ that chaps. ix.-xi. extend from the completion of the Temple and its deliverance during the invasion of Alexander, and from the victories of the Maccabees, to the rejection of the true shepherd and the curse upon the false; and chaps. xi.-xii. "from a future repentance for the death of Christ to the final conversion of the Jews and Gentiles."**

But on the same grounds Eichhorn †† saw in the chapters, not a prediction, but a reflection of the Greek period. He assigned chaps. ix. and x. to an author in the time of Alexander the Great; xi.-xiii. 6 he placed a little later, and brought down xiii. 7-xiv. to the Maccabean period. Böttcher ‡‡ placed the whole in the wars of Ptolemy and Seleucus after Alexander's death; and Vatke, who had at first selected a date in the reign of Artaxerxes Longhand, 464-425, finally decided for the Maccabean period, 170 ff.§§

In recent times the most thorough examination of the chapters has been that by Stade,‖‖ and the conclusion he comes to is that chaps. ix.-xiv. are all from one author, who must have written during the early wars between the Ptolemies and Seleucids about 280 B. C., but employed, especially in chaps. ix., x., an earlier prophecy. A criticism and modification of Stade's theory is given by Kuenen. He allows that the present form of chaps. ix.-xiv. must be of post-exilic origin: this is obvious from the mention of the Greeks as a world-power; the description of a siege of Jerusalem by *all* the heathen; the way in which (chaps. ix. 11 f., but especially x. 6-9) the captivity is presupposed, if not of all Israel, yet of Ephraim; the fact that the House of David are not represented as governing; and the thoroughly priestly character of all the chapters. But Kuenen holds that an ancient prophecy of the eighth century underlies chaps. ix.-xi., xiii. 7-9, in which the several actual phrases of it survive;* and that in their present form xii.-xiv. are older than ix.-xi., and probably by a contemporary of Joel, about 400 B. C.

In the main Cheyne,† Cornill,‡ Wildeboer,§ and Staerk ‖ adhere to Stade's conclusions. Cheyne proves the unity of the six chapters and their date *before* the Maccabean period. Staerk brings down xi. 4-17 and xiii. 7-9 to 171 B. C. Wellhausen argues for the unity, and assigns it to the Maccabean times. Driver judges ix.-xi., with its natural continuation, xiii. 7-9, as not earlier than 333; and the rest of xii.-xiv. as certainly post-exilic, and probably from 432-300. Rubinkam ¶ places ix. 1-10 in Alexander's time, the rest in that of the Maccabees, but Zeydner ** all of it to the latter. Kirkpatrick,†† after showing the post-exilic character of all the chapters, favours assigning ix.-xi. to a different author from xii.-xiv. Asserting that to the question of the exact date it is impossible to give a definite answer, he thinks that the whole may be with considerable probability assigned to the first sixty or seventy years of the Exile, and is therefore in its proper place between Zechariah and "Malachi." The reference to the sons of Javan he takes to be a gloss, probably added in Maccabean times.‡‡

It will be seen from this catalogue of conclusions that the prevailing trend of recent criticism has been to assign "Zech." ix.-xiv. to post-exilic times, and to a different author from chaps. i.-viii.; and that while a few critics maintain a date soon after the Return, the bulk are divided between the years following Alexander's campaigns and the time of the Maccabean struggles.§§

There are, in fact, in recent years only two attempts to support the conservative position of Pusey and Hengstenberg that the whole book is a genuine work of Zechariah the son of Iddo. One of these is by C. H. H. Wright in his Bampton Lectures. The other is by George L. Robinson, now Professor at Toronto, in a reprint (1896) from the *American Journal of Semitic Languages and Literatures,* which offers a valuable history of the discussion of the whole question from the days of Mede, with a careful argument of all the evidence on both sides. The

* ix. 1.
† See above, chap. xxxi.
‡ x. 10.
§ ix. 10, 13, etc.
‖ "Dan. u. Sacharja."
¶ Page 503.
** See Addenda, p. 671.
†† "Einl." in the beginning of the century.
‡‡ "Neue Exeg. krit. Aehrenlese z. A. T.," 1864.
§§ "Einl.," 1882, p. 709.
‖‖ "Z. A. T. W.," 1881, 1882. See further proof of the late character of language and style, and of the unity, by Eckardt, "Z. A. T. W.," 1893, pp. 76 ff.

* § 81, n, 3, 10.
† *Jewish Quart. Review*, 1889.
‡ "Einl."
§ "A. T. Litt."
‖ "Untersuchung über die Komposition u. Abfassungszeit von Zach. 9-14," etc. Halle, 1891 (not seen).
¶ 1892: quoted by Wildeboer.
** 1893: quoted by Wildeboer.
†† "Doctrine of the Prophets," 438 ff., in which the English reader will find a singularly lucid and fair treatment of the question. See, too, Wright.
‡‡ Page 472, Note A.
§§ Kautzsch—the Greek period.

very original conclusion is reached that the chapters reflect the history of the years 518-516 B. C.

In discussing the question, for which our treatment of other prophets has left us too little space, we need not open that part of it which lies between a pre-exilic and a post-exilic date. Recent criticism of all schools and at both extremes has tended to establish the latter upon reasons which we have already stated,* and for further details of which the student may be referred to Stade's and Eckhardt's investigations in the *Zeitschrift für A. T. Wissenschaft* and to Kirkpatrick's impartial summary. There remain the questions of the unity of chaps. ix.-xiv.; their exact date or dates after the Exile, and as a consequence of this their relation to the authentic prophecies of Zechariah in chaps. i.-viii.

On the question of unity we take first chaps. ix.-xi., to which must be added (as by most critics since Ewald) xiii. 7-9, which has got out of its place as the natural continuation and conclusion of chap. xi.

Chap. ix. 1-8 predicts the overthrow of heathen neighbours of Israel, their possession by Jehovah and His safeguard of Jerusalem. Vv. 9-12 follow with a prediction of the Messianic King as the Prince of Peace; but then come vv. 13-17, with no mention of the King, but Jehovah appears alone as the hero of His people against the Greeks, and there is indeed sufficiency of war and blood. Chap. x. makes a new start: the people are warned to seek their blessings from Jehovah, and not from Teraphim and diviners, whom their false shepherds follow. Jehovah, visiting His flock, shall punish these, give proper rulers, make the people strong and gather in their exiles to fill Gilead and Lebanon. Chap. xi. opens with a burst of war on Lebanon and Bashan and the overthrow of the heathen (vv. 1-3), and follows with an allegory, in which the prophet first takes charge from Jehovah of the people as their shepherd, but is contemptuously treated by them (4-14), and then taking the guise of an evil shepherd represents what they must suffer from their next ruler (15-17). This tyrant, however, shall receive punishment, two-thirds of the nation shall be scattered, but the rest, further purified, shall be God's own people (xiii. 7-9).

In the course of this prophesying there is no conclusive proof of a double authorship. The only passage which offers strong evidence for this is chap. ix. The verses predicting the peaceful coming of Messiah (9-12) do not accord in spirit with those which follow predicting the appearance of Jehovah with war and great shedding of blood. Nor is the difference altogether explained, as Stade thinks, by the similar order of events in chap. x., where Judah and Joseph are first represented as saved and brought back in ver. 6, and then we have the process of their redemption and return described in vv. 7 ff. Why did the same writer give statements of such very different temper as chap. ix. 9-12 and 13-17? Or, if these be from different hands, why were they ever put together? Otherwise there is no reason for breaking up chaps. ix.-xi., xiii. 7-9. Rubinkam, who separates ix. 1-10 by a hundred and fifty years from the rest; Bleek, who divides ix. from x.; and Staerk, who separates ix.-xi. 3 from the rest, have been answered by Robinson and others.† On the ground of language, grammar, and syntax, Eckardt has fully proved that ix.-xi are from the same author of a late date, who, however, may have occasionally followed earlier models and even introduced their very phrases.*

More supporters have been found for a division of authorship between chaps. ix.-xi., xiii. 7-9, and chaps. xii.-xiv. (less xiii. 7-9). Chap. xii. opens with a title of its own. A strange element is introduced into the historical relation. Jerusalem is assaulted, not by the heathen only, but by Judah, who, however, turns on finding that Jehovah fights for Jerusalem, and is saved by Jehovah before Jerusalem in order that the latter may not boast over it (xii. 1-9). A spirit of grace and supplication is poured upon the guilty city, a fountain opened for uncleanness, idols abolished, and the prophets, who are put on a level with them, abolished too, where they do not disown their profession (xii. 10-xiii. 6). Another assault of the heathen on Jerusalem is described, half of the people being taken captive. Jehovah appears, and by a great earthquake saves the rest. The land is transformed. And then the prophet goes back to the defeat of the heathen assault on the city, in which Judah is again described as taking part; and the surviving heathen are converted, or, if they refuse to be, punished by the withholding of rain. Jerusalem is holy to the Lord (xiv.). In all this there is more that differs from chaps. ix.-xi., xiii. 7-9, than the strange opposition of Judah and Jerusalem. Ephraim, or Joseph, is not mentioned, nor any return of exiles, nor punishment of the shepherds, nor coming of the Messiah,† the latter's place being taken by Jehovah. But in answer to this we may remember that the Messiah, after being described in ix. 9-12, is immediately lost behind the warlike coming of Jehovah. Both sections speak of idolatry, and of the heathen, their punishment and conversion, and do so in the same apocalyptic style. Nor does the language of the two differ in any decisive fashion. On the contrary, as Eckardt‡ and Kuiper have shown, the language is on the whole an argument for unity of authorship.§ There is, then, nothing conclusive against the position, which Stade so clearly laid down and strongly fortified, that chaps. ix.-xiv. are from the same hand, although, as he admits, this cannot be proved with absolute certainty. So also Cheyne: "With perhaps one or two exceptions, chaps. ix.-xi. and xii.-xiv. are so closely welded together that even analysis is impossible."‖

The next questions we have to decide are whether chaps. ix.-xiv. offer any evidence of being by Zechariah, the author of chaps. i.-viii., and if not to what other post-exilic date they may be assigned.

It must be admitted that in language and in style the two parts of the Book of Zechariah have features in common. But that these have been exaggerated by defenders of the unity there can be no doubt. We cannot infer anything from the fact¶ that both parts contain specimens of clumsy diction, of the repetition of the same word, of phrases (not the same phrases) unused by other writers; ** or that each is lavish in voc-

* Above, pp. 669, f.

† Robinson, pp. 76 ff.

* "Z. A. T. W.," 1893, 76 ff. See also the summaries of linguistic evidence given by Robinson. Kuenen finds in ix.-xi. the following pre-exilic elements: ix. 1-5, 8-10, 13*a* (?); x. 1 f., 10 f.; xi. 4-14 or 17.

† Kuenen.

‡ See above, p. 669, *n.*

§ See also Robinson.

‖ *Jewish Quarterly Review*, 1889, p. 81.

¶ As Robinson, *e. g.*, does.

** *E.g.*, "holy land," ii. 16, and "Mount of Olives," xiv. 4.

atives; or that each is variable in his spelling. Resemblances of that kind they share with other books: some of them are due to the fact that both sections are post-exilic. On the other hand, as Eckardt has clearly shown, there exists a still greater number of differences between the two sections, both in language and in style.* Not only do characteristic words occur in each which are not found in the other, not only do chaps. ix.-xiv. contain many more Aramaisms than chaps. i.-viii., and therefore symptoms of a later date; but both parts use the same words with more or less different meanings, and apply different terms to the same objects. There are also differences of grammar, of favourite formulas, and of other features of the phraseology, which, if there be any need, complete the proof of a distinction of dialect so great as to require to account for it distinction of authorship.

The same impression is sustained by the contrast of the historical circumstances reflected in each of the two sections. Zech. i.-viii. were written during the building of the Temple. There is no echo of the latter in "Zech." ix.-xiv. Zech. i.-viii. picture the whole earth as at peace, which was true at least of all Syria; they portend no danger to Jerusalem from the heathen, but describe her peace and fruitful expansion in terms most suitable to the circumstances imposed upon her by the solid and clement policy of the earlier Persian kings. This is all changed in "Zech." ix.-xiv. The nations are restless; a siege of Jerusalem is imminent, and her salvation is to be assured only by much war and a terrible shedding of blood. We know exactly how Israel fared and felt in the early sections of the Persian period: her interests in the politics of the world, her feelings towards her governors and her whole attitude to the heathen were not at that time those which are reflected in "Zech." ix.-xiv.

Nor is there any such resemblance between the religious principles of the two sections of the Book of Zechariah as could prove identity of origin. That both are spiritual, or that they have a similar expectation of the ultimate position of Israel in the history of the world, proves only that both were late offshoots from the same religious development, and worked upon the same ancient models. Within these outlines there are not a few divergences. Zech. i.-viii. were written before Ezra and Nehemiah had imposed the Levitical legislation upon Israel; but Eckardt has shown the dependence on the latter of "Zech." ix.-xiv.

We may, therefore, adhere to Canon Driver's assertion, that Zechariah in chaps. i.-viii. "uses a different phraseology, evinces different interests, and moves in a different circle of ideas from those which prevail in chaps. ix.-xiv."† Criticism has indeed been justified in separating, by the vast and growing majority of its opinions, the two sections from each other. This was one of the earliest results which modern criticism achieved, and the latest researches have but established it on a firmer basis.

If, then, chaps. ix.-xiv. be not Zechariah's, to what date may we assign them? We have already seen that they bear evidence of being upon the whole later than Zechariah, though they appear to contain fragments from an earlier period. Perhaps this is all we can with certainty affirm.

* *Op. cit.*, 103-109: *cf.* Driver, "Introd.," 354.
† "Introd.," p. 354.

Yet something more definite is at least probable. The mention of the Greeks, not as Joel mentions them about 400, the most distant nation to which Jewish slaves could be carried, but as the chief of the heathen powers, and a foe with whom the Jews are in touch and must soon cross swords,* appears to imply that the Syrian campaign of Alexander is happening or has happened, or even that the Greek kingdoms of Syria and Egypt are already contending for the possession of Palestine. With this agrees the mention of Damascus, Hadrach, and Hamath, the localities where the Seleucids had their chief seats.† In that case Asshur would signify the Seleucids and Egypt the Ptolemies:‡ it is these, and not Greece itself, from whom the Jewish exiles have still to be redeemed. All this makes probable the date which Stade has proposed for the chapters, between 300 and 280 B. C. To bring them further down, to the time of the Maccabees, as some have tried to do, would not be impossible so far as the historical allusions are concerned; but had they been of so late a date as that, viz., 170 or 160, we may assert that they could not have found a place in the prophetic canon, which was closed by 200, but must have fallen along with Daniel into the Hagiographa.

The appearance of these prophecies at the close of the Book of Zechariah has been explained, not quite satisfactorily, as follows. With the Book of "Malachi" they formed originally three anonymous pieces,§ which because of their anonymity were set at the end of the Book of the Twelve. The first of them begins with the very peculiar construction "Massa' Debar Jehovah," "oracle of the word of Jehovah," which, though partly belonging to the text, the editor read as a title, and attached as a title to each of the others. It occurs nowhere else. The Book of "Malachi" was too distinct in character to be attached to another book, and soon came to have the supposed name of its author added to its title.‖ But the other two pieces fell, like all anonymous works, to the nearest writing with an author's name. Perhaps the attachment was hastened by the desire to make the round number of Twelve Prophets.

ADDENDA.

Whiston's work (p. 450) is "An Essay towards restoring the True Text of the O. T. and for vindicating the Citations made thence in the N. T.," 1722, pp. 93 ff. (not seen). Besides those mentioned on p. 669 (see *n.*) as supporting the unity of Zechariah there ought to be named De Wette, Umbreit, von Hoffmann, Ebrard, etc. Kuiper's work (p. 671) is "Zacharia 9-14," Utrecht, 1894 (not seen). Nowack's conclusions are: ix.-xi. 3 date from the Greek period (we cannot date them more exactly, unless ix. 8 refers to Ptolemy's capture of Jerusalem in 320); xi., xiii. 7-9, are post-exilic; xii.-xiii. 6 long after Exile; xiv. long after Exile, later than "Malachi."

CHAPTER XXXIII.

THE CONTENTS OF "ZECHARIAH" IX.-XIV.

FROM the number of conflicting opinions which prevail upon the subject, we have seen how impossible it is to decide upon a scheme of

* ix. 13.
† ix. 1 f.
‡ x. 11. See above, p. 669.
§ See above, pp. 331 ff., for proof of the original anonymity of the Book of "Malachi."
‖ Above, p. 640.

division for "Zech." ix.-xiv. These chapters consist of a number of separate oracles, which their language and general conceptions lead us on the whole to believe were put together by one hand, and which, with the possible exception of some older fragments, reflect the troubled times in Palestine that followed on the invasion of Alexander the Great. But though the most of them are probably due to one date and possibly come from the same author, these oracles do not always exhibit a connection, and indeed sometimes show no relevance to each other. It will therefore be simplest to take them piece by piece, and, before giving the translation of each, to explain the difficulties in it and indicate the ruling ideas.

1. The Coming of the Greeks (ix. 1-8).

This passage runs exactly in the style of the early prophets. It figures the progress of war from the north of Syria southwards by the valley of the Orontes to Damascus, and then along the coasts of Phœnicia and the Philistines. All these shall be devastated, but Jehovah will camp about His own House and it shall be inviolate. This is exactly how Amos or Isaiah might have pictured an Assyrian campaign, or Zephaniah a Scythian. It is not surprising, therefore, that even some of those who take the bulk of "Zech." ix.-xiv. as post-exilic should regard ix. 1-5 as earlier even than Amos, with post-exilic additions only in vv. 6-8.* This is possible. Vv. 6-8 are certainly post-exilic, because of their mention of the half-breeds, and their intimation that Jehovah will take unclean food out of the mouth of the heathen; but the allusions in vv. 1-5 suit an early date. They equally suit, however, a date in the Greek period. The progress of war from the Orontes valley by Damascus and thence down the coast of Palestine follows the line of Alexander's campaign in 332, which must also have been the line of Demetrius in 315 and of Antigonus in 311. The evidence of language is mostly in favour of a late date.† If Ptolemy I. took Jerusalem in 320,‡ then the promise, no assailant shall return (ver. 8), is probably later than that.

In face, then, of Alexander's invasion of Palestine, or of another campaign on the same line, this oracle repeats the ancient confidence of Isaiah. God rules: His providence is awake alike for the heathen and for Israel. "Jehovah hath an eye for mankind, and all the tribes of Israel."§ The heathen shall be destroyed, but Jerusalem rest secure; and the remnant of the heathen be converted, according to the Levitical notion, by having unclean foods taken out of their mouths.

Oracle.

"The Word of Jehovah is on the land of Hadrach, and Damascus is its goal ‖—for Jehovah hath an eye *upon* the heathen,* and all the tribes of Israel—and on† Hamath, *which* borders upon it, Tyre and Sidon, for they were very wise.‡ And Tyre built her a fortress, and heaped up silver like dust, and gold like the dirt of the streets. Lo, the Lord will dispossess her, and strike her rampart§ into the sea, and she shall be consumed in fire. Ashklon shall see and shall fear, and Gaza writhe in anguish, and Ekron, for her confidence‖ is abashed, and the king shall perish from Gaza, and Ashklon lie uninhabited. Half-breeds¶ shall dwell in Ashdod, and I will cut down the pride of the Philistines. And I will take their blood from their mouth and their abominations from between their teeth,** and even they shall be left for our God, and shall become like a clan in Judah, and Ekron shall be as the Jebusite. And I shall encamp for a guard†† to My House, so that none pass by or return, and no assailant again pass upon them, for now do I regard it with Mine eyes."

2. The Prince of Peace (ix. 9-12).

This beautiful picture, applied by the Evangelist with such fitness to our Lord upon His entry to Jerusalem, must also be of post-exilic date. It contrasts with the warlike portraits of the Messiah drawn in pre-exilic times, for it clothes Him with humility and with peace. The coming King of Israel has the attributes already imputed to the Servant of Jehovah by the prophet of the Babylonian captivity. The next verses also imply the Exile as already a fact. On the whole, too, the language is of a late rather than of an early date.‡‡ Nothing in the passage betrays the exact point of its origin after the Exile.

The epithets applied to the Messiah are of very great interest. He does not bring victory or salvation, but is the passive recipient of it.§§ This determines the meaning of the preceding adjective, "righteous," which has not the moral sense of "justice," but rather that of "vindication," in which "righteousness" and "righteous" are so frequently used in Isa. xl.-lv.‖‖ He is "lowly," like the Servant of Jehovah; and comes riding not the horse, an animal for war,

* So Staerk, who thinks Amos I. made use of vv. 1-5.

† ix. 1, אדם, "mankind," in contrast to the tribes of Israel; 3, חרוץ, "gold"; 5, ישב as passive, *cf.* xii. 6; הוביש, Hi. of בּוֹשׁ, in passive sense only after Jeremiah (*cf.* above, p. 661, on Joel); in 2 Sam. xix. 6, Hosea ii. 7, it is active.

‡ See p. 667.

§ ix. 1.

‖ Heb. "resting-place:" *cf.* Zech. vi. 8, "bring Mine anger to rest." This meets the objection of Bredenkamp and others, that מנוחה is otherwise used of Jehovah alone, in consequence of which they refer the suffix to Him.

* The expression "hath an eye" is so unusual that Klostermann, *Theo. Litt. Zeit.*, 1879, 566 (quoted by Nowack), proposes to read for ערי עין, "Jehovah's are the cities of the heathen." For אדם, "mankind," as = "heathen" *cf.* Jer. xxxii. 20.

† So LXX.: Heb "also."

‡ So LXX.: Heb. has verb in sing.

§ *Cf.* Nahum iii. 8; Isa. xxvi. 1.

‖ Read מִבְטָחָה.

¶ Deut. xxiii. 3 (Heb., 2 Eng.).

** The prepositions refer to the half-breeds. Ezekiel uses the term "to eat upon the blood," *i. e.*, meat eaten without being ritually slain and consecrated, for illegal sacrifices (xxxiii. 35: *cf.* 1 Sam. xiv. 32 f.; Lev. xix. 26, xvii. 11-14).

†† מִצָּבָה for מִן־צָבָא; but to be amended to מַצָּבָה, 1 Sam. xiv. 12, "a military post." Ewald reads מְצָבָה, "rampart." LXX. ἀνάστημα = מַצֵּבָה.

‡‡ ix 10, מֹשֵׁל, *cf.* Dan. xi. 4; אפסי ארץ only in late writings (unless Deut. xxxiii. 17 be early)—see Eckardt, p. 80; 12, בצרון is ἅπαξ λεγόμενον; the last clause of 12 is based on Isa. lxi. 7. If our interpretation of צדיק and נושע be right, they are also symptoms of a late date.

§§ נוֹשָׁע (ver. 9): the passive participle.

‖‖ *Cf.* "Isaiah xl.-lxvi." ("Expositor's Bible"), p. 785.

because the next verse says that horses and chariots are to be removed from Israel,* but the ass, the animal not of lowliness, as some have interpreted, but of peace. To this day in the East asses are used, as they are represented in the Song of Deborah, by great officials, but only when these are upon civil, and not upon military, duty.

It is possible that this oracles closes with ver. 10, and that we should take vv. 11 and 12, on the deliverance from exile, with the next.

"Rejoice mightily, daughter of Zion! shout aloud, daughter of Jerusalem! Lo, thy King cometh to thee, vindicated and victorious,† meek and riding on an ass,‡ and on a colt the she-ass' foal.§ And I ‖ will cut off the chariot from Ephraim and the horse from Jerusalem, and the war-bow shall be cut off, and He shall speak peace to the nations, and His rule shall be from sea to sea and from the river even to the ends of the earth. Thou, too,—by thy covenant-blood,¶ I have set free thy prisoners from the pit.** Return to the fortress, ye prisoners of hope; even to-day do I proclaim: Double will I return to thee."††

3. The Slaughter of the Greeks (ix. 13-17).

The next oracle seems singularly out of keeping with the spirit of the last, which declared the arrival of the Messianic peace, while this represents Jehovah as using Israel for His weapons in the slaughter of the Greeks and heathens, in whose blood they shall revel. But Stade has pointed out how often in chaps. ix.-xiv. a result is first stated and then the oracle goes on to describe the process by which it is achieved. Accordingly we have no ground for affirming ix. 13-17 to be by another hand than ix. 9-12. The apocalyptic character of the means by which the heathen are to be overthrown, and the exultation displayed in their slaughter, as in a great sacrifice (ver. 15), betray Israel in a state of absolute political weakness, and therefore suit a date after Alexander's campaigns, which is also made sure by the reference to the "sons of Javan," as if Israel were now in immediate contact with them. Kirkpatrick's note should be read, in which he seeks to prove "the sons of Javan" a late gloss; ‡‡ but his reasons do not appear conclusive. The language bears several traces of lateness.§§

"For I have drawn Judah for My bow, I have charged *it* with Ephraim; and I will urge thy sons, O Zion, against the sons of ‖‖ Javan, and make thee like the sword of a hero. Then will Jehovah appear above them, and His shaft shall go forth like lightning; and the Lord Jehovah shall blow a blast on the trumpet, and travel in the storms of the south.* Jehovah will protect them, and they shall devour (?) † and trample . . . ;‡ and they shall drink their blood§ like wine, and be drenched with it, like a bowl and like the corners of the altar. And Jehovah their God will give them victory in that day. . . ‖ How good it ¶ is, and how beautiful! Corn shall make the young men flourish and new wine the maidens."

4. Against the Teraphim and Sorcerers (x. 1, 2).

This little piece is connected with the previous one only through the latter's conclusion upon the fertility of the land, while this opens with rain, the requisite of fertility. It is connected with the piece that follows only by its mention of the shepherdless state of the people, the piece that follows being against the false shepherds. These connections are extremely slight. Perhaps the piece is an independent one. The subject of it gives no clue to the date. Sorcerers are condemned both by the earlier prophets, and by the later.** Stade points out that this is the only passage of the Old Testament in which the Teraphim are said to speak.†† The language has one symptom of a late period.‡‡

After emphasising the futility of images, enchantments, and dreams, this little oracle says, therefore the people wander like sheep: they have no shepherd. Shepherd in this connection cannot mean civil ruler, but must be religious director.

"Ask from Jehovah rain in the time of the latter rain.§§ Jehovah is the maker of the lightning-flashes, and the winter rain He gives to them—to every man herbage in the field. But the Teraphim speak nothingness, and the sorcerers see lies, and dreams discourse vanity, and they comfort in vain. Wherefore they wander (?) ‖‖ like a flock of sheep, and flee about, ¶¶ for there is no shepherd."

* Why "chariot from Ephraim" and "horse from Jerusalem" is explained in "Hist. Geog.," pp. 329-331.

† See above.

‡ Symbol of peace as the horse was of war.

§ Son of she-asses.

‖ Mass.: LXX. "He."

¶ Heb. "blood of thy covenant," but the suffix refers to the whole phrase (Duhm, "Theol. der Proph.," p. 143). The covenant is Jehovah's; the blood, that which the people shed in sacrifice to ratify the covenant.

** Heb. adds "there is no water in it," but this is either a gloss, or perhaps an attempt to make sense out of a dittography of מבור, or a corruption of "none shall be ashamed."

†† Isa. lxi. 7.

‡‡ "Doctrine of the Prophets," Note A. p. 472.

§§ 14, on תימן see Eckardt; 15, זויות, Aramaism; כבש is late; 17, התנוסס, only here and Psalm lx. 6; נוב, probably late.

‖‖ So LXX.: Heb. reads, "thy sons, O Javan."

* LXX. ἐν σάλῳ τῆς ἀπειλῆς αὐτοῦ, "in the tossing of His threat," בשער גערו (?) or בשער העדו. It is natural to see here a reference to the Theophanies of Hab. iii. 3, Deut. xxxiii. (see above, pp. 596 f.).

† Perhaps וִיכַלּוּ, "overcome them." LXX. καταναλώσουσιν.

‡ Heb. "stones of a sling," אבני קלע. Wellhausen and Nowack read "sons," בני, but what then is קלע?

§ Reading דמם for Heb. והמו, "and roar."

‖ Heb. "like a flock of sheep His people," (but how is one to construe this with the context?) "for (? like) stones of a diadem lifting themselves up (? shimmering) over His land." Wellhausen and Nowack delete "for stones . . . shimmering" as a gloss. This would leave "like a flock of sheep His people in His land," to which it is proposed to add "He will feed." This gives good sense.

¶ Wellhausen, reading טובה, fem. suffix for neuter. Ewald and others "He." Hitzig and others "they," the people.

** Of these *Cf.* "Mal." iii. 5; the late Jer. xliv. 8 ff.; Isa. lxv. 3-5; and, in the Priestly Law, Lev. xix. 31, xx. 6.

†† "Z. A. T. W.," I. 60. He compares this verse with 1 Sam. xv. 23. In Ezek. xxi. 26 they give oracles.

‡‡ חזיז, "lightning-flash," only here and in Job xxviii. 26, xxxviii. 25.

§§ LXX. read: "in season early rain and latter rain."

‖‖ נסעו, used of a nomadic life in Jer. xxxi. 24 (23), and so it is possible that in a later stage of the language it had come to mean to wander or stray. But this is doubtful, and there may be a false reading, as appears from LXX. ἐξηράνθησαν.

¶¶ For יענו read וינעו. The LXX. ἐκακώθησαν read וירעו.

5. Against Evil Shepherds (x. 3-12).

The unity of this section is more apparent than its connection with the preceding, which had spoken of the want of a shepherd, or religious director, of Israel, while this is directed against their shepherds and leaders, meaning their foreign tyrants.*

The figure is taken from Jeremiah xxiii. 1 ff., where, besides, "to visit upon" † is used in a sense of punishment, but the simple "visit" ‡ in the sense of to look after, just as within ver. 3 of this tenth chapter. Who these foreign tyrants are is not explicitly stated, but the reference to Egypt and Assyria as lands whence the Jewish captives shall be brought home, while at the same time there is a Jewish nation in Judah, suits only the Greek period, after Ptolemy had taken so many Jews to Egypt,§ and there were numbers still scattered throughout the other great empire in the north, to which, as we have already seen, the Jews applied the name of Assyria. The reference can hardly suit the years after Seleucus and Ptolemy granted to the Jews in their territories the rights of citizens. The captive Jews are to be brought back to Gilead and Lebanon. Why exactly these are mentioned, and neither Samaria nor Galilee, forms a difficulty, to whatever age we assign the chapter.

The language of x. 3-12 has several late features.‖ Joseph or Ephraim, here and elsewhere in these chapters, is used of the portion of Israel still in captivity, in contrast to Judah, the returned community.

The passage predicts that Jehovah will change His poor leaderless sheep, the Jews, into war-horses, and give them strong chiefs and weapons of war. They shall overthrow the heathen, and Jehovah will bring back His exiles. The passage is therefore one with chap. ix.

"My wrath is hot against the shepherds, and I will make visitation on the he-goats:¶ yea, Jehovah of Hosts will ** visit His flock, the house of Judah, and will make them like His splendid war-horses. From Him the corner-stone, from Him the stay,†† from Him the war-bow, from Him the oppressor—shall go forth together. And in battle shall they trample on heroes as on the dirt of the streets,‡‡ and fight, for Jehovah is with them, and the riders on horses shall be abashed. And the house of Judah will I make strong and work salvation for the house of Joseph, and bring them back,§§ for I have pity for them,* and they shall be as though I had not put them away,* for I am Jehovah their God * and I will hold converse with them.* And Ephraim shall be as heroes,† and their heart shall be glad as with wine, and their children shall behold and be glad: their heart shall rejoice in Jehovah. I will whistle for them and gather them in, for I have redeemed them, and they shall be as many as they once were. I scattered them ‡ among the nations, but among the far-away they think of Me, and they will bring up § their children, and come back. And I will fetch them home from the land of Miṣraim, and from Asshur ‖ will I gather them, and to the land of Gilead and Lebānon will I bring them in, though *these* be not found *sufficient* for them. And they ¶ shall pass through the sea of Egypt,** and He shall smite the sea of breakers, and all the deeps of the Nile shall be dried, and the pride of Assyria brought down, and the sceptre of Egypt swept aside. And their strength †† shall be in Jehovah, and in His Name shall they boast themselves ‡‡—oracle of Jehovah."

6. War upon the Syrian Tyrants (xi. 1-3).

This is taken by some with the previous chapter, by others with the passage following. Either connection seems precarious. No conclusion as to date can be drawn from the language. But the localities threatened were on the southward front of the Seleucid kingdom. "Open, Lebānon, thy doors" suits the Egyptian invasions of that kingdom. To which of these the passage refers cannot of course be determined. The shepherds are the rulers.

"Open, Lebānon, thy doors, that the fire may devour in thy cedars. Wail, O pine-tree, for the cedar is fallen; §§ wail, O oaks of Bashan, for fallen is the impenetrable ‖‖ wood. Hark to the wailing of the shepherds! for their glory is destroyed. Hark how the lions roar! for blasted is the pride ¶¶ of Jordan."

7. The Rejection and Murder of the Good Shepherd (xi. 4-17; xiii. 7-9).

There follows now, in the rest of chap. xi., a longer oracle, to which Ewald and most critics after him have suitably attached chap. xiii. 7-9.

This passage appears to rise from circumstances similar to those of the preceding and from the same circle of ideas. Jehovah's people are His flock and have suffered. Their rulers are their shepherds; and the rulers of other peoples are their shepherds. A true shepherd is sought for Israel in place of the evil ones which have distressed them. The language shows

* There can therefore be none of that connection between the two pieces which Kirkpatrick assumes (p. 669 and note).

† פקד על.

‡ פקד את.

§ See above, p. 667.

‖ x. 5, בוס, Eckardt, p. 82; 6, 12, גִּבֵּר, Pi., *cf.* Eccles. x. 10, where it alone occurs besides here; 5, 11, הבישו in passive sense.

¶ As we should say, "bell-wethers": *cf.* Isa. xiv. 9, also a late meaning.

** So LXX., reading כי־יפקד for כי־פקד.

†† "Corner-stone" as name for a chief: *cf.* Judg. xx. 2; 1 Sam. xiv. 38; Isa. xix. 13. "Stay" or "tent-pin," Isa. xxii. 23. "From Him," others "from them."

‡‡ Read בַּגִּבֹּרִים and כְּטִיט (Wellhausen).

§§ Read וַהֲשִׁבוֹתִים for the Mass. וְהוֹשְׁבוֹתִים, "and I will make them to dwell."

* רחמתים and זנחתים, אלהיהם and אענם, key-words of Hosea i.-iii.

† LXX.; sing. Heb.

‡ Changing the Heb. points which make the verb future. See Nowack's note.

§ With LXX. read וְחִיּוּ for Mass. וְחָיוּ.

‖ See above, p. 669.

¶ So LXX.; Mass. sing.

** Heb. צרה, "narrow sea": so LXX., but Wellhausen suggests מערים, which Nowack adopts.

†† גברתם for גברתים.

‡‡ For יתהלכו read יתהללו, with LXX. and Syr.

§§ Heb. adds here a difficult clause, "for nobles are wasted." Probably a gloss.

‖‖ After the Kerî.

¶¶ *I. e.*, "rankness"; applied to the thick vegetation in the larger bed of the stream: see "Hist. Geog.," p. 484.

traces of a late date.* No historical allusion is obvious in the passage. The "buyers" and "sellers" of God's sheep might reflect the Seleucids and Ptolemies between whom Israel were exchanged for many years, but probably mean their native leaders. The "three shepherds cut off in a month" were interpreted by the supporters of the pre-exilic date of the chapters as Zechariah and Shallum (2 Kings xv. 8-13), and another whom these critics assume to have followed them to death, but of him the history has no trace. The supporters of a Maccabean date for the prophecy recall the quick succession of high priests before the Maccabean rising. The "one month" probably means nothing more than a very short time.

The allegory which our passage unfolds is given, like so many more in Hebrew prophecy, to the prophet himself to enact. It recalls the pictures in Jeremiah and Ezekiel of the overthrow of the false shepherds of Israel, and the appointment of a true shepherd.† Jehovah commissions the prophet to become shepherd to His sheep that have been so cruelly abused by their guides and rulers. Like the shepherds of Palestine, the prophet took two staves to herd his flock. He called one "Grace," the other "Union." In a month he cut off three shepherds—both "month" and "three" are probably formal terms. But he did not get on well with his charge. They were wilful and quarrelsome. So he broke his staff Grace, in token that his engagement was dissolved. The dealers of the sheep saw that he acted for God. He asked for his wage, if they cared to give it. They gave him thirty pieces of silver, the price of an injured slave,‡ which by God's command he cast into the treasury of the Temple, as if in token that it was God Himself whom they paid with so wretched a sum. And then he broke his other staff, to signify that the brotherhood between Judah and Israel was broken. Then, to show the people that by their rejection of the good shepherd they must fall a prey to an evil one, the prophet assumed the character of the latter. But another judgment follows. In chap. xiii. 7-9 the good shepherd is smitten and the flock dispersed.

The spiritual principles which underlie this allegory are obvious. God's own sheep, persecuted and helpless though they be, are yet obstinate, and their obstinacy not only renders God's good-will to them futile, but causes the death of the one man who could have done them good. The guilty sacrifice the innocent, but in this execute their own doom. That is a summary of the history of Israel. But had the writer of this allegory any special part of that history in view? Who were the "dealers of the flock"?

"Thus saith Jehovah my God:§ Shepherd the flock of slaughter, whose purchasers slaughter them impenitently, and whose sellers say,* Blessed be Jehovah, for I am rich!—and their shepherds do not spare them. [For I will no more spare the inhabitants of the land—oracle of Jehovah; but lo! I am about to give mankind † over, each into the hand of his shepherd,‡ and into the hand of his king; and they shall destroy the land, and I will not secure it from their hands.§] And I shepherded the flock of slaughter for the sheep merchants,‖ and I took to me two staves—the one I called Grace, and the other I called Union ¶—and so I shepherded the sheep. And I destroyed the three shepherds in one month. Then was my soul vexed with them, and they on their part were displeased with me. And I said: I will not shepherd you: what is dead, let it die; and what is destroyed, let it be destroyed; and those that survive, let them devour one another's flesh! And I took my staff Grace, and I brake it so as to annul my covenant which I made with all the peoples.** And in that day it was annulled, and the dealers of the sheep,†† who watched me, knew that it was Jehovah's word. And I said to them, If it be good in your sight, give me my wage, and if it be not good, let it go! And they weighed out my wage, thirty pieces of silver. Then said Jehovah to me, Throw it into the treasury ‡‡ (the precious wage at which I §§ had been valued of them). So I took the thirty pieces of silver, and cast them to the House of Jehovah, to the treasury.‖‖ And I brake my second staff, Union, so as to dissolve the brotherhood between Judah and Israel.¶¶ And Jehovah said to me: Take again to thee the implements of a worthless shepherd: for lo! I am about to appoint a shepherd over the land; the destroyed he will not visit, the . . .*** he will not seek out, the wounded he will not heal, the . . .††† he will not

* xi. 5, וָאַעְשִׁר, Hiph., but intransitive, "grow rich;" 6, ממציא; 7, 10, נעם (?); 8, בחל, Aram.; 13, יְקָר, Aram., Jer. xx. 5, Ezek. xxii. 25, Job xxviii. 10; in Esther ten, in Daniel four times (Eckardt); xiii. 7, עמית, one of the marks of the affinity of the language of "Zech." ix.-xiv. to that of the Priestly Code (*cf.* Lev. v. 21, xviii. 20, etc.), but in P it is concrete, here abstract; צעריב; 8, גוע, see Eckardt, p. 85.

† Jer. xxiii. 1-8; Ezek. xxxiv., xxxvii. 24 ff.: *cf.* Kirkpatrick, p. 462.

‡ Exod. xxi. 32.

§ LXX. "God of Hosts."

* Read plural with LXX.

† That is the late Hebrew name for the heathen: *cf.* ix. 1.

‡ Heb. רֵעֵהוּ, "neighbour"; read רֹעֵהוּ.

§ Many take this verse as an intrusion. It certainly seems to add nothing to the sense and to interrupt the connection, which is clear when it is removed.

‖ Heb. לָכֵן עֲנִיֵּי הַצֹּאן, "wherefore the miserable of the flock," which makes no sense. But LXX. read εἰς τὴν Χαναάνιτην, and this suggests the Heb. לכנעני, "to the Canaanites," *i. e.*, "merchants, of the sheep": so in ver. 11.

¶ Lit. "Bands."

** The sense is here obscure. Is the text sound? In harmony with the context עמים ought to mean "tribes of Israel." But every passage in the O. T. in which עמים might mean "tribes" has been shown to have a doubtful text: Deut. xxxii. 8, xxxiii. 3; Hosea x. 14; Micah i. 2.

†† See above, note ‖ on the same mis-read phrase in ver. 7.

‡‡ Heb. הַיּוֹצֵר, "the potter." LXX. χωνευτήριον, "smelting furnace." Read הָאוֹצָר by change of א for י: the two are often confounded.

§§ Wellhausen and Nowack read "thou hast been valued of them." But there is no need of this. The clause is a sarcastic parenthesis spoken by the prophet himself.

‖‖ Again Heb. "the potter," LXX. "the smelting furnace," as above in ver. 13. The additional clause "House of God" proves how right it is to read "the treasury," and disposes of the idea that "to throw to the potter" was a proverb for throwing away.

¶¶ Two codd. read "Jerusalem," which Wellhausen and Nowack adopt.

*** Heb. הַנַּעַר, "the scattered." LXX. τὸν ἐσκορπισμένον.

††† הַנִּצָּבָה, obscure: some translate "the sound" or "stable."

cherish, but he will devour the flesh of the fat and . . .*

"Woe to My worthless† shepherd, that deserts the flock! The sword be upon his arm and his right eye! May his arm wither, and his right eye be blinded."

Upon this follows the section xiii. 7-9, which develops the tragedy of the nation to its climax in the murder of the good shepherd.

"Up, Sword, against My shepherd and the man My compatriot ‡—oracle of Jehovah of Hosts. Smite § the shepherd, that the sheep may be scattered; and I will turn My hand against the little ones.‖ And it shall come to pass in all the land—oracle of Jehovah—that two-thirds shall be cut off in it, and perish, but a third shall be left in it. And I shall bring the third into the fire, and smelt it as *men* smelt silver and try it as *men* try gold. It shall call upon My Name, and I will answer it. And I will ¶ say, It is My people, and it will say, Jehovah my God!"

8. JUDAH *versus* JERUSALEM (xii. 1-7).

A title, though probably of later date than the text,** introduces with the beginning of chap. xii. an oracle plainly from circumstances different from those of the preceding chapters. The nations, not particularised as they have been, gather to the siege of Jerusalem, and, very singularly, Judah is gathered with them against her own capital. But God makes the city like one of those great boulders, deeply embedded, which husbandmen try to pull up from their fields, but it tears and wounds the hands of those who would remove it. Moreover God strikes with panic all the besiegers, save only Judah, who, her eyes being opened, perceives that God is with Jerusalem and turns to her help. Jerusalem remains in her place; but the glory of the victory is first Judah's, so that the house of David may not have too much fame nor boast over the country districts. The writer doubtless alludes to some temporary schism between the capital and country caused by the arrogance of the former. But we have no means of knowing when this took place. It must often have been imminent in the days both before and especially after the Exile, when Jerusalem had absorbed all the religious privilege and influence of the nation. The language is undoubtedly late.††

The figure of Jerusalem as a boulder, deeply bedded in the soil, which tears the hands that seek to remove it, is a most true and expressive summary of the history of heathen assaults upon her. Till she herself was rent by internal dissensions, and the Romans at last succeeded in tearing her loose, she remained planted on her own site.* This was very true of all the Greek period. Seleucids and Ptolemies alike wounded themselves upon her. But at what period did either of them induce Judah to take part against her? Not in the Maccabean.

Oracle of the Word of Jehovah upon Israel.

"Oracle of Jehovah, who stretched out the heavens and founded the earth, and formed the spirit of man within him: Lo, I am about to make Jerusalem a cup of reeling for all the surrounding peoples, and even Judah † shall be at the siege of Jerusalem. And it shall come to pass in that day that I will make Jerusalem a stone to be lifted‡ by all the peoples—all who lift it do indeed wound § themselves—and there are gathered against it all nations of the earth. In that day—oracle of Jehovah—I will smite every horse with panic, and their riders with madness; but as for the house of Judah, I will open its ‖ eyes, though every horse of the peoples I smite with blindness. Then shall the chiefs ¶ of Judah say in their hearts, . . .** the inhabitants of Jerusalem through Jehovah of Hosts their God. In that day will I make the districts of Judah like a pan of fire among timber and like a torch among sheaves, so that they devour right and left all the peoples round about, but Jerusalem shall still abide on its own site.†† And Jehovah shall first give victory to the tents ‡‡ of Judah, so that the fame of the house of David and the fame of the inhabitants of Jerusalem be not too great in contrast to Judah."

* Heb. "and their hoofs he will tear" (?).

† For Heb. האליל read as in ver. 15 האוילי.

‡ עמית: only in Lev. and here.

§ הך. Perhaps we should read אַכֶּה, "I smite," with Matt. xxvi. 31.

‖ Some take this as a promise: "turn My hand towards the little ones."

¶ LXX. Heb. אמרתי, but the ו has fallen from the front of it.

** See above, p. 671.

†† xii. 2, רַעַל, a noun not found elsewhere in O. T. We found the verb in Nahum ii. 4 (see above, p. 586), and probably in Hab. ii. 16 for והערל (see above, p. 595, *n.*): it is common in Aramean; other forms belong to later Hebrew (*cf.* Eckardt, p. 85). 3, שׂרט is used in classic Heb. only of intentional cutting and tattooing of oneself; in the sense of "wounding" which it has here it is frequent in Aramean. 3 has besides אבן מעמסה, not found elsewhere. 4 has three nouns terminating in ־ון, two of them—תמהון, "panic," and עורון, judicial "blindness"—in O. T. only found here and in Deut. xxviii. 28, the former also in Aramean. 7, למען לא is also cited by Eckardt as used only in Ezek. xix. 6, xxvi. 20, and four times in Psalms.

* xii. 6. תחתיה.

† The text reads "against" Judah, as if it with Jerusalem suffered the siege of the heathen. But (1) this makes an unconstruable clause, and (2) the context shows that Judah was "against" Jerusalem. Therefore Geiger ("Urschrift," p. 58) is right in deleting על, and restoring to the clause both sense in itself and harmony with the context. It is easy to see why על was afterwards introduced. LXX, καὶ ἐν τῇ Ἰουδαίᾳ.

‡ Since Jerome, commentators have thought of a stone by throwing or lifting which men try their strength, what we call a "putting stone." But is not the idea rather of one of the large stones half-buried in the earth which it is the effort of the husbandman to tear from its bed and carry out of his field before he ploughs it? Keil and Wright think of a heavy stone for building. This is not so likely.

§ שׂרט, elsewhere only in Lev. xxi. 5, is there used of intentional cutting of oneself as a sign of mourning. Nowack takes the clause as a later intrusion; but there is no real reason for this.

‖ Heb. "upon Judah will I keep My eyes open" to protect him, and this has analogies, Job xiv. 3, Jer. xxxii. 19. But the reading "its eyes," which is made by inserting a ו that might easily have dropped out through confusion with the initial ו of the next word, has also analogies (Isa. xlii. 7, etc.), and stands in better parallel to the next clause, as well as to the clauses describing the panic of the heathen.

¶ Others read אַלְפֵי, "thousands," *i. e.*, "districts"

** Heb. "I will find me"; LXX. εὑρήσομεν ἑαυτοῖς.

†† Hebrew adds a gloss: "in Jerusalem."

‡‡ The population in time of war.

9. Four Results of Jerusalem's Deliverance (xii. 8-xiii. 6).

Upon the deliverance of Jerusalem, by the help of the converted Judah, there follow four results, each introduced by the words that it happened "in that day" (xii. 8, 9, xiii. 1, 2). First, the people of Jerusalem shall themselves be strengthened. Second, the hostile heathen shall be destroyed, but on the house of David and all Jerusalem the spirit of penitence shall be poured, and they will lament for the good shepherd whom they slew. Third, a fountain of sin and uncleanness shall be opened. Fourth, the idols, the unclean spirit, and prophecy, now so degraded, shall all be abolished. The connection of these oracles with the preceding is obvious, as well as with the oracle describing the murder of the good shepherd (xiii. 7-9). When we see how this is presupposed by xii. 9 ff., we feel more than ever that its right place is between chaps. xi. and xii. There are no historical allusions. But again the language gives evidence of a late date.* And throughout the passage there is a repetition of formal phrases which recalls the Priestly Code and the general style of the post-exilic age.† Notice that no king is mentioned, although there are several points at which, had he existed, he must have been introduced.

1. The first of the four effects of Jerusalem's deliverance from the heathen is the promotion of her weaklings to the strength of her heroes, and of her heroes to divine rank (xii. 8). "In that day Jehovah will protect the inhabitants of Jerusalem, and the lame among them shall in that day be like David *himself*, and the house of David like God, like the Angel of Jehovah before them."

2. The second paragraph of this series very remarkably emphasises that upon her deliverance Jerusalem shall not give way to rejoicing, but to penitent lamentation for the murder of him whom she has pierced—the good shepherd whom her people have rejected and slain. This is one of the few ethical strains which run through these apocalyptic chapters. It forms their highest interest for us. Jerusalem's mourning is compared to that for "Hadad-Rimmon in the valley" or "plain of Megiddo." This is the classic battle-field of the land, and the theatre upon which Apocalypse has placed the last contest between the hosts of God and the hosts of evil:‡ In Israel's history it had been the ground not only of triumph but of tears. The greatest tragedy of that history, the defeat and death of the righteous Josiah, took place there;§ and since the earliest Jewish interpreters the "mourning of Hadad-Rimmon in the valley of Megiddo" has been referred to the mourning for Josiah.* Jerome identifies Hadad-Rimmon with Rummâni,† a village on the plain still extant, close to Megiddo. But the lamentation for Josiah was at Jerusalem; and it cannot be proved that Hadad-Rimmon is a place-name. It may rather be the name of the object of the mourning, and as Hadad was a divine name among Phœnicians and Arameans, and Rimmôn the pomegranate was a sacred tree, a number of critics have supposed this to be a title of Adonis, and the mourning like that excessive grief which Ezekiel tells us was yearly celebrated for Tammuz.‡ This, however, is not fully proved.§ Observe, further, that while the reading Hadad-Rimmon is by no means past doubt, the sanguine blossoms and fruit of the pomegranate, "red-ripe at the heart," would naturally lead to its association with the slaughtered Adonis.

"And it shall come to pass in that day that I will seek to destroy all the nations who have come in upon Jerusalem. And I will pour upon the house of David and upon all the inhabitants of Jerusalem the spirit of grace and of supplication, and they shall look to him‖ whom they have pierced; and they shall lament for him, as with lamentation for an only son, and bitterly grieve for him, as with grief for a first-born. In that day lamentation shall be as great in Jerusalem as the lamentation for Hadad-Rimmon¶ in the valley of Megiddo. And the land shall mourn, every family by itself: the family of the house of David by itself, and their wives by themselves; the family of the house of Nathan by itself, and their wives by themselves; the family of the house of Levi by itself, and their wives by themselves; the family of Shime'i ** by itself, and their wives by themselves; all the families who are left, every family by itself, and their wives by themselves."

3. The third result of Jerusalem's deliverance from the heathen shall be the opening of a fountain of cleansing. This purging of her sin follows fitly upon her penitence just described. "In that day a fountain shall be opened for the house of David, and for the inhabitants of Jerusalem, for sin and for uncleanness." ††

4. The fourth consequence is the removal of idolatry, of the unclean spirit, and of the degraded prophets from her midst. The last is especially remarkable: for it is not merely false prophets, as distinguished from true, who shall be removed: but prophecy in general. It is singular that in almost its latest passage the prophecy of Israel should return to the line of its earliest representative, Amos, who refused to call himself prophet. As in his day, the prophets had become mere professional and mercenary oracle-mongers, abjured to the point of death by their own ashamed and wearied relatives.

"And it shall be in that day—oracle of Jehovah of Hosts—I will cut off the names of the

* xii. 10, שפך רוח, not earlier than Ezek. xxxix. 29, Joel iii. 1, 2 (Heb.); תחנונים only in Job, Proverbs, Psalms, and Daniel; המר, an intrans. Hiph.; xiii. 1, מקור, "fountain," before Jeremiah only in Hosea xiii. 15 (perhaps a late intrusion), but several times in post-exilic writings instead of pre-exilic באר (Eckardt); נִדָּה, only after Ezekiel; 3, *cf.* xii. 10, דקר, chiefly, but not only, in post-exilic writings.

† See especially xii. 12 ff., which is very suggestive of the Priestly Code.

‡ "Hist. Geog.," chap. xix. On the name "plain of Megiddo" see especially notes, p. 386.

§ 2 Chron. xxxv. 22 ff.

* Another explanation offered by the Targum is the mourning for "Ahab son of Omri, slain by Hadad-Rimmon son of Tab-Rimmon."

† LXX. gives for Hadad-Rimmon only the second part, ῥοῶν.

‡ Ezek. viii. 14.

§ Baudissin, "Studien z. Sem. Rel. Gesch.," I. 295 ff.

‖ Heb. "Me"; several codd. "him": some read אֵלָיו, "to [him] whom they have pierced;" but this would require the elision of the sign of the acc. before "who." Wellhausen and others think something has fallen from the text.

¶ See above.

** LXX. Συμεών.

†† *Cf.* Ezek. xxxvi. 25, xlvii. 1.

idols from the land, and they shall not be remembered any more. And also the prophets and the unclean spirit will I expel from the land. And it shall come to pass, if any man prophesy again, then shall his father and mother who begat him say to him, Thou shalt not live, for thou speakest falsehood in the name of Jehovah: and his father and mother who begat him shall stab him for his prophesying. And it shall be in that day that the prophets shall be ashamed of their visions when they prophesy, and shall not wear the leather cloak in order to lie. And he will say, No prophet am I! A tiller of the ground I am, for the ground is my possession * from my youth up. And they shall say to him, What are these wounds in† thy hands? and he shall say, What I was wounded with in the house of my lovers!"

10. Judgment of the Heathen and Sanctification of Jerusalem (xiv.).

In another apocalyptic vision the prophet beholds Jerusalem again beset by the heathen. But Jehovah Himself intervenes, appearing in person, and an earthquake breaks out at His feet. The heathen are smitten, as they stand, into mouldering corpses. The remnant of them shall be converted to Jehovah and take part in the annual Feast of Booths. If any refuse they shall be punished with drought. But Jerusalem shall abide in security and holiness: every detail of her equipment shall be consecrate. The passage has many resemblances to the preceding oracles.‡ The language is undoubtedly late, and the figures are borrowed from other prophets, chiefly Ezekiel. It is a characteristic specimen of the Jewish Apocalypse. The destruction of the heathen is described in verses of terrible grimness: there is no tenderness nor hope exhibited for them. And even in the picture of Jerusalem's holiness we have no really ethical elements, but the details are purely ceremonial.

"Lo! a day is coming for Jehovah,§ when thy spoil will be divided in thy midst. And I will gather all the nations to besiege Jerusalem, and the city will be taken and the houses plundered and the women ravished, and the half of the city shall go into captivity, but the rest of the people shall not be cut off from the city. And Jehovah shall go forth and do battle with those nations, as in the day when He fought in the day of contest. And His feet shall stand in that day on the Mount of Olives which is over against Jerusalem on the east, and the Mount of Olives shall be split into halves from east to west by a very great ravine, and half of the Mount will slide northwards and half southwards . . . ,‖ for the ravine of mountains¶ shall extend to 'Aṣal,* and ye shall flee as ye fled from before the earthquake in the days of Uzziah king of Judah,† and Jehovah my God will come and‡ all the holy ones with Him.§ And in that day there shall not be light, . . . congeal.‖ And it shall be one ¶ day—it is known to Jehovah **—neither day nor night; and it shall come to pass that at evening time there shall be light.

"And it shall be in that day that living waters shall flow forth from Jerusalem, half of them to the eastern sea and half of them to the western sea: *both* in summer and in winter shall it be. And Jehovah shall be King over all the earth: in that day Jehovah will be One and His Name One. All the land shall be changed to plain,†† from Geba to Rimmon,‡‡ south of Jerusalem; but she shall be high and abide in her place §§ from the Gate of Benjamin up to the place of the First Gate, up to the Corner Gate, and from the Tower of Hanan'el as far as the King's Winepresses. And they shall dwell in it, and there shall be no more Ban,‖‖ and Jerusalem shall abide in security. And this shall be the stroke with which Jehovah will smite all the peoples who have warred against Jerusalem: He will make their flesh moulder while they still stand upon their feet, and their eyes shall moulder in their sockets, and their tongue shall moulder in their mouth.

["And it shall come to pass in that day, there shall be a great confusion from Jehovah among them, and they shall grasp every man the hand of his neighbour, and his hand shall be lifted against the hand of his neighbour.¶¶ And even Judah shall fight against Jerusalem, and the wealth of all the nations round about shall be swept up, gold and silver and garments, in a very great mass." These two verses, 13 and 14, obviously disturb the connection, which ver. 15 as obviously resumes with ver. 12. They are, therefore, generally regarded as an intrusion.*** But why they have been inserted is not clear. Ver. 14 is a curious echo of the strife between Judah and Jerusalem described in chap. xii.

* Read אֲדָמָה קִנְיָנִי for the Mass. אדם הקנני: so Wellhausen.

† Hed. "between."

‡ But see below, p. 679.

§ לִיהוה; or "belonging to Jehovah;" or like the "Lamed auctoris" or Lamed when construed with passive verbs (see Oxford "Heb.-Eng. Dictionary," pp. 513 and 514, col. 1), "from, by means of, Jehovah."

‖ Heb.: "and ye shall flee, the ravine of My mountains." The text is obviously corrupt. but it is difficult to see how it should be repaired. LXX., Targ. Symmachus and the Babylonian codd. (Baer, p. 84) read וְנִסְתַּם, "ye shall be closed," for וְנַסְתֶּם, "ye shall flee," and this is adopted by a number of critics (Bredenkamp, Wellhausen, Nowack). But it is hardly possible before the next clause, which says the valley extends to 'Aṣal.

¶ Wellhausen suggests the ravine (גיא) of Hinnom.

* אצל, place-name: *cf.* אָצֵל, name of a family of Benjamin, viii. 37 f., ix. 43 f.; and בֵּית הָאֵצֶל, Micah i. 11. Some would read אֵצֶל, the adverb "near by."

† Amos. i. 1.

‡ LXX.

§ LXX.; Heb. "thee."

‖ Heb. Kethibh, יְקָרוֹת יְקִפָּאוּן, "jewels" (? hardly stars as some have sought to prove from Job xxxi. 26) "grow dead" or "congealed." Heb. Ḳerê, "jewels and frost," וְקִפָּאוֹן. LXX. καὶ ψύχη καὶ πάγος, וְקָרוֹת וְקִפָּאוֹן, "and cold and frost." Founding on this Wellhausen proposes to read חוֹם for אוֹר, and renders, "there shall be neither heat nor cold nor frost." So Nowack. But it is not easy to see how חוֹם ever got changed to אוֹר.

¶ "Unique" or "the same"?

** Taken as a gloss by Wellhausen and Nowack.

†† עֲרָבָה, the name for the Jordan Valley, the Ghôr ("Hist. Geog.," pp. 482-484). It is employed, not because of its fertility, but because of its level character. *Cf.* Josephus' name for it, "the Great Plain" (IV. "Wars" viii. 2; IV. "Antt." vi. 1). also 1 Macc. v. 52, xvi. 11.

‡‡ Geba "long the limit of Judah to the north, 2 Kings xxiii. 8" ("Hist. Geog.," pp. 252, 291). Rimmon was on the southern border of Palestine (Josh. xv. 32, xix. 7), the present Umm er Rummamîn N. of Beersheba (Rob., "B. R.").

§§ Or "be inhabited as it stands."

‖‖ *Cf.* "Mal." iii. 24 (Heb.).

¶¶ Ezek. xxxviii. 21.

*** So Wellhausen and Nowack.

They may be not a mere intrusion, but simply out of their proper place; yet, if so, where this proper place lies in these oracles is impossible to determine.]

"And even so shall be the plague upon the horses, mules, camels, and asses, and all the beasts which are in those camps—just like this plague. And it shall come to pass that all that survive of all the nations who have come up against Jerusalem, shall come up from year to year to do obeisance to King Jehovah of Hosts, and to keep the Feast of Booths. And it shall come to pass that whosoever of all the races of the earth will not come up to Jerusalem to do obeisance to King Jehovah of Hosts, upon them there shall be no rain. And if the race of Egypt go not up nor come in, upon them also shall * come the plague, with which Jehovah shall strike the nations that go not up to keep the Feast of Booths. Such shall be the punishment † of Egypt, and the punishment † of all nations who do not come up to keep the Feast of Booths."

The Feast of Booths was specially one of thanksgiving for the harvest; that is why the neglect of it is punished by the withholding of the rain which brings the harvest. But such a punishment for such a neglect shows how completely prophecy has become subject to the Law. One is tempted to think what Amos or Jeremiah or even "Malachi" would have thought of this. Verily all the writers of the prophetical books do not stand upon the same level of religion. The writer remembers that the curse of no rain cannot affect the Egyptians, the fertility of whose rainless land is secured by the annual floods of her river. So he has to insert a special verse for Egypt. She also will be plagued by Jehovah, yet he does not tell us in what fashion her plague will come.

The book closes with a little oracle of the most ceremonial description, connected not only in temper but even by subject with what has gone before. The very horses, which hitherto have been regarded as too foreign,‡ or—as even in this group of oracles §—as too warlike, to exist in Jerusalem, shall be consecrated to Jehovah. And so vast shall be the multitudes who throng from all the earth to the annual feasts and sacrifices at the Temple, that the pots of the latter shall be as large as the great altar-bowls,‖ and every pot in Jerusalem and Judah shall be consecrated for use in the ritual. This hallowing of the horses raises the question, whether the passage can be from the same hand as wrote the prediction of the disappearance of all horses from Jerusalem.¶

"In that day there shall be upon the bells of the horses, Holiness unto Jehovah. And the *very* pots in the House of Jehovah shall be as the bowls before the altar. Yea, every pot in Jerusalem and in Judah shall be holy to Jehovah of Hosts, and all who sacrifice shall come and take of them and cook in them. And there shall be no more any pedlar ** in the House of Jehovah of Hosts in that day."

* So LXX. and Syr. The Heb. text inserts a "not."

† חטאת, in classic Heb. "sin"; but as in Num. xxxii. 23, and Isa. v. 18, "the punishment that sin brings down."

‡ Hosea xiv. 3.

§ ix. 10.

‖ So Wellhausen.

¶ ix. 10.

** Heb. "Canaanite." *Cf.* Christ's action in cleansing the Temple of all dealers (Matt. xxi. 12–14).

JONAH.

"And this is the tragedy of the Book of Jonah, that a Book which is made the means of one of the most sublime revelations of truth in the Old Testament should be known to most only for its connection with a whale."

CHAPTER XXXIV.

THE BOOK OF JONAH.

THE Book of Jonah is cast throughout in the form of narrative—the only one of our Twelve which is so. This fact, combined with the extraordinary events which the narrative relates, starts questions not raised by any of the rest. Besides treating, therefore, of the book's origin, unity, division, and other commonplaces of introduction, we must further seek in this chapter reasons for the appearance of such a narrative among a collection of prophetic discourses. We have to ask whether the narrative be intended as one of fact; and if not, why the author was directed to the choice of such a form to enforce the truth committed to him.

The appearance of a narrative among the Twelve Prophets is not, in itself, so exceptional as it seems to be. Parts of the Books of Amos and Hosea treat of the personal experience of their authors. The same is true of the Books of Isaiah, Jeremiah, and Ezekiel, in which the prophet's call and his attitude to it are regarded as elements of his message to men. No: the peculiarity of the Book of Jonah is not the presence of narrative, but the apparent absence of all prophetic discourse.*

Yet even this might be explained by reference to the first part of the prophetic canon—Joshua to Second Kings.† These Former Prophets, as they are called, are wholly narrative—narrative in the prophetic spirit and written to enforce a moral. Many of them begin as the Book of Jonah does:‡ they contain stories, for instance, of Elijah and Elisha, who flourished immediately before Jonah and like him were sent with commissions to foreign lands. It might therefore be argued that the Book of Jonah, though narrative, is as much a prophetic book as they are, and that the only reason why it has found a place, not with these histories, but among the Later Prophets, is the exceedingly late date of its composition.§

This is a plausible, but not the real, answer to our question. Suppose we were to find the latter by discovering that the Book of Jonah, though in narrative form, is not real history at all, nor pretends to be, but, from beginning to end, is as much a prophetic sermon as any of the other Twelve Books, yet cast in the form of parable or allegory? This would certainly explain the adoption of the book among the Twelve; nor would its allegorical character appear without precedent to those (and they are among the most conservative of critics) who maintain (as

* Unless the Psalm were counted as such. See below, p. 684.

† *Minus* Ruth, of course.

‡ *Cf.* with Jonah i. 1, וַיְהִי Josh. i. 1, 1 Sam. i. 1, 2 Sam. i. 1. The corrupt state of the text of Ezek. i. 1 does not permit us to adduce it also as a parallel.

§ See below. p. 680.

the present writer does not) the allegorical character of the story of Hosea's wife.*

It is, however, when we pass from the form to the substance of the book that we perceive the full justification of its reception among the prophets. The truth which we find in the Book of Jonah is as full and fresh a revelation of God's will as prophecy anywhere achieves. That God has "granted to the Gentiles also repentance unto life"† is nowhere else in the Old Testament so vividly illustrated. It lifts the teaching of the Book of Jonah to equal rank with the second part of Isaiah, and nearest of all our Twelve to the New Testament. The very form in which this truth is insinuated into the prophet's reluctant mind, by contrasting God's pity for the dim population of Nineveh with Jonah's own pity for his perished gourd, suggests the methods of our Lord's teaching, and invests the book with the morning air of that high day which shines upon the most evangelic of His parables.

One other remark is necessary. In our effort to appreciate this lofty gospel we labour under a disadvantage. That is our sense of humour—our modern sense of humour. Some of the figures in which our author conveys his truth cannot but appear to us grotesque. How many have missed the sublime spirit of the book in amusement or offence at its curious details! Even in circles in which the acceptance of its literal interpretation has been demanded as a condition of belief in its inspiration, the story has too often served as a subject for humorous remarks. This is almost inevitable if we take it as history. But we shall find that one advantage of the theory, which treats the book as parable, is that the features, which appear so grotesque to many, are traced to the popular poetry of the writer's own time and shown to be natural. When we prove this, we shall be able to treat the scenery of the book as we do that of some early Christian fresco, in which, however rude it be or untrue to nature, we discover an earnestness and a success in expressing the moral essence of a situation that are not always present in works of art more skilful or more correct.

1. The Date of the Book.

Jonah ben-Amittai, from Gath-hepher‡ in Galilee, came forward in the beginning of the reign of Jeroboam II. to announce that the king would regain the lost territories of Israel from the Pass of Hamath to the Dead Sea.§ He flourished, therefore, about 780, and had this book been by himself we should have had to place it first of all the Twelve, and nearly a generation before that of Amos. But the book neither claims to be by Jonah, nor gives any proof of coming from an eye-witness of the adventures which it describes,‖ nor even from a contemporary of the prophet. On the contrary, one verse implies that when it was written Nineveh had ceased to be a great city.¶ Now Nineveh fell, and was practically destroyed, in 606 B. C.** In all ancient history there was no collapse of an imperial city more sudden or so complete.* We must therefore date the Book of Jonah some time after 606, when Nineveh's greatness had become what it was to the Greek writers, a matter of tradition.

A late date is also proved by the language of the book. This not only contains Aramaic elements which have been cited to support the argument for a northern origin in the time of Jonah himself,† but a number of words and grammatical constructions which we find in the Old Testament, some of them in the later and some only in the very latest writings.‡ Scarcely less decisive are a number of apparent quotations and echoes of passages in the Old Testament, mostly later than the date of the historical Jonah, and some of them even later than the Exile.§ If it could be proved that the Book of Jonah quotes from Joel, that would indeed set it down to a very late date—probably about 300 B. C., the period of the composition of Ezra-Nehemiah, with the language of which its own shows most affinity.‖ This would leave time for its reception

*See above, p. 560.

†Acts xi. 8.

‡*Cf.* Gittah-hepher, Josh. xix. 13, by some held to be El Meshhed, three miles northeast of Nazareth. The tomb of Jonah is pointed out there.

§2 Kings xiv. 25.

‖*Cf.* Kuenen, "Einl.," II. 417, 418.

¶iii. 3: היתה, "was."

**See above, pp. 565 ff., 583 ff.

* *Cf.* George Smith, "Assyrian Discoveries," p. 94; Sayce, "Ancient Empires of the East," p. 141. *Cf.* previous note.

†As, *e. g.*, by Volck, article "Jona" in Herzog's "Real. Encycl.": the use of שֶׁל for אֲשֶׁר, as, *e. g.*, in the very early Song of Deborah. But the same occurs in many late passages: Eccles. i. 7, 11, ii. 21, 22, etc.; Psalms cxxii., cxxiv., cxxxv. 2, 8, cxxxvii. 8, cxlvi. 3.

‡A. Grammatical constructions:—i. 7, בְּשֶׁלְּמִי; 12, בְּשֶׁלִּי: that בשל has not altogether displaced אשר ל: König ("Einl.," 378) thinks a proof of the date of Jonah in the early Aramaic period. iv. 6, the use of לְ for the accusative, *cf.* Jer. xl. 2, Ezra viii. 24: seldom in earlier Hebrew, 1 Sam. xxiii. 10, 2 Sam. iii. 30, especially when the object stands before the verb, Isa. xi. 9 (this may be late), 1 Sam. xxii. 7, Job v. 2; but continually in Aramaic, Dan. ii. 10, 12, 14, 24, etc. The first personal pronoun אני (five times) occurs oftener than אנכי (twice), just as in all exilic and post-exilic writings. The numerals ii. 1, iii. 3, precede the noun, as in earlier Hebrew.

B. Words:—מנה in Pi. is a favourite term of our author, ii. 1, iv. 6, 8; is elsewhere in O. T. Hebrew found only in Dan. i. 5, 10, 18, 1 Chron. ix. 29, Psalm lxi. 8; but in O. T. Aramaic מנא Pi. מַנִּי occurs in Ezra vii. 25, Dan. ii. 24, 49, iii. 12, etc. ספינה, i. 5, is not elsewhere found in O. T., but is common in later Hebrew and in Aramaic. התעשת, i. 6, "to think," for the Heb. השב, *cf.* Psalm cxlvi. 4, but Aram. *cf.* Dan. vi. 4 and Targums. טעם in the sense "to order" or "command," iii. 7, is found elsewhere in the O. T. only in the Aramaic passages Dan. iii. 10, Ezra vi. 1, etc. רִבּוֹ, iv. 11, for the earlier רבבה occurs only in later Hebrew, Ezra ii. 64, Neh. vii. 66, 72, 1 Chron. xxix. 7 (Hosea viii. 12, Kethibh is suspected). שתק, i. 11, 12, occurs only in Psalm cvii. 30, Prov. xxiv. 20. עמל, iv. 10, instead of the usual יגע. The expression "God of Heaven," i. 9, occurs only 2 Chron. xxxvi. 23, Psalm cxxxvi. 26, Dan. ii. 18, 19, 44, and frequently in Ezra and Nehemiah.

§In chap. iv. there are undoubted echoes of the story of Elijah's depression in 1 Kings xix., though the alleged parallel between Jonah's tree (iv. 8) and Elijah's broom-bush seems to me forced. iv. 9 has been thought, though not conclusively, to depend on Gen. iv. 6, and the appearance of יהוה אלהים has been referred to its frequent use in Gen. ii. f. More important are the parallels with Joel: iii. 9 with Joel ii. 14*a*, and the attributes of God in iv. 2 with Joel ii. 13. But which of the two is the original?

‖Kleinert assigns the book to the Exile; Ewald to the fifth or sixth century; Driver to the fifth century ("Introd.," 301); Orelli to the last Chaldean or first Persian age; Vatke to the third century. These assign generally to after the Exile: Cheyne (*Theol. Rev.*, XIV., p. 218: *cf.* art. "Jonah" in the "Encycl. Brit."), König ("Einl."), Rob. Smith, Kuenen, Wildeboer, Budde, Cornill, Farrar, etc. Hitzig brings it down as far as the Maccabean age, which is impossible if the prophetic

into the Canon of the Prophets, which was closed by 200 B. C.* Had the book been later it would undoubtedly have fallen, like Daniel, within the Hagiographa.

2. The Character of the Book.

Nor does this book, written so many centuries after Jonah had passed away, claim to be real history. On the contrary, it offers to us all the marks of the parable or allegory. We have, first of all, the residence of Jonah for the conventional period of three days and three nights in the belly of the great fish, a story not only very extraordinary in itself and sufficient to provoke the suspicion of allegory (we need not stop to argue this), but apparently woven, as we shall see,† from the materials of a myth well known to the Hebrews. We have also the very general account of Nineveh's conversion, in which there is not even the attempt to describe any precise event. The absence of precise data is indeed conspicuous throughout the book. "The author neglects a multitude of things which he would have been obliged to mention had history been his principal aim. He says nothing of the sins of which Nineveh was guilty,‡ nor of the journey of the prophet to Nineveh, nor does he mention the place where he was cast out upon the land, nor the name of the Assyrian king. In any case, if the narrative were intended to be historical, it would be incomplete by the frequent fact, that circumstances which are necessary for the connection of events are mentioned later than they happened, and only where attention has to be directed to them as having already happened." § We find, too, a number of trifling discrepancies, from which some critics‖ have attempted to prove the presence of more than one story in the composition of the book, but which are simply due to the license a writer allows himself when he is telling a tale and not writing a history. Above all, there is the abrupt close to the story at the very moment at which its moral is obvious.¶ All these things are symptoms of the parable—so obvious and so natural, that we really sin against the intention of the author, and the purpose of the Spirit which inspired him, when we wilfully interpret the book as real history.**

3. The Purpose of the Book.

The general purpose of this parable is very clear. It is not, as some have maintained,†† to

canon closed in 200 B. C., and seeks for its origin in Egypt, "that land of wonders," on account of its fabulous character, and because of the description of the east wind as חרישית (iv. 8), and the name of the gourd, קיקיון, Egyptian "kiki." But such a wind and such a plant were found outside Egypt as well. Nowack dates the book after Joel.

* See above, p. 443.

† Below, pp. 687 ff.

‡ Contrast the treatment of foreign states by Elisha, Amos, and Isaiah, etc.

§ Abridged from pp. 3 and 4 of Kleinert's Introduction to the Book of Jonah in Lange's Series of Commentaries. Eng. ed., Vol. XVI.

‖ Köhler, *Theol. Rev.*, Vol. XVI.; Böhme, "Z. A. T. W.," 1887, pp. 224 ff.

¶ Indeed throughout the book the truths it enforces are always more pushed to the front than the facts.

** Nearly all the critics who accept the late date of the book interpret it as parabolic. See also a powerful article by the late Dr. Dale in the *Expositor*, Fourth Series, Vol. VI., July, 1892, pp. 1 ff. *Cf.*, too, C. H. H. Wright, "Biblical Essays" (1886), pp. 34–98.

†† Marck (quoted by Kleinert) said: "Scriptum est magna parte historicum sed ita ut in historia ipsa lateat maximi vaticinii mysterium, atque ipse fatis suis, non minus quam effatis vatem se verum demonstret." Hitzig curiously thinks that this is the reason why it has been placed in the Canon of the Prophets next to the unfulfilled prophecy of God against Edom. But by the date which Hitzig assigns to the book the prophecy against Edom was at least in a fair way to fulfilment. Riehm ("Theol. Stud. u. Krit.," 1862, pp. 413 f.): "The practical intention of the book is to afford instruction concerning the proper attitude to prophetic warnings"; these, though genuine words of God, may be averted by repentance. Volck (art. "Jona" in Herzog's "Real. Encycl.") gives the following. Jonah's experience is characteristic of the whole prophetic profession. "We learn from it (1) that the prophet must perform what God commands him, however unusual it appears; (2) that even death cannot nullify his calling; (3) that the prophet has no right to the fulfilment of his prediction, but must place it in God's hand." Vatke ("Einl.," 688) maintains that the book was written in an apologetic interest, when Jews expounded the prophets and found this difficulty, that all their predictions had not been fulfilled. "The author obviously teaches: (1) since the prophet cannot withdraw from the Divine commission, he is also not responsible for the contents of his predictions; (2) the prophet often announces Divine purposes, which are not fulfilled, because God in His mercy takes back the threat, when repentance follows; (3) the honour of a prophet is not hurt when a threat is not fulfilled, and the inspiration remains unquestioned, although many predictions are not carried out."

To all of which there is a conclusive answer, in the fact that, had the book been meant to explain or justify unfulfilled prophecy, the author would certainly not have chosen as an instance a judgment against Nineveh, because, by the time he wrote, all the early predictions of Nineveh's fall had been fulfilled, we might say, to the very letter.

explain why the judgments of God and the predictions of his prophets were not always fulfilled—though this also becomes clear by the way. The purpose of the parable, and it is patent from first to last, is to illustrate the mission of prophecy to the Gentiles, God's care for them, and their susceptibility to His word. More correctly, it is to enforce all this truth upon a prejudiced and thrice-reluctant mind.*

Whose was this reluctant mind? In Israel after the Exile there were many different feelings with regard to the future and the great obstacle which heathendom interposed between Israel and the future. There was the feeling of outraged justice, with the intense conviction that Jehovah's kingdom could not be established save by the overthrow of the cruel kingdoms of this world. We have seen that conviction expressed in the Book of Obadiah. But the nation, which read and cherished the visions of the Great Seer of the Exile,† could not help producing among her sons men with hopes about the heathen of a very different kind—men who felt that Israel's mission to the world was not one of war, but of service in those high truths of God and of His Grace which had been committed to herself. Between the two parties it is certain there was much polemic, and we find this still bitter in the time of our Lord. And some critics think that while Esther, Obadiah, and other writings of the centuries after the Return represent the one side of this polemic, which demanded the overthrow of the heathen, the Book of Jonah represents the other side, and in the vexed and reluctant prophet pictures such Jews as were willing to proclaim the destruction of the enemies of Israel, and yet like Jonah were not without the lurking fear that God would disappoint their predictions and in His patience leave the heathen

* So even Kimchi; and in modern times De Wette, Delitzsch, Bleek, Reuss, Cheyne, Wright, König, Farrar, Orelli, etc. So virtually also Nowack. Ewald's view is a little different. He thinks that the fundamental truth of the book is that "true fear and repentance bring salvation from Jehovah."

† Isa. xl ff.

room for repentance.* Their dogmatism could not resist the impression of how long God had actually spared the oppressors of His people, and the author of the Book of Jonah cunningly sought these joints in their armour to insinuate the points of his doctrine of God's real will for nations beyond the covenant. This is ingenious and plausible. But in spite of the cleverness with which it has been argued that the details of the story of Jonah are adapted to the temper of the Jewish party who desired only vengeance on the heathen, it is not at all necessary to suppose that the book was the produce of mere polemic. The book is too simple and too grand for that. And therefore those appear more right who conceive that the writer had in view, not a Jewish party, but Israel as a whole in their national reluctance to fulfil their Divine mission to the world.† Of them God had already said: "Who is blind but My servant, or deaf as My messenger whom I have sent? . . . Who gave Jacob for a spoil and Israel to the robbers? Did not Jehovah, He against whom we have sinned? —for they would not walk in His ways, neither were they obedient to His law."‡ Of such a people Jonah is the type. Like them he flees from the duty God has laid upon him. Like them he is, beyond his own land, cast for a set period into a living death, and like them rescued again only to exhibit once more upon his return an ill-will to believe that God had any fate for the heathen except destruction. According to this theory, then, Jonah's disappearance in the sea and the great fish, and his subsequent ejection upon dry land, symbolise the Exile of Israel and their restoration to Palestine.

In proof of this view it has been pointed out that, while the prophets frequently represent the heathen tyrants of Israel as the sea or the sea-monster, one of them has actually described the nation's exile as its swallowing by a monster, whom God forces at last to disgorge his living prey.§ The full illustration of this will be given in chap. xxxvi. on "The Great Fish and What it Means." Here it is only necessary to mention that the metaphor was borrowed, not, as has been alleged by many, from some Greek, or other foreign, myth, which, like that of Perseus and Andromeda, had its scene in the neighbourhood of Joppa, but from a Semitic mythology which was well known to the Hebrews, and the materials of which were employed very frequently by other prophets and poets of the Old Testament.‖

Why, of all prophets, Jonah should have been selected as the type of Israel, is a question hard but perhaps not impossible to answer. In history Jonah appears only as concerned with Israel's reconquest of her lands from the heathen. Did the author of the book say: I will take such a man, one to whom tradition attributes no outlook beyond Israel's own territories, for none could be so typical of Israel, narrow, selfish, and with no love for the world beyond herself? Or did the author know some story about a journey of Jonah to Nineveh, or at least some discourse by Jonah against the great city? Elijah went to Sarepta, Elisha took God's word to Damascus: may there not have been, though we are ignorant of it, some connection between Nineveh and the labours of Elisha's successor? Thirty years after Jonah appeared, Amos proclaimed the judgment of Jehovah upon foreign nations, with the destruction of their capitals; about the year 755 he clearly enforced, as equal with Israel's own, the moral responsibility of the heathen to the God of righteousness. May not Jonah, almost the contemporary of Amos, have denounced Nineveh in the same way? Would not some tradition of his serve as the nucleus of history round which our author built his allegory? It is possible that Jonah proclaimed doom upon Nineveh; yet those who are familiar with the prophesying of Amos, Hosea, and, in his younger days, Isaiah, will deem it hardly probable. For why do all these prophets exhibit such reserve in even naming Assyria, if Israel had already through Jonah entered into such articulate relations with Nineveh? We must, therefore, admit our ignorance of the reasons which led our author to choose Jonah as a type of Israel. We can only conjecture that it may have been because Jonah was a prophet, whom history identified only with Israel's narrower interests. If, during subsequent centuries, a tradition had risen of Jonah's journey to Nineveh or of his discourse against her, such a tradition has probability against it.

A more definite origin for the book than any yet given has been suggested by Professor Budde.* The Second Book of Chronicles refers to a "Midrash of the Book of the Kings"† for further particulars concerning King Joash. A "Midrash"‡ was the expansion, for doctrinal or homiletic purposes, of a passage of Scripture, and very frequently took the form, so dear to Orientals, of parable or invented story about the subject of the text. We have examples of Midrashim among the Apocrypha, in the Books of Tobit and Susannah and in the prayer of Manasseh, the same as is probably referred to by the

* So virtually Kuenen, "Einl.," II. p. 423; Smend, "Lehrbuch der A. T. Religionsgeschichte," pp. 408 f., and Nowack.

† That the book is a historical allegory is a very old theory. Hermann v. d. Hardt ("Ænigmata Prisci Orbis," 1723: *cf.* "Jonas in Carcharia, Israel in Carcathio," 1718, quoted by Vatke, "Einl.," p. 686) found in the book a political allegory of the history of Manasseh led into exile, and converted, while the last two chapters represent the history of Josiah. That the book was symbolic in some way of the conduct and fortunes of Israel was a view familiar in Great Britain during the first half of this century: see the Preface to the English translation of Calvin on Jonah (1847). Kleinert (in his commentary on Jonah in Lange's Series, Vol. XVI. English translation, 1874) was one of the first to expound with details the symbolising of Israel in the prophet Jonah. Then came the article in the *Theol. Review* (XIV., 1877, pp. 214 ff.) by Cheyne, following Bloch's "Studien z. Gesch. der Sammlung der althebräischen Litteratur" (Breslau, 1876); but adding the explanation of "the great fish," from Hebrew mythology (see below). Von Orelli quotes Kleinert with approval in the main.

‡ Isa. xlii. 19–24.

§ Jer. li. 34, 44 f.

‖ That the Book of Jonah employs mythical elements is an opinion that has prevailed since the beginning of this century. But before Semitic mythology was so well known as it is now, these mythical elements were thought to have been derived from the Greek mythology. So Gesenius, De Wette, and even Knobel, but see especially F. C. Baur in Ilgen's *Zeitschrift* for 1837, p. 201. Kuenen ("Einl.," 424) and Cheyne (*Theol. Rev.*, XIV.) rightly deny traces of any Greek influence on Jonah, and their denial is generally agreed in.

Kleinert (*op.cit.*, p. 10) points to the proper source in the native mythology of the Hebrews: "The sea-monster is by no means an unusual phenomenon in prophetic typology. It is the secular power appointed by God for the scourge of Israel and of the earth (Isa. xxvii. 1)"; and Cheyne (*Theol. Rev.*, XIV., "Jonah: a Study in Jewish Folk-lore and Religion") points out how Jer. li. 34, 44 f., forms the connecting link between the story of Jonah and the popular mythology.

* "Z. A. T. W.," 1892, pp. 40 ff.

† 2 Chron. xxiv. 27.

‡ *Cf.* Driver, "Introduction," I. p. 497.

Chronicler.* That the Chronicler himself used the "Midrash of the Book of the Kings" as material for his own book is obvious from the form of the latter and its adaptation of the historical narratives of the Book of Kings.† The Book of Daniel may also be reckoned among the Midrashim, and Budde now proposes to add to their number the Book of Jonah. It may be doubted whether this distinguished critic is right in supposing that the book formed the Midrash to 2 Kings xiv. 25 ff. (the author being desirous to add to the expression there of Jehovah's pity upon Israel some expression of His pity upon the heathen), or that it was extracted just as it stands, in proof of which Budde points to its abrupt beginning and end. We have seen another reason for the latter;‡ and it is very improbable that the Midrashim, so largely the basis of the Book of Chronicles, shared that spirit of universalism which inspires the Book of Jonah.§ But we may well believe that it was in some Midrash of the Book of Kings that the author of the Book of Jonah found the basis of the latter part of his immortal work, which too clearly reflects the fortunes and conduct of all Israel to have been wholly drawn from a Midrash upon the story of the individual prophet Jonah.

4. Our Lord's Use of the Book.

We have seen, then, that the Book of Jonah is not actual history, but the enforcement of a profound religious truth nearer to the level of the New Testament than anything else in the Old, and cast in the form of Christ's own parables. The full proof of this can be made clear only by the detailed exposition of the book. There is, however, one other question, which is relevant to the argument. Christ Himself has employed the story of Jonah. Does His use of it involve His authority for the opinion that it is a story of real facts?

Two passages of the Gospels contain the words of our Lord upon Jonah: Matt. xii. 39, 41, and Luke xi. 29, 30.‖ "A generation, wicked and adulterous, seeketh a sign, and sign shall not be given it, save the sign of the prophet Jonah. . . . The men of Nineveh shall stand up in the Judgment with this generation, and condemn it, for they repented at the preaching of Jonah, and behold, a greater than Jonah is here. This generation is an evil generation: it seeketh a sign; and sign shall not be given it, except the sign of Jonah. For as Jonah was a sign to the Ninevites, so also shall the Son of Man be to this generation."

These words, of course, are compatible with the opinion that the Book of Jonah is a record of real fact. The only question is, are they also compatible with the opinion that the Book of Jonah is a parable? Many say No; and they allege that those of us who hold this opinion are denying, or at least ignoring, the testimony of our Lord; or that we are taking away the whole force of the parallel which He drew. This is a question of interpretation, not of faith. We do not believe that our Lord had any thought of confirming or not confirming the historic character of the story. His purpose was purely one of exhortation, and we feel the grounds of that exhortation to be just as strong when we have proven the Book of Jonah to be a parable. Christ is using an illustration: it surely matters not whether that illustration be drawn from the realms of fact or of poetry. Again and again in their discourses to the people do men use illustrations and enforcements drawn from traditions of the past. Do we, even when the historical value of these traditions is *very* ambiguous, give a single thought to the question of their historical character? We never think of it. It is enough for us that the tradition is popularly accepted and familiar. And we cannot deny to our Lord that which we claim for ourselves.* Even conservative writers admit this. In his recent Introduction to Jonah, Orelli says expressly: "It is not, indeed, proved with conclusive necessity that, if the resurrection of Jesus was a physical fact, Jonah's abode in the fish's belly must also be just as historical."†

Upon the general question of our Lord's authority in matters of criticism, His own words with regard to personal questions may be appositely quoted: "Man, who made Me a judge or divider over you? I am come not to judge . . . but to save." Such matters our Lord surely leaves to ourselves, and we have to decide them by our reason, our common-sense, and our loyalty to truth—of all of which He Himself is the creator, and of which we shall have to render to Him an account at the last. Let us remember this, and we shall use them with equal liberty and reverence. "Bringing every thought into subjection to Christ" is surely just using our knowledge, our reason, and every other intellectual gift which He has given us, with the accuracy and the courage of His own Spirit.

5. The Unity of the Book.

The next question is that of the Unity of the Book. Several attempts have been made to prove from discrepancies, some real and some alleged, that the book is a compilation of stories from several different hands. But these essays are too artificial to have obtained any adherence from critics; and the few real discrepancies of narrative from which they start are due, as we have

* 2 Chron. xxxiii. 18.

† See Robertson Smith, "Old Test. in the Jewish Church," pp. 140, 154.

‡ See above, pp. 681 f.

§ *Cf.* Smend, "A. T. Religionsgeschichte," p. 409, n. 1.

‖ Matt. xii. 40.—"For as Jonah was in the belly of the whale three days and three nights, so shall the Son of Man be in the heart of the earth three days and three nights"—is not repeated in Luke xi. 29, 30, which confines the sign to the preaching of repentance, and is suspected as an intrusion both for this and other reasons, *e. g.*, that ver. 40 is superfluous and does not fit in with ver. 41, which gives the proper explanation of the sign; that Jonah, who came by his burial in the fish through neglect of his duty and not by martyrdom, could not therefore in this respect be a type of our Lord. On the other hand, ver. 40 is not unlike another reference of our Lord to His resurrection, John ii. 19 ff. Yet, even if ver. 40 be genuine, the vagueness of the parallel drawn in it between Jonah and our Lord surely makes for the opinion that in quoting Jonah our Lord was not concerned about quoting facts, but simply gave an illustration from a well-known tale. Matt. xvi. 4, where the sign of Jonah is again mentioned, does not explain the sign.

* Take a case. Suppose we tell slothful people that theirs will be the fate of the man who buried his talent; is this to commit us to the belief that the personages of Christ's parables actually existed? Or take the homiletic use of Shakespeare's dramas—"as Macbeth did," or "as Hamlet said." Does it commit us to the historical reality of Macbeth or Hamlet? Any preacher among us would resent being bound by such an inference. And if we resent this for ourselves, how chary we should be about seeking to bind our Lord by it.

† Eng. trans. of "The Twelve Minor Prophets," p. 172. Consult also Farrar's judicious paragraphs on the subject: "Minor Prophets," 234 f.

seen, rather to the license of a writer of parable than to any difference of authorship.*

In the question of the Unity of the Book, the Prayer or Psalm in chap. ii. offers a problem of its own, consisting as it does almost entirely of passages parallel to others in the Psalter. Besides a number of religious phrases, which are too general for us to say that one prayer has borrowed them from another,† there are several unmistakable repetitions of the Psalms.‡

And yet the Psalm of Jonah has strong features, which, so far as we know, are original to it. The horror of the great deep has nowhere in the Old Testament been described with such power or with such conciseness. So far, then, the Psalm is not a mere string of quotations, but a living unity. Did the author of the book himself insert it where it stands? Against this it has been urged that the Psalm is not the prayer of a man inside a fish, but of one who on dry land celebrates a deliverance from drowning, and that if the author of the narrative himself had inserted it, he would rather have done so after ver. 11, which records the prophet's escape from the fish.§ And a usual theory of the origin of the Psalm is that a later editor, having found the Psalm ready-made and in a collection where it was perhaps attributed to Jonah,‖ inserted it after ver. 2, which records that Jonah did pray from the belly of the fish, and inserted it there the more readily, because it seemed right for a book which had found its place among the Twelve Prophets to contribute, as all the others did, some actual discourse of the prophet whose name it bore.* This, however, is not probable. Whether the original author found the Psalm ready to his hand or made it, there is a great deal to be said for the opinion of the earlier critics,† that he himself inserted it, and just where it now stands. For, from the standpoint of the writer, Jonah was already saved, when he was taken up by the fish—saved from the deep into which he had been cast by the sailors, and the dangers of which the Psalm so vividly describes. However impossible it be for us to conceive of the compilation of a Psalm (even though full of quotations) by a man in Jonah's position,‡ it was consistent with the standpoint of a writer who had just affirmed that the fish was expressly "appointed by Jehovah," in order to save his penitent servant from the sea. To argue that the Psalm is an intrusion is therefore not only unnecessary, but it betrays failure to appreciate the standpoint of the writer. Given the fish and the Divine purpose of the fish, the Psalm is intelligible and appears at its proper place. It were more reasonable indeed to argue that the fish itself is an insertion. Besides, as we shall see, the spirit of the Psalm is national; in conformity with the truth underlying the book, it is a Psalm of Israel as a whole.

If this be correct, we have the Book of Jonah as it came from the hands of its author. The text is in wonderfully good condition, due to the ease of the narrative and its late date. The Greek version exhibits the usual proportion of clerical errors and mis-translations,§ omissions‖ and amplifications,¶ with some variant readings** and other changes that will be noted in the verses themselves.

* The two attempts which have been made to divide the Book of Jonah are those by Köhler in the *Theol. Rev.*, XVI. 139 ff., and by Böhme in the "Z. A. T. W.," VII. 224 ff. Köhler first insists on traits of an earlier age (rude conception of God, no sharp boundary drawn between heathens and the Hebrews, etc.), and then finds traces of a late revision: lacuna in i. 2; hesitation in iii. 1, in the giving of the prophet's commission, which is not pure Hebrew: change of three days to forty (*cf.* LXX.); mention of unnamed king and his edict, which is superfluous after the popular movement; beasts sharing in mourning; also in i. 5, 8, 9, 14, ii. 2, הַדָּגָה, iii. 9, iv. 1-4, as disturbing context; also the building of a booth is superfluous, and only invented to account for Jonah remaining forty days instead of the original three; iv. 6, צל על ראשו להיות for an original לְהַצִּל לוֹ = to offer him shade; 7, "the worm," תולעת, due to a copyist's change of the following בעלות. Withdrawing these, Köhler gets an account of the sparing of Nineveh on repentance following a sentence of doom, which, he says, reflects the position of the city of God in Jeremiah's time, and was due to Jeremiah's opponents, who said in answer to his sentence of doom: If Nineveh could avert her fate, why not Jerusalem? Böhme's conclusion, starting from the alleged contradictions in the story, is that no fewer than four hands have had to deal with it. A sufficient answer is given by Kuenen ("Einl.," 426 ff.), who, after analysing the dissection, says that its "improbability is immediately evident." With regard to the inconsistencies which Böhme alleges to exist in chap. iii. between ver. 5 and vv. 6-9, Kuenen remarks that "all that is needed for their explanation is a little good-will"—a phrase applicable to many other difficulties raised with regard to other Old Testament books by critical attempts even more rational than those of Böhme. Cornill characterises Böhme's hypothesis as absurd.

† "To Thy holy temple," vv. 5 and 8: *cf.* Psalm v. 8. etc. "The waters have come round me to" my very "soul," ver. 6: *cf.* Psalm lxix. 2. "And Thou broughtest up my life," ver. 7: *cf.* Psalm xxx. 4. "When my soul fainted upon me," ver. 8: *cf.* Psalm cxlii. 4, etc. "With the voice of thanksgiving," ver. 10: *cf.* Psalm xlii. 5. The reff. are to the Heb. text.

‡ *Cf.* ver. 3 with Psalm xvii. 7; ver. 4 with Psalm xlii. 8; ver. 5 with Psalm xxxi. 23; ver. 9 with Psalm xxxi. 7, and ver. 10 with Psalm l. 14.

§ Budde, as above, p. 570.

‖ De Wette, Knobel, Kuenen.

* Budde.

† *E.g.*, Hitzig.

‡ Luther says of Jonah's prayer, that "he did not speak with these exact words in the belly of the fish, nor placed them so orderly, but he shows how he took courage, and what sort of thoughts his heart had, when he stood in such a battle with death." We recognise in this Psalm "the recollection of the confidence with which Jonah hoped towards God, that since he had been rescued in so wonderful a way from death in the waves, He would also bring him out of the night of his grave into the light of day."

§ ii. 5, B has *λαόν* for *ναόν*; 1. 9. for עברי it reads עבדי, and takes the ׳ to be abbreviation for יהוה; ii. 7, for בְעדי it reads בעלי, and translates *κάτοχοι*; iv. 11, for יֹשׁ־בָהּ it reads, ישבו, and translates *κατοικοῦσι*.

‖ i. 4, גדולה, perhaps rightly omitted before following גדול; i. 8, B omits the clause באשר to לנו, probably rightly, for it is needless, though supplied by Codd. A. Q; iii. 9, one verb, *μετανοήσει*, for ישוב ונחם, probably correctly, see below.

¶ i. 2, *ἡ κραυγὴ τῆς κακίας* for רעתם; ii. 3, *τὸν θεόν μου* after יהוה; ii. 10, in obedience to another reading; iii. 1, *τὸ ἔμπροσθεν* after קראיה; iii. 8, לאמר.

** iii. 4, 8.

CHAPTER XXXV.

THE GREAT REFUSAL.

JONAH i.

WE have now laid clear the lines upon which the Book of Jonah was composed. Its purpose is to illustrate God's grace to the heathen in face of His people's refusal to fulfil their mission to them. The author was led to achieve this purpose by a parable, through which the prophet Jonah moves as the symbol of his recusant, exiled, redeemed, and still hardened people. It is the Drama of Israel's career, as the Servant of God, in the most pathetic moments of that career. A nation is stumbling on the highest road nation was ever called to tread.

> "Who is blind but My servant,
> Or deaf as My messenger whom I have sent?"

He that would read this Drama aright must remember what lies behind the Great Refusal which forms its tragedy. The cause of Israel's recusancy was not only wilfulness or cowardly sloth, but the horror of a whole world given over to idolatry, the paralysing sense of its irresistible force, of its cruel persecutions endured for centuries, and of the long famine of Heaven's justice. These it was which had filled Israel's eyes too full of fever to see her duty. Only when we feel, as the writer himself felt, all this tragic background to his story, are we able to appreciate the exquisite gleams which he flashes across it: the generous magnanimity of the heathen sailors, the repentance of the heathen city, and, lighting from above, God's pity upon the dumb heathen multitudes.

The parable or drama divides itself into three parts: The Prophet's Flight and Turning (chap. i.); The Great Fish and What it Means (chap. ii.); and The Repentance of the City (chaps. iii. and iv.).

The chief figure of the story is Jonah, son of Amittai, from Gath-hepher in Galilee, a prophet identified with that turn in Israel's fortunes by which she began to defeat her Syrian oppressors, and win back from them her own territories—a prophet, therefore, of revenge, and from the most bitter of the heathen wars. "And the word of Jehovah came to Jonah, the son of Amittai, saying, Up, go to Nineveh, the Great City, and cry out against her, for her evil is come up before Me." But "he arose to flee." It was not the length of the road, nor the danger of declaring Nineveh's sin to her face, which turned him, but the instinct that God intended by him something else than Nineveh's destruction; and this instinct sprang from his knowledge of God Himself. "Ah now, Jehovah, was not my word, while I was yet upon mine own soil, at the time I made ready to flee to Tarshish, this—that I knew that Thou art a God gracious and tender and long-suffering, plenteous in love and relenting of evil?"* Jonah interpreted the Word which came to him by the Character which he knew to be behind the Word. This is a significant hint upon the method of revelation.

It would be rash to say that, in imputing even to the historical Jonah the fear of God's grace upon the heathen, our author were guilty of an anachronism.† We have to do, however, with a greater than Jonah—the nation herself. Though perhaps Israel little reflected upon it, the instinct can never have been far away that some day the grace of Jehovah might reach the heathen too. Such an instinct, of course, must have been almost stifled by hatred born of heathen oppression, as well as by the intellectual scorn which Israel came to feel for heathen idolatries. But we may believe that it haunted even those dark periods in which revenge upon the Gentiles seemed most just, and their destruction the only means of establishing God's kingdom in the world. We know that it moved uneasily even beneath the rigour of Jewish legalism. For its secret was that faith in the essential grace of God, which Israel gained very early and never lost, and which was the spring of every new conviction and every reform in her wonderful development. With a subtle appreciation of all this, our author imputes the instinct to Jonah from the outset. Jonah's fear, that after all the heathen may be spared, reflects the restless apprehension even of the most exclusive of his people—an apprehension which by the time our book was written seemed to be still more justified by God's long delay of doom upon the tyrants whom He had promised to overthrow.

But to the natural man in Israel the possibility of the heathen's repentance was still so abhorrent that he turned his back upon it. "Jonah rose to flee to Tarshish from the face of Jehovah." In spite of recent arguments to the contrary, the most probable location of Tarshish is the generally accepted one, that it was a Phœnician colony at the other end of the Mediterranean. In any case it was far from the Holy Land; and by going there the prophet would put the sea between himself and his God. To the Hebrew imagination there could not be a flight more remote. Israel was essentially an inland people. They had come up out of the desert, and they had practically never yet touched the Mediterranean. They lived within sight of it, but from ten to twenty miles of foreign soil intervened between their mountains and its stormy coast. The Jews had no traffic upon the sea, nor (but for one sublime instance* to the contrary) had their poets ever employed it except as a symbol of arrogance and restless rebellion against the will of God.† It was all this popular feeling of the distance and strangeness of the sea which made our author choose it as the scene of the prophet's flight from the face of Israel's God. Jonah had to pass, too, through a foreign land to get to the coast: upon the sea he would only be among heathen. This was to be part of his conversion. "He went down to Yapho, and found a ship going to Tarshish, and paid the fare thereof, and embarked on her to get away with" her crew‡ "to Tarshish—away from the face of Jehovah."

The scenes which follow are very vivid: the sudden wind sweeping down from the very hills on which Jonah believed he had left his God; the tempest; the behaviour of the ship, so alive with effort that the story attributes to her the feelings of a living thing—"she thought she must be broken"; the despair of the mariners, driven from the unity of their common task to the hopeless diversity of their idolatry—"they cried every man unto his own god"; the jettisoning of the tackle of the ship to lighten her (as we should say, they let the masts go by the

* iv. 2.

† For the grace of God had been the most formative influence in the early religion of Israel (see p. 447), and Amos, only thirty years after Jonah, emphasised the moral equality of Israel and the Gentiles before the one God of righteousness. Given these two premisses of God's essential grace and the moral responsibility of the heathen to Him, and the conclusion could never have been far away that in the end His essential grace must reach the heathen too. Indeed in sayings not later than the eighth century it is foretold that Israel shall become a blessing to the whole world. Our author, then, may have been guilty of no anachronism in imputing such a foreboding to Jonah.

* Second Isaiah. See chap. lx.

† See the author's "Hist. Geog. of the Holy Land," pp. 131–134.

‡ Heb. "them."

board); the worn-out prophet in the hull of the ship, sleeping like a stowaway; the group gathered on the heaving deck to cast the lot; the passenger's confession, and the new fear which fell upon the sailors from it; the reverence with which these rude men ask the advice of him, in whose guilt they feel not the offence to themselves, but the sacredness to God; the awakening of the prophet's better self by their generous deference to him; how he counsels to them his own sacrifice; their reluctance to yield to this, and their return to the oars with increased perseverance for his sake. But neither their generosity nor their efforts avail. The prophet again offers himself, and as their sacrifice he is thrown into the sea.

"And Jehovah cast a wind * on the sea, and there was a great tempest,† and the ship threatened‡ to break up. And the sailors were afraid, and cried every man unto his own god; and they cast the tackle of the ship into the sea, to lighten it from upon them. But Jonah had gone down to the bottom of the ship and lay fast asleep. And the captain of the ship§ came to him, and said to him, What art thou doing asleep? Up, call on thy God; peradventure the God will be gracious to us, that we perish not. And they said every man to his neighbour, Come, and let us cast lots, that we may know for whose sake is this evil *come* upon us. So they cast lots, and the lot fell on Jonah. And they said to him, Tell us now,‖ what is thy business, and whence comest thou? what is thy land, and from what people art thou? And he said to them, A Hebrew am I, and a worshipper of the God of Heaven,¶ who made the sea and the dry land. And the men feared greatly, and said to him, What is this thou hast done? (for they knew he was fleeing from the face of Jehovah, because he had told them). And they said to him, What are we to do to thee that the sea cease *raging* against us? For the sea was surging higher and higher. And he said, Take me and throw me into the sea; so shall the sea cease *raging* against you: for I am sure that it is on my account that this great tempest is *risen* upon you. And the men laboured ** with the oars to bring the ship to land, and they could not, for the sea grew more and more stormy against them. So they called on Jehovah and said, Jehovah, let us not perish, we pray Thee, for the life of this man, neither bring innocent blood upon us: for Thou art Jehovah, Thou doest as Thou pleasest. Then they took up Jonah and cast him into the sea, and the sea stilled from its raging. But the men were in great awe of Jehovah, and sacrificed to Him and vowed vows."

How very real it is and how very noble! We see the storm, and then we forget the storm in the joy of that generous contrast between heathen and Hebrew. But the glory of the passage is the change in Jonah himself. It has been called his punishment and the conversion of the heathen. Rather it is his own conversion. He meets again not only God, but the truth from which he fled. He not only meets that truth, but he offers his life for it.

* So LXX.: Heb. "a great wind."
† Heb. "on the sea.
‡ Lit. "reckoned" or "thought."
§ Heb. "ropes."
‖ The words "for whose sake is this evil *come* upon us" do not occur in LXX. and are unnecessary.
¶ Wellhausen suspects this form of the Divine title.
** Heb. "aug."

The art is consummate. The writer will first reduce the prophet and the heathen whom he abhors to the elements of their common humanity. As men have sometimes seen upon a mass of wreckage or on an ice-floe a number of wild animals, by nature foes to each other, reduced to peace through their common danger, so we descry the prophet and his natural enemies upon the strained and breaking ship. In the midst of the storm they are equally helpless, and they cast for all the lot which has no respect of persons. But from this the story passes quickly, to show how Jonah feels not only the human kinship of these heathen with himself, but their susceptibility to the knowledge of his God. They pray to Jehovah as the God of the sea and the dry land; while we may be sure that the prophet's confession, and the story of his own relation to that God, forms as powerful an exhortation to repentance as any he could have preached in Nineveh. At least it produces the effects which he has dreaded. In these sailors he sees heathen turned to the fear of the Lord. All that he has fled to avoid happens there before his eyes and through his own mediation.

The climax is reached, however, neither when Jonah feels his common humanity with the heathen nor when he discovers their awe of his God, but when in order to secure for them God's sparing mercies he offers his own life instead. "Take me up and cast me into the sea; so shall the sea cease from *raging* against you." After their pity for him has wrestled for a time with his honest entreaties, he becomes their sacrifice.

In all this story perhaps the most instructive passages are those which lay bare to us the method of God's revelation. When we were children this was shown to us in pictures of angels bending from heaven to guide Isaiah's pen, or to cry Jonah's commission to him through a trumpet. And when we grew older, although we learned to dispense with that machinery, yet its infection remained, and our conception of the whole process was mechanical still. We thought of the prophets as of another order of things; we released them from our own laws of life and thought, and we paid the penalty by losing all interest in them. But the prophets were human, and their inspiration came through experience. The source of it, as this story shows, was God. Partly from His guidance of their nation, partly through close communion with Himself, they received new convictions of His character. Yet they did not receive these mechanically. They spake neither at the bidding of angels, nor like heathen prophets in trance or ecstasy, but as "they were moved by the Holy Ghost." And the Spirit worked upon them first as the influence of God's character,* and second through the experience of life. God and life—these are all the postulates for revelation.

At first Jonah fled from the truth, at last he laid down his life for it. So God still forces us to the acceptance of new light and the performance of strange duties. Men turn from these, because of sloth or prejudice, but in the end they have to face them, and then at what a cost! In youth they shirk a self-denial to which in some storm of later life they have to bend with heavier, and often hopeless hearts. For their narrow prejudices and refusals, God punishes them by

* "I knew how Thou art a God gracious."

bringing them into pain that stings, or into responsibility for others that shames, these out of them. The drama of life is thus intensified in interest and beauty; characters emerge heroic and sublime.

> "But, oh the labour,
> O prince, the pain!"

Sometimes the neglected duty is at last achieved only at the cost of a man's breath; and the truth, which might have been the bride of his youth and his comrade through a long life, is recognised by him only in the features of Death.

CHAPTER XXXVI.

THE GREAT FISH AND WHAT IT MEANS—THE PSALM.

JONAH ii.

AT this point in the tale appears the Great Fish. "And Jehovah prepared a great fish to swallow Jonah, and Jonah was in the belly of the fish three days and three nights."

After the very natural story which we have followed, this verse obtrudes itself with a shock of unreality and grotesqueness. What an anticlimax! say some; what a clumsy intrusion! So it is if Jonah be taken as an individual. But if we keep in mind that he stands here, not for himself, but for his nation, the difficulty and the grotesqueness disappear. It is Israel's ill-will to the heathen, Israel's refusal of her mission, Israel's embarkation on the stormy sea of the world's politics, which we have had described as Jonah's. Upon her flight from God's will there followed her Exile, and from her Exile, which was for a set period, she came back to her own land, a people still, and still God's servant to the heathen. How was the author to express this national death and resurrection? In conformity with the popular language of his time, he had described Israel's turning from God's will by her embarkation on a stormy sea, always the symbol of the prophets for the tossing heathen world that was ready to engulf her; and now to express her exile and return he sought metaphors in the same rich poetry of the popular imagination.

To the Israelite who watched from his hills that stormy coast on which the waves hardly ever cease to break in their impotent restlessness, the sea was a symbol of arrogance and futile defiance to the will of God. The popular mythology of the Semites had filled it with turbulent monsters, snakes, and dragons who wallowed like its own waves, helpless against the bounds set to them, or rose to wage war against the gods in heaven and the great lights which they had created; but a god slays them and casts their carcases for meat and drink to the thirsty people of the desert.* It is a symbol of the perpetual war between light and darkness; the dragons are the clouds, the slayer the sun. A variant form, which approaches closely to that of Jonah's great fish, is still found in Palestine. In May, 1891, I witnessed at Hasbeya, on the western skirts of Hermon, an eclipse of the moon.

*For the Babylonian myths see Sayce's Hibbert Lectures; George Smith's "Assyrian Discoveries"; and Gunkel, "Schöpfung u. Chaos."

When the shadow began to creep across her disc there rose from the village a hideous din of drums, metal pots, and planks of wood beaten together; guns were fired, and there was much shouting. I was told that this was done to terrify the great fish which was swallowing the moon, and to make him disgorge her.

Now these purely natural myths were applied by the prophets and poets of the Old Testament to the illustration, not only of Jehovah's sovereignty over the storm and the night, but of His conquest of the heathen powers who had enslaved His people.* Isaiah had heard in the sea the confusion and rage of the peoples against the bulwark which Jehovah set around Israel; † but it is chiefly from the time of the Exile onward that the myths themselves, with their cruel monsters and the prey of these, are applied to the great heathen powers and their captive, Israel. One prophet explicitly describes the Exile of Israel as the swallowing of the nation by the monster, the Babylonian tyrant, whom God forces at last to disgorge his prey. Israel says: ‡ "Nebuchadrezzar the king of Babylon hath devoured me§ and crushed me,§ . . . he hath swallowed me up like the Dragon, filling his belly, from my delights he hath cast me out." But Jehovah replies:‖ "I will punish Bel in Babylon, and I will bring out of his mouth that which he hath swallowed. . . . My people, go ye out of the midst of her."

It has been justly remarked by Canon Cheyne that this passage may be considered as the intervening link between the original form of the myth and the application of it made in the story of Jonah.¶ To this the objection might be offered that in the story of Jonah the "great fish" is not actually represented as the means of the prophet's temporary destruction, like the monster in Jeremiah li., but rather as the vessel of his deliverance.** This is true, yet it only means that our author has still further adapted the very plastic material offered him by this much-transformed myth. But we do not depend for our proof upon the comparison of a single passage. Let the student of the Book of Jonah read carefully the many passages of the Old Testament, in which the sea or its monsters rage in vain against Jehovah, or are harnessed and led about by Him; or still more those passages in which His conquest of these monsters is made to figure His conquest of the heathen powers,††—and the conclusion will appear irresistible that the story of the "great fish" and of Jonah the type of Israel is drawn from the same source. Such a solution of the problem has one great advantage. It relieves us of the grotesqueness which attaches to the literal conception of the story, and of the necessity of those painful efforts for accounting for a miracle which have distorted the common-sense and even the orthodoxy of so many commentators of the book.‡‡ We are dealing, let us remember, with

* Passages in which this class of myths are taken in a physical sense are Job iii. 8, vii. 12, xxvi. 12, 13, etc., etc., and passages in which it is applied politically are Isa. xxvii. 1, li. 9; Jer. li. 34, 44; Psalm lxxiv., etc. See Gunkel, "Schöpfung u. Chaos."

† Chap. xvii. 12-14.

‡ Jer. li. 34.

§ Heb. margin, LXX. and Syr.; Heb. text "us."

‖ Jer. li. 44, 45.

¶ Cheyne, *Theol. Rev.* XIV. See above, p. 682.

** See above, p. 684, on the Psalm of Jonah.

†† Above, p. 687, *n*.

‡‡ It is very interesting to notice how many commentators (*e. g.*, Pusey, and the English edition of Lange) who take the story in its individual meaning, and therefore

poetry—a poetry inspired by one of the most sublime truths of the Old Testament, but whose figures are drawn from the legends and myths of the people to whom it is addressed. To treat this as prose is not only to sin against the common-sense which God has given us, but against the simple and obvious intention of the author. It is blindness both to reason and to Scripture.

These views are confirmed by an examination of the Psalm or Prayer which is put into Jonah's mouth while he is yet in the fish. We have already seen what grounds there are for believing that the Psalm belongs to the author's own plan, and from the beginning appeared just where it does now.* But we may also point out how, in consistence with its context, this is a Psalm, not of an individual Israelite, but of the nation as a whole. It is largely drawn from the national liturgy.† It is full of cries which we know, though they are expressed in the singular number, to have been used of the whole people, or at least of that pious portion of them, who were Israel indeed. True that in the original portion of the Psalm, and by far its most beautiful verses, we seem to have the description of a drowning man swept to the bottom of the sea. But even here, the colossal scenery and the magnificent hyperbole of the language suit not the experience of an individual, but the extremities of that vast gulf of exile into which a whole nation was plunged. It is a nation's carcase which rolls upon those infernal tides that swirl among the roots of mountains and behind the barred gates of earth. Finally, vv. 9 and 10 are obviously a contrast, not between the individual prophet and the heathen, but between the true Israel, who in exile preserve their loyalty to Jehovah, and those Jews who, forsaking their "covenant-love," lapse to idolatry. We find many parallels to this in exilic and post-exilic literature.

"And Jonah prayed to Jehovah his God from the belly of the fish, and said:—

"I cried out of my anguish to Jehovah, and He answered me;
From the belly of Inferno I sought help—Thou heardest my voice.
For Thou hadst ‡ cast me into the depth, to the heart of the seas, and the flood rolled around me;
All Thy breakers and billows went over me.
Then I said, I am hurled from Thy sight:
How § shall I ever again look towards Thy holy temple?
Waters enwrapped me to the soul; the Deep rolled around me;
The tangle was bound about my head.
I was gone down to the roots of the hills;
Earth *and* her bars were behind me for ever.
But Thou broughtest my life up from destruction, Jehovah my God!
When my soul fainted upon me, I remembered Jehovah,
And my prayer came in unto Thee, to Thy holy temple.
They that observe the idols of vanity,
They forsake their covenant-love.
But to the sound of praise I will sacrifice to Thee;
What I have vowed I will perform.
Salvation is Jehovah's.

"And Jehovah spake to the fish, and it threw up Jonah on the dry land."

as miraculous, immediately try to minimise the miracle by quoting stories of great fishes who have swallowed men, and even men in armour, whole, and in one case at least have vomited them up alive!

* See above, pp. 684 f.

† See above, p. 684, *nn*.

‡ The grammar, which usually expresses result, more literally runs, "And Thou didst cast me;" but after the preceding verse it must be taken not as expressing consequence but cause.

§ Read אֵיךְ for אַךְ, and with the LXX. take the sentence interrogatively.

CHAPTER XXXVII.

THE REPENTANCE OF THE CITY.

JONAH iii.

HAVING learned, through suffering, his moral kinship with the heathen, and having offered his life for some of them, Jonah receives a second command to go to Nineveh. He obeys, but with his prejudice as strong as though it had never been humbled, nor met by Gentile nobleness. The first part of his story appears to have no consequences in the second.* But this is consistent with the writer's purpose to treat Jonah as if he were Israel. For, upon their return from Exile, and in spite of all their new knowledge of themselves and the world, Israel continued to cherish their old grudge against the Gentiles.

"And the word of Jehovah came to Jonah the second time, saying, Up, go to Nineveh, the great city, and call unto her with the call which I shall tell thee. And Jonah arose and went to Nineveh, as Jehovah said. Now Nineveh was a city great before God, three days' journey" through and through.† "And Jonah began by going through the city one day's journey, and he cried and said, Forty ‡ days more and Nineveh shall be overturned."

Opposite to Mosul, the well-known emporium of trade on the right bank of the Upper Tigris, two high artificial mounds now lift themselves from the otherwise level plain. The more northerly takes the name of Kujundschik, or "little lamb," after the Turkish village which couches pleasantly upon its northeastern slope. The other is called in the popular dialect Nebi Yunus, "Prophet Jonah," after a mosque dedicated to him, which used to be a Christian church: but the official name is Nineveh. These two mounds are bound to each other on the west by a broad brick wall, which extends beyond them both, and is connected north and south by other walls, with a circumference in all of about nine English miles. The interval, including the mounds, was covered with buildings, whose ruins still enable us to form some idea of what was for centuries the wonder of the world. Upon terraces and substructions of enormous breadth rose storied palaces, arsenals, barracks, libraries, and temples. A lavish water system spread in all directions from canals with massive embankments and sluices. Gardens were lifted into mid-air, filled with rich plants and rare and beautiful animals. Alabaster, silver, gold, and precious stones relieved the dull masses of brick and flashed sunlight from every frieze and battlement. The surrounding walls were so broad that chariots could roll abreast on them. The gates, and especially the river gates, were very massive.§

All this was Nineveh proper, whose glory the Hebrews envied and over whose fall more than

* Only in iii. 1, "second time," and in iv. 2 are there any references from the second to the first part of the book.

† The diameter rather than the circumference seems intended by the writer, if we can judge by his sending the prophet "one day's journey through the city." Some, however, take the circumference as meant, and this agrees with the computation of sixty English miles as the girth of the greater Nineveh described below.

‡ LXX. Codd. B, etc., read "three days"; other Codd. have the "forty" of the Heb. text.

§ For a more detailed description of Nineveh see above on the Book of Nahum, pp. 584 ff.

one of their prophets exult. But this was not the Nineveh to which our author saw Jonah come. Beyond the walls were great suburbs,* and beyond the suburbs other towns, league upon league of dwellings, so closely set upon the plain as to form one vast complex of population, which is known to Scripture as "The Great City." † To judge from the ruins which still cover the ground,‡ the circumference must have been about sixty miles, or three days' journey. It is these nameless leagues of common dwellings which roll before us in the story. None of those glories of Nineveh are mentioned of which other prophets speak, but the only proofs offered to us of the city's greatness are its extent and its population.§ Jonah is sent to three days, not of mighty buildings, but of homes and families, to the Nineveh, not of kings and their glories, but of men, women, and children, "besides much cattle." The palaces and temples he may pass in an hour or two, but from sunrise to sunset he treads the dim drab mazes where the people dwell.

When we open our hearts for heroic witness to the truth there rush upon them glowing memories of Moses before Pharaoh, of Elijah before Ahab, of Stephen before the Sanhedrim, of Paul upon Areopagus, of Galileo before the Inquisition, of Luther at the Diet. But it takes a greater heroism to face the people than a king, to convert a nation than to persuade a senate. Princes and assemblies of the wise stimulate the imagination; they drive to bay all the nobler passions of a solitary man. But there is nothing to help the heart, and therefore its courage is all the greater, which bears witness before those endless masses, in monotone of life and colour, that now paralyse the imagination like long stretches of sand when the sea is out, and again terrify it like the resistless rush of the flood beneath a hopeless evening sky.

It is, then, with an art most fitted to his high purpose that our author—unlike all other prophets, whose aim was different—presents to us, not the description of a great military power: king, nobles, and armed battalions: but the vision of those monotonous millions. He strips his country's foes of everything foreign, everything provocative of envy and hatred, and unfolds them to Israel only in their teeming humanity. ‖

His next step is still more grand. For this teeming humanity he claims the universal human possibility of repentance—that and nothing more.

Under every form and character of human life, beneath all needs and all habits, deeper than despair and more native to man than sin itself, lies the power of the heart to turn. It was this and not hope that remained at the bottom of Pandora's Box when every other gift had fled. For this is the indispensable secret of hope. It lies in every heart, needing indeed some dream of Divine mercy, however far and vague, to rouse it; but when roused, neither ignorance of God, nor pride, nor long obduracy of evil may withstand it. It takes command of the whole nature of a man, and speeds from heart to heart with a violence, that like pain and death spares neither age nor rank nor degree of culture. This primal human right is all our author claims for the men of Nineveh. He has been blamed for telling us an impossible thing, that a whole city should be converted at the call of a single stranger; and others have started up in his defence and quoted cases in which large Oriental populations have actually been stirred by the preaching of an alien in race and religion; and then it has been replied, "Granted the possibility, granted the fact in other cases, yet where in history have we any trace of this alleged conversion of all Nineveh?" and some scoff, "How could a Hebrew have made himself articulate in one day to those Assyrian multitudes?"

How long, O Lord, must Thy poetry suffer from those who can only treat it as prose? On whatever side they stand, sceptical or orthodox, they are equally pedants, quenchers of the spiritual, creators of unbelief.

Our author, let us once for all understand, makes no attempt to record an historical conversion of this vast heathen city. For its men he claims only the primary human possibility of repentance; expressing himself not in this general abstract way, but as Orientals, to whom an illustration is ever a proof, love to have it done—by story or parable. With magnificent reserve he has not gone further; but only told into the prejudiced faces of his people, that out there, beyond the Covenant, in the great world lying in darkness, there live, not beings created for ignorance and hostility to God, elect for destruction, but men with consciences and hearts, able to turn at His Word and to hope in His Mercy—that to the farthest ends of the world, and even on the high places of unrighteousness, Word and Mercy work just as they do within the Covenant.

The fashion in which the repentance of Nineveh is described is natural to the time of the writer. It is a national repentance, of course, and though swelling upwards from the people, it is confirmed and organised by the authorities: for we are still in the Old Dispensation, when the picture of a complete and thorough repentance could hardly be otherwise conceived. And the beasts are made to share its observance, as in the Orient they always shared and still share in funeral pomp and trappings.* It may have been, in addition, a personal pleasure to our writer to record the part of the animals in the movement. See how, later on, he tells us that for their sake also God had pity upon Nineveh.

"And the men of Nineveh believed upon God, and cried a fast, and from the greatest of them to the least of them they put on sackcloth. And word came to the king of Nineveh, and he rose off his throne, and cast his mantle from upon him, and dressed in sackcloth and sat in the dust. And he sent criers to say in Nineveh:—

"By Order of the King and his Nobles, thus: —Man and Beast, Oxen and Sheep, shall not taste anything, neither eat nor drink water. But let them clothe themselves † in sackcloth, both man and beast, and call upon God with power, and turn every man from his evil way and from *every* wrong which they have in hand. Who knoweth but that God may ‡ relent and turn

* רחבות עיר, Gen. x. 11.

† Gen. x. 12, according to which the Great City included, besides Nineveh, at least Resen and Kelach.

‡ And taking the present Kujundschik, Nimrud, Khorsabad, and Balawat as the four corners of the district.

§ iii. 2, iv. 11.

‖ Compare the Book of Jonah, for instance, with the Book of Nahum.

* *Cf.* Herod. IX. 24; Joel i. 18; Virgil, "Eclogue" V., "Æneid" XI. 80 ff.; Plutarch, "Alex." 72.

† LXX.: "and they did clothe themselves in sackcloth," and so on.

‡ So LXX. Heb. text: "may turn and relent, and turn."

from the fierceness of His wrath, that we perish not? *

"And God saw their doings, how they turned from their evil way; and God relented of the evil which He said He would do to them, and did it not."

CHAPTER XXXVIII.

ISRAEL'S JEALOUSY OF JEHOVAH.

JONAH iv.

HAVING illustrated the truth, that the Gentiles are capable of repentance unto life, the Book now describes the effect of their escape upon Jonah, and closes by revealing God's full heart upon the matter.

Jonah is very angry that Nineveh has been spared. Is this (as some say) because his own word has not been fulfilled? In Israel there was an accepted rule that a prophet should be judged by the issue of his predictions: "If thou say in thine heart, How shall we know the word which Jehovah hath not spoken?—when a prophet speaketh in the name of Jehovah, if the thing follow not nor come to pass, that is the thing which Jehovah hath not spoken, but the prophet hath spoken presumptuously, thou shalt have no reverence for him." † Was it this that stung Jonah? Did he ask for death because men would say of him that when he predicted Nineveh's overthrow he was false and had not God's word? Of such fears there is no trace in the story. Jonah never doubts that his word came from Jehovah, nor dreads that other men will doubt. There is absolutely no hint of anxiety as to his professional reputation. But, on the contrary, Jonah says that from the first he had the foreboding, grounded upon his knowledge of God's character, that Nineveh would be spared, and that it was from this issue he shrank and fled to go to Tarshish. In short he could not, either then or now, master his conviction that the heathen should be destroyed. His grief, though foolish, is not selfish. He is angry, not at the baffling of his word, but at God's forbearance with the foes and tyrants of Israel.

Now, as in all else, so in this, Jonah is the type of his people. If we can judge from their literature after the Exile, they were not troubled by the non-fulfilment of prophecy, except as one item of what was the problem of their faith—the continued prosperity of the Gentiles. And this was not, what it appears to be in some Psalms, only an intellectual problem or an offence to their sense of justice. Nor could they meet it always, as some of their prophets did, with a supreme intellectual scorn of the heathen, and in the proud confidence that they themselves were the favourites of God. For the knowledge that God was infinitely gracious haunted their pride; and from the very heart of their faith arose a jealous fear that He would show His grace to others than themselves. To us it may be difficult to understand this temper. We have not been trained to believe ourselves an elect people; nor have we suffered at the hands of the heathen. Yet, at least, we have contemporaries and fellow-Christians among whom we may find still alive many of the feelings against which the Book of Jonah was written. Take the Oriental Churches of to-day. Centuries of oppression have created in them an awful hatred of the infidel, beneath whose power they are hardly suffered to live. The barest justice calls for the overthrow of their oppressors. That these share a common humanity with themselves is a sense they have nearly lost. For centuries they have had no spiritual intercourse with them; to try to convert a Mohammedan has been for twelve hundred years a capital crime. It is not wonderful that Eastern Christians should have long lost power to believe in the conversion of infidels, and to feel that anything is due but their destruction. The present writer once asked a cultured and devout layman of the Greek Church, Why then did God create so many Mohammedans? The answer came hot and fast: To fill up Hell! Analogous to this were the feelings of the Jews towards the peoples who had conquered and oppressed them. But the jealousy already alluded to aggravated these feelings to a rigour no Christian can ever share. What right had God to extend to their oppressors His love for a people who alone had witnessed and suffered for Him, to whom He had bound Himself by so many exclusive promises, whom He had called His Bride, His Darling, His Only One? And yet the more Israel dwelt upon that Love the more they were afraid of it. God had been so gracious and so long-suffering to themselves that they could not trust Him not to show these mercies to others. In which case, what was the use of their uniqueness and privilege? What worth was their living any more? Israel might as well perish.

It is this subtle story of Israel's jealousy of Jehovah, and Jehovah's gentle treatment of it, which we follow in the last chapter of the book. The chapter starts from Jonah's confession of a fear of the results of God's lovingkindness and from his persuasion that, as this spread of the heathen, the life of His servant spent in opposition to the heathen was a worthless life; and the chapter closes with God's own vindication of His Love to His jealous prophet.

"It was a great grief to Jonah, and he was angered; and he prayed to Jehovah and said: Ah now, Jehovah, while I was still upon mine own ground, at the time that I prepared to flee to Tarshish, was not this my word, that I knew Thee to be a God gracious and tender, long-suffering and plenteous in love, relenting of evil? And now, Jehovah, take, I pray Thee, my life from me, for for me death is better than life."

In this impatience of life as well as in some subsequent traits, the story of Jonah reflects that of Elijah. But the difference between the two prophets was this, that while Elijah was very jealous *for* Jehovah, Jonah was very jealous *of* Him. Jonah could not bear to see the love promised to Israel alone, and cherished by her, bestowed equally upon her heathen oppressors. And he behaved after the manner of jealousy and

* The alleged discrepancies in this account have been already noticed. As the text stands the fast and mourning are proclaimed and actually begun before word reaches the king and his proclamation of fast and mourning goes forth. The discrepancies might be removed by transferring the words in ver. 6, "and they cried a fast, and from the greatest of them to the least they clothed themselves in sackcloth," to the end of ver. 8, with a לאמר or ויאמרו to introduce ver. 9. But, as said above (pp. 681, 684, *n*.), it is more probable that the text as it stands was original, and that the inconsistencies in the order of the narrative are due to its being a tale or parable.

† Deut. xviii. 21, 22.

of the heart that thinks itself insulted. He withdrew, and sulked in solitude, and would take no responsibility nor further interest in his work. Such men are best treated by a caustic gentleness, a little humour, a little rallying, a leaving to nature, and a taking unawares in their own confessed prejudices. All these—I dare to think even the humour—are present in God's treatment of Jonah. This is very natural and very beautiful. Twice the Divine Voice speaks with a soft sarcasm: "Art thou very angry?" * Then Jonah's affections, turned from man to God, are allowed their course with a bit of nature, the fresh and green companion of his solitude; and then when all his pity for this has been roused by its destruction, that very pity is employed to awaken his sympathy with God's compassion for the great city, and he is shown how he has denied to God the same natural affection which he confesses to be so strong in himself. But why try further to expound so clear and obvious an argument?

"But Jehovah said, Art thou *so* very angry?" Jonah would not answer—how lifelike is his silence at this point!—"but went out from the city and sat down before it,† and made him there a booth and dwelt beneath it in the shade, till he should see what happened in the city. And Jehovah God prepared a gourd,‡ and it grew up above Jonah to be a shadow over his head. . . .§ And Jonah rejoiced in the gourd with a great joy. But as dawn came up the next day God prepared a worm, and *this* * wounded the gourd, that it perished. And it came to pass, when the sun rose, that God prepared a dry east-wind,† and the sun smote on Jonah's head, so that he was faint, and begged for himself that he might die,‡ saying, Better my dying than my living! And God said unto Jonah, Art thou so very angry about the gourd? And he said, I am very angry—even unto death! And Jehovah said: Thou carest for a gourd for which thou hast not travailed, nor hast thou brought it up, a thing that came in a night and in a night has perished.§ And shall I not care for Nineveh, the Great City,‖ in which there are more than twelve times ten thousand human beings who know not their right hand from their left, besides much cattle?"

God had vindicated His love to the jealousy of those who thought that it was theirs alone. And we are left with this grand vague vision of the immeasurable city, with its multitude of innocent children and cattle, and God's compassion brooding over all.

* The Hebrew may be translated either, first "Doest thou well to be angry?" or second, "Art thou very angry?" Our versions both prefer the *first*, though they put the *second* in the margin. LXX. take the *second*. That the second is the right one is not only proved by its greater suitableness, but by Jonah's answer to the question, "I am very angry, *yea*, even unto death."

† Heb. "the city."

‡ קִיקָיוֹן, the Egyptian kiki, the Ricinus or Palma Christi. See above, p. 680, *n*.

§ Heb. adds "to save him from his evil," perhaps a gloss.

* Heb. "it."

† חֲרִישִׁית. The Targum implies a "quiet," *i. e.*, "sweltering, east wind." Hitzig thinks that the name is derived from the season of ploughing, and some modern proverbs appear to bear this out: "an autumn east wind." LXX. *συγκαίων*. Siegfried-Stade: "a cutting east wind," as if from חרשׁ. Steiner emends to חריסית, as if from חֶרֶס = "the piercing," a poetic name of the sun; and Böhme, "Z. A. T. W.," VI. 256, to חרירית, from חרר, "to glow." Köhler (*Theol. Rev.*, XVI., p. 143) compares חֶרֶשׂ, "dried clay."

‡ Heb.: "begged his life, that he might die."

§ Heb.: "which was the son of a night, and son of a night has perished."

‖ Gen. x. 12.

THE GOSPEL OF ST. MATTHEW

CONTENTS.

THE GOSPEL OF ST. MATTHEW.

BY THE REV. JOHN MONRO GIBSON, M. A., D. D.

CHAPTER I.

THE COMING OF THE CHRIST.

MATTHEW i.

THE New Testament opens appropriately with the four Gospels; for, though in their present form they are all later in date than some of the Epistles, their substance was the basis of all apostolic preaching and writing. As the Pentateuch to the Old Testament, so is the fourfold Evangel to the New.

That there should be a manifold presentation of the great facts which lie at the foundation of our faith and hope, was both to be expected and desired. The Gospel of Jesus Christ, as proclaimed by the first preachers of it, while in substance always the same, would be varied in form, and in number and in variety of details, according to the individuality of the speaker, the kind of audience before him, and the special object he might have in view at the time. Before any form of presentation had been crystallised, there would therefore be an indefinite number of Gospels, each "according to" the individual preacher of "Christ and Him crucified." It is, therefore a marvellous proof of the guidance and control of the Divine Spirit that out of these numerous oral Gospels there should emerge four, each perfect in itself, and together affording, as with the all-round completeness of sculpture, a life-like representation of the Lord Jesus Christ. It is manifestly of great advantage to have these several portraits of our Lord, permitting us to see Him from different points of view, and with varying arrangements of light and shade; all the more that, while three of them set forth in abundant variety of detail that which is more external,—the face, the features, the form, all the expression of that wondrous Life,—the fourth, appropriately called on that account "the Gospel of the heart of Jesus," unveils more especially the hidden riches of His inner Life. But, besides this, a manifold Gospel was needed, in order to meet the wants of man in the many-sidedness of his development. As the heavenly "city lieth four square," with gates on the east, and the west, and the north, and the south, to admit strangers coming from all points of the compass; so must there be in the presentation of the Gospel an open door for all mankind. How this great purpose is attained by the fourfold Gospel with which the New Testament opens can be readily shown; and even a brief statement of it may serve a useful purpose as introductory to our study of that which is known as the First Gospel.

The inscription over the cross was in three languages: Hebrew, Latin, and Greek. These languages represented the three great civilisations which were the final outcome of ancient history—the Jewish, the Roman, the Greek. These three were not like so many nations selected at random, but stood for three leading types of humanity. The Jew was the man of the past. He could claim Moses and the prophets; he had Abraham for his father; his records went back to the Genesis of all things. He represented ancient prerogative and privilege, the conservatism of the East. The Roman was the man of the present. He was master of the world. He represented power, prowess, and victory; and while serving himself heir to the culture which came from the shores of the Ægean Sea, he had combined with it the rude strength and restless activity of the barbarian and Scythian of the North. The Greek was the man of the future. He had lost his political empire, but still retained an empire in the world of thought. He represented humanity, and the ideal, and all the promise which was afterwards to be realised in the culture of the nations of the West. The Jew was the man of tradition, the Roman the man of energy, the Greek the man of thought. Turning now to the Gospels, we find the wants of each of these three types provided for in a wondrous way. St. Matthew addresses himself especially to the Jew with his Gospel of fulfilment, St. Mark to the Roman with "his brief and terse narrative of a three years' campaign," St. Luke to the Greek with that all-pervading spirit of humanity and catholicity which is so characteristic of his Evangel; while for those who have been gathered from among the Jews and Romans and Greeks—a people who are now no longer Jews or Greeks, but are "all one in Christ Jesus," prepared to receive and appreciate the deeper things of Christ—there is a fourth Gospel, issued at a later date, with characteristics specially adapted to them: the mature work of the then venerable John, the apostle of the Christian.

It is manifest that for every reason the Gospel of St. Matthew should occupy the foremost place. "To the Jew first" is the natural order, whether we consider the claims of "the fathers," or the necessity of making it clear that the new covenant was closely linked to the old. ' Salvation is of the Jews;" the Christ of God, though the Saviour of the world, had been in a very special sense "the Hope of Israel," and therefore it is appropriate that He should be represented first from the standpoint of that nation. We have, accordingly, in this Gospel, a faithful setting forth of Christ as He presented Himself to the mind and heart of a devout Jew, "an Israelite indeed, in whom was no guile," rejoicing to find in Him One who fulfilled ancient prophecy and promise, realised the true ideal of the kingdom of God, and substantiated His claim to be Himself the divine Saviour-King for whom the nation and the world had waited long.

The opening words of this Gospel suggest that we are at the genesis of the New Testament, the genesis not of the heavens and the earth, but of Him who was to make for us "new heavens and a new earth, wherein dwelleth righteousness." The Old Testament opens with the thought, "Behold I make all things;" the New Testament with that which amounts to the promise, "Behold I make all things new." It begins with the advent of "the Second Man, the Lord from

Heaven." That He was indeed a "Second Man," and not merely one of the many that have sprung from the first man, will presently appear; but first it must be made clear that He is man indeed, "bone of our bone, flesh of our flesh;" and therefore the inspired historian begins with His historic genealogy. True to his object, however, he does not trace back our Lord's descent, as does St. Luke, to the first man, but contents himself with that which is especially interesting to the Jew, setting Him forth as "the son of David, the son of Abraham." There is another difference between the genealogies, of a more serious kind, which has been the occasion of much difficulty; but which also seems to find readiest explanation in the different object each Evangelist had in view. St. Luke, writing for the Gentile, is careful to give the natural descent, while St. Matthew, writing for the Jew, sets forth that line of descent—diverging from the other after the time of David—which made it clear to the Jew that He was the rightful heir to the kingdom. The object of the one is to set Him forth as the Son of Man; of the other to proclaim Him King of Israel.

St. Matthew gives the genealogy in three great epochs or stages, which, veiled in the Authorised Version by the verse division, are clearly exhibited to the eye in the paragraphs of the Revised Version, and which are summed up and made emphatic at the close of the genealogical tree (ver. 17). The first is from Abraham to David; the second from David to the captivity in Babylon; the third from the captivity to Christ. If we glance at these, we shall find that they represent three great stages in the development of the Old Testament promises which find their fulfilment in the Messiah.

"To Abraham and to his seed were the promises made." As given to Abraham himself, the promise ran thus: "In thy seed shall all the nations of the earth be blessed." As made to David, it indicated that the blessing to the nations should come through a king of his line. These were the two great promises to Israel. There were many others; but these stand out from the rest as constituting the mission and the hope of Israel. Now, after long waiting, both are to be fulfilled in Christ. He is the chosen Seed in Whom all nations shall be blessed. He is the Son of David, who is to sit upon His throne for ever, and reign, not over Israel alone, but over men, as "Prince of Peace" and "King of Glory." But what has the captivity in Babylon to do with it? Very much; as a little reflection will show.

The captivity in Babylon, as is well known, was followed by two great results: (1) it cured the people of idolatry for ever, so that, while politically the kingdom had passed away, in reality, and according to the spirit, it was then for the first time constituted as a kingdom of God. Till then, though politically separate from the Gentile nations, spiritually Israel had become as one of them; for what else than a heathen nation was the northern kingdom in the days of Ahab or the southern kingdom in the time of Ahaz? But after the captivity, though as a nation shattered into fragments, spiritually Israel became and continued to be one. (2) The other great result of the captivity was the Dispersion. Only a small remnant of the people came back to Palestine. Ten of the tribes passed out of sight, and but a fraction of the other two returned. The rest remained in Babylon, or were scattered abroad among the nations of the earth. Thus the Jews in their dispersion formed, as it were, a Church throughout the ancient world,—their eyes ever turned in love and longing to the Temple at Jerusalem, while their homes and their business were among the Gentiles—in the world, but not of it; the prototype of the future Church of Christ, and the soil out of which it should afterwards spring. Thus out of the captivity in Babylon sprang, first, the spiritual as distinguished from the political kingdom, and, next, the world-wide as distinguished from the merely national Church. Clearly, then, the Babylonish captivity was not only a most important historical event, but also a stage in the grand preparation for the Advent of the Messiah. The original promise made to Abraham, that in his seed should all the nations of the earth be blessed, was shown in the time of David to be a promise which should find its fulfilment in the coming of a king; and as the king after God's heart was foreshadowed in David, so the kingdom after the Divine purpose was foreshadowed in the condition of the people of God after the captivity in Babylon, purified from idolatry, scattered abroad among the nations, with their innumerable synagogues (prototypes of our churches) and their peculiarities of faith and life and worship. Abraham was called out of Babylon to be a witness for God and the coming Christ; and, after the long training of centuries, his descendants were taken back to Babylon, to scatter from that world-centre the seed of the coming kingdom of God. Thus it comes to pass that in Christ and His kingdom we see the culmination of that wonderful history which has for its great stages of progress Abraham, David,* the Captivity, Christ.

So much for the earthly origin of the Man Christ Jesus; but His heavenly descent must also be told; and with what exquisite simplicity and delicacy is this done. There is no attempt to make the words correspond with the greatness of the facts. As simple and transparent as clear glass, they allow the facts to speak for themselves. So it is all the way through this Evangel. What a contrast here to the spurious Gospels afterwards produced, when men had nothing to tell, and so must put in their own poor fictions, piously intending sometimes to add lustre to the too simple story of the Infancy, but only with the effect of degrading it in the eyes of all men of taste and judgment. But here there is no need of fiction, no need even of rhetoric or sentiment. The fact itself is so great that the more simply it is told the better. The Holy One of Israel came into the world with no tinsel of earthly pomp; and in strict harmony with His mode of entrance, the story of His birth is told with like simplicity. The Sun of Righteousness rises like the natural sun, in silence; and in this Gospel, as in all the others, passes on to its setting

*To some minds it may present itself as a difficulty that the great name of Moses should not find a place in the series; was not he as much of an epoch-maker as David? The answer is that, from the point of view of prophecy and promise, he was not. This, which lies implicitly in St. Matthew's summary, is set forth explicitly by St. Paul in his epistle to the Galatians, where he shows that the Law, as a stage in the dealings of God with the nation, did not belong to the main course of development, but came in as an episode, was "added because of transgressions" (Gal. iii. 16–19).

through the heaven of the Evangelist's thought, which stands, like that other heaven, "majestic in its own simplicity."

The story of the Incarnation is often represented as incredible; but if those who so regard it would only reflect on that doctrine of heredity which the science of recent years has brought into such prominence, if they would only consider what is involved in the obvious truth that, "that which is born of the flesh is flesh," they would see that it was not only natural but necessary that the birth of Jesus Christ should be "on this wise." Inasmuch as "the first man is of the earth, earthy," "the Second Man" must be "of heaven," or He will be no Second Man at all; He will be sinful and earthy like all the others. But all that is needful is met in the manner so chastely and beautifully set forth by our Evangelist, in words which, angelic in their tone and like the blue of heaven in their purity, so well become the angel of the Lord.

Some wonder that nothing is said here of Nazareth and what took place there, and of the journey to Bethlehem; and there are those who are fain even to find some inconsistency with the third Gospel in this omission, as if there were any need to wonder at omissions in a story which tells of the first year on one page and the thirtieth on the next! These Gospels are not biographies. They are memorials, put together for a special purpose, to set forth this Jesus as the Son of God and Saviour of the world. And the special object, as we have seen, of St. Matthew is to set Him forth as the Messiah of Israel. In accordance with this object we have His birth told in such a way as to bring into prominence those facts only in which the Evangelist specially recognised a fulfilment of Old Testament prophecy. Here again the names give us the main thoughts. Just as Abraham, David, Babylon, suggest the main object of the genealogy, so the names Emmanuel, Jesus, suggest the main object of the record of His birth. "All this was done that it might be fulfilled which was spoken by the prophet."

The first name mentioned is "Jesus." To understand it as St. Matthew did, we must bear in mind that it is the old historic name Joshua, and that the first thought of the Hebrew mind would be, Here is One who shall fulfil all that was typified in the life and work of the two Old Testament heroes who bore that name, so full of hopeful significance.* The first Joshua was Israel's captain on the occasion of their first settlement in the Land of Promise after the bondage in Egypt; the second Joshua was Israel's high priest at their second settlement in the land after the bondage in Babylon. Both were thus associated with great deliverances; but neither the one nor the other had given the rest of full salvation to the people of God (see Heb. iv. 8); what they had done had only been to procure for them political freedom and a land they could call their own,—a picture in the earthly sphere of what the Coming One was to accomplish in the spiritual sphere. The salvation from Egypt and from Babylon were both but types of the great salvation from sin which was to come through the Christ of God. These or such as these must have been the thoughts in the mind of Joseph when he heard the angel's words: "Thou shalt call His name Joshua; for it is He that shall save His people from their sins."

Joseph, though a poor carpenter of Nazareth, was a true son of David, one of those who waited for the salvation of Israel, who had welcomed the truth set forth by Daniel, that the coming kingdom was to be a kingdom of the saints of the Most High,—not of political adventurers, as was the idea of the corrupt Judaism of the time; so he was prepared to welcome the truth that the coming Saviour was One who should deliver, not from the rule of *Rome*, but from the guilt and power and death of *Sin*.

As the name Joshua, or Jesus, came from the earliest times of Israel's national history, the name Emmanuel came from its latest, even out of the dark days of King Ahaz, when the hope of the people was directed to the birth of a Child who should bear this name. Some have thought it enough to show that there was a fulfilment of this hope in the time of Ahaz, to make it evident that St. Matthew was mistaken in finding its fulfilment in Christ; but this idea, like so many others of the same kind, is founded on ignorance of the relation of the Old Testament history to the New Testament times. We have seen that though Joshua of the early times and his successor of the same name did each a work of his own, yet both of them were in relation to the future but prototypes of the Great Joshua who was to come. In the same way exactly, if there was, as we believe, a deliverance in the time of Ahaz, to which the prophet primarily referred, it was, as in so many other cases, but a picture of the greater one in which the gracious purpose of God, manifested in all these partial deliverances, was to be "fulfilled," *i. e.*, filled to the full. The idea in the name "Emmanuel" was not a new one even in the time of King Ahaz. "I will be with you;" "Certainly I will be with you;" "Fear not, for I am with you,"—such words of gracious promise had been echoed and re-echoed all down the course of the history of the people of God, before they were enshrined in the name prophetically used by Isaiah in the days of King Ahaz; and they were finally embodied, incarnated, in the Child born at Bethlehem in the fulness of the time, to Whom especially belongs that name of highest hope, "Emmanuel," "God with us."

If, now, we look at these two names, we shall see that they not only point to a fulfilment, in the largest sense, of Old Testament prophecy, but to the fulfilment of that which we all need most—the satisfaction of our deepest wants and longings. "God is light;" sin is darkness. With God is the fountain of life; "sin when it is finished bringeth forth death." Here shines the star of hope; there lies the abyss of despair. Now, without Christ we are tied to sin, separated from God. Sin is near; God is far. That is our curse. Therefore what we need is God brought near and sin taken away—the very blessings guaranteed in these two precious names of our Lord. As Emmanuel, He brings God near to us, near in His own incarnate person, near in His loving life, near in His perfect sympathy, near in His perpetual presence, according to the promise, "Lo, I am with you alway, even unto the end of the world." As Jesus, He saves us from our sins. How he does it is set forth in the sequel of the Gospel, culminating in the sacrifice of the cross, "to finish the transgression, and to make an end of sins, and to make

*The Hebrew name Joshua, of which Jesus is simply the Greek transliteration, combines the two words Jehovah and Salvation (*cf.* Num. xiii. 16.)

reconciliation for iniquity, and to bring in everlasting righteousness." For He has not only to bring God down to us, but also to lift us up to God; and while the incarnation effects the one, the atonement, followed by the work of the Holy Spirit, is necessary to secure the other. He touches man, the creature, at his cradle; He reaches down to man, the sinner, at His cross—the end of His descent to us, the beginning of our ascent with Him to God. There we meet Him and, saved from sin, we know Him as our Jesus; and reconciled to God, we have Him with us as Emmanuel, God with us, always with us, with us throughout all life's changes, with us in death's agony, with us in the life to come, to guide us into all its wisdom and honour and riches and glory and blessing.

CHAPTER II.

HIS RECEPTION.

MATTHEW ii.

THIS one chapter contains all that St. Matthew records of the Infancy. St. Mark and St. John tell us nothing, and St. Luke very little. This singular reticence has often been remarked upon, and it certainly is most noteworthy, and a manifest sign of genuineness and truthfulness: a token that what these men wrote was in the deepest sense not their own. For if they had been left to themselves in the performance of the task assigned them, they could not have restrained themselves as they have done. The Jews of the time attached the greatest importance to child-life, as is evident from the single fact that they had no less than eight different words to mark the successive stages of development from the new-born babe up to the young man; and to omit all reference to these stages, except the slight notice of the Infancy in this chapter, was certainly not "according to Matthew" the Jew, —not what would have been expected of him had he been left to himself. It can only be explained by the fact that he spoke or was silent according as he was moved or restrained by the Holy Ghost. This view is strikingly confirmed by comparison with the spurious Gospels afterwards published, by men who thought they could improve on the original records with their childish stories as to what the boy Jesus said and did. These awkward fictions reflect the spirit of the age; the simple records of the four Evangelists mirror for us the Spirit of Truth. To the vulgar mind they may seem bare and defective, but all men of culture and mature judgment recognise in their simplicity and naturalness a note of manifest superiority.

Much space might be occupied in setting forth the advantages of this reticence, but a single illustration may suggest the main thought. Recall for a moment the well-known picture entitled, "The Shadow of the Cross," designed and executed by a master, one who might surely be considered qualified to illustrate in detail the life at Nazareth. We have nothing to say as to the merit of the picture as a work of art: let those specially qualified to judge speak of this; but is it not generally felt that the realism of the [illegible]rpenter's shop is most painful? The eye is in[illegible]ctively averted from the too obtrusive de[illegible] while the mind gladly returns from the startling vividness of the picture to the vague impressions made on us by the mere hints in the sacred Scriptures. Was it not well that our blessed Saviour should grow in retirement and seclusion; and if so, why should that seclusion be invaded? If His family life was withdrawn from the eyes of the men of that time, there remains the same reason why it should be withdrawn from the eyes of the men of all time; and the more we think of it, the more we realise that it is better in every way that the veil should have been dropped just where it has been, and that all should remain just as it was, when with unconscious skill the sacred artists finished their perfect sketches of the child Jesus.

Perhaps, however, the question may be asked: If St. Matthew would tell us so little, why say anything at all? What was his object in relating just what he has set down in this chapter? We believe it must have been to show how Christ was received. It seems, in fact, to correspond to that single sentence in the fourth Gospel, "He came unto His own, and His own received Him not;" only St. Matthew gives us a wider and brighter view; he shows us not only how Jerusalem rejected Him, but how the East welcomed Him and Egypt sheltered Him. Throughout the entire Old Testament our attention is called, not merely to Jerusalem, which occupied the centre of the ancient world, but to the kingdoms round about, especially to the great empires of the East and South—the empire of the East represented in succession by Ancient Chaldea, Assyria, Babylonia, Media, and Persia; and that of the South—the mighty monarchy of Egypt, which under its thirty dynasties held on its steady course alongside these. How natural, then, for the Evangelist whose special mission it was to connect the old with the new, to take the opportunity of showing that, while His own Jerusalem rejected her Messiah, her old rivals of the East and of the South gave Him a welcome. In the first chapter the Child Jesus was set forth as the Heir of the promise made to Abraham and his seed, and the fulfilment of the prophecy given to the chosen people; now He is further set forth as the One who satisfies the longings of those whom they had been taught to regard as their natural enemies, but who now must be looked upon as "fellow-heirs" with them of God's heritage, and "partakers of His promise in Christ by the Gospel." It will be seen, then, how the second chapter was needed to complete the first, and how the two together give us just such a view of the Advent as was most needed by the Jews of the period, while it is most instructive and suggestive to men of all countries and of all time. As, then, the last paragraph began with, "Now the birth of Jesus Christ was on this wise," we may regard this as beginning with, "Now the reception of Jesus Christ was on this wise."

According to the plan of these expositions, we must disregard details, and many interesting questions, for the consideration of which it is surely enough to refer to the many well-known and widely-read books on the Life of Christ; and confine ourselves to those general thoughts and suggestions which seem best fitted to bring out the spirit of the passage as a whole.

Let us, then, look first at the manner of His reception by Jerusalem, the city which as Son of David He could claim as peculiarly His own. It was the very centre of the circle of Old Testament illumination. It had all possible advantages, over every other place in the world, for knowing when and how the Christ should come. Yet, when He did come, the people of Jerusalem know nothing about it, but had their first intimation of the fact from strangers who had come from the far East to seek Him. And not only did they know nothing about it till they were told, but, when told, they were troubled (ver. 3). Indifference where we should have expected eagerness, trouble where we should have looked for joy!

We have only to examine the contemporary accounts of the state of society in Jerusalem to understand it thoroughly, and to see how exceedingly natural it was. Those unacquainted with these records can have no idea of the gaiety and frivolity of the Jewish capital at the time. Every one, of course, knows something of the style and magnificence in which Herod the Great lived; but one is not apt to suppose that luxurious living was the rule among the people of the town. Yet so it seems to have been. Dr. Edersheim, who has made a special study of this subject, and who quotes his authorities for each separate statement, thus describes * the state of things: "These Jerusalemites—townspeople as they called themselves—were so polished, so witty, so pleasant. . . . And how much there was to be seen and heard in those luxuriously furnished houses, and at these sumptuous entertainments! In the women's apartments friends from the country would see every novelty in dress, adornments, and jewellery, and have the benefit of examining themselves in looking-glasses. . . . And then the lady-visitors might get anything in Jerusalem, from a false tooth to an Arabian veil, a Persian shawl, or an Indian dress!" Then, after furnishing what he calls "too painful evidence of the luxuriousness at Jerusalem at that time, and of the moral corruption to which it led," he concludes by giving an account of what one of the sacred books of the time describes as "the dignity of the Jerusalemites," mentioning particulars like these: "the wealth which they lavished on their marriages; the ceremony which insisted on repeated invitations to the guests to a banquet, and that men inferior should not be bidden to it; the dress in which they appeared; the manner in which the dishes were served, the wine in white crystal vases; the punishment of the cook who failed in his duty," and so on.

If things of that kind represented the dignity of the people of Jerusalem, we need not ask why they were troubled when they heard that to them had been born in Bethlehem a Saviour who was Christ the Lord. A Saviour who would save them from their sins was the very last thing people of that kind wanted. A Herod suited them better, for it was he and his court that set the example of the luxury and profligacy which characterised the capital. Do not all these revelations as to the state of things in the capital of Israel set off more vividly than ever the pure lustre of the quiet, simple, humble, peaceful surroundings of the Babe of Bethlehem and Boy of Nazareth? Put the "dignity" and trouble of Jerusalem over against the humility and peace of Bethlehem, and say which is the more truly dignified and desirable. When we look at the contrast we cease to wonder that, with the exception of a very few devout Simeons and Annas, waiting for the consolation of Israel, Jerusalem, as a whole, was troubled to hear the rumour of the advent of her Saviour-King.

Herod's trouble we can so readily understand that we need not spend time over it, or over what he did to get rid of it, so thoroughly in keeping as it was with all that history tells us of his character and conduct. No wonder that the one thought in *his* mind was "Away with Him!"

But who are these truly dignified men, who are now turing their backs on rich and gay Jerusalem, and setting their faces to the obscurity and poverty of the village of Bethlehem? They are men of rank and wealth and learning from the far East—representatives of all that is best in the old civilisations of the world. They had only the scantiest opportunities of learning what was the Hope of Israel, and how it should be realised; but they were earnest men; *their* minds were not taken up with gaiety and frivolity; they had studied the works of nature till their souls were full of the thought of God in His glory and majesty; but their hearts still yearned to know if He, Whose glory was in the heavens, could stoop to cure the ills that flesh is heir to. They had heard of Israel's hope, the hope of a child to be born of David's race, who should bring divine mercy near to human need; they had a vague idea that the time for the fulfilment of that hope was drawing near; and, as they mused, behold a marvellous appearance in the heavens, which seemed to call them away to seek Him whom their souls desired! Hence their long journey to Jerusalem and their eager entrance into Bethlehem. Had their dignity been the kind of dignity which was boasted of in Jerusalem, they would no doubt have been offended by the poverty of the surroundings, the poor house with its scanty furniture and its humble inmates. But theirs was the dignity of mind and soul, so they were not offended by the poor surroundings; they recognised in the humble Child the object of their search; they bowed before Him, doing Him homage, and presented to Him gifts as a tribute from the East to the coming King of righteousness and love.

What a beautiful picture; how striking the contrast to the magnificence of Herod the Great in Jerusalem, surrounded by his wealthy and luxurious court. Verily, these were *wise* men from the East, wise with a wisdom not of this world—wise to recognise the hope of the future, not in a monarch *called* "the Great," surrounded by the world's pomp and luxury, but in the fresh young life of the holy heaven-born Child. Learned as they were, they had simple hearts—they had had some glimpse of the great truth that it is not learning the world needs so much as life, new life. Would that all the wise men of the present day were equally wise in heart! We rejoice that so many of them are; and if only all of them had true wisdom, they would consider that even those who stand as high in the learning of the new West as these men did in the learning of the old East, would do themselves honour in bowing low in presence of the Holy Child, and acknowledge that by no effort of the greatest intellect is it possible to reach that truth which can alone meet the deepest wants of men—that there is no other hope for man than the new birth, the fresh, pure, holy life which came into the world when the Christ was born, and which comes into every heart that in simple trustfulness gives Him a welcome as did these

* "Life and Times of Jesus the Messiah," vol. i. p. 130.

wise men of old. There, at the threshold of the Gospel, we see the true relation of science and religion.

> "Let knowledge grow from more to more,
> But more of reverence in us dwell;
> That mind and soul, according well,
> May make one music as before."

All honour to these wise men for bending low in presence of the Holy Child; and thanks be to God for allowing His servant Matthew to give us a glimpse of a scene so beautiful, so touching, so suggestive of pure and high and holy thought and feeling.

The gifts of the East no doubt provided the means of securing a refuge in the South and West. That Egypt gave the fugitives a friendly welcome, and a safe retreat so long as the danger remained, is obvious; but here again we are left without detail. The one thing which the Evangelist wishes to impress upon us is the parallel between the experience of Israel and Israel's Holy One. Israel of the Old Testament, born in Palestine, had to flee into Egypt. When the time was ripe for return, the way was opened for it; and thus the prophet speaks of it in the name of the Lord: "When Israel was a child, then I loved him, and called My son out of Egypt." Now that the Holy One of Israel has come to fulfil old Israel's destiny, the prophetic word, which had been only partially realised in the history of the nation, is fulfilled in the history of the Anointed One. Hence, just as it happened with the nation, so did it happen with the nation's representative and King; born in His own land, He had to flee into Egypt, and remain there till God brought Him out, and set Him in His land again.

Other points of agreement with the prophetic word are mentioned. It is worthy of note that they are all connected with the dark side of prophecy concerning the Messiah. The reason for this will readily appear on reflection. The Scribes and Pharisees were insistent enough on the bright side, the side that favoured their ideas of a great king, who should rescue the people from the Roman yoke, and found a great world-kingdom, after the manner of Herod the Great or of Cæsar the mighty. So there was no need to bring strongly out that side of prophecy which foretold of the glories of the coming King. But the sad side had been entirely neglected. It is this, accordingly, which the Evangelist is prompted to illustrate.

It was, indeed, in itself an occasion of stumbling that the King of Israel should have to flee to Egypt. But why should one stumble at it, who looked at the course of Israel's history as a nation, in the light the prophets threw upon it? It was an occasion of stumbling that His birth in Bethlehem should bring with it such sorrow and anguish; but why wonder at it when so great a prophet as Jeremiah so touchingly speaks of the voice heard in Ramah, "Rachel weeping for her children and would not be comforted,"—a thought of exquisite beauty and pathos as Jeremiah used it in reference to the banished ones of his day, but of still deeper pathos as now fulfilled in the sorrow at Ramah, over the massacre of her innocents, when not Israel but Israel's Holy One is banished from the land of His birth. Again, it was an occasion of stumbling that the King of Israel, instead of growing up in majesty in the midst of the Court and the capital, should retire into obscurity in the little village of Nazareth, and for many years be unheard of by the great ones of the land; but why wonder at it when the prophets again and again represent Him as growing up in this very way, as "a root out of a dry ground," as a twig or "shoot out of the stem of Jesse," growing up "out of His place," and attracting no attention while He grew. Such is the meaning of the words translated, "He shall be called a Nazarene." This does not appear in our language; hence the difficulty which many have found in this reference, there being no passage in any of the prophets where the Christ is spoken of as a Nazarene; but the word to Hebrew ears at once suggests the Hebrew for "Branch," continually applied to Him in the prophets, and especially connected with the idea of His quiet and silent growth, aloof from the throng and unnoticed by the great.

This completes, appropriately, the sketch of His reception. Unthought of by His own, till strangers sought Him; a source of trouble to them when they heard of Him; His life threatened by the occupant, for the time, of David's throne, He is saved only by exile, and on returning to His people passes out of notice: and the great world moves on, all unconscious and unconcerned, whilst its Saviour-King is preparing, in the obscurity of His village home, for the great work of winning a lost world back to God.

CHAPTER III.

HIS HERALD.

MATTHEW iii. 1-12.

THIRTY years have gone since all Jerusalem was in trouble at the rumour of Messiah's birth. But as nothing has been heard of Him since, the excitement has passed away. Those who *were* troubled about it are aging or old or dead; so no one thinks or speaks of it now. There have been several political changes since, mostly for the worse. Judea is now a province of Rome, governed by procurators, of whom the sixth, called Pontius Pilate, has just entered on his office. Society is much the same as before—the same worldliness and luxurious living after the manner of the Greek, the same formalism and bigotry after the manner of the Scribe. There is no sign, in Jerusalem at least, of any change for the better.

The only new thing stirring is a rumour in the street. People are telling one another that a new prophet has arisen. "In the Palace?"—"No." "In the Temple?"—"No." "Surely somewhere in the city?"—"No." He is in the wilderness, clad in roughest garb, subsisting on poorest fare—a living protest against the luxury of the time. He makes no pretence to learning, draws no fine distinctions, gives no curious interpretations, and yet, with only a simple message,—which, however, he delivers as coming straight from God Himself,—is drawing crowds to hear him from all the country side. So the rumour spreads throughout the town, and great numbers go out to see what it is all about; some perhaps from curiosity, some in hope that it may be the dawn of a brighter day for Israel, all of them no doubt more or less stirred with the excitement of the thought that, after so many silent centuries, a veritable prophet has come, like those of old. For it must be remembered that even in gay Jerusalem the deep-rooted feelings of national pride and patriotism had been only overlaid, not superseded, by the veneer of Greek and Roman civilisation, which only seemed for the moment to satisfy the people.

So they go out in multitudes to the wilderness; and what do they see? "A man clothed in fine raiment," like the Roman officials in the palace, which in those degenerate days were Jerusalem's pride? "A reed shaken by the wind," like the time-serving politicians of the hour? Nay, verily; but a true prophet of the Lord, one reminding them of what they have read in the Scriptures of the great Elijah, who suddenly appeared in the wild mountain region of Gilead, at a time when Phœnician manners were making the same havoc in Israel that Greek manners are now making in Jerusalem. Who can he be? He seems to be more than a prophet. Can he be the Christ? But this he entirely disclaims. Is he Elijah then? John probably knew that he was sent "in the spirit and power of Elijah," for so his father had learned from the angel on the occasion of the announcement of his birth; but that was not the point of their question. When they asked, "Art thou Elijah?" they meant "Art thou Elijah risen from the dead?" To this he must, of course, answer, "No." In the same way he must disclaim identity with any of the prophets. He will not trade upon the name of any of these holy men of old. Enough that he comes, a nameless one, before them, with a message from the Lord. So, keeping himself in the background, he puts his message before them, content that they should recognise in it the fufilment of the well-known word of prophecy: "A voice crying in the wilderness, Prepare ye the way of the Lord, make His paths straight."

John wishes it to be distinctly understood that he is not that Light which the prophets of old have told them should arise, but is sent to bear witness to that Light. He has come as a herald to announce the approach of the King, and to call upon the people to prepare for His coming. Think not of me, he cries, ask not who I am; think of the coming King, and make ready for Him,—"Prepare ye the way of the Lord, make *His* paths straight."

How is the way of the Lord to be prepared? Is it by summoning the people to arms all over the land, that they may repel the Roman invader and restore the ancient kingdom? Such a proclamation would no doubt have struck a chord that would have vibrated through all the land. That would have been after the manner of men; it was not the way of the Lord. The summons must be, not to arms, but to *repentance:* "Wash you, make you clean: put away the evil of your doings." So, instead of marching up, a host of warriors, to the Roman citadel, the people troop down, band after band of penitents, to the Jordan, confessing their sins. After all it is the old, old prophetic message over again,—the same which had been sent generation after generation to a back-sliding people, its burden always this: "Turn ye unto Me, saith the Lord of Hosts, and I will turn unto you, saith the Lord of Hosts."

Like many of the old prophets, John taught by symbol as well as by word. The preparation needed was an inward cleansing, and what more fitting symbol of it than the water baptism to which he called the nation? "In that day," it was written in the prophets, "there shall be a fountain opened to the house of David and to the inhabitants of Jerusalem, for sin and for uncleanness." The prophecy was about to be fulfilled, and the baptism of John was the appropriate sign of it. Again, in another of the prophets the promise ran, "Then will I sprinkle clean water upon you, and ye shall be clean; from all your filthiness and from all your idols will I cleanse you . . . and I will put my spirit within you." John knew well that it was not given to him to *fulfil* this promise. He could not grant the real baptism, the baptism of the Holy Ghost; but he could baptise with water; he could give the sign and assurance to the truly penitent heart that there was forgiveness and cleansing in the coming One; and thus, by his baptism with water, as well as by the message he delivered, he was preparing the way of the Lord. All this, we cannot but observe, was in perfect accord with the wonderful prophetic utterance of his father Zacharias, as recorded by St. Luke: "Thou, child, shalt be called the prophet of the Highest: for thou shalt go before the face of the Lord to prepare His ways; to give knowledge of salvation unto His people by the remission of their sins,"—not to give salvation, which only Christ can give, but the knowledge of it. This he did not only by telling of the coming Saviour, and, when He came, pointing to Him as "the Lamb of God that taketh away the sin of the world;" but also by the appropriate sign of baptism, which gave the same knowledge in the language of symbol addressed to the eye.

The summons of the prophet of the wilderness is not in vain. The people come. The throngs increase. The nation is moved. Even the great ones of the nation condescend to follow the multitude. Pharisees and Sadducees, the leaders of the two great parties in Church and State, are coming; many of them are coming. What a comfort this must be to the prophet's soul. How gladly he will welcome them, and let it be known that he has among his converts many of the great ones of the land! But the stern Baptist is a man of no such mould. What cares he for rank or position or worldly influence? What he wants is reality, simplicity, godly sincerity; and he knows that, scarce as these virtues are in the community at large, they are scarcest of all among these dignitaries. He will not allow the smallest admixture of insincerity or hypocrisy in what is, so far, a manifest work of God. He must test these new-comers to the uttermost, for the sin of which they need most to repent is the very sin which they are in danger of committing afresh in its most aggravated form in offering themselves for baptism. He must therefore test their motives; he must at all risks ensure that, unless their repentance is genuine, they shall not be baptised. For their own sakes, as well as for the work's sake, this is necessary. Hence the strong, even harsh language he uses in putting the question *why* they had come. Yet he would not repel or discourage them. He does not send them away as if past redemption, but only demands that they bring forth fruit worthy of the repentance they profess. And lest they should think that there was an easier way of entrance for them than for others, lest they should think that they had claims sufficient because of their descent, he reminds them that God can have his kingdom upon earth, even though every son of Abraham in the world should reject Him: "Think not to say within yourselves, We have Abraham to our father: for I say unto you, that God is able of these stones to raise up children unto Abraham."

It is as if he said, The coming kingdom of righteousness and truth will not fail, even if Pharisees and Sadducees and all the natural children of Abraham refuse to enter its only gate of repentance; if there is no response to the Divine summons where it is most to be expected, then it can be secured where it is least to be expected; if flesh become stone, then stone can be made flesh, according to the word of promise. So there will be no gathering in of mere formalists to make up numbers, no including of those who are only "Jews outwardly." And there will be no half measures, no compromise with evil, no parleying with those who are unwilling or only half willing to repent. A time of crisis has come,—"now also the axe is laid unto the root of the trees." It is not lifted yet. But it is there lying ready, ready for the Lord of the vineyard, when He shall come (and He is close at hand); then, "*every* tree which bringeth not forth good fruit is hewn down and cast into the fire."

Yet not for judgment is He coming,—John goes on to say,—but to fulfil the promise of the Father. He is coming to baptise you with the Holy Ghost and with fire—to purify you through and through and to animate you with a new life, glowing, upward-striving, heaven-aspiring; and it is to prepare you for this unspeakable blessing that I ask you to come and put away those sins which must be a barrier in the way of His coming, those sins which dim your eyes so that you cannot see Him, which stop your ears so that you cannot recognise your Shepherd's voice, that clog your hearts so that the Holy Spirit cannot reach them,—repent, *repent*, and be baptised all of you; for there cometh One after me, mightier than I, whose meanest servant I am not worthy to be,—He shall baptise you with the Holy Ghost and with fire, if you are ready to receive Him; but if you are not, still you cannot escape Him, "Whose fan is in His hand, and He will throughly cleanse His threshing-floor; and He will gather His wheat into the garner, but the chaff He will burn up with unquenchable fire" (R. V.).

The work of John must still be done. It specially devolves upon the ministers of Christ; would they were all as anxious as he was to keep in the background, as little concerned about position, title, official rank, or personal consideration.

CHAPTER IV.

HIS BAPTISM.

MATTHEW iii. 13-17.

"THE baptism of John, was it from Heaven or of men?" This question must have been asked throughout the length and breadth of the land in the days of his mission. We know how it was answered; for even after the excitement had died away, we are told that "all men counted John for a prophet." This conviction would of course prevail in Nazareth as well as everywhere else. When, therefore, the Baptist removed from the wilderness of Judea and the lower reaches of the Jordan to the ford of Bethany, or Bethabara, —now identified with a point much farther north, within a single day's journey of Nazareth,—the people of Galilee would flock to him, as before the people of Judea and Jerusalem had done. Among the rest, as might naturally be expected, Jesus came. It was enough for Him to know that the baptism of John was of Divine appointment. He was in all things guided by His Father's will, to whom He would day by day commit His way. Accordingly, just as day by day He had been subject to His parents, and just as He had seen it to be right to go up to the Temple in accordance with the Law, so He recognised it to be His duty to present Himself, as His countrymen in such large numbers were doing, to receive baptism from John. The manner of the narrative implies that He came, not as if He were some great person demanding special recognition, but as simply and naturally as any of the rest: "Then cometh Jesus from Galilee to the Jordan unto John, to be baptised of him."

John looks at Him. Does he know Him at all? Perhaps not; for though they are cousins, their lives have been lived quite apart. Before their birth their mothers met; but it is doubtful if they themselves have seen each other before, and even if they have, in earlier years, they may both be so changed that recognition is uncertain. The one has had his home in the South; the other in the North. Besides, the elder of the two has spent his life mostly in the desert, so that probably he is a stranger now even to his own townspeople, and his father and mother, both very old when he was born, must be dead and gone long ago. Perhaps, then, John did not know Jesus at all; certainly he did not yet know Him as the Messiah. But he sees something in Him that draws forth the homage of his soul. Or possibly he gathers his impressions rather from what Jesus says. All the rest have confessed sin; He has no sin of His own to confess. But words would no doubt be spoken that would convey to the Baptist how this disciple looked on sin, how the very thought of it filled Him with horror, how His whole soul longed for the righteousness of God, how it was a sacred passion with Him that sin should perish from the hearts of men, and righteousness reign in its place. Whether then, it was by His appearance, the clear eye, the calm face,—an open window for the prophet to look through into His soul, —or whether it was by the words He spoke as He claimed a share in the baptism, or both combined, John was taken aback—surprised a second time, though in just the opposite way to that in which he had been surprised before. The same eagle eye that saw through the mask of Pharisee and Sadducee could penetrate the veil of humility and obscurity; so he said: "I have need to be baptised of Thee, and comest Thou to me?"

Think of the majesty of this John. Remember how he bore himself in presence of the Pharisees and Sadducees; and how he faced Herod, telling him plainly, at the risk of his life, as it afterwards proved, "It is not lawful for thee to have thy brother's wife." Remember that all Judea, and Jerusalem, and Galilee had been bowing down in his presence; and now, when an obscure nameless One of Nazareth comes to him, only as yet distinguished from others by the holiness of His life and the purity of His soul, John would not have Him bow in his presence, but would himself bend low before Him: "I have need to be baptised of Thee, and comest Thou to me?" Oh, for more of that grand combination of lofty courage and lowly reverence! Verily, "among them that are born of women there hath not risen a greater than John the Baptist."

But Jesus answering said unto him, "Suffer it now; for thus it becometh us to fulfil all righteousness" (R. V.). Though about to enter on His Messianic work, He has not yet taken its burden on Him; accordingly He comes, not as Messiah, but in the simplest and most unassuming way; content still, as He has been all along till now, to be reckoned simply as of Israel. This is what we take to be the force of the plural pronoun "us."

On the other hand, it should be remembered that Jesus must have recognised in the summons to the Jordan a call to commence His work as Messiah. He would certainly have heard from His mother of the prophetic words which had been spoken concerning His cousin and Himself; and would, therefore, as soon as He heard of the mission of John, know well what it meant—He could not but know that John was preparing the way before Him, and therefore that His time was close at hand. Of this, too, we have an indication in His answer to the expostulation of John. "Suffer it now," He says; as if to say, I am as yet only one of Israel; My time is at hand, when I must take the position to which I am called, but meantime I come as the rest come: "Suffer it *now;* for thus it becometh us to fulfil all righteousness."

While then Jesus came simply in obedience to the will of God, He must have come with a very heavy burden. His study of the Scriptures must have made Him painfully familiar with the dark prospects before Him. Well did He know that the path of the Messiah must be one of suffering, that He must be despised and rejected, that He must be wounded for the people's transgressions and bruised for their iniquity; that, in a word, He must be the suffering Priest before He can be the reigning King. This thought of His priesthood must have been especially borne in upon Him now that He had just reached the priestly age. In His thirteenth year—the Temple age—He had gone to the Temple, and now at the age when the priest is consecrated to his office, He is summoned to the Jordan, to be baptised by one whom He knows to be sent of God to prepare the way before Him. Those Scriptures, then, which speak of the priestly office the Messiah must fill, must have been very much in His mind as He came to John and offered Himself to be baptised. And of all these Scriptures none would seem more appropriate at the moment than those words of the fortieth Psalm: "Lo, I come: in the volume of the book it is written of Me, I delight to do Thy will, O My God."

At this point we can readily see the appropriateness of His baptism, and also an element in common between it and that of the people. They had come professing to be willing to do the will of God by turning from sin to righteousness. He had no need to turn from sin to do the will of God; but He had to turn from the quiet and peaceful home life at Nazareth, that He might take up the burden laid upon Him as Messiah. So He as well as they had to leave the old life and begin a new one; and in this we can see how fitting it was that He as well as they should be baptised. Then, just as by baptism—the symbol, in their case, of separation from sin and consecration to God—John made "ready a people prepared for the Lord;" so by baptism—the symbol, in His case, of separation from private life and consecration to God in the office of Messiah,—the Lord was made ready for the people. By baptism John opened the door of the new Kingdom. From the wilderness of sin the people entered it as subjects; from the seclusion of private life Jesus entered it as King and Priest. They came under a vow of obedience unto Him; He came under a vow of obedience unto death, even the death of the Cross.

This, then, is the moment of His taking up the Cross. It is indeed the assumption of His royalty as Messiah-King; but then He knew that He must suffer and die before He could enter on His glory; therefore, as the first great duty before Him, He takes up the Cross. In this we can see a still further appropriateness in the words already quoted, as is suggested in the well-known passage in the Epistle to the Hebrews: "Sacrifice and offering thou wouldest not, but a body hast thou prepared me: in burnt offerings and sacrifices for sin thou hast had no pleasure. Then said I, Lo, I come (in the volume of the book it is written of me) to do thy will, O God." Ah, who can understand the love in the heart of Jesus, who can measure the sacrifice He makes, as He bends before John, and is baptised into the name of "the Christ," the Saviour of mankind!

The act of solemn consecration is over. He comes up out of the water. And lo, the heavens are opened, and the Spirit of God descends upon Him, and a voice from heaven calls, "This is My beloved Son, in Whom I am well pleased."

"The heavens were opened." What was the precise natural phenomenon witnessed we can only conjecture, but whatever it was, it was but a symbol of the spiritual opening of the heavens. The heaven of God's love and of all holy Angels, shut from man by sin, was opened again by the Christ of God. Nothing could be more appropriate, therefore, than that just at the moment when the Holy One of Israel had bowed Himself to take up His heavy burden, when for the first time it was possible to say, "Behold the Lamb of God, that taketh away the sin of the world!" the heavens should open to welcome Him, and in welcoming Him, the Sin-bearer, to welcome all whose sins He came to take away.

"And He saw the Spirit of God descending like a dove, and lighting upon Him." This was His anointing for the work He had come to do. The priests of the line of Aaron had been anointed with oil; He was anointed with that of which the oil was but a symbol,—the Holy Spirit descending from the open heaven. From His birth, indeed, He had been guided by the Spirit of God. But up to this time He had, as we have seen, nothing more than was needed to minister to that growth in wisdom which had been going on in private life these thirty years, nothing more than was necessary to guide Him day by day in His quiet, unexacting duties at home. Now He needs far more. Now He must receive the Spirit without measure, in the fulness of His grace and power; hence the organic form of the symbol. The emblem used when the apostles were baptised with the Holy Ghost was tongues of fire, indicating the partial nature of the endowment; here it is the dove, suggesting the idea of completeness and, at the same time, as every one sees, of beauty, gentleness, peace, and love. Again let it be remembered that it is on Him as our representative that the Spirit descends, that His baptism with the Holy Ghost is in order that He may be ready to fulfil the word of John, "He shall baptise you with the Holy Ghost and with fire." Heaven opened above Him means all heavenly blessings prepared for those who follow Him into the new Kingdom. The descent of the Spirit means the bestowment on Him and His of heaven's best gift as an earnest of all the rest.

Last of all there is the voice, "This is My beloved Son, in whom I am well pleased," spoken not merely to Himself individually,—all along, in the personal sense, He was God's beloved Son, in whom He was well pleased,—but to the Messiah, as the Representative and Head of a new redeemed humanity, as the First-born among many brethren, as One who at the very moment was undertaking suretyship on behalf of all who had already received Him or should in the ages to come receive Him as their Priest and King—"*This* is My beloved Son, in whom I am well pleased."

Blessed be the God and Father of our Lord Jesus Christ, who hath blessed us with all spiritual and heavenly blessings in Him: with an open heaven, a present Spirit, a reconciled Father's voice. Blessed be our loving Lord and Saviour that He came so humbly to the Jordan, stooped so bravely to the yoke, took up our heavy Cross, and carried it through these sorrowful years to the bitter, bitter end. And blessed be the Holy Spirit of all grace, that He abode on Him, and abides with us. May the grace of the Lord Jesus Christ, and the love of God, and the communion of the Holy Ghost, be with us all!

CHAPTER V.

HIS TEMPTATION.

MATTHEW iv. 1-11.

MUCH has been written on the possibility of temptation in the experience of a sinless Being. The difficulties which have been raised in this region are chiefly of a metaphysical kind, such as it is possible—for some minds, we might say inevitable—to raise at every point in that mysterious complexity which we call life. Without attempting to enter profoundly into the question, may not an appeal be made to our own experience? Do we not all know what it is to be "tempted without sin,"—without sin, that is, in reference to the particular thing to which we are tempted? Are there not desires in our nature, not only thoroughly innocent, but a necessary part of our humanity, which, nevertheless, give occasion to temptation? But on its being recognised that to follow the impulse, however natural, would lead to wrong-doing, the temptation is instantly repelled and integrity perfectly preserved. In such a case there is temptation, conflict, victory—all without sin. Surely then what is possible to us on occasion, was also possible to our Lord on all occasions, all through His pure and spotless life. His taking our nature indeed involved not only the possibility, but the necessity, of temptation.

The passage before us records what is known as *the* Temptation, by which it is not, of course, meant that it was the only one. Our Lord was all His life exposed to the assaults of the Tempter, which seem indeed to have increased in violence as He approached the end of His life. Why, then, is this attack singled out for special record? The reason seems obvious. It marks the beginning of the life-work of the Messiah. In His quiet home at Nazareth Jesus must have had the ordinary temptations to which childhood and youth are subject. That was the time of quiet preparation for the great campaign. Now the war must begin. He must address Himself to the mighty undertaking of destroying the works of the devil. The great adversary, therefore, wisely endeavours to mar it at the outset, by a deliberately planned series of assaults, directed against all the vulnerable points of that human nature his great antagonism must wear. From this time onward our Lord's whole life was to be a warfare, not against the rage of wicked men only, but against the wiles of the unseen adversary, whose opposition must have been as bitter and relentless as that of his representatives in flesh and blood. From the nature of the case, the conflict waged in the spiritual sphere could not appear in the history. It belonged to that hidden life, of which even the closest disciples could see but very little. We get a hint of it occasionally in certain looks and words betokening inward conflict, and in those frequent retirings to solitary places to pray; but of the actual soul experience we have no record, except in the case of this first pitched battle, so to call it, of the lifelong conflict. It is evident that our Lord Himself must have given His disciples the information on this deeply interesting subject which enabled them to put it on record, for the encouragement and comfort of His people in all time to come. Blessed be His Holy Name, for this unveiling of His hidden life.

The greater portion, indeed, is still veiled. A dark cloud of mystery hangs over the forty days. Nothing else is told of them in this Gospel than that Jesus fasted for that time—an indication of sustained intensity in the life of His spirit. From St. Mark and St. Luke we learn that the temptation lasted throughout the entire period—a fact not at all inconsistent with sustained spiritual elevation, for it is just at such periods that man is most exposed to the assaults of the enemy. We may not penetrate the darkness of these forty days. Like the darkness in Gethsemane, and again, from the sixth to the ninth hour on Calvary, it forbids entrance. These were times when even "the disciple whom Jesus loved" could not be with Him. These are solitudes that can never be disturbed. Only this we know: that it was necessary that our Saviour should pass through these dark "cloud-gates" as He entered on and as He finished His priestly work on earth.

But though we cannot comprehend what our Lord did for us during these forty days, when He "recovered Paradise to all mankind," we may, remembering that He was tempted, not only as our Representative, but as our Exemplar, endeavour with all humility and reverence to enter into this soul-experience of our Lord, so far as the vivid representation of its main features in the inspired record warrants.

It is always difficult to tell the story of soul-experience in such a way as to come home to the common mind and heart of humanity. It will not do to tell it in the language of philosophy or psychology, which none but those familiar with such discussions could understand. It must be addressed to the imagination as well as to the pure reason. If this had been sufficiently kept in view, it might have saved many a difficulty on the part of those who have set themselves to discover exactly what were the outward circumstances of the temptation, forgetting that here especially it is the inward and spiritual with which we have to do, not the outward and physical. It is not what happened to the body of Jesus,—whether it was actually carried to a pinnacle of the Temple or not,—with which we have any concern in connection with the subject of temptation; but what happened to His soul: for it is the soul of man, not his body, which is tempted.

It is above all things necessary to hold firmly to the reality of the temptation. It was no mere sham fight: it was just as real as any we have ever had when most fiercely assailed by the tempter. This will, of course, dispose of the vulgar idea that the devil appeared in recognisable shape, like one of Doré's fiends. Some people cannot rise above the folly of imagining that there is nothing real that is not material, and therefore that our Saviour could have had no conflict with Satan, if Satan had not assumed some material shape. The power of temptation consists of its appearance of being suggested without sinister intent. Our Lord was tempted "like as we are," and therefore had not the advantage of seeing the tempter in his proper person. He may have appeared "as an angel of light," or it may have been only as an invisible spirit that he came. However that may be, it was unquestionably a spiritual experience; and in that consists its reality and value.

In order firmly to grasp the reality of the conflict, we must not only bear in mind that our Lord had to contend with the same invisible adversary whom we must encounter, but that He had to meet him just as we have to meet him—not as God, but as man. The man Christ Jesus was tempted, and in His human nature He triumphed. He had "emptied Himself" of His Divine attributes; and to have had recourse to them when the battle raged too fiercely for His resources as a man, would have been to have acknowledged defeat. What need was there to show that God could triumph over Satan? There needed no Incarnation and no wilderness contest for that. Had it not been as a man that He triumphed there had been no victory at all. It is true that He went into the wilderness in the power of the Spirit; but so may we go into any wilderness or anywhere. It was through Divine strength He triumphed, but only in that strength made perfect in human weakness according to the promise which is valid for us all. Here too "He was tempted like as we are," with the same ways and means of resisting the temptation and overcoming it as are available to us. It follows from all this that we should not look at this temptation scene as something quite foreign to ourselves, but should endeavour to enter into it, and, as far as possible, to realise it.

Observe first the close connection with the baptism. This is made prominent and emphatic in all the three accounts. Evidently, then, it supplies the key to it. The baptism of Christ was His consecration to the work of His Messiahship. And let us not imagine that He had any ready-made plan for the accomplishment of it. His was no stereotyped life-work, such as that which most of us take up, in which we can learn from those who have gone before how they set about it and proceed accordingly. Even with all that advantage most of us have to do not a little hard thinking, before we can lay our plans. Could it be, then, that He who had such a work before Him had no need to think over it, and plan it, and weigh different methods of procedure, and face the difficulties which every one who enters on a new enterprise has to meet? Do not let us forget for a moment that He was a real man, and that in planning the course He would pursue, as in all other points, He was tried like as we are.

Accordingly, no sooner is He baptised, than He withdraws by Himself alone, as Moses and others had done when about to enter on their work, to commune with God and to take counsel with His own thoughts. Was He free from all misgiving? Let us not imagine that it was impossible for Him to doubt. Tempted in all points like as we are, He must have known this sore temptation. One may well suppose, then, that He was visited again and again with misgivings during these forty days, so that it was not at all unnatural that temptation should take the form: "If Thou be the Son of God——"

Look now at the first temptation, and mark the double human weakness to which it was addressed. On the one hand *doubt*—"*If* Thou art the Son of God;" on the other, *hunger*—for He had fasted long and had as strong a craving for bread as any of us would have had in the circumstances. See now the force of the temptation. He is suffering from hunger; He is tempted to doubt. How can He have relief? "If Thou be the Son of God, *command that these stones be made bread.*" Special powers are intrusted to Him for His work as Messiah. Should He not use them now? Why not? So in his subtlety suggests the tempter. In vain. He had taken His place among His brother-men, and would not separate Himself from them. They could not command stones to be made bread; and would He cease to be their brother? What saith the Law? A well-known passage leaps into His memory: "Man shall not live by bread alone, but by every word that proceedeth out of the mouth of God." Man must trust in God, and when he is hungry in the wilderness, as Israel was of old, must look upwards for his help. So must I; so will I. And He bears the hunger, repels the doubt, and conquers His subtle foe.

The thought of the doubt that must exist in other minds if not in His own, gives occasion for a second assault. To have proved His power by commanding the stones to be made bread would only have gratified a personal craving. But would it not advance His work to make some signal display of the powers by which He shall be accredited—do something that would attract universal attention; not in the desert, but in Jerusalem;—why not show to all the people that God is with Him by casting Himself from the pinnacle of the Temple? "If Thou be the Son of God, cast Thyself down; for it is written, He shall give His angels charge concerning

Thee; and in their hands they shall bear Thee up, lest at any time Thou dash Thy foot against a stone." One sees at once the added force of this temptation. The hunger remains, together with the weakness of body and faintness of spirit which always accompany it. And the very weapon He used to repel the first assault is turned against Him now, for His adversary has found a passage of Scripture, which he uses with great effect. Moreover, the appeal seems to be to that very spirit of trustfulness which stood Him in such stead in His first encounter. Is He not hard beset? What then? Does He in this emergency summon to His aid any ally denied to us in similar stress of trial? No: He does exactly what we have to do in the same case: meets Scripture quoted with a bias by other Scripture thought of without prejudice. He recognises that the Scripture first presented to His mind is only a part of the truth which bears on the case. Something more must be had in view, before the path of duty is clear. To meet the distracting thought, this word occurs, "Thou shalt not tempt the Lord thy God." It is one thing to trust, another to tempt. I was trusting when I refused to command the stones to be made bread. But I should be tempting God were I to cast myself down from a pinnacle of the Temple. I should be experimenting upon Him, as did the children of Israel at Meribah and at Massah (for that is the connection of the words He quotes) when they said, "Is the Lord among us or not?" I must not experiment, must not tempt, I must simply trust. Thus victory is gained a second time.

If it is not right to begin His work by any such display as that which the Tempter has just suggested, how shall it be begun? A question surely of unexampled difficulty. The air was full of expectancy in regard to the coming of King Messiah. The whole nation was ready to hail him. Not only so, but even the heathen nations were more or less prepared for His coming. Why not take advantage of this favourable state of things at home and abroad? Why not proclaim a kingdom that will satisfy these widespread expectations, and gather round itself all those enthusiasms; and, after having thus won the people, then proceed to lead them on to higher and better things? Why not? It would be bowing down to the prince of this world. It is clearly a temptation of the Evil One. To yield to it would be to fall down before him and worship him in exchange for the kingdoms of this world and the glory of them. It would be gaining the allegiance of men by methods which are not of God, but of the great adversary. He recognises the device of Satan to lure Him from the path of self-denial which He sees to be the path of duty; accordingly, with energy He says, "Get thee hence, Satan; for it is written, Thou shalt worship the Lord thy God, and Him only shalt thou serve." In establishing My kingdom I must show Myself to be a servant and worshipper of God and of Him only; accordingly, no worldly methods must be used, however promising they may seem to be; the battle must be fought with spiritual weapons, the kingdom must be established by spiritual forces alone, and on truth and love alone must I depend: I choose the path of the Cross. "Get thee hence, Satan."

The crisis is passed. The path of duty and of sorrow lies plain and clear before Him. He has refused to turn aside to the right hand or to the left. The Tempter has been foiled at every point, and so must withdraw, for the time, at least, "Then the devil leaveth Him; and, behold, angels came and ministered unto Him."

CHAPTER VI.

BEGINNING OF HIS GALILEAN MINISTRY.

MATTHEW iv. 12-25.

DID our Lord's ministry begin in Galilee? If so, why did He not Himself set the example of "beginning at Jerusalem"? As a matter of fact we learn from the fourth Gospel that He did begin at Jerusalem; and that it was only after He was rejected there that He changed the scene of His labours to the North. Why then do the three Evangelists not mention this earlier ministry in the South? The answer to this question seems suggested by the stress laid by each of the three on the fact of John's imprisonment, as giving the date after which Christ commenced His work in the North. Here, for example (ver. 12), it is put thus: "Now when He heard that John was delivered up, He withdrew into Galilee." Their idea, then, seems to be that the Judean ministry of Christ belonged rather to the closing months of John's career; and that only after John's mission, the sphere of which had been mainly in the South, had closed, could the special work of Christ be regarded as having begun.

If we review the facts we shall see how natural and accurate was this view of the case. John was sent to prepare the way of the Lord, to open the door of Jerusalem and Judea for His coming. At first the herald meets with great success. Jerusalem and Judea flock out to him for his baptism. The way seems ready. The door is opened. The Messiah has come; and John has pointed Him out as "the Lamb of God that taketh away the sin of the world." Now the Passover is at hand. People will be gathered together from all parts of the land. What better time for the Lord to come to His temple? And, as we are told in the fourth Gospel, Jesus takes the opportunity, goes up to Jerusalem, enters into the Temple, and at once begins to cleanse it. How is He received? As one whose way has been prepared, whose claims have been duly authenticated by a prophet of the Lord, as all acknowledge John to be? Not at all. Forth step the Temple officials and ask Him by what authority He does these things. He has come unto His own; His own receive Him not. He does not, however, too hastily accept their suicidal refusal to receive Him. He gives them time to think of it. He tarries in the neighbourhood, He and John baptising in the same region; patiently waiting, as it would seem, for signs of relenting on the part of the rulers and Pharisees,—one of whom, indeed, has come by night and made inquiries; and who can tell what the result will be—whether this Nicodemus may not be able to win the others over, so that after all there will be waiting for the King the welcome He ought to have, and which He is well entitled to expect after the reception given to His herald? But no: the impression of John's preaching and baptism is wearing off; the hardness of heart returns, and passes into positive bitterness, which reaches such a height that at last Herod finds the tide so turned that he can hazard what a few months before would have been the foolhardy policy of seizing John and shutting him in prison. So ends the mission of John—beginning with largest hope, ending in cruellest disappointment.

The early Judean ministry of Christ, then, as related by St. John, may be regarded as the opportunity which Christ gave to the nation, as represented by the capital and the Temple, to follow out the mission of John to its intended issue—an opportunity which the leaders of the nation wasted and threw away, and which therefore came to nothing. Hence it is that the three Evangelists, without giving any of the details which were afterwards supplied by St. John, sum up the closing months of the forerunner's ministry in the one fact which suggests all, that John was silenced, and shut up in prison. We see, then, that though Jesus did in a sense commence His work in Galilee, He did not do so until He had first given the authorities of the city and the Temple the opportunity of having it begin, as it would seem most natural that it should have begun, in the centre of the old kingdom.

But though it was His treatment in the South which was the immediate cause of this withdrawal to the North and the beginning of the establishment of the new kingdom there, yet this was no unforeseen contingency—this too was anticipated in the prophetic page, for herein was fulfilled the word of Isaiah the prophet, spoken long ago of this same northern land: "The land of Zabulon and the land of Nepthalim, by the way of the sea, beyond Jordan, Galilee of the Gentiles; the people which sat in darkness saw great light; and to them which sat in the region and shadow of death light is sprung up."

It is the old story over again. No room in the inn, so He must be born in a manger; no safety in Judea, so He must be carried to Egypt; no room for Him in His own capital and His Father's house, so He must away to the country, the uttermost part of the land, which men despised, the very speech of which was reckoned barbarous in the polite ears of the metropolitans, a region which was scarce counted of the land at all, being known as "Galilee of the Gentiles," a portion of the country which had been overrun more than any other by the foreign invader, and therefore known as "the region and shadow of death;" here it is that the new light will arise, the new power be first acknowledged, and the new blessing first enjoyed—one of the many illustrations of the Lord's own saying, "Many of the last shall be first, and the first last."

Here, then, our Lord begins the work of setting up His kingdom. He takes up the same message which had seemed to return void to its preacher in the South. John had come saying, "Repent ye; for the kingdom of heaven is at hand." The people of the South had seemed to repent; and the kingdom seemed about to come in the ancient capital. But the repentance was only superficial; and though it still remained true that the kingdom was at hand, it was not to begin in Jerusalem.

So, in the new, and, to human appearance, far less promising field in the North, the work must be begun afresh; and now the same stirring words are ringing in Galilee, as rang a few months before in Judea: "Repent; for the kingdom of heaven is at hand."

It is now in fact close at hand. It is interesting to note its first beginnings. "And Jesus walking by the sea of Galilee,* saw two brethren, Simon called Peter, and Andrew his brother, casting a net into the sea; for they were fishers. And He saith unto them, Follow Me, and I will make you fishers of men. And they straightway left their nets, and followed Him. And going on from thence He saw other two brethren, James the son of Zebedee, and John his brother, in a ship with Zebedee their father, mending their nets; and He called them and they immediately left the ship and their father, and followed Him."

Observe in the first place that, though John is in prison, and to all human appearance failure has been written on the work of his life, the failure is only seeming. The multitudes that had been stirred by his preaching have relapsed into their old indifference, but there are a few whose souls have been permanently touched to finer issues. They are not of the lordly Pharisees or of the brilliant Sadducees; they cannot even claim to be metropolitans: they are poor Galilean fishermen: but they gave heed when the prophet pointed them to the Lamb of God, the Messiah that was to come; and though they had only spent a short time in His company, yet golden links had been forged between them; they had heard the Shepherd's voice: had fully recognised His Kingly claims; and so were ready, waiting for the word of command. Now it comes. The same Holy One of Nazareth is walking by the shores of their lake. He has been proclaiming His kingdom, as now at last beginning; and, though the manner of its establishment is so entirely different from anything to which their thoughts have been accustomed in the past, their confidence in Him is such that they raise no doubt or question. Accordingly, when they see Him coming alone and unattended, without any of the trappings or the suits of royalty, without any badge or sign of office, with a simple word of command,—a word of command, moreover, which demanded of them the sacrifice of all for His sake, the absolute trusting of themselves and all their future to His guidance and care,—they do not hesitate for a single moment; but first Andrew and Simon his brother, and a little further on James and John his brother, straightway leave nets, father, friends, home, everything, and follow Him.

Such was the first exercise of the royal authority of the new King. Such was the constitution of His—Cabinet shall we call it?—or of His Kingdom itself, shall we not rather say? for, so far as we can see, His cabinet at this moment was all the kingdom that he had. Let us here pause a moment and try to realise the picture painted for us in that grey morning time of what we now call the Christian Era. Suppose some of our artists could reproduce the scene for us: in the background the lake with the deserted boats upon the shore, old Zebedee with a half sad, half bewildered look upon his face, wondering what was happening, trying to imagine what he would do without his sons, and what his sons would do without him and the boat and the nets; and, in

* It is worthy of notice that He has had the same experience even in Galilee as before, for He is cast out of His own place Nazareth, so that He cannot really begin there. He gave them the first opportunity in Galilee as He had given Jerusalem first of all, but they too had rejected it, had driven Him out, and hence it is that the beginning was not in the village up in the hills, but down by the lakeside in the midst of the busy life that thronged its shores.

the foreground, the five men walking along, four of them without the least idea of where they were going or of what they had to do. Or suppose that, instead of having a picture of it now, with all the light that eighteen centuries have shed upon it, we could transport ourselves back to the very time and stand there on the very spot and see the scene with our own eyes; and suppose that we were told by some bystander, That man of the five that looks like the leader of the rest thinks himself a king: he imagines he has been sent to set up a kingdom of Heaven upon the earth; and he has just asked these other four to join him, and there they are, setting out upon their task. What should we have thought? If we had had only flesh and blood to consult with, we should have thought the whole thing supremely ridiculous; we should have expected to see the four men back to their boats and nets again in a few days, sadder but wiser men. How far Zebedee had a spiritually enlightened mind we dare not say; perhaps he was as willing that his sons should go, as they were to go; but if he was, it could not have been flesh and blood that revealed it to him; he as well as his sons must have felt the power of the Spirit that was in Christ. But if he did not at all understand it or believe in it, we can fancy him saying to the two young men when they left: "Go off now, if you like; you will be back again in a few days, and foolish as you have been, your old father will be glad to take you into his boat again."

It is worth while for us to try to realise what happened in its veriest simplicity; for we have read the story so often, and are so thoroughly familiar with it, that we are apt to miss its marvel, to fail to recognise that it is perhaps the most striking illustration in all history of the apostle's statement, "God hath chosen the foolish things of the world to confound the wise, and God hath chosen the weak things of the world to confound the things which are mighty, . . . that no flesh should glory in His presence."

Where was ever a weaker thing in this world than the beginning of this kingdom? It would be difficult to imagine any commencement that would have seemed weaker in worldly eyes. Stand by once again and look at it with only human eyes; say, is it not all weakness together?—weakness in the leader to imagine He can set up a kingdom after such a fashion, weakness in the followers to leave a paying business on such a fool's errand. But "the foolishness of God is wiser than men: and the weakness of God is stronger than men." And now that we look back upon that scene, we recognise it as one of the grandest this earth has ever witnessed. If it were painted now, what light must there be in the Leader's eye, what majesty in His step, what glory of dawning faith and love and hope in the faces of the rest—it must needs be a picture of Sunrise, or it would be utterly unworthy of the theme!

Now follow them: where will they go, and what will they do? Will they take arms and call to arms the countryside? Then march on Jerusalem and take the throne of David, and thence to Rome and snatch from Cæsar the sceptre of the world? "And Jesus went about all Galilee, teaching in their synagogues, and preaching the Gospel of the Kingdom, and healing all manner of sickness and all manner of disease among the people." Teaching—preaching—healing: these were the methods for setting up the kingdom. "*Teaching*"—this was the new light; "*preaching* the Gospel of the Kingdom"—this was the new power, power not of the sword but of the Word, the power of persuasion, so that the people will yield themselves willingly or not at all, for there is to be not a shadow of constraint, not the smallest use of force or compulsion, not the slightest interference with human freedom in this new kingdom; and "*healing*,"—this is to be the great thing; this is what a sick world wants, this is what souls and bodies of men alike are crying out for—"healing all manner of sickness and all manner of disease among the people." Heavenly light, heavenly power, heavenly healing—these are the weapons of the new warfare; these the regalia of the new kingdom. "And the report of Him went forth into all Syria; and they brought unto Him all that were sick, holden with divers diseases and torments, possessed with devils, and epileptic, and palsied; and He healed them" (R. V.). Call to mind, for a moment, how in the extremity of hunger He would not use one fraction of the entrusted power for His own behoof. "Himself He cannot save." But see how He saves others. No stinting now of the heavenly power; it flows in streams of blessing: "They brought unto Him all that were sick, . . . and He healed them."

It is daybreak on the shores of Galilee. The Sun of Righteousness has risen with healing in His wings.

CHAPTER VII.

THE GOSPEL OF THE KINGDOM.

("SERMON ON THE MOUNT.")

MATTHEW v., vi., vii.

IT may seem almost heresy to object to the time-honoured title "Sermon on the Mount;" yet, so small has the word "sermon" become, on account of its application to those productions of which there is material for a dozen in single sentences of this great discourse, that there is danger of belittling it by the use of a title which suggests even the remotest relationship to these ephemeral efforts. No mere sermon is this, only distinguished from others of its class by its reach and sweep and power: it stands alone as the grand charter of the commonwealth of heaven; or, to keep the simple title the evangelist himself suggests (iv. 23), it is "The Gospel (or good news) of the Kingdom." To understand it aright we must keep this in mind, avoiding the easy method of treating it as a mere series of lessons on different subjects, and endeavouring to grasp the unity of thought and purpose which binds its different parts into one grand whole.

It may help us to do this if we first ask ourselves what questions would naturally arise in the minds of the more thoughtful of the people, when they heard the announcement, "The kingdom of heaven is at hand." It was evidently to such persons the Lord addressed Himself. "Seeing the multitudes," we read, "He went up into the mountain," perhaps for the purpose of selecting His audience. The idle and indifferent would stay down on the plain; only those who were in some measure stirred in spirit would follow Him as He climbed the steep ascent from the shore of the lake to the plateau above; and in their minds they would in all probability be revolving such questions as these: (1) "What is this kingdom, what advantages does it offer, and who are the people that belong to it?" (2) "What is required of those that belong to it? what are its laws and obligations?" And if these two questions were answered satisfactorily, a third would naturally follow—(3) "How may those who desire to share its privileges and assume its obligations become citizens of it?" These, accordingly, are the three great questions dealt with in succession.

I. The Nature and Constitution of the Kingdom (vv. 2-16: first in itself, and then in relation to the world).

1. *In Itself* ("*The Beatitudes*"), vv. 2-12.

The answer to the questions in the people's hearts is given in no cold didactic way. The truth about the heavenly kingdom comes warm from a loving heart yearning over the woes of a weary and heavy-laden humanity. Its first word is "Blessed"; its first paragraph, Beatitudes. Plainly the King of Heaven has come to bless. There is no thunder nor lightning nor tempest on this mount; all is calm and peaceful as a summer's day.

How high the key-note struck in this first word of the King! The advantages usually associated with the best earthly government are very moderate indeed. We speak of the commonwealth, a word which is supposed to mean the common welfare; but the common welfare is quite beyond the power of any earthly government, which at most can only give protection against those enemies that would hinder the people from doing what they can to secure their own welfare. But here is a kingdom which is to secure the well-being of all who belong to it; and not well-being only, but something far beyond and above it: for "eye hath not seen, nor ear heard, neither have entered into the heart of man, the things which God hath prepared for them that love Him," and which His ambassador wrapped up in that great word "Blessed," the key-note of the Gospel of the Kingdom.

As he proceeds to show wherein this blessedness is to be found, we are struck by the originality of the conception, and its opposition to vulgar ideas. What the ordinary way of thinking on the subject is to this day can be readily seen in that very word "wealth," which in its original significance means welfare, but from the mistaken idea that a man's life consists in the abundance of the things which he possesses has come to mean what it means now. Who can tell the woes that result from the prevalence of this grand mistake—how men are led off in pursuit of happiness in a wrong direction altogether, away from its true source, and set to contending and competing with one another, so that there is constant danger—a danger averted only by the degree in which the truth enshrined in the Beatitudes prevails—that "the common wealth" will become the common woe? What a different world this would be if only the teaching of Christ on this one subject were heartily accepted—not by a few here and there, but by society at large! Then should we see indeed a kingdom of heaven upon earth.

For observe wherein our new King finds the universal weal. We cannot follow the beatitudes one by one; but glancing over them we see, running through them all, this great truth—that blessedness is essentially spiritual, that it depends not so much on a man's condition as on his character, not so much on what he has as on what he is. It needs no great effort of imagination to see that if men in general were to make it their main object and endeavour in life to be what they ought to be, rather than to scramble for what they can get, this earth would speedily become a moral paradise.

In expounding the blessedness of the kingdom the Master has unfolded the character of its members, thus not only explaining the nature of the kingdom and the advantages to be enjoyed under it, but also showing who those are that belong to it. That this was intended seems evident from the first and the last of the beatitudes, both ending with the emphatic words "theirs is the kingdom of heaven." It is as if on the two gates at the hither and farther end of this beautiful garden were inscribed the words, "The truly blessed ones, the citizens of the commonwealth of heaven, are those who are at home here." Originality of conception is again apparent. A kingdom so constituted was an entirely new thing in the world. Previously it had been a matter of race or of place or of forced subjection. The forefathers of these people had belonged to the kingdom of Israel, because they belonged to Israel's race; themselves belonged to the empire of Rome, because their country had been conquered and they were obliged to acknowledge Rome's sway; moreover, they were subjects of Herod Antipas, simply because they lived in Galilee. Here was a kingdom in which race distinctions had no place, which took no account of territorial limits, which made no appeal to force of arms or rights of conquest—a kingdom founded on character.

Yet it is no mere aristocracy of natural virtue. It is not a Royal Academy of the spiritually noble and great. Its line seems rather to stretch down to the lowest, for who else are the poor in spirit? And the mourners and the meek are no elect classes of nature's nobility. On the other hand, however, it runs up to heights even quite out of sight of the easy-going virtue of the day; for those who belong to this kingdom are men full of eager aspirations, bent on heart purity, given to efforts for the good of others, ready even to suffer the loss of all things for truth and righteousness' sake. The line is stretched so far down that even the lowest may enter; yet it runs up so high that those have no place in it who are satisfied with mere average morality, who count it enough to be free from vices that degrade the man, and innocent of crimes that offend the state. Most respectable citizens of an earthly commonwealth such honest men may be; but no kingdom of heaven is open to such as they. The foundations of common morality are of course assumed, as is made specially evident in the next division of the great discourse; but it would have been quite misleading had the Herald of heaven's kingdom said "Blessed are the honest," or "Blessed is the man who tells no lies." The common virtues are quite indispensable; but there must be something beyond these—first a sense of need of something far higher and better, then a hungering and thirsting after it, and as a necessary consequence some attainment of it, in order to citizenship in the kingdom of heaven and enjoyment of its blessedness.

The last beatitude breaks forth into a song of joy. No light-hearted joy, as of those who shut their eyes to the dark things in life, but joy in facing the very worst the world can do: "Blessed are ye when men shall revile you, and persecute you, and shall say all manner of evil against you falsely, for My sake. Rejoice, and be exceeding glad." O wonderful alchemy of heaven, which can change earth's dust and ashes into purest gold! Think, too, what riches and royalty of spirit in place of the poverty with which the series began.

These eight beatitudes are the diatonic scale of heaven's music. Its keynote is blessing; its upper octave, joy. Those who heard it first with quickened souls could no longer doubt that the kingdom of heaven was at hand; indeed, was there on the mountain that day!

2. *In relation to the World* (vv. 13-16).

The original promise to Abraham was twofold: "I will bless thee," "Thou shalt be a blessing" (Gen. xii. 2). The beatitudes correspond to the former, the passage before us to the latter. The beatitudes are, so to speak, the home affairs of the kingdom of heaven; the passage which follows is occupied with foreign relations. Those spoke of blessedness within, this speaks of usefulness without; for the disciples of Christ are known not only by their personal character and disposition, but also by their influence on others.

The relations of the members of the kingdom to "those that are without" is a complex and difficult subject; but the essence of it is set forth with surpassing clearness, comprehensiveness, and simplicity by the use of two unpretentious but most expressive figures, almost infinite in their suggestiveness—salt and light. This is our first experience of a well-known characteristic of the teaching of Christ—viz., His use of the simplest and most familiar objects of nature and circumstances of daily life, to convey highest and most important truth; and at once we recognise the touch of the Master. We cannot fail to see that out of all nature's infinity He has selected the two illustrations,—the only two, which exactly fit and fill the purpose for which He employs them. To the thoughtful mind there is something here which prepares for such tokens of mastery over nature as are found later on in the hushing of the storm and the stilling of the sea.

"Salt" suggests the conservative, "light" the liberal, side of the politics of the kingdom; but the two are not in opposition, they are in fullest harmony, the one being the complement of the other. Christian people, if they are what they profess to be, are all conservatives and all liberals: conservators of all that is good, and diffusers of all that is of the nature of light. Each of these sides of Christian influence is presented in succession.

"*Ye are the salt of the earth.*" The metaphor suggests the sad fact that, whatever tendency to upward development there may be in the world of nature, there is a contrary tendency in the world of men, so far as character is concerned. The world has often made great advances in civilisation; but these, unless counteracted by forces from above, have always been accompanied by a degeneracy in morals, which in course of time has brought about the ruin of mighty states. All that is best and most hopeful in mere worldly civilisation has in it the canker of moral evil,

> "That rotting inward slowly moulders all."

The only possible counteractive is the introduction of an element into society which will hold in check the forces that make for unrighteousness, and be itself an elevating and purifying influence. Such an element Christians were to be in the world.

Such, to a large extent, they have been. That they were the salt of the Roman empire during the evil days of its decline, no student of history can fail to see. Again, in the Dark Ages that followed, we can still trace the sweetening influence of those holy lives which were scattered like shining grains of salt through the ferment and seething of the times. So it has been throughout, and is still. It is true that there is no longer the sharp distinction between Christians and the world which there was in days when it cost something to confess Christ. There are now so many Christians in name who are not so in reality, and, on the other hand, so many in reality who are not so in name, and moreover so many who are Christians neither in name nor in reality, but who are nevertheless unconsciously guided by Christian principles as the result of the wide diffusion of Christian thought and sentiment—that the conservative influence of distinctive Christianity is very difficult to estimate and is far less appreciated than it should be. But it is as real and efficient as ever. If Christianity, as a conservative force in society, were to be suddenly eliminated, the social fabric would fall in ruins; but if only the salt were all genuine, if Christian people everywhere had the savour of the eight beatitudes about them, their conservative power as to all that is good, and restraining influence as to all that is evil, would be so manifest and mighty that none could question it.

If the salt would only keep its savour—there is the weak point. We know and feel it after the experience of all these centuries. And did not our omniscient Lord lay His finger on it at the very outset? He needed not that any one should tell Him what was in man. He knew that there was that in His truth which would be genuinely and efficiently conservative; but He knew equally well that there was that in man which would to a large extent neutralise that conservative power, that the salt would be in constant danger of losing its savour. Hence, after the encouraging words "Ye are the salt of the earth," He gives an earnest warning which necessarily moderates the too sanguine anticipations that would otherwise have been excited.

Alas! with what sad certainty has history proved the need of this warning! The salt lost its savour in the churches of the East, or it would never have been cast out and trodden under foot of the Mohammedan invaders. It lost its savour in the West, or there would have been no papal corruption, growing worse and worse till it seemed as if Western Christendom must in turn be dissolved—a fate which was only averted by the fresh salt of the Reformation revival. In modern times there is ever the same danger, sometimes affecting all the churches, as in the dark days preceding the revival under Whitefield and Wesley, always affecting some of them or some portions of them, as is too apparent on every hand in these days in which we live. There is as much need as ever to lay to heart the solemn warning of the King. It is as pungent as salt itself. "Of what use," He asks, "is tasteless salt? It is fit only to be cast out and trodden under foot of men." Equally useless is the so-called Christian, who has nothing in character or life to distinguish him from the world; who, though he may be honest and truthful and sober, a very respectable citizen of an earthly kingdom, has none of the characteristic marks of the kingdom of heaven, none of the savour of the beatitudes about him. It is only because there are still so many savourless Christians that the value of the Church as a conservative influence on society is so little recognised; and that there are so many critics, not all unintelligent or wilfully unfair, who begin to think it is time that it were cast out and trodden under foot of men.

"*Ye are the light of the world.*" We need not stay to show the liberality of light. Its peculiar characteristic is giving, spending; for this purpose wholly it exists, losing its own life in order to find it again in brightness diffused on all around.

Observe, it is not "Ye carry the light," but "Ye *are* the light." We are apt to think of light in the abstract—as truth, as doctrine, as something to be believed and held and expounded. We quote the familiar words, "Great is the Truth, and it shall prevail," and we imagine they are true. They are true indeed, in the long run, but not as often understood, certainly not in the region of the moral and spiritual. Of course truth in the abstract, especially moral and spiritual truth, ought to prevail; but it never does when men's interests lie, or seem to lie, in the contrary direction. Such truth, to be mighty, must be vitalised; it must glow in human hearts, burn on human tongues, shine in human lives. The King of truth knew this well; and hence He placed the hope of the future, the hope of dispelling the world's darkness, not in abstract truth, but in truth incarnate in the true disciple: "*Ye* are the light of the world."

In the strictest and highest sense, of course, Christ Himself is the Light of the world. This is beautifully set forth in discourses reported by another Evangelist (John viii. 12, ix. 5); and, indeed, it has been already taught by implication in the Evangel before us, where, as we have seen, the opening of Christ's ministry is likened to sunrise in the land of Zebulon and Naphtali (chap. iv. 16). But the personal Christ cannot remain upon the earth. Only for a few years can He be in this way the Light of the world, as He expressly says in one of the passages above referred to (John ix. 5); and He is speaking now not for the next few years, but for the coming centuries, during which He must be represented by His faithful disciples, appointed to be His witnesses (Acts i. 8) to the ends of the earth; so at once He puts the responsibility on them, and says, "Ye are the light of the world."

This responsibility it was impossible to avoid. As a matter of course, the kingdom of heaven must be a prominent object in the sight of men. The mountain of the Lord's house must be established on the top of the mountains (Isa. ii. 2), and therefore may not be inconspicuous: "A city set on a hill cannot be hid." It has been often said, but it will bear repeating, that Christians are the world's Bible. People who never read a word of either Old or New Testament will read the lives of those who profess to draw their inspiration thence, and will judge accordingly. They will form their opinions of Christ and of His kingdom by those who call themselves or are called by others Christians. "A city set on a hill *cannot* be hid." Here we have a truth complementary to that other conveyed in the symbol of salt. It taught that true Christians exert a great deal of silent, unobserved influence, as of salt hidden in a mass; but, besides this, there is their position as connected with the kingdom of heaven which forbids their being wholly hid.

Indeed, it is their duty to see to it that they are not artificially hid: "Neither do men light a lamp, and put it under the bushel, but on the stand; and it shineth unto all that are in the house" (R. V.). How beautifully does the illustration lend itself to the needed caution against timidity, without giving the least encouragement to the opposite vice of ostentation! Why does light shine? Simply because it cannot help it; it is its nature; without effort or even consciousness, and making no noise, it quietly does its duty; and in the doing of it does not encourage but even forbids any looking at itself—and the brighter it is, the more severely does it forbid it. But while there is no ostentatious obtrusiveness on the one hand, there is no ignoble shirking on the other. Who would ever think of kindling a light and then putting it under a bed? Yet how many Christians do that very thing when they are called to work for Christ, to let the light He has given them shine in some of the dark places where it is most needed!

Here, again, our Lord lays His finger on a weak spot. The Church suffers sorely, not only from quantities of savourless salt,—people calling themselves Christians who have little or nothing distinctively Christian about them,—but also from bushel-covered lights, those who are genuinely Christian, but who do all they can to hide it, refusing to speak on the subject, afraid to show earnestness even when they feel it most, carefully repressing every impulse to let their light shine before men, doing everything, in fact, which is possible to render their testimony to Christ as feeble, and their influence as Christians as small, as it can be. How many in all our Christian communities are constantly haunted by a nervous fear lest people should think them forward! For one person who makes a parade of his Christianity there are a hundred or a thousand who want always to shrink into a corner. This is not modesty; it is the sign of an unnatural self-consciousness. The disciples of Christ should act simply, naturally, unconsciously, neither making a display on the one hand nor hiding their light on the other. So the Master puts it most beautifully and suggestively: "Let your light so shine before men, that they may see your good works" (not the worker—that is of no consequences—but the works), "and glorify your Father which is in heaven."

So closes the first great division of the Manifesto of the King. It had begun with "goodwill to men"; it has shown the way of "peace on earth"; it closes with "glory to God in the highest." It is a prolonged echo of the angels' song. The Gospel of the Kingdom, not only as set forth here in these beautiful paragraphs, but in all its length and breadth and depth and height, in all its range and scope and application, is but an expansion of its very first proclamation: "Glory to God in the highest, on earth peace, goodwill to men."

II. The Law of the Kingdom (v. 17-vii. 12).

1. *General Principles* (vv. 17-20).

After blessing comes obligation—after beatitude, law. It is the same order as of old. The old covenant was in its origin and essence a covenant of promise, of blessing. Mercy, not duty, was its key-note. When God called Abraham to the land of promise, His first word was: "I will bless thee, and make thy name great; and thou shalt be a blessing" (Gen. xii. 2). Later on came the obligation resulting, as in Genesis xvii. 1: "Walk before me, and be thou perfect." So in the history of the Nation, the promise came first and the law followed it after an interval of four hundred years—a fact of which special use is made by the Apostle Paul (Gal. iii. 17, 18). The Mosaic dispensation itself began by an acknowledgment of the ancient promise ("I am the God of your fathers"—Ex. iii. 6), and a fresh declaration of Divine mercy ("I know their sorrows, and am come to deliver them"—Ex. iii. 7, 8). When Mount Sinai was reached, the entire covenant was summarised in two sentences, the first reciting the blessing, the second setting forth the resulting obligation: "Thus shalt thou say to the house of Jacob, and tell the children of Israel; Ye have seen what I did unto the Egyptians, and how I bare you on eagles' wings, and brought you unto Myself. Now, therefore, if ye will obey My voice indeed, and keep My covenant, then ye shall be a peculiar treasure unto Me above all people" (Ex. xix. 3-5). The very Decalogue itself is constructed on the same principle; for before a single commandment is given, attention is called to the great salvation which has been wrought on their behalf: "I am the Lord thy God, which brought thee out of the land of Egypt, out of the house of bondage." Thus closely does the proclamation of the new kingdom follow the lines of the old; far above and beyond it in respect of development, in essence it is the same.

It was therefore most appropriate that, in entering on the subject of the law of His kingdom, Christ should begin with the caution, "Think not that I am come to destroy the law or the prophets." On this point there would necessarily be the greatest sensitiveness on the part of the people. The law was their glory—all their history had gathered round it, the prophets had enforced and applied it; their sacred Scriptures, known broadly as "The Law and the Prophets," had enshrined it. Was it, then, to be set aside for new legislation? The feeling was quite natural and proper. It was necessary, therefore, that the new King should set Himself right on a matter so important. He has not come to overturn everything. He accepts the old covenant more cordially and thoroughly than they do, as will presently appear; He will build on it as a sure foundation; and whatever in His legislation may be new grows naturally out of the old. It is, moreover, worthy of notice that while the Mosaic economy is specially in His mind, He does not entirely leave out of consideration the elements of truth in other religious systems; and therefore defines the attitude He assumes as a Legislator and Prophet, in terms of the widest generality: "I am not come to destroy, but to fulfil."

While in the widest sense He came not to destroy, but to fulfil, so that He could with fullest liberality acknowledge what was good and true in the work of all former teachers, whoever and wherever they had been, thus accepting and incorporating their "broken lights" as part of His "Light of the world" (compare John i. 9), He can speak of the old covenant in a way in which it would have been impossible to speak of the work of earth's greatest and best. He can accept it as a whole without any reservation or deduction: "For verily I say unto you, Till heaven and earth pass, one jot or one tittle shall in no wise pass from the law, till all be fulfilled." Observe, however, that this statement is not at all inconsistent with what He teaches concerning the temporary character of much of the Mosaic legislation; it simply makes it clear that whatever passes away, does not pass by destruction, but by fulfilment—*i. e.*, the evolution of its hidden life—as the bud passes into the rose. The bud is there no longer; but it is not destroyed, it is fulfilled in the rose. So with the law as infolded in the Old Testament, unfolded in the New. How well fitted to inspire all thoughtful minds with confidence must have been the discovery that the policy of the new kingdom was to be on the lines, not of brand-new experimental legislation, but of Divine evolution!

Not only does He Himself do homage to the law, but takes order that His followers shall do the same. It is no parting compliment that He pays the old covenant. It is to be kept up both in the doing and in the teaching, from generation to generation, even in its least commandments. Not that there is to be such insistence on very small matters as to exclude altogether from the kingdom of heaven those who do not press every jot and tittle; but that these will be reckoned of such importance, that those who are lax in doctrine and practice in regard to them must be counted among the least in the kingdom; while those who destroy nothing, but seek to fulfil everything, will be the great ones. What a foundation is laid here for reverence of all that is contained in the law and the prophets! And has it not been found that even in the very smallest features of the old covenant, even in the details of the tabernacle worship, for example, there is for the devout and intelligent Christian a treasury of valuable suggestion? Only we must beware of putting jots and tittles in the place that belongs to the weightier matters of the law, of which we have warnings sufficient in the conduct of the scribes and Pharisees. Their righteousness had the appearance of extending to the minutest matters; but, large as it seemed in popular eyes, it was not nearly large enough; and accordingly, in closing this general definition of His relation to the old covenant, our Lord had to interpose this solemn warning: "I say unto you, that except your righteousness shall exceed the righteousness of the scribes and Pharisees, ye shall in no case enter the kingdom of heaven." Theirs was a righteousness as it were of the tips of the fingers, whereas He must have "the whole body full of light"; theirs was a righteousness that tithed mint and anise and cummin, and neglected judgment, mercy, and faith; theirs was in the narrow sphere of the letter, that which He demanded must be in the large and lofty region of the Spirit.

2. *Illustrations from the Moral Law* (vv. 21-48). The selection of illustrative instances is made with consummate skill. Our Lord, avoiding that which is specially Jewish in its interest, treats of matters that are of worldwide importance. He deals with the broadest principles of righteousness as adapted to the universal conscience of mankind, starting at the lowest point of mere earthly morality and rising to the very highest development of Christian character, thus leading up to the magnificent conclusion: "Be ye therefore perfect, even as your Father which is in heaven is perfect."

He begins with the crime which the natural conscience most strongly and instinctively condemns, the crime of murder; and shows that the scribes and Pharisees, and those who had been like them in bygone days, really destroyed the sixth commandment by limiting its range to the muscles, so that, if there were no actual killing, the commandment was not broken; whereas its true sphere was the heart, the essence of the forbidden crime being found in unjustifiable anger, even though no word is uttered or muscle moved, —a view of the case which ought to have been suggested to the intelligent student of the law by such words as these: "Thou shalt not hate thy brother in thine heart" (Lev. xix. 17); or again: "Whoso killeth his neighbour ignorantly, whom he hated not in time past, . . . is not worthy of death, inasmuch as he hated him not in time past" (Deut. xix. 4). Hatred in the heart, then, is murder. How searching! And how terribly severe the sentence! Even in its least aggravated form it is the same as that decreed against the actual shedding of blood. All the three sentences are death-penalties, only there are aggravations in the penalty where there are aggravations in the offence. Such is the Saviour's teaching on the great subject of sin. Yet there are those who imagine that the Sermon on the Mount is all the gospel they need!

The two practical applications which follow press the searching subject home. The one has reference to the Throne of Grace, and teaches that all offences against a brother must be put away before approaching it. The other has reference to the Throne of Judgment, and teaches by a familiar illustration drawn from common experience in the courts of Palestine that it is an awful thing to think of standing there with the memory of a single angry feeling that had not been forgiven and utterly removed (v. 26).

The crime of adultery furnishes the next illustration; and He deals with it on the same lofty principles and with the same terrible severity. He shows that this crime, too, is of the heart—that even a wanton look is a commission of it; and again follows up His searching exposition by a twofold practical application, first showing that personal purity must be maintained at any cost (vv. 29, 30), and then guarding the sacredness of home, by that exaltation of the marriage bond which has secured the emancipation of woman and her elevation to her proper sphere, and kept in check those frightful evils which are ever threatening to defile the pure and sacred spring from which society derives its life and sustenance (vv. 31-32).

Next comes the crime of perjury—a compound sin, which breaks at the same time two commandments of the Decalogue, the third and the ninth. Here, again, our Lord shows that, if only due homage is paid in the heart to reverence and to truth, all swearing is superseded. Let a man habitually live in the fear of the Lord all the day long, and "his word is as good as his oath"—he will always speak the truth, and will be incapable of taking the name of the Lord in vain. It is of course to be remembered that these are the laws of the kingdom of Christ; not laws meant for the kingdoms of this world, which have to do with men of all sorts, but for a kingdom made up of those who hunger and thirst after righteousness, who seek and find purity of heart. This passage accordingly has no bearing on the procedure of secular courts of justice. But, though the use of oaths may still be a necessity in the world, in the kingdom of heaven they have no place. The simple "Yea, yea," "Nay, nay," is quite enough where there is truth in the inward parts and the fear of God before the eyes; and the feeling of reverence, not only for God Himself, but for all the works of His hands, will effectually prevent the most distant approach to profanity.

The sin of revenge furnishes the next illustration. The Pharisaic perversion of the old law actually sanctioned private revenge, on the ground of a statute intended for the guidance of the courts of justice, and given for the sake of curbing the revengeful spirit which without it would lead a prosecutor to demand that his enemy should suffer more than he had inflicted. In this way they really destroyed that part of the Mosaic legislation, whereas He fulfilled it by developing still further,—bringing, in fact, to perfection,—that spirit of humanity which had dictated the law at the first. The true spirit of the Mosaic legislation was to discourage private revenge by assigning such cases to the courts, and curbing it still further by the limitation of the penalty imposed. Was not this spirit most nobly fulfilled, carried to its highest development, when the Saviour laid it down as the law of His kingdom that our revenge is to be the returning of good for evil?

The four practical illustrations (vv. 39-42) have been a source of difficulty, but only to those who forget that our Saviour is all the while warning against "the letter that killeth," and showing the need of catching "the spirit" of a commandment which "giveth life" to it. To deal with these illustrations according to the letter, as telling us exactly what to do in particular cases, is not to fulfil, but to destroy the Saviour's words. The great thing, therefore, is to catch their spirit; then they will be found of use, not for so many specified cases, but for all cases whatever. As an illustration of the difficulties to which we refer, mention may be made of the prejudice against the passage which suggests the turning of the other cheek. on the ground that it encourages a craven spirit. Take it as a definite command, and this would be in many cases the result. It would be the result wherever fear or pusillanimity was the motive. But where is there in all this passage the least trace of fear or pusillanimity? It is all love and magnanimity. It is the very antipodes of the craven spirit. It is the heroism of self-denying love!

The last illustration cuts at the root of all sin

and crime, the tap-root of selfishness. The scribes and Pharisees had made use of those regulations, most needful at the time, which separated Israel from other nations, as an excuse for restricting the range of love to those prepared to render an equivalent. Thus that wonderful statute of the old legislation, "Thou shalt love thy neighbour as thyself," was actually made a minister to selfishness; so that, instead of leading them to a life above the world, it left them not a whit better than the lowest and most selfish of the people. "If ye love them which love you, what reward have ye? Do not even the publicans the same?" Thus was the noble "royal law according to the Scripture" destroyed by the petty quibbling use of the word "neighbour." Our Lord fulfilled it by giving to the word neighbour its proper meaning, its widest extent, including even those who have wronged us in thought or word or deed, "I say unto you, Love your *enemies*, bless them that curse you, do good to them that hate you, and pray for them which despitefully use you, and persecute you."

How lofty, how far beyond the reach of the natural man!—but not impossible, or it would not have been demanded. It is one of the things of the kingdom concerning which the assurance is given later on: "Ask, and ye shall receive; seek, and ye shall find." Still, the Master knows full well that it is no small demand He is making of poor human nature. So at this point He leads our thoughts upward to our Father in heaven, suggesting in that relationship the possibility of its attainment (for why should not a child be like its father?) and the only example possible, for this was a range of righteousness beyond the reach of all that had gone before—He Himself as the Son of the Father would later set it forth before the eyes of men in all its lustre. But that time is yet to come, and meantime He can only point upward to the Highest, and urge them to this loftiest height of righteousness by the tender plea, "That ye may be the children of your Father which is in heaven: for He maketh His sun to rise on the evil and on the good, and sendeth rain on the just and on the unjust."

How beautiful and expressive are these symbols from nature, and how encouraging the interpretation of nature His use of them suggests! And what shall we say of their suggestiveness in the higher sphere of the spirit? Already the Sun of Righteousness is rising with healing in His wings; and in due time the rain of the Spirit will fall in fulness of blessing; so shall His disciples receive all that is needful to raise them to the very highest in character and conduct, in beatitude and righteousness; and accordingly their Master may well finish His whole exposition of the morals of the kingdom with the stirring, stimulating call, "Be ye therefore perfect, even as your Father which is in heaven is perfect."

3. *Illustrations from Religious Duty* (vi. 1-18).

The righteousness of the kingdom is still the great subject; for the reading of the Revised Version in the first verse of the chapter is evidently the correct one. The illustrations of the preceding passage have all come under the head of what we call morality as distinguished from religion, but it is important to observe that our Lord gives no sanction to the separation of the two.

Morality divorced from religion is a flower without root, which may bloom for a while, but in the end must wither away; religion without morality is—nothing at all; worse than nothing, for it is a sham. It is evident, of course, that this great word "righteousness," as used by our Lord, has a far wider scope than is given to it by those who take it merely as the equivalent of truth and honesty, as if a man could in any proper sense of the word be righteous, who was ungenerous to his neighbours, unfilial to God, or not master of himself.

Again, we have a principle laid down: "Take heed that ye do not your righteousness before men, to be seen of them" (R. V.). It is the same great principle as before, though the caution in which it is embodied is different. For if we compare ver. 20 of the preceding chapter, and remember its subsequent development in the verses which follow, we find that it agrees with the warning before us in insisting on righteousness of the heart as distinguished from that which is merely outward. The difference lies in this, that whereas, in the cases already dealt with, external conformity with the law is good so far as it goes, but does not go nearly far enough ("except your righteousness shall exceed," exceed, *i. e.*, by reaching back and down to the deepest recesses of the heart), in the cases now to be taken up external conformity is not good in itself, but really evil, inasmuch as it is mere pretence. Accordingly the caution now must needs be much stronger: "*Be ye not* as the hypocrites."

It is not, however, the being seen which is condemned, otherwise the caution would be at variance with the earnest counsel in chap. v. 16, and would, in fact, amount to a total prohibition of public worship. As before, it is a matter of the heart. It is the hidden motive which is condemned: "Take heed that ye do not your righteousness before men, *to be seen of them*."

The principle is applied in succession to Almsgiving, to Prayer, to Fasting.

Almsgiving is no longer regarded as distinctively a religious duty. Nor can it be put under the head of morality according to the common idea attached to that word. It rather occupies a kind of borderland between them, coming under the head of philanthropy. But whence came the spirit of philanthropy? Its foundation is in the holy mountains. Modern philanthropy is like a great fresh-water lake, on the shores of which one may wander with admiration and delight for great distances without discovering any connection with the heaven-piercing mountains. But such connection it has. The explorer is sure to find somewhere an inlet showing whence its waters come, a bright sparkling stream which has filled it and keeps it full; or springs below it, which, though they may flow far underground, bring the precious supplies from the higher regions, perhaps quite out of sight. If these connections with the upper springs were to be cut off, the beautiful lake would speedily dry up and disappear. Almsgiving, therefore, is in its right place here: its source is in the higher regions of the righteousness of the kingdom. And in these early days the lakes had not been formed, for the springs were only beginning to flow from the great Fountain-head.

The general object our Lord has in view, moreover, leads Him to treat the subject, not in relation to those who receive, but to those who give. There may be good done through the gifts of men who have no higher object in view than the sounding of their own trumpet; but, so far as they themselves are concerned, their giving has no value in the sight of God. Everything depends on the motive: hence the injunction of secrecy. There may indeed be circumstances which suggest or even require a certain measure of publicity, for the sake of the object or cause to which gifts are devoted; but so far as the giver is concerned, the more absolute the secrecy the better. For though it is possible to give in the most open and public way without at all indulging the petty motive of ostentation, yet so weak is human nature on that side of it, that our Lord puts His caution in the very strongest terms, counselling us not only to avoid courting the attention of others, but to refrain from even thinking of what we have done; for that seems to be the point of the striking and memorable words "Let not thy left hand know what thy right hand doeth."

The trumpet-blowing may be a great success. What the Master thinks of that success is seen in the caustic irony of the words "Verily I say unto you, they have their reward." There it is —and you can see just how paltry and pitiful it is; for there is nothing a man is more ashamed of than to be caught in even the slightest attempt to parade himself. But if the praise of men is never thought of, it cannot be said "they have their reward." Their reward is to come; and though it doth not yet appear, it will certainly be worthy of our Father Who seeth in secret.

Under the head of *Prayer* two cautions are given. The one may be dismissed in a few words, not only because it exactly corresponds with the preceding case, but because among us there is scarcely any temptation to that against which it is directed. The danger now is all the other way. The temptation for true children of the kingdom is not to parade their devotion for show, but to conceal it for shame. Still there are some directions in which even yet the caution against ostentation in prayer is needed—as, for instance, by those who in public or social prayer assume affected tones, or try in any way to give an impression of earnestness beyond what is really felt. Of the sanctimonious tone we may say that it has its reward in the almost universal contempt it provokes.

The other caution is directed, not against pretence, but against superstition. It will be seen, however, that the two belong to the same category, and therefore are most appropriately dealt with together. What is the sin of the formalist? It is that his heart is not in his worship. What is the folly of the vain repetitionist? It is the same—that his heart is not in his words. For there is no discouragement of repetition, if it be prompted by genuine earnestness. Our Lord again and again encouraged even importunate prayer, and Himself in the Garden offered the same petition three times in close succession. It is not, then, repetition, but "*vain* repetition,"— empty of heart, of desire, of hope—that is here rebuked; not much prayer, but "much speaking," the folly of supposing that the mere "saying" of prayers is of any use apart from the emotions of the heart in which true prayer essentially consists.

To guide us in a matter so important, our Lord not only cautions against what prayer ought not to be, but shows what it ought to be. Thus, incidentally as it were, He hands to us this pearl of great price, this purest crystal of devotion, to be a possession of His people for ever, never to lose its lustre through millenniums of daily use, its beauty and preciousness becoming rather more and more manifest to each successive generation.

It is given especially as a model of *form*, to show that, instead of the vain repetitions condemned, there should be simplicity, directness, brevity, order—above all, the plain, unadorned expression of the heart's desire. This main object is accomplished perfectly; a whole volume on the form of prayer could not have done it better, or so well. But, besides this, there is instruction as to the *substance* of prayer. We are taught to rise high above all selfish considerations in our desires, seeking the things of God first; and when we come to our own wants, asking nothing more than our Father in heaven judges to be sufficient for the day, while all the stress of earnestness is laid on deliverance from the guilt and power of sin. Then as to the *spirit* of prayer, mark the filial reverence implied in the invocation,—the fraternal spirit called for by the very first word of it, and the spirit of forgiveness we are taught to cherish by the very terms in which we ask it for ourselves. All this and more is superadded to the lesson for the sake of which the model prayer has been given.

The third application is to *Fasting*. In another place (ix. 14) will be found the principle to be followed in regard to times of fasting. Here it is taken for granted that there will be such times, and the principle announced at the beginning of the chapter is applied to the exercise. Let it be done in secret, before no other eye than His Who seeth in secret; thus only can we have the blessed recompense which comes to the heart that is truly humbled in the sight of God.

This principle plainly condemns that kind of fasting which is done only before men, as when in the name of religion people will abstain from certain kinds of food and recreation on particular days or at appointed times, without any corresponding humbling of the heart. The fasting must be before God, or it is a piece of acting, "as the hypocrites," who play a part before men, and when they go home put off the mask and resume their proper life. "Be ye not as the hypocrites;" therefore see that your fasting is before God; and then, if the inward feeling naturally leads to restriction of the pleasures of the table or of society, or to any other temporary self-denial, let it by all means be followed out, but so as to attract just as little attention as possible; and not only so, but if any traces of the secret exercise still remain when the penitential hour with God alone is over, these are to be carefully removed before returning to the ordinary intercourse of life. Our "penitence and prayer" are for ourselves only, and for God. Before men our *light* should shine.

The three illustrations cover by suggestion the whole ground; for prayer may well be understood in that large scriptural sense in which praise is included, and fasting is suggestive of all mortification of the flesh and humbling of the spirit. The first shows true religion in its outgoing, the second in its upgoing, while the third abases self; and all three are mutually helpful, for the higher we soar God-ward in praise and prayer, the lower shall we bend in reverent humility, and the further will our hearts go out in world-wide charity.

All depends on truth in the inward parts, on the secret life of the soul with God. How impressively is this stated throughout the whole passage! Observe the almost rhythmical repetitions: "Be ye not as the hypocrites," three times repeated: "Verily I say unto you, they have their reward," the very words three times repeated; "Let thine alms be *in secret*," "Pray to thy Father which is *in secret*," "That thou appear not unto men to fast, but unto thy Father which is *in secret*"; and once more, three times repeated, "Thy Father which seeth in secret Himself shall reward thee." No vain repetitions these. They press the great lesson home with a threefold force.

4. *Duty in relation to the World and the things of it* (vi. 19-vii. 12).

From this point onwards the plan of the discourse is not so apparent, and some have given up the idea of finding orderly sequence in it; yet there seems to be no insuperable difficulty, when the right point of view is taken. The perplexity seems to have arisen from supposing that at this point an entirely new subject begins, whereas all that follows on to chapter vii. 12, arranges itself easily under the same general head—the Righteousness of the Kingdom. According to this arrangement of the discourse there is an introduction of fourteen verses (v. 3-16), and a concluding passage of almost exactly the same length (vii. 13-27); while the main discussion occupies nearly three chapters, the subject throughout being the Righteousness of the Kingdom, dealt with, first as morality (v. 17-48), second as religion (vi. 1-18), and finally as spirituality (vi. 19-vii. 12), beginning and ending with a general reference to the law and the prophets (v. 17, vii. 12). The first of these divisions had to do with righteousness as between man and man; * the second with righteousness before God alone; while the third, on the consideration of which we now enter, deals with righteousness as between the children of the kingdom and the world in the midst of which it is set up. And just as in the paragraphs already considered we have been shown that our Lord came not to destroy, but to fulfil the code of ethics, and the rules for Divine service in the law and the prophets, so in this it will be made equally apparent that He came not to destroy, but to fulfil the principles involved in the political code by which Israel was separated from the nations of the world to be the Lord's peculiar people.

The subject before us now, therefore, is the relations of the children of the kingdom to the world, and it is dealt with—

(1) *As regards the good things of the world.* From the Beatitudes we have already learned that the blessedness of the children of the kingdom is to consist not in the abundance of the things they possess, but in qualities of soul, possessions in the realm of the unseen. Yet the children of the kingdom cannot do without the good things of this world; what, then, has the law of the kingdom to say in regard to their acquisition and use? The subject is large and difficult; but with amazing clearness and force, comprehensiveness and simple practical utility, it is set forth in a single paragraph, which is also characterised by a surpassing beauty of language. As before, the strait and narrow path is marked off by cautions on the right and on the left. On the one side must be shunned the Scylla of *greed*, on the other the Charybdis of *care*. The one is the real danger of seeking too much, the other the supposed danger of having too little, of "the good things of life."

It is not, however, a question of quantity. As before, it is a question of the heart. On the one hand, it is not the danger of having too much, but of seeking too much; on the other, it is not the danger of having too little, but of fearing that there will not be enough. It is a mistake, therefore, to say that the one caution is for the rich and the other for the poor. True, indeed, the rich are in greater danger of Scylla than of Charybdis, and the poor in more peril from the pool than from the rock; still a rich man may be, often is, a victim of care, while a poor man may readily have his heart far too much set on the yearly or weekly increase of his little store. It seems better, then, to make no distinction of classes, but to look at each caution as needed by all.

(*a*) Against seeking the good things of the world too earnestly (vv. 19-24). It is important to notice the strong emphasis on the word "treasure." This is evident not only from the reduplication of it—for the literal translation would be, "Treasure not for yourselves treasures upon the earth"—but also from the reason against it assigned in ver. 21: "Where thy treasure is, there will thy heart be also." It is clear, then, that there is no prohibition of wealth, but only of making it "thy treasure." But against this the law of the kingdom is in the highest degree decided and uncompromising. The language is exceedingly forcible, and the reasons marshalled are terribly strong. With all faithfulness, and with growing earnestness, the Master shows that to disobey this law is foolish, pernicious, fatal. It is *foolish;* for all earthly treasures are perishable, eaten by moth, consumed by rust, stolen by thieves, while the heavenly treasures of the spiritually-minded are incorruptible and safe for evermore. It is not only foolish, but most *pernicious,*—injurious to that which is most sensitive and most precious in the life, that which is to the soul what the eye is to the body, the darkening of which means the darkening of the whole body, not the mere clouding of the vision, but the condition suggested by the awful words "full of darkness"; while the corresponding deterioration in the lower ranges of the life is indicated by what follows: "If therefore the light that is in thee be darkness, how great is that darkness!" It is not only foolish and most pernicious, but *fatal*, for "No man *can* serve two masters"; so that to set the heart on the world means to give up the kingdom. It is vain to try to satisfy two claimants of the heart. One or other must be chosen: "Ye *cannot* serve God and Mammon."

(*b*) Against anxiety about the things of the world. The Revised Version has, by its correct translation, now removed the difficulty which seemed to lie in the words "Take no thought." To modern ears these words seemed to encourage thoughtlessness and to bless improvidence. Our translators of the seventeenth century, however, had no such idea. It is the result of a

* It is true that under the head of oaths comes the duty of reverence, which scarcely seems to fall under this head: but it will be remembered that this point comes in by way of a very natural suggestion in dealing with falsehood and the regulation of conversation, which evidently belongs to righteousness as between man and man.

change of meaning in a current phrase. At the time the translation was made, "to take thought" meant to be anxious, as will appear from such a passage as that in the first book of Samuel (ix. 5), where Saul says to his servant, "Come and let us return; lest my father leave caring for the asses, and *take thought* for us," evidently in the sense of "be anxious about us." * It is then, manifestly, not against thoughtfulness and providence, but against anxious care that the caution is directed.

Although this evil seems to lie in the opposite direction from that of avarice, it is really the same both in its root and its fruit, for it is due to the estrangement of the heart from our Father in heaven, and amounts, in so far as it prevails, to enslavement to the world. The covetous man is enslaved in one way, the anxious man in another; for does not our common language betray it every time we think or speak of "*freedom* from care"? We need not wonder, then, that our Lord should connect what He is about to say on this evil so closely with what He has said on the other, as He does by the use of the word *therefore*: "Therefore I say unto you, Be not anxious for your life."

But though, like the other, it is slavery, the sin of it is not nearly so great, and hence the difference of tone, which cannot but be observed as this new caution is given. It is no longer strong condemnation, but gentle expostulation; not dark threatening now, but tender pleading. As before, reason after reason is given against yielding to the all too natural weakness of the human heart. We are encouraged to remember what God has given already: the life, with such amazing powers and capabilities; the body, with all its marvellous intricacy and adaptation: and can it be supposed that He is likely to withhold the food to maintain the life, the raiment to clothe the body?—to remember how the little birds of the air and the modest lilies of the field are not forgotten: how then can we think that our Father would forget us, who are of so much more value than they?—to remember that the very fact that we know Him as our Father should be guarantee enough, preventing us from an anxious solicitude pardonable in the heathen, who have no such knowledge of a Father in heaven Who knoweth what His children need;—to remember also how vain and fruitless is our care, seeing we cannot in the very smallest lengthen the life for which we fret, while our times are wholly in the hand of Him Who gave it at first and daily satisfies its wants. Such is a bare outline of the thought in this passage, to attempt to expound or illustrate which would be to spoil it. The best way to deal with such a passage is first to study it carefully to see that its meaning and the point of all its parts are clearly apprehended, and then quietly, slowly, lovingly to read it over and let its heavenly music enter into the soul. Then, when the reading is finished and the great lesson has filled the heart with trustful love, we may look back upon it and observe that not only is a great spiritual lesson taught, but incidentally we are encouraged and directed to interrogate Nature and learn what she has to teach, to gaze on her beauty and lovingly look at what she has to show. Thus we find, as it were by the way, in the simple words of our King, the germ principles of science and of art.

* This complete change of meaning, amounting in fact, to the destruction and almost to the inversion of the sense, is one of many illustrations of the absolute need of revision from time to time of translations, not only to make them more correct, but even to keep them as correct as they were at first.

But these are wayside pearls; no special attention is called to them. These glimpses of nature come so naturally from the Lord of nature that nothing is made of them—they "flash along the chords and go"; and we return to the great lesson which, now that the cautions have been given, can be put in its positive form: "Seek ye first the kingdom of God, and His righteousness; and all these things shall be added unto you" (vi. 33). Seek ye first *His* kingdom, and *His* righteousness. Already as we have seen, this lesson has been implied in the Lord's Prayer; but it is well that it should be expressly set down—this will insure that the treasure is above, that the eye is clear, that the life is one: "and all these things shall be added," so that to-morrow need not trouble you. Trouble there must be in the world, but no one need have more than each day brings: "Sufficient unto the day is the evil thereof."

(2) *As regards the evil in the world.* The transition from the good things of the world to the evil that is in it comes quite naturally from the turn the Master's thought has taken in the close of the preceding paragraph. It is important to observe, however, that the whole subject of the evil in the world is not in view at this point. Has not the evil in the world in the large sense been in view from the beginning throughout; and has not the great subject of righteousness had all along as its background the dark subject of sin? The one point here is this: the attitude of the children of the kingdom to the evil which they cannot but see in the people of the world by whom they are surrounded.

Here, as before, there are two warnings, each against a danger lying in opposite directions: the one, the danger of making too much of the evil we see, or think we see, in others; the other, that of making too little of it.

(*a*) As against making too much of it—the danger of censoriousness (vii. 1-5). Here, again, the language is very strong, and the warning given is solemn and earnest—a sure sign that the danger is real and great. Again, too, considerations are urged, one after another, why we should beware. First, there is so much evil in ourselves, that we should be most careful how we condemn it in others, for "with what judgment ye judge ye shall be judged; and with what measure ye mete, it shall be measured to you again." Moreover, severity is a sign not of purity, but of the reverse: "Why beholdest thou the mote that is in thy brother's eye, but considerest not the beam that is in thine own eye?" Our severity should be applied to ourselves, our charity to others: especially if we would have any success in the correcting of our neighbour's faults: "How wilt thou say to thy brother, Let me cast out the mote out of thine eye; and lo, the beam is in thine own eye?" (R. V.) Otherwise we are hypocrites, and we must thoroughly reform ourselves before we have any idea even how to begin to improve others: "Thou hypocrite, first cast out the beam out of thine own eye; and then shalt thou see clearly to cast out the mote out of thy brother's eye." Of what exceeding value is this teaching just where it stands! The Saviour has been summoning His people not only to pure morality and true godliness, but to lofty spirituality of mind and heart; and knowing what was in man—knowing that dangers lurked on his path at every turn, and that even the highest spirituality has its special danger, its besetting sin—He points it out, paints it in all its blackness, spares not the sin of the saint any more than the sin of the sinner, calls the man that gathers his skirts about him with the word or the thought "I am holier than thou" by the same ugly name with which He brands the poor fools who disfigure their faces that they may be seen of men to fast. Yet, severe as it is, is it not needed? does not our best judgment approve and applaud? and are we not glad and grateful that our Lord has warned us so earnestly and impressively against a danger it might never have occurred to us to fear?

But there is another side to the subject; so we have another warning, in relation to the evil we see in the men of the world. It is—

(*b*) Against making too little of it (ver. 6). Though we may not judge, we must discriminate. It may be wrong to condemn: but it may be necessary to withdraw, otherwise sacred things may be profaned and angry passions stirred, and thus much harm may be done though only good was intended. Such is the manifest purport of the striking caution: "Give not that which is holy unto the dogs, neither cast ye your pearls before swine, lest they trample them under their feet, and turn again and rend you."

The Saviour is now about to close what He has to say on the Righteousness of the Kingdom in its relation to the Law and the Prophets; and He does it by setting forth in most memorable words a great privilege and a compact, comprehensive, portable rule—a privilege which will keep the heart right with God, a rule which will keep the heart right with man (vv. 7-12). The former is of course the more important of the two, so it comes first and has much the larger space. It is the mighty privilege of prayer. When we think of the height and the depth, the length and breadth, of the Righteousness of the Kingdom—when we think of the dangers which lurk on every hand and at every stage in our life-journey—we may well cry, "Who is sufficient for these things?" To that cry of the heart this is the answer: "Ask, and it shall be given you." We have had prayer before; but it was prayer as a part of righteousness, prayer as a religious duty. Now it is prayer as a power, as the one sure and only means of avoiding the terrible evils on every side, and obtaining the unspeakable blessings, the "good things" (ver. 11) of the kingdom of heaven. This being so, it was of the greatest importance that we should have faith to use it. Hence the repeated assurance, and the plain strong language in which it is conveyed; hence, too, the simple, strong, and touching arguments to dispel our doubts and encourage our trust (vv. 9-11).

Here, again, of what priceless value are these few words of our blessed Lord! Just where they are needed most they come, bringing "strength to the fainting heart" in view of the seemingly inaccessible heights of God's holy hill, on which the city of His kingdom is set. Why need we faint or fear, now that we can ask and be sure of receiving, can seek and be sure of finding, can knock at door after door of these halls of Sion, and have them, one after another, opened at our touch?

Again as before, prayer to God is closely connected with our behaviour to men. In the model prayer we were taught to say "Forgive us our debts, as we forgive our debtors"; and not only so, but a special warning was added, that if we do not forgive others, we cannot be forgiven. So here too we are reminded that if we are to expect our Father to act in a fatherly way to us by giving us good things, we must act in a brotherly way to our neighbours. Hence the golden rule which follows, and hence its connection with the prayer-charter by the word "therefore." And now that our relations to God and man have been summed up in the filial relation embodied in prayer, and in the fraternal relation embodied in the Golden Rule, all is complete, and the proof of this is furnished in the appropriate concluding words: "This is the Law and the Prophets."

III. Invitation to Enter the Kingdom. (vii. 13-29).

The Master has now said everything necessary in order to clear away popular misapprehensions, and place the truth about His kingdom fairly before the minds of His hearers. He has explained its nature as inward and spiritual, setting forth the character of those who belong to it, the blessedness they will enjoy, and the influence they will exert on the world around them. He has set forth clearly and fully the obligations that will rest upon them, as summed up in the comprehensive requirement of righteousness ununderstood in a larger and deeper sense than ever before—obligations of such stringency as to make it apparent that to seek the kingdom of God and His righteousness is no holiday undertaking, that it is no easy thing to be a Christian, but that it requires self-restraint, self-humbling, self-denial; and that therefore His kingdom cannot be attractive to the many, but must appeal to those who are earnest-spirited enough to ask and seek and knock for admittance.

Now that all has been fully and faithfully set forth—now that there is no danger of obtaining disciples under misapprehension—the great invitation is issued: *Enter ye in.* It is the free universal invitation of the Gospel, as large and liberal as that later one, "Whosoever will, let him come," though given in such a way as to keep still prominently before the minds of all comers what they may expect, and what is expected of them: "Enter ye in by the narrow gate: for wide is the gate, and broad is the way, that leadeth to destruction, and many be they that enter in thereby. For narrow is the gate, and straitened the way, that leadeth unto life, and few be they that find it" (R. V.).

The terms of this first invitation are very significant. The motives of fear and hope are appealed to; but not directly or specially. In the background lies, on the one hand, the dark doom of "destruction," and on the other the glorious hope of "life"; but neither the one nor the other is made emphatic. The demand for "righteousness" has been elaborated in full, and warnings against sin have been multiplied and pressed with intensest earnestness; but Christ does not now, as on account of the hardness of men's hearts He felt it needful later on to do, set forth in language that appeals vividly to the imagination the fate of those who take the broad way of easy self-indulgence; nor does He endeavour to picture the things which eye hath not seen, nor ear heard, nor heart conceived, which God hath prepared for them that love Him; He simply suggests in the briefest manner, by the use of a single word in each case—and that word characterised not so much by strength as by suggestiveness—what will be the fate of one, the goal of the other. Suggestive as both words are in the highest degree, they are not emphatic, but lie as it were in the background, while the attention is kept on the present alternative: on the one hand the wide gate, the broad way, the many thronging it; on the other, the narrow gate, the straitened way, the few finding it. Our Lord summons not so much to a choice that will pay, as to a choice that will cost; and in so doing makes His appeal to all that is noblest and highest and best in human nature.

Throughout the whole discourse He has been leading up to this point. He has been setting forth no prospect of happiness "to draw the carnal eye," but an ideal of blessedness to win the spiritual heart. He has been unfolding a righteousness, which, while it cannot but be repulsive to man's natural selfishness, profoundly stirs and satisfies his conscience; and now, in strict keeping with all that has gone before, the appeal is made in such a way as shall commend it, not to the thoughtless, selfish crowd, but to those whose hearts have been drawn and whose consciences have been touched by His presentation of the blessedness they may expect and the righteousness expected of them. From all this there is surely to be learned a most important lesson, as to the manner in which the Gospel should usually be presented—not by sensational descriptions of the glories of heaven or the horrors of hell, nor by the mere reiteration of exhortations to "come to Jesus," but by such information of the mind, awakening of the heart, and stirring of the conscience as are found in perfection in this great discourse of the Master.

It is characteristic of the large view our Lord takes of human life that He speaks of only two paths. There seem so many, leading off in all different directions; and so there are on a limited view of life's horizon; but when eternal issues are in sight, there are but two: the easy path of self-indulgence leading down to death, and the difficult path of duty* leading up to life.

It is worthy of remark that there is not a trace of asceticism in our Lord's representation. The straitness referred to is not outward, any more than the righteousness is; so that there is no encouragement given to self-imposed restrictions and limitations, as in the monastic vows of "poverty, chastity, and obedience." The way is strait enough in itself without any effort of ours to make it straiter. It is enough that we set ourselves to keep all the commandments; so shall we have a sufficiency of exercise to toughen our spiritual fibre, to strengthen our moral energies, to make us men and women instead of slaves of lust or tools of mammon. For, be it ever remembered, the way we take leads on naturally and unavoidably to its end. Destruction is no arbitrary punishment for self-indulgence; nor is life an arbitrary reward for self-discipline and surrender to the will of God. The path of self-indulgence "leadeth to destruction," by a law which cannot be annulled or set aside. But the path of self-restraint and self-surrender (for these are what make of us men, and not "blind mouths," as Milton expressively puts it), the path which is entered by the strait gate, and is continued along the narrow way, is one which in the course of natural development "leadeth unto life."

The call to enter is followed by words of solemn warning against certain dangers which might beset even those who wish to enter. First, the danger of false guidance: "Beware of false prophets." The danger lies in the future. Hitherto, while speaking throughout of present duty, there have been backward glances over the past, as our Lord has made it evident, point after point, that the righteousness of His kingdom was not the destruction, but the fulfilment of the law and the prophets. Now, however, He anticipates the time when there will be those claiming to speak in the name of God, or in His own name, whose doctrines will not be a fulfilment, but a destruction of the Truth, and a constant danger to those who may be exposed to their wolf-like ravages. There is manifestly no reference to such differences of opinion as divide real Christians from each other in these days. The doctrine throughout this manifesto is not speculative, but practical; it nowhere brings into prominence matters of opinion, or what are called theological tenets, but everywhere lays stress on that which immediately and powerfully affects the life. So it is here also, as is evident from the criterion suggested for the detection of false teachers: "By their fruits ye shall know them." Besides, the connection in which the caution occurs makes it evident that our Lord had specially in view those teachers who would lead their disciples astray as to the way of life, especially those who would dare to make that easy which he had shown to be "strait," who would set before their hearers or readers a broad path instead of the narrow one which alone leadeth unto life. This is a danger which besets us in these days. There is so strong a sentiment abroad in favour of liberality—and liberality properly so called is so admirable, and has been so much a stranger in times past—that we are in danger of accepting in its name easy-going representations of the Christian life which amount to a total abolition of the strait gate and the narrow way. Let us by all means be liberal enough to acknowledge all who have entered by the strait gate of genuine repentance, and are walking in the narrow way of faith and obedience, however much they may differ from us in matters of opinion, forms of worship, or modes of work; but let us beware how we give even the smallest encouragement to any on the broad road to imagine that they can continue as they are, and find it all right in the end. So to tamper with truth in the guise of liberality is to play the wolf in sheep's clothing.

The test our Lord gives for "discerning the spirits" is one which requires time for its application, but it is the only sure one; and when we remember that the Master is now looking forward into the future history of His kingdom, we can see why He should lay stress on a test whose operation, though slow, was sure. It is of course assumed that the first criterion is the Word of the Lord Himself. This is the law of the kingdom; but, knowing well what was in man, the Lord could not but foresee that

*Duty of course in its largest sense—to God and man and self—including all "righteousness" in the Master's sense of the word.

there would be those who could so twist any words that might be spoken on those great subjects as to lay snares for the unwary; and therefore, besides the obvious appeal "to the law and to the testimony," He supplied a practical test which, though less speedy in its application, was perfectly sure in its results.

The announcement of so important a test leads to the development of the general principle on which its validity depends—viz., the vital connection between essential doctrine and life. In the long run the one is always the outcome of the other. In the spiritual as in the natural world every species brings forth fruit "after its kind." "Do men gather grapes of thorns, or figs of thistles? Even so every good tree bringeth forth good fruit: but a corrupt tree bringeth forth evil fruit. A good tree cannot bring forth evil fruit, neither can a corrupt tree bring forth good fruit." The law being so absolute, making it certain, on the one hand, that where there is truth in the inward parts there will be good fruit in the outward life, and on the other, that where there is corrupt fruit in the outward life there must be that which is corrupt in the hidden man of the heart, it follows that the criterion is so sure as to be without appeal: "Every tree that bringeth not forth good fruit is hewn down, and cast into the fire" (ver. 19), and therefore may well determine the question as to who are trustworthy teachers in the Church: "Wherefore by their fruits ye shall know them."

In the development of the principle the Master's thought has been enlarged so as to include not teachers only, but all His disciples; and His range of view has been extended so as to embrace the last things. The great day of Judgment is before him. He sees the multitudes gathered around the throne. He foresees that there will be many on that great day who will discover, when it is too late, that they have allowed themselves to be deceived, that they have not been careful enough to test their spiritual guides, that they have not been careful enough to try themselves and make sure that their fruits were such that the Lord of the vineyard could recognise them as His own. He is filled with sympathy and sorrow at the prospect; so He lifts up His voice in earnest warning, that, if possible, none of those to whom the words will ever come may allow themselves to fall into so fatal an error: "Not every one that saith unto me, Lord, Lord, shall enter into the kingdom of heaven; but he that doeth the will of My Father which is in heaven."

How naturally, and as it were unconsciously and inevitably, He has passed from the Teacher to the Judge! Not as a personal claim. In His earliest teaching He kept personal claims as much in the background as possible. But now it is impossible to avoid some disclosure of His divine authority. He must speak of the Judgment; and He cannot speak of it without making it appear that He is Judge. The force of this is all the greater that He is, as it were, surprised into it; for He is evidently not thinking of Himself at all, but only of those who then were or would afterwards be in danger of making a most fatal mistake, leading to consequences awful and irreparable. We can well imagine that from this point on to the end there must have been a light on His face, a fire in His eye, a solemnity in His tone, a grandeur in His very attitude, which struck the multitude with amazement, especially at the *authority* (ver. 29) with which He spoke: "Many will say to Me in that day, Lord, Lord, did we not prophesy by Thy name, and by Thy name cast out devils, and by Thy name do many mighty works? And then will I profess unto them, I never knew you: depart from me, ye that work iniquity" (R. V.).

Again, observe the form the warning takes, revealing the consciousness that to depart from Him was *doom*—one of the many tokens throughout this discourse that none else than the Lord of life and glory could possibly have spoken it. Yet how many vainly think that they can accept it without acknowledging Him!

The same solemn and regal tone is kept up throughout the impressive passage which closes all, and presses home the great warning against trusting to any experience short of the surrender of the life to do the will of God as set forth in the words of Christ His Son. The two classes He has now in view are not the two great classes who walk, the one in the broad and the other in the narrow way. They are two classes of *hearers*. Most of those that throng the broad way are not hearers at all; they have no desire or intention of seeking any other than the broad way—they would as little think of going up into a mountain and listening to a discourse on righteousness, as they would of wearing a hair shirt or doing any other kind of penance; but those our Lord has now in view all have the idea of seeking the right way: their very attitude as hearers shows it—they are all of the church-going class, to translate into modern phrase; and what He fears is that some of them may deceive themselves by imagining that because they hear with interest and attention, perhaps admiration, therefore they are in the narrow way. Accordingly He solemnly warns them that all this may amount to nothing: there may be attention, interest, admiration, full assent to all; but if the hearing is not followed by doing, all is in vain.

It may almost go without saying that, after what our Lord has just been teaching as to the vital connection between the faith of the heart and the "fruits" of the life (vv. 15-23), there is no "legalism" here. In fact, the doing is not outward; it is a doing of the heart. The righteousness He has been expounding has, as we have seen, been a righteousness of the heart, and the doing of it, as a matter of course, is a heart-work, having its root in faith, which is the beginning of the doing in every case, according to His own word in another place: "This is the work of God, that ye believe on Him Whom He hath sent."

The illustration with which He presses home the warning is in the highest degree appropriate and forcible. The man who not only hears, but does, makes thorough work, digs deep (as St. Luke puts it in his record), and founds the house he is building for time and eternity upon solid rock; while the man who hears but does not, is one who takes no care as to his foundation, but erects his house just where he happens to be, on loose sand or earth, which the first storm will dislodge and sweep away. Meanwhile testing times are coming—rains, floods, winds—the searching trials of life culminating in the final judgment in the life to come. These all test the work of the builder, and render apparent the wisdom of the man who provided against the coming storm by choosing the rock foundation, for his house abides through all; and the folly of the other, who without a foundation carelessly risked all, for his house gives way before the storm, and great is the fall of it.

Alas for many hearers of the Word! Alas for many admirers of the "Sermon on the Mount"! Where will they be when everything turns on the question "Wert thou a doer of it?"

CHAPTER VIII.

THE SIGNS OF THE KINGDOM.

MATTHEW viii.-ix. 35.

REFERRING to chap. iv. 23, we find the work of Christ at the beginning of His ministry summarised as teaching and preaching and healing all manner of diseases. Of the teaching and preaching we have had a signal illustration in what is called the Sermon on the Mount; now the other great branch of the work is set before us in a group of miracles, filling up almost the whole of the eighth and ninth chapters.

The naturalness of the sequence will be at once apparent. If men had needed nothing more than counsel, guidance, rules of life, then might the Gospel have ended when the Sermon on the Mount was concluded. There are those who think they need nothing more; but if they knew themselves they would feel their need not only of the Teacher's word, but of the Healer's touch, and would hail with gladness the chapters which tell how the Saviour dealt with the poor leper, the man with the palsy, the woman with the fever, those poor creatures that were vexed with evil spirits, that dead damsel in the ruler's house. We may well rejoice that the great Teacher came down from the mountain, and made Himself known on the plain and among the city crowds as the mighty Healer; that His stern demand for perfect righteousness was so soon followed by that encouraging word, so full of comfort, for such as we: "I came not to call the righteous, but sinners" (ix. 13). The healing, then, is quite as essential as the teaching. The Sermon points out the way, unfolds the truth; but in the touch and word of the King Himself is found the life. The Christ of God had come, not as a mere Ambassador from the court of heaven to demand submission to its laws, but as a mighty Saviour, Friend, and Comforter. Hence it was necessary that He should make full proof of His mission in this respect as well as in the other; and accordingly the noble ethics taught on the mount are followed by a series of heavenly deeds of power and lovingkindness done in the plain.

The group in chaps. viii. and ix. is well fitted to give a comprehensive view of Christ's power and willingness to save. If only they were looked at in this intelligent way, how the paltry prejudices against "miracles" (a word, let it be observed, not once to be found in this Gospel) would vanish. Miracles, wonders, prodigies—how incredible in an age of enlightenment! Yes; if they were introduced as miracles, wonders, prodigies; but they are not. They are signs of the kingdom of heaven—just such signs of it as the intelligent reason demands; for how otherwise is it possible for One Who comes to save to show that He is able to do it? How could the people have been expected to welcome Him as a Saviour, unless He had taken some means to make it evident that He had the power as well as the will to save? Accordingly, in consonance with what enlightened reason imperatively demands of such an One as He claims to be, we have a series of "mighty deeds" of love, showing forth, not only His grace, but His power—power to heal the diseases of the body, power over the realm of nature, power over the unseen world of spirit, power to forgive and save from sin, power to restore lost faculties and conquer death itself. Such are the appropriate signs of the kingdom spread before us here.

Let us look first at that which occupies the foremost place,—power to heal disease. The diseases of the body are the outward symptoms of the deep-seated malady of the spirit; hence it is fitting that He should begin by showing in this region His will and power to save. Yet it is not a formal *showing* of it. It is no mere demonstration. He does not seek out the leper, set him up before them, and say, "Now you will see what I can do." All comes about in a most simple and natural way, as became Him Who was no wonder-worker, no worker of miracles in the vulgar use of that word, but a mighty Saviour from heaven with a heart of love and a hand of power.

THE LEPER (viii. 1-4).

"And when He was come down from the mountain, great multitudes followed Him. And behold, there came to Him a leper." What will He do with him? Should He say to him, "Poor man, you are too late—the sermon is done"? or should He give him some of the best bits over again? No, there is not a sentence in the whole of it that would be any answer to that cry, "Lord, if Thou wilt, Thou canst make me clean." What does He do, then? "Jesus put forth His hand, and touched him, saying, I will: be thou clean. And immediately his leprosy was cleansed."

Is it, then, a great stumbling-block in your way, O nineteenth-century critic, that you are expected to believe that the Lord Jesus actually did heal this leper? Would it take the stumbling-block away to have it altered? Suppose we try it, amended to suit the "anti-supernaturalism" of the age. "And behold, there came a leper to Him, saying, Lord, if Thou wilt, Thou canst make me clean. And Jesus put out His hand, and motioned him away, saying, Poor man, you are quite mistaken, I cannot help you. I came to teach wise people, not to help poor wretches like you. There are great laws of health and disease; I advise you to find them out, and obey them: consult your doctor, and do the best you can. Farewell." Oh, what nonsense many wise people talk about the difficulty of believing in Divine power to heal! The fact is, that if Christ had not proved Himself a healer, men could not have believed in Him at all.

There could have been no better introduction to the saving work of the Christ of God. Leprosy was of all diseases the most striking symbol of sin. This is so familiar a thought that it need not be set forth in detail. One point, however, must be mentioned, as it opens up a vein of tender beauty in the exquisite simplicity of the story—the rigorous separation of the leprous from the healthy, enforced by the ceremonial law, which made it defilement to touch a leper. Yet "Jesus stretched forth His hand, and *touched* him." "He was holy, harmless, undefiled, separate from sinners;" therefore He could mingle with them, contracting no stain Himself, but diffusing health around Him. He could take no defilement from the leper's touch; the current was all the other way: "virtue" went out of Him, and flowed in healing streams through the poor leper's veins. O lovely symbol of the Saviour's relation to us sinners! He has in His holy Incarnation touched our leprous humanity; and remaining stainless Himself, has set flowing a fountain of healing for all who will open to Him hearts of faith and let Him touch them with His pure heart of love. Those were most wonderful words spoken on the mount: they touch the conscience to the quick and fire the soul with heavenly aspiration; but this touch of the leper goes to our hearts, for it proves to us that, though the time is coming when He shall sit as Judge and say to all the sinful, "Depart from Me," as yet He is the loving Saviour, saying, "Come unto Me, ye weary," and touching the leprous into health.

That our Saviour was totally averse to anything at all sensational, and determined rather to repress than encourage the mere thirst for marvels, is evident from the directions given to the leper to say nothing about what had happened to him, but to take the appointed method of giving thanks to God for his recovery, at the same time registering the fact, so that while his cure should not be used to gather a crowd, it might be on record with the proper authorities as a witness to the truth of which it was a sign.

The Centurion's Servant (5-13).

This case, while affording another valuable illustration of the Master's willingness and power to save, differs in several important points from the first, so that the lesson is widened. First and chiefly, the application was from a Gentile; next, it was not on his own behalf that the centurion made it, but on behalf of another, and that other his servant; and, further, it was a request to heal a patient out of sight, out of knowledge even, as it would seem. Each of these particulars might suggest a doubt. He has healed this Jew; but will He listen to that Gentile? He has responded to this man's own cry; but will He respond when there is no direct application from the patient? He has cured this man with a touch; but can he cure a patient miles away? The Saviour knew well the difficulties which must have lain in the way of this man's faith. He has evidence, moreover, that his is genuine faith, and not the credulity of superstition. One could readily imagine an ignorant person thinking that it made no difference whether the patient were present, or a thousand miles away: what difference does distance make to the mere magician? But this man is no ignorant believer in charms and incantations. He is an intelligent man, and has thought it all out. He has heard of the kingdom of heaven, and knows that this is the King. Reasoning from what he knows of the Roman kingdom, how orders given from a central authority can be despatched to the outskirts, and be executed there with as great certainty as if the Emperor himself had gone to do it, he concludes that the King of the spiritual world must in like manner have means of communication with every part of His dominion; and just as it was not necessary, even for a mere centurion, to do personally everything he wanted done, having it in his power to employ some servant to do it, so it was unreasonable to expect the King of heaven Himself to come in person and heal his servant: it was only necessary, therefore, that He should speak the word, and by some unseen agency the thing would be done. At once the Saviour recognises the man's thoughtful intelligence on the subject, and, contrasting with it the slowness of mind and heart of those of whom so much more might have been expected, "He marvelled, and said to them that followed, Verily I say unto you, I have not found so great faith, no, not in Israel."

The thought of this immediately suggests to Him the multitudes that shall exercise a similar faith in ages to come, and in lands far off; and, as on the mount, when He looked forward to the great future, His heart yearned over the mere hearers of the word shut out at last; so here He yearns with a great yearning over His unbelieving countrymen, whose exclusion at last from the heavenly kingdom would be felt with all the sharper pain that such multitudes from far less favoured lands were safe within—at home, with the patriarchs of the chosen nation—while they, the natural heirs of the kingdom, were exiles from it for evermore. Hence the wail and warning which follow His hearty appreciation of the centurion's faith: "And I say unto you, that many shall come from the east and the west, and shall sit down with Abraham, and Isaac, and Jacob, in the kingdom of heaven: but the sons of the kingdom shall be cast forth into the outer darkness: there shall be weeping and gnashing of teeth."

How fared it with the centurion's appeal? Was it any hindrance that he was a foreigner, that he made it not for himself but for a servant, and that the patient was so far away? None whatever. As he rightly judged, the King of heaven had resources in abundance to meet the case. Without the least hesitation, Jesus said to the centurion, "Go thy way: and as thou hast believed, so be it done unto thee. And his servant was healed in the selfsame hour."

The Fever Patient (14, 15).

The leprosy and palsy were symbols of sin wholly possessing its victims: the one suggestive of the state of those who are positively defiled by sin, the other of the condition of those who, though sound to all outward appearance, are simply wanting in inward life, paralysed in that part of their being which constitutes life. These two cases, then, were most suitable for setting forth the saving power of the Christ of God as regards the unconverted, be they Jew or Gentile. This third cure is within the circle of the disciples. It is a case of fever in the home of Peter. It therefore fitly suggests the diseases to which those are still liable who have come to Christ and been healed of their leprosy or palsy, the chronic disease which defiled or paralysed them in time past; but who are still liable to contagion, still exposed to attacks of fever, acute diseases which, though temporary, are most dangerous, and, just as certainly as the others, need the touch of the Great Physician for their healing. These fevers separate us from Christ and unfit us for His service; but they need not continue to do this, for if only we allow Him to enter the house and touch us, the fever will cease; and, like this patient in the home of

Peter, we may at once arise and minister unto Him.

The three specific cases which have been so appropriately selected and given in detail are followed by a general enumeration of a number of similar ones dealt with in like manner, "when the even was come"—the whole experience of that eventful day leading to the joyful recognition of the fulfilment of a grand prophetic word spoken long ago of the Messiah that was to come: "Himself took our infirmities, and bare our sicknesses."

The quotation is most suggestive. It raises the question of our Lord's personal relation to disease. We have seen reason to believe that disease could not contaminate His holy flesh; and certainly we never read of His suffering from any sickness of His own. Did He then know nothing personally of disease and fleshly infirmity? If not, how could He be tempted in all points like as we are? The solution seems to lie in this most interesting quotation. It is not a literal citation from the Septuagint, but it is a thoroughly fair and true reproduction of the idea of the prophet; and it clearly suggests to the mind that the Christ's relation to human sickness was of the same kind as His relation to human sin. Though personally He had no sin, yet "He was made sin for us," so that He felt the intolerable weight pressing Him down as in the garden, and the awful darkness wrapping Him round as on the cross. In the same way, even though His flesh may never actually have been subjected to physical disease, He nevertheless could not remove diseases from others without bearing them Himself. Ah! it cost Him far more than we are apt to think, to say, "I will, be thou clean." It was only by the sacrifice of His life that He could take away the sin of the world; and we believe that it was only by the sacrifice of a part of His life that He could take away the disease of a sufferer. When He said, "Somebody hath touched Me, for virtue has gone out of Me," we may be sure it was no mere jostling of the crowd; it was an outflow of His life, a partial shedding, so to speak, of His precious blood. Just as later, in the words of St. Peter, "He bare our sins in His own body on the tree," so already "Himself took our infirmities and bare our sicknesses."

The Impulsive Scribe (18-20).

The two incidents which follow, though at first sight apparently different in character from the great majority of the group, are quite in place among the mighty deeds of the Master, manifesting, as they do, His penetrating insight into character. To all appearance there could have been no better offer than that of the impulsive scribe—"Master, I will follow Thee whithersoever Thou goest"; and, had it been made with a full understanding of all it meant, it would beyond all question have been at once accepted; but He Who "knew what was in man" saw at once what manner of man this was—how he was quite unprepared for the hardships he would have to undergo; and therefore, while by no means declining the offer, He gives him fair warning of what he might expect, in these memorable words: "The foxes have holes, and the birds of the air have nests; but the Son of man hath not where to lay His head." There is infinite pathos in the words. Moreover, the form in which the truth is put, while fitted effectually to deter the selfish and faint-hearted, would be no discouragement to a truly devoted and courageous soul, but would rather fire it with a holier ardour to follow the Son of man anywhere, at whatever cost, rejoicing to be "counted worthy to suffer shame" and loss "for His name."

The Hesitating Disciple (21, 22).

This case is one of the opposite description. Judging from the way in which the scribe had been dealt with, it might have been expected that when this disciple asked to be excused for a time, in order to discharge a duty which seemed so urgent, the answer would have been one not only allowing but even enforcing the delay. But no. Why the difference? Again, because the Master saw "what was in man." This was no impulsive, impetuous nature which needed a word of caution, but one of those hesitating natures which need to be summoned to immediate decision. It would seem also, from the peculiar expression, "Leave *the dead* to bury their own dead" (R. V.), that he belonged to an ungodly family, to associate again with whom at such a critical time in his history would be most prejudicial; and it must be remembered that it would not have been the mere attending of the funeral; there were the laws of uncleanness, which would oblige him, if he went, to stay many days; and meantime the golden opportunity might be gone.

Thus are we guarded against the two opposite dangers—the one besetting the eager and impulsive, the other the halting and irresolute. In neither case are we told what the result was. We may surmise that the scribe disappeared from view, and that the other joined the party in the boat; but "something sealed the lips of that Evangelist"; from which we may perhaps infer that his main object in relating the two incidents was, not to give information of them, but to show forth the glory of the Master as the Searcher of hearts; to signalise the fact that He was no less Master of the minds than of the bodies of men.

The Storm Stilled (23-27).

It was not enough that the Saviour of mankind should have power to grapple with disease and skill to search the hearts of men: He must be Master not only of life, but of its environment too. That He is becomes apparent before the boat which carries the little company reaches the other side of the lake. One of those tempests which often lash the Sea of Galilee into sudden fury has burst upon them, and the little boat is almost covered with the waves. Here is a situation beyond the reach even of the Great Physician, unless indeed He be something more. He is something more. He is Lord of nature, Master of all its forces!

Must He not be? He has come to reveal the unseen God of nature; must He not then make it manifest, now that the occasion calls for it, that winds and waves are "ministers of His, that do His pleasure"? Again, it is no mere "miracle," no mere marvel which He works in the salvation of His terrified disciples—it is a sign, an indispensable sign of the kingdom of heaven.

The story is told with exquisite simplicity, and with all the reality of manifest and transparent truthfulness. "He was asleep"—naturally enough after the fatigues of the day, notwithstanding the howling of the storm; for why should He fear wind or wave? Is there not a promise here for all His followers when tempest-tossed: "So He giveth His beloved sleep"?

His disciples let Him sleep as long as they dare; but the peril is too imminent now. So they come to Him and awake Him, saying, "Save, Lord; we perish!" Though no concern for Himself would ever have disturbed His slumber, the first cry of His disciples rouses Him at once to action. The resources of His human nature, beyond which He never went for the purpose of meeting His own personal needs, had been completely exhausted; but there is no diminution of His power to save those who call upon Him. Without any trace remaining of weariness or weakness, He hastens to relieve them. First,* He quiets the tempest in the disciples' hearts, rebuking their unbelief and calming their fears; then He stills the storm without, rebuking the winds and the sea; "and there was a great calm." It reads like the story of creation. No wonder the astonished disciples exclaimed: "What manner of man is this, that even the winds and the sea obey Him?"

Demons Cast Out (28-34).

Visible nature is not man's sole environment. There is an unseen universe besides; and He Who would be Saviour of mankind must be Master there as well. That this also is sure is now proved beyond a doubt. For it is important to observe that this is not an ordinary case of healing, otherwise its true place would have been with the group of bodily diseases at the beginning of this series. When we consider its salient features, we see that it is just in its right place, closely following, as it does, the stilling of the storm. There are storms in the spiritual world, more terrible by far than any in the realm of nature; and it is necessary that these darker storms be also subject to the control of the Saviour of mankind. "The prince of the power of the air" and all his legions must be subject to the "Son of man." And this subjection, rather than the cure of the individual sufferers, is the salient feature of the passage. It is not the men, but the demons possessing them, who cry out, "What have we to do with Thee, Jesus, Thou Son of God? art Thou come hither to torment us before the time?" Well did these evil spirits know who He was; and well, also, did they know that He was mightier than they, and that the time was coming when they would be put entirely under His feet: "Art Thou come to torment us *before the time?*"

The sequel has been the occasion of much cavil. It has been represented as entirely beyond the bounds of rational belief; but why? The whole subject of demoniacal possession is a most difficult one; but many of the calmest and deepest thinkers, quite apart from the testimony of the Gospel, have found themselves unable to explain a multitude of dark facts in history and experience apart from the reality of demoniacal influence. If a spirit can exercise a malign influence on a man, why not on an animal? Moreover, seeing that the keeping of these swine was an open breach of the law, what difficulty is there in supposing that Christ should allow their destruction, especially when we consider that this transference of the malign influence not only made more apparent His absolute control over the spirits of evil, but taught a most striking and instructive lesson as to their affinities? For certain persons there is no more instructive and no more needful passage in Scripture than this. The difficulty is, that those who prefer to keep their swine will not welcome the mighty Exorcist, but, like these people of old, beseech Him to "depart out of their coasts."

* The order is different in the second and third Gospels; but here only is the order of events noted: "And He saith unto them, Why are ye fearful. O ye of little faith? *Then* He arose."

Sins Forgiven (ix. 1-13).

Master of disease—Searcher of hearts—Master of the forces of nature—Master of the powers of the Unseen: is not this enough? Not yet; He must make it evident that "the Son of man hath power on earth to forgive sins." To heal the diseases of the body was a great and blessed thing to do, but it was not thorough work; for what are all these varied diseases—leprosy, fever, palsy—but symptoms of one great disorder which has its roots, not in the flesh, but in the soul, a disease belonging to that region of the unseen, in which He has now made manifest His power—the dark disease of sin. The time has now come to show that He can deal effectually with it; and immediately on His return to His own side of the lake, the opportunity presents itself. "They brought to Him a man sick of the palsy, lying on a bed."

As a case of palsy, it is not new. The centurion's servant was a palsy case; and though from His treatment of it, as of the leprosy and fever, it might fairly have been inferred that He could deal also with that which was deeper, it was not enough to leave it to inference—it must be made manifest. It may have been that the disease of this man had been in some special manner connected with previous sins, so that his conscience may have been the more exercised as he looked back over his past life; but whether this was so or not, it is obvious that his conscience was at work,—that much as his palsy may have troubled him, his guilt troubled him much more. Why, otherwise, should the Saviour have addressed him as He did, making no reference to the disease, but dealing directly with his spiritual condition? Moreover, the special affection shown in the Saviour's mode of address seems to indicate His recognition of that broken and contrite spirit with which the Lord is well pleased. It would scarcely be too strong to translate it thus: "My dear child, be of good cheer; thy sins are forgiven."

The Saviour is coming closer and closer to human need, dealing more and more thoroughly with the world's want and woe. If we look at it aright, we cannot but recognise it as really a greater thing to heal the deep disease of the soul, than to heal any or all of the diseases of the body, greater even than to still the storm or rule by superior power the spirits of evil. For here there is something more needed than power or skill, even though both be infinite. We have already had a glimpse of the need there was, even in taking away human sickness, that the Healer Himself should suffer. But deeper far is this necessity if the disease of the soul is to be reached. It is only the Lamb of God that can take away the sin of the world. These scribes were right for once when they made more of this claim than of any that had gone before, saying within themselves, "This man blasphemeth;" . . . "Who can forgive sins but God only?"

How could He prove to them His power actually to forgive the man's sins? A demonstration of this is quite impossible; but He will come as near to it as may be. He has already recognised the faith of the bearers, and the penitence of the man himself; just as quickly He discerns the thoughts of the scribes, and gives them proof that He does so by asking them, "Wherefore think ye evil in your hearts?" Then, answering their thought (which was, "He is only saying it"), He replies in effect, "It is indeed as easy to say one thing as another, if saying is all; but that you may be sure that the saying of it is not all, I shall not repeat what I said before, the result of which from the nature of the case you cannot see, but something else, the result of which you shall see presently"; whereupon, turning to the sick of the palsy, He said: "Arise, take up thy bed, and go unto thine house. And he arose, and departed to his house." With characteristic reticence, the sacred historian says nothing of the feelings of the happy man as he hied him home with a double blessing beyond the power of words to tell.

Is it possible to imagine any better proof that could have been given of Christ's authority to forgive sins? Let those who have a horror of anything extraordinary suggest some way in which this assurance could have been given without any manifestation of superhuman power. If they cannot, why continue those unreasoning objections to the kind of proof He did give, when no other proof can be even suggested that would have at all suited the purpose?

The purpose was accomplished, so far at least as the people were concerned. Whether the scribes found some way of evading the conclusion, the Evangelist does not say; but he does say that "when the multitudes saw it, they marvelled," or, as the probably more correct version of the Revisers gives it, "they were afraid." This is true to nature, for now they knew that they stood in the presence of One Who could look them through and through, and touch them in their sorest spot; so it was natural that their first feeling should be one of awe. Still, they could not but be thankful at the same time that there was forgiveness within their reach; so quite consistently the narrative proceeds—And they "glorified God, which had given such power unto men."

Now that His power to deal with sin is made so apparent, it is time to let it be known that all sinners are welcome. Hence most appropriately there follows the call of one from among the most despised class to take a place among His closest followers. We can well understand how the modest Matthew, who never mentions anything else about himself, was glad to signalise the grace of the Master in seeking out the hated and despised publican. Not only does Christ welcome him, but consents to sit at meat with his former associates (ver. 10); and when the self-righteous Pharisee complains, He takes occasion to speak those memorable words, so full of warning to those who think themselves righteous, so full of comfort to those who know themselves sinners: "They that be whole need not a physician, but they that are sick. . . . I am not come to call the righteous, but sinners to repentance."

Death Vanquished (14-26).

The focal point of the passage is the chamber of death in the house of Jairus. There we learn that He Who had shown Himself to be Lord of nature and of human nature, Master of the spirits of evil, and Saviour from sin, is also Conqueror of Death. He needs no preparation for the encounter. The summons comes to Him in the midst of a discourse, yet He asks not a moment's delay, but sets out at once; on the other hand, He is in no haste, for He has time to attend to another sufferer by the way; and there is no exhaustion afterwards, for He deals with another case, and still another, on His way back.

The question with which He was engaged when the summons came was one raised by the disciples of John, who, as we learn from the other accounts, were prompted by the Pharisees in the hope of exciting antagonism between the followers of John and of Jesus. Perhaps also they had the hope of setting Him at variance with Himself, for had He not declared that one jot or one tittle should not pass from the law till all was fulfilled? Why, then, did not His disciples fast? To this it might have been answered that the frequent fasts observed by Pharisees, and also by the disciples of John, were not really appointed by the law, which prescribed only one day of fasting in the year—the great atonement day. But the Saviour gives an answer of much wider scope and farther-reaching significance. There was involved, not the question of fasting only, but of the entire ceremonial law; and He disposes of it all by a series of characteristic illustrations, each of them as good as a volume on the subject could have been. The first of these illustrations sets the true principle of fasting in full, clear light by a simple question —"Can the children of the bridechamber mourn, as long as the bridegroom is with them? but the days will come, when the bridegroom shall be taken away from them, and then shall they fast." There is here much more to think of besides the answering of the question. There is a treasury of valuable suggestion in His calling Himself the Bridegroom, thus applying to Himself the rich imagery of the Old Testament on this theme; while at the same time He adopts the very figure which John himself had used in order to mark his relation to Jesus as the Bridegroom's friend (*cf.* John iii. 29); and it is especially worthy of note how this keeps up the *Gospel* idea,—the great joy, as of a marriage, in the yielding of the heart to Christ. No less striking is His touching reference to the dark days coming, the first distinct foreshadowing of the Cross. It has been well said by a German writer, "What man has ever looked so calmly, so lovingly (*lieblich*), from such a height into such an abyss!" from the position of the Bridegroom of humanity to that of the outcast on the Cross. Ah! the shadow of that Cross is never off Him, not even when He is exulting in His bridegroom joy. But these are only incidental suggestions;

the main idea is the true principle of fasting, which, like all the observances of the New Testament, must be the expression of that which is in the heart. Let the heart only be true, and when the Bridegroom of the heart is present, fasting will be entirely out of the question; but when He is absent no rule will be needed—they will fast as the natural expression of their sorrow.

The two companion illustrations which follow set in the clearest light the large subject of the relation of the new dispensation to the old in respect of forms. As to substance, He had already made it plain that the old was not to be destroyed, nor even superseded, but fulfilled, to its last jot and tittle, as harvest fulfils seed-time. But as to form, the case was entirely different. The new life, while losing nothing which was in the old, was to be larger and freer, and therefore must have new garments to match. To try to piece out and patch the old would be no improvement, but much the reverse, for a worse rent would be the only result. The second illustration, suggested like the first by the associations of the marriage feast (the Saviour's illustrations are never far-fetched—He always finds exactly what He needs close at hand, thus proving Himself Master of the imagination as of all else), is to the same purpose. The new wine of the kingdom of heaven, though it retains all the the excellence of the old vintage, yet having fresh properties of its own, must have fresh skins to hold it, that its natural expansion be not hindered; for to attempt to confine it in the old vessels would be to expose them to destruction and to lose the wine.

What a striking illustration of these suggestive words of warning has been the history of doctrine and of form in those churches which cling to the worn-out ritualism of the Old Testament! Old Testament forms were good in their time; but they are not good to hold the new wine of spiritual life; and to attempt to combine them, as modern ritualists do, is to injure both, to do violence to the forms by subjecting them to a strain for which they were never intended, and to lose the greater part of the life by trying to put it in moulds which were never intended for it. There is now no longer the excuse which our Lord was so ready to make, at that time of transition, for those who were slow to recognise the superiority of the new—a point which is brought out in the pendant to this illustration which the Evangelist Luke records: "No man also having drunk old wine straightway desireth new: for he saith, The old is better;" or rather, according to the more correct reading, "the old is good." Thus, while the true principle was laid down for all time, excuse was made on behalf of John and his disciples, for clinging with a natural fondness to that which had done good service in the past. A very needful lesson this for too ardent reformers, not considerate enough of what is in many respects wholesome and praiseworthy conservatism.

It was in the midst of these important teachings that the message came from the chamber of death, to which we must now again direct our thoughts: "While He spake these things unto them, behold, there came a ruler, and worshipped Him, saying, My daughter is even now dead: but come and lay Thy hand upon her, and she shall live. And Jesus arose, and followed him, and so did His disciples." This promptness is a most precious revelation of the Divine readiness to help at any moment. No need of waiting for a convenient time. Any moment is convenient for Him, to Whom the affairs even of the infinite universe are no burden.

The same lesson is still more strikingly taught by His manner of dealing with the case which met Him on the way to the ruler's house. So hastily had He set out, in response to the ruler's appeal, that one would have thought this of all times the most inconvenient—especially for a chronic invalid—to gain a hearing. Here is a woman who has had a disease for twelve years, and who therefore might surely be asked to wait a few hours at least, till the Physician should be at leisure! And the case is not at all forced on His attention; she does not stand in front of Him, so that He cannot pass without noticing her,—she only "came behind Him"; nor does she take any means that seem likely to arrest His attention,—she only "touched the hem of His garment." But it is enough. Slight as the indication is that some one needs His help, He at once observes it; nor does He exhibit the least sign of impatience or of haste; He turns round, and speaks in the kindest manner, assuring her, as it were, of her right to enjoy the great blessing of health, which had just come to her, for as soon as she had touched Him He had cured her of her long and weary ailment. What encouragement to the most timid soul! And what a revelation of the large sympathy and ever-ready helpfulness of our Saviour Christ, and of our heavenly Father Whom He so gloriously reveals!

The scene is now changed to the chamber of death. There are most interesting details given in the fuller account by the Evangelist Mark, but our scope is large enough here without endeavouring to bring them all in. The maid had been at the point of death when the father left the house; now it is all over, and the room is full of noisy mourners. These clamorous demonstrations were evidently very painful to the sensitive heart of Christ, not only, perhaps, on account of their unreality, but also because of their inappropriateness in view of the better hope which He was bringing into light. For we take it that in these words "Give place: for the maid is not dead, but sleepeth," there was not only a reference to His intention at once to bring the dead one back to life, but to the true nature of death in His kingdom. In it death was to be death no longer—only a sleep, with the prospect of a speedy and blessed awaking. Therefore such heathenish lamentations were to be henceforward out of place. Perhaps, too, He wished to set these people thinking on the great subject of death—what it is, what it means, and whether after all it need be death in the sense in which alone the noisy mourners thought of it. But "they laughed Him to scorn," so they must be "put forth." The Lord of life cannot reveal Himself to such as these. Only the faithful disciples, and the parents whose hearts have been prepared for such a revelation by the discipline of genuine grief, are permitted to be present. It is probable that both parents had their hearts fully opened to the Lord; for though the mother had waited by the daughter's bedside, she had no doubt gone with her husband in spirit on his hopeful errand; and the father's faith must have been greatly confirmed by what had happened on the way back—there was nothing lost by that delay, even though in the meantime the message had come from the house that it was too late. It was not too late: it was well that the damsel had died; for now the Saviour has the opportunity to show that He is no less Master of the last great enemy than of all the other enemies of man. "He took her by the hand, and the maid arose."

Lost Faculties Restored (27-34).

The raising of the dead may be regarded as the culminating point of the series; yet there is a special value in the two that follow in close succession before the series is complete. We have seen already that, occurring, as they do immediately after, they show that His power is not at all exhausted—a token this of the exhaustlessness of the Divine love and helpfulness. But, besides this, are they not resurrections too—the raising again of faculties that had long been dead? Vision is a large part of our natural life; and to lose it is to descend, so far, into the darkness of death. And as the eye is to impression, so is the tongue to expression. The one is the crown of life on its receptive side, the other on its communicative side (*cf.* Psalm lvii. 8; cviii. 1, 2). The eye, then, may well represent life on the one side of it and the tongue on the other; while the two together represent it as completely as it is possible to do. Thus these two cases really come nearer to the idea of spiritual resurrection than even the raising of the dead damsel. In the case of the daughter of Jairus there was no part left alive to make its appeal to the Lifegiver on behalf of the rest; but with the others it was different: the blind men, for example, were able to cry for mercy (ver. 27); and it was possible for the Saviour to say to them, as He touched their eyes, "According to your faith be it unto you" (ver. 29), which He could not have said to the damsel.

Had the series ended with the raising of the daughter of Jairus, it had been made sufficiently apparent that Christ was able and willing to raise the dead; but it had still remained unrevealed by what means a man spiritually dead could secure for himself the resurrection of his lost spiritual powers. Now it is clear. The death of the spirit is parallel, not to the total death of the damsel, but to the partial death of the blind; for though the spirit of a man be dead, his mind remains alive, his heart too, his conscience even, and his body of course; there remains enough of him, so to speak, to imitate the example of these two blind men, to ask the Son of David for mercy, to follow Him till he finds it, to allow Him first to draw out the dormant faculty of faith, and then, having prepared him for the mighty boon, to pour celestial light upon his soul, bestowing on him a life so new and fresh and blessed, that it will seem to him as if it were, and it will in point of spiritual fact really be, life from the dead.

It seems more than likely that it was because He wished to subordinate the physical to the spiritual that He strictly charged them, saying, "See that no man know it." If the main thing had been the restoration of bodily sight, the more who heard of it the better. But His great purpose was far higher,—even to put an end to spiritual blindness and death; therefore He must limit His dealings with natural blindness to those who were prepared to receive the lower blessing without injuring them in their higher nature; and to make known such a case in the way of advertisement through the country-side would have been to descend from His lofty position as Saviour of men and Herald of the kingdom of heaven to that of oculist for the neighbourhood. But, though we can readily see why the Saviour should forbid the publication of the cure, it was natural enough that the men should disobey the order. They probably attributed His injunction to modesty, and thought they were showing a proper appreciation of what had been done for them by publishing it abroad. Blameworthy they certainly were; but not inexcusable.

The other case—the cure of the dumb demoniac—comes, if possible, still closer to the spiritual condition with which it was the work of the Saviour especially to deal. Like the former, it was the loss of a faculty; but, unlike it, it was not the natural loss of it, but the eclipsing of it by the malign presence of a spirit of evil. How closely parallel is this to the case of the spiritually dead. What is it that has destroyed the great faculty by which God is known and worshipped? Is it not sin? Let that demon be cast out, and not only will the eye see, but the tongue will speak; there will be a new song in the mouth, even praise to the Most High.

Furthermore, as the cure of the blind men brought into prominence the power of faith, this brings into prominence the power of Christ to save to the uttermost. For what more helpless case could there be? He could not cry, for he was dumb. He could not follow Christ as the blind men had done, for he had not control of himself; so he must be brought by others. Yet for him, as well as for them, there is full salvation, as soon as he comes into the presence of the Lord of life. No wonder the multitudes marvelled, and said, "It was never so seen in Israel"! and no wonder that the Pharisees, unable in any other way to evade the force of such a succession of manifest signs of the kingdom of heaven, should be driven to the contradictory and blasphemous suggestion, "He casteth out devils through the prince of the devils" (ver. 34).

The series is now complete; and, long as it has been, we could not dispense with a single case. There has been no repetition. Each case reported in detail has had its own special and peculiar value: the leper, the centurion's servant, the mother-in-law of Peter, the dealings with the impulsive scribe and the hesitating disciple, the stilling of the storm and mastery of the unseen legions of evil, the forgiving of sin, and welcoming of repentant sinners, the healing of the chronic invalid by the way, the raising of the dead damsel, and the restoring of sight to the blind and speech to the dumb,—all different, all most precious, all needed to bring out some aspect of the truth concerning Jesus as the Saviour of mankind, all together giving us a most comprehensive presentation of the signs of the kingdom of heaven. And now that the nature of His work has been so fully set forth in its two great departments of teaching and of healing, the rest is left unrecorded, except in the general statement that "Jesus went about all the cities and villages, teaching in their synagogues, and preaching the gospel of the kingdom, and healing every sickness and every disease among the people" (ver. 35).

CHAPTER IX.

THE KING'S AMBASSADORS.

MATTHEW ix. 36-x. 42.

I.—THE MISSION (ix. 36-x. 5).

So far the King Himself has done all the work of the kingdom. But it has grown upon Him, so that He can no longer do it without assistance; He must therefore provide Himself with deputies. His doing so will be the first step in the organisation of His world-wide kingdom. He reveals, however, no plan laid down to meet all possible emergencies. It is enough to provide for necessities as they develop themselves. He constructs no mechanism beforehand into the different parts of which life may be afterwards guided or forced; His only care is about the life, knowing well that if only this be full and strong, the appropriate organisation will be ready when it is needed.

In conformity with this principle He does not make His arrangements, necessary as they manifestly are, without first providing that they shall not be mechanical, but vital, that they shall originate, not as a contrivance of mind, but as an outflow of soul. First, we are informed by the Evangelist that the soul of the Master Himself was stirred with compassion as He looked upon the multitude, and thought how much they needed in the way of shepherding, and how little it was possible for them to have. It was no matter of planning for the extension of His kingdom; it was a great yearning over the sheep that were scattered, and torn (ver. 36, Gk. of oldest MSS.), and lost (x. 6). But it is not enough that the Master's heart should be touched: the disciples also must be moved. So He turns their thoughts in the same direction, urging them to observe how plenteous the harvest, how few the labourers; and therefore to pray that the lack may be speedily supplied. He sets them thinking and praying about it—the only way to lay foundations for that which shall be true and lasting. Let it be observed further, that the two emblems He uses present most strikingly the great motives to missionary work: compassion for the lost, and zeal for the Divine glory. "Sheep having no shepherd,"—this appeals to our human sympathies; the Lord of the harvest deprived of His harvest for want of labourers to gather it in,—this appeals to our love and loyalty to God.

The result of their thought and prayer presently appears; for we read in the next sentence of the setting apart of the twelve disciples to the work. It does not follow, because the narrative is continuous, that the events recorded were; it is probable that an interval elapsed which would be largely spent in prayer, according to the word of the Master.

This is the first mention of the Twelve in this Gospel; but it is evident that the number had been already made up, for they are spoken of as "His twelve disciples." It would appear from the second and third gospels that, immediately before the delivery of the Sermon on the Mount, the Twelve were chosen from the whole number of disciples to be constantly with Him, as witnesses of His works and learners of His doctrine. By this time they had been so far instructed and trained by their companionship with Christ, that they could be safely intrusted with a mission by themselves; accordingly, He for the first time gives them power to do deeds of mercy of the same sort as those which He Himself had been doing, as signs of the kingdom of heaven.

As the apostles have not been mentioned before, their names are appropriately given here. The number "twelve" was no doubt significant, as suggestive of the twelve tribes of Israel; but there was plainly no attempt to have the tribes represented separately. It would seem as if all were Galileans, except one, and that one was Judas Iscariot (*i. e.*, the man of Kerioth, supposed to be a town in Judea). The reason of this almost exclusive choice of Galileans is in all probability to be found in the simple fact that there were none other available. There had been those, in the course of His Judean ministry, who had after a certain fashion believed on Him; but there was not one of them whom He could trust with such work as this (John ii. 23-5). It may be thought, indeed, that surely there might have been some better representative—at least, than Judas proved himself to be—of the southern tribes; but why should we think so? We have no reason to suppose that Judas was a traitor at heart when he was chosen. Perhaps there was in him at that time the making of as grand an apostle as the best of them. It was not long, indeed, before the demon in him began to betray itself to the searching glance of the Master (John vi. 70) but had he only in the power of the Master he followed, cast that demon out of his own heart, as possibly enough he may have helped in this very mission to cast demons out of others, all would have been well. The subsequent fall of the traitor does not by any means show that Christ now made a mistaken choice; it only shows that the highest privileges and opportunities may, by the tolerance of sin in the heart, be not only all in vain, but may lead to a condemnation and ruin more terrible by far than would have been possible without them.

Not only was the apostolate Galilean,—it was plebeian, and that without a solitary exception. It seems to include not a single person of recognised rank or position. Again, we believe that this is to be accounted for by the simple fact that there were none of these available. We cannot suppose that if there had been a disciple like Paul in the ranks, the Master would have hesitated to give him a place in the sacred college; but, seeing there was none, He would not go out of His way to secure a representative of the learned or the great. Had Nicodemus been bold enough to come out decidedly on the Lord's side, or had Joseph of Arimathea developed earlier that splendid courage which he showed when the Master's work on earth was done, we can scarcely doubt that their names might have been included in the roll. But there is no such name; and now, as we look back, was it not better so? Otherwise there could not have been such a wonderful illustration of the great fact that "God hath chosen the weak things of the world to confound the things which are mighty"; there could not otherwise have been the same invincible evidence that the work these men did was not the work of men, but was indeed and in truth the doing of God.

Though they were all from the lower ranks of life, they were characterised by great varieties of gifts and dispositions. Some of them, indeed, are scarcely known to us at all. It may be that they were more or less ordinary men, who made no special mark; but it would be rash to set this down as certain, or even as probable, seeing that our records of the time are so scanty, and are manifestly constructed with the idea, not of giving to every man his due—as would be the poor ideal of a mere writer of history—but of making nothing of the men, and everything of the cause and of the Master in Whose great Personality theirs was merged. But those of them who do appear in the records are men of such varied dispositions and powers that the Twelve might after all have been a fair miniature of the Church at large. Some of the selections seem very strange. We have already referred to Judas the traitor. But there were those among them who must have been far less likely men than he. There were two in particular, the choice of whom seemed to violate all dictates of wisdom and prudence. These were Matthew the publican and Simon the Cananean or Zealot. To have a publican, hated as the whole class was, among the apostles, was apparently to invite the hostility and contempt of the great majority of the nation, and especially of those who were strongly national in feeling. On the other hand, to invite one who was known as a Zealot, a radical and revolutionist in politics, a man who had identified himself with the wildest schemes for the overthrow of the Government, was to provoke the opposition of all the law-abiding and peace-loving people of the time. Yet how could the heavenly King have more effectually shown that His kingdom was not of this world, that the petty party spirit of the day had no place in it whatever, that it mattered not what a man had been, if now he was renewed in the spirit of his mind, and consecrated in heart and soul and life to do the will of God and serve his Master Christ? *

So it has come to pass that, though these twelve men had nothing at all to recommend them to the favour of the world, and though there was very much from every worldly point of view to create the strongest prejudices against them and to militate against their influence, yet they have, by the grace of their Divine Master, so triumphed over all, that when we think of them now, it is not as fishermen, nor as publican or Zealot—even the traitor has simply dropped out of sight—we see before us only "the glorious company of the apostles"!

II.—The Commission (x. 5-42).

"These twelve Jesus sent forth" (in pairs, as we learn elsewhere, and as is indicated here, perhaps, by the grouping in the list), "and charged them." This leads us to look at their commission. It begins with a limitation, which, however, was only to be temporary. The time had not yet come for the opening of the door to the Gentiles. Besides this, we must remember that the Saviour's heart was yearning over His own people. This appears in the tender way He speaks of them as "the lost sheep of the house of Israel." Moreover, the apostles were by no means ready, with all their national prejudices still rank in them, to be intrusted with so delicate and difficult a duty as getting into communication with an alien race. Accordingly their field is strictly limited to their own countrymen.

There seems to have been a limitation also in their message. They had themselves been to some extent instructed in regard to the nature of the kingdom, its blessedness, its righteousness, its leading principles and features; but, though they may have begun to get some glimpse of the truth in regard to these great matters, they certainly had not yet made it their own; accordingly they are given, as the substance of their preaching, only the simple announcement, with which the Baptist had begun his ministry, and with which Christ also commenced His: "The kingdom of heaven is at hand." Though there seems to have been a limitation on the teaching side, there was none on the side of healing, for their Lord empowers them to do the very same things for the relief of their suffering fellow-countrymen as they had seen Himself doing. We have already seen how much teaching there was in these signs of the kingdom; and we can well believe that it was far better, considering the stage of advancement the apostles had reached, that reliance should be placed on the light such deeds of mercy would necessarily throw on the nature of the kingdom, than on any exposition which, apart from their Master, they could at that time have been able to give. Above all it is to be clear that the privileges of the kingdom are free to all; its blessings are to be dispensed without money and without price: "Freely ye have received, freely give."

How, then, were they to be supported? About this they were to give themselves no concern. They were now to put in practice the great command, "Seek ye first the kingdom of God, and His righteousness," relying on the promise, "all these things shall be added unto you." But in no miraculous way are they to look for the provision of their wants. They are to be maintained by those among whom and for whom they labour. This was to be no burden, but a privilege, reserved for those who were found "worthy" (ver. 11). Nor was it to be divided among as many as possible. They were to stay on with the same person who first received them, as the one whom the Master had chosen for the honour; while, if any refused to recognise it as a privilege, there was to be no weak solicitation, but a dignified withdrawal. The regulations throughout are manifestly intended to keep most vividly before their minds that they went not in their own names, nor in their own strength, nor at their own charges,—that they were ambassadors of a King, clothed with His authority, armed with His power, vested with His rights; so that there is a manifest appropriateness in the solemn words with which this part of the commission closes: "Verily I say unto you, It shall be more tolerable for the land of Sodom and Gomorrha in the day of judgment, than for that city" which rejects you (ver. 15).

The part of the charge which follows, and which the limitation of our plan will not allow us to illustrate point by point, bears not so much on the work more immediately before them as on the whole work of their apostolate. It may have been spoken, as some suppose, later on, and only put here as germane to the occasion; for, as we have seen, the arrangement of this gospel is not chronological, but is largely top-

* It is interesting to notice, that, though Matthew here calls himself Matthew the publican, no one else does. To others the publican is lost in the apostle—it is only himself who will not forget the hole of the pit whence he was digged.

ical. Still there seems no very strong reason for supposing that the entire discourse was not spoken at this very time; for why should not the apostles in the very beginning of their way have some idea of what it would cost them to accept the work to which they were now called?

The leading thoughts are these: They must expect to be exposed to trial and suffering in the prosecution of their mission. The Master Himself was sorely tried, and the servant must not expect exemption. He is not indeed to court trials, or to submit to persecutions which are not inevitable: "When they persecute you in this city, flee ye into another." On the other hand, when the path of duty lies evidently through trial or danger, he must not shirk it, but face it boldly; and in all emergencies he is to place implicit confidence in Him Whose servant he is: "When they deliver you up, be not anxious how or what ye shall speak: for it shall be given you in that hour what ye shall speak" (R. V.). "The very hairs of your head are all numbered. Fear ye not, therefore." There is no way of avoiding the cross; and they would be quite unworthy of their Master should they seek to avoid it. Yet there is a great reward for those who bravely take it up and patiently bear it to the end. It is the way to higher honour (ver. 32), and to the only life that is worthy of the name (ver. 39); while to turn away from it is to choose a path which leads to shame (ver. 33) and death (ver. 39).

The passage, taken up, as so much of it has been, with the anticipations of ill-treatment which the apostles will receive in setting out as sheep in the midst of wolves, closes most appropriately and beautifully with a series of blessings on those who will treat them well, ending with the encouraging assurance that even a cup of cold water given to a thirsty disciple will not be forgotten of God.

The lessons on Christian work with which this passage abounds are so numerous that it would be vain to attempt to unfold them. It is not merely a record of facts; it is an embodiment of great principles which are to govern the disciples of Christ in their service to the end of the world. If only the Church as a whole were to think and pray as Christ taught His disciples to think and pray before this great event; and then if the labourers whom God has sent, or would, in answer to the prayers of the Church, immediately send, into His harvest were to act—not necessarily according to the letter, but in every part according to the spirit of these instructions,—using their own faculties with all the wisdom of the serpent, and trusting to Divine grace and power with all the simplicity of the dove—it would not be long before all the scattered sheep were gathered into the fold, all the ripe sheaves garnered for the Lord of the harvest!

CHAPTER X.

THE SHADOW OF THE CROSS.

MATTHEW xi., xii.

I.—DISCOURAGEMENTS (xi).

HITHERTO almost everything has been hopeful and encouraging in our Evangelist's record of the Saviour's ministry. It began like daybreak on the shores of the sea of Galilee. Great multitudes followed Him wherever He went; and those whom He called to be with Him cheerfully responded to the summons. When He preached the Gospel of the kingdom, the people were astonished at His doctrine, and recognised that He "taught them as one having authority, and not as the scribes." His works of healing were warmly welcomed, and to a large extent appreciated by the people generally, though already it was apparent that those whose selfish interests were touched by the progress of the truth were ready to cavil and complain. Notwithstanding this, the work has grown upon Him so that He has found it necessary to arm His twelve disciples with powers like His own, and send them forth as heralds of His kingdom through the land.

But the path of the King is not to be a triumphal progress. It is to be a *via dolorosa,* leading to a cross and a grave. Many prophecies had been already fulfilled, as our Evangelist has shown again and again; but there are others of a different sort which can as little fail of their fulfilment,—like that which speaks of the Messiah as "despised and rejected of men, a man of sorrows, and acquainted with grief." It is not at all to be wondered at, then, that the Evangelist should now give his readers some idea of the discouragements which met the King in the setting up of His kingdom on the earth. The first of these which he mentions comes from a quarter from which least of all it might have been expected.

1. *John in doubt* (vv. 1-15).

It was, indeed, not at all unnatural that John should be in doubt. Think of his character: stern, uncompromising, severe, and bold to rashness. Think of his circumstances: languishing in prison for the truth's sake, without any prospect of rescue;—after all, was Jesus King, or Herod? Remember, too, in what terms he had predicted the coming One: "Now also the axe is laid unto the roots of the trees;" . . . "He that cometh after me is mightier than I;" . . . "Whose fan is in His hand, and He will throughly purge His floor, and gather His wheat into the garner; but He will burn up the chaff with unquenchable fire." Did not this betoken a work which would be swift, severe, thorough,—very different from anything of which he could hear in his prison cell? The coming of the kingdom was too gentle and too slow for the stern, impatient Baptist. Accordingly, "offended" (see ver. 6, R. V.: "finding occasion of stumbling") in his Master, he sends this message, in the hope possibly that it may constrain Him to avow Himself and to bring matters to a crisis: "Art thou He that should come, or do we look for another?"

Though it was natural enough that John should doubt, it was none the less trying to Jesus. The disciples were only children yet. Not one of them could enter into full sympathy with Him. John, the forerunner, was the one strong man, on whom He had reason thoroughly to rely, who had been tried again and again, and always found brave and true. Yet it is he who sends the doubting message. What a shock it must have been to the sensitive heart, what a trial to the faith, of the Man Christ Jesus!

The message must have been a very disturbing and disconcerting one, and fitted, if widely known, to neutralise to a large degree in the minds of the people the witness John had borne to Jesus. It is the last thing the Evangelist would have thought of mentioning, if he had been actuated in the selection of his material by motives of policy; and the fact that this incident is published in two of the Gospels is a striking illustration of what is manifest throughout—the perfect simplicity and candour of the sacred historians.

Have we not reason to be most thankful that they did record it? To the truly thoughtful mind it is no weakening of the testimony of John; while it is full of comfort for the honest doubter, giving him the assurance that even when the most serious questions trouble him—even though the very foundations of his faith seem to be shaken—"there hath no temptation taken" him "but such as is common to man," such as even a brave and true soul like John had to face; full of encouragement also to do just as he did,—go straight to the Master Himself with the doubts, and let Him deal with them—wisely, faithfully, tenderly—as He does here.

How, then, does He deal with them? By a miracle, opening the prison doors, and so making it perfectly plain to him that not Herod, but Jesus, is King? By a sudden outburst of vengeance, destroying hosts of unrepentant sinners and alarming all the country side, and so satisfying the sternest thoughts of the Baptist in his cell? Not at all. He deals with them as He intends to deal with doubters always: points him quietly to the many tokens of His Divine mission—not in the way of judgment wrought on sinners nor of any grand demonstration which will astonish the nation, but in the quiet progress of His helpful, healing, comforting work: "Go, and show John again those things which ye do hear and see: the blind receive their sight, and the lame walk, the lepers are cleansed, and the deaf hear, the dead are raised up, and the poor have the gospel preached to them." Then He encourages him to hold fast the beginning of his confidence firm unto the end, by adding the significant words, "Blessed is he, whosoever shall find none occasion of stumbling in Me" (R. V.). It was far better for John himself that he should be allowed to rally, than that anything special should be done to meet his doubts. He did rally; he did secure the blessing his Master set before him; he was satisfied without any open demonstration, satisfied to wait on and suffer in faith and patience, till at last he sealed the testimony of his magnificent life by a martyr's death.

Those are in some respects to be envied who in childlike simplicity believe without doubt or question; but there is a special blessing for those who by the very force of their nature must wrestle with doubt, yet in the trying hour find no occasion of stumbling in Him. They come out of the conflict more than conquerors through Him that loved them.

The answer sent to John was kind; but there was no flattery in it—not even a word of commendation of his heroic endurance. The Master knew the strength of His disciple, and He dealt with him accordingly. But as soon as the messengers are gone He tells the people what He thinks of him. He in effect deprecates the thought of judging John by a message sent in an hour of weakness and despondency. "Do not imagine for a moment," He seems to say, "that the man you went out into the wilderness to see is feeble as a reed, or soft as a courtier. He is all, and more than all, you took him to be. He is a prophet indeed; and much more, for He is a herald of the heavenly King. Among them that are born of woman there hath not risen a greater than John the Baptist; and though he has not the advantages of even the little ones in the kingdom of heaven, inasmuch as he belongs to the old dispensation, yet, as herald of the new, he occupies a peculiarly honoured place—he stands between the old and the new; for all the prophets and the law prophesied until John; while from the days of John the Baptist until now the kingdom of heaven is preached, and men are pressing into it. He is, in fact, if only you had ears to hear, if only your minds were open to read the Scriptures according to the spirit of them, that very Elijah whose coming your prophet has taught you to expect" (vv. 7-14).

So far we have followed what seems to be the drift of our Saviour's words in regard to John; but there is more than this in them. He is contrasting the feebleness and fickleness of the multitude with the strength and stability of John. There is before His mind, throughout, the thought of the transcendent importance of the events of the time as compared with the thoughtlessness of the people of the time. The question "What went ye out for to see?" was intended not merely to bring into relief the greatness of John, but to search their hearts. The important events of the time had circled first around John the Baptist, then around Himself. The people had not the least idea of the transcendent greatness of John and still less of the infinite greatness of Him to Whom he had borne witness. Jesus did not wish as yet fully to assert His own claims, yet He desired to bring the inconsiderate multitudes to some conception of the things which their eyes saw, to rebuke and, if possible, to correct their thoughtlessness and indifference.

It is to the presence of this underlying thought that some forms of expression are due which otherwise are difficult to understand. This applies in particular to ver. 12, which has been a terrible stumbling-block to expositors. So far as the position of John was concerned, it was enough to say that from his time the kingdom of God was preached (the form found in St. Luke); but in view of the levity and thoughtlessness of the multitudes it is put in such a way as to suggest that it is not your thoughtless, fickle, reed-hunting, sight-seeing people, that get the kingdom, but eager, earnest, "violent" men. The same thought accounts for the manner in which the paragraph closes, indicating that that which had been spoken ought to lead to more serious thought, more intelligent appreciation both of the herald and of the kingdom which in the spirit and power of the Great Elijah he has heralded: "He that hath ears to hear, let him hear."

But would they hear? Alas, no! and this accordingly must be put down as a second and most serious discouragement.

2. *The Unreasonableness of the People* (vv. 16-19).

Unable to recognise the true significance of the events of the time, with deaf ears to the heavenly message which first the herald and then the King had brought them, they fastened their attention on that which was merely incidental: the asceticism of John, the social friendliness of Jesus. Of the first they complained, because it was not like the second; of the second they complained, because it was not like the first. Any excuse for a complaint; no ear to hear nor soul to appreciate the message of either. To what can He liken them? To a set of children, sitting in the market-place indeed, but with no thought of business in their heads: they are there only to amuse themselves; and even in their games they are as unreasonable as they can be. One set proposes to play a wedding, and the rest say, "No, we want a funeral"; then, when the others take it up and start the game of funeral, they change their tune, and say, "No, we prefer a wedding." Nothing will please those who have no intention to be satisfied. Caring nothing for the kingdom which John heralded, the multitude only noticed the peculiarity of his garb, and the stern solitariness of his life, and said he must be a lunatic. When the King Himself comes with no such peculiarity, but mingling on familiar and friendly terms with the people, still caring nothing for the kingdom which He preached, they find fault with Him for the very qualities the absence of which they deprecated in John. If they had acted, not as foolish children, but as wise men, they would have recognised that both were right, inasmuch as each was true to himself and to the position he filled. It was right and fitting that the last of the old prophets should be rugged and stern and solitary, even as the great Elijah, in whose spirit and power he came. It was no less right and fit that the Saviour-King of men should set out on new lines and introduce the new dispensation in a manner suited to its distinctive features of freedom and familiar friendliness. Thus, in the one case, and in the other, "wisdom is justified of her children."

3. *The Unbelief of the Cities* (vv. 20-24).

Though the multitudes which had flocked to hear John might be fickle and thoughtless, surely better things might be expected of those favoured towns by the lake of Galilee, where the signs of the kingdom had been so abundantly exhibited and the truth of the kingdom so earnestly and frequently preached. But no: even they "repented not." They would bring their sick in crowds to get them healed; but they hid as it were their faces from Him. They had not indeed treated Him as the people of Nazareth had done; for Nazareth had cast Him out, and Capernaum had taken Him in. Yet His lamentation is not over Nazareth, but over Capernaum. We can readily see why. What He suffered at Nazareth was a personal indignity. He was so summarily ejected that He had not time or opportunity to set before them the signs of the kingdom. But in Capernaum the time and opportunity had been ample. The truth had been fully told; the signs had been fully wrought. The people had seemed to listen; and all betokened a happy issue. We can imagine the Saviour waiting and hoping and longing (for again, let it be remembered that He was very man, and that this experience discouraged Him as it would discourage any of us), and then tasting all the bitterness of hope deferred, ending in crushing disappointment.

For a long time He continues silent, bearing the heavy burden in His heart, till the fountain of grief could be pent up no longer: "Then began He to upbraid the cities wherein most of His mighty works were done, because they repented not." The words He speaks are very awful; but it is in the last resort. Love and mercy have been His theme from day to day; and it is only because these are obstinately rejected that wrath and judgment must now find a voice. It is not a wrathful voice: there are tears in it. What must it have cost Him to speak these awful words about Capernaum's impending doom! To think that those who were nearest His heart of all, to whom He devoted the freshness of His first days of service, the dew of His youth, so to speak—that they would have none of Him, but preferred to remain in sin with all the woe it necessarily entailed,—oh! it must have been torture to that loving heart. And we may be sure there was no less pathos in this last appeal to Bethsaida, Chorazin, and Capernaum, than there was in the later lamentation over the city of the South.

How does the Saviour bear Himself under these repeated discouragements? The passage which follows will show (vv. 25-30). Some have found a difficulty in the word "answered," because there appears no question with which it is connected. But did not these discouragements require an answer? As we read, first of the doubts of John, then of the thoughtlessness of the multitudes, and then of the impenitence of the favoured cities by the lake, is there not a question in our hearts, becoming more and more urgent as each new discouragement appears, What will He say to this? What can He answer? Thus our minds are well prepared for that which immediately follows: "At that time Jesus answered and said, I thank Thee, O Father." Is it to be a thanksgiving, then, after such a series of disappointments and vexations? Even so. As He has looked to the cities of the plain, His voice has been a wail; now that He looks up to His Father, wailing ceases, and thanksgiving takes its place. So will it always be to faith which is genuine and deep enough. It is only when we look below and around that we are depressed. When we look up we are strong. "I will lift up mine eyes unto the hills, from whence cometh my help. My help cometh from the Lord Who made heaven and earth." Was it the remembrance of this passage at the time of need which suggested the form of His thanksgiving: "I thank Thee, Father, Lord of heaven and earth"?

Surely we have here the living original of that grand apostolic word. "In everything give thanks"; for if "at that season" (R. V.) the Saviour of men found occasion for thanksgiving, we may well believe that at any season, however dark, we may find something to stir our hearts to gratitude; and the very exercise of thanksgiving will bring a deep spiritual joy to set against the bitterest sorrow, even as it was with our Lord, Who, as St. Luke informs us, "rejoiced in spirit" as He lifted up His soul in thanks to God that day.

What, then, does He find to be thankful for? First, He discovers a cause for gratitude in the very limitation which occasions His sorest disappointments: "I thank Thee, . . . because Thou hast hid these things from the wise and prudent, and hast revealed them unto babes." There is of course the cheering thought that amid the general unbelief and rejection there are some childlike souls who have welcomed the truth. Some are fain to make this the sole cause of thankfulness, as if He meant to say, "I thank Thee, that *though* Thou hast hid these things from the wise and prudent, Thou hast revealed them unto babes." But there is no authority for introducing this little word. The Saviour gives thanks, not merely in spite of this hiding, but because of it. It is true, indeed, that He uses the language of resignation, "Even so, Father: for so it seemed good in Thy sight," which makes it evident that the fact that so many of the wise and intelligent rejected His gospel presented a real difficulty to His mind, as it has done to earnest souls in all ages. But while it was no doubt enough for Him to feel sure that it was right in the sight of God, we are not without indication in what follows, that His faith not only led to resignation, but enabled Him to see for Himself that it was wisely ordered. For what is the great object of the Gospel? Is it not to dethrone itself and enthrone God in the hearts of men? It is clear, then, that, if it had in any way appealed to pride and self-sufficiency, it would have defeated its own end. Suppose the revealing of things had been to the wise and prudent as such, what would have been the result? The kingdom of heaven would have become a mere scholarship prize. And however good a thing scholarship may be, and however important that it be encouraged, this is not the work of the Christ of God. His Gospel is for all; so it is addressed not to the great in intellect, which would confine it to the few, but to the lowly in heart, which brings it within reach of all,—for the very wisest and greatest in intellect may be, and ought to be, meek and lowly in heart.

Indeed, is it not to the meek and lowly heart that even the truths of science are disclosed? A man who approaches nature with a preconceived theory, about which his mind is already made up, is sure to miss the mark. To enter into its secrets, prejudices and prepossessions must be laid aside, and things observed with open mind and simple receptiveness. In this conection one sees the special appropriateness of the reference to "the Lord of heaven and earth." The principle is one which is not restricted in its range: it runs all through nature. Still more appropriate is the appeal to the fatherhood of God. It is not for the Father to be partial to his clever children, and leave the less favoured ones to shift for themselves. To Him they are all "babes"; and to them He must be not examiner, nor prize-giver, but above all *Father*, if they would understand and feel His love. So the more one thinks of it, the more in every point of view does it seem good and necessary that these things should not be made known to the "wise and understanding" (R. V.) as such, but should be revealed to "babes," and to those of childlike spirit. It is well. The wisest and most learned may join in the thanksgiving, for it is far better for them to take their places with the rest, as many happily do, and receive the same loving welcome; and those of us who cannot call ourselves wise and learned should surely be most devoutly thankful that, however impossible it may be to compete with these highly favoured ones in obtaining the prizes of earth, we are at no disadvantage in striving for "the prize of the high calling of God in Christ Jesus."

The next great thought which comes to the relief of the Saviour in His discouragement is that, while there are barriers in the heart of man, there is no barrier in the heart of God, no limit whatever to the outpouring of Divine love and grace: "All things are delivered unto Me of My Father." Even at the time when it is borne in upon Him that men will have none of Him, He exults in the thought that He has everything for them. If only they could see it! If only they knew the boundless treasure there was for them in God! If only they knew that God had put all within their reach by sending them His Son! But the Son is unknown except to the Father, who sent Him; and the Father is unknown except to the Son, Who has come to reveal Him. But He *has* come to reveal Him: and with the revealing the way will be opened for all good things to follow. As He thinks of it His heart yearns over the orphaned children of men, and He exults in the thought that He has for them the revelation of the Father's heart and home, with enough and to spare for all His children (ver. 27).

Then follows such an outpouring of heart as there never has been before. He knows that only in the Father can the children of men find rest, and so He says "Come unto Me," and I will lead you to the Father, Who alone knows Me, as I alone know Him; and you, finding Him in Me, shall know Him too, and your hearts shall be at rest.

It is beautiful and most touching to observe how our Lord is, as it were, compelled to make His appeal more personal than He has ever done before. We look in vain through His previous utterances as reported in this Gospel for such reduplication of the personal pronouns as there is here. What is the reason of it? We can see it when we read between the lines. Hitherto His great subject has been the kingdom of heaven. This kingdom He has been preaching through all the country-side, setting forth its purity and blessedness, unfolding its unspeakable riches, and entreating all to enter in by the strait gate, which He has thrown open to receive them. But they will not enter. These things, in spite of all He can say, are hid from them. Well He knows what is the difficulty: it is the hardness of their hearts. If He could only get at these hearts! How can He do it? It can only be by the opening out of all His heart to them; so He will make His pleading a personal entreaty now. Hence the peculiarly winning form His invitation now assumes. It is no longer "Enter ye in at the strait gate"; it is not even, "I have come to call sinners to repentance"; it is the cry of a loving, yearning heart, "Come unto Me." And how tenderly He thinks of them!—no more upbraiding now, no more reproof. He will try to reach the conscience through the heart, and so He does not even think of them as sinners now—He forgets everything but their weariness and woe: "Come unto Me, all ye that labour and are heavy laden, and I will rest you." *

We shall not, however, dwell on the precious words with which this chapter ends. They are as rich and suggestive as they are simple and heart-thrilling; but for this very reason we must not attempt to do more than place them in their setting, which is often missed, for the words

* This is the literal translation, which means more than "give you rest." It is not as if rest were a blessing He could bestow, as a friend would make a present which might be retained after the giver had gone. Rest is not so much what He gives to us as what He is to us; and so He says, not "I will give you rest," but "I will rest you" (*i. e.*, I will *be* your rest).

themselves have attracted so much attention, and so filled the minds and hearts of those who have looked at them that too little has been made of their surroundings. Observe only how nobly the Son of Man comes out of this ordeal of disappointment and discouragement. See the grandeur of His faith. "At that season," when we should expect to see Him in the depths, He rises to the very height of His dignity and majesty. This passage above all others has been cited as an example of the self-assertion of Jesus—say rather His sublime consciousness of Divine dignity, prerogative, and power; yet so entirely natural and unassuming is it all, that in the very same breath He can say, without conveying to the most thoughtful mind the least feeling of incongruity: "I am meek and lowly in heart." Then behold what manner of love! These chilling blasts of doubt, indifference, and unbelief only fan it into a warmer, steadier flame. The sweetest of all His invitations, the most touching of all His appeals, comes from a heart which has just been wounded in its tenderest place, and has tasted the bitterness of cruel disappointment. Who can measure the patient love which "at that season" finds such utterance?

II.—The Contradiction of Sinners (xii.).

The darkness deepens on the Saviour's path. He has now to encounter direct antagonism. There have been, indeed, signs of opposition before. When the man sick of the palsy was forgiven, "certain of the scribes said within themselves, This man blasphemeth" (ix. 3); but it was only "within themselves," they did not venture to speak out. Again, after the feast in the house of Levi, the Pharisees complained, but not to Christ Himself; "they said unto His disciples, Why eateth your Master with publicans and sinners?" (ix. 11). And when the dumb demoniac was cured, the Pharisees muttered, "He casteth out devils through the prince of the devils" (ix. 34), but did not yet say it to His face. But now they are emboldened to attack Him directly. Possibly they saw as clearly as any the discouraging aspect of affairs for the new kingdom. They had, in all probability, heard of the doubts of John, had taken note of the fault-findings of the people (if, indeed, these had not been first suggested by themselves), had observed that even "the cities where most of His mighty works were done repented not" (xi. 20); and having therefore less occasion to fear consequences, they might think it safe to attack one who stood for a rapidly failing cause.

1. Observe, first, the spirit in which our Lord meets the repeated attacks of which the record is given in this chapter. There are four in close succession. The first is the charge of Sabbath-breaking made against the disciples, because they rubbed a few ears of corn in their hands as they passed through the fields on the Sabbath day; and following it, the entangling question put to the Master in the synagogue. Then there is the accusation founded on the healing of the blind and dumb demoniac: "This man doth not cast out devils, but by Beelzebub the prince of the devils" (ver. 24). The third attack is the hypocritical application, "Master, we would see a sign from Thee" (ver. 38), the word "Master" being evidently used in mockery, and the request for "a sign" a scornful way of suggesting that all the signs He was giving were worth nothing. These three attacks were made by the Pharisees, and were most irritating and vexatious, each in its own way. The first was annoying on account of its pettiness, the second because of its bitter malice, while the third was a studied insult; and yet, galling as these repeated attacks must have been, we may well suppose that the keenest wound of all to the gentle spirit of the Son of man would be the last, inflicted by the members of His own family, who seemed at this time as unsympathetic and unbelieving as the Pharisees themselves; for the untimely interruption recorded at the close of the chapter was intended, as we learn from the account in the second gospel, to put Him under restraint as a madman. This last interruption, in which even His mother joined, must have been gall and wormword to that tender heart.

Now "consider Him that endured such contradiction of sinners against Himself" (Heb. xii. 3). How does He bear Himself through these storms of calumny and insult? He bears Himself so that out of this dark chapter of His history there comes to us one of the loveliest portraits of Him to be found anywhere. It had been sketched by one of the old masters as an ideal portrait, and is now at last matched in real life: "Behold My Servant, Whom I have chosen; My Beloved, in Whom My soul is well pleased: I will put My spirit upon Him, and He shall show judgment to the Gentiles. He shall not strive, nor cry; neither shall any man hear His voice in the streets. A bruised reed shall He not break, and smoking flax shall He not quench, till He send forth judgment unto victory. And in His name shall the Gentiles trust" (vv. 18-21). What gentleness and tenderness, yet what strength and majesty!—for, though "He strives not," nor lifts up His voice in angry altercation, while He will not break the bruised reed, nor quench the smoking flax, He will nevertheless declare judgment, and secure victory, and make His name such a power in the earth, that the Gentiles shall hope in Him and the world go after Him. We can fancy the glow on the Evangelist's face as he pauses in the midst of the sad record of these cruel assaults, to look at, and show to us, that lovely portrait of the Son of man. And is it not all the lovelier that it shines out from such a background? Does it not give new significance to the tender words which linger in our ears from the chapter of discouragement before: "Learn of Me; for I am meek and lowly in heart: and ye shall find rest unto your souls"?

2. It would have been a great thing if our Lord had only borne in dignified silence these repeated provocations; but He is too good and kind to leave these misguided people to their own devices without an effort to enlighten their dark minds and arouse their sleeping consciences. How patiently He reasons with them! We may glance at each attack in succession as an illustration of this.

On the charge of Sabbath-breaking He endeavours to set them right by citing appropriate scriptures (vv. 3, 4); appealing to the law itself (ver. 5); furnishing them with a great principle laid down by one of the prophets, the key of the whole position (ver. 7); and concludes by an illustrative act, accompanied by a simple and telling argument, which appeals to the universal conscience and heart (vv. 9-13). Again, how patiently He answers the malicious charge of collusion with Satan, showing them in the clearest manner, and with amazing power, how far they are astray, and what a dangerous path they are treading (vv. 25-37). So, too, in meeting the third attack: though He cannot but sternly rebuke the hypocritical application for "a sign," He yet does it in such a way as to prepare for them in due time, when perhaps they may be ready to appreciate it, a new sign—His death and resurrection—overcoming the difficulty arising from the fact that He could not yet speak of it in plain terms (for it was at a later period than this that He began to speak plainly of it even to His disciples) by veiling it under the figure of "the sign of the prophet Jonas": a way of putting it which had the advantage of being memorable, and at the same time enigmatical enough to veil its meaning till the event should lighten it all up, and bring out its deep suggestiveness; and while thus preparing them for the new sign when it should come, He warns them against that evil state of mind and heart which threatened to render even it of no avail (vv. 38-45). And then, with what marvellous readiness does He use the painful interruption with which the chapter ends for the teaching of truth of the highest and purest and tenderest quality! What patience, what long-suffering, what meekness of wisdom, what faithfulness, what strength and tenderness! Every line of the likeness drawn by the inspired hand of the old master is more than justified (vv. 46-50).

3. Observe, further, that in all His dealings with His bitterest foes He never in the least degree lowers His dignity, but rather asserts it in the boldest and strongest terms. It may be questioned, indeed, if there is any chapter in all the history in which this is more marked. This, again, may be illustrated from all the four occasions.

In the argument on the Sabbath question hear Him as He draws Himself up, in presence of His accusers, and says: "In this place is One greater than the temple" (ver. 6); and again: "The Son of man is Lord even of the Sabbath day" (ver. 8). Must there not have been something heavenly-majestic in His look and bearing when words like these were allowed to pass unchallenged by such men? This consciousness of dignity appears no less in the argument by which the second charge is met. In proof of this we may point to verses 28 and 30; and the same impression is produced by the solemnly repeated "I say unto you" (vv. 31, 36), in each case introducing one of those declarations of judgment to which reference is made in the passage quoted from the prophet (vv. 18-20). Quite as conspicuous is the same feature in the third remonstrance, in which He asserts His superiority to the great ones of the old covenant in language which acquires, from the connection in which it occurs, a strength far beyond the mere terms employed: "Behold, a greater than Jonas, . . . behold, a greater than Solomon, is here" (vv. 41, 42). And in the last of the four sad encounters the same lofty consciousness of peerless dignity is manifest. Son of Mary is He? brother of James and Joses? See Him lift His eyes to heaven, and speak of "*My* Father," and look down the ages, and out to the uttermost bounds of earth, and say, "Whosoever shall do the will of My Father which is in heaven, the same is My brother, and sister, and mother" (ver. 50).

4. We have seen how kindly and patiently the Saviour deals with these cavillers, so as to give them every opportunity of seeing their folly and wickedness, and the beauty and excellence of the truth they are resisting. But He does much more than this. He speaks not only so as to meet their objections, and give them the opportunity of being set right, but so as to provide instruction, warning, and encouragement for all succeeding ages. To show in any satisfactory way how this is done would require separate treatment for each of the four instances; but it may be possible in a very brief way to suggest it.

The first attack gave Him the opportunity of speaking on the Sabbath law. As we have seen, He began to treat the subject from the strictly Jewish standpoint, using the example of David and the ritual of the Temple to correct the misapprehensions and misrepresentations of those with whom in the first instance He had to do. But He does not leave it as a mere Jewish question; He broadens His view, and shows that the day of rest is for humanity at large—not, however, as a burden, but as a blessing, the principle which underlies it being "mercy, and not sacrifice." Thus, out of this conflict there has come to us the Magna Charta of the people's Sabbath, the full text of which is given in the corresponding passage of the second gospel: "The Sabbath was made for man, and not man for the Sabbath: therefore the Son of man is Lord also of the Sabbath." Here we have, on the one hand, the vindication of our rights against those who would deprive us of the day of rest, as if the privilege had been intended only for the Jews, and was abolished when the dispensation closed; and, on the other, the assertion of our liberty against those who, by their petty regulations and restrictions, would make God's precious gift a burden instead of a blessing. And how wisely and beautifully does He confirm to us our privileges by following the charter with an argument which, though coming still under the head of the great principle ("Mercy, and not sacrifice"), is no mere repetition, but illustrates the wider aspect just unfolded, by its freedom from Jewish colour, and its appeal to the conscience and heart of mankind at large: "What man shall there be among you, that shall have one sheep, and if it fall into a pit on the Sabbath day, will he not lay hold on it, and lift it out? How much, then, is a man better than a sheep?" (vv. 11, 12).

The second attack gave Him the opportunity of bringing out with great distinctness and vividness the witness of the Spirit of God to His work as Saviour of mankind. These Pharisees regarded His miracles as mere displays of power, apart altogether from the spirit of purity, mercy, and grace so manifest in them all. It was only this narrowness of view that made it possible for them to imagine that the Spirit of evil, to whom of course no one could deny a certain measure of mere power, was behind them. How completely He answers their blasphemous suggestion by showing that the works He did, judged, not by the mere power they displayed, but by their whole spirit and tendency, were at the very opposite pole from the works of

Satan, we plainly see; but the point now is the permanent value of His reasoning. At first sight it may seem to be quite out of date. Whoever dreams now of disposing of the works of Christ by attributing them to Satan? Let us not be over-hasty, however, in concluding that old objections are out of date. If we look closely at those regarded as the newest, we may find that they are but old ones in a new dress. What of the position taken by some intelligent men in our day, who candidly admit the power of Christianity to elevate and sanctify men, and yet set it down as false?

As an illustration of this, we cannot do better than refer to a recent production* of the Agnostic School, in which there is the most emphatic testimony to the blessed power of Christianity in particular instances, followed by these most candid and generous words: "What needs admitting, or rather proclaiming, by agnostics who would be just, is that the Christian doctrine has the power of elevating and developing saintliness, which has had no equal in any other creed or philosophy." Yet the book in which that sentence occurs assumes throughout that this doctrine, which has had no equal in producing saintliness—a quality which in another place is described as "so lofty, so pure, so attractive, that it ravishes men's souls"—is untrue! Is, then, the argument of our Lord out of date? and is it too late to ask the old question, "Can Satan cast out Satan?"

It does not always follow, of course, that that which is good in its effects in particular cases, is thereby proved to be true. Truth and falsehood are to be determined fundamentally on other grounds than those of proved utility—this applies alike to truth and duty; there is an absolute truth and falsehood quite irrespective of utility, and there is an absolute right and wrong quite irrespective of utility,—but though we cannot in particular cases prove that to be true which appears to be beneficial, yet we cannot but believe that in the end, the true, the good, and the beautiful will be found to coincide; and we maintain that, seeing the effects of genuine Christianity on human character have been tested for nearly two thousand years, and have been found to "make for righteousness," nobility, purity, all that is good and gracious, high and holy, it is too late in the day to set it down to the father of lies. We may be mistaken in our passing judgments, may be misled into accepting as eternally true and right some measure or doctrine which has not yet had time to develop its real nature and character, which may produce good results at first, and then by degrees develop other results of quite a contrary kind—take the history of Monasticism as a case in point; but when there have been ample time and opportunity for testing the fruits of a system, as there has been in the case of Christianity; when we observe that the gospel of Christ has had these wonderful effects through eighteen successive centuries among all ranks and classes, nations and races of men—it ought surely to require something stronger than Agnosticism (which at the worst can only say, "I do not know") to make us believe the outrageously improbable supposition that it is false, and therefore presumably of the kingdom of lies and of unclean things. There have been too many devils cast out of human hearts to make it at all doubtful that in very deed "the kingdom of God has come" among us (ver. 28). There has been too much spoiling of "the strong man's goods" to make it at all doubtful that "a stronger than he" has mastered him and is spoiling his house. "The Son of God was manifested, that He might destroy the works of the devil" (1 John iii. 8); and wherever He has been admitted into human hearts He has done it, setting up His kingdom of "righteousness and peace and joy in the Holy Ghost." The argument is as fresh to-day as the day it was propounded; and it has now all the added strength of centuries of confirmation.

* "The Service of Man," by J. Cotter Morison.

The third attack gave our Lord the opportunity of laying bare the root of unbelief, and setting forth the important truth that, when the heart is estranged from God, mere signs are unavailing. The signs He had given in abundance should have been enough, especially when the only way of evading their force the ingenuity of scepticism could devise had been closed by the powerful argument just delivered. Besides this there was the crowning sign of the resurrection still to come; yet He knew that even that would fail to satisfy—not for reasons intellectual, but because of the spirit of the age, as He points out in that striking and powerful parable (vv. 43-45), and hints in the suggestive term, "an evil and adulterous generation" (ver. 39), the word "adulterous" referring to the well-known, and at that time thoroughly understood, language of the Old Testament, according to which estrangement of heart from God is branded as spiritual adultery. (See Jeremiah iii., Hosea i., ii., and many other passages.)

Herein we see a sufficient explanation of the widespread unbelief of the age in which we live. It is because the heart of this generation is so far estranged from God, so wedded to the earthly and material, so taken up with selfish aggrandisement and the multiplication of the luxuries of life. In many cases of unbelief the individual is not so much to blame as the spirit of the age of which he is the representative. Observe that the Lord does not say, "Ye evil Pharisees," but, "An evil and adulterous generation"; thus making it evident that the spirit of scepticism was not peculiar to themselves, but a something diffused throughout society. Hence it comes that many men, of blameless lives—of whom it would be a breach of charity to say that they loved darkness rather than light, because their deeds were evil—nevertheless declare themselves unsatisfied with the signs of the divine mission of Christ our Lord. Why is this? It is because they are infected with the spirit of the age, engrossed with the material, the sensible, the secular; while their hearts, "swept and garnished" though they be, are "empty" of God: "The god of this world hath blinded the minds of the unbelieving, that the light of the gospel of the glory of Christ, Who is the image of God, should not dawn upon them" (2 Cor. iv. 4, R. V.).

Such persons not only cannot recognise the signs of the kingdom of heaven, but are in a state of heart and mind to which no sign can possibly be given. We are indebted to the fine candour of the late Mr. Darwin for a striking illustration of this. In his Life there is an interesting correspondence with Professor Asa Gray, the great botanist, who, wondering how Darwin could remain unconvinced by the innumerable evidences of design in nature, took the liberty of asking him if he could think of any possible proof which he would consider sufficient. To this Mr. Darwin replied: "Your question, 'What would convince me?' is a poser. If I saw an angel come down to teach us so, and I was convinced, from others seeing him, that I was not mad, I should believe." If he had left it there, it might have been pertinent to ask him whether Christ is not just such an angel come down from heaven to teach us, and whether a sufficient number of persons did not see Him in the flesh, to say nothing of the multitudes who know Him in the spirit, to convince us that we are not mad in believing it. He did not, however, leave it there, but went on to say: "If man was made of brass and iron, and in no way connected with any other organism which had ever lived, I should perhaps be convinced." Nothing could be more candid, or more in keeping with the transparent honesty of this great man. But what an acknowledgment! Man must cease to be man, and become a metal machine, and the universe must cease to be a harmonious whole, before there can be evidence enough for so simple and elementary a principle as design in the universe; and then only a "perhaps"! If all this were done for me, "I should *perhaps* be convinced." Is our Lord's answer to the seekers after a sign out of date? "Verily I say unto you, There shall no sign be given unto this generation" (Mark viii. 12). How could there be?

What will He make of the distressing interruption caused by the interference of His mother and brethren? Knowing their motives and intentions as He did, He could not for a moment yield; and how was it possible to deal with them without a public rebuke, from which, seeing that His mother was involved in it, His heart would instinctively shrink? It was a most painful position; and the more we think of it, and try to imagine possible ways of extrication, the more we must admire the wisdom and kindness shown in the way in which He confronted the difficulty. He makes use of the opportunity for giving a new and most winning view of the kingdom of heaven as a happy family, united each to Himself, and all to the Father by the holiest bonds; thus opening out the paradise of a perfect home to all who choose to enter it, taking the sacred ties involved in the sweet words "brother" and "sister" and "mother," and giving them a range, a dignity, and a permanence they never had before.

In all this there was no word of direct censure; yet the sadly mistaken conduct of His kindred did not pass without implied rebuke; for the effect of His words was to make it clear that, sacred as were, in His eyes, the ties of earth, their only hope of permanence was in alliance with the higher ties of heaven. He has come in the loving Father's name to gather in His wandering children; and if His mother and brethren according to the flesh attempt to hinder Him, He cannot listen to them for a moment, but must steel His heart against their blind appeals, and that, not only for His works' sake, but for theirs also. They are slow to believe; but the least likely way to bring them to faith would be to yield to their unbelief. He will prosecute the path of duty, though it involve the sacrifice of all that cheers and comforts His heart; He must set His face as a flint to finish the work His Father has given Him to do, and they will understand Him by-and-by. There is no doubt they would go home with sore hearts that day; but no very long time would elapse till they would all be most grateful that their foolish, however well-meant, interference had failed of its intent.

The course of events in later times has proved that the gentle rebuke involved in our Lord's reception of the message from His mother was not only necessary at the time and for her, but for the ages to come as well. We have seen that, in each of the attacks recorded before, our Saviour replies in such a way that His words not only meet the objection of the moment, but continue of permanent value to meet similar objections and gainsayings in ages to come. So is it here. It certainly is no fault of Mary herself, whose name should ever be held in the highest respect by all who love the Lord, that a corrupt Church, reversing all the teaching of the Church's Head, not only elevated the earthly relationship far above the spiritual, but in virtue of this relationship put the mother in the place of the Son, and taught an ignorant people to worship her and trust in her as a mediator. But the fact that this was done, and is persisted in to this day, shows that when our Lord set aside the mere earthly relationship as one that must be merged in the spiritual, He was correcting not only a pardonable error of Mary, but a most unpardonable error that afterwards, without any encouragement whatever from her, should be committed in her name.

After all, however, it is not the setting aside of the claims of Mary and the lowering of the earthly relationship in comparison with the heavenly, which is the great thing in the passage; but the Gospel of the Family of God. We have had the Gospel of the Kingdom of God, and glad tidings it has been indeed; but have we not here something even better? It is much to be permitted to hail the Son of God as our King; is it not better still to be encouraged to hail Him as a Brother, to know that all that is sweetest and tenderest in the dear words "brother," "sister," "mother," can be imported into our relation to Him? How it endears the heavenly relationship, and hallows the earthly!

Again, how it rebukes all sectarianism! He "stretches out His hand towards His disciples," and then to all the world by that word "*whosoever.*" And it is not the mere promise of salvation with which this "whosoever" is connected. There are Christians in the present day who can scarcely allow themselves to be sectarian enough to deny that there is salvation out of the Church to which they happen to belong: they are good enough to think that these people who do not follow with them may somehow or other be saved; but the idea of fraternising with them! that is quite another thing. Now listen to the Saviour Himself: "Whosoever shall do the will of My Father which is in heaven" (no question of what Church he belongs to, or anything of that sort), "the same is My brother, and sister, and mother." No arm's-length recognition there; He takes all true disciples to His heart.

Observe, moreover, the emphasis on *doing*, with which we are already familiar. In setting forth the Gospel of the Kingdom, our Lord was careful to warn His hearers: "Not every one that saith unto Me, Lord, Lord, shall enter into the kingdom of heaven; but he that doeth the will of My Father" (vii. 21); and now that He is setting forth the Gospel of the Family the emphasis is still in the same place. It is not "Whosoever shall connect himself with this church or that church;" it is not "Whosoever shall be baptised, and take the sacrament;" it is "Whosoever shall do the will of My Father in heaven." This emphasis on doing, in connection with these endearing relations, is most significant. There must be love among the members of the family; and what else than love is the characteristic of the family ties? But how is love to be shown? How are we to distinguish it from mere sentiment? Our Saviour is careful to teach us; and never is He more careful than in those passages where tender feeling is most prominent—as, for example, in His parting words in the upper room, where again and again He reminds His disciples that obedience is the only sure test of love: "If ye love Me, keep My commandments;" "He that hath My commandments, and keepeth them, he it is that loveth Me" (John xiv. 15, 21). For the same reason obedience is here set forth as the only certain mark of the true disciple: "Whosoever shall do the will of My Father which is in heaven, the same is My brother, and sister, and mother."

CHAPTER XI.

THE PARABLES OF THE KINGDOM.

MATTHEW xiii.

"THE same day went Jesus out of the house, and sat by the sea side." We can well imagine that, after such a series of discouragements and mortifications, the weary and heavy-laden Saviour would long to be alone, to get away from the abodes of men, to some lonely place where silent nature around Him would calm His spirit and furnish a temple in which He might lift up His soul to God. How long He was allowed to be alone we cannot tell; but possibly He may have contrived for a time to remain unobserved. How burdened His spirit must have been! What strength of faith it must have needed to look forward with any hope to the future of His work at such a time of crushing disappointment! We must remember that He was true man, and therefore His heart must have been very sore as He dwelt on the painful experiences through which He had just been passing. The obstacles which lay right in His path must have seemed well-nigh insuperable; and it would have been no wonder if at such a time He had despaired of the prospects of the kingdom of righteousness and peace and joy He had come to set up on the earth. He did not despair; but He did most deeply ponder; and the result of His thinking appears in the series of parables recorded in this chapter, which set forth, on the one hand, the nature of the obstacles the kingdom must meet, and the reason why it must meet them, and on the other, its certain prospect, notwithstanding these, of growth and development onward to its final consummation.

If He was permitted to enjoy His seclusion, it was only for a short time. "He could not be hid," His quiet retreat was discovered; and presently there came to Him great multitudes, so many that the only convenient way to address them all was to get into a boat, and speak to the people gathered on the shore. It is a lovely picture: the multitudes on the shore with the green fields around and the hills behind, and the Master speaking from the little boat. Viewed apart from the sorrowful experience of the past, it would have been full of cheer and hope. What more encouraging sight than such a throng gathered to hear the words of light and hope He had for them? But how can He view it apart from the sorrowful experience of the past? Have not these crowds been around Him day after day, week after week; and what has come of it all?

It is one thing to sow the seed of the kingdom; it is quite another to gather the harvest. The result depends on the soil. Some of it may be hard, so that the seed cannot enter; some of it, though receptive on the surface, yet so rocky underneath, that the fairest shoots will wither in a day; some of it so filled with seeds of thorns and weeds that plants of grace are choked as they attempt to grow; while only a portion, and it may be a small proportion of the whole, can yield a fair or full return. Such were His thoughts as He looked on the field of men before Him, and glanced from it to the fields of the plain of Gennesaret around, in the foreground of which as in a picture the multitudes were set. As He thought, so He spoke, using the one field as a parable of the other, thus veiling, and at the same time beautifully revealing, His thought in a figure, which, simple as it was, demanded some degree of spiritual understanding for its appreciation; and accordingly after speaking the parable He adds the suggestive word, "Who hath ears to hear, let him hear."

There is something very touching in that word. It thrills with the pathos of these preceding chapters of disappointment. He had such a message for them—good tidings of great joy, rest for the weary and heavy laden, words of life and light and hope eternal—if only there were ears to hear. But that sad passage of Isaiah is running in His mind: "By hearing ye shall hear, and shall not understand; and seeing ye shall see, and shall not perceive: for this people's heart is waxed gross, and their ears are dull of hearing, and their eyes they have closed; lest at any time they should see with their eyes, and hear with their ears, and should understand with their heart, and should be converted, and I should heal them." That is the great obstacle, the one hindrance. Oh! if only men would hear; if only they would not close the ears of their souls! "Who hath ears to hear, let him hear."

I. THE PRINCIPLE OF PARABOLIC INSTRUCTION.

The parable is a new style of teaching as compared with that of which the "Sermon on the Mount" was so notable an example. That discourse was not by any means lacking in illustration; still its main lines of thought were of the nature of direct spiritual instruction. But here there is no direct spiritual teaching. It is all indirect; it is parabolic through and through. No wonder the disciples noticed the difference, and came to the Master with the question, "Why speakest Thou unto them in parables?" The answer He gives is a revelation of the thoughts which have been passing in His mind. Of this disclosure we have already availed ourselves in our attempt to picture the scene; but it remains to look at this weighty passage as answering the disciples' question, and so explaining the rise of that form of instruction in which, as in all that He did, He showed himself a perfect Master.

The whole thing turns on the distinction between earnest inquirers and careless hearers. There must have been many of the latter in His audience, for this was no selected company, like that which listened to the Sermon on the Mount. The earnest inquirer has ears to hear; the other has not. The difference this makes is most strikingly set forth in the strong declaration: "Whosoever hath, to him shall be given, and he shall have more abundance: but whosoever hath not, from him shall be taken away even that he hath,"—that is, instead of being the better for what he has heard, he is the worse; not apprehending the truth, he is only perplexed and confused by it, and instead of going away enriched, he is poorer than ever.

What, then, is to be done? If, instead of doing the people good, it only does them harm, why try to teach them at all? Why not let them alone, till they come with ears to hear, ready to receive? Happily this sad alternative is not the only resource. The truth may be put in such a way that it has both a shell and kernel of meaning; and the kernel may be so inclosed in the shell that it can be kept safely there, ready for the time when the inner fruit, which is the true food of the soul, can be used. For this purpose the parable is pre-eminently serviceable. The shell of meaning is so simple and familiar, that even a child can understand it; being of the nature of a story, it is very easily remembered; and connected as it is with that which is frequently observed, it will come up again and again to the minds of those in whom the thought has been lodged; so that, even if, on first hearing it, there is no possibility of understanding its deep spiritual significance, the time may come when it will flash upon the spirit the light which has been concealed within and so preserved from waste.

Take this parable of "The Sower" as an illustration. The disciples, having ears to hear, were ready to get the good of it at once, so to them He expounds it (vv. 18-23) on the spot. The rest were not ready to receive and apply it. Having ears (but not ears to hear), they heard not; but did it follow from this that it was useless, even worse than useless, to give it them? Had the teaching been direct, it would have been so; for they would have heard and rejected, and that would have been the last of it. But put as it was in parabolic form, while they were not prepared to understand and apply it then, they could not but carry it away with them; and, as they walked the fields, and observed the birds picking the seeds from the trodden field-paths, or the tiny plants withering on the rocky ledges, or the springing wheat strangled with rank growths of thorns, or the healthy growing wheat plant, or later in the season the rich golden grain on the good soil, they would have opportunity after opportunity of getting a glimpse of the truth, and finding that which at the first they were so unprepared to receive.

In this we can see the harmony of the passage before us, with its parallels in the second and third Gospels, where the object of speaking in parables is represented as being "that seeing, they might not see, and hearing they might not understand" (see Mark iv. 12, and Luke viii. 10). It is true that the object of the parable was to veil as well as to reveal; and the effect, which was also an intended effect, was to veil it from the unprepared heart and reveal it to the heart prepared; but inasmuch as the heart which is unprepared to-day may be prepared to-morrow, or next month, or next year, the parable may serve, and was intended to serve, the double purpose of veiling it and revealing it to the same person—veiling it from him as long as his heart was gross, but revealing it to him as soon as he should turn to the Lord and be willing to use his spiritual powers of apprehension for the purpose for which they had been given him. Thus, while this method of instruction was of the nature of judgment on the hardhearted for the moment, it was really in the deepest sense a device of love, to prolong the time of their opportunity, to give them repeated chances instead of only one. It was judgment for the moment, with a view to mercy in the time to come. So we find, as always, that even when our Saviour seems to deal harshly with men, His deepest thoughts are thoughts of love; and in His recourse to the parabolic veil, He is once more illustrating the truth of the prophet's description of Him cited in the foregoing chapter: "A bruised reed shall He not break, and smoking flax shall He not quench, till He send forth judgment unto victory."

How many difficulties might have been avoided if expositors had used less of the mere "dry light" of the understanding, and tried more to lay their hearts alongside the beating heart of Christ! "Is not my word like as a fire? saith the Lord." Had this been remembered, and the fire of love in such a passage as this brought to bear upon the heart, before it was used "like a hammer that breaketh the rock in pieces," how different in many cases would have been the result! It is sad to think that this very passage as to the object of the parables has been used as if it simply taught predestination in its hardest sense, dooming the poor misguided soul to hopelessness for ever; whereas, if we enter at all into sympathy with the Saviour's heart in the sad and trying circumstances in which the words were spoken, we find in it no harshness at all, but the yearning of a patient love, seeking if by any means He may reach and gain the lost.

We have, indeed, the evidence on every side that the Saviour's heart was greatly moved at this time. We have already recognised the pathos of the cry, "Who hath ears to hear, let him hear." We have seen the sorrow of His heart in the sad quotation from the prophet Isaiah. On the other hand, what joy He has in those who do see and hear!—"But blessed are your eyes, for they see; and your ears, for they hear. For verily I say unto you, That many prophets and righteous men have desired to see those things which ye see, and have not seen them; and to hear those things which ye hear, and have not heard them." The same satisfaction appears later (ver. 51), when, after finishing the series, He asks His disciples, "Have ye understood all these things?" and they say unto Him, "Yea, Lord." He adds, "Therefore every scribe which is instructed unto the kingdom of heaven is like unto a man that is an householder, which bringeth forth out of his treasure things new and old." The Saviour evidently rejoices in the thought that these disciples, having ears to hear, are making real progress,—so much so that in due time they will be ready to be teachers of others, each having a treasury of his own; and not only will they be in possession of the old, but will have power to strike out new views of sacred truth, and so be prepared with freshness and variety to set forth the glad tidings of the kingdom of heaven. How fully these hopes were realised we have only to look forward to the epistles to see. There we have things old, the very truths the Master taught in the days of His flesh; and not the old alone, for there are things new as well, fresh settings of the old, new aspects, varied applications of the truth—a treasury indeed for the ages to come. The Saviour, then, had good reason to take comfort that some of the seed He was sowing in tears was falling on good soil, and promising a rich and blessed harvest.

But the dark and discouraging side is never long out of sight. Returning to His own country, and teaching in their synagogue, He so impressed the people that they could not but ask certain questions, which, if they had only pondered them, would have led them to the truth: "Whence hath this man this wisdom, and these mighty works?" But the mere outside things that met their eyes so engrossed their attention, that their heads and hearts remained as empty as ever. Instead of pressing the question *Whence?* which would have led them up to heaven and to God, they dwelt upon "*this man*," this common man, this carpenter's son, with a mother called Mary, and brothers with the common names, James and Joseph, Simon and Judas; so, proving themselves to be of the earth earthy, they closed their ears and were "offended in Him." It was very evident that the only hope of reaching people of that kind was to speak in parables, which they could remember without understanding in the meantime, with the hope that by-and-by as they thought of the subject without such prejudices as these which now cause them to stumble, they may at last understand, and receive the truth and inherit eternal life.

II. The Group of Seven.

So far we have dealt with the parabolic method of teaching, and in doing so have glanced at only one of the seven parables the chapter contains, every one of which invites special study; but inasmuch as our plan will not admit of this, we shall attempt nothing more than a general view of the entire group; and to this we restrict ourselves the more willingly that there is a unity in the cluster which is apt to escape notice when they are considered apart, and because by letting go the details we get the prominent features more vividly before our minds.

The arrangement seems to be in three pairs, with a single concluding parable. The first pair —"The Sower" and "The Tares"—set forth the manner of the establishment of the kingdom of heaven, and the obstacles it must encounter. The sphere from which both parables are taken is admirably suited to bring out the radical distinction in regard to the manner of its establishment between the new kingdom and those with which the people were already familiar. They were founded by the sword; this kingdom by the Word. Not force, but persuasion, is to be the weapon; and accordingly there is placed before the mind, not a warrior hasting to battle, but a sower sowing seed. "The field is the world," we are told—the world of men, of human hearts; and the seed is "the word of the kingdom." It is "good seed," and therefore it ought to be welcome; but there are serious obstacles in the way.

The first parable sets forth the obstacles encountered in the soil itself. Sometimes the seed falls on *hard soil,* where it cannot penetrate the surface, and presently birds come and carry it away—representing those hearers of the word who, though they remember it for a short time, have their hearts hardened against it, so that it does not enter, but is presently snatched away by trifling worldly thoughts which come fluttering into the mind. Then there is the *shallow soil,* a little loose earth on the surface, and close under it the hard rock, harder even than the trodden wayside—a kind of soil in which the seed will rapidly take root and spring up, and as rapidly wither away in the noonday heat, and which therefore fitly represents those who are easily impressed, but whose impressions do not last; who make many resolutions indeed, but in so half-hearted and impulsive a way that they are destined to be blighted by the first blast of temptation. Finally, there is the *preoccupied soil,* where thorns and thistles hold the ground and choke the springing plants of grace, representing those who "are choked with cares, and riches and pleasures of this life, and bring no fruit to maturity."

The *good soil* is marked by characteristics which are simply the negatives of these: it is not hard, so the seed enters; not shallow, so it takes root; not preoccupied, so it holds the ground, and springs up and brings forth fruit, "in some thirty, in some sixty, in some a hundred-fold."

There are, however, other obstacles than those found in the nature of the soil. There is the diligence of the enemy, and the impossibility of getting rid of those who have come under his influence, as set forth in the second parable, that of "The Tares of the Field." In this parable the good seed is no longer the word, but "the children of the kingdom"; as if to suggest that Christians themselves are to be to the world what the word has been to them; while the bad seed—sown when men sleep, sown when Christians are asleep—does not remain as mere seed, but embodies itself in "children of the wicked one," who take their places side by side with the true children of the kingdom, and whom it is so difficult to distinguish from them, that the separation may not be attempted till the time of the harvest, when it shall be complete and final, and "the righteous shall shine forth as the sun in the kingdom of their Father."

The second pair—"The Mustard Seed" and "The Leaven"—set forth the growth of the kingdom notwithstanding the many obstacles it must encounter, the one indicating its growth as recognisable to the observant eye, the other its pervasive power as permeating society. This twofold view of the development of the kingdom is in the same line of thought as the illustrations of the light and the salt in the Sermon on the Mount. The prophecy these parables infold is most marvellous, spoken as it was in a time of so deep discouragement. There is true pathos in the thought of the grain of mustard seed, "the least of all seeds," and in the little word "hid," which comes in so significantly in the parable of the Leaven; and there is great strength of faith in the readiness of mind to recognise the hopeful thought of the inherent life and energy hidden in the tiny germ, and working all unseen in the little leaven which literally disappeared in the at first unaltered mass.

The parables of "The Hid Treasure" and "The Pearl" form a third pair, shadowing forth the unsearchable riches of Christ. The reduplication of the thought adds greatly to its impressiveness, and moreover affords the opportunity of suggested variation in the experience of those who find the treasure. The merchantman we naturally think of as representing the rich, and the man finding the treasure in the field as one of the poor in this world's goods. Both alike, however, "buy" their prize at the price of all that they possess, on the principle which underlies all our Lord's teaching as to the way of life: "Whosoever he be of you that forsaketh not all that he hath cannot be My disciple." The one comes upon his treasure unexpectedly; the other finds it in the course of diligent search. Both alike, however, recognise its exceeding value as soon as it is seen; and it is under no constraint, but willingly and gladly—"for joy thereof," as it is put in the case of the man who from his not seeking it might have been thought indifferent to it—that each one sells all that he has and buys it.

The last parable, according to the arrangement we have suggested, stands alone. It is the parable of "The Net," and its subject is the consummation of the Kingdom. Its teaching is indeed to a great extent anticipated in the parable of the tares of the field; but in that parable, though "the end of the world" is pictured in the most impressive imagery, it is not the main thought, as it is here, where the one lesson is, that the present mixed state of things cannot continue for ever, that there must come a time of separation, when those in whose hearts God reigns shall be gathered to a place by themselves, where they shall be satisfied for ever, with their treasure no longer hid, but open in all its immeasurable fulness; while those who refused to allow God to reign in their hearts, and preferred their own selfishness and sin, shall be cast away and consumed, with "wailing and gnashing of teeth."

CHAPTER XII.

THE CRISIS IN GALILEE.

MATTHEW xiv.-xvi. 12.

THE lives of John and of Jesus, lived so far apart, and with so little intercommunication, have yet been interwoven in a remarkable way, the connection only appearing at the most critical times in the life of our Lord. This interweaving, strikingly anticipated in the incidents of the nativity as recorded by St. Luke, appears, not only at the time of our Saviour's baptism and first introduction to His Messianic work, but again at the beginning of His Galilean ministry, which dates from the time when John was cast into prison, and once again as the stern prophet of the desert finishes his course; for his martyrdom precipitates a crisis, to which events for some time have been tending.

The period of crisis, embracing the facts recorded in the two chapters following and in part of the sixteenth, is marked by events of thrilling interest. The shadow of the cross falls so very darkly now upon the Saviour's path, that we may look for some more striking effects of light and shade,—Rembrandt-like touches, if with reverence we may so put it,—in the Evangelist's picture. Many impressive contrasts will arrest our attention as we proceed to touch briefly on the story of the time.

I.—THE BANQUET OF HEROD AND THE FEAST OF CHRIST (xiv. 1-21).

"Among them that are born of woman there hath not risen a greater than John the Baptist." Such was the Saviour's testimony to His forerunner in the hour of his weakness; and the sequel fully justified it. The answer which came to John's inquiry brought him no outward relief. His prison bolts were as firmly fastened as before, Herod was as inexorable, the prospect before Him as dark as ever; but he had the assurance that Jesus was the Christ, and that His blessed work of healing the sick and preaching the gospel to the poor was going on; and that was enough for him. So he was quite content to languish on, resting in the Lord and waiting patiently for Him. We learn from St. Mark that Herod was in the habit of sending for him at times, evidently interested in the strange man, probably to some extent fascinated by him, and possibly not without some lingering hope that there might be some way of reconciling the preacher of righteousness and securing the blessing of so well-accredited a messenger of Heaven. There is little doubt that at these times the way was open for John to be restored to liberty, if only he had been willing to lower his testimony against Herod's sin, or consent to say no more about it; but no such thought ever crossed his noble soul. He had said, "It is not lawful for thee to have her;" and not even in the hour of deepest depression and darkest doubt did he for a moment relax the rigour of his requirements as a preacher of righteousness.

As he had lived, so he died. We shall not dwell on the details of the revolting story. It is quite realistic enough in the simple recital of the Evangelist. One cannot help recalling in this connection four hideous pictures of Salome with the head of John the Baptist recently displayed, all on the line, in the *Salon* at Paris. Of what possible use are such representations? To what sort of taste do they minister? There was no picture of John looking with flashing eyes at the guilty monarch as he said, "It is not lawful for thee to have her." That is the scene which is worthy of remembrance: let it abide in the memory and heart; let the tragic end serve only as a dark background to make the central figure luminous, "a burning and a shining light."

The time of Herod's merciful visitation is over. So long as he kept the Baptist safe (Mark vi. 19, 20) from the machinations of Herodias, he retained one link with better things. The stern prisoner was to him like a second conscience; and so long as he was there within easy reach, and Herod continued from time to time to see him and hear what he had to say, there remained some hope of repentance and reformation. Had he only yielded to the promptings of his better nature, and obeyed the prophet, the way of the Lord would have been prepared, the preacher of righteousness would have been followed by the

Prince of Peace; and the gospel of Jesus, with all its unspeakable blessing, would have had free course in his court and throughout his realm. But the sacrifice of the prophet to the cruelty of Herodias and the folly and wickedness of his vow put an end to such prospects; and the fame of Christ's deeds of mercy, when at last it reached his ears, instead of stirring in him a living hope, aroused the demon of guilty conscience, which could not rid itself of the superstitious fear that it was John the Baptist risen from the dead. Thus passed away for ever the great opportunity of Herod Antipas.

The disciples of John withdrew in sorrow, but not in despair. They had evidently caught the spirit of their master; for as soon as they had reverently and lovingly taken up the mortal remains and buried them, they came and told Jesus.

It must have been a terrible blow to Him,—perhaps even more than it was to them, for they had Him to go to, while He had none on earth to take counsel with: He must carry the heavy burden of responsibility all alone; for even the most advanced of the Twelve could not enter into any of His thoughts and purposes; and certainly not one of them, we might indeed say not all of them together, had at this time anything like the strength and steadfastness of the great man who had just been taken away. We learn from the other accounts that at the same time the Twelve returned from their first missionary journey; so that the question would immediately come up, What was to be done? It was a critical time. Should they stir up the people to avenge the death of their prophet? This would have been after the manner of men, but not according to the counsel of God. Long ago the Saviour had set aside, as quite apart from His way of working, all appeals to force; His kingdom must be a kingdom of the truth, and on the truth He will rely, with nothing else to trust to than the power of patient love. So He takes His disciples away to the other side of the lake, outside the jurisdiction of Herod, with the thoughtful invitation: "Come ye yourselves apart into a desert place, and rest awhile."

What are the prospects of the kingdom now? Sin and righteousness have long been at strife in the court of Galilee; now sin has conquered and has the field. The great preacher of righteousness is dead; and the Christ, to Whom he bore such faithful witness, has gone to the desert. Again the sad prophecy is fulfilled: "He is despised and rejected of men; a man of sorrows, and acquainted with grief." That little boat crossing from the populous shores of Gennesaret to the desert land on the other side—what does it mean? Defeat? A lost cause? Is this the end of the mission in Galilee, begun to the music of that majestic prophecy which spoke of it as daybreak on the hills and shores of Naphtali and Zebulun, Gennesaret and Jordan? Is this the outcome of two mighty movements so full of promise and hope? Did not all Jerusalem and Judea go after John, confessing their sins and accepting his baptism? And has not all Galilee thronged after Jesus, bringing their sick to be healed, and listening, at least with outward respect and often expressed astonishment, to His words of truth and hope? Now John is dead, and Jesus is crossing with His own disciples and those of John in a boat—one boat enough to hold them all—to mourn together in a desert place apart. Suppose we had been sitting on the shore that day, and had watched it getting ever smaller as it crossed the sea, what should we have thought of the prospects? Should we have found it easy to believe in Christ that day? Verily "the kingdom of God cometh not with observation."

The multitudes will not believe on Him; yet they will not let Him rest. They have rejected the kingdom; but they would fain get as much as they can of those earthly blessings which have been scattered so freely as its signs. So the people, noticing the direction the boat has taken, throng after Him, running on foot round the northern shore. When Jesus sees them, sad and weary as He is, He cannot turn away. He knows too well that it is with no pure and lofty devotion that they follow Him; but He cannot see a multitude of people without having His heart moved with a great longing to bless them. So He "went forth, and healed their sick."

He continued His loving work, lavishing His sympathy on those who had no sympathy with Him, till evening fell, and the disciples suggested that it was time to send the people away, especially as they were beginning to suffer from want of food. "But Jesus said unto them, They need not depart: give ye them to eat. And they say unto Him, We have here but five loaves, and two fishes. He said, Bring them hither to Me."

The miracle which follows is of very special significance. Many things point to this. (1) It is the one miracle which all the four Evangelists record. (2) It occurs at a critical time in our Lord's history. There has been discouragement after discouragement, repulse after repulse, despite and rejection by the leaders, obstinate unbelief and impenitence on the part of the people, the good seed finding almost everywhere hard or shallow or thorny soil, with little or no promise of the longed-for harvest. And now a crowning disaster has come in the death of John. Can we wonder that Christ received the tidings of it as a premonition of His own? Can we wonder that henceforth He should give less attention to public preaching, and more to the training of the little band of faithful disciples who must be prepared for days of darkness coming on apace—prepared for the cross, manifestly now the only way to the crown? (3) There is the significant remark (John vi. 4) that "the Passover was nigh." This was the last Passover but one of our Saviour's life. The next was to be marked by the sacrifice of Himself as "the Lamb of God that taketh away the sin of the world." Another year, and He will have fulfilled His course, as John has fulfilled His. Was it not, then, most natural that His mind should be full, not only of thoughts of the approaching Passover, but also of what the next one must bring. This is no mere conjecture; for it plainly appears in the long and most suggestive discourse St. John reports as following immediately upon the miracle and designed for its application.

The feeding of the five thousand is indeed a sign of the kingdom, like those grouped together in the earlier part of the Gospel (viii., ix). It showed the compassion of the Lord upon the hungry multitude, and His readiness to supply their wants. It showed the Lordship of Christ over nature, and served as a representation in miniature of what the God of nature is doing every year, when, by agencies as far beyond our ken as those by which His Son multiplied the loaves that day, He transmutes the handful of seed-corn into the rich harvests of grain which feed the multitudes of men. It taught also, by implication, that the same God Who feeds the bodies of men with the rich abundance of the year is able and willing to satisfy all their spiritual wants. But there is something more than all this, as we might gather from the very way it is told: "And He commanded the multitude to sit down on the grass, and took the five loaves, . . . and looking up to heaven, He blessed, and brake, and gave the loaves to the disciples, and the disciples to the multitude." Can we read these words without thinking of what our Saviour did just a year later, when He took bread and blessed it, and brake it, and gave it to the disciples and said, "Take, eat, this is My body" (xxvi. 26)? He is not, indeed, instituting the Supper now; but it is very plain that the same thoughts are in His mind as when, a year later, He did so. And what might be inferred from the recital of what He did becomes still more evident when we are told what afterwards He said—especially such utterances as these: "I am the bread of life;" "The bread which I will give you is My flesh, which I will give for the life of the world;" "Verily I say unto you, Except ye eat the flesh of the Son of man, and drink His blood, ye have no life in you."

We have, then, here, not a sign of the kingdom only, but a parable of life eternal, life to be bestowed in no other way than by the death to be accomplished at Jerusalem at the next passover, life for thousands, life ministered through the disciples to the multitudes, and not diminished in the ministering, but growing and multiplying in their hands, so that after all are fed there remain "twelve baskets full,"—far more than at the first: a beautiful hint of the abundance that will remain for the Gentile nations of the earth. That passover parable comes out of the anguish of the great Redeemer's heart. Already, as He breaks that bread and gives it to the people, He is enduring the cross and despising the shame of it, for the joy set before Him of giving the bread of life to a hungry world.

One can scarcely fail at this point to contrast the feast in honour of Herod's birthday with the feast which symbolised the Saviour's death. "When a convenient day was come, Herod on his birthday made a supper to his lords, high captains, and chief estates of Galilee; and——" the rest is well known,—the feasting, mirth, and revelry, ending in the dark tragedy, followed by the remorse of a guilty conscience, the gnawing of the worm that dieth not, the burning of the fire that is not quenched. Then think of that other feast on the green grass in the pure air of the fresh and breezy hillside—the hungry multitudes, the homely fare, the few barley loaves and the two small fishes; yet by the blessing of the Lord Jesus there was provided a repast far more enjoyable to these keen appetites than all the delicacies of the banquet to the lords of Galilee—a feast pointing indeed to a death, but a death which was to bring life and peace and joy to thousands, with abundance over for all who will receive it. The one is the feast to which the world invites; the other is the feast which Christ provides for all who are willing to "labour not for the meat that perisheth, but for that which endureth unto eternal life."

II.—Calm on the Mountain and Trouble on the Sea.

We learn from the fourth Gospel that the immediate result of the impression made by our Lord's miraculous feeding of the five thousand was an attempt on the part of the people to take Him by force and make Him a king. Thus, as always, their minds would run on political change, and the hope of bettering their circumstances thereby; while they refuse to allow themselves to think of that spiritual change which must begin with themselves, and show itself in that repentance and hunger and thirst after righteousness, which He so longed to see in them. Even His disciples, as we know, were not now, nor for a long time subsequent to this, altogether free from the same spirit of earthliness; and it is quite likely that the general enthusiasm would excite them not a little, and perhaps lead them to raise the question, as they were often fain to do, whether the time had not at last come for their Master to declare Himself openly, put Himself at the head of these thousands, take advantage of the widespread feeling of irritation and discontent awakened by the murder of John the Baptist, whom all men counted for a prophet (Mark xi. 32), hurl Herod Antipas from the high position he disgraced, and, with all Galilee under His control and full of enthusiasm for His cause, march southward on Jerusalem. This was no doubt the course of action they for the most part expected and wished; and, with One at their head Who could do such wonders, what was there to hinder complete success?

May we not also with reverence suppose that this was one of the occasions on which Satan renewed those assaults which he began in the wilderness of Judea? A little later, when Peter was trying to turn Him aside from the path of the Cross, Jesus recognised it, not merely as a suggestion of the disciple, but as a renewed temptation of the great adversary. We may well suppose, then, that at this crisis the old temptation to bestow on Him the kingdoms of the world and the glory of them—not for their own sake, of course (there could have been no temptation in that direction), but for the sake of the advancement of the interests of the heavenly kingdom by the use of worldly methods of policy and force—was presented to Him with peculiar strength.

However this may have been, the circumstances required prompt action of some kind. It was necessary that the disciples should be got out of reach of temptation as soon as possible; so He constrained them to enter into a boat, and go before Him to the other side, while He dispersed the multitude. And need we wonder that in the circumstances He should wish to be entirely alone? He could not consult with those He trusted most, for they were quite in the dark, and anything they were at all likely to say would only increase the pressure put upon Him by the people. He had only One for His Counsellor and Comforter, His Father in heaven, Whose will He had come to do; so He must be alone with Him. He must have been in a state of great physical exhaustion after all the fatigue of the day, for though He had come for rest He had found none; but the brave, strong spirit conquers the weary flesh, and instead of going to sleep He ascends the neighbouring height to spend the night in prayer.

It is interesting to remember that it was after this night spent in prayer that He delivered the remarkable discourse recorded in the sixth chapter of St. John, in which He speaks so plainly about giving His flesh for the life of the world. It is evident, then, that, if any question had arisen in His mind as to the path of duty, when He was suddenly confronted with the enthusiastic desire of the multitudes to crown Him at once, it was speedily set at rest: He now plainly saw that it was not the will of His Father in heaven that He should take advantage of any such stirring of worldly desire, that He must give no encouragement to any, except those who were hungering and thirsting after righteousness, to range themselves upon His side. Hence, no doubt, the sifting nature of the discourse He delivered the following day. He is eager to gather the multitudes to Himself; but He cannot allow them to come under any false assumption;—He must have spiritually-minded disciples, or none at all: accordingly He makes His discourse so strongly spiritual, directs their attention so far away from earthly issues to the issues of eternity ("I will raise him up at the last day" is the promise He gives over and over again, whereas they wanted to be raised up then and there to high places in the world), that not only did the multitude lose all their enthusiasm, but "from that time many of His disciples went back, and walked no more with Him," while even the Twelve themselves were shaken in their allegiance, as seems evident from the sorrowful question with which He turned to them: "Will ye also go away?" We may reverently suppose, then, that our Lord was occupied, during the early part of the night, with thoughts like these—in preparation, as it were, for the faithful words He will speak and the sad duty He will discharge on the morrow.

Meantime a storm has arisen on the lake—one of those sudden and often terrible squalls to which inland waters everywhere are subject, but which are greatly aggravated here by the contrast between the tropical climate of the lake, 620 feet below the level of the Mediterranean, and the cool air on the heights which surround it. The storm becomes fiercer as the night advances. The Saviour has been much absorbed, but He cannot fail to notice how angry the lake is becoming, and to what peril His loved disciples are exposed. As the Passover was nigh, the moon would be nearly full, and there would be frequent opportunities, between the passing of the clouds, to watch the little boat. As long as there seems any prospect of their weathering the storm by their own exertions He leaves them to themselves; but when it appears that they are making no progress, though it is evident that they are "toiling in rowing," He sets out at once to their relief.

The rescue which follows recalls a former incident on the same lake (viii. 23-27). But the points of difference are both important and instructive. Then He was with His disciples in the ship, though asleep; in their extremity they had only to rouse Him with the cry, "Save, Lord, or we perish!" to secure immediate calm and safety. Now He was not with them; He was out of sight, and beyond the reach even of the most piercing cries. It was therefore a much severer trial than the last, and remembering the special significance of the miracle of the loaves, we can scarcely fail to notice a corresponding suggestiveness in this one. That one had dimly foreshadowed His death; did not this, in the same way, foreshadow the relations He would sustain to His disciples after His death? May we not look upon His ascent of this mountain as a picture of His ascension into heaven—His betaking Himself to His Father now as a shadow of His going to the Father then—His prayer on the mount as a shadow of His heavenly intercession? It was to pray that He ascended; and though He, no doubt, needed, at that trying time, to pray for Himself, His heart would be poured out in pleading for His disciples too, especially when the storm came on. And these disciples constrained to go off in a boat by themselves,—are they not a picture of the Church after Christ had gone to His Father, launched on the stormy sea of the world? What will they do without Him? What will they do when the winds rise and the waves roar in the dark night? Oh! if only He were here, Who was sleeping in the boat that day, and only needed to be roused to sympathise and save! Where is He now? There on the hilltop, interceding, looking down with tenderest compassion, watching every effort of the toiling rowers. Nay, He is nearer still! See that Form upon the waves! "It is a spirit," they cry; and are afraid, very much as, a little more than a year afterward, when He came suddenly into the midst of them with His "Peace be unto you," they were terrified and affrighted, and supposed that they had seen a spirit (Luke xxiv. 37). But presently they hear the familiar voice: "Be of good cheer: it is I; be not afraid." There can be no doubt that the remembrance of that night on the lake of Galilee would be a wondrous consolation to these disciples during the storms of persecution through which they had to pass after their Master had ascended up to heaven; and their faith in the presence of His Spirit, and His constant readiness to help and save, would be greatly strengthened by the memory of that apparently spectral Form they had seen coming across the troubled sea to their relief. Have we not some reason, then, for saying that here, too, we have not only another of the many signs of the kingdom showing our Lord's power over nature and constant readiness to help His people in time of need, but a parable of the future, most appropriately following that parable of life through death set forth in the feeding of the thousands on the day before?

There seems, in fact, a strange prophetic element running all through the scenes of that wondrous time. We have already referred to the disposition on the part even of the Twelve, as manifested next day at the close of the discourse on the "bread of life," to desert Him—to show the same spirit which afterward, when the crisis reached its height, so demoralised them that "they all forsook Him, and fled"; and have we not, in the closing incident, in which Peter figures so conspicuously, a mild foreshadowing of his terrible fall, when the storm of human passion was raging as fiercely in Jerusalem as did the winds and waves on the lake of Galilee that night? There is the same self-confidence: "Lord, if it be Thou, bid me come unto Thee on the water;" the same alarm when he was brought face to face with the danger the thought of which he had braved; then the sinking, sinking as if about to perish, yet not hopelessly (for the Master had prayed for him that his faith should not fail); then the humble prayer, "Lord, save me" ; and the gracious hand immediately stretched out to save. Had the adventurous disciple learnt his lesson well that day, what it would have saved him! May we not say that there is never a great and terrible fall, however sudden it seems, which has not been preceded by warnings, even long before, which, if heeded, would have certainly averted it? How much need have the disciples of Christ to learn thoroughly the lessons their Lord teaches them in His gentler dealings, so that when darker days and heavier trials come they may be ready, having taken unto themselves the whole armour of God to withstand in the evil day, and having done all, to stand.

There are many other important lessons which might be learnt from this incident, but we may not dwell on them; a mere enumeration of some of them may, however, be attempted. It was faith, in part at least, which led the apostle to make this venture; and this is, no doubt, the reason why the Lord did not forbid it. Faith is too precious to be repressed; but the faith of Peter on this occasion is anything but simple, clear, and strong: there is a large measure of self-will in it, of impulsiveness, of self-confidence, perhaps of love of display. A confused and encumbered faith of this kind is sure to lead into mischief,—to set on foot rash enterprises, which show great enthusiasm, and perhaps seem to rebuke the caution of the less confident for the time, but which come to grief, and in the end bring no credit to the cause of Christ. The rash disciple's enterprise is not, however, an entire failure: he does succeed so far; but presently the weakness of his faith betrays itself. As long as the impulse lasted, and his eye was fixed on his Master, all went well; but when the first burst of enthusiasm was spent, and he had time to look round upon the waves, he began to sink. But how encouraging it is to observe that, when put to extremity, that which is genuine in the man carries it over all the rest!—the faith which had been encumbered extricates itself, and becomes simple, clear, and strong; the last atom of self-confidence is gone, and with it all thought of display; nothing but simple faith is left in that strong cry of his, "Lord, save me!"

Nothing could be imagined better suited than this incident to discriminate between self-confidence and faith. Peter enters on this experience with the two well mixed together,—so well mixed that neither he himself nor his fellow-disciples could distinguish them; but the testing process precipitates one and clarifies the other,—lets the self-confidence all go and brings out the faith pure and strong. Immediately, therefore, his Lord is at his side, and he is safe;—a great lesson this on faith, especially in revealing its simplicity. Peter tried to make a grand thing of it: he had to come back to the simple, humble cry, and the grasping of his Saviour's outstretched hand.

The same lesson is taught on a larger scale in the brief account of the cures the Master wrought when they reached the other side, where all that was asked was the privilege of touching His garment's hem, "and as many as touched were made perfectly whole;" not the great ones, not the strong ones, but "as many as touched." Only let us keep in touch with Him, and all will assuredly be well with us both in time and in eternity.

III.—Israel after the Flesh and Israel after the Spirit (xv.).

Issue is now joined with the ecclesiastical leaders at Jerusalem, who send a deputation to make a formal complaint. When Jerusalem was last mentioned in our Gospel it was in connection with a movement of quite a different character. The fame of the Saviour's deeds of mercy in Galilee had then just reached the capital, the result being that many set out at once to find out what new thing this might be: "There followed Him great multitudes of people from Galilee, and from Decapolis, and from Jerusalem, and from Judea, and from beyond Jordan" (iv. 25). That wave of interest in the south had now died down; and instead of eager multitudes there is a small sinister band of cold, keen-witted, hard-hearted critics. It was a sad change, and must have brought new distress to the Saviour's troubled heart; but He is none the less ready to face the trial with His wonted courage and unfailing readiness of resource.

Their complaint is trivial enough. It is to be remembered, of course, that it was not a question of cleanliness, but of ritual; not even of ritual appointed by Moses, but only of that prescribed by certain traditions of their fathers which they held in superstitious veneration. These traditions, by a multitude of minute regulations and restrictions, imposed an intolerable burden on those who thought it their duty to observe them; while the magnifying of trifles had the natural effect of keeping out of sight the weightier matters of the law. Not only so, but the most trivial regulations were sometimes so managed as to furnish an excuse for neglect of the plainest duties. Our Lord could not therefore miss the opportunity of denouncing this evil, and accordingly He exposes it in the plainest and strongest language.

The question with which He opens His attack is most incisive. It is as if He said, "I am accused of transgressing *your* tradition. What is your tradition? It is itself transgression of the law of God." Then follows the striking illustration, showing how by their rules of tradition they put it within the power of any heartless son to escape entirely the obligation of providing even for his aged father or mother —an illustration, be it remembered, which brought out more than a breach of the fifth commandment; for by what means was it that the ungrateful son escaped his obligation? By taking the name of the Lord in vain; for surely there could be no greater dishonour to the name of God than meanly to mark as dedicated to Him ("Corban") what ought to have been devoted to the discharge of an imperative filial duty. Besides, it was not at all necessary that the money or property should be actually dedicated to sacred uses; it was only necessary to say that it was, only necessary to pronounce over it that magic word Corban, and then the mean hypocrite could use it for the most selfish purposes—for any purpose, in fact, he chose, except that purpose for which it was his duty to use it. It is really difficult to conceive such iniquity wrapped up in a cloak of so-called religion. No wonder our Lord was moved to indignation, and applied to His critics the strong language of the prophet: "Ye hypocrites, well did Isaiah prophesy of you, saying, This people honoureth Me with their lips; but their heart is far from Me, . . . teaching as their doctrines the precepts of men" (R. V.). No wonder that He turned away from men who were so deeply committed to a system so vile, and that He explained, not to His questioners, but to the multitude who had gathered round, the principle on which He acted.

There seems, however, to have been more of sorrow than of anger in His tone and manner. How else could the disciples have asked Him such a question as that which follows: "Knowest Thou that the Pharisees were offended, after they heard this saying?" Of course the Pharisees were offended. They had most excellent reason. And the disciples would have known that He had no intention of sparing them in the least, and no concern whether they took offence or not, if His tone had been such as an ordinary person would naturally have put into such an invective. It is probable that He said it all calmly, earnestly, tenderly, without the slightest trace of passion; from which it would not be at all unnatural for the disciples to infer that He had not fully realised how strong His language had been, and into what serious collision He had brought Himself with the leaders in Jerusalem. Hence their gentle remonstrance, the expression of those feelings of dismay with which they saw their Master break with one party after another, as if determined to wreck His mission altogether. Was it not bad policy to give serious offence to persons of such importance at so critical a time?

The Saviour's answer is just what was to be expected. Policy had no place in His plan. His kingdom was of the truth; and whatever was not of truth must go, be the consequences what they might. That system of traditionalism had its roots deeply and firmly fastened in the Jewish soil; its fibres were through it all; and to disturb it was to go against a feeling that was nothing less than national in its extent. But no matter: firmly, deeply, widely rooted though it was, it was not of God's planting, and therefore it cannot be let alone: "Every plant, which My heavenly Father hath not planted, shall be rooted up." It is for all ritualists, ancient and modern, all who teach for doctrines what are only commandments of men, seriously to ponder this most radical utterance by One Whose right it is to speak with an authority from which there is no appeal.

Having thus condemned the ritualistic teaching of the day, He disposes next of the false teachers. This He does in a way which ought to have been a warning to those persecutors and heresy-hunters who, by their unwise use of force and law, have given only larger currency to the evil doctrines they have tried to suppress. He simply says "Let them alone: they be blind leaders of the blind. And if the blind lead the blind, both shall fall into the ditch." Expose their error by all means; root it out if possible; but as for the men themselves, "let them alone."

The principle He sets forth as underlying the whole subject is the same as that which underlies His teaching in the Sermon on the Mount—viz., that "out of the heart are the issues of life." The ritualist lays stress on that which enters into the man—the kind of food which enters his mouth, the objects which meet his eye, the incense which enters his nostril; Christ sets all this aside as of no consequence in comparison with the state of the heart (vv. 16-20). Such teaching as this was not only irreconcilable with that of the scribes and Pharisees from Jerusalem, but it lay at the very opposite pole.

Was it on this account that after this interview Jesus withdrew as far as possible from Jerusalem? He is limited, indeed, in His range to the Holy Land, as He indicates in His conversation with the woman of Canaan; but just as after the death of John He had withdrawn out of the jurisdiction of Herod to the east, so now, after this collision with the deputation from Jerusalem, He withdraws to the far north, to the borders of Tyre and Sidon. And was it only a coincidence that, just as Jerusalem had furnished such sorry specimens of dead formalism, the distant borders of heathen Tyre and Sidon should immediately thereafter furnish one of the very noblest examples of living faith? The coincidence is certainly very striking and most instructive. The leaders from Jerusalem had been dismissed with the condemnation of their own prophet: "This people honoureth Me with their lips, but their heart is far from Me;" while out of far-away heathendom there comes one whose whole heart is poured out to Him in earnest, persevering, prevailing prayer. It is one of those contrasts with which this portion of our Lord's history abounds, the force of which will appear more clearly as we proceed.

The suppliant was "a woman of Canaan," or, as she is described more definitely elsewhere, a Syro-Phœnician woman. Yet she has learned of Jesus—knows Him as the Christ, for she calls Him "Son of David"—knows Him as a Saviour, for she comes to ask that her daughter may be healed. Her application must have been a great solace to His wounded heart. He always loved to be asked for such blessings; and, rejected as He had been by His countrymen, it must have been a special encouragement to be approached in this way by a stranger. That it was so may be inferred from what He said on similar occasions. When the Roman centurion came to have his servant healed, Jesus commended his wonderful faith, and then added: "I say unto you, That many shall come from the east and west, and shall sit down with Abraham, and Isaac, and Jacob, in the kingdom of heaven." So, too, when it was announced to Him that some Greeks desired to see Him, the first effect was to sharpen the agony of His rejection by His own countrymen; but immediately He recovers Himself, looks beyond the cross and the shame to the glory that shall follow, and exclaims, "I, if I be lifted up from the earth, will draw all men unto Me." There can be no doubt that at this time of rejection in Galilee it must have been a similar consolation to receive this visit from the woman of Canaan.

How, then, can we explain His treatment of her? First, He answered her not a word. Then He reminded her that she did not belong to Israel, as if she therefore could have no claim on Him. And when she still urged her suit, in a manner that might have appealed to the hardest heart, He gave her an answer which seems so incredibly harsh, that it is with a feeling of pain one hears it repeated after eighteen hundred years. What does all this mean? It means "praise and honour and glory" for the poor woman; for the disciples, and for all disciples, a lesson never to be forgotten. He Who knew what was in man, knew what was in this noble woman's heart, and He wished to bring it out —to bring it out so that the disciples should see it, so that other disciples should see it, so that generation after generation and century after century should see it, and admire it, and learn its lesson. It cost her some minutes' pain: Him also,—how it must have wrung His heart to treat her in a way so foreign to every fibre of His soul! But had He not so dealt with her, what a loss to her, to the disciples, to countless multitudes! He very much needs a shining example of living faith to set over against the dead formalism of these traditionalists; and here it is: He must bring it out of its obscurity, and set it as a star in the firmament of His gospel, to shine for ever and ever. He tested her to the uttermost, because He knew that at the end of all He could say: "O woman, great is thy faith: be it unto thee even as thou wilt." The heart of the Saviour was never filled with a deeper tenderness or a wiser and more far-seeing love than when He repulsed this woman again and again, and treated her with what seemed at the moment most inexcusable and unaccountable harshness.

The lessons which shine out in the simple story of this woman can only be touched in the slightest manner. We have already referred to the contrast between the great men of Jerusalem and this poor woman of Canaan; observe now how strikingly is suggested the distinction between Israel according to the flesh and Israel according to the spirit. The current idea of the time was that lineal descent from Abraham determined who belonged to the house of Israel and who did not. The Saviour strikes at the root of this error. He does not indeed attack it directly. For this the time has not yet come: the veil of the Temple has not yet been rent in twain. But He draws aside the veil a little, so as to give a glimpse of the truth and prepare the way for its full revealing when the time shall come. He does not broadly say, "This woman of Canaan is as good an Israelite as any of you;" but He says, "I am not sent but unto the lost sheep of the house of Israel"—and heals her daughter notwithstanding. Was it not, then, evident that this poor woman after all did in some sense belong to the lost sheep of the house of Israel whom Jesus came to save?

The house of Israel?—what does Israel mean? Learn at Peniel. See Jacob in sore distress at the brook Jabbok. A man is wrestling with him, —wrestling with him all the night, until the break of day. It is no mere man, for Jacob finds before all is over that he has been face to face with God. The man who wrestled with him indeed was the same as He Who wrestled with this woman of Canaan. The Divine Man struggles to get away without blessing the patriarch. Jacob cries, in the very desperation of his faith, "I will not let Thee go, except Thou bless me!" The victory is won. The blessing is granted, and these words are added: "What is thy name?" "Jacob." "Thy name shall be called no more Jacob, but Israel" (*i. e.*, prince with God): "for as a prince hast thou power with God and with men, and hast prevailed."

Was this woman, then, or was she not, "a prince" with God? Did she, or did she not, belong to the true house of Israel? Let us now look back to vv. 8 and 9: "This people" (*i. e.*, the children of Israel according to the flesh . . . "honoureth Me with their lips; but their heart is far from Me. But *in vain* do they worship Me." In vain do they worship: are they, then, princes with God? Nay, verily; they are only actors before Him, as the Saviour plainly says. Truly they are not all Israel who are of Israel; and just as truly they are not the only Israel who are of Israel, for here is this woman of Canaan who earns the name of Israel by as hard a contest and as great a victory as that of Jacob at the brook Jabbok, when first the name was given.

Another instructive contrast is inevitably suggested between the foremost of the apostles and this nameless woman of Canaan. The last illustration of faith was Peter's venture on the water. What a difference between the strong man and the weak woman! To the strong, brave man the Master had to say "O thou of little faith! wherefore didst thou doubt?" To the weak woman, "O woman, great is thy faith." What an encouragement here to the little ones, the obscure, unnoticed disciples! "Many that are first shall be last, and the last first."

The encouragement to persevering prayer, especially to parents anxious for their children, is so obvious that it need only be named. That silence first, and then these apparent refusals, are trials of faith, to which many earnest hearts have not been strangers. To all such the example of this woman of Canaan is of great value. Her earnestness in making the case of her daughter her own (she does not say, "Have mercy on my daughter;" but, "Have mercy on *me;*" and again, "Lord, help *me*"), and her unconquerable perseverance till the answer came, have been an inspiration ever since, and will be to the end of the world.

The lesson taught by our Lord's dealing with the woman of Canaan is conveyed again on a larger scale by what happened in the region of Decapolis, east of the Sea of Galilee; for it was in that region, as we learn from the more detailed account in the second Gospel, that the events which follow came to pass.

The distance from the one place to the other is considerable, and the route our Lord took was by no means direct. His object at this time seems to have been to court retirement as much as possible, that He might give Himself to the preparation of His disciples—and we may with reverence add, His own preparation also—for the sad journey southward to Jerusalem and Calvary. Besides, His work in the north is done: no more circuits in Galilee now; so He keeps on the far outskirts of the land, passing through Sidon, across the southern ridge of Lebanon, past the base of mighty Hermon, then southward to Decapolis—all the way on border territory, where the people were more heathen than Jewish in race and religion. We can imagine Him on this long and toilsome journey, looking in both directions with strange emotion —away out to the Gentile nations with love and longing; and (with what mingled feelings of pain and eagerness who can tell?) to that Jerusalem, where soon He must offer up the awful sacrifice. When, after the long journey, He came nigh to the Sea of Galilee, He sought seclusion by going up into a mountain. But even in this borderland He cannot be hid; and when the sick and needy throng around Him, He cannot turn away from them. He still keeps within the limits of His commission, as set forth in His reply to the woman of Canaan; but, though He does not go to seek out those beyond the pale, when they seek

Him, He cannot send them away; accordingly, in these heathen or semi-heathen regions, we have another set of cures and another feeding of the hungry multitude.

We need not dwell on these incidents, as they are a repetition, with variations, of what He had done at the conclusion of His work in Galilee. As to the repetition,—strange to say, there are those who cavil, whenever similar events appear successively in the story of the life and work of Christ. As if it were possible that a work like His could be free from repetition! How often does a physician repeat himself in the course of his practice? Christ is always repeating Himself. Every time a sinner comes to Him for salvation, He repeats Himself, with variations; and when need arose in Decapolis—like that which had previously arisen at Bethsaida, only more urgent, for the multitude in the present case had been three days from home, and were ready to faint with hunger—must their wants go unrelieved merely to avoid repetition? As to the telling of it—for this of course might have been avoided, on the ground that a similar event had been related before—was there not most excellent reason for it, in the fact that these people were not of the house of Israel in the literal sense? To have omitted the record of these deeds of mercy would have been to leave out the evidence they afforded that the love of Christ went out not to Jews only, but to all sick and hungry ones.

Sick and hungry—these words suggest the two great needs of humanity. Christ comes to heal disease, to satisfy hunger; in particular, to heal the root disease of sin, and satisfy the deep hunger of the soul for God and life in Him. And when we read how He healed all manner of disease among the multitudes in Decapolis, and thereafter fed them abundantly when they were ready to faint with hunger, we see how He is set forth as a Saviour from sin and Revealer of God beyond the borders of the land of Israel.

It is worth noticing how well this general record follows the story of the woman of Canaan. Just as she—though not of Israel after the flesh—proved herself to be of Israel after the spirit, so these heathen or semi-heathen people of Decapolis forsake their paganism when they see the Christ; for of no heathen deity do they speak: they "glorified the God of Israel" (ver. 31). Thus we have a contrast similar to that which we recognised in the case of the woman of Canaan, between those scribes and Pharisees of Jerusalem—who drew near to the God of Israel with their lips while the heart was far away—and these people of Decapolis, who, though "afar off" in the estimation of these dignitaries of Jerusalem, are in truth "nigh" to the God of Israel. Is there not in the events of the chapter a wondrous light cast on the true meaning of the name Israel, as not according to the flesh, but according to the spirit?

IV.—The Culmination of the Crisis (xvi. 1-12).

All this time Jesus has been keeping as much out of the way of His ungrateful countrymen as the limits of His commission would permit, hovering, as it were, around the northern outskirts of the land. But when in the course of this largest circuit of all His northern journeys, He reaches Decapolis, He is so near home that He cannot but cross the lake and revisit the familiar scenes. How is He received? Do the people flock around Him as they did before? If it had been so, we should no doubt have been told. There seems to have been not a single word of welcome. Of all the multitudes He had healed and blessed, there is no one to cry, "Hosanna to the Son of David!"

His friends, if He has any, have gone back, and walk no more with Him; but His old enemies the Pharisees do not fail Him; and they are not alone now, nor, as before, in alliance only with those naturally in sympathy with them, but have actually made a league with their great opponents, the two rival parties of Pharisee and Sadducee finding in their common hatred of the Christ of God a sinister bond of union.

This is the first time the Sadducees are mentioned in this Gospel as coming in contact with Jesus. Some of them had come to the baptism of John, to his great astonishment; but, beyond this, they have as yet put in no appearance. They were the aristocracy of the land, and held the most important offices of Church and State in the capital. It is therefore the less to be wondered at that up to this time the Carpenter of Nazareth should have been beneath their notice. Now, however, the news of His great doings in the north has at last compelled attention; the result is this combination with the Pharisees, who have already been for some time engaged in the attempt to put Him down. There is indication elsewhere (Mark viii. 15) that the Herodians had also united with them; so we may look upon this as the culmination of the crisis in Galilee, when all the forces of the country have been roused to active and bitter hostility.

The Pharisees and Sadducees, as is well known, were at opposite poles of thought; the one being the traditionalists, the other the sceptics, of the time, so that it was quite remarkable that they should unite in anything. They did, however, unite in this demand for a sign from heaven. Neither of them could deny that signs had been given,—that the blind had received sight, lepers had been cleansed, the lame healed, and deeds of mercy done on every side. But neither party was satisfied with this. Each was wedded to a system of thought according to which signs on earth were of no evidential value. A sign from heaven was what they needed to convince them. The demand was practically the same as that which the Pharisees and scribes had made before (xii. 38), though it is put more specifically here as a sign *from heaven*. The reason why the Pharisees adopted the same method of attack as before is not far to seek. Their object was not to obtain satisfaction as to His claims, but to find the easiest way of discrediting them; and, knowing as they did from their past experience that the demand of a special sign would be refused, they counted on the refusal beforehand, to be used by their new allies as well as themselves as a weapon against Him. They were not disappointed, for our Lord was no respecter of persons; therefore He spoke just as plainly and sternly when the haughty Sadducees were present as He had done before they made their appearance.

The words are stern and strong; but here again it is "more in sorrow than in anger" that He speaks. We learn from St. Mark that, as He gave His answers, "He sighed deeply in His spirit." There had been so many signs, and they were so plain and clear—signs which spoke for themselves, signs which so plainly spelt out the words, "The kingdom of heaven is among you"—that it was unspeakably sad to think that they should be blind to them all, and find it in their heart to ask for something else, which in its nature would be no sign at all, but only a portent, a barren miracle.

We can see in this how determined our Lord was not to minister to the craving for the merely miraculous. He would work no miracle for the mere purpose of exciting astonishment or even of producing conviction, when there was quite enough for all who were at all willing to receive it, in the regular, natural, and necessary development of His work as the Healer of the sick, the Shepherd of the people, the Refuge of the troubled and distressed. Had there been no signs of the times, there might have been some reason for signs in the heavens; but when there were signs in abundance of the kind to appeal to all that was best in the minds and hearts of men, why should these be discredited by resorting to another kind of sign much inferior and far less adapted to the securing of the special object for which the King of heaven had come into the world? The signs of the times were after all far more easily discerned than those signs in the heavens by which they were accustomed to anticipate both fine and stormy weather. There were signs of blessing enough to convince any doubter that the summer of heaven was easily within His reach; on the other hand, in the state of the nation, and the rapidly developing circumstances which were hastening on the fulfilment of the most terrible of the prophecies concerning it, there were signs enough to give far more certain indication of approaching judgment, than when the red and lowering morning gave token of the coming thunderstorm (vv. 2, 3). So He tells them, convicting them of wilful blindness; and then repeats in almost identical terms the refusal He had given to the scribes and Pharisees before: "A wicked and adulterous generation seeketh after a sign; and there shall no sign be given unto it, but the sign of the prophet Jonas" (see xii. 39, and remarks on it on pp. 738-9).

"And He left them, and departed." How sad for Him; how awful for them! Had there been in their hearts one single aspiration for the true and good, He would not have left them so. Where are these Pharisees and Sadducees now? What do they now think of the work of that day?

"He left them, and again entering into the boat departed to the other side" (Mark viii. 13). Did He ever cross the lake again? If He did, there is no record of it. He passed in sight of it in that sorrowful southward journey to Jerusalem which He must presently commence; and He will visit the same shore again after His resurrection to cheer the apostles at their toil; but this seems to have been the last crossing. What a sad one it must have been!—after a beginning so bright that it was heralded as daybreak on Gennesaret's shore, after all His self-denying toil, after all the words of wisdom He has spoken and the deeds of mercy He has done upon these shores, to leave them, as He does now, rejected and despised, an outcast, to all outward appearance a failure. No wonder He is silent in that crossing of the lake; no wonder He is lost in saddest thought, turning over and over in His mind the signs of the times forced so painfully on His attention!

The disciples with Him in the boat had no share in these sad thoughts. Their minds, as it would seem, were occupied for the most part with the mistake they had made in provisioning the boat. Accordingly, when at last He broke silence, He found them quite out of touch with Him. He had been thinking of the sad unbelief of these Pharisees and Sadducees, and of the awful danger of allowing the spirit which was in them to dominate the life; hence the solemn caution: "Take heed, and beware of the leaven of the Pharisees and of the Sadducees." The disciples meantime had been counting their loaves, or rather, looking sadly on the one loaf which, on searching their baskets, they found to be all they had; and when the word *leaven* caught their ear, coupled with a caution as to a particular kind of it, they said one to another, "It is because we have taken no bread!" Another cause of sadness to the Master. He had been mourning over the blindness of Pharisees and Sadducees; He must now mourn over the blindness of His own disciples; and not blindness only, but also forgetfulness of a thrice-taught lesson: for why should the mere supply of bread be any cause of anxiety to them, after what they had seen once and again in these very regions to which they were going?

But these hearts were not shut against Him; theirs was not the blindness of those that will not see; accordingly, the result is very different. He did not leave them and depart; nor, on the other hand, did He explain in so many words what He meant. It was far better that they should find out for themselves. The riddles of nature and of life are not furnished with keys. They must be discerned by thoughtful attention; so, instead of providing them a key to His little parable, He puts them in the way of finding it for themselves by asking them a series of questions which convinced them of their thoughtlessness and faithlessness, and led them to recognise His true meaning (vv. 8-12).

CHAPTER XIII.

THE NEW DEPARTURE.

(FOUNDING OF THE CHURCH.)

MATTHEW xvi. 13-xvii. 21.

THIS conversation at Cæsarea Philippi is universally regarded as marking a new era in the life of Christ. His rejection by "His own" is now complete. Jerusalem, troubled at His birth, had been troubled once again when He suddenly came to His Temple, and began to cleanse it in His Father's name; and though many at the feast were attracted by His deeds of mercy, He could not commit Himself to any of them (John ii. 24): there was no rock there on which to build His Church. He had passed through Samaria, and found there fields white unto the harvest, but the time of reaping was not yet. Galilee had given better promise: again and again it had appeared as if the foundation of the new kingdom would be firmly laid in the land of "Zebulun and Naphtali"; but there had been bitter and crushing disappointment,—even the cities where most of His mighty works were done repented not.

The people had eagerly welcomed His earthly things; but when He began to speak to them of heavenly things they "went back, and walked no more with Him." And though opportunity after opportunity was given them while He hovered on the outskirts, ever and anon returning * to the familiar scenes, they would not repent; they would not welcome or even receive the kingdom of God which Christ came to found. The country has been traversed from the wilderness of Judea, in the far south, even unto Dan; and as there had been no room for the Infant King in the inn, so there was none in all the land for the infant kingdom.

Thus it comes to pass that, with the very small band He has gathered around Him—called in the land indeed, but now of necessity called to come out of it—He withdraws to the neighbourhood of the Gentile town of Cæsarea Philippi; not for seclusion only, but, as the event shows, to found an *Ecclesia*—His Church. The scenery in this region is exceptionally beautiful, and the place was in every way suited for a season of quiet communion with nature and with nature's God. It was, moreover, just outside the land; and in the place and surroundings there was much that must have been suggestive and inspiring. Is not this great mountain, on one of the southern flanks of which they are now resting, the mighty Hermon, the great landmark of the north, rearing its snowy head on high to catch the precious clouds of heaven, and enrich with them the winds that shall blow southward over Palestine? And are not these springs which issue from the rock beside them the sources of the Jordan, the sacred river? As the dew of Hermon, and as the flowing of the water-springs, shall be that Church of the living God, which, as the sequel will unfold, had its first foundation on this rocky hillside and by these river sources.

Into this remote and rocky region, then, the Master has retired with the small band of faithful disciples, on whom alone He can depend for the future. But can He depend even on them? Have they not been tainted with the general apostasy? Does He not already know one of them to be in heart a traitor? (*cf.* John vi. 70). And have not all of them just needed the caution themselves to beware of the leaven of the Pharisees and Sadducees? Are they really strong men of faith, like "faithful Abraham," or are they to be like reeds shaken by the wind? The time has come to test it. This He does, first by asking them what they think of Himself, and then by showing them what they must expect if they still will follow Him. First there must be the test of faith, to ascertain what they have learned from their intercourse with Him in the past; then the test of hope, lest their attachment to Him should be based on expectations doomed to disappointment.

I.—The Christ (xvi. 13-20).

The faith test is a strictly personal one. We have seen how the Master has, so to speak, focussed His gospel in Himself. He had begun by preaching the Gospel of the Kingdom, and calling men to repentance; but as time passed on He found it necessary to make a more personal appeal, pressing His invitations in the winning form, "Come unto Me." When things came to a crisis in Galilee He first in symbol and then in word set Himself before the people as the bread of life, which each one must receive and eat if he would live. Thus He has been making it more and more evident that the only way to receive the Kingdom of God is to welcome Himself as the Son of the living God come to claim the hearts of men for His Father in heaven. How is it with the little band? Is theirs the popular notion, which classes the Son of God as only one among other gifted sons of men, or do they welcome Him in the plenitude of His divine prerogative and power? Hence the first inquiry, which brings out the answer: "Some say that Thou art John the Baptist: some, Elias; and others, Jeremias, or one of the prophets." This is manifestly the popular idea at its highest and best. There were, no doubt, among the people those whose thought already was "Away with Him! away with Him!" But it might well go without saying that the disciples had no sympathy with these. It did, however, remain to be seen whether they were not content, like the rest of the people, to accept Him as a teacher sent from God, a great prophet of Israel, or at most a John the Baptist, the mere herald of the coming King. We can imagine, then, with what intensity of feeling the Master would look into the disciples' eyes as He put the testing question, "But whom say *ye* that I am?" and with what joy He would hail the ready response of their spokesman Peter, when, with eyes full of heavenly light and heart glowing with sacred fire, he exclaimed, "Thou art the Christ, the Son of the living God!"

It would be beyond belief, were it not so sadly familiar a fact, that some, professing honestly to interpret this passage, resolve the answer of the apostle into little or nothing more than the popular idea, as if the Sonship here referred to were only what any prophet or righteous man might claim. He surely must be wilfully blind who does not see that the apostolic answer which the Lord accepts is wide as the poles from the popular notions He so decisively rejects; and this is made peculiarly emphatic by the striking words with which the true answer is welcomed—the Saviour's first personal beatitude (as if to suggest, His is the kingdom of heaven—*cf.* Matt. v. 3, 10): "Blessed art thou, Simon Bar-jona: for flesh and blood hath not revealed it unto thee, but My Father which is in heaven." It will be remembered that, in asserting His own personal relation to the Father, Christ had said: "No man knoweth the Son, but the Father; neither knoweth any man the Father, save the Son, and he to whomsoever the Son will reveal Him" (xi. 27); and now that to one at least the Father has been revealed in the Son, He recognises the fact with joy. These notions of the people about Him were but earth-born notions, the surmisings of "flesh and blood": this faith of the true apostle was born from above; it could have come only from heaven.

Now at last, therefore, the foundation is laid, and the building of the spiritual temple is begun. The words which follow (ver. 18) are quite natural and free from most, if not from

* A touching fulfilment of the Messianic spirit of these prophetic words: "How shall I give thee up, Ephraim? how shall I deliver thee, Israel? how shall I make thee as Admah? how shall I set thee as Zeboim? mine heart is turned within me, my repentings are kindled together." Compare chap, xi. 21-24.

all, the difficulties in which perverse human ingenuity has entangled them, if only we bear in mind the circumstances and surroundings. The little group is standing on one of the huge rocky flanks of mighty Hermon, great boulders here and there around them; and in all probability, well in sight, some great stones cut out of the rock and made ready for use in building, like those still to be seen in the neighbourhood of Baalbec, to the north of Hermon; for this region was famous for its great temples. Now, when we remember that the two words our Lord uses (πέτρος and πέτρα) for "rock" in our version have not precisely the same meaning—the one (Petros, Peter) signifying a piece of rock, a stone, the other (Petra) suggesting rather the great bed-rock out of which these stones are cut and on which they are lying—we can understand that, while the reference is certainly in the first place to Peter himself, the main thing is the great fact just brought out that he is resting, in the strength of faith, on God as revealed in His Son. Thus, while Peter is certainly the piece of rock, the first stone which is laid upon the great underlying foundation on which all the faithful build, and therefore is in a sense—the common popular sense, in fact—the foundation stone, yet the foundation of all is the Bed-Rock, on which the first stone and all other stones are laid. Bearing this well in mind, we further see that there is no inconsistency between this and those other scriptures in which God is represented as alone the Rock of our salvation. The Bed-Rock, "the Rock of Ages," is here, as elsewhere, God as revealed in His Son, and Peter is the first stone "well and truly laid" upon it.

If the surroundings suggest the use of the words "Petros" and "Petra," stone and rock, the circumstances suggest the use of the word Ecclesia, or Church, which is here employed by our Lord for the first time. Up to this time He has spoken always of the kingdom, never of the church. How is this to be explained? Of course the kingdom is the larger term; and now it is necessary that that portion of the kingdom which is to be organised on earth should be distinguished by a specific designation; and the use of the word "church" in preference to the more familiar "synagogue" may be accounted for by the desire to avoid confusion. Besides this, however, the word itself is specially significant. It means an assembly "called out," and suggests the idea of separateness, so appropriate to the circumstances of the little band of outcasts.

To see into this more fully let us recall the recent teaching as to the true Israel (chap. xv.), no longer to be found in the old land of Israel. If there is to be an Israel at all, it must be reconstituted "outside the camp." In view of this, how strikingly significant is it that just as Abraham had to leave his country and go to a strange land to found the old theocracy, so Christ has to leave His country and go with His followers to those remote northern regions to constitute "*the Israel of God*," to inaugurate His Church, the company of those who, like these faithful ones, come out and are separate to be united by faith to Him! Christ with the Twelve around Him is the Israel of the New Testament; and we can imagine that it was on this occasion especially that in the prayers which we know from St. Luke's Gospel He offered in connection with this very conversation, He would find these words of devotion especially appropriate: "Behold, I and the children which God hath given Me" (Heb. ii. 13). The family of God (see chap. xii. 49) are by themselves apart, disowned by those who still bear unworthily the name of Israel; and most appropriate it is that on this occasion our Lord should begin to use that great word, which means first "called out" and then "gathered in": "on this rock I will build My CHURCH."

When we think of the place and the scene and the circumstances, the sad memories of the past and the gloomy forebodings for the future, what sublimity of faith must we recognise in the words which immediately follow: "The gates of hell shall not prevail against it"! Oh! shame on us who grow faint-hearted with each discouragement, when the Master, with rejection behind Him and death before Him, found it encouragement enough after so much toil to make a bare beginning of the new temple of the Lord; and even in that day of smallest things was able to look calmly forward across the troubled sea of the dark future and already raise the shout of final victory!

But that day of victory is still far off; and before it can even begin to come, there must be a descent into the valley of the shadow of death. He is about to tell His disciples that He must go up to Jerusalem and die, and leave them to be the builders of the Church. He cannot continue long to be the Keeper of the keys; so He must prepare them for taking them from His hand when the time shall come for Him to go. Hence the words which follow, appropriately addressed in the first place to the disciple who had first confessed Him: "I will give unto thee the keys of the kingdom of heaven." "Honour to whom honour is due:" the first member of the Church is to be its prime minister as well. When the Master's voice shall be silent, the voice of the rock-disciple (and of the other disciples as well, for the same commission was afterwards extended to them all) shall have the same authority to bind, to loose, to regulate the administration of Church affairs as if He Himself were with them. It is not yet time to tell them how it would be—viz., by the coming and indwelling of His Spirit; it is enough now to give them the assurance that the infant Church shall not be left without authority from above, without power from on high.

The Church is founded; but for a time it must remain in obscurity. The people are not ready; and the gospel, which is to be the power of God unto salvation, is not yet complete, until He shall go up to Jerusalem and suffer many things and die. Till then all that has passed in this sacred northern retreat must remain a secret: "He charged His disciples that they should tell no man that He was the Christ" (R. V.).

II.—THE CROSS (xvi. 21-28).

A still more searching test must now be applied. It is not enough to discover what they have learned from their intercourse with Him in the past; He must find out whether they have courage enough to face what is now impending in the future. Their faith in God as revealed in Christ His Son has been well approved. It remains to be seen whether it is strong enough to bear the ordeal of the cross, to which it must soon be subjected: "From that time forth began Jesus to show unto His disciples how that He must go unto Jerusalem and suffer many things of the elders and chief priests and scribes, and be killed."

Already from time to time He had darkly hinted what manner of death He should die; but it was only from this time that He began to *show* it unto them, to put it before them so that they could not fail to see it. Herein see the wisdom and tender considerateness of "the Son of man." So dark and difficult a lesson would have been too much for them before. The ordeal would have been too severe. Not until their faith has begun with some firmness to grasp His true and proper divinity, can their hope live with such a prospect. There must be some basis for a faith in His rising again, before He can ask them even to look into the dark abyss of death into which He must descend. That basis is found in the confession of the rock-apostle; and relying on it He can trust them by-and-by, if not at once, to look through the darkness of the suffering and death to the rising again, the prospect of which He sets before them at the very same time: "and be raised again the third day." Besides, there was no possibility of their ever beginning to understand the atonement till they had grasped the truth of the incarnation. To this day the one is intelligible only in the light of the other. Those to whom Jesus of Nazareth is only "one of the prophets" cannot begin to see how He *must* suffer and die. Only those who with the apostles rise to the realisation of His divine glory are prepared to understand anything of the mystery of His Cross and Passion.

As yet, however, the mystery is too deep and the prospect too dark even for them, as becomes painfully evident from the conduct of the bravest of them all, who "took Him, and began to rebuke Him, saying, Be it far from Thee, Lord: this shall not be unto Thee."

We naturally and properly blame the presumption of the apostle, who, when he did not understand, might at least have been silent, or have contented himself with some modest question, instead of this unbecoming remonstrance with One Whose Messiahship and Divine Sonship he had just confessed. But, though we may blame him for what he said, we cannot wonder at what he thought and felt. The lesson of the cross is just beginning. The disciples are just entering a higher form in the Master's school; and it does not follow, because they have undergone so well their examination on the great lesson of the past, that they are prepared all at once to take in what must be the great lesson of the future. They have had time for the first: may they not be allowed time for the second? Why, then, is Peter reproved so very severely?

We may say, indeed, that faithfulness to Peter himself required it. The strong commendation with which his noble confession has been greeted, instead of making him humble, as it ought to have done, inasmuch as it reminded him that it was not of himself but from above he had the power to make it, seems to have made him over-confident, trustful to that very flesh and blood to which he had been assured he was, in regard to that confession, in no wise indebted. It was therefore necessary that the warm commendation accorded to the strength of his faith should be balanced by an equally strong condemnation of his unbelief. But there is more than this to be said. Christ is looking at Peter, and speaking to Peter; but he recognises *another*, whom He names and whom in the first place he addresses: "Get thee behind Me, Satan." He recognises the same old enemy, with the same old weapon of assault; for it is the same temptation as that which formed the climax of the conflict in the wilderness, a temptation to prosecute His work by methods which would spare Him the awful agony of the cross. The devil had departed from Him then; but only, as we were informed, "for a season"; and there are frequent indications in the subsequent history that at critical times the great adversary took opportunities of renewing the old temptation. This is one of these occasions. Let us by all means bear in mind that our Lord was true man—that He was "compassed with infirmity," that He was "tempted in all points like as we are," though ever without sin; let us not imagine, then, that His human soul was always on so serene a height that the words of one who loved Him and whom He loved so much would have no effect on Him. It was hard enough for Him to face the awful darkness, without having this new stumbling-block set in His path. It is a real temptation, and a most dangerous one; He may not therefore tamper with it for a moment: He may not allow His affection for His true disciple to blind Him to the real source of it; He must realise with whom He has to deal; He must behind the love of the apostle recognise the malice of the evil one, who is using him as his instrument; accordingly, with His face set as a flint, with His whole being braced for resistance, so that not a hair's-breadth shall be yielded, He says: "Get thee behind Me, Satan: thou art a stumbling-block unto Me" (R. V.)—words which clearly indicate that He had recognised the danger, and summoned the resources of His faith and obedience to put the stumbling-block away.

"Resist the devil, and he will flee from you." We may be sure, therefore, that so soon as the energetic words were spoken *he* was gone: the stumbling-block was out of the way. The words which follow may therefore be regarded as spoken to Peter himself, to bring to his own consciousness the difference between the heavenly faith which had come by revelation from above, and the earthly doubt and denial, which was evidently not of God, though so natural to flesh and blood: "Thou mindest not the things of God, but the things of men" (R. V.).

Thus once more the Christ of God takes up the cross of man. In doing so He not only sets aside the protest, uttered or unexpressed, of His disciples' hearts; but He tells them plainly that they too must take the same dark path if they would follow Him: "Then said Jesus unto His disciples, If any man will come after Me, let him deny himself, and take up his cross, and follow Me." So He tests them to the uttermost. He withdraws nothing He has said about the blessedness of those who welcome the kingdom of heaven; but the time has come to put the necessary condition in its strongest light, so that, if they still follow, it will be not blindly, but with eyes fully open to all that it involves. He has given hints before of the stringency of the Divine requirement; He has spoken of the strait gate and the narrow way; now He goes to the very heart of that hard matter, and unfolds the innermost secret of the kingdom of heaven. "Let him deny himself:" here is the pivot of all—the *crux*.

Be it observed that this is not "self-denial" as currently understood, a term applied to the denial to self of something or other which perhaps self cares very little about, but something much more radical. It is the denial of self involving as its correlative the giving of the life to God. It is the death of self-will, and the birth of God-will,* as the central force of the life.

"Let him deny himself, *and take up his cross*." Each one has "his" cross, some point in which the will of God and self-will come in direct opposition. To the Captain of our salvation the conflict came in its very darkest and most dreadful form. Its climax was in the Garden, when after the great agony He cried: "Not My will, but Thine be done." Our conflict will not be nearly so severe: it may even be on a point that may seem small,—whether or not we will give up some besetting sin, whether or not we will do some disagreeable duty, whether or not we will surrender something which stands between us and Christ,—but whatever that be in which the will of God and our own will are set in opposition, there is our cross, and it must be taken up, and self must be denied that we may follow Christ. "They that are Christ's have *crucified the flesh*."

Is this, then, the great salvation? Does it resolve itself into a species of suicide? Do we enter the kingdom of life by death? It is even so; and the words which follow resolve the paradox: "For whosoever will save his life shall lose it: and whosoever will lose his life for My sake shall find it." It is a surrender of life, certainly, for the giving up of self means the giving up of all; but these words "for My sake" make all the difference. It is a surrender which, in dethroning self, enthrones Christ in the life. It is dying indeed; but it is dying into life: it is an act of faith which puts an end to the old life of the flesh, and opens the gate for the new life of the spirit.

We have seen that all may hinge on some point that may seem quite small, in which case the sacrifice is plainly not to be compared with the compensation; but even when the very greatest sacrifice is demanded, it is folly not to make it: "For what shall a man be profited, if he shall gain the whole world, and forfeit his life?" (R. V.). And, if life is forfeited, how can it be bought back again: "What shall a man give in exchange for his life" (R. V.)? "In Him was life," and in Him is life still; therefore He is more to us than all the world. It is better to suffer the loss of all things for Christ than to have all that flesh and blood could desire without Him.

The world is very large; and the Son of man must have seemed very small and weak that day, as He told them of the coming days when He should suffer so many things at His enemies' hands, and die; but this is only while the time of testing lasts: things will be seen in their true proportion by-and-by, when "the Son of man shall come" (what a golden background this to the dark prospect immediately before them! He *must go;* yes; but He *shall come*) "in the glory of His Father with His angels; then He shall reward every man according to his works." Thus, with the searching test the Saviour gives the reassuring prospect; and lest by reason of its indefinite distance they may fail to find in it all the encouragement they need for the present distress, He gives them the further assurance that, before very long, there shall be manifest tokens of the coming glory of their now despised and slighted King: "Verily I say unto you, There be some standing here, which shall not taste of death till they see the Son of man coming in His kingdom."

* "Our wills are ours, we know not how:
Our wills are ours, *to make them Thine*."

III.—The Glory (xvii. 1-8).

"After six days"—the interval is manifestly of importance, for the three Evangelists who record the event all lay stress on it. St. Luke says "about an eight days," which indicates that the six days referred to by the others were days of interval between that on which the conversation at Cæsarea Philippi took place and the morning of the transfiguration. It follows that we may regard this important epoch in the life of our Lord as covering a week; and may we not speak of it as His passion week in the north? The shadow of the cross was on Him all His life through; but it must have been much darker during this week than ever before. At the beginning of it He had been obliged for the first time to let that shadow fall upon His loved disciples, and the days which followed seem to have been given to thought and prayer, and quiet, unrecorded conversation. Beyond all question their thought would be fixed on the new subject of contemplation which had just been brought before them, and whatever conversation they had with one another and with the Master would have this for its centre. It cannot but have been a very sad and trying week. The first tidings of the approach of some impending disaster is often harder to bear than is the stroke itself when afterwards it falls. To the disciples the whole horizon of the future would be filled with darkest clouds of mystery; for though they had been told also of the rising again and the glory that should follow, they could as yet get little cheer from what lay so far in the dim distance, and was, moreover, so little understood that even after the vision on the mount, the favoured three questioned with each other what the rising from the dead might mean (Mark ix. 10). To the Master the awful prospect must have been much more definite and real; yet even to His human soul it could not have been free from that namelessness of mystery that must have made the anticipation in some respects as bad as the reality, rendering the week to Him a passion week indeed.

No wonder that at the end of it He has a great longing heavenward, and that He should ask the three most advanced of His disciples, who had been with Him in the chamber of death and were afterwards to be witnesses of His agony in the Garden, to go with Him to a high mountain apart. The wisdom of His taking only these three was afterwards fully apparent, when it proved that the experience awaiting them on the mountain-top was almost too much for even them to bear. It is of no importance to identify the mountain; probably it was one of the spurs of the Hermon range, at the base of which they had spent the intervening week. We can perfectly understand the sacred instinct which led the Saviour to seek the highest point which could be readily reached, so as to feel Himself for the time as far away from earth and as near to heaven as possible. When we think of this, what pathos is there in the reference to the height of the mountain and the loneliness of the spot: He "bringeth them up into a high mountain apart"!

We are told by St. Luke that they went up "to pray." It seems most natural to accept this statement as not only correct, but as a sufficient statement of the object our Saviour had in view. The thought of transfiguration may not have been in His mind at all. Here, as always, He was guided by the will of His Father in heaven; and it is not necessary to suppose that to His human mind that will was made known earlier than the occasion required. We are not told that He went up to be transfigured: we are told that He went up to pray.

It seems probable that the idea was to spend the night in prayer. We know that this was a not infrequent custom with Him; and if ever there seemed a call for it, it must have been now, when about to begin that sorrowful journey which led to Calvary. With this thought agree all the indications which suggest that it was evening when they ascended, night while they remained on the top, and morning when they came down. This, too, will account in the most natural manner for the drowsiness of the apostles; and the fact that their Lord felt none of it only proved how much more vivid was his realisation of the awfulness of the crisis than theirs was. We are to think of the four, then, as slowly and thoughtfully climbing the hill at eventide, carrying their *abbas,* or rugs, on which they would kneel for prayer, and which, if they needed rest, they would wrap around them, as is the Oriental custom. By the time they reached the top, night would have cast its veil of mystery on the grandeur of the mountains round about them; while snowy Hermon in the gloom would rise like a mighty giant to heaven, its summit "visited all night by troops of stars." Never before nor since has there been such a prayer meeting on this earth of ours.

A careful reading of all the records leads us to think of the following as the order of events. Having gone up to pray, they would doubtless all kneel down together. As the night wore on, the three disciples, being exhausted, would wrap themselves in their cloaks and go to sleep; while the Master, to whom sleep at such a time was unnatural, if not impossible, would continue in prayer. Can we suppose that that time of pleading was free from agony? His soul had been stirred within Him when Peter had tempted Him to turn aside from the path of the Cross; and may we not with reverence suppose that on that lonely hilltop, as later in the Garden, there might be in His heart the cry, "Father, if it be possible"? If only the way upward were open now! Has not the kingdom of God been preached in Judea, in Samaria, in Galilee, away to the very borderlands? and has not the Church been founded? and has not authority been given to the apostles? Is it, then, absolutely necessary to go back, back to Jerusalem, not to gain a triumph, but to accept the last humiliation and defeat? There cannot but have been a great conflict of feeling; and with all the determination to be obedient even unto death, there must have been a shrinking from the way of the cross, and a great longing for heaven and home and the Father's welcome. The longing cannot be gratified: it is not possible for the cup to pass from Him; but just as later in Gethsemane there came an angel from heaven strengthening him, so now His longing for heaven and home and the smile of His Father is gratified in the gladdening and strengthening experience which followed His prayer—a foretaste of the heavenly glory, so vivid, so satisfying, that He will thenceforth be strong, for the joy that is set before Him, to endure the Cross, despising the shame. For behold, as He prays, His face becomes radiant, the glory within shining through the veil of His mortal flesh. We all know that this flesh of ours is more or less transparent, and that in moments of exaltation the faces of even ordinary men will shine as with a heavenly lustre. We need not wonder, then, that it should have been so with our Lord, only in an immeasurably higher degree: that His face should have shone even "as the sun"; and that, though He could not yet ascend to heaven, heaven's brightness should have descended on Him and wrapped Him round, so that even "His raiment was white as the light." And not only heavenly light is round, but heavenly company; for "behold, there appeared unto them Moses and Elias talking with Him."

The disciples could not sleep through all this. "When they were fully awake, they saw His glory, and the two men that stood with Him" (Luke ix. 32, R. V.). How they recognised them we are not told. It may have been through their conversation, which in part at least they understood; for the substance of it has been preserved in St. Luke's Gospel, where we read that they "spake of His decease (literally, *exodus*) which He should accomplish at Jerusalem." The human soul of Jesus no doubt longed for an exodus here and now, from this very height of Hermon in the presence of God; but He knows this cannot be: His exodus must be accomplished in a very different way, and at Jerusalem. This Moses and Elijah knew; and their words must have brought Him encouragement and strength, and given steadiness and assurance to the wavering hearts of Peter, James, and John.

That the conversation was intended for their benefit as well, seems indicated by the way in which Peter's intervention is recorded: "Then *answered* Peter, and said unto Jesus." What he said is quite characteristic of the impulsive discipline, so ready to speak without thinking. On this occasion he blunders in a very natural and pardonable way. He feels as if he ought to say something; and, as nothing more to the purpose occurs to him, he blurts out his thoughtless proposal to make three tabernacles for their abode. Besides the thoughtlessness of this speech, which is manifest enough, there seems to lurk in it a sign of his falling back into the very error which a week ago he had renounced—the error of putting his Master in the same class as Moses and Elias, reckoning Him thus, as the people of Galilee had done, simply as "one of the prophets." If so, his mistake is at once corrected; for behold a bright luminous cloud—fit symbol of the Divine presence: the cloud suggesting mystery, and the brightness, glory—wraps all from sight, and out of the cloud there comes a voice:

"This is My beloved Son, in Whom I am well pleased; hear ye Him."

We now see how appropriate it was that just these two should be the heavenly messengers to wait upon the Son of man on this occasion. The one represented the law, the other the prophets. "The law and the prophets were until John;" but both are now merged in the gospel of Jesus, Who is all and in all. Moses and Elijah have long had audience of the people of God; but behold a greater than Moses or Elijah is here, and they must withdraw; and accordingly, when the Voice is silent and the cloud has cleared away, Jesus is left alone. No one remains to divide His authority and none to share His sorrow. He must tread the winepress alone. Moses and Elijah return to the world of spirits—Jesus, God's beloved Son, to the world of men. And all His human sympathies were fresh and quick as ever; for, finding His three disciples fallen on their faces for fear, He came and touched them, saying, "Arise, and be not afraid." They no doubt thought their Lord had laid aside His human body, and left them all alone upon the mountain; but with His human hand He touched them, and with His human voice He called them as of old, and with His human heart He welcomed them again. Reassured, they lifted up their eyes, and saw their Lord—the man Christ Jesus as before—and no one else. All is over; and as the world is unprepared for it, the vision is sealed until the Son of man be risen from the dead.

Why were their lips sealed? The more we think of it, the more we shall see the wisdom of this seal of secrecy, even from the other nine; for had they been prepared to receive the revelation, they would have been privileged to witness it. The transfiguration was no mere wonder; it was no sign granted to incredulity: it was one of those sacred experiences for rare spirits in rare hours, which nature itself forbids men to parade, or even so much as mention, unless constrained to it by duty.

It is one of the innumerable notes of truth found, wherever aught that is marvellous is recorded in these Gospels, that the glory on the mount is not appealed to, to confirm the faith of any but the three who witnessed it. Upon them it did produce a deep and abiding impression. One of them, indeed, died a martyr's death so very early that we have nothing from his pen (Acts xii. 2); but both the others have left us words written late in their after life, which show how ineffaceable was the impression produced upon them by what they saw that memorable night. John evidently has it in mind, both in the beginning of his Epistle and of his Gospel, as where he says: "We beheld His glory, the glory as of the only begotten of the Father;" and Peter thus conveys the assurance which the experience of that night left with him to the end: "We have not followed cunningly devised fables, when we made known unto you the power and coming of our Lord Jesus Christ, but were eyewitnesses of His majesty. For He received from God the Father honour and glory, when there came such a voice to Him from the excellent glory, This is My beloved Son, in Whom I am well pleased. And this voice which came from heaven we heard, when we were with Him in the holy mount." But while the impression made upon the three who witnessed it was so deep and abiding, it could not be expected to have any direct evidential value to others; accordingly it remained unused in their dealings with others until their Master's work had been crowned by His resurrection from the dead, which was to be *the* sign, as He had again and again said to those who kept asking Him for a sign from heaven. The transfiguration was indeed a sign from heaven; but it was no sign for a faithless generation: it was only for those who by the strength of their faith and the purity of their devotion were prepared to receive it. Signs fitted to satisfy the doubting heart had been wrought in great abundance (xi. 4, 5); and the crowning sign was to be certified by many infallible proofs, after which it would be time to speak of the experience of that sacred night upon the holy mount.

How fitly the transfiguration closes this memorable week! As we linger with the Lord and His disciples at the sources of the Jordan, we realise that we have reached what we may call the water-shed of doctrine in His training of the Twelve. Slowly have they been rising in their thoughts of Christ, until at last they recognise His true divinity, and make a clear and full confession of it. But no sooner have they reached that height of truth than they are constrained to look down into the dark valley before them, at the bottom of which they dimly see the dreadful cross; and then, to comfort and reassure, there is this vision of the glory that shall follow. Thus we have, in succession, the three great doctrines of the faith: Incarnation, Atonement, Resurrection. There is first the glory of Christ as the Son of God; then His shame as Bearer of our sin; then the vision of the glory that shall follow, the glory given to Him as His reward. For may we not regard that company upon the mount as a miniature of the Church in heaven and on earth? There was the great and glorified Head of the Church, and round Him five representative members: two from the family in heaven, three from the family on earth—those from the Church triumphant, these from the Church still militant—those from among the saints of the old covenant, these the firstfruits of the new. Could there have been a better representation of "the whole family in heaven and on earth"? How appropriate that the passion week of the north, which began with the founding of the Church in the laying of its first stone, should end with a vision of it as completed, which must to some extent have been a fulfilment of the promise, "He shall see of the travail of His soul, and shall be satisfied"!

Observe, too, in quick succession, the great key-words of the new age: The Christ (xvi. 16), The Church (ver. 18), The Cross (ver. 24), The Glory (ver. 27): the latter, as still in the future, made real by the glory on the holy mount. The mediæval interpreters, always on the watch for the symbolism of numbers, especially the number three, regarded Peter as the apostle of faith, James of hope, and John of love. And though we may set this aside as a touch of fancy, we cannot fail to observe that just as the mind, in its grasp of truth, is led from the incarnation to the atonement, and thence to the resurrection and the glory that shall follow; so the cardinal graces of the Christian life are called out in quick succession: first faith with its rock-foundation; then love with its self-sacrificing devotion; and finally hope with its vision of heavenly glory. The whole gospel of Christ, the whole life of the

Christian, is found in this brief passage of the first Evangelist, ending with the suggestive words, "Jesus only."

IV.—The Descent (xvii. 9-21).

Who can tell what each step downward cost the Son of man? If it seemed good to the disciples to be on the mountain-top, what must it have been to the Master! and what utter denial of self and conscious taking up of the cross it must have been to leave that hallowed spot! We have already seen a reason, as regards the disciples, why the vision should be sealed till the time of the end; but was there not also a reason which touched the Master Himself? It was well that He had enjoyed such a time of refreshing—it would be something to look back to in darkest hours; but it must be a memory only: it may not therefore be a subject of conversation—not the glory, but the cross, must now, both for Himself and for His disciples, fill all the near horizon.

This view of the case is confirmed by the manner in which He deals with their question respecting Elijah. It was a very natural question. It was no doubt perplexing in many ways to be absolutely forbidden to tell what they had seen; but it seemed especially mysterious in view of Elijah's appearance, which they not unnaturally regarded as a fulfilment of the prophecy for which the scribes were waiting. Hence their question, "Why, then, say the Scribes that Elias must first come?" Our Lord's answer turned their thoughts to the true fulfilment of the prophecy, which was no shadowy appearance on a lonely hill, but the real presence among the men of the time of a genuine reformer who had come in the spirit and power of Elijah, and who would certainly have restored all things, had not these very scribes and Pharisees, failing to recognise him, left him to the will of the tyrant who had done away with him. Then most significantly He adds, that as it had been with the Elijah, so would it be with the Messiah of the time: "Likewise shall also the Son of man suffer of them." Thus, in showing them where to look for the true fulfilment of the prophecy, He turns their attention as well as His own away from the glory on the mount, which must now be a thing of the past, to that dark scene in the prison cell, which was so painfully impressed upon their minds, and those still darker scenes in the near future of which it was the presage.

At the foot of the mountain there is presented one of those striking contrasts with which, as we have seen, this Gospel abounds. It is very familiar to us through Raphael's great painting; and we shall certainly not make the mistake of attempting to translate into our feeble words what is there seen, and may now be regarded as "known and read of all men." Leaving, therefore, to the imagination the contrast between the glory on the mount and the misery on the plain, let us briefly look at the scene itself. Briefly; for though it well deserves detailed treatment, the proper place for this would be the full record of it in the second Gospel; while the more general way in which it is presented here suggests the propriety of dealing with it in outline only. Without, then, attempting to enter on the striking and most instructive details to be found in St. Mark's Gospel, and without even dealing with it as we have endeavoured to deal with similar cures under the head of the Signs of the Kingdom, it may be well to glance at it in the light of the words used by our Lord when He was confronted with the sorrowful scene: "O faithless and perverse generation, how long shall I be with you? how long shall I suffer you?"

It seems evident from these words that He is looking at the scene, not so much as presenting a case of individual suffering, appealing to His compassion, as a representation in miniature of the helplessness and perverseness of the race of men He has come to save. Remember how well He knew what was in man, and therefore what it must have been to Him, immediately after such a season of pure and peaceful communion on the holy mount, to have to enter into sympathy with all the variety of helplessness and confusion He saw around Him. There is the poor plague-stricken boy in the centre; beside him his agonised father; there, the feeble and blundering disciples, and the scribes (Mark ix. 14) questioning with them; and all around the excited, sympathetic, and utterly perplexed multitude. Yet the kingdom of heaven is so near them, and has been so long proclaimed among them! Alas! alas for the perversity of men, that blinds them to the Sun of Righteousness, already arisen with healing in His wings, and for the unbelief even of the disciples themselves, which renders them, identified though they are with the kingdom, as helpless as all the rest! When we think of all this, need we wonder at the wail which breaks from the Saviour's sorrowful heart, need we wonder that He cries "How long? how long?"

"Bring him hither to Me." Here is the solvent of all. "From that very hour" the boy is cured, the father's heart is calmed and filled with gladness, the cavillers are silenced, the multitudes are satisfied, and the worn-out faith of the disciples is renewed. Out of chaos, order, out of tumult, peace, by a word from Christ. It was a wilder sea than Galilee at its stormiest; but at His rebuke the winds and waves were stilled, and there was a great calm.

So would it be still, if this generation were not perverse and faithless in its turn—the world perverse, the Church faithless. Above the stormy sea of human sin and woe and helplessness, there still is heard the lamentation "How long shall I be with you? how long shall I suffer you?" Here are we groaning and travailing in this late age of the world and of the Church, the worst kind of demons still working their will in their poor victims, the cry of anxious parents going up for lost children, disciples blundering and failing in well-meant efforts to cast the demons out, wise and learned scribes pointing at them the finger of scorn, excited and angry multitudes demanding satisfaction which they fail to get—Oh, if only all could hear the voice of the Son of man as the multitude heard it that day; and if we would only with one consent recognise the majesty of His face and mien as they did (see Mark ix. 15), bring to Him our plague-stricken ones, our devil-possessed, bring to Him our difficulties and perplexities, our vexed questions and our hard problems, would He not as of old bring order out of our chaos, and out of weakness make us strong? Oh, for more faith, faith to take hold of the Christ of God, come down from His holy habitation, and with us even to the end of the world, to bear the infirmities and carry the sorrows and take away the sins of men!—then should we be able to say to this mountain of evil under which our cities groan, "Be thou removed, and be thou cast into the sea," and it would be done. If only the Church of Christ in the world to-day had through all its membership that faith which is the only avenue by which the power of God can reach the need of man, our social problems would not long defy solution—"nothing would be impossible"; for over the millions of London, and the masses everywhere, there broods the same great heart of love and longing which prompted the gracious words, "Come unto Me, *all* ye that labour and are heavy laden, and I will give you rest;" and there is not a wretched one in all the world for whom there is not a blessed ray of hope in this pathetic wail which still proceeds from the loving heart of Him Who is the same yesterday and to-day and for ever. "O faithless and perverse generation, how long shall I be with you? how long shall I suffer you? *bring him hither to Me.*"

"Bring him hither"—this is a work of faith as well as a labour of love. The Church on earth is in the same position now as were the nine when the Master was absent from them on the mountain-top. He has ascended up on high, and the work must be carried on by the members of His body on the earth; and it is only in proportion to their faith that any success can attend them in their work.

Is faith, then, all that is necessary? It is: provided it be genuine living faith. This seems to be the point of the reference to the grain of mustard seed. The little seed, small as it is, is set in true relation to the great life-force of Mother Nature, and therefore out of it by-and-by there comes a mighty tree; and in the same way even feeble faith, if it be genuine, and therefore set in true relation to the power of the Father of our spirits, becomes receptive of a force which in the end nothing can resist. But genuine living faith it must be: there must be the real opening up of the soul to the Spirit of the living God, so that the man's nature becomes a channel through which unobstructed the grace and power of God shall flow. It need scarcely be remarked that the notion which mistakes faith for mere belief of certain doctrines is utterly misleading. In nothing is the perversity of a faithless generation more conspicuous than in the persistency with which this absurd and unscriptural notion of faith holds its ground, even with those who are supposed to be leaders of thought in certain directions. If only that mountain of folly could be cleared away, there would be a decided brightening of the spiritual outlook; for then men everywhere would see that the faith which Christ expects of them, and without which nothing can be accomplished, is no mere intellectual belief, but the laying open and leaving open of the entire nature to the Spirit of Christ. Thus spurious dead faith would be utterly discredited, and genuine living faith would alone be recognised; and while the first effect would be to disclose the exceeding scantiness of the Church's faith, the result would be that even though what stood the test should be small as a grain of mustard seed, it would have in it such vitality and power that by-and-by it would become mighty and all-pervading, so that before it mountains would disappear (ver. 20).

The last words of the paragraph * carry us back to the ultimate necessity for prayer. It is plain that our Lord refers to habitual prayer. We cannot suppose that these nine disciples had utterly neglected this duty; but they had failed to live in an atmosphere of prayer, as was their Master's rule. We may be sure that they had not prayed at the base of the mountain as their Lord had prayed on the summit, or they would certainly not have failed in their attempt to cure the lunatic child. This demand for prayer is not really anything additional to the faith set forth as the one thing needful. There has been a good deal of discussion lately as to whether we can think without words. We shall not presume to decide the question; but it may safely be affirmed that without words we could not think to any purpose. And just as the continuance and development of our thinking are dependent on words, so the continuance and development of our faith are dependent on prayer. Is not the weak spot of our modern Christianity just here? In this age of tear and wear, bustle and excitement, what becomes of prayer? If the amount of true wrestling with God in the daily life of the average Christian could be disclosed, the wonder might be, not that he accomplishes so little, but that God is willing to use him at all.

CHAPTER XIV.

LAST WORDS AT CAPERNAUM.

MATTHEW xvii. 22-xviii. 35.

THE TEMPLE TRIBUTE (xvii. 22-27.)

THE way southward lies through Galilee; but the time of Galilee's visitation is now over, so Jesus avoids public attention as much as possible, and gives Himself up to the instruction of His disciples, especially to impressing upon their minds the new lesson of the Cross, which they find it so very hard to realise, or even to understand. A brief stay in Capernaum was to be expected; and there above all places He could not hope to escape notice; but the manner of it is sadly significant—no friendly greeting, no loving welcome, not even any personal recognition, only a more or less entangling question as to the Temple tax, addressed, not to Christ Himself, but to Peter: "Doth not your Master pay the half-shekel?" (R. V.). The impulsive disciple showed his usual readiness by answering at once in the affirmative. He perhaps thought it was becoming his Master's dignity to show not a moment's hesitation in such a matter; but if so, he must have seen his mistake when he heard what his Lord had to say on the subject, reminding him as it did that, as Son of God, He was Lord of the Temple, and not tributary to it.

Some have felt a difficulty in reconciling the position taken on this occasion with His previous attitude towards the law, notably on the occasion of His baptism, when in answer to John's remonstrance, He said, "It becometh us to fulfil all righteousness"; but it must be remembered that He has entered on a new stage of His career. He has been rejected by those

* They are relegated to the margin in R. V.; but the parallel passage in St. Mark's Gospel is acknowledged to be genuine.

who acknowledged allegiance to the Temple, virtually excommunicated, so that He has been constrained to found His Church outside the commonwealth of Israel; He must therefore assert His own rights and theirs in spiritual things (for it must be remembered that the "half-shekel" was not the tribute to Cæsar, but the impost for the maintenance of the Temple worship). But while asserting His right He would not insist on it: He would stand by His disciple's word, and so avoid putting a stumbling-block in the way of those that were without, and who therefore could not be expected to understand the position He took. While consenting to pay the tax, He would provide it in such a way as not to lower His lofty claims in the view of His disciples, but rather to illustrate them, bringing home, as it must have done, to them all, and especially to the "pilot of the Galilean lake," that all things were under His feet, down to the very "fish of the sea, and whatsoever passeth through the paths of the seas" (Psalm viii. 8, l. 10-12). The difficulty which some feel in regard to this miracle, as differing so much in its character from those wrought in presence of the people as signs of the kingdom and credentials of the King, is greatly relieved, if not altogether removed, by remembering what was the special object in view—the instruction of Peter and the other disciples—and observing how manifestly and peculiarly appropriate it was for this particular purpose.

THE LITTLE ONES (xviii. 1-14).

The brief stay at Capernaum was signalised by some other lessons of the greatest importance. First, *as to the great and the small in the kingdom of heaven.* We learn from the other Evangelists that by the way the disciples had disputed with one another who should be the greatest. Alas for human frailty, even in the true disciple! It is most humiliating to think that, after that week, with its high and holy lessons, the first thing we hear of the disciples should be their failure in the very particulars which had been special features of the week's instruction. Recall the two points: the first was faith in the Christ, the Son of the living God, and over against it we have from lack of faith the signal failure with the lunatic child; the second was self-denial, and over against it we have this unseemly strife as to who should be greatest in the kingdom.

It is startling and most sad; but is it not true to nature? Is it not after the most solemn impressions that we need to be most watchful? And how natural it is, out of what is taught us, to choose and appropriate what is welcome, and, without expressly rejecting, simply to leave unassimilated and unapplied what is unwelcome. The great burden of the instruction for the last eight or ten days had been the Cross. There had been reference to the rising again, and the coming in the glory of the kingdom; but these had been kept strictly in the background, mentioned chiefly to save the disciples from undue discouragement, and even the three who had the vision of glory on the mount were forbidden to mention the subject in the meantime. Yet they let it fill the whole field of view; and though when the Master is with them He still speaks to them of the Cross, when they are by themselves they dismiss the subject, and fall to disputing as to who shall be the greatest in the kingdom!

How patiently and tenderly their Master deals with them! No doubt the same thought was in His heart again: "O faithless and perverse generation, how long shall I be with you? how long shall I suffer you?" But He does not even express it now. He takes an opportunity, when they are quietly together in the house, of teaching them the lesson they most need in a manner so simple and beautiful, so touching and impressive, as to commend it to all true-hearted ones to the end of time. Jesus called a little child to Him, "and set him in the midst of them." Can we doubt that they felt the force of that striking object-lesson before He said a word? Then, as we learn from St. Mark, to whom we always look for minute details, after having set him in the midst of them for them to look at and think about for a while, He took him in His arms, as if to show them where to look for those who were nearest to the heart of the King of heaven.

Nothing could have been more suggestive. It perfectly suited the purpose He had in view; but the meaning and the value of that simple act were by no means limited to that purpose. It most effectually rebuked their pride and selfish ambition; but it was far more than a rebuke—it was a revelation which taught men to appreciate child-nature as they had never done before. It was a new thought the Lord Jesus so quietly introduced into the minds of men that day, a seed-thought which had in it the promise, not only of all that appreciation of child-life which is characteristic of Christendom to-day, and which has rendered possible such poems as Vaughan's "Retreat," and Wordsworth's grand ode on "Immortality," but also of that appreciation of the broadly human as distinguished from the mere accidents of birth or rank or wealth which lies at the foundation of all Christian civilisation. The enthusiasm of humanity is all in that little act done so unassumingly in heedless Capernaum.

The words spoken are in the highest degree worthy of the act they illustrate. The first lesson is, "None but the lowly are in the kingdom:" "Except ye be converted (from the selfish pride of your hearts), and become (lowly and self-forgetful) as little children, ye shall not enter into the kingdom of heaven." A most heart-searching lesson! What grave doubts and questions it must have suggested to the disciples! They had faith to follow Christ in an external way; but were they *really* following Him? Had He not said, "If any man will come after Me, let him deny himself"? Were they denying self? On the other hand, however, we need not suppose that this selfish rivalry was habitual with them. It was probably one of those surprises which overtake the best of Christians; so that it was not really a proof that they did not belong to the kingdom, but only that for the time they were acting inconsistently with it; and therefore, before they could think of occupying any place, even the very lowest in the kingdom, they must repent, and become as little children.

The next lesson is, *The lowliest in the kingdom are the greatest:* "Whosoever therefore shall humble himself as this little child, the same is greatest in the kingdom of heaven." Again a most wonderful utterance, now so familiar to us, that we are apt to regard it as a thing of course; but what a startling paradox it must have been to the astonished disciples that day! Yet, as they looked at the bright, innocent, clear-eyed, self-unconscious little child, so simple, so trustful, there must have come a response from that which was deepest and best within them to their Master's words. And though the thought was new to them at the time, it did come home to them: it passed into their nature, and showed itself afterwards in precious fruit, at which the world still wonders. They did not indeed get over their selfishness all at once; but how grandly were they cured of it when their training was finished! If there is one thing more characteristic of the apostles in their after life than any other, it is their self-forgetfulness, their self-effacement, we may say. Where does Matthew ever say a word about the sayings or doings of Matthew? Even John, who was nearest of all to the heart of the Saviour, and with Him in all His most trying hours, can write a whole gospel without ever mentioning his own name; and when he has occasion to speak of John the Baptist does it as if there were no other John in existence. So was it with them all. We must not forget that, so far as this lesson of self-denial is concerned, they were only beginners now (see xvi. 21); but after they had completed their course and received the Pentecostal seal, they did not disgrace their Teacher any more: they did then really and nobly deny self; and thus did they at last attain true greatness in the kingdom of heaven.

So far we have what may be called the Saviour's direct answer to the question as to the greatest; but He cannot leave the subject without also setting before them the claims of the least in the kingdom of heaven. He has shown them how to be great: He now teaches them how to treat the small. The two things lie very close together. The man who makes much of himself is sure to make light of others; and he who is ambitious for worldly greatness will have little regard for those who in his eyes are small. The lesson, then, would have been incomplete had He not vindicated the claims of the little ones.

It is manifest, from the whole strain of the passage which follows, that the reference is not exclusively to children in years, but quite as much to children in spiritual stature, or in position and influence in the Church. The little ones are those who are small in the sense corresponding to that of the word "great" in the disciples' question. They are those, therefore, that are small and weak, and (as it is sometimes expressed) of no account in the Church, whether this be due to tender years or to slender abilities or to scanty means or to little faith.

What our Lord says on this subject comes evidently from the very depths of His heart. He is not content with making sure that the little ones shall receive as good a welcome as the greatest: they must have a special welcome, just because they are small. He identifies Himself with them—with each separate little one: "Whoso shall receive one such little child in My name receiveth Me." What a grand security for the rights and privileges of the small! what a word for parents and teachers, for men of influence and wealth in the Church in their relations to the weak and poor!

Then follow two solemn warnings, wrought out with great fulness and energy. The first is against putting a stumbling-block in the way of even one of these little ones—an offence which may be committed without any thought of the consequences. Perhaps this is the very reason why the Master feels it necessary to use language so terribly strong, that He may, if possible, arouse His disciples to some sense of their responsibility: "Whoso shall offend one of these little ones which believe in Me, it were better for him that a millstone were hanged about his neck, and that he were drowned in the depth of the sea." How jealously He guards the little ones! Verily he that toucheth them "toucheth the apple of His eye."

From the corresponding passage in St. Mark, it would appear that Christ had in view, not only such differences of age and ability and social position as are found in every community of disciples, but also such differences as are found between one company and another of professing Christians (see Mark ix. 38-42). This infuses a new pathos into the sad lament with which He forecasts the future: "Woe unto the world because of offences! for it must needs be that offences come; but woe to that man by whom the offence cometh!" The solemn warnings which follow, not given now for the first time (see chap. v. 29, 30), coming in this connection, convey the important lesson that the only effectual safeguard against causing others to stumble is to take heed to our own ways, and be ready to make any sacrifice in order to maintain our personal purity, simplicity, and uprightness (vv. 8, 9). How often alas! in the history of the Church has the cutting off been applied in the wrong direction; when the strong, in the exercise of an authority which the Master would never have sanctioned, have passed sentence of excommunication against some defenceless little one; whereas if they had laid to heart these solemn warnings, they would have cut off, not one of Christ's members, but one of their own—the harsh hand, the hasty foot, the jealous eye, which caused them to stumble!

The other warning is: "Take heed that ye despise not one of these little ones." To treat them so is to do the reverse of what is done in heaven. Be their guardian angels rather, if you would have the approval of Him Who reigns above; for their angels are those who always have the place of honour there. Is there not something very touching in this home reference, "*My* Father which is in heaven"?—especially when He is about to refer to the mission of mercy which made Him an exile from His home. And this reference gives Him an additional plea against despising one of these little ones; for not only are the highest angels their honoured guardians, but they are those whom the Son of man has come to seek and to save. The little lamb which you despise is one for whom the heavenly Shepherd has thought it worth His while to leave all the rest of His flock that He may go after it, and seek it on the lonely mountains, whither it has strayed, and over whose recovery He has greater joy than even in the safety of all the rest. The climax is reached when He carries thoughts above the angels, above even the son of man, to the will of the Father (now it is *your* Father; for He desires to bring to bear upon them the full force of that tender relationship which it is now their privilege to claim): "Even so it is not the will of your Father which is in heaven, that one of these little ones should perish."

Trespasses (xviii. 15-35).

The transition is natural from those solemn words in which our Lord has warned His disciples against offending "one of these little ones," to the instructions which follow as to how they should treat those of their brethren who might trespass against them. These instructions, occupying the rest of this chapter, are of perennial interest and value, so long as it must needs be that offences come.

The trespasses referred to are of course real. Much heartburning and much needless trouble often come of "offences" which exist only in imagination. A "sensitive" disposition (often only another name for one that is uncharitable and suspicious) leads to the imputing of bad motives where none exist, and the finding of sinister meanings in the most innocent acts. Such offences are not worthy of consideration at all. It is further to be observed that our Lord is not dealing with ordinary quarrels, where there are faults on both sides, in which case the first step would be not to tell the brother his fault, but to acknowledge our own. The trespass, then, being real, and the fault all on the other side, how is the disciple of Christ to act? The paragraphs which follow make it clear.

"The wisdom that is from above is first pure, then peaceable;" accordingly we are first shown how to proceed in order to preserve the purity of the Church. Then instructions are given with a view to preserve the peace of the Church. The first paragraph shows how to exercise discipline; the second lays down the Christian rule of forgiveness.

"If thy brother shall trespass against thee," —what? Pay no heed to it? Since it takes two to make a quarrel, is it best simply to let him alone? That might be the best way to deal with offences on the part of those that are without; but it would be a sad want of true brotherly love to take this easy way with a fellow-disciple. It is certainly better to overlook an injury than to resent it; yet our Lord shows a more excellent way. His is not the way of selfish resentment, nor of haughty indifference; but of thoughtful concern for the welfare of him who has done the injury. That this is the motive in the entire proceeding is evident from the whole tone of the paragraph, in illustration of which reference may be made to the way in which success is regarded: "If he shall hear thee, thou hast gained thy brother." If a man sets out with the object of gaining his cause or getting satisfaction, he had better let it alone; but if he wishes not to gain a barren triumph for himself, but to gain his brother, let him proceed according to the wise instructions of our Lord and Master.

There are four steps: (1) "Go and tell him his fault between thee and him alone." Do not wait till he comes to apologise, as is the rule laid down by the rabbis, but go to him at once. Do not think of your own dignity. Think only of your Master's honour and your brother's welfare. How many troubles, how many scandals might be prevented in the Christian Church, if this simple direction were faithfully and lovingly carried out! In some cases, however, this may fail; and then the next step is: (2) "Take with thee one or two more, that in the mouth of two or three witnesses every word may be established." The process here passes from private dealing; still there must be no undue publicity. If the reference to two or at most three (see R. V.) fail, it becomes a duty to (3) "tell it unto the church," in the hope that he may submit to its decision. If he decline, there is nothing left but (4) excommunication: "Let him be unto thee as an heathen man and a publican."

The mention of church censure naturally leads to a declaration of the power vested in the church in the matter of discipline. Our Lord had already given such a declaration to Peter alone; now it is given to the church as a whole in its collective capacity: "Verily I say unto you, Whatsoever ye shall bind on earth shall be bound in heaven: and whatsoever ye shall loose on earth shall be loosed in heaven." But the question comes: What is the church in its collective capacity? If it is to have this power of discipline, of the admission and rejection of members —a power which, rightly exercised on earth, is ratified in heaven—it is important to know something as to its constitution. This much, indeed, we know: that it is an assembly of believers. But how large must the assembly be? What are the marks of the true church?

These questions are answered in vv. 19 and 20. It is made very plain that it is no question of numbers, but of union with one another and the Lord. Let it be remembered that the whole discourse has grown out of the strife with one another which should be the greatest. Our Lord has already shown that, instead of ambition to be the greatest, there must be readiness to be the least. He now makes it plain that instead of strife and division there must be agreement, unity in heart and desire. But if only there be this unity, this blending of hearts in prayer, there is found the true idea of the Church. Two disciples in full spiritual agreement, with hearts uplifted to the Father in heaven, and Christ present with them,—there is what may be called the primitive cell of the Church, the body of Christ complete in itself, but in its rudimentary or germinal form. It comes to this, that the presence of Christ with His people and of His spirit in them, uniting them with one another and with Him, is that which constitutes the true and living church; and it is only when thus met in the name of Christ, and acting in the spirit of Christ, that assemblies of believers, whether large or small, have any guarantee that their decrees on earth are registered in heaven, or that the promise shall be fulfilled to them, that what they ask "shall be done for them of My Father which is in heaven."

These words were spoken in the day of small things, when the members of the Church were reckoned by units; therefore it is a mistake to use them as if very small gatherings for prayer were especially pleasing to the great Head of the Church. It does indeed remain true, for the encouragement of the faithful few, that wherever two or three are met in the name of Jesus He is there; but that makes it no less disappointing when the numbers might be reasonably expected to be very much larger. Because our Lord said, "Better two of you agreed than the whole twelve at strife," does it follow that two or three will have the power in their united prayers which two or three hundred would have? The stress is not on the figure, but on the agreement.

The words "There *am I* in the midst of them"

are very striking as a manifestation of that strange consciousness of freedom from limitations of time and place, which the Lord Jesus felt and often expressed even in the days of His flesh. It is the same consciousness which appears in the answer to the cavil of the Jews as to the intimacy with Abraham He seemed to them to claim,—"Before Abraham was, I am." As a practical matter also it suggests that we do not need to ask and wait for the presence of the Master when we are truly met in His name. It is not *He* that needs to be entreated to draw near to us: "There *am I*."

So far the directions given have been with a view to the good of the offending brother and the honour of Christ and His cause. It remains to show how the offended person is to act on his part. Here the rule is very simple: "forgive him." What satisfaction, then, is the offended party to get? The satisfaction of forgiving. That is all; and it is enough.

It will be observed, indeed, that our Lord, in His discourse up to the point we have reached, has said nothing directly about forgiveness. It is fairly implied, however, in the manner of process, in the very first act of it indeed; for no one will go to an offending brother with the object of gaining him, unless he have first forgiven him in his heart. Peter appears to have been revolving this in his mind, and in doing so he cannot get over a difficulty as to the limit of forgiveness. He was familiar, of course, with the rabbinical limit of the third offence, after which the obligation to forgiveness ceased; and, impressed with the spirit of his Master's teaching, he no doubt thought he was showing great liberality in more than doubling the number of times the offence might be repeated and still be considered pardonable: "Lord, how oft shall my brother sin against me, and I forgive him? till seven times?" It has been thought that some of his brethren had been treating Peter badly, so that his patience was sorely tried. Be that as it may, the question was not at all unnatural. But it was founded on a fallacy, which our Lord cleared away by His answer, and thoroughly exposed by means of the striking parable which follows. The fallacy was this: that we have a right to resent an injury, that in refraining from this we are forbearing to exercise our right, and consequently that there is a limit beyond which we have no call to exercise such forbearance. Our Lord by His answer clears away the limit, and makes the obligation unconditional and universal (ver. 22).

The parable shows the reason why there should be no limit—viz., that all believers, or members of the Church, by accepting from God the unlimited forgiveness He has extended to them, are thereby implicitly pledged to extend a like unlimited forgiveness to others. There is no duty on which our Lord insists more strenuously than this duty of forgiving those who trespass against us, always connecting closely together our forgiving and our being forgiven; and in this parable it is set in the strongest light.

The greatest offence of which our fellow-man can be guilty is as nothing to the sins we have committed against God. The proportion suggested is very startling. The larger sum is more than two millions sterling on the lowest computation; the smaller is not much more than four guineas. This is no exaggeration. Seven times altogether for a brother's offences seems almost unpardonable: do we never offend against God as many times in a single hour? Then think of the days, and the years! This is a startling thought on the one side; but how cheering on the other! For the immensity of the debt does not interfere in the slightest with the freeness and fulness and absoluteness of the forgiveness. Verily there is no more satisfying or reassuring presentation of the gospel than this parable, especially these very words, which rang like a knell of doom in the unmerciful servant's ear: "I forgave thee *all that debt*." But just in proportion to the grandeur of the gospel here unfolded is the rigour of the requirement, that as we have been forgiven so must we forgive. While we gladly take the abounding comfort, let us not miss the stern lesson, evidently given with the very strongest feeling. Our Lord paints the picture of this man in the most hideous colours, so as to fill our minds and hearts with a proper loathing of the conduct of those he represents. The same intention is apparent in the very severe terms in which the punishment is denounced: "His lord was wroth, and delivered him to the tormentors." After this how awful is the closing sentence: "So likewise shall My heavenly Father do also unto you, if ye from your hearts forgive not every one his brother their trespasses."

Is that tender name of Father out of place? By no means; for is it not the outraged love of God that cries out against the unforgiving soul? And the words "from your hearts,"—are they not too hard on poor frail human nature? It is easy enough to grant forgiveness with the lips,—but from the heart? Yet so it stands written; and it only shows the need we have, not only of unmeasured mercy, but of unmeasured grace. Nothing but the love of Christ can constrain to such forgiveness. The warning was a solemn one, but it need have no terror for those who have truly learned the lesson of the Cross, and welcomed the Spirit of Christ to reign in their hearts. "I can do all things through Christ Who strengtheneth me."

There is an admirable fulness and harmony in Christ's teaching on this subject, as on every other. The duty of unlimited forgiveness is most plainly enjoined; but not that weak forgiveness which consists simply in permitting a man to trespass as he chooses. Forgiveness and faithfulness go hand in hand. The forgiveness of the Christian is in no case to be the offspring of a weak unmanly indifference to wrong. It is to spring from gratitude and love: gratitude to God, Who has forgiven his enormous debt, and love to the enemy who has wronged him. It must be combined with that faithfulness and fortitude which constrains him to go to the offending party and frankly, though kindly, tell him his fault. Christ's doctrine of forgiveness has not an atom of meanness in it, and His doctrine of faithfulness has not a spark of malice. "The wisdom that is from above is first pure, then peaceable, gentle, and easy to be entreated, full of mercy and good fruits, without partiality and without hypocrisy. And the fruit of righteousness is sown in peace of them that make peace."

CHAPTER XV.

LAST DAYS IN PERÆA.

MATTHEW xix. 1-xx. 16.

THERE were two main roads from Galilee to Jerusalem. One passed through Samaria, on the west of the Jordan, the other through Peræa, east of it. It was by the former that our Lord went northward from Judea to begin His work in Galilee; it is by the other that He now goes southward to complete His sacrifice in Jerusalem. As "He must needs go through Samaria" then, so He must needs go through Peræa now. The main thought in His mind is the journey; but He cannot pass through the large and important district beyond the Jordan without bringing the kingdom of heaven near to the people, and accordingly we read that "great multitudes followed Him, and He healed them there." We learn from St. Luke's Gospel that "He went through the cities and villages teaching, and journeying towards Jerusalem"; and from the details there recorded, especially the mission of the seventy which belongs to that period, it is evident that these circuits in Peræa must have occupied several months. Concerning the work of these months our Evangelist is silent, just as he was silent concerning the earlier work in Judea and Samaria, as recorded by St. John. We are reminded by this of the fragmentariness of these memorials of our Lord; and when we consider how much is omitted in all the narratives (see John xxi. 25) we can understand how difficult it is to form a closely connected history without any gaps between, and with accurately fitted joinings at the intersections of the different accounts.

There is, however, no difficulty here; for by comparison with the third Gospel we find that our Evangelist omits all the circuits in Peræa, and takes up the story again when our Lord is just about to leave that region for Jerusalem. When we take his point of view we can see how natural this was. It was his special calling to give a full account of the work in Galilee. Hence the haste with which he passes from what it was necessary for him to tell of the early years in the south till the work in Galilee began; and in the same way, now that the work in Galilee is done, he hastens to the great crisis in Jerusalem. In following the journey southward he lingers only in two places, each of them associated with special memories. The one is Capernaum, where Jesus, as we have seen, tarried for a few days before taking final leave of Galilee; the other is the place beyond Jordan, in the region where in baptism He had solemnly entered on His work (*cf.* John x. 40), where again He remains for a brief period before going up to Jerusalem for the last time.

MARRIAGE AND DIVORCE (vv. 3-12).

There it was, and then, that the Pharisees came to Him with their entangling question concerning divorce. To know how entangling it was it is necessary to remember that there was a dispute at the time between two rival schools of Jewish theology—the school of Hillel and that of Shammai—in regard to the interpretation of Deut. xxiv. 1. The one school held that divorce could be had on the most trivial grounds; the other restricted it to cases of grievous sin. Hence the question: "Is it lawful for a man to put away his wife for every cause?" The answer Jesus gives is remarkable, not only for the wisdom and courage with which He met their attack, but for the manner in which He availed Himself of the opportunity to set the institution of marriage on its true foundation, and give perpetual security to His followers for the sanctity of home, by laying down in the clearest and strongest manner the position that marriage is indissoluble from its very nature and from its divine appointment (vv 4-6). As we read these clear and strong utterances let us bear in mind, not only that the laxity which unhappily prevailed in Rome had extended to Palestine, but that the monarch of the country through which our Lord was passing was himself one of the most flagrant offenders. How inspiring it is to think that then and there should have been erected that grand bulwark of a virtuous home: "What God hath joined together, let not man put asunder."

The Pharisees must have felt that He spoke with authority; but they are anxious not to lose their opportunity of getting Him into a difficulty, so they press Him with the disputed passage in Deuteronomy: "Why did Moses, then, command to give a writing of divorcement, and to put her away?" Our Lord's answer exposes the double fallacy lurking in the question. "Why did Moses command?" He did not command; he only suffered it—it was not to further divorce, but to check it, that he made the regulation about the "writing of divorcement." And then, not only was it a mere matter of suffrance,—it was a suffrance granted "because of the hardness of your hearts." Since things were so bad among your fathers in the matter of marriage, it was better that there should be a legal process than that the poor wives should be dismissed without it; but from the beginning it was not so—it was not intended that wives should be dismissed at all. Marriage is in itself indissoluble, except by death or by that which in its very nature is the rupture of marriage (ver. 9).

The wide prevalence of lax views on this subject is made evident by the perplexity of the disciples. They were not at all prepared for such stringency, so they venture to suggest that if that is to be the law, better not marry at all. The answer our Lord gives, while it does admit that there are circumstances in which celibacy is preferable, plainly intimates that it is only in quite exceptional cases. Only one of the three cases He mentions is voluntary; and while it is certainly granted that circumstances might arise in which for the kingdom of heaven's sake celibacy might be chosen (*cf.* 1 Cor. vii. 26), even then it must be only in cases where there is special grace, and such full preoccupation with the things of the kingdom as to render it natural; for such seems to be the import of the cautionary words with which the paragraph closes: "He that is able to receive it, let him receive it." How completely at variance with this wise caution have been the Romish decrees in regard to the celibacy of the clergy may go without saying.

THE CHILDREN (vv. 13-15).

"*Then* were there brought unto Him little children"—a happy interruption! The Master has just been laying the solid foundations of the Christian home; and now the group of men by whom He is surrounded is joined by a troop of mothers, some carrying infants in their arms (for the passage in St. Luke expressly mentions infants), and some leading their little ones by the hand, to receive His blessing. The timeousness of this arrival does not seem to have struck the disciples. Their hearts had not yet been opened to the lambs of the fold, notwithstanding the great lesson at Capernaum. With as little regard for the feelings of the mothers as for the rights of the children, they "rebuked those that brought them" (Mark x. 13), and motioned them away. That this wounded the heart of the Saviour appears in His answer, which is stronger, as indicating displeasure, than is shown in our translation; while in the second Gospel it is expressly mentioned that Jesus "was much displeased." How can we thank the Lord enough for that sore displeasure? A distinguished opponent of Christianity has lately been asking whether he is expected to accept the kind and peaceful Jesus, Who smiles in one place, or the stern Judge Who frowns in another—with the evident implication that it is impossible to accept both. How any person of intelligence can find difficulty in supposing that Christ could without inconsistency be either gentle or stern, as the occasion required, is very marvellous; but here is a case in which the sternness and gentleness are blended together in one act; and who will say that there is the least incompatibility between them? He was much displeased with the disciples; His heart was overflowing with tenderness to the children: and in that moment of conflicting feeling He utters that immortal sentence, these noblest and now most familiar of household words, "Suffer little children, and forbid them not, to come unto Me: for of such is the kingdom of heaven."

The rights of woman had been implicitly taught in the law of marriage carried back to the original creation of male and female; the treatment of woman had been vindicated from the rudeness of the disciples which would have driven the mothers away; and this reception of the children, and these words of welcome into the kingdom for all such little ones, are the charter of the children's rights and privileges. It is very plain that Christ has opened the kingdom of heaven, not only to all believers, but to their children as well. That "the kingdom of heaven" is here used in its ordinary sense throughout this Gospel, as referring to the heavenly kingdom which Christ had come to establish upon earth, cannot be denied; but it is a very fair inference from the Saviour's words that, seeing the children are acknowledged as having their place in the kingdom on earth, those of them who pass away from earth in childhood certainly find as sure and cordial a welcome in the kingdom above.

"The holy to the holiest leads,
The kingdoms are but one."

The porch is on earth, the palace is in heaven; and we may be very sure that all whom the King acknowledges in the porch shall be welcome in the palace.

What a rebuke in these words of our Lord to those who deal with children indiscriminately as if they were all dead in trespasses and sins. How it must grieve the Saviour's heart when lambs of his own fold who may have been His from their earliest infancy are taught that they are utterly lost, and must be lost for ever, unless they pass through some extraordinary change, which is to them only a nameless mystery. It is a mistake to think that children as a rule need to be dragged to the Saviour, or frightened into trusting Him: what they need is to be *suffered* to come. It is so natural for them to come that all they need is very gentle leading, and above all nothing done to hinder or discourage them: "Suffer little children, and forbid them not, to come unto Me: for of such is the kingdom of heaven."

The Rich Young Man (vv. 16-22).

Another inference from these precious words of Christ is the importance of seeking to win the children for Christ while yet they are children, ere the evil days come, or the years draw nigh, when they will be apt to say they have no pleasure in Him. It is a sad thing to think how soon the susceptibility of the child-nature may harden into the impenetrability which is sometimes found even in youth. Is there not a suggestion of this in the story of the young man which immediately follows?

There was everything that seemed hopeful about him. He was young, so his heart could not be very hard; of good moral character, amiable in disposition, and stirred with noble aspirations; moreover, he did the very best thing in coming to Christ for guidance. Yet nothing came of it, because of one obstacle, which would have been no hindrance in his childhood, but which proved insurmountable now. Young as he was, his affections had had time to get so intertwined with his worldly possessions that he could not disengage them, so that instead of following Christ "he went away sorrowful."

The manner of our Lord's dealing with this young man is exceedingly instructive. Some have found a difficulty in what seems to them the strange answer to the apparently straightforward and admirable question, "What good thing shall I do, that I may have eternal life?" Why did He not give the same answer which St. Paul afterwards gave to the Philippian jailer? Why did He not only fail to bring himself forward as the way, the truth, and the life, but even disclaim the goodness which the young man had imputed to Him? And why did He point him to the law instead of showing him the Gospel? Everything becomes quite clear when we remember that Christ dealt with people not according to the words they spoke, but according to what He saw to be in their hearts. Had this young man been in a state of mind at all like that of the Philippian jailer when he came trembling and fell down before Paul and Silas, he would no doubt have had a similar answer. But he was in the very opposite condition. He was quite satisfied with his own goodness; it was not salvation he was seeking, but some new merit to add to the large stock he already had: "what good thing shall I do" in addition to all the well-known goodness of my character and daily life? what extra claim can I establish upon the favour of God? Manifestly his idea of goodness was only conventional; it was the goodness which passes muster among men, not that which justifies itself before the all-searching eye of God; and having no higher idea of goodness than that, he of course used it in no higher sense when he addressed Christ as "good Master." There could, then, be no more appropriate or more heart-searching question than this,—"*Why* callest thou Me good?" (it is only in the conventional sense you use the term, and conventional goodness is no goodness at all); "there is none good but One, that is God." Having thus stimulated his easy conscience, He sends him to the law that he may have knowledge of his sin, and so may take the first step towards eternal life. The young man's reply to this reveals the secret of his heart, and shows that Christ had made no mistake in dealing with him as He did. "Which?" he asks, evidently expecting that, the Ten Commandments being taken for granted, there will be something higher and more exacting, the keeping of which will bring him the extra credit he hopes to gain.

The Lord's answer to his question was well fitted to take down his spiritual pride, pointing him as it did to the commonplace Decalogue, and to that part of it which seemed the easiest; for the first table of the law is passed over, and only those commandments mentioned which bear upon duty to man. And is there not special skill shown in the way in which they are marshalled, so as to lead up to the one which covered his weak point? The sixth, the seventh, the eighth, the ninth, the fifth are rapidly passed in review; then the mind is allowed to rest on the tenth, not, however, in its mere negative form, "Thou shalt not covet," but as involved in that positive requirement which sums up the whole of the second table of the Law, "Thou shalt love thy neighbour as thyself." We can imagine how the Saviour would mark the young man's countenance, as one after another the commandments were pressed upon his conscience, ending with that one which should have pierced him as with a two-edged sword. But he is too strongly encased in his mail of self-righteousness; and he only replies, "All these things have I kept from my youth up: what lack I yet?" Clearly it is a surgical case; the medicine of the Commandments will not do; there must be the insertion of the knife: "Go, and sell that thou hast, and give to the poor."

Let us not, however, mistake the tone. "Jesus beholding him loved him" (Mark x. 21); and the love was never warmer than at the moment when He made this stern demand. There was sorrow on His face and in His tone when He told him of the hard necessity; and there was a heart full of love in the gracious invitation which rounded off the sharp saying at the end: "Come, and follow Me." Let us hope that the Saviour's compassionate love was not finally lost on him; that, though he no doubt did lose the great opportunity of taking a high place in the kingdom, he nevertheless, before all was done, bethought him of the Master's faithful and loving words, repented of his covetousness, and so found an open door and a forgiving welcome.

Danger of Riches (vv. 23-26).

So striking an incident must not be allowed to pass without seizing and pressing the great lesson it teaches. No lesson was more needful at the time. Covetousness was in the air; it was already setting its mark on the Hebrew people, who, as they ceased to serve God in spirit and in truth, were giving themselves over more and more to the worship of mammon; and, as the Master well knew, there was one of the twelve in whom the fatal poison was even then at work. We can understand, therefore, the deep feeling which Christ throws into His warning against this danger, and His special anxiety to guard all His disciples against an over-estimate of this world's riches.

We shall not, however, fully enter into the mind of our Lord, if we fail to notice the tone of compassion and charity which marks His first utterance. He is still thinking kindly of the poor rich young man, and is anxious to make all allowance for him. It is as if He said, "See that you do not judge him too harshly; think how hard it is for such as he to enter the kingdom." This will explain how it is that in repeating the statement He found it desirable, as recorded by St. Mark, to introduce a qualification in order to render it applicable to all cases: "How hard is it for them that trust in riches to enter into the kingdom!" But while softening it in one direction, He puts it still more strongly in another: "Again I say unto you, it is easier for a camel to go through the eye of a needle than for a rich man to enter into the kingdom of God." We shall not enter into the trivial discussion as to the needle's eye; it is enough to know that it was a proverbial phrase, probably in common use, expressing in the strongest way the insurmountable obstacle which the possession of riches, when these are trusted in and so put in place of God, must prove to their unfortunate owner.

The disciples' alarm expressed in the question "Who, then, can be saved?" does them much credit. It shows that they had penetration enough to see that the danger against which their Master was guarding them did not beset the rich alone; that they had sufficient knowledge of themselves to perceive that even such as they, who had always been poor, and who had given up what little they had for their Master's sake, might nevertheless not be free enough from the well-nigh universal sin to be themselves quite safe. One cannot help thinking that the searching look, which St. Mark tells us their Lord bent on them as He spoke, had something to do with this unusual quickness of conscience. It reminds us of that later scene, when each one asked, "Lord, is it I?" Is there any one of us, who, when that all-seeing Eye is fixed upon us, with its pure and holy gaze into the depths of our being, can fail to ask, with the conscience-stricken disciples, "Who, then, can be saved?"

The answer He gives does not at all lighten the pressure on the conscience. There is no recalling of the strong words which suggest the idea of utter impossibility. He does not say, "You are judging yourselves too strictly"; on the contrary, He confirms their judgment, and tells them that there they are right: "With men this *is* impossible"; but is there not another alternative? "Who art thou, O great mountain? before Zerubbabel thou shalt become a plain;" "With God all things are possible." A most significant utterance this for those to ponder who, instead of following our Lord's dealing with this case to its close, treat it as if the final word had been "If thou will enter into life, keep the commandments." This favourite passage of the legalists is the one of all others which most completely overthrows his hopes, and shows that so deep are the roots of sin in the heart of man, even of the most amiable and most exemplary, that none can be saved except by the power of divine grace overcoming that which is to men an impossibility. "Behold, God is my salvation."

It is worthy of note that it is as a hindrance to *entering* the kingdom that riches are here stigmatised,—which suggests the thought that the danger is not nearly so great when riches increase to those who have already entered. Not that there is even for them no serious danger, nor need of watching and of prayer that as they increase, the heart be not set upon them; but where there is true consecration of heart the consecration of wealth follows as a natural and easy consequence. Riches are a responsibility to those that are in the kingdom; they are a misfortune only to those who have not entered it.

As on the question of marriage or celibacy, so on that of property or poverty, the Romanist has pushed our Lord's words to an extreme which is evidently not intended. It was plain even to the disciples that it was not the mere possession of riches, but the setting the heart on them, which He condemned. If our Lord had intended to set forth the absolute renunciation of property as a counsel of perfection to His disciples, this would have been the time to do it; but we look in vain for any such counsel. He saw it to be necessary for that young man; but when He applies the case to disciples in general, He does not say "If any man will come after Me, let him sell all that he has, and give to the poor," but contents Himself with giving a very strong warning against the danger of riches coming between man and the kingdom of God. But while the ascetic interpretation of our Lord's words is manifestly wrong, the other extreme of reducing them to nothing is far worse, which is the danger now.

Rewards (xix. 27-xx. 16*).

The thought of sacrifice very naturally suggests as its correlative that of compensation; so it is not at all to be wondered at that, before this conversation ended, the impulsive disciple, so much given to think aloud, should blurt out the honest question: "Behold, we have forsaken all and followed Thee; what shall we have therefore?" He could not but remember that while the Master had insisted on His disciples denying self to follow Him, He had spoken no less clearly of their finding life through losing it, and of their being rewarded according to their deeds (see xvi. 24-27). A more cautious man would have hesitated before he spoke; but it was no worse to speak it than to think it: and then, it was an honest and fair question; accordingly our Lord gives it a frank and generous answer, taking care, however, before leaving the subject, to add a supplementary caution, fitted to correct what was doubtful or wrong in the spirit it showed.

Here, again, we see how thoroughly natural is our Saviour's teaching. "Not to destroy, but to fulfil," was His motto. This is as true of His relation to man's nature as of His relation to the law and the prophets. "What shall we have?" is a question not to be set aside as wholly unworthy. The desire for property is an original element in human nature. It was of God at the first; and though it has swelled out into most unseemly proportions, and has usurped a place which does by no means belong to it, that is no reason why it should be dealt with as if it had no right to exist. It is vain to attempt to root it out; what it needs is moderating, regulating, subordinating. The tendency of perverted human nature is to make "What shall we have?" the first question. The way to meet that is not to abolish the question altogether, but to put it last, where it ought to be. To be, to do, to suffer, to enjoy—that is the order our Lord marks out for His disciples. If only they have it as their first anxiety to be what they ought to be, and to do what they are called to do, and are willing, in order to this, to take up the cross, to suffer whatever may be theirs to suffer, then they may allow as large scope as they please to the desire for possession and enjoyment.

Observe the difference between the young man and the disciples. He was coming to Christ for the first time; and if our Lord had set before him what he would gain by following Him, He would have directly encouraged a mercenary spirit. He therefore says not a word to him about prospects of reward either here or hereafter. Those who choose Christ must choose Him for His own sake. Our Saviour dealt in no other way with Peter, James, and John. When first He called them to follow Him, He said not a word about thrones or rewards; He spoke of work: "Follow Me, and I will make you fishers of men"; and it was not till they had fully committed themselves to Him that He went so far as to suggest even in the most general way the thought of compensation. It would have spoiled them to have put such motives prominently before them at an earlier stage. But it is different now. They have followed Him for months, even years. They have been tested in innumerable ways. They are not certainly out of danger from the old selfishness; but with the exception of one of them, who is fast developing into a hypocrite, all they need is a solemn word of caution now and then. The time had come when their Master might safely give them some idea of the prospects which lay before them, when their cross-bearing days should be over.

The promise looks forward to an entirely altered state of things spoken of as "the regeneration"—a remarkable term, reminding us of the vast scope of our Saviour's mission as ever present to His consciousness even in these days of smallest things. The word recalls what is said in the book of Genesis as to "the generation of the heaven and of the earth," and suggests by anticipation the words of the Apocalypse concerning the regeneration, "Behold, I make all things new," and "I saw a new heaven and a new earth." That the reference is to that final restitution of all things, and not merely to the new dispensation, seems evident from the words which immediately follow: "When the Son of man shall sit on the throne of His glory." Why, then, was the promise given in words so suggestive of those crude notions of an earthly kingdom, above which it was so difficult and so important for the disciples to rise? The answer is to be found in the limitation of human language: "Eye hath not seen, nor ear

*The latter part of ver. 16—"Many be called, but few chosen"—does not properly belong to this passage (see R. V.); its consideration will therefore be postponed till its proper place is reached (see chap. xxii. 14).

heard, neither have entered into the heart of man, the things which God hath prepared for them that love Him"; accordingly, if the promise was to be of any use to them in the way of comfort and encouragement, it must be expressed in terms which were familiar to them then. To their minds the kingdom was as yet bound up with Israel; "the twelve tribes of Israel" was as large a conception of it as their thoughts could then grasp; and it would certainly be no disappointment to them when they afterwards discovered that their relation as apostles of the Lord was to a much larger "Israel," embracing every kindred and nation and people and tribe; and though their idea of the thrones on which they would sit was then and for some time afterwards quite inadequate, it was only by starting with what ideas of regal power they had, that they could rise to those spiritual conceptions which, as they matured in spiritual understanding, took full possession of their minds.

The Lord is speaking, however, not for the apostles alone, but for all His disciples to the end of time; so He must give a word of cheer, in which even the weakest and most obscure shall have a part (ver. 29). Observe that here also the promise is only for those who have left what they had for the sake of Christ. We are not authorised to go with a message after this form: "If you leave, you will get." The reward is of such a nature that it cannot be seen until the sacrifice is made. "Except a man be born again, he cannot see the kingdom of God;" until a man loses his life for Christ's sake, he cannot find it. But when the sacrifice has been made, then appears the compensation, and it is seen that even these strong words are not too strong: "Every one that hath forsaken houses, or brethren, or sisters, or father, or mother, or wife, or children, or lands, for My name's sake, shall receive an hundred-fold, and shall inherit everlasting life." The full consideration of this promise belongs rather to St. Mark's Gospel, in which it is presented without abridgment.

The supplementary caution—"But many that are first shall be last; and the last shall be first" —is administered in apparent reference to the spirit of the apostle's question, which exhibits still some trace of mercenary motive, with something also of a disposition to self-congratulation. This general statement is illustrated by the parable immediately following it, a connection which the unfortunate division into chapters here obscures; and not only is an important saying of our Lord deprived in this way of its illustration, but the parable is deprived of its key, the result of which has been that many have been led astray in its interpretation. We cannot attempt to enter fully into the parable, but shall only make such reference to it as is necessary to bring out its appropriateness for the purpose our Lord had in view. Its main purport may be stated thus: many that are first in amount of work shall be last in point of reward; and many that are last in amount of work shall be first in point of reward. The principle on which this is based is plain enough: that in estimating the reward it is not the quantity of work done or the amount of sacrifice made that is the measure of value, but the spirit in which the work is done or the sacrifice made. The labourers who made no bargain at all, but went to work on the faith of their Master's honour and liberality, were the best off in the end. Those who made a bargain received, indeed, all they bargained for; but the others were rewarded on a far more liberal scale, they obtaining much more than they had any reason to expect. Thus we are taught that those will be first who think least of wages as wages, and are the least disposed to put such a question as, "What shall we then have?" This was the main lesson for the apostles, as it is for all who occupy places of prominence in the kingdom. It is thus put in later years by one of those who now for the first time learned it: "Look to yourselves, that we lose not those things which we have wrought, but that we receive a full reward" (2 John 8). "Look to yourselves," see that your spirit be right, that there be nothing selfish, nothing mercenary, nothing vainglorious; else much good labour and real self-denial may miss its compensation.

Besides the lesson of caution to the great ones, there is a lesson of encouragement to the little ones in the kingdom—those who can do little and seem to themselves to sacrifice little for Christ. Let such remember that their labour and self-denial are measured not by quantity but by quality, by the spirit in which the service, however small it be, is rendered, and the sacrifice, trifling as it seems, is made. Not only is it true that many that are first shall be last; but also that many of the last shall be first. "If there be first a willing mind, it is accepted according to that a man hath, and not according to that he hath not."

Neither in the general statement of our Lord, nor in the parable which illustrates it, is there the slightest encouragement to idlers in the vineyard—to those who do nothing and sacrifice nothing for Christ, but who think that, when the eleventh hour comes, they will turn in with the rest, and perhaps come off best after all. When the Master of the vineyard asks of those who are standing in the market-place at the eleventh hour, "Why stand ye here all the day idle?" their answer is ready, "Because no man hath hired us." The invitation came to them, then, for the first time, and they accepted it as soon as it was given them. Suppose the Master of the vineyard had asked them in the morning, and at the first hour and the second and the third, and so on all the day, and only at the eleventh hour did they deign to notice His invitation, how would they have fared?

CHAPTER XVI.

TO JERUSALEM.

MATTHEW xx. 17-xxi. 17.

I.—THE GOING UP (xx. 17-34).

WE have now reached the last stage of the long and sorrowful journey to Jerusalem. From the corresponding passage in the second Gospel we learn that the disciples were greatly moved by something in their Master's manner: "they were amazed; and as they followed, they were afraid." It would appear, indeed, that they had considerable hesitation in following at all, for it is pointedly mentioned that "Jesus went before them," a hesitation which was no doubt due to the same feeling which prompted Peter, on the first announcement of the journey to

Jerusalem and what it would involve, to say "Be it far from Thee, Lord"; and as then, so now, the Saviour felt it as an obstacle in His onward path which He must resolutely put out of the way; and it was doubtless the new and severe effort required of that heroic will to set it aside, and in doing so to face the gathering storm alone, which explained His unwonted agitation as He addressed Himself to the last stage of the fatal journey.

Still, He longs to have His disciples in sympathy with Him. He knows well that not yet have they fully appreciated what He has said to them; accordingly, at some convenient point on the way, He takes them by themselves and tells them once again, more distinctly and definitely than ever, what must be the issue of the step He is now taking (vv. 17-19). St. Luke tells us that even yet "they understood none of these things." Their minds must have been in a state of great bewilderment; and when we think of this, we may well admire that strong personal devotion to their Master which made them willing, however reluctantly and hesitatingly, still to follow Him into the dark unknown. With the one sad exception, they were thoroughly loyal to their King; they trusted Him absolutely; and though they could not understand why He should be mocked and scourged and crucified in His own capital, they were willing to go with Him there, in the full expectation that, in some way they then could not imagine, He should triumph over his enemies and erect those thrones and bring in that glory of the kingdom of which He had spoken.

This failure of theirs to comprehend the real situation, which one Evangelist mentions, is well illustrated by an incident which happened on the road as recorded by the others—one of those evidently undesigned coincidences which continually meet us, and which, in a higher degree than mere circumstantial agreements, confirm our faith in the accuracy of the sacred writers. "Then came to Him the mother of Zebedee's children with her sons, worshipping Him, and desiring a certain thing of Him,"—the "certain thing," as it turned out, being that the two sons should have the chief places of honour in the kingdom. From the form in which the request was presented it would seem as if it had been founded on a misapprehension of one of His own sayings. In St. Mark's Gospel, where the part which the two sons themselves had in it is related, the very words of the application are given thus: "Master, we would that Thou shouldest do for us whatsoever we shall desire," as if to remind Him of His promise to any two of them who should agree as touching anything they should ask (xviii. 19), and to claim the fulfilment of it. It need not be assumed that the request was a purely selfish one. However vague their ideas may have been as to the days of darkness that awaited them in Jerusalem, we cannot suppose that they left them wholly out of view; and if not, they must have been prepared, or have thought themselves prepared, to take foremost places in the battlefield as well as in the triumph that would surely follow. There may well have been, then, a touch of chivalry along with the grosser motive which, it is to be feared, was their main inspiration.

This makes it easier for us to understand the possibility of their coming with such a request at such a time. We all know how easy it is to justify a selfish proceeding when there is something to offset it. We ourselves know how natural it is to think of those scriptures which suit our purpose, while we conveniently forget for the moment those that do not. Was it, then, unnatural that James and John, forgetting for the moment what their Lord had taught them as to the way to true greatness in His kingdom, should satisfy themselves with the thought that they were at all events taking up their cross in the first place, and as to the ulterior object were certainly acting up to the very plain and emphatic word of the Master Himself: "I say unto you, that if two of you shall agree on earth as touching anything that they shall ask, it shall be done for them."

This view of their state of mind is confirmed by our Lord's way of dealing with them. He first asks them what it is they have agreed upon; and, when the mother tells Him, He quietly shows them that, so far from agreeing together, none of them know what they are asking. They are all using the same words, but the words might as well be in an unknown tongue,—better perhaps, inasmuch as to misunderstand is a degree worse than not to understand at all. He then proceeds to show them that the fulfilment of their request would involve issues for which as yet they were by no means prepared: "Jesus answered and said, Ye know not what ye ask. Are ye able to drink of the cup that I shall drink of?" Their answer confirms the view suggested, that they did not leave out altogether the thought of cross-bearing; but we have only to remember what took place in the course of a week to see that in saying "We are able," they knew as little of what they were promising as they had known of what they were asking. He will not, however, break the bruised reed of their devotion, nor quench the feeblest spark of self-denying courage; accordingly He does not slight their offer, but, in accepting it, He reminds them that the honours of the kingdom of heaven are not for favourites, or for those who may first apply, but only for those who approve themselves worthy in the sight of Him Who seeth all, and who rewards every man according to his deeds (ver. 23).

The ten were not much better than the two. It was natural, indeed, that, when they heard it, they should be "moved with indignation"; but, though natural, it was not Christian. Had they remembered the lesson of the little child, or even thought deeply enough of that very recent one about the last and the first, they would have been moved with something else than indignation. But need any one wonder that selfishness should be so very hard to kill? Is it not true to nature? Besides, the Spirit had not yet been given, and therefore we need not wonder that even the plainest teaching of the Lord Himself failed to cast the selfish spirit out of His disciples then. "*Knowledge* comes, but *wisdom* lingers." On the other hand, think of the marvellous patience of the Master. How disappointing it must have been at such a time to see in all of them a spirit so wholly at variance with all that by precept and example He had been labouring to instil into them! Yet without one word of reproach He teaches them the old lesson once again, gives them liberally the wisdom which they lack, and upbraids them not.

The words of Christ not only meet the case most fully, but reach far beyond the immediate occasion of their utterance. Thus He brings good out of evil, and secures that even the strife of His disciples shall make for "peace on earth." He begins by showing how absolutely in contrast to the kingdoms of the world is the kingdom He has come to establish. In them the great ones "lord it over" (R. V.) others; in it the great ones are those who serve. What a revolution of thought is involved in this simple contrast! of how much that is great and noble has it been the seed! The dignity of labour, the royalty of service, the pettiness of selfish ambition, the majesty of self-sacrificing love; the utter condemnation of the miserable maxim "Every man for himself"; the world's first question "What shall we have?" made the last, and its last question "What shall we give?" made the very first—such are some of the fruits which have grown from the seed our Lord planted in so ungenial soil that day. We are, alas! still very far from realising that great ideal; but ever since that day, as an ideal, it has never been quite out of sight. Early Christianity under the guidance of the apostles strove, though with all too little success, to realise it; the chivalry of the Middle Ages, with its glorification of knighthood,* was an attempt to embody it; and what is the constitutionalism of modern times but the development of the principle in political life, the real power being vested not in the titular monarch, who represents ideally the general weal, but in a *ministry*, so designated to mark the fact that their special function is to minister or serve; the highest position in the realm bearing the humble title of *Prime Minister*, or first servant of the state. It is of value to have the principle before us as an ideal, even though it be buried under the tombstone of a name, the significance of which is forgotten; but when the kingdom of heaven shall be fully established on the earth, the ideal will be realised, not in political life only, but all through society. If only the ambition to serve our generation according to the will of God were to become universal, then would God's kingdom come and His will be done on earth even as it is in heaven.

Of this great principle of the heavenly kingdom the King Himself is the highest illustration: "even as the Son of man came not to be ministered unto, but to minister, and to give His life a ransom for many." There are those who write about "the service of man" as if the thought of it were a development of nineteenth-century enlightenment; but there it is in all its truth and grandeur in the life, and above all in the death of our Lord and Saviour Jesus Christ! His entire life was devoted to the service of man; and His death was but the giving up in one final act of surrender what had all along been consecrated to the same high and holy ministry.

These closing words of the great lesson are memorable, not only as setting before us the highest exemplification of the law of service, which as "Son of Man" Christ gave to the world; but as presenting the first intimation of the purpose of the great sacrifice He was about to offer at Jerusalem. Again and again He had told the disciples that it was necessary; but now for the first time does He give them an idea why it was necessary. It is too soon, indeed, to give a full explanation; it will be time enough to unfold the doctrine of atonement after the atonement has been actually made. Meantime He makes it plain that, while His whole life was a life of ministering as distinguished from being ministered unto, the supreme service He had come to render was the giving of His life as a ransom, something to be rendered up as a price which must be paid to redeem His people. It is plain from this way of putting it, that He viewed the giving up of His life as the means by which alone He could save the "many" who should, as His redeemed or ransomed ones, constitute His kingdom.

On the way to Jerusalem lay the beautiful city of Jericho. The place now called by that name is such a wretched assemblage of miserable hovels that it is difficult for the traveller to realise that the Jericho of the days of our Lord was not only the most luxurious place of resort in Palestine, but one that might vie with its fashionable rivals throughout the Roman Empire. Since the days of Herod the Great it had been the winter residence of the Court. Jerusalem being on the cold hill-top, it was convenient to have within easy reach a warm and sheltered spot in the deep valley of the Jordan; and with a delightful winter climate and a rich and fertile soil, Jericho needed only the lavish expenditure of money to make it into "a little Paradise," as Josephus calls it. With its gardens of roses and groves of palm, it was, even before the time of Herod, so beautiful a place, that, as a gem of the East, Antony bestowed it on Cleopatra as an expression of his devotion; after it passed into the hands of Herod, a theatre was erected and an amphitheatre, and many other noble and costly buildings; and during the season it was thronged by the rich and the great of the land, among whom would be distinguished visitors from foreign parts. What effect would all this grandeur have on Christ and His disciples as they passed through it on their way to Jerusalem? We are not told. Two things only are noted as worthy of record: the salvation of a rich publican (Luke xix. 1-10), and the healing of two poor blind men. Not the gardens and palaces of the city, but its sins and sorrows, engage the Saviour's thoughts and occupy His time.

As a rule, we regard it as waste of time to deal with the "discrepancies" between the different Evangelists; but as one of the most serious of them all has been found here it may be well to look at it to see how much or how little it amounts to. First, the other Gospels speak of the cure of a blind man, and tell his name, Bartimæus; this one says that two blind men were cured, and does not mention any name. If the other Evangelists had said that only one was healed, there would have been a real discrepancy; but they do not. Another "discrepancy" which has been noticed is that St. Matthew says Christ "touched their eyes," while the others do not mention the touch, but only tell us what He said; but surely there is no difficulty in supposing that Christ both touched the eyes and spoke the words at the same time. It is true that the words as recorded by St. Mark and St. Luke are not identical, but they are precisely to the same effect; and it is quite possible that every word which both of them report was actually said and that other words besides were spoken which have not been preserved.

These differences are not discrepancies at all; but there remains one which may fairly enough

*The knight was originally a *Knecht*=a servant or slave.

be so characterised. The first and second Gospel represent the cure as taking place on the way into Jericho; the third puts it on the way out.

Various suppositions, more or less plausible, especially less, have been made to "reconcile" these two representations: such as the fact that there were really two Jerichos, the old and the new, the cure being wrought as the Saviour passed from the one to the other, so that both accounts would be strictly accurate; or again, that cures may have been wrought both in entering and in leaving Jericho. But why should we trouble ourselves to reconcile so small a difference? It is not of the slightest consequence whether the cure took place on the way in or on the way out. If it had been a point on which strict accuracy was essential, care would doubtless have been taken to note the very moment and the very spot where it took place—as, for example, in the case of the cure of the nobleman's son at Capernaum (John iv. 52); but it was not; and therefore we have no more reason to wonder at the variation in so unimportant a detail than at those variations from the accurate text which we continually find in the quotations from the Old Testament Scriptures. The discrepancy does not in the slightest degree affect the credibility of any of the witnesses; it only serves, together with the other variations, to show the independence of the different accounts. How small must be the minds, or how strong the prejudices, of those who find support for their unbelief in discrepancies of which this is acknowledged to be one of the gravest examples!

It so happens, too, that there is no story in all the Gospels which shines more lustrously in its own light. It is full of beauty and pathos in all the versions of it which have come down to us; but most of all in the graphic story of St. Mark, to whose Gospel therefore its illustration may be regarded as belonging by special right.

II.—The Royal Entry (xxi. 1-17).

Travelling from Jericho, it is probable that our Lord reached Bethany on the evening of Friday, a week before His crucifixion. The next day, being the Jewish Sabbath, He would spend in retirement, probably in the house of Lazarus, whom a short time before He had raised from the dead. The following day, the first day of the week, would therefore be the date of His entry into Jerusalem as the Royal Son of David, come to claim His kingdom.

That this entrance into the capital is a most important event in the history of Jesus is evident not only from its nature and consequences, but also from the fact that it is one which all the four Evangelists record. Indeed, it is just at this point that the four narratives converge. The river of the water of life, which "was parted and became four heads" diverging at times in their course, now unites its waters in one channel broad and deep; and all the four Evangelists, though in different accents still, and with variation in the selection of details, combine to tell the same wondrous story of our Saviour's passion, the story of "the decease which He should accomplish at Jerusalem."

This was the first occasion on which our Lord distinctly put forth His claim to royalty. From the beginning of His ministry He had shown Himself to be a "prophet mighty in word and in deed," and to those who followed Him it became manifest that He was the Prophet foretold by Moses, for whose coming they had been taught to look with eager eyes (see Deut. xviii. 15-19). From the beginning of His ministry, too, the Saviour had been proclaiming "the gospel of the kingdom"; but when we examine carefully all He says about it, we find that He never expressly asserts that He Himself is King. Not that He conceals the all-important truth: He speaks of the kingdom in such a way that those who have ears to hear may learn that He is King Himself—as, for instance, when He says, "Suffer the little children to come unto Me, and forbid them not: for of such is the kingdom of heaven." One might quite readily infer from these words that Jesus Himself was King; but the claim is not thereby formally made. Besides, not only is it true that up to this time He did not formally assume the royal title, but He even resisted attempts made to thrust it upon Him (*e. g.*, John vi. 15). For this refusal to be crowned by the multitude there was only too good reason. Their ideas of royalty were entirely different from His. Had He allowed Himself to be borne on the tide of popular favour to royal honours, His kingdom would have been thereby marked as "of this world," it would have been stamped as something very different from the kingdom of "righteousness and peace and joy in the Holy Ghost" He had come to establish. Had He been a mere enthusiast, He would undoubtedly have yielded to such a tidal wave of public excitement; but His unerring wisdom taught Him that He must reach His throne by another path than that of popular favour. Rather must it be through popular rejection—through the dark portals of despite and death; and for that, His hour had not then come.

Now it has come. He has been steadily advancing to Jerusalem for the very purpose of accomplishing that decease which is to be the portal of His royalty. Already fully revealed as Prophet, He is about to be made "perfect through suffering" as our great High Priest. It is time, therefore, that He reveal Himself as King, so that no one may have it afterwards to say that He never really claimed the throne of His father David.

How, then, shall He assert His right? Shall a herald be sent to proclaim with the sound of a trumpet that Jesus of Nazareth is King over Israel in Jerusalem? To take such a course would be to court misunderstanding. It would be to raise the standard of revolt against the Romans. It would stir the city in a very different fashion from that in which the Prince of Peace would have it stirred. It would be the signal for tumult, bloodshed, and disastrous war. The ordinary method is evidently not to be thought of. How, then, shall it be done?

Our Lord is never at a loss for means to accomplish His designs in His own way, which is always the best. He sends to a neighbouring village for a young ass, mounts it, and rides into the city. That is all He does. Not a word said about royalty, no herald, no trumpeter, no proclamation, no royal pomp, nothing whatever to rouse the Roman jealousy or ire—nothing but the very ordinary circumstance of a man riding into the city on an ass's colt, a mode of conveyance not in itself calculated to attract any special notice. What was there, then, in such an act to secure the end? Nothing in itself; but a great deal when taken in connection with a remarkable prophecy in the Book of Zechariah well known to every Jew, and much in the thoughts of all who were looking for the promised Messiah. It is true, indeed, that an ordinary man might have done the same thing and the people have taken no notice of him. But Jesus had become the object of very great interest and attention to large numbers of the people on account of the miracles He had been working—notably that great miracle which still stirred the minds of the whole community, the raising of Lazarus from the dead. The chief priests and scribes, indeed, and the men of influence in Jerusalem, regarded Him with all the greater rancour on account of His miracles of mercy, and they had been specially embittered against Him since the raising of Lazarus; but it was different with the body of the people, especially those who had come or were coming from Galilee and other distant parts of the land to be present at the great Paschal feast. We are told by St. John that a large number of these had gone out the day before to Bethany, both to see Lazarus, who was naturally an object of curiosity, and also to see Jesus Himself; these accordingly were precisely in the state of mind in which they would most readily catch up the idea so naturally suggested by the significant act of our Saviour's riding into the city of David on a colt the foal of an ass. The result, accordingly, was as had been intended, and is thus described by our Evangelist: "The most part of the multitude spread their garments in the way; and others cut branches from the trees and spread them in the way. And the multitudes that went before Him, and that followed, cried, saying, Hosanna to the Son of David; Blessed is He that cometh in the name of the Lord; Hosanna in the highest" (R. V.).

The excellence of the method adopted by our Saviour to set forth His royal claims will still further appear when we consider that it arose quite naturally out of the circumstances in which He was placed. So much was this the case that some have thought He was taken by surprise, that He had no intention of calling forth the testimony of the people to His royal claims, that in fact He was only giving way to a movement He could not well resist; but this shallow view is plainly set aside, not only by what has been already advanced, but also by the answer He gives to the Pharisees who ask Him to rebuke and silence His disciples: "I tell you that if these should hold their peace, the stones would immediately cry out" (Luke xix. 39, 40).

Not only did the means adopted by our Lord rise naturally out of the circumstances in which He and His followers were placed, but they were specially suited to suggest important truths concerning the kingdom He claimed as His own. We have already seen that, if He had entered the city in regal pomp and splendour, it would have conveyed an entirely false idea of the kingdom. The method He did adopt was such as to give a true idea of it.

First, it strikingly suggested the kingliness of lowliness, which, as we have seen, was one of its great distinctive principles. As we look back over His recent instructions to His disciples, we see how very much this thought was in His heart and how great was the importance He attached to it. He had just taught them that the Son of man had come, not to be ministered unto, but to minister and to give His life a ransom for many; and His manner of entering into His capital must be in harmony with the lowly, self-renouncing work He has come to do. Thus He shows in the most impressive way that His kingdom is not of this world. There is no suggestion of rivalry with Cæsar; yet to those who look beneath the surface He is manifestly more of a king than any Cæsar. He has knowledge of everything without a spy (ver. 2); He has power over men without a soldier (ver. 3); He has simply to say "The Lord hath need," and immediately His royal will is loyally fulfilled. Evidently He has the mind of a King and the will of a King: has He not also the heart of a King, of a true Shepherd of the people? See how He bears the burden of their future on His heart, a burden which weighs so heavily upon Him that He cannot restrain His tears (Luke xix. 41-44). There is no kingly state; but was not His a kingly soul, Who in such humble guise rode into Jerusalem that day?

Not less than lowliness is peace suggested as characteristic of His kingdom. First by the manner of His entrance; for while the horse and the chariot were suggestive of war, the ass was the symbol of peace. And then, the prophecy is one of peace. Immediately after the words quoted by the Evangelist there follows this remarkable promise: "I will cut off the chariot from Ephraim, and the horse from Jerusalem, and the battle bow shall be cut off; and He shall speak peace unto the heathen; and His dominion shall be from sea even to sea, and from the river even to the ends of the earth." It would seem, indeed, that some at least in the multitude realised that through the Messiah was to be expected a deeper peace than that between man and man. This deeper peace may have been suggested to their minds by the words following next in the prophecy, which goes on to speak of prisoners of hope rescued from the pit, and turning to the stronghold; or by the Psalm from which their cry "Hosanna in the highest" was taken (Ps. cxviii.); certain it is that their minds did rise to a higher conception of the work of the Messiah than they had given token of before; for the cry of some of them at least was "Peace in heaven, and glory in the highest" (Luke xix. 38). A striking proof this, of the fitness of His manner of entering into His capital to suggest the purest, highest, and best thoughts concerning the kingdom which He claimed as His own.

As Jerusalem was the city of the great King, the Temple was His house, His royal palace, and accordingly He enters it and takes possession in His Father's name. We are told by St. Mark that "when He had looked round about upon all things, it being now eventide, He went out unto Bethany with the twelve." But St. Matthew, who is accustomed to pay more attention to the logical than to the exact chronological sequence of events, proceeds at once to relate the purging of the Temple, which really took place the following day, but which was so plainly the natural sequel of His royal entrance that he very properly gives it in close connection therewith. Besides, what the King did on entering the Temple the next day admirably illustrates the prophecy. For what saith the prophet? "Behold thy King cometh unto thee: He is just, and having salvation." "He is *just*,"—therefore He will not tolerate the unholy traffic in the Temple, but "cast out all them that sold and bought in the Temple, and overthrew the tables of the money-changers and the seats of them that sold the doves; and He saith unto them, My house shall be called a house of prayer; but ye make it a den of robbers" (R. V.): "*and having salvation*"—accordingly, when He sees the blind and the lame in the Temple He does not turn them out, He does not turn away from them, "He healed them." The casting out of the traders illustrated the *righteousness* of the kingdom, the healing of the blind and lame, its *peace*, and the shouts of the children which followed, its *joy*.

This coming of the King to His capital has been familiarly spoken of as "the triumphal entry." The term seems unfortunate and misleading. The waving of palms, the strewing of branches and leaves, the spreading of garments on the way—all this gave it something of the aspect of a triumph; but that it was no triumph none knew better than the man of Sorrows, Who was the centre of it all. There was certainly no triumph in His heart that day. If you wish to look into His heart, watch Him as He comes to the turn of the road where first the great city bursts upon His sight. How it glitters in the sun, its palaces and towers gleaming in the splendour of the day, its magnificent Temple, which had taken nearly half a century to build, rearing its stately head high above all, into the glorious heaven—a city and a temple for a king to be proud of, especially when seen through waving palm branches held in the hands of a rejoicing throng who shout "Hosanna to the Son of David, Hosanna in the highest!" Surely His soul must be thrilled with jubilant emotion!

Ah! but look at Him: look at Him closely. Go up to Him, near enough to see His face and hear what He is saying. Is He jubilant? His eyes are wet with tears; and with tears in His voice He is speaking "the saddest words of tongue or pen": O Jerusalem, "if thou hadst known, even thou, at least in this thy day, the things which belong unto thy peace! but now they are hid from thine eyes. For the days shall come upon thee, that thine enemies shall cast a trench about thee, and compass thee round, and keep thee in on every side, and shall lay thee even with the ground, and thy children within thee; and they shall not leave in thee one stone upon another; because thou knewest not the time of thy visitation." Ah! well the Man of Sorrows knew what all that shouting and rejoicing were worth; not even for a moment was He misled by it; no less certainly now when the plaudits of the multitudes were ringing around Him, than when He had been on the way going up to Jerusalem, did He know that, though He was the rightful King, He should receive no king's welcome, but should suffer many things and die. He knew that it was to no royal palace, but to the bitter cross, He was advancing, as He rode down Olivet, across the Kedron, and up to the city of David. Yet it is not the thought of His own cross that draws the tears from His eyes; it is the thought of the woes impending over those whom He has come to save, but who will have none of Him. O the depth of divine love in these self-forgetful tears!

One thrill of joy the day had for the King of sorrows. It was His welcome from the children. The plaudits of the multitude He seems to have received in silence. Why should He be moved by *hosannas* from the lips of those who, as soon as they shall find out what manner of King He is, will cry "Away with Him"? But the hosannas of the children are genuine music to His soul. The little ones at least are true. There is no guile in their spirits. "Of such is the kingdom of heaven." It is most touching to observe how lovingly the heart of the Saviour goes out to the little ones at this most trying time. The climax of pathos in His lament over Jerusalem is reached when, after speaking of the fate of the city, He adds, "and thy children within thee"; and the same deep sympathy with the little ones is shown in the answer He gives to the mean-spirited priests and scribes who were moved with indignation and tried to silence their sweet voices: "Have ye never read, Out of the mouth of babes and sucklings Thou hast perfected praise?"

"And He left them, and went out of the city into Bethany, and He lodged there,"—not in the house of Lazarus, we may be sure, or He would not have "hungered" when in the morning He returned to the city (ver. 18); no doubt under the open canopy of heaven or at best under some booth erected as a temporary shelter. What were His thoughts, what His feelings, as He looked back on the day and forward to the week?

CHAPTER XVII.

CONFLICT IN THE TEMPLE.

MATTHEW xxi. 18-xxiii.

IT had been written that the Lord should suddenly come to His Temple (Mal. iii. 1); but He would not too hastily assert His rights. The first day He simply "looked round about upon all things" (Mark xi. 11), and then withdrew to Bethany. The second day—without, however, even yet assailing the authority of those in power—He assumed His prerogative as Lord of the Temple by casting out the traffickers, healing the blind and the lame, and accepting the hosannas of the children. The scribes and Pharisees showed some displeasure at all this, and raised objections; but the answer they received silenced, if it did not satisfy them. Thus two days passed without any serious attempt to dispute His authority; but on the third day the conflict began. It was a dark and terrible day, and of its fateful history we have a full account in this Gospel.

The day opens with the sight on the way to the city of the withered fig tree, a sad symbol of the impending fate of Israel, to be decided ere the day closed by their final rejection of their Saviour-King. This was our Lord's single miracle of judgment; many a stern word of warning did He speak, but there is no severity in His deeds: they are all mercy and love. The single exception, if exception it may be called, makes this great fact stand out only the more impressively. It was necessary for love's sake to show that in that arm, which was always strong to save, there was also strength to smite if the sad necessity should come; but so tender-hearted is He that He cannot bear to strike where the stroke can be felt, so He lets it fall on an unconscious tree. Thus to the end He justifies His name of Jesus, Saviour, and illustrates the blessed truth of which His whole life is the expression, that "God is love." "The Son of man is not come to destroy men's lives but to save them." Judgment is His strange work; from the very thought of it He shrinks, as seems suggested to us here by the fact that, in the use He makes of the circumstance in His conversation with the disciples, He refrains from speaking of its dark significance, but rather takes the opportunity of teaching from it an incidental lesson full of hope and comfort regarding the power of faith and the value of prayer (vv. 21, 22).

As soon as on the third day He enters the Temple the conflict begins. It would seem that the interval our Lord had in mercy allowed for calm reflection had been used for no other purpose than to organise a conspiracy for the purpose of entangling Him in His words and so discrediting His authority. We gather this from the carefully framed questions with which He is plied by one party after another. Four successive attacks are recorded in the passage before us: the first by the chief priests and elders of the people demanding His authority; the next by the Pharisees, assisted by the Herodians, who endeavoured by means of the difficulty of the tribute money to embroil Him with the Roman power; this was again immediately followed by a third, in which the prime movers were the Sadducees, armed with what they considered an unanswerable question regarding the life to come; and when that also broke down there was a renewed attack of the Pharisees, who thought to disconcert Him by a perplexing question about the law.

We may not discuss the long sad history of these successive attacks with any fulness, but only glance first at the challenge of our Lord's authority and how He meets it, and next at the ordeal of questions with which it was followed.

I.—The Challenge (xxi. 23-xxii. 14).

"By what authority doest Thou these things? And who gave Thee this authority?" The question was fair enough; and if it had been asked in an earnest spirit Jesus would have given them, as always to the honest inquirer, a kind and satisfying answer. It is not, however, as inquirers, but as cavillers, they approach Him. Again and again, at times and in ways innumerable, by fulfilment of prophecy, by His mighty deeds and by His wondrous words, He had given proof of His Divine authority and established His claim to be the true Messiah. It was not therefore because they lacked evidence of His authority, but because they hated it, because they would not have this man to reign over them, that now they question Him. It was obvious that their only object was to entangle Him; accordingly our Lord showed how in the net they were spreading for Him their own feet were caught.

He meets their question with a counter-question, "The baptism of John, whence was it? from heaven, or of men?" The more we examine this question, the more must we admire the consummate wisdom it displays. We see at once how it turns the tables on His critics; but it is far more important to notice how admirably adapted it was to lead them to the answer of their own question, if only they would follow it out. They dared not repudiate the baptism of John; and had not John baptised Jesus, and solemnly borne repeated testimony to His Messiahship? Had he not most emphatically borne that very testimony to a formal deputation sent by themselves? (John i. 19-27). Finally, were not the ministry and testimony of John closely associated in prophecy with that very coming of the Lord to His Temple which gave them so deep offence: "Behold, I will send My messenger, and he shall prepare the way before Me: and the Lord, whom ye seek, shall suddenly come to His temple: . . . behold, He shall come, saith the Lord of hosts." Our Lord's counter-question, then, was framed with such exquisite skill as to disappoint their malice, while at the same time it was suited to guide the earnest inquirer to the truth.

The propounders of the question were not true men, but hypocrites. A negative answer they *could* not give. An affirmative they *would* not give. So when they refused to answer, our Lord replied, "Neither tell I you by what authority I do these things."

The Lord of the Temple now assumes the offensive, and directs against His opponents a series of parables which He holds up to them as a triple mirror in which from different points of view they may see themselves in their true character, and as a set of danger signals to warn them of their impending doom. He presents them with such marvellous skill that He makes the Pharisees their own judges, and constrains them to pass sentence on themselves. In the first parable He constrains them to declare their own guilt; in the second, He makes them decree their own punishment; in the third, He warns them of the impending fate of the people they were leading to destruction.

We have said that in these parables Christ assumes the offensive; but this is true only in a very superficial sense. In the deepest sense He spoke them not against the Pharisees, but for them. His object was to carry home to their hearts the conviction of sin, and to impress them with a sense of their danger before it was too late. This was what above all they needed. It was their only hope of salvation. And how admirably suited for His purpose were these three parables! Their application to themselves was plain enough after it was stated, but not beforehand; the effect of which was that they were put in a position to give an impartial verdict on their own conduct. It was the same method so effectively employed by Nathan in bringing conviction to the conscience of David. Had Christ charged the sin of the Pharisees directly home upon them they would have been at once thrown on the defensive, and it would have been impossible to reach their conscience through the entanglements of prejudice and personal interest. Christ wishes to disentangle them from all that was darkening their moral vision, and He uses the parable as the most effective means. It is a great mistake, then, to suppose that Jesus contented Himself with turning the tables on them, and carrying the war, so to speak, into the enemy's country. It was with them a war of words, but not with Him. He was seeking to save these poor lost ones. He wished to give them His best for their worst. They had come to entangle Him in His talk. He does His best to disentangle them from the meshes of self-deception. The tone of all three parables is exceptionally severe; but the spirit of them is love.

The Two Sons (vv. 28-32).

The parable of the two sons is exceedingly simple; and the question founded upon it, "Whether of them twain did the will of his father?" admitted of but one answer—an answer which seemed, as it was spoken, to involve only the simplest of all moral judgments; yet how keen the edge of it when once it was disclosed! Observe the emphatic word *did*, suggesting without saying it, that it made comparatively little difference what they *said* (see xxiii. 3). So far as profession went, the Pharisees were all that could be desired. They were the representatives of religion in the land; their whole attitude corresponded to the answer of the second son: "I go, sir." Yet when John—whom they themselves admitted to be a prophet of the Lord—came to them in the way of righteousness, they set his word aside and refused to obey him. On the other hand, many of those whose lives seemed to say "I will not," when they heard the word of John, repented and began to work the works of God. Thus it came to pass that many of these had entered the kingdom, while the self-complacent Pharisee still remained without.

The words with which the parable is pressed home are severe and trenchant; but they are nevertheless full of gospel grace. They set in the strongest light the welcome fact that the salvation of God is for the chief of sinners, for those who have been rudest and most rebellious in their first answers to the divine appeal; and then, while they condemn so very strongly the self-deceiver, it is not for the purpose of covering him with confusion, but in order to open his eyes and save him from the net in which he has set his feet. Even in that terrible sentence which puts him lower down than open and disgraceful sinners, there is a door left still unlatched for him to enter. "The publicans and harlots go into the kingdom of God *before you*"; but you may enter after them. If only you, like them, would "afterward" repent—if you would repent of your hypocrisy and insincerity, as they have repented of their rudeness and rebellion—you would be as gladly welcomed as they into the kingdom of God.

The Husbandmen (vv. 33-46).

The second parable follows hard on the first, and presses the chief priests and Pharisees so closely that they cannot fail to see in the end that it is themselves they have been constrained to judge and condemn (ver. 45). It is indeed difficult to suppose that they had not even from the beginning some glimpse of the intended application of this parable. The vineyard was a familiar symbol with a definite and well-understood meaning, from which our Lord in His use of it does not depart. The vineyard being the nation, the owner is evidently God; the fruit expected, righteousness; the particulars mentioned (the fence, the press, the tower) implying the completeness of the arrangements made by the owner for securing the expected fruit. The husbandmen are the leaders of the people, those who are responsible for their direction and control. The going to a far country represents the removal of God from their sight; so that they are, as it were, put upon their honour, left to act in the matter of the vineyard according to the prompting of their own hearts. All this is contained in the few lines which make up verse 33, and forms the groundwork of this great parable. Thus are set forth in a very striking manner the high privileges and grave responsibilities of the leaders of the Jewish people, represented at the time by the chief priests and Pharisees He was then addressing. How are they meeting this responsibility? Let the parable tell.

It is a terrible indictment, showing in the strongest light the guilt of their fathers, and pointing out to them that they are on the verge of a crime far greater still. Again and again have prophets of righteousness come in the name of the Lord, and demanded the fruits of righteousness which were due. How have they been received? "The husbandmen took his servants, and beat one, and killed another, and stoned another." So have their fathers acted time after time and still the patience of the owner is not exhausted, nor does He even yet give up all hope of fruit from His favoured vineyard; so, as a last resort, He sends His son, saying, "They will reverence my son."

We can imagine the tone in which the Son of God would speak these words. What a sublime consciousness is implied in His use of them! and how touchingly does He in this incidental way give the best of all answers to the question with which His enemies began! Surely the son, the only and well-beloved son,* had the best of all authority to act for the father! In the former parable He had appealed to the recognised authority of John; now He indicates that the highest authority of all is in Himself. If only their hearts had not been wholly shut against the light, how it would have flashed upon them now! They would have taken up the cry of the children, and said, "Hosanna! blessed is He that cometh in the name of the Lord"; and the parable would have served its purpose before it had reached its close. But they are deaf and blind to the things of God; so the awful indictment must proceed to the bitter end.

If there was in the heart of Christ an exalted consciousness of His filial relation to God as He spoke of the sending of the Son, what a pang must have shot through it as He proceeded to depict in such vivid colours the crime they are now all ready to commit, referring successively as He does to the arrest, the handing over to Pilate, and the crucifixion without the gate: "They caught him, and cast him out of the vineyard, and slew him." How apalling it must have been to Him to speak these words! how appalling it ought to have been to them to hear them! That they did feel the force of the parable is evident from the answer they gave to the question, "What will he do to those husbandmen?" and, as we have said, they must surely have had some glimpses of its application to themselves; but it did not disturb their self-complacency, until our Lord spoke the plain words with which He followed up the parable, referring to that very Psalm from which the children's cry of "Hosanna" was taken. From it He selects the symbol of the stone rejected by the builders, but by God made the head of the corner, applying it to Himself (the rejected stone) and them (the builders). The reference was most appropriate in itself; and it had the further advantage of being followed by the very word which it would be their salvation now to speak. "Hosanna" is the word which immediately follows the quotation He makes, and it introduces a prayer which, if only they will make their own, all will yet be well with them. The prayer is, "Save now, I beseech Thee, O Lord"; followed by the words, "Blessed be

* See the accounts in the second and third Gospels.

He that cometh in the name of the Lord." May we not assume that our Lord paused after making His quotation to give them the opportunity of adopting it as their own prayer? His whole heart was longing to hear these very words from them. Have we not the proof of it further on, in the sad words with which He at last abandoned the hope: "I say unto you, ye shall not see Me henceforth till ye shall say, Blessed is He that cometh in the name of the Lord" (xxiii. 39)?

Seeing they will not take the warning of the parable, and that they refuse the opportunity given them while yet under its awe-inspiring influence, to repent and return, He must give sentence against them: "Therefore say I unto you, The kingdom of God shall be taken away from you, and given to a nation bringing forth the fruits thereof." This sentence He follows up by setting before them the dark side of the other symbol: "Whosoever shall fall on this stone shall be broken: but on whomsoever it shall fall, it will grind him to powder." They were stumbling on the stone now, and about to be broken upon it; but the danger that lay before them if they persisted in their present unbelief and sin, would be far greater still, when He Whom they now despised and rejected should be at the head of all authority and power.

But all is vain. Steeling their hearts against His faithful words, they are only the more maddened against Him, and fear alone restrains them from beginning now the very crime against which they have just had so terrible a warning: "When they sought to lay hands on Him, they feared the multitudes, because they took Him for a prophet."

The Marriage Feast (xxii. 1-14).

The manner in which this third parable is introduced leaves room for doubt whether it was spoken in immediate connection with the two preceding. The use of the word "answered" (ver. 1) would rather suggest the idea that some conversation not reported had intervened. But though it does not form part of a continuous discourse with the others, it is so closely connected with them in scope and bearing that it may appropriately be dealt with, as concluding the warning called forth by the first attack of the chief priests and elders. The relation between the three parables will be best seen by observing that the first has to do with their treatment of John; the second and third with their treatment of Himself and His apostles. The second and third differ from each other in this: that while the King's Son, Who is prominent in both, is regarded in the former as the last and greatest of a long series of heavenly messengers sent to demand of the chosen people the fruits of righteousness, in the latter He is presented, not as demanding righteousness, but as bringing joy. Duty is the leading thought of the second parable, privilege of the third; in the one sin is brought home to Israel's leaders by setting before them their treatment of the messengers of righteousness, in the other the sin lies in their rejection of the message of grace. Out of this distinction rises another—viz., that while the second parable runs back into the past, upwards along the line of the Old Testament prophets, the third runs down into the future, into the history of the apostolic times. The two together make up a terrible indictment, which might well have roused these slumbering consciences, and led even scribes and Pharisees to shrink from filling up the measure of their iniquities.

A word may be necessary as to the relation of this parable to the similar one recorded in the fourteenth chapter of St. Luke, known as "The parable of the Great Supper." The two have many features in common, but the differences are so great that it is plainly wrong to suppose them to be different versions of the same. It is astonishing to see what needless difficulties some people make for themselves by the utterly groundless assumption that our Lord would never use the same illustration a second time. Why should He not have spoken of the gospel as a feast, not twice merely, but fifty times? There would, no doubt, be many variations in His manner of unfolding the thought, according to the circumstances, the audience, the particular object in view at the time; but to suppose that because He had used that illustration in Galilee He must be forbidden from reverting to it in Judea is a specimen of what we may call the insanity of those who are ever on the watch for their favourite "discrepancies." In this case there is not only much variation in detail, but the scope of the two parables is quite different, the former having more the character of a pressing invitation, with only a suggestion of warning at the close; whereas the one before us, while preserving all the grace of the gospel as suggested by the figure of a feast to which men are freely invited, and even heightening its attractiveness inasmuch as it is a wedding feast—the most joyful of all festivities—and a royal one too, yet has throughout the same sad tone of judgment which has been characteristic of all these three parables, and is at once seen to be specially appropriate to the fateful occasion on which they were spoken.

As essentially a New Testament parable, it begins with the familiar formula "The kingdom of heaven is like." The two previous parables had led up to the new dispensation; but this one begins with it, and is wholly concerned with it. The King's Son appears now, not as a messenger, but as a bridegroom. It was not the first time that Jesus had spoken of Himself as a bridegroom, or rather as *the* Bridegroom.* The thought was a familiar one in the prophets of the Old Testament, the Bridegroom, be it remembered, being none other than Jehovah Himself. Consider, then, what it meant that *Jesus* should without hesitation or explanation speak of Himself as the Bridegroom. And let us not imagine that He simply took the figure, and applied it to Himself as fulfilling prophecy; let us not fail to realise that He entered fully into its tender meaning. When we think of the circumstances in which this parable was spoken we have here a most pathetic glimpse into the sanctuary of our Saviour's loving heart. Let us try with reverent sympathy to enter into the feeling of the King's Son, come from heaven to seek humanity for His bride, to woo and to win her from the cruel bondage of sin and death, to take her into union with Himself, so that she may share with Him the liberty and wealth, the purity and joy, the glory and the hope of the heavenly kingdom! The King "made

* Another example of the use of the same illustration more than once. See ix. 15.

a marriage for His Son"—where is the bride? what response is she making to the Bridegroom's suit? A marriage for His Son! On Calvary?

It must have been very hard for Him to go on; but He will keep down the rising tide of emotion, that He may set before this people and before all people another attractive picture of the kingdom of heaven. He will give even these despisers of the heavenly grace another opportunity to reconsider their position. So He tells of the invitations sent out first to "them that were bidden"—*i. e.*, to the chosen people who had been especially invited from the earliest times, and to whom, when the fulness of the time had come, the call was first addressed. "And they would not come." There is no reference to the aggravations which had found place in the former parable (xxi. 39). These were connected not so much with the offer of grace, which is the main purport of this parable, as with the demand for fruit, which was the leading thought of the one before. It was enough, then, in describing how they dealt with the invitation, to say, "They would not come"; and, indeed, this refusal hurt Him far more than their buffets and their blows. When He is buffeted He is silent, sheds no tears, utters no wail; His tears and lamentation are reserved for them: "How often would I have gathered thy children together, even as a hen gathereth her chickens under her wings, and ye would not!" "*They would not come.*"

But the love of the King and of His Son is not yet exhausted. A second invitation is sent, with greater urgency than before, and with fuller representations of the great preparations which had been made for the entertainment of the guests: "Again, he sent forth other servants, saying, Tell them which are bidden, Behold, I have prepared my dinner: my oxen and my fatlings are killed, and all things are ready: come unto the marriage." As the first invitation was that which had been already given and which they were now rejecting, the second refers to that fuller proclamation of the gospel which was yet to be made after the work of the Bridegroom-Redeemer should be finished when it could be said, as not before: "All things are ready."

In the account which follows, therefore, there is a foreshadowing of the treatment the apostles would afterwards receive. Many, indeed, were converted by their word, and took their places at the feast; but the people as a whole "made light of it, and went their ways, one to his farm, another to his merchandise: and the remnant took his servants, and entreated them spitefully, and slew them." What was the consequence? Jerusalem, rejecting the gospel of the kingdom, even when it was "preached with the Holy Ghost sent down from heaven," must be destroyed; and new guests must be sought among the nations that up till now had no especial invitation to the feast. This prophetic warning was conveyed in terms of the parable; yet there is a touch in it which shows how strongly the Saviour's mind was running on the sad future of which the parable was but a picture: "When the king heard thereof, he was wroth: and he sent forth his armies, and destroyed those murderers, and burned up their *city.*" Why "city"? There had been no mention of a city in the parable. True; but Jerusalem was in the Saviour's heart, and all the pathos of His lament over it is in that little word. "*Their* city" too, observe,—reminding us of "*your* house" at the close of this sad day (xxiii. 38). In the same way the calling of the Gentiles is most skilfully brought within the scope of the parable, by the use of the peculiar word translated in the Revised Version—"the partings of the highways," which seems to suggest the thought of the servants leaving the city precincts and going out in all directions along the main trunk roads to "the partings of the highways," to carry the gospel to all without distinction, wherever could be found an ear of man to listen, or a human heart to welcome the King's grace and the Bridegroom's love. Thus, after all, the wedding was to be furnished with guests.

The parable, as we have seen, is one of grace; but righteousness too must find a place in it. The demand for fruits of righteousness is no less rigid in the new dispensation than it had been in the old. To make this clear and strong the parable of the Feast is followed by the pendant of the Wedding Garment.

There are two ways in which the heavenly marriage feast may be despised: first, by those who will not come at all; next, and no less, by those who try to snatch the wedding joy without the bridal purity. The same leading thought or motive is recognisable here as in the parable of the two sons. The man without the wedding garment corresponds to the son who said "I go, sir," and went not, while those who refuse altogether correspond to the son who answered "I will not." By bearing this in mind we can understand, what to many has been a serious difficulty—how it is that the punishment meted out to the offender in this second parable is so terribly severe. If we simply think of the parable itself, it does seem an extraordinary thing that so slight an offence as coming to a wedding feast without the regulation dress should meet with such an awful doom; but when we consider whom this man represents we can see the very best of reasons for it. Hypocrisy was his crime, than which there is nothing more utterly hateful in the sight of Him Who desireth truth in the inward parts. It is true that the representation does not at first seem to set the sin in so very strong a light; but when we think of it, we see that there was no other way in which it could be brought within the scope of this parable. It is worthy of notice, moreover, that the distinction between the intruder and the others is not observed till the king himself enters, which indicates that the difference between him and the others was no outward distinction, that the garment referred to is the invisible garment of righteousness. To the common eye he looked like all the rest; but when the all-searching Eye is on the company he is at once detected and exposed. He is really worse than those who would not come at all. They were honest sinners; he was a hypocrite—*at* the feast with mouth and hand and eye, but not *of* it, for his spirit is not robed in white: he is the black sheep in the fold; a despiser within, he is worse than the despisers without.

Even to him, indeed, the king has a kindly feeling. He calls him "Friend," and gives him yet the opportunity to repent and cry for mercy. But he is speechless. False to the core, he has no rallying point within to fall back upon. All is confusion and despair. He cannot even pray. Nothing remains but to pronounce his final doom (ver. 13).

The words with which the parable closes (ver. 14) are sad and solemn. They have occasioned difficulty to some, who have supposed they were meant to teach that the number of the saved will be small. Their difficulty, like so many others, has been due to forgetfulness of the circumstances under which the words were spoken, and the strong emotion of which they were the expression. Jesus is looking back over the time since He began to spread the gospel feast, and thinking how many have been invited, and how few have come! And even among those who have seemed to come there are hypocrites! One He specially would have in mind as He spoke of the man without the wedding garment; for though we take him to be the type of a class, we can scarcely think that our Lord could fail to let His sad thoughts rest on Judas as He described that man. Taking all this into consideration we can well understand how at that time He should conclude His parable with the lamentation: "Many are called, but few chosen." It did not follow that it was a truth for all time and for eternity. It was true for the time included in the scope of the parable. It was most sadly true of the Jewish nation then, and in the times which followed on immediately; but the day was coming, before all was done, when the heavenly Bridegroom, according to the sure word of prophecy, should "see of the travail of His soul, and be satisfied." No creed article, therefore, have we here, but a cry from the sore heart of the heavenly Bridegroom, in the day of His sorrows, in the pain of unrequited love.

II.—The Ordeal of Questions (xxii. 15-46).

The open challenge has failed; but more subtle weapons may succeed. The Pharisees have found it of no avail to confront their enemy; but they may still be able to entangle Him. They will at all events try. They will spring upon Him some hard questions, of such a kind that, answering on the spur of the moment, He will be sure to compromise Himself.

1. The first shall be one of those semi-political semi-religious questions on which feeling is running high—the lawfulness or unlawfulness of paying tribute to Cæsar. The old Pharisees who had challenged His authority keep in the background, that the sinister purpose of the question may not appear; but they are represented by some of their disciples who, coming fresh upon the scene and addressing Jesus in terms of respect and appreciation, may readily pass for guileless inquirers. They were accompanied by some Herodians, whose divergence of view on the point made it all the more natural that they should join with Pharisees in asking the question; for it might fairly be considered that they had been disputing with one another in regard to it, and had concluded to submit the question to His decision as to one who would be sure to know the truth and fearless to tell it. So together they come with the request: "Master, we know that Thou art true, and teachest the way of God in truth, neither carest Thou for any man: for Thou regardest not the person of men. Tell us therefore, What thinkest Thou? Is it lawful to give tribute unto Cæsar, or not?"

But they cannot impose upon Him: "Jesus perceived their wickedness, and said, Why tempt ye Me, ye hypocrites?" Having thus unmasked them, without a moment's hesitation He answers them. They had expected a "yes" or a "no"—a "yes" which would have set the people against Him, or better still a "no" which would have put Him at the mercy of the government. But, avoiding Scylla on the one hand, and Charybdis on the other, He makes straight for His goal by asking for a piece of coin and calling attention to Cæsar's stamp upon it. Those who use Cæsar's coin should not refuse to pay Cæsar's tribute; but, while the relation which with their own acquiescence they sustain to the Roman emperor implied corresponding obligations in the sphere it covered, this did not at all interfere with what is due to the King of kings and Lord of lords, in Whose image we all are made, and Whose superscription every one of us bears: "Render therefore unto Cæsar the things which are Cæsar's; and unto God the things that are God's." Thus He not only avoids the net they had spread for Him, and gives them the very best answer to their question, but, in doing so, He lays down a great principle of far-reaching application and permanent value respecting the difficult and much-to-be-vexed question as to the relations between Church and State. "O answer full of miracle!" as one had said. No wonder that "when they had heard these words they marvelled, and left Him, and went their way."

2. Next come forward certain Sadducees. That the Pharisees had an understanding with them also seems likely from what is said both in ver. 15, which seems a general introduction to the series of questions, and in ver. 34, from which it would appear that they were somewhere out of sight, waiting to hear the result of this new attack. Though the alliance seems a strange one, it is not the first time that common hostility to the Christ of God has drawn together the two great rival parties (see chap. xvi. 1). If we are right in supposing them to be in combination now, it is a remarkable illustration of the deep hostility of the Pharisees that they should not only combine with the Sadducees against Him, as they had done before, but that they should look with complacency on their using against Him a weapon which threatened one of their own doctrines. For the object of the attack was to cast ridicule on the doctrine of the resurrection, which assuredly the Pharisees did not deny.

The difficulty they raise is of the same kind as those which are painfully familiar in these days, when men of coarse minds and fleshly imaginations show by their crude objections their incapacity even to think on spiritual themes. The case they supposed was one they knew He could not find fault with so far as this world was concerned, for everything was done in accordance with the letter of the law of Moses, the inference being that whatever confusion there was in it must belong to what they would call His figment of the resurrection: "In the resurrection whose wife shall she be of the seven? for they all had her."

It is worthy of note that our Lord's answer is much less stern than in the former case. These men were not hypocrites. They were scornful, perhaps flippant; but they were not intentionally dishonest. The difficulty they felt was due to the coarseness of their minds, but it was a real difficulty to them. Our Lord accordingly gives them a kindly answer, not denouncing them, but calmly showing them where they are wrong: "Ye do err, not knowing the Scriptures, nor the power of God."

Ye know not the power of God, or ye would not suppose that the life to come would be a mere repetition of the life that now is, with all its fleshly conditions the same as now. That there is continuity of life is of course implied in the very idea of resurrection; but true life resides not in the flesh, but in the spirit, and therefore the continuity will be a spiritual continuity; and the power of God will effect such changes on the body itself that it will rise out of its fleshly condition into a state of being like that of the angels of God. The thought is the same as that which was afterwards expanded by the apostle Paul in such passages as Rom. viii. 5-11, 1 Cor. xv. 35-54.

Ye know not the Scriptures, or you would find in the writings of Moses from which you quote, and to which you attach supreme importance, evidence enough of the great doctrine you deny. "Have ye not read that which was spoken unto you by God, saying, I am the God of Abraham, and the God of Isaac, and the God of Jacob?" Here, again, Jesus not only answers the Sadducees, but puts the great and all-important doctrine of the life to come and the resurrection of the body on its deepest foundation. There are those who have expressed astonishment that He did not quote from some of the later prophets, where He could have found passages much clearer and more to the point: but not only was it desirable that, as they had based their question on Moses, He should give His answer from the same source; but in doing so He has put the great truth on a permanent and universal basis; for the argument rests not on the authority of Moses, nor, as some have supposed, upon the present tense "I am," but on the relation between God and His people. The thought is that such a relation between mortal man and the eternal God as is implied in the declaration "I am the God of Abraham, and the God of Isaac, and the God of Jacob" is itself a guarantee of immortality. Not for the spirit only, for it is not as spirits merely, but as men that we are taken into relation to the living God; and that relation, being of God, must share His immortality: "God is not the God of the dead, but of the living." The thought * is put in a very striking way in a well-known passage in the Epistle to the Hebrews: "But now they [the patriarchs] desire a better country, that is, an heavenly: *wherefore God is not ashamed to be called their God:* for He hath prepared for them a city."

Our Lord's answer suggests the best way of assuring ourselves of this glorious hope. Let God be real to us, and life and immortality will be real too. If we would escape the doubts of old Sadducee and new Agnostic, we must be much with God, and strengthen more and more the ties which bind us to Him.

3. The next attempt of the Pharisees is on an entirely new line. They have found that they cannot impose upon Him by sending pretended inquirers to question Him. But they have managed to lay their hands on a real inquirer now —one of themselves, a student of the law, who is exercised on a question much discussed, and to which very different answers are given; they will suggest to him to carry his question to Jesus and see what He will say to it. That this was the real state of the case appears from the fuller account in St. Mark's Gospel. When, then, St. Matthew speaks of him as asking Jesus a question, "tempting Him," we are not to impute the same sinister motives as actuated those who sent him. He also was in a certain sense tempting Jesus—*i. e.*, putting Him to the test, but with no sinister motive, with a real desire to find out the truth, and probably also to find out if this Jesus was one who could really help an inquirer after truth. In this spirit, then, he asks the question, "Which is the great commandment in the law?"

The answer our Lord immediately gives is now so familiar that it is difficult to realise how great a thing it was to give it for the first time. True, He takes it from the Scriptures; but think what command of the Scriptures is involved in this prompt reply. The passages quoted lie far apart—the one in the sixth chapter of Deuteronomy, the other in the nineteenth of Leviticus in quite an obscure corner; and nowhere are they spoken of as the first and second commandments, nor indeed were they regarded as commandments in the usually understood sense of the word. When we consider all this we recognise what from one point of view might be called a miracle of genius, and from another a flash of inspiration, in the instantaneous selection of these two passages, and bringing them together so as to furnish a summary of the law and the prophets beyond all praise which the veriest unbeliever, if only he have a mind to appreciate that which is excellent, must recognise as worthy of being written in letters of light. That one short answer to a sudden question—asked indeed by a true man, but really sprung upon Him by His enemies who were watching for His halting—is of more value in morals than all the writings of all the ethical philosophers, from Socrates to Herbert Spencer.

It is now time to question the questioners. The opportunity is most favourable. They are gathered together to hear what He will say to their last attempt to entangle Him. Once more He has not only met the difficulty, but has done so in such a way as to make the truth on the subject in dispute shine with the very light of heaven. There could not, then, be a better opportunity of turning their thoughts in a direction which might lead them, if possible in spite of themselves, into the light of God.

The question Jesus asks (vv. 41-45) is undoubtedly a puzzling one for them; but it is no mere Scripture conundrum. The difficulty in which it lands them is one which, if only they would honestly face it, would be the means of removing the veil from their eyes, and leading them, ere it is too late, to welcome the Son of David come in the name of the Lord to save them. They fully accepted the psalm to which He referred as a psalm of David concerning the Messiah. If, then, they would honestly read that psalm they would see that the Messiah when He comes must be, not a mere earthly monarch, as David was, but a heavenly monarch,

* Compare the same thought in Ps. xvi. 8-11.

one who should sit on the throne of God and bring into subjection the enemies of the kingdom of heaven. If only they would take their ideas of the Christ from the Scriptures which were their boast, they could not fail to see Him standing now before them. For we must remember that they had not only the words He spoke to guide them. They had before them the Messiah Himself, with the light of heaven in His eye, with the love of God in His face; and had they had any love for the light, they would have recognised Him then—they would have seen in Him, whom they had often heard of as David's Son, the Lord of David, and therefore the Lord of the Temple, and the heavenly King of Israel. But they love the darkness rather than the light, because their deeds are evil: therefore their hearts remain unchanged, the eyes of their spirit unopened; they are only abashed and silenced: "No man was able to answer Him a word, neither durst any man from that day forth ask Him any more questions."

III.—The House Left Desolate (xxiii.).

The day of grace is over for the leaders of the people; but for the people themselves there may still be hope; so the Lord of the Temple turns to "the multitude," the general throng of worshippers, mingled with whom were several of His own disciples, and solemnly warns them against their spiritual guides. There is every reason to suppose that many of the scribes and Pharisees were within hearing; for when He has finished what He has to say to the people, He turns round and addresses them directly in that series of terrible denunciations which follow (ver. 13, *seq.*).

His warning is couched in such a way as not in the least degree to weaken their respect for Moses, or for the sacred Scriptures, the exposition of which was the duty of their spiritual guides. He separates sharply between the office and the men who hold it. Had they been true to the position they occupied and the high duties they had been called to discharge, they would have been worthy of all honour; but they are false men: "they say, and do not." Not only so, but they do positive evil, making that grievous for the people which ought to be a delight; and when they do or seem to do the right thing, it is some petty observance, which they exaggerate for the sake of vain display, while their hearts are set on personal pre-eminence. Such are the leading thoughts set forth with great vigour of language and force of illustration, and not without a touch of keen and delicate irony in our Lord's remarkable indictment of the scribes and Pharisees recorded by our Evangelist (vv. 2-7).

Then follows one of those passages of profound significance and far-reaching application which, while admirably suiting the immediate occasions on which they were spoken, prove to be a treasury of truth for the ages to come. At first sight it strikes us as simply an exhortation to cultivate a disposition the reverse of that of the scribes and Pharisees. He has been drawing their portrait; now He says, Be ye not like unto them, but unlike in every respect. But in saying this He succeeds in laying down great principles for the future guidance of His Church, the remembrance of which would have averted most of the evils which in the course of its history have weakened its power, hindered its progress, and marred its witness to the truth. With one stroke He abolishes all claims of men to intervene between the soul and God. "One is your Teacher" (R. V.), "One is your Father," "One is your Master." Who is that One? He does not in so many words claim the position for Himself; but it is throughout implied, and at the end almost expressed; for, while in speaking of the Teacher and the Father He says nothing to indicate who the One is, when He comes to the Master He adds "even the Christ" (R. V.). Standing thus at the end of all, these words suggest that the office of the Christ was to bring God within reach of every soul, so that without any intervention of scribe or Pharisee, priest or pope, each one could go direct to Him for instruction (Teacher), for loving recognition (Father), for authoritative guidance and control (Master).

We must remember, too, that He was speaking to His disciples as well as to the multitude, and to them these words would be full of meaning. When He said, "One is your Teacher," of whom could they possibly think but of Himself? When He said, "One is your Father," they would recall such utterances as "I and My Father are One," and have suggested to them the truth which was so very soon to be plainly stated: "He that hath seen Me, hath seen the Father." It is probable, then, that even before He reached the end, and added the words "even the Christ," the minds of His disciples at least had anticipated Him. Thus we find in these remarkable words an implicit claim on the part of Christ to be the sole Prophet, Priest, and King of His people: their sole Prophet, to teach them by the enlightening and sanctifying grace of the Holy Spirit; their sole Priest, to open up the way of access to a reconciled Father in heaven; their sole King, alone entitled to be the Lord of their conscience and their heart.

If only the Christian Church had been true to all this, how different would her history have been! Then the Word of God would have been, throughout, the only and sufficient rule of faith, and the Holy Spirit dealing directly with the spirits of men its sole authoritative interpreter. Then would there have been no usurping priesthood to stand between the soul of men and their Father in heaven, to bind heavy burdens and grievous to be borne and lay them upon men's shoulders, to multiply forms and observances and complicate what should have been simplest of all—the direct way to the Father in heaven, through Christ the great Priest of humanity. Then would there have been no lordship over men's consciences, no ecclesiastical usurpation, no spiritual tyranny, no inquisition, no persecution for conscience' sake. How inexcusable has it all been! It would seem as if pains had been taken deliberately to violate not only the spirit, but the very letter of the Saviour's words, as, *e. g.*, in the one fact that, while it is expressly written "Call no man your father upon the earth," the Church of Rome has actually succeeded age after age in getting the millions under its usurped spiritual control, to give a man that very title; for the word "pope" is the very word * which our Lord so expressly forbids.

* "*Papa*," pope, is the Latin translation of the Hebrew word for Father.

But all clerical assumption of priestly power is just as certainly and as clearly in violation of this great charter of our spiritual liberties.

"And all ye are brethren." This is the second commandment of the true canon law, like unto the first and springing naturally out of it, as naturally as the love of neighbour springs out of love to God. As soon as the time shall come when all Christians shall own allegiance alike, full and undivided, to the one Lord of mind and heart and conscience, then will there be an end to all ecclesiastical exclusiveness; then shall we see realised and manifested to the world the brotherhood in Christ of all believers.

Turning once again to the scribes and Pharisees, the Lord of the Temple denounces them in words perhaps the most terrible in the whole Bible. It is a very thunderstorm of indignation, with flash after flash of scorn, peal after peal of woe. It is "*the* burden of the Lord," "the wrath of the Lamb." Is this at all inconsistent with the meekness and lowliness of His heart, the love and tenderness of His character? Certainly not! Love is no love at all, unless it be capable of indignation against wrong. Besides, it is no personal wrongs which stir the heart of Jesus, "Who when He was reviled, reviled not again, when He suffered, He threatened not"; but the wrong these hypocrites are doing to the poor sheep they are leading all astray. The occasion absolutely demanded a tempest of indignation. There is this further to be considered, that the Lord Jesus, as Revealer of God, must display His justice as well as His mercy, His wrath as well as His love.

This passage, terrible as it is, commends itself to all that is noblest and best in us. Who is there who does not thank God for this scathing denunciation of that most hateful of all abominations—hypocrisy? See how He brands it in every sentence—"Woe unto you, scribes and Pharisees, hypocrites!"—how piece by piece He shows their miserable life to be a lie. *Hypocrites!* because you profess to sit in Moses' seat, to have the key of knowledge, to know the way of life yourselves, and show it to others; and all this profession is a lie (ver. 13). *Hypocrites!* because your pretended charity is a lie, aggravated by the forms of devotion with which it is masked, while the essence of it is most sordid avarice (ver. 14). *Hypocrites!* because your zeal for God is a lie, being really a zeal for the devil, your converts being perverts worse than yourselves (ver. 15). *Hypocrites!* because your morality is a lie, making the law of God of none effect by your miserable casuistry (vv. 16-22). *Hypocrites!* because your devotion is a lie, consisting merely in punctilious attention to the minutest forms, while the weighty matters of the law you set aside, like those who "strain out the gnat and swallow the camel" (vv. 23, 24, R. V.). *Hypocrites!* because your whole demeanour is a lie, all fair without like a whited sepulchre, while within ye are "full of dead men's bones, and of all uncleanness" (vv. 25-28). *Hypocrites!* because your pretended reverence for the prophets is a lie, for had you lived in the days of your fathers you would have done as they did, as is plain from the way in which you are acting now; for you build the tombs of the dead prophets and put to death the living ones (vv. 29-31).

The sin branded, sentence follows: "Fill ye up then the measure of your fathers." Since you will not be saved, there is nothing for it but that you go on in sin to the bitter end: serpents, "for ever hissing at the heels of the holy," a brood of vipers, with no hope now of escaping the judgment of Gehenna!

As in the Sermon on the Mount (see page 722) so here, when He speaks as Judge He cannot conceal His personal majesty. All throughout He has been speaking with authority, but has, as usual, avoided the obtrusion of His personal prerogative. Even in saying "One is your Master, even the Christ," it is not at all the same as if He had said, even Myself. All it necessarily conveyed was, "One is your master, even the Messiah," whoever he may be. But now He speaks as from His judgment throne. He is no longer thinking of Himself as one of the prophets, or even as the King's Son, but as Lord of all; so He says: "Wherefore, behold, *I* send unto you prophets, and wise men, and scribes: and some of them ye shall kill and crucify; and some of them shall ye scourge in your synagogues, and persecute them from city to city: that upon you may come all the righteous blood shed on the earth," from Abel to Zacharias.* And, again, "Verily *I* say unto you, All these things shall come upon this generation."

But judgment is His strange work. He has been compelled by the fire of His holiness to break forth into this tempest of indignation against the hypocrites, and to pronounce upon them the long-deferred sentence of condemnation and wrath. But there has been a wail in all His woes. His nature and His name is love, and it must have been a terrible strain on Him to keep up the foreign tone so long. "The *wrath* of the *Lamb*" is a necessary but not a natural combination. We may not wonder, then, though well we may adore, when after the tension of these woes, His heart is melted into tenderness as He mourns over the fate which all His love may not avert: "O Jerusalem, Jerusalem, thou that killest the prophets and stonest them which are sent unto thee, how often would I have gathered thy children together, even as a hen gathereth her chickens under her wings, and ye would not!" Again, observe the lofty consciousness shining out in the little pronoun "*I*." He is a young man of little more than thirty; but His personal consciousness runs back through all the ages of the past, through all the times of the killing of the prophets and stoning of the messengers of God, from Abel on to Zachariah: and not only so, but this Son of Israel speaks in the most natural way as the brooding mother of them all through all their generations—what wonders, not of beauty alone, and of exquisite pathos, but of conscious majesty in that immortal lamentation!

Our Saviour's public ministry is closed. He has yet many things to say to His disciples—a private ministry of love to fulfil ere He leave the world and go to the Father; but His public ministry is ended now. Commenced with beatitudes, it ends with woes, because the blessings offered in

*The reason why these two are named is sufficiently obvious, when we remember that the second Book of Chronicles, in which the martyrdom of Zachariah is recorded, was the last book of the Hebrew Scriptures, just as we might say, *All* the promises from Genesis to Revelation. The difficulty which has been made so much of (Barachias *v.* Jehoiada) is of no importance except to those who will not remember that the letter killeth and the spirit giveth life.

the beatitudes have been rudely rejected and trampled underfoot. And now the Lord of the Temple is about to leave it—to leave it to its fate, to leave it as He counselled His disciples to leave any city or house that refused to receive them: shaking the dust off His feet; and in doing so, as He turns from the astonished hierarchs, He utters these solemn words, which close the time of their merciful visitation and leave them to "eat of the fruit of their own way, and be filled with their own devices"; "Behold, your house is left unto you desolate." *Your* house. It was Mine. I was its glory, and would have been its defence; but when I came unto My own, Mine own received Me not; and now it is no longer Mine but yours, and therefore desolate. *Desolate;* and therefore defenceless, a ready prey for the Roman eagles when they swoop on the defenceless brood. "For I say unto you, Ye shall not see Me henceforth till"—till when? Is there still a door of hope? There is, even for scribes and Pharisees—hypocrites; the door ever open here on earth: "Him that cometh unto Me, I will in nowise cast out." The door is closed upon them for ever as leaders of the people; as temple authorities they can never be recognised again,—their house is left to them desolate, but for themselves there is still this door of hope; these awful woes therefore are not a final sentence, but a long, loud, last call to enter ere it be too late. And as if to show, after all the wrath of His terrible denunciation, that judgment is "His strange work" and that He "delighteth in mercy," He points in closing to that still open door, and says, "Ye shall not see Me henceforth, till ye shall say, 'Blessed is He that cometh in the name of the Lord.'"

Why did they not say it then? Why did they not entreat Him to remain? But they did not. So "Jesus went out, and departed from the Temple" (xxiv. 1); and though eighteen hundred years have rolled away since then, the time has not yet come when as a people they have said, "Blessed is He that cometh in the name of the Lord"; accordingly their house is still desolate, and they are "scattered and peeled"—chickens that will not nestle under the mother's wing.

CHAPTER XVIII.

THE PROPHECY ON THE MOUNT.

MATTHEW xxiv., xxv.

WE have seen that though the Saviour's public ministry is now closed, He still has a private ministry to discharge—a ministry of counsel and comfort to His beloved disciples, whom He soon must leave in a world where tribulation awaits them on every side. Of this private ministry the chief remains are the beautiful words of consolation left on record by St. John (xiii.-xvii.), and the valuable words of prophetic warning recorded by the other Evangelists, occupying in this Gospel two long chapters (xxiv., xxv.).

This remarkable discourse, nearly equal in length to the Sermon on the Mount, may be called the Prophecy on the Mount; for it is prophetic throughout, and it was delivered on the Mount of Olives. From the way in which it is introduced (vv. 1-3) we see that it is closely connected with the abandonment of the Temple, and that it was suggested by the disciples calling His attention to the buildings of the Temple, which were in full view of the little group as they sat on the Mount of Olives that memorable day—buildings which seemed stately and stable enough in their eyes, but which were already tottering to their fall before

". . . that eye which watches guilt
And goodness; and hath power to see
Within the green the mouldered tree,
And towers fallen as soon as built."

Thus everything leads us to expect a discourse about the fate of the Temple. The minds of the whole group are full of the subject; and out of the fulness of their hearts the question comes, "Tell us, when shall these things be? And what shall be the sign of Thy coming, and of the end of the world?" From the latter part of the question it is evident that the coming of Christ and the end of the world were closely connected in the disciples' minds with the judgment that was about to come upon the Temple and the chosen people—a connection which was right in point of fact, though wrong in point of time. We shall not be surprised, therefore, to discover that the burden of the first part of the prophecy is that great event to which the attention of all was at that moment so pointedly directed. But since the near as well as the distant event is viewed as the coming of the Son of man, we may give to what may be called the prophecy proper as distinguished from the pictures of judgment that follow, a title which embodies this unifying thought.

I. THE COMING OF THE SON OF MAN (vv. 3-44).

In secular history the destruction of Jerusalem is nothing more than the destruction of any other city of equal size and importance. It is indeed marked out from similar events in history by the peculiarly terrible sufferings to which the inhabitants were subjected before the final overthrow. But apart from this, it is to the general historian an event precisely similar to the destruction of Babylon, of Tyre, of Carthage, or of any other ancient city once the seat of a dominion which now has passed away. In sacred history it stands alone. It was not merely the destruction of a city, but the close of a dispensation—the end of that great age which began with the call of Abraham to come out from Ur of the Chaldees, and be the father of a people chosen of the Lord. It was "the end of the world" (comp. R. V., ver. 3, margin) to the Jews, the end of the world which then was, the passing away of the old to give place to the new. It was the event which bore the same relation to the Jews as the Flood did to the antediluvians, which was emphatically the end of the world to them. If we bear this in mind it will enable us to appreciate the tremendous importance assigned to this event wherever it is referred to in the sacred Scriptures, and especially in this momentous chapter.

But though the destruction of Jerusalem is the primary subject of the prophecy, in its full sweep it takes a far wider range. The Saviour sees before Him with prophetic eye, not only that great event which was to be the end of the world which then was—the close of the dispensation of grace which had lasted two thousand years; but also the end of all things, when the last dispensation of grace—not for Israel alone, but for the whole world—shall have come to a close. Though these two events were to be separated from each other by a long interval of time, yet were they so closely related in their nature and issues that our Lord, having in view the needs of those who were to live in the new dispensation, could not speak of the one without also speaking of the other. What He was then saying was intended for the guidance, not only of the disciples then around Him, and of any other Jews who might from them receive the message, but also for the guidance of the whole Christian Church throughout the world to the end of time,—another marvellous illustration of that sublime consciousness of life and power, infinitely beyond the limits of His mere manhood, which is ever betraying itself throughout this wondrous history. Had He confined Himself to the destruction of Jerusalem, His words would have had no special interest for us, any more, for example, than the burden of Babylon or of Tyre or of Dumah in the Old Testament Scriptures; but when He carries us on to that Last Great Day, of which the day of Jerusalem's destruction (as closing the Old Testament dispensation) was a type, we recognise at once our own personal interest in the prophecy; for we ourselves are individually concerned with that Day—we shall then either be overwhelmed in the ruins of the old, or shall rejoice in the glories of the new; therefore we should feel that this prophecy has an interest for us as personal as it had for those who first heard it on the Mount of Olives.

As might be expected from the nature of its subject, the interpretation of the prophecy in matters of detail is beset with difficulties. The sources of difficulty are sufficiently obvious. One is in the elimination of time. The time of both events is studiously concealed, according to the principle distinctly announced by our Saviour just before His ascension: "It is not for you to know the times or the seasons, which the Father hath put in His own power." There are in each case signs given, by which the approach of the event may be recognised by those who will give heed to them; but anything in the shape of a date is studiously avoided. It is perhaps not too much to say that nine-tenths of the difficulties which have been encountered in the interpretation of this passage have arisen from the unwarrantable attempts to introduce dates into it.

Another difficulty arises from the similarity of the two events referred to, and the consequent applicability of the same language to both of them. This leads to different opinions as to which of the two is referred to in certain places. To show the source of these difficulties is to suggest their solution; for when we consider that one event is the type of the other, that one is as it were the miniature of the other, the same on a much smaller scale, we need not hesitate to apply the same language to both,—it may be literally in the one case and figuratively in the other; or it may be in a subordinate sense in the one case, and in the fullest sense in the other; or it may be in precisely the same sense in both cases. In general, however, it will be observed that the lesser event—the destruction of Jerusalem—stands out in full prominence in the beginning of the prophecy, and the greater event—the Great Day of our Saviour's appearing—in the latter part of it.

Still another source of difficulty is that, while our Saviour's object in giving the prophecy was practical, the object of many who study the prophecy is merely speculative. They come to it to satisfy curiosity, and as a matter of course they are disappointed, for our Lord did not intend when He spoke these words to satisfy so unworthy a desire; and, though His word never returns to Him void, it accomplishes that which He pleases, and nothing else; it prospers in the thing to which He has sent it, but not in the thing to which He has not sent it. He has sent us this, not to satisfy our curiosity, but to influence our conduct; and if we use it not for speculative but for practical purposes—not to find support for any favourite theory, which parcels out the future, giving days and hours, which neither the angels in heaven nor the Son of man Himself could tell (Mark xiii. 32)—but to find food for our souls, then we shall not be troubled with so many difficulties, and we shall certainly not be disappointed.

Before we pass from the difficulties of this prophecy, observe how strong an argument they furnish for its genuineness. Those who deny the divinity of Christ are greatly troubled with this prophecy, so much so that the only way in which they can get rid of its witness to Him is by suggesting that it was really composed after the destruction of Jerusalem, and therefore never spoken by Christ at all. There are difficulties enough of other kinds in the way of such a disposal of the prophecy; but there is one consideration which absolutely forbids it—viz., that any one writing after the event would have avoided all that vagueness of language which gives trouble to expositors. To those who can judge of internal evidence, its obscurity is clear proof that this discourse could not have been produced in the full light of the subsequent history, but must have been what it professes to be, a foreshadowing of coming events.

We may not, with the limits imposed by the plan of these expositions, attempt a detailed explanation of this difficult prophecy, but must content ourselves with giving only a general view. Our Lord first warns His disciples against expecting the crisis too early (vv. 4-14). In this passage He prepares the minds of His disciples for the times of trouble and trial through which they must pass before the coming of "the great and notable day of the Lord" which was at hand: there shall be false Christs and false prophets—there shall be wars and rumours of wars, and shaking of the nations, and famines, and pestilences, and earthquakes in divers places; yet will all these be only "the beginning of sorrows." He also prepares their minds for the gigantic work which must be done by them and by their brother-disciples before that great day: "This gospel of the kingdom shall be preached in all the world for a witness unto all nations; and then shall the end come." Thus are the disciples taught the very important and thoroughly practical truth, that they must pass through a great trial and do a great work before the Day shall come.

He then gives them a certain sign by which they shall know that the event is imminent, when it does approach. This is not equivalent to fixing a date. He gives them no idea how long the period of trial shall last, no idea how long time they shall have for the great work before them—He simply gives them a sign, by observing which they shall not be taken completely by surprise.

but have at least a brief space to make their escape from the condemned city. And so very little time will elapse between the sign and the event to which it points, that He warns them against any delay, and tells them, as soon as it shall appear, to flee at once to the mountains and escape for their lives. It is sufficiently evident, by comparing this passage with the corresponding place in Luke, where our Lord speaks of Jerusalem being compassed with armies, that the "abomination of desolation standing in the holy place" refers to some particular act of sacrilegious impiety committed in the Temple just at the time the Romans were beginning to invest the city. Attempts have been made historically to identify this profanation, but it is doubtful if these have been successful. It is sufficient to know that whether or not the fact has found a place in history, it served its purpose as a sign to the Christians in the city who had treasured up in their hearts their Saviour's warning words.

Having told them what the sign would be, and counselled His disciples to lose no time in making their escape as soon as they should see it, He further warns them, in a few impressive words, of the terrors of those days of tribulation (vv. 19-22), and then concludes this portion of the prophecy by warning them against the supposition—a very natural one in the circumstances —that even then the Son of man should come.

So far we have found the leading ideas to be simple and practical, and all connected with the destruction of Jerusalem. (1) Do not expect that event too early; for you must pass through many trials and do much work before it. (2) As soon as you shall see the sign I give you, expect it immediately, and lose no time in making your escape from the horrors of these awful days. (3) Even then, however, do not expect the personal advent of the Son of man; for though it is a day of judgment, it is only one of those partial judgments which are necessary on the principle that "wheresoever the carcase is, there will the eagles be gathered together." The personal advent of Christ and the day of final judgment are only foreshadowed by, not realised in, the destruction of Jerusalem and the close of the old dispensation.

The three closing verses of this portion of the prophecy refer pre-eminently to the great Day of the coming of the Son of man (vv. 29-31). The word "immediately" has given rise to much difficulty, on account of the hasty conclusion to which some have come that "immediately after the tribulation of those days" must mean immediately after the destruction of Jerusalem; according to which all this must have taken place long ago. It is, indeed, sufficiently obvious that the tribulation of those days began with the destruction, or rather with the besieging, of Jerusalem. But when did it end? As soon as the city was destroyed? Nay. If we wish to get some idea of the duration of those days of tribulation, let us turn to the same place in the same prophecy as given by St. Luke (xxi. 23, 24), where it clearly appears that it embraces the whole period of the Jewish dispersion and of the standing of the Gentile Church. "The tribulation of those days" is going on still, and therefore the events of these verses are still future. We look forward to the Day of the Lord of which that terrible day of judgment, to which their thoughts were first turned, was only a dim foreshadowing—a Day far more august in its nature, far more awful in its accompaniments, far more terrible in its aspect to those who are unprepared for it, yet full of glory and of joy to those who "love His appearing."

Appended to the main prophecy are some additional warnings as to time (vv. 32-44) setting forth in the most impressive manner the certainty, the suddenness, and, to those who are not looking for it, the unexpectedness of the coming of the Day of the Lord. Here again, in the first portion the destruction of Jerusalem, and in the latter portion the Day of the Son of man, is prominent. If we bear this in mind it will remove a difficulty many have found in ver. 34, which seems to say that the events specially referred to in vv. 29-31 would be fulfilled before that generation passed away. But when we remember that the prophecy proper closes with the thirty-first verse, and that the warning as to the imminency of the events referred to commences with ver. 32, the difficulty vanishes; for it is most natural that the practical warning should follow the course of the prophecy itself, referring first to the destruction of Jerusalem, and passing from it to that grand event of which it was the precursor. On this principle vv. 32-35 are quite simple and natural, as well as most impressive, and the statement of ver. 34 is seen to be literally accurate.

The passage from ver. 36 onwards is still quite applicable to the near event, the destruction of Jerusalem; but the language used is evidently such as to carry the mind onward to the more distant event which had been brought prominently forward in the latter part of the prophecy (vv. 36-44). In these verses, again, not only is no date given, but we are expressly told that it is deliberately withheld. What then? Are we to dismiss the subject from our minds? Quite the reverse; for though the time is uncertain, the event itself is most certain, and it will come suddenly and unexpectedly. No time will be given for preparation to those who are not already prepared. True, there will be the sign of the Son of man in heaven, whatever that may be; but, like the other sign which was the precursor of Jerusalem's destruction, it will appear immediately before the event, barely giving time for those who have their lamps trimmed and oil in their vessels with their lamps to arise and meet the Bridegroom; but for those who are not watching, it will be too late—it will be with them as with those who lived at the close of the very first dispensation, who were "eating and drinking, marrying and giving in marriage, until the day that Noah entered into the ark, and knew not until the flood came, and took them all away. . . . Watch therefore: for ye know not what hour your Lord doth come. But know this, that if the goodman of the house had known in what watch the thief would come, he would have watched, and would not have suffered his house to be broken up. Therefore be ye also ready: for in such an hour as ye think not the Son of man cometh."

II. Parables and Pictures of Judgment (xxiv. 45-xxv.).

The remainder of this great prophecy is taken up with four pictures of judgment, very striking and impressive, having for their special object the enforcement of the great practical lesson with which the first part has closed: "Watch therefore" (vv. 42, 43); "Be ye also ready" (ver. 44). In the former portion of the prophecy the destruction of Jerusalem was in the foreground, and in the background the coming of the Son of man to judgment in the end of the world. In this portion the Great Day of the Son of man is prominent throughout.

The four pictures, though similar in their scope and object, are different in their subjects. The first represents those who occupy positions of trust in the kingdom; the second and third, all professing Christians,—the one setting forth inward grace, the other outward activity; the fourth is a picture of judgment on the whole world.

1. *The Servant Set over the Household* (xxiv. 45-51).

As in the case of the man without the wedding garment, a single servant is taken as representing a class; and who constitute this class is made quite clear, not only by the fact that the servant is set over the household, but also by the nature of the service: "to give them their food in due season" (R. V.). The application was evidently first to the apostles themselves, and then to all who in the future should be engaged in the same work of providing spiritual nourishment for those under their charge. The very pointed way in which the parable is introduced, together with the fact that only one servant is spoken of, suggests to each one engaged in the work the most careful self-examination. "Who, then, is a faithful and wise servant?" The underlying thought seems to be that such an one is not very easily to be found; and that therefore there is a special benediction for those who through the trying years are found both "faithful and wise," faithful to their high trust, wise in relation to the momentous issues depending on the manner in which they fulfil it. The benediction on the wise and faithful servant is evidently easy to miss and a great thing to gain.

But there is more to be thought of than the missing of the blessing. There is a fearful doom awaiting the unfaithful servant, of which the picture following gives a terrible presentation. Both offence and punishment are painted in the very darkest colours. As to the former, the servant not only neglects his duty, but beats his fellow-servants, and eats and drinks with the drunken. Here a question arises, What was there to suggest such a representation to the Saviour's mind? Surely it could not be intended specially for those who were sitting with Him on the mount that day. If Judas was among the rest, his sin was not of the nature that would have suggested the parable in this particular form, and certainly there is no reason to suppose that any of the rest were in the slightest danger of being guilty of such cruelties and excesses as are here spoken of. Is it not plain then, that the Judge of all had in His view the dark days to come, when the clergy of a degenerate Church would be actually guilty of cruelties and excesses such as could not be more fitly set forth in parable than by the disgraceful conduct of "that wicked servant"?

This is still further confirmed by the reason given for such recklessness,—the evil servant saying in his heart, "My Lord delayeth His coming." There is reason to suppose that the early Christians expected the return of the Lord almost immediately. In so far as they made this mistake, it cannot be charged against their Master; for, as we have seen, He warns them against this error throughout the whole of the prophecy. It is plain, however, that those who made this mistake were in no danger of saying in their hearts, "My Lord delayeth His coming." But as time passed on, and the expectation of the Lord's speedy return grew fainter, then there would come in all its force the temptation to those who did not watch against it of counting on the Lord's delay. When we think of this, we see how necessary it was that the danger should be set forth in language which may have seemed unnecessarily strong at the time, but which the future history of the Church only too sadly justified.

The punishment is correspondingly severe. The word used to picture it ("shall cut him asunder") is one to make us shudder; and some have felt surprised that our Lord did not shrink from the horror of the word. Ah! but it was the horror of the thing which He dreaded, and wished to avert. It was the infinite pity of His heart that led Him to use a word which might prove the very strongest deterrent. Besides, how significant it is! Think, again, of whom He is speaking,—servants set over His household to give food in due season, who instead of doing this maltreat their fellow-servants and ruin themselves with excess. Think of the duplicity of such conduct. By office in the church "exalted unto heaven," by practice "brought down to hell"! That unnatural combination cannot last. These monsters with two faces and one black heart cannot be tolerated in the universe of God. They shall be *cut asunder;* and then it will appear which of the two faces really belongs to the man: cut asunder, his place shall be appointed with the hypocrites, where shall be weeping and gnashing of teeth (ver. 51).

2 and 3. *The Virgins; The Talents* (xxv. 1-30).

The second and third pictures presented in the form of two parables of the kingdom of heaven, set before us the judgment of Christ at His coming on His professed disciples, distinguishing between real and merely nominal Christians, between the pretended and the true members of the kingdom of heaven. In the former parable this distinction is set before us in the contrast between the wise and the foolish virgins; in the latter it appears in the form of the one faithful and the two unfaithful servants. No special significance need be attached to the respective numbers, which are evidently chosen with a view to the consistency of the parables, not to set forth anything in regard to the actual proportion between hypocrites and true disciples in the visible Church.

The relation between the two parables has been already indicated. The first represents the Church as waiting, the second as working, for her Lord; the first shows the necessity of a constant supply of inward grace, the second the need of unremitting outward activity; the teaching of the first is, "Keep thy heart with all diligence, for out of it are the issues of life"; of the second, "Do good as ye have opportunity," "Be faithful unto death, and I will give thee a crown of life." The parable of the Virgins comes appropriately before that of the Talents, inasmuch as a Christian's inner life should be his first care, the outer life being wholly dependent on it. "Keep thy heart with all diligence," is the first command; "Do thy work with all diligence," the second. The first parable calls aloud to every member of the Church, "Be wise"; the second follows it with another call, as urgent as the first, "Be faithful."

The Parable of the Virgins (vv. 1-13), with its marriage feast, recalls the parable of the marriage of the King's Son, so recently spoken in the Temple. The difference between the two is very clearly indicated by the way in which each parable is introduced: there, "the kingdom of heaven *is* likened"; here, "*then shall* the kingdom of heaven *be* likened." The gospel feast which was the subject of the parable spoken in the Temple was already spread; it was a thing of the present; its word was, "All things are ready: come to the marriage"; its preparation had been the object of the heavenly Bridegroom's first coming. The wedding feast of this parable is yet to be prepared; it is "the marriage supper of the Lamb" to which the Lord will call His people at His second coming.

An interval, therefore, of unknown length must pass meantime; and herein, as the sequel will unfold, lies the test which distinguishes the wise from the foolish virgins. This interval is represented by a night, with great appropriateness, seeing that the heavenly Bridegroom is the Sun of the soul. It being night, all alike grow drowsy and fall asleep. To make this a fault, as some do, is to spoil the parable. Had it been wrong to sleep, the wise virgins would certainly have been represented as keeping awake. If, then, we give a meaning to the sleep, it is not that of spiritual torpor, but rather such occupation with the concerns of the present life as is natural and necessary. As the whole of "the life that now is," up till the coming of the Lord, is represented in the parable by the night, and as sleep is the business of night, we may fairly consider that the sleep of the parable represents the business of the life that now is, in which Christians, however anxious to be ready for the coming of the Lord, must engage, and not only so, but must give themselves to it with an engrossment which for the time may amount to as entire abstraction from distinctively spiritual duties as sleep is an abstraction from the duties of the day. In this point of view we see how reasonable is our Lord's requirement. He does not expect us to be always equally wide awake to spiritual and eternal things. The wise as well as the foolish slumber and sleep.

It is not, then, by the temptation to sleep that the interval tests the virgins, but by bringing out a difference which has existed all the while, though at the first it did not appear. All seemed alike at the beginning of the night. Had not every one of them a lamp, with oil in it, and were not the lights of all the ten brightly burning? Yes; and if the Bridegroom had come at that hour, all would have seemed equally ready. But the Bridegroom tarries, and while He tarries the business of the night must go on. In this way time passes, till at an unexpected moment in the very middle of the night as it were, the cry is heard "Behold the Bridegroom cometh: go ye out to meet Him. Then all those virgins arose and trimmed their lamps." Still no difference: each of the ten lamps is trimmed and lighted. But see, five of them are going out almost as soon as they are kindled! What is the reason? There is no store of oil. Here, then, is the difference between the wise and the foolish, and here lies, therefore, the main point of the parable.

What, then, are we to understand in the spiritual sphere by this distinction? That the wise and the foolish represent the watchful and the unwatchful is plain enough; but is there not something here to let us deeper into the secret of the great difference between the one and the other? In order to get this, it is not at all necessary to ask for the significance of each separate detail—the lamp, the wick, the oil, the oil vessel. The details belong to the drapery of the parable; the essentials are manifestly the light and the source whence it comes. The light is the very familiar symbol of the Christian life; the source whence it comes is Divine grace, abiding unseen in the heart. Now, there is a certain superficial goodness which shines for the moment much as the true light of grace shines, but is connected with no perennial supply; there is no oil vessel from which the lamp can be constantly replenished. There may be a flaring up for a moment; but there is no steady enduring light.

All which points to the conclusion that the foolish virgins represent those professing Christians who have religious emotion enough to kindle their lamp of life and make it glow with a flame which looks marvellously like true devotion, but which is little else than the blazing up of natural feeling; while the wise virgins represent those whose constant habit is devotion, whose grace is something they carry with them always, so that at any moment the light of it may shine, the flame glow, pure, bright, steady, inextinguishable. They may be as much engaged in the business of life as the others, so that no flame of devotion may be seen; but deep down, hidden out of sight, like the oil in the vessel, there is abiding grace, which is only waiting the occasion to burst into a flame, of prayer or praise or joyful welcome of the Bridegroom at whatever moment He may come. The distinction, therefore, is between those worldly Christians, whose devotion is a thing of now and then, and those thorough Christians whose devotion is habitual, not always to be recognised on the surface of their life, not always to be seen of men, not so as to hinder their engrossment in business hours with the ordinary duties of life, but so as to be always *there*, the deep abiding habit of their souls. There is the secret of watchfulness; there the secret of readiness for the coming of the Lord.

This explains why the wise virgins cannot help the foolish. It is not that they are selfish, and will not do it; but that it cannot be done. Some commentators, men of the letter, have puzzled themselves as to the advice to go to them that sell and buy. That, again, belongs to the framework of the parable. The thought conveyed is plain enough to those who think not of the letter but of the spirit. It is simply this, that grace is not transferable. A man may belong to the warmest, devoutest, most gracious community of disciples in all Christendom; but if he himself has been foolish, if he has not lived in communion with Christ, if he has not kept himself in communication with the Fountain of grace, not all the saints in whose company he has passed the night of the Lord's personal absence, however willing they may be, will be able to lend him as much as one drop of the sacred oil.

The same principles are applicable to the solemn close of the parable. The question has been asked, Why did not the Bridegroom open the door? Late though the foolish virgins were, they wished to enter, and why should they not be allowed? Again let us look beyond the letter of the parable to the spirit of it—to the great spiritual facts it pictures for us. If it were the mere opening of a door that would remedy the lateness, assuredly it would be done; but the real fact is, that the lateness is now beyond remedy. *The door cannot be opened.* Ponder the solemn words: "I know you not." It is a question of the union of the life with Christ. The wise virgins had lived a life that was always, even in sleep, hid with Christ in God; the foolish virgins had not: they had lived a life which had transient shows of devotion in it, but no reality—a mistake too fatal to be in any wise remedied by the spasms of a few minutes at the close. It is the old familiar lesson, that cannot be taught too often or taken to heart too earnestly: that the only way to die the death of the righteous is to live the life of the righteous.

The Parable of the Talents deals with the same subjects—viz., the professed disciples of Christ; only instead of searching the reality of their inner life, it tests the faithfulness of their service. As in the former parable so in this, stress is laid on the time that must elapse before the Lord's return. The employer of the servants travels "into a far country"; and it is "after a long time" (ver. 19) that "He cometh, and reckoneth with them." Similarly, in the cognate parable of "the pounds," reported by St. Luke, we are told that it was spoken, "because they thought that the kingdom of God should immediately appear" (Luke xix. 11). It would seem, therefore, that both these parables were intended to guard against the temptation to make the anticipation of the Lord's return an excuse for neglect of present duty.

There is evidence that within a short time some Christians in Thessalonica fell into this very temptation,—so much so as to render it necessary that the apostle Paul should write them a letter, his second epistle, for the express purpose of reproving them and setting them right. His first Epistle to the Thessalonians had laid stress on the suddenness of the Lord's coming, as Christ Himself does again and again throughout this discourse; but the result was that some of them, confounding suddenness with imminence, gave themselves up to idle waiting or feverish expectancy, to the neglect even of the most ordinary duties. To meet this he had to call attention to the Divine ordinance, that "if any would not work, neither should he eat," and to enforce it with all the authority of Christ Himself: "Now them that are such" (viz., those excited "busybodies" "working not at all") "we command and exhort by our Lord Jesus Christ, that with quietness they work, and eat their own bread" (2 Thess. iii. 10-12); following it up with a caution, on the other hand, against allowing the Lord's delay to discourage them in their activity in His service: "But ye, brethren, be not weary in well doing."

All this helps us to see how necessary it was that the parable of waiting should be followed by a summons to work, and to admire the marvellous insight of our Lord into human nature in recognising beforehand where hidden dangers would lurk in His people's path. Unhappily, it is not necessary to go back to the case of the Thessalonians to see how needful it is that the parable of work should go along with the parable of waiting; we have painful illustration of it in our own day. Thanks to the clearness and strength of our Lord's teaching, the great majority of those who in our day look for His almost immediate return are not only diligent in work, but an example and a rebuke to many who do not share their expectations; but on the other hand, there are not a few who have been so far led astray as to give up positions of great usefulness, and discontinue work in which they had been signally blessed, with the idea that the great event being now so near, the sole duty of the believer is to wait for it.

The parable assumes that all disciples are servants of Christ, and that all of them have work for Christ to do. There is no reason, however, for narrowing the field of service to what is in current phrase distinctively spoken of as "Christian work." All the work of Christian people should be Christian work, and is Christian work, if it be done as it ought to be done, "as to the Lord." There must evidently, however, be the desire and purpose to "serve the Lord Christ," whatever the nature of the service be.

The talents signify ability and opportunity. We must beware of using the word in any limited or conventional sense. In ordinary conversation the word is generally applied to abilities above the average, as, for example, when a man of more than ordinary ability is spoken of as "a man of talent," or "a talented man." The word ability, indeed, is used in the same way. "A man of ability," "an able man," means a man able to do more than most people can; whereas, properly speaking, and in the sense of the parable, a man who is able to do anything—to break stones, to write his name, to speak a sentence of sense—is an able man. He is not generally so called, but he really is a talented man, for God has given him, as He has given to every one, certain ability, and according to that ability is the talent for service with which Christ entrusts him. At first sight this phrase "according to his several ability" seems invidious, as if suggesting that Christ was a respecter of persons, and dealt more liberally with the strong than with the weak. But the talents are not merely gifts,—they are trusts involving responsibility; and therefore it is simple justice to graduate them according to ability. As we shall see, there is no respect of persons in appointing the awards. But as respects the talents, involving as they do the burden of responsibility, it is very evident that it would be no kindness to the man of less ability that he should be made responsible for more than he can easily undertake.

The gradations of five, two, one, appropriately correspond to what we speak of as superior, ordinary, and inferior ability. At this point occurs the main distinction between this parable and the similar one of the pounds, spoken at a different time and with a different purpose. Here the servants all differ at first, but the faithful ones are alike in the end, inasmuch as they have done equally well in proportion to their ability. There the servants are all alike at the beginning, but the faithful ones receive different awards, inasmuch as they have differed in the degree of their diligence and faithfulness. The two together bring out with striking clearness and force the great thought that not success, but faithfulness is what the Lord insists on. The weakest is at no disadvantage; he may not only do as well as the strongest, but if the measure of his diligence and faithfulness is higher, he may even excel him.

It is in keeping with the difference in the scope of the two parables that in the one the sums entrusted should be large (talents), in the other, small (pounds). In the parable which has for its main lesson, "Make the most of the little you have," the amounts entrusted are small; while the large sums are fitly found in the parable which emphasises what may be called the other side of the great lesson, "To whom much is given, of them much shall be required."

Confining our attention now to the parable before us, we have first the encouraging side in the cases of two of the servants. The number is evidently chosen as the very smallest that would bring out the truth that where abilities differ the reward will be the same, if only the diligence and faithfulness be equal. It is quite probable, indeed, that the number of servants thought of was more than three, perhaps ten,* to correspond with the number of the virgins, and that only as many cases are taken as were necessary to bring out the truth to be taught.

These two faithful servants lost no time in setting to work. This appears in the Revised Version, where the word "straightway" is restored to its right place, indicating that immediately on receiving the five talents the servant began diligently to use them (ver. 16, R. V.). The servant with the two talents acted "in like manner" (ver. 17). The result was that each doubled his capital, and each received the same gracious welcome and high promotion when their lord returned (vv. 20-23). They had been unequally successful; but inasmuch as this was not due to any difference in diligence, but only to difference in ability, they were equal in welcome and reward. It is, however, worthy of remark that while the language is precisely the same in the one case as in the other, it is not such as to determine that their position would be precisely equal in the life to come. There will be differences of ability and of range of service there as well as here. In both cases the verdict on the past was "faithful over a few things," though the few things of the one were more than double the few things of the other; and in the same way, though the promise for the future was for the one as well as for the other, "I will set thee over many things," it might well be that the many things of the future might vary as the few things of the past had done. But all will be alike satisfied, a thought which is beautifully put by Dante in the third canto of his "Paradise," where the sainted Piccarda, in answer to the question whether those who, like her, have the lower places have no envy of those above them, gives an explanation of which this is the concluding passage:

> "So that as we, from step to step,
> Are placed throughout this kingdom, pleases all,
> Even as our King, Who in us plants His will;
> And in His will is our tranquillity;
> It is the mighty ocean, whither tends
> Whatever it creates and nature makes."

Whereupon Dante himself says:

> "Then saw I clearly how each spot in heaven
> Is Paradise, though with like gracious dew
> The supreme virtue shower not over all."
> —Canto III. 82-90 (Carey).

It is not suggested, however, in the parable that there is not the same gracious dew showering over all. "The joy of the Lord" would appear to be the same for all; but it is significant that the leading thought of heavenly reward is not joy, but rather promotion, promotion in service, a higher sphere and a wider range of work, the "few things" which have been our glad service here exchanged for "many things," of which we shall be masters there—no more failures, no more bungling, no more mortifications as we look back upon work half done or ill done or much of it undone: "I will *set thee over* many things (R. V.)." That is the great reward; the other follows as of course: "Enter thou into the joy of thy Lord."

As in the parable of the virgins, so here, the force increases as we pass from encouragement to warning. The closing scene is solemn and fearful. That the man with one talent should be selected as an illustration of unfaithfulness is very significant—not certainly in the way of suggesting that unfaithfulness is more likely to be found among those whose abilities are slender and opportunities small; but so as to make it plain that, though all due allowance is made for this, it can in no case be accepted as an excuse for want of faithfulness. It is just as imperative on the man with one talent, as on him with five, to do what he can. Had the illustration been taken from one with higher endowments, it might have been thought that the greatness of the loss had something to do with the severity of the sentence; but, as the parable is constructed, no such thought is admissible: it is perfectly clear that it is no question of gain or loss, but simply of faithfulness or unfaithfulness: "Hast thou done what thou couldst?"

The offence here is not, as in the first of the four pictures of judgment, painted in dark colours. There was no beating of fellow-servants or drinking with the drunken, no conduct like that of the unjust steward or the unmerciful creditor who took his fellow-servant by the throat—it was simple neglect: "I was afraid, and went and hid thy talent in the earth." The servant had such a modest estimate of his own abilities that he was even afraid he might do mischief in trying to use the talent he had, so he laid it away and let it alone. The excuse he makes (vv. 24, 25) is very true to nature. It is not modesty after all that is at the root of the idleness of those who hide their talent in the earth; it is unbelief. They do not believe in God as revealed in the Son of His love; they think of Him as a hard Master; they shrink from having anything to do with religion, rather wonder at those who have the assurance to think of *their* serving God, or doing anything for the advancement of His kingdom. They know not the grace of the Lord Jesus Christ, and therefore it is that they hold aloof from Him, refusing to confess Him, declining to employ in His service the talents entrusted to their care.

At this point there is an instructive contrast

* In the parable of the pounds the number of servants is ten, and there, too, only three are selected as examples.

between the parable of the virgins and the one before us. There the foolish virgins failed because they took their duties too easily; here the servant fails because he thinks his duties too hard. Bearing this in mind, we recognise the appropriateness of the Lord's answer. He might have found fault with his excuse, showing him how easily he might have known that his ideas of his Master were entirely wrong, and how if he had only addressed himself to the work to which he was called, his difficulties would have disappeared and he would have found the service easily within his powers; but the Master waives all this, accepts the hard verdict on Himself, admits the difficulties in the way, and then points out that even at the worst, even though he "was afraid," even though he had not courage enough, like the other servants, to go straightway to the work to which he was first called, he might have found some other and less trying form of service, something that would have avoided the risks he had not courage to face, and yet at the same time have secured some return for his Lord (vv. 26, 27). The Master is ready to make all allowance for the weakness of His servants, so long as it does not amount to absolute unfaithfulness; so long as by any stretch of charity it is possible to call the servant "good and faithful." In this case it was not possible. Not faithful, but slothful, was the word; therefore good it cannot be, but—the only other alternative—wicked: "thou wicked and slothful servant."

Then follows doom. Instead of promotion, degradation: "take the talent from him." And in this there is no arbitrary punishment, no penalty needing to be *inflicted*—it comes as the result of a great law of the universe, according to which unused powers fall into atrophy, paralysis, and death; while on the other hand, faithful and diligent use of power enlarges it more and more: "Take therefore the talent from him, and give it unto him which hath ten talents. For unto every one that hath shall be given, and he shall have abundance: but from him that hath not shall be taken away even that which he hath." As the necessary and natural sequel to promotion in service was the joy of the Lord, so the natural and necessary sequel of degradation is the "outer darkness," where "there shall be weeping and gnashing of teeth."

4. *The Final Separation* (xxv. 31-46).

As in the Sermon on the Mount, and again in the last discourse in the Temple, so here, the language rises into a strain of great majesty and sublimity as the prophecy draws to a close. No one can fail to recognise it. This vision of judgment is the climax of the teaching of the Lord Christ. Alike for magnificence and for pathos it is unsurpassed in literature. There is no departure from His wonted simplicity of style. As little here as everywhere else do we recognise even a trace of effort or of elaboration; yet as we read there is not a word that could be changed, not a clause that could be spared, not a thought that could be added with advantage. It bears the mark of perfection, whether we look at it from the point of view of the Speaker's divinity or from the point of view of His humanity. Divine in its sublimity, it is most human in its tenderness. "Truly this was the Son of God." Truly this was the Son of man.

The grandeur of the passage is all the more impressive by contrast with what immediately follows: "And it came to pass, when Jesus had finished all these sayings, He said unto His disciples, Ye know that after two days is the feast of the passover, and the Son of man is betrayed to be crucified." Into such an abyss was the Son of man looking when in language so calm, so confident, so majestic, so sublime, He spoke of sitting on the throne of His glory as the Judge of all mankind. Did ever man speak like this Man?

It is significant that even when speaking of the coming glory He still retains His favourite designation, "the Son of man." In this we see one of the many minute coincidences which show the inner harmony of the discourses recorded in this Gospel with those of a different style of thought preserved by St. John; for it is in one of these we read that "He [the Father] hath given Him authority to execute judgment, because He is the Son of man." Thus the judgment of humanity proceeds out of humanity itself, and constitutes as it were the final offering up of man to God. This on the God-ward side; and, on the other side, there is for those who stand before the Judge, the certainty that as Son of man He knows by experience all the weaknesses of those He judges and the force of the temptations by which they have been beset.

Nothing could be more impressive than the picture set before us of the throne of glory, on which is seated the Son of man with all the angels around Him and all nations gathered before Him. It is undoubtedly the great assize, the general judgment of mankind. No partial judgment can it be, nothing less than the great event referred to in that passage already quoted from St. John's Gospel, where after speaking of judgment being committed to the Son of Man, it is added: "Marvel not at this: for the hour cometh, in which all that are in the graves shall hear His voice, and shall come forth: they that have done good, unto the resurrection of life; and they that have done evil, unto the resurrection of damnation." This view of the passage is supported not only by the universality implied throughout and expressed in the term "all the nations"; * but by every reference to the same subject throughout this Gospel, notably the parables of the Tares and the Net (see Matt. xiii. 39-43, 47-50), the general declaration at Cæsarea Philippi, "The Son of man shall come in the glory of His Father, with His angels; and then shall He reward *every man* according to his works" (Matt. xvi. 27); and especially the earlier reference to the same event in this discourse, in that portion of it which we have spoken of as the prophecy proper, where the mourning of all the tribes of earth, and the gathering together of the elect from the one end of heaven to the other, are connected with one another and with the coming of the Son of man (Matt. xxiv. 30, 31).

It seems quite certain, then, that whatever subsequent unfoldings there may be in the later books of the New Testament as to the order in which judgment shall proceed, there is no intention here of anticipating them. It is true that the preceding parables have each given a partial

* It is not forgotten that the word translated "nations" is commonly applied to the Gentiles as distinguished from the Jews; but clearly there is no such limitation here. No commentator, at least of any note, suggests that the Jews as a nation are not among the nations gathered around the throne.

view of the judgment,—the first as affecting those in office in the Church, the second and third as applied to the members of the Church; but just as those specially contemplated in the first parable are included in the wider scope of the second and third, so these contemplated in the second and third are included in the universal scope of the great judgment scene with which the whole discourse is fitly and grandly concluded.

In this great picture of the final judgment the prominent thought is *separation:* "He shall separate them one from another, as a shepherd divideth his sheep from the goats: and He shall set the sheep on His right hand, but the goats on the left." How easily and with what unerring certainty the separation is made—as easily and as surely as the shepherd divideth the sheep from the goats! Nothing eludes the glance of that all-searching Eye. No need of pleading or counter-pleading, of prosecutor or prisoner's counsel, no hope from legal quibble or insufficient proof. All, all is "naked and opened unto the eyes of Him with Whom we have to do." He sees all at a glance; and as He sees, He divides by a single dividing line. There is no middle position: each one is either on the right or on the left.

The dividing line is one entirely new. All nations are there; but not as nations are they divided now. This is strikingly suggested in the original by the change from the neuter (nations, ἔθνη) to the masculine (them, αὐτοὺς), indicating as by a sudden flash of unexpected light that not as nations, but as individuals, must all be judged. The line is one which crosses all other lines that have divided men from one another, so that of all ranks and conditions of men there will be some on the right and some on the left. Even the family line will be crossed, so that husband and wife, parents and children, brothers and sisters, may be found on opposite sides of it. What, then, is this new and final line of separation? The sentence of the King will mark it out for us.

It is the first and only time that Jesus calls Himself the King. He has displayed His royalty in His acts; He has suggested it in His discourses and His parables; He has claimed it by the manner of His entry into His capital and His Temple; He will afterwards assent when Pilate shall ask Him the plain question; but this is the only place where He uses the title in speaking of Himself. How significant and impressive is this! It is as if He would once for all before He suffered disclose the fulness of His majesty. His royalty, indeed, was suggested at the very beginning by the reference to the throne of His glory; but inasmuch as judgment was the work which lay immediately before Him, He still spoke of Himself as the Son of man; but now that the separation is made, now that the books have been opened and closed, He rises above the Judge and styles Himself THE KING.

We must think of Him now as all radiant with His royal glory—that visage which was "so marred more than any man" now shining with celestial light—that Form which was distorted "more than the sons of men," now seen to be the very "form of God," "the chiefest among ten thousand" of the highest angels round Him, "altogether lovely," the personal embodiment of that glorious kingdom He has been preparing through all the centuries from the foundation of the world—disclosed at last as the answer to every longing soul, the satisfaction of every pure desire,—THE KING.

All this we must realise before we can imagine the awful gulf which lies between these simple words, "Depart" and "Come." That sweet word "Come"—how He has repeated and repeated it through all these ages, in every possible way, with endless variations! Spoken so tenderly with His own human lips, it has been taken up and given forth by those whom He has sent in His name: the Spirit has said "Come"; the Bride has said "Come"; the hearers have said "Come"; whosoever would, has been invited to come. The music of the word has never died away. But now its course is nearly run. Once more it will ring out; but with a difference. No longer now to all. The line of separation has been drawn, and across "the great gulf fixed" the old sweet word of grace can reach no longer. It is to those on the right, and these alone, that now the King says "Come." To those on the left there remains the word, a stranger to His lips before, the awful word, "Depart from Me."

In the contrast between these two words, there already is involved all that follows: all the joy of the welcome—"Come, ye blessed of My Father, inherit the kingdom prepared for you from the foundation of the world"; all the horror of the doom—"Depart from Me, ye cursed, into everlasting fire, prepared for the devil and his angels."

Still the great question remains unanswered, *What is the dividing line?* Inasmuch as this belongs to the hidden man of the heart, to the secrecy of consciousness and conscience, the only way in which it could be made to appear in a picture parable of judgment such as this, is by the introduction of such a conversation as that which follows the sentence in each case. The general distinction between the two classes had been suggested by the simile of the sheep and the goats—the one white, the other black, the one obedient, the other unruly; but it is made much more definite by this dramatic conversation. We call it dramatic, because we regard it as extreme bondage to the letter to suppose this to be a prediction of the words that will actually be used, and therefore look upon it simply as intended to represent, as nothing else could, the new light which both the righteous and the wicked will then see suddenly flashed upon their life on earth, a light so full and clear and self-interpreting that there cannot but be unquestioning acquiescence in the justice of the final award.

There are those who, looking at this conversation in the most superficial way, find in it the doctrine of salvation by works, and imagine that they are warranted on the strength of this passage to set aside all that is written in other parts of Scripture as to the necessity of change of heart, to dismiss from their minds all concern about creed or worship, about doctrine or sacraments or church membership. Be kind to the poor—that will do instead of everything else.

In answer to such a perversion of our Lord's language it should surely be enough to call attention to the fact that all is made to turn upon the treatment of Christ by the one class and by the other. Kindness to the poor comes in, not as in itself the ground of the division, but as furnishing the evidence or manifestation of that devotion to God as revealed in Christ, which forms the real ground of acceptance, and the want of which is the sole ground of condemnation. True it is that Christ identifies Himself with His people, and accepts the kindness done to the poorest of them as done to Himself; but there is obviously implied, what is elsewhere in a similar connection clearly expressed, that the kindness must be done "in the name of a disciple." In other words, love to Christ must be the motive of the deed of charity, else it is worthless as a test of true discipleship. The more carefully the whole passage is read, the more manifest will it be that the great question which determines the separation is this: "How have you treated Christ?" It is only to bring out more clearly the real answer to this question that the other is added: How have you treated Christ's poor? For according to each man's treatment of these will have been his treatment of Christ Himself. It is the same principle applied to the unseen Christ as the apostle applies to the invisible God: "He that loveth not his brother whom he hath seen, how can he love God Whom he hath not seen?"

While there is no encouragement here for those who hope to make up for the rejection of Christ by deeds of kindness to poor people, there is abundant room left for the acceptance at the last of those who had no means of knowing Christ, but who showed by their treatment of their fellow-men in distress that the spirit of Christ was in them. To such the King will be no stranger when they shall see Him on the throne; nor will they be strangers to Him. He will recognise them as His own; and they will recognise Him as the very King of Love for Whom their souls were longing, but Who not till now has been revealed to their delighted gaze. To all such will the gracious words be spoken "Come, ye blessed of My Father"; but they too, as well as all the rest, will be received not on the ground of works as distinguished from faith, but on the ground of a real though implicit faith which worked by love and which was only waiting for the revelation of their King and Lord to make it explicit, to bring it out to light.

Philanthropy can never take the place of faith; and yet no words ever spoken or written on this earth have done so much for philanthropy as these. It were vain to attempt, in so brief a sketch, to bring out even in the way of suggestion the mingled majesty and pathos of the words of the King to the righteous, culminating in that great utterance which touches the very deepest springs of feeling and thrills every fibre of the pure and loving heart: "Inasmuch as ye have done it unto one of the least of these My brethren, ye have done it unto Me." Besides the pathos of the words, what depth of suggestion is there in the thought, as shedding light upon His claim to be the Son of man! As Son of God He is the King, seated on the throne of His glory; as Son of man He is identified with all His brethren, even with the least of them, and with each one of them all over all the world and through all the ages: "Inasmuch as ye have done it unto one of the least of these My brethren, ye have done it unto Me." How the divinity shines, how the humanity thrills, through these great words of the King!

The scroll of this grand prophecy is finished with the awful words: "These shall go away into eternal punishment; but the righteous into eternal life" (R. V.). Eternal punishment, eternal life—such are the issues which hang upon the coming of the Son of man to judgment; such are the issues which hang upon the treatment of the Son of man in these years of our mortal life that are passing over us now. There are those who flatter themselves with the idea that, because the question has been raised by honest and candid interpreters of Scripture whether absolute endlessness is necessarily involved in the word eternal, therefore these words of doom are shorn of much of their terror; but surely this is a pitiful delusion. There is no possible way of reducing the force of the word "eternal" which will bring the awfulness of the doom within the bounds of any finite imagination; and whatever may be said as to what the word necessarily implies, whatever vague surmise there may be that absolute endlessness is not in it, this much is perfectly certain: that there is not the slightest suggestion of hope in the words; no straining of the eyes can discern even the straitest gate out of that eternal punishment into eternal life. Between the one and the other there is "a great gulf fixed." It is the final judgment; it is the final separation; and scarcely with more distinctness could the awful letters have been traced, "Leave every hope behind, all ye who enter here." "These shall go away into eternal punishment; but the righteous"—none but the righteous—"into eternal life."

CHAPTER XIX.

THE GREAT ATONEMENT DAY.

MATTHEW xxvi. 1-xxvii. 56.

WE enter now on the story of the last day of the mortal life of our Lord and Saviour. We have already noticed the large proportionate space given to the Passion Week; but still more remarkable is the concentration of interest on the Passion Day. The record of that single day is very nearly one-ninth of the whole book; and a similar proportion is observed by all the four Evangelists. This proportion of space is very striking even when we bear in mind that, properly speaking, the Gospels are not the record of thirty-three or thirty-four years, but only of three or four. Of the story of the years of the public ministry one-seventh part is given to the last day; and this, too, without the introduction of any lengthened discourse. If the discourse in the upper room and the intercessory prayer as recorded by St. John were added, it would be, not one-seventh, but almost one-fourth of the whole. Truly this must be the Day of days! Unspeakably sacred and precious as is the entire life of our Lord and Saviour, sacred above all and precious above all is His death of shame and agony. The same pre-eminence was evidently given to the dying of the Lord Jesus in the special revelation granted to St. Paul, as is evident from the fact that, in setting forth the gospel he had been commissioned to preach, he spoke of it as the gospel of "Jesus Christ and Him crucified," and put in the foreground, not the incarnate life, great as he recognised it to be (1 Tim. iii. 16), but the atoning death of Christ: "I delivered unto you *first of all* that which I also received, how that Christ died for our sins according to the Scriptures." Here, then, we have the very gospel of the grace of God. Here we enter the inner shrine of the Word, the Holy of Holies of the new covenant. Let us draw near with holy reverence and deep humility, yet with the eye of faith directed ever upwards in reliance on the grace of Him Who searcheth all things, even the deep things of God, and Whose work and joy it is to take of the things of Christ, even those that are among the deepest things of God, and show them unto us.

" After Two Days " (xxvi. 1-19).

This passage does not strictly belong to the history of the one great day, but it is the approach to it. It opens with the solemn announcement " After two days is the feast of the Passover, and the Son of man is betrayed to be crucified"; and without any record of the Saviour's doings in the interval,* it closes with the preparation for the keeping of the feast with His disciples, the directions for which are introduced by the pathetic words, " My time is at hand."

The incident at Bethany (vv. 6-13) seems to be introduced here in connection with the development of treason in the soul of Judas. This connection would not be so apparent were it not for the information given in St. John's account of the feast, that it was Judas especially who objected to what he called " this waste " of the ointment, and that the reason why he was displeased at it was because " he had the bag, and bare what was put therein." With this in mind we can see how natural it was that, having had no occasion before to tell the story of the feast at Bethany, the Evangelist should be disposed to tell it now, as connected in his mind with the traitor's selling of his Lord for thirty pieces of silver.

The two days of interval would extend from the evening following the abandonment of the Temple to the evening of the Passover feast. It is important always, and especially in studying the days of the Passion week, to bear in mind that, according to the Jewish mode of reckoning, each new day began, not with the morning as with us, but with the evening. In this they followed a very ancient precedent: " The evening and the morning were the first day." The two days, then, would be from Tuesday evening till Thursday evening; so that with Thursday evening began the last day of our Lord's Passion. There is no record at all of how He spent the Wednesday; in all probability it was in seclusion at Bethany. Nor have we any account of the doings of the Thursday save the directions given to prepare the Passover, the keeping of which was to be the first act of the last day.

We may think of these two days, then, as days of rest for our Lord, of holy calm and quietude —a sacred lull before the awful storm. What were His thoughts? what His feelings? What passages of Scripture were His solace? Would not the ninety-fourth psalm be one of them? If so, how fondly would He dwell upon that sentence of it, " In the multitude of my thoughts within me Thy comforts delight my soul." If we only had a record of His prayers, how rich it would be! If we had the spiritual history of these two days it would no doubt be full of pleading as rich and precious as the prayer of intercession His disciple heard and one of them recorded for our sakes, and of yearning as tender and touching as His wail over Jerusalem. But the Spirit, Who takes of the things of Christ and shows them unto us, does not invade the privacy of the Saviour's hours of retirement. No diary is published; and beyond doubt it is better so. It may be that in the lives of the saints there has been too much of this—not too much of spiritual communing, but too much unveiling of it. It may be that there is a danger of leading us to seek after such " exercises " as an end in themselves, instead of as mere means to the end of holy and unselfish living. What the world should see is the life that is the outcome of those secret communings with God—it should see the life which *was* with the Father manifested in glowing word and self-forgetting deed. Why have we no need to see into that holy, loving heart during these two sacred days in Bethany? Because it is sufficiently revealed in the story of the day that followed it. Ah! the words, the deeds of that day—what revealings of heart, what manifestations of the life within are there!

The very silence of these two days is strikingly suggestive of repose. We are presently to hear of the awful agony in the Garden; but from the very way in which we shall hear of it we shall be strengthened in the impression, which no doubt is the true one, that the two days of interval were not days of agony, but days of soul rest; and in this we recognise a striking contrast to the restlessness of those who spent the time in plotting His destruction. Contrast, for example, the calm of our Lord's announcement in the second verse, with the uneasy plotting in the palace of the high priest. Without agitation He faces the horror of great darkness before Him; without flinching He anticipates the very darkest of it all: " betrayed "—" crucified "; without a tremor on His lips He even specifies the time: " after two days." Now look at that company in the palace of the high priest, as with dark brows and troubled looks they consult how they may take Jesus by subtlety. Observe how in fear they put it off,—as not safe yet, not for nine days at least, till the crowds at the feast, so many of whom had so recently been shouting " Hosanna to the Son of David! " shall have gone home. " Not for nine days," so they resolve. " After two days," so He has said.

> " Oh, but the counsel of the Lord
> Doth stand, for ever sure."

Christ knew far more about it than if there had been a spy in the palace of the high priest, reporting to Him. He was in communication with One Who doeth according to His will in the armies of heaven and among the inhabitants of the earth. Caiaphas and his fellow-conspirators may plot what they please, it shall be done according to the counsel of the Lord; it shall be so done that an apostle shall be able afterwards with confidence to say: " Him, *being delivered by the determinate counsel and foreknowledge of God*, ye have taken."

The means by which their counsels were overruled was the treason of Judas, into whose dark heart the Bethany incident will afford us a glimpse. Its interest turns upon the different

* The feast in Bethany did not take place during this interval, but some days before (see John xii. 1); in all probability the very day before Christ's entry into Jerusalem.

values attached to a deed of love, by Judas on the one hand, and by Jesus on the other.

To Judas it meant waste. And such a waste! —three hundred pence thrown away on the foolish luxury of a moment! "This ointment might have been sold for much, and given to the poor." Be it remembered that there was a good deal to be said for this argument. It is very easy for us, who have the limelight of our Lord's words on the whole scene, to see how paltry the objection was; but even yet, with this story now published, as our Lord said it would be, all over Christendom, how many arguments are heard of the very same description! It is not so much to be wondered at that the objection of Judas found a good deal of favour with some of the disciples. They could not see the blackness of the heart out of which the suggestion came, nor could they see the beauty of the love which shed from Mary's heart a perfume far more precious than the odour of the ointment. Probably even Mary was startled; and, if her Lord had not at once taken her part, might not have had a word to say for herself.

"But Jesus, perceiving it, said unto them, Why trouble ye the woman? for she hath wrought a good work on Me." He understood her—understood her perfectly, read at once the whole secret of her loving heart, explained her conduct better even than she understood it herself, as we shall presently see. He deals very tenderly with the disciples; for He understood them too, saw at once that there was no treason in their hearts, that though they took up the suggestion of the traitor it was in no sympathy with his spirit, but simply because of their want of insight and appreciation. He, however, does rebuke them—gently; and then He quietly opens their eyes to the surpassing beauty of the deed they had ventured to condemn. "She hath wrought a good work upon Me." The word translated "good" has prominent in it the thought of beauty. And since our Lord has set that deed of Mary in its true light, there is no one with any sense of beauty who fails to see how beautiful it is. The very impulsiveness of the act, the absence of all calculation, the simplicity and naturalness of it, the womanliness of it—all these add to its beauty as an outburst of love. We can well imagine that these words of Jesus may have furnished much of the inspiration which thrilled the soul of the apostle as he wrote to the Corinthians his noble eulogy of love. Certainly its pricelessness could not have been more notably or memorably taught. Three hundred pence to be weighed against a true woman's love! "If a man would give all the substance of his house for love, it would utterly be contemned."

We are led into still more sacred ground as we observe how highly the Saviour values Mary's affection for Himself. "She hath wrought a good work upon *Me*"—"*Me* ye have not always"—"she did it for My burial." Who can reach the pathos of these sacred words? There is no doubt that amid the hate by which Jesus was surrounded, with His knowledge of the treason in the dark soul of Judas, and His keen sense of the want of sympathy on the part of the other disciples, His human heart was yearning for love, for sympathetic love. Oh, how He loved! and how that love of His was going out to all around Him throughout the Passion week —without return! We may well believe, then, that this outburst of love from the heart of Mary must have greatly cheered Him.

"She hath wrought a good work *upon Me*." With the ointment on His head, there had come a far sweeter balm to His wounded heart; for He saw that she was not wanting in sympathy —that she had some idea, however vague it might be, of the pathos of the time. She felt, if she did not quite see, the shadow of the grave. And this presentiment (shall we call it?) not as the result of any special thought about it, but in some dim way, had prompted her to choose this touching manner of showing her love: "In that she hath poured this ointment on My body, she did it for My burial." Verily, a true human heart beats here, welcoming, oh! so gladly, this woman's loving sympathy.

But the Divine Spirit is here too, looking far beyond the needs of the moment or the burdens of the day. No one could more tenderly consider the poor; nothing was nearer to His heart than their necessities,—witness that wonderful parable of judgment with which He finished His public ministry; but He knew well that in that personal devotion which was shown in Mary's loving act was to be found the mainspring of all benevolence, and not only so but of all that was good and gracious; therefore to discourage such personal affection would be to seal up the fount of generosity and goodness; and accordingly He not only commends it, but he lifts it up to its proper dignity, He gives it commendation beyond all other words of praise He ever spoke; looking away down the ages, and out to the ends of the earth, and recognising that this love to Himself, this personal devotion to a dying Saviour, was to be the very central force of the gospel, and thus the hope of the world, He adds these memorable words: "Verily I say unto you, Wheresoever this gospel shall be preached in the whole world, there shall also this, that this woman hath done, be told for a memorial of her."

From "this that this woman hath done" the record passes at once to that which was done by the man who had dared to find fault with it. It also is told wherever the gospel is preached as a memorial of him. Behold, then, the two memorials side by side. Has not the Evangelist shown himself the true historian in bringing them together? The contrast intensifies the light that shines from the love of Mary, and deepens the darkness of the traitor's sin. Besides, the story of the three hundred pence is a most fitting prelude to that of the thirty pieces of silver. At the same time, by suggesting the steps which led down to such an abyss of iniquity, it saves us from the error of supposing that the sin of Judas was so peculiar that no one now need be afraid of falling into it; for we are reminded in this way that it was at bottom the very sin which is the commonest of all, the very sin into which Christians of the present day are in greatest danger of falling.

What was it that made so great a gulf between Judas and all the rest? Not natural depravity; in this respect they were no doubt much alike. When the Twelve were chosen there was in all probability as good material, so to speak, in the man of Kerioth as in any of the men of Galilee. What, then, made the difference? Simply this, that his heart was never truly given to his Lord. He tried throughout to serve God and mammon; and if he had been able to combine the two services, if there had been any fair prospect of these thrones on which the Twelve were to sit, and the honours and emoluments of the kingdom with which his fancy had been dazzled, treason would never have entered his mind; but when not a throne but a cross began to loom before him, he found, as every one finds some time, that he must make his choice, and that choice was what it invariably is with those who try to serve the two masters. The god of this world had blinded him. He not only failed to see the beauty of Mary's loving deed, as some of the other disciples did just at the first, but he had become quite incapable of any spiritual insight, quite incapable of seeing his Master's glory, or recognising His claims. In a certain sense, then, even Judas himself was like the other murderers of Christ in not knowing what he did. Only he might have known, would have known, had not that accursed lust of gold been always in the way. And we may say of any ordinary worshipper of mammon of the present day, that if he had been in Judas' place, with the prospects as dark as they were to him, with only the one course left, as it would seem to him, of extricating himself from a losing concern, he would be in the highest degree likely to do the very same thing.

As the two days draw to a close we see Judas seeking opportunity to betray his Master, and Jesus seeking opportunity to keep His last Passover with His disciples. Again, what a contrast! The traitor must lurk and lie in wait; the Master does not even remain in Bethany or seek some lonely house on the Mount of Olives, but sends His disciples right over into the city, and with the same readiness with which He had found the ass's colt on which He rode into Jerusalem He finds a house in which to keep the feast.

I. The Evening (xxvi. 20-30).

The last day of our Lord's Passion begins at eventide on Thursday with the Passover feast, at which "He sat down with the Twelve."

The entire feast would be closely associated in His mind with the dark event with which the day must close; for of all the types of the great sacrifice He was about to offer, the most significant was the paschal lamb. Most fitting, therefore, was it that towards the close of this feast, when its sacred importance was deepest in the disciples' minds, their Master should institute the holy ordinance which was to be a lasting memorial of "Christ our Passover sacrificed for us." Of this feast, then, with its solemn and affecting close, the passage before us is the record.

It falls naturally into two parts, corresponding to the two great burdens on the Saviour's heart as He looked forward to this feast—the Betrayal and the Crucifixion (see ver. 2). The former is the burden of vv. 21-25; the latter of vv. 26-30. There was indeed very much besides to tell—the strife which grieved the Master's heart as they took their places at the table, and His wise and kindly dealing with it (Luke xxii. 24, *seq.*); the washing of the disciples' feet; the farewell words of consolation; the prayer of intercession (John xiii.-xvii.),—but these are all omitted here, that thought may be concentrated on the two outstanding facts: the unmasking and dismissal of the traitor, and the committing to the faithful ones of the sacred charge, "This do in remembrance of Me."

1. It must have been sorrowful enough for the Master as He sat down with the Twelve to mark their unseemly strife, and sadder still to think that, though for the hour so closely gathered round Him, they would soon be scattered every man to his own and would leave Him alone; but He had the comfort of knowing that eleven were true at heart and foreseeing that after all wanderings and falls they would come back again. "He knoweth our frame, and remembereth that we are dust"; and therefore with the eye of divine compassion He could look beyond the temporary desertion, and find satisfaction in the fidelity that would triumph in the end over the weakness of the flesh. But there was one of them, for whom His heart was failing Him, in whose future He could see no gleam of light. All the guiding and counsel with which he had been favoured in common with the rest had been lost on him,—even the early word of special personal warning (John vi. 70), spoken that he might bethink himself ere it were too late, had failed to touch him. There is now only one opportunity left. It is the last night; and the last word must now be spoken. How tenderly and thoughtfully the difficult duty is done! "As they did eat, He said, Verily I say unto you, that one of you shall betray Me." Imagine in what tones these words were spoken, what love and sorrow must have thrilled in them!

The kind intention evidently was to reach the heart of the one without attracting the attention of the rest. For there must have been a studied avoidance of any look or gesture that would have marked the traitor. This is manifest from the way in which the sad announcement is received. It comes, in fact, to all the eleven as a summons to great searchings of heart, a fitting preparation (1 Cor. xi. 28) for the new and sacred service to which they are soon to be invited; and truly there could have been no better sign than the passing from lip to lip, from heart to heart, of the anxious question, "Lord, is it I?" The remembrance of the strife at the beginning of the feast was too recent, the tone of the Master's voice too penetrating, the glance of His eye too searching, to make self-confidence possible to them at that particular moment. Even the heart of the confident Peter seems to have been searched and humbled under that scrutinising look. If only he had retained the same spirit, what humiliation would have been spared him!

There was one who did not take up the question; but the others were all so occupied with self-scrutiny that no one seems to have observed his silence, and Jesus forbears to call attention to it. He will give him another opportunity to confess and repent, for so we understand the pathetic words which follow: "He that dippeth his hand with Me in the dish, the same shall betray Me." This was no mere outward sign for the purpose of denoting the traitor. It was a wail of sorrow, an echo of the old lament of the Psalmist: "Yea, mine own familiar friend, in whom I trusted, which did eat of my bread, hath lifted up his heel against me." How could the heart even of Judas resist so tender an appeal?

We shall understand the situation better if

we suppose what is more than probable,* that he was sitting very near to Jesus, perhaps next to Him on the one side, as John certainly was on the other. We cannot suppose, from what we know of the customs of the East, that Judas was the only one dipping with Him in the dish; nor would he be the only one to whom "the sop" was given. But if his position was as we have supposed, there was something in the vague words our Saviour used which tended to the singling of him out, and, though not the only one, he would naturally be the first to whom the sop was given, which would be a sufficient sign to John, who alone was taken into confidence at the time (see John xiii. 25, 26), without attracting in any special way the attention of the rest. Both in the words and in the action, then, we recognise the Saviour's yearning over His lost disciple, as He makes a last attempt to melt his obdurate heart.

The same spirit is manifest in the words which follow. The thought of consequences to Himself gives Him no concern; "the Son of man goeth, even as it is written of Him;" it is the awful abyss into which His disciple is plunging that fills His soul with horror: "but woe unto that man by whom the Son of man is betrayed! it had been good for that man if he had not been born." O Judas! Thy treachery is indeed a link in the chain of events by which the divine purpose is fulfilled; but it was not necessary that so it should be. In some other way the counsel of the Lord would have been accomplished, if thou hadst yielded to that last appeal. It was necessary that the Son of man should suffer and die for the world's sin, but there was nothing to compel thee to have thy hand in it.

At last Judas speaks; but in no spirit of repentance. He takes up, it is true, the question of the rest, but not in sincerity—only driven to it as the last refuge of hypocrisy. Moreover, he asks it in so low a tone, that neither it nor the answer to it appears to have been noticed by the general company (see John xiii. 29). And that there is no inclining of the heart to his Lord appears perhaps in the use of the formal title Rabbi, retained in the Revised Version: "Is it I, Rabbi?" Had he repented even at this late hour—had he thrown himself, humbled and contrite, at the Saviour's feet, with the question "Lord, is it I?" struggling to find utterance, or better still, the heart-broken confession, "Lord, it is I"—it would not yet have been too late. He Who never turned a penitent away would have received even Judas back again and forgiven all his sin; and in lowliness of heart the repentant disciple might have received at his Master's hands the symbols of that infinite sacrifice which was sufficient even for such as he. But his conscience is seared as with a hot iron, his heart is hard as the nether millstone, and accordingly without a word of confession, actually taking "the sop" without a sign even of shame, he gave himself up finally to the spirit of evil, and went immediately out—"*and it was night*" (see John xiii. 30). There remain now around the Master none but true disciples.

2. The Passover meal is drawing to a close; but ere it is ended the Head of the little family has quite transfigured it. When the traitor left the company we may suppose that the look of unutterable sadness would gradually pass from the Saviour's countenance. Up to this time the darkness had been unrelieved. As he thought of the lost disciple's fate, there was nothing but woe in the prospect; but when from that dark future he turned to His own, He saw, not the horror of the Cross alone, but "the joy set before Him"; and in view of it He was able with a heart full of thanks and praise to appoint for remembrance of the awful day a feast, to be kept like the Paschal feast by an ordinance for ever (see Ex. xii. 14).

The connection of the new feast with the old is closely maintained. It was "as they were eating" that the Saviour took bread, and from the way in which He is said to have taken "a cup" (R .V.) it is plain that it was one of the cups it was customary to take at the Paschal feast. With this in mind we can more readily see the naturalness of the words of institution. They had been feasting on the body of the lamb; it is time that they should look directly at the Lamb of God, which taketh away the sin of the world; so, taking the new symbol and handing it to them, He says, "Take, eat; this is My body."

How strange that into words so simple there should have been imported anything so mysterious and unnatural as some of the doctrines around which controversy in the Church has raged for weary centuries—doctrines sadly at variance with "the simplicity that is in Christ."* At the first institution of the Passover the directions for eating it close with these words, "It is the Lord's Passover." Does any one for a single moment suppose that in so putting it Moses meant to assert any mysterious identity of two things so diverse in their nature as the literal flesh of the lamb and the historical event known as the Lord's Passover? Why, then, should any one for a moment suppose that when Jesus says, "This is My body," He had any thought of mysterious transference or confusion of identity? Moses meant that the one was the symbol of the other; and in the same way our Saviour meant that the bread was henceforth to be the symbol of His body. The same appropriateness, naturalness, and simplicity, are apparent in the words with which He hands the cup: "This is My blood of the covenant" (R. V. omits *new*, which throws the emphasis more distinctly on *My*) "which is shed"—not, like the blood of the lamb, for a little family group, but—"for many," not as a mere sign (see Heb. x.), but "unto remission of sins."

The new symbols were evidently much more suitable to the ordinance which was to be of world-wide application. Besides, it was no longer necessary that there should be further sacrifice of life. Christ our Passover was sacri-

* See the interesting discussion on the arrangement of the table in Edersheim, "Life and Times of Jesus the Messiah," vol. ii. p. 494.

* The high Sacramentarian view of the Lord's Supper is not only at variance with the simple and obvious meaning of the central words of institution, but seems to disregard in the most wanton manner the plainest statements of the very authority on which the ordinance is based. According to the Gospel it was "as they were eating" that Jesus took the bread and gave it to the disciples; according to the Ritualist it ought to be before anything else has touched the lips. For their mystical act of consecration on the part of the priest, all they can find either in gospel or epistle is the simple giving of thanks (that "blessed" of ver. 26 is the same act precisely is obvious by comparing the corresponding passages in the other Gospels and in the first Epistle to the Corinthians—xi. 24); while in opposition to the emphatic "Drink ye all of it," the cup has been refused by the Church of Rome to the great majority of her communicants!

ficed once for all; and therefore there must be no thought of repetition of the sacrifice; it must be represented only; and this is done both simply and impressively in the breaking of the bread and the pouring of the wine. Nothing could be more natural than the transition from the old to the new Passover feast.

Rising now above all matters of detail and questions of interpretation, let us try humbly and reverently to enter into the mind of Christ as He breaks the bread and pours the wine and institutes the feast of love. As in the earlier part of the evening we had in His dealings with the traitor a touching unveiling of His human heart, so now, while there is the same human tenderness, there is with it a reach of thought and range of vision which manifestly transcend all mortal powers.

Consider first how extraordinary it was that at such a time He should take pains to concentrate the thoughts of His disciples in all time to come upon His death. Even the bravest of those who had been with Him in all His temptations could not look at it now; and to His own human soul it must have seemed in the very last degree repulsive. To the disciples, to the world, it must have seemed defeat; yet He calmly provides for its perpetual celebration as a victory!

Think of the form the celebration takes. It is no mournful solemnity, with dirges and elegies for one about to die; but a *Feast*—a strange way of celebrating a death. It may be said that the Passover feast itself was a precedent; but in this respect there is no parallel. The Passover feast was no memorial of a death. If Moses had died that night, would it ever have occurred to the children of Israel to institute a feast for the purpose of keeping in memory so unutterable a calamity? But a greater than Moses is here, and is soon to die a cruel and shameful death. Is not that a calamity as much more dreadful than the other as Christ was greater than Moses? Why, then, celebrate it by a feast? Because this death is no calamity. It is the means of life to a great multitude that no man can number, out of every kindred and tongue and people and nation. Therefore it is most fitly celebrated by a feast. It is a memorial; but it is far more. It is a feast, provided for the spiritual nourishment of the people of God through all their generations. Think what must have been in the Saviour's mind when He said, "Take, eat"; how His soul must have been enlarged as He uttered the words "shed for many." Simple words, easily spoken; but before they came from these sacred lips there must have risen before His mind the vision of multitudes all through the ages, fed on the strangest food, refreshed by the strangest wine, that mortal man had ever heard of.

How marvellously the horizon widens round Him as the feast proceeds! At first He is wholly engaged with the little circle round the table. When He says, "One of you shall betray Me," when He takes the sop and hands it, when He pours out His last lament over the false disciple, He is the Man of Sorrows in the little upper chamber; but when He takes the bread and again the cup, the horizon widens, beyond the cross He sees the glory that shall follow, sees men of all nations and climes coming to the feast He is preparing for them, and before He closes He has reached the consummation in the heavenly kingdom: "I say unto you, I will not drink henceforth of this fruit of the vine, until that day when I drink it new with you in My Father's kingdom." "Truly this was the Son of God."

Then hear Him singing at the close. How bewildered the disciples, how rapt the Master, must have been! What a scene for the painter, what a study of divine calm and human agitation! The "hymn" they sang was in all probability the latter part of the Great Hallel, which closes with Psalm cxviii. It is most interesting as we read the psalm to think what depths of meaning, into which none of His disciples as yet could enter, there must have been to Him in almost every line.

II. The Night (xxvi. 31-75).

As the little company have lingered in the upper room evening has passed into night. The city is asleep, as Jesus leads the way along the silent streets, down the steep slope of Moriah, and across the Kedron, to the familiar place of resort on the mount of Olives. As they proceed in silence, a word of ancient prophecy lies heavy on His heart. It was from Zechariah, whose prophecy was often * in his thoughts in the Passion week. "Awake, O sword, against My shepherd, and against the man that is My fellow, saith the Lord of hosts: smite the shepherd, and the sheep shall be scattered." It is the last part of it that troubles Him. For the smiting of the Shepherd He is well prepared; it is the scattering of the sheep that makes His heart so sore, and forces Him to break the silence with the sorrowful words, "All ye shall be offended because of Me this night." What pathos in these words "because of Me": how it pained Him to think that what must come to Him should be so terrible to them! And is there not a touch of kind allowance in the words "this night"? "He that walketh in the night stumbleth," and how could they but stumble in such a night? Then the thought of the shepherd and the sheep which fills His mind and suggests the passage He quotes is full of tenderness without even a hint of reproach. Who will blame the sheep for scattering when the Shepherd is smitten? And how trustfully and withal how wistfully does He look forward to the reassembling of the flock in the old home, the sacred region where they gathered first round the Shepherd: "After I am risen again, I will go before you [as the shepherd goes before the flock] into Galilee." Thus after all would be fulfilled His prayer of intercession, so recently offered on their behalf: "Holy Father, keep through Thine own name those whom Thou hast given Me, that they may be one."

The silly sheep were not at all alarmed. This was altogether natural; for the danger was not yet within their sight. Nor was it really at all unnatural that the impulsive Peter should be now at the very opposite pole of feeling from where he stood an hour or two before. Then, sharing the general depression, he joined the rest in the anxious question, "Lord, is it I?" now, having been relieved from the anxiety which for the moment pressed upon him, and having been moreover raised into a glow of feeling and an assurance of faith by his Master's tender and stirring words, and the prayer of intercession which so fitly closed them, he has passed from the depths of self-distrust to the heights of self-confidence,

* See Zech. ix. 9, xi. 12, xiii. 7.

so that he even dares to say, "Though all men shall be offended because of Thee, yet will *I* never be offended."

Ah! Peter, you were safe when you were crying "Lord, is it I?"—you are very far from safe now, when you speak of yourself in so different a tone. Jesus sees it all, and gives him warning in the very plainest words. But Peter persists. He vainly imagines that his Master cannot know how strong he is, how burning his zeal, how warm his love, how steadfast his devotion. Of all this he is himself distinctly conscious. There is no mistake about it. Devotion thrills in every fibre of his being; and he knows, he feels it in his soul, that no torture, not death itself, could move him from his steadfastness: "Though I should die with Thee, yet will I not deny Thee." "Likewise also said all the disciples." Quite natural too. For the moment Peter was the leader of the sheep. They all caught his enthusiasm, and were conscious of the same devotion: why, then, should they not acknowledge it as he had done? They had yet to learn the difference between a transient glow of feeling and abiding inward strength. Only by sad experience can they learn it now; so Jesus lets them have the last word.

And now Gethsemane is reached. The olive trees which in the daytime give a shadow from the heat will now afford seclusion, though the moon is at the full. Here, then, the Son of man will spend some time with God, alone, before He is betrayed into the hands of sinners; and yet, true Son of man as He is, He shrinks from being left alone in that dread hour, and clings to the love and sympathy of those who have been with Him in His temptations hitherto. So He leaves eight of the disciples at the entering in of the olive grove, and takes with Him into the darkness the three most in sympathy with Him —the same three who had been the sole witnesses of His power in raising from the dead the daughter of Jairus, and had alone seen His glory on the holy mount. But even these three cannot go with Him all the way. He will have them as near as possible; and yet He must be alone. Did He think of the passage, "I have trodden the winepress * alone, and of the people there was none with me"?

That solitude may not be invaded. We can only, like the disciples of old, look reverently at it from afar. There are probably many true disciples who can get no nearer than the edge of the darkness; those who are closest in sympathy may be able to obtain a nearer view, but even those who like John have leant on His breast can know it only in part—in its depth it passeth knowledge. Jesus is alone in Gethsemane yet, and of the people there is none with Him.

"Ah! never, never can we know
The depth of that mysterious woe."

While it is not possible for any of us to penetrate the deep recesses of Gethsemane, we have a key to let us in, and open to us something of its meaning. This help is found in that striking passage in the Epistle to the Hebrews, where the experience of the Lord Jesus in the Garden is closely connected with His being "called of God an High Priest after the order of Melchisedec." It is true that at His baptism Jesus entered on His ministry in its largest sense, the Prophet, Priest, and King of men. But there is a sense in which later on, at successive stages, He was "called of God" to each of these offices in succession. At His baptism the voice from heaven was, "This is My Beloved Son, in Whom I am well pleased." On the mount of Transfiguration there was this added, "Hear ye Him," and the withdrawal of Moses and Elias, leaving Jesus alone, indicated that henceforth Me was called of God to be the one prophet of humanity. Similarly, though from the beginning He was King, it was not till after He had overcome the sharpness of death that He was "called of God" to be King, to take His seat on the right hand of majesty in the heavens. At what period, then, in His ministry was it that He was called of God to be an high priest? To this natural question the passage in the Epistle to the Hebrews supplies the answer; and when we take the thought with us we see that it is indeed a torch to lighten for us just a little the darkness of the Garden's gloom.

Is there not something in the very arrangement of the group which harmonises with the thought? Three days ago the Temple had been closed for ever to its Lord. Its shrine was empty now for evermore: "Behold, *your* house is left unto you desolate." But still there is to be a temple, in which shall minister a priest, not of the line of Aaron, rather after the older order of Melchisedec—a temple, not of stone, but of men—of believers, according to the later apostolic word: "*Ye* are the temple of the living God." Of that new and living temple we have a representation in Gethsemane. The eight disciples are its court; the three are in the holy place; into the holiest of all our great High Priest has gone—alone: for the veil is not yet rent in twain.

But why the agony? The difficulty has always been to account for the sudden change from the calmness of the Paschal feast to the awful struggle of Gethsemane. What had happened meanwhile to bring about so great a change? There was light in the upper chamber—it was dark in the Garden; but surely the darkness and the light were both alike to Him; or if to His human heart there was the difference we all are conscious of, it could not be that the mere withdrawal of the light destroyed His peace. It is altogether probable that both the previous nights had been spent on this same mount of Olives, and there is no hint of agony then. It is true that the prospect before Him was full of unutterable horror; but from the time He had set His face to go up to Jerusalem it had been always in His view, and though at times the thought of it would come over Him as a cold wave that made Him shudder for the moment, there had been up to this hour no agony like this, and not a trace of pleading that the cup might pass.

What, then, was the new element of woe that came upon Him in that hour? What was the cup now put for the first time to His sacred lips, from which He shrank as from nothing in all His sad experience before? Is not the answer to be found in the region of thought into which we are led in that great passage already referred to, which speaks of Him as then for the first time "called of God an High Priest," which represents Him, though He was a Son, learning His obedience (as a Priest) by the things which He suffered?

* Gethsemane means "oil-press."

May we not, then, reverently conceive of Him as in that hour taking on Him the sin of the world, in a more intimate sense than He had ever done before? "He bare our sins in His own body on the tree." In a certain sense He had borne the burden all His life, for He had throughout endured the contradiction of sinners against Himself; but in some special sense manifestly He bore it on the tree. When did He in that special sense take the awful burden on Him? Was it not in the Garden of Gethsemane? If so, can we wonder that the Holy One shrank from it, as He never shrank from simple suffering? To be identified with sin—to be "made sin," as the apostle puts it—how His soul revolted from it! The cup of sorrow He could take without a murmur; but to take on Him the intolerable load of the world's sin—from this He shrank with all the recoil of stainless purity, with all the horror of a heart that could not bear the very thought. It was not the weakness of His flesh, but the purity of His spirit, that made Him shrink, that wrung from Him once and again, and yet again, the cry, "Father, if it be possible, let this cup pass from Me." It was a new temptation, three times repeated, like that old one in the wilderness. That assault, as we found, was in close relation to His assumption at His baptism of His work of ministry; this conflict in the Garden was, we believe, as closely connected with His assuming His priestly work, undertaking to make atonement for sin by the sacrifice of Himself. As that followed His baptism, this followed His institution of the holy supper. In that ordinance He had prepared the minds of His disciples to turn from the Paschal lamb of the old covenant, to behold henceforth the Lamb of God which taketh away the sin of the world. From the feast He goes straightway to this lonely garden, and there begins * His dread atoning work.

It must have been a great aggravation of His agony that even the three disciples could not enter into sympathy with Him, even so much as to hold their eyes waking. True, they were very weary, and it was most natural that they should be heavy with sleep; but had they had even a faint conception of what that agony of their Master meant they could not possibly have slept; and we can well fancy that in that hour of anguish the Saviour must have called to mind from the Book of Psalms, with which He was so perfectly familiar, the sad lament: "Reproach hath broken my heart; and I am full of heaviness: and I looked for some to take pity, but there was none; and for comforters, but I found none."

But though He keenly feels His loneliness, His thoughts are far less of Himself than of them. Realising so vividly the horrors now so close at hand, He sees, from the very possibility of their sleeping, how utterly unprepared they are for what awaits them, so He summons them to "watch and pray," to be on the alert against sudden surprise, and to keep in constant touch with God, so that they may not find themselves confronted with temptation which, whatever the devotion of the spirit, may prove too much for the weakness of the flesh. Think of the tender consideration of this second warning, when the first had been so little heeded.

And we cannot but agree with those who see in what He said when He returned for the last time to the three, not irony, no touch of sarcasm, but the same tender consideration He has shown throughout. From the Garden they could easily see the city in the moonlight across the ravine. As yet there was no sign of life about it: all was quiet; there was therefore no reason why they should not for the few moments that might remain to them sleep on now and take their rest. But it can only be for a short time, for "the hour is at hand." We may, then, think of the three lying down to sleep, as the eight had probably been doing throughout, while Jesus, from whose mortal eyes sleep was banished now for ever, would watch until He saw the gleam of lanterns and torches as of men from the city coming down the hill, and then He would wake them and say, "Rise, let us be going: behold, he is at hand that doth betray Me."

* Observe the emphatic word, "*began* to be sorrowful" (ver. 37)

The arrest immediately follows the agony; and with it begin the outward shame and torture of the Passion. The time has now come when all the indignities and cruelties of which Jesus had spoken to His disciples "apart in the way" (see xx. 17-19) shall be heaped upon Him. But none of these things move Him. The inward shame and torture had almost been too much for Him. His soul had been "exceeding sorrowful, even unto death"; so that He was in danger of passing away from the scene of conflict ere yet it would be possible to say "It is finished." Only by "strong crying and tears unto Him that was able to save Him from death" had He obtained the needful strength (Luke xxii. 43) to pass the awful ordeal, and come out of it ready to yield Himself up into the "wicked hands" by which He must be "crucified and slain." But now He is strong. St. Matthew does not tell us that the prayer in the Garden was answered; but we see it as we follow the Son of man along the dolorous way. If He shrank from taking up the load of human sin, He does not flinch in carrying it; and amid all He has to bear at the hands of sinners, He maintains His dignity and self-possession.

When the armed men approach, He goes calmly out to meet them. Even the traitor's kiss He does not resent; but only takes occasion to make one more appeal to that stony heart, "Comrade," * He says, "(do) that for which thou art come" (see R. V.). There is a brokenness in the utterance which makes it difficult to translate, but which is touchingly natural. It would seem as if our Lord, when Judas first appeared, though He knew well for what purpose He had come, and wished to show him that He did, yet shrank from putting it into words. When the traitor had actually done that for which he had come, when he had not only given the traitor's kiss, and that in a shamelessly effusive way, as appears from the strong word used in the account both here and elsewhere, then would come that other appeal which most impressed the eyewitness from whom St. Luke had his informa-

* The word "friend" is too strong. It is not the same word our Lord uses when He says: "I have not called you servants, I have called you friends"; it is a word which indicates not heart-friendship, but that familiar intercourse which is supposed to take place only between friends. The selection of the word is a striking illustration of our Lord's carefulness of the claims of sincerity and truth, while He is anxious, if possible, to use a word that will touch the traitor's heart.

tion: "Judas, betrayest thou the Son of man *with a kiss?*"

At this point probably occurred an incident of the arrest recorded only in the fourth Gospel, the recoil of the mob when Jesus confronted them and acknowledged Himself to be the man whom they were seeking. Though this is not mentioned here, we recognise the effect of it upon the disciples. It would naturally embolden them when, on the second advance, they saw their Master in the hands of these men, to ask, "Lord, shall we smite with the sword?" And it was most characteristic that "one of them" (whom we should have recognised, even though St. John had not mentioned his name) should not wait for the answer, but should smite at once.

All is excitement and commotion. Jesus alone is calm. In such a sea of trouble, behold the Man! See the heart at leisure from itself to care for and to cure the wounded servant of the high priest (Luke xxii. 51). Think of the mind so free at such a time to look out far into the future, using the occasion to lay down the great principle that force, as a weapon which will recoil on those who use it, must not be employed in the cause of truth and righteousness. Look at that spirit, so serenely confident of power with God at the very moment that the frail body is helpless in the hands of men: "Thinkest thou that I cannot now pray to My Father, and He shall presently give Me more than twelve legions of angels?" How it enlarges our souls even to try to enter into that great mind and heart at such a moment. What an outlook of thought! What an up-look of faith! And again, what mastery! What self-annihilation! We have seen His self-repression in the prayer He offered in the Garden; but think of the prayers He did not offer; think what effort, what sacrifice, what self-abnegation it must have been to Him to suppress that prayer for help from the legions of heaven against these bands of the ungodly. But it was enough for Him to remember, "How then shall the Scriptures be fulfilled, that thus it must be?" It was necessary that He should suffer at the hands of men; therefore He allows them to lead Him away, only reminding them that the force which would have been needful for the arrest of some robber desperado was surely quite unnecessary in dealing with One Whose daily practice it had been to sit quietly teaching in the Temple.

The reference to the Scriptures was probably intended not only to explain His non-resistance, but also to support the faith of His disciples when they saw Him bound and carried off. Had they known the Scriptures as under His teaching they might well have known them, not only would they have seen that "thus it must be," but they would have had before them the sure prospect of His rising from the dead on the third day. But in their case the Scriptures were appealed to in vain; they had not the faith of their Master to venture on the sure Word of God; and so, hope failing, "all the disciples forsook Him and fled." Not all finally, however, even for that dark night; for though faith and hope failed, there remained love enough in the hearts of two to make them presently stop and think, and then turn slowly and follow from afar. Only Peter is mentioned here as boing this, because the sequel concerns him; but that John also went to the palace of the high priest we know from his own account (John xviii. 15).

The night is not yet over, and therefore there can be no formal meeting of the Jewish council, according to an excellent law which enacted that all cases involving the death penalty should be tried in the daytime. This law was, quite characteristically, observed in the letter, transgressed in the spirit; for though the formal sentence was deferred till morning (xxvii. 1), the real trial was begun and ended before the dawn. The reference by St. Matthew to both sessions of the council enables us clearly to understand what would otherwise have appeared a "manifest discrepancy" between his account and that of St. Luke, the former speaking of the trial as having taken place in the night, while the latter tells us it only began "as soon as it was day."

Our Evangelist shows himself to be a true historian in that, while disposing of the formal morning session in half a sentence, he gives a full account of the night conclave which really settled all. They proceed in a thoroughly characteristic manner. Having secured their prisoner, they must first agree upon the charge: what shall it be? It was no easy matter; for not only had His life been stainless, but He had shown consummate skill in avoiding all the entanglements which had been set for Him; and besides, it so happened that nothing they could prove conclusively against Him, such as His breaking the letter of the Sabbath law, or rather of their traditions, would suit their purpose, for they would run the risk on the one hand of calling fresh attention to the works of healing which had made so deep an impression on the popular mind, and on the other of stirring up strife between the opposing factions which had entered into a precarious union based solely on their common desire to do away with Him. Hence the great difficulty of securing testimony against Him, and the necessity of having recourse to that which was false.

We may wonder perhaps that a court so unscrupulous should have made so much of the difficulty of getting witnesses to agree. Could they not, for other "thirty pieces of silver," have purchased two that would have served their purpose? But it must be remembered that men in their position had to pay some respect to decency; and from their point of view to pay a man for helping to arrest a criminal was an entirely different transaction from giving money to procure false witness. Besides, there were men of the council who did not "consent to the counsel and deed of them" (see Luke xxiii. 51, and John vii. 50, 51), and they must be careful. It is not probable of course that Joseph of Arimathea and Nicodemus would be present at the secret session in the night; but they would of course be present, or have the opportunity of being present, at the regular meeting in the morning.

When, therefore, the attempt to found a charge on the testimony of witnesses against Him failed, the only hope was to force Him, if possible, to incriminate Himself. The high priest accordingly addresses himself to the prisoner, and attempts to induce Him to say something which might tend to clear up the confusion of the witnesses' testimony. It was evident that something had been said about destroying the Temple and building it in three days—would He not state exactly what it was? "But Jesus held His peace." He would not plead before such a tribunal, or acknowledge the irregular appeal by so much as a single word.

Caiaphas is baffled; but there is one course left to him, a course which for many reasons he would have preferred not to take, but he sees now no other way of setting up a charge that will bear examination in the morning. He therefore appeals to Jesus in the most solemn manner to assert or deny His Messiahship.

Silence is now impossible. The high priest has given Him the opportunity of proclaiming His gospel in presence of the council, and He will not lose it, though it seal His condemnation. "He cannot deny Himself." In the most emphatic manner He proclaims Himself the Christ, the Son of God, and tells them that the time is coming when their positions shall be reversed —He their Judge, they summoned to His bar: "Henceforth ye shall see the Son of man sitting at the right hand of power, and coming on the clouds of heaven" (R. V.). What light must have been in His eye, what majesty in His mien, as He spoke those thrilling words! And who shall limit their power? Who of us shall be surprised to find members of that very conclave among the ransomed of the Lord in the New Jerusalem? They might not heed His words that night, but three days after would they not recall them? And fifty days after that again—who can tell?

Meantime the only result is to produce real or affected horror. "The high priest rent his clothes," thereby expressing in a tragic manner how it tore his heart to hear such "blasphemy"; and with one consent, or at least with no voice raised against it, He is condemned to death.

The council have now done with Him for the night, and He is handed over to the custody of the guard and the servants of the high priest. Then follows that awful scene, which cannot be recalled without a shudder. To think that the Holy One of God should suffer these personal indignities—oh, degradation! It is more dreadful to think of than even the nails and the spear. Alas, even the dregs of the bitter cup of sorrow were wrung out to Him! "Is it nothing to you, all ye that pass by? Behold and see if there be any sorrow like unto My sorrow!"

Where is Peter now? We left Him following afar off. He has summoned up courage enough to follow on into the court of the high priest's palace, and to mingle among the people there. If he had been let alone, he would with John have in some measure retrieved the disgrace of all the disciples forsaking their Master in "that night on which He was betrayed"; but it has been necessary to rally all the remnants of his bravery to come so far, and now he has none of it to spare. Besides, he is very tired, and shivering with cold—in no condition, verily, for anything heroic. Who is there of us will cast the first stone at him? There are those that speak of him in a tone of contempt as "quailing before a servant maid," as if the meanness of the occasion were not the very thing which made it so hard for him. Had he been summoned to the presence of the high priest, with all the eyes of the council fastened on him, his tired feeling would have left him all at once, his pulse would have beat fast, the excitement would have stirred him so that no fire of coals would have been needed to warm him, and he might then have acquitted himself in a manner worthy of the rock-apostle; but to be suddenly met with a woman's question sprung upon him unawares, with nobody he cared for looking on, with nothing to rouse his soul from the prostration into which it had been cast by the suddenness of what looked like overwhelming defeat—that was more than even Peter could bear; and accordingly he fell—fell terribly. Not to the bottom all at once. He tries first to pass the question off with a show of ignorance or indifference: "I know not what thou sayest." But when the first downward step is taken, all the rest follow with terrible rapidity. As we look down into the abyss into which plunged headlong the foremost of the Twelve, and hear these oaths and curses, what force it lends to the warning in Gethsemane: "Watch and pray, that ye *enter not* into temptation"!

What a lesson of charity is here! Suppose for a moment that one of the Marys had been standing near, and heard Peter denying his Master with oaths and curses, what would her thought of him have been? What else could it have been than a thought of sorrowful despair? She would have felt constrained, however reluctantly, to place him, not with the timid ten, but alongside of "Judas who betrayed Him." Yet she would have been wrong; and many good people are quite wrong when they judge disciples of Christ by what they see of them when at their worst. After all Peter was true at heart; and though from such an abyss he could never have recovered himself, he was so linked to his Master by the true devotion of the days of old that he could not fall utterly away. It was quite otherwise with Judas. His heart had been set on his covetousness throughout, while Peter in his inmost soul was loyal and true. His Master has prayed for him that his faith fail not. His courage has failed; and if that faith which is the only sure foundation for enduring courage had utterly failed too, his case would have been hopeless indeed. But it has not; there is still a link to bind him to the Lord, Whom in word he is denying for the moment; and first the crowing of the cock which reminds him of his Master's warning, and then immediately after, that look which was turned full on Peter as Jesus passed him, led across the court, perhaps with jeerings and buffetings at the very moment—that solemn memory and that sad and loving look recall him to himself again, the old true life wells up from the depths of the genuine and noble heart of him, and overflows in tears. So ends the story of that awful night.

III. The Morning (xxvii. 1-26).

The formal meeting of the council in the morning would not occupy many minutes. The death sentence had been already agreed upon, and it only remained to take the necessary steps to carry it into effect. Hence the form in which the Evangelist records the morning session: "All the chief priests and elders of the people took counsel against Jesus to put Him to death." This could not have passed as a minute of the meeting; but it was none the less a true account of it. As, however, the law forbade their inflicting the death penalty, "when they had bound Him, they led Him away, and delivered Him to Pontius Pilate the governor."

This delivering up of Jesus is a fact of the Passion on which special stress is laid in the saered records. It seems, indeed, to have weighed on the mind of Jesus Himself as much as the betrayal, as would appear from the manner in which, as He was nearing Jerusalem, He told His disciples what He should suffer there: "Behold, we go up to Jerusalem; and the Son of man shall be delivered unto the chief priests and scribes, and they shall condemn Him to death, *and shall deliver Him unto the Gentiles* to mock, and to scourge, and to crucify" (Matt. xx. 18, 19; see also Mark x. 33, and Luke xviii. 32). Long before this, indeed, "He came unto His own, and His own received Him not." With the sorrow of that rejection He was only too familiar; but it was a new heartbreak to be delivered up to the Gentiles. It was a second betrayal on a much larger scale. So Stephen puts it in the impassioned close of his defence, where he charges the council with being "the *betrayers* and murderers" of "the Just One"; and indeed the thought is suggested here, not only by the association with what follows in regard to the traitor's end, but by the use of the very same word as applied to the traitor's act; for the word translated "betrayed" in verse 3 is the very same in the original as that translated "delivered up" in verse 2. Judas is about to drop out of sight into the abyss; but the nation is one Judas now.

It may be, indeed, that it was the seeing of his own sin as mirrored in the conduct of the council which roused at last the traitor's sleeping conscience. As he saw his late Master led away bound "as a lamb to the slaughter," these very words may have come back to his memory: "They shall deliver the Son of man to the Gentiles to mock, and to scourge, and to crucify." It is quite possible, indeed, that the man of Kerioth was too good a Jew to have been willing to sell his Master to Pilate directly. But now he sees that that is just what he has done. We have no sympathy with those who imagine that Judas only intended to give his Master an opportunity of displaying His power and asserting His rights in a manner that would secure at once the allegiance of the people; but though we see no evidence of any good intentions, we can readily believe that in the act of betrayal his mind did not go beyond the immediate consequences of his action—on the one hand the money; and on the other what was it but the handing of his Master to the chief priests and elders, who were after all His ecclesiastical superiors; and had they not the right to put Him on His trial? But now that he sees Jesus, Whom by long acquaintance he knows to be without spot or stain, bound as a common criminal and led away to execution, his act appears in a new and awful light, he is smitten with a measureless fear, and can no longer bear to think of what he has done.

"He repented himself," so we read in our version; but that it is no true repentance the more expressive Greek makes plain, for the word is quite distinct from that which indicates "repentance after a godly sort." Had there been in his heart any spring of true repentance its waters would have been unsealed long ere this—at the Table, or when in the Garden he heard his Master's last appeal of love. Not love, but fear, not godly sorrow, but very human terror, is what moves him now; and therefore it is not to Jesus that he flies,—had he even now gone up to Him, and fallen at His feet and confessed his sins, he would have been forgiven,—but to his accomplices in crime. Fain would he undo what he has done; but it is impossible! What he can do, however, he will; so he tries to get the chief priests to take back the silver pieces. But they will have nothing to do with them or with him. To his piteous confession they pay no heed; let him settle his own accounts with his own conscience: "What is that to us? see thou to that."

He is now alone; shut up to himself; alone with his sin. Even the thirty pieces of silver, which had such a friendly sound as he first dropped them in his purse, have turned against him; now he hates the very sight of them, and must be rid of them. As the priests will not take them back, he will cast them "into the sanctuary" (R. V.), and so perhaps find some relief. But oh, Judas! it is one thing to get the silver out of your hands, and quite another to get the stain out of your soul. The only effect of it is to make the solitude complete. He has at last come to himself; and what a self it is to come to! No wonder that he "went and hanged himself."

The chief priests have not yet come to themselves. They will by-and-by, whether after the manner of the prodigal or after the manner of the traitor time will show; but meanwhile they are in the full **career** of their sin, and can therefore as yet consult to very good purpose. It was not at all a bad way of getting out of their difficulty with the money found in the sanctuary, to buy with it a place to bury strangers in; but little did they dream that when the story of it should be told thereafter to the world they would be discovered to have unconsciously fulfilled a prophecy (Zech. xi. 12, 13), which on the one hand gibbeted their crime as a valuing of the Shepherd of Israel at the magnificent price of thirty pieces of silver, and on the other carried with it the suggestion of those awful woes which Jeremiah had pronounced at the very spot they had purchased with the price of blood (Jer. xix.).

From the end of the traitor Judas we return to the issue of the nation's treason. "Now Jesus stood before the governor." The full study of Jesus before Pilate belongs rather to the fourth Gospel, which supplies many most interesting details not furnished here. We must therefore deal with it quite briefly, confining our attention as much as possible to the points touched in the record before us.*

* It is most instructive at this point to note the extreme condensation of this report of the trial before Pilate. This is especially noticeable at the first stage of the trial. In the fuller reports by St. John (xviii. 29-38) we find indeed the question, "Art thou king of the Jews?" (v. 33), and the answer "Thou sayest" (v. 37); but how much more besides! So is it beyond question in many other places where there is not the same opportunity of supplying what has been omitted. If this were always borne in mind in reading the Gospels, we should avoid many difficulties, which have often needlessly perplexed the best of people. There is often much to read between the lines, and not only so, but much between the lines we cannot read, the knowledge of which would make crooked things straight and rough places plain. The difficulty of accurately realising a complex scene from a report of it which, however accurate, is highly condensed, ought to be always present to the minds of readers of the Gospels, and ought to be a check on those who attribute to the "mistakes" of the writers what in all probability is due to the ignorance of the readers—ignorance, it may be, of some little matter of detail, or some comparatively unimportant saying, the knowledge of which would at once clear up a difficulty which to the unaided imagination may appear insoluble.

As before the council, so before Pilate, our Lord speaks, or is silent, according as the question affects His mission or Himself. When asked of His Kingdom, He answers in the most decided manner ("Thou sayest" was a strong affirmation, as if to say "Certainly I am"); for on this depends the only hope of salvation for Pilate—for His accusers—for all. He will by no means disown or shrink from acknowledging the mission of salvation on which His Father has sent Him, though it may raise against Him the cry of blasphemy in the council, and of treason in the court; but when He is asked what He has to say for Himself, in the way of answer to the charges made against Him, He is silent: even when Pilate himself appeals to Him in the strongest manner to say something in His own defence, "He gave him no answer, not even to one word" (R. V.). "Insomuch that the governor marvelled greatly;" for how could he understand? How can a cautious, cunning, time-serving man of the world understand the selflessness of the Son of God?

Pilate had no personal grudge against Jesus, and had sense enough to recognise at once that the claims of Kinghood advanced by his prisoner did not touch the prerogatives of Cæsar—had penetration also to see through the motives of the chief priests and elders (ver. 18), and therefore was not at all disposed to acquiesce in the demand made on him for a summary condemnation. Besides, he was not without fears, which inclined him to the side of justice. He was evidently impressed with the demeanour of his prisoner. This appears even in the brief narrative of our Evangelist; but it comes out very strikingly in the fuller record of the fourth Gospel. His wife's influence, too, was used in the same direction. She evidently had heard something about Jesus, and had taken some interest in Him, enough to reach the conviction that He was a "righteous man." It was as yet quite early in the morning, and she may not have known till after her husband had gone out that it was for the trial of Jesus he was summoned. Having had uneasy dreams, in which the Man Who had impressed her so much was a leading figure, it was natural that she should send him a hasty message, so as to reach him "while he was sitting on the judgment seat" (R. V.). This message would reinforce his fears, and increase his desire to deal justly with his extraordinary prisoner.

On the other hand, Pilate could not afford to refuse point-blank the demand of the Jewish leaders. He was by no means secure in his seat. There had been so many disturbances under his administration, as we learn from contemporary history, that his recall, perhaps something more serious than recall, might be expected from Rome, if he should again get into trouble with these turbulent Jews; so he did not dare to run the risk of simply doing what he knew was right. Accordingly he tried several expedients, as we learn from the other accounts, to avoid the necessity of pronouncing sentence, one of which is here set forth at length (ver. 15, *seq.*), probably because it brings into strong relief the absolute rejection of their Messiah alike by the rulers and by the people.

It was a most ingenious device, and affords a striking example of the astuteness of the procurator. Barabbas may have had some following in his "sedition": but evidently he was no popular hero, but a vulgar robber or bandit, whose release was not at all likely to be clamoured for by the multitude; and it was moreover reasonably to be expected that the chief priests, much as they hated Jesus, would be ashamed to even hint that He was worse than this wretched criminal. But he did not know how deep the hatred was with which he had to deal. "He knew that for envy they had delivered Him;" but he did not know that at the root of that envy lay the conviction that either Jesus must perish or they must. They felt that He was "of purer eyes than to behold evil, and could not look upon iniquity"; and inasmuch as they had made up their minds to keep their iniquity, they must get rid of Him; they must seal up these eyes which searched them through and through, they must silence these tones which, silvery as they were, were to them as the knell of judgment. They had no liking for Barabbas, and, to do them justice, no sympathy whatever with his crimes; but they had no reason to be afraid of him: they could live, though he was free. It must have been a hard alternative even for them; but there is no hesitation about it. Themselves and their emissaries are busy among the mob, persuading them "that they should ask Barabbas, and destroy Jesus."

The multitudes are only too easily persuaded. Not that they had the dark envy, or anything like the rooted hatred, of their leaders; but what will a careless mob not be prepared to do when excitement prevails and passions are inflamed? It is not at all unlikely that some of the same people who followed the multitude in shouting "Hosanna to the Son of David!" only five days before, would join in the cry which some of the baser sort would be the first to raise, "Crucify Him! crucify Him!" Those who know human nature best—at its basest, as in the hatred of the chief priests and elders; at its shallowest, as in the passions of the fickle crowd—will marvel least at the way in which the alternative of Pilate was received. There is no touchstone of human nature like the cross of Christ; and in the presence of the Holy One of God, sin is forced, as it were, to show itself in all its native blackness and enormity; and what sin is there, however small it seem to be, which if allowed to develop its latent possibility of vileness, would not lead on to this very choice—"Not Jesus, but Barabbas"?

And Pilate, you may wash your hands before the multitude, and say, "I am innocent of the blood of this just Person"; but it is all in vain. There is a Searcher of hearts Who knows you through and through. "See ye to it," you say; and so said to Judas the chief priests and elders, using the very same words. But both they and you must see to that which each fain would put aside for ever. Aye, and it will be less tolerable for you and for them than even for the thoughtless crowd who cry, "His blood be upon us and on our children." It was in vain to ask of people like these, "What shall I do, then, with Jesus which is called Christ?" There was only one thing to do: the thing which was right. Failing to do this, you had no alternative but to share in the sin of all the rest. Even Pilate must take a side, as all must do. Neutrality here is impossible. Those who persist in making the vain attempt will find themselves at last on the same side as Pilate took when he "released unto them

Barabbas; but Jesus he scourged and delivered to be crucified."

IV. From the Third to the Ninth Hour (xviii. 27-56).

The cool of the morning was passing into the heat of the day, as the soldiers took Jesus and led Him away to be crucified; and the sun was at the same angle in the western sky when He bowed His head and gave up the ghost. In the six hours between lay the crisis of the world (see John xii. 31, Greek): its judgment, its salvation. The great conflict of the ages is concentrated in these hours of agony. In the brief record of them we have the very core and kernel of the gospel of "Jesus Christ *and Him crucified*."

All we can hope to do is to find some point of view which may afford a general survey of the awful scene; and such point of observation we may perhaps discover in the thought of the marvellous significance of each detail when set in the after light of faith. Most of the incidents are quite simple and natural—what might in every way be expected as concomitants of the deed of blood which darkened the day—and yet the simplest of them is charged with unexpected meaning. The actors in this dark scene are moved by the basest of passions, are destitute of the smallest gleam of insight into what is passing; and yet, in saying what they say and doing what they do, they declare the glory of the Christ of God as signally as if they were saying and doing all by Divine direction. In more senses than one "they know not what they do."

From this point of view we might survey all the four records of the Crucifixion, and find striking illustrations of our thought in each of them. As a specimen of this we may refer in passing to the words of Pilate recorded by St. John alone: "Behold the Man!" and again, "Behold your King!" In these remarkable utterances the procurato- quite unconsciously furnishes the answer to his own as yet unanswered questions (John xviii. 38: Matt. xxvii. 22), and, Balaam-like, becomes a preacher of the gospel, summoning the whole world to admiration and homage, to faith and obedience. But we may not extend our view over the other Gospels; it will be enough to glance at the particulars found in that which lies before us.

The first is the mockery of the soldiers. A brutal set they must have been; and their treatment of their victim, as they intended it, is too revolting even to think of in detail. Yet, had they been inspired by the loftiest purpose, and been able to look into the meaning of what they did with the most penetrating insight, they could not have in a more striking manner illustrated the true glory of His royalty. Ah, soldiers! you may well plait that crown of thorns, and put it on His head; for He is the Prince of Sufferers, the King of Sorrow! On that head are many crowns—the crown of righteousness, the crown of heroism, the crown of life; but of them all the very best is the crown of thorns, for it is the crown of Love.

The next incident is the impressing of Simon of Cyrene to bear His cross. It was intended as an insult. The service was too degrading even for any of the rabble of Jerusalem, so they imposed it on this poor foreigner, coming out of the country. Little did they think that this same man of Cyrene, who probably had provoked them by showing some sympathy with the Sufferer, and might by no means grudge the toil, unjustly forced upon him though it was, should with his two sons Alexander and Rufus (see Mark xv. 21) be a kind of firstfruits of a great multitude of foreigners coming out of all countries, who should consider it the highest honour of their lives to take up and bear after Jesus the cross which Simon had borne for Him.

The very name Golgotha, though derived in all probability from the natural appearance of the eminence on which the crosses were erected, has a certain dreary appropriateness, not only because of the horror of the deed, but because the thought is suggested that death's Destroyer gained His victory on death's own ground; and the offering of the potion usually given to deaden pain gave the pale sufferer an opportunity of showing by His refusal of it that not only was the death which ended all a voluntary act, but that each pang of the passion was borne in the resoluteness of a love-constrained will:

> "Thou wilt feel all, that Thou may'st pity all;
> And rather wouldst Thou wrestle with strong pain,
> Than overcloud Thy soul
> So clear in agony.
>
> . . . .
>
> O most entire and perfect Sacrifice,
> Renewed in every pulse,
> That on the tedious Cross
> Told the long hours of death."

The dividing of the garments among the soldiers was a most natural and ordinary incident; it would seem, indeed, to have been the common practice at crucifixions; and the fulfilment of prophecy would be the very last thing that would enter the men's minds as they did it: even St. Matthew himself, in recording it, does not view it in this light; for, though he evidently made a point of calling attention to all fulfilments of prophecy that struck him, he seems to have omitted this;* yet here again, even in a small but most significant matter of detail, as recorded by St. John (xix. 23, 24), the Scriptures are fulfilled.

The writing on the cross is called "His accusation." So indeed it was; for it was for this he was condemned: no other charge could be made good against Him. But it was not His accusation only,—it was His coronation. In vain the chief priests tried to induce the governor to change it. "What I have written, I have written," was his answer; and there it stood, and a better inscription for the cross the apostles themselves could not have devised. "This is *Jesus*," the Saviour—the name above every name. How it must have cheered the Saviour's heart to know that it was there! "This is Jesus, *the King*," never more truly King than when this writing was His only crown. "This is Jesus, the King *of the Jews*," despised and rejected of them now, but Son of David none the less, and yet to be claimed and crowned, and rejoiced in when at last "all Israel shall be saved." Elsewhere we learn that the inscription was in Hebrew and Greek and Latin,—the first the tongue of the people to whose keeping had been committed the oracles of God, the other two the languages in which God's good tidings of Life through a Crucified Saviour could be best and most quickly carried

* The reference is inserted in our Authorised Version, but without sufficient authority. The Revised Version properly omits it.

"to every creature,"—as if to make the proclamation worldwide.

His position between the two thieves is told as simply as all the rest; yet how full of meaning, not only as fulfilling the Scripture which spoke of Him as "numbered with the transgressors," but as furnishing a most impressive picture of the Friend of Sinners, enduring their revilings, and yet as soon as one of them shows the first signs of coming to a better mind, eagerly granting him forgiveness and eternal life, and receiving him into His kingdom as the first-fruits of His redeemed ones.

Again, the mocking cries of the passers-by are exactly what was to be expected from the coarse natures of the men; yet each one of them, when seen in the after light of faith, becomes a tribute to His praise. As an illustration of this, listen to the cry which comes out of the deepest abyss of hatred. Hear these chief priests mocking Him, with the scribes and elders. With bitter taunt they say, in scorn, "He saved others; Himself He cannot save." With bitter taunt? In scorn? Ah, "fools and blind," you little know that you are making a garland of imperishable beauty to wreathe around His brow! It was indeed most true. It was because He saved others that He could not save Himself. Were He willing to let others perish, were He willing to let you perish—He would this very moment save Himself. But He will bear, not only the cruel nails and spear, but your more cruel mockeries, rather than give up His self-imposed task of saving others by His perfect sacrifice!

It is high noon; but there, at that place of a skull, a deed is being done from which the sun must hide his face for shame. "From the sixth hour there was darkness over all the land until the ninth hour." The simple-hearted Evangelist has no reflections of his own to offer; he simply records the well-remembered fact, with his usual reticence of feeling, which makes the deep, dread meaning of it only more impressive. For there is not only darkness over all the land; there is darkness in the Sufferer's soul. The agony of the Garden is on Him once again. He sees no longer the faces of the crowd, and the mocking voices are now silent, for the people cannot but feel the solemnising effect of the midday gloom. The presence of man is forgotten, and with it the shame, even the pain: the Redeemer of the world is again alone with God.

Alone with God, and the sin of the world is on Him. "He bare our sins in His own body on the tree," therefore is it that He must enter even into the very deepest darkness of the soul, the feeling of separation from God, the sense of forsakenness, which is so appalling to the awakened sinner, and which even the sinless One must taste, because of the burden laid upon Him. To Him it was a pang beyond all others, forcing from these silent lips the lamentable cry, "My God, My God, why hast Thou forsaken Me?" There is no reason indeed to suppose that the Sufferer was really forsaken by God, even for a moment. Never was the love of the Father deeper and stronger than when His Son was offering up the all-atoning sacrifice. Never was the repeated testimony more sure than now—"This is My Beloved Son, in Whom I am well pleased." But none the less was there the *sense* of forsakenness.

This sense of forsakenness seems to have had some mysterious connection with the pains of death. In the Garden, where the experience was similar, He said, "My soul is exceeding sorrowful, *even unto death*," and now that death is on Him, now that His human spirit is about to sink into the unknown abyss, now that darkness is closing over Him on every side, He feels as if He were forsaken utterly: yet His faith fails not; perhaps He thinks of the words, "Yea the darkness hideth not from Thee; but the night shineth as the day: the darkness and the light are both alike to Thee," and though He cannot now say "Father" even, He can at least cry as from the depths, His spirit overwhelmed within Him, "My God, My God." That 22d Psalm which was certainly in His mind must have suggested thoughts of hope and strength, and ere His spirit leaves the tortured body He has reached the triumphant close of it; for as its opening utterance became His cry of agony, its closing word suggests His shout of victory. The shout is mentioned by St. Matthew; the words we learn from St. John: "It is finished."

From the sixth hour to the ninth the darkness lasted, and at the ninth hour Jesus yielded up the ghost. The agony is over. The feeling of separation, of utter loneliness, is gone, for the last word has been, "Father, into Thy hands I commend My Spirit"; and as the spirit of the Son of man returns to the Father's bosom, the gloom is gone, and the sun shines out again upon the earth.

How appropriate the rending of the veil,* the quaking of the earth, the shuddering of the graves, and the visitants from the realm of the unseen greeting the eyes of those for whom heaven was opened now, is all so plain in the light of faith on the Son of God that it needs no pointing out. It was no wonder that even the Roman centurion, unaccustomed as he was to think of such things, could not refrain from exclaiming, "Truly this was the Son of God." Much more may we echo his exclamation when in the light of the glory that has followed we look back on "the things that were done." Recall them,—the crown of thorns, the cross-bearing of Simon, the place of a skull, the parting of the garments, the writing on the cross, the company of the thieves, the mockeries of the people, the darkness of the heavens, the shaking of the earth, the rending of the veil,—is there not profound meaning in it all?

The portents at the close, as was natural, impressed the centurion most; but these are just what make the least impression now, because we do not see them, and those for whom no veil has been rent by the Saviour's sacrifice cannot be expected to recognise them. But think of the other incidents—incidents to which not even the most sceptical can attach a shadow of doubt: observe how utterly unconscious the actors were—the soldiers in plaiting the crown of thorns, Pilate in writing His title, the chief priests in shouting "He saved others; Himself He cannot save"—and yet how these all, viewed in a light that did not shine for them, are seen to have vied with each other in setting forth His glory as the Saviour-King; and then say whether it could all have been the merest chance, whether there be not in it manifestly "the determinate counsel and foreknowledge of God," whether it is pos-

* "From the top to the bottom," rent, therefore, by no human hand.

sible to escape the conviction of the Roman centurion, "Truly this is the Son of God!"

The reference to the "many women," "beholding afar off," forms a pathetic close to the story of the Great Atonement Day.

CHAPTER XX.

THE THIRD DAY.

MATTHEW xxvii. 57-xxviii. 15.

Now that the atoning work of Christ is finished, the story proceeds with rapidity to its close. It was the work of the Evangelist to give the history of the incarnate Son of God; and now that the flesh is laid aside, it is necessary only to give such notes of subsequent events as shall preserve the continuity between the prophetic and priestly work of Christ on earth which it had been His vocation to describe, and the royal work which, as exalted Prince and Saviour, it still remained for Him to do. We need not wonder, then, that the record of the three days should be quite brief, and of the forty days briefer still.

This brevity is a note of truthfulness. The old idea of deliberate falsehood having been quite given up, reliance is placed, by those who wish to discredit the gospel witnesses, on the suggestion that the records of the resurrection are the result of fancy crystallising into so-called fact. But not only was there no time, between the death of Christ and the latest date which can be assigned for the writing of the first Gospel, for the process of crystallisation, but had there been such a process, the result would have been very different. Had fancy, and not observation, been the source, how comes it that nothing is told but what came within the range of actual vision? Why is there not a word about Christ's entry into Paradise, or descent into Hades? What a fruitful field for fancy here!—yet there is not even a hint; for it is not from anything in the Gospels, but solely from a passage in one of the Epistles, that the doctrine of the descent into Hades has been derived. There is not a word or a hint of anything that passed in the unseen; a plain statement of what was done with the body of Jesus is absolutely all. Clearly it is not myth, but history, with which here we have to do.

The Evening of the First Day (vv. 57-61).

Day was passing into evening when Jesus "yielded up His spirit"; for the early evening, according to the Jewish reckoning, began at the ninth hour. It was probably some time after this—perhaps towards the later evening, which began about the twelfth hour (six o'clock)—that Joseph of Arimathea thought of claiming the body to give it honourable burial. Why should such a duty have fallen to a stranger? Where were the eleven? Had none of them so far recovered from their fear? Where was Peter? might not his penitence for the past have impelled him to come forward now? Where was John? He had taken the mother of Jesus to his own home; but why did he not come back to see what he could do for the sacred body? How can they all leave this tender office to a stranger?

It may be thought by some sufficient answer simply to say, So the Lord willed it, and so the Scripture was fulfilled which intimated that He Who had died with the wicked should be "with the rich in His death"; but is there not more than this to be said? Is not the disappearance of the eleven and the coming forward of the two secret disciples (for as we learn from the fourth Gospel, Nicodemus—another secret disciple—appears a little later on the scene) true to human nature? Let us remember that the faith of the eleven, while much superior to that of the two, was from the nature of the case exposed to a counter-current of feeling, of which neither Joseph nor Nicodemus could know anything. They had committed themselves and their all to Jesus, as Joseph and Nicodemus had never done. The consequence was that when the terrible tempest broke on Him, it came with all its force on them too. But Joseph and Nicodemus had not as yet ventured their all—had not, it would appear, as yet ventured anything for Christ. They were looking on at the storm, as it were, from the shore; so they could stand it, as those who were in the very midst of it could not. They could stand beholding. Not having made themselves known, they were not exposed to personal danger, hence were in a position calmly and thoughtfully to watch the progress of events. We can imagine them first looking towards Calvary from afar, and then, as the darkness favoured a timid approach, drawing nearer and nearer, and at last coming within the spell of the Divine Sufferer. As they witnessed His patient endurance, they would become more and more ashamed of their half-hearted sympathy, ashamed to think that though they had not consented to the counsel and deed of the rest (Luke xxiii. 51; John vii. 50, 51), they had not had courage to offer any serious opposition. They would feel, as they thought of this, as if they shared the responsibility of what must now appear to them an awful crime; and so, looking to Him whom they had pierced, they would mourn; and, brought at last to decision by His death (John xii. 32), first Joseph, and after him Nicodemus, came out boldly, the one asking for the body of Jesus, the other joining him in those tender and reverent ministrations which all that was best in them now constrained them to render.

The sad duty hastily, but tenderly and fitly, done, a great stone is rolled to the door of the sepulchre, and they depart. But the sepulchre is not deserted yet. What are these figures in the dusk, these women that advance as the others retire? While the two men were busy they have been keeping at a discreet and respectful distance; but now that all is silent at the tomb, they draw nearer, and though night is coming on apace, they cannot leave it, and the story of the long day ends with this pathetic touch: "And Mary Magdalene was there, and the other Mary, sitting over against the sepulchre."

The Second Day (vv. 62-66).

It was the Jewish Sabbath. The Evangelist for some reason avoids the common designation, preferring to speak of it as "the day after the preparation"—whether it was that he shrank from mentioning the Sabbath in such a connection, or whether it was that the great event of the preparation day had such complete possession of his mind that he must date from it, we shall not attempt to decide.

This is the only record we have of that Sabbath day except that St. Luke tells us that on it the women "rested according to the commandment." But the enemies of Jesus could not rest. They were uneasy and troubled now that the deed was done. They could not but have been impressed with the bearing of their Victim, and with all the portents which accompanied His end. It was natural, therefore, that words of His, which when reported to them before had not seemed worth noticing, should come back to them now with fateful force. "After three days I will rise again" was what He had often said. "What if He should rise? we must see that He does not." It would never do, however, to confess to such a fear; but they may get all needful precautions taken by suggesting that there was danger of the disciples stealing the body, and then saying that He had risen. On this pretext they get a guard from Pilate, and authority to seal the sepulchre. Having thus made all secure, they can sleep in peace.

The Morning of the Third Day (xxviii. 1-15).

The women, having rested on the Sabbath according to the commandment, knew nothing of what had been done at the tomb that day, so, as they set out before daybreak on the third morning, they only thought of the great stone, and wondered how it could be rolled away; but when they came, the sun just rising as they reached the spot, they found the stone already rolled away, and an angel of the Lord at the tomb, so lustrous in the livery of heaven that the keepers had quailed in his presence and were powerless to interfere. The awe with which the sight would naturally inspire the women also was mingled with joy as they heard his kindly greeting and sympathetic words. Altogether worthy of an angel from heaven are the words he is reported to have spoken. There is first the tender response to their looks of dread—"Fear not ye," as if to say, These others well may fear, for there is nothing in common between them and me; but with you it is different; "I know that ye seek Jesus, Which was crucified." Then there is the joyful news: "He is not here; for He is risen, as He said:" and as he observes their look of half-incredulous wonder he kindly adds, to let their sight be helper to their faith, "Come, see the place where the Lord lay." Then he gives them the honour of carrying the glad tidings to the other disciples, and assuring them that the Divine Shepherd will meet them all in Galilee, according to His word.

At this point we encounter one of the chief difficulties to be found in St. Matthew's record of the resurrection. There are indeed several particulars in this Gospel, as well as in the others, which it is difficult to fit into a connected account embracing all the facts; but as every person of even moderate intelligence knows that the same difficulty is met in comparing various truthful accounts of any great event in which details are many and complex, it is only the most unreasoning prejudice that can find in this an excuse for doubting the credibility of the writers. Rather is this feature of the records a distinct note of truthfulness; for, had it been easy to fit each fact into its exact place in all the other accounts, we should have heard from the very same doubters, and with far better reason, that there was every sign of its being a made-up story. All the four accounts are brief and fragmentary; there is evidently no attempt whatever to relate all that took place, and we should need to know all in order to form a complete picture of the entire series of events which glorified the first Easter Day. We must therefore be content with the four vivid pictures given us, without insisting on what with our imperfect knowledge is perhaps the impossible task of so combining them as to have one great canvas embracing all the details in each of the four.

The account before us is the briefest of all, and therefore it would be especially out of place in dealing with this Gospel to attempt to fill up the blanks and construct a consecutive history of all that took place on that eventful day. But there is one point with which it is especially necessary to deal in considering St. Matthew's account of the resurrection—viz., the prominence given to the appearance of the Lord to His disciples in Galilee—whereas in the fuller records of the third and fourth Gospels, not Galilee, but Jerusalem and its vicinity, is the region where He makes Himself known.

Those who are anxious to make the most of this difficulty are much disappointed to find the ninth verse in their way. Wishing to prove a sharp contradiction, as if the one said the Lord appeared only in Galilee, and the other that He appeared only in Jerusalem and its neighbourhood, they are naturally vexed to find one of the Jerusalem appearances actually mentioned here. The attempt has accordingly been made to discredit it; but in vain. It stands there an unquestionable part of the original text. So we must bear in mind that St. Matthew not only does not assert that it was only in Galilee that our Lord appeared, but he expressly mentions one appearance in Jerusalem. On the other hand, while St. Mark mentions no appearance in Galilee, he does mention the Lord's promise to meet His disciples there, and leaves it distinctly to be inferred that it was fulfilled. St. Luke, indeed, makes no mention of Galilee at all; but there is abundance of room for it: for while he occupies almost all his space with the record of one day, he tells us in the beginning of his second volume (Acts i. 3) that Christ "showed Himself alive after His passion by many infallible proofs, *being seen of them forty days*, and speaking of the things pertaining to the kingdom of God." St. John also confines himself to what took place at Jerusalem; but in the interesting appendix to that Gospel there is a striking account of a meeting with the eleven in Galilee—evidently not the same one which is recorded here, but another of the same, affording one more specimen of meetings which were no doubt frequently repeated during the forty days. It is abundantly evident, therefore, that there is no contradiction whatever.

Still the question remains, Why does St. Matthew make so little of what the others make so much of, and so much of what the others make so little of? In answer we might first ask whether this was not in every way to be expected and desired. If, as evidently was the case, there were manifestations of the risen Lord both in the south and in the north, and if we were to have several accounts, was it not desirable that one at least should make it his specialty to bring into prominence the appearances in the north? And if so, who could do it more appropriately than Matthew the publican of Galilee? The favour shown his own northern land had most deeply impressed his mind. It will be remembered that he passed over entirely the early Judean ministry recorded by St. John, and rejoiced in the Galilean ministry as the dawning of the new Day according to the words of ancient prophecy (Matt. iv. 14-16).

Furthermore, there is every reason to suppose that it was not till they met in Galilee that the scattered flock of the disciples was gathered all together. The appearances in Jerusalem were to individuals and to little companies; whereas in Galilee it would seem that He appeared to as many as five hundred at once (1 Cor. xv. 6); and though the Lord appeared to the ten (Thomas being absent), and again to the eleven, before they left Jerusalem, it is not to these occasions, but rather to the meeting on the shore of the lake, that we look for their fresh commission to address themselves again to their work as fishers of men. This will appear more clearly if we bear in mind our Lord's sad reference, as the crisis approached, to the scattering of the flock, and His promise that after He had risen again He would go before them into Galilee (Matt. xxvi. 31, 32). We have here, then (ver. 7), a repetition of the same promise, "He goeth before you" (as the shepherd goes before his flock) "into Galilee," where all the scattered ones shall be gathered round the Shepherd once again, and thence sent out as under-shepherds (see John xxi. 15-17), to gather in the rest of the flock that are scattered abroad.

The conduct of the chief priests and scribes (vv. 11-15) is the natural sequel of their futile attempt to seal the sepulchre. It is in vain to raise the objection, as some do, that it was too clumsy a device for men so astute; for what else could they do? It was indeed a poor evasion; but, baffled as they were, no better was possible for them. Let the critic say what better expedient they could have thought of, before he assigns its poverty as a reason for discrediting the story. That St. Matthew, and he alone, records it, is sufficiently accounted for by the fact that, his being the first written Gospel, and moreover the Gospel for the Jew, it behoved him to deal with a saying "commonly reported among the Jews until this day"; while its being recorded by him was a sufficient reason why no further notice should be taken of it, when there was so much of greater importance to tell.

Looking back on this very brief record of the great events of Easter Day, nothing is more striking than the prominence of the women throughout. It is a note of the new dispensation. It must have been very strange to all the disciples, and not least to the author of this Gospel, that woman, who had been kept so far in the background, treated almost as if her presence would pollute the sacred places, should, now that the veil was rent in twain from the top to the bottom, not only enter into the sacred presence of the risen Lord as the equal of her brother man, but should be there before him,—that a woman's eyes should be the first to see Him, a group of women the first to receive His loving welcome and to fall in adoration at His sacred feet. Yet so it was. Not that there was any partiality. "In Christ Jesus there is neither male nor female." It is not a question of sex; it is a question of love and faith; and it was because the love of these women was deeper, and their fidelity greater, than that of any of the men, that they had this honour. Had the love of John been as all-engrossing as that of Mary of Magdala, he would not have had to wait for the Easter tidings till she had come to tell him. It is not a question of faith alone, but of faith and love. The women's faith had failed them too. It was with no hope of seeing a risen Lord that they had gone to the tomb—it was with spices to finish the embalming of His dead body; but their love, love stronger than death, even in the wreck of faith, kept them near, and so it was that, when light first broke from out the darkness, they were there to see.

CHAPTER XXI.

THE GOSPEL FOR ALL THE NATIONS THROUGH "ALL THE DAYS."

MATTHEW xxviii. 16-20.

THIS brief concluding passage is all St. Matthew gives us of the thirty-nine days which followed the Resurrection and preceded the Ascension. It would seem as if he fully realised that the manifestations of these days belonged rather to the heavenly than to the earthly work of Jesus, and that therefore, properly speaking, they did not fall within his province. It was necessary that he should bear witness to the fact of the Resurrection, and that he should clearly set forth the authority under which the first preachers of the gospel acted. Having accomplished both, he rests from his long labour of love.

That the commission of the eleven was not restricted to this particular time and place is evident from notices in the other Gospels (Mark xvi. 15; Luke xxiv. 48; John xx. 21-23, xxi. 15-17); but we can see many reasons why this occasion was preferred to all others. We have already seen how natural it was that St. Matthew should call the attention of his readers to the appearances of the risen Lord in Galilee rather than to those in Jerusalem and its vicinity; and the more we think of it, the more do we see the appropriateness of his singling out this one in particular. It was the only formally appointed meeting of the Lord with His disciples. In every other case He came unannounced and unexpected; but for this meeting there had been a distinct and definite appointment.

This consideration is one of many which render it probable that this was the occasion referred to by St. Paul when our Lord was seen by above five hundred brethren at once; for on the one hand there was nothing but a definite appointment that would bring so large a company together at any one point, and on the other hand, when such an appointment was made, it is altogether natural to suppose that the news of it would spread far and wide, and bring together, not the eleven only, but disciples from all parts of the land, and especially from Galilee, where the greater number of them would no doubt reside. That St. Matthew mentions only the eleven may be accounted for by the object he has in view—viz., to exhibit their apostolic credentials; but even in his brief narrative there is one statement which is most easily understood on the supposition that a considerable number were present. "Some doubted," he says. This would seem altogether natural on the part of those to whom this was the only appearance; whereas it is difficult to suppose that any of the eleven could doubt after what they had seen and heard at Jerusalem.

In any case, the doubts were only temporary, and were in all probability connected with the mode of His manifestation. As on other occasions, of which particulars are given in other Gospels, the Lord would suddenly appear to the assembled company; and we can well understand how, when first His form was seen, He should not be recognised by all; so that, while all would be solemnised, and bow in adoration, some might not be altogether free from doubt. But the doubts would disappear as soon as "He opened His mouth and taught them," as of old. To make these doubts, as some do, a reason for discrediting the testimony of all is surely the very height of perversity. All the disciples were doubters at the first. But they were all convinced in the end. And the very fact that it was so hard to convince them, when they were first confronted with so unexpected an event as the Lord's appearing to them after His death, gives largely increased value to their unfaltering certainty ever afterwards, through all the persecution and sufferings, even unto death, to which their preaching the fact of the Resurrection exposed them.

As Galilee was the most convenient place * for a large public gathering of disciples, so a mountain was the most convenient spot, not only because of its seclusion, but because it would give the best opportunity for all to see and hear. What mountain it was we can only conjecture. Perhaps it was the mount on which the great Sermon was delivered which gave the first outline sketch of the kingdom now to be formally established; perhaps it was the mount which had already been honoured as the scene of the Transfiguration; but wherever it was, the associations with the former mountain scenes in Galilee would be fresh and strong in the disciples' minds.

The choice of a mountain in the north was moreover suitable as signalising the setting aside of Mount Zion and Jerusalem as the seat of empire. From this point of view we can see still another reason why St. Matthew, the Evangelist for the Jew, should mention the formal inauguration of the new kingdom in the north. The rejection of the Messiah by His own people had gone very deeply to the heart of the author of this Gospel. He certainly never obtrudes his feelings, even when they are strongest, as is most strikingly apparent in his calm record of the Passion itself; but there are many things which show how keenly he felt on this point. Recall how he tells us on the one hand that "Herod the king was troubled, and all Jerusalem with him," when the report was spread abroad that the Christ was born in Bethlehem, and on the other that the wise men from the East "rejoiced with exceeding great joy." Remember how he speaks of "Galilee of the Gentiles" as rejoicing in the great light which had been unnoticed or unwelcome in Jerusalem, and how he calls special attention to "the coasts of Cæsarea Philippi," the utmost corner of the land, as the place where the Church was founded. And now, having recorded the Lord's final and formal entry into the ancient capital to claim the throne of David, only to be despised and rejected, mocked and scourged and crucified, it is natural that, as the Evangelist for the Jew, he should pass away from what he often fondly calls "the holy City," * but which is now to him an accursed place, to those calm regions of the north which were associated in his mind with the first shining of the light, with so many words of wisdom spoken by the Lord, with the doing of most of His mighty deeds, with the founding of the Church, and with the glory of the Transfiguration.

* The number at Jerusalem at the time of the Ascension was only a hundred and twenty (Acts i. 15).

The words of the Lord on this last occasion are worthy of all that has gone before. Let all doubters ponder well the significance of this. Suppose for a moment that the story of the Resurrection had been only "the passion of a hallucinated woman," as Renan puts it, and then consider the position. No one of course denies that up to the moment of death there was a veritable Jesus, whose sayings and doings supplied the material for the history; but now that the hero is dead and gone, where are the materials? The fishermen and publicans are on their own resources now. They have to make everything out of nothing. Surely, therefore, there must be now a swift descent; no more of those noble utterances to which we have been accustomed hitherto—only inventions of the poor publican now. No more breadth of view—only Jewish narrowness now. It was about this very time that the disciples asked, "Lord, wilt Thou at this time restore the kingdom to Israel?" Suppose, then, these men obliged themselves to invent a Great Commission, how narrow and provincial will it be!

Is there, then, such a swift descent? Are not the reported words of the risen Lord—not in this Gospel merely, but in all the Gospels—as noble, as impressive, as divine as any that have been preserved to us, from the years of His life in the flesh? Search through this Gospel, and say if there can be found anywhere an utterance that has more of the King in it, that is more absolutely free from all Jewish narrowness and from all human feebleness, than this Great Commission which forms its magnificent close. It is very plain that these simple artists have their subject still before them. Manifestly they are not drawing from imagination, but telling what they heard and saw.

There is an unapproachable majesty in the words which makes one shrink from touching them. They seem to rise before us like a great mountain which it would be presumption to attempt to scale. What a mighty range they take, up to heaven, out to all the earth, down to the end of time!—and all so calm, so simple, so strong, so sure. If, as He finished the Sermon on the Mount, the multitude were astonished, much more must these have been astonished who first listened to this amazing proclamation.

"All authority hath been given unto Me in heaven and on earth" (R. V.). What words are these to come from One Who has just been put to death for claiming to be the king of the Jews! King of kings and Lord of lords is the title now He claims. And yet it is as Son of man He speaks. He does not speak as God, and say, "All authority is Mine": He speaks as the man Christ Jesus, saying, "All authority has

* St. Matthew alone of the Evangelists uses this designation.

been given unto Me"—given as the purchase of His pain: authority in heaven, as Priest with God—authority on earth, as King of men.

Having thus laid broad and deep and strong the foundations of the new kingdom, He sends the heralds forth: "Go ye therefore, and make disciples of all the nations, baptising them into the name of the Father and of the Son and of the Holy Ghost: teaching them to observe all things whatsoever I commanded you" (R. V.). These are simple words and very familiar now, and a distinct effort is needed to realise how extraordinary they are, as spoken then and there to that little company. "All nations" are to be discipled and brought under His sway,—such is the commission; and to whom is it given? Not to Imperial Cæsar, with his legions at command and the civilised world at his feet; not to a company of intellectual giants, who by the sheer force of genius might turn the world upside down; but to these obscure Galileans of whom Cæsar has never heard, not one of whose names has ever been pronounced in the Roman Senate, who have excited no wonder either for intellect or learning even in the villages and country-sides from which they come,—it is to these that the great commission is given to bring the world to the feet of the crucified Nazarene. Imagine a nineteenth-century critic there, and listening. He would not have said a word. It would have been beneath his notice. A curl of the lip would have been all the recognition he would have deigned to give. Yes, how ludicrous it seems in the light of reason! But in the light of history is it not sublime?

The hidden power lay in the conjunction: "Go ye *therefore*." It would have been the height of folly to have gone on such an errand in their own strength; but why should they hesitate to go in the name and at the bidding of One to Whom all authority had been given in heaven and on earth? Yet the power is not delegated to them. It remains, and must remain with Him. It is not, "All authority is given *unto you*." They must keep in closest touch with Him, wherever they may go on this extraordinary mission. How this may be will presently appear.

The two branches into which the commission divides—"Baptising them into the name of the Father and of the Son and of the Holy Ghost," "Teaching them to observe all things whatsoever I commanded you"—correspond to the twofold authority on which it is based. By virtue of His authority in heaven, He authorises His ambassadors to baptise people of all nations who shall become His disciples "into the name of the Father and of the Son and of the Holy Ghost." Thus would they be acknowledged as children of the great family of God, accepted by the Father as washed from sin through the blood of Jesus Christ His Son, and sanctified by the grace of His Holy Spirit—the sum of saving truth suggested in a single line. In the same way by virtue of His authority on earth, He authorises His disciples to publish His commands so as to secure the obedience of all the nations, and yet not of constraint, but willingly, "teaching them to observe all things whatsoever I have commanded you."

Easily said; but how shall it be done? We can imagine the feeling of bewilderment and helplessness with which the disciples would listen to their marching orders, until all was changed by the simple and sublime assurance at the close: "And lo, I am with you alway, even unto the end of the world." This assurance is perhaps the strangest part of all, as given to a company, however small, who were to be scattered abroad in different directions, and who were commissioned to go to the very ends of the earth. How could it be fulfilled? There is nothing in St. Matthew's narrative to explain the difficulty. We know, indeed, from other sources what explains it. It is the Ascension—the return of the King to the heaven whence He came, to resume His omnipresent glory, by virtue of which alone He can fulfil the promise He has made.

This brings us to a question of considerable importance: Why is it that St. Matthew gives no record of the Ascension, and does not even hint what became of the risen Christ after this last recorded interview with His disciples? It seems to us that a sufficient reason is found in the object which St. Matthew had in view, which was to set forth the establishment of the kingdom of Christ upon earth as foretold by the prophets and expected by the saints of old; and inasmuch as it is Christ's kingdom *on earth* which he has mainly in view, he does not call special attention to His return to heaven, but rather to that earthly fact which was the glorious result of it—viz., His abiding presence with His people on the earth. Had he finished his Gospel with the Ascension, the last impression left on the reader's mind would have been of Christ in heaven at the right hand of God—a glorious thought indeed, but not the one it was his special aim and object to convey. But, concluding as he does, the last impression on the reader's mind is of Christ abiding on the earth, and with all His people even to the end of the world—a most cheering, comforting, and stimulating thought. To the devout reader of this Gospel it is as if his Lord had never left the earth at all, but had suddenly clothed Himself with omnipresence, so that, however far apart His disciples might be scattered in His service, each one of them might at any moment see His face, and hear His voice of cheer, and feel His touch of sympathy, and draw on His reserve of power. Thus was it made quite plain, how they could keep in closest touch with Him to Whom was given all authority in heaven and on earth.

After all, is it quite correct to say that St. Matthew omits the Ascension? What was the Ascension? We think of it as a going up; but that is to speak of it after the manner of men. In the kingdom of heaven there is no geographical "up" or "down." The Ascension really meant the laying aside of earthly limitations and the resumption of Divine glory with its omnipresence and eternity; and is not this included in these closing words? May we not fancy one of these doubting ones (ver. 17), who trembled in the presence of that Form in which the Lord appeared to them upon the mount, recalling afterwards the supreme moment when the words "Lo, I am with you," entered into his soul, in language such as this:

> "Then did the Form expand, expand—
> I knew Him through the dread disguise,
> As the whole God within His eyes
> Embraced me"—

an embrace in which he remained, when the Form had vanished.

The Ascension is all in that wonderful "I am." It is not the first time we have heard it. Among His last words in Capernaum, when the Saviour was thinking of His Church in the ages to come, gathered together in companies in all the lands where disciples should meet in His name, the great thought takes Him for the moment out of the limitations of His earthly life; it carries Him back, or rather lifts Him up, to the eternal sphere from which He has come to earth, so that He uses not the future of time, but the present of eternity: "*There am I* in the midst of them" (xviii. 20). A still more striking example has been preserved by St. John. When on one occasion He spoke of Abraham as seeing His day, the Jews interrupted Him with the question, "Thou art not yet fifty years old, and hast Thou seen Abraham?" Recognising in this a challenge of His relation to that timeless, dateless sphere from which He has come, He promptly replies, "Before Abraham was,* *I am.*" It is as if a foreigner, speaking perfectly the language of the country of his adoption, were suddenly betrayed into a form of expression which marked his origin.

That was a momentary relapse, as it were, into the language of eternity; but this last "I am" marks a change in His relations to His disciples: it is the note of the new dispensation of the Spirit. These forty days were a transition time marked by special manifestations—not wholly material as in the days of the Incarnation, nor wholly spiritual as in the days after Pentecost; but on the borderland between the two, so as to prepare the minds and hearts of the disciples for the purely spiritual relation which was thenceforward to be the rule. Whichever appearance was the last to any disciple would be the Ascension to him. To very many in that large gathering this would be the Saviour's last appearance. It was in all probability the time when the great majority of the disciples bade farewell to the Form of their risen Lord. May we not, then, call this the Ascension in Galilee? And just as the parting on the Mount of Olives left as its deepest impression the withdrawal of the man Christ Jesus, with the promise of His return in like manner, so the parting on the mount in Galilee left as its deepest impression not the withdrawal of the human form, but the permanent abiding of the Divine Spirit—a portion of the truth of the Ascension quite as important as the other, and even more inspiring. No wonder that the great announcement which is to be the Christian's title-deed, for all ages to come, of God's unspeakable gift, should be introduced with a summons to adoring wonder: "*Lo,* I am with you alway, even unto the end of the world."

The Gospel ends by removing from itself all limitations of time and space, extending the day of the Incarnation to "all the days," enlarging the Holy Land to embrace all lands. The times of the Son of man are widened so as to embrace all times. The great name Immanuel (i. 23) is now fulfilled for all the nations and for all the ages. For what is this finished Gospel but the interpretation, full and clear at last, of that great Name of the old covenant, the name Jehovah: "I am," "I am that I am" (Exod. iii. 14)? All of the Old Testament revelation is gathered up in this final utterance, "I am—with you"; and it has in it by anticipation all that will be included in that last word of the risen Saviour: "I am Alpha and Omega, the Beginning and the End, the First and the Last" (Rev. xxii. 13).

This last sentence of the Gospel distinguishes the life of Jesus from all other histories, biographies or "remains." It is the one "Life" in all literature. These years were not spent "as a tale that is told." The Lord Jesus lives in His gospel, so that all who receive His final promise may catch the light of His eye, feel the touch of His hand, hear the tones of His voice, see for themselves, and become acquainted with Him Whom to know is Life Eternal. Fresh and new, and rich and strong, for "all the days," this Gospel is not the record of a past, but the revelation of a present Saviour, of One Whose voice sounds deep and clear across all storms of life: "Fear not: I am the First and the Last: I am He that liveth *and was dead;* and behold I AM ALIVE FOR EVERMORE."

* The full significance of the original can scarcely be given in English. The Greek language, rich in the vocabulary of philosophy, has two verbs corresponding to our "to be," one indicating phenomenal, the other absolute being. It is the former which is used of Abraham; the latter is used by our Lord in speaking of Himself. There is, therefore, more than a difference of tense.

THE GOSPEL ACCORDING TO ST. MARK

CONTENTS.

THE GOSPEL ACCORDING TO ST. MARK.

BY THE VERY REV. G. A. CHADWICK, D. D.

CHAPTER I.

THE BEGINNING OF THE GOSPEL.

MARK i. 1-6 (R. V.).

THE opening of St. Mark's Gospel is energetic and full of character. St. Matthew traces for Jews the pedigree of their Messiah; St. Luke's worldwide sympathies linger with the maiden who bore Jesus, and the village of His boyhood; and St. John's theology proclaims the Divine origin of the Eternal Lord. But St. Mark trusts the public acts of the Mighty Worker to do for the reader what they did for those who first "beheld His glory." How He came to earth can safely be left untold: what He was will appear by what He wrought. It is enough to record, with matchless vividness, the toils, the energy, the love and wrath, the defeat and triumph of the brief career which changed the world. It will prove itself to be the career of "the Son of God."

In so deciding, he followed the example of the Apostolic teaching. The first vacant place among the Twelve was filled by an eye-witness, competent to tell what Jesus did "from the baptism of John to the day when He was received up," the very space covered by this Gospel. That "Gospel of peace," which Cornelius heard from St. Peter (and hearing, received the Holy Ghost) was the same story of Jesus "after the baptism which John preached." And this is throughout the substance of the primitive teaching. The Apostles act as men who believe that everything necessary to salvation is (implicit or explicit) in the history of those few crowded years. Therefore this is "the gospel."

Men there are who judge otherwise, and whose gospel is not the story of salvation wrought, but the plan of salvation applied, how the Atonement avails for us, how men are converted, and what privileges they then receive. But in truth men are not converted by preaching conversion, any more than citizens are made loyal by demanding loyalty. Show men their prince, and convince them that he is gracious and truly royal, and they will die for him. Show them the Prince of Life, and He, being lifted up, will draw all men unto Him; and thus the truest gospel is that which declares Christ, and Him crucified. As all science springs from the phenomena of the external world, so do theology and religion spring from the life of Him who was too adorable to be mortal, and too loving to be disobeyed.

Therefore St. Paul declares that the gospel which he preached to the Corinthians and by which they were saved, was, that Christ died for our sins and was buried and rose again, and was seen of sufficient witnesses (1 Cor. xv. 1-8).

And therefore St. Mark is contented with a very brief record of those wondrous years; a few facts, chosen with a keen sense of the intense energy and burning force which they reveal, are what he is inspired to call the gospel.

He presently uses the word in a somewhat larger sense, telling how Jesus Himself, before the story of His life could possibly be unfolded, preached as "the gospel of God" that "the time is fulfilled, and the kingdom of God is at hand," and added (what St. Mark only has preserved for us), "Repent, and believe in the gospel" (i. 14-15). So too it is part of St. Paul's "gospel" that "God shall judge the secrets of men by Jesus Christ" (Rom. ii. 16). For this also is good news of God, "the gospel of the kingdom." And like "the gospel of Jesus Christ," it treats of His attitude toward us, more than ours toward Him, which latter is the result rather than the substance of it. That He rules, and not the devil; that we shall answer at last to Him and to none lower; that Satan lied when he claimed to possess all the kingdoms of the earth, and to dispose of them; that Christ has now received from far different hands "all power on earth"; this is a gospel which the world has not yet learned to welcome, nor the Church fully to proclaim.

Now the scriptural use of this term is quite as important to religious emotion as to accuracy of thought. All true emotions hide their fountain too deep for self-consciousness to find. We feel best when our feeling is forgotten. Not while we think about finding peace, but while we approach God as a Father, and are anxious for nothing, but in everything by prayer and supplication with thanksgiving make known our requests, is it promised that the peace of God which passeth all understanding shall guard our hearts and our thoughts (Phil. iv. 7). And many a soul of the righteous, whom faith in the true gospel fills with trembling adoration, is made sad by the inflexible demand for certain realised personal experiences as the title to recognition as a Christian. That great title belonged at the first to all who would learn of Jesus: the disciples were called Christians. To acquaint ourselves with Him, that is to be at peace.

Meantime, we observe that the new movement which now begins is not, like Judaism, a law which brings death; nor like Buddhism, a path in which one must walk as best he may: it differs from all other systems in being essentially the announcement of good tidings from above.

Yet "the beginning of the gospel of Jesus Christ" is a profound agitation and widespread alarm. Lest the soothing words of Jesus should blend like music with the slumber of sinners at ease in Zion, John came preaching repentance, and what is more, a baptism of repentance; not such a lustration as was most familiar to the Mosaic law, administered by the worshipper to himself, but an ablution at other hands, a confession that one is not only soiled, but soiled beyond all cleansing of his own. Formal Judaism was one long struggle for self-purification. The dawn of a new system is visible in the movement of all Judæa towards one who bids them throw every such hope away, and come to him for the baptism of repentance, and expect a Greater One, who shall baptise them with the Holy Ghost and with fire. And the true function of the predicted herald, the best levelling of the rugged ways of humanity for the Promised One to traverse, was in this universal diffusion of the sense of sin. For Christ was not come to call the righteous, but sinners to repentance.

In truth, the movement of the Baptist, with its double aspect, gathers up all the teaching of the past. He produced conviction, and he promised help. One lesson of all sacred history is universal failure. The innocence of Eden cannot last. The law with its promise of life to the man who doeth these things, issued practically in the knowledge of sin; it entered that sin might abound; it made a formal confession of universal sin, year by year, continually. And therefore its fitting close was a baptism of repentance universally accepted. Alas! not universally. For while we read of all the nation swayed by one impulse, and rushing to the stern teacher who had no share in its pleasures or its luxuries, whose life was separated from its concerns, and whose food was the simplest that could sustain existence, yet we know that when they heard how deep his censures pierced, and how unsparingly he scourged their best-loved sins, the loudest professors of religion rejected the counsel of God against themselves, being not baptised of Him. Nevertheless, by coming to Him, they also had pleaded guilty. Something they needed; they were sore at heart, and would have welcomed any soothing balm, although they refused the surgeon's knife.

The law did more than convict men; it inspired hope. The promise of a Redeemer shone like a rainbow across the dark story of the past. He was the end of all the types, at once the Victim and the Priest. To Him gave all the prophets witness, and the Baptist brought all past attainment to its full height, and was "more than a prophet" when he announced the actual presence of the Christ, when he pointed out to the first two Apostles, the Lamb of God.

AT THE JORDAN.

Mark i. 7-11 (R. V.).

It was when all men mused in their hearts whether John was the Christ or no, that he announced the coming of a Stronger One. By thus promptly silencing a whisper, so honourable to himself, he showed how strong he really was and how unselfish "a friend of the Bridegroom." Nor was this the vague humility of phrase which is content to be lowly in general, so long as no specified individual stands higher. His word is definite, and accepts much for himself. "The Stronger One than I cometh," and it is in presence of the might of Jesus (whom yet this fiery reformer called a Lamb), that he feels himself unworthy to bend to the dust and unbind the latchets or laces of his shoe.

So then, though asceticism be sometimes good, it is consciously not the highest nor the most effective goodness. Perhaps it is the most impressive. Without a miracle, the preaching of John shook the nation as widely as that of Jesus melted it, and prepared men's hearts for His. A king consulted and feared him. And when the Pharisees were at open feud with Jesus, they feared to be stoned if they should pronounce John's baptism to be of men.

Yet is there weakness lurking even in the very quality which gives asceticism its power. That stern seclusion from an evil world, that peremptory denial of its charms, why are they so impressive? Because they set an example to those who are hard beset, of the one way of escape, the cutting off of the hand and foot, the plucking out of the eye. And our Lord enjoins such mutilation of the life upon those whom its gifts betray. Yet is it as the halt and maimed that such men enter into life. The ascetic is a man who needs to sternly repress and deny his impulses, who is conscious of traitors within his breast that may revolt if the enemy be suffered to approach too near.

It is harder to be a holy friend of publicans and sinners, a witness for God while eating and drinking with these, than to remain in the desert undefiled. It is greater to convert a sinful woman in familiar converse by the well, than to shake trembling multitudes by threats of the fire for the chaff and the axe for the barren tree. And John confessed this. In the supreme moment of his life, he added his own confession to that of all his nation. This rugged ascetic had need to be baptised of Him who came eating and drinking.

Nay, he taught that all his work was but superficial, a baptism with water to reach the surface of men's life, to check, at the most, exaction and violence and neglect of the wants of others, while the Greater One should baptise with the Holy Ghost, should pierce the depths of human nature, and thoroughly purge His floor.

Nothing could refute more clearly than our three simple narratives, the sceptical notion that Jesus yielded for awhile to the dominating influence of the Baptist. Only from the Gospels can we at all connect the two. And what we read here is, that before Jesus came, John expected his Superior; that when they met, John declared his own need to be baptised of Him, that he, nevertheless, submitted to the will of Jesus, and thereupon heard a voice from the heavens which must for ever have destroyed all notion of equality; that afterwards he only saw Jesus at a distance, and made a confession which transferred two of his disciples to our Lord.

The criticism which transforms our Lord's part in these events to that of a pupil is far more wilful than would be tolerated in dealing with any other record. And it too palpably springs from the need to find some human inspiration for the Word of God, some candle from which the Sun of Righteousness took fire, if one would escape the confession that He is not of this world.

But here we meet a deeper question: Not why Jesus accepted baptism from an inferior, but why, being sinless, He sought for a baptism of repentance. How is this act consistent with absolute and stainless purity?

Now it sometimes lightens a difficulty to find that it is not occasional nor accidental, but wrought deep into the plan of a consistent work. And the Gospels are consistent in representing the innocence of Jesus as refusing immunity from the consequences of guilt. He was circumcised, and His mother then paid the offering commanded by the law, although both these actions spoke of defilement. In submitting to the likeness of sinful flesh He submitted to its conditions. He was present at feasts in which national confessions led up to sacrifice, and the sacrificial blood was sprinkled to make atonement for the children of Israel, because of all their sins. When He tasted death itself, which passed upon all men, for that all have sinned, He carried out to the utmost the same stern rule to which at His baptism He consciously submitted. Nor will any theory of His atonement suffice, which is content with believing that His humiliations and sufferings, though inevitable, were only collateral results of contact with our fallen race. Baptism was avoidable, and that without any compromise of His influence, since the Pharisees refused it with impunity, and John would fain have exempted Him. Here at least He was not "entangled in the machinery," but deliberately turned the wheels upon Himself. And this is the more impressive because, in another aspect of affairs, He claimed to be out of the reach of ceremonial defilement, and touched without reluctance disease, leprosy, and the dead.

Humiliating and penal consequences of sin, to these He bowed His head. Yet to a confession of personal taint, never. And all the accounts agree that He never was less conscience-stricken than when He shared the baptism of repentance. St. Matthew implies, what St. Luke plainly declares, that He did not come to baptism along with the crowds of penitents, but separately. And at the point where all others made confession, in the hour when even the Baptist, although filled with the Holy Ghost from his mother's womb, had need to be baptised, He only felt the propriety, the fitness of fulfilling all righteousness. That mighty task was not even a yoke to Him, it was an instinct like that of beauty to an artist; it was what became Him.

St. Mark omits even this evidence of sinlessness. His energetic method is like that of a great commander, who seizes at all costs the vital point upon the battle field. He constantly omits what is subordinate (although very conscious of the power of graphic details), when by so doing he can force the central thought upon the mind. Here he concentrates our attention upon the witness from above, upon the rending asunder of the heavens which unfold all their heights over a bended head, upon the visible descent of the Holy Spirit in His fulness, upon the voice from the heavens which pealed through the souls of these two peerless worshippers, and proclaimed that He who had gone down to the baptismal flood was no sinner to be forgiven, but the beloved Son of God, in whom He is well pleased.

That is our Evangelist's answer to all misunderstanding of the rite, and it is enough.

How do men think of heaven? Perhaps only as a remote point in space, where flames a material and solid structure into which it is the highest bliss to enter. A place there must be to which the Body of our Lord ascended and whither He shall yet lead home His followers in spiritual bodies to be with Him where He is. If, however, only this be heaven, we should hold that in the revolutions of the solar system it hung just then vertically above the Jordan, a few fathoms or miles aloft. But we also believe in a spiritual city, in which the pillars are living saints, an all-embracing blessedness and rapture and depth of revelation, whereinto holy mortals in their highest moments have been "caught up," a heaven whose angels ascend and descend upon the Son of man. In this hour of highest consecration, these heavens were thrown open—rent asunder—for the gaze of our Lord and of the Baptist. They were opened again when the first martyr died. And we read that what eye hath not seen nor ear heard nor heart conceived of the preparation of God for them that love Him, He hath already revealed to them by His Spirit. To others there is only cloud or "the infinite azure," as to the crowd by the Jordan and the murderers of Stephen.

Now it is to be observed that we never read of Jesus being caught up into heaven for a space, like St. Paul or St. John. What we read is, that while on earth the Son of man is in Heaven (John iii. 13),* for heaven is the manifestation of God, whose truest glory was revealed in the grace and truth of Jesus.

Along with this revelation, the Holy Spirit was manifested wondrously. His appearance, indeed, is quite unlike what it was to others. At Pentecost He became visible, but since each disciple received only a portion, "according to his several ability," his fitting symbol was "tongues parting asunder like as of fire." He came as an element powerful and pervasive, not as a Personality bestowed in all His vital force on any one.

So, too, the phrase which John used, when predicting that Jesus should baptise with the Holy Ghost, slightly though it differs from what is here, implies† that only a portion is to be given, not the fulness. And the angel who foretold to Zacharias that John himself should be filled with the Holy Ghost, conveyed the same limitation in his words. John received all that he was able to receive: he was filled. But how should mortal capacity exhaust the fulness of Deity? And Who is this, upon Whom, while John is but an awe-stricken beholder, the Spirit of God descends in all completeness, a living organic unity, like a dove? Only the Infinite is capable of receiving such a gift, and this is He in Whom dwelleth all the fulness of the Godhead bodily. No wonder then that "in bodily form" as a dove, the Spirit of God descended upon Him alone. Henceforward He became the great Dispenser, and "the Spirit emanated from Him as perfume from the rose when it has opened."

At the same time was heard a Voice from heaven. And the bearing of this passage upon the Trinity becomes clear when we combine the manifestation of the Spirit in living Personality, and the Divine Voice, not from the Dove, but from the heavens, with the announcement that Jesus is not merely beloved and well-pleasing, but a Son, and in this high sense the only Son, since the words are literally "Thou art the Son of Me, the beloved." And yet He is to bring many sons unto glory.

Is it consistent with due reverence to believe that this voice conveyed a message to our Lord Himself? Even so liberal a critic as Neander has denied this. But if we grasp the meaning of what we believe, that He upon taking flesh "emptied Himself," that He increased in wisdom during His youth, and that there was a day and hour which to the end of life He knew not, we need not suppose that His infancy was so unchildlike as the realisation of His mysterious and awful Personality would make it. There must then have been a period when His perfect human development rose up into what Renan calls (more accurately than he knows) identification of Himself with the object of His

* *Cf.* the admirable note in Archdeacon Watkins' "Commentary on John."

† By the absence of the article in the Greek.

devotion, carried to the utmost limit. Nor is this period quite undiscoverable, for when it arrived it would seem highly unnatural to postpone His public ministry further. Now this reasonable inference is entirely supported by the narrative. St. Matthew indeed regards the event from the Baptist's point of vision. But St. Mark and St. Luke are agreed that to Jesus Himself it was also said, "*Thou* art My beloved Son." Now this is not the way to teach us that the testimony came only to John. And how solemn a thought is this, that the full certitude of His destiny expanded before the eyes of Jesus, just when He lifted them from those baptismal waters in which He stooped so low.

THE TEMPTATION.

Mark i. 12, 13 (R. V.).

St. Mark has not recorded the details of our Lord's temptations, and lays more stress upon the duration of the struggle than the nature of the last and crowning assaults. But he is careful, like the others, to connect it closely with the baptism of Jesus, and the miraculous testimony then borne to Him.

It is indeed instructive that He should have suffered this affront immediately upon being recognised as the Messiah. But the explanation will not be found in the notion, which Milton has popularised, that only now Satan was assured of the urgent necessity for attacking Him:

"That heard the adversary . . . and with the voice Divine
Nigh thunderstruck, the exalted Man, to whom
Such high attest was given, awhile surveyed
With wonder."

As if Satan forgot the marvels of the sacred infancy. As if the spirits who attack all could have failed to identify, after thirty years of defeat, the Greater One whom the Baptist had everywhere proclaimed. No. But Satan admirably chose the time for a supreme effort. High places are dizzy, and especially when one has just attained them; and therefore it was when the voice of the herald and the Voice from the heavens were blended in acclaim, that the Evil One tried all his arts. He had formerly plunged Elijah into despair and a desire to die immediately after the fire from heaven responded to the prophet's prayer. Soon after this he would degrade Peter to be his mouthpiece just when his noblest testimony was borne and the highest approval of his Lord was won. In the flush of their triumphs he found his best opportunity; but Jesus remained unflushed and met the first recorded temptation, in the full consciousness of Messiahship, by quoting the words which spoke to every man alike, and as man.

It is a lesson which the weakest needs to learn, for little victories can intoxicate little men.

It is easy then to see why the recorded temptations insist upon the exceptional dignity of Christ and urge Him to seize its advantages, while He insists upon bearing the common burden and proves Himself greatest by becoming least of all. The sharp contrast between His circumstances and His rank drove the temptations deep into His consciousness and wounded His sensibilities, though they failed to shake His will.

How unnatural that the Son of God should lack and suffer hunger, how right that He should challenge recognition, how needful (though now His sacred Personality is cunningly allowed to fall somewhat into the background) that He should obtain armies and splendour.

This explains the possibility of temptation in a sinless nature, which indeed can only be denied by assuming that sin is part of the original creation. Not because we are sinful, but because we are flesh and blood (of which He became partaker), when we feel the pains of hunger we are attracted by food, at whatever price it is offered. In truth, no man is allured by sin, but only by the bait and bribe of sin, except perhaps in the last stages of spiritual decomposition.

Now, just as the bait allures, and not the jaws of the trap, so the power of a temptation is not its wickedness, not the guilty service, but the proffered recompense; and this appeals to the most upright man, equally with the most corrupt. Thus the stress of a temptation is to be measured by our gravitation, not towards the sin, but towards the pleasure or advantage which is entangled with that. And this may be realised even more powerfully by a man of keen feeling and vivid imagination who does not falter, than by a grosser nature which succumbs.

Now Jesus was a perfect man. To His exquisite sensibilities, which had neither inherited nor contracted any blemish, the pain of hunger at the opening of His ministry, and the horror of the cross at its close, were not less intense, but sharper than to ours. And this pain and horror measured the temptation to evade them. The issue never hung in the scales; even to hesitate would have been to forfeit the delicate bloom of absolute sinlessness; but, none the less, the decision was costly, the temptation poignant.

St. Mark has given us no details; but there is immense and compressed power in the assertion, only his, that the temptation lasted all through the forty days. We know the power of an unremitting pressure, an incessant importunity, a haunting thought. A very trifling annoyance, long protracted, drives men to strange remedies. And the remorseless urgency of Satan may be measured by what St. Matthew tells us, that only after the forty days Jesus became aware of the pains of hunger. Perhaps the assertion that He was with the wild beasts may throw some ray of light upon the nature of the temptation. There is no intimation of bodily peril. On the other hand it seems incredible that what is hinted is His own consciousness of the supernatural dignity from which

"The fiery serpent fled, and noxious worm;
The lion and fierce tiger glared aloof."

Such a consciousness would have relieved the strain of which their pressure is evidently a part. Nay, but the oppressive solitude, the waste region so unlike His blooming Nazareth, and the ferocity of the brute creation, all would conspire to suggest those dread misgivings and questionings which are provoked by "the something that infects the world."

Surely we may believe that He Who was tempted at all points like as we are, felt now the deadly chill which falls upon the soul from the shadow of our ruined earth. In our nature He bore the assault and overcame. And then His human nature condescended to accept help, such as ours receives, from the ministering spirits which are sent forth to minister to them that shall be heirs of salvation. So perfectly was He made like unto His brethren.

THE EARLY PREACHING AND THE FIRST DISCIPLES.

MARK i. 14-20 (R. V.).

St. Mark has shown us the Baptist proclaiming Christ. He now tells us that when John was imprisoned, Jesus, turning from that Judæan ministry which stirred the jealousy of John's disciples (John iii. 26), "came into Galilee, preaching." And one looks twice before observing that His teaching is a distinct advance upon the herald's. Men are still to repent; for however slightly modern preachers may heal the hurt of souls, real contrition is here taken over into the gospel scheme. But the time which was hitherto said to be at hand is now fulfilled. And they are not only to believe the gospel, but to "believe in it." Reliance, the effort of the soul by which it ceases equally to be self-confident and to despair, confiding itself to some word which is a gospel, or some being who has salvation to bestow, that is belief in its object. And it is highly important to observe that faith is thus made prominent so early in our Lord's teaching. The vitalising power of faith was no discovery of St. Paul; it was not evolved by devout meditation after Jesus had passed from view, nor introduced into His system when opposition forced Him to bind men to Him in a stronger allegiance. The power of faith is implied in His earliest preaching, and it is connected with His earliest miracles. But no such phrase as the power of faith is ever used. Faith is precious only as it leans on what is trustworthy. And it is produced, not by thinking of faith itself, but of its proper object. Therefore Christ did not come preaching faith, but preaching the gospel of God, and bidding men believe in that.

Shall we not follow His example? It is morally certain that Abraham never heard of salvation by faith, yet he was justified by faith when he believed in Him Who justifieth the ungodly. To preach Him and His gospel is the way to lead men to be saved by faith.

Few things are more instructive to consider than the slow, deliberate, yet firm steps by which Christ advanced to the revelation of God in flesh. Thirty years of silence, forty days of seclusion after heaven had proclaimed Him, leisurely intercourse with Andrew and John, Peter and Nathanael, and then a brief ministry in a subject nation, and chiefly in a despised province. It is not the action of a fanatic. It exactly fulfils His own description of the kingdom which He proclaimed, which was to exhibit first the blade, then the ear, then the full corn in the ear. And it is a lesson to all time that the boldest expectations possible to faith do not justify feverish haste and excited longings for immediate prominence or immediate success. The husbandman who has long patience with the seed is not therefore hopeless of the harvest.

Passing by the Sea of Galilee, Jesus finds two fishermen at their toil, and bids them follow Him. Both are men of decided and earnest character; one is to become the spokesman and leader of the Apostolic band, and the little which is recorded of the other indicates the same temperament, somewhat less developed. Our Lord now calls upon them to take a decided step. But here again we find traces of the same deliberate progression, the same absence of haste, as in His early preaching. He does not, as unthinking readers fancy, come upon two utter strangers, fascinate and arrest them in a moment, and sweep their lives into the vortex of His own. Andrew had already heard the Baptist proclaim the Lamb of God, had followed Jesus home, and had introduced his brother, to whom Jesus then gave the new name Cephas. Their faith had since been confirmed by miracles. The demands of our Lord may be trying, but they are never unreasonable, and the faith He claims is not a blind credulity.

Nor does He, even now, finally and entirely call them away from their occupation. Some time is still to elapse, and a sign, especially impressive to fishermen, the miraculous draught of fishes, is to burn into their minds a profound sense of their unworthiness, before the vocation now promised shall arrive. Then He will say, From henceforth ye shall catch men: now He says, I will prepare you for that future, I will make you to become fishers of men. So ungrounded is the suspicion of any confusion between the stories of the three steps by which they rose to their Apostleship.

A little further on, He finds the two sons of Zebedee, and calls them also. John had almost certainly been the companion of Andrew when he followed Jesus home, and his brother had become the sharer of his hopes. And if there were any hesitation the example of their comrades helped them to decide—so soon, so inevitably does each disciple begin to be a fisher of other men—and leaving their father, as we are gracefully told, not desolate, but with servants, they also follow Jesus.

Thus He asks, from each group, the sacrifice involved in following Him at an inconvenient time. The first are casting their nets and eager in their quest. The others are mending their nets, perhaps after some large draught had broken them. So Levi was sitting at the receipt of toll. Not one of the Twelve was chosen to that high rank when idle.

Very charming, very powerful still is the spell by which Christ drew His first apostles to His side. Not yet are they told anything of thrones on which they are to sit and judge the tribes of Israel, or that their names shall be engraven on the foundations of the heavenly city besides being great on earth while the world stands. For them the capture of men was less lucrative than that of fish, and less honourable, for they suffered the loss of all things and were made as the filth of the earth. To learn Christ's art, be made helpful in drawing souls to Him, following Jesus and catching men, this was enough to attract His first ministers; God grant that a time may never come when ministers for whom this is enough, shall fail. Where the spirit of self-devotion is absent how can the Spirit of Christ exist?

TEACHING WITH AUTHORITY.

MARK i. 21, 22 (R. V.).

The worship of the synagogues, not having been instituted by Moses, but gradually developed by the public need, was comparatively free and unconventional. Sometimes it happened that remarkable and serious-looking strangers were invited, if they had any word of exhortation, to say on (Acts xiii. 15). Sometimes one presented himself, as the custom of our Lord was (Luke iv. 16). Amid the dull mechanical tendencies which were then turning the heart of Judaism to stone, the synagogue may often have been a centre of life and rallying-place of freedom. In Galilee, where such worship predominated over that of the remote Temple and its hierarchy, Jesus found His trusted followers and the nucleus of the Church. In foreign lands St. Paul bore first to his brethren in their synagogues the strange tidings that their Messiah had expired upon a cross. And before his rupture with the chiefs of Judaism the synagogues were fitting places for our Lord's early teaching. He made use of the existing system, and applied it, just as we have seen Him use the teaching of the Baptist as a starting-point for His own. And this ought to be observed: that Jesus revolutionised the world by methods the furthest from being revolutionary. The institutions of His age and land were corrupt well-nigh to the core, but He did not therefore make a clean sweep, and begin again. He did not turn His back on the Temple and synagogues, nor outrage Sabbaths, nor come to destroy the law and the prophets. He bade His followers reverence the seat where the scribes and the Pharisees sat, and drew the line at their false lives and perilous examples. Amid that evil generation He found soil wherein His seed might germinate, and was content to hide His leaven in the lump where it should gradually work out its destiny. In so doing He was at one with Providence, which had slowly evolved the convictions of the Old Testament, spending centuries upon the process. Now the power which belongs to such moderation has scarcely been recognised until these latter days. The political sagacity of Somers and Burke, and the ecclesiastical wisdom of our own reformers, had their occult and unsuspected fountains in the method by which Jesus planted the kingdom which came not with observation. But who taught the Carpenter? It is therefore significant that all the Gospels of the Galilean ministry connect our Lord's early teaching with the synagogue.

St. Mark is by no means the evangelist of the discourses. And this adds to the interest with which we find him indicate, with precise exactitude, the first great difference that would strike the hearers of Christ between His teaching and that of others. He taught with authority, and not as the scribes. Their doctrine was built, with dreary and irrational ingenuity, upon perverted views of the old law. The shape of a Hebrew letter, words whereof the initials would spell some important name, wire-drawn inferences, astounding allusions, ingenuity such as men waste now upon the number of a beast and the measurement of a pyramid, these were the doctrine of the scribes.

And an acute observer would remark that the authority of Christ's teaching was peculiar in a farther-reaching sense. If, as seems clear, Jesus said, "Ye have heard that it hath been said" (not "by," but) "to them of old time, but I say unto you," He then claimed the place, not of Moses who heard the Divine Voice, but of Him Who spoke. Even if this could be doubted, the same spirit is elsewhere unmistakable. The tables which Moses brought were inscribed by the finger of Another: none could make him the Supreme arbitrator while overhead the trumpet waxed louder and louder, while the fiery pillar marshalled their journeying, while the mysterious Presence consecrated the mysterious shrine. Prophet after prophet opened and closed his message with the words, "Thus saith the Lord." . . . "For the mouth of the Lord hath spoken it." Jesus was content with the attestation, "Verily, I say unto you." Blessed as a wise builder was the hearer and doer of "these words of Mine." Everywhere in His teaching the centre of authority is personal. He distinctly recognises the fact that He is adding to the range of the ancient law of respect for human life, and for purity, veracity, and kindness. But He assigns no authority for these additions beyond His own. Persecution by all men is a blessed thing to endure, if it be for His sake and the gospel's. Now this is unique. Moses or Isaiah never dreamed that devotion to himself took rank with devotion to his message. Nor did St. Paul. But Christ opens His ministry with the same pretensions as at the close, when others may not be called Rabbi, nor Master, because these titles belong to Him.

And the lapse of ages renders this "authority" of Christ more wonderful than at first. The world bows down before something other than His clearness of logic or subtlety of inference. He still announces where others argue, He reveals, imposes on us His supremacy, bids us take His yoke and learn. And we still discover in His teaching a freshness and profundity, a universal reach of application and yet an unearthliness of aspect, which suit so unparalleled a claim. Others have constructed cisterns in which to store truth, or aqueducts to convey it from higher levels. Christ is Himself a fountain; and not only so, but the water which He gives, when received aright, becomes in the faithful heart a well of water springing up in new, inexhaustible developments.

MIRACLES.

MARK i. 23 (R. V.).

We have just read that Christ's teaching astonished the hearers. He was about to astonish them yet more, for we have now reached the first miracle which St. Mark records. With what sentiments should such a narrative be approached? The evangelist connects it emphatically with Christ's assertion of authority. Immediately upon the impression which His manner of teaching produced, straightway, there was in the synagogue a man with an unclean spirit. And upon its expulsion, what most impressed the people was that as He taught with authority, so "with authority He commandeth even the unclean spirits, and they obey Him."

Let us try whether this may not be a providential clue to guide us amid the embarrassments which beset, in our day, the whole subject of miracles.

A miracle, we are told, is an interference with the laws of nature; and it is impossible, because they are fixed and their operation is uniform. But these bold words need not disconcert any one who has learned to ask, In what sense are the operations of nature uniform? Is the operation of the laws which govern the wind uniform, whether my helm is to port or starboard? Can I not modify the operation of sanitary laws by deodorisation, by drainage, by a thousand resources of civilisation? The truth is, that while natural laws remain fixed, human intelligence profoundly modifies their operation. How then will the objector prove that no higher Being can as naturally do the same? He answers, Because the sum total of the forces of nature is a fixed quantity: nothing can be added to that sum, nothing taken from it: the energy of all our machinery existed ages ago in the heat of tropical suns, then in vegetation, and ever since, though latent, in our coal beds; and the claim to add anything to that total is subversive of modern science. But again we ask, If the physician adds nothing to the sum of forces when he banishes one disease by inoculation, and another by draining a marsh, why must Jesus have added to the sum of forces in order to expel a demon or to cool a fever? It will not suffice to answer, because His methods are contrary to experience. Beyond experience they are. But so were the marvels of electricity to our parents and of steam to theirs. The chemistry which analyses the stars is not incredible, although thirty years ago its methods were "contrary" to the universal experience of humanity. Man is now doing what he never did before, because he is a more skilful and better informed agent than he ever was. Perhaps at this moment, in the laboratory of some unknown student, some new force is preparing to amaze the world. But the sum of the forces of nature will remain unchanged. Why is it assumed that a miracle must change them? Simply because men have already denied God, or at least denied that He is present within His world, as truly as the chemist is within it. If we think of Him as interrupting its processes from without, laying upon the vast machine so powerful a grasp as to arrest its working, then indeed the sum of forces is disturbed, and the complaints of science are justified. This may, or it may not, have been the case in creative epochs, of which science knows no more than of the beginning of life and of consciousness. But it has nothing to say against the doctrine of the miracles of Jesus. For this doctrine assumes that God is ever present in His universe; that by Him all things consist; that He is not far from any one of us, for in Him we live and move and have our being, although men may be as unconscious of Him as of gravitation and electricity. When these became known to man, the stability of law was unaffected. And it is a wild assumption that if a supreme and vital force exist, a living God, He cannot make His energies visible without affecting the stability of law.

Now Christ Himself appeals expressly and repeatedly to this immanent presence of God as the explanation of His "works."

"My Father worketh hitherto, and I work." "The Father loveth the Son, and showeth Him all things that Himself doeth." "I, by the finger of God, cast out devils."

Thus a miracle, even in the Old Testament, is not an interruption of law by God, but a manifestation of God who is within nature always; to common events it is as the lightning to the cloud, a revelation of the electricity which was already there. God was made known, when invoked by His agents, in signs from heaven, in fire and tempest, in drought and pestilence, a God who judgeth. These are the miracles of God interposing for His people against their foes. But the miracles of Christ are those of God carrying forward to the uttermost His presence in the world, God manifest in the flesh. They are the works of Him in Whom dwelleth all the fulness of the Godhead bodily.

And this explains what would otherwise be so perplexing, the essentially different nature of His miracles from those of the Old Testament. Infidelity pretends that those are the models on which myth or legend formed the miracles of Jesus, but the plain answer is that they are built on no model of the kind. The difference is so great as to be startling.

Tremendous convulsions and visitations of wrath are now unknown, because God is now reconciling the world unto Himself, and exhibiting in miracles the presence of Him Who is not far from every one of us, His presence in love to redeem the common life of man, and to bless, by sharing it. Therefore His gifts are homely, they deal with average life and its necessities; bread and wine and fish are more to the purpose than that man should eat angels' food, the rescue of storm-tossed fishermen than the engulfment of pursuing armies, the healing of prevalent disease than the plaguing of Egypt or the destruction of Sennacherib.

Such a Presence thus manifested is the consistent doctrine of the Church. It is a theory which men may reject at their own peril, if they please. But they must not pretend to refute it by any appeal to either the uniformity of law or the stability of force.

Men tell us that the divinity of Jesus was an after-thought; what shall we say then to this fact, that men observed from the very first a difference between the manner of His miracles and all that was recorded in their Scriptures, or that they could have deemed fit? It is exactly the same peculiarity, carried to the highest pitch, as they already felt in His discourses. They are wrought without any reference whatever to a superior will. Moses cried unto the Lord, saying, What shall I do? Elijah said, Hear me, O Lord, hear me. But Jesus said I will . . . . I charge thee come out . . . I am able to do this. And so marked is the change, that even His followers cast out devils in His name, and say not, Where is the Lord God of Israel? but, In the Name of Jesus Christ of Nazareth. His power is inherent, it is self-possessed, and His acts in the synoptics are only explained by His words in St. John, "What things soever the Father doeth, these the Son also doeth in like manner." No wonder that St. Mark adds to his very first record of a miracle, that the people were amazed, and asked, What is this? a new teaching! with authority He commandeth even the unclean spirits and they do obey Him! It was divinity which, without recognising, they felt, implicit in His bearing. No wonder also that His enemies strove hard to make Him say, Who gave Thee this authority? Nor could they succeed in drawing from Him any sign from heaven. The centre and source of the supernatural, for human apprehension, has shifted itself, and the vision of Jesus is the vision of the Father also.

THE DEMONIAC.

MARK i. 23-28 (R. V.).

We have seen that belief in the stability of natural law does not forbid us to believe in miracles.

Special objections are urged, however, against the belief in demoniacal possession. The very existence of demons is declared to be inconsistent with the omnipotence of God, or else with His goodness.

And it may be granted that abstract reasoning in an ideal world, though moving in a vacuum, would scarcely evolve a state of things so far removed from the ideal. This, however, is an argument against the existence, not of demons, but of evil in any shape. It is the familiar insoluble problem of all religions, How can evil exist in the universe of God? And it is balanced by the insoluble problem of all irreligious systems: In a universe without God, how can either good or evil exist, as distinguished from the advantageous and the unprofitable? Whence comes the unquestionable difference between a lie and a bad bargain?

But the argument against evil spirits professes to be something more than a disguised reproduction of this abstract problem. What more is it? What is gained by denying the fiends, as long as we cannot deny the fiends incarnate —the men who take pleasure in unrighteousness, in the seduction and ruin of their fellows, in the infliction of torture and outrage, in the ravage and desolation of nations? Such freedom has been granted to the human will, for even these ghastly issues have not been judged so deadly as coercion and moral fatalism. What presumption can possibly remain against the existence of other beings than men, who have fallen yet farther? If, indeed, it be certainly so much farther. For we know that men have lived, not outcasts from society, but boastful sons of Abraham, who willed to perform the lusts (τὰς ἐπιθυμίας) of their father the devil. Now since we are not told that the wickedness of demons is infinite,* but only that it is abysmal, and since we know that abysses of wickedness do actually exist, what sort of vindication of Deity is this which will believe that such gulfs are yawning only in the bosoms of men?

It alarms and shocks us to think that evil spirits have power over the human mind, and still more that such power should extend, as in cases of possession, even to the body. Evil men, however, manifestly wield such power. "They got rid of the wicked one," says Goethe, "but they could not get rid of the wicked ones." Social and intellectual charm, high rank, the mysterious attraction of strong individuality, all are employed at times to mislead and debase the shuddering, reluctant, mesmerised wills of weaker men and women. And then the mind acts upon the body, as perhaps it always does. Drunkenness and debauchery shake the nerves. Paralysis and lunacy tread hard on the footsteps of excess. Experience knows no reason for denying that when wickedness conquers the soul it will also deal hardly with the body.

But we must not stop here. For the Gospels do not countenance the popular notion that special wickedness was the cause of the fearful wretchedness of the possessed. Young children suffered. Jesus often cautioned a sufferer to sin no more lest worse results should follow than those He had removed; but He is never known to have addressed this warning to demoniacs. They suffered from the tyranny of Satan rather than from his seduction; and the analogies which make credible so frightful an outrage upon human nature, are the wrongs done by despots and mobs, by invading armies and persecuting religionists. Yet people who cannot believe that a demon could throw a child upon the fire are not incredulous of Attila, Napoleon, and the Inquisition.

Thus it appears that such a narrative need startle no believer in God, and in moral good and evil, who considers the unquestionable facts of life. And how often will the observant Christian be startled at the wild insurrection and surging up of evil thought and dark suggestions, which he cannot believe to be his own, which will not be gainsaid nor repulsed. How easily do such experiences fall in with the plain words of Scripture, by which the veil is drawn aside, and the mystery of the spiritual world laid bare. Then we learn that man is not only fallen but assaulted, not only feeble but enslaved, not only a wandering sheep but led captive by the devil at his will.

We turn to the narrative before us. They are still wondering at our Lord's authoritative manner, when "straightway," for opportunities were countless until unbelief arose, a man with an unclean spirit attracts attention. We can only conjecture the special meaning of this description. A recent commentator assumes that "like the rest, he had his dwelling among the tombs: an overpowering influence had driven him away from the haunts of men" (Canon Luckock, *in loco*). To others this feature in the wretchedness of the Gadarene may perhaps seem rather to be exceptional, the last touch in the appalling picture of his misery. It may be that nothing more outrageous than morbid gloom or sullen mutterings had hitherto made it necessary to exclude this sufferer from the synagogue. Or the language may suggest that he rushed abruptly in, driven by the frantic hostility of the fiend, or impelled by some mysterious and lingering hope, as the demoniac of Gadara ran to Christ.

What we know is that the sacred Presence provoked a crisis. There is an unbelief which never can be silent, never wearies railing at the faith, and there is a corruption which resents goodness and hates it as a personal wrong. So the demons who possessed men were never able to confront Jesus calmly. They resent His interference; they cry out; they disclaim having anything to do with Him; they seem indignant that He should come to destroy them who have destroyed so many. There is something weird and unearthly in the complaint. But men are also wont to forget their wrong doing when they come to suffer, and it is recorded that even Nero had abundance of compassion for himself. Weird also and terrible is it, that this unclean spirit should choose for his confession that pure and exquisite epithet, the Holy One of God. The phrase only recurs in the words of St. Peter, "We have believed and know that Thou art the Holy One of God" (John vi. 69, R. V.). Was it not a mournful association of ideas which then led Jesus to reply, "Have I not chosen you

* The opposite is asserted by the fact that one demon may ally himself with seven others worse.

the Twelve, and one of you is a devil?*" But although the phrase is beautiful, and possibly "wild with all regret," there is no relenting, no better desire than to be "let alone." And so Jesus, so gentle with sinful men, yet sometime to be their judge also, is stern and cold. "Hold thy peace—be muzzled," He answers, as to a wild beast, "and come out of him." Whereupon the evil spirit exhibits at once his ferocity and his defeat. Tearing and screaming, he came out, but we read in St. Luke that he did the man no harm.

And the spectators drew the proper inference. A new power implied a new revelation. Something far-reaching and profound might be expected from Him who commanded even the unclean spirits with authority, and was obeyed.

It is the custom of unbelievers to speak as if the air of Palestine were then surcharged with belief in the supernatural. Miracles were everywhere. Thus they would explain away the significance of the popular belief that our Lord wrought signs and wonders. But in so doing they set themselves a worse problem than they evade. If miracles were so very common, it would be as easy to believe that Jesus wrought them as that He worked at His father's bench. But also it would be as inconclusive. And how then are we to explain the astonishment which all the evangelists so constantly record? On any conceivable theory these writers shared the beliefs of that age. And so did the readers who accepted their assurance that all were amazed, and that His report "went out straightway everywhere into all the region of Gal'lee." These are emphatic words, and both the author and his readers must have considered a miracle to be more surprising than modern critics believe they did.

Yet we do not read that any one was converted by this miracle. All were amazed, but wonder is not self-surrender. They were content to let their excitement die out, as every violent emotion must, without any change of life, any permanent devotion to the new Teacher and His doctrine.

A GROUP OF MIRACLES.

Mark i. 29-34 (R. V.).

St. Matthew tells us that on leaving the synagogue they entered into Peter's house. St. Mark, with his peculiar sources of information, is aware that Andrew shared the house with his brother.

Especial interest attaches to the mention of the mother-in-law of Peter, as proving that Jesus chose a married man to be an apostle, the very apostle from whom the celibate ministry of Rome professes to have received the keys. The evidence does not stand alone. When St. Paul's apostolic authority was impugned, he insisted that he had the same right to bring with him in his travels a believing wife which Peter exercised. And Clement of Alexandria tells us that Peter's wife acted as his coadjutor, ministering to women in their own homes, by which means the gospel of Christ penetrated without scandal the privacy of women's apartments.

*The connection would be almost certain if the word "devil" were alike in both. But in all these narratives it is "demon" there being in Scripture but one devil.

Thus the notion of a Zenana mission is by no means modern.

The mother of such a wife is afflicted by fever of a kind which still haunts that district. "And they tell Him of her." Doubtless there were solicitude and hope in their voices, even if desire did not take the shape of formal prayer. We are just emerging from that early period when belief in His power to heal might still be united with some doubt whether free application might be made to Him. His disciples might still be as unwise as those modern theologians who are so busy studying the miracles as a sign that they forget to think of them as works of love. Any such hesitation was now to be dispelled for ever.

It is possible that such is the meaning of the expression, and if so, it has a useful lesson. Sometimes there are temporal gifts which we scarce know whether we should pray for, so complex are our feelings, so entangled our interests with those of others, so obscure and dubious the springs which move our desire. Is it presumptuous to ask? Yet can it be right to keep anything back, in our communion with our Father?

Now there is a curious similarity between the expression "they tell Jesus of her" and that phrase which is only applied to prayer when St. Paul bids us pray for all that is in our hearts. "In nothing be anxious, but in everything by prayer and supplication with thanksgiving let your requests be made known unto God." So shall the great benediction be fulfilled: "The peace of God which passeth all understanding, shall guard your hearts and your thoughts" (Phil. iv. 6, 7). All that is unholy shall be purified, all that is unwise subdued, all that is expedient granted.

If this be indeed the force of St. Mark's phrase, Jesus felt their modest reticence to be a strong appeal, for St. Luke says "they besought Him," while St. Matthew merely writes that He saw her lying. The "Interpreter of St. Peter" is most likely to have caught the exact shade of anxiety and appeal by which her friends drew His attention, and which was indeed a prayer.

The gentle courtesy of our Lord's healings cannot be too much studied by those who would know His mind and love Him. Never does He fling a careless blessing as coarse benefactors fling their alms; we shall hereafter see how far He was from leaving fallen bread to be snatched as by a dog, even by one who would have welcomed a boon thus contemptuously given to her; and in the hour of His arrest, when He would heal the ear of a persecutor, His courtesy appeals to those who had laid hold on Him, "Suffer ye thus far." Thus He went to this woman and took her by the hand and raised her up, laying a cool touch upon her fevered palm, bestowing His strength upon her weakness, healing her as He would fain heal humanity. For at His touch the disease was banished; with His impulse her strength returned.

We do not read that she felt bound thereupon to become an obtrusive public witness to His powers: that was not her function; but in her quiet home she failed not to minister unto Him who had restored her powers. Would that all whose physical powers Jesus renews from sickness, might devote their energies to Him. Would that all for whom He has calmed the fever of earthly passion, might arise and be energetic in His cause.

Think of the wonder, the gladness and gratitude of their humble feast. But if we felt aright the sickness of our souls, and the grace which heals them, equal gratitude would fill our lives as He sups with us and we with Him.

Tidings of the two miracles have quickly gone abroad, and as the sun sets, and the restraint of the sabbath is removed, all the city gathers all the sick around His door.

Now here is a curious example of the peril of pressing too eagerly our inferences from the expressions of an evangelist. St. Mark tells us that they brought "all their sick and them that were possessed with devils. And He healed" (not all, but) "many that were sick, and cast out many devils." How easily we might distinguish between the "all" who came, and the "many" who were healed. Want of faith would explain the difference, and spiritual analogies would be found for those who remained unhealed at the feet of the good Physician. These lessons might be very edifying, but they would be out of place, for St. Matthew tells us that He healed them all.

But who can fail to contrast this universal movement, the urgent quest of bodily health, and the willingness of friends and neighbours to convey their sick to Jesus, with our indifference to the health of the soul, and our neglect to lead others to the Saviour. Disease being the cold shadow of sin, its removal was a kind of sacrament, an outward and visible sign that the Healer of souls was nigh. But the chillness of the shadow afflicts us more than the pollution of the substance, and few professing Christians lament a hot temper as sincerely as a fever.

As Jesus drove out the demons, He suffered them not to speak because they knew Him. We cannot believe that His rejection of their impure testimony was prudential only, whatever possibility there may have been of that charge of complicity which was afterwards actually brought. Any help which might have come to Him from the lips of Hell was shocking and revolting to our Lord. And this is a lesson for all religious and political partisans who stop short of doing evil themselves, but reject no advantage which the evil deeds of others may bestow. Not so cold and negative is the morality of Jesus. He regards as contamination whatever help fraud, suppressions of truth, injustice, by whomsoever wrought, can yield. He rejects them by an instinct of abhorrence, and not only because shame and dishonour have always befallen the purest cause which stooped to unholy alliances.

Jesus that day showed Himself powerful alike in the congregation, in the home, and in the streets, and over evil spirits and physical disease alike.

JESUS IN SOLITUDE.

MARK i. 35-39 (R. V.).

St. Mark is pre-eminently the historian of Christ's activities. From Him chiefly we learn to add to our thought of perfect love and gentleness that of One whom the zeal of God's house ate up. But this evangelist does not omit to tell us by what secret fountains this river of life was fed; how the active labours of Jesus were inspired in secret prayers. Too often we allow to one side of religion a development which is not excessive, but disproportionate, and we are punished when contemplation becomes nerveless, or energy burns itself away.

After feeding the five thousand, St. Mark tells us that Jesus, while the storm gathered over His disciples on the lake, went up into a mountain to pray. And St. Luke tells of a whole night of prayer before choosing His disciples, and how it was to pray that He climbed the mountain of transfiguration.

And we read of Him going into a desert place with His disciples and to Olivet, and oft-times resorting to the garden where Judas found Him, where, in the dead of night, the traitor naturally sought Him.

Prayer was the spring of all His energies, and His own saying indicated the habit of His mortal life as truly as the law of His mysterious generation: "I live by the Father."

His prayers impress nothing on us more powerfully than the reality of His manhood. He, Who possesses all things, bends His knees to crave, and His prayers are definite, no empty form, no homage without sense of need, no firing of blank cartridge without an aim. He asks that His disciples may be with Him where He is, that Simon's strength may fail not, that He may Himself be saved from a dreadful hour. "Such touches," said Godet, "do not look like an artificial apotheosis of Jesus, and they constitute a striking difference between the gospel portrait and the legendary caricature."

The entire evening had been passed in healing the diseases of the whole town; not the light and careless bestowal of a boon which cost nothing, but wrought with so much sympathy, such draining of His own vital forces, that St. Matthew found in it a fulfilment of the prophecy that He should Himself bear our sicknesses. And thus exhausted, the frame might have been forgiven for demanding some indulgence, some prolongation of repose.

But the course of our Lord's ministry was now opening up before Him, and the hindrances becoming visible. How much was to be hoped from the great impression already made; how much to be feared from the weakness of His followers, the incipient envy of priest and Pharisee, and the volatile excitability of the crowd. At such a time, to relieve His burdened heart with Divine communion was more to Jesus than repose, as, at another time, to serve Him was meat to eat. And therefore, in the still fresh morning, long before the dawn, while every earthly sight was dim but the abysses of heaven were vivid, declaring without voice, amid the silence of earth's discord, the glory and the handiwork of His Father, Jesus went into a solitary place and prayed.

What is it that makes solitude and darkness dreadful to some, and oppressive to very many?

Partly the sense of physical danger, born of helplessness and uncertainty. This He never felt, who knew that He must walk to-day and tomorrow, and on the third day be perfected. And partly it is the weight of unwelcome reflection, the searching and rebukes of memory, fears that come of guilt and inward distractions of a nature estranged from the true nature of the universe. Jesus was agitated by no inward discords, upbraided by no remorse. And He had probably no reveries; He is never recorded to soliloquise; solitude to Him was but another name for communion with God His Father; He was never alone, for God was with Him.

This retirement enabled Him to remain undisturbed until His disciples found Him, long after the crowds had besieged their dwelling. They had not yet learned how all true external life must rest upon the hidden life of devotion, and there is an accent of regret in the words, "All are seeking Thee," as if Jesus could neglect in self-culture any true opportunity for service.

The answer, noteworthy in itself, demands especial attention in these times of missions, demonstrations, Salvation Armies, and other wise and unwise attempts to gather excited crowds around the cross.

Mere sensation actually repelled Jesus. Again and again He charged men not to make Him known, in places where He would stay; while in Gadara, which He had to leave, His command to the demoniac was the reverse. Deep and real convictions are not of kin with sightseeing and the pursuit of wonders. Capernaum has now heard His message, has received its full share of physical blessing, is exalted unto heaven. Those who were looking for redemption knew the gospel, and Jesus must preach it in other towns also. Therefore, and not to be the centre of admiring multitudes, came He forth from His quiet home.

Such is the sane and tranquil action of Jesus, in face of the excitement caused by His many miracles. Now the miracles themselves, and all that depends on them, are declared to be the creation of the wildest fanaticism, either during His lifetime or developing His legend afterwards. And if so, we have here, in the action of human mind, the marvel of modern physicists, ice from a red-hot retort, absolute moderation from a dream of frenzy. And this paradox is created in the act of "explaining" the miracles. The explanation, even were it sustained by any evidence, would be as difficult as any miracle to believe.

THE LEPER.

Mark i. 40-45 (R. V.).

The disease of leprosy was peculiarly fearful to a Jew. In its stealthy beginning, its irresistible advance, the utter ruin which it wrought from the blood outward until the flesh was corroded and fell away, it was a fit type of sin, at first so trivial in its indications, but gradually usurping all the nature and corrupting it. And the terrible fact, that the children of its victims were also doomed, reminded the Israelite of the transmission of the taint of Adam.

The story of Naaman and that of Gehazi make it almost certain that the leprosy of Scripture was not contagious, for they were intimate with kings. But, apparently to complete the type, the law gave to it the artificial contagion of ceremonial uncleanness, and banished the unhappy sufferer from the dwellings of men. Thus he came to be regarded as under an especial ban, and the prophecy which announced that the illustrious Man of Sorrows would be esteemed "stricken of God," was taken to mean that He should be a leper. This banishment of the leper was indeed a remarkable exception to the humanity of the ancient law, but when his distress began to be extreme, and "the plague was turned into white," he was released from his uncleanness (Lev. xiii. 17). And this may teach us that sin is to be dreaded most while it is yet insidious; when developed it gives a sufficient warning against itself. And now such a sufferer appeals to Jesus. The incident is one of the most pathetic in the Gospel; and its graphic details, and the shining character which it reveals, make it very perplexing to moderate and thoughtful sceptics.

Those who believe that the charm of His presence was "worth all the resources of medicine," agree that Christ may have cured even leprosy, and insist that this story, as told by St. Mark, "must be genuine." Others suppose that the leper was already cured, and Jesus only urged him to fulfil the requirements of the law. And why not deny the story boldly? Why linger so longingly over the details, when credence is refused to what is plainly the mainspring of the whole, the miraculous power of Jesus? The answer is plain. Honest minds feel the touch of a great nature; the misery of the suppliant and the compassion of his Restorer are so vivid as to prove themselves; no dreamer of a myth, no process of legend-building, ever wrought after this fashion. But then, the misery and compassion being granted, the whole story is practically conceded. It only remains to ask, whether the "presence of the Saintly Man" could work a chemical change in tainted blood. For it must be insisted that the man was "full of leprosy," and not, as one suggests, already far advanced towards cure. The contrast between his running and kneeling at the very feet of Jesus, and the conduct of the ten lepers, not yet released from their exclusion, who stood afar off while they cried out (Luke xvii. 12), is sufficient evidence of this, even if the express statement of St. Luke were not decisive.

Repulsive, and until now despairing, only tolerated among men through the completeness of his plague, this man pushes through the crowd which shrinks from him, kneels in an agony of supplication, and says "If Thou wilt, Thou canst make me clean." If Thou wilt! The cruelty of man has taught him to doubt the heart, even though satisfied of the power of Jesus. In a few years, men came to assume the love, and exult in the reflection that He was "able to keep what 'was' committed to Him," "able to do exceeding abundantly above all that we ask or think." It did not occur to St. Paul that any mention of His will was needed.

Nor did Jesus Himself ask a later suppliant, "Believest thou that I am willing," but "Believest thou that I am able to do this?"

But the charm of this delightful incident is the manner in which our Lord grants the impassioned prayer. We might have expected a shudder, a natural recoil from the loathsome spectacle, and then a wonder-working word. But misery which He could relieve did not repel Jesus; it attracted Him. His impulse was to approach. He not only answered "I will,"—and deep is the will to remove all anguish in the wonderful heart of Jesus,—but He stretched forth an unshrinking hand, and touched that death in life. It is a parable of all His course, this laying of a clean hand on the sin of the world to cleanse it. At His touch, how was the morbid frame thrilled with delightful pulses of suddenly renovated health. And how was the despairing, joyless heart, incredulous of any real will to help him, soothed and healed by the pure delight of being loved.

This is the true lesson of the narrative. St. Mark treats the miraculous cure much more lightly than the tender compassion and the swift movement to relieve suffering. And He is right. The warm and generous nature revealed by this fine narrative is what, as we have seen, most impresses the doubter, and ought most to comfort the Church. For He is the same yesterday and to-day. And perhaps, if the divinity of love impressed men as much as that of power, there would be less denial of the true Godhead of our Lord.

The touch of a leper made a Jew unclean. And there is a surprising theory, that when Jesus could no more openly enter into a city, it was because the leper had disobediently published what implied His ceremonial defilement. As if our Lord were one to violate the law by stealth.

But is it very remarkable that Christ, Who was born under the law, never betrayed any anxiety about cleanness? The law of impurity was in fact an expression of human frailty. Sin spreads corruption far more easily than virtue diffuses purity. The touch of goodness fails to reproduce goodness. And the prophet Haggai has laid stress upon this contrast, that bread or pottage or wine or oil or any meat will not become holy at the touch of one who bears holy flesh in the skirt of his garment, but if one that is unclean by a dead body touch any of these, it shall be unclean (ii. 12, 13). Our hearts know full well how true to nature is the ordinance.

But Christ brought among us a virtue more contagious than our vices are, being not only a living soul, but a life-imparting Spirit. And thus He lays His hand upon this leper, upon the bier at Nain, upon the corpse of the daughter of Jairus, and as fire is kindled at the touch of fire, so instead of pollution to Him, the pureness of healthful life is imparted to the defiling and defiled.

And His followers also are to possess a religion that is vitalising, to be the light of the world, and the salt of the earth.

If we are thus to further His cause, we must not only be zealous, but obedient. Jesus strictly charged the leper not to fan the flame of an excitement which already impeded His work. But there was an invaluable service which he might render: the formal registration of his cure, the securing its official recognition by the priests, and their consent to offer the commanded sacrifices. In many a subsequent controversy, that "testimony unto them" might have been embarrassing indeed. But the leper lost his opportunity, and put them upon their guard. And as through his impulsive clamour Jesus could no more openly enter into a city, but even in desert places was beset by excited crowds, so is He deprived to-day of many a tranquil ministration and lowly service, by the zeal which despises order and quiet methods, by the undisciplined and ill-judged demonstrations of men and women whom He has blessed.

CHAPTER II.

THE SICK OF THE PALSY.

MARK ii. 1 (R. V.).

JESUS returns to Capernaum, and an eager crowd blocks even the approaches to the house where He is known to be. St. Mark, as we should expect, relates the course of events, the multitudes, the ingenious device by which a miracle is obtained, the claim which Jesus advances to yet greater authority than heretofore, and the impression produced. But St. Luke explains that there were "sitting by," having obtained the foremost places which they loved, Pharisees and doctors of the law from every village of Galilee and Judæa, and from Jerusalem itself. And this concourse, evidently preconcerted and unfriendly, explains the first murmurs of opposition recorded by St. Mark. It was the jealousy of rival teachers which so readily pronounced Him a blasphemer.

The crowds besiege the very passages, there was no room, no, not around the door, and even if one might struggle forward, four men bearing a litter might well despair. But with palsied paralysis at stake, they would not be repulsed. They gained the roof by an outer staircase, such as the fugitives from Jerusalem should hereafter use, not going through the house. Then they uncovered and broke up the roof, by which strong phrases St. Mark means that they first lifted the tiles which lay in a bed of mortar or mud, broke through this, and then tore up the poles and light rafters by which all this covering was supported. Then they lowered the sick man upon his pallet, in front of the Master as He taught.

It was an unceremonious act. However carefully performed, the audience below must have been not only disturbed but inconvenienced, and doubtless among the precise and unmerciful personages in the chief seats there was many an angry glance, many a murmur, many a conjecture of rebukes presently to be inflicted on the intruders.

But Jesus never in any circumstances rebuked for intrusion any suppliant. And now He discerned the central spiritual impulse of these men, which was not obtrusiveness nor disrespect. They believed that neither din while He preached, nor rubbish falling among His audience, nor the strange interruption of a patient and a litter intruded upon His discourse, could weigh as much with Jesus as the appeal on a sick man's face. And this was faith. These peasants may have been far enough from intellectual discernment of Christ's Personality and the scheme of salvation. They had, however, a strong and practical conviction that He would make whole their palsied friend.

Now the preaching of faith is suspected of endangering good works. But was this persuasion likely to make these men torpid? Is it not plain that all spiritual apathy comes not from overtrust, but from unbelief, either doubting that sin is present death, or else that holiness is life, and that Jesus has a gift to bestow, not in heaven, but promptly, which is better to gain than all the world? Therefore salvation is linked with faith, which earns nothing but elicits all, like the touch that evokes electricity, but which no man supposes to have made it.

Because they knew the curse of palsy, and believed in a present remedy, these men broke up the roof to come where Jesus was. They won their blessing, but not the less it was His free gift.

Jesus saw and rewarded the faith of all the group. The principle of mutual support and cooperation is the basis alike of the family, the nation, and the Church. Thus the great Apostle desired obscure and long-forgotten men and women to help together with him in their prayers. And He who visits the sins of the fathers upon the children unto the third and fourth generation, shows mercy unto many more, unto thousands, in them that love Him. What a rebuke is all this to men who think it enough that they should do no harm, and live inoffensive lives. Jesus now bestowed such a blessing as awoke strange misgivings among the bystanders. He divined the true burden of that afflicted heart, the dreary memories and worse fears which haunted that sick bed,—and how many are even now preparing such remorse and gloom for a bed of pain hereafter!—and perhaps He discerned the consciousness of some guilty origin of the disease. Certainly He saw there one whose thoughts went beyond his malady, a young soul, with hope glowing like red sparks amid the ashes of his self-reproach, that a teacher so gracious as men reported Jesus, might bring with Him a gospel indeed. We know that he felt thus, for Jesus made him of good cheer by pardon rather than by healing, and spoke of the cure itself as wrought less for his sake than as evidence.

Surely that was a great moment when the wistful gaze of eyes which disease had dimmed, met the eyes which were as a flame of fire, and knew that all its sullied past was at once comprehended and forgiven.

Jesus said to him, "Son, thy sins are forgiven thee." The term of endearment was new to his lips, and very emphatic; the same which Mary used when she found Him in the temple, the same as when He argued that even evil men give good gifts unto their children. Such a relation towards Himself He recognised in this afflicted penitent. On the other hand, the dry argumentative temper of the critics is well expressed by the short crackling unemotional utterances of their orthodoxy: "Why doth this man thus speak? He blasphemeth. Who can forgive sins but one, God." There is no zeal in it, no passion for God's honour, no spiritual insight, it is as heartless as a syllogism. And in what follows a fine contrast is implied between their perplexed orthodoxy, and Christ's profound discernment. For as He had just read the sick man's heart, so He "perceived in His spirit that they so reasoned within themselves." And He asks them the searching question, "Whether is easier to say, Thy sins be forgiven thee, or to say, Arise and walk?" Now which is really easier? It is not enough to lay all the emphasis upon "to say," as if with Jesus the ease of an utterance depended on the difficulty of testing it. There is indeed a certain irony in the question. They doubtless imagine that Jesus was evading their scrutiny by only bestowing what they could not test. To them forgiveness seemed more easily offered than a cure. To the Christian, it is less to heal disease, which is a mere consequence, than sin, which is the source of all our woes. To the power of Jesus they were alike, and connected with each other as the symptom and the true disease. In truth, all the compassion which blesses our daily life is a pledge of grace; and He Who healeth all our diseases forgiveth also all our iniquities. But since healing was the severer test in their reckoning, Jesus does not evade it. He restores the palsied man to health, that they might know that the Son of man hath authority on earth to forgive sins. So then, pardon does not lie concealed and doubtful in the councils of an unknown world. It is pronounced on earth. The Son of man, wearing our nature and touched with our infirmities, bestows it still, in the Scriptures, in the Sacraments, in the ministrations of His servants. Wherever He discerns faith, He responds with assurance of the absolution and remission of sins.

He claims to do this, as men had so lately observed that He both taught and worked miracles, "with authority." We then saw that this word expressed the direct and personal mastery with which He wrought, and which the apostles never claimed for themselves.

Therefore this text cannot be quoted in defence of priestly absolutions, as long as these are hypothetical, and depend on the recipient's earnestness, or on any supposition, any uncertainty whatever. Christ did not utter a hypothesis.

Fortunately, too, the argument that men, priestly men, must have authority on earth to forgive sins, because the Son of man has such authority, can be brought to an easy test. There is a passage elsewhere, which asserts His authority, and upon which the claim to share it can be tried. The words are, "The Father gave Him authority to execute judgment, because He is the Son of man," and they are immediately followed by an announcement of the resurrection to judgment (John v. 27, 29). Is any one prepared to contend that such authority as that is vested in other sons of men? And if not that, why this?

But if priestly absolutions are not here, there remains the certainty that Jesus brought to earth, to man, the gift of prompt effective pardon, to be realised by faith.

The sick man is ordered to depart at once. Further discourse might perhaps be reserved for others, but he may not linger, having received his own bodily and spiritual medicine. The teaching of Christ is not for curiosity. It is good for the greatly blessed to be alone. And it is sometimes dangerous for obscure people to be thrust into the centre of attraction.

Hereupon, another touch of nature discovers itself in the narrative, for it is now easy to pass through the crowd. Men who would not in their selfishness give place for palsied misery, readily make room for the distinguished person who has received a miraculous blessing.

THE SON OF MAN.

Mark ii. 10.

When asserting His power to forgive sins, Jesus, for the first time in our Gospel, called Himself the Son of man.

It is a remarkable phrase. The profound reverence which He from the first inspired restrained all other lips from using it, save only when the first martyr felt such a rush of sympathy from above poured into his soul, that the thought of Christ's humanity was more moving than that of His deity. So too it is then alone that He is said to be not enthroned in heaven, but standing, "the Son of man, standing on the right hand of God" (Acts vii. 56).*

What then does this title imply? Beyond

* The exceptions in the Revelation are only apparent. St. John does not call Jesus the Son of man (i. 13), nor see Him, but only the type of Him, standing (v. 6).

doubt it is derived from Daniel's vision: "Behold there came with the clouds of heaven one like unto a Son of man, and He came even to the Ancient of Days" (vii. 13). And it was by the bold and unequivocal appropriation of this verse that Jesus brought upon Himself the judgment of the council (Matt. xxvi. 64; Mark xiv. 62).

Now the first impression which the phrase in Daniel produces is that of strong and designed contrast between the Son of man and the Eternal God. We wonder at seeing man "brought nigh" to Deity. Nor may we suppose that to be "like unto a Son of man," implies only an appearance of manhood. In Daniel the Messiah can be cut off. When Jesus uses the epithet, and even when He quotes the prophecy, He not only resembles a Son of man, He is truly such; He is most frequently "*the* Son of man," the pre-eminent, perhaps the only one.*

But while the expression intimates a share in the lowliness of human nature, it does not imply a lowly rank among men.

Our Lord often suggested by its use the difference between His circumstances and His dignity. "The Son of man hath not where to lay His head:" "Betrayest thou the Son of man with a kiss," in each of these we feel that the title asserts a claim to different treatment. And in the great verse, God "hath given Him authority to execute judgment, because He is the Son of man," we discern that although human hands are chosen as fittest to do judgment upon humanity, yet His extraordinary dignity is also taken into account. The title belongs to our Lord's humiliation, but is far from an additional abasement; it asserts His supremacy over those whom He is not ashamed to call brethren.

We all are sons of men; and Jesus used the phrase when He promised that all manner of sins and blasphemies shall be forgiven to us. But there is a higher sense in which, among thousands of the ignoble, we single out one "real man;" and in this sense, as fulfilling the idea, Jesus was the Second Man. What a difference exists between the loftiest sons of vulgar men, and the Son of our complete humanity, of the race, "of Man." The pre-eminence even of our best and greatest is fragmentary and incomplete. In their veins runs but a portion of the rich life-blood of the race: but a share of its energy throbs in the greatest bosom. We seldom find the typical thinker in the typical man of action. Originality of purpose and of means are not commonly united. To know all that holiness embraces, we must combine the energies of one saint with the gentler graces of a second and the spiritual insight of a third. There is no man of genius who fails to make himself the child of his nation and his age, so that Shakespeare would be impossible in France, Hugo in Germany, Goethe in England. Two great nations slay their kings and surrender their liberties to military dictators, but Napoleon would have been unendurable to us, and Cromwell ridiculous across the channel.

Large allowances are to be made for the Greek in Plato, the Roman in Epictetus, before we can learn of them. Each and all are the sons of their tribe and century, not of all mankind and all time. But who will point out the Jewish warp in any word or institution of Jesus? In the new man which is after His image there cannot be Greek and Jew, circumcision and uncircumcision, barbarian, Scythian, bondman, freeman, but Christ is all and in all, something of Him represented by each, all of them concentrated in Him. He alone speaks to all men without any foreign accent, and He alone is recognised and understood as widely as the voices of nature, as the sigh of waves and breezes, and the still endurance of the stars. Reading the Gospels, we become aware that four writers of widely different bias and temperament have all found an equally congenial subject, so that each has given a portrait harmonious with the others, and yet unique. It is because the sum total of humanity is in Christ, that no single writer could have told His story.

But now consider what this implies. It demands an example from which lonely women and heroic leaders of action should alike take fire. It demands that He should furnish meditation for sages in the closet, and should found a kingdom more brilliant than those of conquerors. It demands that He should strike out new paths towards new objects, and be supremely original without deviating from what is truly sane and human, for any selfish or cruel or unwholesome joy. It demands the gentleness of a sheep before her shearers, and such burning wrath as seven times over denounced against the hypocrites of Jerusalem woe and the damnation of hell. It demands the sensibilities which made Gethsemane dreadful, and the strength which made Calvary sublime. It demands that when we approach Him we should learn to feel the awe of other worlds, the nearness of God, the sinfulness of sin, the folly of laying up much goods for many years; that life should be made solemn and profound, but yet that it should not be darkened nor depressed unduly; that nature and man should be made dear to us, little children, and sinners who are scorned yet who love much, and lepers who stand afar off—yes, and even the lilies of the field and the fowls of the air; that He should not be unaware of the silent processes of nature which bears fruit of itself, of sunshine and rain, and the fury of storms and torrents, and the leap of the lightning across all the sky. Thus we can bring to Jesus every anxiety and every hope, for He, and only He, was tempted in all points like unto us. Universality of power, of sympathy, and of influence, is the import of this title which Jesus claims. And that demand Jesus only has satisfied, Who is the Master of Sages, the Friend of sinners, the Man of Sorrows, and the King of kings, the one perfect blossom on the tree of our humanity, the ideal of our nature incarnate, the Second Adam in Whom the fulness of the race is visible. The Second Man is the Lord from Heaven. And this strange and solitary grandeur He foretold, when He took to Himself this title, itself equally strange and solitary, the Son of man.

THE CALL AND FEAST OF LEVI.

MARK ii. 13-17 (R. V.).

Jesus loved the open air. His custom when teaching was to point to the sower, the lily, and the bird. He is no pale recluse emerging from

* And this proves beyond question that He did not merely follow Ezekiel in applying to himself the epithet as if it meant a son among many sons of men, but took the description in Daniel for His own. Ezekiel himself indeed never employs the phrase: he only records it.

a library to instruct, in the dim religious light of cloisters, a world unknown except by books. Accordingly we find Him "again by the seaside." And however the scribes and Pharisees may have continued to murmur, the multitudes resorted to Him, confiding in the evidence of their experience, which never saw it on this fashion.

That argument was perfectly logical; it was an induction, yet it led them to a result curiously the reverse of theirs who reject miracles for being contrary to experience. "Yes," they said, "we appeal to experience, but the conclusion is that good deeds which it cannot parallel must come directly from the Giver of all good."

Such good deeds continue. The creed of Christ has re-formed Europe, it is awakening Asia, it has transformed morality, and imposed new virtues on the conscience. It is the one religion for the masses, the lapsed, and indeed for the sick in body as truly as in soul; for while science discourses with enthusiasm upon progress by the rejection of the less fit, our faith cherishes these in hospitals, asylums, and retreats, and prospers by lavishing care upon the outcast and rejected of the world. Now this transcends experience: we never saw it on this fashion; it is supernatural. Or else let scientific atheism produce its reformed magdalens, and its homes for the hopelessly diseased and imbecile, and all "the weakest" who go, as she tenderly assures us, "to the wall."

Jesus now gave a signal proof of His independence of human judgment, His care for the despised and rejected. For such a one He completed the rupture between Himself and the rulers of the people.

Sitting at the receipt of toll, in the act of levying from his own nation the dues of the conqueror, Levi the publican received the call to become an Apostle and Evangelist. It was a resolute defiance of the pharisaic judgment. It was a memorable rebuke for those timid slaves of expediency who nurse their influence, refuse to give offence, fear to "mar their usefulness" by "compromising themselves," and so make their whole life one abject compromise, and let all emphatic usefulness go by.

Here is one upon whom the bigot scowls more darkly still than upon Jesus Himself, by whom the Roman yoke is pressed upon Hebrew necks, an apostate in men's judgment from the national faith and hope. And such judgments sadly verify themselves; a despised man easily becomes despicable.

But however Levi came by so strange and hateful an office, Jesus saw in him no slavish earner of vile bread by doing the foreigner's hateful work. He was more willing than they who scorn him to follow the true King of Israel. It is even possible that the national humiliations to which his very office testified led him to other aspirations, longings after a spiritual kingdom beyond reach of the sword or the exactions of Rome. For his Gospel is full of the true kingdom of heaven, the spiritual fulfilments of prophecy, and the relations between the Old Testament and the Messiah.

Here then is an opportunity to show the sneering scribe and carping Pharisee how little their cynical criticism weighs with Jesus. He calls the despised agent of the heathen to His side, and is obeyed. And now the name of the publican is engraven upon one of the foundations of the city of God.

Nor did Jesus refuse to carry such condescension to its utmost limit, eating and drinking in Levi's house with many publicans and sinners, who were already attracted by His teaching, and now rejoiced in His familiarity. Just in proportion as He offended the pharisaic scribes, so did He inspire with new hope the unhappy classes who were taught to consider themselves castaway. His very presence was medicinal, a rebuke to foul words and thoughts, an outward and visible sign of grace. It brought pure air and sunshine into a fever-stricken chamber.

And this was His justification when assailed. He had borne healing to the sick. He had called sinners to repentance. And therefore His example has a double message. It rebukes those who look curiously on the intercourse of religious people with the world, who are plainly of opinion that the leaven should be hid anywhere but in the meal, who can never fairly understand St. Paul's permission to go to an idolater's feast. But it gives no license to go where we cannot be a healing influence, where the light must be kept in a dark lantern if not under a bushel, where, instead of drawing men upward, we shall only confirm their indolent self-satisfaction.

Christ's reason for seeking out the sick, the lost, is ominous indeed for the self-satisfied. The whole have no need of a physician; He came not to call the righteous. Such persons, whatever else they be, are not Christians until they come to a different mind.

In calling Himself the Physician of sick souls, Jesus made a startling claim, which becomes more emphatic when we observe that He also quoted the words of Hosea, "I will have mercy and not sacrifice" (Matt. ix. 13; Hos. vi. 6). For this expression occurs in that chapter which tells us how the Lord Himself hath smitten and will bind us up. And the complaint is just before it that when Ephraim saw his sickness and Judah saw his wound, then went Ephraim to Assyria and sent to king Jareb, but he is not able to heal you, neither shall he cure you of your wound (Hos. v. 13-vi. 1). As the Lord Himself hath torn, so He must heal.

Now Jesus comes to that part of Israel which the Pharisees despise for being wounded and diseased, and justifies Himself by words which must, from their context, have reminded every Jew of the declaration that God is the physician, and it is vain to seek healing elsewhere. And immediately afterwards, He claims to be the Bridegroom, whom also Hosea spoke of as divine. Yet men profess that only in St. John does He advance such claims that we should ask, Whom makest Thou Thyself? Let them try the experiment, then, of putting such words into the lips of any mortal.

The choice of the apostles, and most of all that of Levi, illustrates the power of the cross to elevate obscure and commonplace lives. He was born, to all appearance, to an uneventful, unobserved existence. We read no remarkable action of the Apostle Matthew; as an Evangelist he is simple, orderly, and accurate, as becomes a man of business, but the graphic energy of St. Mark, the pathos of St. Luke, the profundity of St. John are absent. Yet his greatness will outlive the world.

Now as Christ provided nobility and a career for this man of the people, so He does for all.

"Are all apostles?" Nay, but all may become pillars in the temple of eternity. The gospel finds men plunged in monotony, in the routine of callings which machinery and the subdivision of labour make ever more colourless, spiritless, and dull. It is a small thing that it introduces them to a literature more sublime than Milton, more sincere and direct than Shakespeare. It brings their little lives into relationship with eternity. It braces them for a vast struggle, watched by a great cloud of witnesses. It gives meaning and beauty to the sordid present, and to the future a hope full of immortality. It brings the Christ of God nearer to the humblest than when of old He ate and drank with publicans and sinners.

THE CONTROVERSY CONCERNING FASTING.

Mark ii. 18 (R. V.).

The Pharisees had just complained to the disciples that Jesus ate and drank in questionable company. Now they join with the followers of the ascetic Baptist in complaining to Jesus that His disciples eat and drink at improper seasons, when others fast. And as Jesus had then replied, that being a Physician, He was naturally found among the sick, so He now answered, that being the Bridegroom, fasting in His presence is impossible: "Can the sons of the bridechamber fast while the Bridegroom is with them?" A new spirit is working in Christianity, far too mightily to be restrained by ancient usages; if the new wine be put into such wineskins it will spoil them, and itself be lost.

Hereupon three remarkable subjects call for attention: the immense personal claim advanced; the view which Christ takes of fasting; and, arising out of this, the principle which He applies to all external rites and ceremonies.

I. Jesus does not inquire whether the fasts of other men were unreasonable or not. In any case, He declares that His mere presence put everything on a new footing for His followers who could not fast simply because He was by. Thus He assumes a function high above that of any prophet or teacher: He not only reveals duty as a lamp casts light upon the compass by which men steer; but He modifies duty itself, as iron deflects the needle.

This is because He is the Bridegroom.

The disciples of John would hereupon recall his words of self-effacement; that he was only the friend of the Bridegroom, whose fullest joy was to hear the Bridegroom's exultant voice.

But no Jew could forget the Old Testament use of the phrase. It is clear from St. Matthew that this controversy followed immediately upon the last, when Jesus assumed a function ascribed to God Himself by the very passage from Hosea which He then quoted. Then He was the Physician for the soul's diseases; now He is the Bridegroom, in Whom centre its hopes, its joys, its affections, its new life. That position in the spiritual existence cannot be given away from God without idolatry. The same Hosea who makes God the Healer, gives to Him also, in the most explicit words, what Jesus now claims for Himself. "I will betroth thee unto Me for ever . . . I will even betroth thee unto Me in faithfulness, and thou shalt know the Lord" (ii. 19, 20). Isaiah too declares "thy Maker is thy husband," and "as the bridegroom rejoiceth over the bride, so shall thy God rejoice over thee" (liv. 5; lxii. 5). And in Jeremiah, God remembers the love of Israel's espousals, who went after Him in the wilderness, in a land that was not sown (ii. 2). Now all this is transferred throughout the New Testament to Jesus. The Baptist is not alone in this respect. St. John regards the Bride as the wife of the Lamb (Rev. xxi. 9). St. Paul would fain present his Corinthian Church as a pure virgin to Christ, as to one husband (2 Cor. xi. 2). For him, the absolute oneness of marriage is a mystery of the union betwixt Christ and His Church (Eph. v. 32). If Jesus be not God, then a relation hitherto exclusively belonging to Jehovah, to rob Him of which is the adultery of the soul, has been systematically transferred by the New Testament to a creature. His glory has been given to another.

This remarkable change is clearly the work of Jesus Himself. The marriage supper of which He spoke is for the King's Son. At His return the cry will be heard, Behold the Bridegroom cometh. In this earliest passage His presence causes the joy of the Bride, who said to the Lord in the Old Testament, Thou art my Husband (Hosea ii. 16).

There is not to be found in the Gospel of St. John a passage more certainly calculated to inspire, when Christ's dignity was assured by His resurrection and ascension, the adoration which His Church has always paid to the Lamb in the midst of the throne.

II. The presence of the Bridegroom dispenses with the obligation to fast. Yet it is beyond denial that fasting as a religious exercise comes within the circle of New Testament sanctions. Jesus Himself, when taking our burdens upon Him, as He had stooped to the baptism of repentance, condescended also to fast. He taught His disciples when they fasted to anoint their head and wash their face. The mention of fasting is indeed a later addition to the words "this kind (of demon) goeth not out but by prayer" (Mark ix. 29), but we know that the prophets and teachers of Antioch were fasting when bidden to consecrate Barnabas and Saul, and they fasted again and prayed before they laid their hands upon them (Acts xiii. 2, 3).

Thus it is right to fast, at times and from one point of view; but at other times, and from Jewish and formal motives, it is unnatural and mischievous. It is right when the Bridegroom is taken away, a phrase which certainly does not cover all this space between the Ascension and the Second Advent, since Jesus still reveals Himself to His own though not unto the world, and is with His Church all the days. Scripture has no countenance for the notion that we lost by the Ascension in privilege or joy. But when the body would fain rise up against the spirit, it must be kept under and brought into subjection (1 Cor. ix. 27). When the closest domestic joys would interrupt the seclusion of the soul with God, they may be suspended, though but for a time (1 Cor. vii. 5). And when the supreme blessing of intercourse with God, the presence of the Bridegroom, is obscured or forfeited through sin, it will then be as inevitable that the loyal heart should turn away from worldly pleasures, as that the first disciples should reject these in the dread hours of their bereavement.

Thus Jesus abolished the superstition that grace may be had by a mechanical observance of a prescribed regimen at an appointed time. He did not deny, but rather implied the truth, that body and soul act and counteract, so that spiritual impressions may be weakened and forfeited by untimely indulgence of the flesh.

By such teaching Jesus carried forward the doctrine already known to the Old Testament. There it was distinctly announced that the return from exile abrogated those fasts which commemorated national calamities, so that "the fast of the fourth month, and of the fifth, and of the seventh and of the tenth shall be to the houses of Israel joy and gladness, cheerful feasts" (Zech. vii. 3, viii. 19). Even while these fasts had lasted they had been futile, because they were only formal. "When ye fasted and mourned, did ye at all fast unto me? And when ye eat, and when ye drink, do ye not eat for yourselves, and drink for yourselves?" (Zech. vii. 5, 6). And Isaiah had plainly laid down the great rule, that a fast and an acceptable day unto the Lord was not a day to afflict the soul and bow the head, but to deny and discipline our selfishness for some good end, to loose the bonds of wickedness, to undo the bands of the yoke, and to let the oppressed go free, to deal bread to the hungry, and to bring home the poor that is cast out (Isa. lviii. 5-7).

The true spirit of fasting breathes an ampler breath in any of the thousand forms of Christian self-denial, than in those petty abstinences, those microscopic observances, which move our wonder less by the superstition which expects them to bring grace than by the childishness which expects them to have any effect whatever.

III. Jesus now applies a great principle to all external rites and ceremonies. They have their value. As the wineskin retains the wine, so are feelings and aspirations aided, and even preserved, by suitable external forms. Without these, emotion would lose itself for want of restraint, wasted, like spirit wine, by diffuseness. And if the forms are unsuitable and outworn, the same calamity happens, the strong new feelings break through them, "and the wine perisheth, and the skins." In this respect, how many a sad experience of the Church attests the wisdom of her Lord; what losses have been suffered in the struggle between forms that had stiffened into archaic ceremonialism and new zeal demanding scope for its energy, between the antiquated phrases of a bygone age and the new experience, knowledge, and requirements of the next, between the frosty precisions of unsympathetic age and the innocent warmth and freshness of the young, too often, alas, lost to their Master in passionate revolt against restraints which He neither imposed nor smiled upon.

Therefore the coming of a new revelation meant the repeal of old observances, and Christ refused to sew His new faith like a patchwork upon ancient institutions, of which it would only complete the ruin. Thus He anticipated the decision of His apostles releasing the Gentiles from the law of Moses. And He bestowed on His Church an adaptiveness to various times and places, not always remembered by missionaries among the heathen, by fastidious critics of new movements at home, nor by men who would reduce the lawfulness of modern agencies to a question of precedent and archæology.

THE SABBATH.

MARK ii. 23-28 (R. V.).

Twice in succession Christ had now asserted the freedom of the soul against His Jewish antagonists. He was free to eat with sinners, for their good, and His followers were free to disregard fasts, because the Bridegroom was with them. A third attack in the same series is prepared. The Pharisees now take stronger ground, since the law itself enforced the obligation of the Sabbath. Even Isaiah, the most free-spirited of all the prophets, in the same passage where he denounced the fasts of the self-righteous, bade men to keep their foot from the Sabbath (Isa. lviii. 13, 14). Here they felt sure of their position; and when they found the disciples, in a cornfield where the long stems had closed over the path, "making a way," which was surely forbidden labour, and this by "plucking the ears," which was reaping, and then rubbing these in their hands to reject the chaff, which was winnowing, they cried out in affected horror, Behold, why do they that which is not lawful? To them it mattered nothing that the disciples really hungered, and that abstinence, rather than the slight exertion which they condemned, would cause real inconvenience and unrest.

Perhaps the answer of our Lord has been as much misunderstood as any other words He ever spoke. It has been assumed that He spoke across the boundary between the new dispensation and the old, as One from whose movements the restraints of Judaism had entirely fallen away, to those who were still entangled. And it has been inferred that the Fourth Commandment was no more than such a restraint, now thrown off among the rest. But this is quite a misapprehension both of His position and theirs. On earth He was a minister of the circumcision. He bade His disciples to observe and do all that was commanded from the seat of Moses. And it is by Old Testament precedent, and from Old Testament principles, that He now refutes the objection of the Pharisees. This is what gives the passage half its charm, this discovery of freedom like our own in the heart of the stern old Hebrew discipline, as a fountain and flowers on the face of a granite crag, this demonstration that all we now enjoy is developed from what already lay in germ enfolded in the law.

David and his followers, when at extremity, had eaten the showbread which it was not lawful for them to eat. It is a striking assertion. We should probably have sought a softer phrase. We should have said that in other circumstances it would have been unlawful, that only necessity made it lawful; we should have refused to look straight in the face the naked ugly fact that David broke the law. But Jesus was not afraid of any fact. He saw and declared that the priests in the Temple itself profaned the Sabbath when they baked the showbread and when they circumcised children. They were blameless, not because the Fourth Commandment remained inviolate, but because circumstances made it right for them to profane the Sabbath. And His disciples were blameless also, upon the same principle, that the larger obligation overruled the lesser, that all ceremonial observance gave way to human need, that mercy is a better thing than sacrifice.

And thus it appeared that the objectors were themselves the transgressors; they had condemned the guiltless.

A little reflection will show that our Lord's bold method, His startling admission that David and the priests alike did that which was not lawful, is much more truly reverential than our soft modern compromises, our shifty devices for persuading ourselves that in various permissible and even necessary deviations from prescribed observances, there is no real infraction of any law whatever.

To do this, we reduce to a minimum the demands of the precept. We train ourselves to think, not of its full extension, but of what we can compress it into. Therefore, in future, even when no urgency exists, the precept has lost all beyond this minimum; its sharp edges are filed away. Jesus leaves it to resume all its energy, when mercy no longer forbids the sacrifice.

The text, then, says nothing about the abolition of a Day of Rest. On the contrary, it declares that this day is not a Jewish, but a universal ordinance, it is made for man. At the same time, it refuses to place the Sabbath among the essential and inflexible laws of right and wrong. It is made for man, for his physical repose and spiritual culture; man was not made for it, as he is for purity, truth, and godliness. Better for him to die than outrage these; they are the laws of his very being; he is royal by serving them; in obeying them he obeys his God. It is not thus with anything external, ceremonial, any ritual, any rule of conduct, however universal be its range, however permanent its sanctions. The Sabbath is such a rule, permanent, far-reaching as humanity, made "for man." But this very fact, Jesus tells us, is the reason why He Who represented the race and its interests, was "Lord even of the Sabbath."

Let those who deny the Divine authority of this great institution ponder well the phrase which asserts its universal range, and which finds it a large assertion of the mastery of Christ that He is Lord "even of the Sabbath." But those who have scruples about the change of day by which honour is paid to Christ's resurrection, and those who would make burdensome and dreary, a horror to the young and a torpor to the old, what should be called a delight and honourable, these should remember that the ordinance is blighted, root and branch, when it is forbidden to minister to the physical or spiritual welfare of the human race.

CHAPTER III.

THE WITHERED HAND.

Mark iii. 1-6 (R. V.).

In the controversies just recorded we have recognised the ideal Teacher, clear to discern and quick to exhibit the decisive point at issue, careless of small pedantries, armed with principles and precedents which go to the heart of the dispute.

But the perfect man must be competent in more than theory; and we have now a marvellous example of tact, decision, and self-control in action. When Sabbath observance is again discussed, his enemies have resolved to push matters to extremity. They watch, no longer to cavil, but that they may accuse Him. It is in the synagogue; and their expectations are sharpened by the presence of a pitiable object, a man whose hand is not only paralysed in the sinews, but withered up and hopeless. St. Luke tells us that it was the right hand, which deepened his misery. And St. Matthew records that they asked Christ, Is it lawful to heal on the Sabbath day? thus urging Him by a challenge to the deed which they condemned. What a miserable state of mind! They believe that Jesus can work the cure, since this is the very basis of their plot; and yet their hostility is not shaken, for belief in a miracle is not conversion; to acknowledge a prodigy is one thing, and to surrender the will is quite another. Or how should we see around us so many Christians in theory, reprobates in life? They long to see the man healed, yet there is no compassion in this desire, hatred urges them to wish what mercy impels Christ to grant. But while He relieves the sufferer He will also expose their malice. Therefore He makes His intention public, and whets their expectation, by calling the man forth into the midst. And then He meets their question with another: Is it lawful to do good on the Sabbath day or evil, to save life or to kill? And when they preserved their calculated silence, we know how He pressed the question home, reminding them that not one of them would fail to draw his own sheep out of a pit upon the Sabbath day. Selfishness made the difference, for a man was better than a sheep, but did not, like the sheep, belong to them. They do not answer: instead of warning Him away from guilt, they eagerly await the incriminating act: we can almost see the spiteful subtle smile playing about their bloodless lips; and Jesus marks them well. He looked round about them in anger, but not in bitter personal resentment, for He was grieved at the hardness of their hearts, and pitied them also, even while enduring such contradiction of sinners against Himself. This is the first mention by St. Mark of that impressive gaze, afterwards so frequent in every Gospel, which searched the scribe who answered well, and melted the heart of Peter.

And now, by one brief utterance, their prey breaks through their meshes. Any touch would have been a work, a formal infraction of the law. Therefore there is no touch, neither is the helpless man bidden to take up any burden, or instigated to the slightest ritual irregularity. Jesus only bids him do what was forbidden to none, but what had been impossible for him to perform; and the man succeeds, he does stretch forth his hand: he is healed: the work is done. Yet nothing has been done; as a work of healing not even a word has been said. For He who would so often defy their malice had chosen to show once how easily He can evade it, and not one of them is more free from any blame, however technical, than He. The Pharisees are so utterly baffled, so helpless in His hands, so "filled with madness" that they invoke against this new foe the help of their natural enemies, the Herodians. These appear on the stage because the immense spread of the Messianic movement endangers the Idumæan dynasty. When first the wise men sought an infant King of the Jews, the Herod of that day was troubled. That instinct which struck at His cradle is now re-awakened, and will not slumber again until the fatal day when the new Herod shall set Him at nought and mock Him. In the meanwhile these strange allies perplex themselves with the hard question, How is it possible to destroy so acute a foe?

While observing their malice, and the exquisite skill which baffles it, we must not lose sight of other lessons. It is to be observed that no offence to hypocrites, no danger to Himself, prevented Jesus from removing human suffering. And also that He expects from the man a certain co-operation involving faith: he must stand forth in the midst; every one must see his unhappiness; he is to assume a position which will become ridiculous unless a miracle is wrought. Then he must make an effort. In the act of stretching forth his hand the strength to fetch it forth is given; but he would not have tried the experiment unless he trusted before he discovered the power. Such is the faith demanded of our sin-stricken and helpless souls; a faith which confesses its wretchedness, believes in the good will of God and the promises of Christ, and receives the experience of blessing through having acted on the belief that already the blessing is a fact in the Divine volition.

Nor may we overlook the mysterious impalpable spiritual power which effects its purposes without a touch, or even an explicit word of healing import. What is it but the power of Him Who spake and it was done, Who commanded and it stood fast?

And all this vividness of look and bearing, this innocent subtlety of device combined with a boldness which stung His foes to madness, all this richness and verisimilitude of detail, this truth to the character of Jesus, this spiritual freedom from the trammels of a system petrified and grown rigid, this observance in a secular act of the requirements of the spiritual kingdom, all this wealth of internal evidence goes to attest one of the minor miracles which sceptics declare to be incredible.

THE CHOICE OF THE TWELVE.

Mark iii. 7-19 (R. V.).

We have reached a crisis in the labours of the Lord, when hatred which has become deadly is preparing a blow. The Pharisees are aware, by a series of experiences, that His method is destructive to their system, that He is too fearless to make terms with them, that He will strip the mask off their faces. Their rage was presently intensified by an immense extension of His fame. And therefore He withdrew from the plots which ripen most easily in cities, the hotbeds of intrigue, to the open coast. It is His first retreat before opposition, and careful readers of the Gospels must observe that whenever the pressure of His enemies became extreme, He turned for safety to the simple fishermen, among whom they had no party, since they had preached no gospel to the poor, and that He was frequently conveyed by water from point to point, easily reached by followers, who sometimes indeed outran Him upon foot, but where treason had to begin its wiles afresh. Hither, perhaps camping along the beach, came a great multitude not only from Galilee but also from Judæa, and even from the capital, the headquarters of the priesthood, and by a journey of several days from Idumæa, and from Tyre and Sidon, so that afterwards, even there, He could not be hid. Many came to see what great things He did, but others bore with them some afflicted friend, or were themselves sore stricken by disease. And Jesus gave like a God, opening His hand and satisfying their desires, "for power went out of Him, and healed them all." Not yet had the unbelief of man restrained the compassion of His heart, and forced Him to exhibit another phase of the mind of God, by refusing to give that which is holy to the dogs. As yet, therefore, He healeth all their diseases. Then arose an unbecoming and irreverent rush of as many as had plagues to touch Him. A more subtle danger mingled itself with this peril from undue eagerness. For unclean spirits, who knew His mysterious personality, observed that this was still a secret, and was no part of His teaching, since His disciples could not bear it yet. Many months afterwards, flesh and blood had not revealed it even to Peter. And therefore the demons made malicious haste to proclaim Him the Son of God, and Jesus was obliged to charge them much that they should not make Him known. This action of His may teach His followers to be discreet. Falsehood indeed is always evil, but at times reticence is a duty, because certain truths are a medicine too powerful for some stages of spiritual disease. The strong sun which ripens the grain in autumn, would burn up the tender germs of spring.

But it was necessary to teach as well as to heal. And Jesus showed His ready practical ingenuity, by arranging that a little boat should wait on Him, and furnish at once a pulpit and a retreat.

And now Jesus took action distinctly Messianic. The harvest of souls was plenteous, but the appointed labourers were unfaithful, and a new organisation was to take their place. The sacraments and the apostolate are indeed the only two institutions bestowed upon His Church by Christ Himself; but the latter is enough to show that, so early in His course, He saw His way to a revolution. He appointed twelve apostles, in clear allusion to the tribes of a new Israel, a spiritual circumcision, another peculiar people. A new Jerusalem should arise, with their names engraven upon its twelve foundation stones. But since all great changes arrive, not by manufacture but by growth, and in co-operation with existing circumstances, since nations and constitutions are not made but evolved, so was it also with the Church of Christ. The first distinct and formal announcement of a new sheepfold, entered by a new and living Way, only came when evoked by the action of His enemies in casting out the man who was born blind. By that time, the apostles were almost ready to take their place in it. They had learned much. They had watched the marvellous career to which their testimony should be rendered. By exercise they had learned the reality, and by failure the condition of the miraculous powers which they should transmit. But long before, at the period we have now reached, the apostles had been chosen under pressure of the necessity to meet the hostility of the Pharisees with a counter-agency, and to spread the knowledge of His power and doctrine farther than One Teacher, however endowed, could reach. They were to be workers together with Him.

St. Mark tells us that He went up into the

mountain, the well-known hill of the neighbourhood, as St. Luke also implies, and there called unto Him whom He Himself would. The emphasis refutes a curious conjecture, that Judas may have been urged upon Him with such importunity by the rest that to reject became a worse evil than to receive him.* The choice was all His own, and in their early enthusiasm not one whom He summoned refused the call. Out of these He chose the Twelve, elect of the election.

We learn from St. Luke (v. 12) that His choice, fraught with such momentous issues, was made after a whole night of prayer, and from St. Matthew that He also commanded the whole body of His disciples to pray the Lord of the Harvest, not that they themselves should be chosen, but that He would send forth labourers into His harvest.

Now who were these by whose agency the downward course of humanity was reversed, and the traditions of a Divine faith were poured into a new mould?

It must not be forgotten that their ranks were afterwards recruited from the purest Hebrew blood and ripest culture of the time. The addition of Saul of Tarsus proved that knowledge and position were no more proscribed than indispensable. Yet is it in the last degree suggestive, that Jesus drew His personal followers from classes, not indeed oppressed by want, but lowly, unwarped by the prejudices of the time, living in close contact with nature and with unsophisticated men, speaking and thinking the words and thoughts of the race and not of its coteries, and face to face with the great primitive wants and sorrows over which artificial refinement spreads a thin, but often a baffling veil.

With one exception the Nazarene called Galileans to His ministry; and the Carpenter was followed by a group of fishermen, by a despised publican, by a zealot whose love of Israel had betrayed him into wild and lawless theories at least, perhaps into evil deeds, and by several whose previous life and subsequent labours are unknown to earthly fame. Such are the Judges enthroned over the twelve tribes of Israel.

A mere comparison of the lists refutes the notion that any one Evangelist has worked up the materials of another, so diverse are they, and yet so easily reconciled. Matthew in one is Levi in another. Thaddeus, Jude, and Lebbæus, are interchangeable. The order of the Twelve differs in all the four lists, and yet there are such agreements, even in this respect, as to prove that all the Evangelists were writing about what they understood. Divide the Twelve into three ranks of four, and in none of the four catalogues will any name, or its equivalent, be found to have wandered out of its subdivision, out of the first, second, or third rank, in which doubtless that apostle habitually followed Jesus. Within each rank there is the utmost diversity of place, except that the foremost name in each is never varied; Peter, Philip, and the Lesser James, hold the first, fifth, and ninth place in every catalogue. And the traitor is always last. These are coincidences too slight for design and too striking for accident, they are the natural signs of truth. For they indicate, without obtruding or explaining, some arrangement of the ranks, and some leadership of an individual in each.

Moreover, the group of the apostles presents a wonderfully lifelike aspect. Fear, ambition, rivalry, perplexity, silence when speech is called for, and speech when silence is befitting, vows, failures, and yet real loyalty, alas! we know them all. The incidents which are recorded of the chosen of Christ no inventor of the second century would have dared to devise; and as we study them, we feel the touch of genuine life; not of colossal statues such as repose beneath the dome of St. Peter's, but of men, genuine, simple and even somewhat childlike, yet full of strong, fresh, unsophisticated feeling, fit therefore to become a great power, and especially so in the capacity of witnesses for an ennobling yet controverted fact.

* Lange, "Life of Christ," ii. p. 179.

CHARACTERISTICS OF THE TWELVE.

MARK iii. 14-19 (R. V.).

THE pictures of the Twelve, then, are drawn from a living group. And when they are examined in detail, this appearance of vitality is strengthened, by the richest and most vivid indications of individual character, such indeed as in several cases to throw light upon the choice of Jesus. To invent such touches is the last attainment of dramatic genius, and the artist rarely succeeds except by deliberate and palpable character-painting. The whole story of Hamlet and of Lear is constructed with this end in view, but no one has ever conjectured that the Gospels were psychological studies. If, then, we can discover several well-defined characters, harmoniously drawn by various writers, as natural as the central figure is supernatural, and to be recognised equally in the common and miraculous narratives, this will be an evidence of the utmost value.

We are all familiar with the impetuous vigour of St. Peter, a quality which betrayed him into grave and well-nigh fatal errors, but when chastened by suffering made him a noble and formidable leader of the Twelve. We recognise it when He says, "Thou shalt never wash my feet," "Though all men should deny Thee, yet will I never deny Thee," "Lord, to whom should we go? Thou hast the words of everlasting life." "Thou art the Christ, the Son of the living God," and in his rebuke of Jesus for self-sacrifice, and in his rash blow in the garden. Does this, the best-established mental quality of any apostle, fail or grow faint in the miraculous stories which are condemned as the accretions of a later time? In such stories he is related to have cried out, "Depart from Me, for I am a sinful man, O Lord," he would walk upon the sea to Jesus, he proposed to shelter Moses and Elijah from the night air in booths (a notion so natural to a bewildered man, so exquisite in its officious well-meaning absurdity as to prove itself, for who could have invented it?), he ventured into the empty sepulchre while John stood awe-stricken at the portal, he plunged into the lake to seek his risen Master on the shore, and he was presently the first to draw the net to land. Observe the restless curiosity which beckoned to John to ask who was the traitor, and compare it with his question, "Lord, and what shall this man do?" But the second of these was after the resurrection, and in answer to a prophecy. Everywhere we find a real person and the same, and the vehemence is everywhere that of a warm heart, which could fail signally but could weep bitterly as well, which could learn not to claim, though twice invited, greater love than that of others, but when asked "Lovest thou Me" at all, broke out into the passionate appeal, "Lord, Thou knowest all things, Thou knowest that I love Thee." Dull is the ear of the critic which fails to recognise here the voice of Simon. Yet the story implies the resurrection.

The mind of Jesus was too lofty and grave for epigram; but He put the wilful self-reliance which Peter had to subdue even to crucifixion, into one delicate and subtle phrase: "When thou was young, thou girdedst thyself, and walkedst whither thou wouldest." That self-willed stride, with the loins girded, is the natural gait of Peter, when he was young.

St. James, the first apostolic martyr, seems to have over-topped for a while his greater brother St. John, before whom he is usually named, and who is once distinguished as "the brother of James." He shares with him the title of a Son of Thunder (Mark iii. 17). They were together in desiring to rival the fiery and avenging miracle of Elijah, and to partake of the profound baptism and bitter cup of Christ. It is an undesigned coincidence in character, that while the latter of these events is recorded by St. Matthew and St. Mark, the former, which, it will be observed, implies perfect confidence in the supernatural power of Christ, is found in St. Luke alone, who has not mentioned the title it justifies so curiously (Matt. xx. 20; Mark x. 35; Luke ix. 54). It is more remarkable that he whom Christ bade to share his distinctive title with another, should not once be named as having acted or spoken by himself. With a fire like that of Peter, but no such power of initiative and of chieftainship, how natural it is that his appointed task was martyrdom. Is it objected that his brother also, the great apostle St. John, received only a share in that divided title? But the family trait is quite as palpable in him. The deeds of John were seldom wrought upon his own responsibility, never if we except the bringing of Peter into the palace of the high priest. He is a keen observer and a deep thinker. But he cannot, like his Master, combine the quality of leader with those of student and sage. In company with Andrew he found the Messiah. We have seen James leading him for a time. It was in obedience to a sign from Peter that He asked who was the traitor. With Peter, when Jesus was arrested, he followed afar off. It is very characteristic that he shrank from entering the sepulchre until Peter, coming up behind, went in first, although it was John who thereupon "saw and believed." *

With like discernment, he was the first to recognise Jesus beside the lake, but then it was equally natural that he should tell Peter, and follow in the ship, dragging the net to land, as that Peter should gird himself and plunge into the lake. Peter, when Jesus drew him aside, turned and saw the disciple whom Jesus loved following, with the same silent, gentle, and sociable affection, which had so recently joined him with the saddest and tenderest of all companions underneath the cross. At this point there is a delicate and suggestive turn of phrase. By what incident would any pen except his own have chosen to describe the beloved disciple as Peter then beheld him? Assuredly we should have written, The disciple whom Jesus loved, who also followed Him to Calvary, and to whom he confided His mother. But from St. John himself there would have been a trace of boastfulness in such a phrase. Now the author of the Fourth Gospel, choosing rather to speak of privilege than service, wrote "The disciple whom Jesus loved, which also leaned back on His breast at the supper, and said, Lord, who is he that betrayeth Thee?"

St. John was again with St. Peter at the Beautiful Gate, and although it was not he who healed the cripple, yet his co-operation is implied in the words, "Peter, fastening his eyes on him, *with John*." And when the Council would fain have silenced them, the boldness which spoke in Peter's reply was "the boldness of Peter and John."

Could any series of events justify more perfectly a title which implied much zeal, yet zeal that did not demand a specific unshared epithet? But these events are interwoven with the miraculous narratives.

Add to this the keenness and deliberation which so much of his story exhibits, which at the beginning tendered no hasty homage, but followed Jesus to examine and to learn, which saw the meaning of the orderly arrangement of the graveclothes in the empty tomb, which was first to recognise the Lord upon the beach, which before this had felt something in Christ's regard for the least and weakest, inconsistent with the forbidding of any one to cast out devils, and we have the very qualities required to supplement those of Peter, without being discordant or uncongenial. And therefore it is with Peter, even more than with his brother, that we have seen John associated. In fact Christ, who sent out His apostles by two and two, joins these in such small matters as the tracking a man with a pitcher into the house where He would keep the Passover. And so, when Mary of Magdala would announce the resurrection, she found the penitent Simon in company with this loving John, comforted, and ready to seek the tomb where he met the Lord of all Pardons.

All this is not only coherent, and full of vital force, but it also strengthens powerfully the evidence for his authorship of the Gospel, written the last, looking deepest into sacred mysteries, and comparatively unconcerned for the mere flow of narrative, but tender with private and loving discourse, with thoughts of the protecting Shepherd, the sustaining Vine, the Friend Who wept by a grave, Who loved John, Who provided amid tortures for His mother, Who knew that Peter loved Him, and bade him feed the lambs—and yet thunderous as becomes a Boanerges, with indignation half suppressed against "the Jews" (so called as if he had renounced his murderous nation), against the selfish high-priest of "that same year," and against the son of perdition, for whom certain astute worldlings have surmised that his wrath was such as they best understand, personal, and perhaps a little spiteful. The temperament of John, revealed throughout, was that of August, brooding and warm and hushed and fruitful, with low rumblings of tempest in the night.

It is remarkable that such another family resemblance as between James and John exists be-

* It is also very natural that, in telling the story, he should remember how, while hesitating to enter, he "stooped down" to gaze, in the wild dawn of his new hope.

tween Peter and Andrew. The directness and self-reliance of his greater brother may be discovered in the few incidents recorded of Andrew also. At the beginning, and after one interview with Jesus, when he finds his brother, and becomes the first of the Twelve to spread the gospel, he utters the short unhesitating announcement, "We have found the Messiah." When Philip is uncertain about introducing the Greeks who would see Jesus, he consults Andrew, and there is no more hesitation, Andrew and Philip tell Jesus. And in just the same way, when Philip argues that two hundred pennyworth of bread are not enough for the multitude, Andrew intervenes with practical information about the five barley loaves and the two small fishes, insufficient although they seem. A man prompt and ready, and not blind to the resources that exist because they appear scanty.

Twice we have found Philip mentioned in conjunction with him. It was Philip, apparently accosted by the Greeks because of his Gentile name, who could not take upon himself the responsibility of telling Jesus of their wish. And it was he, when consulted about the feeding of the five thousand, who went off into a calculation of the price of the food required—two hundred pennyworth, he says, would not suffice. Is it not highly consistent with this slow deliberation, that he should have accosted Nathanael with a statement so measured and explicit: "We have found Him, of whom Moses in the law, and the prophets did write, Jesus of Nazareth, the Son of Joseph." What a contrast to Andrew's terse announcement, "We have found the Messiah." And how natural that Philip should answer the objection, "Can any good thing come out of Nazareth?" with the passionless reasonable invitation, "Come and see." It was in the same unimaginative prosaic way that he said long after, "Lord, show us the Father, and it sufficeth us." To this comparatively sluggish temperament, therefore, Jesus Himself had to address the first demand He made on any. "Follow me," He said, and was obeyed. It would not be easy to compress into such brief and incidental notices a more graphic indication of character.

Of the others we know little except the names. The choice of Matthew, the man of business, is chiefly explained by the nature of his Gospel, so explicit, orderly, and methodical, and until it approaches the crucifixion, so devoid of fire.

But when we come to Thomas, we are once more aware of a defined and vivid personality, somewhat perplexed and melancholy, of little hope but settled loyalty.

All the three sayings reported of him belong to a dejected temperament: "Let us also go, that we may die with Him"—as if there could be no brighter meaning than death in Christ's proposal to interrupt a dead man's sleep. "Lord, we know not whither Thou goest, and how can we know the way?"—these words express exactly the same despondent failure to apprehend. And so it comes to pass that nothing short of tangible experience will convince him of the resurrection. And yet there is a warm and devoted heart to be recognised in the proposal to share Christ's death, in the yearning to know whither He went, and even in that agony of unbelief, which dwelt upon the cruel details of suffering, until it gave way to one glad cry of recognition and of worship; therefore his demand was granted, although a richer blessing was reserved for those who, not having seen, believed.

THE APOSTLE JUDAS.

MARK iii. 19.

The evidential value of what has been written about the apostles will, to some minds, seem to be overborne by the difficulties which start up at the name of Judas. And yet the fact that Jesus chose him—that awful fact which has offended many—is in harmony with all that we see around us, with the prodigious powers bestowed upon Napoleon and Voltaire, bestowed in full knowledge of the dark results, yet given because the issues of human freewill never cancel the trusts imposed on human responsibility. Therefore the issues of the freewill of Judas did not cancel the trust imposed upon his responsibility; and Jesus acted not on His foreknowledge of the future, but on the mighty possibilities, for good as for evil, which heaved in the bosom of the fated man as he stood upon the mountain sward.

In the story of Judas, the principles which rule the world are made visible. From Adam to this day men have been trusted who failed and fell, and out of their very downfall, but not by precipitating it, the plans of God have evolved themselves.

It is not possible to make such a study of the character of Judas as of some others of the Twelve. A traitor is naturally taciturn. No word of his draws our attention to the fact that he had gained possession of the bag, even though one who had sat at the receipt of custom might more naturally have become the treasurer. We do not hear his voice above the rest, until St. John explains the source of the general discontent, which remonstrated against the waste of ointment. He is silent even at the feast, in despite of the words which revealed his guilty secret, until a slow and tardy question is wrung from him, not, "Is it I, Lord?" but "Rabbi, is it I?" His influence is like that of a subtle poison, not discerned until its effects betray it.

But many words of Jesus acquire new force and energy when we observe that, whatever their drift beside, they were plainly calculated to influence and warn Iscariot. Such are the repeated and urgent warnings against covetousness, from the first parable, spoken so shortly after his vocation, which reckons the deceitfulness of riches and the lust of other things among the tares that choke the seed, down to the declaration that they who trust in riches shall hardly enter the kingdom. Such are the denunciations against hypocrisy, spoken openly, as in the Sermon on the Mount, or to His own apart, as when He warned them of the leaven of the Pharisees which is hypocrisy, that secret vice which was eating out the soul of one among them. Such were the opportunities given to retreat without utter dishonour, as when He said, "Do ye also will to go away? . . . Did I not choose you the Twelve, and one of you is a devil?" (John vi. 67, 70). And such also were the awful warnings given of the solemn responsibilities of special privileges. The exalted city which is brought down to hell, the salt which is trodden under foot, the men whose sin remained because they can claim to see, and still more plainly, the first that shall be last, and the man for whom it were good that he had not been born. In many besides the last of these, Judas must have felt himself sternly because faithfully dealt with. And the exasperation which always results from rejected warnings, the sense of a presence utterly repugnant to his nature, may have largely contributed to his final and disastrous collapse.

In the life of Judas there was a mysterious impersonation of all the tendencies of godless Judaism, and his dreadful personality seems to express the whole movement of the nation which rejected Christ. We see this in the powerful attraction felt toward Messiah before His aims were understood, in the deadly estrangement and hostility which were kindled by the gentle and self-effacing ways of Jesus, in the treachery of Judas in the garden and the unscrupulous wiliness of the priests accusing Christ before the governor, in the fierce intensity of rage which turned his hands against himself and which destroyed the nation under Titus. Nay, the very sordidness which made a bargain for thirty pieces of silver has ever since been a part of the popular conception of the race. We are apt to think of a gross love of money as inconsistent with intense passion, but in Shylock, the compatriot of Judas, Shakespeare combines the two.

Contemplating this blighted and sinister career, the lesson is burnt in upon the conscience, that since Judas by transgression fell, no place in the Church of Christ can render any man secure. And since, falling, he was openly exposed, none may flatter himself that the cause of Christ is bound up with his reputation, that the mischief must needs be averted which his downfall would entail, that Providence must needs avert from him the natural penalties of evil-doing. Though one was as the signet upon the Lord's hand, yet was he plucked thence. There is no security for any soul anywhere except where love and trust repose, upon the bosom of Christ.

Now if this be true, and if sin and scandal may conceivably penetrate even the inmost circle of the chosen, how great an error is it to break, because of these offences, the unity of the Church, and institute some new communion, purer far than the Churches of Corinth and Galatia, which were not abandoned but reformed, and more impenetrable to corruption than the little group of those who ate and drank with Jesus.

CHRIST AND BEELZEBUB.

MARK iii. 20-27 (R. V.).

While Christ was upon the mountain with His more immediate followers, the excitement in the plain did not exhaust itself; for even when He entered into a house, the crowds prevented Him and His followers from taking necessary food. And when His friends heard of this, they judged Him as men who profess to have learned the lesson of His life still judge, too often, all whose devotion carries them beyond the boundaries of convention and of convenience. For there is a curious betrayal of the popular estimate of this world and the world to come, in the honour paid to those who cast away life in battle, or sap it slowly in pursuit of wealth or honours, and the contempt expressed for those who compromise it on behalf of souls for which Christ died. Whenever by exertion in any unselfish cause health is broken, or fortune impaired, or influential friends estranged, the follower of Christ is called an enthusiast, a fanatic, or even more plainly a man of unsettled mind. He may be comforted by remembering that Jesus was said to be beside Himself when teaching and healing left Him not leisure even to eat.

To this incessant and exhausting strain upon His energies and sympathies, St. Matthew applies the prophetic words, "Himself took our infirmities and bare our diseases" (viii. 17). And it is worth while to compare with that passage and the one before us, Renan's assertion, that He traversed Galilee "in the midst of a perpetual fête," and that "joyous Galilee celebrated in fêtes the approach of the well-beloved." ("Vie de J.," pp. 197, 202). The contrast gives a fine illustration of the inaccurate shallowness of the Frenchman's whole conception of the sacred life.

But it is remarkable that while His friends could not yet believe His claims, and even strove to lay hold on Him, no worse suspicion ever darkened the mind of those who knew Him best than that His reason had been disturbed. Not these called Him gluttonous and a winebibber. Not these blasphemed His motives. But the envoys of the priestly faction, partisans from Jerusalem, were ready with an atrocious suggestion. He was Himself possessed with a worse devil, before whom the lesser ones retired. By the prince of the devils He cast out the devils. To this desperate evasion, St. Matthew tells us, they were driven by a remarkable miracle, the expulsion of a blind and dumb spirit, and the perfect healing of his victim. Now the literature of the world cannot produce invective more terrible than Jesus had at His command for these very scribes and Pharisees, hypocrites. This is what gives majesty to His endurance. No personal insult, no resentment at His own wrong, could ruffle the sublime composure which, upon occasion, gave way to a moral indignation equally sublime. Calmly He calls His traducers to look Him in the face, and appeals to their own reason against their blasphemy. Neither kingdom nor house divided against itself can stand. And if Satan be divided against himself and his evil works, undoing the miseries and opening the eyes of men, his kingdom has an end. All the experience of the world since the beginning was proof enough that such a suicide of evil was beyond hope. The best refutation of the notion that Satan had risen up against himself and was divided was its clear expression. But what was the alternative? If Satan were not committing suicide, he was overpowered. There is indeed a fitful temporary reformation, followed by a deeper fall, which St. Matthew tells us that Christ compared to the cleansing of a house from whence the evil tenant has capriciously wandered forth, confident that it is still his own, and prepared to return to it with seven other and worse fiends. A little observation would detect such illusory improvement. But the case before them was that of an external summons reluctantly obeyed. It required the interference of a stronger power, which could only be the power of God. None could enter into the strong man's house, and spoil his goods, unless the strong man were first bound, "and then he will spoil his house." No more distinct assertion of the personality of evil spirits than this could be devised. Jesus and the Pharisees are not at all at issue upon this point. He does not scout as a baseless superstition their belief that evil spirits are at work in the world. But He declares that His own work is the reversal of theirs. He is spoiling the strong man, whose terrible ascendancy over the possessed resembles the dominion of a man in his own house, among chattels without a will.

That dominion Christ declares that only a stronger can overcome, and His argument assumes that the stronger must needs be the finger of God, the power of God, come unto them. The supernatural exists only above us and below.

Ages have passed away since then. Innumerable schemes have been devised for the expulsion of the evils under which the world is groaning, and if they are evils of merely human origin, human power should suffice for their removal. The march of civilisation is sometimes appealed to. But what blessings has civilisation without Christ ever borne to savage men? The answer is painful: rum, gunpowder, slavery, massacre, small-pox, pulmonary consumption, and the extinction of their races, these are all it has been able to bestow. Education is sometimes spoken of, as if it would gradually heal our passions and expel vice and misery from the world, as if the worst crimes and most flagrant vices of our time were peculiar to the ignorant and the untaught, as if no forger had ever learned to write. And sometimes great things are promised from the advance of science, as if all the works of dynamite and nitro-glycerine, were, like those of the Creator, very good.

No man can be deceived by such flattering hopes, who rightly considers the volcanic energies, the frantic rage, the unreasoning all-sacrificing recklessness of human passions and desires. Surely they are set on fire of hell, and only heaven can quench the conflagration. Jesus has undertaken to do this. His religion has been a spell of power among the degraded and the lost; and when we come to consider mankind in bulk, it is plain enough that no other power has had a really reclaiming, elevating effect upon tribes and races. In our own land, what great or lasting work of reformation, or even of temporal benevolence, has ever gone forward without the blessing of religion to sustain it? Nowhere is Satan cast out but by the Stronger than he, binding him, overmastering the evil principle which tramples human nature down, as the very first step towards spoiling his goods. The spiritual victory must precede the removal of misery, convulsion, and disease. There is no golden age for the world, except the reign of Christ.

"*ETERNAL SIN.*"

MARK iii. 28, 29 (R. V.).

Having first shown that His works cannot be ascribed to Satan, Jesus proceeds to utter the most terrible of warnings, because they said, He hath an unclean spirit.

"All their sins shall be forgiven unto the sons of men, and their blasphemies wherewith soever they shall blaspheme, but whosoever shall blaspheme against the Holy Spirit hath never forgiveness, but is guilty of an eternal sin."

What is the nature of this terrible offence? It is plain that their slanderous attack lay in the direction of it, since they needed warning; and probable that they had not yet fallen into the abyss, because they could still be warned against it. At least, if the guilt of some had reached that depth, there must have been others involved in their offence who were still within reach of Christ's solemn admonition. It would seem therefore that in saying, "He casteth out devils by Beelzebub . . . He hath an unclean spirit," they approached the confines and doubtful boundaries between that blasphemy against the Son of man which shall be forgiven, and the blasphemy against the Holy Spirit which hath never forgiveness.

It is evident also that any crime declared by Scripture elsewhere to be incurable, must be identical with this, however different its guise, since Jesus plainly and indisputably announces that all other sins but this shall be forgiven.

Now there are several other passages of the kind. St. John bade his disciples to pray, when any saw a brother sinning a sin not unto death, "and God will give him life for them that sin not unto death. There is a sin unto death: not concerning this do I say that he should make request" (1 John v. 16). It is idle to suppose that, in the case of this sin unto death, the Apostle only meant to leave his disciples free to pray or not to pray. If death were not certain, it would be their duty, in common charity, to pray. But the sin is so vaguely and even mysteriously referred to, that we learn little more from that passage than that it was an overt public act, of which other men could so distinctly judge the flagrancy that from it they should withhold their prayers. It has nothing in common with those unhappy wanderings of thought or affection which morbid introspection broods upon, until it pleads guilty to the unpardonable sin, for lapses of which no other could take cognizance. And in Christ's words, the very epithet, blasphemy, involves the same public, open revolt against good.* And let it be remembered that every other sin shall be forgiven.

There are also two solemn passages in the Epistle to the Hebrews (vi. 4-6; x. 26-31). The first of these declares that it is impossible for men who once experienced all the enlightening and sweet influences of God, "and then fell away," to be renewed again unto repentance. But falling upon the road is very different from thus falling away, or how could Peter have been recovered? Their fall is total apostasy, "they crucify to themselves the Son of God afresh, and put Him to an open shame." They are not fruitful land in which tares are mingled; they bear only thorns and thistles, and are utterly rejected. And so in the tenth chapter, they who sin wilfully are men who tread under foot the Son of God, and count the blood of the covenant an unholy thing, and do despite (insult) unto the Spirit of grace.

Again we read that in the last time there will arise an enemy of God so unparalleled that his movement will outstrip all others, and be "*the* falling away," and he himself will be "the man of sin" and "the son of perdition," which latter title he only shares with Iscariot. Now the essence of his portentous guilt is that "he opposeth

* "Theology would have been spared much trouble concerning this passage, and anxious timid souls unspeakable anguish, if men had adhered strictly to Christ's own expression. For it is not *a sin* against the Holy Ghost which is here spoken of, but *blasphemy* against the Holy Ghost."—Lange, "Life of Christ," vol. ii. p. 269.

and exalteth himself against all that is called God or that is worshipped": it is a monstrous egotism, "setting himself forth as God," and such a hatred of restraint as makes him "the lawless one" (2 Thess. ii. 3-10).

So far as these passages are at all definite in their descriptions, they are entirely harmonious. They describe no sin of the flesh, of impulse, frailty, or passion, nor yet a spiritual lapse of an unguarded hour, of rash speculation, of erring or misled opinion. They speak not of sincere failure to accept Christ's doctrine or to recognise His commission, even though it breathe out threats and slaughters. They do not even apply to the dreadful sin of denying Christ in terror, though one should curse and swear, saying, I know not the man. They speak of a deliberate and conscious rejection of good and choice of evil, of the wilful aversion of the soul from sacred influences, the public denial and trampling under foot of Christ, the opposing of all that is called God.

And a comparison of these passages enables us to understand why this sin never can be pardoned. It is because good itself has become the food and fuel of its wickedness, stirring up its opposition, calling out its rage, that the apostate cannot be renewed again unto repentance. The sin is rather indomitable than unpardonable: it has become part of the sinner's personality; it is incurable, an eternal sin.

Here is nothing to alarm any mourner whose contrition proves that it has actually been possible to renew him unto repentance. No penitent has ever yet been rejected for this guilt, for no penitent has ever been thus guilty.

And this being so, here is the strongest possible encouragement for all who desire mercy. Every other sin, every other blasphemy shall be forgiven. Heaven does not reject the vilest whom the world hisses at, the most desperate and bloodstained whose life the world exacts in vengeance for his outrages. None is lost but the hard and impenitent heart which treasures up for itself wrath against the day of wrath.

THE FRIENDS OF JESUS.

MARK iii. 31-35 (R. V.).

We have lately read that the relatives of Jesus, hearing of His self-sacrificing devotion, sought to lay hold on Him, because they said, He is beside Himself. Their concern would not be lightened upon hearing of His rupture with the chiefs of their religion and their nation. And so it was, that while a multitude hung upon His lips, some unsympathising critic, or perhaps some hostile scribe, interrupted Him with their message. They desired to speak with Him, possibly with rude intentions, while in any case, to grant their wish might easily have led to a painful altercation, offending weak disciples, and furnishing a scandal to His eager foes.

Their interference must have caused the Lord a bitter pang. It was sad that they were not among His hearers, but worse that they should seek to mar His work. To Jesus, endowed with every innocent human instinct, worn with labour and aware of gathering perils, they were an offence of the same kind as Peter made himself when he became the mouthpiece of the tempter. For their own sakes, whose faith He was yet to win, it was needful to be very firm. Moreover, He was soon to make it a law of the kingdom that men should be ready for His sake to leave brethren, or sisters, or mother, and in so doing should receive back all these a hundredfold in the present time (x. 29, 30). To this law it was now His own duty to conform. Yet it was impossible for Jesus to be harsh and stern to a group of relatives with His mother in the midst of them; and it would be a hard problem for the finest dramatic genius to reconcile the conflicting claims of the emergency, fidelity to God and the cause, a striking rebuke to the officious interference of His kinsfolk, and a full and affectionate recognition of the relationship which could not make Him swerve. How shall He "leave" His mother and his brethren, and yet not deny His heart? How shall He be strong without being harsh?

Jesus reconciles all the conditions of the problem, as pointing to His attentive hearers, He pronounces these to be His true relatives, but yet finds no warmer term to express what He feels for them than the dear names of mother, sisters, brethren.

Observers whose souls were not warmed as He spoke may have supposed that it was cold indifference to the calls of nature which allowed His mother and brethren to stand without. In truth, it was not that He denied the claims of the flesh, but that He was sensitive to other, subtler, profounder claims of the spirit and spiritual kinship. He would not carelessly wound a mother's or a brother's heart, but the life Divine had also its fellowships and its affinities, and still less could He throw these aside. No cold sense of duty detains Him with His congregation while affection seeks Him in the vestibule; no, it is a burning love, the love of a brother or even of a son, which binds Him to His people.

Happy are they who are in such a case. And Jesus gives us a ready means of knowing whether we are among those whom He so wonderfully condescends to love. "Whosoever shall do the will of My Father which is in heaven." Feelings may ebb, and self-confidence may be shaken, but obedience depends not upon excitement, and may be rendered by a breaking heart.

It is important to observe that this saying declares that obedience does not earn kinship; but only proves it, as the fruit proves the tree. Kinship must go before acceptable service; none can do the will of the Father who is not already the kinsman of Jesus, for He says, Whosoever shall (*hereafter*) do the will of My Father, the same is (*already*) My brother and sister and mother. There are men who would fain reverse the process, and do God's will in order to merit the brotherhood of Jesus. They would drill themselves and win battles for Him, in order to be enrolled among His soldiers. They would accept the gospel invitation as soon as they refute the gospel warnings that without Him they can do nothing, and that they need the creation of a new heart and the renewal of a right spirit within them. But when homage was offered to Jesus as a Divine teacher and no more, He rejoined, Teaching is not what is required: holiness does not result from mere enlightenment: Verily, verily, I say unto thee, except a man be born again, he cannot see the kingdom of God. Because the new birth is the condition of all spiritual power and energy, it follows that if any man shall henceforth do God's will, he must already be of the family of Christ.

Men may avoid evil through self-respect, from early training and restraints of conscience, from temporal prudence or dread of the future. And this is virtuous only as the paying of a fire-insurance is so. But secondary motives will never lift any man so high as to satisfy this sublime standard, the doing of the will of the Father. That can only be attained, like all true and glorious service in every cause, by the heart, by enthusiasm, by love. And Jesus was bound to all who loved His Father by as strong a cord as united His perfect heart with brother and sister and mother.

But as there is no true obedience without relationship, so is there no true relationship unfollowed by obedience. Christ was not content to say, Whoso doeth God's will is My kinsman: He asked, Who is My kinsman? and gave this as an exhaustive reply. He has none other. Every sheep in His fold hears His voice and follows Him. We may feel keen emotions as we listen to passionate declamations, or kneel in an excited prayer-meeting, or bear our part in an imposing ritual; we may be moved to tears by thinking of the dupes of whatever heterodoxy we most condemn; tender and soft emotions may be stirred in our bosom by the story of the perfect life and Divine death of Jesus; and yet we may be as far from a renewed heart as was that ancient tyrant from genuine compassion, who wept over the brevity of the lives of the soldiers whom he sent into a wanton war.

Mere feeling is not life. It moves truly; but only as a balloon moves, rising by virtue of its emptiness, driven about by every blast that veers, and sinking when its inflation is at an end. But mark the living creature poised on widespread wings; it has a will, an intention, and an initiative, and as long as its life is healthy and unenslaved, it moves at its own good pleasure. How shall I know whether or not I am a true kinsman of the Lord? By seeing whether I advance, whether I work, whether I have real and practical zeal and love, or whether I have grown cold, and make more allowance for the flesh than I used to do, and expect less from the spirit. Obedience does not produce grace. But it proves it, for we can no more bear fruit except we abide in Christ, than the branch that does not abide in the vine.

Lastly, we observe the individual love, the personal affection of Christ for each of His people. There is a love for masses of men and philanthropic causes, which does not much observe the men who compose the masses, and upon whom the causes depend. Thus, one may love his country, and rejoice when her flag advances, without much care for any soldier who has been shot down, or has won promotion. And so we think of Africa or India, without really feeling much about the individual Egyptian or Hindoo. Who can discriminate and feel for each one of the multitudes included in such a word as Want, or Sickness, or Heathenism? And judging by our own frailty, we are led to think that Christ's love can mean but little beyond this. As a statesman who loves the nation may be said, in some vague way, to love and care for me, so people think of Christ as loving and pitying us because we are items in the race He loves. But He has eyes and a heart, not only for all, but for each one. Looking down the shadowy vista of the generations, every sigh, every broken heart, every blasphemy, is a separate pang to His all-embracing heart. "Before that Philip called thee, when thou wast under the fig-tree, I saw *thee*," lonely, unconscious, undistinguished drop in the tide of life, one leaf among the myriads which rustle and fall in the vast forest of existence. St. Paul speaks truly of Christ "Who loved me, and gave Himself for me." He shall bring every secret sin to judgment, and shall we so far wrong Him as to think His justice more searching, more penetrating, more individualising than His love, His memory than His heart? It is not so. The love He offers adapts itself to every age and sex: it distinguishes brother from sister, and sister again from mother. It is mindful of "the least of these My brethren." But it names no Father except One.

CHAPTER IV.

THE PARABLES.

MARK iv. 1, 2, 10-13 (R. V.).

As opposition deepened, and to a vulgar ambition the temptation to retain disciples by all means would have become greater, Jesus began to teach in parables. We know that He had not hitherto done so, both by the surprise of the Twelve, and by the necessity which He found, of giving them a clue to the meaning of such teachings, and so to "all the parables." His own ought to have understood. But He was merciful to the weakness which confessed its failure and asked for instruction.

And yet He foresaw that they which were without would discern no spiritual meaning in such discourse. It was to have, at the same time, a revealing and a baffling effect, and therefore it was peculiarly suitable for the purposes of a Teacher watched by vindictive foes. Thus, when cross-examined about His authority by men who themselves professed to know not whence John's baptism was, He could refuse to be entrapped, and yet tell of One Who sent His own Son, His Beloved, to receive the fruit of the vineyard.

This diverse effect is derived from the very nature of the parables of Jesus. They are not, like some in the Old Testament, mere fables, in which things occur that never happen in real life. Jotham's trees seeking a king are as incredible as Æsop's fox leaping for grapes. But Jesus never uttered a parable which was not true to nature, the kind of thing which one expects to happen. We cannot say that a rich man in hell actually spoke to Abraham in heaven. But if he could do so, of which we are not competent to judge, we can well believe that he would have spoken just what we read, and that his pathetic cry, "Father Abraham," would have been as gently answered, "Son, remember." There is no ferocity in the skies; neither has the lost soul become a fiend. Everything commends itself to our judgment. And therefore the story not only illustrates, but appeals, enforces, almost proves.

God in nature does not arrange that all seeds should grow: men have patience while the germ slowly fructifies, they know not how; in all things but religion such sacrifices are made, that the merchant sells all to buy one goodly pearl; an earthly father kisses his repentant prodigal; and even a Samaritan can be neighbour to a Jew in his extremity. So the world is constructed: such is even the fallen human heart. Is it not reasonable to believe that the same principles will extend farther; that as God governs the world of matter so He may govern the world of spirits, and that human helpfulness and clemency will not outrun the graces of the Giver of all good?

This is the famous argument from analogy, applied long before the time of Butler, to purposes farther-reaching than his. But there is this remarkable difference, that the analogy is never pressed, men are left to discover it for themselves, or at least, to ask for an explanation, because they are conscious of something beyond the tale, something spiritual, something which they fain would understand.

Now this difference is not a mannerism; it is intended. Butler pressed home his analogies because he was striving to silence gainsayers. His Lord and ours left men to discern or to be blind, because they had already opportunity to become His disciples if they would. The faithful among them ought to be conscious, or at least they should now become conscious, of the God of grace in the God of nature. To them the world should be eloquent of the Father's mind. They should indeed find tongues in trees, books in the running brooks, sermons in stones. He spoke to the sensitive mind, which would understand Him, as a wife reads her husband's joys and sorrows by signs no stranger can understand. Even if she fails to comprehend, she knows there is something to ask about. And thus, when they were alone, the Twelve asked Him of the parables. When they were instructed, they gained not only the moral lesson, and the sweet pastoral narrative, the idyllic picture which conveyed it, but also the assurance imparted by recognising the same mind of God which is revealed in His world, or justified by the best impulses of humanity. Therefore, no parable is sensational. It cannot root itself in the exceptional, the abnormal events on which men do not reckon, which come upon us with a shock. For we do not argue from these to daily life.

But while this mode of teaching was profitable to His disciples, and protected Him against His foes, it had formidable consequences for the frivolous empty followers after a sign. Because they were such they could only find frivolity and lightness in these stories; the deeper meaning lay farther below the surface than such eyes could pierce. Thus the light they had abused was taken from them. And Jesus explained to His disciples that, in acting thus, He pursued the fixed rule of God. The worst penalty of vice is that it loses the knowledge of virtue, and of levity that it cannot appreciate seriousness. He taught in parables, as Isaiah prophesied, "that seeing they may see, and not perceive, and hearing they may hear, and not understand; lest haply they should turn again and it should be forgiven them." These last words prove how completely penal, how free from all caprice, was this terrible decision of our Gentle Lord, that precautions must be taken against the evasion of the consequences of crime. But it is a warning by no means unique. He said, "The things which make for thy peace . . . are hid from thine eyes" (Luke xix. 42). And St. Paul said, "If our gospel is veiled, it is veiled in them that are perishing"; and still more to the point, "The natural man receiveth not the things of the Spirit of God, for they are foolishness unto him; and he cannot know them, because they are spiritually discerned" (2 Cor. iv. 3; 1 Cor. ii. 14). To this law Christ, in speaking by parables, was conscious that He conformed.

But now let it be observed how completely this mode of teaching suited our Lord's habit of mind. If men could finally rid themselves of His Divine claim, they would at once recognise the greatest of the sages; and they would also find in Him the sunniest, sweetest, and most accurate discernment of nature, and its more quiet beauties, that ever became a vehicle for moral teaching. The sun and rain bestowed on the evil and the good, the fountain and the trees which regulate the waters and the fruit, the death of the seed by which it buys its increase, the provision for bird and blossom without anxiety of theirs, the preference for a lily over Solomon's gorgeous robes, the meaning of a red sky at sunrise and sunset, the hen gathering her chickens under her wing, the vine and its branches, the sheep and their shepherd, the lightning seen over all the sky, every one of these needed only to be re-set and it would have become a parable.

All the Gospels, including the fourth, are full of proofs of this rich and attractive endowment, this warm sympathy with nature; and this fact is among the evidences that they all drew the same character, and drew it faithfully.

THE SOWER.

MARK iv. 3-9, 14-20 (R. V.).

"Hearken," Jesus said; willing to caution men against the danger of slighting His simple story, and to impress on them that it conveyed more than met their ears. In so doing He protested in advance against fatalistic abuses of the parable, as if we were already doomed to be hard, or shallow, or thorny, or fruitful soil. And at the close He brought out still more clearly His protest against such doctrine, by impressing upon all, that if the vitalising seed were the imparted word, it was their part to receive and treasure it. Indolence and shallowness *must* fail to bear fruit: that is the essential doctrine of the parable; but it is not necessary that we should remain indolent or shallow: "He that hath ears to hear, let him hear."

And when the Epistle to the Hebrews reproduces the image of land which bringeth forth thorns and thistles, our Revised Version rightly brings out the fact, on which indeed the whole exhortation depends, that the same piece of land might have borne herbs meet for those for whose sake it is tilled (vi. 7).

Having said "Hearken," Jesus added, "Behold." It has been rightly inferred that the scene was before their eyes. Very possibly some such process was within sight of the shore on which they were gathered; but in any case, a process was visible, if they would but see, of which the tilling of the ground was only a type. A nobler seed was being scattered for a vaster harvest, and it was no common labourer, but the true sower, who went forth to sow. "The sower soweth the word." But who was he? St. Matthew tells us "the sower is the Son of man," and whether the words were expressly uttered, or only implied, as the silence of St. Mark and St. Luke might possibly suggest, it is clear that none of His disciples could mistake His meaning. Ages have passed and He is the sower still, by whatever instrument He works, for we are God's husbandry as well as God's building. And the seed is the Word of God, so strangely able to work below the surface of human life, invisible at first, yet vital, and grasping from within and without, from secret thoughts and from circumstances, as from the chemical ingredients of the soil and from the sunshine and the shower, all that will contribute to its growth, until the field itself is assimilated, spread from end to end with waving ears, a corn-field now. This is why Jesus in His second parable did not any longer say "the seed is the word," but "the good seed are the sons of the kingdom" (Matt. xiii. 38). The word planted was able to identify itself with the heart.

And this seed, the Word of God, is sown broadcast as all our opportunities are given. A talent was not refused to him who buried it. Judas was an apostle. Men may receive the grace of God in vain, and this in more ways than one. On some it produces no vital impression whatever; it lies on the surface of a mind which the feet of earthly interests have trodden hard. There is no chance for it to expand, to begin its operation by sending out the smallest tendrils to grasp, to appropriate anything, to take root. And it may well be doubted whether any soul, wholly indifferent to religious truth, ever retained even its theoretic knowledge long. The foolish heart is darkened. The fowls of the air catch away for ever the priceless seed of eternity. Now it is of great importance to observe how Jesus explained this calamity. We should probably have spoken of forgetfulness, the fading away of neglected impressions, or at most of some judicial act of providence hiding the truth from the careless. But Jesus said, "straightway cometh Satan and taketh away the word which hath been sown in them." No person can fairly explain this text away, as men have striven to explain Christ's language to the demoniacs, by any theory of the use of popular language, or the toleration of harmless notions. The introduction of Satan into this parable is unexpected and uncalled for by any demand save one, the necessity of telling all the truth. It is true therefore that an active and deadly enemy of souls is at work to quicken the mischief which neglect and indifference would themselves produce, that evil processes are helped from beneath as truly as good ones from above; that the seed which is left to-day upon the surface may be maliciously taken thence long before it would have perished by natural decay; that men cannot reckon upon stopping short in their contempt of grace, since what they neglect the devil snatches quite away from them. And as seed is only safe from fowls when buried in the soil, so is the word of life only safe against the rapacity of hell when it has sunk down into our hearts.

In the story of the early Church, St. Paul sowed upon such ground as this in Athens. Men who spent their time in the pursuit of artistic and cultivated novelties, in hearing and telling some new thing, mocked the gospel, or at best proposed to hear its preacher yet again. How long did such a purpose last?

But there are other dangers to dread, besides absolute indifference to truth. And the first of these is a too shallow and easy acquiescence. The message of salvation is designed to affect the whole of human life profoundly. It comes to bind a strong man armed, it summons easy and indifferent hearts to wrestle against spiritual foes, to crucify the flesh, to die daily. On these conditions it offers the noblest blessings. But the conditions are grave and sobering. If one hears them without solemn and earnest searching of heart, he has only, at the best, apprehended half the message. Christ has warned us that we cannot build a tower without sitting down to count our means, nor fight a hostile king without reckoning the prospects of invasion. And it is very striking to compare the gushing and impulsive sensationalism of some modern schools, with the deliberate and circumspect action of St. Paul, even after God had been pleased miraculously to reveal His Son in him. He went into seclusion. He returned to Damascus to his first instructor. Fourteen years afterwards he deliberately laid his gospel before the Apostles, lest by any means he should be running or had run in vain. Such is the action of one penetrated with a sense of reality and responsibility in his decision; it is not the action likely to result from teaching men that it suffices to "say you believe" and to be "made happy." And in this parable, our Saviour has given striking expression to His judgment of the school which relies upon mere happiness. Next to those who leave the Seed for Satan to snatch away, He places them "who, when they have heard the word, straightway receive it with joy." They have taken the promises without the precepts, they have hoped for the crown without the cross. Their type is the thin layer of earth spread over a shelf of rock. The water, which cannot sink down, and the heat reflected up from the stone, make it for a time almost a hot bed. Straightway the seed sprang up, because it had no deepness of earth. But the moisture thus detained upon the surface vanished utterly in time of drought; the young roots, unable to penetrate to any deeper supplies, were scorched; and it withered away. That superficial heat and moisture was impulsive emotion, glad to hear of heaven, and love, and privilege, but forgetful to mortify the flesh, and to be partaker with Christ in His death. The roots of a real Christian life must strike deeper down. Consciousness of sin and its penalty and of the awful price by which that penalty has been paid, consciousness of what life should have been and how we have degraded it, consciousness of what it must yet be made by grace—these do not lead to joy so immediate, so impulsive, as the growth of this shallow vegetation. A mature and settled joy is among "the fruits of the spirit:" it is not the first blade that shoots up.

Now because the sense of sin, and duty, and atonement have not done their sobering work, the feelings, so easily quickened, are also easily perverted: "When tribulation or persecution ariseth because of the word, straightway they stumble." These were not counted upon. Neither trouble of mind nor opposition of wicked men was included in the holiday scheme of the life Divine. And their pressure is not counterweighted by that of any deep convictions. The roots have never penetrated farther than temporal calamities and trials can reach. In the time of drought they have *not* enough. They endure, but only for a while.

St. Paul sowed upon just such soil in Galatia. There his hearers spoke of such blessedness that they would have plucked out their eyes for him. But he became their enemy because he told them all the truth, when only a part was welcome. And as Christ said, Straightway they stumble, so St. Paul had to marvel that they were so soon subverted.

If indifference be the first danger, and shallowness the second, mixed motive is the third. Men there are who are very earnest, and far indeed from slight views of truth, who are nevertheless in sore danger, because they are equally earnest about other things; because they cannot resign this world, whatever be their concern about the next; because the soil of their life would fain grow two inconsistent harvests. Like seed sown among thorns, "choked" by their entangling roots and light-excluding growths, the word in such hearts, though neither left upon a hard surface nor forbidden by rock to strike deep into the earth, is overmastered by an unworthy rivalry. A kind of vegetation it does produce, but not such as the tiller seeks: the word becometh unfruitful. It is the same lesson as when Jesus said, "No man can serve two masters. Ye cannot serve God and mammon."

Perhaps it is the one most needed in our time of feverish religious controversy and heated party spirit, when every one hath a teaching, hath a revelation, hath a tongue, hath an interpretation, but scarcely any have denied the world and taken in exchange a cross.

St. Paul found a thorny soil in Corinth which came behind in no gift, if only gifts had been graces, but was indulgent, factious, and selfish, puffed up amid flagrant vices, one hungry and another drunken, while wrangling about the doctrine of the resurrection.

The various evils of this parable are all of them worldliness, differently manifested. The deadening effect of habitual forgetfulness of God, treading the soil so hard that no seed can enter it; the treacherous effect of secret love of earth, a buried obstruction refusing to admit the gospel into the recesses of the life, however it may reach the feelings; and the fierce and stubborn competition of worldly interests, wherever they are not resolutely weeded out, against these Jesus spoke His earliest parable. And it is instructive to review the foes by which He represented His Gospel as warred upon. The personal activity of Satan; "tribulation or persecution" from without, and within the heart "cares" rather for self than for the dependent and the poor, "deceitfulness of riches" for those who possess enough to trust in, or to replace with a fictitious importance the only genuine value, which is that of character (although men are still esteemed for being "worth" a round sum, a strange estimate, to be made by Christians, of a being with a soul burning in him); and alike for rich and poor, "the lusts of other things," since none is too poor to covet, and none so rich that his desires shall not increase, like some diseases, by being fed.

Lastly, we have those on the good ground, who are not described by their sensibilities or their enjoyments, but by their loyalty. They "hear the word and accept it and bear fruit." To accept is what distinguishes them alike from the wayside hearers into whose attention the word never sinks, from the rocky hearers who only receive it with a superficial welcome, and from the thorny hearers who only give it a divided welcome. It is not said, as if the word were merely the precepts, that they obey it. The sower of this seed is not he who bade the soldier not to do violence, and the publican not to extort: it is He who said, Repent, and believe the gospel. He implanted new hopes, convictions, and affections, as the germ which should unfold in a new life. And the good fruit is borne by those who honestly "accept" His word.

Fruitfulness is never in the gospel the condition by which life is earned, but it is always the test by which to prove it. In all the accounts of the final judgment, we catch the principle of the bold challenge of St. James, "Show me thy faith without thy works, and I will show thee my faith by my works." The talent must produce more talents, and the pound more pounds; the servant must have his loins girt and a light in his hand; the blessed are they who did unto Jesus the kindness they did unto the least of His brethren, and the accursed are they who did it not to Jesus in His people.

We are not wrong in preaching that honest faith in Christ is the only condition of acceptance, and the way to obtain strength for good works. But perhaps we fail to add, with sufficient emphasis, that good works are the only sufficient evidence of real faith, of genuine conversion. Lydia, whose heart the Lord opened and who constrained the Apostle to abide in her house, was converted as truly as the gaoler who passed through all the vicissitudes of despair, trembling and astonishment, and belief.

"They bear fruit, thirtyfold and sixtyfold and an hundredfold." And all are alike accepted. But the parable of the pounds shows that all are not alike rewarded, and in equal circumstances superior efficiency wins a superior prize. One star differeth from another star in glory, and they who turn many to righteousness shall shine as the sun forever.

LAMP AND STAND.

Mark iv. 21-25 (R. V.).

Jesus had now taught that the only good ground was that in which the good seed bore fruit. And He adds explicitly, that men receive the truth in order to spread it, and are given grace that they may become, in turn, good stewards of the manifold grace of God.

"Is the lamp brought to be put under the bushel or under the bed, and not to be put on the stand?" The language may possibly be due, as men have argued, to the simple conditions of life among the Hebrew peasantry, who possessed only one lamp, one corn-measure, and perhaps one bed. All the greater marvel is it that amid such surroundings He should have announced, and not in vain, that His disciples, His Church, should become the light of all humanity, "the lamp." Already he had put forward the same claim even more explicitly, saying, "Ye are the light of the world." And in each case, He spoke not in the intoxication of pride or self-assertion, but in all gravity, and as a solemn warning. The city on the hill could not be hid. The lamp would burn dimly under the bed; it would be extinguished entirely by the bushel. Publicity is the soul of religion, since religion is light. It is meant to diffuse itself, to be, as He expressed it, like leaven which may be hid at first, but cannot be concealed, since it will leaven all the lump. And so, if He spoke in parables, and consciously hid His meaning by so doing, this was not to withdraw His teaching from the masses, it was to shelter the flame which should presently illuminate all the house. Nothing was hid, save that it should be manifested, nor made secret, but that it should come to light. And it has never been otherwise. Our religion has no privileged inner circle, no esoteric doctrine; and its chiefs, when men glorified one or another, asked, What then is Apollos? And what is Paul? Ministers through whom ye believed. Agents only, for conveying to others what they had received from God. And thus He Who now spoke in parables, and again charged them not to make Him known, was able at the end to say, In secret have I spoken nothing. Therefore He repeats with emphasis His former words, frequent on His lips henceforward, and ringing through the messages He spoke in glory to His Churches. If any man hath ears to hear, let him hear. None is excluded but by himself.

Yet another caution follows. If the seed be the Word, there is sore danger from false teaching; from strewing the ground with adulterated grain. St. Mark, indeed, has not recorded the Parable of the Tares. But there are indications of it, and the same thought is audible in this saying, "Take heed what ye hear." The added words are a little surprising: "With what measure ye mete it shall be measured unto you, and more shall be given unto you." The last clause expresses exactly the principle on which the forfeited pound was given to him who had ten pounds already, the open hand of God lavishing additional gifts upon him who was capable of using them. But does not the whole statement seem to follow more suitably upon a command to beware what we teach, and thus "mete" to others, than what we hear? A closer examination finds in this apparent unfitness a deeper harmony of thought. To "accept" the genuine word is the same as to bring forth fruit for God; it is to reckon with the Lord of the talents, and to yield the fruit of the vineyard. And this is to "mete," not indeed unto man, but unto God, Who shows Himself froward with the froward, and from him that hath not, whose possession is below his accountability, takes away even that he hath, but gives exceeding abundantly above all they ask or think to those who have, who are not disobedient to the heavenly calling.

All this is most delicately connected with what precedes it; and the parables, hiding the truth from some, giving it authority, and colour, and effect to others, were a striking example of the process here announced.

Never was the warning to be heedful what we hear more needful than at present. Men think themselves free to follow any teacher, especially if he be eloquent; to read any book, if only it be in demand; and to discuss any theory, provided it be fashionable, while perfectly well aware that they are neither earnest inquirers after truth, nor qualified champions against its assailants. For what then do they read and hear? For the pleasure of a rounded phrase, or to augment the prattle of conceited ignorance in a drawing-room.

Do we wonder when these players with edged tools injure themselves, and become perverts or agnostics? It would be more wonderful if they remained unhurt, since Jesus said, "Take heed what ye hear . . . from him that hath not shall be taken even that he hath." A rash and uninstructed exposure of our intellects to evil influences, is meting to God with an unjust measure, as really as a wilful plunge into any other temptation, since we are bidden to cleanse ourselves from all defilement of the spirit as well as of the flesh.

THE SEED GROWING SECRETLY.

MARK iv. 26-29 (R. V.).

St. Mark alone records this parable of a sower who sleeps by night, and rises for other business by day, and knows not how the seed springs up. That is not the sower's concern: all that remains for him is to put forth the sickle when the harvest is come.

It is a startling parable for us who believe in the fostering care of the Divine Spirit. And the paradox is forced on our attention by the words "the earth beareth fruit of herself," contrasting strangely as it does with such other assertions, as that the branch cannot bear fruit of itself, that without Christ we can do nothing, and that when we live it is not we but Christ who liveth in us.

It will often help us to understand a paradox if we can discover another like it. And exactly such an one as this will be found in the record of creation. God rested on the seventh day from all His work, yet we know that His providence never slumbers, that by Him all things consist, and that Jesus defended His own work of healing on a Sabbath day by urging that the Sabbath of God was occupied in gracious provision for His world. "My Father worketh hitherto, and I work." Thus the rest of God from creative work says nothing about His energies in that other field of providential care. Exactly so Jesus here treats only of what may be called the creative spiritual work, the deposit of the seed of life. And the essence of this remarkable parable is the assertion that we are to expect an orderly, quiet, and gradual development from this principle of life, not a series of communications from without, of additional revelations, of semi-miraculous interferences. The life of grace is a natural process in the supernatural sphere. In one sense it is all of God, who maketh His sun to rise, and sendeth rain, without which the earth could bear no fruit of herself. In another sense we must work out our own salvation all the more earnestly because it is God that worketh in us.

Now this parable, thus explained, has been proved true in the wonderful history of the Church. She has grown, not only in extent but by development, as marvellously as a corn of wheat which is now a waving wheat-stem with its ripening ear. When Cardinal Newman urged that an ancient Christian, returning to earth, would recognise the services and the Church of Rome, and would fail to recognise ours, he was probably mistaken. To go no farther, there is no Church on earth so unlike the Churches of the New Testament as that which offers praise to God in a strange tongue. St. Paul apprehended that a stranger in such an assembly would reckon the worshippers mad. But in any case the argument forgets that the whole kingdom of God is to resemble seed, not in a drawer, but in the earth, and advancing towards the harvest. It must "die" to much if it will bring forth fruit. It must acquire strange bulk, strange forms, strange organisms. It must become, to those who only knew it as it was, quite as unrecognisable as our Churches are said to be. And yet the changes must be those of logical growth, not of corruption. And this parable tells us they must be accomplished without any special interference such as marked the sowing time. Well then, the parable is a prophecy. Movement after movement has modified the life of the Church. Even its structure is not all it was. But these changes have every one been wrought by human agency, they have come from within it, like the force which pushes the germ out of the soil, and expands the bud into the full corn in the ear. There has been no grafting knife to insert a new principle of richer life; the gospel and the sacraments of our Lord have contained in them the promise and potency of all that was yet to be unfolded, all the gracefulness and all the fruit. And these words, "the earth beareth fruit of herself, first the blade, then the ear, then the full corn in the ear," each so different, and yet so dependent on what preceded, teach us two great ecclesiastical lessons. They condemn the violent and revolutionary changes, which would not develop old germs, but tear them open or perhaps pull them up. Much may be distasteful to the spirit of sordid utilitarianism; a mere husk, which nevertheless within it shelters precious grain, otherwise sure to perish. If thus we learn to respect the old, still more do we learn that what is new has also its all-important part to play. The blade and the ear in turn are innovations. We must not condemn those new forms of Christian activity, Christian association, and Christian councils, which new times evoke, until we have considered well whether they are truly expansions, in the light and heat of our century, of the sacred life-germ of the ancient faith and the ancient love.

And what lessons has this parable for the individual? Surely that of active present faith, not waiting for future gifts of light or feeling, but confident that the seed already sown, the seed of the word, has power to develop into the rich fruit of Christian character. In this respect the parable supplements the first one. From that we learned that if the soil were not in fault, if the heart were honest and good, the seed would fructify. From this we learn that these conditions suffice for a perfect harvest. The incessant, all-important help of God, we have seen, is not denied; it is taken for granted, as the atmospheric and magnetic influences upon the grain. So should we reverentially and thankfully rely upon the aid of God, and then, instead of waiting for strange visitations and special stirrings of grace, account that we already possess enough to make us responsible for the harvest of the soul. Multitudes of souls, whose true calling is, in obedient trust, to arise and walk, are at this moment lying impotent beside some pool which they expect an angel to stir, and into which they fain would then be put by some one, they know not whom—multitudes of expectant, inert, inactive souls, who know not that the text they have most need to ponder is this: "the earth beareth fruit of itself." For want of this they are actually, day by day, receiving the grace of God in vain.

We learn also to be content with gradual progress. St. John did not blame the children and young men to whom he wrote, because they were not mature in wisdom and experience. St. Paul exhorts us to grow up in all things into Him which is the Head, even Christ. They do not ask for more than steady growth; and their Master, as He distrusted the fleeting joy of hearers whose hearts were shallow, now explicitly bids us not to be content with any first attainment, not to count all done if we are converted, but to develop first the blade, then the ear, and lastly the full corn in the ear.

Does it seem a tedious weary sentence? Are we discontent for want of conscious interferences of heaven? Do we complain that, to human consciousness, the great Sower sleeps and rises up and leaves the grain to fare He knows not how? It is only for a little while. When the fruit is ripe, He will Himself gather it into His eternal garner.

THE MUSTARD SEED.

MARK iv. 30-34 (R. V.).

St. Mark has recorded one other parable of this great cycle. Jesus now invites the disciples to let their own minds play upon the subject. Each is to ask himself a question: How shall we liken the kingdom of God? or in what parable shall we set it forth?

A gentle pause, time for them to form some splendid and ambitious image in their minds, and then we can suppose with what surprise they heard His own answer, "It is like a grain of mustard seed." And truly some Christians of a later day might be astonished also, if they could call up a fair image of their own conceptions of the kingdom of God, and compare it with this figure, employed by Jesus.

But here one must observe a peculiarity in our Saviour's use of images. His illustrations of His first coming, and of His work of grace, which are many, are all of the homeliest kind. He is a shepherd who seeks one sheep. He is not an eagle that fluttereth over her young and beareth them on her pinions, but a hen who gathereth her chickens under her wings. Never once does He rise into that high and poetic strain with which His followers have loved to sing of the Star of Bethlehem, and which Isaiah lavished beforehand upon the birth of the Prince of Peace. There is no language more intensely concentrated and glowing than He has employed to describe the judgment of the hypocrites who rejected Him, of Jerusalem, and of the world at last. But when He speaks of His first coming and its effects, it is not of that sunrise to which all kings and nations shall hasten, but of a little grain of mustard seed, which is to become "greater than all the herbs," and put forth great branches, "so that the birds of the heaven can lodge under the shadow of them." When one thinks of such an image for such an event of the founding of the kingdom of God, and its advance to universal supremacy, represented by the small seed of a shrub which grows to the height of a tree, and even harbours birds, he is conscious almost of incongruity. But when one reconsiders it, he is filled with awe and reverence. For this exactly expresses the way of thinking natural to One who has stooped immeasurably down to the task which all others feel to be so lofty. There is a poem of Shelley, which expresses the relative greatness of three spirits by the less and less value which they set on the splendours of the material heavens. To the first they are a palace-roof of golden lights, to the second but the mind's first chamber, to the last only drops which Nature's mighty heart drives through thinnest veins. Now that which was to Isaiah the exalting of every valley and the bringing low of every mountain, and to Daniel the overthrow of a mighty image whose aspect was terrible, by a stone cut out without hands, was to Jesus but the sowing of a grain of mustard seed. Could any other have spoken thus of the founding of the kingdom of God? An enthusiast over-values his work, he can think of nothing else; and he expects immediate revolutions. Jesus was keenly aware that His work in itself was very small, no more than the sowing of a seed, and even of the least, popularly speaking, among all seeds. Clearly He did not overrate the apparent effect of His work on earth. And indeed, what germ of religious teaching could be less promising than the doctrine of the cross, held by a few peasants in a despised province of a nation already subjugated and soon to be overwhelmed.

The image expresses more than the feeble beginning and victorious issue of His work, more than even the gradual and logical process by which this final triumph should be attained. All this we found in the preceding parable. But here the emphasis is laid on the development of Christ's influence in unexpected spheres. Unlike other herbs, the mustard in Eastern climates does grow into a tree, shoot out great branches from the main stem, and give shelter to the birds of the air. So has the Christian faith developed ever new collateral agencies, charitable, educational, and social: so have architecture, music, literature, flourished under its shade, and there is not one truly human interest which would not be deprived of its best shelter if the rod of Jesse were hewn down. Nay, we may urge that the Church itself has become the most potent force in directions not its own: it broke the chains of the negro; it asserts the rights of woman and of the poor; its noble literature is finding a response in the breasts of a hundred degraded races; the herb has become a tree.

And so in the life of individuals, if the seed be allowed its due scope and place to grow, it gives shelter and blessing to whatsoever things are honest and lovely, not only if there be any virtue, but also if there be any praise.

Well is it with the nation, and well with the soul, when the faith of Jesus is not rigidly restricted to a prescribed sphere, when the leaves which are for the healing of the nations cast their shadow broad and cool over all the spaces in which all its birds of song are nestling.

A remarkable assertion is added. Although the parabolic mode of teaching was adopted in judgment, yet its severe effect was confined within the narrowest limits. His many parables were spoken "as they were able to hear," but only to His own disciples privately was all their meaning expounded.

FOUR MIRACLES.

MARK iv. 39, v. 15, 31, 41 (R. V.).

There are two ways, equally useful, of studying Scripture, as there are of regarding the other book of God, the face of Nature. We may bend over a wild flower, or gaze across a landscape; and it will happen that a naturalist, pursuing a moth, loses sight of a mountain-range. It is a well-known proverb, that one may fail to see the wood foi the trees, losing in details the general effect. And so the careful student of isolated texts may never perceive the force and cohesion of a connected passage.

The reader of a Gospel narrative thinks, that by pondering it as a whole, he secures himself against any such misfortune. But a narrative dislocated often loses as much as a detached verse. The actions of our Lord are often exquisitely grouped, as becometh Him who hath made everything not beautiful only, but especially beautiful in its season. And we should not be content without combining the two ways of reading Scripture, the detailed and the rapid,—lingering at times to apprehend the marvellous force of a solitary verse, and again sweeping over a broad expanse, like a surveyor, who, to map a country, stretches his triangles from mountain peak to peak.

We have reached a point at which St. Mark records a special outshining of miraculous power. Four striking works follow each other without a break, and it must not for a moment be supposed that the narrative is thus constructed, certain intermediate discourses and events being sacrificed for the purpose, without a deliberate and a truthful intention. That intention is to represent the effect, intense and exalting, produced by such a cycle of wonders on the minds of His disciples. They saw them come close upon each other: we should lose the impression as we read, if other incidents were allowed to interpose themselves. It is one more example of St. Mark's desire to throw light, above all things, upon the energy and power of the sacred life.

We have to observe therefore the bearing of these four miracles on each other, and upon what precedes, before studying them one by one.

It was a time of trial. The Pharisees had decided that He had a devil. His relatives had said He was beside Himself. His manner of teaching had changed, because the people should see without perceiving, and hear without understanding. They who understood His parables heard much of seed that failed, of success a great way off, of a kingdom which would indeed be great at last, but for the present weak and small. And it is certain that there must have been heavy hearts among those who left, with Him, the populous side of the lake, to cross over into remote and semi-pagan retirement. To encourage them, and as if in protest against His rejection by the authorities, Jesus enters upon this great cycle of miracles.

They find themselves, as the Church has often since been placed, and as every human soul has had to feel itself, far from shore, and tempest-beaten. The rage of human foes is not so deaf, so implacable, as that of wind and wave. It is the stress of adverse circumstances in the direst form. But Jesus proves Himself to be Master of the forces of nature which would overwhelm them.

Nay, they learn that His seeming indifference is no proof that they are neglected, by the rebuke He speaks to their over-importunate appeals, Why are ye so fearful? have ye not yet faith? And they, who might have been shaken by the infidelity of other men, fear exceedingly as they behold the obedience of the wind and the sea, and ask, Who then is this?

But in their mission as His disciples, a worse danger than the enmity of man or convulsions of nature awaits them. On landing, they are at once confronted by one whom an evil spirit has made exceeding fierce, so that no man could pass by that way. It is their way nevertheless, and they must tread it. And the demoniac adores, and the evil spirits themselves are abject in supplication, and at the word of Jesus are expelled. Even the inhabitants, who will not receive Him, are awe-struck and deprecatory, and if at their bidding Jesus turns away again, His followers may judge whether the habitual meekness of such a one is due to feebleness or to a noble self-command.

Landing once more, they are soon accosted by a ruler of the synagogue, whom sorrow has purified from the prejudices of his class. And Jesus is about to heal the daughter of Jairus, when another form of need is brought to light. A slow and secret decline, wasting the vital powers, a silent woe, speechless, stealthily approaching the Healer—over this grief also He is Lord. And it is seen that neither the visible actions of Jesus nor the audible praises of His petitioners can measure the power that goes out of Him, the physical benefits which encompass the Teacher as a halo envelops flame.

Circumstances, and the fiends of the pit, and the woes that waste the lives of men, over these He has been seen to triumph. But behind all that we strive with here, there lurks the last enemy, and he also shall be subdued. And now first an example is recorded of what we know to have already taken place, the conquest of death by his predicted Spoiler. Youth and gentle maidenhood, high hope and prosperous circumstances have been wasted, but the call of Jesus is heard by the ear that was stopped with dust, and the spirit obeys Him in the far-off realm of the departed, and they who have just seen such other marvels, are nevertheless amazed with a great amazement.

No cycle of miracles could be more rounded, symmetrical, and exhaustive; none could better vindicate to His disciples His impugned authority, or brace their endangered faith, or fit them for what almost immediately followed, their own commission, and the first journey upon which they too cast out many devils, and anointed with oil many that were sick, and healed them.

THE TWO STORMS.

Mark vi. 47-52 (R. V.).

Few readers are insensible to the wonderful power with which the Gospels tell the story of the two storms upon the lake. The narratives are favourites in every Sunday school; they form the basis of countless hymns and poems; and we always recur to them with fresh delight.

In the first account we see as in a picture the weariness of the great Teacher, when, the long day being over and the multitude dismissed, He retreats across the sea without preparation, and "as He was," and sinks to sleep on the one cushion in the stern, undisturbed by the raging tempest or by the waves which beat into the boat. We observe the reluctance of the disciples to arouse Him until the peril is extreme, and the boat is "now" filling. We hear from St. Mark, the associate of St. Peter, the presumptuous and characteristic cry which expresses terror, and perhaps dread lest His tranquil slumbers may indicate a separation betwen His cause and theirs, who perish while He is unconcerned. We admire equally the calm and masterful words which quell the tempest, and those which enjoin a faith so lofty as to endure the last extremities of peril without dismay, witho t agitation in its prayers. We observe the strange incident, that no sooner does the storm cease than the waters, commonly seething for many hours afterwards, grow calm. And the picture is completed by the mention of their new dread (fear of the supernatural Man replacing their terror amid the convulsions of nature), and of their awestruck questioning among themselves.

In the second narrative we see the ship far out in the lake, but watched by One, Who is alone upon the land. Through the gloom He sees them "tormented" by fruitless rowing; but though this is the reason why He comes, He is about to pass them by. The watch of the night is remembered; it is the fourth. The cry of their alarm is universal, for they all saw Him and were troubled. We are told of the promptitude with which He thereupon relieved their fears; we see Him climb up into the boat, and the sudden ceasing of the storm, and their amazement. Nor is that after-thought omitted in which they blamed themselves for their astonishment. If their hearts had not been hardened, the miracle of the loaves would have taught them that Jesus was the Master of the physical world.

Now all this picturesque detail belongs to a single Gospel. And it is exactly what a believer would expect. How much soever the healing of disease might interest St. Luke the physician, who relates all such events so vividly, it would have impressed the patient himself yet more, and an account of it by him, if we had it, would be full of graphic touches. Now these two miracles were wrought for the rescue of the apostles themselves. The Twelve took the place held in others by the lame, the halt, and the blind: the suspense, the appeal, and the joy of deliverance were all their own. It is therefore no wonder that we find their accounts of these especial miracles so picturesque. But this is a solid evidence of the truth of the narratives; for while the remembrance of such actual events should thrill with agitated life, there is no reason why a legend of the kind should be especially clear and vivid. The same argument might easily be carried farther. When the disciples began to reproach themselves for their unbelieving astonishment, they were naturally conscious of having failed to learn the lesson which had been taught them just before. Later students and moralists would have observed that another miracle, a little earlier, was a still closer precedent, but they naturally blamed themselves most for being blind to what was immediately before their eyes. Now when Jesus walked upon the waters and the disciples were amazed, it is not said that they forgot how He had already stilled a tempest, but they considered not the miracle of the loaves, for their heart was hardened. In touches like this we find the influence of a bystander beyond denial.

Every student of Scripture must have observed the special significance of those parables and miracles which recur a second time with certain designed variations. In the miraculous draughts of fishes, Christ Himself avowed an allusion to the catching of men. And the Church has always discerned a spiritual intention in these two storms, in one of which Christ slept, while in the other His disciples toiled alone, and which express, between them, the whole strain exercised upon a devout spirit by adverse circumstances. Dangers never alarmed one who realised both the presence of Jesus and His vigilant care. Temptation enters only because this is veiled. Why do adversities press hard upon me, if indeed I belong to Christ? He must either be indifferent and sleeping, or else absent altogether from my frail and foundering bark. It is thus that we let go our confidence, and incur agonies of mental suffering, and the rebuke of our Master, even though He continues to be the Protector of His unworthy people.

On the voyage of life we may conceive of Jesus as our Companion, for He is with us always, or as watching us from the everlasting hills, whither it was expedient for us that He should go. Nevertheless, we are storm-tossed and in danger. Although we are His, and not separated from Him by any conscious disobedience, yet the conditions of life are unmitigated, the winds as wild, the waves as merciless, the boat as cruelly "tormented" as ever. And no rescue comes: Jesus is asleep: He cares not that we perish. Then we pray after a fashion so clamorous, and with supplication so like demands, that we too appear to have undertaken to awake our Lord. Then we have to learn from the first of these miracles, and especially from its delay. The disciples were safe, had they only known it, whether Jesus would have interposed of His own accord, or whether they might still have needed to appeal to Him, but in a gentler fashion. We may ask help, provided that we do so in a serene and trustful spirit, anxious for nothing, not seeking to extort a concession, but approaching with boldness the throne of grace, on which our Father sits. It is thus that the peace of God shall rule our hearts and minds, for want of which the apostles were asked, Where is your faith? Comparing the narratives, we learn that Jesus reassured their hearts even before He arose, and then, having first silenced by His calmness the storm within them, He stood up and rebuked the storm around.

St. Augustine gave a false turn to the application, when he said, "If Jesus were not asleep within thee, thou wouldst be calm and at rest. But why is He asleep? Because thy faith is asleep," etc. (Sermon lxiii.) The sleep of Jesus was natural and right; and it answers not to our spiritual torpor, but to His apparent indifference and non-intervention in our time of distress. And the true lesson of the miracle is that we should trust Him Whose care fails not when it seems to fail, Who is able to save to the uttermost, and Whom we should approach in the direst peril without panic. It was fitly taught them first when all the powers of the State and the Church were leagued against Him, and He as a blind man saw not and as a dumb man opened not His mouth.

The second storm should have found them braver by the experience of the first; but spiritually as well as bodily they were farther removed from Christ. The people, profoundly moved by the murder of the Baptist, wished to set Jesus on the throne, and the disciples were too ambitious to be allowed to be present while He dismissed the multitudes. They had to be sent away, and it was from the distant hillside that Jesus saw their danger. Surely it is instructive, that neither the shades of night, nor the abstracted fervour of His prayers, prevented Him from seeing it, nor the stormlashed waters from bringing aid. And significant also, that the experience of remoteness, though not sinful, since He had sent them away, was yet the result of their own worldliness. It is when we are out of sympathy with Jesus that we are most likely to be alone in trouble. None was in their boat to save them, and in heart also they had gone out from the presence of their God. Therefore they failed to trust in His guidance Who had sent them into the ship: they had no sense of protection or of supervision; and it was a terrible moment when a form was vaguely seen to glide over the waves. Christ, it would seem, would have gone before and led them to the haven where they would be. Or perhaps He "would have passed by them," as He would afterwards have gone further than Emmaus, to elicit any trustful half-recognition which might call to Him and be rewarded. But they cried out for fear. And so it is continually with God in His world: men are terrified at the presence of the supernatural, because they fail to apprehend the abiding presence of the supernatural Christ. And yet there is one point at least in every life, the final moment, in which all else must recede, and the soul be left alone with the beings of another world. Then, and in every trial, and especially in all trials which press in upon us the consciousness of the spiritual universe, well is it for him who hears the voice of Jesus saying, It is I, be not afraid.

For only through Jesus, only in His person, has that unknown universe ceased to be dreadful and mysterious. Only when He is welcomed does the storm cease to rage around us.

It was the earlier of these miracles which first taught the disciples that not only were human disorders under His control, and gifts and blessings at His disposal, but also the whole range of nature was subject to Him, and the winds and the sea obey Him.

Shall we say that His rebuke addressed to these was a mere figure of speech? Some have inferred that natural convulsions are so directly the work of evil angels that the words of Jesus were really spoken to them. But the plain assertion is that He rebuked the winds and the waves, and these would not become identical with Satan even upon the supposition that he excites them. We ourselves continually personify the course of nature, and even complain of it, wantonly enough, and Scripture does not deny itself the use of ordinary human forms of speech. Yet the very peculiar word employed by Jesus cannot be without significance. It is the same with which He had already confronted the violence of the demoniac in the synagogue, Be muzzled. At the least it expresses stern repression, and thus it reminds us that creation itself is made subject to vanity, the world deranged by sin, so that all around us requires readjustment as truly as all within, and Christ shall at last create a new earth as well as a new heaven.

Some pious people resign themselves much too passively to the mischiefs of the material universe, supposing that troubles which are not of their own making must needs be a Divine infliction, calling only for submission. But God sends oppositions to be conquered as well as burdens to be borne; and even before the fall the world had to be subdued. And our final mastery over the surrounding universe was expressed, when Jesus our Head rebuked the winds, and stilled the waves when they arose.

As they beheld, a new sense fell upon His disciples of a more awful presence than they had yet discerned. They asked not only what manner of man is this? but, with surmises which went out beyond the limits of human greatness, Who then is this, that even the winds and the sea obey Him?

CHAPTER V.

THE DEMONIAC OF GADARA.

MARK v. 1-20 (R. V.).

FRESH from asserting His mastery over winds and waves, the Lord was met by a more terrible enemy, the rage of human nature enslaved and impelled by the cruelty of hell. The place where He landed was a theatre not unfit for the tragedy which it revealed. A mixed race was there, indifferent to religion, rearing great herds of swine, upon which the law looked askance, but the profits of which they held so dear that they would choose to banish a Divine ambassador, and one who had released them from an incessant peril, rather than be deprived of these. Now it has already been shown that the wretches possessed by devils were not of necessity stained with special guilt. Even children fell into this misery. But yet we should expect to find it most rampant in places where God was dishonoured, in Gerasa and in the coasts of Tyre and Sidon. And it is so. All misery is the consequence of sin, although individual misery does not measure individual guilt. And the places where the shadow of sin has fallen heaviest are always the haunts of direst wretchedness.

The first Gospel mentions two demoniacs, but one was doubtless so pre-eminently fierce, and possibly so zealous afterward in proclaiming his deliverance, that only St. Matthew learned the existence of another, upon whom also Satan had wrought, if not his worst, enough to show his hatred, and the woes he would fain bring upon humanity.

Among the few terrible glimpses given us of the mind of the fallen angels, one is most significant and sinister. When the unclean spirit is gone out of a man, to what haunts does he turn? He has no sympathy with what is lovely or sublime: in search of rest he wanders through dry places, deserts of arid sand in which his misery may be soothed by congenial desolation. Thus the ruins of the mystic Babylon become an abode of devils. And thus the unclean spirit, when he mastered this demoniac, drove him to a foul and dreary abode among the tombs. One can picture the victim in some lucid moment, awakening to consciousness only to shudder in his dreadful home, and scared back again into that ferocity which is the child of terror.

> "Is it not very like,
> The horrible conceit of death and night,
> Together with the terror of the place
> . . . .
> Oh! if I wake, shall I not be distraught,
> Environèd with all these hideous fears?"
> —"Romeo and Juliet," iv. 3.

There was a time when he had been under restraint, but "now no man could any more bind him" even with iron upon feet and wrists. The ferocity of his cruel subjugator turned his own strength against himself, so that night and day his howling was heard, as he cut himself with stones, and his haunts in the tombs and in the mountains were as dangerous as the lair of a wild beast, which no man dared pass by. What strange impulse drove him thence to the feet of Jesus? Very dreadful is the picture of his conflicting tendencies; the fiend within him struggling against something still human and attracted by the Divine, so that he runs from afar, yet cries aloud, and worships yet disowns having anything to do with Him; and as if the fiend had subverted the true personality, and become the very man, when ordered to come out he adjures Jesus to torment him not.

And here we observe the knowledge of Christ's rank possessed by the evil ones. Long before Peter won a special blessing for acknowledging the Son of the living God, the demoniac called Him by the very name which flesh and blood did not reveal to Cephas. For their chief had tested and discovered Him in the wilderness, saying twice with dread surmise, If Thou be the Son of God. It is also noteworthy that the phrase, the most High God, is the name of Jehovah among the non-Jewish races. It occurs in both Testaments in connection with Melchizedek the Canaanite. It is used throughout the Babylonian proclamations in the book of Daniel. Micah puts it into the lips of Balaam. And the damsel with a spirit of divination employed it in Philippi. Except once, in a Psalm which tells of the return of apostate Israel to the Most High God (lxxviii. 35), the epithet is used only in relation with the nations outside the covenant. Its occurrence here is probably a sign of the pagan influences by which Gadara was infected, and for which it was plagued. By the name of God then, whose Son he loudly confessed that Jesus was, the fiend within the man adjures Him to torment him not. But Jesus had not asked to be acknowledged; He had bidden the devil to come out. And persons who substitute loud confessions and clamorous orthodoxies for obedience should remember that so did the fiend of Gadara. Jesus replied by asking, What is thy name? The question was not an idle one, but had a healing tendency. For the man was beside himself: it was part of his cure that he was found "in his right mind;" and meanwhile his very consciousness was merged in that of the fiends who tortured him, so that his voice was their voice, and they returned a vaunting answer through his lips. Our Lord sought therefore both to calm His excitement and to remind him of himself, and of what he once had been before evil beings dethroned his will. These were not the man, but his enemies by whom he was "carried about," and "led captive at their will." And it is always sobering to think of "Myself," the lonely individual, apart from even those who most influence me, with a soul to lose or save. With this very question the Church Catechism begins its work of arousing and instructing the conscience of each child, separating him from his fellows in order to lead him on to the knowledge of the individualising grace of God.

It may be that the fiends within him dictated his reply, or that he himself, conscious of their tyranny, cried out in agony, We are many; a regiment like those of conquering Rome, drilled and armed to trample and destroy, a legion. This answer distinctly contravened what Christ had just implied, that he was one, an individual, and precious in his Maker's eyes. But there are men and women in every Christian land, whom it might startle to look within, and see how far their individuality is oppressed and overlaid by a legion of impulses, appetites, and conventionalities, which leave them nothing personal, nothing essential and characteristic, nothing that deserves a name. The demons, now conscious of the power that calls them forth, besought Him to leave them a refuge in that country. St. Luke throws light upon this petition, as well as their former complaint, when he tells us they feared to be sent to "the abyss" of their final retribution. And as we read of men who are haunted by a fearful looking for of judgment and a fierceness of fire, so they had no hope of escape, except until "the time." For a little respite they prayed to be sent even into the swine, and Jesus gave them leave.

What a difference there is between the proud and heroic spirits whom Milton celebrated, and these malignant but miserable beings, haunting the sepulchres like ghosts, truculent and yet dastardly, as ready to supplicate as to rend, filled with dread of the appointed time and of the abyss, clinging to that outlying country as a congenial haunt, and devising for themselves a last asylum among the brutes. And yet there are equally far from the materialistic superstitions of that age and place; they are not amenable to fumigations or exorcisms, and they do not upset the furniture in rushing out. Many questions have been asked about the petition of the demons and our Lord's consent. But none of them need much distress the reverential enquirer, who remembers by what misty horizons all our knowledge is enclosed. Most absurd is the charge that Jesus acted indefensibly in destroying property. Is it then so clear that the owners did not deserve their loss through the nature of their investments? Was it merely as a man, or as the Son of the living God, that His consent was felt to be necessary? And was it any part of His mission to protect brutes from death?

The loss endured was no greater than when a crop is beaten down by hail, or a vineyard devastated by insects, and in these cases an agency beyond the control of man is sent or permitted by God, Who was in Christ.

A far harder question it is, How could devils enter into brute creatures? And again, why did they desire to do so? But the first of these is only a subdivision of the vaster problem, at once inevitable and insoluble, How does spirit in any of its forms animate matter, or even manipulate it? We know not by what strange link a thought contracts a sinew, and transmutes itself into words or deeds. And if we believe the dread and melancholy fact of the possession of a child by a fiend, what reason have we, beyond prejudice, for doubting the possession of swine? It must be observed also, that no such possession is proved by this narrative to be a common event, but the reverse. The notion is a last and wild expedient of despair, proposing to content itself with the uttermost abasement, if only the demons might still haunt the region where they had thriven so well. And the consent of Jesus does not commit Him to any judgment upon the merit or the possibility of the project. He leaves the experiment to prove itself, exactly as when Peter would walk upon the water; and a laconic "Go" in this case recalls the "Come" in that; an assent, without approval, to an attempt which was about to fail. Not in the world of brutes could they find shelter from the banishment they dreaded; for the whole herd, frantic and ungoverned, rushed headlong into the sea and was destroyed. The second victory of the series was thus completed. Jesus was Master over the evil spirits which afflict humanity, as well as over the fierceness of the elements which rise against us.

THE MEN OF GADARA.

MARK v. 14-20 (R. V.).

The expulsion of the demons from the possessed, their entrance into the herd, and the destruction of the two thousand swine, were virtually one transaction, and must have impressed the swineherds in its totality. They saw on the one hand the restoration of a dangerous and raging madman, known to be actuated by evil spirits, the removal of a standing peril which had already made one tract of country impassable, and (if they considered such a thing at all) the calming of a human soul, and its advent within the reach of all sacred influences. On the other side what was there? The loss of two thousand swine; and the consciousness that the kingdom of God was come nigh unto them. This was always an alarming discovery. Isaiah said, Woe is me! when his eyes beheld God high and lifted up. And Peter said, Depart from me, when he learned by the miraculous draught of fish that the Lord was there. But Isaiah's concern was because he was a man of unclean lips, and Peter's was because he was a sinful man. Their alarm was that of an awakened conscience, and therefore they became the heralds of Him Whom they feared. But these men were simply scared at what they instinctively felt to be dangerous; and so they took refuge in a crowd, that frequent resort of the frivolous and conscience-stricken, and told in the city what they had seen. And when the inhabitants came forth, a sight met them which might have won the sternest, the man sitting, clothed (a nice coincidence, since St. Mark had not mentioned that he "ware no clothes,") and in his right mind, even him that had the legion, as the narrative emphatically adds. And doubtless the much debated incident of the swine had greatly helped to reassure this afflicted soul; the demons were palpably gone, visibly enough they were overmastered. But the citizens, like the swineherds, were merely terrified, neither grateful nor sympathetic; uninspired with hope of pure teaching, of rescue from other influences of the evil one, or of any unearthly kingdom. Their formidable visitant was one to treat with all respect, but to remove with all speed, "and they began to beseech Him to depart from their borders." They began, for it did not require long entreaty; the gospel which was free to all was not to be forced upon any. But how much did they blindly fling away, who refused the presence of the meek and lowly Giver of rest unto souls; and chose to be denied, as strangers whom He never knew, in the day when every eye shall see Him.

With how sad a heart must Jesus have turned away. Yet one soul at least was won, for as He was entering into the boat, the man who owed all to Him prayed Him that he might be with Him. Why was the prayer refused? Doubtless it sprang chiefly from gratitude and love, thinking it hard to lose so soon the wondrous benefactor, the Man at whose feet he had sat down, Who alone had looked with pitiful and helpful eyes on one whom others only sought to "tame." Such feelings are admirable, but they must be disciplined so as to seek, not their own indulgence, but their Master's real service. Now a reclaimed demoniac would have been a suspected companion for One who was accused of league with the Prince of the devils. There is no reason to suppose that he had any fitness whatever to enter the immediate circle of our Lord's intimate disciples. His special testimony would lose all its force when he left the district where he was known; but there, on the contrary, the miracle could not fail to be impressive, as its extent and permanence were seen. This man was perhaps the only missionary who could reckon upon a hearing from those who banished Jesus from their coasts. And Christ's loving and unresentful heart would give this testimony to them in its fulness. It should begin at his own house and among his friends, who would surely listen. They should be told how great things the Lord had done for him, and Jesus expressly added, how He had mercy upon thee, that so they might learn their mistake, who feared and shrank from such a kindly visitant. Here is a lesson for these modern days, when the conversion of any noted profligate is sure to be followed by attempts to push him into a vagrant publicity, not only full of peril in itself, but also removing him from the familiar sphere in which his consistent life would be more convincing than all sermons, and where no suspicion of self-interest could overcloud the brightness of his testimony.

Possibly there was yet another reason for leaving him in his home. He may have desired to remain close to Jesus, lest, when the Saviour was absent, the evil spirits should resume their sway. In that case it would be necessary to exercise his faith and convince him that the words of Jesus were far-reaching and effectual, even when He was Himself remote. If so, he learned the lesson well, and became an evangelist through all the region of Decapolis. And where all did marvel, we may hope that some were won. What a revelation of mastery over the darkest and most dreadful forces of evil, and of respect for the human will (which Jesus never once coerced by miracle, even when it rejected Him), what unwearied care for the rebellious, and what a sense of sacredness in lowly duties, better for the demoniac than the physical nearness of his Lord, are combined in this astonishing narrative, which to invent in the second century would itself have required miraculous powers.

WITH JAIRUS.

Mark v. 21-43 (R. V.).

Repulsed from Decapolis, but consoled by the rescue and zeal of the demoniac, Jesus returned to the western shore, and a great multitude assembled. The other boats which were with Him had doubtless spread the tidings of the preternatural calm which rescued them from deadly peril, and it may be that news of the event of Gadara arrived almost as soon as He Whom they celebrated. We have seen that St. Mark aims at bringing the four great miracles of this period into the closest sequence. And so he passes over a certain brief period with the words "He was by the sea." But in fact Jesus was reasoning with the Pharisees, and with the disciples of John, who had assailed Him and His followers, when one of their natural leaders threw himself at His feet.

The contrast is sharp enough, as He rises from a feast to go to the house of mourning, from eating with publicans and sinners to accompany a ruler of the synagogue. These unexpected calls, these sudden alternations all found Him equally ready to bear the same noble part, in the most dissimilar scenes, and in treating temperaments the most unlike. But the contrast should also be observed between those harsh and hostile critics who hated Him in the interests of dogma and of ceremonial, and Jairus, whose views were theirs, but whose heart was softened by trouble. The danger of his child was what drove him, perhaps reluctantly enough, to beseech Jesus much. And nothing could be more touching than his prayer for his "little daughter," its sequence broken as if with a sob; wistfully pictorial as to the process, "that Thou come and lay Thy hands upon her," and dilating wistfully too upon the effect, "that she may be made whole and live." If a miracle were not in question, the dullest critic in Europe would confess that this exquisite supplication was not composed by an evangelist, but a father. And he would understand also why the very words in their native dialect were not forgotten, which men had heard awake the dead.

As Jesus went with him, a great multitude followed Him, and they thronged Him. It is quite evident that Jesus did not love these gatherings of the idly curious. Partly from such movements He had withdrawn Himself to Gadara; and partly to avoid exciting them He strove to keep many of His miracles a secret. Sensationalism is neither grace nor a means of grace. And it must be considered that the perfect Man, as far from mental apathy or physical insensibility as from morbid fastidiousness, would find much to shrink away from in the pressure of a city crowd. The contact of inferior organisations, selfishness driving back the weak and gentle, vulgar scrutiny and audible comment, and the desire for some miracle as an idle show, which He would only work because His gentle heart was full of pity, all these would be utterly distressing to Him who was

> "The first true gentleman that ever breathed,"

as well as the revelation of God in flesh. It is therefore noteworthy that we have many examples of His grace and goodness amid such trying scenes, as when He spoke to Zacchæus, and called Bartimæus to Him to be healed. Jesus could be wrathful, but He was never irritated.

Of these examples one of the most beautiful is here recorded, for as He went with Jairus, amidst the rude and violent thronging of the crowds, moving alone (as men often are in sympathy and in heart alone amid seething thoroughfares), He suddenly became aware of a touch, the timid and stealthy touch of a broken-hearted woman, pale and wasted with disease, but borne through the crowd by the last effort of despair and the first energy of a newborn hope. She ought not to have come thither, since her touch spread ceremonial uncleanness far and wide. Nor ought she to have stolen a blessing instead of praying for it. And if we seek to blame her still further, we may condemn the superstitious notion that Christ's gifts of healing were not conscious and loving actions, but a mere contagion of health, by which one might profit unfelt and undiscovered. It is urged indeed that hers was not a faith thus clouded, but so majestic as to believe that Christ would know and respond to the silent hint of a gentle touch. And is it supposed that Jesus would have dragged into publicity such a perfect lily of the vale as this? and what means her trembling confession, and the discovery that she could not be hid? But when our keener intellects have criticised her errors, and our clearer ethics have frowned upon her misconduct, one fact remains. She is the only woman upon whom Jesus is recorded to have bestowed any epithet but a formal one. Her misery and her faith drew from His guarded lips, the tender and yet lofty word Daughter.

So much better is the faith which seeks for blessing, however erroneous be its means, than the heartless propriety which criticises with most dispassionate clearness, chiefly because it really seeks nothing for itself at all. Such faith is always an appeal, and is responded to, not as she supposed, mechanically, unconsciously, nor, of course, by the *opus operatum* of a garment touched (or of a sacrament formally received), but by the going forth of power from a conscious Giver, in response to the need which has approached His fulness. He knew her secret and fearful approach to Him, as He knew the guileless heart of Nathanael, whom He marked beneath the fig-tree. And He dealt with her very gently. Doubtless there are many such concealed woes, secret, untold miseries which eat deep into gentle hearts, and are never spoken, and cannot, like Bartimæus, cry aloud for public pity. For these also there is balm in Gilead, and if the Lord requires them to confess Him publicly, He will first give them due strength to do so. This enfeebled and emaciated woman was allowed to feel in her body that she was healed of her plague, before she was called upon for her confession. Jesus asked, Who touched my clothes? It was one thing to press Him, driven forward by the multitude around, as circumstances impel so many to become churchgoers, readers of Scripture, interested in sacred questions and controversies until they are borne as by physical propulsion into the closest contact with our Lord, but not drawn thither by any personal craving or sense of want, nor expecting any blessed reaction of "the power proceeding from Him." It was another thing to reach out a timid hand and touch appealingly even that tasselled fringe of His garment which had a religious significance, whence perhaps she drew a semi-superstitious hope. In the face of this incident, can any orthodoxy forbid us to believe that the grace of Christ extends, now as of yore, to many a superstitious and erring approach by which souls reach after Christ?

The disciples wondered at His question: they knew not that "the flesh presses, but faith touches;" but as He continued to look around and seek her that had done this thing, she fell down and told Him all the truth. Fearing and trembling she spoke, for indeed she had been presumptuous, and ventured without permission. But the chief thing was that she had ventured, and so He graciously replied, Daughter, thy faith hath made thee whole; go in peace and be whole of thy plague. Thus she received more than she had asked or thought; not only healing for the body, but also a victory over that self-effacing, fearful, half-morbid diffidence, which long and weakening disease entails. Thus also, instead of a secret cure, she was given the open benediction of her Lord, and such confirmation in her privilege as many more would enjoy if only with their mouth confession were made unto salvation.

While He yet spoke, and the heart of Jairus was divided between joy at a new evidence of the power of Christ, and impatience at every moment of delay, not knowing that his Benefactor was the Lord of time itself, the fatal message came, tinged with some little irony as it asked, Why troublest thou the Teacher any more? It is quite certain that Jesus had before now raised the dead, but no miracle of the kind had acquired such prominence as afterwards to claim a place in the Gospel narratives.

One is led to suspect that the care of Jesus had prevailed, and they had not been widely published. To those who brought this message, perhaps no such case had travelled, certainly none had gained their credence. It was in their eyes a thing incredible that He should raise the dead, and indeed there is a wide difference between every other miracle and this. We struggle against all else, but when death comes we feel that all is over except to bury out of our sight what once was beautiful and dear. Death is destiny made visible; it is the irrevocable. Who shall unsay the words of a bleeding heart, I shall go to him but he shall not return to me? But Christ came to destroy him that had the power of death. Even now, through Him, we are partakers of a more intense and deeper life, and have not only the hope but the beginning of immortality. And it was the natural seal upon His lofty mission, that He should publicly raise up the dead. For so great a task, shall we say that Jesus now gathers all His energies? That would be woefully to misread the story; for a grand simplicity, the easy bearing of unstrained and amply adequate resources, is common to all the narratives of life brought back. We shall hereafter see good reason why Jesus employed means for other miracles, and even advanced by stages in the work. But lest we should suppose that effort was necessary, and His power but just sufficed to overcome the resistance, none of these supreme miracles is wrought with the slightest effort. Prophets and apostles may need to stretch themselves upon the bed or to embrace the corpse; Jesus, in His own noble phrase, awakes it out of sleep. A wonderful ease and quietness pervade the narratives, expressing exactly the serene bearing of the Lord of the dead and of the living. There is no holding back, no toying with the sorrow of the bereaved, such as even Euripides, the tenderest of the Greeks, ascribed to the demigod who tore from the grip of death the heroic wife of Admetus. Hercules plays with the husband's sorrow, suggests the consolation of a new bridal, and extorts the angry cry, "Silence, what have you said? I would not have believed it of you." But what is natural to a hero, flushed with victory and the sense of patronage, would have ill become the absolute self-possession and gentle grace of Jesus. In every case, therefore, He is full of encouragement and sympathy, even before His work is wrought. To the widow of Nain He says, "Weep not." He tells the sister of Lazarus, "If thou wilt believe, thou shalt see the salvation of God." And when these disastrous tidings shake all the faith of Jairus, Jesus loses not a moment in reassuring Him: "Fear not, only believe," He says, not heeding the word spoken: that is to say, Himself unagitated and serene.*

In every case some co-operation was expected from the bystanders. The bearers of the widow's son halted, expectant, when this majestic and tender Wayfarer touched the bier. The friends of Lazarus rolled away the stone from the sepulchre. But the professional mourners in the house of Jairus were callous and insensible, and when He interrupted their clamorous wailing, with the question, Why make ye tumult and weep? they laughed Him to scorn; a fit expression of the world's purblind incredulity, its reliance upon ordinary "experience" to disprove all possibilities of the extraordinary and Divine, and its heartless transition from conventional sorrow to ghastly laughter, mocking in the presence of death—which is, in its view, so desperate —the last hope of humanity. Laughter is not the fitting mood in which to contradict the Christian hope, that our lost ones are not dead, but sleep. The new and strange hope for humanity which Jesus thus asserted, He went on to prove, but not for them. Exerting that moral ascendency, which sufficed Him twice to cleanse the Temple, He put them all forth, as already He had shut out the crowd, and all His disciples but "the elect of His election," the three who now first obtain a special privilege. The scene was one of surpassing solemnity and awe; but not more so than that of Nain, or by the tomb of Lazarus. Why then were not only the idly curious and the scornful, but nine of His chosen ones excluded? Surely we may believe, for the sake of the little girl, whose tender grace of unconscious maidenhood should not, in its hour of reawakened vitality, be the centre of a gazing circle. He kept with Him the deeply reverential and the loving, the ripest apostles, and the parents of the child, since love and reverence are ever the conditions of real insight. And then, first, was exhibited the gentle and profound regard of Christ for children. He did not arouse her, as others, with a call only, but took her by the hand, while He spoke to her those Aramaic words, so marvellous in their effect, which St. Peter did not fail to repeat to St. Mark as he had heard them, Talitha cumi; Damsel, I say unto thee, Arise. They have an added sweetness when we reflect that the former word, though applied to a very young child, is in its root a variation of the word for a little lamb. How exquisite from the lips of the Good Shepherd, Who gave His life for the sheep. How strange to be thus awakened from the mysterious sleep, and to gaze with a child's fresh eyes into the loving eyes of Jesus. Let us seek to realise such positions, to comprehend the marvellous heart which they reveal to us, and we shall derive more love and trust from the effort than from all such doctrinal inference and allegorising as would dry up, into a *hortus siccus*, the sweetest blooms of the sweetest story ever told.

*Unless indeed the meaning be rather, "*over* hearing the word," which is not its force in the New Testament (Matt. xviii. 17, twice).

So shall we understand what happened next in all three cases. Something preternatural, and therefore dreadful, appeared to hang about the lives so wondrously restored. The widow of Nain did not dare to embrace her son until Christ "gave him to his mother." The bystanders did not touch Lazarus, bound hand and foot, until Jesus bade them "loose him and let him go." And the five who stood about this child's bed, amazed straightway with a great amazement, had to be reminded that being now in perfect health, after an illness which left her system wholly unsupplied, something should be given her to eat. This is the point at which Euripides could find nothing fitter for Hercules to utter than the awkward boast, "Thou wilt some day say that the son of Jove was a capital guest to entertain." What a contrast! For Jesus was utterly unflushed, undazzled, apparently unconscious of anything to disturb His composure. And so far was He from the unhappy modern notion, that every act of grace must be proclaimed on the housetop, and every recipient of grace, however young, however unmatured, paraded and exhibited, that He charged them much that no man should know this.

The story throughout is graphic and full of character; every touch, every word reveals the Divine Man; and only reluctance to believe a miracle prevents it from proving itself to every candid mind. Whether it be accepted or rejected, it is itself miraculous. It could not have grown up in the soil which generated the early myths and legends, by the working of the ordinary laws of mind. It is beyond their power to invent or to dream, supernatural in the strictest sense.

This miracle completes the cycle. Nature, distracted by the Fall, has revolted against Him in vain. Satan, intrenched in his last stronghold, has resisted, and humbled himself to entreaties and to desperate contrivances, in vain. Secret and unspoken woes, and silent germs of belief, have hidden from Him, in vain. Death itself has closed its bony fingers upon its prey, in vain. Nothing can resist the power and love which are enlisted on behalf of all who put their trust in Jesus.

CHAPTER VI.

REJECTED IN HIS OWN COUNTRY.

MARK vi. 1-6 (R. V.).

WE have seen how St. Mark, to bring out more vividly the connection between four mighty signs, their ideal completeness as a whole, and that mastery over nature and the spiritual world which they reveal, grouped them resolutely together, excluding even significant incidents which would break in upon their sequence. Bearing this in mind, how profoundly instructive it is that our Evangelist shows us this Master over storm and demons, over too-silent disease, and over death, too clamorously bewailed, in the next place teaching His own countrymen in vain, and an offence to them. How startling to read, at this juncture, when legend would surely have thrown all men prostrate at his feet, of His homely family and His trade, and how He Who rebuked the storm "could there do no mighty work."

First of all, it is touching to see Jesus turning once more to "His own country," just at this crisis. They had rejected Him in a frenzy of rage, at the outset of His ministry. And He had very lately repulsed the rude attempt of His immediate relatives to interrupt His mission. But now His heart leads Him thither, once again to appeal to the companions of His youth, with the halo of His recent and surpassing works upon His forehead. He does not abruptly interrupt their vocations, but waits as before for the Sabbath, and the hushed assembly in the sacred place. And as He teaches in the synagogue, they are conscious of His power. Whence could He have these things? His wisdom was an equal wonder with His mighty works, of the reality of which they could not doubt. And what excuse then had they for listening to His wisdom in vain? But they went on to ask, Is not this the carpenter? the Son of Mary? they knew His brothers, and His sisters were living among them. And they were offended in Him, naturally enough. It *is* hard to believe in the supremacy of one whom circumstances marked as our equal, and to admit the chieftainship of one who started side by side with us. In Palestine it was not disgraceful to be a tradesman, but yet they could fairly claim equality with "the carpenter." And it is plain enough that they found no impressive or significant difference from their neighbours in the "sisters" of Jesus, nor even in her whom all generations call blessed. Why then should they abase themselves before the claims of Jesus?

It is an instructive incident. First of all, it shows us the perfection of our Lord's abasement. He was not only a carpenter's son, but what this passage only declares to us explicitly, He wrought as an artisan, and consecrated for ever a lowly trade, by the toil of those holy limbs whose sufferings should redeem the world.

And we learn the abject folly of judging by mere worldly standards. We are bound to give due honour and precedence to rank and station. Refusing to do this, we virtually undertake to dissolve society, and readjust it upon other principles, or by instincts and intuitions of our own, a grave task, when it is realised. But we are not to be dazzled, much less to be misled, by the advantages of station or of birth. Yet if, as it would seem, Nazareth rejected Christ because He was not a person of quality, this is only the most extreme and ironical exhibition of what happens every day, when a noble character, self-denying, self-controlled, and wise, fails to win the respect which is freely and gladly granted to vice and folly in a coronet.

And yet, to one who reflected, the very objection they put forward was an evidence of His mission. His wisdom was confessed, and His miracles were not denied; were they less wonderful or more amazing, more supernatural, as the endowments of the carpenter whom they knew? Whence, they asked, had He derived His learning, as if it were not more noble for being original.

Are we sure that men do not still make the same mistake? The perfect and lowly humanity of Jesus is a stumbling block to some who will freely admit His ideal perfections, and the matchless nobility of His moral teaching. They will grant anything but the supernatural origin of Him to Whom they attribute qualities beyond parallel. But whence had He those qualities? What is there in the Galilee of the first century which prepares one for discovering there and then the revolutioniser of the virtues of the world, the most original, profound, and unique of all teachers, Him Whose example is still mightier than His precepts, and only not more perfect, because these also are without a flaw, Him Whom even unbelief would shrink from saluting by so cold a title as that of the most saintly of the saints. To ask with a clear scrutiny, whence the teaching of Jesus came, to realise the isolation from all centres of thought and movement, of this Hebrew, this provincial among Hebrews, this villager in Galilee, this carpenter in a village, and then to observe His mighty works in every quarter of the globe, is enough to satisfy all candid minds that His earthly circumstances have something totally unlike themselves behind them. And the more men give ear to materialism and to materialistic evolution without an evolving mind, so much the more does the problem press upon them, Whence hath this man this wisdom? and what mean these mighty works?

From our Lord's own commentary upon their rejection we learn to beware of the vulgarising effects of familiarity. They had seen His holy youth, against which no slander was ever breathed. And yet, while His teaching astonished them, He had no honour in his own house. It is the same result which so often seems to follow from a lifelong familiarity with Scripture and the means of grace. We read, almost mechanically, what melts and amazes the pagan to whom it is a new word. We forsake, or submit to the dull routine of ordinances the most sacred, the most searching, the most invigorating, and the most picturesque.

And yet we wonder that the men of Nazareth could not discern the divinity of "the carpenter," whose family lived quiet and unassuming lives in their own village.

It is St. Mark, the historian of the energies of Christ, who tells us that He "could there do no mighty work," with only sufficient exception to prove that neither physical power nor compassion was what failed Him, since "He laid His hands upon a few sick folk and healed them." What then is conveyed by this bold phrase? Surely the fearful power of the human will to resist the will of man's compassionate Redeemer.

He would have gathered Jerusalem under His wing, but she would not; and the temporal results of her disobedience had to follow: siege, massacre, and ruin. God has no pleasure in the death of him who dieth, yet death follows, as the inevitable wages of sin. Therefore, as surely as the miracles of Jesus typified His gracious purposes for the souls of men, Who forgiveth all our iniquities, Who healeth all our diseases, so surely the rejection and defeat of those loving purposes paralysed the arm stretched out to heal their sick.

Does it seem as if the words "He could not,"

even thus explained, convey a certain affront, throw a shadow upon the glory of our Master? And the words "they mocked, scourged, crucified Him," do these convey no affront? The suffering of Jesus was not only physical: His heart was wounded; His overtures were rejected; His hands were stretched out in vain; His pity and love were crucified.

But now let this be considered, that men who refuse His Spirit continually presume upon His mercy, and expect not to suffer the penalty of their evil deeds. Alas! this is impossible. Where unbelief rejected His teaching, He "could not" work the marvels of His grace. How shall they escape who reject so great salvation?

THE MISSION OF THE TWELVE.

MARK vi. 7-13 (R. V.).

Repulsed a second time from the cradle of His youth, even as lately from Decapolis, with what a heavy heart must the Loving One have turned away. Yet we read of no abatement of His labours. He did not, like the fiery prophet, wander into the desert and make request that He might die. And it helps us to realise the elevation of our Lord, when we reflect how utterly the discouragement with which we sympathise in the great Elijah would ruin our conception of Jesus.

It was now that He set on foot new efforts, and advanced in the training of His elect. For Himself, He went about the villages, whither slander and prejudice had not yet penetrated, and was content to break new ground among the most untaught and sequestered of the people. The humblest field of labour was not too lowly for the Lord, although we meet, every day, with men who are "thrown away" and "buried" in obscure fields of usefulness. We have not yet learned to follow without a murmur the Carpenter, and the Teacher in villages, even though we are soothed in grief by thinking, because we endure the inevitable, that we are followers of the Man of Sorrows. At the same moment when democracies and priesthoods are rejecting their Lord, a king had destroyed His forerunner. On every account it was necessary to vary as well as multiply the means for the evangelisation of the country. Thus the movement would be accelerated, and it would no longer present one solitary point of attack to its unscrupulous foes.

Jesus therefore called to Him the Twelve, and began to send them forth. In so doing, His directions revealed at once His wisdom and His fears for them.

Not even for unfallen man was it good to be alone. It was a bitter ingredient in the cup which Christ Himself drank, that His followers should be scattered to their own and leave Him alone. And it was at the last extremity, when he could no longer forbear, that St. Paul thought it good to be at Athens alone. Jesus therefore would not send His inexperienced heralds forth for the first time except by two and two, that each might sustain the courage and wisdom of his comrade. And His example was not forgotten. Peter and John together visited the converts in Samaria. And when Paul and Barnabas, whose first journey was together, could no longer agree, each of them took a new comrade and departed. Perhaps our modern missionaries lose more in energy than is gained in area by neglecting so humane a precedent, and forfeiting the special presence vouchsafed to the common worship of two or three.

St. Mark has not recorded the mission of the seventy evangelists, but this narrative is clearly coloured by his knowledge of that event. Thus He does not mention the gift of miraculous power, which was common to both, but He does tell of the authority over unclean spirits, which was explicitly given to the Twelve, and which the Seventy, returning with joy, related that they also had successfully dared to claim. In conferring such power upon His disciples, Jesus took the first step towards that marvellous identification of Himself and His mastery over evil, with all His followers, that giving of His presence to their assemblies, His honour to their keeping, His victory to their experience, and His lifeblood to their veins, which makes Him the second Adam, represented in all the newborn race, and which finds its most vivid and blessed expression in the sacrament where His flesh is meat indeed and His blood is drink indeed. Now first He is seen to commit His powers and His honour into mortal hands.

In doing this, He impressed on them the fact that they were not sent at first upon a toilsome and protracted journey. Their personal connection with Him was not broken, but suspended for a little while. Hereafter, they would need to prepare for hardship, and he that had two coats should take them. It was not so now: sandals would suffice their feet; they should carry no wallet; only a staff was needed for their brief excusion through a hospitable land. But hospitality itself would have its dangers for them, and when warmly received they might be tempted to be fêted by various hosts, enjoying the first enthusiastic welcome of each, and refusing to share afterwards the homely domestic life which would succeed. Yet it was when they ceased to be strangers that their influence would really be the strongest; and so there was good reason, both for the sake of the family they might win, and for themselves who should not become self-indulgent, why they should not go from house to house.

These directions were not meant to become universal rules, and we have seen how Jesus afterwards explicitly varied them. But their spirit is an admonition to all who are tempted to forget their mission in personal advantages which it may offer. Thus commissioned and endowed, they should feel as they went the greatness of the message they conveyed. Wherever they were rejected, no false meekness should forbid their indignant protest, and they should refuse to carry even the dust of that evil and doomed place upon their feet.

And they went forth and preached repentance, casting out many devils, and healing many that were sick. In doing this, they anointed them with oil, as St. James afterwards directed, but as Jesus never did. He used no means, or when faith needed to be helped by a visible application, it was always the touch of His own hand or the moisture of His own lip. The distinction is significant. And also it must be remembered that oil was never used by disciples for the edification of the dying, but for the recovery of the sick.

By this new agency the name of Jesus was more than ever spread abroad, until it reached the ears of a murderous tyrant, and stirred in his bosom not the repentance which they preached, but the horrors of ineffectual remorse.

HEROD.

Mark vi. 14-29 (R. V.).

The growing influence of Jesus demanded the mission of the Twelve, and this in its turn increased His fame until it alarmed the tetrarch Herod. An Idumæan ruler of Israel was forced to dread every religious movement, for all the waves of Hebrew fanaticism beat against the foreign throne. And Herod Antipas was especially the creature of circumstances, a weak and plastic man. He is the Ahab of the New Testament, and it is a curious coincidence that he should have to do with its Elijah. As Ahab fasted when he heard his doom, and postponed the evil by his submission, so Herod was impressed and agitated by the teaching of the Baptist. But Ahab surrendered his soul to the imperious Jezebel, and Herod was ruined by Herodias. Each is the sport of strong influences from without, and warns us that a man, no more than a ship, can hope by drifting to come safe to haven.

No contrast could be imagined more dramatic than between the sleek seducer of his brother's wife and the imperious reformer, rude in garment and frugal of fare, thundering against the generation of vipers who were the chiefs of his religion. How were these two brought together? Did the Baptist stride unsummoned into the court? Did his crafty foemen contrive his ruin by inciting the Tetrarch to consult him? Or did that restless religious curiosity, which afterwards desired to see Jesus, lead Herod to consult his forerunner? The abrupt words of John are not unlike an answer to some feeble question of casuistry, some plea of extenuating circumstances such as all can urge in mitigation of their worst deeds. He simply and boldly states the inflexible ordinance of God: It is not lawful for thee to have her.

What follows may teach us much.

1. It warns us that good inclinations, veneration for holiness in others, and ineffectual struggles against our own vices, do not guarantee salvation. He who feels them is not God-forsaken, since every such emotion is a grace. But he must not infer that he never may be forsaken, or that because he is not wholly indifferent or disobedient, God will some day make him all that his better moods desire. Such a man should be warned by Herod Antipas. Ruggedly and abruptly rebuked, his soul recognised and did homage to the truthfulness of his teacher. Admiration replaced the anger in which he cast him into prison. As he stood between him and the relentless Herodias, and "kept him safely," he perhaps believed that the gloomy dungeon, and the utter interruption of a great career, were only for the Baptist's preservation. Alas, there was another cause. He was "much perplexed": he dared not provoke his temptress by releasing the man of God. And thus temporising, and daily weakening the voice of conscience by disobedience, he was lost.

2. It is distinctly a bad omen that he "heard him gladly," since he had no claim to well-founded religious happiness. Our Lord had already observed the shallowness of men who immediately with joy receive the word, yet have no root. But this guilty man, disquieted by the reproaches of memory and the demands of conscience, found it a relief to hear stern truth, and to see from far the beauteous light of righteousness. He would not reform his life, but he would fain keep his sensibilities alive. It was so that Italian brigands used to maintain a priest. And it is so that fraudulent British tradesmen too frequently pass for religious men. People cry shame on their hypocrisy. Yet perhaps they less often wear a mask to deceive others than a cloak to keep their own hearts warm, and should not be quoted to prove that religion is a deceit, but as witnesses that even the most worldly soul craves as much of it as he can assimilate. So it was with Herod Antipas.

3. But no man can serve two masters. He who refuses the command of God to choose whom he will serve, in calmness and meditation, when the means of grace and the guidance of the Spirit are with him, shall hear some day the voice of the Tempter, derisive and triumphant, amid evil companions, when flushed with guilty excitements and with sensual desires, and deeply committed by rash words and "honour rooted in dishonour," bidding him choose now, and choose finally. Salome will tolerate neither weak hesitation nor half measures; she must herself possess "forthwith" the head of her mother's foe, which is worth more than half the kingdom, since his influence might rob them of it all. And the king was exceeding sorry, but chose to be a murderer rather than be taken for a perjurer by the bad companions who sat with him. What a picture of a craven soul, enslaved even in the purple—and of the meshes for his own feet which that man weaves, who gathers around him such friends that their influence will surely mislead his lonely soul in its future struggles to be virtuous. What a lurid light does this passage throw upon another and a worse scene, when we meet Herod again, not without the tyrannous influence of his men of war.

4. We learn the mysterious interconnection of sin with sin. Vicious luxury and self-indulgence, the plastic feebleness of character which half yields to John, yet cannot break with Herodias altogether, these do not seem likely to end in murder. They have scarcely strength enough, we feel, for a great crime. Alas, they have feebleness enough for it, for he who joins in the dance of the graces may give his hand to the furies unawares. Nothing formidable is to be seen in Herod, up to the fatal moment when revelry, and the influence of his associates, and the graceful dancing of a woman whose beauty was pitiless, urged him irresistibly forward to bathe his shrinking hands in blood. And from this time forward he is a lost man. When a greater than John is reported to be working miracles, he has a wild explanation for the new portent, and his agitation is betrayed in his broken words, "John, whom I beheaded, he is risen." "For," St. Mark adds with quiet but grave significance, "Herod himself had sent forth and laid hold upon John, and bound him." Others might speak of a mere teacher, but the conscience of Herod will not suffer it to be so; it is his victim; he has learnt the secret of eternity; "and therefore do these powers work in him." Yet Herod was a Sadducee.

5. These words are dramatic enough to prove themselves; it would have tasked Shakespeare to invent them. But they involve the ascription

from the first of unearthly powers to Jesus, and they disprove, what sceptics would fain persuade us, that miracles were inevitably ascribed, by the credulity of the age, to all great teachers, since John wrought none, and the astonishing theory that he had graduated in another world, was invented by Herod to account for those of Jesus. How inevitable it was that such a man should set at naught our Lord. Dread, and moral repulsion, and the suspicion that he himself was the mark against which all the powers of the avenger would be directed, these would not produce a mood in which to comprehend One who did not strive nor cry. To them it was a supreme relief to be able to despise Christ.

Elsewhere we can trace the gradual cessation of the alarm of Herod. At first he dreads the presence of the new Teacher, and yet dares not assail Him openly. And so, when Jesus was advised to go thence or Herod would kill Him, He at once knew who had instigated the crafty monition, and sent back his defiance to that fox. But even fear quickly dies in a callous heart, and only curiosity survives. Herod is soon glad to see Jesus, and hopes that He may work a miracle. For religious curiosity and the love of spiritual excitement often survive grace, just as the love of stimulants survives the healthy appetite for bread. But our Lord, Who explained so much for Pilate, spoke not a word to him. And the wretch, whom once the forerunner had all but won, now set the Christ Himself at naught, and mocked Him. So yet does the god of this world blind the eyes of the unbelieving. So great are still the dangers of hesitation, since not to be for Christ is to be against Him.

6. But the blood of the martyr was not shed before his work was done. As the falling blossom admits the sunshine to the fruit, so the herald died when his influence might have clashed with the growing influence of his Lord, Whom the Twelve were at last trained to proclaim far and wide. At a stroke, his best followers were naturally transferred to Jesus, Whose way he had prepared. Rightly, therefore, has St. Mark placed the narrative at this juncture, and very significantly does St. Matthew relate that his disciples, when they had buried him, "came and told Jesus."

Upon the path of our Lord Himself this violent death fell as a heavy shadow. Nor was He unconscious of its menace, for after the transfiguration He distinctly connected with a prediction of His own death the fact that they had done to Elias also whatsoever they listed. Such connections of thought help us to realise the truth, that not once only, but throughout His ministry, He Who bids us bear our cross while we follow Him, was consciously bearing His own. We must not limit to "three days" the sorrows which redeemed the world.

BREAD IN THE DESERT.

MARK vi. 30-46 (R. V.).

The Apostles, now first called by that name, because now first these "Messengers" had carried the message of their Lord, returned and told Him all, the miracles they had performed, and whatever they had taught. From the latter clause it is plain that to preach "that men should repent," involved arguments, motives, promises, and perhaps threatenings which rendered it no meagre announcement. It is in truth a demand which involves free will and responsibility as its bases, and has hell or heaven for the result of disobedience or compliance. Into what controversies may it have led these first preachers of Jesus! All was now submitted to the judgment of their Master. And happy are they still who do not shrink from the healing pain of bringing all their actions and words to Him, and hearkening what the Lord will speak.

Upon the whole, they brought a record of success. And around Him also were so many coming and going that they had no leisure so much as to eat. Whereupon Jesus draws them aside to rest awhile. For the balance must never be forgotten between the outer and the inner life. The Lord Himself spent the following night in prayer, until He saw the distress of His disciples, and came to them upon the waves. And the time was at hand when they, who now rejoiced that the devils were subject unto them, should learn by sore humiliation and defeat that this kind goeth not forth except by prayer. We may be certain that it was not bodily repose alone that Jesus desired for his flushed and excited ambassadors, in the hour of their success. And yet bodily repose also at such a time is healing, and in the very pause, the silence, the cessation of the rush, pressure, and excitement of every conspicuous career, there is an opportunity and even a suggestion of calm and humble recollection of the soul. Accordingly they crossed in the boat to some quiet spot, open and unreclaimed, but very far from such dreariness as the mention of a desert suggests to us. But the people saw Him, and watched His course, while outrunning him along the coast, and their numbers were augmented from every town as they poured through it, until He came forth and saw a great multitude, and knew that His quest of solitude was baffled. Few things are more trying than the world's remorseless intrusion upon one's privacy, and subversions of plans which one has laid, not for himself alone. But Jesus was as thoughtful for the multitude as He had just shown Himself to be for His disciples. Not to petulance but to compassion did their urgency excite Him; for as they streamed across the wilderness, far from believing upon Him, but yet conscious of sore need, unsatisfied with the doctrine of their professional teachers, and just bereaved of the Baptist, they seemed in the desert like sheep that had no shepherd. And He patiently taught them many things.

Nor was He careful only for their souls. We have now reached that remarkable miracle which alone is related by all the four Evangelists. And the narratives, while each has its individual and peculiar points, corroborate each other very strikingly. All four mention the same kind of basket, quite different from what appears in the feeding of the four thousand. St. John alone tells us that it was the season of the Passover, the middle of the Galilean spring-time; but yet this agrees exactly with St. Mark's allusion to the "green grass" which summer has not yet dried up. All four have recorded that Jesus "blessed" or "gave thanks," and three of them that He looked up to heaven while doing so. What was there so remarkable, so intense or pathetic in His expression, that it should have won this three-fold celebration? If we remember the symbolical meaning of what He did, and that as

His hands were laid upon the bread which He would break, so His own body should soon be broken for the relief of the hunger of the world, how can we doubt that absolute self-devotion, infinite love, and pathetic resignation were in that wonderful look, which never could be forgotten?

There could have been but few women and children among the multitudes who "outran Jesus," and these few would certainly have been trodden down if a rush of strong and hungry men for bread had taken place. Therefore St. John mentions that while Jesus bade "the people" to be seated, it was the men who were actually arranged (vi. 10 R. V.). Groups of fifty were easy to keep in order, and a hundred of these were easily counted. And thus it comes to pass that we know that there were five thousand men, while the women and children remained unreckoned, as St. Matthew asserts, and St. Mark implies. This is a kind of harmony which we do not find in two versions of any legend. Nor could any legendary impulse have imagined the remarkable injunction, which impressed all four Evangelists, to be frugal when it would seem that the utmost lavishness was pardonable. They were not indeed bidden to gather up fragments left behind upon the ground, for thrift is not meanness; but the "broken pieces" which our Lord had provided over and above should not be lost. "This union of economy with creative power," said Olshausen, "could never have been invented, and yet Nature, that mirror of the Divine perfections, exhibits the same combination of boundless munificence with truest frugality." And Godet adds the excellent remark, that "a gift so obtained was not to be squandered."

There is one apparent discord to set against these remarkable harmonies, and it will at least serve to show that they are not calculated and artificial.

St. John represents Jesus as the first to ask Philip, Whence are we to buy bread? whereas the others represent the Twelve as urging upon Him the need to dismiss the multitude, at so late an hour, from a place so ill provided. The inconsistency is only an apparent one. It was early in the day, and upon "seeing a great company come unto Him," that Jesus questioned Philip, who might have remembered an Old Testament precedent, when Elisha said "Give unto the people that they may eat. And his servitor said, What? shall I set this before an hundred men? He said, again . . . they shall both eat and shall also leave thereof." But the faith of Philip did not respond, and if any hope of a miracle were excited, it faded as time passed over. Hours later, when the day was far spent, the Twelve, now perhaps excited by Philip's misgiving, and repeating his calculation about the two hundred pence, urge Jesus to dismiss the multitude. They took no action until "the time was already past," but Jesus saw the end from the beginning. As surely the issue taught them not to distrust their Master's power. Now the same power is for ever with the Church; and our heavenly Father knoweth that we have need of food and raiment.

Even in the working of a miracle, the scantiest means vouchsafed by Providence are not despised. Jesus takes the barley-loaves and the fishes, and so teaches all men that true faith is remote indeed from the fanaticism which neglects any resources brought within the reach of our study and our toil. And to show how really these materials were employed, the broken pieces which they gathered are expressly said to have been composed of the barley-loaves and of the fish.

Indeed it must be remarked that in no miracle of the Gospel did Jesus actually create. He makes no new members of the body, but restores old useless ones. "And so, without a substratum to work upon He creates neither bread nor wine." To do this would not have been a whit more difficult, but it would have expressed less aptly His mission, which was not to create a new system of things, but to renew the old, to recover the lost sheep, and to heal the sick at heart.

Every circumstance of this miracle is precious. That vigilant care of the weak which made the people sit down in groups, and await their turn to be supplied, is a fine example of the practical eye for details which was never, before or since, so perfectly united with profound thought, insight into the mind of God, and the wants of the human race.

The words, Give ye them to eat, may serve as an eternal rebuke to the helplessness of the Church, face to face with a starving world, and regarding her own scanty resources with dismay. In the presence of heathenism, of dissolute cities, and of semi-pagan peasantries, she is ever looking wistfully to some costly far-off supply. And her Master is ever bidding her believe that the few loaves and fishes in her hand, if blessed and distributed by Him, will satisfy the famine of mankind.

For in truth He is Himself this bread. All that the Gospel of St. John explains, underlies the naratives of the four. And shame on us, with Christ given to feed and strengthen us, if we think our resources scanty, if we grudge to share them with mankind, if we let our thoughts wander away to the various palliatives for human misery and salves for human anguish, which from time to time gain the credence of an hour; if we send the hungry to the country and villages round about, when Christ the dispenser of the Bread of souls, for ever present in His Church, is saying, They need not depart, give ye them to eat.

The sceptical explanations of this narrative are exquisitely ludicrous. One tells us how, finding themselves in a desert, "thanks to their extreme frugality they were able to exist, and this was naturally" (what, naturally?) "regarded as a miracle." This is called the legendary explanation, and every one can judge for himself how much it succeeds in explaining to him. Another tells us that Jesus being greater than Moses, it was felt that He must have outstripped him in miraculous power. And so the belief grew up that as Moses fed a nation during forty years, with angels' food, He, to exceed this, must have bestowed upon five thousand men one meal of barley bread.

This is called the mythical explanation, and the credulity which accepts it must not despise Christians, who only believe their Bibles.

Jesus had called away His followers to rest. The multitude which beheld this miracle was full of passionate hate against the tyrant, upon whose hands the blood of the Baptist was still warm. All they wanted was a leader. And now they would fain have taken Jesus by force to thrust this perilous honour upon Him. Therefore He sent away His disciples first, that ambition and hope might not agitate and secularise their minds; and when He had dismissed the multitude He Himself ascended the neighbouring mountain, to cool His frame with the pure breezes, and to refresh His Holy Spirit by communion with His Father. Prayer was natural to Jesus; but think how much more needful is it to us. And yet perhaps we have never taken one hour from sleep for God.

"JESUS WALKING ON THE WATER."

MARK vi. 47-52 (R. V.).

(See iv. 36, pp. 847-849.)

UNWASHEN HANDS.

MARK vi. 53-vii. 13 (R. V.).

THERE is a condition of mind which readily accepts the temporal blessings of religion, and yet neglects, and perhaps despises, the spiritual truths which they ratify and seal. When Jesus landed on Gennesaret, He was straightway known, and as He passed through the district, there was a hasty bearing of all the sick to meet Him, laying them in public places, and beseeching Him that they might touch, if no more, the border of His garment. By the faith which believed in so easy a cure, a timid woman had recently won signal commendation. But the very fact that her cure had become public, while it accounts for the action of these crowds, deprives it of any special merit. We only read that as many as touched Him were made whole. And we know that just now He was forsaken by many even of His disciples, and had to ask His very Apostles, Will ye also go away?

Thus we find these two conflicting movements: among the sick and their friends a profound persuasion that He can heal them; and among those whom He would fain teach, resentment and revolt against His doctrine. The combination is strange, but we dare not call it unfamiliar. We see the opposing tendencies even in the same man, for sorrow and pain drive to His knees many a one who will not take upon his neck the easy yoke. Yet how absurd it is to believe in Christ's goodness and power, and still to dare to sin against Him, still to reject the inevitable inference that His teaching must bring bliss. Men ought to ask themselves what is involved when they pray to Christ and yet refuse to serve Him.

As Jesus moved thus around the district, and responded so amply to their supplication that His very raiment was charged with health as if with electricity, which leaps out at a touch, what an effect He must have produced, even upon the ceremonial purity of the district. Sickness meant defilement, not for the sufferer alone, but for his friends, his nurse, and the bearers of his little pallet. By the recovery of one sick man, a fountain of Levitical pollution was dried up. And the harsh and rigid legalist ought to have perceived that from his own point of view the pilgrimage of Jesus was like the breath of spring upon a garden, to restore its freshness and bloom.

It was therefore an act of portentous waywardness when, at this juncture, a complaint was made of His indifference to ceremonial cleanness. For of course a charge against His disciples was really a complaint against the influence which guided them so ill.

It was not a disinterested complaint. Jerusalem was alarmed at the new movement resulting from the mission of the Twelve, their miracles, and the mighty works which He Himself had lately wrought. And a deputation of Pharisees and scribes came from this centre of ecclesiastical prejudice, to bring Him to account. They do not assail His doctrine, nor charge Him with violating the law itself, for He had put to shame their querulous complaints about the Sabbath day. But tradition was altogether upon their side: it was a weapon ready sharpened for their use against one so free, unconventional, and fearless.

The law had imposed certain restrictions upon the chosen race, restrictions which were admirably sanitary in their nature, while aiming also at preserving the isolation of Israel from the corrupt and foul nations which lay around. All such restrictions were now about to pass away, because religion was to become aggressive, it was henceforth to invade the nations from whose inroads it had heretofore sought a covert. But the Pharisees had not been content even with the severe restrictions of the law. They had not regarded these as a fence for themselves against spiritual impurity, but as an elaborate and artificial substitute for love and trust. And therefore, as love and spiritual religion faded out of their hearts, they were the more jealous and sensitive about the letter of the law. They "fenced" it with elaborate rules, and precautions against accidental transgressions, superstitiously dreading an involuntary infraction of its minutest details. Certain substances were unclean food. But who could tell whether some atom of such substance, blown about in the dust of summer, might adhere to the hand with which he ate, or to the cups and pots whence his food was drawn? Moreover, the Gentile nations were unclean, and it was not possible to avoid all contact with them in the market-places, returning whence, therefore, every devout Jew was careful to wash himself, which washing, though certainly not an immersion, is here plainly called a baptism. Thus an elaborate system of ceremonial washing, not for cleansing, but as a religious precaution, had grown up among the Jews.

But the disciples of Jesus had begun to learn their emancipation. Deeper and more spiritual conceptions of God and man and duty had grown up in them. And the Pharisees saw that they ate their bread with unwashen hands. It availed nothing that half a population owed purity and health to their Divine benevolence, if in the process the letter of a tradition were infringed. It was necessary to expostulate with Jesus, because they walked not according to the tradition of the elders, that dried skin of an old orthodoxy in which prescription and routine would ever fain shut up the seething enthusiasms and insights of the present time.

With such attempts to restrict and cramp the free life of the soul, Jesus could have no sympathy. He knew well that an exaggerated trust in any form, any routine or ritual whatever, was due to the need of some stay and support for hearts which have ceased to trust in a Father of souls. But He chose to leave them without excuse by showing their transgression of actual precepts which real reverence for God would have respected. Like books of etiquette for people who have not the instincts of gentlemen; so do ceremonial religions spring up where the instinct of respect for the will of God is dull or dead. Accordingly Jesus quotes against these Pharisees a distinct precept, a word not of their fathers, but of God, which their tradition had caused them to trample upon. If any genuine reverence for His commandment had survived, it would have been outraged by such a collision between the text and the gloss, the precept and the precautionary supplement. But they had never felt the incongruity, never been jealous enough for the commandment of God to revolt against the encroaching tradition which insulted it. The case which Jesus gave, only as one of "many such things," was an abuse of the system of vows, and of dedicated property. It would seem that from the custom of "devoting" a man's property, and thus putting it beyond his further control, had grown up the abuse of consecrating it with such limitations that it should still be available for the owner, but out of his power to give to others. And thus, by a spell as abject as the taboo of the South Sea islanders, a man glorified God by refusing help to his father and mother, without being at all the poorer for the so-called consecration of his means. And even if he awoke up to the shameful nature of his deed, it was too late, for "ye no longer suffer him to do aught for his father or his mother." And yet Moses had made it a capital offence to "speak evil of father or mother." Did they then allow such slanders? Not at all, and so they would have refused to confess any aptness in the quotation. But Jesus was not thinking of the letter of a precept, but of the spirit and tendency of a religion, to which they were blind. With what scorn He regarded their miserable subterfuges, is seen by His vigorous word, "full well do ye make void the commandment of our God that ye may keep your traditions."

Now the root of all this evil was unreality. It was not merely because their heart was far from God that they invented hollow formalisms; indifference leads to neglect, not to a perverted and fastidious earnestness. But while their hearts were earthly, they had learned to honour God with their lips. The judgments which had sent their fathers into exile, the pride of their unique position among the nations, and the self-interest of privileged classes, all forbade them to neglect the worship in which they had no joy, and which, therefore, they were unable to follow as it reached out into infinity, panting after God, a living God. There was no principle of life, growth, aspiration, in their dull obedience. And what could it turn into but a routine, a ritual, a verbal homage, and the honour of the lips only? And how could such a worship fail to shelter itself in evasions from the heart-searching earnestness of a law which was spiritual, while the worshipper was carnal and sold under sin?

It was inevitable that collisions should arise. And the same results will always follow the same causes. Wherever men bow the knee for the sake of respectability, or because they dare not absent themselves from the outward haunts of piety, yet fail to love God and their neighbour, there will the form outrage the spirit, and in vain will they worship, teaching as their doctrines the traditions of men.

Very completely indeed was the relative position of Jesus and His critics reversed, since they had expressed pain at the fruitless effort of His mother to speak with Him, and He had seemed to set the meanest disciple upon a level with her. But He never really denied the voice of nature, and they never really heard it. An affectation of respect would have satisfied their heartless formality: He thought it the highest reward of discipleship to share the warmth of His love. And therefore, in due time, it was seen that His critics were all unconscious of the wickedness of filial neglect which set His heart on fire.

CHAPTER VII.

THINGS WHICH DEFILE.

MARK vii. 14-23 (R. V.).

WHEN Jesus had exposed the hypocrisy of the Pharisees, He took a bold and significant step. Calling the multitude to Him, He publicly announced that no diet can really pollute the soul; only its own actions and desires can do that: not that which entereth into the man can defile him, but the things which proceed out of the man.

He does not as yet proclaim the abolition of the law, but He surely declares that it is only temporary, because it is conventional, not rooted in the eternal distinctions between right and wrong, but artificial. And He shows that its time is short indeed, by charging the multitude to understand how limited is its reach, how poor are its effects.

Such teaching, addressed with marked emphasis to the public, the masses, whom the Pharisees despised as ignorant of the law, and cursed, was a defiance indeed. And the natural consequence was an opposition so fierce that He was driven to betake Himself, for the only time, and like Elijah in his extremity, to a Gentile land. And yet there was abundant evidence in the Old Testament itself that the precepts of the law were not the life of souls. David ate the showbread. The priests profaned the Sabbath, Isaiah spiritualised fasting. Zechariah foretold the consecration of the Philistines. Whenever the spiritual energies of the ancient saints received a fresh access, they were seen to strive against and shake off some of the trammels of a literal and servile legalism. The doctrine of Jesus explained and justified what already was felt by the foremost spirits in Israel.

When they were alone, "the disciples asked of Him the parable," that is, in other words, the saying which they felt to be deeper than they understood, and full of far-reaching issues. But Jesus rebuked them for not understanding what uncleanness really meant. For Him, defilement was badness, a condition of the soul. And therefore meats could not defile a man, because they did not reach the heart, but only the bodily organs. In so doing, as St. Mark plainly adds, He made all meats clean, and thus pronounced the doom of Judaism, and the new dispensation of the Spirit. In truth, St. Paul did little more than expand this memorable saying. "Nothing that goeth into a man can defile him," here is the germ of all the decision about idol meats—"neither if 'one' eat is he the better, neither if he eat not is he the worse." "The things which proceed out of a man are those which defile the man," here is the germ of all the demonstration that love fulfils the law, and that our true need is to be renewed inwardly, so that we may bring forth fruit unto God.

But the true pollution of the man comes from within; and the life is stained because the heart is impure. For from within, out of the heart of men, evil thoughts proceed, like the uncharitable and bitter judgments of His accusers—and thence come also the sensual indulgences which men ascribe to the flesh, but which depraved imaginations excite, and love of God and their neighbour would restrain—and thence are the sins of violence which men excuse by pleading sudden provocation, whereas the spark led to a conflagration only because the heart was a dry fuel—and thence, plainly enough, come deceit and railing, pride and folly.

It is a hard saying, but our conscience acknowledges the truth of it. We are not the toy of circumstances, but such as we have made ourselves; and our lives would have been pure if the stream had flowed from a pure fountain. However modern sentiment may rejoice in highly coloured pictures of the noble profligate and his pure-minded and elegant victim; of the brigand or the border ruffian full of kindness, with a heart as gentle as his hands are red; and however true we may feel it to be that the worst heart may never have betrayed itself by the worst actions, but many that are first shall be last, it still continues to be the fact, and undeniable when we do not sophisticate our judgment, that "all these evil things proceed from within."

It is also true that they "further defile the man." The corruption which already existed in the heart is made worse by passing into action; shame and fear are weakened; the will is confirmed in evil; a gap is opened or widened between the man who commits a new sin, and the virtue on which he has turned his back. Few, alas! are ignorant of the defiling power of a bad action, or even of a sinful thought deliberately harboured, and the harbouring of which is really an action, a decision of the will.

This word, which makes all meats clean, ought for ever to decide the question whether certain drinks are in the abstract unlawful for a Christian.

We must remember that it leaves untouched the question, what restrictions may be necessary for men who have depraved and debased their own appetites, until innocent indulgence *does* reach the heart and pervert it. Hand and foot are innocent, but men there are who cannot enter into life otherwise than halt or maimed. Also it leaves untouched the question, as long as such men exist, how far may I be privileged to share and so to lighten the burden imposed on them by past transgressions? It is surely a noble sign of religious life in our day, that many thousands can say, as the Apostle said, of innocent joys, "Have we not a right? . . . Nevertheless we did not use this right, but we bear all things, that we may cause no hindrance to the gospel of Christ."

Nevertheless the rule is absolute: "Whatsoever from without goeth into the man, it cannot defile him." And the Church of Christ is bound to maintain, uncompromised and absolute, the liberty of Christian souls.

Let us not fail to contrast such teaching as this of Jesus with that of our modern materialism. "The value of meat and drink is perfectly transcendental," says one. "Man is what he eats," says another. But it is enough to make us tremble, to ask what will issue from such teaching if it ever grasps firmly the mind of a single generation. What will become of honesty, when the value of what may be had by theft is transcendental? How shall armies be persuaded to suffer hardness, and populations to famish within beleaguered walls, when they learn that "man is what he eats," so that his very essence is visibly enfeebled, his personality starved out, as he grows pale and wasted underneath his country's flag? In vain shall such a generation strive to keep alive the flame of generous self-devotion. Self-devotion seemed to their fathers to be the noblest attainment; to them it can be only a worn-out form of speech to say that the soul can overcome the flesh. For to them the man *is* the flesh; he is the resultant of his nourishment; what enters into the mouth makes his character, for it makes him all.

There is that within us all which knows better; which sets against the aphorism, "Man is what he eats;" the text "As a man thinketh in his heart so is he;" which will always spurn the doctrine of the brute, when it is boldly confronted with the doctrine of the Crucified.

THE CHILDREN AND THE DOGS.

MARK vii. 24-30 (R. V.).

THE ingratitude and perverseness of His countrymen have now driven Jesus into retirement "on the borders" of heathenism. It is not clear that He has yet crossed the frontier, and some presumption to the contrary is found in the statement that a woman, drawn by a fame which had long since gone throughout all Syria, "came out of those borders" to reach Him. She was not only "a Greek" (by language or by creed as conjecture may decide, though very probably the word means little more than a Gentile), but even of the especially cursed race of Canaan, the reprobate of reprobates. And yet the prophet Zechariah had foreseen a time when the Philistine also should be a remnant for our God, and as a chieftain in Judah, and when the most stubborn race of all the Canaanites should be absorbed in Israel as thoroughly as that which gave Araunah to the kindliest intercourse with David, for Ekron should be as a Jebusite (ix. 7). But the hour for breaking down the middle wall of partition was not yet fully come. Nor did any friend plead for this unhappy woman, that she loved the nation and had built a synagogue; nothing as yet lifted her above the dead level of that paganism to which Christ, in the days of His flesh and upon earth, had no commission. Even the great champion and apostle of the Gentiles confessed that His Lord was a minister of the circumcision by the grace of God, and it was by His ministry to the Jews that the Gentiles were ultimately to be won. We need not be surprised therefore at His silence when she pleaded, for this might well be calculated to elicit some expression of faith, something to separate her from her fellows, and so enable Him to bless her without breaking down prematurely all distinctions. Also it must be considered that nothing could more offend His countrymen than to grant her prayer, while as yet it was impossible to hope for any compensating harvest among her fellows, such as had been reaped in Samaria. What is surprising is the apparent harshness of expression which follows that silence, when even His disciples are induced to intercede for her. But theirs was only the softness which yields to clamour, as many people give alms, not to silent worth, but to loud and pertinacious importunity. And they even presumed to throw their own discomfort into the scale, and urge as a reason for this intercession, that she crieth after *us*. But Jesus was occupied with His mission, and unwilling to go farther than He was sent.

In her agony she pressed nearer still to Him when He refused, and worshipped Him, no longer as the Son of David, since what was Hebrew in His commission made against her; but simply appealed to His compassion, calling Him Lord. The absence of these details from St. Mark's narrative is interesting, and shows the mistake of thinking that his gospel is simply the most graphic and the fullest. It is such when our Lord Himself is in action; its information is derived from one who pondered and told all things, not as they were pictorial in themselves, but as they illustrated the one great figure of the Son of man. And so the answer of Jesus is fully given, although it does not appear as if grace were poured into His lips. "Let the children first be filled, for it is not meet to take the children's bread, and to cast it to the dogs." It might seem that sterner words could scarcely have been spoken, and that His kindness was only for the Jews, who even in their ingratitude were to the best of the Gentiles as children compared with dogs. Yet she does not contradict Him. Neither does she argue back,—for the words, "Truth, Lord, but . . ." have rightly disappeared from the Revised Version, and with them a certain contentious aspect which they give to her reply. On the contrary she assents, she accepts all the seeming severity of His view, because her penetrating faith has detected its kindly undertone, and the triple opportunity which it offers to a quick and confiding intelligence. It is indeed touching to reflect how impregnable was Jesus in controversy with the keenest intellects of Judaism, with how sharp a weapon He rent their snares, and retorted their arguments to their confusion, and then to observe Him inviting, tempting, preparing the way for an argument which would lead Him, gladly won, captive to a heathen's and a woman's importunate and trustful sagacity. It is the same Divine condescension which gave to Jacob his new name of Israel because He had striven with God and prevailed.

And let us reverently ponder the fact that this pagan mother of a demoniacal child, this woman whose name has perished, is the only person who won a dialectical victory in striving with the Wisdom of God; such a victory as a father allows to his eager child, when he raises gentle obstacles, and even assumes a transparent mask of harshness, but never passess the limit of the trust and love which He is probing.

The first and most obvious opportunity which He gives to her is nevertheless hard to show in English. He might have used an epithet suitable for those fierce creatures which prowl through Eastern streets at night without any master, living upon refuse, a peril even to men who are unarmed. But Jesus used a diminutive word, not found elsewhere in the New Testament, and quite unsuitable to those fierce beasts, a word "in which the idea of uncleanness gives place to that of dependence, of belonging to man and to the family." No one applies our colloquial epithet "doggie" to a fierce or rabid brute. Thus Jesus really domesticated the Gentile world. And nobly, eagerly, yet very modestly she used this tacit concession, when she repeated His carefully selected word, and inferred from it that her place was not among those vile "dogs" which are "without," but with the domestic dogs, the little dogs underneath the table.

Again, she observed the promise which lurked under seeming refusal, when He said, "Let the children first be filled," and so implied that her turn should come, that it was only a question of time. And so she answers that such dogs as He would make of her and hers do not fast utterly until their mealtime after the children have been satisfied; they wait under the table, and some ungrudged fragments reach them there, some "crumbs."

Moreover, and perhaps chiefly, the bread she craves need not to be torn from hungry children. Their Benefactor has had to wander off into concealment, they have let fall, unheeding, not only crumbs, although her noble tact expresses it thus lightly to their countryman, but far more than she divined, even the very Bread of Life. Surely His own illustration has admitted her right to profit by the heedlessness of "the children." And He *had* admitted all this: He had meant to be thus overcome. One loves to think of the first flush of hope in that trembling mother's heavy heart, as she discerned His intention and said within herself, "Oh, surely I am not mistaken; He does not really refuse at all; He wills that I should answer Him and prevail." One supposes that she looked up, half afraid to utter the great rejoinder, and took courage when she met His questioning inviting gaze.

And then comes the glad response, no longer spoken coldly and without an epithet: "Oh, woman, great is thy faith." He praises not her adroitness nor her humility, but the faith which would not doubt, in that dark hour, that light was behind the cloud; and so He sets no other limit to His reward than the limit of her desires: "Be it unto thee even as thou wilt."

Let us learn that no case is too desperate for prayer, and perseverance will surely find at last that our Lord delighteth to be gracious. Let us be certain that the brightest and most confiding view of all His dealings is the truest, and man, if only he trusts aright, shall live by every word that proceedeth out of the mouth of God.

Thus did Jesus declare, in action as in word, the fading out of all distinction between the ceremonially clean and unclean. He crossed the limits of the Holy Land: He found great faith in a daughter of the accursed race; and He ratified and acted upon her claim that the bread which fell neglected from the table of the Jew was not forbidden to the hunger of the Gentile. The history of the Acts of the Apostles is already here in spirit.

THE DEAF AND DUMB MAN.

MARK vii. 31-37 (R. V.).

There are curious and significant varieties in the methods by which our Saviour healed. We have seen Him, when watched on the Sabbath by eager and expectant foes, baffling all their malice by a miracle without a deed, by refusing to cross the line of the most rigid and ceremonial orthodoxy, by only commanding an innocent gesture, Stretch forth thine hand. In sharp contrast with such a miracle is the one which we have now reached. There is brought to Him a man who is deaf, and whose speech therefore could not have been more than a babble, since it is by hearing that we learn to articulate; but of whom we are plainly told that he suffered from organic inability to utter as well as to hear, for he had an impediment in his speech, the string of his tongue needed to be loosed, and Jesus touched his tongue as well as his ears, to heal him.

It should be observed that no unbelieving theory can explain the change in our Lord's method. Some pretend that all the stories of His miracles grew up afterward, from the sense of awe with which He was regarded. How does that agree with effort, sighing, and even gradation in the stages of recovery, following after the most easy, astonishing, and instantaneous cures? Others believe that the enthusiasm of His teaching and the charm of His presence conveyed healing efficacy to the impressible and the nervous. How does this account for the fact that His earliest miracles were the prompt and effortless ones, and as time passes on, He secludes the patient and uses agencies, as if the resistance to His power were more appreciable? Enthusiasm would gather force with every new success.

All becomes clear when we accept the Christian doctrine. Jesus came in the fulness of the love of God, with both hands filled with gifts. On His part there is no hesitation and no limit. But on the part of man there is doubt, misconception, and at last open hostility. A real chasm is opened between man and the grace He gives, so that, although not straitened in Him, they are straitened in their own affections. Even while they believe in Him as a healer, they no longer accept Him as their Lord.

And Jesus makes it plain to them that the gift is no longer so easy, spontaneous, and of public right as formerly. In His own country He could not do many mighty works. And now, returning by indirect routes, and privately, from the heathen shores whither Jewish enmity had driven Him, He will make the multitude feel a kind of exclusion, taking the patient from among them, as He does again presently in Bethsaida (chap. viii. 23). There is also, in the deliberate act of seclusion and in the means employed, a stimulus for the faith of the sufferer, which would scarcely have been needed a little while before.

The people were unconscious of any reason why this cure should differ from former ones. And so they besought Jesus to lay His hand on him, the usual and natural expression for a conveyance of invisible power. But even if no other objection had existed, this action would have meant little to the deaf and dumb man, living in a silent world, and needing to have his faith aroused by some yet plainer sign. Jesus therefore removes him from the crowd whose curiosity would distract his attention—even as by affliction and pain He still isolates each of us at times from the world, shutting us up with God.

He speaks the only language intelligible to such a man, the language of signs, putting His fingers into his ears as if to break a seal, conveying the moisture of His own lip to the silent tongue, as if to impart its faculty, and then, at what should have been the exultant moment of conscious and triumphant power, He sighed deeply.

What an unexpected revelation of the man rather than the wonder worker. How unlike anything that theological myth or heroic legend would have invented. Perhaps, as Keble sings, He thought of those moral defects for which, in a responsible universe, no miracle may be wrought, of "the deaf heart, the dumb by choice." Perhaps, according to Stier's ingenious guess, He sighed because, in our sinful world, the gift of hearing is so doubtful a blessing, and the faculty of speech so apt to be perverted. One can almost imagine that no human endowment is ever given by Him Who knows all, without a touch of sadness. But it is more natural to suppose that He Who is touched with the feeling of our infirmities, and Who bare our sickness, thought upon the countless miseries of which this was but a specimen, and sighed for the perverseness by which the fulness of His compassion was being restrained. We are reminded by that sigh, however we explain it, that the only triumphs which made Him rejoice in Spirit were very different from displays of His physical ascendancy.

It is interesting to observe that St. Mark, informed by the most ardent and impressible of the apostles, by him who reverted, long afterwards, to the voice which he heard in the holy mount, has recorded several of the Aramaic words which Jesus uttered at memorable junctures. "Ephphatha, Be opened," He said, and the bond of his tongue was loosed, and his speech, hitherto incoherent, became plain. But the Gospel which tells us the first word he heard is silent about what he said. Only we read, and this is suggestive enough, that the command was at once given to him, as well as to the bystanders, to keep silent. Not copious speech, but wise restraint, is what the tongue needs most to learn. To him, as to so many whom Christ had healed, the injunction came, not to preach without a commission, not to suppose that great blessings require loud announcement, or unfit men for lowly and quiet places. Legend would surely have endowed with special eloquence the lips which Jesus unsealed. He charged them that they should tell no man.

It was a double miracle, and the latent unbelief became clear of the very men who had hoped for some measure of blessing. For they were beyond measure astonished, saying He doeth all things well, celebrating the power which restored the hearing and the speech together. Do we blame their previous incredulity? Perhaps we also expect some blessing from our Lord, yet fail to bring Him all we have and all we are for blessing. Perhaps we should be astonished beyond measure if we received at the hands of Jesus a sanctification that extended to all our powers.

CHAPTER VIII.

THE FOUR THOUSAND.

MARK viii. 1-10 (R. V.).

WE now come upon a miracle strangely similar to that of the Feeding of the Four Thousand. And it is worth while to ask what would have been the result, if the Gospels which contain this narrative had omitted the former one. Scepticism would have scrutinised every difference between the two, regarding them as variations of the same story, to discover traces of the growth of the myth or legend, and entirely to discredit it. Now, however, it is plain that the events are quite distinct; and we cannot doubt but that information as full would clear away as completely many a perplexity which still entangles us. Archbishop Trench has well shown that the later narrative cannot have grown out of the earlier, because it has not grown at all, but fallen away. A new legend always "outstrips the old, but here . . . the numbers fed are smaller, the supply of food is greater, and the fragments that remain are fewer." The latter point is, however, doubtful. It is likely that the baskets, though fewer, were larger, for in such a one St. Paul was lowered down over the wall of Damascus (Acts ix. 25). In all the Gospels the Greek word for baskets in the former miracle is different from the latter. And hence arises an interesting coincidence; for when the disciples had gone into a desert place, and there gathered the fragments into wallets, each of them naturally carried one of these, and accordingly twelve were filled. But here they had recourse apparently to the large baskets of persons who sold bread, and the number seven remains unaccounted for. Scepticism indeed persuades itself that the whole story is to be spiritualised, the twelve baskets answering to the twelve apostles who distributed the Bread of Life, and the seven to the seven deacons. How came it then that the sorts of baskets are so well discriminated, that the inferior ministers are represented by the larger ones, and that the bread is not dealt out from these baskets but gathered into them?

The second repetition of such a work is a fine proof of that genuine kindness of heart, to which a miracle is not merely an evidence, nor rendered useless as soon as the power to work it is confessed. Jesus did not shrink from thus repeating Himself, even upon a lower level, because His object was not spectacular but beneficent. He sought not to astonish but to bless.

It is plain that Jesus strove to lead His disciples, aware of the former miracle, up to the notion of its repetition. With this object He marshalled all the reasons why the people should be relieved. "I have compassion on the multitude, because they continue with Me now three days, and have nothing to eat: and if I send them away fasting to their home, they will faint in the way; and some of them are come from far." It is the grand argument from human necessity to the Divine compassion. It is an argument which ought to weigh equally with the Church. For if it is promised that "nothing shall be impossible" to faith and prayer, then the deadly wants of debauched cities, of ignorant and brutal peasantries, and of heathenisms festering in their corruptions—all these, by their very urgency, are vehement appeals instead of the discouragements we take them for. And whenever man is baffled and in need, then he is entitled to fall back upon the resources of the Omnipotent.

It may be that the disciples had some glimmering hope, but they did not venture to suggest anything; they only asked, Whence shall one be able to fill these men with bread here in a desert place? It is the cry of unbelief—*our* cry, when we look at our resources, and declare our helplessness, and conclude that possibly God may interpose, but otherwise nothing can be done. We ought to be the priests of a famishing world (so ignorant of any relief, so miserable), its interpreters and intercessors, full of hope and energy. But we are content to look at our empty treasuries, and ineffective organisations, and to ask, Whence shall a man be able to fill these men with bread?

They have ascertained, however, what resources are forthcoming, and these He proceeds to use, first demanding the faith which He will afterwards honour, by bidding the multitudes to sit down. And then His loving heart is gratified by relieving the hunger which it pitied, and He promptly sends the multitude away, refreshed and competent for their journey.

THE LEAVEN OF THE PHARISEES.

MARK viii. 11-21 (R. V.).

Whenever a miracle produced a deep and special impression the Pharisees strove to spoil its effect by some counter-demonstration. By so doing, and at least appearing to hold the field, since Jesus always yielded this to them, they encouraged their own faction, and shook the confidence of the feeble and hesitating multitude. At almost every crisis they might have been crushed by an appeal to the stormy passions of those whom the Lord had blessed. Once He might have been made a king. Again and again His enemies were conscious that an imprudent word would suffice to make the people stone them. But that would have spoiled the real work of Jesus more than to retreat before them, now across the lake, or, just before, into the coasts of Tyre and Sidon. Doubtless it was this constant avoidance of physical conflict, this habitual repression of the carnal zeal of His supporters, this refusal to form a party instead of founding a Church, which renewed incessantly the courage of His often-baffled foes, and led Him, by the path of steady ceaseless self-depression, to the cross which He foresaw, even while maintaining His unearthly calm, amid the contradiction of sinners against Himself.

Upon the feeding of the four thousand they demand of Him a sign from heaven. He had wrought for the public no miracle of this peculiar kind. And yet Moses had gone up, in the sight of all Israel, to commune with God in the mount that burned; Samuel had been answered by thunder and rain in the wheat harvest; and Elijah had called down fire both upon his sacrifice and also upon two captains and their bands of fifty. Such a miracle was now declared to be the regular authentication of a messenger from God, and the only sign which evil spirits could not counterfeit.

Moreover the demand would specially embarrass Jesus, because He alone was not accustomed to invoke heaven: His miracles were wrought by the exertion of His own will. And perhaps the challenge implied some understanding of what this peculiarity involved, such as Jesus charged them with, when putting into their mouth the words, This is the heir, come, let us kill Him. Certainly the demand ignored much. Conceding the fact of certain miracles, and yet imposing new conditions of belief, they shut their eyes to the unique nature of the works already wrought, the glory as of the Only-begotten of the Father which they displayed. They held that thunder and lightning revealed God more certainly than supernatural victories of compassion, tenderness, and love. What could be done for moral blindness such as this? How could any sign be devised which unwilling hearts could not evade? No wonder that hearing this demand, Jesus sighed deeply in His spirit. It revealed their utter hardness; it was a snare by which others would be entangled; and for Himself it foretold the cross.

St. Mark simply tells us that He refused to give them any sign. In St. Matthew He justifies this decision by rebuking the moral blindness which demanded it. They had material enough for judgment. The face of the sky foretold storm and clear weather, and the process of nature could be anticipated without miracles to coerce belief. And thus they should have discerned the import of the prophecies, the course of history, the signs of the times in which they lived, so plainly radiant with Messianic promise, so menacing with storm-clouds of vengeance upon sin. The sign was refused moreover to an evil and adulterous generation, as God, in the Old Testament, would not be inquired of at all by such a people as this. This indignant rejoinder St. Mark has compressed into the words, "There shall no sign be given unto this generation"—this which has proof enough, and which deserves none. Men there were to whom a sign from heaven was not refused. At His baptism, on the Mount of Transfiguration, and when the Voice answered His appeal, "Father, glorify Thy name," while the multitude said only that it thundered—at these times His chosen ones received a sign from heaven. But from those who had not was taken away even that which they seemed to have; and the sign of Jonah availed them not.

Once more Jesus "left them" and crossed the lake. The disciples found themselves with but one loaf, approaching a wilder district, where the ceremonial purity of food could not easily be ascertained. But they had already acted on the principle which Jesus had formally proclaimed, that all meats were clean. And therefore it was not too much to expect them to penetrate below the letter of the words, "Take heed, beware of the leaven of the Pharisees, and the leaven of Herod." In giving them this enigma to discover, He acted according to His usage, wrapping the spiritual truth in earthly phrases, picturesque and impressive; and He treated them as life treats every one of us, which keeps our responsibility still upon the strain, by presenting new moral problems, fresh questions and trials of insight, for every added attainment which lays our old tasks aside. But they understood Him not. Some new ceremonial appeared to them to be designed, in which everything should be reversed, and the unclean should be those hypocrites, the strictest observers of the old code. Such a mistake, however blameworthy, reveals the profound sense of an ever-widening chasm, and an expectation of a final and hopeless rupture with the chiefs of their religion. It prepares us for what is soon to come, the contrast between the popular belief and theirs, and the selection of a rock on which a new Church is to be built. In the meantime the dire practical inconvenience of this announcement led to hot discussion, because they had no bread. And Jesus, perceiving this, remonstrated in a series of indignant questions. Personal want should not have disturbed their judgment, remembering that twice over He had fed hungry multitudes, and loaded them with the surplus of His gift. Their eyes and ears should have taught them that He was indifferent to such distinctions, and His doctrine could never result in a new Judaism. How was it that they did not understand?

Thereupon they perceived that His warning was figurative. He had spoken to them, after feeding the five thousand, of spiritual bread which He would give, even His flesh to be their food. What then could He have meant by the leaven of the Pharisees but the imparting of *their* religious tendencies, their teaching, and their insincerity?

Was there any real danger that these, His chosen ones, should be shaken by the demand for a sign from heaven? Did not Philip presently, when Christ spoke of seeing the Father, eagerly cry out that this, if it were granted, would suffice them? In these words he confessed the misgiving which haunted their minds, and the longing for a heavenly sign. And yet the essence of the vision of God was in the life and the love which they had failed to know. If they could not see Him in these, He must for ever remain invisible to them.

We too require the same caution. When we long for miracles, neglecting those standing miracles of our faith, the gospel and the Church: when our reason is satisfied of a doctrine or a duty, and yet we remain irresolute, sighing for the impulse of some rare spiritual enlightenment or excitement, for a revival, or a mission, or an oration to lift us above ourselves, we are virtually asking to be shown what we already confess, to behold a sign, while we possess the evidence.

And the only wisdom of the languid, irresolute will, which postpones action in hope that feeling may be deepened, is to pray. It is by the effort of communion with the unfelt, but confessed Reality above us, that healthy feeling is to be recovered.

MEN AS TREES.

MARK viii. 22-26 (R. V.).

When the disciples arrived at Bethsaida, they were met by the friends of a blind man, who besought Him to touch him. And this gave occasion to the most remarkable by far of all the progressive and tentative miracles, in which means were employed, and the result was gradually reached. The reasons for advancing to this cure by progressive stages have been much discussed. St. Chrysostom and many others have conjectured that the blind man had but little faith, since he neither found his own way to Jesus, nor pleaded his own cause, like Bartimæus. Others brought him, and interceded for him. This may be so, but since he was clearly a consenting party, we can infer little from details which constitutional timidity would explain, or helplessness (for the resources of the blind are very various), or the zeal of friends or of paid servants, or the mere eagerness of a crowd, pushing him forward in desire to see a marvel.

We cannot expect always to penetrate the motives which varied our Saviour's mode of action; it is enough that we can pretty clearly discern some principles which led to their variety. Many of them, including all the greatest, were wrought without instrumentality and without delay, showing His unrestricted and underived power. Others were gradual, and wrought by means. These connected His "signs" with nature and the God of nature; and they could be so watched as to silence many a cavil; and they exhibited, by the very disproportion of the means, the grandeur of the Worker. In this respect the successive stages of a miracle were like the subdivisions by which a skilful architect increases the effect of a *façade* or an interior. In every case the means employed were such as to connect the result most intimately with the person as well as the will of Christ.

It must be repeated also, that the need of secondary agents shows itself, only as the increasing wilfulness of Israel separates between Christ and the people. It is as if the first rush of generous and spontaneous power had been frozen by the chill of their ingratitude.

Jesus again, as when healing the deaf and dumb, withdraws from idle curiosity. And we read, what is very impressive when we remember that any of the disciples could have been bidden to lead the blind man, that Jesus Himself drew Him by the hand out of the village. What would have been affectation in other cases was a graceful courtesy to the blind. And it reveals to us the hearty human benignity and condescension of Him Whom to see was to see the Father, that He should have clasped in His helpful hand the hand of a blind suppliant for His grace. Moistening his eyes from His own lips, and laying His hands upon him, so as to convey the utmost assurance of power actually exerted, He asked, Seest thou aught?

The answer is very striking: it is such as the knowledge of that day could scarcely have imagined; and yet it is in the closest accord with later scientific discovery. What we call the act of vision is really a two-fold process; there is in it the report of the nerves to the brain, and also an inference, drawn by the mind, which previous experience has educated to understand what that report implies. For want of such experience, an infant thinks the moon as near him as the lamp, and reaches out for it. And when Christian science does its Master's work by opening the eyes of men who have been born blind, they do not know at first what appearances belong to globes and what to flat and square objects. It is certain that every image conveyed to the brain reaches it upside down, and is corrected there. When Jesus then restored a blind man to the perfect enjoyment of effective intelligent vision, He wrought a double miracle; one which instructed the intelligence of the blind man as well as opened his eyes. This was utterly unknown to that age. But the scepticism of our century would complain that to open the eyes was not enough, and that such a miracle would have left the man perplexed; and it would refuse to accept narratives which took no account of this difficulty, but that the cavil is anticipated. The miracle now before us refutes it in advance, for it recognises, what no spectator and no early reader of the marvel could have understood, the middle stage, when sight is gained but is still uncomprehended and ineffective. The process is shown as well as the completed work. Only by their motion could he at first distinguish living creatures from lifeless things of far greater bulk. "He looked up," (mark this picturesque detail,) "and said, I see men; for I behold them as trees, walking."

But Jesus leaves no unfinished work: "Then again laid He His hands upon his eyes, and he looked steadfastly, and was restored, and saw all things clearly."

In this narrative there is a deep significance. That vision, forfeited until grace restores it, by which we look at the things which are not seen, is not always quite restored at once. We are conscious of great perplexity, obscurity, and confusion. But a real work of Christ may have begun amid much that is imperfect, much that is even erroneous. And the path of the just is often a haze and twilight at the first, yet is its light real, and one that shineth more and more unto the perfect day.

THE CONFESSION AND THE WARNING.

MARK viii. 27-32 (R. V.).

We have now reached an important stage in the Gospel narrative, the comparative withdrawal from evangelistic effort, and the preparation of the disciples for an approaching tragedy. We find them in the wild country to the north of the Lake of Galilee, and even as far withdrawn as to the neighbourhood of the sources of the Jordan. Not without a deliberate intention has Jesus led them thither. He wishes them to realise their separation. He will fix upon their consciousness the failure of the world to comprehend Him, and give them the opportunity either to acknowledge Him, or sink back to the lower level of the crowd.

This is what interests St. Mark; and it is worthy of notice that he, the friend of Peter, mentions not the special honour bestowed upon him by Christ, nor the first utterance of the memorable words "My Church."

"Who do men say that I am?" Jesus asked. The answer would tell of acceptance or rejection, the success or failure of His ministry, regarded in itself, and apart from ultimate issues unknown to mortals. From this point of view it had very plainly failed. At the beginning there was a clear hope that this was He that should come, the Son of David, the Holy One of God. But now the pitch of men's expectation was lowered. Some said, John the Baptist, risen from the dead, as Herod feared; others spoke of Elijah, who was to come before the great and notable day of the Lord; in the sadness of His later days some had begun to see a resemblance to Jeremiah, lamenting the ruin of his nation; and others fancied a resemblance to various of the prophets. Beyond this the Apostles confessed that men were not known to go. Their enthusiasm had cooled, almost as rapidly as in the triumphal procession, where they who blessed both Him, and "the kingdom that cometh," no sooner felt the chill of contact with the priestly faction, than their confession dwindled into "This is Jesus, the prophet of Nazareth." "But Who say ye that I am?" He added; and it depended on the answer whether or not there should prove to be any solid foundation, any rock, on which to build His Church. Much difference, much error may be tolerated there, but on one subject there must be no hesitation. To make Him only a prophet among others, to honour Him even as the first among the teachers of mankind, is to empty His life of its meaning, His death of its efficacy, and His Church of its authority. And yet the danger was real, as we may see by the fervent blessing (unrecorded in our Gospel) which the right answer won. For it was no longer the bright morning of His career, when all bare Him witness and wondered; the noon was over now, and the evening shadows were heavy and lowering. To confess Him then was to have learned what flesh and blood could not reveal.

But Peter did not hesitate. In answer to the question, "Who say *ye?* Is your judgment like the world's?" He does not reply, "We believe, we say," but with all the vigour of a mind at rest, "Thou art the Christ;" that is not even a subject of discussion: the fact is so.

Here one pauses to admire the spirit of the disciples, so unjustly treated in popular exposition because they were but human, because there were dangers which could appal them, and because the course of providence was designed to teach them how weak is the loftiest human virtue. Nevertheless, they could part company with all they had been taught to reverence and, with the unanimous opinion of their native land, they could watch the slow fading out of public enthusiasm, and continue faithful, because they knew and revered the Divine life, and the glory which was hidden from the wise and prudent.

The confession of Peter is variously stated in the Gospels. St. Matthew wrote for Jews, familiar with the notion of a merely human Christ, and St. Luke for mixed Churches. Therefore the first Gospel gives the explicit avowal not only of Messiahship, but of divinity; and the third Gospel implies this. "Thou art the Christ, the Son of the living God"—"the Christ of God." But St. Mark wrote for Gentiles, whose first and only notion of the Messiah was derived from Christian sources, and steeped in Christian attributes, so that, for their intelligence, all the great avowal was implied in the title itself, Thou art the Christ. Yet it is instructive to see men insisting on the difference, and even exaggerating it, who know that this Gospel opens with an assertion of the Divine sonship of Jesus, and whose theory is that its author worked with the Gospel of St. Matthew before his eyes. How then, or why, do they suppose the confession to have been weakened?

This foundation of His Church being secured, His Divine Messiahship being confessed in the face of an unbelieving world, Jesus lost no time in leading His apostles forward. They were forbidden to tell any man of Him: the vain hope was to be absolutely suppressed of winning the people to confess their king. The effort would only make it harder for themselves to accept that stern truth which they were now to learn, that His matchless royalty was to be won by matchless suffering. Never hitherto had Jesus proclaimed this truth, as He now did, in so many words. It had been, indeed, the secret spring of many of His sayings; and we ought to mark what loving ingenuity was lavished upon the task of gradually preparing them for the dread shock of this announcement. The Bridegroom was to be taken away from them, and then they should fast. The temple of His body should be destroyed and in three days reared again. The blood of all the slaughtered prophets was to come upon this generation. It should suffice them, when persecuted unto death, that the disciple was as His Master. It was still a plainer intimation when He said that to follow Him was to take up a cross. His flesh was promised to them for meat and His blood for drink. (Chap. ii. 20; John ii. 19; Luke xi. 50; Matt. x. 21, 25; 38; John vi. 54.) Such intimations Jesus had already given them, and doubtless many a cold shadow, many a dire misgiving had crept over their sunny hopes. But these it had been possible to explain away, and the effort, the attitude of mental antagonism thus forced upon them, would make the grief more bitter, the gloom more deadly, when Jesus spoke openly the saying, thenceforth so frequently repeated, that He must suffer keenly, be rejected formally by the chiefs of His creed and nation, and be killed. When He recurs to the subject (ix. 31), He adds the horror of being "delivered into the hands of men." In the tenth chapter we find Him setting His face toward the city outside which a prophet could not perish, with such fixed purpose and awful consecration in His bearing that His followers were amazed and afraid. And then He reveals the complicity of the Gentiles who shall mock and spit upon and scourge and kill Him.

But in every case, without exception, He announced that on the third day He should arise again. For neither was He Himself sustained by a sullen and stoical submission to the worst, nor did He seek so to instruct His followers. It was for the joy that was set before Him that He endured the cross. And all the faithful who suffer with Him shall also reign together with Him, and are instructed to press toward the mark for the prize of their high calling. For we are saved by hope.

But now, contrast with the utmost courage of the martyrs, who braved the worst, when it emerged at last suddenly from the veil which mercifully hides our future, and which hope can always gild with starry pictures, this courage that looked steadily forward, disguising nothing, hoping for no escape, living through all the agony so long before it came, seeing His wounds in the breaking of bread, and His blood when wine was poured. Consider how marvellous was the love, which met with no real sympathy, nor even comprehension, as He spoke such dreadful words, and forced Himself to repeat what must have shaken the barb He carried in His heart, that by-and-by His followers might be somewhat helped by remembering that He had told them.

And yet again, consider how immediately the doctrine of His suffering follows upon the confession of His Christhood, and judge whether the crucifixion was merely a painful incident, the sad close of a noble life and a pure ministry, or in itself a necessary and cardinal event, fraught with transcendent issues.

THE REBUKE OF PETER.

MARK viii. 32-ix. 1 (R. V.).

The doctrine of a suffering Messiah was strange in the time of Jesus. And to the warm-hearted apostle the announcement that his beloved Master should endure a shameful death was keenly painful. Moreover, what had just passed made it specially unwelcome then. Jesus had accepted and applauded a confession which implied all honour. He had promised to build a new Church upon a rock; and claimed, as His to give away, the keys of the kingdom of heaven. Hopes were thus excited which could not brook His stern repression; and the career which the apostle promised himself was very unlike that defence of a lost cause, and a persecuted and martyred leader, which now threatened him. The rebuke of Jesus clearly warns Peter that he had miscalculated his own prospect as well as that of his Lord, and that he must prepare for the burden of a cross. Above all, it is plain that Peter was intoxicated by the great position just assigned to him, and allowed himself an utterly strange freedom of interference with his Master's plans. He "took Him and began to rebuke Him," evidently drawing Him aside for the purpose, since Jesus "turned about" in order to see the disciples whom He had just addressed. Thus our narrative implies that commission of the keys to him which it omits to mention, and we learn how absurd is the infidel contention that each evangelist was ignorant of all that he did not record. Did the appeal against those gloomy forebodings of Jesus, the protest that such evil must not be, the refusal to recognise a prophecy in His fears, awaken any answer in the sinless heart? Sympathy was not there, nor approval, nor any shade of readiness to yield. But innocent human desire for escape, the love of life, horror of His fate, more intense as it vibrated in the apostle's shaken voice, these He assuredly felt. For He tells us in so many words that Peter was a stumbling-block to Him, although He, walking in the clear day, stumbled not. Jesus, let us repeat it again and again, endured not like a Stoic, deadening the natural impulses of humanity. Whatever outraged His tender and perfect nature was not less dreadful to Him than to us; it was much more so, because His sensibilities were unblunted and exquisitely strung. At every thought of what lay before Him, his soul shuddered like a rudely touched instrument of most delicate structure. And it was necessary that He should throw back the temptation with indignation and even vehemence, with the rebuke of heaven set against the presumptuous rebuke of flesh, "Get thee behind Me. . . . for thou art mindful not of the things of God, but the things of men."

But what shall we say to the hard word, "Satan"? Assuredly Peter, who remained faithful to Him, did not take it for an outbreak of bitterness, an exaggerated epithet of unbridled and undisciplined resentment. The very time occupied in looking around, the "circumspection" which was shown, while it gave emphasis, removed passion from the saying.

Peter would therefore understand that Jesus heard, in his voice, the prompting of the great tempter, to whom He had once already spoken the same words. He would be warned that soft and indulgent sentiment, while seeming kind, may become the very snare of the destroyer.

And the strong word which sobered him will continue to be a warning to the end of time.

When love of ease or worldly prospects would lead us to discourage the self-devotion, and repress the zeal of any convert; when toil or liberality beyond the recognised level seems a thing to discountenance, not because it is perhaps misguided, but only because it is exceptional; when, for a brother or a son, we are tempted to prefer an easy and prosperous life rather than a fruitful but stern and even perilous course, then we are in the same danger as Peter of becoming the mouthpiece of the Evil One.

Danger and hardness are not to be chosen for their own sake; but to reject a noble vocation, because these are in the way, is to mind not the things of God but the things of men. And yet the temptation is one from which men are never free, and which intrudes into what seems most holy. It dared to assail Jesus; and it is most perilous still, because it often speaks to us, as then to Him, through compassionate and loving lips.

But now the Lord calls to Himself all the multitude, and lays down the rule by which discipleship must to the end be regulated.

The inflexible law is that every follower of Jesus must deny himself and take up his cross. It is not said, Let him devise some harsh and ingenious instrument of self-torture: wanton self-torture is cruelty, and is often due to the soul's readiness rather to endure any other suffering than that which God assigns. Nor is it said, Let him take up My cross, for the burden Christ bore devolves upon no other; the fight He fought is over.

But it speaks of some cross allotted, known, but not yet accepted, some lowly form of suffering, passive or active, against which nature pleads, as Jesus heard His own nature pleading when Peter spoke. In taking up this cross we must deny self, for it will refuse the dreadful burden. What it is, no man can tell his neighbour, for often what seems a fatal besetment is but a symptom and not the true disease; and the angry man's irritability, and the drunkard's resort to stimulants, are due to remorse and self-reproach for a deeper hidden evil gnawing the spiritual life away. But the man himself knows it. Our exhortations miss the mark when we bid him reform in this direction or in that, but conscience does not err; and he well discerns the effort or the renouncement, hateful to him as the very cross itself, by which alone he can enter into life.

To him, that life seems death, the death of all for which he cares to live, being indeed the death of selfishness. But from the beginning, when God in Eden set a barrier against lawless appetite, it was announced that the seeming life of self-indulgence and of disobedience was really death. In the day when Adam ate of the forbidden fruit he surely died. And thus our Lord declared that whosoever is resolved to save his life—the life of wayward, isolated selfishness—he shall lose all its reality. the sap, the sweetness, and the glow of it. And whosoever is content to lose all this for the sake of the Great Cause, the cause of Jesus and His gospel, he shall save it.

It was thus that the great apostle was crucified with Christ, yet lived, and yet no longer he, for Christ Himself inspired in his breast a nobler and deeper life than that which he had lost, for Jesus and the gospel. The world knows, as the Church does, how much superior is self-devotion to self-indulgence, and that one crowded hour of glorious life is worth an age without a name. Its imagination is not inflamed by the picture of indolence and luxury, but by resolute and victorious effort. But it knows not how to master the rebellious senses, nor how to insure victory in the struggle, nor how to bestow upon the masses, plunged in their monotonous toils, the rapture of triumphant strife. That can only be done by revealing to them the spiritual responsibilities of life, and the beauty of His love Who calls the humblest to walk in His own sacred footsteps.

Very striking is the moderation of Jesus, Who does not refuse discipleship to self-seeking wishes but only to the self-seeking will, in which wishes have ripened into choice, nor does He demand that we should welcome the loss of the inferior life, but only that we should accept it. He can be touched with the feeling of our infirmities.

And striking also is this, that He condemns not the vicious life only: not alone the man whose desires are sensual and depraved; but all who live for self. No matter how refined and artistic the personal ambitions be, to devote ourselves to them is to lose the reality of life, it is to become querulous or jealous or vain or forgetful of the claims of other men, or scornful of the crowd. Not self-culture but self-sacrifice is the vocation of the child of God.

Many people speak as if this text bade us sacrifice the present life in hope of gaining another life beyond the grave. That is apparently the common notion of saving our "souls." But Jesus used one word for the "life" renounced and gained. He spoke indeed of saving it unto life eternal, but His hearers were men who trusted that they had eternal life, not that it was a far-off aspiration (John vi. 47, 54).

And it is doubtless in the same sense, thinking of the freshness and joy which we sacrifice for worldliness, and how sadly and soon we are disillusionised, that He went on to ask, What shall it profit a man to gain the whole world and forfeit his life? Or with what price shall he buy it back when he discovers his error? But that discovery is too often postponed beyond the horizon of mortality. As one desire proves futile, another catches the eye, and somewhat excites again the often baffled hope. But the day shall come when the last self-deception shall be at an end. The cross of the Son of man, that type of all noble sacrifice, shall then be replaced by the glory of His Father with the holy angels; and ignoble compromise, aware of Jesus and His words, yet ashamed of them in a vicious and self-indulgent age, shall in turn endure His averted face. What price shall they offer then, to buy back what they have forfeited?

Men who were standing there should see the beginning of the end, the approach of the kingdom of God with power, in the fall of Jerusalem, and the removal of the Hebrew candlestick out of its place.

CHAPTER IX.

THE TRANSFIGURATION.

MARK ix. 2-8 (R. V.).

THE Transfiguration is an event without a parallel in all the story of our Lord. This breaking forth of unearthly splendour in a life of self-negation, this miracle wrought without suffering to be relieved or want supplied, and in which He seems to be not the Giver of Help but the Receiver of Glory, arrests our attention less by the greatness of the marvel than by its loneliness.

But if myth or legend had to do with the making of our Gospels, we should have had wonders enough which bless no suppliant, but only crown the sacred head with laurels. They are as plentiful in the false Gospels as in the later stories of Mahomed or Gautama. Can we find a sufficient difference between these romantic tales and this memorable event—causes enough to lead up to it, and ends enough for it to serve?

An answer is hinted by the stress laid in all three narratives upon the date of the Transfiguration. It was "after six days" according to the first two. St. Luke reckons the broken portions of the first day and the last, and makes it "about eight days after these sayings." A week has passed since the solemn announcement that their Lord was journeying to a cruel death, that self-pity was discordant with the things of God, that all His followers must in spirit endure the cross, that life was to be won by losing it. Of that week no action is recorded, and we may well believe that it was spent in profound searchings of heart. The thief Iscariot would more than ever be estranged. The rest would aspire and struggle and recoil, and explain away His words in such strange ways, as when they presently failed to understand what the rising again from the dead should mean (ver. 10). But in the deep heart of Jesus there was peace, the same which He bequeathed to all His followers, the perfect calm of an absolutely surrendered will. He had made the dread announcement and rejected the insidious appeal; the sacrifice was already accomplished in His inner self, and the word spoken, Lo, I come to do Thy will, O God. We must steadily resist the notion that the Transfiguration was required to confirm His consecration; or, after six days had passed since He bade Satan get behind Him, to complete and perfect His decision. Yet doubtless it had its meaning for Him also. Such times of more than heroic self-devotion make large demands upon the vital energies. And He whom the angels more than once sustained, now sought refreshment in the pure air and solemn silence of the hills, and above all in communion with His Father, since we read in St. Luke that He went up to pray. Who shall say how far-reaching, how all-embracing such a prayer would be? What age, what race may not hope to have shared its intercessions, remembering how He once expressly prayed not for His immediate followers alone. But we need not doubt that now, as in the Garden, He prayed also for Himself, and for support in the approaching death-struggle. And the Twelve, so keenly tried, would be especially remembered in this season. And even among these there would be distinctions; for we know His manner, we remember that when Satan claimed to have them all, Jesus prayed especially for Peter, because his conversion would strengthen his brethren. Now this principle of benefit to all through the selection of the fittest, explains why three were chosen to be the eyewitnesses of His glory. If the others had been there, perhaps they would have been led away into millennarian day-dreams. Perhaps the worldly aspirations of

Judas, thus inflamed, would have spread far. Perhaps they would have murmured against that return to common life which St. Peter was so anxious to postpone. Perhaps even the chosen three were only saved from intoxicating and delusive hopes by the sobering knowledge that what they had seen was to remain a secret until some intervening and mysterious event. The unripeness of the others for special revelations was abundantly shown, on the morrow, by their failure to cast out a devil. It was enough that their leaders should have this grand confirmation of their faith. There was among them, henceforth, a secret fountain of encouragement and trust, amid the darkest circumstances. The panic in which all forsook Him might have been final but for this vision of His glory. For it is noteworthy that these three are the foremost afterwards in sincere though frail devotion: one offering to die with Him, and the others desiring to drink of His cup and to be baptised with His baptism.

While Jesus prays for them, He is Himself made the source of their revival. He had lately promised that they who willed to lose their life should find it unto life eternal. And now, in Him who had perfectly so willed, they beheld the eternal glory beaming forth, until His very garments were steeped in light. There is no need of proof that the spirit has power over the body; the question is only of degree. Vile passions can permanently degrade human comeliness. And there is a beauty beyond that of line or colour, seen in vivid hours of emotion, on the features of a mother beside her sleeping babe, of an orator when his soul burns within him, of a martyr when his face is as the face of an angel, and often making fairer than youthful bloom the old age that has suffered long and been kind. These help us, however faintly, to believe that there is a spiritual body, and that we may yet bear the image of the heavenly. And so once, if only once, it is given to sinful men to see how a perfect spirit can illuminate its fleshly tabernacle, as a flame illuminates a lamp, and what the life is like in which self-crucifixion issues. In this hour of rapt devotion His body was steeped in the splendour which was natural to holiness, and which would never have grown dim but that the great sacrifice had still to be carried out in action. We shall best think of the glories of transfiguration not as poured over Jesus, but as a revelation from within. Moreover, while they gaze, the conquering chiefs of the Old Testament approach the Man of Sorrows. Because the spirit of the hour is that of self-devotion, they see not Abraham, the prosperous friend of God, nor Isaiah whose burning words befit the lips that were touched by fire from an unearthly altar, but the heroic law-giver and the lion-hearted prophet, the typical champions of the ancient dispensation. Elijah had not seen death; a majestic obscurity veiled the ashes of Moses from excess of honour; yet these were not offended by the cross which tried so cruelly the faith of the apostles. They spoke of His decease, and their word seems to have lingered in the narrative as strangely appropriate to one of the speakers; it is Christ's "exodus." *

But St. Mark does not linger over this detail, nor mention the drowsiness with which they struggled; he leans all the weight of his vivid narrative upon one great fact, the evidence now given of our Lord's absolute supremacy.

For at this juncture Peter interposed. He "answered," a phrase which points to his consciousness that he was no unconcerned bystander, that the vision was in some degree addressed to him and his companions. But he answers at random, and like a man distraught. "Lord, it is good for us to be here," as if it were not always good to be where Jesus led, even though men should bear a cross to follow Him. Intoxicated by the joy of seeing the King in His beauty, and doubtless by the revulsion of new hope in the stead of his dolorous forebodings, he proposes to linger there. He will have more than is granted, just as, when Jesus washed his feet, he said "not my feet only, but also my hands and my head." And if this might be, it was fitting that these superhuman personages should have tabernacles made for them. No doubt the assertion that he wist not what to say, bears specially upon this strange offer to shelter glorified bodies from the night air, and to provide for each a place of separate repose. The words are incoherent, but they are quite natural from one who has so impulsively begun to speak that now he must talk on, because he knows not how to stop. They are the words of the very Peter whose actions we know so well. As he formerly walked upon the sea, before considering how boisterous were the waves, and would soon afterwards smite with the sword, and risk himself in the High Priest's palace, without seeing his way through either adventure, exactly so in this bewildering presence he ventures into a sentence without knowing how to close it.

Now this perfect accuracy of character, so dramatic and yet so unaffected, is evidence of the truth of this great miracle. To a frank student who knows human nature, it is a very admirable evidence. To one who knows how clumsily such effects are produced by all but the greatest masters of creative literature, it is almost decisive.

In speaking thus, he has lowered his Master to the level of the others, unconscious that Moses and Elijah were only attendants upon Jesus, who have come from heaven because He is upon earth, and who speak not of their achievements, but of His sufferings. If Peter knew it, the hour had struck when their work, the law of Moses and the utterances of the prophets whom Elijah represented, should cease to be the chief impulse in religion, and without being destroyed, should be "fulfilled," and absorbed in a new system. He was there to whom Moses in the law, and the prophets bore witness, and in His presence they had no glory by reason of the glory that excelleth. Yet Peter would fain build equal tabernacles for all alike.

Now St. Luke tells us that he interposed just when they were departing, and apparently in the hope of staying them. But all the narratives convey a strong impression that his words hastened their disappearance, and decided the manner of it. For while he yet spake, as if all the vision were eclipsed on being thus misunder-

* Once besides in the New Testament this phrase was applied to death. That was by St. Peter speaking of his own, when the thought of the transfiguration was floating in his mind, and its voices lingered unconsciously in his memory (2 Pet. i. 15, *cf.* ver. 17). The phrase, though not unclassical, is not common.

stood, a cloud swept over the three—bright, yet overshadowing them—and the voice of God proclaimed their Lord to be His beloved Son (not faithful only, like Moses, as a steward over the house), and bade them, instead of desiring to arrest the flight of rival teachers, hear Him.

Too often Christian souls err after the same fashion. We cling to authoritative teachers, familiar ordinances, and traditional views, good it may be, and even divinely given, as if they were not intended wholly to lead us up to Christ. And in many a spiritual eclipse, from many a cloud which the heart fears to enter, the great lesson resounds through the conscience of the believer, Hear Him !

Did the words remind Peter how he had lately begun to rebuke his Lord? Did the visible glory, the ministration of blessed spirits and the voice of God teach him henceforth to hear and to submit? Alas, he could again contradict Jesus, and say Thou shalt never wash my feet. I never will deny Thee. And we, who wonder and blame him, as easily forget what we are taught.

Let it be observed that the miraculous and Divine Voice reveals nothing new to them. For the words, This is My beloved Son, and also their drift in raising Him above all rivalry, were involved in the recent confession of this very Peter that He was neither Elijah nor one of the prophets, but the Son of the Living God. So true is it that we may receive a truth into our creed, and even apprehend it with such vital faith as makes us "blessed," long before it grasps and subdues our nature, and saturates the obscure regions where impulse and excitement are controlled. What we all need most is not clearer and sounder views, but the bringing of our thoughts into subjection to the mind of Jesus.

THE DESCENT FROM THE MOUNT.

MARK ix. 9-13 (R. V.).

In what state of mind did the apostles return from beholding the glory of the Lord, and His ministers from another world? They seem to have been excited, demonstrative, ready to blaze abroad the wonderful event which ought to put an end to all men's doubts.

They would have been bitterly disappointed, if they had prematurely exposed their experience to ridicule, cross-examination, conjectural theories, and all the controversy which reduces facts to logical form, but strips them of their freshness and vitality. In the first age as in the nineteenth, it was possible to be witnesses for the Lord without exposing to coarse and irreverent handling all the delicate and secret experiences of the soul with Christ.

Therefore Jesus charged them that they should tell no man. Silence would force back the impression upon the depths of their own spirits, and spread its roots under the surface there.

Nor was it right to make such a startling demand upon the faith of others before public evidence had been given, enough to make scepticism blameworthy. His resurrection from the dead would suffice to unseal their lips. And the experience of all the Church has justified that decision. The resurrection is, in fact, the centre of all their miraculous narratives, the sun which keeps them in their orbit. Some of them, as isolated events, might have failed to challenge credence. But authority and sanction are given to all the rest by this great and publicly attested marvel, which has modified history, and the denial of which makes history at once untrustworthy and incoherent. When Jesus rose from the dead, the whole significance of His life and its events was deepened.

This mention of the resurrection called them away from pleasant day-dreams, by reminding them that their Master was to die. For Him there was no illusion. Coming back from the light and voices of heaven, the cross before Him was as visible as ever to His undazzled eyes, and He was still the sober and vigilant friend to warn them against false hopes. They, however, found means of explaining the unwelcome truth away. Various theories were discussed among them, what the rising from the dead should mean, what should be in fact the limit to their silence. This very perplexity, and the chill upon their hopes, aided them to keep the matter close.

One hope was too strong not to be at least hinted to Jesus. They had just seen Elias. Surely they were right in expecting his interference, as the scribes had taught. Instead of a lonely road pursued by the Messiah to a painful death, should not that great prophet come as a forerunner and restore all things? How then was murderous opposition possible?

And Jesus answered that one day this should come to pass. The herald should indeed reconcile all hearts, before the great and notable day of the Lord came. But for the present time there was another question. That promise to which they clung, was it their only light upon futurity? Was not the assertion quite as plain that the Son of Man should suffer many things and be set at nought? So far was Jesus from that state of mind in which men buoy themselves up with false hope. No apparent prophecy, no splendid vision, deceived His unerring insight. And yet no despair arrested His energies for one hour.

But, He added, Elias had already been offered to this generation in vain; they had done to him as they listed. They had re-enacted what history recorded of his life on earth.

Then a veil dropped from the disciples' eyes. They recognised the dweller in lonely places, the man of hairy garment and ascetic life, persecuted by a feeble tyrant who cowered before his rebuke, and by the deadlier hatred of an adulterous queen. They saw how the very name of Elias raised a probability that the second prophet should be treated "as it is written of" the first.

If then they had so strangely misjudged the preparation of His way, what might they not apprehend of the issue? So should also the Son of man suffer of them.

Do we wonder that they had not hitherto recognised the prophet? Perhaps, when all is made clear at last, we shall wonder more at our own refusals of reverence, our blindness to the meaning of noble lives, our moderate and qualified respect for men of whom the world is not worthy.

How much solid greatness would some of us overlook, if it went with an unpolished and unattractive exterior? Now the Baptist was a rude and abrupt person, of little culture, unwelcome in kings' houses. Yet no greater had been born of woman.

THE DEMONIAC BOY.

MARK ix. 14-29 (R. V.).

Peter soon had striking evidence that it would not have been "good" for them to linger too long upon the mountain. And our Lord was recalled with painful abruptness from the glories of transfiguration to the scepticism of scribes, the failure and shame of disciples, and the triumph of the powers of evil.

To the Twelve He had explicitly given authority over devils, and even the Seventy, venturing by faith to cast them out, had told Him of their success with joy. But now, in the sorrow and fear of these latter days, deprived of their Master and of their own foremost three, oppressed with gloomy forebodings, and infected with the worldliness which fails to pray, the nine had striven in vain. It is the only distinct repulse recorded, and the scribes attacked them keenly. Where was their Master at this crisis? Did not they profess equally to have the necessary power? Here was a test, and some failed, and the others did not present themselves. We can imagine the miserable scene, contrasting piteously with what passed on the summit of the hill. And in the centre were an agonised father and a tortured lad.

At this moment the crowds, profoundly moved, rushed to meet the Lord, and on seeing Him, became aware that failure was at an end. Perhaps the exceeding brightness lingered still upon His face; perhaps it was but the unearthly and victorious calm of His consecration, visible in His mien; what is certain is that they were greatly amazed, and ran to Him and did homage.

Jesus at once challenged a renewal of the attack which had been too much for His apostles. "What question ye with them?" But awe has fallen upon the scribes also, and misery is left to tell its own tale. Their attack by preference upon the disciples is very natural, and it by no means stands alone. They did not ask Him, but His followers, why He ate and drank with sinners, nor whether He paid the half-shekel (Mark ii. 16; Matt. xvii. 24). When they did complain to the Master Himself, it was commonly of some fault in His disciples: Why do Thy disciples fast not? Why do they on the Sabbath day that which is not lawful? Why do they eat with defiled hands? (Mark ii. 18, 24; vii. 5). Their censures of Himself were usually muttered or silent murmurings, which He discerned, as when He forgave the sins of the palsied man; when the Pharisee marvelled that He had not washed His hands; when He accepted the homage of the sinful woman, and again when He spoke her pardon (Mark ii. 8; Luke xi. 38; vii. 39-49). When He healed the woman whom a spirit of infirmity had bent down for eighteen years, the ruler of the synagogue spoke to the people, without venturing to address Jesus (Luke xiii. 14).

It is important to observe such indications, unobtrusive, and related by various evangelists, of the majesty and impressiveness which surrounded our Lord, and awed even His bitter foes.

The silence is broken by an unhappy father, who had been the centre of the group, but whom the abrupt movement to meet Jesus has merged in the crowd again. The case of his son is among those which proved that demoniacal possession did not imply the exceptional guilt of its victims, for though still young, he has suffered long. The demon which afflicts him is dumb; it works in the guise of epilepsy, and as a disease it is affected by the changes of the moon; a malicious design is visible, in frequent falls into fire and water, to destroy him. The father had sought Jesus with him, and since He was absent had appealed to His followers, but in vain. Some consequent injury to his own faith, clearly implied in what follows, may possibly be detected already, in the absence of any further petition, and in the cold epithet, "Teacher," which he employs.

Even as an evidence the answer of Jesus is remarkable, being such as human ingenuity would not have invented, nor the legendary spirit have conceived. It would have seemed natural that He should hasten to vindicate His claims and expose the folly of the scribes, or else have reproached His followers for the failure which had compromised Him.

But the scribes were entirely set aside from the moment when the Good Physician was invoked by a bleeding heart. Yet the physical trouble is dealt with deliberately, not in haste, as by one whose mastery is assured. The passing shadow which has fallen on His cause only concerns Him as a part of the heavy spiritual burden which oppresses Him, which this terrible scene so vividly exhibits.

For the true importance of His words is this, that they reveal sufferings which are too often forgotten, and which few are pure enough even to comprehend. The prevalent evil weighed upon Him. And here the visible power of Satan, the hostility of the scribes, the failure of His own, the suspense and agitation of the crowd, all breathed the spirit of that evil age, alien and harsh to Him as an infected atmosphere. He blames none more than others; it is the "generation," so faithless and perverse, which forces Him to exclaim: "How long shall I be with you? how long shall I bear with you?" It is the cry of the pain of Jesus. It bids us to consider Him Who endured such contradiction of sinners, who were even sinners against Himself. So that the distress of Jesus was not that of a mere eye-witness of evil or sufferer by it. His priesthood established a closer and more agonising connection between our Lord and the sins which tortured Him.

Do the words startle us, with the suggestion of a limit to the forbearance of Jesus, well-nigh reached? There *was* such a limit. The work of His messenger had been required, lest His coming should be to smite the world. His mind was the mind of God, and it is written, Kiss the Son, lest He be angry.

Now if Jesus looked forward to shame and anguish with natural shrinking, we here perceive another aspect in which His coming Baptism of Blood was viewed, and we discover why He was straitened until it was accomplished. There is an intimate connection between this verse and His saying in St. John, "If ye loved Me, ye would rejoice, because I go unto My Father."

But swiftly the mind of Jesus recurs to the misery which awaits help; and He bids them bring the child to Him. Now the sweet influence of His presence would have soothed and mitigated any mere disease. It is to such influence that sceptical writers are wont to turn for an explanation, such as it is, of the works He wrought. But it was the reverse in cases of possession. There a wild sense of antagonism and revolt was wont to show itself. And we might learn that this was something more than epilepsy, even were it left doubtful otherwise, by the outburst of Satanic rage. When he saw Him, straightway the spirit convulsed him grievously, and he fell wallowing and foaming.

Yet Jesus is neither hurried nor agitated. In not one of His miracles does precipitation, or mere impulse, mingle with His grave and self-contained compassion. He will question the scribes while the man with a withered hand awaits His help. He will rebuke the disciples before quelling the storm. At Nain He will touch the bier and arrest the bearers. When He feeds the multitude, He will first command a search for loaves. He will stand still and call Bartimæus to Him. He will evoke, even by seeming harshness, the faith of the woman of Canaan. He will have the stone rolled away from the sepulchre of Lazarus. When He Himself rises, the grave-clothes are found folded up, and the napkin which bound His head laid in a place by itself, the last tribute of mortals to His mortality not being flung contemptuously aside. All His miracles are authenticated by the stamp of the same character—serene, not in haste nor tardy, since He saw the end from the beginning. In this case delay is necessary, to arouse the father, if only by interrogation, from his dull disappointment and hopelessness. He asks therefore "How long time is it since this came upon him?" and the answer shows that he was now at least a stripling, for he had suffered ever since he was a child. Then the unhappy man is swept away by his emotions: as he tells their sorrows, and thinks what a wretched life or miserable death lies before his son, he bursts into a passionate appeal. If Thou canst do anything, do this. Let pity for such misery, for the misery of father as well as child, evoke all Thy power to save. The form is more disrespectful than the substance of his cry; its very vehemence is evidence that some hope is working in his breast; and there is more real trust in its wild urgency than in many a reverential and carefully weighed prayer.

Yet how much rashness, self-assertion, and wilfulness (which is really unbelief) were mingled with his germinant faith and needed rebuke. Therefore Christ responded with his own word: "If *thou* canst: thou sayest it to Me, but I retort the condition upon thyself: with thee are indeed the issues of thine own application, for all things are possible to him that believeth."

This answer is in two respects important. There was a time when popular religion dealt too much with internal experience and attainent. But perhaps there are schools among us now which verge upon the opposite extreme. Faith and love are generally strongest when they forget themselves, and do not say "I am faithful and loving," but "Christ is trustworthy, Christ is adorable." This is true, and these virtues are becoming artificial, and so false, as soon as they grow self-complacent. Yet we should give at least enough attention to our own attainments to warn us of our deficiencies. And wherever we find a want of blessedness, we may seek for the reason within ourselves. Many a one is led to doubt whether Christ "can do anything" practical for him, since private prayer and public ordinances help him little, and his temptations continue to prevail, whose true need is to be roused up sharply to the consciousness that it is not Christ who has failed; it is he himself: his faith is dim, his grasp on his Lord is half-hearted, he is straitened in his own affections. Our personal experiences should never teach us confidence, but they may often serve to humble and warn us.

This answer also impresses upon us the dignity of Him who speaks. Failure had already come through the spiritual defects of His disciples, but for Him, though "meek and lowly of heart," no such danger is even contemplated. No appeal to Him can be frustrated except through fault of the suppliant, since all things are possible to him that believeth.

Now faith is in itself nothing, and may even be pernicious; all its effect depends upon the object. Trust reposed in a friend avails or misleads according to his love and his resources; trust in a traitor is ruinous, and ruinous in proportion to its energy. And since trust in Jesus is omnipotent, Who and what is He?

The word pierces like a two-edged sword, and reveals to the agitated father the conflict, the impurity of his heart. Unbelief is there, and of himself he cannot conquer it. Yet is he not entirely unbelieving, else what drew him thither? What impulse led to that passionate recital of his griefs, that over-daring cry of anguish? And what is now this burning sense within him of a great and inspiring Presence, which uges him to a bolder appeal for a miracle yet more spiritual and Divine, a cry well directed to the Author and Finisher of our faith? Never was medicine better justified by its operation upon disease, than the treatment which converted a too-importunate clamour for bodily relief into a contrite prayer for grace. "I believe, help Thou mine unbelief." The same sense of mixed imperfect and yet real trust should exist in every one of us, or else our belief being perfect should be irresistible in the moral sphere, and in the physical world so resigned, so confident in the Love which governs, as never to be conscious of any gnawing importunate desire. And from the same sense of need the same cry of help should spring.

Miraculous legends have gathered around the lives of many good and gracious men within Christendom and outside it. But they cannot claim to weigh against the history of Jesus, until at least one example can be produced of such direct spiritual action, so profound, penetrating, and effectual, inextricably interwoven in the tissue of any fable.

All this time the agitation of the people had increased. A multitude was rushing forward, whose excitement would do more to distract the father's mind than further delay to help him. And Jesus, even in the midst of His treatment of souls, was not blind to such practical considerations, or to the influence of circumstances. Unlike modern dealers in sensation, He can never be shown to have aimed at religious excitement, while it was His custom to discourage it. Therefore He now rebuked the unclean spirit in the lad, addressing it directly, speaking as a superior. "Thou deaf and dumb spirit, I command thee, come out of him," and adding, with explicitness which was due perhaps to the obstinate ferocity of "this kind," or perhaps was intended to help the father's lingering unbelief, "enter no more into him." The evil being obeys, yet proves his reluctance by screaming and convulsing his victim for the last time, so that he, though healed, lies utterly prostrate, and "the more part said, He is dead." It was a fearful exhibition of the disappointed malice of the pit. But it only calls forth another display of the power and love of Jesus, Who will not leave the sufferer to a gradual recovery, nor speak, as to the fiend, in words of mere authority, but reaches forth His benign hand, and raises him, restored. Here we discover the same heart which provided that the daughter of Jairus should have food, and delivered her son to the widow of Nain, and was first to remind others that Lazarus was encumbered by his grave-clothes. The good works of Jesus were not melodramatic marvels for stage effect: they were the natural acts of supernatural power and love.

JESUS AND THE DISCIPLES.

MARK ix. 28-37 (R. V.).

When the apostles had failed to expel the demon from the child they gave a very natural expression to their disappointment. Waiting until Jesus was in private and in the house, they said, "We for our parts were unable to cast it out." They take no blame to themselves. The tone is rather of perplexity and complaint because the commission formerly received had not held good. And it implies the question which is plainly expressed by St. Matthew, Why could we not cast it out? Their very unconsciousness of personal blame is ominous, and Jesus replies that the fault is entirely their own. They ought to have stimulated, as He did afterwards, what was flagging but not absent in the father, what their failure must have daunted further in him. Want of faith had overcome them, says the fuller account: the brief statement in St. Mark is, "This kind [of demon] can come out by nothing but by prayer"; to which fasting was added as a second condition by ancient copyists, but without authority. What is important is to observe the connection between faith and prayer; so that while the devil would only have gone out if they had prayed, or even perhaps only if they had been men of prayer, yet their failure was through unbelief. It plainly follows that prayer is the nurse of faith, and would have strengthened it so that it should prevail. Only in habitual communion with God can we learn to trust Him aright. There, as we feel His nearness, as we are reminded that He bends to hear our cry, as the sense of eternal and perfect power blends with that of immeasurable love, and His sympathy becomes a realised abiding fact, as our vainglory is rebuked by confessions of sin, and of dependence, it is made possible for man to wield the forces of the spiritual world and yet not be intoxicated with pride. The nearness of God is inconsistent with boastfulness of man. For want of this, it was better that the apostles should fail and be humbled, than succeed and be puffed up.

There are promises still unenjoyed, dormant and unexercised powers at the disposal of the Church to-day. If in many Christian families the children are not practically holy, if purity and consecration are not leavening our Christian land, where after so many centuries license is but little abashed and the faith of Jesus is still disputed, if the heathen are not yet given for our Lord's inheritance nor the uttermost parts of the earth for His possession—why are we unable to cast out the devils that afflict our race? It is because our efforts are so faithless. And this again is because they are not inspired and elevated by sufficient communion with our God in prayer.

Further evidences continued to be given of the dangerous state of the mind of His followers, weighed down by earthly hopes and fears, wanting in faith and prayer, and therefore open to the sinister influences of the thief who was soon to become the traitor. They were now moving for the last time through Galilee. It was a different procession from those glad circuits, not long before, when enthusiasm everywhere rose high, and sometimes the people would have crowned Him. Now He would not that any man should know it. The word which tells of His journey seems to imply that He avoided the main thoroughfares, and went by less frequented by-ways. Partly no doubt His motives were prudential, resulting from the treachery which He discerned. Partly it was because His own spirit was heavily weighed upon and retirement was what He needed most. And certainly most of all because crowds and tumult would have utterly unfitted the apostles to learn the hard lesson, how vain their daydreams were, and what a trial lay before their Master.

We read that "He taught them" this, which implies more than a single utterance, as also perhaps does the remarkable phrase in St. Luke, "Let these sayings sink into your ears." When the warning is examined, we find it almost a repetition of what they had heard after Peter's great confession. Then they had apparently supposed the cross of their Lord to be such a figurative one as all His followers have to bear. Even after the Transfiguration, the chosen three had searched for a meaning for the resurrection from the dead. But now, when the words were repeated with a naked, crude, resolute distinctness, marvellous from the lips of Him Who should endure the reality, and evidently chosen in order to beat down their lingering evasive hopes, when He says "They shall kill Him, and when He is killed, after three days He shall rise again," surely they ought to have understood.

In fact they comprehended enough to shrink from hearing more. They did not dare to lift the veil which covered a mystery so dreadful; they feared to ask Him. It is a natural impulse, not to know the worst. Insolvent tradesmen leave their books unbalanced. The course of history would have run in another channel, if the great Napoleon had looked in the face the need to fortify his own capital while plundering others. No wonder that these Galileans recoiled from searching what was the calamity which weighed so heavily upon the mighty spirit of their Master. Do not men stifle the voice of conscience, and refuse to examine themselves whether they are in the faith, in the same abject dread of knowing the facts, and looking the inevitable in the face? How few there are, who bear to think, calmly and well, of the certainties of death and judgment?

But at the appointed time the inevitable arrived for the disciples. The only effect of their moral cowardice was that it found them unready, surprised and therefore fearful, and still worse, prepared to forsake Jesus by having already in heart drawn away from Him, by having refused to comprehend and share His sorrows. It is easy to blame them, to assume that in their place we should not have been partakers in their evil deeds, to make little of the chosen foundation stones upon which Christ would build His New Jerusalem. But in so doing we forfeit the sobering lessons of their weakness, who failed, not because they were less than we, but because they were not more than mortal. And we who censure them are perhaps indolently refusing day by day to reflect, to comprehend the meaning of our lives and of their tendencies, to realise a thousand warnings, less terrible only because they continue to be conditional, but claiming more attention for that very reason.

Contrast with their hesitation the noble fortitude with which Christ faced His agony. It was His, and their concern in it was secondary. Yet for their sakes He bore to speak of what they could not bear to hear. Therefore to Him there came no surprise, no sudden shock; his arrest found Him calm and reassured after the conflict in the Garden, and after all the preparation which had already gone forward through all these latter days.

One only ingredient in His cup of bitterness is now added to those which had been already mentioned: " The Son of man is delivered up into the hands of men." And this is the same which He mentioned in the Garden: " The Son of man is betrayed into the hands of sinners."

It was that from which David recoiled when he said, " Let me fall into the hands of God, but let me not fall into the hands of men." Suffering has not reached its height until conscious malice designs the pang, and says, " So would we have it." Especially true was this of the most tender of all hearts. Yet this also Jesus foreknew, while He steadfastly set His face to go toward Jerusalem.

Faithless inability to grapple with the powers of darkness, faithless unreadiness to share the cross of Jesus, what was to be expected next? Estrangement, jealousy, and ambition, the passions of the world heaving in the bosom of the Church. But while they fail to discern the spirit of Judas, the Lord discerned theirs, and asked them in the house, What were ye reasoning in the way? It was a sweet and gentle prudence, which had not corrected them publicly nor while their tempers were still ruffled, nor in the language of severe rebuke, for by the way they had not only reasoned but disputed one with another, who was the greatest.

Language of especial honour had been addressed to Peter. Three had become possessed of a remarkable secret on the Holy Mount, concerning which hints on one side, and surmises on the other, may easily have excited jealousy. The failure of the nine to cast out the devil would also, as they were not humbled, render them irritable and self-asserting.

But they held their peace. No one asserted his right to answer on behalf of all. Peter, who was so willingly their spokesman at other times, did not vindicate his boasted pre-eminence now. The claim, which seemed so reasonable while they forgot Jesus, was a thing to blush for in His presence. And they, who feared to ask Him of His own sufferings, knew enough to feel the contrast between their temper, their thoughts and His. Would that we too by prayer and self-examination, more often brought our desires and ambitions into the searching light of the presence of the lowly King of kings.

The calmness of their Lord was in strange contrast with their confusion. He pressed no further His inquiry, but left them to weigh His silence in this respect against their own. But importing by His action something deliberate and grave, He sat down and called the Twelve, and pronounced the great law of Christian rank, which is lowliness and the lowliest service. " If any man would be the first, he shall be the least of all, and the servant of all." When Kaisers and Popes ostentatiously wash the feet of paupers, they do not really serve, and therefore they exhibit no genuine lowliness. Christ does not speak of the luxurious nursing of a sentiment, but of that genuine humility which effaces itself that it may really become a servant of the rest. Nor does He prescribe this as a penance, but as the appointed way to eminence. Something similar He had already spoken, bidding men sit down in the lowest room, that the Master of the house might call them higher. But it is in the next chapter, when despite this lesson the sons of Zebedee persisted in claiming the highest places, and the indignation of the rest betrayed the very passion it resented, that Jesus fully explains how lowly service, that wholesome medicine for ambition, is the essence of the very greatness in pursuit of which men spurn it.

To the precept, which will then be more conveniently examined, Jesus now added a practical lesson of amazing beauty. In the midst of twelve rugged and unsympathetic men, the same who, despite this action, presently rebuked parents for seeking the blessing of Christ upon their babes, Jesus sets a little child. What but the grace and love which shone upon the sacred face could have prevented this little one from being utterly disconcerted? But children have a strange sensibility for love. Presently this happy child was caught up in His arms, and pressed to His bosom, and there He seems to have lain while John, possibly conscience-stricken, asked a question and received an unexpected answer. And the silent pathetic trust of this His lamb found its way to the heart of Jesus, who presently spoke of " these little ones who believe in Me" (v. 42).

Meanwhile the child illustrated in a double sense the rule of greatness which He had laid down. So great is lowliness that Christ Himself may be found in the person of a little child. And again, so great is service, that in receiving one, even one, of the multitude of children who claim our sympathies, we receive the very Master; and in that lowly Man, who was among them as He that serveth, is manifested the very God: whoso receiveth Me receiveth not Me but Him that sent me.

OFFENCES.

Mark ix. 38-50 (R. V.).

When Jesus spoke of the blessedness of receiving in His name even a little child, the conscience of St. John became uneasy. They had seen one casting out devils in that name, and had forbidden him, " because he followeth not us." The spirit of partisanship which these words betray is somewhat softer in St. Luke, but it exists. He reports "because he followeth not (Jesus) with us."

The behaviour of the disciples all through this period is unsatisfactory. From the time when Peter contradicted and rebuked Jesus, down to their final desertion, there is weakness at every turn. And this is a curious example of it, that immediately after having failed themselves,* they should rebuke another for doing what their Master had once declared could not possibly be an evil work. If Satan cast out Satan his house was divided against itself: if the finger of God was there no doubt the kingdom of God was come unto them.

It is interesting and natural that St. John should have introduced the question. Others were usually more forward, but that was because he was more thoughtful. Peter went first into the sepulchre; but he first, seeing what was there, believed. And it was he who said "It is the Lord," although Peter thereupon plunged into the lake to reach Him. Discerning and grave; such is the character from which his Gospel would naturally come, and it belongs to him who first discerned the rebuke to their conduct implied in the words of Jesus. He was right. The Lord answered, "Forbid him not, for there is no man which shall do a mighty work in My name, and be able quickly to speak evil of Me:" his own action would seal his lips; he would have committed himself. Now this points out a very serious view of human life, too often overlooked. The deed of to-day rules to-morrow; one is half enslaved by the consequences of his own free will. Let no man, hesitating between two lines of action, ask, What harm in this? what use in that? without adding, And what future actions, good or evil, may they carry in their train?

The man whom they had rebuked was at least certain to be for a time detached from the opponents of truth, silent if not remonstrant when it was assailed, diluting and enfeebling the enmity of its opponents. And so Christ laid down the principle, "He that is not against us is for us." In St. Luke the words are more plainly pointed against this party spirit, "He that is not against you is for you."

How shall we reconcile this principle with Christ's declaration elsewhere, "He that is not with Me is against Me, and he that gathereth not with Me scattereth"?

It is possible to argue that there is no contradiction whatever, for both deny the existence of a neutral class, and from this it equally follows that he who is not with is against, and he who is not against us is with us. But this answer only evades the difficulty, which is, that one passage reckons seeming neutrality as friendship, while the other denounces it as enmity.

A closer examination reveals a more profound reconciliation. In St. Matthew, Christ announced His own personal claim; in St. Mark He declares that His people must not share it. The manifestation of God was not made to be criticised or set aside: He loves them who love Him; He demands the hearts He died for; and to give Him less is to refuse Him the travail of His soul. Therefore he that is not with Christ is against Him. The man who boasts that he does no harm, but makes no pretence of religion, is proclaiming that one may innocently refuse Christ. And it is very noteworthy that St. Matthew's aphorism was evoked, like this, by a question about the casting out of devils. There the Pharisees had said that He cast out devils by Beelzebub. And Jesus had warned all who heard, that in such a controversy, to be indifferent was to deny Him. Here, the man had himself appealed to the power of Jesus. He had passed, long ago, the stage of cool semi-contemptuous indifference. Whether he was a disciple of the Baptist, not yet entirely won, or a later convert who shrank from the loss of all things, what is plain is that he had come far on the way towards Jesus. It does not follow that he enjoyed a saving faith, for Christ will at last profess to many who cast out devils in His name, that He never knew them. But intellectual persuasion and some active reliance were there. Let them beware of crushing the germs, because they were not yet developed. Nor should the disciples suppose that loyalty to their organisation, although Christ was with them, was the same as loyalty to Him. "He that is not against *you* is for you," according to St. Luke. Nay more, "He that is not against *us* is for us," according to St. Mark. But already He had spoken the stronger word, "He that is not for *Me* is against Me."

No verse has been more employed than this in sectarian controversy. And sometimes it has been pressed too far. The man whom St. John would have silenced was not spreading a rival organisation; and we know how the same apostle wrote, long afterwards, of those who did so: "If they had been of us, they would have continued with us; but they went out that they might be made manifest how all they are not of us" (1 John ii. 19). This was simply a doer of good without ecclesiastical sanction, and the warning of the text is against all who would use the name of discipline or of order to bridle the zeal, to curb the energies, of any Christian soul. But it is as least as often the new movement as the old organisation that would silence all who follow not with it.

But the energies of Christ and His gospel can never be monopolised by any organisation whatsoever. Every good gift and every perfect gift, wherever we behold it, is from Him.

All help, then, is to be welcomed; not to hinder is to speed the cause. And therefore Jesus, repeating a former saying, adds that whosoever, moved by the name of Christ, shall give His followers one cup of water, shall be rewarded. He may be and continue outside the Church; his after life may be sadly inconsistent with this one action: that is not the question; the sole condition is the genuine motive—one impulse of true respect, one flicker of loyalty, only decided enough to speed the weary ambassador with the simplest possible refreshment, should "in no wise lose its reward." Does this imply that the giver should assuredly enter heaven? Alas, no! But this it says, that every spark of fire in the smoking flax is tended, every gracious movement is answered by a gift of further grace, to employ or to abuse. Not more surely is the thirsty disciple refreshed, than the feverish worldliness of him who just attains to render this service is fanned and cooled by breezes from heaven, he becomes aware of a deeper and nobler life, he is melted and drawn towards better things. Very blessed, or very

* That the event was recent is implied in the present tense; "he followeth not": "forbid him not"; the matter is still fresh.

miserable is he who cannot remember the holy shame, the yearning, the sigh because he is not always thus, which followed naturally upon some deed, small in itself perhaps, but good enough to be inconsistent with his baser self. The deepening of spiritual capacity is one exceeding great reward of every act of loyalty to Christ.

This was graciously said of a deed done to the apostles, despite their failures, rivalries, and rebukes of those who would fain speed the common cause. Not, however, because they were apostles, but "because ye are Christ's." And so was the least, so was the child who clung to Him. But if the slightest sympathy with these is thus laden with blessing, then to hinder, to cause to stumble one such little one, how terrible was that. Better to die a violent and shameful death, and never sleep in a peaceful grave.

There is a worse peril than from others. We ourselves may cause ourselves to stumble. We may pervert beyond recall things innocent, natural, all but necessary, things near and dear and useful to our daily life as are our very limbs. The loss of them may be so lasting a deprivation that we shall enter heaven maimed. But if the moral evil is irrevocably identified with the worldly good, we must renounce it.

The hand with its subtle and marvellous power may well stand for harmless accomplishments now fraught with evil suggestiveness; for innocent modes of livelihood which to relinquish means crippled helplessness, yet which have become hopelessly entangled with unjust or at least questionable ways; for the great possessions, honestly come by, which the ruler would not sell; for all endowments which we can no longer hope to consecrate, and which make one resemble the old Chaldeans, whose might was their god, who sacrificed to their net and burned incense to their drag.

And the foot, with its swiftness in boyhood, its plodding walk along the pavement in maturer age, may well represent the caprices of youth so hard to curb, and also the half-mechanical habits which succeed to these, and by which manhood is ruled, often to its destruction. If the hand be capacity, resource, and possession, the foot is swift perilous impulse, and also fixed habitude, monotonous recurrence, the settled ways of the world.

Cut off hand and foot, and what is left to the mutilated trunk, the ravaged and desolated life? Desire is left; the desire of the eyes. The eyes may not touch the external world; all may now be correct in our actions and intercourse with men. But yet greed, passion, inflamed imagination may desecrate the temple of the soul. The eyes misled Eve when she saw that the fruit was good, and David on his palace roof. Before the eyes of Jesus, Satan spread his third and worst temptation. And our Lord seems to imply that this last sacrifice of the worst because the deepest evil must be made with indignant vehemence; hand and foot must be cut off, but the eye must be cast out, though life be half darkened in the process.

These latter days have invented a softer gospel, which proclaims that even the fallen err if they utterly renounce any good creature of God, which ought to be received with thanksgiving; that the duty of moderation and self-control can never be replaced by renunciation, and that distrust of any lawful enjoyment revives the Manichean heresy. Is the eye a good creature of God? May the foot be received with thanksgiving? Is the hand a source of lawful enjoyment? Yet Jesus made these the types of what must, if it has become an occasion of stumbling, be entirely cast away.

He added that in such cases the choice is between mutilation and the loss of all. It is no longer a question of the full improvement of every faculty, the doubling of all the talents, but a choice between living a life impoverished and half spoiled, and going complete to Gehenna, to the charnel valley where the refuse of Jerusalem was burned in a continual fire, and the worm of corruption never died. The expression is too metaphorical to decide such questions as that of the eternal duration of punishment, or of the nature of the suffering of the lost. The metaphors of Jesus, however, are not employed to exaggerate His meaning, but only to express it. And what He said is this: The man who cherishes one dear and excusable occasion of offence, who spares himself the keenest spiritual surgery, shall be cast forth with everything that defileth, shall be ejected with the offal of the New Jerusalem, shall suffer corruption like the transgressors of whom Isaiah first used the tremendous phrase, "their worm shall not die, neither shall their fire be quenched," shall endure at once internal and external misery, as of decomposition and of burning.

Such is the most terrible menace that ever crossed the lips into which grace was poured. And it was not addressed to the outcast or the Pharisee, but to His own. They were called to the highest life; on them the influence of the world was to be as constant and as disintegrating as that of the weather upon a mountain top. Therefore they needed solemn warning, and the counter-pressure of those awful issues known to be dependent on their stern self-discipline. They could not, He said in an obscure passage which has been greatly tampered with, they could not escape fiery suffering in some form. But the fire which tried would preserve and bless them if they endured it; every one shall be salted with fire. But if they who ought to be the salt of the world received the grace of God in vain, if the salt have lost its saltness, the case is desperate indeed.

And since the need of this solemn warning sprang from their rivalry and partisanship, Jesus concludes with an emphatic charge to discipline and correct themselves and to beware of impeding others: to be searching in the closet, and charitable in the church: to have salt in yourselves, and be at peace with one another.

CHAPTER X.

DIVORCE.

MARK x. 1-12 (R. V.).

IT is easy to read without emotion that Jesus arose from the scene of His last discourse, and came into the borders of Judæa beyond Jordan. But not without emotion did Jesus bid farewell to Galilee, to the home of His childhood and sequestered youth, the cradle of His Church, the centre of nearly all the love and faith He had awakened. When closer still to death, His heart reverted to Galilee, and He promised that when He was risen He would go thither before His disciples. Now He had to leave it. And we must not forget that every step He took towards Jerusalem was a deliberate approach to His assured and anticipated cross. He was not like other brave men, who endure death when it arrives, but are sustained until the crisis by a thousand flattering hopes and undefined possibilities. Jesus knew precisely where and how He should suffer. And now, as He arose from Galilee, every step said, Lo, I come to do Thy will, O God.

As soon as He entered Peræa beyond Jordan, multitudes came to Him again. Nor did His burdened heart repress His zeal: rather He found relief in their importunity and in His Father's business, and so, "as He was wont, He taught them again." These simple words express the rule He lived by, the patient continuance in well-doing which neither hostilities nor anxieties could chill.

Not long was He left undisturbed. The Pharisees come to Him with a question dangerous in itself, because there is no conceivable answer which will not estrange many, and especially dangerous for Jesus, because already, on the Mount, He had spoken upon this subject words at seeming variance with His free views concerning Sabbath observance, fasting, and ceremonial purity. Most perilous of all was the decision they expected when given by a teacher already under suspicion, and now within reach of that Herod who had, during the lifetime of his first wife, married the wife of a living man. "Is it lawful for a man to put away his wife for every cause?" It was a decision upon this very subject which had proved fatal to the forerunner.

But Jesus spoke out plainly. In a question and answer which are variously reported, what is clear is that He carefully distinguished between a command and a permission of Moses. Divorce had been allowed; yes, but some reason had been exacted, whatever disputes might exist about its needful gravity, and deliberation had been enforced by demanding a legal document, a writing of divorcement. Thus conscience was bidden to examine its motives, and time was gained for natural relentings. But after all, Jesus declared that divorce was only a concession to their hardness of heart. Thus we learn that Old Testament institutions were not all and of necessity an expression of the Divine ideal. They were sometimes a temporary concession, meant to lead to better things; an expedient rather than a revelation.

These words contain the germ of St. Paul's doctrine that the law itself was a schoolmaster, and its function temporary.

To whatever concessions Moses had been driven, the original and unshaken design of God was that man and woman should find the permanent completion of their lives each in the other. And this is shown by three separate considerations. The first is the plan of the creation, making them male and female, and such that body and soul alike are only perfect when to each its complement is added, when the masculine element and the feminine "each fulfils defect in each . . . the two-celled heart beating with one full stroke life." Thus by anticipation Jesus condemned the tame-spirited verdict of His disciples, that since a man cannot relieve himself from a union when it proves galling, "it is not good" to marry at all. To this he distinctly answered that such an inference could not prove even tolerable, except when nature itself, or else some social wrong, or else absorbing devotion to the cause of God, virtually cancelled the original design. But already He had here shown that such prudential calculation degrades man, leaves him incomplete, traverses the design of God Who from the beginning of the creation made them male and female. In our own days, the relation between the sexes is undergoing a social and legislative revolution. Now Christ says not a word against the equal rights of the sexes, and in more than one passage St. Paul goes near to assert it. But equality is not identity, either of vocation or capacity. This text asserts the separate and reciprocal vocation of each, and it is worthy of consideration, how far the special vocation of womanhood is consistent with loud assertion of her "separate rights."

Christ's second proof that marriage cannot be dissolved without sin is that glow of heart, that noble abandonment, in which a man leaves even father and mother for the joy of his youth and the love of his espousals. In that sacred hour, how hideous and base a wanton divorce would be felt to be. Now man is not free to live by the mean, calculating, selfish afterthought, which breathes like a frost on the bloom of his noblest impulses and aspirations. He should guide himself by the light of his highest and most generous intuitions.

And the third reason is that no man, by any possibility, can undo what marriage does. They two are one flesh; each has become part of the very existence of the other; and it is simply incredible that a union so profound, so interwoven with the very tissue of their being, should lie at the mercy of the caprice or the calculations of one or other, or of both. Such a union arises from the profoundest depths of the nature God created, not from mean cravings of that nature in its degradation; and like waters springing up from the granite underneath the soil, it may suffer stain, but it is in itself free from the contamination of the fall. Despite of monkish and of Manichean slanders, impure dreams pretending to especial purity, God is He Who joins together man and woman in a bond which "no man," king or prelate, may without guilt dissolve.

Of what followed, St. Mark is content to tell us that in the house, the disciples pressed the question further. How far did the relaxation which Moses granted over-rule the original design? To what extent was every individual bound in actual life? And the answer, given by Jesus to guide His own people through all time, is clear and unmistakable. The tie cannot be torn asunder without sin. The first marriage holds, until actual adultery poisons the pure life in it, and man or woman who breaks through its barriers commits adultery. The Baptist's judgment of Herod was confirmed.

So Jesus taught. Ponder well that honest unshrinking grasp of solid detail, which did not overlook the physical union whereof is one flesh, that sympathy with high and chivalrous devotion forsaking all else for its beloved one, that still more spiritual penetration which discerned a Divine purpose and a destiny in the correlation of masculine and feminine gifts, of strength and grace, of energy and gentleness, of courage and long-suffering—observe with how easy and yet firm a grasp He combines all these into one overmastering argument—remember that when He spoke, the marriage tie was being relaxed all over the ancient world, even as godless legislation is to-day relaxing it—reflect that with such relaxation came inevitably a blight upon the family, resulting in degeneracy and ruin for the nation, while every race which learned the lesson of Jesus grew strong and pure and happy—and then say whether this was only a Judæan peasant or the Light of the World indeed.

CHRIST AND LITTLE CHILDREN.

Mark x. 13-16 (R. V.).

This beautiful story gains new loveliness from its context. The disciples had weighed the advantages and disadvantages of marriage, and decided in their calculating selfishness, that the prohibition of divorce made it "not good for a man to marry." But Jesus had regarded the matter from quite a different position; and their saying could only be received by those to whom special reasons forbade the marriage tie. It was then that the fair blossom and opening flower of domestic life, the tenderness and winning grace of childhood, appealed to them for a softer judgment. Little children (St. Luke says "babes") were brought to Him to bless, to touch them. It was a remarkable sight. He was just departing from Peræa on His last journey to Jerusalem. The nation was about to abjure its King and perish, after having invoked His blood to be not on them only, but on their children. But here were some at least of the next generation led by parents who revered Jesus, to receive His blessing. And who shall dare to limit the influence exerted by that benediction on their future lives? Is it forgotten that this very Peræa was the haven of refuge for Jewish believers when the wrath fell upon their nation? Meanwhile the fresh smile of their unconscious, unstained, unforeboding infancy met the grave smile of the all-conscious, death-boding Man of Sorrows, as much purer as it was more profound.

But the disciples were not melted. They were occupied with grave questions. Babes could understand nothing, and therefore could receive no conscious intelligent enlightenment. What then could Jesus do for them? Many wise persons are still of quite the same opinion. No spiritual influences, they tell us, can reach the soul until the brain is capable of drawing logical distinctions. A gentle mother may breathe softness and love into a child's nature, or a harsh nurse may jar and disturb its temper, until the effects are as visible on the plastic face as is the sunshine or storm upon the bosom of a lake; but for the grace of God there is no opening yet. As if soft and loving influences are not themselves a grace of God. As if the world were given certain odds in the race, and the powers of heaven were handicapped. As if the young heart of every child were a place where sin abounds (since he is a fallen creature, with an original tendency towards evil), but where grace doth not at all abound. Such is the unlovely theory. And as long as it prevails in the Church we need not wonder at the compensating error of rationalism, denying evil where so many of us deny grace. It is the more amiable error of the two. Since then the disciples could not believe that edification was for babes, they naturally rebuked those that brought them. Alas, how often still do the beauty and innocence of childhood appeal to men in vain. And this is so, because we see not the Divine grace, "the kingdom of heaven," in these. Their weakness chafes our impatience, their simplicity irritates our worldliness, and their touching helplessness and trustfulness do not find in us heart enough for any glad response.

In ancient times they had to pass through the fire to Moloch, and since then through other fires: to fashion when mothers leave them to the hired kindness of a nurse, to selfishness when their want appeals to our charities in vain, and to cold dogmatism, which would banish them from the baptismal font as the disciples repelled them from the embrace of Jesus. But He was moved with indignation, and reiterated, as men do when they feel deeply, "Suffer the little children to come unto Me; forbid them not." And He added this conclusive reason, "for of such," of children and childlike men, "is the kingdom of God."

What is the meaning of this remarkable assertion? To answer aright, let us return in fancy to the morning of our days; let our flesh, and all our primitive being, come back to us as those of a little child.

We were not faultless then. The theological dogma of original sin, however unwelcome to many, is in harmony with all experience. Impatience is there, and many a childish fault; and graver evils develop as surely as life unfolds, just as weeds show themselves in summer, the germs of which were already mingled with the better seed in spring. It is plain to all observers that the weeds of human nature are latent in the early soil, that this is not pure at the beginning of each individual life. Does not our newfangled science explain this fact by telling us that we have still in our blood the transmitted influences of our ancestors the brutes?

But Christ never meant to say that the kingdom of heaven was only for the immaculate and stainless. If converted men receive it, in spite of many a haunting appetite and recurring lust, then the frailties of our babes shall not forbid us to believe the blessed assurance that the kingdom is also theirs.

How many hindrances to the Divine life fall away from us, as our fancy recalls our childhood. What weary and shameful memories, base hopes, tawdry splendours, envenomed pleasures, entangling associations vanish, what sins need to be confessed no longer, how much evil knowledge fades out that we never now shall quite unlearn, which haunts the memory even though the conscience be absolved from it. The days of our youth are not those evil days, when anything within us saith, My soul hath no pleasure in the ways of God.

When we ask to what especial qualities of childhood did Jesus attach so great value, two kindred attributes are distinctly indicated in Scripture.

One is humility. The previous chapter showed us a little child set in the midst of the emulous disciples, whom Christ instructed that the way to be greatest was to become like this little child, the least.

A child is not humble through affectation, it never professes nor thinks about humility. But it understands, however imperfectly, that it is beset by mysterious and perilous forces, which it neither comprehends nor can grapple with. And so are we. Therefore all its instincts and experiences teach it to submit, to seek guidance, not to put its own judgment in competition with those of its appointed guides. To them, therefore, it clings and is obedient.

Why is it not so with us? Sadly we also know the peril of self-will, the misleading power of appetite and passion, the humiliating failures which track the steps of self-assertion, the distortion of our judgments, the feebleness of our wills, the mysteries of life and death amid which we grope in vain. Milton anticipated Sir Isaac Newton in describing the wisest

> "As children gathering pebbles on the shore."
> —"Par. Reg.," iv. 330.

And if this be so true in the natural world that its sages become as little children, how much more in those spiritual realms for which our faculties are still so infantile, and of which our experience is so rudimentary. We should all be nearer to the kingdom, or greater in it, if we felt our dependence, and like the child were content to obey our Guide and cling to Him.

The second childlike quality to which Christ attached value was readiness to receive simply. Dependence naturally results from humility. Man is proud of his independence only because he relies on his own powers; when these are paralysed, as in the sickroom or before the judge, he is willing again to become a child in the hands of a nurse or of an advocate. In the realm of the spirit these natural powers are paralysed. Learning cannot resist temptation, nor wealth expiate a sin. And therefore, in the spiritual world, we are meant to be dependent and receptive.

Christ taught, in the Sermon on the Mount, that to those who asked Him, God would give His Spirit as earthly parents give good things to their children. Here also we are taught to accept, to receive the kingdom as little children, not flattering ourselves that our own exertions can dispense with the free gift, not unwilling to become pensioners of heaven, not distrustful of the heart which grants, not finding the bounties irksome which are prompted by a Father's love. What can be more charming in its gracefulness than the reception of a favour by an affectionate child. His glad and confident enjoyment is a picture of what ours might be.

Since children receive the kingdom, and are a pattern for us in doing so, it is clear that they do not possess the kingdom as a natural right, but as a gift. But since they do receive it, they must surely be capable of receiving also that sacrament which is the sign and seal of it. It is a startling position indeed which denies admission into the visible Church to those of whom is the kingdom of God. It is a position taken up only because many, who would shrink from any such avowal, half-unconsciously believe that God becomes gracious to us only when His grace is attracted by skilful movements upon our part, by conscious and well-instructed efforts, by penitence, faith, and orthodoxy. But whatever soul is capable of any taint of sin must be capable of compensating influences of the Spirit, by Whom Jeremiah was sanctified, and the Baptist was filled, even before their birth into this world (Jer. i. 5; Luke i. 15). Christ Himself, in Whom dwelt bodily all the fulness of the Godhead, was not therefore incapable of the simplicity and dependence of infancy.

Having taught His disciples this great lesson, Jesus let His affections loose. He folded the children in His tender and pure embrace, and blessed them much, laying His hands on them, instead of merely touching them. He blessed them not because they were baptised. But we baptise our children, because all such have received the blessing, and are clasped in the arms of the Founder of the Church.

THE RICH INQUIRER.

MARK x. 17-22 (R. V.).

The excitement stirred by our Lord's teaching must often have shown itself in a scene of eagerness like this which St. Mark describes so well. The Saviour is just "going forth" when one rushes to overtake Him, and kneels down to Him, full of the hope of a great discovery. He is so frank, so innocent and earnest, as to win the love of Jesus. And yet he presently goes away, not as he came, but with a gloomy forehead and a heavy heart, and doubtless with slow reluctance.

The authorities were now in such avowed opposition that to be Christ's disciple was disgraceful, if not dangerous, to a man of mark. Yet no fear withheld this young ruler who had so much to lose; he would not come by night, like Nicodemus before the storm had gathered which was now so dark; he openly avowed his belief in the goodness of the Master, and his own ignorance of some great secret which Jesus could reveal.

There is indeed a charming frankness in his bearing, so that we admire even his childlike assertion of his own virtues, while the heights of a nobility yet unattained are clearly possible for one so dissatisfied, so anxious for a higher life, so urgent in his questioning, What shall I do? What lack I yet? That is what makes the difference between the Pharisee who thanks God that he is not as other men, and this youth who has kept all the commandments, yet would fain be other than he is, and readily confesses that all is not enough, that some unknown act still awaits achievement. The goodness which thinks itself upon the summit will never toil much farther. The conscience that is really awake cannot be satisfied, but is perplexed rather and baffled by the virtues of a dutiful and well-ordered life. For a chasm ever yawns between the actual and the ideal, what we have done and what we fain would do. And a spiritual glory, undefined and perhaps undefinable, floats ever before the eyes of all men whom the god of this world has not blinded. This inquirer honestly thinks himself not far from the great attainment; he expects to reach it by some transcendent act, some great deed done, and for this he has no doubt of his own prowess, if only he were well directed. What shall I do that I may have eternal life, not of grace, but as a debt—that I may inherit it? Thus he awaits direction upon the road where heathenism and semi-heathen Christianity are still toiling, and all who would purchase the gift of God with money or toil or merit or bitterness of remorseful tears.

One easily foresees that the reply of Jesus will disappoint and humble him, but it startles us to see him pointed back to works and to the law of Moses.

Again, we observe that what this inquirer seeks he very earnestly believes Jesus to have attained. And it is no mean tribute to the spiritual elevation of our Lord, no doubtful indication that amid perils and contradictions and on His road to the cross the peace of God sat visibly upon His brow, that one so pure and yet so keenly aware that his own virtue sufficed not and that the kingdom of God was yet unattained, should kneel in the dust before the Nazarene, and beseech this good Master to reveal to him all his questioning. It was a strange request, and it was granted in an unlooked for way. The demand of the Chaldean tyrant that his forgotten dream should be interpreted was not so extravagant as this, that the defect in an unknown career should be discovered. It was upon a lofty pedestal indeed that this ruler placed our Lord.

And yet his question supplies the clue to that answer of Christ which has perplexed so many. The youth is seeking for himself a purely human merit, indigenous and underived. And the same, of course, is what he ascribes to Jesus, to Him who is so far from claiming independent human attainment, or professing to be what this youth would fain become, that He said, "The Son can do nothing of Himself. . . . I can of Mine own self do nothing." The secret of His human perfection is the absolute dependence of His humanity upon God, with whom He is one. No wonder, then, that He repudiates any such goodness as the ruler had in view.

The Socinian finds quite another meaning in His reply, and urges that by these words Jesus denied His Deity. There is none good but one, That is God, was a reason why He should not be called so. Jesus, however, does not remonstrate absolutely against being called good, but against being thus addressed from this ruler's point of view, by one who regards Him as a mere teacher and expects to earn the same title for himself. And indeed the Socinian who appeals to this text gasps a sword by the blade. For if it denied Christ's divinity it must exactly to the same extent deny also Christ's goodness, which he admits. Now it is beyond question that Jesus differed from all the saints in the serene confidence with which He regarded the moral law, from the time when He received the baptism of repentance only that He might fulfil all righteousness, to the hour when He cried, "Why hast Thou forsaken Me?" and although deserted, claimed God as still His God. The saints of to-day were the penitents of yesterday. But He has finished the work that was given Him to do. He knows that God hears Him always, and in Him the Prince of this world hath nothing. And yet there is none good but God. Who then is He? If this saying does not confess what is intolerable to a reverential Socinian, what Strauss and Renan shrank from insinuating, what is alien to the whole spirit of the Gospel, and assuredly far from the mind of the evangelists, then it claims all that His Church rejoices to ascribe to Christ.

Moreover Jesus does not deny even to ordinary men the possibility of being "good."

A good man out of the good treasure of his heart bringeth forth good things. Some shall hear at last the words, Well done, good and faithful servant. The children of the kingdom are good seed among the tares. Clearly His repugnance is not to the epithet, but to the spirit in which it is bestowed, to the notion that goodness can spring spontaneously from the soil of our humanity. But there is nothing here to discourage the highest aspirations of the trustful and dependent soul, who looks for more grace.

The doctrinal importance of this remarkable utterance is what most affects us, who look back through the dust of a hundred controversies. But it was very secondary at the time, and what the ruler doubtless felt most was a chill sense of repression and perhaps despair. It was indeed the death-knell of his false hopes. For if only God is good, how can any mortal inherit eternal life by a good deed? And Jesus goes on to deepen this conviction by words which find a wonderful commentary in St. Paul's doctrine of the function of the law. It was to prepare men for the gospel by a challenge, by revealing the standard of true righteousness, by saying to all who seek to earn heaven, "The man that doeth these things shall live by them." The attempt was sure to end in failure, for, "by the law is the knowledge of sin." It was exactly upon this principle that Jesus said "Keep the commandments," spiritualising them, as St. Matthew tells us, by adding to the injunctions of the second table, "Thou shalt love thy neighbour as thyself," which saying, we know, briefly comprehends them all.

But the ruler knew not how much he loved himself: his easy life had met no searching and stern demand until now, and his answer has a tone of relief, after the ominous words he had first heard. "Master," and he now drops the questionable adjective, "all these have I kept from my youth;" these never were so burdensome that he should despair; not these, he thinks, inspired that unsatisfied longing for some good thing yet undone. We pity and perhaps blame the shallow answer, and the dull perception which it betrayed. But Jesus looked on him and loved him. And well it is for us that no eyes fully discern our weakness but those which were so often filled with sympathetic tears. He sees error more keenly than the sharpest critic, but he sees earnestness too. And the love which desired all souls was attracted especially by one who had felt from his youth up the obligation of the moral law, and had not consciously transgressed it.

This is not the teaching of those vile proverbs which declare that wild oats must be sown if one would reap good corn, and that the greater the sinner the greater will be the saint.

Nay, even religionists of the sensational school delight in the past iniquities of those they honour, not only to glorify God for their recovery, nor with the joy which is in the presence of the angels over one sinner that repenteth, but as if these possess through their former wickedness some passport to special service now. Yet neither in Scripture nor in the history of the Church will it appear that men of licentious revolt against known laws have attained to usefulness of the highest order. The Baptist was filled with the Holy Ghost from his mother's womb. The Apostle of the Gentiles was blameless as touching the righteousness of the law. And each Testament has a special promise for those who seek the Lord early, who seek His kingdom and righteousness first. The undefiled are nearest to the throne.

Now mark how endearing, how unlike the stern zeal of a propagandist, was Christ's tender and loving gaze; and hear the encouraging promise of heavenly treasure, and offer of His own companionship, which presently softened the severity of His demand; and again, when all failed, when His followers doubtless scorned the deserter, ponder the truthful and compassionate words, How hard it is!

Yet will Christ teach him how far the spirit of the law pierces, since the letter has not wrought the knowledge of sin. If he loves his neighbour as himself, let his needier neighbour receive what he most values. If he loves God supremely, let him be content with treasure in the hands of God, and with a discipleship which shall ever reveal to him, more and more profoundly, the will of God, the true nobility of man, and the way to that eternal life he seeks.

The socialist would justify by this verse a universal confiscation. But he forgets that the spirit which seizes all is widely different from that which gives all freely: that Zacchæus retained half his goods; that Joseph of Arimathea was rich; that the property of Ananias was his own, and when he sold it the price was in his own power; that St. James warned the rich in this world only against trusting in riches instead of trusting God, who gave them all richly, for enjoyment, although not to be confided in. Soon after this Jesus accepted a feast from his friends in Bethany, and rebuked Judas, who complained that a costly luxury had not been sold for the benefit of the poor. Why then is his demand now so absolute? It is simply an application of his bold universal rule, that every cause of stumbling must be sacrificed, be it innocent as hand or foot or eye. And affluent indeed would be all the charities and missions of the Church in these latter days, if the demand were obeyed in cases where it really applies, if every luxury which enervates and all pomp which intoxicates were sacrificed, if all who know that wealth is a snare to them corrected their weakness by rigorous discipline, their unfruitfulness by a sharp pruning of superfluous frondage.

The rich man neither remonstrated nor defended himself. His self-confidence gave way. He felt that what he could not persuade himself to do was a "good thing." And he who came running went away sorrowful, and with a face "lowering" like the sky which forebodes "foul weather." That is too often the issue of such vaunting offers. Yet feeling his weakness, and neither resisting nor upbraiding the faithfulness which exposes him, doubtless he was long disquieted by new desires, a strange sense of failure and unworthiness, a clear vision of that higher life which had already haunted his reveries. Henceforward he had no choice but to sink to a baser contentment, or else rise to a higher self-devotion. Who shall say, because he failed to decide then, that he persisted for ever in the great refusal? Yet was it a perilous and hardening experience, and it was easier henceforward to live below his ideal, when once he had turned away from Christ. Nor is there any reason to doubt that the inner circle of our Lord's immediate followers was then for ever closed against him.

WHO THEN CAN BE SAVED?

MARK x. 23-31 (R. V.).

As the rich man turned away with the arrow in his breast, Jesus looked round about on His disciples. The Gospels, and especially St. Mark, often mention the gaze of Jesus, and all who know the power of an intense and pure nature silently searching others, the piercing intuition, the calm judgment which sometimes looks out of holy eyes, can well understand the reason. Disappointed love was in His look, and that compassionate protest against harsh judgments which presently went on to admit that the necessary demand was hard. Some, perhaps, who had begun to scorn the ruler in his defeat, were reminded of frailties of their own, and had to ask, Shall I next be judged? And one was among them, pilfering from the bag what was intended for the poor, to whom that look of Christ must have been very terrible. Unless we remember Judas, we shall not comprehend all the fitness of the repeated and earnest warnings of Jesus against covetousness. Never was secret sin dealt with so faithfully as his.

And now Jesus, as He looks around, says, "How hardly shall they that have riches enter into the kingdom of God." But the disciples were amazed. To the ancient Jew, from Abraham to Solomon, riches appeared to be a sign of the Divine favour, and if the pathetic figure of Job reminded him how much sorrow might befall the just, yet the story showed even him at the end more prosperous than at the beginning. In the time of Jesus, the chiefs of their religion were greedily using their position as a means of amassing enormous fortunes. To be told that wealth was a positive hindrance on the way to God was wonderful indeed.

When Jesus modified His utterance, it was not to correct Himself, like one who had heedlessly gone beyond His meaning. His third speech reiterated the first, declaring that a manifest and proverbial physical impossibility was not so hard as for a rich man to enter the kingdom of God, here or hereafter. But He interposed a saying which both explained the first one and enlarged its scope. "Children" He begins, like one who pitied their inexperience and dealt gently with their perplexities, "Children, how hard is it for them that trust in riches to enter into the kingdom of God." And therefore is it hard for all the rich, since they must wrestle against this temptation to trust in their possessions. It is exactly in this spirit that St. James, who quoted Jesus more than any of the later writers of Scripture, charges the rich that they be not highminded, nor trust in uncertain riches, but in the living God. Immediately before, Jesus had told them how alone the kingdom might be entered, even by becoming as little children; lowly, dependent, willing to receive all at the hands of a superior. Would riches help them to do this? Is it easier to pray for daily bread when one has much goods laid up for many years? Is it easier to feel that God alone can make us drink of true pleasures as of a river, when a hundred luxuries and indulgences lull us in sloth or allure us into excess? Hereupon the disciples perceived what was more alarming still, that not alone do rich men trust in riches, but all who confound possessions with satisfaction, all who dream that to have much is to be blessed, as if property were character. They were right. We may follow the guidance of Mammon beckoning from afar, with a trust as idolatrous as if we held his hand. But who could abide a principle so exacting? It was the revelation of a new danger, and they were astonished exceedingly, saying, Then who can be saved? Again Jesus looked upon them, with solemn but reassuring gaze. They had learned the secret of the new life, the natural impossibility throwing us back in helpless appeal to the powers of the world to come. "With men it is impossible, but not with God, for all things are possible with God."

Peter, not easily nor long to be discouraged, now saw ground for hope. If the same danger existed for rich and poor, then either might be encouraged by having surmounted it, and the apostles had done what the rich man failed to do—they had left all and followed Jesus. The claim has provoked undue censure, as if too much were made out of a very trifling sacrifice, a couple of boats and a paltry trade. But the objectors have missed the point; the apostles really broke away from the service of the world when they left their nets and followed Jesus. Their world was perhaps a narrow one, but He Who reckoned two mites a greater offering than the total of the gifts of many rich casting in much, was unlikely to despise a fisherman or a publican who laid all his living upon the altar. The fault, if fault there were, lay rather in the satisfaction with which Peter contemplates their decision as now irrevocable and secure, so that nothing remained except to claim the reward, which St. Matthew tells us he very distinctly did. The young man should have had treasure in heaven: what then should they have?

But in truth, their hardest battles with worldliness lay still before them, and he who thought he stood might well take heed lest he fell. They would presently unite in censuring a woman's costly gift to Him for Whom they professed to have surrendered all. Peter himself would shrink from his Master's side. And what a satire upon this confident claim would it have been, could the heart of Judas then and there have been revealed to them.

The answer of our Lord is sufficiently remarkable. St. Matthew tells how frankly and fully He acknowledged their collective services, and what a large reward He promised, when they should sit with Him on thrones, judging their nation. So far was that generous heart from weighing their losses in a worldly scale, or criticising the form of a demand which was not all unreasonable.

But St. Mark lays exclusive stress upon other and sobering considerations, which also St. Matthew has recorded.

There is a certain tone of egoism in the words, "Lo, we . . . what shall we have?" And Jesus corrects this in the gentlest way, by laying down such a general rule as implies that many others will do the same; "there is no man" whose self-sacrifice shall go without its reward.

Secondary and lower motives begin to mingle with the generous ardour of self-sacrifice as soon as it is careful to record its losses, and inquire about its wages. Such motives are not absolutely forbidden, but they must never push into the foremost place. The crown of glory animated and sustained St. Paul, but it was for Christ, and not for this, that he suffered the loss of all things.

Jesus accordingly demands purity of motive. The sacrifice must not be for ambition, even with aspirations prolonged across the frontiers of eternity: it must be altogether "for My sake and for the gospel's sake." And here we observe once more the portentous demand of Christ's person upon His followers. They are servants of no ethical or theological system, however lofty. Christ does not regard Himself and them, as alike devoted to some cause above and external to them all. To Him they are to be consecrated, and to the gospel, which, as we have seen, is the story of His Life, Death, and Resurrection. For Him they are to break the dearest and strongest of earthly ties. He had just proclaimed how indissoluble was the marriage bond. No man should sever those whom God had joined. But St. Luke informs us that to forsake even a wife for Christ's sake, was a deed worthy of being rewarded an hundredfold. Nor does He mention any higher being in whose name the sacrifice is demanded. Now this is at least implicitly the view of His own personality which some profess to find only in St. John.

Again, there was perhaps an undertone of complaint in Peter's question, as if no compensation for all their sacrifices were hitherto bestowed. What should their compensation be? But Christ declares that losses endured for Him are abundantly repaid on earth, in this present time, and even amid the fires of persecution. Houses and lands are replaced by the consciousness of inviolable shelter and inexhaustible provision. "Whither wilt thou betake thyself to find covert?" asks the menacing cardinal; but Luther answers, "Under the heaven of God." And if dearest friends be estranged, or of necessity abandoned, then, in such times of high attainment and strong spiritual insight, membership in the Divine family is felt to be no unreal tie, and earthly relationships are well recovered in the vast fraternity of souls. Brethren, and sisters, and mothers, are thus restored an hundredfold; but although a father is also lost, we do not hear that a hundred fathers shall be given back, for in the spiritual family that place is reserved for One.

Lastly, Jesus reminded them that the race was not yet over; that many first shall be last and the last first. We know how Judas by transgression fell, and how the persecuting Saul became not a whit behind the very chiefest apostle. But this word remains for the warning and incitement of all Christians, even unto the end of the world. There are "many" such.

Next after this warning comes yet another prediction of His own suffering, with added circumstances of horror. Would they who were now first remain faithful? or should another take their bishopric?

With a darkening heart Judas heard, and made his choice.

[Mark x. 32-34. See Mark viii. 31, p. 867.]

CHRIST'S CUP AND BAPTISM.

Mark x. 35-40 (R. V.).

We learn from St. Matthew that Salome was associated with her sons, and was indeed the chief speaker in the earlier part of this incident.

And her request has commonly been regarded as the mean and shortsighted intrigue of an ambitious woman, recklessly snatching at an advantage for her family, and unconscious of the stern and steep road to honour in the kingdom of Jesus.

Nor can we deny that her prayer was somewhat presumptuous, or that it was especially unbecoming to aim at entangling her Lord in a blindfold promise, desiring Him to do something undefined, "whatsoever we shall ask of Thee." Jesus was too discreet to answer otherwise than, "What would ye that I should do for you?" And when they asked for the chief seats in the glory that was yet to be their Master's, no wonder that the Ten, hearing of it, had indignation. But Christ's answer, and the gentle manner in which He explains His refusal, when a sharp rebuke is what we would expect to read, alike suggest that there may have been some softening, half-justifying circumstance. And this we find in the period at which the daring request was made.

It was on the road, during the last journey, when a panic had seized the company; and our Lord, apparently out of the strong craving for sympathy which possesses the noblest souls, had once more told the Twelve what insults and cruel sufferings lay before Him. It was a time for deep searching of hearts, for the craven to go back and walk no more with Him, and for the traitor to think of making His own peace, at any price, with His Master's foes.

But this dauntless woman could see the clear sky beyond the storm. Her sons shall be loyal, and win the prize, whatever be the hazard, and however long the struggle.

Ignorant and rash she may have been, but it was no base ambition which chose such a moment to declare its unshaken ardour, and claim distinction in the kingdom for which so much must be endured.

And when the stern price was plainly stated, she and her children were not startled, they conceived themselves able for the baptism and the cup; and little as they dreamed of the coldness of the waters, and the bitterness of the draught, yet Jesus did not declare them to be deceived. He said, Ye shall indeed share these.

Nor can we doubt that their faith and loyalty refreshed His soul amid so much that was sad and selfish. He knew indeed on what a dreadful seat He was soon to claim His kingdom, and who should sit upon His right hand and His left. These could not follow Him now, but they should follow Him hereafter—one by the brief pang of the earliest apostolic martyrdom, and the other by the longest and sorest experience of that faithless and perverse generation.

1. Very significant is the test of worth which Jesus propounds to them: not successful service, but endurance; not the active, but the passive graces. It is not *our* test, except in a few brilliant and conspicuous martyrdoms. The Church, like the world, has crowns for learning, eloquence, energy; it applauds the force by which great things are done. The reformer who abolishes an abuse, the scholar who defends a doctrine, the orator who sways a multitude, and the missionary who adds a new tribe to Christendom,—all these are sure of honour. Our loudest plaudits are not for simple men and women, but for high station, genius, and success. But the Lord looketh upon the heart, not the brain or the hand; He values the worker, not the work; the love, not the achievement. And, therefore, one of the tests He constantly applied was this, the capability for noble endurance. We ourselves, in our saner moments, can judge whether it demands more grace to refute a heretic, or to sustain the long inglorious agonies of some disease which slowly gnaws away the heart of life. And doubtless among the heroes for whom Christ is twining immortal garlands, there is many a pale and shattered creature, nerveless and unstrung, tossing on a mean bed, breathing in imperfect English loftier praises than many an anthem which resounds through cathedral arches, and laying on the altar of burnt sacrifice all he has, even his poor frame itself, to be racked and tortured without a murmur. Culture has never heightened his forehead nor refined his face: we look at him, but little dream what the angels see, or how perhaps because of such an one the great places which Salome sought were not Christ's to give away except only to them for whom it was prepared. For these, at last, the reward shall be His to give, as He said, "To him that overcometh will I give to sit down with Me upon My throne."

2. Significant also are the phrases by which Christ expressed the sufferings of His people. Some, which it is possible to escape, are voluntarily accepted for Christ's sake, as when the Virgin mother bowed her head to slander and scorn, and said, "Behold the servant of the Lord, be it unto me according to Thy word." Such sufferings are a cup deliberately raised by one's own hand to the reluctant lips. Into other sufferings we are plunged: they are inevitable. Malice, ill-health, or bereavement plies the scourge; they come on us like the rush of billows in a storm; they are a deep and dreadful baptism. Or we may say that some woes are external, visible, we are seen to be submerged in them; but others are like the secret ingredients of a bitter draught, which the lips know, but the eye of the bystander cannot analyse. But there is One Who knows and rewards; even the Man of Sorrows Who said, The cup which My heavenly Father giveth, shall I not drink it?

Now it is this standard of excellence, announced by Jesus, which shall give high place to many of the poor and ignorant and weak, when rank shall perish, when tongues shall cease, and when our knowledge, in the blaze of new revelations, shall utterly vanish away, not quenched, but absorbed like the starlight at noon.

3. We observe again that men are not said to drink of another cup as bitter, or to be baptised in other waters as chill, as tried their Master; but to share His very baptism and His cup. Not that we can add anything to His all-sufficient sacrifice. Our goodness extendeth not to God. But Christ's work availed not only to reconcile us to the Father, but also to elevate and consecrate sufferings which would otherwise have been penal and degrading. Accepting our sorrows in the grace of Christ, and receiving Him into our hearts, then our sufferings fill up that which is lacking of the afflictions of Christ (Col. i. 24), and at the last He will say, when the glories of heaven are as a robe around Him, "I was hungry, naked, sick, and in prison in the person of the least of these."

Hence it is that a special nearness to God has ever been felt in holy sorrow, and in the pain of hearts which, amid all clamours and tumults of the world, are hushed and calmed by the example of Him Who was led as a lamb to the slaughter.

And thus they are not wrong who speak of the Sacrament of Sorrow, for Jesus, in this passage, applies to it the language of both sacraments.

It is a harmless superstition even at the worst which brings to the baptism of many noble houses water from the stream where Jesus was baptised by John. But here we read of another and a dread baptism, consecrated by the fellowship of Christ, in depths which plummet never sounded, and into which the neophyte goes down sustained by no mortal hand.

Here is also the communion of an awful cup. No human minister sets it in our trembling hand; no human voice asks, "Are ye able to drink the cup that I drink?" Our lips grow pale, and our blood is chill; but faith responds, "We are able." And the tender and pitying voice of our Master, too loving to spare one necessary pang, responds with the word of doom: "The cup that I drink ye shall drink; and with the baptism that I am baptised withal shall ye be baptised." Even so: it is enough for the servant that he be as his Master.

THE LAW OF GREATNESS.

MARK x. 41-45 (R. V.).

When the Ten heard that James and John had asked for the chief places in the kingdom, they proved, by their indignation, that they also nourished the same ambitious desires which they condemned. But Jesus called them to Him, for it was not there that angry passions had broken out. And happy are they who hear and obey His summons to approach, when, removed from His purifying gaze by carelessness or wilfulness, ambition and anger begin to excite their hearts.

Now Jesus addressed them as being aware of their hidden emulation. And His treatment of it is remarkable. He neither condemns, nor praises it, but simply teaches them what Christian greatness means, and the conditions on which it may be won.

The greatness of the world is measured by authority and lordliness. Even there it is an uncertain test; for the most real power is often wielded by some anonymous thinker, or by some crafty intriguer, content with the substance of authority while his puppet enjoys the trappings. Something of this may perhaps be detected in the words, "They which are accounted to rule over the Gentiles lord it over them." And it is certain that "their great ones exercise authority over them." But the Divine greatness is a meek and gentle influence. To minister to the Church is better than to command it, and whoever desires to be the chief must become the servant of all. Thus shall whatever is vainglorious and egoistic in our ambition defeat itself; the more one struggles to be great the more he is disqualified: even benefits rendered to others with this object will not really be service done for them but for self; nor will any calculated assumption of humility help one to become indeed the least, being but a subtle assertion that he is great, and like the last place in an ecclesiastical procession, when occupied in a self-conscious spirit. And thus it comes to pass that the Church knows very distinctly who are its greatest sons. As the gift of two mites by the widow was greater than that of large sums by the rich, so a small service done in the spirit of perfect self-effacement,—a service which thought neither of its merit nor of its reward, but only of a brother's need, shall be more in the day of reckoning than sacrifices which are celebrated by the historians and sung by the poets of the Church. For it may avail nothing to give all my goods to feed the poor, and my body to be burned; while a cup of cold water, rendered by a loyal hand, shall in no wise lose its reward.

Thus Jesus throws open to all men a competition which has no charms for flesh and blood. And as He spoke of the entry upon His service, bearing a cross, as being the following of Himself, so He teaches us, that the greatness of lowliness, to which we are called, is His own greatness. "For verily the Son of Man came not to be ministered unto but to minister." Not here, not in this tarnished and faded world, would He Who was from everlasting with the Father have sought His own ease or honour. But the physician came to them that were sick, and the good Shepherd followed His lost sheep until He found it. Now this comparison proves that we also are to carry forward the same restoring work, or else we might infer that, because He came to minister to us, we may accept ministration with a good heart. It is not so. We are the light and the salt of the earth, and must suffer with Him that we may also be glorified together.

But He added another memorable phrase. He came "to give His life a ransom in exchange for many." It is not a question, therefore, of the inspiring example of His life. Something has been forfeited which must be redeemed, and Christ has paid the price. Nor is this done only on behalf of many, but in exchange for them.

So then the crucifixion is not a sad incident in a great career; it is the mark towards which Jesus moved, the power by which He redeemed the world.

Surely, we recognise here the echo of the prophet's words, "Thou shalt make His soul an offering for sin . . . by His knowledge shall My righteous servant justify many, and He shall bear their iniquities" (Isa. liii. 10, 11).

The elaborated doctrine of the atonement may not perhaps be here, much less the subtleties of theologians who have, to their own satisfaction, known the mind of the Almighty to perfection. But it is beyond reasonable controversy that in this verse Jesus declared that His sufferings were vicarious, and endured in the sinners' stead.

BARTIMÆUS.

MARK x. 46-52 (R. V.).

There is no miracle in the Gospels of which the accounts are so hard to reconcile as those of the healing of the blind at Jericho.

It is a small thing that St. Matthew mentions two blind men, while St. Mark and St. Luke are only aware of one. The same is true of the demoniacs at Gadara, and it is easily understood that only an eyewitness should remember the obscure comrade of a remarkable and energetic man, who would have spread far and wide the particulars of his own cure. The fierce and dangerous demoniac of Gadara was just such a man, and there is ample evidence of energy and vehemence in the brief account of Bartimæus. What is really perplexing is that St. Luke places the miracle at the entrance to Jericho, but St. Matthew and St. Mark, as Jesus came out of it. It is too forced and violent a theory which speaks of an old and a new town, so close together that one was entered and the other left at the same time.

It is possible that there were two events, and the success of one sufferer at the entrance to the town led others to use the same importunities at the exit. And this would not be much more remarkable than the two miracles of the loaves, or the two miraculous draughts of fish. It is also possible, though unlikely, that the same supplicant who began his appeals without success when Jesus entered, resumed his entreaties, with a comrade, at the gate by which He left.

Such difficulties exist in all the best authenticated histories: discrepancies of the kind arise continually between the evidence of the most trustworthy witnesses in courts of justice. And the student who is humble as well as devout will not shut his eyes against facts, merely because they are perplexing, but will remember that they do nothing to shake the solid narrative itself.

As we read St. Mark's account, we are struck by the vividness of the whole picture, and especially by the robust personality of the blind man. The scene is neither Jerusalem, the city of the Pharisees, nor Galilee, where they have persistently sapped the popularity of Jesus. Eastward of the Jordan, He has spent the last peaceful and successful weeks of His brief and stormy career, and Jericho lies upon the borders of that friendly district. Accordingly something is here of the old enthusiasm: a great multitude moves along with His disciples to the gates, and the rushing concourse excites the curiosity of the blind son of Timæus. So does many a religious movement lead to inquiry and explanation far and wide. But when he, sitting by the way, and unable to follow, knows that the great Healer is at hand, but only in passing, and for a moment, his interest suddenly becomes personal and ardent, and "he began to cry out" (the expression implies that his supplication, beginning as the crowd drew near, was not one utterance but a prolonged appeal), "and to say, Jesus, Thou Son of David, have mercy on me." To the crowd his outcry seemed to be only an intrusion upon One Who was too rapt, too heavenly, to be disturbed by the sorrows of a blind beggar. But that was not the view of Bartimæus, whose personal affliction gave him the keenest interest in those verses of the Old Testament which spoke of opening the blind eyes. If he did not understand their exact force as prophecies, at least they satisfied him that his petition could not be an insult to the great Prophet of Whom just such actions were told, for Whose visit he had often sighed, and Who was now fast going by, perhaps for ever. The picture is one of great eagerness, bearing up against great discouragement. We catch the spirit of the man as he inquires what the multitude means, as the epithet of his informants, Jesus of Nazareth, changes on his lips into Jesus, Thou Son of David, as he persists, without any vision of Christ to encourage him, and amid the rebukes of many, in crying out the more a great deal, although pain is deepening every moment in his accents, and he will presently need cheering. The ear of Jesus is quick for such a call, and He stops. He does not raise His own voice to summon him, but teaches a lesson of humanity to those who would fain have silenced the appeal of anguish, and says, Call ye him. And they obey with a courtier-like change of tone, saying, Be of good cheer, rise, He calleth thee. And Bartimæus cannot endure even the slight hindrance of his loose garment, but flings it aside, and rises and comes to Jesus, a pattern of the importunity which prays and never faints, which perseveres amid all discouragement, which adverse public opinion cannot hinder. And the Lord asks of him almost exactly the same question as recently of James and John, What wilt thou that I should do for thee? But in his reply there is no aspiring pride: misery knows how precious are the common gifts, the every-day blessings which we hardly pause to think about; and he replies, Rabboni, that I may receive my sight. It is a glad and eager answer. Many a petition he had urged in vain; and many a small favour had been discourteously bestowed; but Jesus, Whose tenderness loves to commend while He blesses, shares with him, so to speak, the glory of his healing, as He answers, Go thy way, thy faith hath made thee whole. By thus fixing his attention upon his own part in the miracle, so utterly worthless as a contribution, but so indispensable as a condition, Jesus taught him to exercise hereafter the same gift of faith.

"Go thy way," He said. And Bartimæus "followed Him on the road." Happy is that man whose eyes are open to discern, and his heart prompt to follow, the print of those holy feet.

CHAPTER XI.

THE TRIUMPHANT ENTRY.

MARK xi. 1-11 (R. V.).

JESUS had now come near to Jerusalem, into what was possibly the sacred district of Bethphage, of which, in that case, Bethany was the border village. Not without pausing here (as we learn from the fourth Gospel), yet as the next step forward, He sent two of His disciples to untie and bring back an ass, which was fastened with her colt at a spot which He minutely described. Unless they were challenged they should simply bring the animals away; but if any one remonstrated, they should answer, "The Lord hath need of them," and thereupon the owner would not only acquiesce, but send them. In fact they are to make a requisition, such as the State often institutes for horses and cattle during a campaign, when private rights must give way to a national exigency. And this masterful demand, this abrupt and decisive rejoinder to a natural objection, not arguing nor requesting, but demanding, this title which they are bidden to give to Jesus, by which, standing thus alone, He is rarely described in Scripture (chiefly in the later Epistles, when the remembrance of His earthly style gave place to the influence of habitual adoration), all this preliminary arrangement makes us conscious of a change of tone, of royalty issuing its mandates, and claiming its rights. But what a claim, what a requisition, when He takes the title of Jehovah, and yet announces His need of the colt of an ass. It is indeed the lowliest of all memorable processions which He plans, and yet, in its very humility, it appeals to ancient prophecy, and says unto Zion that her king cometh unto her. The monarchs of the East and the captains of the West might ride upon horses as for war, but the King of Sion should come unto her meek, and sitting upon an ass, upon a colt, the foal of an ass. Yet there are fitness and dignity in the use of "a colt whereon man never sat," and it reminds us of other facts, such as that He was the firstborn of a virgin mother, and rested in a tomb which corruption had never soiled.

Thus He comes forth, the gentlest of the mighty, with no swords gleaming around to guard Him, or to smite the foreigner who tramples Israel, or the worse foes of her own household. Men who will follow such a King must lay aside their vain and earthly ambitions, and awake to the truth that spiritual powers are grander than any which violence ever grasped. But men who will not follow Him shall some day learn the same lesson, perhaps in the crash of their reeling commonwealth, perhaps not until the armies of heaven follow Him, as He goes forth, riding now upon a white horse, crowned with many diadems, smiting the nations with a sharp sword, and ruling them with an iron rod.

Lowly though His procession was, yet it was palpably a royal one. When Jehu was proclaimed king at Ramoth-Gilead, the captains hastened to make him sit upon the garments of every one of them, expressing by this national symbol their subjection. Somewhat the same feeling is in the famous anecdote of Sir Walter Raleigh and Queen Elizabeth. And thus the disciples who brought the ass cast on him their garments, and Jesus sat thereon, and many spread their garments in the way. Others strewed the road with branches; and as they went they cried aloud certain verses of that great song of triumph, which told how the nations, swarming like bees, were quenched like the light fire of thorns, how the right hand of the Lord did valiantly, how the gates of righteousness should be thrown open for the righteous, and, more significant still, how the stone which the builders rejected should become the head-stone of the corner. Often had Jesus quoted this saying when reproached by the unbelief of the rulers, and now the people rejoiced and were glad in it, as they sang of His salvation, saying, "Hosanna, blessed is He that cometh in the name of the Lord, Blessed is the kingdom that cometh, the Kingdom of our father David, Hosanna in the highest."

Such is the narrative as it impressed St. Mark. For his purpose it mattered nothing that Jerusalem took no part in the rejoicings, but was perplexed, and said, Who is this? or that, when confronted by this somewhat scornful and affected ignorance of the capital, the voice of Galilee grew weak, and proclaimed no longer the advent of the kingdom of David, but only Jesus, the prophet of Nazareth; or that the Pharisees in the temple avowed their disapproval, while contemptuously ignoring the Galilean multitude, by inviting Him to reprove some children. What concerned St. Mark was that now, at last, Jesus openly and practically assumed rank as a monarch, allowed men to proclaim the advent of His kingdom, and proceeded to exercise its rights by calling for the surrender of property, and by cleansing the temple with a scourge. The same avowal of kingship is almost all that he has cared to record of the remarkable scene before His Roman judge.

After this heroic fashion did Jesus present Himself to die. Without a misleading hope, conscious of the hollowness of His seeming popularity, weeping for the impending ruin of the glorious city whose walls were ringing with His praise, and predicting the murderous triumph of the crafty faction which appears so helpless, He not only refuses to recede or compromise, but does not hesitate to advance His claims in a manner entirely new, and to defy the utmost animosity of those who still rejected Him.

After such a scene there could be no middle course between crushing Him, and bowing to Him. He was no longer a Teacher of doctrines, however revolutionary, but an aspirant to practical authority, Who must be dealt with practically.

There was evidence also of His intention to proceed upon this new line, when He entered into the temple, investigated its glaring abuses, and only left it for the moment because it was now eventide. To-morrow would show more of His designs.

Jesus is still, and in this world, King. And it will hereafter avail us nothing to have received His doctrine, unless we have taken His yoke.

THE BARREN FIG-TREE.

Mark xi. 12-14, 20-25 (R. V.).

No sooner has Jesus claimed His kingdom, than He performs His first and only miracle of judgment. And it is certain that no mortal, informed that such a miracle was impending, could have guessed where the blow would fall. In this miracle an element is predominant which exists in all, since it is wrought as an acted dramatised parable, not for any physical advantage, but wholly for the instruction which it conveys. Jesus hungered at the very outset of a day of toil, as He came out from Bethany. And this was not due to poverty, since the disciples there had recently made Him a great feast, but to His own absorbing ardour. The zeal of God's house, which He had seen polluted and was about to cleanse, had either left Him indifferent to food until the keen air of morning aroused the sense of need, or else it had detained Him, all night long, in prayer and meditation out of doors. As He walks, He sees afar off a lonely fig-tree covered with leaves, and comes if haply He might find anything thereon. It is true that figs would not be in season for two months, but yet they ought to present themselves before the leaves did; and since the tree was precocious in the show and profusion of luxuriance, it ought to bear early figs. If it failed, it would at least point a powerful moral; and, therefore, when only leaves appeared upon it, Jesus cursed it with perpetual barrenness, and passed on. Not in the dusk of that evening as they returned, but when they passed by again in the morning the blight was manifest, the tree was withered from its very roots.

It is complained that by this act Jesus deprived some one of his property. But the same retributive justice of which this was an expression was preparing to blight, presently, all the possessions of all the nation. Was this unjust? And of the numberless trees that are blasted year by year, why should the loss of this one only be resented? Every physical injury must be intended to further some spiritual end; but it is not often that the purpose is so clear, and the lesson so distinctly learned.

Others blame our Lord's word of sentence, because a tree, not being a moral agent, ought not to be punished. It is an obvious rejoinder that neither could it suffer pain; that the whole action is symbolic; and that we ourselves justify the Saviour's method of expression as often as we call one tree "good" and another "bad," and say that a third "ought" to bear fruit, while not much could be "expected of" a fourth. It should rather be observed that in this word of sentence Jesus revealed His tenderness. It would have been a false and cruel kindness never to work any miracle except of compassion, and thus to suggest the inference that He could never strike, whereas indeed, before that generation passed away, He would break His enemies in pieces like a potter's vessel.

Yet He came not to destroy men's lives but to save them. And, therefore, while showing Himself neither indifferent nor powerless against barren and false pretensions, He did this only once, and then only by a sign wrought upon an unsentient tree.

Retribution fell upon it not for its lack of fruit, since at that season it shared this with all its tribe, but for ostentatious, much-professing fruitlessness. And thus it pointed with dread significance to the condition of God's own people, differing from Greece and Rome and Syria, not in the want of fruit, but in the show of luxuriant frondage, in the expectation it excited and mocked. When the season of the world's fruitfulness was yet remote, only Israel put forth leaves, and made professions which were not fulfilled. And the permanent warning of the miracle is not for heathen men and races, but for Christians who have a name to live, and who are called to bear fruit unto God.

While the disciples marvelled at the sudden fulfilment of its sentence, they could not have forgotten the parable of a fig-tree in the vineyard, on which care and labour were lavished, but which must be destroyed after one year of respite if it continued to be a cumberer of the ground.

And Jesus drove the lesson home. He pointed to "this mountain" full in front, with the gold and marble of the temple sparkling like a diadem upon its brow, and declared that faith is not only able to smite barrenness with death, but to remove into the midst of the sea, to plant among the wild and storm-swept races of the immeasurable pagan world, the glory and privilege of the realised presence of the Lord. To do this was the purpose of God, hinted by many a prophet, and clearly announced by Christ Himself. But its accomplishment was left to His followers, who should succeed in exact proportion to the union of their will and that of God, so that the condition of that moral miracle, transcending all others in marvel and in efficacy, was simple faith.

And the same rule covers all the exigencies of life. One who truly relies on God, whose mind and will are attuned to those of the Eternal, cannot be selfish, or vindictive, or presumptuous. As far as we rise to the grandeur of this condition we enter into the Omnipotence of God, and no limit need be imposed upon the prevalence of really and utterly believing prayer. The wishes that ought to be refused will vanish as we attain that eminence, like the hoar frost of morning as the sun grows strong.

To this promise Jesus added a precept, the admirable suitability of which is not at first apparent. Most sins are made evident to the conscience in the act of prayer. Drawing nigh to God, we feel our unfitness to be there, we are made conscious of what He frowns upon, and if we have such faith as Jesus spoke of, we at once resign what would grieve the Spirit of adoption. No saint is ignorant of the convicting power of prayer. But it is not of necessity so with resentment for real grievances. We may think we do well to be angry. We may confound our selfish fire with the pure flame of holy zeal, and begin, with confidence enough, yet not with the mind of Christ, to remove mountains, not because they impede a holy cause, but because they throw a shadow upon our own field. And, therefore, Jesus reminds us that not only wonder-working faith, but even the forgiveness of our sins requires from us the forgiveness of our brother. This saying is the clearest proof of how much is implied in a truly undoubting heart. And this promise is the sternest rebuke of the Church, endowed with such ample powers, and yet after nineteen centuries confronted by an unconverted world.

THE SECOND CLEANSING OF THE TEMPLE.

MARK xi. 15-19 (R. V.).

With the authority of yesterday's triumph still about Him, Jesus returned to the temple, which He had then inspected. There at least the priesthood were not thwarted by popular indifference or ignorance: they had power to carry out fully their own views; they were solely responsible for whatever abuses could be discovered. In fact the iniquities which moved the indignation of Jesus were of their own contrivance, and they enriched themselves by a vile trade which robbed the worshippers and profaned the holy house.

Pilgrims from a distance needed the sacred money, the half-shekel of the sanctuary, still coined for this one purpose, to offer for a ransom of their souls (Exod. xxx. 13). And the priests had sanctioned a trade in the exchange of money under the temple roof, so fraudulent that the dealers' evidence was refused in the courts of justice.

Doves were necessary for the purification of the poor, who could not afford more costly sacrifices, and sheep and oxen were also in great demand. And since the unblemished quality of the sacrifices should be attested by the priests, they had been able to put a fictitious value upon these animals, by which the family of Annas in particular had accumulated enormous wealth.

To facilitate this trade, they had dared to bring the defilement of the cattle market within the precincts of the House of God. Not indeed into the place where the Pharisee stood in his pride and "prayed with himself," for that was holy; but the court of the Gentiles was profane; the din which distracted and the foulness which revolted Gentile worship were of no account to the average Jew. But Jesus regarded the scene with different eyes. How could the sanctity of that holy place not extend to the court of the stranger and the proselyte, when it was written, Thy house shall be called a house of prayer for all the nations? Therefore Jesus had already, at the outset of His ministry, cleansed His Father's house. Now, in the fulness of His newly asserted royalty, He calls it My House: He denounces the iniquity of their traffic by branding it as a den of robbers; He casts out the traders themselves, as well as the implements of their traffic: and in so doing He fanned to a mortal heat the hatred of the chief priests and the scribes, who saw at once their revenues threatened and their reputation tarnished, and yet dared not strike, because all the multitude was astonished at His teaching.

But the wisdom of Jesus did not leave Him within their reach at night; every evening He went forth out of the city.

From this narrative we learn the blinding force of self-interest, for doubtless they were no more sensible of their iniquity than many a modern slavedealer. And we must never rest content because our own conscience acquits us, unless we have by thought and prayer supplied it with light and guiding.

We learn reverence for sacred places, since the one exercise of His royal authority which Jesus publicly displayed was to cleanse the temple, even though upon the morow He would relinquish it for ever, to be "your house"—and desolate.

We learn also how much apparent sanctity, what dignity of worship, splendour of offerings, and pomp of architecture may go along with corruption and unreality.

And yet again, by their overawed and abject helplessness we learn the might of holy indignation, and the awakening power of a bold appeal to conscience. "The people hung upon Him, listening," and if all seemed vain and wasted effort on the following Friday, what fruit of the teaching of Jesus did not His followers gather in, as soon as He poured down on them the gifts of Pentecost.

Did they now recall their own reflections after the earlier cleansing of the temple? and their Master's ominous words? Thev had then remembered how it was written, The zeal of thine house shall eat Me up. And He had said, Destroy this temple, and in three days I shall raise it up, speaking of the Temple of His body, which was now about to be thrown down.

THE BAPTISM OF JOHN, WHENCE WAS IT?

MARK xi. 27-33 (R. V.).

The question put to Jesus by the hierarchy of Jerusalem is recorded in all the synoptic Gospels. But in some respects the story is most pointed in the narrative of St. Mark. And it is natural that he, the historian especially of the energies of Christ, should lay stress upon a challenge addressed to Him, by reason of His masterful words and deeds. At the outset, he had recorded the astonishment of the people because Jesus taught with authority, because "Verily I say" replaced the childish and servile methods by which the scribe and the Pharisee sustained their most wilful innovations.

When first he relates a miracle, he tells how their wonder increased, because with authority Jesus commanded the unclean spirits and they obeyed, respecting His self-reliant word "I command thee to come out," more than the most elaborate incantations and exorcisms. St. Mark's first record of collision with the priests was when Jesus carried His claim still farther, and said "The Son of man hath authority" (it is the same word) "on earth to forgive sins." Thus we find the Gospel quite conscious of what so forcibly strikes a careful modern reader, the assured and independent tone of Jesus; His bearing, so unlike that of a disciple or a commentator; His consciousness that the Scriptures themselves are they which testify of Him, and that only He can give the life which men think they possess in these. In the very teaching of lowliness Jesus exempts Himself, and forbids others to be Master and Lord, because these titles belong to Him.

Impressive as such claims appear when we awake to them, it is even more suggestive to reflect that we can easily read the Gospels and not be struck by them. We do not start when He bids all the weary come to Him, and offers them rest, and yet declares Himself to be meek and lowly. He is meek and lowly while He makes such claims. His bearing is that of the highest rank, joined with the most perfect graciousness; His great claims never irritate us, because they are palpably His due, and we readily concede the astonishing elevation whence He so graciously bends down so low. And this is one evidence of the truth and power of the character which the Apostles drew.

How natural is this also, that immediately after Palm Sunday, when the people have hailed their Messiah, royal and a Saviour, and when He has accepted their homage, we find new indications of authority in His bearing and His actions. He promptly took them at their word. It was now that He wrought His only miracle of judgment, and although it was but the withering of a tree (since He came not to destroy men's lives but to save them), yet was there a dread symbolical sentence involved upon all barren and unfruitful men and Churches. In the very act of triumphal entry, He solemnly pronounced judgment upon the guilty city which would not accept her King.

Arrived at the temple, He surveyed its abuses and defilements, and returned on the morrow (and so not spurred by sudden impulse, but of deliberate purpose), to drive out them that sold and bought. Two years ago He had needed to scourge the intruders forth, but now they are overawed by His majesty, and obey His word. Then, too, they were rebuked for making His Father's house a house of merchandise, but now it is His own—"My House"—but degraded yet farther into a den of thieves.

But while traffic and pollution shrank away, misery and privation were attracted to Him; the blind and the lame came and were healed in the very temple; and the centre and rallying-place of the priests and scribes beheld His power to save. This drove them to extremities. He was carrying the war into the heart of their territories, establishing Himself in their stronghold, and making it very plain that since the people had hailed Him King, and He had responded to their acclaims, He would not shrink from whatever His views of that great office might involve.

While they watched, full of bitterness and envy, they were again impressed, as at the beginning, by the strange, autocratic, spontaneous manner in which He worked, making Himself the source of His blessings, as no prophet had ever done since Moses expiated so dearly the offence of saying, Must we fetch you water out of the rock? Jesus acted after the fashion of Him Who openeth His hands and satisfieth the desire of every living thing. Why did He not give the glory to One above? Why did He not supplicate, nor invoke, but simply bestow? Where were the accustomed words of supplication, "Hear me, O Lord God, hear me," or, "Where is the Lord God of Israel?"

Here they discerned a flaw, a heresy; and they would force Him either to make a fatal claim, or else to moderate His pretensions at their bidding, which would promptly restore their lost influence and leadership.

Nor need we shrink from confessing that our Lord was justly open to such reproach, unless He was indeed Divine, unless He was deliberately preparing His followers for that astonishing revelation, soon to come, which threw the Church upon her knees in adoration of her God manifest in flesh. It is hard to understand how the Socinian can defend his Master against the charge of encroaching on the rights and honours of Deity, and (to borrow a phrase from a different connection) sitting down at the right hand of the Majesty of God, whereas every priest standeth ministering. If He were a creature, He culpably failed to tell us the conditions upon which He received a delegated authority, and the omission has made His Church ever since idolatrous. It is one great and remarkable lesson suggested by this verse: if Jesus were not Divine, what was He?

Thus it came to pass, in direct consequence upon the events which opened the great week of the triumph and the cross of Jesus, that the whole rank and authority of the temple system confronted Him with a stern question. They sat in Moses' seat. They were entitled to examine the pretensions of a new and aspiring teacher. They had a perfect right to demand "Tell us by what authority thou doest these things." The works are not denied, but the source whence they flow is questioned.

After so many centuries, the question is fresh to-day. For still the spirit of Christ is working in His world, openly, palpably, spreading blessings far and wide. It is exalting multitudes of ignoble lives by hopes that are profound, far-reaching, and sublime. When savage realms are explored, it is Christ Who hastens thither with His gospel, before the trader in rum and gunpowder can exhibit the charms of a civilisation without a creed. In the gloomiest haunts of disease and misery, madness, idiotcy, orphanage, and vice, there is Christ at work, the good Samaritan, pouring oil and wine into the gaping wounds of human nature, acting quite upon His own authority, careless who looks askance, not asking political economy whether genuine charity is pauperisation, nor questioning the doctrine of development, whether the progress of the race demands the pitiless rejection of the unfit, and selection only of the strongest specimens for survival. That iron creed may be natural; but if so, ours is supernatural, it is a law of spirit and life, setting us free from that base and selfish law of sin and death. The existence and energy of Christian forces in our modern world is indisputable: never was Jesus a more popular and formidable claimant of its crown; never did more Hosannas follow Him into the temple. But now as formerly His credentials are demanded: what is His authority and how has He come by it?

Now we say of modern as of ancient inquiries, that they are right; investigation is inevitable and a duty.

But see how Jesus dealt with those men of old. Let us not misunderstand Him. He did not merely set one difficulty against another, as if we should start some scientific problem, and absolve ourselves from the duty of answering any inquiry until science had disposed of this. Doubtless it is logical enough to point out that all creeds, scientific and religious alike, have their unsolved problems. But the reply of Jesus was not a dexterous evasion, it went to the root of things, and, therefore, it stands good for time and for eternity. He refused to surrender the advantage of a witness to whom He was entitled: He demanded that all the facts and not some alone should be investigated. In truth their position bound His interrogators to examine His credentials; to do so was not only their privilege but their duty. But then they must begin at the beginning. Had they performed this duty for the Baptist? Who or what was that mysterious, lonely, stern preacher of righteousness who had stirred the national heart so profoundly, and whom all men still revered? They themselves had sent to question him, and his answer was notorious: he had said that he was sent before the Christ: he was only a voice, but a voice which demanded the preparation of a way before the Lord Himself, Who was approaching, and a highway for our God. What was the verdict of these investigators upon that great movement? What would they make of the decisive testimony of the Baptist?

As the perilous significance of this consummate rejoinder bursts on their crafty intelligence, as they recoil confounded from the exposure they have brought upon themselves, St. Mark tells how the question was pressed home, "Answer Me!" But they dared not call John an impostor, and yet to confess him was to authenticate the seal upon our Lord's credentials. And Jesus is palpably within His rights in refusing to be questioned of such authorities as these. Yet immediately afterwards, with equal skill and boldness, He declared Himself, and yet defied their malice, in the story of the lord of a vineyard, who had vainly sent many servants to claim its fruit, and at the last sent his beloved son.

Now apply the same process to the modern opponents of the faith, and it will be found that multitudes of their assaults on Christianity imply the negation of what they will not and dare not deny. Some will not believe in miracles because the laws of nature work uniformly. But their uniformity is undisturbed by human operations; the will of man wields, without cancelling, these mighty forces which surround us. And why may not the will of God do the same, if there be a God? Ask them whether they deny His existence, and they will probably declare themselves Agnostics, which is exactly the ancient answer, "We cannot tell." Now as long as men avow their ignorance of the existence or non-existence of a Deity, they cannot assert the impossibility of miracles, for miracles are simply actions which reveal God, as men's actions reveal their presence.

Again, a demand is made for such evidence, to establish the faith, as cannot be had for any fact beyond the range of the exact sciences. We are asked, Why should we stake eternity upon anything short of demonstration? Yet it will be found that the objector is absolutely persuaded, and acts on his persuasion of many "truths which never can be proved"—of the fidelity of his wife and children, and above all, of the difference between right and wrong. That is a fundamental principle: deny it, and society becomes impossible. And yet sceptical theories are widely diffused which really, though unconsciously, sap the very foundations of morality, or assert that it is not from heaven but of men, a mere expediency, a prudential arrangement of society.

Such arguments may well "fear the people," for the instincts of mankind know well that all such explanations of conscience do really explain it away.

And it is quite necessary in our days, when religion is impugned, to see whether the assumptions of its assailants would not compromise time as well as eternity, and to ask, What think ye of all those fundamental principles which sustain the family, society, and the state, while they bear testimony to the Church of Christ.

CHAPTER XII.

THE HUSBANDMEN.

MARK xii. 1-12 (R. V.).

THE rulers of His people have failed to make Jesus responsible to their inquisition. He has exposed the hollowness of their claim to investigate His commission, and formally refused to tell them by what authority He did these things. But what He would not say for an unjust cross-examination, He proclaimed to all docile hearts; and the skill which disarmed His enemies is not more wonderful than that which in their hearing answered their question, yet left them no room for accusation. This was achieved by speaking to them in parables. The indifferent might hear and not perceive: the keenness of malice would surely understand but could not easily impeach a simple story; but to His own followers it would be given to know the mysteries of the kingdom of God.

His first words would be enough to arouse attention. The psalmist had told how God brought a vine out of Egypt, and cast out the heathen and planted it. Isaiah had carried the image farther, and sung of a vineyard in a very fruitful hill. The Well-beloved, Whose it was, cleared the ground for it, and planted it with the choicest vine, and built a tower, and hewed out a wine-press, and looked that it should bring forth grapes, but it had brought forth wild grapes. Therefore He would lay it waste. This well-known and recognised type the Lord now adopted, but modified it to suit His purpose. As in a former parable the sower slept and rose, and left the earth to bring forth fruit of itself, so in this, the Lord of the vineyard let it out to husbandmen and went into a far country. This is our Lord's own explanation of that silent time in which no special interpositions asserted that God was nigh, no prophecies were heard, no miracles startled the careless. It was the time when grace already granted should have been peacefully ripening. Now we live in such a period. Unbelievers desire a sign. Impatient believers argue that if our Master is as near us as ever, the same portents must attest His presence; and, therefore, they recognise the gift of tongues in hysterical clamour, and stake the honour of religion upon faith-healing, and those various obscure phenomena which the annals of every fanaticism can rival. But the sober Christian understands that, even as the Lord of the vineyard went into another country, so Christ His Son (Who in spiritual communion is ever with His people) in another sense has gone into a far country to receive a kingdom and to return. In the interval, marvels would be simply an anachronism. The best present evidence of the faith lies in the superior fruitfulness of the vineyard He has planted, in the steady advance to rich maturity of the vine He has imported from another clime.

At this point Jesus begins to add a new significance to the ancient metaphor. The husbandmen are mentioned. Men there were in the ancient Church, who were specially responsible for the culture of the vineyard. As He spoke, the symbol explained itself. The imposing array of chief priests and scribes and elders stood by, who had just claimed as their prerogative that He should make good His commission to their scrutiny; and none would be less likely to mistake His meaning than these self-conscious lovers of chief seats in the synagogues. The structure of the parable, therefore, admits their official rank, as frankly as when Jesus bade His disciples submit to their ordinances because they sit in Moses' seat. But He passes on, easily and as if unconsciously, to record that special messengers from heaven had, at times, interrupted the self-indulgent quietude of the husbandmen. Because the fruit of the vineyard had not been freely rendered, a bondservant was sent to demand it. The epithet implies that the messenger was lower in rank, although his direct mission gave him authority even over the keepers of the vineyard. It expresses exactly the position of the prophets, few of them of priestly rank, some of them very humble in extraction, and very rustic in expression, but all sent in evil days to faithless husbandmen, to remind them that the vineyard was not their own, and to receive the fruits of righteousness. Again and again the demand is heard, for He sent "many others;" and always it is rejected with violence, which sometimes rises to murder. As they listened, they must have felt that all this was true, that while prophet after prophet had come to a violent end, not one had seen the official hierarchy making common cause with him. And they must also have felt how ruinous was this rejoinder to their own demand that the people should forsake a teacher when they rejected him. Have any of the rulers or of the Pharisees believed on Him? was their scornful question. But the answer was plain, As long as they built the sepulchres of the prophets, and garnished the tombs of the righteous, and said, If we had been in the days of our fathers, we would not have been partakers with them in the blood of the prophets, they confessed that men could not blindly follow a hierarchy merely as such, since they were not the official successors of the prophets but of those who slew them. The worst charge brought against them was only that they acted according to analogy, and filled up the deeds of their fathers. It had always been the same.

The last argument of Stephen, which filled his judges with madness, was but the echo of this great impeachment. Which of the prophets did not your fathers persecute? and they killed them which showed before of the coming of the Righteous One, of Whom ye have now become the betrayers and murderers.

That last defiance of heaven, which Stephen thus denounced, his Master distinctly foretold. And He added the appalling circumstance, that however they might deceive themselves and sophisticate their conscience, they really knew Him Who He was. They felt, at the very least, that into His hands should pass all the authority and power they had so long monopolised: "This is the Heir; come let us kill Him and the inheritance shall be ours." If there were no more, the utterance of these words put forth an extraordinary claim.

All that should have been rendered up to heaven and was withheld, all that previous messengers had demanded on behalf of God without avail, all "the inheritance" which these wicked husbandmen were intercepting, all this Jesus announces to be His own, while reprehending the dishonesty of any other claim upon it. And as a matter of fact, if Jesus be not Divine, He has intercepted more of the worship due to the Eternal, has attracted to Himself more of the homage of the loftiest and profoundest minds, than any false teacher within the pale of monotheism has ever done. It is the bounden duty of all who revere Jesus even as a teacher, of all who have eyes to see that His coming was the greatest upward step in the progress of humanity, to consider well what was implied, when, in the act of blaming the usurpers of the heritage of God, Jesus declared that inheritance to be His own. But this is not all, though it is what He declares that the husbandmen were conscious of. The parable states, not only that He is heir, but heir by virtue of His special relationship to the Supreme. Others are bondservants or husbandmen, but He is the Son. He does not inherit as the worthiest and most obedient, but by right of birth; and His Father, in the act of sending Him, expects even these bloodstained outlaws to reverence His Son. In such a phrase, applied to such criminals, we are made to feel the lofty rank alike of the Father and His Son, which ought to have overawed even them. And when we read that "He had yet one, a beloved Son," it seems as if the veil of eternity were uplifted, to reveal a secret and awful intimacy, of which, nevertheless, some glimmering consciousness should have controlled the most desperate heart.

But they only reckoned that if they killed the Heir, the inheritance would become their own. It seems the wildest madness, that men should know and feel Who He was, and yet expect to profit by desecrating His rights. And yet so it was from the beginning. If Herod were not fearful that the predicted King of the Jews was indeed born, the massacre of the Innocents was idle. If the rulers were not fearful that this counsel and work was of God, they would not, at Gamaliel's bidding, have refrained from the Apostles. And it comes still closer to the point to observe that, if they had attached no importance, even in their moment of triumph, to the prediction of His rising from the dead, they would not have required a guard, nor betrayed the secret recognition which Jesus here exposes. The same blind miscalculation is in every attempt to obtain profit or pleasure by means which are known to transgress the laws of the all-beholding Judge of all. It is committed every day, under the pressure of strong temptation, by men who know clearly that nothing but misery can result. So true is it that action is decided, not by a course of logic in the brain, but by the temperament and bias of our nature as a whole. We need not suppose that the rulers roundly spoke such words as these, even to themselves. The infamous motive lurked in ambush, too far in the background of the mind perhaps even for consciousness. But it was there, and it affected their decision, as lurking passions and self-interests always will, as surely as iron deflects the compass. "They caught Him and killed Him," said the unfaltering lips of their victim. And He added a circumstance of pain which we often overlook, but to which the great minister of the circumcision was keenly sensitive, and often reverted, the giving Him up to the Gentiles, to death accursed among the Jews; "they cast Him forth out of the vineyard."

All evil acts are based upon an overestimate of the tolerance of God. He had seemed to remain passive while messenger after messenger was beaten, stoned, or slain. But now that they had filled up the iniquity of their fathers, the Lord of the vineyard would come in person to destroy them, and give the vineyard to others. This last phrase is strangely at variance with the notion that the days of a commissioned ministry are over, as, on the other hand, the whole parable is at variance with the notion that a priesthood can be trusted to sit in exclusive judgment upon doctrine for the Church.

At this point St. Mark omits an incident so striking, although small, that its absence is significant. The by-standers said, "God forbid!" and when the horrified exclamation betrayed their consciousness of the position, Jesus was content, without a word, to mark their self-conviction by His searching gaze. "He looked upon them." The omission would be unaccountable if St. Mark were simply a powerful narrator of graphic incidents; but it is explained when we think that for him the manifestation of a mighty Personage was all in all, and the most characteristic and damaging admissions of the hierarchy were as nothing compared with a word of his Lord. Thereupon he goes straight on to record that, besides refuting their claim by the history of the past, and asserting His own supremacy in a phrase at once guarded in form and decisive in import, Jesus also appealed to Scripture. It was written that by special and marvellous interposition of the Lord a stone which the recognised builders had rejected should crown the building. And the quotation was not only decisive as showing that their rejection could not close the controversy; it also compensated, with a promise of final victory, the ominous words in which their malice had seemed to do its worst. Jesus often predicted His death, but He never despaired of His kingdom.

No wonder that the rulers sought to arrest Him, and perceived that He penetrated and despised their schemes. And their next device is a natural outcome from the fact that they feared the people, but did not discontinue their intrigues; for this was a crafty and dangerous attempt to estrange from Him the admiring multitude.

THE TRIBUTE MONEY.

MARK xii. 13-17 (R. V.).

The contrast is very striking between this incident and the last. Instead of a challenge, Jesus is respectfully consulted; and instead of a formal concourse of the authorities of His religion, He is Himself the authority to Whom a few perplexed people profess to submit their difficulty. Nevertheless, it is a new and subtle effort of the enmity of His defeated foes. They have sent to Him certain Pharisees who will excite the popular indignation if He yields anything to the foreigner, and Herodians who will, if He refuses, bring upon Him the colder and deadlier vengeance of Rome. They flatter, in order to stimulate, that fearless utterance which must often have seemed to them so rash: "We know that Thou art true, and carest not for any one, for Thou regardest not the person of men, but of a truth teachest the way of God." And they appeal to a higher motive by representing the case to be one of practical and personal urgency. "Shall we give, or shall we not give?"

Never was it more necessary to join the wisdom of the serpent to the innocence of the dove, for it would seem that He must needs answer directly, and that no direct answer can fail to have the gravest consequences. But in their eagerness to secure this menacing position, they have left one weak point in the attack. They have made the question altogether a practical one. The abstract doctrine of the right to drive out a foreign power, of the limits of authority and freedom, they have not raised. It is simply a question of the hour, Shall we give or shall we not give?

And Jesus baffled them by treating it as such. There was no longer a national coinage, except only of the half shekel for the temple tax. When He asked them for a smaller coin, they produced a Roman penny stamped with the effigy of Cæsar. Thus they confessed the use of the Roman currency. Now since they accepted the advantages of subjugation, they ought also to endure its burdens: since they traded as Roman subjects, they ought to pay the Roman tribute. Not He had preached submission, but they had avowed it; and any consequent unpopularity would fall not upon Him but them. They had answered their own question. And Jesus laid down the broad and simple rule, "Render (pay back) unto Cæsar the things that are Cæsar's, and unto God the things that are God's. And they marvelled greatly at Him." No wonder they marvelled, for it would be hard to find in all the records of philosophy so ready and practical a device to baffle such cunning intriguers, such keenness in One Whose life was so far removed from the schools of worldly wisdom, joined with so firm a grasp on principle, in an utterance so brief, yet going down so far to the roots of action.

Now the words of Jesus are words for all time; even when He deals with a question of the hour, He treats it from the point of view of eternal fitness and duty; and this command to render unto Cæsar the things which are Cæsar's has become the charter of the state against all usurpations of tyrannous ecclesiastics. A sphere is recognised in which obedience to the law is a duty to God. But it is absurd to pretend that Christ taught blind and servile obedience to all tyrants in all circumstances, for this would often make it impossible to obey the second injunction, and to render unto God the things which are God's,—a clause which asserts in turn the right of conscience and the Church against all secular encroachments. The point to observe is, that the decision of Jesus is simply an inference, a deduction. St. Matthew has inserted the word "therefore," and it is certainly implied: render unto Cæsar the things which you confess to be his own, which bear his image upon their face.

Can we suppose that no such inference gives point to the second clause? It would then become, like too many of our pious sayings, a mere supplement inappropriate, however excellent, a make-weight, and a platitude. No example of such irrelevance can be found in the story of our Lord. When, finding the likeness of Cæsar on the coin, He said, Render, therefore, unto Cæsar the things that are Cæsar's, and unto God the things that are God's, He at least suggested that the reason for both precepts ran parallel, and the image of the higher and heavenlier Monarch could be found on what He claims of us. And it is so. He claims all we have and all we are. "The earth is the Lord's, and the fulness thereof:" and "I have made thee, thou art Mine." And for us and ours alike the argument holds good. All the visible universe bears deeply stamped into its substance His image and superscription. The grandeur of mountains and stars, the fairness of violet and harebell, are alike revelations of the Creator. The heavens declare His glory: the firmament showeth His handiwork: the earth is full of His riches: all the discoveries which expand our mastery over nature and disease, over time and space, are proofs of His wisdom and goodness, Who laid the amazing plan which we grow wise by tracing out. Find a corner on which contrivance and benevolence have not stamped the royal image, and we may doubt whether that bleak spot owes Him tribute. But no desert is so blighted, no solitude so forlorn.

And we should render unto God the things which are God's, seeing His likeness in His world. "For the invisible things of Him since the creation of the world are clearly seen, being perceived through the things which are made, even His everlasting power and divinity."

And if most of all He demands the love, the heart of man, here also He can ask, "Whose image and superscription is this?" For in the image of God made He man. It is sometimes urged that this image was quite effaced when Adam fell. But it was not to protect the unfallen that the edict was spoken "Whoso sheddeth man's blood, by man shall his blood be shed, for in the image of God made He man." He was not an unfallen man of whom St. Paul said that he "ought not to have his head veiled, forasmuch as he is the image and glory of God;" neither were they unfallen, of whom St. James said, "We curse men which are made after the likeness of God" (Gen. ix. 6; 1 Cor. xi. 7; James iii. 9). Common men, for whom the assassin lurks, who need instruction how to behave in church, and whom others scorn and curse, these bear upon them an awful likeness; and even when they refuse tribute to their king, He can ask them, Whose is this image?

We see it in the intellect, ever demanding new worlds to conquer, overwhelming us with its victories over time and space. "In apprehension how like a God." Alas for us! if we forget that the Spirit of knowledge and wisdom is no other than the Spirit of the Lord God.

We see this likeness far more in our moral nature. It is true that sin has spoiled and wasted this, yet there survives in man's heart, as nowhere else in our world, a strange sympathy with the holiness and love of God. No other of His attributes has the same power to thrill us. Tell me that He lit the stars and can quench them with a word, and I reverence, perhaps I fear Him; yet such power is outside and beyond my sphere; it fails to touch me, it is high, I cannot attain unto it. Even the rarer human gifts, the power of a Czar, the wisdom of Bacon, are thus beyond me, I am unkindled, they do not find me out. But speak of holiness, even the stainless holiness of God, undefiled through all eternity, and you shake the foundations of my being. And why does the reflection that God is pure humble me more than the knowledge that God is omnipotent? Because it is my spiritual nature which is most conscious of the Divine image, blurred and defaced indeed, but not obliterated yet. Because while I listen I am dimly conscious of my birthright, my destiny, that I was born to resemble this, and all is lost if I come short of it. Because every child and every sinner feels that it is more possible for him to be like his God than like Newton, or Shakespeare, or Napoleon. Because the work of grace is to call in the worn and degraded coinage of humanity, and as the mint restamps and reissues the pieces which have grown thin and worn, so to renew us after the image of Him that created us.

CHRIST AND THE SADDUCEES.

MARK xii. 18-27 (R. V.).

Christ came that the thoughts of many hearts might be revealed. And so it was, that when He had silenced the examination of the hierarchy, and baffled their craft, the Sadducees were tempted to assail Him. Like the rationalists of every age, they stood coldly aloof from popular movements, and we seldom find them interfering with Christ or His followers, until their energies were roused by the preaching of His Resurrection, so directly opposed to their fundamental doctrines.

Their appearance now is extremely natural. The repulse of every other party left them the only champions of orthodoxy against the new movement, with everything to win by success, and little to lose by failure. There is a tone of quiet and confident irony in their interrogation, well befitting an upper-class group, a secluded party of refined critics, rather than practical teachers with a mission to their fellow-men. They break utterly new ground by raising an abstract and subtle question, a purely intellectual problem, but one which reduced the doctrine of a resurrection to an absurdity, if only their premises can be made good. And this peculiarity is often overlooked in criticism upon our Lord's answer. Its intellectual subtlety was only the adoption by Christ of the weapons of his adversaries. But at the same time, He lays great and special stress upon the authority of Scripture, in this encounter with the party which least acknowledged it.

Their objection, stated in its simplest form, is the complication which would result if the successive ties for which death makes room must all revive together when death is abolished. If a woman has married a second time, whose wife shall she be? But their statement of the case is ingenious, not only because they push the difficulty to an absurd and ludicrous extent, but much more so because they base it upon a Divine ordinance. If there be a Resurrection, Moses must answer for all the confusion that will ensue, for Moses gave the commandment, by virtue of which a woman married seven times. No offspring of any union gave it a special claim upon her future life. "In the Resurrection, whose wife shall she be of them?" they ask, conceding with a quiet sarcasm that this absurd event must needs occur.

For these controversialists the question was solely of the physical tie, which had made of twain one flesh. They had no conception that the body can be raised otherwise than as it perished, and they rightly enough felt certain that on such a resurrection woeful complications must ensue.

Now Jesus does not rebuke their question with such stern words as He had just employed to others, "Why tempt ye Me, ye hypocrites?" They were doubtless sincere in their conviction, and at least they had not come in the disguise of perplexed inquirers and almost disciples. He blames them, but more gently: "Is it not for this cause that ye err, because ye know not the Scriptures, nor the power of God?" They could not know one and not the other, but the boastful wisdom of this world, so ready to point a jibe by quoting Moses, had never truly grasped the meaning of the writer it appealed to.

Jesus, it is plain, does not quote Scripture only as having authority with His opponents: He accepts it heartily: He declares that human error is due to ignorance of its depth and range of teaching; and He recognises the full roll of the sacred books "the Scriptures."

It has rightly been said that none of the explicit statements, commonly relied upon, do more to vindicate for Holy Writ the authority of our Lord than this simple incidental question.

Jesus proceeded to restate the doctrine of the Resurrection and then to prove it; and the more His brief words are pondered, the more they will expand and deepen.

St. Paul has taught us that the dead in Christ shall rise first (1 Thess. iv. 16). Of such attainment it is written, Blessed and holy is he that hath part in the first Resurrection (Rev. xx. 6).

Now since among the lost there could be no question of family ties, and consequent embarrassments, Jesus confines His statement to these happy ones, of whom the Sadducee could think no better than that their new life should be a reproduction of their existence here,—a theory which they did wisely in rejecting. He uses the very language taken up afterwards by His apostle, and says, "When they shall rise from the dead." And He asserts that marriage is at an end, and they are as the angels in heaven. Here is no question of the duration of pure and tender human affection, nor do these words compromise in any degree the hopes of faithful hearts, which cling to one another. Surely we may believe that in a life which is the outcome and resultant of this life, as truly as the grain is of the seed, in a life also where nothing shall be forgotten, but on the contrary we shall know what we know not now, there, tracing back the flood of their immortal energies to obscure fountains upon earth, and seeing all that each has owed half unconsciously to the fidelity and wisdom of the other, the true partners and genuine helpmeets of this world shall for ever drink some peculiar gladness, each from the other's joy. There is no reason why the close of formal unions which include the highest and most perfect friendships should forbid such friendships to survive and flourish in the more kindly atmosphere of heaven.

What Christ asserts is simply the dissolution of the tie, as an inevitable consequence of such a change in the very nature of the blessed ones as makes the tie incongruous and impossible. In point of fact, marriage as the Sadducee thought of it, is but the counterpoise of death, renewing the face which otherwise would disappear, and when death is swallowed up, it vanishes as an anachronism. In heaven "they are as the angels," the body itself being made "a spiritual body," set free from the appetites of the flesh, and in harmony with the glowing aspirations of the Spirit, which now it weighs upon and retards. If any would object that to be as the angels is to be without a body, rather than to possess a spiritual body, it is answer enough that the context implies the existence of a body, since no person ever spoke of a resurrection of the soul. Moreover, it is an utterly unwarrantable assumption that angels are wholly without substance. Many verses appear to imply the opposite, and the cubits of measurement of the New Jerusalem were "according to the measure of a man, that is of an angel" (Rev. xxi. 17), which seems to assert a very curious similarity indeed.

The objection of the Sadducees was entirely obviated, therefore, by the broader, bolder, and more spiritual view of a resurrection which Jesus taught. And by far the greater part of the cavils against this same doctrine which delight the infidel lecturer and popular essayist of to-day would also die a natural death, if the free and spiritual teaching of Jesus and its expansion by St. Paul were understood. But we breathe a wholly different air when we read the speculations even of so great a thinker as St. Augustine, who supposed that we should rise with bodies somewhat greater than our present ones, because all the hair and nails we ever trimmed away must be diffused throughout the mass, lest they should produce deformity by their excessive proportions ("De Civitate Dei," xxii. 19). To all such speculation, he who said, To every seed his own body, says, Thou fool, thou sowest not that body that shall be. But though Jesus had met these questions, it did not follow that His doctrine was true merely because a certain difficulty did not apply. And, therefore, He proceeded to prove it by the same Moses to whom they had appealed, and whom Jesus distinctly asserts to be the author of the book of Exodus. God said, "I am the God of Abraham, and the God of Isaac, and the God of Jacob. He is not the God of the dead, but of the living: ye do greatly err."

The argument is not based upon the present tense of the verb *to be* in this assertion, for in the Greek the verb is not expressed. In fact the argument is not a verbal one at all; or else it would be satisfied by the doctrine of the immortality of the spirit, and would not establish any resurrection of the body. It is based upon the immutability of God, and, therefore, the imperishability of all that ever entered into vital and real relationship with Him. To cancel such a relationship would introduce a change into the Eternal. And Moses, to whom they appealed, had heard God expressly proclaim Himself the God of those who had long since passed out of time. It was, therefore, clear that His relationship with them lived on, and this guaranteed that no portion, even the humblest, of their true personality should perish. Now the body is as real a part of humanity as the soul and spirit are, although a much lowlier part. And therefore it must not really die.

It is solemn to observe how Jesus, in this second part of His argument, passes from the consideration of the future of the blessed to that of all mankind; "as touching the dead that they are raised." With others than the blessed, therefore, God has a real though a dread relationship. And it will prove hard to reconcile this argument of Christ with the existence of any time when any soul shall be extinguished.

"The body is for the Lord," said St. Paul, arguing against the vices of the flesh, "and the Lord for the body." From these words of Christ he may well have learned that profound and far-reaching doctrine, which will never have done its work in the Church and in the world, until whatever defiles, degrades, or weakens that which the Lord has consecrated is felt to blaspheme by implication the God of our manhood, unto Whom all our life ought to be lived; until men are no longer dwarfed in mines, nor poisoned in foul air, nor massacred in battle, men whose intimate relationship with God the Eternal is of such a kind as to guarantee the resurrection of the poor frames which we destroy.

How much more does this great proclamation frown upon the sins by which men dishonour their own flesh. "Know ye not," asked the apostle, carrying the same doctrine to its utmost limit, "that your bodies are the temples of the Holy Ghost?" So truly is God our God.

THE DISCERNING SCRIBE.

MARK xii. 28-34 (R. V.).

The praise which Jesus bestowed upon this lawyer is best understood when we take into account the circumstances, the pressure of assailants with ensnaring questions, the sullen disappointment or palpable exasperation of the party to which the scribe belonged. He had probably sympathised in their hostility: and had come expecting and desiring the discomfiture of Jesus. But if so, he was a candid enemy; and as each new attempt revealed more clearly the spiritual insight, the self-possession and balanced wisdom of Him Who had been represented as a dangerous fanatic, his unfriendly opinion began to waver. For he too was at issue with popular views: he had learned in the Scriptures that God desireth not sacrifice, that incense might be an abomination to Him, and new moons and sabbaths things to do away with. And so, perceiving that He had answered them well, the scribe asked, upon his own account, a very different question, not rarely debated in their schools, and often answered with grotesque frivolity, but which he felt to go down to the very root of things. Instead of challenging Christ's authority, he tries His wisdom. Instead of striving to entangle Him in dangerous politics, or to assail with shallow ridicule the problems of the life to come, he asks, What commandment is the first of all? And if we may accept as complete this abrupt statement of his interrogation, it would seem to have been drawn from him by a sudden impulse, or wrenched by an over-mastering desire, despite of reluctance and false shame.

The Lord answered him with great solemnity and emphasis. He might have quoted the commandment only. But He at once supported the precept itself and also His own view of its importance by including the majestic prologue, "Hear, O Israel; the Lord our God, the Lord is one; and thou shalt love the Lord thy God with all thy heart, and with all thy soul, and with all thy mind, and with all thy strength."

The unity of God, what a massive and reassuring thought! Amid the debasements of idolatry, with its deification of every impulse and every force, amid the distractions of chance and change, seemingly so capricious and even discordant, amid the complexities of the universe and its phenomena, there is wonderful strength and wisdom in the reflection that God is one. All changes obey His hand which holds the rein; by Him the worlds were made. The exiled patriarch was overwhelmed by the majesty of the revelation that his father's God was God in Bethel even as in Beer-sheba: it charmed away the bitter sense of isolation, it unsealed in him the fountains of worship and trust, and sent him forward with a new hope of protection and prosperity. The unity of God, really apprehended, is a basis for the human will to repose upon, and to become self-consistent and at peace. It was the parent of the fruitful doctrine of the unity of nature which underlies all the scientific victories of the modern world. In religion, St. Paul felt that it implies the equal treatment of all the human race, when he asked, "Is He the God of Jews only? Is He not the God of Gentiles also? Yea, of Gentiles also, if so be that God is one" (Rom. iii. 29 R. V.). To be one, he seems to say, implies being universal also. And if it thus excludes the reprobation of races, it disproves equally that of individual souls, and all thought of such unequal and partial treatment as should inspire one with hope of indulgence in guilt, or with fear that his way is hid from the Lord.

But if this be true, if there be one fountain of all life and loveliness and joy, of all human tenderness and all moral glory, how are we bound to love Him. Every other affection should only deepen our adoring loyalty to Him Who gives it. No cold or formal service can meet His claim, Who gives us the power to serve. No, we must love Him. And as all our nature comes from Him, so must all be consecrated: that love must embrace all the affections of "heart and soul" panting after Him, as the heart after the water-brooks; and all the deep and steady convictions of the "mind," musing on the work of His hand, able to give a reason for its faith; and all the practical homage of the "strength," living and dying to the Lord. How easy, then, would be the fulfilment of His commandments in detail, and how surely it would follow. All the precepts of the first table are clearly implied in this.

In such another commandment were summed up also the precepts which concerned our neighbour. When we love him as ourselves (neither exaggerating his claims beyond our own, nor allowing our own to trample upon his), then we shall work no ill to our neighbour, and so love shall fulfil the law. There is none other commandment greater than these.

The questioner saw all the nobility of this reply; and the disdain, the anger, and perhaps the persecution of his associates could not prevent him from an admiring and reverent repetition of the Saviour's words, and an avowal that all the ceremonial observances of Judaism were as nothing compared with this.

While he was thus judging, he was being judged. As he knew that Jesus had answered well, so Jesus saw that he answered discreetly; and in view of his unprejudiced judgment, his spiritual insight, and his frank approval of One Who was then despised and rejected, He said, Thou art not far from the kingdom of God. But he was not yet within it, and no man knows his fate.

Sad, yet instructive, it is to think that he may have won the approval of Christ, and heard His words, so full of discernment and of desire for his adherence, and yet never crossed the invisible and mysterious boundary which he then approached so nearly. But we also may know, and admire, and confess the greatness and goodness of Jesus, without forsaking all to follow Him.

His enemies had been defeated and put to shame, their murderous hate had been denounced, and the nets of their cunning had been rent like cobwebs; they had seen the heart of one of their own order kindled into open admiration, and they henceforth renounced as hopeless the attempt to conquer Jesus in debate. No man after that durst ask Him any questions.

He will now carry the war into their own country. It will be for them to answer Jesus.

DAVID'S LORD.

MARK xii. 35-40 (R. V.).

Jesus, having silenced in turn His official interrogators and the Sadducees, and won the heart of His honest questioner, proceeded to submit a searching problem to His assailants. Whose son was the Messiah? And when they gave Him an obvious and shallow answer, He covered them with confusion publicly. The event is full of that dramatic interest which St. Mark is so well able to discern and reproduce. How is it then that he passes over all this aspect of it, leaves us ignorant of the defeat and even of the presence of the scribes, and free to suppose that Jesus stated the whole problem in one long question, possibly without an opponent at hand to feel its force?

This is a remarkable proof that his concern was not really for the pictorial element in the story, but for the manifestation of the power of his Master, the "authority" which resounds through his opening chapters, the royalty which he exhibits at the close. To him the vital point is that Jesus, upon openly claiming to be the Christ, and repelling the vehement attacks which were made upon Him as such, proceeded to unfold the astonishing greatness which this implied; and that after asserting the unity of God and His claim upon all hearts, He demonstrated that the Christ was sharer of His throne.

The Christ, they said, was the Son of David, and this was not false: Jesus had wrought many miracles for suppliants who addressed Him by that title. But was it all the truth? How then did David call Him Lord? A greater than David might spring from among his descendants, and hold rule by an original and not merely an ancestral claim: He might not reign as a son of David. Yet this would not explain the fact that David, who died ages before His coming, was inspired to call Him *My* Lord. Still less would it satisfy the assertion that God had bidden Him sit beside Him on His throne. For the scribes there was a serious warning in the promise that His enemies should be made His footstool, and for all the people a startling revelation in the words which follow, which the Epistle to the Hebrews has unfolded, making this Son of David a priest for ever, after another order than that of Aaron.

No wonder that the multitude heard with gladness teaching at once so original, so profound, and so clearly justified by Scripture.

But it must be observed how remarkably this question of Jesus follows up His conversation with the scribe. Then He had based the supreme duty of love to God upon the supreme doctrine of the Divine Unity. He now proceeds to show that the throne of Deity is not a lonely throne, and to demand, Whose Son is He Who shares it, and Whom David in Spirit accosts by the same title as his God?

St. Mark is now content to give the merest indication of the final denunciation with which the Lord turned His back upon the scribes of Jerusalem, as He previously broke with those of Galilee. But it is enough to show how utterly beyond compromise was the rupture. The people were to beware of them: their selfish objects were betrayed in their very dress, and their desire for respectful salutations and seats of honour. Their prayers were a pretence, and they devoured widows' houses, acquiring under the cloak of religion what should have maintained the friendless. But their affected piety would only bring upon them a darker doom.

It is a tremendous impeachment. None is entitled to speak as Jesus did, who is unable to read hearts as He did. And yet we may learn from it that mere softness is not the meekness He demands, and that, when sinister motives are beyond doubt, the spirit of Jesus is the spirit of burning.

There is an indulgence for the wrongdoer which is mere feebleness and half compliance, and which shares in the guilt of Eli. And there is a dreadful anger which sins not, the wrath of the Lamb.

THE WIDOW'S MITE.

Mark xii. 41-44 (R. V.).

With words of stern denunciation Jesus for ever left the temple. Yet He lingered, as if reluctant, in the outer court; and while the storm of His wrath was still resounding in all hearts, observed and pointed out an action of the lowliest beauty, a modest flower of Hebrew piety in the vast desert of formality. It was not too modest, however, to catch, even in that agitating hour, the eye of Jesus; and while the scribes were devouring widows' houses, a poor widow could still, with two mites which make a farthing, win honourable mention from the Son of God. Thus He ever observes realities among pretences, the pure flame of love amid the sour smoke which wreathes around it. What He saw was the last pittance, cast to a service which in reality was no longer God's, yet given with a noble earnestness, a sacrifice pure from the heart.

1. His praise suggests to us the unknown observation, the unsuspected influences which surround us. She little guessed herself to be the one figure, amid a glittering group and where many were rich, who really interested the all-seeing Eye. She went away again, quite unconscious that the Lord had converted her two mites into a perennial wealth of contentment for lowly hearts and instruction for the Church, quite ignorant that she was approved of Messiah, and that her little gift was the greatest event of all her story. So are we watched and judged in our least conscious and our most secluded hours.

2. We learn St. Paul's lesson, that, "if the readiness is there, it is acceptable according as a man hath, and not according as he hath not."

In war, in commerce, in the senate, how often does an accident at the outset blight a career for ever. One is taken in the net of circumstances, and his clipped wings can never soar again. But there is no such disabling accident in religion. God seeth the heart. The world was redeemed by the blighted and thwarted career of One Who would fain have gathered His own city under His wing, but was refused and frustrated. And whether we cast in much, or only possess two mites, an offering for the rich to mock, He marks, understands, and estimates aright.

And while the world only sees the quality, He weighs the motive of our actions. This is the true reason why we can judge nothing before the time, why the great benefactor is not really pointed out by the splendid benefaction, and why many that are last shall yet be first, and the first last.

3. The poor widow gave not a greater proportion of her goods, she gave all; and it has been often remarked that she had still, in her poverty, the opportunity of keeping back one half. But her heart went with her two mites. And, therefore, she was blessed. We may picture her return to her sordid drudgery, unaware of the meaning of the new light and peace which followed her, and why her heart sang for joy. We may think of the Spirit of Christ which was in her, leading her afterwards into the Church of Christ, an obscure and perhaps illiterate convert, undistinguished by any special gift, and only loved as the first Christians all loved each other. And we may think of her now, where the secrets of all hearts are made known, followed by myriads of the obscure and undistinguished whom

her story has sustained and cheered, and by some who knew her upon earth, and were astonished to learn that this was she. Then let us ask ourselves, Is there any such secret of unobtrusive lowly service, born of love, which the future will associate with me?

CHAPTER XIII.

THINGS PERISHING AND THINGS STABLE.

Mark xiii. 1-7 (R. V.).

Nothing is more impressive than to stand before one of the great buildings of the world, and mark how the toil of man has rivalled the stability of nature, and his thought its grandeur. It stands up like a crag, and the wind whistles through its pinnacles as in a grove, and the rooks float and soar about its towers as they do among the granite peaks. Face to face with one of these mighty structures, man feels his own pettiness, shivering in the wind, or seeking a shadow from the sun, and thinking how even this breeze may blight or this heat fever him, and how at the longest he shall have crumbled into dust for ages, and his name, and possibly his race, have perished, while this same pile shall stretch the same long shadow across the plain.

No wonder that the great masters of nations have all delighted in building, for thus they saw their power, and the immortality for which they hoped, made solid, embodied and substantial, and it almost seemed as if they had blended their memory with the enduring fabric of the world.

Such a building, solid, and vast, and splendid, white with marble, and blazing with gold, was the temple which Jesus now forsook. A little afterwards, we read that its Roman conqueror, whose race were the great builders of the world, in spite of the rules of war, and the certainty that the Jews would never remain quietly in subjection while it stood, "was reluctant to burn down so vast a work as this, since this would be a mischief to the Romans themselves, as it would be an ornament to their government while it lasted."

No wonder, then, that one of the disciples, who had seen Jesus weep for its approaching ruin, and who now followed His steps as He left it desolate, lingered, and spoke as if in longing and appeal, "Master, see what manner of stones, and what manner of buildings."

But to the eyes of Jesus all was evanescent as a bubble, doomed and ab ut to perish: "Seest thou these great buildings, there shall not be left here one stone upon another that shall not be thrown down."

The words were appropriate to His solemn mood, for He had just denounced its guilt and flung its splendour from Him, calling it no longer "My house," nor "My Father's house," but saying, "Your house is left unto you desolate." Little could all the solid strength of the very foundations of the world itself avail against the thunderbolt of God. Moreover, it was a time when He felt most keenly the consecration, the approaching surrender of His own life. In such an hour no splendours distract the penetrating vision; all the world is brief and frail and hollow to the man who has consciously given himself to God. It was the fitting moment at which to utter such a prophecy.

But, as He sat on the opposite slope, and gazed back upon the towers that were to fall, His three favoured disciples and Andrew came to ask Him privately when should these things be, and what would be the sign of their approach.

It is the common assertion of all unbelievers that the prophecy which followed has been composed since what passes for its fulfilment. When Jesus was murdered, and a terrible fate befell the guilty city, what more natural than to connect the two events? And how easily would a legend spring up that the sufferer foretold the penalty? But there is an obvious and complete reply. The prediction is too mysterious, its outlines are too obscure; and the ruin of Jerusalem is too inexplicably complicated with the final visitation of the whole earth, to be the issue of any vindictive imagination working with the history in view.

We are sometimes tempted to complain of this obscurity. But in truth it is wholesome and designed. We need not ask whether the original discourse was thus ambiguous, or they are right who suppose that a veil has since been drawn between us and a portion of the answer given by Jesus to His disciples. We know as much as it is meant that we should know. And this at least is plain, that any process of conscious or unconscious invention, working backwards after Jerusalem fell, would have given us far more explicit predictions than we possess. And, moreover, that what we lose in gratification of our curiosity, we gain in personal warning to walk warily and vigilantly.

Jesus did not answer the question, When shall these things be? But He declared, to men who wondered at the overthrow of their splendid temple, that all earthly splendours must perish. And He revealed to them where true permanence may be discovered. These are two of the central thoughts of the discourse, and they are worthy of much more attention from its students than they commonly receive, being overlooked in the universal eagerness "to know the times and the seasons." They come to the surface in the distinct words, "Heaven and earth shall pass away, but My words shall not pass away."

Now, if we are to think of this great prophecy as a lurid reflection thrown back by later superstition on the storm-clouds of the nation's fall, how shall we account for its solemn and pensive mood, utterly free from vindictiveness, entirely suited to Jesus as we think of Him, when leaving for ever the dishonoured shrine, and moving forward, as His meditations would surely do, beyond the occasions which evoked them? Not such is the manner of resentful controversialists, eagerly tracing imaginary judgments. They are narrow, and sharp, and sour.

1. The fall of Jerusalem blended itself, in the thought of Jesus, with the catastrophe which awaits all that appears to be great and stable. Nation shall rise against nation, and kingdom against kingdom, so that, although armies set their bodies in the gap for these, and heroes shed their blood like water, yet they are divided among themselves and cannot stand. This prediction, we must remember, was made when the iron yoke of Rome imposed quiet upon as much of the world as a Galilean was likely to take

into account, and, therefore, was by no means so easy as it may now appear to us.

Nature itself should be convulsed. Earthquakes should rend the earth, blight and famine should disturb the regular course of seed-time and harvest. And these perturbations should be the working out of a stern law, and the sure token of sorer woes to come, the beginning of pangs which should usher in another dispensation, the birth-agony of a new time. A little later, and the sun should be darkened, and the moon should withdraw her light, and the stars should "be falling" from heaven, and the powers that are in the heaven should be darkened. Lastly, the course of history should close, and the affairs of earth should come to an end, when the elect should be gathered together to the glorified Son of Man.

2. It was in sight of the ruin of all these things that He dared to add, My word shall not pass away.

Heresy should assail it, for many should come in the name of Christ, saying, I am He, and should lead many astray. Fierce persecutions should try His followers, and they should be led to judgment and delivered up. The worse afflictions of the heart would wring them, for brother should deliver up brother to death, and the father his child, and children should rise up against parents and cause them to be put to death. But all should be too little to quench the immortality bestowed upon His elect. In their sore need, the Holy Ghost should speak in them: when they were caused to be put to death, he that endureth to the end, the same shall be saved.

Now these words were treasured up as the utterances of One Who had just foretold His own approaching murder, and Who died accordingly amid circumstances full or horror and shame. Yet His followers rejoiced to think that when the sun grew dark, and the stars were falling, He should be seen in the clouds coming with great glory.

It is the reversal of human judgment: the announcement that all is stable which appears unsubstantial, and all which appears solid is about to melt like snow.

And yet the world itself has since grown old enough to know that convictions are stronger than empires, and truths than armed hosts. And this is the King of Truth. He was born and came into the world to bear witness to the truth, and every one that is of the truth heareth His voice. He is the Truth become vital, the Word which was with God in the beginning.

THE IMPENDING JUDGMENT.

Mark xiii. 8-16 (R. V.).

When we perceive that one central thought in our Lord's discourse about the last things is the contrast between material things which are fleeting, and spiritual realities which abide, a question naturally arises, which ought not to be overlooked. Was the prediction itself any more than a result of profound spiritual insight? Are we certain that prophecy in general was more than keenness of vision? There are flourishing empires now which perhaps a keen politician, and certainly a firm believer in retributive justice governing the world, must consider to be doomed. And one who felt the transitory nature of earthly resources might expect a time when the docks of London will resemble the lagoons of Venice, and the State which now predominates in Europe shall become partaker of the decrepitude of Spain. But no such presage is a prophecy in the Christian sense. Even when suggested by religion, it does not claim any greater certainty than that of sagacious inference.

The general question is best met by pointing to such specific and detailed prophecies, especially concerning the Messiah, as the twenty-second Psalm, the fifty-third of Isaiah, and the ninth of Daniel.

But the prediction of the fall of Jerusalem, while we have seen that it has none of the minuteness and sharpness of an after-thought, is also too definite for a presentiment. The abomination which defiled the Holy Place, and yet left one last brief opportunity for hasty flight, the persecutions by which that catastrophe would be heralded, and the precipitating of the crisis for the elect's sake, were details not to be conjectured. So was the coming of the great retribution, the beginning of His kingdom within that generation, a limit which was foretold at least twice besides (Mark ix. 1 and xiv. 62), with which the "henceforth" in Matthew xxvi. 64 must be compared. And so was another circumstance which is not enough considered: the fact that between the fall of Jerusalem and the Second Coming, however long or short the interval, no second event of a similar character, so universal in its effect upon Christianity, so epoch-making, should intervene. The coming of the Son of man should be "in those days after that tribulation."

The intervening centuries lay out like a plain country between two mountain tops, and did not break the vista, as the eye passed from the judgment of the ancient Church, straight on to the judgment of the world. Shall we say, then, that Jesus foretold that His coming would follow speedily? and that He erred? Men have been very willing to bring this charge, even in the face of His explicit assertions. "After a long time the Lord of that servant cometh. . . . While the bridegroom tarried they all slumbered and slept. . . . If that wicked servant shall say in his heart, My Lord delayeth His coming."

It is true that these expressions are not found in St. Mark. But instead of them stands a sentence so startling, so unique, that it has caused to ill-instructed orthodoxy great searchings of heart. At least, however, the flippant pretence that Jesus fixed an early date for His return, ought to be silenced when we read, "Of that day or that hour knoweth no one, not even the angels of heaven, nor the Son, but the Father."

These words are not more surprising than that He increased in wisdom and marvelled at the faith of some, and the unbelief of others (Luke ii. 52; Matt. viii. 10; Mark vi. 6). They are involved in the great assertion that He not only took the form of a servant, but emptied Himself (Phil. ii. 7). But they decide the question of the genuineness of the discourse; for when could they have been invented? And they are to be taken in connection with others, which speak of Him not in His low estate, but as by nature and inherently, the Word and the Wisdom of God; aware of all that the Father doeth; and

Him in Whom dwelleth all the fulness of the Godhead bodily (John i. 1; Luke xi. 49; John v. 20; Col. ii. 9).

But these were "the days of His flesh;" and that expression is not meant to convey that He has since laid aside His body, for He says, "A spirit hath not flesh . . . as ye see Me have" (Heb. v. 7; Luke xxiv. 39). It must therefore express the limitations, now removed, by which He once condescended to be trammelled. What forbids us, then, to believe that His knowledge, like His power, was limited by a lowliness not enforced, but for our sakes chosen; and that as He could have asked for twelve legions of angels, yet chose to be bound and buffeted, so He could have known that day and hour, yet submitted to ignorance, that He might be made like in all points to His brethren? Souls there are for whom this wonderful saying, "the Son knoweth not," is even more affecting than the words, "The Son of man hath not where to lay His head."

But now the climax must be observed which made His ignorance more astonishing than that of the angels in heaven. The recent discourse must be remembered, which had asked His enemies to explain the fact that David called Him Lord, and spoke of God as occupying no lonely throne. And we must observe His emphatic expression, that His return shall be that of the Lord of the House (ver. 35), so unlike the temper which He impressed on every servant, and clearly teaching the Epistle to the Hebrews to speak of His fidelity as that of a Son over His house, and to contrast it sharply with that of the most honourable servant (iii. 6).

It is plain, however, that Jesus did not fix, and renounce the power to fix, a speedy date for His second coming. He checked the impatience of the early Church by insisting that none knew the time.

But He drew the closest analogy between that event and the destruction of Jerusalem, and required a like spirit in those who looked for each.

Persecution should go before them. Signs would indicate their approach as surely as the budding of the fig-tree told of summer. And in each case the disciples of Jesus must be ready. When the siege came, they should not turn back from the field into the city, nor escape from the housetop by the inner staircase. When the Son of man comes, their loins should be girt, and their lights already burning. But if the end has been so long delayed, and if there were signs by which its approach might be known, how could it be the practical duty of all men, in all the ages, to expect it? What is the meaning of bidding us to learn from the fig-tree her parable, which is the approach of summer when her branch becomes tender, and yet asserting that we know not when the time is, that it shall come upon us as a snare, that the Master will surely surprise us, but need not find us unprepared, because all the Church ought to be always ready?

What does it mean, especially when we observe, beneath the surface, that our Lord was conscious of addressing more than that generation, since He declared to the first hearers, "What I say unto you I say unto all, Watch"? It is a strange paradox. But yet the history of the Church supplies abundant proof that in no age has the expectation of the Second Advent disappeared, and the faithful have always been mocked by the illusion, or else keen to discern the fact, that He is near, even at the doors. It is not enough to reflect that, for each soul, dissolution has been the preliminary advent of Him who has promised to come again and receive us unto Himself, and the Angel of Death is indeed the Angel of the Covenant. It must be asserted that for the universal Church, the feet of the Lord have been always upon the threshold, and the time has been prolonged only because the Judge *standeth* at the door. The "birth-pangs" of which Jesus spoke have never been entirely stilled. And the march of time has not been towards a far-off eternity, but along the margin of that mysterious ocean, by which it must be engulfed at last, and into which, fragment by fragment, the beach it treads is crumbling.

Now this necessity, almost avowed, for giving signs which should only make the Church aware of her Lord's continual nearness, without ever enabling her to assign the date of His actual arrival, is the probable explanation of what has been already remarked, the manner in which the judgment of Jerusalem is made to symbolise the final judgment. But this symbolism makes the warning spoken to that age for ever fruitful. As they were not to linger in the guilty city, so we are to let no earthly interests arrest our flight,—not to turn back, but promptly and resolutely to flee unto the everlasting hills. As they should pray that their flight through the mountains should not be in the winter, so should we beware of needing to seek salvation in the winter of the soul, when the storms of passion and appetite are wildest, when evil habits have made the road slippery under foot, and sophistry and selfwill have hidden the gulfs in a treacherous wreath of snow.

Heedfulness, a sense of surrounding peril and of the danger of the times, is meant to inspire us while we read. The discourse opens with a caution against heresy: "Take heed that no man deceive you." It goes on to caution them against the weakness of their own flesh: "Take heed to yourselves, for they shall deliver you up." It bids them watch, because they know not when the time is. And the way to watchfulness is prayerfulness; so that presently, in the Garden, when they could not watch with Him one hour, they were bidden to watch and pray, that they enter not into temptation.

So is the expectant Church to watch and pray. Nor must her mood be one of passive idle expectation, dreamful desire of the promised change, neglect of duties in the interval. The progress of all art and science, and even the culture of the ground, is said to have been arrested by the universal persuasion that the year One Thousand should see the return of Christ. The luxury of millennarian expectation seems even now to relieve some consciences from the active duties of religion. But Jesus taught His followers that on leaving His house, to sojourn in a far country, He regarded them as His servants still, and gave them every one his work. And it is the companion of that disciple to whom Jesus gave the keys, and to whom especially He said, "What, couldest thou not watch with Me one hour?" St. Mark it is who specifies the command to the porter that he should watch. To watch is not to gaze from the roof across the distant roads. It is to have girded loins and a kindled lamp; it is not measured by excited expectation, but by readiness. Does it seem to us that the world is no longer hostile, because persecution and torture are at an end? That the need is over for a clear distinction between her and us? This very belief may prove that we are falling asleep. Never was there an age to which Jesus did not say Watch. Never one in which His return would be other than a snare to all whose life is on the level of the world.

Now looking back over the whole discourse, we come to ask ourselves, What is the spirit which it sought to breathe into His Church? Clearly it is that of loyal expectation of the Absent One. There is in it no hint, that because we cannot fail to be deceived without Him, therefore His infallibility and His Vicar shall for ever be left on earth. His place is empty until He returns. Whoever says Lo, here is Christ, is a deceiver, and it proves nothing that he shall deceive many. When Christ is manifested again, it shall be as the blaze of lightning across the sky. There is perhaps no text in this discourse which directly assails the Papacy; but the atmosphere which pervades it is deadly alike to her claims, and to the instincts and desires on which those claims rely.

CHAPTER XIV.

THE CRUSE OF OINTMENT.

Mark xiv. 1-9 (R. V.).

Perfection implies not only the absence of blemishes, but the presence, in equal proportions, of every virtue and every grace. And so the perfect life is full of the most striking, and yet the easiest transitions. We have just read predictions of trial more startling and intense than any in the ancient Scripture. If we knew of Jesus only by the various reports of that discourse, we should think of a recluse like Elijah or the Baptist, and imagine that His disciples, with girded loins, should be more ascetic than St. Anthony. We are next shown Jesus at a supper gracefully accepting the graceful homage of a woman.

From St. John we learn that this feast was given six days before the passover. The other accounts postponed the mention of it, plainly because of an incident which occurred then, but is vitally connected with a decision arrived at somewhat later by the priests. Two days before the passover, the council finally determined that Jesus must be destroyed. They recognised all the dangers of that course. It must be done with subtlety; the people must not be aroused; and therefore they said, Not on the feast-day. It is remarkable, however, that at the very time when they so determined, Jesus clearly and calmly made to His disciples exactly the opposite announcement. "After two days the passover cometh, and the Son of man is delivered up to be crucified" (Matt. xxvi. 2). Thus we find at every turn of the narrative that their plans are over-ruled, and they are unconscious agents of a mysterious design, which their Victim comprehends and accepts. On one side, perplexity snatches at all base expedients; the traitor is welcomed, false witnesses are sought after, and the guards of the sepulchre bribed. On the other side is clear foresight, the deliberate unmasking of Judas, and at the trial a circumspect composure, a lofty silence, and speech more majestic still.

Meanwhile there is a heart no longer light (for He foresees His burial), yet not so burdened that He should decline the entertainment offered Him at Bethany.

This was in the house of Simon the leper, but St. John tells us that Martha served, Lazarus sat at meat, and the woman who anointed Jesus was Mary. We naturally infer some relationship between Simon and this favoured family: but the nature of the tie we know not, and no purpose can be served by guessing. Better far to let the mind rest upon the sweet picture of Jesus, at home among those who loved Him: upon the eager service of Martha; upon the man who had known death, somewhat silent, one fancies, a remarkable sight for Jesus, as He sat at meat, and perhaps suggestive of the thought which found utterance a few days afterwards, that a banquet was yet to come, when He also, risen from the grave, should drink new wine among His friends in the kingdom of God. And there the adoring face of her who had chosen the better part was turned to her Lord with a love which comprehended His sorrow and His danger, while even the Twelve were blind—an insight which knew the awful presence of One upon his way to the sepulchre, as well as one who had returned thence. Therefore she produced a cruse of very precious ointment, which had been "kept" for Him, perhaps since her brother was embalmed. And as such alabaster flasks were commonly sealed in making, and only to be opened by breaking off the neck, she crushed the cruse between her hands and poured it on His head. On His feet also, according to St. John, who is chiefly thinking of the embalming of the body, as the others of the anointing of the head. The discovery of contradiction here is worthy of the abject "criticism" which detects in this account a variation upon the story of her who was a sinner. As if two women who loved much might not both express their loyalty, which could not speak, by so fair and feminine a device; or as if it were inconceivable that the blameless Mary should consciously imitate the gentle penitent.

But even as this unworthy controversy breaks in upon the tender story, so did indignation and murmuring spoil that peaceful scene. "Why was not this ointment sold for much, and given to the poor?" It was not common that others should be more thoughtful of the poor than Jesus.

He fed the multitudes they would have sent away; He gave sight to Bartimæus whom they rebuked. But it is still true, that whenever generous impulses express themselves with lavish hands, some heartless calculator reckons up the value of what is spent, and especially its value to "the poor;" the poor, who would be worse off if the instincts of love were arrested and the human heart frozen. Almshouses are not usually built by those who declaim against church architecture; nor is utilitarianism famous for its charities. And so we are not surprised when St. John tells us how the quarrel was fomented. Iscariot, the dishonest pursebearer, was exasperated at the loss of a chance of theft, perhaps of absconding without being so great a loser at the end of his three unrequited years. True that the chance was gone, and speech would only betray his estrangement from Jesus, upon Whom so much good property was wasted. But evil tempers must express themselves at times, and Judas had craft enough to involve the rest in his misconduct. It is the only indication in the Gospels of intrigue among the Twelve which even indirectly struck at their Master's honour.

Thus, while the fragrance of the ointment filled the house, their parsimony grudged the homage which soothed His heart, and condemned the spontaneous impulse of Mary's love.

It was for her that Jesus interfered, and His words went home.

The poor were always with them: opportunities would never fail those who were so zealous; and whensoever they would they could do them good,—whensoever Judas, for example, would. As for her, she had wrought a good work (a high-minded and lofty work is implied rather than a useful one) upon Him, Whom they should not always have. Soon His body would be in the hands of sinners, desecrated, outraged. And she only had comprehended, however dimly, the silent sorrow of her Master; she only had laid to heart His warnings; and, unable to save Him, or even to watch with Him one hour, she (and through all that week none other) had done what she could. She had anointed His body beforehand for the burial, and indeed with clear intention "to prepare Him for burial" (Matt. xxvi. 12).

It was for this that His followers had chidden her. Alas, how often do our shrewd calculations and harsh judgments miss the very essence of some problem which only the heart can solve, the silent intention of some deed which is too fine, too sensitive, to explain itself except only to that sympathy which understands us all. Men thought of Jesus as lacking nothing, and would fain divert His honour to the poor; but this woman comprehended the lonely heart, and saw the last inexorable need before Him. Love read the secret in the eyes of love, and this which Mary did shall be told while the world stands, as being among the few human actions which refreshed the lonely One, the purest, the most graceful, and perhaps the last.

THE TRAITOR.

MARK xiv. 10-16 (R. V.).

It was when Jesus rebuked the Twelve for censuring Mary, that the patience of Judas, chafing in a service which had grown hateful, finally gave way. He offered a treacherous and odious help to the chiefs of his religion, and these pious men, too scrupulous to cast blood-money into the treasury or to defile themselves by entering a pagan judgment hall, shuddered not at the contact of such infamy, warned him not that perfidy will pollute the holiest cause, cared as little then for his ruin as when they asked what to them was his remorseful agony; but were glad, and promised to give him money. By so doing, they became accomplices in the only crime by which it is quite certain that a soul was lost. The supreme "offence" was planned and perpetrated by no desperate criminal. It was the work of an apostle, and his accomplices were the heads of a divinely given religion. What an awful example of the deadening power, palsying the conscience, petrifying the heart, of religious observances devoid of real trust and love.

The narrative, as we saw, somewhat displaced the story of Simon's feast, to connect this incident more closely with the betrayal. And it now proceeds at once to the passover, and the final crisis. In so doing, it pauses at a curious example of circumspection, intimately linked also with the treason of Judas. The disciples, unconscious of treachery, asked where they should prepare the paschal supper. And Jesus gave them a sign by which to recognise one who had a large upper room prepared for that purpose, to which he would make them welcome. It is not quite impossible that the pitcher of water was a signal preconcerted with some disciple in Jerusalem, although secret understandings are not found elsewhere in the life of Jesus. What concerns us to observe is that the owner of the house which the bearer entered was a believer. To him Jesus is "the Master," and can say "Where is My guest-chamber?"

So obscure a disciple was he, that Peter and John required a sign to guide them to his house. Yet his upper room would now receive such a consecration as the Temple never knew. With strange feelings would he henceforth enter the scene of the last supper of his Lord. But now, what if he had only admitted Jesus with hesitation and after long delay? We should wonder; yet there are lowlier doors at which the same Jesus stands and knocks, and would fain come in and sup. And cold is His welcome to many a chamber which is neither furnished nor made ready.

The mysterious and reticent indication of the place is easily understood. Jesus would not enable His enemies to lay hands upon Him before the time. His nights had hitherto been spent at Bethany; now first it was possible to arrest Him in the darkness, and hurry on the trial before the Galileans at the feast, strangers and comparatively isolated, could learn the danger of their "prophet of Galilee." It was only too certain that when the blow was struck, the light and fickle adhesion of the populace would transfer itself to the successful party. Meanwhile, the prudence of Jesus gave Him time for the Last Supper, and the wonderful discourse recorded by St. John, and the conflict and victory in the Garden. When the priests learned, at a late hour, that Jesus might yet be arrested before morning, but that Judas could never watch Him any more, the necessity for prompt action came with such surprise upon them that the arrest was accomplished while they still had to seek false witnesses, and to consult how a sentence might best be extorted from the Governor. It is right to observe at every point, the mastery of Jesus, the perplexity and confusion of His foes.

And it is also right that we should learn to include, among the woes endured for us by the Man of Sorrows, this haunting consciousness that a base vigilance was to be watched against, that He breathed the air of treachery and vileness.

Here then, in view of the precautions thus forced upon our Lord, we pause to reflect upon the awful fall of Judas, the degradation of an apostle into a hireling, a traitor, and a spy. Men have failed to believe that one whom Jesus called to His side should sink so low.

They have not observed how inevitably great goodness rejected brings out special turpitude, and dark shadows go with powerful lights; how, in this supreme tragedy, all the motives, passions, moral and immoral impulses are on the tragic scale; what gigantic forms of baseness, hypocrisy, cruelty, and injustice stalk across the awful platform, and how the forces of hell strip themselves, and string their muscles for a last desperate wrestle against the powers of heaven, so that here is the very place to expect the extreme apostasy. And so they have conjectured that Iscariot was only half a traitor. Some project misled him of forcing his Master to turn to bay. Then the powers which wasted themselves in scattering unthanked and unprofitable blessings would exert themselves to crush the foe. Then he could claim for himself the credit deserved by much astuteness, the consideration due to the only man of political resource among the Twelve. But this well-intending Judas is equally unknown to the narratives and the prophecies, and this theory does not harmonise with any of the facts. Profound reprobation and even contempt are audible in all the narratives; they are quite as audible in the reiterated phrase, "which was one of the Twelve," and in almost every mention of his name, as in the round assertion of St. John that he was a thief and stole from the common purse. Only the lowest motive is discernible in the fact that his project ripened just when the waste of the ointment spoiled his last hope from apostleship,—the hope of unjust gain, and in his bargaining for the miserable price which he still carried with him when the veil dropped from his inner eyes, when he awoke to the sorrow of the world which worketh death, to the remorse which was not penitence.

One who desired that Jesus should be driven to counter-measures and yet free to take them, would probably have favoured His escape when once the attempt to arrest Him inflicted the necessary spur, and certainly he would have anxiously avoided any appearance of insult. But it will be seen that Judas carefully closed every door against his Lord's escape, and seized Him with something very like a jibe on his recreant lips.

No, his infamy cannot be palliated, but it can be understood. For it is a solemn and awful truth, that in every defeat of grace the reaction is equal to the action; they who have been exalted unto heaven are brought down far below the level of the world; and the principle is universal that Israel cannot, by willing it, be as the nations that are round about, to serve other gods. God Himself gives him statutes that are not good. He makes fat the heart and blinds the eyes of the apostate. Therefore it comes that religion without devotion is the mockery of honest worldlings; that hypocrisy goes so constantly with the meanest and most sordid lust of gain, and selfish cruelty; that publicans and harlots enter heaven before scribes and pharisees; that salt which has lost its savour is fit neither for the land nor for the dung-hill. Oh, then, to what place of shame shall a recreant apostle be thrust down?

Moreover it must be observed that the guilt of Judas, however awful, is but a shade more dark than that of his sanctimonious employers, who sought false witnesses against Christ, extorted by menace and intrigue a sentence which Pilate openly pronounced to be unjust, mocked His despairing agony, and on the resurrection morning bribed a pagan soldiery to lie for the Hebrew faith. It is plain enough that Jesus could not and did not choose the apostles through foreknowledge of what they would hereafter prove, but by His perception of what they then were, and what they were capable of becoming, if faithful to the light they should receive.

Not one, when chosen first, was ready to welcome the purely spiritual kingdom, the despised Messiah, the life of poverty and scorn. They had to learn, and it was open to them to refuse the discipline. Once at least they were asked, Will ye also go away? How severe was the trial may be seen by the rebuke of Peter, and the petition of "Zebedee's children" and their mother. They conquered the same reluctance of the flesh which overcame the better part in Judas. But he clung desperately to secular hope, until the last vestige of such hope was over. Listening to the warnings of Christ against the cares of this world, the lust of other things, love of high places and contempt of lowly service, and watching bright offers rejected and influential classes estranged, it was inevitable that a sense of personal wrong, and a vindictive resentment, should spring up in his gloomy heart. The thorns choked the good seed. Then came a deeper fall. As he rejected the pure light of self-sacrifice, and the false light of his romantic daydreams faded, no curb was left on the baser instincts which are latent in the human heart. Self-respect being already lost, and conscience beaten down, he was allured by low compensations, and the apostle became a thief. What better than gain, however sordid, was left to a life so plainly frustrated and spoiled? That is the temptation of disillusion, as fatal to middle life as the passions are to early manhood. And this fall reacted again upon his attitude towards Jesus. Like all who will not walk in the light, he hated the light; like all hirelings of two masters, he hated the one he left. Men ask how Judas could have consented to accept for Jesus the blood-money of a slave. The truth is that his treason itself yielded him a dreadful satisfaction, and the insulting kiss, and the sneering "Rabbi," expressed the malice of his heart. Well for him if he had never been born. For when his conscience awoke with a start and told him what thing he had become, only self-loathing remained to him. Peter denying Jesus was nevertheless at heart His own; a look sufficed to melt him.

For Judas, Christ was become infinitely remote and strange, an abstraction, "the innocent blood," no more than that. And so, when Jesus was passing into the holiest through the rent veil which was His flesh, this first Antichrist had already torn with his own hands the tissue of the curtain which hides eternity.

Now let us observe that all this ruin was the result of forces continually at work upon human hearts. Aspiration, vocation, failure, degradation—it is the summary of a thousand lives. Only it is here exhibited on a vast and dreadful scale (magnified by the light which was behind, as images thrown by a lantern upon a screen) for the instruction and warning of the world.

THE SOP.

MARK xiv. 17-21 (R. V.).

In the deadly wine which our Lord was made to drink, every ingredient of mortal bitterness was mingled. And it shows how far is even His Church from comprehending Him, that we think so much more of the physical than the mental and spiritual horrors which gather around the closing scene.

But the tone of all the narratives, and perhaps especially of St. Mark's, is that of the exquisite Collect which reminds us that our Lord Jesus Christ was contented to be betrayed, and given up into the hands of wicked men, as well as to suffer death on the cross. Treason and outrage, the traitor's kiss, and the weakness of those who loved Him, the hypocrisy of the priest and the ingratitude of the mob, perjury and a mock trial, the injustice of His judges, the brutal outrages of the soldiers, the worse and more malignant mockery of scribe and Pharisee, and last and direst, the averting of the face of God, these were more dreadful to Jesus than the scourging and the nails.

And so there is great stress laid upon His anticipation of the misconduct of His own.

As the dreadful evening closes in, having come to the guest chamber "with the Twelve"—eleven whose hearts should fail them and one whose heart was dead, it was "as they sat and were eating" that the oppression of the traitor's hypocrisy became intolerable, and the outraged One spoke out. "Verily I say unto you, One of you shall betray Me, even he that eateth with Me." The words are interpreted as well as predicted in the plaintive Psalm which says, "Mine own familiar friend in whom I trusted, which did also eat of My bread, hath lifted up his heel against Me." And perhaps they are less a disclosure than a cry.

Every attempt to mitigate the treason of Judas, every suggestion that he may only have striven too wilfully to serve our Lord by forcing Him to take decided measures, must fail to account for the sense of utter wrong which breathes in the simple and piercing complaint "one of you . . . even he that eateth with Me." There is a tone in all the narratives which is at variance with any palliation of the crime.

No theology is worth much if it fails to confess, at the centre of all the words and deeds of Jesus, a great and tender human heart. He might have spoken of teaching and warnings lavished on the traitor, and miracles which he had beheld in vain. What weighs heaviest on His burdened spirit is none of these; it is that one should betray Him who had eaten His bread.

When Brutus was dying he is made to say—

> "My heart doth joy, that yet, in all my life,
> I found no man, but he was true to me."

But no form of innocent sorrow was to pass Jesus by.

The vagueness in the words "one of you shall betray Me," was doubtless intended to suggest in all a great searching of heart. Coming just before the institution of the Eucharistic feast, this incident anticipates the command which it perhaps suggested: "Let a man examine himself, and so let him eat." It is good to be distrustful of one's self. And if, as was natural, the Eleven looked one upon another doubting of whom He spake, they also began to say to Him, one by one (first the most timid, and then others as the circle narrowed), Is it I? For the prince of this world had something in each of them,—some frailty there was, some reluctance to bear the yoke, some longing for the forbidden ways of worldliness, which alarmed each at this solemn warning, and made him ask, Is it, can it be possible, that it is I? Religious self-sufficiency was not then the apostolic mood. Their questioning is also remarkable as a proof how little they suspected Judas, how firmly he bore himself even as those all-revealing words were spoken, how strong and wary was the temperament which Christ would fain have sanctified. For between the Master and him there could have been no more concealment.

The apostles were right to distrust themselves, and not to distrust another. They were right, because they were so feeble, so unlike their Lord. But for Him there is no misgiving: His composure is serene in the hour of the power of darkness. And His perfect spiritual sensibility discerned the treachery, unknown to others, as instinctively as the eye resents the presence of a mote imperceptible to the hand.

The traitor's iron nerve is somewhat strained as he feels himself discovered, and when Jesus is about to hand a sop to him, he stretches over, and their hands meet in the dish. That is the appointed sign: "It is one of the Twelve, he that dippeth with Me in the dish," and as he rushes out into the darkness, to seek his accomplices and his revenge, Jesus feels the awful contrast between the betrayer and the Betrayed. For Himself, He goeth as it is written of Him. This phrase admirably expresses the co-operation of Divine purpose and free human will, and by the woe that follows He refutes all who would make of God's fore-knowledge an excuse for human sin. He then is not walking in the dark and stumbling, though men shall think Him falling. But the life of the false one is worse than utterly cast away: of him is spoken the dark and ominous word, never indisputably certain of any other soul, "Good were it for him if that man had not been born."

"That man!" The order and emphasis are very strange. The Lord, who felt and said that one of His chosen was a devil, seems here to lay stress upon the warning thought, that he who fell so low was human, and his frightful ruin was evolved from none but human capabilities for good and evil. In "the Son of man" and "that man," the same humanity was to be found.

For Himself, He is the same to-day as yesterday. All that we eat is His. And in the most especial and far-reaching sense, it is His bread which is broken for us at His table. Has He never seen traitor except one who violated so close a bond? Alas, the night when the Supper of the Lord was given was the same night when He was betrayed.

BREAD AND WINE.

MARK xiv. 22-25 (R. V.).

How much does the Gospel of St. Mark tell us about the supper of the Lord? He is writing to Gentiles. He is writing probably before the sixth chapter of St. John was penned, certainly before it reached his readers. Now we must not undervalue the reflected light thrown by one Scripture upon another. Still less may we suppose that each account conveys all the doctrine of the Eucharist. But it is obvious that St. Mark intended his narrative to be complete in itself, even if not exhaustive. No serious expositor will ignore the fulness of any word or action in which later experience can discern meanings, truly involved, although not apparent at the first. That would be to deny the inspiring guidance of Him who sees the end from the beginning. But it is reasonable to omit from the interpretation of St. Mark whatever is not either explicitly there, or else there in germ, waiting underneath the surface for other influences to develop it. For instance, the "remembrance" of Christ in St. Paul's narrative may (or it may not) mean a sacrificial memorial to God of His Body and His Blood. If it be, this notion was to be conveyed to the readers of this Gospel hereafter, as a quite new fact, resting upon other authority. It has no place whatever here, and need only be mentioned to point out that St. Mark did not feel bound to convey the slightest hint of it. A communion, therefore, could be profitably celebrated by persons who had no glimmering of any such conception. Nor does he rely, for an understanding of his narrative, upon such familiarity with Jewish ritual as would enable his readers to draw subtle analogies as they went along. They were so ignorant of these observances that he had just explained to them on what day the passover was sacrificed (ver. 12).

But this narrative conveys enough to make the Lord's Supper, for every believing heart, the supreme help to faith, both intellectual and spiritual, and the mightiest of promises, and the richest gift of grace.

It is hard to imagine that any reader would conceive that the bread in Christ's hands had become His body, which still lived and breathed; or that His blood, still flowing in His veins, was also in the cup He gave to His disciples. No resort could be made to the glorification of the risen Body as an escape from the perplexities of such a notion, for in whatever sense the words are true, they were spoken of the body of His humiliation, before which still lay the agony and the tomb.

Instinct would revolt yet more against such a gross explanation, because the friends of Jesus are bidden to eat and drink. And all the analogy of Christ's language would prove that His vivid style refuses to be tied down to so lifeless and mechanical a treatment. Even in this Gospel they could discover that seed was teaching, and fowls were Satan, and that they were themselves His mother and His brethren. Further knowledge of Scripture would not impair this natural freedom of interpretation. For they would discover that if animated language were to be frozen to such literalism, the partakers of the Supper were themselves, though many, one body and one loaf, that Onesimus was St. Paul's very heart, that leaven is hypocrisy, that Hagar is Mount Sinai, and that the veil of the temple is the flesh of Christ (1 Cor. x. 17; Philem. ver. 12; Luke xii. 1; Gal. iv. 25; Heb. x. 20). And they would also find, in the analogous institution of the paschal feast, a similar use of language (Exod. xii. 11).

But when they had failed to discern the doctrine of a transubstantiation, how much was left to them. The great words remained, in all their spirit and life, "Take ye, this is My Body . . . this is My Blood of the Covenant, which is shed for many."

(1) So then, Christ did not look forward to His death as to ruin or overthrow. The Supper is an institution which could never have been devised at any later period. It comes to us by an unbroken line from the Founder's hand, and attested by the earliest witnesses. None could have interpolated a new ordinance into the simple worship of the early Church, and the last to suggest such a possibility should be those sceptics who are deeply interested in exaggerating the estrangements which existed from the first, and which made the Jewish Church a keen critic of Gentile innovation, and the Gentiles of a Jewish novelty.

Nor could any genius have devised its vivid and pictorial earnestness, its copious meaning, and its pathetic power over the heart, except His, Who spoke of the Good Shepherd and of the Prodigal Son. And so it tells us plainly what Christ thought about His own death. Death is to most of us simply the close of life. To Him it was itself an achievement, and a supreme one. Now it is possible to remember with exultation a victory which cost the conqueror's life. But on the Friday which we call Good, nothing happened except the crucifixion. The effect on the Church, which is amazing and beyond dispute, is produced by the death of her Founder, and by nothing else. The Supper has no reference to Christ's resurrection. It is as if the nation exulted in Trafalgar, not in spite of the death of our great Admiral, but solely because he died; as if the shot which slew Nelson had itself been the overthrow of hostile navies. Now the history of religions offers no parallel to this. The admirers of the Buddha love to celebrate the long spiritual struggle, the final illumination, and the career of gentle helpfulness. They do not derive life and energy from the somewhat vulgar manner of his death. But the followers of Jesus find an inspiration (very displeasing to some recent apostles of good taste) in singing of their Redeemer's blood. Remove from the Creed (which does not even mention His three years of teaching) the proclamation of His death, and there may be left, dimly visible to man, the outline of a sage among the sages, but there will be no longer a Messiah, nor a Church. It is because He was lifted up that He draws all men unto Him. The perpetual nourishment of the Church, her bread and wine, are beyond question the slain body of her Master and His blood poured out for man.

What are we to make of this admitted fact, that from the first she thought less of His miracles, His teaching, and even of His revelation of the Divine character in a perfect life, than of the doctrine that He who thus lived, died for the men who slew Him? And what of this, that Jesus Himself, in the presence of imminent death, when men review their lives and set a value on their achievements, embodied in a solemn ordinance the conviction that all He had taught and done was less to man than what He was about to suffer? The Atonement is here proclaimed as a cardinal fact in our religion, not worked out into doctrinal subtleties, but placed with marvellous simplicity and force, in the forefront of the consciousness of the simplest. What the Incarnation does for our bewildering thoughts of God, the absolute and unconditioned, that does the Eucharist for our subtle reasonings upon the Atonement.

(2) The death of Christ is thus precious, because He Who sacrificed for us can give Himself away. "Take ye" is a distinct offer. And so the communion feast is not a mere commemoration, such as nations hold for great deliverances. It is this, but it is much more, else the language of Christ would apply worse to that first supper whence all our Eucharistic language is derived, than to any later celebration. When He was absent, the bread would very aptly remind them of His wounded body, and the wine of His blood poured out. It might naturally be said, Henceforward, to your loving remembrance this shall be my Body, as indeed, the words, As oft as ye drink it, are actually linked with the injunction to do this in remembrance. But scarcely could it have been said by Jesus, looking His disciples in the face, that the elements were then His body and blood, if nothing more than commemoration were in His mind. And so long as popular Protestantism fails to look beyond this, so long will it be hard pressed and harassed by the evident weight of the words of institution. These are given in Scripture solely as having been spoken then, and no interpretation is valid which attends chiefly to subsequent celebrations, and only in the second place to the Supper of Jesus and the Eleven.

Now the most strenuous opponent of the doctrine that any change has passed over the material substance of the bread and wine, need not resist the palpable evidence that Christ appointed these to represent Himself. And how? Not only as sacrificed for His people, but as verily bestowed upon them. Unless Christ mocks us, "Take ye" is a word of absolute assurance. Christ's Body is not only slain, and His Blood shed on our behalf; He gives Himself *to* us as well as *for* us; He is ours. And therefore whoever is convinced that he may take part in "the sacrament of so great a mystery" should realise that he there receives, conveyed to him by the Author of that wondrous feast, all that is expressed by the bread and wine.

(3) And yet this very word "Take ye," demands our co-operation in the sacrament. It requires that we should receive Christ, as it declares that He is ready to impart Himself, utterly, like food which is taken into the system, absorbed, assimilated, wrought into bone, into tissue, and into blood. And if any doubt lingered in our minds of the significance of this word, it is removed when we remember how belief is identified with feeding, in St. John's Gospel. "I am the bread of life: he that cometh to Me shall not hunger, and he that believeth on Me shall never thirst. . . . He that believeth hath eternal life. I am the bread of life." (John vi. 35, 47, 48.) If it follows that to feed upon Christ is to believe, it also follows quite as plainly that belief is not genuine unless it really feeds upon Christ.

It is indeed impossible to imagine a more direct and vigorous appeal to man to have faith in Christ than this, that He formally conveys, by the agency of His Church, to the hands and lips of His disciples, the appointed emblem of Himself, and of Himself in the act of blessing them. For the emblem is food in its most nourishing and in its most stimulating form, in a form the best fitted to speak of utter self-sacrifice, by the bruised corn of broken bread, and by the solemn resemblance to His sacred blood. We are taught to see, in the absolute absorption of our food into our bodily system, a type of the completeness wherewith Christ gives Himself to us.

That gift is not to the Church in the gross, it is "divided among" us; it individualises each believer; and yet the common food expresses the unity of the whole Church in Christ. Being many we are one bread.

Moreover, the institution of a meal reminds us that faith and emotion do not always exist together. Times there are when the hunger and thirst of the soul are like the craving of a sharp appetite for food. But the wise man will not postpone his meal until such a keen desire returns, and the Christian will seek for the Bread of life, however his emotions may flag, and his soul cleave unto the dust. Silently and often unaware, as the substance of the body is renovated and restored by food, shall the inner man be strengthened and built up by that living Bread.

(4) We have yet to ask the great question, what is the specific blessing expressed by the elements, and therefore surely given to the faithful by the sacrament? Too many are content to think vaguely of Divine help, given us for the merit of the death of Christ. But bread and wine do not express an indefinite Divine help, they express the body and blood of Christ, they have to do with His Humanity. We must beware, indeed, of limiting the notion overmuch. At the Supper He said not "My flesh," but "My body," which is plainly a more comprehensive term. And in the discourse when He said "My Flesh is meat indeed," He also said "I am the bread of life. . . . He that eateth Me, the same shall live by Me." And we may not so carnalise the Body as to exclude the Person, who bestows Himself. Yet is all the language so constructed as to force the conviction upon us that His body and blood, His Humanity, is the special gift of the Lord's Supper. As man He redeemed us, and as man He imparts Himself to man.

Thus we are led up to the sublime conception of a new human force working in humanity. As truly as the life of our parents is in our veins, and the corruption which they inherited from Adam is passed on to us, so truly there is abroad in the world another influence, stronger to elevate than the infection of the fall is to degrade; and the heart of the Church is propelling to its utmost extremities the pure life of the Second Adam, the Second Man, the new Father of the race. As in Adam all die, even so in Christ shall all be made alive; and we who bear now the image of our earthy progenitor shall hereafter bear the image of the heavenly. Meanwhile, even as the waste and dead tissues of our bodily frame are replaced by new material from every meal, so does He, the living Bread, impart not only aid from heaven, but nourishment, strength to our poor human nature, so weary and exhausted, and renovation to what is sinful and decayed. How well does such a doctrine of the sacrament harmonise with the declarations of St. Paul: "I live, and yet no longer I, but Christ liveth in me." "The Head, from whom all the body being supplied and knit together through the joints and bands, increaseth with the increase of God" (Gal. ii. 20; Col. ii. 19).

(5) In the brief narrative of St. Mark there are a few minor points of interest.

Fasting communions may possibly be an expression of reverence only. The moment they are pressed further, or urged as a duty, they are strangely confronted by the words, "While they were eating, Jesus took bread."

The assertion that "they all drank," follows from the express commandment recorded elsewhere. And while we remember that the first communicants were not laymen, yet the emphatic insistence upon this detail, and with reference only to the cup, is entirely at variance with the Roman notion of the completeness of a communion in one kind.

It is most instructive also to observe how the far-reaching expectation of our Lord looks beyond the Eleven, and beyond His infant Church, forward to the great multitude which no man can number, and speaks of the shedding of His blood "for many." He, who is to see of the travail of His soul and to be satisfied, has already spoken of a great supper when the house of God shall be filled. And now He will no more drink of the fruit of the vine until that great day when the marriage of the Lamb having come, and His Bride having made herself ready, He shall drink it new in the consummated kingdom of God.

With the announcement of that kingdom He began His gospel: how could the mention of it be omitted from the great gospel of the Eucharist? or how could the Giver of the earthly feast be silent concerning the banquet yet to come?

THE WARNING.

Mark xiv. 26-31 (R. V.).

Some uncertainty attaches to the position of Christ's warning to the Eleven in the narrative of the last evening. Was it given at the supper, or on Mount Olivet; or were there perhaps premonitory admonitions on His part, met by vows of faithfulness on theirs, which at last led Him to speak out so plainly, and elicited such vainglorious protestations, when they sat together in the night air?

What concerns us more is the revelation of a calm and beautiful nature, at every point in the narrative. Jesus knows and has declared that His life is now closing, and His blood already "being shed for many." But that does not prevent Him from joining with them in singing a hymn. It is the only time when we are told that our Saviour sang, evidently because no other occasion needed mention; a warning to those who draw confident inferences from such facts as that "none ever said He smiled," or that there is no record of His having been sick. It would surprise such theorists to observe the number of biographies much longer than any of the Gospels, which also mention nothing of the kind. The Psalms usually sung at the close of the feast are cxv. and the three following. The first tells how the dead praise not the Lord, but we will praise Him from this time forth for ever. The second proclaims that the Lord hath delivered my soul from death, mine eyes from tears, and my feet from falling. The third bids all the nations praise the Lord, for his merciful kindness is great and His truth endureth for ever. And the fourth rejoices because, although all nations compassed me about, yet I shall not die, but live and declare the works of the Lord; and because the stone which the builders rejected is become the head stone of the corner. Memories of infinite sadness were awakened by the words which had so lately rung around His path: "Blessed is He that cometh in the name of the Lord;" but His voice was strong to sing, "Bind the sacrifice with cords, even to the horns of the altar;" and it rose to the exultant close, "Thou art my God, and I will praise Thee: Thou art my God, I will exalt Thee. O give thanks unto the Lord for He is good, for His mercy endureth for ever."

This hymn, from the lips of the Perfect One, could be no "dying swan-song." It uplifted that more than heroic heart to the wonderful tranquillity which presently said, "When I am risen, I will go before you into Galilee." It is full of victory. And now they go unto the Mount of Olives.

Is it enough considered how much of the life of Jesus was passed in the open air? He preached on the hill side; He desired that a boat should be at His command upon the lake; He prayed upon the mountain; He was transfigured beside the snows of Hermon; He oft-times resorted to a garden which had not yet grown awful; He met His disciples on a Galilean mountain; and He finally ascended from the Mount of Olives. His unartificial normal life, a pattern to us, not as students but as men—was spent by preference neither in the study nor the street.

In this crisis, most solemn and yet most calm, He leaves the crowded city into which all the tribes had gathered, and chooses for His last intercourse with His disciples, the slopes of the opposite hill side, while overhead is glowing, in all the still splendour of an Eastern sky, the full moon of Passover. Here then is the place for one more emphatic warning. Think how He loved them. As His mind reverts to the impending blow, and apprehends it in its most awful form, the very buffet of God Who Himself will smite the Shepherd, He remembers to warn His disciples of their weakness. We feel it to be gracious that He should think of them at such a time. But if we drew a little nearer, we should almost hear the beating of the most loving heart that ever broke. They were all He had. In them He had confided utterly. Even as the Father had loved Him, He also had loved them, the firstfruits of the travail of His soul. He had ceased to call them servants and had called them friends. To them He had spoken those affecting words, "Ye are they which have continued with me in My temptations." How intensely He clung to their sympathy, imperfect though it was, is best seen by His repeated appeals to it in the Agony. And He knew that they loved Him, that the spirit was willing, that they would weep and lament for Him, sorrowing with a sorrow which He hastened to add that He would turn into joy.

It is the preciousness of their fellowship which reminds Him how this, like all else, must fail Him. If there is blame in the words, "Ye shall be offended," this passes at once into exquisite sadness when He adds that He, Who so lately said, "Them that Thou gavest Me, I have guarded," should Himself be the cause of their offence, "All ye shall be caused to stumble because of Me." And there is an unfathomable tenderness, a marvellous allowance for their frailty in what follows. They were His sheep, and therefore as helpless, as little to be relied upon, as sheep when the shepherd is stricken. How natural it was for sheep to be scattered.

The world has no parallel for such a warning to comrades who are about to leave their leader, so faithful and yet so tender, so far from estrangement or reproach.

If it stood alone it would prove the Founder of the Church to be not only a great teacher, but a genuine Son of man.

For Himself, He does not share their weakness, nor apply to Himself the lesson of distrustfulness which He teaches them; He is of another nature from these trembling sheep, the Shepherd of Zechariah, "Who is My fellow, saith the Lord of Hosts." He does not shrink from applying to Himself this text, which awakens against Him the sword of God (Zechariah xiii. 7).

Looking now beyond the grave to the resurrection, and unestranged by their desertion, He resumes at once the old relation; for as the shepherd goeth before his sheep, and they follow him, so He will go before them into Galilee, to the familiar places, far from the city where men hate Him.

This last touch of quiet human feeling completes an utterance too beautiful, too characteristic to be spurious, yet a prophecy, and one which attests the ancient predictions, and which involves an amazing claim.

At first sight it is surprising that the Eleven who were lately so conscious of weakness that each asked was he the traitor, should since have become too self-confident to profit by a solemn admonition. But a little examination shows the two statements to be quite consistent. They had wronged themselves by that suspicion, and never is self-reliance more boastful than when it is reassured after being shaken. The institution of the Sacrament had invested them with new privileges, and drawn them nearer than ever to their Master. Add to this the infinite tenderness of the last discourse in St. John, and the prayer which was for them and not for the world. How did their hearts burn within them as He said, "Holy Father, keep them in Thy name whom Thou hast given Me." How incredible must it then have seemed to them, thrilling with real sympathy and loyal gratitude, that they should forsake such a Master.

Nor must we read in their words merely a loud and indignant self-assertion, all unworthy of the time and scene. They were meant to be a solemn vow. The love they professed was genuine and warm. Only they forgot their weakness; they did not observe the words which declared them to be helpless sheep, entirely dependent on the Shepherd, whose support would speedily seem to fail.

Instead of harsh and unbecoming criticism, which repeats almost exactly their fault by implying that we should not yield to the same pressure, let us learn the lesson, that religious exaltation, a sense of special privilege, and the glow of generous emotions, have their own danger. Unless we continue to be as little children, receiving the Bread of Life without any pretence to have deserved it, and conscious still that our only protection is the staff of our Shepherd, then the very notion that we are something, when we are nothing, will betray us to defeat and shame.

Peter is the loudest in his protestations; and there is a painful egoism in his boast, that even if the others fail, he will never deny Him. So in the storm, it is he who should be called across the waters. And so an early reading makes him propose that he alone should build the tabernacles for the wondrous Three.

Naturally enough, this egoism stimulates the rest. For them, Peter is among those who may fail, while each is confident that he himself cannot. Thus the pride of one excites the pride of many.

But Christ has a special humiliation to reveal for his special self-assertion. That day, and even before that brief night was over, before the second cock-crowing ("the cock-crow" of the rest, being that which announced the dawn) he shall deny his Master twice. Peter does not observe that his eager contradictions are already denying the Master's profoundest claims. The others join in his renewed protestations, and their Lord answers them no more. Since they refuse to learn from Him, they must be left to the stern schooling of experience. Even before the betrayal, they had an opportunity to judge how little their good intentions might avail. For Jesus now enters Gethsemane.

IN THE GARDEN.

MARK xiv. 32-42 (R. V.).

All Scripture, given by inspiration of God, is profitable; yet must we approach with reverence and solemn shrinking the story of our Saviour's anguish. It is a subject for caution and for reticence, putting away all over-curious surmise, all too-subtle theorising, and choosing to say too little rather than too much.

It is possible so to argue about the metaphysics of the Agony as to forget that a suffering human heart was there, and that each of us owes his soul to the victory which was decided, if not completed, in that fearful place. The Evangelists simply tell us how He suffered.

Let us begin with the accessories of the scene, and gradually approach the centre.

In the warning of Jesus to His disciples there was an undertone of deep sorrow. God will smite Him, and they will all be scattered like sheep. However dauntless be the purport of such words, it is impossible to lose sight of their melancholy. And when the Eleven rejected His prophetic warning, and persisted in trusting the hearts He knew to be so fearful, their professions of loyalty could only deepen His distress, and intensify His isolation.

In silence He turns to the deep gloom of the olive grove, aware now of the approach of the darkest and deadliest assault.

There was a striking contrast between the scene of His first temptation and His last; and His experience was exactly the reverse of that of the first Adam, who began in a garden, and was driven thence into the desert, because he failed to refuse himself one pleasure more beside ten thousand. Jesus began where the transgression of men had driven them, in the desert among the wild beasts, and resisted not a luxury, but the passion of hunger craving for bread. Now He is in a garden, but how different from theirs. Close by is a city filled with foemen, whose messengers are already on His track. Instead of the attraction of a fruit good for food, and pleasant, and to be desired to make one wise, there is the grim repulsion of death, and its anguish, and its shame and mockery. He is now to be asailed by the utmost terrors of the flesh and of the spirit. And like the temptation in the wilderness, the asault is three times renewed.

As the dark "hour" approached, Jesus confessed the two conflicting instincts of our human nature in its extremity—the desire of sympathy, and the desire of solitude. Leaving eight of the disciples at some distance, He led still nearer to the appointed place His elect of His election, on whom He had so often bestowed special privilege, and whose faith would be less shaken by the sight of His human weakness, because they had beheld His Divine glory on the holy mount. To these He opened His heart. "My soul is exceeding sorrowful, even unto death; abide ye here and watch." And He went from them a little. Their neighbourhood was a support in His dreadful conflict, and He could at times return to them for sympathy; but they might not enter with Him into the cloud, darker and deadlier than that which they feared on Hermon. He would fain not be desolate, and yet He must be alone.

But when He returned, they were asleep. As Jesus spoke of watching for one hour, some time had doubtless elapsed. And sorrow is exhausting. If the spirit do not seek for support from God, it will be dragged down by the flesh into heavy sleep, and the brief and dangerous respite of oblivion.

It was the failure of Peter which most keenly affected Jesus, not only because his professions had been so loud, but because much depended on his force of character. Thus, when Satan had desired to have them, that he might sift them all like wheat, the prayers of Jesus were especially for Simon, and it was he when he was converted who should strengthen the rest. Surely then he at least might have watched one hour. And what of John, His nearest human friend, whose head had reposed upon His bosom? However keen the pang, the lips of the Perfect Friend were silent; only He warned them all alike to watch and pray, because they were themselves in danger of temptation.

That is a lesson for all time. No affection and no zeal are a substitute for the presence of God realised, and the protection of God invoked. Loyalty and love are not enough without watchfulness and prayer, for even when the spirit is willing, the flesh is weak, and needs to be upheld.

Thus, in His severest trial and heaviest oppression, there is neither querulousness nor invective, but a most ample recognition of their good will, a most generous allowance for their weakness, a most sedulous desire, not that He should be comforted, but that they should escape temptation.

With His yearning heart unsoothed, with another anxiety added to His heavy burden, Jesus returned to His vigil. Three times He felt the wound of unrequited affection, for their eyes were very heavy, and they wist not what to answer Him when He spoke.

Nor should we omit to contrast their bewildered stupefaction, with the keen vigilance and self-possession of their more heavily burdened Lord.

If we reflect that Jesus must needs experience all the sorrows that human weakness and human wickedness could inflict, we may conceive of these varied wrongs as circles with a common centre, on which the cross was planted. And our Lord has now entered the first of these; He has looked for pity, but there was no man; His own, although it was grief which pressed them down, slept in the hour of His anguish, and when He bade them watch.

It is right to observe that our Saviour had not bidden them to pray with Him. They should watch and pray. They should even watch with Him. But to pray for Him, or even to pray with Him, they were not bidden. And this is always so. Never do we read that Jesus and any mortal joined together in any prayer to God. On the contrary, when two or three of them asked anything in His name, He took for Himself the position of the Giver of their petition. And we know certainly that He did not invite them to join His prayers, for it was as He was praying in a certain place that when He ceased, one of His disciples desired that they also might be taught to pray (Luke xi. 1). Clearly then they were not wont to approach the mercy seat hand in hand with Jesus. And the reason is plain. He came directly to His Father; no man else came unto the Father but by Him; there was an essential difference between His attitude towards God and ours.

Has the Socinian ever asked himself why, in this hour of His utmost weakness, Jesus sought no help from the intercession of even the chiefs of the apostles?

It is in strict harmony with this position that St. Matthew tells us, He now said not Our Father, but My Father. No disciple is taught, in any circumstances to claim for himself a monopolised or special sonship. He may be in his closet and the door shut, yet must he remember his brethren and say, Our Father. That is a phrase which Jesus never addressed to God. None is partaker of His Sonship; none joined with Him in supplication to His Father.

THE AGONY.

MARK xiv. 34-42 (R. V.).

SCEPTICS and believers have both remarked that St. John, the only Evangelist who was said to have been present, gives no account of the Agony.

It is urged by the former, that the serene composure of the discourse in his Gospel leaves no room for subsequent mental conflict and recoil from suffering, which are inconsistent besides with his conception of a Divine man, too exalted to be the subject of such emotions.

But do not the others know of composure which bore to speak of His Body as broken bread, and seeing in the cup the likeness of His Blood shed, gave it to be the food of His Church for ever?

Was the resignation less serene which spoke of the smiting of the Shepherd, and yet of His leading back the flock to Galilee? If the narrative was rejected as inconsistent with the calmness of Jesus in the fourth Gospel, it should equally have repelled the authors of the other three.

We may grant that emotion, agitation, is inconsistent with unbelieving conceptions of the Christ of the fourth Gospel. But this only proves how false those conceptions are. For the emotion, the agitation is already there. At the grave of

Lazarus the word which tells that when He groaned in spirit He was troubled, describes one's distress in the presence of some palpable opposing force (John xi. 34). There was, however, a much closer approach to His emotion in the garden, when the Greek world first approached Him. Then he contrasted its pursuit of self-culture with His own doctrine of self-sacrifice, declaring that even a grain of wheat must either die or abide by itself alone. To Jesus that doctrine was no smooth, easily announced theory, and so He adds, "Now is My soul troubled, and what shall I say? Father, save Me from this hour. But for this cause came I unto this hour" (John xii. 27).

Such is the Jesus of the Fourth Gospel, by no means that of the modern analysts. Nor is enough said, when we remind them that the Speaker of these words was capable of suffering; we must add that profound agitation at the last was inevitable, for One so resolute in coming to this hour, yet so keenly sensitive of its dread.

The truth is that the silence of St. John is quite in his manner. It is so that he passes by the Sacraments, as being familiar to his readers, already instructed in the gospel story. But he gives previous discourses in which the same doctrine is expressed which was embodied in each Sacrament,—the declaration that Nicodemus must be born of water, and that the Jews must eat His flesh and drink His blood. It is thus that instead of the agony, he records that earlier agitation. And this threefold recurrence of the same expedient is almost incredible except by design. St. John was therefore not forgetful of Gethsemane.

A coarser infidelity has much to say about the shrinking of our Lord from death. Such weakness is pronounced unworthy, and the bearing of multitudes of brave men and even of Christian martyrs, unmoved in the flames, is contrasted with the strong crying and tears of Jesus.

It would suffice to answer that Jesus also failed not when the trial came, but before Pontius Pilate witnessed a good confession, and won upon the cross the adoration of a fellow-sufferer and the confession of a Roman soldier. It is more than enough to answer that His story, so far from relaxing the nerve of human fortitude, has made those who love Him stronger to endure tortures than were emperors and inquisitors to invent them. What men call His weakness has inspired ages with fortitude. Moreover, the censure which such critics, much at ease, pronounce on Jesus expecting crucifixion, arises entirely from the magnificent and unique standard by which they try Him; for who is so hard-hearted as to think less of the valour of the martyrs because it was bought by many a lonely and intense conflict with the flesh?

For us, we accept the standard; we deny that Jesus in the garden came short of absolute perfection; but we call attention to the fact that much is conceded to us, when a criticism is ruthlessly applied to our Lord which would excite indignation and contempt if brought to bear on the silent sufferings of any hero or martyr but Himself.

Perfection is exactly what complicates the problem here.

Conscious of our own weakness, we not only justify but enjoin upon ourselves every means of attaining as much nobility as we may. We "steel ourselves to bear," and therefore we are led to expect the same of Jesus. We aim at some measure of what, in its lowest stage, is callous insensibility. Now that word is negative; it asserts the absence or paralysis of a faculty, not its fulness and activity. Thus we attain victory by a double process; in part by resolutely turning our mind away, and only in part by its ascendency over appreciated distress. We administer anodynes to the soul. But Jesus, when He had tasted thereof, would not drink. The horrors which were closing around Him were perfectly apprehended, that they might perfectly be overcome.

Thus suffering, He became an example for gentle womanhood, and tender childhood, as well as man boastful of his stoicism. Moreover, He introduced into the world a new type of virtue, much softer and more emotional than that of the sages. The stoic, to whom pain is no evil, and the Indian laughing and singing at the stake, are partly actors and partly perversions of humanity. But the Good Shepherd is also, for His gentleness, a lamb. And it is His influence which has opened our eyes to see a charm unknown before, in the sensibility of our sister and wife and child. Therefore, since the perfection of manhood means neither the ignoring of pain nor the denying of it, but the union of absolute recognition with absolute mastery of its fearfulness, Jesus, on the approach of agony and shame, and who shall say what besides, yields Himself beforehand to the full contemplation of His lot. He does so, while neither excited by the trial nor driven to bay by the scoffs of His murderers, but in solitude, in the dark, with stealthy footsteps approaching through the gloom.

And ever since, all who went farthest down into the dread Valley, and on whom the shadow of death lay heaviest, found there the footsteps of its conqueror. It must be added that we cannot measure the keenness of the sensibility thus exposed to torture. A physical organisation and a spiritual nature fresh from the creative hand, undegraded by the transmitted heritage of ages of artificial, diseased, and sinful habit, unblunted by one deviation from natural ways, undrugged by one excess, was surely capable of a range of feeling as vast in anguish as in delight.

The sceptic supposes that a torrent of emotion swept our Saviour off His feet. The only narratives he can go upon give quite the opposite impression. He is seen to fathom all that depth of misery, He allows the voice of nature to utter all the bitter earnestness of its reluctance, yet He never loses self-control, nor wavers in loyalty to His Father, nor renounces His submission to the Father's will. Nothing in the scene is more astonishing than its combination of emotion with self-government. Time after time He pauses, gently and lovingly admonishing others, and calmly returns to His intense and anxious vigil.

Thus He has won the only perfect victory. With a nature so responsive to emotion, He has not refused to feel, nor abstracted His soul from suffering, nor silenced the flesh by such an effort as when we shut our ears against a discord. Jesus sees all, confesses that He would fain escape, but resigns Himself to God.

In the face of all asceticisms, as of all stoicisms, Gethsemane is the eternal protest that every part of human natutre is entitled to be heard, provided that the spirit retains the arbitration over all.

Hitherto nothing has been assumed which a reasonable sceptic can deny. Nor should such a reader fail to observe the astonishing revelation of character in the narrative, its gentle pathos, its intensity beyond what commonly belongs to gentleness, its affection, its mastery over the disciples, its filial submission. Even the rich imaginative way of thinking, which invented the parables and sacraments, is in the word "this cup."

But if the story of Gethsemane can be vindicated from such a point of view, what shall be said when it is viewed as the Church regards it? Both Testaments declare that the sufferings of the Messiah were supernatural. In the Old Testament it was pleasing to the Father to bruise Him. The terrible cry of Jesus to a God who had forsaken Him is conclusive evidence from the New Testament. And if we ask what such a cry may mean, we find that He is a curse for us, and made to be sin for us, Who knew no sin.

If the older theology drew incredible conclusions from such words, that is no reason why we should ignore them. It is incredible that God was angry with His Son, or that in any sense the Omniscient One confused the Saviour with the sinful world. It is incredible that Jesus ever endured estrangement as of lost souls from the One Whom in Gethsemane He called Abba Father, and in the hour of utter darkness, My God, and into Whose Fatherly hands He committed His Spirit. Yet it is clear that He is being treated otherwise than a sinless Being, as such, ought to expect. His natural standing-place is exchanged for ours. And as our exceeding misery, and the bitter curse of all our sin fell on Him, Who bore it away by bearing it, our pollution surely affected His purity as keenly as our stripes tried His sensibility. He shuddered as well as agonised. The deep waters in which He sank were defiled as well as cold. Only this can explain the agony and bloody sweat. And as we, for whom He endured it, think of this, we can only be silent and adore.

Once more, Jesus returns to His disciples, but no longer to look for sympathy, or to bid them watch and pray. The time for such warnings is now past: the crisis, "the hour" is come, and His speech is sad and solemn. "Sleep on now and take your rest, it is enough." Had the sentence stopped there, none would ever have proposed to treat it as a question, "Do ye now sleep on and take your rest?" It would plainly have meant, "Since ye refuse My counsel and will none of My reproof, I strive no further to arouse the torpid will, the inert conscience, the inadequate affection. Your resistance prevails against My warning."

But critics fail to reconcile this with what follows, "Arise, let us be going." They fail through supposing that words of intense emotion must be interpreted like a syllogism or a lawyer's parchment.

"For My part, sleep on: but your sleep is now to be rudely broken: take your rest so far as respect for your Master should have kept you watchful; but the traitor is at hand to break such repose, let him not find you ignobly slumbering. 'Arise, he is at hand that doth betray Me.'"

This is not sarcasm, which taunts and wounds. But there is a lofty and profound irony in the contrast between their attitude and their circumstances, their sleep and the eagerness of the traitor.

And so they lost the most noble opportunity ever given to mortals, not through blank indifference nor unbelief, but by allowing the flesh to overcome the spirit. And thus do multitudes lose heaven, sleeping until the golden hours are gone, and He who said, "Sleep on now," says, "He that is unrighteous, let him be unrighteous still."

Remembering that defilement was far more urgent than pain in our Saviour's agony, how sad is the meaning of the words, "the Son of man is betrayed into the hands of sinners," and even of "the sinners," the representatives of all the evil from which He had kept Himself unspotted.

The one perfect flower of humanity is thrown by treachery into the polluted and polluting grasp of wickedness in its many forms; the traitor delivers Him to hirelings; the hirelings to hypocrites; the hypocrites to an unjust and sceptical pagan judge; the judge to his brutal soldiery; who expose Him to all that malice can wreak upon the most sensitive organisation, or ingratitude upon the most tender heart.

At every stage an outrage. Every outrage an appeal to the indignation of Him who held them in the hollow of His hand. Surely it may well be said, Consider Him who endureth such contradiction; and endured it from sinners against Himself.

THE ARREST.

MARK xiv. 43-52 (R. V.).

ST. MARK has told this tragical story in the most pointed and the fewest words. The healing of the ear of Malchus concerns him not, that is but one miracle among many; and Judas passes from sight unfollowed: the thought insisted on is of foul treason, pitiable weakness, brute force predominant, majestic remonstrance and panic flight. From the central events no accessories can distract him.

There cometh, he tells us, "Judas, one of the Twelve." Who Judas was, we knew already, but we are to consider how Jesus felt it now. Before His eyes is the catastrophe which His death is confronted to avert—the death of a soul, a chosen and richly dowered soul for ever lost—in spite of so many warnings—in spite of that incessant denunciation of covetousness which rings through so much of His teaching, which only the presence of Judas quite explains, and which His terrible and searching gaze must have made like fire, to sear since it could not melt—in spite of the outspoken utterances of these last days, and doubtless in spite of many prayers, he is lost: one of the Twelve.

And the dark thought would fall cold upon Christ's heart, of the multitudes more who should receive the grace of God, His own dying love, in vain. And with that, the recollection of many an hour of lovingkindness wasted on this familiar friend in whom He trusted, and who now gave Him over, as he had been expressly warned, to so cruel a fate. Even toward Judas, no unworthy bitterness could pollute that sacred heart, the fountain of unfathomable compassions, but what speechless grief must have been there, what inconceivable horror. For the outrage was dark in form as in essence. Judas apparently conceived that the Eleven might, as they had promised, rally around their Lord; and he could have no perception how impossible it was that Messiah should stoop to escape under cover of their devotion, how frankly the good Shepherd would give His life for the sheep. In the night, he thought, evasion might yet be attempted, and the town be raised. But he knew how to make the matter sure. No other would as surely as himself recognise Jesus in the uncertain light. If he were to lay hold on Him rudely, the Eleven would close in, and in the struggle, the prize might yet be lost. But approaching a little in advance, and peaceably, he would ostentatiously kiss his Master, and so clearly point Him out that the arrest would be accomplished before the disciples realised what was being done.

But at every step the intrigue is overmastered by the clear insight of Jesus. As He foretold the time of His arrest, while yet the rulers said, Not on the feast day, so He announced the approach of the traitor, who was then contriving the last momentary deception of his polluting kiss.

We have already seen how impossible it is to think of Judas otherwise than as the Church has always regarded him, an apostate and a traitor in the darkest sense. The milder theory is at this stage shattered by one small yet significant detail. At the supper, when conscious of being suspected, and forced to speak, he said not, like the others, "Lord," but "Rabbi, is it I?" Now they meet again, and the same word is on his lips, whether by design and in Satanic insolence, or in hysterical agitation and uncertainty, who can say?

But no loyalty, however misled, inspired that halting and inadequate epithet, no wild hope of a sudden blazing out of glories too long concealed is breathed in the traitor's Rabbi!

With that word, and his envenomed kiss, the "much kissing," which took care that Jesus should not shake him off, he passes from this great Gospel. Not a word is here of his remorse, or of the dreadful path down which he stumbled to his own place. Even the lofty remonstrance of the Lord is not recorded: it suffices to have told how he betrayed the Son of man with a kiss, and so infused a peculiar and subtle poison into Christ's draught of deadly wine. That, and not the punishment of that, is what St. Mark recorded for the Church, the awful fall of an apostle, chosen of Christ; the solemn warning to all privileged persons, richly endowed and highly placed; the door to hell, as Bunyan has it, from the very gate of heaven.

A great multitude with swords and staves had come from the rulers. Possibly some attempt at rescue was apprehended from the Galileans who had so lately triumphed around Jesus. More probably the demonstration was planned to suggest to Pilate that a dangerous political agitation had to be confronted.

At all events, the multitude did not terrify the disciples: cries arose from their little band, "Lord, shall we smite with the sword?" and if Jesus had consented, it seems that with two swords the Eleven whom declaimers make to be so craven, would have assailed the multitude in arms.

Now this is what points the moral of their failure. Few of us would confess personal cowardice by accepting a warning from the fears of the fearful. But the fears of the brave must needs alarm us. It is one thing to defy death, sword in hand, in some wild hour of chivalrous effort—although the honours we shower upon the valiant prove that even such fortitude is less common than we would fain believe. But there is a deep which opens beyond this. It is a harder thing to endure the silent passive anguish to which the Lamb, dumb before the shearers, calls His followers. The victories of the spirit are beyond animal strength of nerve. In their highest forms they are beyond the noble reach of intellectual resolution. How far beyond it we may learn by contrasting the excitement and then the panic of the Eleven with the sublime composure of their Lord.

One of them, whom we know to have been the impulsive Simon, showed his loss of self-control by what would have been a breach of discipline, even had resistance been intended. While others asked should they smite with the sword, he took the decision upon himself, and struck a feeble and abortive blow, enough to exasperate but not to disable. In so doing he added, to the sorrows of Jesus, disobedience, and the inflaming of angry passion among His captors.

Strange it is, and instructive, that the first act of violence in the annals of Christianity came not from her assailants but from her son. And strange to think with what emotions Jesus must have beheld that blow.

St. Mark records neither the healing of Malchus nor the rebuke of Peter. Throughout the events which now crowd fast upon us, we shall not find Him careful about fulness of detail. This is never his manner, though he loves any detail which is graphic, characteristic, or intensifying. But his concern is with the spirit of the Lord and of His enemies: he is blind to no form of injustice or insult which heightened the sufferings of Jesus, to no manifestation of dignity and self-control overmastering the rage of hell. If He is unjustly tried by Caiaphas, it matters nothing that Annas also wronged Him. If the soldiers of Pilate insulted Him, it matters nothing that the soldiers of Herod also set Him at nought. Yet the flight of a nameless youth is recorded, since it adds a touch to the picture of His abandonment.

And therefore he records the indignant remonstrance of Jesus upon the manner of His arrest. He was no man of violence and blood, to be arrested with a display of overwhelming force. He needed not to be sought in concealment and at midnight.

He had spoken daily in the Temple, but then their malice was defeated, their snares rent asunder, and the people witnessed their exposure. But all this was part of His predicted suffering, for Whom not only pain but injustice was foretold, Who should be taken from prison and from judgment.

It was a lofty remonstrance. It showed how little could danger and betrayal disturb His consciousness, and how clearly He discerned the calculation of His foes.

At this moment of unmistakable surrender, His disciples forsook Him and fled. One young man did indeed follow Him, springing hastily from slumber in some adjacent cottage, and wrapped only in a linen cloth. But he too, when seized, fled away, leaving his only covering in the hands of the soldiers.

This youth may perhaps have been the Evangelist himself, of whom we know that, a few years later, he joined Paul and Barnabas at the outset, but forsook them when their journey became perilous.

It is at least as probable that the incident is

recorded as a picturesque climax to that utter panic which left Jesus to tread the winepress alone, deserted by all, though He never forsook any.

BEFORE CAIAPHAS.

Mark xiv. 53-65 (R. V.) .

We have now to see the Judge of quick and dead taken from prison and judgment, the Preacher of liberty to the captives bound, and the Prince of Life killed. It is the most solemn page in earthly story; and as we read St. Mark's account, it will concern us less to reconcile his statements with those of the other three, than to see what is taught us by his especial manner of regarding it. Reconciliation, indeed, is quite unnecessary, if we bear in mind that to omit a fact is not to contradict it. For St. Mark is not writing a history, but a Gospel, and his readers are Gentiles, for whom the details of Hebrew intrigue matter nothing, and the trial before a Galilean Tetrarch would be only half intelligible.

St. John, who had been an eye-witness, knew that the private inquiry before Annas was vital, for there the decision was taken which subsequent and more formal assemblies did but ratify. He therefore, writing last, threw this ray of explanatory light over all that the others had related. St. Luke recorded in the Acts (iv. 27) that the apostles recognised, in the consent of Romans and Jews, and of Herod and Pilate, what the Psalmist had long foretold, the rage of the heathen and the vain imagination of the peoples, and the conjunction of kings and rulers. His Gospel therefore lays stress upon the part played by all of these. And St. Matthew's readers could appreciate every fulfilment of the prophecy, and every touch of local colour. St. Mark offers to us the essential points: rejection and cruelty by His countrymen, rejection and cruelty over again by Rome, and the dignity, the elevation, the lofty silence, and the dauntless testimony of his Lord. As we read, we are conscious of the weakness of His crafty foes, who are helpless and baffled, and have no resort except to abandon their charges and appeal to His own truthfulness to destroy Him.

He shows us first the informal assembly before Caiaphas, whither Annas sent Him with that sufficient sign of his own judgment, the binding of His hands, and the first buffet, inflicted by an officer, upon His holy face. It was not yet daylight, and a formal assembly of the Sanhedrim was impossible. But what passed now was so complete a rehearsal of the tragedy, that the regular meeting could be disposed of in a single verse.

There were confusion and distress among the conspirators. It was not their intention to have arrested Jesus on the feast day, at the risk of an uproar among the people. But He had driven them to do so by the expulsion of their spy, who, if they delayed longer, would be unable to guide their officers. And so they found themselves without evidence, and had to play the part of prosecutors when they ought to be impartial judges. There is something frightful in the spectacle of these chiefs of the religion of Jehovah suborning perjury as the way to murder; and it reminds us of the solemn truth, that no wickedness is so perfect and heartless as that upon which sacred influences have long been vainly operating, no corruption so hateful as that of a dead religion. Presently they would cause the name of God to be blasphemed among the heathen, by bribing the Roman guards to lie about the corpse. And the heart of Jesus was tried by the disgraceful spectacle of many false witnesses, found in turn and paraded against Him, but unable to agree upon any consistent charge, while yet the shameless proceedings were not discontinued. At the last stood up witnesses to pervert what He had spoken at the first cleansing of the Temple, which the second cleansing had so lately recalled to mind. They represented Him as saying, "I am able to destroy this temple made with hands,"—or perhaps, "I will destroy" it, for their testimony varied on this grave point—"and in three days I will build another made without hands." It was for blaspheming the Holy Place that Stephen died, and the charge was a grave one; but His words were impudently manipulated to justify it. There had been no proposal to substitute a different temple, and no mention of the temple made with hands. Nor had Jesus ever proposed to destroy anything. He had spoken of their destroying the Temple of His Body, and in the use they made of the prediction they fulfilled it.

As we read of these repeated failures before a tribunal so unjust, we are led to suppose that opposition must have sprung up to disconcert them; we remember the councillor of honourable estate, who had not consented to their counsel and deed, and we think, What if, even in that hour of evil, one voice was uplifted for righteousness? What if Joseph confessed Him in the conclave, like the penitent thief upon the cross?

And now the high priest, enraged and alarmed by imminent failure, rises in the midst, and in the face of all law cross-questions the prisoner, Answerest Thou nothing? What is it which these witness against Thee? But Jesus will not become their accomplice; He maintains the silence which contrasts so nobly with their excitement, which at once sees through their schemes and leaves them to fall asunder. And the urgency of the occasion, since hesitation now will give the city time to rise, drives them to a desperate expedient. Without discussion of His claims, without considering that some day there *must* be some Messiah (else what is their faith and who are they), they will treat it as blasphemous and a capital offence simply to claim that title. Caiaphas adjures Him by their common God to answer, Art Thou the Christ, the Son of the Blessed? So then they were not utterly ignorant of the higher nature of the Son of David: they remembered the words, Thou art My Son, this day have I begotten Thee. But the only use they ever made of their knowledge was to heighten to the uttermost the Messianic dignity which they would make it death to claim. And the prisoner knew well the consequences of replying. But He had come into the world to bear witness to the truth, and this was the central truth of all. "And Jesus said, I am." Now Renan tells us that He was the greatest religious genius who ever lived, or probably ever shall live. Mill tells us that religion cannot be said to have made a bad choice in pitching on this Man as the ideal representative and guide of humanity. And Strauss thinks that we know enough of Him to assert that His consciousness was unclouded by the memory of any sin. Well, then, if anything in the life of Jesus is beyond controversy, it is this, that the sinless Man, our ideal representative and guide, the greatest religous genius of the race, died for asserting upon oath that He was the Son of God. A good deal has been said lately, both wise and foolish, about Comparative Religion: is there anything to compare with this? Lunatics, with this example before their eyes, have conceived wild and dreadful infatuations. But these are the words of Him whose character has dominated nineteen centuries, and changed the history of the world. And they stand alone in the records of mankind.

As Jesus spoke the fatal words, as malice and hatred lighted the faces of His wicked judges with a base and ignoble joy, what was His own thought? We know it by the warning that He added. They supposed themselves judges and irresponsible, but there should yet be another tribunal, with justice of a far different kind, and there they should occupy another place. For all that was passing before His eyes, so false, hypocritical, and murderous, there was no lasting victory, no impunity, no escape: "Ye shall see the Son of man sitting at the right hand of power and coming with the clouds of heaven." Therefore His apostle Peter tells us that in this hour, when He was reviled and reviled not again, "He committed Himself to Him that judgeth righteously" (1 Peter ii. 23).

He had now quoted that great vision in which the prophet Daniel saw Him brought near unto the Ancient of Days, and invested with an everlasting dominion (Dan. vii. 13, 14). But St. Matthew adds one memorable word. He did not warn them, and He was not Himself sustained, only by the mention of a far-off judgment: He said they should behold Him thus "henceforth." And that very day they saw the veil of their temple rent, felt the world convulsed, and remembered in their terror that He had foretold His own death and resurrection, against which they had still to guard. And in the open sepulchre, and the supernatural vision told them by its keepers, in great and notable miracles wrought by the name of Jesus, in the desertion of a great multitude even of priests, and their own fear to be found fighting against God, in all this the rise of that new power was henceforth plainly visible, which was presently to bury them and their children under the ruins of their temple and their palaces. But for the moment the high-priest was only relieved; and he proceeded, rending his clothes, to announce his judgment, before consulting the court, who had no further need of witnesses, and were quite content to become formally the accusers before themselves. The sentence of this irregular and informal court was now pronounced, to fit them for bearing part, at sunrise, in what should be an unbiassed trial; and while they awaited the dawn Jesus was abandoned to the brutality of their servants, one of whom he had healed that very night. They spat on the Lord of Glory. They covered His face, an act which was the symbol of a death sentence (Esther vii. 8), and then they buffeted Him, and invited Him to prophesy who smote Him. And the officers "received Him" with blows.

What was the meaning of this outburst of savage cruelty of men whom Jesus had never wronged, and some of whose friends must have shared His super-human gifts of love? Partly it was the instinct of low natures to trample on the fallen, and partly the result of partisanship. For these servants of the priests must have seen many evidences of the hate and dread with which their masters regarded Jesus. But there was doubtless another motive. Not without fear, we may be certain, had they gone forth to arrest at midnight the Personage of whom so many miraculous tales were universally believed. They must have remembered the captains of fifty whom Elijah consumed with fire. And in fact there was a moment when they all fell prostrate before His majestic presence. But now their terror was at an end: He was helpless in their hands; and they revenged their fears upon the Author of them.

Thus Jesus suffered shame to make us partakers of His glory; and the veil of death covered His head, that He might destroy the face of the covering cast over all peoples, and the veil that was spread over all nations. And even in this moment of bitterest outrage He remembered and rescued a soul in the extreme of jeopardy, for it was now that the Lord turned and looked upon Peter.

THE FALL OF PETER.

MARK xiv. 66-72 (R. V.).

The fall of Peter has called forth the easy scorn of multitudes who never ran any risk for Christ. But if he had been a coward, and his denial a dastardly weakness, it would not be a warning for the whole Church, but only for feeble natures. Whereas the lesson which it proclaims is this deep and solemn one, that no natural endowments can bear the strain of the spiritual life. Peter had dared to smite when only two swords were forthcoming against the band of Roman soldiers and the multitude from the chief priests. After the panic in which all forsook Jesus, and so fulfilled the prediction "ye shall leave Me alone," none ventured so far as Peter. John indeed accompanied him; but John ran little risk, he had influence and was therefore left unassailed, whereas Peter was friendless and a mark for all men, and had made himself conspicuous in the garden. Of those who declaim about his want of courage few indeed would have dared so much. And whoever misunderstands him, Jesus did not. He said to him, "Satan hath desired to have you (all) that he may sift you like wheat, but I have prayed for thee (especially) that thy strength fail not." Around him the fiercest of the struggle was to rage, as around some point of vantage on a battlefield; and it was he, when once he had turned again, who should establish his brethren (Luke xxii. 31, 32).

God forbid that we should speak one light or scornful word of this great apostle! God grant us, if our footsteps slip, the heart to weep such tears as his.

Peter was a loving, brave, and loyal man. But the circumstances were not such as human bravery could deal with. Resistance, which would have kindled his spirit, had been forbidden to him, and was now impossible. The public was shut out, and he was practically alone among his enemies. He had come "to see the end," and it was a miserable sight that he beheld. Jesus was passive, silent, insulted: His foes fierce, unscrupulous, and confident. And Peter was more and more conscious of being alone, in peril, and utterly without resource. Moreover sleeplessness and misery lead to physical languor and cold,* and as the officers had kindled a fire, he was drawn thither, like a moth, by the double wish to avoid isolation and to warm himself. In thus seeking to pass for one of the crowd, he showed himself ashamed of Jesus, and incurred the menaced penalty, "of him shall the Son of man be ashamed, when He cometh." And the method of self-concealment which he adopted only showed his face, strongly illuminated, as St. Mark tells us, by the flame.

If now we ask for the secret of his failing resolution, we can trace the disease far back. It was self-confidence. He reckoned himself the one to walk upon the waters. He could not be silent on the holy mount, when Jesus held high communion with the inhabitants of heaven. He rebuked the Lord for dark forebodings. When Jesus would wash his feet, although expressly told that he should understand the act hereafter, he rejoined, Thou shalt never wash my feet, and was only sobered by the peremptory announcement that further rebellion would involve rejection. He was sure that if all the rest were to deny Jesus, he never should deny Him. In the garden he slept, because he failed to pray and watch. And then he did not wait to be directed, but strove to fight the battle of Jesus with the weapons of the flesh. Therefore he forsook Him and fled. And the consequences of that hasty blow were heavy upon him now. It marked him for the attention of the servants: it drove him to merge himself in the crowd. But his bearing was too suspicious to enable him to escape unquestioned. The first assault came very naturally, from the maid who kept the door, and had therefore seen him with John. He denied indeed, but with hesitation, not so much affirming that the charge was false as that he could not understand it. And thereupon he changed his place, either to escape notice or through mental disquietude; but as he went into the porch the cock crew. The girl, however, was not to be shaken off: she pointed him out to others, and since he had forsaken the only solid ground, he now denied the charge angrily and roundly. An hour passed, such an hour of shame, perplexity, and guilt as he had never known, and then there came a still more dangerous attack. They had detected his Galilean accent, while he strove to pass for one of them. And a kinsman of Malchus used words as threatening as were possible without enabling a miracle to be proved, since the wound had vanished: "Did I myself not see thee in the garden with Him?" Whereupon, to prove that his speech had nothing to do with Jesus, he began to curse and swear, saying, I know not the man. And the cock crew a second time, and Peter remembered the warning of his Lord, which then sounded so harsh, but now proved to be the means of his salvation. And the eyes of his Master, full of sorrow and resolution, fell on him. And he knew that he had added a bitter pang to the sufferings of the Blessed One. And the crowd and his own danger were forgotten, and he went out and wept.

It was for Judas to strive desperately to put himself right with man: the sorrow of Peter was for himself and God to know.

What lessons are we taught by this most natural and humbling story? That he who thinketh he standeth must take heed lest he fall. That we are in most danger when self-confident, and only strong when we are weak. That the beginning of sin is like the letting out of water. That Jesus does not give us up when we cast ourselves away, but as long as a pulse of love survives, or a spark of loyalty, He will appeal to that by many a subtle suggestion of memory and of providence, to recall His wanderer to Himself.

And surely we learn by the fall of this great and good apostle to restore the fallen in the spirit of meekness, considering ourselves lest we also be tempted, remembering also that to Peter Jesus sent the first tidings of His resurrection, and that the message found him in company with John, and therefore in the house with Mary. What might have been the issue of his anguish if these holy ones had cast Him off?

* "By the fire the children sit
Cold in that atmosphere of death."
—"In Memoriam," xx.

CHAPTER XV.

PILATE.

MARK xv. 1-20 (R. V.).

WITH morning came the formal assembly, which St. Mark dismisses in a single verse. It was indeed a disgraceful mockery. Before the trial began its members had prejudged the case, passed sentence by anticipation, and abandoned Jesus, as one condemned, to the brutality of their servants. And now the spectacle of a prisoner outraged and maltreated moves no indignation in their hearts.

Let us, for whom His sufferings were endured, reflect upon the strain and anguish of all these repeated examinations, these foregone conclusions gravely adopted in the name of justice, these exhibitions of greed for blood. Among the "unknown sufferings" by which the Eastern Church invokes her Lord, surely not the least was His outraged moral sense.

As the issue of it all, they led Him away to Pilate, meaning, by the weight of such an accusing array, to overpower any possible scruples of the governor, but in fact fulfilling His words, "they shall deliver Him unto the Gentiles." And the first question recorded by St. Mark expresses the intense surprise of Pilate. "Thou," so meek, so unlike the numberless conspirators that I have tried,—or perhaps, "Thou," Whom no sympathising multitude sustains, and for Whose death the disloyal priesthood thirsts, "Art *Thou* the King of the Jews?" We know how carefully Jesus disentangled His claim from the political associations which the high priests intended that it should suggest, how the King of Truth would not exaggerate any more than understate the case, and explained that His Kingdom was not of this world, that His servants did not fight, that His royal function was to uphold the truth, not to expel conquerors. The eyes of a practised Roman governor saw through the accusation very clearly. Before him, Jesus was accused of sedition, but that was a transparent pretext; Jews did not hate Him for enmity to Rome: He was a rival teacher and a successful one, and for envy they had delivered Him. So far all was well. Pilate investigated the charge, arrived at the correct judgment, and it only remained that he should release the innocent man. In reaching this conclusion Jesus had given him the most prudent and skilful help, but as soon as the facts became clear, He resumed His impressive and mysterious silence. Thus, before each of his judges in turn, Jesus avowed Himself the Messiah and then held His peace. It was an awful silence, which would not give that which was holy to the dogs, nor profane the truth by unavailing protests or controversies. It was, however, a silence only possible to an exalted nature full of self-control, since the words actually spoken redeem it from any suspicion or stain of sullenness. It is the conscience of Pilate which must henceforth speak. The Romans were the lawgivers of the ancient world, and a few years earlier their greatest poet had boasted that their mission was to spare the helpless and to crush the proud. In no man was an act of deliberate injustice, of complaisance to the powerful at the cost of the good, more unpardonable than in a leader of that splendid race, whose laws are still the favourite study of those who frame and administer our own. And the conscience of Pilate struggled hard, aided by superstitious fear. The very silence of Jesus amid many charges, by none of which His accusers would stand or fall, excited the wonder of His judge. His wife's dream aided the effect. And he was still more afraid when he heard that this strange and elevated Personage, so unlike any other prisoner whom he had ever tried, laid claim to be Divine. Thus even in his desire to save Jesus, his motive was not pure, it was rather an instinct of self-preservation than a sense of justice. But there was danger on the other side as well; since he had already incurred the imperial censure, he could not without grave apprehensions contemplate a fresh complaint, and would certainly be ruined if he were accused of releasing a conspirator against Cæsar. And accordingly he stooped to mean and crooked ways, he lost hold of the only clue in the perplexing labyrinth of expediencies, which is principle, and his name in the creed of Christendom is spoken with a shudder—"crucified under Pontius Pilate!"

It was the time for him to release a prisoner to them, according to an obscure custom, which some suppose to have sprung from the release of one of the two sacrificial goats, and others from the fact that they now celebrated their own deliverance from Egypt. At this moment the people began to demand their usual indulgence, and an evil hope arose in the heart of Pilate. They would surely welcome One who was in danger as a patriot: he would himself make the offer; and he would put it in this tempting form, "Will ye that I release unto you the King of the Jews?" Thus would the enmity of the priests be gratified, since Jesus would henceforth be a condemned culprit, and owe His life to their intercession with the foreigner. But the proposal was a surrender. The life of Jesus had not been forfeited; and when it was placed at their discretion, it was already lawlessly taken away. Moreover, when the offer was rejected, Jesus was in the place of a culprit who should not be released. To the priests, nevertheless, it was a dangerous proposal, and they needed to stir up the people, or perhaps Barabbas would not have been preferred.

Instigated by their natural guides, their religious teachers, the Jews made the tremendous choice, which has ever since been heavy on their heads and on their children's. Yet if ever an error could be excused by the plea of authority, and the duty of submission to constituted leaders, it was this error. They followed men who sat in Moses' seat, and who were thus entitled, according to Jesus Himself, to be obeyed. Yet that authority has not relieved the Hebrew nation from the wrath which came upon them to the uttermost. The salvation they desired was not moral elevation or spiritual life, and so Jesus had nothing to bestow upon them; they refused the Holy One and the Just. What they wanted was the world, the place which Rome held, and which they fondly hoped was yet to be their own. Even to have failed in the pursuit of this was better than to have the words of everlasting life, and so the name of Barabbas was enough to secure the rejection of Christ. It would almost seem that Pilate was ready to release both, if that would satisfy them, for he asks, in hesitation and perplexity, "What shall I do then with Him Whom ye call the King of the Jews?" Surely in their excitement for an insurgent, that title, given by themselves, will awake their pity. But again and again, like the howl of wolves, resounds their ferocious cry, Crucify Him, crucify Him.

The irony of Providence is known to every student of history, but it never was so manifest as here. Under the pressure of circumstances upon men whom principle has not made firm, we find a Roman governor striving to kindle every disloyal passion of his subjects, on behalf of the King of the Jews,—appealing to men whom he hated and despised, and whose charges have proved empty as chaff, to say, What evil has He done? and even to tell him, on his judgment throne, what he shall do with their King; we find the men who accused Jesus of stirring up the people to sedition, now shamelessly agitating for the release of a red-handed insurgent; forced moreover to accept the responsibility which they would fain have devolved on Pilate, and themselves to pronounce the hateful sentence of crucifixion, unknown to their law, but for which they had secretly intrigued; and we find the multitude fiercely clamouring for a defeated champion of brute force, whose weapon has snapped in his hands, who has led his followers to the cross, and from whom there is no more to hope. What satire upon their hope of a temporal Messiah could be more bitter than their own cry, "We have no king but Cæsar"? And what satire upon this profession more destructive than their choice of Barabbas and refusal of Christ? And all the while, Jesus looks on in silence, carrying out His mournful but effectual plan, the true Master of the movements which design to crush Him, and which He has foretold. As He ever receives gifts for the rebellious, and is the Saviour of all men, though especially of them that believe, so now His passion, which retrieved the erring soul of Peter, and won the penitent thief, rescues Barabbas from the cross. His suffering was made visibly vicarious.

One is tempted to pity the feeble judge, the only person who is known to have attempted to rescue Jesus, beset by his old faults, which will make an impeachment fatal, wishing better than he dares to act, hesitating, sinking inch by inch and like a bird with broken wing. No accomplice in this frightful crime is so suggestive of warning to hearts not entirely hardened.

But pity is lost in sterner emotion as we remember that this wicked governor, having borne witness to the perfect innocence of Jesus, was content, in order to save himself from danger, to watch the Blessed One enduring all the horrors of a Roman scourging, and then to yield Him up to die.

It is now the unmitigated cruelty of ancient paganism which has closed its hand upon our Lord. When the soldiers led Him away within the court, He was lost to His nation, which had renounced Him. It is upon this utter alienation, even more than the locality where the cross was fixed, that the Epistle to the Hebrews turns our attention, when it reminds us that "the bodies of those beasts whose blood is brought into the holy place by the high priest as an offering for sin, are burned without the camp. Wherefore Jesus also, that He might sanctify the people through His own blood, suffered without the gate." The physical exclusion, the material parallel, points to something deeper, for the inference is that of estrangement. Those who serve the tabernacle cannot eat of our altar. Let us go forth unto Him, bearing His reproach. (Heb. xii. 10-13).

Renounced by Israel, and about to become a curse under the law, he has now to suffer the cruelty of wantonness, as He has already endured the cruelty of hatred and fear. Now, more than ever perhaps, He looks for pity and there is no man. None responded to the deep appeal of the eyes which had never seen misery without relieving it. The contempt of the strong for the weak and suffering, of coarse natures for sensitive ones, of Romans for Jews, all these were blended with bitter scorn of the Jewish expectation that some day Rome shall bow before a Hebrew conqueror, in the mockery which Jesus now underwent, when they clad Him in such cast-off purple as the Palace yielded, thrust a reed into His pinioned hand, crowned Him with thorns, beat these into His holy head with the sceptre they had offered Him, and then proceeded to render the homage of their nation to the Messiah of Jewish hopes. It may have been this mockery which suggested to Pilate the inscription for the cross. But where is the mockery now? In crowning Him King of sufferings, and Royal among those who weep, they secured to Him the adherence of all hearts. Christ was made perfect by the things which He suffered; and it was not only in spite of insult and anguish, but by means of them, that He drew all men unto Him.

CHRIST CRUCIFIED.

MARK xv. 21-32 (R. V.).

At last the preparations were complete and the interval of mental agony was over. They led Him away to crucify Him. And upon the road an event of mournful interest took place. It was the custom to lay the two arms of the cross upon the doomed man, fastening them together at such an angle as to pass behind His neck, while his hands were bound to the ends in front. And thus it was that Jesus went forth bearing His cross. Did He think of this when He bade us take His yoke upon us? Did He wait for events to explain the words, by making it visibly one and the same to take His yoke and to take up our cross and follow Him?

On the road, however, they forced a reluctant stranger to go with them that he might bear the cross. The traditional reason is that our Redeemer's strength gave way, and it became physically impossible for Him to proceed; but this is challenged upon the ground that to fail would have been unworthy of our Lord, and would mar the perfection of His example. How so, when the failure was a real one? Is there no fitness in the belief that He who was tempted in all points like as we are, endured this hardness also, of struggling with the impossible demands of human cruelty, the spirit indeed willing but the flesh weak? It is not easy to believe that any other reason than manifest inability would have induced his persecutors to spare Him one drop of bitterness, one throb of pain. The noblest and most delicately balanced frame, like all other exquisite machines, is not capable of the rudest strain: and we know that Jesus had once sat wearied by the well, while the hardy fishers went into the town, and returned with bread. And this night our gentle Master had endured what no common victim knew. Long before the scourging, or even the buffeting began, His spiritual exhaustion had needed that an angel from heaven should strengthen Him. And the utmost possibility of exertion was now reached: the spot where they met Simon of Cyrene marks this melancholy limit; and suffering henceforth must be purely passive.

We cannot assert with confidence that Simon and his family were saved by this event. The coercion put upon him, the fact that he was seized and "impressed" into the service, already seems to indicate sympathy with Jesus. And we are fain to believe that he who received the honour, so strange and sad and sacred, the unique privilege of lifting some little of the crushing burden of the Saviour, was not utterly ignorant of what he did. We know at least that the names of his children, Alexander and Rufus, were familiar in the Church for which St. Mark was writing, and that in Rome a Rufus was chosen in the Lord, and his mother was like a mother to St. Paul (Rom. xvi. 13). With what feelings may they have recalled the story, "him they compelled to bear His cross."

They led Him to a place where the rounded summit of a knoll had its grim name from some resemblance to a human skull, and prepared the crosses there.

It was the custom of the daughters of Jerusalem, who lamented Him as He went, to provide a stupefying draught for the sufferers of this atrocious cruelty. "And they offered Him wine mixed with myrrh, but He received it not," although that dreadful thirst, which was part of the suffering of crucifixion, had already begun, for He only refused when He had tasted it.

In so doing He rebuked all who seek to drown sorrows or benumb the soul in wine, all who degrade and dull their sensibilities by physical excess or indulgence, all who would rather blind their intelligence than pay the sharp cost of its exercise. He did not condemn the use of anodynes, but the abuse of them. It is one thing to suspend the senses during an operation, and quite another thing by one's own choice to pass into eternity without consciousness enough to commit the soul into its Father's hands.

"And they crucify Him." Let the words remain as the Evangelist left them, to tell their own story of human sin, and of Divine love which many waters could not quench, neither could the depths drown it.

Only let us think in silence of all that those words convey.

In the first sharpness of mortal anguish, Jesus saw His executioners sit down at ease, all unconscious of the dread meaning of what was passing by their side, to part His garments among them, and cast lots for the raiment which they had stripped from His sacred form. The Gospels are content thus to abandon those relics about which so many legends have been woven. But indeed all through these four wonderful narratives the self-restraint is perfect. When the Epistles touch upon the subject of the crucifixion they kindle into flame. When St. Peter soon afterwards referred to it, his indignation is beyond question, and Stephen called the rulers betrayers and murderers (Acts ii. 23, 24; iii. 13, 14; vii. 51-53) but not one single syllable of complaint or comment mingles with the clear flow of narrative in the four Gospels. The truth is that the subject was too great, too fresh and vivid in their minds, to be adorned or enlarged upon. What comment of St. Mark, what mortal comment, could add to the weight of the words "they crucify Him"? Men use no figures of speech when telling how their own beloved one died. But it was differently that the next age wrote about the crucifixion; and perhaps the lofty self-restrain of the Evangelists has never been attained again.

St. Mark tells us that He was crucified at the third hour, whereas we read in St. John that it was "about the sixth hour" when Pilate ascended the seat of judgment (xix. 14). It seems likely that St. John used the Roman reckoning, and his computation does not pretend to be exact; while we must remember that mental agitation conspired with the darkening of the sky, to render such an estimate as he offers even more than usually vague.

It has been supposed that St. Mark's "third hour" goes back to the scourging, which, as being a regular part of Roman crucifixion, he includes, although inflicted in this case before the sentence. But it will prove quite as hard to reconcile this distribution of time with "the sixth hour" in St. John, while it is at variance with the context in which St. Mark asserts it.

The small and bitter heart of Pilate keenly resented his defeat and the victory of the priests. Perhaps it was when his soldiers offered the scornful homage of Rome to Israel and her monarch that he saw the way to a petty revenge. And all Jerusalem was scandalised by reading the inscription over a crucified malefactor's head, The King of the Jews.

It needs some reflection to perceive how sharp the taunt was. A few years ago they had a king, but the sceptre had departed from Judah; Rome had abolished him. It was their hope that soon a native king would for ever sweep away the foreigner from their fields. But here the Roman exhibited the fate of such a claim, and professed to inflict its horrors not upon one whom they disavowed, but upon their king indeed. We know how angrily and vainly they protested; and again we seem to recognise the solemn irony of Providence. For this was their true King, and they, who resented the superscription, had fixed their Anointed there.

All the more they would disconnect themselves from Him, and wreak their passion upon the helpless One whom they hated. The populace mocked Him openly: the chief priests, too cultivated to insult avowedly a dying man, mocked Him "among themselves," speaking bitter words for Him to hear. The multitude repeated the false charge which had probably done much to inspire their sudden preference for Barabbas, "Thou that destroyest the temple and buildest it again in three days, save Thyself and come down from the cross."

They little suspected that they were recalling words of consolation to His memory, reminding Him that all this suffering was foreseen, and how it was all to end. The chief priests spoke also a truth full of consolation, "He saved others, Himself He cannot save," although it was no physical bar which forbade Him to accept their challenge. And when they flung at Him His favourite demand for faith, saying "Let the Christ, the King of Israel, now come down from the cross, that we may see and believe," surely they reminded Him of the great multitude who should not see, and yet should believe, when He came back through the gates of death.

Thus the words they spoke could not afflict Him. But what horror to the pure soul to behold these yawning abysses of malignity, these gulfs of pitiless hate. The affronts hurled at suffering and defeat by prosperous and exultant malice are especially Satanic. Many diseases inflict more physical pain than torturers ever invented, but they do not excite the same horror, because gentle ministries are there to charm away the despair which human hate and execration conjure up.

To add to the insult of His disgraceful death, the Romans had crucified two robbers, doubtless from the band of Barabbas, one upon each side of Jesus. We know how this outrage led to the salvation of one of them, and refreshed the heavy laden soul of Jesus, oppressed by so much guilt and vileness, with the visible firstfruit of His passion, giving Him to see of the travail of His soul, by which He shall yet be satisfied.

But in their first agony and despair, when all voices were unanimous against the Blessed One, and they too must needs find some outlet for their frenzy, they both reproached Him. Thus the circle of human wrong was rounded.

The traitor, the deserters, the forsworn apostle, the perjured witnesses, the hypocritical pontiff professing horror at blasphemy while himself abjuring his national hope, the accomplices in a sham trial, the murderer of the Baptist and his men of war, the abject ruler who declared Him innocent yet gave Him up to die, the servile throng who waited on the priests, the soldiers of Herod and of Pilate, the pitiless crowd which clamoured for His blood, and they who mocked Him in His agony,—not one of them whom Jesus did not compassionate, whose cruelty had not power to wring His heart. Disciple and foeman, Roman and Jew, priest and soldier and judge, all had lifted up their voice against Him. And when the comrades of His passion joined the cry, the last ingredient of human cruelty was infused into the cup which James and John had once proposed to drink with Him.

THE DEATH OF JESUS.

MARK xv. 33-41 (R. V.).

Three hours of raging human passion, endured with Godlike patience, were succeeded by three hours of darkness, hushing mortal hatred into silence, and perhaps contributing to the penitence of the reviler at His side. It was a supernatural gloom, since an eclipse of the sun was impossible during the full moon of Passover. Shall we say that, as it shall be in the last days, nature sympathised with humanity, and the angel of the sun hid his face from his suffering Lord?

Or was it the shadow of a still more dreadful eclipse, for now the eternal Father veiled His countenance from the Son in whom He was well pleased?

In some true sense God forsook Him. And we have to seek for a meaning of this awful statement—inadequate, no doubt, for all our thoughts must come short of such a reality, but free from prevarication and evasion.

It is wholly unsatisfactory to regard the verse as merely the heading of a psalm, cheerful for the most part, which Jesus inaudibly recited. Why was only this verse uttered aloud? How false an impression must have been produced upon the multitude, upon St. John, upon the penitent thief, if Jesus were suffering less than the extreme of spiritual anguish. Nay, we feel that never before can the verse have attained its fullest meaning, a meaning which no experience of David could more than dimly shadow forth, since we ask in our sorrows, Why have we forsaken God? but Jesus said, Why hast Thou forsaken Me?

And this unconsciousness of any reason for desertion disproves the old notion that He felt Himself a sinner, and "suffered infinite remorse, as being the chief sinner in the universe, all the sins of mankind being His." One who felt thus could neither have addressed God as "My God," nor asked why He was forsaken.

Still less does it allow us to believe that the Father perfectly identified Jesus with sin, so as to be "wroth" with Him, and even "to hate Him to the uttermost." Such notions, the offspring of theories carried to a wild and irreverent extreme, when carefully examined impute to the Deity confusion of thought, a mistaking of the Holy One for a sinner or rather for the aggregate of sinners. But it is very different when we pass from the Divine consciousness to the bearing of God toward Christ our representative, to the outshining or eclipse of His favour. That this was overcast is manifest from the fact that Jesus everywhere else addresses Him as My Father, here only as My God. Even in the garden it was Abba Father, and the change indicates not indeed estrangement of heart, but certainly remoteness. Thus we have the sense of desertion, combined with the assurance which once breathed in the words, O God, Thou art my God.

Thus also it came to pass that He who never forfeited the most intimate communion and sunny smile of heaven, should yet give us an example at the last of that utmost struggle and sternest effort of the soul, which trusts without experience, without emotion, in the dark, because God is God, not because I am happy.

But they who would empty the death of Jesus of its sacrificial import, and leave only the attraction and inspiration of a sublime life and death, must answer the hard questions, How came God to forsake the Perfect One? Or, how came He to charge God with such desertion? His follower, twice using this very word, could boast that he was cast down yet not forsaken, and that at his first trial all men forsook him, yet the Lord stood by him (2 Cor. iv. 9; 2 Tim. iv. 16, 17). How came the disciple to be above his Master?

The only explanation is in His own word, that His life is a ransom in exchange for many (Mark x. 45). The chastisement of our peace, not the remorse of our guiltiness, was upon Him. No wonder that St. Mark, who turns aside from his narrative for no comment, no exposition, was yet careful to preserve this alone among the dying words of Christ.

And the Father heard His Son. At that cry the mysterious darkness passed away; and the soul of Jesus was relieved from its burden, so that He became conscious of physical suffering; and the mockery of the multitude was converted into awe. It seemed to them that His Eloi might indeed bring Elias, and the great and notable day, and they were willing to relieve the thirst which no stoical hardness forbade that gentlest of all sufferers to confess. Thereupon the anguish that redeemed the world was over; a loud voice told that exhaustion was not complete; and yet Jesus "gave up the ghost." *

Through the veil, that is to say His flesh, we have boldness to enter into the holy place; and now that He had opened the way, the veil of the temple was rent asunder by no mortal hand, but downward from the top. The way into the holiest was visibly thrown open, when sin was expiated, which had forfeited our right of access.

And the centurion, seeing that His death itself was abnormal and miraculous, and accompanied with miraculous signs, said, Truly this was a righteous man. But such a confession could not rest there: if He was this, He was all He claimed to be: and the mockery of His enemies had betrayed the secret of their hate; He was the Son of God.

"When the centurion saw. . . . There were also many women beholding." Who can overlook the connection? Their gentle hearts were not to be utterly overwhelmed: as the centurion saw and drew his inference, so they beheld, and felt, however dimly, amid sorrows that benumb the mind, that still, even in such wreck and misery, God was not far from Jesus.

When the Lord said, It is finished, there was not only an end of conscious anguish, but also of contempt and insult. His body was not to see corruption, nor was a bone to be broken, nor should it remain in hostile hands.

Respect for Jewish prejudice prevented the Romans from leaving it to moulder on the cross, and the aproaching Sabbath was not one to be polluted. And knowing this, Joseph of Arimathæa boldly went in to Pilate and asked for the body of Jesus. It was only secretly and in fear that he had been a disciple, but the deadly crisis had developed what was hidden; he had opposed the crime of his nation in their council, and in the hour of seeming overthrow he chose the good part. Boldly the timid one "went in," braving the scowls of the priesthood, defiling himself moreover, and forfeiting his share in the sacred feast, in hope to win the further defilement of contact with the dead.

Pilate was careful to verify so rapid a death; but when he was certain of the fact, "he granted the corpse to Joseph," as a worthless thing. His

* The ingenious and plausible attempt to show that His death was caused by a physical rupture of the heart has one fatal weakness. Death came too late for this; the severest pressure was already relieved.

frivolity is expressed alike in the unusual verb * and substantive: he "freely bestowed," he "gave away" not "the body" as when Joseph spoke of it, but "the corpse," the fallen thing, like a prostrated and uprooted tree that shall revive no more. Wonderful it is to reflect that God had entered into eternal union with what was thus given away to the only man of rank who cared to ask for it. Wonderful to think what opportunities of eternal gain men are content to lose; what priceless treasures are given away, or thrown away as worthless. Wonderful to imagine the feelings of Joseph in heaven to-day, as he gazes with gratitude and love upon the glorious Body which once, for a little, was consigned to his reverent care.

St. John tells us that Nicodemus brought a hundred pound weight of myrrh and aloes, and they together wrapped Him in these, in the linen which had been provided; and Joseph laid Him in his own new tomb, undesecrated by mortality.

And there Jesus rested. His friends had no such hope as would prevent them from closing the door with a great stone. His enemies set a watch, and sealed the stone. The broad moon of Passover made the night as clear as the day, and the multitude of strangers, who thronged the city and its suburbs, rendered any attempt at robbery even more hopeless than at another season.

What indeed could the trembling disciples of an executed pretender do with such an object as a dead body? What could they hope from the possession of it? But if they did not steal it, if the moral glories of Christianity are not sprung from deliberate mendacity, why was the body not produced, to abash the wild dreams of their fanaticism? It was fearfully easy to identify. The scourging, the cross, and the spear, left no slight evidence behind, and the broken bones of the malefactors completed the absolute isolation of the sacred body of the Lord.

The providence of God left no precaution unsupplied to satisfy honest and candid inquiry. It remained to be seen, would He leave Christ's soul in Hades, or suffer His Holy One (such is the epithet applied to the body of Jesus) to see corruption?

Meantime, through what is called three days and nights—a space which touched, but only touched, the confines of a first and third day, as well as the Saturday which intervened, Jesus shared the humiliation of common men, the divorce of soul and body. He slept as sleep the dead, but His soul was where He promised that the penitent should come, refreshed in Paradise.

CHAPTER XVI.

CHRIST RISEN.

MARK xvi. 1-18 (R. V.).

THE Gospels were not written for the curious, but for the devout. They are most silent therefore where myth and legend would be most garrulous, and it is instructive to seek, in the story of Jesus, for anything similar to the account of the Buddha's enlightenment under the Bo tree. We read nothing of the interval in Hades; nothing of the entry of His crowned and immortal body into the presence chamber of God; nothing of the resurrection. Did He awake alone? Was He waited upon by the hierarchy of heaven, who robed Him in raiment unknown to men? We are only told what concerns mankind, the sufficient manifestation of Jesus to His disciples.

And to harmonise the accounts a certain effort is necessary, because they tell of interviews with men and women who had to pass through all the vicissitudes of despair, suspense, rapturous incredulity,* and faith. Each of them contributes a portion of the tale.

From St. John we learn that Mary Magdalene came early to the sepulchre, from St. Matthew that others were with her, from St. Mark that these women, dissatisfied with the unskilful ministrations of men (and men whose rank knew nothing of such functions), had brought sweet spices to anoint Him Who was about to claim their adoration; St. John tells how Mary, seeing the empty sepulchre, ran to tell Peter and John of its desecration; the others, that in her absence an angel told the glad tidings to the women; St. Mark, that Mary was the first to whom Jesus Himself appeared. And thenceforth the narrative more easily falls into its place.

This confusion, however perplexing to thoughtless readers, is inevitable in the independent histories of such events, derived from the various parties who delighted to remember, each what had befallen himself.

But even a genuine contradiction would avail nothing to refute the substantial fact. When the generals of Henry the Fourth strove to tell him what passed after he was wounded at Aumale, no two of them agreed in the course of events which gave them victory. Two armies beheld the battle of Waterloo, but who can tell when it began? At ten o'clock, said the Duke of Wellington. At half-past eleven, said General Alava, who rode beside him. At twelve according to Napoleon and Drouet; and at one according to Ney.

People who doubt the reality of the resurrection, because the harmony of the narratives is underneath the surface, do not deny these facts. They are part of history. Yet it is certain that the resurrection of Jesus colours the history of the world more powerfully to-day than the events which are so much more recent.

If Christ were not risen, how came these despairing men and women by their new hope, their energy, their success among the very men who slew Him? If Christ be not risen, how has the morality of mankind been raised? Was it ever known that a falsehood exercised for ages a quickening and purifying power which no truth can rival?

From the ninth verse to the end of St. Mark's account it is curiously difficult to decide on the true reading. And it must be said that the note in the Revised Version, however accurate, does not succeed in giving any notion of the strength of the case in favour of the remainder of the Gospel. It tells us that the two oldest manuscripts omit them, but we do not read that in one of these a space is left for the insertion of something, known by the scribe to be wanting there. Nor does it mention the twelve manuscripts of almost equal antiquity in which they

* *I. e.*, in the New Testament, where it occurs but once besides.

* Can anything surpass that masterstroke of insight and descriptive power, "they still disbelieved for joy" (Luke xxiv. 41).

are contained, nor the early date at which they were quoted.

The evidence appears to lean towards the belief that they were added in a later edition, or else torn off in an early copy from which some transcribers worked. But unbelief cannot gain anything by converting them into a separate testimony, of the very earliest antiquity, to events related in each of the other Gospels.

And the uncertainty itself will be wholesome if it reminds us that saving faith is not to be reposed in niceties of criticism, but in a living Christ, the power and wisdom of God. Jesus blamed men for thinking that they had eternal life in their inspired Scriptures, and so refusing to come for life to Him, of Whom those Scriptures testified. Has sober criticism ever shaken for one hour that sacred function of Holy Writ?

What then is especially shown us in the closing words of St. Mark?

Readiness to requite even a spark of grace, and to bless with the first tidings of a risen Redeemer the love which sought only to embalm His corpse. Tender care for the fallen and disheartened, in the message sent especially to Peter. Immeasurable condescension, such as rested formerly, a Babe, in a peasant woman's arms, and announced its Advent to shepherds, now appearing first of all to a woman "out of whom He had cast seven devils."

A state of mind among the disciples, far indeed from that rapt and hysterical enthusiasm which men have fancied, ready to be whirled away in a vortex of religious propagandism (and to whirl the whole world after it), upon the impulse of dreams, hallucinations, voices mistaken on a misty shore, longings which begot convictions. Jesus Himself, and no second, no messenger from Jesus, inspired the zeal which kindled mankind. The disciples, mourning and weeping, found the glad tidings incredible, while Mary who had seen Him, believed. When two, as they walked, beheld Him in another shape, the rest remained incredulous, announcing indeed that He had actually risen and appeared unto Peter, yet so far from a true conviction that when He actually came to them, they supposed that they beheld a spirit (Luke xxiv. 34, 37). Yet He looked in the face those pale discouraged Galileans, and bade them go into all the world, bearing to the whole creation the issues of eternal life and death. And they went forth, and the power and intellect of the world are won. Whatever unbelievers think about individual souls, it is plain that the words of the Nazarene have proved true for communities and nations, He that believeth and is baptised has been saved, He that believeth not has been condemned. The nation and kingdom that has not served Christ has perished.

Nor does any one pretend that the agents in this marvellous movement were insincere. If all this was a dream, it was a strange one surely, and demands to be explained. If it was otherwise, no doubt the finger of God has come unto us.

THE ASCENSION.

Mark xvi. 19-20 (R. V.).

We have reached the close of the great Gospel of the energies of Jesus, His toils, His manner, His searching gaze, His noble indignation, His love of children, the consuming zeal by virtue of which He was not more truly the Lamb of God than the Lion of the tribe of Judah. St. Mark has just recorded how He bade His followers carry on His work, defying the serpents of the world, and renewing the plague-stricken race of Adam. In what strength did they fulfil this commission? How did they fare without the Master? And what is St. Mark's view of the Ascension?

Here, as all through the Gospel, minor points are neglected. Details are only valued when they carry some aid for the special design of the Evangelist, who presses to the core of his subject at once and boldly. As he omitted the bribes with which Satan tempted Jesus, and cared not for the testimony of the Baptist when the voice of God was about to peal from heaven over the Jordan, as on the holy mount he told not the subject of which Moses and Elijah spoke, but how Jesus Himself predicted His death to His disciples, so now He is silent about the mountain slope, the final benediction, the cloud which withdrew Him from their sight, and the angels who sent back the dazed apostles to their homes and their duties. It is not caprice nor haste that omits so much interesting information. His mind is fixed on a few central thoughts; what concerns him is to link the mighty story of the life and death of Jesus with these great facts, that He was received up into Heaven, that He there sat down upon the right hand of God, and that His disciples were never forsaken of Him at all, but proved, by the miraculous spread of the early Church, that His power was among them still. St. Mark does not record the promise, but he asserts the fact that Christ was with them all the days. There is indeed a connection between his two closing verses, subtle and hard to render into English, and yet real, which suggests the notion of balance, of relation between the two movements, the ascent of Jesus and the evangelisation of the world, such as exists, for example, between detachments of an army co-operating for a common end, so that our Lord, for His part, ascended, while the disciples, for their part, went forth and found Him with them still.

But the link is plainer which binds the Ascension to His previous story of suffering and conflict. It was "then," and "after He had spoken unto them," that "the Lord Jesus was received up." In truth His ascension was but the carrying forward to completion of His resurrection, which was not a return to the poor conditions of our mortal life, but an entrance into glory, only arrested in its progress until He should have quite convinced His followers that "it is I indeed," and made them understand that "thus it is written that the Christ should suffer, and rise again from the dead the third day," and filled them with holy shame for their unbelief, and with courage for their future course, so strange, so weary, so sublime.

There is something remarkable in the words, "He was received up into heaven." We habitually speak of Him as ascending, but Scripture more frequently declares that He was the subject of the action of another, and was taken up. St. Luke tells us that, "while they worshipped, He was carried up into heaven," and again "He was received up. . . . He was taken up" (Luke xxiv. 51; Acts i. 2, 9). Physical interference is not implied: no angels bore Him aloft; and the narratives make it clear that His glorious Body, obedient to its new mysterious nature, arose unaided. But the decision to depart, and the choice of a time, came not from Him: He did not go, but was taken. Never hitherto had He glorified Himself. He had taught His disciples to be contented in the lowest room until the Master of the house should bid them come up higher. And so, when His own supreme victory is won, and heaven held its breath expectant and astonished, the conquering Lord was content to walk with peasants by the Lake of Galilee and on the slopes of Olivet until the appointed time. What a rebuke to us who chafe and fret if the recognition of our petty merits be postponed.

"He was received up into heaven!" What sublime mysteries are covered by that simple phrase. It was He who taught us to make, even of the mammon of unrighteousness, friends who shall welcome us, when mammon fails and all things mortal have deserted us, into everlasting habitations. With what different greetings, then, do men enter the City of God. Some converts of the death bed perhaps there are, who scarcely make their way to heaven, alone, unhailed by one whom they saved or comforted, and like a vessel which struggles into port, with rent cordage and tattered sails, only not a wreck. Others, who aided some few, sparing a little of their means and energies, are greeted and blessed by a scanty group. But even our chieftains and leaders, the martyrs, sages, and philanthropists whose names brighten the annals of the Church, what is their influence, and how few have they reached, compared with that great multitude whom none can number, of all nations and tribes and peoples and tongues, who cry with a loud voice, Salvation unto our God who sitteth upon the throne, and unto the Lamb. Through Him it pleased the Father to reconcile all things unto Himself, through Him, whether things upon the earth or things in the heavens. And surely the supreme hour in the history of the universe was when, in flesh, the sore-stricken but now the all-conquering Christ re-entered His native heaven.

And He sat down at the right hand of God. The expression is, beyond all controversy, borrowed from that great Psalm which begins by saying, "The Lord said unto my Lord, Sit thou at My right hand," and which presently makes the announcement never revealed until then, "Thou art a Priest for ever after the order of Melchizedec" (Ps. cx. 1, 4). It is therefore an anticipation of the argument for the royal Priesthood of Jesus which is developed in the Epistle to the Hebrews. Now priesthood is a human function: every high priest is chosen from among men. And the Ascension proclaims to us, not the Divinity of the Eternal Word, but the glorification of "the Lord Jesus;" not the omnipotence of God the Son, but that all power is committed unto Him Who is not ashamed to call us brethren, that His human hands wield the sceptre as once they held the reed, and the brows then insulted and torn with thorns are now crowned with many crowns. In the overthrow of Satan He won all, and infinitely more than all, of that vast bribe which Satan once offered for His homage, and the angels for ever worship Him who would not for a moment bend His knee to evil.

Now since He conquered not for Himself, but as Captain of our Salvation, the Ascension also proclaims the issue of all the holy suffering, all the baffled efforts, all the cross-bearing of all who follow Christ.

His High Priesthood is with authority. "Every high priest standeth," but He has for ever sat down on the right hand of the throne of the majesty in the heavens, a Priest sitting upon His throne (Heb. viii. 1; Zech. vi. 13). And therefore it is His office, Who pleads for us and represents us, Himself to govern our destinies. No wonder that His early followers, with minds which He had opened to understand the Scriptures, were mighty to cast down strongholds. Against tribulation and anguish and persecution and famine and nakedness and peril and sword they were more than conquerors through Him. For He worked with them and confirmed His word with signs. And we have seen that He works with His people still, and still confirms His gospel, only withdrawing signs of one order as those of another kind are multiplied. Wherever they wage a faithful battle, He gives them victory. Whenever they cry to Him in anguish, the form of the Son of God is with them in the furnace, and the smell of fire does not pass upon them. Where they come, the desert blossoms as a rose; and where they are received, the serpents of life no longer sting, its fevers grow cool, and the demons which rend it are cast out.